Dictionary of

WOMEN ARTISTS

Dictionary of

WOMEN ARTISTS

VOLUME I

Introductory Surveys
Artists, A–I

Editor
DELIA GAZE

Picture Editors
MAJA MIHAJLOVIC
LEANDA SHRIMPTON

FITZROY DEARBORN PUBLISHERS
LONDON AND CHICAGO

Copyright © 1997 by
FITZROY DEARBORN PUBLISHERS

FITZROY DEARBORN PUBLISHERS
70 East Walton Street
Chicago, Illinois 60611
USA

or

11 Rathbone Place
London WIP IDE
England

British Library Cataloguing in Publication Data
Dictionary of women artists
   1. Women artists – Dictionaries
   I. Gaze, Delia
   709.2'2

ISBN 1–884964–21–4

Library of Congress Cataloging in Publication Data is available.

First published in the USA and UK 1997

Typeset by Lorraine Hodghton, Radlett, Herts, UK
Printed in Great Britain by the Bath Press

Cover illustration:
Self-Portrait in Profile Facing Left, Drawing by Käthe Kollwitz, 1933

Frontispieces:
vol.1: Jacoba van Heemskerck in her studio, 1915
vol.2: *In the Studio* by Asta Nørregaard, 1883

CONTENTS

EDITOR'S NOTE

The *Dictionary of Women Artists* contains substantial entries on artists working in a wide variety of media from the Middle Ages to the present day, in countries throughout Europe as well as America and Australasia. To set the work and careers of the individual artists in context, introductory essays examine training opportunities and the changing conditions of work for women since the medieval period. A survey on women as artists in the Middle Ages assesses the evidence for women's participation in the arts in earlier periods, both in the West and in Byzantium.

The book is the fruit of the extensive scholarly interest in the subject of women artists that has been manifested since the 1970s, as part of a wider re-examination of women's history. While there are already very useful works of reference in the field, no previously published dictionary has covered such a wide-ranging historical and geographical span with such detailed entries. The list of artists was initially drawn up in consultation with the advisers whose names are listed on page xi. It was expanded and refined through the suggestions of contributors. For practical reasons, certain firm parameters were established at the outset: the project would be concerned only with the Western tradition in art, and it would exclude women born after 1945; the emphasis would be historical rather than contemporary, and no attempt would be made to cover architecture, interior or garden design, or fashion.

Major themes of the book are the problems women encountered in trying to obtain adequate training, and their endeavours to gain professional recognition and status comparable to that of men; the concentration is thus on the "fine" arts of painting and sculpture. But the areas in which women have traditionally been employed are by no means neglected. Survey essays on printmakers and copyists shed light on the activities of those who operated on the margins of the official art world, and there are entries, for example, on 16th- and 17th-century printmakers, 18th-century textile designers and goldsmiths, and 19th-century ceramists. For the most part, however, the contribution of women to the applied arts was anonymous, or at least poorly documented, and therefore unsuited to the format of the entries included here. For continuity with the earlier periods, there are also entries on the most innovative 20th-century artists and designers working in the fields of ceramics, textiles and metalwork, including important women members of the Wiener Werkstätte and the Bauhaus. But these professional women were not the only ones who aspired to be artists, and although professionalism is perhaps the most dominant theme in the book, attention is also given to the many women whose artistic activity was confined to the domestic sphere: the amateur artists from the middle and upper classes, whose work was regarded as a mere "accomplishment" and a social skill.

The selection of entrants never ceased to be problematic. Only a minority would satisfy those most obvious criteria for inclusion in a reference book: contemporary reputation or posthumous fame. And of those who do qualify on these grounds – the women artists mentioned by Lodovico Guicciardini in the 16th century, for instance – only a handful are adequately documented or have left behind a sufficient corpus of work to warrant an individual entry; hence, Levina Teerlinc is included, but Susanna Horenbout is not, and only one of the 17th-century French academicians – Elisabeth-Sophie Chéron – has her own entry, although others are discussed in the context of the introductory surveys.

In a book dealing with such an area as this, it is perhaps inadvisable to talk of "criteria for inclusion" in any conventional sense at all; in many cases, the race was as important as the prize, and failure no ground for exclusion. A case in point is Anne Forbes: her derivative and rather mediocre work would in no way qualify her for inclusion in a dictionary of artists judged according to traditional art-historical norms, but her career, illuminated by surviving correspondence, offers a fascinating insight into the difficulties an 18th-century woman painter experienced in trying to establish herself. Thus in many ways this *Dictionary* may be regarded as an anthology, the entries demonstrating the extremely wide range of artistic activities in which women have been engaged; the roles accorded to them in a patriarchal society; and their responses to the constraints imposed upon them.

The book contains examples of artists who worked in the context of the convent, court or city; who were active as members of a family workshop or married into one; who were pupils, relatives, lovers or wives of well-known artists; who were representative practitioners within the genres traditionally associated with women: portraiture, still life, flower painting and genre; who established successful businesses, or who were amateur artists; who had exhibiting careers and gained some degree of professional recognition; who enjoyed popular success; who were educators or campaigners for women's artistic advancement; whose art and writings influenced other artists; who were associated with an avant-garde group, movement or trend; who were instrumental in the diffusion of modernism; who were themselves pioneers; whose work was or is pertinent to women's concerns; who explored issues of gender, race and identity; and artists who followed independent paths and cannot be categorised.

With only 600 entries, the *Dictionary* is inevitably selective, but the inclusion of one name at the expense of another who may have equal claims is an unavoidable consequence of the process of putting a book of this sort together and should not be taken to imply that the list of entries constitutes some kind of canon. We endeavoured to maintain an international balance, but there is an inescapable – although not intentional – Anglo-American bias, which largely stems from the abundance of literature on the subject in these areas. In the selection process, priority was weighted towards the earlier artists, to those who have attracted critical comment in at least their own language, those whose work was particularly relevant to women's issues and, for the more recent artists, those with a strong exhibiting career and public profile.

Artists are listed under their professional name – the one that they first or most frequently worked or exhibited under – in a form current in their lifetime; cross-references are provided from alternative names that the reader is likely to come across in the literature. The entries contain basic biographical information, a list of exhibitions (where appropriate), a bibliography and a signed critical essay contributed by a specialist on the artist concerned. The headnote points to the main areas of an artist's activity; she would, for example, be described as a writer only if this formed an integral part of her work as an artist. The outline biography is intended to provide a framework for the critical discussion of the artist's work in the essay. Major awards are mentioned here, unless they accompany an exhibition cited in the list below. Every effort has been made to ensure that the information provided is accurate. In many cases, the contributor's own archival research produced results that differed considerably from published sources; dates of birth proved particularly fluid.

The list of exhibitions is intended to convey the character of the artist's exhibiting career. Posthumous exhibitions are not listed, with the exception of a major retrospective held soon after an artist's death; important later exhibitions are signposted by the inclusion of the catalogue(s) in the bibliography. For most artists with post-war careers, only individual exhibitions are listed; important group shows are either mentioned in the biography or essay, or alluded to by the presence of the catalogue in the bibliography. Exhibitions are listed in chronological order; the venue is followed by the year(s) of a show's opening. For regularly occurring group exhibitions, such as the Paris Salon and the Royal Academy, the years of participation are cited; "occasionally" points to a break, but is no comment on the frequency of showing. For touring exhibitions, only the first venue is named.

The bibliography is arranged chronologically, to give the reader an indication of the historiography of the subject. Survey books and dictionaries are rarely cited, since they appear in the general bibliography. Exhibition catalogues are listed under their title, with the first venue and the year of opening; authors are given when a single entry or essay is cited in a more general work. English-language editions of books are provided wherever possible. Any writings by an artist are listed separately, under the heading "Selected Writings"; such lists include books, as well as articles that shed light on the entrant's work as an artist. Writings that appear in a broader context, such as statements in exhibition catalogues, are listed in the bibliography. Significant manuscript collections are noted at the end of the bibliography. In the essays, references to works in the bibliography are given as follows: author and date for books and articles, venue (i.e. town/city) and date for exhibition catalogues. The locations of works are provided wherever possible; otherwise, a reference is given to a published illustration (abbreviation: "repr.").

Acknowledgments

I am indebted to many people for the successful completion of this project. I would like to thank the advisers and all those who wrote for the book for their patience and help, which far exceeded what was asked of them; those who gave advice in the initial stages – Lorne Campbell, Elizabeth Clegg, Cecile Johnson, Ann Jones, Helen Langdon, Lesley Stevenson, Liz Stubbs and Ruth Thackeray – as well as the many friends who encouraged me throughout; and those who translated, assisted with the foreign-language entries, proof-read or otherwise helped with the book: Richard Aronowitz-Mercer, Kate Bomford, Antonia Boström, Anne Charvet, Tracy Chevalier, Nicola Coleby, Lucinda Collinge, Sara Dodd, Jacqueline Griffin, Julie Berger Hochstrasser, Justyna Jameson, Carol Jones, Ute Krebs, David McDuff, Valerie Nunn, Alette Rye Scales, Ines Schlenker, Marjorie Trusted, Clare Turner, Philip Ward-Jackson and Sebastian Wormell. I should also like to thank the staff of the National Art Library, the Witt, Conway and book libraries at the Courtauld Institute of Art, the Warburg Institute, the Tate Gallery, the British Library, the Women's Art Library and the Westminster Central Library, and Jill Heberden for the loan of books. Particular thanks are due to my colleagues at Fitzroy Dearborn for their support and help, Joanna Banham, Kate Berney, Mark Hawkins-Dady and Lesley Henderson, and especially to the picture editors, Leanda Shrimpton and Maja Mihajlovic, for their hard work and imaginative suggestions. Above all, I would like to thank Daniel Kirkpatrick, the publisher, who not only commissioned the book but also undertook the most mundane of tasks, for his undaunted optimism and humour.

DELIA GAZE

ADVISERS

Kathleen Adler
Shulamith Behr
Annemarie Weyl Carr
Nicola Coleby
Judith Collins
Estrella de Diego
Ann Eatwell
Michelle Facos
Tamar Garb
Sara F. Matthews Grieco
Janice Helland
Alison McNeil Kettering

Anne Kirker
Nancy Mowll Mathews
Jennifer Hawkins Opie
Gill Perry
Griselda Pollock
Wendy Wassyng Roworth
Mary Schoeser
Jane Sellars
Philip Ward-Jackson
Genevieve Warwick
Mara R. Witzling

CONTRIBUTORS

Mary Jo Aagerstoun
Marianne Aav
Jane Abdy
Kathleen Adler
Kent Ahrens
David Alexander
David Alston
Janet A. Anderson
Janice Anderson
Ruth Pérez Antelo
Bruce Arnold
Julie Aronson
Kate Baden Fuller
Christina Barton
Danuta Batorska
Karen A. Bearor
Marion Beckers
Shulamith Behr
Irene Below
Carl Belz
Marianne Berardi
Renate Berger
Avis Berman
Henriette Bessis

Jon Bird
Emily Black
Peter Black
Whitney Blausen
Marja Bloem
Ulrike Bolte
Kate Bomford
Antonia Boström
Patrick Bourne
Nicola Gordon Bowe
John E. Bowlt
Christine Boydell
Bettina Brandt
Patricia Brauch
Clare A. A. Brisby
Xanthe Brooke
Betty Ann Brown
Candice Bruce
William Buchanan
Georgina Buckland
Ariella Budick
Bernard Bumpus
Judith Bumpus
Janine Burke

Martha B. Caldwell
Susan Havens Caldwell
Vivian P. Cameron
Franca Trinchieri Camiz
Lucia Cappellozza
E. A. Carmean, Jr
Flavio Caroli
Annemarie Weyl Carr
Susan P. Casteras
Ruta Čaupova
Madeline H. Caviness
Mary Ann Caws
Mary Chan
Robin M. Chandler
Liana De Girolami Cheney
Anja Cherdron
Charlotte Christensen
Hazel Clark
Trinkett Clark
Sue Clegg
Margot Coatts
Georgiana M. M. Colvile
Emmanuel Cooper
John Crabbe
Elizabeth Cropper
Bridget Crowley
Elizabeth Cumming
Penelope Curtis
Sabine Dahmen
Carol Damian
Brenda Danilowitz
John A. Day
Katy Deepwell
Lea Rosson DeLong
Patricia de Montfort
Danielle Derrey-Capon
Jutta Dick
Estrella de Diego
Carol Diethe
Terence Diggory
Sara M. Dodd
Claire Doherty
Siobhan Dougherty
Lamia Doumato
Douglas Dreishpoon
Charles Dumas
Marilyn Dunn
Diana C. du Pont
Elizabeth Eastmond
Ann Eatwell
Sarah Edge
Bridget Elliott
Elaine Hirschl Ellis
Erika Esau
Michael Evans
Gabriele Fabiankowitsch
Michelle Facos
Betsy Fahlman
Constance A. Fairchild
Alicia Craig Faxon

Madeleine Fidell-Beaufort
Phylis Floyd
Jeana K. Foley
Mary F. Francey
Kathleen M. Friello
Anne Ganteführer
Tamar Garb
Andrea Garrihy
Lola B. Gellman
Margherita Giacometti
Linda Gill
Pat Gilmour
Deborah A. Goldberg
Catherine J. Golden
Saundra Goldman
Helen Goodman
Elizabeth Goring
Sylvia Gosden
Louise Govier
Trudie Grace
Jeffrey D. Grove
Nina Guryanova
Mona Hadler
Catherine Hall-van den Elsen
Lesley Halliwell
Catherine Harding
Helga H. Harriman
Beth Harris
Rosemary Harris
Ruth Hayden
Lisa Heer
Janice Helland
Nancy G. Heller
Cecilia Fajardo Hill
Jane Hill
Mike Hill
Patricia Hills
Alison Hilton
Julie Berger Hochstrasser
Lena Holger
Denise Hooker
Jeremy Howard
Caro Howell
Rosella M. Huber-Spanier
William Hull
Kristina Huneault
Shannon Hunter Hurtado
Jane Hylton
Jo Anna Isaak
Margaret Iversen
Fredrika H. Jacobs
Lynn F. Jacobs
Christopher M. S. Johns
Cecile Soliz Johnson
Deborah Jean Johnson
Heather Johnson
Alexa M. Johnston
Amelia Jones
Ann Jones
Britta Kaiser-Schuster

Janet A. Kaplan
Elyse Zorn Karlin
S.B. Kennedy
Alison McNeil Kettering
Catherine King
Elaine A. King
Julie King
Anne Kirker
Els Kloek
George Knox
Baerbel Kovalevski
Harry J. Kraaij
Miriam Kramer
Ute Krebs
John P. Lambertson
Cecily Langdale
Doïna Lemny
Sabina Lessmann
Mary Tompkins Lewis
Elisabeth Lidén
Marcelo Lima
Evelyn Lincoln
Anna Lena Lindberg
Stephen Lloyd
Dominique Lobstein
Christina Lodder
Sarah M. Lowe
Joe Lucchesi
Natalie Luckyj
Heidrun Ludwig
Margaret F. MacDonald
Linda F. McGreevy
Catherine MacKenzie
Duncan Macmillan
Sarat Maharaj
Alyce Mahon
Valerie Mainz
Marietta Mautner Markhof
Jan Marsh
Nancy-Clay Marsteller
Joan M. Marter
Brenda Martin
Nancy Mowll Mathews
Janelle Mellamphy
Marsha Meskimmon
Kathryn Metz
Barbara L. Michaels
Lillian B. Miller
Claudine Mitchell
Adelina Modesti
Pamela Dawson Moffat
Laurie J. Monahan
Gerta Moray
John Morrison
Elizabeth Mulley
Anke Münster
Caroline P. Murphy
Joan Murray
Carola Muysers
Carol A. Nathanson

Jane Necol
Pamela Gerrish Nunn
Kathy O'Dell
John N. O'Grady
Annika Öhrner
Gloria F. Orenstein
Martina Padberg
Melinda Boyd Parsons
Anthony Parton
Pamela A. Patton
Martha Moffitt Peacock
Juliet Peers
Phyllis Peet
Lydia M. Peña
Karina Marotta Peramos
Gill Perry
Catherine Phillips
Clare Phillips
Pamela Potter-Hennessey
Alan Powers
Elizabeth Prelinger
Nancy Proctor
Erich Ranfft
Beate Reese
Christopher Reeve
Hildegard Reinhardt
Leslie Reinhardt
Elizaveta Renne
Jacqueline Riding
Ann Roberts
Roxana Robinson
Barley Roscoe
Peter Rose
Martin Rosenberg
N.K.A. Rothstein
Wendy Wassyng Roworth
Veronika Rüther-Weiss
Wendy R. Salmond
Marina Sassenberg
Gill Saunders
Alette Rye Scales
Ines Schlenker
Eva Schmitt
Edith Schoeneck
Hrafnhildur Schram
Birgit Schulte
Miriam Seidel
Jane Sellars
Harriet F. Senie
Jane A. Sharp
Mary D. Sheriff
Nicola J. Shilliam
Pippa Shirley
Wendy Slatkin
Kim Sloan
Helen E. Smailes
Mary Smart
Elizabeth A.T. Smith
Richard J. Smith
John Somerville

Domenica Spadaro
Virginia B. Spivey
Lesley Stevenson
Katlijne Van der Stighelen
Karin Stober
Mary Towley Swanson
Katharina Sykora
Verena Tafel
Ailsa Tanner
Tara Leigh Tappert
Dorcas Taylor
Paula Terra Cabo
Birgit Thiemann
Alison Thomas
Margo Hobbs Thompson
Joanna Thornberry
Anniken Thue
Marina Vaizey
Debra Wacks
Neil Walker
Susan Waller

Esmé Ward
Cynthia R. Weaver
Michelle L. Weber
Nina Weibull
Julia Weiner
Sigrid Wortmann Weltge
James A. Welu
Barbro Werkmäster
Helen Weston
Anne Wichstrøm
Colin Wiggins
Beth Elaine Wilson
Sarah Wilson
Sarah Wimbush
Audur H. Winnan
Mara R. Witzling
Amy J. Wolf
Jeryldene M. Wood
Alison Yarrington
Charlotte Yeldham
Myriam Zerbi

ALPHABETICAL LIST
OF ARTISTS

VOLUME I

Magdalena Abakanowicz
Louise Abbéma
Berenice Abbott
Carla Accardi
Eileen Agar
Anni Albers
Gretchen Albrecht
Helen Allingham
Laura Alma-Tadema
Tarsila do Amaral
Anna Ancher
Sophie Anderson
Sofonisba Anguissola
Rita Angus
Eleanor Antin
Ida Applebroog
Diane Arbus
Pauline Auzou
Josefa d'Ayala de Óbidos
Gillian Ayres

Harriet Backer
Caroline Bardua
Hannah and Florence Barlow
Wilhelmina Barns-Graham
Jennifer Bartlett
Glenys Barton
Marie Bashkirtseff
Hester Bateman
Gudrun Baudisch
Mary Beale
Lady Diana Beauclerk
Cecilia Beaux
Clarice Beckett
María Eugenia de Beer
Vanessa Bell
Benedetta
Lynda Benglis
Teresa Benincampi
Mme Benoist
Charlotte Berend-Corinth
Ella Bergmann-Michel

Sarah Bernhardt
Mme Léon Bertaux
Elsa Beskow
Henryka Beyer
Aenne Biermann
Anna Bilińska-Bohdanowicz
Vivienne Binns
Isabel Bishop
Dorrit Black
Elizabeth Blackadder
María Blanchard
Tina Blau
Lucienne Bloch
Sandra Blow
Anna Blunden
Anna Boch
Barbara Leigh Smith Bodichon
Bona
Rosa Bonheur
Lee Bontecou
Gesina ter Borch
Marie-Geneviève Bouliar
Louise Bourgeois
Margaret Bourke-White
Joanna Boyce
Olga Boznańska
Marie Bracquemond
Norah Braden
Marianne Brandt
Louise-Catherine Breslau
Eleanor Fortescue Brickdale
Elena Brockmann
Romaine Brooks
Lucy Madox Brown
Henriette Browne
Trude Brück
Jaroslava Brychtová
Beverly Buchanan
Kate Bunce
Lady Butler

Margherita Caffi
Claude Cahun
Julia Margaret Cameron

Gabrielle Capet
Anne Marie Carl Nielsen
Margaret Carpenter
Emily Carr
Rosalba Carriera
Carrington
Leonora Carrington
Maria Caspar-Filser
Mary Cassatt
Elizabeth Catlett
Hanna Cauer
Marie Cazin
Vija Celmins
Emilie Charmy
Constance Charpentier
Barbara Chase-Riboud
Elisabeth-Sophie Chéron
Judy Chicago
Chryssa
Fanny Churberg
Lygia Clark
Edna Clarke Hall
Camille Claudel
Franciska Clausen
Florence Claxton
Joyce Clissold
Prunella Clough
Marie-Anne Collot
Ithell Colquhoun
Susie Cooper
Maria Cosway
Louisa Courtauld
Suor Maria Eufrasia della Croce
Lena Cronqvist
Imogen Cunningham

Louise Dahl-Wolfe
Anne Seymour Damer
Natalya Danko
Hanne Darboven
Anna Julia De Graag
Dorothy Dehner
Elaine de Kooning
Mary Delany
Sonia Delaunay
Virginie Demont-Breton
Evelyn De Morgan
Siri Derkert
Maria Oakey Dewing
Teresa Díaz
Barbara Regina Dietzsch
Jessica Dismorr
Suor Maria de Dominici
Rita Donagh
Marion Dorn
Victoria Dubourg
Ruth Duckworth
Natalia Dumitrescu
Susanna Duncombe
Françoise Duparc

Amalia Duprè
Susan Durant
Sofya Dymshits-Tolstaya

Susan Macdowell Eakins
Joan Eardley
Abastenia St Leger Eberle
Mary Beth Edelson
Marie Ellenrieder
Rebeccah Emes
Ende
Gutte Eriksen
Eléonore Escallier
Alexandra Exter

Jacqueline Fahey
Claire Falkenstein
Félicie de Fauveau
Sheila Fell
Sonja Ferlov
Jackie Ferrara
Lucrina Fetti
Leonor Fini
Janet Fish
Audrey Flack
Gerda Flöckinger
Mathilde Flögl
Mary Sargant Florence
Lavinia Fontana
Anne Forbes
Elizabeth Forbes
Raquel Forner
Gela Forster
Ethel Fox
Fernanda Francés y Arribas
Helen Frankenthaler
Elizabeth Frink
Harriet Whitney Frishmuth
Elizabeth Fritsch
Meta Vaux Warrick Fuller

Wanda Gág
Fede Galizia
Elizabeth Gardner
Anna Maria Garthwaite
Giovanna Garzoni
Wilhelmina Geddes
Artemisia Gentileschi
Marguerite Gérard
Margaret Gillies
Caterina Ginnasi
Gluck
Elizabeth Godfrey
Hilde Goldschmidt
Anna Golubkina
Natalya Goncharova
Eva Gonzalès
Dora Gordine
Sylvia Gosse
Mary Grant

Helen Lundeberg
Vivian Lynn

Dora Maar
Molly Macalister
Frances Macdonald
Margaret Macdonald
Norah McGuinness
Loren MacIver
Isabel McLaughlin
Mary Louise McLaughlin
Mary Fairchild MacMonnies
Bessie MacNicol
Anne Madden
Bea Maddock
Elena Makovskaya-Luksch
Marie von Malachowski
Anita Malfatti
Maruja Mallo
Jeanne Mammen
Sylvia Plimack Mangold
Diana Mantuana
Marcello
Marevna
Marisol
Theresa Concordia Maron-Mengs
Agnes Martin
Mary Martin
Maria Martins
Jacqueline Marval
Enid Marx
Alice Trumbull Mason
Louisa Matthiasdóttir
Constance Mayer
Else Meidner
Margaret Mellis
Louisa Anne Meredith
Maria Sibylla Merian
Anna Lea Merritt
Annette Messager
Lee Miller
Lizinka de Mirbel
Mary Miss
Joan Mitchell
Lisette Model
Paula Modersohn-Becker
Tina Modotti
Lucia Moholy
Louise Moillon
Marg Moll
Berthe Morisot
Jacqueline Morreau
May Morris
Ree Morton
Mary Moser
Anna Mary Robertson Moses
Marlow Moss
Marie-Louise von Motesiczky
Vera Mukhina
Gabriele Münter

Elizabeth Murray

Hanna Nagel
Alice Neel
Plautilla Nelli
Louise Nevelson
Jessie Newbery
Elisabet Ney
Winifred Nicholson
Vera Nilsson
Astrid Noack
Asta Nørregaard
Elizabeth Nourse
Gunnel Nyman
Jenny Nyström

Georgia O'Keeffe
Maria van Oosterwijck
Meret Oppenheim
Olga Oppenheimer
Princess Marie Christine d'Orléans
Chana Orloff
Emily Mary Osborn
Anna Ostroumova-Lebedeva
Gerta Overbeck

Ana Maria Pacheco
María Luisa Pacheco
Gina Pane
Lygia Pape
Isabella Catanea Parasole
Mimi Parent
Vilma Parlaghy
Ulrica Fredrica Pasch
Magdalena van de Passe
Anna Claypoole and Sarah Miriam Peale
Clara Peeters
Amelia Peláez
Beverly Pepper
I. Rice Pereira
Lilla Cabot Perry
Deanna Petherbridge
Howardena Pindell
Eunice Pinney
Katharine Pleydell-Bouverie
Elena Polenova
Lyubov Popova
Beatrix Potter
Mary Potter
Jane Poupelet
Alexandra Povorina
Lotte B. Prechner
Margaret Preston
Hans Anton Prinner
Dod Procter
Sarah Purser

Henrietta Rae
Alice Rahon
Yvonne Rainer

Carol Rama
Wendy Ramshaw
Clara von Rappard
Gwen Raverat
Katharine Read
Vinnie Ream
Anne Redpath
Anita Rée
Ruth Reeves
Regina
Paula Rego
Anne Estelle Rice
Germaine Richier
Lucie Rie
Bridget Riley
Clara Rilke-Westhoff
Faith Ringgold
Coba Ritsema
Christina Robertson
Suze Robertson
Adelaide Alsop Robineau
Marietta Robusti
Dorothea Rockburne
Emy Roeder
Geertruydt Roghman
Luisa Roldán
Henriëtte Ronner-Knip
Margaretha Roosenboom
Martha Rosler
Properzia de' Rossi
Susan Rothenberg
Olga Rozanova
Sophie Rude
Rachel Ruysch
Hannah Ryggen

Betye Saar
Kay Sage
Niki de Saint Phalle
Kyllikki Salmenhaara
Charlotte Salomon
Josefa Sánchez
Susanna Maria von Sandrart
Angeles Santos Torroella
Augusta Savage
Miriam Schapiro
Mira Schendel
Helene Schjerfbeck
Carolee Schneemann
Anna Maria van Schurman
Ethel Schwabacher
Thérése Schwartze
Kathleen Scott
Janet Scudder
Louise Seidler
Zinaida Serebryakova
Ellen Wallace and Rolinda Sharples
Aleksandra Shchekatikhina-Pototskaya
Amrita Sher-Gil
Elizabeth Eleanor Siddal

Renée Sintenis
Elisabetta Sirani
Monica Sjöö
Marta Skulme
Sylvia Sleigh
Clarissa Sligh
Agnes Slott-Møller
Grace Cossington Smith
Jaune Quick-to-See Smith
Pamela Colman Smith
Joan Snyder
Rebecca Solomon
Marie Spartali
Jo Spence
Lilly Martin Spencer
Nancy Spero
Louisa Starr
Emma Stebbins
Milly Steger
Pat Steir
Varvara Stepanova
Alice Barber Stephens
Irma Stern
Florine Stettheimer
May Stevens
Margaret Olrog Stoddart
Marianne Stokes
Gunta Stölzl
Zofia Stryjeńska
Michelle Stuart
Jane Sutherland
Júlíana Sveinsdóttir
Betty Swanwick
Mary Swanzy
Annie Swynnerton

Sophie Taeuber-Arp
Agnes Tait
Dorothea Tanning
Lenore Tawney
Janice Tchalenko
Levina Teerlinc
Ellen Thesleff
Alma W. Thomas
Mary Thornycroft
Anna Ticho
Charley Toorop
Toyen
Phoebe Traquair
Nína Tryggvadóttir
Tilsa Tsuchiya

Nadezhda Udaltsova

Suzanne Valadon
Nanine Vallain
Anne Vallayer-Coster
Remedios Varo
Gertrud Vasegaard
Pablita Velarde

Paule Vézelay
Maria Elena Vieira da Silva
Elisabeth Vigée-Lebrun
Caterina Vigri
Anna Roemersdochter and Maria Tesselschade Visscher
Bessie Onahotema Potter Vonnoh
Ursula von Rydingsvard
Charmion von Wiegand

Ethel Walker
Kay WalkingStick
Cecile Walton
Henrietta Ward
Louisa, Marchioness of Waterford
Caroline Watson
June Wayne
Bertha Wegmann
Ruth Weisberg
Rosario Weiss
Clara Pauline Barck Welles
Marianne Werefkin

Candace Wheeler
Anne Whitney
Gertrude Vanderbilt Whitney
Joyce Wieland
Vally Wieselthier
Maria Wiik
Hannah Wilke
Evelyn Williams
Jackie Winsor
Ann Wolff
Marta Worringer
Michaelina Woutier
Denise Wren

Marya Yakunchikova
Vera Yermolayeva

Dana Zámečniková
Eva Zeisel
Marguerite Thompson Zorach
Unica Zürn

CHRONOLOGICAL LIST
OF ARTISTS

active 975	Ende
1098–1179	Hildegard of Bingen
active c.1178–c.1196	Herrad
active c.1316	Teresa Díaz
c.1413–1463	Caterina Vigri
c.1510/20–1576	Levina Teerlinc
active 1514–29	Properzia de' Rossi
1523–1588	Plautilla Nelli
1528–after 1565	Catharina van Hemessen
c.1532–1625	Sofonisba Anguissola
c.1547–1612	Diana Mantuana
1552–1614	Lavinia Fontana
1552–1638	Barbara Longhi
c.1552/60–1590	Marietta Robusti
c.1578–c.1630	Fede Galizia
1584–1651	Anna Roemersdochter Visscher
active 1585–1625	Isabella Catanea Parasole
1590–1660	Caterina Ginnasi
1592–1649	Maria Tesselschade Visscher
1593–1652/3	Artemisia Gentileschi
1597–1676	Suor Maria Eufrasia della Croce
1600–1670	Giovanna Garzoni
1600–1637	Magdalena van de Passe
active 1603–50	Margaretha de Heer
1607–1678	Anna Maria van Schurman
1609–1660	Judith Leyster
1609/10–1696	Louise Moillon
active 1611–21	Clara Peeters
active 1614–73	Lucrina Fetti
1625–1651	Geertruydt Roghman
1630–1693	Maria van Oosterwijck
c.1630–1684	Josefa d'Ayala de Óbidos
active 1630s–1652	María Eugenia de Beer
1631–1690	Gesina ter Borch
1633–1699	Mary Beale
1638–1665	Elisabetta Sirani
active 1639–49	Josefa Sánchez
active 1642–59	Michaelina Woutier
1645–1703	Suor Maria de Dominici
1647–1717	Maria Sibylla Merian
1648–1711	Elisabeth-Sophie Chéron
c.1650–1710	Margherita Caffi
1652–1706	Luisa Roldán
1658–1716	Susanne Maria von Sandrart

1664–1750	Rachel Ruysch
1675–1757	Rosalba Carriera
1681–1747	Giulia Lama
1690–1763	Anna Maria Garthwaite
1693–1723	Margareta Haverman
1700–1788	Mary Delany
1706–1783	Barbara Regina Dietzsch
1709–1794	Hester Bateman
1713–1783	Anna Rosina Lisiewska
active c.1720–58	Elizabeth Godfrey
1721–1782	Anna Dorothea Lisiewska-Therbusch
1723–1778	Katharine Read
1725–1812	Susanna Duncombe
1725–1808	Theresa Concordia Maron-Mengs
1726–1778	Françoise Duparc
1729–1807	Louisa Courtauld
1734–1808	Lady Diana Beauclerk
1735–1796	Ulrica Fredrica Pasch
active 1737–79	Marie Anne Loir
1741–1807	Angelica Kauffman
1743–1813	Maria Margaretha La Fargue
1744–1819	Mary Moser
1744–1818	Anne Vallayer-Coster
1745–1834	Anne Forbes
1748–1821	Marie-Anne Collot
1748–1828	Anne Seymour Damer
1749–1803	Adélaïde Labille-Guiard
1754–1820	Marie-Victoire Lemoine
1755–1842	Elisabeth Vigée-Lebrun
1760–1838	Maria Cosway
1760/61–1814	Caroline Watson
1761–1818	Gabrielle Capet
1761–1837	Marguerite Gérard
1763–1825	Marie-Geneviève Bouliar
1767–1849	Constance Charpentier
1768–1826	Mme Benoist
1769–1849	Ellen Wallace Sharples
1770–1849	Eunice Pinney
1775–1835	Pauline Auzou
1775–1821	Constance Mayer
1778–1830	Teresa Benincampi
1781–1864	Caroline Bardua
1782–1855	Henryka Beyer
active 1785–1810	Nanine Vallain

1786–1866	Louise Seidler	1845–1932	Harriet Backer
1791–1863	Marie Ellenrieder	1845–1916	Tina Blau
1791–1878	Anna Claypoole Peale	1845–1892	Fanny Churberg
1793–1872	Margaret Carpenter	1845–1927	Maria Oakey Dewing
1793–1838	Rolinda Sharples	1845–1909	Louisa Starr
1796–1849	Lizinka de Mirbel	1846–1933	Lady Butler
1796–1854	Christina Robertson	1846–1901	Kate Greenaway
1797–1867	Sophie Rude	1846–1928	Madeleine-Jeanne Lemaire
1800–1885	Sarah Miriam Peale	1847–1939	Mary Louise McLaughlin
1801–1886	Felicie de Fauveau	1847–1914	Vinnie Ream
1803–1887	Margaret Gillies	1847–1926	Bertha Wegmann
active 1808–c.1829	Rebeccah Emes	active 1847–73	Susan Durant
1809–1895	Mary Thornycroft	1848–1926	Helen Allingham
1812–1895	Louisa Anne Meredith	1848–1936	Anna Boch
1813–1839	Princess Marie Christine d'Orléans	1848–1933	Lilla Cabot Perry
1814–1891	Amalia Lindegren	1848–1943	Sarah Purser
1814–1843	Rosario Weiss	1849–1883	Eva Gonzalès
1815–1879	Julia Margaret Cameron	1850–1898	Elena Polenova
1815–1882	Emma Stebbins	1851–1916	Hannah Bolton Barlow
1818–1891	Louisa, Marchioness of Waterford	1851–1938	Susan Macdowell Eakins
1819–1881	Elisabeth Jerichau Baumann	1851–1918	Thérèse Schwartze
1821–1909	Henriëtte Ronner-Knip	1852–1909	Laura Alma-Tadema
1821–1915	Anne Whitney	1852–1934	Gertrude Käsebier
1822–1899	Rosa Bonheur	1852–1936	Phoebe Traquair
1822–1865	Clementina, Viscountess Hawarden	1853–1933	Asta Nørregaard
1822–1902	Lilly Martin Spencer	1853–1928	Jane Sutherland
1823–1903	Sophie Anderson	1853–1928	Maria Wiik
1825–1909	Mme Léon Bertaux	1854–1946	Jenny Nyström
1827–1891	Barbara Leigh Smith Bodichon	1855–1909	Florence Elizabeth Barlow
1827–1888	Eléonore Escallier	1855–1942	Cecilia Beaux
1827–1923	Candace Wheeler	1855–1919	Evelyn De Morgan
1829–1915	Anna Blunden	1855–1940	Ellen Day Hale
1829–1901	Henriette Browne	1855–1931	Frida Hansen
1829–1862	Elizabeth Eleanor Siddal	1855–1922	Suze Robertson
1830–1908	Harriet Hosmer	1855–1927	Marianne Stokes
1831–1861	Joanna Boyce	1856–1927	Louise-Catherine Breslau
1831–1908	Mary Grant	1856–1927	Kate Bunce
1831–1867	Adelaide Ironside	1856–1942	Anna Klumpke
1832–1886	Rebecca Solomon	1857–1893	Anna Bilińska-Bohdanowicz
1832–1924	Henrietta Ward	1857–1954	Mary Sargant Florence
1833–1907	Elisabet Ney	1857–1912	Clara von Rappard
1834–after 1908	Emily Mary Osborn	1858–1927	Louise Abbéma
1836–1879	Marcello	1858–1946	Mary Fairchild MacMonnies
1837–1922	Elizabeth Gardner	1858–1932	Alice Barber Stephens
1840–1916	Marie Bracquemond	1859–1935	Anna Ancher
1840–after 1879	Florence Claxton	1859–1935	Virginie Demont-Breton
1840–1926	Victoria Dubourg	1859–1912	Elizabeth Forbes
1841–1895	Berthe Morisot	1859–1938	Elizabeth Nourse
1842–1928	Amalia Duprè	1859–1928	Henrietta Rae
1843–1894	Lucy Madox Brown	1860–1884	Marie Bashkirtseff
1843–1933	Louise Jopling	1860–1935	Oda Krohg
1843–1914	Kitty Kielland	1860–1961	Anna Mary Robertson Moses
1843–1896	Margaretha Roosenboom	1860–1938	Marianne Werefkin
1843–1927	Marie Spartali	1861–1951	Ethel Walker
1844–1923	Sarah Bernhardt	1862–1944	Hilma af Klint
1844–1926	Mary Cassatt	1862–1939	Fernanda Francés y Arribas
1844–1924	Marie Cazin	1862–1938	May Morris
1844–1930	Anna Lea Merritt	1862–1946	Helene Schjerfbeck
1844–1933	Annie Swynnerton	1862–1937	Agnes Slott-Møller
c.1844–after 1911	Edmonia Lewis	1863–1945	Anne Marie Carl Nielsen

1863–1955	May Guinness	1879–1979	Edna Clarke Hall
1863–1923	Vilma Parlaghy	1879–1970	Ida Kerkovius
1864–1943	Camille Claudel	1880–1967	Charlotte Berend-Corinth
1864–1927	Anna Golubkina	1880–1980	Harriet Whitney Frishmuth
1864–1940	Hanna Hirsch Pauli	1880–1943	Marie von Malachowski
1864–1952	Frances Benjamin Johnston	1881–1932	María Blanchard
1864–1933	Margaret Macdonald	1881–1962	Natalya Goncharova
1864–1948	Jessie Newbery	1881–1968	Sylvia Gosse
1865–1940	Olga Boznańska	1881–1948	Milly Steger
1865–1941	Elizaveta Kruglikova	1881–1965	Marta Worringer
1865–1929	Adelaide Alsop Robineau	1882–1949	Alexandra Exter
1865–1934	Margaret Olrog Stoddart	1882–1931	Norah Neilson Gray
1865–1938	Suzanne Valadon	1882–1978	Mary Swanzy
1866–1932	Jacqueline Marval	1883–1976	Imogen Cunningham
1866–1943	Beatrix Potter	1883–1956	Marie Laurencin
1867–1945	Käthe Kollwitz	1884–1945	Thérèse Lessore
1867–1940	Janet Scudder	1884–1977	Marg Moll
1868–1953	Grace Henry	1884–1967	Zinaida Serebryakova
1868–1965	Clara Pauline Barck Welles	1885–1979	Sonia Delaunay
1869–1947	Frances Hodgkins	1885–1939	Jessica Dismorr
1869–1958	Lucy Kemp-Welch	1885–1948	Sigrid Hjertén
1869–1945	Else Lasker-Schüler	1885–1966	Malvina Hoffman
1869–1904	Bessie MacNicol	1885–1963	Alexandra Povorina
1869–1954	Ellen Thesleff	1885–1957	Gwen Raverat
1870–1902	Marya Yakunchikova	1885–1933	Anita Rée
1871–1945	Emily Carr	1886–1973	Tarsila do Amaral
1871–1955	Anna Ostroumova-Lebedeva	1886–1963	Sofya Dymshits-Tolstaya
1871–1944	Florine Stettheimer	1886–1941	Olga Oppenheimer
1872–1945	Eleanor Fortescue Brickdale	1886–1918	Olga Rozanova
1872–1952	Ethel Fox	1886–1961	Nadezhda Udaltsova
1872–1955	Bessie Onahotema Potter Vonnoh	1887–1935	Clarice Beckett
1873–1921	Frances Macdonald	1887–1955	Wilhelmina Geddes
1874–1953	Elsa Beskow	1887–1968	Valentine Hugo
1874–1970	Romaine Brooks	1887–1986	Georgia O'Keeffe
1875–1949	Jessie M. King	1887–1968	Marguerite Thompson Zorach
1875–1963	Margaret Preston	active 1887–96	Elena Brockmann
1875–1942	Gertrude Vanderbilt Whitney	1888–1973	Siri Derkert
1876–1923	Jacoba van Heemskerck	1888–1979	Vera Nilsson
1876–1973	Anna Vaughn Hyatt Huntington	1888–1954	Astrid Noack
1876–1939	Gwen John	1888–1968	Chana Orloff
1876–1907	Paula Modersohn-Becker	1888–1965	Renée Sintenis
1876–1961	Coba Ritsema	1889–1978	Hannah Höch
1877–1924	Anna Julia De Graag	1889–1964	Anita Malfatti
1877–1968	Meta Vaux Warrick Fuller	1889–1953	Vera Mukhina
1877–1913	Elena Guro	1889–1924	Lyubov Popova
1877–1970	Laura Knight	1889–1966	Júliana Sveinsdóttir
1877–1962	Gabriele Münter	1889–1943	Sophie Taeuber-Arp
1877–1967	Lotte B. Prechner	1890–1956	Nina Hamnett
1877–1959	Anne Estelle Rice	1890–1976	Jeanne Mammen
1878–1968	Maria Caspar-Filser	1890–1958	Marlow Moss
1878–1974	Emilie Charmy	1890–1971	Emy Roeder
1878–1942	Abastenia St Leger Eberle	1890–1962	Marta Skulme
1878–1964	Letitia Hamilton	1891–1951	Dorrit Black
1878–1963	Sella Hasse	1891–1964	Katharina Heise
1878–1967	Elena Makovskaya-Luksch	1891–1976	Zofia Stryjeńska
1878–1932	Jane Poupelet	1891–1978	Alma W. Thomas
1878–1954	Clara Rilke-Westhoff	1891–1955	Charley Toorop
1878–1947	Kathleen Scott	1891–1956	Cecile Walton
1878–1951	Pamela Colman Smith	1891–1979	Denise Wren
1879–1961	Vanessa Bell	1892–1942	Natalya Danko

1892–1957	Gela Forster	1900–1988	Louise Nevelson
1892–1980	Dorothy Johnstone	1900–1981	Mary Potter
1892–1967	Sarra Lebedeva	1900–1983	Charmion von Wiegand
1892–1984	Marevna	1901–	Norah Braden
1892–1972	Dod Procter	1901–1994	Dorothy Dehner
1892–1966	Ruth Reeves	1901–1983	Gertrude Hermes
1892–1962	Augusta Savage	1901–1967	Alexandra Luke
1892–1967	Aleksandra Shchekatikhina-Pototskaya	1901–1987	Else Meidner
1892–1984	Grace Cossington Smith	1901–1983	Lisette Model
1892–1984	Paule Vézelay	1902–1988	Isabel Bishop
1893–1983	Marianne Brandt	1902–1992	Trude Brück
1893–1932	Carrington	1902–1989	Hanna Cauer
1893–1958	Mathilde Flögl	1902–1995	Susie Cooper
1893–1946	Wanda Gág	1902–1987	Raquel Forner
1893–1982	Florence Henri	1902–1994	Louise Henderson
1893–1971	Maria Likarz-Strauss	1902–1995	Maruja Mallo
1893–1981	Winifred Nicholson	1902–	Enid Marx
1893–1938	Vera Yermolayeva	1902–1971	I. Rice Pereira
1894–1954	Claude Cahun	1902–1983	Hans Anton Prinner
1894–1955	Evie Hone	1902–1959	Germaine Richier
1894–1989	Lucia Moholy	1902–1995	Lucie Rie
1894–1974	Regina	1902–1980	Toyen
1894–1970	Hannah Ryggen	c.1902–1955	María Izquierdo
1894–1958	Varvara Stepanova	1903–1982	Joyce Clissold
1894–1966	Irma Stern	1903–1975	Barbara Hepworth
1894–1981	Agnes Tait	1903–1980	Norah McGuinness
1894–1980	Anna Ticho	1903–	Isabel McLaughlin
1895–1971	Ella Bergmann-Michel	1903–1984	Ethel Schwabacher
1895–1989	Louise Dahl-Wolfe	1904–1971	Margaret Bourke-White
1895–1978	Gluck	1904–1956	Gertrude Greene
1895–1975	Alice Halicka	1904–1982	Nadia Khodossievitch
1895–1965	Dorothea Lange	1904–1971	Alice Trumbull Mason
1895–1985	Katharine Pleydell-Bouverie	1904–1987	Alice Rahon
1895–1965	Anne Redpath	1905–	Lois Mailou Jones
1895–1945	Vally Wieselthier	1906–1988	Ithell Colquhoun
1896–1964	Marion Dorn	1906–1977	Lea Grundig
1896–1990	Lotte Jacobi	1906–1996	Marie-Louise von Motesiczky
1896–1942	Tina Modotti	1906–	Eva Zeisel
1896–1968	Amelia Peláez	1907–1982	Gudrun Baudisch
1897–1977	Benedetta	1907–1954	Frida Kahlo
1897–1980	Hilde Goldschmidt	1907–	Dora Maar
1897–1944	Mainie Jellett	1907–1969	Mary Martin
1897–1983	Gunta Stölzl	1907–1977	Lee Miller
1898–1991	Berenice Abbott	1907–1975	Hanna Nagel
1898–1933	Aenne Biermann	1907–	Lenore Tawney
1898–1951	Katarzyna Kobro	1908–1970	Rita Angus
1898–1993	Lotte Laserstein	1908–	Claire Falkenstein
1898–1980	Tamara de Lempicka	1908–1996	Leonor Fini
1898–1977	Gerta Overbeck	1908–1984	Lee Krasner
1898–1963	Kay Sage	1908–	Helen Lundeberg
c.1898–1991	Dora Gordine	1908–1963	Remedios Varo
1899–1991	Eileen Agar	1908–1992	Maria Elena Vieira da Silva
1899–1994	Anni Albers	1909–	Lucienne Bloch
1899–1986	Franciska Clausen	1909–1970	Marion Greenwood
1899–1973	Majlis Grotell	1909–1961	Lisbet Jobs
1899–1981	Grethe Jürgens	1909–	Loren MacIver
1899–1940	Elfriede Lohse-Wächtler	1909–1948	Gunnel Nyman
1900–1957	Erika Giovanna Klien	1910–	Dorothea Tanning
1900–1973	Maria Martins	1911–	Louise Bourgeois
1900–1984	Alice Neel	1911–1984	Sonja Ferlov

1912–	Wilhelmina Barns-Graham	1930–	Niki de Saint Phalle
1912–	Agnes Martin	c.1930–	Lygia Pape
1912–	Angeles Santos Torroella	1931–	Elizabeth Blackadder
1913–1988	Marie-Anne Lansiaux	1931–	Lee Bontecou
1913–1985	Meret Oppenheim	1931–1979	Sheila Fell
1913–1941	Amrita Sher-Gil	1931–	Audrey Flack
1913–1968	Nína Tryggvadóttir	1931–	Vivian Lynn
1913–	Gertrud Vasegaard	1931–	Bridget Riley
1914–	Anita Hoy	1931–	Joyce Wieland
1914–1996	Gocken Jobs	1932–	Anne Madden
1914–	Margaret Mellis	1932–1984	Tilsa Tsuchiya
1915–	Elizabeth Catlett	1933–	Chryssa
1915–	Natalia Dumitrescu	1933–	Betty LaDuke
1915–1981	Kyllikki Salmenhaara	1933–	Michelle Stuart
1915–1989	Betty Swanwick	1934–	Sheila Hicks
1916–	Sylvia Sleigh	1934–	Bea Maddock
1916–1970	Unica Zürn	1934–	Yvonne Rainer
1917–	Leonora Carrington	1934–	Dorothea Rockburne
1917–	Louisa Matthiasdóttir	1934–1992	Jo Spence
1917–1943	Charlotte Salomon	c.1934–	Mary Beth Edelson
1918–	Gutte Eriksen	1935–	Eleanor Antin
1918–	Carol Rama	1935–	Gwyn Hanssen Pigott
1918–	Pablita Velarde	1935–	Paula Rego
1918–	June Wayne	1935–	Kay WalkingStick
1919–	Prunella Clough	1936–1970	Eva Hesse
1919–1989	Elaine de Kooning	1936–	Joan Jonas
1919–	Ruth Duckworth	1936–	Kim Lim
1919–	Maria Lassnig	1936–	Gillian Lowndes
1919–1982	María Luisa Pacheco	1936–1977	Ree Morton
1919–1988	Mira Schendel	1937–	Tess Jaray
1920–1988	Lygia Clark	1937–	Ann Wolff
1920–1960	Joy Hester	1938–	Vija Celmins
1920–1979	Molly Macalister	1938–	Lena Cronqvist
1921–1963	Joan Eardley	1938–	Janet Fish
1921–1993	Ghisha Koenig	1938–	Ulrica Hydman-Vallien
1922–	Grace Hartigan	1938–	Sylvia Plimack Mangold
1923–1971	Diane Arbus	1938–	Monica Sjöö
1923–	Miriam Schapiro	1939–	Barbara Chase-Riboud
1924–	Carla Accardi	1939–	Judy Chicago
1924–	Jaroslava Brychtová	1939–	Rita Donagh
1924–	Mimi Parent	1939–	Liliane Lijn
1924–	Beverly Pepper	1939–1990	Gina Pane
1924–	May Stevens	1939–	Deanna Petherbridge
1925–	Sandra Blow	1939–	Wendy Ramshaw
1926–	Bona	1939–	Carolee Schneemann
1926–1992	Joan Mitchell	1939–	Clarissa Sligh
1926–	Jacqueline Morreau	1940–	Vivienne Binns
1926–	Betye Saar	1940–	Beverly Buchanan
1926–	Nancy Spero	1940–	Elizabeth Fritsch
1927–	Gerda Flöckinger	1940–1995	Nancy Graves
1928–	Helen Frankenthaler	1940–	Elizabeth Murray
1929–	Ida Applebroog	1940–	Jaune Quick-to-See Smith
1929–	Jacqueline Fahey	1940–	Joan Snyder
1929–	Jackie Ferrara	1940–	Pat Steir
1929–	Evelyn Williams	1940–1993	Hannah Wilke
1930–	Magdalena Abakanowicz	1941–	Jennifer Bartlett
1930–	Gillian Ayres	1941–	Lynda Benglis
1930–1993	Elizabeth Frink	1941–	Hanne Darboven
1930–	Marisol	1941–	Mary Kelly
1930–	Faith Ringgold	1941–	Jackie Winsor

1942–	Susan Hiller	1943–	Martha Rosler
1942–	Joyce Kozloff	1944–	Glenys Barton
1942–	Janice Tchalenko	1944–	Harmony Hammond
1942–	Ursula von Rydingsvard	1944–	Rebecca Horn
1942–	Ruth Weisberg	1944–	Mary Miss
1943–	Gretchen Albrecht	1945–	Maggi Hambling
1943–	Diana Hobson	1945–	Valerie Jaudon
1943–	Annette Messager	1945–	Barbara Kruger
1943–	Ana Maria Pacheco	1945–	Susan Rothenberg
1943–	Howardena Pindell	1945–	Dana Zámečniková

PREFACE

Why a dictionary of women artists at this time?

This dictionary embodies the vast shift that has occurred over the past 25 years concerning our knowledge and interpretation of women as artistic producers. By its size, scope, depth and breadth it obviates the question asked by Linda Nochlin in 1971: "Why have there been no great women artists?"[1] Even a cursory glance through its pages reveals that since the Middle Ages women have, indeed, been active makers of art in diverse media and geographical locales. Our purpose here is to consolidate and make available to both researchers and students the wealth of information that has been uncovered and recovered, as scholars have attempted to write women artists back into art history.

The scope of this work is limited to the Western tradition, from the medieval to the modern periods, including persons born before 1945; those born later have been omitted for practical reasons. Several hundred artists are presented in individual entries of varying lengths, incorporating details of their biographies and assessment of their art, as well as basic bibliographical information and exhibition chronology. The *Dictionary* also contains some 20 introductory surveys in order to contextualise these individual entries. These surveys differ somewhat in purpose and scope, depending on their subject. While the dictionary includes entries on women photographers and those who worked in the so-called applied arts, its emphasis is most definitely on painters and sculptors. Architects and interior designers, for example, have been omitted, not because of some judgement about the worthiness of their contribution, but rather to keep the scope of the project manageable. Likewise, the inclusion of only a few women who have worked in the more traditionally "female" areas such as needlework should be interpreted as the result of logistical constraints.

Our primary aim in this volume is historical, not theoretical. Nevertheless, it would be useful to present, at the outset, a brief overview of the process by which women artists and their artistic productions have been made visible over the past 25 years. In her discussion of the multi-faceted impact of writing women into history, Joan Wallach Scott said that "the effort goes far beyond the naive search for the heroic ancestors of the contemporary women's movement to a re-evaluation of established standards of historical significance".[2] While the first investigations by art historians mostly consisted of the search for "lost" women artists, as in analogous research by historians and literary critics, subsequent analyses have questioned or revised the basic paradigms of art history. Their primary purpose was the collection of information that established women as producers of art, and these early endeavours accepted as given a fixed "canon" of artists, a traditional subdivision of art-historical "periods" and conventional categories of appropriate artistic practice. Such an approach illustrates the limitations of the process of recovery, according to Scott, which fails to bring about any real change in the conventional historical (or in this case art-historical) narrative.[3] As Peggy McIntosh has asserted, this historical method is problematic because it "assumes that the discipline is perfect as constructed" and that "women don't count" except for those few who have achieved within it.[4]

Subsequent analyses looked to social factors that might have accounted for women's exclusion from the art-historical canon. One critical stance emphasised women's hardships and exclusions – their "struggles" as they pursued the "obstacle race".[5] In the introduction to her book of this title, Germaine Greer says that her intention is to show how women artists as a "group" were "tormented by the same conflicts of motivation and the same practical difficulties, the obstacles both external and surmountable, internal and insurmountable of the race for achievement".[6] At this stage, women artists were perceived as a universal cohort whose difference from the "norm" was constructed as a liability. Their differing position was problematic: the disadvantages of women artists were stressed and women artists were perceived as "victims" of a misogynistic system. One drawback of this stage of historical analysis is that it leads to anger and resentment,[7] and while observation of the cultural barriers to women's achievement encourages us to question the construction of the canon, it does not necessarily revise it. Instead, it tends to ghetto-ise women's accomplishments, still considering them as exceptions, as outside the norm.

Like their counterparts in historical and literary analysis, more recent art-historical reassessments have focused on the social construction of gender, the "comparative location and activities of men and women … [and] what representations of sexual difference suggest about the structure of social, economic and political authority".[8] Critics and historians have emphasised the actual achievements of women artists, understanding that "since there have always been women artists, the issue is … how they worked despite these restraints".[9] Taking into account that women's cultural positions differed from those of their male counterparts, researchers have identified how artists adopted "enabling strategies" that allowed them to work when they found their gender in conflict with accepted conventions about the nature of art and its culturally sanctioned producers.[10] Furthermore, when viewed from this perspective, the production of women artists, which often differed from that of canonical male artists, forces contemporary scholars to reassess that canon and its assumptions. Scott's discussion regarding the "usefulness" of gender as a historical category is absolutely to the point here. As she says:

> feminist desires to make woman a historical subject cannot be realized simply by making her the agent or principal character of a historical narrative. To discover where women have been throughout history it is necessary to examine what gender and sexual difference have had to do with the workings of power.

She continues:

> the realization of the radical potential of women's history comes in the writing of narratives that focus on women's experience and analyze the ways in which politics construct gender and gender constructs politics. Female agency then becomes not the recounting of great deeds performed by women, but the exposure of the often silent and hidden operations of gender which are nonetheless present and defining forces of politics and political life.[11]

While this volume, with its chronological orientation, its periodic surveys and its biographical organisation might seem to be a product of the older approach in which women are made "historical subjects" and their "great deeds" are emphasised, in actuality it exemplifies the more sophisticated methodology in which discrete events are carefully examined through the lens of gender. No attempt has been made to "fit" the artists discussed herein into a pre-packaged canon of artistic "greats". No attempt is made to create an alternative canon of "great" women artists. While the canon itself is not questioned from a polemical stance, the essays in this volume look at the specifics of the circumstances under which women engaged in art. In that way the presence of women practitioners is written back into the history of art. And at the same time a more accurate sense of such questions as how the art market functioned, or what standards were prevalent at different times, is communicated.

Thus, one could say that simply by its weight the information herein challenges conventional readings of art history. First, the *Dictionary* makes very clear that women always were involved in the production of art in some way. It is also clear that there were a good number of women artists and patrons who achieved a certain amount of repute during their lifetimes. Furthermore, the analyses are specific and take their subjects on their own terms, without trying to fit the artists into a pre-existing paradigm. By considering, instead, the specific circumstances under which women made art they conclude, along with Annemarie Weyl Carr regarding women as artists during the Middle Ages, that the "dark is light enough". The forceful, but previously unacknowledged presence of women during that allegedly unenlightened period provides a good illustration of how the work encompassed in this volume expands our understanding of the role of women in the production of art. Contrary to popular misconception, during the medieval period many women were prominent cultural patrons. Furthermore, although a signature need not imply authorship in the way we would conceive it, at that time patrons played a more active role in the conception of works of art. As Carr and her associates also point out, the materials of high art differed during that period, so that two sisters noted for their work in gold and gems were not "minor" artists, as a contemporary bias would seem to indicate; rather they were working with the most valued media of their time. Additionally, women's names appear in guild lists consistently, particularly those associated with the production of textiles, also not merely a "decorative" art. By looking beyond the established art-historical preconceptions of what constituted art and art-making, the actual contributions of numerous women artists can now be chronicled.

But if women artists were there all along, how could it be that their accomplishments are only now being recovered? This volume also helps to answer and explain this predicament. Although women did play a more active role in the production of art than they have been traditionally granted – and many achieved high status within their lifetimes – this volume documents the very real cultural and institutional impediments that have prevented women as a group from being on "equal" terms with their male counterparts. Women could not study from live models until the end of the 19th century, so they were precluded from practising history painting, then viewed as the ultimate in the hierarchy of artistic worthiness.[12] The woman who was able to have access to the necessary education to compete in that arena was the exception. This explains why, as Nochlin observed at the outset, so many early women artists were the daughters of artists who were able to learn their crafts through their fathers. In all centuries from the 15th through the 18th there are instances of women who gained access to artistic education through the position and influence of their fathers (or other family members), which opened a route that would not have been otherwise available to them. The necessity for male protection or patronage continued, actually, into the 20th century, when women artists gained access to public forums through the influence of a spouse or a lover whose high status in the art world helped her career to progress.

Although, in actuality, women produced art during all post-medieval periods, their presence as creators with authority equivalent to that of their male counterparts was only grudgingly acknowledged in the public discourse. Women artists were constructed as "different" from their male colleagues, who constituted the norm while the woman of achievement was considered exceptional. The complicated and persistent attempts to exclude women from the academies or to limit their membership, as discussed in the survey on Academies of Art, provide an excellent case in point. The academies were agencies of both education and legitimisation, whose "overriding concern was to raise the dignity of the profession". Women were excluded from full participation in most major European academies from the Renaissance through the 19th century via several different strategies. When women were allowed membership in an academy at all their fellow academicians took steps to ensure that they would comprise only a small fraction of the membership, as in the Académie Royale de Peinture et de Sculpture in France, which agreed in 1770 to receive no more than four women at one time (and hastened to point out that they were in no way obliged to fulfil that entire number). Furthermore, women were often accorded different status that prohibited them from being perceived as "true" members that held the same standards as their male counterparts. In the French Academy, for example, female academicians were not allowed to take the same public oaths as men, and were thus perceived as "foreign in some fashion to its constitution".

The gendered nature of artistic practice has also hindered the ability of women to produce art with significant impact in the public sphere. The post-Renaissance construction of the concept of "artist" has been gendered as male, whether conceived in Renaissance terms as the genius reflecting God's genius or in the 19th-century context of the bohemian who expresses his scorn for the bourgeoisie by having numerous sexual exploits.[13] According to the 18th-century system of aesthetics, the work of women was delicate – the pleasing – whereas that of men was powerful – the sublime. The nature of high art has also been gendered, as has the classification of the relative worthiness of various genres of painting. From the 16th to the 19th centuries paintings whose subjects were drawn from history and mythology were deemed to be more "important" art productions than landscapes, portraiture or still lifes, lesser subjects because they focused on the specific, the individual or the domestic. When this model changed during the latter part of the 19th century, and artists were exhorted to find their subject matter in "modern life", for the most part that implied the modern city to which women did not have the same access as men. During the 20th century abstraction, "pure art", was given a higher worth than art with residual narrative content; this way of seeing was also gendered. Finally, as time progressed from the Middle Ages to the present day, the rift between high art and the so-called crafts has widened. Those areas in which women had long excelled – such as needlework – were devalued accordingly. The Arts and Crafts movements of the later part of the 19th century were a solid attempt to return to a more medieval convention, not only in stylistic motifs, but in terms of recognising the "artfulness" that could characterise various objects of use.

These very real impediments explain how a conventional history of art that excluded the presence of women could have been written. Because the contributors to this *Dictionary* have taken a nuanced regard of history, a picture of women's place within it is allowed to emerge: "the rich world that is revealed when you look at women's lives starting from women's own ground, rather than assuming that we are victims or deprived".[14] The space in which women were active as creators, patrons and entrepreneurs in a variety of traditional and non-traditional media is opened up and made visible. In so doing, a different response to Nochlin's question is provided, one that makes clear that perhaps the long-accepted parameters for assessing "great" art and artists are not strictly or unilaterally valid, nor do they give the most full and subtle interpretation of the historical data.

MARA R. WITZLING

Notes

[1] Linda Nochlin, "Why have there been no great women artists?", *Woman in Sexist Society: Studies in Power and Powerlessness,* ed. Vivian Gornick and Barbara K. Moran, New York: Basic Books, 1971; reprinted in *Women, Art and Power and Other Essays,* New York: Harper, and London: Thames and Hudson, 1988, pp.145–78. Nochlin's essay and the question it asks has stood as a benchmark for the feminist reassessment of art history. Numerous subsequent writers have used this question as the starting point of their investigations, which over the years have pushed its boundaries, showing why other questions need to be asked. Nochlin herself has pointed out that other questions are more relevant and productive. None the less, if one could cite a starting point for the project on which all others are based – this is it.

[2] Joan Wallach Scott, "Women in history: The modern period", *Past and Present,* no.101, November 1983, p.145.

[3] *ibid.,* p.147.

[4] Peggy McIntosh, "Interactive phases of curricular re-vision: A feminist perspective", *Traditions and Translations: Women's Studies and a Balanced Curriculum,* conference held at Claremont College, CA, February 1983, p.26.

[5] Germaine Greer, *The Obstacle Race: The Fortunes of Women Painters and Their Work,* London: Secker and Warburg, and New York: Farrar Straus, 1979. Greer mentions Nochlin's essay specifically, and says that it asks a "false question". According to Greer, the real questions are "What is the contribution of women to the visual arts?" "If there were any women artists, why were there not more?" "If we can find one good painting by a woman, where is the rest of her work?" "How good were the women who earned a living by painting?"

[6] *ibid.,* p.6.

[7] McIntosh op. cit., p.27.

[8] Scott op. cit., p.153.

[9] Rozsika Parker and Griselda Pollock, *Old Mistresses: Women, Art and Ideology,* London and New York: Routledge, 1981. Parker and Pollock make this statement in response to Nochlin's assertion, as they characterise it, that "institutional restraints were responsible for women's 'problems' in art practice".

[10] Griselda Pollock's essay "Modernity and the spaces of femininity" in *Vision and Difference: Femininity, Feminism and the Histories of Art* (London and New York: Routledge, 1988) is an early example of a study of women artists' positional negotiations. The term "enabling strategies" is used by Bridget Elliot and Jo-Ann Wallace in *Women Artists and Writers: Modern (Im)Positionings* (London and New York: Routledge, 1994) with reference to the "diverse strategies" developed by women artists "for negotiating what were unequal, and thus frequently uneasy, relationships with their male modernist counterparts" (p.17).

[11] Scott op. cit., p.156.

[12] Nochlin calls attention to this institutional barrier in her germinal article cited above: "By examining in detail a single deprivation or disadvantage, the unavailability of the nude model, I have suggested that it was indeed made institutionally impossible for women to achieve artistic excellence or success on the same footing as men" (p.176).

[13] For a history of the conflation of genius and masculinity that extends back to the Roman empire, see Christina Battersby, *Gender and Genius: Towards a Feminist Aesthetic,* Bloomington: Indiana University Press, 1989.

[14] McIntosh op. cit., p.32.

GENERAL BIBLIOGRAPHY

Compiled by Michelle L. Weber

1. General Reference (dictionaries, bibliographies and indices)

Aa, Abraham Jacob van der, *Biographisch woordeboek der Nederlanden*, Haarlem: Van Brederode, 1852–78; reprinted Amsterdam: Isräel, 1969

AHIP, *Getty Union List of Artists Names (ULAN)*, Vocabulary Coordination Group, Getty Art History Information Program, Boston: Hall, 1994

AKL, *Allgemeines Künstlerlexikon: Die bildenden Künstler aller eiten und Völker*, Leipzig: Seemann, 1983–

Aldana Fernández, Salvador, *Guía abreviada de artistas valencianos*, Valencia: Ayuntamiento de Valencia, 1970

Allgemeine deutsche Biographie, Leipzig: Duncker und Humbolt, 1875–1912

American Art Annual, 37 vols, New York and Washington, DC: American Federation of Arts, 1898–1948 (vol.27, 1930: *Biographical Directories of Craftsmen and Designers and Pictorial Photographers*; vol.30, 1933: *Biographical Directory of American Painters and Sculptors*)

American Women: 1500 Biographies, New York: Mast Crowell Kirkpatrick, 1897; reprinted Detroit: Gale Research, 1973

Andresen, Andreas, *Der deutsche Peintre-Graveur, oder, Die deutschen Maler als Kupferstecher, nach ihrem Leben und ihren Werken, von dem letzten Drittel des 16. Jahrhunderts bis zum Schluss des 18. Jahrhunderts, und in Anschluss an Bartsch's Peintre-graveur*, 5 vols, Leipzig: Weigel Danz, 1864–78; reprinted New York: Collectors' Editions, 1969; Hildesheim: Olms, 1973

Archibald, Edward H.H., *Dictionary of Sea Painters*, 2nd edition, Woodbridge, Suffolk: Antique Collectors' Club, 1989

Arntz, Wilhelm F., *Verzeichnis der seit 1945 erschienenen Werkkataloge zur Kunst des 20. Jahrhunderts*, The Hague: Arntz-Winter, 1975

Artists Directory, Covering Painters, Sculptors and Engravers, New Delhi: Lalit Kala Akademi, 1966[?]

Artists in Canada: A Union List of Artists' Files/Artistes au Canada: Une liste collective des dossiers d'artistes, Ottawa: Library, National Gallery of Canada, 1988

Australian Art: Artists Working Names Authority List, Canberra: Australian National Gallery, 1990

Auvray, Louis and Emile Bellier de la Chauvignerie, *Dictionnaire général des artistes de l'école française*, 2 vols, Paris: Renouard, 1882–5; supplement, 1887; reprinted New York: Garland, 1979

Bailey, Joyce W., ed., *Handbook of Latin American Art/Manual de arte latino americano*, 2 vols, Oxford and Santa Barbara, CA: ABC-Clio Information Services, 1984

Balteau, J., Michel Barroux and M. Prévost, eds, *Dictionnaire de biographie française*, Paris: Letouzey et Ane, 1933–

Bartsch, Adam von, *Le Peintre graveur*, 21 vols, Vienna: Degen, 1803–21; reprinted Leipzig: Barth, 1854–76; Hildesheim: Olms, 1970

Baudicour, Prosper de, *Le Graveur français continué, ou catalogue raisonné des estampes gravées par les peintres et les dessinateurs de l'école française nés dans le XVIIIe siècle*, 2 vols, Paris: Bouchard Huzard Rapilly, 1859–61; reprinted Paris: de Nobele, 1967

Bazin, Germain and others, eds, *Kindler's Malereilexikon*, 6 vols, Zürich: Kindler, 1964–71

Bellori, Giovanni P., *Le vite de' pittori, scultori et architetti moderni*, Turin: Einaudi, 1976

Bénézit, Emmanuel, *Dictionnaire critique et documentaire des peintres, sculpteurs, dessinateurs et graveurs*, revised edition, 10 vols, Paris: Librairie Gründ, 1976

Berko, Patrick and Vivian Berko, *Dictionary of Belgian Painters Born Between 1750 and 1875*, Brussels: Laconti, 1981

Berman, Esmé, *Art and Artists of South Africa: An Illustrated Biographical Dictionary and Historical Survey of Painters and Graphic Artists Since 1875*, Cape Town and Rotterdam: Balkema, 1974

Bernt, Walther, *Die niederländischen Maler und Zeichner des 17. Jahrhunderts*, Munich: Bruckmann, 1979–80

Bessone-Aurelj, Antonietta M., *Dizionario degli scultori ed architetti italiani*, Genoa: Alighieri, 1947

——, *Dizionario dei pittori italiani*, 2nd edition, Milan: Lapi, 1928

Bihalji-Merin, Oto and Tomasevic Nebebojsa-Bato, *World Encyclopedia of Naive Art: A Hundred Years of Naive Art*, London: Muller, 1984

The Biographical Cyclopaedia of American Women, vol.1, compiled by Mabel Ward Cameron, New York: Halvord, 1924; vol.2, compiled by Erma Conkling Lee, New York: Lee, 1925; reprinted Detroit: Gale Research, 1974

Biographie nationale publiée par l'Académie royale des sciences, des lettres et des beaux-arts de Belgique, Brussels: Thiry-van Buggenhoudt, 1866–

Biro, Adam and René Passeron, eds, *Dictionnaire générale du surréalisme et de ses environs*, Fribourg: Office du Livre, 1982

Blas, J.I. de, ed., *Pintores españoles contemporáneos desde 1881, nacimiento de Picasso: Diccionario*, Madrid: Estiarte, [1972]

Blättel, Harry, *International Dictionary Miniature Painters, Porcelain Painters, Silhouettists/Internationales Lexikon Miniatur-Maler, Porzellan-Maler, Silhouettisten/Dictionnaire international peintres miniaturistes, peintres sur porcelaine, silhouettistes*, Munich: Art & Antiques, 1992

Bonafons, Louis A. [Abbé de Fontenai], *Dictionnaire des artistes*, 2 vols. Paris: Vincent, 1776; reprinted Geneva: Minkoff, 1972

Bradley, John W., *A Dictionary of Miniaturists, Illuminators, Calligraphers and Copyists, with References to Their Works and Notices of Their Patrons, from the Establishment of Christianity to the Eighteenth Century*, New York: Franklin, 1958

Breeze, George, *Society of Artists in Ireland, Index of Exhibits, 1765–1780*, Dublin: National Gallery of Ireland, 1985

Brenzoni, Raffaello, *Dizionario di artisti veneti: Pittori, scultori, architetti, ecc. dal XIII al XVIII secolo*, Florence: Olschki, 1972

British Artists Authority List, Developed by the Yale Center for British Art, Photograph Archive, New Haven: Yale Center for British Art, Photograph Archive, 1988

British Printmakers, 1855–1955: A Century of Printmaking from the Etching Revival to St Ives, Wiltshire: Garton/Scolar Press, 1992

Browne, Turner and Elaine Partnow, *Macmillan Biographical Encyclopedia of Photographic Artists and Innovators*, New York and London: Macmillan, 1983

Brun, Carl, *Schweizerisches Künstlerlexikon*, 4 vols, Frauendeld: Huber, 1905–17; reprinted New York and Nendeln, Liechtenstein: Kraus, 1982

Bryan, Michael, *A Biographical and Critical Dictionary of Painters and Engravers*, 2 vols, London: Carpenter, 1816

——, *Dictionary of Painters and Engravers*, ed. George Williams, 5 vols, New York: Macmillan, 1903

Bryant, Mark and Simon Heneage, *Dictionary of British Cartoonists and Caricatures, 1730–1980*, Aldershot: Scolar Press, 1994

Burbidge, Robert Brinsley, *Dictionary of British Flower, Fruit and Still-Life Artists*, 2 vols, Leigh-on-Sea, Essex: Lewis, 1974

Buscombe, Eve, *Artists in Early Australia and Their Portraits: A Guide to the Portrait Painters of Early Australia*, Sydney: Eureka Research, 1978

Busse, Joachim, *Internationales Handbuch aller Maler und Bildhauer des 19. Jahrhunderts*, Wiesbaden: Busse Kunst Dokumentation, 1977

Camard, Jean-Pierre and Anne-Marie Belfort, *Dictionnaire des peintres et sculpteurs provençaux, 1880–1950*, [n.p.]: Bendor, [1975]

Campbell, Jean, *Australian Watercolour Painters*, Sydney: Eureka Research, 1983

Campoy, Antonio Manuel, *Diccionario crítico del arte español contemporáneo*, Madrid: Ibérico Europea, 1973

Caplan, Hillier H., *The Classified Directory of Artists' Signatures, Symbols and Monograms*, revised edition, Detroit: Gale Research, 1982

Ceán Bermudez, Juan A., *Diccionario histórico de los más ilustres profesores de las bellas artes en España*, 6 vols, Madrid: Ibarra, 1800; reprinted New York and Nendeln, Liechtenstein: Kraus, 1965

Cederholm, Theresa Dickason, *Afro-American Artists: A Bio-Bibliographical Directory*, Boston: Trustees of the Boston Public Library, 1973

Columbia University Libraries, Avery Architectural Library, *Avery Obituary Index of Architects and Artists*, 2nd edition, Boston: Hall, 1980

Comanducci, Agostino Mario, *Dizionario illustrato dei pittori, disegnatori e incisori italiani moderni e contemporanei*, Milan: Petruzzi, 1970–74

——, *I pittori italiani dell'ottocento: Dizionario critico e documentario*, 2 vols, Milan: Casa Editrice Artisti d'Italia, 1934; reprinted Milan: San Gottardo, 1991

Crespi, Luigi, *Vite de' pittori bolognesi*, Rome: Carlo Emmanuele III, 1769

Crookshank, Anne and the Knight of Glin, *The Painters of Ireland, c.1600–1920*, London: Barrie and Jenkins, 1978; 2nd edition, 1979

Cummings, Paul, *Dictionary of Contemporary American Artists*, New York: St Martin's Press, 1988

Darmstaedter, Robert, *Reclam's Künstlerlexikon*, Stuttgart: Reclam, 1979

Davis, Lenwood G. and Janet L. Sims, *Black Artists in the United States: An Annotated Bibliography of Books, Articles and Dissertations on Black Artists, 1779–1979*, Westport, CT: Greenwood Press, 1980

Dawdy, Doris Ostrander, *Artists of the American West: A Biographical Dictionary*, Chicago: Swallow Press, 1974–85

Delteil, Loÿs, *Le Peintre-graveur illustré*, 31 vols, Paris: Delteil, 1906–30

Dicionário brasileiro de artistas plásticos, 4 vols, Brasília: Instituto Nacional do Livro, 1973–80

Dick, Jutta and Marina Sassenberg, *Jüdische Frauen im 19. und 20. Jahrhundert*, Reinbek bei Hamburg: Rowohlt, 1993

Dictionary of American Biography, New York: Scribner, 1928–

Dictionary of International Biography, London: Dictionary of International Biography, 1963–

The Dictionary of National Biography, Oxford: Oxford University Press, 1917–

Dictionnaire biographique des artistes belges de 1830 à 1970, Brussels: Arto, 1978

Dictionnaire biographique du Canada, Toronto: University of Toronto Press, 1966

Dictionnaire biographique illustré des artistes en Belgique depuis 1830, Brussels: Arto, 1978

Dictionnaire universel de la peinture, Paris: Le Robert, 1975

Dizionario biografico degli italiani, Rome: Istituto dell'enciclopedia italiana, 1960–

Dizionario degli artisti italiani del XX secolo, Turin: Bolaffi, 1979

Dizionario enciclopedico Bolaffi dei pittori e degli incisori italiani, dall'XI al XX secolo, Turin: Bolaffi, 1972–6

Dolman, Bernard, *A Dictionary of Contemporary British Artists*, 2nd edition, London: Art Trade Press, 1929; reprinted Woodbridge, Suffolk: Antique Collectors' Club, 1981

Edouard-Joseph, René, *Dictionnaire biographique des artistes contemporains, 1910–1930*, 3 vols, Paris: Art et Edition, 1931–3; supplement, 1936

Emanuel, Muriel and others, eds, *Contemporary Artists*, 2nd edition, New York and London: Macmillan, 1983

Engen, Rodney K., *Dictionary of Victorian Engravers, Print Publishers and Their Works*, Cambridge: Chadwyck-Healey, 1979

——, *Dictionary of Wood Engravers*, Cambridge: Chadwyck-Healey, 1985

Fielding, Mantle, *Mantle Fielding's Dictionary of American Painters, Sculptors and Engravers*, revised edition, ed. Glenn B. Opitz, Poughkeepsie, NY: Apollo, 1987

Findlay, James A., *Modern Latin American Art: A Bibliography*, Westport, CT, and London: Greenwood Press, 1983

Fisher, Stanley W., *A Dictionary of Watercolour Painters, 1750–1900*, London and New York: Foulsham, 1972

Fleming, John and Hugh Honour, *The Penguin Dictionary of Decorative Arts*, London: Allen Lane, 1977

Flippo, Willem G., *Lexicon of the Belgian Romantic Painters*, Antwerp: International Art Press, 1981

Forschungsunternehmen der Fritz Thyssen Stiftung, *Bibliographie zur Kunstgeschichte des 19. Jahrhunderts: Publikationen der Jahre 1940–1966*, ed. Hilda Lietzmann, Munich: Prestel, 1968

——, *Bibliographie zur Kunstgeschichte des 19. Jahrhunderts: Publikationen der Jahre 1967–1979, mit Nachträgen zu den Jahren 1940–1966*, ed. Marianne Prause, Munich: Prestel, 1984

Foskett, Daphne, *A Dictionary of British Miniature Painters*, London: Faber and Faber, 1972

Frick Art Reference Library, New York, *Spanish Artists from the Fourth to the Twentieth Century: A Critical Dictionary*, Boston: Hall, 1994–

Fuchs, Heinrich, *Register zu den österreichischen Malern des 19. Jahrhunderts*, Vienna: Fuchs, 1988

Gealt, Adelheid M., *Painting of the Golden Age: A Biographical Dictionary of Seventeenth-Century European Painters*, Westport, CT, and London: Greenwood Press, 1993

Gelsted, Otto, *Gelsteds kunstner-leksikon, 1900–1942*, Copenhagen: Jensens, 1942

Genaille, Robert, *Dictionnaire des peintres flamands et hollandais*, Paris: Larousse, 1967

Germaine, Max, *Artists and Galleries of Australia and New Zealand*, 2nd edition, Brisbane: Boolarong, 1994

Goldstein, Franz, *Monogramm-Lexikon: Internationales Verzeichnis der Monogramme bildenen Künstler seit 1859*, Berlin: de Gruyter, 1964

Gorina, Tatiana N. and Oskar E. Voltsenburg, *Khudozhniki narodov SSSR, Biobibliograficheskii slovar*, Moscow: Iskusstvo, 1970

Gould, John, *Biographical Dictionary of Painters, Sculptors, Engravers and Architects*, 2 vols, London: Wilson, 1835

Gowing, Lawrence, *A Biographical Dictionary of Artists*, New York and London: Macmillan, 1983

Gran, Henning and Peter Anker, *Illustrert norsk kunstnerleksikon: Stemmeberettigede, malere, grafikere/tegnere, billedhoggere*, 2nd edition, Olso: Broen, 1956

Grant, Maurice Harold, *A Dictionary of British Sculptors from the XIIth Century to the XXth Century*, London: Rockliff, 1953

Graves, Algernon, *The British Institution, 1806–1867: A Complete Dictionary of Contributors and Their Work from the Foundation of the Institution*, 1875; reprinted Bath: Kingsmead Press Reprints, 1969

——, *A Dictionary of Artists Who Have Exhibited Works in the Principal London Exhibitions from 1760 to 1904*, 3rd edition, London: Graves, 1901; reprinted Bath: Kingsmead Press Reprints, 1984

——, *The Royal Academy of Arts: A Complete Dictionary of Contributors and Their Work from Its Foundation in 1769 to 1904*, 8 vols, London: Graves, 1905–6; reprinted New York: Franklin, 1972; Bath: Kingsmead Press Reprints; Calne, Wiltshire: Hilmarton Manor Press, 1989

——, *Royal Academy Exhibitors, 1905–1970*, 6 vols, London: E.P. Publishing, 1973–82

——, *The Society of Artists of Great Britain, 1760–1791, and The Free Society of Artists, 1761–1783: A Complete Dictionary of Contributors and Their Work from the Foundation of the Societies to 1791*, London: Bell, 1907; reprinted Bath: Kingsmead Press Reprints, 1969

Groce, George C. and David Wallace, eds, *New-York Historical Society's Dictionary of Artists in America, 1564–1860*, New Haven, CT: Yale University Press, 1957

Gunnis, Rupert, *Dictionary of British Sculptors, 1660–1851*, London: Abbey Library, 1968

Halsby, Julian, *Scottish Watercolours, 1740–1940*, London: Batsford, 1989

——, *Dictionary of Scottish Painters, 1600–1690*, Edinburgh and Oxford: Phaidon/Bourne Fine Art, 1990

Harper, J. Russell, *Early Painters and Engravers in Canada*, Toronto: University of Toronto Press, 1970

Havlice, Patricia P., *Index to Artistic Biography*, Metuchen, NJ: Scarecrow Press, 1973; first supplement, 1981

Hazan, Fernand, ed., *Dictionary of Italian Painting*, New York: Tudor, 1964

Hollstein, F.W.H., *Dutch and Flemish Etchings, Engravings and Woodcuts, ca.1450–1700*, Amsterdam: Hertzberger, 1949

—, *German Engravings, Etchings and Woodcuts, ca.1400–1700*, Amsterdam: Hertzberger, 1954

Horne, Alan, *The Dictionary of Twentieth-Century British Book Illustrators*, Woodbridge, Suffolk: Antique Collectors' Club, 1994

Houfe, Simon, *The Dictionary of British Book Illustrators and Caricaturists, 1800–1914*, Woodbridge, Suffolk: Antique Collectors' Club, 1978

Hymans, Henri S., *Près de 700 biographies d'artistes belges, parues dans La Biographie nationale, dans l'art flamand et hollandais, dans Le Dictionnaire des Drs Thieme et Becker et dans diverses publications du pay et de l'étranger*, Brussels: Hayez, 1920

Igoe, Lynn M. and James Igoe, *250 Years of Afro-American Art: An Annotated Bibliography*, New York: Bowker, 1981

Jakovsky, Anatole, *Peintres naïfs: Dictionnaire des peintres naïfs du monde entier*, Basel: Basilius-Presse, 1976

James, Edward T., ed., *Notable American Women, 1607–1950*, 3 vols, Cambridge, MA: Belknap Press of Harvard University Press, 1971

Johnson, Jane and A. Greutzner, *The Dictionary of British Artists, 1880–1940*, Woodbridge, Suffolk: Antique Collectors' Club, 1980

Jørgenen, Svend P., *Munksgaard kunstnerleksikon*, Copenhagen: Munksgaard, [1962]

Karpel, Bernard, *Arts in America: A Bibliography*, 4 vols, Washington, DC: Smithsonian Institution Press, 1979

Kay, Ernest, ed., *Dictionary of Scandinavian Biography*, Cambridge, UK: International Biographical Centre, 1976

Kerr, Joan, ed., *The Dictionary of Australian Artists: Painters, Sketchers, Photographers and Engravers to 1870*, Oxford and Melbourne: Oxford University Press, 1992

Koie, Tove, *Kunstnerleksikon*, Copenhagen: AOF, 1985

Koroma, Kaarlo, *Suomen kuvataiteilijat: Suomen taiteilijaseutan julkaisema elämäkerrasto*, Borgå: Söderström, 1962

Kraam, Christiaan, *De levens en werken der Hollandsche en Vlaamsche kunstschilders, beeldhouwers, graveurs en bouwmeesters*, Amsterdam: Gebroeders Diederichs, 1857–64; reprinted Amsterdam: Isräel, 1974

Krantz, Les, ed., *American Artists: An Illustrated Survey of Leading Contemporary Americans*, New York and Oxford: Facts on File Publications, 1985

Lami, Stanislas, *Dictionnaire de sculpteurs de l'école française au dix-huitième siècle*, 2 vols, Paris: Champion, 1910

—, *Dictionnaire de sculpteurs de l'école française au dix-neuvième siècle*, 4 vols, Paris: Champion, 1916

Lanzi, Luigi A., *Storia pittorica dell'Italia dal risorgimento delle belle arti fin presso al fine del XVIII secolo*, 3rd edition, 3 vols, Bassano da Grappa: Remondini, 1809; English edition, 6 vols, 1828

Laperrière, Charles Baille de, ed., *Royal Academy Exhibitors, 1826–1990*, 4 vols, Calne, Wiltshire: Hilmarton Manor Press, 1991

Lewis, Frank, *British Historical Painters*, Leigh-on-Sea, Essex: Lewis, 1979

Lexikon der Frau, 2 vols, Zürich, 1953–4

Lexicon der zeitgenössischen schweizer Künstler, Frauenfeld: Huber, 1981

Lilja, Gösta and others, *Svenskt konstnärs lexikon: Tiotusen svenska konstnärers liv och verk*, 5 vols, Malmö: Allhems Förlag, 1952–67

Lister, Raymond, *Prints and Printmaking: A Dictionary and Handbook of the Art in Nineteenth-Century Britain*, London: Methuen, 1984

McCulloch, Alan, *Encyclopedia of Australian Art*, Hawthorne, Victoria, and London: Hutchinson, 1984

MacDonald, Colin S., *Dictionary of Canadian Artists*, Ottawa: Canadian Paperbacks, 1967–

McEwan, Peter J.M., *Dictionary of Scottish Art and Architecture*, Woodbridge, Suffolk: Antique Collectors' Club, 1994

Mackenzie, Ian, *British Prints: Dictionary and Price Guide*, Woodbridge, Suffolk: Antique Collectors' Club, 1988

Maere, Jan de and Marie Wabbes, *Illustrated Dictionary of Seventeenth-Century Flemish Painters*, ed. Jennifer A. Martin, 3 vols, Brussels: La Renaissance de Livre, c.1994

Mallalieu, Huon L., *The Dictionary of British Watercolour Artists up to 1920*, 3 vols, Woodbridge, Suffolk: Antique Collectors' Club, 1988

Mallett, Daniel Trowbridge, *Mallett's Index of Artists, International-Biographical: Including Painters, Sculptors, Illustrators, Engravers and Etchers of the Past and the Present*, New York: Bowker, 1935; reprinted Bath: Kingsmead Press Reprints, 1976

—, *Supplement to Mallett's Index of Artists, International-Biographical: Including Painters, Sculptors, Illustrators, Engravers and Etchers of the Past and the Present*, New York: Bowker, 1935; reprinted Bath: Kingsmead Press Reprints, 1977

Marini, Giuseppe Maria, *Bolaffi, catalogo della pittura italiana dell'ottocento*, Turin: Mondadori, 1981

Mathews, Oliver, *Early Photographs and Photographers: A Survey in Dictionary Form*, London: Reedminster, 1973

Mayer, Leo A., *Bibliography of Jewish Art*, Jerusalem: Magnes, 1967

Mazalic, Doko, *Leksikon umjetnika: Slikara, vajara, graditelja, zlatara, kaligrafa i drugih koji su radili u Bosni i Hercegovini*, Sarajevo: Veselin Maslesa, 1967

Milner, John, *A Dictionary of Russian and Soviet Artists, 1420–1970*, Woodbridge, Suffolk: Antique Collectors' Club, 1993

Mitchell, Sally, *Dictionary of British Equestrian Artists*, Woodbridge, Suffolk: Antique Collectors' Club, 1985

Molhuysen, Philip Christiaan, *Nieuw Nederlandisch biografisch woordenboek*, London: Sijthoff, 1911–37; reprinted Amsterdam: Isräel, 1974

Murray, Peter and Linda Murray, *Dictionary of Art and Artists*, London: Penguin, 1988

Nagler, Georg K., *Die Monogrammisten und diehenigen bekannten und unbekannten Künstler aller Schulen*, 5 vols, Munich: Franz, 1858–79; reprinted Nieuwkoop: De Graaf, 1966

—, *Die Monogrammisten*, Munich: Hirths, 1919

—, *Neues allgemeines Künstler-Lexikon*, 2 vols, Munich, 1836–52; reprinted Leipzig: Schwarzenberg & Schumann, 1924

Nahum, Peter, *Monograms of Victorian and Edwardian Artists*, London and New York: Foulsham, 1976

Naylor, Colin, ed., *Contemporary Artists*, 3rd edition, London: St James Press, and New York: St Martin's Press, 1989

Neue deutsche Biographie, Berlin: Duncker und Humbolt, 1953–85

Neumann, Wilhelm, *Lexikon baltischer Künster*, Riga: Jonck & Doliewsky, 1908; reprinted Hannover-Döhren: Hirschheydt, 1972

Newall, Christopher, *The Grosvenor Gallery Exhibitions: Change and Continuity in the Victorian Art World*, Cambridge: Cambridge University Press, 1995

Norsk kunstner leksikon: Bildende kunstnere, arkitekter, kunsthaandverkere, Oslo: Universitetsforlaget, 1982–6

O'Neil, A., *A Dictionary of Spanish Painters: Comprehending That Part of Their Biography Immediately Connected with the Arts from the Fourteenth Century to the Eighteenth*, London: O'Neil, 1833–4

Opitz, Glenn B., *Dictionary of American Sculptors*, Poughkeepsie, NY: Apollo, 1984

Osborne, Harold, *The Oxford Companion to Art*, Oxford: Clarendon Press, 1970

—, *The Oxford Companion to the Decorative Arts*, Oxford: Clarendon Press, 1975

Ossorio y Bernard, Manuel, *Galería biográfica de artistas españoles del siglo XIX*, Madrid: Moreno y Rojas, 1883–4; reprinted Madrid: Librería Gaudí, 1975

Österreichisches biographisches Lexikon, 1815–1950, Graz: Boehlaus Nachfolger, 1957

Osterwalder, Marcus, *Dictionnaire des illustrateurs, 1800–1914 (Illustrateurs, caricaturistes et affichistes)*, Neuchâtel: Ides et Calendes, 1989

Pamplona, Fernando de, *Dicionário de pintores e escultores portugueses ou que trabalharam em Portugal*, Porto: Livraria Civilização Editora, 1987–8

Pascoli, Lione, *Vite de' pittori, scultori ed architetti moderni*, 2 vols, Rome: de Rossi, 1730–36; reprinted Rome: Calzone, 1933

Pavière, Sydney Herbert, *Dictionary of British Sporting Painters*, Leigh-on-Sea, Essex: Lewis, 1968

—, *A Dictionary of Flower, Fruit and Still-Life Painters*, 4 vols, Leigh-on-Sea, Essex: Lewis, 1962–4

Peppin, Brigid and Lucy Micklethwait, *Dictionary of British Book Illustrators of the Twentieth Century*, London: Murray, 1983

Pilkington, Matthew, *A General Dictionary of Painters*, 2 vols, London: McLean, 1824

Platts, Una, *Nineteenth-Century New Zealand Artists*, Christchurch: Avon Fine Prints, 1979

Plüss, Eduard and Hans Christoph von Tavel, *Künstlerlexikon der Schweiz: XX. Jahrhundert*, 2 vols, Frauenfeld: Huber, 1958–67

Pontual, Roberto, *Dicionário das artes plásticas no Brasil*, Rio de Janeiro: Civilização Brasileira, [1969]

Prut, Constantin, *Dictionar de arta moderna*, Bucharest: Albatross, 1982

Pyke, E.J., *A Biographical Dictionary of Wax Modellers*, Oxford: Clarendon Press, 1973

Ráfols, José F., *Diccionario de artistas de Cataluña, Valencia y Baleares*, 5 vols, Barcelona: Ediciones Catalanes y La Gran Enciclopedia Vasca, 1980–81

—, *Diccionario biográfica de artistas de Cataluña desde la época roman a hasta nuestros días*, Barcelona: Milla, 1951–4

Rainov, Bogomil N., *Portreti*, Sofia: Bulgarski pisatel, 1975

Redgrave, Samuel, *A Dictionary of Artists of the English School: Painters, Sculptors, Architects, Engravers and Ornamentists, with Notices of Their Lives and Works*, revised edition, ed. Frances M. Redgrave, London: Bell, 1878; reprinted Bath: Kingsmead Press Reprints, 1970

Rees, T. Mardy, *Welsh Painters, Engravers and Sculptors, 1527–1911*, Caernarvon: Welsh Publishing Company, [1912]

Samuels, Peggy and Harold Samuels, *The Illustrated Biographical Encyclopedia of Artists of the American West*, Garden City, NY: Doubleday, 1976

Sartin, Stephen, *British Narrative Painters*, Leigh-on-Sea, Essex: Lewis, 1978

Scheen, Pieter A., *Lexicon Nederlandse beeldende Kunstenaars, 1750–1950*, 2 vols, The Hague: Scheen, 1981

Schidlof, Leo, *The Miniature in Europe in the 16th, 17th, 18th and 19th Centuries*, 4 vols, Graz: Akademische Druck- und Verlagsanstalt, 1964

Schmidt, Rudolf, *Österreichisches Künstlerlexikon: Von den Anfangen bis zur Gegenwart*, Vienna: Tusch, 1974–

Seyn, Eugène M.H. de, *Dessinateurs, graveurs et peintres des anciens Pays-Bas: Ecoles flamande et hollandaise*, Turnhout: Brépols, [1949]

Smith, Ralph Clifton, *A Biographical Index of American Artists*, Baltimore: Williams and Wilkins, 1930; reprinted Charleston: Garnier, 1967; New York: Olana Gallery, [198–]

Smith, Veronica Babington, *Dictionary of Contemporary Artists*, Oxford and Santa Barbara, CA: ABC-Clio Information Services, 1981

—, *International Directory of Exhibiting Artists*, Oxford and Santa Barbara, CA: ABC-Clio Information Services, 1983

Soria, Regina, *American Artists of Italian Heritage, 1776–1945: A Biographical Dictionary*, London and Toronto: Associated University Press, 1993

Spalding, Frances, *Dictionary of British Art*, iv: *Twentieth-Century Painters and Sculptors*, Woodbridge, Suffolk: Antique Collectors' Club, 1990

Spooner, Shearjashub, *A Biographical History of the Fine Arts*, 4th edition, 2 vols, New York: Leypoldt and Holt, c.1865

Stewart, Ann M., *Royal Hibernian Academy of Arts, Index of Exhibitors, 1826–1979*, 3 vols, Dublin: Manton, 1985–7

Strickland, Walter G., *Dictionary of Irish Artists*, 2 vols, Dublin and London: Maunsel, 1913; reprinted Shannon: Irish University Press, and New York: Hacker, 1969

Svenska konstnärer: Biografisk handbok, Stockholm: Nybloms, 1982

Svenski konstnärslexikon, Malmö: Allhems Foerlag, 1952–67

Tannock, Michael, *Portuguese Twentieth-Century Artists: A Biographical Dictionary*, Chichester: Phillimore, 1978

Taveres Chico, Mário, *Dicionário da pintura portuguesa*, Lisbon: Estúdios Cor, 1973

Thieme, Ulrich and Becker, Felix, *Allgemeines Lexikon der bildenden Künstler*, Leipzig: Seemann, 1907–50

Toman, Prokop H., *Dodatky, Ke slovniku: Ceskoslovenskych vytvarnych umelcu*, Prague: Kanladatelstvi krásné literatury, hudby a umeni, 1955

Turner, Jane, ed., *The Dictionary of Art*, 34 vols, London and New York: Grove, 1996

Uglow, Jennifer S., ed., *The International Dictionary of Women's Biography*, New York: Continuum, 1982

Villani, Carlo, *Stelle femminili: Dizionario bio-bibliografico*, 2 vols, Naples: Albrighi, 1915–16

Vollmer, Hans, *Allgemeines Lexikon der bildenden Künstler des XX. Jahrhunderts*, 6 vols, Leipzig: Seemann, 1953–62

——, *Künstler-Lexikon des zwanzigsten Jahrhunderts*, Leipzig: Seemann, 1953–62

Waller, François Gérard, *Biographisch woordenboek van noord Nederlandse graveurs*, The Hague: Nijhoff, 1938; reprinted Amsterdam: Isräel, 1974

Waterhouse, Ellis Kirkham, *Dictionary of British Eighteenth-Century Painters in Oils and Crayons*, Woodbridge, Suffolk: Antique Collectors' Club, 1981

——, *Dictionary of Sixteenth- and Seventeenth-Century British Painters*, Woodbridge, Suffolk: Antique Collectors' Club, 1988

Waters, Grant M., *Dictionary of British Artists Working 1900–1950*, 2 vols, Eastbourne: Eastbourne Fine Art, 1975

Weilbach, Philip, *Weilbachs kunstnerleksikon*, 3rd edition, Copenhagen: Aschehoug, 1947–52

Who Was Who, London: A. & C. Black, 1920–

Who Was Who: A Cumulated Index, 1897–1990, London: A. & C. Black, 1991

Who Was Who in America, Chicago: Marquis Who's Who, 1943–

Who Was Who in American Art, Madison, CT: Sound View Press, 1985

Who Was Who in American History, Arts and Letters, Chicago: Marquis Who's Who, 1975

Who Was Who in the Soviet Union, Metuchen, NJ: Scarecrow Press, 1972

Who's Who: An Annual Biographical Dictionary, London: A. & C. Black, 1849–

Who's Who in American Art, New York: Bowker, 1936/7–

Who's Who in Art, London: Art Trade Press, 1927–

Who's Who in Austria, Montreal: Intercontinental Book and Publishing Company, 1954–

Who's Who in France, Paris: Lafitte, 1955–

Who's Who in Germany, Munich: Intercontinental Book and Publishing Company, 1956–

Who's Who in Graphic Art, Zürich: Amstutz and Herdeg Graphic Press, 1962–

Who's Who in the Arts: A Biographical Encyclopedia Containing some 15,000 Biographies and Addresses of Prominent Personalities, Organizations, Associations and Institutions Connected with the Arts in the Federal Republic of Germany, Austria and Switzerland, Wörthsee: Who's Who Book and Publishing Company, 1978

Who's Who of American Women, Chicago: Marquis, 1959–

Wilson, Arnold, *A Dictionary of British Marine Painters*, revised edition, Leigh-on-Sea, Essex: Lewis, 1980

Wingfield, Mary Ann, *Dictionary of Sporting Artists, 1650–1990*, 3rd edition, 2 vols, Woodbridge, Suffolk: Antique Collectors' Club, 1995

Witt Library, *A Checklist of Painters, c.1200–1994, Represented in the Witt Library, Courtauld Institute of Art, London*, London: Mansell Information Publishing, and Chicago: Fitzroy Dearborn, 1995

Woman's Who's Who of America, New York: American Commonwealth Company, 1914–15; reprinted Detroit: Gale Research, 1976

Wood, Christopher, *The Dictionary of British Art*, iv: *Victorian Painters*, 2 vols, Woodbridge, Suffolk: Antique Collectors' Club, 1995

——, *The Dictionary of Victorian Painters*, 2nd edition, Woodbridge, Suffolk: Antique Collectors' Club, 1978

Wood, Jeremy, *Hidden Talents: A Dictionary of Neglected Artists Working 1880–1950*, Billinghurst: Jeremy Wood Fine Art, 1994

Wood, John Clairmont, *Dictionary of British Animal Painters*, Leigh-on-Sea, Essex: Lewis, 1973

The World Who's Who of Women, 3rd edition, Cambridge, UK: International Biographical Centre, 1973–

Wright, Christopher, *Paintings in Dutch Museums: An Index of Oil Paintings in Public Collections in the Netherlands by Artists Born Before 1870*, London: Sotheby-Parke Bernet, 1980

Wurzbach, Alfred von, ed., *Niederländisches Künstler-Lexikon auf Grund archivalischer Forschung*, Vienna: Halm, 1906–11; reprinted Amsterdam: Isräel, 1974

Young, William, ed., *A Dictionary of American Artists, Sculptors and Engravers from the Beginnings Through the Turn of the Twentieth Century*, Cambridge, MA: Young, 1968

Zador, Anna and Genthon Istvan, *Müveszeti lexikon*, 4 vols, Budapest: Akademiai Kiado, 1965–8

Zampetti, Pietro, *A Dictionary of Venetian Painters*, 5 vols, Leigh-on-Sea, Essex: Lewis, 1969–79

2. Women Artists: Dictionaries and Bibliographies

Anderson, Janet A., *Women in the Fine Arts: A Bibliography and Illustration Guide*, Jefferson, NC: McFarland, 1991

Bachmann, Donna G. and Sherry Piland, *Women Artists: An Historical, Contemporary and Feminist Bibliography*, Metuchen, NJ: Scarecrow Press, 1978; revised edition, 1994

Bowes, Marie, *Women Artists: A Directory and Bibliography of Women in the Visual Arts and Related Fields*, Berkeley, CA: Women's History, 1971

Chiarmonte, Paula, *Women Artists in the United States: A Selective Bibliography and Resource Guide on the Fine and Decorative Arts, 1750–1986*, Boston: Hall, 1990

Collins, Jim L., *Women Artists in America: Eighteenth Century to the Present*, 2 vols, Chattanooga: University of Tennessee, Art Department, 1973–5

Collins, Jim L. and Glenn B. Opitz, eds, *Women Artists in America: Eighteenth Century to the Present (1780–1980)*, revised edition, Poughkeepsie, NY: Apollo, 1980

Dunford, Penny, *A Biographical Dictionary of Women Artists in Europe and America since 1850*, Philadelphia: University of Pennsylvania Press, 1989; Hemel Hempstead, Herts: Harvester Wheatsheaf, 1990

Föreningen Svenska konstnärinnor, 1910–1990, Stockholm: Jubileumsåret, 1990

Germaine, Max, *A Dictionary of Women Artists of Australia*, Roseville East: Craftsman House, 1991

Gubitosi, Vincenzo, ed., *Enciclopedia nazionale la donna nell'arte*, Rapallo: Ipotesi, 1982–

Heller, Jules and Nancy G. Heller, eds, *North American Women Artists of the Twentieth Century: A Biographical Dictionary*, New York: Garland, 1995

Hill, Vicki Lynn, ed., *Female Artists, Past and Present*, Berkeley, CA: Women's History Research Center, 1974 (directory and bibliography)

Kerr, Joan, ed., *Heritage: The National Women's Art Book*, Sydney: Dictionary of Australian Artists / Craftsman House, 1995

Krichbaum, Jörg and Zondergeld, Rein A., *Künstlerinnen: Von der Antike bis zur Gegenwart*, Cologne: DuMont, 1979

Langer, Cassandra, *Feminist Art Criticism: An Annotated Bibliography*, Boston: Hall, 1993

Moe, Louisa, ed., *International Women's Year Supplement*, Berkeley, CA: Women's History Research Center, 1975 (supplement to Hill 1974)

Muysers, Carola and others, eds, *Käthe, Paula und der ganze Rest: Ein Nachschlagewerk*, Berlin: Berlinische Galerie, 1992

Palmquist, Peter E., *A Bibliography of Writings By and About Women in Photography, 1850–1950*, Arcata, CA: Palmquist, 1990

Petteys, Chris, *Dictionary of Women Artists: An International Dictionary of Women Artists Born Before 1900*, Boston: Hall, 1985

Prather-Moses, Alice Irma, *The International Dictionary of Women Workers in the Decorative Arts*, Metuchen, NJ: Scarecrow Press, 1981

Roake, JoAnne, *Women Artists: A Selected Bibliography*, Bibliographic Series no.19, Sacramento, CA: Library, California State University, 1977

Scheen, Pieter A., *Lexicon Nederlandse beeldende kunstenaars, 1750–1880*, The Hague: Scheen, 1981

Tufts, Eleanor, *American Women Artists, Past and Present: A Selected Bibliographic Guide*, 2 vols, New York: Garland, 1984–9

Williams, Ora, *American Black Women in the Arts and Social Sciences: Bibliographic Survey*, Metuchen, NJ: Scarecrow Press, 1973

Wolff-Thomsen, Ulrike, *Lexicon Schleswig-Holsteinischer Künstlerinnen*, Heide: Boysen, c.1994

Women Artists and Women in the Arts: A Bibliography of Art Exhibition Catalogues, Boston, MA: Worldwide Books, 1978

3. Women Artists: Surveys

Alesson, Jean, *Les Femmes artistes au salon de 1878 et l'exposition universelle*, Paris: Au bureau de la gazette des femmes, 1878

Alpha Kappa Alpha, Beta Iota Omega Chapter, Negro Heritage Committee, *Afro-American Women in Art: Their Achievements in Sculpture and Painting*, Greensboro, NC: The Committee, 1969

Ambrus, Caroline, *Australian Women Artists: First Fleet to 1945: History, Hearsay and Her Say*, Woden, Australia: Irrepressible Press, 1992

Ambrus, Caroline, ed., *The Ladies' Picture Show: Sources on a Century of Australian Women Artists*, Sydney: Hale and Iremonger, 1984 (bibliographic citations of Australian women artists pre-1945)

Anderson, Dorothy May, *Women, Design and the Cambridge School*, West Lafayette, IN: PDA, 1980

Anonymous Was a Woman: A Documentation of the Women's Art Festival: A Collection of Letters to Young Women Artists, Valencia, CA: Feminist Art Program, California Institute of the Arts, 1974

Anscombe, Isabelle, *A Woman's Touch: Women in Design from 1860 to the Present Day*, London: Virago, and New York: Viking, 1984

Apostolos-Cappadona, Diana and Lucinda Ebersole, eds, *Women, Creativity and the Arts: Critical and Autobiographical Perspectives*, New York: Continuum, 1995

Ashburn, Elizabeth, *Lesbian Art: An Encounter with Power*, Roseville East, Australia: Craftsman House (in preparation)

Askey, Ruth and Laura Brunsman, eds, *Modernism and Beyond: Women Artists of the Pacific Northwest*, New York: Midmarch, 1993

Bank, Mirra, *Anonymous Was a Woman*, New York: St Martin's Press, 1979 (critical discussion of the anonymous productions of women artists)

Barber, Fionna, *Contemporary Irish Women Artists*, Dublin: Attic, 1989

Battersby, Christine, *Gender and Genius: Towards a Feminist Aesthetic*, Bloomington: Indiana University Press, 1989

Beckett, Wendy, *Contemporary Women Artists*, Oxford: Phaidon, 1988

Behr, Shulamith, *Women Expressionists*, Oxford: Phaidon, and New York: Rizzoli, 1988

Benjamin, Samuel Green Wheeler, *Our American Artists*, Boston, MA: Lothrop, 1881 (includes "Lady illustrators", chapter 10)

Benoust, Madeline, *Quelques femmes peintres*, Paris: Stock, 1936

Benstock, Shari, *Women of the Left Bank: Paris, 1900–1940*, Austin: University of Texas Press, 1986; London: Virago, 1987

Berger, Renate, *Malerinnen auf dem Weg ins 20. Jahrhundert: Kunstgeschichte als Sozialgeschichte*, Cologne: DuMont, 1982

——, *"Und ich sehe nichts, nichts als die Malerei": Autobiographische Texte von Künstlerinnen des 18.–20. Jahrhunderts*, Frankfurt am Main: Fischer, 1987

Blair, Karen J., *The Torchbearers: Women and Their Amateur Arts Associations in America, 1890–1930*, Bloomington: Indiana University Press, 1994

Boccaccio, Giovanni, *De claris mulieribus* (c.1370); as *Concerning Famous Women*, ed. G.A. Guarino, New Brunswick, NJ: Rutgers University Press, [1963] (includes a discussion of Pliny's mention of women artists)

Borzello, Frances and Natacha Ledwidge, *Graphic Guide: Women Artists*, London: Camden Press, 1986

Bosma, Y., *De vrouwelijke kunstacademie-student en haar beroepsloopbaan*, Amsterdam: Stichting Centrum voor Onderwijs-onderzoek (SCO), 1989

Bowers, Susan and Ronald Dotterer, eds, *Gender, Culture and the Arts: Women, the Arts and Society*, London and Toronto: Associated University Presses, 1993

Brafford, C.J. and Laine Thom, eds, *Dancing Colors: Paths of Native American Women*, San Francisco: Chronicle, 1992

Breitling, Gisela, *Die Spuren des Schiffs in den Wellen: Eine autobiographische Suche nach en Frauen in der Kunstgeschichte*, Berlin: Oberbaum, 1980

Broude, Norma and Mary D. Garrard, eds, *Feminism and Art History: Questioning the Litany*, New York: Harper, 1982

——, *The Expanding Discourse: Feminism and Art History*, New York: Icon, 1992

——, *The Power of Feminist Art: The American Movement of the 1970s*, New York: Abrams, and London: Thames and Hudson, 1994

Brown, Betty Ann and Arlene Raven, *Exposures: Women and Their Art*, Pasadena, CA: NewSage Press, 1989

Buckley, Cheryl, *Potters and Paintresses: Women Designers in the Pottery Industry, 1870–1955*, London, Women's Press, 1990

Burke, Janine, *Australian Women Artists, 1840–1940*, Collingwood, Victoria: Greenhouse, 1980

Burkhauser, Jude, ed., *Glasgow Girls: Women in Art and Design, 1880–1920*, 2nd edition, Edinburgh: Canongate, and Cape May, NJ: Red Ochre, 1993

Callen, Anthea, *Angel in the Studio: Women in the Arts and Crafts Movement, 1870–1914*, London: Astragal, 1979; as *Women Artists of the Arts and Crafts Movement, 1870–1914*, New York: Pantheon, 1979

Campos, Adalgisa Arantes and others, *Mulher e arte*, Belo Horizonte, Brazil: UFMG / Nucleo de Estudos e Pesquisas sobre a Mulher, 1988

Cavé, Marie Elisabeth Blavot Boulanger, *La Femme aujourd'hui, la femme d'autrefois*, Paris: Plon, 1863 (discusses the education of women, including the training of women artists)

Caws, Mary Ann, ed., *Surrealism and Women*, Cambridge: Massachusetts Institute of Technology Press, 1991

Chadwick, Whitney, *Women, Art and Society*, London and New York: Thames and Hudson, 1990; revised edition, 1996

——, *Women Artists and the Surrealist Movement*, Boston: Little Brown, and London: Thames and Hudson, 1985

Chadwick, Whitney and Isabelle de Courtivron, eds, *Partnership*, London and New York: Thames and Hudson, 1993

Cherry, Deborah, *Painting Women: Victorian Women Artists*, London and New York: Routledge, 1993

Clayton, Ellen C., *English Female Artists*, 2 vols, London: Tinsley, 1876

Clement, Clara Erskine, *Women in the Fine Arts from the Seventh Century BC to the Twentieth Century AD*, Boston: Houghton Mifflin, 1904; reprinted New York: Hacker, 1974

Clement, Clara Erskine and Laurence Hutton, *Artists of the Nineteenth Century and Their Work*, 2 vols, Boston: Houghton Osgood, and London: Trübner, 1879; reprinted New York: Arno Press, 1969

Collins, Georgia and Renee Sandell, *Women, Art and Education*, Reston, VA: National Art Education Association, 1984

Contemporary American Women Artists, San Rafael, CA: Cedco, 1991

Contemporary American Women Sculptors, Phoenix, AZ: Oryx Press, 1986

The Creative Woman: A Report of the Committee on the Arts and Humanities, Washington, DC: National Commission for the Observance of International Women's Year, 1976

Dahms, Gustav, *Der Existenzkampf der Frau im modernen Leben*, Berlin: Tändler, 1885–96 (includes the section: "Die Frauen in der Kunst" by Georg Voss)

Deepwell, Katy, ed., *New Feminist Art Criticism: Critical Strategies*, Manchester: Manchester University Press, 1995

Dewhurst, C. Kurt, Betty MacDowell and Marsha MacDowell, *Artists in Aprons: Folk Art by American Women*, New York: Dutton, 1979

Diego, Estrella de, *La mujer y la pintura del XIX español*, Madrid: Universidad Complutense de Madrid, 1987

Eastmond, Elizabeth and Merimeri Penfold, *Women and the Arts in New Zealand: Forty Works, 1936–86*, Auckland: Penguin, 1986

Ecker, Gisela, ed., *Feminist Aesthetics*, London: Women's Press, 1985; Boston: Beacon Press, 1986

Eiblmayer, Silvia, *Kunst mit Eigen-Sinn: Aktuelle Kunst von Frauen*, Vienna: Locker, 1985

Ellet, Elizabeth Fries Lummis, *Women Artists in All Ages and Countries*, New York: Harper, 1859

Elliot, Maud Howe, ed., *Art and Handicraft in the Woman's Building of the World's Columbian Exposition, Chicago, 1893*, Paris and New York: Goupil, 1893; Chicago: Rand McNally, 1894

Elliott, Bridget and Jo-Ann Wallace, *Women Artists and Writers: Modern (Im)Positionings*, London and New York: Routledge, 1994

Emmy, Elsa, *Donna, arte, Marxisme: Con un'autoanalisi sullo sviluppo della creatività*, Rome: Bulzoni, 1977

Eschwey, Maymie, *Women in Limning: Yesterday and Today*, Minneapolis: Maymie Eschwey, 1993 (examines women portrait miniaturists)

Evers, Ulrika, *Deutsche Künstlerinnen des 20. Jahrhunderts: Malerei, Bildhauerei, Tapisserie*, Hamburg: Schultheis, 1983

Faxon, Alicia Craig and Sylvia Moore, eds, *Pilgrims and Pioneers: New England Women in the Arts*, New York: Midmarch, 1987

Festival Nacional das mulheres nas artes, São Paulo: Revista NOVA, 1982 (first festival, 3–12 September 1982)

Fidière, Octave, *Les Femmes artistes à l'Académie Royale de Peinture et de Sculpture*, Paris: Charavay Frères, 1885

Fine, Elsa Honig, *Women and Art: A History of Women Painters and Sculptors from the Renaissance to the 20th Century*, Montclair, NJ: Allanheld and Schram, and London: Prior, 1978

Frueh, Joanna, Cassandra L. Langer and Arlene Raven, eds, *New Feminist Criticism: Art, Identity, Action*, New York: HarperCollins, 1994

Frym, Gloria, *Second Stories: Conversations with Women Whose Artistic Careers Began after Thirty-Five*, San Francisco: Chronicle, 1979

Furniss, Harry, *Some Victorian Women: Good, Bad and Indifferent*, New York: Dodd Mead, 1923 (includes the chapter: "Some women artists")

Garb, Tamar, *Sisters of the Brush: Women's Artistic Culture in*

Late Nineteenth-Century Paris, New Haven and London: Yale University Press, 1994

—, *Women Impressionists*, Oxford: Phaidon, and New York: Rizzoli, 1986

García de Carpi, Lucía, *La pintura surrealista española (1924–1936)*, Madrid: Ediciones ISTMO, 1986

Gesellschaft Schweizerischer Malerinnen Bildhauerinnen und Kunstgewerblerinnen, *Berner Künstlerinnen gestern + heute, 1909–1987/Artistes bernoises hier et aujourd'hui, 1909–1987*, Bern: Die Gesellschaft, 1987

Glanville, Phillipa and Jennifer Faulds Goldsborough, *Women Silversmiths, 1685–1845: Works from the Collection of the National Museum of Women in the Arts, Washington, DC*, London: Thames and Hudson, 1990

Gover, C. Jane, *The Positive Image: Women Photographers in Turn of the Century America*, Albany, NY: State University of New York Press, 1988

Greer, Germaine, *The Obstacle Race: The Fortunes of Women Painters and Their Work*, London: Secker and Warburg, and New York: Farrar Straus, 1979

Griffin, Gabriele, ed., *Difference in View: Women and Modernism*, Bristol, PA: Taylor and Francis, 1994

Guhl, Ernst, *Die Frauen in die Kunstgeschichte*, Berlin: Guttentag, 1858

Gwyn, Sandra, *Women in the Arts in Canada*, Ottawa: Royal Commission on the Status of Women in Canada, 1971

Hanaford, Phebe A., *Daughters of America*, Augusta, ME: True, 1873 (includes the chapter: "Women artists")

Harthy, Marsden, *Adventures in the Arts*, New York: Boni and Liveright, 1921 (includes the chapter: "Some women artists")

Hayes, Dannielle B., *Women Photograph Men*, New York: Morrow, 1977

Hedges, Elaine and Ingrid Wendt, *In Her Own Image: Women Working in the Arts*, New York: McGraw Hill, 1980

Heller, Nancy G., *Women Artists: An Illustrated History*, New York: Abbeville, 1987; revised edition, 1991

Henkes, Robert, *The Art of Black American Women: Works by Twenty-Four Artists of the Twentieth Century*, Jefferson, NC: McFarland, 1993

Hess, Thomas B. and Elizabeth C. Baker, eds, *Art and Sexual Politics: Women's Liberation, Women Artists and Art History*, New York and London: Macmillan, 1973

Hildebrandt, Hans, *Die Frau als Künstlerin*, Berlin: Mosse, 1928

Hubert, Renée Riese, *Magnifying Mirrors: Women, Surrealism and Partnership*, Lincoln: University of Nebraska Press, 1994

Jaffé, Patricia, *Women Engravers*, London: Virago, 1988

Juno, Andrea and V. Vale, *Angry Women*, no.13, San Francisco: Re/Search Publications, 1991 (16 women performance artists discuss a wide range of topics concerning social and political inequalities)

Karas, Maria, *The Woman's Building, Chicago 1893/The Woman's Building, Los Angeles, 1973*, Los Angeles: Woman's Graphic Center, 1975

Kavaler-Adler, Susan, *The Compulsion to Create: A Psychoanalytic Study of Women Artists*, London and New York: Routledge, 1993

Keener, Frederick M. and Susan E. Lorsch, eds, *Eighteenth-Century Women and the Arts*, Westport, CT, and New York: Greenwood Press, 1988

Kimball, Gayle, ed., *Women's Culture: The Women's Renaissance of the Seventies*, Metuchen, NJ: Scarecrow Press, 1981 (includes the section: "The visual arts")

King-Hammond, Leslie, *Gumbo ya ya: Anthology of Contemporary African-American Women Artists*, New York: Midmarch Arts Press, 1995

Kirby, Sandy, *Sight Lines: Women's Art and Feminist Perspectives in Australia*, Sydney: Craftsman House/Gordon and Breach, 1992

Kirker, Anne, *New Zealand Women Artists: A Survey of 150 Years*, Auckland, New Zealand: Reed Methuen, 1986; 2nd edition, Tortola, BVI: Craftsman House, 1993

Kirkland, Frances and Winifred Kirkland, *Girls Who Became Artists*, New York: Harper, 1934

Klinger, Linda and Wayne Kurie, *International Women in Design*, Washington, DC: Supon Design Group, 1993

Kluge, Helen Lait and others, *Billedet som kampmiddel: Kvindebilleder mellem 1968 og 1977*, Copenhagen: Information Forlag, 1977

Kramer, Jack, *Women of Flowers: A Tribute to Victorian Women Illustrators*, New York: Stewart Tabori and Chang, 1996

Krull, Edith, *Women in Art*, London: Studio Vista, 1989 (German original, 1984)

LaDuke, Betty, *Africa Through the Eyes of Women Artists*, Trenton, NJ: Africa World Press, 1991

—, *Compañeras: Women, Art and Social Change in Latin America*, San Francisco: City Lights, 1985

—, *Women Artists: Multi-Cultural Visions*, Trenton, NJ: Red Sea Press, 1992

Lambton, Gunda, *Stealing the Show: Seven Women Artists in Canadian Public Art*, Montreal and New York: McGill-Queen's University Press, 1994

Lang, Gladys Engel and Kurt Lang, *Etched in Memory: The Building and Survival of Artistic Productivity*, Chapel Hill: University of North Carolina Press, 1990 (includes the chapter: "The case of the disappearing lady etchers")

Lauter, Estella, *Women as Mythmakers: Poetry and Visual Art by Twentieth-Century Women*, Bloomington: Indiana University Press, 1984

Lindberg, Anna Lena and Barbro Werkmäster, eds, *Kvinnor som konstnärer*, Stockholm: Liber, 1975

Lippard, Lucy R., *From the Center: Feminist Essays on Women's Art*, New York: Dutton, 1976

—, *The Pink Glass Swan: Selected Essays on Feminist Art*, New York: New Press, 1995

Loeb, Judy, *Feminist Collage: Educating Women in the Visual Arts*, New York: Teachers College, Columbia University, 1979

Lyle, Cindy, Sylvia Moore and Cynthia Navaretta, eds, *Women Artists of the World*, New York: Midmarch, 1984

McCarthy, Kathleen D., *Women's Culture: American Philanthropy and Art, 1830–1930*, Chicago: University of Chicago Press, 1991

McQuiston, Liz, *Women in Design: A Contemporary View*, New York: Rizzoli, 1988

Mandel, William M., *Soviet Women*, Garden City, NY:

Doubleday / Anchor, 1975 (includes the chapter: "Artists and sports")

Marsh, Jan and Pamela Gerrish Nunn, *Women Artists and the Pre-Raphaelite Movement*, London: Virago, 1989

Meskimmon, Marsha and Shearer West, eds, *Visions of the "Neue Frau": Women and the Visual Arts in Weimar Germany*, Aldershot: Scolar Press, 1995

Miller, Lynn F. and Sally S. Swenson, *Lives and Works: Talks with Women Artists*, Metuchen, NJ: Scarecrow Press, 1981

Miner, Dorothy, *Anastaise and Her Sisters: Women Artists of the Middle Ages*, Baltimore: Walters Art Gallery, 1974

Möbius, Helga, *Women of the Baroque Age*, Montclair, NJ: Schram, 1984 (includes the chapter: "Women artists")

Moore, Catriona, ed., *Dissonance: Feminism and the Arts, 1970–90*, St Leonards, NSW: Allen and Unwin; Woolloomooloo, NSW: Artspace, 1994

Moutoussamy-Ashe, Jeanne, *Viewfinders: Black Women Photographers*, New York: Dodd Mead, 1986

Munro, Eleanor, *Originals: American Women Artists*, New York: Simon and Schuster, 1979

Munsterberg, Hugo, *A History of Women Artists*, New York: Clarkson Potter, 1975

Nabakowski, Gislind, Helke Sander and Peter Gorsen, *Frauen in der Kunst*, 2 vols, Frankfurt am Main: Suhrkamp, 1980

National Museum of Women in the Arts, New York: Abrams, 1987 (catalogue of the permanent collection)

1990 Collection: A Portfolio of Australian Women Artists, The New South Wales Cancer Council, 1990

Nochlin, Linda, *Women, Art and Power, and Other Essays*, New York: Harper, 1989

Nunn, Pamela Gerrish, *Canvassing Women: Recollections by Six Victorian Women Artists*, London: Camden, 1986

—, *Victorian Women Artists*, London: Women's Press, 1987

Opfell, Olga S., *Special Visions: Profiles of Fifteen Women Artists from the Renaissance to the Present Day*, Jefferson, NC: McFarland, 1991

Orr, Clarissa Campbell, ed., *Women in the Victorian Art World*, Manchester: Manchester University Press, 1995

Oulmont, Charles, *Les Femmes peintres du dix-huitième siècle*, Paris: Les Editions Rieder, 1928

Palmquist, Peter E., *A Directory of Women in California Photography before 1901*, Arcata, CA: Palmquist, 1990

—, *A Directory of Women in California Photography, 1900–1920*, Arcata, CA: Palmquist, 1991

Parada y Santin, José, *Las pintoras españolas: Boceto histórico-biográfico y artístico*, Madrid: Imprenta del Asilo de Huérfanos del sagrado Corazón de Jesús, 1903

Parker, Rozsika and Griselda Pollock, *Old Mistresses: Women, Art and Ideology*, London and New York: Routledge, 1981

—, *Framing Feminism: Art and the Women's Movement, 1970–1985*, London and New York: Pandora, 1987

Perry, Gill, *Women Artists and the Parisian Avant-Garde*, Manchester: Manchester University Press, and New York: St Martin's Press, 1995

Petersen, Karen and J. J. Wilson, *Women Artists: Recognition and Reappraisal from the Early Middle Ages to the Twentieth Century*, New York: Harper, 1976; London: Women's Press, 1978

Plakolm-Forsthuber, Sabine, *Künstlerinnen in Österreich,*

1897–1938: Malerei, Plastik, Architektur, Vienna: Picus, 1994

Pollock, Griselda, *Avant-Garde Gambits, 1888–1893: Gender and the Colour of Art History*, London and New York: Thames and Hudson, 1992

—, *Vision and Difference: Femininity, Feminism and the Histories of Art*, London and New York: Routledge, 1988

Ragg, Laura M., *The Women Artists of Bologna*, London: Methuen, 1907

Raven, Arlene, *Crossing Over: Feminism and Art of Social Concern*, Ann Arbor, MI: UMI Research Press, c.1988

Rheinische Expressionistinnen, Schriftenreihe des Vereins August Macke-Haus, no.10, Bonn, 1993

Robbins, Trina, *A Century of Women Cartoonists*, Northampton, MA: Kitchen Sink Press, 1993

Robinson, Hilary, ed., *Visibly Female: Feminism and Art, An Anthology*, New York: Bantam, 1974

Rosenberg, Judith Pierce, *A Question of Balance: Artists and Writers on Motherhood*, Watsonville, CA: Papier-Mâché Press, 1995

Rosenblum, Naomi, *A History of Women Photographers*, New York: Abbeville, 1994

Roth, Moira, *The Amazing Decade: Women and Performance Art in America, 1970–80*, Los Angeles: Astro Artz, 1983

Rubinstein, Charlotte Streifer, *American Women Artists from Early Times to the Present*, Boston: Hall, 1982

—, *American Women Sculptors: A History of Women Working in Three Dimensions*. Boston: Hall, 1990

Ruddick, Sara and Pamela Daniels, *Working It Out: 23 Women Writers, Artists, Scientists and Scholars Talk about Their Lives and Work*, New York: Pantheon, 1977

Russell, Beverly, *Women of Design: Contemporary American Interiors*, New York: Rizzoli, 1992

Sachs, Hannelore, *The Renaissance Women*, ed. D. Talbot Rice, New York: McGraw Hill, 1971 (includes the chapter: "The practice of art"; German original)

Salaman, Naomi, ed., *What She Wants: Women Artists Look at Men*, London and New York: Verso, 1994

Scheffler, Karl, *Die Frau und die Kunst*, Berlin: Bard, 1908

Schmidt, Margit and Sabine Schutz, eds, *Selbstlaut: Autobiographische Aspekte in der Kunst von Frauen*, Cologne: Richter, 1993

Setting the Pace: The Women's Art Movement, 1980–1983, Adelaide, South Australia: Women's Art Movement, 1984

Sheppard, Alice, *Cartooning for Suffrage*, Albuquerque: University of New Mexico Press, 1994

Sherman, Claire Richter and Adele M. Holcomb, eds, *Women as Interpreters of the Visual Arts, 1820–1979*, Westport, CT: Greenwood Press, 1981

Sills, Leslie, *Inspirations: Stories about Women Artists*, Niles, IL: Albert Whitman, 1989

Skiles, Jacqueline, *The Women Artists' Movement*, Pittsburgh: KNOW, 1972

Skiles, Jacqueline and Janet McDevitt, *A Documentary Herstory of Women Artists in Revolution*, Pittsburgh: KNOW, 1971

Slatkin, Wendy, *Women Artists in History: From Antiquity to the Twentieth Century*, Englewood Cliffs, NJ: Prentice Hall, 1985; revised as *Women Artists in History: From Antiquity to the Present*, 3rd edition, Upper Saddle River, NJ: Prentice Hall, 1997

Snyder-Ott, Joelynn, *Women and Creativity*, Millbrae, CA: Les Femmes, 1978

Spacks, Patricia Ann Meyer, *The Female Imagination*, New York: Avon Books, 1976

Sparrow, Walter Shaw, ed., *Women Painters of the World from the Time of Caterina Vigri (1413–1463) to Rosa Bonheur and the Present Day*, London: Hodder and Stoughton, and New York: Stokes, 1905; reprinted New York: Hacker, 1976

Spencer, Samia I., *French Women and the Age of Enlightenment*, Bloomington: Indiana University Press, 1984 (includes the section: "Creative women and women artists")

Steele, Valerie, *Women of Fashion: Twentieth-Century Designers*, New York: Rizzoli, 1991

Stofflet, Mary, *American Women Artists: The Twentieth Century*, New York: Harper, 1979

Sullivan, Constance, ed., *Women Photographers*, New York: Abrams, 1990

Tippett, Maria, *By A Lady: Celebrating Three Centuries of Art by Canadian Women*, Toronto: Viking, 1992

Topliss, Helen, *Modernism and Feminism: Australian Women Artists, 1900–1940*, Roseville East: Craftsman House, 1996

Torelli, Vieri, *Pittrici e scultrici italiane d'oggi*, [Bologna]: Fiammenghi, [1953]

Tucker, Marcia and others, *Espaces de l'art: Feminisme, art et histoire de l'art*, Paris: Ecole nationale superieure des Beaux-Arts, 1994

Tufts, Eleanor, *Our Hidden Heritage: Five Centuries of Women Artists*, New York and London: Paddington Press, 1974

Urquidi, José Macedonio, *Bolivianas ilustres: Heróinas escritoras, artistas: Estudios, biográficos y críticos*, La Paz: Escuela Tipográfica Salesiana, 1918

Vachon, Marius, *La Femme dans l'art, des protectrices des arts, les femmes artistes*, 2 vols, Paris: Rouan, 1893

Van Wagner, Judy K. Collischan, *Lines of Vision: Drawings by Contemporary Women*, New York: Hudson Hills Press, 1989

—, *Women Shaping Art: Profiles of Power*, New York: Praeger, 1984

Véquard, Yves, *The Women Painters of Mathila*, New York: Hacker, 1986

Voight, Anna, *New Visions, New Perspectives: Voices of Contemporary Australian Women Artists*, Roseville East: Craftsman House, 1996

Von Blum, Paul, *Other Visions, Other Voices: Women Political Artists in Greater Los Angeles*, Lanham, MD: University Press of America, 1994

Waller, Susan, *Women Artists in the Modern Era: A Documentary History*, Metuchen, NJ: Scarecrow Press, 1991

Weese, Maria and Doris Wild, *Die Schweizer Frau in Kunstgewerbe und bildender Kunst*, Zürich: Fussli, 1928

Weiermair, Peter, ed., *Male Nudes by Women: An Anthology*, Zürich: Stemmle, 1995

Weiman, Jeanne Madeline, *The Fair Women*, Chicago: Academy Chicago, 1981

Weiss, Andrea, *Paris Was a Woman: Portraits from the Left Bank*, San Francisco: Harper, 1995 (women artists and writers)

Weltge, Sigrid Wortmann, *Bauhaus Textiles: Women Artists and the Weaving Workshop*, London: Thames and Hudson, 1993; as *Women's Work: Textile Art from the Bauhaus*, San Francisco: Chronicle, 1993

Wheeler, Kenneth W. and Virginia Lee Lussier, *Women, the Arts and the 1920s in Paris and New York*, New Brunswick and London: Transaction, 1982

Wichstrøm, Anne, *Kvinner ved staffeliet: Kvinnelige malere i Norge før 1900*, Oslo: Universitetsforlaget, 1983 (revised edition in preparation)

Wiesenfeld, Cheryl and others, *Women See Woman*, New York: Crowell, 1976

Wilding, Faith, *By Our Own Hands: The Women Artist's Movement, Southern California, 1970–1976*, Santa Monica: Double X, 1977

Williams, Val, *Woman Photographers: The Other Observers, 1900 to the Present*, London: Virago, 1986; as *The Other Observers: Women Photographers in Britain, 1900 to the Present*, 1991

Wilson, Shirley Cameron, *From Shadow into Light: South Australian Women Artists Since Colonisation*, Adelaide: Delmont, 1988

Witzling, Mara R., ed., *Voicing Our Visions: Writings by Women Artists*, New York: Universe, 1991; London: Women's Press, 1992

—, *Voicing Today's Visions: Writings by Contemporary Women Artists*, New York: Universe, 1994

Wolf-Graaf, Anke, *Die Verborgene Geschichte der Frauenarbeit: Eine Bildchronik*, Basel: Beltz, 1983

Yablonskaya, M.N., *Women Artists of Russia's New Age, 1910–1935*, New York: Rizzoli, and London: Thames and Hudson, 1989

Yeldham, Charlotte, *Women Artists in Nineteenth-Century France and England: Their Art Education, Exhibition Opportunities and Memberships in Exhibiting Societies and Academies with an Assessment of the Subject Matter of Their Work and Summary Biographies*, 2 vols, New York: Garland, 1984

4. Women Artists: Exhibition Catalogues

Catalogue, International Exhibition, 1879: Official Catalogue, Part III, Women's Pavilion at the Philadelphia Centennial Exhibition, 1876

The Work of Women Etchers of America: An Exhibition, Union League Club, New York, and elsewhere, 1888

Catalogue of a Collection of Engravings, Etchings and Lithographs by Women, Grolier Club, New York, 1901

Die Kunst der Frau: XXXVII. Austellung der Vereiningung Bildender Künstler Österreichs Secession, Wien: 1. Ausstellung der Vereinigung Bildender Künstlerinnen Österreichs, Wiener Secession, Vienna, 1910

Catalog of an Exhibition of Paintings, Sculpture, Drawings and Prints by the New York Society of Women Artists [bound with] *Catalog of an Exhibition of Paintings and Sculpture by the Society of Swedish Women Artists*, Brooklyn Museum, NY, 1931

Les Femmes artistes d'Europe exposent au Musée de Paume,

Musée des Ecoles Etrangères contemporaines du Jeu de Paume des Tuileries, Paris, and elsewhere, 1937

Fiftieth Anniversary Exhibition 1889–1939: National Association of Women Painters and Sculptors, American Fine Arts Building, New York, 1939

International Women Painters, Sculptors, Gravers, Riverside Museum, New York, 1940

Famous British Women Artists, Graves Art Gallery, Sheffield, 1953

Women Printmakers, Philadelphia Museum of Art, 1956

Die Frau als Künstlerin: Werke aus vier Jahrhunderten, Helmhaus, Zürich, 1958

Paintings and Drawings by Some Women War Artists, Imperial War Museum, London, 1958

Women Artists in America Today, Dwight Art Memorial, Mount Holyoke College, South Hadley, MA, 1962

Women in Contemporary Art, Woman's College Gallery, Duke University, Durham, NC, 1963

Women Artists of America, 1707–1964, Newark Museum, NJ, 1965

The American Woman as Artist, 1820–1965, Pollock Galleries, Southern Methodist University, Dallas, 1966

The Pennsylvania Academy and Its Women: 1850–1885: Portraits and Still Life, Peale Museum, Baltimore, 1967

Fotografinnen, Folkwang Museum, Essen, 1970

Twenty-Six Contemporary Women Artists, Aldrich Museum of Contemporary Art, Ridgefield, CT, 1971

Women Artists Series, Mabel Smith Douglass Library, Douglass College, Rutgers University, New Brunswick, 1971– (annual exhibition of women artists)

American Woman Artist Show, Kunsthaus Hamburg, 1972

A New Vitality in Art: The Black Woman, John and Norah Warbeke Gallery, Mount Holyoke College, South Hadley, MA, 1972

Invisible / Visible: Twenty-One Artists, Long Beach Museum of Art, CA, 1972

New York Women Artists, University Art Gallery, State University of New York at Albany, 1972

Old Mistresses: Women Artists of the Past, Walters Art Gallery, Baltimore, 1972

Unmanly Art, Suffolk Museum, Stony Brook, NY, 1972

The White Marmorean Flock: Nineteenth-Century American Women Neoclassical Sculptors, Vassar College Art Gallery, Poughkeepsie, NY, 1972

Womanhouse, Feminist Art Program, California Institute of the Arts, Valencia, 1972

Women: A Historical Survey of Works by Women Artists, Salem Fine Arts Center, Winston-Salem, NC, 1972

Fourteen American Women Printmakers of the '30s and '40s, Mount Holyoke College Art Museum, South Hadley, MA, 1973

Les Femmes peintres au XVIIIe siècle, Musée Goya, Castres, 1973

The Pennsylvania Academy and Its Women, 1850–1920, Pennsylvania Academy of the Fine Arts, Philadelphia, 1973

Women Choose Women, New York Cultural Center, 1973

In Her Own Image, Fleisher Mar Memorial, Philadelphia, 1974

Women's Work: American Art 1974, Museum of the Philadelphia Civic Center, Philadelphia, 1974

Deutsche bildende Künstlerinnen von der Geithezeit bis zur Gegenwart, Nationalgalerie, Staatliche Museen zu Berlin, 1975

La Femme peintre et sculpteur du 17e siècle au 20e siècle, Grand Palais, Paris, 1975

Frauen-Kunst: Neue Tendenzen, Galerie Krinzinger, Innsbruck, 1975

From Women's Eyes: Women Painters in Canada, Agnes Etherington Art Centre, Kingston, Ontario, 1975

Kvinnfolk, Malmö Konsthall, Malmö, 1975

Kvinnor som målat, Nationalmuseum, Stockholm, 1975

Some Canadian Women Artists, National Gallery of Canada, Ottawa, 1975

Son & Others: Women Artists See Men, Queens Museum, Flushing, NY, 1975

Women Artists: A Review of the Permanent Collection, San Francisco Fine Arts Museum, 1975

Women of Photography: An Historical Survey, San Francisco Museum of Art, and elsewhere, 1975

Works on Paper: Women Artists, Brooklyn Museum, Print Gallery, NY, 1975

The Year of the Woman: Reprise, Bronx Museum of the Arts, NY, 1975

American Artist '76: A Celebration, Marion Koogler McNay Art Institute, San Antonio, TX, 1976 (an exhibition of work by women artists)

7 American Women: The Depression Decade, Vassar College Art Gallery, Poughkeepsie, NY, 1976

Combative Acts, Profiles and Voices: An Exhibition of Women Artists from Paris, AIR Gallery, New York, 1976

From Women's Eyes: Women Painters in Canada, Agnes Etherington Art Centre, Kingston, Ontario, 1976

The Ladies, God Bless 'em: The Women's Art Movement in Cincinnati in the Nineteenth Century, Cincinnati Art Museum, 1976

Nineteenth-Century American Women Artists, Whitney Museum of American Art, Downtown Branch, New York, 1976

Some Forgotten … Some Remembered: Women Artists of South Australia, Sydenham Gallery, Norwood, South Australia, 1976

West of Scotland Women Artists: 25th Anniversary Loan Exhibition, 1951–1976, Victoria Hall, Helensburgh, Scotland, 1976

Women Artists, 1550–1950, Los Angeles County Museum of Art, and elsewhere, 1976

The Woman Artist in the American West, 1860–1960, Muckenthaler Cultural Center, Fullerton, CA, 1976

Frauen machen Kunst, Galerie Magers, Bonn, 1977

Kunst in der Kornschutte: "Eine Gelbe und eine Violette Frau", Rathaus Luzern, Switzerland, 1977

Künstlerinnen International, 1877–1977, Neue Gesellschaft für Bildende Kunst, Berlin, 1977

National Association of Women Artists, 1889–1977: 88th Annual Exhibition, National Academy of Design, New York, 1977

Women Painters and Poets, Loeb Student Center, Contemporary Arts Gallery, New York University, 1977

Hommage à Goya: Eine Ausstellung der GEDOK, Verband

der Gemeinschaft der Künstlerinnen und Kunstfreunde, Kunsthaus, Hamburg, 1978

Women Artists '78: Metropolitan Area: New York, New Jersey, Connecticut, Graduate Center of the City University of New York, 1978

Artists in Aprons: Folk Art by American Women, Museum of American Folk Art, New York, 1979

Colorado Women in the Arts, Arvada Center for the Arts and Humanities, Arvada, CO, 1979

Feministische Kunst Internationaal, Haags Gemeentemuseum, The Hague, 1979

Künstlerinnen der russischen Avantgarde/Women Artists of the Russian Avant-Garde, 1910–1930, Galerie Gmurzynska, Cologne, 1979

Masculin, feminin, Neue Galerie am Landesmuseum Jaanneum, Graz, 1979

Recollections: Ten Women of Photography, International Center of Photography, New York, and elsewhere, 1979

Umrisse: Bilder, Objeckte, Videos, Filme von Künstlerinnen, Kunsthalle zu Kiel, 1979

Women Artists in Washington Collections, University of Maryland Art Gallery, College Park, 1979

Danske kvindelige kunstnere fra det 19. og 20. århundrede / Women Artists of the 19th and 20th Centuries in the Collection of the Royal Museum of Fine Arts, Royal Museum of Fine Arts, Copenhagen, 1980

First International Festival of Women Artists, Carlsberg Glyptotek, Copenhagen, 1980

L'altra metà dell'avanguardia, 1910–1940: Pittrici e scultrici nei movimenti delle avanguardie storiche, Palazzo Reale, Milan, and elsewhere, 1980

La Femme artiste d'Elisabeth Vigée-Lebrun à Rosa Bonheur, Musée Despiau-Wlerick, Donjon Lacataye, Mont-de-Marsan, 1981

Forever Free: Art by African-American Women, 1862–1980, Center for the Visual Arts Gallery, Illinois State University, Normal, and elsewhere, 1981

Home Work: The Domestic Environment Reflected in Work by Contemporary Women Artists, National Women's Hall of Fame, Seneca Falls, NY, 1981

Künstlerinnen aus Mexiko: Fiona Alexander...[et al.], Kunstlerhaus Bethanien, Berlin, and elsewhere, 1981

Målarinnor från Finland: Seitsemän suomalaista taiteilijaa, Nationalmuseum, Stockholm, and elsewhere, 1981

Transformations: Women in Art '70s–'80s, New York Coliseum, 1981

Typisch Frau, Bonner Kunstverein und Galerie Magers, Bonn, 1981

Art et féminisme, Musée d'art contemporain, Montreal, 1982

A Centenary Exhibition to Celebrate the Founding of the Glasgow Society of Lady Artists in 1882, Collins Gallery, Glasgow, 1982

Homage to Women Artists of the Americas: A Selection of Works from the Permanent Collection of the Museum of Modern Art of Latin America, Museum of Modern Art of Latin America, Washington, DC, 1982

Kvinners bilder: Malerinner i Norge før 1900, Kunstnerforbundet, Oslo, 1982

Views by Women Artists: Sixteen Independently Curated Theme Shows Sponsored by the New York Chapter of the Women's Caucus for Art, New York Chapter of the Women's Caucus for Art, New York, 1982 (umbrella catalogue)

Women's Art Show, 1550–1970, Nottingham Castle Museum, 1982

Latin American Women Artists, Bronx Museum of the Arts, NY, 1982

Frauen und Kunst im Mittelalter, Städtische Gallery, Wolfsburg, 1983

L'Avant-garde au féminin: Moscou—Saint-Petersbourg—Paris, 1907–1930, Centre d'art plastique contemporain, Paris, 1983

Women Artists from Puerto Rico, Cayman Gallery, New York, 1983

Women Artists: Selected Works from the Collection, Herbert F. Johnson Museum of Art, Cornell University, Ithaca, NY, 1983

The Feminine Gaze: Women Depicted by Women, 1900–1930, Whitney Museum of American Art, New York, 1984

Utopia, Frauen Museum, Bonn, 1984

Schweizer Künstlerinnen heute, Helmhaus, Zürich, 1984

Die Rationale: Rationale Konzepte von Künstlerinnen, 1915–1985, Frauen Museum, Bonn, 1985

Kunst Mit Eigen-Sinn: Aktuelle Kunst von Frauen: Texte und Dokumentation, Museum Moderner Kunst, Vienna, and Museum des 20. Jahrhunderts, Munich, 1985

Women Artists of South Africa/Vrouekunstenaars in Suid-Afrika, South African National Gallery, Cape Town, 1985

Women Stained Glass Artists of the Arts and Crafts Movement, William Morris Gallery, London, 1985

A Graphic Muse: Prints by Contemporary American Women, Mount Holyoke College Art Museum, South Hadley, MA, and elsewhere, 1987

American Women Artists, 1830–1930, National Museum of Women in the Arts, Washington, DC, 1987

Das Verborgene Museum I: Dokumente von Frauen in Berliner öffentlichen Sammlungen, Akademie der Künste, Berlin, 1987

The Genius of the Fair Muse: Paintings and Sculpture: Celebrating Women Artists, 1875–1945, Grand Central Art Galleries, New York, 1987

Irish Women Artists from the Eighteenth Century to the Present Day, National Gallery of Ireland, Dublin, and elsewhere, 1987

La Femme et le surréalisme, Musée Cantonal des Beaux-Arts, Lausanne, 1987

Standing Ground: Sculpture by American Women, Contemporary Arts Center, Cincinnati, 1987

De drogo till Paris: Nordiska konstnärinnor på 1880-talet, Liljevalchs Konsthall, Stockholm, 1988

Women Artists of the New Deal Era, National Museum of Women in the Arts, Washington, DC, 1988

Women's Works: Paintings, Drawings, Prints and Sculpture by Women Artists in the Permanent Collection: Walker Art Gallery, Liverpool, Lady Lever Art Gallery, Port Sunlight, Sudley Art Gallery, Liverpool, National Museums and Galleries on Merseyside, Liverpool, 1988

Bloemen uit de kelder, Gemeentemuseum, Arnhem, 1989

Making Their Mark: Women Artists Move into the Mainstream, Cincinnati Art Museum, and elsewhere, 1989

Rooms with a View: Women's Art in Norway, 1880–1990, Royal Norwegian Ministry of Foreign Affairs, Oslo, 1989

Three Generations of Greek Women Artists: Figures, Forms and Personal Myths, National Museum of Women in the Arts, Washington, DC, 1989

Künstlerinnen des 20. Jahrhunderts, Museum Wiesbaden, 1990

La mujer en México / Women in Mexico, Centro Cultural / Arte Contemporáneo Mexico, Mexico City, and National Academy of Design, New York, 1990

Artystki polskie, National Museum, Warsaw, 1991

Voices of Freedom: Polish Women Artists and the Avant-Garde, National Museum of Women in the Arts, Washington, DC, 1991

Den fries kvindelige kunstnere, 1891, Kvindemuseet, Århus, and Skagens Museum, Skagen, 1991

Domesticity and Dissent: The Role of Women Artists in Germany, 1918–1938, Leicester Museum and Art Gallery, and elsewhere, 1992

Profession ohne Tradition: 125 Jahre Verein der Berliner Künstlerinnen, Berlinische Galerie, Berlin, 1992

Ten Decades: Careers of Ten Women Artists Born 1897–1906, Norwich Gallery, Norfolk Institute of Art and Design, Norwich, 1992

A Century of Australian Women Artists: 1840s–1940s, Deutscher Fine Art, Melbourne, 1993

Important Australian Women Artists, Melbourne Fine Arts Gallery, Melbourne, 1993

Regardes de femmes, Musée d'art moderne, Liège, 1993

Ultra Modern: The Art of Contemporary Brazil, National Museum of Women in the Arts, Washington, DC, 1993

A Struggle for Fame: Victorian Women Artists and Authors, Yale Center for British Art, New Haven, 1994

"Den otroliga verkligheten": 13 kvinnliga pionjärer , Prins Eugens Waldermarsudde, Stockholm, and elsewhere, 1994

South Australian Women Artists: Paintings from the 1890s to the 1940s, Art Gallery of South Australia, Adelaide, 1994

At Century's End: Norwegian Artists and the Figurative Tradition, Henie-Onstad Art Center, Høvikodden, Norway, and National Museum of Women in the Arts, Washington, DC, 1995

Frauen im Aufbruch? Künstlerinnen im deutschen Südwesten, 1800–1945, Städtische Galerie, Karlsruhe, 1995

Latin American Women Artists/Artistas Latinoamericanas: 1915–1995, Milwaukee Art Museum, WI, and elsewhere, 1995

Muse küsst Muse: Eine zeitgenössische Reflexion über historische Künstlerinnen, Lindenau-Museum, Altenberg, 1995

31 Women Artists from 31 Danish Art Museums, Women's Museum, Denmark, 1995

5. Women's Art Periodicals and Special Issues
Women's Art Periodicals

At the Crossroads: Black Women's Art Magazine
Toronto, Ontario, Canada
Current: 1994–

The Blatant Image
Wolfcreek, OR, USA
Ceased: 1981–3

Calyx: A Journal of Art and Literature by Women
Corvalis, OR, USA
Current: 1976–

Camera Obscura: A Journal of Feminism and Film Theory
Berkeley, CA, USA
Current: 1976–

Chrysalis: A Magazine of Women's Culture
Los Angeles, USA
Ceased: 1977–80

Creative Woman
Arlington Heights, IL, USA
Current: 1977–

FAN: Feminist Arts News
Birmingham, UK
Ceased: 1980–93

Feminist Art Journal
Brooklyn, NY, USA
Ceased: 1972–7

Frauen-Kunst-Wissenschaft
Marburg an der Lahn, Germany
Current: 1987–

Gallerie: Women Artists Monograph
(Formerly: *Gallerie: Women's Art*)
North Vancouver, BC, Canada
Current: 1988–

Helicon Nine: A Journal of Women's Art and Letters
Kansas City, USA
Ceased: 1979–89

Heresies: A Feminist Publication on Art and Politics
New York, USA
Ceased: 1977–96

Hot Flashes
c/o Guerrilla Girls, New York, USA
Ceased: 1993–95
(New on-line format: http://www.voyagerco.com/gg/)

Kalliope, A Journal of Women's Art
Florida Community College, Jacksonville, FL, USA
Current: 1979–

Kassandra: Feministische zeitschrift fur die visuellen Kunste
Berlin, Germany
Ceased[?]: 1977–

Lapis
Milan, Italy
Current[?]: 1987–

Leggere Donna
Ferrara, Italy
Current: 1980–

Lip: Australian Feminist Art Journal
Carlton, Victoria, Australia
Ceased[?]: 1976–

Matriart
Women's Art Resource Centre

Toronto, Ontario, Canada
Current: 1990–

N. Paradoxa
http://web.ukonline.co.uk/members/n.paradoxa/index.htm
Current: 1996–

Ruimte: Vrouw en Kunst
Amsterdam, Netherlands
Current: 1992–

Sibyl-Child: A Woman's Arts and Culture Journal
Silver Spring, MD, USA
Ceased: 1975–88

Spirale
London, Ontario, Canada
Ceased: 1981–3

Womanart
Brooklyn, NY, USA
Ceased: 1976–8

Woman's Art Journal
Knoxville, TN, USA
Current: 1980–

Womanspace Journal
Los Angeles, USA
Ceased: 1973

Women Artists News
(Formerly: *Women Artists Newsletter*)
New York, USA
Current: 1975–

Women in the Arts
National Museum of Women in the Arts, Washington, DC,
   USA
Current: 1987–

Women in the Arts Bulletin
Women in the Arts Foundation, New York, USA
Ceased: 1973–93

Women in Photography
Los Angeles, USA
Current: 1980–

Women's Art Magazine
(Formerly: *Women Artists Slide Library Journal*)
London, UK
Current: 1985–

Women's Art Registry of Minnesota (WARM) Journal
Minneapolis, USA
Current: 1980–

Special Issues

Art Criticism
vol.1, no.2 (1979)
"Women's art: A series of four articles"

Art Education
(November 1975)
Entire issue devoted to the subject of women in the arts

Art Journal
vol.35, no.4 (Summer 1976)

Entire issue devoted to the subject of women in the arts

Art Magazine
vol.5, no.15 (Fall 1973)
"5th anniversary issue: A survey of women in art"
vol.7, no.24 (December 1975)
"In celebration of women's year in Canada"

Art News
vol.69, no.9 (January 1971)
"Women's liberation, women artists and art history: A special
   issue"
vol.70, no.8 (October 1980)
"Where are the great men artists?"

Artes Visuales
(January–March 1976)
"Mujeres / arte / femineidad"

Arts in Society
vol.11, no.1 (Spring–Summer 1974)
"Women and the arts"

Artweek
vol.8, no.4 (22 January 1977)
"Women artists throughout history"
vol.8, no.6 (5 February 1977)
"Women artists, 1800–1950"

Connexions: An International Women's Quarterly
no.24 (Fall 1987)
"Visual arts"

Dada/Surrealism
no.18 (1989)
"Surrealism and women"

Exposure
vol.19, no.3 (1981)
"Women in photography"

Fotozoom
vol.11, no.131 (August 1986)
"Mujeres × mujeres"

Meanjin Quarterly
vol.34, no.4 (December 1975)
"Women in the arts"

The Mentor
vol.2 (16 March 1914)
"Famous American women painters"
vol.6 (1 February 1919)
"Women sculptors of America"

National Sculpture Review
vol.24, nos 2–3 (Summer–Fall 1975)
"American women sculptors: part 1"
vol.24, no.4 (Winter 1975–6)
"American women sculptors: part 2"

Obliques
no.14–15 (1977)
"La femme surréaliste"

Opus International
vol.88 (Spring 1983)
"L'apport la part des femmes"

Sage: A Scholarly Journal on Black Women
vol.4, no.1 (Spring 1987)
"Artists and artisans"

The Southern Quarterly: A Journal of Arts in the South
vol.17, no.2 (Winter 1979)
"Art and feminism"

Southwest Art
vol.10, no.11 (April 1981)
Entire issue devoted to the subject of women in the arts
vol.25, no.6 (November 1995)
"Women in the arts"

Take One
vol.3, no.2 (February 1972)
"Women in film"

Village Voice
vol.32, no.40 (6 October 1987)
Special section: "What do women artists want?"

Visual Dialog
vol.1, no.2 (Winter 1975–6)
vol.2, no.3 (Winter 1976–7)
"Women in the visual arts"

Women Studies
vol.6, no.1 (1978)
"Women artists on women artists"

6. Indices

Allen, Martha Leslie, ed., *Index Directory of Women's Media*, Women's Institute for Freedom of the Press, 1972–
Brownmiller, Sara, *An Index to Women's Studies Anthologies: Research Across the Disciplines, 1980–1984*, Boston: Hall, 1994
Cardinale, Susan, *Anthologies By and About Women: An Analytical Index*, Westport, CT: Greenwood Press, 1982
Herman, Kali, *Women in Particular: An Index to American Women*, Phoenix, AZ: Oryx Press, 1984
Ireland, Norma Olin, *Index of Women of the World from Ancient to Modern Times*, Westwood, MA: Faxon, 1970
Women's Studies Index, Boston: Hall, 1991–
Women's Studies on CD-ROM, Boston: Hall, 1995–

7. Resource Centres

Archive of Women Artists
c/o Chris Petteys
309 Delmar Street
Sterling, CO 80751
USA

Archives of Women Sculptors
Blagg-Huey Library, Special Collections
Texas Women's University
PO Box 23715
Denton, TX 76204
USA

Archives on Women Artists
Art Reference Library
Brooklyn Museum
188 Eastern Parkway
Brooklyn, NY 11238
USA

Archives on Women Artists
Library and Research Center
National Museum of Women in the Arts
1250 New York Avenue, NW
Washington, DC 20005
USA

The Faucett Library
London Guildhall University
Calcutta House, Old Castle Street
London E1 7NT
UK

Frauen Museum
im Krausfeld 10
5300 Bonn 1
Germany

International Women Artists Archive (IWAA)
PO Box 600
Hadley, MA 01035
USA

Mabel Smith Douglass Library
Rutgers University
Chapel Drive
New Brunswick, NJ 08903
USA

New York Feminist Art Institute Archive
91 Franklin Street
New York, NY 10013
USA

Resource Centre
Museum of Women's Art
Second Floor North
55/63 Goswell Road
London EC1V 7EN
UK

Stichting Vrouwen in de Beeldende Kunst
Keizersgracht 10
1015 CN Amsterdam
Netherlands

The Arthur and Elizabeth Schlesinger Library on the History of Women in America
Radcliffe College
10 Garden Street
Cambridge, MA 02138
USAWomen Artists' Archive
300 Riverside Drive
New York, NY 10025
USA

Women Artists' Archive
Ruben Salazar Library
Sonoma State University
Rohnert Park, CA 94928
USA

Women's Art Library
(Formerly: Women Artists Slide Library)
Fulham Palace
Bishops Avenue

London SW6 6EA
UK

Women's Art Register
Carringbush Regional Library
415 Church Street
Richmond, Victoria 3121
Australia

Women's Art Resource Centre
80 Spadina Avenue, Suite 506
Toronto, Ontario M5V 2J3
Canada

8. Miscellaneous
Relating to Women in the Arts

Fine, Elsa Honig, Lola B. Gellman and Judy Loeb, *Women's Studies and the Arts*, Philadelphia: Women's Caucus for Art, 1978

Garrard, Mary D., *Slides of Works by Women Artists: A Source Book*, New York: College Art Association, Women's Caucus, 1974

Landon, Ann R., *Women Visual Artists You Might Like to Know: A Quick Reference Guide for Teachers and Others*, Hamden, CT: Women in the Arts, 1990

Navaretta, Cynthia, *Guide to Women's Art Organizations and Directory for the Arts*, New York: Midmarch, 1982

Relating to Women

Dickstein, Ruth, Victoria A. Mills and Ellen J. Waite, eds, *Women in LC's Terms: A Thesaurus of Library of Congress Subject Headings Relating to Women*, Phoenix, AZ: Oryx Press, 1988

Doss, Martha Merrill, *Women's Organizations: A National Directory*, Garrett Park, MD: Garrett Park Press, 1986

Hinding, Andrea, ed., *Women's History Sources: A Guide to Archives and Manuscript Collections in the United States*, New York: Bowker, 1979

Lerner, Gerda, *Women are History: A Bibliography in the History of American Women*, Madison: Graduate Program in Women's History, Department of History, University of Wisconsin, 4th edition, 1986

National Women's Studies Association Directory of Women's Studies Programs, Women's Centers and Women's Research Centers, College Park, MD: National Women's Studies Association, 1990

Women's Studies Encyclopedia, ii: *Literature, Arts and Learning*, ed. Helen Tierney, Westport, CT, and New York: Greenwood Press, 1990

Women Artists On-line

Guerrilla Girls
http://www.voyagerco.com/gg/
Isis: Art and Culture of Women of the African Diaspora
http://www.netdiva.com/isis.html
Women Artists: An On-line Art Index
http://sunsite.unc.edu/cheryb/women
Women Artists Archive
http://www.sonoma.edu/library/special/waa

Women's Studio Workshop
http://www.webmark.com/wsw/wswhome.htm
The World's Women On-Line
http://wwol.inre.asu.edu/isa.html

Frequently Cited Institutions (with translations)

Academia de Bellas Artes
Academy of Fine Arts

Académie Royale de Peinture et de Sculpture
Royal Academy of Painting and Sculpture

Accademia di Belle Arti
Academy of Fine Arts

Allgemeiner Deutscher Frauenverein
General Germany Women's Association

Bund Deutscher und Österreichischer Künstlerinnenvereine
Union of German and Austrian Women Artists' Associations

Damenakademie des Münchner Künstlerinnenvereins
Ladies' Academy of the Munich Association of Women Artists

Das Junge Rheinland
The Young Rhineland

Deutsche Akademie der Künste
German Academy of Art

Deutsche Gesellschaft für Photographie
German Photographic Society

Deutscher Künstlerbund
German Artists' Association

Deutscher Werkbund
German Work Association

Ecole des Beaux-Arts
School of Fine Arts

Ecole Gratuite de Dessin pour les Jeunes Filles
Free Drawing School for Young Girls

Escuela de Artes y Oficios
School of Arts and Crafts

Escuela de Bellas Artes
School of Fine Arts

Escuela Especial de Pintura, Escultura y Grabado
Special School of Painting, Sculpture and Printmaking

Exposiciones Nacionales de Bellas Artes
National Fine Arts Exhibitions

Frauenkunstverband
League of Women's Art

Freie Secession
Free Secession

GEDOK (Gemeinschaft Deutscher und Österreichischer Künstlerinnen)
Association of German and Austrian Women Artists

Grossherzogliche Sächsische Hochschule für Bildende Kunst
Grand Duke of Saxony High School for the Visual Arts

Handwerker- und Kunstgewerbeschule, Hannover
School of Artisans and Applied Art, Hannover

Hochschule für Angewandte Kunst, Berlin-Weissensee
High School of Applied Art, Berlin-Weissensee

Institut für höheren weiblichen Zeichenunterricht
Institute for Higher Female Instruction in Drawing

Kunstgewerbeschule
School of Applied Art

Kunstgewerbliche Werkstätte
Applied Art Workshop

Kunstschule für Frauen und Mädchen, Vienna
Vienna Art School for Women and Girls

Kunstverein
Artists' Association

Malerinnenschule
Women Painters School

Münchener Neue Secession
Munich New Secession

Neue Künstlervereinigung München (NKVM)
New Artists' Association, Munich

Österreichischer Werkbund
Austrian Work Association

Schule für Kunststickerei
School for Needlework

Società delle Giovani Italiane per Promuovere la Coltura delle
  Lettere, delle Arti e delle Altre Virtù nella Donna
Society of Young Italian Women for Promoting the Cultivation
  of Literature, Arts and Other Virtues in Women

Société des Aquarellistes
Society of Watercolour Painters

Société des Femmes Artistes
Society of Women Artists

Société Nationale des Beaux-Arts
National Society of Fine Arts

Staatliche Kunstschule Berlin
State Art School, Berlin

Union des Femmes Peintres et Sculpteurs
Union of Women Painters and Sculptors

Verband Bildender Künstler der DDR
Association of Artists of the GDR

Verein der Künstlerinnen und Kunstfreundinnen zu Berlin
Association of Berlin Women Artists and Amateurs of Art

Verein der Künstlerinnen zu Berlin
Association of Berlin Women Artists

Wiener Frauenkunst
Vienna Women Art

Wiener Kunstschule für Frauen und Mädchen
Vienna Art School for Women and Girls

Wiener Werkstätte
Vienna Workshop

Zeichen- und Malschule des Vereins der Künstlerinnen und
  Kunstfreundinnen zu Berlin
School of Drawing and Painting of the Association of Berlin
  Women Artists and Amateurs of Art

INTRODUCTORY SURVEYS

Women as Artists in the Middle Ages
"The Dark Is Light Enough"

This essay surveys the evidence of women as artists in the Western and Byzantine Middle Ages in the centuries between about 600 and 1400. Dorothy Miner's *Anastaise and Her Sisters* (1974) laid the foundation for current inquiry into medieval women's art.[1] Much of the data that she – and indeed that we today – rely upon was noted already in 19th- and early 20th-century sources.[2] Our task has been its assembly and, more importantly, its interpretation. Composing a fabric within which to understand the widely scattered women whom we discover challenges many of our preconceptions about the production, the consumption and indeed the very definition of art in the Middle Ages. The job of interpreting women as artists has been enriched by recent insights into women's prominent role as cultural patrons in the Middle Ages.[3] The work of women as creators of rich and significant artefacts takes its place within this broader rediscovery of women as arbiters of medieval culture.

Inevitably the search for medieval women artists depends to a fair extent upon the search for signed works. But signatures are notoriously slippery in medieval art. Although medieval works are more often signed than we generally imagine (see Bergmann 1985 and Legner 1985, both with bibliographies), names do not necessarily appear in the same contexts or carry the same messages as they do in more modern arts, and they lead less often to the agonistic heroes of self-expression whom groups in search of a history hunger to own. Signatures are problematic not only because of the longstanding reluctance of modern scholars to credit women with the production of the works on which their names actually appear, but because of a genuine ambiguity in medieval attributions of authorship. Craftsperson, designer, entrepreneur and patron may all be identified as the one who "made" a work, and the presence of a name is no guarantee that it singles out the person closest to the modern conception of that work's "creator". Questions of gender more often complicate than clarify this situation. Thus the embroidery of the superb 13th-century Göss vestments in the Museum für Kunst und Industrie, Vienna, is traditionally attributed to the Kunigunde whose name is inscribed in purple silk on the pluvial: "Heavenly Mother receive the gift of Kunigunde, may the pluvial with an alb be pleasing to you, heavenly patron" (*celi matrona Chunegundis suscipe dona, casula cum cappa placeat tibi celica [patrona]*; Bock 1856–71, ii, pp.47 and 296). Had the inscription named a man, he would have been read at once as the vestment's donor; Kunigunde was imagined as an artist because more women than men are known by name as embroiderers. Today scholars regard

Kunigunde, too, as the donor. But should this attribution imply the same relationship to the work that we would assume for a man? Might women, whose names appear with such notable frequency as donors of fine textiles, have been more closely involved and so have assumed more authority than men in the design of such works? Can we assume that they had equal access to the cultural resources that are deployed in the often intricate iconographic programmes of these works? Might they, indeed, have had even greater access to images than men, as Herrin (1982) and Hamburger (1989 and 1991) both suggest, the one for Byzantium, the other for the West?

Such issues of interpretation lead us to search beyond the testimony of signatures to the contexts of medieval luxury production. Legal texts – guild and tax lists, cases at law, deeds of contract, inheritance and sale – have proved to be especially informative about the ways in which work was distributed and valued, but texts that lurk on the edge of legend can offer insights into mentality, as well. Thus, the 9th-century *Vita* of the sainted 7th-century Mosan sisters Harlinde and Renilde is well known for its claim that the sisters wrote and copied so much that it would be laborious for robust men (Eckenstein 1896, p.231). It is less often cited for the way in which it describes their surviving works: a book sparkling with new gold and shining gems, and an embroidery ornate with gold and jewels. The sisters were embroiderers in precious materials, then, as well as scribes; moreover, their work in both media is described with nearly the same words: both are luminous with gold and precious stones. That the "new gold and shining gems" seem in the case of the book to refer to a new, 9th-century cover and not to the sisters' pages is unimportant; what matters in the *Vita* is that golden splendour characterises all their work. It is an aesthetic attribute, a way of conferring greatness. Luminous materials assumed great power in the medieval eye, and metalwork and embroidery were the media that deployed such materials in their purest and most compelling form. Even monumental media such as architecture and sculpture were affected by this. From the silver- and gem-clad chapels of the Merovingians and Byzantines (literally called *soroi* – "reliquaries" – in Constantinople) to the glazed and mosaiced churches of the later medieval West, buildings were assimilated to the quality of fine metalwork and its dazzling, mobile manifestation in the pliant coats of embroidered gold that vested clergy, rulers and ritual spaces. As Dodwell (1982) has shown so vividly, works in gold and gems were the high arts of the Middle Ages. This is precisely what their *Vita* attributes to the sisters Harlinde and Renilde. Their scribal labour was virtuous; their work in gold was great.

These examples illustrate some of the challenges of interpretation that confront one in the quest for women artists in the Middle Ages. There is the question of the extent to which women and women's work were distinct from men and their work; there is the question of women's access to cultural resources; there is the question of what – in the medieval scheme of value – most nearly corresponds to a conception of art and of the artist that we can accept; and there is the question of modes of production and their relation to the names that do appear in inscriptions, documents and narrative sources.

The most explicit documentation on the distribution of labour within the trades comes from the guild lists that survive from Paris, Cologne and London (Uitz 1990; Baron 1968; Michaëlsson 1951). It is probable that the essentially urban and workshop patterns implied in guild organisation characterised Constantinople throughout the period covered in this chapter. In the West, on the other hand, guild lists appear only towards the end of the period treated here, from the 1290s onwards. Relating their testimony to the patterns of production that preceded them has not been done on a systematic basis for women's work. The implications for women of the mature guild system, in turn, extend well beyond the period covered here (for the Netherlands, see Guilds and the Open Market survey). Two things are striking in the evidence offered by the guild lists. One is the pervasiveness of women's presence: women figure in 108 of the 321 professions found in Paris in the years around 1300 (Uitz 1990, p.52). In addition to the guilds engaged in the production of silk and linen cloth that were limited in law or in practice to women alone, we find women in many other trades, including those of painter, glazier, sculptor and metalworker, where they may comprise as many as 12 per cent of the names (Lillich 1985, pp.80–82). Many of the women who appear are widows who inherited their husbands' shops. But others were masters in their own right, and Edith Ennen (1989, p.186) has suggested that the incomes of employed wives helped to finance their husbands' engagement in the otherwise unpaid offices of civic government. If women appear pervasively in the lists, however, the guild lists are equally notable for the numerical dominance they give to men, especially as masters. Both phenomena must to some extent reflect the patterns of work that preceded the guilds during the centuries that dominate this chapter, but it is far from clear just how.

The guilds bring out a fact of medieval evidence: where names appear, women's names appear among them. Book art and textile arts are the skills in which one can most consistently find women named, and so it is in these that one can best ponder the issues of women's artistic productivity. This essay will focus heavily upon these media, examining the evidence for women as artists in textiles and then book arts in the medieval West, and turning thereafter to these same media in Byzantium to see the degree to which patterns prevalent in the West were valid there, as well. This said, it remains to be ascertained to what extent women in fact gravitated to the skills in which their names appear, or whether their names appear in these skills simply because more names of all types are associated with them.

Western Europe

Textile arts

The association of women with textiles and especially needlework is found too persistently throughout the Middle Ages to have escaped commentary, though this commentary, as Rozsika Parker has shown (Parker 1984, pp.13–59), has varied widely, from the Victorian adulation of the myth of cloistered womanhood through the affirmative interest of Parker herself to the opprobrium of Germaine Greer (1979, pp.151–68), who saw in it a confinement of women's ingenuity to a minor and repressive craft. Textiles that bear attributions are characteristically the great ones – large and intricate floor or wall coverings or opulent embroideries in gold and precious gems. Works such as these were exceptional in their own time for their high cost in both materials and labour, and the people associated with them are often of correspondingly elite social status, making it difficult to distinguish patronage from active participation in the design and production of the works: one wonders how many of the 20 crowned women cited in Franz Bock's index (Bock 1856–71, ii, pp.363–77) actually themselves made the gold-gorgeous textiles assigned by legend or inscription to their hands (though see Dodwell 1982, p.70, on Edith, queen of Edward the Confessor of England). None the less, there is enough evidence to make it clear that the association of women and fine textiles was neither a figment of Victorian imagination nor a matter simply of women's exile from the major arts into the realm of craft. This association was as characteristic of Byzantium as it was of the West.

Already in the 5th century, the *Notitia dignitatum*, a Roman inventory of the empire's cities, referred to cloth-manufactories as "gynaecea"; the term continues in the early medieval centuries, and it is as gynaecea that Paul Grimm identifies two rooms at the Ottonian palace at Tilleda in which loom weights and foundations for upright looms were found (Grimm 1963). Their name implies that these were staffed by women, and indeed one hears in 9th-century Augsburg of an estate that employed 24 women in a cloth workshop and at Reichenau of taxes paid in kind with *textura feminae* – women's textile work (Uitz 1990, pp.18–19). There is no evidence that the gynaecea produced fine textiles, but the production of fine textiles, too, is associated with women from the very beginning of the Middle Ages. Caesarius of Arles in 6th-century France and the Council of Clovesho of 747 in England both objected to the amount of time spent by nuns in the production of fine embroidery (such complaints are so frequent that they must be a topos: see Dodwell 1982, p.57, and Eckenstein 1896, p.226), and references to gifts of fine textiles by women are frequent in the early Church.

This is especially true in England, where women figure recurrently in early saints' lives as the source of fine textiles. Thus, the silken shroud of St Wilfrid (d. 709 or 710) and the fine shroud of St Guthlac (d. 715) were both provided by abbesses, and St Cuthbert (d. 687) is said by the *Liber Eliensis* to have received silks magnificently embroidered with gold and precious gems by St Etheldreda of Ely (Dodwell 1982, p.49, though he doubts the report on Etheldreda since it is not recorded by Bede; Eckenstein 1896, p.225). Etheldreda belonged to the royal elite of the realm, and it is around such noble figures that reports of wondrous works of textile art cluster most richly. We see this at Etheldreda's Ely itself. We hear not only of Etheldreda's skill in the 7th century, but later of Aelfflaed, widow of Byrhtnoth, earldorman of Ely (d. 991 at the Battle of Maldon), who gave the abbey church of Ely a woven or embroidered hanging that was figured with her dead husband's deeds (Budny 1991; Dodwell 1982, p.135). A generation later Aethelswitha, daughter of King Canute, refused marriage and retired to a dwelling near Ely, where, *cum puellulis* – with a group of young girls – she devoted herself to the production of gold embroidery for the abbey; a headband made with her own hands still survived in the late 12th century (Bock 1856–71, i, p.153; Dodwell 1982, p.70). These accounts from Ely embrace lay and cloistered women, large works and small, and sacred and secular subject matter. All, however, are recorded because of their splendour. How impressive such pieces could be is indicated by the account of an altar frontal embroidered in 1016 by Aethelswitha's mother, Queen Aelgiva, which was so richly studded with gold, pearls and gems that it was said to resemble the monumental medium of gold mosaic (Thieme and Becker 1907–50, i, p.96). The surviving stole of St Cuthbert (Durham Cathedral Treasury; repr. Dodwell 1982, pl.F; Staniland 1991, fig.5), produced between 909 and 916 at the instigation of Queen Aethelfleda, can still give an impression of this work. Who actually made the Cuthbert stole is unknown, but we know of queens commissioning such work from other women. Thus, in 1083 Matilda, queen of William the Conqueror, gave to her foundation of La Trinité at Caen a chasuble embroidered at Winchester by Alderet's wife (Staniland 1991, p.8). A married woman and therefore clearly a lay person, Alderet's wife must have been a professional embroiderer like two women cited in the great inventory of 1086–7 recording property in England known as Domesday Book: Leofgyd, who held an estate in Wiltshire "because she used to make, and still makes, the embroidery of the King and Queen", and Aelfgyd, given land by the sheriff of Buckinghamshire "on condition of her teaching his daughter embroidery work" (*idem*).

The examples cited are assembled from different kinds of evidence, but they are striking in the fact that – as Budny notes – the surviving evidence for the Anglo-Saxon period names women – not men – in conjunction with the production of fine textiles (1991, p.272); women of various social levels practised this work. Their skill is clear; their authority is more complicated. Many of these people probably worked to designs developed by men; we hear, for instance, of the artistically gifted St Dunstan in the 10th century providing a design for a noble lady named Aethelwynn, who embroidered it in gold and jewels (Dodwell 1982, p.70). But in other instances women must have worked to their own designs. The case of Aelfflaed is especially tantalising, for her hanging for Ely anticipates that other great textile war-narrative, the Bayeux Tapestry. A 70-metre-long embroidered narrative of the Norman Conquest of England of 1066 (Wilson 1985; Bernstein 1986), the Bayeux Tapestry is often claimed for women. It can illuminate the question of authorship. Bernstein has traced many of its motifs persuasively to manuscript sources at Canterbury, and so to male designers. Like Queen Matilda, they very probably relied on professional embroiderers – including women – associated with Canterbury to execute their designs (Parker 1984, p.27). A large number of the motifs, however, derive ultimately from

the early 9th-century Utrecht Psalter (Bibliotheek der Rijksuniversiteit te Utrecht, MS 32), which in 1066 was in the great (male) monastic library at Christ Church, Canterbury. But it is important to remember that its exceptionally rich visual imagery has suggested to modern scholars that it was initially made for a woman, the Carolingian queen Judith (McKitterick 1990, p.311). If such books were indeed made for them, early medieval women would scarcely have lacked the iconographic repertoire to design elaborately figured textiles such as Aelfflaed's.

It seems clear that early medieval women participated extensively in the production of fine textiles, and that aristocratic women must have commanded both the craft and the iconographic resources required for the creation of remarkable designs. Evidence from the early medieval Continent only corroborates the role of women as producers of fine textile art. The so-called battle flag of Gerberga of *c*.962 survives as concrete testimony (Backes and Dölling 1971, pp.198–9). A square of silk (33 × 33 cm.) preserved in the treasury of Cologne Cathedral, it is embroidered in gold with figures of Christ, the Archangels and saints, to whom a prostrate Count Ragenardus is shown praying. Beneath him in large letters are the words GERBERGA ME FECIT (Gerberga made me). The name – clearly that of a woman – lies close to his form, suggesting that Gerberga was his wife; if so, she was assuredly a noblewoman.

Women's names continue to appear in conjunction with fine textiles as one moves into the 12th and 13th centuries. At this point, however, the more complex and costly types of production were increasingly dominated by professional ateliers. This is certainly the case with the technique of the knotted carpet, seen in a sequence of 12th-century survivals in Germany culminating in the famous carpet at St Servatius, Quedlinburg, which bears in a metric inscription the name of Agnes of Meissen (d. 1203), noble abbess of the Ottonian imperial convent of Quedlinburg (Wilckens 1992; Stuttgart 1977, i, pp.641–4, ii, figs 597–8). It is unlikely that her nuns themselves practised the new and specialised craft of the pile carpet. But Agnes probably was responsible for the carpet's learned theme, which repeats the subject of Martianus Capellus's *Marriage of Mercury to Philology* already used earlier in a carpet of 995 given by the nun Hedwig to the monastery of St Gall (Eckenstein 1896, p.233).

Mounting professionalism affected both lay and monastic production. In the urban world of lay craftspeople it generated ever-greater specialisation. This is demonstrated in the realm of gold embroidery. Associated particularly with England, as the generic term *opus anglicanum* indicates, gold embroidery was practised in a number of urban centres by the end of the 13th century (see London 1963; Brel-Bordaz 1982; Cologne 1985, ii, pp.140–45). Earlier, as our examples from Ely have shown, costly production had gathered into monastic centres: it may well have been among such groups as the *puellulae* of Ely that the lay embroiderers mentioned in the Domesday Book were trained. In the first half of the 12th century we hear of the pope acquiring embroidery from the mystic and nun Christina of Markyate (Eckenstein 1896, p.227). The signed embroideries by Abbess Iohanna of Beverly in England (an altar frontal of *c*.1290–1340, signed on the back DOMNA IOHANNA BEVERLAI MONACA ME FECIT; London 1963; see illustration), and those

Iohanna of Beverly, embroidered altar frontal, *c.*1290–1320; Victoria and Albert Museum, London

from 13th-century Cologne by the Abbess Iulia (a horizontal border embroidered DOMINA IVLIA ABBATISA; Kunstgewerbe-museum, Berlin; Cologne 1985, ii, pp.441, 443, no.F82) and by Odelia (a border of *c.*1290–1340 signed ODILIA ME FECIT; Victoria and Albert Museum, London; *ibid.*, p.441), who was probably also a nun, although she does not give a title, show that convents continued to produce fine work. Monasteries did, too, as demonstrated by the embroiderers John of Thanet (active 1300–20; Staniland 1991, p.58; London 1963) and Thomas of Selmiston (d. 1419; Parker 1984, p.44).

In 1246, on the other hand, when the pope was impressed by the splendid vestments of the English clergy and sent to England to acquire comparable ones, his request was turned over to the merchants of London (Staniland 1991, pp.10–12). It is to them, also, that the extraordinarily prodigal patronage of the court was committed in the 13th and 14th centuries. Among the embroiderers were many women; their names – most notably that of Mabel of Bury St Edmunds, embroiderer for King Henry III – appear in contracts (*ibid.*, p.10; Lancaster 1972, pp.83–5). But alongside the women were many men: men and women belonged together to long-lived family dynasties of needleworkers, such as the Settere family, and one cannot in any sense designate embroidery as a gender-specific task of women; it was a professional speciality. Thus, Mabel's work was judged by "discreet men and women with knowledge of embroidery"; 112 people – 70 men and 42 women – were engaged in 1330 to embroider counterpanes for Queen Philippa of England (Staniland 1991, pp.13–14, 23); and more men than women are named in the London court records known as the Hustings Rolls from the years around 1300 (Fitch 1976, pp.288–96; Brel-Bordaz 1982, p.21).

One by one, women of real authority who worked as master embroiderers and weavers emerge from these documents: we find women taking on apprentices (Parker 1984, p.47) and occasionally being sued (for a suit against one Katherine Duchewoman who was accused of weaving a tapestry deceptively in 1374, see Amt 1993, p.205). Some tasks seem to have been dominated by women: in Paris the ribbon-makers and braid-makers were all women (Uitz 1990, p.51). But specialisation was not wholly conducive to the woman artist. One notes in the contract for Queen Philippa's counterpanes that the women were paid two-thirds what the men were; moreover, men and women alike worked not to their own designs but to those of professional artists who were hired at twice the needleworkers' wages. Major works were contracted not with the embroiderers themselves but with entrepreneurs who assembled the requisite teams of artists and craftspeople; their exploitative and often biased behaviour is illustrated vividly in

the case brought in 1286 against the Douai wool merchant Jehan Boinebroke by 40 employees including the dyer, Agnes li Patiniere, for defrauding her and a number of other women (Gies and Gies 1978, pp.165–74), and only rarely do women seem to have assumed the status of merchant entrepreneur: just one woman – Rose of Burford, wool merchant and wife of a London wool merchant – is known among those who managed the lucrative embroidery trade in London (Parker 1984, pp.47–8). The statutes of Parisian embroiderers of 1316 – in which nearly half of the 200 names are women's – and the guild lists of Cologne both corroborate the English evidence that women were prominent in the craft of fine textiles; at the same time they confirm the close interaction of men and women, and the very high degree of specialisation that tended to make needlework a craft pursued in hired groups, anonymously, under the hegemony of named artists and commercial entrepreneurs.

Urbanisation and the attendant professional specialisation of trades had an effect upon monastic production as well, and especially upon the urban convents founded with increasing bourgeois support under the aegis of the mendicant and reformed orders. Here, the effect was less specialisation as such than self-sufficiency. One can study this especially in Germany, where Catholic convents were often passed on to Protestant sodalities and so escaped destruction. Recent catalogues on the urban development of Osnabrück, Freiburg, Cologne and Nuremberg all give remarkable vistas into the richness and intensity of the visual culture in the local convents (Braunschweig 1985, Freiburg im Breisgau 1970, Cologne 1985 and Schraut 1987, respectively). Textiles – though unsigned – are prominent. Both the *Ancren riwle*, a devotional text composed around 1200 in England for women anchorites, and the great secular writer Christine de Pisan (or Pizan) around 1400 spoke of nuns producing woven or embroidered objects for sale to help support their houses (Parker 1984, p.43). In the same period we find nuns producing within their own communities the beautiful textiles that outfitted their churches: wall hangings, huge curtains to veil the sanctuary during Lent (*Fastentücher*), garments for their devotional figures of Christ, the Virgin and the saints, and covers for the choir benches. Varied techniques were used – a 14th-century border for an altar that survives at, and was probably produced in, the convent of Isenhagen is entirely embroidered in beads of coral, pearls and other semi-precious stones, recalling Queen Aelgiva's altar frontal in its mosaic-like opulence (Braunschweig 1985, i, pp.472–3, no.389). But the most characteristic technique is the brightly coloured wool embroidery known significantly as *Klosterstich* – that is, convent stitch.[4] A late but fully documented picture of this work is offered by the Saxon convent of Lüne, where some 85 square metres of colourful woollen embroidery were produced by the sisters of the community in the 16 years between 1492 and 1508. Seventeen sisters took part in shifting groups of six to nine at once, signing their work with initials that can – in the one case of Margarete Rosenhagen – be matched with a name in the task-book (Appuhn 1983, p.12). There were celebrations when a piece was finished, but the work was undertaken as a form of devotion and reflects the devotional themes of the sisters' spiritual life. The surviving records at Lüne post-date our period, but big, beautifully embroidered *Fastentücher* survive at Lüne from as early as the beginning of the 14th century, and it seems likely that they, too, were produced internally by members of the convent (*ibid.*, p.21). (The 13th-century *Fastentuch* of Richmod von Adocht, formerly in the church of the Holy Apostles, Cologne, and recorded in the sketchbook of Matthias Joseph de Noël, had the prominent praying figure of a nun in the lower border; repr. Cologne 1985, ii, pp.196–7, no.E15.) How pervasive this model of self-sufficient convent production actually was is debated, as illustrated especially clearly by Moessner's considered treatment of the rich legacy of embroideries – including the famous late 14th-century Tristan tapestry – preserved at the Cistercian convent of Wienhausen (Moessner 1987). In the mid-15th century, however, it is clear that a number of houses – including Wienhausen itself, St Katherine's and the Clarissan convent in Nuremberg, and Heilig Grab in Bamberg – had become significant purveyors of fine textiles, not only adorning their own buildings but filling commissions for secular institutions in their cities.[5] The nine-part tapestry of 1508 (Diözesanmuseum, Bamberg) with its tiny marginal image of nuns at their great upright loom offers a pictorial signature of this kind of convent-industrial women's art (Baumgärtel-Fleischmann 1983, pp.54–5).

The evidence of fine textiles is both rich and elusive. It confirms the fact that, as noted, where names appear, women's names appear among them. Neither types of work nor roles within them – patron, entrepreneur, master, labourer – are gender-segregated. Creative authority, on the other hand, remains harder to assign.

Book arts

Book art is another area in which names – and with them women's names – appear in fair number. It can cast further light on questions posed by the evidence of textiles: of the degree of authority assumed by women in works associated with them, of the relation of women and women's work to men and their work, of the role of monastic as opposed to secular life in women's expression, and of the relative importance of different media.

Testimony to the role of women in the production of books, like that in the production of fine textiles, runs back in hagiographic sources to the very beginning of our period, when the 6th-century Caesaria of Arles is reported both to have copied books and to have trained her nuns to do so, especially the works of her brother Caesarius (Heinrich 1924, p.149; Casa 1993). Already more than a century earlier St Melania had made fair copies of the biblical commentaries and translations of her mentor St Jerome; again later, in the 8th century, we hear

of St Boniface giving Eadburg, Abbess of Thanet, a silver stylus so that she could produce books for him, including a copy of the Epistle of Peter in gold (Heinrich 1924, p.150; for Eadburg's embroidery for Boniface, see Dodwell 1982, p.57). Writing in gold was an activity requiring highly developed skill and judgement. At the same time, however, these accounts indicate that women's scribal work, like that with textiles, was dominated from the beginning by utility.

The earliest surviving group of books that can be assigned to women is the cluster of 13 codices attributed to the convent of Charlemagne's sister, Gisela, at Chelles (Bischoff 1957). Among the 13 is a three-volume copy of Augustine's commentary on the Psalms (Cologne, Dombibliothek, MSS 63, 65 and 67) that preserves the signatures of nine of its ten scribes; all are women. Like the career of Gisela herself, a correspondent and confidante of the scholar Alcuin, the books reflect a learned community. There are no painted ornaments in these volumes, but Bernhard Bischoff (*ibid.*, p.401) would like to attribute to Chelles, as well, the superbly illuminated Gelassy Sacramentary (Biblioteca Apostolica Vaticana, MS Reg.lat. 316). This would not automatically assure its illumination by a woman, for Chelles was a double monastery, twinned with a male institution. We know, however, that women did paint such books. This is indicated by the Gelassy Sacramentary's famous contemporary, the Gellone Sacramentary (Paris, Bibliothèque Nationale, MS lat.12048), produced around 800 at Meaux. The Gellone Sacramentary itself is signed in one of its initials by a man, David. However, its sister manuscript (Cambrai, Bibliothèque Municipale, MS 300), a codex of 198 folios incorporating St Augustine's *De trinitate*, contains in an initial on folio 155r the similar signature of one Madalberta, clearly a woman (*ibid.*, p.410; Lowe 1934–72, v, p.12, no.739; see illustration). Women no less than men moved from calligraphy to design in their manual meditations on sacred Scripture (on the manual meditations of great scribes, see Lewis 1980).

The manuscripts from Chelles confirm the high calligraphic accomplishment at least of a very elite community of early medieval women; they also alert us to key themes of our quest. One is its scribes' role as nuns; Harlinde and Renilde, too, were nuns, and the books of nuns figure throughout the history of medieval women's art. No less significant, however, is its nuns' contact with male religious. Chelles was a double monastery, and Gisela received spiritual advice from Alcuin. Recurrently, we find male spiritual writers turning to women to replicate their works (and so to assure their fame): like Melania and Caesaria, so in the 12th century we find Irmgard and Regelinde of Admont copying the Admont scholar Irembert's commentary on Joshua, Judges and Ruth, a work of more than 1000 pages, and a certain Brother Idung sent his work to be "clearly copied and diligently edited" by the nuns of Niedermünster in Regensburg (Heinrich 1924, p.151). Conversely, the women who were educated in these circumstances became educators of women, and the double monastery plays repeatedly through the history of the medieval bookwoman.

The earliest surviving cycle of figural paintings securely associated with a woman is the rich illumination of the Spanish Beatus of Girona (Girona Cathedral, MS 7), signed in 975 by the scribe Señor and the painters Emeterius and Ende (q.v.). Ende was most probably a nun. Efforts to isolate Ende's

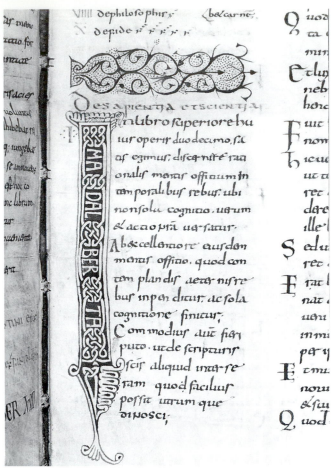

Initial I with the name Madalberta, c.800; Cambrai, Bibliothèque Municipale, MS 300, fol.155r

contribution to this magnificent book have been fraught on the one hand by efforts to distinguish some inherently "female" quality in her art, and on the other by a deep reluctance to credit the colophon's clear statement that a woman was a painter. This reluctance runs recurrently – though not always so ill-advisedly – through the scholarship of the middle third of the 20th century in particular.

The Girona Apocalypse was produced in the double monastery of Tábara in León, and it may well be that Ende lived there. We do, however, know of nuns who worked for houses other than their own. This is the case with the Spanish Benedictine, Londegonda, nun of Bobadilla, who in 912 produced a compilation of monastic rules for the monastery of Samos (cited in Marques Casanovas, Dubler and Neuss 1962, p.71, note 1, quoting Francisco de Asis de Bofarull y Sans, *Conferencias publicas relativas a la Exposición Universal de Barcelona*, Barcelona, 1889). This surely also applies to the elusive German nun, Diemud of Wessobrunn, who produced some 45 manuscripts in the years between 1075 and her death around 1130. Cited as a contemporary of Pope Gregory VII (1073–85) in a manuscript account of the Abbots of Wessobrunn, Diemud is described more fully in the text of an anonymous 16th-century monk of Wessobrunn, who writes of her:

Diemudis was formerly a most devout nun of this our monastery of Wessobrunn. For our monastery was formerly double, or divided into two parts – that is to say, of monks and nuns … This virgin was most skilful in the art of writing. For though she is not known to have composed any work, yet she wrote with her own hand many volumes in a most beautiful and legible character, both for divine service and for the public library of the monastery, which are enumerated in a list written by herself in a certain plenarius. For in that list the following books pertaining to divine service are enumerated … [translated in Maitland 1844, pp.419–20].

There follows a list of five missals, some with Epistles, Gospels, a gradual and sequences for the entire year, two books of offices, two Gospel books and a book of Epistles. One of the missals is listed as having been given to the Bishop of Trier, and the large number of missals suggests that Diemud took orders for them. After the service books, the account goes on to list a further 35 volumes of biblical and patristic texts by Diemud, of which one, a bible in two volumes, was given in exchange for an estate of land in Pisinberch. The Anonymous concludes:

These are the volumes written with her own hand by the aforesaid handmaid of God, Diemudis … But at what period she lived I could never discover, since, in all the books (we charitably hope from humility), she omitted to mention her name and the time when she finished.

The account of the Wessobrunn monk is as interesting for its evaluation as for its enumeration of Diemud's books: while admiring her labour as a copyist he notes that she did not compose texts. As with Harlinde and Renilde, her scribal work was more virtuous than great. None the less, his account has captivated historians, who have hoped to find surviving evidence of Diemud's work. Volumes signed by "Diemud" have, indeed, emerged – volumes not only written but painted in a beautiful and legible character. One of them (Munich, Bayerische Staatsbibliothek, clm.23056) has a picture of a nun named Diemud (repr. Greer 1979, p.157), but belongs to the 13th century; a second, a handsomely illuminated missal of the 12th century (Bayerische Staatsbibliothek, clm.11004), bears an enigmatic colophon usually believed to identify Diemud as the scribe but in fact stating that "pious Diemud made the material of the book" (Swarzenski 1908–13, p.62, gives the colophon as: *Materiam libri fecit Diemuod pia scribi / Seo Rudberto celi pro munere certo / Celestis vite scribuntur in ordine scribe*). This book has been the subject of extensive debate; rather late in character for our Diemud, it contains a text arranged for Salzburg use, and the nun of its colophon – whatever her role – may have been Diemud, Abbess of Nonnberg in Salzburg (d. 1136; *idem*). Yet a third Diemud appears in a 12th-century manuscript (Bayerische Staatsbibliothek, clm.23044) that came to Munich from Wessobrunn (*ibid.*, p.63).

Diemud (Demut) – that is, Humility – is in fact a frequent monastic name. Also at Admont, noted for its learned women, we find among the necrologies one "Diemud, member of our congregation and scribe" (*Diemudis conversa nostrae congregationis et scriptrix*; Heinrich 1924, p.151). Whether or not the Diemud described by the Anonymous of Wessobrunn will ever be identified, her name has proved to be a mine of generosity. In the first place, her name has yielded not just one but in fact four or even five bookwomen: the scribe of Admont, the illuminator of clm.23056, the nun in the colophon of clm.11004, the scribe of clm. 23044 and the scribe of the Wessobrunn Anonymous. The copyist-nun thus emerges in striking numbers. In the second place, Diemud illuminates a modern preoccupation. The Anonymous described Diemud as a scribe. All the books that have jockeyed for her name, however, have been illuminated. Like the Anonymous, who had hesitated to lend the aura of fame to a "mere" copyist, we, too, demand more than "mere" calligraphy of an artist.

The colophon page of a manuscript in Strasbourg (Bibliothèque du Grand Séminaire, MS 78; repr. Alexander 1992, pl.28; Cologne 1985, iii, p.245, no.B44) may be a medieval dialogue on this very issue. A voluminous martyrology, it was copied in 1154 by an excellent calligrapher, the nun Guta of Schwarzenthann. She has given her name – prominently written and highlighted with colours – in an elaborate, full-page colophon. She does not include the name of the book's more modestly skilled illuminator, Sintram, a monk at Marbach, Schwarzenthann's brother monastery. Sintram, however, had his own way of claiming pre-eminence. In the miniature that accompanies the colophon it is he, and not the scribe Guta of the proud text, who stands at the right hand of the Virgin.

The pride of achievement that radiates from both Guta's colophon and Sintram's miniature finds a compelling expression in the well-known self-portrait of the nun Guda, who stands, her artist's right hand large before her breast, in an initial on folio 110v of a 12th-century homiliary (see illustration; Cologne 1985, iii, p.244, no.43; Legner 1985, p.213). Her banderole tells us that she both copied the volume and illuminated it with initials. Only two of the initials contain figures, but they show vividly how the skilled bookwoman could assume expressive and even self-expressive control of her craft, turning her products into statements of her own creative power. Diemud of Wessobrunn had not signed her books, as was usual for monastic labour; Guda's eloquent initial forces one to stop and ask how many other unsigned medieval initials are the work of women, since women obviously were scribes, and some like Ende and Guta had the opportunity to develop very high levels of skill and self-awareness.

Guda makes visible a kind of creative engagement that unquestionably existed also in textile work but has been harder to demonstrate there. A second major conceptual model that emerges with particular clarity in book art is offered by the works of the famous 12th-century abbesses, Hildegard of Bingen (q.v.) and Herrad (q.v.). Both were women of encyclopaedic learning; both owed their education to their monastic upbringing; and both composed books unique in their own time in which images played a central role. Neither book has survived in the original: Hildegard's *Scivias* described, interpreted and illustrated 35 of her complex, powerful visions; Herrad's *Hortus deliciarum* was a pictorial encyclopaedia for her nuns at Hohenbourg that traced the history of salvation through 636 elaborately glossed images. Neither author illuminated the finished book with her own hand, and several quite different hands appear in the *Hortus deliciarum*. None the less, it must have been the authors themselves who conceived the exceptional interdependence of image and text in

Guda, self-portrait, 12th-century; Frankfurt am Main, Stadt- und Universitätsbibliothek, MS Barth. 42, fol.110v

their books and directed its realisation. As such, they emerge as towering visual innovators. Madeline Caviness's vigorous claim for Hildegard's status as a great artist is one of the most significant contributions to this *Dictionary*.

The image of the artist that these two great figures present is a distinctively medieval one, given its clearest definition, perhaps, by Sandra Hindman in her book on that great secular woman intellectual and author, Christine de Pisan (1364–1431):

Christine seems to have been involved to a considerable degree in the make-up of the pictorial cycle. The degree of her involvement fully justifies claims that the illuminators worked under Christine's direction, following her verbal instructions. It is clear, moreover, that she gave explicit instructions in the form of the purple rubrics to the illuminators. She certainly supervised the illustration.

Evidence concerning manuscript production in Paris suggests that this sort of involvement on the part of the author may have been common. Christine's own writings on art show her to have been more outspoken in the role of the artist than her contemporaries and, further, to have perceived the artist as an imitator of reality, not an inventor of pictures. A study of the various pictorial sources for the Epistre reveals that probably the author, not the miniaturists, studied related illuminated manuscripts and selectively adapted their models to the Epistre. In some cases, such as the Ovide, these models were close to Christine's ends and therefore were retained unchanged. In many other cases modifications were introduced so as to express the themes emphasized in the text …

> We can now turn to these manuscripts, confident that the overall characteristics and the individual details of their particular programs were worked out by Christine, not by her illuminators [Hindman 1986, pp.98–9].

It must be in much the same way that the *Scivias* and the *Hortus deliciarum* were produced. The acknowledgement of the formative role of their authors in the conception and design of their novel, imaginative illumination and the recognition of them as artists open valuable vistas on to artistic invention in the domain of textiles, too: how many major patrons – such as Kunigunde or Agnes of Meissen – directed their craftspeople in this formative way? It also opens up new realms of historical inquiry into the way the intellectual imagination of the great medieval woman of learning was furnished. Several scholars have concluded that richly imaged books were associated especially closely with the education of women and with women's devotional practices in the Middle Ages, as has been intimated already in the reference to the Utrecht Psalter (McKitterick 1990, p.311; Hamburger 1991; Camille 1985, pp.41–2). A vast pictorial encyclopaedia such as Herrad's would thus assume a logical place in a convent noted for its learned women, as was Hohenbourg. Herrad's mentor and predecessor as abbess, Reglindis, is variously associated with the convents of Bergen and Admont, famous for their learned communities and bound by close mutual ties (Cames 1971, p.138; Radspieler 1962). Hohenbourg's intellectual roots thus run back to the great double monastery of Admont; it is perhaps time to study the genealogy of its visual culture, as well.

This image of the artist as instigator unites three of the most brilliant names among medieval women. More than 200 years stretch between them, Hildegard and Herrad in the 12th century and Christine in the late 14th. It has been a source of consternation, even anger, that these centuries have not yielded more visible women of their stature. Major developments in the patterns of production occurred in these centuries and each has been blamed for this dearth. On the one hand, during these centuries production was urbanised, as attested by the guilds. The guild lists of painters and illuminators, like those of embroiderers, show a steady if less numerous flow of women's names. In Italy before the 15th century professional women almost always figure as scribes (Frugoni 1992, p.400, cites Montanaria, a scribe, wife of Onesto, who received a contract from a Florentine named Bencivenne in 1271–2; Antonia, a scribe, daughter of Rodolfo del fu Gandolfo, 1275; Allegra, a scribe, wife of Ivano, 1279; Flandina di Tebaldino, scribe, active 1268; Uliana di Beneventu da Faenza, scribe, 1289; and Branca, scribe, 1329, wife of the scribe Anastasio). But the guild list of 1339 for the Florentine painters' guild, the Compagnia di San Luca, does imply the membership of women, though they paid only two-thirds the dues of the male members (Los Angeles 1976, p.15), and a few women emerge in other documents to assert their presence: Donatella miniatrix, wife of a miniaturist, is cited in a document in Bologna in

1271 (*ibid.*, p.14; Miner 1974, p.11); a Florentine woman identified as "the woman [or, Domina] the wife of Acco the painter" is documented in 1295 when she took a (male) apprentice for four years (the Latin is *domina uxore Acci pictoris*. "Domina" may be a proper name, or simply "the woman"; London 1989, p.9), and a portrait of *St Francis* in San Francesco a Ripa, Rome, was attributed in the 17th century to a Lady Jacoba (Cook 1994, pp.23–4).

In Paris, on the other hand, ten of the 229 painters and sculptors in the guild lists from the decades around 1300 were women (Baron 1968, nos 1, 2, 19, 29, 74, 79, 146, 160bis, 215 and 219); in the lists of painters in Bruges Farquhuar found that 12 per cent in 1454 and by 1480 nearer to 25 per cent of those named were women (cited in Miner 1974, p.24). Five of the women in the Paris lists are associated with deceased husbands of the same trade and so may have been heirs rather than practitioners of the husband's business: one notes in the self-portrait (1512) of the illuminator Nicholaus Bertschi with his wife, Margaret (Stuttgart, Württembergische Landesbibliothek, MS mus.1, fol.65 [fol.236v], repr. Alexander 1992, pl.50), that he alone paints, while she serves him. Others, however, were unquestionably professionals, either living by themselves or married to men with different trades. (See in Baron 1968: no.2, Aalis *l'ymagiere* [=sculptor?, see pp.40–41], married to Thybaut the carpenter; no.74, Eremboure, *enlumineresse*; no.215, Thiephaine, *peintresse*, and Thomasse, *enluminerresse* and *taverniere*, all cited without spouses; for a review of the evidence for women as master illuminators in Paris, see Farber 1993, p.37, note 2.) Even within marriage, as the textile trades have shown, crafts were family specialities and not the personal career of the male alone. So, for instance, we saw the Florentine *domina* taking on a (male) apprentice quite independently of her painter husband. More famous, if not as yet traced to identifiable work, was Bourgot, daughter of the painter Jehan de Noir. Cited as an *enlumineresse* in a contract of her father's in 1353, she went on to share his commissions for the courts of France and Berry (Meiss 1969, p.168; Miner 1974, pp.18–19). In Bourgot we encounter the pattern so familiar from the post-medieval world, of the painter who is the daughter of a painter.

These data leave no doubt that women practised as professional painters in the late medieval cities of Europe. Among them was the title figure of Dorothy Miner's essay, the painter Anastaise, of whom Christine de Pisan wrote: "she is so skillful and experienced in painting borders and miniatures of manuscripts that no one can cite an artist in the city of Paris … who in these endeavors surpasses her" (quoted in Miner 1974, p.8). What Christine praised Anastaise for were her borders and backgrounds, though, and not her creative initiative. As Hindman's reconstruction of Christine's own methods of book design show, it is as trained producers rather than as inventors of illuminations that guild members of either sex generally worked. Here as in the realm of fine textiles it is certain that a portion of the artfulness of late medieval art – its consummate skill and sophisticated beauty – was due to the highly professional women who made it. Women who took projects in hand as conceptual overseers, as Christine herself did, remained rare.

The women who do emerge as candidates for this role in the later medieval centuries are monastic. They can be found particularly in Germany and the Low Countries. Cistercian, Clarissan and especially Dominican houses in the wake of the wide-ranging Dominican reform movement of the late 14th and 15th centuries produced many books, culminating in the great 15th-century library of 500 volumes at the Dominican convent of St Katherine, Nuremberg: repeated Dominican proscriptions of women's copying must reflect its vitality rather than its absence.[6] Christian von Heusinger (1959) has identified almost a dozen Dominican convents in south Germany with active scriptoria, and Elisabeth Schraut (1988) has identified a range of volumes produced in Cistercian houses. Women illuminators are fewer than scribes – among its many scribes, St Katherine's produced only one illuminator who is known by name and oeuvre. This is Barbara Gwichtmacherin (d. 1491), known to have illuminated a gradual of 1459 (Nuremberg, Stadtbibliothek, MS Cent.V, App.34q) not because of her own signature but from the records of the book's binder (Fischer 1928, pp.69–70; Schraut 1991, pp.100–01; Schraut also attributes Stadtbibliothek, MS Cent.V 10a to Gwichtmacherin). Women illuminators do appear throughout the later Middle Ages, though, both in decorated documents like the indulgence of 1363 at Herkenrode (Oliver 1995) and a charter of 1362 at St Katherine's itself (now Nuremberg, Stadtarchiv, Alte Urkunden, no.234; repr. Schraut 1987, no.52, pl.5), and in illuminated books. Especially impressive is Gisle von Kerzenbroeck, named in an inscription at the beginning of a magnificently written and illuminated gradual (Osnabrück, Gymnasium Carolinum and Bischöfliches Generalvikariat MS) from the Cistercian convent of Rulle near Osnabrück: "The venerable and devout virgin Gisle of Kerzenbroeck wrote, illuminated, notated, paginated and decorated with pictures and golden initials this excellent book in her own memory. In the year of Our Lord 1300 her soul rested in holy peace. Amen."[7] Gisle herself appears in two of the volume's sonorous initials (see illustration), confirming its close connection with her. Despite the carefully inventoried inscription, however, her authorship has been challenged, for both script and painting display the work not of one but of several hands. Oliver has argued in response that these may belong to Gisle's monastic sisters under her direction. The convent did engage in book work – four scribe-nuns are known there, including the prolific Cristina von Haltern, who signed the two-volume Rulle Bible (Osnabrück, Gymnasium Carolinum MS 90) in 1278 (Oliver 1997, notes 20 and 22) – and it is possible that one or more sisters in such a community also practised illumination at a professional level of skill.

This possibility is demonstrated by the convent of the Poor Clares in Cologne. Members of the convent produced a number of musical manuscripts in the 13th and early 14th centuries, among them several with very beautiful illuminations (Galley 1961). Of these, a gradual (Cologne, Wallraf-Richartz Museum, Graphische Sammlung Inv. Nrs 67–71) of the 1330s copied by Sister Gertrude van dem Uorst may have been illuminated in the scriptorium of the Franciscan friary of Cologne, where in 1299 a Brother Johannes von Valkenburg "*scripsi et notavi et illu[m]i[n]avi*" two handsome graduals (Cologne, Diözesanbibliothek, MS 1B; Bonn, Universitätsbibliothek, MS 384; Oliver 1997, note 13). A cluster of comparably fine musical manuscripts from the 1350s, on the other hand, are signed by the Clarissan sister Loppa de Speculo.

Among them an antiphonary (Stockholm, Kungl. Bibliothek, MS 172A), contains, on folio 106, the explicit inscription: "Sister Jutta Alfter paid for this book with her money and alms; pray for her and for those she remembers. Sister Loppa de Speculo completed it, writing, ruling, notating, illuminating it so that she would not be excluded from your hearts ...".[8] Like her Franciscan counterpart, Johannes, Loppa lists her responsibilities in the book. That she herself provided the illuminations as well as the filigree initials has been challenged: not only are they of professional calibre, but the missals attributed to Loppa (Cologne, Domarchiv, MS 149; Brussels, Bibliothèque Royale, MSS 209, 212) were made for use not in her own convent, but elsewhere (Beer 1965, p.150). Nuns' production for other monastic houses is long-attested, however: in 1366, at much the time that Loppa was working, we find the Cistercian monk Jacob of Lindau ordering an antiphonary (Heidelberg, MS Sale IX 66) from Sister Catherine de Brugg of Rothenmünster near Lake Konstanz, who is portrayed in a large initial at the beginning of the book in what may be a self-portrait (Wattenbach 1875, p.376). Moreover, as Galley (1961, pp.16 and 18) has shown, among Loppa's sisters was one with the same family name as the Franciscan painter Johannes von Valkenburg, and it seems entirely plausible that the children of highly skilled professional clans would have brought their family skills with them into their monastic houses. Italy, too, yields painter-nuns in the 14th century, such as Sister Giovanna Petroni of the Sienese convent of Santa Maria (Bradley 1887–9, iii, p.61). Gisle, Loppa and Giovanna suggest that, if women are to be identified as initiators of major painting projects, they should be sought in the religious life.

During the 13th century there was an escalation in the number and intensity of women seeking a spiritual life, either in cloistered monasticism or in a form such as that of the beguine movement, which was more integrated into secular life (Oliver 1988, pp.130–32; Oliver 1997, p.106). Beguines were lay women who gathered in devotional associations only loosely recognised by the established Church. The religious community thus acquired a vitality that made it a major focus of women's artistic production. Here as in textile work the convent responded to the shifting conditions of late medieval production, developing a self-sufficient answer to its distinctive needs. Convents carried on – as male monasteries rarely did – the earlier medieval model of the self-contained, in-house scriptorium (Oliver 1997, p.116). That convents produced illuminated books in the Gothic centuries has been widely recognised, as the currency of the term *Nonnenbücher* proves. Like the word *Klosterstich*, encountered in embroidery, it is a German term, identifying the area most richly informative about these works. And like the term *Klosterstich* it is dismissive in tone, indicating a technical and often an iconographic simplicity that looks painfully naive next to the sophisticated productions of urban professionals. Yet it is precisely in this area of convent production that the most vividly interesting scholarship on medieval women artists is being done.

Indicative of the interest of this material is the seemingly exiguous fact that the later medieval manuscripts discussed so far have been almost entirely musical manuscripts; so, too, is the exuberantly decorated manuscript (Bornem, Abdij Sint Bernardus, MS 1) produced in 1244 at the convent of Nazareth

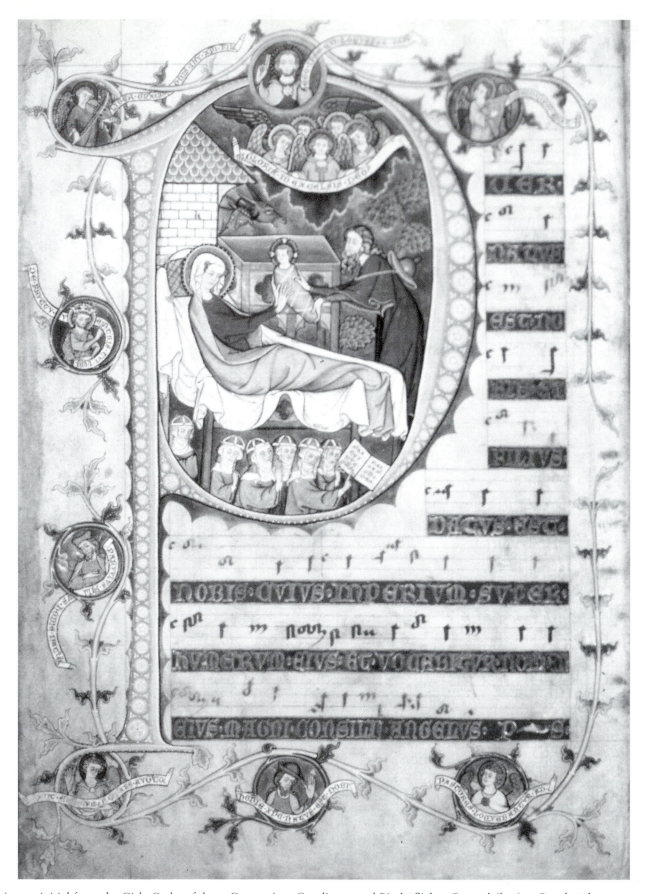

Christmas initial from the Gisle Codex, fol.25; Gymnasium Carolinum und Bischöfliches Generalvikariat, Osnabrück

in Lier, Belgium, and notated by a nun named Christina, perhaps the sister of the great Nazareth mystic, Beatrice (Oliver 1997, p.106). Already Wilhelm Wattenbach in 1875 had noted the association of women and musical manuscripts (p.376), observing that musical manuscripts need to be made by the musicians who know and use their music. The musical manuscripts are, in short, a sign that these books by nuns were intimately woven into their lives and worship. This is even truer of the psalter, the great devotional book of the Middle Ages. In the 12th century the devotional psalter had emerged as one of the major recipients of illumination. Already at this time the owners of these luxurious books were predominantly women,[9] and women continue in the ensuing centuries to appear repeatedly as the owners of devotional psalters (Oliver 1992). Psalters, in turn, as Oliver has shown, appear with striking frequency among books made by women's religious groups (Oliver 1997, p.106). She notes the 13th-century psalters produced at the Cistercian convent of Engelsberg in Switzerland (Beer 1959, pp.25–6), the group of psalters from mid-13th-century Liège in Belgium that she attributes to beguines of that city, and the bequest left in 1266 by a Liège beguine to fund the production of psalters. Liturgical books, in turn, dominate the later Cistercian book production that Schraut examines (1988, p.49), and here again it is a musical book – an antiphonary (Stuttgart, Württembergischer Landes-bibliothek, HB XVII 17), copied and illuminated in 1344 with numerous signatures by Alheid Quidenbeumen at Billigheim – that bears the fullest illumination (*ibid.*, pl.I).

The books produced by women's communities prove to be not only closely bound to their religious life, but illuminated in ways that cast a unique light upon that life. Oliver (1997, pp.111–16) has shown this particularly finely in her analysis of a type of ornament that recurs in books associated with women's communities. In books as widely varied as Gisle von Kerzenbroeck's gradual discussed above, and a modest little homiliary (Baltimore, Walters MS W148; repr. Miner 1974, figs 4–5) redecorated in the early 14th century, she finds rich adornment, often recalling gold and coloured embroidery, applied to particular words that play a strategic role in the performance of the liturgy. This sort of liturgically based embellishment is not usual in manuscripts made in male communities, but it does reflect the practice of pious reading, *lectio divina*, that characterised monastic life. It permeates especially the writings of Mechtild of Hackeborn (d. 1298), whose *Book of Special Grace* dwells with delectation upon individual words and their many resonances of meaning and instruction. As Oliver notes:

> Words were thus laden individually with great spiritual merit and Mechtild visualized them as jewels. On the feast of Saint Agnes, Christ and the saint appeared to Mechtild in red robes. All the saint's words (that is, the text of her office) were embroidered in golden letters on Christ's robe and gave off light which entered the hearts of the choir singing the psalms ... At the memorial service for Abbess Gertrude, Mechtild saw the apostles bearing large, richly ornamented books, acknowledging the abbess' apostolic calling as spiritual teacher of her nuns. Abbess Gertrude herself appeared adorned in a vestment of green embellished with innumerable golden stars, its seams studded with white pearls and small

rubies. Such splendor immediately recalls embroidery, the art form in which German nuns excelled in the Gothic period ... [1997, p.115].

The white pearls and little rubies recall the pearl- and coral-studded embroidery from Isenhagen. In the rich pages of the nuns' manuscripts, *lectio divina*, illumination and embroidery come together in a luminous visual feast, a spiritual delectation that was distinctive to women's expression. It was a women's art.

Hamburger (1990), in turn, has begun to explore the figural images in such books. Often decried – by Greer (1979), for example – because they remained inbred and out of fashion, copied and recopied over many decades without stylistic or qualitative modification (e.g. the pages discussed in Oliver 1997, p.107, fig.54), the miniatures in nuns' books none the less bear a particular weight of significance in Hamburger's view (1989 and 1991), for in the later medieval centuries especially, images were regarded as peculiarly appropriate to women and their ways of thinking. Thus, images assumed an expressive licence that they rarely had in men's institutions. Formulated by women to speak to women of the powerful affections of their own hearts in devotion, the images in women's devotional books often carry an intensity of content that is unique and uniquely tailored to them. While certainly not claiming all women's devotional imagery for women artists, Hamburger has nevertheless found many miniatures that were painted by women, opening up a whole class of devotional book that has been neglected by historians seeking art as traditionally defined. The devotional intensity of Hamburger's images will lend a new interest to the distinctive themes of women's textile art, as well, leading historians to look beyond the cheerful simplicity of their *Klosterstich* to the devotional impetus behind it.

Monumental arts

In the figures of Guda with her vigorous, self-expressive craft, of Hildegard, Herrad and Christine with their creative authority, and of the anonymous artists of the *Nonnenbücher* with their intense expressive imagery, the art of the book has given clear formulation to types of women artists known also, if less clearly, from textiles. Only in tapestry, however, have these media yielded evidence of women as creators of art on a monumental scale. Where names appear in the Middle Ages, women's names appear among them, but names are extremely rare in the monumental arts of the Middle Ages, and women are correspondingly elusive. The only reasonably securely identified woman monumental artist is Teresa Díaz (q.v.), named in the inscription in the choir frescoes of *c.*1316 at Santa Clara in Toro (Zamora) in Spain and presented for the first time by Pamela Patton in this *Dictionary*. The inscription, TERESA DIEÇ ME FECIT, repeats exactly that of Gislebertus on the tympanum at Autun; to query it would require considering the possibility – as only few have done – that Gislebertus, too, was a patron, not a sculptor. Díaz's signature may have bearing on fresco cycles like those from the 14th century in the convent church at Wienhausen in Germany that have traditionally been attributed to nuns. It also reinforces insights offered by other media: Lillich's evidence from the guild lists of Paris glaziers, where 12 per cent of those named are women (1985, pp.80–82); the women, Aalis and Perronelle, listed between 1292 and 1316 as *imagiere* – sculptor – in Paris (Baron 1968, nos 2 and 19); and Alexander Neckham's report from his own late 12th-century London of women goldsmiths (Amt 1993, p.198). In addition, there is a tantalising inscription on a reliquary cross (*c.*1150–70; Metropolitan Museum of Art, New York; [IN HO]NORE: S[AN]C[T]I; SALVATORIS: SANCCIA: GUIDISALVI: ME; FECIT; New York 1993) from the church of San Salvador de Fuentes (Asturias) in Spain, which may point to a woman goldsmith, although its similarity to donors' inscriptions is problematic. These scanty data imply that here as elsewhere, women joined in their families' craft. The greatest woman sculptor of the Middle Ages, however – Sabine, daughter of Erwin von Steinbach, the late 13th-century master builder of Strasbourg Cathedral – has been shown in a remarkable deconstruction by Geyer (1989) to be a component of her father's florid, high Romantic myth.

Conclusions

The evidence assembled here has treated women as artists in the medieval West. More extensive than evidence from Byzantium, where names are rarely given, it offers certain rules of thumb to use in assessing the place of women in medieval art. At no time in the Middle Ages were women excluded from the media in which their society forged its visual imagery of faith and prestige. Fine textiles were the most consistent and costly medium in which their work is found: kings and priests were vested in these fabrics; saints were propitiated; spaces were made numinous; and the stories of husbands and heroes were consecrated to history. But women are attested, too, as scribes and illuminators, goldsmiths and glaziers, sculptors and mural painters. Media as such offer few barriers to women.

Corollary to this is the rarity of gender-specific tasks. While textile work seems in the early Middle Ages to have been associated especially with women, the medieval guilds show both men and women engaged in most aspects of cloth-making and working; women, in turn, practised even heavy tasks like glass-making and stone-carving alongside their husbands and brothers in family businesses. Even monastic production is most visible in the double monasteries – Chelles, San Salvatore, Marbach/Schwarzenthann, Wessobrunn, Admont – where male and female religious often worked together on major projects. The tendency to look for women's enclaves, whether in segregated secular tasks or cloistered retreats, is rewarded only rarely and then at the chronological extremes of the Middle Ages, at the beginning or the end.

Authority itself is hard to divide on gendered lines. The medieval divisions of responsibility in creative tasks do not coincide with our own, and this makes it difficult for us to assign artistic authority. At all points in the Middle Ages, however, it is clear that women functioned in a vast range of different capacities, and no one definition of "artist" will embrace a critical cross-section of them.

If media and métier in themselves offered few barriers to women, however, it is also true that patterns of greater and lesser visibility play across the data that are offered here. The convent recurs in every period discussed and obviously offered contexts conducive to women's art. At the same time, it is notable how heavily weighted the evidence is towards Germany and the Low Countries. Spain, Italy and even France make far more reticent appearances.[10] While survival of documentation may condition this distribution, especially in the later Middle Ages when the passage of German convents to Protestant sodalities protected their contents and continuity, it very probably reflects genuine conditions of medieval existence, as well. Both the canonical houses with their double monasteries and the reformed mendicant houses in the later Middle Ages were stronger in Germany than elsewhere; the canonical double houses had been discouraged in the Carolingian territories already under Louis the Pious in the early 9th century. It is the double monasteries in particular that come to the forefront of the evidence about women as artists. This suggests the rule that it is not monasticism itself but the *type* of monasticism available to women that affected their opportunities for artistic expression.[11]

After the monasteries, the lists of the medieval urban guilds are the most valuable resource we have for tracing women's roles in the production of fine things, and they expand the monastic evidence especially in the range of media represented. There are many media, including glazing and sculpture, in which women are known only from the guild lists, and it is Alexander Neckham's observations of his own urban surroundings that yield our most concrete testimony to women as metalworkers. The testimony of the cities makes it clear that women worked in most media that we embrace in the broad category of art. None the less, the distribution of evidence across media remains uneven. Conspicuously slim throughout most of the Middle Ages is evidence of women's participation in the seasonal arts of masonry, mural painting and monumental sculpture; rare, too, are the extremely expensive arts such as work in precious metals, for which – until cities created an ongoing demand – the need in any one place was limited and artists were engaged only sporadically over the span of centuries. If gender as such offered little impediment to women's participation, it may be that itinerancy did: that except where flourishing monastic houses or urban development offered steady employment that removed the need for itinerancy, the seasonal and sporadic arts were not practised widely by women.

The urbanisation of production reflected by the guilds, on the other hand, shows an extensive engagement of women in the professions: as indicated, few tasks were closed to them. The growth of the towns thus can certainly be seen as offering opportunities to women, engaging them in the sophisticated and excellently regulated skilled labour that distinguishes so much of later medieval art. At the same time, it is true that the entrepreneurial patterns of urban production favoured male control of both families and businesses. It can be no accident that the types of women's artistic expression most defined by gender – the late medieval cloister arts – occurred as a counterpoint to the late medieval city, for all its large numbers of working women.

Byzantium

The observations suggested by surveying women's art in the Western Middle Ages can be of help when one turns to Byzantium.[12] The search for individual artists is more difficult in Byzantium than in the West. A far smaller percentage of Byzantine art survives to us than remains from the medieval

West; moreover, the Byzantine world observed the etiquette of humility – and especially of monastic humility – far more scrupulously than any other medieval culture (Wendel 1950). Accordingly, artists' names of any kind are scarcely known, and the names of women artists do not survive at all. Here, then, one cannot turn to tangible works of art to trace the role of women. Instead, one must turn to oblique evidence: to monastic constitutions; to wills and inventories; to inscriptions in surviving manuscripts attesting to convent libraries; to eulogies and biographies of women; and to hagiographic material.

The evidence yielded by these sources is meagre. It can be shown that Western patterns appear in Byzantium, as well. In Byzantium, too, women appear among the major cultural patrons throughout the Middle Ages, from the great Late Antique imperial women of the Theodosian house and the 6th-century Anicia Juliana to the 15th-century Anna Notaras.[13] As in the West, the production of books and fine textiles provides the most generous source of craftswomen, and they appear in these media in both lay and monastic contexts. Johnstone has found the names of both lay and monastic women – albeit very late – as embroiderers (1967, pp.59–62). In the realm of the book, too, the names of both lay and monastic women can be found. Five women's scribal signatures are known. Two are monastic – Anna, scribe of a 13th-century manuscript containing sermons of John Chrysostom and Cyril of Alexandria (El Escorial, MS gr.530; see de Andrés 1963–7, iii, p.168), and Maria in a 14th-century manuscript (Moscow, Historical Museum, S268 343/CCCXXX; Vogel and Gardthausen 1909, p.288). Two were lay people – Eirene, daughter of the late 13th-century professional calligrapher Theodore Hagiopetrites (Carr 1981), and Sophia, daughter of Rikos Kontoioannes, who signed Athos, Simonopetra 1377 in 1469 (Vogel and Gardthausen 1909, p.401). The scholarly work of the fifth, the Constantinopolitan scholar and patron Theodora Raoulaina (c.1240-1300), who copied Biblioteca Apostolica Vaticana, MS gr.1189, embraces both the lay and the monastic phases of her life (Kugéas 1907).[14] As in the West, finally, the emergence of the named independent lay professional is accompanied by the appearance of the father-and-daughter team. This is illustrated by Eirene, the daughter of the calligrapher Theodore Hagiopetrites, cited above. Her work is known from a Heirmologion of 1309 (Sinai MS 1256), whose musical notation seems to have been furnished by no less a person than the great composer-monk, John Koukouzeles. Again, three centuries later in the expatriate Greek community in Paris, we find another such team in the Vergikios family of Cretan calligraphers: Angelos Vergikios's edition of Manuel Philes's description of animals (1564; Oxford, Bodleian Library, MS Auct. F4 15) may owe its miniatures to his daughter (Harlfinger 1977, p.337; Oxford 1966, no.66).

These examples show that patterns seen in the West were also valid in Byzantium. They do not, however, show how far this validity extended. The Eastern examples are at present radically fewer and more isolated. This is particularly noticeable in the realm of the scribe and illuminator. Byzantium is poor in names and does not begin to yield the splendid patina of painters that highlights the roster of Western bookwomen. Given the convention of scribal humility in the East, it is not surprising that signed books are extremely rare. Far less expected, on the other hand, has been the dearth of oblique

evidence offered by the Byzantine women's monasteries: monastic constitutions, saints' lives, library lists and ex-libris. The scant evidence of women as producers of books cannot be dismissed as a testimony to female illiteracy in Byzantium. Most middle- and upper-class women in Byzantium seem to have been literate, at least in the Greek of common and religious use (Grosdidier de Matons 1965–7, iii, p.29; Kazhdan 1978, p.55): even in the distant province of Cappadocia, for instance, Annabel Wharton (1988, p.17) has noted that some of the pilgrim graffiti in the churches are by women, and among the legal documents preserved on Mount Athos, though fewer women than men are involved, the percentage of those signing their own names – as opposed to "x"ing a signature written for them – is virtually the same as for men (gathered from a survey in Lemerle, Guillou and Svoronos 1970). Saints' lives throughout the history of Byzantium state that their subjects learned their letters from their mothers, and a number of Byzantine intellectuals cite the importance of their mothers to their education. Both the 9th-century Theodore of Stoudios and the 11th-century Michael Psellos corresponded extensively with their mothers (see Diehl 1939, pp.111–32, 291–316), and Psellos speaks poignantly of the learning of both his sister and his daughter (Kyriakis 1976). These women emerge as persons of great mental energy. They poured this energy into household, prayer and charitable works, and the mothers of both Theodore and Psellos turned, when their children were grown, to lives of fiercely ascetic monasticism. In this phase of their lives they fall into a pattern found consistently also in the Vitae of women saints: they pray fervently, lapse into ecstasy, are fearless in the defence of moral rectitude, and work with a driving, mortifying intensity to help the poor. They do not read or write. Such behaviour is a commonplace in Byzantine female hagiography. Finely honed intellectual activity, by contrast, seems not to have been a template available for the presentation of women's lives, even – or perhaps more correctly, especially – within the context of the religious life. Not even satire offers a place in Byzantine literature to the woman of learning. Our challenge is to glimpse the truth that lies behind such patterns.

The exclusion of women from the image of learning was certainly fostered by the gulf that prevailed in the empire between the common Greek of daily life and piety on the one hand and the classicising pure Greek of learned and bureaucratic discourse on the other. The Katharevousa of courtly learning was a jealously guarded male preserve to which women gained access only rarely and through male instruction. None the less, one does find a sequence of genuinely literary women in court circles: in the 9th century the caustic nun, poet and musician Kassia (or Kassiane), author both of scathing classical epigrams – some decrying the fate of being a woman – and of some of the greatest hymns of the Orthodox Church (Rochow 1967, p.59 and passim; Trypolitis 1992); in the 12th century the princess Anna Komnene, historian and Aristotelian philosopher, and the Sevastokratorissa Eirene Komnene, patron of Byzantium's most innovative secular literature in the period of the Crusades (Jeffreys 1981); and in the 13th century the scholar-princess Theodora Raoulaina all exemplify this group. Socially, intellectually and creatively, these are figures of an excellence comparable to Hildegard, Herrad and Christine de Pisan in the West. What may be notable is the fact that they afford no evidence at all that their education was acquired in a convent. On the contrary, they cite lay teachers, and those who entered convents brought their habit of learning with them from lay into monastic life. Thus, Anna Komnene began her tutelage by making secret arrangements with a court eunuch (Darrouzès 1970, pp. 220–323; Browning 1962; Buckler 1929); Kassia and the later learned abbess, Eirene-Eulogia Choumnaina (1291–c.1355), were taught to some extent by their fathers (Rochow 1967, p.31; Hero 1985, p.147); and Michael Psellos gives no indication that the tutors he hired for his daughter were nuns (Kyriakis 1976, p.85). Even in the lives of these highly literate women, then, the convent as a likely locus of women's learning remains elusive.

The surviving women's monastic constitutions (called typika) do little to ameliorate this impression.[15] These documents are, as Laiou so tellingly points out, the works of women well acquainted with the economy of running a large household. The administrative affairs – as exemplified by the typikon drawn up by Anna Komnene's mother, the empress Eirene Doukaina (c.1066–1123), for the convent of the Virgin Kecharitomene (Gautier 1985) – are meticulously spelled out, and they plainly presuppose a community of women well able to read, write and keep accounts. Eirene herself was a fluent reader at least of devotional literature: her daughter Anna describes how she devoted her time to books, often appearing at table with a volume of mystic theology still in hand (Sewter ed., 1969, pp.110–11, 178–9). Yet Eirene made no provision in her typikon for a library, a glaring omission in the face of aristocratic male foundations. She did prescribe manual work, but it does not seem to have been of an intellectual or literary nature. Its charitable function suggests that it was perhaps weaving and sewing (Laiou 1985, p.83). One nun was to read while the others worked, and readings were also conducted during meals. But intellectual work as such is not acknowledged. In the 14th-century typikon formulated by Eirene-Eulogia Choumnaina, too, though there were two levels of sisters, one devoted to psalmody and one to common chores, the pursuit of intellectual work is not touched upon, and education is confined to those young girls who would remain in the convent – the schooling of seculars was proscribed (ibid., p.91). This is characteristic. Theodora Raoulaina, who herself entered a convent, left her library to the small Aristine Monastery that she founded for her friend in learning, the patriarch Gregory II of Cyprus. Thus, the surviving typika give no insight into women as producers of books. Ex-libris reinforce this image. Women clearly owned books: illuminated volumes belonging to women appear even among the provincial codices of the late 12th- and 13th-century "decorative style" group (Carr 1987, cat.no.25, Athos, Stauronikita 56, a Gospel Book bearing the ex-libris of a nun, Euphrosyne; cat.no.96, Paris, Bibliothèque Nationale, MS gr.97, probably made for the woman, Olympia, whose name appears on several pages). But books whose ex-libris indicate membership of a convent library are remarkably rare (Carr 1985, pp.12–13; Volk 1955). If the book arts illumine the role of Byzantine convents in fostering women's production only palely, the evidence of textiles is even more elusive. Both weaving and embroidery were practised extensively by nuns, but tangible evidence of their work survives only from the post-Byzantine centuries (Johnstone 1967, pp.59–62).

The convent in Byzantium, then, does not provide so clear a context for women as cultural arbiters as it does in the West. This fact brings home the conclusion that had emerged from the evidence of the medieval West: that the role of the monastery in cultivating women's art depends less on monasticism as such than upon the kind of monasticism available to women. The role of the Byzantine convent in the cultivation of scribes, artists and scholars may have been conditioned by the availability of other avenues for the education of women; it surely responded to the fact that women's houses – to a far greater extent than male ones – were located in cities and so were able to draw upon urban professionals in a way that Western houses could not or did not do (Talbot, "A comparison …", 1985). Yet the elusiveness of the convent must also depend upon our own difficulty in identifying the evidence. This is indicated by Irmgard Hutter's examination (1995) of the Typikon (Oxford, Lincoln College, MS gr.35) drafted in stages during the early 14th century for the Constantinopolitan convent of the Theotokos Bebaios Elpidos (Virgin of Sure Hope) by Theodora Synadene and her daughter Euphrosyne. Theodora was a lay person most of her life; Euphrosyne grew up as a nun in the convent her mother had founded for her; but both were literate, as their lives demanded. Like the vast majority of women's monasteries in Byzantium, the Bebaios Elpidos was an urban institution; thus, it had access to the ample scribal and artistic resources of the capital, and this may well account for the accomplished calligraphy and fine miniatures in its Typikon. The composite character of the manuscript, however, with additions and deletions, led Hutter to the conclusion that – though the miniatures were probably provided by a hired professional – the text itself was produced in the convent by the nuns. We know that Kassia, Anna Komnene and Theodora Raoulaina used their years of claustration to write, and it seems probable that women's houses, if less likely to have taken the initiative in developing the learned arts than their counterparts in the West, none the less did offer a context in which the educated woman could exercise the skills she grew up with. Hutter's study should encourage closer examination of other books associated with convents.

Outside the convent, names of craftswomen do not survive. To a far greater extent than in the West, however, Byzantium was an urban culture. Constantinople was the empire's foremost city, but by the 12th century we know that Thessaloniki, Athens, Thebes, Corinth, Arta and the coastal cities of Asia Minor were industrially active, as well. If convents offered a less receptive context for the development of women as artists, cities must have offered a far more conducive one in Byzantium than they did during much of the Middle Ages in the West. The guild records no longer survive here, but we know for sure that women played a major role in the centuries-old silk industry. An icon cover preserved in the Moscow Kremlin attests to one face of this work: namely, as an aspect of Byzantine diplomacy (Moscow 1991, pp.60–61, no.17). Circles of cultivated needlewomen must have travelled with noble emissaries and especially with women to maintain the elaborate wardrobes so crucial to the state presence of a great Byzantine bride or statesman. The icon cover was embroidered by the women who attended the princess Helen Stephanovna in late 15th-century Moscow, and it actually portrays the women themselves gathered with the princess in celebration before the icon their work was made to cover. It represents a far older tradition. Behind this one example must lie many other such women's works.

On a more middle-class level, too, women are cited as skilled in the production of luxury textiles. Textiles and especially silk production yielded the livelihoods of many families in the cities of Greece, and it was the women silk weavers whom the Normans carried off as booty when they sacked the Greek city of Thebes in 1147 (Brand 1993). Likewise in Constantinople the famous imperial silks were woven in home-based workshops. This, as we know from the later evidence of urbanisation in the West, is a very probable setting for women's active participation. The likelihood of their importance is given tantalising support by Angeliki Laiou's remarkable reconstruction of a women's guild of textile workers in 11th-century Constantinople (1986). The membership of a 12th-century confraternity in Thebes casts interesting light upon professional women in Byzantium, for it includes the names of three women, none of them wives of members and all of them levied the same fees and duties as men, implying their professional independence (Nesbitt and Wiita 1975, p.369). This equality stands in striking contrast to the guild records of Florence cited above, in which women were assessed only two-thirds the dues charged to men. As far away as medieval Georgia, in fact, during the reign of the 13th-century Queen Tamar, Shavla Rustaveli included in his epic poem *The Man in the Panther's Skin* a vivid description of the social power and visibility of the wife of a president of a merchants' guild. This woman not only oversaw business and extended hospitality and entertainment to the members, but she led the guild of merchants' wives, to whom their husbands entrusted their affairs while they were away (Uitz 1990, p.38).

The testimony of painting is more elusive. The fairly extensive evidence of mural and icon painting that survives from the 12th century in Cyprus, the Peloponnesus and Macedonia indicates that these arts were practised in a number of cases by itinerant painters, who supplied both the murals and the icons for the churches they adorned. Illuminated manuscripts from the provinces, too, have yielded strikingly little evidence for settled ateliers of miniaturists outside Constantinople. Such painters as appear in these contexts must have been itinerant. Here, as in the West, itinerancy may well have been a deterrent to women's participation. In Constantinople itself, on the other hand, there is ample evidence that lay and monastic production interpenetrated, and that paintings were supplied to lay and monastic patrons alike by lay painters working from their own homes. This is the case with the early 11th-century painter Pantoleon: recipient of a miracle that occurred while he was at work in his home in Constantinople on an icon commissioned by a great abbot, Pantoleon seems also to have been the main miniaturist of the magnificently illuminated Menologion (Biblioteca Apostolica Vaticana, MS gr.1613) commissioned by the emperor Basil II (Sevcenko 1972). Apparently, he was a prominent lay professional whose home was his atelier, and who took on commissions in various media for lay and religious patrons alike. These are precisely the conditions that fostered the dynasties of specialised male and female professionals in the West, and it is hard to believe that in Byzantium, too, they would not have produced women as well as men who were artists. The scribes cited at the beginning of this section –

Eirene, daughter of Theodore Hagiopetrites, and Sophia, daugher of Rikos Kontoioannes – confirm this pattern.

Although it differs significantly in its social and institutional distribution, then, the meagre evidence for women as artists in Byzantium tends to confirm the broad conclusions suggested by the testimony of the West. Women were active in most areas in which men were, though social proscriptions – against itinerancy, for instance, or against learning the pure language of official power – must have curtailed their access to authority. Cities, with their patterns of family production and their steady clientele, seem to have fostered the participation of women, and in Byzantium as in the West it is in the luxury trades such as silk-making, embroidering and the book arts that individuals – among them women – acquire visibility. Women of creativity and at times of real economic prominence and authority certainly contributed to these arts with their superbly controlled level of professional skill and taste. The number of women who assumed initiative as masters in these enterprises is harder to assess, however, in both cultures. In both cultures the conduciveness of monasticism to women's artistic development seems to have depended less upon monasticism as such than upon the kind of monasticism available to them. In both cultures, moreover, it seems that women's activity most usually developed in conjunction with, and not separately from, the work of men. Where names occur, women's names appear among them.

ANNEMARIE WEYL CARR
with the help of ANNE DERBES (Hood College, Frederick, MD),
PAULA GERSON (International Center of Medieval Art, New York),
JUDITH H. OLIVER (Colgate University, Hamilton, NY) and
PAMELA A. PATTON (Southern Methodist University, Dallas)

Notes

[1] See since then Carr 1976 and 1985; Ludwigshaven 1983; Parker 1984; Schraut 1987; Chadwick 1990; Yawn-Bonghi 1992; Oliver 1997; Hamburger (in preparation). I owe my thanks to Professor Eleanor Tufts, who first engaged me in the issue of women as artists, to Dr Alice-Mary Maffrey Talbot, who encouraged my work on Byzantine women, and to Maria Hopewell, who introduced me to the literature on Sabine von Steinbach.

[2] See especially Maitland 1844; Bock 1856–71; Wattenbach 1875; Bradley 1887–9; Eckenstein 1896; Thieme and Becker 1907–50; Heinrich 1924.

[3] As an *entré* into this by now very richly documented material, see Bell 1982; Berman 1985; Sekules 1987; Caviness 1993; Jeffreys 1980; Laiou 1981.

[4] See Kroos 1970; Freiburg im Breisgau 1970; Braunschweig 1985; Cologne 1985; Schraut 1987; and, with colour plates, Appuhn 1963.

[5] For Wienhausen, see Appuhn 1983, p.13, and Moessner 1987; for Nuremberg, see Schraut 1991, pp.94, 106–10; for Heilig Grab, see Baumgärtel-Fleischmann 1983, p.54.

[6] The literature on these houses is by now quite extensive. For the beguines, see Oliver 1988; for the Cistercians, see Schraut 1988; for the Clarissans, see Galley 1961, Schraut 1991 and Steingräber 1952; for the Dominicans, see Fischer 1928; Raspe 1905, pp.10–31; Schraut 1987 and Heusinger 1959; for the oeuvre of a group of Brigittine or Cistercian nuns in Westphalia, see Oliver 1997. For the Dominican proscriptions against women's production of books, in 1249, 1254 and again in 1263, see Oliver 1997.

[7] *Istu[m] egregiu[m] libru[m] scripsit, ill[um]inavit, notavit, i[m]paginavit, aureis litteris et imaginibus pulchris decoravit venerabilis ac devota virgo Gysela de Kerzenbroeck i[n] sui memoria[m].*

Anno d[omi]ni MCCC cui[us] a[n]i[m]a req[ui]escat i[n] s[an]c[t]a pace; on the Gisle Codex, see Kroos 1973; and Oliver 1997, where she translates the inscription, p.109, and reproduces it, fig.56.

8   *Soror Jutta de Alft[er] p[er]solvit ist[um] lib[rum] cu[m] suis expe[n]sis et el[eemosyn]is orate p[ro] ea et p[ro] q[ui]b[u]s devote i[n]te[n]d[i]t et Soror Loppa de Spec[u]lo p[er]fecit scr[i]bendo, liniando, nota[n]do, illu[m]i[n]ando q[ui]a n[on] excludatis ex cordib[us] v[est]ris ...*; Galley 1961; among the other manuscripts attributed to Loppa, in addition to the Stockholm antiphonary and the missals cited below, is a fragmentary antiphonary, Cologne, Wallraf-Richartz Museum, inv. nos 56 and 66.

9   Thus the earliest of the devotional psalters with their distinctive full-page multiple frontispieces and calendars were made for women, identified currently as Christina of Markyate and Queen Melisende of Jerusalem, and women continue to be prominent among their owners. For the kind of text included in these books, see the woman's psalter and commentary published in Gregory 1990.

10   Thus see Bomford in London 1989, who comments, p.9: "As far as is known, the painters in medieval Italy were nearly all men ... Unlike Northern painting, there are no illustrations from Italy of women at the easel". Of Spain, Patton wrote in notes for this project: "I found no literature treating the topic of women artists in Spain ... One area which I had hoped might yield evidence of artistic activity by women was that of textile arts ... I found no indication that the possibility of female artists had even been considered". Even in England the number of women known in the book arts is scant in the later centuries; hence the interest with which Mary C. Erler (book review in *Scriptorium*, xlviii, 1994, p.350) noted Christopher de Hamel's attribution of one of the early 15th-century prayer books from Syon Abbey to its owner, Anna Kaarlsdottir, in *Syon Abbey ... 1991*.

11   For the impact of varied types of monasticism, see Wemple 1990.

12   On women in Byzantium, see Galatariotou 1988; Grosdidier de Matons 1967; Herrin 1983; Laiou 1981; Laiou 1993; Talbot, "A comparison ...", 1985; and the dedicated volume, *Byzantinische Forschungen*, ix, 1985, which includes articles by Dorothy DeF. Abrahamse, Annemarie Weyl Carr, Angela Hero, Angeliki E. Laiou and Alice-Mary Maffrey Talbot.

13   See Holum 1982; Harrison 1989; Jeffreys 1980; Nunn 1986.

14   Nelson and Lowden 1991 have challenged the attribution to Theodora's patronage of the large "Palaiologina Group" of often outstanding illuminated manuscripts from around 1300 that had been proposed by Buchthal and Belting 1978.

15   For two views of these as documents of women, see Galatariotou 1988 and Laiou 1985.

Bibliography

The West

Christine de Pisan (1364–1431), *The Book of the City of Ladies*, New York: Persea, 1982

S[amuel] R[offey] Maitland, *The Dark Ages: Essays Illustrating the State of Religion and Literature in the Ninth, Tenth, Eleventh and Twelfth Centuries*, London: Rivington, 1844; reprint, with introduction by Frederick Stokes, Port Washington, NY: Kennikat Press, 1969

Franz Bock, *Geschichte der liturgischen Gewänder des Mittelalters*, 3 vols, Bonn: Henry & Cohen, 1856–71; reprinted Graz: Akademische Druck- und Verlagsanstalt, 1970

Wilhelm Wattenbach, *Das Schriftwesen im Mittelalter*, Leipzig: Hirzel, 1875

John W. Bradley, *A Dictionary of Miniaturists, Illuminators, Calligraphers and Copyists*, 3 vols, London: Quaritch, 1887–9

Lina Eckenstein, *Woman under Monasticism: Chapters on Saint-Lore and Convent Life Between AD 500 and AD 1500*, Cambridge: Cambridge University Press, 1896; reprinted New York: Russell and Russell, 1963

Theodor Raspe, *Studien zur deutschen Kunstgeschichte: Die Nürnberger Miniaturmalerei bis 1515*, Studien zur deutschen Kunstgeschichte, 60, Strasbourg: Heitz, 1905

Ulrich Thieme and Felix Becker, *Allgemeines Lexikon der bildenden Künstler von der Antike bis zur Gegenwart*, 37 vols, Leipzig: Seeman, 1907–50

Georg Swarzenski, *Die Salzburger Malerei*, 2 vols, Leipzig: Hiersemann, 1908–13

Maria Pia Heinrich, *The Canonesses and Education in the Early Middle Ages*, PhD dissertation, Catholic University of America, Washington, DC, 1924

Karl Fischer, *Die Buchmalerei in den beiden Dominikanerklöstern Nürnbergs*, Nuremberg, 1928

E. A. Lowe, ed., *Codices latini antiquiores: A Palaeographical Guide to the Ninth Century*, 2nd edition, 11 vols, Oxford: Clarendon Press, 1934–72

Karl Michaëlsson, "Le livre de la taille de Paris, l'an de grace 1313", *Göteborgs Högskolas Årsskrift*, lvii/3, 1951, pp.1–349

Erich Steingräber, "Neun Miniaturen einer Franziskus-Vita", *Zeitschrift für schweizerischen Architektur und Kunstgeschichte*, xiii, 1952, pp.237–45

Bernhard Bischoff, "Die Kölner Nonnenhandschriften und das Skriptorium von Chelles", *Karolingische und Ottonische Kunst: Werden, Wesen, Wirkung*, Forschungen zur Kunstgeschichte und christlichen Archäologie, 3, Wiesbaden: Steiner, 1957, pp.395–411

Ellen Beer, *Beiträge zur oberrheinischen Buchmalerei in der erste Hälfte des 14. Jahrhunderts, unter besonderer Berücksichtigung der Initialornamentik*, Basel: Birkhauser, 1959

Christian von Heusinger, "Spätmittelalterliche Buchmalerei im oberrheinischen Frauenklostern", *Zeitschrift für die Geschichte des Oberrheins*, new series, lxviii (=cvii), 1959, pp.136–60

Eberhard Galley, "Miniaturen aus dem Kölner Klarissenkloster: Ein Kapitel rheinischen Buchmalerei des 14. Jahrhunderts", *Aus der Welt des Bibliothekars (Festschrift für Rudolf Juchhoff)*, ed. Kurt Ohly, Cologne: Greven, 1961, pp.15–28

Jaime Marques Casanovas, César E. Dubler and Wilhelm Neuss, *Sancti Beati a Liebana in Apocalypsin: Codex Gerundensis*, 2 vols, Oltun: Graf, 1962

H. Radspieler, "Reglind aus Admont, Abtissin von Bergen und Hohenburg", *Neuburger Kollektaneenblatt*, cxv, 1962, pp.33–48

Horst Appuhn, *Meisterwerke der niedersächsischen Kunst des Mittelalters*, Bad Honnef Rhein: Peters, 1963

Paul Grimm, "Zwei bemerkenswerte Gebäude in der Pfalz Tilleda: Eine zweite Tuchmacherei", *Prähistorische Zeitschrift*, xli, 1963, pp.62–82

Opus anglicanum: English Medieval Embroidery, exh. cat., Arts Council at the Victoria and Albert Museum, London, 1963

Ellen Beer, "Literaturbericht: Gotische Buchmalerei. Literatur von 1945 bis 1961", *Zeitschrift für Kunstgeschichte*, xxviii, 1965

Françoise Baron, "Enlumineurs, peintres et sculpteurs parisiens des XIIIe et XIVe siècle d'après les rôles de la taille", *Bulletin Archéologique du Comité des Travaux Historiques et Scientifiques*, iv, 1968, pp.37–121

Millard Meiss, *French Painting in the Time of Jean de Berry*, 2 vols, 2nd edition, London: Phaidon, 1969

Renate Kroos, *Niedersächsische Bildstickereien des Mittelalters*, Berlin: Deutscher Verlag für Kunstwissenschaft, 1970

Kunstepochen der Stadt Freiburg: Ausstellung zur 850-Jahrfeier, exh. cat., Städtliche Museen, Freiburg im Breisgau, 1970

Magnus Backes and Regine Dölling, *Art of the Dark Ages*, New York: Abrams, 1971

Gérard Cames, *Allégories et symboles dans l'Hortus deliciarum*, Leiden: Brill, 1971

R. Kent Lancaster, "Artists, suppliers, clerks: The human factors in the art patronage of King Henry III", *Journal of the Warburg and Courtauld Institutes*, xxxv, 1972, pp.81–107

Renate Kroos, "Der Codex Gisle I: Forschungsbericht und Datierung", *Niederdeutsche Beiträge zur Kunstgeschichte*, xii, 1973, pp.117–34

Dorothy Miner, *Anastaise and Her Sisters: Women Artists of the Middle Ages*, Baltimore: Walters Art Gallery, 1974

Annemarie Weyl Carr, "Women as artists in the Middle Ages", *Feminist Art Journal*, v, 1976, pp.5–9, 26

Marc Fitch, "The London makers of *opus anglicanum*", *Transactions of the London and Middlesex Archaeological Society*, xxvii, 1976, pp.228–96

Women Artists, 1550–1950, exh. cat., Los Angeles County Museum of Art, and elsewhere, 1976

Die Zeit der Staufer: Geschichte, Kunst, Kultur, 5 vols, exh. cat., Württembergisches Landesmuseum, Stuttgart, 1977

Frances Gies and Joseph Gies, *Women in the Middle Ages*, New York: Crowell, 1978

Germaine Greer, *The Obstacle Race: The Fortunes of Women Painters and Their Work*, London: Secker and Warburg, and New York: Farrar Straus, 1979

Suzanne Lewis, "Sacred calligraphy: The chi rho page in the Book of Kells", *Traditio*, xxxvi, 1980, pp.139–59

S.G. Bell, "Medieval women book owners: Arbiters of lay piety and ambassadors of culture", *Signs*, vii, 1982, pp.742–68

Odile Brel-Bordaz, *Broderies d'ornements liturgiques XIIIe–XIVe siècles*, Paris: Nouvelles Editions Latines, 1982

C.R. Dodwell, *Anglo-Saxon Art: A New Perspective*, Ithaca, NY: Cornell University Press, and Manchester: Manchester University Press, 1982

Horst Appuhn, *Bildstickereien des Mittelalters in Kloster Lüne*, Dortmund: Harenberg, 1983

Renate Baumgärtel-Fleischmann, *Ausgewählte Kunstwerke aus dem Diözesanmuseum Bamberg*, Bamberg: Bayerische Verlagsanstalt, 1983

Frauen und Kunst im Mittelalter, exh. cat., Wilhelm-Hack-Museum, Ludwigshaven, 1983

Rozsika Parker, *The Subversive Stitch: Embroidery and the Making of the Feminine*, London: Women's Press, 1984; New York: Routledge, 1989

Ulrike Bergmann, "PRIOR OMNIBUS AUCTOR – an höchster Stelle aber steht der Stifter", *Ornamenta ecclesiae: Kunst und Künstler der Romanik*, 3 vols, exh. cat., Schnütgen-Museum, Cologne, 1985, i, pp.117–48

Constance H. Berman, "Women as donors and patrons to southern French monasteries in the twelfth and thirteenth centuries", *The Worlds of Medieval Women: Creativity, Influence, Imagination*, ed. Constance H. Berman and others, Morgantown: West Virginia University Press, 1985, pp.53–68

Michael Camille, "Seeing and reading: Some visual implications of medieval literacy and illiteracy", *Art History*, viii, 1985, pp.26–49

Anton Legner, "Illustres Manus", *Ornamenta ecclesiae: Kunst und Künstler der Romanik*, 3 vols, exh. cat., Schnütgen-Museum, Cologne, 1985, i, pp.187–230

Meredith Parsons Lillich, "Gothic glaziers: Monks, Jews, taxpayers, Bretons, women", *Journal of Glass Studies*, xxvii, 1985, pp.72–92

Ornamenta ecclesiae: Kunst und Künstler der Romanik, 3 vols, exh. cat., Schnütgen-Museum, Cologne, 1985

Stadt im Wandel: Kunst und Kultur des Bürgertums in Norddeutschland, 1150–1650, 4 vols, exh. cat., Herzog Anton Ulrich-Museum, Braunschweig, 1985

David M. Wilson, *The Bayeux Tapestry: The Complete Tapestry in Colour*, London: Thames and Hudson, and New York: Knopf, 1985

David J. Bernstein, *The Mystery of the Bayeux Tapestry*, London: Weidenfeld and Nicolson, 1986; Chicago: University of Chicago Press, 1987

Sandra L. Hindman, *Christine de Pizan's "Epistre d'Othéa": Painting and Politics at the Court of Charles VI*, Toronto: Pontifical Institute of Mediaeval Studies, 1986

V. Moessner, "The medieval embroideries of Convent Wienhausen", *Studies in Cistercian Art and Architecture*, iii, 1987, pp.161–77

Elisabeth Schraut, ed., *Stifterinnen und Künstlerinnen im mittelalterlichen Nürnberg*, Nuremberg: Selbstverlag der Stadt Nürnberg, 1987

Veronica Sekules, "Women and art in England in the thirteenth and fourteenth centuries", *Age of Chivalry*, exh. cat., Royal Academy, London, 1987, pp.41–8

Judith H. Oliver, *Gothic Manuscript Illumination in the Diocese of Liège, c.1250–1330*, 2 vols, Leuven: Peeters, 1988

Elisabeth Schraut, "Zum Bildungszustand fränkischer Zisterzienserinnenkonvente", *Württembergische Franken*, lxxii, 1988, pp.42–67

Art in the Making: Italian Painting Before 1400, exh. cat., National Gallery, London, 1989

Edith Ennen, *The Medieval Woman*, Oxford: Blackwell, 1989

Marie-Jeanne Geyer, "Le mythe d'Erwin de Steinbach", *Exposition de bâtisseurs de cathédrals gothiques*, exh. cat., Strasbourg, 1989, pp.322–9, 477–9

Jeffrey Hamburger, "The visual and the visionary: The image in late medieval monastic devotions", *Viator*, xx, 1989, pp.161–82

Whitney Chadwick, *Women, Art and Society*, New York and London: Thames and Hudson, 1990

Stewart Gregory, ed., *The Twelfth-Century Psalter Commentary in French for Laurette d'Alsace (An Edition of Psalms, I–L)*, 2 vols, London: Modern Humanities Research Association, 1990

Jeffrey F. Hamburger, *The Rothschild Canticles: Art and Mysticism in Flanders and the Rhineland circa 1300*, New Haven and London: Yale University Press, 1990

Rosamond McKitterick, ed., *The Uses of Literacy in Early Mediaeval Europe*, Cambridge and New York: Cambridge University Press, 1990

Erika Uitz, *The Legend of Good Women: Medieval Women in Towns and Cities*, Mt Kisco, NY: Moyer Bell, 1990; as *Women in the Medieval Town*, London: Barrie and Jenkins, 1990 (German original, 1988)

Suzanne Fonay Wemple, "Female monasticism in Italy and its comparison with France and Germany from the ninth through the eleventh centuries", *Frauen in Spätantike und Frühmittelalter*, ed. Werner Affeldt, Sigmaringen: Thorbecke, 1990, pp.291–310

Mildred Budny, "The Byrhtnoth tapestry or embroidery", *The Battle of Maldon, AD 991*, ed. Donald Scragg, Oxford: Blackwell, 1991, pp.263–78

Jeffrey Hamburger, "A *Liber Precum* in Silestat and the development of the illustrated prayer book in Germany", *Art Bulletin*, lxxiii, 1991, pp.209–36

Elisabeth Schraut, "Überlegungen zu den Möglichkeiten der Frauen im mittelalterlichen Kunstbetrieb am Beispiel Nürnberg", *Auf der Suche nach der Frau im Mittelalter: Fragen, Quellen, Antworten*, ed. Bea Lundt, Munich: Fink, 1991, pp.81–114

Kay Staniland, *Embroiderers*, London: British Museum Press, and Toronto: University of Toronto Press, 1991

Syon Abbey: The Library of the Brigettine Nuns and Their Peregrinations after the Reformation: An Essay by Christopher de Hamel, with the Manuscript at Arundel Castle, Otley: Roxburghe Club, 1991

Jonathan J.G. Alexander, *Medieval Illuminators and Their Methods of Work*, New Haven and London: Yale University Press, 1992

C. Frugoni, "The imagined woman", *A History of Women in the West, II: Silences of the Middle Ages*, ed. Christiane Klapisch-Zuber, Cambridge, MA: Harvard University Press, 1992

Jeffrey F. Hamburger, "Art, enclosure and the 'Cura Monialium': Prolegomena in the guise of a postscript", *Gesta*, xxxi, 1992, pp.108–34

Judith Oliver, "Devotional psalters and the study of beguine spirituality", *Vox Benedictina*, ix, 1992, pp.198–225

Leonie von Wilckens, "The Quedlinburg carpet", *Hali*, xiv/5, 1992, pp.97–128

Lila Yawn-Bonghi, "Medieval women artists and modern historians", *Medieval Feminist Newsletter*, xii, 1992, pp.10–19

Emilie Amt, ed., *Women's Lives in Medieval Europe: A Sourcebook*, New York and London: Routledge, 1993

The Art of Medieval Spain, AD 500–1200, exh. cat., Metropolitan Museum of Art, New York, 1993

Lorena Casa, *Religious Women as Scribes and Artists in Early Anglo-Saxon England*, MA thesis, University of London, 1993

Madeline H. Caviness, "Patron or matron: A Capetian bride and a *vade mecum* for her marriage", *Speculum*, lxviii, 1993, pp.333–63

Allen S. Farber, "Considering a marginal master: The work of an early fifteenth-century Parisian manuscript decorator", *Gesta*, xxxii, 1993, pp.21–39

William Cook, "Early images of St Francis of Assisi in Rome", *Exegisti monumentum aere perennius: Essays in Honor of John Frederick Charles*, ed. Bruce R. Baker and John E. Fischer, Indianapolis: Guild Press of Indiana, 1994

Judith Oliver, "The Herkenrode indulgence, Avignon and pre-Eyckian painting of the mid-fourteenth-century Low Countries", *Flanders in a European Perspective: Manuscript Illumination around 1400 in Flanders and Abroad: Proceedings of the International Colloquium, Leuven, 7–10 September 1993*, ed. M. Smeyers and B. Cardon, Leuven: Peeters, 1995, pp.187–206

——, "The Walters homiliary and Westphalian manuscripts", *Journal of the Walters Art Gallery*, liv, 1996, pp.69–85

——, "Worship of the word: Some Gothic Nonnenbücher in their devotional context", *Women and the Book: Assessing the Visual Evidence*, ed. Jane Taylor and Lesley Smith, London: British Library, and Toronto: University of Toronto, 1997

Jeffrey Hamburger, *Nuns as Artists: The Visual Culture of a German Convent at the End of the Middle Ages* (in preparation)

Byzantium

Anna Comnena (1083–1153), *The Alexiad*, ed. E. R. A. Sewter, Harmondsworth: Penguin, 1969

S. Kugéas, "Zur Geschichte der Münchner Thukydideshandschrift Augustanus F", *Byzantinische Zeitschrift*, xvi, 1907, pp.590–609

Marie Vogel and Victor Gardthausen, *Die griechischen Schreiber des Mittelalters und der Renaissance*, Beihefte zum zentralblatt für Bibliothekswesen, 33, Leipzig, 1909; reprinted Hildesheim: Olms, 1966

Georgina Buckler, *Anna Comnena: A Study*, London: Oxford University Press, 1929

Charles Diehl, *Figures byzantines*, Paris: Colin, 1939

C. Wendel, "Die ΤΑΡΕΙΠΟΤΗΣ des griechischen Schreibermönches", *Byzantinische Zeitschrift*, xliii, 1950, pp.259–66

Otto Volk, *Die byzantinischen Klosterbibliotheken von Konstantinopel, Thessalonike und Kleinasien*, PhD dissertation, Ludwig-Maximilians-Universität, Munich, 1955

Robert Browning, "An unpublished funeral oration on Anna Comnena", *Proceedings of the Cambridge Philological Society*, new series, viii, 1962, pp.1–12

Gregorio de Andrés, *Catàlogo de los códices griegos de la Biblioteca de El Escorial*, 3 vols, Madrid, 1963–7

José Grosdidier de Matons, "La femme dans l'empire byzantin", *Histoire mondiale de la femme*, 4 vols, Paris: Nouvelle Librairie de France, 1965–7, iii, pp.11–43

Greek Manuscripts in the Bodleian Library, exh. cat., Bodleian Library, Oxford, 1966

Pauline Johnstone, *The Byzantine Tradition in Church Embroidery*, London: Tiranti, and Chicago: Argonaut, 1967

Ilse Rochow, *Studien zu der Person, den Werken und dem Nachleben der Dichterin Kassia*, Berliner byzantinishe Arbeiten, 38, Berlin: Akademie, 1967

Jean Darrouzès, *Georges et Démétrios Tornikès: Lettres et discours*, Paris: Editions du Centre Nationale de Recherche Scientifique, 1970

Paul Lemerle, André Guillou and Nicolas Svoronos, *Actes de Lavra, première partie: Des origines à 1204. Archives del'Athos, v, i, et album*, Paris: Lethielleux, 1970

Ihor Sevcenko, "On Pantoleon the painter", *Jahrbuch der österreichischen Byzantinistik*, xxii, 1972, pp.241–9

John Nesbitt and John Wiita, "A confraternity of the Comnenian era", *Byzantinische Zeitschrift*, lxviii, 1975, pp.360–84

Michael J. Kyriakis, "Medieval European society as seen in two eleventh-century texts of Michael Psellos", *Byzantine Studies/Etudes Byzantines*, iii/2, 1976, pp.77–106

Dieter Harlfinger, "Zu griechischen Kopisten und Schriftsteller des 15. und 16. Jahrhunderts", *La Paléographie grecque et byzantine*, Paris: Editions du Centre Nationale de Recherche Scientifique, 1977, pp.327–39

Hugo Buchthal and Hans Belting, *Patronage in Thirteenth-Century Constantinople: An Atelier of Late Byzantine Book Illumination and Calligraphy*, Washington, DC: Dumbarton Oaks, 1978

Alexander Kazhdan, *Byzanz und seine Kultur*, Darmstadt: Wissenschaftliche Buchgesellschaft, 1978

Elizabeth M. Jeffreys, "The Comnenian background to the *Romans d'antiquité*", *Byzantion*, l, 1980, pp.455–86

Annemarie Weyl Carr, "A note on Theodore Hagiopetrites", *Scriptorium*, xxxv, 1981, pp.287–90

Elizabeth M. Jeffreys, "The Sevastokratorissa Eirene as literary patroness: The monk Iakovos", *Jahrbuch der österreichischen Byzantinistik*, xxxii/2, part 3, 1981, pp.63–71

Angeliki E. Laiou, "The role of women in Byzantine society", *Jahrbuch der österreichischen Byzantinistik*, xxxi/1, 1981, pp.233–60

Judith Herrin, "Women and the faith in icons in early Christianity", *Culture, Ideology and Politics: Essays for Eric Hobsbawm*, ed. Raphael Samuel and Gareth Stedman Jones, London: Routledge, 1982, pp.56–83

Kenneth G. Holum, *Theodosian Empresses: Women and Imperial Dominion in Late Antiquity*, Berkeley: University of California Press, 1982

Judith Herrin, "In search of Byzantine Women: Three avenues of approach", *Images of Women in Antiquity*, ed. Averil Cameron and Amelie Kuhrt, Detroit: Wayne State University Press, and London: Croom Helm, 1983, pp.167–89; revised edition, London: Routledge, 1993

Dorothy DeF. Abrahamse, "Women's monasticism in the Middle Byzantine period: Problems and prospects", *Byzantinische Forschungen*, ix, 1985, pp.35–58

Annemarie Weyl Carr, "Women and monasticism: Introduction from an art historian", *Byzantinische Forschungen*, ix, 1985, pp.1–15

Paul Gautier, "Le Typikon de la Theotokos Kécharitômenè", *Revue des Etudes Byzantines*, xliii, 1985, pp.5–165

Angela Hero, "Irene-Eulogia Choumnaina Palaiologina, abbess of the convent of Philanthropos Soter in Constantinople", *Byzantinische Forschungen*, ix, 1985, pp.119–47

Angeliki E. Laiou, "Observations on the life and ideology of Byzantine women", *Byzantinische Forschungen*, ix, 1985, pp.59–102

Alice-Mary Maffrey Talbot, "A comparison of the monastic experience of Byzantine men and women", *Greek Orthodox Theological Review*, xxx, 1985, pp.1–20

——, "Late Byzantine nuns: By choice or necessity?" *Byzantinische Forschungen*, ix, 1985, pp.103–18

Angeliki E. Laiou, "The festival of 'Agathe': Comments on the life of Constantinopolitan Women", *Byzantion: Aphieroma ston Andrea N. Strato*, 2 vols, Athens: Nia A. Stratos, 1986, i, pp.111–22

Valerie Nunn, "The encheirion as adjunct to the icon in the Middle Byzantine period", *Byzantine and Modern Greek Studies*, x, 1986, pp.73–102

Annemarie Weyl Carr, *Byzantine Illumination, 1150–1250: The Study of a Provincial Tradition*, Chicago: University of Chicago Press, 1987

Catia Galatariotou, "Byzantine women's monastic communities: The evidence of the Typika", *Jahrbuch der österreichischen Byzantinistik*, xxxviii, 1988, pp.263–90

Annabel Jane Wharton, *Art of Empire: Painting and Architecture of the Byzantine Periphery: A Comparative Study of Four Provinces*, University Park: Pennsylvania State University Press, 1988

R. Martin Harrison, *A Temple for Byzantium: The Discovery and Excavation of Anicia Juliana's Palace-Church in Istanbul*, Austin: University of Texas Press, and London: Harvey Miller, 1989

Medieval Pictorial Embroidery: Byzantium, Balkans, Russia, exh. cat., Eighteenth International Congress of Byzantinists at the Moscow Kremlin State Museums, Moscow, 1991

Robert S. Nelson and John Lowden, "The Palaeologina group: Additional manuscripts and new questions", *Dumbarton Oaks Papers*, xlv, 1991, pp.59–68

Antonia Trypolitis, ed., *Kassia: The Legend, the Woman and Her Work*, New York: Garland, 1992

Charles Brand, "Some women of Thebes – and elsewhere", *To*

Hellenikon: Studies in Honor of Speros Vryonis, Jr, 2 vols, New Rochelle, NY: Caratzas, 1993, i, pp.59–68

Angeliki E. Laiou, ed., *Consent and Coercion to Sex and Marriage in Ancient and Medieval Societies*, Washington, DC: Dumbarton Oaks, 1993

Irmgard Hutter, "Die Geschichte des Lincoln College Typikons", *Jahrbuch der österreichischen Byzantinistik*, xlv, 1995, pp.79–114

Thalia Gouma-Peterson, Bibliography on women in Byzantium: http:www.wooster.edu/art/wb.html

Convents

Before the Council of Trent (1545–63)

From the earliest ages of monasticism through the later Middle Ages, women were involved in the making of works of art to be used in or to adorn their communities. For both male and female religious communities, the making of works of art on religious themes satisfied the monastic ideals of work and prayer. On many occasions the production of works of art enabled communities to support themselves. Yet the making of works of art in religious communities of women has been little studied, because historians of monasticism have focused on masculine production, and historians of art have marginalised the art forms most frequently made in women's convents.

The study of convent artists has its own difficulties. There are few survivals of works of art made by nuns, and the documentary references to the activity of women as artists in convents are often unclear. The materials that do survive are often difficult of access, tucked away in hard-to-reach parts of museums, or still within enclosed convents. Even objects with a known provenance are hard to contextualise because so few convents of women are well published.

By far the largest literature on this subject concerns nuns as makers of books. This literature has been produced mostly by palaeographers and bibliographers interested in the origins and contexts for the making of manuscripts, so that the identification of women's production is a by-product of their researches rather than the principal goal. There are, for example, good studies of the books produced in such places as St Katherine's, Nuremberg, and the Benedictine convent of Ebstorf in Saxony, as well as studies of the production of manuscripts from specific regions, such as Lüneburg and Switzerland. Neither historians of monasticism nor historians of art, however, have attempted to integrate the surviving production from women's convents into mainstream histories. The art produced in convents often falls outside the stylistic norms with which regions and periods have been associated; it thus fails to be integrated into period or regional studies. There has also been a tendency to classify "nuns' work" (*Nonnenarbeit*) as something other than fine arts, and thus to marginalise it further. When surviving production from women's houses takes the form of small reliquary shrines, silk flowers or garments for statues, it eludes art-historical categories completely.

None the less, there have been some efforts at outlining the history of convent artists' production. Lina Eckenstein's classic work, *Woman under Monasticism* (1896), synthesised some of these bibliographic studies, and brought together scattered references to other art forms. Dorothy Miner's essay on women illuminators, *Anastaise and Her Sisters* (1974), updated this information, and was an important source for Annemarie Weyl Carr's essay on "Women as artists in the Middle Ages" (1976). The general surveys of women artists that began to appear in the 1970s often begin with the 16th century, leaving the convent artists of the Middle Ages out of the picture; of these, Germaine Greer's overview of women artists (1979) brought together many of the scattered references buried in art-historical literature in her chapter on "The cloister", but this book must be used with care. The most convenient summary of the literature on nuns as artists and patrons, especially in the German regions, is the prodigious synthesis provided by Jeffrey Hamburger's "Art, enclosure and the 'Cura Monialium'" (1992). Examples of convent artists' production before Trent may also be found in the catalogue of the exhibition *Le Jardin clos de l'âme* held in Brussels in 1994.

During the late Middle Ages there was an increase in the number of communities of women in para-religious organisations, such as beguines, pinzochere and tertiaries. These groups used some of the same strategies for supporting themselves as the regular houses of religious women, so that the term "convent artist" becomes somewhat more fluid in the later medieval period. The Council of Trent forced most of these communities into enclosure, making their lives more like those of their professed sisters in regular houses.

Conditions of production

Several factors created special conditions for the practice of making art in women's convents. Women's houses were often less fiscally secure than male houses, resulting in a limited access to materials for women artists. As a result, works of art produced by nuns are often made of simple and inexpensive materials. After the issuance of the Decretal *Periculoso* in 1298, which required that women's convents enforce *clausura* (or enclosure), the access of convent artists to the study of techniques, or to see works outside their convents, was further curtailed. This development coincided with a shift in the making of books from monastic to secular workshops in major urban centres. The increasing professionalisation of many trades at the end of the Middle Ages, for example in book illumination and textiles, made it more difficult for women to make and market their works, as guild regulations often forbade women's participation and guild leaders used legal remedies to restrict nuns' access to markets, particularly in the textile trades. (In 1456, for example, the silk workers of Cologne petitioned for restrictions against the beguines of that city.)

As they were, at least in theory, enclosed, the women had little or no access to training at professional levels. There were several ways for nuns to master artistic techniques: they were either self-taught, or they were the daughters of artists who learned their craft before entering the convent, or they were taught by senior sisters in their convents. There is documentary evidence that some religious men taught artistic techniques to nuns; for example, the Dominican friar Giovanni Dominici, whose many letters (c.1396–1406) written to the sisters of Corpus Domini in Venice discuss aspects of making books (Gilbert 1984). It is also known from documents that at the end of the 15th century a female illuminator of Bruges, named Margriete or Grietkin Scheppers, taught illumination to the nuns of the Carmelite convent of Sion. From accomplished artists within the convent other women would learn artistic skills; this was the case, for example, in the 15th century at St Katherine's in Nuremberg, and in the 16th century at the Dominican convent of Santa Caterina di Siena in Florence, where Plautilla Nelli (q.v.) taught a number of pupils.

Despite the ideal of enclosure, however, women were not entirely cut off from artistic currents in the world: just as nuns maintained commerce with the world in financial and political terms, they were also often brought into contact with secular artists through donors to convents and family relations of the nuns. For example, the Poor Clares of Monteluce in Perugia commissioned Raphael to execute an altarpiece of the *Coronation of the Virgin* (1505; Pinacoteca Vaticana, Rome) for the high altar of their church. It was for the refectory of the Benedictine convent of Sant'Apollonia in Florence that Andrea del Castagno executed his *Last Supper* (1447); because this was part of the enclosed precinct of the convent, it is likely that few secular artists in 15th-century Florence ever saw the fresco. In Bruges the painter Gerard David painted an altarpiece of the *Virgo inter virgines* (1509; Musée des Beaux-Arts, Rouen) for the Carmelite convent of Sion, which he gave to this community. The entrance of such works of art into the precincts of the convent surely encouraged convent artists' own production.

At various points throughout the Middle Ages, religious movements to reform monastic life stimulated artistic production. Reformed communities placed a greater emphasis on the prayer cycles of the *opus dei* than convents that had modified their practices, and thus they demanded more accurate and standardised books. For example, when the Benedictine convent at Ebstorf was reformed in 1469 its whole library had to be replaced. At the same time, the ideals of the reformers usually stressed economic self-sufficiency and aesthetic simplicity. These notions encouraged the making of liturgical books and other objects within reformed communities, although books were also acquired from secular workshops. Groups of reformed houses created administrative links that encouraged close ties between them; this led to artists from one community working for others in the same order.

The Reformation led to the dismantling of convents as centres of production; in Germany, the Netherlands and England convents were closed (though some in Germany were converted to sodalities), convent properties were redistributed and works of art were scattered or destroyed. The Catholic Counter-Reformation responded by enforcing very restrictive regulations regarding the proper activities and opportunities for nuns (see "After the Council of Trent" below).

Book arts

Many libraries in Europe and America preserve manuscripts whose colophons indicate that the books were manufactured or embellished by nuns. While there is no general study as yet that brings together or analyses all the references to medieval nuns' production of books, much can be learned from the bibliographic and palaeographic literature. This literature is especially rich for the German-speaking regions of Europe. Of this category, by far the most renowned examples are the *Hortus deliciarum* of Herrad (q.v.) and the manuscripts of the *Scivias* of Hildegard of Bingen (q.v.).

As members of religious communities, nuns needed books. While of course some of the books used in women's houses were made in professional scriptoria and either purchased for or given to the convent, the making of books in the convent or the amending of books obtained from elsewhere were common practices. There is good evidence for women's activity as scribes from the earliest Middle Ages (with the scriptorium at Chelles the best-studied example; see "Women as artists in the Middle Ages" survey). This activity continued into the Renaissance. There is also evidence for women as illuminators or decorators of books. Some of this evidence can be found in colophons or inscriptions in books: the signature of Ende (q.v.) on the Beatus of Girona (Girona Cathedral, MS 7) is the most familiar example. The occasional self-portrait included in manuscripts, such as the portrait of Guda in a homiliary in Frankfurt am Main (Stadt- und Universitätsbibliothek, MS Barth.42; see illustration, p.9), provides further evidence of nuns' activities in this field. In this example the figure holds a banderole with a text that reports: "Guda, sinful woman, wrote and painted this book". The inscription "Handmaid of Jesus Christ, Maria the daughter of Orman, written 1453" accompanies the self-portrait of a nun in a Florentine breviary now in Vienna (Österreichische Nationalbibliothek, MS 1923).

Many of these books are simply adorned with vegetal or figural motifs rendered in line drawings with simple washes. The forms themselves are often untutored in style, with little awareness of the stylistic factors that dominate the professionally made illuminations. The books are often made with simple yet bright colours, rather than the expensive blues and golds that characterise the most lavish manuscripts. As in books produced in secular workshops, the styles of works by women vary from region to region and period to period.

Few books on secular themes have been connected with convent production; the bulk of books made by nuns were religious in nature, and liturgical in function, such as missals and breviaries. At St Katherine's in Nuremberg, in the mid-15th century, Sister Barbara Gwichtmacherin decorated numerous books (most Stadtbibliothek, Nuremberg) that Sister Margareta Kartauserin signed as scribe (Heusinger 1959). The Poor Clares convent of Corpus Domini in Bologna still preserves a breviary illuminated by Caterina Vigri (q.v.), whose work as an artist is attested by her contemporary biography. Some private prayer books or books intended for meditation were also the work of nuns, as is a translation of the *Life of St Francis* illustrated by the German Franciscan Sibylla de Bondorff in 1478 (London, British Library, Add. MS 15,710). A large number of illustrated prayer books from German convents await further study. Certain genres of books continued to be made in convents long after the printing press replaced the manuscript; these tended to be larger-format choral books, such as graduals and antiphonals, and specialised texts for in-house use.

Textiles

The traditional feminine accomplishment of needlework entered the convent with the women who were professed there. Women's work in the convent often meant making textiles, either for personal or communal use, or for sale to other institutions. Evidence from church councils, such as the council held at Clovesho in England in 747, suggests that some religious communities spent more time at the needle than at the *opus dei*. Many of these communities specialised in liturgical vestments and altar cloths, for themselves and for others. The most famous genre of needlework from the Middle Ages, *opus anglicanum*, is often discussed as the product of convent workshops, but current thinking is that this kind of embroidery was usually the product of professional, lay workshops of either men or women. None the less, the only signed English embroidery to survive from the Middle Ages is an altar frontal (c.1290–1340; see illustration, p.6), worked with heraldic images, which bears the inscription DOMNA IOHANNA BEVERLAI MONACA ME FECIT. Furthermore, there is a great deal of documentary evidence for nuns all over Europe supporting their houses with their needlework. Hagiographies of early medieval saints often describe their activities as needlewomen, especially in the making of liturgical textiles. The Cistercian nuns of the convent of Bijloke in Ghent specialised in such embroideries, which were sold to churches in the town in the mid-14th century; in the 1440s the Benedictine nuns of Sant'Apollonia provided other churches in Florence with embroideries. Certain techniques of needlework were practised in specific regions, for example, the white-on-white embroideries known as *opus teutonicum*, which were the speciality of medieval German convents (several whitework examples of the 14th and 15th centuries are preserved at the Cistercian convent of Wienhausen). Study of these materials is hampered by the great losses sustained.

For certain regions, there is also evidence that nuns worked in tapestry. When in 1454–5 Johannes Meyer, a Dominican of Basel, translated a Dominican guide for the duties of various officers of the convent (Humbert of Romans's *Instructiones de officiis ordinis*), he declined to elaborate on the work that would be known by all, which was enumerated as: "writing, sewing, embroidery, tapestry weaving, spinning, crocheting, combing and carding the wool, hooking and weaving cloth". This text, written for German Dominican nuns, presupposes that nuns were familiar with textile arts, including tapestry weaving. A large number of tapestries have survived that point to origins in the convent, from centres such as Nuremberg, Freiberg and Bamberg. In some of these textile works, the nuns depicted themselves working at looms (e.g. the *Passion* tapestry in Bamberg Cathedral Treasury, repr. A. Cavallo, *Medieval Tapestries in the Metropolitan Museum*, New York, 1993, fig.85), or otherwise in the role of donors. For both embroidery and tapestry, it is often assumed that patterns and designs for the nuns' work were supplied from outside the convent, but although this phenomenon is demonstrable in some cases, it is not possible to make generalisations.

Prints

Closely related to both book illustration and textile arts is the medium of printmaking, which appears as an art form in women's convents in the 15th century. Convents such as Bethany in Mechelen (Belgium), Wienhausen in Germany and St Katherine's, Nuremberg, have all left traces of their activities as the supplier of individual woodcut or metal-cut prints to pilgrims or visitors to their houses. Many manuscripts made in the Nuremberg convent still have single woodcut images pasted into them. It is uncertain whether the nuns carved the blocks from which the images were printed, but it seems that they did the printing and selling. The Dominican convent of San Jacopo di Ripoli in Florence added a printing press to its active scriptorium, producing some 70 editions between 1470 and 1484. These are largely devotional texts, but the list does also include some secular books.

Panel and wall painting

The evidence for women as panel painters is mounting; some of this evidence is documentary, some of it within the works themselves. A notice in a chronicle for the Cistercian convent of Wienhausen indicates that the walls of the nuns' choir were painted by members of the community late in the 15th century. A panel depicting the *Virgin Enthroned* (Pinacoteca Malaspina, Pavia) is signed "the work of the reverend lady Andriole de Baracchis abbess of this convent 1489". The convent in question is the Benedictine house of San Felice in Pavia, where other pictures – including frescoes – have been associated with the artist. To the Franciscan Caterina Vigri have been attributed several different panels. Vasari described the large-scale work by the Dominican Plautilla Nelli of Florence both on panel and on canvas; Nelli's sisters at Santa Caterina di Siena in Florence also painted in these media. The biographies of early 16th-century Dominican nuns in Lucca describe their efforts at both book illustration and panel painting. Similarly, sources describe the paintings of the Dominican Sister Tommasina del Fiesco of Genoa, who died in 1534. Most of the work described in the sources has not survived. Several panels from the convent of San Domenico, Pisa, now in the museum there, appear to be the work of sisters in this community, where miniature painting was also practised.

Conclusions

The activities of nuns in the making of art is but one aspect of their contribution to the development of European artistic traditions. Nuns were important patrons of the arts throughout the Middle Ages, an issue also being reconsidered by scholars in recent years. One of the most fascinating topics being examined is the important role that nuns played in using works of art – both as a means to express and explore their spirituality and as a means to attract donations and respect from the laity for their vocations. Jeffrey Hamburger's work in this area has shown that many of the forms of art, if not their uses, that the laity adopted in the later Middle Ages had their origins in the spiritual exercises and forms of piety that were practised by nuns in late medieval convents. We still have far to go to measure the contribution of medieval nuns to the history of art.

ANN ROBERTS

After the Council of Trent (1545–63)

As the production of art became increasingly secularised during the Renaissance, monasteries and convents were no longer the centres of art that they had been in the Middle Ages. In the 15th century women artists continued to be nuns, but the first professional female artists who emerged in the 16th century were from the secular world. The knowledge and training necessary for the Renaissance artist was not available in the isolation of the convent. The societal expectations of female comportment and restrictions on studying from the nude that circumscribed the sphere of artistic activity of even secular women artists was compounded in the closed atmosphere of the convent. Among the reforms of the Catholic Church that resulted from the Council of Trent (1545–63) was the enforcement of a strict enclosure for female convents. Enclosure and the regime of cloistered life were not conducive to the development of artistic talent, yet nun-artists continued to exist. Religious communities welcomed and used their talents. The artistic production of post-Tridentine nuns must be understood in the context of the spiritual ambience in which it was created.

A dowry was required of all nuns in order to provide for their maintenance in the convent. It was intended to provide adequate material support so that the nuns could devote themselves to spiritual perfection and to the particular work of their institution. Edicts of Church authorities and constitutions of religious communities closely regulated the daily and spiritual life of the cloistered nuns. While individual convents varied, in a generic sense a nun's day was occupied by the recitation of the divine office together in the choir, attendance at Mass, adoration of the Eucharist, prayer, consumption of devotional literature for spiritual inspiration – either read silently or aloud by an appointed nun during their common meals – communal work for the benefit of the convent, and periods of "religious recreation". Silence was maintained throughout much of the day. Choir nuns, for whom literacy was required, recited the divine office, while lay nuns served in a more manual capacity. Convents were regarded as centres of sanctity of spiritual benefit for their cities. Nuns performed a vital function in the Church through their prayers for the salvation of souls and the conversion of heretics and infidels.

Absolute separation from the world was regarded by the Church as necessary if nuns were to pursue spiritual perfection. They were permitted to speak with lay people only through the grilles in the parlour and listened to Mass from within the nuns' choir, viewing the Eucharist through a grille, their only communication with the public space of the church attached to their convent. Communion was received through a small communion window generally located in the tribune wall. St Charles Borromeo in his *Instructiones fabricae* (Milan, 1577) prescribed norms for convents of cloistered nuns. Rules regarding cloister and the isolation of the nuns from the outside world were amplified and reiterated frequently throughout the next two centuries. Contact with the people and affairs of the secular world was viewed by Church authorities as obstructing the nuns' attainment of spiritual perfection.

While obsessive concerns about enclosure reflect the paternalistic and anti-feminine attitudes of the time, the conditions of the cloister were not solely male-imposed. Participating in the renewal of religious spirit of the Counter-Reformation, women played an active role in the Church. Ecclesiastical patronage had traditionally been a sphere of public activity that embraced women. Numerous women in the 16th and 17th centuries founded or supported both male and female religious institutions. Women founders favoured reformed orders and their endeavours helped propagate the tenets of the Counter-Reformation. Asceticism and mysticism were religious currents in many post-Tridentine convents. Such mystical saints as Teresa of Ávila and Maria Maddalena de' Pazzi were inspirations for other nuns.

In addition to their contemplative life, many convents in this era performed an active mission in providing education for young women from the noble and middle classes to prepare them for the convent or for marriage. Their curriculum provided a basic education in reading, writing, some arithmetic, domestic arts and Christian doctrine. Fees from students helped to supplement convents' income while equipping women to serve either the Church or their families as good Christians.

Although the Counter-Reformation Church tried to guard against the forced vocations that had often been practised by families who could not afford marriage dowries for their daughters, this still sometimes occurred or was more subtly effected by the practice of placing young girls for education in the convent where they became disposed to the religious life from an early age. On the other hand, many women desired a religious life. There are numerous accounts of spiritually inclined women who were forced by their families into marriages of dynastic advantage against their wishes. The fact that such an exceptionally ascetic order as the Turchine founded by Maria Vittoria Fornari Strata in Genoa in 1604 rapidly expanded and attracted women from prestigious noble families in spite of the arduous life it offered, and the fact that its dowry was higher than most convents, attests to the attraction that the cloister and devotional life held for women.

Post-Tridentine convents exhibit a complexity of character. They could be centres of devotion populated with women of great spirituality. Yet the convent also represented a microcosm of the secular society that the nuns had left outside the cloister wall. Rules were not always followed to perfection. More contact with the world was maintained than Church officials and even some of the nuns desired. Frequent abuses were nuns spending too much time chatting with visitors in the parlour and visits by noblewomen, some of whom took up residence in convents. The complex, even contradictory character of post-Tridentine convents is reflected in the relation of nuns to the art produced by and for them.

A significant problem affecting nun artists was a lack of access to training and exposure to current artistic trends. Instructors from outside the cloister were not permitted. Many nuns who were artists had received some training before entering the convent. Typical of the pattern of female access to artistic instruction in this era, they came from either artistic families or the upper classes. Such was the case of Lucrina Fetti (q.v.), a nun in the Franciscan convent of Sant'Orsola in Mantua. Sister of the painter Domenico Fetti, she studied with him, and her art was heavily influenced by his style. When he was called to Mantua by his patron, Ferdinando IV Gonzaga, his family accompanied him. Impressed by Lucrina's virtue and

Gaspar de Crayer: *St Lutgard Embraced by the Crucified Christ,* 1653; Convent of the Zwartzusters, Antwerp

talent as an artist, the duke provided her with a dowry when she was professed in the convent of Sant'Orsola, founded by his aunt Margherita in 1599. Fetti painted several works for her convent including a full-length *St Mary Magdalene* (now San Martino, Mantua) that was part of an iconographic programme celebrating female saints who dedicated themselves to the service of Christ. She also executed a series of portraits of noble Gonzaga women (Palazzo Ducale, Mantua) who were patrons of the convent, demonstrating a skill in handling decorative details of costume typical of late 16th- and early 17th-century portraiture.

The Neapolitan nun Luisa Capomazza (d. 1646) was well educated and had the opportunity to study paintings in her own home and receive drawing and painting lessons from respected artists, who perhaps included a renowned female painter of the time, Mariangiola Criscuolo. Capomazza dedicated herself to painting and became a nun in order to avoid marriage. Religious life apparently afforded her the opportunity to concentrate on her art and she produced many sacred images that served to inspire the devotions of her fellow nuns and other devout persons who placed them in their homes. In addition, she produced several public altarpieces, including ones for the churches of Gesù e Maria and Santa Chiara in Naples. Although her biographer, Bernardo De Dominici, criticised her lack of perfection in drawing, he noted that she continuously improved as an artist and always had clients.

In France, four sisters of the artist Laurent de La Hyre, nuns at Sainte-Perrine de la Villette, were noted for their talent in drawing and painting. Sister Sainte-Madeleine, daughter and student of Quentin Varin, designed paintings (1647) for her church of the Ursulines in Amiens. Before entering the convent of the Visitation in Chaillot, the Palatine princess Louise had received lessons from the Caravaggesque painter Gerrit van Honthorst, while Anne-Marie-Renée Strésor (1651–1713), daughter of the portraitist Henri Strésor, had established a reputation as a painter before entering the convent of Chaillot. Within the convent, artistically talented nuns sometimes instructed their fellow nuns.

Nuns were to read devotional literature as a source of spiritual inspiration. Visual images in convents also contributed to this end. Communal spaces of the convent such as the nuns' choir, refectory, staircases and corridors were decorated with paintings and sculpture. Nuns kept devotional images in their cells, even though these were not to be regarded as personal property. Some of these images were prints while others were paintings, such as the crucifixes painted on canvas by Sister Bernardina Ruschi for her Dominican convent of San Giorgio in Lucca. The Discalced Carmelite nun Maria Eufrasia della Croce (q.v.), who painted a *Nativity of Christ* (untraced) for her church of San Giuseppe a Capo le Case in Rome, also embellished the interior spaces of the adjoining convent with mural paintings (oil on plaster), the iconography of which was keyed to their location and reflected the mysticism of the reformed Carmelite saints Teresa of Ávila and Maria Maddalena de' Pazzi. Such images provided models for the nuns, confirmed the validity of their vocation and encouraged their devotions. The effective power of images is illustrated in Gaspar de Crayer's *St Lutgard Embraced by the Crucified Christ* (1653; see illustration), painted for an altarpiece in the Cistercian abbey of Nazareth in Lier, in which an image of

Christ adored by the saintly nun literally comes to life. In Spain two other Discalced Carmelite nuns, Cecilia Sobrino (1570–1646) and her sister María Sobrino, produced devotional paintings of the *Ecce Homo*, *Salvador Mundi* and *Christ as Man of Sorrows* at their convent of La Concepción, Valladolid. These are the only extant works by Spanish painter nuns although several other nuns are recorded. The Sobrino nuns found some of their artistic sources in prints. The conditions under which they painted illustrate some of the difficulties faced by artist nuns. Their order embraced a strict monastic poverty that seemed to extend even to the materials available to them since the supports of the paintings are composed of mismatched pieces of fabric, and the pigment is of poor quality. Given their busy devotional commitments and the convent's work of embroidering vestments, the Sobrino sisters had little time to devote to their painting, but their skills were admired by their contemporaries.

Although their artistic talent tended to be regarded as a novelty, artist nuns did gain recognition. In the early 18th century a German nun, Catherine von Kreitmair from the Bridgettine convent in Altomünster, was famed for her miniatures not only in Germany but also in Rome, where each year one of her productions was sent to an appreciative Pope Clement XI. Her abbess Candida Schmid was also reportedly a clever artist. The skills of talented nuns were appreciated by their convents. In France some superiors sought to attract artistically talented women to their convents in order both to avoid admitting lay artists and artisans into the convent and paying for works. Among the numerous Italian Dominican nuns who were artists was Sister Chiara Alberti (d. 1664), who was chosen by Francesca Baglioni Orsini, founder of the Roman convent of Santa Maria dell'Umiltà, because of her ability as a painter. She provided the convent with many copies in oil of other paintings and since she was skilled in perspective she created scenery for the Christmas crèche and convent plays, diversions that were extremely popular among nuns.

Although convents were not the major centres of embroidery that they had been in the Middle Ages, nuns continued to be involved in this art form. Needlework formed part of a young woman's education in domestic arts, which were taught in the convent, and presumably was included in the manual labour that was part of a nun's daily routine. Chiara Alberti was involved in the manufacture of an embroidered antependium decorated with birds and flowers for the Dominican fathers at Santa Maria sopra Minerva in Rome as well as other embroideries for her own convent. Another nun at Santa Maria dell'Umiltà, Maria Gabriella Bianchini (d. 1679), was noted for her skill in design and embroidery. Nuns at La Concepción in Valladolid executed a magnificent set of vestments with biblical scenes designed by Philip II's artists at El Escorial. The Bridgettines at Altomünster and nuns in the southern Netherlands are noted as producing embroidery and lace. Nuns in several French convents also excelled in these art forms. Their production supplied not only their own convents but was also sometimes sold and served as an important source of revenue. Yet by the 17th century nuns were also the patrons of textile decorations for their churches, commissioning works from male artisans, as did nuns at San Bernardino ai Monti, Rome (1677–84). Many convents were richly endowed with various types of liturgical furnishings that were often either produced or commissioned by the nuns.

An extension of textile arts were reliquary assemblages combining figures of wax or reconstructed bones of saints dressed in rich fabrics that nuns in some convents were adept at constructing. The art of artificial flower-making was popular in French cloisters such as those of the Ursulines of Quimperlé and the Visitandines of Carpentras. Nuns also decorated cloister grottoes and hermitages used for private devotions, sometimes encrusting the surfaces with shells and mosaics of fragments of glass and pottery.

Nuns' involvement with art extended beyond that of producers to that of patrons, participating in a long tradition of female ecclesiastical patronage. In the 17th and 18th centuries nuns played a significant role in this capacity. Some of the most outstanding ecclesiastical decorations of baroque Rome, for instance, were commissioned by female convents, which managed to attract leading artists to embellish their churches and convents. Domenico Maria Canuti and Enrico Haffner's *quadratura* vault at Santi Domenico e Sisto (1674–5), a *tour de force* of illusionistic ceiling painting, is an example of their patronage. In Rome and other parts of Europe as well, most artists commissioned were male, although as previously discussed some artist nuns provided decorations. While female convents were under the supervision of a cardinal protector and a board of male deputies who oversaw their business affairs, the nuns and their abbesses still possessed considerable authority to initiate and carry out decorative projects. Sometimes these were financed from the general patrimony of a convent derived from property, dowries and investments in government bond issues and long-term loans. Such revenues did not provide surplus money, however, and convents' potential to commission works of art was augmented by the contributions of individual nuns. Many nuns came from noble families who provided them with allowances to be used for their religious needs. These allowances empowered the nuns to become patrons of decorations in their churches and convents. The vow of poverty was maintained because technically a nun's allowance was supervised by her abbess and was considered the convent's property. Yet documents confirm that nuns were willing to employ their allowances for church projects.

The reconstruction and decorations that transformed Santa Marta al Collegio Romano in Rome from a crumbling ruin to an exquisite gem was due almost entirely to the generosity of individual nuns. Sister Maria Scolastica Colleoni, who possessed a private income inherited from her brother, paid for a new vault decorated with gilded stuccoes and frescoes designed by Giovanni Battista Gaulli (1671). Ultimately the project included six new lateral chapels and their decoration. Among the other nuns who contributed to the decorations was the abbess Maria Eleonora Boncompagni, who spent a considerable sum on sculpture and paintings for the tribune. The theme of Guglielmo Cortese's high altarpiece, *Christ in the House of Mary and Martha* (1673), alluded both to the contemplative life of the Augustinian nuns and to their active mission in providing education.

A pattern of individual nuns' functioning as patrons is evident throughout 17th- and 18th-century Rome. The Benedictine church of Sant'Ambrogio della Massima was also rebuilt and decorated in the 17th century through the patronage of its noblewomen nuns. Beatrice Torres, assisted by her brother Cardinal Ludovico Torres, initiated the reconstruction of the church in 1606 on the designs of Carlo Maderno. During a later phase of the project she acted as building supervisor. She was not the only nun to be actively involved in the architecture of her convent. Another Benedictine, Angela Targona, abbess of Santa Cecilia in Trastevere, frustrated by the poor design of an addition to the convent in 1637, redesigned the project herself. Several French nuns are also recorded as architects. Working either independently or assisted by a lay or ecclesiastic male expert, they designed their convents and supervised construction. Such involvement helped to ensure that the spaces of the cloister were truly appropriate for the nuns.

Nuns frequently directed their patronage to the decoration of chapels that manifested their devotion to saints special to their order and church and sometimes honoured their families as well. The nuns at Sant'Ambrogio della Massima placed their family coats of arms in prominent positions in their chapels, as did the noblewomen nuns who decorated chapels between 1632 and 1652 at Santi Domenico e Sisto. Not only did family money and status empower nuns as patrons, but their noble families sometimes provided access to leading artists.

Even when convent economic conditions were strained, nuns employed their allowances for the embellishment of their churches. Around the time that the Franciscan nuns of San Bernardino ai Monti were petitioning for relief for their impoverished convent, Sister Maria Chiara Caroli undertook the decoration of the tribune (1663) with money inherited from her brother. The embellishment of their churches and convents with art works and liturgical objects was clearly a priority. Within the private spaces of the cloister, art works potently expressed and inspired spiritual devotion. In the public space of the church, which the nuns did not enter, the embellishments they commissioned gave these cloistered women a public voice. Thematically their decorations celebrated the saints special to their order and their particular church. The Virgin, female saints, virtues and depictions of nuns were often emphasised. Although some reformed orders espoused a severity of decoration, for many convents in the baroque age the lavish display of beauty was a sincere expression of religious devotion and brought honour to the church and convent.

Since much art created by nuns is no longer extant or was produced anonymously, it is difficult to assess their work critically. But evidence in contemporary lives of artists and convent documents attests to the activity of nuns as producers and patrons of art in the post-Tridentine era. This art was an expression of their spirituality and played a crucial role in their devotional lives.

MARILYN DUNN

Bibliography

Carlo Borromeo, *Instructiones fabricae et supellectiles ecclesiaticae*, Milan, 1577

Antonio Seneca, "Prattica del governo spirituale e temporale de monasterii delle monache secondo regole e constitutioni de Santi Padri loro fondatori e del Sacro Concilio di Trento e di Somma Pontifici", manuscript, 1604, Archivio Segreto Vaticano, Archivum Arcis, n.6492

Bernardo De Dominici, *Vite dei pittori, scultori ed architetti napole-tani*, iii–iv, Naples, 1742–5

Vincenzo Marchese, *Memorie dei più insigni pittori, scultori ed architetti domenicani*, 2 vols, Florence: Parenti, 1845–6

Lina Eckenstein, *Woman under Monasticism: Chapters on Saint-Lore and Convent Life Between AD 500 and AD 1500*, Cambridge: Cambridge University Press, 1896; reprinted New York: Russell and Russell, 1963

A. Hauber, "Deutsche Handschriften in Frauenklöstern des späteren Mittelalters", *Zentralblatt für Bibliothekswesen*, xxxi, 1914, pp.341–73

Christian von Heusinger, "Spätmittelalterliche Buchmalerei im ober-rheinischen Frauenklöstern", *Zeitschrift für die Geschichte des Oberrheins*, new series, lxviii (=cvii), 1959, pp.136–60

Raymond Creytens, "La riforma dei monasteri femminili dopo i decreti tridentini", *Il Concilio di Trento e la riforma tridentina*, i, Rome, 1965, pp.45–84

Carla Russo, *I monasteri femminili di clausura a Napoli nel secolo XVII*, Naples: Università di Napoli, Istituto di Storia Medioevale e Moderna, 1970

Dorothy Miner, *Anastaise and Her Sisters: Women Artists of the Middle Ages*, Baltimore: Walters Art Gallery, 1974

Annemarie Weyl Carr, "Women as artists in the Middle Ages", *Feminist Art Journal*, v, 1976, pp.5–9, 26

Women Artists, 1550–1950, exh. cat., Los Angeles County Museum of Art, and elsewhere, 1976

Raymond Creytens, *Cultural and Intellectual Heritage of the Italian Dominican Nuns*, Summit, NJ: Dominican Nuns Monastery of Our Lady of the Rosary, 1977

Luigi Fiorani, "Monache e monasteri romani nell'età del quietismo", *Ricerche per la storia religiosa di Roma*, i, 1977, pp. 63–111

Germaine Greer, *The Obstacle Race: The Fortunes of Women Painters and Their Work*, London: Secker and Warburg, and New York: Farrar Straus, 1979

Ernest Persoons, "Lebensverhältnisse in den Frauenklöstern der windesheimer Kongregation in Belgien und in den Nierderlanden", *Klösterliche Sachkultur des Spätmittelalters*, ed. H. Appelt, Vienna, 1980, pp.73–111

Creighton Gilbert, "Tuscan observants and painters in Venice ca.1400", *Interpretazioni veneziane: Studi di storia dell'arte in onore di Michelangelo Muraro*, ed. David Rosand, Venice: Arsenale, 1984, pp.109–20

Mindy N. Taggard, "Cecilia and María Sobrino: Spain's golden-age painter-nuns", *Woman's Art Journal*, vi/2, 1985–6, pp.15–19

Victoria Joan Moessner, "The medieval embroideries of Convent Wienhausen", *Studies in Cistercian Art and Architecture*, ed. Meredith P. Lillich, Cistercian Studies Series, 89, Kalamazoo, MI: Cistercian Publications, 1987, pp.161–77

Geneviève Reynes, *Couvents de femmes: La Vie des religieuses clôitrées dans la France des XVIIe et XVIIIe siècles*, Paris: Fayard, 1987

Ann Roberts, "North meets south in the convent: The altarpiece of Saint Catherine of Alexandria in Pisa", *Zeitschrift für Kunstgeschichte*, l, 1987, pp.187–206

Marilyn Dunn, "Nuns as art patrons: The decoration of S. Marta al Collegio Romano", *Art Bulletin*, lxx, 1988, pp.451–77

Thérèse B. McGuire SSJ, "Monastic artists and educators of the Middle Ages", *Woman's Art Journal*, ix/2, 1988–9, pp.3–9

Philippe Bonnet, "La pratique des arts dans les couvents de femmes au XVIIe siècle", *Bibliothèque de l'Ecole des Chartres*, cxlvii, 1989, pp.433–72

Myriam Zerbi Fanna, "Lucrina Fetti pittrice", *Civiltà Mantovana*, new series, no.23–4, 1989, pp.35–53

Gabriella Zarri, "Recinti sacri: Sito e forma dei monasteri femminili a Bologna tra '500 e '600", *Luoghi sacri e spazi della santità*, ed. Sofia Boesch Gajano and Lucetta Scaraffia, Turin: Rosenberg & Sellier, 1990, pp.381–96

Kay Staniland, *Embroiderers*, London: British Museum Press, and Toronto: Toronto University Press, 1991

Jeffrey F. Hamburger, "Art, enclosure and the 'Cura Monialium': Prolegomena in the guise of a postscript", *Gesta*, xxxi, 1992, pp.108–34

Carolyn Valone, "Roman matrons as patrons: Various views of the cloister wall", *The Crannied Wall: Women, Religion and the Arts in Early Modern Europe*, ed. Craig A. Monson, Ann Arbor: University of Michigan Press, 1992, pp.49–72

Marilyn Dunn, "Piety and patronage in seicento Rome: Two noble-women and their convents", *Art Bulletin*, lxxvi, 1994, pp.644–63

Le Jardin clos de l'âme: L'Imaginaire des religieuses dans les Pays-Bas du Sud, depuis le 13e siècle, exh. cat., Palais des Beaux-Arts, Brussels, 1994

Ann Roberts, "Chiara Gambacorta of Pisa as patroness of the arts", *Creative Women in Medieval and Early Modern Italy*, ed. E. Ann Matter and John Coakley, Philadelphia: University of Pennsylvania Press, 1994, pp.120–54

Carolyn Valone, "Women on the Quirinal Hill: Patronage in early modern Rome", *Art Bulletin*, lxxvi, 1994, pp.129–46

Jeryldene M. Wood, "Breaking the silence: The Poor Clares and the visual arts in fifteenth-century Italy", *Renaissance Quarterly*, xlviii, 1995, pp.262–86

——, *Women, Art and Spirituality: The Poor Clares of Early Modern Italy*, Cambridge: Cambridge University Press, 1996

Franca Trinchieri Camiz, "'Virgo-non sterilis': Nuns as artists in 17th-century Rome", *Picturing Women in Renaissance and Baroque Italy*, ed. Sara Matthews Grieco and Geraldine Johnson (in preparation)

Jeffrey Hamburger, *Nuns as Artists: The Visual Culture of a German Convent at the End of the Middle Ages* (in preparation)

Guilds and the Open Market
The Example of the Netherlands

15th and 16th centuries

In the 15th and 16th centuries art production in the Netherlands primarily came not from monastic or court centres, but from lay artists working within guild structures. Artists' guilds – which in the Low Countries arose mainly in the 14th century – were a form of craft guild, that is, a city-based labour organisation grouped according to a particular trade (or trades). The purpose of the guilds was to protect their members by controlling production and sales within their métiers; hence guild regulations typically limited membership to citizens of the town, charged entrance fees, regulated the quality of the product, established procedures regarding apprenticeships and forbade non-members from selling their wares. In the Netherlands, guild regulations did not prohibit membership for women, and indeed records of the artists' guilds in particular show that women did join them. One study estimates that the percentage of women in the painters' guild of Bruges was about 12 per cent in 1454 and about 25 per cent in the 1480s (Miner 1974, p.24), figures that presumably resulted from the heavy participation of women within manuscript illumination, an important art industry in Bruges. The presence of women within the St Luke's guild of Antwerp (which included painters, sculptors and illuminators as well as other sorts of artisans) is confirmed by a guild document of 1537 in which one article is addressed to "whatever man or woman" is in the guild (van der Straelen 1855, p.43). Nevertheless the number of women included in the *Liggeren*, that is, the registers of the Antwerp St Luke's guild, is very low: only one woman is listed as a free master in the period 1453–1500, Magriete van Mere, identified as a *verlichtersse*, a female manuscript illuminator, and only about three others appear in the listings for 1500–50, a time when Antwerp art production was at its peak (Rombouts and van Lerius 1864–76, i, pp.20, 71, 77 and 85).

Most of the women who entered the guilds came from families involved in art production. One of the best-known examples is that of Agnes van den Bossche, the daughter and sister of painters active in Ghent, who became a free master in the Ghent painters' guild in 1468 (Wolfthal 1985) and received a number of commissions from the city of Ghent for painted flags. Another example is Kateline van Ruysbroeck, also called Katherine van den Berge, who is recorded as entering the Brussels stone-carvers' guild (which contained sculptors, architects and masons) in 1490, the only woman documented within this guild during the 14th and 15th centuries (Duverger 1933, p.72): her father as well as numerous other male relatives also appear to have been members of the stone-carvers' guild. Within the *Liggeren* of the Antwerp St Luke's guild of 1509, the name of the free master Lysbeth Laureys is entered, identified not by her craft specialisation as was common, but as the "daughter of Jan" (Rombouts and van Lerius 1864–76, i, p.71). The most common way in which women became members of the guilds, however, was as widows of guild members: until they remarried, widows inherited the guild rights of their late husbands, and were allowed to run their shops and even take on apprentices. During his visit to Antwerp in 1526, Albrecht Dürer reported witnessing a guild procession that included a large troop of widows (Hutchison 1990, 137–8). Most of the women listed in the Antwerp *Liggeren* between 1550 and 1600 are identified as widows, including some listed in association with apprentices, such as the widow Lansman, a printer (Rombouts and van Lerius 1864–76, i, p.199); records of guild payments for 1585–6 even contain a special section for the numerous widows in the guild (*ibid.*, pp.307–8). In some cities, women who were separated from guild-member spouses – not just widows – had the same rights as their estranged husbands, as is evident from the case of Digne Zierix: although legally separated from a painter in the Antwerp St Luke's guild, Zierix nevertheless had her rights to hire assistants and run a painting workshop upheld in a legal proceeding of 1488 (van der Stock 1993, pp.47–8). Whether she or any of the widows who were members of the guild were active as artists as well as entrepreneurs is not fully clear, nor is it known how large a percentage of widows or estranged wives actually availed themselves of their guild rights (Ann Sutherland Harris in Los Angeles 1976, p.14, argues that the cases of such women participating in and/or running the workshop in the absence of their spouse were rare). The fact that Zierix was never listed as a guild member in the *Liggeren* – though she stated explicitly in court that she had paid her guild dues every year and indeed her guild rights were held to be valid upon continued payment of her dues – indicates that not all women members of the guild were listed in the *Liggeren*. Thus the extent of women's involvement in the Antwerp St Luke's guild may be significantly under-reported.

It should be noted, however, that women's participation in art production did not necessarily require guild membership. Women could have worked, for example, as assistants (called *cnapen*, *knechten* or *compagnons*) who did not have to register in the guilds. But more probably, women worked as artists in informal ways, helping out within the family business. Such activities are difficult to verify due to a lack of documentation: indeed the existence of Margaret van Eyck, who was once said to have painted alongside her famous brothers Jan and Hubert, has been called into question (Wolfthal 1985, p.8). Nevertheless, there is evidence within Germany of a mother assisting her son within the printing trade, and of daughters working at their father's Nuremberg press (Landau and Parshall 1994, pp.12 and 375, note 37). Such situations must have existed in the Netherlands as well: in particular, Susanna Horenbout (1503–45) of Ghent may have illuminated some pages within books produced by her father, the well-known miniaturist Gerard Horenbout (Malibu 1983, p.121). Susanna did not, however, work solely in the shadow of her father, for when she was 18 years old Dürer actually purchased one of her miniatures during his stay in Antwerp (Hutchison 1990, p.167). She later attained renown as a portrait miniaturist in England after she (with her family, most probably) left the Low Countries to reside there (Malibu 1983, p.118). While in England, she was active at the court of Henry VIII, and married a royal official, John Parker (Hutchison 1990, p.167; Campbell and Foister 1986, pp.725–7).

Women played their most active role within the art industry, however, not as guild masters producing art, but as sellers of art works. There is considerable evidence to indicate that Netherlandish artists often had their wives and daughters managing the sale of their works. Payment records that include separate allocations for the wives of the artists may form one source of evidence: for example, in 1511 the abbey of Averbode paid Laureys Keldermans for a *Passion* altarpiece, and also designated additional small sums, both for Keldermans's assistant and for his wife (Lefèvre 1935, p.51). The practice of giving payments to artists' wives was not uncommon either in the Netherlands or Germany, and there is even one record of a payment, in 1459, to the wife of Rogier van der Weyden for an altarpiece in Cambrai (Huth 1967, p.92, note 51). Such payments may simply represent a form of courtesy to the artist, but quite possibly they indicate that these women actually assisted in the negotiations for the sale of the art works in question. And although the exact significance of such payments is still uncertain, other documents clearly show that the wives of Netherlandish artists – like the wife of Dürer who went to the Frankfurt fairs to sell her husband's prints (Hutchison 1990, p.83) – took their husbands' art to the fairs of Brabant, the major market outlet for art in the Low Countries during the 15th and 16th centuries. For example, in 1436 in Antwerp, four men legally registered their debt to Katlijne van der Stoct, wife of the Brussels painter Jan van der Stoct, for an altarpiece that they had bought for the church of Rumst, near Antwerp (Asaert 1972, p.47, document 4);

Katlijne must have effected this sale by taking her husband's work to the Antwerp fairs, since Brussels' art products could only be legally sold in Antwerp at the open markets held during fair times. Female relatives of another Brussels artist, the polychromer Jan van der Perssen, are documented as selling his works both at the Antwerp fairs and those of the nearby town of Bergen-op-Zoom. One document records the purchase of an altarpiece by a priest in Bergen-op-Zoom from "joncffrouwe Wendelmoeden van der Peersschen" of Brussels (Slootmans 1963, p.32, note 86); this Wendelmoet van der Perssen probably was the daughter of the artist, not his wife, since the term "joncffrouwe" indicates an unmarried young woman. A second document, this time an Antwerp document of 1479, records a purchase of an altarpiece by Jacop Nemery of Maasdam (in present-day Holland) from a woman identified as Wendelmoet van der Borch, widow of the late Jan van der Perssen of Brussels (Asaert 1972, p.58, document 27); in this case, the widow appears to have been liquidating the left-over stock of her late husband at the Antwerp market.

Indeed widows were particularly active in the selling of art at markets. The *pand*-markets of the Netherlands, where artists rented stalls for selling their wares, frequently included widows among the lists of renters. In the early 16th century widows constituted between about 14 and 18 per cent of the total of those renting stalls in the Bruges *pand* to sell paintings, for there were 3 painters' widows and 14 painters renting during the period 1512–19, and 2 widows and 12 painters from 1520 to 1526 (Wilson 1983, pp.477–8). The Antwerp *pand*-records show that between 1543 and 1560 five widows and one daughter rented stalls there in addition to some 48 male artists (Ewing 1990, pp.572–3). In many of these instances, however, widows were concerned only to dispose of the remains of the business, rather than to continue it: this practice is suggested by the testament of Vrancke van der Stockt (before 1424–95), a Brussels painter, who bequeathed his unfinished paintings and design drawings to his sons – presumably to be used to continue the business – but left his finished pictures to his wife, presumably to be sold (Campbell 1976, p.195). Indeed, in Bruges, the records indicate that none of the widows continued renting stalls in the *pand* longer than four years, thereby suggesting that they either left the business relatively quickly (perhaps due to remarriage or death) or found other sales outlets for their wares (Wilson 1983, p.479). Similarly, in Antwerp, four of the five widows renting at the *pand* kept their stalls for only four years or less (Ewing 1990, pp.572–3).

Nevertheless some women – both widows and others – do appear to have been engaged in an active and ongoing manner as art dealers. The widow of the painter Aert Alleyns, for example, continued to rent a stall at the Antwerp *pand* for at least ten years after her husband's death (*ibid.*, p.572). One woman who appears to have been especially active as an art dealer is Lysbette Lambrechts of Antwerp, who, as recorded in an Antwerp document of 1513, purchased two sculpted altarpieces from Jan vander Zijpe, at her house, during the Antwerp fairs, for the price of 22 Flemish pounds; the document further notes that she was planning to sell these altarpieces in England (Doehaerd 1962–3, p.114, no.2903). The circumstances of this purchase indicate that Lambrechts was quite deeply involved in the art trade: the transaction took place in her house, a sign

that she already had a business established there, involved the purchase of two pieces of art, thereby suggesting that she dealt in bulk, and required payment of a sum, which – though not excessive for altarpieces of this sort – nevertheless represented a capital investment worth over four years' salary for the average Antwerp labourer. Moreover, in selling these works in England, Lambrechts was operating within the most sophisticated branch of mercantile capitalism, the export trade. The conditions of sale even included the provision that if the altarpieces were lost or burned in transport, Lambrechts would be responsible to pay only half the purchase price to vander Zijpe, an advantageous arrangement for her, since it partially insured her property at his expense. Such records indicate that women's participation in the open market for art was not always limited to smaller-scale, family-related businesses, but could extend into the arena of larger-scale, international commerce.

LYNN F. JACOBS

17th and 18th centuries

In 1633 the brewer's daughter Judith Leyster (q.v.) was enrolled as a painter in the Haarlem guild of St Luke. A year later it was recorded that she had accordingly paid her contribution of four stuivers. One year later still, in 1635, her name again appears in the guild registers, this time in connection with a conflict with the painter Frans Hals. Willem Woutersz., a student of Leyster's, had run away after only four days to become a pupil of Hals. Leyster felt that she had the right to the apprenticeship fee, which was more than three months overdue, from Willem's mother. Both women had to appear before the guild directors, and reached an agreement with the following stipulations: Willem's mother had to pay four guilders in past-due tuition to Leyster; Leyster was to instruct her servant to see to it that Willem's things were returned home; and Hals was to send the boy home because he was not allowed to take in a pupil of another guild member. Moreover, Leyster had to pay a penalty of 12 stuivers for failure to report an apprentice. She quickly took this opportunity to report that she had two other pupils; apparently she was afraid of incurring still more fines (Ellen Broersen in Worcester 1993, p.20).

From this incident we can deduce that at that time in the Netherlands it was quite normal for female artists to become members of the guild of St Luke, to have their own workplace and to take on apprentices. This impression seems to be strengthened by the fact that there are many women artists from the 17th-century Netherlands known by name. But it is unknown whether these were all self-supporting artists like Leyster. And although the young Leyster may well have achieved a striking level of independence within the circle of Haarlem artists, this self-sufficient status did not last long. In 1636, not long after the conflict, she married the painter Jan Miense Molenaer. Thereafter little more is heard of Leyster the painter, although it does appear from documents that she was involved with Molenaer's activities as an art dealer. The question remains whether the status of Leyster as an autonomous master painter, with her own workplace and apprentices, was so common after all. What opportunities were really open to

Leonard Bramer: "*Paintings for Sale*", drawing; Prentenkabinet der Rijksuniversiteit Leiden women within the regulations of the guild of St Luke? Could they pursue an artist's training and become members of the guild? What precisely was women's share in the production and trade of art in the Dutch golden age, and how was their art sold?

Guilds and their regulations

From the late Middle Ages onwards, every town in the Netherlands had trade guilds. Originally these were religious organisations of craft workers from various professions; members would maintain a common altar under the banner of the guild. Besides this religious purpose, the guilds also provided for the material needs of their members. The guild functioned by way of its statutes as a regulatory body over the relevant trades. With that authority the members were protected against moonlighting and other forms of unprofessional work and market infringement. After the Reformation the guilds in the Northern Netherlands lost their religious function, and survived thereafter as purely secular professional organisations.

Painters belonged to the local guild of St Luke. But guilds almost always contained more than one group of workers, and which trades these were varied from town to town. Moreover, groups could divide up. The Amsterdam guild of St Luke, for example, consisted in 1621 of painters, art dealers, glass-makers, embroiderers and their sales people, bookbinders and booksellers, carvers, tapestry-makers, compass-makers, coffin-makers and "all others who make their living with pen, brush or with paint". Around 1660 the compass-makers and the bookbinders and booksellers separated off to form their own guild (van Eeghen 1969, pp.66–7). In Haarlem the book printers were not included, but the coppersmiths, potters, goldsmiths (split off in 1639) and second-hand dealers (Miedema 1985, p.80; Aikema and others 1975, p.134) were. Yet, however diverse the composition of the guilds of St Luke may have been, as a rule artists were the authoritative group within them. They consistently occupied several administrative posts. It goes without saying that women artists never played such a role. In that regard the Pauline commandment that women in the church should be silent still enjoyed an all-too-universal social validity.

In the ordinances issued by the guilds' board of directors, the rights and privileges of the members were firmly established. Naturally there were also all sorts of local variations with regard to this, but broadly speaking the guilds of St Luke shared the following regulations. Only members of the guild were permitted to practise the trades organised within the guild. Often every possible regulation was instituted against concurrent production and trade from outside the town. So in general the sale of goods that fell under the auspices of the guild by non-guild members was forbidden, and sale by outsiders was permitted only at the annual fairs, held in most towns twice a year. Guild members had to be citizens of the town or married to a burgher's daughter; they had to pay a set entry fee; they had to have spent a certain period of time in training (and sometimes they were also required to submit a masterpiece) before being established as an independent master and being able to open their own shop; they were permitted only a certain number of apprentices and servants; they had to register their apprentices; and they had to provide burial for

their guild brothers and sisters. Apprentices were required to serve the specified period of apprenticeship and to pay to their master the apprentice's fees stipulated. And as for women? It is remarkable that really nothing is laid down in the ordinances about the comings and goings of women as such in the affairs of the guilds. As a group they received no separate rulings of their own. They were of course named as guild sisters who were also to be buried by the guild brothers, but this rule had no bearing on working conditions. The only rule that did explicitly address women in this context was that of the rights of widows. This established mainly that after the death of her husband a widow could continue his business and remain a member of the guild, sometimes on the condition that she took a foreman into her service. Widows retained this right until such time as they remarried someone from another trade. At that point their rights expired. Furthermore, the daughters of masters were usually registered separately as possible candidates for marriage to incoming guild members: the latter would then be able to pay reduced initiation fees. For the rest the ordinances of the guilds of St Luke are silent on the rights and duties of women. It was implicitly clear that men never had women in mind in the training of artists. In the rules regarding training, for example, mention is made only of *leer-jongens* (boy apprentices), and of "sons" of tradesmen who were permitted to apprentice with their "fathers" without charge. Only in connection with the obligations of masters is there mention at one point of the *meestersvrouwen* (masters' wives).

All in all, from the ordinances of the various guilds of St Luke one cannot make out much about the place that was granted to women in the painter's profession. We must conclude that in fact nothing formally stood in the way of a woman becoming an independent master-painter. But in practice it would not have been easy for a woman to establish herself. Raising a child to become a fully trained painter had to be done under the tutelage (and in the home) of at least one master. Usually a student followed up his first period of training with lessons with another teacher. That meant that the parents had to pay tuition for years – often as long as five or six. This was an investment that parents would rarely make at that time for a daughter.

For some guilds of St Luke, parts of the registers of members or of membership records have been preserved. Minutes have also sometimes survived from meetings of the executive committee of the guild in which the names of active painters (such as that of Judith Leyster) appear. These sources confirm that women were guild members, but the number of women painters is exceptionally small. Take, for example, the master books and accounts of the Delft St Luke's guild for the years 1613–1714. Two women (of which one was a widow who "continued") were named among the 352 painters, 1 woman as (fine art) printer, 1 woman among the 16 stonemasons, 3 women among the 31 pottery-painters, 3 women among the 30 chair-painters, 4 women among the 146 glass-vendors and glass-engravers (the women were always indicated in the feminine, as *glasverkoopsters*), 12 women among the 56 "lamplighters, art dealers and book dealers" and 6 of the 12 shopkeepers (Obreen 1877–90, I, xxx; Montias 1982, appendix). In brief, from the documents that are preserved from the Delft guild, we must conclude that women were seldom members of the guild as practising artists, though they were strikingly present in the merchandising of the various crafts brought together by the guild of St Luke. This impression is strengthened by research into the St Luke's guilds of other towns. Overall, what few women guild members there were seem to have been occupied primarily with the sale of goods (namely second-hand dealers and the sale of earthenware). Sometimes widows are named as masters of an atelier, but then as a rule in the context of back-due membership fees or as party to the completion of a student's contract. It is indicative that in apprenticeship contracts women are never named as the lesson-taking party, but rather as the lesson-giving party (de Jager 1990; Miedema 1986). The female master was now responsible, even if she had taken over the atelier from her deceased husband and had taken a foreman into her service for the actual painting work.

Women artists in the Northern Netherlands

The almost total absence of women artists from the guild archives in the Northern Netherlands does not necessarily mean that women did not make art. It does not explain why we can only find women in two social sectors: in the milieu of painters themselves, and in the circle of (upper-class) dilettantes.

That women painters appeared in the milieu of other, male painters is not surprising. A girl with talent from the family of a painter could be trained for nothing by her father or another close relation; guild members were free to teach their sons the trade without having to set up a separate teaching contract for them and without having to register them as apprentices, and it was not written anywhere that it would have to be different for daughters. So a good many daughters, sisters and nieces with connections in painters' families must have been inspired to learn the craft; in any case it cost the family virtually nothing. According to the artists' biographer Arnold Houbraken, the father of Adriana van Spilberg (1650–?), who was himself a painter, was so impressed by the talent of his daughter that he wanted her to marry someone inside the profession, so that she could continue painting (Houbraken 1753, iii, p.45). Indeed, there must also have been strong opposition to the artistic development of daughters. This can be deduced from Houbraken's observation that Maria Sybilla Merian (q.v.), whose father and stepfather were both artists, regularly infuriated her mother because as a girl she would rather occupy herself with the brush than with domestic pursuits (ibid., p.220).

Because these women all found themselves in a painter's milieu anyway, very few of them would have taken the trouble to set themselves up independently. Why should a young woman start an atelier if her father, brother or uncle already had one? This explains why we seldom come across these women painters (or printmakers) in the guild archives: most were simply hidden within the membership of a family member. Only the very best of them would have been able to make a name for herself, or would therefore have signed her work. One example for whom signed work survives is Maria de Grebber (c.1602–80). She was the eldest daughter of the Haarlem painter Frans Pietersz. de Grebber; two of her brothers were also painters. She herself married a potter from Enkhuizen, and it is not known whether she was still connected

to the painters' milieu. We do know that she was still painting immediately after her wedding. The two surviving portraits painted by her (one in Rijksmuseum Het Catharijne convent, Utrecht, the other untraced) date in fact from about a year after her marriage. When her husband died five years later, she was taken into the home and care of two single women and a widower. Although for a long time nothing is heard about her connections with the painter's art world, in 1649 her only daughter Isabella married none other than the Leiden-Amsterdam painter Gabriel Metsu (Irene van Thiel-Stroman in Worcester 1993, pp.228–9). She still therefore had contacts with other artists. This example must suffice, but it is striking that for the Northern Netherlands in the 17th and 18th centuries many more women from artistic families are known for whom some work survives (Geertruydt Roghman, q.v. Magdalena van de Passe, q.v., Margaretha de Heer, q.v., Adriana van Spilberg, Suzanna van Steenwijk-Gaspoel, Gesina ter Borch, q.v., Henriette Wolters-Van Pee, Alida Withoos, Sara Troost, Cornelia de Rijck, Cornelia Cuyck, Maria van der Laeck, Maria Margaretha La Fargue, q.v.).

There are also a number of artists from painters' families whose existence is known only from the fact that they are named in various artists' dictionaries under the entries of their fathers, brothers or spouses. For example, the three brothers Glauber had a painting sister, Diana, of whom it was said that she "made fine pictures and portraits with the brush", but no work of hers survives. Houbraken did know enough to add that she later went blind. So long as no work from these female artists is known, they are of little art-historical importance. It might be interesting to investigate to what extent it was just such active daughters and sisters who formed the link between the various artists' families of the Northern Netherlands. Because one thing is certain: artists' families were frequently related to each other through marriage. The craft may then in theory and in practice have passed primarily from father to son, yet for the "networking" by way of marriages within one's own milieu women were genuinely indispensable. It could well have been that daughters with talent had an advantage in that respect over their sisters without talent.

Quite a few names of artists also survive from the circle of dilettantes. This can be explained by the fact that the humanistic educational ideals of the time in the Northern Netherlands favoured a broad education in order that children might develop their talents, and this principle applied also to girls. It was therefore quite common for girls from good circles to learn not only reading, writing, arithmetic, music and poetry, but also drawing, painting in oils, watercolour, glass engraving, embroidery, etc. Interestingly, these burghers' daughters also came in contact with professional painters from their town, because they took lessons with them. So we know that Gerard van Honthorst in The Hague gave lessons to children from prominent circles, including girls (Bok and de Meijere 1985, p.300). The father of Rachel Ruysch (q.v.) arranged for her to take lessons with Willem van Aelst, and the Dordrecht amateur painter Margaretha van Godewijck (1627–77) took lessons from, among others, Nicolaas Maes. Anna Maria van Schurman (q.v.) studied in the atelier of Crispijn van de Passe – but what is nice about this last case is that she probably took her lessons from Magdalena van de Passe (van der Stighelen 1992, p.67).

For most of these women artistic work remained no more than a hobby, and – as in the case of van Schurman and van Godewijck – not even the most important one. Literature and poetry were more highly regarded. Godewijck made this clear with her little poem on a small portrait painted by an anonymous woman: "The painter, with the brush / captures but the smallest bit / The noblest of the maid / is where she bears her head" (Schotel 1841, p.62). Some of these girls were so deft in the handling of the brush that they developed into well-known professional artists. A good example is Maria van Oosterwijck (q.v.). She remained a painter her entire life, together with her serving maid Geertje Pieters, who had also dedicated herself to art. Interestingly Houbraken observed that the servant had become so good at painting that after the death of her mistress she lived by it; he does not report this for van Oosterwijck, who is known to have offered her works for sale by way of a middleman for good money. In Houbraken's eyes she was too much of a "dilettante" (and perhaps also too rich). She never married. According to Houbraken, the painter Willem van Aelst was still pressing for her hand in his old age, but she held out by demanding that he must be at his easel every day for an entire year (their ateliers faced each other). This anecdote illustrates how closely amateurs could be related to the world of professional painters. If an amateur was highly respected, a guild could even make her an honorary member, as in the case of Anna Maria van Schurman in Utrecht and Rachel Ruysch in The Hague. But this honour could also be extended to a painter's daughter. In 1777 Cornelia van Cuyck became "master" and honorary member of The Hague painters' confraternity. Then too we must realise that the distinction between the milieux was in some cases all too artificial. For example, the professor's daughter Rachel Ruysch married a painter, the portrait painter Juriaen Pool II. It is said that he felt himself so inferior to his wife that after her death he stopped painting and started a lace business (Gram 1882, p.42). This anecdote, nice as it sounds, cannot be true: he died before his wife.

Many more women artists could be named for the 17th and 18th centuries combined: some 150 altogether. Undoubtedly some further searching in the various dictionaries would yield greater numbers. Yet this number is high compared with the number of female artists in other countries. But is it also high when we consider it in the Netherlandish context? Art historians and historians are presently occupied with the question of how much art was actually produced in the Republic; obviously in this context they are also trying to estimate how many active artists there were. The historian van der Woude has suggested that in the 17th century about 3200 painters must have been active, and in the 18th century some 1900. He concludes moreover that these numbers comprised only men (van der Woude 1991, p.36). Montias comes up with about the same numbers. Based on these figures we must conclude that women played a modest part in the art production of the time. Modest, perhaps, but women artists did at least exist. The question is whether this fact is to be explained by the prominent position of women in the Northern Netherlands that registers so often remark upon and historians still often propose. But the explanation may be simpler: in an art-loving climate in which many men were painting, women too were inspired more than elsewhere.

Women, the art trade and the market

"It is astonishing how little systematic study the subject of this article has received since the early 1900s." With this sober statement Montias (1988, p.244) opened his article on art dealers in the 17th-century Netherlands. If that is true in general, then certainly there is very little to say about the affairs of women in the art trade. Were women involved in the art trade? And how did women artists themselves operate in it?

As mentioned previously, several female art dealers were enlisted among the Delft guild members. Also in the membership lists of other guilds of St Luke, such as those of The Hague, Haarlem and Middelburg, several women art dealers appear. Moreover women are named as "shopkeepers", which could refer to the shop belonging to a painter's atelier (though mostly they dealt with the sale of earthenware – apparently suitable work for women). There must have been widows of painters who kept their shop. How often this happened is hard to say. The biggest question is whether much art was actually sold through painters' shops. It could not have been easy for a painter's widow to carry on the business. The Antwerp merchant's daughter Antoinette Houwaart, for example, gave it up shortly after the death of her husband, the Amsterdam painter Jan (Krabbetje) Asselijn. This successful painter died in 1652, aged about 42, and left Antoinette with four children in a rented house in Amsterdam. Three years later the household inventory was made up on account of non-payment of rent. From this it appears that Antoinette had sub-let the front room to the painter Cornelis van Nerveu. Another room was rented to an embroidery-worker. In Nerveu's room were found 46 paintings (which were by him, as was explicitly stated in the notarial acts), while in the rest of the house only decorations and poor paintings were to be found. The shop inventory was done by hand by the chamber for insolvent estates, for 23 guilders. Meanwhile Antoinette absconded.

A somewhat less unfortunate, but nevertheless remarkable story is that of Lucretia de Beauvois. She was probably 18 years old when she married the painter and art dealer Herman Saftleven in 1626 in Rotterdam. He died one year later, leaving her with three stepchildren (of whom the eldest son was about the same age as she). In the year after her husband's death she travelled with her serving maid to Leiden, Haarlem and Gouda to sell paintings from her inheritance at the markets. She was spared neither expense nor difficulties: with costs only for travel, food and lodgings she was already 57 guilders short. But then she also sold a good many paintings in the short year that she was active. The reason is clear: although as the widow of a guild member she had the right to carry on his business, it was agreed with the stepchildren that the shop and business should be sold. This explains why for only eight months or so Lucretia had sold paintings so fanatically. Nothing else is known about her except for the year of her death: 1638 (Obreen 1877–90, ii, pp.115–27). A younger brother was named as her heir. He was a painter, and apprenticed to no less a person than Cornelis Saftleven, the eldest stepchild of his sister.

As has been stated, probably only a small share of the sale of art took place in the shops of the members of the guild (Montias 1982, p.194). Paintings, prints and other art were sold in the aforementioned yearly markets, too. Documents also make mention of women who walk around selling paintings (Weijerman 1769). Besides the markets, artists could also offer up their work at official public sales. Painters themselves even organised auctions or lotteries of their work. The role of women in these various forms of art trade has not yet been researched, but it was probably not very great. Naturally the spouses of art dealers sometimes also had an understanding of their affairs, but we do not find traces of them in the sources. Judith Leyster, for example, was undoubtedly involved in her husband's art trade, but her involvement is evident only from a few references. The only women who stood out were the junk-dealers, but their share in the art trade would have been limited to the cheap paintings they sold in auctions (Montias 1982, p. 205). It is worth mentioning here that some women also appear as booksellers. In this sector women certainly played their part in the art trade – they sold prints.

The question of how women artists themselves sold their work remains to be considered. In general it is difficult to say anything until some systematic research is done. Presumably women from the milieu of painters tried to sell their work in just the same way as their fathers, brothers, uncles and/or husbands. Perhaps some of these women let their work pass for that of their husband, father or brother because that brought more money, but when a woman had made a name for herself, she would naturally sell her work under her own name. Some women would also have done work on commission. The dilettante Agnes Block, who collected paintings of flowers and vegetables, had Maria Sybilla Merian, Alida Withoos and Maria Moninks all work for her on commission (van de Graft 1943, pp.118–20). The architectural painter Suzanna van Steenwijk-Gaspoel also painted on commission; she got 600 guilders for her painting of the Leiden Lakenhal (1642; *Catalogus van de schilderijen en tekeningen* 1983, pp.321–2). Some women artists made such a name for themselves that they would sell their work in court circles outside the Netherlands, as did Maria van Oosterwijck, Rachel Ruysch, Adriana Spilberg and Henriette Wolters-van Pee among others. Moreover, van Oosterwijck also tried to sell her work on her own initiative: in 1672 she commissioned an art dealer in Amsterdam to sell her work in Germany (Montias 1982, pp.218–19). Because contemporaries found it so exceptional that a woman artist could sell her work for large sums, the prices are frequently recorded as well. Of the Rotterdam papercutting artist Elisabeth Ryberg it was recorded in 1710 that 600 guilders were asked for the smallest piece (Uffenbach 1753, pp.266–7). On the less prominent artists, who for example earned their money making copies after Dutch masters or giving drawing lessons, as did Maria Margaretha La Fargue, sources as a rule offer far less information.

Conclusion

The success stories of women artists of international fame speak to the imagination, and so they did in earlier times. That is the reason they have survived. But in general it holds true that we know almost nothing of the lives and careers of the many women artists who must have been active in the Netherlands in the 17th and 18th centuries. Of course that was also the case – albeit to a lesser extent – for many of their male colleagues. The women painted, drew, did watercolours, paper-cuttings or engravings, because they were inspired to do

so at home. They did so either because they enjoyed it as a pastime (the amateurs) or because they could earn a living from it (the professional artists). For some both motives were concurrent. More biographical research into the lesser-known artists is needed. Some stopped on their marriage, as did some male painters as soon as they married a rich woman. Others – like Judith Leyster – occupied themselves with the art trade and were otherwise hidden by the work of their spouse. There were also women who could not give up painting, as well as others who were not allowed to stop. If more life stories of Dutch women artists (and men too) are collected, perhaps patterns will emerge that will shed light not only on the life of the artist and the art trade in general in the Netherlands in the 17th and 18th centuries, but also of the place of women in that world.

ELS KLOEK

Bibliography

Arnold Houbraken, *De groote schouburgh der Nederlantsche konstschilders en schilderessen* [The great theatre of Dutch male and female painters], 3 vols, 2nd edition, Amsterdam, 1753

Zacharias Conrad von Uffenbach, *Merckwürdige Reisen durch Niedersachsen, Holland und Engelland*, 3 vols, Ulm und Memmigen, 1753

Jacob Campo Weijerman, *De grote schouburg: Levensbeschrijvingen der Nederlandsche Konstschilders en Konstschilderessen* [The great theatre: Biographies of Dutch male and female painters], 1769

G.D.J. Schotel, *Letter- en oudheidkundige avondstonden* [Literary and archaeological evenings], Dordrecht, 1841

Jan Baptist van der Straelen, *Jaerboek der vermaerde en kunstryke gilde van Sint Lucas binnen de stad Antwerpen* [Yearbook of the renowned and art-rich guild of St Luke in the city of Antwerp], Antwerp: Peeters-van Genechten, 1855

Philippe Felix Rombouts and Theodore van Lerius, *De Liggeren en andere historische archieven der Antwerpsche Sint Lucasgilde* [The registers and other historical archives of the Antwerp St Luke's guild], 2 vols., 1864–76; reprinted Amsterdam: Israel, 1961

Fr D.O. Obreen, *Archief Nederlandsche Kunstgeschiedenis* [Archive of Dutch art history], 7 vols, Rotterdam: Hengel en Eeltjes, 1877–90; reprinted Soest: Davaco, 1976

Johan Gram, *De schildersconfrerie Pictura en Hare Academie van Beeldende Kunsten te 's Gravenhage* [The painter's confraternity Pictura and the Academy of Fine Arts in The Hague], Rotterdam: Elsevier, 1882

Jozef Duverger, *De brusselsche steenbickeleren: Beeldhouwers, bouwmeesters, metselaars enz. der XIVe en XVe eeuw* [The stone-chippers of Brussels: Sculptors, architects, bricklayers, etc., of the 14th and 15th centuries], Ghent: Vyncke, 1933

P. Lefèvre, "Textes concernant l'histoire artistique de l'abbaye d'Averbode", *Revue Belge d'Archéologie et d'Histoire de l'Art*, v, 1935, pp.45–58

C. Catharina van de Graft, *Agnes Block: Vondels nichts en vriendin* [Agnes Block: Vondel's niece and friend], Utrecht: Bruna & Zoon, 1943

G.J. Hoogewerff, *De geschiedenis van de Lucasgilden in Nederland* [The history of the guild of St Luke in the Netherlands], Amsterdam: van Kampen, 1947

Renée Doehaerd, *Etudes anversoises: Documents sur le commerce international à Anvers, 1488–1514*, 3 vols, Paris: SEVPEN, 1962–3

Korneel J.F. Slootmans, "Les marchands brabançons et, plus spécialement, les marchands bruxellois aux foires de Berg-op-Zoom, d'après les données des archives de Berg-op-Zoom", *Cahiers Bruxellois*, viii, 1963, pp.13–64

Hans Huth, *Künstler und Werkstatt der Spätgotik*, 2nd edition, Darmstadt: Wissenschaftliche Buchgesellschaft, 1967

Isabella H. van Eeghen, "Het Amsterdamse Sint Lucasgilde in de 17de eeuw" [The Amsterdam guild of St Luke in the 17th century], *Amstelodamum*, lxi, 1969, pp.65–102

Gustaaf Asaert, "Documenten voor de geschiedenis van de beeldhouwkunst te Antwerpen in de XVe eeuw" [Documents for the history of sculpture in Antwerp in the 15th century], *Jaarboek van het Koninklijk Museum voor Schone Kunsten Antwerpen*, 1972, pp.43–86

Dorothy Miner, *Anastaise and Her Sisters: Women Artists of the Middle Ages*, Baltimore: Walters Art Gallery, 1974

Aikema and others, "Schilderen is een Ambacht als een Ander" [Painting is a trade like any other], *Proef*, 1975, pp.124–44

Lorne Campbell, "The art market in the Southern Netherlands in the fifteenth century", *Burlington Magazine*, cxviii, 1976, pp.188–98

Women Artists, 1550–1950, exh. cat., Los Angeles County Museum of Art, and elsewhere, 1976

Hessel Miedema, *De archiefbescheiden van het St Lukasgilde te Haarlem, 1497–1798* [The archival records of the guild of St Luke in Haarlem, 1497–1798], 2 vols, Alphen aan den Rijn: Canaletto, 1980

John Michael Montias, *Artists and Artisans in Delft: A Socio-Economic Study of the Seventeenth Century*, Princeton, NJ: Princeton University Press, 1982

Catalogus van de schilderijen en tekeningen [Catalogue of paintings and drawings], Leiden: Stedelijk Museum De Lakenhal, 1983

Renaissance Painting in Manuscripts: Treasures from the British Library, exh. cat., J. Paul Getty Museum, Malibu, 1983

Jean C. Wilson, "The participation of painters in the Bruges 'pandt' market, 1512–1550", *Burlington Magazine*, cxxv, 1983, pp.476–79

Marten Jan Bok and Jos de Meijere, "Schilderes aan haar ezel: Nieuwe gegevens over het schilderij van Gerard van Honthorst" [Painter at her easel: New facts about the painting of Gerard van Honthorst], *Maandblad Oud-Utrecht*, lviii, 1985, pp.298–303

Hessel Miedema, "De St Lucasgilden van Haarlem en Delft in de zestiende eeuw" [The guilds of St Luke of Haarlem and Delft in the 16th century], *Oud Holland*, xcix, 1985, pp.77–91

Diane Wolfthal, "Agnes van den Bossche: Early Netherlandish painter", *Woman's Art Journal*, vi/1, 1985, pp.8–11

Lorne Campbell and Susan Foister, "Gerard, Lucas and Susanna Horenbout", *Burlington Magazine*, cxxviii, 1986, pp.719–27

Hessel Miedema, "Over vakonderwijs aan kunstschilders in de Nederlanden tot de zeventiende eeuw" [On professional education for painters in the Netherlands in the 17th century], *Leids Kunsthistorisch Jaarboek*, v–vi, 1986–7, pp.268–82

——, "Kunstschilders, gilde en Academie: Over het probleem van de emancipatie van de kunstschilders in de Noordelijke Nederlanden" [Painters, guilds and the Academy: The problem of the emancipation of painters in the Northern Netherlands], *Oud Holland*, ci, 1987, pp.1–33, 141–7

John Michael Montias, "Cost and value in seventeenth-century Dutch art", *Art History*, x, 1987, pp.455–66

——, "Art dealers in the seventeenth-century Netherlands", *Simiolus*, xviii, 1988, pp.244–56

Marten Jan Bok, "'Nulla dies sine linie': De opleiding van schilders in Utrecht in de eerste helft van de zeventiende eeuw" ["Not a day without a line": The training of painters in Utrecht in the first half of the 17th century], *De Zeventiende Eeuw*, vi, 1990, pp.58–68

Dan Ewing, "Marketing art in Antwerp, 1460–1560: Our Lady's pand", *Art Bulletin*, lxxii, 1990, pp.558–84

Jane Campbell Hutchison, *Albrecht Dürer: A Biography*, Princeton: Princeton University Press, 1990

Ronald de Jager, "Meester, leerjongen, leertijd: Een analyse van zeventiende-eeuwse Noord-Nederlandse leerlingcontracten van kunstschilders, goud- en zilversmeden" [Master, apprentice, apprenticeship: An analysis of 17th-century North Netherlandish apprenticeship contracts of painters, gold- and silversmiths], *Oud Holland*, civ, 1990, pp.69–111

John Michael Montias, "Estimates of the number of Dutch master-painters, their earnings and their output in 1650", *Leidschrift*, vi, 1990, pp.59–74

Marten Jan Bok and Gary Schwartz, "Schilderen in opdracht in Holland in de 17e eeuw" [Painting on commission in Holland in the 17th century], *Holland*, xxiii, 1991, pp.183–95

Bram Kempers, "Opdrachtgevers, verzamelaars en kopers: Visies op kunst in Holland tijdens de Republiek" [Patrons, collectors and buyers: Visions of art in Holland during the Republic], *Holland*, xxiii, 1991, pp.196–209

A.M. van der Woude, "De schilderijenproduktie in Holland tijdens de Republiek: Een poging tot kwantificatie" [The production of paintings in Holland during the Republic: An effort at quantification], *Kunst-zaken: Particulier initiatief en overheidsbeleid in de wereld van de beeldende kunst* [The business of art, private enterprise and government policy in the world of the visual arts], Kampen: Kok Agora, 1991, pp.18–50

Katlijne van der Stighelen, "'Et ses artistes mains (…)': De kunstzinnigheid van Anna Maria van Schurman" ["And her artistic hands (…): The artistry of Anna Maria van Schurman], *Anna Maria van Schurman, 1607–1678: Een uitzonderlijk geleerde vrouw* [Anna Maria van Schurman: An exceptionally learned woman], ed. Mirjam de Baar and others, Zutphen: Walburg, 1992, pp.61–74

Judith Leyster: A Dutch Master and Her World, Frans Halsmuseum, Haarlem, and Worcester Art Museum, MA, 1993 (especially Ellen Broersen, "'Judita Leystar': A painter of 'good, keen sense'", pp.15–38; Els Kloek, "The case of Judith Leyster: Exception or paradigm?", pp.55–68; and Irene van Thiel-Stroman, "Maria de Grebber", pp.228–33)

Jan van der Stock, "De organisatie van het beeldsnijders- en schildersatelier te Antwerpen: Documenten, 1480–1530" [The organisation of the carvers' and painters' ateliers in Antwerp: Documents, 1480–1530], *Antwerpse retabels 15de–16de eeuw*, exh. cat., Museum voor Religieuze Kunst Antwerpen, Antwerp, 1993, ii, pp.47–53

David Landau and Peter Parshall, *The Renaissance Print, 1470–1550*, New Haven and London: Yale University Press, 1994

Els Kloek, Catherine Peters Sengers and Esther Tobé, eds, *Vrouwen en het kunstenaarsleven in de Republiek: Een overzicht* [Women and the life of artists in the Dutch Republic: A survey], Utrechtse Historische Cahiers (in preparation)

Court Artists

The position of court artist can be traced back to the mid-13th century when a court culture emerged that was separate from the work of the monasteries and when certain individual artists were given titles, regular salaries and special privileges. Initially appointed as a *varlet de chambre*, *Kammerdiener* or *familiaris*, the artist entered the personal service of his ruler and, as a reward for service and loyalty, was granted favours and expenses by his sovereign. The court artist was not paid on a piecework basis as to cost of materials or hours of labour but was awarded, as a sign of princely *liberalitas*, a pension or salary to cover expenses. Thus, in 1427, Jan van Eyck was retained in the service of Philip the Good of Burgundy not on account of a particular task, but to be available when required and so as to serve to the best of his ability as a diligent and loyal subject (Warnke 1993, p.134).

Further reward for the duty of service was in the form of exemption from artists' guilds and from the obligations and fiscal payments that membership of such civic institutions entailed. The court artist was valued for his personal talent, and recognition of an individual's abilities as an artist could occasionally lead to ennoblement, although this was comparatively rare and, as in the celebrated case of Velázquez, usually not achieved without some difficulty. With the possible exception of Rubens, the court artist never achieved the same high status as that of the international elite with which he came into contact, but he nevertheless achieved fame for his own talents from within an aristocratic circle and crucially contributed to an ethos of grandeur and culture of urbane humanism that could be fostered there.

Women court artists first emerged in Western Europe in the 16th century. To a far greater extent than their male counterparts, they remained within the personal sphere of the house and household of the sovereign and detached from the more public affairs of government and rulership. This essay will consider the position of the woman court artist from the 16th to the 19th centuries and indicate why, at a particular court and at a particular time, a woman artist may have been preferred.

In some cases distinctions between the appointed and salaried court artist and those artists who worked for the court on a commission basis can be misleading. Court standards varied, court protocol was not permanently fixed and frames of reference shifted from court to court. In 18th-century France, for instance, several prominent women artists – Anne Vallayer-Coster (q.v.), Elisabeth Vigée-Lebrun (q.v.), Adélaïde Labille-Guiard (q.v.) – worked very successfully on commission for the French court and had close social ties and contacts with it. Labille-Guiard was even given the title of *Peintre des Mesdames* (the King's aunts) and awarded a pension of 1000 livres, but she did not work and reside at Versailles nor did she belong to a household there. She was awarded the pension in lieu of studio lodgings in the Louvre to which she was entitled but from which she was excluded on account of the large number of female pupils that were attached to her studio (Passez 1973, pp.301–3). There was no provision for the position of female court artist within the official structures of the French court comparable to those that were provided by, say, the organisations of some of the smaller German courts, and the case of Anna Dorothea Lisiewska-Therbusch (q.v.) is instructive in this respect.

After successfully providing decorative works for a hall of mirrors at the court of Duke Karl Eugen von Württemberg in Stuttgart, Therbusch travelled to Mannheim and in 1763 was awarded the title of court painter there by the Elector Palatine Karl Theodor (Berckenhagen 1987). The position of the female court artist was well established in the Palatinate where the promotion of both artists and musicians added prestige to a court that was relatively impotent on the wider international and political scene. After her success at Mannheim, Therbusch attempted to establish herself both in Paris and with the court at Versailles. Although she was accepted as a member of the French Académie Royale in 1767, she never obtained a French royal commission or any official appointment at the French court, in spite of several strenuous and vain attempts to do so (Paris 1984, pp.358–63). In terms of the progress of her career, therefore, the appointment at Mannheim must be seen as providing only a hoped-for but ultimately unfulfilled opportunity for further advancement and official recognition.

Obtaining an appointment

Most women artists in this period emerged out of family workshops and women court artists often came from a family and/or workshop that had established close ties and connections with a court. Susanna Horenbout, her father Gerard and her brother Lucas were all painters in the service of Henry VIII, and Susanna's first marriage, during the 1520s, was to John Parker, Yeoman of Henry's Wardrobe of Robes and Keeper of the Palace of Westminster (Campbell and Foister 1986). Levina Teerlinc (q.v.) was the daughter of a well-known Flemish miniature painter Simon Bening and was married to George Teerlinc who, as a Gentleman Pensioner at the burial of Henry VIII, was also a member of the English royal household (Auerbach 1954, p.51). Similar dynastic networks continue into the 18th century. Both Anna Dorothea Lisiewska-Therbusch and her sister Anna Rosina Lisiewska (q.v.) were trained in the studio of their father, the portraitist George Lisiewski, who had arrived in Berlin from Poland in 1692 as part of the entourage of the court architect, Eosander. In 1741 Anna Rosina married the Prussian court painter and copyist David Matthieu; he was the widower of another Lisiewski sister, and a son from this previous marriage, Georg David Matthieu, and two of Anna Rosina's children, Rosina and Leopold Matthieu, also went on to become painters (Berlin 1987, pp.113–18). Anna Rosina was appointed court painter at Braunschweig in 1777, when her second husband and friend of Lessing, Ludwig de Gasc, was named professor of French language and literature there.

Anne Killigrew was both a painter and a poet although only two portraits by her hand are known: a full-length *Self-Portrait* (Berkeley Castle, Trustees) and a similarly full-length portrait of *James II* (see illustration). She is famous today chiefly because Dryden, who was himself at the time keen to curry favour at court, composed an ode to her shortly after her death in her mid-twenties from smallpox in June 1685. The poem is

Anne Killigrew: *James II*, Royal Collection, © Her Majesty Queen Elizabeth II

a celebration of the *ut pictura poesis* tradition in which painting and poetry were praised as liberal and sister arts and because these activities both ennobled and were ennobling (Hooker and Swedenberg, Jr, eds, 1969, iii, pp.317–18). Killigrew's appointment at court as maid-of-honour in the household of Mary of Modena, wife of James II, can, however, also be linked to the strong loyalties and patronal networks of the family into which she had been born.

When the French princess Henrietta Maria came to England to marry Charles I, she brought with her a large retinue of French servants; many of these French servants were soon dismissed and replaced by English courtiers who were overt supporters of the English monarchy. Sir Robert Killigrew was Queen Henrietta Maria's vice-chamberlain until his death in 1633 and in 1629 Anne's uncle, Sir Thomas Killigrew, was appointed vice-chancellor to this queen's household; he then went on to become groom to the bedchamber of Charles II and master of the revels (Hibbard, "The role of a queen consort", in Asch and Birke 1991, pp.393–414). Anne's father, Dr Henry Killigrew, had been chaplain to Charles I and was rewarded for his royalist loyalty during the Commonwealth and Protectorate by being appointed master of the Savoy Hospital, a prebendary of Westminster and almoner to James, then Duke of York; Anne's brother, Henry, was a naval captain and became an admiral (Hooker and Swedenberg, Jr, eds, 1969, iii, pp.317–18). Given this family background, we can situate Anne's appointment within a context of powerful, dynastic networks of patronage and the promotion of distinct factions, allegiances and favourites at a time of great internal division and turmoil in the country at large.

Often some powerful protector or patron at court, or with close links to court society, was the agency and intermediary whereby a woman artist achieved a position at court. Thus it was on the recommendation of the Duke of Alba and after painting his portrait in 1558 that Sofonisba Anguissola (q.v.) was invited to the court of Philip II of Spain (Perlingieri 1992, p.109). The favour that Louise Seidler (q.v.) enjoyed at Weimar developed out of her friendship and close personal contact with Goethe, while the influential and powerful protection and advice of Ignaz Heinrich, Freiherr von Wesenberg, were important stimuli for Marie Ellenrieder (q.v.) at the outset of her career.

An appointment as court artist usually involved travel to and residence at the court in question. The opportunity to travel should not, however, necessarily be seen as a mark of independence and freedom of action. Indeed, women may sometimes have been chosen to hold positions at court on account of a noted virtue, chastity and obedience; this may well have been the case with Sofonisba Anguissola in the 16th century, with Anne Killigrew in the 17th century and with Marie Ellenrieder in the 19th century, all of whom were unmarried when first appointed at court.

Although marriage seems to have temporarily hindered the career of Anna Dorothea Lisiewska-Therbusch, who appears to have had an enforced break as an artist after her marriage to the painter/inn proprietor Ernst Friedrich Therbusch and the birth of her children, there is no evidence that the career of Rachel Ruysch (q.v.), appointed court painter by the Elector Palatine Johann Wilhelm in 1708, was hindered by her

marriage to the portrait painter Juriaen Pool II in 1693, or by the subsequent birth of her ten children.

For an unmarried woman, entry at court as an artist also rested on the support of her father. Amilcare Anguissola, father of Sofonisba, seems even and rather exceptionally to have promoted his daughter's career as court painter with some assiduity. Writing in September 1559 from Milan to the king of Spain, he accepted the appointment of his daughter at the court and in the service and household of Her Serene Highness, the Queen. In his letter he stressed his own obedience and devotion, apologised for being unable to accompany his daughter and thereby personally pay his own homage as a good subject and admitted that he was consoled by the knowledge that his daughter would be in service to the most powerful Catholic and Christian King in the world, whose house was famed as a religious monastery (*ibid.*, p.112).

Women artists were, however, sometimes prevented from taking up court appointments, and this could be on account of the important contributions they made to the family business. Marietta Robusti (q.v.) was prevented from taking up a court appointment after having been invited first by the Emperor Maximilian and then by Philip II of Spain, because of her participation in the workshop of her father, Tintoretto; she was, instead, betrothed to the goldsmith Mario d'Augusta on condition that she did not leave her father's household in his lifetime (Chadwick 1990, p.16). In 1734 Anna Rosina Lisiewska had also apparently initially turned down a probable position as court painter in Dresden due to the wishes of her father.

The role of women artists at court

Baldassare Castiglione's influential *Il libro del cortegiano* was first published in 1528. It contains a series of fictionalised discussions between members of the household of Elisabetta Gonzaga, Duchess of Urbino, about the characteristics of the perfect courtier and includes chapters devoted to the nature and pursuits of the female courtier. The lady was presented in terms of an appropriate propriety and her behaviour was to be of a gentle delicacy and dignified modesty. She was to be excluded from the profession of arms, certain recreational pursuits and the playing of loud instruments that were considered to be too manly and unbecoming for women, but in many other respects her accomplishments were to be similar to those of the male courtier. In the absence of her husband, she was to manage his estate and household and her attainments, alongside those of the male courtier, had a strong humanities bias and required knowledge of literature and painting, music, dance and conversation. It is from within such a cultural context that the activities of the woman court artist can, initially, be addressed.

The painter Catharina van Hemessen (q.v.) was, for instance, married to the musician and organist of Antwerp Cathedral, Chrétien de Morien, and she is listed alongside other court functionaries as "kleine Catheline", lady-in-waiting to Mary of Hungary, in a household ordinance of 20 November 1555 (Zwolle 1993, p.189). In 1556 the couple travelled to Spain as part of the queen's retinue. Mary of Hungary, the younger sister of the emperor Charles V, became governor-general of the Netherlands in 1531 after the death of her aunt Margaret of Austria and the earlier death of her husband, Louis II of Hungary. Her court was noted for its humanism and for the wide range of artistic activity it promoted. The architect and sculptor Jacques Dubroeucq created, for instance, the castles of Binche and Mariemont and these were filled with large collections of books and paintings; 24 paintings by Titian from these castles also accompanied the queen to Spain after the abdication of Charles V in 1555 (Trevor-Roper 1976, p.41). While it would be wrong to suggest that the journey to Spain in the 16th century of a Flemish painter and her musician husband was as a direct result of a particular publication or of a single specific influence, the evidence of such a journey is indicative of the cultivation of music and painting that took place from within a royal household and as part of an aristocratic setting in which such arts were considered as liberal arts and as the appropriate accompaniments for enlightened rulers.

The woman court artist was often assigned to the female household of the court to which she belonged and she mostly produced the one-off easel painting that could be supplied without a large back-up in facilities and of labour. Catharina van Hemessen depicted herself working at her easel in just this way. In her annotated *Self-Portrait* (1548; Kunstmuseum, Basel) the artist shows herself in the act of painting a face at the same time as she looks out with some confidence towards the spectator. She is handsomely costumed, but in a respectable rather than luxurious and extravagant fashion and, with a quiet realism and self-assurance, she holds the attributes of her profession. The skill and diligence that the use of the *mahlstick* implies are complemented by the pride and self-affirmation that this self-portrait presents us with. Her status here is obviously not that of a mere artisan, but neither is it that of a high-born aristocrat or a "great" man in the grand manner tradition of high art.

The career of Sofonisba Anguissola provides us with further evidence of the special nature and status of the woman court artist. Anguissola arrived in Spain just before Philip II returned to Madrid with his new, young bride. Philip was 32 and had been married twice before; Elisabeth (or Isabel) de Valois was just 13 and came from the much less strict environment of the French court. Anguissola was more mature, well over 25, and had an established reputation both on account of her skills as a painter and on account of her nobility, grace and virtue. Italian artists were highly valued and sought after in both France and Spain, but Anguissola's appointment as lady-in-waiting to the queen of Spain could well also have been for reasons of propriety. In the only firmly dated and attributed self-portrait that she produced while in service at the Spanish court (1561; Althorp, Northampton, Collection Earl Spencer) the painter shows herself in sober costume, cultivating the gracious, liberal art of music and in contrast to the appearance of her own servant, whose more rugged facial features imply physically harder and rougher forms of labour. The portrait also carries an inscription indicating that the painting has been produced by the virgin Sofonisba Anguissola for her father.

The principal activity undertaken by the woman court artist was the painting of portraits, and her subjects were often the female members of the particular household to which she belonged. Portraiture can involve quite a close and intimate personal contact between sitter and artist, sovereign and servant, and this may well have been a factor in the selection of a woman artist for service in the female court household. The portraiture that was produced commemorated the ruling dynasty and validated the role and function of women at court in general – as the bearers of future generations to the court, as the possessors of sentiment and affection at the court and as the ornament and beauty of the court.

In Marie Ellenrieder's major group portrait of the *Grand Duchess Sophie von Baden with Her Five Children* (completed 1834; private collection, ex-Zähringersammlung, Neues Schloss, Baden-Baden) the wife and children of the ruler, Grand Duke Leopold I, are shown in careful harmony and with a degree of intimacy. It should, though, also be noted that while the Grand Duchess balances the youngest son Prince Karl on her knee in a pose of gentle and concerned motherhood and her eldest child, Alexandrine, stands behind her and looks to her mother as a model, the eldest son, Ludwig, is seated on the opposite side of the composition. In the absence of his father, he looks out at the spectator with a clear and far-sighted gaze and with an open book resting on his knees. In the distance, as part of the landscape background, there can be seen the silhouetted outlines of the city of Karlsruhe, as seat of the court and as evidence of its dominion. While the propagandistic element of this image is perhaps muted, the participation of women at the court is certainly envisaged here as the combination of nature with nurture and beauty with sentiment.

As a maid of honour or lady-in-waiting the woman artist often participated in some of the more general activities that sustained the cultivated circle to which she belonged, not necessarily just as a specialist portrait painter but also as a fitting companion. Susanna Horenbout was, for instance, sent as a gentlewoman and companion to attend to Anne of Cleves on her journey to England and she was at Calais in 1539 helping to teach Anne the card game of cent (Campbell and Foister 1986). Particularly in the case of foreign-born consorts and their households, such companionship may have been highly prized and very necessary.

Drawing and painting were valued accomplishments for ladies at court, and women artists were sometimes employed to give instruction in these pursuits. In a letter of 1561 to Duke Guglielmo Gonzaga, Girolamo Negri reported that Sofonisba Anguissola had commented favourably on the life-likeness of the queen's attempts at painting (Perlingieri 1992, p.120). In 1823, and in a more formal and official capacity, Louise Seidler was appointed drawing teacher to the Princesses of Sachsen-Weimar.

The fact that portraiture in one form or another – there was, for instance, a strong miniature tradition in England – was the major form of production for the woman court artist does not mean that only portraiture was produced by women court artists. Indeed, particularly in later periods and partly as a result of outside commissions, their output could be quite varied. Ellenrieder received several important commissions for altarpieces and religious works; Lisiewska-Therbusch produced paintings of mythological and genre subjects; and Seidler became a history painter of both religious and literary topics. However, even though many still-life painters were women, the appointment of specialist still-life painters in the Palatinate – first Rachel Ruysch and then Katrina Treu – was atypical and has to be placed within the patronal preferences and traditions of a particular court.

Katrina Treu was born in Bamberg in 1743, came from a family of painters and was a pupil in the studio of her father, Marquard Treu (Thieme and Becker 1933). She was appointed cabinet painter in Mannheim in 1769 and her appointment there could well be linked to the genre of art she practised. An earlier Elector of the Palatinate, Johann Wilhelm, had appointed the celebrated and well-known still-life painter Rachel Ruysch to his court at Düsseldorf where he had also created a large princely collection of 17th-century Netherlandish, Flemish and Italian paintings. As a later successor to the title of Elector Palatine, Karl Theodor may well have wished not only to emulate his predecessor as an enlightened patron of the arts, but to outdo him. He spent huge sums on opera and theatre – more than 200,000 gulden a year – and in 1761 he brought to Mannheim, where his court was now located, much of the painting collection that Johann Wilhelm had amassed. There it was housed in a new purpose-built gallery and greatly enlarged with additional purchases of paintings and of hundreds of prints, maps and drawings, and the gallery and a special prints and drawings room were opened to the public (Grotkamp-Schepers 1980, pp.12–23). In 1766 and through the intervention of Karl Theodor, Katrina Treu also became the first female professor at the Düsseldorf Academy (Berlin 1987, p.20). Karl Theodor can, thus, be ranked as a generous benefactor of the arts and, in his promotion of Treu, he can also now be seen to be the promoter of a more national and local German talent.

The woman court artist who practised sculpture was also an exception. Only two such sculptors can be identified: Luisa Roldán (q.v.) was trained in the studio of a celebrated father, Pedro Roldán, married another sculptor and received the title of Sculptor to the Bedchamber (*Escultora de Cámara*) of the Spanish king Charles II in 1692; Marie-Anne Collot (q.v.), together with her father-in-law Etienne-Maurice Falconet, worked at the court of Catherine II in St Petersburg and in 1779 became, jointly with Falconet, court sculptor to the Stadtholder William V in The Hague. That there were no real facilities at court for the woman sculptor is borne out by the petitions Luisa Roldán addressed first to Charles II, then to Queen Mariana of Neuberg and then to Philip V in which there are repeated requests for an appropriate salary, clothes, food and accommodation (Proske 1964, pp.128–32).

While male court artists could be made responsible for entire schemes of interior decoration, less permanent yet still costly and labour-intensive court pageantries, festivities, ceremonial and a whole host of other attendant administrative and bureaucratic tasks, women court artists worked in less public spheres. They were not placed in charge of teams of workers, large studio workshops or projects that required elaborate, collaborative and hierarchical organisation. Excluded from the life class and thus with little or no experience of drawing and sketching from the live male nude model, they were not employed to contribute to and work on the complex allegorical imagery and iconography of the absolutist state. They also received no formal training in mathematics and perspective and did not practise architecture.

Salaries and rewards

The permanent position of salaried court artist might bring very real material rewards, although this was not always the case. Petitions for greater financial remuneration were not uncommon despite the fact that such petitioning could also bring about an increase in expected duties, for the security that a regular pension or salary provided also brought with it certain demands and obligations. After successfully petitioning for an increased pension in 1830, Marie Ellenrieder had, for instance, to supply a major *Pflichtbild* every other year (Berlin 1987, p.135; a *Pflichtbild* was a painting that had to be produced as part of the duties incumbent on a court artist).

Sometimes, particularly in earlier periods, ties of loyalty and of service might be expressed not only by the promise of regular financial payments but also by an exchange of gifts. Thus in 1563, in addition to her annuity of £40 and in her capacity as gentlewoman, Levina Teerlinc received two gilt spoons from Queen Elizabeth of England as a New Year's gift; while in a New Year's Roll of 1553 she was recorded as having presented a small picture of the *Trinity* to Queen Mary and as having received in exchange a gilt "salte" weighing six ounces (Auerbach 1954, pp.91, 103–4). In donating a work as a voluntary present an artist could attract attention and also thereby gain special favours. Teerlinc appears to have been particularly successful in gaining special favours: even after her death, and in a document under the privy seal of the queen, her husband was awarded a special gift of £10 on her behalf.

Gifts could function as substitutes for financial recompense, offsetting some of the costs necessitated by attendance at court. Susanna Horenbout was mentioned in the Privy Purse accounts of Princess Mary in August 1544 for having received 12 yards of black satin (Campbell and Foister 1986). Proper court dress was an obligatory accoutrement of life at court and a gift like this has to be considered as part of the expenses that were inevitably incurred in and required by service at court.

Such exchanges must be seen as a part of larger systems of awards and rewards that underpinned the ways in which the court as a whole functioned and was constituted. In exchange for certain privileges, titles, honours and material recompense, the subject had a duty of service and loyalty to her sovereign and special, additional gifts might act as signs of particular favour and of particularly good service. This certainly seems to have been the case with Sofonisba Anguissola, who was left 3000 ducats and a piece of brocade in Isabel de Valois's will of 1566 and who was then given an additional 3000 ducats for her dowry by Philip II in 1569 provided that she resided in a royal palace in Castile or in some equivalent (Perlingieri 1992, p.152). Court artists were, in addition, generally exempt from the payment of taxes and customs duties. A letter to Philip II from Anguissola claimed such an exemption after she had been compelled to pay customs duty in Pisa on some silver, clothing and personal effects (*ibid.*, p.141); it also provides us with evidence that exemptions like these could be of very real financial advantage. However, by accepting such pensions, salaries, special gifts and exemptions, the court artist also thereby relinquished a certain amount of independence and freedom of action. Even as late as 1782 Angelica Kauffman (q.v.) turned down the opportunity of becoming court painter to the Kingdom of Naples on the grounds that she would thereby lose her freedom (Zimdars, "Angelika Kauffmann – Notizen zu Leben und Werk", in Konstanz 1992, pp.13–25).

There were further ways to reward the work and loyalty of the successful court artist, for the system that enabled the courts to function was also underpinned by the granting and acknowledgement of honour. Besides the granting of titles, honour could be expressed in a variety of other, quite tangible forms. The portrait of *Rachel Ruysch* (North Carolina Museum of Art, Raleigh) by Constantine Netscher shows the woman court artist nobly seated and with the medal she had received in 1710 from the Elector Palatine Johann Wilhelm prominently displayed hanging from her neck on a blue ribbon. Although Marie Ellenrieder had withdrawn from the court at Karlsruhe, 20 years later in 1862 and a year before her death, she received a visit from the young Grand Duke Friedrich I because she had been unable to pay her respects and attend on her new sovereign due to her own ill health. This personal visit was a matter of great honour for the artist (Berlin 1987, p.135).

Catharina van Hemessen was one of four famous living women artists mentioned by Lodovico Guicciardini in a text that was first published in 1567 (Guicciardini 1588, pp.130–31). This writer also praises Susanna Horenbout as an excellent painter and illuminator, who had found the highest favour at the court of Henry VIII in England (Campbell and Foister 1986). Although no known works have been firmly attributed to Horenbout, the fact that these named women artists are singled out for praise in a contemporary account and in relation to the honours that courts could bestow is evidence of the high profile that women court artists could acquire. In the second edition (1568) of Vasari's *Vite* Sofonisba Anguissola is marked out on account of both her grace as a lady and her abilities as a painter. Women were not awarded noble status, but service at court as an artist could mark out a woman for special mention, honour and privileges and on account of her achievements, talent and ability. It is also worth noting that of the relatively few women known to have had successful careers as artists in the 16th and 17th centuries, a significant proportion had salaried court appointments. The first two out of the four living women artists mentioned by Guicciardini were, for instance, singled out as successful artists at court.

While the granting of appointments, titles, privileges and rewards to some women painters at court reveals aspects of the underlying systems and structures that sustained such institutions, it also shows the extent to which women were, nevertheless, still generally confined to the orbit of the private and the domestic. Court culture provided limited opportunity for personal artistic responses and on the whole it is not possible to distinguish any particularly feminine forms or styles of artistic expression as emerging from out of this culture. Rather it is in the scope and range of her activities that the female court artist can be distinguished. The subject of female court patronage is also one that should provide rich scope for future research.

VALERIE MAINZ

Bibliography

Baldassare Castiglione, *Il libro del cortegiano*, 1528; as *The Book of the Courtier*, 1561

Lodovico Guicciardini, *Descrittione di tutti i paesi bassi, altrimenti detti Germania Inferiore*, Antwerp, 1567; 2nd edition, 1588

Giorgio Vasari, *Le vite de' più eccellenti pittori, scultori ed architettori*, Florence, 1568; ed. Gaetano Milanesi, 9 vols, Florence: Sansoni, 1878–85, v, p.81; vi, pp.498–502; vii, p.133; as *Lives of the Most Eminent Painters, Sculptors and Architects*, 10 vols, London: Macmillan-Medici Society, 1912–15; reprinted New York: AMS, 1976

U. Thieme and F. Becker, *Allgemeines Lexikon der bildenden Künstler von der Antike bis zur Gegenwart ...*, xxxiii, 1933

W.H. Bruford, *Germany in the Eighteenth Century: The Social Background of the Literary Revival*, Cambridge: Cambridge University Press, 1935

Erna Auerbach, *Tudor Artists: A Study of Painters in the Royal Service and of Portraiture from the Accession of Henry VIII to the Death of Elizabeth I*, London: Athlone Press, 1954

Beatrice Gilman Proske, "Luisa Roldán at Madrid", *Connoisseur*, clv, 1964, pp.126–32, 199–203, 269–73

Edward Miles Hooker and H.T. Swedenberg, Jr, eds, *The Works of John Dryden*, iii, Berkeley: University of California Press, 1969

Michael Levey, *Painting at Court*, London: Weidenfeld and Nicolson, and New York: New York University Press, 1971

Anne-Marie Passez, *Adélaïde Labille-Guiard (1749–1803): Biographie et catalogue raisonné de son oeuvre*, Paris: Arts et Métiers Graphiques, 1973

H.R. Trevor-Roper, *Princes and Artists: Patronage and Ideology at Four Habsburg Courts, 1517–1633*, London: Thames and Hudson, and New York: Harper, 1976

Women Artists, 1550–1950, exh. cat., Los Angeles County Museum of Art, and elsewhere, 1976

A.G. Dickens, ed., *The Courts of Europe: Politics, Patronage and Royalty, 1400–1800*, London: Thames and Hudson, and New York: McGraw Hill, 1977

Jonathan Brown and J.H. Elliott, *A Palace for a King: The Buen Retiro and the Court of Philip IV*, New Haven and London: Yale University Press, 1980

Barbara Grotkamp-Schepers, *Die Mannheimer Zeichnungsakademie (1756/69–1803) und die Werke der ihr angeschlossenen Maler und Stecher*, Frankfurt am Main: Haag & Herchen, 1980

Jennifer M. Fletcher, "The glory of the female sex: Women artists, c.1500–1800", *The Women's Art Show, 1550–1970*, exh. cat., Nottingham Castle Museum, 1982, pp.8–10

Norbert Elias, *The Court Society*, New York: Pantheon, and Oxford: Blackwell, 1983 (German original)

Artists of the Tudor Court: The Portrait Miniature Rediscovered, 1520–1620, exh. cat., Victoria and Albert Museum, London, 1983

Diderot et l'art de Boucher à David, exh. cat., Paris, 1984

Lorne Campbell, *The Early Flemish Pictures in the Collection of Her Majesty the Queen*, Cambridge and New York: Cambridge University Press, 1985

Lorne Campbell and Susan Foister, "Gerard, Lucas and Susanna Horenbout", *Burlington Magazine*, cxxviii, 1986, pp.719–27

Ekhart Berckenhagen, "Anna Dorothea Therbusch", *Zeitschrift des Deutschen Vereins für Kunstwissenschaft*, xli, 1987, pp.118–60

Das Verborgene Museum I: Dokumentation der Kunst von Frauen in Berliner öffentlichen Sammlungen, exh. cat., Akademie der Künste, Berlin, 1987

Siân Evans, ed., *The Memoirs of Elisabeth Vigée-Le Brun*, Bloomington: Indiana University Press, and London: Camden, 1989

Edith Krull, *Women in Art*, London: Studio Vista, 1989 (German original)

Whitney Chadwick, *Women, Art and Society*, New York and London: Thames and Hudson, 1990

Ronald G. Asch and Adolf M. Birke, eds., *Princes, Patronage and the Nobility: The Court at the Beginning of the Modern Age, c.1450–1650*, Oxford and New York: Oxford University Press, 1991

Ekhart Berckenhagen, "Anna Rosina Lisiewska-Matthieu-de Gasc", *Niederdeutsche Beiträge zur Kunstgeschichte*, xxxi, 1992, pp.77–114

Ilya Sandra Perlingieri, *Sofonisba Anguissola: The First Great Woman Artist of the Renaissance*, New York: Rizzoli, 1992

"... und hat als Weib unglaubliches Talent" (Goethe): Angelika Kauffmann (1741–1807), Marie Ellenrieder (1791–1863), exh.

cat., Rosgartenmuseum, Konstanz, 1992

Maria van Hongarije, 1505–1558: Koningin tussen keizers en kunstenaars [Mary of Hungary, 1505–1558: Queen among emperors and artists], exh. cat., Waanders Uitgevers, Zwolle, 1993

Martin Warnke, *The Court Artist: On the Ancestry of the Modern Artist*, Cambridge and New York: Cambridge University Press, 1993

Academies of Art

Italy

The first academies of painting and sculpture were founded in Italy during the second half of the 16th century. Formed under the protection of a prince or state, art academies were intended as instruments of artistic reform, and their members included scholars, art lovers and art patrons as well as painters, sculptors and architects. They were modelled on literary and scientific academies, societies of humanist scholars and gentlemen who shared an interest in ancient culture. Part of the purpose of art academies was to free artists from the exclusive control of the guilds to which they had traditionally belonged (painters to the Arte de' Medici e Speziali, sculptors and architects to the Università dei Fabbricanti). Nevertheless, they continued to share many of the same functions and aims, and the first art academies co-existed with the system of guilds and artists' confraternities (Compagnia di San Luca). There were also private academies that were less formal associations of artists who trained and worked together, such as the Accademia degli Incamminati founded by the Carracci in Bologna (1584). But both public and private academies differed from guilds and medieval workshops in their focus on art theory and classical ideals in addition to studio practice.

As practical institutions, academies set standards, laid down rules and regulations for the business of art production and provided instruction; however, their overriding concern was to raise the dignity of the profession. This emphasis on the intellectual foundations of the visual arts, the application of the mind as well as the hand in the perfect union of theory and practice, was the fundamental principle underlying the academic programme. According to academic theory, the artist's idea or concept was developed and perfected through *disegno*, a term that meant both drawing and design.

By the middle of the 17th century a hierarchy of the arts became institutionalised in academies. The fine arts of painting, sculpture and architecture with their intellectual basis in *disegno* were considered superior to the manually produced mechanical arts and crafts. The art of painting was itself subdivided into higher and lesser categories, with history painting considered the highest because its purpose was to provide instruction and delight to the mind through the representation of morally uplifting themes. Based on Leon Battista Alberti's concept of *historia* (*De pictura*, 1435), history paintings portrayed significant human actions in narratives taken from biblical and classical literature and history. Its didactic purpose distinguished it from less lofty subjects that simply imitated nature in order to please the eye and lacked moral values: portraiture, themes from everyday life (genre), landscape and still-life painting. This division of the arts into higher and lower categories, with their attendant qualities of social and intellectual status, had consequences for the position of women within the profession.

Both the theoretical and practical programmes of art academies made life drawing from nude models one of their primary activities; in fact, the term "academy" still signifies life drawing. Proficiency in drawing the human figure in action and knowledge of anatomy were essential for training as a history painter. Young artists began to develop these skills by copying old master paintings and engravings. Parts of bodies, limbs and faces were practised first, followed by whole figures, and eventually the student moved on to three-dimensional objects in the form of sculptures or casts of antique statuary. Only after these were fully mastered could an artist advance to life studies from the draped and nude model. Women artists could follow the early stages of study by copying paintings, prints, statuary or plaster casts, which might include nude or nearly nude figures, but at this level of training, when male artists advanced to life classes, women were left behind. Drawing directly from the nude, especially the male nude, was thought to be unsuitable for them. The very idea of a woman artist taking the male prerogative to study living nude figures, male or female, and to create them herself, her pencil or brush stroking the portrayed flesh, could be construed as both titillating and distracting to the male students. Thus, the academic emphasis on the male nude made it difficult for women to pursue history painting and restricted most of them to the lesser genres of portraiture and still life.

The first formal art academy, the Accademia del Disegno, was created in Florence in 1563 under the inspiration of the artist-writer Giorgio Vasari and with the support of Cosimo I de' Medici, Grand Duke of Tuscany. Its members were selected from among the best painters, sculptors and architects in Florence, and its statutes were drawn up by a group of artists and humanist scholars. The curriculum they developed aimed to provide a broad liberal education for artists, and included mathematics, perspective, anatomy, life drawing and natural philosophy.

During its first 50 years the Accademia del Disegno had no women members. In 1616 Artemisia Gentileschi (q.v.) was accepted as the first female academician, although she and her husband had been permitted to use the facilities for the previous two years. Gentileschi's acceptance was undoubtedly tied to the patronage and support she received from the Medici family. Later in the 17th century the names of three more women appear in academy records: Rosa Maria Setterni (1662), Caterina Angiola Corsi Pierozzi (1691) and Colomba Agrani (1691).

In Rome the Accademia di San Luca, dedicated to St Luke, the patron saint of artists, was founded in 1593 by the painter and theorist Federigo Zuccari with the support of Cardinal Federigo Borromeo. As in the Florentine academy, Zuccari's principal aim was to promote the intellectual basis of art, *disegno*, and also to enhance the status and respectability of artists in society. The Academy set standards for admission, collected dues from members, held exhibitions and competitions (*concorsi*), and awarded prizes, which were a mark of official approval for young artists. The basic activity of the academy was the training of artists, so facilities for copying paintings, a study collection of plaster casts of antique sculpture and models for life drawing were provided. There was to be an ambitious programme of lectures and theoretical debates on various subjects such as the meaning of *disegno*, decorum in composition, the rendering of human movements in painting and the qualities of architecture.

Although membership of the Academy was not at first a prerequisite for a successful artistic career, if artists joined they had to abide by its regulations. These included restrictions on selling work below a fixed price, painting licentious subjects, attracting other artists' pupils and keeping a model. Members were required to present the Academy with one of their works, a reception piece. It is not entirely clear, however, whether such rules, which were rewritten several times during the course of the 17th century, were ever fully operational.

According to the rules of the Accademia di San Luca of 1607, women could be elected to membership but were prohibited from attending meetings. Caterina Ginnasi (q.v.), one of the few female members, is recorded in 1638 as having paid dues for the annual banquet held by the academicians in honour of St Luke. The name of the still-life painter Giovanna Garzoni (q.v.) appears on a list of academicians created in April 1633. Although this list is not considered reliable, she may have been admitted under the informal procedures of the 1620s and 1630s. After 1654 Garzoni is also noted on six occasions as a contributor to the annual celebration feast for the patron saint. In 1656, and later in 1669–70, she was treated to the special cakes that were customarily given to members who were ill. At her death she bequeathed her belongings to the Academy (Harris in Los Angeles 1976, p.15). After 1617 members of the nobility, scholars and distinguished foreign artists, including women, could be nominated for honorary membership as "accademici d'onore e di grazia" or "accademico di merito", to distinguish them from the local professional members.

In the 18th century more women were elected to membership in academies, but they were primarily foreigners who had established themselves as accomplished artists before coming to Italy. On 10 October 1762, just a few months after her arrival in Florence, the Swiss-born Angelica Kauffman (q.v.), already a celebrated artist at the age of 21, was elected to the Accademia del Disegno. Payment of her entrance fee was recorded several days later; however, her membership was more of an honour than an expectation of full participation in academy business. The Italian-born British painter Maria Cosway (q.v.) was similarly elected to membership in the Florentine Accademia del Disegno before the age of 20 on 27 September 1778. Kauffman was also honoured in 1762 with membership in the Accademia Clementina in Bologna (founded in 1709), and almost 20 years later, on her return to Italy from England in 1781, she was made an honorary member of the Accademia delle Belle Arti in Venice, which had been founded in 1750 as the first public art school in that city.

The Venetian Rosalba Carriera (q.v.) was elected Accademica di Merito in the Roman Accademia di San Luca on 27 September 1705. As a reception piece for their collection, she presented the institution with a small painting on ivory representing *Innocence*. When Kauffman became a member on 17 November 1765, she donated an allegorical painting of *Hope*. Other women artists listed as members in the 18th century, most of whom were either foreigners or related to important male artists by birth or marriage, include Luisa Roldán (q.v., 1706), Maria Tibaldi Subleray (1742), Veronika Stern (1742), Maria Maini, daughter of the painter Giovanni Battista Maini (no date), Maria Vien, wife of the Director of the French Academy in Rome (1757), Caterina Preziado, "daughter of a prince" (1760), Theresa Concordia Maron-Mengs (q.v., 1766) and Elisabeth Vigée-Lebrun (q.v., 1790). Despite their increasing numbers, women were still not allowed to vote or to draw from nude models.

Women artists and academies of art in Rome

The exclusion of women from full participation in the Roman Academy was due primarily to its continuing emphasis on life drawing, although the academy's stress on the theoretical basis of art and the supremacy of history painting also played a part. In reality, during much of the 17th and the 18th centuries in Rome, drawing from models took place in private studios rather than in the Accademia di San Luca, which did not consistently provide classes. One place at which artists could draw from nude models was the Académie de France, the French Academy in Rome, which had been founded in 1666 as a branch of the Parisian Academy and where life drawing classes were held every day. In any case, models were generally male, for although female models were occasionally used in Italian academies, this did not become standard practice until the 19th century (see Bignamini in Boschloo 1989). In 1754 Pope Benedict XIV established the Accademia del Nudo in Rome as a place for art students to draw from nude and draped models on a regular basis without paying a fee. Members of the Accademia di San Luca, to which the school was affiliated, took turns supervising classes, posing models and correcting students' work. Competitions (*concorsi*) were held at the end of each year for the best drawing and sculpted figure, and medals were awarded. Women, who were excluded from these classes, were at a distinct disadvantage in the advancement of their careers, especially those who aspired to pursue history painting. In 1752 the British painter Katharine Read (q.v.) was in Italy to further her artistic training. Her situation was described in a letter from one of her patrons (Abbé Grant): "... was it not for the restrictions her sex obliges her to be under, ... she would shine wonderfully in history painting, too, but it is impossible for her to attend public academies or even design or draw from nature ...".

Among Kauffman's early sketches made in Rome in the early 1760s are a few nude or nearly nude male figures. One drawing (Kupferstichkabinett, Berlin, repr. Baumgärtel 1990, p.81), proudly and perhaps defiantly signed "Designée par moi Marianne Angélique Kauffman l'an 1763", represents a nude man tied to a tree trunk with a sweep of drapery behind him. The figure's pose, as if viewed from slightly below, his left side towards the picture plane, resembles a standard life-class attitude with one arm behind his back and the other outstretched. While it is conceivable that Kauffman drew from a live model, perhaps in the privacy of her own studio, it is much more likely that this was copied from a drawing by another artist. She did in fact copy at least one nude study from an engraving after a drawing by the French artist Fragonard (c.1760; Städelsches Kunstinstitut und Städtische Galerie, Frankfurt am Main, repr. Baumgärtel 1990, p.85). She knew many artists in Rome, including Nathaniel Dance and Gavin Hamilton, who may well have allowed her to copy their studies.

Academies of art outside Florence and Rome

With the support of Church and State, the Accademia del Disegno in Florence and the Accademia di San Luca in Rome remained the most important and influential art academies in Italy. During the 17th and 18th centuries dozens of new public and private academies modelled on those of Florence and Rome were founded in other Italian cities such as Bologna, Milan, Lucca, Parma and Venice. The intellectual ideals and emphasis on life drawing and the study of antiquities also inspired the formation of academies in other European cities, including Haarlem, Utrecht, Amsterdam, Paris, Nuremberg, Berlin, Dresden, Munich, Vienna, Copenhagen, Edinburgh, Dublin, Lisbon, Madrid and St Petersburg, although most remained provincial (see Pevsner 1940).

Artists from all over Europe, including such women as Anne Forbes (q.v.), whose trip abroad was financed by subscription among friends and relations in Edinburgh, continued to travel to the artistic centres of Italy, especially Florence and Rome, to learn from the art of the "old masters" and classical antiquity. Some women artists were able to participate in exhibitions and competitions in the newer academies, and a few even became members. Nevertheless, the only academy that could rival the Florentine Accademia del Disegno and the Roman Accademia di San Luca in influence and prestige was the French Académie Royale de Peinture et de Sculpture, and it was in the Academy in Paris that the role of women as artists was seriously challenged.

WENDY WASSYNG ROWORTH

France

The Académie Royale de Peinture et de Sculpture was founded in France in 1648 during the reign of Louis XIV. In contrast to the artists' guild or Maîtrise, the Academy stressed its honorific, rather than commercial function. Academicians could not keep a shop or display works for sale in their studios, and their regulations stressed decorum and learning. The Crown, moreover, gave the newly formed Academy the privilege of posing the nude (male) model for public instruction and provided a system of government patronage that would make the Académie Royale into a powerful arts institution. The finance minister Colbert was the first official protector of the Academy, and he used this position not only to ensure the flow of government patronage, but also to control art production in the interests of the state.

In 1737 the Academy solidified its control over the visual arts by holding official art exhibitions, known as Salons, in the Salon carrée of the Louvre in the autumn, in alternate years. Although the Academy had earlier sponsored sporadic exhibitions, in 1737 the Salon was regularised as a biennial event. Only academicians could show their works at the Salon, which was one of the very few public exhibition spaces in 18th-century Paris. The Salon grew increasingly important as the exhibitions encouraged a flowering of art criticism, which increased as the century progressed.

Acceptance procedures and the admission of women

It was during Colbert's tenure of office, on 14 April 1663, that the Academy accepted its first woman member: Cathérine Duchemin, wife of the sculptor François Girardon. The painter Charles Le Brun presented to the academicians a flower painting by Duchemin, and "the Company, affected by their esteem for this work and recognising the merit of this young woman, resolved to give her the position of Académicienne" (Procès-verbaux, i, pp.222–3). The institution's official rationale for accepting Duchemin rested on interpreting the king's intention in founding the Academy. In assessing her case for admission, the academicians deemed it their duty to abide by the king's wish to honour "all those who excel in the arts of painting and sculpture and those judged worthy, regardless of their sex" (idem). But women were not honoured in the same way as their male contemporaries. For example, at the same meeting in which Duchemin was accepted, the company also received 14 male artists. Whereas she was sent letters of appointment, they were ordered to take the oath in which they swore to uphold "religiously" the rules and statutes of the Academy. Oath-taking in France during the Ancien Régime formalised and added force to commitments, but women were banned from swearing them, excepting, of course, the vow of marriage. Beyond requiring oath-taking, in the 17th century admission procedures were not regularised nor were admissions systematically recorded. Later, however, the differences between the admissions of men and women became more evident.

Male painters usually went through the Academy's training programme, which they concluded by presenting for evaluation a work of their choice. If the work was accepted, they entered the Academy as a provisional member or agréé, with the evaluated work designated as their morceau d'agrément. To obtain final acceptance, the aspiring academician completed a second "masterpiece" called the morceau de réception. The subject of this work was usually assigned by the Academy, which gave the artist a specific period of time, normally a year, to complete it. These procedures governed the admission of nearly all male artists, although a few were excepted from them in one way or another. The morceau de réception was especially important since its subject determined the category in which a painter was received. Once received as a painter of a particular genre, the artist could never change his or her designated place. At the top of the academic hierarchy was history painting (subjects drawn from history, myth, religion as well as allegory) and below that portraiture, genre painting, landscape and still life. Although the system of apprenticeship and admission was regularised by the 18th century, women were never received in the "normal" way. The Academy usually made them *agréée* and *académicienne* on the same day. Most, although not all, brought to the session several paintings from which the academicians could "find" appropriate reception pieces.

Women and the status of the Academy

The acceptance of women moved the Académie Royale de Peinture et de Sculpture closer to the Maîtrise than to the other honorific institutions, such as the Académie des Sciences and the Académie Française, which did not admit women. This partly explains why women were kept in an equivocal position within the arts institution. The presence of women in the corporation bespoke a lowered status and evoked the mixed body of the guild, which admitted not only women but also art dealers and artisans. The Academy was also anxious to stress its difference from the Maîtrise since on several other counts the two functioned in a similar way. For example, both encouraged a long apprenticeship for students in the atelier of an established master and both asked for a masterpiece (which the Academy called a *morceau de réception*). Most significantly, both institutions (like all other guilds) gave preference to the sons of its members, and some consideration to their daughters and widows. For the history of women in the Academy this last point is significant, especially since family connections seem to have played a role in opening the Academy to women. Indeed, the first three women received into the Academy were the daughters or wives of academicians. After Cathérine Duchemin, Geneviève and Madeleine Boulogne, daughters of Louis Boulogne, were accepted in 1669. In total, one-third of all women admitted were relatives of academic artists. Marie-Thérèse Reboul, wife of Joseph Vien, was accepted in 1754, and Marie-Suzanne Giroust, wife of Alexandre Roslin, in 1770.

Although the Academy could not exclude women entirely, it could maintain them in an equivocal position – as foreign elements – since they were not allowed to swear allegiance to the institution and its rules. The Academy records suggest that it was never eager to admit women and always did so as "exceptions". This was the case even though women were admitted infrequently and comprised a very small proportion of the membership. Indeed, between 1648 and 1792, when the Academy was disbanded and reorganised, the royal institution admitted more than 450 artists. Of that number, 15 (3 per cent) were women. The collective anxiety about these women is encoded in certain phrases that appear repeatedly in the *Procès-verbaux*; specifically, those indicating that the acceptance of a particular woman was not meant to set a precedent. For example, in 1680 Dorothée Massée was accepted "in the position of academician, without allowing her to be a precedent for the future" (*Procès-verbaux*, ii, pp.175–6). In 1682 the admission of Cathérine Pérot was qualified with the phrase: "ce sans tirer consequence" (*ibid.*, ii, p.215), which appeared again in recording the election of Rosalba Carriera in 1720 (*ibid.*, iv, p.303). In 1722 the same phrase marks the record of admitting a second foreign woman, Margareta Haverman (q.v., *ibid.*, iv, p.328). Although it was another 32 years before the next woman was admitted, the Academy still felt compelled to point out that the admission of Madame

Vien, on 30 July 1754, was not to set a precedent (*ibid.*, vii, p.41).

These standards of recording the admission of women are punctuated in the Academy's history by the record of official efforts to restrict the number of women who could enter the academic body. On 25 September 1706 the *Procès-verbaux* recorded only one item of business at the regular meeting: "Règlement général que l'on ne recevra aucune Damoiselle en qualité d'Académicienne". The rule was allegedly prompted by the fact that the Academy had learned that "several ladies who have applied themselves to painting have planned to present themselves to be received as académiciennes". After "une sérieuse réflexion" the company decided to forestall the presentations of these women by resolving that henceforth they would receive no woman as academician and that this resolution would serve as the "règlement général" (*ibid.*, iii, p.34). This rule may also have been promoted because in 1706 six women – the largest group at any one time – were current members of the Academy. Besides the sisters Boulogne, in 1672 the Academy had received Elisabeth-Sophie Chéron (q.v.), the first woman admitted who was not the wife or daughter of an academician. Chéron, not incidentally, was the most distinguished and learned woman artist of 17th-century France, one whose works the academicians distinguished as "very exceptional and surpassing the ordinary power (force) of her sex" (*ibid.*, i, p.388). Three other women had also been admitted: Anne Strésor in 1677, Dorothée Massée in 1680 and Cathérine Pérot in 1682. The rule of 1706 that closed the Academy to women, however, was not long-lasting; it was enacted without the king's order and did not have the force of law. Fourteen years later the resolution was broken and two foreign women were received: the Italian Carriera (1720) and the Dutchwoman Haverman (1722). Foreign women might have been doubly alien to the French Academy, but they were much less threatening than local ones. The foreigner was usually passing through; she did not disrupt the established circuits of patronage, or challenge male monopolies over academic enterprise.

Between 1706, when the first rule for prohibiting the admission of women was enacted, and 1770, when a second one was suggested, the Academy admitted women sporadically. With one notable exception, all the women admitted during this period were either foreigners, such as Carriera, Haverman and the Prussian Terbouche (1767), or artists' wives, such as Madame Vien (1757) and Madame Roslin (1770). The exception was Mlle Vallayer (q.v.), also admitted in 1770, whose father was goldsmith to the king. Two months after her admission on 28 September 1770, Pierre, the first painter, proposed another *Règlement pour l'admission des femmes l'Académie*:

> Although [the Academy] is pleased to encourage talent in women by admitting some into our body, nevertheless, these admissions, foreign in some fashion to its constitution must not be repeated too often. [The Academy] has agreed that it will receive no more than four women. It will, however, receive women only in cases in which their extraordinarily distinguished talents lead the Academy to wish, with a unanimous voice, to crown them with particular distinction. The Academy does not pretend to oblige itself always to fill the number of four, reserving

for itself the right to choose only those whose talents are truly distinguished [*Procès-verbaux*, vii, p.53].

Like the resolution of 1706, however, Pierre's regulation lacked the official sanction of the Crown, and it was not until 13 years later that the Academy obtained officially the longed-for limitation on the number of women. This came in conjunction with the acceptance, in 1783, of two women, the last who would ever be members of that royal institution: Elisabeth Vigée-Lebrun (q.v.) and Adélaïde Labille-Guiard (q.v.). The decree limiting the number of women is inseparable from the controversy that surrounded the admission of one of those women, Vigée-Lebrun. Because she was married to an art dealer, the Academy, represented by its director d'Angiviller, held her in violation of the statute forbidding artists from engaging in commerce, and refused to admit her. At the request of the queen, Marie-Antoinette, the king ordered an exception to the rule, which opened the way for the artist to be accepted as *académicienne*. In contrast to this example, on the same day the academicians conducted and recorded the acceptance of Labille-Guiard according to the practices established for accepting women. But the double admission did more than stress the differences in how the two candidates were admitted. Receiving Labille-Guiard brought the number of women in the Academy to four (the other two were Mme Vien and Mme Vallayer-Coster). Moreover, four was precisely the number that Pierre had selected as the appropriate limit for women more than a decade before. In addition to the order admitting Vigée-Lebrun, d'Angiviller persuaded the king to give a second order, "limiting to four the number of women who can, in the future, be admitted into the Academy". The academicians responded by sending "a letter of thanks to M. d'Angiviller for having preserved the rights of the Academy and the force of its statutes, and for having fixed the number of women academicians at four" (*Procès-verbaux*, ix, p.153). The director's justification for limiting the number of women to four was as follows: "this number is sufficient to honour their talent; women can not be useful to the progress of the arts because the modesty of their sex forbids them from being able to study after nature and in the public school established and founded by your Majesty" (*ibid.*, ix, p.157). What d'Angiviller meant by the progress of the arts was, of course, the progress of history painting.

Women and academic training in France

It has been more than two decades since Linda Nochlin (1971) argued in her ground-breaking work that women were excluded from the highest achievements in painting because they could not receive the necessary academic training. Women were excluded from two learning situations – drawing after nature and attending the Academy school. Modesty dictated that women should not look at the nude male body, which is what study after nature meant in this context. Posing the male model was the only life drawing sanctioned in the Academy, and it was this privilege that distinguished the Academy from the Maîtrise. Modesty kept women from other aspects of artistic education, as well. They could not attend schools such as the Ecole Royale des Elèves Protégés, where aspiring artists not only learned the finer points of practice, but also acquired intellectual knowledge in subjects thought essential to history painting: geography, history, literature, anatomy and

perspective. This exclusion exemplifies the general situation in France where young men and women were educated separately and learned different kinds of subjects and skills thought *convenable* to their sex.

In comparison to the noble genre of history painting, the lesser genres were theoretically feminised since their only function was to please. History paintings, on the other hand, were made to instruct, to edify, to instil virtue and to capture *gloire*. A fear of the emasculating effect of women was one factor in the prevention of women – always foreign to the academic body – from entering the Académie Royale in too great a number. Too many women would dilute the proportion of history painters, which was one measure of the Academy's manliness. It was not, d'Angiviller argued, in society's interests to promote women as members of such institutions as the Académie Royale. Women, he implies, would impede the progress of art by taking academic positions that might otherwise be filled by (male) history painters. But this is a specious argument – there was no limit on the number of academicians, and so an alteration in the ratio of male to female artists entering the Academy could not affect the "progress of the arts".

At the same time that d'Angiviller was working to close admission to the Academy to women, other avenues for women's advancement in the arts were also being closed. For example, women had formerly been allowed to train in the studios of academic painters who had their lodgings and ateliers in the Louvre (an atelier in the Louvre was one of the rewards available to academicians). Only one woman artist, Vallayer-Coster, had lodgings there and the pains taken over them show that she, like Vigée-Lebrun, had a powerful protector in Marie-Antoinette. D'Angiviller, moreover, had no reason to fear that Vallayer-Coster (then Mlle Vallayer) might pose a threat to the "decency" of the Louvre. He wrote to her that, as director of the Academy, he wanted her to have an apartment where she could "cultivate in peace" her distinguished talents (Michel 1970). When a second woman, Labille-Guiard, asked for lodgings in the Louvre, however, d'Angiviller was not so accommodating. She was not asking for solitude, but for a place to hold her art school for young women. In a letter of November 1785 to the king concerning Labille-Guiard's request for lodgings in the Louvre, d'Angiviller points out that because the artist "has a school for young students of her sex", allowing her to bring her studio and students to the Louvre would present great dangers. He reminds the king that "all the artists have their lodging in the Louvre and as one only gets to all these lodgings through vast corridors that are often dark, this mixing of young artists of different sexes would be very inconvenient for morals and for the decency of your majesty's palace" (Passez 1973, p.301). The point, of course, ignores the fact that the Louvre already housed a mixed-sex community, because artists had wives and daughters and other women relatives living there. But perhaps d'Angiviller could accept this mixing because the women residing there were located firmly under the roof of male authority (of a father or husband).

Even more pernicious than denying Labille-Guiard's request for lodgings was d'Angiviller's order prohibiting artists from teaching women students in the Louvre. He was so adamant about the issue that in 1785 he went so far as to get an official order from the king forbidding these classes (Guiffrey 1874). It is important to bear in mind that it was through such private lessons that many young women artists, Vigée-Lebrun for example, received their early education. Thus d'Angiviller closed an important avenue for the training of women artists who were not the wives or daughters of academicians. The director's zeal in enforcing the ban is evident in the letters exchanged in 1787 between d'Angiviller and the artists Jacques-Louis David and Joseph-Benoît Suvée who had taken on women students in their ateliers. D'Angiviller reminded both artists that the Louvre was a "place where it is particularly necessary that decency should reign, so we cannot allow ourselves to close our eyes to this abuse" (19 July 1787; Silvestre de Sacy 1953, p.176). Even when one of the girls' guardians wrote to d'Angiviller, he received a curt and officious reply. D'Angiviller told him in no uncertain terms that his daughter's exclusion was not motivated by a mistaken impression of her conduct, but by a general consideration of the trouble that could follow from holding a school for girls. He said quite bluntly that even if all precautions possible were taken to ensure decency, this would not justify a departure from the rule (ibid., p.177). One suspects that the rule was meant to ensure something other than decency.

Women, Academy, Revolution

Labille-Guiard's attempts to gain for women students an official training-ground at the Louvre were thwarted by d'Angiviller. During the Revolutionary period her attempts to gain other privileges for women also failed, this time thwarted by the leader of the so-called "progressive" painters, Joseph Vien. In 1790 the Academy would use the same strategies to keep women in an equivocal position that they had used a century earlier. The oath again became a point that separated the women from the men.

In 1790 the officers banned women from discussions about re-organising the Academy because they had not taken the oath. That this ban followed Labille-Guiard's attempts to gain for women an unlimited number of seats in the Academy is significant. It demonstrates again that when under threat from women – as it had been already in 1706 and 1783 – the Academy would act to limit their role, even though the records and reports suggest that the academicians were by no means unanimous in their resolve to keep women out. Moreover, the timing of this ban also supports the historian Geneviève Fraisse's argument that the ideology of liberty and equality fostered by the Revolution raised in a glaring way the problem of women's rights (La Raison des femmes, Paris: Plon, 1992, pp.49–62). Indeed, an appeal to the new principles fuelled Labille-Guiard's attempts to gain equality for women.

Little about these attempts is recorded in the Academy's Procès-verbaux, but more is suggested in the memoirs of the engraver Wille. His entry for 23 September 1790 begins: "Madame Guiard, seated next to me, made a very well justified speech on the admission of women artists to the Academy and proved that accepting an unlimited number must be the only admissible rule" (Duplessis 1857, ii, p.268). Wille also described a second motion made by Labille-Guiard and supported by the painter Vincent that would allow some women to be distinguished with particular honours. Labille-Guiard justified the request by arguing that because women could neither participate in the governance of the Academy nor be professors in its schools, there was no way in which they could elevate themselves within the existing hierarchy. Commenting on the fate of the proposal, Wille wrote: "This article, despite the opposition of M. LeBarbier, was approved and passed the vote, as did the first" (idem). Again we see that the members of the Academy were by no means united in their opposition to women, and it was left to the officers to stop their efforts to gain more equal power. And it shows that the admission of artists' wives and daughters was by no means a cue that those academicians supported women's rights. For the artist who seems to have led the move to suppress Labille-Guiard's efforts was none other than Vien, whose wife had been admitted to the Academy in 1757.

Although the minutes in the Procès-verbaux do not record the meeting cited by Wille, the record does include a letter dated 23 September 1790 from the officers to the academicians that refers to the meeting. The officers – and chief among them Vien – seem to have separated themselves from the academicians for the purpose of enacting new statutes. To justify the move they argued that it was impossible to continue work with the entire Assembly because, among other things, several members supported their opinions with a "chaleur immodéré" and because:

> … we do not find it appropriate that women mix themselves in a work that is foreign to them, it being only a question of redrafting the Statutes, which do not concern them at all since they have not submitted to them, never having taken the oath to obey them [Procès-verbaux, x, p.81].

How convenient that women are foreign to the Academy because they have not taken the oath! Oath-taking, it seems, both in the Ancien Régime and during the Revolution, was a male prerogative. After all the revolutionary dust had settled and the Academy was reorganised, there were no more exceptional women in that corporate body, for the Academy had closed its doors to them.

MARY D. SHERIFF

Nordic countries

The Nordic countries dealt with in this essay – Denmark, Sweden, Norway and Finland – are in many ways closely related, particularly in the sphere of art. During the 18th century, Sweden and Finland were under one monarchy, as were Denmark and Norway. The Danish Academy in Copenhagen and its Swedish counterpart in Stockholm were both established in the 1730s, with the Parisian Academy as their principal model.

For reasons both practical (the need for efficient artists) and economic (the strengthening of national abilities), the Royal Danish Academy of Fine Arts in Copenhagen was founded in 1738 and opened for instruction two years later with two artists brought from France and Italy as professors: Louis-Augustin Le Clerc and Hieronimo Miani. Signing the statutes after a visit to the Academy on his birthday in 1754, the absolute monarch Frederik V claimed that it was founded by him on this very date. In Sweden, the Royal Academy of Fine Arts sprang from similar circumstances. Foreign artists, in this case from France, were needed for the construction and decoration of a new royal castle, and in 1735 the original Kongl. Ritareakademien (Royal Drawing Academy) was founded there under the direction of Guillaume Taraval in order to provide a means of regular training for Swedish artists. The Academy was established as the Kongl. Målare- och Bildhuggare-Academien (Royal Academy of Painters and Sculptors), but its statutes were signed by Gustaf III only in 1773. Norway did not have a national academy until 1909, but the Kongelige Tegne- og Kunstskole (Royal Drawing- and Art School) in Christiania (Oslo) provided a precedent from 1818. Norwegian artists meanwhile completed their studies at the Copenhagen Academy, while Finnish artists went to Stockholm, at least until drawing schools were established in Finland, in Åbo (1830) and Helsinki (1848).

At first, women as well as men took part in exhibitions and became members of the two early Nordic academies. The vital access to academic training, however, was gendered from the very start, although both Danish and Swedish statutes are silent on the subject of who was allowed to study at the academy and who was not. In practice, this free training was available to men only. Neither academy was open to female students before 1864 (Stockholm) and 1888 (Copenhagen). In addition, the crucial monopoly of life drawing was a staggering blow to anyone aspiring to be an artist outside the academic institutions. The consistent exclusion of women students meant that the knowledge needed for the highest-regarded genre of history painting was entirely confined to men.

Like their counterparts in continental Europe, the two Nordic academies were founded to raise the status of artists by means of theoretical claims intended to elevate them above simple craftsmen and thus to snatch the visual arts out of the hands of the guilds. In their early years, however, the parameters between craftsmen and painters, amateurs and professionals, were not clear-cut. The Academy exhibitions in Stockholm, for instance, where from 1794 students and members showed their works alongside amateurs (both men and women) and foreign artists, all sorts of entries could be found – not only the traditional genres such as painted or engraved portraits and landscapes but works in a variety of techniques and different materials. Admission was free, and visitors could marvel at drawings and models representing mechanical innovations, such as a proposal for a wooden bridge, or architectural projects, such as triumphal arches. Pictures were sometimes sewn on white silk, sometimes carved in ebony, and sculptures were quite often made of wax. A study of these entries reveals, however, that gender affected the possible choices. Male artists or architects – whether professionals or amateurs – would put forward all kinds of work except embroideries, while the female register was restricted to drawings, paintings and needlework.

The first members of the Swedish Academy were chosen as soon as it was awarded its statutes, in 1773. In a group of 15, one woman was invited, the portrait painter Ulrica Fredrica Pasch (q.v.). Recent research has pointed to her prolific activity that enabled her not only to earn her own living from early on, but also to support her father in his old age. An unusual portrait of c.1790 (Royal Academy of Fine Arts, Stockholm) representing Pasch in a dressing gown reinforces the impression of an established and self-assured artist who managed to co-exist alongside her male colleagues. Whether this painting is a self-portrait or emanates from the hand of her brother, Lorens Pasch the Younger, is difficult to ascertain, but since sitters often chose the way in which they were represented, this distinction is irrelevant. Pasch is set against a neutral background and wears a white tulle cap over her short curly hair. The black hooded garment is lined with blue and, judging by the graceful folds, made of a fine material. There seems to be no other painting of the period depicting a woman dressed in this way, although there are several portraits of men – and quite often of artists – dressed in a similar fashion. By thus representing themselves in the informal clothing used in portraits of wealthy merchants, professors, noblemen and gentlemen of the 18th century, artists were placing themselves in a higher social position than that usually ascribed to them. This particular dress, as Patricia Cunningham has noted ("Eighteenth-century nightgowns: The gentleman's robe in art and fashion", *Dress: Journal of the Costume Society of America*, x, 1984, pp.2–11), may be an indication of the fairly recent status accorded to artists, approaching that of writers, scholars and other intellectuals.

The use of the "undress formula" by a woman artist was an innovation that emphasises Pasch's position as an established artist and member of the Academy of Fine Arts. However, membership of the academies in both Stockholm and Copenhagen was accorded not only to professional artists but also to amateurs and patrons. This is one possible reason why women artists, who were excluded from regular training, have since been treated as amateurs. The two Danish artists who obtained member status in the later 18th century were both to a large degree self-taught: the royal flower painter Magdalene Margrethe Bärens, née Schäffer, who became a member in 1780, and Cathrina Maria Møller, who was elected in 1790. The engraver Marie Jeanne Clemens, née Crévoisier, who learned her trade from her husband, the artist Johann Friederich Clemens, was elected an *agréée* in Copenhagen in 1782; she would have been elected a full member on submission of a reception piece, but this never happened.

Bärens, who in her lifetime enjoyed being called the "first and best Danish flower painter", tried her fortune in London for two years in the late 1780s, but the competition there was evidently too stiff. She painted free compositions in gouache, mixing flowers from different seasons, based on her collection of sketches. She also made natural-looking sewn and painted fruit sculptures. Møller's reception pieces for membership of the Danish Academy were two embroideries in black thread on white silk, imitating copperplate engravings after paintings by Raphael. Such signed sewn pictures, appearing alongside paintings and sculptures, represent a transitional stage in the fast-changing 18th-century art world, at a time when the strict, hierarchical classification into higher and lower genres was not yet totally dominant, and copying from old masters was still a legitimate artistic occupation. The vulnerable status of these women artists, whose subjects and techniques were soon to be outranked, is emphasised by comparison with Johanna Marie Fosie (wife of a priest, Jens Eriksen Westengaard), who was only one generation older. Born in 1726, the daughter of the engraver Jacob Fosie, she mainly made landscapes, often taking Dutch paintings as models. But she also made still lifes, religious scenes and such curiosities as a rhinoceros from life, which she proudly signed "Johanna Fosie ad vivum delin et fec". A leather-bound and gold-stamped *album amicorum* (Det kongelige Bibliotek, Copenhagen), full of pictures and poems dedicated to Fosie by prominent artist-friends, suggests that she enjoyed a more prominent role than her women colleagues of a few decades later.

The Academy in Copenhagen served both Denmark and its subject country Norway. When the Norwegian amateur artist Catharine Hermine Kølle (b. 1788) was in her formative years and in need of training, the full effect of the sorted academy system had already come into force. As a woman she could neither enter the academy nor join a workshop of the disappearing guild system. It is illuminating to compare her situation with that of a contemporary, the Norwegian landscape painter Johan Christian Dahl, who was trained as a craftsman painter. With the help of sponsors, he soon got the opportunity of studying at the Royal Danish Academy of Fine Arts in Copenhagen, and thus managed to become a free artist and a professor at the Dresden Academy – and a Norwegian national hero. While Dahl became a professional artist, Kølle remained an exceptional amateur, painting exquisite watercolours and *vedute* of her mountain travels and walks to Italy and back, but restricted to showing her pictures to those who visited her at home. In effect, the art world in the Nordic countries was entirely structured by gender conventions and closed to women for a long time.

ANNA LENA LINDBERG

Britain

A state-sponsored academy of art was not established in Britain until 1768. The history of the formation of the Royal Academy of Arts and its forerunners, which included private academies run by artists themselves and societies of artists who banded together to produce public art exhibitions, must be seen as part of a search for a national identity in the arts that was closely tied to the commercial concerns of British artists who decried the lack of a native school of art and the importation of continental art and artists (see Bignamini 1989).

In the latter years of the 17th century a few private art academies set up for both professional and amateur artists provided training through the study of antique statuary and live models. Although traditional studios and workshops continued to provide training on an individual basis, by the middle of the 18th century a few academies were established to foster common artistic goals and standards under the guidance of a single instructor. A number of British artists, many of whom had travelled on the Continent and observed artistic training there, felt the need to organise life drawing classes along the lines of Italian and French theory and practice. The most important academic predecessor of the Royal Academy in London was the Academy in St Martin's Lane (1735–68), in which William Hogarth played a major role. Outside London, academies developed in Edinburgh (1729 and 1760), Dublin (1742), Birmingham (1754) and Glasgow (1754), providing instruction through the copying of paintings, prints and casts.

A unique feature of British academies was the regular employment of both female and male nude models in the life class. Since the Renaissance, European artists had studied from female models in the privacy of their studios, and they were occasionally used in some of the early Italian and German academies, but they did not become part of regular academic practice in Europe and America until the 19th century. In fact, throughout the 17th and 18th centuries the Académie Royale in Paris and the Académie Française in Rome forbade the use of naked female models at the same time that study of the nude male was the essential foundation of artistic theory and practice. For artists who could not afford to hire a woman to model in private, female anatomy was studied from antique sculpture and old master paintings, engravings or drawing books. Ironically, the British, who were so late in the development of an official academy, led the way in the systematic study of female anatomy through living models (see Nottingham and London 1991).

Societies for the promotion of the arts

The Society for the Encouragement of Arts, Manufactures and Commerce (Society of Arts), founded in London in 1754 to encourage inventions and improvements in the "Arts and Sciences", awarded premiums (prizes) for the best paintings in different categories, such as history or landscape, and to boys and girls under the age of 16 who produced the best drawings. In 1759 they also offered premiums for drawings from "Living Models at the Academy of Artists in St Martin's Lane ... by young men under 24 years". The practice of drawing from the live human figure, which was becoming standard practice for young male artists, was not considered appropriate for young women.

In the years just preceding the creation of the Royal Academy of Arts several groups of artists came together for the purposes of promoting contemporary British art through public exhibitions and raising money through admissions and the sale of catalogues. In 1760 the Society for the Encouragement of Arts, Manufactures and Commerce provided a room in London for an exhibition by one such group; however, the independent-minded artists wanted more autonomy than the Society was willing to allow in the charging of admission fees and the selection and hanging of their pictures, so in 1762 they broke away to form the Free Society of Artists and held their own exhibitions until 1783. Several women, such as Angelica Kauffman (1765, 1766 and 1783), were among the exhibitors. This group also formed a charitable fund to help artists and their families in times of need. Another breakaway rival group, the Society of Artists of Great Britain (1761), which became the Incorporated Society of Artists in 1765, held their own exhibitions until 1791, and these also included works by women artists such as Mary Moser (q.v.) and Katharine Read (q.v.).

Foundation of the Royal Academy of Arts

After this long and sometimes bitter campaign by different factions of British artists, on 10 December 1768 the Royal Academy of Arts was founded under the protection of George III (see Bignamini and Hutchison in Boschloo 1989). The *Instrument of Foundation* laid down regulations for membership of the Academy and its governance under a Council and an elected President, a position first filled by Joshua Reynolds. During his presidency (1768–92) Reynolds delivered a series of lectures, later published as *Discourses on Art*, in which he laid out his ideas for the theory and practice of academic art. The *Instrument of Foundation* also specified how business should be conducted, the establishment of an annual public exhibition of paintings, sculptures and designs, and a programme of instruction patterned on the Italian and French academies that stressed mathematics and perspective, as well as anatomy studied from the antique and from living models. Instruction in the Academy schools was supervised by artists called Visitors who were elected from the membership, in addition to professors of anatomy, perspective and geometry, painting and architecture. A Keeper of the Royal Academy fulfilled the responsibility of providing life models, books, casts and other items essential for artistic education. Admission to the school was restricted to students who could demonstrate their abilities to the Visitors, the Keeper and the Council.

Membership in the Royal Academy consisted of 40 painters, sculptors and architects. After the initial appointment of the founding members, all future vacancies were to be filled by election from among the participants in the annual exhibitions, which were open to "all Artists of distinguished merit", as judged by a committee of academicians. After 1770 a separate category called Associates of the Royal Academy was established. This was limited to 20 in number and was originally intended as a way to add more engravers to the membership, albeit with lesser status. Another adjunct group were honorary members, which included antiquaries and professors of ancient literature and history.

Women in the Royal Academy

Among the 40 founding members were two highly accomplished women artists, Kauffman and Moser, the latter the daughter of the first Keeper of the Royal Academy, George Moser. The Swiss-born and Italian-trained Kauffman had arrived in London just two years earlier, but had already made a major impression on a number of influential artists and patrons. Although a foreigner, Kauffman's background and skills as a history painter, the highest category of painting, which Reynolds and others hoped to promote, made her a valuable asset in the struggle to cultivate patrons and to gain recognition for art produced in Britain. The fact that she was a woman and a foreigner seemed less important than her status as a history painter who could serve as role model for the type of artist Britain needed. Among the founding members, Moser was one of only two flower painters, a much lower rank in the hierarchy of painting; however, the combination of her father's influence and her precocious talent gained her a place within this elite group. She had been awarded a silver prize by the Society of Arts in 1759, at the age of 15.

While Kauffman and Moser were not expected to attend meetings, they did take part in the judging for gold medals and travelling scholarships by sending in marked lists. They also voted in elections. Kauffman mailed her votes in the form of letters to the President, but between 1779 and 1810 Moser often attended general assemblies and participated in Academy proceedings. No doubt inspired by the two female academicians, the Incorporated Society of Artists, which continued to exist as a separate body, elected several women to honorary memberships in 1769. These were the painters Read, Mary

Grace, Mary Benwell, Eliza Gardiner and Mary Black, the last a skilful copyist of old master paintings.

Before the mid-19th century there seems to have been an unofficial limit on the admission of women to the Academy schools. There was, in fact, by that time a separate government Female School of Art and Design (1843) to which the Academy contributed money, a factor that discouraged women applicants to the Royal Academy Schools. Nevertheless, in 1860 a female artist, Laura Anne Herford, was admitted to the Antique School by judges who did not suspect she was a woman because her drawings had been identified only by her initials. Soon after, a few more women students were accepted, including Louisa Starr (q.v.), who won medals in 1865 and 1867. With the admission of even a limited number of women students, the Council acted to ensure observation of the strictest propriety.

Women artists and the life class

The best-known early representation of the Royal Academy is Johann Zoffany's informal group portrait of 1771–2 (see illustration) in which the members are portrayed in Old Somerset House, London, the first home of the Academy. Casts of antique statues are arranged along the wall behind the artists, but the primary function of this room was life drawing, an activity central to the Academy's programme. All the artists can be identified, and include the painter Zoffany at the far left and the first President, Sir Joshua Reynolds, who stands near the centre of the picture with his characteristic ear trumpet. He is one of the few figures who does not direct his attention towards the two male models at the far right of the picture, one disrobing in the foreground and the other posing under the direction of the Keeper, George Moser. The two female founding members of the Royal Academy are physically absent from this scene and are represented only by their portraits hanging on the wall above the male models. Despite Kauffman's and Moser's participation in just about every function of the Academy, as Linda Nochlin observed in her essay "Why have there been no great women artists?" (1971), Zoffany's decision to set the scene in the life class made their marginalisation very apparent.

The Royal Academy held winter and summer terms for the "Academy of Living Models, men and women of different characters" provided by the Keeper. Four male models were employed daily to sit for two hours, the established practice in European academies, holding the same pose aided by a rope or staff, as seen in Zoffany's picture. A female model sat three nights a week, every other week. They were better paid than the men but were regarded with curiosity and suspicion, considered no better than prostitutes, which many of them may have been. To ensure proper decorum no unmarried men under the age of 20 were permitted to draw from the female nude, and no others except members of the royal family were admitted during the time the model was sitting. Women artists were not allowed to draw from the nude model in the Royal Academy until 1893, when the partially draped figure was introduced into the female life class.

Under these circumstances Moser and Kauffman did not attend life class; nevertheless, an unusual drawing by Moser of a full-length standing female nude (Fitzwilliam Museum, Cambridge, repr. Nottingham 1982, p.45) suggests that she

Johann Zoffany: *Life Class at the Royal Academy*, 1771–2; Royal Collection, © Her Majesty Queen Elizabeth II

may have had the opportunity to study from a female model, perhaps at the St Martin's Lane Academy, where her father had provided models as he did in his later role as Keeper of the Royal Academy. However, this drawing may simply have been copied from the work of a male colleague. Similarly, Kauffman managed to overcome the obstacle of exclusion from the life class – a serious drawback for a history painter – by copying academy drawings by other artists, casts of Classical sculpture, and the heads and limbs of clothed living models.

In later years malicious rumours suggested that Kauffman had disguised herself as a man so that she could slip into the Academy to attend the life class, or that she hired male models to pose in the privacy of her studio. J.T. Smith wrote in *Nollekens and His Times* (London, 1824) that he asked the model Charles Cranmer, the same man who sat for Reynolds, if this were true. Cranmer assured him that although he had modelled for Kauffman many years earlier, her father was always present, and he had only bared his arms, shoulders and legs for her to draw. Kauffman's biographer had decried a similar method and insisted that she always adhered to the strictest propriety in her work. Women artists were forced to tread a fine line between mastering necessary academic skills and maintaining their reputations.

Frances Reynolds, the sister of Sir Joshua Reynolds and a painter herself, was said to have expressed the opinion that it was a great pity drawing from nude models should be a necessary part of the education of a painter. Her view was noted by James Northcote, Joshua Reynolds's pupil and assistant, in a letter dated 21 December 1771, in which he added: "Miss Reynolds drew all her figures clothed except infants". In Northcote's own opinion, it was "impossible to make a good history painter and not know the human figure well, for many great painters drew the outlines of the body always before they did the drapery on them" (Whitley 1928, ii, p.287).

Women in the Royal Academy exhibitions in the 18th century

The Academy annual exhibitions continued to grow so that by 1779 more than 400 works were shown. The hanging committee was quite strict in their control over the appropriateness of submissions. The "high" arts of painting and sculpture were favoured over the "low" arts and crafts, and while any professional or amateur was allowed to submit work, the standard was biased in favour of academically trained artists. Needlework, artificial flowers and models in coloured wax were displayed in other contemporary exhibitions, but after 1771 they were specifically excluded from the Royal Academy. In 1791 a Miss Lane tried to submit a picture made of hair but was rejected. Other types of art excluded from consideration were drawings copied after paintings, and in some cases engravings after works of art were not allowed. This emphasis on originality and academic training made it almost impossible for most women artists to gain acceptance even though they were not officially excluded by the rules.

Despite these rigid restrictions some women artists apart from the academicians Kauffman and Moser were able to show their work at the annual exhibitions. One of them was the prodigy Helen Beatson, who in 1779 exhibited a picture at the tender age of eleven years. Read was also a frequent exhibitor, and Maria Cosway (q.v.) showed 42 portraits and subject paintings from mythology and literature between 1781 and 1801.

Frances Reynolds exhibited two pictures at the Royal Academy in 1774, *Children Going to Bed* (no.354) and *The Garland, from Prior* (no.355). They are officially identified as by "A Lady" with no indication of her name, but we know that they were hers because a reviewer commented on no.354:

> We do not remember ever to have seen a prettier subject for the exercise of a lady's pencil ..., nor could it perhaps be better made use of in the hands of a more experienced artist ... The public are indebted for this picture to Miss Reynolds, sister to the President of the Royal Academy.

The following year she exhibited *Lace Makers* (no.382), a miniature, described by a critic as "a pretty, elegant, feeling picture". Unfortunately, her brother's view was that her pictures made him cry and others laugh (Whitley 1928, i, pp.297–8). Unlike Kauffman, Moser and Cosway, who pursued painting as a profession and were taken more or less seriously, Frances Reynolds felt herself relegated to amateur status by her brother's attitude and social aspirations, which restricted her to the role of a proper gentlewoman and frustrated her artistic ambitions. She confessed in a letter to a friend that she "envyd the female competitors in the exhibition" and pointed out that there were "other female competitors besides those who made it a profession" (Wendorf 1996, pp.80–81).

Kauffman exhibited numerous portraits and history paintings during her years in London and even after her return to Italy in 1781, often sending in as many as five or six a year. In 1771 the artist Mrs Delany wrote: "This morning we have been to see Mr [Benjamin] West's and Mrs Angelica's paintings ... My partiality leans to my sister painter. She certainly has a great deal of merit, but I like her history still better than her portraits" (*The Autobiography and Correspondence of Mary Granville, Mrs Delany*, ed. Lady Llanover, 6 vols, London: Bentley, 1861–2; reprinted New York: AMS Press, 1974). Kauffman generally received very favourable notices for her works, especially history paintings. The reviewers' high regard may be interpreted as expressions in support of that genre's importance as much as praise for Kauffman herself. In addition, even positive reviews were sometimes moderated by criticism of certain weaknesses, especially the "effeminacy" of the male characters. With their smooth contours and covered limbs, her painted men may have reflected her lack of study of male anatomy, or they could have been deliberately modelled to resemble the Roman relief sculptures of beautiful young men so admired by antiquarians.

In 1775 a notorious incident involving Kauffman caused a stir in the Academy. Another artist, Nathaniel Hone, sent a painting to the annual exhibition called *The Conjuror* (National Gallery of Ireland, Dublin). This picture showed an old bearded magician waving his wand over a group of engravings of famous old master paintings, while a little girl leaned coyly on his knee looking at a large open book. Viewers recognised it immediately as a satiric attack on Reynolds's method of borrowing motifs from well-known works of art to incorporate into his compositions, and the little girl may have been understood to represent his friend and inspiration, Kauffman. However, the reason it was finally removed from public view in the Royal Academy was Kauffman's written objection to what she believed was a small nude female figure intended to represent her. The figure in question was in the background among a group of artists waving paintbrushes towards St Paul's Cathedral, an allusion to a decorative project in which Kauffman was to take part. After a group from the Royal Academy tried to persuade her to allow Hone's picture, she wrote indignantly with threats to remove her own paintings if *The Conjuror* remained. In the end Kauffman won, the painting was removed and the offending figure painted out.

Kauffman's decorative paintings for the Royal Academy

In 1780 the Academy moved to new quarters in Somerset House in the Strand, and plans were developed for a series of allegorical ceiling paintings to represent the theoretical basis of academic art. Kauffman, who was included in this important scheme, was assigned four oval paintings of allegorical images to represent the four parts of painting: *Invention, Composition, Design* and *Colour*. They were set into the ceiling of the Council Chamber around a central painting by Benjamin West that represented *Nature*, the *Three Graces* and the *Four Elements*. Kauffman's complex and subtle female personifications characterise the theory of art as expressed in Reynolds's lectures, which were originally delivered in this room. In 1837 the paintings were moved to the library of the Academy's new premises in Trafalgar Square. Since 1899 these paintings and the ones by West have been on the ceiling of the entrance hall of the Royal Academy's current home in Burlington House.

Women academicians after Kauffman and Moser

The status and respect granted to Kauffman and Moser as female academicians were never real issues within the Royal Academy, but it was a very long time before another woman was elected to their ranks. In 1879 the admission of women to membership of the Royal Academy was seriously considered when Lady Butler (q.v.) missed election by a narrow margin. The Council decided that since the *Instrument of Foundation* (1768) had specified that members must be "men of fair moral character" as well as artists of "high reputation in their profession" – the historical status of Kauffman and Moser notwithstanding – women were ineligible. Nevertheless, at the request of the General Assembly a resolution was put forward to allow for the election of women but with limited "privileges". In fact no female members were elected until Annie Swynnerton (q.v.) and Laura Knight (q.v.) became Associates, in 1922 and 1927 respectively. Knight achieved full status as Royal Academician in 1936, more than 150 years after the two women founding members.

WENDY WASSYNG ROWORTH

Bibliography

General

Nikolaus Pevsner, *Academies of Art Past and Present*, Cambridge: Cambridge University Press, and New York: Macon, 1940; reprinted New York: Da Capo, 1973 (important study of the history of academies of art with extensive bibliography)

Linda Nochlin, "Why have there been no great women artists?", *Woman in Sexist Society: Studies in Power and Powerlessness*, ed. Vivian Gornick and Barbara K. Moran, New York: Basic Books, 1971; reprinted New American Library, 1972, pp.480–510

Ann Sutherland Harris, "Introduction", *Women Artists, 1550–1950*, exh. cat., Los Angeles County Museum of Art, and elsewhere, 1976, pp.15–44

Jennifer M. Fletcher, "The glory of the female sex: Women artists, c.1500–1800", *The Women's Art Show, 1550–1970*, exh. cat., Nottingham Castle Museum, 1982, pp.8–10

Cynthia E. Roman, "Academic ideals of art education", *Children of Mercury: The Education of Artists in the Sixteenth and Seventeenth Centuries*, exh. cat., Brown University, Providence, RI, 1984, pp.81–95

Laura Olmstead Tonelli, "Academic practice in the sixteenth and seventeenth centuries", *ibid.*, pp.95–107

Anton W.A. Boschloo and others, eds, *Academies of Art Between Renaissance and Romanticism*, The Hague: SDU, 1989 (an important source, with extensive bibliographies on academies in Europe, although there is no specific discussion of women)

Bettina Baumgärtel, *Angelika Kauffmann (1741–1807): Bedingungen weiblicher Kreativität in der Malerei des 18. Jahrhunderts*, Weinheim and Basel, 1990 (Kauffman and other women artists in academies)

Italy

Melchior Missirini, *Memorie per servire alla storia della Romana Accademia di San Luca fino alla morte di Antonio Canova*, Rome, 1823

Jean Arnaud, *L'Académie de Saint-Luc à Rome (Considerations historiques depuis son origine jusqu'à nos jours)*, Rome: Loescher, 1886

Vincenzo Golzio, *La galleria e le collezioni dell'Accademia di San Luca in Rome*, Rome: La Libreria dello Stato, 1966

Italo Faldi, "Dipinti di figura dal rinascimento al neoclassicism", *L'Accademia Nazionale di San Luca*, ed. C. Petrangeli and others, Rome: De Luca, 1974, pp.158–70 (paintings by Rosalba Carriera and Angelica Kauffman in the Accademia di San Luca, Rome)

Stefano Susinno, "I ritratti degli academici", *ibid.*, pp.201–70 (portraits and self-portraits of various women artists in the Accademia di San Luca, Rome)

A. Cipriani, "L'Accademia di San Luca dai Concorsi dei Giovani ai Concorsi Clementini" in Boschloo 1989, pp.61–76

France

Georges Duplessis, ed., *Mémoires et journal de J.G. Wille*, 2 vols, Paris: Renouard, 1857

J.J. Guiffrey, "Ecoles de demoiselles dans les ateliers de David et de Suvée au Louvre", *Nouvelles Archives de l'Art Français*, 1874–5, pp.396–7

Procès-verbaux de l'Académie Royale de Peinture et de Sculpture, ed. Anatole de Montaiglon, 11 vols, Paris: J. Baur and Charavay Frères, 1875–92; reprinted Paris: Nobele, 1972 (minutes of meetings of the French Academy; invaluable source for information on women in the Academy)

Octave Fidière, *Les Femmes artistes à l'Académie Royale de Peinture et de Sculpture*, Paris: Charavay Frères, 1885 (factual overview of women in the French Academy based on primary sources)

Etienne Charavay, "Réception de Mmes Vigée-Lebrun et Guiard à l'Académie de peinture", *Nouvelles Archives de l'Art Français*, vi, 1890, Paris: Dumolin, pp. 181–2

J.J. Guiffrey, *Histoire de l'Académie de Saint-Luc*, published as vol.ix of *Archives de l'Art Français*, Paris: Champion, 1915 (history of the painters' guild, the Académie de Saint-Luc, which included many women artists)

Jacques Silvestre de Sacy, *Le Comte d'Angiviller, dernier Directeur Général des Bâtiments du Roi*, Paris: Plon, 1953

Marianne Roland Michel, *Anne Vallayer-Coster, 1744–1818*, Paris: CIL, 1970 (contains extensive discussion of Vallayer-Coster's association with the Academy)

Anne-Marie Passez, *Adélaïde Labille-Guiard (1749–1803): Biographie et catalogue raisonné de son oeuvre*, Paris: Arts et Métiers Graphiques, 1973 (includes substantial discussion of Labille-Guiard and Vigée-Lebrun in relation to the Academy)

Elisabeth Vigée-Lebrun, *Souvenirs*, ed. Claudine Herrmann, 2 vols, Paris: Des Femmes, 1984

Thomas E. Crow, *Painters and Public Life in Eighteenth-Century Paris*, New Haven: Yale University Press, 1985 (no specific discussion of women, but considers many other aspects of academic practice from the founding of the Academy to the French Revolution; particularly strong on relation between Academy and political events)

Albert Boime, *The Academy and French Painting in the Nineteenth Century*, revised edition, New Haven, Yale University Press, 1986 (although there is no specific analysis of women in the Academy, this book provides a full discussion of academic practices in the 19th century)

Candace Clements, "The Academy and the other: Les graces and le genre galant", *Eighteenth-Century Studies*, xxv, 1992, pp.469–94 (discusses practices of life drawing in the Academy)

Reed Benhamou, *Public and Private Art Education in France*, published as volume of *Studies on Voltaire and the Eighteenth Century*, Oxford: Siden Press, 1993 (discusses all aspects of artistic education throughout France, including both the Académie Royale and provincial academies; extensive bibliography)

Mary D. Sheriff, *The Exceptional Woman: Elisabeth Vigée-Lebrun and the Cultural Politics of Art*, Chicago: University of Chicago Press, 1996 (includes analysis of the Academy's attitudes towards women artists and a short history of women in the Academy; extensive bibliography)

Nordic countries

Hans Jorgen Birch, *Billedgallerie for Fruentimmer, indeholdende Levnetsbeskrivelser over beromte og larde danske, norske og udenlandske Fruentimmere* [Picture gallery for women, containing biographies of famous and learned Danish, Norwegian and foreign women], 3 vols, Copenhagen, 1793–5

Ludvig Looström, *Den svenska Konstakademien under första århundradet af hennes tillvaro, 1735–1835* [The Swedish Academy of Fine Arts during its first century, 1735–1835], Stockholm: Looström & Komp, 1887

Else Kai Sass, "Kvinden som skabende kunstner" [Woman as creative artist], *Kvinden i Danmark*, ed. Lisbet Hindsgaul and Kate Fleron, Odense: Skandinavisk Bogforlag, 1942, pp.693–748

Torben Holck Colding and others, *Akademiet og Guldalderen, 1750–1850* [The Academy and the golden age, 1750–1850], Dansk Kunsthistorie, billed Kunst og Skulptur, 3, Copenhagen: Politiken, 1972

Borgerkunst: Hos familien Fosie på Ostergade omkring 1750 [Bourgeois art: At the family Fosie in East Street around 1750], exh. cat., Kobenhavns bymuseum, Copenhagen, 1977

Bengt von Bonsdorff and others, *Konsten i Finland från medeltid till nutid* [Art in Finland from the Middle Ages to the present day], Helsinki: Schildt, 1978

Anna Lena Lindberg and Barbro Werkmäster, "Kvinnliga konstnärer i Norden" in Germaine Greer, *Hinderloppet: Kvinnans väg genom konsten* [The obstacle race: The fortunes of women painters and their work], Uppsala: Brombergs, 1980, pp.328–44

Christina Granroth, *Margareta Capsia: Biografiska uppgifter och tre bibliska motiv* [Margareta Capsia: Biography and three biblical motifs], dissertation, Helsinki University, Institute of Art History, 1985

Anka Ryall and Jorunn Veiteberg, *En kvinnelig oppdagelsereisende i det unga Norge: Catharine Hermine Kølle* [A woman explorer in the young Norway: Catharine Hermine Kølle], Oslo: Pax, 1991

Magne Malmanger, "Fra klassisisme til tidlig realisme, 1814–1870" [From classicism to realism, 1814–1870], *Norges malerkunst: Fra hoymiddelalderen til 1900* [The art of painting in Norway: From the High Middle Ages to 1900], i, ed. Knut Berg, Oslo: Gyldendal Norsk Forlag, 1993, pp.187–350

Margareta Willner-Rönnholm, *Åbo ritskola, 1830–1981: En konstskolas utveckling, verksamhetsbetingelser och roll under olika skeden* [Åbo/Turku drawing school, 1830–1981: The development, requirements and significance of an art school], dissertation, Åbo/Turku Academy Institute of Art History, 1993

Anna Lena Lindberg, "Ulrica Fredrica Pasch and the 'Eternal Feminine'", *Woman's Art Journal*, xv/2, 1994–5, pp.3–8

——, "'One and onlies': Capsia, Pasch and Kølle and the artist profession in early modern northern Europe", *Konsthistorisk tidskrift* (in preparation)

Britain

G. Baretti, *A Guide Through the Royal Academy*, London, 1781 (includes description of ceiling paintings by Angelica Kauffman)

Algernon Graves, *The Royal Academy of Arts: A Complete Dictionary of Contributors and Their Work from Its Foundation in 1769 to 1904*, 8 vols, London: Graves, 1905–6; reprinted New York: Franklin, 1972

William T. Whitley, *Artists and Their Friends in England, 1700–1799*, 2 vols, London, 1928; reprinted New York: Blom, 1968

M. Butlin, "An eighteenth-century art scandal: Nathaniel Hone's 'The Conjuror'", *Connoisseur*, clxxiv, 1970, pp.1–9 (includes Kauffman's correspondence with the Royal Academy with her objections to this satirical painting)

Sidney C. Hutchison, *The History of the Royal Academy, 1768–1986*, 2nd edition, London: Royce, 1986

John Newman, "Reynolds and Hone: 'The Conjuror'", *Reynolds*, exh. cat., Royal Academy, London, 1986, pp.344–54 (discussion of satirical painting attacking Reynolds and Kauffman)

Ilaria Bignamini, "'The 'Academy of Art' in Britain before the foundation of the Royal Academy" in Boschloo 1989, pp.434–50

Sidney C. Hutchison, "The Royal Academy of Arts in London: Its history and activities" in Boschloo 1989, pp.451–63

The Artist's Model: Its Role in British Art from Lely to Etty, exh. cat., University Art Gallery, Nottingham, and Iveagh Bequest, Kenwood, London, 1991 (examines British artists' use of life models and antique statuary in academies and private studios)

Richard Wendorf, *Sir Joshua Reynolds: The Painter in Society*, Cambridge, MA: Harvard University Press, 1996 (on Frances Reynolds; also Reynolds's friendship with Kauffman)

Copyists

Copies and the reproductive arts

Throughout the early modern period, copies played an important reproductive role in the visual culture of Western Europe. Although prints could and did duplicate the subject matter and format of an image, the colour, style and particular qualities of the original medium were absent. Before the 19th-century development of planographic and photo-mechanical techniques of reproduction, copying a painting in the same medium as the original was one of the few viable means to achieve a close replication of all its qualities. The copy and copying were thus important both to the practices of the consumers who commissioned or purchased such images and to those of the artists who made them.

During the Renaissance, as paintings became greatly esteemed for their aesthetic qualities, political or ideological significance, and as costly, class-marking commodities, the demand for copies of acclaimed works of art grew quickly. Copies enabled the development of a unique identity for each individual painting and also allowed the dissemination of the image to a wider audience. Regardless of the particular organising principle motivating the patron or collector – indexical, historical, monographic, geographic or purely decorative – copies served to fill important lacunae in the collections of many important connoisseurs. As northern Europeans from France, Britain and the German and Nordic countries sought to emulate the opulent habits of the picture-collecting Italian nobility, copies enabled an exact appropriation of many of the visual components of this culture. Indeed, copies were in many ways preferable to original paintings in that they had the added value of illustrating the published histories and theoretical texts that formed the basis of a pan-European polite discourse on art. Moreover, they maintained reference to the contextual significance of the original as well as to those of the entire network of other similar copies. Well into the 19th and 20th centuries, this pattern of cultural arrogation continued to be an important model for the *nouveau riche* of the Americas and other European colonies who sought acceptance from the cultural mainstream of Europe. Once installed within these new colonial contexts, copies, particularly those of important religious paintings, royal or official portraits, or ideologically-charged history paintings, contributed greatly to the processes of acculturation and control imposed upon subservient nations.

For the artist, copying was a primary step in his or her training. Academic theory dictated that the student first learn to draw by copying prints and drawings before taking models from life. When facility in drawing had been attained, students then learned an understanding of colour and the application of paint by copying the work of their teachers as well as that of famous masters. Students were frequently restricted to copying until they had attained the necessary skill and command of their master's technique and style. They were then judged able and ready to challenge or surpass the accomplishments of their predecessors with their own unique vision. Many artists continued to copy throughout their lifetimes in order to practise, to learn from or to pay homage to other masters' work. Even though modernist ideologies of artistic production privileged original work above all else, copying and the graphic reproductive arts continued to be important (although often concealed) elements of the workshop practices of many prominent artists until well into the 19th century. Consumer demand for versions or replications of the master's more popular works was the economic foundation of most workshops, especially those of portrait painters. Many artists followed the examples set by Raphael, Titian and Rubens, who had all recognised the importance of artistic reproduction for the augmentation and propagation of their reputations. The work and reputation of women artists in particular have been intimately tied to both the production and the concept of the copy from the Renaissance until the recent past.

Copying and the education of the artist

Traditional academic practice advocated that both male and female students should learn drawing by first copying, from other drawings or prints, the simplest outlines of bodily components such as heads, eyes, hands, limbs, etc. Once these were mastered and synthesised into entire bodies, the student advanced to the copying of finished drawings, prints and plaster casts, while at the same time developing expertise in the techniques of shading, working in ink, chalk or pastel, and painting in washes. Only then did the student draw from life or raw nature. Female art students often completed these early stages of artistic training only to be discouraged from continuing their studies at the next level – that of figure drawing. Women were prevented on the grounds of morality from participating in these drawing classes, which, in general, focused on the study of the nude male body, and were deemed the basis for the expressive portrayal of human thought and action in that highest genre of subject matter, history painting. Such classes were sponsored and regulated by the many academies of art established throughout Europe during the 17th, 18th and 19th centuries, and which were generally structured to favour male over female students (see Academies of Art survey). Female participation was not only prohibited in the life-drawing class, but was also increasingly discouraged or rigidly controlled in many of the other aspects of the curriculum, prize-givings or exhibitions institutionalised by most academies of art. Ambitious women attempted to circumvent this restriction by copying other students' figure studies, by moving on to the next stage of training (which consisted of learning the theory and application of paint and colour by copying from pre-existing paintings), or by surreptitiously hiring their own models. However, as authentic knowledge of the human body was considered essential for the skilled artist, critics held this lack of training against women artists, regardless of their real ability or accomplishment. Consequently, many women were prevented from taking the educational steps that would enable them to rise from the immature status of the journeyman or amateur to the level of the professional artist fully legitimised with academic credentials.

Workshop practices

Copying was an important component of the work performed in the collaborative system of the studio, *bottega* or workshop, the most prevalent structure for the production of paintings in Europe before the 20th century. Headed by a prominent master who was personally unable to supply the demand for his pictures, these workshops served both to educate and employ other artists who were collectively responsible for its production of images. Such studios not only provided for the reproduction of the master's original work but also the continued care and conservation of images that had already left the workshop. Women artists often participated in these collaborations, either as students or as assistants. The actual division of labour within such organisations varied; masters either assigned work as it was needed or contracted skilled individuals to specialise in particular tasks. Such responsibilities included the preparation of pigments and canvases, the blocking-in and underpainting of the figures, the painting of costumes, landscape elements, draperies and backgrounds, the cleaning and conservation of older works, and the production of studio copies. Portrait studios in particular were responsible for a tremendous number of copies and versions of a master's work (or those of other artists). Studio work would then be finished (perhaps) and signed by the master whose signature attested to a certain standard of style or execution.

An easily exploitable workforce – both inexpensive and available – for the studio of a painter was that of his female relatives. Several women artists of the early modern period received their training in the arts as a result of being related to male artists. Some managed to become independent and professional artists in their own right, but many remained as assistants in the studios of their fathers, brothers or husbands. Marriages between the daughters or sisters of artists and other artists served not only to form familial as well as professional bonds between various workshops, but also to transfer skills and labour from one studio to another. Many of these daughters, sisters and wives specialised in the reproductive aspects of the workshop's practice, freeing their male relations for more creative work. These women not only painted, but also often drew, etched and engraved, in full-scale or miniature, their copies of the more popular images of the master. While an artist's male offspring were also frequently trained to follow in their father's footsteps, they would eventually be expected to challenge, surpass and leave behind their parent/teachers; daughters by training and social convention were not expected to advance to this stage of creative autonomy. The best that many could expect to accomplish was to imitate their fathers' style and technique so expertly and closely as to be indistinguishable from them. The work of these women was thus marked with the identity of their male relatives and not their own. Marietta Robusti (q.v.), the daughter of Tintoretto, worked in a style so closely modelled on her father's that only one picture is today attributed to her. The "faithful" and exact copyist whose work could not be distinguished from that of her father became a *topos* for the praise of daughter-artists such as Anne Louise de Deyster (1690–1747) who further merged her identity with that of her father by becoming his biographer as well as his copyist. Indeed, it was by no means unusual for male artists to appropriate the works of their talented female relatives; both Orazio Gentileschi and Johann Joseph Kauffman claimed to have done paintings actually produced by their daughters, Artemisia Gentileschi and Angelica Kauffman (both q.v.).

The inclusion of wives, daughters and sisters in the family business (albeit in the more mechanical aspects of it) was typical throughout Europe during the 16th, 17th and even 18th centuries. As most middle-class businesses were conducted on the same premises as domestic life, women of the early modern period often contributed to a broader range of the family's business activities than mere care of the family. Preparation of canvases, the laying-in of backgrounds, the painting of drapery or landscape elements, as well as responsibility for the reproduction of the studio's more popular or important works, were frequently the province of female family members. In Italy, Agnese Dolci (d. 1689) was trained by her father Carlo to be a successful copyist in his style; other less-known daughter-artists include Vittoria Farinato and Rosalia Novelli who both copied for their fathers. In Spain, Dorotea Joanes (d. 1609) and Margarita Joanes (d. 1613) collaborated with their father Vicente Juan Macip, as did Isabel Sanchez Coello (1564-1612), who produced the tremendous number of copies of the royal portraits painted by her father, Claudio Coello, for the Spanish court. In England, Susanna Penelope Rosse, the daughter of the court dwarf/painter Richard Gibson, was instructed by her father in watercolour and oil painting and her copies in miniature of many of the paintings in the royal collection were highly praised by contemporary critics. In the later 18th century, Maria Cosway (q.v.) reproduced much of her husband's work for him in soft-ground etching. In France, Madelaine Hérault (1635–82), daughter of the landscape painter, Antoine Hérault, was trained by her father and served as a copyist first for his studio and then, after her marriage to Noël Coypel, for her husband's studio. Her sister Antoinette was a successful copyist in miniature of old master paintings whose marriage to Guillaume Chastel provided an important connection for her family with the prestigious engraving family. Their niece Marie Cathérine, daughter of their painter-brother Charles Antoine, also married a painter, Silvestre le Jeune, who was called to Dresden to serve as court painter to Augustus II. There, Marie Cathérine, like many of the other women of her family, helped her husband with the preliminary tasks of the workshop as well as with the numerous copies required of the official court portraits. Their daughter Marie Maximilienne Silvestre (1708–97) continued the family tradition by copying in the workshops of her male relatives as had her female forebears. In Florence, Anna Bacherini Piattoli (1720–88), wife and mother to two other painters, Gaetano and Giuseppe Piattoli, served as a court painter specialising in pastel and miniature portraits and religious scenes, many of which seem to have been copies of other masters' works. Her work is known today only through three self-portraits, one of which was completed in 1776 for the famous Medici collection of self-portraits. Here she modestly portrays herself at her work table, copying Andrea del Sarto's *Madonna del Sacco* in miniature. A most extreme example of family collaboration was that of the Edinburgh Nasmyth family, in the early 19th century. Alexander Nasmyth trained and employed all of his four sons and his daughters Anne, Barbara, Charlotte, Elizabeth, Jane and Margaret in his combined drawing school/picture manufactory. While the sons were trained as professional painters within the academic system, each of the daughters was put to work teaching drawing to ladies or in the mass production of the generic "Claudian" Scottish landscape paintings associated with the family. This familial organisation of studio labour continued well into the 19th century: Lucy Madox Brown (q.v.) and her sister Catherine (later Mrs Hueffer), daughters of the painter Ford Madox Brown, did preparatory work and produced copies for their father.

For many artists, skill in the arts was the only training they could give their daughters to ensure their future living. Teaching art also became a professional option as watercolour painting and drawing developed during the 18th century into important drawing-room accomplishments for young women of the upper classes. Mary Black, the daughter of Thomas Black, served as an assistant to the portrait painter Allan Ramsay and supported herself as a portrait painter, as a copyist of contemporary portraits and old master paintings, and as a teacher of painting for fashionable young women. Another of Ramsay's studio assistants, Philip Reinagle, trained his two daughters Fanny and Charlotte in miniature copying and both displayed their work at the Royal Academy and British Institution exhibitions. The sister of the painter Hugh Douglas Hamilton, Maria Bell (later Lady Bell), as well as his daughter Harriott Hamilton (later Mrs John Way), were both successful copyists of old master paintings and contemporary portraits. Anne Forbes (q.v.), the granddaughter of William Aikman, was trained as a portrait painter and copyist and served as the copyist of old master paintings in the Roman studio of the Neo-classical painter Gavin Hamilton between c.1768 and 1771.

Not all women copyists served as useful and convenient appendages to the practices of their families. Mary Beale (q.v.) was the daughter of John Cradock, a Suffolk parson and enthusiastic amateur painter from whom she may have received some early training. She married Charles Beale, a Deputy Clerk in the Patents Office, in 1652 and the young couple settled in Covent Garden, the centre for London's artistic community from which they made several friends. Mary took a more serious interest in painting at this point, studying with Walker, and possibly Lely, two of the most prominent portrait painters of the day. By 1670 Charles's career in the Patents Office had faltered and Mary began painting professionally in order to support her young family. Her social connections among the clergy formed the basis for a clientele and her artist-friends obliged her by throwing other commissions and much copying work in her way. She soon became the centre of a busy studio modelled closely upon those of her male associates. Her husband, Charles, stretched canvases, ground colours and served as her business manager by keeping records of her work and acting as her public intermediary. Her two sons, Charles and Bartholomew, both trained by their mother, assisted her by painting backgrounds and draperies. She also took students, including two young women, Keaty Tioche and Sarah Curtis. Curtis, who married the Revd Benjamin Hoadley in 1701, modelled her own professional practice (focused for the most part on portraiture and copying) after that of her teacher and soon became a rival. Both women attracted attention through their unusual career choices. Mary Beale's work was studied with great interest and curiosity by the art chroniclers George Vertue and Horace Walpole, who wrote favourably concerning her style and production during the mid-18th century. Beale's success was due not only to her talent, but also because she never challenged or stepped over contemporary boundaries constraining male and female social spheres. Her genteel social class provided her with a clientele, the scale of her work was small and not very costly, she frequently took as sitters children, women and servants (subjects not threatening to her male rivals), and was not overly fastidious about accepting excess work from other artists' studios. Moreover, she modestly allowed her husband to represent her in the more public aspects of the business. Throughout the 18th and 19th centuries, women such as Mary

Beale with artistic talent turned to copying as a marginal, but viable profession.

Within the studios of those women artists who achieved a modicum of fame, such as the Swiss painter Angelica Kauffman, copying still played an important role. Kauffman, like most of her male contemporaries, spent a considerable period of training in Italy, copying in the leading collections there. Even after establishing herself as one of the leading history painters in London, she was frequently requested by her clientele to copy not only her own work but that of other masters as well. Several decorative programmes undertaken by Kauffman included copies after artists such as Titian, Guercino, Domenichino and Guido Reni as well as her own work. Kauffman's decorative work in particular found favour with her fashionable clientele; in order to take advantage of the popularity of her work, Kauffman worked closely with print-makers and publishers of reproductive prints. Several of her designs were reproduced in Matthew Boulton's and Francis Eginton's "Mechanical Paintings" project (1770s-80s), and used as decorative panels on furniture or in architecture.

Amateur painting

During the 18th and 19th centuries, the growing perception of painting as a drawing-room accomplishment for young ladies encouraged many women of the upper and middle classes to participate in the arts (see Amateur Artists survey). Such activities filled leisure hours, served as an entertainment, provided a means of documenting personal experience, and allowed young women to participate knowledgeably in the fashionable discourses of art. As in the training of the professional artist, the young lady learned much of her skill by copying the works of others. The models for such endeavours could range from prints and drawings to the paintings from the family collection. Amateur artists noted for their copying included Mrs Anne Carlisle, a protégée of King Charles I; Mrs Rhoda Astley (1725-57), whose copies were hung at Seaton Delavel, Northumberland; Mrs Eglinton Margaret Pearson (d. 1823), who made two sets of copies after the Raphael Cartoons; Lady Helena Percival, daughter of the 1st Earl of Egremont; and Lady Caroline Stanhope, a relative of the Earl of Harrington whose copy of the portrait of *Mary, Queen of Scots* hung in the family seat in Derbyshire.

For many amateurs, copying the works of the old masters or other artists was the height of their ambition, and their work would be displayed in family rooms to demonstrate their "accomplishment". For others, the copies they made themselves, acquired from friends or purchased from professional artists often allowed them to form small art collections or to decorate their personal apartments. George Vertue reports that Lady Burlington made copies of her husband's collection for her boudoir, and that Miss Da Costa copied paintings by Rubens, van Dyck and others for her "ladys Cabinet". The Boudoir at Wardour Castle, Wiltshire, the seat of Lord Arundell was richly decorated with a collection of drawings and miniatures, many of them copies after Guido Reni, Raphael and Pannini. A Mrs Corbet decorated the ante-drawing-room of Sundorne Castle in Shropshire with her own copies after Cuyp, Vandevelde, Barroccio and Raphael.

One of the best-known amateur painters of the 18th century, Mary Delany (q.v.), was an avid copier of paintings.

Sophie von la Roche described her as a "remarkable lady close to 90 years" seated in a room decorated with pictures from galleries in Italy, the Netherlands and France, "abundant evidence of her noble industry and intellect". She also records Mrs Delany as stating: "There are no masterpieces you see there, merely copies I made while on my travels." Mrs Delany's high birth and court connections gave her access to many important collections from which she borrowed and copied extensively, including paintings by Veronese, Lely, Claude, Soldi, Guido Reni, Salvator Rosa, Rembrandt, Correggio and Hogarth. Copying seems to have functioned for her as an opportunity for close repeated analysis and meditation on either the subject of the representation itself or of the skill and technique of the original artists. Upon finishing a copy of a Veronese in 1744, she wrote to a friend: "I have finished it as high as possible for me to finish, because it will be a sort of study for me when I can't get better pictures to copy." Often copying served as a basis for experiencing nostalgic memories of times past; in 1745 she wrote: "I have copied in large one of the sketches of Dovedale that I took when we were there together. How many tender ideas did it raise whilst I was drawing it." Many of the copies she produced went as gifts to her women friends. She gave her copy of Hogarth's *Sigismunda* to the Duchess of Portland, a half-length of the Duchess of Mazarin to a Miss Bushe, and a copy of her mother's portrait to her close friend Mrs Dawes. Her will, dated 22 February 1788, distributed her remaining pictures, for the most part copies, among her circle of women friends

Many women lacking training or painting materials translated such paintings into other materials. Particularly popular at the end of the 18th century were needlework pictures, many of which were copies of old master and contemporary paintings. Mary Linwood, Harriet Frankland and Anne Morritt all made and exhibited pictures in needlework, that most acceptable of female leisure activities. The high critical acclaim they received was as much in response to their audacious appropriation of male masterpieces into a medium heavily associated with female domesticity as for the skill of their undertaking. Harriet Frankland's copy in needlework of Tenier's *Prodigal Son* was exhibited at the tenth Spring Gardens exhibition of the Society of Artists in 1769. Mary Linwood's copies after Morland, Reynolds, Stubbs, Gainsborough and Raphael went on display in an exhibition touring London and the surrounding counties at the end of the 18th century. Anne Eliza Morritt's tapestry copies after Zuccarelli, Poussin, Pietro da Cortona, Rubens, Annibale Carracci and Salvator Rosa were exhibited in York and highly praised by Arthur Young in his account of *A Six Month's Tour Through the North of England* (1771). This translation of creative and artistic work into an acceptable feminine medium allowed these women to participate in cultural and intellectual matters that might otherwise have rendered them unfeminine, or "unnatural" in the eyes of their contemporaries.

For many young women of the leisured classes, the drawing-room accomplishments of painting and drawing could also provide them with a marketable skill should they need it. Ellen Sharples (q.v.) was not born into an artistic family, but instead was trained in painting and drawing as amateur activities befitting a young woman of the gentry. However, after marrying her drawing master James Sharples around 1787, Ellen soon put her training in a "ladies accomplishment" to profitable use in her husband's practice. The couple journeyed to America with their young children between 1794 and 1801 and again between 1809 and 1811. There, they travelled through the new country as itinerant artists, offering their services as portraitists and copyists to elite patrons. Their miniature portraits of *George Washington* (of which more than 40 were produced, including at least 6 copies by Ellen) and other prominent members of American society were in great demand and proved to be extremely remunerative. Upon the family's return to England, Ellen continued to produce both original and copies of miniature portraits on ivory and even exhibited at the Royal Academy in 1807. After the death of her husband in 1811, she returned with her family to Bristol, where, with her son James, she continued to be a mainstay of the family business. Ellen was also responsible for the artistic education of her young daughter Rolinda, whose talent and training soon enabled her to study with Philip Reinagle and to become a professional artist in her own right.

The feminisation of the copy

With the growth of the middle classes and the industrialisation of Western Europe during the 19th century, European society was increasingly divided into gender-based spheres of activity. The male realm was that of public interaction, politics and manufacture, one in which male identity was defined by the individual's production, speech and action. The female domain was defined by reproduction, passivity, silence and a domestic economy in which women became the major consumers of the products of mass culture manufactured by men. Unacknowledged, but essential to such ideological constructions was the importance of woman's reproductive capacity to the filiation and kinship ties between men. Women were responsible not only for the biological continuation of their class/race/species, but also for the cultural reproduction and transmission of social ideologies through their maintenance of the family and their responsibility for the moral indoctrination and education of the young. Such larger ideological concerns shaped modern conceptions of creativity, the role of the artist, and notions of originality.

The feminisation and marginalisation of the copy played an important role in the modernist notion of the male artist as a creative genius, a conception constructed and institutionalised in the 19th-century art market and academic practice. The autonomy and reputation of the modern artist was threatened by the dominance of the classical canon and the market's reiteration of that canon through copies and prints. The most frequent mode for classifying the copy with "after" yielded identity, authority and financial gain to the name of the original master rather than that of the copyist. During the 18th century the definition of taste was transformed from the ability to recognise and discuss the subject of the representation to the recognition and discussion of the singularity of the artist. Originality and authenticity became the criteria for selection or judgement in order to protect such concepts of intellectual property. The elevation of the modern artist was enabled by the exclusion of artisans and certain practices within the institutions of museum and academy. Throughout Europe, academic regulations maintained the practice of copying, but only in

a marginal capacity. Copying was increasingly discouraged except by: 1) students for whom copying was important to the process of learning through emulation; 2) the reproductive arts such as printmaking where replication was an inherent part of the processes of production; 3) artisans or failed artists who were pushed by lack of talent to the margins of the profession; and 4) women whose access to original art was increasingly limited, whose training was frequently halted at the stage of the copy, and whose basic social role was considered to be innately "reproductive". Moreover, the discourse of the copy takes on a connotation of amateurism and femininity just as the making of the copy is devalued as an occupation. The access to the copy allowed to women artists both in the making of images and habits of consuming them tends to contribute to and reinforce this depreciation.

During the 19th century, copying thus became a legitimate career for women artists once it had been discarded as an appropriate activity for the male artist. While women's access to the academic stages of training that enabled originality were limited, their access to institutions where copying was approved became fairly easy. Organisations founded to enable student study of the old masters (such as the British Institution in London) and museums such as the National Gallery in London and the Louvre in Paris were constantly filled with copyists, often with waiting lists for the more popular paintings. Women were a significant presence among these painters, both as students learning from the old masters and as professional copyists producing copies either for private collectors or public institutions. In France during the Second Empire, a special government office sponsored a large number of copies after official portraits or history paintings for display in various state institutions. It also commissioned copies of religious paintings for distribution to provincial churches, according to an agreement made between Church and State. Women artists were considered equally capable of providing such copies as male artists, and several such as Juliette de Ribeiro, Zoe Laura de Chatillon, Ernestine Froidure de Pelleport, Henriette and Clara Fournier, and Justine de Janvry received regular and well-paid commissions from the government to paint the required images.

While copying did allow women access to a realm of male activity and knowledge and did at times enable them to form their own intimate spheres of intellect and conversation, their association with a discourse of copying and reproduction prohibited or made their creativity extremely difficult on a professional level. Stopped at an adolescent stage in the training of the artist, women were discouraged from expressing their subjectivity and autonomy in their work, and their copying served most strongly to contrast with male originality and genius. Indeed, as an act of study, translation or interpretation, copying was seen as transforming the woman artist into an ideal spectator or audience for the appreciation of male genius. This conception is best illustrated in Nathaniel Hawthorne's character of Hilda in his novel *The Marble Faun* (1860). Hilda, a young virginal American artist, travels to Rome to study from the art of the past. There she is so overwhelmed by her confrontation with the old masters that she discards all ambition to conceive "great pictures" with her "feminine mind". She shuts herself away in a tower where she is untarnished by any authentic experience, her identity completely subsumed by the paintings she copies, feeling rather than intellectualising her response; through her copying she thus becomes the perfect receptor for the male artist:

> Hilda had ceased to consider herself as an original artist … she had the gift of discerning and worshipping excellence in a most unusual measure. She saw – no, not saw, but felt – through and through a picture … she went straight to the central point, in which the master had conceived his work. Thus, she viewed it, as it were, with his own eyes, and hence her comprehension of any picture that interested her was perfect.

She thus becomes the "handmaid of Raphael". Her role is again that of reproduction, her copying of a great work "by patient faith and self-devotion … multiplied it for mankind".

The 20th century

By the 20th century the copy had become so completely marginal within the practices of art that it was generally equated with failure, poor judgement, unsavoury market practices, and the fraudulence and deceit of forgery. The ideologies of modernism dictated that the artist strive to be of the avant-garde and to express only those original and unique aspects of his (or her) personal vision. The reproductive functions of the copy were relegated to photography, while the previous importance placed on copying to learn was now seen as antithetical to the development of originality and personal expression in the neophyte artist. Women artists, like the male artists of the 18th century, abnegated the copy in order to avoid its contamination of their reputations and ambitions and to validate their tenuous position as professionals. The copy was allowed a partial legitimacy through Pop Art, but only as kitsch or a tongue-in-cheek reference on the part of the superiorly-placed, informed artist to his or her position relative to the traditions of representation and the art of the past. However, recent feminist critique and revision of modernism (its gendered constructions of originality and genius in particular) has challenged many women artists to address these aspects in their work. The post-modern work of artists such as Sherrie Levine, Cindy Sherman and Dottie Attie questions how patriarchal assumptions and the traditions of art structure their roles as both artists and women. Dottie Attie's small copies of sections of paintings by past masters are reassembled and re-contextualised by text panels through which the artist imposes her own personal narrative and interpretation of the Western art tradition. Sherrie Levine has re-photographed the work of Walker Evans, Edward Weston, Andreas Feininger and Eliot Porter in order to examine the importance our culture places on originality and intellectual property. Cindy Sherman's work, in which she photographs herself appropriating the forms of advertising, film images and old masters, probes Western conventions of representing women as well as her own position as an artist within a tradition that has previously privileged only men.

LISA HEER

Bibliography

Nathaniel Hawthorne, *The Marble Faun*, Boston: Ticknor and Fields, 1860

Lady Llanover, ed., *The Autobiography and Correspondence of Mary Granville, Mrs Delany*, 6 vols, London: Bentley, 1861–2; reprinted New York: AMS Press, 1974

Bea Howe, "Pioneer of the woolwork picture", *Country Life*, cxi, March 1952, pp.656-8

"The Excellent Mrs Mary Beale", exh. cat., Geffrye Museum, London, and elsewhere, 1975

Germaine Greer, *The Obstacle Race: The Fortunes of Women Painters and Their Work*, London: Secker and Warburg, and New York: Farrar Straus, 1979

Rozsika Parker and Griselda Pollock, *Old Mistresses: Women, Art and Ideology*, London and New York: Routledge, 1981

Paul Duro, *The Copy in French Nineteenth-Century Painting*, PhD dissertation, University of Essex, 1983

Rozsika Parker, *The Subversive Stitch: Embroidery and the Making of the Feminine*, London: Women's Press, 1984; New York: Routledge, 1989

Charlotte Yeldham, *Women Artists in Nineteenth-Century France and England*, 2 vols, New York: Garland, 1984

Rosalind E. Krauss, *The Originality of the Avant-Garde and Other Modernist Myths*, Cambridge: Massachusetts Institute of Technology Press, 1985

Griselda Pollock, "Art, artschool, culture: Individualism after the death of the author", *Block*, no.11, 1985–6, pp.8-18

Paul Duro, "The *Demoiselles à Copier* in the Second Empire", *Woman's Art Journal*, vii/1, Spring–Summer 1986, pp.1–7

Andreas Huyssen, *After the Great Divide: Modernism, Mass Culture, Postmodernism*, Bloomington: Indiana University Press, 1986

Leonore Davidoff and Catherine Hall, *Family Fortunes: Men and Women of the English Middle Class, 1780–1850*, London: Hutchinson, and Chicago: University of Chicago Press, 1987

Susan Lambert, *The Image Multiplied: Five Centuries of Printed Reproductions of Paintings and Drawings*, London: Trefoil, 1987

Griselda Pollock, *Vision and Difference: Femininity, Feminism and the Histories of Art*, London and New York: Routledge, 1988

Wendy Steiner, *Pictures of Romance: Form Against Context in Painting and Literature*, Chicago: University of Chicago Press, 1988

Christine Battersby, *Gender and Genius: Towards a Feminist Aesthetic*, Bloomington: Indiana University Press, and London: Women's Press, 1989

Retaining the Original: Multiple Originals, Copies and Reproductions, Studies in the History of Art, 20, Washington, DC: National Gallery of Art, 1989

Whitney Chadwick, *Women, Art and Society*, London and New York: Thames and Hudson, 1990; revised edition, 1996

Ann Bermingham, "The origins of painting and the ends of art: Wright of Derby's *Corinthian Maid*", *Painting and the Politics of Culture: New Essays on British Art, 1700–1850*, ed. John Barrell, Oxford and New York: Oxford University Press, 1992, pp.135–65

Susan P. Casteras, "Excluding women: The cult of the male genius in Victorian painting", *Rewriting the Victorians: Theory, History and the Politics of Gender*, ed. Linda M. Shires, New York and London: Routledge, 1992

Wendy Wassyng Roworth, ed., *Angelica Kauffman: A Continental Artist in Georgian England*, London: Reaktion, 1992

Deborah Cherry, *Painting Women: Victorian Women Artists*, London and New York: Routledge, 1993

Gill Perry and Michael Rossington, eds, *Femininity and Masculinity in Eighteenth-Century Art and Culture*, Manchester: Manchester University Press, 1994

A Struggle for Fame: Victorian Women Artists and Authors, exh. cat., Yale Center for British Art, New Haven, 1994

Lisa Heer, *Problems in Copies: The Production, Consumption and Criticism of Copies after the Old Masters in Eighteenth-Century England*, PhD dissertation, Bryn Mawr College, 1995

Kathryn Metz, "Ellen and Rolinda Sharples: Mother and daughter painters", *Woman's Art Journal*, xvi/1, 1995, pp.3–11

Printmakers

From the first days of printmaking, following the development of the woodcut in the 15th century, women have been involved in the print trade as members of printmaking families. It is easily forgotten that in the past printmaking had a primary function in transmitting information, whether religious, technical, commercial, artistic or scientific, and that much printmaking was only secondarily an artistic activity in its own right. Nuns in the Low Countries who were involved in the cutting and printing of religious woodcuts in the 15th century would not have considered themselves to be artists. Women were crucial to certain aspects of the print trade; for example, the colouring of prints was often done by women and their children, and women often ran shops or stalls selling prints. Many women continued their husbands' workshops as widows, employing journeymen to carry out tasks that were beyond their abilities or strengths. There were many strenuous activities connected with printmaking, especially plate printing; thus there were physical barriers against the entry of women into printmaking in addition to the cultural obstacles that prevented them from making independent careers; these did not begin to be surmounted until the end of the 19th century.

Reproductive printmakers of the early modern period

The first identifiable women printmakers were members of families involved in engraving; their unpaid skill could be used to strengthen the family as an economic unit and reduce the need to employ strangers who might be disruptive or disloyal as well as expensive. Although on occasion a daughter might show sufficient artistic ability to repay the effort of additional training, this had to be balanced against the likelihood that when she married her skills would be lost, possibly to a rival family of engravers. Sometimes, however, a young woman would show such exceptional skill or initiative that her work had to be recognised and her name allowed to appear on the plates. The best-known woman engraver in Renaissance Italy was Diana Mantuana (q.v.), daughter of an engraver and stucco-worker in Mantua who worked for Giulio Romano and who also made engravings of Romano's works to promote his reputation. She learned from her father to do likewise and signed 46 plates; these were either engraved to promote the work of living artists or to provide plates to inform others about antique works of art; in other words they were primarily bought for their information. This is not to deny that they might have additional value because they were well engraved, but the plates made by reproductive printmakers were initially bought as images of works of art.

In northern Europe Magdalena van de Passe (q.v.) was trained in Utrecht by her father Crispijn van de Passe the Elder, as were her three brothers. Her name is on 25 plates, a small output even for a relatively short life, and she probably assisted family members on others. A generation later in Paris the Flemish family of van der Stella produced an able woman engraver, Claudine Bouzonnet (Lyon, 1636–Paris, 1698). With two brothers and two sisters she trained as a painter under her uncle, the painter Jacques de Stella, but she concentrated on etching and engraving. She produced 125 plates, in particular after Poussin and her uncle, whose name she later took. In Spain María Eugenia de Beer (q.v.), daughter of the Flemish engraver Cornelio de Beer, produced engravings for illustrated books.

Painter-etchers

The women discussed above worked as reproductive engravers, but there are also women who used printmaking for original work. In Amsterdam there was Geetruydt Roghman (q.v.), daughter of the engraver Hendrik Lambertz. Roghman and great-niece of the painter and etcher Roelant Saverij. She signed only 13 plates, including a few landscapes designed and initially etched by her brother Roelant, but she also designed and engraved five interesting prints of women engaged in domestic tasks. They are perhaps the first example both of a woman designing prints and also making prints of specifically female subjects. These were issued by the Amsterdam engraver and publisher Claes Jansz. Visscher, and the fact that they were engraved rather than etched would have meant that, if there was a demand for the prints, large editions could be printed.

17th-century Italy

In Italy there continued to be women printmakers drawn from artistic families. Teresia del Po, daughter of the painter Pietro del Po, learned painting from her father and became a member of the Roman Accademia di San Luca in 1678. He also taught her printmaking; her best-known print was an engraving of one of his *Nativity* pictures. She died in Rome in 1716, and was roughly contemporary with the long-lived Suor Isabella Piccini (Venice, 1644–?1735), daughter of an engraver of the second rank, Jacopo Piccini. She became a nun, using her skills, such as they were, to engrave portraits of eminent Italians for G.B. Fabri's *Conchilia celeste* (Venice, 1690), as well as a number of religious prints; some of these are important because they were distributed by Antonio Remondini, whose inexpensive prints reached all over Europe.

Very different from Suor Isabella was Elisabetta Sirani (q.v.), daughter of Giovan Andrea Sirani, an assistant of Guido Reni and contemporary of the important painter-etcher Simone Cantarini. She trained as a painter and attracted early attention; she also, like so many painters of the time, tried her hand at etching and her 14 known prints stand comparison with the best of her contemporaries. Her best-known print, a memorable *Holy Family* after her own design, was done at the age of 19.

18th-century France

In the 18th century it was in Paris that much of the most important printmaking in Europe took place. The tradition of line engraving produced singly issued prints of portraits and history paintings of superb quality as well as elegant book illustrations; at the same time there were opportunities for painter-etchers. There were many important families of engravers and many of these had female members who showed engraving skills. Three Hortheemels sisters, whose brother was the engraver Frederic, were all printmakers: Louise Madeleine married the reproductive engraver Charles Nicolas Cochin the Elder, and did a great deal to help the career of their son, who became a celebrated designer and etcher, famous for his portrait medallions of well-known figures. She engraved several of his works as well as providing plates for J.B. Monicart's *Versailles immortalisé* (1720). Marie Anne married the engraver Nicolas Tardieu, and Marie Nicolle married the painter Alexis Simon Belle.

Among women of the next generation one can single out Renée Elisabeth Lepicie, wife of the engraver Bernard Lepicie, and Cathérine Cousinet, who studied engraving under L. Cars and Etienne Fessard before her marriage to the engraver L.S. Lempereur; like several other women she continued to sign plates with her maiden name after her marriage. As the century went on there were increasing numbers of women engaged in printmaking in Paris; admittedly most worked only on an intermittent basis and generally on plates of secondary importance, but their total output is impressive. Some women, however, did receive academic recognition, which was crucial given the very regimented and centralised organisation of engraving in Paris. Anne Philiberte Coulet, a pupil of Aliamet and Lempereur, who became known for her landscape prints, was received at the Vienna Academy in 1770. The short-lived Cathérine Deschamps was another well-regarded figure, who engraved both before and after her marriage in 1761 to her instructor, the engraver Jacques-Firmin Beauvarlet. Among those working immediately before the Revolution were Marguerite Hemery, sister of the engraver François-Antoine Hemery; she married Nicolas Ponce – one of the leading engravers of the *estampe galante* that pictured the life of the rich – and made a name for herself with her book illustrations; her sister Thérèse Eléonore, who married the engraver C.L. Lingée, and whose artistic talents were recognised by membership of the Marseille Academy, was successful in the crayon manner, developed to produce decorative facsimiles of drawings; Marie Catherine Riollet, who was the third wife of Beauvarlet, publisher of her *Mauvaise Riche* after Teniers; and Marie Rosalie Bertaud, pupil of Augustin Saint-Aubin and Pierre Philippe Choffard, who engraved a number of landscapes after Joseph Vernet.

All these women can be classed as reproductive engravers; there was little market for etchings by unknown artists, and one of the few women of the time who showed the freedom of handling associated with the painter-etcher was Marguerite Gérard (q.v.). She studied both painting and etching under her brother-in-law Jean-Honoré Fragonard, and in 1779 etched his drawing *Au génie de Franklin*. This was perhaps the most important print by a woman made in 18th-century Paris, and admirably conveyed all the force and drama of the original, and was well received by collectors of etchings. Gérard was sufficiently talented to have a successful career as a painter and etched only six prints, all after Fragonard and all done in her early years. By their nature etchings of this kind had only a limited sale and much valuable painting time could be spent trying to sell them. The process of etching was of course easier than engraving and it is therefore no surprise that it was taken up by artistic amateurs, as well as by a few professional artists, notably Saint-Aubin and Jean Baptiste Le Prince.

French amateurs

The prints made by amateurs were generally distributed privately among friends and acquaintances, though the fame of their makers might occasionally attract a more general curiosity. The most celebrated exponent was the Marquise de Pompadour, mistress of Louis XV, who made nearly 80 prints, mostly in the 1750s, and her lead was followed by others. This was by no means the first time that leisured women had amused themselves making prints. The accomplished Anna Maria van Schurman (q.v.), savante and musician, made half a dozen prints, and her contemporary the Dutch poet Anna Maria de Koker etched some ten landscapes in the style of Jan van Goyen and others. Others who experimented included royalty, notably Queen Christina of Sweden, who abdicated on converting to Catholicism and settled in Rome. Often amateurs left the messy side of printmaking, such as biting and proving, to their professional teachers, who would often, openly or surreptitiously, improve the plates, so that it is difficult for posterity to be able to judge the artistic abilities of, say, Madame de Pompadour; at least one of her plates was retouched by Charles Nicolas Cochin. On the other hand there can be no doubting the talents of Maria Anna, Archduchess of Austria, who had a wide interest in the arts and sciences. She studied under the painter Friedrich August Brand and became a member of the Imperial Academy of copperplate-engravers in the year following its foundation in 1767. In 1772 she issued a series of landscapes and genre scenes, *Sechzehn radirte Blätter*.

Angelica Kauffman

The constraints upon women meant that very few had genuinely independent careers as artists. Most of the printmakers, it is clear, were members of families of engravers engaged in reproductive work, and did not use printmaking for their personal artistic expression. In the 18th century the most remarkable example of a woman who did make her own way was Angelica Kauffman (q.v.). Her formative years were spent in Italy, where the tradition of the painter-etcher was the most powerful in Europe. She took up etching in her early twenties and made a number of plates, some after other painters but others after her own designs. Initially these were distributed privately, but after she went to London in 1766 she took advantage of the great interest she aroused and herself published a set of prints for a guinea (£1 1s.). She continued to make etchings for sale. When she left England for Italy she sold her plates, many of which were re-issued by the important London printseller John Boydell and therefore became widely known.

British amateurs

Kauffman's example helped to encourage fashionable women, many of whom had taken drawing lessons, to take up printmaking. This had in fact already been given encouragement by the fledgling Society of Arts; its primary purpose was to encourage the arts of design for commercial reasons, and it offered "premiums" (prizes) for drawing, but it also advertised premiums for etchings made by women. The motive may have been to secure the goodwill towards the Society from the families of the nobility and gentry whose daughters were most likely to be able to compete. One keen amateur was Lady Louisa Greville, daughter of the Earl of Warwick, whose many etchings after landscapes by the Carracci, Salvator Rosa and Marco Ricci, as well as figure studies after Guercino, are mostly dated 1758–62, before her marriage to William

Churchill in 1770. Public exhibitions began in 1760 and she exhibited one etching, a landscape after Salvator Rosa, at the Free Society in 1762. Unlike the Royal Academy, founded in 1768, the Society of Artists and the breakaway Free Society both allowed prints to be exhibited, though only a few women took advantage of this opportunity. As in France such prints were not usually sold but were instead given away or exchanged in aristocratic circles. Horace Walpole, who tended to exaggerate the talents of well-born artists, assembled two albums of etchings (Lewis Walpole Library, Farmington) by men and women who etched as a pastime, as did another collector, Richard Bull (two albums in the British Museum, London). Among the few amateur prints that were sold were aquatints by Catherine Maria Fanshawe, who did a number of charming studies of children around 1800, and sold some prints in aid of charitable causes. Aquatint was a form of tonal etching introduced in the 1770s for the reproduction of wash drawings; it was more difficult than traditional etching, which simply called for the design to be scratched with a needle through the hard ground coating the copper plate, and was therefore seldom used by amateurs.

Drawing masters now started to teach etching; prominent among these was William Austin, who actually advertised that he taught etching; among the women who were probably taught by him was Miss Catherine St Aubin who made several etchings and whose drawings of her family home, St Michael's Mount, Cornwall, were etched by Austin. One woman who advertised as a teacher of etching was Mary Darly, wife of the designer and etcher Matthew Darly. It is difficult to separate their work; together they etched and published the political satires of George Townshend, who pioneered the combination of personal caricature and political satire. Darly kept a shop – as did many engravers' wives – in the early 1760s and her name appears as publisher on a number of satires, mostly directed against the Scots-born minister Lord Bute. In 1762 she published a booklet: *A Book of Caricatures, on 60 Copper Plates, with the Principles of Designing ... with Sundry Ancient & Modern Examples ... for the Use of Young Gentlemen and Ladies.*

Professional women engravers in Britain

There were very few professional women engravers in Britain, and those there were generally did not sign many plates. Angélique Ravenet, daughter of a French-born line engraver, may have been instructed by her father; after her marriage to the engraver V.-M. Picot she exhibited a mezzotint of *Cervetti* (the cellist G. Basseri) at the Society of Artists (1771), but did not sign many other plates and, although she may have assisted her husband, she was probably engaged in the printselling side of his business. At the Society of Artists Miss Elizabeth Judkins exhibited mezzotints after Joshua Reynolds in 1772 and 1775; she was undoubtedly instructed by her uncle, the mezzotint engraver James Watson, but did not become a professional engraver. It was Watson's daughter Caroline (q.v.) who became the only British-born woman professional; she did not engrave in mezzotint but in the new technique of stipple or dotted manner, which was developed out of the French crayon manner and was initially used in Britain from the mid-1770s to reproduce drawings by Kauffman. It was very difficult, in Britain as elsewhere, for a young woman to learn printmaking

as a career except within the family. The only British engraver who appears to have had female apprentices was John Raphael Smith, who took on Ann Probin and Caroline Kirkley in 1789; they were probably engaged to learn print colouring rather than engraving, though Kirkley did sign one mezzotint. A few other women signed occasional stipples, for example Mary Ann Rigg, who was probably taught by Edmund Scott, whom she married. Later on Marie Anne Bourlier engraved a considerable number of stipples between 1806, when she engraved ten of the *Portraits ... of the Royal Family* (Abbey 1952, "Life" 278), published by E. Harding, and about 1815. There were also a few line engravers, notably Elisabeth Ellis and Letitia Byrne, who assisted her father, the engraver William Byrne, and became an accomplished etcher. These two women both had their names on many plates; this was not so in the case of the daughters of Isaac Taylor, the line engraver who trained his daughters alongside his apprentices. Their talents lay elsewhere as writers and they did not progress to signing plates; we only know of their training because Mary Taylor mentions it in her autobiography (*Autobiography and Other Memorials of Mrs Gilbert*, ed. Josiah Gilbert, London: King, 1874, i, p.103).

One last professional engraver in 18th-century Britain remains to be mentioned: Maria Catherine Hull, who married the engraver Theophilus Prestel in Nuremberg in 1769 and assisted him, initially on the crayon manner facsimiles he made of drawings and later with his aquatints. She left him in 1786 and went to London, which had taken over from Paris as the most important centre of printmaking. In the eight years remaining to her she engraved some very large and impressive landscape plates, which, like many London prints of the time, had a wide sale in Germany and the rest of continental Europe.

Women were becoming more important as buyers of prints by the end of the 18th century, and there was a greater market for prints with a feminine appeal. The best example of this is perhaps the edition of Mary Robinson's poem *The Winter Day* published in 1804 by Rudolph Ackermann with aquatint plates by Caroline Watson after designs by Maria Cosway (q.v.). Ackermann had in 1800 published *Imitations in Chalk* etched by Cosway, a drawing book of softground etchings by Maria of sketches by her husband Richard Cosway. Another group of etchings that she made were of eight paintings in the Louvre, sketched on a short visit to Paris following the Peace of Amiens in 1802, and originally intended to illustrate a description of the Louvre and its new treasures which had been commandeered from all the newly conquered lands.

The introduction of lithography

Until the early 19th century printmaking was, except for relief methods of woodcut and wood-engraving, done on copper, using intaglio methods whereby the image was printed from ink retained on the plate in lines or rough areas produced mechanically or by acid. The first planographic technique, lithography, involved drawing on limestone – which repelled ink when wet – with a wax crayon whose marks held the ink.

Ackermann was one of the first printsellers to take an interest in lithography, or "polyautography" as the process was initially called following its discovery in 1798 by a German, Aloys Senefelder. He visited London in 1800–01, and, after he obtained a patent, several lithographs drawn on the stone by various artists were published in 1803 as *Specimens of*

Polyautography. The artists included one woman amateur, Lady Cawdor, née Caroline Howard, who contributed two pen lithograph landscapes. The same year Ackermann issued *Twelve Views of Scotland* by Miss F. Waring, which were chalk lithographs; their extreme rarity today suggests they did not sell very well, and the interest in lithography did not really develop in Britain until after Ackermann published an English edition of Senefelder's *Complete Course in Lithography* (1819). It was in fact in Munich and then Paris that the earliest commercial lithographs were made. When interest was revived in Britain it opened up much greater opportunities for women printmakers, as it was much easier to work on stone than with the etching needle. There are numerous examples made by women, several of whom illustrated their own travel books with lithographs.

There were few women who could be called professional lithographers. There is little doubt that the prejudice against "trade" in 19th-century Europe inhibited many women from taking up such a career. Therefore most lithographs made by women were either by amateurs, such as Princess Charlotte Bonaparte, whose work included a series of American landscapes, or by women painters, such as Elise Journet, who made lithographs of some of her paintings for publication in *L'Artiste*. One French professional was Cécile Marechal Marchand, who assisted her lithographer husband Jacques Marchand and signed at least 36 lithographs herself. The most important woman lithographer was Fanny Palmer, who turned to the process as a way of supporting her family after it ran into financial trouble. Her earliest lithographs were made in Leicester in 1842 (Abbey 1952, "Scenery" 199), but in 1844 she and her family emigrated from Britain to the USA. There she first worked as an independent lithographer, but she was before long recruited by the publisher Nathaniel Currier and became one of the mainstays of the firm of Currier & Ives; she is credited with some 200 lithographs, drawn on the stone by herself, between 1849 and 1868. Most of the purchasers of these popular prints, which give such an evocative picture of America, were quite unaware that she was a woman since she simply signed herself "F. F. Palmer".

The "etching revival"

Despite the interest in and ease of lithography, etching remained a popular pastime. In Britain the list of amateurs was headed by Queen Victoria, who had lessons from George Hayter, who became her Painter in Ordinary in 1841. A number of British women made prints in distant parts of the Empire; for example, in 1826, Countess Amherst, wife of the Governor-General of India, made an etching of Sir Charles D'Oyly's painting room in Patna (Sir Charles himself later took up lithography and involved several British women in his Bihar Lithographic Press). In Paris the painter Frédérique O'Connell began in 1853 to teach art, including etching, to ladies and produced several etchings herself.

It was in Paris that the Etching Revival began, and major artists began to take a new interest in producing prints. The most active printmaker was the American painter Mary Cassatt (q.v.), who made 220 etchings and 2 lithographs from about 1878; among these her colour etchings, many of them of women and children, attracted most notice. Her example seems to have encouraged Berthe Morisot (q.v.), but, although the latter made a few drypoints and a lithograph based on existing drawings, she did not maintain her interest. Another important artist who made prints was Suzanne Valadon (q.v.). She made some 30 etchings and drypoints, mostly studies of women, but they were largely unknown until her later fame as a painter aroused interest in them. In Britain the growing status of etching was reflected by the foundation in 1880 of the Society of Painter-Etchers, which was to have many women members (after the Society received a royal charter members were denoted as "RE" and associates "ARE"). Among the first full members was Mary Nimmo Moran, who, with Cassatt, was one of the main exhibitors in a display of the *Work of Women Etchers of America* at the Museum of Fine Arts, Boston, in 1887–8. One of the most influential of women etchers was Constance Pott, known for her landscape prints, who became a full member of the Society in 1898. She was assistant to Frank Short, one of the leading printmakers of his day, at the Royal College of Art, London, where a number of women trained, such as Mary Anne Sloane. Other women, such as Margaret Kemp-Welch, ARE, were taught printmaking at the art school at Bushey run by the painter and printmaker Herbert Herkomer.

The etching boom

There could hardly be a greater contrast between the pastoral, often cosy subject matter of much British and American printmaking and the prints produced by Käthe Kollwitz (q.v.). She turned to printmaking principally to express her distress about the condition of the poor, which she saw as the wife of a Berlin doctor, but she also produced some extraordinarily powerful self-portraits. Kollwitz worked in a number of techniques and after World War I also took up woodcut, influenced by the powerful work of Ernst Barlach. However, the European public was not really interested in work of such a disturbing nature as she produced – after the horrors of the war more reassuring images were in demand.

During the immediate post-war period there was a tremendous surge of demand for etchings on both sides of the Atlantic, and many women artists were ready to respond, from painters such as Laura Knight (q.v.) with her etchings of the stage or of circus life, to Berthe Jacques, who was one of the founders of the Chicago Society of Etchers. Chicago emerged as an important centre for printmaking, and etchers from all over the world sent prints to its annual exhibitions. Among the most interesting women etchers in Britain were those influenced by Walter Sickert, such as Edna Clarke Hall (q.v.); his pupils included Sylvia Gosse, RE (q.v.) and Wendela Boreel, ARE. In 1920 the Society of Graphic Artists was founded, with annual exhibitions held until 1940, when it had 46 women members, many of them printmakers.

Colour prints

The colour etchings produced by Mary Cassatt have already been mentioned: in the early years of the 20th century there was a great vogue for colour prints of various kinds. There was a resurgence in colour lithography in Paris in the 1890s in which women played little part, but women played a major part in the production of colour prints that had their inspiration in Japanese art, in particular in colour woodcuts. In the USA Arthur Wesley Dow, who taught in New York, was a central figure, and those who produced colour prints as a result, either directly or indirectly, of his example included Helen Hyde and Georgia O'Keeffe (q.v.).

In Britain an important influence was Mabel Royds, who was inspired by Japanese colour woodblocks and began to produce colour prints just before World War I. She taught the American printmaker Norma Bassett Hall, who was the sole woman founding member of the Prairie Print Makers, a society that distributed an annual gift print to its members between 1931 and 1965, five of them by women. Colour woodcuts were also popular in Australia, largely through the example and teaching of Thea Proctor.

The boldness inherent in woodcut had already made its impact on the Continent, most notably at the fifth exhibition of the Vienna Secession in 1899. Among those who turned to the colour woodcut as a consequence was Norbertine von Bresslern-Roth, who made an impact with her colour wood-cuts of animals. One prolific exponent of the woodcut was Emma Boorman, who also trained in Vienna. After World War I she travelled extensively, not only in Europe but also in Asia, and made many powerful prints, many of which are on a large scale, and mostly of the cities she visited. She was one of the printmakers who was not deterred by the Depression of the 1930s; the collapse of the boom was most felt by traditional etchers and many of those who produced colour prints continued in work. One individual talent who emerged at the time was Elyse Ashe Lord, who made many distinctive colour prints, many with drypoint, under the influence of Chinese painting.

Another technique that attracted interest despite the Depression was the colour linocut. This was pioneered by Claude Flight, who taught at the Grosvenor School of Modern Art, London, from 1926; among his pupils, and a major exhibitor at the annual British Lino-Cut exhibitions of the Grosvenor School's students held from 1930, was Sybil Andrews, whose work, influenced by Futurism, seemed appropriately "modern". In Australia several women, notably Ethleen Palmer, used linocut very effectively.

Wood engraving

If women were in the clear minority as artists in previous centuries, there was one specialised area in which they held the lead during the 20th century: wood-engraving. The greatest of the group trained in London was Clare Leighton, who studied under Noel Rooke at the Central School and was one of the early members of the Society of Wood Engravers founded in 1920. Some of her prints, notably those in her book *Four Hedges* (1935), have an important part in the British pastoral tradition. She settled permanently in the USA in 1939. Gertrude Hermes (q.v.), Agnes Miller Parker, Gwen Raverat (q.v.) and Joan Hassall all became well known, largely because so much of their work was reproduced by means of photolithography as book illustrations.

Printmaking and the avant-garde

Most of the British wood-engravers were traditional in their aims and subject matter, but Hermes was a more radical artist and was one of six women printmakers who were included in an exhibition at the British Museum of avant-garde printmakers, the others being Sybil Andrews, Eileen Agar (q.v.), Gillian Ayres (q.v.), Prunella Clough (q.v.) and Lill Tschudi. Bringing such a list up to date would lead to the addition of such artists as Paula Rego (q.v.). In the 20th century printmaking has everywhere moved into a more central position in contemporary art, becoming a means of expression for many major artists. Nowhere is this seen more powerfully than in the USA, where the important artists who have been printmakers include such figures as Isabel Bishop (q.v.) and Peggy Bacon. Many artists have come to printmaking thanks to the establishment of printing workshops: Tamarind, for example, was important for Anni Albers (q.v.), Louise Nevelson (q.v.) and Miriam Schapiro (q.v.). Universal Limited Art Editions, sustained for so long by Tatyana Grosman, helped the careers of several artists, such as Mary Callery, Grace Hartigan (q.v.) and Helen Frankenthaler (q.v.).

DAVID ALEXANDER

Bibliography

(excluding references to artists with their own entries in the *Dictionary*)

General

Adam von Bartsch, *Le Peintre-graveur*, 21 vols, Vienne, 1803–21

Charles Le Blanc, *Manuel de l'amateur d'estampes, 1550–1820*, 4 vols, Paris: Bouillon, 1854–89

Catalogue of a Collection of Engravings, Etchings and Lithographs by Women, exh. cat., The Grolier Club, New York, 1901

Malcolm C. Salaman, *The New Woodcut*, London: The Studio, and New York: Boni, 1930

Timothy A. Riggs, *The Print Council Index to Oeuvre-Catalogues of Prints by European and American Artists*, Millwood, NY: Kraus, 1983

Allgemeines Kunstler-Lexikon, Munich: Saur, 1990–

Elizabeth Harvey-Lee, *Mistresses of the Graphic Arts: Famous and Forgotten Women Printmakers, c.1550–c.1950*, dealer's cat., North Aston, Oxford, 1995

Italy

Alexandre de Vesme, *Le Peintre-graveur italien*, Milan: Hoepli, 1906

Donne artiste nelle collezioni del Museo di Bassano, exh. cat., Museo Civico di Bassano di Grappa, 1986

Italian Etchers of the Renaissance and Baroque, exh. cat., Museum of Fine Arts, Boston, 1989

The Netherlands

F. W. H. Hollstein, *Dutch and Flemish Etchings, Engravings and Woodcuts, c.1450–1700*, Amsterdam: Hertzberger, 1949–

"Dames Gaan Voor": De Vrouw in de prentkunst, 1500–1800 ["Ladies first": Women in printmaking, 1500–1800], exh. cat., Museum Boymans-van Beuningen, Rotterdam, 1975

Printmaking in the Age of Rembrandt, exh. cat., Museum of Fine Arts, Boston, 1980

Germany and Austria

Andreas Andresen, *Der Deutsche Peintre-Graveur*, 5 vols, Leipzig: Weigel, 1864–78

F. W. H. Hollstein, *German Engravings, Etchings and Woodcuts, c.1400–1700*, Amsterdam: Hertzberger, 1954–

France

Inventaire du Fonds Français: Graveurs du XVIIe siècle, 11 vols, Paris: Bibliothèque Nationale, 1939–

Inventaire du Fonds Français: Graveurs du XVIIIe siècle, 14 vols, Paris: Bibliothèque Nationale, 1939–69

Inventaire du Fonds Français: Graveurs après 1800, 14 vols, Paris: Bibliothèque Nationale, 1930–77

Britain

Harold J. Wright, "The lithographs of Ethel Gabain", *Print Collector's Quarterly*, x, 1923, pp.254–87

C.A. Nicholson, "The etchings of Orovida [Pisarro]", *Print Collector's Quarterly*, xii, 1926, pp.176–202

Clare Stuart Wortley, "Amateur etchers", *Print Collector's Quarterly*, xix, 1932, pp.189–

J.R. Abbey, *Scenery of Great Britain and Ireland in Aquatint and Lithography, 1770–1860, from the Library of J.R. Abbey*, London: Curwen Press, 1952; reprinted Folkestone: Dawsons, 1972, and San Francisco: Wofsy, 1991

George Mackley, *Monica Poole: Wood-Engraver*, Biddenden, Kent: Florin Press, 1984

Garton and Cooke, Catalogue 28, dealer's cat., London, 1984 (with a full list of the colour woodcuts of Mabel Royds)

David Chambers, *Joan Hassall: Engravings and Drawings*, Pinner: Private Libraries Association, 1985

Patricia Jaffé, *Women Engravers*, London: Virago, 1988 (wood-engravers only)

British Avante-Garde Printmaking, exh. cat., British Museum, London, 1990

James Hamilton, *Wood Engraving and the Woodcut in Britain, c.1890–1990*, London: Barrie and Jenkins, 1994

Stephen Coppel, *Linocuts of the Machine Age: Claude Flight and the Grosvenor School*, Aldershot: Scolar Press, 1995

North America

George C. Groce and David H. Wallace, *The New-York Historical Society's Dictionary of Artists in America, 1564–1860*, New Haven: Yale University Press, 1957

Mary B. Cowdrey, "Fanny Palmer, an American lithographer", *Prints: Thirteen Illustrated Essays on the Art of the Print*, ed. Carl Zigrosser, New York: Holt Rinehart, 1962, pp.218–34

Richard S. Field and Ruth E. Fine, *A Graphic Muse: Prints by Contemporary American Women*, New York: Hudson Hills Press, 1987

Esther Sparks, *Universal Limited Art Editions: A History and Catalogue, the First Twenty-Five Years*, Chicago: Art Institute, 1989

Arthur Wesley Dow and His Influence, exh. cat., Herbert F. Johnson Museum of Art, Cornell, Ithaca, 1990

Mary Evans O'Keefe Gravalos and Carol Pulin, *Bertha Lum*, Washington, DC: Smithsonian Institution Press, 1991

Tim Mason and Lynn Mason, *Helen Hyde*, Washington, DC: Smithsonian Institution Press, 1991

Martha R. Severens, *Alice Ravenel Huger Smith: An Artist, a Place and a Time*, Charleston, SC: Carolina Art Association, 1993

C.S. Rubinstein, "Fanny Palmer", *The Dictionary of Art*, ed. Jane Turner, xxiii, London and New York: Grove, 1996

Australia

Sydney by Design: Wood and Linoblock Prints by Sydney Women Artists Between the Wars, exh. cat., National Gallery of Australia, Canberra, 1995

Amateur Artists

Amateur art as a social skill and a female preserve

16th and 17th centuries

Any discussion of amateur art must begin with a definition of the term. According to the *Encyclopaedia Britannica*, the original meaning of the word "amateur" is "someone who participates in any art, craft, game, sport or other activity solely for pleasure and enjoyment". Indeed, the root of the word derives from the Latin *amare* (to love) and *amatorem*, which means essentially "one who has a taste for anything". The second meaning of the word is more judgemental: it indicates "a person of inferior or superficial skill, ability or proficiency, as compared with others who specialise in and are expert in any field". Those who practise art for pleasure are distinguished from those who practise the same art for other reasons, to which category belong the specialists or experts, who are motivated by professional ambition rather than by love of the field.

In practice, the term amateur usually has a double meaning. An art amateur is someone who practises the arts for his or her pleasure and does this without explicitly specialising. This implies that he or she does not apply him or herself professionally, and practises the arts alongside other activities. As far as we know, the term was first used at the court of Louis XIV (1642–1715) to indicate "a connoisseur of the fine arts". It was apparently initially used in the literal sense of the word: an amateur loves the arts and in this sense is a "connoisseur". The term is also encountered with the same meaning in 18th-century England. In 1784 the word "amateur" was used for "one who appreciated the polite arts of painting and music". This introduction may make it clear that the use of the term "amateur artists" for the 16th and 17th centuries is an anachronism. However, the absence of the term during this period does not imply that the phenomenon now associated with it did not exist.

"Amateur" or "Amateuse"?

Both the interpretations of "amateurs" quoted above have to do with men, and it is worthy of note that the word spread only in its masculine form. The feminine variant *amateuse* is not found in France, Britain or the Netherlands. How can one come to an understanding of the content of the term that is applicable to women as well? Were women active as amateurs in the visual arts? The following perspectives enable the profile of the amateur to be defined with greater exactitude.

1. An amateur is someone who is not professionally involved with the arts. Consequently, the amateur activity is practised alongside other activities that may or may not be professional. This expression seems to imply that amateurs could not be members of professional organisations, such as the guilds of St Luke.

2. The status of "amateur" assumes a certain socio-economic situation. Someone who practises the arts for pleasure has no intention of providing a living for himself or herself with this activity. Thus amateurs are found primarily in the upper social classes. An abundance of free time is required for it.

3. An important exception must be made for women who came from artist families. The practice of art on a non-professional basis then takes place in the context of the family. Here artistic practice is the result of having an atelier at hand and of possible "natural" aptitude. That an artist has a daughter who develops into an amateur artist is in this

case the result of practical circumstances. Here we are dealing with "circumstantial" amateur artists.

4. The practice of the arts as a hobby was often the result of an educational process whereby handicraft skills were practised alongside music, dancing and horseback riding. The practice of the arts by the dilettante thus fits within a broader notion of the upbringing thought necessary for women if they were to prepare for a role in society. These one might call "intentional" amateur artists.

5. The practice of the arts as a hobby is sometimes also classified as "amateurish" on the basis of the genre employed. The more decorative genres (the minor arts, flower-pieces, still lifes, etc.) were associated with amateurism more than was history painting. Copying after the models of the "great masters" was likewise seen as a mark of dilettantism. Sometimes also copying took place as a means of schooling when teachers were lacking.

The origins of the phenomenon

Important in this context is the question of the origin of the phenomenon. From what point was amateur artistic practice a criterion for the evaluation of a woman's upbringing?

Among the Greeks and Romans little intellectual ambition was attributed to women. The woman's education stopped in the gynaeceum, from which point she was occupied with the administration of the household. In the early Renaissance this thread was taken up once more. Leon Battista Alberti wrote in his treatise *Della famiglia*: "women are by nature timid, soft, slow, and therefore more useful when they watch over things". Alberti does not say that they should benefit from this opportunity to practise the skills of handicrafts. When Baldassare Castiglione published *Il libro del cortegiano* in 1528, he also paid a great deal of attention to the role women had to fulfil in the milieu of the court. A woman must not be intelligent so much as modest and courteous in conversation. It was also good if she could dance, play a musical instrument and have some schooling in painting. While a number of exceptionally learned women are known about in detail, information about their artistic activities is rarely found. An exception is Isabella d'Este, who spoke Latin, Greek and various "modern" languages, danced well, and played both the clavecimbel and the lute. We are told that she designed objects for embroidery work and also executed these herself.

Instruction versus the "interests of conversation"

The 16th-century French poet Louise Labé, who opened the first bourgeois salon in France, spoke several languages and learned dancing and horseback riding, music and handicrafts. Painting or drawing were apparently not among her accomplishments. Margaret, one of the daughters of Sir Thomas More, was still more versatile: she studied logic, arithmetic, physics and philosophy; she, too, played music. The most important advocate of a "total education" for women was Juan Luis Vives, who was the tutor of, among others, Mary Tudor, daughter of Catherine of Aragon, to whom he dedicated his treatise on the education of women in 1523; the English translation, *Instruction of a Christian Woman*, appeared in 1540. Certainly, some education of girls could do no harm, but what was taught had to conform to the housewifely tasks of women. Neither Erasmus nor Vives was an advocate of "the fashionable court lady of the Italian mode". In their eyes, such women, who aspired to appropriate a social role at court, had forsaken the necessary modesty. There is no mention of explicit artistic training.

The "industrial" arts such as spinning and weaving on the other hand could indeed have a certain practical utility. In Catholic lands the upbringing of girls was managed by prominent orders of nuns such as the Ursulines. In 1596 the first French convent of the order was founded in Avignon. Here girls from both the upper and lower classes went to school. Sewing was almost always on the programme. For less wealthy girls, a craft such as lace-making was sometimes also taught. The girls recruited from better social ranks also learned some Latin and Italian and were instructed in dancing and music.

The composition of the programme indicates that the upbringing of girls was still inspired by the Renaissance ideal as articulated by Castiglione. Both in England and in France the education of women was focused on the *arts d'agrément*, which were intended to turn women into socially useful partners. Inspired by the example of the early 15th-century writer Christine de Pisan in her *Livre de la Cité des Dames*, by the beginning of the 17th century a discussion had originated on the supposed inferiority of women. "Male and female are the same creature, with the same capabilities", wrote Marie Le Jars de Gournay in 1622. The Netherlandish Anna Maria van Schurman (q.v.) answered in 1641 with a treatise on the question of whether it was fitting for the Christian woman to occupy herself with the study of literature. She also held that condemning women to the needle and the scissors was the result of custom and nothing else. The English translation of van Schurman's text (1659) inspired the linguist Bathshua Makin to write the *Essay to Revive the Ancient Education of Gentlewomen in Religion, Manners, Arts and Tongues* (1673). Van Schurman also maintained contact with Madeleine de Scudéry. In one of the ten parts of *Le Grand Cyrus* (Paris, 1649–53) the latter wrote:

> Is there anything more bizarre than to see how one approaches the education of women. One does not wish them to become coquettes, and yet one permits them to learn carefully all that is appropriate to coquetry without allowing them to learn anything that could occupy their mind or fortify their virtue … Up to now, with rare exceptions, the education of girls goes no further than reading, writing, dancing and singing.

Madeleine de Scudéry comes out in favour of a broader intellectual training in which the "musical" plays only a limited role. In that province, according to her, there were already plenty of opportunities. Thus de Scudéry apparently felt that artistic activities did not contribute to the upbringing of women. One encounters precisely the same point of view from Mary Astell, who in *An Essay in Defence of the Female Sex* (1696) considers painting as one of those

> mindless occupations that kept women from real learning. [Men] have endeavoured to train us up altogether to Ease and Ignorance … about the age of six or seven [the sexes] begin to be separated, and the boys are sent to the Grammar school and the girls to Boarding Schools, and other places, to learn needlework, Dancing, Singing, Music, Drawing, Painting and other Accomplishments

... Reading and Writing are the main Interests of Conversation, though Music and Painting may be allow'd to contribute something toward it, as they give us an Insight into the Arts that make up a great Part of the Pleasures and Diversions of Mankind.

Astell sees artistic occupation as a social skill and not as something that can enrich women as such. According to Iain Pears (1988), the number of women active as amateur artists in 17th-century England was significantly greater than the number of men who knew how to ply the brush. Nevertheless, he assumes that the phenomenon of the woman dilettante was fully developed only during the course of the 18th century. Painting and drawing were decent pastimes for women, because they were clearly more useful to them than the other specifically feminine occupations. For men this was quite obviously not the case.

On the basis of the views of both de Scudéry and Astell one deduces that "intentional" amateur artists are to be sought in a privileged aristocratic milieu that was anything but feminist in its inspiration. Women with some feminist engagement reacted against this form of "pastime" because they functioned expressly to stereotype the sexes.

Nevertheless, there were also "intentional" amateur artists who drew an emphatic distinction between the traditional feminine pastimes such as weaving and embroidery and the more explicitly artistic ones of drawing, painting and sculpture. The real discussion in which women also took part did not take place until the 17th century. Anna Maria van Schurman, for example, recommended these last media together with a whole range of minor arts as a sensible and emancipatory occupation. It cannot be determined with certainty whether the type of the "intentional" woman dilettante with great artistic versatility is found earlier than the 17th century. "Circumstantial" female artists were certainly to be found earlier, in the antique prototypes that had played their own role in the thinking about women and art from the early Renaissance. No indication of any expressly "amateur" women artists can be found in Pliny the Elder's *Historia naturalis* of AD 70. In his paragraph on *Pinxere et mulieres* he indicates five different women artists, of whom at least two belong to the category of circumstantial artists. They include Timarete, daughter of Micon the younger; Irene, daughter and pupil of the painter Cratinus; Aristarete, daughter of the painter Nearchus, as the teacher of Autubulus; and finally Iaia of Cyzicus, who was active as an unmarried woman in Rome and painted primarily portraits. Pliny further remarks that she – living at the time with Marcus Varro – asked prices for her portraits that were as high as those of such prominent painters as Sopolis and Dionysus. As far as we know, this last woman cannot in any way be described as an amateur.

Examples

In order to elucidate the complex concept of amateur artist, two case-studies are presented here. For the 16th century Catharina van Hemessen (q.v.; see also Court Artists survey), who came from a trade milieu and applied herself to painting, exemplifies the "circumstantial" amateur artist. Anna Maria van Schurman, who was situated in an aristocratic-humanist environment and cultivated the ambition of absolute versatility, functions as an example of the "intentional" amateur artist

for the 17th century. The selection is justified by the fact that the careers of both women are relatively well documented. Both their position and their work make clear how difficult it is to articulate and apply the distinction between professional and non-professional.

Catharina van Hemessen was born in 1528 as the daughter of Jan Sanders van Hemessen and Barbe de Fevre. Four years earlier her father had become a member of the Antwerp Guild of St Luke. She herself appears not to have had relations with the painters' guild. Her known oeuvre is limited in number, and all her known works date from the years 1548–55. Among her most attractive paintings are her self-portrait at the easel of 1548 (Kunstmuseum, Basel) and the portrait of a 22-year-old woman at the clavier from the same year (Wallraf-Richartz-Museum, Cologne); the portraits were probably originally pendants. Van Hemessen married the musician Chrétien de Morien, who in 1552 had become the organist for the Onze-Lieve-Vrouwekerk in Antwerp. In 1556 the couple was invited to the court of Mary of Hungary in Spain, but it is not known how long they stayed there.

Van Hemessen was not a guild member and, as far as we know, produced very little. Her sitters seem to have been recruited from her immediate surroundings and there are several reasons to suppose that she practised the arts explicitly as an amateur. Mary of Hungary provided the couple with a pension at her death, but this does not in itself necessarily imply that van Hemessen was active as an artist at the Spanish court. On the other hand it is indeed remarkable that she is still expressly mentioned in the first edition of Lodovico Guicciardini's *Descrittione di tutti i paesi bassi, altrimenti detti Germania Inferiore* (1567) as among

the most outstanding women in this art [of painting] that are still alive today … Catharine daughter of the most outstanding master Jan van Hemssen, housewife of Kerstiaen, the very excellent player of instruments: so that they both have practised their great virtues and arts for the Queen of Hungary in Spain and she has even provided them both with good support for the rest of their lives after her death.

As the daughter of an amateur artist, van Hemessen may be compared with Susanna, the daughter of Gerard Horenbout. Albrecht Dürer met this painter-miniaturist, among others, when he was living in Antwerp in 1521. In his daybook he noted: "Item master Gerhart, illuminist, has a daughter 18 years old, named Susanna, who has illuminated a little plate, a Saviour, for which I have given her one guilder". His judgement at once praises and deprecates: "It is a wonder that a Woman's picture can be of such quality". Given that little more is known about the woman, one can assume that her amateurish skill left no historical trace.

Like many of her Italian contemporaries, van Hemessen was taught by her father. An analysis of women artists known by name in the period between the 15th century and the 19th shows that some three-quarters came from an artistic milieu. Their activities in surroundings where several family members were also active as artists often make it difficult to distinguish their works from those of their family. This distinction was made only exceptionally in the past, largely because it was professional production that was evaluated – and not the

The Patini Family, engraving after a portrait by Noël III Jouvenet; Bibliothèque royale Albert Ier, Brussels

amateur work of daughters or spouses. On the other hand, Alison Kettering's *Drawings from the Ter Borch Studio Estate in the Rijksmuseum* (2 vols, The Hague: Staatsuitgeverij, 1988) demonstrates that through fundamental detailed study the drawings can be attributed to Gerard, Harmen, Moses, Anna and Gesina ter Borch (q.v.).

The female amateur artists examined here did not practise the arts because their fathers prized the educational value of drawing and/or painting. The training happened as it were by itself. Experience taught and stimulated. So it is no surprise that in his *Gulden Cabinet vande edel vry schilderconst* (Golden cabinet of the noble free art of painting; 1661) Cornelis de Bie refers emphatically to the daughters of great artists:

In Brabant Fame also praises the beautiful minds
Of the fragile women who pawn their spirits
To the pleasant Brush, wherein they are experienced
As shown to us by the art of the Daughter of Pepijn,
Of d'Egmont, and Van Dijck, so elegant, clever and
  powerful
Vigorous and colourful, and wondrously masterful …

Sofonisba Anguissola (q.v.) was the oldest daughter of an impoverished nobleman from Cremona. In accord with Italian custom, the daughters, of whom there were six in the family, received instruction in drawing and music. When Anna Maria van Schurman was born in Cologne in 1607 to a father who had come from Antwerp and a noble German mother, a "humanist" education for the girl was to be expected. In an autobiographical apologia entitled *Eukleria seu melioris partis electio*, published in 1673, she tells of her lessons in Latin, music and various arts to verify herself finally as a linguist, theologian, philosopher and artist. She experimented with an array of arts. She virtually invented the pastel portrait in the Netherlands and also made portraits in graphite and wash, on ivory and buckskin. There are decoratively written pages and also runners preserved from her hand, as well as exceptionally skilful cuttings, etchings and embroidery.

In her dissertation about whether or not the Christian woman should become a scholar, van Schurman recommends the arts and sciences. Yet she finds that not all women are suited to take up this invitation. Only women of at least average intelligence and with adequate free time would be considered eligible. This last implies an unmarried state or sufficient financial means to employ servants. According to van Schurman, mathematics, poetry, painting and "other fine arts" not listed further formed a suitable "feminine pastime".

With this she smoothed a path that must have ensured the peace of mind of women who were both Christian and creative. She herself was the role model. Her self-portraits were unusually popular as prints. At an advanced age she joined the sect of the Genevan reformer Jean de Labadie, through which her intellectual and artistic activities received a severe blow.

The exception: Being amateur without being artist

The term amateur artist indicates practitioners at the margin of the official artistic circuit. In this same margin lay the art critics, who in the 17th century were also connoisseurs. "Intentional" dilettantes and connoisseurs of art were often in the same circle, though it must be remarked here that women were seldom to be found among the recognised connoisseurs. The humanist tradition itself invited but few 17th-century women to take part in a discourse in which art became an intellectual affair. Even Schurman in her *Dissertatio* – despite her extensive philosophical schooling – does not go so far as to discuss the theory of art.

For this reason one is surprised by the initiative of Carola Catharina Patina, who published a luxurious folio written in Latin: *Tabellae selectae ac explicatae* (1694). She was the daughter of the famous Paris-born doctor and numismatist Carolus Patin who became professor of medicine in Padua in 1676. She was at home in history, mathematics and archaeology, and spoke Latin as well as French and Italian. The book contained a selection of paintings elucidated by her, primarily by Italian masters who are all also portrayed in print. In 1684 the Rouen artist Noël III Jouvenet did a portrait of the learned family. The print after this portrait (see illustration) ends the *Tabellae selectae*, and the accompanying commentary is particularly detailed. Patina emphasises the simplicity of her own hairdo in contrast to the fashionable coiffures of her mother and sister, who were likewise intellectually active: *Sexum nostrum reprehendebat vetus quidam; autor, comuntur, plectuntur, annus est*. Patina found that she used her time well; she certainly did not need a "year" to do her make-up and her hair! A clearer proof of distinction can scarcely be given. This difference becomes still more evident through the celestial globe in her right hand, an attribute about which her parents had some doubt. Patina responds, however, with a quote from a letter written by Thomas More to his daughter Margaret in which he specifically advises the study of the *sphaera*. Earlier in the book Patina also discusses Holbein's portrait of More's family, in which the oldest daughter is naturally included.

So the circle is complete: one learned woman becomes the inspirational example for another. The importance of connoisseurship would become more widely recognised only in the course of the 18th century. Women connoisseurs remained rare even then. Carola Catharina Patina constitutes a rare early example of a dilettante who was indeed delighted but was herself not artistically active.

KATLIJNE VAN DER STIGHELEN

18th and 19th centuries

The classification of many women artists of the 18th and 19th centuries as "amateur" rather than "professional" is extremely problematic and generally involves the imposition of 20th-century categorisations of artistic quality on work produced by women operating within a very different cultural milieu. The categories of "amateur" and "professional" were not always clearly defined for the male artists of this period, let alone for women seeking access to or parity in a male-dominated field. Today, the term "amateur" takes much of its meaning from its opposition to "professional", and often implies a performance of marginal proficiency practised by those who lack commitment, are partially trained, or want in talent. In the past, art historians have often relegated many women artists to amateur status because the "professional" conditions of production have, since the early modern period, been defined by the artist's ability to claim a certain level of training and expertise, to receive some monetary compensation for his or her work, or, better still, to make a living or reputation because of the high level of skill and knowledge in the realm in which he or she "professed" expertise. These expectations were generally attainable for the men who specified such criteria, but often extremely difficult to realise for women whose other social roles prevented them from partaking in such activities. Equally problematic have been recent attempts to compensate for the past neglect of women artists by over-stressing the professional status or quality of work produced by women who were not necessarily as concerned with such qualifications as we are today.

During the 18th century, the term "amateur" also connoted another – perhaps more important – meaning, one that lingers in today's usage and which is important for an understanding of the situation of many "amateur" women artists of earlier periods. In the early modern period, "amateur" had come to indicate a member of the upper classes, one who loved, who had a passionate, even obsessive interest in art but primarily as a connoisseur – a collector or expert in the knowledge of art. Members of this class needed no recompense for the practice of art and, in general, preferred not to dirty or disfigure their hands with manual labour. The "professional" making of art was stigmatised as a lower- or middle-class activity, and upper-class amateurs of this sort learned the practice of art only in so far as it advanced their expertise in the understanding and knowledge of artistic matters. Since the Renaissance, many women, such as Isabella d'Este and Queen Christina of Sweden, had taken great delight in the arts and, participating as patrons, collectors and connoisseurs in the artistic cultures of their periods, had qualified as "amateurs" according to this usage of the term. During the 18th century, this royal model for the amateur was continued with Sophie Albertine, Princess of Sweden; Christiane Louise, Countess of Solms-Laubach and the wife of Prince Friedrich Carl Ludwig von Hohenlohe-Kirchberg; and Caroline Luise, Margravine of Baden. Certainly, the love of and desire for knowledge in artistic matters continued to be a major motivation for many women artists through the 19th and 20th centuries.

The term "amateur" began to take on a more marginal connotation towards the end of the 18th century. Seeking to elevate their profession and to ensure their autonomous control over the production and interpretation of art, the men regulating the professional status of male artists through institutions such as art schools and academies protected their occupation by increasingly placing limitations on various types of artists and the works they produced. As well as male amateurs and practitioners of non-academic genre and media, upper- and middle-class women (many of whom were receiving a greater education in art and art-related matters than they had previously) were restricted from partaking in the privileges of such professional organisations. For example, in 1770 the French Académie Royale decreed that no more than four women at a time could be members, and although two women artists were among the founding members of the Royal Academy in England in 1768, no others were accorded such privileges until well into the 20th century (see Academies of Art survey). Many women, whose skills and knowledge might have qualified them to work on a level consistent with their male counterparts, were thus denied the professional certification and access to the modes of training, production and marketing that would have potentially enabled them to compete as equals. Consequently, women artists, save for an exceptional few, were unable to rise above the amateur level. In addition, the association of women with this status had a reciprocal feminising and marginalising effect on social perceptions of amateur work in general.

Cultural constructions of gender and contemporary definitions of women's social and biological functions and acceptable behaviour and activities contributed greatly to perceptions of women as "professional" or "amateur" during the 18th and 19th centuries. The ideologies of gender delineated by contemporary philosophers and cultural critics such as Jean-Jacques Rousseau stressed that a woman's "natural" place, because of her child-bearing capability, was linked to the private and domestic sphere – the home – this being the site of motherhood and the care of the family. Just as a woman's place was thus restricted to the privacy of her home, the male's place was to provide for her by labouring in the public world. The industrial revolution and capitalism encouraged the growth of professionalism throughout most male occupations of the bourgeois classes. This concept of professionalism encouraged the individual (usually one of male gender) to declare an avocation for a particular activity, to seek education in the necessary "science" and skills and, finally, to have his validity endorsed and accredited by the certifying institutions of university or academy. Indeed, such systems were inherently dependent upon a division of labour in which the male professional worked for a wage in the public world while his female dependants remained at home providing for the domestic needs of the family. These divisions of public and private spheres according to differences in gender were increasingly manifested and promoted throughout Western Europe and America by changes in the urban fabric, particularly in the separation of the home from the place of work. The situation differed from that of periods before industrialisation, when work and domestic life frequently shared the same space and women might take part as vital participants in various aspects of a family business. Even in the exceptional case that a woman artist was talented and received adequate training, she was generally expected to relegate her artistic interests to a position secondary to her domestic duties, especially after marriage and the birth of children. Consequently many women artists were, by definition, not professional and therefore amateur and, despite their relative skill or knowledge, able to practise art only as an interest ancillary to their basic social function or their domestic roles as daughters, mothers and wives.

18th century

Both the making of art objects and connoisseurship became widespread and acceptable "amateur" activities for upper-class women to fill their free time during this period. The economic prosperity, diversity of consumer goods and services, and greater leisure time generated by agricultural innovation and the growing industrialism and commerce of the 18th century enabled well-born men and women to pursue and develop a variety of educated interests and skills. At this time art and connoisseurship also became important components of the cultural exchange among and throughout the greater European community. As more and more members of the upper classes took advantage of the new transportation and mobility and travelled through the major cities of Western Europe for reasons of pleasure, business or education (institutionalised as the Grand Tour), the knowledge of and the ability to discuss art, architecture and archaeology became important indications of upper-class status and heritage while abroad. Seeing the appropriate monuments and collections, learning to discuss personal experiences and responses in a seemly and knowledgeable manner, and collecting souvenirs and art objects to attest to their travels on their return home became the goal of many Grand Tourists. Although the personal pleasure and educational development of individual women were seldom the motivating factors for this type of travel as they were for young gentlemen, many women accompanied their male relatives on such journeys and were subject to and influenced by these cultural preoccupations and "amateur" activities no less than their male companions. An exceptional few, such as Elizabeth Percy, Duchess of Northumberland, who assembled a small collection of paintings for herself during her tour of the Netherlands in 1771, were able to make purchases according to their own tastes only if in possession of their own fortunes or generous allowances. In general, however, very few women had the personal economic resources that enabled them to indulge their interests to quite the same extent as men. They were able to view those important monuments that were considered appropriate for their sight. Ancient art and archaeology, linked with the male dominion of classical language and literature, were often deemed inappropriate topics for women to study. "Modern" art (art made during and after the 16th century) was considered more comprehensible for female understanding as long as the subject matter was not too violent or sexual, and women could acquire an extensive knowledge of this material in the public and private collections they saw during their travels, thus qualifying as "amateurs" in one of the contemporary usages of the term.

In the expatriate circles in which Grand Tourists found themselves during their travels abroad, class restrictions normally observed at home became more relaxed and there were greater mobility and interchange between people of different classes. Rome, with its rich treasures of art and architecture from both ancient and modern eras, was a primary goal not only for aristocratic tourists but also for artists. Many young artists of different nationalities journeyed there in order to study the art of the past, to advance their reputations and to make themselves known to potential patrons. In this foreign context, men and women of the upper classes mingled socially and shared interests with artists of their own nationalities as well as with those of their host country. The patronage and purchase of art – particularly portraits and landscapes commemorative of their experiences – were also important activities that brought these two segments of society together. Indeed, social visits to the ateliers of the leading masters became desirable tourist attractions, integral components of the spectacle of the Grand Tour, and further stimulus for developing general interest and connoisseurship in the arts. These connections and intellectual pursuits, both amateur and professional, were carefully maintained and nurtured by both artists and patrons on their return home. Once at home, women as well as male "amateurs" developed similar relationships of patronage and intellectual exchange with the artists of their localities. Viewing habits that had developed on the Grand Tour were continued on their return; the commissioning of portraits and other genres of painting, visits to artists' studios, and attendance at collections, exhibitions, museums and picture-auctions all continued to be popular entertainments. In France during the early to mid-18th century, such women amateurs played important roles as purveyors of culture through the new social convention of the salon. Within the public rooms and boudoirs of many great Parisian houses, the *salonnières* – educated upper-class hostesses, many of whom qualified as amateurs because of their strong intellectual interests in the arts – brought together artists, writers, *philosophes* and scientists with members of the upper classes for entertainment, polite conversation and intellectual exchange. The *salonnières'* pursuit and encouragement of the arts were reflected not only by the hospitality they offered to artists, architects and connoisseurs, but also in the patronage they extended in their careful and elaborate decoration of the salons and boudoirs in which such assemblies and conversations were held.

For upper-class art lovers, the motivation to understand and be knowledgeable about artistic matters led to their experimentation with the actual making of images and objects. Authority over the arts for both connoisseurs and artists was divided between those who claimed expertise in the *scientia* – the science or knowledge of art – and *arte* – the technical skill and dexterity necessary for the production of art. Artists claimed both distinctions, and consequently amateurs often extended their study to the actual production of images and objects in order both to enhance and validate their critical judgement and expertise. Many women amateurs began their practice of art for just such reasons. An excellent example of this type of female amateur was Caroline Luise, Margravine of Baden. She was born Landgravine of Hesse-Darmstadt, and in 1751 married Margrave Carl Friedrich of Baden-Durlach. Her interest in collecting art led her to study painting with Liotard and she became known as the Hessian Minerva. She was made a member of the Royal Danish Academy of Fine Arts in 1763 and of the Accademia degli Arcadi in Rome in 1776. Another amateur similarly motivated was Jeanne Poisson, Marquise de Pompadour, the mistress of Louis XV, whose interests in philosophy, music, architecture and the arts led her to the extensive study and patronage of a variety of arts and artists. Her intellectual passions also induced her to become first an accomplished draughtswoman, and later to develop proficiencies in painting and printmaking as well. Such women were true "amateurs" in every aspect of the 18th-century usage of the word; their connoisseurship and strong interests in the history and discourse of art were passionately combined and manifested in their physical and personal involvement with the actual creative feat. Indeed, Mme de Pompadour's myriad interests, personal expertise and the connections she nurtured within the cultural milieu enabled her to be a powerful mediator between the king, court and contemporary intellectuals and artists, and transformed her patronage and favour into an influential force in the Parisian art world.

The ability to manoeuvre successfully within elite circles, to have sufficient knowledge of the cultural concerns of this stratum of society in order to engage in polite conversation, led many of the upper classes to provide their daughters with at least rudimentary skills in the visual arts, music, literature and contemporary languages. Concerning amateur painting and other "harmless amusements for young people", the amateur artist Mary Delany (q.v.) noted in 1753: "*Painting has fewer objections, and generally leads people into much better company.*" In England, several women of the upper classes were noted for their artistic work, including Lady Diana Beauclerk (q.v.); Lady Anson (née Lady Elizabeth Hardwick), whose painting was praised by Mrs Delany; Mrs Rhoda Astley, whose portraits of family members were displayed at Seaton Delavel, Northumberland, and commented upon by Bishop Pococke in 1760; Lady Fitzwilliam, whose work was displayed at Wentworth House; Lady Caroline Stanhope, a relative of the Earl of Harrington, whose paintings hung at Elvaston Castle, Derbyshire; and Margaret, Countess of Lucan, whose miniature work was commented upon by both Horace Walpole and Sir Joshua Reynolds.

Artistic "accomplishments", as ladies' amateur art work came to be called, were considered desirable and encouraged for several reasons. As noted above, these activities provided women of the leisured classes with entertainment, an outlet for their creative impulses and intellectual curiosity, served as busy work or diversion to fill excess time, or escapist solace for those whose personal life was unhappy. For the widowed Mrs Delany, painting and drawing not only occupied much of her day but also complemented and augmented her intellectual interest in the art she saw (and frequently borrowed for further study) in the collections of her friends and relatives. The talented Maria Cosway (q.v.), forbidden from painting professionally by her jealous husband, the miniaturist Richard Cosway, distracted herself from her unhappy marriage in the private pursuit of painting and music. But painting was also a social activity that many women practised in the company of other women. Commenting upon a visit from a young friend, Mrs Delany wrote:

> I am happy to have her; she has spread before me some of her drawings that she has done since I saw her, and they are charming. I lent her some prints of Claude, that she has copied to great perfection; and now we shall paint and draw and chatter together as fast as our hands, eyes and tongues can go.

Women amateurs gathered not only to work together, but to discuss art and to show one another their works. Many women hung their own work in the rooms set aside for their use, and

Mary Delany: flower collage, 1774–88; British Museum, London

this served several functions. No formal or public venue for the display of amateur achievements existed for either men or women; many women lacked the economic resources to purchase works by professional artists and thus decorated empty domestic spaces with their own work; others were thereby enabled to inject an element of self-expression or to assert personal control over their immediate environment. In these boudoirs, drawing-rooms and informal workrooms, women visited, discussed and exchanged work with one another. Mrs Delany, whose rooms were decorated with her own work ("abundant evidence of her noble industry and intellect", as the diarist Sophie von la Roche commented), shared her artistic interests with Lady Andover, also an amateur painter; the Duchess of Leeds brought Lady Vanburgh and then later Lady Cardigan and Lady Westmorland to see her pictures. She herself became an attraction or curiosity for well-connected foreign tourists, including Sophie von la Roche, to visit when in London. At her death in 1788, most of her work was willed to various friends, many of whom were noble-women who had shared her interests. Indeed, the amateur context of women's drawing-rooms extended beyond the discussion and making of art to the trade and exchange of pictures as well. Elizabeth Percy, Duchess of Northumberland, described her visit while touring the Netherlands to see the "fine pictures" of a Mme Boshart: "she is a woman of fashion but notwithstanding, would (which is almost the case in general here) part with them for a good price."

While the knowledge and practice of art were important mechanisms of social bonding for many women, they could also operate as exclusionary tactics as well. Ladies' "accomplishments" served to provide a basis of class differentiation from the encroachment of the increasingly wealthy middle classes who sought affiliation with the aristocracy. Knowledge of the arts, the ability to perform, to purchase and to converse appropriately, constituted a constantly changing coded system of taste controlled by the upper classes who had the time and resources to participate in such activities. To a certain degree, the free time of upper-class women, the leisure activities and hobbies with which they filled that free time, and the changing criteria for women's education during this period served as exclusionary devices to shut out those who wished to enter higher social circles. Attempts by the middle classes to cross class boundaries were thwarted by subtle strategic changes within these cultural codes, which served to exclude those who might have the wealth and leisure time, but who had not been born, raised or educated within the class that regulated cultural practices. Women, as well as men, had increasingly decisive roles in this process, and the well-born, educated lady "amateur" thus served as an important component in the maintenance of class distinctions.

Within the elite circles of the aristocracy, the development of women's interest and education in the arts served another important social function, that of making the lady amateur a more attractive commodity in the matrimonial marketplace. Not only were her accomplishments, social graces and leisure activities capable of reflecting and augmenting her husband's social status, but as romantic love and mutual attraction rather than the unification of political and landed interests became the basis of matrimonial choice during the 18th century, the lady amateur made an attractive companion for the gentleman amateur, whose interests and education her knowledge complemented. Within the ritual of courtship, the performative spectacle of the young woman dancing, drawing, singing or playing a musical instrument allowed male attention to be focused on her person, while "maidenly modesty" was maintained in a socially acceptable manner through her concentration and preoccupation with her immediate task. In her absence, the exhibition of a young lady's accomplishments – by means of musical instruments, drawings, watercolours, needlework and other "busy" work within the public rooms of her family's residence – formed an important element in the process of her debut into society and the proclamation of her marriageability. For example, the early 18th-century English art chronicler George Vertue reported that when the Princess Augusta arrived in London to marry Frederick, Prince of Wales, her paintings were prominently displayed to the court for a year after her marriage. Such exhibitions of a young lady's artistic skill and accomplishment also served as important models for imitation within the descending ranks of the aristocracy, gentry and middle classes who sought to prepare their daughters for socially advantageous marriages by having them trained in fashionable accomplishments; Vertue also noted that the paintings of Miss Da Costa (the daughter of a London merchant and businessman) decorated an entire cabinet of her family's house.

As the knowledge and practice of art became important social assets, art training became an important part of women's education. Young women were often trained in the practice of art on an individual basis at home and by private instructors. These tutors were artists who were employed by great noble families to care for their various artistic needs, including the maintenance and restoration of collections, decoration and the painting of portraits as well as the artistic education of the younger members of the family, or they were artists who were either desirous of supplementing their income (as did Bernard Lens with Mrs Delany, the Misses Da Costa and Lady Helena Percival, the daughter of the 1st Earl of Egremont) or unable to subsist from the sale of their own work and thus reduced to teaching in order to earn a living. The daughters of families less wealthy or prominent received art instruction within the confines of one of the many new boarding and finishing schools often founded towards the end of the century by impoverished gentlewomen. In this context, drawing, languages, music and dancing were supplements to the regular curriculum and required additional fees. Women with economic means, previous training and a strong commitment to the arts could also seek instruction from more prominent artists if any were willing to accept female students; thus Mary Delany studied with William Hogarth and Mme de Pompadour with Boucher.

Women's training in the arts differed greatly from that of male artists. Distinct media and techniques for women's practice were stressed: line-drawing, crayon, watercolour, pastel and occasionally miniature painting on ivory were advocated as the most seemly media for women's performance; their perceived qualities of delicacy, meticulous execution and preciosity were considered to be innately feminine. In general, women, even those of the upper classes, seldom had the privilege of a specially assigned room to serve as their studio; the spaces for both their domestic duties and their amusements had to overlap and be multi-functional. The cleanliness and daintiness of the female hands and body had to be maintained as well. Consequently, amateur women artists sought and were encouraged to pursue artistic recreations that had a certain ease of execution, were tidy, and that used easily prepared, fast-drying materials such as ready-to-use watercolours and tube paint. Besides requiring compact workspace, these artistic activities had to employ equipment that was limited in quantity, portable and easily stored away so that such personal occupations would not interfere with the other activities of the family. Work in pastel was perceived to be especially appropriate for women because it was associated with the work of the Venetian artist Rosalba Carriera (q.v.), a woman artist who had excelled in the technique. Its light palette was also reminiscent of the rococo interiors dominated by the female *salonnières*; its delicacy of touch was viewed as akin to that of lacework (the production of which had long been the domain of women) and its chalk pigments were similar to those used in women's make-up. Miniature painting, with its costly materials and minutely detailed finish, was not only seen as jewel-like in its execution and scale, but was frequently enframed by gems and metalwork and functioned as jewellery for the adornment of the female body. It, too, became a highly popular medium for women's amateur work.

Many exceptional women did work on a grander scale in the messier, smellier and technically more complicated medium of oil-painting, such as Mrs Delany (who had a servant to grind and mix colours and to clean up after her); printmaking, as practised by Mme de Pompadour and Isabella Howard (the second wife of the 3rd Earl Howard); and even in sculpture, in which Anne Seymour Damer (q.v.) excelled. But these media were seen as requiring an education, intelligence and physical strength not believed to be present in the female body. Moreover, painting and sculpture, especially in the genres of history and figure painting, were increasingly privileged as high art and elevated above other media, techniques and subject matter by the institutions of academy and museum, both dominated by professional male artists. For women to work at this level was felt during the late 18th century to demonstrate an ambition that was both defeminising and "unnatural".

Much of the artistic training that women received was by no means intended to prepare them to work at a level commensurate with that of male professionals. Frequently, women's training followed that of their male counterparts only through the earliest stages of the usual curriculum, deliberately leaving them at an adolescent level of expertise, which, to a large degree, pre-determined their amateur status. Instruction for both men and women began with the learning of draughtsmanship. Starting with pen or pencil, novices learned first to draw by copying simple shapes and outlines, advancing from these to more complicated forms using the techniques of chiaroscuro and colouring with crayon, pastel or watercolour washes. Whereas male students then usually progressed to working in oil or stone, the training for most women stopped at this intermediary stage and most lady amateurs continued to work only in these "lesser" media. Indeed, when the French Academy limited the number of female academicians to four in 1770, it concurrently opened its enrolment of women amateurs in its drawing classes. Not only were drawing and watercolour

often ranked as preliminary stages in the training of artists, they also continued to be used by professional artists for working up preparatory designs and sketches before beginning the final finished product in oil and stone. This also contributed to the perception of the media most frequently used by women as preparatory and peripheral.

Apart from the more traditional media of "high art", women artists worked in a variety of materials and methods ranging from embroidery and needlework, wax modelling, shell and beadwork, cut-paper work and collage, the painting of fans, china, small furniture and other decorative objects, to the construction of jewellery and other artistic *objets* with unusual material such as hair and feathers. Mrs Delany, who spent most of her artistic life painting, is better known today for the delicate paper mosaic flower studies she made in the latter years of her life. She also produced several shellwork pictures as well as silhouettes, embroidered pictures and featherwork. Several of these media – particularly textile work – were considered to be appropriate for female practice because of their applicability to the functioning or decoration of the domestic context. Their focus on small minute detail also called forth – and served to display – the female virtues of patience, diligence and perseverance. Indeed, many of these techniques and materials – such as pastel portraiture and watercolour washes – came to be seen as rather feminine activities because of their marked popularity with women practitioners.

For many women amateurs, however, the choice of odd materials or techniques was simply an ingenious and imaginative way to provide for creative aspirations within their limited contexts. In general, women amateurs demonstrated a remarkable ability to compensate for their lack of resources in the assembly, reshaping and personalisation of their immediate visual experience. The techniques of collage and *découpage* – the piecing together of images appropriated from other sources – particularly satisfied amateur desires for both viewing and making images and reached their most monumental manifestation in the late 18th-century decorative fad, the "print room". A selection of reproductive prints was pasted directly on to the walls of a special room or cabinet in imitation of picture galleries and then framed with engraved or cut-out paper swags, bows, medallions and borders. Lady Louisa Conolly constructed a print room (the Small Dining-Room) in the 1760s and 1770s at Castletown (Co. Kildare, Ireland); the Countess of Egremont (wife of the 3rd Earl) decorated the Great North Dressing-Room at Petworth, Sussex, in this manner around 1801; Mrs Chute and her nieces were responsible for pasting up the print room at The Vyne, Hampshire, in 1815. For amateurs such as these, the print room offered a relatively inexpensive way of practising the aesthetic judgements of connoisseurship in the collecting, indexing and arranging of important works of art; for other women, the design, assembly and decoration of the spaces around the prints provided them with a means for creative expression. Collage and the print room gave women the opportunity to appropriate and make their own the images and ideas generally controlled by men; similarly, the choice of the new and strange materials that many employed in their work allowed women artists to carve out their own sphere of artistic production. Moreover, women's artistic skills displayed in "marginal" materials (beads, shells, hair, etc.) were more acceptable in that they did not compete with the work of male artists on either a professional or an amateur level.

Subject matter as well as media took on gendered implications as certain genres were both favoured by women and advocated for their use. Women, even those who excelled in the early stages of their training, were effectively prevented from progressing to professional status by their prohibition from attending the life-drawing classes, as many scholars have noted. Up to this point in the artist's education, the student learned first by copying earlier masters' works, or from drawing subjects within the minor genres of still-life, landscape and animal painting. Life-drawing classes, in which the student learned to draw the human body from a nude live model, was conducted and regulated by the official art schools and academies that were dedicated to the production of professional artists. Female students were banned from attending these classes on moral grounds. As the understanding of and proficiency in the depiction of the workings of the human body were deemed essential to an artist's ability to manipulate the expressive potential of the figure in history painting, the highest of genres, women were effectively prevented from participating in this domain. Lack of life-class training discouraged women from figure drawing except on an amateur basis. Moreover, critics generally held women's lack of this crucial step in the training of the professional artists against them regardless of whatever their real skill or achievement might be. Instead, both professional and amateur women artists produced works in the lower genres of still-life, flower-painting, landscape, domestic topics and portraiture. This limiting range of subject matter both contributed and responded to contemporary polarisations of female and male spheres that in turn were linked to the gendered opposition of the feminine nature and emotion versus masculine culture and reason. Women's art was on a small, precious and intimate scale, portraying their personal, particular experience of botanical subjects, animals, landscape and the "natural" human topics found in the home, while men's art was more typified by the generalising, intellectualising, philosophically elevated "grand style" of history painting.

19th century

During the 19th century women of the elite classes continued to draw and paint much as they had during the 18th. Princess Eugenie of Sweden, Princess Marie Christine d'Orléans (q.v.) and Queen Victoria and her daughters were all committed amateur artists as were many women of the aristocracy, such as Louise de Broglie, Comtesse d'Haussonville; Catherine Maria, Countess of Charleville; and Louisa, Marchioness of Waterford (q.v.). However, as men of mercantile or professional occupation attained greater wealth and independence, many from the middle classes sought to demonstrate their new social mobility through imitation of upper-class behaviour and patterns of consumption. Their wives and daughters were encouraged to partake in the leisure activities of aristocratic women (albeit on a more limited basis) and to become accomplished in the arts. Indeed, the disciplined instruction of most women of the higher classes in drawing and painting, regardless of their personal inclination or skill, resulted in much art of mediocre quality, which contributed to the deflating value of

amateur work during the 19th century. Social biases against women earning their living remained and became even stronger during this period as women's roles became more entrenched within the domestic context. However, their artistic training did allow women a marginally acceptable professional option if they were orphaned, widowed or faced with destitution. In such circumstances, most women with a modicum of education and possessing some accomplishment sought employment as governesses. Book illustration, decorative painting, the hand-colouring of prints and the teaching of art also offered semi-professional options to make a living, of which many in such situations took advantage. Emily Mary Osborn's painting *Nameless and Friendless* (1857; for illustration, see p.1053) depicts one such woman, accompanied by her young son, forced by widowhood or poverty to leave her "proper" domestic context. She has ventured into the public marketplace, in the attempt to sell the paintings or drawings previously produced solely for her own or her husband's amusement. Mary P. Harrison, an amateur painter of flower pictures, eventually supported her invalid husband and three children with botanical illustration. Clara Maria Wheatley Pope illustrated botanical texts following the death of her painter husband in 1801, and even after remarrying continued to teach painting to young women, including Princess Sophia of Gloucester and the Duchess of St Albans. For the most part, however, amateur work was the only completely legitimised artistic activity for women, and women amateur painters proliferated during the 19th century.

Middle-class women of the Victorian period were increasingly held responsible for the consumption of material goods for their family's immediate needs as well as for the decoration and maintenance – "the arranging" – of the family domicile. With the greater restrictions on the resources, leisure time and domestic environment of the middle-class woman, much of her effort was expended upon artistic activities that affected her family's lifestyle, the early training and education of her children, and the decoration of her clothing and domestic environment. Indeed, many of the earliest art schools were established to train women for employment, such as the French Ecole Gratuite de Dessin pour les Jeunes Filles (opened in 1803), which focused on teaching the design and decoration of feminine and domestic artefacts such as textiles, painted wallpaper, lace, artificial flowers, fans, lampshades, cameos, vignettes, ceramic and enamel painting, book bindings and tapestries. The watercolours of the Irish artist Louisa Payne Gallway depicted a variety of topics and were set in a screen that was entitled *Memoirs of Old Haunts and Happy Days* (1867) and given as a present to her cousin. Idleness in women, even those of the leisured classes, was a social vice to be avoided or masked by the artistic construction or improvement of such functional objects. This linkage of female work with the design and decoration of functional household items would contribute to the marginalisation of "craft" (as opposed to "art") that underpins evaluations of much of Western visual culture. Wives and daughters were encouraged to spend a portion of their day in the parlour or the morning-room at the small worktables assigned to their personal use. Pencil or pen-and-ink sketching, watercolour and gouache remained popular media for women's work as they had in the late 18th century.

Even within the privacy of the home, a woman's work was

not conducted without scrutiny or restriction. She was schooled to be sensitive and submissive to those around her. Many women served as amateur assistants to their husbands and fathers, as did the British woman Jane Webb Loudon, who illustrated her husband's *Encyclopaedia of Gardening* (1834), or as Lady Wilkinson did with her husband, Sir Gardiner Wilkinson, in his *Desert Plants of Egypt*. The time, expenditure and even the choice of subject matter of many amateur women artists were often closely supervised and regulated by their husbands or fathers. Amateur art was for the most part anonymously produced, and frequently, if exhibited or published, ascribed as "By a Lady". The American flower painter Susan Fenimore Cooper published her illustrated *Rural Hours by a Lady* in 1850 anonymously; her name is never given, but her father, James Fenimore Cooper, is frequently credited as "The Author of *The Deerslayer*". Consequently, much amateur work has been ignored because of the difficulty of attributing it to any specific artist.

Nineteenth-century attitudes concerning women held that their natural emotional and responsive sensitivities equipped them to play a central and refining role within the family and the home – and by extension society in general. Female accomplishments, even on an amateur level, served not only as entertainment for themselves, but also to provide a comfortable and elegant home for the benefit of the husband and children. As women's lives became increasingly restricted to the domestic and the interior, their role within this limited context was to respond to the emotional, physical and material needs of the members of their household. As in the 18th century, painting and sketching were social activities, undertaken in the company of other women, usually a sister, mother, daughter or close personal friend. Many women practised art only during their childhood and adolescence, abandoning these activities when they married and had children, while others kept up their interests throughout their lifetime. Even those who had received an excellent and advanced education in the arts and had briefly attempted to paint on a professional standing, such as Edma Pontillon, sister of Berthe Morisot, often practised only on an amateur level after marriage. The resulting drawings and paintings depict the specific places and activities with which women associated themselves and manifest the boundaries placed upon their social experience and domain. The watercolours of the English artist Mary Ellen Best recorded the rooms of the house she lived in, depicting the furnishings, occupants and activities of each, as did an entire album produced by Charlotte Bosanquet and the pen-and-ink washes produced by the Irish artist Caroline Hamilton. Much of women's amateur art was characterised by a more personal, intimate and particularised response to their individual situation, focusing on their emotive response to the everyday circumstances of domestic family life and to their restricted views of nature. Moreover, 19th-century ideologies of gender held that women were innately closer to nature. Local landscape, domestic animals and garden plants and flowers were easily accessible and, as in earlier centuries, popular choices as subject matter for amateur women artists. Studies of vegetable and animal matter were also easily adapted to textile design and interior decoration. Paintings of flowers, in particular, became highly popular and feminised with a poetical and sentimental language of their own. For many women, however,

close study of animals and flowers led to a greater intellectual interest and knowledge of natural history, zoology, entomology and botany – topics of inquiry not usually encouraged in women. English amateurs such as Priscilla Susan Bury, Elizabeth Twining, Lady Harriet Anne Hooker Thiselton Dyer, Beatrix Potter (q.v.) and Marianne North; Americans such as Susan Fenimore Cooper and Mrs E.W. Wirt; the Irish amateurs Lydia Shackleton and Lady Blake; the French amateur Natalie, Baronne Renaud; and the Australian Louisa Anne Meredith (q.v.) all became renowned naturalists through their amateur artistic study, and several became published authors and illustrators.

Domestic subject matter was also deemed singularly appropriate for women artists, besides being that which was most readily available for study. Genre paintings of the rituals of a woman's life – household work, courtship, motherhood, family life and children – or cautionary tales warning against the transgression of these norms, were extremely popular with both professional and amateur women artists throughout the 19th century. Such topics both reiterated the "natural" domestic sphere of femininity, and painters such as the four Hayllar sisters, Edith and Jessica in particular, produced and exhibited images depicting a serene and highly ordered domesticity in which the preferred female roles were carefully represented. Although these women could and did at times exhibit at venues such as the Royal Academy, they were considered to offer little or no challenge to the subject matter, techniques and economic success of male artists of professional status. By means of their sketched notes of family life, many women became responsible for the unofficial recording of family memory, thereby extending their genetic and reproductive functions into the artistic context. Portraits of relatives or close connections, such as those produced by Cassandra Austen of her sister Jane (c.1810), by Amelia Curran of Percy Bysshe Shelley (1819) and by Adèle Hugo in 1838 of her children, helped to document family likenesses, connections and lineage. Not only were the appearances of their family members and immediate environment preserved, but women's amateur sketching recorded the events of day-to-day home life, special occasions, or journeys both local and abroad and further served to form an archive of family memory.

Of growing popularity through the course of the 19th century was the organisation of women's drawings, designs and vignettes into sketchbooks and albums. These collections of small pictures were usually arranged according to a general organising principle: they held only a particular type of image, such as portraits of family members, or a record of botanical study, studies from other artists' work, or they served as a souvenir by recording a particular event or journey. Sometimes the work was by a single artist, while at other times such albums brought together samples of others' work as well. Either way, they served as small-scale records of taste and personal response on the part of an individual woman. Many albums were simple sketchbooks while others could be richly-bound compilations of watercolours, sketches, drawings and portraits made by their owners together with similar images exchanged with other amateur artists. They also frequently contained reproductive prints, postcards and images drawn from the popular press.

After the development of photography, such women

amateurs as Julia Margaret Cameron (q.v.) and Clementina, Viscountess Hawarden (q.v.), practised the new technology as well as collecting the images that were most often housed in such albums. When Adolphe Alfonse Diseri introduced the relatively inexpensive *carte-de-visite* portrait photographs in the mid-19th century, the collection of these small, easily exchangeable images in albums became a tremendous fad, quickly replacing the collections of drawn and painted portraits, and eventually developing into the traditional photograph album. In Switzerland, the Russian Marguerite de Krüdener brought her paintings and drawings of her home, holidays and portraits of her family members in discrete albums, while her sister Marie included in hers a *mélange* of materials including pen and ink drawings, watercolours, maps, photographs, prints, pressed flowers and butterflies. Such accretions, in which female "amateur" response to the visual environment and artistic culture was collaged on to the pages of a book, bear a resemblance to the 18th-century print rooms. Both allowed women to imitate the larger collections of old masters and ancient sculpture in which their male relatives were able to indulge themselves. The difference in scale between such collections as the print room and the album reflects both the increased restriction on women's activities during the 19th century as well as the extension of such activities for women from the upper classes to the small-scale endeavours of the middle classes. In such albums female response was easily contained, privatised or stored away, to be brought out later for display and discussion in the company of other women, with male admirers, or for the amusement of visitors and relatives. Many albums were frequently exchanged or given away as gifts to female family members and close friends. Albums and the types of images they contained became a peculiarly feminine genre of art production that in turn largely shaped the art made for them. Julia Margaret Cameron, for example, produced her photographs as unique objects, but always with an eye to their inclusion in the albums she presented to her friends and family. The containment and concealment of women's artistic work within such albums point to the relative unimportance of their particular vision frozen on paper and indicates instead the greater importance placed on the spectacle or display of the lady artists as they sketched, painted or looked at these albums under the gaze of their male relations or acquaintances.

Many of the educational strategies for teaching young women proper accomplishments – private drawing masters, governesses and finishing schools – remained the same from the 18th century to the mid-19th. However, the middle classes were not always able to afford these more expensive forms of training for their daughters. In such cases, responsibility for teaching drawing and painting to the young girls of a household often fell to their mother or another female family member who had some skill in such matters. The Barker sisters, Leila, Octavia and Lucette, all amateur painters of animals, flowers and landscape topics, were taught to draw by their father, Thomas Barker, a Yorkshire vicar who objected to their working for recompense. By the end of the 18th century, a burgeoning trade in popular literature for female audiences had developed, and it continued to expand in the 19th century. Drawing manuals and "how-to" books such as *The Lady's Drawing Book and Compleat Florist* of 1755 and *The*

Student's Treasure, A New Drawing Book ... of 1804, ladies' magazines and periodicals ranging from Rudolph Ackermann's *Repository of Arts* and the *Ladies Monthly Museum* to *Gazette des Femmes* and *La Mode Illustrée* provided elementary lessons in drawing and watercolour, instructions in the appropriate response to and appreciation of art, and frequently household hints, botanical information, sewing and embroidery patterns, fashion plates and social gossip. Entrepreneurs such as Ackermann, who capitalised on the popularity of his own magazine by opening a London shop of the same name, specialised in art supplies, prints, art books and other commodities to exploit the women's market for art goods. Such literature and resources not only helped to provide an inexpensive education in the arts, but also enabled women to work within the seclusion of their own homes, thereby preserving domestic sanctity.

In general, speciality or professional training for women artists went against bourgeois definitions of feminine respectability. In Britain (as was typical of most Western nations) women were not allowed into the Royal Academy schools until the late 1850s, after a long feminist campaign. Meanwhile, many women attended the informal ateliers or academies founded by artists of both sexes who wished to profit from the tremendous amateur demand for instruction. Young women from both Britain and America whose parents could support their ambitions both financially and ideologically travelled to Paris and Rome, where masters were accepting of female students and society was less concerned with the transgressions of foreigners. Others took advantage of the local and national schools of design that, starting in the 1840s, were established to train and make employable women without other means of support, in the more mundane aspects of commercial design and illustration. Women who wished to practise art on the more serious basis associated with male professionalism agitated for art schools modelled after those for men – including carefully monitored life classes – and were quick to differentiate their goals from those of their amateur sisters.

Art classes conducted for amateurs allowed women an option to leave their domestic environments in order to extend their social circle and to participate in the public sphere on a limited basis. Another opportunity to leave the safe environment of the home was membership in one of the many amateur sketching and watercolour societies that were founded during the 19th century. These clubs, whose organisation ranged from the local to the national levels, brought amateur ladies, or ladies and gentlemen, together for the "mutual improvement in painting and drawing and the cultivation of a taste for art" (as was stated by the founders of the Irish Amateur Drawing Society). Apart from offering convivial social advantages, these groups brought together people of similar interests for lectures, discussion and sketching expeditions, disseminated interest in art, dispensed instruction for their members, and also provided opportunities for exhibition.

Exhibition became increasingly difficult for both male and female amateur painters over the course of the 19th century. While women were not completely banned from showing works even in venues as prestigious as the Paris Salon or the Royal Academy's annual exhibition, amateur work in general was increasingly marginalised in order to protect the primacy of the male professionals. With the mid-19th-century foundation of academies for the serious training of professional women artists throughout Western Europe and America, women artists also attempted to control and elevate their position in the art world to match the standards of male professional artists. Like the male academicians of the previous century, they, too, sought to emphasise the legitimacy of their occupation through the certification of their members and dissociation from the mediocrity connoted by the female amateur tradition. Young women whose strongest motivation for the study of art was to become "accomplished" according to social convention, or to develop a moderate interest in a pleasurable time-filling activity, became known as "academy belles". Their tenuous commitment, undeveloped or lack of talent, and conventional taste for predictable subject matter (often of sentimental or domestic topics) led to their ostracism first by male artists, and then by their more committed sisters who sought to separate themselves from this marginalised group. Outside the venue of their own amateur associations, women amateurs were frequently either charged to exhibit with their professional colleagues or ostracised completely.

As the system of workshop and private patronage typical of early modern artistic production was replaced by galleries and the public exhibition of art as the primary conduits through which an artist's work could become known, the institutions that sponsored and regulated such displays increasingly restricted both female and male amateur painters. The economic exigencies of the life of the professional artist necessitated the ability to seek out and woo patrons, dealers and publicity, and involved aggressive qualities that contradicted the virtues of womanly modesty and were deemed socially unacceptable as well as actively discouraged. Women, even those who had overcome the difficulties of obtaining professional instruction, were pushed back into amateur status by the denial of access to the major venues of visual consumption and profitable exchange: academic exhibitions and gallery salerooms. Amateur women artists, particularly those of the upper classes, could and did exhibit or donate their work for charitable causes. Lady Waterford designed the cartoons for the stained-glass windows of the church of Clonegan and produced a series of frescoes for a Northumberland village school; the Princess Royal contributed one of her etchings to an auction benefiting the Crimean War effort; and Francesca Alexanders sold a series of her Tuscan drawings to benefit charity (New Haven 1994, pp.18–19). Such attempts generally only contributed to the association of amateur work with charitable and community volunteerism.

Towards the end of the 19th century, the domestic subject matter and focus of most amateur women's work found a legitimate place with the Arts and Crafts Movement. Sponsored by male aesthetes such as the members of the Pre-Raphaelite group and William Morris, this movement promulgated a return to a pre-industrial artisanship in which art, design and function were to be integrally united in the making of the craft object. Ornamental needlework, crewelwork, lace-making, wood-engraving, wallpaper design, ceramic tiles and pottery were revived and produced in the Morris firm, helped by the female members of his family, his wife Jane, his daughter May Morris (q.v.), his sister-in-law Elizabeth and others. This workshop and the many that imitated it not only provided many women with professional work, but also helped to give a greater dignity, aesthetic and monetary value to the feminine "arranging" of household interior decoration for which amateur women had long been held responsible.

By the end of the 19th century a clear qualitative differentiation had been made between amateur and professional status for women as well as men. The term had come to connote a level of mediocrity, domesticity, lack of commitment and an association with volunteerism and the social hobbies of the leisured woman. For women engaged seriously in the production of art, "amateur" had become a label carefully to be avoided.

LISA HEER

Bibliography

Baldassare Castiglione, *Il libro del cortegiano*, 1528; as *The Book of the Courtier*, 1561

M.A. Vente, "De illustre Lieve-Vrouwe Broederschay te 's Hertogenbosch, 1541–1615" [The illustrious brotherhood of Our Lady in 's Hertogenbosch, 1541–1615], *Tidschrift van de Vereniging voor Nederlandse muziekgeschiedenis*, xix, 1960–61, pp.32–43

Carola Catharina Patina, *Tabellae selectae ac explicatae*, Patavii [Padua], 1691

Christian Gottlieb Jöcher, *Allgemeines Gelehrten-Lexikon*, iii, Leipzig, 1715, columns 1300–01

Elizabeth Percy, Duchess of Northumberland, *A Short Tour Made in the Year One Thousand Seven Hundred and Seventy-One*, London, 1775

J.P. Neale, *Views of the Seats of Noblemen and Gentlemen in England, Wales, Scotland and Ireland*, London, 1818

The Autobiography and Correspondence of Mary Granville, Mrs Delany, ed. Lady Llanover, 6 vols, London: Bentley, 1861–2; reprinted New York: AMS Press, 1974

Edmond Vander Straeten, *La Musique aux Pays-Bas avant le XIXe siècle*, vii, Brussels: Van Trigt, 1885, p.426

George Vertue, "The Vertue note books" in *The Walpole Society*, xviii, xx, xxii, xxiv, xxvi and xxix, London: Oxford University Press, 1929–47

Claire Williams, ed., *Sophie in London, 1786: Being the Diary of Sophie von la Roche*, London: Cape, 1933

Ruth Kelso, *Doctrine for the Lady of the Renaissance*, Urbana: University of Illinois Press, 1956; reprinted 1978

M.A. Vente, "De illustre Lieve- Vrouwe Broederschay te 's Hertogenbosch, 1541–1615", *Tidschrift van de Vereniging voor Nederlandse muziekgeschiedenis*, xix, 1960–61, pp.32–43

Women Artists, 1550–1950, exh. cat., Los Angeles County Museum of Art, and elsewhere, 1976

Ian Maclean, *Woman Triumphant: Feminism in French Literature, 1610–1652*, Oxford: Clarendon Press, 1977

Desmond Guinness, "The revival of the print room", *Antique Collector*, vi, 1978, pp.88-91

Phyllis Stock, *Better than Rubies: A History of Women's Education*, New York: Putnam, 1978

Anthea Callen, *Angel in the Studio: Women in the Arts and Crafts Movement, 1870–1914*, London: Astragal, 1979; as *Women Artists of the Arts and Crafts Movement*, New York: Pantheon, 1979

Germaine Greer, *The Obstacle Race: The Fortunes of Women Painters and Their Work*, London: Secker and Warburg, and New York: Farrar Straus, 1979

Ruth Hayden, *Mrs Delany: Her Life and Her Flowers*, London: British Museum Publications, 1980; revised as *Mrs Delany's Flower Collages*, 1992

Rozsika Parker and Griselda Pollock, *Old Mistresses: Women, Art and Ideology*, London: Routledge, 1981

Rozsika Parker, *The Subversive Stitch: Embroidery and the Making of the Feminine*, London: Women's Press, 1984; New York: Routledge, 1989

Linda Woodbridge, *Women and the English Renaissance: Literature and the Nature of Womankind, 1540 to 1620*, Urbana: University of Illinois Press, 1984

Charlotte Yeldham, *Women Artists in Nineteenth-Century France and England*, 2 vols, New York: Garland, 1984

R.J. Schoeck, "Margaret More", *Contemporaries of Erasmus: A Biographical Register of the Renaissance and Reformation*, 3 vols, Toronto: University of Toronto Press, 1985–7, ii, pp.455–6

Stevie Davies, *The Idea of Woman in Renaissance Literature: The Feminine Reclaimed*, Brighton: Harvester, 1986

Karel Moens, "De vrouw in de huismuziek: Een iconografische studie naar 16de- en 17de-eeuwse schilderijen en prenten uit de Nederlanden" [Women in family music-making: An iconographical study of 16th- and 17th-century paintings and prints from the Netherlands], *Jaarboek van het Vlaams Centrum voor Oude Muziek*, ii, 1986, pp.43–63

Leonore Davidoff and Catherine Hall, *Family Fortunes: Men and Women of the English Middle Class, 1780–1850*, London: Hutchinson, and Chicago: University of Chicago Press, 1987

Gilpin to Ruskin: Drawing Masters and Their Manuals, exh. cat., Fitzwilliam Museum, Cambridge, 1987

Iain Pears, *The Discovery of Painting: The Growth of Interest in the Arts in England, 1680–1768*, New Haven and London: Yale University Press, 1988

Whitney Chadwick, *Women, Art and Society*, London and New York: Thames and Hudson, 1990; revised edition, 1996

Anne Higonnet, "Secluded vision: Images of feminine experience in nineteenth-century Europe", *The Expanding Discourse: Feminism and Art History*, ed. Norma Broude and Mary D. Garrard, New York: HarperCollins, 1992, pp.170–85

Ann Pullen, "*Conversations on the Arts*: Writing a space for the female viewer in the *Repository of Arts*, 1809–15", *Oxford Art Journal*, xv/2, 1992, pp.15–26

Ann Bermingham, "The aesthetics of ignorance: The accomplished woman in the culture of connoisseurship", *Oxford Art Journal*, xvi/2, 1993, pp.3–20

Deborah Cherry, *Painting Women: Victorian Women Artists*, London and New York: Routledge, 1993

Wayne E. Franits, *Paragons of Virtue: Women and Domesticity in Seventeenth-Century Dutch Art*, Cambridge and New York: Cambridge University Press, 1993

Gerda Lerner, *The Creation of Feminist Consciousness: From the Middle Ages to Eighteen-Seventy*, New York and Oxford: Oxford University Press, 1993

Anne Crookshank and the Knight of Glin, *The Watercolours of Ireland*, London: Barrie and Jenkins, 1994

Els Kloek, Nicole Teeuwen and Marijke Huisman, *Women of the Golden Age: An International Debate on Women in Seventeenth-Century Holland, England and Italy*, Hilversum: Verloren, 1994

A Struggle for Fame: Victorian Women Artists and Authors, exh. cat., Yale Center for British Art, New Haven, 1994

Mirjam de Baar and others, eds, *Choosing the Better Part: Anna Maria van Schurman, 1607–1678*, Dordrecht and London: Kluwer Academic Publishers, 1996 (Dutch original, 1992)

Jack Kramer, *Women of Flowers: A Tribute to Victorian Women Illustrators*, New York: Stewart Tabori and Chang, 1996

Training and Professionalism

19th and 20th centuries

1. Britain and Ireland

19th century

The professional female artist emerged in 19th-century Britain as an apparently new feature of the domestic art scene. Seeming to be preceded only by a few individuals such as Angelica Kauffman (q.v.), she was a product of the developments that made the 19th century a different era from the 18th: that is to say, first of industrialisation and urbanisation, and subsequently of the women's rights movement and the commodification of art. Although little remarked upon before the 1840s, she posed a challenge to the economy of art and the assumed role and character of high culture and to the sexual politics of Victorian society. The controversy about women's ability to achieve in this field and the propriety and convenience of her attempting to do so was huge, lasting beyond the end of the century, although census figures suggest the ranks of female artists to have been small and the growth in their numbers to have slowed steadily after the middle of the century (e.g. 1841: 278; 1851: 548; 1861: 853; 1871: 1069).

1800–1837

During the first decades of the 19th century, the upper- and middle-class woman was expected to treat creative work as a hobby or accomplishment, making no distinction between, say, musical performance, embroidery and painting, while the working-class woman was presumed to possess neither creativity nor cultural aspirations. All women were expected to have a capacity for needlework and a taste for the decorative, but they were equally assumed to possess no ambition for public acknowledgement, no originality of thought and little intellectual or physical rigour. The tradition of amateurism, typified by copies and miniature portraits, obscured the fact that such activities were carried on professionally by such women artists as the Sharpe sisters. The only female artist with a national reputation was the portraitist Margaret Carpenter (q.v.), though professional families such as the landscapist Nasmyths and Rayners included women. Confounding the stereotype of the delicate watercolourist animated by personal associations, all these women produced a steady output of oil paintings on commission.

Anon.: *Life Class at the Female School of Art*, from *Illustrated London News*, June 1868, p.616

Obtaining a fine-art training was difficult. Although there was no systematic art education for women, some fine-art institutions in provincial cities had an educational arm and might admit women, though they had about them the aura of upper-class amateurism. Relatives in the profession and private drawing teachers were the readiest source of fine-art instruction for women. The establishment of provincial art exhibitions from the 1820s on allowed women to gain some local exposure, reputation and professional standing, depending on the liberalism of the civic leaders in the region: thus, for instance, Rolinda Sharples (q.v.) gained a great reputation in Bath and Bristol, and women were allowed to participate in the exhibitions of the Royal Hibernian Academy in Dublin from their inception in 1829. Where women were allowed to participate in these new arenas, however, their position was usually signalled as an aberration from an implied male norm: the Society of Painters in Watercolours, or Old Watercolour Society (established 1804; Royal Watercolour Society from 1881), classed women as "lady members", which it saw as synonymous with "honorary members", a status imposed on women also by the Society of British Artists (established 1823).

1838–1869

The practice of art was one that middle-class women, socialised into a feminine amateurism in artistic activities, increasingly tried to turn to professional use. Their motivation ranged from the need of an income to the search for greater fulfilment or independence than convention allowed them. Since Victorian ideology restricted all respectable women's usefulness to the family, home and factory, and yet economic and demographic reality made such ghettoisation difficult to sustain, the issues raised by the increase in numbers and visibility of women artists were not only aesthetic but social and political. They pivoted on the division of activity and experience into private and public spheres and the alleged symbiosis between the domestic and the professional worlds. The specific questions debated from the 1850s against a background of the "woman question" were of woman's innate abilities, her proper or desired roles in society generally and culture in particular, her moral probity and her intellectual worth. Prejudices concerning woman's natural and necessary nature and function remained persuasive to a large number of Victorians, whose society exaggerated sexual difference wherever it could.

The development of Realism, with its emphasis on observation and rejection of classical learning, opened art up to female practitioners, and Pre-Raphaelitism in particular promised validation of the genres to which women commonly had greater access: still life, landscape, portraiture and scenes of mundane reality. The growth in popularity of genre – anecdotal scenes of everyday life – was significant for women, whose social immobility and poor training opportunities left them generally ill-equipped for the traditionally prestigious types of work, such as history painting. Convention allowed that the domestic world, along with still life, portraiture and landscape, was a legitimate subject for women artists.

The most prestigious sources of fine-art education – the Royal Academy of Arts in London, the Royal Scottish Academy in Edinburgh and the Royal Hibernian Academy in Dublin – either prohibited or did not welcome women students. A campaign to open the educational opportunities offered by the Royal Academy to women on an equal basis with men was launched by women artists, writers and social reformers in 1859 and was partially successful by 1861, when female students were conditionally accepted.

All other training options were second best. They included the Government Schools of Design, established from the 1840s throughout Britain and Ireland and including a Female School in London (threatened with closure in 1859), although these institutions offered an applied-art training meant to raise the aesthetic level of manufacture rather than preparation for the career of painter, sculptor or architect. It was, indeed, much easier to get a design training than a fine-art one, even when the demand among middle-class women for marketable skills was reluctantly recognised: the Queen's Institute for the Training and Employment of Educated Women was set up in Dublin in 1861 for this express purpose, but went along the road to fine art only as far as still-life and landscape painting. Some private art schools such as Cary's or Leigh's (both London) accepted women, though their aim of preparing students for application to the Royal Academy Schools limited their relevance to female students until 1861. Another possibility was the drawing teacher who was privately employed to teach in the pupil's home or his/her own rooms. Even more dependent on the availability of family finance was tuition in the schools or studios of such continental centres as Paris, Munich and Rome; academies were closed to women throughout Europe, but the atelier system functioning in other European countries, though little favoured in Britain, depended only on a woman finding a practising artist willing to teach female students, as Anna Mary Howitt and Jane Benham found when seeking an art education in Munich in 1850. Self-help was a widespread source of training for women, which could include learning from instruction manuals, copying from private or public art collections, arranging private study from the life (the Society of Female Artists attempted some collective self-help in respect of this particular problem) or sketching excursions.

In the absence of reliable accessible training provision, it was women in artistic families who could most easily become artists themselves, whether in painting, engraving or sculpture. Certainly, nearly all the women artists who became best known in this period, such as Henrietta Ward (q.v.), Mary Thornycroft (q.v.), Rebecca Solomon (q.v.) and Joanna Boyce (q.v.), were daughters, wives or sisters of male artists. Although the family gave practical assistance and access to professional networks, it could also predetermine and restrict the kind of work a woman practised and keep her in the shadow of her male relatives through their shared name. The categorisation in the census of 1861 of artists as professionals would have encouraged such female artists as these to claim their identity, though deterring others still bound by the etiquette of "fine-ladyism".

Exhibition and membership of exhibiting bodies was often categorically denied to women (e.g. the Glasgow Institute of Fine Arts, established in 1861). Exhibition opportunity depended in most cases on membership of the exhibiting body, and the establishment in London in 1857 of the Society of Female Artists was a response to the discriminatory, restrictive membership generally allowed to women. Anti-academic and anti-institutional feeling grew from the middle of the century, giving rise to the Free Exhibition (established 1848, later the National Institution), more accessible to women because less costly, the Dudley Gallery (established 1865), more congenial to women because it favoured watercolour and had no membership system, and others. Photographic societies and exhibitions were set up in the 1850s, and appear to have been generally open to women, though not necessarily welcoming. The exposure sought by women graphic artists was, of course, of a different kind, and several female illustrators such as Mary Ellen Edwards and Adelaide and Florence Claxton (q.v.) established themselves as regular contributors to medium-range weeklies, monthlies and annuals.

Women were active in art writing at most levels. Anna Jameson and Elizabeth (Lady) Eastlake became prominent in the 1850s for their learned books and articles, while many lesser-known women published art history for adults and for children, translations of art-historical classics, biographies, handbooks and manuals. The feminist press obviously offered express opportunities for female journalists. Art critics, however, were nearly all men until the 1880s, and tended to treat women's work with condescension or paternalism if they did not simply ignore it as unimportant, unskilled and unoriginal. Though a liberal trend of sincere encouragement was discernible on the establishment of the Society of Female Artists, this tailed off in the mid-1860s. The inferior status of women's art was generally perpetuated in all kinds of writing about art, whether by men or women, typified by the common journalistic habit of reviewing women's exhibits as a separate category even where they were not in fact hung together.

The rise of such commercial dealers as Ernest Gambart and Henry Wallis in the 1850s and 1860s brought little advantage to female artists as a group, although a few crowd-pleasing individuals whose novelty value could command high prices (the French painter Rosa Bonheur, q.v., stands out) did find success with a wide public in this way. Women who were construed as semi-amateur, such as the landscapist Barbara Bodichon (q.v.) and the photographer Julia Margaret Cameron (q.v.), were, perversely, as likely to be given solo shows in this milieu, no doubt because they were neither serious challengers for the patronage that men guarded jealously nor claiming more than a marginal role for women in the delineation of mainstream taste and trends. While old master (sic) collections, private and public, contained hardly any women's work, the principal collectors of contemporary art, such as Richard Vernon, also bought very little work by women, with isolated examples by the portraitist Margaret Carpenter, landscapists the Nasmyth sisters, topographer Louise Rayner and the history painter Henrietta Ward being the exceptions that proved the rule. This generalisation applies also to the avant-garde taste for Pre-Raphaelitism. Few women were in command of the wealth needed to form an art collection, and those who are documented, such as Queen Victoria, the heiress Angela Burdett-Coutts and Ruskin's friend Ellen Heaton, showed no partiality for (though no prejudice against) women's work. Royal patronage was premised on a conventional sexual division of labour that allocated to sculptor Mary Thornycroft, for example, the portrayal of the royal babies in statuette form. A more fruitful source of patronage for women artists were the Art Unions, whose prizewinners, though routinely castigated as possessing low-brow, narrow taste, looked for works at the cheaper end of the market. Public commissions such as the interior decorations of the Palace of Westminster and statues of local worthies did not go to women.

1870–1900

In her book *Modern Painters and Their Paintings* (1874) Sarah Tytler remarked:

> I may observe, in proof of the difficulty which the technicalities of art must present to women, that of all the women painters whom I have chronicled, I am not aware of one … who did not overcome the difficulty, by the advantage of an early familiarity with art, from having been the daughter of a painter, or, at least, of an engraver.

This was a situation reflected by the case studies in Ellen Clayton's *English Female Artists* (1876), but it became less so as, with improving opportunities and a greater general resignation to the fact of women artists, preparing for a career in painting (still much more feasible than sculpture) was less of a challenge to convention and propriety. The best-known women artists of this period, Lady Butler (q.v.), Henrietta Rae (q.v.), Kate Greenaway (q.v.) and Helen Allingham (q.v.), had no family connection to the profession. One of the factors behind this change in climate was the opening in 1871 of the Slade School of Fine Art, London, which, in distinguishing itself from the Royal Academy Schools, promised better opportunities for women from the start.

Although Louisa Starr (q.v.) and Jessie McGregor appeared to have proved the case for women by winning the gold medal for history painting at the Royal Academy Schools in 1867 and 1872 respectively, the Royal Academy continued to limit women's training with special regulations until 1893, when a life class for women was introduced (and when the Royal Hibernian Academy finally admitted women students), and to deny women membership of the Academy itself until 1923. Women continued to seek art training abroad, especially if looking for modern art: an example is Sarah Purser (q.v.), whose French connections became an important influence in late 19th-century Irish art. The retardataire wish to see women content with the less prestigious and arguably amateur pursuits classed as applied arts was evidenced in the reception of the Royal School of Art Needlework (established 1872) and the Ladies' Work Society (established 1875), which attempted to play the emergence of women as creative talents and the contemporary revival of the "arts and crafts" off against each other to conservative purpose. The Arts and Crafts Movements in Scotland and Ireland, by contrast, effected a broadening of the spectrum of women's creativity, bringing prominence to individual female artists and craftswomen alike.

The revival of classicism established by the late 1860s and pre-eminent by the 1880s, though unsuited to women's education and experience, attracted many ambitious women artists by its cultural cachet, especially after their access to improved fine-art training gave them greater confidence in tackling the nude. Even as the Royal Academy tried to reassert its importance through the classical revival, independent exhibition fora proliferated and the Grosvenor Gallery (established in 1877 by Sir Coutts and Lady Lindsay) was by contrast welcoming to female artists, who, like the male exhibitors, were hand-picked. But independent initiatives did not necessarily exhibit progressive sexual politics, and the same range of attitudes to women could be seen towards the end of the 19th century as at the middle: the Watercolour Society of Ireland (founded in 1870 as the Amateur Drawing Society) was dominated by women; the Old Watercolour Society elected its first woman member in 1890; but the Dublin Art Club (established 1886) categorised women still as "lady members" and the Glasgow Art Club (established 1880), the Art Workers' Guild (established 1884) and the New English Art Club (established 1886) were for men only. Thus there was still an argument for women-only organisations such as the Glasgow Society of Lady Artists (established 1882). In the commercial sector, Elizabeth Thompson, later Lady Butler, and Helen Allingham were made conspicuous by solo shows at the Fine Art Society, though the most famous female artist of the period, Kate Greenaway, found success in the less weighty field of illustration, made more feminine by her specialisation in material for children.

Female journalists became common in this period. The poet Alice Meynell and the columnist Florence Fenwick-Miller were among the women whose writings displayed a special interest in art during the last two decades of the 19th century. Reviews of the Society of Female Artists (renamed the Society of Lady Artists in 1874), the only regular exhibition where women's work was in the majority, became fewer and more cursory in this period as an anti-feminist backlash manifested itself in the 1880s, remobilising the misogynistic arguments of the mid-19th century. There was a revival of interest in Kauffman and her French contemporaries such as Elisabeth Vigée-Lebrun (q.v.), which set them up as the exemplars of a feminine art. A similarly retrogressive use was made of Princess Louise's much-publicised example of upper-class amateurism, which extended to exhibition while eschewing professionalism.

Collectors, whether mainstream or avant-garde, such as Edmund Davies, Mr and Mrs George McCulloch and George Holt, showed greater willingness to purchase women's work though usually via one favourite individual artist. Some progress in public patronage was marked by Amelia Paton Hill's statue of *David Livingstone* in Princes Street, Edinburgh, described on its erection in 1876 as "the first public work of the kind to be executed by a woman". The first purchases of women's work for a public institution occurred in the Liverpool Corporation's acquisition in 1871 of the painting *Elaine* by Sophie Anderson (q.v.), and in 1873 of Louisa Starr's *Sintram*, and for a national institution in the Chantrey Bequest's acquisition in 1890 of *Love Locked Out* by Anna Lea Merritt (q.v.) for the new Tate Gallery. The persistence and escalation of the women's rights movement in the 1890s, embodied for many in the "New Woman", ensured that the century ended on a note of challenge and resistance as strong as when women artists first emerged as an issue in mid-century.

Pamela Gerrish Nunn

20th century

The visibility of women artists in Britain and Ireland in the 20th century is marked by a contradiction – a seemingly steady increase in the number of women working in all areas of art and design work matched by a corresponding decrease in their appearance in art-history books until the 1970s, when feminist art historians started to look again at women's work. At the centre of this problem is the representation of women in modern art collections (e.g. Tate Gallery, London; Arts Council Collection) and standard modernist art history books (e.g. Charles Harrison's *English Art and Modernism, 1900–1939*, Denis Farr's *English Art, 1870–1940* and Frances Spalding's *British Art since 1900*) of 10–20 per cent, while their representation within contemporary art exhibitions in the course of the century has fluctuated between 25 and 50 per cent. The representation of women artists' work in art criticism and art history needs to be separated from the actual patterns of social and historical change in order to reassess women's position as artists. Two contributory factors to this picture of social and historical change in the 20th century are the expansion and development of general education (from which women benefited as both pupils and teachers) and women's changing status in the labour market (where the numbers of women, single and married, has steadily increased in the course of the century).

Since the 1890s women have formed the majority of students educated in British and Irish art schools, fluctuating between 50 and 75 per cent of all art students. This pattern varies considerably from school to school: at the Royal Academy Schools in London, for instance, women students formed less than 25 per cent of the student intake between 1901 and 1914, whereas at the Slade School of Fine Art, London (from its foundation in 1871 to 1945), the ratio was reversed, with women students forming 75 per cent of the student intake. In the same period, at the Glasgow School of Art, women students formed a fluctuating 33 to 47 per cent of the intake, rising to 50 per cent after 1920. If access to art education was no longer the major obstacle to women that it had been in the 19th century, access to institutions did not equate with equality of opportunity within the art school or in professional life.

While certain Victorian and Edwardian stereotypes about the lady amateur were abandoned in the 20th century, the suspicion persisted until well into the 1960s that the large numbers of women in art education were merely filling in time between school and marriage. The low expectations of many male lecturers in fine art (from Professor Tonks to Reg Butler) about the lack of seriousness of women students are matched by the frequency of accounts in autobiographies of women artists who had to "prove" their commitment to male tutors (e.g. Laura Knight, q.v., Nina Hamnett, q.v.). By 1910 the nude, rather than the draped model, which had been so central to any form of academic training in the 19th century, was offered to women as an object of study in life-drawing classes in most London art schools, but many provincial art schools continued the convention of the draped model in the name of "propriety" until 1945. Women were largely taught in sex-segregated classes until 1918 and this fashion continued in some art schools until 1945.

During the period 1900–18 art education became increasingly diversified as the distinctions between fine art and the applied and commercial arts became more marked. At the turn of the century, particularly in the applied arts under the impetus of the Arts and Crafts Movement, more enlightened educators such as W. R. Lethaby (Central School of Art, London) and Francis Newbery (Glasgow School of Art) encouraged women students as professional artists and designers while maintaining that certain areas of design were more suited to women; they thus perpetuated a different form of gender stereotyping of women's abilities at the same time as opening up opportunities for women. Val Williams (1986, p.90) has emphasised the role a formal training played in enabling women to pursue a career in photography, and the ways in which studio portrait photography and providing editorial coverage for "women's interests" in magazines were seen as the means to earn a living in photography. A similar argument was made by Lorna Green (1990) about the role of art schools in providing limited and specialised opportunities for women to work in certain areas of sculpture.

As education remained fee-paying, these prejudices were also reinforced by the pattern that emerged in most schools of a predominance of fee-paying "daughters of educated men" studying in day classes, when compared with the large number of men enrolled in part-time evening classes after a day's work elsewhere. Working-class women also entered the art and design fields through evening classes and so gained opportunities to develop as designers. Scholarships were highly prized, especially the Prix de Rome, which was first awarded to a woman, Winifred Knights (Monnington), in 1920, and many women benefited from the opportunities offered by county or school scholarships and medals. In 1933 the diversity of diplomas and teaching certificates offered by individual schools was replaced first by the Art Teacher's Diploma, then in 1946 by the National Diploma of Design; this was followed in 1961 by the Diploma of Art and Design, and in the 1970s by the introduction of degrees, equivalent in academic status to those of universities. The expansion of private secondary education for middle- and upper-class girls since the 1870s, followed by the expansion of state provision and the slow raising of the school-leaving age in the first half of the 20th century, also contributed to the increasing general extension of women's education into higher education, particularly into teacher training. In 1918, when women were partially enfranchised for the first time, the universities (with the exception of Cambridge) opened their doors to women. Art education, as with higher education in general, became more than a finishing school for middle-class women – it was a means to a "room of one's own", an independent income and professional status.

The high number of women students in art education was not mirrored by the number of women teachers and lecturers in higher education – and this remains one of the foremost problems of inequality in art education. No woman taught at the Royal Academy Schools before the 1960s, a reflection of the fact that only four women were elected to its ranks between 1922 and 1945. At the Slade, only one woman teacher was employed before 1945, Margaret Alexander (who taught

Winifred Knights: *The Deluge*, 1920; oil on canvas; Tate Gallery, London

there 1928–46). By contrast, the Glasgow School of Art, in the period 1892–1920, employed 27 women artists: 7 in painting and drawing, and 20 in the applied-arts section, among them Jessie M. King (q.v.), Ann Macbeth, Frances Macdonald (q.v.) and Dorothy and Olive Carleton Smyth. The same pattern can be found at the Metropolitan School of Art in Dublin, where Alice Jacob headed the Design School (c.1900–21), and where women students, alongside lace and needlework, excelled in the applied arts of enamelling and stained glass. By the 1960s art schools offered diplomas in an increasingly wide and more highly specialised variety of fields from textiles to jewellery, printmaking to pottery, graphic design to fine art, film and photography. While the opportunities to teach in art schools remained highly limited until 1945, many women ran their own schools and classes, for example Mainie Jellett (q.v.), Lucy Kemp-Welch (q.v.) and Sylvia Gosse (q.v.). Education continued to play a crucial role in the large number of independent workshops established by women in the first half of the 20th century, such as those of Evelyn Gleeson, Evie Hone (q.v.) and Susie Cooper (q.v.). By the 1960s an increasing number of

women artists could be found lecturing in art schools and participating in what has become the dominant model of the (male) fine artist, who both exhibits and teaches.

A further aspect to women's education is the frequency with which women artists trained or studied abroad. Paris remained a magnet for aspiring artists before 1945 and the main opportunity to meet and learn about modernist artists and to live *la vie bohème* (e.g. Mainie Jellett, Eileen Agar, q.v., Nina Hamnett). There have, however, been many prominent women artists both pre- and post-1945 who have not taught or held posts in art schools (e.g. Barbara Hepworth, q.v., Eileen Agar), a pattern in direct contrast to the "norm" for male artists in the 20th century, and it is within the art school system – and its particular relationship to the art market – that a "structural" discrimination against women has been both established and maintained.

While most of the well-known women artists who trained in the 1900s and 1910s were middle- or upper-class women who were able to continue their practice either because of a private income or through the support of family or husband, this pattern changed in the 1920s as a more diverse cross-section of the daughters of "professional and educated men" entered the labour market. Career books for girls and young women written between the 1900s and 1930s encouraged those interested in fine art to consider both teacher training and a specialism in an area of craft, design or applied arts as the most likely means through which a woman could find employment. This "realism" was both a reflection of knowledge about women's actual employment prospects and the generally low aspirations of women's abilities. A large number of women trained at art school went to work in the expanding primary and secondary education system as the state both raised the school-leaving age and made primary education compulsory. Equal pay was not introduced until 1945 and women were forced to leave their teaching jobs on marriage by law. The work of women artists in this sector included both major reforms and innovations in the training of children and the development of art in schools (e.g. Evelyn Gibbs, Nan Youngman) but its generally low status did not change until the Depression in the 1930s increasingly encouraged men to start seeking employment in schools.

Negative stereotyping of women artists in the press is another characteristic between 1900 and 1960, and the legacy of this continues to mar the perception of women's considerable achievements as artists today. Women were frequently told in the late 19th and early 20th centuries that they must choose between a career and marriage (with the presumption of motherhood) and that it was impossible to combine the two. While the reputations of many women artists have in the 20th century been overshadowed by that of their partners, their lives and careers show that this "choice" has been increasingly refused in so far as many women artists married and, of these, some, but by no means all, had children. Married women, in general, have entered the wage-labour market in increasing numbers throughout the 20th century but the social prejudices against women continuing to work once married continued – an ideology reinforced in the 1920s and 1930s by legal dismissal on marriage in both teaching and the civil service. This general social prejudice, which has its more positive characterisations in the 1950s as "housewife as career", has contributed to some of the most marked prejudices of the 20th century against women who were known to be partners of male artists, trivialising their labour as a "hobby" , the result of "frustrated maternity" (Brighton and Morris 1977, p.228), or by characterising women's work as simply derivative of their male partners, rather than the result of mutual exchanges.

During the course of the 20th century the "ideology" of separate and appropriate spheres of public activity for men and private/domestic activity for women has shifted from the separation of home and work into more complex patterns of horizontal and vertical segregation amongst women and men at work. These patterns of segregation, where women are either confined to particular areas of labour (horizontal) or "cluster" at the bottom of the profession with only a select minority rising to the top (vertical), are typical of women artists' careers when compared to their male peers, both in terms of their limited entry into a hierarchical and increasingly segmented and specialised fine-art market, and the clustering of women in often devalued branches of the arts, crafts and design industries. If one also bases an assessment of sex discrimination upon the marks of recognition given by the art world to its leading artists, a pattern of belated recognition is also visible in terms of the granting of awards, prizes or one-person exhibitions at prestigious galleries to men earlier and more frequently than their women colleagues. Discrimination along gender lines is also reflected in the actual market values for the works of women artists, which have generally sold for lower prices than equivalent works by their male peers.

The diversity of work undertaken by women artists through the course of the 20th century is one of the key indicators of women's ingenuity, since wherever opportunities opened up women artists have taken them. The rise in women in other professions such as architecture, law, medicine, even engineering, is used repeatedly as an indication of this general trend. Fine-art printmaking is one area where women's participation grew rapidly (Gertrude Hermes, q.v., Clare Leighton) – a pattern at odds with the almost exclusively male-dominated commercial printers. Women nevertheless continued to find opportunities to exhibit, while keeping their eye on possibilities to work as graphic artists, illustrators, craftspersons or designers. Vanessa Bell (q.v.), Nina Hamnett, Frances Hodgkins (q.v.) and Gertrude Hermes all worked as applied artists and designers alongside the exhibition of their paintings. Banners, posters, illustrations and applied art were made for the fight for the vote, for example, the work of Sylvia Pankhurst for the Women's Social and Political Union; of the Artists Suffrage League (from 1907, chaired by Mary Lowndes); and the Suffrage Atelier (from 1909).

In the 1920s and 1930s the four women artists' exhibiting groups – the Society of Women Artists, the Women's International Art Club, the Glasgow Society of Women Artists and the Scottish Society of Women Artists – all offered their members the opportunity to exhibit both paintings and sculpture alongside craft objects in recognition of this aspect of women artists' work. At a time when the fine-art market was increasingly specialised into print, painting, sculpture and drawing exhibitions, the mixing of fine art and craft brought only the rebuke that these exhibitions were not professional enough, regardless of the fact that the same women artists sent their fine-art exhibits to other major group exhibitions. The Royal Academy, which separated art forms, abolished the display of miniatures in 1940 – one area in which women artists *had* dominated.

At the turn of the 19th and 20th centuries the dominant model of the fine artist was centred on regular participation in large group exhibitions and selection to membership of prestigious artists' groups. London remained the largest community of artists and the centre of the art market in contemporary art. Flourishing art communities could also be found throughout Britain and Ireland with the combination of an art school, a local academy and competing groups of younger or more avant-garde artists, as in Glasgow, Edinburgh, Manchester and Dublin, and more rural communities, such as Newlyn and St Ives in Cornwall. The submission of works to large-scale metropolitan exhibitions attracted commissions as well as building critical reputations and would be supplemented by one-person exhibitions at individual London dealers and auction houses (even the few exhibitions of Gwen John, q.v., in London, for example, fit this pattern). Between 1900 and 1930 women artists gained considerably both in the numbers participating in these exhibition forums and the numbers elected to these large artists' groups, which averaged between 25 and 33 per cent in the inter-war years – a figure directly opposed to their majority presence as students. The election of the first four women to the Royal Academy can be seen in this light, but the minority of women selected has remained tiny as women formed only 10 per cent of all Associates (ARA) and Academicians (RA) by the 1980s and tokenistic, when compared with the London Group, where women's participation in the exhibitions reached 50 per cent by 1930 but their membership was confined to 30 per cent. The Royal Academy did host a rare prize in its open exhibition for women sculptors, the Lady Feodora Gleichen memorial prize (Gleichen had been a sculptor and bequested the money) from 1926 to the 1940s.

Women artists were given war commissions in both world wars, in the schemes initiated by the British Government, though the scale and the type of commission was never on the same terms as those of their male counterparts. Anna Airy was the only woman offered commissions of munitions factories on the same basis as men in World War I. The remaining commissions came from the Women's War Committee (1918–20), set up to document and celebrate women's contribution to the war effort, and these were displayed during the 1920s at the Imperial War Museum as a separate part of the collection, the Women's Section. Art works by women artists form 5 per cent of the First World War Collection and 10 per cent of the Second World War Collection at the Imperial War Museum, London. The Second World War collection was commissioned by Kenneth Clark under the War Artists Advisory committee. Laura Knight, Evelyn Gibbs and Evelyn Dunbar were among the women who received commissions.

By the 1930s artists no longer relied on large group exhibitions to build their critical reputation and instead concentrated on the public exhibition of their work in one-person or small peer-group exhibitions organised by dealers. Large-scale group exhibitions became increasingly criticised for the inconsistent and poorly arranged hanging of the exhibits, which drowned the few decent works considered to be on show. This criticism has to be seen in the context of the belated arrival in Britain of both the dealer-critic system from France and a growing interest in modernism, where small exhibitions of one artist or a small group demonstrating their shared and common interests were becoming a more formidable method of gaining critical attention. The establishment of the Irish Living Art exhibitions in 1943 is another extension of this "modernist" pattern. While many women artists did exhibit over a long period with one particular dealer (Ethel Walker, q.v., at Redfern; Laura Knight at the Leicester Galleries; Barbara Hepworth at Gimpel Fils and Marlborough, all in London), a consistent long-term relationship with one dealer is frequently what marks out those who are considered the most prominent and successful women of the period. The development of modernist groups, such as the Seven and Five Society and the English Surrealist group, did little to promote women artists into their ranks, and the numbers of women in these groups remained very small (around 10 per cent). The emergence of modernism in the 1930s in Britain was combined with a deep recession in the art market following the slump. In this context, the exclusion of women could be seen as one means through which a newly emergent modernist and male-dominated group could assert its

"professionalism", but it is also possible to recognise sexist practices within the ideology of modernism. There have, however, been many notable women dealers in this period. Peggy Guggenheim had galleries in both London and Manchester in the 1930s, and after World War II Halima Nalech and Annely Juda. In the post-1945 expansion of the art market and publicly funded gallery system, there has been a steady rise in women's participation in the art world as administrators and curators. By the early 1990s women formed 75 per cent of arts administrators, although the inequality of vertical segregation remains an issue.

Art criticism in contemporary art journals and newspapers was until the 1960s a male-dominated endeavour, although there were some notable women art critics before World War II, for example, Gwen Raverat (q.v., *Time and Tide*), Myfanwy (née Evans) Piper (*Axis*), E.H. Ramsden and Mary Chamot (also a curator at the Tate Gallery). Many women artists also participated in the production of avant-garde journals and publications (e.g. Jessica Dismorr, q.v., Eileen Agar and Barbara Hepworth).

The art infrastructure in Britain changed considerably in 1945 with the establishment of the Arts Council of Great Britain. While the dealer-critic system continued to develop, it did so in relationship to a new network of both private and publicly funded art centres and institutions that showed contemporary art independently of the city art museums and galleries established in the Victorian era. The art centre movement of the 1960s and the growth since the 1970s of sculpture parks and temporary site-specific art works are two other factors in the expansion of opportunities to show work in the regions in a context other than a large group exhibition. Increasingly exhibition internationally either under the aegis of the British Council's touring exhibitions or representation at the Venice or São Paulo Biennales or through reciprocal relationships with galleries in Paris or New York became an important feature of an artist's profile. The selection of women artists to represent Britain has been poor with some notable exceptions, for example Barbara Hepworth and Bridget Riley (q.v.); the Irish sent two women painters, Norah McGuinness (q.v.) and Nano Reid, to the Venice Biennale in 1950, and a woman sculptor, Hilary Heron, in 1956. Another factor in the development of post-war exhibition was the model of exhibition and catalogues set by the Museum of Modern Art in New York. Whereas before 1945 most exhibitions were accompanied by a short essay and/or a hand-list, during the 1950s and 1960s increasingly well-illustrated catalogues with extended critical essays became the norm. Few women artists have benefited from this kind of scholarly attention and the representation of women in large-scale retrospectives is both mixed and very poor. Only eight one-person shows of women artists were held at the Tate Gallery between 1910 and 1986 compared with 214 for men. Although several women have been short-listed for the Turner Prize, introduced in the 1980s by the Tate, Rachel Whiteread has been the only woman to win in a decade. Institutions of contemporary art such as the Whitechapel Art Gallery and the Institute of Contemporary Arts in London, or publicly funded galleries such as the Camden Arts Centre in London, Ikon in Birmingham, Arnolfini in Bristol, Cornerhouse in Manchester and others, have since the 1950s become increasingly important as venues for both thematic presentations of contemporary art and retrospectives of mid-career artists. It is generally in their shows that increasing numbers of contemporary women artists can be seen, and many feminist exhibitions were held at these venues in the 1970s and 1980s.

While the women's movement has brought women together for many different initiatives in the visual arts since the early 1970s, access to resources (both material and intellectual) and institutional recognition remain key problems for many women. Insights from feminist art theory and history have challenged many assumptions about values in the critical assessment of art practices and initiated new directions in art practice. But the question of who gets written into the history books remains.

KATY DEEPWELL

Bibliography

Vrynwy Biscoe, *300 Careers for Women*, London: Lovat, Fraser and Nicholson, 1932

Winifred Kirkland and Frances Kirkland, *Girls Who Became Artists*, New York and London: Harper, 1934

Mary Chamot, *Modern Painting in England*, London: Country Life, and New York: Scribner, 1937

Stuart Macdonald, *The History and Philosophy of Art Education*, London: University of London Press, 1970

Grant M. Waters, *Dictionary of British Artists Working 1900–1950*, 2 vols, Eastbourne: Eastbourne Fine Art, 1975

Jane Johnson and A. Greutzner, *The Dictionary of British Artists, 1880–1940*, Woodbridge, Suffolk: Antique Collectors' Club/Baron, 1976

Janet Minihan, *The Nationalization of Culture: The Development of State Subsidies to the Arts in Great Britain*, London: Hamish Hamilton, and New York: New York University Press, 1977

Andrew Brighton and Lynda Morris, eds, *Towards Another Picture*, Nottingham: Midland Group, 1977

Anthea Callen, *Angel in the Studio: Women in the Arts and Crafts Movement, 1870–1914*, London: Astragal, 1979; as *Women Artists of the Arts and Crafts Movement, 1870–1914*, New York: Pantheon, 1979

Germaine Greer, *The Obstacle Race: The Fortunes of Women Painters and Their Work*, London: Secker and Warburg, and New York: Farrar Straus, 1979

Carol Dyhouse, *Girls Growing Up in Late Victorian and Edwardian England*, London and Boston: Routledge 1981

Grant Longman, *The Herkomer Art School and Subsequent Developments, 1901–1918*, Bushey Reference Paper no.2, Bushey: Longman, 1981

AIA: The Story of the Artists' International Association, 1933–1953, exh. cat., Museum of Modern Art, Oxford, 1983

Jane Lewis, *Women in England, 1870–1950: Sexual Divisions and Social Change*, Brighton: Wheatsheaf, and Bloomington: Indiana University Press, 1984

Charlotte Yeldham, *Women Artists in Nineteenth-Century France and England*, 2 vols, New York: Garland, 1984

Chris Petteys, *An International Dictionary of Women Artists Born Before 1900*, Boston: Hall, 1985

Pamela Gerrish Nunn, ed., *Canvassing Women: Recollections by Six Victorian Women Artists*, London: Camden, 1986

Val Williams, *Women Photographers: The Other Observers, 1900 to the Present*, London: Virago, 1986; as *The Other Observers: Women Photographers in Britain, 1900 to the Present*, 1991

Gail Braybon and Penny Summerfield, *Out of the Cage: Women's Experiences in Two World Wars*, London and New York: Pandora, 1987

Jane Beckett and Deborah Cherry, *The Edwardian Era*, London: Phaidon, 1987

Irish Women Artists from the Eighteenth Century to the Present Day, exh. cat., National Gallery of Ireland, Dublin, and elsewhere, 1987

Pamela Gerrish Nunn, *Victorian Women Artists*, London: Women's Press, 1987

Rozsika Parker and Griselda Pollock, *Framing Feminism: Art and the Woman's Movement, 1970–1985*, London and New York: Pandora, 1987

Robert Radford, *Art for a Purpose: The Artists' International Association, 1933–1953*, Winchester: Winchester School of Art Press, 1987

Lisa Tickner, *The Spectacle of Women: Imagery of the Suffrage Campaign, 1907–1914*, London: Chatto and Windus, 1987; Chicago: University of Chicago Press, 1988

Pauline Barrie, "The art machine", *Women Artists Slide Library Journal*, no.20, December 1988–January 1989, p.9

Deirdre Beddoe, *Back to Home and Duty: Women Between the Wars, 1918–1939*, London and Boston: Pandora, 1989

Jan Marsh and Pamela Gerrish Nunn, *Women Artists and the Pre-Raphaelite Movement*, London: Virago, 1989

Cheryl Buckley, *Potters and Paintresses: Women Designers in the Pottery Industry, 1870–1955*, London: Women's Press, 1990

Mary Ann Caws, *Women of Bloomsbury: Virginia, Vanessa and Carrington*, New York and London: Routledge, 1990

Penny Dunford, *A Biographical Dictionary of Women Artists in Europe and America since 1850*, New York and London: Wheatsheaf, 1990

Lorna Green, *The Position and Attitudes of Contemporary Women Sculptors in Britain, 1987–1989*, M.Phil. dissertation, Department of Fine Art, Leeds University, 1990

Ten Decades: Careers of Ten Women Artists Born 1897–1906, exh. cat., Norwich Gallery, Norfolk Institute of Art and Design, Norwich, 1992

Jude Burkhauser, ed., *Glasgow Girls: Women in Art and Design, 1880–1920*, 2nd edition, Edinburgh: Canongate, and Cape May, NJ: Red Ochre, 1993

Deborah Cherry, *Painting Women: Victorian Women Artists*, London and New York: Routledge, 1993

Sybil Oldfield, ed., *This Working-Day World: Women's Lives and Culture(s) in Britain, 1914–1945*, London: Taylor and Francis, 1994

A Struggle for Fame: Victorian Women Artists and Authors, exh. cat., Yale Center for British Art, New Haven, 1994

Clarissa Campbell Orr, ed., *Women in the Victorian Art World*, Manchester: Manchester University Press, 1995

2. France

19th century

During the 19th century all the world looked to France for leadership in the fine arts. For the professional artist of either sex, the opportunities for training, exhibiting and selling art in Paris were unrivalled. For women, the highly competitive atmosphere of this art capital meant that they faced extreme obstacles in training and professional activities, but at the same time it propelled such ambitious women as Elisabeth Vigée-Lebrun (q.v.), Rosa Bonheur (q.v.), Marie Bashkirtseff (q.v.), Berthe Morisot (q.v.) and Mary Cassatt (q.v.) to rare international fame.

In the century ushered in by Napoleon, there were seen the blossoming of a government-sponsored system for the production of art during the early decades and then, at the mid-point, the growth of a free art market to displace it. Both systems helped large numbers of artists to attain the status of such professionals as doctors, lawyers and professors in terms of education and income. But neither system could support all those who aspired to be artists, particularly as the high status of the arts attracted an increasing number of applicants from outside as well as inside France. Women found that they could be easily eliminated from competition for the many reasons that kept them out of professional life in general, but women's desire to participate in the arts was so great that persistence and politicking allowed many of them to force open the closed door.

The central obstacle for women artists in France was their exclusion from the Ecole des Beaux-Arts, the primary training facility for the inner circle of artists whose careers would be assured by government and private patronage. The school was run by the French government for the purpose of testing and refining the most promising students and ultimately sending the best each year to study at the French Academy in Rome. Although many men such as Gustave Courbet were rejected from this prestigious school and went on to become successful artists, not even being allowed to apply roused the ire of women artists all through the century. The admission of women to the Ecole des Beaux-Arts was finally granted in 1897 as the direct result of the efforts of the sculptor Mme Léon Bertaux (q.v.) and the Union des Femmes Peintres et Sculpteurs, which she had founded in 1881.

Until that victory was won, however, women found other avenues of artistic training. For the most part this meant private lessons, but an important state art school, the Ecole Gratuite de Dessin pour les Jeunes Filles, was opened in 1803, assuring talented women without money a basic level of artistic training. As Charlotte Yeldham (1984) points out, the schools of design for boys and girls in Paris, as well as the provincial schools that followed, were primarily established to train budding artists in the decorative and industrial arts, but they also provided courses in drawing, painting and sculpture. With fine-art training, a young woman could move on to more advanced work in a private studio or she could turn to teaching in one of the many public grammar schools. Rosa Bonheur was the most famous of the directors of the Ecole Gratuite de Dessin pour les Jeunes Filles during her tenure from 1848 to 1859.

The women who rose to prominence in the Paris art world, however, tended to have the means and the connections to study in the private studios of the greatest artists of their day. The women in the early 19th century who exhibited regularly in the Salons (opened to women in 1791) and who received the patronage of the emperors, kings and the wealthiest collectors of that era learned their craft from such masters as David (Mme Benoist, q.v.), Regnault (Pauline Auzou, q.v.), Greuze (Constance Mayer, q.v.) and Fragonard (Marguerite Gérard, q.v.). Adélaïde Labille-Guiard (q.v.), one of the most successful women artists of the 18th century, was also a teacher of important artists of the early 19th century, such as Gabrielle Capet (q.v.). Mme Benoist, Pauline Auzou and Lizinka de Mirbel (q.v.) followed in her footsteps by opening their own ateliers for women students. An example of women handing down their skills through several generations is that of Marie Godefroid, a portraitist from a prominent artistic family, who taught at an exclusive girls' school outside Paris run by Mme Jeanne Campan. An American student of Mme Campan later set up her own school in Pittsburgh and taught Mary Cassatt's mother, who was in turn instrumental in promoting her daughter's career.

By far the most dominant figure of the first decades of the 19th century was Vigée-Lebrun, whose rise to the top epitomises the unusual paths that women often followed to achieve rare international fame. She was a child prodigy. Her father provided her earliest training, and by the age of 15 she was able to support the family with her commissions for copies and portraits. She married one of the most active art dealers of the day who promoted her work. When her patron, Queen Marie-Antoinette, was beheaded in 1790, she spent the next decade painting all over Europe in exile from France. Forever identified with Mme de Staël's novel *Corinne; ou, L'Italie* (1807) because of her portrait of de Staël in the guise of her heroine (1808; Musée d'Art et d'Histoire, Geneva), Vigée-Lebrun published her memoirs of her own peripatetic life in 1835. Her example, primarily transmitted through her writings, influenced many women in the 19th century to pursue careers in the arts, including the young Rosa Bonheur.

Vigée-Lebrun thus combined all the strategies of the marginalised woman artist to circumvent the system: she used the influence of her father and husband, she found success abroad, she capitalised on the sensationalism of one of the most popular novels of her day, and she assured her legacy by publishing her own account of her life. Few women could afford to be quite so independent, but most found that success came from marketing their art outside the bureaucracy that served the interests of male artists more than their own.

By mid-century, the new emperor Napoleon III began to have a profound influence on the French art world. Napoleon's belief in the importance of visual symbols of power not only transformed the city of Paris into an impressive display of monumental buildings and sweeping boulevards, but it created an unprecedented demand for public art of all kinds. Painters, sculptors, printmakers and decorative artists found work making portraits and religious scenes to spread the glory of Napoleon's reign throughout France. The industry of making copies alone kept dozens of artists on the government payroll. While the most prestigious commissions went to male artists, there were sufficient jobs on the lower levels to bring increasing numbers of women into the fold. In addition, the government enthusiasm for art also spurred the cosmopolitan population of Paris to collect privately. By the accounting of Harrison and Cynthia White (1965), about 200,000 paintings were being produced each year. The Whites estimated that approximately one third of the artists were women.

By and large the women at mid-century trained and conducted their careers in the same manner that women had in the early 19th century. They studied in the ateliers of prominent artists, exhibited at the Salon and used their connections to attract government and private commissions. The primary difference was the spirit in which women approached art. Social movements and feminist groups such as the St Simonistes that were underway by the 1830s protested at the exclusion of women from the workplace and the resulting inability of women to improve their circumstances by honest labour. The dilemma was most keenly felt by educated middle-class women who were barred from the professional world inhabited by their brothers and husbands. For these women art

Anna Klumpke: *Rosa Bonheur*, 1898; oil on canvas; 117.2 × 98.1 cm.; Metropolitan Museum of Art, New York; Gift of the artist in memory of Rosa Bonheur, 1922 (22.222)

became a viable alternative to the genteel servitude of being a governess. Flora Tristan, the social activist and grandmother of Paul Gauguin, was apprenticed in a lithography shop. The novelist George Sand tried her hand at painting to support herself during the 1830s.

Art continued to be thought of as a source of income for the gentlewoman in reduced circumstances in novels throughout the 19th century, such as Emile Zola's Comtesse de Beauvilliers and her daughter Alice in *L'Argent*, first published in 1891: "Behind the thin muslin curtains she could vaguely distinguish the figure of the Countess, who was mending some linen, whilst Alice was busy with some water-colour sketches, which she painted hurriedly by the dozen and secretly sold" (*Money*, 1894, p.233). This image of the woman artist working behind the scenes for much-needed money was a far cry from Mme de Staël's romantic Corinne.

Rosa Bonheur, the most famous woman artist at mid-century, was equally far from the idol of her youth, Vigée-Lebrun. Although she also trained with her father and owed much of her worldwide fame to the efforts of a dealer, the Belgian Ernest Gambart, rather than to the French academic system, Bonheur's fame rested on her down-to-earth hard work as opposed to the cosmopolitan glamour of Vigée-Lebrun. Her ten years as director of the Ecole Gratuite de Dessin pour les Jeunes Filles endorsed the prosaic side of studying and teaching art. Bonheur's speciality, monumental animal paintings, was gender-neutral, as were her studies in the stables and abattoirs of Paris. The Empress Eugénie celebrated Bonheur's neutrality by saying, as she bestowed the red ribbon of the Légion d'Honneur on her in 1865: "Genius has no sex".

In the 1860s the old system of private study in the atelier of an established artist began to give way to a new method of learning. Increasingly the young art student could enrol in a class, sometimes organised by a prominent artist, but more often at a new type of "academy". Beginning in 1862 young women could attend a school of decorative arts in Paris that had numerous branches, called Les Ecoles Professionelles d'Elisa Lemonnier. In painting, starting in 1868, both men and women could attend classes at the Académie Julian. For the next ten years, until they were separated into their own classes, there existed in Paris the unique opportunity for women to receive their training alongside men.

Rodolphe Julian, who had studied with Cabanel and Cogniet but had not been accepted at the Ecole des Beaux-Arts, accurately gauged the demand for training created by the burgeoning of the arts during the Second Empire. He was especially canny in opening the doors of his school to women since they had so few other choices. Women made up a growing percentage of his first mixed classes, but the price they paid for studying from the nude model "side by side with the Frenchmen" was high. May Alcott Nieriker (1879) described the patience that women in those classes had to have to endure the gazing of the men:

> One remembers the brave efforts made by a band of American ladies ... who supported one another with such dignity and modesty, in a steadfast purpose under this ordeal, that even Parisians, to whom such a type of womanly character was unknown and almost incomprehensible, were forced into respect and admiration of the

simple earnestness and purity which proved a sufficient protection from even their evil tongues.

Julian found that although some women were steadfast enough to brave the harassment, most found it too uncomfortable – particularly the Frenchwomen who probably understood more of the insults. Once he separated the sexes the school flourished; although the peace women gained was mitigated by the fact that they paid higher fees and felt they received less rigorous instruction. In spite of these complaints, the Salon success of the women who studied at Julian's was undeniable, and the determined student received a high level of professional training.

In addition to the Académie Julian, classes for women were offered by such artists as Charles Chaplin, Carolus-Duran and William Bouguereau in Paris and Thomas Couture in his studio in suburban Villiers-le-Bel. Of the women who would be prominent in Paris in the second half of the 19th century, Eva Gonzalès (q.v.) and Mary Cassatt studied with Chaplin, Cassatt went on to study with Couture, and Marie Bashkirtseff studied at the Académie Julian. From that same generation, Berthe Morisot sought the advice of a number of teachers including Corot, and Marie Bracquemond (q.v.) was a pupil of Ingres.

Women seeking instruction in sculpture had fewer choices apart from the Ecole Gratuite de Dessin. In 1873 Mme Léon Bertaux began holding classes, and in 1879 she built her own sculpture school in the avenue de Villiers. Bertaux's influence extended far beyond her own classes, however. In 1881 she founded the first professional organisation for women artists in Paris, the Union des Femmes Peintres et Sculpteurs. Taking Rosa Bonheur as their model, just as Bonheur had taken Vigée-Lebrun, the women who flocked to the Union sought equal opportunities. To this end they began petitioning the Ecole des Beaux-Arts for women's classes, they instituted the first annual exhibitions for women and, in 1890, founded their own journal, the *Gazette des Femmes*. As Tamar Garb (1994) points out, the organisation grew to 450 members by the end of the 19th century and the exhibitions were as large as 1000 works. All the women artists in Paris benefited from the activism of this group whether they chose to participate or not. Some of the better-known members and exhibitors were Eva Gonzalès, Marie Bashkirtseff, and Virginie Demont-Breton (q.v.), who became the second president of the Union.

However, the organisation's adherence to the professional structure of the French government system – training at the Ecole des Beaux-Arts and pursuit of medals in the Salon – set it at odds with the more modern system of art production and distribution that had been gaining ground since the mid-19th century. After the fall of the Second Empire in 1870, government support of the arts declined precipitously. Without this centralised patronage, the stylistic standards for government works of art as well as the monolithic Ecole des Beaux-Arts and the Salon began to succumb to the pressures of the large and unruly community of artists, patrons and dealers that had assembled in Paris. The conservative art style and professional strategy promoted by the Union des Femmes Peintres et Sculpteurs represented only one of many options available to women in the later 19th century.

The growth of private art dealers and the proliferation of exhibiting societies in Paris increased artists' exposure to the buying public. Instead of using the Salon as the annual clearing-house in which artists proved themselves to collectors, dealers and government juries, artists in the 1870s began to seek such opportunities more often and in a variety of settings. The new art-buying public was extraordinarily diverse, from the newly rich to the foreign tourist to the modest middle-class professional. Thus works of art for sale began to appear in "exhibitions" in business offices, restaurants, jewellery stores and art-supply shops in addition to art dealers and auction houses. Naturally the diversity of audience spawned a diversity of styles unheard of in the past.

The most famous outgrowth of this chaotic period in French culture was the style known as Impressionism. One of many exhibition societies that sprang up in the 1870s, the Impressionist group gained attention because of its link to contemporary naturalist literature, notably that of Zola, which brought their art an intellectual and avant-garde audience. The presence of three highly visible women in the group, Berthe Morisot, Mary Cassatt and Marie Bracquemond, accentuated the "modern" image they wanted to project. To show their total freedom from the old government art systems, they vowed not to exhibit at the Salon. Instead they trusted their fate to journalists and newspaper art critics and an interested dealer, Paul Durand-Ruel, to help get their paintings into the hands of collectors. At certain times, when he could afford it, Durand-Ruel offered his artists a regular income in exchange for a regular flow of paintings to the gallery. He handled the work of the women in the group as well as the men and for Mary Cassatt he eventually became exclusive dealer. When the old French academic system finally collapsed after the turn of the 19th and 20th centuries, the Impressionist women, unlike most of their sister artists who had tied their fate to the traditional style, became the only women from their period to achieve lasting fame.

The welter of styles, exhibiting groups and dealers continued to increase as the century drew to a close. The presence of many foreign artists and art collectors in Paris contributed to the instability of the situation. Training was less a matter of lengthy study in one atelier or *académie* and more a sampling of approaches that could be gained from private lessons, study at Julian's or at the Académie Colarossi, which had recently opened to women, or attendance at one of the small art schools set up by women for women students. Study of the nude model, both male and female, was *de rigueur*. Some women, such as Suzanne Valadon (q.v.), were able to begin as models and then take up painting. Women had the choice of exhibiting at either the government Salon or the new Salon of the Société Nationale des Beaux-Arts. Furthermore, an annual exhibition of Indépendants was hung without jury selection. As Garb (1994) points out, women could also show their work in the private exhibitions of such societies as the Société des Aquarellistes, Paris, or in one of the numerous groups just for women, such as the Société des Femmes Artistes, the Association des Femmes Artistes Américaines, the Femmes Pastellistes and Les XII.

An example of the successful woman at the end of the 19th century is Camille Claudel (q.v.), a sculptor who studied at the Académie Colarossi, in a co-operative studio with other women, and finally with Rodin. Her work was promoted by several dealers including Samuel Bing and Eugéne Blot and she

had a crowning Salon success in 1893. She concentrated on small-scale sculptures that would have a wider market among collectors, and she allied herself with the Symbolist intelligentsia with her themes of love and death. By 1900 she was hailed as one of the greatest sculptors of her day. Claudel did not have the benefit of the Ecole des Beaux-Arts, nor was her income secure through large-scale public sculptures. She advanced her career instead by training in the best schools and ateliers available to her and reached the public primarily through the efforts of a dealer even though she continued to show at the Salons. As the successful women throughout the 19th century had done, she patched together both conventional and unconventional elements from the array available to her to appeal to the tastes and desires of her own time.

NANCY MOWLL MATHEWS

20th century

1900–1930

> Lady art students of the present day are going to Paris in increasing numbers. That the life they lead there differs from that led by their male companions, both as regards its freedom and its strenuousness, goes without saying; but it is sufficiently Bohemian for the most enterprising feminine searcher after novelty.

Thus wrote the reviewer Clive Holland in *The Studio* of December 1903. Despite the social constraints of gender that are acknowledged here, at the beginning of the 20th century Paris offered women artists better opportunities for exhibiting and training than those available in most provincial French towns and in many other European art centres. The capital attracted many aspiring women artists from the French provinces, from Europe and America, who came to study and exhibit their work, and who subsequently settled in the city. This group, which includes French names such as Marie Laurencin and Jacqueline Marval, as well as Tamara de Lempicka and Sonia Delaunay from Russia and María Blanchard (all q.v.) from Spain, forms part of a broader international artistic culture, shared by both male and female artists, for whom Paris had become an undisputed artistic centre and the cradle of so-called avant-garde developments. Many other women artists came to Paris for shorter periods to work, study, and/or exhibit. Among the better-known names are Paula Modersohn-Becker, Käthe Kollwitz, Gabriele Münter and Marianne Werefkin from Germany, and Natalya Goncharova and Lyubov Popova from Russia (all q.v.).

Although the Ecole des Beaux-Arts was fully open to women by 1900 (when they were finally allowed to enter the ateliers), its influence was already on the wane. Increasingly, public interest and critical attention seem to have shifted from the official, government-sponsored salons and art schools towards the more commercial arena of the private galleries and academies and the independent exhibiting societies. For artists of both sexes who were interested in pursuing more "progressive" forms of art that could feed the growing network of private galleries, dealers and collectors, the many private Parisian academies were a popular training ground. Between 1900 and 1914 a large number of such academies were springing up under the leadership of well-known or established artists, including the Académie Matisse (founded by Henri

Matisse), the Académie de la Palette (whose teachers included Amédée Ozenfant and Dunoyer de Segonzac) and the Académie Ranson (whose teachers included Paul Sérusier and Maurice Denis). The Académie Russe, a school founded exclusively for Russian art students in Paris, attracted many women who worked alongside other emigré artists such as Soutine and Zadkine.

Most of these institutions admitted women and included large numbers of foreign students. By 1900 the Académie Colarossi was competing with the Académie Julian as one of the most popular art schools for women students, attracting a truly international clientele. Clive Holland described a morning class at Colarossi's in 1903, in which

> there were five girls and half a score of men working on sketches of a Spaniard in matador costume: except that 50 per cent of the men were Americans, there was scarcely another instance of two of the same workers being of the same nationality.

As Colarossi's became one of the most popular venues for foreign students, conditions could be crowded. The Russian artist Marevna (q.v.), who moved to Paris in 1912, has provided a vivid description of a mixed life-drawing class that she joined one evening that year:

> The crowd there was thicker still; the building was filled with a whole army of young students of all nationalities, and all the rooms were packed. In the one where we were drawing from the nude the air was stifling, because of an inferno permeated by the strong smell of perspiring bodies mixed with scent, fresh paint, damp waterproofs and dirty feet; all this was intensified by the thick smoke from cigarettes and the strong tobacco of pipe smokers. The model under the electric light was perspiring heavily and looked at times like a swimmer coming up out of the sea. The post was altered every five minutes, and the enthusiasm and industry with which we all worked had to be seen to be believed [*Life in Two Worlds*, 1962, p.122].

Women's access to the growing number of private academies also provided a context within which they might be associated with, or become aware of, some of the early modernist groups and networks. Although the educational culture and the conditions of artistic production continued to favour a male-dominated profession, the atmosphere of the private academies – and some of the bohemian artistic circles associated with them – helped to expand the educational and artistic alternatives for women during the first decade of the century. Many of these institutions increased the possibilities for acquiring less "academic" forms of training, and allowed women to work alongside male artists who have now come to be seen as "heroes" of the Parisian avant-garde. For example, Kees van Dongen's influence on many of his female students who graduated from the Académie Vitti is now well known, encouraging a widespread pursuit of "Fauve" interests during this period. And in 1907 Georges Braque, who had been a fellow pupil with Laurencin at the Académie Humbert, first introduced her to Picasso and his circle of friends around the Bateau Lavoir.

Access to exhibiting space and the support of a dealer were, of course, crucial factors in the establishment of a career in art.

For women seeking such a career during the first two decades of the 20th century, there were still professional obstacles to be overcome. However, the success of the so-called "independent" salons during this period helped to make available more exhibiting opportunities for both male and female artists. Since its foundation in 1884, the Salon des Indépendants had provided an outlet for those artists whose work did not meet the more traditional standards required in the official salons. Moreover, the Indépendants was open to anyone, and (in theory at least) did not employ a jury system. This encouraged submissions from women who might otherwise have been thwarted by professional prejudice. This society became one of the most important exhibiting spaces for women during the first two decades of the 20th century, when Jacqueline Marval, Emilie Charmy (q.v.), Laurencin, Suzanne Valadon (q.v.) and others showed there regularly. Valadon was well known for her outspoken support of the "open" exhibiting policies of the society, although she deplored what she saw as its decline in the late 1910s. Most of the women associated with the Cubist movement, including Sonia Delaunay, Alice Halicka (q.v.), Marevna and Blanchard, showed regularly at the Indépendants during the 1910s.

Another outlet popular with lesser known artists was the Salon d'Automne, founded in 1903. Unlike the Salon des Indépendants, admissions were controlled by an elected jury, but in its early years it encouraged submissions from "beginners" and "those modern artists who found it so difficult to gain the publicity they deserved" (Franz Jourdain, first president, 1905). Many women artists working on the fringes of the Fauve movement, including Charmy and Marval, submitted regularly to the annual Salon d'Automne show. In fact, both women had exhibits in the famous Salon d'Automne of 1905 and 1906 (seminal shows in the history of Fauve painting), although their works were hung separately from the now notorious Fauve galleries. In terms of their aesthetic interests both women were producing canvases that would now qualify as Fauve, but they did not participate directly within the Fauve circle that exhibited together. Evidence from catalogues and reviews suggests that this circle was organised into a recognisable exhibiting group largely by Matisse, and that its self-image as a group of "radical" artists involved a sense of predominantly masculine creative roles. Thus the many women painters who adopted similar styles and technical interests were rarely represented in the group hanging space or seldom participated in collective studio activity.

With the growth of the commercial market during the pre-war period, the support of a dealer became a vital source of economic and professional security for artists. Powerful dealers such as Bernheim-Jeune, Ambroise Vollard and Daniel Kahnweiler played significant roles in the sale and promotion of work by artists such as Matisse, Derain, Picasso and Braque, who are now seen as key figures in the early history of modernism. Although the work of many women artists was taken up by dealers, and some received contracts, memories and accounts by several women suggest that relationships between female artists and male dealers were often vulnerable to exploitation by the latter. In her autobiography *Life in Two Worlds* Marevna expressed her anger at the sexually exploitative relationships that were often on offer (to her) in return for a dealer's support.

By the 1920s, however, increasing numbers of women had entered the male-dominated profession of dealer. These included Berthe Weill, Jeanne Bucher, Blanche Guillot, Colette Weil and Katia Granoff. Weill, who first established her famous gallery in 1901, made her name as one of the first dealers to buy the work of Picasso and Matisse. She was continually dogged by financial problems and lacked the capital resources of major dealers such as Vollard, but her commitment to promote the work of young and little-known artists involved the patronage of several women artists who were beginning to achieve limited success in the 1900s, 1910s and 1920s, including Marval, Charmy, Laurencin, Valadon and Halicka. But in her accounts of her days as a dealer Weill continually complains about the difficulties that she experienced as a woman trying to survive in a competitive and predominantly masculine world, writing in 1917: "A woman's struggle is hard and requires an exceptionally strong will."

A more conventional way in which women could relate (as patrons) to the world of culture at the beginning of the 20th century was as hostesses of artistic "salons", a form of patronage that echoed the wealthy salonnières of the 18th century, and which was traditionally dominated by women from the haute bourgeoisie or aristocracy. During the period before World War I the influx of many wealthy American women to Paris began to swell the ranks of this group of female patrons and collectors, of whom the best known is probably Gertrude Stein. While Stein became a key figure within those bohemian avant-garde groups that flourished around the now mythical figure of Picasso, and an important collector of Cubist works, she showed little interest in the work of contemporary women artists. Although her public display of an unconventional lesbian sexuality and her committed pursuit of a career as a professional writer undermined certain masculine codes of artistic and sexual behaviour, she seems to have shown little concern to promote the roles of other women artists and writers.

Public perceptions of such roles were closely tied up with contemporary ideas (moral, social, political and aesthetic) on what constituted a desirable femininity. The increasing numbers of women entering the profession during the first decade of the 20th century helped to generate a critical discourse on the most desirable forms of art practice for les femmes peintres (a distinct category that clearly separated women from the largely male notion of peintre). The improvement in educational and exhibiting possibilities for women, and their increased visibility within professional spaces, also provoked a misogynistic fear (in some quarters) that they were somehow destabilising the profession. In his book Parisiennes de ce temps, published in 1910, Octave Uzanne wrote:

> Women authors, painters and musicians have multiplied during the last twenty years in bourgeois circles, and even in the demi monde. In painting especially they do not meet with the violent opposition they endured in former times. One may even say that they are too much in favour, too much encouraged by the pride and ambition of their families, for they threaten to become a veritable plague, a fearful confusion, and a terrifying stream of mediocrity. A perfect army of women painters invades the studios and the Salons, and they have even opened an

exhibition of "women painters and sculptors" where their works monopolise whole galleries.

Much of the critical writing that surrounded the activities of women painters in the first three decades of the century reveals a concern to categorise some notion of "feminine" art, which is defined according to a set of assumptions about the "stronger" or more "intellectual" qualities of "masculine" art. Women's traditional association with the decorative arts, especially in areas such as fabric design, fashion design and embroidery, itself affected public perceptions of what might constitute "women's art", and encouraged notions of "feminine" art as somehow more decorative or "delicate". But such stereotypes have long and complicated histories, which can be traced back to 18th- and 19th-century characterisations of women's roles and artistic practices. Such categories were subject to constant re-negotiation and debate during the first decades of the 20th century, when increasing numbers of women were engaging with modernist concerns in painting, and competing with men for comparable professional status.

Public perceptions of the nature and status of women's art was, of course, directly affected by its visibility in the influential salons and private galleries. During World War I, when many male artists were mobilised, women's names are (not surprisingly) more visible on exhibition lists. Although larger salons such as the Indépendants and the Salon d'Automne closed for the duration of the war, many private dealers continued to buy and sell. After the initial slump of the first year of the war, business picked up, and several important exhibitions of modern art were organised. Perhaps the most publicised of these was the famous Salon d'Antin of July 1916, which was titled "L'Art moderne en France", and organised by André Salmon, an influential critic of avant-garde art. The show included Picasso's notorious Les Demoiselles d'Avignon of 1907 and works by Matisse, Derain, van Dongen, Max Jacob, Fernand Léger, Gino Severini and Giorgio De Chirico. Unusually for a show that claimed to represent the avant-garde, around one-fifth of the exhibits were by women artists, including Marevna, Blanchard, Marval and Marie Vassiliev.

GILL PERRY

1930–1945

There is no distinct break in the story of women artists and their training in Paris after 1930, at least before World War II. Unfortunately, much basic archival work on less prominent figures remains to be done, and this account can only begin to build up a picture through contrasting examples. Certain figures became more prominent in the mid-1930s, such as the dealer Jeanne Bucher, whose stable included the female artists of the already international movement of geometric abstract painting and sculpture called Abstraction-Création – women such as Sophie Taeuber-Arp, wife of Jean Arp, Paule Vézelay and Marlow Moss (all q.v.). Abstraction-Création, taking the name Réalités Nouvelles from an exhibition at the Galerie Charpentier in 1939, transformed itself into the Salon des Réalités Nouvelles after World War II. The changes in the prestige of "modernism" as such in the 1930s of course had an impact. As life and art in the Soviet Union became more repressive, dealers such as Katia Granoff came to Paris, where she ran a very successful gallery through to the 1960s and beyond.

Another ambitious young Russian woman was Nadia Khodossievitch (q.v.). Having trained with Malevich and the leader of the so-called Polish Unists, Wladislaw Streminski, in Russia, Khodossievitch was horrified by the turn from Suprematism to "productionism" and resolved to abandon an increasingly utilitarian ethos to work in Paris under Fernand Léger. Escaping via marriage to Stanislas Grabowski, she met Léger at the Académie Moderne with Ozenfant and her fellow Russian, Alexandra Exter (q.v.), in 1924. Paradoxically, as she acquired greater prestige, changing from pupil to teacher in Léger's academy, which she ran for him during his trips to America in the late 1930s, her work responded to the Communist call for realism and she exhibited realist works in the left-wing venue that opened in 1934, the Maison de la Culture.

The 1930s was a time of severe economic crisis in France, especially for artists whose market, with the exception of figures such as Picasso, collapsed. It is interesting that one of the chief organisers of the Communist-orientated Association des Ecrivains et des Artistes Révolutionnaires, Boris Taslitzky, the companion of Amrita Sher-Gil (q.v.), came as she did from Lucien Simon's atelier in the Ecole des Beaux-Arts. However, under the auspices of the Maison de la Culture, which absorbed the AEAR organisation, a new strain of autodidactic painters came to a certain prominence, such as Edouard Pignon and André Fougeron; their working-class origins meant that they frequented the "Université Nouvelle" or "Université Ouvrière" for political instruction, and at the same time evening drawing classes (such as the one in the working-class *arrondissement* of Belleville) and copied in the Louvre – a practice recommended by Léger and Jacques Lipchitz, both of whom ran open studios of a kind under the auspices of the AEAR. The ethos of the "worker" and "proletarian painting" was, however, very masculine, despite the presence of women artists such as Gisèle Delsinne, Andrée Viollis and Nadia Khodossievitch, and influential younger art historians such as Agnès Humbert, whose book on *David* was one of the first to offer a "Marxist" vision of the revolutionary artist. This was the time of Popular Front reform and democratisation of art structures and institutions in general. Madeleine Rousseau was a driving force, along with Georges-Henri Rivière, of the Association Populaire des Amis des Musées. The photographer Gisèle Freund politicised her art, with photocollages such as *La Misère de Paris* shown at the third Exposition d'Habitation at the Salon des Art Menagers in 1936; while the glamorous Charlotte Perriand, who visited the Soviet Union in 1934 to supervise the construction of Le Corbusier's Centrosoya building, worked on the Popular Front-inspired Centre Rural with Léger for the Paris Exposition Internationale of 1937, and would help Le Corbusier with the design of the working-class kitchen for his Maison d'Habitation in Marseille after the war.

The anti-fascist, pro-Communist movement of the 1930s was international, Parisian organisations having their counterparts in London or Amsterdam. Thus the artists Kowalska, Yvette Guibert and the Swede Greta Knutson (wife of Tristan Tzara) were among those who sent works from Paris to the Artists' International Association anti-fascist exhibition in London in 1935, while reciprocally Nan Youngman, Misha Black, Elisabeth Watson and Betty Rea came from the London AIA to Paris to work on James Holland's statistically-orientated murals for the League of Nations room and the International Peace Campaign room in the Peace Pavilion at the Paris Exposition Internationale of 1937: here the political tensions were massively intensified in the light of the Spanish Civil War and the bombing of Guernica. Ironically, the most memorable of all sculptures at the exhibition was the gigantic industrial worker and peasant woman, brandishing hammer and sickle respectively, atop the Russian Pavilion, a sculpture by Vera Mukhina (q.v.), who had trained with Rodin's epigone, Emile Bourdelle, and at the Académie de la Grande Chaumière before 1914.

After 1945

The generation of female artists of the 1940s continued to espouse traditional techniques and the ethos of the School of Paris. Painters such as the Romanian Natalia Dumitrescu (q.v.) and the Portuguese Maria Elena Vieira da Silva (q.v.) continued with traditional easel paintings, conventional formats and the emphasis on *belle peinture*, the sensuality of the *tache* (dab) of paint, respecting the conventions of their pre-war training. Vieira da Silva had trained at La Grande Chaumière, the Académie Fernand Léger and Stanley William Hayter's Atelier 17 (for engraving); now a new and vertiginous sense of dissolving depths and perspectives gave her work a contemporary "existentialist" feel. The division of the Parisian scene into a series of conflicting styles with their own Salons continued: the Salon des Tuileries, the Salon des Indépendants, the Salon des Réalités Nouvelles, which started up again in 1946 for abstract geometric art and was international in scope (663 exhibits from 16 countries by 1948); the new and more eclectic Salon de Mai, founded in 1945, at first under an existentialist aegis (the writings of Camus and Sartre were exhibited), later a forum for new works by Matisse and Picasso as well as the host of epigones. The Salon des Moins de Trente Ans, founded during the German occupation, was a forum for young talent with a sense of political commitment: together with such artists as Bernard Buffet, female artists, totally forgotten today, such as Angèle Macles-Herment, exhibited there, while Mireille Miailhe came to prominence in 1948 at this salon with the vengeful widows of *Les Veuves* in 1946; her satirical painting, *La Visite de l'atelier (les amateurs)*, was again the star of the salon in 1948. A generation of painters affected by the impact of the Communist Resistance after 1941 and the electoral success of the Party in 1944 – very often either trained to paint figuratively, or autodidacts – joined the wave of realist painters with socialist-realist themes that, surprisingly enough, started to dominate the Salon d'Automne, former birthplace of Fauvism, from 1947–8. Despite accusations of an art controlled and directed by Stalin's cultural spokesman A.A. Zhdanov, many artists such as Geneviève Zondervan and Marie-Anne Lansiaux (q.v.) exhibited canvases with themes such as unemployment, strikes, protest marches, in good faith, until the situation changed to become one of deliberate provocation. In 1951 the French police removed seven canvases from the Salon d'Automne, including Lansiaux's *1 May 1951*, of the Communist protest marches; this gave symbolic dimensions to the Party's confrontation with the government over policy. Major exhibitions such as *Algérie 52*, sponsored by the French Communist Party, demonstrated the importance of painting as a medium in this kind of debate, a medium more effective at the time than journalism, cinema or television, still a luxury in France. Mireille Miailhe continued the tradition of orientalist painters in *Algérie 52* (which she shared with Boris Taslitzky) in the steps of her 20th-century female orientalist precursors. Before 1939 women such as Lucie Ranvier-Chartier, Elisabeth Faure, Jeanne Thil or the remarkable official sculptor Anna Quinquaud had received their training, commissions and honours from the French state. Miailhe, too, ventured into the far-flung reaches of French colonial territory, but to report on resistance, political rebellion and shocking poverty, adopting the djellabah in order to penetrate sequestered female spaces and to sketch more inconspicuously. Special exhibitions aside, realism, to a greater or lesser extent politically engaged, continued to dominate the Salon d'Automne until 1953; the Salon des Moins de Trente Ans metamorphosed (inevitably!) into the Salon de la Jeune Peinture in 1953, which would become the hotbed of the politically engaged post-Stalinist "New Figuration" movement in the 1960s (again a "macho" movement with less scope for female painters).

The Communists and the Surrealists were long-standing ideological enemies in France; one confrontation that exemplifies attitudes towards style and technique was their differing interpretation of the poet Lautréamont's famous maxim: "Poetry should be made by all and not by one". For the Communists, this meant a democratisation of art involving easy legibility of style and a clear "message". Often, alas, a "levelling down" was involved, and paintings of great banality were produced. For the Surrealists, however, Lautréamont's dictum was translated as performative: everyone should *make* art. Though so many painters who ended up as Surrealists were professionally trained, the "Surrealist object" in combination, later, with Marcel Duchamp's "ready-made", vitiated both the purpose and the necessity for such training. While Eileen Agar (q.v.), for example, was trained as a painter at the Slade, her two versions of *Angel of Anarchy*, exhibited at the International Surrealist exhibitions in Amsterdam and London in 1938 and 1940 respectively, were examples of *bricolage*: improvisations (over a classical cast) using silk, feathers, diamanté, and in homage to Surrealism's inspirations of ethnographic origin, Oceanic art "fetishes", cowrie shells and African bark. Surrealism was marketed in many private galleries in Paris in the 1940s but, as always, had no Salon. International Surrealist exhibitions, however, were held again in 1947, 1959 and 1965. Importantly, the renewal of Surrealism in Paris coincided with the discovery of so-called psychopathological art in Paris, shown at the Sainte-Anne psychiatric hospital in 1946 and on an international scale in 1950, and, at the same time, Jean Dubuffet's promotion of Art Brut, art by "outsiders", the untrained, the mentally ill. Many Art Brut artists who now have a "classic" status were discovered for the first time in this post-war period at the Sainte-Anne hospital, at the exhibition *Art Brut préféré aux arts culturels* at the Galerie René Drouin in 1947, and the great retrospective at the Musée des Arts Décoratifs in 1967. These shows included such women as "Aloyse", the medium Jeanne Tripier, and the British woman Madge Gill, while in the international Surrealist exhibition devoted to Eros at the Galerie Daniel Cordier in 1957 slightly "deranged" artists such as Leonora Carrington (q.v.) and Hans Bellmer's companion Unica Zürn (q.v.), who figured alongside the Art Brut artist

Aloyse. Carrington had been academically trained in Italy and London, while Zürn became severely mentally disturbed, discovered the chance technique of decalcomania independently from the Surrealists, and produced automatic drawings as well as superb anagrammatic poetry. Meret Oppenheim's "cannibal feast" at the opening, a living woman bedecked with food, prone on the banquet table, epitomised the Surrealist attitude to Eros; no training was necessary here.

These important changes in sensibility, which involved a fundamental shift regarding notions of both "modernism" and "professionalism" transform one's understanding of major artists of the 1960s such as Niki de Saint Phalle (q.v.). Genuinely successful professional women artists in the postwar period were few: Vieira da Silva and Germaine Richier (q.v.) come most strongly to mind; the dealers Jeanne Bucher to 1947, Collete Allendy, Denise René – who has promoted abstract geometric art (including Aurélie Nemours) in her gallery since 1945, and in the 1960s Iris Clert, doyenne for the Nouveaux Réalistes, had extremely important roles. In a situation of such stylistic plurality, various registers of realism coexisted: Bernard Buffet, Francis Gruber, Balthus, Jean Hélion were important artists remote from the socialist realist arguments. Moreover, in a context of political attacks on abstraction (as incomprehensible and elitist), "modernism" by this time – not a term used in post-war France as it is today – was a historical concept. The "second" modernism, in the Greenbergian sense, of the New York School was yet to have its impact in France. Certainly the figurative work of Germaine Richier, in bronze, with its deliberate evocation not only of her 16th-century precursor Filigier Richier but also the great tradition exemplified and continuing with Rodin and Bourdelle, has nothing to do with "modernism" and everything to do with continuity, from her use of Rodin's model Nardone to her use of the same skilled families, Rudier, Valsuani and Susse, to cast her pieces.

Turning to Niki de Saint Phalle, who was initially so insecure about her lack of training, it was precisely the "extraprofessional" sources that gave her work its strength and uniqueness and, in turn, one could argue, reinvigorated the "canon" itself, as the work of Jean Dubuffet had done before her. Hence she joined no school or immediate artistic community, but with encouragement retained her essentially autodidact style, reinforced by the eccentricity of Gaudí's ceramics (discovered in 1955) and the Palais du Facteur Cheval – a Surrealist favourite. To what extent is the evocation of such "female" qualities as abundance, decorativeness, hysteria and "schizophrenia" in her work deliberate? Such works include: the *Joan of Arc* door (1959); the "home-made" aspect of *St Sebastian or Portrait of My Lover*, with "ready-made" shirt and dartboard; the "kitchen" element of the first meat-cleaver assemblages and the *Tirs* (shooting paintings) of spaghetti, eggs and tomatoes that spilled out of the ruptured plaster; and the fertility goddess Nanas, covered in plastic fruit and flowers as well as children's toys – out of the 16th-century painter Arcimboldo but certainly recalling Oppenheim's living "cannibal feast". As always when the ratios are so imbalanced, Niki's status within the Nouveau Réaliste group of Arman, César, Gérard Deschamps and Martial Raysse, Raymond Hains, Daniel Spoerri and the *affichistes* (torn poster artists) Raymond Hains and Jacques de la Villéglé was that of a female "supplement", a mascot. More telling of the overwhelming ideological and institutional odds facing women artists – who in ateliers and even the large Salons were quite numerous, is the proportional statistics of men to women artists in the retrospective *72 pour 72: Douze ans d'art contémporain* held in Paris in 1972, which purported to summarise the achievements of the last 12 years – the liberated 1960s, no less. Seventy men were exhibited; there were two women artists, Niki de Saint Phalle and the Nebraska-born textile artist Sheila Hicks (q.v.). Niki's great supporter Pontus Hulten continued this stance in his quasi-millennial survey *Territorium artis*, which opened at the Kunst- und Ausstellungshalle in Bonn in 1992, which showed 4 female artists and 106 men! The show was topped on the upper and roof garden with Niki's retrospective – again a demonstration of the curious "supplementary" status of the woman artist. While Niki's collaborative works with the Swiss kinetic sculptor Jean Tinguely were hugely successful, such reciprocity was extremely rare: one has only to mention the cramping effect of Picasso on the independence of the photographer Dora Maar (q.v.) or the painter Françoise Gilot; even Roland Penrose – hardly a great painter – dampened the *élan* of the American photographer Lee Miller (q.v.), who became wife, cook, hostess – and the aggression revealed in the themes of the later work of Dorothea Tanning (q.v) expresses to some extent the mixed emotions she experienced, living perpetually in the orbit of Max Ernst.

It is the lesser-known artists whose careers are sometimes the most informative of the lost stories of the institutions of artistic practice beyond the commercial gallery world. In Marie-Anne Lansiaux's archives, for example, are documents relating to official purchases by the French State: in 1947 the Ministère de l'Education Nationale, Direction Générale des Arts et des Lettres, bought *A Little Kitchen* (*c.*1942) for 4,000 francs; in 1951, at the height of her political engagement, the same education ministry acting for Arts et Lettres, Direction de l'Enseignement et de la Production Artistique, bought *The Yard*, exhibited at the Salon Populiste, for 30,000 francs, and the Communist municipality of Saint-Denis bought a political work, *Departure of a Peace Demonstration in the Suburbs*, for 60,000 francs; in 1953 a still life was bought after being exhibited at the Salon des Indépendants for the State for 20,000 francs, and *The Street* from the Salon Populiste by the Ville de Paris for 100,000 francs. Lansiaux's contemporary and friend Geneviève Zondervan served on the committee and continued to exhibit in the international Biennale des Femmes Peintres et Sculpteurs: 108 salons took place between 1882, when Mme Léon Bertaux (q.v.) launched the first, and 1992. One third of the 230 women exhibiting in that last Salon did so for the first time. The president, Janine Canault, declared: "This Salon has existed since 1882, and yet ... There are still too few women painters in the galleries, little interest in their work in the media, a hesitant attitude on the part of speculators and art amateurs as far as they are concerned."

While immense contrasts exist between countries, between the now-equalising opportunities for training at least in the affluent West, it is significant that the most "equal" of democracies, America, should have spawned the Guerrilla Girls: "a bunch of masked avengers", who "fight sexism and racism in the art world with facts, humour and fake fur". They materialised in their gorilla masks "mysteriously in the dark night of 1988" in response to "An international survey of painting and sculpture" at the Museum of Modern Art in New York, a show in which a mere 13 of the 169 artists were women. No single woman has yet come forward to betray an identity behind the mask: they call themselves Romaine Brooks, Frida Kahlo, Tina Modotti, Gertrude Stein; they campaign on political issues as well as art. Lee Krasner declared: "We secretly suspect that all women are born Guerrilla girls. It's just a question of helping them discover it ... " Guerrilla Girls have travelled to Barcelona, Basel, Berlin, Dublin, Graz, Helsinki, Oslo and Vienna in Europe: they have featured recently in the review *Blocnotes* in Paris. Will they make a difference?

SARAH WILSON

Bibliography

Madame de Staël (Anne Louise Germaine), *Corinne; ou, L'Italie,* 1807; English translation, New Brunswick, NJ: Rutgers University Press, 1987

Louise-Elisabeth Vigée-Lebrun, *Souvenirs de Mme Louise-Elisabeth Vigée Lebrun*, 3 vols, Paris: Fournier, 1835–7; as *Memoirs of Madame Vigée Lebrun*, ed. Lionel Strachey, New York: Doubleday, 1903; London: Grant Richards, 1904; abridged edition with introduction by John Russell, New York: Braziller, 1989

May Alcott Nieriker, *Studying Art Abroad and How To Do It Cheaply*, Boston: Roberts, 1879

E. Somerville, "An 'atelier des dames'", *Magazine of Art*, 1886, pp.152–7

Marie Bashkirtseff, *Le Journal de Marie Bashkirtseff*, ed. A. Theuriet, 2 vols, Paris, 1887; as *The Journal of Marie Bashkirtseff*, London: Cassell, 1890; ed. Rozsika Parker and Griselda Pollock, London: Virago, 1985

Emile Zola, *L'Argent*, 1891; as *Money*, 1894

Octave Uzanne, *Parisiennes de ce temps*, Paris: Mercure de France, 1910

Berthe Weill, *Pan! dans l'oeil! (Ou trente ans dans les coulisses de la peinture contemporaine, 1900–1930)*, Paris: Lipschutz, 1933

Ambroise Vollard, *Recollections of a Picture Dealer*, Boston: Little Brown, and London: Constable, 1936; reprinted New York: Dover, 1978

Deux peintres et un poète retour d'Algérie: Boris Taslitzky, Mireille Miailhe et Jacques Dubois, Paris: Editions Cercle d'Art, 1952

Marevna Vorobëv, *Life in Two Worlds*, London and New York: Abelard Schuman, 1962

Harrison C. White and Cynthia A. White, *Canvases and Careers: Institutional Change in the French Painting World*, New York: Wiley, 1965

Women Artists, 1550–1950, exh. cat., Los Angeles County Museum of Art, and elsewhere, 1976

Sharon Flescher, "Women artists at the Paris Salon of 1870: An avant-garde view", *Arts Magazine*, lii/3, 1977, pp.99–101

Abstraction-Création, 1931–1936, exh. cat., Westfälisches Landesmuseum, Münster, and Musée d'Art Moderne de la Ville de Paris, 1978

Iris Clert, *Iris-Time: L'artventure*, Paris: Denoel, 1978

L'altra metà dell'avanguardia, 1910–1940: Pittrici e scultrici nei movimenti delle avanguardie storiche, exh. cat., Palazzo Reale, Milan, and elsewhere, 1980

Malcolm Gee, *Dealers, Critics and Collectors of Modern Painting: Aspects of the Parisian Art Market Between 1910 and 1930*, New York: Garland, 1981

Katia Granoff, *Ma vie et mes rencontres*, Paris: Bourgeois, 1981

Paris-Paris, 1937–1957: Créations en France, exh. cat., Centre Georges Pompidou, Paris, 1981

J. Diane Radycki, "The life of lady art students: Changing art education at the turn of the century", *Art Journal*, xlii, Spring 1982, pp.9–13

AIA: The Story of the Artists' International Association, 1933–1953, exh. cat., Museum of Modern Art, Oxford, 1983

Carte blanche à Denise Réné: Aventure géométrique et sinétique, exh. cat., Paris Art Center, 1984

Charlotte Yeldham, *Women Artists in Nineteenth-Century France and England*, 2 vols, New York: Garland, 1984

Guy Vighnot, *La Jeune Peinture, 1941–1961*, Paris: Edition Terre des Peintres, 1985

Paul Duro, "The 'Demoiselles à Copier' in the Second Empire", *Woman's Art Journal*, vii/1, 1986, pp.1–7

Shari Benstock, *Women of the Left Bank: Paris, 1900–1940*, Austin: University of Texas Press, 1986; London: Virago, 1987

Michèle Lefrançais, "Art et aventure au féminin", *Coloniales, 1920–1940*, exh. cat., Musée Municipale, Boulogne-Billancourt, 1989, pp.53–66

Marina Sauer, *L'Entrée des femmes à l'Ecole des Beaux-Arts, 1880–1923*, Paris: Ecole Nationale Supérieure des Beaux-Arts, 1990

Catherine Millet, *Conversations avec Denise René*, Paris: Biro, 1991

Biennale des femmes peintres et sculpteurs, 1882–1992: 108ème Salon, exh. cat., Grand Palais, Paris, 1992

Hommage à Nadia Léger: Retrospective, 1967–1992, exh. cat., Musée National Fernand Léger, Biot, 1992

Catherine Fehrer "Women at the Académie Julian in Paris", *Burlington Magazine*, cxxxvi, 1994, pp.752–7

Tamar Garb, *Sisters of the Brush: Women's Artistic Culture in Late Nineteenth-Century Paris*, New Haven and London: Yale University Press, 1994

Jeanne Bucher: Une galerie d'avant-garde, 1925–1946, exh. cat., Les Musées de la Ville de Strasbourg, 1994

Nancy Mowll Mathews, *Mary Cassatt: A Life*, New York: Villard, 1994

Gill Perry, *Women Artists and the Parisian Avant-Garde*, Manchester: Manchester University Press, and New York: St Martin's Press, 1995

Sarah Wilson, "Femininities/Mascarades", *Rrose is a Rrose is a Rrose: Gender Performance in Photography*, exh. cat., Solomon R. Guggenheim Museum, New York, 1997

3. Germany, Austria and Switzerland

The fact that so little is known about the history of women artists has to do with the way in which women have been perceived and evaluated. With a few exceptions, art made by women in the German-speaking countries was not purchased in any quantity, collected systematically or carefully preserved; it was not accurately labelled in collections or made the subject of scholarly research. It has thus been difficult to identify the body of art created by women, so that our knowledge of their legacy is incomplete.

The study of women artists did not form part of the usual art-historical syllabus at universities, and interest in the subject increased only with the advent of the modern women's movement. In the mid-1970s exhibitions were organised, beginning with *Künstlerinnen international, 1877–1977*, held at the Neue Gesellschaft für Bildende Kunst in Berlin (1977), and for the first time there were scholarly discussions about women artists and the way in which women were perceived and represented by (male) artists, especially at the congresses of female art historians held in Marburg (1983), Zürich (1984), Vienna (1986), Berlin (1988), Hamburg (1991) and Trier (1995). The first Frauenmuseum was founded in 1981, in Bonn, but it lacked the resources and the opportunities available to an established museum to make acquisitions. At first women artists were regarded as guarantors of female authenticity and less as parts of a context to be reconstructed, so there was concentration on biographical information. Since the political context of work by women (including artistic work) was fundamentally different from the work opportunities for men, a lengthy process of research was required for each period, each country, and each region.

The problems involved in working closely with the received biographical data, of keeping in view the basic differences in the circumstances of female and male artists, and the examination of the conventions and deficits of art history have led to the recognition that ways of seeing can be just as "constructed" as relationships. A critical reassessment of the methodology is needed if we are to grasp the underlying structures of power and patterns of argument behind the testimonies of oppression, silence, and the falsification and marginalisation of female creativity.

In the early 19th century the ideas of the Enlightenment took on a particular significance for women artists who had been born in the previous century. These were mainly the daughters of artist families, whose talents were recognised and encouraged by their fathers or by other relatives. In this way women surmounted the first hurdle in a career as a court artist or a respectable portrait painter that was often carefully planned. Women artists of the 18th century not only provided proof of their talent and their mobility, but they were also sought after, so long as they could be identified as an "exception", that is, distinct from other women, and could be controlled in their ambitions. Not infrequently, male "encouragement" concealed a substantial financial interest; the income might go to the artist's father or husband, for example, or she might have to provide for a family without male support. Even Angelica Kauffman (q.v.) ended up complaining that she was "tired of painting for sale" (quoted in Bremen 1993, p.46), an indication of artistic ambition that rebelled against the expectations of relatives and patrons.

The international status and the high esteem that women artists of previous eras had enjoyed seem to have vanished from the collective consciousness by the beginning of the 19th century. For young girls in the German-speaking world, the only role model of any significance was Angelica Kauffman (*ibid.*, pp.41–4; Memoirs of Johanna Schopenhauer, "Jugendleben und Wanderbilder" (1848) in Berger 1987, pp.60–64). In art centres such as Weimar, Dresden, Berlin, Munich, Vienna, Paris, London and Rome the fame of admired women artists survived longer than elsewhere through commissions, contacts and works accessible to the public. But of greater importance for prospective women artists, who had the greatest difficulty in appealing to female precursors, were the conditions for training in a middle-class environment. Here girls were perceived in terms of their future usefulness as wives or mothers, and any desire that deviated from this and reached beyond narrow utility received a reprimand. If a woman's appearance made her future role as a wife seem unlikely, then her wish to be trained as an artist might be taken seriously, and she would be encouraged, within limits (as Käthe Kollwitz, q.v., was by her father). In Goethe's circle Caroline Bardua (q.v.), Louise Seidler (q.v.) and Julie von Egloffstein, and in

Konstanz Marie Ellenrieder (q.v.), belong to this category. To be taken seriously in their desire to work as artists, especially if they did not come from artistic families, such women had to flatter and win over famous men or women patrons, and rely on aristocratic or middle-class patronage.

The art academies and their life classes were closed to women, who instead had to rely on over-priced and unsystematic private lessons, and on scholarships and patronage with conditions attached, which seldom allowed them to pursue their own interests and often kept them in the role of permanent petitioners. Women artists had to acquire skills by studying for themselves, but they found that the results of their inadequate training were used to support the thesis that they were a deficient sex unsuited for art. Those who sought to escape from these attitudes by going abroad, leaving behind the provincialism of the little courts in the hope of finding the freedom to develop, discovered, as did Anna Dorothea Lisiewska-Therbusch (q.v.) in the 18th century, that male artists at their destinations also held these double standards. As Diderot wrote with obvious sympathy for Lisiewska-Therbusch:

> She does not lack the talent to arouse interest in a country like ours, she lacks youth, beauty, modesty, coquetterie. She could have been enthusiastic about the merits of our great artists, taken lessons from them, had more bosom and a handsome posterior and have had to offer both to the artists [quoted in Bremen 1993, p.54].

How strongly envy and competitiveness determined the judgement of male colleagues is shown by a remark made by Daniel Chodowiecki in relation to Lisiewska-Therbusch's attempt to go beyond the areas traditionally allotted to women – portraiture and copies of old masters – when she turned to mythological subjects:

> It was especially when she had the notion to arouse voluptuous ideas that she was insufferable, particularly when I reflected that this was an old woman who wished to arouse these ideas in order to earn money [ibid., p.51].

Both these sources show that already in the 18th century sexual attitudes were being cited to ward off female competition: members of the French Académie Royale had rejected Lisiewska-Therbusch's *Jupiter Transforms Himself into Pan to Surprise the Sleeping Antiope* on the grounds that it was "obscene". The fact that one of these academicians was Boucher, who openly and without scruple catered for the sexual proclivities of his clientele in his choice of themes, shows clearly that male and female artists were measured by two different standards (*idem*; Nobs-Greter 1984, pp.121–45). This tendency increased in the 19th century. To get training, women artists from middle-class backgrounds who did not come from artist families and who had to rely on patrons, such as Ellenrieder, Bardua and Seidler, had to submit to excessive, constantly monitored respectability. For a woman artist the loss of her reputation meant the loss of everything. Forced into the role of petitioner, she had to earn for herself every concession, every "support", however modest, however wounding to her self-respect. Flattery and a pupil's imitation of a "master" were the tributes that women had to pay in order to gain a minimum of professional attention. If a woman was without youth and beauty – or at least the signals of sexual subjugation

– interest in a female artist, as Diderot correctly observed, remained cerebral and unfledged, or else turned to rejection mixed with competitive envy and resentment. The young sculptor Elisabet Ney (q.v.) experienced this when she fought her way from provincial Westphalia to a place as a student at the Munich Academy; as an "exception" she was taken into the circle of Varnhagen von Ense, Rahel Varnhagen's widower, and once Christian Daniel Rauch had accepted her as a pupil, she was one of the few women sculptors of her time to obtain public commissions; she made portrait busts of such politicians as *Otto von Bismarck* and *Giuseppe Garibaldi*, of scientists, intellectuals and *Arthur Schopenhauer*, who was impressed by her appearance. Women artists such as Ney found that, as a matter of survival, they had to use their phase of youthful beauty to get themselves professionally established. Beauty, the knack of attracting people's interest, and being prepared to move around – not only on tours to France, England, Greece, Italy, Spain or Egypt, but also from town to town, court to court, pursuing commissions and keeping up contacts – were essential ingredients of success (Emily Fourmy Cutrer, *The Art of the Woman: The Life and Work of Elisabet Ney*, Lincoln: University of Nebraska Press, 1988).

Women artists of the early 19th century found some support and limited patronage in the social circles of sisters and women friends, and – like Seidler or Ellenrieder – in the strict fulfilment of duties and in religiosity. It was to sisters or female friends – such as Bettina von Arnim and Karoline von Günderode – that they felt bound spiritually, in response to their desire to experience the world directly, and to give this experience an appropriate form, one that was not imposed and censored from the outside (Bremen 1993, pp.31–41). Goethe had set an example when he fled to Italy to escape the restrictions of home. In the succeeding decades Rome became the longed-for destination. Those women artists who through grants or commissions were able to make their way there and make contact with other artists (for example, some of the Nazarenes) were mostly noblewomen. Although there is evidence of women taking lodgings together, no circle of women artists at this period made its presence felt in Rome as a corporate body.

It is apparent that in the early 19th century contemporaries and critics were incapable or unwilling to separate the gender of the artist from artistic achievement. What was reviewed was not the work but the gender of its maker. The high-minded and uninhibited treatment of such questions such as Diderot had shown (he posed in the nude for his friend Lisiewska-Therbusch) was to be the exception. Women were measured by conventions; their deficiencies, the result of their lack of education and training, were held against them as part of their "nature". The mental anguish created by these contradictory demands has left traces in the diaries, letters and memoirs of individual women artists (Berger 1987).

The "surplus of women" created by the waves of emigration after 1848 meant that there were fewer and fewer women in the educated middle classes and *petite bourgeoisie* who could be supported by their families. The existing ban on training and a career for members of the middle classes made it increasingly hard to conceal this difficulty by work at home. The Allgemeiner Deutscher Frauenverein, founded in 1865 in the consciousness that women had no political rights, thus concentrated on obtaining access to educational institutions and paid public work to enable women to support themselves.

Women artists were invariably excluded from lucrative commissions because of their poor training, and only a few fields, such as portrait painting and work as copyists, were open to them. Under the pretext of decency they were kept away from life classes, and they were also prevented from displaying their work in public. The extensive network of relationships that characterised the courtly and bourgeois salon culture did, however, enable women to obtain not only a livelihood but also a modest reputation (Susanne Jensen, "'Wo sind die weiblichen Mäzene … ?' Private Kunstförderung im Verein der Künstlerinnen und Künstfreundinnen zu Berlin", in Berlin 1992, pp.299–310; Petra Wilhelmy-Dollinger, 'Die Berliner Salons und der Verein der Künstlerinnen und Künstfreundinnen zu Berlin", *ibid.*, pp.339–52). But the drive towards greater professionalism brought new problems.

If industrialisation had exposed women and girls of the lower classes to the extremes of physical hardship and marginalisation, women from the educated middle classes, *petite bourgeoisie* and the office-holding nobility had a different problem: once they were seen publicly to be contributing to the financial support of a family that could no longer support itself, they found that not only was their own respectability damaged, but also that of their relatives. Unstintingly committed to a pattern of life that only a tiny upper class could maintain, they had to preserve the appearance of leisure without being able to be leisured.

Women's handiwork, which had largely lost its practical function in the family and had degenerated to a status symbol, now took on a new value. In a society that had only recently introduced universal compulsory schooling for girls, without making provision for any further, vocational training, women's handicrafts became a means of survival: the work could be done under family control without having to leave the house, and agencies could be used in order to preserve anonymity – that is, to conceal the fact that women were relying on their earnings. The collapse of such conditions was only a question of time. Numerous women from the middle classes attempted to earn their living without loss of respectability, drawing on their meagre and unsystematic education, which gave them only a basic knowledge of music, drawing, painting and languages. Since they could not be distinguished from the more affluent female amateurs, this was a fatal kind of competition. From now on any woman artist was under suspicion of amateurism, which was the more perfidious when male artists were doing their utmost to keep female competition to a minimum by excluding women from the academies and charging huge training fees.

From 1865, the year in which the organised women's movement emerged with the Allgemeiner Deutscher Frauenverein, Berlin developed into a centre for efforts to create public and paid work for women from middle-class backgrounds. Almost all the professions that were "appropriate to their status" were developed from the range of duties of "higher daughters". The first training centres were aimed at governesses and female amateurs. Among them was the Lette-Verein, founded in 1865. Its liberal founder was a severe opponent of women's emancipation, but in order to mitigate the worst poverty the association offered unmarried women training in painting, sculpture,

graphics, illustration and pattern-drawing. The orientation towards the applied arts at the Lette-Verein was also apparent at the Institut für höheren weiblichen Zeichenunterricht, which opened in 1867; in courses for women at the Berlin Gewerbemuseum; and at the Schule für Kunststickerei founded in 1879, which sought to professionalise women's handiwork.

Competition to these institutions, which reacted to the boom in the applied arts, arose with the creation in 1868 of the Zeichen- und Malschule des Vereins der Künstlerinnen und Kunstfreundinnen zu Berlin. This coming together of women artists and society ladies, influential feminists and women patrons, was to continue for many years. The encouragement of young women artists was just as important to them as the task of organising exhibitions, sales and scholarships. Although the school also opened a section for women drawing teachers and employed respected women artists such as Jeanne Bauck and Käthe Kollwitz as teachers, it could not offer the full training programme of an academy.

Meanwhile the art academies followed the common principle of reserving the admission of women not as a right but merely as a favour – if at all (a summary sketch is given in Lehman 1914); their admission was seen mainly in terms of its advantage to the men from uneducated classes who were studying there, and whose cultural level could be raised through a female presence, and not in terms of the well-being of the young women artists (Wolff-Arndt 1929, pp.8, 60–63). The undignified manoeuvring of the academicians can be explained not least as stemming from the anxiety that they might lose the sinecure of their private schools that were crowded with "ladies", women who came almost exclusively from the privileged classes, and who could provide valuable contacts and commissions. (These academicians were mostly young artists who, after finishing their academic training at low cost – set to enable men from the lower classes to study at the academies – opened "schools" in order to finance their own artistic careers.) Such schools also represented a marriage market for rising or older artists (such as Lovis Corinth and Rodolphe Julian), in which the pupils' dowries were as welcome as their social contacts or their organisation of the artist's household. Many teachers were concerned with eliminating competition or attracting female imitators without any prospects. The innumerable secondary intentions of such teachers would have made a meaningful programme of study difficult or impossible.

Marriage in general, and – perversely enough – marriage to artists in particular, endangered the artistic development of women artists more than any other way of life. Celibacy was therefore to be recommended. Yet it was not just young aspiring women artists who were thrust into a contemptuous light by their new freedom of movement in the public and bohemian worlds. The mockery of writers, critics and male artists who drew for such magazines as *Simplicissimus* and *Jugend* was directed indiscriminately against young women, whose beauty was interpreted as lack of seriousness, against "Malweiber" and "Ölschwestern" or the "third sex" (lesbians), who made no secret of their rejection of "unfair" men, but imitated them in their dress and gestures.

In works such as Otto Weininger's *Geschlecht und Character* (1903) writers, academics, philosophers and politicians reveal an ideology of contempt for or hatred of women –

and artists of all movements provided a visual affirmation of this. Many caricatures were concerned with the life classes. An unspoken motive of the academicians in excluding female students from life study concerned the sexual relationships that they and their students had with female models. Life study stood at the summit of the academic hierarchy of training, and its highest level was marked by the sexual use made of the model by the teacher and advanced students. The mere presence of female students would have exposed the sexual camaraderie between professors and pupils as well as the double standards of the academicians, who were so severe in their criticism of women.

Three institutions sought to oppose these appalling conditions: the Zeichen- und Malschule der Künstlerinnen und Kunstfreundinnen in Berlin, founded in 1868; the Damenakademie des Münchner Künstlerinnenvereins, established in 1882; and the Malerinnenschule in Karlsruhe, founded in 1885. Although such institutions did not have the means to offer a fully comprehensive academic programme, they were credible and successful as far as professionalism was concerned. They offered women artists the opportunity to teach, and provided their pupils with female role models. The experience of organising such schools, of maintaining the teaching programme and putting on exhibitions and festivals also stood women artists in good stead, since it gave teachers and pupils the opportunity of breaking through the traditional connection between creativity and masculinity and of concentrating on what mattered. Since the schools had to finance themselves through members' subscriptions, school fees, exhibitions and donations, they inevitably recorded a high turnover of younger teachers, who often used them as a springboard for posts in the state-financed and opulently equipped academies or else to build up an independent livelihood. The art academies in Germany and Austria (Switzerland had no art academy) remained exclusively for men until almost the end of the 19th century, and some even into the early 20th century. Here, unlike the USA, the few academically orientated women's schools failed to provide an alternative. The same applies to the three above-mentioned art schools for women if they are compared to academies, but it is notable that some of the best-known women artists emerged from such schools, including Käthe Kollwitz and Paula Modersohn-Becker (q.v.).

The number of women from the middle classes who could no longer be supported by their families must have been considerable; this is the most likely explanation for the demand for the few existing educational opportunities on offer. If women artists were tormented by being placed on the same level as lazy or inept dilettanti, Alfred Lichtwark, the director of the Hamburger Kunsthalle, attempted to play female amateurs against women artists and use them for his own purposes. Lichtwark saw the meagre artistic training of the middle-class male as a reason for the uncompetitiveness of applied art manufactures on an international level. Like his mentors – Justus Brinckmann, director of the Museum für Kunst und Gewerbe in Hamburg, who was married to the painter Henriette Hahn, and Julius Lessing, the head of the Berlin Kunstgewerbemuseum and its school – Lichtwark was in favour of the strict limitation of artistic work for women. He was attracted by the potential of leisured, well-to-do women amateurs, who in his view constituted a high-ranking

public. Lichtwark's understanding of art history was slight, and his knowledge of important women artists of earlier centuries even slighter; any serious art not controlled by male interests was regarded with suspicion not only by Lichtwark, but also by the directors of large museums and by critics such as Karl Scheffler (Berger 1982, pp.78–87, 66–72). Since Lichtwark believed that through rich female dilettanti he could gain influence over their husbands, he gave them a programme in the hope of raising the standard of German applied art.

Schools of applied art and organisations of amateurs also had their status in Austria, before the Zeichenschule of the Wiener Frauen-Erwerbs-Verein was founded in 1867 with the aim of "raising taste" and providing women with "new sources of income through drawing and painting" (Plakolm-Forsthuber 1994, pp.32, 39–44). Rudolf von Eitelberger ensured that attached to the K.K. Museum für Kunst und Industrie, established in 1864, was a Kunstgewerbeschule, founded in 1867 and also open to selected young women. He was concerned with the use of culture in the formation of a national identity. In this framework even women who would not otherwise have had the opportunity had a modest "place", though one that was always being questioned. Here parallels with German developments are clear. Craftwork and applied art had a high national status in the consciousness of the reformers. The admission of female students remained restrictive, and for important specialist subjects it was purely a matter of rhetoric. Eitelberger's strategy of keeping women away from the specialist classes was successful – as was the later attempt by Gropius at the Bauhaus. Like Lichtwark, Eitelberger believed that "the vocation of women to high art is very limited" (ibid., p.42).

Although here it was only a matter of commercial application and not fine art, women realised to their amazement that the same arguments that had excluded them from the art academies were being directed against them in the sphere of applied art, and they were exposed to the same irritation, scepticism and mockery that they had met from fine artists. The Viennese academy even reinforced the rejection of female pupils. As in Germany, here too there were arrangements between the heads of schools regarding relations with women artists or craftswomen. In the 1880s consideration was even given to excluding women from schools that had just started to accept female pupils.

Twenty years later the rising generation of female craftworkers in Austria profited from a development that in 1900 had led to Austrian handicrafts being presented for the first time in international competition, at the 8th Secession Exhibition in Vienna. The growing demand led in 1903 to the founding of the Wiener Werkstätte. This offered young craftswomen the opportunity of contributing designs that would then be marketed under the firm's name or issued by leading artists as their own work. The strong involvement of trainees/new recruits soon led to the accusation of "feminisation". The assumption so often formulated for art, that male artists were creative and women artists imitative, was transferred in full to applied art and aimed as a reproach against women. Yet they made no official protests against the second-class status assigned to them in the hierarchy of the sexes, and contributed considerably to the success of the Wiener Werkstätte. The poor wages there and the economic hardship

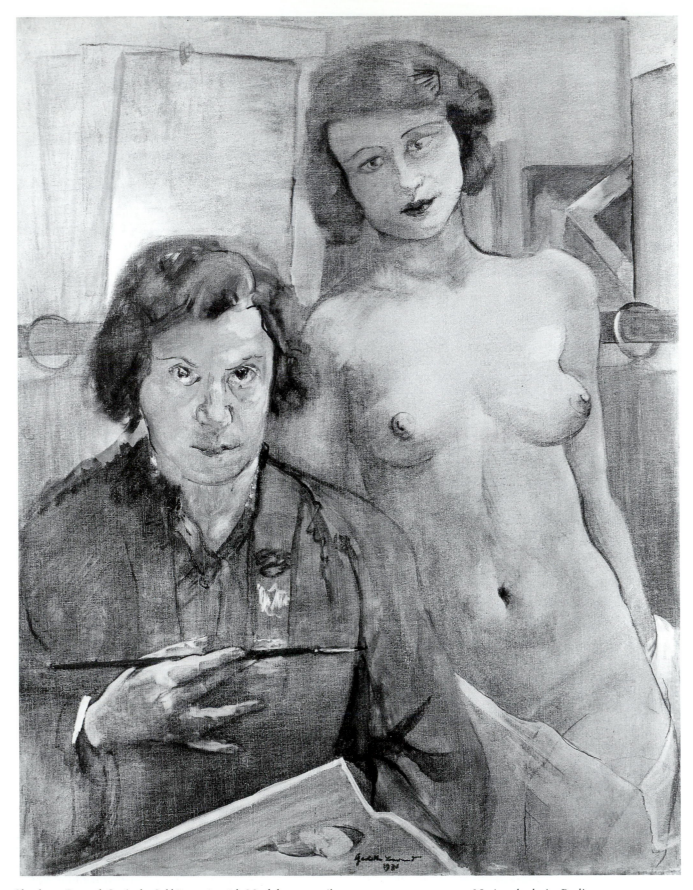

Charlotte Berend-Corinth: *Self-Portrait with Model*, 1931; oil on canvas; 90 × 70.5 cm.; Nationalgalerie, Berlin

that followed World War I, and which lasted until the early 1930s, led to many craftswomen becoming independent. They set up studios and workshops. Emmy Zweybrück-Prochaska established the Kunstgewerbliche Werkstätte in 1913, and in 1915 she combined it with a Kunstgewerbliche Privat-lehranstalt, where she trained female pupils – as did Elfriede Berbalk in her Metallwerkstätte. To some critics, women's involvement in craftwork, with its practical use, was merely a modern version of amateurism, and this too damaged the reputation of women artists who had been forced to earn their living in the applied arts in order to survive.

Such foundations, however, marked the first commercial successes. The only parallels elsewhere were in the world of photography. Since 1890, one section of the Lette-Verein had consisted of female photographers, and in Munich the Fotoatelier Elvira (1887–1908), run by Sophia Goudstikker and Anita Augspurg, set standards for portrait, court and society photography for years and brought in its wake comparable firms also run by female photographers. In Vienna Dora Kallmus at the Atelier d'Ora (1907–27) built up a similar clientele consisting of intellectuals, artists, dancers, women writers, etc., and it was to be only a few years before the first women photo-journalists – such as Gerta Taro in the Spanish Civil War – moved beyond the framework of portrait and fashion photography to new areas of work.

Austrian women artists went abroad, to the Munich Damenakademie, for instance, to study or to teach. In 1897, the year in which the Vienna Secession was founded, the Wiener Kunstschule für Frauen und Mädchen was opened. Unlike Germany, here the initiative came not from an association of women artists, but from a painter, Olga Prager. Among the founder-members of the Damenakademie was the Austrian artist Bertha Tarnoczy; later Tina Blau (q.v.) and Carola von Bär-Mathes taught there. On the strength of her experience as a teacher in Munich, Blau, a landscape painter, was recruited as one of the first teachers at the new schools in Vienna. The supporting association was proud of its low student fees. Other teachers were "secessionists and artists of second quality" (ibid., pp.52–3).

Many aspiring women artists lost energy in struggles with their families, with sceptical teachers, with husbands who undermined their work (as Justus Brinckmann did when as a museum director he forbade his wife, Henriette Hahn, to paint) or who allotted them second place (as Lovis Corinth did to Charlotte Berend-Corinth, q.v.), and with art dealers and critics who did not believe that works by women were worthy of any serious consideration (as Philippine Wolff-Arndt describes in her memoirs). Such prejudices encroached on their own thoughts and feelings (Wolff-Arndt 1929, pp.49, 50–52, 64–5, 96). It was hard to escape the chorus of "important" artists, dignitaries and official representatives who were constantly evoking female incapacity and valued women only as their public or as paying guests, as patrons and copyists.

How were women to keep away from family life, the petty competition for the favour of self-proclaimed "masters" in private ateliers, the chaos of state-imposed restrictions, and actually achieve something? How could young women artists use their money sensibly? How could they gain space for experiments, and develop beyond the barren discussions about the "place" of women artists? How were they to evade the guidance of content, the censorship, the control and the gossip of the "masters" on whom they had to rely for basic training? These and similar questions became all the more pressing as the patronage of the aristocracy and the churches declined in importance. Dora Hitz must have discovered just how difficult it was to go back to the experiences of earlier centuries when she went to the court of Princess Elisabeth of Romania (who had published poetry under the pseudonym of Carmen Sylva and supported the training of women). Neither the court nor the church offered opportunities to gain access to the avant-garde, so Hitz gave up her life at court for the freedom of Paris, where she could study the newest artistic developments.

Before 1900 very few Austrian women made use of the advantages of Paris. Munich had remained the preferred destination for them: it provided respected private ateliers, the Damenakademie and the opportunity on summer courses at the Neu-Dachauto school to study from the nude and to concentrate on landscape painting. Rome had been the destination favoured by German women artists in the early 19th century, but from the late 1860s and early 1870s into the early 20th century German and Swiss women artists sought opportunities in the French capital.

Artists, men and women, from all over Europe and America, went to Paris for the training available there. As far as access to the institutions went, the situation for women hardly differed from that at home: the Ecole des Beaux-Arts was as closed to them as were the academies at home. Here too there was the most undignified struggle, which reached its climax in a public protest organised by students against the presence of the first female students, when in 1897 they were driven out of the school building with a howl of "Down with women!" (Garb 1994, p.103). Private ateliers such as the Académie Julian provided a separate ladies' class, but women had to pay twice as much as men. Nevertheless, Paris offered something that hardly any other city could offer: a lively art scene delighting in innovation, an international body of students, more effective private schools and, as well as exhibitions and publications, participation in the most recent developments in painting and sculpture.

In 1881 French women artists had founded the Union des Femmes Peintres et Sculpteurs, and under the direction of Mme Léon Bertaux (q.v.) and Virginie Demont-Breton (q.v.) had waged a relentless struggle for opportunities in training, exhibitions and commissions. In Paris the Salon des Femmes was founded, as was the Journal des Femmes Artistes. The alternation of galanterie and contempt with which female students from all over the world were treated at the Académie Julian or Académie Colarossi did not prevent women artists from spending the most productive time of their lives there.

With its descriptions of the teaching at the Académie Julian, the journal of Marie Bashkirtseff (q.v.), which circulated in various versions and translations, also made an impact in Germany. It presented problems of identity with which young women artists such as Paula Modersohn-Becker and Clara Rilke-Westhoff (q.v.) were already familiar from their own experience, before they set off for Paris at the turn of the 20th century. The journals also show that it was not so much the teachers who were the students' role models as their fellow pupils, such as Louise Breslau (q.v.), because of their professionalism and determination to achieve something.

Ambition, the struggle for prizes and state commissions, for official recognition and support – all this could be experienced and assessed on the spot, in contact with teachers, colleagues, French feminists and fellow pupils from all over the world. Towards the end of the 19th century Paris was more than the sum of the talents assembled there. It offered few opportunities for integration, but rather a sense of alienation, of loneliness and of being unrecognised, which resulted in some of the best works by German and Austrian women artists.

The oeuvre of women artists in the 19th century was created outside the world of academies. Artists, academicians, museum directors, politicians and publicists comprised a network of contacts that women artists as a group were unable to penetrate, and only in isolated instances were they able to set up something in opposition. The women artists of the 19th century could not count on pertinent critique, one that did not lead into a review of the "feminine", on an appropriate reception or on the correct storage of their works; Ernst Guhl (1858), Karl Scheffler (1908) and Hans Hildebrandt (1928) represented the level on which the "discussion" or approach to a "historiography" of female cultural achievements was played. A feature in common among critics was the repetition of clichés, the assertion that women were in principle incapable and the stereotyped pointing to the "place" of women – unattractive, contemptible areas away from interesting developments. Women were suspect as a sex, so no trust was put in their art, and there was no issue that was not sexualised. In 1908 women had joined together in the Bund Deutscher und Österreichischer Künstlerinnenvereine; some were able to exhibit in the Hagenbund, from 1906, or, like Charlotte Berend-Corinth and Käthe Kollwitz, were appointed to the committee and jury of the Berlin Secession; and in 1913 a Frauenkunstverband was planned in order to create an equivalent to the Verein Berliner Künstler, which did not accept female members. But despite such steps forward it is obvious that the struggle of the art academies against women artists was successful. Ironically, when the historic moment for women to enter the academies as students and teachers arrived, the institutions suffered the most radical loss of importance in their history.

One exception to this was the Bauhaus, which flourished during the years of the Weimar Republic (1919–33). Its locations – Weimar, Dessau and Berlin – also marked stages in its internal development. The Bauhaus was linked to democratic hopes. According to its founding programme, it was to be a modern training centre combining the strengths of handicraft, art and industry and, in contrast to the traditional academies, it was to be innovative. The rules adopted in 1919 stipulated that the Bauhaus must accept female students. In the post-war period many young women artists took advantage of this opportunity, although female handicraft traditions were foreign to industrial production (see Anja Baumhoff, "Zwischen Berufung und Beruf: Frauen am Bauhaus" in Berlin 1992, pp.113–120).

There could be no talk of the conquest of new fields. The tolerance of women students was paid for with a strict restriction to "feminine" areas of activity: weaving. It was the architecture departments of traditional academies and technical high schools that trained the first women architects, and in the open market they were initially tied down to interior design,

especially for kitchens. Later such women architects as Margarete Schütte-Lihotzky, Liane Zimbler, Friedl Dicker, Ella Briggs-Baumfeld and Lucy Hillebrand concentrated on the building of housing estates and residential projects, and set great store on answering the architectural needs of working women (Plakolm-Forsthuber 1994, pp.237–65; Berlin 1991).

Women artists appeared late as teachers at academies and art schools, occasionally in the 1920s and following World War II; in the 1940s the sculptor Renée Sintenis (q.v.) and the tapestry-maker Woty Werner were appointed to the Hochschule der Künste in Berlin, which succeeded the old Berlin Academy. National Socialism marked a break, with the dissolution of feminist organisations, the exiling of Jewish women artists and the exclusion of "degenerate" women artists. The proscribing of the existing associations of the women's movement, and an ideology that reduced women to motherhood, meant that everything that women artists had hitherto attained was now in doubt: the way ahead was indicated by the exclusion of such renowned figures as Käthe Kollwitz and Renée Sintenis from the Prussian Academy. Women sculptors such as Hanna Cauer (q.v.) profited from their accommodation to the new regime; others passed their lives as unobtrusively as possible in impoverished conditions or in opposition. The most eloquent testimony of these years was left by the Jewish woman painter Charlotte Salomon (q.v.) in a series of drawings *Leben? oder Theater? Ein autobiographisches Singspiel*. Everything that had been built up with infinite struggle was wiped out within a few years. Further damage was done by the bombs of World War II; they destroyed not only the studios of women artists and the work of lifetimes, but also such valuable material as the original diary of Paula Modersohn-Becker.

From the last years of the 19th century until the 1930s there were repeated attempts to raise public awareness of the situation of women as subjects and objects of art through exhibitions, a tradition that was taken up again by the modern women's movement. In 1977 the first survey exhibition *Künstlerinnen international, 1877–1977* was held in Berlin, in Vienna the exhibition *Kunst mit Eigensinn: Aktuelle Kunst von Frauen* (1985) and in Wiesbaden *Künstlerinnen des 20. Jahrhunderts* (1990). Attempts were made to address the museum policies that had been so disastrous for women artists in the past, a task that the Verborgenes Museum in Berlin took up in 1987 with its *Dokumente von Frauen in Berliner öffentlichen Sammlungen*, assuming the long-overdue reappraisal of the Verein der Künstlerinnen und Kunstfreundinnen zu Berlin with the exhibition *Profession ohne Tradition*. In addition to such thematic exhibitions, there was also a desire to foster co-operation between women artists and women art historians in approaching women artists of the past, and two exhibitions in which female artists and art historians worked together were held in Berlin: *Ich bin nicht ich, wenn ich sehe* (1991) and *Muse küsst Muse* (1995). This was preceded by autobiographical declarations by Judy Chicago (q.v.) in *Through the Flower: My Struggles as an Artist* (1975) and Gisela Breitling in *Die Spuren des Schiffs in den Wellen: Eine autobiographische Suche nach den Frauen in der Kunstgeschichte* (1980), the resonance of which can be compared with the journals of Marie Bashkirtseff.

To sum up, it can be said that the continuum of the history

of women artists lies in discontinuity: in ever-new attempts to overcome obstacles, to develop a world view and to give it public value. In the 19th century the function of great patrons, male and female, was gradually assumed by members of the family, friends, salon ladies and organised female connoisseurs of art. Instead of small, educated circles that knew how to assess and encourage art, there soon emerged a new public shaped by the media. The expanding press offered many new opportunities for those opposed to women artists to air their views; this was, however, linked with a rapid decline in the standard of art criticism.

Despite all this, it is all the more surprising to see what and how much was achieved. One explanation is that there was one place in which women artists could think, dream, experiment, give an account of themselves – in their writings (Berger 1987, pp.15–32). In diaries, letters, memoirs, autobiographies, poems and novels a picture emerged of what women artists hoped to become in spite of hostility and contempt, a picture of themselves and a picture of the world seen through their eyes. The written word leaves room for visual imaginings, wishes and hopes, self-doubt and certainties, room for the future. Here – sometimes more strongly than in the world of images created by women artists – what was unseen, un-experienced and new had its first anchoring in reality. For women artists writing meant survival. The writings left by women artists gain in significance in the 19th century. They not only provide clarification but also reflect the attempt to escape alien control, male directives and androcentric systems.

In the midst of the everyday challenges and demands with which women artists had to reckon as women, their publicly silenced voice finds expression in a record for posterity. Without these writings, without the hidden knowledge behind the publicly displayed consciousness, nothing of significance could be created; the diary was necessary for this to become reality. Diaries contain formulations of what threatens the creation of art: external and internal resistance, conventions, prejudices, anti-feminism and – yet more dangerous – trivialisation. Diaries are at once the trace of a life and a warning: "To die, oh God, to die having left nothing behind!" wrote Marie Bashkirtseff. "To die like a dog!!! To die like hundreds of thousands of other women, whose names can barely be read on their gravestones" (ibid., p.170). The autobiographical writings left by women artists of the 19th and 20th centuries delineate a topography of genesis, which the scant visual material that survives can reveal to us only occasionally.

RENATE BERGER

Bibliography

General

Ernst Guhl, *Die Frauen in der Kunstgeschichte*, Berlin: Guttentag, 1858

Georg Voss, *Die Frauen in der Kunst*, Berlin, 1895

Karl Scheffler, *Die Frau und die Kunst*, Berlin: Bard, 1908

Henni Lehmann, *Das Kunststudium der Frauen: Ein Vortrag gehalten zu Frankfurt am Main*, Darmstadt: Koch, 1914

Lu Märten, *Die Künstlerin*, Munich: Langen, 1919

Hans Hildebrandt, *Die Frau als Künstlerin*, Berlin: Mosse, 1928

Maria Weese and Doris Wild, *Die Schweizer Frau in Kunstgewerbe und bildender Kunst*, Zürich and Leipzig, 1928

Künstlerinnen international, 1877–1977, exh. cat., Neue Gesellschaft für Bildende Kunst, Berlin, 1977

Germaine Greer, *The Obstacle Race: The Fortunes of Women Painters and Their Work*, London: Secker and Warburg, and New York: Farrar Straus, 1979

Gislind Nabakowski, Helke Sander and Peter Gorsen, *Frauen in der Kunst*, 2 vols, Frankfurt am Main: Suhrkamp, 1980

Renate Berger, *Malerinnen auf dem Weg ins 20. Jahrhundert: Kunstgeschichte als Sozialgeschichte*, Cologne: DuMont, 1982

Grethe Jürgens, *Gerta Overbeck: Bilder der zwanziger Jahre*, exh. cat., Bonner Kunstverein, Bonn, 1982

Ulrika Evers, *Deutsche Künstlerinnen des 20. Jahrhunderts: Malerei, Bildhauerei, Tapisserie*, Hamburg: Schultheis, 1983

Cordula Bischoff and others, eds, *Frauen Kunst Geschichte: Zur Korrektur des herrschenden Blicks*, Giessen: Anabas, 1984 (transactions of a conference held in Marburg, 1983)

Ruth Nobs-Greter, *Die Künstlerin und ihr Werk in der deutschsprachigen Kunstgeschichtsschreibung*, Zürich: Juris, 1984

Silvia Eiblmayr and others, eds, *Kunst mit Eigensinn: Aktuelle Kunst von Frauen: Texte und Dokumentation*, Vienna: Löcker, 1985

Hof-Atelier Elvira, 1887–1928: Ästheten, Emanzen, Aristokraten, exh. cat., Stadtmuseum, Munich, 1985

Verena Dietrich, *Architektinnen: Ideen, Projekte, Bauten*, Stuttgart: Kohlhammer, 1986

Ilsebill Barta and others, eds, *Frauen, Bilder, Männer, Mythen: Kunsthistorische Beiträge*, Berlin: Reimer, 1987 (transactions of a conference held in Vienna, 1986)

Renate Berger, *"Und ich sehe nichts, nichts als die Malerei": Autobiographische Texte von Künstlerinnen des 18.–20. Jahrhunderts*, Frankfurt am Main: Fischer, 1987

Das Verborgene Museum I: Dokumente von Frauen in Berliner öffentlichen Sammlungen, exh. cat., Akademie der Künste, Berlin, 1987

Denise Noël, *L'Académie Julian: Les Ateliers pour dames, 1868–1907*, thesis, Sorbonne, Paris, 1988

Heidemarie Seblatnig, ed., *Einfach den Gefahren ins Auge sehen: Künstlerinnen im Gespräch*, Vienna: Böhlau, 1988

Edith Krull, *Women in Art*, London: Studio Vista, 1989 (German original)

Ines Lindner and others, eds, *Blick-Wechsel: Konstruktionen von Männlichkeit und Weiblichkeit in Kunst und Kunstgeschichte*, Berlin: Reimer, 1989 (transactions of a conference held in Berlin, 1988)

Christiane Müller, *Bildende Künstlerinnen in der DDR – Soziales Umfeld und Werk: Versuch einer Situationsanalyse zu Beginn der 80er Jahre*, dissertation, Humboldt University, Berlin, 1989

Künstlerinnen des 20. Jahrhunderts, exh. cat., Museum Wiesbaden, 1990

Theresa Georgen and others, eds, *Ich bin nicht ich, wenn ich sehe: Dialoge: Ästhetische Praxis in Kunst und Wissenschaft von Frauen*, Berlin: Reimer, 1991

Domesticity and Dissent: The Role of Women Artists in Germany, 1918–1938, exh. cat., Leicester Museum and Art Gallery, and elsewhere, 1992

Renate Herter, *Visuelle Dialoge: Zum Verhältnis von Weiblichkeit und Kunst*, Berlin: Orlanda Frauenverlag, 1992

Medaillenkünstlerinnen in Deutschland: Kreativität in Geschichte und Gegenwart, exh. cat., Staatliche Galerie Moritzburg, Halle, 1992

Carola Muysers and others, eds, *Käthe, Paula und der ganze Rest: Ein Nachschlagewerk*, Berlin: Berlinische Galerie, 1992

Profession ohne Tradition: 125 Jahre Verein der Berliner Künstlerinnen, exh. cat., Berlinische Galerie, Berlin, 1992

Gunther Salje, Ulrike Schaz and Bernhard Watka, *Bildende Künstlerinnen heute: Lebenslage und Selbstverständnis*, Frankfurt am Main: Lang, 1992

"... und hat als Weib unglaubliches Talent" (Goethe): Angelika Kauffmann (1741–1807), Marie Ellenrieder (1791–1863), exh. cat., Rosgartenmuseum, Konstanz, 1992

Silvia Baumgart and others, eds, *Denkräume zwischen Kunst und Wissenschaft, no.5: Kunsthistorikerinnentagung in Hamburg*, Berlin: Reimer, 1993 (transactions of a conference held in Hamburg, 1991)

Frauen Kunst Geschichte, Forschungsgruppe Marburg, ed., *Feministische Bibliografie zur Frauenforschung in der Kunstgeschichte*, Pfaffenweiler: Centaurus, 1993

"… ihr werten Frauenzimmer, auf!": Malerinnen der Aufklärung, exh. cat., Roselius-Haus, Bremen, 1993

Rheinische Expressionistinnen, Schriftenreihe des Vereins August Macke-Haus, no.10, Bonn, 1993

Tamar Garb, *Sisters of the Brush: Women's Artistic Culture in Late Nineteenth-Century Paris*, New Haven and London: Yale University Press, 1994

Sabine Plakolm-Forsthuber, *Künstlerinnen in Österreich, 1897–1938: Malerei, Plastik, Architektur*, Vienna: Picus, 1994

Marsha Meskimmon and Shearer West, eds, *Visions of the "Neue Frau": Women and the Visual Arts in Weimar Germany*, Aldershot: Scolar Press, 1995

Muse küsst Muse: Eine zeitgenössische Reflexion über historische Künstlerinnen, exh. cat., Lindenau-Museum, Altenberg, 1995

Individuals
(excluding references to artists with their own entries in the *Dictionary*)

Hermione von Preuschen, *Der Roman meines Lebens: Ein Frauenleben um die Jahrhundertwende*, Berlin: 1926

Philippine Wolff-Arndt, *Wir Frauen von einst: Erinnerungen einer Malerin*, Munich: Reinhardt, 1929

Ida Dehmel, exh. cat., Staats- und Universitätsbibliothek, Hamburg, 1970 (founder of GEDOK, an association of women artists in Germany with local clubs)

Sabine Lepsius, *Ein Berliner Künstlerleben um die Jahrhundertwende*, Munich: Muller, 1972

Gisela Breitling, *Die Spuren des Schiffs in den Wellen: Eine autobiographische Suche nach den Frauen in der Kunstgeschichte*, Berlin: Oberbaum, 1980

Ulrike Rosenbach, *Videokunst-Foto-Aktion/Performance, Feministische Kunst*, Frankfurt am Main: Rosenbach, 1982

Maria Slavona, 1865–1931: Eine deutsche Impressionistin, exh. cat., Sammlung Bröhan, Berlin, 1982

Gisela Breitling, "Sprechen und Stummsein: Die künstlerische Rede: Gedanken über Redekonventionen und weibliches Selbstverständnis", *Die Horen*, no.132, 1983

Monika Faver, *Madame d'Ora: Wien-Paris: Portraits aus Kunst und Gesellschaft, 1907–1957*, Vienna and Munich: Brandstetter, 1983

Johanna Ey und ihr Künstlerkreis: Zum 120. Geburtstag der Düsseldorfer Kunsthändlerin, exh. cat., Galerie Remmert und Barth, Düsseldorf, 1984

Gisela Breitling, Stuttgart: Parkland, 1987

Margarete Geiger, *Briefe der Malerin aus Würzburg, Bamberg, München und Wien an ihre Familie in Schweinfurt, 1804–1809*, ed. Friederike Kotuc, Nuremberg: Spätlese, 1987

Madame d'Ora, Vienna and Paris, 1907–1957: The Photography of Dora Kallmus, exh. cat., Vassar College Art Gallery, Poughkeepsie, 1987

Carmen Oberst, *Kairos: Der günstige Augenblick*, Hamburg: Blauflug, 1987

Helen Ernst, 1904–1948: Berlin, Amsterdam, Ravensbrück: Stationen einer antifaschistischen Künstlerin, exh. cat., Das Verborgene Museum, Berlin, 1988

Anita Prammer, *Valie Export: Eine multimediale Künstlerin*, Vienna: Wiener Frauenverlag, 1988

Johannes Grützke, *Gisela Breitling: Szenen aus dem Leben einer Malerin*, Berlin: Ladengalerie, 1989

Marta Astfalck-Vietz: Photographien, 1922–1935, exh. cat., Berlinische Galerie, 1991

Raum-Spiel: Spiel-Räume: Lucy Hillebrand, exh. cat., Das Verborgene Museum, Berlin, 1991

Annegret Rittmann, ed., *Ida Gerhardi (1862–1927): Eine westfälische Malerin zwischen Paris und Berlin*, Münster: Ardey, 1993

Brigitte Doppagne, *Ottilie Reyländer: Stationen einer Malerin*, Worpswede: Worpsweder Verlag, 1994

Irme Schaber, *Gerta Taro, Fotoreporterin im Spanischen Bürgerkrieg: Eine Biografie*, Marburg: Jonas, 1994

4. Italy

Many are familiar with one of the opening scenes of Madame de Staël's novel, *Corinne; ou, L'Italie* (1807), in which an Anglo-Italian woman is cheered by an adoring crowd on her way to the Campidoglio in Rome to be crowned for her artistic and literary achievements. The author implies that this Italian support of a woman artist's career is unique to its time, remarking: "There can be nothing more hostile to the habits and opinions of an Englishman than any great publicity given to the career of a woman … " (p.18, trans. Isabel Hill, London: Bentley, 1833).

Perhaps surprisingly, Corinne's triumph may have been based on factual events. Carlo Villani records in his *Stelle femminili* (1915) that in the late 18th century Teresa Bandettini, author and *improvvisatrice*, was publicly recognised by a ceremony on the Campidoglio. Indeed, this was the standard practice for members of the Accademia Nazionale di San Luca until 1844, when the festivities were transferred to the Academy's present campus in via di Ripetta (Gaetana Scano, *L'Accademia Nazionale di San Luca*, Rome: De Luca, 1974, pp.31–3).

Women artists were recognised in similar ceremonies as members of the Accademia Nazionale di San Luca and its prototypical organisations from the beginning of the 18th century, enjoying an earlier sustained academic recognition in Italy than in most of the rest of Europe and the USA (see Academies of Art survey). A steady trickle of women artists had joined the Accademia di San Luca throughout the 18th and 19th centuries; the earliest female members in the 19th century included the miniaturists Sofia Clerc in 1801 and Marianna Waldstein in 1807, and the portrait painter Faustina Bracci Armellini in 1811.

It is striking that the few women who did join the Italian academies of art seem not to have threatened the male membership enough to provoke the explicit exclusion of females, as happened in France and Britain. Nevertheless, few Italian women ever became academicians or, indeed, professional artists. This would indicate that other cultural barriers were at work to discourage women from the field and its professional ranks, obviating the necessity for direct prohibitions. Furthermore, while women were not explicitly barred from study of the nude in Italian academies, the genres that most Italian women painters pursued – portraiture and the miniature – indicate that the implicit conventions of gender operated in Italy as elsewhere to discourage women artists from undertaking the more prestigious figure and history painting, or sculpture.

None the less, as early as 1873 the new Italian monarch, Vittorio Emmanuele II, redrafted the charter of the Florentine Accademia di Belle Arti, explicitly stating in Title II, Article 3: "Among the academicians of merit ['of merit' being an honorific title] women may also be admitted, and without limit to their numbers" (Luigi Biagi, *L'Accademia di belle arti di Firenze*, Florence: Le Monnier, 1941, p.151; my translation).

Nor were women artists denied access to study of the nude within the guidelines of this charter, as indeed they never had been explicitly prohibited under the wording of earlier charters. Alberto Riccoboni even makes an – unconfirmed – claim that Teresa Benincampi (q.v.), student of Canova, was actually a professor at the Accademia di Belle Arti in Florence (*Roma nell'arte: La scultura nell'evo moderno, dal quattrocento ad oggi*, Rome: Casa Editrice Mediterranea, 1942).

As in France and Britain, most successful women artists in Italy before the rise of the academies and even after were trained at home by their fathers (as was the case with Amalia Duprè, q.v., who was trained by her father Giovanni Duprè) and/or husbands who were artists, or by close family friends. At least one 18th-century woman artist, Felicità Sartori, was trained by an older woman artist, Rosalba Carriera (q.v.). The Church was also an important supporter for women artists throughout the centuries, both by providing informal training and a venue for painters within cloistered communities (see Convents survey), and by offering commissions to women artists whose femininity was seen as consistent with religious purity and zeal. By the 19th century, as in most of Europe and the USA, upper-class Italian women were receiving "accomplishment art" training as a standard part of their preparation for marriage and genteel society, but they were not encouraged to pursue their training beyond amateurism. Natalie Harris Bluestone cites the case of the 19th-century art historian Carolina Bonafede, whose tract *Cenni biografici e ritratti d'insigni delle donne bolognese* (1845) recounted the life of the 16th-century sculptor Properzia de' Rossi (q.v.) not to inspire contemporary women to pursue similar careers, but to "fill them with civic and gender pride". But most of all Bonafede, using dubious reasoning, concludes that the sculptor's example should lead women "to study hard and, above all, to encourage their men folk" (Natalie Harris Bluestone, "The female gaze: Women's interpretations of the life and work of Properzia de' Rossi, Renaissance sculptor", *Double Vision: Perspectives on Gender and the Visual Arts*, London and Toronto: Associated University Presses, 1995, p.47).

At the same time, however, the 19th-century interest in women's accomplishments that led to the publication of historical surveys of women's achievements in the USA and Britain, such as Elizabeth Fries Ellet's *Women Artists in All Ages and Countries* (New York: Harper, 1859; London: Bentley, 1860), had its parallel in Italy among works more explicitly designed to encourage excellence and ambition among young Italian women: Carlo Villani's *Stelle femminili* cited above, Maria Domenica Crety's *Le donne celebri di Terra d'Otranto* (1913); M. Francesco Serdonati's *Giunta alle donne illustri italiane di M. Giovanni Boccaccio* (1906), Cesare Conti's *La donna nell'arte* (Turin: Sten, n.d) and Virginia Olper Monis's "La veneziana nell'arte e nella vita" (1914). Individual women artists were treated in fiction as well, among them Contessa Anita Zappa Bovanelli's drama *La Tintoretto* (Milan: de Mohr, n.d.) about the 16th-century painter Marietta Robusti (q.v.).

Many female leaders of the Risorgimento, such as Anna Maria Mozzoni, had combined the rhetoric of national liberation with that of female emancipation, calling for the immediate incorporation of women as full citizens in the new nation. The voices of these pivotal women players in Italian unification were difficult to ignore in post-unification restructurings of government and educational institutions. The explicit support for women artists' training, such as the charter of 1873 for the Florentine Accademia di Belle Arti, was accompanied by an unprecedented number of women art students. In addition to the academies of Florence and Rome, important centres for the training of women artists in the 19th century included the Accademia in Venice and the new Istituto di Belle Arti in Naples. Many women art students went on to teach art, for the most part in primary and secondary schools. Italian unification was accompanied by the formation of numerous progressivist societies, some specifically for women's advocacy, that offered venues for national and international contacts and professional recognition. There was, for example, the Istituto Italiano per lo Sviluppo Generale del Progresso, which gave awards for artistic achievement. The Società delle Giovani Italiane per Promuovere la Coltura delle Lettere, delle Arti e delle Altre Virtù nella Donna, "with competitions and prizes", included foreign members and thus provided opportunities for international contact among women artists. The increase in the visibility of women in the arts led not only to more female participation in national art competitions, particularly those in Turin and the Mostre della Secessione Romana, but also, in the last decade of the 19th century, to special exhibitions for women artists only: the *Beatrice* in Florence in 1890, and the Esposizioni d'Arte Femminile in Florence in 1899 and 1900. In 1915 three women artists from Italy participated in the Panama-Pacific Exposition in San Francisco: the flower-painter Sofia de Muralt, the engraver Matilde Festa Piacentini and the painter Emma Ciardi; the latter two both received gold medals.

By the turn of the 20th century the Galleria Nazionale d'Arte Moderna in Rome had acquired Maria Ippolito's painting *Crepuscolo gelido* (exhibited in 1829 at the Esposizione di Venezia), and other museums had begun to acquire works by earlier women artists: works by Artemisia Lomi were to be found in the Museo di Napoli and the Palazzo Pitti, Florence, while the collections of the Galleria di Ravenna, the Pinacoteca di Forlì and the Museo di Brera in Milan included paintings by Barbara Longhi (q.v.). Antonetta Maria Bessone Aurelj, also a poet, dramatist and author of the *Dizionario dei pittori italiani* (Città di Castello: Lapi, 1915), was named miniaturist to the queen mother, Margherita of Savoy, in 1910; and works by Felicità Sartori, protégée of Rosalba Carriera, were collected by the royal family. Cesare Vivaldi, in the introduction to Simona Weller's *Il complesso di Michelangelo* (1976), describes the years from 1910 to 1930 as a "golden period" for Italian women artists with respect to the preceding centuries, but notes that the onset of fascism took its toll, primarily on young and emerging women artists. Even though Valentine de Saint-Point and a few other women, such as Benedetta (q.v.) and Regina (q.v.), maintained a high profile among the Italian Futurists, neither the anti-feminist mood of the movement nor de Saint-Point's *Manifesto of the Futurist Woman* did much to encourage women artists to seek equal access to educational opportunities, claiming that "To grant equal rights to woman is to make her lose all of her fertile power" (Katz 1986–7, p.13). Indeed, according to Weller, it was not until the 1960s that Italian women artists began to enter art training and the profession in numbers comparable to those of other European countries.

NANCY PROCTOR

Bibliography

M. Francesco Serdonati, *Giunta alle donne illustri italiane di M. Giovanni Boccaccio*, Florence, 1906

Laura M. Ragg, *The Women Artists of Bologna*, London: Methuen, 1907

Maria Domenica Crety, *Le donne celebri di Terra d'Otranto*, Lecce: Guida, 1913

Virginia Olper Monis, "La veneziana nell'arte e nella vita", *Varietas*, xi, July 1914

Carlo Villani, *Stelle femminili: Dizionario bio-bibliografico*, 2 vols, Naples: Albrighi, 1915–16

Vieri Torelli, *Pittrici e scultrici italiane d'oggi*, Bologna: Fiammenghi, 1953

Simona Weller, *Il complesso di Michelangelo: Ricerca sul contributo dato dalla donna all'arte italiana del Novecento*, Pollenza: La Nuova Foglio, 1976

Luciano Rubino, *Le spose del vento: La donna nelle arti e nel designo degli ultimi cento anni*, Verona: Bertani, 1979

Vincenzo Gubitosi, ed., *Enciclopedia nazionale la donna nell'arte*, Rapallo: Ipotesi, 1982–

Segni di donna: L'arte al femminile in Umbria, 1915–1984, exh. cat., Palazzo Cesi, Acquasparta, 1984

M. Barry Katz, "The women of Futurism", *Woman's Art Journal*, vii/2, 1986–7, pp.3–13

Dal salotto agli ateliers: Produzione artistica femminile a Milano, 1880–1920, exh. cat., Museo di Milano, Milan, 1989

Rita Giordano, "Le artiste bolognesi del XVIII secolo", *Carrobbio*, xviii, 1992, pp.196–206

E. Ann Matter and John Coakley, eds, *Creative Women in Medieval and Early Modern Italy*, Philadelphia: University of Pennsylvania Press, 1994

5. The Netherlands

In the Netherlands at the end of the 20th century the doors of the academies of art and design stand open to all those who have followed a secondary school education and possess artistic talent. Future artists, whether male or female, have equal opportunities in this respect, as they do in the appointment policies for directorial positions in museums, cultural commissions and teaching. The selection must not be influenced by gender – official discussions do not allow any misunderstanding on this matter. Art is purchased with the one and only criterion that the work must satisfy norms of quality. But this present, relatively rosy social position of women artists has had to be fought for, over a period of almost two centuries. And how rosy is that position at the end of the 1990s on closer inspection?

19th century

At the beginning of the 19th century the population of the Netherlands was recovering from French domination. The French Revolution had little or no liberating effect on the position of women (Posthumus-van der Goot 1948). Their place was at home, while men worked outside. This was in contrast to the conditions of earlier times, when a painter's working and living spaces were integrated – relatives were then involved in the work, and prospective women artists could learn the

profession in the atelier of a relative, and possibly also begin to practise alongside them. However, the separation of working and living spaces became complete in the 18th century with the result that aspiring female artists had difficulties in obtaining a training in the trade (Lindenburg 1978). Women were not admitted to academies of the visual arts until around 1870, although there had been an academy at The Hague since 1682 (Reynaerts 1994).

Elementary schools for boys and for girls had existed since the beginning of the 18th century, and it was considered good breeding for girls, of what we would now refer to as secondary-school age, from well-to-do circles, to receive instruction in, among other subjects, handicrafts, dancing, singing and piano playing, as well as drawing and painting, in a domestic environment or at a girls' boarding school (Brandt Corstius 1978). Moreover, some artistically talented individuals took additional private lessons in the atelier of a painter with whom they were on good terms. This did not alter the fact that in the early 19th century Dutch women stayed at home.

But alongside this another development was taking place. After 1800 the population of the Netherlands became poorer. This social problem gradually opened the door for women to move beyond the home in order to acquire an income. Female members of a painter's family helped, as in earlier times, in the workplace or the atelier; other women became governesses or schoolteachers. The demand for teachers increased with the improvement and greater accessibility of elementary education. In 1827 a state examination for schoolteachers was instituted, with such trades as handicrafts and drawing on the curriculum (Posthumus-van der Goot 1948). (The law about secondary education for girls was not passed until 1863.)

Most women painters of the period, such as Cornelia Lamme, Henriëtte Geertruij Knip and Elisabeth A. Haanen, or still later Gerardina J. van de Sande Bakhuyzen, learned painting from their fathers (Scheen 1981). Henriëtte Geertruij Knip pursued further studies in Paris and for about three years (1802–5) took lessons there in the atelier of a painter born in the Netherlands. This is in contrast to the artistic education of her brother and colleague who was six years older: he too was initially taught by his father and then went to Paris to continue his studies, but he spent seven years in Paris and then a few years in Italy (Posthumus-van der Goot 1948). Nevertheless, Knip had a successful career, despite the contemporary prejudice against professional women painters. When in 1827 a painting of hers was bought by the queen, the commentary in the *Journal des Dames et des Modes* remarked that such a sale must remain an exception, in consideration of "the common good".

Women had no particular problems when it came to exhibiting; they could do so, for instance, in the Felix Meritis society in Amsterdam. But there was no question of women's membership, even though regulations did not expressly prohibit this. In the first quarter of the 19th century it was only too obvious that upper-class women did not step out of line. Women could also show their work at the sales exhibitions of one of the largest and best-known artists' associations, the Amsterdam society of Arti et Amicitiae, founded in 1834. They were, however, still excluded from membership of a jury. Until 1849 a woman could only be an amateur member; thereafter she could be a professional one. But it was not until after 1900

W.B. Tholen: *Drawing Lesson of the Painter's Society Pulchri in the The Hague*, 1889; Stedelijk Museum, Amsterdam

that female and male members had the same rights (Brandt Corstius 1978). The records of the biennial *Tentoonstelling van levende meesters* (Exhibition of living masters) held in Amsterdam from 1834 reveal the number of art-works made by women. In this exhibition a total of at least 575 works were shown, of which there were only 25 by (16 different) women painters. About half of the 25 works were still lifes. Women very rarely practised the highly esteemed genre of history painting (*ibid.*).

A somewhat more liberal period began in the Netherlands in 1848. Industrialisation, improvements in the standard of living, the education of the poor and increasing attention to healthcare all combined to create a climate in which the contributions of women were accepted, and women obtained more freedom of movement. In 1865 the first school of industrial skills for female pupils was founded in Amsterdam. Included in the curriculum were drawing, lithography, wood-engraving, needlework and the use of the sewing machine (Posthumus-van der Goot 1948). Although women were still unable to pursue a professional training at an academy of art, female pupils could prepare for the art certificate for secondary education at The Hague Academy from 1863. Increasing numbers of women applied to do this, so it was only natural that special women's classes were formed as a result (Reynaerts in Amsterdam 1994, p.90). In the mid-19th century academies in the Netherlands were still primarily drawing academies where students drew from plaster casts, mostly in the evenings. But Sientje Mesdag-van Houten and Maria Ph. Bilders-van Bosse,

both of whom belonged to well-to-do circles in The Hague, received only private lessons. The education of women painters was still somewhat more limited than that of their male colleagues and they had far fewer opportunities to maintain professional contacts. Both these artists, as well as many others, married painters, which brought them some relief from their artistic isolation (Arnhem 1989). Moreover, as a result, they had more access to sales exhibitions, both domestic and foreign. Women artists born some ten years later, Margaretha Roosenboom (q.v.) and Thérèse Schwartze (q.v.), also received their initial instruction in the ateliers of their fathers – they both came from painters' families. Both later gave private lessons themselves in their ateliers. Schwartze pursued her education in Munich and Paris. She belonged to the generation of women who could take lessons at the Rijksacademie in Amsterdam (*ibid.*).

From the last quarter of the 19th century women artists had increasing opportunities to qualify in their profession on an equal basis with men. Aspiring women artists could receive instruction in drawing at the Rotterdam Academy from 1861; at the Rijksacademie in Amsterdam from 1863; while in 1872 the Academy in The Hague started a course for female pupils: "Wednesdays and Saturdays from three to five o'clock". Male and female students still did not take lessons together (Brandt Corstius 1978). Yet the Netherlands were at the forefront in comparison with the admissions policies of other European academies. Those in Antwerp, Paris (the Ecole des Beaux-Arts) and Munich admitted women students in 1888, 1897 and

1919 respectively. Moreover, at the end of the 19th century academies in the Netherlands were no longer restricted to drawing instruction but offered an expanded programme that included painting. Wally Moes, who was one of the first female students at the Rijksacademie in Amsterdam, wrote about these improved conditions in her memoirs:

> to become comfortable with colours, letting the brush gradually become a part of the hand … and along with this the nourishing chatter and teasing of other students; where or how is this offered more completely and more naturally than in an academy? [Reynaerts in Amsterdam 1994].

Suze Robertson (q.v.), who in 1877 took her proficiency examinations at The Hague Academy and at first gave lessons in Rotterdam, managed to arrange to take the course in drawing from the nude model at the art academy there in the evenings. As she herself recalled, never before had a woman been permitted to attend the nude class (The Hague 1984). From 1895 onwards the aspiring women painters of the Rijksacademie in Amsterdam were permitted to form a class to work from the nude model (Reynaerts in Amsterdam 1994).

Exhibitions exclusively of women's work were organised. One of the first was held in 1871, organised by the association Arbeid Adelt (Work ennobles), an offshoot of the Algemene Nederlandsche Vrouwenvereniging (General Association of Dutch Women). The exhibits not only comprised products of the applied arts made by the less well-off, but also paintings, by Thérèse Schwartze among others. *De Nationale tentoonstelling van vrouwenarbeid* (National exhibition of women's work) at The Hague was held on the occasion of Queen Wilhelmina's coronation in 1898, an exhibition also partly inspired by the Woman's Building at the World's Columbian Exposition held five years earlier in Chicago. The Hague show was such a success that it encouraged women to work in the area of the arts and crafts (Posthumus-van Goot 1948).

20th century

After the turn of the 20th century, women's rights and opportunities increased thanks to the efforts of the first feminist wave. In 1919, for example, women obtained the right to vote. In 1913 women's organisations again held a great exhibition, now in Amsterdam: *De Vrouw, 1813–1913* (Women, 1813–1913). At the centre of the exhibition was the Pavilion of Statistics, where it was reported that up to that time 93 women physicians had completed their studies since their champion Aletta Jacobs had succeeded in this field 30 years earlier; also that a considerable number of other women academics had completed their doctoral examinations (The Hague 1984). The number of professional women painters and sculptors had likewise increased dramatically. (In fact, there was much greater conflict over the admittance of women students to university than to the academies.) The Visual Arts section of the exhibition received 667 submissions, of which 37 were sculptures (*ibid.*).

As a result of the contacts made at the academy, women artists around 1900 often grouped themselves with others they had met there. Such mutual contact had a very stimulating effect on the practice of their profession. Thus there were the circles of the Amsterdamse Joffers (Amsterdam Ladies), to whom belonged Coba Ritsema (q.v.), trained at the Rijksacademie in Amsterdam, and the Haagse Joffers, among whom was Anna Julia de Graag (q.v.), schooled at The Hague Academy (Venema 1977; Zwolle 1991, p.82; Heyting 1994). Moreover, women artists were often members of more than one artists' society and were tolerated in the related social clubs. As a result, professional contacts, with art dealers among others, became much easier. Women painters such as Jacoba van Heemskerck (q.v.), Else Berg, Charley Toorop (q.v.) and Lou Loeber, working in altogether different styles, all maintained relations with circles of artists both in the Netherlands and abroad (Hermes 1991; Haarlem 1989). For many women artists there was now the opportunity to become fully qualified in their profession and to maintain contacts with colleagues, and thus be in touch with contemporary trends. Interest in their work was shown not only by art dealers, but also by critics and museum curators. The way in which critics wrote about the work of women and the presentation of their work in museums still often left a lot to be desired, however, and remained an important feminist issue.

The damaging effects of World War II had been overcome by the 1960s, and the time was ripe for a revision of the established order. In the 1960s and 1970s, with the second feminist wave, the position of women improved still further; to take just one example, it became increasingly a matter of course for women to study and work (Metz 1995). The number of women students who pursued an education at the academies of fine arts increased substantially. There was a general growth in the number of women students training in the professions, but the percentage of women in professional fine-arts education was significantly higher still. From 1981 onwards women formed the largest group of day students at the academies. The duration of studies and results were the same for female as for male students. A comparable increase was perceptible in the professional field. In 1971, out of a total of 20,600 artists (painters, sculptors, industrial designers, photographers, filmmakers), 16 per cent were women; in 1985, out of 30,000 artists, 27 per cent were women (Bosma 1989). At the beginning of the 1990s, 45 per cent of those active in the visual arts professions were women (Gorlee 1992).

In the 1970s it had been thought that women artists should seek their own explicit feminine identity; by the 1990s this idea was abandoned (Halbertsma 1978; Halbertsma 1979). The career of artist (autonomous or applied artist and teacher) was not, however, yet experienced in the same way by women and men. Research reveals that after their academy training women found work later than their male colleagues, more often worked part-time, and on average earned less. In addition there seemed to be typical women's professions, such as fashion, textile and ceramic design. Women artists were strongly represented in the area of video art (Gorlee 1992). Women tended to teach more in centres for artistic design, men in elementary and secondary education, which is better paid (Bosma 1989).

Even in the 1980s and 1990s, the works of women have been usually severely under-represented in museums, in the more prestigious exhibitions and in art periodicals (Top 1994; van Hamersveld 1987; Korporaal 1989). A few commercial galleries (e.g. Galerie Oele, Amsterdam) and museums (e.g. Museum for Modern Art, Arnhem) pursue an equal opportunities policy. Fellowships, subsidies and prizes are not conferred equally on men and women (Gorlee 1992). Many discussions on this topic become mired in the quality argument – a moot point because the criteria of quality in art are not fixed but are subject to individual preferences at any given moment. One of the reasons for such under-representation is that women have not yet adequately penetrated the higher reaches of society. Stichting Amazone (Amazon Foundation; established 1977) and Stichting Vrouwen in de Beeldende Kunst or SVBK (Foundation for Women in the Visual Arts; established 1978), both started in Amsterdam, were an attempt to improve the social position of women artists (*Vrouwen, kunst en media* 1988). Target group networks that form a part of the Landelijke Stichting Vrouwennetwerk Nederland (National Foundation Women's Network of the Netherlands) are supported by the state. At issue is how women's achievements may be broadened. Apart from the fact that consciousness-raising demands support, more women need to take part in arts management. Professionalism needs to be stimulated, among other ways, through greater subsidies for child care and postgraduate education. The state of progress of emancipation in the Netherlands is demonstrated by the fact that three women artists (and no men) were chosen to represent the country at the Venice Biennale in 1995. The co-ordinator of the exhibition in the Netherlands Rietveld-pavilion made his choice in the conviction that "their work now sets the tone for the academies". He called women "the bohemians of the end of the 20th century, strong and pugnacious" (Vermeyden 1995). However positive, his choice of work by women only, and his words, still show signs of an undesirable distinction between male and female artists.

ROSELLA M. HUBER-SPANIER

Bibliography

W.H. Posthumus-van der Goot, *Van moeder op dochter* [From mother to daughter], Leiden: Brill, 1948

Adriaan Venema, *De Amsterdamse Joffers* [The Amsterdam ladies], Baarn: Wereldvenster, 1977

Marlite Halbertsma, "Vrouw en Kunstakademie" [Women and the Academy of Art], *Nieuwsbulletin Stichting Vrouwen in de Beeldende Kunst (SVBK)*, i/3, 1978

Rosa Lindenburg "Kunst is vrouwelijk: Over de vrouw in de beeldende kunst" [Art is feminine: On women in the visual arts], *Openbaar Kunstbezit*, ii/4, 1978, pp.147–57

Liesbeth Brandt Corstius in *ibid.*, pp.158–67

Marlite Halbertsma, "Tweede Nationale Vrouwenakademiedag 17 maart Academie Sint-Joost Breda" [Second National "Women in the Academy" Day, 17 March, Academy Saint Justus, Breda], *Nieuwsbulletin Stichting Vrouwen in de Beeldende Kunst (SVBK)*, ii/2, 1979

Pieter A. Scheen, *Lexicon Nederlandse beeldende kunstenaars, 1750–1880* [Dictionary of Dutch women artists], The Hague: Scheen, 1981

Suze Robertson, exh. cat., Gemeentemuseum, The Hague, 1984

I. van Hamersveld, "Cijfers", *Ruimte*, iv/4–5, 1987, pp.56–60

Vrouwen, kunst en media: Advies over de positie van de vrouwen op het terrein van de cultuur [Women, art and media: Notice on the position of women in the realm of culture], ii, 57/88, The Hague: Emancipatieraad, 1988

Else Berg: Schilderijen, aquarellen en tekeningen [Else Berg: Oils, watercolours and drawings], exh. cat., Frans Hals Museum, Haarlem, 1989

Bloemen uit de kelder [Flowers from the cellar], exh. cat., Gemeentemuseum, Arnhem, 1989

Y. Bosma, *De vrouwelijke kunstacademie-student en haar beroepsloopbaan* [Women students of the art academy and their careers], Amsterdam: Stichting Centrum voor Onderwijs-onderzoek (SCO), 1989

L. Korporaal, "Aandacht voor vrouwen in de kunsttijdschriften" [Attention to women in art periodicals], *Ruimte*, vi/4, 1989, pp.34–7

Nio Hermes, ed., *Met verve* [With fervour]: *Charley Toorop, Lizzy Ansingh, Jacoba van Heemskerck, Lou Loeber, Sorella, Adya van Rees-Dutilh*, Amsterdam: Furie, 1991

De schilders van tachtig: Nederlandse schilderkunst, 1880–1895 [Painters of the 1880s: Dutch painting, 1880–1895], exh. cat., Waanders Uitgevers, Zwolle, and elsewhere, 1991 (especially essay by Jenny Reynaerts, pp.88–107)

Loes Gorlee, "Gelijke kansen" [Equal opportunity], *Stichting Amazone en Beroepsvereniging van Beeldende Kunstenaars* (BBK) [The Amazon Foundation and Professional Association of Visual Artists], Amsterdam: IJKpunt, 1992

Lien Heyting, *De wereld in een dorp: Schilders, schrijvers en wereldverbeteraars in Laren en Blaricum, 1880–1920* [The world in a village: Painters, writers and starry-eyed idealists, 1880–1920], Amsterdam: Meulenhoff, 1994

Titia Top, *Art and Gender: Creative Achievement in the Visual Arts*, dissertation, i, Groningen, 1994

Tracy Metz, "Feminisme in het fin de siècle" [Feminism at the end of the century], *NRC Handelsblad*, 24 June 1995 (Saturday supplement)

Marianne Vermeyden, "De Nederlandse inzending op de Biennale van Venetië" [The Netherlands' submission to the Venice Biennale], *NRC Handelsblad*, 2 June 1995 (Cultural supplement)

6. Nordic countries

19th century

The dominant feature of the professional lives of Nordic women artists in the 19th century was their struggle to enter the state-run training institutions. As elsewhere, their exclusion from the academies was based on the undesirability of women attending life classes and drawing from the nude. The prevailing moral code that managed to hold women outside the academic world also barred them from the most prestigious field of the visual arts – sculpture – as well as the highest-ranking genre of painting – history painting.

Exclusion from the academies of art not only meant that women had no access to prize competitions and the ensuing publicity, but also – and mainly – they had no opportunity of receiving remuneration in the form of stipends, scholarships and the all-important study trips to the Continent. In spite of the fact that the academies did not admit women, in both Denmark and Sweden there were privately trained artists who managed to have satisfactory careers. *Weilbachs Kunstnerleksikon* (1947–52), the encyclopedia of Danish artists, lists around 200 women artists born between 1800 and 1884. Those who rose above amateur status in the first part of the 19th century were almost exclusively still-life artists, concentrating on the highly popular genre of flower painting. One of them, Hanne Hellesen, even received instruction at the Academy in addition to her private training with the prominent male flower painter of the day, Johan Laurentz Jensen.

Women painters were permitted to participate in Denmark's

only official art exhibitions, held by and at the Royal Danish Academy at the Charlottenborg Palace in Copenhagen, and their financial success could be appreciable. Hermania Neergaard showed a total of 116 works at 41 Charlottenborg exhibitions; while Emma Thomsen, another pupil of Jensen's, exhibited 130 paintings in a total of 49 shows. She received the coveted Neuhausen prize in 1861, for a work that was bought by an influential collector, Count A.W. Moltke. Christine Løvmand studied with the flower painter Johannes Ludvig Camradt and with the history and portrait painter Christoffer Wilhelm Eckersberg; in 1842 she received a travel grant from Christian VIII. Women were not excluded from royal patronage, and Løvmand sold eight paintings to the royal family. Still lifes by these artists, who all came from the upper-middle classes and remained single, were also bought by the national gallery and included in the acquisitions of the Kunstforeningen (Artists' Society). This association was founded in 1825 to promote contemporary art through exhibitions and an annual lottery as well as prize contests, and to remedy the decline of official patronage of the arts by Church and State. In the nascent art criticism women artists were neglected in favour of history painters, portraitists, landscape and genre painters – all male, academy-trained artists. Two women from a middle-class background managed, however, to rise above flower painting: Bolette Puggaard, née Hage, who exhibited landscapes at Charlottenborg, and the illegitimate daughter of an army officer, Eleonore Tscherning, who painted portraits and landscapes and worked at one of the earthenware manufactories, P. Ipsen (c.1868–84). The porcelain and ceramic manufactories provided work for many women artists who were unable to construct a career for themselves in the fine arts, while later in the 19th century photography gave them new opportunities. The only Danish painter to attain international fame was Elisabeth Jerichau Baumann (q.v.), the Polish-born wife of the sculptor Jens Adolf Jerichau.

There was also a handful of women artists in Sweden who trained privately and managed to sustain themselves as painters. Sophie Adlersparre received instruction in Léon Cogniet's atelier in Paris in 1839–40. Thanks to the patronage of Queen Josefina of Sweden, she managed to overcome antagonism towards her artistic efforts. Maria Röhl came to Stockholm as an orphan, intending to earn her living as a governess. Her talents were spotted by a professor at the Academy, the engraver Christian Forssell, who undertook her artistic education; subsequently, she became a well-known portraitist. In 1853 she too was in Paris, studying under Cogniet. Unequalled success as a genre painter was achieved by Amalia Lindegren (q.v.) with her picturesque scenes of the Dalecarlia region of Sweden. She was among the four women who in 1849 enjoyed the exceptional opportunity of studying at the Royal Academy of Fine Arts in Stockholm, provided through the efforts of a professor there, Carl Gustaf Qvarnström, an advocate of female integration in the institution. Another of these privileged women, Lea Ahlborn, became the first woman civil servant in Sweden when she was appointed to the Royal Mint on the death of her father in 1855. She went on to design most medals produced in Sweden during her lifetime, all its mint money as well as Norwegian and Finnish coins. Nevertheless, she was discriminated against when it came to her pension, which was lower than that

accorded to men; she therefore decided not to resign. A third member of the quartet, Agnes Börjesson, went on to study with Constantin Hansen in Denmark and later joined the large contingent of Norwegian and Swedish painters at the Düsseldorf Academy. She specialised in 16th- and 17th-century interiors with figures. In the 1860s Munich became the most popular destination for studies abroad; both the Swedish artist Jeanna Bauck and the Dane Bertha Wegmann (q.v.), who were mainly active as portrait painters, studied there.

As early as 1864 a "Section for Women" was established at the Royal Academy of Fine Arts in Stockholm, with 18 students in attendance in its first year. The first generation of female students took great care not to adopt the bohemian lifestyle of their male fellow students, but in the 1870s an easy camaraderie reigned between the sexes. They worked and studied together, went on summer vacations and on study trips abroad.

Under the directorship of Vilhelm Klein, a Drawing and Applied Arts School for Women was set up in Copenhagen in 1875. The intention was to provide women with the necessary knowledge and skills to work commercially, mainly in the porcelain and terracotta manufactories and as etchers and wood-engravers. One quarter of the 800 students who had attended the school by 1900 found employment, so the school could be reckoned a success, but, as the painter Johanne Krebs vehemently pointed out, it was very expensive. The fees of the male students at the Academy were lower, even though they had more hours on their curriculum, a fact that also hampered women when they studied abroad. (The Académie Julian in Paris, for instance, charged women much higher fees than their male colleagues.) Krebs's lobbying led to the establishment, in 1888, of a women's school as an official part of the Royal Danish Academy of Fine Arts, although in a separate building in Copenhagen and with segregated classes. The puritanical ban on attending life classes with men was not lifted until the 1920s. Krebs was the leader of the school until 1907, and the female students were lucky in getting progressive, junior teachers in contrast to the very old professors who taught the young men. But Krebs was also aware of the problems involved in entering an institution on the decline: the best of the younger generation of male artists had already established themselves in a private academy run by the most prominent realist painters, away from the ossified academy. Krebs reckoned, though, that the benefits in terms of influence, scholarships, travel stipends and opportunities to exhibit at the Charlottenborg shows should also be available to women. But the dilemma was there to stay, and grew in proportion to the diminishing influence of academies all over the world.

In Norway only a few women embarked on an artistic career before the late 19th century. Asta Hansteen received her professional training in Copenhagen, Düsseldorf and Paris, and her self-portrait of 1844 is the first known painting by a woman in Norway. She recalled the time when she painted "in deep solitude as the only female painter of Christiania [Oslo]". Most Norwegian women painters were born after 1850 and had careers starting around 1880, at the time of the emergent Norwegian emancipation movement. Some of these artists were linked with the movement, and Asta Hansteen, together with the writer Camilla Collett, helped pave the way for debates on women's rights. The painter Kitty Kielland (q.v.)

Fanny Churberg: *Waterfall*, 1877; oil on canvas; 30.5 × 48.5 cm.; Museum of Finnish Art Ateneum, Helsinki

established herself in Germany and France as a landscape painter, but spent her summers in Norway. Like many of her Nordic contemporaries, she exhibited at the Paris Salons and various World Fairs, which were surprisingly open to showing women's work, when compared with the important biennales and museum shows of the 20th century. Kielland was among the founders of the Norwegian women's movement in 1884, and advocated the rights of unmarried women against the strictures of the Norwegian State Church. As elsewhere in the Nordic countries, Norwegian women painters before 1900 were born into the upper levels of society, being mostly daughters of civil servants and wealthy businessmen. Most of them remained single, while some married fellow artists and ceased to be painters in their own right. One of those who gave up her own career was Sofie Thomesen, a Munich-trained portrait and figure painter who married Erik Werenskiold in 1882 and whose later activities in the arts consisted mainly in embroideries after her husband's designs. The foremost Norwegian painter in the Impressionist vein, Harriet Backer (q.v.), decided to pursue her own career, which precluded marriage and children. Among the Danish women who gave up their careers to assist their husbands in the arts was Anna Gabriele Rohde, who married the sculptor Niels Hansen Jacobsen. She became his helpmate in the studio as well as his model, lying immobile on the floor for hours on end during his work on *Death and the Mother* after Hans Christian Andersen. Rohde received a teacher's degree in 1887, and in addition studied French to

support her family, at the same time as creating works in the applied arts that were sold to the Museum für Kunst und Gewerbe in Hamburg, among other institutions. At Jacobsen's retrospective at the breakaway art show Den frie udstilling (Free exhibition) in Copenhagen in 1901, Rohde exhibited a few pieces herself.

Women artists were relatively numerous in Finland in the 19th century, when the country was under Russian rule. Women were allowed to enrol in the drawing school of the Finnish Artists' Association from its foundation in 1848. Its permissive co-education can be explained by its lack of life classes, so that both male and female students had to look elsewhere for artistic training. Several women went to Düsseldorf, where they worked as private students, because there were no women's classes at the Academy. Among them were Augusta E. Soldan, Viktoria Åberg, Alexandra Frosterus-Såltin, as well as the highly gifted Fanny Churberg (q.v.), who gave up painting in 1880.

The first group of Finnish women to attain general recognition, but often also adverse criticism, comprised Amélie Lundahl, Maria Wiik (q.v.), Helena Westermarck and Elin Danielson-Gambogi. They all attended the drawing school of the Artists' Association, as well as the private academy of the Düsseldorf-trained Adolf von Becker in Helsinki. Westermarck received a travel grant from the Senate; the three others went to France on government grants. Lundahl lived for a while in Brittany, while Westermarck and Danielson painted at

Concarneau. Westermarck also worked at Pont-Aven, but due to tuberculosis virtually gave up painting for literature, art criticism and the advocacy of women's rights. The outstanding artist, and child prodigy, within this group is Helene Schjerfbeck (q.v.), who in contrast to the other Finnish women painters aspired to become a history painter.

Finnish women artists were not among the Fennoman landscape painters of the 1890s, but they did contribute to the Symbolist movement, notably Beda Stjernschantz, who painted some of her most remarkable pictures in Estonia, and Ellen Thesleff (q.v.). Although Finnish women were the first in Europe to be enfranchised, in 1906, their presence gradually disappeared from the visual arts. Only Churberg had pointed to another sphere of activity, with her support for the revival of Finnish handicrafts. Schjerfbeck, who respected Churberg, also made designs for tapestries, and Finnish women artists throughout the 20th century have contributed extensively to the applied arts of their country.

Apart from the struggle to enter the artistic establishment at home, the most important part of the lives of women artists in the last third of the 19th century would often be their time as students in Paris, where almost all of them went at one time or another. They rented studios together and shared the cost, and attended life classes at the Académie Julian or the Académie Colarossi, alongside students from elsewhere in Europe and the USA. The cost of living in Paris was comparatively low, and even more so was life at the artists' colonies in Brittany and such villages as Gréz-sur-Loing, where the Nordic artists spent their summers painting in oil and watercolours. These included, in the 1880s, the Norwegians Harriet Backer, Kitty Kielland and Signe Scheel, a pupil of Christian Krohg's, as well as Asta Nørregaard (q.v.), who executed an altarpiece for Gjøvik Church during her stay, in 1882–3, the only major official commission from a Norwegian woman artist before 1900. From Denmark Anna Ancher (q.v.) studied under Puvis de Chavannes and went on to occupy a secure position in the ranks of Realist painters at the Charlottenborg exhibitions, while Marie Triepcke, who in 1889 had married her former teacher Peder Severin Krøyer, the most celebrated Danish painter of the day, soon gave up her own career. For a while she resigned herself to motherhood and interior decoration, but then eloped from the Danish artists' colony at Skagen with the Swedish composer Hugo Alfven. Her life as an artist in her own right was definitely over, and the marriage ended unhappily for her.

Among the Swedish painters in Paris was Hanna Hirsch Pauli (q.v.), who was also to face difficulties as the wife of a well-known artist, Georg Pauli. Her failure to obtain important commissions after her return home was a disappointment that she shared with many of her generation. Karin Bergöö was forced to turn to the "minor" arts after her marriage to Carl Larsson, and decorated their famous home in Sundborn, Dalecarlia, while Eva Bonnier, of the wealthy publishing dynasty, committed suicide. A few Nordic women undertook an even harder challenge and became sculptors; the first among them was Anne Marie Carl Nielsen (q.v.).

If women were to gain equality with men, they had increasingly to antagonise society by taking part in the rebellions against the very institutions they had fought to enter for such a long time. On the initiative of the Swedish painter Ernst Josephson, a movement named Opponenterna (The opponents) demanded reform of the Royal Academy of Fine Arts in 1885. The petition signed by 84 artists, six of them women, was rejected. A breakaway show entitled *Från Seinens strand* (From the banks of the River Seine) was held the same year, and in 1886 the Konstnärsförbundet (Artists' Association) was founded, which in 1890 had two women on its governing board. But soon the Swedish artists were to segregate the women from their ranks: when the avant-garde group De unga (Young ones) was established in 1907, their statutes specified that only men could be members. Such declared antagonism within Swedish artistic circles led to the founding, in 1910, of the Svenska konstnärinnors förening (Association of Swedish Women Artists), which held its first exhibition in 1911.

The rebels against the Royal Danish Academy of Fine Arts had formed their own breakaway group, Den frie udstilling (Free exhibition), in 1891. Five women were among the founder-members: Johanne Krebs, Edma Frølich Stage, Agnes Slott-Møller (q.v.), Susette Skovgaard Holten and Marie Krøyer. Two of them were daughters of eminent artists (Peter Christian Skovgaard and Lorenz Frølich), and both Krøyer and Slott-Møller were married to well-known painters. Slott-Møller is the only one who attained lasting fame in her own lifetime, on account of important official commissions.

20th century

The victories gained at the turn of the 20th century turned out, to a great degree, to be Pyrrhic. The financial benefits to be had from positions within the official art institutions – cheap studios at the academies and stipends – were still important to women who wanted to make a living in the visual arts, but as modernism gained ground the situation became increasingly bewildering. The role accorded to the artist in the jargon of art criticism, as well as in the minds of museum directors and collectors, was a rebel with a cause (like Picasso), a seer (like van Gogh or Munch) or an analyst of the fundamentals of the visual arts, almost a scientist (like Kandinsky); all roles difficult for women to fill. Critical vocabulary took its most laudatory epithets from the language of warfare, giving special applause to the avant-garde, bravely advancing into unknown territory. Women not only fell victim to these wars of words and ideas, but they were much disadvantaged by such movements as Cubism, Dada and Surrealism. Even though women have been in the midst of most 20th-century art movements, only the Russian experiments saw them in the first rank.

Although women attained a general acceptance of their careers within the visual arts, the obstacles remained the same, with the additional burden of the difficulty of being allowed to break away from mainstream naturalism. Women continued as portrait painters, and a few even as sculptors. The Danish sculptor Helen Schou, a pupil of the painter Agnes Jensen (who was married to Edvard Weie) and the sculptor Carl Nielsen, executed the large equestrian monument of *Christian X* in Århus, as well as the gigantic *Jutlandish Stallion* in Randers, both technical achievements in the classical tradition. But women still had to stand back when they married, and personal tragedies were still a risk to them. The Swede Sigrid Hjertén (q.v.), a pupil of Matisse and the wife of the painter Isaac Grünewald, ended by giving up painting, whereas the early modernism of Franciska Clausen (q.v.) was followed by half a lifetime spent portrait painting in her homeland of Southern Jutland. Late recognition came to some Nordic painters with the women's liberation movement in the 1960s, such as Clausen and the Surrealist Rita Kernn-Larsen in Denmark, followed by a new wave of acquisitions by museums and public institutions . In Sweden the outstanding painter Vera Nilsson (q.v.) was the first woman to be elected to the Royal Academy of Fine Arts (1954) since 1889, and she immediately set to work towards the election of Siri Derkert (q.v) and Greta Knuttson-Tzara. Nilsson still awaits proper international recognition as an artist, having fallen outside the concept of the avant-garde.

Perhaps erroneously seen as a pioneer of modernism, since the 1980s Hilma af Klint (q.v.) has been included in important museum shows in the USA and Europe. The generation born around 1940–45 in the Nordic countries did make themselves seen and heard in the wake of the women's movement, whether or not they themselves were connected to it. Even though the statistics regarding official sales, museum acquisitions, the large number of women graduating from art schools and the small number sitting on governmental bodies have not changed a great deal, some women artists have made a lasting mark on the Nordic art scene: Marie-Louise Ekman (de Geer), who was also a professor at the Konsthögskolan (School of Art) in Stockholm from 1984 to 1991, and Lena Cronqvist (q.v.), a prominent painter who, like Ekman, also had experience of working as a stage designer. A generation of very powerful Finnish women artists came to the fore in the 1970s: Chris af Enehielm, who attended the Free Art School in Helsinki and worked for a while as stage designer, Leena Luostarinen, Marika Mäkelä, Silja Rantanen and Raili Tang. During the 1980s in Denmark a formidable number of women designers began to work in the theatre, while the neo-abstract expressionism brought a new generation of women artists into prominence.

The artistic life of the Faroe islands, Iceland and Greenland has been quite distinct. Traditionally linked with Copenhagen, Icelandic artists studied at the Royal Danish Academy until the 1960s, when they made connections all over the world. Júlíana Sveinsdóttir (q.v.) studied with the landscape painter Thórarinn Benedikt Thorlaksson in 1908 and went on to study in Copenhagen, graduating from the Royal Danish Academy in 1917. She continued to exhibit at the Charlottenborg shows, and settled in Denmark. The landscape tradition was continued in a modernist version by Gudrún Kristjánsdóttir. Of great importance for artistic training in Greenland was the foundation of the Workshop for Graphic Artists, founded in Nuuk in 1972 under the direction of Hans Lynge. It was later expanded into an academy, the School of Art of Greenland; here Aka Høegh became the first woman to fulfil an important role in the development of the visual arts of the country.

CHARLOTTE CHRISTENSEN

Bibliography

Anna Lena Lindberg and Barbro Werkmäster, eds, Kvinnor som konstnärer [Women as artists], Stockholm: Liber, 1975

Danske kvindelige kunstnere fra det 19. og 20. århundrede repræsenteret på Statens Museum for Kunst [Danish women artists from the 19th and 20th centuries represented in the State Art Museum], exh. cat., Statens Museum for Kunst, Copenhagen, 1980

Anna Lena Lindberg and Barbro Werkmäster, "Kvinnliga konstnärer i Norden" in Germaine Greer, Hinderloppet: Kvinnans väg genom konsten [The obstacle race: The fortunes of women painters and their work], Uppsala: Brombergs, 1980, pp.328–44

Målarinnor från Finland/Seitsemäri suomalaista taiteilijaa [Women painters from Finland], exh. cat., Nationalmuseum, Stockholm, and elsewhere, 1981

Ingrid Ingelman, Kvinnliga konstnärer i Sverige [Women artists in Sweden], Uppsala, 1982 (A study of the pupils of the Royal Academy of Fine Arts, admitted 1864–1924)

Kvinners bilder: Malerinner i Norge før 1900 [Women painters in Norway before 1900], exh. cat., Kunstnerforbundet, Oslo, 1982

Karin Moe, Kvinne & kunstner [Woman and artist], Oslo, 1983

Anne Wichstrøm, Kvinner ved staffeliet: Kvinnelige malere i Norge før 1900 [Women at the easel: Women painters in Norway before 1900], Oslo: Universitetsforlaget, 1983 (revised edition in preparation)

Göran M. Silfverstolpe, Vera Nilsson, Uddevalla, 1986

De drogo till Paris: Nordiska konstnärinnor på 1880–talet [They went to Paris: Nordic women artists in the 1880s], exh. cat., Liljevalchs Konsthall, Stockholm, 1988

Den fries kvindelige kunstnere, 1891 [Den frie's women artists, 1891], exh. cat., Kvindemuseet, Århus, and Skagens Museum, Skagen, 1991

Riitta Konttinen, Totuus enemmän kuin kauneus: Naistaiteilija, realismi ja naturalismi, 1880-luvulla: Amelie Lundahl, Maria Wiik, Helena Westermarck, Helene Schjerfbeck ja Elin Danielson [Truth before beauty: The woman artist, Realism and Naturalism in the 1880s ...], Helsinki: Otava, 1991

Markku Valkonen, Finnish Art over the Centuries, Helsinki, 1992

Ingamaj Beck, Vingspeglar: Möten med samtida konstnärer [Contemporary Swedish artists], Stockholm, 1993

At Century's End: Norwegian Artists and the Figurative Tradition, 1880/1990, exh. cat, Henie-Onstad Art Center, Høvikodden, and National Museum of Women in the Arts, Washington, DC, 1995

Marianne Sørensen, 31 Women Artists from 31 Danish Art Museums, Ministry of Culture and Women's Museum in Denmark, 1995

7. Russia

Modernity and the industrial era came several decades later to Russia, which was retarded by the institution of serfdom (abolished in 1861) and a population split between a tiny educated class and a vast illiterate peasantry. In the 19th century the call for women's rights to education and equality emerged in the 1860s, when wider issues of social and political reform were being debated. It was not until the 1870s that a first generation of professional women artists appeared in Russia (the earliest artist included in this Dictionary, Elena Polenova, was born in 1850). As their opportunities improved, women emerged as crucial participants in the art movements of the late imperial and early Soviet periods, to a degree unparalleled in other countries. The cultural and political extremes that marked Russian life in the second half of the 19th century contributed to the radicalisation of educated women, many of whom became active participants in women's education, the populist and revolutionary movements, and social reform. These earlier precedents may help to explain why a relatively large proportion of major Russian artists of the early 20th century were women, and why women were accustomed to leadership roles within the artistic community as patrons, collectors, entrepreneurs and organisers of a wide range of cultural endeavours.

Ekaterina Khilkova: *View of the Women's Section of the St Petersburg Drawing School for Auditors,* 1855; State Russian Museum, St Petersburg

Before 1842

After centuries of seclusion in the *terem* (women's chamber), bound by the feudal teachings of the *Domostroy* (a 16th-century tract on family life), and restricted in their creative outlets to the production of ecclesiastical embroideries, upper-class Russian women found their lives fundamentally changed by the reforms of Peter the Great (1689–1725). Peter's rapid westernisation of Russian society brought women into public life and offered them the rudiments of education. For most of the 18th century Russia was ruled by a succession of three powerful women – Anna (1730–40), Elizabeth (1741–62) and Catherine (1762–96) – and it was during their reigns that the major art institutions were established – the Imperial Porcelain Factory (1744) and the Academy of Fine Arts (1757) – as well as the imperial art collections that helped to form Western taste in Russia. But while it was possible by the end of the 18th century for a few women to make a mark in the world of letters and humanities, as did Princess Ekaterina Dashkova, President of the Academy of Sciences, in the more profession-

ally oriented visual arts girls from the nobility learned just enough proficiency in drawing and watercolour as was appropriate to a finishing-school education, in institutes such as the Smolny Institute for Noble Girls in St Petersburg (established 1764). The only women artists to attain any professional acclaim in Russia during this period were both foreigners: Elisabeth Vigée-Lebrun (q.v.), who spent six years in St Petersburg portraying members of the Russian aristocracy, and Christina Robertson (q.v.), a Scotswoman who was much sought after in the 1840s for her society portraits at the court of Nicholas I. Russian women of good family were expected rather to follow the example of the Empress Marya Fyodorovna, the German-born wife of Paul I, whose skill as a medallionist and silhouettist established a tradition of respectable and proficient amateurism. At the other end of the social spectrum, some serf women could expect to be trained in a number of luxury handicrafts (lace, weaving, beading, embroidery) at their owner's behest, for his or her personal consumption and profit. (Male serfs were more likely to be sent to the Academy of Fine Arts in St Petersburg for training in architecture, painting, sculpture and the applied arts.)

1842–1861

An institutional art training first became available to Russian women in the 1840s, as a direct result of a new governmental campaign to stimulate industrial growth by improving the industrial arts through the spread of art education. The new emphasis on developing the taste of artist and consumer alike made it possible for middle-class women to consider professions in the handicrafts and as drawing teachers. The first two drawing schools to be established in Russia outside the Academy of Fine Arts both offered limited professional training to women from the working and lower-middle classes. In 1842 a women's section was added to the small drawing school that the Ministry of Finance had set up in St Petersburg three years earlier. Located in the Customs House building and known as the School at the Stock Exchange (*Shkola na Birzhe*), the Women's Drawing Classes subsequently became part of the School of the Society for the Encouragement of the Arts (established 1857), the institution at which the majority of Russian women received their art education until the end of the 19th century. In Moscow, beginning in 1843, women were admitted to the Women's Drawing Section of the Drawing School Related to the Arts and Crafts (established 1825), later renamed the Stroganov School of Technical Drawing. Here the curriculum for women was limited to drawing flowers, ornament, landscapes and in exceptional cases the human head. The student body (40 in the first year) was divided between young girls from the lower classes who were trained for professional work in handicrafts and ladies "from the upper class" who had no such practical goals in mind and were taught separately. Of the former group a handful became certified drawing teachers and some also distinguished themselves as painters. Among noblewomen only the most energetic went beyond cultivating art as a social grace, such as Princess Marya Volkonskaya, who organised a small drawing circle where she and her friends painted saints and church ornament under the tutelage of the academician Fyodor Solntsev. On the other hand, throughout the 19th century those with administrative abilities could use them in the capacity of president or honorary patron of cultural organisations, as did Grand Duchess Marya Nikolayevna, who was president of both the Society for the Encouragement of the Arts and the Academy of Fine Arts, and Countess Praskovya Uvarova, who succeeded her husband as president of the Moscow Archaeological Society on his death in 1885.

By the mid-19th century limited access to the Academy of Fine Arts became available to women, as higher education in general came within their reach. In 1858 Alexander II approved the establishment of gymnasia for girls and the following year women were admitted as auditors to university courses. By the 1850s women could also audit drawing classes at the Academy and take part in its exhibitions in the categories open to them. The academic hierarchy of genres allowed women to work in portraiture, landscape, still-life and genre painting. In 1854 Sofya Sukhovo-Kobylina won the academy's first-class gold medal for a landscape, an event that she recorded for posterity in a painting of 1859, now in the Tretyakov Gallery, Moscow. Another Academy pupil and the daughter of an artist, the 12-year-old Vera Meyer, received a silver medal in 1859 for her self-portrait, but after her marriage to the academician Pavel Chistyakov, a popular drawing teacher for many women artists, she gave up painting altogether.

1861–1891

Opportunities for women to study, exhibit and make a living from art improved during the reigns of Alexander II (1855–81) and Alexander III (1881–94), but they did so against a background of political and social upheaval that fundamentally affected the way in which women saw their role as artists in relation to society as a whole. By the 1870s there was already a recognisable group of "lady artists" from the upper classes who operated on the periphery of the Academy, restricted in medium to watercolour, drawing and pastel, and in subject to genre, landscape, portraiture and still life. But there was also an alternative group of women who rejected the idea of art for its own sake and in its traditional forms as a selfish indulgence. For these "women of the sixties" the ideal of personal freedom and collective work, embodied in Vera Pavlovna, the heroine of Nikolai Chernyshevsky's novel *Chto delat?* (What is to be done? 1863), inspired them to place their talents at the service of the public good. In this context prejudices against the applied arts held less sway as the relevance of "high art" to the common people came into question. The artist Elena Polenova (q.v.) typified this spirit of self-sacrifice throughout the 1870s, serving as a nurse in the Russo-Turkish war, training as a governess, and volunteering to teach drawing and dressmaking in a St Petersburg charity school before she finally enrolled in majolica and watercolour courses at the School of the Society for the Encouragement of the Arts in 1880. Others became professional drawing teachers or opened their own schools, as did the Kharkov artist Marya Rayevskaya-Ivanova, who also published her own primer, *Azbuka risovaniya dlya semi i dlya shkoly* (A drawing ABC for family and school), in 1879. Still others, mostly the wives of landowners with estates in the provinces, laid the foundation for a nationwide revival of peasant arts and crafts when they established training workshops on their estates, in the hope of winning peasants away from the cities and factories and back to their abandoned handicrafts with the promise of a steady income. Elizaveta Mamontova, wife of the railway magnate and maecenas Savva Mamontov, guaranteed the success of her Abramtsevo workshop for peasant boys (established 1876) when Polenova became its artistic director, designing art furniture based on folk ornament, in 1885.

The most vocal supporter of women artists during these years was the critic Vladimir Stasov (brother of the feminist Nadezhda Stasova), whose protégées included Elizaveta Bem, the sculptor Marya Ditrikh, Varvara and Aleksandra Shneyder, and Tatyana Semechkina. The most professionally active of these was Elizaveta Bem, whose silhouettes and watercolours of children in national garb won her a national and international reputation in the 1870s and 1880s. Stasov hailed her as "part of an emerging generation of women artists" at a time when "there are very few women [in Russia] who contemplate getting involved in anything but family affairs and everyday trivia" (V.V. Stasov, "Novyye khudozhestvennyye izdaniya" [New art publications], *Sobraniye sochineniy* [Collected works], St Petersburg, 1894, ii, p.298). For women seeking other forms of employment in the art world he encouraged serious collecting and scholarship in areas of national art traditionally considered a woman's domain. Thus, Natalya Shabelskaya's collection of Russian textiles and women's work was unparalleled in its breadth and quality, while Sofya Davydova pioneered the study of Russian lacemaking and was responsible for the foundation of the Mariynsky Lace School in St Petersburg in 1883.

The number of women seeking a formal art training increased in the 1870s, in step with the general movement for higher education that culminated in the inauguration in 1878 of the Bestuzhev Women's Higher Courses, which provided university-level training in medicine, the natural sciences, history and mathematics. With full equality in the Academy still denied them (access to live models was off-limits as was eligibility to study abroad as an Academy pensioner), women gravitated in growing numbers to the schools of industrial art. Not only did these schools offer an increasingly rigorous art education, modelled on the best industrial arts schools of Europe, but because the emphasis on decoration rather than intellectual content coincided with existing ideas about femininity they placed fewer restrictions on women than did the more prestigious fine arts schools. In his exhibition reviews of the 1870s Stasov particularly stressed the attainments of women students, noting that they excelled in "one of the most difficult architectural projects", the design of church iconostases (icon screens), whereas before "they knew only how to draw flowers, or at best sentimental landscapes and smarmy portraits". At the same time, however, women were still taught separately from men and until the end of the 19th century their fees continued to be twice those of the male students.

A major challenge to the authority and hierarchy of the Academy was the foundation in 1870 of the Association of Travelling Exhibitions, whose members (the Wanderers or Peredvizhniki) championed the painting of contemporary Russian life and its problems. The Association members Ivan Kramskoy, Ivan Shishkin and Kirill Lemokh became influential teachers at the School of the Society for the Encouragement of the Arts and a number of their women students, such as Polenova, went on to become professional artists, as did some of their own daughters and wives, for example, Sofya Yunker (née Kramskaya), Olga Lagoda-Shishkina and Elena Makovskaya-Luksch (q.v.). While the Association allowed women to take part in its annual exhibitions, however, it drew the line at granting them full membership.

The first arts association to be established by women was the First Ladies' Art Circle, founded in St Petersburg in 1882 by Pelagya Kuriar as a charitable organisation to support needy artists, but also to "develop artistic aspirations among Russian lady amateurs, allowing them to benefit from the advice of various artists, to observe them at work and to work themselves under their supervision during the circle's Wednesday meetings". With a membership dominated by such upper-class amateurs as Baronesses Marya von der Pahlen and Elena Vrangel, the circle provided women with exhibition opportunities and its charitable goals guaranteed sales for the exhibitors, primarily among members of the imperial family and the aristocracy. But it also reinforced condescending attitudes towards the "lady artist" as a "frequently bored, relatively rich, not terribly well educated, not overly cultivated woman" flirting with art to kill time and *ennui*.

Since study in one of the great European art centres was considered essential to an artist's education and women were not eligible to be Academy pensioners in Rome or Paris, only those with some financial resources could afford to travel independently to Europe to see the museums or to study with an acknowledged master. Thus, Marya Rayevskaya-Ivanova studied in Dresden with Professor Ergardt, the sculptor Teresa Ris both studied and eventually settled in Vienna, Sofya Kramskaya spent several months in Paris where she could draw from the live model, and Marya von der Pahlen spent a year in Paris studying under Trelat, Gérôme and Léon Bonnard. It was not until 1879 that the School of the Society for the Encouragement of the Arts sent its first pensioner, Polenova, to Paris to study ceramics.

1891–1905

After three decades in which liberal ideals and reform gave way to anarchism and harsh reaction, during the 1890s many younger Russian artists turned away from social concerns and realism to the world of subjective states, intuition and emotion. These were spheres of experience universally associated with female psychology and they were considered most fully expressed in the non-narrative genres of landscape, still life, portraiture and ornament, also the acknowledged domain of women. After eight years working for the Abramtsevo workshop, for example, in 1893 Polenova abandoned her work with peasant boys and turned increasingly to symbolic paintings, the illustration of fairy tales in the style of Walter Crane, and to ornamental designs that conveyed complex "musical" emotions. Her close friend Marya Yakunchikova (q.v.) also experimented throughout the decade with ways to express the inexpressible, using pyrogravure, woodcut and appliqué embroidery, as well as oil painting, to convey such moods as anxiety, euphoria and nostalgic longing. The expanded opportunities for experimenting with new media typical of the Symbolist era also worked to women's advantage. Art embroidery became not only acceptable in progressive art circles like the Mir Iskusstva (World of Art) and Blue Rose groups, but as practised by Natalya Davydova, Agnessa Lindeman, Tatyana Lugovskaya-Dyagileva, Vera Wulf and others it epitomised the aesthetic ideals of Symbolism with its emphasis on flatness, stylisation and expressive line. Classes in the stylisation of flowers and plants were added to the curriculum of the leading industrial arts schools and all offered classes in porcelain painting, majolica and ceramics where many of the teachers as well as the students were women. In the commercial, guild-controlled field of gold- and silver-work a number of women owned and operated successful workshops, usually the legacy of a deceased father or husband. Among the most prominent were Marya Adler, whose Moscow firm employed 74 workers and had its own drawing school, Evdokya Sazikova, Marya Semyonova and Pavla Mishukova.

In 1891 the Academy of Arts admitted the first class of women to be eligible for the title of Artist (first class). The teachers most supportive of women were Nikolai Dubovskoy, Dmitry Kardovsky and Ilya Repin, who was a member of the Association of Travelling Exhibitions with strong sympathies for progressive trends in painting and for women – Marianne

Werefkin (q.v.), Anna Ostroumova-Lebedeva (q.v.) and Zinaida Serebryakova (q.v.) were all his pupils. Even so, in 1896 only 34 of the Academy's 388 pupils were women, compared to 84 of the 189 at the Stieglitz (Shtiglits) school (established 1876) in St Petersburg. The most prestigious rival fine arts school was the Moscow School of Painting, Sculpture and Architecture, whose more liberal faculty attracted students disillusioned with academicism and realism alike. Yet as the biographies in this *Dictionary* seem to suggest, the Moscow school did not admit large numbers of full-time women students, perhaps because few of them had the foundation training needed to pass the gruelling entrance exams. Instead, most women artists in this period moved frequently between private studios and public schools, from the provinces to the capitals, and from Russia to Europe and back again. Particularly popular was the Moscow studio of Konstantin Yuon and Ivan Yudin, which prepared students for the Moscow School entrance exams, but affordable alternatives were also provided by other women. In 1893 Princess Marya Tenisheva opened the Tenisheva School in St Petersburg, with Repin as its foremost teacher and Marya Chembers, Elena Makovskaya-Luksch and Serebryakova among its pupils. In 1899 Elizaveta Zvantseva, herself a former Repin pupil at the Academy, opened a school in Moscow (moved to St Petersburg in 1906) where men and women worked together from nude models and whose graduates included Sofya Dymshits-Tolstaya (q.v.), Elena Guro (q.v.), Olga Rozanova (q.v.) and Margarita Sabashnikova (later the wife of the poet Max Voloshin). Study abroad also became easier and more acceptable for women artists. Ostroumova-Lebedeva, Yakunchikova and Anna Golubkina (q.v.) all studied with important teachers in Paris, and Elizaveta Kruglikova (q.v.) and Olga Mechnikova were co-founders of the Montparnas society (1903), an organisation that informed Russian artists who had recently arrived in Paris about study and exhibition opportunities.

A handful of women attained varying degrees of success in the traditionally masculine field of sculpture, in genres other than the portrait busts for which a woman's powers of observation were thought best suited. One of the first women sculptors in Russia was the academy-trained Marya Dillon, who specialised in portraits, allegorical figures and monuments on literary themes and in whose studio Natalya Danko (q.v.) worked. Teresa Ris, initially an auditor at the Moscow School, won the Karl Ludwig medal in 1896 for her plaster figure *Lucifer*. And despite her peasant origins, Anna Golubkina was able to obtain an excellent training at the Moscow School and the Academy of Arts, followed by two periods of study in Paris. Her reputation was confirmed in 1901 when she was commissioned to sculpt a panel in high relief (*The Wave*) for the entrance of the new Moscow Art Theatre.

By the beginning of the 20th century only the architectural profession still remained beyond the reach of women, although courses in architectural ornament and styles had long been an important component of the curriculum in the industrial arts schools. It was not until 1904 that a Society to Investigate Avenues for the Technical Education of Women was formed in St Petersburg by Praskovya Aryan and in 1906 the Women's Polytechnic Courses were opened, with an architecture department whose faculty included the leading architects of the day. Two years later women were finally admitted to the architecture department of the Academy of Fine Arts, and the same year E. Bagayeva opened her own four-year Women's Architectural Courses (from 1913 the Women's Polytechnical Institute).

The rise of merchant-class art patronage affected women artists as well as men by the turn of the 19th and 20th centuries. Throughout the 1890s Pavel Tretyakov collected work by Polenova and Yakunchikova, as well as by such lesser-known women as Emilya Shanks, Ekaterina Yunge (daughter of the sculptor Count Fyodor Tolstoy) and Marya Fyodorova, all of whom specialised in intimate genre scenes or mood landscapes. Women also became influential collectors and patrons themselves. Marya F. Yakunchikova (Marya Yakunchikova's sister-in-law) was one of Valentin Serov's first patrons, but was best known for her Solomenko embroidery workshops in Tambov province, where peasant women produced both traditional and modernised embroideries designed by Polenova, Yakunchikova and Natalya Davydova. Princess Marya Tenisheva, initially an aspiring singer who had also studied art at the Académie Julian in Paris, utilised the resources of her wealthy industrialist husband in a number of artistic and philanthropic enterprises. She assembled a collection of watercolours; founded an excellent museum of Russian antiquities in Smolensk; co-funded the art journal *Mir iskusstva* (World of Art) with Savva Mamontov; and at Talashkino, her estate in Smolensk province, she created both a summer colony for visiting artists and a network of workshops where peasant crafts were revived and sold through a store in Moscow.

With the spread of literacy and the growth of a consumer economy, women who specialised in the graphic arts and illustration found employment in various branches of the publishing industry, from designing covers for such popular magazines as *Niva* (e.g. Elena Samokish-Sudkovskaya), to illustrating postcards for the series put out by the Red Cross and the Community of St Evgeny (Rimma Braylovskaya, Marya Chembers, Agnessa Lindeman, Anna Ostroumova-Lebedeva, Aleksandra Shneyder and even Grand Duchess Olga Alexandrovna, sister of Nicholas II). Thanks to the World of Art group's special affection for the art of the book, the design of graphic elements such as the *ex-libris*, vignette, silhouette and cover-page became acceptable, even innovative genres in which many women trained in the industrial arts excelled.

1905–1917

By the year of the First Russian Revolution in 1905 the old centres of artistic authority – the Academy and the Association of Travelling Exhibitions – had lost all credibility with a younger generation of Russian artists. Not until 1916 did the Academy give way to the inevitable by electing four uncontroversial women artists to the rank of academician – Serebryakova, Ostroumova-Lebedeva, Olga Della-Vos-Kardovskaya and the flower painter Aleksandra Shneyder. While many women gladly took advantage of these new privileges, others still preferred the freedom of frequent moves between art schools and private studios at home and abroad. With its well-equipped workshops and close ties to Moscow industries, the Stroganov School offered such students as Lyudmila Mayakovskaya, Rozanova and Varvara Stepanova (q.v.) the design skills and practical training that each would draw on in the Soviet period. In 1906 the School of the Society for the Encouragement of the Arts adopted many of the Stroganov's innovations, under the directorship of Nicholas Roerich and new faculty such as Agnessa Lindeman (art embroidery) and Ivan Bilibin, whose graphic arts students included two women whom he would later marry: Marya Chembers and Aleksandra Shchekatikhina-Pototskaya (q.v.). The quality and number of provincial art schools also improved during this period and many women received a solid training before moving to the capitals, for example Alexandra Exter (q.v.) and Evgenya Pribylskaya at the Kiev Art Institute, Stepanova at the Kazan Art School and Danko at the Vilnius Art School.

Russian women continued to study abroad until the outbreak of World War I. While some gravitated towards Munich where a small Russian community studied at the Ažbè and Hollosy Schools (Marianne Werefkin), the studios of pre-war Paris (La Grande Chaumière, La Palette, Académie Ranson, Académie Julian) became the mecca for aspiring women painters such as Lyubov Popova (q.v.) and Nadezhda Udaltsova (q.v.). In 1908 the painter Marya Vasileva established her own art school in Paris (the Académie Russe or Académie Vassiliev), which became the centre of cultural life for Russians. Even the Academy of Fine Arts sent its first woman pensioner (Elena Kiseleva) to Paris in 1907.

Young women artists figured with unprecedented prominence in the avant-garde art circles that formed and reformed during this period. With their rejection not simply of artistic conventions but often of the entire social and philosophical structure that supported them, the close-knit groups of the pre-revolutionary decade offered women an equality and visibility rarely found in contemporary Russian society. The experiments with modern French art of Natalya Goncharova (q.v.) placed her beyond the pale of acceptable behaviour for artists and women alike, giving her an outsider status that she cultivated by her active participation in the Cubo-Futurists' face-painting, public performances and cabaret culture of the pre-war era. Women were particularly active in the Supremus group formed by Kazimir Malevich during the war years (seven of the 14 artists who took part in the *First Futurist Exhibition: 0.10* in 1915 were women). With interests ranging far beyond the pursuit of abstract painting for its own sake, Rozanova, Popova and Exter applied the principles of Malevich's Suprematism to the decoration of women's accessories, theatre design, and experimental typography and book illustration. Women also continued to play important entrepreneurial and organisational roles during the war years. For example, between 1911 and 1919 Natalya Dobychina's Bureau in Petrograd was Russia's leading private commercial gallery, hosting the *0.10* exhibition in 1915–16.

After 1917

When the Russian Empire toppled in 1917, many of the values and institutions it had maintained fell with it. The official equality of women was proclaimed and so too was the right of all citizens to an art education free of academic elitism and authoritarianism. The central organisation in charge of all art issues was Narkompros (the People's Commissariat of Enlightenment), and the women who had been so active in the avant-garde groups of the war years immediately stepped into positions of authority, reorganising the decimated industrial

arts centres, restructuring the education system and teaching in the new State Free Art Studios (Svomas) and Higher State Artistic and Technical Workshops (Vkhutemas), setting up museums and organising exhibitions, public spectacles and propaganda. In Kiev Exter was an influential teacher and organiser, and in Smolensk and Vitebsk Vera Yermolayeva (q.v.) and Nina Kogan were active members of Unovis (Affirmers of the New in Art), teaching a new generation of artists in which women were offered the same rights and opportunities as men.

With studio art and easel painting temporarily discredited as bourgeois and elitist, it was those artists who embraced the tenets of Constructivism and production art who shaped Soviet culture during the first half of the decade. Popova and Stepanova used stage and costume design as a laboratory for their very successful work as textile and clothing designers, and joined forces with proponents of the folk art revival (Evgenya Pribylskaya, Natalya Davydova), the couturier Nadezhda Lamanova and the sculptor Vera Mukhina (q.v.) to create new clothing prototypes for the Soviet woman. The promotion of literacy and political awareness gave print media (magazines, posters, advertising, books) an unprecedented social importance that women artists accustomed to working in these formerly minor areas quickly exploited. Outside the Constructivist camp more palatable images of Soviet culture were created by women working in porcelain, a medium whose potential for disseminating powerful ideological messages that were also decorative and accessible was quickly recognised. Danko and Shchekatikhina-Pototskaya were both considered important revolutionary artists, a sign that political change had indeed brought about a re-evaluation of artistic values. The zenith of women's contributions to early Soviet art and art policy was undoubtedly the Soviet contribution to the Paris Exposition des Arts Décoratifs et Industriels Modernes of 1925. But as political control over cultural life tightened in the late 1920s and the fine arts and realism were proclaimed the principal repositories of Soviet values, women once again found themselves part of a monolithic, academy-controlled art world that perpetuated sex-role stereotypes even as they proclaimed female emancipation (e.g. Mukhina's *Industrial Worker and Collective Farm Girl* of 1939). As for all those who rejected the Revolution or could not endure its consequences. emigration was the only alternative. Some women left for Berlin or Paris immediately in 1917 (Rimma Braylovskaya, Princess Tenisheva), others participated fully in Soviet artistic life for several years before deciding to leave for uncertain futures in the West (Exter, Ksenya Boguslavskaya, Serebryakova, Shchekatikhina-Pototskaya).

WENDY R. SALMOND

Bibliography

Aleksandr Somov, "Zhenshchiny-khudozhnitsy" [Women artists], *Vestnik iziashchnikh iskusstv*, no.1, 1883, pp.517–24

Isabel F. Hapgood, "Russian women, 1", *Chautauguan*, xxxii/6, March 1901, pp.589–94

Nina Moleva and E.M. Belyutin, *Russkaya khudozhestvennaya shkola vtoroy poloviny XIX–nachala XX veka* [The Russian art school of the second half of the 19th century to the beginning of the 20th], Moscow: Iskusstvo, 1967

Richard Stites, *The Women's Liberation Movement in Russia:*

Feminism, Nihilism and Bolshevism, 1860–1930, Princeton, NJ: Princeton University Press, 1978

Künstlerinnen der russischen Avantgarde/Russian Women Artists of the Avant-Garde, 1910–1930, exh. cat., Galerie Gmurzynska, Cologne, 1979

Alison Hilton, "'Bases of the new creation': Women artists and Constructivism", *Arts Magazine*, October 1980, pp.142–5

Nina Smurova, "Iz istoriy vysshego zhenskogo arkhitekturnogo obra-zovaniya v Rossiy" [From the history of women's higher architectural education in Russia], *Problemy istoriy sovetskoy arkhitektury (Sbornik nauchnykh trudov)* [Problems of the history of Soviet architecture (collection of scholarly papers)], Moscow: TsNIIT gradostroitelstva, 1980, pp.110–18

M.N. Yablonskaya, *Women Artists of Russia's New Age, 1900–1935*, New York: Rizzoli, and London: Thames and Hudson, 1990

D.Ya. Severyukhin and O.L. Leykind, *Khudozhniki russkoy emigrat-siy (1917–1941): Biograficheskiy slovar* [Artists of the Russian emigration (1917–1941): Biographical dictionary], St Petersburg: Chernysheva, 1994

Alison Hilton, "Domestic crafts and creative freedom: Russian women's art", *Russia – Women – Culture*, ed. Helena Goscilo and Beth Holmgren, Bloomington: Indiana University Press, 1996

Wendy R. Salmond, *Arts and Crafts in Late Imperial Russia: Reviving the Kustar Art Industries, 1870–1917*, Cambridge and New York: Cambridge University Press, 1996

8. Spain

The situation of women artists in Spain during the 19th and 20th centuries was in many ways more discouraging than that of their European counterparts, with whom they shared many problems. To the usual historical barriers were added those peculiar to Spain, isolated from developments during the years that were crucial to the consolidation of feminism, when the country was under the dictatorship of General Franco. This situation also led to the late incorporation of gender theory in art history in Spain, the main reason for the lack of monographs or research into this subject. This makes it difficult to evaluate the production of women artists, although the arduous path taken by Spanish women artists can be traced through the few existing pieces of research. It is only since the late 1970s that the situation of women artists in Spain has been rectified.

During the 19th century the social structure of Spain, like that of other countries, underwent a series of transformations. These were reflected in the arts and had undeniable repercussions on the work of women artists and its reception by society. The incorporation of a new social group, the bourgeoisie, led to the taste for history painting being replaced by that for genre, still-life and portrait painting. This not only fitted in better with the pictorial traditions of women – who historically had been excluded from the great themes of painting – but the smaller sizes of the pieces meant that young women artists could work at home without needing to have the studio that was vital for history painting. In other words, it enabled women painters, who, in a typically 19th-century manner, were frequently called "amateur" artists, to play a greater part in the art world. Although very few 19th-century works by women artists are preserved, making a critical analysis extremely difficult, the titles of the exhibited works enable the

most common themes to be reconstructed. Not only did these include flower paintings and still lifes, as is to be expected, but genre painting and a few portraits also appeared. Contributions by women artists to history painting are minimal and, when they do appear, very late.

Certainly, the emergence of the "dilettante" or "amateur", a figure that grew in popularity in Spain, as in the rest of Europe, during the 19th century, led to the formation of a more informed group of people who bought and sold works of art or who visited exhibitions. This was sometimes perceived as the "democratisation of art" as well as a symptom of decadence, frequently commented on by critics in Spain. (The discussion of the levels of artistic perception is a recurring theme in art criticism from the late 1860s. A classic example is José García y Serrano, *Las bellas artes en España*, Madrid: Ansart, 1867; among others, Domingo Malpica, *De arte moderno: Breves reflexiones sobre el arte de la pintura*, Madrid: González, 1874, refers to the "plebification of art".) The term "amateur", however, was also applied to those who painted as a pastime rather than as a profession; this was an idea intimately connected with the 19th-century notion of the middle-class woman's work. This concept enjoyed such popularity among the critics who referred to this so-called decadence during the second half of the 19th century that some of them even accused the working classes and women of being the cause of such degradation in the arts. (The critic Antonio Danvila, for example, stated: "the advances of culture have introduced the cultivation of art among even one-horse towns and the gentler sex, who are responsible for many of the artistic sacrileges that draw our attention", *¿Estamos en decadencia?*, *Historia y Arte*, May 1896, p.144.)

This particular reading by the critics reveals a certain degree of concern about the growing participation of women on the artistic scene, which is witnessed by the noticeable numbers of women artists taking part in the Exposiciones Nacionales de Bellas Artes. In fact, the catalogues of these exhibitions are almost the only means of studying the contribution of women artists even in the early 20th century and despite the progressive disfavour of these exhibitions (for the Exposiciones Nacionales de Bellas Artes, see Pantorba 1980; for the participation of women in these exhibitions, see Diego 1987). Women had little influence on the life of the academies in the 18th and early 19th centuries, when they were invited to become members more often on account of their social position than their artistic skill (Pérez-Neu de Robla 1964). (Parada y Santin 1903 contains, pp.67–9, a long list of women academicians, all of whom were members of the nobility; for the problem of women in the 18th century, who were particularly handicapped in the sphere of education, see Fernandez Quintanilla 1981.). By contrast, there was an avalanche of women participating in the Exposiciones Nacionales – more than 400 women artists are documented between 1860 and 1910, with a far higher proportion of painters than sculptors. It should be pointed out that these figures include one-off participants; otherwise, one might think that the desire to take part in the outside world and not to restrict painting to a strictly family environment implied a desire for "professionalisation", a central point of the discussion concerning women artists in the 19th century.

This proposition leads on to the following question: how

Margarita Arosa: *La Baigneuse*, 1887

many women really became "professional" and, even more important, how many achieved fame or a place within the "history of art"? First, as mentioned above, in Spain monographs on women artists are still lacking, in many cases because work has consistently been lost, which makes it difficult to situate them in the context to which they might hypothetically belong. An even stronger argument is that many men tried to open up a path for themselves in the art world during the 19th century, but very few have survived in history.

Whatever the true situation, all aspects of the careers of women artists, even in the 19th century, were conditioned by their art education, although perhaps it would be more pertinent to speak of the omissions in that education. During the early years of the 19th century there was a discernible desire to provide an artistic education for young working-class girls in an institutional rather than a religious context. This was related to a certain degree of "professionalisation" and was thus very different to earlier attempts to provide a "decorative" artistic education for young girls from the wealthier classes, who were often taught by private teachers. The former initiative, the Estudios de Niñas (young girls), took place in 1818 at the Academia de Bellas Artes de San Fernando in Madrid, and aimed to provide young girls with a means of

earning their living through painting, or rather through its application to the so-called industrial arts:

> ... with drawing, women can apply themselves to beautiful embroidery, to etching and engraving landscapes on fans, cards and regular prints such as those executed by the Académica de Mérito Doña Maria del Carmen Saíz; other women can illustrate these works, others can give drawing classes to young girls in their homes, others can become fashion designers creating clothes and new things, others can become florists or make different children's games with varied inventions [*Informe sobre los alumnos de Dibujo de la Real Junta de Caridad en la Merced y Fuencarral*, 11 January 1818, Archivo de la Real Academia de San Fernando, Madrid, 1–33/16].

This experiment was subject to a number of mishaps and crises, caused not least by its poor reception by the families of the students enrolled on the course. After spreading through the social classes, it was finally abandoned in 1854, partly due to the irregular attendance of the students.

The collapse of this course poses another question, which is difficult to answer. Without taking into account the well-known religious instruction or private classes, particularly in the case of the daughters, sisters or wives of artists, where were official art classes provided for women between 1854 and the 1880s, when women's names first begin to appear among the graduates of the Escuela Especial de Pintura, Escultura y Grabado, now the Escuela de Bellas Artes? Until the academic year of 1878–9, no women's names appear on any of the surviving documents, and even from this year they are few and women were excluded from some of the basic classes such as pictorial anatomy and composition. Such exclusion, which was prevalent throughout Europe, disqualified women *a priori* from "great painting". However, the discrimination against them did not end there: to enter the Escuela Especial, male artists needed only to apply to the director, whereas women artists had to present a prize certificate at the Escuela de Artes y Oficios, an institution that filled the academic gap during the 1860s and 1870s – and even later – even though the classes there were clearly close to the applied arts. Young women at the Escuela Especial also had to sit different examinations, of which there were two kinds, one for history painting and one for landscape painting (for the former, women students sat an identical examination to their male colleagues, with the exclusion of pictorial anatomy). On the course of 1878–9, there were only 5 women compared to 164 men studying landscape painting, drawing from the antique and perspective, and only 2 of these, Adela Ginés and Teresa Madasin, appeared again at later dates in the century. (Ginés was the first woman to be awarded a prize at the Escuela Especial (1894), and also achieved a certain degree of fame and several mentions and awards at the Exposiciones Nacionales.) In the early 20th century there was a slight increase in the proportion of women artists – 17 women compared to 167 men – and, in 1901, among the few documents preserved, the first few names of women artists begin to appear on the pictorial anatomy course, with many of the prizes being awarded to women from that year on.

The small number of women artists registered on courses compared to the huge number entering the Exposiciones

Nacionales indicates that there were alternative ways of receiving an art education, although this would often have been very precarious. As has been noted, one possibility may have been the Escuela de Artes y Oficios, private schools or colleges of education, religious education or private classes with artists who were often of the second rank. The proliferation of treatises, books and drawing methods specially planned for "young ladies", which gave the rudiments of drawing – directed, above all, towards embroidery or the applied arts – also points towards the possibility of training "without a teacher". To some extent, the treatises continued the tradition of the drawing manuals that were so popular in the 19th century, frequently stating that they were concerned with works conceived for either sex (Diego 1986). This fact is interesting, for it endorses the impression of women's artistic training as, on the one hand, a means of making a living and, on the other, as pure "enthusiasm" or a hobby, at a time when, because of new social fashions, the paint brush replaced the needle. The idea that women artists were not professionals even penetrated male iconography, and in the 1830s Pedro Sáez presented a picture that showed an attractive young woman painting a canvas with the disheartening title of *The Amateur*.

The education system clearly perceived women painters as amateurs; its exclusions lead to the suspicion that there was something more at stake than just the supposed saving of morality. In some of the general treatises for women compiled by some of the most reactionary female writers the idea of the "amateur" reappears. A good example of this is in the writings of Maria Pilar Sinués de Marco, perhaps one of the most celebrated writers of books on women's education in the 1880s. One of her books explains how this "decorative education" can eventually help a woman to earn her living, always associated with moral values. The writer explains:

> Fortunate is the woman who, endowed with so much talent, so much sympathy, so much renowned beauty and integrity, when she finishes a picture, a musical composition or a book, is able to find reasonable and constant buyers who wish to acquire her work for a fair remuneration and acquire it with true satisfaction [Sinués de Marco 1880, p.76].

In any case, such a training was never seen as a means of becoming independent, but merely as a way of making a living in cases where the family finds itself in difficult economic circumstances. Other female writers of a more liberal disposition, such as Concepción Arenal, nevertheless argued that women artists found themselves relegated to painting copies or fans because of their lack of training (Arenal 1895).

Despite this social animosity towards the professionalisation of women artists, some of them tried to take their works out of the family environment through the Exposiciones Nacionales, such private exhibitions as those of the Círculo de Bellas Artes and the Sala Parés of Barcelona – which, from the last few years of the 19th century, often held shows of work by women – and associations such as the Sociedad de Acuarelistas (watercolour artists). They also attempted to sell them. A few price lists are preserved, showing that there was not much difference in price between works by women artists and those by second-rank male artists. Some notices of purchase also survive, printed in the newspapers, although the very appearance of these notices of purchase of works by women artists makes it seem that this was exceptional. Purchases by the State were rare, given that only works awarded prizes in the Exposiciones Nacionales were acquired. The few women awarded prizes – and thus of the few paintings acquired – helps to explain the difficulty of locating works by women artists.

Thus, judging from the barely noticeable effect of the 400 documented women painters, and even taking into account the fact that future research and the hypothetical discovery of missing works may throw new light on the problem, the substitution of the paint brush for the needle seems to have been incidental in Spain at that time. Many of the ways in which the teaching of drawing manifested itself were reflected in industry but, as Rozsika Parker and Griselda Pollock have stated (*Old Mistresses: Women, Art and Ideology*, New York, Pantheon, and London: Routledge, 1981), the general attitude made it clear that what was done was not as important as who did it.

Despite the progress of education in the 19th century and the attempts at professionalisation, no significant changes seem to have been brought about in the early years of the 20th century. The arrival of the so-called avant-garde and its inherent restructuring of the art world meant that with a few exceptions women were unable to become fully integrated, revealing how their admission to the "life-drawing" class did not signify a war that had been won, but instead a battle that had not been lost. In fact, training continued to be confused with applied knowledge, as can be seen by comparing the numbers of women students at the Escuela Especial de Pintura, Escultura y Grabado, which during the first 30 years did not rise above 5 per cent, with those at the Escuelas de Artes y Oficios, which reached up to 38 per cent (Capel Martinez 1986). With regard to private education, very few women trained with established, well-known artists.

If the situation is evaluated on the basis of the systems of distribution, the overall picture is quite depressing. Despite the fact that in the early part of the 20th century several private galleries began to flourish, particularly in Barcelona – the Dalmau gallery, for instance, showed, among others, Salvador Dalí, as well as organising the Associació d'Artistes Indépendents in 1936, in which several women participated – the majority of women artists continued to show their work at the by-then discredited Exposiciones de Bellas Artes, which were stagnating in 19th-century parameters. Nor did women actively participate in the associations and groups of artists that were so popular at the time (Jaime Brihuega, *Las vanguardias artisticas en Espana, 1900–1936*, Madrid: Itsmo, 1981, pp.99ff.).

Thus, in the salon of Artistas Ibéricos of 1925, which aimed to show avant-garde trends, there were very few female participants, and even fewer have survived in art history. In general, only a small number of women were really committed to the avant-garde, and of these only four Spanish women were able to compete with their colleagues: María Blanchard (q.v.), Maruja Mallo (q.v.), Remedios Varo (q.v.) and Angeles Santos (q.v.). Furthermore, all these women carried out their activity outside the country: the first in Paris and the second in Argentina, while Remedios Varo left Spain after meeting Benjamin Péret, and Angeles Santos eventually abandoned painting.

The succeeding generations, by then integrated into a more egalitarian education system, met with similar problems. However, from the 1970s onwards women began to exhibit regularly, reflecting the general cultural modernisation of the country. In the last few years, sculpture has begun to enjoy popularity among women artists, although the previously discussed late incorporation of gender theory into the history of art has meant that it was only in the late 1980s that the young generation was able to adopt fully a commitment to feminist art.

ESTRELLA DE DIEGO

Bibliography

María Pilar Sinués de Marco, *La dama elegante*, Madrid: Martin, 1880

Concepción Arenal, "Estado de la mujer en España", *Boletín de la Institución Libre en Enseñanza*, 21 August 1895; reprinted in *La emancipación de la mujer en España*, Madrid: Jucar, 1974, p.30

José Parada y Santín, *Las pintoras españolas: Boceto histórico-biográfico y artístico*, Madrid: Imprenta del Asilo de Huérfanos del sagrado Corazón de Jesús, 1903

Bernardino de Pantorba, *Historia y crítica de las Exposiciones Nacionales de Bellas Artes celebradas en España*, Madrid, 1948; revised edition, Madrid: Garcia-Rama, 1980

Carmen Pérez-Neu de Robla, *Galería universal de pintoras*, Madrid: Nacional, 1964

Paloma Fernández-Quintanilla, *La mujer ilustrada en la España del siglo XVIII*, Madrid: Ministerio de Cultura, 1981

Rosa Capel Martinez, *El trabajo y la educación de la mujer en España (1900–1930)*, revised edition, Madrid: Ministerio de Cultura, 1986

Estrella de Diego, "Aprendar a dibujar sin maestro", *Goya*, no.192, 1986, pp.355–61

——, *La mujer y la pintura del XIX español*, Madrid: Universidad Computense de Madrid, 1987

9. Australasia

1840–1880

The assessment of the achievements of women artists in Australasia (Australia and New Zealand) before 1900 is still fluid, as research continually refines limiting stereotypes. In the 1840s women with professional training – rather than amateur sketchers – were among the increasing numbers of "free" migrants (i.e. not associated with convict settlement) to Australia. Whether they publicly deployed their skills depended on personal choice and family dictates rather than a definable historical pattern. While Georgiana McCrae's husband forbade her from augmenting the family finances through painting sales in the 1840s, her contemporary Mary Morton Allport – of a comparable social rank – freely advertised for commissions in the Hobart press and published lithographs as probably the first Australian woman printmaker. Lithography also provided an early public forum for the New Zealand artist Martha King of Wanganui, four of whose drawings were circulated as illustrations to E.J. Wakefield's *Illustrations to Adventure in New Zealand* (1845). In this early period, the issue of professional versus amateur was not so strictly divided on gender lines as it was in Europe, because

circumstances forced many male artists, both free-settler and convict, to practise their art only part-time or as a pastime.

Broad parallels can be drawn among women working in several Australian colonies during the 1840s, for example McCrae, Allport, Louisa Ann Meredith (q.v.), Martha Berkeley and Teresa Walker. Both their choice of media – wax, watercolours, miniatures – and their stylistic approach reflected the marketplace options available to women in early Victorian Britain. Before emigration, these women had shown occasionally at the Royal Academy in London, the competitions of the Society of Arts and other such organisations in Britain. Often small in scale, delicate, but undeniably skilled, their works show a poetic sentiment and sweet grace of gesture that holds its own against the obvious claims of large-scale oil paintings by male artists. The portrait watercolours of the New Zealander Sarah Greenwood show a similarly fine execution and sympathetic observation of dress and mores as the work of her Australian contemporaries, although little is known about her early professional experience in England. The South Australian-based artist Martha Berkeley is now regarded as a significant painter of the 1840s; her portrait watercolours reflect fashionable mannerisms, yet a faintly naive focus on dress and millinery gives them a surprisingly tough, even glamorous edge. In 1840 Berkeley's sister, the wax modeller Teresa Walker, was the first artist of either gender to send works back to the Royal Academy exhibitions from an Australian studio. Previously, Australian subjects had been brought to England by artists returning there, and were often completed outside Australia from sketches made while travelling.

Outside upper-class cultural circles, the professional art/craft options for women diversified during the years 1800–80. Family workshops gave access to varied skills. Women managed taxidermy, photography and silversmith studios in colonial Sydney, for example. Widows frequently maintained their husbands' businesses successfully. Even in the fine arts women who exhibited widely were often, but not always, the daughters and sisters of male professionals. In New Zealand, for example, Edith Halcombe first copied the drawings of her father, William Swainson, and then produced original works, including lithographed views of Manawatu to illustrate her husband's book about that district.

From the earliest white settlement in New South Wales, free and convict women practised sewing, millinery and dress designing, traditional female specialisations. Some British prostitutes sentenced to transportation were former milliners or seamstresses. The embroidery, appliqué and design skills revealed on the few securely identified productions of convict women – for example, the quilt (1841; National Gallery of Australia, Canberra) made by convicts on the ship *Rajah* or the presentation basket (1838; Tasmanian Museum and Art Gallery, Hobart) to Lady Franklin – are fashionable rather than naive in style, indistinguishable from work by middle-class amateurs. Likewise, Aboriginal Australian girls and women were trained under the influence of missionaries and philanthropists in plain and fancy sewing, quilt making and whitework, reflecting the standards of design, technique and execution expected from all white Anglo-Australian women.

Natural history provided a niche for women in both Australia and New Zealand, yet it also conveniently disenfranchised women with regard to bohemian constructions of (male) genius. In the 1840s Martha King drew exquisite botanical studies that are now highly regarded as important colonial New Zealand art works. Caroline Atkinson wrote and illustrated nature articles for the Sydney press in the 1860s, as well as writing novels and painting for its own sake. The Scott sisters, Helena and Harriet, dominated scientific illustration in Sydney in the 1860s and 1870s, occasionally also taking on decorative commissions including graphics and medals displaying "Ruskinian" natural ornament. Margaret Forrest, the wife of a West Australian premier, was a botanical artist and committee member of Perth's early professional artists' guilds.

The flower painter Ellis Rowan refused to be marginalised, directly engaging male wrath. She had the highest international profile of any Australian artist of either gender, winning medals at exhibitions across Europe including Russia. While few women could match Rowan's self-consciously piquant feminine heroism – she imaged herself in a long white dress, menaced by crocodiles on a tropical river – Emily Harris demonstrated how a dedicated artist could push botanical painting to the parameters of professionalism accorded to women in Australasia. She sent flower studies from New Zealand to the Melbourne International Exhibition of 1880 and to the Indian and Colonial Exhibition of 1886 in London, but like many women at this period, she presented her studies on textiles and as screens, as well as in "high art" formats. Harris may have been hemmed in by the expectations of her contemporaries – she and her sister kept house for their widowed father – yet her own writings of the mid-1880s (a rare first-hand voice for a late 19th-century Australasian woman artist; quoted in Kirker 1987) express her frustration at the way in which teaching and housework encroached on her time, her annoyance at critics describing her work as "pretty" – a word she regarded as inimical to "Art" or serious aspirations – and her exertions in painting landscapes, even getting up at 6 a.m. Harris had distinct economic goals: she supplemented the family income by selling flower paintings, decorated furniture and drapes, taught at an infant school with her sisters and also took on private art pupils. It is no surprise that contemporaries regarded her with some seriousness, and an album of her studies of New Zealand plants was published in 1890.

1880–1920

Advanced British culture of the 1870s and 1880s made a distinct impact on the colonies. A mildly radical plein-air school drawn from Bastien-Lepage and the Newlyn School in Cornwall rather than Monet was established in Australia around 1885. Both Australians (e.g. Dora Serle in 1902) and New Zealanders (e.g. Dorothy Richmond c.1898) studied at Newlyn with Elizabeth Forbes (q.v.) and Stanhope Forbes when overseas. Institutions – galleries, art schools and strictly regulated art societies – rapidly developed in Australian and New Zealand cities, including the Auckland Society of Arts (established 1869), the Victorian Academy of the Arts, Melbourne (established 1870), and Otago Art Society (established 1875). The emergence by the 1880s of cohesive progressive artistic factions created an increasingly uncomfortable milieu for women. It was difficult for them to obtain first-hand knowledge of the avant-garde. Moreover, in an artistic climate dominated by charismatic leadership figures and where British aestheticism was eagerly emulated, women rarely gained the strategic respect accorded to male artists, although conditions varied from centre to centre. Women in South Australia enjoyed a particularly high level of involvement in professional art and at the Central School of Arts and Crafts, from the appointment of Elizabeth Armstrong as teacher. The foundation of the distinguished Launceston Art Society (Tasmania) in 1891 was solely due to women artists. In New Zealand Dorothy Richmond was acclaimed as an influential force in Wellington intellectual life; she was elected to the council of the New Zealand Academy of Fine Arts in 1904 and was mentor and teacher to the art community of her home city. Richmond, who made several trips to Britain in the last three decades of the 19th century, studied at the Slade School of Fine Art in London (1873–5) and, among New Zealanders, was acquainted with the cultural developments of the 1880 – aestheticism, design and Whistlerian impressionism – that were championed by the Australian plein-air movement.

During the last two decades of the 19th century the suffrage movement became a prominent social force in both Australia and New Zealand. New Zealand women were the first in the British Empire to be granted the vote, in 1893, with South Australia following in 1894. The feminist movement influenced the professional lives of women artists both indirectly and specifically. Access to tertiary education and the professions created a widening public forum for women, enabling them to gain financial independence. Art was one of many vocations that were championed and facilitated by feminists. Large exhibitions formed a key strategy in the publicising of women's art, such as the Women's Arts and Industrial Exhibition in Sydney (1888), Australian exhibits in the Woman's Building at the World's Columbian Exposition in Chicago (1893) and the First Exhibition of Australian Women's Work, Melbourne (1907), which included art and craft exhibits sent by women from many overseas countries. Information on a number of high-profile professional women artists in Europe was disseminated throughout Australasia by journalists with mild commitments to feminism. Both the Canterbury *Times* and the Melbourne *Sun* featured articles on Rosa Bonheur (q.v.) and Lady Butler (q.v.), among others, as well as providing further commentaries on women at the Royal Academy and the Paris Salons during the 1890s. In Australia, the radical left circles who promoted nationalism and independence often reacted adversely to feminism, creating a climate in which the public and cultural achievements of women were mocked savagely – such conflicts are reflected in the extreme reactions that Ellis Rowan encountered throughout her working life.

Further specific links between the feminist movement and the increasing profile of women as artists could be traced. Three of the first six female medical students enrolled at the University of Melbourne in 1886 had sisters who were professional artists. Following the example of women in other professions, artists formed cultural groupings. The Austral Salon was founded in 1891 by female journalists associated with the plein-air movement, but at first prominent male artists were included in its activities, and its later focus was on music. Two women's art organisations were founded in the early years of the 20th century. The Melbourne Society of Women Painters and Sculptors, established in 1902, was less overtly feminist, concentrating until the 1960s on women artists who enjoyed a high reputation among their peers, independent of political stance. The Sydney Society of Women Painters was founded in 1910, a response to jury discrimination in the male-dominated art societies. It made public statements, such as protesting against gender bias in museum purchases, but barely lasted two decades – even after changing its name (and aims) to the Women's Industrial Art Society – while the MSWPS is still in existence. The Lyceum Clubs and affiliates throughout Australasia represented women in the professions, especially university graduates, but also regarded visual artists as suitably qualified for membership. In 1904 the London Lyceum Club offered to accept paintings sent to London by New Zealand women and to forward them to public exhibitions if they displayed an appropriate level of skill.

Art students worked through a curriculum based on the British Schools of Design. Teaching staff regarded colonial students of either gender as unsuited for advanced training. During the 1870s the National Gallery of Victoria School in Melbourne – then the most formalised art academy in Australasia – relegated both male and female painting students to the copying of gallery exhibits. Eleanor Ritchie Harrison left in disgust after six months of copying and went to the South Kensington Schools in London in 1875, and later to Parisian ateliers. By c.1880 ambitious students demanded curriculum reforms, but while male students generally defined themselves as professionals, their female classmates were assumed to be satisfied with the mediocre standards. The few women who were accepted by the progressive faction often bore the brunt of the authorities' attacks on the reformers. They would swiftly punish any misconduct, especially towards male students – as in the case of Clara Collins, who was dismissed for rowdy behaviour in class in 1880 – or moves towards self-promotion – as in 1886, when Alice Chapman showed by invitation with a professional male art society. Male students who exhibited with the same society as Chapman escaped without censure.

The period 1890–1910 is marked by women's increasing success at government art schools, especially when the clearly misogynist director of the National Gallery School, George Folingsby, was replaced by Bernard Hall in 1892. The National Gallery of Victoria School, Melbourne, was regarded as the best in Australasia from the 1880s to the 1930s, attracting artists from across the country, including Vida Lahey from Queensland. By 1910 women students leaving the school could establish considerable local reputations – and economic independence – as academic artists, as did Dora Wilson for her street scenes, Alice Bale as a flower painter, Jo Sweatman as a landscapist and Aileen Dent as a portraitist. The pastels of Janet Cumbrae Stewart, the most securely "out" lesbian in Australian art history, attracted comment from about 1910 onwards. She spent the inter-war years in Europe, exhibiting and selling her female nudes in London. Around 1910–14 the plein-air painter Clara Southern achieved something of the reputation of male landscape painters, although her work was not as original in outlook as that of her contemporaries Jane Sutherland (q.v.), Jane Price and the portraitist Violet Teague. Teague painted in a consciously "grand" manner and won certificates and medals at the Paris Salon (1898 and 1921) and at the Panama-Pacific Exposition in San Francisco (1915) with full-length portraits sent over from Melbourne.

The Melbourne Gallery School also attracted many New Zealand students. Grace Joel, who won first prize for painting from the nude in 1893, was perhaps the earliest female student to capture some contemporary fame in Melbourne, disquieting Australian male artists by displaying a vigour of execution deemed typically masculine. She moved between Australia and New Zealand in the 1890s and later travelled overseas – there is some intriguing evidence to suggest that Renoir and Isaac Israels were colleagues, although her later works posit more academic influences. Her high profile in expatriate circles – she was well placed in Salon and other exhibitions – anticipated the success of Frances Hodgkins (q.v.), and led Australians to "claim" her as their own.

The cultures of Australia and New Zealand overlapped more closely around 1900 than they do today. The New Zealand awareness of plein-air painting, for example, was substantially drawn from artists previously resident in Australia, whereas the foundations of professional art circles in New Zealand had at first been thoroughly "steeped in the English watercolour tradition". Influences, however, were mutual; the work of the Queenslander Bessie Gibson strongly reflected the early watercolour style of her teacher Frances Hodgkins. Kit Turner, an esteemed Arts and Crafts metalworker in Melbourne in the 1920s, was already a trained artist/craft worker in New Zealand before enrolling at the Melbourne Gallery School in 1913. Adelaide Perry, winner of the travelling scholarship of 1920, spent her youth and adolescence in New Zealand and received her first art training there. Another major Australian artist who had been an active exhibitor while living in New Zealand during her adolescence was Dora Meeson. She subsequently worked in London, where she provided art works for the suffrage movement, including a banner (1908; Parliament House, Canberra). Several New Zealand expatriate women made an impact on the art scene in Sydney between the wars, from Maud Sherwood, one of the most professionally successful members of the Sydney Society of Women Painters, to the younger modernist Helen Stewart.

After World War I, New Zealand art schools attained a level of professionalism that made study trips across the Tasman increasingly unnecessary. The La Trobe scheme was set up in 1920 to bring professionally trained teachers from Britain to New Zealand to develop art courses there. New Zealand cultural life between the wars was enriched by the emergence of two equally strong regional traditions, influenced by the particular strengths of their art colleges, the Elam School of Auckland and the Canterbury School of Arts (the Ilam School) in Christchurch. Canterbury nurtured landscape painting whereas Auckland favoured figuration. The latter, under the influence of the teachers Archibald Fisher and Lois White, eschewed academic schemas, stressing instead the formalist rhythm and construction of Renaissance and Baroque art. Canterbury was often regarded as the leading art centre in New Zealand during the 1920s. While these colleges both provided work for a select number of talented women as teachers, correlating statistics suggest that women have always formed the majority of students, although even as late as 1991 Elam could boast only three women on the full-time staff. The few women employed there in the 20th century, however, have a credible record of achievement. Ida Eise (1920s–50s) and Lois White (late 1940s–early 1960s) spent long years at

Auckland. Canterbury employed Margaret Stoddart (q.v.) in the early 1900s, Rata Lovell-Smith from 1924 to 1945, Louise Henderson (q.v.) from 1925, and Evelyn Page in the 1930s, part-time, and Doris Lusk and Eileen Mayo after World War II.

Private art schools were also viable options for artists in Australasia. With an eye on financial independence, women in the 19th century could exploit and service the desire of middle-class families for their daughters to display genteel "accomplishments", including art and craft skills. The production of some teachers and governesses was extremely professional and extended to large oils and figurative works. Berthe Mouchette and Marie Lion were young French sisters, professionally trained artists and occasional Salon exhibitors who ran a fashionable ladies' school in Melbourne in the 1880s, producing some fine beaux-arts style works. In New Zealand, Dorothy Richmond and Frances Hodgkins ran a private art school before the latter moved to Europe, frustrated by the provincial community in which she found herself. By the 1920s increasing interest in art and design sustained private classes and studio teaching. Schools and drawing groups of various degrees of formality were organised by many women including Jessie Traill, the sculptor Ola Cohn, Esther Paterson, Thea Proctor, Adelaide Perry and Dorrit Black (q.v.). Frances Ellis from New Zealand started as a pupil at the notable Dattilo Rubbo School in Sydney and was promoted to assistant teacher before taking over the helm at Rubbo's retirement in 1941 (until 1949). She displayed a more radical, less illustrative approach to form and colour than her mentor.

In the years 1880–1939 many Australians and New Zealanders lived and worked for extended periods overseas. Frances Hodgkins was the most widely respected and successful expatriate artist. Iso Rae painted for more than four decades in Etaples, France, where her Australian family had settled in 1887. Flora Scales, a long-term French resident, was interned during World War II as a subject of the British empire, losing work through looting. A few artists went to America, where Constance Jenkins Mackey established herself on the faculty of the College of Arts and Crafts, Oakland, California, and at the San Francisco Institute of Fine Arts by c.1944, and Mary Cecil Allen worked at colleges on the East Coast during the 1930s. For some, travel provided the opportunity to gain supplementary qualifications from overseas schools. For others it was a conscious (and often permanent) break with parochial constraints. The stagnation of the modernist Edith Collier's career through familial responsibilities after her return home to New Zealand documents the forces that compelled women to travel: a painting and many studies from the nude, produced in England, were burned on her father's insistence. Clarice Beckett (q.v.) juggled solo exhibitions with the nursing of aged parents and housekeeping – a typical fate facing middle-class spinster daughters in both Australia and New Zealand during the early 20th century.

Mina Arndt studied in Germany under Lovis Corinth, but the outbreak of World War I dislocated her permanently from artistic sources in central Europe. Arndt returned home, under-appreciated in New Zealand, and her works – like those of Clarice Beckett of Melbourne – received appropriate recognition only decades after her death. By 1914 Hilda Rix Nicholas had established herself in France, painting formal figurative

oils and sketching Parisian street life in pastel. The death of her close family – mother, sister and husband – during World War I encouraged an intensely patriotic edge to her post-war art, expressed in recognisably mainstream terms: grand pastoral landscapes, studies of Australian country people and the "bush" – paralleling the public catharsis and testament of war-related traumas in conservative Australian official art of the 1920s and 1930s. Kate O'Connor from Perth lived in Paris, but although her experiments with the emotional and ambient effects of light on her subjects were appreciated by Vuillard, she lacked both money and wealthy patrons, and made no effective impression on art circles; during the 1920s she supported herself by painting fabrics for department stores and couture houses, including Poiret. She suffered the fate of many expatriates, too foreign to make an impact in France, yet exotically French when she returned to Australia, continually an alien. The Adelaide-born Stella Bowen did cross the threshold of "legendary" Paris in the 1920s, but, despite her talent, as the mistress of Ford Madox Ford rather than as an Australian artist. Flamboyant and radical, Mary Cockburn Mercer from Victoria acted as translator at the Académie Lhôte in the late 1920s and had some standing in cosmopolitan leisured society on the Côte d'Azur as well as on the fringes of the School of Paris.

1920–1945

Modern art, including Futurism, was discussed in the Australian press before World War I, though local experiments were based upon limited personal observations and imported reproductions and magazines. Modernism existed outside official cultural institutions in both New Zealand and Australia during the inter-war period, and women were crucial to its dissemination. For example, Norah Simpson's memories and collection of European reproductions introduced a group of students at the Dattilo Rubbo School in Sydney to modernism. Grace Cossington Smith (q.v.) built upon Simpson's lead, painting works that illustrate Australian life during World War I. Margaret Preston (q.v.) operated at the highest levels of the Sydney art world as a lecturer, theorist and advocate of modern art, as did Thea Proctor. In Melbourne Isabel Hunter Tweddle performed something of the same role, but unlike Preston and Proctor she never committed her ideas to writing and is therefore generally left out of standard accounts. Her gestural expressionist paintings, however, undoubtedly influenced not only younger, and now more acknowledged women artists – including Sybil Craig, Peggie Crombie, Lina Bryans and Joy Hester (q.v.) – but also the male "stars" of the 1940s, many of whom knew Tweddle's art well, but failed to acknowledge her.

Women were the stalwarts of The Group in Christchurch, the first New Zealand forum, founded in 1927, for more progressive art than that promoted by the established art societies. Helen Crabb, observing the proselytising activities of her friends, the Australian modernists Thea Proctor and Dorrit Black, was outspoken and direct in her support of New Zealand women's access to progressive art. The tuition that she provided for women with children and aspiring artists with little practical connection with modernism emphasised psychological observation and haptic energy. From her classes there emerged a number of women who would later gain some status as artists in New Zealand.

By the later 1920s the process of transmission was more certain. Australians and New Zealanders wishing to "go modern" would travel overseas (if they could afford it) and study at either the Grosvenor School of Modern Art in London or the Académie Lhôte in Paris. Through her work in Sydney in the 1930s, Helen Stewart, a New Zealander who had trained at the Académie Lhôte, was a direct link between New Zealand's lively modernist scene and the influential yet idiosyncratic modernism of Australia. Her high, clear colours, often deployed as shifting surface planes of patterning, correspond more to the work of New Zealand-based artists such as Rita Angus (q.v.), Rata Lovell-Smith and May Smith than the Fry and Cubist-based formalist line and construction of many Australian artists. In Australia in the 1920s modern style was acceptable in certain contexts – especially fashion and the decorative arts – but not in "serious" painting and sculpture. This distinction created a broad gender divide, with the significant conservative, nationalist images being painted mostly by men, leaving modernism and design as a forum for women.

While the inter-war identification of women with decoration may have been superficial and limiting, since the 1890s, when Ruskin and William Morris had had a great impact in Australia, design and craft had provided more opportunities for women artists than the high arts. These interests could be pursued to some length. Eirene Mort studied in London at the National Art Training School and the Royal College of Needlework, and later worked for Liberty's before returning to Australia to produce stencil designs, painted and embroidered textiles and graphic design in a fine Art Nouveau style, often incorporating – as did many contemporaries – Australian flora and fauna. China painting provided a reliable income for women through sales, and also fostered a network of private teaching opportunities in the various art and craft media, whereby unmarried professional artists supported themselves by promoting classes for young girls. Some students painted as a pastime, others (on their teacher's advice) went on to attend government schools with the ambition of pursuing professional careers. Wood carving found many followers, including Nellie Payne in Tasmania, whose commissioned work featured widely in church and school interiors. But the crafts were not a quaint dead end. When the French-born artist Louise Henderson arrived in New Zealand from Paris, she brought a professionalism to the teaching of embroidery and textiles there in the 1930s, teaching at the Canterbury School of Art and publishing instruction books on this craft. Her paintings, following study with Jean Metzinger in Paris in 1952, represent a significant step towards the development of a non-figurative idiom in New Zealand art. Such ideas were expressed with equal effectiveness in her tapestry designs and stained glass.

Sculpture, under the impetus of the British New Sculpture movement, which stressed modelling, small scale and personal expression, was pursued enthusiastically by Australasian women from the 1890s onwards. Margaret Thomas had earlier worked as a sculptor in the 1870s, but she turned to art criticism and writing in London in the 1880s. In the 1890s two Australians, Theo Cowan and Margaret Baskerville, aimed for professional recognition. Cowan received a commission from the Art Gallery of New South Wales in 1896, leading to questions in Parliament about the wisdom of spending public money in this way. Margaret Butler of New Zealand and the Australian Dora Barclay studied under Bourdelle in Paris, and Butler's sculptures were exhibited at the Royal Academy in London and the Paris Salon, as well as in solo exhibitions in Vienna and elsewhere during the 1920s and 1930s.

In the inter-war period, Australian printmaking, especially of modernist relief prints, was dominated by women, notably Margaret Preston, Dorrit Black and Maud Sherwood. Here is a point of distinction between Australia and New Zealand, where it was not until the 1970s that women achieved a comparable level of acknowledgement as esteemed printmakers (this fact neatly cuts across the implication that printmaking was a "lighter" form of modernism, ideally suited to women). Connie Lloyd of Auckland was a rare example of an early woman etcher in New Zealand between the wars, albeit overshadowed by her father, the etcher and illustrator Trevor Lloyd. Both Maud Sherwood and Thea Proctor were praised by conservative critics for avoiding "expected" female pitfalls of "weak" drawing and form. The crisply rhythmic linocuts of the Australians Dorrit Black, Ethel Spowers and Eveline Syme and the New Zealander Eileen Mayo reflect their studies under Claude Flight at the Grosvenor School of Modern Art in London. Others, such as Helen Ogilvie, learned the technique through observation and manuals, while in Sydney many women were taught by Adelaide Perry, who ran her own art school. Likewise Hilda Wiseman introduced Ida Eise to linocutting in Auckland. Australian etching was conservative, dominated by males working in the painter-etcher tradition, although the most original inter-war etcher was Jessie Traill, a pupil of Frank Brangwyn. Her industrial subjects, including her famous series – watercolours and drawings as well as prints – of the construction of the Sydney Harbour Bridge have been raised by historians to iconic status. Mina Arndt of New Zealand also attended Brangwyn's classes in the early 1900s. Beatrix Darbyshire of Perth was an effective etcher in the conservative landscape style.

Women worked widely as commercial artists in the inter-war period. Francis (Frankie) Payne supported herself and her child in Sydney in the 1920s. Covers for the elegant society journal, *The Home*, brought fame to Thea Proctor, Hera Roberts and other women. The "flapper" generation expressed itself through a surprising number of female cartoonists, whose work was published in magazines of both upper-class and popularist milieux. The savage, cynical wit has survived well, with the stylish Betty Paterson working in an Art Deco style, and later Edith Wall, influenced in the 1930s by the British magazine *Punch*.

In the 1930s art-based careers greatly diversified. The artist Frances Derham was famed as an educationalist and an advocate for "child art". Frances Burke, whose screen-printed fabric was popular in fashionable circles, promoted industrial design as a discipline in Australia from the 1930s onwards. The printmaker Eileen Mayo also worked with typography and designed publications and postage stamps in both New Zealand and Australia. Aboriginal Australian motifs became a fashionable pivot for a developing local progressive design, purged of Art Nouveau and Pre-Raphaelite influences. The popularity of "Aboriginal motifs" allowed the Hermansberg Mission resident Cordula Ebatarinja to gain a profile as an exhibiting artist from the 1940s onwards. New Zealanders

Hilda Rix Nicholas: *The Fair Musterer*, 1935; oil on canvas; 102.3 × 160.4 cm.; Queensland Art Gallery, Brisbane; purchased 1971

adapted Maori motifs to modernism, as seen in Lorna Reyburn Waller's linocut *Kia Ora New Zealand* and Hilda Wiseman's Maori carving in a woodcut bookplate of 1927. New Zealanders viewed Maori art as a valid design source and a statement of (white) national identity and pride at least a generation earlier than the re-evaluation in white Australia of Aboriginal artefacts as more than anthropological curiosities.

Many early art dealers were women. Margaret McLean of Melbourne handled prominent radical and conservative artists of both genders throughout the 1920s and 1930s, and Treania Smith was co-director with Mary Turner of the Macquarie Galleries, the major Sydney dealers. Jeanette Sheldon opened the first commercial gallery in Brisbane (1921), showing art from other Australian centres and overseas, as well as promoting local artists. Alannah Coleman, an Australian artist, gained a solid reputation as a dealer and gallery associate in London after World War II. The first dealer to specialise in contemporary New Zealand painting was Helen Hitchings, who founded her gallery in Wellington in 1951. Women had been art writers as early as the 1890s when the Hobart-Melbourne sisters Edith Reverdy (married to Gustave Courbet's nephew) and Marie Therese Loureiro worked as art critics for *The Age* in Melbourne. Mary Tripe published a particularly solid oeuvre of writing in *Art in New Zealand* during the 1920s and 1930s.

European-trained refugees made Australia aware of art history as an academic discipline. Gertrude Langer and Ursula Hoff became influential in Australian art circles in the 1940s.

The consolidation of national identity and self-purpose in the visual arts that was characteristic of Australia in the 1880s and 1890s coincided with the arrival of inter-war modernism in New Zealand. The overturning of stale formulae by the 20th-century avant-garde empowered Regionalist ambition to image New Zealand without resorting to British "conventions". Progressive New Zealand landscape painting expressed practical as well as metaphysical issues, "proving" that mature artists could be trained in New Zealand – without a "requisite" overseas trip. The vision of such women as Rata Lovell-Smith, their engagement with painting the ordinary, yet vivid, everyday views, directly shaped and confirmed the effectiveness of this changing vision of New Zealand life and scenery. Rita Angus's *Rutu* (1951; see illustration) expressed a profoundly serious and wide-ranging programme to personify and characterise the specific cultural and historical identity of New Zealand, acknowledging elements of European and Polynesian belief.

After 1945

The post-war period brought profound and ever-accelerating

Rita Angus: *Rutu*, 1951; Museum of New Zealand Te Papa Tongarewa, Wellington (B31439)

changes in the cultural outlook of Australia and New Zealand. By this date, the discussion of both cultures as a unity presents an artificial delimiting construction. The contemporary cultural relationship between Australia and New Zealand is undoubtedly fruitful, but far more volatile, fluctuating and dark than it was two generations earlier, when developments in the two countries followed broadly parallel lines within the British Empire.

In the 1950s a new confidence in Australian contemporary art among both establishment and corporate buyers was noticeable. By 1962, with the exhibition of Australian art at the Whitechapel Gallery, London, Australia had developed a significant presence on the British contemporary scene. Women, however, were virtually excluded from this new taste for antipodean art. Only one woman, Mary Durack, whose art reflected the dramatic "outback" themes identified with Australian male artists, was included in the Whitechapel show. The final blossoming of critical awareness and confidence in the work of the New Zealand-based artist Rita Angus in the 1960s equally betokened a conceptual shift in attitudes towards regional-based artists and aesthetics. Art with an avowed local programme ranked in significance alongside, if not above, foreign-based styles as an embodiment of a mature contemporary culture. A local artist could "mean" and say as much as any import.

At the same time women actively advocated a more internationally based, non-figurative style. Such Australian women artists as Grace Crowley, Dawn Sime, Yvonne Audette and Erica McGilchrist were all painting and exhibiting abstract works by the late 1950s. Audette, who had worked and studied in New York, where she had some contact with the Abstract Expressionist movement, performed the familiar role of translating overseas developments. Similarly Jean Horsley of New Zealand, based in London in the 1960s, spent time in New York, which confirmed the primacy of abstraction for her. In 1966 the New Vision Gallery in Auckland staged a joint exhibition of her work with Louise Henderson's abstracts.

Abstraction had become the central stylistic language of sculpture by the early 1960s, and women received a surprisingly large number of opportunities in Australasia in the movement to decorate civic and corporate spaces with monumental abstract sculptures – despite the continuing stereotyping of women as trite and unduly imitative in professional art circles. In 1969, within months of her graduation from art school, Marté Szirmay won the Smirnoff Sculpture award, with a work still standing in Newmarket, Auckland. Norma Redpath and Inge King were foundation members of the Centre Five group, which sought to promote abstract sculpture in Australia. The American-born and trained Margel Hinder created early examples of kinetic sculpture in Australia and later became especially renowned as a fountain designer.

Due to the post-war emphasis on fashionable male artists, the activities of women artists in Australia and New Zealand are relatively low key in comparison to the explosion that took place in the mid-1970s. The Women's Art Movement and the catalysing effect in Australasia of Women's Liberation and American feminist art have been documented in published sources, so only a brief outline will be given here. A crucial pattern across Australasia was the tendency for women to organise bodies, such as the Women's Art Forum (1975) in Melbourne and the Women's Art Movement in Adelaide, that promoted consciousness-raising, advocacy, politics, as well as help with practical issues such as technical instruction, exhibition opportunities, equity of representation and exhibition spaces. Factional disputes and/or limitations in financial or managerial resources meant that some of these well-intentioned organisations foundered. Some, such as the Women's Art Register (slide library and archive, Melbourne, established 1975) and the Association of Women Artists (Auckland, founded in the 1980s), still survive. The richness of the emotional and professional legacy of crucial bodies such as the Women's Gallery in Wellington (1980–84) meant, however, that their influence extended far beyond their period of operation. Likewise, certain exhibitions and events had a long-lasting resonance, including the *Mothers' Memories, Others' Memories* of Vivienne Binns (q.v.), the exhibition *Mothers* at the Women's Gallery, Wellington (1981), and the *Commonwealth Quilt*, a collaborative project of Carole Shepheard, Toi Maihi, Luseane Koloi and more than 60 other women at the Auckland Festival of 1990. Norms of art-market practices were scrutinised, interrogated and confronted at every possible level. Historians brought out paintings from storage and consciously intervened in sexist tertiary and secondary educational discourses. Collaborative and politicised work challenged politically neutral, but chic investment art. The boundaries of art and craft were melted to bring personal, diaristic and expressive elements into "high" art. Domestic life, childbirth, violence against women, discrimination, lesbian identity, union and industrial issues were brought into the public arena alongside traditional masculinist public iconographies of religion, politics, philosophy and nationalism.

Yet the positive achievements of feminist art often were (and are) enacted to a converted audience of women, against a broader pattern of institutionalised scepticism. Statistics compiled by, for example, Anna Waldman, Caroline Ambrus and Merren Ricketson in Australia and Anne Kirker and Janet Paul in New Zealand during the 1980s and 1990s document discrepancies in many areas of art practice: representation in exhibitions – only 11 artists were female out of a total of 82 included in *Two Centuries of New Zealand Art* at the Auckland City Gallery in 1990; grants – women received $71,900 out of a total disbursement of $177,000 in 1985 from the Queen Elizabeth II Arts Council of New Zealand; employment – with 39 men as opposed to 11 women teaching art full-time in New South Wales technical colleges in 1981; and gallery purchases – only 15 per cent of contemporary Australian paintings purchased by the Art Gallery of New South Wales, Sydney, in 1981 were by women. Art politics declared that feminism was out of fashion in the 1980s, and younger women often echoed women of earlier generations in stressing that they were professional, not women artists.

Yet, ironically, artists who reject the overtly feminist art of the 1970s and early 1980s still operate in an art market that has been unmistakably broadened by the initiatives of 1970s feminism: the rapprochement of art and craft, installations, video and film, performance, textual commentaries/diaristic expression in exhibitions, posters, cheap ephemeral media and politicised race- and/or gender- conscious art. French-based feminist theories have returned women's art to the forefront of debate, re-opening the issues for a new generation. A vernacular interest in survey and historical shows based upon the vastly successful *Completing the Picture*, which toured Australia in 1992–3, and the many women's exhibitions, historic and contemporary, that commemorated the centenary of New Zealand Women's Suffrage in 1993 provide a *de facto* popular cross reference and extension of contemporary feminisms. Girlie feminisms have reclaimed such previously taboo subjects as Barbie dolls, Parisian catwalks and S&M dungeons, while collaborative, community and trade-union-based art projects are still organised. The various branches of the Embroiderers' Guild in Australia collaborated on a series of panels for the new Australian Federal Parliament House in Canberra (1984–8), as did New Zealand embroiderers for a curtain for the New Globe Theatre, London. Yet other women are working effectively at the highest echelons of contemporary culture, winning prestigious grants and commissions, and gaining senior and professorial ranking at universities and art colleges. The controversial choice of a woman, Jenny Watson, as sole Australian representative at the Venice Biennale of 1994 would have been unthinkable a decade earlier.

Issues of race and gender are being constantly renegotiated. Anthropological stereotypes placed a particular burden on New Zealand Maori and Australian Aboriginal artists, condemning women's role to that of traditional craftworkers, lauding de-politicised older "authentic" women and denying the experience of younger, urban-based artists who had studied at art colleges rather than with "elders" and "aunties". The Haeata Maori Women's Art Collective was specifically organised to counteract the invisibility of women in high-profiled international touring shows of Maori art. In the 1990s Australia and New Zealand found new synchronicity and relationship in a growing awareness of their common histories as white colonising nations and in the newly focused sense of regional identity within the Asia-Pacific region, when contemporary culture is no longer the prerogative of white artists who studied in London or New York. Mediterranean, Middle Eastern, African, Indian, Vietnamese, Polynesian and Melanesian experiences and inheritances, as well as Islamic, Buddhist, Hindu and other beliefs, are encompassed to varying degrees within the Australasian cultural vernacular.

In the mid-1990s many practitioners display advanced levels of skill and professionalism; there is an enthusiastic audience for women's work; funding bodies such as the Australia Council and the Queen Elizabeth II Arts Council of New Zealand have vastly improved the statistical balance in their funding. Equality within institutional contexts of the public gallery and the canon of national "masterpieces" will surely follow under pressure from the ever-vigilant audience and art makers.

JULIET PEERS, with ANNE KIRKER
(with the help of Pamela Gerrish Nunn)

Bibliography

Janine Burke, *Australian Women Artists, 1840–1940*, Collingwood, Victoria: Greenhouse, 1980

Roger Butler and Jan Minchin, *Thea Proctor: The Prints*, Sydney: Resolution Press, 1980

Mothers, exh. cat., Women's Gallery, Wellington, 1981

Caroline Ambrus, ed., *The Ladies' Picture Show: Sources on a Century of Australian Women Artists*, Sydney: Hale and Ironmonger, 1984 (bibliographic citations of Australian women artists pre-1945)

Judith Brett, "Australia and New Zealand", *Meanjin*, no.3, 1985, pp.328–30

Elizabeth Eastmond and Merimeri Penfold, *Women and the Arts in New Zealand: Forty Works, 1936–86*, Auckland: Penguin, 1986 (full-page colour plates for all artists)

Margaret Hazzard and Helen Hewison, *Flower Paintings of Ellis Rowan: From the Collection of the National Library of Australia*, revised edition, Canberra: National Library of Australia, 1987

Anne Kirker, "Women and art", *Public and Private Worlds: Women in Contemporary New Zealand*, ed. Shelagh Cox, Wellington: Allen and Unwin/Port Nicholson Press, 1987, pp.83–102

M. Evans, Bridie Long and Tilly Lloyd, eds, *A Woman's Picture Book: 28 Women Artists of New Zealand*, Wellington: Government Printing Office, 1988

Bruce James, *Grace Cossington Smith*, Sydney: Craftsman House, 1990

Eileen Mayo: Painter, Designer, exh. cat., National Library of New Zealand, Wellington, 1992

Victoria Hammond and Juliet Peers, *Completing the Picture: Women Artists and the Heidelberg Era*, 2nd edition, Hawthorn East: Artmoves, 1992

Sandy Kirby, *Sight Lines: Women's Art and Feminist Perspectives in Australia*, Sydney: Craftsman House/Gordon and Breach, 1992

By the Waters of Babylon: A. Lois White, exh. cat., Auckland City Gallery, 1993

Anne Kirker, *New Zealand Women Artists: A Survey of One Hundred and Fifty Years*, 2nd edition, Tortola, BVI: Craftsman House, 1993

Juliet Peers, *More Than Just Gumtrees: A Personal, Social and Artistic History of the Melbourne Society of Women Painters and Sculptors*, Melbourne Society of Women Painters and Sculptors in association with Dawn Revival Press, 1993

White Camellias: A Century of Women's Artmaking in Canterbury, exh. cat., Robert McDougall Art Gallery, Canterbury, 1993

Artlink: Australian Contemporary Art Quarterly, xiv/1, Autumn 1994 (survey issue: "Art and the feminist project", especially Christina Barton, "Making (a) difference: Suffrage year celebrations and the visual arts in New Zealand", pp.62–4, and Anne Kirker, "Re-orienting feminism in Aotearoa", pp.65–7)

Creators and Inventors, exh. cat., National Gallery of Victoria, Melbourne, 1994

Maryanne Dever, ed., *Wallflowers and Witches: Women and Culture in Australia, 1910–1945*, St Lucia: University of Queensland Press, 1994

Jeanette Hoorn, ed., *Strange Women: Studies in Art and Gender*, Melbourne: University of Melbourne Press, 1994

Therese Kenyon, *Under a Hot Tin Roof: Art, Passion and Politics at the Tin Sheds Art Workshop*, Sydney: State Library of New South Wales in Association with Power Publications, 1995

Joan Kerr, ed., *Heritage: The National Women's Art Book*, Sydney: Dictionary of Australian Artists/Craftsman House, 1995 (500 entries on Australian-based women artists, including some New Zealand artists with substantial Australian associations, c.1780s–1955)

A l'ombre des jeunes filles et des fleurs (sic): *A Guide to Women Artists in the Benalla Art Gallery Collection, pre-1960*, exh. cat., Benalla Art Gallery, Victoria, 1995

10. North America

19th century

USA

In the 19th century women artists in the USA found themselves in a different situation from that in Europe. Unlike France, the country lacked a strong centralised government that used the arts as a propaganda tool. And unlike Europe in general, it lacked an upper class with a long tradition of art patronage. Therefore, the training and professional opportunities for women were stereotypically American: regional, pragmatic and entrepreneurial.

Three major art centres on the East Coast – Philadelphia, New York and Boston – vied for leadership in the American fine arts, yet many important women artists emerged from Chicago, Cincinnati, St Louis, San Francisco and many lesser art centres across the country. Not one but two academies arose to train the country's elite artists – the Pennsylvania Academy of the Fine Arts in Philadelphia (1805) and the National Academy of Design in New York (1808) – but training on an equally effective level could be gained from many other institutions and individual teachers. Clubs, exhibiting societies and galleries could be found in every reasonably-sized town. Furthermore, American artists took full advantage of European training and professional opportunities when the offerings of their own country no longer satisfied them. The multiplicity of training and professional organisations available in 19th-century America was a sign of the earnestness with which local arts communities organised themselves to bring culture to a nation of modest artistic patronage.

Unlike France, where a professional class of fine artists could be supported by a combination of government and private patrons, artists in America were forced to be entrepreneurial – offering to the general public a combination of fine, reproductive and decorative art skills, while teaching on the side. As in Europe, the few artists who attained the highest status and greatest fame in the fine arts were men, but, below that small group, both men and women had to take advantage of whatever opportunities came their way. Those American women who could truly claim to have succeeded as fine artists, such as Harriet Hosmer (q.v.), Elizabeth Gardner (q.v.) and Mary Cassatt (q.v.), tended to live abroad.

In spite of these difficulties, women throughout the 19th century pieced together sufficient training and financial support to be able to practise as artists on a number of levels. In some regions, such as the state of Maine, they accounted for 50 per cent of the professional artists recorded during that period. The cultural patterns and institutions changed, but the desire of American women to find employment in art was constant. In the early part of the 19th century an upper class of British descent still held power in the USA, despite the War of Independence (1776–81) from Britain. Artists who had trained in Britain, such as Gilbert Stuart, Charles Willson Peale and Thomas Sully, set the standards for portraiture, both private and official. They in turn paved the way for some of the first prominent women artists of the century, Jane Stuart (Gilbert Stuart's daughter), Sarah Miriam and Anna Claypoole Peale (q.v., daughters of the miniaturist James Peale and nieces of Charles Willson Peale) and Jane Sully (daughter of Thomas Sully). These women trained with their fathers and found many doors open to them. Jane Stuart practised mainly as a copyist filling the seemingly endless demand for her father's famous portraits of *George Washington*, but Sarah Peale shaped an impressive career for herself as a portraitist and still-life painter in Baltimore and later St Louis. Peale and her sister Anna Claypoole were the first women to be elected

academicians of the Pennsylvania Academy of the Fine Arts in 1824, and their friend, Jane Sully, was elected in 1831.

Women were also instrumental in shaping a very different type of art that was prominent in the early 19th century and is very popular today: "naive" or "schoolgirl" art. These images were either painted in watercolour or worked in embroidery, but the bold patterns and exaggerations of form gave them a distinctive style. Although called "naive", the style was taught in private girls' schools through a process of copying engravings of famous paintings, many by Angelica Kauffman (q.v.), simplifying and flattening the composition, and adding dramatic colouring. That these works were highly regarded is signalled by the care taken in framing and preserving the finest examples. Some of the best-known artists who continued to paint in this style were Eunice Pinney (q.v.) and Mary Ann Willson. Because biblical and other religious imagery was especially effective, related watercolours can be found in the art of religious sects such as the Shakers where it was practised primarily by women. The influence of this type of folk art may be equated with the popular "Images d'Epinal" of France.

But the more typical women artists of the early 19th century were neither daughters of famous male artists nor practitioners of a "folk" style, but women such as Sophia Peabody Hawthorne or Susannah Paine whose careers encompassed a range of art endeavours. Hawthorne studied with the best Boston painters, Chester Harding, Thomas Doughty and Washington Allston, in the 1820s. She developed a modest market for her own landscape paintings as well as copies of Doughty's. However, after her marriage to the writer Nathaniel Hawthorne, who encouraged her art, she did not hesitate to paint such mundane objects as fire screens and lampshades when necessary to help support the family. Susannah Paine became an artist when a divorce left her on her own. With only the training she acquired in a private school, she developed a career as a portraitist in Portland, Maine, and travelled around the state as an itinerant artist.

A similar pioneering spirit could be found in Lilly Martin Spencer (q.v.), one of the first women to achieve national recognition. Spencer developed her skills among local artists in the small town of Marietta, Ohio, where she held her first exhibition at the age of 19. She later studied in Cincinnati and at the National Academy of Design in New York. Her fame was spread throughout the country in the 1850s and 1860s by means of reproductive engravings that were distributed by subscription to a large middle-class audience.

The generation of American women who came of age in the late 1840s was strongly affected by the emergence of feminist activism that culminated in the Women's Rights Convention, Seneca Falls, New York, in 1848. As in Europe, a woman's right to earn a living was part of the feminist platform, and the arts were perceived as a worthy field to enter. The first training schools for women in the decorative and industrial arts were founded in this spirit, including the Philadelphia School of Design for Women (1844), the Cooper Union Free Art School, New York (1854), and the Pratt Institute, Brooklyn (1877). Many other schools were founded for men and women, but women quickly assumed as high as 80 per cent of the student body. These included the Yale School of the Fine Arts, New Haven (1867), the College of Fine Arts, Syracuse University (1873, which became the John Crouse Memorial College for

Women in 1889), and the Massachusetts Normal Art School, Boston (for the training of art teachers, 1873). In addition to the other arts that women could practise as a trade at this time – design and decoration of household objects, sewing and fashion design, reproductive printmaking (lithography and wood-engraving, illustration) – came the invention of photography in 1839. As the first commercially successful photographic processes swept the world, women set up their own businesses as practitioners and teachers.

Ambitious women were also inspired by the women's movement of the 1840s and 1850s to strive for greater success in the fine arts. The example of Rosa Bonheur (q.v.) in France fired the imagination of more than one American woman, including the most colourful and effective of this consciously feminist generation of American artists, Harriet Hosmer. After studying with the sculptor Paul Stephenson in Boston, Hosmer studied anatomy in the Missouri Medical College, St Louis, and then returned home to Massachusetts to set up her own sculpture studio in 1851. Convinced that she needed to go beyond the resources of her own country, she travelled to Rome to study with the British sculptor John Gibson. Through Gibson she developed an English clientele and had her first success in Britain. She executed monumental marble sculptures as well as small-scale garden pieces and, when she became financially pressed, she created an appealing version of *Puck* sitting on a toadstool that was so popular that she supported herself well for years with commissions for copies. She was at the centre of a group of foreign women sculptors in Rome, mostly Americans, who attracted attention in the international art community. Hosmer and another American sculptor, Louise Lander, were the models for the main characters in Nathaniel Hawthorne's *The Marble Faun* (1860), in which he eulogised the woman artist as the epitome of the independent modern woman.

The phenomenon of women sculptors in Rome acting as a group or, as Henry James referred to them, "a white marmorean flock", was repeated in other centres where American women artists congregated. In Boston, students of the painter William Morris Hunt, who held art classes for women between 1868 and 1879, formed a well-known, if informal circle of professional painters and teachers who exhibited together in 1888. In New York, the Ladies Art Association was founded in 1867 to promote women artists through exhibitions and instruction. They also established a studio building in 1881 for women to live and work and had branches in Washington, DC, and Paris. They were succeeded by the National Association of Women Artists in 1889 and by numerous similar associations across the country including the Sketch Club of San Francisco, founded in the 1880s, and the Plastic Club of Philadelphia in 1895.

The most important outcome of women organising to promote their work in the middle decades of the 19th century was the Women's Pavilion at the Centennial Exposition held in Philadelphia in 1876. Organised and funded by women across the country, this building, located on the centennial fair grounds, exhibited women's achievements in such fields as journalism, medicine, science, literature, inventions, teaching, business, social work and art. Women's art ranged from the industrial to the decorative to the fine arts. Sculptures were shown by several members of the women sculptors' group in Rome, including Harriet Hosmer, Blanche Nevins, Florence Freeman and Margaret Foley. Members of the Ladies Art Association, such as Eliza Greatorex, also sent work, as did such prominent Philadelphia artists as Emily Sartain, who became principal of the Philadelphia School of Design for Women. Since the decentralised American art world did not allow any one group to hold national, much less international exhibitions of women artists – as did the Union des Femmes Peintres et Sculpteurs in Paris – the Women's Pavilion offered a rare opportunity for women from all over the country to be united.

The Women's Pavilion also marked the end of an era. After the Civil War (1861–5) a group of women emerged who had inherited the gains made by their activist mothers; they took professionalism in the arts as their right. Instead of attempting to solve societal problems through art education or activism, these women were less willing to settle for design, decorative or industrial arts and more interested in strategies for a successful fine art career. They tended not to join associations of women artists, but concentrated on the bastions of male authority in the arts – exclusive academies and prestigious exhibitions. They also had the means and desire to spend long periods abroad and occasionally expatriated to benefit their own careers rather than work for the betterment of women artists at home. They represented only a small segment of the total number of women making a living in the arts in the late 19th century, but their influence was enormous. Of this group the best known today are Elizabeth Gardner and Mary Cassatt.

Gardner and Cassatt continued an American tradition of artist expatriation beginning with Benjamin West in the 18th century. Like their predecessors and their contemporaries, Whistler and Sargent, they found that the opportunities for recognition in the fine arts were more plentiful in a world art capital such as Paris. Although Gardner followed a Salon career path and Cassatt joined the Impressionists, they each found a niche in Paris that did not exist at home. Elizabeth Gardner was inspired to become an artist by her art teacher at boarding school, Imogene Robinson, with whom she later taught at the Worcester School of Design and Fine Arts in Massachusetts. When their school closed in 1864 because of the Civil War, they went to Paris to become professional painters. Gardner quickly gravitated to the polished academic style of William Bouguereau and studied with Jean-Baptiste-Ange Tissier and Hughes Merle as well as in a women's co-operative studio. In 1871 she moved to an artist's enclave on the rue Notre-Dame des Champs where she was the neighbour of William Bouguereau and by 1879 announced her engagement to him. She concentrated on moving up in the Salon hierarchy, exhibiting frequently after 1868, winning an honourable mention in 1879, which made her *hors concours* (able to enter pictures without submitting to the jury), and medals in the Salon of 1887 (third-class) and the Exposition Universelle of 1889 (bronze). But her success in the Salon world was not enough to promote and sustain her in the public eye. In order to support herself she also executed and sold copies of paintings in the Louvre, painted portraits and "pot boilers" (inexpensive paintings on popular themes) for American tourists, wrote articles on events in Paris for American newspapers, held a weekly "afternoon" in her studio, and facilitated the sale of

Alice Barber Stephens: *The Women's Life Class at the Pennsylvania Academy of the Fine Arts*, *c*.1879; oil on cardboard (grisaille); 30.5 × 35.6 cm.; Pennsylvania Academy of the Fine Arts, Philadelphia; Gift of the artist

French paintings, including works by Bouguereau, to American collectors. She was the entrepreneurial American woman artist transplanted to Paris.

In comparison Mary Cassatt had her earliest art training in private schools in France and Germany before the age of 11, and studied at the elite Pennsylvania Academy of the Fine Arts for four years before arriving in Paris in late 1865. In Paris she attended Charles Chaplin's well-known class for women and had lessons from Jean-Léon Gérôme. She also began exhibiting at the Salon in 1868 but, rather than relying exclusively on an official career, by 1871 she began placing works with dealers in New York (Goupil) and Philadelphia (Bailey's jewellery store and Ernst Teubner). She cultivated art critics to receive greater attention in the press and sought out mentors among European artists in France, Italy and Spain. Her interest in contemporary trends in art led her to the Impressionists, among whom she formed many lasting friendships and a mentor relationship with Degas. In 1879 she withdrew from Salon competitions and began participating in the annual Impressionist exhibitions, highly publicised forums in which she could show as many works as she wanted. The Impressionist exhibitions also introduced her to a French circle of patrons that few American artists succeeded in attracting. Her work was handled by such French dealers as Durand-Ruel and Alphonse Portier and eventually Ambroise Vollard, and by 1894 her earnings allowed her to purchase a country house. Like Elizabeth Gardner, she also painted copies, pot boilers and portraits, and advised American collectors on purchases of French art.

The many other American women who established fine art careers abroad in the late 19th century represent variations on the themes established by Gardner and Cassatt. Elizabeth

Boott Duveneck, Mary MacMonnies (q.v.), Elizabeth Nourse (q.v.), Anna Klumpke (q.v.), Lilla Cabot Perry (q.v.), Sarah Dodson and Anna Lea Merritt (q.v.) are a few who became identified with artists and movements in Europe. The many American women who came to Paris just to study at the *académies* Julian, Colarossi and others are too numerous to count.

In the USA at this time, the traditional fine arts institutions were changing under pressure from the artists who had studied abroad. While the Pennsylvania Academy of the Fine Arts had admitted women as members as early as 1824 and the National Academy of Design in New York soon after in 1826, their classes remained the few that still restricted female attendance. In the 1860s only 20 per cent of the students were women (as opposed to 75 per cent at the Yale School of the Fine Arts) and life classes were closed to women at the Pennsylvania Academy until 1868 and at the National Academy of Design until 1871. In 1875 the Art Students League was founded in New York to oppose the conservative policies of the National Academy of Design and promote equal opportunities for men and women. In 1877 women spearheaded the founding of the Society of American Artists, which offered an alternative exhibiting opportunity for the women excluded from the National Academy.

In 1893 another truly international exhibition of women's art was held in the Woman's Building of the World's Columbian Exposition in Chicago. This was modelled on the Women's Pavilion of the Philadelphia Centennial Exposition of 1876, and its organisers displayed the talents of women artists in all media with a nod to the newly successful American women in the fine arts. The design of the building, by Sophia Hayden, provided for monumental decorations in painting and sculpture as well as exhibition halls for industrial, decorative and fine arts. Taking as its theme "women gathering fruits from the tree of knowledge", the display emphasised the role of newly improved educational opportunities in making women an effective force in modern society. When Elizabeth Gardner declined the commission to paint the key murals illustrating this theme, the two opposing subjects, *Primitive Woman* and *Modern Woman*, were given to Mary MacMonnies and Mary Cassatt. Sculptors for the architectural decorations included Alice Rideout, Enid Yandell and Anne Whitney (q.v.). In addition to the Woman's Building, the work of American women artists could be seen in the Department of Fine Arts of the fair as well as throughout the pavilions erected by each state.

In 1895 Cecilia Beaux (q.v.) became the first full-time teacher at the Pennsylvania Academy of the Fine Arts. She had studied with Catherine Drinker, Adolf Van der Wielan and William Sartain in Philadelphia before entering the Académie Julian, Paris, in 1888 as an established artist. In 1890 she set up her studio in Philadelphia as a portraitist and in 1899 moved to New York where she had gained the support of New York artists around Helena de Kay Gilder, a founder of the Society of American Artists, and her husband Richard Watson Gilder, publisher of the *Century* magazine. With her contacts in the press and exhibitions she established not only a powerful private clientele but a public presence. By the turn of the 20th century she was the most famous woman in the fine arts in the USA.

When modernist art theories swept the American art world in the early 20th century, most of the women who had gained a foothold in the fine arts were unceremoniously dropped from histories of American art. The only woman positioned to keep her place in a modernist re-writing of the 19th century was the Impressionist Mary Cassatt who, unlike her contemporaries, has held public attention to this day. Apart from this accident of taste and values, Cassatt should not be isolated from the field of women artists produced by the USA in the 19th century. As a group they showed a high level of talent, dedication and common sense to make careers for themselves out of the patchwork of opportunities and avenues that were open to them.

NANCY MOWLL MATHEWS

Canada

Women artists in 19th-century Canada shared many of the same entrepreneurial and pragmatic traits as their American sisters, but the dual heritage of France and Britain produced a unique cultural hybrid. In Quebec, the model of centralised patronage in the form of the French Catholic Church predominated; elsewhere, in the Maritimes, Ontario and the western provinces, British institutional models were dominant. In addition, irregular settlement patterns across western Canada resulted in variable conditions for cultural pursuits, which in many cases mirrored their American counterparts.

Instruction in the fine arts as well as handicrafts had been a regular feature of the Ursuline missions in Quebec since the 17th century. Elsewhere, some of the earliest evidences of art instruction and female cultural entrepreneurship are found in Halifax, with the opening of Mrs Thresher's private ladies school (1821) and Maria E. Morris's School of Drawing and Painting (1833). By the mid-19th century comparable developments could be found throughout Ontario in small ladies academies and private schools. It was here that the first official art school in Canada, the Ontario School of Art, opened in 1876. Although women students were in the minority, the presence of Mrs Charlotte Schreiber – the sole female founding member of the Royal Canadian Academy in 1880 and the only woman to gain full RCA membership until 1933 – as the school's only female instructor validated teaching as a profession for women. Over the next 20 years new art schools in such metropolitan centres as Toronto, Montreal and Halifax increased access to professional training and in certain instances provided teaching positions. Women were often instrumental in these initiatives: Miss Westmacott founded and taught at the Associated Art School in Toronto (1886); Mrs Anna Leonowens established the Victoria School of Art and Design in Halifax (1887); and Miss Mary Phillips opened her Montreal School of Art and Applied Design in 1891. Modelled on the South Kensington School of Art, these schools incorporated applied and industrial arts alongside fine arts with the goal of better employment opportunities for their female students.

Despite such enterprises, women seeking access to life drawing were required to study abroad. Florence Carlyle, Laura Muntz, Sidney Strickland Tully, Sophie Pemberton, Lucille Casey MacArthur and Emily Carr (q.v.) all trained outside Canada, in London, New York or the Parisian academies. Some, like Tully and Muntz, returned to offer classes modelled on Parisian ateliers. Others, like Lucille MacArthur, divided time between Europe and Canada. Success abroad, measured by Salon awards, school prizes and participation in international exhibitions, was essential for establishing professional status at home. Until the 1870s, provincial exhibitions, local agricultural fairs and occasional student exhibitions, such as the Halifax exhibition of William Eager's students in 1838, provided women artists with their primary exhibition venue. However, with the establishment of professional artist organisations – Ontario Society of Artists (1872) and Royal Canadian Academy (1880) – a few women artists did exhibit their work alongside male professionals. Many also participated successfully in the international exhibitions in Philadelphia (1876), Chicago (1893) and London (1886).

Parallel with these developments in the fine arts, many women chose photography as a profession. Although most were employed as photographic assistants, by 1891 as many as 135 professional women photographers had opened studios across Canada. In Winnipeg, Rossetta E. Carr employed two women in her staff of four. Most began as assistants to fathers, husbands and brothers and only later managed independent studios. Art journalism provided another professional avenue for women. Major newspapers and magazines printed articles by the painter Harriet Ford and the journalists Mrs Margaret Fairbairn, Madame Josephine Dandurand and Agnes Machar on a wide range of cultural topics. By the end of the 19th century, notwithstanding the restrictive and exclusionary practices within art academies, camera clubs and art schools, women had established themselves in Canada as professional artists, teachers, photographers, art critics and cultural activists.

NATALIE LUCKYJ

20th century

Critics have noted the emergence of a new female type in North American literary fiction of the 1890s. Invented by such authors as Kate Chopin, this woman drank, smoked, spoke her mind and moved about freely. A result of the commingling of politics and art, she was a caricature of contemporary feminists, and she lived a life of unprecedented personal freedom. This new heroine did not in any way reflect the reality of women's lives or feminist concerns; she signals, however, that women's lives were changing. While female social and familial roles remained constant (and continue to resist change even today), women had won a new visibility in the public sphere. If she were white and wealthy, a woman could obtain a sound education. By 1890, fully 10 per cent of all American graduate students were women, and by 1910 the American Census Bureau logged more than 9000 female physicians.

As part of this general phenomenon, most major North American art academies were open to women, though instruction of men and women was rarely comparable. By the third quarter of the 19th century, even life drawing classes, previously available only to men, began to admit women. This accommodation equalised a critical aspect of academic art training, but came at a time when the importance and influence of traditional academic training had permanently waned. Moreover, there were significant exceptions. At the National Academy of Design in New York, for example, it was not until

1903 that women were allowed to compete for the prestigious Prix de Rome, and the Academy continued to bar women from anatomy classes until 1914.

The National Academy was America's answer to the official art schools and exhibition networks of Europe. During the high point of academic influence in the 19th century, entrée into the European academies could establish artistic reputation; thus, it was training abroad in either the academies or the studios of recognised masters that remained the ambition of talented American and, especially, Canadian artists throughout the 19th century. Consistently lagging behind American art schools in equal opportunity, European academies were largely closed to women. In 1896 the Union des Femmes Peintres et Sculpteurs in Paris, established for just this purpose, stormed Europe's leading art institution, the Ecole des Beaux-Arts, and won the admission of women. Even when European training was available to women, however, it, too, was typically in a more compromised form than that offered to men, or in the studios of minor artists.

In response, women set about establishing options for themselves and others. The most extraordinary and vital alternative to traditional academic art instruction was the Art Students League of New York, founded in 1875 by, among others, the painter Helena de Kay Gardner. The ASL was characterised by strong liberal leanings from its founding, including women not only as fully matriculating students, but as faculty and policy makers on its governing boards. For the first several decades of operation, women effectively dominated the Board of Control and, through such artists as Alice Beach Winter and Cornelia Barnes, associated the institution with radical women's causes from suffrage to birth control. Rather than a formal curriculum, the ASL provided studios in which students could train with established artists for as long or as little as they chose. Isabel Bishop (q.v.) remembers the ASL in the 1920s as still "exciting! The students were arguing in the lunchroom. The teachers were having feuds ... And you could study whatever you wanted, pay for a month and go where you wished" (Munro 1979, p.148). Although the sculptor Marisol (q.v.) remembered the ASL as somewhat tired by the time of her matriculation in the 1950s, at least through World War II it remained a leading centre of progressive art teaching and governance. It is in operation to this day, and counts among its alumnae almost every major American woman artist of the first half of the 20th century, from Georgia O'Keeffe (q.v.) to Lee Krasner (q.v.), and many significant women artists, American and Canadian, thereafter.

Official support networks were equally closed to women. America's National Institute of Arts and Letters, founded in 1898, did not count a woman among its 250 members until 1907, when Julia Ward Howe, author of *The Battle Hymn of the Republic*, was elected. It took 19 years for a second woman to be admitted, the writer Mary Deland in 1926. Women visual artists were not represented until 1927, and according to statistics available in 1980, there were still only 12 living female artist-members, and seven deceased. That same year (1980), the American Academy, founded in 1905 with 50 members, could count among its living female artist-members only Georgia O'Keeffe and Isabel Bishop. Similarly, though women exhibited at the Royal Academy of Arts in Canada from its inception in 1880, women were not admitted to membership until well into the 20th century, and remain sparsely represented on its governing board.

Once again, in the absence of recognition and collegiality, women established their own alternatives. Occasionally, a cohesive group of artist-friends, both men and women, could serve as the kind of community that male artists had enjoyed since the time of the medieval guilds. Such was the case with the New York "14th Street Gang" of urban realists in the 1930s, also known as the Union Square group. Students and alumni of the ASL inspired by the teacher Kenneth Hayes Miller, the group counted among its numbers Minna Citron and Isabel Bishop. In Canada, a tradition of local, gender-blind artist-societies became the basic unit of Canadian arts organisations otherwise resistant to unification on a national or regional level. These have ranged in type from artists' groups such as the Painters Eleven in Ontario in the early 1950s to the more structured Emma Lake art camp in northern Saskatchewan in the late 1950s through the 1960s.

The integration of women into these groups was atypical, none the less. A more reliable community for women artists – and one that had persisted in female-dominated form since the 18th century – was the private salon. Social gatherings of like-minded people, salons provided male and female participants, as well as women organisers, with a much-needed sense of context. Without such a structure, the isolation and reticence that women artists experienced in each other's company could be numbing, as Miriam Schapiro (q.v.) recalled in 1975: "[Women] never discussed problems of ambition and ruthlessness. The spirit of the times did not permit such frankness … When Helen [Frankenthaler, q.v.] and I were together … we never discussed our paintings. We were in the same gallery and didn't discuss our work" (San Diego 1975, p.11).

In contrast, Romaine Brooks (q.v.) and Natalie Barney, together in Paris from 1915, made their salon famous for its commitment to serious art debate, as well as providing a special haven for lesbian artists. The New York salon of Florine Stettheimer (q.v.) became not only a gathering place for the international avant-garde, but the only site where she would exhibit her new work. The Whitney Studio Club, conducted from 1918 to 1930 in the Greenwich Village studios of Gertrude Vanderbilt Whitney (q.v.), served to gather and promote both male and female artists. Isabel Bishop remembered its impact in 1927: "I had no artist friends. No art life. Eventually, however, the Whitney Studio Club run by Gertrude Whitney was a resource … I became a member and showed my still lifes there" (Munro 1979, p.150). Bishop also recalled the salon of the women's rights activist Katherine Dreier: "There was the Société Anonyme, where Katherine Dreier held forth … The place was an inspiration" (ibid., p.148).

The salonnières were usually women of wealth and culture, and their contacts with artists transformed several into keen and influential patrons. In the depths of the Depression and after, these women founded the most significant museums of modern art in the world, completely transforming the North American art scene. Katherine Dreier was one of the major impresarios of the avant-garde in the 1920s, and an advanced painter in her own right. Her exhibitions of radical European art were the first of their kind, and her establishment of the Société Anonyme collection, now at the Yale University Art Gallery in New Haven, functioned as North America's first museum of modern art. Similarly, the artist and patron Gertrude Vanderbilt Whitney became the founder of the Whitney Museum of American Art, established expressly to provide a stage for neglected modern American artists. In the 1940s Peggy Guggenheim's gallery cum salon, Art of this Century, became the birthplace of the Abstract Expressionist movement, and often provided these artists' only source of income. When Guggenheim moved to Venice in 1946, the museum she established there served as the first introduction of contemporary North American art to Europe.

Many other women contributed to this trend, thereby extending into our own time women's historical role as patrons of the arts. Most notably, Baroness Hilla Rebay became the driving force behind the creation of the Guggenheim Museum of Non-Objective Art in New York; the collection of Lillie Bliss became the core of the Museum of Modern Art, also in New York; and Etta and Dr Claribel Cone established the Cone Wing at the Baltimore Museum of Art. In this way, women who were not artists exercised a decisive impact on world art.

It is not inevitable, however, that female entrepreneurs will support female artists. None of the women cited above promoted art by women exclusively, or even aggressively. Hilla Rebay's collection was notably weak in work by women, and Peggy Guggenheim, though organising such important exhibitions as 31 Women in 1943, was recorded as being hostile to women artists. This phenomenon was not restricted in time or place. When Jackson Pollock left Betty Parsons's stable of artists in the 1940s, she summarily dropped his wife, Lee Krasner, having given her exhibitions only grudgingly in the first place. As late as 1989, at least one major New York art dealer, Mary Boone, openly refused to handle women artists, citing the absence of collectors of "women's work".

During the first half of the 20th century, the most active promoter of art by women may have been Alfred Stieglitz in his New York galleries: 291, An Intimate Gallery and An American Place. Even before his well-known association with Georgia O'Keeffe, he had exhibited the work of such avant-garde women artists as Marguerite Thompson Zorach (q.v.), and a full range of women photographers, including Annie Brigman, Gertrude Käsebier (q.v.) and Jan Reece. His policies could hardly be described as gender-blind, however. He is reported to have remarked to Anita Pollitzer, who had brought him O'Keeffe's drawings: "Finally a woman on paper!" and continued to conflate sexuality and creativity as his relationship with O'Keeffe grew. He must be held at least partially accountable for the sexualised readings of O'Keeffe's work, since he often showed them alongside his own subtly erotic photographs of her. At one point, as O'Keeffe summered without him in New Mexico, he was said to have found "another young woman artist" to be his bright new star in her absence. Finally, although he gave O'Keeffe one-person shows each year for at least 20 years, he did not sell her work eagerly. When she once remarked to him that she "would like to make a living this year", he simply refused to part with her work. Stieglitz also stood in the way of O'Keeffe's decision to paint a mural for the Radio City Music Hall, New York, during the 1930s. She seems to have accepted these impediments resignedly, explaining in a later interview: "You try arguing with him and see where it gets you" (O'Keeffe 1977).

By the eve of World War I, women artists had broken down

most institutional barriers to equal education. The Armory Show, the controversial watershed exhibition of avant-garde European and American art held in New York in 1913, had included more than 40 women artists. Among them, Marguerite Zorach was recognised as producing the most radical paintings in America to that date; Edith Dimmock Glackens sold all eight of her exhibited paintings; and Ethel Myers and Abastenia St Leger Eberle (q.v.) attracted significant critical attention. That same year, these women and several others formed the artists' contingent in the suffrage parade down Fifth Avenue, led by Eberle and joined by hundreds of female (and male) workers and professionals. Like the progressive political policies of the Art Students League, the professional lives of women artists were often inseparable from – or at least circumscribed by – issues of gender in both the private and public spheres.

During this same period, O'Keeffe was living a typical female, middle-class American life, characterised by expanded educational opportunities and internalised gender limitations. She received her first art instruction as a routine part of the girls' curriculum at a convent school in Madison, Wisconsin. By 1905, with the youthful dream of "being an artist" and the encouragement of her art teacher, Elizabeth May Willis, she attended specialised classes at the Art Institute of Chicago. She described her first experience in the life drawing class there in terms that recreate the psycho-social barriers with which young women struggled: the male model was "... naked except for a small loincloth. I was surprised – I was shocked – blushed a hot and uncomfortable blush – didn't look around in my embarrassment and don't remember anything about the anatomy lesson. It was a suffering" (Slatkin 1993, p.217).

In 1907, with uneven training, O'Keeffe moved to New York to enrol at the Art Students League. She joined the studio of William Merritt Chase, who had established an environment particularly sympathetic to women. None the less, two years later, O'Keeffe still did not regard herself as an artist. With her family in financial crisis in Virginia and disillusionment about her abilities, she left New York for a position in Chicago as a commercial artist. This episode marked a major shift in her ambitions. In 1911 she returned to the family home, eyes weakened by a recent bout of measles, and prepared to abandon her dream of "being an artist". From the start, this notion had been predicated on masculinist ideas of "genius" for which there were almost no female role models. Once in Virginia, O'Keeffe turned her attention to teaching, the single career option for educated middle-class North American women at the beginning of the 20th century. Over the next several years, she taught at institutions in Virginia, South Carolina and Texas. As a sideline, she continued to study, pressed by her sisters and inspired by the principles of Arthur Wesley Dow, whose theories of abstract design and the expression of emotion renewed her interest in art. None the less, in 1915, when Stieglitz agreed to show her work, O'Keeffe wrote to Anita Pollitzer from South Carolina that she worried "there wasn't any use ruining good paper", that she "wasn't even sure that [she] had anything worth expressing" and that she had "almost decided never to try anymore" (Witzling 1991, p.213). O'Keeffe continued to be burdened by doubt throughout her life, as when she took to her bed following every major exhibition at Stieglitz's gallery, or when she was hospitalised in the 1930s for "nervous exhaustion". On the occasion of her retrospective at the Museum of Modern Art in 1946 (the first for a woman at that institution), O'Keeffe was asked what the primary requirement for an artist was; she replied: "Nerve" (Rubinstein 1982, p.185).

The first exhibition of O'Keeffe's work at Stieglitz's gallery in 1916 – a remarkable opportunity for a 29-year-old female artist – was a personal as well as a professional turning point. In 1917 she stopped teaching; more importantly, she later recalled:

> I found myself saying to myself – I can't live where I want to – I can't go where I want to – I can't do what I want to – I can't even say what I want to ... I decided I was a very stupid fool not to at least paint as I wanted to ... as that seemed to be the only thing ... that didn't concern anybody [Witzling 1991, p.222].

While O'Keeffe was apparently wilful from a young age, she also had within her family a number of self-sufficient, independent female role models: both her grandmothers had been frontier women who had raised their families alone, and two unmarried aunts had professional careers. At crucial points in her life, it was women to whom she turned, or who provided critical support: Elizabeth May Willis, her first art teacher and mentor; her sisters, who had urged her to return to study following her depression of 1911; her friend, Anita Pollitzer, who offered help and advice over several decades; and later, Mabel Dodge Luhan, who introduced her to New Mexico and provided both comfort and stimulation. It was Luhan whom she contacted when the press response to her work began to revolve around the perception of sexuality, and asked her for a piece of written criticism: "A woman might say something that a man can't – I feel there is something unexplored about woman that only a woman can explore" (ibid., p.225).

O'Keeffe's strong identity precluded the stereotype of the quiescent female. To the charge by a critic that her flowers were imitations of Stieglitz's photographs, she countered that while they occasionally worked with similar motifs, she had influenced Stieglitz at least as much as he had influenced her. At the height of the political battle for the passage of the Equal Rights Amendment in the 1940s, she wrote to Eleanor Roosevelt, who opposed the bill: "The ERA would write into the highest law of our land, legal equality for all. At present women do not have it and I believe we are considered – half the people" (ibid., p.228). Perhaps one of the surest indicators of O'Keeffe's independence – and one of the few uncharacteristic aspects of her education – is her disregard of European art and training; she did not even begin to travel abroad until late in life.

Of all women artists in the 20th century, O'Keeffe has been the most readily accepted into the mainstream canon of art history. Her first major retrospective (outside Stieglitz's galleries) was held in 1943 at the Art Institute of Chicago, followed by the Museum of Modern Art in 1946, and the Whitney Museum of American Art in 1970. The Whitney retrospective propelled her to star-status, and from that point on she was both well-exhibited and well-published, regarded as the *grande dame* of American painting. Also in 1970, she was awarded the prestigious gold medal for painting by the National Institute of Arts and Letters, a thoroughly male-based institution. None the less, neither O'Keeffe nor any other woman artist was mentioned in Horst W. Jansen's standard *History of Art* textbook, which was reprinted throughout the 1970s. Jansen opined in 1979 that he had "not been able to find a woman artist who clearly belongs in a one volume history of art" (Broude and Garrard 1994, p.16).

Following World War I, mounting feminist activity culminated in the passage of women's suffrage in Canada in 1918, and in America in 1920. Perhaps as a result, the decade of the 1920s has been seen as one of extraordinary female liberation. In fact, unprecedented numbers of American women moved out of the home and into the female labour force, which grew in this decade by 26 per cent to slightly more than two million. Despite this, there is little evidence that a real revolution occurred in women's economic or social roles; the employment statistics reflected a primary increase in traditional, low-paying, clerical and domestic occupations. Women who had been employed in non-gender-based positions during the war were quickly demobilised after it, and between 1910 and 1930 the number of female physicians in America actually declined from 9015 to 6825.

One theory holds that this failure of economic and social progress was the result of the decline of feminist activism following the victory of suffrage. This may also help to explain the decreased numbers of large-scale mural commissions offered to women at the end of the 1920s in anticipation of the World's Fairs from those offered on the occasion of the Panama-Pacific Exposition in 1915: by the later date, feminist agitation was simply not in evidence. The phenomenon of the "flapper" of the 1920s, a kind of materialisation of the "liberated" fantasies of 19th-century pulp fiction writers, obscured the stagnation into which American women had slipped. Newly stringent immigration quotas, the sanctioning of racist organisations and practices, and a dead halt to legislation positively effecting the status of women were all related issues in this decade.

In both Canada and the USA, female art students turned increasingly for their training to institutions that stressed "practical" employment, such as the School of Applied Design for Women in New York. The School prepared women for commercial fields from interior design to needlework, thus supporting traditionally female domestic arts and crafts. While women attended these and other art schools in growing numbers, however, very few made the transition from amateur, or student status, to professional artist. This transition was facilitated in America in the 1930s with progressive federal legislation meant to combat the economic crisis of the Depression. The best that can be said of the status of women artists in the 1920s is that the decade produced an army of well-trained young women prepared to take on the challenges of professionalism offered during the presidency of Franklin Delano Roosevelt.

The variety of work-relief programmes developed by the Roosevelt administration during the Depression, known generally as the Works Progress Administration (WPA), was remarkable on at least two levels. To begin with, they acknowledged artists as workers, were committed to supporting them, and thereby established the first systematic episode of public patronage in North American history. Second, by all accounts, official and anecdotal, the federal programmes were

gender-neutral. The first Canadian programme to present this level of national, bias-free support was established only in 1957 as the Canada Council, though it is now stronger than its contemporary American counterpart, the National Endowment for the Arts and the Humanities.

An individual qualified for the WPA art unit, the Federal Art Project, by taking a general exam or submitting proof of professional activities. Not only were large numbers of female art students automatically qualified, those women unable or unwilling to participate in higher education could still display expertise. Artists who met the additional qualification of financial need (roughly 90 per cent) submitted their work on a monthly basis to regional supervisors and were provided with regular salaries. Ten per cent were admitted on the basis of skill alone, and were almost invariably placed in the Mural Division of the programme. Major mural commissions were then awarded from anonymous competitions of unsigned sketches. Isabel Bishop, Alice Neel (q.v.), Louise Nevelson (q.v.), Lucienne Bloch (q.v.) and Lee Krasner, among others, won their first major commissions through the mural division of the WPA. Krasner had abandoned painting in 1933 at the peak of the Depression to pursue a more practical occupation: she enrolled in a teacher-training course at the City College of New York. Like many artists, she was able to return to painting in 1935 due to FAP support.

It is probable that Eleanor Roosevelt was responsible for the non-discriminatory policies of the WPA, just as she was responsible for the influx of female government officials around the President. Women comprised 41 per cent of all artists on work-relief, not only as practitioners, but also as teachers and, importantly, administrators. The photographer Berenice Abbott (q.v.) was supervisor of the Photography Division; the African-American artists Augusta Savage (q.v.) and Gwendolyn Bennett were directors of the Harlem Art Center, New York, a pulse point for the Harlem Renaissance; Ruth Reeves (q.v.) was national co-ordinator of the Index of American Design, a permanent archive of American folk arts directly benefiting anonymous work by women and African-Americans; Lee Krasner, Elizabeth Olds and Helen Lundeberg (q.v.) were local supervisors; and Audrey McMahon was the New York regional director of the Federal Art Project. This position gave McMahon supreme authority over the biggest and most productive art-producing region in North America: almost half of all American artists lived in New York. While many women were engaged in political activity through these government positions, others worked outside official networks by returning to earlier female traditions of unionisation and group activism: Alice Neel aided in the founding of the Unemployed Artists Association, Bernarda Bryson was one of the founders of the Artists' Union, and Margaret Bourke-White (q.v.) was vice-chairman of the American Artists Congress.

Women experienced in this period an unprecedented opportunity to work at their art as professionals. Commenting on this in the context of the Art Students League, Isabel Bishop remarked: "There was absolutely no feeling in those days … about my being a girl. It just didn't come up" (Munro 1979, p.148). The assumption of professionalism and the spirit of camaraderie facilitated an explosion of work by women. These factors may also have helped to generate the phenomenon of

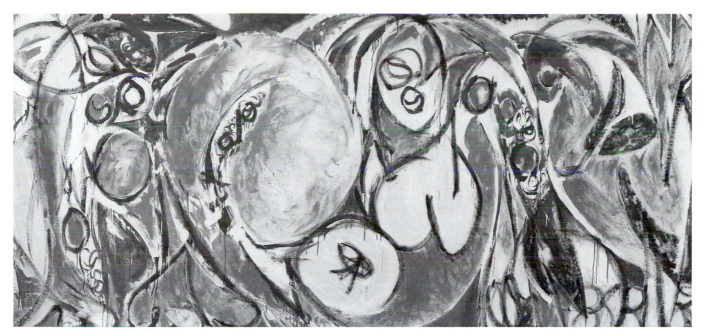

Lee Krasner: *The Seasons*, 1957; oil on canvas; 235.6 × 517.3 cm.; Whitney Museum of American Art, New York; purchased with funds from Frances and Sydney Lewis (by exchange), the Mrs Percy Uris Purchase Fund and the Painting and Sculpture committee

the egalitarian art colony during and after the period of government support. In Woodstock, New York, Provincetown and Gloucester, Massachusetts, Ogunquit, Maine, Laguna Beach, California, and Taos, New Mexico, women artists played an equal role and benefited equally from the support and friendship these communities offered. Similarly, the founding of American Abstract Artists (AAA) in New York during this period, ostensibly to provide a context for artists working outside the dominant realist trend, provided an unusual number of women artists and artist couples with shared visibility and responsibility. It was at AAA, for example, that Lee Krasner secured her reputation as a major player in the American abstract art movement.

None the less, it would be naive to suggest that gender-bias and discrimination could be exorcised from the individual consciousness through legislation. In fact, there had been a dark underbelly to the support of working women in the 1930s, ironically promoted by Roosevelt's female Secretary of Labor, Frances Perkins, who called throughout her tenure for the return of married women to the home. This idea dominated the later 1940s, and remained a key obstacle to the acceptance and advancement of the working wife and mother, both socially and psychologically.

The generation of women artists to come to maturity before World War II was the first to have experienced equal access to artistic training and professional support. In 1943, when federal programmes were terminated to focus energy on the war, these women lost the firm footing of government patronage. Almost simultaneously, the dominance of the New York School of painters, later known as the Abstract Expressionists and predicated on the machismo mystique of explosive genius, served to undercut women further. The rejection of women artists by the New York School was both individual and programmatic; it was supported by reactionary social trends

following World War II, and quickly snapped shut the window of opportunity for women opened by the Depression. Throughout this period, the painter Lee Krasner was in a unique position as an artist of reputation and the wife of the leading star of the New York School, Jackson Pollock.

Krasner's training was rigorous and systematic. Recognised as a prodigy, she won a scholarship to the Women's Art School of Cooper Union, an institution whose popularity grew rapidly after World War II, and later entered the traditional National Academy of Design. In 1934 she joined the Federal Art Project, studied at the Art Students League, and from 1937 to 1940 painted in the studio of Hans Hofmann. Throughout the 1930s and 1940s, Hofmann's School of Fine Arts trained several of the soon-to-be prominent painters of the New York School. He also became a popular teacher to many of the most gifted women of the period. The sculptor Louise Nevelson, fresh from the Art Students League, travelled to Munich in 1931 to study with him, and joined him again in New York after his emigration. Krasner remained a devotee, despite what she described as his straightforward male chauvinist posture. She recalled his critiques of her work as the same back-handed praise that earlier women artists had experienced: "This painting is so good you'd never know it was done by a woman!" (Chadwick 1990, p.302).

These attitudes extended beyond professional contacts into art-social networks. The 8th Street Club, with the Cedar Bar, the two major meeting places for the New York School painters, admitted women only as audience. Women were effectively silenced – excluded from active participation in the intense discussions with critics and curators that the male artists found so inspiring. Women were never allowed to attend board meetings or policy discussions, even as non-participants. At the Cedar, Krasner remembered being told by Barnett Newman: "we don't need dames", and felt that women were generally "treated like cattle" (ibid., p.303). For women working in non-traditional media, the sense of threat on the part of male artists could be even greater. Nevelson was told by a colleague that she "had to have balls to be a sculptor" (Slatkin 1993, p.250). More significantly, she received press critiques such as the following: "We learned the artist was a woman in time to check our enthusiasm. Had it been otherwise, we might have hailed these sculptural expressions as by surely a great figure amongst the moderns" (Chadwick 1990, p.308).

Interestingly, two female members of the group loosely identified as the second generation of Abstract Expressionists – though they were painting alongside their male colleagues in the first generation – do not recollect any significant bias. Helen Frankenthaler wrote: "It was a relatively trusting and beautiful period ... there seemed to be little that was motivated, threatening, or contaminating ... It was lucky to be in one's early 20s with a group of painters to argue painting with" (Munro 1979, p.216). It is difficult to contextualise Frankenthaler's perceptions, but she came to the group with many of the traditional accoutrements by which females seemed benign even while trespassing in a man's world: she was both wealthy and attractive; she had not yet made a significant artistic reputation (especially relative to a figure such as Krasner); and she was introduced into these circles by her close friend, the "Kingmaker" (sic) of critics, Clement Greenberg.

Grace Hartigan (q.v.), who corroborated Frankenthaler's impressions with her own, could not be characterised as similarly non-threatening. In 1952 she became one of the first artists of this generation to earn an international reputation when her painting, *Persian Jacket*, was purchased by the Museum of Modern Art in New York. Hartigan may have compensated by presenting herself as "one of the boys", painting for a brief period under the name of George and severing ties with her husband and children. As in centuries past, the neutering of one's female identity was not an uncommon strategy: the painter Gertrude Greene (q.v.) also adopted a male persona, Peter G. Greene, and Elaine de Kooning (q.v.) and Lee Krasner (whose real name was Lenore, not the androgynous Lee) signed their paintings only with their initials. Alice Neel and Louise Nevelson, who, like Hartigan, could not juggle the pressures of their art with those of motherhood, also gave up their children. Nevelson even felt compelled to promote her machismo by responding to the remark about her lack of "balls" with the protest: "I have balls!"

Following Hartigan, Frankenthaler was the next woman artist of this period to win widespread recognition. By the early 1960s, Frankenthaler had been featured in *Life*, *Look* and *Time*, attaining a prominence that was climaxed in 1969 by one of the first full-scale retrospectives of a woman artist at the Whitney. In contrast, such artists as Krasner and Nevelson, who came into the New York School as artistic contenders, did not fare so well. It was only in 1978 with the Whitney Museum exhibition *Abstract Expressionism: The Formative Years* that Krasner was restored to her pivotal place as a leading abstractionist of the early 1940s. Following a flurry of rediscovery, she received a long-overdue retrospective one year before her death, declaring it "too late". Similarly, Nevelson fell into obscurity during the Abstract Expressionist episode and worked for long periods in isolation and neglect. At one point,

she had not sold a piece for more than 30 years and, for lack of space, burned much of the contents of her studio. Since the 1970s and the purposeful reclamation of women artists, Nevelson has been recognised as one of the leading sculptors of the 20th century.

As in the 1930s, the appropriateness of combining family and career became a crucial issue for many female artists of this generation. Early in the century, ambitious, educated women often made the self-conscious decision not to marry. Between 1877 and 1924, 75 per cent of all American women who earned the PhD were single; in 1920, 88 per cent of all professional women were single, and the female workforce itself was overwhelmingly dominated by unmarried women under 25 until World War II. Those career women who married usually gave up their ambitions at this time, or certainly with the arrival of a baby. Marjorie Organ Henri's transition from painter to "muse" is characteristic of the early part of the century. After marrying the prominent Ash Can School painter, Robert Henri, she spent most of her time posing for him. When asked about her own work, she said that she did not have "the extra grain of ego she needed" to persevere and that if she had, she "might have spoiled her understanding disposition" (Rubinstein 1982, p.168). She referred to her husband as "The Boss", asserted that he had enough ego for both of them, and that his art was simply more important than hers.

Forty years later, Lee Krasner was still significantly derailed as an artist by her marriage. Despite her memories of shabby treatment by the New York School coterie, Krasner insisted that her husband Jackson Pollock was neither misogynist nor chauvinist. None the less, she said of their relationship: "he was the important thing. I couldn't do enough for him" and admitted that her own work began to seem "irrelevant" (Cincinnati 1989, p.28). She found corroboration for this view all around her. In 1949 Krasner and Pollock showed their work together in an exhibition at the Sidney Janis Gallery, *Artists: Man and Wife*. Predictably, the exhibition title defined her role as dependent and subsidiary. This experience, and subsequent reviews, discouraged Krasner from exhibiting again until 1951, and she later destroyed most of her works from this period. She did not recover her pre-Pollock productivity until his death.

Even Georgia O'Keeffe, who remained consistently committed to painting throughout her life, struggled with the tension of her public and private roles. Between 1917 and 1937 she posed for more than 500 photographs by her husband, a task that drained her of time and energy. In the 1930s, as her independence grew, she met with increasing resistance from Stieglitz. She wrote in 1932: "I am divided between my man and a life with him ... I have to get along with my divided self the best way I can" (Slatkin 1993, p.227). In contrast, the African-American artist Alma Thomas (q.v.) described the freedoms her choice to remain childless and unmarried allowed: "I paint when I feel like it. I didn't have to come home. Or I could come home late and there was nobody to interfere with what I wanted ... It was what I wanted, and no argument. That is what allowed me to develop" (Munro 1979, pp.195–6).

Nevertheless, a woman artist's professional life could be compromised by the demands of daily life without the additional complications of family. The Canadian painter Emily

Carr (q.v.) was a promising young art student and, like many Canadians, especially from the West Coast, she looked for training abroad. Between 1890 and 1911 she studied in San Francisco, London and Paris. On her return to British Columbia, she decided to run a boarding house as a means of support while devoting herself to her art. Ironically, domestic duties overwhelmed her, and she entered a long period of artistic dormancy. It was only when she was "discovered" by the director of the National Gallery in Ottawa in 1927 that she was relieved of major economic concerns and returned fully to creative life. Loosely affiliated with the Group of Seven, and encouraged by them, Carr was a prolific painter until a stroke ten years later, when she transferred her attention primarily to writing. Carr's circuitous path was characteristic of the necessarily erratic lives of many women professionals, married or single.

For many of these artists, the decision not to marry, not to have children, or to abandon either or both, was based not only in practicality but in the deeply ingrained belief that a woman was fundamentally circumscribed by her social and biological roles. This, in turn, was supported by social legislation. In 1940, for example, a married woman could not hold her own earnings in 11 US states and could not make contracts in 16 US states. In several states, she could be divorced if she were not a virgin upon marriage, could be sued for damages in the case of adultery, could not sue for child support, did not have guardianship rights, and could not serve on juries. By the 1950s, through the new medium of television, the image of woman as solely devoted wife and mother in such programmes as *The Donna Reed Show* and *Father Knows Best* became iconic. The sculptor Louise Bourgeois (q.v.) wrote: "I have had a guilt complex about pushing my art, so much so that every time I was about to show I would have some sort of attack. So I decided it was better simply not to try … the work was done and hidden away" (Munro 1979, p.156).

The conflict of homemaker and career woman, while still a challenge for many women, was a significant impediment well into the 1960s. The oeuvre of Eva Hesse (q.v.) was produced just before her premature death in 1970, and she is an important transitional figure on many levels. On the one hand, like so many women before her, Hesse received formative training at the Art Students League. She also studied at the Pratt Institute of New York and Yale University, two rigorously professional institutions whose popularity at this point placed them among the most competitive contemporary art schools. Hesse was an aggressive and successful student. In the matter of separate identity, however, she struggled as had older women artists:

> I think at the time I met the man I married, I shouldn't say I went backwards, but I did, because he was a more mature and developed artist. He would push me in his direction and I would be unconsciously somewhat influenced by him. Yet when I met him, I had already had a drawing show which was much more me [Cincinnati 1989, p.269].

There was increasing recognition in Hesse's self-analysis that this conflict was at least partly pre-determined by socially constructed gender roles. According to Alice Neel, women artists of the 1940s and 1950s did not care "to fight the fight

in the streets" (*ibid.*, p.40). With Hesse's generation, the fight for recognition, like that prior to 1920, became political.

In 1966 NOW (National Organization for Women) was founded in acknowledgement of the need for a watchdog organisation to monitor gender bias. Three years later, this awareness led to the first organised protests against racism and sexism in the American art world, initially and specifically aimed at the three leading American art museums: the Metropolitan Museum of Art, the Museum of Modern Art and the Whitney Museum of American Art in New York. Throughout the 1970s, artist/activist groups such as WAR (Women Artists in Revolution), Where We At, Black Women Artists, WSBAL (Women, Students and Artists for Black Art Liberation), the Ad Hoc Women Artists Group, Women in the Arts, the Los Angeles Council of Women Artists, Ariadne and the Women's Caucus for Art conducted political actions demanding equal representation in schools, exhibitions and legislative bodies. The most successful Canadian counterpart, CAR (Canadian Artists' Representation), founded in 1968, successfully lobbied the government to legislate protection from unfair or unremunerated exploitation of both male and female artists' names and works. By 1981 there were more than 40 artist-run co-operatives in Canada, several of which, such as the Women's Cultural Building in Toronto, Womanspirit in London, Ontario, Manitoba Women in the Arts, Powerhouse in Montreal and Vancouver Women in Focus maintain a specifically feminist orientation.

As conceded by one Whitney curator, the pressure was effective. The activists Betye Saar (q.v.) and Barbara Chase-Riboud (q.v.) were included in the first major exhibition of African-American women at the Whitney in 1970; the percentage of women artists shown in the Whitney Annual exhibition rose from 15 per cent in 1969 to 22 per cent in 1970; the percentage of solo exhibitions by women artists in New York galleries rose from an average of 9 per cent in 1970 to 24 per cent by 1980; and supportive services such as the international liaison network, WEB (West-East Bag), the Women's Art Registry of slides, and the Women's Caucus's Job Roster were established across the country. These developments were not restricted to the USA. The end of the 1970s represented a high point in the exhibiting, critical discussion and the recognition of North American women artists in general. It is not coincidental that renewed feminist visibility at this time, combined with institutional fiscal crises, led to the shift towards co-education on the part of many gender-segregated American and Canadian colleges and universities.

As they had in the past, women also set about establishing options to traditional educational and professional venues, especially of a feminist nature. Judy Chicago (q.v.) organised the first feminist art curriculum at the California State College at Fresno in 1970, a model programme providing context, support and training by and for women. She wrote: "I realized that if the art community as it existed could not provide me with what I needed in order to realize myself, then I would have to commit myself to developing an alternative" (Slatkin 1993, p.284). In 1971 Chicago and her colleague Miriam Schapiro expanded the programme and re-established it at the California Institute of the Arts, a cutting-edge institution on the West Coast well-known for its progressive ideas and policies. Although Chicago resigned in 1973 in protest against

CalArts' failure to provide adequate financial support, and Schapiro resigned in 1975 to return to New York, the programme left an enduring educational, artistic and social legacy. In 1973 Chicago, Sheila de Bretteville and Arlene Raven founded the Woman's Building, which remained an active force in Los Angeles until 1991, housing the Feminist Studio Workshop and a women's art gallery, Womanspace. In 1975 Chicago also published her autobiography *Through the Flower*. This ground-breaking text recorded the development of Chicago's personal and artistic maturity from the point of view of feminist awareness. That same year Chicago began a work that is widely acknowledged as the first piece of feminist art, *The Dinner Party*, created as a collaborative project reclaiming the lives of forgotten women in history.

Chicago had previous experience with collaboration and workshop practice in a project that became the most significant component of the CalArts programme, Womanhouse. Here, Chicago, Schapiro and a group of female graduate students rehabilitated a dilapidated Los Angeles mansion, utilising the spaces as exhibition sites for installation and performance art. These media had begun to emerge in Los Angeles in the 1960s, ultimately derived from the 1950s concepts of the Happening and multi-media presentation. The latter had been developed, in particular, at Black Mountain College, North Carolina, a short-lived, post-World War II art school where many of the most exciting inter-disciplinary collaborations among students, teachers and professional artists first occurred.

Throughout the 1970s women not only dominated the performance and installation genres, but were its leaders. Issues specific to women's bodies and experience were explored through subjects such as the goddess, female sexuality, fertility and gender roles, and paralleled the international trend towards "écriture feminine", or "writing the female body". Similarly, many women in this period also attempted to recover women's traditional "craft" media for high art, resulting in stylistic episodes known as Pattern and Decoration, Femmage and the resurgence of collage, assemblage and photo-montage.

Some of the most innovative work in this context was produced by Faith Ringgold (q.v.). As a middle-class, African-American female, Ringgold knew at a young age that she would need to work to live, but, more importantly, her mother – a fashion designer – expected her to "be somebody" (*Faith Ringgold* 1991). Ringgold was aware of her artistic ambitions in her early teens, but does not recall specific encouragement from her teachers. In fact, she was once told that she did not know how to draw; it was from that moment, she says, that she knew she was an artist, because no one had the power to delimit who she could be. Ringgold enrolled at the City College of New York, and since the liberal arts programme was closed to women, she majored in education, receiving an undergraduate degree in 1955 and a master's degree in 1959. From 1955 she taught in the New York City public schools, resigning only in 1973 to devote herself full-time to her art.

Ringgold had begun to work seriously as an independent artist in the early 1960s, turning her dining room into studio space. By the late 1960s, she was politically active in both the African-American and women's rights movements, founding a series of organisations including Where We At and WSBAL. She also produced several of the most significant, politically

charged paintings of this period in the Pop mode. None the less, like the lives of so many artists, hers was a balancing act. She said of this time:

> Had it not been for Mother taking the girls [Ringgold's daughters] to Europe that summer, I would not have been able to complete those paintings … That was why I walked out [from her marriage] … I didn't want to spend my summer cleaning the house and cooking … I spent my days at the gallery painting till well into the night. At the end of the summer [her husband] had left. Who could blame him? I needed him, but I needed my freedom too … If I called him now he would just say, "Don't let those girls go away alone. Keep them with you. Give up the art" [Slatkin 1993, p.366].

Shortly after this period, Ringgold became deeply interested in African culture, teaching courses on African art and integrating African motifs into her compositions. The difficulty of transporting her work led her to soft, cloth supports and inspired by a family – and cultural – tradition of story-telling, she began to produce story quilts in the early 1980s. The use of fabric brought personal, ethnic and political identification to her art. Her mother had worked with fabric all her life, and the quilt had been an early African-American woman's medium. Like Chicago in *The Dinner Party*, Ringgold was consciously aware that she was blurring the traditional boundaries between craft – "female art" – and fine art – "male art". When asked if people called her sewn pieces "crafts", she answered: "Claes Oldenburg's soft typewriters are sewn pieces, and I never heard anyone call them craft. It's who's doing it that makes it craft" (*ibid.*, p.322).

Throughout the 1970s, women played a catalytic role in redirecting mainstream art currents. Not only did women artists introduce new genres, techniques and subject matter, they effectively brought to a close the "pure painting" movements that had dominated modernism since about 1870. As artists working from female experience, they went far in completing the historical record, moving women out of the role of passive theme into that of active speaker. One author has written that, in the past: "it has been possible to construct a history of mainstream art without women. In the future, this will not be so, in large part because of the contributions made during this period" (Randy Rosen in Cincinnati 1989, p.22). None the less, there is significant evidence that the 1980s brought with it a reactionary trend like that documented in Susan Faludi's broad socio-cultural study, *Backlash* (1991).

The emergence of the American New Right – the Moral Majority – at the end of the 1970s renewed the conflict around the "appropriate" role of women, and was founded at least in part on a platform of anti-feminism. Although during the decade the barriers in law, and even custom, to a woman's autonomy were substantially eliminated, the female role of child-bearer and family caretaker became a prominent issue once again. Reflecting the social climate, a number of the most important New York galleries refused to carry the work of women, citing the absence of collectors, or the likelihood of an artist's distracting pregnancies. Museum statistics reflect a similar trend. Throughout the 1980s, there was a marked decline of women artists included in the Whitney Biennial, experiencing an initial rapid drop from 32 per cent in 1979 to

20 per cent in 1981. In 1984, when the Museum of Modern Art opened its new facilities with the exhibition *An International Survey of Painting and Sculpture*, only 13 of 164 artists were women. This clearly had an impact on an artist's earning capacity. During the period 1980–85, 40 per cent of those classifying themselves as professional artists in the USA were women; during the same period, a National Endowment for the Arts survey recorded the average annual income from art of men at $13,000 compared to $5700 for women.

It was in response to the Museum of Modern Art's exhibition that a group of artists and art historians came together to form an activist group known as the Guerrilla Girls. Concealing their identities in gorilla costumes, they post data throughout the art districts of Manhattan documenting, among other issues, sexism and racism in New York galleries and museums. They insist upon the profound and often damaging connection between a woman artist's professional life and gender role expectations on the part of society. They have kept "the fight in the streets" by picketing art institutions, attracting the news media with information-based performances and promoting their activities through sets of slides and videos. In the arena of mainstream art developments, the opening of the National Museum of Women in the Arts in 1987 in Washington, DC, has also served to impede the backlash. Although criticised as exclusive and exclusionary, it is the first museum in North America to be solely devoted to art by women, and founded by a private collector, Wilhelmina Cole Holliday, it has kept alive the tradition of female patronage of the arts.

Women artists have struggled inordinately with the conflicting demands of female identity and artistic identity. Throughout the 1960s, at least, art has exacted a high psychic toll on women: in the 20th century, this would include the depressions and alcoholism of Alice Trumbull Mason (q.v.); Alice Neel's breakdowns and suicide attempts; Nevelson's persistent but never-acted-upon desire to kill herself; Grace Hartigan's relinquishing of her name and children; even Georgia O'Keeffe's "nervous exhaustion" following exhibitions. Perhaps the greatest shift for women in the final decade of the 20th century – despite resistance to the contrary – is the decline of institutionalised scorn towards the working wife and mother. Consequently, young women artists do not document the same intensity of conflicting social roles with which earlier artists were so heavily burdened. Even now, however, a gap separates ideals of equal opportunity from realities of economic discrimination. Along with new freedoms, the feminisation of poverty in North America has also grown. Fully 70 per cent of the adult poor are women, and women artists continue to earn less than 50 per cent of the income of male counterparts.

DEBORAH JEAN JOHNSON

Bibliography

Elizabeth Fries Ellet, *Women Artists in All Ages and Countries*, New York: Harper, 1859; London: Bentley, 1860

"Woman's position in art", *The Crayon*, viii, 1861, pp.25–8

H.W., "Lady-artists in Rome", *Art Journal*, v, 1866, pp.177–8

Harriet Ford, "The Royal Canadian Academy of Arts", *Canadian Magazine*, iii, 1894, p.48

M.E. Dignam, "Canadian women and the development of art",

Women of Canada: Their Life and Work, Toronto: National Council of Women, 1900; reprinted 1975

Anna Lea Merritt, "A letter to artists: Especially women artists", *Lippincott's Monthly Magazine*, lxv, 1900, pp.463–9; reprinted in *Love Locked Out: The Memoirs of Anna Lea Merritt*, ed. Galina Gorokhoff, Boston: Museum of Fine Arts, 1982

Newton MacTavish, "Laura Muntz and her art", *Canadian Magazine*, xxxvii, 1911, pp.419–24

31 Women, exh. cat., Art of the Century, New York, 1943

Jane C. Giffen, "Susanna Rowson and her academy", *Magazine Antiques*, xcviii, 1970, pp.436–40

Paul Duval, *Four Decades: The Canadian Group of Painters and Their Contemporaries, 1930–1970*, Toronto: Clarke Irwin, 1972

Doris Cole, *From Tipi to Skyscraper: A History of Women in Architecture*, Boston: I Press, 1973

Francis V. O'Connor, ed., *Art for the Millions: Essays from the 1930s by Artists and Administrators of the WPA Federal Art Project*, Greenwich, CT: New York Graphic Society, 1973

Judy Chicago, *Through the Flower: My Struggle as a Woman Artist*, New York: Doubleday, 1975; 2nd edition, New York: Doubleday, and London: Women's Press, 1982

From Women's Eyes: Women Painters in Canada, exh. cat., Agnes Etherington Art Centre, Kingston, 1975

Miriam Schapiro: The Shrine, the Computer and the Dollhouse, exh. cat., Mandeville Art Gallery, University of California at San Diego, 1975

Some Canadian Women Artists, exh. cat., National Gallery of Canada, Ottawa, 1975

Judith Paine, "The Women's Pavilion of 1876", *Feminist Art Journal*, iv/4, 1975–6, pp.5–12

7 American Women: The Depression Decade, exh. cat., Vassar College Art Gallery, Poughkeepsie, NY, 1976

Jane C. Nylander, "Some print sources of New England schoolgirl art", *Magazine Antiques*, cx, 1976, pp.292–301

Women Artists, 1550–1950, exh. cat., Los Angeles County Museum of Art, and elsewhere, 1976

Marie Elwood, "The state dinner service of Canada, 1898", *Material History Bulletin*, Spring 1977, p.41

O'Keeffe, video, produced and directed by Perry Miller Adato, WNET 13 Production, 1977

Guy Robert, *L'Art au Québec depuis 1940*, Montreal: La Presse, 1977

Women in American Architecture: A Historic and Contemporary Perspective, exh. cat., Whitney Library of Design, 1977

Abstract Expressionism: The Formative Years, exh. cat., Herbert F. Johnson Museum of Art, Ithaca, NY, and elsewhere, 1978

Terry Fenton and Karen Wilkin, *Modern Painting in Canada*, Edmonton: Hurtig, 1978

Great Expectations: The European Vision of Nova Scotia, 1749–1848, exh. cat., Mount Saint Vincent Art Gallery, Halifax, 1978

Anthea Callen, *Angel in the Studio: Women in the Arts and Crafts Movement, 1870–1914*, London: Astragal, 1979; as *Women Artists of the Arts and Crafts Movement, 1870–1914*, New York: Pantheon, 1979

Eleanor Munro, *Originals: American Women Artists*, New York: Simon and Schuster, 1979

Painters Eleven in Retrospect, exh. cat., Robert McLaughlin Gallery, Oshawa, Ontario, 1979

Julie Graham, "American women artists' groups: 1867–1930", *Woman's Art Journal*, i/1, 1980, pp.7–12

Martha J. Hoppin, "Women artists in Boston, 1870–1900: The pupils of William Morris Hunt", *American Art Journal*, xiii/1, 1981, pp.17–46

Evelyn de R. McMann, *Royal Canadian Academy of Arts: Exhibitions and Members, 1880–1979*, Toronto: University of Toronto Press, 1981

Charlotte Streifer Rubinstein, *American Women Artists from Early Times to the Present*, Boston: Hall, 1982

Mary Ann Stankiewicz, "The creative sister: An historical look at women, the arts, and higher education", *Studies in Art Education*, xxiv/1, 1982, pp.49–55

Kenneth W. Wheeler and Virginia Lee Lussier, eds, *Women, the Arts and the 1920s in Paris and New York*, New Brunswick, NJ: Transaction, 1982

Robert Bringhurst and others, eds, *Visions: Contemporary Art in Canada*, Vancouver: Douglas and McIntyre, 1983

Lee Krasner: A Retrospective, exh. cat., Museum of Fine Arts, Houston, and elsewhere, 1983

Rediscovery: Canadian Women Photographers, 1841–1941, exh. cat., London Regional Art Gallery, London, Ontario, 1983

Social Concern and Urban Realism: American Painting of the 1930s, exh. cat., Boston University Art Gallery, 1983

Madeleine Fidell-Beaufort, "Elizabeth Jane Gardner Bouguereau: A Parisian artist from New Hampshire", *Archives of American Art Journal*, xxiv/2, 1984, pp.2–9

David Rubinstein, *Before the Suffragettes: Women's Emancipation in the 1890s*, Brighton: Harvester, and New York: St Martin's Press, 1986

American Women Artists, 1830–1930, exh. cat., National Museum of Women in the Arts, Washington, DC, and elsewhere, 1987

Paula Blanchard, *The Life of Emily Carr*, Vancouver: Douglas and McIntyre, and Seattle: University of Washington Press, 1987

Alicia Faxon and Sylvia Moore, eds, *Pilgrims and Pioneers: New England Women in the Arts*, New York: Midmarch Arts Press, 1987

Helen Goodman, "Emily Sartain: Her career", *Arts Magazine*, lxi, 1987, pp.61–5

——, "Women illustrators of the golden age of American illustration", *Woman's Art Journal*, viii/1, 1987, pp.13–22

American Women of the Etching Revival, exh. cat., High Museum of Art, Atlanta, 1988

Wendy Beckett, *Contemporary Women Artists*, New York: Universe, and Oxford: Phaidon, 1988

Sally L. Kitch, "'As a sign that all may understand': Shaker gift drawings and female spiritual power", *Winterthur Portfolio*, xxiv, 1989, pp.1–28

Making Their Mark: Women Artists Move into the Mainstream, 1970–85, Cincinnati Art Museum, and elsewhere, 1989

Whitney Chadwick, *Women, Art and Society*, New York and London: Thames and Hudson, 1990; revised edition, 1996

Dangerous Goods: Feminist Visual Art Practices, exh. cat., Edmonton Art Gallery and elsewhere, 1990

Frances Anne Hopkins, 1838–1919: Canadian Scenery, exh. cat., Thunder Bay National Exhibition Centre, 1990

Nancy Mowll Mathews, "American women artists at the turn of the century: Opportunities and choices", *Lilla Cabot Perry: An American Impressionist*, exh. cat., National Museum for Women in the Arts, Washington, DC, 1990, pp.105–14

Doris Shadbolt, *Emily Carr*, Vancouver: Douglas and McIntyre, and Seattle: University of Washington Press, 1990

Patricia Dunlavy Valenti, "Sophia Peabody Hawthorne: A study of artistic influence", *Studies in the American Renaissance*, 1990, pp.1–21

William Chafe, *American Women in the 20th Century*, New York: Oxford University Press, 1991

Hélène Cixous, "The laugh of the Medusa", *Feminisms: An Anthology of Literary Theory and Criticism*, ed. Robyn R. Warhol and Diane Price Herndl, New Brunswick, NJ: Rutgers University Press, 1991

Betsy Fahlman, "Women art students at Yale, 1869–1913", *Woman's Art Journal*, xii/1, 1991, pp.15–23

Faith Ringgold: The Last Story Quilt, video, created and produced by Linda Freeman, L and S Video Enterprises, Inc., 1991

Mara R. Witzling, ed., *Voicing Our Visions: Writings by Women Artists*, New York: Universe, 1991; London: Women's Press, 1992

Maria Tippett, *By a Lady: Celebrating Three Centuries of Art by Canadian Women*, Toronto: Viking, 1992

Whitney Chadwick and Isabelle de Courtivron, eds, *Significant Others: Creativity and Intimate Partnership*, New York and London: Thames and Hudson, 1993

Wendy Slatkin, ed., *The Voices of Women Artists*, Englewood Cliffs, NJ: Prentice Hall, 1993 Norma Broude and Mary D. Garrard, eds, *The Power of Feminist Art: The American Movement of the 1970s*, New York: Abrams, and London: Thames and Hudson, 1994

Nancy Mowll Mathews, *Mary Cassatt: A Life*, New York: Villard, 1994

Maria Tippett, *Emily Carr: A Biography*, revised edition, Toronto: Stoddard, 1994

Stephanie Walker, *This Woman in Particular: Biographical Images of Emily Carr*, Waterloo, Ontario: Wilfrid Laurier University Press, 1996

Modernism and Women Artists

Modernism remains a vexed and slippery term designating a cultural field usually defined by various combinations of the following: 1) particular notions of periodisation; 2) relationships to broader philosophical and historical conceptions of modernity; and 3) the rise of various avant-garde groups and/or innovative cultural practices that paradoxically break with and perpetuate Western traditions. This essay will outline some of the theoretical problems posed by women working in various visual fields during the years between 1890 and 1945. It will, however, also address the continued legacy of modernist paradigms during the heyday of Abstract Expressionism in the 1940s and 1950s and during the feminist movements of the 1960s and 1970s.

The period opens with the first wave of women's suffrage activity and the growing fragmentation of an increasingly competitive cultural marketplace for both sexes. It also encompasses the outbreak of World War II, during which there was not only a reorientation of the art market from Paris and London to New York, but also significant shifts in the perception of gender roles as career opportunities for women first expanded during the war, then disappeared as part of a reinscription of domestic femininity in the late 1940s and the 1950s. It should be stressed that there are wide divergences between pre- and post-war conceptions of modernism. Before the war, during the period often called "early modernism" (Butler 1994), the term was a fluid one that was widely debated by a number of writers, artists and critics, particularly those associated with the avant-garde. During and after the war, especially during the 1950s, 1960s and 1970s, the term modernism in the visual arts was used in increasingly narrow ways by critics such as Alfred Barr and Clement Greenberg who, drawing upon the earlier writings of philosophers such as Immanuel Kant and critics such as Roger Fry and Clive Bell, redefined the avant-garde project as one of formalist innovation. As numerous art historians have pointed out, their redefinition of the term was achieved by overlooking the complex socio-political agendas of earlier generations. Such an ostensibly apolitical construction of modernism appealed to champions of a newly emerging American avant-garde whose cultural "freedoms" were celebrated as democratic alternatives to Stalinist Socialist Realism during the Cold War (see, for example, the essays by Kozloff, Cockcroft, Guilbaut, and Schapiro and Schapiro, collected together in Frascina 1985). As Barr's and Greenberg's accounts of modernism achieved ascendency in the North American art world and became associated with the increasingly marketable and narrowly formalist movements of post-painterly abstraction and minimalism, a second wave of cultural critics, including many feminists, challenged its limitations as well as some of the more conservative ways it had become institutionalised. Such critiques have often been associated (more or less problematically) with the emergence of post-modern cultural forms and practices during the 1980s and 1990s.

In some senses it might be argued that feminist analyses of modernism have contributed to and built upon the growing critique of artistic autonomy mounted by literary critics, social historians of art and by post-modern, post-colonial and queer studies critics. Recent discussions of modernism by such critics as T.J. Clark (1973), Peter Bürger (1984), Matei Calinescu (1987), Raymond Williams (1989), Susan Buck-Morss (1989), Kenneth E. Silver (1989) and Jeffrey Weiss (1994) – a selective list – have attempted to restore some of modernism's lost socio-political complexities by returning to more politicised accounts of modernism by early 20th-century critics such as Bertold Brecht, Walter Benjamin and Theodor Adorno. While some individuals have been more attentive to gender issues than others, such criticism has been characterised by explorations of the social, political, racial and psychic stakes in cultural production under what David Harvey (1989), Raymond Williams (1989) and others have characterised as the conditions of modernity. Some of the widely acknowledged structural conditions that characterise the modern period are: the ambivalent relationship to Enlightenment promises of liberation through the scientific domination of nature and the rational ordering of society; tensions between national and international perspectives in an age of continuing colonial expansion; a compressed sense of time and space; rapid urbanisation; the rise of the mass media and industrial models of mass production, contributing to an extensive commodification of the cultural marketplace; the breakdown and/or rejection of traditional systems of representation and the proliferation of experimental avant-garde groups; and, last but not least, the emergence of socialist, feminist and anti- or post-colonial politics. As we shall see, feminist critics concentrating on questions related to women's artistic production have generated different (albeit sometimes interrelated) problematics and historical points of focus.

Feminist politics of one sort or another has played a central role in recent studies of women's relationship to modernism and modernity, in shaping the questions that are posed and/or fixing the historical ground to be covered. Not surprisingly, given the respective sizes of the disciplines of literary studies and art history, surveys recuperating women's participation in literary modernism have been more numerous. Although such surveys have tended to concentrate on women artists only as their work and lives relate to those of women writers, they have generated interesting insights into alternative and/or transgressive models of creativity, as well as a shared experimentation with identities, lifestyles, communities, motifs, genres, media, stylistic conventions and audiences (see, for example, Hanscombe and Smyers 1987; Benstock 1986; Gilbert and Gubar 1988–94; Kime 1990 and 1995). Of course, there have been many more focused literary studies addressing problematics that often spill over into visual forms of cultural production. Citing only a few examples, one could list: the operation of sexual difference and figures of the feminine in literary texts (Jardine 1985), the marginalisation of sentimental discourses (Clark 1991), the figures of the grotesque (Russo 1995) and the primitive (Torgovnick 1990), as well as the cultural transcription of political desires that range from progressive (DeKoven 1991) to conservative (Light 1991).

Surveys of women's visual work during this period are less numerous and have usually taken the form of exhibition catalogues (Paris 1983), documentary sources (Waller 1991; Witzling 1991), monographs on individual artists and studies focusing on women involved with particular artistic movements. Useful introductory overviews of the activities of women artists during the period 1900–40/45 are provided in a number of more general studies (see, for example, chapters in Fine 1978, Chadwick 1990 and Slatkin 1997). Useful reproductions of their work can be found in the exhibition catalogue *Women Artists, 1550–1950* (Los Angeles County Museum of Art, 1976) and biographical profiles and interviews with a number of important American women artists in Eleanor Munro's *Originals: American Women Artists* (New York: Simon and Schuster, 1979).

Although these introductory texts vary in the ways in which they organise the material, which can be grouped by nationality (e.g. European and American), artistic movement or media, the central figures are largely the same. Käthe Kollwitz (q.v.) and Paula Modersohn-Becker (q.v.) are usually discussed in relation to German Expressionism, although the politically committed "realism" of the former and the self-consciously "primitivising" maternal imagery of the latter strike out in new directions. More recent studies of women associated with German Expressionism (e.g. Behr 1988) have also explored the work of Marianne Werefkin (q.v.) and Gabriele Münter (q.v.) in more detail as well as introducing a number of less well-known artists. Women associated with movements that critically explored various notions of the decorative include Sonia Delaunay (q.v.) with her Orphist and Dada connections, and Vanessa Bell (q.v.) with her work for the Omega Workshops. Both of these artists provide fascinating examples of an integrated art practice that crosses the divisions of high/low, art/craft as well as abstract/decorative. Other examples of such border crossing can be found in the Russian Constructivist work of Lyubov Popova (q.v.) and Varvara Stepanova (q.v.) and the textile work of Gunta Stölzl (q.v.), who was part of the Bauhaus weaving workshop. While the important contribution of Hannah Höch (q.v.) to collage and photo-montage is connected with Dada, her exploration of the relation of the "new woman" to the consumerist ideology of mass culture has a slightly different focus (see Lavin 1993).

In her intriguing studies of women artists connected with the Parisian avant-garde between 1900 and the late 1920s (Maria Gutiérriez Blanchard, Alice Halicka, Marie Laurencin,

Jacqueline Marval, Suzanne Valadon, all q.v., and others) Gill Perry explores how gender inflected their relations with the Cubist and Fauve movements as well as their training, the marketing of their work under a "feminised" School of Paris label and their representations of other women and female nudes. Another book that usefully situates women's production both inside and outside a leading avant-garde movement is Whitney Chadwick's study (1985) of Surrealist women artists (Meret Oppenheim, Frida Kahlo, Dorothea Tanning, Leonora Carrington, Leonor Fini, Kay Sage, all q.v., and others), which considers how they ambivalently negotiated the Surrealists' fascination with Woman as a figure of repressed irrational and natural powers and their fetishistic celebration of the *femme-enfant* by turning to different sources of identification and inspiration. Other important European painters such as the British portraitist Gwen John (q.v.) cannot be so easily situated in the context of any particular movement, although her life was typical of many expatriate women artists working in Paris.

In the USA some of the most frequently discussed women artists of the early 20th century include Romaine Brooks (q.v.), Georgia O'Keeffe (q.v.) and Florine Stettheimer (q.v.). Brooks was an expatriate who produced most of her work in Paris, and is best known for her striking portraits of members of the lesbian coterie surrounding the American poet Natalie Barney. Through her marriage to Alfred Stieglitz O'Keeffe was closely associated with his 291 circle in New York, but she nevertheless established her own highly distinctive style and developed large-format flower paintings and highly abstracted cityscapes and desert landscapes. Florine Stettheimer's eccentrically decorative compositions are also hard to connect to any artistic group and belong instead to her own wealthy upper-class milieu of New York that she often parodied in her paintings.

The extensive excavation and appreciation of women's artistic activity from the early 20th century was assisted by the work of a feminist art criticism during the 1970s that discussed the limitations of those modernist paradigms that had prevailed up to that point. In particular, this feminist critique rejected the fetishisation of a limited canon of formally innovative work that had neglected or dismissed much of women's artistic production described in the last few paragraphs. Lillian Robinson and Lise Vogel (1971) noted that modernist critics tended to focus on the autonomy of the work of art, broadly detaching culture from history and ignoring the "contextual" considerations of race, sex and class. Using a similar logic, Carol Duncan (1973) stressed that the much-vaunted bohemian "freedoms" of the early 20th-century avant-garde were often based on the sexual exploitation of female models in both representational and material terms. During the same period, Linda Nochlin (1971) wondered about the criteria that excluded women artists from being considered "great", and Lucy Lippard (1976) explored the sorts of imagery and issues that she felt characterised women's art. For many writers in the 1970s, a feminist perspective offered a welcome escape from the sterility of the modernist mainstream. In Lucy Lippard's words:

> Feminism's greatest contribution to the future of art has probably been its lack of contribution to modernism. Feminist methods and theories have instead offered a socially concerned alternative to the increasingly

mechanical "evolution" of art about art [Lippard 1984, p.149].

Continuing this critique of Greenbergian modernism in the early 1980s, artists such as Mary Kelly and art historians such as Rozsika Parker and Griselda Pollock drew attention to the production and valuing of gendered positions across a wide range of institutional sites. Drawing upon semiotic and psychoanalytic theories, these writers argued that meanings were produced not only by the artist in her/his studio but also by a network of other commentators, including dealers, critics, teachers and members of the general public. The fact that these writers placed a strong material emphasis on socially and psychically situating artistic statements meant that they refuted any notions of female, feminine or feminist essentialisms. As Parker and Pollock explained: "(r)ather we are concerned to discover the relationships between women artists and the institutions of art and ideology throughout historical shifts and changes" (Parker and Pollock 1981, p.136; see also Kelly 1981). In more recent work, Pollock has continued to explore the constructed nature of gender categories, asserting that the "practices which constitute the most visible feminist interventions in culture are not to be defined according to the gender of their expressive subject" (1992, pp.152–3).

The refusal of fixed, stable and biologically rooted feminine identities has characterised the work of many post-structuralist/anti-essentialist feminist critics, including Judith Butler who argues that such terms as "women" must be understood as performative constructions and permanent sites of political contest. She stresses that although it might be tactically expedient to identify oneself provisionally as a "woman" in local struggles, it is important to remain aware of the term's limitations and exclusions (Butler 1993, pp.222–3). Butler's observations can help us come to terms with some of the more acrimonious and problematic generational debates between those feminist artists, critics, theorists and historians who launched various critiques of modernism during the 1970s and 1980s. Many critics from the 1970s have subsequently defended themselves against charges of naive essentialism by accusing critics from the 1980s of taking up "male" theory and abandoning political activism. As Amelia Jones has pointed out, the overly reductive nature of this debate becomes apparent when one situates the particular struggles of the different generations historically. Such false divisions between mind and body, theory and activism, and different generations, cannot be sustained when one realises that the theoretical arguments of the 1980s have had material consequences and that many writers and artists of the 1970s were already theoretically sophisticated, even if their terminology and paradigms were not those of the 1980s (see Jones 1995; Broude and Garrard 1994; Pollock 1993). I, too, have argued that the modernist period can be more productively reassessed by considering how women from earlier generations conceptualised their artistic and interpretive agencies and horizons in ways that acknowledge late 20th-century theoretical agendas without invoking them as judgemental criteria (Elliott 1996).

One of the most important contributions of post-structuralist feminism has been the realisation that women artists are not the only ones interested in the discursive manipulation and destabilisation of gendered identities and signifiers. Many recent studies have demonstrated that certain male artists and writers belonging to various sub-cultural groups have also disrupted the binary logic of gender construction (see, for example, Jardine 1985; Jones 1994; Reed 1991; Werth 1990; Chave 1994). While such developments have radically extended the scope of feminist inquiry, a number of critics have worried that the necessary theoretical gap between discursive and experiential femininities might once again result in the marginalisation of women artists and writers who often have fewer resources and less room to manoeuvre than many of their male counterparts (Jardine 1985, p.37; see also Huyssen 1986 and Suleiman 1990). Because social, ideological and psychic inequalities have persisted well into the late 20th century, when conservative governments in many Western countries are reversing the movement towards equality and widening the gender gap by repealing equity legislation and down-sizing social services, it is essential for those pursuing feminist political agendas to relate discursive configurations of femininity to the material possibilities that exist for women at any given historical moment. Although in this essay I am focusing on writing that deals with women artists, it is important to relate this material to other feminist interrogations of modernist gender construction. Again, it is worth stressing that I am uncomfortable with hierarchical manoeuvres that set theorising about visual and rhetorical constructions of gender above and against gathering historical information about women artists. Both activities need to be at once theoretically informed *and* historically grounded. Finally, given the enormous amount of activity in the modernist field, I am only able to introduce a few important areas of research and cite a limited number of sources.

Much interesting work has focused on the first wave of feminist activism surrounding the issues of women's suffrage and the demands of the "New Woman" that emerged in the 1890s and continued through the 1930s. Lisa Tickner's richly detailed and theoretically sophisticated study (1987) of the British suffrage movement is essential reading. Tickner addresses not only the formation and day-to-day operation of suffrage artists' ateliers, but also considers the way in which women manipulated existing representations of femininity to forge new political meanings and identities. In the USA Ellen Wiley Todd (1993) has explored representations of the "New Woman" in the work of several New York artists, including Isabel Bishop (q.v.), during the 1920s and 1930s. It should be stressed that controversies over the "New Woman" often touched upon questions of sexual orientation and the problematic figure of the mannish lesbian woman. This issue is raised in Maud Lavin's study of Hannah Höch (1993), which broadly explores the crisis of gendered identities in the context of Weimar Germany, and also by Emmanuel Cooper (1994), who provides a chapter on the "New Woman" that looks at the work of artists such as Tamara de Lempicka (q.v.; see also Diana Souhami's monograph of 1988 on the British artist Gluck, q.v.). Susan Fillin-Yeh (1995) has also recently addressed women's dandyism through case studies of Georgia O'Keeffe and Florine Stettheimer. Susan Gubar (1981) and Marjorie Garber (1992) have also theorised the complicated politics of women's cross-dressing.

Another important area of activity has been an exploration of women artists' relationships to the various avant-garde groups and theories. Addressing revisionist accounts of the

politics of French Impressionist painting made by social historians of art such as T.J. Clark (1973), Griselda Pollock (1988) examined how the spaces of modernity were differently configured for women and women artists such as Berthe Morisot (q.v.) and Mary Cassatt (q.v.). Building on Janet Wolff's notion of the invisible *flâneuse*, Pollock points out that the avant-garde's fetishisation of Baudelaire's notion of the artist as *flâneur* marginalises women's experiences of modernity. Instead, Pollock conceptualises cultural mobility and agency in new ways that take questions of gender into account (see her essay "Modernity and the spaces of femininity" in Pollock 1988). Elizabeth Wilson (1995) has addressed the limitations of Wolff's notion of the invisible *flâneuse* by pointing out that women experienced increasing social mobility during the period. Recent studies that also address women's agency in relation to modernist avant-garde movements and discourses have been published by Gill Perry (1993 and 1995) and by Bridget Elliott and Jo-Ann Wallace (1994). Perry, as mentioned earlier, focuses on women artists working in Paris from c.1900 to the late 1920s, critically addressing how constructions of femininity were constantly negotiated in the professional context of the atelier, the exhibition and in various sites of critical discourse as well as in the practice of executing portraits and female nudes. Focusing on the collaboration of women artists and writers (e.g. Romaine Brooks, Vanessa Bell, Marie Laurencin, Nina Hamnett and Djuna Barnes) in the same period in France and England, Elliott and Wallace identify several key modernist discourses, including those of avant-gardism, professionalism, genius and purity. In particular, they consider how women artists were differently positioned (e.g. wealthy, poor, immigrant, lesbian, heterosexual) and how this positioning inflected their artistic practice, particularly in the areas of self-portraiture and portraits of other women. Another book that spans the literary and visual is a collection of essays edited by Gabriele Griffin (1994), which looks at Djuna Barnes, Leonora Carrington, Susan Hiller (q.v.) and Lee Krasner (q.v.). At the time of writing, two further edited collections of essays addressing women artists and modernism, by Katy Deepwell, and Caroline Howlett and Hugh Stevens, are in press.

Taking a different tack and criticising much recent poststructuralist feminist theorising, a study by Christine Battersby (1989) focuses more closely on the issue of genius, which she feels needs to be reappropriated in order to generate a feminist aesthetic that is based upon great, individual female artists. In a wide-ranging book that moves from Surrealism to women's writing and artistic production during the 1980s, Susan Suleiman (1990) explores the subversive figures of the female body and the laughing mother, arguing that certain post-modern women artists (e.g. Leonora Carrington, Barbara Kruger, q.v., Cindy Sherman, Jenny Holzer) and writers have continued the more radical and irreverent spirit of the historical avant-gardes. Johanna Drucker (1994) similarly explores how post-modern women artists have critically engaged with the legacy of modernist subjectivity in a discussion of the works of Sherrie Levine, Cindy Sherman and Barbara Kruger. Three other articles that offer intriguing insights into how notions of avant-gardism have been rhetorically gendered are Andreas Huyssen's study of modernism and mass culture, Anne Wagner's study (1989) of Lee Krasner's contradictory positioning in the modernist and feminist canons, and Lisa Tickner's essays (1993 and 1994) on masculinity and modernism in which she looks at the work of Gwen John, Vanessa Bell, Kate Lechmere and Helen Saunders.

All of the sources I have cited in my discussion of women and the avant-garde have relied on Western European and North American case studies. As Jo-Anna Isaak has pointed out (1989), another set of theoretical assumptions might be extrapolated from a different range of case studies, such as the work of women artists associated with various sectors of the Russian avant-garde (see Briony Fer's helpful introduction of 1993 to some of these issues) and Latin America (see Baddeley and Fraser 1989). As Isaak rightly notes, most theorising about modernism is usually based on a limited Eurocentric perspective, often privileging England and France. Certainly, given spatial constraints and my own area of research, the same limitations frame this essay.

Also of crucial importance is a growing body of research exploring the ways in which women artists secured access to training, patronage, exhibiting space, models, critical reviews and other kinds of support networks. Since I cannot do justice to the huge volume of research in this field, I will mention only a handful of recent studies that, in addition to unearthing new historical information, also offer new insights into women's agency in the modernist cultural field. In terms of the Victorian art world, one might turn to the studies of Deborah Cherry (1993), Clarissa Campbell Orr (1995) and Janice Helland (1996), who show how women's day-to-day working conditions and institutional affiliations affected their representational practices. Turning to late 19th-century France, Tamar Garb's study (1994) of the Union des Femmes Peintres et Sculpteurs provides invaluable insights into various intersecting discourses of art and femininity, as does Debora Silverman's (1989), which examines how the rhetoric of femininity played an integral role in the decorative Art Nouveau movements of France. Pen Dalton (1995) discusses the ways in which a traditional modernist bias has shaped more recent art education. (See also the studies exploring the relationships between women artists and their models by Betterton 1987; Mathews 1991; Garb 1993; Elliott 1996; and others.)

An interest in the decorative or applied arts has traditionally been associated with women, as Rozsika Parker (1984), Anthea Callen (1979) and other feminist critics have observed. Here I will discuss only a few sources that address these areas of activity in relation to modernist artistic production. Both Nancy Troy (1991) and Christopher Reed (1991) have published studies that broadly address the function of the decorative and domestic in modernist artistic discourses. Although neither study offers a sustained analysis of the works of women artists, both explore the gendered inflections of a new, increasingly consumer-oriented aesthetic. More specifically on the subject of fashion, one should refer to Elizabeth Wilson's analysis (1985) of fashion and modernity, which not only deals with women as workers in the fashion industry but also looks at them as highly sophisticated urban consumers. Also important is Peter Wollen's analysis (1993) of the role that such concepts as fashion, orientalism and decoration played in modernist discourses. More broadly considering women's involvement in the sphere of design is Judy Attfield and Pat Kirkham's collection of essays (1989), which includes not only

fashion but also furniture and interior design, architecture and town-planning. Further explorations of fashion and architecture can be found in a collection of essays compiled by Lynne Walker (1994), which are drawn from a conference organised by the Design History Society. (The extensive literature on theoretical questions related to the practices of women photographers and film-makers is too complex to raise here.)

Finally, it seems useful to conclude this brief overview of modernism and women artists by considering how questions of racial and cultural difference are reshaping the field. Certainly, there is much evidence to suggest that certain women artists adopted self-consciously "primitive" references and styles of painting, as Gill Perry analyses in the case of Paula Modersohn-Becker. Whether women artists mobilised "primitive" sources in ways that differed from their male counterparts awaits further investigation. If white women artists were usually excluded from early formulations of the modernist canon, women artists of colour were almost invisible. Much has changed over the past few years as an emerging body of criticism by writers such as Bell Hooks (1995), Maud Sulter (1990) and Rasheed Araeen (London 1989) discuss the political and cultural agendas of artists including Carrie Mae Weems, Alison Saar, Emma Amos, Mona Hatoum, Lubaina Himid and Sonia Boyce. Although this "other story" focuses on contemporary practices that are usually considered more "post-modern" than "modernist", there are important links between this work and that of earlier artists such as Meta Vaux Warrick Fuller (q.v.) who was part of the Harlem Renaissance (Driskell 1987). As increasingly sophisticated and multivalent critical paradigms are applied to investigations of modernism, many of its continuities and affinities with post-modernism will become more evident.

BRIDGET ELLIOTT

Bibliography

Alfred H. Barr, Jr, *Cubism and Abstract Art*, New York: Museum of Modern Art, 1936; reprinted Cambridge, MA: Harvard University Press, 1986

Clement Greenberg, *Art and Culture: Critical Essays*, Boston: Beacon Press, 1961

——, "Modernist painting", *Art and Literature*, iv, Spring 1965, pp.193–201

Walter Benjamin, *Illuminations*, ed. Hannah Arendt, New York: Harcourt Brace, 1968; London: Collins, 1973 (German original)

Linda Nochlin, "Why have there been no great women artists?", *Woman in Sexist Society: Studies in Power and Powerlessness*, ed. Vivian Gornick and Barbara K. Moran, New York: Basic Books, 1971; reprinted New American Library, 1972, pp.480–510

Lillian S. Robinson and Lise Vogel, "Modernism and history", *New Literary History*, iii/1, 1971–2, pp.177–99

T. J. Clark, *Image of the People: Gustave Courbet and the 1848 Revolution*, London: Thames and Hudson, 1973; Princeton: Princeton University Press, 1982

Carol Duncan, "Virility and domination in early 20th-century vanguard painting", *Artforum*, December 1973, pp.30–39

Lucy R. Lippard, *From the Center: Feminist Essays on Women's Art*, New York: Dutton, 1976

Elsa Honig Fine, *Women and Art: A History of Women Painters and Sculptors from the Renaissance to the 20th Century*, Montclair, NJ: Allanheld and Schram, and London: Prior, 1978

Anthea Callen, *Angel in the Studio: Women in the Arts and Crafts Movement, 1870–1914*, London: Astragal, 1979; as *Women*

Artists of the Arts and Crafts Movement, 1870–1914, New York: Pantheon, 1979

Roger Fry, *Vision and Design*, ed. J.B. Bullen, London and New York: Oxford University Press, 1981 (first published 1920)

Susan Gubar, "Blessings in disguise: Cross-dressings as redressing for female modernists", *Massachusetts Review*, xxii, 1981, pp.477–508

Rozsika Parker and Griselda Pollock, *Old Mistresses: Women, Art and Ideology*, London: Routledge, 1981

Mary Kelly, "Re-viewing modernist criticism", *Screen*, no.22, Autumn 1981, pp.41–62

L'Avant-garde au feminin: Moscou, Saint-Petersbourg, Paris, 1907–1930, exh. cat., Centre d'art plastique contemporain, Paris, 1983

Peter Bürger, *Theory of the Avant-Garde*, Minneapolis: University of Minnesota Press, 1984 (German original, 1974)

Lucy R. Lippard, "Sweeping exchanges: The contribution of feminism to the art of the 1970s", *Get the Message? A Decade of Art for Social Change*, New York: Dutton, 1984

Rozsika Parker, *The Subversive Stitch: Embroidery and the Making of the Feminine*, London: Women's Press, 1984; New York: Routledge, 1989

Whitney Chadwick, *Women Artists and the Surrealist Movement*, Boston: Little Brown, and London: Thames and Hudson, 1985

Francis Frascina, ed., *Pollock and After: The Critical Debate*, New York: Harper, 1985

Alice Jardine, *Gynesis: Configurations of Woman and Modernity*, Ithaca, NY: Cornell University Press, 1985

Elizabeth Wilson, *Adorned in Dreams: Fashion and Modernity*, London: Virago, 1985

Shari Benstock, *Women of the Left Bank, Paris 1900–1940*, Austin: University of Texas Press, 1986

Andreas Huyssen, *After the Great Divide: Modernism, Mass Culture, Postmodernism*, Bloomington: Indiana University Press, 1986

Rosemary Betterton, "How do women look? The female nude in the work of Suzanne Valadon", *Looking On: Images of Femininity in the Visual Arts and Media*, ed. Rosemary Betterton, London and New York: Pandora, 1987, pp.217–34 (expanded version of article first published in *Feminist Review*, no.19, March 1985)

Matei Calinescu, *Five Faces of Modernity: Modernism, Avant-Garde, Decadence, Kitsch, Postmodernism*, Durham: Duke University Press, 1987 (revised edition of *Faces of Modernity*, 1977)

David Driskell, "The Flowering of the Harlem Renaissance: The art of Aaron Douglas, Meta Warrick Fuller, Palmer Hayden and William H. Johnson", *The Harlem Renaissance: Art of Black America*, exh. cat., Studio Museum in Harlem, New York, 1987, pp.105–54

Gillian Hanscombe and Virginia L. Smyers, *Writing for Their Lives: The Modernist Women, 1910–1940*, London: Women's Press, 1987

Lisa Tickner, *The Spectacle of Women: Imagery of the Suffrage Campaign, 1907–14*, London: Chatto and Windus, 1987; Chicago: University of Chicago Press, 1988

Shulamith Behr, *Women Expressionists*, Oxford: Phaidon, and New York: Rizzoli, 1988

Griselda Pollock, *Vision and Difference: Femininity, Feminism and the Histories of Art*, London: Routledge, 1988

Diana Souhami, *Gluck, 1895–1978: Her Biography*, London: Pandora, 1988

Sandra M. Gilbert and Susan Gubar, *No Man's Land: The Place of the Woman Writer in the Twentieth Century*, 3 vols, New Haven: Yale University Press, 1988–94

Judy Attfield and Pat Kirkham, eds, *A View from the Interior: Feminism, Women and Design*, London: Women's Press, 1989

Oriana Baddeley and Valerie Fraser, *Drawing the Line: Art and Cultural Identity in Contemporary Latin America*, London and New York: Verso, 1989

Christine Battersby, *Gender and Genius: Towards a Feminist Aesthetic*, Bloomington: Indiana University Press, and London: Women's Press, 1989

Susan Buck-Morss, *The Dialectics of Seeing: Walter Benjamin and the Arcades Project*, Cambridge: Massachusetts Institute of Technology Press, 1989

David Harvey, *The Condition of Postmodernity: An Enquiry into the Origins of Cultural Change*, Oxford and Cambridge, MA: Blackwell, 1989

Jo-Anna Isaak, "Representation and its (dis)contents [a review of Griselda Pollock's *Vision and Difference*]", *Art History*, xii, 1989, pp.362–6

The Other Story: Afro-Asian Artists in Post-War Britain, exh. cat., South Bank Centre, London, 1989

Kenneth E. Silver, *Esprit de Corps: The Art of the Parisian Avant-Garde and the First World War, 1914–1925*, Princeton: Princeton University Press, 1989

Debora Silverman, *Art Nouveau in Fin-de-Siècle France: Politics, Psychology and Style*, Berkeley: University of California Press, 1989

Anne Wagner, "Lee Krasner as L.K.", *Representations*, no.25, 1989, pp.42–57

Raymond Williams, *The Politics of Modernism: Against the New Conformists*, ed. Tony Pinkney, London: Verso, 1989

Whitney Chadwick, *Women, Art and Society*, London and New York: Thames and Hudson, 1990

Bonnie Scott Kime, ed., *The Gender of Modernism: A Critical Anthology*, Bloomington: Indiana University Press, 1990

Susan Rubin Suleiman, *Subversive Intent: Gender, Politics and the Avant-Garde*, Cambridge, MA: Harvard University Press, 1990

Maud Sulter, ed., *Passion: Discourses on Blackwomen's Creativity*, Hebden Bridge, Yorks: Urban Fox Press, 1990

Marianna Torgovnick, *Gone Primitive: Savage Intellects, Modern Lives*, Chicago: University of Chicago Press, 1990

Margaret Werth, "Engendering imaginary modernism: Henri Matisse's *Bonheur de vivre*", *Genders*, no.9, November 1990, pp.49–74

Suzanne Clark, *Sentimental Modernism: Women Writers and the Revolution of the Word*, Bloomington: Indiana University Press, 1991

Marianne DeKoven, *Rich and Strange: Gender, History, Modernism*, Princeton: Princeton University Press, 1991

Alison Light, *Forever England: Femininity, Literature and Conservatism Between the Wars*, London: Routledge, 1991

Patricia Mathews, "Returning the gaze: Diverse representations of the nude in the art of Suzanne Valadon", *Art Bulletin*, lxxiii, 1991, pp.415–30

Christopher Reed, "Bloomsbury bashing: Homophobia and the politics of criticism in the eighties", *Gender*, no.11, 1991, pp.58–80

Nancy J. Troy, *Modernism and the Decorative Arts in France: Art Nouveau to Le Corbusier*, New Haven: Yale University Press, 1991

Susan Waller, *Women Artists in the Modern Era: A Documentary History*, Metuchen, NJ: Scarecrow Press, 1991

Mara R. Witzling, ed., *Voicing Our Visions: Writings by Women Artists*, New York: Universe, 1991; London: Women's Press, 1992

Marjorie Garber, *Vested Interests: Cross Dressing and Cultural Anxiety*, New York: Routledge, 1992

Griselda Pollock, "Painting, feminism, history", *Destabilizing Theory: Contemporary Feminist Debates*, ed. Michèle Barrett and Anne Phillips, Stanford: Stanford University Press, 1992

Judith Butler, *Bodies that Matter: On the Discursive Limits of "Sex"*, New York: Routledge, 1993

Deborah Cherry, *Painting Women: Victorian Women Artists*, London and New York: Routledge, 1993

Briony Fer, "The language of construction", *Realism, Rationalism, Surrealism: Art Between the Wars*, New Haven and London: Yale University Press/Open University, 1993, pp.87–169

Tamar Garb, "Gender and representation", *Modernity and Modernism: French Painting in the Nineteenth Century*, New

Haven and London: Yale University Press/Open University, 1993, pp.219–90

Maud Lavin, *Cut with the Kitchen Knife: The Weimar Photomontages of Hannah Höch*, New Haven and London: Yale University Press, 1993

Gill Perry, "Primitivism and the 'Modern'", *Primitivism, Cubism, Abstraction: The Early Twentieth Century*, New Haven and London: Yale University Press/Open University, 1993, pp.3–85

Lisa Tickner, "Now and then: The hieratic head of Ezra Pound", *Oxford Art Journal*, xvi/2, 1993, pp.55–61

Ellen Wiley Todd, *The "New Woman" Revised: Painting and Gender Politics on Fourteenth Street*, Berkeley: University of California Press, 1993

Peter Wollen, "Out of the past: Fashion/orientalism/the body", *Raiding the Icebox: Reflections on Twentieth-Century Culture*, Bloomington: Indiana University Press, and London: Verso, 1993, pp.1–34

Griselda Pollock, "The politics of theory: Generations and geographies", *Genders*, no.17, Fall 1993, pp.99–119

Norma Broude and Mary D. Garrard, eds, *The Power of Feminist Art: The American Movement of the 1970s*, New York: Abrams, and London: Thames and Hudson, 1994

Christopher Butler, *Early Modernism: Literature, Music and Painting in Europe, 1900–1916*, Oxford: Clarendon Press, 1994

Anna C. Chave, "New encounters with *Les Demoiselles d'Avignon*: Gender, race and the origins of Cubism", *Art Bulletin*, lxxvi, 1994, pp.597–611

Emmanuel Cooper, *The Sexual Perspective: Homosexuality and Art in the Last 100 Years in the West*, 2nd edition, London and New York: Routledge, 1994

Johanna Drucker, *Theorizing Modernism: Visual Art and the Critical Tradition*, New York: Columbia University Press, 1994

Bridget Elliott and Jo-Ann Wallace, *Women Artists and Writers: Modernist (Im)positionings*, London: Routledge, 1994

Tamar Garb, *Sisters of the Brush: Women's Artistic Culture in Late Nineteenth-Century Paris*, New Haven and London: Yale University Press, 1994

Gabriele Griffin, ed., *Difference in View: Women and Modernism*, London: Taylor and Francis, 1994

Amelia Jones, *Postmodernism and the En-gendering of Marcel Duchamp*, Cambridge and New York: Cambridge University Press, 1994

Lisa Tickner, "Men's work? Masculinity and modernism", *Visual Culture: Images and Interpretations*, ed. Norman Bryson, Michael Ann Holly and Keith Moxey, Hanover, NH: University Press of New England, 1994, pp.42–82

Lynne Walker, ed., *Cracks in the Pavements: Gender/Fashion/Architecture*, London: Sorella Press, 1994

Jeffrey S. Weiss, *The Popular Culture of Modern Art: Picasso, Duchamp and Avant-Gardism*, New Haven: Yale University Press, 1994

Pen Dalton, "Modernism, art education and sexual difference", *New Feminist Art Criticism: Critical Strategies*, ed. Katy Deepwell, Manchester: Manchester University Press, 1995

Susan Fillin-Yeh, "Dandies, marginality and modernism: Georgia O'Keeffe, Marcel Duchamp and other cross-dressers", *Oxford Art Journal*, xviii/2, 1995, pp.33–44

Bell Hooks, *Art on My Mind: Visual Politics*, New York: New Press, 1995

Amelia Jones, "Power and feminist art (history) [a review of Norma Broude's and Mary D. Garrard's *The Power of Feminist Art: Emergence, Impact and Triumph of the American Feminist Art Movement*]", *Art History*, xvi, 1995, pp.435–43

Bonnie Scott Kime, *Refiguring Modernism*, i: *The Women of 1928*, Bloomington: Indiana University Press, 1995

Clarissa Campbell Orr, ed., *Women in the Victorian Art World*, Manchester: Manchester University Press, 1995

Gill Perry, *Women Artists and the Parisian Avant-Garde*, Manchester: Manchester University Press, and New York: St Martin's Press, 1995

Mary Russo, *The Female Grotesque: Risk, Excess and Modernity*, New York: Routledge, 1995

E. Wilson, "The invisible *flâneur*", *Postmodern Cities and Spaces*, ed. Sophie Watson and Katherine Gibson, Oxford and Cambridge, MA: Blackwell, 1995, pp.59–79

Bridget Elliott, "'The strength of the weak' as portrayed by Marie Laurencin", *On Your Left: New Historical Materialism in the 1990s*, ed. Ann Kibbey and others, New York: New York University Press, 1996, pp.69–109

Janice Helland, *The Studios of Frances and Margaret Macdonald*, Manchester: Manchester University Press, 1996

Wendy Slatkin, *Women Artists in History: From Antiquity to the Present*, 3rd edition, Upper Saddle River, NJ: Prentice Hall, 1997

Katy Deepwell, ed., *Women and Modernism* (in preparation)

Caroline Howlett and Hugh Stevens, eds, *Borderlines: Gender, Sexuality and the Margins of Modernism* (in preparation)

Feminism and Women Artists

An important difference between art produced by earlier women artists and by those who have been active since the 1970s is that, in recent years, many women artists have been engaged in a deliberate dialogue with the Western art-historical tradition. Despite their widely differing goals and means of attaining them, most of these artists have sought to redress, through their art, fissures and lacunae in the Western canon – particularly with regard to women's positioning within it. While many contemporary women artists have been influenced by the feminist movement and have identified themselves as "feminists", their work has assumed diverse forms and has encompassed a variety of different strategies to achieve so-called feminist goals. In fact, in speaking of developments from this period, it is more accurate to refer to "feminisms" in the plural, rather than to a monolithic "feminist" agenda.

This essay will present an overview of art produced in response to contemporary feminism, beginning with the so-called first generation of feminist artists in the early 1970s, continuing through their successors in the 1980s and early 1990s. Some critics have found it expedient to subdivide the major developments in the art of this period into two "waves", each proscribed by a corresponding decade, the first wave of the 1970s perceived as more "activist" and the second wave of the 1980s as more "theoretical", thus tending to polarise the aims of these "generations" (e.g. Cincinnati 1989, pp.19–20). While feminist artistic interventions of the 1970s might seem to have had more overtly political motivations than those of later years, there is no clear-cut division based on chronology. As a case in point, two of the pieces most definitively associated with each methodology – Judy Chicago's *Dinner Party* (1974–9) and Mary Kelly's *Post-Partum Document* (1973–9) – are almost exactly contemporaneous. It is more useful, instead, to define the differences in terms of contrasting, but not mutually exclusive strategies employed in order to achieve a similar end: art that "represents" the point of view of its female creators more effectively than that produced in the past.

During the late 1960s and early 1970s there was a resurgence of feminist consciousness, combined with an increase in specific political activities, the era of (so-called) Women's Liberation. Numerous women artists active during this period, including May Stevens, Mary Kelly, Judy Chicago, Harmony Hammond and Monica Sjöö (all q.v.), have acknowledged the impact of the political feminist movement on the direction of their art. These artists and others, in both Britain and the USA, participated in feminist collectives, exhibition spaces and discussion groups. The same political phenomena influenced the future development of art history, both in the birth of so-called feminist art history and in the subsequent "deconstruction" of the received art-historical canon, under the influence of post-modernist thought. Mary Kelly's group in London, for example, included such important theorists as Laura Mulvey and Griselda Pollock. Linda Nochlin's germinal article "Why have there been no great women artists?" appeared in 1971, calling for a critique that would reformulate "the crucial questions of the discipline" (Nochlin 1971, p.146). This process has taken place ever since through the work of feminist art historians and other scholars who have attempted to restructure the field of art history, and through feminist artists themselves who have brought about changes to the canon through their art.

Judy Chicago's early work constitutes an excellent example of the strategies and concerns of some women artists who sought to fulfil an overtly polemical agenda through their art. As she has documented in her autobiography *Through the Flower*, Chicago felt herself alienated from the Western art-historical tradition by the assumption that "to be a woman and an artist was contradictory" (Chicago 1975, p.43). She came to realise that she was forced to hide "the real content" of her art, a sentiment that was shared by other artists during the early 1970s including Harmony Hammond, who described her understanding that "if [she] wanted to be taken seriously as an artist [she] had to paint what the boys painted" (quoted in Witzling 1994, p.249) and, as a result, painted herself out of her own work.

Chicago set out to find a visual structure that would allow her to express her "femininity" through her art, and ended up formulating the much touted but little understood concept of vaginal iconography. Chicago, along with Miriam Schapiro (q.v.) with whom she collaborated, asserted that in the work of diverse earlier women artists they had observed "a frequent use of the central image ... sometimes surrounded by folds or undulations, as in the structure of the vagina" (Chicago 1975, p.143). In her own work, in paintings such as *Big Ox, No.2* (1968), Schapiro had also begun to seek a centripetal structure. The art critic Lucy Lippard further defined the recurring elements of "central core" imagery as "the preponderance of circular forms, central focus, inner space" (Lippard 1976, pp.49, 143–5). Schapiro and Chicago were particularly impressed with women artists' use of the central space as "the framework for an imagery which allows for the complete reversal of the ways in which women are seen in the culture" (Chicago 1975, pp.143–4). In order to effect this perceptual reversal, Chicago worked with Schapiro, and with students in their class at the California Institute of the Arts, on the environmental *Womanhouse* whose motifs were identified during the process of "consciousness raising". Issues involved with domesticity, with women's traditional culture, with the repetitive nature of women's traditional lives were explored. Following this period, in *The Dinner Party*, her *magnum opus*, Chicago represented 39 important women in history through ceramic plates that epitomise central core imagery, and runners embellished with embroidery styles typical of the periods in which these women lived. Chicago described this work, based on both the triangle, an ancient symbol of female power, and the iconography of the Last Supper, as "a people's history – the history of women in Western civilization" (quoted in Witzling 1991, p.380).

Many other women artists who did not necessarily accept the premise that there was a particular pictorial construct based on "female" experience sought to establish a dialogue with the Western tradition by posing alternative approaches to representing the female body. Joan Semmel, for example, in her paintings and her writings explored a female erotic, consisting of undulating transparent layers, stimulated by the female body as literally seen from the point of view of its possessor. In *Hand Down*, for example, the viewer looks past folds of breasts and belly, to a female hand reaching between its owner's crotch. Semmel said that she wanted to create "an imagery that would respond to female feelings" rather than one that stemmed from male sexual fantasies. She continued: "My paintings deal with communication, how a hand touches a body ... sensuality with the power factor eliminated" (quoted in Seiberling 1974, p.55). Hannah Wilke (q.v.) began making wall hangings of undulating layers of pink latex, and then went on to explore her "starification series": vaginal forms, made from such malleable materials as chewing gum and kneaded erasers, adhered first to the artist's body and then to photographs. She described her art as "a very female thing ... about multilayered forms ... organic like flowers" (*ibid.*, p.58). Hammond similarly identified "a feeling of touching oneself [that] is directly connected to women's art-making" ("A sense of touch", quoted in Witzling 1994, p.254). For her, this feeling was expressed in sculptures made by obsessively wrapping layers of fabric, a sensual experience, "pushing out from the center" ("Spiral", quoted in *ibid.*, p.256). Although these artists did not claim that they were influenced by her writings, during the same period the film critic Laura Mulvey wrote her influential essay "Visual pleasure and narrative cinema" (1975), in which she characterised the "determining male gaze" through which women's image has "continually been stolen". The projects of the artists discussed above offered methods of redressing the situation identified by Mulvey, or of taking back what the critic Lisa Tickner slightly later referred to as "colonized territory" by reversing the usual situation in which the female body is the object of art produced by male artists for a masculine audience (Tickner 1978, p.239).

Performance and environmental art provided women artists with other strategies to wrest the female body from the controlling male gaze and to enable its inhabitant to become a speaking subject. The live performances and films of Carolee Schneemann (q.v.), the earliest of which actually predate the feminist movement, were born from a desire to "make a gift of [her] body to other women: giving our bodies back to ourselves" (*ibid.*, p.247). In *Eye Body* (1963) she placed snakes on her naked body, suggestive of Minoan rituals; in *Meat Joy* (1964) she and several other actors, both male and female, engaged in an orgy involving pieces of raw meat. *Interior Scroll* (1975), in which she appeared on stage nude and proceeded to pull a scroll from her vagina and read from it, in particular spoke to the issue of women's ownership of their own bodies as a source of sexual pleasure. After painting on her body and establishing a correlation with the idea of a painter's live model, Schneemann read from the scroll in which "a happy man/a structuralist film-maker" says: "don't ask us/to look at your films ... /there are certain films/we cannot look at/the personal clutter/the persistence of feeling ..." (quoted in Broude and Garrard 1994, p.163). In this work, as in others, Schneemann asserted the right to present the female body in its own terms, unmediated by the male gaze.

Several other women performance artists used their bodies as a site of artistic activity during the 1970s. In her early work the German Rebecca Horn (q.v.) manipulated and extended parts of her body during such performances and installations as *Cornucopia: Seance for Two Breasts* (1970) and *Finger-Gloves: An Instrument to Extend the Manual Sensibilities* (1972). In France, Gina Pane (q.v.) evolved several performances that challenged the stereotypical view of the female body as a site of pleasure by their stress on pain. In *Escalade non anaesthesié* (1971; for illustration, see p.1065) she climbed up and down a ladder decked with sharp protrusions until her bare hands and feet were bleeding; in other works she transformed herself into a slab of meat (*Sentimental Action*, 1973) or chewed raw meat until she vomited. More recently, the Prague-born artist Jana Sterbak created performances that played upon the metaphorical identification of meat and the female body. In *Vanitas: Flesh Dress for an Albino Anorectic* (1987) she clothed a female body in a "dress" composed of 60 pounds of rotting flank steak. Eleanor Antin (q.v.) performed *Carving* (1973) over a period of a month during which she lost ten pounds, documenting the change through daily photographs.

Change to the actual body of the artist through weight loss has also been explored by Adrian Piper and more recently by Faith Ringgold (q.v.) in her several story quilts on that subject. Earlier, Piper had participated in a series of street performances called *Catalysis* (1970), in which she altered her physical appearance to depart radically from socially acceptable norms of personal comportment as, for example, when she rode on a subway train in New York garbed in clothing saturated with stale vinegar, eggs and milk. Martha Rosler (q.v.) performed and videotaped numerous works that challenged the acceptance of the objectification of the female body. In *Vital Statistics of a Citizen, Simply Obtained* (1973), for example, a woman (Rosler herself) was stripped, interrogated, her body measured and then videotaped while preparing food in a kitchen. More recently, in her videos, performances and installations, the Lebanese-born Mona Hatoum has gone beyond exploration of the external bodily surface. *Corps étranger* (1994) provides the viewer with a video tour of her interior vital organs, which are viewed on a screen on the floor of a dark circular booth, thanks to the technique of endoscopy.

Another approach adopted by women performance artists during the 1970s was to use their bodies in rituals that asserted women's strength and power through identification with imagery associated with prehistoric goddess worship. Cuban-born Ana Mendieta made several series of images, which she documented photographically, in which she covered her body with mud, flowers or burned her silhouette into the earth. "My art is the way I re-establish the bonds that unite me to the universe", she wrote. "It is a return to the maternal source. Through my earth/body sculptures I become one with the earth" (Gadon 1989, p.278). Through several performances and their photographic documentation, Mary Beth Edelson (q.v.) sought to establish links with traditional sites and images of the goddess. She used her own image as a "stand-in" for the goddess in private rituals at various coastal sites – Montauk, Long Island, the Outer Banks of North Carolina and the Neolithic Grapçeva cave, off the coast of the former Yugoslavia. She enhanced the photographic records of these events with drawing and collage, as the energy waves that radiate from her head in *Woman Rising* from North Carolina. Of her pilgrimage to the Yugoslavian cave where she surrounded her body, submerged to the waist, with a "fire ring" she said: "I felt like the center of the universe..." (*ibid.*, p.273).

In recent decades numerous other women artists have sought to re-establish a positive image of female power through the depiction of the goddess in her many guises. An early example of a work that illustrates such concerns was the temporary environmental sculpture *La Hon* ("She" in Swedish), built by Niki de Saint Phalle (q.v.) in collaboration with Jean Tinguely and installed at the Moderna Museet in Stockholm in 1966. Viewers were able to enter and exit this brightly painted, colossal, recumbent female figure through a vaginal portal, reiterating prehistoric reverence for the sacred feminine by recreating the primal experiences of birth and death, of moving from womb to tomb. A milk bar was housed in one breast and a cinema in her head. Like many of Saint Phalle's smaller *Venus* and *Nana* figures, the shape of this figure echoed the bulbous, fecund forms of the many prehistoric sculptures of women believed by some to be depictions of maternal deities. Soon after, Monica Sjöö painted a controversial image of *God Giving Birth* (1968; for illustration see p.1277), a black woman silhouetted against the sky with a baby's head emerging from her vulval area. This was the earliest of many images of the goddess made by Sjöö, a writer concerned with the lost tradition of the goddess, who has made numerous pilgrimages to various sacred sites, which she has incorporated into her paintings and drawings. Likewise Meinrad Craighead, who lived for 14 years as a cloistered nun in a Benedictine abbey, published a book, *The Mother's Songs* (1986), containing 40 of her paintings of the great Mother in which the maternal principle is associated with the continuous, generative power of the earth. In her scrolls Nancy Spero (q.v.) has used repeating images of powerful female deities such as the Celtic Shelagh-na-gig (*Chorus Line I*, 1985) and the Egyptian Nut (*To the Revolution*, 1983), images of "freedom from every kind of physical, mental and social constraint; a freedom we don't possess but need to nurture, as an idea of a feeling..." (Gadon 1989, p.338). Audrey Flack, a leading photo-realist painter, turned to sculpting images of "contemporary goddesses for a new age" (Gouma-Peterson's phrase in Los Angeles 1992) – reinterpreting traditional figures such as Medusa and Athena and creating hybrids such as the *Egyptian*

Rocket Goddess and *Islandia: Goddess of Healing Waters*, images that celebrate women's strength and power.

Other artists in the 1970s employed political strategies in their attempts to insert a female presence into the history of art. To this end, Sylvia Sleigh (q.v.) created paintings in which the traditional relationship between artist (male) and subject (female) was deliberately reversed. In such paintings as *Reclining Nude: Paul Rossano*, *Philip Golub Reclining* and most especially *Turkish Bath* (1973), a parody of Ingres's work of the same title, Sleigh placed the image of naked males in poses that were typical of those of the female nude in the post-Renaissance tradition. In a moving essay, May Stevens argued that "art should be taken to the revolution" (quoted in Witzling 1994, pp.71–3), a position that she had exercised in her own work for several decades, beginning in the 1970s with her series of "Big Daddy" images. In these works, based on a caricatured image of her father seated watching television with his pug dog on his lap, Stevens expressed her outrage at the militaristic, racist and patriarchal oppression that had become characteristic of American culture. During the 1980s she explored her matrilineage in a series of images juxtaposing the "ordinary" life of her mother with the "extraordinary" life of the radical Rosa Luxemburg, both of whom had been silenced by the patriarchy. Sleigh and Stevens both painted heroised images of their female contemporaries, and Sleigh, with four other artists, contributed paintings to the never-constructed "Sister Chapel", a recreation of the Sistine Chapel celebrating heroic women.

Some feminist artists sought to differentiate themselves and their works from the approaches chronicled above, considering them to be manifestations of "essentialism", in that, as in the past, women appeared to be designated in terms of their biological characteristics. Works that stressed a vaginal iconography were chided for once more defining women by their body parts. Likewise, performance art has been criticised as an ambiguous strategy, at risk for "the recuperation of the female body to the patriarchal spectacle" (Nead 1992, p.68). Similar accusations have been made against the movement to reclaim great goddess imagery, which critics see as based on the misguided belief that there is such a thing as a "feminine essence". Although it can be argued that looking back to cultures in which female strength was celebrated rather than denigrated hardly constitutes the acceptance of an essential femininity (as does Gloria Orenstein in *The Reflowering of the Goddess*, 1990), there has been a mounting chorus of voices that refuse to accept any universal construction of the category "woman".

Many feminist artists believe that because the female image has been over-determined in Western culture all representations of women are doomed to recreate stereotypes. This stance has been aligned with other post-modernist deconstructions of the history of art, and its practitioners have adopted strategies that subvert the common construction of the sign "woman" in the Western tradition. Mary Kelly, an American who did much of her early work in London, was an important proponent of this approach, which "uses multiple representational modes" (Owens 1983, p.491) by combining text, artefacts and natural fragments, presented as if on exhibition at an anthropological museum, to allow viewers to construct their own images. In *Post-Partum Document*, her first mature work,

she examined the mother-child relationship, and particularly the construction of motherhood and loss of maternal authority, by presenting a series of "mother's artefacts" including stained nappy liners, hand prints and recordings of early speech utterances. She avoided "the literal figuration of mother and child" as a "historical strategy...to cut across the predominant representation of the look...and to picture the woman as the subject of her own desire" (Kelly 1983, pp.xxvii–xxviii). In her next major work, *Interim* (1984–9), Kelly confronted the problem of "representing" the middle-aged woman, no longer useful in the patriarchy as a sex object or child-bearer, by offering the viewer a variety of textual narratives interspersed with images of women's clothing, graphs and advertising fragments. Here, too, she avoided the literal depiction of the female figure, allowing, instead, for multiple possible readings. Similarly, the French artist Annette Messager (q.v.) mixes various media – objects such as dolls, photographs and textual fragments – to encourage the viewer to examine critically cultural definitions of gender. Working in series, in small books (as in *My Jealousies* or *My Approaches*) or mixed-media installations (*Histories of Dresses*), Messager forces the viewer to piece together "ethnological" fragments, to reconstruct bodily experience, without depending on stereotyped images of femininity. Rosemarie Trockel, in Germany, also used fetishised imagery to encourage the viewer to construct "the feminine" through mechanically embroidered objects of clothing – hats, tights and "dead-pan" drawing.

Like other post-modern authors and artists, Kelly challenges viewers to construct the meaning of her works from shifting, unstable signifiers that often subvert accepted visual expectations. In this, her endeavour is similar to that of several American photographers. Lorna Simpson, like Kelly, "refuses the literal figuration" of her subject, often a black female, by presenting her figures from the rear without allowing us to see their faces and, like Kelly, accompanies her images with destabilising textual elements, as in *Twenty Questions (A Sampler)* (1986), where the accompanying text asks: "Is she pretty as a picture/Or clear as crystal/or pure as a lily/or black as coal/or sharp as a razor"? Of course, these questions have no simple answers, if any at all. Barbara Kruger (q.v.) collects "found" commercial photographic images and pairs them with provocative phrases built of "pronominal shifters" (I, we, you, they) that disrupt the power imbalance associated with the gaze in Western culture while at the same time revealing that "masculinity and femininity are not stable identities, but subject to exchange" (*ibid.*, p.499). Kruger has stated that one major goal in her work is "to welcome a female spectator into the world of men", which she achieves by inserting a female presence as the speaking and seeing subject, in such works as an untitled photograph of a stone face, affixed with the phrase "your gaze hits the side of my face". Sherrie Levine rephotographs works by such famous photographers as Walker Evans and Edward Weston, subverting the modernist and masculinist concept of the "great author". In her early photographs Cindy Sherman used her own image as model, mimicking "stills" from movies of the 1940s and 1950s, depicting stereotyped images of women, making "self-portraits" that destabilised the selfhood of their author, and reveal the extent to which "femininity is a masquerade" in this popular culture (*idem*). In her more recent work, Sherman has

Barbara Kruger: *Untitled (Your Gaze Hits the Side of My Face)*, 1981; photograph; 139.7 × 104.1 cm.

made huge coloured images of dismembered female figures, accompanied by such images of pollution as used condoms, rubbish and dildos. In these works Sherman contradicts the stereotyped image of women – glossy, contained, antiseptic.

While acknowledging how strategies such as Kelly's "explore desire and identity without colluding in the objectification of women", Lynda Nead also points out that the bodily norm Kelly assumes is one that is "both valued and exhibited within patriarchal culture". She continues:

> Denying visibility to "the female body" as a universal category perpetuates the invisibility of women whose bodies do not conform to the ideals of the dominant culture and who may be struggling for the right to physical and public visibility [Nead 1992, p.76].

Thus, some women artists have recently presented aspects of the female body that make visible what has been considered an "inappropriate" image of femininity. For example, the images of the British photographer Jo Spence (q.v.) "concern a working-class woman, aging and with a scarred body". Particularly in *Narratives of Dis-ease*, Spence explores some of her "feelings and experiences since being diagnosed and treated for breast cancer" (*ibid.*, p.80). Spence's process of making visible what has been taboo is related to the work of the young American sculptor Kiki Smith, most of whose works focus on the body in the process of breaking its boundaries of containment: bleeding, crying, lactating, defecating, birthing. Smith chose the theme of "the open, protruding, extended, secreting body" because she believes that "our bodies are basically stolen from us" and she "wanted to reclaim one's own turf" (Schliefer 1991, p.86).

One other tactic used by women artists to recast history with women's perspective included is related to the process of story-telling. This is a significant process, because so many stories in the Western tradition are deficient in female protagonists, both in sheer number and in how they are permitted to act. By telling stories in which women and other oppressed groups are given full voice as protagonists, artists "challenge the pervasive 'master narratives' of the culture that would contain them" (Lippard 1990, p.57). Artists and writers see that "speaking from the margins" can be a strategy of resistance to cultural obliteration (Hooks 1990, p.145). The African-American artist Faith Ringgold exemplifies this process in her story quilts, combining visual images and narrative text in a single frame, each spoken from the point of view of an African-American female protagonist. In *Tar Beach*, for example, Ringgold tells the story of eight-year-old Cassie Louise Lightfoot, a girl from Harlem, a segregated New York ghetto, who claims the George Washington Bridge, Union Hall and an ice-cream factory simply by flying over them, concluding that "anyone can fly". In her subsequent series *The French Collection*, Ringgold constructs a protagonist, Willia Marie Simone, a black American painter living in Paris, whose story "intersects" with many of the major monuments and practitioners of modern art history. Like the work of many earlier artists, this series of quilts by Ringgold is a deliberate attempt to insert a female – and in this case – an African-American presence into the standard historical narrative.

The de-centring, de-stabilising aim of feminist artistic practice has been compared to similar practices in post-modernism.

Just as post-modern artists and writers have challenged the hegemony of Western culture and its master narratives, so too have feminist artists questioned the Western privileging of the authority of the visible and its equation with "maleness" (cf. Owens 1983). But one way in which feminist projects are distinguished from other post-modern endeavours is that, despite their "deconstruction" of entrenched ways of seeing, rather than closing off possibilities through ambiguity they seek to open them up. Barbara Kruger "welcome[s] a female spectator" into the visible by giving the previously objectified female a voice with which to "talk back", to speak. Thus, it could be argued that much of the work described above is "reconstructive" in that its goal in subverting the Western tradition is to offer more balanced, less monolithic, more inclusive means of representing the visible world.

MARA R. WITZLING

Bibliography

Linda Nochlin, "Why have there been no great women artists?", *Woman in Sexist Society: Studies in Power and Powerlessness*, ed. Vivian Gornick and Barbara K. Moran, New York: Basic Books, 1971; reprinted New American Library, 1972, pp.480–510
John Berger, *Ways of Seeing*, New York: Viking, 1973
Judy Chicago and Miriam Schapiro, "Female imagery", *Womanspace Journal*, i/1, Summer 1973, pp.11–17
Dorothy Seiberling, "The female view of Erotica", *New York*, 14 February 1974
Judy Chicago, *Through the Flower: My Struggle as a Woman Artist*, New York: Doubleday, 1975; 2nd edition, New York: Doubleday, and London: Women's Press, 1982
Laura Mulvey, "Visual pleasure and the narrative cinema", *Screen*, no.16, Autumn 1975, pp.6–18; reprinted in *Visual and Other Pleasures*, Bloomington: Indiana University Press, and London: Macmillan, 1989
Cindy Nemser, *Art Talk: Conversations with 12 Women Artists*, New York: Scribner, 1975
Lucy R. Lippard, *From the Center: Feminist Essays on Women's Art*, New York: Dutton, 1976
Sara Ruddick and Pamela Daniels, *Working It Out: Twenty-Three Women Writers, Artists, Scientists and Scholars Talk about Their Lives and Work*, New York: Pantheon, 1977
Lisa Tickner, "The body politic: Female sexuality and women artists since 1970", *Art History*, i, 1978, pp.236–49; reprinted in *Looking On: Images of Femininity in the Visual Arts and Media*, ed. Rosemary Betterton, London and New York: Pandora, 1987
Judy Chicago, *The Dinner Party: A Symbol of Our Heritage*, New York: Doubleday, 1979
Eleanor Munro, *Originals: American Women Artists*, New York: Simon and Schuster, 1979
Carolee Schneemann, *More than Meat Joy: Complete Performance Works and Selected Writings*, ed. Bruce McPherson, New Paltz, NY: Documentext, 1979
The Ancient Religion of the Great Cosmic Mother of All, edited and extended by Barbara Mor, Trondheim, Norway: Rainbow Press, 1981; revised as *The Great Cosmic Mother: Rediscovering the Religion of the Earth*, San Francisco: Harper, 1987; 2nd edition, 1991
Rozsika Parker and Griselda Pollock, *Old Mistresses: Women, Art and Ideology*, London: Routledge, 1981
Charlotte Streifer Rubinstein, *American Women Artists from Early Times to the Present*, Boston: Hall, 1982
Mary Kelly, *Post-Partum Document*, London: Routledge, 1983
Craig Owens, "The discourse of others: Feminists and postmodernists", *The Anti-Aesthetic: Essays on Postmodern Culture*, ed. Hal Foster, Port Townsend: Bay Press, 1983; reprinted in Broude and Garrard 1992

Moira Roth, *The Amazing Decade: Women and Performance Art in America, 1970–80*, Los Angeles: Astro Artz, 1983

Art after Modernism: Rethinking Representation, exh. cat., New Museum of Contemporary Art, New York, 1984

Harmony Hammond, *Wrappings: Essays on Feminism, Art and the Martial Arts*, New York: TSL Press, 1984

Meinrad Craighead, *The Mother's Songs*, Mahwah, NJ: Paulist Press, 1986

Rozsika Parker and Griselda Pollock, *Framing Feminism: Art and the Women's Movement, 1970–85*, London and New York: Pandora Press, 1987

Griselda Pollock, *Vision and Difference: Femininity, Feminism and the Histories of Art*, London: Routledge, 1988

Christine Battersby, *Gender and Genius: Towards a Feminist Aesthetic*, Bloomington: Indiana University Press, and London: Women's Press, 1989

Elinor Gadon, *The Once and Future Goddess: A Symbol for Our Time*, San Francisco: Harper, and Wellingborough: Aquarian, 1989

Making Their Mark: Women Artists Move into the Mainstream, 1970–85, exh. cat., Cincinnati Art Museum, and elsewhere, 1989

Whitney Chadwick, *Women, Art and Society*, London and New York: Thames and Hudson, 1990; revised edition, 1996

Bell Hooks, *Yearning: Race, Gender and Cultural Politics*, Boston: South End Press, 1990

Mary Kelly: Interim, exh. cat., New Museum of Contemporary Art, New York, and elsewhere, 1990

Lucy R. Lippard, *Mixed Blessings: New Art in a Multicultural America*, New York: Pantheon, 1990

Gloria Feman Orenstein, *The Reflowering of the Goddess*, Oxford: Pergamon Press, 1990

Susan Rubin Suleiman, *Subversive Intent: Gender, Politics and the Avant-Garde*, Cambridge, MA: Harvard University Press, 1990

Suzi Gablik, *The Reenchantment of Art*, New York and London: Thames and Hudson, 1991

Faith Ringgold, *Tar Beach*, New York: Crown, 1991

Kristen Brooke Schliefer, "Inside and out: An interview with Kiki Smith", *Print Collector's Newsletter*, July 1991, pp.84-7

Mara R. Witzling, ed., *Voicing Our Visions: Writings by Women Artists*, New York: Universe, 1991; London: Women's Press, 1992

Breaking the Rules: Audrey Flack: A Retrospective, 1950–1990, exh. cat., Frederick S. Wight Art Gallery, University of California, Los Angeles, and elsewhere, 1992

Norma Broude and Mary D. Garrard, eds, *The Expanding Discourse: Feminism and Art History*, New York: Icon, 1992

Lynda Nead, *The Female Nude*, London and New York: Routledge, 1992

Norma Broude and Mary D. Garrard, eds, *The Power of Feminist Art: The American Movement of the 1970s*, New York: Abrams, and London: Thames and Hudson, 1994

Joanna Frueh, Cassandra L. Langer and Arlene Raven, eds, *New Feminist Criticism: Art, Identity, Action*, New York: HarperCollins, 1994

Mara R. Witzling, ed., *Voicing Today's Visions: Writings by Contemporary Women Artists*, New York: Universe, 1994

ARTISTS

A

Abakanowicz, Magdalena

Polish sculptor and graphic artist, 1930–

Born in Falenty, 20 June 1930. Studied at School of Fine Art, Sopot, 1949–50; Academy of Fine Arts, Warsaw, 1950–54. Married Jan Kosmowski, 1956. First travelled to the West, 1958, to the USA and Mexico, 1970–71, to Australasia and the Far East, 1976. Taught at the Academy of Fine Arts, Poznań, 1965–90. Recipient of gold medal, São Paulo Bienal, 1965; Grand Prize, World Crafts Council, New York, 1974; Gottfried-von-Herder Foundation prize, Vienna, 1979; Polonia Restituta medal, 1980; Alfred Jurzykowski Foundation award, New York, 1983; Francis Greenburger Foundation award, 1990; award for Distinction in Sculpture, Sculpture Center, New York, 1993; honorary doctorates from Royal College of Art, London, 1974, and Rhode Island School of Design, Providence, 1993. Chevalier, Ordre des Arts et Lettres, France, 1985. Lives in Warsaw.

Selected Individual Exhibitions

Galerie Kordegarda, Warsaw: 1960
Galerie Dautzenberg, Paris: 1962
Galerie Alice Pauli, Lausanne: 1967, 1969, 1971, 1975, 1977, 1979
  (retrospective), 1981, 1983, 1985
Kunstindustrimuseet, Oslo: 1967 (touring)
Stedelijk van Abbemuseum, Eindhoven: 1968–9 (touring)
Kunsthalle, Mannheim: 1969
Konsthall, Södertälje, Sweden: 1970
Pasadena Art Museum, CA: 1971
Kunstverein für die Rheinlande und Westfalen, Düsseldorf: 1972
Muzeum Sztuki, Łódź: 1974, 1991
Whitechapel Art Gallery, London: 1975
Art Gallery of New South Wales, Sydney: 1976 (touring, organised
  by Australian Council for the Arts)
Konsthall, Malmö: 1977 (*Organic Structures*, touring)
Polish Pavilion, Venice Biennale: 1980
Museum of Contemporary Art, Chicago: 1982–4 (touring retrospective)
Xavier Fourcade, New York: 1985
Palace of Exhibitions, Mücsarnok, Budapest: 1988
Städelsches Kunstinstitut und Städtische Galerie, Frankfurt am Main:
  1989
Marlborough Gallery, New York: 1989, 1992, 1993, 1994
Sezon Museum of Art, Tokyo: 1991 (touring)
Institute for Contemporary Art, PS 1 Museum, Long Island City, NY:
  1993

Bibliography

Judith Bumpus, "Rope environments", *Art and Artists*, ix, October
  1974, pp.36–41
Magdalena Abakanowicz, exh. cat., Museum of Contemporary Art,
  Chicago, and elsewhere, 1982
Hunter Drohojowska, "Magical mystery tours", *Art News*, lxxxiv,
  September 1985, pp.108–13
Leslie Milosky, "Art essay: Magdalena Abakanowicz", *Feminist
  Studies*, xiii, Summer 1987, pp.363–78
Magdalena Abakanowicz: Skulpturen, 1967–90, exh. cat.,
  Städelsches Kunstinstitut und Städtische Galerie, Frankfurt am
  Main, 1989
Magdalena Abakanowicz, exh. cat., Richard Gray Gallery, Chicago,
  1990 (contains bibliography)
Nancy Princenthal, "Abakanowicz: Memories and monuments", *Art
  in America*, lxxviii, March 1990, pp.178–83
Douglas Dreishpoon, "Monumental intimacy: An interview with
  Magdalena Abakanowicz", *Arts Magazine*, lxv, December 1990,
  pp.45–9
Michael Brenson, "Survivor art", *New York Times Magazine*, 29
  November 1992, pp.46–54
Magdalena Abakanowicz: Recent Sculpture, exh. cat., Museum of
  Art, Rhode Island School of Design, Providence, and elsewhere,
  1993
Magdalena Abakanowicz: War Games, exh. cat., Institute for
  Contemporary Art, PS 1 Museum, Long Island City, NY, 1993
Barbara Rose, *Magdalena Abakanowicz*, New York: Abrams, 1994
  (contains bibliography)
Mara R. Witzling, ed., *Voicing Today's Visions: Writings by
  Contemporary Women Artists*, New York: Universe, 1994
Michael Brenson, "Magdalena Abakanowicz's 'Abakans'", *Art
  Journal*, liv, Spring 1995, pp.56–61

Magdalena Abakanowicz entered the art world through the back door, so to speak, when she exhibited, in 1962, at the first Biennale International de la Tapisserie, in Lausanne, Switzerland. Even as a so-called weaver, she consciously defied traditional rules and techniques, eventually transforming this humble craft into some of the most memorable sculptures ever made. Defying rules has always been the artist's *modus operandi*, and the work that she has produced over the past 33 years – beginning with the *Abakans* and including her numerous rope installations, various *Heads*, *Seated Figures*, *Crowds*, *Backs*, *Embryology*, site-specific commissions and *War Games* – asks existential questions at the same time as it posits resolute truths. Her sculpture takes nothing for granted, except the human condition, with its foibles and contradictions, resilience and potential for change.

Abakanowicz: *Ancestor*, from the *War Games* series, 1989; wood and iron; 150 × 630 × 100 cm.; Courtesy Marlborough Gallery, New York

Abakanowicz described herself to the critic Michael Brenson as a "gypsie" who could "work in any place and in any part of the world" (Brenson 1992, p.50). She also told him that she wanted her work to affect everyone in some way, to "touch universal problems". However, despite her cosmopolitan intentions and the work's archetypal implications, the artist acknowledges that she and her art are by-products of a particular cultural history. As a young girl living in Poland, she survived World War II and, subsequently, a series of political upheavals that dramatically altered her world view. Her work is inextricably bound to these unsettling circumstances. And still, as an expression rich in levels of meaning, her sculpture transcends the autobiographical.

From the outset of her career, Abakanowicz stretched the limits of whatever her medium was. In the early 1960s she rebelled against the technical constraints of the loom and experimented with disparate materials, weaving together composite wall hangings whose designs recalled earlier paintings – an enchanted world she referred to as "my rain forest" – but whose surface density pushed towards the third dimension. These were trying times for the artist, who laboured long hours in the cramped quarters of Maria Laszkiewicz's Warsaw studio. It did not take long, however, to realise the sculptural potential of her circumstances. She recalled in an interview: "It was becoming clear to me that I could build a three-

dimensional reality; soft, full of secrets, protecting me, being a shield to me, and at the same time being my own creation, an integral part of myself. So the *Abakans* came into being" (Dreishpoon 1990, p.47).

The *Abakans*, begun around 1967, set the tenor for many of Abakanowicz's subsequent cycles. No one had ever used the loom to produce such monumental, free-standing entities, whose pliable constitution questioned traditional sculptural values. Massive beings with multiple personalities, these hollow personages possess a sense of mystery and association that distinguishes most of Abakanowicz's ideas regardless of medium. "Like all of Abakanowicz's cycles", wrote Michael Brenson, "the 'Abakans' lead outward, away from what they might appear to represent, into psychology and history, toward fundamental links between human beings and nature that are always waiting to be recognised and explored by the imagination" (Brenson 1995, p.58).

Whether one is confronting an installation of *Abakans*, *Standing Figures* or the more recent series of *War Games*, inside/outside is an apt metaphor for the multiple ways in which Abakanowicz's work can be perceived. Inside signifies the work's psychological centre, an allusive spirit, a place of refuge. Outside denotes its public persona, phenomenology, the way it interacts with viewers, its place in history. Whereas inside implies a personality that is shy, self-effacing and humble, outside suggests a more resilient, confident and ambitious entity. Such characterisations, however, are relative. That they coexist and are often interchangeable within any given piece reinforces its complex nature.

Early on Abakanowicz moved beyond weaving. Her rope installations at the Södertälje Konsthall in Sweden and the Nationalmuseum in Stockholm (both in 1970), as well as at the Pasadena Art Museum in California and the Malmö Konsthall in Sweden, in 1971 and 1977 respectively, were a *tour de force*. They transformed their environment, like theatre, and introduced a narrative dimension as well. Rope had a special place in the artist's material repertoire. Composed of many intertwined fibres or threads, rope could symbolise unitary strength and community. When twisted into convoluted knots, it signified chaos and disorder. Rope had multiple meanings for Abakanowicz, whose installations, when compared with contemporaneous work being done by Eva Hesse (q.v.) and Jackie Winsor (q.v.) in the USA, were by far the most ambitious in terms of their monumentality and scope.

By the late 1970s Abakanowicz was well known in international art circles. But it was not until 1980, when she represented Poland at the Venice Biennale, that her career accelerated. The work she exhibited there, a series of free-standing burlap figures, finally liberated her from what she called the "ghetto of weavers" (Brenson 1992, p.50), and since then her sculpture has developed in a number of directions. Never one to limit the ideological extensions of her ideas, she uses whatever materials and techniques seem appropriate for a given project. A series of *Sagacious Heads* (1989) was cast in bronze. For an installation in the Negev desert, in 1987, she carved seven huge disks out of limestone. Some of her standing figures (*Crowds*, 1986–91) were also cast in bronze, while others – a remarkable series of *Backs* begun in 1976 – were assembled with burlap and glue. The *War Games* (1989) are disregarded tree trunks stripped of their bark, whose extremities are capped with steel or bandaged with burlap. Materials are selected for their associative potential – fibre and burlap signify vulnerability and impermanence; bronze and stone strength and durability; wood and steel the collision between nature and technology – and their ability to embody grand themes (*Ancestor*, 1989; see illustration). The same can be said of her subjects, which gravitate between images of dissolution, death and disfigurement, and the possibility of rebirth, growth and perseverance. Her simple, iconic forms, posed alone or in communities, traverse a vast metaphorical terrain – isolation and solitude, meditation and prayer, ritual, judgement and incarceration – and straddle the line between abstraction and representation. Ultimately, her work can be seen as part of a vitalist tradition extending back to Henry Moore, Alberto Giacometti, Constantin Brancusi and Auguste Rodin. Within this sculptural continuum, Abakanowicz creates her own analogues for an ever-changing human condition.

Abakanowicz's work is represented in numerous international collections, including the Art Institute of Chicago; Detroit Institute of the Arts; Hirshhorn Museum, Washington, DC; Metropolitan Museum of Art and Museum of Modern Art, New York; Stedelijk Museum, Amsterdam; Centre Georges Pompidou, Paris; National Museum, Warsaw; National Museum of Modern Art, Kyoto; and the National Gallery of Australia, Canberra.

DOUGLAS DREISHPOON

Abbéma, Louise
French painter, printmaker and sculptor, 1858–1927

Born in Etampes, Seine-et-Oise, 30 October 1858. Studied in Paris under Charles Chaplin, Louis Dévedeux, Jean-Jacques Henner and Emile-Auguste Carolus-Duran. Several close friendships with women, notably with Sarah Bernhardt (q.v.). Recipient of merit award in art, Saxe-Coburg-Gotha, 1883; Palmes académiques, 1887. Chevalier, Légion d'Honneur, 1906. Died in Paris, July 1927.

Principal Exhibitions

Paris Salon: occasionally 1874–1926 (honourable mention 1881)
Galerie Georges Petit, Paris: 1889, 1890, 1891, 1892, 1893, 1899, 1901, 1902 (all individual)
Woman's Building, World's Columbian Exposition, Chicago: 1893
Exposition Universelle, Paris: 1900 (bronze medal)

Bibliography

Frédéric Chevalier, "Le Salon de 1877: L'Impressionisme au Salon", *L'Artiste*, July 1877
Louis Enault, *Paris: Salon 1885*, Paris, 1885
Angelo Mariani, *Figures contemporaines: Tirées de l'album Mariani*, Paris: Floury, 1899
Harispe, "Louise Abbéma", *Revue Illustrée*, i, 1907, pp.113–21
Gérald Schurr, *Les Petits Maîtres de la peinture, 1820–1920*, i, Paris: Editions de l'Amateur, 1975
P. Comte, *Ville de Pau: Musée des Beaux-Arts: Catalogue raisonné des peintures*, Pau, 1978
The Romantics to Rodin: French Nineteenth Century Sculpture from North American Collections, exh. cat., Los Angeles County Museum of Art and elsewhere, 1980
La Femme artiste d'Elisabeth Vigée-Lebrun à Rosa Bonheur, exh. cat., Musée Despiau-Wlerick, Donjon Lacataye, Mont-de-Marsan, 1981

"Je veux" ("I will") was the motto printed on Louise Abbéma's writing paper and this wilful formula guided her life and career for nearly 70 years. She was born into a wealthy, art-loving family with parents who moved in artistic circles, which led to her encounter at just 13 with Sarah Bernhardt (q.v.). The two women were to maintain a close friendship and, until her death, Bernhardt exerted much influence over Abbéma, affecting both her personality and the development of her artistic ideas. Abbéma's several friendships with women were the butt of snide remarks, especially from Robert de Montesquiou.

From 1874 Abbéma was included in the Salon with a portrait of *Mme ****, her mother (Salon cat. 1874, no.1; untraced). She obtained her first public success in 1876 with a full-length portrait of *Sarah Bernhardt* (Salon cat. 1876, no.1; private collection, Paris). Two years later she exhibited a medal (Salon cat. 1878, no.3990; Musée d'Orsay, Paris) made in 1875, which depicted the profile of her friend, entitled *Portrait of Mlle Sarah Bernhardt, Member of the Comédie Française*; the following year Bernhardt responded with a marble bust entitled *Portrait of Mlle Louise Abbéma* (Salon cat. 1879,

Abbéma: *Lunch in the Conservatory*, 1877; oil on canvas; 194 × 308 cm.; Musée des Beaux-Arts, Pau

no.4794; Musée d'Orsay). Abbéma did no more sculpture and devoted herself henceforth to a prolific output of work in her Paris studios, first at 91 rue Blanche and then, from 1876, at 47 rue Laffitte. Her work can be divided schematically into three broad categories according to technique: paintings, pastels and watercolours; large-scale decorative work; and engravings.

Abbéma began her painting career with portraits, and above all with many bust-length representations of actors and actresses at the Comédie Française (Comédie Française and Musée Carnavalet, Paris; e.g. *Mlle Jeanne Samary*, 1879; *Mlle B. Baretta*, 1880), depicted in their costumes. With rapid touches, she aimed above all to capture the spirit of the sitters. She remained faithful to this type of picture, which was to ensure her continued success. Some of her portraits, such as those of *Ferdinand de Lesseps* (Salon cat. 1884, no.1; untraced) and *Comtesse de Martel, Known as Gyp* (Salon cat. 1892, no.1; sold Neuilly, 14 November 1990) were shown at the annual Salons of the Société des Artistes Français. Others were private commissions that went straight from Abbéma's studio to their new home (portrait of *Mme Lucien Guitry*, 1876; sold Christie's, New York, 27 May 1993). Some are known today only from contemporary references, for example the portraits of the painters *Henner* and *Carolus-Duran* and of the architect *Charles Garnier*. At the Société des Artistes Français in 1922 she exhibited another portrait, of *Sarah Bernhardt in Her Studio at Belle-Isle-en-Mer* (Salon cat. 1922, no.1; untraced). After Bernhardt's death in 1923 Abbéma

offered the painting, in homage to her departed friend, to the curators of the Musée du Luxembourg and the Musée de Versailles, but without success.

From 1881 Abbéma developed a variety of techniques, using oil paint, pastels and watercolours, reflecting the influence of Japanese painting and her taste for flowers and animals. Some of her works at that time were painted on fans (*Sarah Bernhardt in Her Japanese Garden*, c.1885; Jane Voorhees Zimmerli Art Museum, New Brunswick; *Flowers in front of the Snow-Covered Tuileries Gardens*, sold Drouot-Richelieu, Paris, 3 April 1992). Her prolific output also included genre scenes as well as a few outdoor scenes, which are in effect portraits transported into the countryside, or often to the seaside, beginning in 1874 with *M. and Mme de Grièges, Baron de Dourdan and the Dog Molda at Tréport* (private collection, Paris) and again at the Salon of 1909 with *By the Sea* (Salon cat. 1909, no.1; untraced). Indoor scenes are more common, for example *Lunch in the Conservatory* (1877; see illustration), in which she painted the dramatic actor Emile de Najac, her parents and sister Jeanne and Sarah Bernhardt. This painting was described by one critic as "a great canvas reminiscent of Bazille in the earnestness of its execution, the authority of its composition and of Manet in its range of greys and the violence of its brush strokes" (Schurr 1975, p.12). Another indoor scene is *Song of the Afternoon* (Salon cat. 1885, no.2; sold Sotheby's, New York, 24 May 1995).

As a result of the building of town halls for the Paris arrondissements, Abbéma received commissions for decorative panels in several buildings: the Hôtels de Ville for the 7th, 10th (1902) and 20th arrondissements. She also executed work for other buildings in Paris: *Gismonda and the Woman of Samaria*, exhibited at the Salon of 1904, and *Magpie*, shown at the Salon of 1907, for the Théâtre Sarah Bernhardt (now Théâtre de la Ville); a *Joan of Arc* for the church of Notre-Dame-de-Lorette; and allegorical subjects for the Musée de l'Armée and the hall of the Société Nationale d'Horticulture de France. In the provinces, Abbéma was involved in a number of projects including the decoration of Fécamp Abbey, for which she provided a panel (Salon cat. 1899, no.1); and for the Grande Salle of the Hôtel de Ville in Redon she painted a portrait of *Anne, Duchess of Brittany* (1911). Outside France she executed a panel for the Governor's Palace in Dakar, Senegal. Lastly, Abbéma was a talented and well-known watercolourist, a regular contributor to journals such as the *Gazette des Beaux-Arts*, *L'Art* and *L'Art et la Mode*, as well as an illustrator who provided the engravings for René Maizeroy's *La Mer*.

The mixture of academic influences and impressionistic handling in Abbéma's work that had charmed critics before 1880 no longer found favour with many journalists after 1900, and her great social success went hand-in-hand with increasingly unfavourable reviews and relative obscurity after World War I. The contents of her studio were dispersed in 1937.

DOMINIQUE LOBSTEIN

Abbott, Berenice

American photographer, 1898–1991

Born in Springfield, Ohio, 17 July 1898. Attended Ohio State University, Columbus, 1917–18; received some training in journalism at Columbia University, New York, 1918. Studied sculpture independently in New York, 1918–21, then in the Paris studios of Emile Bourdelle and Constantin Brancusi, 1921–3, and at the Kunstschule, Berlin, 1923. Worked as studio assistant to Surrealist photographer Man Ray in Paris, 1923–5; introduced to the work of photographer Eugène Atget, 1925; opened own studio in Paris, 1926. Purchased prints and negatives from Atget's estate after his death in 1927. Returned to USA, 1929. Worked for *Fortune* and *Life* magazines, and for the Works Progress Administration Federal Art Project (WPA/FAP), 1935–9. Instructor in photography, New School for Social Research, New York, 1935–58. Worked for Physical Science Study Committee of Educational Services Inc., New York, 1958–61. Left New York for Maine, 1968. Recipient of honorary doctorates from University of Maine, Orono, 1971; Smith College, Northampton, Massachusetts, 1973; New School for Social Research, 1981; Bates College, Lewiston, Maine, 1981; Bowdoin College, Brunswick, Maine, 1982. Died in Monson, Maine, 9 December 1991.

Selected Individual Exhibitions
Julian Levy Gallery, New York: 1932
Museum of the City of New York: 1934, 1937
Yale University, New Haven: 1934 (touring), 1937
Springfield Museum of Fine Arts, MA: 1935
Massachusetts Institute of Technology, Cambridge: 1941, 1959, 1985
Galérie l'Epoque, Paris: 1947
Art Institute of Chicago: 1951
San Francisco Museum of Modern Art: 1953
Currier Gallery of Art, Manchester, NH: 1955, 1960
Toronto Art Museum: 1956
Smithsonian Institution, Washington, DC: 1960 (*Image of Physics*, touring), 1969 (retrospective), 1982
Museum of Modern Art, New York: 1970 (retrospective)
Witkin Gallery, New York: 1973
Marlborough Gallery, New York: 1976 (touring)
Galerie Zabriskie, Paris: 1977 (with Eugène Atget)
International Center of Photography, New York: 1981–2 (*The 20's and 30's*, touring)
New York Academy of Sciences: 1987
New York Public Library: 1989–90 (touring retrospective)

Selected Writings
"Eugène Atget", *Creative Art*, v, 1929, pp.651–6; reprinted in *Photography, Essays and Images: Illustrated Readings in the History of Photography*, ed. Beaumont Newhall, New York: Museum of Modern Art, 1980
A Guide to Better Photography, New York: Crown, 1941; revised as *New Guide to Better Photography*, 1953
The View Camera Made Simple, Chicago: Ziff-Davis, 1948
"What the camera and I see", *Art News*, l, September 1951, pp.36–7, 52
"The image of science", *Art in America*, xlvii/4, 1959, pp.76–9
The World of Atget, New York: Horizon, 1964

Bibliography
Elizabeth McCausland, *Changing New York*, New York: Dutton, 1939; reissued as *New York in the Thirties*, New York: Dover, and London: Constable, 1973
——, "Berenice Abbott – realist", *Photo Arts*, ii, Spring 1948, pp.46–50
Henry W. Lanier, *Greenwich Village Today and Yesterday*, New York: Harper, 1949
E.G. Valens, *Magnet*, Cleveland: World, 1964; London: Longman, 1970
——, *Motion*, Cleveland: World, 1965; London: Longman, 1970
Nathan Lyons, ed., *Photographers on Photography*, Englewood Cliffs, NJ: Prentice Hall, 1966
Chenoweth Hall, *A Portrait of Maine*, New York: Macmillan, 1968
E.G. Valens, *The Attractive Universe*, Cleveland: World, 1969
Anne Tucker, ed., *The Woman's Eye*, New York: Knopf, 1973
Women of Photography, exh. cat., San Francisco Museum of Art and elsewhere, 1975
Berenice Abbott, exh. cat., Marlborough Gallery, New York, and elsewhere, 1976
Alice C. Steinbach, "Berenice Abbott's point of view", *Art in America*, lxiv, November–December 1976, pp.77–81
Margaretta K. Mitchell, *Recollections: Ten Women of Photography*, New York: Viking, 1979
Berenice Abbott: Documentary Photographs of the 1930s, exh. cat., New Gallery of Contemporary Art, Cleveland, 1980
Michael G. Sundell, "Berenice Abbott's work in the thirties", *Prospects: An Annual of American Cultural Studies*, v, 1980, pp.269–92
Berenice Abbott: The 20's and 30's, exh. cat., International Center of Photography, New York, and elsewhere, 1981
Avis Berman, "The unflinching eye of Berenice Abbott", *Art News*, lxxx, January 1981, pp.86–93
Hank O'Neal, *Berenice Abbott: American Photographer*, New York: McGraw-Hill, 1982; as *Berenice Abbott: Sixty Years of Photography*, London: Thames and Hudson, 1982

Abbott: *Newsstand, 32nd Street and 3rd Avenue, 19 November 1935*, from *Changing New York*; New York Public Library, Photography Collection, Miriam and Ira D. Wallach Division of Art, Prints and Photographs, Astor Lenox and Tilden Foundation

David M. Maxfield, "Berenice Abbott: A photographer of the twentieth century", *Arts in Virginia*, xxiv/1–2, 1983–4, pp.30–39

Julia van Haaften, ed., *Berenice Abbott*, New York: Aperture, 1988

Berenice Abbott, Photographer: A Modern Vision, exh. cat., New York Public Library and elsewhere, 1989

David Vestal and others, *Berenice Abbott: Photographer*, 2nd edition, Washington, DC: Smithsonian Institution Press, 1990 (first published as exh. cat., Museum of Modern Art, New York, 1970)

Joann Prosyniuk, ed., *Modern Arts Criticism*, ii, Detroit: Gale Research, 1992

Although Berenice Abbott made her mark as a documentary photographer, she originally trained as a sculptor with Emile Bourdelle and Constantin Brancusi in Paris and Berlin. After deciding to devote her life to photography, she became Man Ray's photographic assistant in 1923, and in 1926 she opened her own portrait studio in Paris. For three years she photographed creative celebrities including James Joyce, Neil Fujita, Jean Cocteau, André Gide, Marie Laurencin (q.v.), André Siegfried and Eugène Atget. She also photographed many of the expatriate American artists and writers who were

in Paris in this period. Her first exhibition of portrait photographs was held at the Au Sacre du Printemps gallery in Paris in 1926.

Abbott had encountered Atget's documentary photographs of Paris in 1925 and was immediately captivated by his work, so different from her own. Her embracing of his aesthetic marked a watershed in her career: exposed to the authority of his visual conception and purity of form, she appeared to refute the exotic and Surrealist influence evident in her earlier portraits. After Atget's death, in 1927, she determined to save his work and to bring it to international attention. With the financial backing of the New York art dealer Julian Levy, in 1928 she purchased 5000 of Atget's photographs from his estate.

In 1929 Abbott visited New York and was so impressed by the city's complexity and vitality that she decided to close her Paris studio and return there to live. She brought with her a portion of Atget's oeuvre, and in 1930 she arranged publication of a book, *Atget Photographe de Paris*. The effect of Atget's straightforward, uninflected documentary style is evident in her photographic work after her return to the USA. By the mid-1930s Abbott, with Edward and Brett Weston, Charles Sheeler and Paul Outerbridge, spearheaded the American Realist photographic style.

Deeply affected by Atget's style and by his commitment to recording the streets of historical Paris, Abbott determined to undertake a comprehensive portrait of New York, to document its changing appearance and interpret its vital spirit through the camera. She worked alone on this project, using an 8 × 10-inch (20.3 × 25.4 cm.) camera. In contrast to her exploration of human character in the Paris portraits, in urban landscapes she eliminated the human face wherever possible, attempting to produce compositions devoid of sentimentality and psychological overtones. A selection of early images was shown at the Museum of the City of New York in 1932, and a major one-woman exhibition of her photographs was held there in 1934. As arts funding was scarce in this period – there was no official patronage – in 1935 Abbott applied to the Works Progress Administration (WPA), and obtained support through the US government's New Deal program. In her proposal to the WPA Abbott wrote:

> To photograph New York City means to seek to catch in the sensitive and delicate photographic emulsion the spirit of the metropolis, while remaining true to its essential fact, its hurrying tempo, its congested streets, the past jostling the present. The concern is not with an architectural rendering of detail, the buildings of 1935 overshadowing everything else, but with a synthesis which shows the skyscraper in relation to the less colossal edifices which preceded it ...

Abbott's images from this period of Manhattan shop windows, such as *Chicken Market, 55 Hester Street* (1937), *Blossom Restaurant, 103 Bowery* (1935) and *Bread Store, 259 Bleecker Street* (1937) reveal a visual sensibility reminiscent of Atget. She always denied the influence of Atget's photographs of French culture, however, citing her inclusion of printed texts as well as her treatment of the diffused reflections of mirrored objects. In many of the New York photographs the words become part of a larger object and carry more impact than their original, literal meaning. During a period of nine years she took hundreds of photographs of New York, recording streets, residences, commercial buildings, windows, parks, bridges, roads, cemeteries and civic monuments. Among the best known are *Newsstand, 32nd Street and 3rd Avenue, 19 November 1935* (see illustration) and *Father Duffy, Times Square* (1937), both of which use a wealth of detail to describe the subject as well as the moment of recording. Throughout the work the story is one of contrast and change: old is next to new; decay invades beauty.

Abbott's photographs of New York have become a valuable historical resource, because many of the landmarks she documented no longer exist. In 1939 a book of her photographs titled *Changing New York* was published under the auspices of the Federal Art Project, with captions by Elizabeth McCausland. The negatives and a set of master prints from the project are housed in the Museum of the City of New York.

Much of Abbott's work in the 1940s and 1950s was devoted to scientific experimental photography. She published an instruction manual, *A Guide to Better Photography*, in 1941, a book of photographs titled *Greenwich Village Today and Yesterday* in 1949 and *A New Guide to Better Photography* in 1953. Her studies of motion and light contributed to the understanding of physical laws and the properties of liquids and solids. A series of photographs she made between 1958 and 1961 for Educational Services Inc. was circulated as an exhibition, the *Image of Physics*, by them and the Smithsonian Institution. Other scientific books for which she provided photographs included *Magnet* (1964) and *Motion* (1965), both by E. G. Valens.

Abbott continued to promote Atget's work in this period. She produced 100 copies of the *Eugène Atget Portfolio*, a selection of prints made from his original glass negatives, in 1956, and her *World of Atget* was published in 1964. Her efforts to secure his reputation culminated in the sale to the Museum of Modern Art, New York, in 1968 of the vast collection of Atget photographs, which became known as the Abbott-Levy Collection; four exhibitions from the Collection were later held there. Two books of Abbott's own photographs were published in the late 1960s: *A Portrait of Maine* (1968) and *The Attractive Universe* (1969). A retrospective exhibition of her work was held at the Museum of Modern Art in 1970. She was also awarded several honorary doctoral degrees. Despite her long and prolific career, Berenice Abbott will be remembered mainly for her distinctive architectural record of New York in the 1930s and her powerfully revealing portraits of American expatriates and the fashionable/intellectual world of Paris in the 1920s.

ELAINE A. KING

Accardi, Carla
Italian painter, 1924–

Born in Trapani, Sicily, 9 October 1924. Studied at the Accademia delle Belle Arti in Palermo and then studied in Florence. Settled in Rome, 1946; met the artists Antonio Sanfilippo, Giulio Turcato, Pietro Consagra and Ugo Attardi, and went with them to Paris. Co-founder of Forma group, 1947. Married Sanfilippo, 1949; daughter born 1951. Included in the exhibitions *Individualità d'oggi* at Galleria Spazio, Rome, and *Individualità d'aujourd'hui* at Galerie Rive Droite, Paris, organised by French critic Michel Tapié, 1955, and received international recognition. Joined Continuità group, 1961. Became active in the feminist movement, 1970s. Lives in Rome.

Selected Individual Exhibitions
Libreria Age d'Or, Rome: 1950
Libreria Salto, Milan: 1951 (with Antonio Sanfilippo)
Galleria San Marco, Rome: 1955
Galerie Stadler, Paris: 1956, 1965
Galleria dell'Ariete, Milan: 1957, 1966
Galleria La Salita, Rome: 1958, 1959, 1961
Galleria Notizie, Turin: 1959, 1960, 1964, 1966
Venice Biennale: 1964, 1988
Loggetta Lombardesca, Pinacoteca Communale, Ravenna: 1983
Padiglione d'Arte Contemporanea, Milan: 1983
Ex-Convento di San Carlo, La Salerniana, Erice: 1983 (retrospective)
Istituto Italiano di Cultura, Madrid: 1985

Galleria Civica, Modena: 1989 (retrospective)
Museo Civico, Gibellina: 1990 (retrospective)
Museo d'Arte Contemporanea, Rivoli: 1994 (retrospective)

Bibliography

Maurizio Vallarino, "Luminous marks", *Art and Artists*, no.75, June 1972, pp.30–35

L'altra metà dell'avanguardia, 1910–1940: Pittrici e scultrici nei movimenti delle avanguardie storiche, exh. cat., Palazzo Reale, Milan, and elsewhere, 1980

Carla Accardi, exh. cat., Padiglione d'Arte Contemporanea, Milan, 1983

Carla Accardi, exh. cat., Istituto Italiano di Cultura, Madrid, 1985

Italian Art in the 20th Century: Painting and Sculpture, 1900–1988, exh. cat., Royal Academy, London, and elsewhere, 1989

Rosma Scuteri, "Carla Accardi", *Flash Art*, no.152, 1990, pp.134–7 (interview)

Robert C. Morgan, "Carla Accardi", *Tema Celeste*, no.30, 1991, pp.52–5

Carla Accardi, exh. cat., Museo d'Arte Contemporanea, Rivoli, 1994

Cesare Pavese said that when he wrote he always took off from where his last piece had ended. Carla Accardi read Pavese's notes as a young child, and has made a career of emulating his artistic model. Since she first began to paint in the mid-1940s, she has with unwavering consistency explored aspects of non-figurative abstract art, every period of her oeuvre expanding on or incorporating aspects of earlier periods.

Accardi's early work, which echoed post-Cubist language, was among the first forays into abstract art in Italy. She was a founding member of Forma, a group of young abstract artists that formed in 1947 as a contrast to the gestural-abstractionist group Informel. After an early period of works that Accardi considers to be mostly studies or experiments, and which culminated in a crisis of anxiety in 1953, she re-emerged in 1954 having arrived at what she saw as "a personal style" (Vallarino 1972, p.30). She began researching linear rhythms and developed an automatic script-like sign, likened to the works of Mark Tobey. This new, mature style of painting began with a series of large-scale, organic web-like patterns of clearly delineated white script on monochrome black backgrounds. The choice of black-and-white palette was influenced by her passion for the cinema and her interest in the role of photography in the modern era. Furthermore, for Accardi these two colours represented absolutes: absolute light against a total absence of light.

Over time Accardi began incorporating areas of grey into her paintings, as in *Materico con grigi* (1954; Rosangela Cochran Collection, Turin), where the overlapping lines of slender black script are complemented with staccato arcs of various hues of grey. Accardi progressed to the addition of first muted, then increasingly saturated colour, as in *Labirinto con settora* (1957; Luciano Pistoi Collection, Rome). This work demonstrates the manner in which Accardi moves between periods in a single painting, being in many ways typical of the earlier black-and-white paintings. Yet it also anticipates her optical works, in the replacement of white tempera with red enamel in two subdivisions of the canvas, and also in the incorporation of black-on-white signs, which create visual push-and-pull between the positive and negative space.

In 1961 Accardi had completed the black-and-white painting series and confronted colour in earnest. She joined the

Accardi: *Millenaria*, 1988

group Continuità and, in accordance with its tenets, introduced greater order and deliberation into her work, in part as a reaction against the group Informel. The script-like signs she had developed in her earlier work broadened to more precise interlocked shapes, more homogeneous than in her earlier work, and sometimes presented in a series of repeated groups, as in *Panel in Plexiglass and Fluorescent Paint* (1965; Galleria Marlborough, Rome). The signs are coloured with solid hues that have the same essential, defined quality and the strength of black and white. Through the juxtaposition of two or three high-contrast – though not necessarily complementary – colours of equal intensity, Accardi developed a style of optical painting that emphasised the radiance of colour and light.

The works of the early to mid-1960s can be seen as a continuation of the positive/negative space ambiguity studies of the 1950s, with an accent on the chromatic value. In *L'est* (1964; Galerie Stadler, Paris) she painted alternating areas of thick and thin calligraphic forms in dark crimson on a muted olive ground, creating an over-sized chequerwork grid pattern. The all-over patterning of small curved and circular red shapes in irregular lines creates an equally intricate negative pattern in the complementary base colour. These colour contrast paintings led to more overt experiments in optical image fluctuation, as in *Bianco Bianco* (1967; Galleria Notizie, Rome), where two semicircles of small S-shaped strokes expand in a rippling pattern across the canvas, creating the illusion of a bending frame.

Wanting to explore the luminosity of colour without the distraction of an opaque support, Accardi began in the mid-1960s to paint with fluorescent pigment on clear plastic sico-foil. The transparency of the support allows the works to react with the light of the surrounding space, which emphasises the optical vibrations of the colour-sign patterns. She then began creating spatial objects, the most complex of which is *Triplice tenda* (1970; Galleria Qui-Arte Contemporanea, Rome), one of a series of objects inspired by Arab tents. Accardi constructed three fragile, freestanding tents of stretched plastic covered in regular oblique lines of pink tilde-shaped strokes. The tents are placed one outside the other, each one larger than the last, with the maximum height reaching over 4 metres. The rippling effect of the painted patterns on the transparent plastic is complemented by the actual vibration of the three tents, which respond to the slightest movement near them. The spectator participates in this flux in the most intimate way, as she or he is able to walk into the art work and become a part of it.

In the 1970s Accardi immersed herself in the Italian feminist political movement, an immersion that influenced her art. She felt the need for structure, and began working again in black, white and a variety of shades of grey. Her mark-making became more repetitive, more anonymous, and was eventually abandoned in a series of transparent woven works in which the expressive element of the artist's hand was completely eliminated.

Accardi suffered another period of artistic crisis in 1979. From this, she emerged to create a series of shaped canvases, in which she approached painting from the edges, concentrating on the stretcher bars. As she gradually began painting again, she moved in a new direction using unprimed canvas as she had used black in the black-and-white works and as she had used the plastic: the raw canvas constituted colour in her works as much as the vinyl paints had done. While she explored a new way of painting in this period, Accardi continued to incorporate aspects of her earlier work in the new. In *Broad Daylight and Deep Night* (1985; artist's collection), for example, the script-signs she developed in the 1950s and used throughout her career have simply grown in size and definition. As biomorphic shapes of flat colour outlined in a contrasting colour, they could be the non-figurative equivalent of Keith Haring's work. Accardi continued to play with the effects of complementary colours, creating a frame within the frame of *Daylight* by changing the central blue forms outlined in red to green forms outlined in orange on the outer 20 centimetres of the canvas. The ambivalence between positive and negative space also remains, raw canvas creating textured shapes between patches of solid vinyl colour. In the later 1980s Accardi began to allow traces of her mark-making to remain on her finished canvases. In *Twigs, Birches, Crocuses* (1988; Galleria Pieroni, Rome) she allows for slight fluctuation in brightness of her surface colour. In *Dittico Lilla* (1988; artist's collection) there are visible brush strokes and even drippings on the canvas.

The new period of experimentation in which Accardi is still immersed incorporates techniques from a number of her past periods. Works such as *Per gli stretti spazi No.2* (1988; artist's collection) have a grey background painted in a variety of subtle hues and traversed by large signs of muted colour, on top of which is thick, painterly calligraphy in a vibrant hue.

JANELLE MELLAMPHY

Affry, Adèle d' *see* Marcello

Agar, Eileen
British painter, 1899–1991

Born in Buenos Aires, Argentina, 1 December 1899. Moved to England, 1906. Attended weekly classes at Byam Shaw School of Art, London, 1919–20; studied at Leon Underwood School of Painting and Sculpture, London, 1920–21; Slade School of Fine Art, London, 1922–4. Father died, leaving her a private income, 1925. Eloped to France with fellow student Robin Bartlett, 1925; divorced 1929. Lived with Hungarian writer Joseph Bard from 1926; married him 1940; he died 1975. Lived in France, 1928–30; studied briefly under Cubist painter Frantisek Foltyn in Paris, returning to London in 1930. Contributed to literary magazine the *Island*, edited by Bard, 1930–31. Joined London Group, 1933. Affair with Paul Nash, 1935–40. Spent summer of 1937 in Mougins with Nash, Nusch Eluard and Picasso. Included in *International Surrealist Exhibition*, New Burlington Galleries, London, 1936; also participated in International Surrealist exhibitions in New York (1936), Tokyo (1937), Paris (1938), Amsterdam (1938) and London (1940). Ceased painting during World War II. Lived in Kensington, London, from 1957, often spending winters in Canary Islands. Associate member, Royal Academy, 1990. Died in London, 17 November 1991.

Selected Individual Exhibitions
Bloomsbury Gallery, London: 1933
Redfern Gallery, London: 1942 (with Michael Rothenstein)
Leger Gallery, London: 1947
Hanover Gallery, London: 1949, 1951
Obelisk Gallery, London: 1957
Brook Street Gallery, London: 1962, 1964 (retrospective)
Galleria Billico, Rome: 1963
Commonwealth Art Gallery, London: 1971 (retrospective)
New Art Centre, London: 1975, 1976, 1978, 1981, 1983, 1984
Birch and Conran Fine Art, London: 1987 (retrospective)

Selected Writings
"Womb magic", *Island*, December 1931
A Look at My Life, London: Methuen, 1988 (with Andrew Lambirth)

Bibliography
International Surrealist Exhibition, exh. cat., New Burlington Galleries, London, 1936
Herbert Read, ed., *Surrealism*, London: Faber, and New York: Harcourt Brace, 1936
Eileen Agar: Retrospective, exh. cat., Commonwealth Art Gallery, London, 1971
Dada and Surrealism Reviewed, exh. cat., Arts Council of Great Britain, London, 1978

Agar: *Autobiography of an Embryo*, 1933–4; oil on board; Tate Gallery, London

Thirties: British Art and Design Before the War, exh. cat., Arts Council of Great Britain, London, 1979

Dawn Ades, "Notes on two women Surrealist painters: Eileen Agar and Ithell Colquhoun", *Oxford Art Journal*, iii/1, 1980, pp.36–42

Eileen Agar: Paintings and Drawings, exh. cat., New Art Centre, London, 1981

Whitney Chadwick, *Women Artists and the Surrealist Movement*, London: Thames and Hudson, and Boston: Little Brown, 1985

A Salute to British Surrealism, 1930–1950, exh. cat., The Minories, Colchester, and elsewhere, 1985

Angels of Anarchy and Machines for Making Clouds: Surrealism in Britain in the Thirties, exh. cat., Leeds City Art Galleries, 1986

Eileen Agar: A Retrospective, exh. cat., Birch and Conran Fine Art, London, 1987

La Femme et le surréalisme, exh. cat., Musée Cantonal des Beaux-Arts, Lausanne, 1987

Teresa Grimes, Judith Collins and Oriana Baddeley, *Five Women Painters*, London: Lennard, 1989

Andrew Wilson, "The spirit of Surrealism", *Art Line Magazine*, 1989 (special supplement, with Birch and Conran Gallery, London)

Gill Houghton and Pauline Barrie, "Eileen Agar", *Women Artists Slide Library Journal*, no.27, February–March 1989, pp.5–7; no.28, April–May 1989, pp.20–21

Judith Young Mallin, "Eileen Agar", *Surrealism and Women*, ed. Mary Ann Caws and others, Cambridge: Massachusetts Institute of Technology Press, 1991, pp.213–27

Lillian Gethic, "Blazing a trail", *Feminist Art News*, iv/4, 1992, pp.8–9

Ten Decades: Careers of Ten Women Artists Born 1897–1906, exh. cat., Norwich Gallery, Norfolk Institute of Art and Design, Norwich, 1992

Brigitte Libmann, "British women Surrealists: Deviants from deviance", *This Working Day World: Social, Political and Cultural History of Women's Lives, 1914–45*, ed. Sybil Oldfield, London: Taylor and Francis, 1994, pp.156–8

Eileen Agar has the distinction of being the only British woman painter included in the International Surrealist exhibition of 1936, which launched Surrealism in Britain. With Emmy Bridgwater and Edith Rimmington, she remained one of the few women members of the British Surrealist Group organised around E.L.T. Mesens during the late 1930s and early 1940s. She survived the notorious argument in 1940 at the Barcelona Restaurant in London, when Mesens demanded that members exhibit only in Surrealist shows, because she alone was allowed dual membership of the Surrealist Group and the London Group. Many other artists, including Ithell Colquhoun (q.v.), Toni del Renzio, Grace Pailthorpe and Reuben Mednikoff left at this point. Agar's adherence to Surrealist principles has resulted in her work appearing in nearly every retrospective and overview of British Surrealism since the 1930s.

Agar's early work of the late 1920s consisted of portraits and self-portraits produced in a loosely post-Impressionist style (e.g. *Self-Portrait*, 1927; National Portrait Gallery, London). Her early training was with Leon Underwood, where her peers included Henry Moore, Gertrude Hermes (q.v.) and the architect Rodney Thomas. She then moved to the Slade, and in 1925 eloped with a fellow student, Robin Bartlett, escaping her family and travelling to Paris and then Spain before settling in Normandy for the brief time that the marriage lasted. In 1926 she met Joseph Bard, a Hungarian writer and poet, moving to Paris with him in 1929. Here she studied briefly with the Cubist painter Foltyn, and met many avant-garde artists and writers. In the early 1930s she began experimenting with abstraction and the representation of space, producing such works as *Movement in Space* (1930–31), and began using collage and paper cut-outs in her work (*Three Symbols*, 1930; Tate Gallery, London). In her short essay "Womb magic" (1931) Agar discussed the dominance of a feminine type of imagination:

> Apart from rampant and hysterical militarism, there is no male element left in Europe, for the rational and intellectual conception of life has given way to a more miraculous creative interpretation and artistic imaginative life is under the sway of womb magic [quoted in Wilson 1989].

Many of the themes in her article are realised in *Autobiography of an Embryo* (1933–4; see illustration), which mixes imagery of womb, egg and foetus and the languages of procreation and creation yet retains an organised classical structure. *Quadriga*

(1935; Collection Roland Penrose) uses the horse motif from a Greek frieze, repeating the motif in each of the four divisions of the canvas and modulating the treatment of each.

Agar was selected for the Surrealist exhibition of 1936 by Paul Nash and Herbert Read, who were both "enchanted by the rare quality of her talent, the product of a highly sensitive imagination and a feminine clairvoyance" (Ades 1980, p.37). She showed three paintings and five objects at this exhibition. *Modern Muse* (1931), for example, offers a pictographic merging of male and female active and passive elements, linking both sexual and artistic imagery. She had met Nash in Swanage in the summer of 1935, and through him she developed her long-standing interest in the study of shells, fossils, plant life and the symbolic function of the natural world. Agar's *Seashore Monster* is a found object – an encrusted anchor chain – but it becomes a metaphor for Surrealist artistic creativity, created by nature, chance and man in equal combination.

In the late 1930s Agar made other experiments with found objects. Her work, including the first version of *Angel of Anarchy* (1937; destroyed), was illustrated in the *London (Gallery) Bulletin* and shown in the International Surrealist exhibition in Amsterdam in 1938. The second version (1940; Tate Gallery) has become widely reproduced as an iconic Surrealist object. In both, a plaster cast of Bard's head is transformed, in the first case through the addition of paint, feathers and collage, while in the second version the face is entirely wrapped in silk fabric and beads with additional feathers both "luxuriant and vaguely threatening". Other Surrealist objects include *Marine Object* (1939; Tate Gallery), *Ceremonial Hat for Eating Bouillabaisse* (1936; artist's estate) and *Fishbaskets* (1965; Tate Gallery). Collage and chance effects were also increasingly incorporated into her painting, as in *Battle Cry/Bullet-Proof Painting* (1938; Collection Gordon Onslow Ford), which uses lead paint and plaster on a metal surface, and *Precious Stones* (1936; Leeds City Art Galleries).

Agar's work was interrupted by the war effort, and she had great difficulty in re-establishing herself after it ended. In 1957 she painted *Bomber* (repr. London 1981), a memory of a holiday spent in the Canary Islands in the early 1950s, the first of many painting trips there. After 1965 she began painting in acrylics rather than oils and on a larger scale (122 × 152 cm. as opposed to 50 × 76 cm.), as in *Creatures of the Sea*, *Room with a View of the Moon*, *War Bride* and *Sleepwalkers*, all of which were exhibited in Agar's retrospective of 1987 that revived her career in the late 1980s, although *Slow Movement* (1970; Scottish National Gallery of Modern Art, Edinburgh) is executed in oil and pencil on canvas. Agar's works are often described as depending on auto-suggestion. She also represents the abstract wing of Surrealist painting. Her affairs with Nash and Eluard and her contact with most of the Surrealist circle in Paris during the 1930s have led to her characterisation as an archetypal Surrealist muse or "free and adored" woman. Although she was an independent woman with a private income, she nevertheless retained her commitment to painting throughout her life.

KATY DEEPWELL

Albers, Anni
German designer, weaver and graphic artist, 1899–1994

Born Annelise Fleischmann in Berlin, 12 June 1899. Studied art in Berlin under Martin Brandenburg, 1916–19. Studied at Kunstgewerbeschule, Hamburg, 1919–20; Bauhaus in Weimar, 1922–5, in Dessau, 1925–9 (Bauhaus diploma 1930). Worked independently in Dessau then Berlin, 1930–33; also part-time instructor and acting director of the Bauhaus weaving workshop. Married artist Josef Albers, 1925; he died 1976. Emigrated to USA, November 1933; became US citizen, 1937. Assistant professor of art, Black Mountain College, North Carolina, 1933–49. Moved to New York, 1949; first weaver to have a solo exhibition at Museum of Modern Art. Moved to New Haven, on Josef Albers's appointment to Chair of Design at Yale University, 1950. Turned to printmaking, 1963. Recipient of medal for craftsmanship, American Institute of Architects, 1961; fellowship, Tamarind Lithography Workshop, Los Angeles, 1964; gold medal for "uncompromising excellence", American Crafts Council, 1980; honorary doctorates from Maryland Institute College of Art, Baltimore, 1972; York University, Toronto, 1973; Philadelphia College of Art, 1976; University of Hartford, Connecticut, 1979; Rhode Island School of Design, Providence, 1990; Royal College of Art, London, 1990. Died 9 May 1994.

Selected Individual Exhibitions
Museum of Modern Art, New York: 1949, 1990
Wadsworth Atheneum, Hartford: 1953
Massachusetts Institute of Technology, Cambridge: 1959
Carnegie Institute, Pittsburgh: 1959
Yale University Art Gallery, New Haven: 1959
Colorado Springs Fine Arts Center: 1959
Contemporary Art Museum, Houston: 1960
Kunstmuseum der Stadt, Düsseldorf: 1975
Bauhaus-Archiv, Museum für Gestaltung, Berlin: 1975
Brooklyn Museum, NY: 1977
Queen's College Library, New York: 1979
Galerie Denise René, Paris: 1984
Renwick Gallery, National Museum of American Art, Smithsonian Institution, Washington, DC: 1985–6 (touring retrospective)
Mary Ryan Gallery, New York: 1989
Villa Stuck, Munich: 1989 (with Josef Albers)

Selected Writings
"Work with material", *Black Mountain College Bulletin*, v, 1938; reprinted in *College Art Journal*, iii, January 1944, pp.51–4
"Handweaving today: Textile work at Black Mountain College", *Weaver*, vi, January–February 1941, pp.3–7
"We need crafts for their contact with materials", *Design*, xlvi, December 1944, pp.21–2
"Fabrics", *Arts and Architecture*, lxv, March 1948, p.33
"Weavings", *Arts and Architecture*, lxvi, February 1949, p.24
"Ben Nicholson: Paintings, reliefs, drawings ... 1948", *Magazine of Art*, xliii, January 1950, p.36 (review)
"Fabric: The pliable plane", *Craft Horizons*, xviii, July–August 1958, pp.15–17
On Designing, New Haven: Pellango Press, 1959
On Weaving, Middletown, CT: Wesleyan University Press, 1965; London: Studio Vista, 1966

*Pre-Columbian Mexican Miniatures: The Josef and Anni Albers
Collection*, New York: Praeger, and London: Lund Humphries,
1970

Bibliography

Bauhaus, 1919–1928, exh. cat., Museum of Modern Art, New York,
1938; reprinted New York: Arno Press, and London: Secker and
Warburg, 1975

Josef and Anni Albers: Paintings, Tapestries and Woven Textiles, exh.
cat., Wadsworth Atheneum, Hartford, 1953

Anni Albers: Pictorial Weavings, exh. cat., Massachusetts Institute of
Technology, Cambridge, 1959

Nell Welliver, "A conversation with Anni Albers", *Craft Horizons*,
xxv, July–August 1965, pp.17–21, 40–45

Wall Hangings, 2 vols, exh. cat., Museum of Modern Art, New York,
1969

Louise Bourgeois, "The fabric of construction", *Craft Horizons*,
xxix, March–April 1969, pp.30–31

Eckhard Neumann, *Bauhaus and Bauhaus People*, New York: Van
Nostrand Reinhold, 1970

Martin Duberman, *Black Mountain: An Exploration in Community*,
New York: Dutton, 1972; London: Wildwood House, 1974

Nicholas Fox Weber, "Anni Albers and the printerly image", *Art in
America*, lxiii, July–August 1975, p.89

Hans M. Wingler, *The Bauhaus: Weimar, Dessau, Berlin, Chicago*,
3rd edition, Cambridge: Massachusetts Institute of Technology
Press, 1976 (German original)

Anni Albers: Drawings and Prints, exh. cat., Brooklyn Museum, NY,
1977

Anni Albers: Prints and Drawings, exh. cat., University Art Gallery,
University of California, Riverside, 1980

Mildred Constantine and Jack Lenor Larsen, *The Art Fabric:
Mainstream*, New York: Van Nostrand Reinhold, 1980

Nicholas Fox Weber, "Weaving wonders", *House and Garden*, clvii,
July 1985, pp.58–63

The Woven and Graphic Art of Anni Albers, exh. cat., Renwick
Gallery, National Museum of American Art, Smithsonian
Institution, Washington, DC, and elsewhere, 1985 (contains
extensive bibliography)

Howard Dearstyne, *Inside the Bauhaus*, ed. David Spaeth, New
York: Rizzoli, and London: Architectural Press, 1986

*Bauhaus Weaving Workshop: Source and Influence for American
Textiles*, exh. cat., Philadelphia College of Textiles and Science,
1987

Mary Emma Harris, *The Arts at Black Mountain College*,
Cambridge: Massachusetts Institute of Technology Press, 1987

Karl Taube, *The Albers Collection of Pre-Columbian Art*, New York:
Hudson Hills Press, 1988

Anni und Josef Albers: Eine Retrospektive, exh. cat., Villa Stuck,
Munich, 1989

Sigrid Wortmann Weltge, *Bauhaus Textiles: Women Artists and the
Weaving Workshop*, London: Thames and Hudson, 1993; as
Women's Work: Textile Art from the Bauhaus, San Francisco:
Chronicle, 1993

In 1922, when the world seemed to her "a tangle of hopelessness" and "undirected energy", Anni Albers, newly arrived at
the Bauhaus in Weimar, recognised that here was a place for
"taking chances", for experimentation, which, though often
"groping and fumbling", had purpose and direction. In the ten
years that followed, Annelise Fleischmann, neophyte and
student, grew to be Anni Albers, artist, designer and teacher.
Her early sense of the order and clarity that art offered crys-
tallised into a clear comprehension of the primacy and potential of materials and of the enduring aesthetic power of good
design. In 1984, towards the end of a creatively rich, varied
and eventful working life, she would write: "... to comprehend

Albers: *Untitled Wall Hanging*, 1924; silk triple weave;
182.9 × 121.9 cm.; Busch-Reisinger Museum, Harvard
University, Cambridge, Massachusetts

art is to confide in a constant" (Washington 1985, p.13).
Although she did not choose it, once assigned to the Bauhaus
weaving workshop, Albers quickly recognised that weaving
was a medium that, far from being "sissy" and weak as she
had suspected, engaged the artist in an intense struggle.
Weaving started from a zero point. Its material, the thread, was
a simple yet infinite line. Unlike a line drawn or painted on a
surface it was tangible. Its matrix, the loom – a simple structure of lines and intervals (warp and weft) – challenged and
teased the artist into "building a fabric out of thread" (*On
Designing* 1959, p.14). Weaving provided "the stimulation and
source for inventiveness that may come in the course of struggling with a hard-to-handle material" (*ibid.*, p.63).

Albers's weavings from the Bauhaus period, and the delicate, intricately beautiful designs in gouache on graph paper on
which they were based, reveal a clear and logical development.
The relative simplicity of an early piece such as *Untitled Wall
Hanging* (1924; see illustration) – with its flat, symmetrical,
undifferentiated bands of muted beiges and greys – soon
evolved into the complexity of the originally brilliantly
coloured, though now faded, triple weave *Black-White-Red*

(1927; private collection, Germany). A limited edition of five reproductions was made in 1964 (example in Bauhaus-Archiv, Berlin). As the eye scrutinises such works as *Black-White-Red* and *Black-White-Grey* (1927; Bauhaus-Archiv, Berlin), it searches to reconstruct the underlying patterns. The seeming clarity of composition is undercut by the tantalising and elusive configurations that defy easy assimilation. An apparently ordered, rectilinear arrangement turns out to be a challenging visual exploration. The viewer is held to attention and not let off the hook lightly. For her diploma project at the Bauhaus in 1930 Albers produced a drapery fabric of cotton chenille and cellophane to be used as a stage curtain in the Bundeschule auditorium in Bernau. This innovative material was not simply a demonstration of virtuosity but in perfect accord with the function of the drapes. The outer shiny surface reflected light into the auditorium, while the sound-absorbent underside concealed behind-the-stage noises from the audience.

In the USA, at Black Mountain College from 1933 to 1949, and then in New Haven, Albers continued to teach, to write about her work and to test the limits of her art. She revered the ancient textile artists of Peru whose work she studied, collected and treasured. It provided lessons in versatility and inventiveness that she regarded as the essence of hand-weaving. By the 1940s, however, she believed that the increasing mechanisation of industrial production was seriously diminishing the weaver's capacity for invention. Although advanced technology had produced marvellous, sparkling synthetic fibres and finishes as well as newly brilliant colours, "the spontaneous shaping of a material has been lost and the blueprint has taken over" (*ibid.*, p.13). To counteract the resulting "barrenness in today's weaving", Albers advocated a rapprochement between hand-weaving and industrial production. The revolutionary fibres would benefit from innovative methods of construction that only the hand-weaver could develop. Her own work was a practical demonstration of these beliefs. She pioneered the use of non-traditional materials. Working with textile manufacturers, she executed architectural commissions – among them the design of drapery materials of cotton chenille, copper Lurex and white plastic thread (1944) for Philip Johnson's Rockefeller Guest House in Manhattan, and draperies and bedspreads for dormitory rooms in Walter Gropius's Harvard Graduate Center (1949–50). Similar ground-breaking fabrics were shown in the exhibition of her work at the Museum of Modern Art in 1949. Convinced of the links between well-designed textiles and architecture – between the aesthetic and the practical – Albers had her materials fashioned into room-dividing screens. These, uniquely, combined complicated open-weave patterns, shimmering synthetic fibres and dust-repellent finishes. At the same time she took her more private work in a new direction and made "pictorial weavings" – small-scale pieces that asserted their own integrity as complete works of art. In *Development in Rose II* (1952; Art Institute of Chicago) a subtle and delicate range of coloured linen threads – beiges, pinks, greys, blacks and touches of green – unfolds in a virtuoso array of weaving patterns. Tightly woven borders are juxtaposed with an irregular open-weave matrix traversed by horizontal lines tied together by looping threads – all in a small (63 × 45cm.) format. Stacks of horizontal lines created by looped weft threads first appeared in *Ancient Writing* (1936; National Museum of American Art, Smithsonian Institution,

Washington, DC) and Albers developed the calligraphic associations of the woven line further in a pair of small works, *Haiku* and *Code* (both 1961; Josef and Anni Albers Foundation, Orange), and in the large composite *Six Prayers* (1967; Jewish Museum, New York).

In 1963, at the Tamarind Lithography Workshop in California, Albers made her first prints. In 1947 she had created gouaches in which magnified, intricately looped images of threads were delineated against a painterly background. Now she translated these into a pair of lithographs, *Enmeshed I* and *II*, and a pair of screenprints *Untitled I* and *II*. These were followed in 1964 by a portfolio of seven *Line Involvements*. Freed from the constraints of warp and weft Albers could now, in Paul Klee's phrase, "take a line for a walk". As she had done in her weaving, Albers produced prints of great spatial and textural complexity from a deliberately limited vocabulary of forms. In the *Meander* prints (repr. Washington 1985, pl.40) the ancient motif is repeated and superimposed in subtly modulated tones to create an abstract surface that continually invites the eye to explore depth and surface. In the screenprints *Camino Real* (1967–9; *ibid.*, pl.35), *GRI* and other related series, she used simple repeated triangles and the intervals between them to conjure dynamic symphonies of colour, form and space in which background and foreground are linked in pulsating relationships. In *Orchestra I* (1979; *ibid.*, fig.85) and *Letter* (1980; *ibid.*, fig.86) it is the outlines of the familiar triangles that serve as musical and calligraphic metaphors. Whether weaving, drawing or making prints, Anni Albers was a fearless artist, living and working according to her own stated tenets: "We learn courage from art work ... We learn to dare to make a choice, to be independent" (*On Designing* 1959, p.31).

BRENDA DANILOWITZ

Alberti, Chiara *see* Convents survey

Albrecht, Gretchen

New Zealand painter, 1943–

Born in Onehunga, Auckland, 7 May 1943. Studied at University of Auckland School of Fine Arts, 1960–63 (diploma in painting); Auckland Secondary Teachers' Training College, 1966. Worked in various factories and as a relief art teacher, 1967. Head of art department, Kelston Girls' High School, 1968–71; teaching fellow in painting, University of Auckland School of Fine Arts, 1972–3. Taught private art class for women, 1974–5. Spent 13 months in USA and Europe, 1978–9; many subsequent visits. Travelled to Britain to assist with touring performances of *Hotspur: A Ballad for Music*, 1981. Frances Hodgkins fellow, University of Otago, 1981–2. Worked at Gertrude Street Studios, Melbourne, 1984. Married artist James Ross, 1970 (second marriage); son from previous marriage born 1961. Recipient of first prize, Tokoroa art award, 1972; first Zonta award,

1973; first prize, Pakuranga art award, 1976; Queen Elizabeth II Arts Council grants 1976, 1978 and 1986. Lives in Grey Lynn, Auckland.

Selected Individual Exhibitions

Ikon Gallery, Auckland: 1964
Barry Lett Galleries, Auckland: 1967, 1970, 1972, 1974, 1975, 1977
Holdsworth Galleries, Sydney: 1970
Brooke/Gifford Gallery, Christchurch: 1975, 1984, 1994
Bosshard Galleries, Dunedin: 1977, 1981
Peter Webb Galleries, Auckland: 1978, 1980, 1981
Dunedin Public Art Gallery: 1981
Janne Land Gallery, Wellington: 1983
Dowse Art Gallery, Lower Hutt: 1985
Sue Crockford Gallery, Auckland: 1985, 1986, 1987, 1988, 1989, 1990, 1991, 1993, 1994
Auckland City Art Gallery: 1985 (*Seasonal*, artist's project)
Hamilton Centre for Contemporary Art: 1986
Sarjeant Gallery, Wanganui: 1986 (retrospective)
Todd Gallery, London: 1988, 1990
Clare Hall Gallery, Cambridge University, UK: 1992

Bibliography

Kurt von Meier, "Contemporary painting in New Zealand", *Art and Australia*, ii–iii, December 1964, pp.190–202
Jim Barr and others, *Contemporary New Zealand Painters*, i, Martinborough: Taylor, 1980
Phillida Bunkle and Beryl Hughes, eds, *Women in New Zealand Society*, Auckland: Allen and Unwin, 1980
W. H. Oliver and others, eds, *The Oxford History of New Zealand*, Wellington, Oxford and New York: Oxford University Press, 1981
Seven Painters: The Eighties, exh. cat., Sarjeant Gallery, Wanganui, 1982
Priscilla Pitts, "Gretchen Albrecht: The early years", *Art New Zealand*, no.26, 1983, pp.36–7
Gordon McLauchlan, ed., *New Zealand Encyclopaedia*, Auckland: Bateman, 1984
NZ/NY, exh. cat., 22 Wooster Gallery, New York, 1985
Francis Pound, *Forty Modern New Zealand Paintings*, Auckland: Penguin, 1985
Seasonal/Four Paintings, exh. cat., Auckland City Art Gallery, 1985
AFTERnature: A Survey: 23 Years, exh. cat., Sarjeant Gallery, Wanganui, 1986
Elizabeth Eastmond and Merimeri Penfold, *Women and the Arts in New Zealand: Forty Works, 1936–86*, Auckland: Penguin, 1986
Gretchen Albrecht: Collages, 1988–89, exh. cat., Hamilton Centre for Contemporary Art, 1986
Gil Docking and Michael Dunn, *Two Hundred Years of New Zealand Painting*, 2nd edition, Auckland: Bateman, 1990
Michael Dunn, *A Concise History of New Zealand Painting*, Auckland: Bateman, 1991
Candy Elsmore, *Aspects of the Work of Gretchen Albrecht*, MFA dissertation, University of Auckland, 1991
Linda Gill, *Gretchen Albrecht*, Auckland: Random Century, 1991
Anne Kirker, *New Zealand Women Artists: A Survey of 150 Years*, 2nd edition, Tortola, BVI: Craftsman House, 1993
Reclaiming the Madonna: Artists and Mothers, exh. cat., Usher Gallery, Lincoln, UK, and elsewhere, 1994

Among New Zealand artists Gretchen Albrecht is pre-eminent as a colourist, known for the splendour and lyricism of her painting. Emerging from art school in 1963, she belongs to the first generation of New Zealand artists to move away from regionalist concerns, responding instead to the stimulus of international modernism, particularly the abstract painters of the New York School. Since the early 1970s she has consistently explored the expressive possibilities of line, shape and colour, using different abstract "languages" – gestural brush stroke, colour-field saturation, geometric hard edge – to arrive at a unique vocabulary, a supple synthesis of abstractions. Unlike the modernists, Albrecht has used this vocabulary to refer not only to itself but also to nature, the mainspring of her work. She chose the title *AFTERnature* for a survey exhibition of 1986, and the titles of individual paintings reinforce this connection: *Winged Spill* (1974), *Florabunda* (1984), *Cataract* (1988) and *Poesia Nocturne* (1990). Her work is notable for the coherence and vigour of its focus, its powers of distillation and, at the same time, the development of ever more complex layers of connotation, drawn from the art and architecture of the past, from literature and music. Modernism is inflected by strategies that take account of Albrecht's position as both a New Zealand and a woman artist.

Albrecht's work ranges in scale from small watercolours, posters, paper pulps and lithographs to the monumentality of her stage sets for opera and ballet. Most of her paintings – she is primarily a painter – relate to the height of the human figure and the stretch of the arms, two metres wide or high. Her printmaking has always been in association with excellent technicians, the images relating closely to the paintings she was doing at the time. In 1982, for example, she made lithographs at the Beehive Press in Adelaide, South Australia; in 1983 and 1994 she worked on paper pulps at the Exeter Press, SoHo, New York, and in 1994 produced further lithographs at Limeworks, Christchurch, New Zealand. Albrecht was commissioned to design sets for two chamber operas, *Tristan and Iseult* (1978) and *Hotspur: A Ballad for Music* (1980) by the New Zealand composer Gillian Whitehead, the latter with words by the New Zealand poet Fleur Adcock. In 1988 she made sets for the ballet *Now is the Hour* by the New Zealand dancer and choreographer Douglas Wright. These stage sets were all large, painterly backdrops of canvas using Albrecht's distinctive colour harmonies and abstract language. Like her prints they related closely to her painted images.

Albrecht's earliest paintings were figurative. At art school, she developed a private mythology of enigmatic figures through which she dealt with urgent autobiographical material. A decade before feminist ideas had arrived in New Zealand, Albrecht was deconstructing the nude and traditional themes such as Susannah and the Elders. After leaving art school she took images from contemporary life and transformed them into almost surreal arrangements of colour and shape. *Wizzo the Magician* (1963), one of her autobiographical paintings, and *Wooden Horse* (1967), based on a newspaper photograph of a polo player practising, were both bought by the Auckland City Art Gallery – early recognition of an outstanding new talent. In the four years between these two paintings Albrecht had moved from thickly applied oil paint to washes of acrylic, which has remained her main medium.

During the 1970s Albrecht's work shifted away from autobiographical material to an engagement with the outer world. With it went an enlargement of scale from easel painting to two-metre canvases, stretched and unprimed, that had to be laid on the floor. On to these Albrecht manipulated overlapping transparent acrylic washes to form billowing organic shapes, suggestive of the gardens, the land-, sky- and seascapes she observed around her in Auckland. The American artists

Albrecht: *Nocturne (The Spiral Unwinds)*, 1991; acrylic and oil on canvas on oval stretcher; 154 × 244.5 cm.; Sarjeant Gallery, Wanganui, New Zealand

Helen Frankenthaler (q.v.) and Morris Louis were important influences at this time, although Albrecht did not share either Frankenthaler's emphasis on chance or the Greenbergian purism of Louis's abstraction.

Painting for Albrecht is a "felt response" to the visual world, engaging the emotions, the mind and the body. In such works of the 1970s as *Indian Summer* (National Gallery, Wellington) and *Golden Cloud* (Auckland City Art Gallery) the sense of physical involvement with her materials matches the passion of her response to natural beauty. There is also an intellectual focus on the two-dimensional nature of painting, and the power of colour to create space and movement.

The experience of travel to the USA and Europe in 1978–9, her first journey beyond Australasia, was finally distilled into a new shape, a semicircle made out of two quadrants bolted together. For the following decade Albrecht explored the symbolic potential of this shape, which she has always called a "hemisphere", implying "space, a shape to contain the feeling". The hemisphere, besides signifying modernist interest in the shaped canvas, referred to her experience of European painting in its architectural setting, to the barrel vaults, tympana and lunettes of Romanesque and Renaissance buildings. Its left and right sides can suggest contrast and duality and, since the radius of each half is roughly the length of the arm, it retains a relationship with the human body.

Describing some of the developments that took place within this form, Francis Pound wrote:

> … in Albrecht's hemispheres from 1981 to 1983, invariably, one half is one colour and the other half is another, in a colloquy of colours, speaking one to another across that central vertical split … [see *Cardinal*, 1981; Dunedin Public Art Gallery, New Zealand]. Next, the central fissure opens, thickens, is engorged, to become lips, hymen, vagina, petalled lip [see *The Fire and the Rose*, 1984; Sarjeant Gallery, Wanganui]. It's as if the hemisphere, the seed capsule of colour, has opened at the moment of ripeness, by a parting of its valves … to a kind of productive tearing of colour. Then, in 1984, a new possibility arises: across the central fissure the colours begin to fuse, so that the whole lunette becomes one coloured, or so that its various colours flow as arched bands across the whole of its surface … [Wanganui 1986, p.29].

In *Seasonal*, an artist's project at the Auckland City Art Gallery (1985–6), Albrecht showed four majestic hemispheres, *Arbour* (artist's collection), *Blossom* (Waikato Museum of Art and History, Hamilton), *Orchard (for Keats)* (Fletcher Challenge Collection, Auckland) and *Exile* (Collection Erika and Robin Congreve, Auckland), each alluding to a season and its associated metaphors, but avoiding overt reference to the European spring, summer, autumn and winter, since these do not apply to the sub-tropical climate of Auckland, however deeply rooted in the New Zealand colonial consciousness. The Auckland climatic reality is of abundance, fertility and strong colour, all spectacularly conveyed in these four paintings. Sweeping arcs of high-key colour became the ground for almost figurative shapes, thickly painted in oil around the meeting-point between the two quadrants of the hemisphere.

Since 1989 an even more richly suggestive shape, the oval, has become the "container" for Albrecht's ideas. The horizontal oval, apart from its art-historical associations with landscape painting, is the cartographic convention used for depicting the whole world, and it is also the egg, the beginning of life. Within its wholeness it retains the hemisphere's two halves. Albrecht exploits this greater range of meaning with impressive confidence. Her colour has darkened and deepened. Black has become a constant, sweeping round the edge of the oval, sometimes lit by trails of gold, framing a glowing centre of deep purple, blue or red formed by multiple layers of thin acrylic. The swirling rhythms are punctuated by hard-edged rectangles of opaque colour, thick oil paint applied within a stencil, looking like a strip of canvas collaged on to the surface. There are usually two of these rectangles, placed in each half of the oval, horizontally or vertically, their colour sharply contrasting with the body of the painting, or barely emerging from it. These "nomadic geometries" (a phrase Albrecht has borrowed from the poem "San Ildefonso Nocturne" by Octavio Paz) vary in size and set up complex spatial relations, both with each other and the rest of the painting. The title of *Nocturne (The Spiral Unwinds)* (1991; see illustration) refers to the section in the same poem that describes a firework display, but Albrecht's painting arouses the deeper emotions associated with elemental events, the whirling of galaxies in the cosmos or the moment of conception within the egg.

Each new phase of Albrecht's painting career, each new painting, proceeds organically from what has gone before, subsuming past discoveries and pushing on to make new ones. The paintings become a metaphor for the progress of a life, with its accumulated layers of experience and knowledge, its celebration of beauty, its search for meaning by imposing – or discovering – form.

LINDA GILL

Alletit *see* Bertaux

Allingham, Helen

British painter and illustrator, 1848–1926

Born Helen Paterson in Swadlincote, near Burton-on-Trent, Derbyshire, 26 September 1848; father a physician. Received her first art education at Unitarian Boarding School for Girls, Altrincham, Cheshire, founded by her grandmother, Sarah Smith Herford. Studied drawing and painting at the Birmingham School of Design, 1862–5 (several awards). Stayed in London with her aunt, the artist Laura Herford, and studied at the Royal Female School of Art, Bloomsbury, 1866–7; Royal Academy Schools, 1868–72; Slade School of Fine Art, evening classes, 1872–4. While studying, also provided illustrations for popular journals: *Once a Week*, *Cassell's Magazine*, *Little Folks*, *Aunt Judy* and *Cornhill*. First permanent position, *The Graphic*, 1870–74. Married Irish poet William Allingham, 1874; three children (two sons, one daughter), born 1875, 1877 and 1882; husband died 1889. Moved from Chelsea to Sandhills, near Witley, Surrey, 1881; returned to London, settling in Hampstead, 1888. Associate member, Society of Painters in Watercolours, 1875; first woman member, Royal Watercolour Society, 1890. Died in Haslemere, Surrey, 28 September 1926.

Principal Exhibitions

Dudley Gallery, London: from 1870
Royal Academy, London: 1874, 1878
Society of Painters in Watercolours (later Royal Watercolour Society), London: occasionally 1874–1925
Exposition Universelle, Paris: 1878, 1900 (honourable mention)
Fine Art Society, London: 1886, 1887 (twice), 1891, 1904 (all individual)
Exposition Internationale, Brussels: 1897 (silver medal)
Columbian Exhibition, Chicago: 1902 (bronze medal)

Selected Writings

Editor, *William Allingham: A Diary*, London: Macmillan, 1907; reprinted 1985 (with D. Radford)
Editor, *Letters to William Allingham*, London: Longman, 1911 (with Mrs E. Baumer Williams)

Bibliography

Ellen C. Clayton, *English Female Artists*, 2 vols, London: Tinsley, 1876
Alfred Lys Baldry, "The work of Mrs Allingham", *Magazine of Art*, xxiii, 1899, pp.355–61
Marcus B. Huish, *Happy England as Painted by Helen Allingham, RWS*, London: Adam and Charles Black, 1904; reprinted as *The Happy England of Helen Allingham*, London: Bracken, 1985
Stewart Dick, *The Cottage Homes of England Illustrated by Helen Allingham*, London: Arnold, 1909
Cottages of Yester-Year: Watercolours by Helen Allingham RWS (1848–1926), exh. cat., Guildford House Gallery, 1988
Christopher Wood, *Paradise Lost: Paintings of English Country Life and Landscape, 1850–1914*, London: Barrie and Jenkins, 1988; North Pomfret, VT: Trafalgar Square, 1989
Helen Allingham and Hampstead, London: Hampstead Museum, 1990
Ina Taylor, *Helen Allingham's England*, Exeter: Webb and Bower, 1990
Nature into Art: English Landscape Watercolours, exh. cat., North Carolina Museum of Art, Raleigh, 1991
Victorian Landscape Watercolours, exh. cat., Yale Center for British Art, New Haven, 1992
Deborah Cherry, *Painting Women: Victorian Women Artists*, London and New York: Routledge, 1993

Despite gender restrictions imposed on women artists in the 19th century, Helen Allingham achieved prominence as one of Britain's finest watercolourists. Best known for her picturesque views of a rustic life remote to late 19th-century industrialised Britain, she also painted charming domestic interiors, landscapes, portraits of children and friends. Her nostalgic visions

Allingham: *Henry at the Cottage Gate*, 1886; watercolour; 19 × 17.8 cm.; Nancy-Clay Marsteller Collection, Cleveland

of rural England reflect not only the changing roles of countrywomen, but also the desire of an urbanised middle class for an idyllic country retreat.

Frederick Walker, whom she met at the Royal Academy, was an early influence on Allingham's art, encouraging her to work in watercolours. With its large, graceful figure in a typical landscape setting, Allingham's *Raking Hay* (c.1875; Richard Hagen Fine Paintings, Worcestershire) emulates his

work both in medium and composition. At the age of 22 she began exhibiting at the Dudley Gallery in London, but in order to earn an income she was forced to work as a freelance graphic artist illustrating serial stories in magazines. She drew scenes from Mrs Ewing's novels for *Aunt Judy* as well as illustrating the serial version of Thomas Hardy's *Far from the Madding Crowd* in 1873 for *Cornhill*. Her first permanent post was as a reporter/illustrator for *The Graphic* in 1870, but social conventions did not allow her to roam city streets like her male colleagues. She wrote on fashions and provided social vignettes instead, thus developing a lifelong technique of making rapid sketches on site and carefully finishing work in the studio.

After her marriage to the poet William Allingham in 1874, when she had no further need to support herself financially, she ceased working in black and white and concentrated on watercolours. She and her husband moved in the social circle of Alfred, Lord Tennyson, Thomas Carlyle and Dante Gabriel Rossetti. She painted exquisite informal portraits of artistic and literary friends, such as *Thomas Carlyle* (c.1876; Scottish National Portrait Gallery, Edinburgh), as well as her family. Also during the late 1870s Allingham began painting on family holidays and produced quiet interior scenes reminiscent of 17th-century Dutch domestic genre painting. *The Lessons* (1885; Phillips, London) portrays a cosy and well-organised middle-class home.

In the early 1880s Allingham lightened her palette and began using the scratching-out method instead of Chinese white. According to her biographer, Marcus Huish, her small paint box contained ten colours in moist cake form ranging from cobalt to sepia (Huish 1904, p.194). Darker colours were obtained by washing a solution of gum arabic over the dry painted surface. Always sketching in plein air, Allingham outlined scenes with light blue or brown instead of a pencil (Taylor 1990, p.98). Figures, animals and small details were later added in her studio.

The family moved to Sandhills, near the artists' colony of Witley, Surrey, in 1881. There Allingham was inspired by rural life. She met the watercolourist Myles Birket Foster and the horticulturalist and garden designer Gertrude Jekyll. She began to paint quaint scenes of thatched cottages under Foster's influence, but her figures were smaller in scale and the cottage became the central motif (*Redlynch, Wiltshire*; Christopher Wood Gallery, London). These paintings also reflect agrarian changes in England, when women were no longer hired for fieldwork but instead became more home-oriented. Allingham depicted women engaged in ordinary daily occupations – pegging out laundry (*Clothesline*, 1879; Hampstead Museum, London), tending children and chatting by a cottage gate. Her models, however, were not local people but her own children or professional models from London. A particularly charming painting, *Henry at the Cottage Gate* (1886; see illustration), features her young son standing at the garden gate backed by a thatched cottage. The harmonious integration of cottage, figures and flowers, produced by tonal hues and scale, constitute the essence of Allingham's painting.

She was influenced by Jekyll, who was not only a garden designer, but was also concerned with the preservation of old cottages and promoted the picturesque cottage garden. Allingham's pictures of cottage gardens derive from sketches and studies of both her own and Jekyll's flower-beds. She also made numerous flower studies, such as *Study of Pansies* (Maas Gallery, London). To the 19th-century collector, Allingham reinforced and preserved traditional English values of home and hearth. Rooted in 18th-century notions of the picturesque, the cottage vernacular embodied a sense of pride and prosperity. Pre-industrialised man was seen as living in harmony with nature; the countryside thus represented a rural idyll lost to the present. In addition to this nostalgic view, the countryside also represented a place of retreat.

Allingham continued to work in plein air after the family's move to Hampstead in 1888, taking the train for day excursions into the countryside and describing the fleeting scenes framed by the train windows in her paintings. The year 1890 was professionally a benchmark for Allingham when she was the first woman to be elected to full membership of the Royal Watercolour Society. By this date, she could expect to earn around 50 guineas for her cottage scenes. She also expanded her repertoire with illustrations of grand manor houses owned by friends and Kent landscapes (*Harvest Field, Kent*, 1895–1900; Whitworth Gallery, University of Manchester). In the desire to expand her subject matter, Allingham visited Italy in 1901 and 1902. There she painted seascapes (*Venetian Sunset*, 1901–2; Hampstead Museum), flower gardens and village markets with women standing in stalls. Sixty of these Italian scenes were hung in her solo exhibition *Country Life and Venice* at the Fine Art Society in 1904, but her public was not receptive to any deviation from her trademark renderings of cottage life.

Allingham continued to exhibit a few paintings in group shows at the Fine Art Society until 1925, using drawings from her old sketchbooks and models posed in her studio (Taylor 1990, p.92). With World War I, her popularity waned. Her visions of an idyllic countryside and rural life seemed too imaginary and irrelevant for 20th-century society.

NANCY-CLAY MARSTELLER

Alma-Tadema, Laura

British painter, 1852–1909

Born Laura Theresa Epps in London, April 1852, the youngest of three artistic sisters; father a physician. Also an accomplished musician, but became increasingly interested in drawing. Studied at Bedford College, London, and, on the advice of Ford Madox Brown, studied the ancient material at the British Museum. Studied under Lawrence Alma-Tadema, 1870; married him, 1871; two step-daughters, Laurence and Anna, the latter also a professional artist. Lived in London, but travelled abroad throughout her married life, particularly in the Low Countries. Died in London, 15 August 1909.

Principal Exhibitions

Paris Salon: 1873–4, 1877, 1881
Royal Academy, London: occasionally 1873–1909
Royal Glasgow Institute: 1875, 1878, 1881, 1885, 1891
Internationale Kunstausstellung, Berlin: 1876 (gold medal)
Exposition Universelle, Paris: 1878 (silver medal), 1900 (silver medal)
Royal Scottish Academy, Edinburgh: 1879–81, 1885, 1889
Grosvenor Gallery, London: 1880–85, 1887
New Gallery, London: 1889
World's Columbian Exposition, Chicago: 1893 (silver medal)
Fine Art Society, London: 1910 (retrospective)

Selected Writings

"The appeal against female suffrage: A rejoinder", *Nineteenth Century*, xxvi, 1889, pp.347–54

Alma-Tadema: *Sweet Industry*, exhibited 1904; Manchester City Art Galleries

Bibliography

Henry Blackburn in *Grosvenor Notes*, London, 1881, p.18; 1882, p.45; 1883, p.8

Alice Meynell, "Laura Alma-Tadema", *Art Journal*, November 1883, pp.345–7

Clara Erskine Clement, *Women in the Fine Arts*, Boston: Houghton Mifflin, 1904; reprinted New York: Hacker, 1974

Lady Alma-Tadema, exh. cat., Fine Art Society, London, 1910

Kathleen Fisher, *Conversations with Sylvia: Sylvia Gosse, Painter, 1881–1968*, ed. Eileen Vera Smith, London: Skilton, 1975

Vern G. Swanson, *Sir Lawrence Alma-Tadema*, London: Ash and Grant, 1977

Women's Art Show, 1550–1970, exh. cat., Nottingham Castle Museum, 1982

Susan P. Casteras, *Victorian Childhood*, New York: Abrams, 1986

Pamela Gerrish Nunn, *Victorian Women Artists*, London: Women's Press, 1987

Painting Women: Victorian Women Artists, exh. cat., Rochdale Art Gallery, 1987

Deborah Cherry, *Painting Women: Victorian Women Artists*, London and New York: Routledge, 1993

The work of Laura Alma-Tadema focuses on Dutch-inspired domestic scenes – children at play and motherhood, with

occasional excursions into pastel portraiture and flower painting. Her training began with drawing lessons at home,
followed by study at the British Museum, on the advice of Ford
Madox Brown. A decision in 1870 to study with Lawrence
Alma-Tadema, the Dutch-born painter of classical set-pieces,
began her serious training as a painter. Indeed, Alma-Tadema's
concern for detail and historical accuracy echoes that of her
master (later her husband). Frequent visits to the Low
Countries enabled her to study de Hooch and Vermeer, while
exhibitions of Dutch Masters and works by such contemporary genre artists as Maris, Israels and B.J. Blommers were an
established feature of the London art calendar. Alma-Tadema's
first success at the Paris Salon in 1873, *The Mirror* (1872), was
followed by *A Still Life* (1872; both Mesdag Museum, The
Hague). Such subjects may have been encouraged by Lawrence
Alma-Tadema, who apparently regarded "the study of still life
to be of the utmost importance" (Meynell 1883, p.346). Later,
Alma-Tadema developed interests in genre and landscape,
exhibiting with distinction at the Royal Academy, the Paris
Salon and the Grosvenor Gallery. Her landscape subjects
comprise small-scale oil panels, mostly painted around Rome,
Mentone and Castellamare. These were intensely private
works, for few were exhibited before her death.

Writing of Alma-Tadema, Meynell noted the increasingly
specialised approach of 19th-century historians towards differing historic periods. "The result", she wrote, "must be the
increased concentration of the power of some mental faculties
and the suspension of others; but it is the natural result of the
accumulation of facts which has fallen on the heads of the
present generation" (*ibid.*, p.345). Alma-Tadema's art borrowed the trappings of domestic life in 17th-century Holland to
construct a world largely peopled by women and children,
whose dress may have been 17th century but whose relationship to the viewer was unmistakably Victorian. Childhood was
a common theme amongst artists in the 19th century, from
John Everett Millais to Emily Mary Osborn (q.v.). An enduring cult of childhood presented children to an adult audience
as bearers of moral lessons and purveyors of lost innocence. As
Susan Casteras has suggested, Victorian society sanctioned
adults to re-experience childhood in ways "not fully understood in pre-Freudian times" (Casteras 1986, p.6).

Alma-Tadema's images focus mostly on Victorian middle-
class childhood, whose domain was sharply delineated from
the adult world. Works such as *May I Come In?* (1883; repr.
Meynell 1883, p.345) and *Always Welcome* (1887; Russell-
Cotes Art Gallery, Bournemouth) portray children faced with
the realities and social conventions of adulthood. In *Always
Welcome* a young girl attends her bedridden mother and learns
moral lessons of humility and compassion. The painting also
offered didactic value to young women, according to Victorian
ideals of nurturing, submissive femininity. Furthermore, in an
era of high infant and maternal mortality, sickness was a well-
established symbol of Christian fortitude and acceptance, and
a recurrent theme in art. In *Always Welcome*, the message is
doubly potent – the mother, upholder of the spiritual fabric of
society, rests, watched over by the female child, symbol of
moral purity. On the other hand, in *Airs and Graces* (date
unknown; Mesdag Museum) childish uncertainty combines
with innocent abandonment to depict the middle-class ritual of
acquiring the social graces.

Alma-Tadema often depicted women in domestic settings,
working at occupations suitable for middle-class women. In
Sweet Industry (exh. 1904; see illustration) a needlewoman in
17th-century costume sits in the parlour, absorbed in her task
rather than the brightly lit world beyond her window. As
Deborah Cherry has noted, Alma-Tadema and contemporaries
such as Alice Havers reworked the idea of motherhood during
a period in which historians were discovering "in the Dutch
Republic of the seventeenth century ... not only precedents for
the class dominance of the bourgeoisie, colonial and imperial
rule, but also the ideologies of the separate spheres and domestic womanhood" (Rochdale 1987, p.27).

That her figures function within a Dutch-inspired bourgeois
domesticity corresponds with descriptions of the Alma-
Tademas' meticulously furnished studio houses at Regent's
Park and, later, Grove End Road, St John's Wood. One visitor
remarked that to enter any of the rooms at Grove End Road
"was apparently to walk into a picture ... Lady Tadema's
studio, for instance, might have been a perfect Dutch interior
by Vermeer or de Hooch" (Swanson 1977, p.27). Furthermore,
a racial aspect to Victorian fondness for Dutch art infuses
Meynell's estimation of Alma-Tadema. She wrote:

> By too much straining after the grace of the Latin
> nations, the German part of the English race has been led
> to neglect, and has thus forfeited, the Gothic grace which
> had a value and a beauty apart, eminently fitting and
> harmonious for us. In the details of domestic life, Dutch
> habits, Dutch furniture, and Dutch dress of the gentler
> and more courtly sort in the seventeenth century, Mrs
> Alma-Tadema has found unconventional honest, and ...
> homely grace, which Latinised eyes might never have
> discovered [Meynell 1883, p.345].

Meynell perceives a robust simplicity and picturesqueness in
17th-century Dutch life analogous with Alma-Tadema's art.

In 1889 Alma-Tadema signed an appeal against women's
suffrage published in the *Nineteenth Century*. The appeal
claimed that the most desirable role for woman was not as an
individual, prescribing change for society, but as defender of its
essential fabric – the family group. "In her hands", it asserted,
"rests the keeping of a pure tone in society ... She is often not
alive to her power, and if her power became conscious, it
would lose much of its potency" (p.354). This idea of woman
as an organic, nurturing creature juxtaposes comfortably with
Alma-Tadema's domestic scenes, in which the figure forms an
integral part of the surroundings. Content to identify with
established codes of Victorian womanhood, she used a domestic arena to convey an order and harmony comparable with
Lawrence Alma-Tadema's classical set-pieces.

PATRICIA DE MONTFORT

Amaral, Tarsila do
Brazilian painter, 1886–1973

Born on a farm in Capivari, in the interior of São Paulo state,
1886. Studied painting in São Paulo, 1916–17, and at the
Académie Julian, Paris, 1920–21. Formed Grupo dos Cinco

in São Paulo, 1922. Further studies in Paris under André Lhôte, Fernand Léger and Albert Gleizes, 1922 and 1922–3. Joined Pau-Brasil group to explore artistic heritage of Brazil, 1923. Married poet Oswald de Andrade in São Paulo, 1926; divorced 1930. Visited Soviet Union, 1931. Represented Brazil at Venice Biennale, 1960. Died in São Paulo, 1973.

Selected Individual Exhibitions

Galerie Percier, Paris: 1926, 1928
Museum of Modern Western Art, Moscow: 1931
Museu de Arte Moderna, São Paulo: 1950 (retrospective)
São Paulo Bienal: 1963
Museu de Arte Moderna, Rio de Janeiro: 1969–70 (touring retrospective)

Bibliography

Oswald de Andrade, "Manifesto da Poesia Pau-Brasil", *Correo da Manha* (Rio de Janeiro), 18 March 1924
——, "Manifesto Antropofago", *Revista de Antropofagia* (São Paulo), no.1, 1928
Mário de Andrade and others, *Revista Academica: Homenagem a Tarsila*, Rio de Janeiro, 1940
Sérgio Milliet, *Tarsila do Amaral*, São Paulo: Artistas Brasileiros Contemporaneos, 1953
Aracy Amaral, *Desenhos de Tarsila*, São Paulo: Cultrix, 1971
——, *Tarsila: Sua obra e seu tempo*, 2 vols, São Paulo: Perspectiva, 1975
Tarsila: Obras, 1920/1930, exh. cat., IBM do Brasil, São Paulo, 1982
Nadia Batella Gotlib, *Tarsila do Amaral: A musa radiante*, São Paulo: Editora Brasiliense, 1983
Carlos Lemos and others, *The Art of Brazil*, New York: Harper, 1983
Marcos A. Marcondes, *Tarsila*, São Paulo: Art, 1986
Art of the Fantastic: Latin America, 1920–1987, exh. cat., Indianapolis Museum of Art and elsewhere, 1987
Art in Latin America: The Modern Era, 1820–1980, exh. cat., South Bank Centre, London, and elsewhere, 1989
Oriana Baddeley and Valerie Fraser, *Drawing the Line: Art and Cultural Identity in Contemporary Latin America*, London and New York: Verso, 1989
Stella de Sá Rego, "Pau-Brasil: Tarsila do Amaral", *Latin American Art*, ii, Winter 1990, pp.18–22
Latin American Artists of the Twentieth Century, exh. cat., Museum of Modern Art, New York, 1993

It was in Paris that the Brazilian artist Tarsila do Amaral awakened to the significance of exotic and primitive subject matter for the avant-garde and realised that she could look to her own country for inspiration. Tarsila do Amaral and her future husband, the poet Oswald de Andrade, went to Paris for the first of many visits in 1920, when the fascination with the exotic cultures and art forms of the New World and Africa was at its height. It was a period dominated by the masters of Cubism, Futurism and Expressionism, and Tarsila took advantage of her stays in Paris to study with Fernand Léger and Albert Gleizes. She learned the basic tenets of abstract composition and how to create flat arrangements of pictorial construction.

In 1923 Amaral and Andrade returned to São Paulo, where a young group of artists and intellectuals had already begun to question the realities of Brazil's identity and the controlling forms of European art and culture that had little to do with the country in the 20th century. Their activism and desire for renewal in Brazilian culture encouraged the first movement towards modernism in the country and the use of new forms of

Amaral: *EFCB (Estrada de Ferro Central do Brasil/Brazilian Central Railway)*, 1924; oil on canvas; 142 × 126.8 cm.; Museu de Arte Contemporânea da Universidade de São Paulo, Brazil

technique and expression outside the rules of the academic system. Inspired by their message, the two artists became active in this burgeoning avant-garde and the highly creative environment of São Paulo in the 1920s. In keeping with the group's interest in Brazil's indigenous culture, Amaral and Andrade were determined to explore their own land, its vibrant ethnic mixture, the colonial architecture, festivals and African rhythms. In 1924 they embarked on a voyage of discovery that took them from Carnival in Rio to the gold-filled colonial churches of Minas Girais to the remote interior. Filled with a new visual aesthetic, Amaral wanted to apply the lessons of European modernism to create a unique vocabulary based on Brazilian nativist themes and subjects. In 1924 Andrade wrote the "Manifesto da Poesia Pau-Brasil" presenting their avant-garde attitudes regarding the popular and nativist culture of the country. Pau-Brasil is a reference to the indigenous dyewood (Brazilwood) that gave the country its name and was the first important resource for export in colonial trade. Amaral gave artistic form to Andrade's words by creating paintings celebrating the landscape, the impact of industrialisation and modernisation, and the traditions of the indigenous people. The first of her Pau-Brasil paintings is *EFCB (Estrada de Ferro Central do Brasil/Brazilian Central Railway)* (1924; see illustration). The industrialised city with its railway spans, telephone lines and traffic signals is reduced to flat patterns of bright colours and given a Brazilian flavour by the addition of palm trees and the silhouette of a colonial church on the horizon. The intense colours of the tropics, the festivals and folk arts and crafts contrast vividly with the heavy black contours symbolising industrialisation and make an obvious comment about the duality of living in a tropical/primitivist environment that is also modern. Rapidly perfecting a method of stylised representation of Brazilian subjects set within solid Cubist compositions, Amaral incorporated tropical flora and fauna, the *mestizo* and black populations of the small towns, rural villages and city boundaries in an intense palette based on the popular arts and crafts of the people. She painted a number of cityscapes and landscapes during this period, including *Hillside of Shanty Towns* (1924; private collection) and *São Paulo* (1924; private collection), that are specific to São Paulo, with its colonial city sprawling outwards to incorporate the shanty towns (*favelas*) crawling up its hillsides with their predominantly Afro and mulatto populations.

After her marriage to Andrade in 1926, Amaral began the next series of works, a tropical-surrealist approach to her nativist aesthetic described as Antropofagia. The Antropofagia movement occupied the São Paulo avant-garde in the mid-1920s and stood for artistic independence from European domination. Tarsila's first work in the series was a present to her husband entitled *Abaporú* (1928; Collection Maria Anna and Raul de Souza Dantas Forbes, São Paulo). Translated "man who eats" from the Tupi-Guarani Indian language, *Abaporú* is a huge solitary figure with enormous feet sitting on a bright green patch of land and leaning his tiny head on his hand. Behind him a blazing lemon-slice moon and simplified cactus plant dominate the landscape. Rooted to the soil with his foot, he may be an imaginary descendant of mythical creatures called *sciapods* described in classical mythology as members of monstrous races that entered into the lore of the voyages of exploration and became conflated with stories of cannibals. Amaral used the image as a symbol of the primordial people rooted in the earth and inspired Andrade to publish his "Manifesto Antropofagia" or "Cannibalist Manifesto" two months later, initiating a more aggressive attitude towards nativist subjects for both of them. As a metaphor for Brazil's dependency on European culture, the cannibal represents the conquering, not the conquered people, and calls for Brazilians to revolt against those elements that represent European aesthetics, past and present. The sequel painting, *Antropofagia* (1929; Foundation José and Paulina Nemirovsky), celebrates the fertility of the land with the *Abaporú* entwined with a female creature whose enlarged breast hangs over his knee. Tropical plants, banana leaves and cacti frame the background and the lemon-slice sun shines benevolently above. Rendered with the utmost simplicity, devoid of all extraneous details, the canvas is painted with smooth strokes and minimal colours, placing emphasis on the iconography of the land that is inseparable from its creatures. The same attention to a fantasy landscape with surreal creatures and distortions is present in *Setting Sun* (1929; Collection Jean Boghici, Rio de Janeiro). The world of nature appears untouched by human beings and sways with rhythmic grace as the flora and fauna come to life under the watchful gaze of the setting sun. Five Amazon otters (*ariranhas*) swim placidly through the water, the only occupants of the dreamlike scene.

Amaral's surreal representations of the land pay tribute to the beauty of the Brazilian environment and make a prophetic statement about the disastrous consequences of man's careless exploitation of nature, 50 years before the destruction of Brazil's rain forests was an issue of international concern. The same message appears as a subtle undercurrent in *Forest* (1929; Museu de Arte Contemporánea da Universidade de São Paulo), in which the pristine and elemental forces of nature are reduced to four abstract elements: eggs, trees, land and dead tree trunks. Each one is symbolic in the cycle of nature, from the fertility of the land represented by the egg to its death and destruction represented by the dead tree trunks. The contrast between life and death, before and after, is a powerful statement about the value of nature. The dead trunks, standing like sentinels on the horizon, fade into the distance of the desolate landscape, marking the future of the eggs in time and space.

In 1931 Amaral visited the Soviet Union to organise an exhibition in Moscow and was deeply affected by the social conditions suffered by the Russian people. On her return to Brazil she began a series of works based on social commentary. The faces of the people change with the palette as she captures Russian poverty in *2nd Class* (1931; Collection Fanny Feffer, São Paulo). Working with the same sensitivity she applied to representations of the people of Brazil, Tarsila paints a portrait of dejection and sadness of universal significance. After her divorce from Andrade in 1930 interrupted the production of her painting, Amaral continued with themes of social realism in her paintings of the late 1930s and 1940s. The 1950s were years of widespread acceptance with successful exhibitions in Brazil, and in 1960 she represented Brazil at the Venice Biennale. She worked in the country outside São Paulo until her death.

The paintings of Tarsila do Amaral represent more than a break from rigid and conservative academic standards. As one of the most important early modernists of South America, she sought themes and subjects based on her own land and people and depicted them according to contemporary systems of abstraction and expression. She worked with a sincerity of purpose and unique vision and style to create an image of an ideal, invented world that was quintessentially Brazilian.

CAROL DAMIAN

Ancher, Anna
Danish painter, 1859–1935

Born Anna Kirstine Brøndum in Skagen, 18 August 1859; father a hotelier. Studied drawing and colour theory at Vilhelm Kyhn's academy in Copenhagen, winters 1875–8. Married painter Michael Ancher, 1880; daughter Helga, also a painter, born 1883; husband died 1927. Visited Göteborg, Sweden, 1881; Germany and Vienna, 1882; Paris, Amsterdam and Belgium, 1885. Spent winter of 1888–9 in Paris; studied under Puvis de Chavannes in Léon Bonnat's studio. Trips to Berlin and the Netherlands, 1891; Italy, 1897 and 1924; Germany (Berlin, Dresden), 1900. Recipient of first-class medal, Royal Danish Academy of Fine Arts, Copenhagen, 1903; second-class Eckersberg medal, Copenhagen, 1904; Ingenio et Arti medal, Copenhagen,

1913. Member of Academy Plenum Assembly (Plenarforsamling), Copenhagen, 1904. Died in Skagen, 15 April 1935.

Principal Exhibitions

Charlottenborg, Copenhagen: 1880–1927, 1929–35 (salons), 1935 (retrospective)

Exposition Universelle, Paris: 1889 (silver medal), 1900 (medal)

Kunstforening, Copenhagen: 1890 (*En samling moderne dansk kunst* [A collection of modern Danish art])

Internationale Kunstausstellung, Berlin: 1891 (honourable mention)

World's Columbian Exposition, Chicago: 1893

Industriforeningen, Copenhagen: 1895 (*Kvindernes udstilling – fra fortid til nutid* [Women's exhibition – from the past to the present])

Guildhall, London: 1907 (*Works by Danish Painters*)

Landsudstilling (National Exhibition), Århus: 1909

Esposizione Internazionale, Rome: 1911

Public Art Galleries, Brighton, Sussex: 1912 (*Modern Danish Artists*)

Den frie udstillingsbygning, Copenhagen: 1920 (*Kvindelige kunstneres retrospektive udstilling* [Women artists' retrospective]), 1930 (*Kvindelige kunstneres Samfund* [Society of Women Artists])

Brooklyn Museum, NY: 1927 (*Danish National Exhibition of Paintings, Sculpture, Architecture and Applied Art*)

Jeu de Paume, Paris: 1928 (*L'Art danois*)

Selected Writings

Breve fra Anna Ancher [Letters from Anna Ancher], ed. Knud Voss, Copenhagen: Herluf Stokholm, 1984

Bibliography

Alba Schwartz, *Skagen: Den svundne tid i sagn og billeder* [Skagen: Legends and pictures of times gone by], 1912; revised edition, Skagen: Skagens Museum, 1992

—, *Skagen: Før og nu* [Skagen: Before and now], 1913; revised edition, Skagen: Skagens Museum, 1992

Karl Madsen, *Skagens malere* [Skagen painters], Copenhagen: Gyldendal, 1929

Walther Schwartz, "Skagens datter" [Skagen's daughter], *Politiken*, 1939; reprinted in *De glade farvers fest* [Festival of gay colours], Copenhagen: Schwartz & Fisker, 1989, pp.41–53

Ernst Mentze, *P.S. Krøyer*, Copenhagen: Det Schønbergske Forlag, 1969

Knud Voss, *Skagensmaleren Anna Ancher, 1859–1935* [The Skagen painter Anna Ancher], Tølløse: Stok-Art, 1974

Margrethe Loerges, *Et solstrejf i en stue i Skagen: Portræt af Anna Ancher* [Flickering sunlight in a room in Skagen: A portrait of Anna Ancher], Copenhagen: Hernov, 1978

Henri Usselmann, *Complexité et importance des contacts des peintres nordiques avec l'impressionisme*, PhD dissertation, University of Göteborg, 1979

Danske kvindelige kunstnere fra det 19. og 20. århundrede repræsenteret på Statens Museum for Kunst [Danish women artists from the 19th and 20th centuries represented in the Statens Art Museum], exh. cat., Statens Museum for Kunst, Copenhagen, 1980

Knud Voss, *Mennesker og kunst på Skagen* [People and art in Skagen], Skagen: Skagens Museum, 1982

Bente Scavenius, *Fremsyn – snæversyn: Dansk Dagbladskunstkritik, 1880–1901* [Forward looking – inward looking: Danish newspaper art criticism, 1880–1901], Copenhagen: Borgen, 1983

Margrethe Loerges, *Anna Ancher*, Copenhagen: Andersen, 1984

1880-årene i nordisk maleri [The 1880s in Nordic painting], exh. cat., Nasjonalgalleriet, Oslo, and elsewhere, 1985

Dreams of a Summer Night: Scandinavian Painting at the Turn of the Century, exh. cat., Arts Council of Great Britain, London, 1986

Kvindelige kunstnere på Skagen: Anna Ancher, Oda Krohg, Marie Krøyer [Women artists in Skagen], exh. cat., Moss (Oslo), Skagens Museum, Skagen, and elsewhere, 1987

Ole Wivel, *Anna Ancher*, Tølløse: Stok-Art, 1987 (in Danish and English)

De drogo till Paris: Nordiska konstnärinnor på 1880-talet [They went to Paris: Nordic women artists in the 1880s], exh. cat., Liljevalchs Konsthall, Stockholm, 1988

Kirk Varnedoe, *Northern Light: Nordic Art at the Turn of the Century*, New Haven and London: Yale University Press, 1988

Alessandra Comini, "Nordic luminism and the Scandinavian recasting of Impressionism", *World Impressionism: The International Movement, 1860–1920*, ed. Norma Broude, New York: Abrams, 1992, pp.274–313

Elisabeth Fabritius, *Michael Anchers ungdom, 1865–1880* [Michael Ancher's youth], 2 vols, Skagen: Helga Anchers Fond, 1992– (second volume in preparation)

Hans Dam Christensen, "Anna Ancher og den kunsthistoriske litteratur" [Anna Ancher and the art historical literature], *Periskop*, i/1, June 1993, pp.9–23

Anna Ancher, 1859–1935, exh. cat., Niedersächsisches Landesmuseum, Hannover, and elsewhere, 1994

Anna Ancher occupies a special place in Danish art. She was the only accomplished woman painter and native *Skagener* in the influential colony of artists that flourished in Skagen, Denmark's northernmost peninsula, during the 1880s and early 1890s. As a summer destination, Skagen attracted artists from all over Scandinavia who came to practise the radical new French figure and plein-air painting in the brilliant northern light and to exchange ideas from their foreign travels. From the time that P.S. Krøyer – the only member of the colony with an international reputation – returned from his extensive foreign travels in 1882, the nucleus of the colony was formed by Anna, her husband Michael Ancher and Krøyer. Michael Ancher had left the Academy in Copenhagen without a diploma and gone to Skagen in search of primitivist motifs in 1874. His heroic portrayals of Skagen fishermen and Krøyer's impressionistic paintings of artists' lunch parties and evening strolls on beaches have created a mythology for the area. Ancher was at the centre of this mythology, the pivot around which the drama of the artists' lives was wound, who managed to find time to paint in between her duties as wife, hostess, mother and daughter. She observed from nature and absorbed from her male colleagues what she needed in order to find her own expressive voice. Her artistic independence was remarkable. and all the more remarkable is the modernity of her idiom, with its reduced, abstracting forms and bold expressive colours, singling her out as one of the most innovative painters of her generation, exceeding most of her male colleagues, including her husband.

Her achievements and contribution to the modern breakthrough in Danish art were recognised during her lifetime. In Paris she was awarded medals for her entries in the Expositions Universelles of 1889 and 1900, when she was one of only two Danish painters to be mentioned favourably by the French critics. She won medals at other international exhibitions and in Denmark, where she regularly entered her work for the Charlottenborg exhibitions and at the various other venues that began to appear from the early 1890s; she was generally well reviewed. She was awarded membership of the Academy Plenum Assembly and in 1913 she received the Ingenio et Arti medal from the Danish king. She won the respect and

Ancher: *Maid in the Kitchen*, 1883–6; oil on canvas; 87.7 × 68.5 cm.; Hirschsprung Collection, Copenhagen

admiration of her male colleagues for the sincerity of her human portrayal as well as the simplified form and light-suffused colour that lend mood and atmosphere to her mostly small and intimate oil paintings. Her increasing interest in mood and Symbolism is reflected in a small number of interiors and landscapes that are empty of human presence, but the human figure remained central to her work. Her family and the working people of her immediate surroundings provided her with subject matter.

After Ancher's death her reputation waned. After the discovery, in the artist's family house in Skagen in 1964, of a chest full of unknown works by her – mainly studies and sketches in oil – a renewed interest manifested itself in a number of exhibitions over the next three decades, culminating in a major retrospective mounted in Germany in 1994 and touring to Copenhagen and Skagen in 1995.

There has been a consistent failure to address seriously the issues of gender and representation that affected Ancher's work, yet the issue of gender is important in a critical appraisal of it. As a woman she would never have become a painter if it were not for her exceptional circumstances. At a time when Danish women did not have the vote and were barred from entry to the Academy schools, it was unthinkable for a woman outside an inner circle to pursue art professionally. Prevailing prejudices combined with women's own internalised expectations and demands made it difficult and frightening for women to compete as equals with men. The fact that Ancher was born and brought up in Brøndum's Inn, Skagen, owned by her family and later to win fame as a home and meeting place for artists, gave her an unusual entrée to the exclusive male domain of art. In her own home she was able to learn from the visiting artists, watch them work and see their copies of the great masters brought home from foreign trips. She received drawing lessons from Karl Madsen, who was to become an influential critic and the Skagen Museum's first director, and at the age of 16 she became engaged to Michael Ancher. From then on his support and encouragement were crucial to Ancher's development, although she never allowed him or anyone else to influence her to the exclusion of her own inner vision. When she married Michael Ancher on her 21st birthday she had spent three successive winters in Copenhagen taking classes in drawing and colour theory at the school run by the academic professor and landscape painter Vilhelm Kyhn, who had little faith in her talent and advised her to give up painting and devote herself to her domestic responsibilities as a wife. Kyhn's lack of support was compensated for by her husband's encouragement. The painting *Assessing the Day's Work* (1883; Statens Museum for Kunst, Copenhagen), on which both artists worked, is an exceptional visual record of a husband-and-wife team of painters. Without Michael's support, it is doubtful that Ancher would have had the confidence and courage to exhibit her works at the Charlottenborg exhibitions in Copenhagen – the Danish equivalent of the Paris Salon. Most of the women who exhibited at the Academy were flower painters. As such, they were acknowledged as professional artists but were not valued highly by the critics.

Ancher, on the other hand, enjoyed critical and popular acclaim from an early age. Aged only 19 she had her exhibition début at the Academy (Charlottenborg) with a rather naive composition of an old couple in a landscape. It was, somewhat mercifully, ignored by the critics, but the following year she had her first excellent review for the portrait of *Lars Gaihede Whittling a Stick* (1880; Skagens Museum). Its detailed drawing and mixed browns and blues show the influence of Michael Ancher, but the psychological depth of the characterisation exceeded Michael's own portrayals of the same sitter. Ancher did not pursue the style, however, but was far more attracted to the new French ideas introduced to her by Krøyer and the Norwegian painter Christian Krohg, friend of the Impressionists in Paris and teacher and mentor of Edvard Munch. Krøyer's lighter palette and fine understanding of figure and light as well as Krohg's fuller and more vibrant use of colour and the way he cut his compositions at the edges became part of Ancher's vocabulary.

The winter she spent in Paris (1888–9) increased her confidence. She won a silver medal at the Exposition Universelle and spent much time absorbing impressions of Paris. She enjoyed watching the faces of the customers when dining in a coachmen's café and was altogether enchanted, as she wrote, with the indigenous working people who reminded her of her favourite characters in Zola's novels. Sadly, the only work that has come to light from this extended visit to Paris is a portrait of the Norwegian woman painter *Kitty Kielland* (1889; Michael og Anna Anchers Hus, Skagen), which excels in the psychological depth of its characterisation. Ancher enrolled for classes with Puvis de Chavannes at a studio run by Léon Bonnat, a favourite with the Nordic artists. Her interest in modern colour theory and Symbolism would account for this choice; Puvis's colour treatment was considered very modern by Danish critics. When painting her subsequent group compositions, the best of which is *A Funeral* (1890; Statens Museum for Kunst), composed in clear pinks and dark blues, Ancher may have been influenced by Puvis. But her contact with French Impressionism exerted an even greater influence. It has been said that she was deeply impressed with the work of Manet, Degas and the other Impressionists. *Sunshine in the Blue Room* (1891; Skagens Museum), painted not long after her return from Paris, can be seen as an important Impressionist breakthrough in Skagen. It depicts a domestic interior with a child: a rhapsody of colour and light in which the room and the little girl, sitting in a chair below the window, are subordinated to the colours of the light that falls in from the window, across the girl's blonde hair on to the wall and the carpet. The colours are applied directly on to the canvas, not mixed first. Coloured light guides our gaze from the detailed yellows, gold and blues of the window side of the composition across to the wall and down to the solitary little figure in her chair, where the pale blues of the reflected light on the wall are echoed on the back of her dress.

The sitter for the painting was Ancher and Michael's only child, Helga. When she was born in 1883 Ancher had recently started painting the *Maid in the Kitchen* (1883–6; see illustration), but she did not finish it until three years later. Its colours are brilliant and vibrant: the kitchen interior is bathed in a warm, diffused sunlight, filtered through a yellow curtain that highlights the contrasting red and black of the clothes worn by the maid, who is shown from the back. Ancher had seen works by Vermeer and de Hooch in Vienna before starting the painting, but although the picture owes a debt to the Dutch masters, her experience of motherhood during the intervening years may have given her a heightened awareness of the isolation of the woman's sphere that may account for the quiet melancholy of the composition. The ray of light from the window creates the same sense of distinction between the exterior and the interior that is such a strong feature of the painting she had done the previous year, *Sunshine in the Blind Woman's Room* (1885; Den Hirschsprungske Samling). The sense of remoteness and isolation created by this distinction between the public and private spheres is a recurrent feature of Ancher's paintings of women in interiors. From *Young Girl Arranging Flowers* (1885; Aarhus Kunstmuseum, Århus) and *Young Girl Before a Lamp* (1887) to *Young Girl in front of a Mirror* (1899; both Skagens Museum), Ancher depicts women who seem remote, isolated and evasive as subjects. Portrayed from the back, looking down or with their faces hidden, they are never part of the light and joy that Ancher always locates outside their sphere.

Nevertheless, there is in all these interiors also a poignant sense of intimacy, created by the way the end wall of the composition is always parallel to the picture plane, reminding us that these are flat surfaces of paint. After the turn of the century, Ancher's concern with the surface of the canvas led her to paint increasingly reduced forms and to use bolder colours. The interiors that she now painted are often empty of people and she attempted landscapes, which are rare among her oeuvre and hardly count for anything in her reputation as an artist. She seems to compose in abstract masses of colour and light. *Interior with Chair and Plant* (undated) reveals her awareness of both Fauvism and Expressionism, as do the two empty interiors *Midday Hour, Interior* (1914) and *Interior with Sunlight and Red Door* (1918; all Skagens Museum). In her late landscapes there is a strong atmospheric quality; one senses the midday heat of the burning golden-reds of the quiet street in *Daphnesvej, Motif from Skagen Østerby* (c.1915), in which the narrow shadow effect on the right confirms the time of day, while the cooler, violet tones of the long shadows cast by the houses on the left side of the composition in *Østerbyvej in Skagen-Østerby* (1915; both Skagens Museum) suggest the still mood of late afternoon.

The only known self-portrait by Anna Ancher is a tiny painting in three-quarter profile (c.1877–8; Helga Anchers Fond, Skagen). It reveals a strong face with a full, sensuous mouth, a slightly crooked nose and a pair of large, piercing dark eyes. Characteristically, her gaze does not meet ours. She is evasive as a subject – as she was in character. The colours are rich and the facial expression determined and spirited. She was a sensual, not an intellectual artist. She sought in her art to create a synthesis of Naturalism and a kind of Symbolism that was not really Symbolism, since its point of departure was always an observation of her immediate surroundings; but it suggested an atmosphere. This synthesis, combined with the simple perception and the painterly emphasis on the surface, anticipates later Danish modernist painting and singles out Anna Ancher as one of the most forward-looking painters of her generation.

ALETTE RYE SCALES

See also Noack

Anderson, Sophie

French painter, 1823–1903

Born Sophie Gengembre in Paris, 1823; father an architect. Left for USA with her family, 1848. Married British artist Walter Anderson, c.1849. Settled in England, 1854. Moved to Isle of Capri, Italy, for health reasons, late 1860s or early 1870s. Returned to England and settled in Falmouth, Cornwall, 1894. Died 1903.

Principal Exhibitions

Royal Society of British Artists, London: 1855–7, 1863–6, 1868–9, 1890
Royal Academy, London: occasionally 1855–96
National Academy of Design, New York: 1860
British Institution, London: 1864–5
Liverpool Autumn Exhibition: 1870
Grosvenor Gallery, London: 1878–80, 1882–3, 1885–7

Bibliography

Ellen C. Clayton, *English Female Artists*, 2 vols, London: Tinsley, 1876

Christopher Forbes, *The Royal Academy (1837–1901) Revisited: Victorian Paintings from the Forbes Magazine Collection*, New York: privately printed, 1975

Pamela Gerrish Nunn, *Victorian Women Artists*, London: Women's Press, 1987

Jane Sellars, *Women's Works: Paintings, Drawings, Prints and Sculpture by Women*, Liverpool: National Museums and Galleries on Merseyside, 1988

Deborah Cherry, *Painting Women: Victorian Women Artists*, London and New York: Routledge, 1993

A Struggle for Fame: Victorian Women Artists and Authors, exh. cat., Yale Center for British Art, New Haven, 1994

Little has been written about Sophie Anderson, a French-born artist who showed remarkable resilience not only in creating a career and earning money as an artist, but also by sustaining her profession in America, Britain and from the Isle of Capri. The offspring of an English mother and a French architect father, she was brought up mostly in rural France until the late 1840s. From an early age she drew and at the age of 20 studied very briefly in the atelier of the history painter Baron Charles Auguste de Steuben before his departure for Russia. In general, however, she was virtually self-taught. She left Paris with her parents in the wake of the Revolution of 1848. Her family moved to the USA, settling first in Cincinnati and then in Manchester, Pennsylvania. During this time Sophie Gengembre earned a living producing portraits, possibly for sitters who lived in the Pittsburgh area. Moreover, she worked for Louis Prang and Company, a well-known purveyor of American popular imagery in chromolithograph form. She also contributed five book illustrations to *Historical Collections of the Great West* (1852) by Henry Howe. In the USA she met and married the British artist Walter Anderson, and the couple moved to Britain in 1854. Anderson's first exhibited work there was *An American Market Basket*, which was exhibited at the Society of British Artists and purchased by a Mr Fallowes of Manchester. The couple lived intermittently for several years in London, Dalston and Bramley, but for reasons of her ill health in the late 1860s or early 1870s they moved for almost 20 years to live and work on the Isle of Capri. By the early

Anderson: *Elaine*, exhibited 1870; Walker Art Gallery, Liverpool

1890s Anderson returned to Britain and settled in Falmouth, Cornwall, continuing to paint and exhibit well into her last years as a septuagenarian.

Her history of exhibitions and productivity confirm that after her marriage Anderson continued to paint in what has been described by Pamela Gerrish Nunn (1987) as one of many Victorian "painting partnerships" that allowed women both to create art and to earn money with their artistic spouses. It is known, for example, that Anderson's commanding *Elaine* (see illustration) was priced at £420 at the Liverpool Autumn Exhibition of 1870. When it was purchased in 1871, this Tennysonian literary interpretation and pictorial *tour de force* was the first painting to be bought from the Liverpool public purse as well as the first one to enter a civic gallery there. In this respect Anderson was among the relatively few women who saw their paintings become acquisitions at the large municipal museums. From the outset she managed to earn a living with a degree of commercial success, not only in America but also in Britain, and works like her *Christmas Time* were engraved for magazines with wide circulation such as the *Illustrated London News* and *The Graphic*. Among her private patrons was the noted Pre-Raphaelite collector Thomas E. Plint.

Her contributions at the Royal Academy ranged in content from her inaugural *Virgin and Child* in 1855 to Classical subject matter such as *Evoe, evoe Bacche* in 1883. Many entries were typically figural or narrative subjects with titles such as the *Day of Rest*, *Nuggets*, *London Street Flowers* and *Roasting the Pine Cones*. During her long career she also exhibited at the National Academy of Design in New York, the British Institution, the Royal Society of British Artists and in the 1880s at the avant-garde Grosvenor Gallery in London. At the last she was among a select group of women artists (including Louise Jopling, Louisa Starr, Marie Spartali, Louisa, Marchioness of Waterford, and Evelyn De Morgan, all q.v.) who received remarkably enlightened treatment by the founders of this controversial gallery.

In addition to her smaller-scale genre pictures, Anderson also painted numerous relatively large-scale historical compositions and neo-classicising canvases such as her arcadian *Song* (Wolverhampton Art Gallery) of 1881. Until recently, however, she has been known primarily for her domestic or narrative pictures, notably *No Walk Today* (private collection, Lady Scott, repr. Graham Reynolds, *Victorian Painting*, revised edition, New York: Harper, 1987, pl.73), as well as for other charming genre pictures such as *Guess Again* (Forbes Magazine Collection) and *Children's Story-Book* (Birmingham City Museum and Art Galleries). Most of her paintings are in private collections, although some were acquired from the mid-1980s by major museums both in Britain and America.

SUSAN P. CASTERAS

Anguissola, Lucia *see under* Anguissola, Sofonisba

Anguissola, Sofonisba
Italian painter, *c.*1532–1625

Born in Cremona, *c.*1532, into a noble family; her sisters Elena (died after 1584), Anna Maria (died after 1585) and Lucia (died ?1565) were also painters. Studied in Cremona under Bernardino Campi, *c.*1546–9, and Il Sojaro, 1549–*c.*1552/3. Lady-in-waiting and portrait painter at the Spanish court in Madrid, 1559–73. Married (1) Don Fabrizio de Moncado, brother of the viceroy of Sicily, after August 1569; later resided in Palermo; (2) Orazio Lomellino, a Genoese nobleman, 1579 or 1580; living in Genoa by October 1583. Living in Palermo by 1624, when Anthony van Dyck made a sketch of her (British Museum, London), recording that her eyesight was weakened. Buried in San Giorgio dei Genovesi, Palermo, 16 November 1625; survived by Orazio, who dedicated the inscription on her tomb, 1632.

Bibliography
Giorgio Vasari, *Le vite de' più eccellenti pittori, scultori ed architettori*, Florence, 1568; ed. Gaetano Milanesi, 9 vols, Florence: Sansoni, 1878–85, v, p.81; vi, pp.498–502; vii, p.133; as *Lives of the Most Eminent Painters, Sculptors and Architects*, 10 vols, London: Macmillan-Medici Society, 1912–15; reprinted New York: AMS, 1976

Giambattista Zaist, *Notizie istoriche de' pittori, scultori ed architetti cremonesi, con un appendice d'altre notizie, il discorso di Alessandro Lamo intorno alla scoltura, e pittura …* (1584), 2 vols, Cremona, 1774; reprinted Cremona, 1975

Antonio Campi, *Cremona fedelissima città et nobilissima colonia de Romani …*, Cremona, 1585; reprinted Bologna: Forni, 1974

Raffaello Soprani, *Le vite de' pittori, scolturi ed architetti genovesi …*, Genoa, 1674; 2nd edition, 2 vols, ed. Carlo Giuseppe Ratti, Genoa, 1768–9; reprinted Genoa, 1965

Filippo Baldinucci, *Notizie de' professori del disegno da Cimabue in qua*, Florence, 1681–1728; reprint, ed. F. Ranalli and Paola Barocchi, 7 vols, Florence, 1974–5

M. Fournier-Sarlovèze, "Sofonisba Anguissola et ses soeurs", *Revue de l'Art Ancien et Moderne*, v, 1899, pp.313–24, 379–92

Charles de Tolnay, "Sofonisba Anguissola and her relations with Michelangelo", *Journal of the Walters Art Gallery*, iv, 1941, pp.115–19

Women Artists, 1550–1950, exh. cat., Los Angeles County Museum of Art, and elsewhere, 1976

Flavio Caroli, *Sofonisba Anguissola e le sue sorelle*, Milan: Mondadori, 1987

Rossana Sacchi, "Documenti per Sofonisba Anguissola", *Paragone*, xxxix/457, 1988, pp.73–89

María Kusche, "Sofonisba Anguissola en España: Retrattista en la corte de Felipe II junto a Alonso Sánchez Coello y Jorge de la Rúa", *Archivo Español de Arte*, lxii/248, 1989, pp.391–420 (with English summary)

Lionello Puppi, "Un tassello archivistico (e un quesito) per la biografia di Sofonisba Anguissola", *Paragone*, xl/473, 1989, pp.105–8

Flavio Caroli, "Aggiunte a Sofonisba Anguissola e Fede Galizia", *Notizie da Palazzo Albani*, xx, 1991, pp.143–8

María Kusche, "Sofonisba Anguissola: Vuelta a Italia: Continuación de sus relaciónes con la corte Española", *Paragone*, xliii/513, 1992, pp.10–35

Ilya Sandra Perlingieri, *Sofonisba Anguissola: The First Great Woman Artist of the Renaissance*, New York: Rizzoli, 1992

Sofonisba Anguissola e le sue sorelle, exh. cat., Centro Culturale, Cremona, and elsewhere, 1994

Mary Garrard, "Here's looking at me: Sofonisba Anguissola and the problem of the woman artist", *Renaissance Quarterly*, xlvii, 1994, pp.556–622

Fredrika Jacobs, "Woman's capacity to create: The unusual case of Sofonisba Anguissola", *ibid.*, pp.74–101

Sofonisba Anguissola: A Renaissance Woman, exh. cat., National Museum of Women in the Arts, Washington, DC, 1995

Of the nearly 40 women now known to have been active in visual arts professions in Italy during the 16th century, Sofonisba Anguissola holds a singular place. Internationally renowned in her lifetime, she, in contrast to other women artists, never fell from critical grace. In the history of art, Anguissola's name has appeared with regularity since Marco Gerolamo Vida counted her among the most significant painters in his *Cremonensium Orationes III adversus Papienses in controversia Principatus* (1550) and Giorgio Vasari included her in the second edition of his *Vite* (1568). It was only in 1994, however, that the major retrospective *Sofonisba Anguissola e le sue sorelle* brought together a significant number of her works.

While critical acknowledgement has accorded this artist an unusual position in the annals of art history, there is much about her early career that strikes a familiar chord. The oldest in a family of six daughters and one son, Sofonisba Anguissola was born to parents of Cremonese nobility – Amilcare Anguissola and Bianca Ponzone. In her early teens, she and her sister Elena were sent to study painting with Bernardino Campi. If the association, which lasted from *c.*1546 to 1549, was not typically that of apprentice to master but resembled more the relationship of paying guest to instructional host, Anguissola's artistic training seems to have followed conventional lines. She was taught the fundamentals of materials and technique which she practised with copying exercises. The compositional affinity of Anguissola's early works to those of Campi indicates the orthodoxy of her training. Contemporary discussions of other women, such as Lucrezia Quistelli and Suor Plautilla Nelli (q.v.), suggest that this was the *modus operandi* for women. The recent attribution by Giulio Bora (Cremona 1994) of seven studies of figures in diverse poses (one in Kupferstichkabinett, Berlin; six in Louvre, Paris), all of which have been squared for transfer, points out that she, like her male peers, was also schooled in the essential principles of *l'arte del disegno*. These drawings also reveal her exposure to and assimilation of Leonardo da Vinci's classically idealising manner via such artists as Bernardino Luini. Campi's departure for Milan in 1549 resulted in Anguissola's approximate three-year affiliation with Bernardino Gatti, called Il Sojaro. It was through Il Sojaro, who tempered Correggio's fluid Emilian style with that of Pordenone's hardened Mannerism, that Anguissola was exposed to the Parmesan mode of imaging. Sometime around 1554 she arrived in Rome. Her exposure to Roman Mannerism reinforced what she had learned from Il Sojaro, as is evident in the attenuated figure of the languidly posed Virgin in *Holy Family* (1559; Accademia Carrara, Bergamo).

Anguissola: *Bernardino Campi Painting a Portrait of Sofonisba Anguissola*, late 1550s; oil on canvas; Pinacoteca Nazionale, Siena

The extant correspondence between Amilcare Anguissola and an array of influential humanists and potential patrons reveals the role of promoter played by Sofonisba's father. Letters to Michelangelo also disclose Amilcare's paternal zeal in securing the best possible guidance for his artist-daughter. In a letter to Michelangelo dated 7 May 1557 Amilcare thanks the master for the "innate courtesy and goodness" that prompted him "in the past to introduce her" to art. He goes on to request Michelangelo "to guide her again" and to ask that he send to Sofonisba "one of your drawings that she may colour it in oil, with the obligation to return it to you faithfully finished by her own hand". Given Michelangelo's acknowledged assistance to other artists, it is more than reasonable to assume his willingness to grant Amilcare this favour. While no image has been identified in connection with this specific request, Anguissola's drawing of *Asdrubale Bitten by a Crayfish* (late 1550s; Museo di Capodimonte, Naples) links her name to that of Michelangelo. In a letter to Cosimo de' Medici dated 20 January 1562, Tomaso Cavalieri explained his gift of the Capodimonte drawing in the following terms: "…

the divine Michelangelo having seen a drawing done by [Sofonisba's] hand of a smiling girl, said that he would have liked to see a weeping boy as a subject more difficult to draw" (Tolnay 1941, p.117). *Asdrubale Bitten by a Crayfish* not only meets the challenge, it goes one better, juxtaposing the smiling girl with the weeping boy.

Cavalieri's coupling of Anguissola's name with that of Michelangelo, a pairing that is also found in Vasari's life of Anguissola, is, perhaps, understandable. While Michelangelo was singular as *Il divino*, Anguissola was unique among 16th-century women artists in being praised as men's creative equal. Certainly, she was a much sought-after painter. Paintings by her hand were requested by and subsequently entered the collections of Pope Julius III and members of the Este, Farnese, Medici and Borghese families. By 1559 her reputation had spread beyond the Italian peninsula. In that year she entered the Spanish court as lady-in-waiting and portrait painter to the queen, Isabel of Valois. She would remain in Spain until 1573, sharing with Antonis Mor and Alonso Sanchez Coello the prestige of being a member of the triumvirate of Spanish court painters.

While Anguissola executed a few devotional panels during her tenure in Spain, most of her time was devoted to painting portraits of members of the royal court and family, including *Philip II* and *Anne of Austria* (both Prado, Madrid), *Isabel of Valois* (Kunsthistorisches Museum, Vienna) and *Infanta Isabella Clara Eugenia* (Spanish Embassy, Paris, property of the Prado). In keeping with the decorum of courtly taste and reflecting the austerity of the religious climate, these portraits are marked by an almost formulaic restraint in composition, colour and light. Because other artists at the Spanish court not only painted similarly restrained images but also reproduced some of Anguissola's portraits, questions of attribution have arisen. Comparison of problematical works with those securely attributed to Sofonisba combined with technical examination have in recent years clarified most of these questions. Despite the reserved formality, poised elegance and almost petrified stiffness of Anguissola's Spanish works, qualities found also in paintings by Mor and Sanchez Coello, the physiognomies that Sofonisba recorded reveal distinctive personalities behind the decorous mask, or what Leonardo da Vinci called "the motions of the mind". In this respect, Anguissola's roots in Lombard traditions, specifically the mimetic melding of unidealised naturalism with a calculated style so evident in the works of Moretto da Brescia and Giovanni Moroni, are clearly visible. While such critics as Baldinucci and Zaist may be guilty of hyperbole in their praise of Anguissola as the equal of Titian in the art of portraiture, there can be little doubt that she mastered the art of capturing a sitter's psyche. Nowhere is this more apparent than in her more casual portrait conversation pieces.

As Vasari observed when he visited the Anguissola home in 1566, the enlivened individuality seen in Sofonisba's portraits of Italian and Spanish nobility had been given free rein in images of family members, or so-called portrait conversation pieces. Indeed, such paintings as *Amilcare Anguissola with His Son Asdrubale and Daughter Minerva* (Nivaagaards Malierisamling, Nivaa) and *The Artist's Sisters Playing Chess* (Muzeum Narodowe, Poznań) are intimate and perceptive studies of the complexities of interpersonal relationships and arrested motion. Compositionally ambitious, these portraits are particularly notable for their inventiveness, specifically Anguissola's sympathetic unification of multiple figures through a shared feeling; familial devotion in the former, jocularity and wit in the latter. In this regard, they display the vitality and freshness of her drawings *Asdrubale Bitten by a Crayfish* and the *Old Woman and Young Girl Studying the Alphabet* (Uffizi, Florence), which was subsequently engraved by Jacob Bos. On the one hand, these images reflect Flemish precedent modulated by Leonardo's concern with the symbiotic relationship of action-to-reaction; on the other, they look forward to Caravaggio's early profane works (e.g. *Boy Bitten by a Lizard*, c.1597; Fondazione Roberto Longhi, Florence).

The more than a dozen self-portraits by Anguissola stand midway between the reserve of her formal presentations of Italian nobility and Spanish royalty and her engaging portrait conversation pieces. Most, such as *Self-Portrait Before an Easel* (Muzeum Zamek, Lancut) and *Self-Portrait Before a Spinet* (Museo di Capodimonte), are images of self-fashioning in accordance with contemporary prescriptions for the ideal lady. *Bernardino Campi Painting a Portrait of Sofonisba Anguissola* (late 1550s; see illustration) is, by contrast, an ingenious double-portrait inversion of the usual male mentor/female protégée relationship. Standing in front of a portrait of Anguissola resting on an easel, Campi, his right hand steadied by a mahlstick, turns to gaze at the artist who, of course, is Anguissola. So positioned, Anguissola holds a double place, at once within the pictorial frame as object yet also outside the pictorial space as the objectifier. Ultimately and most importantly, she assumes all agency, an assumption made clear by the greater vivacity she has imparted to Campi's countenance in comparison to the static and stiff image he has supposedly painted of her. Given Anguissola's occupation, an occupation that one contemporary humanist described as "the profession of gentlemen", this image can only be viewed as the statement of an assured and self-possessed artist.

Following her return to Italy, Anguissola resided in Palermo and Genoa. Early sources indicate that her late oeuvre consisted primarily of devotional panels. Although many of these works have yet to be identified, those that do survive, such as the *Virgin Nursing Her Child* (1588; Museum of Fine Arts, Budapest) and *Holy Family with St Anne and the Young John the Baptist* (1592; Lowe Art Museum, Coral Gables), suggest that she responded to the impress of Counter-Reformation sobriety and the influence of Luca Cambiaso's use of chiaroscuro and nocturnal luminosity. As is the case with her early figure studies, these panels also attest to her awareness of current trends in late 16th-century art theory. As Cardinal Gabriele Paleotti advised, Anguissola rendered her subjects in a manner that delights (*dilettare*), teaches (*insegnare*) and moves (*movere*) the viewer to feelings of devotion.

Sofonisba was not the only Anguissola daughter to receive artistic training and to gain renown as a painter. Like Sofonisba, Elena studied with Campi and Gatti. The third sister, Lucia, who was probably taught by her oldest sister, had the potential, according to Filippo Baldinucci, to "become a better artist than even Sofonisba" had she not died so young. Lucia's signed portrait of *Dr Pietro Manna* (c.1560; Prado) suggests that she was at least her sister's equal in pictorial realism. Not only did Lucia capture the physician's probing mind through the rendering of his penetrating gaze, the Aesculapian snake coiled around the staff he holds in his left hand has been identified as the type (*Coluber viridiflavus*) most commonly found in Lombardy.

FREDRIKA H. JACOBS

See also Court Artists survey

Angus, Rita

New Zealand painter, 1908–1970

Born Henrietta Catherine Angus in Hastings, North Island, 12 March 1908; grew up in Hawke's Bay and Manawatu district. Studied intermittently at Canterbury College School of Art, Christchurch, under Leonard Booth and Cecil Kelly, 1927–33; attended lectures at Elam School of Art, Auckland, 1930. Married commercial artist Alfred Cook, 1930; divorced 1934. Worked as an illustrator for the *Press Junior*, Christchurch, 1934–7. Joined Peace Pledge Union, 1939; avoided work connected with the war effort. Patient in psychiatric hospital, 1949–50. Worked in both North Island and South Island, settling in a cottage in Thorndon, Wellington, in 1953; spent several months each year with her parents in Napier during 1960s. Travelled to Europe on a New Zealand Art Societies fellowship, 1958–9. Suffered from ill health after a back injury in 1962. Died in Wellington, 26 January 1970.

Principal Exhibitions

Individual
Centre Gallery, Wellington: 1957, 1961, 1963, 1964, 1967 (with Jean and Tim Angus)
Victoria University Library, Wellington: 1968
National Art Gallery, Wellington: 1983–4 (touring retrospective)

Group
Canterbury Society of Arts, Christchurch: occasionally 1930–65
Auckland Society of Arts: occasionally 1932–68
The Group Show, Christchurch: occasionally 1932–69
New Zealand Academy of Fine Arts, Wellington: occasionally 1932–63 (annuals), 1969 (*Five New Zealand Painters*)
Centennial Pavilion, Wellington: 1940 (*National Centennial Exhibition of New Zealand Art*)
Auckland City Art Gallery: 1957 (*Eight New Zealand Painters*), 1958 (*Five New Zealand Watercolourists*), 1960 (*New Zealand Realist Tradition*), 1960 (*Contemporary New Zealand Painting*)
Commonwealth Institute, London: 1965 (*Contemporary Painting in New Zealand*)
Smithsonian Institution, Washington, DC: 1969 (*New Zealand Modern Art*)

Writings

Text in *Year Book of the Arts*, no.3, 1947, pp.67–8

Bibliography

Gordon H. Brown, *New Zealand Painting, 1920–1940: Adaption and Nationalism*, Wellington, 1975
"Rita Angus: Impressions by some friends", *Art New Zealand*, no.3, 1976–7, pp.12–20, 43
Ronald Brownson, *Rita Angus*, MA thesis, University of Auckland, 1977
Gordon H. Brown, *New Zealand Painting, 1940–1960: Conformity and Dissension*, Wellington: Queen Elizabeth II Arts Council, 1981
Gordon H. Brown and Hamish Keith, *An Introduction to New Zealand Painting, 1839–1980*, 2nd edition, Auckland: Collins, 1982
Rita Angus, exh. cat., National Art Gallery, Wellington, and elsewhere, 1983 (contains bibliography)
Janet Paul, "What makes Rita Angus different?", *Art New Zealand*, no.26, 1983, pp.28–31
Elizabeth Eastmond and Merimeri Penfold, *Women and the Arts in New Zealand: Forty Works, 1936–86*, Auckland: Penguin, 1986
Laurence Simmons, "'Tracing the self': The self-portraits of Rita Angus", *ANTIC*, no.4, October 1988, pp.39–51
Gil Docking and Michael Dunn, *Two Hundred Years of New Zealand Painting*, 2nd edition, Auckland: Bateman, 1990
Michael Dunn, *A Concise History of New Zealand Painting*, Auckland: Bateman, 1991
Francis Pound, "Nationalism, the goddess and the landscape of maternal embrace", manuscript, 1992, Elam School of Fine Arts Library, University of Auckland
Anne Kirker, *New Zealand Women Artists: A Survey of 150 Years*, 2nd edition, Tortola, BVI: Craftsman House, 1993

Rita Angus Papers, 1399, 1937–1970, are in the Alexander Turnbull Library, Wellington.

Rita Angus's reputation as New Zealand's leading Regionalist artist is largely based on her major touring retrospective of 1983–4 and the accompanying publication *Rita Angus* (Wellington 1983). Previously, there had been little detailed critical commentary on the work of this artist, who was active from the late 1920s to the late 1960s. Her significance for New Zealand art history has now been reassessed and her influence has impacted on a number of recent and contemporary New Zealand artists. Angus's Regionalism was part of the dominant strand of New Zealand art practice, yet her contribution, while in part exemplary of the movement, also provided a unique and different voice in certain respects. Her self-portraits, for instance, where symbolism is incorporated, and especially her goddess "portraits" lie outside mainstream Regionalism's emphasis on landscape.

The social and artistic contexts in which Angus worked were neither altogether conducive to life as an artist nor, more specifically, to that of a woman artist and a "separated" woman: New Zealand's major exhibiting venues over this period were few and largely dominated by the Art Societies; the one arts magazine, *Art in New Zealand*, while including some coverage of Angus, was somewhat limited, while the rigid gender roles prescribed by society made it difficult, except for the most determined women artists, to follow a career in the arts. A clear awareness of inequalities was articulated by the artist herself in an early image, a bookplate, where she depicts herself as Cleopatra confronting a snake, with a dagger above her head and her hands bound by a heavy ball and chain (private collection, Christchurch, repr. Wellington 1983, p.17). They are also expressed in writing, on the subject of "Divorce" (she divorced after four years of marriage to the painter Alfred Cook), where she stated that as a result of "the female half of the population emotionally frustrated, religiously unsublimated, disappointed in her liberty, weaned of her employment, there is present a restlessness and a resentment (all the more massive because repressed)" (Alexander Turnbull Library, Wellington, MS Papers 1399:3/3).

Angus: *Self-Portrait*, 1936–7; Dunedin Public Art Gallery, New Zealand

Despite these difficulties, and often living frugally and in isolation, Angus produced a substantial oeuvre over four decades. She studied at the Canterbury College School of Art, held her first solo exhibition at the age of 49 and lived and worked in both the South and North Islands. She wrote of her aims in art: "... as a woman painter I work to represent love of humanity and faith in mankind, in a world, which is, to me, richly variable and infinitely beautiful ..." (*Year Book of the Arts*, 1947).

Her style, variations of which she used throughout her career, depends on crisp outline, an emphasis on structure, often iconic in its arrangement, rich colour and detailed brushwork, whose seamlessness reveals little of its application. Such emigrant British painters as Christopher Perkins advocated a clarity of style in opposition to the then prevailing diluted form of Impressionism, together with a focus on "modern" subjects. And local literary figures such as A.R.D. Fairburn noted how, in New Zealand: "There is no golden mist in the air, no merlin in our woods ... We must learn to draw rather than paint, even if we are using a brush, or we shall not be perfectly truthful" (*Some Aspects of New Zealand Art and Letters*, London, 1934). Other factors important for the formation of Angus's characteristically chiselled style included Chinese art, Early Renaissance Italian art and the work of such old masters as Vermeer, accessible to her through reproductions.

While she produced a substantial number of highly lyrical watercolours over her career – *Untitled (Kapiti from Waikanae)* (1951; Auckland City Art Gallery) is one, and the O'Keeffian close-focus purple flower, *Untitled (Passionflower)*

(1943; Rita Angus Loan Collection, Museum of New Zealand, Wellington) is another – Angus's reputation largely rests on her larger-scale oils. Of landscape subjects, the early *Cass* (1936; Robert McDougall Art Gallery, Christchurch) has become emblematic of the notion of the "invention of New Zealand". It depicts a tiny rural railway station in central, iconic fashion within the typically isolated mountainous South Island landscape. A pile of timber suggests construction in progress, while the small size of the lone figure in relation to the landscape speaks of the dominance of the land in relation to the efforts of a descendant of the European pioneer settlers. While specific in their detail, later landscapes such as *Central Otago* (1954–6/1969; Museum of New Zealand) in fact artfully combine disparate views into one composite image. Other later landscapes, while continuing a naturalistic attention to detail, demonstrate a play on Cubist and Surrealist pictorial strategies: *Landscape with Arum Lily* (1953; private collection, Wellington, repr. Wellington 1983, p.178) and *Untitled (Two Stones in Landscape)* (1966; Rita Angus Loan Collection, Museum of New Zealand) are two such works. Both contain, like so many of Angus's landscapes, the simplified shape of a dwelling, suggesting, as with Georgia O'Keeffe's shelter/habitats, a womb-like container within a landscape arguably gendered feminine. Certainly New Zealand poets of the period saw it in such terms when they addressed "Fairest earth ... let us come to you barefoot, as befits love, as the boy to the trembling girl ..." (A.R.D. Fairburn, "The Dominion", 1938, quoted in an unpublished text by Francis Pound).

Painted at the same period as *Cass*, Angus's *Self-Portrait* (1936–7; see illustration) is one of many variations on self-representation by this artist. Here she presents herself gloved, holding a cigarette and gazing out with an unsettlingly direct and acerbic look. The emphatic, contoured style has much in common with the portraiture of Wyndham Lewis, while there is an unusual connection here of "woman" with notions of culture (rather than the more usual nature) in the deployment of an urban setting, together with strong suggestions of the iconography of the "new woman" in the prominence of the motif of the cigarette and absence of signs of conventional femininity. Other portraits from this earlier stage of her career include portraits of children, for instance the double portrait *Fay and Jane Birkinshaw* (1938; Rita Angus Loan Collection, Museum of New Zealand) – *Fay* later to be the novelist Fay Weldon – and the important *Portrait (Betty Curnow)* (1942; Auckland City Art Gallery), depicting Betty Curnow, wife of the poet Allen Curnow and mother of the contemporary New Zealand critic Wystan Curnow. This work was produced soon after the Centennial Exhibition of New Zealand (1940), for which Allen Curnow had been commissioned to write "Landfall in Unknown Seas". Painted at a time when the history of New Zealand was being reassessed, this powerful portrait of a significant figure is given further resonance through the use of symbolism and telling detail and has come to be seen as a portrait of a New Zealand generation.

Most unusual iconographically in the context of New Zealand Regional realist portraiture, and within the wider context of Regional realism in other countries, are three "goddess portraits" by Rita Angus: *A Goddess of Mercy* (1946–7; Robert McDougall Art Gallery), *Sun Goddess* (1949; private collection, Christchurch, repr. Wellington 1983, p.117) and *Rutu* (1951; for illustration, see p.130). Each sets a female figure, variously garbed and with varying attributes suggesting mysticism and peace, and whose features recall those of Angus, before a landscape setting. *Rutu* depicts a blond-haired, dark-skinned woman, a sun/halo behind her head against a tropical setting, her hands gently touching a lotus. Both a play on the Maori version of her name and recalling the biblical Ruth, this hieratic representation denotes spirituality and, in the signs of racial mix, a clearly positivist, utopian view, from the 1950s, of the melding of the two dominant races within Aotearoa/ New Zealand, the indigenous Maori with the European, or Pakeha. Within the context of contemporary New Zealand where bi-culturalism is a major political issue, it functions as a particularly bold and provocative image.

ELIZABETH EASTMOND

Antin, Eleanor
American artist, 1935–

Born Eleanor Fineman in New York, 27 February 1935. Studied creative writing and art at the College of the City of New York (BA 1958); phenomenology at New School for Social Research, New York; also studied at the Tamara Daykarhanova School for the Stage, New York, 1954–6. Professional actress under the name Eleanor Barrett, 1955–8. Married poet David Antin, 1961; one son. Visiting lecturer, 1974–5, assistant professor, 1975–8, and associate professor, 1978–9, University of California, Irvine; professor of visual arts, University of California, San Diego, from 1979. Recipient of National Endowment for the Arts (NEA) grant, 1979; Pushcart prize for *A Romantic Interlude*, 1982; Vesta award for performance, Los Angeles, 1984; Dorothy Arzner Special Recognition Crystal award for film direction, *The Man Without a World*, Beverly Hills, 1992. Lives in Solana Beach, California.

Selected Individual Exhibitions
Long Island University, Brooklyn, NY: 1968
Gain Ground Gallery, New York: 1970
California Institute of the Arts, Valencia: 1972
United States Postal Distribution: 1972 (*100 Boots*, distributed through the mail)
Museum of Modern Art, New York: 1973
University of California, Irvine: 1974
The Clocktower, New York: 1976
La Jolla Museum of Contemporary Art, CA: 1977
Whitney Museum of American Art, New York: 1978
Ronald Feldman Fine Arts, New York: 1979, 1980, 1983, 1986, 1995
Franklin Furnace, New York: 1979
Los Angeles Institute of Contemporary Art: 1981
MAG Galleries, Los Angeles: 1988
Artemisia, Chicago: 1989 (retrospective)
San Diego Museum of Contemporary Art, La Jolla, CA: 1991 (*Man Without a World*, touring)

Selected Writings
Before the Revolution, Santa Barbara, CA: Santa Barbara Museum of Art, 1979
Being Antinova, Los Angeles: Astro Artz, 1983
The Eleanora Antinova Plays, Los Angeles: Sun and Moon, 1993

Bibliography
Lucy R. Lippard, *Six Years: The Dematerialization of the Art Object from 1966 to 1972*, New York: Praeger, 1973
Cindy Nemser, *Art Talk: Conversations with 12 Women Artists*, New York: Scribner, 1975
The Angel of Mercy, exh. cat., Museum of Contemporary Art, La Jolla, CA, 1977
Arlene Raven and Deborah Marrow, "Eleanor Antin: What's your story?", *Chrysalis*, viii, Summer 1978, pp.43–51
Eleanor Munro, *Originals: American Women Artists*, New York: Simon and Schuster, 1979
Nancy Bowen, *Profile: Eleanor Antin*, Chicago: School of the Art Institute, Video Data Bank, i/4, 1981
Moira Roth, *The Amazing Decade: Women and Performance Art in America, 1970–80*, Los Angeles: Astro Artz, 1983
Sandra Agalidi, "Antin/Antinova: The self as art medium", *Michigan Quarterly Review*, xxiii, Winter 1984, pp.49–56
Kim Levin, *Beyond Modernism: Essays on Art from the 70s and 80s*, New York: Harper, 1988
Henry M. Sayre, *The Object of Performance: The American Avant-Garde since 1970*, Chicago: University of Chicago Press, 1989
Lucy Lippard, *The Pink Glass Swan: Selected Essays on Feminist Art*, New York: New Press, 1995

The art of Eleanor Antin is not easily confined to a singular classification. Described as conceptual, feminist and performance, Antin's work centres on the exploration of the self. She pursues these concerns by using her body as a medium for expression, often incorporating autobiography and the creation of other personas to blur the distinction between reality and artistic creation. While theatre is a vital component of her work, Antin also employs photography, assemblage, happenings and literature to develop the issues she confronts.

Antin worked as a professional actress before turning to the visual arts in the 1960s. Early Dadaist-style paintings gave way to her first fully developed work, *Blood of a Poet's Box* (1965–8), a green slide box filled with blood samples that she had collected from 100 poets. After moving with her husband and son to California in the latter part of the decade, Antin produced *Consumer Goods* pieces: *California Lives* (exh. Gain Ground Gallery, New York, 1970) and *Portraits of Eight New York Women* (exh. Chelsea Hotel, New York, 1971). Motivated by her awareness of the ubiquitous commercial presence in the country, these works each assembled four to nine objects purchased from a Sears catalogue. Antin conceived them as portraits in which the collected items provided clues to the subject's identity. In their attention to the relationship between societal influences and the perception of identity, the *Consumer Goods* foreshadow the dominant themes in Antin's oeuvre.

The exhaustion of travelling across the country to exhibit her work in New York led to Antin's frustration with the distribution system imposed by the art establishment. She responded with *100 Boots Move On* (1972; see illustration). Using photographs, Antin documented the adventures of 100 rubber boots on their journey from California to New York, where they were exhibited at the Museum of Modern Art. Postcards depicting the boots at such places as a carnival, supermarket and the Brooklyn Bridge were sent to art critics and others on a list of 1000 names as a way of distributing the work without relying on the traditional gallery system.

Antin: *100 Boots Move On*, Sorrento Valley, California, 24 June 1972, 8.50 a.m.

Through her periodic mailings, Antin's narrative unfolded over the course of two years.

In the early 1970s Antin began using her body as a medium to explore better the cultural and psychic construction of the self. By focusing on the female body to examine these issues, she inscribed feminist concerns into her work. In *Carving: A Traditional Sculpture* (1971) Antin used 148 photographs of her naked body to document the minute physical changes that occurred over a 36-day period when she lost 4.5 kilograms. The images provide a visual text recording the creative process of "sculpting" a figure that was more closely aligned with the ideal aesthetic of Classical art. Similarly, in *Representational Painting* (1972), Antin used video to depict her transformation from her natural self into a glamorous woman through the application of make-up. In addition to providing a narrative framework for these images, the use of photographic documentation distanced Antin in her role as artist from her position as the created object. In this way, photography helps give her work an authority that obscures the line between creator and created, reality and fiction.

This distinction was further explored around 1974 when Antin's focus on the physical self shifted to a closer examination of psychological considerations of identity. Through the creation of various personas, she has been able to examine herself in relation to society, not as a single identity but rather in multiple roles that are open to the individual. Her original

figures of the King, the Nurse, the Ballerina and the Black Movie Star have split and changed over the years; for example, the Black Movie Star has been absorbed by the other personalities. These personas are presented to the audience through the media of photography, video and live events. By supplementing her performance with photographic and literary documentation, Antin provides a history of her characters that lends them a legitimacy that blurs the lines between reality and their fictional existence.

This difference is examined within the performances as well. In *Recollections of My Life with Diaghilev* (first presented 1980, Ronald Feldman Fine Arts, New York) Antin assumes the role of Eleanora Antinova, the aged black ballerina who had starred in Diaghilev's famous Ballets Russes. Photographs from her past surround the diva who sits in a chair, sipping sherry, while she reads from her memoirs. As the narrative progresses, the viewer is challenged not only by the figure of Antinova as a creation of the artist, but also by the ambiguities in Antinova's memories, suggesting a blurring of "real" and imaginary within the ballerina's recognition of her own identity. The work succeeds in acknowledging the incongruities between the psychic and public construction of self.

In *Loves of a Ballerina* (first presented 1986, Ronald Feldman Fine Arts) film offers a chance to look into Antinova's public and private life as it is projected on screen. Antin's portrayal of Antinova uses the romantic idea of the ballerina to explore the fine line between caricature and archetype. Through her use of film, the pervading tension between reality and fiction in her work is augmented by the viewer's perspective outside Antinova's world. Likewise, Antin removes her characters from the conventional realm of the art gallery to question these boundaries. The king would often walk around his domain of Solano Beach to visit his subjects, and in 1987 Antin published *Being Antinova*, in which she recorded her experiences over a three-week period when she assumed the ballerina's identity while presenting performances in New York.

Antin's use of the body and creation of alternate personas have allowed her to convey the personal and social aspects in the individual's construction of identity. A recognition of the ambiguity inherent in film and photography has enabled Antin to advance her themes by altering the viewer's perspective to obscure lines of reality and fiction. Through her experimentation with various media, Antin continues to develop new ideas for expressing herself through her art.

VIRGINIA B. SPIVEY

Applebroog, Ida
American painter, 1929–

Born Ida Horowitz in the Bronx, New York, 1929; adopted the name Applebroog after 1973. Studied at the New York Institute of Applied Arts and Sciences, 1948–50, and School of the Art Institute of Chicago, 1965–8. Taught at University of California, San Diego, 1973–4. Moved to New York, 1974. Recipient of National Endowment for the Arts (NEA) grants, 1980 and 1985; Creative Artists Public Service (CAPS) grant, New York State Council on the Arts, 1983; Guggenheim fellowship, 1990; Milton Avery Professorship, Bard College, Annandale-on-Hudson, New York, 1991–2; Lifetime Achievement award, College Art Association, 1995. Married: three children. Lives in New York.

Selected Individual Exhibitions

Whitney Museum of American Art, New York: 1978 (film and video)
Williams College Museum of Art, Williamstown, MA: 1979
Ronald Feldman Fine Arts, New York: 1980, 1981, 1982, 1984, 1986, 1987, 1989, 1991, 1994
Printed Matter Windows, New York: 1980
Douglass College, Rutgers University, New Brunswick: 1981
Spectacolor Board, Times Square, New York: 1983
Chrysler Museum, Norfolk, VA: 1984
Institute of Contemporary Art, University of Pennsylvania, Philadelphia: 1986
Matrix Gallery, Wadsworth Atheneum, Hartford, CT: 1987
Seibu, Seed Hall, Tokyo: 1990
Contemporary Arts Museum, Houston, TX: 1990 (*Happy Families*, touring)
Riverside Studios, London: 1990
Exhibition Hall, Avtozavodskaya, Moscow: 1991
Ulmer Museum, Ulm: 1991–2 (touring)
Brooklyn Museum, NY: 1993
Orchard Gallery, Derry, Ireland: 1993 (touring)

Bibliography

Lucy Lippard, "Taking liberties", *Village Voice*, 23 November 1982, pp.121, 136
Ronny H. Cohen, "Ida Applebroog: Her books", *Print Collector's Newsletter*, xv, 1984, pp.49–51
Linda F. McGreevy, "Under current events: Ida Applebroog's *Inmates and Others*", *Arts Magazine*, lix, October 1984, pp.128–31
Ida Applebroog, exh. cat., Institute of Contemporary Art, University of Pennsylvania, Philadelphia, 1986
Linda F. McGreevy, "Ida Applebroog's latest paradox: Dead-ends = new beginnings", *Arts Magazine*, lx, April 1986, pp.29–31
Ida Applebroog, exh. cat., Ronald Feldman Fine Arts, New York, 1987
Ida Applebroog: Art at the Edge, exh. cat., High Museum of Art, Atlanta, and elsewhere, 1989
Ida Applebroog, exh. cat., Seibu, Seed Hall, Tokyo, 1990
Ida Applebroog: Happy Families: A Fifteen-Year Survey, exh. cat., Contemporary Arts Museum, Houston, 1990
Melissa Harris, "Ida Applebroog", *Interview*, xx, February 1990, p.36
Mira Schor, "*Medusa redux*: Ida Applebroog and the spaces of post-modernity", *Artforum*, xxviii, March 1990, pp.116–22
Ida Applebroog: Bilder, exh. cat., Ulmer Museum, Ulm, and elsewhere, 1991
Ida Applebroog, exh. cat., Orchard Gallery, Derry, and elsewhere, 1993
Katy Deepwell, "The menace of the spoken word", *Women's Art*, no.56, January–February 1994, pp.22–3
Max Kozloff, "The cruelties of affection", *Art in America*, lxxxiii, September 1995, pp.82–7

With their leached monochromes and precise outlining, Ida Applebroog's paintings maintain an air of ostensible neutrality serving to trap the viewer. Lured by their enigmatic pseudo-narratives, the unwary are likely to fall into the amber depths of the artist's nightmarish scenarios. These fragmented, interrupted stories have become more complicated and allusive in the years since Applebroog changed her concentration from minimalistic sculpture to figurative painting in the mid-1970s. This mutation of medium became part of a complete alteration in the artist's persona, following hard upon her adoption of the name that survived the strangled silences of a mid-life crisis. "Ap...broogs", the sole sounds uttered by the erstwhile sculptress Ida Horowitz during a lengthy depression, became Ida Applebroog's new signature when the new-born painter emerged to grapple with society's demons.

Re-entering the art world in the mid-1970s with a series of lithographed books (*Galileo Works* and *A Performance*, 1979; *Blue Books*, 1981) sent surreptitiously through the mail to a selected audience, the freshly reconstituted Applebroog established her Critical Realist approach with a sardonic blend of simplified linear figuration owing a debt to Pop Art's spare iconography, and punctuated by terse, startling statements implying a contradictory narrative with serio-comic undertones. Men and women embroiled in the emotional quagmires of power struggles inhabit these little picture books, their sequential titles redolent of the impotence resulting from an absurdly banal – and all-too-familiar – battle of the sexes.

Poised to engage in a more public confrontation with power, Applebroog encountered her first brush with notoriety in 1982 with *Past Events*, a simple installation sponsored by Creative Time for the Great Hall in the New York Chamber of Commerce, a boardroom lined with portraits of the city's all-male leadership. Marking a return to the sculptural mode that

Applebroog: *Camp Compazine*, 1988; oil on canvas; four panels, 218.4 × 355.6 cm.

would culminate in a series of tiny cast-lead figures seated on park benches that same year, she placed a Rococo flower girl in the centre of the polished conference table. Surmounted by a comic-book thought balloon, this deceptively charming sylph expressed the artist's main motif: "Gentlemen, America is in trouble". The Mellons and Rockefellers on the walls seemed to generate more Applebroogian commentary on the situation: "Is Capitalism Necessary?", "You Can Never Be Too White", and the saucy "Underneath I'm Naked". De-installed within hours, the censored *Past Events* none the less announced the presence of a subversive voice, a new provocateur with a few axes to grind on the flanks of the American Dream.

Applebroog has consistently implicated the common fantasy of an ideal society – equal, rational, comfortable, uniform and safe – in her increasingly complex imagery. From her Rhoplex *Illuminated Manuscripts* (private collection) and vellum "window-shade" drawings, wherein figures indulge their clandestine desires (the inadvertent self-lynching of thrill-seeking teenagers in *Trinity Towers*; private collection) or suffer from indifference (the women inhabiting lonely rooms and single beds in *Hotel Taft* and *Boardwalk Regency*), to the smaller translucent strips that extend the narratives into what appear to be film-clip fragments, Applebroog began a scathing commentary, tempered by moral compassion, on the futility of emotional contact. These little story-boards have the brittle quality of shed snake-skin, an attribute lent to her scenarios by the toxic rhoplex.

Applebroog soon found the traditional medium of oil on canvas more amenable to her intentions, and in the mid-1980s she switched from the tiny, translucent panels to larger linen supports. Initially these canvases were singular, but within a year smaller canvas panels had begun to abut their edges, complicating the narratives with contrapuntal "sub-plots". Using combinations of thin washes and scraping with a palette knife (an approach similar to that of Leon Golub), Applebroog found that she could replicate the desirable qualities of rhoplex, combining them with the suggestive grain of the canvas to create effects that simulated stained linen bandages. In 1984 she exhibited her first series of large-scale single-panel paintings, the titles of which – *Lovelace Clinic* (Collection Martin Sklar), *Hillcrest State* (Collection Idette Weber), *Riverdale Home for the Aged* and *Wentworth Gardens* (artist's collection) – ground their scenarios in institutional indifference, educational collusion and geriatic depression.

In yet another series immediately following the first, a quartet of *Women* (all subtitled *After de Kooning*; all in private collections) rendered in acidic green hues faces a variety of social constraints, from corseting to political torture. This group of works not only introduced specific feminist subjects but also gave Applebroog opportunities to explore the history of recent art with a wickedly apt imitation of one of Willem de Kooning's patently monstrous women. All the components of her full-fledged style were now in place, including the deployment of small vignettes whose characters behave in transgressive fashion. In accord with her earlier self-advice to "try to keep a kind of obscure realism" in place to allow interpretive flexibility, the artist launched an ongoing series of complex polyptychs. Incorporating the earlier medievalist manuscript illuminations, these new altarpieces to the collapse of empathy also increased Applebroog's assaults on the debilitated powers of transcendent modernism. Each of these multi-panelled works centres on a field; at once literal landscapes of decay (fruit rotting beneath overladen trees in *Emetic Fields*; artist's collection) and fields of inaction that mock the heroic spaces of the Abstract Expressionists, these works are voids in the heart where protagonists hesitate and stumble. Surrounded by Applebroog's cast of powerful and powerless characters, some of whom offer terse comments on the situations at the centre of each polyptych, while others execute wan embraces or repetitious tasks, all narrative grinds to an effective – and affective – halt.

Although she frequently quotes Goya, as in *Camp Compazine* (1988; see illustration) – named for an anti-emetic drug – which is flanked by an enormous child-eating daddy akin to the Spanish painter's *Saturn* (Prado, Madrid), this artist's demons are far more often monsters of a very modern hell. Like Sartre, Ida Applebroog would probably find hell residing in other people's indifference – and she would no doubt agree with the insight of Walt Kelly's Pogo: "We have met the enemy and he is us".

LINDA F. McGREEVY

Arbus, Diane

American photographer, 1923–1971

Born Diane Nemerov in New York, 14 March 1923; sister of the poet Howard Nemerov. Took a short course in basic photographic techniques under Berenice Abbott (q.v.), 1943; later studied photography under Alexey Brodovitch, 1954, then under Lisette Model (q.v.) at the New School for Social Research, New York. Married fashion photographer Allan Arbus, 1941; two daughters; separated 1959; divorced. Initially worked as assistant to husband, then as his partner; pursued independent career from 1957. Photographer for *Harper's Bazaar*, *Show*, *Glamour*, *Vogue* and various other fashion magazines, as well as the *New York Times*. Part-time instructor at Parsons School of Design, New York, 1965–6; Cooper Union, New York, 1968–9; Rhode Island School of Design, Providence, 1970–71. Lived and taught at Westbeth, an artists' cooperative in New York, 1970–71. Recipient of Guggenheim fellowships, 1963 and 1966; Robert Leavitt award, New York, 1970. First American photographer to be given an individual exhibition at the Venice Biennale, posthumously 1972. Committed suicide in New York, 26 July 1971.

Principal Exhibitions

Museum of Modern Art, New York: 1967–75 (*New Documents*, with Garry Winogrand and Lee Friedlander, touring), 1971 (*New Photography USA*, touring), 1972–5 (touring retrospective)
Seibu Museum, Tokyo: 1973–9 (touring retrospective)

Selected Writings

"The full circle", *Harper's Bazaar*, November 1961
"Mae West: Emotion in motion", *Show*, January 1965, pp.42–5
"Tokyo Rose is home", *Esquire*, May 1969, pp.168–9

Bibliography

Diane Arbus, exh. cat., Museum of Modern Art, New York, and elsewhere, 1972
Doon Arbus and Marvin Israel, eds, *Diane Arbus*, Millerton, NY: Aperture, 1972; London: Allen Lane, 1974
Amy Goldin, "Diane Arbus: Playing with conventions", *Art in America*, lxi, March–April 1973, pp.72–5
Max Kozloff, "The uncanny portrait: Sander, Arbus, Samaras", *Artforum*, xi, June 1973, pp.58–66
Ian Jeffrey, "Diane Arbus and American freaks", *Studio International*, clxxxvii, 1974, pp.133–4
Judith Goldman, "Diane Arbus: The gap between intention and effect", *Art Journal*, xxxiv, Fall 1974, pp.30–35
Susan Sontag, *On Photography*, New York: Farrar Straus and Giroux, 1977; London: Allen Lane, 1978
Shelley Rice, "Essential differences: A comparison of the portraits of Lisette Model and Diane Arbus", *Artforum*, xviii, May 1980, pp.66–71
Diana Hulick, *The Photography of Diane Arbus*, PhD dissertation, Princeton University, 1982
Doon Arbus and Marvin Israel, eds, *Diane Arbus: Magazine Work*, Millerton, NY: Aperture, 1984; London: Bloomsbury, 1992
Patricia Bosworth, *Diane Arbus: A Biography*, New York: Knopf, 1984
Patrick Roegiers, *Diane Arbus, ou, le rêve du naufrage*, Paris: Chêne, 1985
Catherine Lord, "What becomes a legend most? The short, sad career of Diane Arbus", *The Contest of Meaning: Critical Histories of Photography*, ed. Richard Bolton, Cambridge: Massachusetts Institute of Technology Press, 1990, pp.111–23
James Guimond, *American Photography and the American Dream*, Chapel Hill: University of North Carolina Press, 1991
Diana Emery Hulick, "Diane Arbus's women and transvestites: Separate selves", *History of Photography*, xvi/1, 1992, pp.34–9
Jane Livingston, *The New York School: Photographs, 1936–1963*, New York: Stewart, Tabori and Chang, 1992
Carol Armstrong, "Biology, destiny, photography: Difference according to Diane Arbus", *October*, no.66, Fall 1993, pp.29–54
"Diane Arbus", *History of Photography*, xix/2, 1995 (special issue; contains extensive bibliography)
Doon Arbus and Yolanda Cuomo, eds, *Diane Arbus: Untitled*, New York: Aperture, 1995

In the late 1950s and early 1960s Diane Arbus used her camera as a critical tool to undermine many of America's most sacredly held values and beliefs. Critics, reading backwards from her suicide in 1971, have tended to discuss Arbus as an expressionist who voiced her own existential angst through the suffering and alienation of her subjects. But Arbus's oeuvre also offers an incisive and profound commentary on the social, cultural and political realities of America in the years around 1960.

Arbus's professional career began around 1943, when she and her husband, Allan Arbus, started a fashion photography business together. While Allan actually shot and developed the pictures, she choreographed them – set the scene, acquired the props, chose and posed the models. Their fashion work, while not artistically interesting, heightened her sensitivity to the camera's ability to falsify and invent, and it was from these years that Arbus retained the directorial conventions of carefully posing her subjects in relatively static compositions and

Arbus: *Retired Man and His Wife at Home in a Nudist Camp One Morning, New Jersey, 1963*; gelatin-silver print; 38.5 × 37.5 cm.; Museum of Modern Art, New York; Purchase © 1972 Estate of Diane Arbus, New York

illuminating them with a flash. Almost all her later pictures show a studied intentionality, a calculated effect of confrontational, monumental symmetry that differs radically from the spontaneity valued by such contemporary street photographers as Garry Winogrand and Lee Friedlander.

Between 1956, when her partnership with Allan was winding down, and about 1961, Arbus experimented with a 35 mm. camera, favoured by Henri Cartier-Bresson, William Klein and Robert Frank. Ultimately, though, she preferred 2¹/₄-inch cameras like the Rolleiflex and Mamiyaflex, which

permitted a greater range of detail and nuance; the waist-level viewfinder enabled her to engage more intensely with her subjects, and the large, square format allowed more darkroom control (Diana Hulick, "Diane Arbus's expressive methods", *History of Photography*, 1995, p.107).

Arbus's most famous works were published in an Aperture monograph in 1972, the year after her death. The book, which includes pictures taken between 1962 and 1971, is not organised chronologically and invites a thematic analysis. In 1984 Aperture published another collection entitled *Diane Arbus:*

Magazine Work, which features images (including some that also appear in the monograph) taken on assignment for such glossy magazines as *Esquire* and *Harper's Bazaar*. Arbus, whose commercial fashion photographs had appeared in *Glamour* and *Vogue*, and who continued to rely on popular magazines as both outlets and sources of income, straddled the divide between the market-place and the museum. Her work was included in the *New Documents* exhibition (1967) at the Museum of Modern Art in New York and many of her "mass-market" photographs resurfaced in the museum's retrospective of her career in 1972.

In the mid- or late 1950s Arbus studied photography with Lisette Model (q.v.), known for her unsentimental images of often ungainly, disfigured men and women, of gamblers and drunks. Under Model's tutelage, she found the subjects who really interested her: outsiders, freaks, transvestites, the self-invented – "singular people", she wrote, "who appear like metaphors somewhere further out than we do" ("The full circle", 1961). She became fascinated with those at the margins of society, but also revealed the hidden eccentricities of "normal people", pinpointing what she called "the gap between intention and effect" – the difference between the way people see themselves and the way that they are perceived by others (Arbus and Israel 1972, p.2).

Arbus began photographing transvestites in 1957, suggesting – at a time when *Life* magazine was able to cite a battery of experts to the effect that sex roles were exclusively biological in origin – that one's gender is a matter of personal choice. Even in the following decade, her work continued to comment on the rigidity of gender roles and the ideology of domesticity that she herself had rejected as a career woman in the 1950s. Among many other works, *Naked Man Being a Woman* (1968; *ibid.*), a picture of a male nude wearing make-up, his penis tucked between his legs and out of sight, implies that gender can be adopted, taken on or off at the whim or will of the individual and cannot be absolutely dictated by society.

The idealised images of the nuclear family that had been so popular in the 1950s also became targets of Arbus's mordant wit, metamorphosing, in her interpretations, into pictures of estranged parents and bizarre children. Her grotesque version of a Madonna and Child, *Woman with Her Baby Monkey, NJ* (1971; *ibid.*), cuts to the quick of American culture's veneration of motherhood (Guimond 1991, p.223). The woman preens with maternal pride as she cradles the monkey in her arms. In *A Jewish Giant at Home with His Parents* (1970; *ibid.*) the father gazes straight ahead while the mother tentatively confronts her outsized progeny. Images such as these challenged the prevalent ideologies of domesticity and "togetherness" that had been promoted both in the popular press and in such exhibitions as Edward Steichen's *Family of Man* at the Museum of Modern Art (1955).

Arbus used art-historical references to examine critically aspects of American culture. In *Retired Man and His Wife at Home in a Nudist Camp One Morning, New Jersey, 1963* (see illustration), one of a series of photographs of nudists, she takes aim at traditional representations of Adam and Eve, re-imagining them standing, awkward and unglamorously naked, in the thin, scraggly woods of New Jersey. Her visual allusion to the graceful figures of Dürer and Michelangelo heightens the disparity between today's and yesterday's paradise. Arbus wrote about the nudist colonies:

> There is an empty pop bottle or rusty bobby pin underfoot, the lake bottom oozes mud in a particularly nasty way ... It is as if way back in the Garden of Eden ... Adam and Eve had begged the Lord to forgive them; and God, in his boundless exasperation, had said, 'all right, then. STAY. Stay in the Garden, Get civilized. Procreate. Muck it up.' And they did ["Notes on the nudist camp" in Arbus and Israel 1984, p.69].

The nudists in this series emerge as literal embodiments of contemporary American cultural utopianism. They are, like America itself, ingenuous and open, but also bloated and corrupt, searching vainly for a lost innocence.

Towards the end of her life, between 1969 and 1971, Arbus moved outdoors, photographing at residences for the mentally retarded. In these last works, known as the *Untitled* series, she rejected the characteristic stillness of her portraiture in order to capture the expressive gestures of human bodies – albeit still strange bodies – in motion. These subjects, free of the constraints of ideology and culture, are both mysterious and pure.

ARIELLA BUDICK

Armstrong, Elizabeth *see* Forbes, Elizabeth

Arp, Sophie *see* Taeuber-Arp

Auzou, Pauline
French painter, 1775–1835

Born Jeanne Marie Catherine Desmarquest in Paris, 24 March 1775; adopted by a cousin, added La Chapelle to her last name and used Pauline as her first. Studied under Jean-Baptiste Regnault, a contemporary of Jacques-Louis David. Married paper merchant Charles Marie Auzou, 1793; at least five children, four surviving infancy: two sons, one born in 1794; two daughters. Maintained a studio for female students for over 20 years after 1800. Died in Paris, 15 May 1835.

Principal Exhibitions

Paris Salon: 1793, 1795–6, 1798–1800, 1802, 1804, 1806, 1808, 1810, 1812, 1814, 1817, 1830 (medal of honour 1807)

Bibliography

Joachim LeBreton, *Rapport à l'empereur et roi sur les Beaux-Arts*, Paris, 1808, p.82

Vivian Cameron, "Portrait of a musician by Pauline Auzou", *Currier Gallery of Art Bulletin*, no.2, 1974, pp.1–17.

Women Artists, 1550–1950, exh. cat., Los Angeles County Museum of Art, and elsewhere, 1976

Auzou: *Arrival of the Archduchess Marie-Louise in the Gallery of the Château of Compiègne, 28 March 1810*; Palais de Versailles, Paris

Germaine Greer, *The Obstacle Race: The Fortunes of Women Painters and Their Work*, London: Secker and Warburg, and New York: Farrar Straus, 1979

Marie Claude Chaudonneret, *Fleury Richard et Pierre Révoil: La Peinture troubadour*, Paris: Arthena, 1980 (pp.26 and 37, note 126, for reference to medal of 1807)

La Femme artiste d'Elisabeth Vigée-Lebrun à Rosa Bonheur, exh. cat., Musée Despiau-Wlerick, Donjon Lacataye, Mont-de-Marsan, 1981

Vivian Cameron, *Woman as Image and Image-Maker in Paris During the French Revolution*, PhD dissertation, Yale University, 1983

Claire Constans, *Musée National du Château de Versailles: Les Peintures*, 2 vols, Paris: Réunion des Musées Nationaux, 1995

Recognised by her peers as a dedicated and talented painter, Pauline Auzou exhibited works tenaciously at the Paris Salons from 1793 until 1814. An ambitious artist, she exhibited not only portraits and genre scenes but also history paintings illustrating mythological, classical, medieval and contemporary themes.

In the late 1780s or early 1790s Auzou, then Desmarquest, became a student of Jean-Baptiste Regnault. As part of her training, she made studies of drawings, sculptures and paintings, including those of figures in Regnault's *Perseus and Andromeda* (Hermitage, St Petersburg) and his *Alcibiades and Socrates* (Louvre, Paris). More surprisingly, she also made academic studies of nude, or almost nude figures, male as well as female (private collection, Paris, repr. Cameron 1983, pl.13). One of her inaugural pieces at the Salon of 1793 was a *Bacchante* (private collection, Paris, *ibid.*, pl.17), showing a half-length figure of a young woman, naked above the waist, encircling a bust of Bacchus with grapes and leaves. With the focus on the mythological female nude and the *genre gracieux* (see Christopher Sells, "Jean-Baptiste Regnault in Louisville", *Bulletin of the J.B. Speed Art Museum*, xxvii/2, April 1973, p.11), Auzou showed that she had absorbed much of Regnault's style and themes. At the same time she was able to demonstrate her own capabilities in painting a nude figure, modelled probably after another of Regnault's female students (see Madame Clement-Hemery, *Souvenirs de 1793 et 1794*, Cambrai, 1832, p.10). In the 1790s the artist exhibited a number of paintings illustrating figures from the Antique, either historical, such as *Alcibiades and Timandra* (exh. Salon 1796) and *Dinomache, Mother of Alcibiades, Crying over the*

Ashes of Clinias, Her Husband (exh. Salon 1796), or mytho-logical, such as *Hebe* (exh. Salon 1799; untraced). Thematically, these were indebted to Regnault.

Auzou also painted numerous genre scenes that included *Young Women Making Music* (exh. Salon 1796), *Young Girl Hesitating to Open a Letter* (exh. Salon 1798), *A Young Girl Reading* (exh. Salon 1799) and *A Young Woman Playing a Prelude on the Piano* (exh. Salon 1800; all untraced). By 1804, when she exhibited *First Sentiment of Coquetry*, she demon-strated other stylistic interests, exploring the effects of chiaroscuro upon the girl, bedecked with mother's jewellery and make-up, and illuminated by a roaring fire in the fireplace behind her (private collection, Paris, repr. Los Angeles 1976, ill.71). Such domestic scenes were perhaps initially influenced by the popularity of works by Greuze and his followers, such as Philiberte Ledoux. They were also more suited to the expanding bourgeois market of the early 1800s. Unlike Greuze, Auzou celebrates the girl's ascendance to adult status, situating her between childhood, designated by the ball on the floor, and womanhood, noted by the pin-cushion and needle and thread on the mantle. The colours, smooth handling of paint and concern for details are all characteristic of Auzou's work. Another work entitled *Departure for the Duel* (untraced; sketch in private collection, Paris), exhibited in 1806, employed life-sized figures to represent a father leaving his family to resolve a matter of honour. The scale of the paint-ing together with a "subject closest to our customs" (as Denon expressed it in his critique of the painting; see *Quatrième lettre sur le Salon de 1806, à M. Denon*, Collection Deloynes, xl, no.1071, p.15), its harmony of colours and sure paint strokes earned her a great deal of attention. It was probably for this work that she earned a medal of honour the following year.

Auzou also exhibited a number of portraits, including one of *Regnault* (untraced) at the Salon of 1800. Her *Portrait of a Musician* (Currier Gallery of Art, Manchester, NH, repr. Cameron 1974, fig.1), dated 1809, combines the influence of Regnault, in the mass of the figure as well as the modelling of the face, with that of Ingres, expressed in the shallow space, chair with curving back and tilted sheet music. It also shows how well she was able to depict both the external appearance and the character of the sitter. Her expertise at portraiture is best seen in a formidable late *Self-Portrait* (private collection, Paris, repr. Cameron 1983, fig.8), which Ingres is said to have admired.

In the 1800s Auzou turned to troubadour painting, which had become increasingly popular with the patronage of the Empress Josephine (see François Pupil, *Le Style troubadour; ou, La Nostalgie du bon vieux temps*, Nancy: Presses Universitaires, 1985, p.498), and illustrated themes of the abandoned wife or troubadour lovers, which were extremely fashionable. In 1808 she exhibited *Agnès de Méranie*, a paint-ing representing the third wife of Philippe-Auguste with her two children, at a private altar, giving a letter to the Comtesse de Barres to give to the king (see Charles Landon, *Salon de 1808*, i, part 2, Paris 1808, p.97 and pl.57). The work was appreciated for its composition (Landon), the expression of the dying Agnès, the brilliant and harmonious colours and the beauty of the details (see *Examen critique et raisonné des tableaux des peintres vivans, formant l'exposition de 1808*, Paris, 1808, in Collection Deloynes, xliii, no.1143, pp.62–3,

and Pupil, *op. cit.*, p.516). Other paintings of this nature followed, including *Diane de France and Montmorency*, exhib-ited at both the Salons of 1812 and 1814 (see Charles Landon, *Salon de 1812*, i, Paris, 1812, p.22 and pl.8); *Noves and Alix de Provence* and *Boucicault and Mlle de Beaufort* (untraced), both exhibited at the Salon of 1817.

In 1810 Auzou exhibited the first of two works dealing with Napoleonic propaganda, supporting Napoleon's second marriage to the 18-year-old Marie-Louise of Austria. The *Arrival of the Archduchess Marie-Louise in the Gallery of the Château of Compiègne, 28 March 1810* (see illustration) repre-sents the princess, dressed in red velvet, by the side of her new husband, Napoleon, receiving flowers of welcome from French girls dressed in white. Such contemporary history painting allowed Auzou to combine her talents as a portraitist with her interest in children (e.g. *A Child at His Lunch*, exh. Salon 1804) as well as genre scenes. One critic (*Le Moniteur Universel*, 6 February 1811, p.143) wrote that she had success-fully captured the candour and naiveté of the girls and that she had also happily surmounted the difficulties of capturing the nuances of white in their dresses. She followed this at the Salon of 1812 with a painting entitled *Her Majesty the Empress, Before Her Marriage and at the Moment of Leaving Her Family, Distributing Diamonds to Her Family* (Château, Versailles, repr. Greer 1979, p.302). Royalty becomes domesti-cated here in "a charming scene" with children of various ages, some accepting the gifts, others trying on the jewellery, their poses deemed "gracious and natural", their expressions "sweet and affectionate" (*Le Moniteur Universel*, 10 March 1813, p.257). It was presumably in connection with her studio for women artists that Auzou produced a work entitled *Têtes d'Etudes*, published in Paris by Didot in the 1800s.

VIVIAN P. CAMERON

Ayala de Óbidos, Josefa d'

Portuguese painter and printmaker, c.1630–1684

Born in the parish of San Vicente, Seville, c.1630, to Baltasar Gómes Figueira, painter, and his Spanish wife Catalina de Ayala. Moved with her family to Óbidos, central Portugal, April 1634. Educated at the Augustinian convent of Santa Ana, Coimbra, from 1644. Returned to Óbidos, 1653; lived both at the family home in Rua Nova and on a farmstead, Casal da Capeleira, just outside the town's medieval walls, until her death, 22 July 1684.

Bibliography

Manuel Barreto da Silveira, "Informaçao que tirei das egrejas de Santa M. e S. Pedro da Villa de Óbidos", 20 February 1693, Bibliothèque Nationale, Paris, MS Portuguese 32, fols 237–9

Felix Da Costa, *Antiguidade da arte da pintura*, Lisbon, 1696; as *The Antiquity of the Art of Painting*, ed. George Kubler, New Haven: Yale University Press, 1967, p.467

Damião Froes Perym, *Theatro heroino, abecedario histórico e catál-ogo das mulheres illustres en armas, letras accoens heróicas, e artes liberais*, i, Lisbon, 1734, pp.493–5

Luiz Xavier da Costa, *Uma águafortista do século XVII: Josefa d'Ayala*, Coimbra, 1931

Esposicão das pinturas de Josefa de Óbidos (Ayala), exh. cat., Museo Nacional de Arte Antiga, Lisbon, 1949

Luís Reis-Santos, *Josefa d'Óbidos (Ayala)*, Lisbon [1956] (first comprehensive study, with list of signed and dated works)

José Hernández Díaz, *Josefa de Ayala: Pintora ibérica del siglo XVII*, Seville, 1967

Edward J. Sullivan, "Josefa de Ayala: A woman painter of the Portuguese Baroque", *Journal of the Walters Art Gallery*, xxvii, 1978, pp.22–35

——, "Obras de Josefa de Ayala", *Archivo Español de Arte*, liv, 1981, pp.87–93

Luís de Moura Sobral, "Três *bodegones* do Museu de Evora: Algumas considerações", *Colóquio: Artes*, no.55, 1982, pp.5–13

Edward J. Sullivan, "*Herod and Salome with the Head of John the Baptist* by Josefa de Ayala", *Source*, ii/1, 1982, pp.26–9

Luís de Moura Sobral, "Un nuevo cuadro de Josefa de Ayala", *Archivo Español de Arte*, lvii, 1984, pp.386–7

Vitor Serrão, "Josefa d'Ayala e a pintura portuguesa do século XVII", *Estudos de Pintura Maneirista e Barroca*, Lisbon: Caminho, 1986, pp.181–203

Josefa de Óbidos e o Tempo Barroco, exh. cat., Galeria de Pintura do Rei D. Luis, Lisbon, 1991

Josefa d'Ayala's career coincided with Portugal's struggle to free itself from Spanish control. Even her parentage underlines the artistic and economic links of the two countries. Her father Baltasar Gómes Figueira trained as a painter in Seville before returning to his home town of Óbidos in central Portugal with his Spanish wife and Josefa, aged four. He became a noted painter of tenebrist altarpieces and still lifes. Josefa's maternal uncle was probably Bernabé Ayala, a follower of the Spaniard Francisco de Zurbarán; her godfather was Seville's leading painter of religious art, Francisco Herrera the Elder; her Sevillian grandfather had a large picture collection; and one of her sisters married a Portuguese painter.

Ayala began working in 1646 from the convent of Santa Ana in the university town of Coimbra, producing engravings of half-length saints and then painting intimate devotional scenes, on a similar small scale, on copper. For the latter she used Flemish and Dutch prints as a compositional design source. Together with a hot colouring with a distinctive use of pinks, lilacs and oranges, decorative textiles and idiosyncratic doll-like faces with arched eyebrows, they remained her trademarks. She continued to produce engravings (e.g. *Insignia of the University of Coimbra*, 1653, frontispiece to the University's *Estatutos* of 1654; repr. Sullivan 1978, fig.2) and religious paintings on copper throughout the 1650s, branching out in the 1660s into larger-scale altarpieces on canvas and the still lifes on which her reputation now rests. St Catherine, her mother's name saint, was a favourite figure of Ayala's. Her earliest etching, dated 1646 (private collection, Lisbon, *ibid.*, fig.1), was a bust-length version of the saint, and her first major commission (1661) was for five canvases for the altar of St Catherine of Alexandria in Santa Maria, Óbidos (*in situ*). The Zurbaránesque paintings set into a two-storeyed columned altarpiece around a statue of St Catherine show an unusual iconography, combining typical themes such as her *Mystic Marriage* with the less common *Coronation of St Catherine* and also half-lengths of the *Penitent Magdalene* and the *Inspiration of St Teresa of Ávila*.

Ayala's Sevillian-style naturalistic tenebrism was probably learned from her father and it has been suggested that the *Month of March* (private collection, Lisbon, *ibid.*, fig.13 as

Alenquer), one of a series of large *Months* painted in 1668, was a collaborative work between them, Josefa painting the foreground still life and her father the beach landscape behind. Her father's still lifes were influenced by those he had seen by Zurbarán in Seville and possibly even by the now lost still lifes of Herrera the Elder. Although she followed her father's compositional style, Ayala employed a different technique, revealed by X-rays, preferring a spontaneous brushwork to her father's preparatory underdrawing.

The Baltimore *Paschal Lamb* (1660–70; Walters Art Gallery) has become Ayala's best-known still life, perhaps because it is her only known work outside Portugal and compositionally close to Zurbarán's treatment of the subject (1635–40; San Diego Museum of Fine Arts). The painting is untypically stark: most of her other versions (Igrega dos Congregados, Braga; private collection, Estoril; Museo Regional, Evora (two versions; see illustration); Paco dos Duques de Bragança, Guimarães) of this iconic image of the sacrificial, bound Lamb of God are garlanded with flowers. Her practice of adding bouquets of flowers to religiously symbolic motifs may have been influenced by Spanish paintings, or reflected the common Iberian practice of decorating altars with bouquets on feast days.

By the 1670s, her most productive decade, Ayala's reputation had spread and she gained numerous major commissions from churches and religious houses. Large altarpieces were never her strength. Several show evidence of slack design, perhaps through pressure of work engendered by economic responsibilities for her mother and two nieces after her father's death in 1674. Her skill was better expressed in the naturalistic details of dress, jewellery, books and papers that furnish the saint's study in *St Teresa Inspired by the Holy Spirit* for the altarpiece of the *Life of St Teresa* (1672; Our Lady of the Assumption, Cascais) for the Discalced Carmelites of Cascais. Such altarpieces were public statements of Counter Reformation orthodoxy for which Ayala used conventional imagery. Appropriately she reserved more inventive iconography for single easel paintings, probably private commissions. She was always more at ease on an intimate scale, producing some of her best devotional work in small scenes, often candlelit, worthy of Northern Caravaggesque artists, such as the *Mary Magdalene* (1653; Museu de Machado de Castro, Coimbra). In her tender candle-lit *Holy Family* (1674; Museu Regional, Évora, on deposit in Portuguese Embassy, Brazil), a small easel painting probably for a private patron, a toddler Christ Child blesses the simple peasant meal of fish and radishes in front of the praying family. Ayala minutely described the table setting with the eye of a consummate still-life artist.

Ayala's modern reputation rests on her still lifes. In contrast, the earliest description of her work, in her compatriot Felix Da Costa's *Antiguidade da arte da pintura* of 1696, makes only a brief and tangential reference to them, and they were not mentioned at all in the more fulsome biographical entry in Froes Perym's *Theatro heroino* of 1734. This probably reflects the low status of the genre among art theorists. Perym's entry accompanies those on regal, aristocratic, religious and legendary women and eulogises her art, devotion and international fame. His account suggests that her curiosity value as a woman artist attracted commissions from ladies visiting the

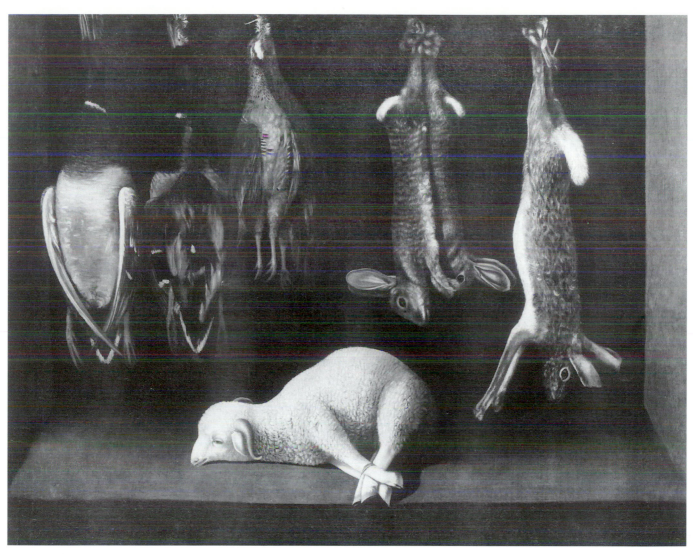

Ayala de Óbidos: *Paschal Lamb*, Museu de Evora, Portugal

fashionable royal spa at nearby Caldas da Rainha. Perym particularly mentioned a visit by Queen Maria Francisca for the portrait of her daughter Isabel, but the portraits of the queen and infanta, once considered Ayala's (Museu do Coches, Lisbon), are now attributed to other Portuguese artists. The one portrait firmly attributed to Ayala, of the *Beneficiado Faustino das Neves* (*c.*1670; Museu Municipal, Óbidos), is of a distinguished member of the Colegiada of Santa Maria in Óbidos, and shows that she was one of Portugal's leading portraitists.

Ayala's early celebrity, and her status as the only Portuguese woman artist remembered in print in the 17th and 18th centuries, followed by the decline of her fame in the early 20th century, may have both clouded and exaggerated her significance. The fact that Portuguese Baroque painting was until recently an unknown quantity has added to the confusion. Only recently have biographical details been clarified, a corpus of paintings identified and her work evaluated. Her artistic development was further confused by the assumption that Óbidos was a provincial backwater. In fact it had important contacts with the court and ecclesiastical hierarchy, as it lay on the lands of the rich and culturally powerful royal monastery of Alcobaça, which commissioned works from both father and daughter. Ayala used those links, her father's connections and her devout reputation to gain religious and court patronage. The habitual reference to Óbidos in her signature, "Josepha em Óbidos", may also have enhanced her reputation, adding a rural cachet to her still lifes. The solemn, later literary descriptions of Ayala as pious, solitary and mystic are contradicted by contemporary legal documents that show her as an active landowner who affectionately named three of her cows Elegant, Cherry and Beauty.

XANTHE BROOKE

Ayres, Gillian
British painter, 1930–

Born in Barnes, London, 3 February 1930. Studied at Camberwell School of Arts and Crafts, 1946–50; selected for first *Young Contemporaries* exhibition in final year, 1950. Married Henry Mundy, 1951; two sons, born 1958 and 1966. Worked part-time at Artists International Association Gallery, London, 1951–9; began to exhibit with London Group, 1951. Taught at Bath Academy of Art, Corsham, 1959–65; St Martin's School of Art, London 1966–78 (senior lecturer 1976); head of painting, Winchester School of Art, 1978–81. Participated in the exhibitions *Situation*, 1960, and *New London Situation*, 1961, both in London. Spent summers on Luing Isle, Scotland, 1972–9; moved to North Wales, 1981; to south-west England, 1987. Recipient of Japan International Art Promotion Association award, Tokyo Biennale, 1963; bursary, 1975, and purchase award, 1979, Arts Council of Great Britain; second prize, John Moore's exhibition, Liverpool, 1982; Charles Wollaston award, 1989, and Critics' prize, 1990, Royal Academy summer exhibition; gold medal, Seventh Triennale-India, 1991. Associate, 1982, and member, 1991, Royal Academy. Order of the British Empire (OBE), 1986. Lives in Gooseham, near Bude, Cornwall.

Selected Individual Exhibitions
Gallery One, London: 1956
Redfern Gallery, London: 1958
Molton Gallery, London: 1960 (with Anthea Alley), 1962
Hamilton Gallery, London: 1963
Arnolfini Gallery, Bristol: 1964, 1989 (touring)
Kasmin Gallery, London: 1965, 1966, 1969
Hayward Gallery, London: 1971 (*Large Paintings – Three Painters*, with John Golding and Alan Gouk)
Women's Interart Center, New York: 1976
Kettle's Yard Gallery, Cambridge: 1978
Knoedler Gallery, London: 1979, 1982, 1984, 1987, 1988
Museum of Modern Art, Oxford: 1981 (touring)
Serpentine Gallery, London: 1983–4 (touring retrospective, organised by Arts Council of Great Britain)
M. Knoedler & Co., New York: 1985
Fischer Fine Art, London: 1990
Seventh Triennale-India: 1991–4 (touring, organised by British Council)
Purdy Hicks Gallery, London: 1993
Royal Academy, London: 1997

Selected Writings
"Notes on paintings", *Fine Art Letter*, no.2, December 1980
"Pablo Picasso, 1881–1973: A centenary celebration", *Fine Art Letter*, no.4, July 1981

Bibliography
Gillian Ayres: Paintings. Anthea Alley: Sculpture, exh. cat., Molton Gallery, London, 1960
Gillian Ayres: Paintings, exh. cat., Molton Gallery, London, 1962
Gillian Ayres, exh. cat., Galerie Alvarez, Porto, Portugal, 1977
Gillian Ayres: Recent Paintings, exh. cat., Kettle's Yard Gallery, Cambridge, 1978
Matthew Collings, "Gillian Ayres", *Flash Art*, no.94–5, January–February 1980
Gillian Ayres: Paintings, exh. cat., Museum of Modern Art, Oxford, and elsewhere, 1981
Gareth Williams, "Contrast, continuity, coherence: The paintings of Gillian Ayres", *Art International*, xxiv, March–April 1981, pp.98–104, 160
Gillian Ayres, exh. cat., Arts Council of Great Britain, London, 1983 (contains bibliography)
Jamie Rasaad, "Gillian Ayres", *Artscribe*, no.43, October 1983, pp.43–6
Gillian Ayres, exh. cat., Arnolfini Gallery, Bristol, and elsewhere, 1989
Gillian Ayres, exh. cat., Fischer Fine Art, London, 1990
Gillian Ayres, British Council exh. cat., Seventh Triennale-India, 1991
Judith Bumpus, "The experience of India: New paintings by Gillian Ayres", *Contemporary Art*, Summer 1993, pp.20–23

Gillian Ayres first became known as one of a younger generation of post-war abstract artists who established themselves as leaders of a British avant-garde. Determined from youth to be a painter, Ayres left school at the earliest opportunity and applied to the Slade School of Fine Art in 1946. She was accepted, but told that at 16 she was too young to enrol and advised to start her professional training at the Camberwell School of Arts and Crafts. Camberwell's painting school was dominated by former members of the Euston Road School of Drawing and Painting, most of whom taught a peculiarly English brand of uncompromising realism. The only teacher among them to whom Ayres has acknowledged any debt was Victor Pasmore, whose poetic landscapes of the early 1940s she admired. Pasmore was one of the founders of the Euston Road School, but his thinking was already changing in the second half of the 1940s in favour of a return to international modernism. At Camberwell Ayres joined his Saturday painting class where she was stimulated into finding a more personal and expressive alternative to objective realism. The formation of her developing ideas owed much to Albert Halliwell's influential classes in industrial design, which made her aware of Bauhaus concepts, of Le Corbusier and Sonia Delaunay (q.v.), among others, as well as to her own excited discovery in the school's library of a copy of *Unit One: The Modern Movement in English Architecture, Painting and Sculpture* (1934). William Johnstone, Camberwell's enlightened principal, further encouraged her in her convictions, as did the experience of frequent visits to Paris to look at French painting.

On leaving Camberwell in 1950, Ayres worked at the Galleries of the Artists International Association where she shared a part-time job with Henry Mundy, a fellow-student from Camberwell, whom she married in 1951. There she also met a number of mostly older artists with similar sympathies, among them Roger Hilton and Adrian Heath. In this animating company she had begun by 1953 to paint abstract compositions. The work of the American painters Mark Rothko, Joan Mitchell (q.v.), Sam Francis and, in particular, Jackson Pollock offered continual inspiration at this time. In the late 1950s she saw the publication of photograms from Hans Namuth's documentary film showing Pollock dripping paint over huge canvases laid on the floor. Enthused by his liberating example, she experimented with working on the floor, causing astonished reactions to her unconventional and frenzied procedures. In 1957 she received a commission to paint a 2.4-metre mural in four large panels for the dining room of South Hampstead High School for Girls, London. She found that she was able to master the huge scale and to cover the prepared boards with speed by pouring and flinging the paint over them, and allowing areas of colour to run into one another. The same year she exhibited the earliest of her hardboard paintings in a large mixed exhibition at the Redfern Gallery in London,

Ayres: *Ultima Thule*, 1978–80; oil on canvas; 225 × 354 cm.; Arts Council Collection, Hayward Gallery, London

Metavisual, Tachiste, Abstract: Painting in England Today. She was the youngest artist and, as on many subsequent occasions, the only woman to be selected. The context for this show supported her own leanings, which were as much in sympathy with the Parisian post-war school of Tachisme as with the parallel New York aesthetic of Abstract Expressionism. This tendency continued in such paintings as *Distillation* (1958; Tate Gallery, London), but Ayres now worked the liquid paint into a loosely assembled construction of ragged and irregular patches. A characteristic feature of her early work was the use of *Ripolin*, a high-grade French house enamel, in emulation of Picasso's nonchalant use of this same paint.

With the New York School of Abstract Expressionism and the Parisian Tachiste painters Ayres shared the belief that a mark spontaneously applied to the canvas could be the starting point for a painterly creation that had no reference to anything outside itself. This new aesthetic whereby the artist is "in the painting", as Ayres put it, determining the outcome by his or her own choice of actions, was closely allied to existentialist beliefs. Nothing is preconceived. Ayres described her own working method as "a process of looking for something to happen in the painting". It did not involve preliminary drawings, but evolved out of a chaos of paint, often put on with her hands, and worked with other tools and materials, although never with the palette knife.

Ayres's reputation was established by her presence in two group shows, which were organised and financed by the exhibiting artists to provide a much-needed opportunity to display large abstract work, and which have acquired historic importance in British post-war modernism: *Situation* in 1960, where she hung *Cumuli* (1959; artist's collection), *Trace* and *Muster*, and *New London Situation* the following year. On both occasions Ayres's canvases were noticeably painterly in contrast to the dominant trend among British artists towards "hard-edge" abstraction. The two canvases she showed in *New London Situation*, *Scud* (1961; whereabouts unknown) and *Blimps* (1961; Annely Juda), and a similar canvas, *Break-Off* (1961; Tate Gallery), were spare, thinly painted compositions of roughly drawn forms and ovals, the "blimps" of the title, floating on an open ground. In a statement Ayres gave an extraordinary insight into the emotional and imaginative activity that accompanied the physical mark-making: "A shape – a relationship – a body – oddness – shock – mood – cramped – isolated – acid – sweet – encroaching – pivoting – fading – bruised …".

In the early 1960s Ayres began experimenting with the newly available acrylic pigments. In a sequence of canvases, such as *Piranha* (1963), she painted hard-edged "ribbons" of colour, turning in the last years of the decade to explore the effect of vivid beads and blobs suspended in a field of colour. The length of these last grew to some six to nine metres and were covered with increasingly abstract dots. In later works such as *Weddell* (1972; artist's collection) Ayres produced dense and unfathomable surfaces running with streams of paint. Dissatisfied finally with the flat, inert look achieved with acrylics, she returned in 1976 to the medium of oil paint, and its lustrous range of vibrant colours.

The canvases of the mid-1970s were also characterised by surfaces thickly covered with broken brush marks and it was with these works that Ayres's mature artistic personality began to emerge. *Orlando Furioso* (1977–9; Arts Council Collection), *Ultima Thule* (1978–80; see illustration) and *Mons Graupius* (1979–80; Rochdale Art Gallery) were typical of a lavish impasto that would be built up, scraped down and repainted in a procedure that often lasted a considerable period. The finished compositions emerged slowly out of a dense mêlée of coloured marks "skidding" into one another, each with its own internal logic and poetic structure. The titles given to her paintings, *Angelus ad Pastores* (1980–81; private collection), *Where Phoebus First Did Daphne Love* (1982) and the later triptych *Green Grow the Rushes, O!* (1990), frequently had, and indeed still have, fanciful literary or musical references but these, Ayres insists, have never been more than useful labels.

On a visit to Florence in 1979 the impression made on her by Renaissance tondos merged with her admiration for the radiant splendour of rose windows in the great Gothic cathedrals, and the association occasioned a series of circular paintings. She first explored the idea in *Ah Mine Heart* (1979–81; British Council) on the unprimed surface of a large mahogany table top, but from then on she had special circular stretchers made. Increasingly she worked on different coloured grounds, opening up the impenetrable surfaces of the late 1970s and creating a more dynamic sense of space by the introduction of discrete forms. The richly decorative quality of these paintings was enhanced by a sumptuousness and luminosity of colour absorbed from the Venetian school, but its inspiration was also related to Orphism and Sonia Delaunay's experiments in colour and movement. This new-found clarity, together with an exultant sense of freedom expressed in such paintings as *Antony and Cleopatra* (1982; Tate Gallery), may well have been generated by her decision to move in November 1981 to the north-west coast of Wales, where she could paint without distraction. In 1987 she moved again, this time to the south of England on the boundary between Devon and Cornwall. The dramatic oppositions set up by a predominance of black in much of her work in the late 1980s suggested that a further range of responses and emotions was driving her ideas. For the first time more clearly defined imagery, such as suns, stars, crescents and flowers, started to play a subconscious role in her painterly configurations, producing a tension between purely geometric marks or abstract drawing, and organic forms. One of the resulting canvases, the very large and gestural *Full Fathom Five* (1988; private collection, USA), won the Charles Wollaston award for the most distinguished work in the Royal Academy Summer Exhibition in 1989, crowning this period of intense work and achievement. The following January Ayres went to Jaipur at the invitation of the British Council to paint some canvases for the Seventh Triennale-India of 1991. She was sole British representative and winner of the gold medal. *Indian Summer* (1990; British Council, New Delhi), with its hot pinks and acid greens, is charged with a sense of India. The experience of that visit has since been fully absorbed into Ayres's abstract language.

JUDITH BUMPUS

B

Backer, Harriet

Norwegian painter, 1845–1932

Born in Holmestrand, 21 January 1845; father a wealthy ship owner. Moved with her family to Christiania (Oslo), 1857. Studied painting in Christiania under Johan Fredrik Eckersberg, 1861–5, and Christen Brun, 1867–8; in Bergen under Knud Bergslien, 1872–4. Private student of Norwegian painter Eilif Peterssen in Munich, 1874–8. Lived in Paris, 1878–88, studying briefly under Léon Bonnat, Jean-Léon Gérôme and Jules Bastien-Lepage; spent most summers in Norway; stayed in Brittany 1881 and 1882; on Fleskum in Bærum, 1886. Returned to Norway, 1888. Lived in Sandvika, 1889–93, then settled in Christiania. Ran painting school, 1889–1912. Friend of Kitty Kielland (q.v.). Recipient of National scholarship, 1886–7; King's gold medal of merit, 1908; state pension, 1921. Member, board of directors of National Gallery, Christiania, 1898–1918; honorary member, Royal Academy of Fine Arts, Stockholm, 1930. Knight of First Class, Royal Order of St Olav, 1925. Died in Oslo, 25 March 1932.

Principal Exhibitions

Individual

Kunstforeningen, Christiania: 1907, 1925
Kunstnerforbundet, Christiania: 1914, 1922
Kunstforeningen, Bergen: 1916
Konstnärshuset, Stockholm: 1925
Kunstnernes Hus, Oslo: 1933 (retrospective)

Group

Christiania Kunstforening (Art Association): 1877–8, 1887, 1891
München Kunstverein, Munich: 1877–8, 1891
Bergen Kunstforening (Art Association): 1877–8, 1886
Paris Salon: 1880–82 (honourable mention 1880)
Høstutstillingen (Autumn Salon), Christiania/Oslo: occasionally 1884–1930
Exposition Universelle, Paris: 1889 (silver medal), 1900
Munich: 1890 (*Münchener II Jahresausstellung*), 1895 (*Nordische Ausstellung*)
World's Columbian Exposition, Chicago: 1893
Internationale Kunstausstellung, Berlin: 1896
Stockholm: 1897 (*Allmänna konst- och industriutställningen* [Universal art and industry exhibition])
Internationale Ausstellung, Munich: 1901
Berlin Secession: 1904
Vienna: 1913 (*Sezession Norwegische Kunst*)

Bibliography

Erling Lone, *Harriet Backer*, Christiania: Aschehoug, 1924

K. Haug, "Norway's great woman artist", *American-Scandinavian Review*, 1925, pp.735–40

Henning Alsvik and Leif Ostby, *Norges Billedkunst* [Norwegian painting], i, Oslo, 1951

Else Christie Kielland, *Harriet Backer, 1845–1932*, Oslo: Aschehoug, 1958

Harriet Backer, exh. cat., Kunstnernes Hus, Oslo, and elsewhere, 1964

U. Hamran, "Harriet Backer og Kitty L. Kielland på Bosvik sommeren 1885" [Harriet Backer and Kitty L. Kielland in Bosvik in the summer of 1885], *Aust-Agder arv: Aust-Agder Museum Årbok*, 1977, pp.117–26

R. Bowman, "The art of Harriet Backer", *Scanorama*, October–November 1978

Anne Wichstrøm, "Blant likemenn: Søkelys på Harriet Backers og Kitty L. Kiellands karrierer" [Among equals: Spotlight on the careers of Harriet Backer and Kitty L. Kielland], *Den skjulte tradisjon* [The hidden tradition], Bergen, 1982, pp.172–91

Harriet Backer, 1845–1932, Kitty L. Kielland, 1843–1914, exh. cat., Stiftelsen Modums Blaafarvevaerk, Drammen, 1983

Anne Wichstrøm, *Kvinner ved staffeliet: Kvinnelige malere i Norge før 1900* [Women at the easel: Women painters in Norway before 1900], Oslo: Universitetsforlaget, 1983 (revised edition in preparation)

Michele Vishny, "Harriet Backer: A 'northern light'", *Arts Magazine*, lvii, May 1983, pp.78–80

1880-årene i nordisk maleri [The 1880s in Nordic painting], exh. cat., Nasjongalleriet, Oslo, and elsewhere, 1985

Marit Lange, *Harriet Backer*, Oslo: Norske Klassikere, 1985

Dreams of a Summer Night: Scandinavian Painting at the Turn of the Century, exh. cat., Arts Council of Great Britain, London, 1986

De drogo till Paris: Nordiska konstnärinnor på 1880-talet [They went to Paris: Nordic women artists in the 1880s], exh. cat., Liljevalchs Konsthall, Stockholm, 1988

Kirk Varnedoe, *Northern Light: Nordic Art at the Turn of the Century*, New Haven and London: Yale University Press, 1988

Marit Lange, "Et nyoppdaget maleri av Harriet Backer" [A recently discovered painting by Harriet Backer], *Kunst og Kultur*, lxxii, 1989, pp.244–7

Alessandra Comini, "Nordic luminism and the Scandinavian recasting of Impressionism", *World Impressionism: The International Movement, 1860–1920*, ed. Norma Broude, New York: Abrams, 1992, pp.274–313

Knut Berg, "Naturalisme og nyromanrikk" [Naturalism and Neoromanticism], *Norges Malerkunst*, ed. Knut Berg, Oslo: Gyldendal, 1993

Anne Wichstrøm, "At century's end: Harriet Backer, Kitty Kielland, Asta Nørregaard", *At Century's End: Norwegian Artists and the Figurative Tradition, 1880/1990*, exh. cat, Henie-Onstad Art

Center, Høvikodden, and National Museum of Women in the Arts, Washington, DC, 1995, pp.21–67

Marit Lange, *Harriet Backer* (in preparation)

Harriet Backer belonged to the National Romantic generation of Norwegian artists and intellectuals. In the 1880s she was a pioneer in developing a moody style of painting that corresponded to the emotional resonances sought by National Romantics. As their country had been dominated for several centuries by Denmark, and since 1814 by Sweden, 19th-century Norwegian intellectuals struggled to define a uniquely Norwegian national identity. While linguistics and literature were the primary fora for these inquiries, towards the end of the century painters, too, became active participants. Where many National Romantic painters concentrated on unique or typical aspects of the Nordic landscape, Backer focused on interiors. Her works are typically small in scale, appropriately unpretentious for the village cottages and churches she so often depicted. During her own lifetime, Backer was hailed as the greatest Norwegian woman artist, and the technical virtuosity of her substantial oeuvre supports this estimation. Her paintings are distinguished by an interest in the effects of light, both natural and artificial. *By Lamplight* (1890; Nasjonalgalleriet, Oslo) depicts a woman seated at a sewing table and concentrating on threading a needle by candlelight. The drawn window shade is aglow with a yellow light, and details of the woman's face and clothing are illuminated. Backer sought to adapt the principles of outdoor painting to interior scenes. *By Lamplight* is executed in the sketchy brush strokes of Naturalism, with far greater attention to lighting effects than to descriptive detail.

Backer began experimenting with Naturalism during the decade she spent in Paris (1878–88), where she associated with the large colony of Nordic expatriates. Within the group were many women artists, and they formed strong bonds of friendship. In 1879 Backer, with the Norwegian painters Hildegard Thorell, Anna Norstedt and Julia Beck, rented a studio in

Backer: *By Lamplight*, 1890; oil on canvas; 73.4 × 100.6 cm.; Rasmus Meyers Collection, Bergen Kommune

Montparnasse where the French academicians Léon Bonnat and Jules Bastien-Lepage came to criticise their work. Although these teachers practised a traditional, hard-edged realistic style characteristic of the venerable Ecole des Beaux-Arts, Backer evidenced greater interest in the looser styles of such artists as Claude Monet, whose works she saw at the Impressionist exhibitions. In 1880 the acceptance of *Solitude* (1878; untraced) at the Paris Salon confirmed for her the critical merit of her work. Although progressive French artists eschewed this time-honoured annual exhibition of painting and sculpture, the Salon was still the place where foreign artists proved their worth. While the interior in *Solitude* was executed in 1878, the figures were not added until 1880, at the behest of Bonnat. This modification produced an emotional tenor suited to Backer's increasing desire for works expressing her subjective response to a motif.

Backer's preference for rendering Norwegian village life may have been nurtured by her attachment to her home town of Holmestrand, but it was reinforced by other factors. Since 1814, when Norway had been ceded to Sweden, a strong impetus had emerged to define a Norwegian national identity. For Norwegian intellectuals, this identity resided in traditional village life and customs, which they zealously fought to preserve. In this context, Backer's placid images of daily rituals, peasant interiors and handicraft assumed ideological significance. She recorded the kinds of places and activities that socially ambitious, modern Norwegians were anxious to leave behind. The gentle emotional tenor of her works is intended to evoke a nostalgic longing for, and appreciation of, Norwegian folk life – to revalue that which was considered old fashioned and lower class. This intra-cultural specificity is a hallmark of National Romanticism and is found in the works of other Nordic artists, including Kitty Kielland (q.v.) and Hanna Hirsch Pauli (q.v.).

Peasant interiors were also popular in the circle of Munich artists around Wilhelm Leibl. It was there that Backer painted *Solitude*, and studied from 1874 to 1878, when Leibl was at the height of his career. The painstaking detail of his imagery found its way into Backer's early paintings, and the unassuming simplicity of his peasant interiors established a formula that she subsequently used in her own work.

In the 1890s Backer painted the series of "blue interiors" for which she is best known. This was the decade of mood painting (*stämningsmaleri*) in Norway, a time when artists sought to represent aspects of Scandinavian nature that were either unique or typical. They fastened on the pervasive blue tonalities of Nordic summer evenings, when a Whistlerian harmony softened the contours of objects that coalesced in a decorative unity. Another *By Lamplight* (1890; see illustration) is perhaps the best known of these works. Here a lone woman sits reading at a kitchen table in front of a lit heating stove. Although the table is set before a large window, it is dark outside, and the only light comes from an oil lamp on the table. Her face is brightly illuminated and the single light source creates dramatic contrasts of light and shadow. While the room's furnishings are quite spartan, this is clearly a middle-class interior, as indicated by the high ceilings, large window, heating stove and Rococo-style chair. *By Lamplight* combines an atmosphere of dignity and seriousness with one of cosiness and security.

In the last 20 years of her life Backer, who never married, painted sunny landscapes and still lifes in addition to interior scenes. Most of these are in private collections. Always working in a small scale, her reserved subjects reflected the modest ambitions considered appropriate for women artists in conservative Norwegian society. Her penultimate painting, *Music* (1917; private collection), depicts a young girl deeply absorbed in her piano playing in the living room of the village parish house in Loiten, where Backer was visiting her friend, the poet Ivar Mortensson Egnund. Backer's works can be found in all major Norwegian public collections, as well as in many other public collections in Scandinavia.

MICHELLE FACOS

Baracchis, Andriole de *see* Convents survey

Barber, Alice *see* Stephens

Barck Welles, Clara Pauline *see* Welles

Bardua, Caroline
German painter, 1781–1864

Born in Ballenstedt, in the duchy of Anhalt-Bernburg, 11 November 1781. Studied under Johann Heinrich Meyer at the Weimar drawing school, 1805–7; became a friend of Johanna Schopenhauer. Received private lessons from Gerhard von Kügelgen in Dresden, 1808–12; from 1811 alongside Louise Seidler (q.v.). Came into close contact with Anton Graff and Caspar David Friedrich. Worked as a portrait painter in Halberstadt, Halle, Magdeburg and Leipzig, 1814–19. Lived in Berlin, 1819–29; visited Paris, 1829; lived in Frankfurt am Main, 1829–32; in Berlin, 1832–52. Remained unmarried and lived with her sister Wilhelmine; her circle of friends included the sculptors Gottfried Schadow and Christian Rauch, and the poets Friedrich Heinrich Karl de la Motte Fouqué, Adelbert von Chamisso and Bettina von Arnim. Received an annual salary from the Berlin Academy from 1839. Founded the first literary and artistic circle for unmarried women in Berlin, the "Kaffeter", 1843. Retired from Berlin to her home town of Ballenstedt, 1852. Died there, 7 June 1864.

Principal Exhibitions
Weimar Academy: 1805–7, 1811

Bardua: *Caspar David Friedrich*, 1810; oil on canvas; 76.5 × 60 cm.; Nationalgalerie, Berlin

Dresden Academy: 1810–12, 1814
Berlin Academy: 1820, 1822, 1826, 1830, 1834, 1838, 1840, 1846

Bibliography

"Verkehr einer deutschen Malerin mit Goethe", *Morgenblatt für gebildete Leser*, no.28, 9 July 1862

Walter Schwartz (pseudonym of Wanda von Dallwitz), *Jugendleben der Malerin Caroline Bardua*, Breslau, 1874

Wilhelm von Kügelgen, *Jugenderinnerungen eines alten Mannes*, Leipzig, 1924

Johannes Werner, *Die Schwestern Bardua*, Leipzig, 1929

Neue Deutsche Biographie, i, Berlin, 1953

Margrit Bröhan, "Die Malerin Caroline Bardua in Berlin", *Der Bär von Berlin*, 1984, pp.25–59 (contains numerous illustrations)

Das Verborgene Museum I: Dokumente von Frauen in Berliner öffentlichen Sammlungen, exh. cat., Akademie der Künste, Berlin, 1987

"... ihr werten Frauenzimmer, auf!": Malerinnen der Aufklärung, exh. cat., Roselius-Haus, Bremen, 1993

Bärbel Kovalevski, "Goethe: Förderer und Modell von Malerinnen", *HB – Kunstführer Thüringen*, no.57, 1995

In order to encourage her many artistic talents, as a young girl in Ballenstedt Caroline Bardua received singing, guitar and drawing lessons. Through her friends she was able to continue her education at the drawing school in Weimar. On the recommendation of Goethe she was taken on there in 1805 as a pupil of Johann Heinrich Meyer, who advised her to draw freely after nature. Bardua took the opportunity to paint portraits of such well-known Weimar personalities as *Goethe, Johannes Daniel Falk, Fernow* and *Johanna Schopenhauer* (all Goethe Museum, Weimar). These early portraits reveal a vivacious painter who created works with a firm brush stroke, although her drawing technique and the characterisation of the sitters were not yet fully developed. During the three years she spent in Weimar, Bardua belonged to the close circle of friends around Goethe and Johanna Schopenhauer. The intellectual conversations about art, literature and creative work of this "tea-society" (music, literature, drawing, silhouette, *tableaux vivants*) stimulated her mind and imagination. Goethe advised Bardua to continue her way on the "military road of art" and gave her a letter of recommendation for the classical history and portrait painter Gerhard von Kügelgen.

Bardua's training under Kügelgen in Dresden was based on the copying of his works and those in the Dresden gallery under his instruction and supervision. It also included drawing practice in the antiquities hall, like art students at the Academy. Bardua lived and worked in the house and studio of "her master". Her parents had allowed three years for Bardua's education as a portrait painter. In 1810 she returned to Ballenstedt after participating successfully in the art exhibition of the Dresden Academy and in 1811–12 she again stayed in Dresden, where she met Kügelgen's new pupil Louise Seidler (q.v.). At the Dresden Academy exhibitions, Bardua introduced herself as a history and portrait painter. Her paintings *St Cecilia* and the *Virgin with the Christ Child* (both 1811; untraced) demonstrate her talent and courage in making her debut in the genre of history painting. In her drawing and use of colour Kügelgen's influence can be clearly seen. The unconventional composition of the *St Cecilia* was regarded as a "mistake" by contemporary critics. The artist had painted herself as Cecilia, idealised and with a guitar instead of the usual attribute of an organ. Bardua then exhibited a *St Cecilia* with organ and angels in the traditional manner at the Dresden exhibition of 1814, for which she received much praise, although she was criticised for an *Amor* (untraced), which was seen as too bold and naturalistic, representing as it did a boy beneath flowers (*Journal des Luxus und der Moden*, Weimar, 1810, 1811 and 1814). Her portraits also showed an independence of conception. In 1810 the unusual manner of her self-portrait and especially the large portrait of *Caspar David Friedrich* (see illustration) were much admired. The half-length portrait of Friedrich against a wide landscape background, shown confronting the viewer, mirrors the contemporary characterisation of Friedrich's pure and childish disposition in his clear expression and lit-up face. Bardua abstained from further attributes in order to convey the painter's personality and instead concentrated on a spiritual understanding of his character through his countenance. The portrait conveys the sitter's talent for observation as well as his self-assurance. In this painting of 1810 there is a stronger emphasis on realism than in the idealised portraits of her master Kügelgen.

Bardua's travels as a portrait painter led her to the German cities of Halberstadt, Halle, Magdeburg, Leipzig and Berlin. She was always looking for commissions in order to earn not only her own livelihood but also that of her sister, as well as pay for her brother's education. The museums of these towns still own some of Bardua's portraits of their citizens. Her energetic and realistic sense influenced her view of the sitter, as shown, for instance, in the portraits of *A.H. Niemeyer*, principal of Halle University, and of the Halle theologian *Christian G. Knapp* (both 1816; in store at Franckesche Stiftung, Halle). They testify to the indirect influence of the distinguished Dresden portrait painter Anton Graff, who recorded the new self-confidence of the middle classes in his paintings.

In order to secure a lasting livelihood as a portrait painter, in 1819 Bardua risked a move to Berlin with her sister Wilhelmine, in the hope that the flourishing Prussian capital with its royal family, nobility, civil servants, scientists and artists would offer opportunities for portrait commissions. After a few early difficulties, Bardua managed to establish herself as one of the most sought-after portrait painters in the city, despite competition from other artists. She painted many portraits of artists and scholars in Berlin (e.g. *Carl Maria von Weber*, 1822; Museen Preussischer Kulturbesitz, Musik-instrumentenmuseum). At her social gatherings she also arranged performances in the new art form, *tableaux vivants*, with much success. She showed many portraits at the Berlin art exhibitions of 1820–22, ranging from simple head portraits to group ones. Among these was a representative image of the ruling duchess, *Julie von Anhalt-Köthen* (1822; Institut für Kunst- und Kulturgut, Schloss Wernigerode), against a romantic landscape background. Bardua also sent some history and allegorical paintings to the Berlin exhibitions. The *Madonna under the Rainbow* (1826; lost World War II) is replete with the spirit of Romanticism. In an original conception the painting shows a little girl's sadness over flowers destroyed in a thunderstorm. Her sadness is combined with hope, symbolised by the young John the Baptist, who invisibly raises them again. In the middle ground the Virgin and the Christ Child smile above the scene. The divine soul of nature thus becomes a symbol of comfort in the face of sudden disaster, making this a didactic work of the parables of Christianity. Bardua, however, lacked both time and commissions for continued work on larger compositions.

In 1839 she travelled to Dresden and painted a second portrait of *Caspar D. Friedrich* (Anhaltische Gemäldegalerie Schloss Georgium, Dessau). The full-length portrait shows the sick and lonely artist in an interior with a romantic view of the Elbe out of the window with the symbolic addition of a bridge with a crucifix, a ship behind the bridge bathed in bright light and a landscape background. Next to the bent seated figure of the artist is a cleaned, unused palette, which gives the painting an atmosphere of melancholy. The portrait is exquisitely executed in its treatment of theme and colouring. It is not well known, being in storage at the Anhaltische Gemäldegalerie, Dessau, together with Bardua's noteworthy portrait of the violinist *Paganini* (1829).

Bardua's knowledge of the fine arts, music and literature was employed in the first literary-artistic women's club in Berlin, the "Kaffeter", which she founded with her sister Wilhelmine. The circle became a cultural event for educated unmarried women in Berlin between 1843 and 1848. At the meetings members contributed artistic pieces of their own invention. After the revolutionary events of 1848, life in Berlin became too exciting for the aging Bardua sisters. In quiet Ballenstedt Bardua continued to paint until the end of her life, producing such works as the portrait of the *Duchess Friederike von Sachsen-Anhalt* (Heimatmuseum Ballenstedt) in the style of a Biedermeier portrait.

Bardua's life is a rare example of the independent career of a female painter in the first half of the 19th century. Her travels from town to town, confident in her abilities and finding work as a painter despite her lack of protection, show great strength of character and courage. She achieved modest wealth solely through her portrait painting, while other important portrait painters, such as Anton Graff, had to earn money by copying paintings by Raphael and Pompeo Batoni. Bardua's works, however, are scattered in private collections or hidden in the stores of museums, still partly unknown because she did not always sign them. Her attempts to recreate traditional subjects with unusual compositions were – as mentioned above – rejected by the public at the beginning of her career. Without backing in an artistic community, her great talent and her efforts to achieve status in history painting ebbed away under the constant pressure to earn money from portrait painting.

As a portrait painter Bardua belongs to the traditions of the realistic portrait art of the Biedermeier. A fine example from her late period is the portrait of the *Daughters of Rabe* (1849; Berlin Museum), a senior civil servant. In the tradition of a friendship painting, Bardua here emphasises the loving relationship of the sisters, bound together through their common experience of nature. Man and Nature are the main subjects of fine art, represented in classicism with an idealised antique appearance, in Romanticism with emotional feeling and in the time of radical technical changes during the Biedermeier period with increasing realism. It is in this artistic development that Caroline Bardua and her work played a part.

BAERBEL KOVALEVSKI

Barlow, Hannah Bolton, 1851–1916, and Florence Elizabeth, 1855–1909
British ceramists and sculptors

Hannah Bolton Barlow Born in Essex, 2 November 1851. Studied at Lambeth School of Art, London, from 1868. Employed by Doulton & Co., Lambeth, London, 1871–1913. Died in London, 16 November 1916.

Principal Exhibitions
International Exhibition, South Kensington, London: 1871, 1872, 1873
Weltausstellung, Vienna: 1873
Centennial Exposition, Philadelphia: 1876
Exposition Universelle, Paris: 1878
Royal Academy, London: 1881, 1883–6, 1889–90

Florence Elizabeth Barlow Born in Essex, 17 April 1855. Studied at Lambeth School of Art, London, from c.1870. Employed by Doulton & Co., London, 1873–1909. Died in London, 1909.

Principal Exhibitions
Royal Academy, London: 1884–5

Bibliography
Ellen C. Clayton, *English Female Artists*, 2 vols, London: Tinsley, 1876
Geoffrey H. Godden, "Hannah B. Barlow", *Apollo*, lxvi, 1957, pp.22–3
Doulton Stoneware Pottery, part 1, exh. cat., Richard Dennis, London, 1971
Desmond Eyles, *The Doulton Lambeth Wares*, London: Hutchinson, 1975
Anthea Callen, *Angel in the Studio: Women in the Arts and Crafts Movement, 1870–1914*, London: Astragal, 1979; as *Women Artists of the Arts and Crafts Movement*, New York: Pantheon, 1979
The Doulton Story, exh. cat., Victoria and Albert Museum, London, 1979
Peter Rose, *Hannah Barlow: A Pioneer Doulton Artist, 1815–1916*, London: Dennis, 1985
—, "Florence Elizabeth Barlow", *Royal Doulton International Collectors' Club Magazine*, vi/3, 1986, pp.18–20
—, "The Barlow family of pottery decorators", *Ceramic Review*, no.101, 1986, pp.30–32
Cheryl Buckley, *Potters and Paintresses: Women Designers in the Pottery Industry, 1870–1955*, London: Women's Press, 1990

A working career devoted to the decoration of ornamental vases might, at first sight, appear to offer limited scope for creative expression. Yet, over a period of more than 40 years, both Hannah and Florence Barlow managed to produce many thousands of pottery pieces, each possessing, in some degree, striking originality of design and quality of craftsmanship. The Barlow sisters grew up in a large, prosperous, happy family living in style at The Grange, Hatfield, Essex, comprising an estate of some 250 hectares. Their father was a bank manager in Bishop's Stortford; it was his sudden and untimely death that plunged the 15-year-old Hannah, her brothers and sisters into the turbulent world of commerce.

The circumstances of the Barlows' employment, together with several hundred other women at the pottery works of

Hannah Barlow: *Vase with Wolves Attacking Deer, c.1872–3*

Doulton & Co., Lambeth, London, marked a significant shift in the status and working environment of women in late 19th-century Britain. Although the Barlow family at Doultons (including briefly a third sister, Lucy, and, until his early death, a brother, Arthur) stood out and were much praised in contemporary accounts, they worked alongside a number of other highly accomplished women artist decorators. (The male decorators, far fewer in number, but including the sculptor George Tinworth, worked in separate studios.) The Art Pottery section at Doultons, a firm previously noted mainly for its utilitarian wares, was revolutionary in many respects. The studios flourished from 1870 onwards, providing the employees with model working conditions that even now appear both liberal and enlightened. The firm encouraged originality and individuality, in striking contrast to the general trend towards standardisation and mass production. At first each artist-decorated piece of work was unique, never to be reproduced in that exact form again. Pairs of vases were, however, relatively common; later, cheaper multiple lines were introduced.

Hannah Barlow had a passion for the teeming animal and bird life of the countryside and showed an early talent for lively sketches of these creatures. It was therefore a natural development to exploit this talent by moving to London to study at Lambeth School of Art. She stayed with friends of her parents, the woodcarver W. G. Rogers and his family. By good fortune, the headmaster of Lambeth School of Art was John C. L. Sparkes, one of the leading art educationalists of the 19th century, who had encouraged Henry Doulton to undertake the experiment of manufacturing art pottery and consequently providing employment for large numbers of Lambeth Art School students. Hannah's studies took a very direct and active course, in marked contrast to the restrictive copying that found favour in official circles. She worked freely in her sketchbooks using pen and pencil, taking every opportunity to draw birds and animals in their natural habitat. She was able to visit Bushy Park, Teddington; Windsor, where she attended a cattle show; the Crystal Palace where, among its many splendours, dog shows were held; periodically she returned to the Essex countryside to stay with her mother and younger brothers and sisters, now living in much reduced circumstances but still able to maintain a varied menagerie of domestic animals. In a lecture given to the Society of Arts some years after Hannah had become established at Doultons, John Sparkes enthused over her ability to capture the essence of her subject: "she possesses a certain Japanese facility of representing the largest amount of fact in the fewest lines, all correct and all embodying in a high degree the essential character of her subject" (lecture at Society of Arts, reprinted in John C.L. Sparkes, "Notes on Lambeth stoneware", Doulton & Co., 1880). It was this quality above all others that characterised Hannah Barlow's ceramic work.

There is no evidence that Hannah and her female associates had anything to do with the techniques of clay preparation, pot making and the later process of firing, but the designing of the pot shapes was sometimes undertaken by women. The early production at Doultons consisted exclusively of salt-glazed stoneware, and the preferred decoration comprised a combination of incised outlines of patterns and pictorial motifs on the unfired clay, which later would be filled with coloured slips and embellished with clay beading, stars and similar additions by assistants under the supervision of the "Head of Studio". In this fully developed phase of the enterprise, Hannah and Florence, both of whom were in the most senior rank of artist-decorators, continued to share a studio, sometimes working in collaboration but more often independently with their own assistants on call to complete the decoration. In the early years, before this system was fully developed, there were a simplicity, consistency and direct vigour in the pots that stemmed from the single-handed approach of the small band of artists, including Hannah and Florence, who pioneered the technique. The work of this early period was never surpassed, although methods became more sophisticated and varied and the chemistry of the firing better understood and controlled.

Works by both Hannah and Florence were regularly displayed publicly, particularly at the major international exhibitions. The first exhibition to show Hannah's work was the International Exhibition at South Kensington in 1871, followed in 1872 and 1873 by similar displays. In 1872 a cabinet (Victoria and Albert Museum, London) designed by Charles Bevan for Gillow & Co. with 14 tile plaques by Hannah Barlow were exhibited. Work was also shown at the Weltausstellung in Vienna in 1873, the Centennial Exhibition in Philadelphia in 1876, and elsewhere. Apart from the work carried out as employees of Doultons, both Florence and Hannah exhibited at major London galleries. Florence exhibited watercolours of birds, her favourite subjects, while Hannah showed sculptural pieces in the form of terracotta reliefs of animal subjects, of which no fewer than eleven were exhibited at the Royal Academy during the 1880s. She also exhibited at the Dudley Gallery, Society of British Artists and various provincial galleries including the Walker Art Gallery in Liverpool.

Both Hannah and Florence Barlow remained unmarried and with their sister Lucy, who acted as housekeeper, maintained a comfortable establishment in Clapham, south London. Hannah's work continued into the 20th century virtually unchanged by fashion, although her dexterity with the inscribing tool was increasingly affected by rheumatism of the right hand. Florence, however, moved with the times, adopting the new techniques of tube-lining as an alternative to inscribing or using her preferred method of *pâte-sur-pâte*. She had adopted this last technique early on, perhaps to distinguish her work from that of her sister, who seldom employed the method. At the turn of the 19th and 20th centuries, Florence's designs became more formalised and Art Nouveau in style – she was more adaptable than Hannah and faced up to changes in taste, which were accompanied by an inexorable decline in demand. Both sisters are, however, inseparably linked with the earlier production of unique artist-designed salt-glazed pots that are as prized today as during their own lifetimes.

PETER ROSE

Barns-Graham, Wilhelmina

British painter, 1912–

Born in St Andrews, Fife, 8 June 1912. Studied at Edinburgh College of Art, 1932–7 (diploma in painting). Studio in Edinburgh, 1936–40. Awarded Andrew Carnegie travelling scholarship and moved to St Ives, Cornwall, 1940. Joined Newlyn Society of Artists, 1942; member of St Ives Society of Artists, 1942–9; first meetings of Crypt Group in her studio, 1946 (exhibited with Crypt Group, 1947–8); founder-member of Penwith Society of Artists, 1949. Trips to Switzerland, 1948–52. Married David Lewis, 1949; divorced 1963. Worked in Italy, 1954–5; won Italian Government travelling scholarship, 1955. Taught at Leeds School of Art, 1956–7. Worked in Spain, France and the Balearics, 1958. Studio in London, 1961–3; subsequently worked in Scotland and St Ives; in Orkney, 1984–5. Lives in Balmungo, near St Andrews.

Selected Individual Exhibitions

Downing Gallery, St Ives, Cornwall: 1947, 1949, 1954
Redfern Gallery, London: 1949, 1952
St Ives Festival: 1951
Roland, Browse and Delbanco, London: 1954
Scottish Gallery, Edinburgh: 1956, 1960, 1981, 1989
Marjorie Parr Gallery, London: 1971
Wills Lane Gallery, St Ives: 1976
Crawford Centre, St Andrews: 1982, 1992
Henry Rothschild Exhibition, Germany: 1982
Pier Arts Centre, Stromness, Orkney: 1984
Gillian Jason Gallery, London: 1987
City Art Centre, Edinburgh: 1989–90 (touring retrospective, organised by Scottish Arts Council)

Bibliography

Denys Val Baker, text in *Cornish Review*, no.1, 1949

J.P. Hodin, text in *Art News and Review*, iv/2, 1952
R.H. Wilenski, *The Modern Movement in Art*, 4th edition, London: Faber, and New York: Yoseloff, 1957
W. Barns-Graham: Recent Gouaches and Spanish Drawings, exh. cat., Scottish Gallery, Edinburgh, 1960
W. Barns-Graham: Paintings and Drawings, exh. cat., LYC Museum and Art Gallery, Cumbria, 1981
W. Barns-Graham: Paintings and Drawings, exh. cat., Crawford Centre, St Andrews, 1982
Homage to Herbert Read, exh. cat., Canterbury College of Art, 1984
St Ives, 1939–64: Twenty-Five Years of Painting, Sculpture and Pottery, exh. cat., Tate Gallery, London, 1985
W. Barns-Graham: Paintings and Drawings, exh. cat., Gillian Jason Gallery, London, 1987
W. Barns-Graham: Retrospective, 1940–1989, exh. cat., Scottish Arts Council, Edinburgh, 1989
Scottish Art since 1900, exh. cat., Scottish National Gallery of Modern Art, Edinburgh, and elsewhere, 1989
W. Barns-Graham at 80: A New View, exh. cat., William Jackson Gallery, London, 1992
Peter Davies, *St Ives Revisited: Innovators and Followers*, Abertillery, Gwent: Old Bakehouse Publications, 1994

In *The Modern Movement in Art* R.H. Wilenski illustrated a work by Wilhelmina Barns-Graham. He sought to define what he considered were fundamental principles governing modern art. Painting, he felt, consisted of two opposed schools of thought: the one was subject-centred and content-driven; the other, and preferred approach, concentrated instead on the investigation and distillation of visual axioms of formal structure. It was to illustrate this latter, "architectural" category of modern art that he used a work by Barns-Graham.

By 1952, when Wilenski's work was first published, Barns-Graham had been a resident of St Ives in Cornwall, and a very active member of its community of artists, for 12 years. She had continued to work in Edinburgh after her graduation from Edinburgh College of Art until 1940. In that year, and as much for her delicate health as for the astute conviction that she would blossom professionally there, Herbert Wellington, the principal of the college, recommended that she should base herself in St Ives. Barns-Graham settled there in March 1940. Inevitably she is associated with major figures of the St Ives group – most often Ben Nicholson, whom she accompanied on sketching trips in the early 1950s. Other parallels might be drawn between aspects of her work and that of Barbara Hepworth (q.v.) and Terry Frost. Whatever her allegiances and influences, the central concerns that have driven her have remained constant throughout her long career. Drawing is at the core of her process. It is through the crisp, clear line drawings, which she looks upon as a mental discipline, that the artist seeks to identify and evoke fundamental principles governing the observed world. Her art is rooted in these outdoor studies, with the visual relationships evolved in the drawings becoming the basis for often more abstract, studio-based works. In a manner perhaps akin to Mondrian's, Barns-Graham seeks to order and codify the complexity of nature into a series of formal principles, while at the same time maintaining a sense of the mystery, harmony and power of the natural world. She explained: "Abstraction is a wide field and is not all necessarily 'abstract'. Abstraction is a refinement and greater discipline to the idea; truth to the medium perfects the idea" (*Freeing the Spirit*, exh. cat., Crawford Centre, St Andrews, 1988).

Barns-Graham: *Blue Drop* 2, 1978; gouache; 101.5 × 81 cm.; Government Collection: Department of the Environment

The order of the studio work is partially imposed through the use of a grid of pencil-drawn lines upon which the dynamic elements of the composition are imposed. This grid not infrequently survives into the finished piece. Sometimes, as in *Movement Over Sand* (1980; gouache on paper; artist's collection), it survives as ghostly pentimenti; sometimes the grid of lines takes its place within an overall constructive design of linear elements, as in *Upper Glacier* (1950; oil on canvas; British Council) and *Blue Drop 2* (1978; see illustration). Order also derives from free improvisations made on proportional relationships. In this manner the golden section determines the compositional divisions of *Spanish Island, Under Over* (1960; gouache on paper; artist's collection). This should not, however, indicate a mechanistic or overly formulaic approach: improvisational methods are not infrequently adopted. *Spanish Island* contains passages of strong gestural handling; *Lime and Flame* (1958; gouache on paper; artist's collection) has areas of splashed and running paint. Irrespective of this a strong graphic quality is always maintained, together with a sense of intellectual control, of analysis and structure.

In form and content there are works that are strongly reminiscent of Ben Nicholson, such as *White Relief Horizontal, No.2* (1955; oil on board; artist's collection). In form, *Rocks, St Mary's, Scilly Isles* (1953; oil on board; artist's collection) recalls Barbara Hepworth's organic sculpture of the 1930s and 1940s. Barns-Graham's own vision is best seen not in the examination of individual pieces but in the continuity of her work. She returns persistently to subjects illustrative of, or recalling, dynamic natural phenomena such as fire, tides, winds and waves. Titles frequently evoke movement. *Expanding Forms, Movement over Sand* (1980; oil on canvas; Bank of Scotland), an abstract composition of coloured triangles intruding from the left side of the painting, stresses both the active and the organic nature of the subject. Similar observations might be made concerning *Celebration of Fire* (1992; gouache; artist's collection). Works that have minimalist abstract titles, such as *Eight Lines, White on Blue* (1988; acrylic on paper; artist's collection), irresistibly recall kinetic natural phenomena, in this case waves and beach.

This interest in the processes of nature seems less obvious in the series of images of rock formations. Varying from directly representational line drawings to schematically reduced paintings, these works seem more concerned with the manipulation of shape and space. They appear static and solid with little of the fluid energy of the wave/fire pieces. In fact they too are best understood in terms of natural creation/destruction. If the glacier paintings of the early 1950s – *Glacier Grindelwald* (1950; oil on canvas; Arts Council of Great Britain) – and the Lanzarote lava images of the late 1980s and early 1990s are used as intermediaries, then the rock-form pieces can be seen as process also. A work such as *Three Rocks* (1952; oil on canvas; Leeds City Art Gallery) seeks to analyse the means by which these forms arise. The creation and metamorphosis of the stuff of the planet itself are deconstructed and systematised. All of the natural world, to which Barns-Graham devotes so much time drawing, is seen as dynamic progression. From this intellectualised world there ultimately emerges an understated and emotionally cool art, aseptic rather than harmonious.

JOHN MORRISON

Bartlett, Jennifer (Losch)
American painter, sculptor and printmaker, 1941–

Born Jennifer Losch in Long Beach, California, 14 March 1941. Studied at Mills College, Oakland (BA 1963); Yale University School of Art and Architecture, New Haven (BFA 1964; MFA 1965). Married Edward Bartlett, mid-1960s; divorced. Instructor, University of Connecticut, Storrs, 1968–72; visiting artist, Art Institute of Chicago, autumn 1972; instructor, School of Visual Arts, New York, 1972–7. Recipient of Creative Artists Public Service (CAPS) grant, 1974; Harris prize, Art Institute of Chicago, 1976 and 1986; Lucas visiting lecturer award, Carleton College, Northfield, Minnesota, 1979; Creative Arts award, Brandeis University, Waltham, Massachusetts, 1983; American Academy and Institute of Arts and Letters award, 1983; M.V. Kohnstamm award, 1986; American Institute of Architects award, 1987. Member, New York Institute of Humanities. Lives in New York.

Selected Individual Exhibitions
Mills College, Oakland, CA: 1963
Paula Cooper Gallery, New York: 1974, 1976, 1977, 1979, 1981, 1982, 1983, 1985, 1987, 1988, 1990, 1991, 1992, 1994, 1995
Wadsworth Atheneum, Hartford, CT: 1977
San Francisco Museum of Modern Art: 1978
Baltimore Art Museum: 1978
Galerie Mukai, Tokyo: 1980, 1989, 1992
Albright-Knox Gallery, Buffalo: 1980
Joslyn Art Museum, Omaha: 1982
Tate Gallery, London: 1982
Walker Art Center, Minneapolis: 1985–6 (*Rhapsody*, touring)
Cleveland Museum of Art: 1986
Contemporary Art Gallery, Seibu, Japan: 1988
Milwaukee Art Museum: 1988
Institute of Fine Arts, Santa Fe: 1993
Orlando Museum of Art: 1993–5 (touring retrospective)

Selected Writings
Cleopatra I–IV, New York: Adventures in Poetry, 1971
Texts in *The World: Autobiography Issue*, 1973
History of the Universe, New York: Moyer Bell, 1985 (novel)

Bibliography
John Russell, "On finding a bold new work", *New York Times*, 16 May 1976
Sally Webster, "Jennifer Bartlett", *Feminist Art Journal*, v/3, Fall 1976, pp.37–8
Roberta Smith, "Bartlett's *Swimmers*", *Art in America*, lxvii, November 1979, pp.93–7
Jennifer Bartlett: Selected Works, exh. cat., Albright-Knox Gallery, Buffalo, 1980
Mario Amaya, "Artist's dialogue: A conversation with Jennifer Bartlett", *Architectural Digest*, xxxviii, December 1981, pp.50–60
Jennifer Bartlett: At the Lake; Up the Creek; In the Garden, exh. cat., Tate Gallery, London, 1982

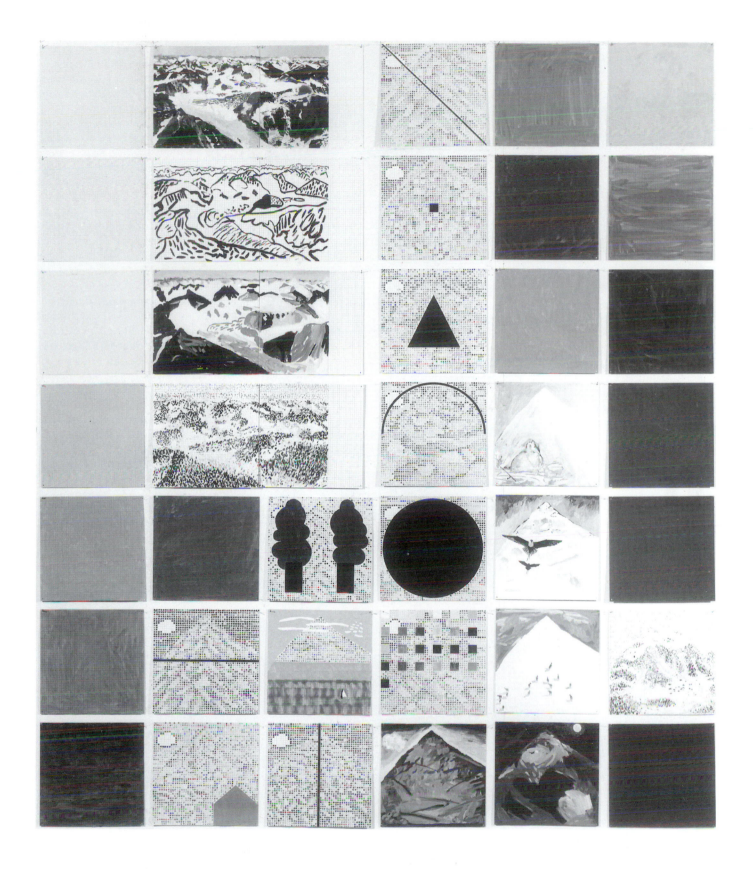

Bartlett: *Rhapsody (Detail No.6), 1975–6*; baked enamel and silkscreen grid on 16-gauge steel, enamel; 988 plate piece, each 30.5 × 30.5 cm., overall 2.29 × 46.86 m.; private collection

John Russell, *Jennifer Bartlett: In the Garden*, New York: Abrams, 1982

Nan Robertson, "In the garden with Jennifer Bartlett", *Art News*, lxxxii, November 1983, pp.72–7

Jeff Perrone, "Jennifer Bartlett: New paintings", *Arts Magazine*, lviii, December 1983, pp.68–9

Richard S. Field, "Jennifer Bartlett: Prints, 1978–1983", *Print Collector's Newsletter*, xv, 1984, pp.1–6

Roberta Smith, *Rhapsody: Jennifer Bartlett*, New York: Abrams, 1985

Calvin Tomkins, "Profiles: Getting everything in", *New Yorker*, 15 April 1985, pp.50–68

Holland Cotter, "The Bartlett variations", *Art in America*, lxxiv, May 1986, pp.124–31

Marge Goldwater, Roberta Smith and Calvin Tomkins, *Jennifer Bartlett*, 2nd edition, New York: Abbeville, 1989

Holland Cotter, "Art in review: Jennifer Bartlett", *New York Times*, 3 October 1992, p.C29

Jennifer Bartlett: A Print Retrospective, exh. cat., Orlando Museum of Art, and elsewhere, 1993

Ever since her ground-breaking exhibition at the Paula Cooper Gallery in 1976, Jennifer Bartlett has been a major force on the American and international art scenes. Known mainly for her complex, multi-part works made of enamel paint on steel plates, Bartlett has spent the past 20 years revising, refining and expanding this signature approach. Her obsession with making countless variations on a few simple motifs links her to the Impressionist masters, but the computer-generated look and the jagged rhythms of her compositions place her firmly at the end of the 20th century. This paradox is typical of Bartlett's work, which is at once passionate and controlled.

At Mills College Bartlett became good friends with fellow art student Elizabeth Murray (q.v.) and at Yale she was strongly influenced by Jack Tworkov, the departmental chair. Like most progressive art courses of the time, that at Yale stressed Abstract Expressionism, a style that Bartlett had already been employing for several years. But Tworkov also encouraged his students to explore other means of expression – notably Pop Art, to which Bartlett was exposed through such guest teachers as James Rosenquist and Jim Dine. Bartlett's concern with everyday objects, and her interest in combining two and three dimensions within a single art work, may well have its roots in her days at Yale – and in earlier discussions with Murray.

As soon as she could, Bartlett moved to New York. Fulfilling a childhood dream, she rented a SoHo loft and joined the crowd of ambitious young artists living and working in that as yet unfashionable quarter. After a brief flirtation with "process art" (which, in her case, involved the display of cheap plastic bowls that had been subjected to various kinds of torture), in 1968 Bartlett started making abstract drawings with coloured dots on graph paper – inspired, she has said, by the tiled signs in the New York subways. From that point she quickly progressed to using brightly coloured *Testors* enamel (the paint used for model aeroplanes) on flat steel plates that had been painted white and overlaid with a grid. After a half-dozen exhibitions of these works she showed *Rhapsody* (1975–6; see illustration), a piece that filled the entire Paula Cooper Gallery with its 988 plates, each 30.5 centimetres square, fastened to the walls. The critic John Russell (1976) called *Rhapsody* "the most ambitious single work of art that has come my way since I started to live in New York".

Like most of Bartlett's works, *Rhapsody* is difficult to characterise and interpret. Although it is clearly related to the repetitive modules of such minimalist artists as Sol Lewitt, Donald Judd and Carl André, Bartlett's composition is neither cold, severe nor mechanical. On the contrary, *Rhapsody* is a sort of visual encyclopedia of every imaginable variation on the artist's favourite themes – a house, a tree, a mountain, clouds – plus several simple geometric forms. Some of the painted squares are smooth, others are filled with aggressive, irregular textures; some feature cheery, childlike drawings, while others are sophisticated aerial views; the materials used and the scales of the images vary as much as the styles with which they are portrayed. Moreover, the meaning of *Rhapsody* eludes the viewer. Critics disagree on whether these apparently simplistic images should be interpreted ironically or otherwise. Bartlett herself maintains that her work contains no symbolism, reinforcing this stance by means of steadfastly neutral titles.

An important related work from 1979–80 is *In the Garden*, another multi-part construction made up of images based on the view from the dining-room of a house in southern France where Bartlett lived for one winter. During her stay Bartlett became so intrigued with the small garden and its cracked swimming pool that she made nearly 200 drawings, as well as a series of paintings, of this subject. Like Monet with his waterlilies, Bartlett recorded the garden at every time of day, from various perspectives and on different scales, using many different styles and a wide range of materials and techniques. (For another, later example, see *Air: 24 Hours*, 1992, three segments of which, *One AM*, *Five AM* and *Five PM*, are in the Metropolitan Museum of Art, New York.) The resulting ensemble of images was displayed at Bartlett's New York gallery, Paula Cooper, in 1981. This led to a number of private and corporate commissions, for which Bartlett's enamel-and-steel format proved to be particularly well suited.

From the beginning Bartlett had stated that she favoured this unlikely medium because of its practicality – such works were durable, fireproof and portable. Moreover, this way of working encouraged her to be flexible: since few individuals had the space to accommodate Bartlett's gigantic installations, she often created entirely new variations on particular themes. One such example is the nine-part *In the Garden* that Bartlett made for a London collector's home (1981; Doris and Charles Saatchi). This work combines oil on canvas with fresco, painting on glass and mirrors, collage and a lacquered wooden screen. In her commission of 1980 for the Institute for Scientific Information, Philadelphia, Bartlett made another large mural version of *In the Garden*, and dispersed a copy of that painting – divided into 54 separate fragments – throughout the building. Other corporate commissions include *Swimmers: Atlanta* (1979), an enormous mural – half oil on canvas and half painted steel plates – for the Federal Building in the Georgia state capital. This work is organised around an ovoid, disc-like shape: Bartlett's stylised "swimmer", which also appears in a number of her other projects, such as the triptych *Swimmers at Dawn, Noon and Dusk* (1979; Walker Art Center, Minneapolis).

Bartlett began experimenting with sculpture in 1984, with her commission for Volvo's corporate headquarters in Göteborg, Sweden. Here, for the first time, she created three-dimensional versions of several characteristic subjects – houses and boats – made of metal and wood, in several different sizes. This work, which includes potentially functional granite tables and chairs, blurs the traditional distinction between "sculpture" and "furniture" – an important issue for many artists of Bartlett's generation. Her Swedish work is related to the miniature cast-iron houses of Joel Shapiro and the stone and wood constructions of Richard Artschwager and Scott Burton.

Since the mid-1980s Bartlett has frequently exhibited paintings on a wall with three-dimensional objects displayed in front of them, for example, *Fire/Nasturtiums* (1988–9; oil on canvas; Walker Art Center), a painting of a table paired with an actual wooden table. She continues to explore various printmaking techniques and to exhibit extensively in the USA and abroad. Always ready to take on new artistic challenges, in 1986 Bartlett accepted an invitation to design a garden in the Battery Park City section of Manhattan – and two years later she designed the sets and costumes for the Paris Opéra's production of a work by Janáček.

NANCY G. HELLER

Barton, Glenys
British sculptor, 1944–

Born in Stoke-on-Trent, Staffordshire, 24 January 1944. Studied at the Royal College of Art, London, 1968–71. Visiting lecturer, Camberwell School of Arts and Crafts, London, 1971–6 (part-time tutor from 1977); Fine Art Department, Portsmouth Polytechnic, 1971–4; Royal College of Art, 1975–6. Artist in residence, Josiah Wedgwood & Co., Staffordshire, 1976–7. Shared studio with Jacqui Poncelet, 1971–5; subsequently studio in Wandsworth, London, 1975–84, and in Burnham-on-Crouch, Essex, from 1984. Recipient of British prize, International Ceramics Exhibition, 1972. Lives in Halstead, Essex.

Selected Individual Exhibitions
Waterloo Place Gallery, London: 1973 (with Jacqui Poncelet)
Kunstindustrimuseet, Copenhagen: 1973
Oxford Gallery, Oxford: 1973
Angela Flowers Gallery, London: 1974, 1981, 1983, 1986, 1994
Galerie Het Kapelhuis, Amersfoort, and Princessehof Museum, Leeuwarden: 1976
Crafts Advisory Committee Gallery, London: 1977
Flowers East, London: 1990, 1993, 1996
Northern Centre for Contemporary Art, Sunderland: 1991

Selected Writings
"A search for order", *Ceramic Review*, no.34, 1975, pp.4–6
"Sculptors in limbo?", *Crafts*, no.33, July–August 1978, pp.32–3
"Idols and images", *Art Review*, xlv, February 1994, pp.48–9

Bibliography
Fiona Adamceski, "Outside tradition", *Crafts*, no.2, May–June 1973, pp.20–23
Ceramic Forms: Recent Work by Seven British Potters, exh. cat., Crafts Council, London, 1974
New Ceramics, exh. cat., Ulster Museum, Belfast, 1974
Elizabeth Fritsch, "Glenys Barton", *Crafts*, no.12, January–February 1975, p.48
Glenys Barton at Wedgwood, exh. cat., Crafts Advisory Committee Gallery, London, 1977
Stephen Bayley, "Glenys Barton at Wedgwood: Review", *Crafts*, no.27, July–August 1977, p.47
British 20th Century Studio Ceramics, exh. cat., Christopher Wood Gallery, London, 1980
Emmanuel Cooper, "Glenys Barton: Sculptures and reliefs", *Ceramic Review*, no.85, 1984, pp.10–11
Artists and Green Warriors, exh. cat., Flowers East Gallery, London, 1990
Glenys Barton: New Sculpture, exh. cat., Flowers East Gallery, London, 1993
Oliver Watson, *Studio Pottery: Twentieth-Century British Ceramics in the Victoria and Albert Museum Collection*, London: Phaidon, 1993 (originally published as *British Studio Pottery*, Oxford: Phaidon, 1990)

Glenys Barton, sculptor, was part of the renaissance within the crafts that took place in Britain in the 1970s. This questioned and rejected traditional perceptions in favour of an eclectic, post-modern use of processes and techniques that could be used to push at and transgress conventional art and craft boundaries.

With makers such as Elizabeth Fritsch (q.v.), Jacqui Poncelet and Jill Crowley, Barton studied at the Royal College of Art at a time of expansion and experiment. Under the enlightened guidance of David Queensberry, Professor of Ceramics, and the thoughtful teaching of Hans Coper, students were encouraged to rethink what craft could do, with many opting to use hand-building rather than throwing on the potter's wheel, and to experiment with bright colour rather than with the subdued and muted tones of stonewares. Most significantly, they were interested in producing objects as part of an artistic statement rather than as utilitarian products. At a time when fine artists were rejecting skills such as life drawing in favour of found and appropriated images of Pop Art, craft was seen as accessible and humanistic, an alternative to the growing anonymity and impersonality of fine art. Far from being rejected, skill was seen as an intrinsic part of craft objects.

From the start, Barton was attracted by the hard-edged and precise qualities of such industrial methods as slip-casting and transfer decoration. After designing a set of stacking tableware for Habitat, she used industrial techniques to good effect in such conceptual pieces as pyramid forms and sets of cubes, cast in bone china and decorated with silk-screened patterns dividing up and articulating the surface. Crisp making was intrinsic to the aesthetic of the objects, and Barton ground the surfaces of the cubes to achieve the precision and sharpness she wanted. Using primary colours, she created cubes that resonate with a Piet Mondrian-like sense of form and colour, and reveal a contemporary interest in hard-edged abstraction. In Barton's small-scale cubes, each little more than a few centimetres in size, the effect is of sculptural components that can be arranged in a wide variety of ways. Other work at this time was more figurative, and much of it was made in collaboration with Wedgwood. Barton was able to make use of the skilled making techniques in use at the factory, particularly with bone china, a material notoriously difficult to control. Limited editions, created by Barton and manufactured by Wedgwood, represent an unusual instance of a successful collaboration between an artist and industry.

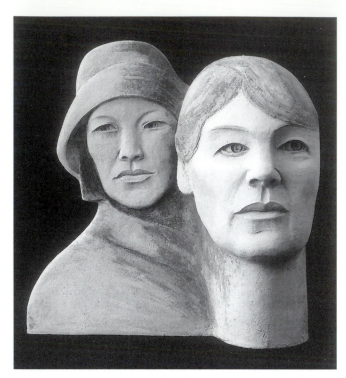

Barton: *Glenda Jackson*, 1993; National Portrait Gallery, London

Inspired by the writing of J.G. Ballard, Barton began considering the significance of the figure in modern life, an interest that continues in her current work. *Lady with Three Faces* (1980; private collection) depicts a naked but faceless standing female figure with a mask lying at her feet with three faces on it, posing the question, which one, if any, is appropriate? The precise making and the clear statement of intent are fundamental parts of the sculpture. This work can be seen as autobiographical, with the female being offered or rejecting the different and often conflicting roles of woman, mother and artist.

In her near-life-sized portrait heads, Barton moved in a direction that was both more adventurous and more familiar, seeking to suggest the timelessness and power of the human face. Some, such as *Ozymandias* (1979; private collection), have a monumental quality that matches the scale and scope of the subject. The modelling is minimal, but the evocation of a powerful, almighty king is ingeniously expressed. In more recent work Barton has created flattened forms with careful modelling to give the illusion of three dimensions, which increases as the head is viewed from different angles.

In portraits of named people, Barton uses a similar method of low relief to capture the appearance and character of the subject. Notable successes include *Glenda Jackson* (1993; see illustration) and a series of portrait heads, some no more than 10 centimetres tall, of *Jean Muir* (private collection), whose striking features, surrounded by a mass of dark hair, are well suggested. Flattened in form, the relief modelling has sufficient detail to evoke the temperament and character of the distinguished designer without seeking to be a conventional portrait.

Barton's continued use of clay to create her sculptures makes full use of the expressive qualities of the material, with some pieces finished to bring out the qualities of the clay, while others are glazed and occasionally sand-blasted to enhance the matt, non-reflective qualities of the surface. Important collections include the Victoria and Albert Museum, London, the Crafts Council and Portsmouth City Museum and Art Gallery.

Through her continued involvement with clay and her exploration of the qualities the material can offer, Barton bridges the world of art and craft with beguiling ease. The objects she creates are about the times in which we live – faces and figures that can only be a part of the late 20th century.

EMMANUEL COOPER

Bashkirtseff, Marie
Russian painter, 1860–1884

Born in Havrontsi, Poltava province, Ukraine, 11 November (Old Style calendar)/23 November (New Style calendar) 1860. Travelled widely with her mother and family after 1870, settling in Paris in 1877. Studied in the women's class at the Académie Julian under Tony Robert-Fleury and later Jules Bastien-Lepage. Visited Spain, 1881. Contributed articles to the feminist journal *La Citoyenne* under the pseudonym Pauline Orell. Member, Union des Femmes Peintres et Sculpteurs, Paris. Died in Paris from tuberculosis, 31 October 1884. (In 1908 Bashkirtseff's mother donated works to the Russian Museum, St Petersburg; these were exhibited in 1930.)

Principal Exhibitions

Paris Salon: 1880–81, 1883–5
Union des Femmes Peintres et Sculpteurs, Paris: 1884, 1885 (retrospective)

Selected Writings

Le Journal de Marie Bashkirtseff, ed. A. Theuriet, 2 vols, Paris, 1887; as *The Journal of Marie Bashkirtseff*, London: Cassell, 1890; ed. Rozsika Parker and Griselda Pollock, London: Virago, 1985
Les Lettres de Marie Bashkirtseff, ed. François Coppée, Paris, 1891; as *Letters*, London: Cassell, 1891
I Kiss Your Hands: The Letters of Guy de Maupassant and Marie Bashkirtseff, London: Rodale Press, 1954

Bibliography

Marie Bashkirtseff, exh. cat., Union des Femmes Peintres et Sculpteurs, Paris, 1885
Mathilde Blind, "A study of Marie Bashkirtseff", *Jules Bastien-Lepage and His Art*, ed. A. Theuriet, London: Unwin, 1892, pp.149–90 (French original, 1892)
M.L. Breakell, "Marie Bashkirtseff: The reminiscence of a fellow-student", *Nineteenth Century and After*, lxii, 1907, pp.110–25
P. Borel, "L'idyll mélancolique, histoire de Maria Bashkirtseff et de Jules Bastien-Lepage", *Annales Politiques et Littéraires*, lxxviii, 1922, pp.535–6, 563–5, 591–2, 617–18, 643–4
Albéric Cahuet, *Moussia: The Life and Death of Marie Bashkirtseff*, New York: Macaulay, 1929 (French original, 1926)
Dormer Creston [D.J. Baynes], *Fountains of Youth: The Life of Marie Bashkirtseff*, London: Butterworth, 1936; New York: Dutton, 1937; as *The Life of Marie Bashkirtseff*, London: Eyre and Spottiswoode, 1943

Doris Langley Moore, *Marie and the Duke of H.: The Daydream Love Affair of Marie Bashkirtseff*, London: Cassell, and Philadelphia: Lippincott, 1966

Women Artists, 1550–1950, exh. cat., Los Angeles County Museum of Art, and elsewhere, 1976

Charlotte Yeldham, *Women Artists in Nineteenth-Century France and England*, 2 vols, New York: Garland, 1984

Colette Cosnier, *Marie Bashkirtseff: Un Portrait sans retouches*, Paris: Horay, 1985

Tamar Garb, "'Unpicking the seams of her disguise': Self-representation in the case of Marie Bashkirtseff", *Block*, xiii, 1987–8, pp.79–86; reprinted in *The Block Reader in Visual Culture*, London and New York: Routledge, 1996

John Milner, *The Studios of Paris: The Capital of Art in the Late Nineteenth Century*, New Haven and London: Yale University Press, 1988

Mara R. Witzling, ed., *Voicing Our Visions: Writings by Women Artists*, New York: Universe, 1991; London: Women's Press, 1992

Bashkirtseff: *The Meeting*, 1884; Musée d'Orsay, Paris

Tamar Garb, *Sisters of the Brush: Women's Artistic Culture in Late Nineteenth-Century Paris*, New Haven and London: Yale University Press, 1994

John O'Grady, *The Life and Work of Sarah Purser*, Dublin: Four Courts Press, 1996

Manuscript volumes of Bashkirtseff's journals are in the Bibliothèque Nationale, Paris.

Naturalist painter, feminist sympathiser, art critic, sculptor, amateur musician and renowned diarist, Marie Bashkirtseff was an extraordinary 19th-century woman. Born of Russian aristocratic parents who were surrounded by scandal (her mother was separated, her father mysteriously absent), she spent most of her childhood and adolescence travelling in various Italian and French cities until settling eventually in Paris. She died at an early age after having suffered from tuberculosis for some years, but her posthumously published journals were widely recognised as an extraordinary document of the life and aspirations of a 19th-century woman artist and *femme du monde*. First published in France in 1887 and in Britain in 1890, the journal was one of the first published documents to articulate the stresses under which aspirant women professionals lived as they tried to reconcile the demands of a socially constructed "femininity" with the exigencies of a life devoted to art and the pursuit of public recognition. Indeed, Bashkirtseff's serious attitude to her art permeated her diaries and was reflected in the substantial output of work that she managed to produce between 1877 (when she decided to become an artist) and 1884 (the year of her death).

In the year after her death Bashkirtseff was honoured with a posthumous retrospective at the annual exhibition of the Union des Femmes Peintres et Sculpteurs, of which she had been a member. Two rooms containing some 230 pastels, paintings and sculptures were devoted to her alone. To mark the occasion, the Union published a dossier of critical writings containing extracts from some 42 articles that had commented on Bashkirtseff's work and a number of obituaries that had appeared in the general as well as the art and feminist press. From these it is apparent that Bashkirtseff was one of the best-known women artists of her time in Paris, one who was widely regarded as a woman of precocious talent and a suitably "feminine" sensibility. Critics such as Paul de Charry, writing for *Le Pays* in 1883, urged her not to be frightened of raising herself above the standards usually reached by women. She, he believed, had the talent and intelligence to pit herself against her male contemporaries (*Le Pays*, 7 May 1883).

Committed to naturalistic pictorial principles, Bashkirtseff set out to give a "truthful" rendering of contemporary life, painting everyday scenes and people. She identified with such Salon naturalists as Jules Bastien-Lepage and those painters of contemporary life who preferred smoothly polished surfaces and a high degree of finish. She chose to show her work at the Paris Salon and at women-only exhibitions. Most famous among Bashkirtseff's works was her highly polished rendering of a life class in the women's studio at the Académie Julian, exhibited under the pseudonym Mlle Andrey at the Salon of 1881 and now in the Hermitage, St Petersburg; her rendering of a group of Paris street urchins, *The Meeting* (see illustration), shown at the Salon of 1884 and again at the Bashkirtseff retrospective in 1885, when it was purchased by the State; and her *Self-Portrait with a Palette* (Musée Cheret, Nice).

In *The Meeting* Bashkirtseff turns her gaze on to the urban poor with all the unselfconscious detachment of a wealthy woman. Exoticised as representatives of "local colour", her youthful subjects are glamorised, even sentimentalised in the smoothly licked, highly finished surface of the oil painting. It was precisely this palatable and prettified poverty that appealed to contemporary audiences, and the painting was highly acclaimed. In the self-portrait Bashkirtseff shows herself soberly attired, palette in hand, her gaze purposefully directed at the viewer. Her professional identity is stressed here, undermined only by the insertion of a harp behind her, which threatens the seriousness of her painting by making it signify as one among a number of female accomplishments. As her journals show, Bashkirtseff was painfully aware of the difficulties a woman faced in embracing a professional identity. She knew that success was always at some cost to her femininity. Her need to retain the aura of a desirable woman, a suitably feminine woman, at the same time as realising her professional goals, remained a source of continued anxiety for her throughout her short life.

Bashkirtseff's commitment to women's advancement went far beyond the norm for fashionable society artists. Unlike the majority of women of her time, she was sympathetic to the call for female suffrage. She wrote for the important feminist journal *La Citoyenne* under the pseudonym Pauline Orell. Under this name she not only wrote art criticism, on one occasion even offering a critique of one of her own works that she had exhibited under the name of Mlle Andrey, but also important analyses of the constraints on women's art education. She was a vociferous campaigner for the opening of the Ecole des Beaux-Arts to women and a fierce defender of women's capacities and talents. It was not only for the feminist press that she wrote; she also became a regular correspondent for a St Petersburg daily, *Nouveau Temps*, with her articles on contemporary Paris painters.

Bashkirtseff's significance goes far beyond her output as a painter. Hailed as a *cause célèbre* during and just after her lifetime, she has functioned subsequently as an important model and type for successive critics and chroniclers interested in the changing construction of "femininity" in modern times.

TAMAR GARB

Bateman, Hester
British goldsmith and silversmith, 1709–1794

Born in London, 1709. Married John Bateman, a gold chain-maker, 1730; five children; husband died 1760. Entered her first mark as a smallworker at Goldsmiths' Hall, 1761; retired from business, 1790. Died in London, 16 September 1794.

Bibliography
David S. Shure, *Hester Bateman, Queen of English Silversmiths*, New York: Doubleday, and London: W.H. Allen, 1959

Eric J.G. Smith, "Women silversmiths", *Antique Dealer and Collectors' Guide*, xxiii, May 1969, pp.67–71, 81; September 1969, pp.81–7

Philippa Glanville and Jennifer Faulds Goldsborough, *Women Silversmiths, 1665–1845: Works from the Collection of the National Museum of Women in the Arts, Washington, DC*, London: Thames and Hudson, 1990

Arthur Grimwade, *London Goldsmiths, 1697–1837: Their Marks and Lives*, 3rd edition, London: Faber, 1990

Hester Bateman, an illiterate woman, found herself at the age of 51 a goldsmith's widow. From this unpropitious beginning, building on the business that her husband had already established and calling upon the talent of her family (two of her sons were qualified goldsmiths), Bateman successfully expanded both the range and the quantity of the goods that she produced to supply a largely middle-class market using the latest, most cost-efficient manufacturing processes. The firm's deliberate use of new ideas and technology enabled it to compete with the cheap silver and Sheffield plate from Birmingham and Sheffield. Bateman, who must be credited with the energy and foresight to pursue this strategy, was able to build her family business into one of the most successful medium-sized manufactories of its day.

From the surviving contemporary evidence it would seem that Hester's father Thomas Needham and his third wife, Ann, were poor. Hester, unable to sign her name in later life, probably had no formal education. Her first marriage to John Bateman in 1730 was a Fleet ceremony (an inexpensive but often clandestine affair conducted through the auspices of the Fleet Prison clergy), another indication of lack of resources. In 1732 the couple married again, but this time in church. John Bateman as a wire drawer and gold chainmaker did not need to register a mark at Goldsmiths' Hall. His health was not good and Hester may have been involved with the business for some time before he died of consumption in 1760. Her first mark was registered in 1761 and it is probable that it was with the help of her sons, John and William, and the firm's apprentice, John Linney, that she was able to resume manufacturing. The type of products produced in the earliest years of her business were small silver articles such as spoons, wine labels, buttons and seals. On registering her third (1774), fifth (1776), sixth (1778) and seventh (1781) marks she called herself a spoon maker, although as early as 1774 she had used the more general title of plateworker.

Surviving examples of her workshops' production before the late 1770s are comparatively rare, and it has been suggested that she was supplying other goldsmiths who marked the silver as their own before sale. Pieces from the last two decades of the 18th century, stamped for Hester Bateman, are much more common, which suggests increasing output and range of product. Largely in the Neo-classical style, the silver is almost exclusively for domestic use, and includes coffee pots, tea urns, cruets, teapots and salvers among the larger items, as well as smaller objects, for example snuffer trays, goblets, salts, mustards and sugar tongs. At its best the workmanship combined simple manufacturing and decorating techniques to form an elegant if repetitious effect. It used easily worked sheet silver and a repertoire of bright cut, pierced or beaded ornament that could be repeated or recombined in unlimited variations. The Bateman style was not high fashion but it was fashionable. In particular, the middle class appreciated the cost-conscious value of using thin gauge metal and less time-consuming manufacturing methods.

The firm continued to invest in new technology to increase the competitive pricing of its own production. A flatting mill for the working of sheet metal was introduced the year after Hester retired from the business, enabling the Batemans to dispense with the need to buy in sheet and perhaps recoup their investment by supplying other workshops. A steam engine to power the manufacturing processes had been added by 1802, ten years ahead of the most prestigious business of the time, Rundell, Bridge & Rundell, the Royal Goldsmiths. The willingness to exploit the latest technology to produce good-quality silver of a standardised design, which had been the foundation of Bateman's success, ensured the survival of the firm into the mid-19th century.

ANN EATWELL

Baudisch, Gudrun
Austrian ceramist and sculptor, 1907–1982

Born in Pöls, Styria, 17 March 1907. Studied at the Österreichische Bundeslehranstalt für das Baufach und Kunstgewerbe (Austrian State School for Engineering and Arts and Crafts), Graz, 1922–6. Worked under Josef Hoffmann in ceramics department of Wiener Werkstätte, Vienna, 1926–30. Shared a workshop with Mario von Pontoni in Vienna, 1930–36. Married (1) engineer Leopold Teltscher, 1931; (2) Karl Heinz Wittke, 1940. Lived in Berlin, 1936–42. Own pottery in Hallstatt, 1943; became master potter, 1947. Co-founder, with Wittke, of Keramik Hallstatt, 1946; handed over management of business to Erwin Gschwandtner, 1977. Worked with Gmund den Keramik from 1968; founded group "H". Died in Salzburg, 16 October 1982.

Principal Exhibitions
Österreichisches Museum für Kunst und Industrie, Vienna: 1930 (*Werkbundausstellung*)
Milan Triennale: 1957 (gold medal)
International Ceramics Exhibition, Prague: 1964 (silver medal)
Brussels World's Fair: 1965
Faenza Triennale: 1965 (gold medal)
Oberösterreichisches Landesmuseum and Schlossmuseum, Linz: 1967 (individual)
Exposition Universelle et Internationale (Expo '67), Montreal: 1967

Bibliography
L. W. Rochowanski, *Ein Führer durch das österreichische Kunstgewerbe*, Vienna, 1930

Gudrun Baudisch: Keramik, exh. cat., Oberösterreichisches Landesmuseum and Schlossmuseum, Linz, 1967

Die Wiener Werkstätte: Modernes Kunsthandwerk von 1903–1932, exh. cat., Österreichisches Museum für angewandte Kunst, Vienna, 1967

Waltraud Neuwirth, *Wiener Keramik: Historismus-Jugendstil-Art Deco*, Braunschweig: Klinkhardt & Biermann, 1974

Otto Wutzel, *Gudrun Baudisch: Keramik: Von der Wiener Werkstätte zur Keramik Hallstatt*, Linz: OLV, 1980

Waltraud Neuwirth, *Die Keramik der Wiener Werkstätte*, i: *Originalkeramiken, 1920–1931*, Vienna: Neuwirth, 1981

Isabelle Anscombe, *A Woman's Touch: Women in Design from 1860 to the Present Day*, London: Virago, and New York: Viking, 1984

Werner J. Schweiger, *Wiener Werkstätte: Designs in Vienna, 1903–1932*, New York: Abbeville, and London: Thames and Hudson, 1984 (German original, 1982)

Astrid Gmeiner and Gottfried Pirhofer, *Der Österreichische Werkbund*, Salzburg: Residenz, 1985

Wiener Werkstätte: Atelier viennois, 1903–1932: Europalia, exh. cat., Brussels, 1987

E. Michitsch, *Frauen-Kunst-Kunsthandwerk: Künstlerinnen der Wiener Werkstätte*, diploma dissertation, University of Vienna, 1993

S. Plakolm-Forsthuber, *Künstlerinnen in Österreich, 1897–1938*, Vienna: Picus, 1994

Manuscript collection is in the Archiv der Wiener Werkstätte, Österreichisches Museum für angewandte Kunst, Vienna.

Gudrun Baudisch's first artistic training, which made a significant impression on her, was in Graz, in Professor W. Grösser's sculpture classes, which was followed by three years in Professor H. Adametz's pottery classes. Later she combined these two branches of art and applied art and made them her own. Pottery was "her" medium and she stayed faithful to it, creating ever-different variants of it, throughout her artistic life. Her father, a doctor in Styria, encouraged her talents and arranged for her to be trained in Vienna. Through the agency of Vally Wieselthier (q.v.), the leading woman potter of the 1920s, in 1926 Baudisch started at the Wiener Werkstätte on a voluntary basis. Josef Hoffmann soon recognised her exceptional gifts and took her on to the workforce permanently. Aged only 19, Baudisch was the youngest member of the Wiener Werkstätte, but was soon noticed for her independent yet conformist work, which followed the Expressionist trend of the times. This independence manifested itself above all in a vigorous strength not only of form but also of expression and colour. According to W. Mrazek, what really counted was: "not just mastering the current style of the moment and of a particular workshop in form and colour – Expressionism – but also being true to one's own personality".

The circle of ceramists in which it was important to assert and establish oneself consisted of around 60 artists, and since 1920 the ceramics department had been one of the most innovative and productive branches of the Werkstätte. Baudisch's first piece of work, on 3 December 1926, was a figurative composition – a boy holding a bowl festooned with lamps in his upraised arms, flanked by candlestick-shaped forms. This composition, 29 centimetres in height and with a restricted colour scheme of red and blue, shows resolution and a preference for autonomous small sculptures. These qualities were intensified in Baudisch's larger sculptures. She always kept to a limited palette of colours.

Baudisch said of her three years with the Wiener Werkstätte: "I loved doing loads and loads of designs: vases, lamp bases, figures, heads, hollow garden statues …". The inventory in the archives of the Wiener Werkstätte contains more than 80 models. Those she made herself have a stability of character that at first seems far removed from Viennese lightness and ease. Baudisch preferred to model women's heads, torsos and figures, and also animals, taking no particular care to render naturalistic proportions. She combined vessels as bowls with heads on top, or added horses to them to make vases for flowers. Her individual vessels are characterised by simple basic shapes with geometric, irregular decoration, partly in relief, and a lively surface texture. She managed to blend function and pure decoration in a harmonious fashion.

Baudisch's recognition within the Werkstätte reached a high point when she helped to create the catalogue celebrating its 25th anniversary in 1928: *Die Wiener Werkstätte, 1903 bis 1928: Modernes Kunstgewerbe und sein Weg*. Together with Wieselthier she designed an embossed book cover in black and red that united text and figures in a geometric grid in the shape of tiles. Wieselthier did the front cover and Baudisch the back.

The last work that Baudisch made with the Werkstätte, in December 1929, was a kneeling female nude, which was a great success at the Österreichische Werkbundausstellung of 1930. The construction and character of the figure point towards her sculptures in Ankara. The Ankara commission, one of the first she received independently, was to create three terracotta figures for the courtyard and some stucco ceilings for the palace of Kemal Atatürk. She obtained this commission, and later some others in Bregenz and Vienna, through the architect C. Holzmeister.

In 1936 Baudisch moved to Berlin, where she specialised in relief work and sculpture for interiors. With C. Jamöck, an Austrian stucco artist, she created the ornamental ceiling of what became the East German Ministry for Culture (formerly the Reichsmünze), with many small decorations, reminiscent of Dagobert Peche. Subsequent commissions for ceilings included the Quartier Napoléon, the winter garden of the Italian Embassy and the banqueting hall of the Spanish Embassy. Her main themes, which recurred again and again, were plants, flowers, animals and historical coats of arms, mainly in a geometric grid.

In 1946, with her second husband, Baudisch founded Keramik Hallstatt. Here she was able to develop her artistic potential fully once more – the making of hand-made pottery freed her creativity. This creative balance was characteristic of her later years. Everyday pottery, small sculptures and wall decorations in relief were central to her repertoire. In her last few years she worked in her own studio in Salzburg. Baudisch received many commissions for interiors in Salzburg, including the stucco ceiling in the Kammer für Arbeiter und Angestellte, terracottas for the Felsenreitschule and numerous decorations in the Grosses Festspielhaus and in hotels.

GABRIELE FABIANKOWITSCH

Baumann, Elisabeth *see* Jerichau Baumann

Beale, Mary
British painter, 1633–1699

Born Mary Cradock in Barrow, near Bury St Edmunds, Suffolk, eldest child of John Cradock BD, Rector of Barrow, and Dorothy Brunton (or Brinton); baptised 26 March 1633. Married Charles Beale, 8 March 1652; three sons (the first died 1654, two others born 1656 and 1660). Moved to Covent Garden, London, by 1656. Began career as a professional portrait painter, 1670; assisted by husband and sons Charles and Bartholomew. Had two pupils in 1681; later taught Sarah Curtis (Mrs Hoadley). Died at home in Pall Mall; buried at St James's, Piccadilly, London, 8 October 1699.

Bibliography

Sir William Sanderson, *Graphice: The Use of the Pen and Pencil; or, the Most Excellent Art of Painting*, London, 1658

C.H. Collins Baker, *Lely and the Stuart Portrait Painters*, 2 vols, London: Warner, 1912

Gery Milner-Gibson-Cullum, "Mary Beale", *Suffolk Institute of Archaeology and Natural History*, xvi, 1918, pp.238–51; as *Mary Beale*, Ipswich: Harrison, 1918

George Vertue, *Note Books*, i–v; index volume, Oxford: Walpole Society, 1930–55

Elizabeth Walsh, "Mrs Mary Beale, paintress", *Connoisseur*, cxxxi, 1953, pp.3–8

——, "Charles Beale 3ᵈ Book, 1680", *Connoisseur*, cxlix, 1962, pp.248–52

Daphne Foskett, *British Portrait Miniatures*, London: Methuen, 1963

"The Excellent Mrs Mary Beale", exh. cat., Geffrye Museum, London, and elsewhere, 1975

Mary Edmond, "Bury St Edmunds: A seventeenth-century art centre", *Volume of the Walpole Society*, liii, 1987, pp.106–18

Mrs Mary Beale, Paintress, 1633–1699, exh. cat., Manor House Museum, Bury St Edmunds, 1994

Charles Beale's notebook for 1677 is in the Bodleian Library, Oxford (MS Rawl 8° 572); his notebook for 1681, Richard Jeffree's *Mary Beale* and miscellaneous documentary material are in the National Portrait Gallery Archives, London.

Mary Beale was the most prolific and successful of the small number of professional female painters working in Britain in the 17th century. She is also one of the best documented of all 17th-century artists as a result of the extant notebooks in which her husband Charles Beale recorded her portrait commissions, payments, working practice and much other incidental information. Her success was due to various factors, including the help she received from her husband and father, both of whom were amateur artists, the support of a wide circle of friends and the encouragement of the court painter Sir Peter Lely; but, more importantly, her own determination to make painting not just a hobby, as it was for many gentlewomen of the period, but a serious career.

Beale's father John Cradock, Rector of Barrow, Suffolk, must initially have instructed her in the rudiments of drawing and oil painting. He obviously did not consider that she would pursue the interest, because he bequeathed his painting materials to his nephew, the professional artist Nathaniel Thach. Beale's interest would also have been stimulated by the circle of professional artists with whom her father was acquainted, including Thach, Robert Walker and Matthew Snelling. In 1652 she married Charles Beale and it seems likely that she had already become a semi-professional painter by 1656, when the couple were living in Covent Garden, London. Her husband recorded that she was being supplied with artists' colours, and she is included among the small number of female artists in Sir William Sanderson's *The Most Excellent Art of Painting*, published in 1658. Early attributed works, *Lady Penelope Hervey* (c.1655; Manor House Museum, Bury St Edmunds) and *"Catherine Gage"* (c.1658; Christchurch Mansion, Ipswich), are in the style of Anthony van Dyck and suggest the

Beale: *Self-Portrait*, c.1675–80; oil on sacking; 89.5 × 74.3 cm.; Manor House Museum, Bury St Edmunds, Suffolk

influence of Robert Walker, thought to have been Beale's tutor, but, as they do not relate clearly to her mature style, they remain problematic. The earliest references to individual portraits are recorded in the journals of Samuel Woodforde of 1664–5, but no firmly attributed works are known before the small head-and-shoulders portrait of her husband (National Portrait Gallery, London), which can be dated c.1663. Around this time the Beales became friendly with Thomas Flatman, who probably instructed Mary in the art of miniature painting; a few examples survive, two of which are signed "MB" (private collections, repr. London 1975). The frequently illustrated three-quarter-length *Self-Portrait* (National Portrait Gallery), in which the artist is represented holding a canvas depicting her two sons, can be dated c.1666. The likely companion portrait of her husband (Manor House Museum) is the most eloquent and ambitious of the many extant portraits of him, and conveys a sensual charm and relaxed mood that tend to set it apart from the usual formal male portraiture of the period.

In 1670, after Charles had lost his lucrative job as Deputy Clerk in the Patents Office, Beale set herself up as a professional portrait painter, living and working in Pall Mall. In a role reversal not common in the 17th century, she now became the family bread-winner, Charles acting as her assistant, dealing with clients, accounts and artists' materials. She seems rapidly to have acquired a successful practice, with clients from the aristocracy and landed middle-classes and, in particular, the Protestant clergy, many of whom were personal friends of the Beales. One of the earliest of the numerous portraits of clergymen that she painted throughout her career is *John*

Wilkins DD (*c.*1670; Bodleian Library, Oxford). The three-quarter-length seated figure proved a popular formula and was repeated in later portraits of bishops.

It is not known how the Beales became acquainted with Sir Peter Lely, but by 1672 Charles was recording that Lely had visited Mary in her studio, and praised her work. Later he lent her paintings from his extensive collection of old masters, including a van Dyck, to copy and even allowed her to watch him at work in order to study his technique. Beale also built up a lucrative trade making copies of Lely's portraits as well as using his poses in her own compositions, for example *Jane Fox, Lady Leigh, as a Shepherdess* (*c.*1676; Manor House Museum). Her success is indicated by the earnings carefully recorded in her husband's notebooks, which rose from £202 5s. 0d. in 1672 to a peak of £429 for 83 commissions in 1677. Her fees, £5 for head and shoulders and £10 for three-quarter lengths, are similar to those of the lesser male artists of the period.

Although Lely's influence was financially advantageous, it tended to force Beale's talent into a mould for which it was not best suited, and the resulting figures often appear awkward and doll-like as well as being derivative. The same criticism does not apply to the head-and-shoulders portraits for which she is now best known. Painted in warm brown tones and with a characteristic feigned stone oval cartouche surround, the formula can be tediously repetitive, but the sitters are presented in a straightforward and honest manner and with considerable charm. The largest single collection of this type is in the Manor House Museum, Bury St Edmunds. Other examples are at Temple Newsam House (Leeds City Council), Felbrigg Hall, Norfolk (National Trust), and various Cambridge colleges.

In between commissions Beale experimented with portraits of family and friends "for study and improvement", using more informal poses and replacing expensive artists' canvas with sacking and bed ticking. These are among her finest works and include the elegant *Self-Portrait* (*c.*1675–80; see illustration), painted in bright hues and with a decorative style influenced by William Wissing. Her sensitive and noted portrayal of children and adolescents is apparent, for example, in the fancy portrait *Child as Bacchus* (*c.*1679; Manor House Museum) and the profile study of a young girl, possibly Keaty Trioche, one of several studio assistants (*c.*1682; Tate Gallery, London). Beale's practice tended to decline after Lely's death, but she continued to produce works full of character until the end of her career, for instance, *Samuel Woodforde DD* (1692; private collection, repr. London 1975, p.40).

Although Beale was a well-patronised artist in her lifetime, and favourably compared with her male competitors by the 18th-century art historian George Vertue, her reputation subsequently declined, and she has been derided by 20th-century critics for a slavish dependence on Lely. It is apparent that the necessity of having to conform to his style in order to support her family did not allow her to develop her talents fully. The exhibition *"The Excellent Mrs Mary Beale"* held at the Geffrye Museum, London, in 1975 and the more individual and distinguished works that have subsequently come to light have served to enhance her current status.

CHRISTOPHER REEVE

See also Copyists survey

Beauclerk, Lady Diana

British amateur artist, 1734–1808

Born Lady Diana Spencer in London, 24 March 1734, the eldest daughter of Charles Spencer, 3rd Duke of Marlborough. Married (1) Frederick St John, 2nd Viscount Bolingbroke, 1757; divorced 1768; (2) Topham Beauclerk, 1768; one son, two daughters; husband died 1780. Appointed lady-in-waiting to Queen Charlotte, 1761. Died in Twickenham, Middlesex, August 1808.

Bibliography

Beatrice Caroline [Mrs Steuart] Erskine, *Lady Diana Beauclerk: Her Life and Work*, London: Fisher Unwin, 1903

—, "Lady Di's scrap-book", *Connoisseur*, vii, 1903, pp.33–7, 92–8

A. de Vesme and A. Calabi, *Francesco Bartolozzi*, Milan: Modiano, 1928

F. W. Hilles and P. B. Daghlian, eds, *Anecdotes of Painting in England, 1760–1795 … Collected by Horace Walpole: Volume the Fifth*, London and New Haven: Yale University Press, 1937

Martin Hardie, *Water-Colour Painting in Britain*, ed. Dudley Snelgrove, i, London: Batsford, 1966

Hanns Hammelmann, *Book Illustrators in Eighteenth-Century England*, ed. T. S. R. Boase, London and New Haven: Yale University Press, 1975

The Genius of Wedgwood, exh. cat., Victoria and Albert Museum, London, 1995

Lady Diana Beauclerk, designer of figurative subjects, was the best known of the aristocratic artists who achieved fame in late 18th-century Britain, through prints after her works, the use of her designs by Wedgwood and the puffery of her friend Horace Walpole.

"Lady Di", as she was known in her circle, was the eldest daughter of the 3rd Duke of Marlborough, and her talents as a draughtswoman were clear from an early age, one of her brothers preserving a pastel sketch after Rubens that she made at Blenheim Palace aged 11. In 1757 she married the 2nd Viscount Bolingbroke, and in 1764–5 was painted as *Lady Bolingbroke* by Joshua Reynolds, who later got to know her and praised her work. After Bolingbroke obtained a divorce by Act of Parliament in 1768 she immediately married Topham Beauclerk; he was known as a wit and book collector and was one of Dr Johnson's younger friends, and his wife was soon acting as hostess to the leading literary and artistic figures of the day. Shortly after their marriage they moved into a villa on Muswell Hill near London, situated where Alexandra Palace now stands. They fitted this out extremely elegantly and it attracted so many visitors that they had to issue tickets, just as Horace Walpole did at Strawberry Hill, Twickenham. In 1773 they also took a house in Robert Adam's new Adelphi Terrace, London; later they moved their country residence to Little Marble Hill, Twickenham, in which Lady Diana painted some of the walls with flowers and infant bacchanals. This move brought them nearer to Walpole who had become a great admirer of Lady Diana's accomplishments. After her husband's death in 1780 she had, however, to exchange her two residences for a modest, if charming cottage in Richmond, Surrey.

Beauclerk was exceptionally adept with the pencil and she dashed off numerous spirited sketches, particularly of children, which were much appreciated by her extensive network of

Beauclerk: *Gypsies and Female Rustics*, 1783; Victoria and Albert Museum, London

friends and relations. She also worked in watercolour and pastel and made a few etchings. Her first undertaking outside her family circle appears to have been a set of seven large drawings in "soot water", black wash, painted for Walpole to illustrate his tragedy, the *Mysterious Mother* (1768), a work that was kept private for some time because it featured incest. The drawings were hung at Strawberry Hill in a specially designed hexagonal closet built in 1776, which was called the Beauclerk Tower. He added other works by her, including large watercolours (cf. the large *Gypsies and Female Rustics*; see illustration), and the room became a part of the house that he particularly enjoyed showing people. In the fifth volume of his *Anecdotes of Painting*, published in 1780, Walpole paid her some absurd compliments, ranking her with Shakespeare: "is there a pencil in a living hand as capable of pronouncing the passions as our unequalled poet; a pencil not only inspired by his insight into nature, but by the graces and taste of Grecian artists". In an unpublished appreciation he wrote of her genius in music, her ability to draw caricatures and cut them out in paper, and her modelling in wax, which she took up in 1774.

During the 1780s Beauclerk's work became known to a wider public through the use of her designs on Wedgwood pottery and through prints of her drawings. The first of these was a sketch of *Georgiana, Duchess of Devonshire*, engraved in 1778 by Francesco Bartolozzi, the leading stipple engraver, the plate being paid for by her brother the Duke of Marlborough (Vesme and Calabi 1928, no.1066). In 1780 Bartolozzi engraved a charming portrait of Beauclerk's two daughters (*ibid.*, no.1212). In 1791 the printseller W. Dickinson published three more prints by Bartolozzi after her drawings: *Cupids* (*ibid.*, no.400) and a pair both entitled *Children at Play* (*ibid.*, nos 1251–2).

During the 1780s many of her designs, notably of bacchanalian boys, appeared on Wedgwood's productions, from vases to medallions, and some of her designs may have been used even earlier. Wedgwood was very conscious of the prestige attached to the work of well-born amateur artists; his Catalogue of 1789 boasted that "Lady Diana Beauclerk and Lady Templeton, whose exquisite taste is universally acknowledged, have honoured me with the liberty of copying their designs". In 1783 Walpole had an ebony cabinet made for the Beauclerk Tower which was decorated with Wedgwood medallions and 17 of her drawings.

From Wedgwood's wording it is unlikely that he paid for these designs; indeed it seems that Beauclerk, in common with other amateurs, sent him unsolicited drawings. It is possible, however, that the artist, who was short of money in her widowhood, earned something from her illustrations for an edition of Gottfried Augustus Burgher's ballad *Leonora*, published in 1796. These plates were mostly engraved by Bartolozzi and no doubt the artist's drawings were, like those of most amateurs, considerably improved in the engraver's studio, even if they were at the same time robbed of some of their spontaneity (*ibid.*, nos 1687–91). The considerable success of this publication, which reflected the growing taste for gothic romanticism, led to a second, *The Fables of John Dryden* (1797), for which 16 drawings she had made in the early 1790s were engraved by Bartolozzi and others (*ibid.*, nos 1708–20). By the end of the decade Beauclerk appears to have become too infirm to have executed much; a final group of prints after her drawings of infant Bacchuses and similar fancy subjects, issued in colour in 1801–3 by Mariano Bovi, are presumably based on earlier drawings.

DAVID ALEXANDER

Beaux, (Eliza) Cecilia
American painter and graphic artist, 1855–1942

Born in Philadelphia, Pennsylvania, 1 May 1855. Studied under Catharine Ann Drinker, 1871–2; studied at the Van der Wielen School under Francis Adolf Van der Wielen, 1872–4; Pennsylvania Academy of the Fine Arts, 1876–8; National Art Training School under Camille Piton, 1879; under William Sartain, 1881–3, all in Philadelphia; studied at Académie Julian, Paris, under Tony Robert-Fleury, William Bouguereau and Benjamin Constant, 1888–9; under Thomas Alexander Harrison and Charles Lasar in Concarneau, summer 1888; at Académie Colarossi, Paris, under Gustave Courtois and P.A.J. Dagnan-Bouveret, 1889. Subsequently taught at the Pennsylvania Academy of the Fine Arts, 1895–1916, and in The Portrait Class, New York, managed by Elizabeth Cady (Stanton) Blake, 1918–28. Lived in Philadelphia until 1898, then divided the year between apartment in New York and summer home and studio, Green Alley, in Gloucester, Massachusetts. Member, Society of American Artists, 1893; Associate member, 1894, and Member, 1902, National Academy of Design; founder-member, Plastic Club, Philadelphia, 1897; Associée, Société Nationale des Beaux-Arts, Paris, 1900; member, National Institute of Arts and Letters, 1930; American Academy of Arts and Letters, 1933; honorary life member, Arts Club of Washington, DC, 1941. Elected one of the 12 most eminent American women, National League of Women Voters, 1922. Recipient of honorary degrees from University of Pennsylvania, Philadelphia, 1908, and Yale University, New Haven, 1912; lifetime achievement awards from American Academy of Arts and Letters, 1926; National Institute of Arts and Letters, 1941. Died in Gloucester, Massachusetts, 17 September 1942.

Principal Exhibitions

Individual

St Botolph Club, Boston: 1897, 1904
Durand-Ruel Galleries, New York: 1903
Macbeth Gallery, New York: 1910
Corcoran Gallery of Art, Washington, DC: 1912
M. Knoedler & Co., New York: 1915, 1917, 1925
Syracuse Museum of Fine Art, NY: 1931 (retrospective)
American Academy of Arts and Letters, New York: 1935 (retrospective)

Group

Pennsylvania Academy of the Fine Arts, Philadelphia: occasionally 1879–1935 (Mary Smith prize 1885, 1887, 1891 and 1892, Temple gold medal 1900)
Paris Salon: occasionally 1887–1923
Exposition Universelle, Paris: 1889, 1900 (gold medal)
Art Club of Philadelphia: 1891–4 (gold medal 1892)
National Academy of Design, New York: occasionally 1892–1934 (Dodge prize 1893, Saltus gold medal 1914, Proctor portrait prize 1915)
World's Columbian Exposition, Chicago: 1893
Carnegie Institute, Pittsburgh: occasionally 1896–1940 (bronze medal 1896, gold medal 1899)
International Society of Painters, Sculptors and Gravers, London: 1897–1900, 1908
Art Institute of Chicago: 1899, 1921 (Logan gold medal), 1932, 1934
Pan-American Exposition, Buffalo, NY: 1901 (gold medal)
Louisiana Purchase Exposition, St Louis: 1904 (gold medal)
Corcoran Gallery of Art, Washington, DC: occasionally 1907–39
Panama-Pacific Exposition, San Francisco: 1915 (medal of honour)

Selected Writings

"Uncle John's coat", *St Nicholas: An Illustrated Magazine for Young Folk*, xii, 1885, p.203
"Why the girl art student fails", *Harper's Bazar*, xlvii, May 1913, pp.221, 249
"Professional art schools", *Art and Progress*, vii/1, November 1915, pp.3–8
"What should the college AB course offer to the future artist?", *American Magazine of Art*, vii, 1916, pp.479–84
"Sargent", *Boston Transcript*, 2 May 1925
Background with Figures: An Autobiography, Boston: Houghton Mifflin, 1930

Bibliography

"'The Century's American artist series: Cecilia Beaux", *Century Magazine*, n.s., xxvi, 1894, pp.797–8
William Walton, "Cecilia Beaux", *Scribner's Magazine*, xxii, 1897, pp.477–85
Mrs Arthur Bell, "The work of Cecilia Beaux", *International Studio*, viii, 1899, pp.215–22
Pauline King, "Cecilia Beaux", *Harper's Bazar*, xxxii, 11 March 1899, pp.208–9
——, "The paintings of Cecilia Beaux", *House Beautiful*, xi, February 1902, pp.175–81
Homer Saint Gaudens, "Cecilia Beaux", *Critic and Literary World*, xlvii, July 1905, pp.38–9
Hildegarde Hawthorne, "A garden of the Heart: 'Green Alley', the home of Miss Cecilia Beaux", *Century Magazine*, n.s., lviii, 1910, pp.581–7
Leila Mechlin, "The art of Cecilia Beaux", *International Studio*, xli/161, July 1910, pp.iii–x
Anne O'Hagan, "Miss Cecilia Beaux", *Harper's Bazar*, xlv, March 1911, p.119
Gutzon Borglum, "Cecilia Beaux: Painter of heroes", *Delineator*, xcviii, June 1921, pp.16–17

Allison Gray, "The extraordinary career of Cecilia Beaux", *American Magazine*, xcvi, October 1923, pp.61–3, 195–8

Carlyle Burrows, "The portraits of Cecilia Beaux", *International Studio*, lxxxv, 1926, pp.74–80

Alice Booth, "America's twelve greatest women: Cecilia Beaux, who has given back to the world almost as much beauty as she has received from it", *Good Housekeeping*, xciii/6, December 1931, pp.34–5, 165–7

Thornton Oakley, *Cecilia Beaux*, Philadelphia: Biddle, 1943

Henry S. Drinker, *The Paintings and Drawings of Cecilia Beaux*, Philadelphia: Pennsylvania Academy of the Fine Arts, 1955

Catherine Drinker Bowen, *Family Portrait*, Boston: Little Brown, 1970

Elizabeth Graham Bailey, "The Cecilia Beaux Papers", *Archives of American Art Journal*, xiii/4, 1973, pp.4–19

Cecilia Beaux: Portrait of an Artist, exh. cat., Pennsylvania Academy of the Fine Arts, Philadelphia, 1974

Judith E. Stein, "Profile of Cecilia Beaux", *Feminist Art Journal*, iv/4, Winter 1975–6, pp.25–31, 33

Cecilia Beaux: Early Drawings, exh. cat., Alfred J. Walker Fine Art, Boston, 1985

Tara L. Tappert, "Cecilia Beaux: A career as a portraitist", *Women's Studies: An Interdisciplinary Journal*, xiv, 1988, pp.389–411

Cecilia Beaux, exh. cat., Alfred J. Walker Fine Art, Boston, 1990

Tara L. Tappert, *Choices: The Life and Career of Cecilia Beaux: A Professional Biography*, PhD dissertation, George Washington University, 1990

Sarah Burns, "The 'earnest, untiring worker' and the 'magician of the brush': Gender politics in the criticism of Cecilia Beaux and John Singer Sargent", *Oxford Art Journal*, xv/1, 1992, pp.36–53

Cecilia Beaux and the Art of Portraiture, exh. cat., National Portrait Gallery, Smithsonian Institution, Washington, DC, 1995

Tara Leigh Tappert, *Out of the Background: Cecilia Beaux and the Art of Portraiture* (in preparation)

Cecilia Beaux Papers are in the Archives of American Art, Smithsonian Institution, Washington, DC, and in the Archives, Pennsylvania Academy of the Fine Arts, Philadelphia.

At the turn of the 19th and 20th centuries, contemporary art critics identified the international style, grand manner portraits of American upper-class men, women and children painted by Cecilia Beaux as eminently effective expressions analogous to those by John Singer Sargent and William Merritt Chase. Beaux's position as "the one woman in a thousand who has no man standing between her and her productions" (Saint Gaudens 1905, p.39) was based on her recognisable impressionistic style and sympathetic approach to her sitters.

In the 1870s Beaux's initial art training had prepared her for a career in the decorative arts. Her earliest commissions included the execution of carefully drawn lithographs, *Brighton Cats* (1874; private collection, repr. Philadelphia 1974, p.43) and *Cionondon Arctatus* (1875; repr. Ferdinand V. Hayden, *Report of the United States Geological Survey of the Territories*, ii, 1875, see Tappert 1988, p.396); the portrayal of small children on china plates, *Clara Hoopes* (1882; private collection, repr. Tappert 1988, p.396) and *Margaretta Wood* (c.1887; private collection, repr. *Philadelphia: Three Centuries of American Art*, exh. cat., Philadelphia Museum of Art, 1976, pp.426–7); and the creation of copy portraits from photographs, using crayon, watercolour and charcoal, *Frances Morton McCullough* (1883; private collection, repr. Tappert 1990, p.491) and *Edmund James Drifton Coxe* (1886; Pennsylvania Academy of the Fine Arts, Philadelphia). While this work perfected Beaux's drawing skills and developed her abilities in various artistic media, her broad interest in depicting figurative images equally prepared her for a career as a high-style portraitist.

During the 1880s, following training at the Pennsylvania Academy of the Fine Arts, where she refused to study with Thomas Eakins, and after work in a private class, with instruction from William Sartain, Beaux began painting portraits from her own stylistic perspective. Her earliest award-winning portrait, *Les Derniers Jours d'enfance* (1883–4; see illustration), a painting of her sister and nephew, displays the cumulative influences of the Philadelphia art training and indicates an awareness of the art styles in vogue in the 1880s. Her drawing experiences with Van der Wielen and her work as a lithographer are evident in the meticulous details of the setting, while the two artfully arranged flower sprigs in the vase on the table suggest an awareness of Oriental art gained from study with Catharine Ann Drinker, Camille Piton and Sartain. Her understanding of the Aesthetic movement's abstract approach to painting, popularised by James McNeill Whistler, is evident in the portrait's formal arrangement of masses, colours and tones, while her portrayal of a heart-rending moment between mother and child acknowledges her appreciation of the psychological realism employed by Eakins. Beaux's portraits in the 1880s exhibited either the "art for art's sake" tenets of the Aesthetic movement (*Ethel Page as Undine*, 1885; private collection, repr. Tappert 1990, p.506), the realist's documentation of everyday life (*Reverend William Henry Furness*, 1886; First Unitarian Church, Philadelphia) or the decorative artist's incorporation of various techniques – the impasto of china painting in the background of *George Burnham* (1886; Philadelphia Museum of Art) and the reliance on the accuracy of photography in *Fanny Travis Cochran* (1887; Pennsylvania Academy of the Fine Arts).

Even though Beaux was emerging as a gifted portraitist in Philadelphia in the 1880s, she decided to spend the year 1888–9 in France, enhancing her artistic credentials. She pursued formal art training in Paris at the Académie Julian and Académie Colarossi, executing life studies such as *Figure Study, Standing Male* (1888–9; private collection, repr. Tappert 1990, p.508) and rendering biblical configurations such as *Supper at Emmaus* (1888–9; Pennsylvania Academy of the Fine Arts), work that taught her anatomy and composition. She further augmented her academy studies with copy work at the Louvre, creating her own version (1888; untraced) of Velázquez's *Infanta Marguerite*. During the summer of 1888 Beaux worked in the art colony at Concarneau on the Brittany coast, painting in a plein-air style under the tutelage of Thomas Alexander Harrison and Charles Lasar. In *Twilight Confidences* (1888; private collection; studies for this painting repr. in Philadelphia 1974, p.63) and the portrait of *Thomas Alexander Harrison* (1888; private collection, repr. Carter Ratcliff, "Americans Abroad", *Art & Auction*, October 1994, p.123) her palette brightened, her brushwork became more fluid and she experimented with colour values and light. While Beaux also produced a few landscapes and figure studies that summer, her overriding interest in painting "heads" helped her to recognise that her talents were best applied to portraiture.

The first painting that she made after this decision was the idealised, Aesthetic-style and dark-toned portrait of *Louise Kinsella* (1889; untraced), which was layered with

Beaux: *Les Derniers Jours d'enfance*, 1883–4; oil on canvas; 116.8 × 137.2 cm.; Museum of American Art of the Pennsylvania Academy of the Fine Arts, Philadelphia: Gift of Cecilia Drinker Saltonstall

autobiographical meaning. Beaux had rejected a marriage proposal that summer and had decided to pursue an art career single-mindedly, a commitment that she examined in her portrayal of the ethereal blonde. Created for the Paris Salon of 1889, this picture is one of the few instances in Beaux's oeuvre where she clearly addressed the personal and professional issues of her own life. Before returning to Philadelphia in the summer of 1889 Beaux travelled to Cambridge, England, to fulfil portrait commissions for members of the Darwin family. While there she discovered pastel as a medium especially good for women's portraits (*Maud (Du Puy) Darwin*, 1889; private collection, repr. Tappert 1990, p.519), a medium that she continued to use for a few years after she returned to Philadelphia (*Helen Biddle Griscom*, 1893; Pennsylvania Academy of the Fine Arts).

In the 1890s the numerous portraits that Beaux painted of various members of her family solidified her style and provided her with opportunities not only to portray "likeness" but also to embed into her paintings the prevailing roles and characteristics of American upper-class men, women and children. While the serene portrayal of her sister, *Aimée Ernesta (Beaux) Drinker* (1891; private collection, repr. Philadelphia 1974, p.71), and the cocky image of her nephew, *Cecil* (1891; Philadelphia Museum of Art), recall the precise dark-toned paintings of the 1880s, the incorporation of underlying messages regarding the proper demeanour of a thriving matron and the self-confidence of a well-bred boy suggest a new thematic direction. By the time Beaux painted portraits of her niece, *Ernesta with Nurse* (1894; Metropolitan Museum of Art, New York), and a cousin, *Sita and Sarita* (1894; Musée d'Orsay, Paris), a facile impressionistic style had emerged, as had even more sophisticated thematic content. These two paintings capture the moment an innocent toddler is in the safe guidance of a protective nurse, and portray the timeless contemplation of a beguiling beauty and her enigmatic cat. The following year, in the painting *New England Woman* (1895; Pennsylvania Academy of the Fine Arts), a portrait of an older second cousin, Beaux executed a bravura display of the various hues in the colour white, and a convincing portrayal of a self-lessly devoted woman dedicated to the values of a bygone era. Beaux experimented with perspective and the illustration of a dimly rendered background setting in *Ernesta and Philip* (1897; private collection, repr. Bowen 1970, p.42), a double portrait of her niece and nephew that conveys the relationship of an older sister to a younger brother. Beaux also painted *At Home* or *Man with a Cat* (1898–9; National Museum of American Art, Smithsonian Institution, Washington, DC), another brilliant white painting of her brother-in-law, Henry Sturgis Drinker, depicted as a genteel man at leisure.

The lessons that Beaux learned in painting portraits of her family were applied throughout the 1890s to the numerous images she created of Philadelphia's genteel upper class. Similar issues of beauty, intelligence and sexuality are embedded in *The Dreamer* (1894; Butler Institute of American Art, Youngstown, OH), a companion piece to *Sita and Sarita*, which displays the artist's skill in the use of the colour white and her ability to create perspective in a dimly sketched background space. *Mrs Thomas A. Scott* (1897; private collection, repr. Tappert 1990, p.575), a portrait of a wealthy Philadelphia matron surrounded by colonial furnishings, recalls the old-fashioned values associated with *New England Woman*. The double portrait of two young sisters, *Gertrude and Elizabeth Henry* (1898–9; Pennsylvania Academy of the Fine Arts), is painted from the same high-point perspective as *Ernesta and Philip*, while the bright green parrot perched on Gertrude's finger adds an Aesthetic colour note similar to the dash of red on the cane in *Cecil* and the pink hat in *Ernesta with Nurse*.

In addition to the individual sitters that Beaux portrayed in the 1890s, she also painted several double portraits that reveal some of her own attitudes and biases. *Mrs Beauveau Borie and Her Son Adolphe* (1896; Amon Carter Museum, Fort Worth) is an ambivalent rendition on the mother and child theme that displays the artist's conflicted feelings about motherhood. The regal presentation, *Mrs Clement A. Griscom and Daughter Frances Canby* (1898; Pennsylvania Academy of the Fine Arts), a portrait of an aristocratic mother and debutante daughter, focuses on the sumptuous fur cloaks worn for a social event rather than the relationship of the two women. The portrait of *Dorothea and Francesca* (1898; Art Institute of Chicago), Beaux's aesthetic interpretation of sisterhood, captures the elegant dance steps of the children of Richard Watson Gilder, editor of *Century Magazine*, and is also one of the finest examples of her ability to combine portraiture and narrative.

Around 1900 Beaux's clientele widened to include sitters in Boston, New York and Washington, DC, and when she built Green Alley in 1905 people throughout the USA began coming to her for their portraits. She preferred to paint studies of people that she knew, but as her clientele expanded beyond her own social world she began to rely on the genre's current styles and conventions. While she still incorporated the Aesthetic, Impressionist and academic styles, she also added the classical elements of 18th-century British grand manner portraiture, for which there was then a resurgent interest. Her portraits were filled with identifiable references to lineage, race, status and proper gender roles, as well as her own preoccupations with beauty, intelligence and social or professional standing. Her particular expertise was an ability to balance the sitter's characteristics – both personal and societal – with the costumes and settings to create a straightforward presentation.

In the first decade of the 20th century Beaux explored different stylistic approaches and fitting narrative messages. Her portraits in the manner of John Singer Sargent, *Harriet Sears Amory* (1903; private collection, repr. Tappert 1990, p.569) and *Henry Parsons (Jimmy) King, Jr* (1905; Cape Ann Historical Museum, Gloucester, MA), were depictions of pure and innocent children – a shy young girl in a rich kimono and a self-assured boy of seven in a lavish interior. She created canvases of young women in their roles as hostesses and debutantes – the sumptuous *Mrs Larz Anderson* (1900; The Society of the Cincinnati, Anderson House), the elegant *Bertha Vaughn* (1901; Radcliffe College) and the Reynolds-like *Dorothy Perkins* (1909; Butler Institute of American Art). She dramatised maternal affection in the Whistler-inspired rendition of the elongated *Mrs Alexander Sedgwick and Daughter Christina* (1902; private collection, repr. *Background with Figures* 1930, p.258) and in the impressionistic interpretation of *Mrs Theodore Roosevelt and Daughter Ethel* (1902; private collection, *ibid.*, p.228). Beaux portrayed older women as society matrons – the glowing *Mrs Richard Low Divine* (1907; Columbus Museum of Art), selflessly devoted maiden aunts – the nearly abstract *Aunt Eliza Leavitt* (1905; private collection, repr. Philadelphia 1974, p.103) and unmarried professional women committed to their vocations – the monochromatic study of *Nurse M. Adelaide Nutting* (1906; Alan Mason Chesney Medical Archives, Johns Hopkins Medical Institutions, repr. Tappert 1990, p.577). The men that she depicted were manly (*A. Piatt Andrew*, 1902–3; Cape Ann Historical Museum) and thoughtful (*Richard Watson Gilder*, 1902–3; private collection, repr. *Background with Figures* 1930, p.210).

During the 1910s Beaux fulfilled portrait commissions for various institutions and individuals and also executed a number of paintings for her own satisfaction. In the official commissions, which were generally formal renditions, she regularly incorporated emblematic elements. The intelligent leadership of *Honorable Sereno E. Payne* (1912; US Capitol, Office of the Architect of the Capitol, House Ways and Means Committee, US House of Representatives, Washington, DC) was indicated by the magnificent, boldly lit head, while the educational career of *Dean Andrew Fleming West* (1916; Princeton University Art Museum) was highlighted by accoutrements of his profession – an academic robe and a marble bust in the background. Her lofty ambitions in the sketches of *Henry James* (1911; National Portrait Gallery, Washington, DC) and *George Arliss* (1913; American Academy of Arts and Letters) were to capture the soulful essence of a creative thinker and the theatrical élan of a vibrant actor. In fulfilling a promise to her nephew, Henry Sandwith Drinker, to paint a portrait of him and his bride when he married, Beaux completed *Portraits in Summer* (1911; private collection, repr. Tappert 1990, p.543). This picture – styled after 18th-century British grand manner portraits – suggests the beginning of a day and a new life together. Twenty years after Beaux painted

Sita and Sarita and *The Dreamer*, she again returned to the theme of the modern woman, painting two of her finest portraits, *After the Meeting* (1914; Toledo Museum of Art), a highly patterned picture depicting the purposeful Dorothea Gilder at the close of a suffragist meeting, and *Ernesta* (1914; Metropolitan Museum of Art), a cool image of Ernesta Drinker as an ideal of regal privilege and elegant simplicity.

In the years surrounding World War I Beaux expressed patriotic sentiment through a variety of artistic renditions. On the eve of the war she painted *The Portent* (1914; Bryn Mawr College Art Collection), a classical feminine idealisation of liberty and patriotism. In *Lieutenant Leslie Buswell* (1918; private collection, repr. *Exhibition of Paintings and Sculpture Contributed by the Founders of the Galleries*, exh. cat., Grand Central Galleries Painters and Sculptors Gallery Association, New York, 1923, no.203) she paid recognition to a neighbour in Gloucester, Massachusetts, memorialising his war service as an ambulance driver for the American Field Service, representing him in a khaki Red Cross uniform with the Croix de Guerre that he had been awarded in 1915 in full display on his jacket. At the end of the war she was one of eight American artists commissioned by the National Art Committee to paint "portraits of all the great men of this war – those who have led up to a military success and led up to peace". Beaux travelled to Europe to fulfil this assignment, painting the portraits of *Cardinal Desiré Joseph Mercier* (1919), *Admiral Sir David Beatty* (1919–20) and *Premier Georges Clemenceau* (1920; all National Museum of American Art), formal images infused with a sense of political idealism.

In the 1920s and 1930s, while the initial waves of modernism were making an impact on American art, Beaux continued to paint portraits in her established style. An accident on the streets of Paris in 1924 – Beaux broke her hip – significantly slowed her production. The following year she completed a sombre painting of herself, a *Self-Portrait No.4* (1925; Uffizi, Florence), surrounded by paint pots and palette, the accoutrements of her profession. Her last public commission was the portrait of *Dr Rufus Ivory Cole* (1933; Rockefeller Institute for Medical Research), an airy interpretation of the man in his laboratory coat.

TARA LEIGH TAPPERT

Beckett, Clarice

Australian painter, 1887–1935

Born in Casterton, Victoria, 21 March 1887. Studied at the National Gallery Art School, Melbourne, under L. Bernard Hall and Frederick McCubbin, 1914–16; studied in the studio of Max Meldrum, *c*.1917. Moved to Beaumaris, a suburb of Melbourne, 1919; lived there for the rest of her life, caring for her aging parents. Taught briefly at a girls' school at Mount Macedon, *c*.1927. Died of pneumonia, 6 July 1935.

Principal Exhibitions

Society of Twenty Melbourne Painters: from 1917

Athenaeum Gallery, Melbourne: 1924–32 (annuals), 1936 (retrospective)

Melbourne Society of Women Painters and Sculptors: from 1926

Bibliography

Clarice Beckett: Memorial Exhibition, exh. cat., Athenaeum Gallery, Melbourne, 1936

Arnold Shore, "Australia's early women artists", *The Herald* (Melbourne), 1 June 1957

Homage to Clarice Beckett, exh. cat., Rosalind Humphries Gallery, Melbourne, 1971

Rosalind Hollinrake, *Clarice Beckett: The Artist and Her Circle*, Melbourne: Macmillan, 1979

Janine Burke, *Australian Women Artists, 1840–1940*, Collingwood, Victoria: Greenhouse, 1980

Caroline Ambrus, *The Ladies' Picture Show: Sources on a Century of Australian Women Artists*, Sydney: Hale and Iremonger, 1984

M.A. McGuire, "Life and your imagining: The art of Clarice Beckett", *Australian Journal of Art*, v, 1986, pp.90–103

Mary Eagle, *Australian Modern Painting Between the Wars, 1914–1939*, Sydney and London: Bay, 1989

Important Australian Women Artists, exh. cat., Melbourne Fine Art Gallery, 1993

Clarice Beckett, exh. cat., Ivan Dougherty Gallery, Sydney, 1995

Joan Kerr, ed., *Heritage: The National Women's Art Book*, Sydney: Dictionary of Australian Artists/Craftsman House, 1995

The artist Colin Colahan once likened Clarice Beckett to Jane Austen, but one might think more readily of a character from a novel by Anita Brookner – quiet lives lived desperately. Clarice Beckett lived an ordered life in suburban Melbourne, caring for her elderly parents. She existed on the periphery of a somewhat bohemian circle of artists and writers, followers of the artist and teacher Max Meldrum. The group was shunned by most of the art community because of its adherence to an unfashionable style that favoured the application of paint to a point of near abstraction. Her work, mainly exhibited at the Athenaeum in Melbourne between 1924 and 1932, was not well received and few works were sold in her lifetime. Despite these setbacks, she continued to paint in her own way and did not bend to pressure. Under the influence of Meldrum, Beckett learned that "painting resulted from a series of optical truths based on tonal relations" (Hollinrake 1979, p.11). Meldrum taught that there was an order to natural perception; that, if allowed, the eye would notice shapes and space and their tonal values.

Beckett's style varied little in the years she was painting and exhibiting – a fact for which she has been repeatedly criticised. The main shift occurred in the late 1920s and early 1930s, as in *Sandringham Beach* (*c*.1935; see illustration), when she began to add touches of brighter, sharper colour to her work. At first glance her work would seem to be monotonous but this is because it requires a surrender in the viewer that, once given, generates instead a sensation like that of meditation. Her paintings have a serenity about them both in their pictorialist vision – blurred and soft, without hard edges – and in their commonplace subject matter. They capture something so transient we are hardly sure that we have seen it. A moment of beauty, which, if we blink, is suddenly gone.

Early mornings shrouded in mist; twilight landscapes in the dusk; summer fields where a mirage of glaring light hangs over the land and trees seem to hover over grass; a wet, watery street – nothing special – just an impression; sunset in Port

Beckett: *Sandringham Beach*, c.1935; oil on canvas; 55.8 × 50.9 cm.; National Gallery of Australia, Canberra

Phillip Bay, children and mothers bathing, their bodies fusing with their watery reflections; a boat lying moored in the shallows; the end of the garden where the fence has started to collapse and chickens run free; another sunset with a point of land almost disappearing; an old boat shed, men idly sitting; a rainy evening in the city, commuters hurrying through wet streets; a beach sunrise, the sand and sea and sky an orange ambrosia; a velvety, misty evening of blue haze; the beach – white sand and touches of delicious blues and yellows and greens; once more, night reflections of lights on the watery streets. They are moments so brief, so fleeting; they are memories, glimpsed and caught, and for that reason contain a poignancy that is hard to locate. There is a loneliness, a sadness that suffuses her work. Her titles, too, were briefly descriptive of mood: *Early Morning Beaumaris* (c.1925), *Naringal Landscape* (c.1925), *Shallows* (c.1927), *Smoke Haze Beaumaris* (c.1931; all private collections, repr. Hollinrake 1979). Most works are neither signed nor dated. (There are examples of Beckett's work in many Australian public collections, including the National Gallery of Australia, Canberra.)

Rising early, Beckett would go down to the bay at Beaumaris, a seaside suburb of Melbourne, to paint. Travelling with a cart that held the small wooden box containing all her brushes, boards and paints, the lid performing the dual role of easel for her boards, she would paint quickly, catching the elusive effects of light and mood. She thinned the paint to the consistency of watercolour and it is partly this that gives her work its softly luminous look. Describing her aim as an attempt to give "an exact illusion of reality", they are, as Mary Eagle has written "a form of visual poetry", hovering tentatively over the canvas (Eagle 1989, p.97). And hovering too is that sense of an ever-present melancholy: a vulnerability mixed with a calm that, even if one were in total ignorance of the details of the artist's life, would still be felt. According to accounts of her death by pneumonia at the age of 48, caught while painting one stormy night, she appeared to have made no struggle to survive.

CANDICE BRUCE

Beer, María Eugenia de
Flemish painter and printmaker, active 1630s–1652

Daughter of the painter and printmaker Cornelio de Beer, who came to Spain from Utrecht in the 1630s. Active in Madrid, Murcia and Lorca. Died after 1652.

Bibliography
Juan A. Ceán Bermudez, *Diccionario de los más ilustres profesores de las bellas artes en España*, 6 vols, Madrid: Ibarra, 1800; reprinted New York: Kraus, 1965

Carmen G. Pérez-Neu, *Galéria universal de pintoras*, Madrid: Nacional, 1964

Matilde López Serrano, *Presencia femenina en las artes del libro español*, Madrid: Fundación Universitaria Española, 1976

J. Carrete and J. Maluquer, *Cuaderno de aves para un príncipe*, Barcelona: Gili, 1982

A.E. Pérez Sánchez, "Las mujeres 'pintoras' en España", *La imagen de la mujer en el arte español: Actas de las terceras jornadas de investigación interdisciplinaria*, Madrid: Universidad Autónoma de Madrid, 1984, pp.73–86

Juan Carrete and others, *El grabado en España (siglos XV al XVIII)*, Summa Artis, xxxi, Madrid: Espasa-Calpe, 1988

Like most women artists of her time, María Eugenia de Beer became an artist because of her family ties, belonging to a group that constituted an important element in Spanish Baroque engraving. Because of the absence of professional engravers in Spain, the demand for foreign skills led to the arrival of a significant number of French, German and Flemish artists, accompanied by their families. In this way the field of the printed Spanish book was opened up for women engravers, among whom were such fine artists as Ana de Heylan and Beer herself. She was a dominant figure in the field of Spanish Baroque engraving, surpassing in this field her father and teacher Cornelio. Ceán Bermudez (i, pp.123–4) described her as a "pupil of her father Cornelio. Lived in Madrid in the mid-17th century, engraving with delicacy several works worthy of the capital".

Two tendencies are evident in Baroque art: the intellectual humanism seen in emblems and *impresas*, and the scientific empiricism of art as a way of recording nature. The work of Beer is demonstrably part of the humanism of Spanish Baroque, as seen particularly in her illustrations for books such as the extraordinary *Cuaderno de aves para el príncipe* (Banco de España, Madrid), undertaken during the 1630s for Prince Baltasar Carlos. The *Cuaderno*, her best-known work, unites prints of 23 different species of birds in a work unique of its kind in Spain. Although some scholars have regarded it as one of the rare instances of the scientific empiricism of the Baroque in Spain, all of Beer's work can be seen rather as forming part of the predominant humanist movement in the world of book illustration in Spanish circles, linked to emblems and *impresas*. The dedication explains the allegorical character of the chosen birds, according to their symbolic meanings: crane, peacock, owl. The intention of the album – to give enjoyment to the young prince – is clear from this, and from Beer's words in the dedication: "Judge now with the birds, until you kill lions". The work finds its origins in the moralising context of the Spanish ornithologist and friar, Ferrer de Valdecebro, *Govierno General, Moral y Político, hallado en las aves más generosas y nobles, sacado de sus generales virtudes y propiedades*. Beer's scientific illustrations are characterised by their Northern precision.

A series of frontispieces and illustrations survive by Beer (all Biblioteca Nacional, Madrid), some designed by herself, others drawn by renowned painters, such as the portrait by Juan Bautista Maino de Diego de Narbona for his book *Annales tractatus iuris* (1642). In Madrid in 1640 the second volume of *Los oprobios que en el árbol de la Cruz oyó Cristo cuando dijo las siete palabras* by Fray Francisco de Rojas has a frontispiece by de Beer; under the title is an olive tree from whose branches hang portraits of *Philip IV*, his son *Baltasar Carlos* and the *Conde Duque*, which seem to be inspired by those by Velázquez. Beer also carried out the frontispieces of Francisco Aguado's *Sumo Sacramento de la Fe, Tesoro del Nombre Christiano* (1640) and Fray Gaspar de la Cruz's *Patria del Hijo de Dios y dicha de sus gloriosos solares Bethlem y Jerusalem* (1642). In 1643 Don Gregorio de Tapia y Salcedo's *Exercicios de la gineta* was published, illustrated with 28 plates by Beer, influenced by the so-called *Telas Reales* by Mazo y Pareja, in a somewhat naïve style contrasting with the delicacy and elegance of her portrait of *Prince Baltasar Carlos*. In the same year she engraved the *Guerra de Flandes*, translated by Basilio Varen. She also undertook a complicated frontispiece with allegorical and biblical scenes for the *Praxis totius moralis Parochis* (1644) by José Rocafull. In 1645 Diego Tovar Valderrama dedicated to the Prince his *Instituciones políticas*, which included a portrait of him executed by María Eugenia. In the same year she engraved the coat of arms of Gabriel Pérez de Barrio "Iustitia administratur trabaxo virtutes quibus recte". Her last known work is a portrait of the venerable *Alfonso Rodríguez* for *Vida, hechos y doctrina del venerable Alfonso Rodríguez* (1652), written by Father Francisco Colin.

MARÍA RUTH PÉREZ-ANTELO

Bell, Vanessa
British painter and designer, 1879–1961

Born Vanessa Stephen in London, 30 May 1879; daughter of Leslie Stephen and sister of Virginia Woolf. Studied under Sir Arthur Cope RA at his school in Kensington, London, 1896–1900; under John Singer Sargent at Royal Academy Schools, London, 1901–4; briefly attended Slade School of Fine Art, London, 1904. First visited Italy, 1902. Moved to 46 Gordon Square, Bloomsbury, 1904. Organised Friday Club, 1905 (resigned 1914). Married writer Clive Bell, 1907; sons Julian born 1908 (killed in Spain, 1937), Quentin born 1910; separated from husband. Moved to Charleston, Firle, Sussex, with Duncan Grant, 1916; daughter Angelica born 1918. Contributed to Roger Fry's Omega Workshops, London, 1913–19. Member of London Group, 1919. Taught at Euston Road School, London, from 1938. Visited Paris frequently from c.1920. Rented La Bergère, near Cassis, southern France, 1927–39. Lived at Charleston, 1939–45; in Islington, London, 1949–55; also travelled widely. Member, Society of Mural Painters, 1950. Died at Charleston, 7 April 1961.

Principal Exhibitions

Individual
Independent Gallery, London: 1920 (with Duncan Grant and Robert Lotiron), 1922
Cooling Galleries, London: 1930
Thomas Agnew and Sons, London: 1932 (with Duncan Grant and Keith Baynes)
Lefevre Galleries, London: 1934, 1937
Leicester Galleries, London: 1941 (with Frank Dobson and Algernon Newton)
Adams Gallery, London: 1956, 1961 (retrospective)
Arts Council Gallery, London: 1964 (retrospective)

Group
London Salon of the Allied Artists Association: 1908, 1912
New English Art Club, London: from 1909
Alpine Club Gallery, London: 1910–12 (with Friday Club), 1913–14 (with Grafton Group)
Grafton Galleries, London: 1912 (*Second Post-Impressionist Exhibition*)
Galerie Barbazanges, Paris: 1912 (*Quelques indépendants anglais*)

Whitechapel Art Gallery, London: 1914 (*Twentieth-Century Art*)
Mansard Gallery, Heal & Sons, London: 1917 (*New Movement in Art*)
Kunsthaus, Zürich: 1918 (*Englische Moderne Malerei*)
London Group: from 1919
London Artists Association: 1926
Marie Sterner Galleries, New York: 1928 (*Modern English Pictures*)

Selected Writings
Notes on Virginia's Childhood: A Memoir, ed. Richard F. Schaubeck, Jr, New York: Hallman, 1974
Vanessa Bell's Family Album, ed. Quentin Bell and Angelica Garnett, London: Norman and Hobhouse, 1991
The Selected Letters of Vanessa Bell, ed. Regina Marler, London: Bloomsbury, and New York: Pantheon, 1993

Bibliography
Recent Paintings by Vanessa Bell, exh. cat., London Artists Association, 1930 (foreword by Virginia Woolf)
Catalogue of Recent Paintings by Vanessa Bell, exh. cat., Lefevre Galleries, London, 1934
Quentin Bell and Stephen Chaplin, "The ideal home rumpus", *Apollo*, lxxx, 1964, pp.284–91
Vanessa Bell: A Memorial Exhibition of Paintings, exh. cat., Arts Council of Great Britain, London, 1964
Quentin Bell, *Virginia Woolf: A Biography*, 2 vols, London: Hogarth Press, and New York: Harcourt Brace Jovanovich, 1972
Vanessa Bell: Paintings and Drawings, exh. cat., Anthony d'Offay Gallery, London, 1973
Richard Cork, *Vorticism and Abstract Art in the First Machine Age, 1: Origins and Development*, London: Gordon Fraser Gallery, and Berkeley: University of California Press, 1976
Vanessa Bell, 1879–1961: An Exhibition to Mark the Centenary of Her Birth, exh. cat., Mappin Art Gallery, Sheffield, 1979
Diane Filby Gillespie, "Vanessa Bell, Virginia Woolf and Duncan Grant: Conversation with Angelica Garnett", *Modernist Studies: Literature and Culture*, iii, 1979, pp.151–8
Vanessa Bell, 1879–1961: A Retrospective Exhibition, exh. cat., Davis and Long, New York, 1980
Simon Watney, *English Post-Impressionism*, London: Studio Vista, 1980
Colin Franck Ball, *Vanessa Bell: A Bibliography*, Canterbury: Canterbury College of Art, 1983
Frances Spalding, *Vanessa Bell*, London: Weidenfeld and Nicolson, and New Haven, CT: Ticknor and Fields, 1983
Vanessa Bell, 1879–1961, exh. cat., Vassar College Art Gallery, Poughkeepsie, NY, and elsewhere, 1984
Gillian Elinor, "Vanessa Bell and Dora Carrington: Bloomsbury painters", *Woman's Art Journal*, v/1, 1984, pp.28–34
The Omega Workshops: Alliance and Enmity in English Art, 1911–1920, exh. cat., Anthony d'Offay Gallery, London, 1984
Diane Filby Gillespie, *The Sisters' Arts: The Writings and Paintings of Virginia Woolf and Vanessa Bell*, Syracuse, NY: Syracuse University Press, 1988
Mary Ann Caws, *Women of Bloomsbury: Virginia, Vanessa and Carrington*, New York and London: Routledge, 1990
Jane Dunn, *A Very Close Conspiracy: Vanessa Bell and Virginia Woolf*, London: Cape, and Boston: Little Brown, 1990
Gillian Naylor, ed., *Bloomsbury: Its Artists, Authors and Designers by Themselves*, London: Pyramid, and Boston: Little Brown, 1990
Richard Shone, *Bloomsbury Portraits: Vanessa Bell, Duncan Grant and Their Circle*, 2nd edition, London: Phaidon, 1993
Lisa Tickner, "The 'left-handed marriage': Vanessa Bell and Duncan Grant", *Significant Others: Creativity and Intimate Partnership*, ed. Whitney Chadwick and Isabelle de Courtivron, New York and London: Thames and Hudson, 1993, pp.65–81
Jan Marsh, *Bloomsbury Women: Distinct Figures in Life and Art*, London: Pavilion, 1995

Hermione Lee, *Virginia Woolf*, London: Chatto and Windus, 1996

Vanessa Bell e Virginia Woolf: Disegnare la vita, exh. cat., Civiche Gallerie d'Arte Moderna e Contemporanea, Ferrara, 1996

See also numerous articles in *Charleston Newsletter*, 1982–9; *Charleston Magazine*, 1990–; and catalogues produced by Bloomsbury Workshop, London, 1988–. The Charleston Papers are in the Tate Gallery Archives, London.

Vanessa Bell is thought of mainly as a "Bloomsbury" artist, from that intellectual and witty group gathered around Virginia and Leonard Woolf, Vanessa and Clive Bell in London, and Duncan Grant in Sussex, in the early and middle years of the 20th century, with Roger Fry as the mediator between things and arts French and English. Her work seemed sometimes overshadowed, for others and for herself, by her lifelong association with the prolific painter Duncan Grant, and sometimes by the extraordinary fame of her sister Virginia Woolf. Bell was an artist with a very remarkable family, life and talent: that the last has waited until the late 20th century to be recognised is due, to a large extent, to the vivid and celebrated details of the collective biography of Bloomsbury, as well as to the widespread passion for Virginia Woolf's writing and being.

Desperately and lengthily loved by the critic and painter Roger Fry, whose acknowledged praise of her work contrasts with his lukewarm support of Carrington (q.v.), the other woman painter in the Bloomsbury group, Bell herself had an abiding and frequently selfabasing love for the homosexual Duncan Grant, which is thought of as a major consideration in her own attitude to her work. She did much of her painting at Charleston, a home that she shared with her husband Clive Bell and Grant and, at times, his various lovers; her particular torment over her necessarily unequal love affected her work. It meant that she took ultimate refuge in that work, which, like her life, was rich in aesthetic relations of all sorts, whether at Charleston or in the south of France, where she painted at Cassis alongside Duncan (whose family had a home there), overcome by the light and colours in contrast to the dark of England. About her long love of and problematic relationship with Duncan Grant, she was endlessly courageous and self-denying ("It seems better not to feel more than one can help", she said to him on 5 February 1930), determining to go on with her work as the only solution to living "without getting upset". As she wrote in a letter to Roger Fry: "It will be an odd life … but it seems to me it ought to be a good one for painting." There is a sense of melancholy hanging over the finest of her pictures, a sense of loneliness, frequently even a sense of exile, of not being at one with her surroundings.

As for the public reaction to her work, it was certainly at a high point in the 1930s, when she had several solo exhibitions, accepted a commission to paint panels for the liner *Queen Mary* and did the sets for ballets by Frederick Ashton and Ethel Smyth. Bell was no longer experimenting with pure abstraction, as she had earlier, nor was she associated with the avant-garde movements of her time, such as Surrealism; she was and remained something of a quiet classic. She is perhaps best known, however, for her very simple designs for the jacket covers of many of Virginia Woolf's books for the Hogarth Press, such as *Jacob's Room* (1922), *To the Lighthouse* (1927), *Three Guineas* (1938), *Granite and Rainbow* (1938) and *Between the Acts* (1941). These designs show not only a profound understanding of the works, but a sense of colour and design all her own. She was also gifted at collaborative work: with Roger Fry's Omega Group she decorated tables and other furniture; with Duncan Grant she decorated houses and the little church at Berwick.

Her own work has many parts to it. Her whole life long, she did portraits, among which her faceless portrait of her sister in an armchair at Asheham (*Virginia Woolf*, 1912) stands out as singularly close to the spirit of Virginia Woolf. After a first period of figurative painting, Bell experimented with a non-representational series of decorations and paintings that may seem, to some, the highlight of her career of portraitist, mural painter, set designer and still-life painter. Her still lifes are among her most successful works, in large part because of her extreme sensitivity to colours and forms. That sensitivity is visible in such paintings as *46 Gordon Square* (1911; Charleston, East Sussex), with the three greenishyellow apples arranged in a long octagonal Chinese platter, the space around them emphasising the sparseness and a kind of discretion. This still life is set diagonally in the lower left-hand corner of the painting, on a ledge bordered by an iron-work railing between whose upright poles a fence outside can be glimpsed, with some thin brownish branches of the tree behind it just visible above – this opening of the inside on to the world beyond being central to the picture. The strange and plunging perspective remains somehow as quiet as the colours, subtle as the play of inside and out. It is often true that Bell experiments more with the oddness of perspective in her earlier works than in her later ones, which are altogether less abstract. On many occasions she painted further pictures of windows, revealing her fascination with the interplay between inner and outer scenes (e.g. *Garden Window, Roquebrune*, 1960; Royal West of England Academy, Bristol).

The British critic Simon Watney, regretting the return of Bell and Grant from their abstract experimental paintings of, say, 1911–14, to a more classical tradition, blames this to some extent on their great interest in France and in such French painters as Cézanne and Matisse. They could have remained at home in their influences, he said, and not treated Britain and British art as a lesser thing than France and French art.

Bell's immense and permanent attraction to France includes the light of the south, of Provence, as well as French art. Writing to Roger Fry on 24 March 1920, she explains what he knows already, that "one is always convinced one must live in France when one gets there. So many things that have to be repressed in one seem to expand and develop" there. The connections with France and French art cannot be overstated. Bell's attachment to Cézanne in particular ("the holy man of Aix") was notable – she would rush over to Paris to see an exhibition, she said to Duncan, because "before long you will have to go to Finland and Germany to see him". Although in her eyes Matisse, Segonzac and Picasso were all wonderful, Cézanne represented for her, as for all the Bloomsbury group, the pinnacle of art: his apples, his mountains, his eye – he is "so extraordinarily solid and alive" (letter to Roger Fry, 3 April 1918).

That, of course, is the way enthusiasts may well feel about Vanessa Bell the person and the painter. The preservation of solidity, interestingly enough, may be one of the most crucial things about her art, for, as she wrote to Roger Fry on 19 September 1923, when there had been the most intense excitement about colour a few years previously, so that many artists were tempted to change everything into colour: "It certainly made me inclined also to destroy the solidity of objects, but I wonder whether now one couldn't get more of that sort of intensity of colours without losing solidity of objects and space."

In any case, Bell was always addicted to the colourful, in her art and her life, setting off her own beauty with an Italian blue hat that would have been out of place in London, say, or enjoying a pair of red espadrilles in Provence precisely for their hue. When Duncan sent her a basket of oranges and lemons, for instance, she immediately reacted as a painter, defying contemporary custom:

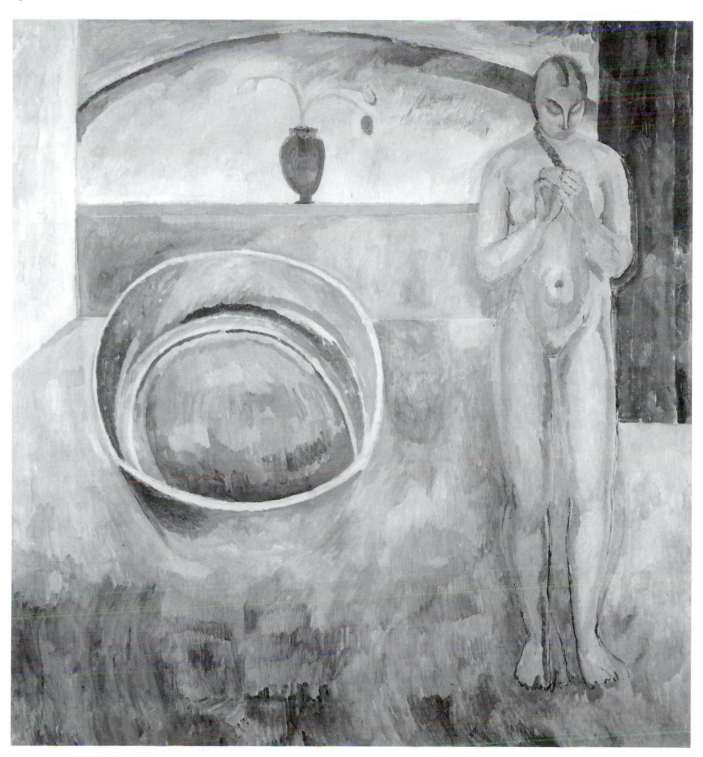

Bell: *The Tub*, 1917; oil and gouache on canvas; Tate Gallery, London

They were so lovely that against all modern theories I suppose I stuck some into my yellow Italian pot and at once began to paint them. I mean one isn't supposed nowadays to paint what one thinks beautiful. But the colour was so exciting that I couldn't resist it [25 March 1914].

Her feeling for colour was intense; but her feeling for feeling is what sets her apart from other equally talented colourists. Writing to Leonard Woolf on 22 January 1913, she entered the argument about significant form (a term used by Roger Fry, and Clive Bell after him) with her own point of view clearly stated: "it can't be the object of a great artist to tell you facts at the cost of telling you what he feels about them". And indeed the greatest of her paintings are perhaps those slightly mysterious scenes with female figures, lending themselves to multiple readings, for example *Studland Beach* (1912; Tate Gallery, London), with the hieratic tall figure standing against the sea, observed by figures faceless and crouching; *The Conversation* (1913–15; Courtauld Institute Galleries, London), with its three women conversing in the frame of a window; and *The Tub* (1917; see illustration), Bell's response to the long pictorial tradition of women bathers, especially the tub paintings of Edgar Degas and, nearer home, Duncan Grant's several paintings of women standing or crouching in their tubs. In Bell's painting the naked woman stands meditatively, with the three flowers in the background against the windowsill, analysed by some commentators as representing Vanessa's difficult position with Duncan and his lover then at Charleston. The almost circular tub stands upended in the empty interior, its top circular line echoing the arch of the window opening, against which stands the vase. It is oddly reminiscent of the series of Carpaccio's *St Ursula* paintings in Venice, of which John Ruskin was so enamoured: the lily on the window ledge a sort of symbol of the Annunciation here, as there; a sense of a self-involvement mysterious in its import; and the Oriental quality of the woman's face, as she plaits her blond hair. Although the naked woman is modelled on Mary Hutchinson, Clive Bell's mistress, and originally wore a shirt, the present statement comes over as a mixture of solitude and the kind of brave stance that requires a self-aware meditation. The strength of feeling comes through inescapably in the figure of the woman alone, standing, with a clarity of profile stark against the background.

Fry, who never stopped loving or admiring Bell, found her art far more valid and lively than his own, praised her sense of colour, calling her a realist by contrast with Grant, whose vision, he said, came from within. In fact, her vision appears to come as much from within as from without, but this is not immediately apparent. There seems visible in her work a certain kind of compassion, as well as strength. These qualities were also present in her dealings with others, as demonstrated in her letter to Carrington the painter, who was very much in Bell's situation, loving and living with the homosexual Lytton Strachey. After his death Bell wrote, in a letter of 25 January 1932, that Carrington should come and "talk to us, for we loved him very much, enough to understand ... But I know it is useless. I know that the many people who loved him cannot help you, who loved him more, and perhaps it is selfish to write, but I think you will forgive me and understand." Although Carrington was to kill herself six weeks later, the

sincerity of Bell's feelings and, indeed, her ability to understand, are visible.

It has often been said that Bell's tormented relationship with Grant provoked her self-denigration and excessive humility towards her own work, which Grant seems often to have valued more than she herself did. Already in 1911, Vanessa Bell wrote to Roger Fry: "But all my pictures are failures now I'm very much depressed about them". Yet her self-doubt gives depth to her self-portraits without detracting from the strength and shine of her best work.

MARY ANN CAWS

Benedetta
Italian painter and writer, 1897–1977

Born Benedetta Cappa in Rome, 1897, into a family of the Waldensian sect. Took a diploma as a kindergarten teacher, and wrote poetry from an early age. Studied in the studio of painter Giacomo Balla, where c.1919 she met Filippo Tommaso Marinetti, the founder of Futurism. Married Marinetti, 1923; three daughters. Lived in Milan until 1925, then settled in Rome, making trips with Marinetti to Paris, Egypt, Argentina and Brazil. Ceased painting after husband's death in 1944, and dedicated herself to the promotion and diffusion of the works of Futurism. Died in Venice, 15 May 1977.

Principal Exhibitions

Venice Biennale: 1926, 1930, 1932, 1934, 1936
Galleria Pesaro, Milan: 1927 (*34 pittori futuristi*)
Casa del Fascio, Bologna: 1927 (*Grande Mostra dei pittori futuristi*)
Imola: 1928 (*Grande Mostra d'arte futurista*)
Palazzo delle Esposizioni, Rome: 1929 (*Arte Marinara*)
Quadriennale d'Arte Contemporanea, Rome: 1931, 1935, 1939
Circolo Artistico, Trieste: 1931 (*Aeropittura futurista*)
Galleria Promotrice, Turin: 1932 (*Amici dell'arte*)
Galerie de la Renaissance, Paris: 1932 (*Prampolini et les aeropeintres futuristes italiens*)
Palazzo Strozzi, Florence: 1967 (*Arte moderna italiana, 1915–1935*)

Selected Writings

Le forze umane, Foligno: Campitelli, 1924 (novel)
Viaggio di Gararà: Romanzo cosmico per teatro, Milan: Morreale, 1931 (novel)
Astra e il sottomarino: Vita trasognata, Naples: Casella, 1935; reprinted Montepulciano: Grifo, 1991 (novel)
"Le futurisme", *Cahiers d'Arts*, xxv, 1950, pp.9–16

Bibliography

F. Orestano, *Opera letteraria di Benedetta*, Rome: Edizioni futuriste di "Poesia", 1936
B. G. Sanzin, *Benedetta, aeropoetessa e pittrice futurista*, Rome: Rassegna Nazionale, 1939
Enrico Crispolti, *Il mito della macchina e altri temi del futurismo*, Trapani: Celebes, 1969
Simona Weller, *Il complesso di Michelangelo*, Pollenza: La Nuova Foglio, 1976
Künstlerinnen international, 1877–1977, exh. cat., Schloss Charlottenburg, Berlin, 1977

Benedetta: *Great X*, 1930; Museé d'Art Moderne de la Ville de Paris

L'altra metà dell'avanguardia, 1910–1940: Pittrici e scultrici nei movimenti delle avanguardie storiche, exh. cat., Palazzo Reale, Milan, and elsewhere, 1980

E. Crispolti, "Benedetta", *Ricostruzione futurista dell'universo*, exh. cat., Turin, 1980

Claudia Salaris, *Le futuriste: Donne e letteratura d'avanguardia in Italia (1909–1944)*, Milan: Edizione delle Donne, 1982

Any evaluation of the life and work of Benedetta must take into consideration her link with Marinetti, although it would be misleading to see her as entirely subservient to him in her career as an artist. She seems in fact to have been an independent figure of great importance in Second and Late Futurism, both in the literary and the artistic spheres; according to the critics, she was among the most creative figures of the avantgarde. In 1934 Marinetti summed up his wife's artistic personality in some verses dedicated to her: "Beny has already taken the tonality of the infinite/and the same airy and serene agility/of a brush that animates the canvas, in the breeze, aeroplane ..." (*Poesie a Beny*, Turin: Einaudi, 1971).

Benedetta's early interest in psychology and teaching are expressed in her earliest *tavole tattili* (tactile pictures), created in the years 1918–20, at the beginning of her relationship with Marinetti. These works represent a singular poetic experiment in which the imagination is stimulated by surfaces made up of diverse materials. This transgressive synthesis between poetry and art, which fitted in well with the typographical revolution proposed by Italian Futurism, inspired Marinetti to write the "Manifesto del tattilismo" (1921), in which he sought a fusion between art, poetry and life through art action.

In the first numbers of the review *Dinamo* (Rome, year 1, nos 1–12, 1919) Benedetta published a composition entitled *Spicologia* (sic) *di un uomo* and *Salotto + Strada, Compenetrazione*. The work uses "free words", in which logical discourse is dis-coordinated, thus disrupting all the conventions of traditional printing. In 1923 Benedetta officially joined the Futurist Movement and occupied herself with a review of Marinetti's novel *Gli indomabili*. Her writing debut was in 1924, when she published the novel *Le forze umane*. Although this work contains autobiographical material, this never declines into the psychologising but rather becomes sublimated, by means of purely graphic signs determined by the development of the narrative, into a spiritual conception of reality and of art, from which emerges the myth of Woman as Creator.

Also in 1924 Benedetta produced her first pictorial works, *Speeding Train by Night* (repr. Pontus Hulten, *Futurismo e futurismi*, Milan, 1986, p.326) and *Speed of a Motorboat* (repr. Florence 1967, p.300), in which the teaching of Giacomo Balla is evident: according to the principle of trajectory, lines of force and action are expressed by spirals and triangles, but although the colours are strong, emphasising the sense of motion, they are also soft and translucent, indicative of the sensitive and lyrically evocative woman that Benedetta revealed herself to be.

In 1927 Benedetta signed, with Marinetti, Azari and Fillia, a crucial document for the mechanical art of Second Futurism: the manifesto in the catalogue of the Futurist exhibition held at the Galleria Pesaro, Milan. The consequent "new Futurist sensibility", which was centred on a "passion for profundity, for life, for liberty and for complexity", was accompanied by an ever-more intensive use of many different materials, although Benedetta did not herself follow this course.

With the signing of the Futurist Airpainting Manifesto in 1929, a new chapter opened in Benedetta's artistic career. She was now impelled to research into the dynamic simultaneity produced by figurative and geometric forms when seen through aerial perspective. Her pictures *Rhythms of Rocks and Sea* (ibid., p.300), the *Great X* (1930; see illustration) and, successively, *Taking Quota* (repr. exh. cat., Venice Biennale, 1932, pl.94) and *Lyricism of Flight* (ibid., pl.95), offer a diverse recomposition of panoramic fragments through movement, light and geometric figures; the controversial and difficult Futurist painting of the period is here dissolved into a suggestive lyricism. To an even greater extent, Benedetta's contemporaneous paintings of panoramic North African landscapes – *The Desert* and *Algerian Salt Lakes* – give a sense of the infinite: apparent reality is transfigured in a new pictorial atmosphere, and the forms are oriented dynamically in space, so that they lose their naturalistic connotations and become enriched with strong emotional content.

The art of Benedetta pays particular attention to the psychology of colour and of form, qualities that are found also in her second literary work, *Viaggio di Gararà* of 1931, in which art as Creation is placed at the summit of her conceptual journey. Allegory and symbol here correspond to the sonorous, graphic and chromatic signs examined by Expressionism and Surrealism.

By this time Benedetta had achieved artistic independence, and was creating light, fluid compositions. In the second half of the 1930s she detached herself from attempts to render the dynamics of motion, and moved to a magical-fantastic painting more clearly derived from the work of Prampolini, and which was directed to a mystic and cosmic vision of the landscape. The paintings *Meeting with the Island* (private collection, repr. Maurizio Calvesi, *Il futurismo*, Milan: Fabbri, 1967, p.165) and *Mystic Interpretation of the Landscape* (repr. Milan 1980, p.123) lead to the complex imaginative orchestration of her wall paintings for the Palazzo delle Poste, Palermo. Her novel *Astra e il sottomarino* (1935), from the same period, is a pure meditation on the phantasm of love, in which reality, the imaginary, the unconscious and the dream follow and intersect one another. This mysticism is clear also in her painting *Mount Tabor* of 1935, in which the contemplative element is complemented by the charm of the colour.

Benedetta also made ceramic reproductions of her own paintings, and her set designs for Marinetti's theatrical works (*L'oceano del cuore*, 1927; *I prigionieri e l'amore*, 1925; *Simultanina*, 1930) demonstrate other aspects of her innovative imagination. In spite of the inaccessibility of her works – most of which are scattered in private collections or "hidden" in ministries and public organisations – her reserved and retiring nature – she never sought solo exhibition opportunities – and the complexities of her writings, Benedetta reveals herself as a subtle, refined, yet vital artist of uncommon audacity. In her works she avoided the aridity often imputed to the Futurists, through the translucency and softness of her colours and the appeal to the senses, but above all through her entirely feminine interior perspective.

LUCIA CAPPELLOZZA

Benglis, Lynda
American sculptor, 1941–

Born in Lake Charles, Louisiana, 25 October 1941. Studied at H. Sophie Newcomb Memorial College for Women, Tulane University, New Orleans, under Ida Kohlmeyer, 1960–64 (BFA in painting); Yale University Summer School, Norfolk, 1963; Brooklyn Museum Art School, New York, 1964–5; New York University (teaching certificate 1965). Married painter Gordon Hart, 1965; divorced 1970. Assistant professor of sculpture, University of Rochester, New York, 1970–72; assistant professor, Hunter College, New York, 1972–3; visiting professor, California Institute of the Arts, Valencia, 1974 and 1976; Princeton University, 1975; visiting artist, Kent State University, Ohio, 1977; Skowhegan School of Painting and Sculpture, Maine, 1979; visiting professor, University of Arizona Department of Art, Tucson, 1982; School of Visual Arts, Fine Arts Workshop, New York, 1985–7, 1991 and 1992. Visited Greece frequently from 1952, India from 1979. Recipient of Guggenheim fellowship, 1975; Australian Arts Council award, 1976; National Endowment for the Arts (NEA) grants, 1979 and 1990; National Council of Arts Administration grant, 1989. Lives in New York, East Hampton and Ahmadabad, India.

Selected Individual Exhibitions
University of Rhode Island, Kingston: 1969
Paula Cooper Gallery, New York: 1970, 1971, 1973, 1974, 1975, 1978, 1980, 1982, 1984, 1987, 1990, 1994
Hayden Gallery, Massachusetts Institute of Technology, Cambridge: 1971
Hansen-Fuller Gallery, San Francisco: 1972, 1973, 1974, 1977
Texas Gallery, Houston: 1973, 1975, 1979, 1980, 1981, 1984
The Clocktower, New York: 1973
Margo Leavin Gallery, Los Angeles: 1977, 1980, 1982, 1985, 1987, 1989, 1991
Fuller Goldeen Gallery, San Francisco: 1979, 1982, 1986
Dart Gallery, Chicago: 1979, 1981, 1983, 1985
Galerie Albert Baronian, Belgium: 1979, 1981
University of South Florida, Tampa: 1980 (touring retrospective)
Heath Gallery, Atlanta: 1980, 1985, 1991, 1992, 1994
Museum of Art, University of Arizona, Tucson: 1981 (retrospective)
Tilden-Foley Gallery, New Orleans: 1984, 1986, 1989, 1991
Alexandria Museum of Art, LA: 1987 (retrospective, with Keith Sonnier)
Richard Gray Gallery, Chicago: 1990, 1993
High Museum of Art, Atlanta: 1991 (*Dual Natures*, touring retrospective)
Auckland City Art Gallery, New Zealand: 1993
Harwood Foundation Museum, Taos, NM: 1994–5 (*Chimera*, touring)

Selected Writings
"Why have there been no great women artists: Social conditions can change", *Art News*, lxix, January 1971, p.43

Bibliography
Klaus Kertess, "Foam structures: The recent work of Lynda Benglis", *Art and Artists*, vii, May 1972, pp.32–7
Robert Pincus-Witten, "Lynda Benglis: The frozen gesture", *Artforum*, xiii, November 1974, pp.54–9
Hermine Freed, "Video and Abstract Expressionism", *Arts Magazine*, xlix, December 1974, pp.67–9
Cindy Nemser, "Four artists of sensuality", *Arts Magazine*, xlix, March 1975, pp.73–5
Barbara Baracks, "Artpark: The new esthetic playground", *Artforum*, xv, November 1976, pp.28–33
Tennessee Williams, "Lynda Benglis", *Parachute*, Spring 1977, pp.7–11
Lucy R. Lippard, "Report from New Orleans: You can go home again: Five from Louisiana", *Art in America*, lxv, July–August 1977, pp.22–5
"Interview: Lynda Benglis", *Ocular: The Directory of Information and Opportunities for the Visual Arts*, iv, Summer 1979, pp.30–43
Donald B. Kuspit, "Cosmetic transcendentalism: Surface-light in John Torreano, Rodney Ripps and Lynda Benglis", *Artforum*, xviii, October 1979, pp.38–40
Robert James Coad, *Between Painting and Sculpture: A Study of the Work and Working Process of Lynda Benglis, Elizabeth Murray, Judy Pfaff and Gary Stephan*, PhD dissertation, New York University, 1984
Lynda Benglis, Keith Sonnier: A Ten-Year Retrospective, 1977–1987, exh. cat., Alexandria Museum of Art, LA, 1987
Robert C. Morgan, "American sculpture and the search for a referent", *Arts Magazine*, lxii, November 1987, pp.20–23
Lynda Benglis: Dual Natures, exh. cat., High Museum of Art, Atlanta, and elsewhere, 1991
Amy Jinkner-Lloyd, "Materials girl: Lynda Benglis in Atlanta", *Arts Magazine*, lxv, May 1991, pp.52–5
Marcia E. Vetrocq, "Knots, glitter and funk", *Art in America*, lxxix, December 1991, pp.92–7
Lynda Benglis: From the Furnace, exh. cat., Auckland City Art Gallery, 1993

Lynda Benglis studied painting with Ida Kohlmeyer as an undergraduate art student, and her mature work resists classification as either painting or sculpture. Her first series of objects, begun in 1966, erased the distinction between figure and ground and recorded the artist's process of applying the medium, wax and pigment, to the support, a narrow, vertical masonite panel. *Excess* (1971; Walker Art Center, Minneapolis) is typical of these wax paintings. Using a brush the same width as the masonite, Benglis stroked layers of coloured beeswax from the centre of the panel out to its rounded ends, allowing the thick medium to separate into organic shapes that reveal successive layers of colour. Benglis makes reference to the human body, in the scale of the piece (an arm's length), its labial central form where the brush strokes originated, and the translucent, skin-like surface of the wax. The repetitive, sensuous gestures traced in the wax subtly inform the work as an investigation of feminine sexuality.

In the late 1960s Benglis did away with the problem of support and ground altogether in a series of poured latex floor works. Contemporary critics situated such works as *Bounce* (1969; private collection, repr. *Artforum*, viii, September 1969, p.60) at the intersection of painting and sculpture, outside the modernist concern of purity in medium. That the latex hardened where it flowed, an apparent record of the process of making the work, led to Benglis's association with Process artists, an alignment she resisted. She asserted that she was interested in the qualities of the rubber medium itself, and that her production was more complex than her interpretation of "process" as a series of steps, executed consecutively in a predetermined order. A photo spread in *Life* magazine (27 February 1970) overtly linked Benglis's technique to Jackson Pollock's drip paintings, while Benglis herself evoked her

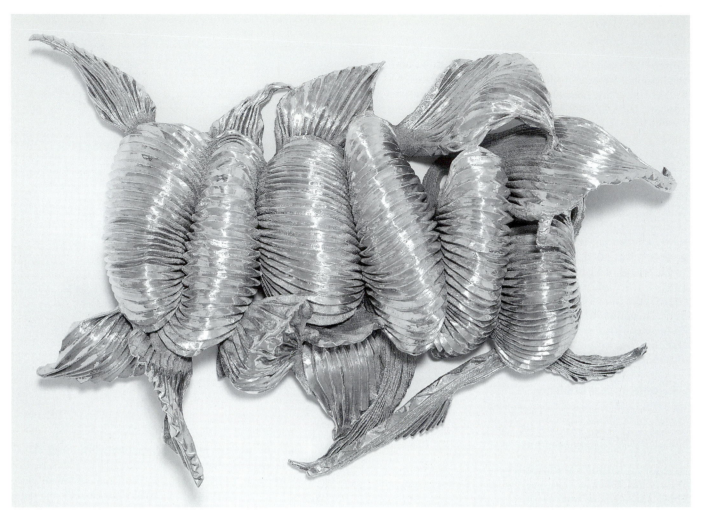

Benglis: *Chubasco*; aluminium, stainless steel; 193 × 248.9 × 61 cm.

Abstract Expressionist forebears in *Odalisque (Hey, Hey Frankenthaler)* (1969; artist's collection).

In the early 1970s Benglis resolved sculptural and pictorial issues in objects made of polyurethane foam that occupied space on the floor or extended into a room from a wall. In *For Carl André* (1970; Modern Art Museum of Fort Worth, TX) she filled the corner of a room with layers of grey foam. Like the work of that Minimalist sculptor, this piece is located assertively on the floor, with the sculptural base eliminated. In 1971 she constructed on-site a series of temporary multiple wall sculptures, which extended aggressively into the viewer's space. She establishes a tension between the nature of the foam that tends to flow, and the residual shape of the wood and wire armature. These cantilevered shapes, such as *Adhesive Products* (1971; Walker Art Center, destroyed, repr. Kertess 1972, p.36), are pictorial and sculptural at once in their concern with surface and occupation of space.

Benglis continued her investigation of the relation of surface and structure in her series of *Sparkle Knots*, beginning in 1972. Like the earlier works, the process of production can be traced in the final piece. In *Epsilon* (1972; Philadelphia Museum of Art) the cotton bunting that wraps the aluminium-screen tubular form is visible at the loose ends of the knot, and unpainted plaster is left showing on the surfaces not covered with paint and glitter. That the *Sparkle Knots* are decorative, even kitschy in their gaudy colours and glitter, and made of mundane materials invites comparison with the desire of some contemporary feminist artists to articulate an essentially feminine art vocabulary. Benglis's knotted forms, however, insistently deny the appearance of a central void, the "core imagery" identified by Judy Chicago (q.v.), Miriam Schapiro (q.v.) and others as a characteristic of art made by women. But in the cosmetic artifice of their surfaces, the knots do foreshadow later feminist theorising of femininity as masquerade.

Benglis made videotapes concurrently with the knots, between 1972 and 1976. She explored the formal qualities of the medium by layering several generations of video images and using video static as part of her vocabulary of images. In *Mumble* (1972; Video Data Bank, Chicago) she thematises the contingency of reality by playing narrative tricks on the viewer: there is an evident disjunction between what Benglis as narrator says is happening on screen and what we see, and her description of what is happening off screen is unreliable and ultimately unverifiable.

Benglis's investigation of artifice in terms of gender is made graphic in the staged self-portraits that adorn invitations and advertisements for her solo exhibitions in 1974. Although she claims empathy with the women's movement of the time, in her collaboration with the sculptor Robert Morris for a pair of announcements (in her own, she poses with her back to the camera, in platform shoes with jeans around her ankles) she risked feminist accusations that she was permitting herself to be sexually exploited. Benglis claimed to be the master of her own sexual identity, posing nude and holding an outsized dildo in an *Artforum* advertisement (November 1974). Mocking the idea that an artist needs a penis to win critical acclaim, she incited criticism that engaged with contemporary feminist debates over pornography. Benglis in each of these instances also critically examined the cult of celebrity that made the artist more important than the work she produces.

Beginning in 1975, Benglis made larger knots covered with metallic flecks. Lighting was important both for its effects on the surfaces of the knots and for the shadows cast on the wall around them in the installation of *7 Come 11* (1976; repr. Kuspit 1979, p.38). In the late 1970s she untied her forms to make a series of wall objects whose scale and shape evoke the female body. *Megesti* (1978; private collection, repr. *Arts Magazine*, January 1979, p.14) is hourglass-shaped, covered with gold leaf. Benglis's decision to use gold was inspired by the spike in gold prices in 1974, and these works are ironic in their reference to the preciousness of the metal, and of fine art. They are all about cosmetic beauty, as light plays across the gilded surfaces of the objects.

Benglis continued to be concerned with the effects of light on a metallic surface in the pleated forms that she made in the 1980s. The regularly folded support is twisted into knots or fans, and sprayed with gold or silver, then bronze, copper and chrome after the market value of the precious metals dipped. The complex shiny surface diffuses light, which makes a regular shape indefinite, as in *One Dime Blues* (1980; private collection, repr. Atlanta 1991, p.91), or a convoluted form such as *Twin Coach* (1988; *ibid.*, p.98) more baroque. The later pleated objects set up a tension between feminine and masculine qualities: they seem to be made of a fabric that billows or drapes, although the material is hard and rigid.

It is too easy, though, to identify an artist's problematic as simply centred on the issue of gender because she is female. With its gaudy complexity, *Diablo* (1990; repr. *Artforum*, xxix, November 1990, p.168), one of a series of pleated aluminium wall sculptures called *Trophies* (1990), makes ironic comment on the acquisition of works of art as a marker of cultural acumen. Benglis's production over the course of her career has investigated formal issues of painting and sculpture, the distinction between high and low art forms, and the preciousness of the art object.

MARGO HOBBS THOMPSON

Benincampi, Teresa
Italian sculptor, 1778–1830

Born in Rome, 1778. Studied under the Neo-classical sculptor Antonio Canova. Associate member, Accademia di San Luca, Rome; member (as poet), Accademia degli Arcadi. Died in Rome, 22 February 1830.

Bibliography

Charlotte Eaton, *Rome in the Nineteenth Century*, 3 vols, Edinburgh, 1820

David Silvagni, *La corte e la società romana nei secoli XVIII e XIX*, 3 vols, Florence and Rome, 1881–5; as *Rome: Its Princes, Priests and People*, 3 vols, London: Stock, 1885–7

Valentino Martinelli and Carlo Pietrangeli, *La Protomoteca Capitolina*, Rome, 1955

Although little is known about Teresa Benincampi's sculptural oeuvre, which consisted largely of terracotta and marble portrait busts signed "Teresa Benincampi Romana", it is clear from contemporary testimony that she was considered to be one of the leading portrait sculptors of early 19th-century Italy. During her sojourn in Rome in the years following the restoration of Pope Pius VII in 1814, that indefatigable travel writer Charlotte Eaton praised Benincampi's bust portrait of the poet *Caesino* (untraced) and various other works by the artist that, alas, she does not specifically name. In describing the sculptural profession in Restoration Rome, Eaton ranks Antonio Canova, Bertel Thorvaldsen and Johann Gottfried Schadow as the most famous practitioners, but from the myriad students and imitators of these three leading artists in the Eternal City she singles out only Benincampi for discussion:

> I shall mention only ... the Signora Teresa Benincampé [sic], whose beautiful bust of Caesino, and many of her other works, need only to be seen to be admired; I cannot, at the same time, refrain from offering my sincere tribute of respect, to her distinguished talents and independent mind, or expressing my fervent wish, that her success may be proportional to her deserts [Eaton 1820, iii, p.315].

Like the French sculptor Marie-Anne Collot (q.v.), Benincampi's gender limited her professional options to the "lesser" genre of portraiture. Women sculptors were extremely rare in early 19th-century Italy, and her precedent was no doubt of great importance to such American sculptors as Anne Whitney (q.v.) and Harriet Hosmer (q.v.), who both practised sculpture in Rome in the middle decades of the century.

During the early years of the 19th century, and under official papal sponsorship, Benincampi's teacher Canova initiated a hall of fame series of bust-length sculptural portraits of the heroes of Italian culture to be placed around the walls of the Pantheon. The degradation of the Papacy, the flight of many nobles and all the cardinals and the exactions of the French occupation of 1808–14 had created tremendous financial hardships for the Roman artistic community, and with this series Canova hoped to provide employment for the numerous impoverished sculptors in the city. The Pantheon project led to the creation of Teresa Benincampi's most important sculpture, the *Aldo Manuzio*, executed c.1815–16. Manuzio, a Venetian philologist and publisher who died in Rome in 1597, was chosen as a subject for a Pantheon bust by a consultative committee of the Accademia di San Luca, of which Canova was Principe and Benincampi an associate member. The slight tilt of Manuzio's head and the rather taut facial features convey a strong sense of intellectual power and confidence. The portrait was commissioned from Benincampi by the Roman publisher Filippo De Romanis, who wished to do honour to his illustrious predecessor. It was very probably

Canova who suggested Benincampi to De Romanis for the commission.

By 1820 there were more than 60 busts of Italian cultural worthies crowding the walls of the Pantheon, so Pope Pius VII and Ercole Consalvi, the Cardinal Secretary of State, decreed that a new museum, the Protomoteca Capitolina, be established on the Capitoline Hill as an adjunct of the Capitoline Museum to house the collection. Benincampi's *Aldo Manuzio* was admitted by the Capitoline Conservators decree of 17 February 1821, the first bust to be so honoured (Martinelli and Pietrangeli 1955, pp.11–13).

In addition to her professional artistic activities, Benincampi was a leading figure of the Roman intelligentsia and also a well-known poet. A friend of the celebrated salon hostess Maria Pizzelli, Benincampi read verses in praise of her friend at a posthumous, polylingual *accademia* held in Pizzelli's honour on 16 September 1806. As a leading poet, Benincampi was a member of the famous Accademia degli Arcadi that had been established at the end of the 17th century by Queen Christina of Sweden (Silvagni 1881–5, ii, pp.566–7).

CHRISTOPHER M.S. JOHNS

Benoist, Mme
French painter, 1768–1826

Born Marie Guillemine Leroulx-Delaville in Paris, 18 December 1768; father a government official. Studied first with Elisabeth Vigée-Lebrun, from 1781 or 1782, then trained under Jacques-Louis David, from 1786. Married royalist lawyer Pierre Vincent Benoist, 1793; two sons, born 1794 and 1796, one daughter, born 1801. Honorary member, Société des Arts de Gand (Ghent), 1809. Died in Paris, 8 October 1826.

Principal Exhibitions
Exposition de la Jeunesse, Paris: 1784–8, 1791
Paris Salon: 1791, 1795–6, 1800, 1802, 1804 (gold medal), 1806, 1810, 1812

Bibliography
Marie-Juliette Ballot, *Une élève de David: La Comtesse Benoist, L'Emilie de Demoustier, 1768–1826*, Paris: Plon, 1914
Women Artists, 1550–1950, exh. cat., Los Angeles County Museum of Art, and elsewhere, 1976
Elsa Honig Fine, *Women and Art: A History of Women Painters and Sculptors from the Renaissance to the 20th Century*, Montclair, NJ: Allanheld and Schram, and London: Prior, 1978
Germaine Greer, *The Obstacle Race: The Fortunes of Women Painters and Their Work*, London: Secker and Warburg, and New York: Farrar Straus, 1979
La Femme artiste d'Elisabeth Vigée-Lebrun à Rosa Bonheur, exh. cat., Musée Despiau-Wlerick, Donjon Lacataye, Mont-de-Marsan, 1981
Vivian Cameron, *Woman as Image and Image-Maker in Paris During the French Revolution*, PhD dissertation, Yale University, 1983
Susan Waller, *Women Artists in the Modern Era: A Documentary History*, Metuchen, NJ: Scarecrow Press, 1991
Claire Constans, *Musée National du Château de Versailles: Les Peintures*, 2 vols, Paris: Réunion des Musées Nationaux, 1995

Madame Benoist, best known for her *Portrait of a Negress* (see illustration), dared to produce and exhibit history painting of a high quality at a time when women were not deemed capable of executing such work. Daughter of a Parisian administrative official, Marie Guillemine Leroulx-Delaville began her career as a painter at a young age, becoming a pupil of Elisabeth Vigée-Lebrun (q.v.), who was accepted into the Academy in 1783. In 1784 Leroulx-Delaville exhibited her first works, a portrait of her father and two pastel studies of heads, at the Exposition de la Jeunesse. In 1786 she, her sister and another female student were transferred to Jacques-Louis David's studio while Vigée-Lebrun had a new studio constructed for herself. Under David, Leroulx-Delaville's style changed. The softer modelling and paler colours favoured by Vigée-Lebrun were replaced by a more rigorous linear style combined with more intense colouring. An early *Self-Portrait* (private collection, France, repr. Ballot 1914, pp.34–6 and ill. opposite p.32), exhibited in 1786, is an intermediary work, showing the influence of both. The ambitious artist joined history painting with portraiture as she depicted herself in classical garb, her right shoulder bare, her hair loosely bound with a ribbon. As she paints a copy of Belisarius and his youthful attendant on the canvas to her left, she looks at the viewer, who occupies the space of David's study for his *Belisarius Begging for Alms* (for a reproduction of the study, presumably by David, see Antoine Schnapper and others, *Jacques-Louis David, 1748–1825*, Paris: Réunion des Musées Nationaux, 1989, fig.48). With that Classical costume, the artist represented not only herself but also La Pittura. In this self-image, she combined the influence of Vigée-Lebrun – in the soft lighting and shading, pale colours and sweeping strokes of paint – with that of David, visible in the weighty drapery folds, which accentuate certain anatomical parts, such as the belly and thigh. Although this portrait has been compared to that of *Vigée-Lebrun with Her Daughter* (1789), a closer comparison can be made with Andromache in David's *Andromache Mourning Hector* (both Louvre), although Leroulx-Delaville's figure is not as robust. Both share, however, the same drapery, a tan material with a quite similar border, also to be found on Sabina in David's *Oath of the Horatii* (Louvre). The frankness and intensity of this ambitious self-portrait earned her much critical acclaim from the *Journal de Paris* as well as the *Mercure de France*, which praised its "grace" as well as its "nobility" (Ballot 1914, p.38).

At the Exposition de la Jeunesse of 1787, Leroulx-Delaville exhibited an even more ambitious work, a genre scene taken from Samuel Richardson's *Clarissa*, which had been the favourite novel of Vigée-Lebrun. In *Clarissa Harlowe at Archer's* (untraced) the heroine, on her knees before a table loaded with letters, expresses both sorrow and courage, a complexity of emotions highly lauded by the reviewer of the *Mercure de France* (23 June 1787, p.189). Like the novel, and like history painting, the work offered several moral messages: warnings against the male sex who made specious offers; against women preferring men of pleasure to men of probity; against "mésalliances"; against the excessive authority of parents. The pendant to this work, entitled the *Visit that Captain Morden, Presented by Belfort, Makes to Clarissa the Eve Before Her Death* (untraced), exhibited in 1788, won further attention by its complexity. Morden, with his expression of indignant sorrow, was much appreciated, but the reviewer, wanting Clarissa awake and frightened, failed to understand that sleep expressed her withdrawal from life, her only possible escape from her dreadful situation (*Mercure de France*, 7 June 1788, pp.44–5).

Like Vigée-Lebrun, who had executed history paintings, Leroulx-Delaville was ambitious, and took the next step forward into history painting. The topics of her subsequent works dealt with the liminal state of a young woman either passing from her family into a sexual or marital relationship, or choosing between that relationship and a career. For one painting, she drew on Apuleius' *Golden Ass*. The *Farewell of Psyche to Her Family* (untraced) was first exhibited in July 1791 at the gallery of Monsieur Lebrun (the husband of Vigée-Lebrun, who had emigrated), and then in September 1791 at the Salon, thrown open for the first time to all artists. A drawing in a private collection represents Psyche weeping in the arms of her mother while her father folds his arms in resignation; behind this group Psyche's sisters sob with grief next to the chariot that will transport her to her bridegroom. Although metaphorically the work was about the approaching union of the soul with love, more literally it represented the departure of a daughter/sister, with all of that scene's attendant emotions. One critic was rapturous about the painting: "I thought that women were hardly capable of composing history painting and especially with this degree of perfection. How everything talks in your painting! how interesting your beautiful and unhappy Psyche is!" (*La Béquille de Voltaire au Salon*, Paris [1791], Deloynes Collection, xvii, no.438, pp.292–3). But, for another (*Lettres analytiques, critiques et philosophiques*, Paris, 1791, Deloynes Collection, xvii, no.441, pp.422–3), the exhibition of this painting offered an occasion to condemn works by female artists. For this critic, the quality of the painting meant that others had had to retouch it; that is, it was, according to him, painted by "thirty-six hands". Furthermore, in this arch-conservative critic's opinion, to achieve this level of expertise the artist had had to be in compromising situations, studying with boys and from male models, all of which made her morally unacceptable, even to the worst libertine.

Such vituperative criticism may well have been caused by the fact that Leroulx-Delaville exhibited *two* history paintings at the Salon of 1791. Her other subject was a feminist reworking of the theme of *Hercules at the Crossroads* (or *Hercules Between Virtue and Vice*), a theme popularised in the 18th century through the publication of the Earl of Shaftesbury's commentary in *Characteristiks*. In *Innocence Between Virtue and Vice* (repr. Ballot 1914, ill. opposite p.64; detail in Los Angeles 1976, ill.7) a young blonde woman, classically garbed, resists the advances of the virile and handsome man who represents Vice (the perennial attribute of a snake representing evil is at his feet, as are roses, the flowers of love) and flees to the protecting arms of the rather stern female figure of Virtue, who points the difficult way to a temple of glory or immortality. In its conception, in the expert handling of both male and female figures, which are decidedly Davidian in appearance, in the rich and varied colouring, as well as in the complicated landscape, Leroulx-Delaville demonstrated a remarkable expertise for an artist only 21 years old. Nevertheless, the unsold work remained within the family.

Two years later, married to Pierre Vincent Benoist, a royalist lawyer from Angers, Leroulx-Delaville missed the Salon of 1793, spending that year and the following one escaping Terrorist authorities. In 1795 she obtained a studio at the Louvre and exhibited at the Salon of that year a portrait of a man, as well as another *Self-Portrait* (private collection, France, repr. Ballot 1914, frontispiece) and two paintings representing *Sappho*, the last history works that she exhibited. Although these remain untraced, sketches in an unpublished album (private collection, Paris) indicate that in one work the poetess, holding a lyre, was seated under a tree; in the other, her dead body, lying on the ground, was surrounded by mourners. Other sketches of 1804–6 of such subjects as *Regulus Returning from Carthage* indicate that Benoist was still interested in history painting.

In late 1797–8, relatively poor, Benoist was reduced to illustrating books translated by her husband, which included *Marie or the Unhappiness of Being a Woman* (ibid., p.145) and *Memoirs of Miss Bellamy*. She missed exhibiting at the Salon of 1798, but returned in 1799 with further portraits. Her renowned *Portrait of a Negress*, exhibited at the Salon of 1800, was possibly inspired by Girodet's portrait of *Jean-Baptiste Belley* (Château, Versailles), exhibited at the Salon of 1798. Benoist's painting represents a woman probably encountered at the home of her brother-in-law Benoist-Cavy, a naval officer who had married in Guadeloupe and travelled to Guyana. Its formal counterpart in David's work is his portrait of *Anne-Marie Thelusson* (Alte Pinakothek, Munich). Benoist's picture is a study of dark and light, a picture of contrasts with the black woman dressed in a white costume, turbaned in white, with one breast exposed, while gazing serenely at the viewer. Although one critic applauded the gracious attitude, the correct drawing and pose – particularly the beautifully drawn right arm – as well as the gracefully arranged drapery, he was far less sanguine about the choice of sitter, since he felt that African faces were ugly ([Baron Jean-Baptiste Boutard], "Salon de l'an VIII", *Journal des Débats*, Collection Deloynes, xxii, no.632, pp.684–5). Unfortunately he was not alone in his prejudice (see, for example, *La Vérité au Museum ...*, Paris, 1800, Deloynes Collection, xxii, no.623, p.309). He further complained that "the air could not circulate around her", that is, the effect of painting this woman was to flatten the picture, make it more abstract, an attitude shared by Benoist's biographer, Marie Ballot (1914, pp.149–50).

During Napoleon's reign in the 1800s, Benoist not only exhibited portraits and genre paintings at the Salons, but also executed a number of official portraits. In 1803 she received her first commission to paint a portrait of *Napoleon* (Palais de Justice, Ghent) as first Consul for the city of Ghent, a work apparently quite similar to Ingres's *Portrait of Bonaparte as the First Consul* (Musée des Beaux-Arts, Liège). In the following years she did other portraits of Napoleon for the cities of Brest, Le Mans and Angers. For the Minister of the Interior in 1804 she executed a portrait of his mother. Other commissions followed, including portraits of *Maréchal Brune* (destroyed) for the Tuileries, *Princess Borghese* (Versailles, repr. Constans 1995, i, p.81) and the phrenologist *Dr Gall* (private collection, France, ibid., ill. opposite p.192).

Benoist's genre subjects included sentimental themes dealing with children, such as *Two Young Children with a Bird's Nest*

Benoist: *Portrait of a Negress*, exhibited Salon of 1800; Musée d'Orsay, Paris

(exh. Salon 1806; private collection, France), executed in a hard, linear style. This represents a seated young boy looking at the viewer, while a young girl, seen in profile, kneels and reaches towards a nest in his lap. In the opinion of one critic, the painting was full of "spirit and grace" (*Journal des Débats*, 7 November 1806, p.1). At the Salon of 1810, she offered a more moral, Greuzian theme, the *Reading of the Bible* (Musée Municipal, Louviers, repr. Ballot 1914, ill. opposite p.224), showing an old Swiss soldier with his granddaughter on his lap while his daughter reads the Bible. The work was proclaimed to be "painted with truth" (*Le Moniteur Universel*, 6 February 1811, p.143), and a scene in which the costumes, figures and scenes were all "in harmony" ([Pierre Gueffier], *Entretien sur les Ouvrages de Peinture, Sculpture et Gravure*, Paris, 1811, p.62). For the Salon of 1812, the last at which she exhibited, Benoist included with two portraits a work entitled *Fortune Teller* (Musée des Beaux-Arts, Saintes, repr. Mont-de-Marsan 1981, pl.12). In this moderately sized canvas (1.95 × 1.14 m.), in front of a fountain and rural landscape (painted by M. Mongin), an old woman, looking attentively at a young shepherdess, tells her fortune while the recipient casts her eyes down, reflecting on her words. By the side of the fountain a young man listens attentively to her prognostications. In this theme, undertaken earlier by a Madame d'Anne for the Salon of 1806 (untraced) and later by David, Benoist returned to the sub-themes of her earlier paintings of *Psyche* and *Innocence Between Virtue and Vice*, focusing on a pivotal moment in a young woman's life when her future remains in the balance and her life will be changed. On the succession of Louis XVIII to the throne and her husband's promotion to Conseiller d'Etat, Benoist was prohibited from exhibiting at the Salons.

VIVIAN P. CAMERON

Berend-Corinth, Charlotte

German painter, 1880–1967

Born Charlotte Berend in Berlin, 25 May 1880. Studied at the Staatliche Kunstschule, Berlin, under Eva Stort and Max Schäfer, and at the Unterrichtsanstalt des Berlin Kunstgewerbemuseums (School of the Berlin Arts and Crafts Museum), from 1898; studied at Lovis Corinth's private art school from 1901. Married Corinth, 1903; son born 1904, daughter born 1909; husband died 1925. Member, 1906, and board member, 1922, Berlin Secession. Published Lovis Corinth's autobiography, 1926–7. Head of a school of painting in Berlin from 1927. Trips to Italy, 1932–9; emigrated to USA, 1939. Opened the Charlotte Berend School of Painting in Santa Barbara, California, 1943. Died in New York, 10 January 1967.

Principal Exhibitions

Individual

Galerie Nierendorf, Berlin: 1930 (retrospective)
Museum, Saarbrücken: 1932
Davenport Municipal Art Galleries, IO: 1935
Everhart Museum of Art, Scranton, PA: 1936
Kleemann Galleries, New York: 1940

Faulkner Art Memorial Galleries, Santa Barbara, CA: 1940
Museum of the Legion of Honor, San Francisco: 1942
Van Diemen Galleries, New York: 1948
Schaeffer Galleries, New York: 1955
Rathaus Reinickendorf, Berlin: 1956
Städtische Galerie, Munich: 1957
Galerie Alex Voemel, Düsseldorf: 1960
Selected Artists Galleries, New York: 1960, 1967
Galerie Vonderbank, Frankfurt am Main: 1961
Staatliche Museen zu Berlin, Nationalgalerie, Berlin: 1967 (retrospective)

Group

Berlin Secession: from 1906
Verein der Künstlerinnen zu Berlin: 1928
Association of Women Painters and Sculptors, Argent Galleries, New York: 1935

Selected Writings

Editor, *Lovis Corinth: Selbstbiographie*, Leipzig, 1926
Reisetage in Spanien, Leipzig, 1926
Mein Leben mit Lovis Corinth, Hamburg: Strom, 1948
Als ich ein Kind war, Hamburg, 1950
Corinth: Sein Leben mit mir, Munich, 1958
Die Gemälde von Lovis Corinth, Munich: Bruckmann, 1958 (with Hans Konrad Röthel)

Bibliography

Monty Schultzmann, *Die Malerin Charlotte Berend-Corinth*, Munich: Bruckmann, 1966
Charlotte Berend-Corinth: Gemälde, Graphik, exh. cat., Staatliche Museen zu Berlin, Nationalgalerie, Berlin, 1967
Irmgard Wirth, *Charlotte Berend-Corinth*, Berlin, 1969
Charlotte Berend-Corinth: Eine Ausstellung zum 100. Geburtstag der Künstlerin, exh. cat., Kunstverein, Erlangen, and elsewhere, 1980
Carola Hartlieb, "Bildende Künstlerinnen zu Beginn der Moderne: Die Künstlerinnen der 'Berliner Secession'", *Profession ohne Tradition: 125 Jahre Verein der Berliner Künstlerinnen*, exh. cat., Berlinische Galerie, Berlin, 1992, pp.59–72

In Germany in the 1920s Charlotte Berend-Corinth became known for her work connected with the Berlin Secession. From 1915 she became a member of the board and jury of the Secession, joining Käthe Kollwitz (q.v.), an indication of the increasing participation of women in arts institutions. Despite the strong influence of her teacher and husband Lovis Corinth, she developed artistic independence, mainly through portraits and work for the theatre and music world of Berlin. As part of the first generation of professionally trained female artists, she was able to draw regularly from the nude, and this suggested a new way of looking at the female body (*Self-Portrait with Model*, 1931; for illustration, see p.102).

The daughter of a Hamburg merchant, Berend began her art studies in Berlin. In 1901 at the age of 21 she entered the private art school of Lovis Corinth, who was then 43 and at the height of his career. They married in 1903 and began working in adjoining studios in Berlin. Berend continued to sign work with her maiden name. She first showed one of her works publicly in 1905 (*Woman in Labour* or *Difficult Hour*; untraced). Corinth reported the reaction of the Secession jury: "Your picture won applause from all sides. Liebermann thinks the subject matter is daring ... Slevogt was appreciative" (Schultzmann 1966, p.7).

Berend's association with the Berlin Secession, which she joined in 1906, was the most important stage in her career. Her search for new means of expression and experiments with Expressionist technique and subject matter were curtailed, however, when her husband had a stroke. The pressure of caring for Corinth and supporting their children led her to escape into illusory worlds: the fairy tales of Hans Christian Andersen, whose *Little Mermaid* she illustrated, and the Berlin Metropol Theatre, with portraits including the dancers *Valeska Gert* and *Anita Berber* and the singer *Fritzi Massary*. She created numerous works, mainly graphic, before 1920, for example the *Max Pallenberg Portfolio* (1918; five colour lithographs 1/100; private collection, Neuss) and the *Anita Berber Portfolio* (1919; cover and eight pages, lithograph; private collection, New York). Detailed and naturalistic painting techniques distinguish her work of this period. At the same time, in the lithographs of the *Pallenberg Portfolio*, for example, she succeeded in capturing the glittering world of the theatre with a few quick strokes of colour.

After Corinth's death in 1925, Berend at first devoted herself to her husband's oeuvre. She arranged his estate, published his autobiography and in 1926 conceived the first major Corinth exhibition in Berlin. Through her activities as a board member, she contributed substantially to the consolidation of the Berlin Secession. From 1927 she headed her own painting school, and she was drawn back to her own work by study trips to Italy and Turkey (1927), Egypt (1928) and Denmark (1929–30). She developed a graphic sign language, particularly in uncommissioned works, such as *Negro Harvesting Dates* (1928; oil on canvas; Pommern Foundation, Kiel) and *Chess Players in Lovis Corinth's Sickroom, 1925 in Amsterdam* (1929 or 1930; oil on canvas; Galerie Bassenge, Berlin). She had solo exhibitions in Germany and abroad in the latter half of the 1920s and in 1930 had her first major retrospective, at the Galerie Nierendorf in Berlin. Just when Berend had firmly established herself in the Berlin art scene, she had to leave Germany due to the rise of National Socialism. After a period in Italy, she followed her son, who had left Germany in 1931, to settle in New York in 1939.

The watercolours that she executed in New York reflect her new surroundings and search for a new home (*On the Roofs of New York*, 1939; Galerie Bassenge). Her preference for net-like forms is evident (*Harbor in Martha's Vineyard with Nets*, 1955; pencil and watercolour on Japanese paper; Neue Galerie, Kassel), as well as a darker palette, which slowly brightened after the war. As in other watercolours, here she exploited the particular quality of Japanese paper to achieve the lightness of oriental ink drawings, in which the materials and the pictorial atmosphere are interrelated. Her watercolour style mirrored her method of narration, according to her biographer Monty Schultzmann: "lively, adding idea to idea, short, poignant allusions that give the essentials but leave room for the imagination to fill in the missing parts."

After World War II Berend published autobiographical writings and a catalogue raisonné of Corinth's oil paintings. Exhibitions of her work were held in American galleries and museums in the 1940s and 1950s; the first exhibition in post-war Germany was held in 1956. She died in 1967, just before the opening of an exhibition at the Berlin Nationalgalerie where her work was shown in the rooms in which her husband's work had been displayed in 1926.

MARINA SASSENBERG

Bergmann-Michel, Ella
German graphic artist, photographer and film-maker, 1895–1971

Born Ella Bergmann in Paderborn, 20 October 1895. Studied at the Grossherzogliche-Sächsische Hochschule für Kunst und Gewerbe, Weimar, 1915–18. Married artist Robert Michel, 1919; son born 1920, daughter born 1927. Moved to Vockenhausen near Frankfurt am Main, 1920. Member of the association Das Neue Frankfurt; associate member of the group Die Abstrakten, Berlin, 1930. Prohibited from exhibiting under the National Socialists. Much of her work destroyed in bombing, 1945. Founder of the Film-Studio, Frankfurt am Main, 1949. Died in Vockenhausen, 8 August 1971.

Principal Exhibitions

Individual
(all with Robert Michel)
Schloss Morsbroich, Leverkusen: 1963
Waddell Gallery, New York: 1968, 1971
Galerie Loehr, Düsseldorf: 1971
Annely Juda Fine Art, London: 1972 (retrospective)
Kunsthalle, Hamburg: 1974 (retrospective)

Group
Nassauischer Kunstverein, Wiesbaden: 1923
Kunsthalle, Mannheim: 1926
Mart-Stam-Haus, Stuttgart: 1927 (*Werkbund*)
Société Anonyme, New York: 1928 (touring)
Frankfurt am Main: 1929 (*Abstrakte und Surrealistische Malerei und Plastik*, touring)
Das Neue Frankfurt, Frankfurt am Main: 1932 (*Abstrakte Kunst*)
Musée St Etienne, Paris: 1964 (*Cinquante ans de collages*)
Städtische Galerie im Lenbachhaus, Munich: 1967 (*Collage '67*)
Institut für Moderne Kunst, Nuremberg: 1968 (*Von der Collage zur Assemblage*)
Kunstverein Frankfurt, Frankfurt am Main: 1968 (*Collagen aus sechs Jahrzehnten*, touring)
Annely Juda Fine Art, London: 1970 (*The Non-Objective World*)

Selected Writings
"Geist der zwanziger Jahre in Frankfurt", *Egoist*, ed. Adam Seide, no.10, Darmstadt, 1966, pp.2–5

Bibliography
Hans Hildebrandt, *Die Frau als Künstlerin*, Berlin, 1928
Herta Wescher, *Die Collage*, Cologne, 1968
Ella Bergmann-Michel und Robert Michel, exh. cat., Kunsthalle, Hamburg, 1974
Künstlerinnen international, 1877–1977, exh. cat., Schloss Charlottenburg, Berlin, 1977
L'altra metà dell'avanguardia, 1910–1940: Pittrici e scultrici nei movimenti delle avanguardie storiche, exh. cat., Palazzo Reale, Milan, and elsewhere, 1980
Ella Bergmann-Michel, exh. cat., Zabriskie Gallery, New York, 1984
Heinz Hirdina, *Neues Bauen, Neues Gestalten: Das Neue Frankfurt*, Berlin, 1984

Ella Bergmann-Michel: Retrospektive Fotografie, exh. cat., Düsseldorf, 1986

Ella Bergmann, Robert Michel: Pioniere der Bildcollage, exh. cat., Städtische Galerie, Paderborn, 1988

Katharina Sykora, "Weg mit allem Dekorativen heisst und hiess es immer für mich", *Der Kairos der Fotografie*, iv/3–4, 1989, pp.72–9

Ella Bergmann-Michel, exh. cat., Sprengel Museum, Hannover, 1990

Künstlerinnen des 20. Jahrhunderts, exh. cat., Museum Wiesbaden, 1990

Ella Bergmann-Michel was an important modern German artist who experimented with a wide range of media, producing innovative work that repeatedly challenged generic conventions over a period of nearly 60 years.

She received an academic art training at the Grossherzogliche-Sächsische Hochschule für Kunst und Gewerbe in Weimar (1915–18). Her nude drawings from this period are conventional, but with her Expressionist wood- and linocuts, which already reveal a refined feeling for the depiction of light, she drew away from academicism. From 1917 she experimented intensively with material collages and assemblages. In the earliest surviving example, *Sunday for Everybody* (1917; Städtische Galerie Paderborn), circles and segments of circles in ink or paper surround a rectangular configuration of small wooden slats, painted yellow or russet. A slat fixed beneath at an angle supported a piece of rabbit fur (now missing). The coloured discs evoke the merry air of the Libori Fair in Paderborn, where Bergmann collected materials for the assemblage. The circular signs distributed across the picture suggest eye symbols and, combined with the phrases torn from magazines that promise "something for everybody on Sundays", they make a witty comment on visual pleasures. Bergmann's assemblage surpassed the contemporary collages of the Berlin Dadaists and anticipated Kurt Schwitters's experiments by two years.

In 1919, with Robert Michel, whom she had met in 1917, she decided to leave the Hochschule and work independently; they married and moved to the countryside near Frankfurt am Main. She soon developed a radical abstract method, interspersing constructivist elements with biomorphic parts. Formulations of this combination appeared in her work over a period of almost 30 years, as in *Big Miracle Picture* (1926; collage and spray technique, Sprengel Museum, Hannover) and *Big Jumping Form* (1954; ink, pencil, watercolour and oil; Sprengel Museum).

Around 1923 Bergmann-Michel began to explore ways of representing the physical properties of light, corresponding to a number of artistic experiments – from Expressionism to Orphism – concerning light. Her sphere pictures, or *Portraits de Rayon*, combine colour spectra cut from physics textbooks with ink lines and light watercolour planes. *My Spectrum* (1926; see illustration) is among the most beautiful examples of her non-symbolic, lyrical-constructive use of light. The two narrow vertical colour scales in blue and pink are composed of bands pasted individually. The rectangles, horizontal and vertical lines and the convex form seem to spread prismatically the beams that hit them. Thus the background dissolves into finely nuanced shades of beige.

Both in technique and content the sphere pictures foreshadowed the artist's involvement with photography, from 1927,

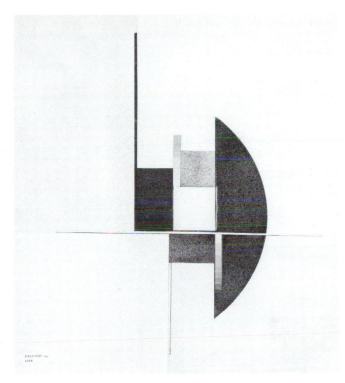

Bergmann-Michel: *My Spectrum (Mein Spektrum)*, 1926; 73.5 × 69.5 cm.; Städtische Galerie Paderborn

and with film, from 1929–30. This shift in media was also prompted by external factors: the movement of artists, architects and typographers originating in the idea of the "Werkbund", which formed in the 1920s in Frankfurt am Main, where Bergmann-Michel had her studio. Her sympathy with social reform led her to collaborate closely with Das Neue Frankfurt, and she organised numerous screenings of contemporary avant-garde films for the Arbeitsgemeinschaft für den unabhängigen Film. The modernist reconstruction of Frankfurt and its effect on the people were the main subjects of her photographic and film work of these years. Several series of photographs document the building complexes that were erected in the spirit of the avant-garde architectural movement Das Neue Bauen: the main emphasis is on the relationship of the people to their changed environment, yet formally the photographs were influenced by the aesthetics of the Neues Sehen (New Vision), with its extreme camera angles. Bergmann-Michel's films employ a didactic political method of narration. *Where Do Old People Live?* (1931–2) introduced a newly built old people's home as exemplary of humane architecture, while *Unemployed Cook for Unemployed* (1932) documents the initiative of Frankfurt's unemployed. It is significant that her last film, the *Last Election* (1932–3), which already showed the National Socialists' domination of Frankfurt streets, was never completed. From 1933 the political left and the avant-garde art of the 1920s were branded as decadent or bolshevist by the National Socialists. Bergmann-Michel was forbidden to exhibit, and six of her works were confiscated. She worked secretly during this period; her pictorial language became uncertain and she took refuge in symbolic, figurative works. Her diary indicates that her artistic work almost entirely ceased during World War II.

Bergmann-Michel did not resume her photographic and film work after the war, although she did continue film screening and lecturing. Her public lectures on modern art and avant-garde film as well as her programming at the Frankfurt Film-Studio, of which she was co-founder, helped to reintroduce modern art to Germany. In her art, she returned to a modified form of collage technique, with combinations of delicate Japanese paper that refer to her sphere pictures. She achieved colour effects similar to her spectrum pictures in the transparent, pastel-coloured layers, for example in *Japanese Paper Collage* (1964; Sprengel Museum).

The real innovation of Bergmann-Michel's late work was the thread collage, in which she continued the exploration of colour and light refraction of the prism pictures of the 1920s. She stretched threads of various colours across the surface of the picture, which was covered with very fine paper strips, thus introducing two planes of lines that are not level with the painting support: the real threads and their shadows. In *Quiet Sleep* (1968; thread collage and spray technique; Sprengel Museum), for example, she reached a new peak of innovation by relying on the most important aspects of her early work. On a finely structured collage of coloured paper, brown, beige and blue threads are stretched horizontally, their shadows crossing the picture with hard, dark lines. In two places the light silhouettes of the phrase fragment "uhiger chlaf", which provide the picture's title, emerge from the midnight-blue depth, like a distant sign from her first brave material collages.

KATHARINA SYKORA

Bernhardt, Sarah

French actress, sculptor and painter, 1844–1923

Born Henriette Rosine Bernard in Paris, 22 October 1844, the natural child of Edouard Bernard, a young law student from Le Havre, and Judith van Hard, a Dutch girl who later became a fashionable courtesan. Brought up by a Breton nurse; educated at Auteuil, then at the convent of Grandchamps, Versailles. Studied acting at the Conservatoire, Paris, where she was a prize-winning student, 1859–63. Engaged by the Comédie Française, 1863, but left after a quarrel. Son by the Belgian prince Henri de Ligne born 1864. Brilliant career at Théâtre de l'Odéon, Paris, 1866–72. Re-engaged by the Comédie Française, 1872; star of their first London visit in 1879; left after another quarrel, established her own troupe and made the first of many triumphal tours to America, 1880. Leased her own theatre, the Théâtre Sarah Bernhardt, Paris, in 1900; acted there for the rest of her life. Chevalier, Légion d'Honneur, 1914. Died in Paris, 21 March 1923.

Principal Exhibitions

Paris Salon: 1874–6, 1878–81, 1885–6 (silver medal 1876)
William Russell Galleries, London: 1879 (individual)
Union League Club, New York: 1880 (individual)
World's Columbian Exposition, Chicago: 1893
Exposition Universelle, Paris: 1900

Selected Writings

Dans les nuages: Impressions d'une chaise, Paris: Charpentier, 1878
My Double Life, London: Heinemann, 1907 (French original, 1907); reprinted London: Owen, 1977
The Art of the Theatre, New York: Dial Press, 1925
The Memoirs of Sarah Bernhardt: Early Childhood Through the First American Tour, and Her Novella "In the Clouds", ed. Sandy Lesberg, New York: Peeble Press, 1977

Bibliography

Tom Taylor in *The Times*, 16 June 1879
La Plume, December 1900
Reynaldo Hahn, *Sarah Bernhardt: Impressions*, London: Mathews and Marrot, 1932 (French original, 1930)
Ernest Pronier, *Sarah Bernhardt: Une vie au théâtre*, Geneva: Jullien, 1942
Cornelia Otis Skinner, *Madame Sarah*, Boston: Houghton Mifflin, and London: Joseph, 1967
Gerda Taranow, *Sarah Bernhardt: The Art Within the Legend*, Princeton: Princeton University Press, 1972
Sarah Bernhardt, 1844–1923, exh. cat., Ferrers Gallery, London, 1973
Joanna Richardson, *Sarah Bernhardt and Her World*, New York: Putnam, and London: Weidenfeld and Nicolson, 1977
The Romantics to Rodin: French Nineteenth-Century Sculpture from North American Collections, exh. cat., Los Angeles County Museum of Art, and elsewhere, 1980
La Femme artiste d'Elisabeth Vigée-Lebrun à Rosa Bonheur, exh. cat., Musée Despiau-Wlerick, Donjon Lacataye, Mont-de-Marsan, 1981
Jane Abdy, "Sarah Bernhardt's role in art", *Christie's Review of the Year*, London, 1986
Robert Fizdale and Arthur Gold, *The Divine Sarah: A Life of Sarah Bernhardt*, New York: Knopf, 1991; London: HarperCollins, 1992
Theatergottinnen: Inszenierte Weiblichkeit: Clara Ziegler, Sarah Bernhardt, Eleonora Duse, exh. cat., Munich, 1994

Sarah Bernhardt was a sculptor of most original talent. The hours she spent in the atelier were far more than a diversion from her demanding roles on the stage. From those sculptures that survive today, and others of which photographs exist, her work shows great skill, and at its most imaginative makes a fascinating contribution to the history of Art Nouveau.

So far 50 sculptures by Bernhardt have been traced from contemporary accounts and photographs, and the whereabouts of some 25 are known today. There must be many more, for she began to sculpt around 1872, and always kept a studio both in Paris and at her holiday home at Belle-Ile, where she spent two months every summer. Throughout her life she lived in an artistic milieu, and her two closest friends were the painters Georges Clairin and Louise Abbéma (q.v.), who both made famous portraits of her in 1876 (portrait by Clairin in Musée du Petit Palais, Paris; that by Abbéma untraced). It was natural that this highly gifted woman, who designed her own clothes and worked hand-in-hand with her stage designers, should be tempted to experiment with painting and sculpture; and so she did when in the early 1870s she found that – star of the Comédie Française though she was – she still had abundant time for what she saw as a possible second career.

Her earliest works tend to be unadventurous and correct. She took as teachers two staid, successful Salon sculptors, Mathieu Meusnier and Franchesci. She began by modelling portrait busts of her friends, which included *Louise Abbéma*

Bernhardt: *Self-Portrait as Sphinx Inkwell*, 1880; height 31.5 cm.

(Musée d'Orsay, Paris), the dramatist *Sardou* (Musée du Petit Palais, Paris) and *Mlle Hocquigny* (private collection, London), her old companion and ally when she ran a hospital during the siege of Paris in 1870. Soon she had the courage to enter her work at the Salon, where she exhibited regularly from 1875 to 1886.

In 1876 Bernhardt sent in her most ambitious work, a huge plaster group depicting an elderly Breton fisherwoman cradling her drowned grandson on her lap, which she called *After the Storm*. She took great pains with this work, even purchasing a skeleton and taking lessons in anatomy to achieve verisimilitude. Great was her pride when *After the Storm* won an honourable mention, and fame for the artist. She carved two smaller versions in marble, and sold the casting rights to the dealer Gambart for 10,000 francs. The size of the bronze edition is not known, but several casts have appeared on the market (see Sotheby's, New York, 26 May 1994, lot 47). The original plaster is untraced, and so are the two small marble versions, although one of these appeared in the sale of her collection in 1923.

It must be admitted that Bernhardt saw the publicity value of her alternative career. Postcards were sold of her working at her plasters, wearing a delightful "sculpting suit" she had specially designed. This consisted of a trouser suit tailored in white satin; at the neck was a huge jabot adorned with a posy of flowers, and her cuffs were trimmed with frills of lace. She worked late into the night, wearing an impromptu candelabrum attached to her head. She also painted, but although her pictures are pleasing they do not rise above amateur status, and lack the vivacity of her sculpture. About 20 works are known, somewhat in the style of Alfred Stevens and Gustave

Doré, who both taught her. Most of the canvases date from the 1870s (e.g. *Palm Seller*, repr. *My Double Life* 1907, p.252; *Return from Church*, Holloway College, Surrey).

When Bernhardt first came to London with the Comédie Française in 1879, she took the opportunity of showing her sculpture to the British public. She hired a gallery in Piccadilly, and offered her guests champagne. The little show was a sensation: it was visited and admired by Gladstone, and Queen Victoria's son Prince Leopold bought a painting. All ten sculptures were sold. On her tour of America the following year she held an equally publicised show at the Union League Club in New York.

The year 1880 was a pivotal one: with one extraordinary work Bernhardt shed the art of the Salon for that of the Symbolists. She made a self-portrait representing herself as a sphinx holding an inkwell between her paws (see illustration). It is an amazing and compelling object. The symbolism is compounded by the bat's wings and mermaid's tail. One is reminded of Gustave Moreau, and it may also be relevant that Bernhardt had acted in *Le Sphinx* in 1874. It is her most important sculpture, and an edition of perhaps ten was cast by Thiébaut Frères. One example has a matching quill pen bearing her initials in diamonds (private collection, Paris). She gave examples to several admirers, including the Prince of Wales (Royal Collection, Sandringham House). In the following year she carved a most beautiful bas-relief bust of *Ophelia*, depicted life size. It demonstrates the skill that Bernhardt had acquired in handling marble. Ophelia's tresses are entwined with rippling waves in a harmonious pattern. Bernhardt gave this sculpture as a present to the Royal Theatre in Copenhagen, a city that she loved. It is on permanent exhibition in the foyer.

In the 1890s Bernhardt was the chief patron of two of the greatest Art Nouveau artists, Alphonse Mucha and René Lalique. The latter designed jewellery for several of her plays, and is also said to have encouraged her to make some bronzes of sea plants with strange incrustations (two examples in private collection, Paris) – works of strange beauty. At the same time she made some bronzes of leaping fish that have extraordinary verve. Her sojourns at Belle-Ile no doubt provided her with models. A group of these marine bronzes was shown at the Exposition Universelle of 1900; at the same time Bernhardt was electrifying audiences every evening in her performance as Napoleon's son in *L'Aiglon*.

JANE ABDY

Bertaux, Mme Léon

French sculptor, 1825–1909

Born Hélène Pilate in Paris, 4 July 1825. Studied under her stepfather, the sculptor Pierre Hébert, and Augustin Dumont. Married (1) Alletit, c.1847; one son; separated from husband before his death; (2) Léon Bertaux. Founder, 1881, and first president, 1881–94, Union des Femmes Peintres et Sculpteurs (UFPS), Paris. Officier de l'Académie, 1881; officier de l'Instruction Publique, 1888. Died at Château de Lassay, Saint-Michel-de-Chavaignes, Sarthe, 20 April 1909.

Principal Exhibitions

Paris Salon: 1849 (under the name Alletit), occasionally 1857–1909 (honourable mention 1863, medals 1864, 1867 and 1873, exemption from jury 1873)

Royal Academy, London: 1874 (bronze medal)

Exposition des Arts Décoratifs, Paris: 1877 (first-class medal)

Union des Femmes Peintres et Sculpteurs, Paris: from 1882

Exposition Universelle, Paris: 1889 (gold medal), 1900

Woman's Building, World's Columbian Exposition, Chicago: 1893

Bibliography

Maria Lamer de Vits, *Les Femmes sculpteurs, graveurs et leurs oeuvres*, 1905

A. D[alligny], obituary, *Journal des Arts*, 24 April 1909, p.3

Edouard Lepage, *Une conquête féministe: Mme Léon Bertaux*, Paris: Dangon, 1911

Tamar Garb, "*L'art féminin*: The formation of a critical category in late nineteenth-century France", *Art History*, xii, 1989, pp.39–65

Susan Waller, *Women Artists in the Modern Era: A Documentary History*, Metuchen, NJ: Scarecrow Press, 1991

Tamar Garb, *Sisters of the Brush: Women's Artistic Culture in Late Nineteenth-Century Paris*, New Haven and London: Yale University Press, 1994

In an article published in the literary and cultural journal *Le Papillon* in March 1883, Mme Léon Bertaux was heralded as "the best and most brilliant living proof that genius has no sex". Such a position could be occupied, claimed this writer, as much by a woman as by a man. Claims such as this surrounded Mme Bertaux's life and career. Famous during her lifetime as a sculptor, educator and indefatigable campaigner for women's artistic advancement, her name was regularly invoked at discussions on public acknowledgement for women's achievements. And yet Mme Bertaux occupies a strange position in relation to the question of "art" and "sex". Committed, as were many ambitious women artists, to traditional skills and values in art, she defended these in the name of her "feminine mission", convinced that she, as a woman, had a particular role to play in the preserving of time-honoured skills and techniques, now more than ever threatened by the onslaught of modernity. She became therefore a spokesperson for the institutional advancement of her sex while invoking women's natural conservatism as their strength. Nothing was beyond a woman's capacities, claimed Mme Bertaux, but it was *as a woman* that she should make her contribution, neither reneging on her "nature" nor selling short her female destiny. It was women's duty to harness their natural womanly skills – their tenderness, sensitivity, caution and respect for tradition – to the elevated task of Art. Art needed their protection and they needed Art's transcendent mission to elevate and give meaning to their lives.

As a sculptor, Mme Bertaux had a considerable career. She first exhibited at the Salon in 1849 under the name of Alletit but from 1857 signed her work Bertaux. (She, like a number of artists, had married her student, but, in a telling inversion of convention, in this case it was the "master" who took on the name of the student not the reverse, as like all 19th-century French women she accepted her husband's name as her own.) She was a regular exhibitor at public exhibitions and a number of her works were acquired by the State relatively early on in her career. Important examples include the *Assumption of the Virgin*, shown in the Salon of 1861 and bought in 1868, and

Young Gallic Prisoner, bought in 1867. She received a number of State commissions, notably for *Young Girl Bathing*, shown in the Salon of 1876 and at the Exposition Universelle of 1878, and executed prestigious works for the city of Paris and numerous churches. Her works are to be seen on the exteriors of the churches of Saint-Laurent and Saint François-Xavier, on the façade of the Hôtel de Ville (for which she executed a bust of the painter *Chardin*), at the "palais du Sénat", the Opéra, the Musée du Luxembourg and the Petit Palais. She received numerous awards in her long career including the prestigious Médaille d'Or at the Exposition Universelle of 1889. In 1892 she put her name forward as a candidate for the recently vacated seat in the all-male Académie des Beaux-Arts, fourth class of the Institut de France; she was not elected, although her candidature provoked heated debate. Many critics were convinced that had she been a man, she would have had no difficulty in being elected.

Three works, all in public collections, serve to illustrate the ambition and achievement of Mme Bertaux's work as a sculptor. Her *Young Gallic Prisoner* (1867; see illustration) shows a rare instance of a woman artist broaching the subject of the male nude, a theme that was, for the most part, forbidden to female artists, who found it extremely difficult to find opportunity to work from the naked figure, particularly the male model. Propriety, decorum and the preservation of both female modesty and male dignity were thought to be at stake in these debates. Most importantly, the entry of women into the life class threatened to expose the repressed sexuality of the life room, which was hailed as a space in which the spiritual and transcendent values of art overshadowed the earthly and base desires of the flesh. Mme Bertaux was not the type to be deterred by such considerations. Rather than seeing herself as a threat to the potential spiritual nature of Art, she felt especially well equipped as a woman to safeguard it, and her highly skilled traditional rendering in marble of a naked young man was, appropriately, purchased by the State for the respectable sum of 5000 francs. The idealised rendering of the body, its non-specificity and illegibility as a specific person (it reads as the generic body of "Art", not a living contemporary man) clothe it in a protective sheath that diffuses its power as a sexualised body. It stands for Youth, France, Innocence, Purity and the Ideal, qualities that, according to Mme Bertaux, were intuitively understood by women. Mme Bertaux's *Young Girl Bathing* of nearly ten years later is a more sensual and titillating exercise in the nude. The model in plaster of this work was shown at the Salon of 1873 and was acquired by the State for 3500 francs in that year. The marble version was installed in the "palais du Sénat" and the sculpture later appeared in bronze at the Salon of 1882 and at the Exposition Universelle of 1889. The sculpture is of a pubescent woman, a typical nymph or bather, with elongated back, graceful gestures, nubile body and self-conscious demeanour, sitting on a grassy bank with a small snail crawling slowly up her back. The slimy trail of the insect is suggested if not depicted and serves to draw attention to the surface of the body, invoking its tactility. But the invitation to touch here borders on an invitation to caress, the body of the woman and the surface of the sculpture becoming one in this moment. The work cannot help but be a sexualised object, notwithstanding the critics' determined claims for its spirituality and pure transcendent value. It was in these terms that the critics greeted Mme Bertaux's most famous work, her *Psyché sous l'empire du mystère*, first exhibited at the Salon of 1889, shown in the same year at the Exposition Universelle and repeatedly shown and reproduced thereafter. Once again, Mme Bertaux turns her hand to the pubescent female nude, here producing the standing figure of a young woman, idealised, remote and abstracted. Highly skilled as an academic sculptor, Mme Bertaux found in the traditional language of sculpture a means of demonstrating her talent while remaining, she contended, true to her mission as a woman. The fact that there were some critics who thought that the aspirations of Mme Bertaux and other women artists to "Grand Art" was unbecoming for French women, who should content themselves with humbler aspirations and traditional women's genres and media, served only to fuel her ambitions and strengthen her resolve to combine a life that was at one time devoted to the elevation of Art and the amelioration of women's lot.

In this context, Mme Bertaux could not confine herself to the life of a practising artist alone. Her activities as a teacher and campaigner were crucial to the project that she had set herself. In 1873 she had opened the "ateliers d'études", courses in sculpture for young girls and women, having become aware of the paltry training facilities available to aspirant women sculptors in Paris. The success of these led her, in 1879, to build a sculpture school for women. She later became an indefatigable campaigner for the entry of women into the Ecole des Beaux-Arts, seeing this as the only acceptable channel for becoming a respectable artist in France. It was through her involvement with her students and her awareness of the difficulties that aspiring women artists faced that she conceived of the idea of an organisation that could represent the interests of all serious women artists and facilitate the exhibition of their work, irrespective of the level of competence they had reached. To this end she founded the first all-women's exhibition society in France, the Union des Femmes Peintres et Sculpteurs, in 1881, and remained president of this organisation from its inception until 1894, when she was succeeded by the younger naturalist painter Virginie Demont-Breton (q.v.). The Union was a unique organisation devoted to the display and sale of its members' works at its annual exhibitions, but it also set up a support network for women. It published a fortnightly journal, provided a meeting place for women artists, which was located at Mme Bertaux's home, and was at the forefront of campaigns for professional representation of women, women's educational campaigns and the advancement of women's reputation throughout the 1880s and 1890s. Mme Bertaux envisaged the Union as a non-competitive exhibiting forum for women. She remained resolutely opposed to jury selection, hierarchical hanging of shows and elitism of any kind, and envisaged an inclusive, eclectic and catholic organisation that would help women to counter some of the disadvantages that they faced in a generally hostile art world. As such she was unique, and although her strong personality and personal conviction formed the basis of Union policy in the early years, the pervasive ethos of individualism and competition gradually inserted itself into the Union's policy-making. By the time Mme Bertaux resigned as president of the Union, it was a well-established and prestigious exhibition forum with nearly 1000 works on show at its sumptuous annual exhibitions. Openings were

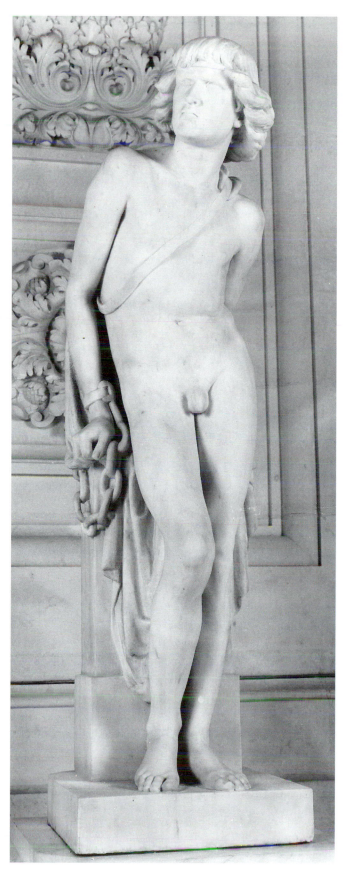

Bertaux: *Young Gallic Prisoner*, 1867; marble; height 1.61 m.; Musée des Beaux-Arts, Nantes

glittering affairs attended by well-known artists, politicians and members of the press. Mme Bertaux had been a tireless promoter of women's art, ensuring extensive critical coverage of the exhibitions. She had even managed to persuade the State to include the Salons des Femmes as one of the annual exhibition forums from which they chose State purchases.

Mme Bertaux was devoted to women's professional advancement but in many ways remained a political and ideological conservative. She never embraced the more far-reaching feminist campaigns, such as the agitation for political rights currently on the agenda in French political circles, nor could she stomach the changes in artistic style and technique that modernism had heralded. She set her sights on traditional institutions and markers of excellence, making the Ecole des Beaux-Arts, the Salon jury, the French Academy and the French School in Rome the focus of her institutional campaigns.

In retrospect it would be easy to construct her as a strangely misguided figure, one who backed the wrong causes and has therefore been relegated, legitimately, to the margins of history. Such a reading does not do justice to the complex situation in which Mme Bertaux and women artists of her time functioned. Excluded for so long from traditional positions of power and privilege, they had learned to believe that it was via such channels that their redemption lay. That these routes have been historically discredited and shown to be marginal to the central project of a society relentlessly bent on modernisation makes them no less worthy of our scholarly attention.

TAMAR GARB

Beskow, Elsa
Swedish illustrator, 1874–1953

Born Elsa Maartmen in Söder, Stockholm, 11 February 1874; father a businessman whose fortunes fluctuated until his death in 1889. Trained as a drawing teacher at the Apprentice School, Stockholm, from 1890; received an annual scholarship that kept her at the School despite her ambitions to study at the Academy. Taught drawing at Anne Whitlock's school, Stockholm, 1894–7. Met painter Natanael Beskow, 1892; married him in 1897, after he had given up painting and become a doctor of divinity; six children, one the artist Bo Beskow. Wrote and illustrated 29 children's books after 1897. Died 1953.

Bibliography

Edvard von Krusenstjerna, *Natanael och Elsa Beskow: Studier och minnesbilder* [Natanael and Elsa Beskow: Studies and commemorative pictures], Stockholm, 1954 (contains extensive bibliography)

Stina Hammar, *Elsa Beskow: En biografi* [Elsa Beskow: A biography], Stockholm, 1958

Tove Jansson, "Sagan inom verkligheten" [The fairy tale within reality], *Bonniers Litterära Magasin*, xxviii, 1959, pp.419–20

Sven Sandström, "Vänlighetens och lekens slott" [The castle of kindness and play], *ibid.*, pp.421–3

Eva von Zweigbergk, *Barnboken i Sverige, 1750–1950* [Children's books in Sweden, 1750–1950], Stockholm, 1965

Elsa Beskow, 1874–1953: En minnesutställning [Elsa Beskow, 1874–1953: A commemorative exhibition], exh. cat., Nationalmuseum, Stockholm, 1974

Blomster fra Sans og Samling [Bewildered flowers], exh. cat., Kunstindustrimuseet, Copenhagen, 1990

Charlotte Christensen, "The flowers' metamorphoses", *Flowers into Art: Floral Motifs in European Painting and Decorative Arts*, ed. Vibeke Woldbye, The Hague: SDU, 1991, pp.107–15

Fatherless at an early age, Elsa Beskow was brought up by her mother and two aunts. She received her professional training at the Apprentice School of Stockholm in the early 1890s, while at the same time attending classes at an academy of applied arts. She could have studied at the Swedish Academy of Fine Arts, where a regular department for female students had been inaugurated in 1864, but she had to settle for a lower level of artistic education, and found employment as a drawing mistress at Anne Whitlock's school in Stockholm between 1894 and 1897, when she married Natanael Beskow. Among her six children, one boy was to become an artist in his own right: Bo Beskow.

Beskow's work as an artist consists almost exclusively of illustrations for books and magazines and for her tales, often in rhyme, for young children, adorned by her own watercolours. Her first artistic endeavours appeared in Christmas magazines and on book covers, and in 1897 she published the first of her 29 books, *Sagan om den lilla, lilla gumman* (The tale of the very little old woman). As a child, Elsa Beskow had been particularly fond of the fairy tales of Hans Christian Andersen and a close observer of Swedish flora, but it was an exhibition of the works of Walter Crane at the Konstnärsförbundet (Artists' Society) in Stockholm in 1896 that defined for her the road to follow as an artist. Not just the style of the graphic works by Crane, but also the ethos of the Arts and Crafts movement that aimed to produce valuable works of art for the people, such as the eminently affordable "sixpenny books", appealed to the Beskows.

In Beskow's stories we find animated flowers, berries and funghi and other impersonations of the Swedish woodland and rural countryside. She belongs to a tradition pioneered by Jean Ignace Grandville in France with his illustrations for *La Vie privée et publique des animaux* (1842–4) and *Les Fleurs animées*, which appeared posthumously in 1847. Grandville in his turn influenced Hans Christian Andersen and Walter Crane, particularly in the latter's *Flora's Feast: A Masque of Flowers* (1899). Other predecessors were Kate Greenaway (q.v.) and Randolph Caldecott, as the great British children's books of the last decades of the 19th century were well known in Scandinavia. Beskow's personal contribution to the genre lies in her powerful evocation of the idyllic long, long days of the Nordic summer, of the open air and the Scandinavian folklore that was so important to artists and preservationists alike around 1900. While she was painting her watercolours, traditional handicraft traditions were being revived, and open-air museums created in memory of the vanishing rural environment.

Beskow had an intense feeling for landscape and her images comprise charming, ethereal glimpses of sunlit meadows and dark, but not gloomy spruce forests, peopled with elf-like, benevolent creatures. This style is already evident in the early works *Puttes äventyr i blåbärsskogen* (Putte's adventures in the

Beskow: *Tomtebobarnen*, 1910; illustration from *Desmä Skovnisser*

blueberry wood) of 1901, as well as in *Tomtebobarnen* (Tomtebo children; 1910; see illustration) and *Pelles nya kläder* (Pelle's new clothes; 1912). A later story, *Tant Grön, tant Brun och tant Gredelin* (Aunt Green, Aunt Brown and Aunt Purple), which was published in 1918, is located in a Biedermeier setting. In spite of its being written during World War I, it has a similarly amiable tone to the rest of her production, not far from the tales of Beatrix Potter (q.v.), but distinctively opposed to the horrors of the Grimm Brothers or the psychological abysses of Lewis Carroll. Beskow's children's books, which have been reprinted for every generation of Swedish children, centre on the beauties of Creation, not on its darker aspects. She also illustrated the works of others, including the *Blommornas bok* (Book of flowers; 1905) by the congenial Swedish artist Jeanna Oterdahl, and Andersen's fairy tale *Thumbelina* (1908). Andersen's *Little Ida's Flowers* had been a childhood favourite, and probably provided the inspiration for her own first animated figures from the vegetable world that appeared in an illustration to a poem in the 1900 edition of the Christmas magazine *Jultomten* (Father Christmas). In Sweden the artist Ottilia Adelborg had been a predecessor in this field, with her alphabet of flowers, *Prinsarnas blomsteralfabet*, as well as the poster for the first major exhibition of women artists in Sweden in 1911, the Föreningen Svenska Konstnärinnor. Beskow was friendly not only with Ottilia Adelborg, but also with the two most internationally renowned Swedish artists of her time, Anders Zorn and Carl Larsson. Beskow shares with Zorn and Larsson the ability to create a pictorial world that sums up Sweden at its Sunday best for the rest of the world: not the existentialist drama inside Strindberg's brain, but the humane and caring, rural and enchanted never-never land of great wide spaces and mystical woods of spruce fir.

CHARLOTTE CHRISTENSEN

Beyer, Henryka
Polish painter, 1782–1855

Born Henrietta Maria Zofia Minter in Szczecin, 7 March 1782. Studied painting in Szczecin under Peter Schmidt; studied flower and still-life painting in Berlin under Gottfried Wilhelm Völcker, 1805–11. Settled in Warsaw, 1811. Married Jan Bogumił Beyer, 1813; three sons; husband died 1819. Studied painting under Antoni Brodowski in Warsaw from 1819. Gave private drawing and painting lessons. Opened the

Beyer: *Bouquet of Flowers in a Vase*, 1827; oil on canvas; 85 × 66 cm.; National Museum, Warsaw

Salon of Drawing and Painting Flowers, Warsaw, the first art school for women in Poland, 1824; director, 1824–33; continued to teach after 1833. Died in Chrzanów, near Warsaw, 24 October 1855.

Principal Exhibitions

Exhibition of Fine Arts, Warsaw: 1821–45 (bronze medal 1821, third-class gold medal 1823, second-class gold medal 1825, honourable mention 1828)

Bibliography

Edward Rastawiecki, *Słownik malarzów polskich* [Dictionary of Polish painters], iii, Warsaw, 1857, pp.134–5

Katalog retrospektywnej wystawy nieżyjących malarzy polskich [Catalogue of the retrospective exhibition of dead Polish painters], Warsaw, 1898, nos 80, 252

Marja Gerson-Dąbrowska, *Polscy artyści: Ich życie i dzieła* [Polish artists: Their lives and works], 2nd edition, Warsaw, 1930

Tadeusz Dobrowolski, *Nowoczesne malarstwo polskie* [Modern Polish painting], i, Wrocław, 1960

Stefan Kozakiewicz, *Malarstwo warszawskie w latach, 1815–1850: Podłoże rozwoju* [Warsaw painting, 1815–1850: Background to development], vi, Warsaw: National Museum, 1962

Sztuka Warszawska: Katalog wystawy jubileuszowej od średniowiecza do połowy XX wieku [Warsaw art: Catalogue of a jubilee exhibition of art from the Middle Ages to the first half of the the 20th century], exh. cat., National Museum, Warsaw, 1962

Janina Wiercińska, "Henryka Beyer", *Słownik artystów polskich i obcych w Polsce działających: Malarze, rzeźbiarze i graficy, sub voce* [Dictionary of Polish and foreign artists working in Poland: Painters, sculptors and graphic artists, *sub voce*], i, Warsaw, 1971, p.145

Stefan Kozakiewicz, *Malarstwo polskie: Oświecenie, klasycyzm, romantyzm* [Polish painting: The age of Reason, Classicism, Romanticism], Warsaw, 1976

La Peinture polonaise du XVIe au début du XXe siècle, Warsaw: National Museum, 1979

Alicja Okońska, *Żywoty pań malujących* [The lives of women painters], Warsaw, 1981

Antoni Brodowski: Życie i dzieło [Antoni Brodowski: Life and work], exh. cat., National Museum, Warsaw, 1985

J. Szulc and E. Szulc, *Cmentarz Ewangelicko-Reformowany w Warszawie: Zmarli i ich rodziny* [Evangelical-Reformed Cemetery in Warsaw: The deceased and their families], Warsaw, 1989

Artystki polskie [Polish women artists], exh. cat., National Museum, Warsaw, 1991

Polish Women Artists and the Avant-Garde: Voices of Freedom, exh. cat., National Museum of Women in the Arts, Washington, DC, 1991

Henryka Beyer is known mainly for her still-life paintings of flowers and fruit. The subject relied on Dutch 17th-century paintings, which had become popular among the middle classes in the 19th century. Beyer's paintings, especially the floral arrangements, in which numerous insects can be seen, are notable for their delicacy of execution, sensitivity of colour, botanical exactness and mastery of technique. She was known for her frequent visits to botanical gardens where she studied diverse vegetation and insects. An excellent example is the *Bouquet of Flowers in a Vase* (see illustration), signed and dated *Hte Beyer pinxit 1827*. Most of her work is in oil, of cabinet size. She was also adept at watercolours; a sheet with butterflies and other insects in the National Museum, Warsaw, shows her mastery of the medium. The insects are represented with great delicacy, realism and scientific exactness. Beyer also

frequently depicted birds (National Museum). She was an excellent lithographer as well, her talents exemplified by a bunch of flowers in this medium in the National Museum. In addition, Beyer painted portrait busts surrounded by wreaths of flowers, which were also influenced by 17th-century Netherlandish art. A good example is the portrait of *Jan Kochanowski* (Muzeum Jana Kochanowskiego, Czarnolas), a renowned Polish renaissance poet. The influence of Beyer on Polish women artists cannot be under-estimated. Not only did she open the first art school for women in Warsaw, she was also one of the first professional Polish artists to maintain herself entirely from the sale of her works. At her death, her former students attended her funeral and covered the casket and chapel with the flowers that she loved.

DANUTA BATORSKA

Biermann, Aenne

German photographer, 1898–1933

Born Anna Sibilla Sternefeld in Goch, on the Lower Rhine, 3 March 1898, into a prosperous Jewish family. Self-taught in photography. Married businessman Herbert Joseph Biermann, 1920; daughter born 1920, son born 1923. Lived in Gera, near Leipzig, 1922–33. Member, Deutscher Werkbund, c.1928–33; Deutsche Gesellschaft für Photographie, 1932–3. Died of a liver disease in Gera, 14 January 1933.

Principal Exhibitions

Kunstkabinett, Munich: 1929 (individual)
Deutscher Werkbund, Stuttgart: 1929 (*Film und Foto*, touring)
Museum Folkwang, Essen: 1929 (*Fotografie der Gegenwart*, touring)
Munich: 1930 (*Das Lichtbild*, touring)
Basel: 1931 (*Die neue Fotografie*)
Palais des Beaux-Arts, Brussels: 1932 (*Exposition internationale de la photographie*, touring)

Selected Writings

"Von der photographischen Darstellung im Allgemeinen und vom photographischen Unterricht im Besonderen", *Thüringen: Eine Monatsschrift für alte und neue Kultur*, v/5, 1929, p.81

Bibliography

Franz Roh, "Fotos von Aenne Biermann (Gera)", *Das Kunstblatt*, no.12, October 1928, pp.306–8

——, *Aenne Biermann: 60 Fotos*, Berlin, 1930 (in German, English and French)

Rudolf Hundt, "Zum Gedenken an Aenne Biermann", *Geraer Kulturspiegel*, no.4, 1947

Ute Eskildsen, *Aenne Biermann: Photographs, 1925–1933*, London: Nishen, 1988 (German original, 1987)

Domesticity and Dissent: The Role of Women Artists in Germany, 1918–1938, exh. cat., Leicester Museum and Art Gallery, and elsewhere, 1992

Jutta Dick and Marina Sassenberg, eds, *Jüdische Frauen im 19. und 20. Jahrhundert: Lexikon zu Leben und Werk*, Reinbek bei Hamburg: Rowohlt, 1993

Aenne Biermann started taking photographs as a young mother; her first subjects were her daughter Helga, born in

Biermann: *Rubber Plant, c.*1927; Museum Folkwang, Essen

1920, and her son Gerd, born in 1923. These photographs were private mementoes, taken without any professional training or object in view. The earliest were taken in 1921, probably with a 6 × 9 cm. hand-held camera. They show the technical difficulties of the amateur, but the difference between atmospheric observation and the consciously posed picture is already apparent. From 1926 Biermann's intellectual attitude to the medium of photography is clearly visible. The photographs take the observer's view into account in the composition of the pictures, but the technical problems that this self-taught photographer had with the medium are obvious.

The Bauhaus, situated at Dessau from 1926, was the centre of the political-cultural avant-garde in the region where Biermann and her husband lived. This is demonstrated by, among others, commissions to Thilo Schoder, a pupil of van de Velde, for the fitting of private and business rooms. In 1928 the first German exhibition of modern photography in the Jenaer Kunstverein, Jena, reflected the spirit of the age. Although Biermann's photographs were not represented in it, she no doubt visited this exhibition, which was only 45 kilometres from her home town of Gera.

Around this time Biermann began working with the geologist Rudolf Hundt. This placed demands on her that she could no longer fulfil with her rudimentary use of the camera. In 1929 she wrote: "About two years ago a geologist asked me to try to take some high-definition pictures of minerals in which the important thing was to ensure that certain details came out clearly. This made me take more account of the technical stipulations of high-quality prints" ("Von der photographischen Darstellung …", 1929). For Biermann, achieving high-quality pictures was also a matter of endowing objects with a new life of their own, revealing, through the effect of light on different surfaces, a new play of shadows and surprising contrasts. Ute Eskildsen (1988) has interpreted Biermann's entry into photography as "an endeavour to approach the situations and things of the everyday world with a camera". The photographs of her children are to be understood in this context, of seeking contact.

While she was working for Hundt, Biermann also took a series of photographs of plants (see illustration). It should be noted that at the exhibition in Jena there was a whole room dedicated to the works of Albert Renger-Patzsch, who in 1923–4 described plant photographs as seeing with insects' eyes. Biermann saw the connection between her geological and her plant photographs in the architectural structure of plants, which made them particularly interesting from a photographic point of view.

Biermann worked in isolation, but nevertheless, as her photographs show, she was bound up in the contemporary discourse. She had to read countless technical photographic journals. With her secure upper-middle-class background she had the most advanced technology at her disposal: she worked with Voïgtländer and Zeiss object lenses and with Vakublitz and Hauff-Leonar products. She had a photographic studio with a close-up camera. A reproduction dating from 1929 refers to the use of gas-light papers: in this case silver chloride papers, which are less light-sensitive than pure silver bromide emulsions. These papers were popular because, unlike the cool tones of silver bromide papers, they soon took on the warm tinges of the previous reproduction papers. With gas-light papers, photographs that had been lit and developed in the normal way took on a brownish-black tone that was hard to stabilise (see Ludwig David, *Photographisches Praktikum, Lehrbuch der Photographie*, Halle, 1924, pp.349–51). Because of their reduced light sensitivity, these papers were particularly popular with beginners, as they could be worked on in a relatively bright darkroom light.

Biermann took photographs with different formats of negative, from around 8 × 10 to 13 × 18 cm. In 1929 her work was mainly produced in formats up to 13 × 18 cm. and later chiefly 18 × 24 cm., while pictures for exhibition were enlarged up to 50 × 60 cm. Nearly all her known photographs bear a consecutive negative numbering, mainly on the back of the card. She preferred to stick her photographs on to a greyish-white card on which she generally signed her name and wrote the title of the photograph. From the very beginning, it seems to have been important to her to show her authorship directly beneath the photograph, as demonstrated by examples of her work as early as 1926–7. Eskildsen interpreted this gesture as an old-fashioned hangover from the days of art photography, but it is quite possible that this signature created an essential identity for Biermann in her specific life and work situation.

JUTTA DICK and MARINA SASSENBERG

Bilińska-Bohdanowicz, Anna
Polish painter, 1857–1893

Born Anna Bilińska in Złotopole, Ukraine, 1857. Studied drawing in Wiatka under Michael Elviro Andiriolli, 1869–71; studied at music conservatory in Warsaw, 1875–7; studied painting under Wojciech Gerson in Warsaw, 1877; gave private music and art lessons and established own studio. Studied in the women's studio at Académie Julian, Paris, under Julian and Tony Robert-Fleury from 1882; gave private art lessons and established own studio; took anatomy lessons at the Ecole des Beaux-Arts, April 1883; studied under Oliver Merson in order to overcome the limitations of the studio for women, May 1883. Suffered severe rheumatic fever, 1883. In 1884, due to exceptional talent and poverty, was exempt from tuition fees at Académie Julian, and won second prize in general competition there; became supervisor (*massière*) of painting studio, June 1886. Married physician Antoni Bohdanowicz, 1892; moved back to Warsaw, intending to open first art academy for women. Died of rheumatic fever and heart disease in Warsaw, 8 April 1893.

Principal Exhibitions
Society for the Encouragement of the Fine Arts, Warsaw: 1876, 1888 (first prize)
Paris Salon: 1884–5, 1887–8, 1892 (silver medal 1887)
Universal Exhibition of Art, Kraków, 1887 (honorary diploma)
Grosvenor Gallery, London: 1888
Exposition Blanc et Noir, Lyon: 1888
Royal Academy, London: 1888–92 (gold medal 1890)
Exposition Universelle, Paris: 1889 (gold medal and exemption from jury)
Internationale Kunstausstellung, Berlin: 1891 (gold medal)

Bilińska-Bohdanowicz: *Portrait of a Lady with Opera Glasses*, 1884; oil on canvas; 91 × 72 cm.; National Museum, Warsaw

Galerie Georges Petit, Paris: 1892
Galerie Desaix, Paris: 1892

Bibliography

Wielka Encyklopedia Powszechna Ilustrowana [Great general illustrated encyclopedia], vii–viii C, Warsaw, 1892

Exposition rétrospective d'oeuvres des peintres polonais, exh. cat., Galerie Georges Petit, Paris, 1900

Katalog Muzeum Narodowego w Krakowie [Catalogue of the National Museum in Kraków], Kraków, 1902

Sto pięćdziesiąt lat malarstwa polskiego w szkicach [150 years of Polish paintings in essays], exh. cat., Warsaw, 1918

Edward Niewiadomski, *Malarstwo polskie XIX i XX wieku* [Polish painting in the 19th and 20th centuries], Warsaw, 1926

Antoni Bohdanowicz, *Anna Bilińska, podług jej dziennika, listów i recenzyj prasy* [Anna Bilińska according to her diary, letters and press reviews], Warsaw: Dom Książki Polskiej, 1928

Zbiory Polskiego Muzeum Narodowego w Rapperswilu: Katalog XXV [Collection of the Polish National Museum in Rapperswil: Catalogue of the 25th TOnZP exhibition], Warsaw, 1928

Marja Gerson-Dabrowska, *Polscy artyści: Ich życie i dzieła* [Polish artists: Their lives and works], Warsaw, 1930

Polski słownik biograficzny [Polish biographical dictionary], ii, Kraków: Polska Akademia Umiejętności, 1936

Tadeusz Dobrowolski, *Nowoczesne malarstwo polskie* [Modern Polish painting], ii, Wrocław, 1960

Słownik Artystów Polskich i Obcych [Dictionary of Polish and foreign artists], i, Wrocław: Zaklad narodowy imienia Ossolinskich, 1971

Wiesław Juszczak, *Teksty o malarzach: Antologia polskiej krytyki artystycznej, 1890–1918* [Writings on painters: Anthology of Polish art criticism, 1890–1918], Wrocław, 1976

Jens Christian von Jensen, ed., *Polnische Malerei von 1830 bis 1914*, Cologne: DuMont, 1978

La Peinture polonaise du XVIe au début du XXe siècle, Warsaw: National Museum, 1979

Symbolism in Polish Painting, 1890–1914, exh. cat., Detroit Institute of Arts, 1984

Andrzej Ryszkiewicz, *Malarstwo polskie: Romantyzm, historyzm, realizm* [Polish painting: Romanticism, historicism, realism], Warsaw: Auriga, 1985

Nineteenth-Century Polish Painting, exh. cat., National Academy of Design, New York, and elsewhere, 1988

The Julian Academy, Paris, 1868–1939, exh. cat., Shepherd Gallery, New York, 1989

Artystki polskie [Polish women artists], exh. cat., National Museum, Warsaw, 1991

Polish Women Artists and the Avant-Garde: Voices of Freedom, exh. cat., National Museum of Women in the Arts, Washington, DC, 1991

Anna Bilińska, like all women in Poland of the time, had no access to an art academy, and in 1882 was the first Polish artist, man or woman, to study in Paris, rather than in Munich as was then the vogue. In 1882, before her trip to Paris, she travelled in Italy, Austria and Germany, studying works of art in museums. She was inspired by Titian and Tintoretto in Italy, and by Rembrandt, Rubens and Murillo in Munich. In Vienna she studied drawings at the Albertina, and at the Academy sketched casts of works by Michelangelo, Jacopo Sansovino and Donatello. After her arrival in Paris, her initial intention was to be a history painter, but she soon abandoned the idea, deciding instead to create a cycle depicting a woman in her different roles; she believed that her art could influence women and felt a responsibility to help them. In order to survive she concentrated on portraiture, but also painted a variety of other subjects. She was an excellent draughtswoman, and painted in oils and watercolours; most of her pictures are of average size. She was able to overcome the prejudice against women portraying nude male figures, as exemplified by an oil study of a partially covered male figure of c.1885 (National Museum, Warsaw).

With her fiancé Wojciech Grabowski, Bilińska planned to establish an academy of art for women in Poland, but after his premature death from tuberculosis in 1885 and the death of her father and best friend Klimcia (Klementyna) Krassowska a year earlier, she fell into severe depression. In 1885, accompanied by her friend Maria Gażycz, she spent time at Pourville-les-Bains, and concentrated on landscapes and seascapes. Her grief for Grabowski was intense and long-lasting, and in her *Self-Portrait* (1887; National Museum, Kraków) she portrayed herself in black mourning dress. She gained international success and recognition through this picture, while her financial independence was assured by Krassowska's will, which freed her from giving lessons and allowed her to concentrate fully on her art.

Bilińska's works exemplify Robert-Fleury's advice to her to observe nature, to paint with a loose brush stroke and to avoid adding unnecessary details. Whether in her *Self-Portrait* of 1887 or the genre scene *At the Seashore* (1886; oil on cardboard; National Museum, Warsaw) she used minimal means to balance the composition and to capture the essential qualities of her subjects, imparting their emotional state. In the latter picture, especially, she conveyed a feeling of intimacy between the mother and her child.

Bilińska was often advised by the renowned Polish romantic painter Józef Chełmoński, one of her friends in Paris. Many of his works depict genre subjects of the Polish countryside, or of the lands that were part of Poland before its partition in the 18th century, and may have influenced her interest in the folklore of Podole and the Ukraine (all works untraced). In 1888, at the Grosvenor Gallery in London, she exhibited a series of genre pictures of Ukrainian peasants and a pastel *Self-Portrait in Ukrainian Costume*, which was purchased by the Gallery. Only a few of her watercolours are known, among them the *Coast of Brittany* (1889; National Museum). The sea is indicated with broad brush strokes; the white waves pound the shore as the dark clouds of an impending storm appear in the sky. The painting comes closer to Turner's early work than to the school of realism, but the feeling of desolation suggests Bilińska's own emotional state.

Bilińska's friendship with the wealthy Kossowski family and Chełmoński brought her into contact with the elite of the Polish expatriate community. She painted portraits of *Ignacy Paderewski* and *Josef Hoffmann*, the latter for the American collector Corning Clark, and of *George Grey Barnard*, a young American sculptor; she also made a drawing for Helena Modrzejewska's album (all untraced). In 1892 Ignacy Korwin-Milewski, a collector of self-portraits of renowned artists, commissioned her to paint her own portrait. The *Unfinished Self-Portrait* of 1893 was donated by her husband to the National Museum, Warsaw; although ill and dying she represented herself unidealised and almost full length against a plain background. Yet her *Portrait of a Lady with Opera Glasses* (1884; see illustration) is the quintessence of elegance and refinement, and the sitter appears to be unaware of the intrusion into her privacy. It is also an excellent example of Bilińska's mastery of composition, texture, colour, drawing and anatomy.

It is difficult to assess Bilińska's oeuvre, because so many of her works, known from the reviews published in Wieslaw Juszczak's anthology, are untraced. Although her letter of 18 January 1884 to Grabowski shows that she thought Manet's paintings lacked merit, in some of her own works she appears to have assimilated many of the new trends. For instance, at the Blanc et Noir exhibition of 1889, her painting *White Elder* (untraced) was described as a symphony of pearl greys, silver whites and transparent shadows; it was shown in London with a study of a girl in a Japanese dress of grey-blue. Both works suggest a change in her approach to colour, and a probable contact with pictures by Whistler. The new sensitivity to the nuances of colour and delicate tonalities is exemplified by the *Street of Unter den Linden in Berlin* (1890; oil on canvas; National Museum). In this winter scene, Bilińska's treatment of space and atmosphere relates to the Impressionists rather than to the school of realism with which she is usually associated. Her untimely death not only cut short her progress as a painter, but also left her intention of establishing an art academy for women in Warsaw unrealised. This would have been modelled on the French academies, but she also intended to extend its curriculum and to give women a well-rounded education. Her death was mourned in Poland by the most eminent people, including her friend Chełmoński and the great poet Maria Konopnicka, both of whom devoted essays to her.

DANUTA BATORSKA

Bingen, Hildegard of *see* Hildegard of Bingen

Binns, Vivienne

Australian artist, 1940–

Born in Wyong, New South Wales, 6 December 1940. Studied at the National Art School, Sydney (diploma 1962), and on the Community Training Program, Bowral, New South Wales, 1982. Acted as consultant to many groups and organisations in Australia, initiating community arts projects from 1972. Projects include *Mothers' Memories, Others' Memories*, Blacktown Municipality, New South Wales, 1979–81; *Full Flight*, rural New South Wales, 1981–3; and *Tower of Babel*, an ongoing work open to contributors by invitation, Sydney, 1989. Member of Women's Art Movement (WAM) and Women's Art Register, Sydney, 1974–8; Women's Art Group, Sydney University, 1974–8; vice-chair, National Association for the Visual Arts (NAVA), 1988–90. Recipient of Order of Australia medal for service to art and craft, 1983; Ros Bower Memorial award for visionary contribution to community art, 1986; Australian Artists Creative fellowship, 1990. Lives in Canberra and in Lawson, New South Wales.

Principal Exhibitions

Watters Gallery, Sydney: 1967, 1991 (both individual)
Westpoint Shopping Plaza, Blacktown: 1981 (*Mothers' Memories, Others' Memories*, final exhibition in tour)
Art Gallery of New South Wales, Sydney: 1981 (*Australian Perspecta*), 1982 (*Vision in Disbelief*, 4th Biennale of Sydney)
Sutton Gallery, Melbourne: 1992 (individual)
Bellas Gallery, Brisbane: 1993 (individual)

Selected Writings

"Mothers' memories, others' memories", *Lip*, no.7, 1980, pp.38–45
"A brief history of an art practice in community contexts", *Artlink*, x, Spring 1990, pp.70–73
Editor, *Community and the Arts: History, Theory, Practice: Australian Perspectives*, Sydney: Pluto, 1991

Bibliography

Lucy R. Lippard, "Out of control: Australian art on the left", *Village Voice*, October 1982
Janine Burke, *Field of Vision: A Decade of Change: Women's Art in the Seventies*, Ringwood, Victoria: Viking, 1990
Bernard Smith and Terry Smith, *Australian Painting, 1788–1990*, 3rd edition, Melbourne: Oxford University Press, 1991
Julie Ewington, "Enduring patterns: The art of Vivienne Binns", *Art Monthly* (Australia), no.51, July 1992, pp.3–5
Sandy Kirby, *Sight Lines: Women's Art and Feminist Perspectives in Australia*, Roseville East, NSW: Craftsman House, 1992
Joan Kerr, "The art of Vivienne Binns", *Art and Australia*, xxx, 1993, pp.337–45

In the Australian journal *Artlink* Vivienne Binns stated that she regarded herself as being a "craftswoman-artist" (1990). She sees her art practice as relating strategically to high culture and professional excellence as much as to low culture, an engagement with the community at large, and with feminism. In 1983 Binns received an Order of Australia medal for her service to art and craft and, as further acknowledgment of her achievements and continuing potential, the Australian Artists Creative fellowship (1990). Trained as a painter at the National Art School, Sydney, Binns subsequently also explored enamelling, silk-screen printing, collaborative sculpture and, to a lesser degree, performance. Aspects of her work practice connect directly with a broad cross-section of people who have not necessarily received formal art training. Significantly, she was general editor of the key publication *Community and the Arts* (1991). Indeed it can be claimed that Vivienne Binns, in her role as artist-in-community and her commitment to the marginalised medium of craft, was a pioneer in the field.

Binns's personal creative explorations have often anticipated issues that have become pivotal for the development of Australian art. An early example was her first solo exhibition at Watters Gallery, Sydney, in 1967, which predated the women's art movement in the country by several years. Comprising paintings with explicit and symbolic representations of genitalia, the show included a vivid, decorative painting entitled *Vag dens* (1966; National Gallery of Australia, Canberra), which has become something of an icon in Australian art history. The title is a diminutive of "Vagina dentata", the toothed vagina. For Binns, who at the time knew nothing of this anti-patriarchal symbol, her image was primarily one of strength and realisation. The psychedelic colours and sinuous lines of the composition locate it specifically with the funky as well as the political energy of Sydney in the mid-1960s.

When the Sydney Women's Art Group was formed in 1974, based very much on the American model (Lucy Lippard visited Australia at this period), Binns was a founding member. She also became an early supporter of the Artworkers Union and generally became recognised as a leading activist for artists' rights. As a central figure in the development of community arts in Australia, she undertook the project *Mothers' Memories, Others' Memories* (1979–81) while she was resident artist at the University of New South Wales and then as artist-in-community at Blacktown. Reporting in the

Binns: *Surfacing in the Pacific*, 1993; acrylic on canvas; 172 × 162 cm.; courtesy Sutton Gallery, Melbourne, and Bellas Gallery, Brisbane

Melbourne-based feminist journal *Lip* (1980, p.39), Binns stated that *Mothers' Memories, Others' Memories* was arrived at

> Through the participation of all kinds of people, the lives of women were recalled and their means of creative expression in the domestic sphere examined. Memories, family albums, artefacts and memorabilia were collected, presented in various forms and interpreted in a variety of ways. There was needlework, crochet work and knitting, as well as the more traditional arts of painting, drawing and pottery, gardening, cooking, homecare and decoration; diaries, albums and letters revealed their importance as expressive media. All this material was drawn from the lives of participants themselves or the lives of their mothers, aunts and grandmothers.

Subsequent community projects that Binns has initiated include *Full Flight* (1981–3), a comprehensive Central Western Arts scheme in New South Wales that focused on lifestyles and the relationship of people to their environment; *Country-City Connection* (1986–8) with the Municipality of North Sydney; and *Tower of Babel*, an ongoing work begun in 1989. The "Tower" comprises small wooden box assemblages made by Binns and other known artists as well as by untutored friends and acquaintances. In recognising the importance of the "amateur" artist and moving beyond the boundaries of contemporary aesthetic canons, Binns has tapped the often overlooked creativity of "ordinary Australians".

Binns's exhibition history encompasses some 30 years, including solo exhibitions at the staunchly supportive Watters Gallery, Sydney, and participation in high-profile events, namely *Australian Perspecta* of 1981 and the Biennale of Sydney (1982) with instances of her collaborative works. In tandem with the artist's travels to Southeast Asia, Japan and, more recently, the South Pacific, she has started exhibiting paintings, works on paper and photographs ("pics") that reflect not only her interest in working across diverse cultural contexts in Australia but an awareness of that country's geographical position in Asia and the Pacific. Her acrylic on canvas *Surfacing in the Pacific* (1993; see illustration) revises an 18th-century painting by William Hodges, an artist on Cook's second voyage to the Pacific, and draws also on tapa cloth patterning (from Tonga). Operating within the politics of a post-colonial Pacific region, and extraordinarily adept at collapsing the divide between craft and fine art, and between dissimilar cultures, through this painting Binns allows for a celebration of the romantic vision of the early explorers yet confronts its imperialism fulsomely, allowing space for indigenous expression.

In a comprehensive article on the artist for *Art and Australia* (1993) Joan Kerr described Binns as "a lifelong iconoclast", someone who has always pursued unfashionable positions in her art practice, whether through the sheer energy and courage of her painting, the pursuit of so-called minor arts or the genuine equality of her collaboration projects. This robust talent has been inspirational for many Australian women artists and more generally for its challenge to a restricted notion of the avant-garde.

ANNE KIRKER

Bishop, Isabel
American painter, 1902–1988

Born in Cincinnati, Ohio, 3 March 1902. Studied illustration at the New York School of Applied Design for Women, 1918–20; painting at the Art Students League, New York, under Kenneth Hayes Miller, 1920–24. Travelled to Europe with Miller, Reginald Marsh and Edward Laning, 1931. Established studio in Union Square, New York, 1934. Married neurologist Harold G. Wolff, 1934; son born 1940; husband died 1962. Lived in Riverdale, New York, after marriage, but continued to work at Union Square studio until 1984. Taught at Art Students League, New York, 1936–7 (the only full-time woman member of staff); Skowhegan School of Painting and Sculpture, Maine, 1956–8 and 1963; Yale University School of Fine Arts, New Haven, 1963. Recipient of numerous awards and prizes, including American Academy of Arts and Letters award, 1943; National Arts Club gold medal, 1968 and 1970; Purchase prize, Mount Holyoke College Art Museum, South Hadley, Massachusetts, 1974; Creative Arts award medal, Brandeis University, Waltham, Massachusetts, 1975; Outstanding Achievement in the Arts award, presented by President Jimmy Carter, 1979; gold medal for painting, American Academy and Institute of Arts and Letters, 1987; honorary doctorates from Moore College of Art, Philadelphia, 1954; Bates College, Lewiston, Maine, 1979; Syracuse University, New York, 1982; Mount Holyoke College, 1983. Associate Member, 1940, and Member, 1941, National Academy of Design; member, 1944, and vice-president, 1946, National Institute of Arts and Letters (first woman officer since 1898); Benjamin Franklin fellow, Royal Society of Arts, London, 1964; member, American Academy of Arts and Letters, New York, 1971. Died in the Bronx, New York, 19 February 1988.

Selected Individual Exhibitions
Midtown Galleries, New York: 1933, 1935, 1936, 1939, 1942, 1949, 1955, 1960, 1967, 1974, 1984, 1986
Herbert Institute, Atlanta: 1939
Smithsonian Institution, Washington, DC: 1945
Berkshire Museum, Pittsfield, MA: 1957
Virginia Museum of Fine Arts, Richmond: 1960
Wood Art Gallery, Montpelier, VT: 1972
University of Arizona Museum of Art, Tucson: 1974–5 (touring retrospective)
Associated American Artists Gallery, New York: 1981 (retrospective)
St Gaudens Museum, St Gaudens, NH: 1983
Laband Art Gallery, Loyola Marymount University, Los Angeles: 1985

Selected Writings
"Concerning edges", *Magazine of Art*, xxxviii, May 1945, pp.168–73
"Kenneth Hayes Miller", *Magazine of Art*, April 1952, pp.162–9

Bibliography
Patricia Paull Newsom, "Isabel Bishop", *American Artist*, xlix, September 1925, pp.42–5, 90
Dorothy Seckler, "Bishop paints a picture", *Art News*, l, November 1951, pp.38–41, 63–4
Fairfield Porter in *The Nation*, 21 May 1960

Bishop: *Subway Scene*, 1957–8; egg tempera and oil on composition board; 101.6 × 71.1 cm.; Whitney Museum of American Art, New York (Purchase, 58.55)

Ernest Harms, "Light is the beginning: The art of Isabel Bishop", *American Artist*, xxv, February 1961, pp.28–33, 60–62

Isabel Bishop: Prints and Drawings, 1925–1964, exh. cat., Brooklyn Museum, NY, 1964

Isabel Bishop, exh. cat., University of Arizona Museum of Art, Tucson, and elsewhere, 1974

Lawrence Alloway, "Isabel Bishop: The grand manner and the working girl", *Art in America*, lxiii, September–October 1975, pp.61–5

Karl Lunde, *Isabel Bishop*, New York: Abrams, 1975

Sheldon Reich, "Isabel Bishop: The 'ballet' of everyday life", *Art News*, lxxiv, September 1975, pp.92–3

Cindy Nemser, "Conversation with Isabel Bishop", *Feminist Art Journal*, no.5, Spring 1976, pp.14–20

Eleanor Munro, *Originals: American Women Artists*, New York: Simon and Schuster, 1979

Mahonri Sharp Young, "The Fourteenth Street School", *Apollo*, cxiii, 1981, pp.164–71

Isabel Bishop: The Affectionate Eye, exh. cat., Laband Art Gallery, Loyola Marymount University, Los Angeles, 1985

Susan Pirpiris Teller, ed., *Isabel Bishop: Etchings and Aquatints: A Catalogue Raisonné*, 2nd edition, New York: Associated American Artists, 1985

Helen Yglesias, *Isabel Bishop*, New York: Rizzoli, 1989 (contains bibliography)

Ellen Wiley Todd, "Isabel Bishop: The question of difference", *Smithsonian Studies in American Art*, iii/4, 1989, pp.24–41

——, *The "New Woman" Revised: Painting and Gender Politics on Fourteenth Street*, Berkeley: University of California Press, 1993

Had Stephen Sondheim never heard of Georges Seurat, he might very well have been attracted to the idea of writing a Broadway musical about the work of Isabel Bishop, frequently referred to as America's best woman painter. He would have had to shift the focus somewhat, since for this artist "color was not the original motif for me. My fundamentals are form, space and light", but emphases on the painstakingly slow crafting of an image and the structural importance of the human figure, moving or resting in New York's Union Square or subways rather than on La Grande Jatte, could have remained the same. Guided by the artist's recorded thoughts, the revised version of *Sunday in the Park with George* could have maintained its relative lack of interest in situating art within a specific social context. Appealing as this idea might be, however, much of what can be said about Bishop, the first woman to have held an executive position in the National Institute of Arts and Letters, would be lost, just as it was with Seurat.

Bishop, educated at the Art Students League under the tutelage of Kenneth Hayes Miller, clearly came to see herself as a "painter's painter". Her now highly prized drawings and etchings were created only to serve the handful of small gessoed panels produced each year. She resisted any pressure she might have felt from her contemporaries to turn her figurative art towards direct social criticism and, as a woman, felt no compunction whatsoever in affiliating herself with the European tradition of the female nude. Whatever may now be said about issues of representation, she is responsible for an impressive oeuvre, many formal qualities of which were brilliantly summarised by Fairfield Porter in a passage on her *Subway Scene* (1957–8; see illustration):

> The materiality of the box that frames the mirror is bright, strong, ugly, the girl herself is passing, but her image, her sublimation, of the thinnest substance of all,

holds you by its subtlety ... Her paradox consists in saying that the part of art which represents the outer world, and which criticism associates with reality, is a sublimation; and that the abstract part that represents nothing, and that criticism associates with non-objectivity, is the part that stands for reality, for the object, for being awake [*The Nation*, 21 May 1960].

These words, which resist the many "realist" analyses offered by critics, apply equally well to any of her paintings from the 1940s on, as can be seen in such works as *Preparation* (1944; Marjorie and Charles Benton Collection, repr. Yglesias 1989, p.61), depicting a massive yet opalescent female nude cutting her toenails, and *Self-Portrait* (1986; Collection Mr and Mrs McCauley Conner; *ibid.*, p.41), in which the somewhat ghost-like, aged artist brings to mind Titian's fragile *Pope Julius III* (Capodimonte, Naples).

Attempts to describe Bishop's panels almost invariably include references to European painting of the 16th to 18th centuries, and this is as she would have wanted. Her nudes often evoke the work of Rubens or Rembrandt, the artist she appreciated above all, and the carefully constructed unfinished/worn appearance of her surfaces are suggestive of many pasts. Yet the word "timeless" sometimes used in conjunction with her work is only part of the story. Just as important are the changes in her picturing of the resolutely white America she observed for decades.

After leaving Miller's classroom in 1923, Bishop struggled alone for a number of years in a rented studio to find her own voice which, by the early 1930s, led her to abandon the crowded, often frieze-like urban scenes that were among Miller's specialities. Unable to persuade those she called the "bums" of Union Square to serve as her models, she settled on the working-class women of the area for her principal subjects – in some respects literally, as she spoke of having "corralled them" into her studio. They were monumentalised, singly or in pairs, in even their most mundane moments and were set within milky-grey spaces bearing few specific indicators of location. As has been convincingly argued by Ellen Wiley Todd (1993), Bishop's young women fulfilled the expectations of the office worker defined in the 1920s and 1930s; they were fashionably attired, modest in their aspirations and showed little of the exhaustion one might have anticipated in a period during which working hours increased and wages declined. *At the Noon Hour* (1939; tempera and pencil on composition board; Museum of Fine Arts, Springfield, MA) offered an appealing image of two healthy, if slightly rumpled female office workers leaning against a wall, alert and engaged in an intimate and obviously pleasurable conversation. Some of the paintings from the early 1940s seem to anticipate the verbal intervention of a viewer: the woman wiping lipstick from her teeth in *Tidying Up* (1941; Indianapolis Museum of Art) is like a friend who, when finished, will turn and ask "did I get it all?", while the open-mouthed *Girl with Frankfurter* (1945; Collection Harold William Brown, repr. Yglesias 1989, p.104) depends on someone to warn her of any impending ketchup spills.

Bishop's women remained in fashion as they moved through the 1950s and 1960s, but were even less tied to the immediate environs of the workplace. Generally in profile, they travelled through the subways or streets, eventually losing not only their recognisable identities as a class of employees, but also the intimacy of contact with one another. *Five Women Walking, No.2* (1967; Edwin A. Ulrich Museum of Art, Wichita State University, KS) contains a grouping of three at its centre, but one that is formed by the exigencies of motion rather than any desire for companionship. By 1970 her women had once again become classifiable "workers". They had metamorphosed into mini-skirted and be-jeaned students who, with their male peers, walked or sat reading in apparent isolation, knit together only by their placement in a variegated web of horizontal striations that sometimes resulted in surfaces reminiscent of crazy-quilts (*High School Students, No.3*, 1974; *ibid.*, p.138).

If Bishop's female figures had been separated from one another by the mid-1960s, shortly to become equal participants in a Seurat-like world of the non-verbal, another associated change can also be observed. Withdrawn from the female viewer was what Todd has characterised as a privileged invitation to enter the spaces of friendship forged by the young office workers of the 1930s and 1940s. The implied, though class-blind, camaraderie of female artist, subject and viewer had dissipated. Bishop lived long enough to witness the collective spirit of second-wave feminism, cautiously inserting herself into some of its activities, but chose to ignore it in her production. Possible explanations for the disappearance of a special place for women in and before her art are numerous, ranging from the personal – an artist no longer requiring from her subjects evidence of the intimacy she believed herself to have been deprived of by a father whose fortunes had fallen and by a distant, suffragist mother – to the aesthetic – the by-then unquenchable nature of her search for a way of articulating the actuality of movement, of physical and social becoming, in all human beings. The unique blend of tradition and modernism that constituted the formal character of Bishop's work erased neither the human figure nor its participation in some form of everyday drama, and her paintings still elicit more questions than answers about what those changing images of the social signified for and about her.

CATHERINE MACKENZIE

Bisschop-Robertson, Suze *see* Robertson, Suze

Black, Dorrit

Australian painter and printmaker, 1891–1951

Born Dorothea Foster Black in Burnside, Adelaide, 23 December 1891. Attended classes at South Australian School of Arts and Crafts, Adelaide, *c.*1910. First visited Europe, 1911–12. Studied at Sydney Art School, 1915–23; studied linocut printmaking under Thea Proctor in Sydney, 1927. Studied at Grosvenor School of Modern Art, London, under Claude Flight and Iain MacNab, 1927; Académie Lhôte, Paris, 1927; André Lhôte summer school, Mirmande, south of France, 1928; took lessons in Paris studio of Albert Gleizes, 1929. Returned to Sydney, late 1929; founder and first director, Modern Art Centre, Sydney, 1932. Visited Europe again, 1934–5. Settled in Adelaide, 1935; taught at South Australian School of Arts and Crafts from 1940. Founder-member and vice-chair, Contemporary Art Society of South Australia, 1942. Established modernist Group 9, comprising nine associate members of Royal South Australian Society of Arts, 1944. Died after a road accident, 13 September 1951.

Principal Exhibitions

Individual
Macquarie Galleries, Sydney: 1930, 1936
Modern Art Centre, Sydney: 1932
Royal South Australian Society of Arts Gallery, Adelaide: 1938, 1945, 1949, 1952 (memorial)

Group
Society of Artists, Sydney: 1916–20, 1926, 1933
Anthony Hordern's Fine Art Gallery, Sydney: 1921 (*Paintings and Drawings by Eleven Australian Women*)
Younger Group of Australian Artists, Sydney: 1924–5
Salon des Indépendants, Paris: 1929
Redfern Gallery and Ward Gallery, London: 1929–31, 1933–7 (*British Linocuts*, all organised by Claude Flight)
Macquarie Galleries, Sydney: 1930 (*A Group of Seven*)
Modern Art Centre, Sydney: 1932 (*Progressive Art*), 1932 (*Seventeen Artists*), 1933 (*Prints*), 1933 (*Drawings*)
Contemporary Group, Sydney: 1933–4, 1936, 1938–9, 1941–7, 1950
Royal South Australian Society of Arts, Adelaide: 1937, 1939–43, 1945–51
Contemporary Art Society of Victoria, Melbourne: 1940–44
Contemporary Art Society of South Australia, Adelaide: 1944, 1946, 1948–51
Group 9, Adelaide: 1944–6, 1948–9, 1951

Bibliography

Some Forgotten … Some Remembered: Women Artists of South Australia, exh. cat., Sydenham Gallery, Adelaide, 1976
Ian North, *The Art of Dorrit Black*, Adelaide: Art Gallery Board of South Australia, 1979 (contains extensive bibliography)
Stephen Coppel, "Claude Flight and his Australian pupils", *Print Quarterly*, xi, 1985, pp.263–83
Shirley Cameron Wilson, *From Shadow into Light: South Australian Women Artists since Colonisation*, St Peter's, South Australia: Delmont, 1988
Adelaide Angries: South Australian Painting of the 1940s, exh. cat., Art Gallery of South Australia, Adelaide, 1989
Mary Eagle, *Australian Modern Painting Between the Wars, 1914–1939*, Sydney and London: Bay, 1989
South Australian Women Artists: Paintings from the 1890s to the 1940s, exh. cat., Art Gallery South Australia, Adelaide, 1994
Joan Kerr, ed., *Heritage: The National Women's Art Book*, Sydney: Dictionary of Australian Artists/Craftsman House, 1995

As a mature artist in her fifties Dorrit Black became one of the most influential figures in South Australian art. Her study overseas and its subsequent remarkable influence on her work led to the development of a style that is unique in the history of Australian art.

Black first studied art in Adelaide with H.P. Gill and Gwen Barringer, from whom she gained a solid but conservative grounding. She studied linocut printing in Sydney with Thea Proctor, and in 1927 travelled overseas to study at the Grosvenor School of Modern Art in London, where she was

Black: *Olive Plantation*, 1946; oil on canvas; 63.5 × 86.5 cm.; Art Gallery of South Australia, Adelaide; Bequest of the Artist, 1952

taught by Iain MacNab, learning much about the solidity of form from his neo-classical style of painting. The major influence on Black's work, however, came from her time in France with the Cubist teachers André Lhôte and Albert Gleizes, with whom she studied in the company of her fellow Australian artists, Grace Crowley and Anne Dangar. While studying with Lhôte these three women painted views of Mirmande, a small village in the south of France, and it is interesting to compare their individual responses to their teachers' Cubist approach. The influence of Lhôte and Gleizes on Black's work is very much evident in *Still Life* (*c*.1928; Art Gallery of South Australia, Adelaide), in which she flattened form and dissected the picture plane with diagonals in order to describe visually the essential construction of the objects depicted. While it is a competent work, it does not yet show the unique and solid style that she later developed in Australia.

When Black returned to Sydney in late 1929 she was soon inspired, as were so many artists, to paint the monumental construction of the Sydney Harbour Bridge, the daily growth of which dominated the Sydney skyline. In *The Bridge* (1930; Art Gallery of South Australia) she employed all the Cubist principles she had adopted from her teachers in France, dividing the picture surface with diagonals and defining form

through angles and flattened surfaces, avoiding a central focus in her brilliant blue view of the Harbour. While in Sydney, Black became actively involved in the contemporary art circles there, establishing the Modern Art Centre in 1932. In 1934 she returned to Europe, this time travelling widely and further absorbing many European influences before returning permanently to Adelaide in 1935.

Black became one of the strongest local forces during the 1940s, a crucial decade in South Australian art, both as a teacher and as an artist of exceptional talent. She brought to Adelaide a style of broadly informed European modernism, and became the most influential teacher at the South Australian School of Arts and Crafts. She was one of the most prolific exhibitors among the artists of Adelaide, showing both linocuts and paintings. She exhibited regularly at the Royal South Australian Society of Arts and, in 1942, became the inaugural vice-chair of the Contemporary Art Society of South Australia, which was formed as a result of revolutionary disquiet among the young artists of Adelaide. In 1944 she established Group 9 to facilitate the showing of modernist work in Adelaide. As an artist who had travelled and studied abroad extensively, the 1940s became a time of distillation and selection when she could produce her own regional style away from external influences. She depicted her beloved South Australian landscape with a robust solidity unparalleled in the work of any other artist, as in *Olive Plantation* (1946; see illustration), depicting an orchard at Magill near her home in the Adelaide foothills, *Coast Road* (1942) and *Cliffs at Second Valley* (c.1949), both on the coast south of Adelaide. This feeling for sculptural form can also be found in her figure compositions. Rounded, solid shapes make highly original cubistic compositions in *Ballet Rehearsal* (1947) and *Sketch Club* (1942; all Art Gallery of South Australia).

Black was also one of Australia's foremost modernist printmakers. Her colour linocuts of the late 1920s show some influence from her teacher, the British artist Claude Flight. The figure compositions *Music*, *The Acrobats* and *Wings*, all of 1927 and probably the first linocuts she made, are characterised by a remarkable vitality, with elements of Art Deco design evident in the compositions. Later works in this medium show a stylistic individuality exceptional in Australian printmaking, and her prints of the early 1930s were among the most advanced executed in Australia at that time. During the 1940s the solidity of form and strength of composition seen in her paintings also appear in her linocuts. One of the most outstanding late works is *Naval Funeral* (c.1949), executed in South Australia. All Black's prints are represented in the Art Gallery of South Australia, Adelaide.

JANE HYLTON

Blackadder, Elizabeth
British painter, 1931–

Born in Falkirk, Scotland, 24 September 1931. Studied at Edinburgh University and Edinburgh College of Art, under William Gillies, 1949–54 (MA). Awarded Andrew Carnegie travelling scholarship and visited Yugoslavia, Greece and Italy, 1954; post-graduate scholarship year in Italy, 1955–6. Married painter John Houston and began part-time teaching at Edinburgh College of Art, 1956. Took teacher-training course, 1958–9. Librarian, Fine Art Department, Edinburgh University, 1959–61; lecturer, School of Drawing and Painting, Edinburgh College of Art, 1962–86. Travelled widely with husband, throughout Europe and to USA and Japan. Recipient of Guthrie award, Royal Scottish Academy, 1962; joint winner, Watercolour Foundation award, Royal Academy Summer Exhibition, 1962; honorary doctorates from Heriot-Watt University and University of Edinburgh. Member, Royal Scottish Society of Painters in Watercolour; Society of Scottish Artists; Royal Glasgow Institute; Royal Incorporation of Architects in Scotland; honorary member, Royal West of England Academy; Royal Society of Painters in Watercolour. Associate member, 1963, and member, 1972, Royal Scottish Academy; Associate, 1971, and member, 1976, Royal Academy. Order of the British Empire (OBE), 1982. Lives in Edinburgh.

Selected Individual Exhibitions
57 Gallery, Edinburgh: 1959
Aitken Dott, Edinburgh: 1961, 1966, 1972, 1974
Mercury Gallery, London: 1965, 1967, 1969, 1971, 1973, 1976, 1978, 1980, 1982, 1984, 1988, 1991, 1993, 1994, 1996
Reading Art Gallery and Museum: 1967
Vaccarino Gallery, Florence: 1970
Loomshop Gallery, Lower Largo, Fife: 1971, 1974, 1976, 1981
Middlesbrough Art Gallery: 1977
Stirling Gallery, Stirling: 1977
Yehudi Menuhin School, Stoke D'Abernon, Surrey: 1978
Bohun Gallery, Henley-on-Thames: 1981
Scottish Arts Council, Edinburgh: 1981–2 (touring retrospective)
Theo Waddington Gallery, Toronto: 1982
Mercury Gallery, Edinburgh: 1982, 1985
Lillian Heidenberg Gallery, New York: 1983, 1986
Henley-on-Thames Festival of Music and Arts: 1987
Glasgow Print Studio Gallery: 1987 (with John Houston), 1993
Aberystwyth Arts Centre: 1989 (touring retrospective, organised by Welsh Arts Council)
Abbot Hall, Kendal: 1990 (retrospective)
Durham Light Infantry Museum, Durham: 1992 (retrospective)
Scottish Gallery, Edinburgh: 1994

Selected Writings
Introduction, *The Plant: Images of Plants, from the Scientifically Accurate to the Purely Imaginative, Selected from Artists Working since the War and Closely Connected with Scotland*, exh. cat., Scottish Arts Council, Edinburgh, 1987 (with Dr Brinsley Burbidge)

Bibliography
T. Elder Dickson, "Scottish painting: The modern spirit", *The Studio*, clxvi, 1963, pp.236–43
Douglas Hall, "Elizabeth Blackadder", *Scottish Art Review*, ix/4, 1964, pp.9–12, 31
Elizabeth Blackadder, exh. cat., Scottish Arts Council, Edinburgh, 1981
Elizabeth Blackadder and John Houston, exh. cat., Glasgow Print Studio Gallery, 1987
Philip Vann, "RA travel: Eastern Eden. Elizabeth Blackadder RA tells Philip Vann of her Japanese inspirations", *RA Magazine*, no.15, 1987, pp.46–8
Judith Bumpus, *Elizabeth Blackadder*, Oxford: Phaidon, 1988
Elizabeth Blackadder, exh. cat., Aberystwyth Arts Centre and Welsh Arts Council, 1989
Scottish Art since 1900, exh. cat., Scottish National Gallery of Modern Art, Edinburgh, and elsewhere, 1989
Deborah Kellaway, *Favourite Flowers: Watercolours by Elizabeth Blackadder*, London: Pavilion, 1994

Elizabeth Blackadder's paintings of landscape, still life and figures won her a prominent place in the 1960s among a younger generation of Scottish artists that included her husband, John Houston. Her treatment of these subjects, while it followed a vigorously Scottish tradition of realism, was also fully cognisant of developments in European modern art and American Abstract Expressionism. By the mid-1960s the ideas that she had been exploring since at least the beginning of the decade began to make a new and significant contribution to forms of 20th-century still-life composition. Most characteristically, her work in oil and watercolour combined abstract themes with a continuing regard for the integrity of the object. She sought to fuse the economy of expression of oriental calligraphy and painting with a Westerner's vision of reality. The full development of these ideas in the 1970s distinguished Blackadder as the first modern artist to relate a long tradition

Blackadder: *Fragment of an Anthology*, 1996; watercolour; 48.3 × 78.8 cm.; Mercury Gallery, London

of Western still life to the aesthetics of an even longer oriental tradition of painting.

Blackadder was educated at Edinburgh College of Art and the University of Edinburgh, gaining a combined first-class Master's degree in Fine Art. Her mentor at the College was the landscape artist William Gillies, head of the painting school, under whom she subsequently began a long teaching career and association with the College. The many distinctions that she won as a student and emerging artist culminated in 1962 when her large oil painting *White Still Life, Easter* (1962; private collection) won the Guthrie award for the best work displayed by a young artist at the Royal Scottish Academy. The imaginative interpretation of her subject revealed the extent to which Blackadder had already defined her pictorial language. Despite its title, the choice and arrangement of small objects was associative rather than realistic. Its theme was seasonally suggestive, not religious. Regular opportunities to travel with Houston during the College vacations provided a wealth of new pictorial ideas, and her landscapes of this period, such as the watercolour *House and Fields, Mykonos* (1962; Scottish National Gallery of Modern Art, Edinburgh) and the thinly painted oil *Church at Ericeira* (1969; Robert Fleming Holdings Ltd), demonstrated the similarity between the compositional devices she used for still lifes and for those used for inhabited landscapes. The arresting qualities of her work derived from her ability to isolate the strongest and essential elements of her subject, to sense the mood and atmosphere of a particular locality, and to render the sensations she received from it with expressive brushwork.

In 1963 the move to a house in Edinburgh with a small garden renewed Blackadder's childhood fascination with flowers, and further stimulated her interest in observing and recording plants, and the natural world in general – animals, birds, butterflies and moths. It was at this time, too, that her delight in collecting bric-a-brac and curiosities expanded in new directions as she discovered decorative kitsch objects and exotic novelties in the London shops. By the end of the decade she had amassed an ever-expanding treasury of fans, toys, boxes and paper kites and flowers, which triggered elaborate configurations such as *Still Life with Japanese Puzzles* (1969; watercolour on paper; City of Edinburgh Art Centre). Besides these artefacts, the pictorial vocabulary of Chinese and Japanese art gave fresh impetus to her painting, either from direct experience of it or mediated through the work of the Western abstract artists Sam Francis, Mark Tobey, Adolph Gottlieb and Jules Bissier. The influence was apparent in such sparingly constructed landscapes as *Broadford, Skye* (1970; watercolour on paper; private collection) and in her near-abstract still lifes of the early 1970s. The traditional still-life support was barely hinted at in *Grey Table* (1970–71; oil on canvas; private collection), and for the rest of the decade Blackadder experimented with a variety of framing and organising devices for stabilising her free-floating imagery. By 1974 naturalistic elements had reappeared in the shape of decorative flower heads. She began to try out the textured Japanese papers that had become available, making use of their qualities and mastering the care needed to control the flow of colour on to their absorbent surfaces.

The 1970s was a productive and successful decade in which Blackadder was the first woman to be elected an Academician in both the Royal Scottish Academy and in the Royal Academy in London. The Houstons bought a larger house and well-stocked garden in south Edinburgh in 1975 and there they developed their horticultural interests in earnest, cultivating, in particular, varieties of iris, tulip and lily. In still-life arrangements of vases, flowers were frequently accompanied, and complemented, by the three cats Blackadder also acquired at this time. From the middle of the decade she worked almost exclusively in watercolours. In 1978 she began to observe and record plants with greater attention to detail, painting her first botanical study, *Amaryllis and Crown Imperial*, in 1979 (watercolour on paper; John Houston). The precision and vitality of Blackadder's paintings of these and other species, in particular the orchid, have drawn enormous popular and professional esteem.

In 1985 Blackadder's admiration for oriental art was given further stimulus by the first of many visits to Japan. Direct experience was influential in formulating her uniquely personal approach to still life. The paper surface, extended horizontally in emulation of scroll paintings, provided an arena for elaborate compositions of Japanese objects ornamented with gold leaf. *Still Life, Kurashiki* (1986; watercolour; private collection), over 1.5 metres long, was one of her most impressively ambitious experiments with pictorial space.

In 1987 a commission from the Scottish National Portrait Gallery to paint a portrait of the children's writer *Mollie Hunter* (Scottish National Portrait Gallery, Edinburgh), and a subsequent portrait of *Naomi Mitchison* (1987–8; National Portrait Gallery, London), the Edinburgh-born novelist, playwright and children's writer, revived Blackadder's use of oil paint. Since then she has worked in the media of both watercolour and oil on a variety of subjects (e.g. *Fragment of an Anthology*, 1996; see illustration). As the range of her activities has continued to develop through the 1980s and 1990s, she has extended her exploration of printmaking and made decorative designs for ceramics and, in 1995, for a set of Royal Mail postage stamps.

JUDITH BUMPUS

Blanchard, María (Gutiérriez)
Spanish painter, 1881–1932

Born in Santander, 6 March 1881; physically disabled due to a pre-natal accident. Studied art privately in Madrid from age 18. Received a study grant from Santander and moved to Paris, 1909; studied at the Académie Vitti under Kees van Dongen and Spanish painter Hermén Anglada Camarasa; also visited Brussels for the first time. Settled permanently in Paris, 1916; associated with Cubist Section d'Or group. Died in Paris, 15 April 1932.

Principal Exhibitions
Exposición Nacional de Bellas Artes, Madrid: 1906, 1908 (third-class medal), 1910 (medal)

Salón de Arte Moderno, Madrid: 1915 (*Pintores integros*)
Galerie Rosenberg, Paris: 1919 (individual)
Salon des Indépendants, Paris: 1920–22
Salon d'Automne, Paris: 1921
Ceux de Demain, Brussels: 1923, 1927 (both individual)
Salon des Tuileries, Paris: 1924

Bibliography
Maurice Raynal, *Anthologie de la peinture en France de 1906 à nos jours*, Paris: Montaigne, 1927
Waldemar George, *María Blanchard*, Brussels: Ceux de Demain, 1928
Isabelle Rivière, *María Blanchard*, Paris: Correa, 1934
Pierre Cabanne, *L'Epopée du cubisme*, Paris: Table Ronde, 1942
Hommages à María Blanchard, exh. cat., Musée Municipal de Limoges, 1965
L'altra metà dell'avanguardia, 1910–1940: Pittrici e scultrici nei movimenti delle avanguardie storiche, exh. cat., Palazzo Reale, Milan, and elsewhere, 1980
María Blanchard, exh. cat., Museo Español de Arte Contemporáneo, 1982
Liliane Caffin Madaule, *María Blanchard, 1881–1932: Catalogue Raisonné*, 2 vols, London: Caffin Madaule, 1992–4
Gill Perry, *Women Artists and the Parisian Avant-Garde*, Manchester: Manchester University Press, and New York: St Martin's Press, 1995

In recent years the work of María Blanchard has enjoyed a revival of interest. In the early 1990s the Musée d'Art Moderne de la Ville de Paris, which owns a substantial collection of her canvases, devoted a small room to the exhibition of her Cubist paintings. This coincided with the publication of a substantial two-volume catalogue raisonné of her work by Liliane Caffin Madaule. Partly inspired by an increasing curatorial interest in France in the work of the so-called *femmes peintres* of the pre-war period, this revival of interest is also associated with the growth of art-historical research into the work of fringe members of the Cubist circle, including the figurative Cubism of André Lhôte, Roger de la Fresnaye and Jean Metzinger, all artists with whom Blanchard became friendly while working in Paris in the 1910s.

Blanchard's Spanish father encouraged her early interest in art, taking her to Madrid at the age of 18 to study drawing with Emilio Sola. After her father's death in 1904, her family moved to Madrid, and she studied there with various private tutors, before leaving for Paris in 1909. The Parisian environment had a significant effect on her artistic outlook, and after being encouraged to pursue a Fauve style by her friend Kees van Dongen, by 1911 Blanchard was immersed in Cubist painting, encouraged – and perhaps influenced – by her close friendship with Juan Gris, another Spaniard working in Paris. After returning to Spain in 1915 to take up a teaching post, she settled again in Paris in 1916, when she became associated with the Cubist exhibiting group, the Section d'Or.

Although she is perhaps best known for her figurative Cubist works of the 1920s, which were often based on domestic or maternal themes, in the 1910s she also produced many compositions and still lifes that developed some of the techniques of both Analytical and Synthetic Cubism. These works reveal an artist directly engaged with some of the problems of representation that preoccupied her better-known male contemporaries.

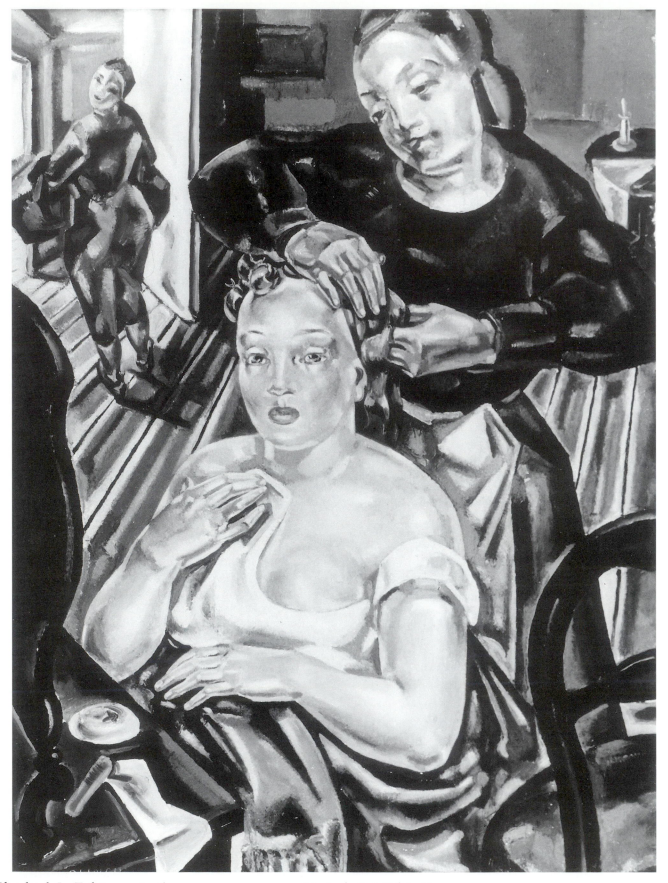

Blanchard: *La Toilette*, 1928; oil on canvas; 100 × 73 cm.; Musée du Petit Palais, Geneva

For example, these paintings often have a collage-like appearance, for Blanchard painted parts of the canvas surface to simulate the appearance of wallpaper or wood grain, a form of visual "game-playing" that also appears in collages of the mid-1910s by Picasso, Braque and Gris (see, for example, her *Child with a Hoop*, c.1915; Musée du Petit Palais, Geneva, repr. Perry 1995, pl.40). Many of these works contain visual clues that evoke the familiar Cubist still-life objects of bottle, glass, newspaper, woman, etc., and some include references to domestic images, such as children and mothers. Such images become a feature of Blanchard's later, more figurative works of the 1920s. During this period she produced many canvases in which spatial ambiguities and angular planes are employed in the depiction of figures acting out domestic scenes, such as *La Toilette* (1928; see illustration), *Mother and Child* and *Washing* (both Musée d'Art Moderne de la Ville de Paris).

Blanchard's adoption of such domestic subjects, in particular her repetition of the mother and child theme, may have contributed to the marginalisation – disappearance – of her work in histories of Cubism. The theme was also easily appropriated into the category of "women's art" and seen as part of the intimate repertoire of the *femmes peintres*. Many early accounts of her work represent a qualitatively different practice of Cubism from that of her male contemporaries, suggesting that the full-blown analytical work of the movement was somehow in conflict with her "feminine" nature.

However, one of the first art critics to see Cubism as a key modern movement, Maurice Raynal, devoted a chapter of his influential book *Anthologie de la peinture en France de 1906 à nos jours* (1927) to her work. He argued that while Blanchard devoted herself to Cubism, she was able to renounce some of the forms of expression that the movement had imposed on its immediate disciples, identifying this as a positive development. He saw her art as occupying a unique position between the movements of Cubism and what he called "la tendance réaliste":

> María Blanchard is gifted with a refined sensibility that could not remain indifferent to a new conception – to the representation of objectivity – which constitutes Cubism. With courage and a remarkable impartiality, from 1914 María gave free rein to her sensitive imagination. She constructed works of great purity and rhythm, a rhythm that is alternatively harsh and supple, and that is always animated by a noble and especially serene daring [pp.65–6].

Raynal's sense of the artist's "sensibility" is somewhat ambivalently constructed in relation both to her physical vulnerabilities (she suffered from physical disabilities due to a pre-natal accident) and to her artistic skills, but is less concerned with the gendered associations of these characteristics than some contemporary commentators. As opposed to seeing hers as a feminised form of Cubism, he attributes her interest in "réalisme" to a pursuit of some of the traditional "raisons plastiques" of art. Raynal's support of Blanchard's work seems to have done little to ensure her status within histories of Cubism. And although Léonce Rosenberg bought up many of her Cubist works from the late 1910s, there is little evidence that he actively promoted them.

GILL PERRY

Blau, Tina
Austrian painter, 1845–1916

Born in Vienna, 15 November 1845, into a Jewish family; father a dentist attached to the Austrian army. Studied under Anton (Antal) Hanély, a pupil of Waldmüller, from the age of 14; under August Schaefer of the Vienna Academy, learning to draw from nature, 1859–69; under Wilhelm von Lindenschmit the younger in Munich, from 1869. Returned to Vienna, 1874; shared a studio with Emil Schindler and visited the Netherlands, 1875. Visited Paris, 1883. Married German animal painter Heinrich Lang, 1883; he died 1891. Settled in Munich after marriage, returning to Vienna in 1894. Co-founder, Kunstschule für Frauen und Mädchen, Vienna, 1897; taught classes to 1915. Died in Vienna, 31 October 1916.

Principal Exhibitions
Genossenschaft der bildenden Künstler Wiens (Vienna Art Association), Künstlerhaus, Vienna: from 1869
Paris Salon: 1883 (honourable mention)
Exposition Universelle, Paris: 1889 (medal)
Münchener Kunstverein, Munich: 1890 (touring)
World's Columbian Exposition, Chicago: 1893 (medal)

Bibliography
Karoline Murau, *Wiener Malerinnen*, Dresden: Piersen, 1895
Max Eisler, "Tina Blau, Malerin", *Westermann's illustrierte deutsche Monatshefte*, June 1916, pp.469–79
Alexandra Ankwicz, "Tina Blau, eine österreichische Malerin", *Frauenbilder aus Österreich*, Vienna: Obelisk, 1955, pp.245–71
Tina Blau, 1845–1916: Eine Wiener Malerin, exh. cat., Österreichische Galerie im Oberen Belvedere, Vienna, 1971
Annelie Roser-DePalma, *Die Landschaftsmalerin Tina Blau*, dissertation, University of Vienna, 1971
Helga H. Harriman, "Olga Wisinger-Florian and Tina Blau: Painters in *fin-de-siècle* Vienna", *Woman's Art Journal*, x/2, 1989–90, pp.23–8
Horst Uhr, "Impressionism in Austria and Germany", *World Impressionism: The International Movement, 1860–1920*, ed. Norma Broude, New York: Abrams, 1992, pp.334–69

In 1882 Tina Blau entered a painting entitled *Spring in the Prater* (see illustration) in the prestigious Künstlerhaus exhibition. This large canvas, depicting well-dressed Viennese enjoying the much-frequented nature park on the outskirts of their city, attracted considerable commentary at the time for its especially light palette, relatively loose brushwork and luminosity. In fact, the selection panel, still adhering to the standards of academic art, only reluctantly accepted its inclusion in the show, despite its basically realistic conception. The painting was judged by some observers as the first Impressionist work by an Austrian.

In assessing Blau's originality, one must recognise that *Freilichtmalerei* (plein-air painting), influenced by the French Barbizon School, had been developing steadily in Austria since the 1850s. According to Horst Uhr (1992, p.336), the roots of Austrian Impressionism were "entirely indigenous". Already in the early 1870s, Blau was associated with a group of Austrian landscape painters known as *Stimmungsimpressionisten* ("mood impressionists"). Preferring picturesque effects and mixed colours, they produced paintings substantially different

Blau: *Spring in the Prater*, exhibited 1882; oil on canvas; 214 × 291cm.; Österreichische Galerie, Vienna

from those of the French Impressionists of the same decade. At the forefront of a revolutionary movement, Blau belies the stereotypical notion that women artists typically lag behind their male colleagues in accepting innovation.

During her long and successful professional career, extending from 1869, when she sold her first painting, to her death in 1916, Blau executed over 200 oil paintings. They were predominantly landscapes, small in scale and only occasionally including human figures, and done largely out of doors. She also completed flower studies (e.g. *Blossom Branch*, c.1894; repr. Vienna 1971, ill.20). Many of her works reveal some attention to detail in the style of *Spring in the Prater*. A case in point is *Bridlepath in the Prater* (1885; private collection, *ibid.*, ill.14). She also, however, painted with a more avant-garde approach, in which structure is reduced to essentials and suggested principally by colour, applied with thick brush strokes, not by line. Examples of this style are *Prater Motif: Krieau* (1882; Historisches Museum der Stadt Wien, Vienna), *In the Tuileries, Sunny Day* (1883; Österreichische Galerie, Vienna) and *Old Court in Vienna* (1910; Galerie Helmut Klewan, Vienna). Blau completed Hungarian, Italian, Dutch, German and French landscapes, but her primary interest centred on Austrian ones, particularly scenes in the Prater, where she had her studio from 1877 until the end of her life.

HELGA H. HARRIMAN

Bloch, Lucienne
American painter, 1909–

Born in Geneva, Switzerland, 5 January 1909; father the composer Ernest Bloch. Emigrated with her family to USA, 1917. Studied at Cleveland School of Art, Ohio, 1924–5 (scholarship). Studied in Paris under André Lhôte and Antoine Bourdelle, and attended drawing and anatomy classes at the Ecole Nationale des Beaux-Arts, 1925–9. Visited Florence and Rome, 1926. Assistant to Diego Rivera at Detroit Institute of Arts, Rockefeller Center and New Workers' School, New York, 1932–4. Employed on Federal Emergency Relief Administration (FERA) art project and mural division of Works Progress Administration Federal Art Project (WPA/FAP), 1935–9. Married former Rivera assistant

Stephen Pope Dimitroff, 1936; two sons, one daughter. Collaborated with Dimitroff after marriage. Lived in Flint, Michigan, during World War II, teaching at Flint Institute of Arts; moved to Mill Valley, California, 1948; subsequently to Gualala, California. Taught fresco painting at University of Michigan School of Architecture and Art, Ann Arbor, 1980s. Lives on a farm in northern California.

Principal Exhibitions

Individual
Delphic Studios, New York: 1933
Flint Institute of Arts, MI: 1983
Benham Studio/Gallery, Seattle: 1995
Arts Centre, Gualala, CA: 1995 (retrospective)

Group
Exposition Internationale, Paris: 1937 (gold medal)
New York World's Fair: 1939
San Francisco Art Festival: 1950 (prize)

Selected Writings
"Murals for use" (c.1936), *Art for the Millions*, ed. F.V. O'Connor, Greenwich, CT: New York Graphic Society, 1973, pp.76–7
"Impressions of Ernest Bloch", *The Spiritual and Artistic Odyssey of Ernest Bloch: A Centenary Retrospective*, Charleston, SC: Piccolo Spoleto, 1980
"On location with Diego Rivera", *Art in America*, lxxiv, February 1986, pp.102–20, 123

Bibliography
Anita Brenner, "Lucienne Bloch: Product of the WPA", *Brooklyn Daily Eagle*, 2 February 1936, pp.12–13C
Bertram D. Wolfe, *The Fabulous Life of Diego Rivera*, New York: Stein and Day, 1963
Richard D. McKinzie, *The New Deal for Artists*, Princeton, NJ: Princeton University Press, 1973
7 American Women: The Depression Decade, exh. cat., Vassar College Art Gallery, Poughkeepsie, NY, 1976
Greta Berman, *The Last Years: Mural Painting in New York City under the Works Progress Administration's Federal Art Project, 1935–1940*, New York: Garland, 1978
Charlotte Streifer Rubinstein, *American Women Artists from Early Times to the Present*, Boston: Hall, 1982
Michele Vishny, "Lucienne Bloch: The New York City murals", *Woman's Art Journal*, xiii/1, 1992, pp.23–8

The year 1995 was an active one for Lucienne Bloch, with the 86-year-old artist having her first solo photography exhibition (Benham Studio/Gallery, Seattle) and a retrospective (Arts Centre, Gualala) of the work that she and Stephen Dimitroff, her companion and mural associate of some 60 years, had created. Both exhibitions, the former featuring images of Frida Kahlo (q.v.) and Diego Rivera, as well as of the hungry children of car workers in Depression-era Detroit, spoke of an artist whose mature career has been profoundly affected by the values and the techniques of the mural movement of the 1930s.

The daughter of the eminent composer Ernest Bloch, Lucienne was educated in art first in Cleveland and then in Paris, and seemed destined for a career in sculpture, her designs for the Dutch Royal Leerdam Glassworks having secured admiration from the likes of Frank Lloyd Wright. She returned to the USA in 1929, but while considering Wright's offer of a teaching position at Taliesen East, a chance meeting with Rivera in New York led to her joining the ranks of those who

apprenticed with the controversial Mexican muralist. Working with him in Detroit and in New York (on the fresco *Man at the Crossroads Looking with Hope and High Vision to the Choosing of a New and Better Future* of 1933 for the RCA Building, which Nelson Rockefeller ordered to be destroyed before completion), Bloch was instructed in every facet of fresco painting, from the painstaking grinding of colours to the application of pigment to surfaces of wet lime plaster. Her experiences with this apprenticeship are recorded in a lively article ("On location with Diego Rivera", 1986), which includes not only her invaluable photographs of the RCA project, but also technical insight into an art-form that, until she met Rivera, Bloch was convinced no living artist actually practised.

By 1934, with her future husband Dimitroff, who had been a technical assistant for Rivera, Bloch had embarked upon her own mural projects. Her first major commission, funded by the Works Progress Administration (WPA), was for a women's detention house in New York; this 14.8-square-metre fresco, which prompted the magazine *Vanity Fair* immediately to nominate her for their "Hall of Fame" of 1935, received a great deal of attention, positive and negative, for its attempt to reconcile the objectives of publicly funded art with the perceived needs of a specific, female audience. Bloch's solution (repr. Berman 1978, fig.2), which she arrived at after consulting the prison psychiatrist and some of the inmates, was to design a simple, brightly coloured composition, the central portion of which showed children of different races at play in a tenement-area clearing. By focusing on readily identifiable facets of the lives of the incarcerated women rather than on morally elevating motifs, Bloch hoped to create art that acted as a "healthy tonic" for her captive viewers.

One suspects that Bloch empathised deeply with these imprisoned women, many of whom would have been separated from their offspring. For much of her career she has been a highly respected illustrator of children's books (see her illustrations for Mary Louise Downer's *Flower*, 1955); during the 1940s and 1950s she accepted mural commissions for a series of institutions dedicated to the care or education of children; and she has often painted egg tempera portraits of small children, including her own. An especially compelling example of the last, a panel entitled *The Barn* (1946; see illustration), shows her young son Pencho standing in front of a barn and proudly clutching a cat as he stares with a child's wondrous triumph towards his mother and the viewer.

If such works as the detention home mural and *The Barn* display something of a naive approach to the rendering of both objects and human beings, Bloch was also perfectly capable of producing designs that demonstrated a sophisticated understanding of modernist strategies. For the music room of the George Washington High School in New York, she worked from 1936 to 1937 on the the second of her WPA fresco projects: four large and three small sections, totalling 60.4 square metres, which document the evolution of music (repr. Vishny 1992, figs 2–5). These strong evocations of the "primitive, oriental, medieval/classical and modern" contributions to the development of music were built around bold, abstracted sound waves, on to and behind which appeared accurate renderings of musical instruments from various cultures, as well as solo and group performers. Their radical disregard for

Bloch: *The Barn*, 1946; tempera on board; 18.4 × 21 cm.; Flint Institute of Arts, Michigan: Gift of Mrs R. S. Bishop

rational proportions and placement, clearly articulating Bloch's familiarity with the Cubist vocabulary that she and many other women had been introduced to in their Parisian classes with André Lhôte, may have been the impetus behind the school principal's attempt to bring the project to a halt. Only her decision to fight his plastering over of the early phases of the murals ensured the completion of what is now considered a stellar example of modernist public art funded through the WPA.

Leaving New York in 1942, Bloch moved first to Flint, where Dimitroff had been brought up from the age of ten, and then on to California in 1948. With Bloch responsible for the design process and Dimitroff acting as technical director, the couple has been responsible for some 40 projects since their westerly moves. A variety of mural techniques have been explored, and the design work has shown a remarkable adaptability to the needs of the commissioners. For one of Eric

Mendelsohn's last buildings, the Temple Emanuel in Grand Rapids, Michigan (repr. W. von Eckardt, *Eric Mendelsohn*, 1960, illus. 92 and 94), Bloch created in 1953 a massive oil and gold-leaf mural, on which sheaves of wheat, grapevines and symbols from her Jewish faith were woven into a gentle tapestry, enlivened by shots of red. A major commission of 1957 for the exterior of the Advanced Research Building for IBM in San Jose resulted in several hundred metres of orange, brown and yellow ceramic tiles arranged into simple abstract patterns, while four fresco panels for the Kit Stewart Chapel of the Calvary Presbyterian Church in San Francisco (1963; repr. *San Francisco Examiner*, 30 June 1963, 3C) featured strongly drafted portraits, 3.9 metres high, of Martin Luther, John Calvin, John Knox and Huldrych Zwingli, based on careful research into depictions by the contemporaries of these Protestant "fathers". Using only four colours (vine black, raw sienna, viridian and venetian red), Bloch's palette took into account the colours that would be cast on to her frescoes by the newly installed stained-glass windows. *Tree for All Seasons* (1989; 2.13 × 2.29 m.; sketch included in the dedication pamphlet, Flint Institute of Arts archives), commissioned for the Flint Institute of Arts in memory of an important supporter, is remarkably simple in composition: the fresco consists of a large, almost crudely drawn tree set on a small patch of grass, perhaps a reference to a motif that her father, who had been fascinated by the camera, once spent several months figuring out how to photograph, discussing at length this problem with his artist-daughter.

Bloch's willingness to adapt her work to the needs of her patrons is no accident. As an ardent proponent of mural art, she has taught and lectured widely on the fresco technique, and more recently has been involved in a number of projects designed to preserve the artistic legacy of Rivera. These activities, however, are approached with more than the passion of an historian: in Bloch's view, art is something that belongs to everyday life and as such needs to satisfy and be comprehended by those with whom it dwells. A fully trained and professionally accomplished artist, she does not consider it even remotely beneath her to speak to audiences on such topics as "Art in the Home", giving counsel on how to select paintings, sculpture and crafts, as well as how to display them to advantage.

CATHERINE MACKENZIE

Blow, Sandra

British painter, 1925–

Born in London, 14 September 1925. Studied at St Martin's School of Art, London, under Ruskin Spear, 1942–6; Royal Academy Schools, London, 1946–7; Accademia delle Belle Arti, Rome, 1947–8. Travelled in Spain and France, 1949–50. Settled in London, 1950. Rented a cottage in Zennor, north Cornwall, 1957–8; subsequently made frequent visits to the area, moving to St Ives in 1995. Associate member, Penwith Society of Artists, 1958. Visiting tutor, Royal College of Art, London, 1961–75. Recipient of International Guggenheim award, Young Artists section, Venice Biennale, 1960; second prize, John Moore's exhibition, Liverpool, 1961; Arts Council of Great Britain purchase award, 1965. Associate, 1971, and member, 1978, Royal Academy. Honorary fellow, Royal College of Art, 1983. Lives in St Ives, Cornwall.

Selected Individual Exhibitions

Gimpel Fils, London: 1953, 1960, 1962
Saidenberg Gallery, New York: 1957
New Art Centre, London: 1966, 1968, 1971, 1973
Clare College, Cambridge: 1968
Royal Academy, London: 1979, 1994
Francis Graham-Dixon Gallery, London: 1991

Bibliography

Edward Lucie-Smith, "Art as something public", *Studio International*, clxxi, 1966, pp.71–3
Pierre Rouve, "Sandra Blow", *Arts Review*, xviii, 5 February 1966, p.41
Hayward Annual '68, exh. cat., Arts Council of Great Britain, London, 1968
Sandra Blow, exh. cat., Royal Academy, London, 1979
St Ives, 1939–64: Twenty-Five Years of Painting, Sculpture and Pottery, exh. cat., Tate Gallery, London, 1985
Sandra Blow: Recent Work, exh. cat., Francis Graham-Dixon Gallery, London, 1991
Judith Bumpus, "Resolving chaos", *RA Magazine*, no.41, Winter 1993, pp.44–7
Sandra Blow, exh. cat., Royal Academy, London, 1994

In the late 1950s and 1960s Sandra Blow won national and international recognition as one of the leading artists responsible for the revival of abstract painting in Britain after World War II. Her work of this period, exemplified by *Winter* (1956; Museum of Modern Art, New York) and *Space and Matter* (1958; Tate Gallery, London), was characterised by a feeling for texture, often achieved by mixing sand or grit, straw and chaff, with her paint, or by applying rough sacking to the canvas. By these means she set up tensions between the fabric of her paintings, the gestural movement expressed in their making and the impression of space created on a flat canvas. If Blow's titles suggest a visual source, she has always denied that her ideas spring from observed reality, although she concedes that things seen and felt may, transmuted, enter her work in some unconscious or unacknowledged way.

Blow's early work was figurative, and her assurance in depicting observed reality gained her entry to St Martin's School of Art at the age of 17. There her talent for figure painting and portraiture flourished under Ruskin Spear and, in 1946, she was admitted to the Royal Academy Schools. However, the precise realism demanded by William Dring's teaching in the academic tradition did not suit her more subjective, painterly approach. Despite Dring's strictures, her student work was hung in the Academy's Summer Exhibitions of 1946 and 1947. While on holiday in Rome in 1947 she met two artists who influenced the development of her ideas profoundly: the American Nicolas Carone, a student of Hans Hofmann, and the Italian Alberto Burri. Through them Blow was introduced to purely abstract concepts and, greatly stimulated, she took leave of absence from the Academy Schools, never to return. She spent the next year travelling round Italy with Burri, who opened her eyes to the abstract principles underlying the art and architecture of the Italian Renaissance. Unable to work in the shadow of Burri's powerful personality, Blow painted virtually nothing in his company. Leaving him, she struggled independently for a further year in order to realise her own ideas of abstract composition. In 1952 she was given the first of several successive solo exhibitions with Gimpel Fils, one of the few London galleries showing abstract art at the time.

Among other artists moving towards abstraction were Alan Davie, Terry Frost, William Gear, Ivon Hitchens, Peter Lanyon, Roger Hilton and Patrick Heron. These last four were associated with a community of artists working in the coastal town of St Ives in Cornwall in south-west England. In 1957 Blow visited St Ives with Roger Hilton, spending a year in Zennor and painting outside, using a palette of natural colours, mostly browns, greys, creams and white. Although the outstanding beauty of the landscape never seduced her from her abstract purpose, Blow insisted that her finished canvases should be

Blow: *Green and White*, 1969; Tate Gallery, London

able to hold their own when set against the strong light, firm contours and wide expanses of the Cornish scene. The many small drawings she made at the time and the continuing use of line in such paintings as *Black, White and Brown; Concrete and Sawdust* (1961; Norwich Castle Museum) owe something to Hilton's linear marks and to his spatial structures. Measurable success came when two of her larger canvases were bought for public collections. The Museum of Modern Art in New York purchased *Winter* and the Tate Gallery in London, *Space and Matter*. Regular appearances in group shows abroad, culminating in 1960 at the Venice Biennale where she won the International Guggenheim award in the Young Artists section, brought her to prominence as the youngest of a generation of British artists demonstrating new trends.

The following year Blow was appointed a visiting tutor at the Royal College of Art, where she was drawn into the new vogue for acrylic paint. After the weighty, often sombre imagery of the 1950s and early 1960s her experiments with tea, ash and acrylic in the mid-1960s were spare in the extreme. Their unexpected clarity and lightness gave the impression that Blow was dealing for the first time with pure space, unencumbered by matter. Although the first two materials were chosen partly for economy, the change introduced a new mood into her work. By the late 1960s Blow's forms, still thinly painted in acrylic, had taken on more colour and, suspended in airy, atmospheric spaces, were held in precarious, but elegant, balance. The satisfying resolution of one of her most notable compositions of this period, the 3-metre-square canvas *Green and White* (1969; see illustration), was provided by accident, and the improvised means by which she successfully completed the work are characteristic of her resourcefulness and imagination. Large, drifting forms appear tethered with a collaged line. In fact, the strip of applied canvas covered a long vertical slash made by a wilful visitor to her studio.

Through the 1970s Blow experimented with more obviously three-dimensional forms, making constructional reliefs out of metal and plastics, and a series of softly sculptured collages. By the following decade she had returned to a more purely painterly manner. Spiralling forms erupted across expanses of white canvas or, in the exuberant gestures of *Vivace* (1988; artist's collection), exploded in spattered paint and fragments of collaged canvas. Her adventurous and forceful use of space, described by resounding sweeps of colour, owed much to her continuing admiration for Hofmann's ideas. On the other hand, her disposal of brilliant splinters of colour recalled Burri's handling of it in the small tempera paintings he was making in the late 1940s. By contrast with the expansive outbursts in *Vivace* and *Glad Ocean* (1989; artist's collection), the absorbed, meditative mood and the quiet containment of such paintings as *Brilliant Corner II* (1993) and the sombre *Selva Oscura* (1994; both artist's collection) are deceptive. Even an image as apparently aimless as *Sea Drift* (1992; private collection) is only arrived at after a long and passionate involvement with the canvas and many reworkings.

In some of Blow's canvases of the 1990s there are formal echoes of earlier work: *Tranquillo* (1993; artist's collection), for example, carries an impression of *Sphere, Alabaster* (1961; Walker Art Gallery, Liverpool). Since Blow's return to St Ives in 1995, memories of her first visit reverberate in her re-awakened experience of the landscape and the startling clarity of the Cornish light (*Soft Sand Inlet, Porthmeor*, 1995; artist's collection). Sandra Blow has sustained a remarkably individual – and not always duly acknowledged – presence in the history of British post-war abstraction. The vigour and strength of her achievement are all the more admirable given the very large scale on which she generally works, and her intuitive, improvised methods.

JUDITH BUMPUS

Blunden, Anna (Elizabeth)

British painter, 1829–1915

Born in St John's Square, London, 22 December 1829; father a Clerkenwell bookbinder. Moved to Exeter with her family, 1833. Trained as a governess in Babbacombe, Devon; soon abandoned this career, receiving parental permission to study art in London. Attended classes at Leigh's Academy, Newman Street; also studied independently in British Museum and National Gallery. Lived with her sister in Exeter, 1855–67; corresponded with John Ruskin, 1855–62. Signed petition for women's entry to the Royal Academy Schools, 1859. Went abroad, 1867, spending time in Switzerland and Germany before setting up a studio in Rome. Returned home in April 1872 after her sister Emily's death; married brother-in-law Francis Richard Martino, a Birmingham manufacturer of Italian origin, December 1872; brought up his two children; own child born 1874. Died in Birmingham, 1915.

Principal Exhibitions

Society of British Artists, London: 1854–66, 1868, 1876–7
Royal Academy, London: 1854, 1856–9, 1862–4, 1866–7, 1872
Society of Female Artists, London: 1857–9
British Institution, London: 1860
Birmingham Society of Artists: from 1861
Dudley Gallery, London: 1865–75, 1877 (watercolour), 1868 (oil)

Bibliography

Henry Wreford, "Studios of Rome", *Art Journal*, 1870, pp.141–2
Ellen C. Clayton, *English Female Artists*, 2 vols, London: Tinsley, 1876
Virginia Surtees, ed., *Sublime and Instructive: Letters from John Ruskin to Louisa, Marchioness of Waterford, Anna Blunden and Ellen Heaton*, London: Joseph, 1972
Pamela Gerrish Nunn, "Ruskin's patronage of women artists", *Woman's Art Journal*, ii/2, 1981–2, pp.8–13
Charlotte Yeldham, *Women Artists in Nineteenth-Century France and England*, 2 vols, New York: Garland, 1984
Hard Times: Social Realism in Victorian Art, exh. cat., Manchester City Art Gallery, 1987
Pamela Gerrish Nunn, *Victorian Women Artists*, London: Women's Press, 1987
Jan Marsh and Pamela Gerrish Nunn, *Women Artists and the Pre-Raphaelite Movement*, London: Virago, 1989
Deborah Cherry, *Painting Women: Victorian Women Artists*, London and New York: Routledge, 1993
Beth Harris, *"For the Needle She?": Images of the Seamstress in the 1840s*, PhD dissertation, City University of New York, Graduate Center (in preparation)

Despite the gains that women artists fought for and made in the 1850s, Anna Blunden's work, like that of so many of her colleagues, has been lost and neglected. From the little of her work that does survive, and from exhibition records, it is clear that she began her career in the early 1850s as a figure painter. Two early ambitious paintings, a scene from *Uncle Tom's Cabin* (1853; repr. Marsh and Nunn 1989, fig.4) and a painting of an underpaid and overworked seamstress (1854; see illustration) demonstrate Blunden's desire, at least at the beginning of her career, to paint serious and reform-minded "modern life" subjects, a genre that had emerged in the 1840s, popularised by such artists as Richard Redgrave and G.F. Watts.

Blunden's painting of an impoverished seamstress formed her exhibition debut at the Society of British Artists in 1854. The painting was exhibited with four lines from Thomas Hood's popular poem of 1843, "The Song of the Shirt". Seamstresses had been a favourite topic with artists, writers and journalists (many of them women) since 1843, when a Parliamentary Report exposed horrible abuses in the employment of women in the clothing industry. Blunden's

Blunden: *Song of the Shirt*, 1854; oil on canvas; 47 × 39.5 cm.; Yale Center for British Art, New Haven, Paul Mellon Fund (B1993.23)

painting employs all the standard iconography of the subject (the garret window with its view of the city, the sewing implements on the table), yet she improved on Redgrave's prototypical image (*The Sempstress*, 1844; Forbes Magazine Collection, New York). She emphasised the seamstress's sense of entrapment and desperate plea for release by focusing solely on the upper body of the figure, which is now framed by – instead of simply sitting beside – an open window, whose wooden slats read like the bars of a prison. Blunden, who had given up a career as a governess to paint, and who needed to support herself through her efforts as an artist, may have seen the subject as one that could earn her both recognition and income. The poet of "The Song of the Shirt" had resurfaced in the minds of the public in 1854 as journalists debated a monument to its author, Hood. Blunden's efforts were rewarded when the painting was engraved and appeared in the *Illustrated London News* in 1854 and in the *Penny Illustrated Paper* in 1862.

Seamstresses had been widely described as the "white slaves of England", a fact that connects the painting described above with one painted a year earlier illustrating a scene from Harriet Beecher Stowe's novel about the evils of slavery, *Uncle Tom's Cabin* (1852). Blunden represents the moment when the saintly Eva puts her hand on Topsy's shoulder and tells her that she loves her. It is this expression of love, the first that Topsy has ever heard, that breaks her pattern of wickedness (which others had seen as inherent and unchangeable).

Women are the subject of both these early paintings by Blunden. In the scene from *Uncle Tom's Cabin* a brave young woman recognises a cruel and unjust system and seeks to undo its dehumanising effects, and in the painting of a seamstress, we witness a woman who is the victim of (what was seen to be) a similarly heartless system. Together, the iconography of the two pictures suggests that Blunden may have been offering a critique of the hypocrisy of nominally Christian nations that do not live by Christian principles of charity and love. In addition, she may be suggesting that the desire for wealth and luxury breeds moral indifference. Both of these themes were prominent in Stowe's novel as well as in literature on seamstresses. Like the painting of a seamstress, Blunden's painting of Topsy and Eva was timely, dating from the same year as Stowe's tour of England.

The titles of other works exhibited by Blunden in the 1850s, such as *Past and Present* (exh. Royal Academy 1858; untraced), which the *Art Journal* described as a scene of two children playing with flowers by the ruins of a mansion, and *Mother's Tale* (exh. Society of British Artists 1855; untraced), suggest that she was also painting sentimental genre paintings of the type that was enormously popular with Victorian audiences. These saleable paintings, along with a portrait painting practice that Blunden maintained in Exeter, and copies of old master paintings commissioned by the critic John Ruskin, seem to have paid the bills. Blunden had studied painting at Leigh's Academy in London, where women had the rare opportunity of studying anatomy, yet she was clearly aware of the limited opportunities for women artists. In 1859 she joined 37 other women in petitioning the Royal Academy for entry into their schools.

In the autumn of 1855 Blunden initiated a correspondence with Ruskin that lasted seven years. Her obsessive amorous

interest in the annoyed and uninterested Ruskin may have allowed him to exert an undue influence on her career. His advice to her in 1862 to "give up figures at once, because you will never be able to sell one", is probably the reason for Blunden's abandonment of figure painting after that date in favour of Pre-Raphaelite-style landscapes (Surtees 1972, p.140). It may also be related to the "nervous illness" (Clayton 1876, p.208) that Blunden complained of, and which prompted her to go abroad in 1867. Indeed their relationship, although existing almost entirely on paper, seems to have involved a good deal of sado-masochism for both. Ruskin wrote to Blunden that she would be better off having "any popular hack or an artist" choose her landscape subjects since "no subject that you choose yourself will ever sell, for years to come". He did, however, recognise her talent in his *Academy Notes* of 1858 and 1859, and his precept of "truth to nature" had a lasting effect on both Blunden's figure paintings and landscapes. Blunden continued to exhibit landscapes in London until her marriage in 1872. After that date, she exhibited only in local exhibitions in Birmingham (where she had settled with her husband) until her death in 1915.

BETH HARRIS

Boch, Anna
Belgian painter, 1848–1936

Born in Saint-Vaast near La Louvière, Hainaut, 10 February 1848; daughter of Frédéric-Victor Boch, a founder of the ceramics factory Boch-Keramis set up in La Louvière in 1841; sister of the landscape painter Eugène Boch; cousin of Octave Maus, founder and secretary of the exhibiting groups Les XX and La Libre Esthétique, and editor of *L'Art Moderne* (1881–1914). Studied under the landscape painters Pierre-Louis Kuhnen and Euphrosine Beernaert, 1866–76; also advised by Isidore Verheyden, a friend for 30 years, and Theo van Rysselberghe, whom she met in 1886. Only female member of Les XX, Brussels, 1885; guest member, La Libre Esthétique, Brussels; founder-member, Vie et Lumière, Brussels, 1904; honorary member, Les Amis de l'Art, La Louvière, 1908. Also active as a promoter and collector of modern art. Chevalier, 1903, and Officier, 1928, Ordre de Léopold; Officier, Ordre de la Couronne, 1919. Lived in rue de l'Abbaye, Ixelles, Brussels, from 1903. Died there, 25 February 1936.

Principal Exhibitions

Individual
Cercle Artistique et Littéraire, Brussels: 1884, 1907, 1923
Galerie Druet, Paris: 1908
Galerie Georges Giroux, Brussels: 1930
Galerie Artes, Brussels: 1932
Petite Galerie, Brussels: 1934

Group
Salon Triennal, Brussels: from 1884
Les XX, Brussels: 1886–93
La Libre Esthétique, Brussels: 1894–7, 1899, 1901–2, 1905, 1907–11, 1913
Vie et Lumière, Brussels: 1904–14

Selected Writings

Souvenirs d'une vie, Brussels, 1935

Bibliography

"Nos femmes-artistes: Mlle Anna Boch", *Bruxelles-Féminin*, Brussels, 1903; Dossier Presse Libre Esthétique, Archives de l'Art Contemporain en Belgique, Brussels

"Les Salons: Anna Boch, G.M. Stevens: Au cercle artistique", *La Belgique Artistique et Littéraire*, vi, 1907, pp.444–7

Octave Maus, "Peintres belges: Anna Boch", *L'Art Moderne*, 13 December 1908, pp.395–6

Lucien Jottrand, *Remembrances*, 1900, pp.21–4 (unidentified periodical, published between 1926 and 1936, Dossier Boch, Archives de l'Art Contemporain en Belgique, Brussels)

Paul Colin, *Anna Boch*, Brussels: Ferain, 1928

Lucien Jottrand, "In memoriam Anna Boch", *La Flandre Libérale*, 12 April 1936

Succession de Mlle Anna Boch, artiste-peintre, sale cat. of works from the artist's studio and collection, Galerie Le Roy, Brussels, 15 December 1936

Thérèse Faider-Thomas, "Anna Boch: Bildnis einer Malerin", *Keramos Werkzeitschrift Villeroy & Boch*, no.6, 1967, pp.10–11

—, "Anna Boch et le groupe des XX", *Miscellanea Professor J. Duverger*, i, Ghent, 1968, pp.402–13

Anna Boch und Eugène Boch: Werke aus den Anfängen der Modernen Kunst, exh. cat., Moderne Galerie, Saarbrücken, 1971

Thérèse Faider-Thomas, "Anna Boch, peintre et mécène", *150 Ans de création et de tradition faïencières: Boch Keramis, La Louvière, 1841–1991*, La Louvière, 1991, pp.73–103

Hommage à Anna et Eugène Boch, exh. cat., Musée de Pontoise, 1994

There are documents in the Bibliothèque royale Albert 1er and Archives de l'Art Contemporain en Belgique, and Musées royaux des Beaux-Arts de Belgique, Brussels.

Having received ten long years of training from teachers who were themselves products of the conventional landscape tradition and who left no significant trace on the history of Belgian art, Anna Boch could have practised painting as other women practised embroidery, taking no pleasure in it and treating it simply as a way of passing the time. Fortunately, however, despite a frail and delicate appearance, an elegant figure and a rather unprepossessing face, Boch showed herself to be a determined young woman with intelligence and a lively, curious gaze. She was motivated by an unquenchable thirst for recognition of her talent in her own right. Having the indisputable advantage of belonging to a wealthy and cultured family, she had the additional advantages of an enterprising cousin, Octave Maus, and of crossing the paths of two talented artists.

The first, Isidore Verheyden, "disciple" of Théodore Baron, introduced her to realism and plein-air painting, taught her to express her emotions, to take a freer approach, to build up her composition and to handle colour. Despite considerable progress, especially in terms of seriousness and robustness of handling, her work of the years 1880–85 still lacks luminosity, movement and relief. The still lifes and interiors, as much as the seascapes or landscapes, still manifest Verheyden's influence. In later canvases, however, a sort of "rebellion" begins to break through, which takes the form of an impressionistic line, with scattered clouds where the broken brush strokes suggest the separation of tones.

In *Isidore Verheyden in His Studio* (*c.*1884; 70 × 60 cm.; private collection, Belgium, repr. Pontoise 1994, p.27) Boch

attempts, in the manner of Courbet, Fantin-Latour or the early Impressionists, the technique of "a picture within a picture". The artist is represented in the act of retouching an impressive landscape in a gold frame which stands on the ground. While she painted this important portrait of her teacher, Verheyden offers us a very pleasing vision of the woman who in his eyes was above all sweetness and romance: *Anna Boch with Sunshade* (*c.*1884–5; Collection Villeroy & Boch, Mettlach). A member of Les XX in November 1884, Verheyden resigned "for personal reasons" in 1888. Did he fear the excessive daring of Impressionism or was he jealous of the influence that Theo van Rysselberghe was henceforth to exert over his pupil? For it is true that in the competitive atmosphere created by her association with van Rysselberghe, the members of Les XX and their guests, Boch blossomed and went on developing. Introduced to Seurat's ideas, she strengthened her line, lightened her palette, divided, dotted, learned to play with light, to model form and produced some really important works such as *The Sideboard* (1889; see illustration), a very lovely still life with a flowered screen, dominated by a range of blues in brush strokes separated to excellent effect, and *Harvest in Flanders* (*c.*1889–90; 83 × 121 cm.; private collection, Belgium, *ibid.*, p.37), an interesting experiment in tonal division applied to a traditional theme of Belgian art.

Like many other painters during the 1890s, Boch extended, spread and merged her brush strokes, as in *Woman in a Landscape* (*c.*1890–92; 101 × 76 cm.; Stedelijk Museum, Amsterdam), which has all the charm of a Monet seen through pointillist eyes. She then moved to a broader approach, spreading areas of colour in the manner of van Rysselberghe, Finch or Signac, using the same violet-mauve and orange colour ranges that they also favoured. In this last manner she painted the interesting series *Brittany Coasts* (1900–02), of which the most well-known is that purchased by the Belgian government in 1902 (108 × 147 cm.; Musées royaux des Beaux-Arts de Belgique, Brussels).

Over and above all other considerations, the explanation of van Rysselberghe's great success as a "teacher" probably lies in his superb portrait of *Anna Boch in Her Studio* (*c.*1889–90; Museum of Fine Arts, Springfield, MA). Where Verheyden had seen a charming young woman, van Rysselberghe portrays an artist. In no way idealising the femininity of his model – though he allows it a certain melancholy – he imbues her with the real strength and determination suited to an outstanding personality who was at one and the same time artist, musician, a patron of the *haute bourgeoisie* and great traveller. Its success was such that, following in the footsteps of her brother, who was immortalised in a yellow jacket against a backdrop of a starry sky by his friend van Gogh (*Eugène Boch*, 1888; Musée d'Orsay, Paris), Boch owed her international fame in some degree to this picture.

With the break-up of Les XX the heyday when Boch was at the forefront of the avant-garde seems to have come to an end. The setting up of La Libre Esthétique, with its overwhelming diversity, its plethora of associates and techniques, cannot be compared to the tight-knit circle of Les XX. Van Rysselberghe, moreover, moved away, first of all travelling and then settling in Paris (1898) and later in the Midi. And like all intense people, who no longer hear the buzzing of the hive around them, Boch retreated bit by bit to known ground, returning to

Boch: *The Sideboard*, 1889; private collection, Musée de Pontoise

impressionist principles while trying to assert her own style: bringing together a frank, haughty, ambitious handling with a light palette, both gentle and sensitive, and fluid, unobtrusive modelling.

When she became involved with Vie et Lumière, Boch was no doubt hoping to recover the enthusiasm of Les XX, but such exceptional moments are rare. So, between two journeys, she organised exhibitions and musical soirées at her home, went on believing in her painting and painted what she liked: pleasant flower pictures, seascapes touched by pointillism and not without interest, street scenes recalling those of Guillaume Vogels, but also numerous rather unfocused landscapes. She exhibited and was popular with those critics who feared revolutionaries, preferring a more refreshing and reassuring art in those troubled times.

More and more sedentary after 1914, Boch often withdrew to her estate at Ohain, where she took up still-life painting again and turned to portrait painting, something she had practised but little hitherto. Her portrait of *Blanchette Dudicourt and Betty Janssens* (1918; 190×129cm.; private collection, Belgium, repr. Pontoise 1994, p.49), seated in a garden, seems particularly successful, revealing Boch, woman *and* artist who, in life, never mixed her styles, playing a single card, painting and accepting only the best; practising, according to Octave Maus (1908): "a pleasing and likeable art, with a bent for happiness, all the more charming in that the manliness of the handling is united with the delicacy and grace of a feminine spirit."

Active to the end, Boch never stopped trying to win her rightful place in the art of her time and, more unusually, did all she could to help her friends do the same. For Boch, like her brother, also played an important role in the art world, getting work for some, buying paintings from others and furthering relations between artists and art lovers. In 1927 she gave James Ensor's *Russian Music* (1881) to the Musées royaux des Beaux-Arts de Belgique, Brussels, to which she was to bequeath Signac's *Rocky Inlet* (1906), Seurat's *La Seine à la Grande Jatte* (1888) and Gauguin's *Conversation in the Fields* (1888). Works by Bernard, Marquet, Lemmen, Finch, Toorop, Vogels, Jefferys, Artan, de Groux and van Gogh (most notably his *Red Vine*, now in the Pushkin Museum, Moscow) were also in her collection. These examples suffice to demonstrate, in addition to her generosity, her eclecticism and her perspicacity.

DANIELLE DERREY-CAPON

Bodichon, Barbara Leigh Smith
British painter, 1827–1891

Born Barbara Leigh Smith in Watlington, Sussex, 8 April 1827, the eldest illegitimate child of Benjamin Leigh Smith, Unitarian and radical MP for Norwich, and Anne Longden, milliner. Studied art as a child, then law and political economy, but mainly art, at Ladies' College, Bedford Square,

London, 1849. Founded Portman Hall School, pioneering the education of children from different classes and religious backgrounds, 1854. Formed friendships with Bessie Rayner Parkes, Anna Mary Howitt, Dante Gabriel Rossetti and George Eliot, 1840s–50s; travelled across Europe unchaperoned with Parkes in 1850. Began career as writer and feminist reformer with publication of *A Brief Summary of the Most Important Laws of England Concerning Women*, 1854; founded the *English Woman's Journal*, 1858. Co-founder, with Emily Davies, of Girton College, Cambridge, 1872. Relationship with John Chapman, editor of the *Westminster Review*, 1854–5. Married Eugène Bodichon, a French anthropologist and physician resident in Algiers, 1857; toured North America with him, meeting leading abolitionists and members of the American Women's Rights Movement; subsequently divided time between Algiers and England, also visiting France to study art under Corot and Daubigny. Died at Scalands, near Robertsbridge, Sussex, 11 June 1891.

Principal Exhibitions

Royal Academy, London: occasionally 1850–72
Society of British Artists, London: occasionally 1851–74
Crystal Palace, London: occasionally 1856–78
National Academy of Design, New York: 1857–8 (*American Exhibition of British Art*, touring)
Society of Female (later Lady) Artists, London: 1858–9, 1866–77, 1880–81
French Gallery, Pall Mall, London: 1859, 1861, 1864 (all individual)
Birmingham Society of Artists: occasionally 1863–81
Dudley Gallery, London: 1865–6, 1869–73, 1875–81
Liverpool Autumn Exhibition: 1871–5

Selected Writings

A Brief Summary of the Most Important Laws of England Concerning Women, Together with a Few Observations Thereon, London, 1854
Women and Work, London, 1857
Editor, *Algeria Considered as a Winter Residence for the English* by Eugène Bodichon, London: English Woman's Journal Office, 1858
Objections to the Enfranchisement of Women Considered, London, 1866
Reasons For and Against the Enfranchisement of Women, London, 1872
An American Diary, 1857–8, ed. Joseph W. Reed, Jr, London: Routledge, 1972

Bibliography

Ellen C. Clayton, *English Female Artists*, 2 vols, London: Tinsley, 1876
The Times, 15 June 1891 (obituary)
Hester Burton, *Barbara Bodichon, 1827–1891*, London: Murray, 1949
John Crabbe, "An artist divided", *Apollo*, cxiii, 1981, pp.311–13
Jacquie Matthews, "Barbara Bodichon: Integrity in diversity", *Feminist Theorists*, ed. Dale Spender, London: Women's Press, and New York: Pantheon, 1983, pp.90–123
Sheila R. Herstein, *A Mid-Victorian Feminist: Barbara Leigh Smith Bodichon*, New Haven and London: Yale University Press, 1985
Candida Ann Lacey, ed., *Barbara Leigh Smith Bodichon and the Langham Place Group*, New York and London: Routledge, 1986 (contains reprints of Bodichon's writings on women's rights, slavery, etc.)
Christopher Newall, *Victorian Watercolours*, Oxford: Phaidon, 1987
John Crabbe, "Feminist with a paintbrush", *Journal of Women Artists Slide Library*, no.22, April–May 1988, pp.8–9
——, "Wild weather in watercolour", *Country Life*, clxxxiii, 2 March 1989, pp.100–01
Gerald M. Ackerman, *Les Orientalistes de l'école britannique*, Courbevoie, Paris: ACR, 1991
Barbara Bodichon, 1827–1891, exh. cat., Girton College, Cambridge, 1991
John Crabbe, "Hidden by history", *Watercolours, Drawings and Prints*, vi/2, Spring 1991, pp.13–17
Barbara Bodichon: Victorian Painter and Feminist, exh. cat., University of Hull, 1992
Victorian Landscape Watercolours, exh. cat., Yale Center for British Art, New Haven, and elsewhere, 1992
Deborah Cherry, *Painting Women: Victorian Women Artists*, London and New York: Routledge, 1993
Pam Hirsch, "Barbara Leigh Smith Bodichon: Artist and activist", *Women in the Victorian Art World*, ed. Clarissa Campbell Orr, Manchester: Manchester University Press, 1995, pp.167–86

More than a century after her death, Barbara Leigh Smith Bodichon is in the unusual position for an artist of being more widely known to social historians than to art lovers. In 1854 she initiated a campaign to reform British law as it applied to women, leading in time to a series of Married Women's Property Acts, and in 1866 she organised the first mass-petition to Parliament in favour of female suffrage. Bodichon also urged an expansion of women's working options and a radical advance in their access to higher education. Yet despite a life spent battling for such causes, she once declared that her primary duty was to be an artist, and over a 30-year period she exhibited more than 300 pictures at some 80 events. Her work was frequently praised in the press and sold well, but she saved the income from her paintings and eventually used it to serve her feminist ideals by bequeathing it to Girton College at Cambridge, which she had helped to found.

One might have expected Bodichon's art to reflect her social concerns, but apart from *Ireland 1846* (Whitworth Art Gallery, Manchester, repr. Hull 1992, p.8), a picture inspired by the potato famine, and a few cartoon-like sketches and a drawing of a prohibited footpath, this did not happen. Landscape was her forte; human figures were rarely granted more than a token role in pictures dominated by hills, trees, coasts, mountains, clouds, ruins, sunsets and moving water. Her love of these things seems to have stemmed from wide-ranging childhood holidays and long stays in Sussex, while there was never any shortage of family encouragement to record them with pencils or paint.

William Henry Hunt provided her first drawing lessons, her grandfather (a patron of the Norwich School) once took the young Barbara to see Turner at work, and later she studied with or was advised by David Cox, Prout, Peter De Wint and one of the Varleys. She then had a period of instruction under Francis Cary at the Ladies' College, Bedford Square, mingled with the Pre-Raphaelites, picked up hints from the seascapist Henry Moore and received continual encouragement from Hercules Brabazon. Bodichon was thus well steeped in English watercolour traditions, which provided the foundations of her art, but in her thirties she also studied in France with Belloc, Daubigny and Corot. Daubigny's plein-air philosophy was especially congenial to her, and the Frenchman became a personal friend. Her friends also included various women artists with whom she exchanged ideas over the years: Helen Allingham (q.v.), Laura Herford, Anna Mary Howitt,

Bodichon: *Roman Aqueduct near Cherchell*, 1861; watercolour with scraping out; 26 × 73 cm.

Marianne North and Emily Osborn (q.v.), the last of whom became her portraitist.

Of her early mentors, she seems to have particularly valued Cox. Something of his style when depicting heavily overcast scenes can be detected in *View of Snowdon with a Stormy Sky* (1854; Yale Center for British Art, New Haven, repr. Crabbe 1989, p.100), while his penchant for representing winds and driving rain was certainly echoed in pictures such as *Near the Lands End* (1875) and *Sea at Hastings III* (both Girton College, Cambridge, repr. Cambridge 1991, p.19). The latter, a masterly amalgam of overbearing weather and tiny beach figures, is one of a long succession of Sussex coastal scenes. These range from the picturesque *Hastings Beach with Fishing Boats* (c.1850; private collection, repr. Crabbe 1981, p.313), via vigorous wave-studies such as *Fishing Boats Coming In*, to the almost eerily static *Sea at Hastings I* (both Girton College), a scene enveloped in mistily diffused light that has been seen as hinting at Whistler.

Bodichon's work has also been linked to that of her friends of the Pre-Raphaelite Brotherhood, which it could sometimes resemble with a suggestion of a leafy or rocky detail. W.M. Rossetti referred to the imposing cliff-top view called *Ventnor Isle of Wight* (1856; private collection, repr. Newall 1987, p.61) as being "full of real Pre-Raphaelitism", yet from time to time the praise accorded by other critics was leavened with remarks about her "unfinished" style. In truth, she was variable, both painstaking and what she called "dashy", and her awareness of this, together with lingering doubts about the quality of her draughtsmanship, probably explains an inclination to append the word "sketch" to the titles of pictures that pose no problem for the modern eye. There is no problem, either, in sensing in her work the eager love of nature that Dante Gabriel Rossetti famously described as motivating her scenic quests, undertaken "in the sacred name of pigment".

That pigment could be pure watercolour, but was usually augmented with bodycolour and sometimes strengthened with gum, while on rare occasions she turned to oils. Most of her pictures were under 61 centimetres in width, although she tended to favour elongated proportions when handling expansive subjects, as in *Roman Aqueduct near Cherchel* (1861; see illustration). In this regard she could resort to extremes, so that

the width of *Château Gaillard on the Seine* (1870; w. 127 cm.; Girton College, repr. Cambridge 1991, p.21) pushes the watercolour medium to its expressive limits. Yet Bodichon was also an accomplished miniaturist, who could accommodate an exquisite sepia-wash scene on a pocket-sized sketchbook page: *Tree by a Lake* (1850; private collection, repr. Crabbe 1991, p.13).

Trees were a perennial love, whether captured in proud clusters as in *At the Edge of a Pinewood* (Fogg Art Museum, Harvard University, ibid., p.15), moulded by the wind in an open field (*Sketch in Sussex I*; Girton College, repr. Cambridge 1991, p.13) or glistening impressionistically in a shifting light (*Trees with Haystacks*, c.1850; private collection, repr. Crabbe 1981, p.312). Flowers occur less frequently – except for the blossoms on countless aloes in the Algerian pictures – but one striking example is an oil, *Study of Sunflowers* (1875; Girton College, repr. Cambridge 1991, p.9), which neatly provides a sunset backcloth. Another notable oil is *Shepherd and Sheep* (Girton College, ibid., p.17), an Algerian scene of biblical tone set on a wild hillside.

The North African connection came with her marriage in 1857 to Dr Bodichon of Algiers, after which her maiden insignia "BLS" usually became "BLSB" or "BLS Bodichon". After an American honeymoon during which she painted *Louisiana Swamps* (for a newspaper engraving, see Hirsch 1995, p.182, and Crabbe 1991, p.16) and *Rapids above Niagara* (1858; Girton College, repr. Cambridge 1991, p.15), she usually spent her winters in Algeria. These sojourns generated a steady flow of exotic pictures that eventually totalled over half of her exhibited work, from which *A Sketch in the Hydra Valley* (1859; Girton College, ibid., cover) and *A Scene near Algiers* (Hastings Museum, repr. Ackerman 1991, p.35) could join the Roman ruin illustrated here to provide a fair selection.

Bodichon's European trips also had artistic offshoots, notably *Château Gaillard* described above and a moonlit *Eruption of Vesuvius* (1855; private collection, repr. Hirsch 1995, p.175), while another corner of her output not to be missed involved flights of fancy. Most remarkable of these is the innocently titled *Afternoon, a Sketch* (Girton College, repr. Cambridge 1991, p.15), which depicts trilithons resembling

Stonehenge, situated on a beach by the sea. In one sense a mere capriccio, this achieves a hauntingly beautiful meeting of images not unlike that offered by the decayed aqueduct reproduced here, and it was difficult to decide for illustration purposes which best represents Barbara Bodichon's rather lonely art.

JOHN CRABBE

Bologna, Catherine of *see* Vigri

Bona

Italian painter and collage artist, 1926–

Born Bona Tibertelli de Pisis in Rome, 12 September 1926. Attended Istituto d'Arte Adolfo Venturi, Modena, 1939; studies interrupted by outbreak of World War II. Took classes at Accademia delle Belle Arti, Venice, 1946, and studied with her uncle, the painter Filippo de Pisis. Went to Paris with de Pisis, 1947; met the poet André Pieyre de Mandiargues and through him the Surrealists; participated in subsequent Surrealist exhibitions. Married Mandiargues, 1950, settling in Paris; daughter born 1967; divorced, then remarried, 1967; husband died 1991. Subsequently travelled widely, visiting Mexico (1958, 1966 and 1980), the Far East (1963) and Japan (1979), residing in Geneva (1982) and frequently returning to Italy. Lives in Paris.

Selected Individual Exhibitions
Galerie Berggruen, Paris: 1952
Il Milione, Milan: 1953
Galleria la Saletta, Modena: 1953
Galleria Chiurazzi, Rome: 1954
Galerie Craven, Paris: 1955
Galerie La Baleine, Cairo: 1955
Galleria Selecta, Rome: 1956
Galeria Antonio da Souza, Mexico City: 1958, 1966
Galerie la Cour d'Ingres, Paris: 1960
Kuapik Gallery, New York: 1960
Galerie du XXème siècle, Paris: 1965
Galleria del Cavallino, Venice: 1967
Galerie 3+2, Paris: 1970
Galleria San Sebastianello, Rome: 1973
Galerie de Seine, Paris: 1974 (retrospective), 1976
Aoki Gallery, Tokyo: 1979
Galeria Arvil, Mexico City: 1980
Galerie de L'Hôtel de Ville, Geneva: 1982, 1986
Quartz, Brest: 1990 (retrospective)
Arenthon, Paris: 1990
Galleria Grafica Tokio, Tokyo: 1991
Galerie La Hune-Brenner, Paris: 1994
Muleta Gallery, Tokyo: 1994

Selected Writings
"L'art du Nouristan", *Los Armandans* (Mallorca), 1964; reprinted in *Bonaventure*, 1977
La Cafarde, Paris: Mercure de France, 1967 (novella)
Bonaventure, Paris: Stock, 1977 (with Alain Vircondelet; autobiography)

"L'attimo felice", *Filippo de Pisis*, Verona, 1978
"Il poeta dell'attimo", *Undici più uno*, Rome, 1980
A moi-même, Paris: Fata Morgana, 1988 (poems)
"Les complaintes de Sérafin", *Drailles*, no.10, 1988, pp.113–21

Bibliography
André Pieyre de Mandiargues, *Bona: L'Amour et la peinture*, Geneva: Skira, 1971
Bona, exh. cat., Galerie de Seine, Paris, 1974
Bona: Vingt-cinq ans d'imagination et de création, exh. cat., Galerie de Seine, Paris, 1976
Obliques, no.14–15, 1977 (special issue: *La Femme surréaliste*)
La Femme et le surréalisme, exh. cat., Musée Cantonal des Beaux-Arts, Lausanne, 1987
Bona: Assemblages et peintures, exh. cat., Quartz, Brest, 1990
Bona, exh. cat., Arenthon, Paris, 1990
Georgiana M.M. Colvile, "Images et mots d'elles", *Regard d'écrivain, parole de peintre*, ed. Monique Chefdor and Dalton Krauss, Nantes: Joca Séria, 1994, pp.93–109

Growing up in Italy, in a highly cultivated milieu, Bona was able to develop her exceptional talent for draughtsmanship early and to master various painting techniques, using her country's great masters, such as Giotto and Giorgio de Chirico, as models. Her uncle Filippo de Pisis remained the strongest influence on her life as an artist, introducing her to the literary and artistic intelligentsia of the period. When she joined the Surrealist group in Paris around 1947, André Breton's poetic principles provided her with an outlet for her own oneiric fantasy world, and much later, in 1958, on her first trip to Mexico, a country of intense creative inspiration for her, she accidentally discovered a unique corresponding medium with which to express it: she began working with fabric, using it for the patchwork collages she now calls ragarts. In the catalogue of Bona's exhibition of 1990 in Brest, Morwena Novion described how the artist experienced that particular revelation by taking a man's jacket apart and discovering a piece of material hidden and imprisoned between the outer garment and the lining. To her delight, Bona then learned that this secret piece was called *l'âme* (the soul, heart or core). One of the joys of ragarts is that of undoing something, tearing it apart and subsequently reconstructing something completely different, like Marcel Duchamp's recontextualisation of objects with his ready-mades, Cubist metonymic fragmentation and Surrealist juxtaposition of seemingly disconnected elements, in order to trigger the spark of an uncanny image.

Although she has proved to be a gifted writer and has produced some important surrealist texts, Bona remains first and foremost a plastic artist. As such, she has mainly explored two domains: portraiture and erotic drawings. Like most of the women Surrealists, Bona has painted many self-portraits over the years. One of the early ones (1956; oil on canvas; private collection) is especially Surrealist, incorporating the artist's profiled bust and head into a rocky landscape, while her very flesh, in Magritte fashion, appears to be made of bricks. The twin portraits of herself (see illustration) and her husband *André Pieyre de Mandiargues* (1968; repr. Pieyre de Mandiargues 1971) in acrylic use lavish colours, hers creating a smooth effect and emphasising her beauty, while his appears to be openly fragmented, seeming to imitate the collage/assemblage technique. A much later collage self-portrait, *Bona in Mexico City* (1990; artist's collection), takes on a tone of

Bona: *Self-Portrait,* 1968

caricature and self-derision, suggesting premature ageing and loss of beauty.

Other portraits include one of her daughter, *Sybille in the Studio* (1982–3; artist's collection), and several of famous writers and artists, frequently Surrealists, the latest being a posthumous portrait of *André Breton* (1994; private collection). A striking example is the portrait of the schizophrenic Surrealist painter and writer Unica Zürn (q.v.), Hans Bellmer's companion, who committed suicide in 1970 (*Unica*, 1986; fabric assemblage; private collection, repr. Brest 1990). Zürn's split personality is cleverly conveyed by representing her as two asymmetrical halves hugging each other; in the background scattered numbers allude to Zürn's obsession with arithmetic and anagrams, while a miniature portrait of a little girl evokes the surrealist myth of the "femme-enfant" or child-woman. This portrait, too, has an uncanny male twin: *L'Homme jasmin (homage to Henri Michaux)* (1986; private collection, *ibid.*), which bears the same title as Zürn's autobiographical narrative based on her experience of psychiatric institutions, addressed to a benign male *alter ego*, now known to be the poet Henri Michaux. Among Bona's portraits there are also two collages of *Apollinaire* and one in oils of *Ezra Pound* (1970; artist's collection), looking like Moses. The likenesses are always quite remarkable (unless the character is schematised and caricatured, as in *Unica Zürn*), yet rendered somewhat magical or dreamlike by daring colour associations and the assemblage-ragarts technique. An article of 1970 on Bona by Olivier Perrelet (quoted in Brest 1990) is aptly titled "Songes en lambeaux de Bona" ("Bona's tattered/shredded dreams"), which conveys the astonishing effect created by her ragarts of being simultaneously fragmented and harmoniously whole. Such an overt antinomy makes Bona a true Surrealist.

The delightful "erotic" drawings are more playful than obscene. Their masterful technique is reminiscent of Hans Bellmer's draughtsmanship, while their mischievous content, or rather its tone, evokes the surrealist humour of Leonora Carrington (q.v.), perhaps as emanating more from the latter's fiction than her painting. These works bear the mark of the snail that Bona has chosen as a kind of totem. The catalogue of Bona's exhibition of 1974 at the Galerie de Seine includes a hand-written inscription by the artist: "The big snail urging me to paint, sometimes drools with rage, but more often with love" (my translation). The male figures in these drawings (her rage) are few, old, ridiculous and almost never naked; the women (clearly symbols of love), usually tangled together, are nude, beautiful and seductive ingénues, involved in *caracolages*. The latter word speaks the unspoken Freudian *Witz* emerging from these pictures: "caracol" in Spanish signifies snail and together with "col(l)age" (the very technique *not* used here) produces the French word "caracolage", meaning capering and gambolling about, like Bona's naked ladies. The latter often sport snail-like attributes, such as spiral patterns.

Furthermore, as Morwena Novion also pointed out, the snail represents the solitary, private and mentally androgynous aspects of Bona's own character. This reserve or shyness, as well as the long years spent in the shadow of de Pisis and Mandiargues (although both were very supportive of her art), have often prevented her from getting the recognition she deserves. Fortunately, she is now offered more and more exhibitions, both in Paris and abroad. She has even been given an informal show of her erotic drawings in a restaurant in Regent Street, London. Bona should indeed be considered as an important Surrealist of the last generation, those who joined Breton's group after World War II; today, however, her unique achievement through ragarts stands out as her very own and she no longer needs to belong to any school.

GEORGIANA M. M. COLVILE

Bonheur, Rosa
French painter and sculptor, 1822–1899

Born in Bordeaux, 16 March 1822, to Raymond Bonheur, drawing instructor and landscape painter, and his wife Sophie. Moved to Paris with her family, 1829. Trained by her father, copying from casts at the Louvre. Met Natalie Micas, who became close friend and companion, 1836. Made sketching trips to the Auvergne, 1846 and 1847, to the Pyrenees, 1850; visited London, Birmingham and Scotland and met Edwin Landseer, 1856. Directed the state-sponsored Ecole Gratuite de Dessin pour les Jeunes Filles, assisted by her sister Juliette (later Juliette Peyrol), 1848–59. Retired with Micas to the Château de By, near Fontainebleau, 1860; spent summers in the south of France, 1875–89. Micas died, 1889. Met Anna Klumpke (q.v.), 1889; Klumpke became her companion at By, 1898. Cross of Légion d'Honneur conferred by the Empress Eugénie, 1865; member, Order of San Carlos of Mexico, 1865; member, Institut d'Anvers (Antwerp), 1868; Commander's cross, Royal Order of Isabella the Catholic, Spain, 1880; Order of Merit for Fine Arts, Saxe-Coburg-Gotha, 1885; Order of Saint-Jacques of Portugal, 1890 (nominated officer 1894); Officier, Légion d'Honneur, 1894; honorary president, Union des Femmes Peintres et Sculpteurs, Paris. Died at Château de By, Seine-et-Marne, 25 May 1899.

Principal Exhibitions

Paris Salon: 1841–50, 1853, 1867, 1899 (third-class medal 1845, gold medal 1848, exemption from jury 1853)

Rouen Salon: 1843 (bronze medal), 1845 (silver medal), 1847 (silver medal)

Brussels Salon: 1851, 1858, 1881

Exposition Universelle, Paris: 1855 (gold medal), 1867 (second-class medal), 1889

German Gallery, London: 1860 (individual)

Society of Female Artists, London: 1861–2, 1865, 1867, 1870, 1873

New Society of Painters in Watercolours, London: 1867–8, 1875

Royal Academy, London: 1869

Lefevre Gallery, London: 1881, 1882, 1896 (all individual)

Woman's Building, World's Columbian Exposition, Chicago: 1893

Galerie Georges Petit, Paris: 1897 (individual), 1900 (retrospective)

Selected Writings

"Fragments of my autobiography", *Magazine of Art*, xxvi, 1902, pp.531–6

Bibliography
John Forbes-Robertson, "Rosa Bonheur", *Magazine of Art*, v, 1882, pp.45–50

Henry Bacon, "Rosa Bonheur", *Century Magazine*, xxviii (new series vi), 1884, pp.833–40

L. Roger-Miles, *Rosa Bonheur: Sa vie, son oeuvre*, Paris: Société d'Edition Artistique, 1900

Anna Klumpke, *Rosa Bonheur: Sa vie, son oeuvre*, Paris: Flammarion, 1908

Theodore Stanton, ed., *Reminiscences of Rosa Bonheur*, London: Melrose, and New York: Appleton, 1910; reprinted New York: Hacker, 1976

Anna Klumpke, *Memoirs of an Artist*, ed. Lilian Whiting, Boston: Wright and Potter, 1940

Women Artists, 1550–1950, exh. cat., Los Angeles County Museum of Art, and elsewhere, 1976

Danielle Digne, *Rosa Bonheur ou l'insolence: L'Histoire d'une vie, 1822–1899*, Paris: Denoël/Gonthier, 1980

Dore Ashton, *Rosa Bonheur: A Life and Legend*, New York: Viking, and London: Secker and Warburg, 1981

Albert Boime, "The case of Rosa Bonheur: Why should a woman want to be more like a man?", *Art History*, iv, 1981, pp.384–409

La Femme artiste d'Elisabeth Vigée-Lebrun à Rosa Bonheur, exh. cat., Musée Despiau-Wlerick, Donjon Lacataye, Mont-de-Marsan, 1981

Rosalia Shriver, *Rosa Bonheur, with a Checklist of Works in American Collections*, Philadelphia: Art Alliance Press, 1982

Charlotte Yeldham, *Women Artists in Nineteenth-Century France and England*, 2 vols, New York: Garland, 1984

Rosa Bonheur: Selected Works from American Collections, exh. cat., Meadows Museum, Southern Methodist University, Dallas, and elsewhere, 1989

Susan Waller, *Women Artists in the Modern Era: A Documentary History*, Metuchen, NJ: Scarecrow Press, 1991

Mara R. Witzling, ed., *Voicing Our Visions: Writings by Women Artists*, New York: Universe, 1991; London: Women's Press, 1992

Tamar Garb, "*L'art feminin*: The formation of a critical category in late nineteenth-century France", *The Expanding Discourse: Feminism and Art History*, ed. Norma Broude and Mary D. Garrard, New York: HarperCollins, 1992, pp.207–30

James M. Saslow, "Disagreeably hidden: Construction and constriction of the lesbian body in Rosa Bonheur's *Horse Fair*", *ibid.*, pp.187–206

Whitney Chadwick, "The fine art of gentling: Horses and women and Rosa Bonheur in Victorian England", *The Body Imaged: The Human Form and Visual Culture since the Renaissance*, ed. Kathleen Adler and Marcia Pointon, Cambridge and New York: Cambridge University Press, 1993, pp.89–107

Wendy Slatkin, *The Voices of Women Artists*, Englewood Cliffs, NJ: Prentice Hall, 1993

Rosa Bonheur correspondence is in the Jake and Nancy Hamon Arts Library, Southern Methodist University, Dallas.

Rosa Bonheur was not only the first woman artist to be awarded the Légion d'Honneur, which was established by Napoleon I to honour the most accomplished French citizens, but also the most prominent woman artist in Europe and America of her time, an example for women artists of a younger generation.

Bonheur was the oldest child of Raymond Bonheur, an artist, drawing instructor and follower of Saint-Simon, whose utopian theories questioned traditional social structures, including gender norms, and his wife Sophie, the child of a middle-class Bordeaux family and a former student of her husband. After Sophie Bonheur's untimely death in 1833, Rosa Bonheur found solace and affection in the Micas family; Natalie Micas would become her lifelong friend and companion. Bonheur's father initially sent her to the school at which he taught and later attempted to apprentice her to a seamstress; she, however, wanted to become a painter, and eventually her father relented, at first teaching her himself and later sending her to the Louvre to copy. He held up Elisabeth Vigée-Lebrun (q.v.) as the model of a successful woman artist and allowed his daughter to bring animals into the family studio so that she could study them. When Bonheur determined to become an *animalier*, she went to the slaughter-house at Roule to study animal anatomy.

Bonheur made her debut at the Salon in 1841 with two paintings, including *Rabbits Nibbling Carrots* (Musée des Beaux-Arts, Bordeaux). In 1845 she was awarded a third-class medal and three years later received a first-class medal. In 1849 she exhibited *Ploughing at Nivernais* (Musée Nationale du Château de Fontainebleau), which had been commissioned by the government of the Second Republic. This monumental work was said to be inspired by the opening chapter of George Sand's novel, *La Mare au diable*. Two teams of oxen strain forward as they draw ploughs through the rich red soil, their scale and power overshadowing their four handlers. As an evocation of rural productivity, the painting was welcomed by government officials and critics. In 1851 Bonheur began preparations for another ambitious work with twice-weekly visits to the Paris horse market. *The Horse Fair* (1853; see illustration) depicts a line of percherons at the market at the Boulevard de l'Hôpital near Salpêtrière. Under a blue sky, a great wheel of rearing and lunging horses surges past as grooms struggle to control them. In the centre of the canvas a rider in blue cap astride one of the horses looks out at the viewer: it has been suggested that this androgynous figure is a self-portrait that Bonheur inserted into the composition as a way of publicly questioning and resisting conventional feminine gender roles.

When it was exhibited at the Salon of 1853 *The Horse Fair* was widely admired. It recalled the work of Théodore Géricault and the frieze of the Parthenon, and Bonheur's precise naturalism and painstaking technique set her apart from other artists who painted the French countryside – particularly the group that included Millet, Théodore Rousseau and Constant Troyon and which came to be known as the Barbizon School. The painting found favour with such conservative critics as Etienne Delécluze, but others argued that her transcription of nature was too literal, that in contrast to Troyon, she merely copied nature. At the close of the exhibition, Bonheur and another woman artist were awarded *hors concours* status and granted the privilege of exhibiting whatever they wished in future Salons, a privilege that after 1852 had been reserved for members of the Légion d'Honneur and the Académie des Beaux-Arts. Although the percheron horses, native to Normandy, were particularly favoured by Louis Napoléon, who used them in his imperial coaches, the large work was not purchased by the government. It was exhibited in Bordeaux and Ghent and purchased by Ernest Gambart, a dealer of prints and paintings who had established a gallery in London to exhibit works by French artists. Gambart arranged for Bonheur to visit Britain while the painting was on view and introduced her to Charles Eastlake, the President of the Royal Academy; Elizabeth Rigby, the discerning art critic married to Eastlake; John Ruskin; and Edwin Landseer, Britain's foremost *animalier*, whom Bonheur greatly respected.

Bonheur's visit to Britain, which also introduced her to new breeds of animals and new subjects, led to such works as

Bonheur: *The Horse Fair*, 1853; oil on canvas; 244.5 × 506.7 cm.; Metropolitan Museum of Art, New York: Gift of Cornelius Vanderbilt, 1887 (87.25)

Gathering for the Hunt (1856; Haggin Museum, Stockton, CA), which represents a group of horses, dogs and riders in the early morning countryside. Ruskin complained that Bonheur's animals lacked the "gleam of humanity, a flash of light through which their life looks out and up to our great mystery of command over them" (quoted in Ashton 1981, p.112). For British audiences especially, representations of animals served as a symbolic zone of mediation between the natural and the human. Horses in particular were often endowed with qualities similar to those considered characteristic of women – docility, patience, courage, perseverance, strength – and representations of horse training thus evoked complex meanings about unruly nature subjected to man's will.

Bonheur's popularity in Britain and the USA enabled her dealers – Gambart and the Tedesco brothers – to place most of her works with collectors, and she had little need to participate in exhibitions in France. She sent *Haymaking at Auvergne* (Musée National du Château de Fontainebleau) to the Exposition Universelle in Paris in 1855, where it was hung as a pendant to *Ploughing at Nivernais* and received a gold medal. This, however, was the last Salon she participated in until the Exposition Universelle of 1867. In 1865 she was visited by the Empress Eugénie – the empress was temporarily acting as regent in Louis Napoléon's absence and she took advantage of the powers conferred on her to award Bonheur the red ribbon of the Légion d'Honneur with the feminist slogan: "Genius has no sex".

Bonheur did not sentimentalise or anthropomorphise her subjects but portrayed them in their natural habitat. *Stag Listening to the Wind* (1867; Vassar College Art Gallery, Poughkeepsie, NY) represents a deer standing on the slope of a hillside where open fields give way to heavy woods: the beast is poised looking towards the field as though ready at the first suspicious noise to dash for cover in the woods. It contrasts markedly with Landseer's popular and much reproduced *Monarch of the Glen* (1851; John Dewar and Sons Ltd), in which a stag turns to confront the viewer, his antlers silhouetted against the distant mountain horizon. In many of Bonheur's works, as in *Returning from the Fields* (1851; Columbus Museum of Art, OH), which shows two ox-drawn carts, and *Pastoral Landscape with Cattle* (Philadelphia Museum of Art), animals are represented standing or travelling down a road, isolated against a flat, open landscape that allows a clear view of Bonheur's careful study of their physiognomy. Bonheur's letters suggest her strong identification with animals: she frequently refers to herself or her correspondents as "my poor little wren" or "your old animal of a sister".

In order to study the animals at the Paris markets and slaughter-houses Bonheur routinely entered highly masculine environments: perhaps as early as the 1840s, and certainly by the early 1850s, when she was preparing *The Horse Fair*, she adopted a form of masculinised dress – trousers and a loose smock (*blouse*). Her preferred costume may have owed something to Saint-Simonian utopian dress experiments, but it was most similar to the dress of male peasants and the studio dress worn by many male artists. By the 1850s this had become her habitual costume in the studio and at home, and she obtained necessary police permission to wear masculine clothing in public. Although she wore *blouse* and trousers in informal photographs, she avoided having formal photographs or portraits made of her in this dress, which she maintained she wore largely for convenience. For more public occasions she developed a style of provincial dress that she wore when necessary, and continually complained that it was uncomfortable.

Edouard Dubufe's portrait of *Rosa Bonheur at 34* (1857; repr. Ashton 1981, p.75) showed her with her arm resting on the shoulders of a bull, dressed in a full skirt and velvet jacket with lace collar.

A public precedent had been established for cross-dressing in the 1830s by George Sand, who had adopted upper-class male dress – a dark suit – when she wanted to attend the theatre. Sand had been satirised in the press for her costume; Bonheur, although she admired Sand, shunned such notoriety. In the 1860s, when her transvestism became a matter of public knowledge, critics treated Bonheur's *blouse* and trousers with amusement as the dress of an absent-minded but well-meaning eccentric whose studio-stable with its stalls for horses and sheep was known from a lithographic view (*ibid.*, p.72). By the end of the century, however, her costume came to be viewed with hostility and she was called a "masculinised" woman. As increasing numbers of young women entered studios where they could work from the nude model, exhibited at the Salon and embarked on careers that called into question traditional feminine roles, attitudes towards Bonheur's resistance to conventional constraints on feminine behaviour became more complex and conflicted. At the Salon of 1893, Mme Achille Fould represented Bonheur in her studio in male dress, surrounded by well-known works and other signs of her professional status and accomplishment (see Garb 1992, p.219), but in such magazines as *Le Monde Illustré* she was satirised and her dress ridiculed (see Saslow 1992, p.194). Bonheur was greatly admired by such younger artists as Virginie Demont-Breton (q.v.), who in her memoirs recalled the day in her childhood when she learned that the famous artist Rosa Bonheur was a woman, and by the American Anna Klumpke (q.v.), who had been given a Rosa Bonheur doll as a child. An account of Bonheur's visit to Britain was included in the *English Woman's Journal*, one of the earliest feminist journals, in 1858; in the 1890s she participated occasionally in the exhibitions of the Union des Femmes Peintres et Sculpteurs and was honoured by the organisation by being named honorary life president.

In 1860, as Bonheur's markets in Britain and the USA became well established, she bought an estate with a château at By, near the forest of Fontainebleau. There she established a household with Natalie and Mme Micas that she called a "domain of perfect friendship". This woman-centred household provided the three women with emotional and practical support and was in keeping with Bonheur's resistance to the traditional constraining roles assigned to women by French law and convention. Although in the later 19th century sexologists would formulate theories of homosexuality and gender variance to explain long-term, highly romanticised relationships between women, earlier in the century such commitments were frequently idealised as a form of elevated and passionate friendship. Bonheur was deeply saddened at the death of Natalie Micas in 1889, but in her later years was consoled by a close association with Anna Klumpke, a young painter who eventually shared her home and studio and who edited and published her memoirs.

Bonheur's estate also provided a home for her collection of animals. In the 1860s most of her paintings represented the deer, horses and dogs from the preserve at By; in the 1870s she turned her attention to lions – some of which she raised on her estate and others that she studied in zoological gardens. These became the subjects of oil paintings and watercolours, such as *Royalty at Home* (1885; Minneapolis Institute of Arts). In her notebooks Bonheur recorded multiple views of animals; as she explained: "I would study an animal and draw it in the position it took, and when it changed to another position I would draw that" (quoted in Ashton 1981, p.98). In her later years she turned to subjects from the American West. When Buffalo Bill Cody brought his Wild West show to Paris for the Exposition Universelle of 1889, she visited the encampment, making sketches of Native Americans and buffalo that would become the basis for such paintings as *Buffalo Hunt* (1889; *ibid.*, pl.155). Her friendship with Cody was commemorated in a portrait of him on horseback, *"Buffalo Bill" Cody* (1889; Whitney Gallery of Western Art, Cody, WY). In Bonheur's final years Anna Klumpke helped her to take up *Wheat Threshing at the Camargue* (Musée National de Château du Fontainebleau), a monumental canvas of a group of fiery horses that she wanted to represent "an infernal waltz". She had begun the painting in 1864 as a companion to the *Horse Fair*, but later set it aside. It remained unfinished at her death.

SUSAN WALLER

Bontecou, Lee

American sculptor and graphic artist, 1931–

Born in Providence, Rhode Island, 15 January 1931. Studied at the Art Students League, New York, under William Zorach and John Hovannes, 1952–5; Skowhegan School of Art, Maine, 1954; studied in Rome on Fulbright fellowships, 1955–9. Taught in art department, Brooklyn College, New York. Recipient of Louis Comfort Tiffany award, 1959; Competition award, Corcoran Gallery of Art Biennial, Washington, DC, 1963; first prize, National Institute of Arts and Letters, 1966. Has one daughter. Lives in western Pennsylvania.

Selected Individual Exhibitions

G Gallery, New York: 1959
Leo Castelli Gallery, New York: 1960, 1962, 1966, 1971
Galerie Ileana Sonnabend, Paris: 1965
Museum Boymans-van Beuningen, Rotterdam: 1968
Städtisches Museum Schloss Morsbroich, Leverkusen: 1968 (touring)
Kunstverein, Berlin: 1968
Museum of Contemporary Art, Chicago: 1972 (retrospective)
Davison Art Center, Wesleyan University, Middletown, CT: 1975
Hawthorne Gallery, Skidmore College, Saratoga Springs, NY: 1977 (retrospective)
Museum of Contemporary Art, Los Angeles: 1993–4 (touring)

Bibliography

Americans 1963, exh. cat., Museum of Modern Art, New York, 1963
Dore Ashton, "Illusion and fantasy: Lee [Magica fantasia di Lee]", *Metro*, no.8, April 1963, pp.28–33
New American Sculpture, exh. cat., Pasedena Art Museum, CA, 1964
Recent American Sculpture, exh. cat., Jewish Museum, New York, 1964

John Coplans, "Higgins, Price, Chamberlain, Bontecou, Westermann", *Artforum*, ii, April 1964, pp.38–40

Lee Bontecou, exh. cat., Galerie Ileana Sonnabend, Paris, 1965

Donald Judd, "Lee Bontecou", *Arts Magazine*, xxxix, April 1965, pp.17–21

Lee Bontecou, exh. cat., Städtisches Museum Schloss Morsbroich, Leverkusen, and elsewhere, 1968

Lee Bontecou: Sculpturen, tekeningen, litho's, exh. cat., Museum Boymans-van Beuningen, Rotterdam, 1968

"Lee Bontecou, untitled", *Bulletin of the Cleveland Museum of Art*, lvi, February 1969, pp.78–80

Tony Towle, "Two conversations with Lee Bontecou", *Print Collector's Newsletter*, ii, 1971, pp.25–8

James R. Mellow, "Bontecou's well-fed fish and malevolent flowers", *New York Times*, 6 June 1971, D19

Lee Bontecou, exh. cat., Museum of Contemporary Art, Chicago, 1972

Lincoln F. Johnson, "A diversity of approaches in contemporary art: Rauschenberg, Bontecou and Noland", *Honolulu Academy of Arts Journal*, i, 1974, pp.51–67

Prints and Drawings by Lee Bontecou, exh. cat., Davison Art Center, Wesleyan University, Middleton, CT, 1975

Eleanor Munro, *Originals: American Women Artists*, New York: Simon and Schuster, 1979

The Sculptural Membrane, exh. cat., Sculpture Center, New York, 1986

Charlotte Streifer Rubinstein, *American Women Sculptors*, Boston: Hall, 1990

Terry R. Myers, "From the junk aesthetic to the junk mentality", *Arts Magazine*, lxiv, February 1990, pp.60–64

Mona Hadler, "Lee Bontecou: Heart of a conquering darkness", *Source: Notes in the History of Art*, xii, Fall 1992, pp.38–44

Elizabeth A. T. Smith, "Abstract sinister", *Art in America*, lxxxi, September 1993, pp.82–7

Mona Hadler, "Lee Bontecou's 'Warnings'", *Art Journal*, liii, Winter 1994, pp.56–61

The work of the American artist Lee Bontecou was widely acclaimed, collected and exhibited in the USA and Europe during the 1960s and early 1970s. Hailed as one of the most promising young sculptors of her generation, Bontecou created a startlingly original body of work that has stood apart from the art historical mainstream and remains little known from a contemporary perspective.

One of the few women artists to achieve broad recognition in the 1960s, Bontecou first distinguished herself in 1959 with a body of small to mid-sized abstract constructions of salvaged canvas and burlap stretched over welded steel frames, held in place by pieces of twisted wire (*Untitled*, 1959; see illustration). In 1960, the year that her work was first shown at Leo Castelli Gallery, Bontecou markedly increased the size and three-dimensionality of many of these predominantly wall-mounted works. She also began to incorporate into her sculpture an array of materials such as rope, denim, leather and black velvet – the last used to create the backdrops for deep voids constructed within many of the works. In untitled pieces of 1961 and 1962, found metal parts and objects ranging from fan blades and industrial saw-tooth components to war-surplus materials such as gas masks and helmets came to be positioned within and across the surfaces of the increasingly eccentrically configured canvas and steel armatures.

While remaining emphatically non-specific, the objects embedded within Bontecou's sculpture endow it with over-tones of figurative and mechanistic imagery. In many of these resolutely abstract and persistently disquieting sculptures, a

Bontecou: *Untitled*, 1959; 251 × 148 × 80 cm.; Moderna Museet, Stockholm

strongly implied human presence – heads, gaping mouths, eye sockets and teeth evoked by deep openings often containing jagged saw-toothed blades and metal grilles – is consistently countered by a seemingly random dispersal of visual detail and an almost cubistic fragmentation of form. The intense three-dimensionality of the works imparts a map-like quality; their relatively vast expanses and deep voids seem also to indicate environmental scale and significance.

Co-existent with the dominant tendencies of the late 1950s to early 1970s – Abstract Expressionism, assemblage, Minimalism, Pop Art and eccentric abstraction – Bontecou's sculpture resists categorisation. Furthermore, the often heroic scale, commanding physicality and brutal quality of her work attracted particular attention because these characteristics seemed at odds with the conventionally defined products of a "feminine" sensibility. Yet discussion of her sculpture often revolved around its perceived sensuality and pointedly female sexuality; critics frequently interpreted the persistent circular openings within the work as body cavities and even as symbolic "vagina dentata" due to their threatening containment of objects. Such allusions rarely acknowledged either the presence or implications of the more substantially representational aspects of Bontecou's sculpture, nor the heterogeneous, multivalent quality of its imagery and overall sculptural character.

To a contemporary viewer, the presence in many of the works of small machines, guns, zippers, rivets, metal grates, gas masks and helmets clearly refers to the materials and activities of war, and more broadly to destruction, brutality and annihilation. Although Bontecou consistently declined to explain the sources of her imagery, she alluded early on to a "concern to build things that express our relation to this country – to other countries – to this world – to other worlds – in terms of myself" (New York 1963, p.12). Not until much later in her career did she expressly reveal that a need to respond to the menacing spectres of war and global destruction had, in part, given shape to much of her early work.

The visual and visceral power of Bontecou's sculpture of the 1960s extends to a body of work on paper produced in tandem with it. Often rendered in almost hyper-realistic detail and configured in dense, all-over compositions, the drawings give evidence of a fascination with relationships between forms and images, particularly in terms of mutation or transformation between the natural and the man-made. Here, the military imagery that found its way obliquely into certain sculptures can be more easily discerned; for example, a highly detailed drawing of 1961 (D26; pencil on paper, Menil Collection, Houston) shows eerily anthropomorphic gas masks dispersed across the emptiness of a white background.

Bontecou's sculpture of the mid-1960s departs from the brutal character of much of her earlier work. Formally more complex in terms of three-dimensionality and texture, this body of work incorporates a wide range of tonalities from black to red to gold to ivory. Using epoxy to build up certain key parts of the works, Bontecou further developed her tendency towards painterly effects that she had previously achieved by shading and modelling form with soot. Invoking a palpable sensation of dynamism and organic profusion, these sculptures (e.g. *Untitled*, 1966; mixed media; 81 × 81 × 45.7cm.; private collection) present a florid preponderance of faceted, overlapping parts; references to flora and fauna and to such images as billowing sails are apparent in both sculptures and drawings (*Untitled*, 1967; pencil and pen and ink on flocked paper; Hirshhorn Museum and Sculpture Garden, Washington, DC) executed between 1965 and 1967. Exuberant and disarmingly lyrical, these works posed an even greater challenge to critics than Bontecou's earlier works in their lack of both an identifiable content and an affinity to recognisable styles and movements.

In the late 1960s and early 1970s Bontecou's work took a frankly figurative turn. Strongly evoking but without directly representing actual species, she sculpted in vacuum-formed plastic and drew startling images of fish and flowering plants, such as *Three Fish* (1970; chalk on black paper; Museum of Modern Art, New York). Combining elements of crystalline physical perfection with qualities of sinister decrepitude, these figurative pieces share other essential characteristics with Bontecou's earlier work, such as a fascination with processes of transformation and with personification of phantasmagoria –

whether observed, remembered or felt. The implicit savagery of these works also functioned as a kind of social and political statement about Bontecou's environmental concerns.

Commingling the organic and inorganic in form, imagery and technique, Bontecou's sculpture and drawings address mutation and transformation within and outside the domain of the human body. The conceptual and visual relationships between a medieval helmet and a flower, the mechanistic teeth of an industrial saw blade and those of a fish, the wretched twist of a piece of wire precariously joining a corner of canvas to a bent steel frame and the sleek, metallic mechanical parts of a found automobile engine, the stencilled name of an identifiable army private on a piece of canvas duffel bag and the abstract, even cosmic implications of blackness at the bottom of a crater-like void function as resonant elements of Bontecou's highly personal artistic vocabulary. One writer noted of Bontecou's compelling, disturbing and profoundly authentic body of work: "The best thing about her work when it hits is that it has nothing to do with anything. It is suffocating, which is the best praise I can give" (John Perreault, "Art", *Village Voice*, 10 June 1971, p.28).

Since the 1970s Bontecou has continued to work two-dimensionally while teaching in the art department of Brooklyn College. Since her recent retirement, she has once again begun to make sculpture but has exhibited very little, living and working quietly in western Pennsylvania. Her work is represented in numerous museum collections, including the Museum of Modern Art, Whitney Museum of American Art and Solomon R. Guggenheim Museum, New York; Art Institute of Chicago; Walker Art Center, Minneapolis; Museum of Fine Arts, Houston; Hirshhorn Museum and Sculpture Garden, Washington, DC; Moderna Museet, Stockholm; and the Stedelijk Museum, Amsterdam.

ELIZABETH A.T. SMITH

Borch, Gesina ter
Dutch amateur painter, 1631–1690

Born in Deventer, 15 November 1631, the daughter of Gerard ter Borch the Elder, and half-sister of Gerard ter Borch the Younger. Resided all her life in Zwolle, except for visits to Gerard the Younger in Deventer and several stays with her sister Jenneken Schellinger in Amsterdam. After Jenneken's death in 1675, the three children of the Schellinger family came to live with her in Zwolle. Died 16(?) April 1690.

Bibliography

M.E. Houck, "Mededelingen betreffende Ter Borch en anderen, benevens aantekeningen omtrent hunne familieleden" [Information concerning Ter Borch and others, with notes on members of his family], *Verslagen en Mededelingen van de Vereeniging tot Beoefening van Overijsselsch Regt en Geschiedenis*, xx, 1899, pp.1–172

S.J. Gudlaugsson, *Katalog der Gemälde Gerard ter Borchs, sowie biographisches Material*, 2 vols, The Hague: Nijhoff, 1959–60

Alison M. Kettering, *Drawings from the Ter Borch Studio Estate in the Rijksmuseum*, 2 vols, The Hague: Staatsuitgeverij, 1988

G. Luijten, "De *Triomf van de Schilderkunst*: Een titeltekening van Gesina ter Borch en een toneelstuk" [The *Triumph of Painting*: A frontispiece by Gesina ter Borch and a stage play], *Bulletin van het Rijksmuseum*, xxxvi, 1988, pp.283–314 (English summary, pp.354–6)

H. Luijten, "Swiren vol van leer, amblemsche wijs geduijt: Een opmerkelijk zeventiende-eeuws poëzie-album van Gesina ter Borch" [Elegancies replete with lessons, shown emblematically: A remarkable 17th-century poetry album by Gesina ter Borch], *ibid.*, pp.315–42 (English summary, pp.356–7, 360)

Alison M. Kettering, "Ter Borch's ladies in satin", *Art History*, xvi, 1993, pp.95–124

Gesina ter Borch was an illustrator and painter of scenes of everyday life, who enjoyed some local recognition. Her less-professional orientation to painting in watercolour led her to explore a variety of subjects and approaches largely unhindered by the conventions of contemporary fine art. Her responsiveness to the more popular artistic currents of her day meant the survival of a considerable body of material reflecting Dutch domestic taste, both visual and literary. Not least among her contributions was the preservation of many drawings by family members, among them drawings by her well-known half-brother, Gerard the Younger.

Like so many girls from artistic families during the early modern period, Gesina ter Borch took advantage both of the intellectual stimulation and the materials available in the parental home. Her father, Gerard the Elder, who had given up an artistic career to become Licence Master of Zwolle (receiver of import and export duties), encouraged the artistic education of his three sons far more vigorously than that of his daughters. Instead, Gesina developed her skills at handwriting (*schoonschrijfkunst*), probably under the supervision of the Zwolle schoolmaster. She preserved her earliest exercises – beautifully penned poems and aphorisms copied from various sources – in a *Materi-Boeck* (Theme book; begun 1646; Rijksmuseum, Amsterdam). Nevertheless, the booklet quickly turned into an album for watercolour drawings and poem illustrations, anticipating Gesina's focus on pictorial art rather than calligraphy in the years ahead. One of these sheets bears the sign of her father's approval, his annotation of the date of execution. (By contrast, Gerard the Elder annotated hundreds of juvenile drawings by his sons.)

Despite the restrictions imposed on young women at the time, Gesina proved to be strongly motivated to develop her artistic talents. She essentially learned to draw by the side of her younger brothers Harmen and Moses. In 1652, shortly after her 21st birthday, she began work on an ambitious album (Rijksmuseum) for her favourite poems, which she illustrated with delicate watercolours, heightened with gold and silver, a medium considered at the time more suitable for women than oil painting. Many of these were fully worked miniatures, loosely based on the illustrations in such contemporary song-books and emblem collections as J.H. Krul's *Eerlyke Tytkorting* (Honourable pastime; 1634) and Jacob Cats's

Borch: *Arrival at a Country House*, 1661; Rijksmuseum, Amsterdam

Spiegel vanden ouden ende nieuwen tijdt (Mirror of old and new times; 1632). Such books were the sources, as well, for the poems she copied into her album. Her selection from this literary material was quite diverse, although Petrarchan love themes predominated: songs featuring lovelorn suitors of hard-hearted beauties. In addition, laudatory poems written in Gesina's honour were entered into the poetry album, most significantly, those by Henrik Jordis, her possible suitor.

Jordis added the dedicatory verses to the poetry album just as Gesina was completing it in 1660. His contribution to Gesina's largest endeavour, the "Art Book" (begun 1660; Rijksmuseum), as he named it, is even more significant. An experienced writer of occasional verse, Jordis was an Amsterdam merchant with connections to literary circles. To this Art Book he contributed an original allegorical play, the *Triomphe der Schilderconst over de Doodt* (Triumph of painting over death), as well as the iconographical programme for Gesina's large title drawing directly based on the play. By 1662 no trace of Gesina's friendship with Jordis remained and she never did marry.

Gesina's major work in the Art Book dates from the 1660s. In a bold style she chronicled the manners, customs and costumes of small-town life in full-size watercolours that provide a wealth of detail about contemporary society and its attitudes (*Arrival at a Country House*, 1661; see illustration). After about 20 pages she transformed the album into a scrapbook. Here can be found many drawings by her brothers and family memorabilia.

The artistic relationship between Gerard the Younger and Gesina was especially close between c.1648 and the mid-1660s. These were the years during which she frequently modelled for his paintings, and they also corresponded to the most intense period of her own artistic activity. Just as Gerard the Younger appears to have encouraged her art, Gesina's very choice of love poetry may have provided inspiration in turn for his genre paintings. During the mid-1660s Gesina also tried oil painting. The most conspicuous example of her efforts can be seen in the posthumous portrait of *Moses ter Borch* (c.1668; Rijksmuseum), on which she collaborated with Gerard.

The local acclaim that Gesina ter Borch enjoyed for her artistic accomplishments is conveyed through the many laudatory poems written in the albums by her admirers. Here the vividness of her personality and character emerge, her cleverness, quickness of mind and devotion to the pursuit of art and knowledge. She can also be credited with preserving the Ter Borch family's work on paper. She stipulated in her will that none of these drawings would leave the family. When the last of the descendants died in 1886, the Rijksmuseum in Amsterdam was able to buy nearly the entire estate intact. This also allowed the rediscovery of an amateur's works, a rare occurrence among 17th-century women amateurs.

ALISON MCNEIL KETTERING

Bouguereau, Elizabeth Gardner *see* Gardner

Bouliar, Marie-Geneviève
French painter, 1763–1825

Born in Paris, 1763; father a tailor. Studied under Joseph Siffred (Siffrein) Duplessis. Died at Château d'Arcy, Saône-et-Loire, 1825.

Principal Exhibitions
Paris Salon: 1791 (prix d'encouragement), 1793, 1795–6, 1798, 1802, 1804, 1812, 1814, 1817

Bibliography
Deloynes Collection, Bibliothèque Nationale, Paris, xviii, nos 488–9, 491 and 493

Marianne Roland-Michel, Etude XX, Archives de la Seine, Boulevard Morland, Paris, n.d.

Henry Jouin, *Mademoiselle Marie-Geneviève Bouliard*, Paris, 1891 (gives incorrect birth dates)

Les Femmes peintres au XVIIIe siècle, exh. cat., Musée Goya, Castres, 1973

Trésors des musées du nord de la France: La Peinture française, 1770–1830, exh. cat., Musée d'Arras and elsewhere, 1975

Women Artists, 1550–1950, exh. cat., Los Angeles County Museum of Art, and elsewhere, 1976

Vivian Cameron, *Woman as Image and Image-Maker in Paris During the French Revolution*, PhD dissertation, Yale University, 1983

La Révolution française et l'Europe, 1789–1799, exh. cat., Grand Palais, Paris, 1989

Marie-Geneviève Bouliar was an accomplished Parisian portraitist whose career spanned more than 30 years. Documentary evidence about her is sparse, but Salon guidebooks show that she exhibited there between 1791 and 1817, thriving professionally during the Revolution. Bouliar took full advantage of the open exhibition policies that operated during the 1790s: this is the period when most of her recorded works were produced, and from which nearly all of her extant work is found.

Little is known of Bouliar's family background and training, but some pertinent details have been confirmed (F. Maison in Arras 1975, p.46). Bouliar was the only daughter of a tailor, a class status ideally suited to success in the anti-aristocratic years of the Revolution. She did not marry, a factor that may account for the initially high level of her production and that encourages a tentative feminist reading of her most ambitious work, *Aspasia* (1794; see illustration), discussed below. Her only documented teacher was Joseph Siffred (Siffrein) Duplessis, noted in the Salon guides for 1796 and 1798. His influence can be seen in Bouliar's work from the late 1790s: for example, the *Woman with a Black Veil* (1798; untraced; shown at the *Exhibition des femmes peintres*, Paris, 1926, photograph in Witt Library, Courtauld Institute of Art, London) focuses on the representation of fabric, a skill for which Duplessis was renowned. Bouliar's pensive subject gathers an exquisitely rendered transparent black veil around her. In general, Bouliar's work is more informal than that of Duplessis, which suggests that another artist was responsible for her initial training. She reached a high standard early in her career, as can be seen in the portrait of M. *Olive, Treasurer of the State of Brittany, and His Family* (Musée des Beaux-Arts, Nantes), which dates from the period 1785–9. Grouped in poses strongly reminiscent of paintings of the Holy Family with John the Baptist, the Olives are a radiant example of the 18th-century family ideal. They embrace their two children, the younger of whom has probably been breast-fed (signalled by Mme Olive's loose chemise). The older child offers him grapes, echoing the action of John the Baptist, and emphasising the fruitfulness of the marriage.

Official recognition for Bouliar's work came at the Salon of 1791, the first to give non-members of the Académie the chance to exhibit at the Louvre. She won a prix d'encouragement of 1000 livres for *Young Woman Crowned with Roses* (Salon cat. no.324), which could be the extant simple frontal portrait of 1791 (private collection, Paris, repr. *Gazette de l'Hôtel Drouot*, 19 December 1986), but it is perhaps more likely to be the more complex painting of 1785 that was exhibited in Paris in 1926 (untraced after three sales: Rothan Sale, Petit Palais, May 1890; Hôtel Drouot, 16 June 1904 and 19 March 1906; photograph in Witt Library). Its earlier date suggests that it was perhaps a favourite work, submitted because it displayed Bouliar's talents so well.

Although the critics tell us little more about Bouliar's public reception, her submissions to the Salons indicate a steady success. In 1793 she showed seven portraits and drawings, including the charming portrait of the *de With Children* (two works, private collection, Paris, repr. Jean-François Heim and Philippe Heim, *Les Salons de peintures de la Révolution française, 1789–1799*, Paris: CAC, 1990, p.151). Many of her commissions came from the artistic community. In 1796 her 13 Salon exhibits included the portraits of *Chevalier Alexandre-Marie Lenoir* and his wife, *Adélaïde Binart* (Musée Carnavalet, Paris). These are affectionate images of two artists, Binart shown here in her work attire. Lenoir was famous for founding the Musée Nationale des Monuments Français (to save "unrevolutionary" but artistically valuable works of public art from destruction), and his unconventional pose shows him leaning on the corner of its huge catalogue. Bouliar also painted the *Children of C. Vernet, Painter, Their Arms Around Each Other*, exhibited at the Salon of 1798 (Salon cat. no.63; private collection, France, repr. *Revue de l'Art*, February 1924).

The prize won in 1791, however, did more than bring new clients. By providing financial aid and a recognised platform for development, it also offered Bouliar the chance to try the elevated genre of the allegorical history portrait. *Aspasia* was shown at the Salon of 1795, its notation as a "Travail d'encouragement" indicating its origin in an earlier prize (see B. Gallini on the confusion caused by the notation of these awards in Paris 1989, iii, pp.831 and 855; *Aspasia* did not itself win a prize). Its subject is the most famous *hetaira* (high-class courtesan) of Classical Athens. Aspasia was both highly intelligent and exceptionally beautiful, and was influential in male spheres of power: she was Pericles' mistress and adviser from 445BC until his death in 429BC (see Plutarch, *Life of Pericles*, xxiv, 34.3). According to Plato, she also tutored Socrates in rhetoric (*Menexenus*, 236b–c). In Bouliar's intriguing, large-scale work Aspasia is seated alone in a grand Classical interior, watched over by a bust of Pericles. Both her beauty and intellect are represented allegorically, but with the emphasis on her physical charms. She looks into a mirror, as if temporarily distracted from the text on the scroll in her left hand and on the table (the text consists of neat but meaning-

Bouliar: *Aspasia*, 1794; Musée des Beaux-Arts, Arras

less Greek characters, perhaps copied by Bouliar without being understood). The globe on the table shows constellations and the signs of the zodiac (a symbol of science), and is decorated with garlands of flowers (Maison interprets these as a reference to Julie d'Angennes, emblem of the *précieuses* and like Aspasia the hostess of a brilliant milieu; see Arras 1975, pp.47–8).

That Bouliar chose to depict such an exceptional, powerful and sexual woman is surely significant. Her decision to focus on Aspasia's beauty and to expose her breast has led to some discussion of what Bouliar wanted to communicate (contrast Ann Sutherland Harris in Los Angeles 1976, pp.203–4, with Cameron 1983, pp.332–3). If she intended some kind of proto-feminist message about the capabilities of women, it is indeed shrouded in the veils of allegorical painting. This is, however, only to be expected of a painting produced in the Paris of 1792–4, when female political activity was suppressed almost as soon as it started (see Olwen H. Hufton, *Women and the Limits of Citizenship in the French Revolution*, Toronto: University of Toronto Press, 1992).

The critics did not react favourably to this work: several commented on *Aspasia* when it was re-exhibited in 1796. Both *Polyscope* and the critic of the *Mercure de France* wrote that this was not Bouliar's best work, although *Polyscope* asserted that she was the best woman artist of the day (Deloynes Collection, xviii, nos 491 and 493). More damaging may have been the offensive personal observations made by the anonymous author of the *Critique du Salon ou les tableaux en vaude-*

villes, who twice commented on Aspasia's ugliness, joking that the artist took herself as a model (*ibid.*, nos 488–9). Perhaps these negative reviews, combined with the relative commercial unviability of this genre, dissuaded Bouliar from working on similar subjects (the only exception is the love-themed *Erminia Carving Tancred's Name on a Tree*, sent to the Salon of 1802; untraced). All the works sent to later Salons were unidentified portraits.

In her *Self-Portrait* of 1792 (Musée des Beaux-Arts, Angers) Bouliar looks at us with a hint of a smile, her hair slightly wind-blown. This was clearly a signature self-portrait: there are replicas of this image in Paris (Musée des Arts Décoratifs), Dijon (Musée des Beaux-Arts), and in private collections in France and the USA. The only self-portrait to show Bouliar working is a lively charcoal drawing (exh. Frérault, Paris, 1928, no.10; photograph in Witt Library), in which she stands at an easel, looking back over her shoulder. In addition to one attributed work, the *Marquis de Cubières as a Child* (Musée des Beaux-Arts, Nantes), there are other works by Bouliar that are now lost but visible on photograph (Witt Library; Frick Art Reference Library, New York; Louvre Service de Documentation, Paris). Most are unidentified portraits of women, but the Louvre Service de Documentation has a photograph of a portrait of *Theresia Cabarrus*, the influential wife of the revolutionary Tallien, shown in classical dress and holding a sheet of music. The Witt Library holds a photograph of a portrait of *Talleyrand* (last recorded at Hôtel Drouot, Paris, 2 March 1911). A rare portrait of a single man, it is nevertheless typical of Bouliar's style: a smiling young man presented in a simple, almost frontal pose. The emphasis is firmly on the man and not his status, which is only discreetly indicated by the Légion d'Honneur insignia on his jacket.

LOUISE GOVIER

Bourgeois, Louise
American sculptor, 1911–

Born in Paris, France, 25 December 1911; naturalised US citizen 1951. Studied in Paris at Sorbonne University, 1932–5 (baccalaureate); Ecole du Louvre, 1936–7; Ecole des Beaux-Arts, 1936–8; Atelier Bissière, 1936–7; Académie de la Grande Chaumière, 1937–8; Atelier Fernand Léger, 1938. Married American art historian Robert Goldwater, 1938; three sons; husband died 1973. Moved to New York, 1938; studied at Art Students League under Vaclav Vytlacil, 1939–40. Taught at Great Neck public schools, New York, 1960; Brooklyn College, New York, 1963 and 1968; Pratt Institute, Brooklyn, 1965–7; Maryland Art Institute, Baltimore, 1984; New School for Social Research, New York, 1987. Recipient of National Endowment for the Arts (NEA) grant, 1973; Outstanding Achievement award, Women's Caucus for Art, 1980; Skowhegan medal for sculpture, 1985; Distinguished Artist award, 1987, and Lifetime Achievement award, 1989, College Art Association; gold medal of honor, National Arts Club, 1987; Creative Arts medal award, Brandeis University, Waltham, 1989; Award for Distinction in Sculpture, Sculpture Center, New York, 1990; Lifetime Achievement award, International Sculpture Center, Washington, DC, 1991; Grand Prix National de Sculpture, French Ministry of Culture, 1991; honorary doctorates from Yale University, New Haven, 1977; Bard College, Annandale-on-Hudson, 1981; Massachusetts College of Art, Boston, 1983; Maryland Art Institute, Baltimore, 1984; New School, New York, 1987; Pratt Institute, Brooklyn, 1993; Art Institute of Chicago, 1995. Officier de l'Ordre des Arts et Lettres, French Ministry of Culture, 1984. Fellow for Life, Metropolitan Museum of Art, New York, 1987. Fellow, American Academy of Arts and Sciences, 1981. Member, American Academy and Institute of Arts and Letters, 1983; Sculptors Guild; American Abstract Artists; College Art Association. Lives in New York.

Selected Individual Exhibitions
Bertha Schaefer Gallery, New York: 1945
Norlyst Gallery, New York: 1947
Peridot Gallery, New York: 1949, 1950, 1953
Rose Fried Gallery, New York: 1963
Stable Gallery, New York: 1964
112 Greene Street, New York: 1974
Xavier Fourcade Gallery, New York: 1978, 1979, 1980
Max Hutchinson Gallery, New York: 1980
Robert Miller Gallery, New York: 1982, 1984, 1986, 1987, 1988, 1989, 1991
Museum of Modern Art, New York: 1982–3 (touring retrospective), 1994–5 (touring)
Daniel Weinberg Gallery, Los Angeles: 1984
Serpentine Gallery, London: 1985
Maeght-Lelong, Paris and Zürich: 1985 (retrospective)
Taft Museum, Cincinnati: 1987–9 (touring)
Museum Overholland, Amsterdam: 1988
Henry Art Gallery, University of Washington, Seattle: 1988
Sperone-Westwater Gallery, New York: 1989
Frankfurter Kunstverein, Frankfurt am Main: 1989–91 (touring retrospective)
Galerie Karsten Greve, Paris: 1992
American Pavilion, Venice Biennale: 1993
Brooklyn Museum, NY: 1993–6 (touring retrospective)
Musée d'Art Moderne de la Ville de Paris: 1995 (retrospective)
Museum of Modern Art, Oxford: 1995–6 (touring)

Selected Writings
"Freud's toys", *Artforum*, January 1990, pp.111–13
"Louise Bourgeois", *Balcon* (Madrid), no.8–9, 1992, pp.44–50

Bibliography
Lucy R. Lippard, "Louise Bourgeois: From the inside out", *Artforum*, xiii, March 1975, pp.26–33; reprinted in Lucy R. Lippard, *From the Center: Feminist Essays on Women's Art*, New York: Dutton, 1976
Louise Bourgeois, exh. cat., Museum of Modern Art, New York, and elsewhere, 1982
Robert Storr, "Louise Bourgeois: Gender and possession", *Art in America*, lxxi, April 1983, pp.128–37
Donald Kuspit, "Louise Bourgeois: Where angels fear to tread", *Artforum*, xxv, March 1987, pp.115–20
Bourgeois, New York: Avendon/Vintage Contemporary Artists, 1988 (interview with Donald Kuspit)
Louise Bourgeois Drawings, exh. cat., Robert Miller Gallery, New York, and Galerie Lelong, Paris, 1988
Stuart Morgan, "Taking cover: Louise Bourgeois interviewed", *Artscribe International*, no.67, January–February 1988, pp.30–34
Louise Bourgeois, exh. cat., Frankfurter Kunstverein, Frankfurt am Main, and elsewhere, 1989

Robert C. Morgan, "Eccentric abstraction and Postminimalism", *Flash Art*, no.144, January–February 1989, pp.73–81

Alain Kirili, "The passion for sculpture: A conversation with Louise Bourgeois", *Arts Magazine*, lxiii, March 1989, pp.68–75

Parkett, no.27, March 1991 (special issue)

Christiane Meyer-Thoss, *Louise Bourgeois: Konstruktionen für den freien Fall (Designing for Free Fall)*, Zürich: Ammann, 1992

Holland Cotter, "Dislocating the modern", *Art in America*, lxxx, January 1992, pp.100–06

David Deitcher, "Art of the installation plan", *Artforum*, xxx, January 1992, pp.78–84

Lisa Liebmann, "Mr Hoet's holiday", *Artforum*, xxxi, September 1992, pp.87–9

Paul Gardner, *Louise Bourgeois*, New York: Universe, 1993

Louise Bourgeois: The Locus of Memory, Works, 1982–1993, exh. cat., Brooklyn Museum, NY, and elsewhere, 1993

Andrew Graham-Dixon, "Totem and taboo", *Vogue* (UK), June 1993, pp.132–7

Connie Butler, "Terrible beauty and the enormity of space", *Art & Text*, no.46, September 1993, pp.60–65

Deborah Wye and Carol Smith, *The Prints of Louise Bourgeois*, New York: Museum of Modern Art, and London: Thames and Hudson, 1994

Francesco Bonami, "Louise Bourgeois: In a strange way, things are getting better and better", *Flash Art*, no.174, January–February 1994, pp.36–9

Ann Gibson, "Louise Bourgeois's retroactive politics of gender", *Art Journal*, liii, Winter 1994, pp.44–7

Louise Bourgeois, exh. cat., Musée National d'Art Moderne Centre Georges Pompidou, and Musée d'Art Moderne de la Ville de Paris, 1995

Marie-Laure Bernadac, *Louise Bourgeois*, Paris: Flammarion, 1996

Louise Bourgeois was born in Paris in 1911. The following year the family moved their tapestry gallery to Choisy-le-Roi and then later settled in the Parisian suburb of Antony on the River Bièvres, where her father established a workshop for restoring old tapestries. Bourgeois's childhood was, in her own account, dominated by her father's ten-year relationship with the children's English nurse, Sadie, and her own feelings of anger and rejection. Initially, she studied mathematics at the Sorbonne (1932) and then enrolled at the Ecole des Beaux-Arts, but she found the academic structure too conservative for her developing artistic interests and took to frequenting the numerous private studios and drawing academies, being taught by, among others, Paul Colin, André Lhôte, Yves Brayer and Fernand Léger. Bourgeois also studied art history at the Ecole du Louvre and lectured in the museum. In 1938 she married the art historian Robert Goldwater and together they joined the flow of refugee artists fleeing Europe for America who were to exert such a profound influence upon American modernism.

Such are the basic historical facts of Bourgeois's early biography. However, as Roland Barthes has observed, history tends to be naturalised by the processes of myth. Artists' lives have always provided a mythic structure for the idealisation of the individual, the cult of the genius describing a range of subject positions from a privileged marginality, through bohemian counter-cultures, to the possession of visionary "truths". Mostly these narratives have inscribed a specific, gendered identity, and have focused upon moments of biography as the keys with which to decipher the hermeneutic code of artistic production: "lives of the artist" that read the passage of experience off and into the works of art. The repetitive tropes of artistic biography partly define the humanistic impulse in Western culture. Bourgeois, as much as any other living artist, has been the subject of such mythic constructions; indeed, she appears to be a willing participant in the narrativisation of experience as mythic moments that symbolically invest the forms and relationships of her art.

The contradictions of childhood, of imaginary completeness and terrible loss, the domestic space as both secure and threatening and the vividness of the Oedipal drama explicitly and recurrently figured in works of catharsis and disavowal, describe an artistic identity constructed at the margins of the avant-garde and across geographical and linguistic boundaries, until the recognition and acclaim for her work that has grown since the beginning of the 1980s. (For example, childhood memory figures prominently in such works as *Cell (Choisy)*, 1990–93; Collection Ydessa Hendeles Foundation, Tokyo, repr. Paris 1995, p.184, where a guillotine presides ominously over the paternal mansion, while the explicit expression of murderous rage occurs in the installation *Destruction of the Father*, 1974; artist's collection, *ibid.*, p.130.) However, her antagonism towards paternal figures and the repressive metaphors of feminine sexuality that characterised Surrealist representations provided the context for a powerful expression of sublimated sexuality in her own work. These themes are worked out in the drawings, paintings and prints she made in the period between her arrival in New York until she began experimenting with sculptural materials a decade later. Their immediacy, graphic range and narrative qualities – a working out and a working through of memory and desire – have been a corollary to her sculptural practice and her increasingly large-scale installations for almost half a century.

The repetitive motif of this period is the combination of a female lower body grafted on to the childlike image of a building that forms the torso and head of the figure: the *Femme Maison* series. The most familiar of the series is the drawing of 1947 (Solomon R. Guggenheim Museum, New York), the image used for the cover illustration of the critic Lucy Lippard's collection of essays *From the Center* (1976). A schematically rendered nude figure faces the viewer, the hips surmounted by a multi-storeyed house with arms attached, the right hand upraised, perhaps in greeting. The ambivalence of this hybrid form, of femininity constrained by the cage of domesticity or, alternatively, emerging from the home into a wider and more public arena, combines themes that repeat throughout Bourgeois's subsequent oeuvre. Perhaps the most characteristic element in her drawings is the repeated patterning of parallel and cross-hatched strokes – of a line that has the quality of the trace of hair or cotton, saturated in ink and drawn or flicked across the surface of the paper. A diary entry records: "Hair in water, hair in flames, hair that dries before the fire …", and an early memory she recounts is of repairing the frayed edges of the Gobelin tapestries in her father's workshop, replacing the excised genitals of cupids (removed by her mother in recognition of the preferences of collectors) with flowers.

As Bourgeois's life spans most of the 20th century, her meetings, associations and friendships map the major artistic currents of Western modernism. She recalls conversations with Brancusi and Giacometti, collaborations with Duchamp and arguments with André Breton. She was one of the few women

Bourgeois: *Untitled (With Foot, "Do You Love Me?")*, 1989; pink marble; 76.2 × 66 × 53.3 cm.

artists to attend meetings held by the Abstract Expressionists and was a member of their group, the "Irascibles". She participated in the anti-war activities of the 1960s, had discussions with Minimalist artists, was associated with Arte Povera, and her work has consistently, though problematically, occupied a pivotal position in feminist art history and theory. (In Robert Mapplethorpe's 1982 photograph of her, dressed in furs and clutching an oversized phallus – her sculpture *Fillette* (1968; Museum of Modern Art, New York) – and laughing at the viewer, Bourgeois adopts the very image of a "bad mother", mocking patriarchal authority.) Myths and fables have a long tradition of connection to the feminine. The curiosity attributed to women that, in the narratives of Eve or Pandora carry a negative connotation, frequently revolves around the forbidden or the secretive. Bourgeois has always been drawn to the socially repressed and the taboo, looking in those secret places and recesses where the knowledge of the self is intimately related to sexuality and the body.

During the 1950s and early 1960s her predominant sculptural form was the vertical – structures that revolve around a central axis or spine to produce totems or pillars that refer to the figure in isolation or in groupings that suggest familial or communal relations (e.g. *Femme Volage*, 1951; Solomon R. Guggenheim Museum; *Quarantania*, 1947–53; Museum of Modern Art, New York). Wood, patinated bronze or plaster are the working materials, the clustering forms, often the subject of compositional readjustment, figure masculinity across a range from aggressive virility to the threat of castration. As she experimented with other materials – plaster, latex and the recurrent use of marble – the sexual body flows between the poles of gender in a palpable materialisation of flesh and skin, interiority and exteriority, attesting to the mutability of sexual identity. Frequently figured as nests, layers and orifices, the constant play of binary terms: masculine/ feminine, interior/exterior, penis/breast, hard/soft, open/closed, rough/smooth, etc., create formal and symbolic relationships and oppositions suggesting both the possibilities of antithesis and the longing for merger. Phallic forms soften into breasts, implode into sexually charged recesses and inner volumes, inscribe the body as the metaphor for plural genders and identities, charting the difficult play between sameness and difference (*Le Regard*, 1966; artist's collection, repr. Paris 1995, p.103; *Janus Fleuri*, 1968; bronze; artist's collection, *ibid.*, p.47; *Cumul*, 1969; marble; Musée National d'Art Moderne, Centre Georges Pompidou, Paris). Bourgeois's female imagery describes the boundaries of the feminine-masculine and masculine-feminine, hybrid spaces and surfaces that symbolise the attraction and repulsion between the sexes, and the loss that prefigures desire. For example, in *Nature Study* (1984; versions exist in red wax, plaster and bronze, the last in Whitney Museum of American Art, New York) sexual difference collapses in the figure of a crouching animal, possibly a griffin, which displays both male and female attributes. A fetishistic expression of polymorphous sexuality, the animal's truncated neck suggests a dismembered phallus, cut-off at the tip. For Bourgeois, fantasy is just another way of connecting reality and history.

In the 1980s Bourgeois started to produce the series of installations called *Cells*, works that combine found objects with carved or cast forms and which create spaces for the enactment of the dramas of family life. Again the influence of her association with the Surrealist movement comes through in the unlikely juxtaposition of objects, combinations that create new and deeper meanings, that tap the source of fantasy and desire. These works are the artist's attempt to manage the emotional traumas that underlie her most profound physical and psychological experiences – obsession, love, hate, tenderness, cruelty; the expression of identity in the recognition of the other: "I love you, do you love me?" Messages of love and pain are inscribed across the surfaces of these assemblages: "Love makes the world go round", "Fear makes the world go round" on the shutters of *Bullet Hole* (1992; repr. Paris 1995, pp.202–3); "Je t'aime" sewn into the cover of the bed supporting the arched body in *Cell (Arch of Hysteria)* (1992–3; artist's collection, *ibid*., p.206) and embroidered across the pillow in the child's bedroom in *Red Rooms* (1994); "Do you love me?" carved into the marble base of *Untitled (With Foot, "Do You Love Me?")* (1989; see illustration). A cell is an enclosed space with either religious or penal connotations, a micro-organism or the component of a battery. Cells are building blocks, transmitters of energy, or places of containment. Condensed, emotionally charged, populated with part-objects (eyes, hands, ears, breasts, in marble, glass, wood and bronze), in these domestic spaces history clings to the architectural remnants that enclose and support the objects that embody memory as a material reality.

Bourgeois's application of technique to material emphasises the craft of making, of hand-skills and co-ordination at the service of the imagination, but with her an imagination that consistently challenges the viewer to reflect upon vision as both an aesthetic and an ethical experience. If this is "woman's work", then it is a conjoining of the pleasure and the pain that accompany gender roles and divisions in order to undo our cultural stereotypes. The giant needles that pierce space (*Needle (Fuseau)*, 1992; *ibid*., p.201), the repetitive piercing of latex or wooden forms (*Articulated Lair*, 1986; Museum of Modern Art), are constant reminders of the social violence that threatens the feminine in the fantasy of castration. These elements are combined in *Cell (Arch of Hysteria)*. Old and weathered shuttering encloses a claustrophobic space in which two objects are juxtaposed – a disused industrial bandsaw that menaces the bronze cast of a headless, arched male body upon a bed covered with a cloth bearing, in red, the repeated phrase "Je t'aime". This extraordinary image of anger and desire, of castration and unbearable longing, expresses the violence of representation in the wish to incorporate and destroy the other. Bourgeois's consummate technical ability, her control over materials most evident in carved stone, suggests a kind of deception – that the stone has abandoned its intransigent materiality to become viscous, flowing into the shapes and volumes that define the final form. This fluidity might be taken as a metaphor for the rhythms and pulsions of the sexual body, the

dissolution of boundaries that has been particularly associated with the maternal body. Bourgeois has herself spoken of the fluids of the body as metaphors of the unconscious – sweat, tears, saliva, urine, milk – and of the corporeal rites of passage that mark the stages of womanhood. The huge installation *Precious Liquids*, first shown at Documenta IX in Kassel (1992), and acquired by the Centre Georges Pompidou, Paris, is a complex arrangement of glass containers attached to stands suggesting something between an alchemical experiment and a surgical operation: of the processes of transformation and renewal.

Glass has become, since the early 1980s, a crucial material for Bourgeois, possessing as it does the qualities of resistance, fragility and strength in its solid state, and of extreme flexibility when molten. Glass can be densely opaque, translucent to the point of invisibility, or reflective when silvered. The mirrors, glass balls, containers – or the rich scarlet blown and cast forms in the *Red Rooms* (the colours of the body's interior spaces and the connotation of passion or danger) – are, for Bourgeois, the material expression of the self's complex identities. In *Cell (Glass Spheres and Hands)* (1990–93; National Gallery of Victoria, Melbourne) the compartment houses five large, clear glass spheres placed on chairs and stools surrounding a table that provides the surface for two hands, carved in white marble. Again the dialectic of pleasure and pain shifts the meanings between the tenderness expressed in the gesture of the touching hands and an allegory of the isolated and alienated self – the emptiness of the spheres. In many of the other installations, the presence of mirrors signifies, for Bourgeois, the acceptance of the real. But mirrors also mark the imaginary, the narcissistic identification with an image that conceals absence, or loss. The viewer is invited into spaces suffused with melancholy and the objects of desire. These spaces recode the domestic setting as both secure and dangerous, as refuge and incarceration, spaces for the giving and the withholding of love. A caress is shadowed by the objects that affirm the pressure of the past upon the present: the prison-house of memory.

The work of Louise Bourgeois, spanning the century as it does, has become increasingly and profoundly emblematic of the emotional and social landscapes that define the formation of our identities in the passage from childhood into a tenuous and fragile adulthood. History, as both personal experience and public memory, determines who we are and, in what Julia Kristeva describes as a deeply psychotic culture, Bourgeois's recognition that "self-knowledge is the only reward" constantly returns her and the viewer to the fundamental need for acceptance, and the acceptance of what is.

JON BIRD

Bourke-White, Margaret
American photographer, 1904–1971

Born Margaret White in New York, 14 June 1904; appended mother's maiden name Bourke, 1927. Attended Columbia University, New York, for one semester, studying photography under Clarence H. White, 1921–2 (left after father's death). Studied at University of Michigan, Ann Arbor,

1922–3; Purdue University, Lafayette, Indiana, 1924; Case Western Reserve University, Cleveland, 1925; Cornell University, Ithaca, New York, 1926–7 (BA). Married (1) Everett Chapman, 1924, divorced 1926; (2) writer Erskine Caldwell, 1939, divorced 1942. Freelance photographer with studio in Cleveland, 1927; in Chrysler Building, New York, 1930; decided to abandon advertising photography, 1936. Associate editor and staff photographer, *Fortune* magazine, New York, 1929–35. Staff photographer for *Life* magazine, New York, 1936–40, 1941–2 and 1945–69 (semi-retired 1957). Chief photographer for Ralph Ingersoll's magazine *PM*, New York, 1940. Travelled to Germany and Soviet Union, 1930 (first foreign photographer permitted to take pictures of Soviet industry); Soviet Union again, 1931 and 1932; Czechoslovakia and Hungary, 1938; London, Romania, Turkey, Syria and Egypt, 1939–40; China and Soviet Union, 1941. First woman war correspondent, US Air Force, 1942; assignments in Britain, North Africa, Italy and Germany, 1942–5. Trips to India, 1946 and 1947; South Africa, 1949–50; Japan and Korea, 1952–3. Recipient of honorary doctorates from Rutgers University, New Brunswick, New Jersey, 1948; University of Michigan, Ann Arbor, 1951; Achievement award, *US Camera*, 1963; Honor Roll award, American Society of Magazine Photographers, 1964. First symptoms of Parkinson's disease, 1953; operations 1959 and 1961. Died in Darien, Connecticut, 27 August 1971.

Principal Exhibitions

Individual

John Becker Gallery, New York: 1931 (*Photographs by Three Americans*, with Ralph Steiner and Walker Evans)
Annual Exhibition of Advertising Art, New York: 1931 (with Anton Bruehl; art works by others)
Little Carnegie Playhouse, New York: 1932
Rockefeller Center, New York: 1934
Art Institute of Chicago: 1956
Syracuse University, NY: 1966
Carl Siembab Gallery, Boston: 1971
Witkin Gallery, New York: 1971
Andrew Dickson White Museum of Art, Cornell University, Ithaca: 1972 (retrospective)

Group

Museum of Modern Art, New York: 1949 (*Six Women photographers*), 1951 (*Memorable Life Photographs*)

Selected Writings

Eyes on Russia, New York: Simon and Schuster, 1931
Photographs of the USSR with an Introduction by the Artist, Albany, NY: Argus Press, 1934
"Dust changes America", *Nation*, cxl, 22 May 1935, pp.597–8
"Photographing this world", *Nation*, cxlii/3685, 1936, pp.217–18
You Have Seen Their Faces, New York: Viking, 1937 (with Erskine Caldwell); reprinted Athens: University of Georgia Press, 1995
North of the Danube, New York: Viking, 1939 (with Erskine Caldwell)
"How the pictures were made", *Popular Photography*, ii, March 1939, pp.15–16, 94–5
Say, Is This the USA? New York: Duell Sloan and Pearce, 1941 (with Erskine Caldwell)
Shooting the Russian War, New York: Simon and Schuster, 1942; reprinted as *The Taste of War*, ed. Jonathan Silverman, London: Century, 1985

"Photographer in Moscow", *Harper's Bazaar*, clxxxiv, March 1942, pp.414–20
They Called It "Purple Heart Valley": A Combat Chronicle of the War in Italy, New York: Simon and Schuster, 1944
"Dear Fatherland, Rest Quietly": A Report on the Collapse of Hitler's "Thousand Years", New York: Simon and Schuster, 1946
Halfway to Freedom: A Report on the New India in the Words and Photographs of Margaret Bourke-White, New York: Simon and Schuster, 1949; as *Interview with India in Words and Pictures*, London: Phoenix House, 1950
A Report on the American Jesuits, New York: Farrar Straus and Cudahy, 1956 (with John La Farge)
"Assignments for publication", *Encyclopedia of Photography*, ii, New York, 1963, pp.274–80
Portrait of Myself, New York: Simon and Schuster, 1963 (autobiography)

Bibliography

Winifred and Frances Kirkland, *Girls Who Became Artists*, New York: Harper, 1934
T. Otto Nall, "The camera is a candid machine: An interview with Margaret Bourke-White", *Scholastic*, 15 May 1937
Rosa Reilly, "Why Margaret Bourke-White is at the top", *Popular Photography*, July 1937
"American aces: Margaret Bourke-White", *US Camera*, May 1940
Lesley Blanch, "At the other end of the lens", *Vogue* (UK), January 1943
Etna M. Kelley, "Margaret Bourke-White", *Photography*, xxxi, August 1952, pp.34–43, 85
"Bourke-White's twenty-five years", *Life*, xxxviii, 16 May 1955, pp.16–18
Robert E. Hood, *Twelve at War: Great Photographers under Fire*, New York: Putnam, 1967
Margaret Bourke-White: Photojournalist, exh. cat., Andrew Dickson White Museum of Art, Cornell University, Ithaca, NY, 1972
Sean Callahan, ed., *The Photographs of Margaret Bourke-White*, Greenwich, CT: New York Graphic Society, 1972 (contains extensive bibliography)
Margaret Bourke-White: The Cleveland Years, 1928–1930, exh. cat., New Gallery of Contemporary Art, Cleveland, 1976
Margaret Bourke-White: The Deco Lens, exh. cat., Joe and Emily Lowe Art Gallery, Syracuse University, NY, 1978
Margaret Bourke-White: The Humanitarian Vision, exh. cat., Joe and Emily Lowe Art Gallery, Syracuse University, NY, 1983
Jonathan Silverman, *For the World to See: The Life of Margaret Bourke-White*, New York: Viking, and London: Secker and Warburg, 1983
Vicki Goldberg, *Margaret Bourke-White: A Biography*, New York: Harper, 1986; London: Heinemann, 1987
David E. James, "Estheticizing the Machine Age", *Artweek*, xviii, 3 October 1987
Margaret Bourke-White, exh. cat., Jane Corkin Gallery, Toronto, 1988
Bourke-White: A Retrospective, exh. cat., International Center of Photography, New York, and elsewhere, 1988
Double Exposure: The Story of Margaret Bourke-White, 94-minute video, Turner Home Entertainment, 1989
Jozef Gross, "Changing the world", *British Journal of Photography*, cxxxvi, 6 April 1989, pp.16–19
Jeanette Ross, "Transcending personality", *Artweek*, xxi, 11 January 1990
Val Williams, *Warworks: Women, Photography and the Iconography of War*, London: Virago, 1994

Manuscripts and correspondence are in the George Arents Research Library for Special Collections, Syracuse University, NY.

Margaret Bourke-White's work presents a definitive vision of mid-20th-century American photographic practice, bringing

Bourke-White: Chrysler Building gargoyle, New York, 1930

together the two primary directions of the medium from the 1920s through the 1940s – the overtly modernist conception that emphasises abstract design with the creation of an elegant and luscious formal visual surface, and the development of socially conscious documentary intended to provoke sympathy for (and ultimately action on behalf of) its disadvantaged subjects. The fusion of these two very different approaches to photography creates an almost intractable tension that is very nearly resolved in some of her finest work.

Her first major contribution to visual culture was her invention of the genre of industrial photography. After graduating from Cornell University in 1927, she settled in Cleveland, the home of steel mills and other heavy industry that captivated her imagination. Working primarily as an architectural photographer, she developed her contacts with the business community to gain entry to the Otis Steel Mill, where she learned through much trial and error how to negotiate the technical difficulties of photographing the pouring of red hot molten metal in a nearly pitch-black interior. Bourke-White brought to this undertaking some early training with the photographer Clarence H. White, who emphasised abstract design and composition. With this approach and the new technical advances of faster film speed, higher contrast paper and magnesium flare lighting, she was able to create beautiful, abstract images of the plant in all its dramatic, fiery glory. Her success at the Otis Mill drew an avalanche of clients seeking her unexpectedly glamorous photographs of industry for use in their advertisements and annual reports. Her work for the Republic Steel Corporation in 1929 quickly caught the eye of Henry Luce, publisher of *Time* magazine, who was just launching *Fortune*, a new magazine aimed at the business world. Bourke-White's photographs of everything from bank vaults to hog slaughtering, reproduced in fine detail, were to become the visual signature of the magazine, and launched her career as a photo-journalist as well.

Moving to New York in 1930, Bourke-White divided her time between *Fortune* and private advertising clients. She leased space for her studio in the Chrysler Building, which she had documented as it was under construction. She was particularly taken with the aluminium gargoyles (translated from Chrysler car ornaments) placed at the four corners of the building on the 61st floor, and made certain that her studio overlooked two of them. Her photograph of one of these gargoyles (see illustration) rings with her belief in the power and beauty of modern industry as she saw it transforming the world. This vision made her extremely popular with corporate clients, who clamoured for her time and talents to provide convincing, formally elegant pictures to elevate their images.

The development of sympathetic human interest in her work grew out of her dissatisfaction with the increasingly ludicrous demands of advertising work, and a growing sense that she wanted to be in touch with "real life". In 1936 she grasped the opportunity to collaborate with Erskine Caldwell (author of *Tobacco Road*) on a book documenting the destitute conditions of share-croppers in the South. *You Have Seen Their Faces*, published in 1937, was widely hailed as a social document of the time. Although she was never employed by the Farm Security Administration (FSA), Bourke-White's work with Caldwell accommodates the themes and general approach found in the contemporary social documentary work of such

photographers as Dorothea Lange (q.v.), Walker Evans and Marion Post Wolcott. She shared with them the belief that if only the ills of the world could be made known through the camera, society would necessarily act to correct them.

Bourke-White carried her new-found human interest into her assignments for *Life* magazine, which Henry Luce founded in 1936. Her photograph of the Fort Peck dam, a WPA project in Montana, with its monumental, repeated concrete towers, graced the cover of the first issue. Inside, her story on the raucous night life of the local boom-town workers caught even the magazine's editors by surprise. With the wealth of material she had sent back to New York, they organised what was probably the first true photo-essay ever published.

With the outbreak of World War II, Bourke-White was inexorably drawn to cover the conflict, beginning in Russia just before and during the German invasion of June 1940. She recounted her experiences, illustrated with her photographs, in her book *Shooting the Russian War* (1942). Continuing as a *Life* correspondent in Europe for the duration of the war, she captured one of her best-known images in 1945 at Buchenwald concentration camp. A line of emaciated, grimy camp survivors in what remains of their tattered, striped uniforms stare with vacant expressions towards the viewer, as they press up feebly against the grid of a welded-wire fence. The photograph is cropped off at either side, so it seems as though these few individuals represent just a small piece of an interminable line of survivors, multiplying the horror indefinitely. The tension arising from the contrast of the deep pathos of the men's faces and the starkly abstract design created by the fence makes this one of Bourke-White's most unforgettable photographs.

The objectification of her subjects through her intensely aesthetic gaze provides one of the greatest points of criticism for her documentary work. On assignment in apartheid South Africa in 1950, Bourke-White accompanied gold miners into the sweltering heat over a mile beneath the surface of the earth, where she reported feeling as though she were operating "in slow motion", rendered unable to speak by the oppressive conditions. There she photographed two miners, sweat glinting beautifully off their black skin as they fill the frame, their safety helmets and bodies carefully forming a repetitive, undulating abstract pattern across the image. The sheer aesthetic beauty of this photograph threatens to overwhelm the fundamental humanity of the bold, forthright gazes that they turn towards the camera, and, as a result, the grotesque working conditions and social inequities forced upon these men become almost detached from history. Grappling with the contradictions inherent in both the medium and her own artistic vision, Margaret Bourke-White's work thus provides a quintessential summary of American photography on the cusp of its shift during the 1950s into the subjective, candid snapshot-mode of such artists as Helen Leavitt and Robert Frank.

As virtually all of her photographs were made for publication, the number of vintage and/or "artistic" prints of Bourke-White's work is rather small. Most of the negatives and prints for *Life* magazine are held in the Time-Warner archives, New York. Other collections of note include the George Arents Research Library for Special Collections, Syracuse University,

New York, and the private collection of her brother, Roger White.

BETH ELAINE WILSON

Boyce, Joanna (Mary)
British painter, 1831–1861

Born in Maida Hill, London, 7 December 1831; father a pawnbroker and former wine merchant. Sister of watercolour painter George Price Boyce, an associate of the Pre-Raphaelites. Studied in London at Cary's Academy, 1849, and at Leigh's Academy, c.1852; also attended John Marshall's lectures on anatomy for artists. Visited Paris with her father, spring 1852. Again in Paris, studying in Thomas Couture's studio, winter 1855–6. Trip to Italy, 1857–8; married painter Henry T. Wells in Rome, December 1857, after a long engagement. Died after giving birth to her third child, 15 July 1861.

Principal Exhibitions
Society of British Artists, London: 1853
Royal Academy, London: 1855–7, 1859–62
Society of Female Artists, London: from 1857

Bibliography
Art Journal, 1861, p.273 (obituary)
English Woman's Journal, viii/43, 1861, pp.143–4 (obituary)
Athenaeum, 20 July 1861, p.89 (obituary)
Sarah Tytler, *Modern Painters and Their Paintings*, London: Strahan, 1873; Boston: Roberts, 1874
Clara Erskine Clement and Laurence Hutton, *Artists of the Nineteenth Century and Their Work*, 2 vols, Boston: Houghton Osgood, and London: Trübner, 1879; reprinted New York: Arno Press, 1969
Henrietta Mary Ada Ward [Mrs E.M. Ward], *Memories of Ninety Years*, ed. Isabel G. McAllister, London: Hutchinson, 1924; New York: Holt, 1925
An Exhibition of Paintings by Joanna Mary Boyce (Mrs H.T. Wells), 1831–1861, exh. cat., Tate Gallery, London, 1935
Charlotte Yeldham, *Women Artists in Nineteenth-Century France and England*, 2 vols, New York: Garland, 1984
Pamela Gerrish Nunn, *Victorian Women Artists*, London: Women's Press, 1987
Jan Marsh and Pamela Gerrish Nunn, *Women Artists and the Pre-Raphaelite Movement*, London: Virago, 1989
Deborah Cherry, *Painting Women: Victorian Women Artists*, London and New York: Routledge, 1993
A Struggle for Fame: Victorian Women Artists and Authors, exh. cat., Yale Center for British Art, New Haven, 1994

Joanna Boyce's artistic career was a distinguished and promising one, albeit one cut short by her death from post-puerperal complications after the birth of her third child. In her case as with many of her female peers, family connections proved crucial in her early development, and her elder brother George Price Boyce was also an artist as well as an early supporter of her artistic endeavours. The third of five children, Boyce was filling sketchbooks with ideas and impressions by her early teens and in 1849 attended Cary's Academy. She and George were especially close in their earlier years and sketched together on family holidays, notably in 1849. While her brother gave her counsel and some introductions to the art world, their father also encouraged her artistic pursuits by chaperoning her to galleries, lectures and the homes of private collectors. In 1852 she was studying art at another institution, Leigh's, and attending John Marshall's anatomical lectures. She also made the acquaintance of other notable contemporary artists such as William Powell Frith, Henrietta and Edward Matthew Ward, Augustus Egg, Frank Stone and Charles Landseer.

An earnest and ambitious young artist, Boyce constantly sketched and took notes on the world around her and was a well-read and intellectual woman of her time. She was in Paris in the spring of 1852, but the death of her father the following year exerted a somewhat dampening temporary effect on her career. None the less, contact with the Pre-Raphaelite circle through her brother's connections was an important influence during these years, as was meeting numerous other young women painters such as Bertha Farwell and Anna Mary Howitt at art classes and elsewhere.

In 1855 Boyce gained some public recognition of her talent when her single figure of *Elgiva* (private collection, repr. Marsh and Nunn 1989, pl.2) was accepted at the Royal Academy. No less a figure than the powerful critic John Ruskin in *Academy Notes* (1855) praised such qualities as its "beautiful imagination" and "pure colour", which placed this picture "among those of the very highest power and promise". Ruskin went so far as to suggest that Boyce "might entertain the hope of taking the place in the very first rank of painters", while a Pre-Raphaelite associate, Ford Madox Brown, hailed *Elgiva* as having "the best head in the Rooms" (Virginia Surtees, ed., *The Diary of Ford Madox Brown*, New Haven and London: Yale University Press, 1981, p.138). During that same year Boyce struggled with more personal issues, for her independence and even radical beliefs were challenged by her feelings for fellow artist Henry Tanworth Wells and his proposal of marriage. Boyce had grave doubts about the institution of marriage, writing to him of the "slavery" to which it reduced women as wives and mothers and of her own "intense love of independence". In the autumn of 1855 she returned to Paris, where she planned to ask Rosa Bonheur (q.v.) to accept her as a student, although she then decided to enroll in the women's classes in Thomas Couture's atelier, where she was able to study from the nude model. While in France, she admired certain contemporary French artists such as Delacroix and Vernet, and while abroad also wrote a few columns on the Paris Exposition Universelle of 1855 for the *Saturday Review*. Her admiration for Pre-Raphaelite canvases and tenets also surfaced in those same articles, and some of her portraiture of the late 1850s in particular reflected a Pre-Raphaelite penchant for vivid colours and highly delineated fabrics, settings and surfaces.

As was the case with numerous other women artists, Boyce's works were sometimes received with back-handed praise about how she could allegedly paint as well as a man. Her oil single figure of *La Veneziana* (1860; destroyed), for example, earned her such accolades, and one critic commented in general of her canvases that "... to unbounded enthusiasm for art, to masculine and vigorous powers of mind were united in Mrs Wells an unmistakably feminine character" (obituary, *The Critic*, 27 July 1861, p.109). Significantly, in *La Veneziana* and other

Boyce: *Mulatto Woman*, 1861; oil on paper on linen; 17.1 × 13.6 cm.; Yale Center for British Art, New Haven, Paul Mellon Fund (B1991.29)

extant works such as *Gretchen* of 1861 (unfinished; Tate Gallery, London) and the incisive portrait of a *Mulatto Woman* (see illustration) of the same date, Boyce reveals her strong and sensitive skill in depicting women of character and strength from the realms of history, literature and imagination, far from merely decorative middle-class ladies.

In late 1857 Boyce, whose career as an artist and critic was established at this point, finally married Wells, with whom she had gone with friends on an extended trip to Italy earlier that year. She used this opportunity to visit and produce art based on visits to Rome, Florence and Naples and also learned Italian for the trip. She continued to paint after marriage, depicting her children, friends and servants in such compositions as *Peep-bo!* (1861; destroyed in World War II, repr. Cherry 1993, pl.25) with its idyllic vision of domesticity and maternal playfulness (in this case with baby daughter Alice). Before her death, the artist left among her papers (private collections, Britain) a list of at least 30 other projects that she had hoped to create – with titles such as *Undine, Autumn, from Keats, Sybil* and *King Cophetua and the Beggar Maid*, the last attesting to the Pre-Raphaelite tendency sometimes evident in aspects of her subject matter and style. Although she also produced some landscapes and genre pictures, from a modern perspective her individual portraits and combined historical/ costumed images of women convey compelling visual power.

During her lifetime Boyce exhibited at the Royal Academy and the Society of British Artists, as well as somewhat problematically (due to issues of quality and a desire to exhibit in mainstream venues such as the Royal Academy) at the Society of Female Artists. Selected examples of her work were included in a few exhibitions beyond her own time – and at the Tate Gallery in 1935 and at Birmingham in 1937, but the paucity of surviving material limits full appreciation of her gifts as a painter.

SUSAN P. CASTERAS

Boznańska, Olga
Polish painter, 1865–1940

Born in Kraków, 15 April 1865. Received first drawing lessons from her mother, an amateur artist; later studied drawing under Józef Siedlecki and painting under Hipolit Lipiński. Taught drawing by Kazimierz Pochwalski, 1883. Attended Adrian Baraniecki's Advanced Courses for Women in Kraków, 1884–6; teachers included Siedlecki, Antoni Piotrowski and art historian Konstanty M. Górski. Studied in Munich under Karl Kricheldorf, October 1886; under landscape and genre painter Wilhelm Dürr, 1888. Established own studio in Munich, 1889. Acting head of Hummel School of Painting in Munich, as substitute for genre and landscape painter Theodor Hummel, 1896. Settled in Paris, 1898. Rejected offer to direct women's studies at Academy of Fine Arts, Kraków, 1896; declined offer of professorship at Warsaw Academy of Fine Arts, 1914. Member, 1898, associate president, 1912, and president, 1913, Society of Polish Artists (Sztuka). President, Society of Polish Women Artists, Kraków, 1899; Polish Literary-Art Society in Paris, 1915.

Sociétaire, Société Nationale des Beaux-Arts, Paris, 1904; member, International Society of Sculptors, Gravers and Painters, 1906; founder-member, Society of Polish Artists in Paris, 1911. Recipient of Porbus Barczewski, Polish Academy, Kraków, 1908; city of Warsaw art prize, 1934; Polonia Restituta Order, 1938. Chevalier, Légion d'Honneur, France, 1912. Died in Paris, 26 October 1940.

Principal Exhibitions

Individual
Galerie Georges Thomas, Paris: 1898 (with Daniel Mordant)
Society of Friends of Fine Arts, Kraków: 1931
Venice Biennale: 1938

Group
Society of Polish Artists, Kraków: from 1886
Society for the Encouragement of the Fine Arts, Warsaw: occasionally 1892–1925 (second prize 1895, honourable mention 1925)
Kunstgenossenschaft, Munich: 1893 (gold medal)
Internationale Kunstausstellung, Vienna: 1894 (gold medal)
Universal National Exhibition, Lwów: 1894 (silver medal)
Society of Portrait Painters, New Gallery, London: 1894 (honourable mention), 1900 (gold medal)
Société Nationale des Beaux-Arts, Paris: occasionally 1896–1926
Society of Polish Artists (Sztuka): from 1898
Exposition Universelle, Paris: 1900 (honourable mention)
Earl's Court, London: 1901 (*Women's Exhibition*, gold medal)
Carnegie Institute, Pittsburgh: occasionally 1901–29 (silver medal 1907)
Internationale Kunstausstellung, Munich: 1905 (gold medal)
International Exhibition, Amsterdam: 1912 (silver medal)
International Art Union, Galerie Roger Levesque, Paris: 1912 (Whitney Hoff Museum prize)
Exposition Internationale, Paris: 1937 (grand prix)

Bibliography

R.L. [Lewandowski], "Olga Boznańska", *Przegląd tygodnia*, no.43, 1895, p.485

H. Piątkowski, *Polskie malarstwo współczesne* [Modern Polish painting], St Petersburg, 1895, pp.179–83

Exposition des oeuvres de Mlle Boznańska (Peintures) et de M. Daniel Mordant (Gravures), exh. cat., Galerie Georges Thomas, Paris, 1898

Clara Erskine Clement, *Women in the Fine Arts*, Boston: Houghton Mifflin, 1904; reprinted New York: Hacker, 1974

Walter Shaw Sparrow, *Women Painters of the World*, London: Hodder and Stoughton, 1905; reprinted New York: Hacker, 1976

A.D. Defries, "Olga de Boznańska", *American Magazine of Art: Art and Progress*, October 1917

J. Rais, "Art polonais contemporain", *Art et Décoration: Revue Mensuelle d'Art Moderne*, xxv/236, August 1921

M. Turwid, "Wieczór u Olgi Boznańskiej", *Tęcza*, no.7, 1937, p.42

Helena Blumówna, *Olga Boznańska, 1865–1940: Materiały do monografii* [Olga Boznańska, 1865–1940: Material for a monograph], Warsaw: Wydawnictwo Państwowego Instytutu Historii Sztuki, 1949

Olga Boznańska (1865–1940), exh. cat., National Museum, Kraków, 1960

Tadeusz Dobrowolski, "Malarstwo portretowe Olgi Boznańskiej" [The portrait painting of Olga Boznańska], *Przegląd Artystyczny*, 1963, no.1, pp.16–27

Helena Blum, *Olga Boznańska: Zarys życia i twórczości* [Olga Boznańska: Sketch of life and work], Kraków: Wydawnictwo Literackie, 1964

Słownik Artystów Polskich i Obcych [Dictionary of Polish and foreign artists], i, Wrocław: Zakład narodowy imienia Ossolinskich, 1971

Helena Blum, *Olga Boznańska*, Warsaw: Prasa-Książka-Ruch, 1974

Wiesław Juszczak, *Teksty o malarzach: Antologia polskiej krytyki artystycznej, 1890–1918* [Writings on painters: Anthology of Polish art criticism, 1890–1918], Wrocław, 1976

La Peinture polonaise du XVIe au début du XXe siècle, catalogue of National Museum, Warsaw, 1979

Symbolism in Polish Painting, 1890–1914, exh. cat., Detroit Institute of Arts, 1984

Nineteenth-Century Polish Painting, exh. cat., National Academy of Design, New York, and elsewhere, 1988

Artystki polskie [Polish women artists], exh. cat., National Museum, Warsaw, 1991

Polish Women Artists and the Avant-Garde: Voices of Freedom, exh. cat., National Museum of Women in the Arts, Washington, DC, 1991

Although Olga Boznańska was a contemporary of the Impressionists, with whom she shared an interest in colour and light, she never considered herself to be a member of the group, and differed from them in both technique and the interpretation of subject, which was based on her own personal vision. This is evident in all her paintings, but especially in the portraits that constitute the majority of her oeuvre.

The brown tonality and composition of *In the Atelier* (1886; oil on canvas; private collection), one of Boznańska's earliest known works, are typical of the Munich school. Soon, however, she began to work with colour, and was particularly influenced by the paintings of Velázquez, especially his light brush strokes, and by the work of Vuillard. Japanese art influenced the vantage-point and perspective of *Grandma's Saint's Day* (1888–9; National Museum, Warsaw). Boznańska's tendency to isolate the figures is already apparent in this early work – instead of a tender scene between a grandmother and granddaughter, each figure is encased in her own psychological world. Boznańska's interest in Japanese art was fleeting, however, and her encounter with the works of Manet played a more important role in her formation. In the portrait of *Paul Nauen* (1893; National Gallery, Kraków) the dark figure of the painter is silhouetted against a plain background and the colours are flat. As early as 1889 Whistler's influence can be seen in the limited palette of *From the Walk* (National Gallery, Kraków). Boznańska now began to limit her colour scheme and to explore colour values and tonalities, as exemplified by *A Girl with Chrysanthemums* (1894; National Museum, Kraków), in which the girl is seen against a plain background. Boznańska's preoccupation with colour is already indicated in such works; she stated: "I have more talent for colour than for form" (Blum 1964).

By the time Boznańska moved to Paris in 1898 her style was already established, and by 1914 it had reached full maturity. Line was unimportant – she transposed the visible world into colour. She was a good draughtswoman, however, and denied that she had anything in common with the Impressionists. She painted almost exclusively in oils, except for a brief period in 1893 when she did some work in pastels. After 1893 she nearly always painted on cardboard rather than canvas. Her technique remained the same – an exploration of colour, at times monochromatic, of its values and half-values, creating a feeling of mystery, as if in a mist. She herself observed: "the subjects are separated from the viewer by a light barrier" (*ibid.*).

Boznańska excelled in perspective, as demonstrated in a rare view of a building, *Pisa Cathedral* (1905; National Museum,

Boznańska: *Henryk Sienkiewicz*, 1913; National Museum, Kraków

Kraków), seen in the moonlight from the southwest. The subtle synchronisation of the blues of the sky with the greys of the cathedral is masterly; it is a night vision, not an exploitation of sunlight on colour. This is the closest that Boznańska ever came to the Impressionists, although she appreciated their work because she owned a catalogue of an exhibition of Claude Monet.

The portrait of her father, *Adam Nowina Boznański* (1904; National Museum, Kraków), shows his physique, personality and psyche with great honesty. The sitter is painted in thick earth tonalities that dematerialise the form; the technique is related to that of earlier masters, but at the same time it clearly demonstrates Boznańska's innovation. In the portrait of *Feliks Jasieński* (1907; National Museum, Kraków) the sitter is shown almost full length, seated in a chair against a plain background. The space of the room is carefully indicated, with the foreground distinguished from the background. Another notable work of the period, the portrait of *Henryk Sienkiewicz* (1913; see illustration), depicts the Polish historical novelist who was awarded the Nobel prize in 1905. The writer is seated, his hands resting on the arms of his chair; he is isolated from the viewer, his gaze directed into a vision of his own. One hand is relaxed and the other tense, the only indication of the active aspect of his personality. This is not an image of the man who was involved in reviving and nourishing the spirit of Polish independence; instead, Boznańska depicted a man who lives in his own world, unaware of those around him. This existentialist quality reappears in nearly all her later works.

Boznańska's personal life had a profound influence on the perception of her subjects, and she herself commented: "I am accused of painting sad figures, but this is how I feel the subject" (ibid., p.108). Her love for Józef Czajkowski, a noted Polish architect, persisted even after he broke off their engagement in 1900 when she refused to join him in Kraków, preferring to remain in Paris; her father's death in 1906 was another severe blow, and her only sister's suicide in 1934 was a traumatic shock from which she never recovered. After 1900 she fell into a state of depression that lasted for the rest of her life, never changed her style of dress and eventually became a recluse, concentrating only on her work. Boznańska appears aloof in a pastel Self-Portrait of 1906 (National Museum, Warsaw), regarding the viewer as an intruder into her privacy and creating an emotional barrier that cannot be breached. The tendency towards complete isolation and aloofness is intensified in the succeeding self-portraits, which come close to existentialism.

In the portraits of the 1920s, and especially of the 1930s, Boznańska concentrated more on the head of the sitter; the figure occupies nearly the entire picture surface and the background is barely visible. The emotional state of the sitter is no longer individualised but takes on that of the artist, exemplified in the portrait of Mrs Gościeński (1925; National Museum, Kraków). Around this time Boznańska stated: "all passes and disappears and only a human being exists". She interpreted the subject in her own way, according to her own vision: "I paint only a sitter whom I find interesting", explaining: "art is not a question of the fashionable; art is above time; and the artist feels the interdependence of colour" (ibid.). She progressively abandoned the definition of form by contour and the representation of depth. The space and architecture of In My Study (1913; National Museum, Warsaw) are established only with colour. Similarly, Still Life (1918; National Museum, Warsaw) is seen as a pure play of colour values in which form and space are almost completely dissolved.

Approximately 80 per cent of Boznańska's extant oeuvre consists of portraits; there are a few still lifes, mostly of flowers, intimate interior views, mainly of her studio, and one or two pictures of Paris street scenes. It is difficult to estimate how many interior views and still lifes she created, because she would often give them away on request. She seldom dated her works, making it difficult to establish a chronology and to trace the development of her style. Many of Boznańska's pictures are in unknown European and American private collections, but most of her works are located in the National Museum, Kraków, to which she bequeathed all the pictures in her possession.

DANUTA BATORSKA

Bracquemond, Marie
French painter, 1840–1916

Born Marie Quiveron at Argenton near Quimper, Brittany, 1 December 1840; her father, a sea captain, died soon after her birth, and her mother remarried. Spent youth in the Jura, in Switzerland and the Auvergne before settling with her family in Etampes, south of Paris. Studied under a local restorer, M. Wassor; later in Ingres's studio in Paris. Married Félix Bracquemond, 1869; son Pierre, also an artist, born 1870; husband died 1914. Moved to Sèvres after Félix appointed artistic director of the Haviland porcelain works, Auteuil, 1871. Abandoned professional career, 1890. Died in Sèvres, 1916.

Principal Exhibitions
Paris Salon: 1857, 1874–5
Exposition Universelle, Paris: 1878 (faience tile panels)
Impressionist group, Paris: 1879, 1880, 1886
Dudley Gallery, London: 1881
Exposition des Peintre-Graveurs, Paris: 1890
Galerie Bernheim-Jeune, Paris: 1919 (retrospective, organised by Pierre Bracquemond)

Bibliography
Pierre Bracquemond, "La vie de Félix et Marie Bracquemond", undated manuscript, private collection, Paris

Gustave Geffroy, La Vie artistique, Paris: Floury, 1894, pp.268–74

Clara Erskine Clement, Women in the Fine Arts, Boston: Houghton Mifflin, 1904; reprinted New York, Hacker, 1974

Oeuvres de Marie Bracquemond (1841–1916), exh. cat., Galerie Bernheim-Jeune, Paris, 1919

Félix Bracquemond: Gravures, dessins, céramiques; Marie Bracquemond: Tableaux, exh. cat., Mortagne, 1972

The Crisis of Impressionism, 1878–1882, exh. cat., University of Michigan Museum of Art, Ann Arbor, 1979

Elizabeth Kane, "Marie Bracquemond: The artist time forgot", Apollo, cxvii, 1983, pp.118–21

Jean-Paul Bouillon and Elizabeth Kane, "Marie Bracquemond", Woman's Art Journal, v/2, 1984–5, pp.21–7

Tamar Garb, Women Impressionists, Oxford: Phaidon, and New York: Rizzoli, 1986

Marie Bracquemond was one of the four women artists associated with the Impressionists. With Berthe Morisot (q.v.) and Mary Cassatt (q.v.) she exhibited in the Impressionist exhibitions, showing altogether three times, in 1879, 1880 and 1886. (Eva Gonzalès, q.v., like her mentor Manet, preferred not to use this forum of display.) Unlike the other three "women Impressionists", however, she did not come from a prosperous, cultured milieu. As a young woman she was admitted to Ingres's studio where she gained the reputation of being one of his most intelligent pupils. In 1869 Marie married the successful engraver Félix Bracquemond, who introduced her to his own circle of friends comprising important contemporary artists and critics. This enabled the young artist to make important contacts. Ironically, the marriage seems also to have inhibited her development as an artist and she has come to be seen as the archetypal female casualty of an oppressive husband.

Bracquemond's own interests led her away from the stylistic conservatism of her husband towards the plein-air painting that was becoming popular among younger artists. Influenced

Bracquemond: *On the Terrace at Sèvres with Fantin-Latour*, 1880; oil on canvas; 88 × 115 cm.; Musée du Petit Palais, Geneva

by Monet and Renoir, she became increasingly committed to the Impressionist aesthetic of rendering contemporary life in unmodulated colour and painterly brush marks. Light became her obsession, and she experimented with different light effects, moving from pictures that explore natural daylight, such as *Tea Time* (1880; Petit Palais, Paris), to essays in artificial light, as in *Under the Lamp* (1887; private collection). To her husband's disapproval, Marie Bracquemond was a fervent defender of Impressionism to the end of her life. "Impressionism has produced … not only a new, but a very useful way of looking at things. It is as though all at once a window opens and the sun and air enter your house in torrents", she declared when Félix attacked what he termed the "folly" of painting out of doors.

Tea Time is a typical Impressionist portrait. The sitter is a young woman placed in a garden setting. The quiet domestic scene, so typical of bourgeois suburban life as portrayed by the artists of the Third Republic, was the perfect subject for a woman artist seeking plein-air subjects. It provided a fitting context for the exploration of natural light effects but provided none of the threats to safety or propriety of more ambitious

landscape painting. Here the artist and her model can proceed unchaperoned in the context of the home and still produce interesting and technically adventurous work.

Bracquemond's sitters were usually her family members or friends. Her son, sister and close friends are her most common models. The intimate relationship between artist and sitter presented particular problems for women artists, especially with male sitters. For a woman artist to scrutinise the face and body of a man she needed to overcome the cultural prohibitions against women looking intently and to cast aside the demure and modest glancing that was deemed appropriate for bourgeois women. This was more easily done with a family member or friend than with a stranger. *Under the Lamp* depicts Alfred Sisley and his wife who were regular guests at the Bracquemond home and formed part of the intimate circle of family and friends that surrounded them in the 1880s.

Despite the "Impressionist" appearance of works executed between 1880 and 1890, Bracquemond prepared her paintings in the traditional way, producing many preparatory drawings and sketches before starting on the canvas. A finished painting such as the ambitious, sun-filled *On the Terrace at Sèvres with*

Fantin-Latour (1880; see illustration) is no spontaneous sketch. Like many of her Impressionist colleagues, the effect of spontaneity and immediacy that Bracquemond strove to achieve was hard won. It was the product of slow and deliberate work.

In 1890 the domestic conflict that her painting provoked resulted in Marie Bracquemond's giving up painting almost completely (except for a few watercolours and drawings). Throughout her married life, she had been a committed mother and home-maker and was constantly aware of the conflicts between these roles and her wish to be an artist. Eventually these were too much to bear and she relinquished her role as an artist to devote herself to being the wife that her husband wanted. It was her son Pierre who documented his mother's life in an unpublished manuscript, "La vie de Félix et Marie Bracquemond". In it he records the pain and difficulties that his mother suffered because of the conflicting demands of her responsibilities as a wife and her needs as an artist. He records, too, his father's jealousy of his mother's talent and his inability to accept her criticism. Bracquemond, the artist, became a casualty of her marriage, spending the last two decades of her life as a virtual recluse in the family home at Sèvres, rarely visiting Paris and never exhibiting her work in public again.

TAMAR GARB

Braden, Norah

British potter, 1901–

Born 1901. Studied book illustration at the Central School of Arts and Crafts, London, 1919–21, then painting at the Royal College of Art, London, 1921–5 (diploma). Worked at Bernard Leach's pottery, St Ives, Cornwall, 1925. Joined Katharine Pleydell-Bouverie (q.v.) at Coleshill, Berkshire, 1928. Left Coleshill and taught at Brighton School of Art, 1936. Stopped working as a potter, c.1939. Did some teaching at Brighton and Central Schools of Art after World War II. Lives in Sussex.

Bibliography

W. A. Thorpe, "English stoneware pottery by Miss K. Pleydell-Bouverie and Miss D. K. N. Braden", *Artwork*, vi, 1930, pp.256–65

Ernest Marsh, "Studio potters of Coleshill, Wilts: Miss K. Pleydell-Bouverie and Miss D. K. N. Braden", *Apollo*, xxxviii, 1943, pp.162–4

R. G. Cooper, *The Modern Potter*, London: Tiranti, 1947

Bernard Leach, *A Potter's Portfolio*, London: Lund Humphries, and New York: Pitman, 1951

George Wingfield Digby, *The Work of the Modern Potter in England*, London: Murray, 1952

Muriel Rose, *Artist-Potters in England*, 2nd edition, London: Faber, 1970

Thirties: British Art and Design Before the War, exh. cat., Arts Council of Great Britain, London, 1979

Isabelle Anscombe, *A Woman's Touch: Women in Design from 1860 to the Present Day*, London: Virago, and New York: Viking Penguin, 1984

Oliver Watson, *Studio Pottery: Twentieth-Century British Ceramics in the Victoria and Albert Museum Collection*, London: Phaidon, 1993 (originally published as *British Studio Pottery*, Oxford: Phaidon, 1990)

Elspeth Moncrieff, "A talent lain dormant", *Weekend Telegraph*, 9 July 1994

Writing in *A Potter's Portfolio* (1951), Bernard Leach described Norah Braden as "the most sensitive and critical of potters", and he often spoke of her as one of his finest pupils. Given that Braden made pots only for a relatively short period – of little more than 12 years – her pots, thrown and turned on the wheel and fired in a wood-burning kiln in a reduction atmosphere, have come to be recognised as among the most delicate and sensual of the pots made within the "Leach tradition".

Talented as a musician as well as an artist, Braden initially set out to study painting. At the Royal College of Art she transferred from painting to pottery, a subject then being taught by Dora Billington, an energetic potter from Stoke-on-Trent. Impressed by an exhibition of pots by Bernard Leach that she saw in London, possibly at Paterson's Gallery in 1923, Braden persuaded Leach to take her as a student at St Ives, arriving following a letter of recommendation from Professor Sir William Rothenstein, head of the Royal College of Art, who had written: "I am sending you a genius".

In 1925 the Leach Pottery, set up in 1920, was still a relatively small concern, desperately trying to establish itself as financially viable. The mood within the small team at the pottery was relaxed and friendly, with the use of nicknames creating an intimate and warm atmosphere. Ada Mason, another student, was known as Peter, Leach himself was known as Rik, and Norah Braden as Lise, while Braden's predecessor Katharine Pleydell-Bouverie (q.v.) was known as Beano. Pleydell-Bouverie had stayed only one year, spending much of the time researching high-temperature ash glazes under the tutelage of the Japanese potter Tsuronosuke Matsubayashi, known as Matsu, who had a wide knowledge of the technical aspects of pottery, experience that was later to prove useful to Braden in the development of her ideas.

Pleydell-Bouverie and Braden struck up a close friendship, and after her three years at the Leach Pottery Braden moved to Pleydell-Bouverie's family home at Coleshill, where the mill cottage had been converted into a pottery. With the help of Matsu, Pleydell-Bouverie had built a high-temperature, wood-fired kiln with two chambers, one for glazed ware, the other utilising waste heat from the first chamber for biscuit firing. The kiln took 36 hours of continuous stoking to fire, and consumed about two tonnes of wood. Not surprisingly, it was fired only four or five times a year, limiting the extent to which pots could be made as experiments. Wealthy and aristocratic, Pleydell-Bouverie was able to make use of the family estate, which not only had convenient buildings that could be used for a studio, but also grew a wide range of woods which could be burned and experiments made with the resulting wood ash.

The kiln proved to be ideal for the sort of pots Braden wished to make. Its long, slow firing enabled an extended period of maturation when clay body and glaze could achieve maximum depth and richness. Like Pleydell-Bouverie, Braden was fascinated by the strength and simplicity of classical Chinese Song Dynasty forms, and by the range and variety of glazes that could be made from different sorts of wood ash. Sketches and notebooks kept in this period record the detailed

Braden: Stoneware pot, *c*.1930

trials they made, the intricate wood-ash glazes, using a great variety of types of ash combined with feldspar and Devon ball clay, and the details of the various firings.

With their mutual interest in Song pots, those made by Braden and Pleydell-Bouverie often look alike, a fact that Pleydell-Bouverie noted: "Lise has taken to making very tall pots ... and I've taken to making very squat ones ... but when we don't adopt such violent means you can't tell t'other from which" (letter to Bernard Leach, Crafts Study Centre, Bath). In fact, Braden was a superb potter with her own distinctive style. Her small bowls, simple and strong in shape, were used to try out the various ash glazes, while the more technically ambitious and often monumental forms such as narrow-necked bottles some 60 centimetres tall, covered jars and round, full-bellied vases had a rare feeling of wholeness and unity. Exhibitions of her pots in London were well-reviewed, being described on one occasion as of "Unfailing good taste and a steady technical progress" (*The Times*, 22 May 1930). Braden's pots were acquired for national collections, such as those at the Victoria and Albert Museum, London, and the Fitzwilliam Museum and Kettle's Yard, Cambridge.

An independent artist, Braden was as critical of her own work as she was of others, and had firm views on what pots should be. At the Leach pottery, she argued with Leach, and far from being in awe of her distinguished teacher, criticised him and the pots he made. Her own pots were decorative rather than utilitarian and were intended to be appreciated as objects in their own right. The importance of form and shape was emphasised, and any decoration was minimal, often consisting of bold brush strokes well integrated into the surface of the glaze and the form of the pot.

After a highly productive eight years, Braden left Coleshill to return to her home county of Sussex to care for her elderly mother. She set up a pottery studio, and taught at Brighton School of Art until the late 1940s. By this time she had stopped potting, and eventually severe arthritis prevented her using the kick wheel. Her greatest pots were made at Coleshill, and are a unique combination of a strong understanding of form, an appreciation of the Oriental aesthetic, and the importance of hand-making as a part of the modernist response to the growing anonymity and impersonality of industrial production. A major sale of her work of the 1930s, held at Bonham's, London, on 13 July 1994, again revealed their strength and integrity.

EMMANUEL COOPER

Brandt, Marianne
German designer and photographer, 1893–1983

Born Marianne Liebe in Chemnitz, 6 October 1893. Studied painting and sculpture at Grossherzogliche Sächsische Hochschule für Bildende Kunst, Weimar, under Fritz Mackensen and Richard Engelmann, 1911–17. Independent artist in Weimar, 1917–23. Spent time in Norway and France after her marriage to Norwegian painter Erik Brandt in 1919; separated 1926; divorced 1935. Studied at the Bauhaus, Weimar, then Dessau, from 1924; deputy head of metal workshop, 1928; Bauhaus diploma, 1929. Subsequently worked with architect Walter Gropius in Berlin. Head of design department, Ruppelwerk hardware factory, Gotha, 1929–33. Member, Deutscher Werkbund. Independent artist in Chemnitz, 1933–49. Teacher for Industrial Design, Staatliche Hochschule für Werkkunst (State High School for Industrial Art), Dresden, under Mart Stam, 1949–51. Collaborated with Stam at the Institut für Industrielle Gestaltung (Institute for Industrial Design), Hochschule für Angewandte Kunst, Berlin-Weissensee, 1951–4. Organised *Deutsche Angewandte Kunst* (German applied art) exhibition in Peking and Shanghai, China, 1953–4. Independent artist in Chemnitz (Karl-Marx-Stadt) from 1954; in Kirchberg, Saxony, from 1976. Died in Kirchberg, 16 June 1983.

Principal Exhibitions
Galerie Gerstenberger, Chemnitz: 1918 (individual)
Deutscher Werkbund, Stuttgart: 1929 (*Film und Foto*, touring)
Bauhaus-Archiv, Berlin: 1993 (retrospective)

Selected Writings
"Bauhausstil", *Bauhaus*, iii/1, 1929, p.21
"Modelle für die Serie", *Form & Zweck*, xi/3, 1979, pp.68–70
"Brief an die junge Generation", *Bauhaus und Bauhäusler*, ed. Eckhard Neumann, Cologne: DuMont, 1985, pp.156–61

Bibliography
Gisela Schulz and Hans-Peter Schulz, "Marianne Brandt", *Bauhaus 2, 6*, exh. cat., Galerie am Sachsenplatz, Leipzig, 1977, pp.8–9
Drei Künstler aus dem Bauhaus, exh. cat., Kupferstichkabinett der Staatlichen Kunstsammlungen, Dresden, 1978
L'altra metà dell'avanguardia, 1910–1940: Pittrici e scultrici nei movimenti delle avanguardie storiche, exh. cat., Palazzo Reale, Milan, and elsewhere, 1980

Brandt: *Self-Portrait in Studio, Bauhaus, Dessau,* Winter 1928–9; Bauhaus Archiv, Berlin

Karsten Kruppa, "Gestalten – ohne an Kunst zu denken", *Bildende Kunst*, xxxi, 1983, pp.373–5

——, "Marianne Brandt: Annäherung an ein Leben", *Die Metallwerkstatt am Bauhaus*, exh. cat., Bauhaus-Archiv, Berlin, 1992, pp.48–55

Anne-Kathrin Weise, *Leben und Werk von Marianne Brandt*, PhD dissertation, Humboldt-Universität, Berlin, 1995

In the 1920s, while she was working at the Bauhaus metal workshop, Marianne Brandt created her famous constructive designs for everyday items: ashtrays, tea and coffee sets, and tea-extract pots. She developed types of lamps that were put into production and thus realised Gropius's programme for the development of standard types in collaboration with industry. At the Bauhaus Brandt also occupied herself with a thorough study of the photographic medium. Like most of the Bauhaus photographers, she was self-taught – there were no regular classes in photography at the Bauhaus before 1929. It was above all her self-portraits, in which she reflected her identity as a woman at the Bauhaus, and her still-life compositions, which are closely connected to the Neues Sehen (New Vision), that became famous. Reflection, distortion, close-up views and cut-outs are typical of these photographs, in which Brandt experimented with the effects of alienation. In her numerous collages and photo-montages, which in their representation of simultaneity are comparable with the work of the Berlin Dadaists, she made a critical statement not so much about purely political matters as about the situation of women in modern society and in the context of current issues.

In 1911 Brandt began her painting studies at the Grossherzogliche Sächsische Hochschule für Bildende Kunst in Weimar under Fritz Mackensen. In 1917 she obtained a studio of her own for the first time. Her early pictures bore an Expressionist stamp and were mainly female and mother-and-child portraits. They shared a general basic mood of suppression and melancholy as, for example, in her picture *Pietà* and the early *Self-Portrait* (1917–19; photograph in Bauhaus-Archiv, Berlin). In 1918 Brandt displayed her work for the first time at the Galerie Gerstenberger in Chemnitz. After her marriage to the Norwegian painter Erik Brandt, who had also studied in Weimar, the couple lived in Norway and France, returning to Weimar in 1921.

Brandt entered the Bauhaus on 1 January 1924, when she was 31 years old; she left her academic work behind her – in fact, she burned most of it. On her preliminary course she learned about works and materials from Josef Albers and László Moholy-Nagy. She studied artistic creation under Wassily Kandinsky and Paul Klee. Her study on the subject of *Relationships Between the Primary Colours and the Basic Shapes – Circle, Triangle, Square* (1924; Musée Nationale d'Art Moderne, Paris) survives from her classes with Kandinsky on "elementary instruction in form".

In 1924, following Moholy-Nagy's advice, Brandt was accepted as an apprentice in the silversmiths' and metal workshop – the work in the carpenters' shop was too heavy for her and she was not interested in weaving, which was the proper "women's department" at the Bauhaus. At first she had to carry out subordinate tasks; she was the only woman in the workshop and the men did not like her being there. She nevertheless produced her first prototypes and models for metal objects to be manufactured by machine. Her first executed design was a simple, small hand-chased ashtray (1924; Bauhaus-Archiv). For herself, she made an inkstand with pen-rest out of sheet copper plated with argentine (1924; Bauhaus-Archiv), which showed strong modernist influence, reflecting her studies under Moholy-Nagy. In 1924 alone Brandt produced an amazing quantity of lamps, pots and small pieces of equipment from different materials. Teapots, for example, appeared in a wide variety of different styles (such as her tea-extract pot, *MT49*). She made spherical models with lids set in at an angle and then, in the same year, she made the style that became famous – hemispherical in shape, with a smooth, sharp-edged top and a similarly round off-centre lid with a wooden knob. The handle was a semicircular slice of wood; the body of the pot rested on cross-pieces rather than on the usual circular stand. This model, in its consistent limitation to almost exclusively geometric shapes, was made in many versions and in a wide range of different materials; it became a veritable incunabulum of modernist Bauhaus work (in silver; 1924; British Museum, London). The silver tea and coffee service (*MT50–55a*; 1924; Bauhaus-Archiv), probably the most expensive item that Brandt produced in the metal shop, and requiring the most work, was made for her friend Marli Ehrmann, a weaver at the Bauhaus. The individual vessels were based on geometric shapes: the cylinder, sphere, circle and cross.

Brandt's designs for ashtrays also explore these basic ideas; the ashtray with triangular lid-opening (*MT36*; 1924; Bauhaus-Archiv) is a variant on the shape of the teapot. The categorisation with model number indicates that the objects were sold as products from the metal workshop of the Bauhaus company. Between 1924 and 1929 Brandt developed 31 practical metal utensils for industrial manufacture, 28 lamps, as well as stools and cupboards. The objects she made from 1926 onwards were of course noticeably more conventional; the avant-garde shape was given up in favour of an extremely simple and functional one (e.g. milk jug, *ME11*; 1926; Bauhaus-Archiv).

After an intervening six-month stay in Paris (1926–7), where she made numerous photo-collages, such as *Paris Impressions* (1926; repr. Leipzig 1977), Brandt joined the metal workshop as a full member of staff. She led technical trials for lamp production and made contacts in the lighting industry, particularly with the firms of Körting & Mathiesen (Kandem) in Leipzig and Schwintzer & Gräff in Berlin for the purpose of adapting and developing functional lighting for industrial production. In 1928, with Hin Bredendieck, she designed the mass-produced Kandem bedside lights and writing-desk lamps (Bauhaus-Archiv).

In 1925 the programmatic Bauhaus book *Malerei, Photographie, Film* by Moholy-Nagy appeared. This stimulated Brandt's photographic activity, which resulted especially in self-portraits and still-life pictures. She repeatedly depicted reflections in glass and metal, and also included her self-portrait, as in the self-portrait with camera, *Reflections Between the Doors of the Bauhaus in Dessau* (c.1926; Bauhaus-Archiv). Her profile *Self-Portrait with Jewellery in the Hair and Around the Neck at the Metallic Festival* (1929; Bauhaus-Archiv) also plays with reflected light. Another strikingly frequent motif is that of reflections in a glass ball. Georg Muche introduced this idea to Weimar in 1921 and Brandt used it in numerous pictures, such as *Self-Portrait in Studio* (1928–9; see illustration). The factor common to all of these photographs is a serious expression of self-questioning, but this is an honest documentation of Brandt's own position in life.

In the international exhibition of the Deutscher Werkbund, *Film und Foto*, or *FiFo* (1929), Brandt, among others, represented the Neues Sehen at the Bauhaus with five photographs. These included the still-life *Clock with Ball* and *Street in the Thaw* (1928–9; Bauhaus-Archiv). Her photomontages were not exhibited. After she left the Bauhaus, Brandt took *Self-Portrait in Double Exposure* (1930–31; Bauhaus-Archiv) while she was working as a designer at the metal factory in Gotha. It shows her in her office, wearing her work clothes, with an expression of extreme self-doubt.

Under the influence of Moholy-Nagy, Brandt was also confronted with the Dadaist principle of collage, which offered her a counterbalance to the strictness of her design activities. In her collages, which she started to create from 1923 onwards, she devoted herself to themes that concerned her as a woman, and worked out her role as the only woman in the Bauhaus metal workshop: the photo-montage *Me* (*c*.1927–8; Bauhaus-Archiv) shows the artist on the periphery of her metal lampshade under the eye of her teacher Moholy-Nagy. The title defines the identification of object and person. The montage *Help Me!* (1926; Staatliche Kunstsammlungen, Dresden) is dominated by the portrait of a modern woman who seems to be casting a critical gaze on the dubious achievements of progress and technology. In the collage *Our Irritating City* (1926; Galerie Berinson, Berlin) Brandt presents a completely different type of city woman – one represented by a 1920s beauty who stares wide-eyed and annoyed at the viewer. After she left the Bauhaus, during her undoubtedly unsatisfying spell in Gotha, Brandt still continued to express her feelings and wishes on the theme of the male/female relationship through the medium of collage. *Captive Balloon* (1931; Staatliche Kunstsammlungen, Dresden) contains in the form of facets a picture of a couple kissing. The man smiles tenderly and the young woman presses a bunch of roses dreamily to her bosom. After 1933 Brandt stopped using the photo-collage technique; in the 1930s the themes of the 1920s – progress, speed, the city, and technology in connection with the new role of women – ceased to stir her.

In 1928–9, after Moholy-Nagy's departure, Brandt had become deputy head of the Bauhaus metal workshop. She resigned in July 1929 because Hannes Meyer had merged the carpentry, wall-painting and metalwork departments into a new consolidated workshop. On 10 September 1929 she left the Bauhaus, receiving a Bauhaus diploma issued by Meyer and Albers as evidence of her completed studies in the metal workshop. The diploma testified to her great creative gifts, her thoroughness and energy, as well as to her feel for organic relationships, linked to a healthy sense of the practical. Brandt subsequently worked in Gropius's architect's practice, where she designed furniture and interior fittings, particularly for housing estates. Gropius, too, acknowledged her inventive gifts, first-rate technical knowledge and outstanding personal qualities.

At the end of 1929 Brandt became head of the design department in the Ruppelwerk hardware factory in Gotha, where she took on and improved the quality of design and colour of mass-produced utensils to such an extent that she was able to exhibit the products at the Grassi-Messe trade fair in Leipzig. During this period she created designs for gift and everyday items that were necessarily unspectacular and constrained to follow the style of the firm. Of these, the writing set with a spherical inkpot and the functional tea-warmer in red-lacquered sheet steel (both 1930–33; Bauhaus-Archiv) are worthy of special notice; these are in the same mould as Brandt's Bauhaus designs.

Because of the world slump, Brandt had to give up this post in 1933 and was forced for financial reasons to return to her parents' house in Chemnitz. As a Norwegian citizen and a former member of the Bauhaus she had very little chance of finding another job. She divorced Erik Brandt at his request in 1935 (they had been separated since 1926). Moholy-Nagy tried to stand up for her in the mid-1930s, and encouraged her to take up designing again, but no lasting link with industry developed, although through Moholy-Nagy she did obtain, in 1932, a design contract with the firm Schweizerische Wohnbedarf AG, who took a design of hers of 1928 for a shallow bowl (Bauhaus-Archiv).

In the 1930s and 1940s Brandt lived with her family; after her parents' death she lived with her sister. During this period she was isolated from her fellow artists and spent her time painting, drawing and weaving. After World War II she tried to get a foothold in the newly founded art schools of East Germany as a designer, first in Dresden and later in Berlin-Weissensee. Her endeavours were unsuccessful, however, because her conception of products, which was based on functionalist principles, was regarded as formalism and therefore undesirable.

In 1947 Moholy-Nagy recommended Brandt as head for the metal workshop in the Staatliche Hochschule für Werkkunst, and in April 1949 she took up this post under Mart Stam. She was responsible for creating industrial designs for the metal, ceramic and wooden-toy workshops, and Stam got her to work on light-fittings as well. Some examples of her work from around 1950 survive: simple jewellery made out of bent wire and perforated sheet brass (1950; Sammlungen Bauhaus Dessau) and some earthenware pottery (1950; Sammlung Industrielle Gestaltung, Berlin, and Sammlungen Bauhaus Dessau).

In 1951 Brandt followed Stam to the Hochschule für Angewandte Kunst in Berlin-Weissensee with its associated Institut für Industrielle Gestaltung (Institute for Industrial Design), where simple but beautiful everyday items were to be designed. Brandt's sketches for shoes, buckles, bags and wallpaper – and for the gavel of the president of the Volkskammer – survive, but the items were never made. The "discussion of formalism" soon put an end to design that owed anything to functionalism, and Stam was sacked in 1952. Marianne Brandt went to China for a year as curator of the exhibition *Deutsche Angewandte Kunst*. She then returned to Chemnitz (Karl-Marx-Stadt), where she lived in complete isolation, able only to work as a painter, sculptor and weaver.

BRITTA KAISER-SCHUSTER

Breslau, (Marie) Louise-Catherine
German painter, 1856–1927

Born in Munich, 6 December 1856, into a family of physicians attached to the court. Grew up in Zürich, where her father had a university post; obtained Swiss nationality, 1892. Studied under Tony Robert-Fleury at Académie Julian, Paris, 1878–81. Visited Brittany, 1881; subsequently travelled to Italy, Germany, the Netherlands and Britain. Moved to Neuilly-sur-Seine with close friend and fellow student Madeleine Zillhardt, c.1886. Sociétaire, Société Nationale des Beaux-Arts, 1890. Chevalier, Légion d'Honneur, 1901. Died in Neuilly-sur-Seine, 12 May 1927.

Principal Exhibitions

Individual
Künstlerhaus, Zürich: 1901
Galerie Georges Petit, Paris: 1904, 1911
Galeries Durand-Ruel, Paris: 1910, 1926
Galerie Brame, Paris: 1921
Ecole des Beaux-Arts, Paris: 1928 (retrospective)

Group
Paris Salon: 1879–89 (honourable mention 1880)
Royal Academy, London: 1882
Union des Femmes Peintres et Sculpteurs, Paris: 1884
Exposition Universelle, Paris: 1889 (gold medal), 1900 (gold medal)
Société Nationale des Beaux-Arts, Paris: from 1890
Exposition Universelle, Bern: 1900 (gold medal)

Bibliography

Robert de Montesquiou, "Un maître femme: Mademoiselle Breslau", *Art et Décoration*, xv, April 1904, pp.133–42
Emile Hovelaque, "Mlle Louise Breslau", *Gazette des Beaux-Arts*, 3rd series, xxxiv, 1905, pp.195–206
Gustave Kahn, "A propos d'une exposition de portraits d'enfants", *Gazette des Beaux-Arts*, 4th series, iv, 1910, pp.316–19
Charles Saunier, "Une exposition de Mlle Louise C. Breslau", *Les Arts*, no.99, March 1910, pp.12–17
Emile William Brandt, "Une artiste suisse à Paris: Visite à Louise-Catherine Breslau", *Les Etrennes Helvétiques*, 1913, pp.13–17
Gustave Kahn, "Louise Breslau", *Beaux-Arts*, no.6, 15 March 1926, pp.93–5
Arsène Alexandre, *Louise C. Breslau*, Paris, 1928
Madeleine Zillhardt, *Louise-Catherine Breslau et ses amis*, Paris, 1932

Breslau: *Chez soi*, or *Intimacy*, exhibited Salon of 1885; Musée d'Orsay, Paris

Ernst W. Bressendorft, "Louise Breslau", *Brigitte*, no.3, 1978, p.199

Charlotte Yeldham, *Women Artists in Nineteenth-Century France and England*, 2 vols, New York: Garland, 1984

John O'Grady, *The Life and Work of Sarah Purser*, Dublin: Four Courts Press, 1996

In the 1870s Paris was the only city where a woman artist could hope to have the advantage of a thorough training and appropriate conditions for the appreciation of her work. And so from 1876 onwards Louise-Catherine Breslau was to be found at the Académie Julian, where for several years she attended the classes of Tony Robert-Fleury. She never forgot how much she owed to this master and always referred to him in Salon catalogues as her only teacher. Like him, she painted a genre scene with a literary title, *"And This Too Shall Pass Away"* (Salon cat. 1879, no.408; untraced), as her first submission to the Salon in 1879. The following year she submitted two works, a genre scene, the *Recall of the Shoemaker* (Salon cat. 1880, no.482; untraced), and a portrait of *Monseigneur Viard* (no.481; untraced), a work that indicates the acknowledged position she now held in Parisian society.

Other arts personalities were to entrust their portraits to Louise Breslau's brush, for example the writer *Michael Georg Conrad* (1882; Historisches Museum, Baden, Switzerland), the sculptor *Jean Carriès* (Salon cat. 1887, no.342; Musée du Petit Palais, Paris), depicted in his studio, and the Swedish painter *Ernst Josephson* (Castle Museum, Gripsholm, Sweden). Her portrait of the English poet *Henry Davison* brought her to the attention of Edgar Degas, who did not scruple to express his admiration for the artist on several occasions. Breslau also provoked the interest of Jean-Louis Forain and Henri Fantin-Latour.

Her submissions to the Salon de la Société des Artistes Français up to 1889, the last year she exhibited there, were mainly composed of portraits and episodes from everyday life. Thus to the Salon of 1885 she sent in a picture called *Chez soi* or *Intimacy* (Salon cat. 1885, no.362; see illustration), depicting Catharina and Bernardina Breslau, which was immediately purchased by the State. The painting shows the artist's pensive mother and her sister leaning over her embroidery, while only the dog, in the foreground to the right, stares out at the viewer. The restrictive nature of the organisation of the Société des Artistes Français and its refusal to recognise the awards made in the foreign sections induced a certain apathy among many painters, who were quick to subscribe to the project for a Société Nationale des Beaux-Arts, which was to be run on more flexible lines. Breslau was a founder-member of the society, joining in 1890, and exhibited work there regularly until late in her life. For her first submission she sent no less than seven works, one painting and six pastels, the latter all portraits. Up to 1895 her submissions were almost entirely portraits, including numerous ones of children, which were to contribute in large measure to her success – around 1900 Breslau was the most famous and sought-after painter of portraits of women and children.

Over the years Breslau's well-organised compositions with their bright colours, on which Impressionism left only the faintest trace in the handling of light and brush strokes, were to give way to an art that borrowed widely from contemporary artistic trends: composition, perspective, palette all came under review in an altogether darker oeuvre, which seems both more anxious and more questioning, and where one feels that the sitters are wrapped up in their own reverie. From 1896 onwards flower paintings took up a growing place in Breslau's output and also won her many plaudits, exemplified by Robert de Montesquiou's comment: "Madame Lemaire, an admirable flower painter, paints faces like petals; Mademoiselle Breslau, a careful portrait painter, depicts flowers like women" (de Montesquiou 1904).

Public success followed social success and around 1900 the museums of her homeland (Switzerland), and those of her country of adoption (France), acquired a number of her works: *Portrait of Friends* of 1881 was bought by the Musée d'Art et d'Histoire, Geneva; *Five o'clock Tea* in 1883 by the Kunstmuseum, Bern; *Reflective Life* (Société Nationale des Beaux-Arts cat. 1908, no.167), a double portrait of the painter and Madeleine Zillhardt, by the Musée Cantonal des Beaux-Arts, Lausanne; and the portrait of *Adelina Poznanska* (1896) by the Louvre, Paris. In her *Self-Portrait* in pastels of 1904 (Musée des Beaux-Arts, Nice) Breslau painted herself turning her back on the world to concentrate on a canvas, as if foreseeing the last years of her career, which were to to be spent in relative artistic isolation. During World War I she abandoned portraits of women and children and instead did a number of portraits of officers, including that of *Guynemer* (pastels; untraced). After the war, and with the sudden arrival on the artistic scene of the Expressionists and the Fauves, her art faded from view. She managed, however, to attract critical attention one last time with her portrait of *Anatole France* (1921; Musée de Versailles et des Trianons). She disappeared from the art scene in the last years of her life, which she spent as an invalid at Neuilly, where she died in 1927 attended by Madeleine Zillhardt. In 1977 a retrospective of her work was held at the Historisches Museum im Landvotgeischloss, Baden, Switzerland.

DOMINIQUE LOBSTEIN

Brickdale, (Mary) Eleanor Fortescue

British painter and illustrator, 1872–1945

Born at Birchamp Villa, Beulah Hill, Upper Norwood, Surrey, 25 January 1872, to Matthew Inglett Fortescue Brickdale, a senior lawyer, and Sarah Anna, daughter of a county court judge. Studied at the local Crystal Palace School of Art under Herbert Bone, then at the Royal Academy Schools, 1897–1900 (prize for lunette design 1897). Moved with her family to Kensington, London, after her father's death (1894); acquired own studio at 11 Holland Park Road, *c*.1902. Often travelled abroad, particularly to Italy and the south of France. Taught at the Byam Shaw School of Art, London, from its foundation in 1911. First woman member, Institute of Painters in Oils, 1902; associate member, 1902, and member, 1920, Royal Society of Painters in Watercolours. Suffered increasing blindness and ill health after 1923; stroke, 1938; died in London, 10 March 1945.

Brickdale: *Little Foot Page*, 1905; Walker Art Gallery, Liverpool

Principal Exhibitions

Individual

Dowdeswell Galleries, London: 1901, 1905, 1909
Leighton House, London: 1902, 1904
Leicester Galleries, London: 1911, 1915, 1920

Group

Royal Academy, London: occasionally 1896–1939
Royal Society of Painters in Watercolours, London: from 1902

Selected Writings

Text in *Women's Employment*, 15 January 1932, p.27

Bibliography

E.B.S, "Eleanor F. Brickdale: Designer and illustrator", *The Studio*, xiii, 1898, pp.103–8

Walter Shaw Sparrow, "On some watercolour pictures by Miss Eleanor Fortescue-Brickdale", *The Studio*, xxiii, 1901, pp.31–44

Canon H. Scott Holland, *Commonwealth*, vii, July 1901, p.224

Centenary Exhibition of Works by Eleanor Fortescue-Brickdale, 1872–1945, exh. cat., Ashmolean Museum, Oxford, 1972

Women Stained Glass Artists of the Arts and Crafts Movement, exh. cat., William Morris Gallery, London, 1985

Jane Sellars, *Women's Works: Paintings, Drawings, Prints and Sculpture by Women*, Liverpool: National Museums and Galleries on Merseyside, 1988

The Last Romantics: The Romantic Tradition in British Art: Burne-Jones to Stanley Spencer, exh. cat., Barbican Art Gallery, London, 1989

Jan Marsh and Pamela Gerrish Nunn, *Women Artists and the Pre-Raphaelite Movement*, London: Virago, 1989

Catheryn H.G. Spence, *A Lady of Real Genius: The Painting of Eleanor Fortescue-Brickdale RWS (1872–1945)*, MA thesis, University of London, 1994

Born in Surrey, the daughter of a successful lawyer with family connections in the West of England, Eleanor Fortescue Brickdale was educated at home and trained in art at the Crystal Palace School of Art under Herbert Bone and at the Royal Academy Schools, where she was awarded a prize for lunette design. Her early work was mainly illustrative and her Royal Academy debut in 1896 was with black-and-white Arthurian subjects. For her first publication, *A Cotswold Village* (1898), she provided 17 vignettes to text by J.A. Gibbs; this was followed by illustrations to Walter Scott's *Ivanhoe* (1898). At the same time she began exhibiting oils at the Royal Academy on literary-narrative subjects (*Pale Complexion of True Love*, exh. 1899; *Deceitfulness of Riches*, exh. 1901; *Rosamund*, exh. 1903; all private collections). Thereafter Brickdale (or Fortescue-Brickdale, as she is often known) pursued a dual career as a painter and illustrator of fine colour-printed editions of well-known literary texts, being one of the first women to work closely with dealers in this enterprise. In later years she also designed for stained glass and some examples of sculpture. Her characteristic practice, alongside one or two oil works annually, was to produce a sequence of similarly sized and framed watercolours for exhibition, which at the same time were reproduced in colour in large-format illustrated books in what appear to have been joint gallery and publisher ventures; between 1905 and 1927 she held eight exhibitions and produced 16 titles of this kind, including selections from Tennyson and Browning, as well as anthologies, such as Palgrave's *Golden Treasury of English Verse*, and a number of religious works, for example, *A Child's Life of Christ* (1906) and *Saint Elizabeth of Hungary* (1912).

In both subject matter and style, Brickdale's work is typical of late or "neo" Pre-Raphaelitism, in the manner also favoured by J.L. Byam Shaw, Brickdale's contemporary and colleague, in whose art school she taught. Her work is characterised by decisive drawing, close observation of natural detail and solid colour; typically, it features single figures in rooms or gardens, often unconventionally selected and composed (see, for example, *Wise Virgins*, 1901, with predella; Durban Art Gallery). In the manner of the time she was given to representations of angels and winged figures of Love, but her use of gender imagery is sometimes unexpected and anti-romantic. Generally, her work displays strength and boldness, qualities often lacking in contemporary illustrations; weaknesses include occasional whimsy, especially in costume pieces. The depiction of landscape is frequently attractive. In later years her handling became broader and more straightforward, reflecting both changing taste and the artist's failing eyesight. She also produced a number of works in plaster, mainly on sacred subjects. Pictures in public collections include *Little Foot Page* (1905; see illustration) and *Enid and Geraint* (1905; Walker Art Gallery, Liverpool). Due to family connections with the aviator Charles Rolls, she took an interest in aeroplane technology, manifested in such works as *Guardian Angel* (1910; untraced, but also published as a colour lithograph by the Medici Society, copy in British Museum, London) and *The Forerunner* (1920; Lady Lever Art Gallery, Port Sunlight), showing Leonardo da Vinci demonstrating his flying machine.

A devout Christian, Brickdale also painted for churches (see Lady Chapel triptych, All Saints, Newland, Glos) and designed more than 20 stained-glass windows (usually for Burlison and Grylls), especially post-World War I memorials. Commissions include those at Bristol House of Charity (1914), St Mary's, Taunton (1920), Bristol Cathedral (1927), Brixham Old Church, Devon (1927), and Mayfield Convent School, Sussex (1935). Major painting commissions in later years included *Knightly Service* (1928) for Winchester College, Hampshire, and *Prospero and Ariel* (1931; untraced) for BBC Broadcasting House, London. During World War I she also designed posters for the government departments of Information and Child Welfare, and this coincided with a move to flat colour and outline illustrations in place of the earlier fully detailed watercolours, a development also seen in the work of Jessie M. King (q.v.). Brickdale did not marry, living all her life in London with her mother and sister. Her professional career, already declining, was closed in 1938 by a stroke.

Her reputation today rests largely on her watercolour illustrations, of which there are a considerable number, but rediscovery of her large oils is underway. A retrospective with a small catalogue was held in 1972 at the Ashmolean Museum, Oxford, which holds several works and studies from the artist's studio.

JAN MARSH

Brockmann, Elena

Spanish painter, active 1887–96

Born in Madrid. Studied under Juan Llanos, José Benlliure and Joaquín Sorolla.

Principal Exhibitions

Exposición Nacional de Bellas Artes, Madrid: 1887 (honourable mention), 1892 (third-class medal), 1895
Bienal, Círculo de Bellas Artes, Madrid: 1896

Bibliography

Enrique Segovia Rocaberti, *Catálogo humorístico de la Exposición Nacional de Bellas Artes*, Madrid, 1887
Fernanflor, "Exposición Nacional de Bellas Artes", *La Ilustración Española y Americana*, 15 July 1887
J.O. Picon, "Exposición Nacional de Bellas Artes", *Historia y Arte*, 1895
Catálogo provisional del Museo de Arte Moderno, Madrid, 1899
Carmen G. Pérez-Neu, *Galéria universal de pintoras*, Madrid: Nacional, 1964
Estrella de Diego, *La mujer y la pintura del XIX español*, Madrid: Cátedra, 1987

It is difficult to comprehend how the trail of Elena Brockmann, whose success as a female artist in the Exposiciones Nacionales de Bellas Artes during the 19th century was outstanding, almost completely disappears in the 20th century. Brockmann studied under two exceptional artists, José Benlliure and Joaquín Sorolla, specialising primarily, as they did, in genre painting. She stands out from her female contemporaries, however, through her choice of other, more complex themes and compositions, such as history painting, where the human figure always appears, demanding a format superior to that used by most other women artists of the time.

An understanding of the extreme restrictions of the time testifies to the merit of this painter: until the 1880s there were no female artists enrolled in the Escuela Especial de Diseño, one of the official institutions of art education. The well-known exclusion of women from life classes continued beyond that date: the register excluded the pictorial anatomy class. A woman could go right through the School without ever drawing a human figure. This selective process – only 12 history paintings were produced by Spanish women artists during this time – increases the importance of Brockmann's work *Philip II Receiving News of the Loss of the Invincible*

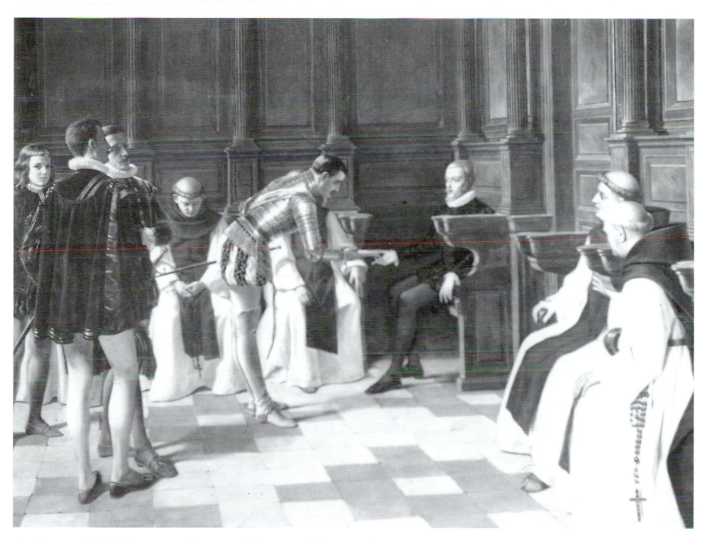

Brockmann: *Philip II Receiving the News of the Loss of the Invincible Armada*, 1895; private collection

Armada (1895; see illustration). Thirty years earlier, such a subject would have been an enormous triumph for a Spanish female painter. In 1895, the year it appeared, the art critics had just declared the official demise of history painting as a genre. Only if the tardy development of female painting is taken into account is it possible to understand Brockmann's incursion into a genre that was already practically abandoned. The complexity of the composition, the number of figures and the predominance of large formats make this painting a *tour de force* and reveal the artist as less concerned with genre than with competence. History painting represented the pinnacle of achievement for 19th-century painting.

Contemporary critics recognised Brockmann's outstanding skill; Fernanflor (1887) described the characteristics displayed in her work as "more male than female, for their serious nature and the quality of the emotions represented. If she is not one of the most brilliant artists, it seems that, by developing her skills, she is one of those who could reach the greatest heights". It may have been that the State was of the same opinion when it acquired *Patio of a Parador* (untraced) for 3000 pesetas; the painting had been awarded only a third-class medal, and the value of the second-class prizes was between 2500 and 4000 pesetas. The state also acquired *Procession Passing Through the Cloister of San Juan de los Reyes* (1892; untraced), and Brockmann was also awarded prizes in the Exposiciones Nacionales. Two of her paintings, the *Philip II* mentioned above and *La Chocara*, appeared on the art market in the mid-1980s (Sotheby's, Madrid, 19 December 1985, lot 18, and 22 May 1986, lot 72, respectively).

MARÍA RUTH PÉREZ-ANTELO

Brodersen, Anne Marie *see* Carl Nielsen

Brooks, Romaine
American painter, 1874–1970

Born Beatrice Romaine Goddard in Rome, Italy, 1874, to Ella Waterman and Major Harry Goddard of Philadelphia. Joined mother and brother St Mar in London, 1886; subsequently educated in north Italy and Switzerland. Studied voice in Neuilly, 1895–6, and Paris, 1896–8; painting at La Scuola Nazionale and Circolo Artistico, Rome, 1898–9, and Académie Colarossi, Paris, 1899–1900. Rented studio on island of Capri, *c.*1900–02; also lived in Nice and Villa Grimaldi, Menton. Inherited a fortune after deaths of mother and brother, 1902. Brief marriage of convenience to pianist and homosexual dilettante John Ellingham Brooks, 1902. Lived in London, 1902–4, spending time in St Ives, Cornwall. Returned to Paris and studied briefly in studio of Gustave Courtois, 1905. Met Gabriele D'Annunzio, 1910, Natalie Clifford Barney, 1915. Set up studio in Venice, 1916. Exhibited at Salon des Indépendants, Paris, 1923. Visited New York briefly in 1925; rented studio in Carnegie Hall, New York, 1935–6. Living on French Riviera with Barney at

outbreak of World War II. Purchased Villa Sant'Agnese, Florence, 1940; lived there until mid-1950s, when she bought Villa Gaia, Fiesole. Moved to studio apartment in Nice, 1967. Croix, Légion d'Honneur, France, 1920. Died in Nice, 7 December 1970.

Selected Individual Exhibitions
Galeries Durand-Ruel, Paris: 1910
Goupil Gallery, London: 1911
Galerie Jean Charpentier, Paris: 1925
Alpine Club Gallery, London: 1925
Wildenstein Galleries, New York: 1925
Galerie Th. Briant, Paris: 1931
Arts Club of Chicago: 1935
National Museum of American Art, Washington, DC: 1971 (retrospective)

Selected Writings
"No pleasant memories" and "A war interlude", undated manuscripts, National Archives of American Art, Smithsonian Institution, Washington, DC
"No pleasant memories", *Life and Letters Today*, xviii/12, Summer 1938, pp.38–44
"The convent", *Life and Letters Today*, xix/18, 1938, pp.14–30

Bibliography
Romaine Brooks, exh. cat., Galeries Durand-Ruel, Paris, 1910
Robert de Montesquiou, "Cambrioleur d'âmes", *Le Figaro*, May 1910
Gustave Kahn, "Romaine Brooks", *L'Art et les Artistes*, xxxvii, May 1923, pp.3, 7 and 14
John Usher, "True painter of personality", *International Studio*, lxxxiii, 1926, pp.46–50
Romaine Brooks, exh. cat., Arts Club of Chicago, 1935
Elisabeth de Gramont, *Romaine Brooks: Portraits, Tableaux, Dessins*, Paris: Braun, 1952; reprinted New York: Arno Press, 1975
Michel Desbruères, "Commentaires", *Bizarre*, xliv, March 1968, pp.13–48
Romaine Brooks: "Thief of Souls", exh. cat., National Museum of American Art, Washington, DC, 1971; reissued with revised essay by Adelyn D. Breeskin, 1986
Meryle Secrest, *Between Me and Life: A Biography of Romaine Brooks*, New York: Doubleday, 1974; London: Macdonald and Jane's, 1976
Pierre de Montera, "Gabriele D'Annunzio, Romaine Brooks et Natalie Barney", *D'Annunzio e il simbolismo europeo*, Milan: Il Saggiatore, 1976
Women Artists, 1550–1950, exh. cat., Los Angeles County Museum of Art, and elsewhere, 1976
Susan Gubar, "Blessings in disguise: Cross-dressing as re-dressing for female modernists", *Massachusetts Review*, xxii/3–4, Autumn 1981, pp.477–508
Giuditta Villa, *Romaine Brooks, (1874–1970)*, PhD dissertation, Università degli Studi, Rome, 1983
Shari Benstock, *Women of the Left Bank: Paris, 1900–1940*, Austin: University of Texas Press, 1986; London: Virago, 1987
Romaine Brooks, 1874–1970, exh. cat., Musée Sainte-Croix, Poitiers, 1987
Catherine Texier, *Analyse et recherche iconographique de l'oeuvre de Romaine Brooks*, PhD dissertation, Université de Paris VIII – Vincennes à Saint-Denis, 1987
Karla Jay, *The Amazon and the Page: Natalie Clifford Barney and Renée Vivien*, Bloomington: Indiana University Press, 1988
Françoise Werner, *Romaine Brooks*, Paris: Plon, 1990
Natalie Barney, *Adventures of the Mind*, New York: New York University Press, 1992 (French original, 1929)

Bridget Elliott and Jo-Ann Wallace, *Women Artists and Writers: Modernist (im)positionings*, London and New York: Routledge, 1994

Catherine McNickle Chastain, "Romaine Brooks: A new look at her drawings", *Woman's Art Journal*, xvii/2, 1996–7, pp.9–14

Joe Lucchesi, *Romaine Brooks' Self-Portraits and the Performance of Lesbian Identity*, PhD dissertation, University of North Carolina (in preparation)

Romaine Brooks was a wealthy American expatriate who specialised in portraiture. After training briefly at the Scuola Nazionale in Rome and the Académie Colarossi in Paris, she began an artistic career that took her through some of the most privileged cultural circles of early 20th-century Europe: the Anglo-American artistic and intellectual colony on Capri; the Parisian society of Comte Robert de Montesquiou, so-called Prince of Aesthetes; the literary Left Bank community of American writer Natalie Barney. Despite her continuous participation in a variety of cultural realms, Brooks cultivated the image of the *lapidé*, the outcast, and this image added rhetorical force to the psychologically penetrating, slightly mocking and judgmental character that critics discovered in her portraits.

The large fortune that Brooks inherited after the death of her mother and brother in 1902 allowed her to begin her continually shifting movements through these rarefied European social realms. A series of self-portraits spanning her career charts both her development as a portraitist and her changing social, intellectual and artistic concerns. These images explore a theme that becomes a leitmotif in Brooks's work: an interior sense of self-identity that also continually references the role external appearances, and particularly clothing, play in constructing a "coherent" and legible internal self. In her first *Self-Portrait* (c.1905; private collection, repr. Poitiers 1987, p.103) she presents herself in an elaborately layered black costume and enormous veiled hat typical of the refined circles of Parisian *mondaines*. By contrast, in *Artist on the Seashore* (1912) Brooks appears in a turbulent and windswept seaside landscape. The painting is imbued with a romantic symbolism that coincides with her close association with the Italian aesthetic poet Gabriele D'Annunzio, whom Brooks portrayed in an identical format as the *Poet in Exile* (both Musée National d'Art Moderne, Paris). By 1923 she had replaced this airy romanticism with a psychologically acute and powerfully androgynous self-presentation (see illustration). Here Brooks wears an oversized riding hat whose brim partially shadows her challenging and unflinching gaze, and her masculinely tailored outfit reflects that of her contemporary lesbian associates.

Brooks also produced a series of photographic self-portraits, visually sophisticated and compositionally complex images in which she specifically addresses the self-conscious construction of identities through clothing and external signifiers (1910–20; private collection, *ibid.*, pp.65–73). Brooks models in various poses and elegant costumes. Some photographs resemble the contemporary fashionable portraits of her friend the British pictorialist photographer Baron de Meyer, while in others she photographs herself reflected and refracted in an array of mirrors, always including the camera apparatus in the picture and often her own paintings reflected in the background.

Around 1900 Brooks settled on Capri and became part of the expatriate community that formed around the British male homosexuals, such as her friend Somerset Maugham, who had fled the backlash against homosexuality after Oscar Wilde's sodomy trial (1895). Soon after meeting there James McNeill Whistler's patron, the American industrialist Charles Lang Freer, Brooks moved to London, took a Tite Street studio near Whistler's and developed her extremely nuanced colour sense, eventually settling on modulations of black, white and greys that reviewers often called "Whistlerian". Her painting of a young girl absorbed by music, *The Piano* (1910; National Museum of American Art, Washington, DC), employs this trademark palette and also resonates with Whistler's aestheticised symbolism. Similarly, her early portraits of such *mondaines* as the Chilean hostess *Mme Errazuris* (c.1908; National Museum of American Art) and *Princess Lucien Murat* (c.1910; private collection, *ibid.*, p.114) follow closely Whistler's tradition of elegant society portraiture.

When she moved to France in 1905, Brooks entered the aristocratic, intellectual salons of Paris through her brief lesbian relationship with the art patron Winnaretta Singer, Princesse de Polignac. De Montesquiou soon became an ardent supporter of her painting. He was the undisputed leader of this cultural milieu, and his poetry and essays typify the refined, esoteric and literary symbolism associated with "the Aesthetes". Brooks's contemporary work shows the influence of this symbolist sensibility. Her first one-woman exhibition at the prestigious Galeries Durand-Ruel consisted entirely of female genre figures – charwomen, a young consumptive, girls in fashionable dresses – executed in refined colour harmonies and delicate handling that matched contemporary "Aesthetic" tastes. An underlying sobriety and a lack of idealisation, however, suggested unseen layers of meaning behind the anonymous faces of the models, prompting de Montesquiou, in his published review of the exhibition, to give Brooks the nickname *cambrioleur d'âmes* ("thief of souls") for her ability to capture "inner truths" behind outward appearances.

Distinctly Symbolist underpinnings and a pervasive psychological exposure also inform her contemporary portraits. Her subjects appear in dark, atmospheric settings, and Brooks often included small objects existing in ambiguous relation to the sitter. In *The Debutante* (1910–11; National Museum of American Art) a turkey statuette stands near an awkward, oddly dressed girl whom Brooks herself described as "ugly". In the portrait of the decorator *Elsie de Wolfe* (c.1914; Musée National d'Art Moderne, Paris) the sitter shares space with a small, delicate porcelain goat that bears a slight resemblance to her. Similarly, Brooks painted the young Jean Cocteau on her studio balcony with the Eiffel Tower looming behind him. In these portraits a connection between object and sitter is suggested but never explained, adding a mysterious and slightly surreal note to otherwise faithful representations.

Apart from several male portraits, Brooks's paintings focus exclusively on women. With the haunting and enigmatic figure of Ida Rubinstein as her model, around 1910 Brooks began to infuse the female body with a dense symbolic iconography and to explore both the erotic possibilities of the female nude and the performative nature of continually shifting identities. Through de Montesquiou, Brooks met Rubinstein, a Russian dancer who had appeared in several Parisian Ballets Russes

Brooks: *Self-Portrait*, 1923; oil on canvas; 117 × 68.3 cm.; National Museum of American Art, Smithsonian Institution, Washington, DC

productions as exotic, tragic – and always erotic – characters, including Salome, Cleopatra and Zobéïde in *Schéhérazade*. Her expressive, attenuated limbs and ghostly pale skin furnished Brooks with a visual icon of female sexuality that continued the tradition of late 19th-century Symbolists. Brooks's themes range from the association of feminine sexuality with death in *The Journey* (1912; National Museum of American Art), where Rubinstein's extremely emaciated and cadaverous figure floats in an inky void; to the *femme fatale* of *White Azaleas* (1910; National Museum of American Art), in which she reclines seductively on a couch, her gaze shrouded by murky shadows. Brooks continues her reading of the female body in explicitly sexual terms in her portrait of the eccentric *Marchesa Luisa Casati* (1920; private collection, repr. Desbruères 1968, pp.46–7), the only major nude not inspired by Rubinstein. In contrast to Rubinstein, the Marchesa Casati is presented as the Symbolist feminine virago, a Medusa figure whose huge eyes stare balefully from beneath her writhing, flame-like corona of auburn hair and whose thin body emerges from a loosely flung purplish cloak.

Rubinstein also appeared in more elaborately allegorical paintings permeated with themes of female sexuality and erotic desire. In a collaborative project with Barney, Brooks painted Rubinstein as the *Weeping Venus* (1916–17; Musée Sainte-Croix, Poitiers), and Barney's accompanying poem makes explicit the interconnection between female eroticism and death that appeared regularly in Symbolist literature and painting. The more enigmatic *Masked Archer* (1910–11; destroyed, repr. Poitiers 1987, p.121) presents Rubinstein's nude form bound to a post, the target of an arrow already released by a male figure. Brooks intended the archer to represent D'Annunzio, and the painting is her response to his drama *The Martyrdom of St Sebastian*, written for Rubinstein and performed in Paris in 1911. The play is an arcane mixture of androgynous sensuality and symbolic Christian melodrama whose underlying gender ambiguity infuriated the Catholic Church and intrigued Parisian audiences. Brooks's painting reworks the gendered themes of ambiguity and power embedded in *St Sebastian*. Rubinstein's exposed, listless and effete Sebastian awaits the arrow shot by the masked, active, yet dwarfish D'Annunzio. In contrast to these images, Brooks also painted Rubinstein as a personification of French war-time courage and duty in *La France croisée* (1915; Museum of American Art), wearing the uniform of a Red Cross nurse and standing defiantly in a decimated landscape before a burning city. D'Annunzio wrote four accompanying poems of explicitly Symbolist allegory, and both were exhibited as part of a fund-raising effort that earned Brooks a medal from the Légion d'Honneur after World War I.

Brooks continued to explore these issues of feminine identity in a portrait series that she produced during the early 1920s. The overt eroticism and sensuality of her earlier nudes, however, is replaced by an iconoclastic androgyny. During World War I Brooks met and began a 50-year personal and professional collaboration with Natalie Barney, who had long been a leader of the Parisian lesbian community, maintaining an openly lesbian lifestyle in the face of public disapproval and censure. Brooks's subsequent sitters reflect not only her closer involvement in a "lesbian *haute monde*", as the British painter Gluck (q.v.) called them, but also a heightened self-consciousness about the public aesthetics of an ambiguously gendered identity.

Apart from her own self-portrait, Brooks's subjects included *Una, Lady Troubridge, Gluck*, the Italian pianist *Renata Borgatti* and the French writer *Elisabeth de Gramont, duchesse de Clermont-Tonnerre* (all 1920–25; National Museum of American Art). Although the mood of the portraits varied – from the austere gravity of Gluck's portrayal to the satiric overtones of Una Troubridge – each woman appears against minimal and spatially compressed backgrounds, and each is dressed in similar, masculinely tailored costumes. Brooks exhibited Gluck's portrait under the name *Peter, a Young English Girl*, a title that suggests the contradictory and oscillating terms under which the portrait constructs an identity for the sitter. Peter's androgynous figure slips across the codes and boundaries of gendered representation, referencing both masculinity and femininity but settling on neither. Brooks installs this same sense of powerful ambiguity in *Una Troubridge*. A play with appearances is everywhere evident, from the rigidity of her exaggeratedly arch collar, binding cravat and oversized monocle, to the stereotypical feminine accents of her large pin curls, delicate pearl earrings and pink lipstick. Brooks often referred to the humour she found in Troubridge's outfits, suggesting both an underlying irony and a self-consciousness about this rhetoric of androgynous self-presentation.

With these portraits Brooks records a sartorial strategy that many lesbians used in order to gain increased cultural visibility in early 20th-century Europe, a visual interpretation and recoding of the so-called "mannish woman" that the pseudo-scientific discourse of sexologists attempted to diagnose and cure. As exhibition reviews suggest, however, these paintings were not necessarily self-evident lesbian representations, and in fact a more complex network of cultural discourses intersected them. On the one hand, the wearing of masculinely tailored jackets, pants and tuxedos enjoyed considerable vogue associated with the fashionable and problematic "modern woman", largely a heterosexual, bourgeois phenomenon that upset traditionally assigned gender roles. On the other hand, both this clothing style and the portraits themselves echo the traditional iconography of the aristocratic dandy. Gluck's incisive comment indicates the crucial vector of class that inflected Brooks's cultural associations, patrons, subjects and self-image. The elevated class status of these women afforded them more social freedoms than their bourgeois counterparts but, paradoxically, subjected them to more intricate and firmly established rituals of public performance and propriety. Much of the visual tension of Brooks's portraits derives from the dilemma of women caught within this social and sexual rubric.

During the late 1920s Brooks's primary artistic interest shifted from painting to drawing, and after producing only two portraits in the 1930s (during a trip to New York) she stopped painting altogether. The drawings are constructed from a continuous line that wanders across the page and is then reformed into various objects and figures. The elegant, fluid arabesques and complex patterns of Brooks's drawings often weave together multiple figures in tortuous and inextricable masses, like the snout-nosed, vaporous creatures and the female figure they menace in *Caught* (1930; National Museum of American Art). Although these works have a broad thematic range, subject matter usually revolves around familial images

(*Sorrow of Rebirth, or Les Parents entraînent leurs enfants*), death (*Dead Too Long*) and conflicts between terrestrial and spiritual forces (*Mother Nature*; all before 1935; National Museum of American Art). Her drawings share stylistic and conceptual ground with contemporary Surrealist automatic writing, and Brooks underlined the connection to an unconscious process of production when, in the preface to the catalogue of her exhibition in Chicago (1935), she described these drawings as "inevitable", and consistently characterised them as attempts to exorcise the nightmares of a difficult early life.

The autobiographical impulse that motivated Brooks's drawings became explicit when she produced 13 works that illustrate her unpublished manuscript "No pleasant memories" (extracts in Secrest 1974 and Werner 1990), a text that she wrote and revised for over 20 years. In this text Brooks represents her life as primarily a struggle against her domineering and nearly demonic mother. As this extraordinary document recounts in excruciating detail the continuous conflicts and oppression of the young artist in trying to sever her family ties, the tone and imagery that Brooks employs wavers between objective, autobiographical description and the fantastic and surreal evocations of a fairy tale. In later chapters she summarily treats her artistic career and personal life; a second volume, "A war interlude", recounts her life in Florence with Natalie Barney during World War II. This volume mixes lengthy accounts of the women's daily activities with affirmations of the Fascist ideology that Brooks fostered through her relationship with D'Annunzio, who in later years became an Italian nationalist hero.

Throughout her career and through the changes in style, themes and personal and professional allegiances, Romaine Brooks's primary artistic interest remained the exploration of identities. Her portraits and drawings are visual resolutions of the socio-psychological and sexual factors that constitute identities and often focus on the performative artifice of visible identities. Her work is a provocative exploration of the links between portraiture, visual imagery, the creation of gendered identities and the problem of the "homosexual subject" in early 20th-century Europe.

JOE LUCCHESI

Brown, Lucy Madox
British painter, 1843–1894

Born in Paris, 19 July 1843, to the artist Ford Madox Brown and his first wife Elizabeth Bromley. Educated at her aunt's school, Milton Lodge, Gravesend, Kent, after her mother's death in 1846; later boarded with Maria Rossetti, who took pupils in her home. Trained in London by her father, alongside her half-sister Catherine Madox Brown (later Mrs Hueffer), her brother Oliver, and Marie Spartali (q.v.). Travelled to Belgium and Cologne with William Morris and his wife, 1869; to Italy in a group that included art writer William Michael Rossetti, 1873. Married Rossetti, 1874; five children, born 1875, 1877, 1879 and 1881 (twins). Spent most winters abroad after tuberculosis diagnosed in 1885, and began to write. Died in San Remo, Italy, April 1894.

Principal Exhibitions
Dudley Gallery, London: 1869–72
Royal Academy, London: 1870

Selected Writings
"Ford Madox Brown", *Magazine of Art*, xiii, 1890, pp.289–96
(as L.M. Rossetti), *Mrs Shelley*, London: Allen, 1890

Bibliography
Ellen C. Clayton, *English Female Artists*, 2 vols, London: Tinsley, 1876
William M. Hardinge, "A reminiscence of Mrs W.M. Rossetti", *Magazine of Art*, xviii, 1895, pp.341–6
Ford Madox Hueffer [Ford Madox Ford], *Ford M. Brown: A Record of His Life and Work*, London and New York: Longman, 1896
——, "The younger Madox Browns", *Artist*, xix, February 1897, pp.49–56
William Michael Rossetti, *Some Reminiscences*, 2 vols, London: Brown Langham, and New York: Scribner, 1906
Elsa Honig Fine, *Women and Art*, Montclair, NJ: Allenheld and Schram, and London: Prior, 1978
Virginia Surtees, ed., *The Diary of Ford Madox Brown*, New Haven and London: Yale University Press, 1981
Charlotte Yeldham, *Women Artists in Nineteenth-Century France and England*, 2 vols, New York: Garland, 1984
Jan Marsh and Pamela Gerrish Nunn, *Women Artists and the Pre-Raphaelite Movement*, London: Virago, 1989

Lucy Madox Brown worked as a professional painter for only a few years, painting and exhibiting regularly between 1869 and 1874, shortly after her marriage to the art critic W.M. Rossetti, brother of the artist Dante Gabriel Rossetti and a champion of the Pre-Raphaelite movement. She studied under her father, Ford Madox Brown, a leading member of the Pre-Raphaelites and an influential teacher. Until she was 25 she considered herself only as an assistant to her father, painting copies of his more popular works. But when his chief assistant Albert Goodwin was unable to continue work she took over and began to paint more on her own. In an article that Lucy Madox Brown wrote on her father in the *Magazine of Art* (1890), she offered this definition of art: "I mean by art the noble inspirations of genius – not the geometrical and technical teachings, which invaluable as they may be for some aspects of the human mind, are not the true means of spreading art – that is only handed from artist to artist." Indeed, as an artist's daughter, she was able to circumvent the usual educational disadvantages for women. Her paintings are simple and direct, and represent a range of historical periods. They show an ability to handle colour, light and fabric, as well as some ambitious compositional devices.

Brown's earliest known exhibited works were mostly watercolours. *Painting*, exhibited at the Dudley Gallery in 1869, shows a young woman seated at an easel working on a picture, depicting an old woman with a bundle of firewood. Her half-sister Catherine was the model for the artist in this picture, as well as for the watercolour *Après le Bal*, exhibited at the Dudley Gallery in 1871. Set in the 18th century, the scene shows two young girls (the other was modelled on Marie Spartali, q.v.) who have retired after a ball; dawn is visible through the window and then reflected in the looking-glass. One girl is asleep on the ottoman in the drawing-room, the other is trying to wake her and induce her to come to bed. Brown also exhibited a watercolour at the Royal Academy in

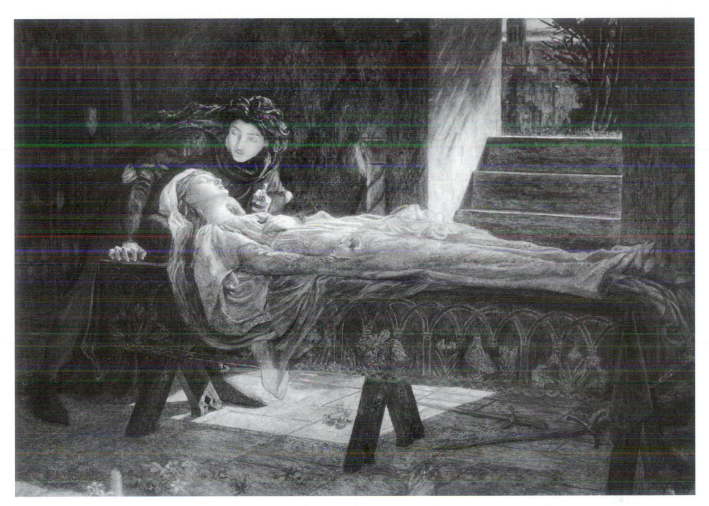

Brown: *Romeo and Juliet in the Tomb*, 1870; National Trust, Wightwick Manor, Madox Rossetti Collection

1870: *The Duet*, which shows a stylishly dressed young woman playing the spinet and singing a duet with her lover. On the spinet is a painting of Orpheus taming the beast with his lyre.

The subject of Romeo in Juliet's tomb was one that Brown painted several times. One of the first versions, a watercolour exhibited at the Dudley Gallery in 1871, shows Juliet lying on her bier in the vault, while Romeo bends over her with the poison phial in his hand. On the floor are the swords of Romeo and Paris. The scene is lit by the moon, whose silvery rays stream through the open door of the vault; they are then reflected from Juliet's snow-white robes on to Romeo's face. There is an uncertainty about the moment – is this death or a temporary suppression of consciousness? In 1895, after the artist's death, a version in oils, showing her mature handling of the medium, was exhibited at the Guildhall Exhibition, London. Brown's attention to light effects is also shown in the watercolour *Cornelius Agrippa Showing the Fair Geraldine in a Magic Mirror to the Earl of Surrey*, in which a magician has drawn aside a curtain, showing Geraldine in the mirror seated in a pleasure garden. The full yet delicate light diffused over this suddenly revealed scene contrasts with the sombre glow of lamplight within the chamber.

Like so many women artists, Brown used those models that were available to her. In an oil of 1871, *Ferdinand and*

Miranda (private collection, Britain, repr. Marsh and Nunn 1989, pl.5), a scene from Shakespeare's *The Tempest*, her brother Oliver Madox Brown was the model for Ferdinand, her sister Catherine for Miranda and her future husband, William Rossetti, for Prospero. Her father was the king. Perhaps the most personal of her works is *Margaret Roper Receiving the Head of Her Father, Sir Thomas More, from London Bridge* (1873; oil on canvas; St Thomas More, Burford), a subject that appears to be unique to her. The scene is grim but dramatic. The devoted daughter stands with outstretched arms in a barge, under the shadow of Old London Bridge, while the head of More, wrapped in its white swathings, is lowered in a basket by friendly, unseen hands. The boatman, perhaps Roper's husband, steadies the boat. The sombre scene is illuminated by mellow beams of moon in the clouded sky. The picture surely reveals something of the artist's feelings about the prominence of her father in her life.

Although Lucy Madox Brown painted only for a short time, she had patrons and her work was bought as well as exhibited. It is clear, however, that being the daughter of a well-known painter was as much a hindrance as an asset to any professional art interests she may have had. After her marriage to Rossetti, she channelled her considerable energies into feminist reform causes until the first signs of tuberculosis in 1885 forced her to reduce her activities and spend several winters abroad. She died in San Remo only six months after her father's death.

ELAINE HIRSCHL ELLIS

Browne, Henriette
French painter, 1829–1901

Born Sophie Bouteiller in Paris, 16 June 1829. Received drawing lessons from Emile Perrin from 1849; studied under Charles Chaplin from 1851. Exhibited under the pseudonym Henriette Browne from 1853. Married diplomat Comte Jules de Saux, 1853; no children; he died 1879. Travelled widely with her husband: to the Netherlands and Italy by late 1850s; Constantinople, 1860; Morocco, 1864(?); Egypt and Syria, winter 1868–9. Visited the artist Wilhelm Leibl in Munich and invited him to Paris, October 1869. One of the three female founder-members of the Société Nationale des Beaux-Arts, Paris, 1862; honorary member, Royal Institute of

Painters in Watercolours, London, 1894. Died in Paris, early 1901.

Principal Exhibitions

Paris Salon: 1853, 1857, 1859, 1861, 1863–70, 1872–8 (second-class medal 1861, third-class medals 1857, 1859 and 1863, the last for engraving)
Exposition Universelle, Paris: 1855 (third-class medal), 1867
French Gallery, Pall Mall, London: occasionally 1856–95 (annuals of French School of Fine Arts), 1859 (individual)
International Exhibition, London: 1862
Society of Female Artists, England: 1867
Royal Academy, London: 1871–2, 1875, 1879
International Colonial Exhibition, Amsterdam: 1883 (silver medal)

Bibliography

A.B., "Madame Henriette Browne", *English Woman's Journal*, v, 1 April 1860, pp.85–92
Charles Kingsley, "Henrietta Browne's picture of the Sisters of Charity", *Fine Arts Quarterly Review*, i, May–October 1863, pp.299–307
Pierre Larousse, *Grand dictionnaire universel du XIXe siècle*, Paris, 1867

Browne: *The Puritans (La Lecture de la Bible)*, 1857; Robert McDougall Art Gallery, Christchurch, New Zealand

T. Chasrel, "Henriette Browne", *L'Art Revue Hebdomadaire Illustrée*, ix, 1877, pp.97–103

Clara Erskine Clement and Laurence Hutton, *Artists of the Nineteenth Century*, 2 vols, Boston: Houghton Osgood, 1879; reprinted New York: Arno Press, 1969

G. Vapereau, *Dictionnaire universel des contemporains*, Paris: Hachette, 1893

Charlotte Yeldham, *Women Artists in Nineteenth-Century France and England*, 2 vols, New York: Garland, 1984

Pamela Gerrish Nunn, *Victorian Women Artists*, London: Women's Press, 1987

Henriette Browne acquired a fashionable reputation in France and Britain in the mid-19th century. Her painting had popular appeal, fetched high prices and attracted influential patrons. She exhibited regularly at the Paris Salon from 1853, the year in which she married, until 1878, the year before her husband's death. In the 1850s her genre painting gained the patronage of the emperor Napoleon III and the empress Eugénie, and in the following decade she gained a certain renown for orientalist painting. From the mid-1850s she exhibited in Britain, where her work was greatly admired in the Victorian period for its sentimental moralising and accomplished technique.

Browne inherited a privileged position in society through her father, the Comte de Bouteiller, a descendant of an old Breton family. Her sex and social position made her choice of profession unusual, and the influence and support of her mother were crucial to her development as an artist. After receiving rudimentary training from a drawing master, Emile Perrin, she attended the female classes of Charles Chaplin where she worked from the live model. Browne's connection with government circles after her marriage to Jules de Saux, a diplomat and secretary to the Comte de Walewski, a Minister in the Second Empire, played an influential part in her career and possibly led to her initial choice of religious genre, a category of painting that appealed to official taste under the Second Empire.

Browne's capacity for realism was evident at the beginning of her career in *A Brother of the Christian Schools* (1855; Manchester City Art Galleries), exhibited at the Exposition Universelle, Paris. Her technical dexterity and skill in layering transparent glazes were revealed in the handling of textures and light effects in *The Puritans* (1857; see illustration), also known as *La Lecture de la Bible*. Browne's religious genre was often constructed on an impressive scale using bold compositions with figures placed towards the front of the picture: *The Puritans* and *Sisters of Charity* (1859; Kunsthalle, Hamburg). These qualities, combined with a preference for idealised naturalism and sentimental moralising in keeping with the taste of the period, assured her popularity with visitors to the Salon. *Sisters of Charity* was acclaimed at the Salon of 1859 and bought for 12,000 francs as a prize in a charity lottery. *The Puritans* was acquired by the empress Eugénie for 6000 francs. Despite Browne's successes, academic recognition was limited and she received only second- and third-class medals.

It was the dealer Gambart who, seeing her work at the Exposition Universelle of 1855, went on to promote Browne at the French Gallery in London, and in 1862 she was ranked among the established French naturalists, Jules Breton, Gustave Brion and Octave Tassaert (*Art Journal*, i, 1862, p.166). Sarah Tytler (*Modern Painters and Their Paintings*, London: Strahan, 1873; Boston: Roberts, 1874) described her as "a gifted and accomplished contemporary painter, holding – not indeed so high a place as Rosa Bonheur, but an honourable place among her brother artists and becoming well known and appreciated in this country". She was among a select group of French artists visited by Elizabeth Thompson, later Lady Butler (q.v.), in 1874. Browne's professional achievements assumed particular significance during the Victorian period in the debate about women's participation in art. In contrast to Rosa Bonheur (q.v.), Browne was perceived as a model of femininity and her painting as an expression of womanly virtue. According to Charles Kingsley, she was said to possess "a heart pure, noble, charitable, and pious" (Kingsley 1863, p.306). In the *English Woman's Journal* she was described as "of a remarkably modest and retiring disposition, devoted to her family and her home" (A.B., 1860, p.85).

In the 1860s Browne exhibited numerous paintings with orientalist themes in which she drew on her experience as a woman traveller in the East. This gave her painting an added interest: *A Visit (Harem Interior, Constantinople, 1860* (untraced), based on her visit to Constantinople, attracted considerable attention at the Salon of 1861. In 1877 she was ranked by T. Chasrel alongside Fromentin and Gérôme, acknowledged leaders in orientalist painting (Chasrel 1877, p.103).

In 1879, when Browne largely gave up exhibiting, she had enjoyed a successful career as a professional artist, specialising in genre painting and orientalism, as well as in portraiture and engraving. While numerous works remain untraced, the number surviving in public collections testifies to her popularity. In England, these include *The Nun* (1859; Sudley Art Gallery, Liverpool), *A Girl Writing* (c.1875: Victoria and Albert Museum, London), *A Greek Captive* (Tate Gallery, London) and *Moorish Girl with Parakeet* (Russell-Cotes Art Gallery and Museum, Bournemouth).

JULIE KING

Bruce, Kathleen *see* Scott

Brück, Trude

German graphic artist and painter, 1902–1992

Born in Breslau, 2 August 1902. Moved to Dortmund with her family, 1912. Studied at the Düsseldorf Academy from 1921, at first in the women's art school. Member of Das Junge Rheinland group from 1922. Travelled to south of France and Algeria with her professor, Heinrich Nauen, 1924. Taught art in a girls' school in Saarbrücken from 1928. Married Dr Ernst Werle in Berlin, 1931; marriage failed, partly due to husband's support of the National Socialist party; divorced 1939. Moved to Munich, 1941; remarried. Ceased work after studio destroyed in an air raid in 1943; became a picture restorer at the Munich Academy. Died in Hersching, 7 August 1992.

Principal Exhibitions
Messepalast, Cologne: 1924 (*Grosse Düsseldorfer Kunstausstellung*)
Galerie Johanna Ey, Düsseldorf: 1925 (individual, twice)
Saarländische Künstlergruppe, Saarbrücken: from 1928
Stadtmuseum, Düsseldorf: 1981 (individual), 1992 (retrospective)

Bibliography
Trude Brück: Gemälde, Graphiken, exh. cat., Stadtmuseum, Düsseldorf, 1981
Peter Barth, *Johanna Ey und ihr Künstlerkreis*, Düsseldorf: Galerie Remmert und Barth, 1984
Am Anfang: Das Junge Rheinland: Zur Kunst- und Zeitgeschichte einer Region, 1918–1945, exh. cat., Städtische Kunsthalle, Düsseldorf, 1985
Das Junge Rheinland: Druckgraphik, exh. cat., Galerie Remmert und Barth, Düsseldorf, 1985
Anke Münster, "Künstlerinnen in Köln und Düsseldorf von 1918 bis 1933", typescript, Giessen, 1991
Trude Brück zum 90. Geburtstag, exh. cat., Stadtmuseum, Düsseldorf, 1992
Rheinische Expressionistinnen, Schriftenreihe Verein August Macke Haus, no.10, Bonn, 1993

Trude Brück was rediscovered in the 1980s, about 40 years after she stopped working as an artist in 1943, when she lost almost all her work. Born at the beginning of the 20th century, she belonged to a new, self-confident generation of women artists. She trained as an artist against her parents' will, but soon saw that at the conservative Düsseldorf Academy she would only be taught technical knowledge. Her contact with the artists' group Das Junge Rheinland was very important to her artistic development. From 1922 onwards she was in the inner circle of this group, who set themselves up against "out-moded models" and "the routine painter's job" in the Rhineland area. With publications and exhibitions in which Max Ernst and Otto Dix took part, they created a forum for contemporary art in that region.

Brück was the only woman in the inner circle of the group. She was very friendly with the organisers, the artists Gert H. Wollheim and Karl Schwesig. They met to work together at the house of Johanna Ey. The gallery owner, sometimes referred to as the "artists' mother" due to the care she took of them, put her exhibition rooms in Düsseldorf permanently at the disposal of the Junges Rheinland artists. Brück held two solo exhibitions there in 1925, but she did not take part in the numerous group exhibitions held by Das Junge Rheinland.

Most of Brück's extant work is now in the Stadtmuseum, Düsseldorf, and it is thanks to the museum's director, Wieland Koenig, that she was rediscovered. Barely two dozen oil paintings, watercolours and engravings survived World War II; these were all created between 1921 and 1928 and thus document only seven years of her artistic activity. Like many Junges Rheinland artists, Brück worked intensively with printmaking, particularly engravings. Some of these are believed to have been made in Karl Schwesig's studio. For Brück, the spidery, fine-veined dry-point etching played the part of a seismograph, tracing the situation of people in the difficult times after World War I. An example of this is the early, small-format work *Alcoholic Family* (1922; see illustration), which clearly shows Brück's antipathy to the academic drawing courses she was attending at the time. As in her depictions of other social-critical themes, Brück placed the figures into a dramatic milieu.

Brück: *Alcoholic Family (Trinkerfamilie)*, 1922; 24.7 × 16.8 cm.; Stadtmuseum, Düsseldorf

She described a vanished engraving from this period in the following terms:

> prominently positioned in the foreground of a city street [was] a drunken, slightly swaying workman wearing a floppy hat. On his arm was an anxious, delicate, heavily pregnant woman gazing straight ahead, while with his left hand he held a passing buxom prostitute tight; she was turned to face him and they were both smiling at each other. Underneath were the printed words "Before the cock crows, you will have denied me thrice!"

This aggressive work almost got Brück expelled from the academy. Other extant engravings from this early period are *No Work* (1924) and *Blinded in the War* (1922; both Stadtmuseum, Düsseldorf), which bears the words: "Curse the war! Curse the work of weapons!" At the same time Brück also painted a version of the theme in oils, but this picture was destroyed in the war.

In addition to these engravings on the subject of human suffering in the post-war years, Brück also produced a series of portraits using the same technique. These include two pictures of her artist friends, *Karl Schwesig* and *Gert H. Wollheim* (both 1922; Stadtmuseum, Düsseldorf). Wollheim, with whom she shared a passion for music and poetry, is shown as a violinist on a perspective plane with spidery lines that suggest sound oscillations. The deformed rendering of the artist's body is noteworthy: joints bend outwards, the hand on the neck of the violin, unlike that holding the bow, is crude, the individual fingers undifferentiated. The representation of Schwesig is the antithesis of this. Brück shows the diminutive, hunchbacked painter in sharp profile with a jutting chin that makes him look simultaneously aggressive and vulnerable. None of her other engravings is as precisely detailed and finished. She also painted a watercolour of the painter *Gert H. Wollheim* (*c*.1925; Stadtmuseum, Düsseldorf), choosing a similar profile view to the portrait of *Schwesig*. In the watercolour, however, Wollheim has his eyes closed, his mouth slightly open, and his complexion is tinged with blue – he looks like a corpse.

In 1924 Brück painted four watercolours on a trip to Algeria with her teacher, the painter Heinrich Nauen. They show everyday scenes that bear a stamp of fascination and the impressions of the journey, for example, *Algerian Street Scene* (1924; Stadtmuseum, Düsseldorf). They stand out from the artist's other work by virtue of their effects of light and shade.

The three extant oil paintings (all Stadtmuseum, Düsseldorf) can give no more than a fragmentary impression of Trude Brück as a painter. Two of the works are self-portraits, the third is the portrait of a fellow-painter, *Loy Walter* (1928). In her self-portraits Brück shows herself as a self-assured young woman, but not as an artist. In *Self-Portrait, Half-Naked* (1925) she takes the woman's best-known rôle in painting – that of the seductive, nude artist's model. The self-portrait she painted a year later shows less physical beauty than intensity of expression.

No work – not even in photographs – survives from the years that Brück spent in the Saarland and then Munich. She described her development as an artist in the following terms: "My compositions and forms became firmer and clearer, as did the colours". In her choice of subject matter she showed her rejection of the Nazi regime; she painted victims of attack, people who were being spied upon, threatened and murdered. Because she worked in secret, these pictures could not endanger her. Years after her studio was destroyed, Trude Brück took up picture restoring and ceased producing her own work.

ANKE MÜNSTER

Brychtová, Jaroslava
Czech glass artist and designer, 1924–

Born in Zelezny Brod, in northern Bohemia, 18 July 1924. Studied applied sculpture at Academy of Applied Arts, Prague, under Karel Stipl, 1944–7; also experimented with *pâte de verre* in collaboration with her father, the sculptor Jaroslav Brychta. Studied at the Academy of Fine Arts, Prague, under Josef Lauda, 1947–52. Married (1) Milos Zahradník, 1947; three children, born 1947, 1951 and 1954; divorced 1962; (2) glass artist Stanislav Libenský, 1963. Founder and director of "Glass for Architecture" department, Nationalfirm Zeleznobrodské Sklo (Zelezny Brod glassworks), 1950–83. Large-scale sculptural work carried out in collaboration with various artists from 1952; collaborated with Libenský from 1955. Artist-in-residence, with Libenský, at Pilchuck Glass School, Stanwood, near Seattle, Washington, 1982 (returned on several occasions, 1982–90). Established own studio in Zelezny Brod, 1984. Recipient of Grand Prix, Exposition Universelle et Internationale, Brussels, 1958; gold medal, São Paulo Bienal, 1965; gold medal and Bavarian State prize, Munich Craft Fair, 1967 and 1995; gold medal, International Design Exhibition, Stuttgart, 1967; City of Prague prize for window in St Wenceslas chapel, Prague Cathedral, 1968; gold medal, glass section, Stuttgart Craft Fair, 1969; prize of honour, 1977, and honourable mention, 1985, International Glass Prize, Coburg; special prize, Glaskunst 81, Kassel, 1981; Rakow award for Excellence in the Art of Glass, Corning Museum of Glass, New York, 1984 (all with Stanislav Libenský). Chevalier, Ordre des Arts et des Lettres, France, 1989. Lives and works with Libenský in Prague and Zelezny Brod.

Selected Individual Exhibitions
(all with Stanislav Libenský)

Galerie Ceskoslovensky Spisovatel (Czech Writers building), Prague: 1962
Museu de Arte Moderna, Rio de Janeiro: 1966
Suomen Lasimuseo (Finnish Glass Museum), Riihimäki: 1983–4 (touring retrospective)
Habitat Galleries, Lathrup Village, MI: 1984
Mestske Museum, Zámek, Mnichovo Hradliště: 1985 (retrospective)
Habitat Galleries, Bay Harbor Islands, FL: 1986
Galerie Clara Scremini, Paris: 1988, 1992
Heller Gallery, New York: 1988, 1990, 1993
Valdsteinská Jízdárna, Prague: 1989 (retrospective, organised by National Gallery and Museum of Decorative Arts, Prague)
Sanske Galerie, Zürich: 1990
Galerie Gottschalk-Betz, Frankfurt am Main: 1990 (with Dana Zámečniková)
Museum Bellerive, Zürich: 1990–91 (touring retrospective)
Nakama Gallery, Tokyo: 1992
Corning Museum of Glass, New York: 1994 (retrospective)

Bibliography
Glass 1959: A Special Exhibition of International Contemporary Glass, exh. cat., Corning Museum of Glass, New York, 1959
Contemporary Glass: Czechoslovakia and Italy, exh. cat., Museum of Contemporary Crafts of the American Craftsmen's Council, New York, 1964
Modernes Glas aus Amerika, Europa und Japan, exh. cat., Museum für Kunsthandwerk, Frankfurt am Main, 1976
Coburger Glaspreis 1977 für moderne Glasgestaltung in Europa, exh. cat., Kunstsammlungen der Veste, Coburg, 1977
New Glass: A Worldwide Survey, exh. cat., Corning Museum of Glass, New York, 1979
Czechoslovakian Glass, 1350–1980, exh. cat., Corning Museum of Glass, New York, 1981
William Warmus, "The art of Libenský and Brychtová", *New Glass Review*, vi, 1985, pp.30–42
Zweiter Coburger Glaspreis für moderne Glasgestaltung in Europa 1985, exh. cat., Kunstsammlungen der Veste, Coburg, 1985
S. Libenský, J. Brychtová, exh. cat., Galerie Clara Scremini, Paris, 1988
Stanislav Libenský, Jaroslava Brychtová: Tvorba z let 1945–1989, exh. cat., Národní Galerie, Prague, 1989
Neues Glas in Europa: 50 Künstler, 50 Konzepte, exh. cat., Kunstmuseum, Düsseldorf, 1990

Sylva Petrová, "The Prague première of the life work of Stanislav Libenský and Jaroslava Brychtová", *Glass Review*, xlv/3, 1990, pp.16–23

Skulpturen aus Glas: Stanislav Libenský und Jaroslava Brychtová, Prag: Eine Retrospektive, 1945–1990, exh. cat., Museum Bellerive, Zürich, 1990

Glassculpturen: Stanislav Libenský en Jaroslava Brychtová, exh. cat., Centrum voor Kunst en Cultuur, St Pieterplein, Ghent, 1991

Ales Vasícek, "An interview with Stanislav Libenský and Jaroslava Brychtová", *Glasswork* (Kyoto), no.10, October 1991, pp.10–19 (in Japanese and English)

Stanislav Libenský, Jaroslava Brychtová: A 40-Year Collaboration in Glass, exh. cat., Corning Museum of Glass, New York, 1994

Prostor svetlo sklo [Space light glass], exh. cat., Mícovna Prazského Hradu, Prague, 1995

Jaroslava Brychtová belongs to the first generation of Czech artists after World War II who devoted themselves to glass art and played a decisive role in the development of new forms of expression with the material. Her most significant contribution is the development of the *pâte de verre* technique (the moulding of glass objects from glass powder and fragments which are heated to melting point in specially designed moulds) for large-scale sculptures, reliefs and windows, which were novelties in Czech glass art. This ancient Egyptian technique was rediscovered in 1882 by the French sculptor and wax modeller Henri Cros, who used it for the modelling of polychrome figural reliefs. From then on the process was one of the characteristic glass techniques of Art Nouveau and Art Deco in France. From 1932 to 1970 windows were made by François Decorchement from *pâte de verre* elements combined with concrete. In Czechoslovakia, Ludwig Moser in Karlovy Vary was the first glass manufacturer to work with *pâte de verre*, and a contract for its design, production and sale was agreed between 1921 and 1931 with the French artist Gabriel Argy-Rousseau in Paris.

The first homespun *pâte de verre* production in Czechoslovakia was developed by the sculptor and glass artist Jaroslav Brychta and his daughter Jaroslava Brychtová. Polychrome brooches and small tiles with figural motifs number among the early *pâte de verre* objects that the artist created between 1944 and 1947, while studying applied sculpture at the Academy of Applied Arts in Prague. From 1947 onwards, small sculptures and relief-decorated glass vessels with a reduced emphasis on figural representation appeared. In their simplicity and spontaneity they are close to the forms of expression in the works of primitive art with which Brychtová became acquainted during a study trip to Paris. Her artistic involvement in the national enterprise Zeleznobrodské Sklo in Zelezny Brod, which was set up in 1948 and whose special department "Glass for Architecture" she built up and led, was an essential qualification for her later large-scale, architecturally orientated works. This activity ran parallel with the final stage of her second degree in sculpture, at the Academy of Fine Arts in Prague under Josef Lauda. After 1952 she created – sometimes in collaboration with Vilem Dostrašil or Igor Korčak – large-scale walls and lattice-works that were composed of relief-decorated *pâte de verre* elements.

From 1955 onwards Brychtová worked with Stanislav Libenský, who in 1954 had been appointed director and teacher of glass painting on hollow glassware and sheet-glass at the Technical College for Glass in Zelezny Brod. His figural glass paintings show, in contrast to her works, a more generous, gestural style and a more extensive stylisation, in which the later step towards abstraction seen in the joint work of these two artists has already begun. Their first piece of joint work was Brychtová's plastic, three-dimensional execution of a bowl design that Libenský had drawn as a head with the profile relief of a young woman. The underlying creative principle here, namely "design sketches by Libenský – plastic rendition by Brychtová", did not remain the basis for their later collaborations. The translation of a graphic design into large-scale three-dimensionality holds numerous creative possibilities whose artistic weight can balance that of the original concept in the overall execution of the sculpture. The question of the precise status of each individual's creative contribution cannot be answered, because – according to statements made by both artists – the definitive design and the three-dimensional model were developed simultaneously in dialogue with each other.

Architecturally related designs dominate their collaborative efforts, which have continued for 40 years, and this architectural activity was an essential part of Brychtová's work as early as 1952. The artists received significant international recognition for the first time at the Exposition Universelle et Internationale, Brussels, in 1958 for their first screen made up of individual pieces of coloured *pâte de verre* with stylised animal motifs. Brychtová herself received a further award for a wall of colourless glass that she had created in collaboration with Igor Korcak. The enormous success of Czech glass art when it was first shown at international exhibitions, at the Milan Triennale in 1957 and in Brussels in 1958, is unthinkable without the pioneering personality of the artist Josef Kaplicky, who had shown commitment to a link with the developments in European art during his time as a teacher at the Academy of Applied Arts in Prague from 1945 to 1962. The international attention that Czech glass art received in turn created a basis for the continuation of a relatively liberal artistic development under the communist regime in Czechoslovakia, which was keen to encourage an increase in exports to Western countries. Brychtová and Libenský, who had been awarded the Grand Prix in 1958, first made the breakthrough to pure abstraction in 1961 with the crystal glass partition wall *Crocodile* for the state-run Hotel International in Brno, after a transitional phase of gradual stylisation. Until the end of the 1970s, however, Brychtová produced both figural and abstract compositions.

The amount of large, publicly commissioned works increased considerably after Libenský's appointment to the Academy of Applied Arts in Prague, where he became the successor to his tutor Josef Kaplicky, who had died in 1962. All works by the two artists were executed under Brychtová's direction at Zeleznobrodské Sklo in Zelezny Brod until 1984, and individual large-scale works still are to this day. While working on 12 relief windows for the stairwell of the Union Internationale de Chemin de Fer (UIC) administration building in Paris (1962–4), the artists for the first time developed their characteristic monochrome relief work for larger surfaces. The first piece of sculpture with purely stereometric inner and outer forms in colourless crystal glass appeared in 1970. The same theme received intensive treatment once again between 1977 and 1982. With the establishment of Brychtová's own studio in

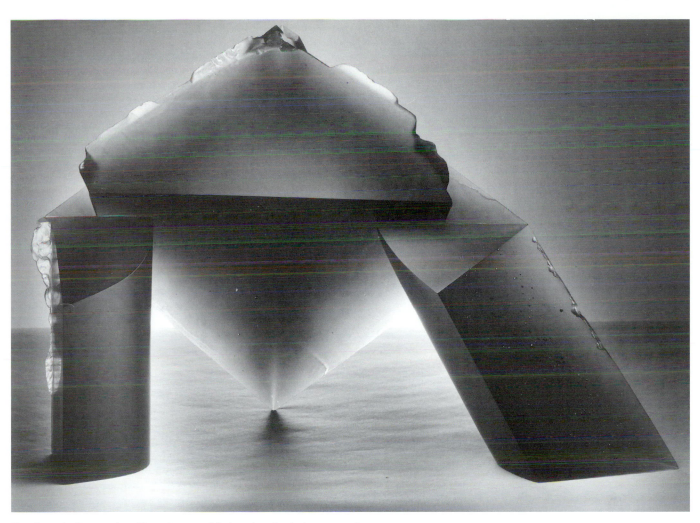

Brychtová: *Coronation II*, 1989; moulded and melted glass; 50 × 80 cm.

1984, coloured glass achieved renewed significance, for example, the gold-bearing glass known as Safirin, whose brick-brown colouring appears blue when held up to the light. Until 1989, abstract variations on the themes "head", "queen" and "table" predominated, culminating in 1988–9 in ominous, snarling figures in such sculptures as *Mankurt* and *Silhouette of the Town I–III* (both artists' collection). A fundamental element of the late coloured glass designs is the subtle use of a smooth wash of colour that fades to a colourlessness dissolving the piece's material presence at the edges, edges whose accidental structures originated in the moulding process of the forms and are increasingly incorporated into the design. Between 1989 and 1992 they produced flat, seemingly folded and stereometrically constructed sculptures that express spirituality; these have a central incision that enlivens the walls like an air shaft. The artists' contemplative gaze also dominates the *Green Eye of the Pyramid*, commissioned for the administration building of Corning Inc. in Corning, New York (1993). This intensely and radiantly green sculpture, which is in the shape of a broken triangle, incorporates a pointed oval eye form in its upper half. This design is close to the old Christian symbol for the "Eye of God", an idea that is expressed by an eye inside a triangle. Common to all the groups of works is an examination of the intrinsic material beauty of glass, glass that

the artists integrate as a natural component into their formal statements.

Examples of Brychtová's work may be found in the collections of the Corning Museum of Glass, New York; Glasmuseum Hentrich in Kunstmuseum Ehrenhof, Düsseldorf; National Museum of Modern Art, Kyoto; Victoria and Albert Museum, London; Metropolitan Museum of Art, New York; and the Museum of Decorative Arts, Prague.

EVA SCHMITT

Buchanan, Beverly

American painter and sculptor, 1940–

Born in Fuquay, North Carolina, 8 October 1940. Studied at Bennett College, Greensboro, North Carolina (BS 1962); Columbia University, New York (MS in parasitology 1968; MPH in public health 1969). Worked as a medical technologist and public health educator in New York and New Jersey while studying at the Art Students League, New York, under Norman Lewis in the mid-1970s. Moved to Georgia to devote full attention to career as an artist, 1977. Artist-in-residence, Nexus Press, 1987–8. Recipient of Guggenheim fellowship, 1980; National Endowment for the Arts (NEA) grants, 1980 and 1994; Pollock-Krasner Foundation grant, 1994. Lives in Athens, Georgia.

Selected Individual Exhibitions

Cinque Gallery, New York: 1972
Truman Gallery, New York: 1978
Heath Gallery, Atlanta: 1981, 1986, 1987
Southeastern Center for Contemporary Art (SECCA), Sculpture Garden, Winston-Salem, NC: 1989
Bernice Steinbaum Gallery, New York: 1990, 1991
Hoffman Gallery, Oregon School of Arts and Crafts, Portland: 1991
Greenville County Museum of Art, SC: 1991
Schering-Plough Corporation, Madison, NJ: 1992
Three Rivers Arts Festival, Pittsburgh: 1992 (organised by Carnegie Museum of Art, Pittsburgh)
Chrysler Museum of Art, Norfolk, VA: 1992
Steinbaum Krauss Gallery, New York: 1993
Montclair Museum of Art, NJ: 1994–6 (*Shackworks*, touring retrospective)

Bibliography

Lucy R. Lippard, *Overlay: Contemporary Art and the Art of Prehistory*, New York: Pantheon, 1983
Judy K. Collischan van Wagner, *Lines of Vision: Drawings by Contemporary Women*, New York: Hudson Hills Press, 1989
Chaney, Goodman and Schwerner: The Mississippi Three: The Struggle Continues, exh. cat., Soho 20, New York, 1990
Conwill, Kinshasha Holman, *New History: Beverly Buchanan, Mel Edwards, Maren Hassinger: Sculptural Installations*, exh. brochure, Atlanta College of Art, 1990
The Decade Show: Frameworks of Identity in the 1980s, exh. cat., Museum of Contemporary Hispanic Art, New York, and elsewhere, 1990
Lucy R. Lippard, *Mixed Blessings: New Art in Multicultural America*, New York: Pantheon, 1990
Next Generation: Southern Black Aesthetic, exh. cat., Southeastern Center for Contemporary Art (SECCA), Winston-Salem, NC, 1990
A Sense of Place: Seven Contemporary Southern Artists, exh. cat., Montgomery Museum of Fine Arts, AL, 1990
Bertoia, Buchanan, Edwards, Mitchel: Sculpture Update, exh. cat., Winston-Salem State University, NC, 1991
Conflict and Transcendence: African-American Art in South Carolina, exh. cat., Columbia Museum of Art, SC, 1992
The Black Family, exh. cat., Patrick and Beatrice Haggerty Museum of Art, Marquette University, Milwaukee, 1993
Dolls in Contemporary Art: A Metaphor of Personal Identity, exh. cat., Patrick and Beatrice Haggerty Museum of Art, Marquette University, Milwaukee, 1993
Beverly Buchanan: Shackworks, a 16-Year Survey, exh. cat., Montclair Museum of Art, NJ, and elsewhere, 1994
House and Home: Spirits of the South, exh. cat., Addison Gallery of American Art, Andover, MA, 1994
Memories of Childhood ... So We're Not the Cleavers or the Brady Bunch, exh. cat., Steinbaum Krauss Gallery, New York, 1994
Sharing the Dream, exh. cat., Sangre De Cristo Art Center, Pueblo, CO, 1994
Leslie King-Hammond, ed., *Gumbo ya ya: Anthology of Contemporary African-American Women Artists*, New York: Midmarch Arts Press, 1995
Lucy R. Lippard, *The Pink Glass Swan: Selected Essays on Feminist Art*, New York: New Press, 1995

As they chronicle an inherent fact of life at the close of the 20th century, the drawings, sculptures and characters of Beverly Buchanan embrace a variety of traditions – both aesthetic and cultural – ultimately making powerful observations about the strength of the human spirit. Blending the visually potent with a natural facility for story-telling, Buchanan addresses a sociological phenomenon – both agrarian and urban in nature – that is global in scale as she pays tribute to the tenacious resolve and undaunted spirit of the "shack dweller". Her vision is made even more trenchant when one considers the fragile cardboard sanctuaries harbouring the homeless in cities throughout the world. Confronting these grim realities, Buchanan incorporates basic tenets culled from Abstract Expressionism, the art of assemblage, folk art, and architecture. To these she adds her innate ability for telling tales and her genuine fascination with people. This fusion creates an aesthetic vehicle that makes an emphatic comment as it imparts an exhilaration and pride in the resiliency of human nature.

Buchanan's shacks suggest the makeshift structures punctuating the generic landscape – particularly, in the artist's case, those found in the southeastern USA. Often uninhabited or abandoned, these improvised, ramshackle dwellings nobly assert the reserve and dignity of an economically and sociologically disenfranchised people. They are the physical embodiment of the survival instinct of a society for whom life has been continuously arduous and intolerant. It is the shack dweller's intrepid determination to overcome adversity that Buchanan documents and hails.

The innocence, courage and wit of the shacks' imaginary inhabitants are infused into Buchanan's oeuvre; these elements are evident in her exuberant palette, spontaneously agitated line and skewed perspective, and in her rough-hewn, tumble-down structures and cock-eyed figures. The sagacious integrity of these people is evoked in the legends that Buchanan writes to accompany her work. She relies on both memory and imagination, bringing to life some of the remarkable figures she has encountered.

Buchanan grew up on the campus of South Carolina State College, Orangeburg, where her father was dean of the Department of Agriculture and an agricultural agent for the state. He advised tenant farmers and sharecroppers, often accompanied by his daughter. Inheriting her father's interest in science and psychology, Buchanan studied medical technology at Bennett College before pursuing two master's degrees, in public health and parasitology at Columbia University. As a medical technologist and public health educator in New York and New Jersey, she exercised her instinctive curiosity about people. During this time she studied at the Art Students League under Norman Lewis, who, with Romare Bearden, served as an artistic mentor and provided her with the impetus to create art. By 1977 she had moved to Georgia, giving up her position in public health in favour of a career as an artist.

From the beginning, Buchanan was concerned with structures and utilised whatever materials were accessible, including clay, concrete, stones, tin, copper and wood. In the 1970s she constructed "walls" that echoed her keen interest in textures and surfaces (*Black Wall Painting*, 1977; acrylic on canvas; 203 × 152 cm.; artist's collection). Her next focus was to construct free-standing, fragmented abstractions with distressed surfaces. Buchanan's first sculptures suggested a mystical, ancestral presence, as well as the artist's intuitive interest in the architecture associated with poverty (*Blue*

Stones, 1985; artist's collection). These primeval, block-like forms convey a sense of ritual and mystery: this metaphysical character still tempers the work she executes today, making it profound and reliquary in nature.

By the late 1980s Buchanan's art had evolved from abstract, organic forms into the expressionistic work for which she is known. In animated works on paper, Buchanan's shacks dance and tilt with jaunty grace in a dense, layered atmosphere (*Fences*, 1991; see illustration). The colours clash daringly, combining the unfettered, exhilarated palette of Henri Matisse and the Fauves with the spontaneous, rhythmic gestures of Hans Hofmann and Joan Mitchell (q.v.).

Buchanan: *Fences*, 1991; oil pastel; 106.7 × 97.8 cm.; Chrysler Museum of Art, Norfolk, Virginia

The insouciance and joy reflected in most of Buchanan's two-dimensional works have not always been as obvious in her sculptures. Most of her shacks manifest an august, sacred presence and the poignant, evocative narratives accentuate the pervasive, sanctified feeling (*Shack South Inside Out*, 1990; cedar, pine, tin, cardboard; 442 × 198 × 77 cm., plus related elements; Steinbaum Krauss Gallery, New York). She brings the fictitious residents to life with her accompanying legends. In *Hastings' House* (1989; wood, tin; 24 × 23 cm.; Collection Roslyn Bernstein), for instance, the artist truly captures the indomitable spirit of Mr Hastings:

> Brunson Earthly Hastings lived by the rules of hard work, no liquor, and one woman. His 10 sons were smart, hardworking farm boys but Anna, his only girl, was his heart. He was blind when she graduated but smiled proudly when he heard them call out, Dr Anna Hastings.

Buchanan's legends add further resonance to her shacks with their vivid imagery and language. Through her succinct yet sensitive writing, the artist endows these imaginary personae with life. Each sympathetic description provides a greater understanding of the shack dweller.

Buchanan builds on her own memories when making these crude, yet compelling sculptures. Her works serve as visual metaphors for the poverty, struggles and ingenuity of a culture that is commonly held in disregard and contempt. The artist makes powerful statements about destitution, inequality and personal triumph. Often Buchanan's shacks symbolise an angry defiance as they address and challenge sociological problems of our time. This concern for social change has propelled Buchanan into a new phase in her work, bringing more of her imaginary inhabitants' personal taste into light with such details as the flowers surrounding the structures, as seen in *Orangeburg County* (1995), and giving it renewed hope and energy. Recycling materials has always played a crucial role in the artist's work, but this exercise has now assumed a more emphatic role, as demonstrated by the bottle caps, glass bottles, buttons, licence plates and other elements that have found their way into her most recent structures. Combined with brilliant colours and words, these items are now a vivid part of Buchanan's sculptural vocabulary. Although sorrow and hardship are unquestionably ingredients in Buchanan's shacks, her works are not icons representing misery and hopelessness, but rather they are joyful elegies that celebrate the integrity, resilience and resolution of the shack dwellers.

TRINKETT CLARK

Bunce, Kate (Elizabeth)

British painter, 1856–1927

Born in Edgbaston, Birmingham, 1856; father John Thackray Bunce, editor of the *Birmingham Daily Post* and chair of the municipal art gallery and art school; sister Myra also an artist. Studied at Birmingham School of Art under E.R. Taylor, 1880s. Lived at home in Edgbaston. Associate member, Royal Birmingham Society of Artists, 1888; founder-member of the Birmingham-based Society of Painters in Tempera, 1901. Died December 1927.

Principal Exhibitions

Royal Academy, London: 1887, 1890, 1892, 1901
New Gallery, London: 1901
Coronation Exhibition, Birmingham: 1911

Bibliography

Birmingham Daily Post, 22 December 1927 (obituary)
By Hammer and Hand: The Arts and Crafts Movement in Birmingham, exh. cat., Birmingham Museums and Art Gallery, 1984
Jan Marsh and Pamela Gerrish Nunn, *Women Artists and the Pre-Raphaelite Movement*, London: Virago, 1989
The Last Romantics: The Romantic Tradition in British Art: Burne-Jones to Stanley Spencer, exh. cat., Barbican Art Gallery, London, 1989
Pamela Norris, ed., *Sound the Deep Waters: Women's Romantic Poetry in the Victorian Age*, Boston: Little Brown, 1991 (illustrations only)

The daughter of a local dignitary, Kate Bunce was a prize-winning student at the Birmingham School of Art in the 1880s, where she studied alongside her sister Myra Louisa Bunce, a metalworker and watercolourist. A staunch Anglo-Catholic, she remained in Birmingham throughout her life and did not marry. Her two best-known works, *Melody* (c.1895; Birmingham Museum and Art Gallery) and *The Keepsake* (1901; see illustration), and her association with the Arts and Crafts circle in Birmingham have led to her work being characterised as essentially decorative, but paintings that have more recently come to light evince a more dramatic and forceful approach. The hall-marks of her art are strong, if static figure drawing and firm, clear colour. She exhibited from 1887 to 1912, in Birmingham, Liverpool, Manchester and London; thereafter she specialised in large-scale works, in the style of mural painting, for church interiors, in both Britain and Canada. Most of these are for specific sites and several were produced in conjunction with her sister's metalwork, as reredoses, etc. Some line drawings and book illustrations also survive. A full-scale study of Bunce's career has yet to be produced; at the time of writing several of her exhibited works are still unlocated.

As far as can be ascertained, Bunce's earliest work was in the honest, well-drawn manner of the Birmingham Art School of the time. Her earliest known picture, a large watercolour called *The Sitting-Room* (1887; Birmingham Museum and Art Gallery), is an interior scene with a woman reading. She was soon drawn towards the Pre-Raphaelite mode, however, as represented by the work of Rossetti and Burne-Jones, and especially to Rossettian subject matter, derived as much from his poems as from his pictures. Thus her Royal Academy debut *How May I, When He Shall Ask* (1887; untraced) depicts the dying Ophelian singer in Rossetti's ballad "An Old Song Ended", and the *Day Dream* (exh. Royal Academy 1892; untraced) refers to his poem and picture of the same title, exhibited in 1883.

In 1893 Bunce was among the artists invited to contribute to a sequence of eleven historical pictures commemorating the city's past, to hang in Birmingham Town Hall; her two works (both untraced) depicted a medieval guild and a 16th-century

Bunce: *The Keepsake*, 1901; Birmingham Museum and Art Gallery

charity. In 1901 *The Keepsake* was chosen as "picture of the year" at the New Gallery. Again allusive of Rossetti's verse ("The Staff and Scrip") this is a decorative, medievalising image showing a seated woman with three attendants, in a shallow space before a tapestry loom ornamented with a crucifix; painted in tempera, it has a stylised quality, elongated figures and much Arts and Crafts detail. *Melody*, in oil, is similar in style, showing a single allegorical figure in an embroidered red and green velvet gown, fingering an inlaid lute and seated before a silver mirror and bowl of apple blossom; in composition this resembles Rossettian figures with flowers (e.g. *La Ghirlandata*), but the handling is distinctly non-carnal. A complementary picture is the recently discovered *Knight* (private collection, Scotland; ex-Christie's, London, 6 November 1995, lot 218), a half-length male figure, bareheaded and with surcoat over chainmail, bearing a chased shield and long lance. This, as befits its subject, is imbued with vigorous masculinity, firm brushwork and absence of decorative detail.

Bunce's most ambitious known easel work is *Chance Meeting* (1907; private collection, USA, repr. Norris 1991), showing the encounter between Beatrice and Dante from *La vita nuova*, a favourite late-Victorian motif tackled also by Rossetti and Henry Holiday. Bunce's two main figures are at the centre of a detailed composition that includes a richly dressed mother and child, a workman and a serving girl, all in historical costume. One of its antecedents would appear to be Jane Benham Hay's *Bonfire of the Vanities* (1867; Homerton College, Cambridge).

According to her obituary in the *Birmingham Daily Post*, Bunce's pictures were "all characterised by beautiful feeling for line and detail, but her best work was done in church painting for which as a deeply religious and spiritual woman she was temperamentally well equipped". Among the best of this work is the reredos at Longworth, Oxfordshire (1904), a triptych depicting the *Virgin and Child* flanked by the *Crucifixion* and *Descent from the Cross* in blues and pinks, set with pearls and within Myra Bunce's silver repoussé frame. Impressive both in size and conception are the four works in yellows and browns (*Annunciation*, *Adoration*, *Crucifixion* and *Entombment*, c.1906) for SS Mary and Ambrose, Egbaston. By 1914 Bunce's style was distinctly old-fashioned and she herself nearing 60. She continued painting until her death, however, allocating money in her will for the completion of her current picture, of the patronal saint for St Alban's Cathedral, Saskatoon, Canada; this forms the third panel of an altar triptych.

Bunce's church decoration may be compared with that of Phoebe Traquair (q.v.) in Scotland in its use of half-stylised sacred figures whose aurcoles glow in golden rows through the crepuscular setting. Her easel work, while not innovative, is stronger, larger and more varied than previously believed. Her class position, religious faith and private income prevented her from seeking public recognition as an artist, although her exhibition schedule and church work show that she painted for public rather than private consumption. Her career is representative of many in her generation with talent and application who were enabled to pursue professional training by the widening opportunities offered to British women from the 1870s onwards, in particular the municipal art schools and exhibition societies, but who failed to join the fully professional ranks and whose work has languished in obscurity for most of the 20th century. To date, her work has received little critical attention, although individual pictures are often chosen for decorative purposes.

JAN MARSH

Butler, Arlene H. *see* Wilke

Butler, Lady

British painter, 1846–1933

Born Elizabeth Southerden Thompson in Lausanne, Switzerland, 3 November 1846. Brought up with her sister

Alice (the poet Alice Meynell) in England and various other European countries. Studied privately under William Standish in London, then attended the Female School of Art, South Kensington, 1861–3 and 1866–70; independent study in Italy, 1869–70. Exhibited widely from 1867. Became nationally famous after *Calling the Roll after an Engagement, Crimea* was bought by Queen Victoria, 1874. Converted to Catholicism with her mother and sister, 1873. Married Irish Catholic Major William Butler (later General Sir William Butler GCB, KCB), 1877; three sons, three daughters; first surviving child born 1879; became Lady Butler when husband knighted, 1886; he died 1910. Travelled in Europe, 1878; subsequently resided where her husband's regiment was stationed: Devonport, 1881–4; Egypt, 1885, 1890–91 and 1892; Brittany, 1886–8; Aldershot, 1893–5; South Africa, 1899, and elsewhere; acquired home at Delgany, Co. Wicklow, Ireland, 1888; returned to Britain, 1901; moved to Bansha Castle, Co. Tipperary, on Butler's retirement in 1905; to Gormanston Castle, Co. Meath, 1922. Proposed for election to the Royal Academy, 1879; narrowly defeated. Painted for war charities during World War I. Died at Gormanston Castle, 2 October 1933.

Principal Exhibitions

Dudley Gallery, London: 1867, 1871–4 (watercolour); 1868, 1872–3 (oil); 1872, 1874 (black and white)
Society of Female (later Lady) Artists, London: 1867–9, 1871–5, 1877
Royal Academy, London: occasionally 1873–1905
New Society of Painters in Watercolours, London: 1874–7
Fine Art Society, London: 1877 (individual)
Exposition Universelle, Paris: 1878
Egyptian Hall, Piccadilly, London: 1881 (individual)
Royal Hibernian Academy, Dublin: 1892, 1899, 1929–30
Paris Salon: 1894
New Gallery, London: 1896
Leicester Galleries, London: 1912, 1915, 1917, 1919 (all individual)

Selected Writings

Letters from the Holy Land, London: A. & C. Black, 1903
From Sketch-Book and Diary, London: A. & C. Black, 1909
An Autobiography, London: Constable, 1922; Boston: Houghton Mifflin, 1923

Bibliography

John Oldcastle, "Our living artists: Elizabeth Butler (née Thompson)", *Magazine of Art*, ii, 1879, pp.257–62
Wilfrid Meynell, "The life and work of Lady Butler", *Art Annual*, xviii, 1898, pp.1–31
Chronique des Arts, no.39, 10 December 1898, pp.355–6
The Times, 4 October 1933 (obituary)
Great Victorian Pictures: Their Paths to Fame, exh. cat., Arts Council of Great Britain, London, 1978
Mathew Paul Lalumia, "Lady Elizabeth Thompson Butler in the 1870s", *Woman's Art Journal*, iv/1, 1983, pp.9–14
Charlotte Yeldham, *Women Artists in Nineteenth-Century France and England*, 2 vols, New York: Garland, 1984
Joan Hichberger, *Military Themes in British Painting, 1815–1914*, PhD dissertation, University of London, 1985
Pamela Gerrish Nunn, *Canvassing: Recollections by Six Victorian Women Artists*, London: Camden Press, 1986
Lady Butler, Battle Artist, 1846–1933, exh. cat., National Army Museum, London, 1987
Paul Usherwood, "Elizabeth Thompson Butler: The consequences of marriage", *Woman's Art Journal*, ix/1, 1988, pp.30–34
——, "Elizabeth Thompson Butler: A case of tokenism", *Woman's Art Journal*, xi/2, 1990–91, pp.14–18
Wendy Slatkin, *The Voices of Women Artists*, Englewood Cliffs, NJ: Prentice Hall, 1993

Butler: *The Roll Call: Calling the Roll after an Engagement, Crimea*, 1874; oil on canvas; Royal Collection © Her Majesty Queen Elizabeth II

Elizabeth Thompson, later Lady Butler, was by the end of the 19th century the most famous woman artist in Britain. She achieved such visibility because she was the first known woman battle painter. Previously, women artists had tended to work in genres considered feminine and/or in which the female figure and experience provided the main theme. In addition, Butler worked on a large scale, which was still not usual for women painters. In a period in which nationalism became imperialism, she drew patriotic support although she claimed to be critical of some aspects of the military establishment and army life.

From her first exhibition appearances, Elizabeth Thompson showed a preference for military subject matter and, though she vowed in 1876 to abjure such themes in favour of religious topics, this was a specialism to which she adhered throughout her career. Her first commission, *Calling the Roll after an Engagement, Crimea*, familiarly known as *The Roll Call* (1874; see illustration), was an overnight success and one of the most popular paintings in the history of the Royal Academy exhibitions. It set the tone for all her major works: a medium-large canvas showing numerous less-than-life-size figures of rank-and-file soldiers in an exterior setting on or near the battlefield. Her emphasis on the soldier rather than the officer was not only new in the genre, but coincided with the Cardwell Reforms of the British Army, begun in 1870. The artist's command of her subject was marvelled at, the sentiment of her scene approved and her technical excellence admired. While Queen Victoria was an immediate admirer, feminists could also hold up Thompson as an example of what women could achieve in fine art. Her gallery-going public was augmented by the engraving of her annual exhibits, which brought the artist considerable copyright fees, greater than any woman artist before her had been able to command.

Though a keen observer from her student days, Butler had leaned considerably on the example of 19th-century French battle painting for her early work. Marrying a military man in 1877, she was able to deepen her observation of army psychology, battle locations and historical details. Her realism was tempered with an eye for the dramatic and the sentimental that gave her best works, such as *Balaclava* (1876; Manchester City Art Galleries) and *Scotland for Ever!* (1880–81; Leeds City Art Gallery), formal impact and emotional conviction. These works were complimented simultaneously for being equal to those of a man and for displaying a womanly sensibility. This perceived combination of masculine excellences and feminine virtues assured her sales and success with a wide range of viewers until the early 1880s. For nearly a decade she produced annual military dramas for the Academy or for solo exhibition with the Fine Art Society: *Quatre Bras* (1875; National Gallery of Victoria, Melbourne), *Balaclava* (1876), *Return from Inkerman* (1877; Ferens Art Gallery, Hull), *Remnants of an Army* (1879; Tate Gallery, London), *Scotland for Ever!* (1880–81), *Defence of Rorke's Drift* (1880–81; Royal Collection), *Floreat Etona!* (1882; private collection, Britain, repr. London 1987, pl.9). The impression she made with her set-piece celebrations of British soldiery was such that her admirers within the Academy put her up for election to membership of that body in 1879, even though women were not officially eligible.

By the 1880s Butler was working in conscious opposition to the aesthetic, anti-academic art that had grown up at the Grosvenor Gallery, representing what she believed were the virtues of realism and moral purpose in art. *Scotland for Ever!* was meant as a deliberate counter to a trend that she despised, but in which she perhaps foresaw the displacement of her own aesthetic. Although in 1883 the writer John Ruskin declared Butler to have converted him, with *The Roll Call* and *Quatre Bras*, to the belief that women could paint, her following waned in this decade, as French battle painters such as Alphonse de Neuville were taken up by her erstwhile audience and her own work declined technically, becoming predictable and florid. The demands of Butler's married life undermined her earlier absorption in the London art world, removing her to the provinces and various foreign outposts and diffusing her concentration, energy and application. It can be supposed that her husband's idiosyncratically liberal views on military matters, which brought him into conflict with the authorities, also confused her interpretation of her subject matter. Her rare attempts to broaden her base, such as *To the Front: French Cavalry Leaving a Breton City on the Declaration of War* (1889; private collection, *ibid.*, pl.11) and *Evicted* (1890; University College Dublin), the only major works in which she included female characters, were not well received.

Through the 1890s Butler concentrated on producing paintings and watercolours of the Napoleonic Wars. The political climate brought her renewed commercial success with these works, though critics attended less and less to her exhibits. Several British male artists had by this time established themselves in battle painting, and were seen to perform better in this genre, which men would always claim as essentially theirs. This became emphatically the case during World War I, which Butler commemorated in watercolours, mostly exhibited in solo shows at the Leicester Galleries, such as her *Waterloo Centenary* exhibition in 1915 and *Some Records of the World War* in 1919. Butler lived in Ireland after the war's end, and by her death in 1933 she had become a figure of the past.

PAMELA GERRISH NUNN

C

Caffi, Margherita

Italian painter, c.1650–1710

Born c.1650, probably in Milan. Daughter of Francesco Volò, a still-life painter active in Milan, and his wife Veronica. Married Ludovico Caffi, also a still-life painter, in Cremona, 1668; at least four children. Settled in Piacenza, 1670. Died in Milan aged 60, 20 September 1710.

Bibliography

G.B. Carboni, *Le pitture e sculture di Brescia che sono esposte al pubblico con un'appendice de alcune private gallerie*, ed. Luigi Chizzola, Brescia, 1760

Giovan Battista Zaist, *Notizie istoriche de' pittori, scultori ed architetti cremonesi, con un appendice d'altre notizie, il discorso di Alessandro Lamo intorno alla scoltura, e pittura ...* (1584), 2 vols, Cremona, 1774; reprinted Cremona, 1975 (vol.ii, p.124)

Luigi Malvezzi, *Le glorie dell'arte Lombarda, ossia illustrazione storica delle più belle opere che produssero i lombardi in pittura, scultura ed architettura dal 1590 al 1850*, Milan, 1882

G. De Logu, *Pittori minori Liguri, Lombardi, Piemontesi del seicento e del settecento*, Venice, 1931

Alfonso Emilio Pérez-Sánchez, *Pintura italiana del siglio XVII en España*, Madrid, 1965

A. Barigozzi Brini and G. Fiori, entry in *Dizionario biografico degli italiani*, xvi, Rome: Istituto dell'Enciclopedia Italiana, 1973

Gli ultimi Medici: Il tardo barocco a Firenze, 1670–1743/The Twilight of the Medici: Late Baroque Art in Florence, 1670–1743, exh. cat., Detroit Institute of Arts and Palazzo Pitti, Florence, 1974

Women Artists, 1550–1950, exh. cat., Los Angeles County Museum of Art, and elsewhere, 1976

Vittorio Caprara, "Nuovi documenti su Stefano Maria Legnani, 'Il Legnanino'", *Paragone*, xxxi/363, 1980, pp.94–104

Pintura española de Bodegónes y Floreros de 1600 a Goya, exh. cat., Prado, Madrid, 1983

Luigi Salerno, *La natura morta italiana, 1560–1805/Still Life Painting in Italy, 1560–1805*, Rome: Bozzi, 1984

Marco Bona Castellotti, *La pittura lombarda del '600*, Milan, 1985

J. Celani Casolo, entry in *Floralia: Florilegio dalla collezioni fiorentine del Sei-Settecento*, exh. cat., Palazzo Pitti, Florence, 1988, pp.107–11

A. Morandotti in *La natura morta in Italia*, ed. F. Zeri and Francesco Porzio, 2 vols, Milan: Electa, 1989

Facts concerning Margherita Caffi and her life are few. Until very recently the dates of her birth and death were unknown, but her death certificate has now been discovered in Piacenza showing that she died in Milan in 1710, aged 60 (Caprara 1980, p.104, note 52). Both public documents and old inventories state that she came from Milan and there are indeed pictures, particularly one signed and dated 1681 (private collection), where inscriptions also bear out that fact. There are also many pictures by her in collections not only in Milan but throughout Lombardy. The misreading and consequent misinterpretation of certain signed and inscribed paintings has in part confused her place of origin by implying that she came from Vicenza, but it now seems more likely that the inscriptions "VICENCINA" and "VINCENCINA" that are appended to her signature on several known paintings (Morandotti 1989, pls 294, 298–9 and p.247; Brini and Fiori 1973, p.271) should be seen as some allusion or reference to Caffi's probable apprenticeship in the workshop of Vincenzo Volò, to whom she was related through her father Francesco Volò. That workshop was probably then taken over by the still-life painter Giuseppe Vicenzino who had adopted the name "Vicenzino" to associate himself professionally with his and Caffi's former master Vincenzo Volò.

By 1668 Margherita was in Cremona where she married the still-life painter Ludovico Caffi, but in 1670 they were both banished from the city and went instead to Piacenza. Over the next 12 years her name appears regularly there in documents. Margherita clearly did not remain in Piacenza all the time, as the numerous paintings found in old collections throughout the region and elsewhere (e.g. a group of paintings originally made for the Medici villa at Poggio a Caiano and now divided between the Pitti and Uffizi galleries in Florence) testify.

Caffi's compositions are crowded with numerous elements, often in receding planes of activity. They are elegant, exuberant and intensely decorative. Caffi employed a generous application of paint with successive layers of glazes, akin to the Roman tradition of still-life painting of which Mario Nuzzi, the most influential and famous flower painter of 17th-century Italy, was the chief exponent. While it appears that Caffi's compositions are casual and unforced, this effect is in fact achieved by very careful preparation and planning of the compositional schemes, where the flowers invariably appear naturally and without vases or other supports. Her vibrant brush strokes override the traditional discipline of *disegno*, and this is why she was long considered to be of the Venetian school or tradition, until recent archival research showed it to be otherwise. The mistaken belief that she came from Vicenza, itself in the Veneto, only reinforced this erroneous notion. This idea of a Venetian origin or activity was encouraged, too, by the fact that the work of Margherita's female contemporary Elizabetta Marchioni, who came from Rovigo in the Veneto, is not so very different in technique from Caffi, and uses similar compositional devices.

Most of Caffi's paintings are in private collections, but there are examples in the Museo Civico, Cremona; Galleria Palatina, Florence; and in Madrid at the Real Academia de San Fernando, the Fundación Santa Marca and Palacio Real.

JOHN SOMERVILLE

Cahun, Claude

French photographer, mixed-media artist and writer, 1894–1954

Born Lucy Schwob in Nantes, 25 October 1894, into a Jewish intellectual family; daughter of Maurice Schwob, publisher of the newspaper *Le Phare de la Loire*, and niece of Symbolist writer Marcel Schwob. Distanced herself from her famous family by adopting the sexually ambiguous name Claude Cahun, 1918; published under this name in *Mercure de France*, reporting on the trial of Oscar Wilde. Moved from Nantes to Paris with stepsister and lifelong lover Suzanne Malherbe, also an artist. Befriended writer-publishers Adrienne Monnier and Sylvia Beach, and poet-artists Robert Desnos, Henri Michaux and Pierre Morhange; wrote for a variety of journals, including *Philosophies*, *Disque Vert* and the avant-garde homosexual review, *L'Amitié*. Joined Association des Ecrivains et Artistes Révolutionnaires (AEAR), 1932; left the following year, disenchanted with its close affiliation to the French Communist Party (PCF) and hostility to any aesthetic other than social realism. Joined anti-fascist Contre-Attaque group founded by Georges Bataille and André Breton, 1934. Left Paris permanently by 1938, moving to the Schwob family summer retreat on Jersey, Channel Islands. Active in the Resistance during the Nazi occupation; arrested and condemned to death, 1944; spared with the island's liberation, 1945; never recovered from incarceration. Continued to live in Jersey with Malherbe. Visited Paris, 1953. Died in Jersey, 8 December 1954.

Principal Exhibitions

Galerie Charles Ratton, Paris: 1936 (*Exposition surréaliste d'objets*)

Selected Writings

"La Salomé d'Oscar Wilde: Le procès Billing et les 47.000 pervertis du Livre noir", *Mercure de France*, no.481, 1 July 1918
"Heroïnes", *Mercure de France*, no.639, February 1925
Aveux non avenus, Paris: Carrefour, 1930
"Réponse à l'enquête: 'Pour qui écrivez-vous?'", *Commune*, no.4, December 1933
Les Paris sont ouverts, 1934 (tract)
"Prenez garde aux objets domestiques", *Cahiers d'Art*, i, ii, 1936

Bibliography

Edouard Jaguer, *Les Mystères de la chambre noire: Le Surréalisme et la photographie*, Paris: Flammarion, 1982

L'Amour Fou: Photography and Surrealism, exh. cat., Corcoran Gallery of Art, Washington, DC, and elsewhere, 1985
Nanda van den Berg, *Claude Cahun*, doctoral dissertation, Moderne Kunst, Utrecht, 1987
Sidra Stich, ed., *Anxious Visions*, New York: Abbeville, 1990
Paris des années 30: Le Surréalisme et le livre, exh. cat., Galerie Zabriskie, Paris, and elsewhere, 1991
François Leperlier, "Dossier Claude Cahun", *Pleine Marge*, no.14, December 1991
——, *Claude Cahun: L'Ecart et la métamorphose*, Paris: Michel Place, 1992
Honor Lasalle and Abigail Solomon-Godeau, "Surrealist confession: Claude Cahun's photomontages", *Afterimage*, xix, March 1992
Therese Lichtenstein, "A mutable mirror: Claude Cahun", *Artforum*, xxx, April 1992, pp.64–7
Mise en scène, exh. cat., Institute of Contemporary Arts, London, 1994
Le Rêve d'une ville: Nantes et le surréalisme, exh. cat., Musée des Beaux-Arts and Bibliothéque Municipale, Nantes, 1994
Claude Cahun photographe, exh. cat., Musée d'Art Moderne de la Ville de Paris, 1995 (includes extensive bibliography and catalogue raisonné)
François Leperlier, *Claude Cahun, 1894–1954*, Paris: Michel Place, 1995

Issues of gender and identity troubles may be taken to frame the work of the writer/artist/photographer Claude Cahun. Active in the prominent literary and artistic circles in Paris between the two world wars, Cahun produced a wide range of Surrealist-inspired objects, collages, photographs and writings that explored gender and identity by focusing on her own image and autobiography. Ironically, at the onset of World War II, Cahun fell into complete obscurity. Indeed, her identity became so uncertain that for a time it was unclear whether she was male or female; her works were attributed to an anonymous artist; and the circumstances of her life were essentially unknown. It is, then, a further irony that the first extensive scholarly work on Cahun should be a biography (Leperlier 1992), for if Cahun's entire oeuvre was devoted to investigating the very notion of a stable subject position through her own autobiographical inquiry, Leperlier – drawing on an interesting array of unpublished letters, manuscripts and documents – sought to fix the identity of Claude Cahun by explaining her through those very ambiguities she took up as her own critical project.

As early as 1919 Cahun consciously spurned conventions of femininity by shaving her head, and then took to dyeing in pink or green the crewcut that was sometimes allowed to sprout; she stained her skin and wore outlandish batiked, vaguely orientalised clothing. The Surrealist Marcel Jean noted in his memoirs that Cahun's appearance – "her face like that of a small bird of prey" – with her companion Malherbe at her side at the Café Cyrano was enough to drive André Breton into temporary exile, forcing him to give up his favourite café and regular meeting place.

The uneasy tension that Cahun inspired was as much cultural as it was personal, and linked to a more general anxiety around identity itself. In this respect, Cahun's work engages current feminist concerns as well as providing an opportunity to examine the ways in which her own avant-garde aspirations converge and intersect with contemporary debates around sexuality and identity.

Cahun: *Self-Portrait (Blue-Beard's Wife: Double Portrait),* 1929; black-and-white photograph; private collection, Musée des Beaux-Arts, Nantes

The strength and difficulty of Cahun's work are still sensed in her self-portraits from this period. For example, in a photograph appearing in an issue of Ribemont-Dessaigne's *Bifur* in 1930, Cahun depicts herself in stark profile, her expression cold, almost menacing; harsh lighting underscores her severe, unadorned appearance, stripped of any mediating "props" – including hair – that might soften her image. This portrait aggressively militates against the "normative ideals" of femininity and, more broadly, exposes the viewer's expectations of intelligible identity as they are grounded, specifically, in gender. Cahun made it her business to keep the question "So who is this, anyway?" constantly in play by exposing her "self" as nothing but a series of constructions.

Cahun takes her own subjectivity as the means of revealing the very impossibility of fixing the self: her texts and images speak to its dissolution, fragmentation and transformations, and biography itself becomes suspect, one more mask among many. Cahun's writings suggest that without a mask there can be no identity – not even human form. Or, alternatively, the self is nothing but masks, a point reiterated in a photo-montage in *Aveux non avenus* where we see a series of faces – all Cahun's – in various guises, springing from a single neck and framed by

the handwritten words: "Under this mask, another mask. I will never finish removing all these faces". The succession of painted eyes and lips underscores the artifice and versatility of a single face, becoming a series of masks that in and of themselves obscure their own "identities": male here, female there, and elsewhere impossible to determine. In any case, revealing is never to be confused with knowing: Cahun insisted that the mystery of the masks remain intact.

Cahun's constantly shifting and transforming self sought to make gender itself ambiguous. Her work revels in the uncertainties afforded by the fluidity of "womanliness"; it was precisely through this indistinct subject-position that the coherence of the "self" was most vulnerable, and therein lay the revolutionary potential of subjectivity itself. Cahun's constructed, shifting identities were but a prelude to the radical dissolution of the individual subjectivity itself – a desire to dissolve the body, to become nothing but a heartbeat. To reach Cahun's imaginary centre, recognisable features are transformed, effaced, producing a subjectivity that turns on its own ambiguities and then, through these, attempts to transcend its own limits. The viewer, too, is asked to engage in this process: a striking self-portrait from the late 1920s underscores Cahun's sexual ambiguity, forcing the viewer to consider the elements comprising gender and identity through an ostensibly transparent and revealing means – the photographed self-portrait. Cahun's expression conveys a certainty of purpose, as determined as her commitment to obscure her own identity. She appears androgynous, her features made artificial with the black liner outlining an invented hairline, a single eyebrow or the tinted flesh of her arms. And beyond the confusion provoked in the viewer in her attempts to "place" Cahun, the image suggests that the viewer herself is implicated in the uncertainties of identity, something that is reinforced by the reflective orb she holds. Appearing as a convex mirror, the sphere reveals obscure light and shadows, rather than a clear reflection, which furthers the sense of disorientation. And even where Cahun depicts herself in particularly gendered roles (e.g. the dandy, the sailor, the debutante), the certainties on which we claim knowledge of gender and sexuality are destabilised. Thus, when she appears in feminine guise – as, for example, in a self-portrait from the early 1930s, where her bared shoulders evoke vulnerability, her expression is tentative and her eyes averted – she counters these elements with the jarring effect of her distorted and shaved head. The conventional feminine pose is transformed by her alien appearance, as though this figure could not be of this world.

In what might seem paradoxical, the individual became the site on which a kind of "collectivity" was to be founded – but only through a radical re-conceptualisation, a being deconstructed through its own self-scrutiny. Not alone in this desire to "dematerialise" the limits of the self, Cahun joined other contemporary leftist intellectuals who sought alternatives to the straightforward political agitation advocated by the Communist Party. For them, a potential space of disruption was the subjective transcending its own bounds; in a society where the coherent subject was central to social stability – its structure, moral codes, rules – a radical re-conceptualisation of the self promised fundamental and profound change. To this end, Cahun began exploring the radical possibilities inherent in material objects and the viewer's relationship to them, an interest she shared with the Surrealists. Exhibiting with them in 1936, Cahun included two objects that sought to create disjunctures through juxtapositions of "found objects" and, on occasion, the addition of texts. Her *Un air de famille* – known only through photographs – consisted of a doll's bed filled with a variety of miniature toys and what appear to be matchbooks, enclosed within a veil. A cryptic message appears on a small sign tacked on to a mock bedpost, reading "dANGEr – *manger* – m Ange z – menge – je mens – mange – gé manje". The words, taken in their entirety, make no sense, although the fragments are suggestive: danger, angel, to eat, my angel, I am lying, etc. The impulse is to make sense of these words through associations with the objects, thereby creating narrative links that make the objects more comprehensible. And yet this is precisely what Cahun's objects refuse. The space of safety and comfort is transformed into a potentially menacing and dangerous one, but the dangers and lies that the text indicates are elusive and unknown. Here the process of viewing parallels that of observing Cahun's self-portraits: one is forced to examine one's own conceptions against the image presented, a comparison that is inevitably disrupted. Cut loose from the literary, narrative elements that struggle to make sense of the world, Cahun's objects emphasise the disparate and disjunctive. Reinforcing this sense of disorder is Cahun's *Qui ne craint pas le grand méchant loup remet la barque sur sa quille et vogue à la dérive*, a variation on her lost *Souris valseuses* from the exhibition of 1936. Nestled in the jaws of an unidentified animal, small unrelated toys are crammed into the skeletal "boat": a tiny doll, a small model church, a light bulb, a pacifier and a menacing humming bird comprise a modern variant of the nonsensical ship of fools. At the base of the bones a caterpillar emerges from its cocoon, perhaps reappearing as the butterfly at the bow of the "ship", about to fly away. Although this aspect of escape and rebirth verges on sentimental cliché, it is offset by the sinister effect produced through the chaotic jumble of toys, many perched precariously on the skeletal jaws. The boat appears ominous rather than whimsical, and the seemingly childlike world is transformed into a space of potential nightmare. The mirror on which the object is placed, encircled with peacock feathers suggestive of non-seeing eyes, reinforces the impression that the sense of the object eludes the viewer, revealing nothing but the surface of appearance.

The ways in which Cahun's contemporary "external" world impinged on her personal experience were no doubt most sizeable: as a woman, as a lesbian, as a Jew, her own identity was particularly circumscribed by existing social labels and stereotypes. Yet while these categories imposed constraints, the fact that they were themselves somewhat unstable and ambiguous allowed Cahun to imagine a radically re-configured identity, grounded not only in her experience as a woman but as a lesbian as well: if the "experts" were baffled in their attempts to define "woman", then the gay woman was an even more vexing issue. Being a lesbian – separate from the "norms" of heterosexuality – enabled Cahun to produce work that so insistently turned on gender ambiguities. In this sense, although Cahun never directly addressed her personal sexuality, her own experience in this ambiguous space as a lesbian was very much an impetus for her artistic production. Furthermore, the fact that lesbian women were a prominent presence in Paris (some of the most fashionable literary circles of the inter-war period

were made up of "notorious" lesbians) provided both a community and an avenue for public expression. Yet, at the same time, this heightened visibility invited what Michel Foucault termed "the policing of sex". If lesbians were able finally to come out of the closet, this also occasioned an opportunity to categorise, study and then control them further. The seemingly permissive culture was quick to reassert control with rising unemployment, declining birth rate and war on the horizon. By the early 1930s the period of cultural flexibility seemed to be coming to a close, and Cahun herself produced far fewer of her enigmatic self-portraits, turning instead to the production of objects.

To shift from the confines of the individual into a space that may be described only through negation – a world without barriers, where identity itself becomes impossible to distinguish – could this exist in any space other than the imaginary? For Cahun, the point was not to imagine what this might "look like" as a reality, but simply to indicate its possibilities, as she clarified in her texts on writing as revolutionary practice. Her access to this revolutionary space was made through the instabilities embodied in her own identity configured around gender and sexuality; she believed that these might lead to a radical re-thinking of the subject, beyond regulatory constraints of gender.

In an age in which identification with a particular group or cause too often replaces revolutionary political and radical thought, Cahun's example is still instructive, encouraging us to imagine a different kind of world in which identity does not fix and freeze the individual, but rather radically transforms the culture that would define her or him.

LAURIE J. MONAHAN

Cameron, Julia Margaret
British photographer, 1815–1879

Born Julia Margaret Pattle in Calcutta, India, 11 June 1815, to James Pattle, an East India Company official, and Adeline de l'Etang. Educated in Europe, living with her maternal grandmother in Versailles; returned to Calcutta, 1834. Married Charles Hay Cameron, jurist and member of the Supreme Council of India, 1838; several children. Returned to England on husband's retirement in 1848, settling in Tunbridge Wells, Kent, before moving to Surrey, 1850; spent time on the Isle of Wight from 1860. Given first camera by her daughter, 1863. Elected member of the Photographic Societies of London and Scotland, 1864. Moved with husband to family plantation in Ceylon, 1875; visited England briefly, 1878. Died in Ceylon, 26 January 1879.

Principal Exhibitions

Individual
French Gallery, Pall Mall, London: 1865
Colnaghi's Gallery, London: 1865
German Gallery, London: 1868
9 Conduit Street, London: 1873

Group
Photographic Society of London: from 1864

Berlin International Photographic Exhibition: 1865 (bronze medal),
1866 (gold medal)
International Exhibition, Dublin: 1865 (honourable mention)
Exposition Universelle, Paris: 1867 (honourable mention)
Photography Exhibition, Groningen, Netherlands: 1869 (bronze
medal)
International Exhibition, London: 1871, 1872, 1873
Weltausstellung, Vienna: 1873 (medal)
Centennial Exposition, Philadelphia: 1876 (medal)

Bibliography

Coventry Patmore, "Mrs Cameron's photographs", *Macmillan's
Magazine*, xiii, January 1866, pp.230–31
Peter Henry Emerson, "Mrs Cameron", *Sun Artists*, no.5, 1890,
pp.33–43
Frederick H. Evans, "Exhibition of photographs of Julia Margaret
Cameron", *Amateur Photographer*, xl, 21 July 1904, pp.43–4
Alvin Langdon Coburn, "The old masters of photography", *The
Century*, xc, 1915, pp.909–20
Una Taylor, *Guests and Memories: Annals of a Seaside Villa*,
London: Oxford University Press, 1924
Victorian Photographs of Famous Men and Fair Women, London:
Leonard and Virginia Woolf, and New York: Harcourt Brace,
1926; revised editon, ed. Tristram Powell, London: Hogarth Press,
1973
Brian Hill, *Julia Margaret Cameron: A Victorian Family Portrait*,
London: Owen, and New York: St Martin's Press, 1973
Charles W. Millard, "Julia Margaret Cameron and Tennyson's *Idylls
of the King*", *Harvard Library Bulletin*, xxi, 1973, pp.187–201
Mrs Cameron's Photographs from the Life, exh. cat., Stanford
University Museum of Art, CA, 1974
Colin Ford, *The Cameron Collection: An Album of Photographs
Presented to Sir John Herschel*, Wokingham and New York: Van
Nostrand Reinhold, 1975
Helmut Gernsheim, *Julia Margaret Cameron: Her Life and
Photographic Work*, 2nd edition, London: Gordon Fraser, and
Millerton, NY: Aperture, 1975
Graham Ovenden, ed., *A Victorian Album: Julia Margaret Cameron
and Her Circle*, London: Secker and Warburg, and New York: Da
Capo Press, 1975
Margaret Harker, *Julia Margaret Cameron*, London: Collins, 1983
Golden Age of British Photography, exh. cat., Victoria and Albert
Museum, London, and elsewhere, 1984
Mike Weaver, *Julia Margaret Cameron, 1815–1879*, Boston: Little
Brown, and London: Herbert Press, 1984 (expanded Italian
edition, Rome, 1985)
Cameron: Her Work and Career, exh. cat., International Museum of
Photography at George Eastman House, Rochester, NY, and else-
where, 1986
Amanda Hopkinson, *Julia Margaret Cameron*, London: Virago, 1986
Whisper of the Muse: The Overstone Album and Other Photographs,
exh. cat., J. Paul Getty Museum, Malibu, CA, 1986
Jan Marsh and Pamela Gerrish Nunn, *Women Artists and the Pre-
Raphaelite Movement*, London: Virago, 1989
A. N. Wilson, *Eminent Victorians*, London: BBC Books, 1989; New
York: Norton, 1990
Whisper of the Muse: The World of Julia Margaret Cameron, exh.
cat., Royal Photographic Society, London, 1990
Pam Roberts, "Julia Margaret Cameron: A triumph over criticism",
The Portrait in Photography, ed. Graham Clarke, London:
Reaktion, and Seattle: University of Washington Press, 1992,
pp.47–70
For My Best Beloved Sister, Mia: An Album of Photographs, exh.
cat., University of New Mexico Art Museum, Albuquerque, 1994
Carol Armstrong, "Cupid's pencil of light: Julia Margaret Cameron
and the maternalization of photography", *October*, no.76, Spring
1996, pp.115–41
*In Focus: Julia Margaret Cameron: Photographs from the J. Paul
Getty Museum*, Getty Trust Publications, 1996

Cameron: *Ellen Terry*, *c*.1864; carbon print; diameter 24 cm.;
Royal Photographic Society, Bath

Julia Margaret Cameron's life, and what we would now call
her career, was set firmly in the tradition of High Victorian
amateurism that in her period transformed the practices of
both the sciences and the arts. She was an amateur in two
senses: first, she had no professional training, was an autodidact, and did not support herself or others in her family by
her "professional" activity as a photographer; second, in the
love, perhaps even obsession, she had for the practice of
photography. She has left behind a legacy of influential
portraits of her peers – the mandarins of Empire and of
government, writers, scholars, politicians, historians and poets.
To a very real extent, her work has defined for us what we take
to be the appearance of the grandees of Victorian Britain, while
other Victorian attitudes are presented with careful artifice in
what are now her period pieces of exquisitely contrived set
tableaux – "art" photographs in which both servants and the
eminent were pressed into hard-held poses by the force of her
formidable will.

Cameron was born in Calcutta, her father, James Pattle, a
member of the Bengal civil service, the family an integral and
integrated part of the imperial ruling classes of the British
Empire; her six sisters also married well, and of their seven
husbands, a jurist, a general, an aristocrat, a landowner among
them, the majority have been commemorated in the *Dictionary
of National Biography*, as has Mrs Cameron herself. Julia was
said not to be as beautiful as her half-dozen sisters; at 22 she
married the very rich and distinguished 45-year-old Charles
Hay Cameron who owned vast plantations in Ceylon, was a
member of the Council of India, and an eminent jurist who
codified the Indian legal system. Plain, plump, overwhelmingly
charming and determined, Julia was for a while the leading
British hostess in India, by virtue of her husband's position and
her own social energy.

Ten years after the marriage the Camerons came to live in England, finally settling at Freshwater on the Isle of Wight. Her family connections provided a strikingly artistic and intellectual milieu; her sister was married to Thoby Prinsep and the Prinseps' salon at Little Holland House in London in the 1840s included the Pre-Raphaelites, while the artist in residence was G.F. Watts, husband of the actress Ellen Terry. Watts painted Julia Margaret Cameron, as well as Terry (*Choosing*), while Mrs Cameron photographed Terry (*Alithea*). The interchanges could be complex: Cameron translated Burger's romantic poem *Leonore*, which was published with illustrations by Daniel Maclise; Maclise also illustrated Tennyson, and his illustration for the dying King Arthur influenced Cameron's photograph the *Passing of Arthur*; in 1874 Cameron made a set of photographs as illustrations for Tennyson's *Idylls of the King* and other poems, at the poet's request. Cameron was generally acknowledged as benevolent, even overwhelmingly so; with unusual energy, enthusiasm and high spirits that were apparently unquenchable, she could also be almost impossibly high-handed. Her very excesses became virtues when faced with the technical complexities of the mechanics of early portrait photography.

Cameron began serious photography in her fiftieth year, her eventful life three-quarters over – her memorable achievement must give hope to all late starters. It was the present of a big camera from her daughter that spurred her interest and energy in this new direction. She transformed an old glazed hen-house on the Cameron property into her studio – the coalhouse was the darkroom – and learned by hard hours of trial and error; she coerced and bullied her sitters. Servants, locals and relatives posed for illustrative tableaux, related to the subject pictures so beloved of the Victorians, and celebrity friends and acquaintances were not only integrated into these set pieces but were persuaded to sit for their individual portraits. She was successful, professionally, in her own life; she had a solo exhibition of her photographs at the art dealer, Colnaghi's, in London in 1865, and the gallery suggests that it was Colnaghi's publications of prints after the old masters that influenced Mrs Cameron's art photography.

A great deal of her work has survived. Of about 3000 images, the photographic historian Helmut Gernsheim estimated that some 60 are outstanding, milestones in Victorian portraiture. There are various significant accounts of her character, personality and working methods – for this we must thank her huge acquaintanceship and network of friends and relations, although surprisingly there is no substantial late 20th-century biography of her. A vivid, even picturesque if somewhat inaccurate account of Cameron was published in 1926 with a selection of her photographs (*Victorian Photographs of Famous Men and Fair Women*) by Virginia Woolf, Cameron's great-niece, accompanied by a fine appreciation of her photography by the Bloomsbury critic, curator and painter Roger Fry. From Woolf we learn of Cameron's indefatigable letter writing (to one friend, Sir Henry Taylor, she wrote every day), her half-realised ambitions to write fiction – she certainly specialised in her "art" photography in the portrayal of visual fiction – and her immense generosity. Taylor observed that Cameron had a great genius, and that "she lives upon superlatives as upon her daily bread".

Perhaps her enthusiasm and energy were excessive, but she could and did exercise extraordinary patience; the elaborate chemical processes of the wet collodion process, which required not only lengthy sittings but the immediate development of the image on a wet glass plate – probably a large surface, 12×15 inches (30×38 cm.) – were handled by Cameron with uncustomary grace. She worked "fruitlessly but not hopelessly", as she said herself of her early experiments.

Her portraits were among the first photographs to challenge the painted image. According to Tennyson, her photographs of him destroyed his anonymity. Tennyson brought the American poet Longfellow to sit for Cameron, telling him that he would have to obey the imperious artist. Thomas Carlyle, who thought his photographic image "terrifically ugly and woebegone", Charles Darwin, the classical scholar Benjamin Jowett, Robert Browning, the painters Holman Hunt and G.F. Watts, and the actress Ellen Terry (see illustration) were among her sitters. The portraits of men are usually comparatively straightforward. The bulk of her work was not composed of portraiture, however, but of illustrations, to Tennyson's poetry, to Shakespeare and to allegorical scenes of her own devising, with women and girls posing as characters and heroines. Her heroes were usually middle-aged even elderly great men, typically posed so that their hair acted as a kind of aureole. Her compositions were heavily influenced by the biblical and historical scenes of the Pre-Raphaelite artists, and other relatively contemporary painters, as well as the old masters. For example, Sir Joshua Reynolds's portrait of *Mrs Siddons as the Tragic Muse* was a direct precursor of Cameron's *Hark, Hark*. But there was also a Zeitgeist at work: Cameron's own *Call, I Follow, I Follow, Let Me Die* pre-dates Dante Gabriel Rossetti's *Beata Beatrix*.

Cameron's generosity, combined with the decline in revenue from Charles Cameron's estates in Ceylon, added to her husband's intense desire to revisit the East. In 1875, accompanied by their two coffins, in case Ceylon did not provide such necessities, they set sail; Cameron revisited England in the spring of 1878; seven months later, she was to die in the East, back in Ceylon. She had continued her photography in the East, photographing for instance *Marianne Thornton*, the indefatigable traveller (and E.M. Forster's aunt), whose paintings on glass of horticultural subjects are housed in a special museum at Kew. But her work in Ceylon did not match the quality of her work executed in England.

Julia Margaret Cameron's portraits of "Famous Men and Fair Women" demonstrated the powerful personalities of her selected subjects, and her own personality. Creatively turning disadvantage to advantage, the awkwardness, difficulty and long time-span of early photographic techniques, Cameron deployed technical imperfections into interesting evidence of character. She liked imperfection; she deliberately refused to refine her focus. It is this bravura, dramatic element in her portraiture that has lifted that aspect of her work beyond reportage.

MARINA VAIZEY

Canziani, Louisa *see* Starr

Capet, Gabrielle
French painter, 1761–1818

Born in Lyon, 6 September 1761; father a servant. Trained by Adélaïde Labille-Guiard (q.v.). Lived with Labille-Guiard (and with François-André Vincent after 1792) until Labille-Guiard's death in 1803, then with Vincent until his death in 1816. Recipient of honourable mention, Commission des Artistes, 1801. Died in Paris, 1 November 1818.

Principal Exhibitions

Exposition de la Jeunesse, Paris: 1781–5
Salon de la Correspondance, Paris: 1785, 1786
Paris Salon: 1791, 1795, 1798–1802, 1804, 1806, 1808, 1810, 1812, 1814

Bibliography

Arnauld Doria, *Gabrielle Capet*, Paris: Les Beaux-Arts, 1934

Anne-Marie Passez, *Adélaïde Labille-Guiard (1749–1803): Biographie et catalogue raisonné de son oeuvre*, Paris: Arts et Métiers Graphiques, 1973

Women Artists, 1550–1950, exh. cat., Los Angeles County Museum of Art, and elsewhere, 1976

Germaine Greer, *The Obstacle Race: The Fortunes of Women Painters and Their Work*, London: Secker and Warburg, and New York: Farrar Straus, 1979

Les Femmes au temps de la Révolution française/Vrouwen in de Franse Revolutie, exh. cat., Banque Bruxelles Lambert, Brussels, 1989

Gabrielle Capet was an artist who worked in pastel, watercolour and oil, executing mostly modest-sized portraits as well as miniatures. Only during the last years of her career did she venture into more ambitious projects, executing a large conversation piece in 1808 and trying history painting in 1814.

The circumstances that led this daughter of a servant from Lyon to Paris remain unknown, nor are we familiar with her early training. In Paris by 1781, she became a student of Adélaïde Labille-Guiard (q.v.) and at the age of 20 began exhibiting at the Exposition de la Jeunesse. The most remarkable of her early works is a *Self-Portrait* (private collection, Paris, repr. Doria 1934, pl.2), signed and dated 1784, which represents the artist equipped with brush and palette, staring out at her male sitter (situated where the spectator stands) while she works on his portrait on the easel at the left of the painting. Possibly as a result of this work, the *Journal de Paris* (no.170, 18 June 1784, p.733) signalled her as an artist "who, among the female virtuosos, has the surest touch and drawing". Capet's pose, her fine costume and hat with a curved brim that shades her forehead are indebted to Labille-Guiard's *Self-Portrait* (Metropolitan Museum of Art, New York), then in production, to be exhibited at the Salon of 1785. Capet herself figures in that work as one of Labille-Guiard's admiring students. By 1785 the reviewer for the *Mercure de France* (cxlix, 11 June 1785, p.85), finding Capet's works so skilful, thought that she had outgrown the Exposition de la Jeunesse. In that year, she also began exhibiting at Pahin de la Blancherie's Salon de la Correspondance.

During these early years Capet's sitters included a brigadier, the *Marquis de Vauborel* (untraced, repr. Doria 1934, p.70), the wife of the intendant of Fontainebleau, *Madame de Longrois* (Musée National du Château de Versailles, *ibid.*,

pl.5), and the superior-general of the Oratoire, the *Reverend Father Moisset* (untraced, *ibid.*, pl.50). When Labille-Guiard was commissioned by Louis XVI's aunts to paint their portraits in 1785–6, Capet must have accompanied her, for she too portrayed them. Her profile drawings of *Madame Adélaïde* and *Madame Victoire* were engraved by S.C. Miger (*ibid.*, pls. 49 and 50). She also painted a miniature of either Madame Elisabeth, Louis XVI's sister, or his daughter Marie-Thérèse, known as Madame Royale (Louvre, Paris, *ibid.*, pl. 22; see also Pierrette Jean-Richard, *Inventaire des miniatures sur ivoire conservées au Cabinet des dessins, Musée du Louvre et Musée d'Orsay*, Paris: Réunion des Musées Nationaux, 1994, no.81). Other royal portraits included a charming miniature of the *Dauphin* holding a wheelbarrow, probably done in 1792 (private collection, Paris, repr. Doria 1934, pl.20). In 1791 she completed a miniature of the *Princesse de Caraman-Chimay* (untraced), but such royalist patronage vanished in the year 1793.

When the Salons were thrown open to all in 1791, Capet exhibited a number of miniatures, praised for their truthfulness as well as their fresh colour (*ibid.*, p.73). Subsequent exhibited works would be equally lauded for their verisimilitude. In 1791 miniatures were all she had available, having had little time to execute oils and pastels, since she was studio assistant to Labille-Guiard, then overloaded with projects and commissions (*ibid.*, p.20). In exchange for that assistance, Capet was given room and board by Labille-Guiard. Economics were probably a factor in Capet's focus on miniatures, providing her with an income she might otherwise not have received. But she was extremely talented in this area and justly won critical acclaim. In 1801, for instance, Capet exhibited two large miniatures, one of her mother (untraced), the other, inspired by Labille-Guiard's portrait of *Pajou* (repr. Passez 1973, p.280 and pl.XXVII), representing the *Sculptor Houdon Working on a Bust of Voltaire* (stolen from museum in Caen, repr. Doria 1934, pl.17). One critic, reporting on this Salon, wrote that Capet, together with Isabey, offered "models of perfection" in miniature (cited in *ibid.*, p 59). For these, the Commission des Artistes awarded her honourable mention (*Journal des Arts, des Sciences, et de Littérature*, no.170, 10 Frimaire an 10, p.334).

In addition to miniatures, Capet exhibited pastels and oils at the Salons from 1795. At the same time a number of pastel portraits, not exhibited, were privately commissioned, including that of the rather dour *Etienne Elias* (private collection, France, repr. Doria 1934, pl.7), the parliamentary lawyer *Pierre-Nicolas Berryer* (Palais de Justice, *ibid.*, pl.6) and the dramatist and member of the Tribunat *Marie-Joseph Chénier* (Stanford University Art Gallery, CA, *ibid.*, pl.10). In the last, Capet has successfully conveyed the solidity of the figure seated in three-quarters view and its position in space, as well as a wonderful sense of character. Several other works merit special attention, including the pastel of the history painter *Charles Meynier* (Ecole des Beaux-Arts, Paris, *ibid.*, pl.12), signed and dated 1799, perhaps exhibited at the Salon of that year (listed as Mesnier under no.706). Leaning on a portfolio, Meynier pauses to reflect on his sketch of an antique subject on the canvas behind him. It was an opportunity for Capet to extend her repertoire into history painting, albeit in outline form. In an oil painting of an unidentified woman (private

Capet: *Studio Interior*, exhibited 1808; oil on canvas; 69 × 83.5 cm.; Neue Pinakothek, Munich

collection, Paris, *ibid.*, pl.11) Capet interpreted the portrait as a genre scene with a still life, since the woman, elegantly adorned with amethyst earrings and necklace, abandons the Pleyel sonata resting on the pianoforte behind her and takes a moment to water her flowers, while she looks out at the spectator.

Capet's *chef d'oeuvre*, showing Madame Vincent – formerly Labille-Guiard – in her studio executing a portrait of the artist-Senator Vien (see illustration), earned Capet the title of history painter (see Charles Landon, *Salon de 1808*, ii, cited in *ibid.*, p.65). Exhibited at the Salon of 1808, this oil painting with many figures included Labille-Guiard (who had died in 1803) painting; Capet herself loading Labille-Guiard's palette; M. Vincent (Labille-Guiard's teacher, friend and eventual husband) close to the painter; the sitter, Vien (Vincent's teacher), as well as his son and his wife; and Vincent's students including Louis Mérimée. This conversation piece, representing a scene in the past and made dramatically even more

important by the presence of Vien's son and Vincent's students, celebrates the idea of genealogy, but most especially artistic genealogy, with Vien representing Capet's artistic great-grand-father since he was a teacher of Vincent, who in turn taught Mérimée and others, including Labille-Guiard, who trained Capet.

At the Salon of 1814, the last in which Capet exhibited, with several portraits of artillery officers, she included her only history painting, a mythological work representing *Hygeia, Goddess of Health* (untraced), which she presented to Dr Moreau de la Sarthe, perhaps for successfully treating her. Her last portraits date from 1815.

VIVIAN P. CAMERON

Capomazza, Luisa *see* Convents survey

Carl Nielsen, Anne Marie

Danish sculptor, 1863–1945

Born Anne Marie Brodersen in Thygesminde, South Jutland, 21 June 1863; father a wealthy farmer. Studied woodcarving in Schleswig, Germany, 1880; also studied anatomy with a local veterinary surgeon. Briefly attended Vilhelm Klein's private School of Drawing and Applied Art for Women, Copenhagen, 1882, then from November 1882 studied under August Saabye, professor of sculpture at the Royal Danish Academy of Fine Arts. One of the first students to enrol at the Academy's School of Drawing and Applied Art for Women, where she held a scholarship, 1889–90. Trips to the Netherlands and Belgium, 1889; Paris, 1889–91; Italy, 1899–1900; Athens and Constantinople, 1903; Greece, 1904–5; Greece and Egypt, 1928. Married Danish composer Carl Nielsen in Paris, 1891; two daughters, born 1891 and 1893 (the painter Anne Marie Telmányi), one son, born 1895; husband died 1931. Member, Den frie udstilling (Free Exhibition); founder member, Women Artists' Society, 1916; Sociétaire, Salon des Beaux-Arts, Paris, 1933; honorary member, Danish Sculptors' Society, 1943; member, Academy Council, 1912–14. Recipient of Ingenio et Arti medal, Copenhagen, 1927; Thorvaldsen medal, Copenhagen, 1932. Died in Copenhagen, 22 February 1945.

Principal Exhibitions

Individual

Kunstforening, Copenhagen: 1895
Galerie Cassirer, Berlin: 1907
Den frie udstillingsbygning, Copenhagen: 1931, 1946 (retrospective)

Group

Charlottenborg, Copenhagen: 1884, 1886–90, 1895, 1907–9 (salons), 1888 (*Den Nordiske udstilling* [Nordic exhibition])
Exposition Universelle, Paris: 1889 (bronze medal)
Den frie udstilling (Free exhibition), Copenhagen: occasionally 1892–1944
World's Columbian Exposition, Chicago: 1893
Industriforeningen, Copenhagen: 1895 (*Kvindernes udstilling – fra fortid til nutid* [Women's exhibition – from the past to the present])
Berlin: 1910 (*Dänische Ausstellung*)
Esposizione Internazionale, Rome: 1911
Public Art Galleries, Brighton, Sussex: 1912 (*Modern Danish Artists*)
Den frie udstillingsbygning, Copenhagen: 1920 (*Kvindelige kunstneres retrospektive udstilling* [Women artists' retrospective])
Brooklyn Museum, NY: 1927 (*Danish National Exhibition of Paintings, Sculpture, Architecture and Applied Art*)
Société Nationale des Beaux-Arts, Paris: 1933
Berlin Olympiad: 1936

Bibliography

Einar Utzon-Frank, *Anne Marie Carl Nielsen: Skitser og statuetter* [Anne Marie Carl Nielsen: Sketches and figurines], 1943
Anne Marie Carl Nielsen, exh. cat., Royal Danish Academy of Fine Arts, Copenhagen, 1946
Anne Marie Telmányi, *Mit barndomshjem* [My home], Copenhagen: Thaning & Appel, 1965
Anne Marie Telmányi, ed., *Anne Marie Carl Nielsen*, Copenhagen: Gyldendal, 1979
Torben Schousboe, ed., *Carl Nielsen: Dagbøger og brevveksling med Anne Marie Carl Nielsen* [Carl Nielsen: Diaries and correspondence with Anne Marie Carl Nielsen], Copenhagen: Gyldendal, 1983
Grethe Holmen, "Anne Marie Carl Nielsen and Anne Marie Telmányi: Mother and daughter", *Woman's Art Journal*, v/2, 1984–5, pp.28–33
Esther Nyholm, *Anne Marie Carl Nielsen: Skitser* [Anne Marie Carl Nielsen: Sketches], 1994

Born on a farm in Jutland to a couple of prosperous, hard-working farmers, Anne Marie Brodersen had to put up a determined fight in order to overcome her father's strong resentment of her choice of vocation. She started making her first clay sketches of animals around the age of ten, and was very reluctantly granted permission to take a three-month wood-carving course in the German town of Schleswig in 1880. Being a good rider from the age of five, and familiar with all the animals of the farm, she seemed destined to marry a well-to-do landowner, but against the desires of her parents she went to Copenhagen to study to become a sculptor.

At the time of her first artistic education, the Royal Danish Academy of Fine Arts was not open to women, but Brodersen's mother had been persuaded to finance her daughter's studies with her personal "egg money" and in 1882 she started at the Klein School and began an apprenticeship with the sculptor August Saabye. Brodersen soon started exhibiting at the traditional Charlottenborg spring exhibition in Copenhagen, where she entered a bust in 1884; in 1887 she received one of the prizes given by the Academy for her relief of *Thor and the Serpent of Midgard* (bronze; Municipality, Hørsholm). Her first study trip to Paris took place in 1889, and in 1890 she returned for a longer stay. One of the few foreign sculptors to influence Brodersen was Rodin, whom she was later to meet in person. Apart from a few early evidences of her acquaintance with the Symbolist style in the work of her Danish contemporaries, the painter and sculptor J.F. Willumsen and Harald and Agnes Slott-Møller (q.v.) who were among the founders of the Secessionist artists' association Den frie, her work is seemingly conservative and lies outside the modernist tradition.

In Paris Brodersen met the Danish musician and composer Carl Nielsen, at whose official debut she had been present a few years earlier. They married soon after, and left on a honeymoon to Italy; in the same year, 1891, their first daughter was born. The second, Anne Marie (later Telmányi), was to become a distinguished portrait painter, but their last child, a son born in 1895, was retarded and sent away from home to be nursed in the country. The marriage between Anne Marie Carl Nielsen and her composer husband was a union of two widely different temperaments, and in the years 1914–22 a deep crisis separated the couple, although they subsequently managed to reconcile their careers and their private feelings once more, and for life.

Brodersen had had her first important show at the great Nordiske udstilling in Copenhagen in 1888, which admitted a large number of women artists, and in 1889 she was allowed to enter two studies of calves, which were remembered by Rodin, at the Exposition Universelle in Paris. She also exhibited at the World's Columbian Exposition in Chicago in 1893, and her copies of Archaic Greek sculptures, which she had studied in Greece in 1903, were exhibited in 1905 and acquired by the Altes Museum in Berlin and the Leipzig museum. In 1907 she had a one-woman show at Galerie

Carl Nielsen: *Queen Dagmar*, statue at Ribe

Cassirer in Berlin, and her entry for a competition in Copenhagen for the monument to the Danish physicist Niels Finsen, a pioneer in the treatment of tuberculosis, won first prize – although the execution of the monument fell to the sculptor Rudolph Tegner.

In 1908 she won a closed competition for an equestrian monument to the Danish king *Christian IX*, to be placed in front of the Christiansborg Palace in Copenhagen, and as the first woman sculptor in Denmark she was also given the commission for the memorial. Work on the national monument went on for many years, and the statue, bronze and life-sized, was unveiled in 1927. Carl Nielsen's equestrian monument lies within the Danish tradition of dignified, tranquil representations of monarchs, from Jacques-François-Joseph Saly's *Frederik V* at the Amalienborg palaces to Herman Vilhelm Bissen's memorial to *Frederik VII* on the opposite side of the Christiansborg Palace, but has even less of the rhetoric of power than these two monuments. Her close observation of animals, which found expression in a great many small wax studies, is evident in the exquisitely balanced horse that carries Christian IX.

Carl Nielsen, who had attended classes at the Royal Danish Academy's School for Women after 1889 (the school opened in 1888), became in 1914 the first woman to become a director of the Academy. While occupied with the equestrian monument, she also did statues of animals and portraits (e.g. bronze bust of *Chief Surgeon Kraft*, 1929; Frederiksberg Hospital; plaster of the zoologist *J.E.V. Boas*, 1919; Academy of Veterinarians, Copenhagen), but also a large bronze statue of *Queen Dagmar* (see illustration), one of Denmark's medieval queens well-known from literature as an embodiment of female wisdom. The statue, set high on a small hill overlooking the marshlands surrounding the city of Ribe, shows the queen standing at the prow of a ship, her clothes billowing in the wind.

Carl Nielsen was commissioned to create two memorials in bronze to *Carl Nielsen*: one, a shepherd boy playing a pipe on a pedestal bearing a profile portrait of the composer, was erected at his birthplace, Nørre Lyndelse (1933); the second, a naked youth on a (wingless) Pegasus was erected near the exhibition building of Den frie, where she exhibited at the association's annual shows, in 1939. The idea for an equestrian monument to the Danish queen *Margrethe I*, which had first been shown as a sketch in 1897, was to occupy Carl Nielsen at different times in her career, but was not made into a large-scale statue. At her death she left a clay model for the horse for such a monument, larger than life-size. It could not be preserved, but her occupation with this strong woman ruler is likely to have had a personal significance. The principal collections of her work are at the Carl Nielsen Museet, Odense; Kunstmuseet Trapholt, Kolding; and Det Danske Kunstindustrimuseum, Copenhagen.

CHARLOTTE CHRISTENSEN

Carolrama *see* Rama

Carpenter, Margaret (Sarah)
British painter, 1793–1872

Born Margaret Sarah Geddes in Salisbury, Wiltshire, 1 February 1793, to Alexander Geddes, a retired army officer, and Harriet Easton. Moved with her family to a farm at nearby Alderbury, 1798. Taught to paint in oils by Thomas Guest in Salisbury, *c.*1805, then copied old masters in the Earl of Radnor's collection at Longford Castle near her family home. Visited London, 1810–12; received financial help from Lord Radnor to move there permanently, 1813. Awarded silver medal, 1812, lesser gold medal, 1813, and principal gold medal, 1814, Society of Arts. Married William Hookham Carpenter, son of Bond Street bookseller and art dealer James Carpenter, 1817; eight children, only five surviving infancy, of whom three, William, Percy and Henrietta, also became artists. Husband appointed Keeper of Prints and Drawings, British Museum, 1845; lived in museum residence,

1852–66; received pension after his death in 1866. Died in London, 13 November 1872.

Principal Exhibitions

Royal Academy, London: 1814–25, 1828–63, 1865–6
British Institution, London: 1814–17, 1819–24, 1826–33, 1835, 1837–40, 1842–53
Royal Institution, Edinburgh: 1822–9
Paris Salon: 1827
Society of British Artists, London: 1831–6
Exposition Universelle, Paris: 1855
Art Treasures Exhibition, Manchester: 1857
Society of Female Artists, London: 1858, 1863
National Portrait Exhibition, London: 1868

Bibliography

Ellen C. Clayton, *English Female Artists*, 2 vols, London: Tinsley, 1876

Walter Shaw Sparrow, ed., *Women Painters of the World*, London: Hodder and Stoughton, and New York: Stokes, 1905; reprinted New York: Hacker, 1976

Donald C. Whitton, *The Grays of Salisbury*, San Francisco: Whitton, 1976

Charlotte Yeldham, *Women Artists in Nineteenth-Century France and England*, 2 vols, New York: Garland, 1984

Catherine Peters, *The King of Inventors: A Life of Wilkie Collins*, London: Secker and Warburg, 1991; Princeton: Princeton University Press, 1993

Margaret Carpenter Bicentenary Exhibition, exh. cat., Salisbury Museum, 1993

Richard J. Smith, *Margaret Sarah Carpenter (1793–1872): A Brief Biography*, Salisbury: Salisbury Museum, 1993

——, "Margaret Carpenter (1793–1872): A Salisbury artist restored", *Hatcher Review*, iv/36, 1993, pp.2–32

Carpenter: *The Young Artist*, 1829; oil on canvas; 108 × 84 cm.; private collection

Margaret Carpenter's career bridges what some historians call the "vacuum" in British art between the Georgian school of portrait painters, culminating in Thomas Lawrence, and the later Victorian schools, from the Pre-Raphaelites onwards. She was at her peak during the 1830s and 1840s, when she was seen by many as the natural successor to Lawrence. This timing, as well as the fact that she was a somewhat lone figure and a woman, helps to account for her quite unjustified neglect ever since her death.

Even as a child, Margaret showed a prodigious talent for drawing portraits, and was in demand from families in the surrounding area. Her parents were not especially artistic, and apart from some limited instruction from Thomas Guest in Salisbury she was largely self-taught. The Earl of Radnor recognised her talent and allowed her to copy the old masters in his collection at Longford Castle. In her early days in London, she was part of a circle of young artists that included William Collins (her future brother-in-law and father of novelist Wilkie), the Scottish painter Andrew Geddes (no relation), David Wilkie and James Stark. Her oil portrait of *James Stark* (c.1814–19; Castle Museum, Norwich) shows a confidence and quality also seen in the smaller oil portrait of her future husband *William Carpenter* (1816; National Portrait Gallery, Bodelwyddan) and the watercolours of herself and William (1817; British Museum, London). The claim that Thomas Lawrence was her teacher has not been fully substantiated. She was, however, influenced by his work and that of Reynolds,

although she spoke with an individual voice and was never accused of imitating either.

Lord Radnor's early patronage was important, but Carpenter's determination and ambition, combined with her talent, ensured that she continued to build on it all through her life. Her Account Book (copy in National Portrait Gallery, London) lists almost 600 clients from all walks of life – and even that is not exhaustive: in all she produced more than 1100 pictures, mostly portraits in oils, but many in chalks, and some watercolour landscapes. There were also subject pictures, many of which she exhibited at the British Institution. Two good examples are *A Gleaner* (1820; South London Gallery, Camberwell) and *The Young Artist* (1829; see illustration), showing a young girl drawing her dog.

In her day Carpenter was one of the few women painting full-scale canvases, as opposed to miniatures, and it is remarkable how she managed to obtain her commissions. As a woman she could not call upon the nobility and gentry, as her brother-in-law used to do, although occasionally Collins recommended her. Yet in spite of marriage and several children, her professional output rarely flagged. With an unbusiness-like husband, and the need to help support her poverty-stricken parents, money was a crucial factor; but Carpenter's work was also driven by a streak of compulsiveness, resulting in conflict with her family responsibilities, which attracted critical comment. In 1825 John Constable noted that her painting was clearly giving her physical problems, and he suspected that her children were neglected for it (John Constable, *Correspondence*, ed. Ronald Brymer Beckett, iv, London: HMSO, 1966, p.137). Not only that, for most of her career she earned more than her husband.

Eton College was a fruitful source of work, through the influence of the Revd Edward Coleridge, for many years an assistant master. Carpenter painted up to 26 "leaving portraits" of boys, which are now in the official College collection, besides some 60 small oil panels for Coleridge himself. After his death, these were dispersed to the families of the sitters; a good example is *The 6th Duke of Roxburghe* (1831; Floors Castle, Kelso).

Carpenter's subjects all have a straightforward reality and energy. She concentrates on bringing the face, and especially the eyes, to the fore. She lights the forehead and hair, and softens the mouth and chin to give the whole face a warmth of personality. It is almost as if she and the sitter were having an animated conversation while she worked. She was also a superb draughtswoman; her small paintings often have the qualities of a miniature, while she could capture equally the swagger of a full-length portrait. From a small panel such as *John Tregonwell* (1833; 25.5 × 20.3 cm.; Russell-Cotes Gallery, Bournemouth) to the magnificent portrait of *Ada, Countess of Lovelace* (1836; 213 × 122 cm.; Government Art Collection, London), she is in total command of her medium. Her qualities were neatly summed up by Walter Shaw Sparrow: "[she is] among those quiet unpretentious portrait-painters whose thoughts are so wrapped up in their determination to be true that they never think of striving after exhibition-room effects." We see "the character of her sitters, and not technical displays of her own cleverness" (Sparrow 1905, p.60).

After Lawrence's death in 1830, Carpenter's career reached new heights. Her work was constantly praised in the art press as being "unaffectedly natural", "gracefully managed", "of classic simplicity". Her pictures of women and children, for example, *The Sisters*, a portrait of her two daughters Henrietta and Jane (1839; Victoria and Albert Museum, London), and *Spring Nosegay* (1831; Castle Museum, Nottingham), found especial favour. Her children are always natural and engaged in their own activities – a spontaneity born of the artist's years of observation of her five siblings and of her own children, unstifled by academic schooling. Over and over again, reviewers asked why she was not a member of the Royal Academy (she exhibited 156 pictures there, more than almost any other woman artist in the 19th century). Eventually in 1844 she was nominated, but as the only woman among some 60 candidates for two vacancies, she never really stood a chance.

Of the tiny fraction of Carpenter's work hanging in public galleries today, most are portraits of men. Of these, the portrait of the sculptor *John Gibson* (1857; National Portrait Gallery, Bodelwyddan) is very fine, but the posthumous portrait of the painter *Richard Bonington* (c.1833; National Portrait Gallery, London) is disappointing and untypical. Most of Carpenter's portraits of women and children are still with the families who commissioned them, but among those in collections open to the public are the beautiful *Lady Musgrave* (1825; Dalemain, Cumbria), the striking *Lady Eastnor* (1828; Eastnor Castle, Herefordshire), the softly delicate *Lady Mary Vyner* (1836; Newby Hall, Yorkshire), *Mrs John Marshall and Her Son* (1838; Leeds City Art Gallery), *Anna Maria Theobald* (1840)

and her sister *Georgiana Thellusson* (1850; both Brodsworth Hall, Yorkshire), *Henrietta Baillie* (1845; Royal College of Physicians, London), two lovely portraits of members of the Frewen family (1846 and 1853; Brickwall House, Northiam, Sussex) and *Mrs Collins*, the mother of William Collins, RA (1826; National Gallery of New Zealand, Wellington). No pupils or "followers" of Carpenter have been identified, apart from her daughter Henrietta, although she probably influenced a number of her contemporaries. Often misattributed, Carpenter's work is gradually coming to light, to show her true stature and importance.

RICHARD J. SMITH

Carr, Emily
Canadian painter, 1871–1945

Born in Victoria, British Columbia, 13 December 1871. Attended California School of Design, San Francisco, 1890–93. Taught art to children in Victoria, 1893–5. First visited Northwest Coast Indian villages, 1899. Studied at Westminster School of Art, London, 1900–03, leaving to paint in St Ives, Cornwall, and in Hertfordshire. Spent 15 months in a sanatorium in England, 1903–4. Returned to Victoria, 1904. Lived in Vancouver, c.1906–10. Attended Académie Colarossi, Paris, 1910. Recuperated from illness in Sweden and painted in Brittany and Concarneau, 1911. Returned to Vancouver and opened studio at 1465 West Broadway, 1912. Built a studio and apartment house, "The House of All Sorts", in Victoria, 1913; later ran it as a boarding house (sold 1936). Visited New York, 1930. Lived with sister Alice after second heart attack, 1940. Died at St Mary's Priory, Victoria, 2 March 1945. Recipient of posthumous honorary doctorate, University of British Columbia, 1945.

Principal Exhibitions

Individual
1465 West Broadway, Vancouver: 1912
Drummond Hall, Vancouver: 1913
Women's Canadian Club, Crystal Gardens Gallery, Victoria: 1930
Seattle Art Museum: 1930, 1943
Lyceum Club and Women's Art Association, Toronto: 1936, 1941
Art Gallery of Toronto: 1937, 1940, 1943
Vancouver Art Gallery: 1938, 1939, 1940, 1941, 1943
University of British Columbia, Vancouver: 1938, 1939, 1940
National Gallery of Canada, Ottawa: 1945 (touring retrospective)

Group
Studio Club, Vancouver: 1907–9, 1912
British Columbia Society of Fine Arts: 1909–10, 1929, 1936–43
Salon d'Automne, Paris: 1911
Island Arts and Crafts Club, Victoria: occasionally 1911–37
National Gallery of Canada, Ottawa: 1927 (*Canadian West Coast Art: Native and Modern*, touring), 1928, 1930–33 (annuals), 1933 (*Contemporary Canadian Painting*, touring)
Group of Seven, Toronto: 1930, 1931
Ontario Society of Artists, Toronto: 1930, 1931
Baltimore Museum of Art: 1931 (*Baltimore Pan-American Exhibition*, touring)
Canadian Group of Painters, Toronto (touring): 1933, 1936–9, 1942
Stedelijk Museum, Amsterdam: 1933 (*Works by Women Artists*)

Selected Writings

"Modern and Indian art of the West Coast", *McGill News* (supplement), June 1929, pp.18–22

Klee Wyck, Toronto: Oxford University Press, 1941

The Book of Small, Toronto: Oxford University Press, 1942; London: Oxford University Press, 1943

The House of All Sorts, Toronto: Oxford University Press, 1944

Growing Pains: The Autobiography of Emily Carr, Toronto: Oxford University Press, 1946

The Heart of a Peacock, ed. Ira Dilworth, Toronto: Oxford University Press, 1953

Pause: A Sketch Book, Toronto: Clarke Irwin, 1953

Hundreds and Thousands: The Journals of Emily Carr, Toronto: Clarke Irwin, 1966

Fresh Seeing: Two Addresses by Emily Carr, Toronto: Clarke Irwin, 1972

Dear Nan: Letters of Emily Carr, Nan Cheney and Humphrey Toms, ed. Doreen Walker, Vancouver: University of British Columbia Press, 1990

Bibliography

Lawren Harris, "Emily Carr and her work", *Canadian Forum*, no.21, December 1941, pp.277–8

Emily Carr: Her Paintings and Sketches, exh. cat., National Gallery of Canada, Ottawa, and elsewhere, 1945

Carol Pearson, *Emily Carr as I Knew Her*, Toronto: Clarke Irwin, 1954

Edythe Hembroff-Schleicher, *M.E.: A Portrayal of Emily Carr*, Toronto: Clarke Irwin, 1969

William Wylie Thom, *The Fine Arts in Vancouver, 1886–1930: An Historical Study*, MA thesis, Department of Fine Arts, University of British Columbia, 1969

Emily Carr: A Centennial Exhibition, exh. cat., Vancouver Art Gallery and elsewhere, 1971; 2nd edition, 1975

Northrop Frye, *The Bush Garden: Essays on the Canadian Imagination*, Toronto: Anansi, 1971

Maria Tippett and Douglas Cole, *From Desolation to Splendour: Changing Perceptions of the British Columbia Landscape*, Toronto: Clarke Irwin, 1977

Edythe Hembroff-Schleicher, *Emily Carr: The Untold Story*, Saanichton, BC: Hancock House, 1978

Doris Shadbolt, *The Art of Emily Carr*, Vancouver: Douglas and McIntyre, and Seattle: University of Washington Press, 1979

Russell Keziere, "Emily Carr: Kultur der Neuen Welt und Widersprüche der Alten Welt", *OKanada*, exh. cat., Akademie der Künste, Berlin, 1982, pp.80–87

Paula Blanchard, *The Life of Emily Carr*, Vancouver: Douglas and McIntyre, and Seattle, University of Washington Press, 1987

The Expressionist Landscape: North American Modernist Painting, 1920–1947, exh. cat., Birmingham Museum of Art, AL, 1988

Ruth Ann Stevens Appelhof, *Emily Carr: Canadian Modernist*, PhD dissertation, Syracuse University, NY, 1988

Terry Goldie, *Fear and Temptation: The Image of the Indigene in Canadian, Australian and New Zealand Literatures*, Kingston: McGill-Queen's University Press, 1989

Doris Shadbolt, *Emily Carr*, Vancouver: Douglas and McIntyre, and Seattle: University of Washington Press, 1990

Emily Carr in France/Emily Carr en France, exh. cat., Vancouver Art Gallery, 1991

Marcia Crosby, "Construction of the imaginary Indian", *Vancouver Anthology: The Institutional Politics of Art*, ed. Stan Douglas, Vancouver: Talonbooks, 1991, pp.272–6

The True North: Canadian Landscape Painting, 1896–1939, exh. cat., Barbican Art Gallery, London, 1991

Scott Watson, "Disfigured nature: The origins of the modern Canadian landscape", *Eye of Nature*, exh. cat., Walter Phillips Gallery, Banff, 1991, pp.103–12

Mara R. Witzling, ed., *Voicing Our Visions: Writings by Women Artists*, New York: Universe, 1991; London: Women's Press, 1992

Gerta Moray, *Northwest Coast Native Culture and the Early Indian Paintings of Emily Carr, 1899–1913*, PhD dissertation, University of Toronto, 1993

Maria Tippett, *Emily Carr: A Biography*, revised edition, Toronto: Stoddard, 1994

Robert Linsley, "Landscapes in motion: Lawren Harris, Emily Carr and the heterogeneous modern nation", *Oxford Art Journal*, xix/1, 1996, pp.80–95

Stephanie Walker, *This Woman in Particular: Contexts for the Biographical Image of Emily Carr*, Waterloo, Ont.: Wilfrid Laurier University Press, 1996

Emily Carr is one of the most celebrated figures in Canadian culture, a position due equally to her outstanding modernist landscape paintings and to her writings. Daughter of a successful English importer-wholesaler who brought his family to British Columbia in 1858, Carr was orphaned in her mid-teens. With the decline of the family's fortunes, she saved her earnings as an art teacher to pursue further art training in Britain and France. She travelled boldly into frontier areas of the province to record the villages and totem poles of the Northwest Coast native peoples. From 1928 on she forged a distinctive modern idiom in paintings of the landscape of British Columbia, which have ever since defined its image in Canadian consciousness.

Carr has attained almost legendary status, as a "little old woman on the edge of nowhere" who transcended local rejection of her modern paintings to achieve national fame, as an eccentric spinster landlady who kept a household of animals (a monkey, parrots, dogs, a pet rat and various wild creatures she tamed), and as a mystic who communed with nature and "lived among the Indians". She contributed substantially to her own legend with seven volumes of autobiographical tales and with her journals and letters (most published posthumously). This has tended to occlude the fact that she was a highly professional and dedicated artist who maintained contact with avant-garde developments after her training in France through available books and magazines and through correspondence with fellow artists.

Carr's landscape paintings eventually won her a place alongside the Group of Seven, the eastern Canadian painters who from 1911 developed images of wilderness landscape that were seen as the expression of a modern Canadian national identity. In oil paintings such as *Indian War Canoe, Alert Bay* (1912; Museum of Fine Arts, Montreal) Carr had independently applied the Post-Impressionist colouring and Fauve linear arabesques she learned in France to the landscape of British Columbia and to the villages and totem poles of the Northwest Coast native peoples. By the time of her death in 1945, Carr was acclaimed as a Canadian van Gogh, and the memorial exhibition mounted of her work became the largest exhibition ever held for a Canadian artist.

Carr has since also been recognised as a significant contributor to the first generation of modernism in North America (see Appelhof in Birmingham 1988). From a feminist art-historical perspective, she emerges as a figure comparable to Georgia O'Keeffe (q.v.), whom she met briefly on her only visit to New York in 1930. As with O'Keeffe, Carr's critical reception has recurrently emphasised her affinity as a woman artist with nature, the expression in her work of a personal and sexual symbology, and her search for spiritual meaning

Carr: *Gwayasdoms d'Sonoqua*, 1928–30; oil on canvas; 100.3 × 65.4 cm.; Art Gallery of Ontario, Toronto: Gift from the Albert H. Robson Memorial Subscription Fund, 1942

through art. She has been claimed as a precursor of feminist spirituality and ecological consciousness (Walker 1996).

Early in her career, Carr's interests diverged from the types of painting expected from women artists at the time. Like Rosa Bonheur (q.v.) and Lady Butler (q.v.), she is a woman artist whose ambition caused her to be characterised as "painting like a man". She focused her attention on two main concerns, to render the specific qualities of the Northwest Coast landscape and to record the visible legacy of aboriginal culture there. Carr's periods of study abroad kindled her interest first of all in the French-derived naturalism of the St Ives and Newlyn artists during her stay in England, and then in the Post-Impressionist and Fauve techniques she learned from English-speaking teachers in France (the Scot J.D. Fergusson, the English Henry Phelan Gibb and the Australian Frances Hodgkins, q.v., all followers of Gauguin and Matisse). Her resulting interest in strong colour and rhythmic brushwork can be seen in *Autumn in France* (1911; oil on cardboard; National Gallery of Canada, Ottawa), which was exhibited at the Paris Salon d'Automne. Her experience in Europe, however, strongly confirmed Carr's Canadian loyalties and her ambition to make a significant artistic contribution to her home province of British Columbia.

Critics and art historians have seen in Carr an artist whose vision was rooted in a formal language and a spiritual wisdom she learned through "deep understanding" of a "vanishing" Indian culture (Shadbolt 1979). As the Canadian painter Lawren Harris exclaimed: "Her art in subject matter has no contact with white peoples. It is an art whose full sustenance is drawn from the soil and the sea ... [I]t embodies an almost primitive oneness with nature, identical one feels with the Indian sympathy with nature" (Harris 1941). This image of the artist as "gone Indian" and inheriting the aborigine's bond to the land is now seen as an example of a recurrent myth in colonial literatures (Goldie 1989, p.16). Carr's representation of Northwest Coast native culture has come under critical scrutiny with the recent awareness that images of aboriginal peoples have reflected Eurocentric, imperialist and often racist attitudes (Crosby 1991, Moray 1993). It is significant that Carr's work gained its first wide recognition in 1927, when it was co-opted for the Canadian National Gallery's exhibition, *Canadian West Coast Art: Native and Modern*. The curators' agenda was to show off Northwest Coast native artefacts as a Canadian national treasure and as a resource for Canadian artists and designers. Their discovery of the aesthetic properties of these artefacts came at an historical moment when decades of aggressively assimilationist Canadian state policy had rendered illegal native social institutions such as the potlatch, had enforced residential schooling for native children, and in 1927 had declared null and void the land claims that British Columbia's aboriginal tribes had been pursuing since the province's entry into Confederation. In this context, the validation of native artefacts as aesthetic objects and their preservation for the white community were further acts of colonial appropriation.

Carr's own earlier paintings and her involvement with Indian subjects were, however, more complex and ambiguous. Their full implications at a time when the "Indian problem" was a heated local social and political issue, as Carr was well aware, have only recently been realised (Moray 1993). Carr had first decided to specialise in documenting aboriginal culture when she was establishing her career in the competitive climate of the new art community of Vancouver. Between 1907 and 1913 she undertook an extensive project to make watercolours and oils of "totem poles in their own village settings, as complete a collection of them as I could" (*Growing Pains* 1946, p.211). Through her contact with modernist primitivism in Paris, Carr became convinced that native carvings had high artistic merit, and she studied their forms carefully in her documentary sketches and paintings, most of which are now in the Vancouver Art Gallery and the British Columbia Archives and Records Service. She made sketching trips during summer breaks from teaching, including a long journey in 1912 among the Kwakiutl islands at the northern end of Vancouver Island, to Gitksan villages on the Skeena River, and to Haida settlements in the Queen Charlotte Islands. By 1913 she was able to mount a huge exhibition with over 200 documentary paintings in a large assembly hall in Vancouver that she hired at her own expense.

An unpublished "Lecture on totems", which Carr delivered at this exhibition to explain aspects of native culture to her white Vancouver audience, shows that during the course of her project she developed great sympathy and respect for the native people, and formed a picture of their culture as a system in which villages, way of life and landscape were interconnected, and many links with the past still maintained. Though not always free herself from the patronising language of her own times, Carr's writings and paintings assert a critical view of the contempt shown by many missionaries and administrators towards native traditional culture, which they represented as a dark and superstitious past. Carr deliberately contested this picture, usually showing the villages as living entities, peopled with figures in contemporary dress, with washing lines between the houses (e.g. *Totem Poles, Kitseukla*, 1912; oil on canvas; Vancouver Art Gallery) or, in the case of the Haida villages that had been abandoned because of smallpox epidemics, as tragic and defiant ruins (e.g. *Tanoo, Queen Charlotte Islands*, 1913; oil on canvas; British Columbia Archives and Records Service). She stated that she intended her documentary record as much for the natives' future as for the settler community. She did her work, she said, "for the honor of the Indian". She usually exhibited the sketches she had made in the native villages before leaving, and made copies for people there who wanted them. In 1912 she approached the Government of British Columbia to support and acquire her record for the provincial museum and art gallery that was being developed in Victoria. Nothing came of this, partly because an economic depression hit the province in 1913, and partly because Carr's testimonies to the value, the past achievements and the presence of the province's native population were not welcome at a moment when increasingly active presentation of native land claims and grievances was causing anxiety to the settler community.

Unlike her American contemporaries – William S. Taylor, who made sketches and photographs for the murals at the American Museum of Natural History, and Edward S. Curtis of Seattle, who made his Northwest Coast photographs for volume 10 of *The North American Indian* in Kwakiutl territory in the same years as Carr did her paintings there – Carr did not seek to recreate the image of an apparently authentic native life unaffected by contact with Europeans. In her paintings, and even more in her later stories, Carr always acknowledged the tensions between tradition and change. The fact that Carr's documentary project gained no effective support either from the provincial government or from private patrons in British Columbia at this time was due to her refusal to conform to popular museological and artistic conventions, as well as to her modernist style, which was ahead of the local climate of taste. This led to a period of acute discouragement and financial difficulty for Carr, and she virtually ceased painting between the years 1913 and 1926. When her professional career resumed in 1927, she turned away from documentation to convey what she saw as the underlying spirit of native culture. Potlatch figures and totem poles were now rendered in close-up with dramatic scale and three-dimensional volume, to make "strong talk" of their owners' pride in lineage. Carr's choice of motifs fitted her own subjective concerns, such as her admiration for native women as mothers, seen in *Totem Mother, Kitwancool* (1928; oil on canvas; Vancouver Art Gallery). She was fascinated by the Kwakiutl mythical figure Dsonokwa, a wild woman of the woods, both frightening and beneficent, whom she celebrated in several paintings such as *Gwayasdoms d'Sonoqua* (1928–30; see illustration) and adopted as a guardian spirit (see Carr's story "Dsonoqua" in *Klee Wyck* 1941).

After 1930 Carr concentrated primarily on landscape painting. Entering a new phase of formal experiment, she drew on elements from a variety of available sources, including books by Ralph Pearson, Jay Hambidge and Katherine Dreier. The overlapping planes and rhythmic repetitions that she found in reproductions of Cubism and the multiplication of stylised elements used in native design are found in a series of oil paintings that use dark colours and heavy, sculpted forms, such as *Indian Church* (1929; Art Gallery of Ontario, Toronto). Carr often projected anthropomorphic and emotional associations on to natural forms, as in *Grey* (1930; private collection, repr. Shadbolt 1979), where a young tree is shown enfolded in a sombre, womb-like forest interior. Because of the darkness, density and power she gave to these images of the forest, they were seen as expressing the "malignant and somber nature" that Northrop Frye (1971) has argued characterises Canadian experience.

By the mid-1930s Carr had developed a special sketching technique in oil on paper that enabled her to paint more freely and spontaneously. She worked on large sheets of inexpensive manila paper, in oil paints thinned with white house paint and gasoline. *Tree (Spiralling Upward)* (1932–3; Vancouver Art Gallery) shows how, in this quick drying medium, she developed a calligraphic brush stroke that could indicate a variety of local forms and textures, unified by a dominant rhythmic flow. As an avid reader of Walt Whitman and follower of syncretic religious currents, Carr now thought of her paintings as the expression of the omnipresence of God, and of the forces of growth and life in nature. She extended her subjects from trees and forest interiors to the movement of the sky, then to the open spaces of the seashore and of tree-clothed hillsides, and occasionally to the massive forms of the coastal mountains. An extraordinary variety of expressive effects are generated by the flow of calligraphic marks that structure the entire surface plane of her late paintings, such as *Stumps and Sky* (1934–5; Art Gallery of Ontario).

GERTA MORAY

Carrick, Ethel *see* Fox

Carriera, Rosalba
Italian painter, 1675–1757

Born in the parish of San Basilio, Venice, 7 October 1675, to Andrea Carriera, clerk, and his wife Alba Foresti, a lacemaker. Admitted to the Accademia di San Luca, Rome, 1705. Stayed in Paris, 1720–21; elected member of the Académie Royale, 1720. Stayed in Modena, 1723. Visited Vienna to work for Emperor Charles VI, 1730. Assisted by her younger sister Giovanna (d.1737). Elected member of the Bologna Academy, 1720. Went blind during the last decade of her life. Died in the parish of SS Vito e Modesto, Venice, 15 April 1757.

Selected Writings

Journal de Rosalba Carriera: Pendant son séjour à Paris en 1720 et 1721, ed. Albert Sensier, Paris: Techeur, 1865

Rosalba's Journal and Other Papers, ed. Austin Dobson, London: Chatto and Windus, 1915; reprinted Freeport, NY: Books for Libraries Press, 1970

Lettere, diari, frammenti, ed. Bernardina Sani, 2 vols, Florence: Olschki, 1985

Bibliography

Antonio Maria Zanetti, *Della pittura veneziana e delle opere pubbliche de' veneziani maestri*, 5 vols, Venice, 1771; reprinted Venice: Filippi, 1972

P. J. Mariette, *Abecedario*, i, 1851, pp.329–32

Vittorio Malamani, "Rosalba Carriera", *Le gallerie nazionali italiani*, iv, 1899, pp.27–149

Emilie von Hoerschelmann, *Rosalba Carriera: Die Meisterin der Pastellmalerei, und Bilder aus der Kunst- und Kulturgeschichte des 18. Jahrhunderts*, Leipzig, 1908

Rosalba Carriera, exh. cat., Istituto Italiano d'Arti Grafiche, Bergamo, 1910 (contains abridged version of Malamani 1899)

Carlo Jeannerat, "Le origini del ritratto a miniatura in avorio", *Dedalo*, year 11, ii, 1931, pp.767–81

Torben Holck Colding, *Aspects of Miniature Painting: Its Origins and Development*, Copenhagen: Munksgaard, 1953

Francesco Cessi, *Rosalba Carriera*, Milan: Fabbri, 1965

Gabriella Gatto, "Per la cronologia di Rosalba Carriera", *Arte Veneta*, xxv, 1971, pp.182–93

Eleanor Tufts, *Our Hidden Heritage: Five Centuries of Women Artists*, New York and London: Paddington Press, 1974

Women Artists, 1550–1950, exh. cat., Los Angeles County Museum of Art, and elsewhere, 1976

Angelo Walther, "Zu den Werken der Rosalba Carriera in der Dresdener Gemäldegalerie", *Beiträge und Berichte der Staatlichen Kunstsammlungen Dresden, 1972–1975*, Dresden: Staatliche Kunstsammlungen Dresden, 1978, pp.65–90

Franca Zava Boccazzi, "Un disegno inedito di Rosalba Carriera", *Arte Veneta*, xxxiii, 1979, pp.146–8

Bernard Aikema, "The 1733 art exhibition at San Rocco in Venice", *Mededelingen van het Nederlands Instituut te Rome*, xliii, 1981, pp.143–8

Franca Zava Boccazzi, "Per Rosalba Carriera e famiglia: Nuovi documenti veneziani", *Arte Veneta*, xxxv, 1981, pp.217–26

Bernardina Sani, "Pastelli e miniature di Rosalba Carriera nella collezione di Giovanni Guglielmo Pfalz", *Itinerari contributi alla storia dell'arte in memoria di Maria Luisa Ferrari*, ed. Antonio Boschetto, ii, Florence: SPES, 1981, pp.133–43

Franco Moro, "Un ritratto di Rosalba Carriera nella pinacoteca di Cremona e un problema inerente la grafica", *Arte Veneta*, xli, 1987, pp.155–8

J. de Bruijn Kops, "Een portretminiatuur door Rosalba Carriera (1675–1757) en de oorsprong van haar schilderkunst op ivoor" [A portrait miniature by Rosalba Carriera and the origin of her painting on ivory], *Bulletin van het Rijksmuseum*, xxxvi, 1988, pp.181–210, 268–71 (with English summary)

Bernardina Sani, *Rosalba Carriera*, Turin: Allemandi, 1988

Wendy Slatkin, *The Voices of Women Artists*, Englewood Cliffs, NJ: Prentice Hall, 1993

The Glory of Venice: Art in the Eighteenth Century, exh. cat., Royal Academy, London, and National Gallery of Art, Washington, DC, 1994

Michael Levey, *Painting in Eighteenth-Century Venice*, 3rd edition, New Haven and London: Yale University Press, 1994

Rosalba Carriera, one of the most successful of all women artists, holds an important position in the history of 18th-century portraiture. She introduced a new intimate elegance in her work, which gave a significant stimulus to that genre of painting, particularly in France, where she was greatly admired. With her original and innovative exploration of the pastel medium, applied with new freedom and delicacy of touch, she was able to catch the flavour and character of the age. Her portraits and allegories were collected all over Europe by enthusiastic patrons and connoisseurs.

Carriera's artistic formation is poorly documented and still quite uncertain. With her two sisters Giovanna and Angela she received a humanist education at home by studying French, history, literature and music. According to Mariette (1851), she started painting snuff boxes and miniatures on ivory. Her correspondence, dating from 1700 onwards, reveals that she was personally acquainted with the painters Antonio Balestra and Federico Bencovich, whose work definitely had some influence on her early production. She also knew the late 17th-century Italian tradition of pastel drawing, represented by such artists as Baldassare Franceschini called il Volterrano and the Florentines Benedetto Luti and Domenico Tempesti, the latter a pupil of Robert Nanteuil. This is clearly shown by her first documented pastel, the portrait of *Anton Maria Zanetti the Younger* (c.1700; Nationalmuseum, Stockholm). This work reveals a light and soft touch, but still a precise and firm underdrawing that makes it quite similar to an oil painting. In the following years Carriera's technique gradually attained a supreme delicacy and finesse for which her style was unique among her contemporaries. She was also inspired by the Rococo artists who were active in Venice in the first decade of the 18th century, in particular Sebastiano Ricci and her brother-in-law Giovanni Antonio Pellegrini. Their lighter palette and new technical freedom determined the development of her style.

Alongside her pastels, the Venetian artist produced an extensive range of miniatures that, from the beginning of her career, made her name famous in Italy and abroad. Even in this genre she was able to render the lightness and softness of the Rococo with an accomplished technique that was her own personal invention. It was with a miniature as a reception piece that Carriera was accepted as a member of the Accademia di San Luca, Rome, in 1705. This work, depicting a *Girl Holding a Dove* (Accademia di San Luca), a white figure on a blue background, is painted in tempera on ivory, with minute, loose brush strokes and subtle light effects that aroused great admiration among the Academicians. This miniature was followed by many others, the intimate or allegorical subjects of which reveal the artist's acute perception of the life and culture of her century. In fresh and delicate sketches reflecting Rococo sensibility and frivolity, she portrayed a *Lady at Her Dressing Table* (Cleveland Museum of Art), *Flute Player* (Hermitage, St Petersburg) and *The Gardener* (Bayerisches Nationalmuseum, Munich).

Carriera's work was appreciated and collected all over Europe. At first her major commissions came from the German princes. Maximilian of Bavaria, during his stay in Venice in 1704, had his portrait made and commissioned those of the most beautiful women in Venice. Duke Christian Ludwig of Mecklenburgh commissioned several miniatures in 1706 and Frederick IV of Denmark, in Venice in the winter of 1708–9, sat for his portrait and commissioned pastels and miniatures. Another very important patron was the Elector Palatine Johann Wilhem von der Platz, a great admirer and collector of Italian Rococo painting, who in 1706 invited Carriera to his court in Düsseldorf. She did not accept, but between 1706 and 1713 produced for him a series of miniatures of arcadian subjects (Bayerisches Nationalmuseum) that reflect contemporary taste; among them is *The Gardener* mentioned above. Carriera's activity for the Elector Palatine is recorded in detail by her regular correspondence with his secretary, Giorgio Maria Rapparini. Her greatest admirer, however, was the Prince Elector of Saxony, later Augustus III of Poland, who first sat for his portrait in 1713, and then acquired Carriera's work throughout his reign. By the end of his life he owned over 150 pastels by her, all displayed in a gallery dedicated to the Venetian artist at his court in Dresden. They then became an important nucleus of the Dresden Gemäldegalerie.

In 1707, in Venice, Carriera met the French artist Nicolas Vleughels, whose pastel drawings, heads in particular, executed with a high degree of finish, had some influence on her. Her contact with Vleughels helped to keep her in touch with contemporary French portraiture and might have drawn her attention to the work of Watteau, who was to have a significant impact on her style, especially after her visits to his studio during her stay in Paris. Carriera's interest in French painting was also encouraged by her friendship with the connoisseurs and collectors Pierre Crozat, who visited Venice in 1715, and Pierre-Jean Mariette, who arrived in 1718.

Another significant contribution to Carriera's artistic development in these years was made by the work of the 16th-century artist Federico Barocci, whose luminous and graceful pastel drawings were much admired in the 18th century and were certainly present in contemporary Venetian collections. The influence of French portraiture, and of Nicolas de Largillière in particular, combined with Barocci's luministic approach, is shown for example in the portrait of a *Venetian*

Carriera: *Self-Portrait as an Old Woman*, 1740s; Royal Collection © Her Majesty Queen Elizabeth II

Procurator (Gemäldegalerie, Dresden). Carriera depicts the sitter in a formal pose appropriate to his social position, but at the same time she reveals his inner personality. The pastels are used with extreme subtlety, using broader and looser strokes for the procurator's sumptuous robe and minute and delicate ones for the face, whose character is rendered by an effective play of light and shadow. The realistic depiction of the face contrasts with the powdery white whig, which enhances the official presentation of the sitter.

A crucial experience for the further development of Carriera's style was her trip to Paris, where she stayed as the guest of the banker Pierre Crozat, from April 1720 to March 1721. There she visited all the major collections and met several leading painters, including Jean François de Troy, Joseph Vivien, Hyacinthe Rigaud, Nicolas de Largillière, Antoine and Charles Coypel, and Watteau. At the same time, the delicate and subtle flattery of her informal portraits and miniatures was greatly appreciated by Parisian society, then reacting strongly against the stiff formality promoted by Louis XIV and his court. Carriera dutifully recorded in her diary the important commissions that she received from the French court and aristocracy, almost competing for their portraits or little mythological pictures. She portrayed the Prince Regent, Philippe d'Orléans, and the young king himself several times, in pastel and miniature. The portrait of *Louis XV* (Gemäldegalerie) is painted with great spontaneity, aiming at rendering the youth and lively personality of the boy much more than his royal state. His formal attire is given a fresh and vivacious note by the sparkling contrast between the bright red of the embroidered jacket and the luminous transparent white of the lace jabot.

In the portrait of *Mademoiselle de Clermont* (Musée Condé, Chantilly) Carriera catches in a rapid impression the refined, mundane and frivolous culture of 18th-century Parisian high society. The attention is focused on the lovely young face, which looks straight at us with confidence and grace, while the girl's fresh beauty is given a sensuous note by the transparent veil just covering her bosom and a frivolous one by the delicate little flowers embellishing her curly hair. Rosalba's Parisian success was officially confirmed by her admission to the Académie Royale in October 1720, only four months after her arrival. When, after leaving Paris in March 1721, she sent a *Nymph* to the Academy as her reception piece, the *Mercure Galant* of February 1722 published an "Eloge de Rosalba Carriera", praising her work for the "gracefulness" of the image, the "lightness" of touch and the gemlike quality of the colour. Never before had the technical possibilities of pastel been exploited with such original invention and finesse. In France Carriera established a fashion for pastel portraits that not only characterised French Rococo painting but also persisted in the 19th century. Her technical innovations were taken up and perfected by several French artists, such as Maurice Quentin de la Tour, Charles Natoire, Jean-Baptiste Perroneau, the German Anton Raphael Mengs and the Swiss Jean Etienne Liotard.

After her return to Venice, Carriera seems to have reflected on and assimilated the French experience, achieving a further evolution and maturity in her art. The portraits painted in the 1730s reveal a deeper psychological insight and judgement of character, while still flattering the sitters. These aspects of her style are largely due to a renewed study of Watteau, most probably also encouraged by the publication of the *Figures de différents caractères, de paysage et d'études dessinées d'après nature par Antoine Watteau*, which Jean de Julienne sent to Carriera in 1728. Superb examples of these "psychological" portraits are the works painted during Rosalba's stay in Vienna in 1730, such as the portrait of *Amalia of Austria*, the little portrait of *Metastasio* (both Gemäldegalerie, Dresden) and the portrait of *Count Daniele Antonio Bertoli* (Badoglio Rota collection, Flambruzzo, Udine). In these works Carriera depicts her subjects with acute and sober realism, rendering their physiognomy with crystalline purity, yet preserving a few subtle details that suggest their distinguished social or intellectual standing. The unattractiveness of the Empress Amalia is tempered by her soft and intelligent gaze and the superb jewels decorating her dress; the poet Metastasio, who was then enjoying great success in Vienna, looks confidently out of the picture, expressing his lively creative genius; the Italian count, Superintendent of the Galleries of Emperor Charles VI in Vienna, appears in all his distinguished and sober elegance. In the last portrait in particular Carriera's technique achieves a spectacular effect by contrasting the luminous head and upper bust of the sitter with a dark background and a dark supporting drapery. The count's face is modelled with a subtle play of chiaroscuro, his powdered hair seems to float softly around his face and the fine texture of his lace jabot is suggested by dragging the flat edge of white chalk lightly over a finished underdrawing of darker tones.

Another significant series of portraits painted in the 1730s and 1740s was commissioned by the numerous British tourists who visited Venice during their Italian grand tour. Carriera's informal representations appealed in particular to the intellectual English aristocrats who were seeking a new, truthful, yet seducing image of themselves. Among them, *Charles Sackville, 2nd Duke of Dorset* (Lord Sackville's Collection, Sevenoaks, Kent), who participated in the intense Venetian social scene in 1730, is impressively portrayed in all his charming youth, wearing a preciously patterned brocade silk jacket and the typical Venetian hat called "tricorno".

In the 1740s two female figures reflect poignantly Carriera's extraordinary power of observation and understanding of the human character. Her moving *Self-Portrait as an Old Woman* (see illustration), painted for another great friend and patron, Joseph Smith, from 1744 British Consul in Venice, a few years before she went blind, shows the artist gazing beyond the observer, withdrawn into a world of her own, her lips firmly set. The prevailing sombre mood of the picture, conveyed by the dark fur robes that the artist is wearing, is just broken by her sparkling earrings and the fine lace that softens her décolleté. An entirely different character dominates the portrait of *Caterina Sagredo Barbarigo* (see illustration), an eccentric, widely travelled noblewoman and a skilled horsewoman, well known in Venice for her beauty. She looks directly out of the picture, in a lively and flirtatious way, her little hat worn daringly askew over her right ear. Her beautiful face is given shape by a subtle chiaroscuro, while fashionable pearls adorn her ears and neck. In this extraordinary portrait Carriera conveys the whole wordly and refined mood of the Settecento. In 1746 Carriera lost her sight, and this sad

Carriera: *Caterina Sagredo Barbarigo*, 1740s; pastel; 42 × 33 cm.; Gemäldegalerie Alte Meister, Staatliche Kunstsammlungen, Dresden

condition afflicted her for the last ten years of her life, putting a premature end to her long artistic career.

MARGHERITA GIACOMETTI

Carrington

British painter and designer, 1893–1932

Born Dora de Houghton Carrington in Hereford, 29 March 1893. Studied at the Slade School of Fine Art, London, under Henry Tonks and Fred Brown, 1910–14 (Slade scholarship 1912). Worked for Roger Fry's Omega Workshops, c.1914–17, and Hogarth Press, 1917 and 1921. Sold work regularly through Birrell and Garnett bookshop, Bloomsbury, London, c.1923–32. Met Lytton Strachey, writer and member of Bloomsbury Group, 1915; lived with him at Tidmarsh Mill, near Pangbourne, Berkshire, 1917–24, then at Ham Spray House, Wiltshire. Married Ralph Partridge, 1921. Shot herself at Ham Spray, 11 March 1932, soon after Strachey's death.

Principal Exhibitions

New English Art Club, London: 1913, 1916
London Group: 1920
Grosvenor Galleries, London: 1921 (*Nameless Exhibition of Modern British Painting*)

Selected Writings

Carrington: Letters and Extracts from Her Diaries, ed. David Garnett, London: Cape, 1970; New York: Holt Rinehart, 1971

Bibliography

Noel Carrington, *Carrington: Paintings, Drawings and Decorations*, 2nd edition, London and New York: Thames and Hudson, 1980

Frances Partridge, *Memories*, London: Gollancz, 1981; as *Love in Bloomsbury: Memories*, Boston: Little Brown, 1981

Gillian Elinor, "Vanessa Bell and Dora Carrington: Bloomsbury painters", *Woman's Art Journal*, v/1, 1984, pp.28–34

Gretchen Gerzina, *Carrington: A Life of Dora Carrington*, London: Murray, and New York: Norton, 1989

Teresa Grimes, Judith Collins and Oriana Baddeley, *Five Women Painters*, London: Lennard, 1989

Mary Ann Caws, *Women of Bloomsbury: Virginia, Vanessa and Carrington*, New York and London: Routledge, 1990

Jane Hill, *The Art of Dora Carrington*, London: Herbert Press, and New York: Thames and Hudson, 1994

Michael Holroyd, *Lytton Strachey: A Critical Biography*, revised edition, London: Chatto and Windus, 1994; New York: Farrar Straus, 1995

Jan Marsh, *Bloomsbury Women: Distinct Figures in Life and Art*, London: Pavilion, 1995

Dora Carrington's decision to be known always by her surname; the notorious arrangement of her "Triangular trinity of happiness" with Lytton Strachey and her husband Ralph Partridge; her changeling appearance in the mythology of her generation; and her suicide before she was 40 have helped to obscure the contribution of a dedicated artist with a streak of creative genius.

Carrington was a conspicuous, prize-winning student at the Slade School of Fine Art (*Standing Nude*, 1913; oil on canvas; University College London, repr. Hill 1994, p.22) and a dramatic character, repeatedly portrayed in fiction of the day. Although the spirit of the age dictated that artists find their role models in continental Europe, Carrington remained remote from these impulses. Her work was informed by Cézanne but inspired by the English pastoral tradition. She believed that William Blake had made all the advances credited to Matisse (*The Feetbathers*, 1919; watercolour on paper; private collection, *ibid.*, p.116). She was a poetic realist and a quintessentially English artist. She painted several inn signs and wrote that painting signboards for Pangbourne shopkeepers was "a greater honour than becoming a member of the London Group" (*The Greyhound*, 1921; *ibid.*, p.66). She rarely signed, dated or exhibited her work and became an isolated worker.

At the Slade Carrington headed a revival in fresco painting. Her first commission was to provide a larger-than-life-size mural in true fresco for the library of Lord Brownlow's 19th-century gothic palace, Ashridge House, Berkhamsted, Hertfordshire. Local bucolic scenes were chosen and rendered in Pre-Raphaelite detail (*Hoeing*, 1912; *ibid.*, p.49).

Her work was inherently autobiographical; she painted the places, people and possessions she loved. Drawing and watercolour were considered preparations for painting on canvas (an explanation for the ubiquitous folds found in Carrington's works on paper) and have a very different sensibility to finished oils. Her fascination with the abstract forms of landscape created intimate place portraits. Her fish-eye image of the *Hill in Snow at Hurstbourne Tarrant* (1916; watercolour on paper; private collection, *ibid.*, p.27), "like the bony ridge of the backbone of a whale", is an accurate rendition as well as a lyrical study, whereas her depiction of what Gerald Brenan called his "yellow oxhide land" in *Yegen "Landscape"* (1924; oil on canvas; private collection, *ibid.*, p.78), of which she wrote: "I am trying a new plan, an entire underpainting in brilliant colours", is a visionary improvisation on a store of remembered images from Spain. *Farm at Watendlath* (1921; oil on canvas; Tate Gallery, London, *ibid.*, p.77) has a similar psychological power and ingeniously employs Lilliputian figures as a foil to balance the picture. *Fishing Boat in the Mediterranean* (c.1929; oil on canvas; private collection, *ibid.*, p.114) has different concerns. Carrington jettisoned line in favour of an exquisite procession of colours that define form and suggest the depths of the sea.

Carrington wrote: "the discovery of a person, of an affection, of a new emotion is to me next to my painting, the greatest thing I care about". She had a watchful temperament and she painted people perceptively, treating subjects according to the role they played in her life. She painted *Lytton Strachey* (1916; oil on canvas; private collection, *ibid.*, p.56) in loving detail with warm squirrel reds, echoed in the roof tiles of *Tidmarsh Mill* (c.1918; see illustration). She drew her own image in a *Self-Portrait* (c.1910; pencil on paper; private collection, *ibid.*, p.18) that was utterly without vanity and unusually revealing. With the exception of Strachey, Carrington's finest portraits are of women of character and she painted a Cornish farmer, *Mrs Box* (1919; oil on canvas; private collection, *ibid.*, p.73), as if she were a Gypsy queen from the New Forest. She also made a frankly erotic drawing of *Julia Strachey* (c.1925; pencil on paper; private collection, *ibid.*, p.103), which hinted

Carrington: *Tidmarsh Mill, c.*1918; oil; private collection

at her sexual duality. Julia was one of Paul Poiret's famously slender models. Carrington, however, pictured her as she fantasised: "very fat, and like a Veronese beauty".

Carrington's introduction to the decorative arts began around 1914 when she worked for Roger Fry's Omega Workshops, decorating objects in the "new" style, providing everything needed for the home but unlike anything ever seen there before. This ephemeral legacy of her taste was established when she decorated her Wiltshire home, Ham Spray, like a bower-bird, with the accumulated souvenirs of her life. Her eclectic collection of "treasures" furnished her with objects for paintings in the vanitas tradition (*Tulips in a Staffordshire Jug, c.*1921; oil on canvas; private collection, *ibid.*, p. 55). Her quest for variety was tireless. She painted tiles and tea sets, made patchwork quilts, each one a calendar of her life; marbled papers for bookbinding; discovered a new technique for patterning on leather; printed book-plates from woodblocks and provided illustrations for five books, establishing a distinguishing feature for the Hogarth Press with her woodcuts for its first publication (*The Servant Girl*, 1917; *ibid.*, p.45). Her skills extended to film-making, and in all these media she explored the themes that preoccupied her contemporaries.

Carrington's decorations of furniture often involved complete transformations. An *HMV Gramophone Cabinet* (1927; Portsmouth City Museum and Art Gallery, *ibid.*, p.115)

was painted with an odalisque, a serpent and a cornet; sportive youths, pages and greyhounds cavorted on a tin trunk and the base of a sewing machine formed the mount for a Rococo fantasy of shells. Working from squared-up drawings and templates she made a full-scale classical decoration (1928; *ibid.*, p.126) for George Rylands, brightening his bleak north-facing rooms at King's College, Cambridge, with colours that complemented his collection of Crown Derby china. Her scheme for Faith Henderson's Wiltshire cottage (since painted out) was bold and fanciful with tumbling cornucopias, entwining vines and orange peacocks on mauve door panels edged with jambs in green. Oddities such as cut oranges were used to apply paint, on top of which she scratched and marked patterns.

Julia Strachey described Carrington as being "by nature a lover of marvels" and her love of theatricality can be seen in the false bookcase that she devised for Strachey's library with titles such as *False Appearances by Dora Wood*. Carrington painted a *trompe-l'oeil* picture of a ghostly *Cook and the Cat* (1931; *ibid.*, p.128) in a blind window of Biddesden, a Vanbrugh-Hawksmoor-style house. The tableau curtains were a recurrent theme in Carrington's seemingly alchemical paintings on glass, backed with silver sweet papers, like moons. Carrington listed some of her subjects: "Flowerpieces, boxers, balloons, volcanoes, tightrope dancers, Victorian beauties, soldiers, tropical botanical flowers, birds and fruits", which she sold, in the 1920s, at the Birrell and Garnett bookshop in Bloomsbury.

Carrington's tinselled pictures ("*Rouen Ware*", c.1923; oil, ink and silver foil on glass; private collection, *ibid.*, p.54) were in the same tradition of popular art as the ornamental opulence of the saloon bar and the costume of the Pearly Kings and Queens. They were inspired by the "demountable baroque" of the fairground, the scrim-shandy work of mariners and the rose and castle of canal boats (fireplace tiles painted for the marriage of Alec and Frances Penrose, 1930; private collection, *ibid.*, p.72). Carrington's appreciation of local peculiarities was before her time. They all gave form to her love of things made for country needs and tastes.

Carrington was a poet-painter. Her vivid, painterly, illuminated letters became a vehicle for focusing her mind for painting (*Gamekeeper's Sons*, 1919; Harry Ransom Humanities Research Center, University of Texas at Austin, *ibid.*, p.99). They have a quirkiness and wit that became the signature of her work and life. In the 1920s, as the bias of her friendships was with writers, Carrington lost the stimulation and encouragement of painters. Incapable of self-praise she became diffident about her work, writing: "It's rather maddening to have the ambition of Tintoretto and to paint like a diseased dormouse". Her artist's discipline was eroded as it became hopelessly undermined by her devotion to Strachey's talent above her own. Concern for his welfare, combined with running their home, left increasingly scant reserves for her work. Despite the fact that Carrington knew that the "vexations of life" disappeared when she was in her studio, conflicting emotions destroyed her purpose. She felt she was "not strong enough to live in this world of people and paint", and lost the facility to work out the harmony that can exist in living, loving and creating. Carrington was constantly conceiving ideas for paintings, walking on the Hampshire downs, plucking visions from the air, but they were not always realised. She rejected many paintings and invariably took completed canvases off the stretchers, ostensibly to use them again (she painted thinly, using a dry mixture without much oil; consequently paintings on rolled canvases are friable). Her identity had become so fragile that it depended upon Lytton's knowledge of her existence. When Lytton died, her own lights went out. Yet when Iris Tree said of Carrington: "you are like a tin of mixed biscuits, your parents were Huntley and Palmers", it was a tribute to her industriousness and the diversity of her work and vision.

JANE HILL

Carrington, Leonora

British painter and writer, 1917–

Born in Clayton Green, Lancashire, 6 April 1917. Educated in England, Florence and France; debutante at court of George V, 1935. Studied drawing and painting at Amedée Ozenfant Academy, London, 1936–7. Met Max Ernst, followed him to Paris and joined André Breton's Surrealist group, 1937; exhibited with the Surrealists in Paris (1938), Amsterdam (1938), New York (1942) and Paris (1947).

Settled in Saint-Martin d'Ardèche with Ernst, 1938. Fled to Spain after his second internment as an enemy alien, and admitted to a mental asylum in Santander after a nervous breakdown, 1940. Escaped to New York after marrying Mexican diplomat Renato Leduc in Lisbon, 1941; renewed association with Surrealists in New York and contributed to *View* and *VVV* magazines. Settled in Mexico City in 1942, divorced Leduc and joined group of European Surrealists. Met her first collector, Edward James, in 1944. Married Hungarian newspaper photographer Emerico (Chiki) Weisz in Mexico, 1946; two sons, born 1946 and 1947. Joined a Gurdjieff group, and with Remedios Varo (q.v.) experimented with alchemy, witchcraft and dream interpretation, 1950s. Left Mexico for a year in protest against government repression of student unrest, 1968. Studied under exiled Tibetan lama in Canada and Scotland, 1971. After 1985, divided her time between Mexico City and USA (New York, Chicago and Richmond, Virginia).

Selected Individual Exhibitions

Pierre Matisse Gallery, New York: 1948
Galería Clardecor, Mexico City: 1950
Galería de Arte Mexicano, Mexico City: 1952
Galería Antonio Souza, Mexico City: 1957
Instituto Nacional de Bellas Artes, Sala Nacional, Mexico City: 1960 (retrospective)
Galería de Arte Mexicano and Instituto Cultural Anglo-Mexican, Mexico City: 1965
Galería de Arte Mexicano/Florencia, Mexico City: 1969
Alexander Iolas Gallery, New York: 1975
Center for Inter-American Relations, New York: 1976 (touring retrospective)
Brewster Gallery, New York: 1978, 1988, 1995
Space Mirage, Tokyo: 1988
Museo Nacional de la Estampa INBA, Mexico City: 1989
Serpentine Gallery, London: 1991–2 (touring retrospective)
Mexican Museum, San Francisco: 1991
Museo de Arte Contemporáneo de Monterrey, Mexico: 1994 (retrospective)

Selected Writings

La Maison de la peur, Paris: Parisot, 1938 (booklet, illustrated by Max Ernst; first written in English, 1937)
La Dame ovale, Paris: GLM, 1939 (illustrated by Max Ernst; first written in English, 1938)
"Down Below", *VVV*, no.4, 1944; as *En Bas*, Paris: Fontaine, 1945; 2nd edition, Paris: Eric Losfeld, 1973; English version, Chicago: Black Swan Press, 1983
"Pénélope", *Les Quatre vents*, vi, Paris, 1946 (play)
Une chemise de nuit de flanelle, Paris: Librairie Les Pas Perdus, 1951 (play)
El mundo mágico de los Mayas, Mexico City: Instituto Nacional de Antropologia y Historia, 1964 (with Andrés Medina and Laurette Séjourné)
Le Cornet acoustique, Paris: Flammarion, 1974; as *The Hearing Trumpet*, New York: St Martin's Press, 1976; London: Routledge, 1977; reprinted London: Virago, 1991
The Oval Lady and Other Stories: Six Surreal Stories, Santa Barbara: Capra, 1975
La Porte de pierre, Paris: Flammarion, 1976; as *The Stone Door*, New York: St Martin's Press, 1977; London: Routledge, 1978
Le Septième Cheval, Montpellier: Coprah, 1977 (first written in English, 1941)
Pigeon vole/contes retrouvés, ed. Jacqueline Chénieux-Gendron, Paris: Le Temps Qu'Il Fait, 1986 (short stories)

The House of Fear: Notes from Down Below, New York: Dutton, 1988; London: Virago, 1989

The Seventh Horse and Other Stories, New York: Dutton, 1988; London: Virago, 1989

Bibliography

André Breton, *Le Surréalisme et la peinture, 1928–1965*, Paris: Gallimard, 1965

——, *Anthologie de l'humour noir, 1896–1966*, Paris: Pauvert, 1966

Gloria Feman Orenstein, "Leonora Carrington: Another reality", *MS*, iii, August 1974, pp.27–31

Leonora Carrington: A Retrospective Exhibition, exh. cat., Center for Inter-American Relations, New York, and elsewhere, 1976

Bettina Knapp, "Leonora Carrington's whimsical dreamworld: Animals talk, children are gods, a black swan lays an Orphic egg", *World Literature Today*, li, 1977, pp.525–30

Obliques, no.14–15, 1977 (special issue: *La Femme surréaliste*)

Gloria Feman Orenstein, "Leonora Carrington's visionary art for the New Age", *Chrysalis*, no.3, 1977, pp.66–77

Jacqueline Chénieux-Gendron, "Les contes de Leonora Carrington: Le tissage d'une intersubjectivité", *Le Surréalisme et le roman, 1922–1950*, Lausanne: L'Age d'Homme, 1983, pp.254–63

Whitney Chadwick, *Women Artists and the Surrealist Movement*, Boston: Little Brown, and London: Thames and Hudson, 1985

La Femme et le surréalisme, exh. cat., Musée Cantonal des Beaux-Arts, Lausanne, 1987

Janice Helland, "Surrealism and esoteric feminism in the paintings of Leonora Carrington", *Canadian Art Review*, xvi, 1989, pp.53–61

Susan Rubin Suleiman, *Subversive Intent: Gender, Politics and the Avant-Garde*, Cambridge, MA: Harvard University Press, 1990

Sonia Assa, "Gardens of earthly delight or, what's cookin? Leonora Carrington in the kitchen", *Studies in Twentieth-Century Literature*, xv, 1991, pp.213–27

Leonora Carrington, exh. cat., Serpentine Gallery, London, and elsewhere, 1991

Leonora Carrington: The Mexican Years, 1943–1985, exh. cat., Mexican Museum, San Francisco, 1991

Mary Ann Caws and others, eds, *Surrealism and Women*, Cambridge: Massachusetts Institute of Technology Press, 1991 (essays on Carrington by Peter Christensen, Georgiana M.M. Colvile and Madeleine Cottenet-Hage)

Mara R. Witzling, ed., *Voicing Our Visions: Writings by Women Artists*, New York: Universe, 1991; London: Women's Press, 1992

Leonora Carrington: Uno retrospectiva, exh. cat., Museo de Arte Contemporáneo de Monterrey, Mexico, 1994

Whitney Chadwick, *Leonora Carrington*, Mexico City: Consejo Nacional de la Cultura y los Artes, Ediciones ERA, 1994

Renée Riese Hubert, *Magnifying Mirrors: Women, Surrealism and Partnership*, Lincoln: University of Nebraska Press, 1994

Leonora Carrington, exh. cat., Brewster Gallery, New York, 1995

Leonora Carrington was barely 20 when she encountered Surrealism in the person of Max Ernst. Her youth, eccentricity and wild imagination prompted André Breton and his cohorts to consider her as a perfect example of the "femme-enfant" or child-woman, the Alice-in-Wonderland figure that they were forever looking for. Unlike Alice Rahon (q.v.), however, Carrington soon transgressed that role. Her rebellion against her English upper-class upbringing was the first sign of her need to establish her individual freedom, so that she could develop her talents as a painter and writer. As a child, her love of painting animals and such eccentric practices as mirror-writing were already manifest, and during her finishing school years in Florence and Paris she discovered not only the Italian masters but also Hieronymus Bosch, whose influence is most clearly expressed in her remarkable *Temptation of St Antony*

(1947; oil on canvas; private collection, repr. Monterrey 1994). There, as in so many of her pictures, Carrington achieves a surreal, uncanny effect by juxtaposing the fantastic proportions of the content (St Anthony's face and beard are tripled like Russian dolls within the gigantic, umbrella-shaped folds of his cloak; tiny delicately painted figures surround him; and the water that one of them pours from an amphora becomes a huge river beneath the holy man's feet) with a classical, well-mastered drawing technique and a subtle sense of colour. The strange blending of the protagonist's clothing with the raw material constituting the background landscape of the world around him and the figure of St Anthony himself evoke the affinity between Carrington and Remedios Varo (q.v.) in Mexico, leading to certain similarities in their styles of painting from the mid-1940s until Varo's death in 1963.

In the early, pre-Mexican years Carrington experimented with portraits and self-portraits (the latter genre being especially characteristic of the Surrealist women artists), in which she metamorphosed and occulted the figures represented, usually giving them a semi-animal form. In childhood, Carrington and her brothers were generally confined to the nursery and entrusted to the care of servants they disliked, which led them to seek out the company of animals. The young Leonora's totem creature was undoubtedly the horse. Her two early self-portraits, *Inn of the Dawn Horse (Self-Portrait)* (1936–7; oil on canvas; 65 × 81.2 cm.; Collection Pierre Matisse, repr. New York 1976) and *Woman and Bird* (1937; oil on canvas; 38 × 31 cm.; private collection, repr. London 1991), both represent Carrington in equine form. The first accentuates her mane-like hair and riding breeches and provides her with a triple animal *alter ego*: a face-on female hyena (this beast reappears in the story "The debutante" of 1939 as the autobiographical girl protagonist's unpresentable smelly animal "id", which ruins a debutante ball), a rocking-horse reminiscent of the nursery and a live horse seen through the window in the background, galloping away to freedom. In the second self-portrait Carrington's head and neck are those of a horse, with her human features and expression. Not only did the young Carrington love to ride horses, but her imagination also fed on the folk tales told by her Irish nanny, including several about the Celtic goddess who could take on any animal shape and about the mare-goddess Epona. In the colours of alchemy, like the other two, the portrait of *Max Ernst* (1939; see illustration) depicts the latter, with his normal human head, hands and feet, as a kind of seahorse shaman in an arctic landscape, clad in a strange merman-shaped fur coat of purplish red, holding a green lantern containing a miniature prancing horse, a representation of Carrington perhaps, with a large white iceberg horse behind him. Several of Carrington's early stories, such as "The House of Fear" (1937), "The Oval Lady" (1938) and "The Seventh Horse" (1941) include horse-people and other hybrid creatures.

Surrealism provided a context for Carrington's fantasy world. At Saint-Martin d'Ardèche, she and Ernst produced plastic and literary works abundantly, in a mutually inspirational close collaboration, including a jointly painted oil *Meeting* (1940; Collection François Petit, Paris), portraits of each other and fantastic tales by Carrington, illustrated by Ernst. After her traumatising experience of mental illness (1940), described in her novella *Down Below* (1944),

Leonora Carrington: *Max Ernst*, 1939; Young-Mallin Archive Collection, New York

Carrington's visionary perception of both her inner and outer worlds was sharpened and intensified. Mexico, which Breton called "The Surrealist country par excellence", added new landscapes, faces and folk tales to those of her Irish heritage, although those early influences continued to dominate Carrington's art, reinforced by a careful study of Robert Graves's book *The White Goddess* (1948). When Carrington was commissioned to paint a large mural, the *Magical World of the Maya* (1963; casein on panel; 2.1 × 4.6 m.; Museo Regional, Tuxtla Gutiérrez, Mexico), celebrating the beliefs of the Chiapas Indians, whose culture and mores she studied closely during several stays in southern Mexico, she nevertheless produced a work that appears far more influenced by Celtic myths of rainbows, unicorns, dragons, animal-drawn

chariots etc. than by those of Mexico. As Whitney Chadwick put it: "she herself has characterized her sensibility as caught between Catholic and Celtic" (Chadwick 1985, p.75).

While Frida Kahlo (q.v.) revived and secularised the old Mexican religious tradition of the *retablo*, Carrington discovered and adopted a medieval technique, consisting of using egg tempera on gessoed wooden panels (Chadwick 1994), thus highlighting the delicacy of her miniature forms in numerous Bosch-influenced compositions, such as *Tuesday* (1946; Collection Isaac Lif), *Palatine Predella* (1946; George Nader Gallery) and *Dog Child of Monkton Priori* (1950; private collection, repr. San Francisco 1991). In later years Carrington continued to use both oil painting and egg tempera, occasionally watercolour, as well as acrylic. She has made lithographs from some of her best paintings, for example *Tuesday* (1987; Collection Georgiana Colvile) and *Crookhey Hall* (oil painting, 1947; private collection, repr. Monterrey 1994; lithograph, 1987; Collection Whitney Chadwick).

Carrington alludes to her friendship and creative collaboration with Remedios Varo in her novel *Le Cornet acoustique* (1974). The two women shared the Parisian and then the Mexican Surrealist experience, a strong interest in magic, alchemy, dreams and culinary experiments. As Sonia Assa has shown (1991), cooking plays an important part and acquires a magic aura in Carrington's work. In some of her stories, such as "White Rabbits" and "The Sisters", eating tends to be a carnivorous and even cannibalistic practice, whereas the feasting creatures in her paintings more often than not seem to be peaceful vegetarians, as in the oils *Edwardian Hunt Breakfast* (1956; private collection, repr. New York 1976) and *Lepidoptera* (1969; private collection, Mexico, *ibid.*).

During the 1970s Carrington became interested in Tibetan culture, thus adding a new mystical facet to her art, and she also expressed a strong solidarity with the various women's movements. *The Godmother* (1970; oil on canvas; Collection Mr and Mrs Nesuhi Ertegun, *ibid.*) portrays a rotund goddess figure in the colours of alchemy, with a dark owl-like head and shoulders, birds perching on her branch-like arms, a globe in her middle, her body made up of the heads of golden-haired women. The culinary motif recurs in a tribute to her mother, *Grandmother Moorhead's Aromatic Kitchen* (1975; oil on canvas; Charles B. Goddard Center for Visual and Performing Arts, Ardmore, Oklahoma). Most of the figures in her later paintings are female, and her later work deals increasingly with the theme of women's old age, as in *The Magdalenes* (1986; egg tempera on panel; private collection). Carrington's later work includes drawings, statuettes (e.g. *Old Magdalena*, 1988; bronze; Brewster Gallery, New York) and tapestries, all alive with magic, exotic colours, dreamlike situations, mythical personae and an indomitable sense of humour. She no longer considers herself to be a Surrealist, although she has expressed and continues to express an alternative fantasy world, which goes further afield even than the work of Ernst or Breton. The exhibition at the Serpentine Gallery, London, in 1991 was her first long-overdue European retrospective and at last revealed her highly original work to her fellow countrymen and women, but she remains to date far better known in Mexico and the USA than in Britain or even France.

GEORGIANA M. M. COLVILE

Caspar-Filser, Maria
German painter, 1878–1968

Born Maria Filser in Riedlingen, 7 August 1878. Studied at the academies in Stuttgart and Munich under Friedrich von Keller, Gustav Igler and Ludwig von Herterich, 1896–1903. Married painter Karl Caspar, 1907; daughter Felizitas, also an artist, born 1917; husband died 1956. Member, 1909, and member of management committee, 1927, Deutscher Künstlerbund; only woman founder-member of the artists' association SEMA, Munich, 1911, and of Münchener Neue Secession, 1913; member, Berlin Secession, 1916; founder-member of the artists' association Die Mappe (Portfolio), Munich, 1918; first female artist to obtain the title professor of visual arts, 1925. Paintings and graphic works declared "degenerate" and removed from public collections, 1937; much work destroyed. Munich apartment destroyed by bombing, 1944. Founder-member of Neue Gruppe, Munich, 1947; founder-member of the newly constituted Deutscher Künstlerbund, Berlin, 1950; member, Bayerische Akademie der Schönen Künste (Bavarian Academy of Fine Arts), 1951; honorary member, Bayerische Akademie der Bildenden Künste (Bavarian Academy of Visual Arts), Munich, 1958. Recipient of Munich art prize, 1947; Upper Swabian art prize, 1952 (with Karl Caspar); Great Distinguished Service Cross of the Federal Republic of Germany, 1959; silver medal, city of Paris, 1961; Cultural prize, city of Rosenheim, 1962; Burda prize, 1963. Died in Brannenburg, 12 February 1968.

Principal Exhibitions

Individual
Galerie Thannhauser, Munich: 1911 (with Karl Caspar), 1922
Galerie Caspari, Munich: 1913 (with Karl Caspar), 1918, 1925
Kestner-Gesellschaft, Hannover: 1916
Kunsthaus Schaller, Stuttgart: 1919, 1937 (both with Karl Caspar)
Museum der Stadt, Ulm: 1924, 1929 (both with Karl Caspar)
Kunstverein, Munich: 1929, 1956 (with Karl Caspar)
Württembergische Staatsgalerie, Stuttgart: 1951 (with Karl Caspar, touring)
Kunstverein, Rosenheim: 1952 (with Karl Caspar), 1957
Kunstverein, Stuttgart: 1959 (touring)
Kunstverein, Ulm: 1960
Galerie Altes Theater, Ravensburg: 1968 (retrospective)

Group
Munich Secession: 1905–13
Sonderbund exhibition, Cologne: 1912
Münchener Neue Secession, Munich: 1913–33
Venice Biennale: 1924, 1926, 1928, 1948
Munich: 1937 (Entartete Kunst)
Neue Gruppe, Munich: 1947–68

Bibliography

Julius Baum, *Die Stuttgarter Kunst der Gegenwart*, Stuttgart, 1913
Fritz Nemitz, *Deutsche Malerei der Gegenwart*, Munich, 1948
Julius Baum, *Die Schwäbische Kunst im 19. und 20. Jahrhundert*, Stuttgart, 1952
Karl Gustav Gerold, *Deutsche Malerei unserer Zeit*, Munich, 1956
Maria Caspar-Filser: Gedächtnisausstellung, exh. cat., Galerie Altes Theater, Ravensburg, 1968
Franz Roh, *German Art in the Twentieth Century: Painting, Sculpture, Architecture*, London: Thames and Hudson, and Greenwich, CT: New York Graphic Society, 1968 (German original, 1958)
Herbert Schindler, *Bayerische Symphonie*, ii, Munich, 1968
Stefan Ott, *Oberschwaben: Gesicht einer Landschaft*, Ravensburg, 1971
Maria Caspar-Filser, 1878–1968, exh. cat., Städtische Galerie, Albstadt, 1978
Das Landschaftsbild der Schwäbischen Alb I, exh. cat., Städtische Galerie, Albstadt, 1980
Rainer Zimmermann, *Die Kunst der verschollenen Generation: Deutsche Malerei des Expressiven Realismus von 1925–1975*, Düsseldorf, 1980
Günther Wirth, *Kunst im deutschen Südwesten von 1945 bis zur Gegenwart*, Stuttgart: Hatie, 1982
Maler in Oberschwaben und am Bodensee, 1933–1945: "Entartet" – verfemt, exh. cat., Städtische Galerie, Saulgau, 1983
Kunst der Moderne in der Landschaft Bodensee-Oberschwaben, exh. cat., Galerie Bodenseekreis, Friedrichshafen, 1984
Maria Caspar-Filser, 1878–1968, exh. cat., Landesgirokasse, Stuttgart, 1986
Deutscher Künstlerbund: 1936 – verbotene Bilder, exh. cat., Sprengel Museum, Hannover, 1986
Das Landschaftsbild der Schwäbischen Alb II, exh. cat., Städtische Galerie, Albstadt, 1987
Günther Wirth, *Verbotene Kunst, 1933–1945: Verfolgte Künstler im deutschen Südwesten*, Stuttgart: Hatie, 1987
Maria Caspar-Filser, exh. cat., Landratsamt Zollern-Alb-Kreis, Balingen, 1988
Deutsche und französische Gemälde des 19. und frühen 20. Jahrhunderts, exh. cat., Kunsthaus Bühler, Stuttgart, 1988
Karl Caspar, Maria Caspar-Filser, Felizitas Köster-Caspar, exh. cat., Landkreis, Rosenheim, 1990
Maria Caspar-Filser, Karl Caspar: Verfolgte Bilder, exh. cat., Städtische Galerie, Albstadt, 1994

In the vanguard of artistic activities until the late 1930s, Maria Caspar-Filser was one of the most important German artists of her time. She was a member or founding member of numerous artists' groups and associations, participating in the Cologne Sonderbund exhibition of 1912, which made modern art successful in Germany, and was the first female German artist to become a professor. Like other artists of her "lost generation", however, she has been largely forgotten. Her career was cruelly interrupted by the rise of National Socialism: branded "degenerate", her work was removed from museums, and she was prohibited from exhibiting. She and her husband went into internal exile, settling in Brannenburg.

Caspar-Filser's oeuvre consists mainly of oil paintings: landscapes, still lifes, flower pieces and figural scenes. Her style has often been compared retrospectively to works by Cézanne, Gauguin, van Gogh, Matisse or Munch, but this ignores the originality of her achievement. She was a strong, independent artist of rich colours and powerful compositions, whose use of colour and form was inspired by the experience of reality. Motifs are taken from her immediate surroundings. Nature is an inexhaustible source of inspiration for her, and new analyses of familiar motifs yield ever different depictions. The development of her work is characterised by the shift from emphasis on the motif to freedom in colour and compositions. *Schalksburg in Winter* (1906; Oberschwäbische Elektrizitätswerke, repr. Balingen 1988, p.27) is in the Swabian Impressionist tradition taught at the Stuttgart Academy: realistic, plein-air painting emphasising links with the native land. While *Autumn in the Swabian Alb* (1908; Landkreis Biberach,

Caspar-Filser: *Melting Snow*, 1909; oil; Städtische Galerie Albstadt, Germany

Galerie des Landratsamtes, *ibid.*, p.29) introduces a more expressionist style with colourful, vibrant forms, *Melting Snow* (1909; see illustration) again faithfully documents the familiar Swabian landscape.

Gradually, Caspar-Filser relinquished realistic depiction. Individual forms in *Swabian Autumn Landscape* (*Apple Harvest near Balingen*; 1910; Städtische Galerie Albstadt, repr. Albstadt 1987, p.45) are composed of abstract planes of colour or defined by an emphatic outline. Trees protectively frame the harvesters, giving the impression of a tranquil village idyll, the security of a traditional way of life. Harvesting carries a symbolic meaning, man gratefully accepting the gift of nature. A lonely castle balances precariously on top of a hill in *Schloss Baldern – Autumn Evening* (1918; private collection, repr. Albstadt 1978, p.69). A path winding dynamically uphill seems almost alive.

The illusion of depth in *Ipf near Bopfingen* (1918; private collection, *ibid.*, p.39) is achieved by progressively subduing the colours and losing the contours of the forms. There is no distinction of detailed, identifiable objects in the foreground. Seen in isolation, the dynamic foreground would form an abstract colour composition; it is only in the context of the whole picture that the landscape emerges. *Summer Morning in Baldern* (1922; private collection, repr. Stuttgart 1986, p.57) goes further along the path to abstraction. The picture cannot be "read", it must impress the viewer as a whole. Parts cannot be interpreted individually without rendering other parts meaningless, simple splashes of colour. Caspar-Filser never, however, fully translates the world of objects into the realm of the abstract.

While the Brannenburg landscapes tend to show the immediate surroundings, often with a tree barring the view (e.g. *Apple Tree with House and Studio*, 1949; artist's estate, repr. Albstadt 1978, p.85), her Italian landscapes offer wide vistas. The subject matter of *Sestri Harbour* (1939; artist's estate, *ibid.*, p.55) is not a vehicle for atmosphere or emotion, but an incentive for a colour composition. The houses are almost dissolved in the pattern of forms. *Thunderstorm over Florence* (1951; artist's estate, *ibid.*, p.84) still shows the influence of Cézanne in its treatment of the landscape as a formal problem. Painted long after her stay at the Villa Romana in Florence (1913–4), the work shows how vivid its memory remained.

Caspar-Filser's flower paintings reveal her masterful use of colour. She determined the colour composition by carefully arranging every object in the still life, closely observing nature for each formulation. For her, the construction of the composition lay in the structure of the still life; composing and depicting were simultaneous processes. The compositions express her closeness to everyday objects and her delight in them. Rich in colours and contrast, *Bunch of Wild Flowers* (1927; private collection, *ibid.*, p.73) seems to move, swaying gently before a green background. *Inn Pikes* (1937; private collection, *ibid.*, p.78) were not arranged by the artist – her interest was aroused spontaneously by their accidental order. Its appeal lies less in the composition than in the transformation of colour.

During the 1940s Caspar-Filser's compositions became lighter, more spacious, transparent and static, with fewer objects (e.g. *Cherries, Strawberries and Small Bunch of Roses*, 1943; artist's estate, *ibid.*, p.83). In *Smoker's Still Life* (1949; private collection, repr. Stuttgart 1986, p.116) the objects are almost isolated; selective perception and the additive combination of detail enable her to devote more attention to each object. In a constant dialogue with nature, Caspar-Filser created works out of a sensuous enjoyment of colour, refreshingly free from dogmatism. Far from banal naturalism, her pictures instead are songs of praise to the magnificence of the earth, its richness and blessings. Above the cold, bleak, snowy *Winter Landscape with Sun* (1958; artist's estate, repr. Albstadt 1978, p.87) a warm sky suggests a promising future. She infuses the exterior with interior familiarity, inner harmony and warmth to get through hard times.

INES SCHLENKER

Cassatt, Mary
American painter and printmaker, 1844–1926

Born in Allegheny City (now part of Pittsburgh), Pennsylvania, 22 May 1844; father a banker; eldest brother Alexander Johnston became president of Pennsylvania Railroad (1899). Travelled in Europe with her family, attending schools in Paris, Heidelberg and Darmstadt, 1851–5. Studied at the Pennsylvania Academy of the Fine Arts, Philadelphia, 1860–64. Went to Europe for further art training, 1865; remained there for the rest of her life, with return trips to USA in 1870–71, 1875, 1898 and 1908. Studied under Charles Chaplin and Jean-Léon Gérôme in Paris, 1866; Edouard Frère, Paul Soyer and other masters in art colonies at Courances and Ecouen, 1867–8; Thomas Couture at Villiers-le-Bel near Ecouen, 1868 and 1874; Charles Bellay in Rome, 1870; friend of Degas. Also made sketching trip to Piedmont, 1869; worked in Parma, Madrid and Seville, 1872–3; visited the Netherlands and Belgium, 1873; Rome again, 1874. Settled in Paris, 1874; joined there by her parents and sister Lydia, 1877. Purchased château at Mesnil-Beaufresne, north of Paris, 1894. Travelled to Italy, 1893; to Italy and Spain on collecting trip with friends Henry O. and Louisine Elder Havemeyer, 1901. Lived in Grasse, near Nice, during the winters of 1912–24 and during World War I. Chevalier, Légion d'Honneur, France, 1904. Died at Mesnil-Beaufresne, 14 June 1926.

Principal Exhibitions

Individual
Galeries Durand-Ruel, Paris: 1891, 1893 (retrospective), 1908, 1914
F. Keppel and Co., New York: 1891
Durand-Ruel Gallery, New York: 1895, 1898, 1903, 1907, 1927
Philadelphia: 1927 (memorial)
Chicago: 1927 (memorial)
New York: 1927 (memorial)
Galerie A.-M. Reitlinger, Paris: 1927, 1931 (retrospective)

Group
Paris Salon: 1868, 1870, 1872–6
National Academy of Design, New York: 1874, 1878 (annuals), 1886 (Impressionist group, special exhibition)
Pennsylvania Academy of the Fine Arts, Philadelphia: 1876–9, 1885, 1898–1907, 1910–12, 1915–17, 1920
Society of American Artists, New York: from 1879
Impressionist group, Paris: 1879, 1880, 1881, 1886
Dowdeswell Galleries, London: 1883 (*Impressionist Art*)
Exposition des Peintre-Graveurs, Paris: 1889, 1890
Woman's Building, World's Columbian Exposition, Chicago: 1893
M. Knoedler, New York: 1915 (*Suffrage Loan Exhibition*)

Selected Writings

Cassatt and Her Circle: Selected Letters, ed. Nancy Mowll Mathews, New York: Abbeville, 1984

Bibliography

Joris-Karl Huysmans, *L'Art moderne*, Paris: Charpentier, 1883
Rambaud Yveling, "Miss Cassatt", *L'Art dans les deux mondes*, no.1, 22 November 1890, p.7
Félix Fénéon, "Cassatt, Pissarro", *Le Chat Noir*, 11 April 1891; reprinted in *Félix Fénéon: Oeuvres plus que complètes*, ed. Joan Halperin, Geneva: Droz, 1970
Exposition Mary Cassatt, exh. cat., Galeries Durand-Ruel, Paris, 1893
Achille Ségard, *Mary Cassatt: Un peintre des enfants et des mères*, Paris: Ollendorff, 1913
George Biddle, "Some memories of Mary Cassatt", *The Arts*, August 1926, pp.107–11
Adelyn Dohme Breeskin, *The Graphic Work of Mary Cassatt: A Catalogue Raisonné*, New York: Bittner, 1948; reissued as *A Catalogue Raisonné of the Graphic Work*, Washington, DC: Smithsonian Institution Press, 1979
Anna Thorne, "My afternoon with Mary Cassatt", *School Arts*, May 1960, pp.10–12
Frederick A. Sweet, *Miss Mary Cassatt, Impressionist from Pennsylvania*, Norman: University of Oklahoma Press, 1966
Adelyn Dohme Breeskin, *Mary Cassatt: A Catalogue Raisonné of the Oils, Pastels, Watercolors and Drawings*, Washington, DC: Smithsonian Institution Press, 1970
Patricia T. Davis, *End of the Line: Alexander J. Cassatt and the Pennsylvania Railroad*, New York: Neale Watson, 1978
Nancy Mowll Mathews, *Mary Cassatt and the "Modern Madonna" of the Nineteenth Century*, PhD dissertation, New York University, 1980
Griselda Pollock, *Mary Cassatt*, New York: Harper, and London: Jupiter, 1980
Mary Cassatt and Philadelphia, exh. cat., Philadelphia Museum of Art, 1985
The New Painting: Impressionism, 1874–1886, exh. cat., Fine Arts Museums of San Francisco, 1986
Frances Weitzenhoffer, *The Havemeyers: Impressionism Comes to America*, New York: Abrams, 1986
Nancy Mowll Mathews, *Mary Cassatt*, New York: Abrams, 1987
Mary Cassatt: The Color Prints, exh. cat., National Gallery of Art, Washington, DC, and elsewhere, 1989

Louisine Havemeyer, *Sixteen to Sixty: Memoirs of a Collector*, ed. Susan Alyson Stein, revised edition, New York: Ursus, 1993

Nancy Mowll Mathews, *Mary Cassatt: A Life*, New York: Villard, 1994 (contains bibliography)

——, *Cassatt: A Retrospective*, New York: Levin, 1996

Best known for her participation in the French Impressionist group and for her paintings of mothers and children, Mary Cassatt is one of the few women artists to have gained an international reputation during her lifetime and to have kept it to the present day. Since it is hard for women to rise to the top of this field and harder still for them to be remembered by posterity, her success offers an object lesson to all. The ingredients contributing to her success were these: a family that was financially and emotionally supportive; a deep reserve of intelligence, energy and talent; an instinct for styles and subjects that was both fresh and lasting; and strong friendships with artists and writers who could both enrich her art and promote it to the outside world. Cassatt marshalled these resources to navigate an entrenched art establishment and to create an art that would inspire artists and amateurs the world over.

Cassatt practised as an artist for more than 50 years, beginning her formal art studies at the Pennsylvania Academy of the Fine Arts in 1860. Romanticism was still the dominant style in the USA during her student days and in some ways can be seen in her approach to subject matter throughout her career. Her earliest endeavours culminated in such paintings as the *Mandolin Player* (private collection, on loan to Philadelphia Museum of Art), which was exhibited at the Paris Salon of 1868. This painting shows the theme of love as expressed by a single monumental figure of a contemplative woman – an interest that would be eventually translated into the mother and child subject and continue into Cassatt's later years.

Women of Cassatt's generation were extremely fortunate in that the wave of feminism that had swept Europe and the USA in the 1840s opened many professional doors for them. Cassatt took advantage of the new educational opportunities, particularly in art academies that from the mid-19th century accepted increasing numbers of women. The availability of high-level training in the fine arts corresponded to the newly co-educational colleges and public universities such as Oberlin and the University of Michigan as well as the founding of women's colleges such as Vassar (1865), Smith (1871) and Wellesley (1875). Cassatt and her friends were outspoken advocates of equal rights all their lives. They campaigned for equal travel scholarships in their student days in the 1860s and campaigned for the vote in their old age in the 1910s. While it is hard to see such clear political statements of women's rights in Cassatt's art, there is no question that she painted women with dignity and the suggestion of a rich inner life.

In addition to confronting the feminist issues of her day, Cassatt also thought deeply about issues of modern art and came to her own conclusions about the reforms that were needed. From the unfair exclusion of women from the official Ecole des Beaux-Arts to the failings of the Salon jury system, Cassatt addressed in impassioned diatribes the wrongs of the French art establishment that set international standards in the 1860s and 1870s. As for the current trends in painting, she felt that acknowledged masters such as Bonnat and Cabanel misinterpreted the old masters and produced work that was "washy, unfleshlike, and grey", as she wrote to her friend Emily Sartain. During the first ten years that she painted in Europe (1866–76) she tried to adapt what teachers called her natural "talent of the brush" to current styles of costume genre painting and fashionable portraiture. She became, however, increasingly interested in the new techniques developed by the Impressionists and found that her own experiments with a lightened palette and a more spontaneous, sketch-like approach were quickly rejected by the Salon juries she was still trying to please in 1875, 1876 and 1877.

Cassatt's reputation as an outspoken critic of the establishment brought her to the attention of the Impressionists and, in 1877, Edgar Degas invited her to exhibit with the group. Her debut among these radical artists took place two years later in the fourth Impressionist exhibition held in a temporary gallery on the avenue de l'Opéra. Cassatt had studied the work of her new colleagues, particularly Degas, Berthe Morisot (q.v.) and Auguste Renoir, and developed a new style that translated her contemplative women from costumed "folk" into modern Parisians enacting the rituals of 19th-century society. Now, instead of showing veiled Spanish women on a balcony during Carnival, she captured well-dressed young Parisians on a balcony at the Théâtre Français. Ritual flirtation was still her theme, but she adjusted her style to show the ephemeral world of contemporary romance and popular entertainment.

From 1879 to 1886 Cassatt was an active member of the Impressionist group both professionally and socially. Her friendships with Degas and Morisot as well as the Impressionist dealer Paul Durand-Ruel and such patrons and supporters as M. and Mme Paul Bérard and Stéphane Mallarmé attest to her integration into rarefied Parisian intellectual and cultural circles – an unusual feat for an American. She was also friendly with both Whistler and Sargent as well as the many other American painters who visited Paris regularly, even though she made it a habit to avoid the American "colony". Thus her art references both French and American values in a mix that defies neat national categorisation. A painting such as *The Loge* (National Gallery of Art, Washington, DC), for example, mixes the French tradition of the *cocotte* with a stolid American innocence.

During the years that Cassatt exhibited with the Impressionists, she also turned her eye to her own family for scenes of contemporary Parisian life. Using a sketchbook approach, she captured her parents and older sister Lydia (who had left Philadelphia in 1877 to live with her in Paris) in their quiet domestic pursuits in their elegant fifth-floor apartment on the avenue Trudaine near the Place Clichy. These good-natured, privileged Americans often found themselves "exposed" on the walls of exhibitions or studied by collectors coming to Cassatt's studio to make a purchase. Cassatt used her family extensively in a series of etchings and drypoints she produced in 1879–80, such as *Lydia and Her Mother at Tea* (1880; National Gallery of Art, Washington, DC). This sudden foray into printmaking was inspired by Degas and the prospect of a new art journal, to be called *Le Jour et la nuit*, which would include original prints by the Impressionists. Although the journal was never published, Cassatt nevertheless came out of the experience with a significant body of new work and polished skills in a new medium.

Cassatt's experiments with printmaking gave her a new respect for the craft of drawing, which, given her natural

Cassatt: *Hélène de Septeuil*, *c*.1889; pastel; 65.7 × 41.9 cm.; Louise Crombie Beach Memorial Collection, William Benton Museum of Art, University of Connecticut

facility with a brush, had never interested her enough to become an accomplished draughtswoman. Even as she continued to work within the Impressionist context, however, she began to emphasise the linear structure of her painting and, towards the mid-1880s, a new, more tightly composed style took the place of her earlier, freer Impressionist works. The spare depiction of her mother's cousin, Mary Dickinson Riddle, in a work called *Lady at the Tea Table* (1883; Metropolitan Museum of Art, New York) marks Cassatt's growing fascination with the power of line. The delicate web Cassatt spins to portray the elderly woman's hand curved lightly but masterfully around the handle of a teapot conveys Mrs Riddle's age, social status and personality in a single gesture. It was at this time that Cassatt also developed her own technique in pastel, which she would alternate with painting from that point on.

With Cassatt's search for a stable, linear structure to her compositions came a similar desire to simplify her subject matter. In the late 1880s she confined herself either to portraits or the mother and child theme. Symbolist trends in art and literature brought back into modern painting many subjects drawn from religious art, such as the Virgin and Child, the Temptation of Eve and the Crucifixion. For the most part, these images were derived from peasant life studied by artists of all nationalities in the villages throughout Europe, from Pont-Aven to Murnau. But although Cassatt often painted in the country during the summer months, she found her own idiom for her "modern Madonna" that combined the Impressionist insistence on modern life with a simplified, monumental composition. She adapted her highly developed devices for depicting the contemplative woman (shadowed face, eyes turned away, calm pose) to the intertwined relationship of woman and child. *Hélène de Septeuil* (see illustration) is a pastel based on studies made of a child model from Septeuil where Cassatt spent the summer of 1889. The simple costume of the "mother" (in reality, Cassatt's maid Mathilde Valet) and the golden brim of the child's hat encircling her head suggest the images of peasant "Madonnas" painted by such contemporaries as the Frenchman Charles Filiger and the American Gari Melchers. But Cassatt's references are seldom so obvious. Many others suggest old master sources from Botticelli to Rubens or are so openly portrait-like that it seems futile to search for sources at all. Regardless of art-historical references, Cassatt's calm, thoughtful treatment of the subject – so different from the melodrama of her main Parisian rival, Eugène Carrière – made a woman's relationship with a child one of the most compelling images to come out of this period.

From the first, these mother and child compositions were enthusiastically received by critics and collectors alike, affirming Cassatt's direction and setting her on a lifelong path that she was not always sure she wanted to follow. At this time Cassatt's business relationship with the dealer Paul Durand-Ruel was regularised, giving him exclusive rights to her annual output. This meant that he made her work readily available to the public in Paris, both in group and one-person shows as well as through his frequent publications. In 1886 Durand-Ruel began to have an annual presence in New York through large exhibitions and, by 1890, he had opened a branch of his Paris gallery on Fifth Avenue. Durand-Ruel benefited from Cassatt's connections to the art-buying public in the USA and, in turn,

he promoted Cassatt on both sides of the Atlantic. The relationship had its occasional rough spots as with any artist and dealer, but, for the most part, each was crucial to the long-term success of the other. While it is probably true that Durand-Ruel encouraged Cassatt to continue painting the mother and child subject long after she had exhausted its possibilities, nevertheless it was he who gave her the professional and financial support to bring the theme to its first full flowering and opened the door for her lasting fame.

Not long after Cassatt had begun to explore the mother and child theme, she embarked on a series of large-scale colour prints modelled after the immensely popular portfolios of Japanese *ukiyo-e* woodblocks. The series included ten images (four were mother and child subjects) that followed Parisian women through a typical day of bathing and dressing, performing errands around town via the omnibus, visiting the dressmaker and entertaining at home. There are two major models depicted, and the viewer becomes acquainted with each as she appears in changing settings.

Cassatt was in the forefront of artists who were just turning to colour prints as a new means of expression. They were partly inspired by Japanese prints and partly by such popular graphic images as posters and other advertising. The small black-and-white images so popular during the "Etching Revival" of the 1860s and 1870s were associated with the print connoisseur, whereas in the more democratic 1890s artists, including Cassatt, wanted to reach a larger audience. With the work of Toulouse-Lautrec, Henri Rivière and others, colour prints in a variety of graphic media began to appear. Although inspired by woodblock prints, Cassatt chose to draw her composition in a clear drypoint line and then apply areas of colour by using aquatint tones from a second and third plate. The delicacy of the colours she achieved, along with the decorative patterning and the sinuous lines, heighten the senses of touch in such tender scenes as *Maternal Caress* and even of taste as the woman licks the envelope in *The Letter* (1890–91; see illustration).

The ten colour prints were presented in 1891 in what constituted Cassatt's first solo exhibition at Durand-Ruel's gallery in Paris. Although Pissarro complained that her prints were not fully appreciated, they were well reviewed and were quickly in demand among collectors in France and the USA. A review by Félix Fénéon in *Le Chat Noir* was highly complimentary, noting that the large, masculine hands that Cassatt loves to give her women help to make the composition flow in long, linear arabesques.

The following year Cassatt went from this print project to a painting project that was just as demanding of her creative and physical energies as the prints had been. Now considered one of the most important American women painters, she was asked to paint one of two central murals for the Woman's Building of the World's Columbian Exposition of 1893. These two murals defined the overarching theme of the pavilion: women's rise from slavery and ignorance in primitive times to her current state of education and accomplishment in the modern day. The mural *Primitive Woman* was commissioned from Mary Fairchild MacMonnies (q.v.), a younger American who had recently taken up residence in Paris with her husband, the sculptor Frederick MacMonnies. The mural *Modern Woman* was commissioned from the 48-year-old Cassatt. Both

Cassatt: *The Letter*, 1890–91; drypoint and aquatint on colour, State III; Metropolitan Museum of Art, New York: Gift of Paul J. Sachs, 1916

murals are now known only from photographs (repr. Maud Howe Elliott, *Art and Handicraft in the Woman's Building of the World's Columbian Exposition, Chicago, 1893*, Chicago and New York: Rand McNally, 1894, p.35), since the original canvases dropped out of sight in the early 20th century. Nevertheless, the scope of the undertaking and the originality of the designs make them a constant object of study. MacMonnies's *Primitive Woman* was the more successful of the two at the time since she strove for and achieved the effect of, as she called it, "glorified wallpaper". Cassatt's mural, on the other hand, used jarring colours and small isolated figures engaged in activities that were somewhat hard to understand. She had chosen to portray "women picking fruit from the Tree of Knowledge", as she wrote to the organiser Berthe Palmer. On the sides were scenes showing young girls pursuing fame and women and the arts. Both the daring colours and symbolist subject matter were out of context in Chicago, but were well appreciated by those who saw the mural or photographs of it in Paris. Cassatt's reference to women's pursuit of knowledge and fame was both timely in light of the advances in women's education and personal, considering her own open desire for public recognition.

As the century drew to a close, Cassatt found herself increasingly drawn back into the art world of her own country. After giving her a major retrospective in Paris in 1893, Durand-Ruel held a similar exhibition of her work in New York in 1895. Three years later he held another exhibition in New York, tempting her at long last to voyage back home. In the more than 20 years since she had been to the USA much had changed, but she was particularly gratified to learn that her art was firmly rooted there among artists, collectors and critics. She had even begun to have a popular presence in such magazines as *Frank Leslie's Popular Monthly* – a fate that she would never have foreseen given her radical beginnings.

Outside the families of her two brothers in Philadelphia, Cassatt was closest to Louisine and Harry Havemeyer, wealthy New York collectors whom she had known since the 1870s. In the late 1880s the Havemeyers began coming regularly to Paris to study and purchase art of all kinds, old master to modern, Asian and Western. Cassatt was happy to share her knowledge of modern French painting and led them to some extraordinary purchases of Impressionist and realist paintings over the next 30 years. After Harry Havemeyer's death in 1907, the two best friends continued to shape the collection together, combining the best of the old and the new into one of the most significant early 20th-century American collections, most of which was bequeathed to the Metropolitan Museum of Art. Because of Cassatt's work with the Havemeyers and a few other American collectors such as the Alfred Popes, the John Whittemores and her own brother, Alexander, she has been given credit for much of the Impressionist art now found in the USA. It may be more correct to say that her role as an adviser, as well as her own presence as an Impressionist artist, made an important contribution to the development of American taste at a time when major public and private collections were being formed.

Cassatt practised as an artist until 1914 when cataracts and a series of unsuccessful operations drastically impaired her vision. But in the last ten years before she put away her brushes she created a large body of work that included monumental mothers and children based on her new interest in old master

painting, portraits of friends and family, and a series of studies of children, which set a new standard for popular child portraiture that continues to the present. She vehemently rejected modernist reforms of painting as developed by Matisse and the Cubists, even though her own colours became more brilliant and she used bold decorative patterning in her later work such as *Sleepy Baby* (c.1910; Dallas Museum of Fine Arts). Encouraged by her dealers, the stalwart Paul Durand-Ruel and the newcomer Ambroise Vollard, Cassatt painted subjects that appealed to the more conservative taste of the emerging new American art public. She loved her chosen subjects but even she could see that she was pushed to do work that was no longer fresh; she later said to an American visitor: "I sold my soul to the dealers".

Nevertheless, her reputation grew to international proportions during these years and she was lauded by both French and American critics. Her financial success was such that it enabled her to maintain three residences – an apartment in Paris, a château at Mesnil-Beaufresne and a villa in Grasse. Even after she stopped painting she was a well-known figure at exhibitions and the object of many an art student's pilgrimage. During her lifetime her works entered such major museum collections as the Musée du Luxembourg (now the Louvre) and the Petit Palais in Paris, the Metropolitan Museum of Art, New York, the Philadelphia Museum of Art and many more in the USA. Today these four museums are the primary repositories of her work, with the National Gallery of Art, Washington, DC, the Art Institute of Chicago and the Museum of Fine Arts, Boston. Cassatt died in 1926, but her art has never fallen from public estimation, nor has the number of exhibitions or publications diminished in the intervening years. Contemporary judgements range from suspicion towards her stereotypical female subject matter to respect for her heroic struggle for recognition and belief in the radical art of the Impressionists. But at either end of the scale, Cassatt is accorded a place of prominence shared by very few.

NANCY MOWLL MATHEWS

See also Training and Professionalism survey 10

Castiglione Colonna, Duchess of *see* Marcello

Catherine of Bologna *see* Vigri

Catlett, Elizabeth
American sculptor and printmaker, 1915–

Born in Washington, DC, 15 April 1915; naturalised Mexican citizen, early 1960s. Married (1) printmaker Charles White, 1941; divorced; (2) painter and printmaker Francisco Mora, 1947; three sons. Studied at Howard University School of

Art, Washington, DC (BS cum laude 1937); University of Iowa, Iowa City, under Grant Wood (MFA 1940). Subsequently studied ceramics at Art Institute of Chicago, 1941; lithography at Art Students League, New York, 1942–3; wood-carving under José L. Ruiz and ceramic sculpture under Francisco Zuniga at Escuela de Pintura y Escultura, Esmeralda, Mexico, 1947–8; also studied privately with Ossip Zadkine in New York, 1943. Head of art department, Dillard University, New Orleans, 1940–42; instructor, Hampton Institute, Virginia, 1943; George Washington Carver School, New York, 1944–5; professor of sculpture, 1958–76, and head of sculpture department, 1959–76, Escuela Nacional de Bellas Artes, Universidad Nacional Autonoma de Mexico, Mexico City; artist-in-residence, University of Michigan, Ann Arbor, 1990. Recipient of first prize, American Negro Exposition, Chicago, 1941; Tlatilco prize, 1962, and Xipe Totec prize, 1964, Sculpture Biennial, Mexico; first prize in sculpture, Atlanta University annual, 1965; first purchase prize, National Print Salon, Mexico, 1969; Alumni award, Howard University, Washington, DC, 1979; outstanding achievement award, National Women's Caucus for Art, San Francisco, 1981; James Van der Zee award, Philadelphia Museum of Art, 1983; honoree, National Sculpture Conference: Works by Women, Cincinnati, 1987; Amistad Research Center award, New Orleans, 1990; Candace award for art, National Coalition of 100 Black Women, New York, 1991; honorary doctorate, Morgan State University, Baltimore, 1993. Lives in Cuernavaca, Mexico, and New York.

Selected Individual Exhibitions

Barnett-Aden Gallery, Washington, DC: 1947
National School of Fine Arts (San Carlos), Mexico City: 1962
Museo de Arte Moderno, Mexico City: 1970
Brockman Gallery, Los Angeles: 1971
Studio Museum in Harlem, NY: 1971
National Center of Afro-American Artists, Dorchester, MA: 1972
Howard University Galleries, Washington, DC: 1972, 1984
Fisk University, Nashville: 1973
Scripps College, Claremont: 1975
Tobey Moss Gallery, Los Angeles: 1981 (with Lynd Ward)
Gallery Tanner, Los Angeles: 1982
New Orleans Museum of Art: 1983
Spelman College, Atlanta: 1985
Mississippi Museum of Art, Jackson: 1986, 1990–92 (*A Courtyard Apart*, with Francisco Mora, touring)
Montgomery Museum of Art, AL: 1991
Hampton University Museum, VA: 1993 (touring retrospective)
June Kelly Gallery, New York: 1993
Isobel Neal Gallery, Chicago: 1994 (*In the Hemisphere of Love*, with Francisco Mora)

Selected Writings

(as Elizabeth Catlett Mora) "The Negro people and American art", *Freedomways*, no.1, Spring 1961, pp.74–80
"The role of the black artist", *Black Scholar*, vi, June 1975, pp.10–14

Bibliography

Elton C. Fax, *Seventeen Black Artists*, New York: Dodd Mead, 1971
Samella Lewis and Ruth Waddy, *Black Artists on Art*, ii, Los Angeles: Contemporary Crafts, 1971
Charlotte Streifer Rubinstein, *American Women Artists from Early Times to the Present*, Boston: Hall, 1982
Shifra Goldman, "Six women artists of Mexico", *Woman's Art Journal*, iii/2, 1982–3, pp.1–9
Thalia Gouma-Peterson, "Elizabeth Catlett: The power of human feeling and of art", *Woman's Art Journal*, iv/1, 1983, pp.48–56
Samella Lewis, *The Art of Elizabeth Catlett*, Claremont, CA: Hancraft Studios, 1984
Freida High Tesfagiorgis, "Afrofemcentrism and its fruition in the art of Elizabeth Catlett and Faith Ringgold", *SAGE*, iv, Spring 1987, pp.25–32
A Courtyard Apart: The Art of Elizabeth Catlett and Francisco Mora, exh. cat., Mississippi Museum of Art, Jackson, and elsewhere, 1990
Samella Lewis, *Art: African American*, revised edition, Los Angeles: Hancraft Studios, 1990
"Elizabeth Catlett: Sculptor, printmaker", *Artist and Influence*, x, 1991, pp.1–27 (interviews by Glory Van Scott, Cuernava, Mexico, 8 December 1981, and Camille Billops, 1 October 1989, New York)
Mara R. Witzling, ed., *Voicing Our Visions: Writings by Women Artists*, New York: Universe, 1991; London: Women's Press, 1992
Romare Bearden and Harry Henderson, *A History of African-American Artists from 1792 to the Present*, New York: Pantheon, 1993
Elizabeth Catlett: Works on Paper, 1944–92, exh. cat., Hampton University Museum, VA, and elsewhere, 1993
Freida High Tesfagiorgis, "Elizabeth Catlett", *Black Women in America: An Historical Encyclopedia*, i, ed. Darlene Clark Hine, Elsa Barklay Brown and Rosalyn Terborg-Penn, New York: Carlson, 1993
Patricia Hills, "Interview with Elizabeth Catlett", unpublished audiotape, 3 June 1995

To African Americans and to Mexicans, although not necessarily to the New York art world, Elizabeth Catlett for many decades has had a secure place in the history of American art – as a teacher, a progressive thinker, a sculptor and a printmaker. That she is not better known to patrons of the commercial art world is hardly surprising, given her independent thinking and her desire to reach the masses of everyday people with her public sculpture and her prints.

Brought up in a poor, but middle-class home in Washington, DC, Catlett distinguished herself at high school as a talented artist. Her ambitions to pursue her art training at the Carnegie Institute of Technology in Pittsburgh were dashed when her scholarship was revoked because of her race (Bearden and Henderson 1993, p.419). She then enrolled at Howard University, the black college in her home town, which provided her with a supportive environment in which to develop her skills. She studied design for two years under Lois Mailou Jones (q.v.) and then switched to painting with James Porter. Her art history professor, James V. Herring, introduced her to African sculpture. Inspired by Diego Rivera, she attempted to paint a mural for a restaurant near the campus (Hills 1995), and she was briefly on the Federal Art Project of the Works Progress Administration (FAP/WPA).

Like many educated African-American women, Catlett went into teaching after graduation, spending two years in the segregated school system in Durham, North Carolina, where she became controversial by raising such issues as the inequities of educational facilities for African-American children and pay differentials between the black and the white teachers (Fax 1971, pp.18–19). The next year she enrolled in

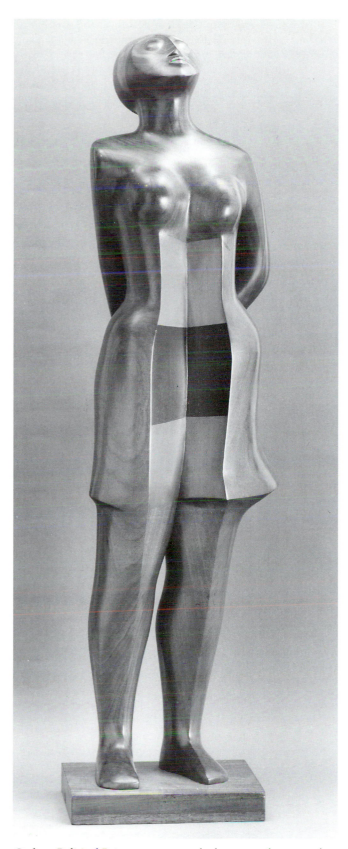

Catlett: *Political Prisoner*, 1971; polychrome sculpture, cedar wood; Art and Artifacts Division, Schomburg Center for Research in Black Culture, New York Public Library-Astor, Lenox and Tilden Foundations

the graduate programme at the University of Iowa, and studied with the regionalist painter Grant Wood. Wood encouraged her to achieve competence in all artistic media, and she began making sculpture. He also urged her to express in her art her own personal experiences, including her racial identification with issues of the black community.

Her career took off in 1941 when the judges of the American Negro Exposition awarded her first prize in sculpture for her Iowa Master's thesis sculpture, *Mother and Child* (1939; repr. Bearden and Henderson 1993, p.420). After teaching briefly at a black college, Prairie View College in Texas, Catlett was called to Dillard University, a black college in New Orleans, to direct their art department (*ibid.*, p.421). When she returned to Chicago in the summer of 1941 to take a course in ceramics at the Art Institute, she met Charles White, whom she later married. After two years at Dillard, Catlett and White moved to New York where Catlett began taking private lessons with the modernist, figurative French sculptor Ossip Zadkine, then in exile there. Zadkine had great vitality, and the older sculptor encouraged her to approach art from a "humanistic international viewpoint". She recalled to Bearden: "I felt the contrary – that it should begin as a nationalistic experience and be projected towards international understanding, as our blues and spirituals do. They are our experience, but they are understood and felt everywhere" (*ibid.*, p.420).

In 1943 Catlett joined the teaching staff of the Hampton Institute, Virginia, when White received a commission to paint a mural. Returning to New York the following year, she began working for the George Washington Carver School, a progressive community art centre, run on a shoestring, that emerged to fill the vacuum when the art centres of the government's WPA had folded. She taught sculpture and dressmaking, and that experience of working with the poor, proud and struggling people of Harlem made a lasting impression on her. During the second year of her employment at the Carver School she supported herself with a Julius Rosenwald Fund fellowship, a fellowship renewed in 1946 only on the condition that she devote herself full time to her art.

In 1946 she and White moved to Mexico, where she embarked on her Rosenwald project, *Negro Woman*, a series of 15 linocuts (Tesfagiorgis 1993, p.230). She took up printmaking with the Taller de Gráfica Popular, a collective of artists, and studied the work of the great Mexican muralists, Diego Rivera, David Siqueiros and José Clemente Orozco. Having divorced Charles White, Catlett married the painter and printmaker Francisco Mora and settled into life in Mexico. She brought up her three sons and enjoyed working collectively with other artists. As she recalled to Bearden: "I learned that art is not something that people learn to do individually, that who does it is not important, but its use and its effects on people are what is most important" (quoted in Bearden and Henderson 1993, p.423). In 1956 she began to study with the sculptors Francisco Zuniga, José Elarese and José L. Ruiz, and in 1958 was employed as a professor of sculpture at the Escuela Nacional de Bellas Artes, Universidad Nacional Autonoma de Mexico. Promoted to head of the sculpture department, she remained at the Escuela Nacional until her retirement in 1976.

Always sympathetic to the travails of poor people and the injuries of class, she and her husband moved within radical, artistic and literary circles in Mexico. During the mid-1950s she found herself harassed by government officials hunting "subversives" and was even jailed for two nights (Hills 1995). When she eventually became a Mexican citizen, the United States government would not issue her with a visa to enter the country, a ban not lifted until her exhibition at the Studio Museum in Harlem in 1971. Always outspoken in her views, Catlett delivered a speech, "The Negro people and American art", to a conference of the National Congress of Negro Artists held in Washington, DC, in 1961. She felt that black artists could contribute to the struggles against discrimination through their subject matter, and exhorted her fellow black artists to shun segregated exhibitions and to make art that would reach a large audience: "If we are to reach the mass of Negro people with our art, we must learn from them; then let us seek inspiration in the Negro people – a principal and never-ending source" (p.80).

Catlett's sculptures are sometimes carved from wood and sometimes cast in bronze. When she chooses single women or mother and child pairings, she uses a modernist, reductive vocabulary of simplified planes and curves that imparts to the pieces a serenity, quiet sensuality and grace: smoothly carved body types of broad hips, rounded bellies, tapering legs, prominent foreheads, generalised hair and symmetrical faces. Yet she has also done moving political works, such as *Homage to My Young Black Sisters* (1968; private collection, repr. Bearden and Henderson 1993, p.420), wherein a female figure lifts up her head and raises her fist in the gesture of solidarity. *Target* (1970; Amistad Research Center, Tulane University, *ibid.*, p.425), inspired by the civil rights struggles, consists of a realistic head of a black man facing an enlarged circular metal band intersected by a metal cross-bar – the enlarged sight from a gun barrel – as if he were the target. *Political Prisoner* (1971; see illustration) is an over-life-size standing female figure, dressed in a stylised shift, who looks upwards with her arms manacled behind her. Her mid-section is gently folded open to reveal equal bands of black, red and green – the flag used to designate Black Power in the 1960s and 1970s – now unfurled to declare her identity.

Some of Catlett's large sculpture pieces are in public spaces: *Olmec Bather* (1966) is placed at the National Polytechnical Institute in Mexico; *Phillis Wheatley* (1973) is at Jackson State College in Mississippi; *Louis Armstrong* (1975–6) is in New Orleans; *People of Atlanta* (1989–91) in City Hall, Atlanta.

In almost all of her linocut prints and lithographs Catlett has been concerned with representing powerful images of black people, the workers of Mexico or political figures. *Sharecropper* (1970; colour linocut; repr. Hampton 1993, cover) depicts a white-haired African-American woman with strongly chiselled features and wearing a straw hat, looking up and over her shoulder. The large safety-pin that holds her coat together hints at the poverty concealed by her proud visage. *Malcolm X Speaks for Us* (1969; colour linocut; *ibid.*, p.20) uses the repeating heads of three images, which surround the face of Malcolm. *Negro Es Bello II* (1969; lithograph; *ibid.*, p.21) represents two mask-like faces of Africans facing rows of Black Panther buttons inscribed "Black is Beautiful", a slogan of the Black Power movement of the 1960s. More recent prints have been less political and explore themes of African-American music and dance.

In the mid-1990s both Catlett and her husband continue to work in Mexico. A tall, handsome woman with a commanding presence and a deep, sonorous voice, Catlett has never flagged in her passion to present the truth of the many facets of the black experience. Her integrity and professionalism have inspired younger artists through both her art and her example.

PATRICIA HILLS

Cauer, Hanna
German sculptor, 1902–1989

Born in Bad Kreuznach, 8 March 1902, into a family of sculptors that spanned three generations. Studied painting at the Berlin Academy under Spiegel and Max Slevogt, 1919; continued studies in Munich, then from 1921 in Hamburg under her uncle Leopold von Kalckreuth. Became interested in sculpture on return to Berlin, stimulated by her father Ludwig Cauer and by the sculptors Ebbinghaus and Hugo Lederer. First woman to receive Rome prize from the Prussian Academy, 1930; spent a year at the Villa Massimo, Rome, studying ancient sculpture, 1930–31. Went to Paris, 1931. Awarded State prize, 1933. Returned to Bad Kreuznach after her Berlin studio was destroyed in an air raid, 1945. Died 16 May 1989.

Principal Exhibitions

Exposition Internationale, Paris: 1937 (gold medal)
Mainz: 1950 (*Vier Generationen der Bildhauerfamilie Cauer*)
Schlosspark-Museum, Bad Kreuznach: 1977 (retrospective)

Bibliography

Herbert Eulenberg, "Hanna Cauer", *Rheinische Heimatblätter*, ix, 1932, pp.264–6

Ernst Wurm, "Bildhauerinnen der Gegenwart", *Kunst im Deutschen Reich*, viii/6–7, June–July 1944, pp.145–52

R. Rossbach, *Hanna Cauer*, Cologne, 1968

Anne Tesch, *Die Bildhauerfamilie Cauer*, Bad Kreuznach: Harrach, 1977

Das Verborgene Museum I: Dokumentation der Kunst von Frauen in Berliner öffentlichen Sammlungen, exh. cat., Akademie der Künste, Berlin, 1987

Elke Masa, *Die Bildhauerfamilie Cauer*, Berlin: Mann, 1989 (contains catalogue raisonné)

Magdalena Bushart, "Der Formsinn des Weibes: Bildhauerinnen in den zwanziger und dreissiger Jahren", *Profession ohne Tradition: 125 Jahre Verein der Berliner Künstlerinnen*, exh. cat., Berlinische Galerie, Berlin, 1992, pp.135–50

Manuscript collection is in the Schlosspark-Museum, Bad Kreuznach.

Hanna Cauer's artistic education began during the Weimar Republic, when the majority of woman sculptors worked in Berlin. Unlike other female sculptors in the city, such as Emy Roeder (q.v.) and Katharina Heise (q.v.), she did not incorporate the late Expressionist or neo-objective tendencies of the 1920s in her oeuvre. Her early work was in the neo-classical style specific to Berlin, exemplified by her father, Ludwig Cauer, and by Hugo Lederer, whose master class she entered in 1928, after a period of painting and life-drawing.

Cauer's early sculptures in plaster, such as the portrait of her brother *Eduard Cauer* (1927; Schlosspark-Museum, Bad Kreuznach), are in this tradition. An independent style is evident in other works, for example the portrait bust of *Gerhard Wolff* (1923; family estate, Kreuznach, repr. Masa 1989, no.8), in which the face is reduced to a few rounded forms, with simplified details, yet the physiognomy is fully captured. The bronze portrait of *Lina Hilger* (1932; Lina-Hilger-Gymnasium, Bad Kreuznach) is enlivened by surface modelling with light and shadow. Portrait busts continued to occupy a special place in Cauer's oeuvre. In a bust of her father made in 1943 (family estate, Kreuznach, *ibid.*, no.35) she roughened the surface to show the effects of age. Direct and at the same time dignified, it is one of her most expressive portraits and reveals her mastery of a broad spectrum of formal means.

Apart from portraits, Cauer's principal subject was the nude, usually female. Early examples include two figurines, *Kneeling Woman* (1920–28; Schlosspark-Museum) and *Crouching Woman* (1927; family estate, Kreuznach, *ibid.*, no.93), in which the female figures are depicted in self-contained, unaffected and "natural" poses. The stimulation of her stay in Italy, made possible by a Rome scholarship from the Prussian Academy, is evident in *Grotto Nymph* (c.1932; untraced, *ibid.*, no.98). The floor-length garment reveals the contours of the individual parts of the body, while the pinned-up hairstyle recalls representations of women in classical antiquity. From Rome, in 1931, Hanna Cauer went to Paris. Works from the following period show the influence of Aristide Maillol. The robust bodies of the women, defined by clear outlines, in the reliefs *Two Bathers* (three reliefs, 1931–2; Schlosspark-Museum) and *Fish Market* (1931–2; Galerie Lange, Berlin) resemble Maillol's monumental female figures, yet the extreme simplification of the faces, perhaps partly explained by the softness of the material used (limestone), is striking. While in the last two works the figures are arranged in flat relief in a confined space, Cauer tried to suggest depth through the extreme differences in the size of the male figures in the relief *Fisher* (c.1930–32; untraced, repr. Eulenberg 1932, p.265). In the reliefs *Music* (1932; Staatsbad, Bad Dürkheim) and *Greek Deities* (three reliefs; 1934; ex-Kronprinzenpalais, Berlin, repr. Masa 1989, no.168), created in Berlin shortly afterwards, the artist turned to a more naturalistic rendering of the human figure. While the upright seated posture of the figure and the drapery around the hips in the relief *Music* still refer back to classical reliefs, the classical attributes of the robust figures in *Greek Deities* have the effect of staffage. From this time onwards Cauer's work shows strong classical influence. The almost life-size bronze *Floating Goddess* (1935; Oranienpark, Bad Kreuznach) is closely linked to classical statues. As the figure touches down against the wind, the drapery presses against her legs and bulges out over her back, reminding one of the wind-blown garments of victories, for example the famous *Winged Nike of Samothrace*.

Also around this time Cauer created two life-size bronze nude figures, *Allegro-Andante* (1934–5; titled *Allegretto and Moderato* in Bushart 1992, p.149), commissioned by the city of Nuremberg for the interior of the refurbished opera house. The allegorical roles of the figures are indicated only by their postures; their gestures are not obviously linked to music but could be seen as coquettish. The softly modelled, harmonious rendering of the female nude is closely related to the allegorical depiction of women in National Socialist sculpture. Cauer showed one of these figures at the Paris Exposition Internationale of 1937, in a section intended to present internationally the "best contemporary" German art (Adolf Ziegler, "Bildende Kunst in Deutschland", *Internationale Ausstellung Paris 1937 für Kunst und Technik*, Paris, 1937, p.51). The international jury of the exhibition, which included the German "State sculptor" Arno Breker (see Mortimer G. Davidson, *Kunst in Deutschland, 1933–45*, i, Tübingen, 1988, p.427), awarded her one of the numerous prizes for German artists. In addition to this piece, Cauer's works at sites programmed by National Socialist art policy included the *Olympia Fountain* (1935; destroyed, repr. Masa 1989, no.104) in front of the Red Town Hall, Berlin, flanked by muscular athletes, and the goddess of wisdom, *Pallas Athena* (1938–9; destroyed, *ibid.*, no.107), at the Reich Ministry of the Interior. Cauer was one of the most successful female sculptors of the Third Reich. Contemporary art criticism supported a manner of depiction closely linked to the model and "pronounced empathy" as specific to female artistic creation. Her sculpture was considered "characteristic of the nature of female artistry" (Wurm 1944, p.148).

The end of World War II was a turning-point in Cauer's artistic work because her Berlin studio and most of her works had been destroyed. Having returned to Bad Kreuznach, she could not execute major sculptures due to the shortage of materials and a lack of commissions. From this time she used mostly plaster and clay (some cast in bronze) and her manner of representation became freer. Thus the drapery and body of the figurine of the dancer *Ruth Boin* (1949; family estate, Kreuznach, repr. Masa 1989, no.134) are treated homogeneously with a summary light surface modelling.

In some sculptures, for example the plaster statue *Atalanta* (1979; family estate, Kreuznach, *ibid.*, no.159), the surface is rough and cracked, the first attempts at an abstract form. This tendency is more marked in reliefs of the 1970s, such as *Reclining Couple* (1976) and *Pan and Nymph* (c.1975; both Schlosspark-Museum), in which Cauer introduced linear incisions in the contours of the fine-limbed figures. The anatomical structure is barely hinted at and the compositions are blurred. In these late works, Cauer distanced herself considerably from the Classical tone predominant in her oeuvre.

ANJA CHERDRON

Cazin, Marie

French sculptor and painter, 1844–1924

Born Marie Guillet in Paimbeuf, Loire Inférieure, 1844. Studied at the Ecole de Dessin, Paris, under Mme Peyrol, sister of Rosa Bonheur (q.v.), then under painter Jean-Charles Cazin. Married Cazin, 1860s; one son; husband died 1901. Sociétaire, Société Nationale des Beaux-Arts, 1891. Maintained a studio in the Latin quarter of Paris until World War I, then retired to Equihen, Pas-de-Calais. Died in Equihen, 1924.

Principal Exhibitions

Royal Academy, London: 1874, 1878
Paris Salon: occasionally 1876–87
Exposition Universelle, Paris: 1889 (gold medal), 1900 (silver medal)
Société Nationale des Beaux-Arts, Paris: 1891–9, 1901–5, 1909, 1911, 1913–14
World's Columbian Exposition, Chicago: 1893
Les Quelques (independent women artists' association), Paris: 1908–13
Brussels Salon: 1914
Panama-Pacific International Exposition, San Francisco: 1915

Bibliography

Gustave Geffroy, *La Vie artistique*, 8 vols, Paris: Floury, 1892–1903
Louis de Fourcaud, "Les Arts décoratifs aux salons", *Revue des Arts Décoratifs*, xiii, 1893, p.384; xv, 1895; xvii, 1897, pp.375–7
Roger Marx, "Les salons", *Le Voltaire*, May 1893
Raoul Sertat, "Revue artistique", *Revue Encylopédique*, June 1893, pp.3 and 6
Claude Bienne, "Beaux-Arts", *Revue Hebdomadaire*, July 1893, p.139
M.M., "Le Monument de Berck-sur-Mer", *Illustration*, 26 August 1893, p.172
André Michel, "La sculpture décorative aux salons", *Art et Décoration*, vi, 1899, pp.33–41
Firmin Javel, "Société Nationale", *Art Français*, May 1899
Roger Marx in *Revue Encyclopédique*, July 1899
Maurice Demaison, "La décennale", *Revue de l'Art Ancien et Moderne*, 10 August 1900, pp.123–5
Paul Vitry, "La sculpture aux Salons", *Art et Décoration*, xvi, 1904, pp.21–34
Maria Lomer de Vits, *Les Femmes sculpteurs*, Paris, 1905
Henri Malo, *Critique sentimentale*, 2nd edition, Paris, 1922
Madeleine Zillhardt, *Louise-Catherine Breslau et ses amis*, Paris, 1932
La Femme artiste d'Elisabeth Vigée-Lebrun à Rosa Bonheur, exh. cat., Musée Despiau-Wlerick, Donjon Lacataye, Mont-de-Marsan, 1981
Odilon Redon, *A Soi-Même: Journal, 1867–1915*, revised edition, Paris: Corti, 1985 (diary entry for May 1885)
Les Sculptures sortent de leur réserve, exh. cat., Musée de Tours, 1988
Octave Mirbeau, *Combats ésthetiques*, Paris: Séguier, 1993

On the esplanade of Berck-sur-Mer, a medical centre and sea resort in northern France, there stands a bronze sculpture featuring two draped female figures attending to a sick child (see illustration). Well loved by the inhabitants who call it "Marianne", it is thought to represent the founder of Berck, an old woman who had a mysterious gift for curing children. That Marie Cazin had conceived it as "Science and Charity", part of a memorial to Doctors Cazin and Perrochaud inaugurated in 1893, has long been lost to the popular collective memory. Marie Cazin's present reputation in Berck is an appropriate emblem of the position accorded to her in French culture during her lifetime: present and significant, but with a somewhat veiled identity.

What established Cazin's career in the public arena were the annual Paris Salons where, first exhibiting as a painter in the late 1870s, she soon made her reputation as a sculptor. Her nomination as Sociétaire of the Société Nationale des Beaux-Arts in 1891, a function that entailed being one of the jury with Rodin, marked the recognition of her distinguished professional status. The Ministère des Beaux-Arts promoted her by exhibiting the bronzes of *David* (1883) and *Young Girls*

Cazin: *Science and Charity*, upper section of the former monument to Drs Perrochaud and Cazin, inaugurated 1893; bronze; Berck-sur-Mer

(purchased 1899) in the Musée du Luxembourg, Paris. Although she was the wife of the eminent painter Jean-Charles Cazin, the originality of her work, as a sculptor, was never put in question. Besides small-scale sculptures sold to private collectors she designed large-scale works for public spaces. She saw sculpture as belonging to social spaces when contributing memorials, funerary sculptures, sculptural reliefs, frescoes and drawings for civic buildings.

There is one theme that frequently recurs in the diversity and range of Cazin's oeuvre: defining the social function of women. *The School* (1893; Musée de Tours, repr. Tours 1988, no.10), a bronze high relief, features a schoolmistress kneeling by a bench, teaching a child to read. The teacher's juvenile features and hair, subtly chiselled to describe a soft substance tightened into a bun, connote an overall gentleness and delicacy in strong contrast to the severity of the dress, buttoned up to the top of its high collar. In such details Cazin explains that woman's professional identity is perceived ideologically as care, concern and duty. This scene takes place outside and in rural settings. Cazin's portrayal of a schoolmistress forms part of a series of sculptures and drawings on the subject of woman and work, the *Child Nurse* (1915; pastel; bought by the State for the cruiser *Waldeck-Rousseau*; destroyed), *Working-Class Woman* (1891; fresco; untraced) and her homage to women's domestic work, *Vie Obscure*, exhibited in a drawing in 1885 and as a bronze high relief in 1901 (untraced), which Louise Breslau (q.v.) described as "representing several women occupied in domestic work … a remarkable masterpiece" (Zillhardt 1932, p.247). *Helping the Sick* (1893; Musée de Tours, repr. Tours 1988, no.11) features a midwife seated on the ground, holding in her lap the new babe she has just washed. The mother is chiselled in the background, lying in a four-poster bed in a modest rural home. In detailing the dress of the "visitors" Cazin qualifies their status as middle-class and provincial. This work was known under several titles: *Helping the Sick* (1891; plaster) presented the scene as an homage to philanthropy, while *The Crib*, also called *Visiting the New Mother* (1893; bronze), shifted attention to the modernised nativity subject transposed in the context of rural France, where the midwife played an important role. *Children of Berck Hospital* (bronze high relief; destroyed) documents the taking over of institutionalised medical science. It features a nurse in lay uniform bringing the children under her care to the daily visits conducted by Doctors Perrochaud and Cazin. In the Berk memorial Marie Cazin gave the place of precedence to the double female character of *Science and Charity*, one shown in her professional role, seated and applying a dressing to the arm of a sick boy, the other in her maternal role, kneeling on the ground to keep close contact with the child.

At the time that Cazin adopted these themes in her sculpture, they occupied the powerful battleground of the Republican state, which had initiated the "free and compulsory" school system and subsidised the creation of "L'assistance publique". French feminists of that period focused their activity on the issues of education, employment, maternity as a social function and the re-evaluation of domestic work. The political dimensions of Cazin's works were not easy to assess simply because she contextualised her subject in rural France, stage-managing moments of domestic experience that confuse public and collective concerns with the depiction of family relationships. On the Parisian cultural scene Cazin's works were always reviewed with respect, the terms most frequently used being "melancholy", "mysterious charm", "poised", "tender", displaying "care", "concern" and "compassion". Originally formulated to describe the female characters represented in her sculpture, these terms build up a fixed image of the woman artist's persona.

Cazin created sculptures on the theme of death's omnipresence, or the precariousness of existence, on the importance of mental and private experiences, subjects favoured in symbolist art. Odilon Redon, in his endeavour to promote an art of mental experience singled out Cazin's *Regret* (bronze; then belonging to H. Adam) as an outstanding achievement. *Regret* featured a woman, her head draped, bending forwards, thoughtful, supporting her head in her hands. Redon explained it as a poetical meditation opening up the idea of melancholy in a chain of associated ideas (Redon 1985, pp.85–7), the representation of a collective state of mind rather than the expression of a woman's nature. Cazin's masks (e.g. *Sadness*, 1882; bronze; untraced), the draped kneeling figures of *Regret* and *Charity*, the frontal, inward-looking female figures shown down to the waist (e.g. *Fragment of Decoration*, 1897; plaster in Musée de Tours as *Autumn*) and *Young Girls* (State purchase 1899; bronze; Musée de Saint-Quentin) extended the imagery of Renaissance and Roman funerary art to sculptures that could find a suitable environment in civic buildings or the homes of private collectors.

In the later part of her career, partly to finance her Paris studio, which she kept until 1915, Cazin undertook proportionally more commissions for decorative designs, including

Fresco, Decorative Subject for a Nursery School (1910; untraced) and cartoons for the State's Tapisserie des Gobelins, *Diane* (1912) and *Venus* (1913). Her last major project was her memorial to *Jean-Charles Cazin*, for which she realised a full standing figure in the guise of a naturalist painter, in 1904. The memorial was finally unveiled in Bormes in 1924, the year of Marie Cazin's death in her eighties.

CLAUDINE MITCHELL

Celmins, Vija
American painter, 1938–

Born in Riga, Latvia, 25 October 1938. Moved into Germany with her family, 1944, eventually settling in a Latvian refugee camp near Esslingen in the Western Sector. Emigrated to USA, 1948, settling in Indianapolis. Studied at John Herron Art Institute, Indianapolis, 1955–62 (BFA); attended Yale University Summer School, 1961; studied painting at University of California, Los Angeles, 1963–5 (MFA). Instructor of painting and drawing, University of California, Los Angeles, 1965–6; University of California, Irvine, 1967–72; California Institute of the Arts, Valencia, 1976 and 1977. Studied Buddhism, 1975–6. Lived in Venice Beach, California, 1962–80, then moved to New York. Taught at Cooper Union, New York, 1984, and Yale University Graduate School, New Haven, 1987. Recipient of National Endowment for the Arts (NEA) grants, 1971 and 1976; Guggenheim fellowship, 1980. Lives in New York.

Selected Individual Exhibitions
Dickson Art Center, University of California, Los Angeles: 1965
David Stuart Galleries, Los Angeles: 1966
Riko Mizuno Gallery, Los Angeles: 1969, 1973
Whitney Museum of American Art, New York: 1973
Felicity Samuel Gallery, London: 1975
Broxton Gallery, Los Angeles: 1975
Newport Harbor Art Museum, Newport Beach, CA: 1979–80 (touring retrospective)
David McKee Gallery, New York: 1983, 1988, 1992
Pence Gallery, Santa Monica, CA: 1990
Institute of Contemporary Art, Philadelphia: 1992–4 (touring retrospective)
University Gallery, University of Massachusetts, Amherst: 1993
Cirrus, Los Angeles: 1994 (retrospective)

Bibliography
J. Livingston, "Four Los Angeles artists", *Art in America*, lviii, May 1970, pp.126–31
Max Kozloff, "Vija Celmins", *Artforum*, xii, March 1974, pp.52–3
Susan C. Larsen, "A conversation with Vija Celmins", *Journal of the Los Angeles Institute of Contemporary Art*, no.20, October–November 1978, pp.36–40
Vija Celmins: A Survey Exhibition, exh. cat., Newport Harbor Art Museum, Newport Beach, CA, and elsewhere, 1979 (contains bibliography)
Richard Armstrong, "Of earthly objects and stellar sights: Vija Celmins", *Art in America*, lxix, May 1981, pp.100–07
Kenneth Baker, "Vija Celmins: Drawings without withdrawing", *Artforum*, xxii, November 1983, pp.64–5

Carter Ratcliffe, "Vija Celmins: An art of reclamation", *Print Collector's Newsletter*, xiv, 1984, pp.193–6

William S. Bartman, ed., *Vija Celmins*, Los Angeles: ART Press, 1992 (interview with Chuck Close)

Vija Celmins, exh. cat., Institute of Contemporary Art, Philadelphia, and elsewhere, 1992

Sheena Wagstaff, "Vija Celmins", *Parkett*, no.32, 1992, pp.6–19

Lynne Cooke, "Vija Celmins", *Burlington Magazine*, cxxxv, 1993, p.238

Brooks Adams, "Visionary realist", *Art in America*, lxxxi, October 1993, pp.102–9

Vija Celmins has been important in the USA since the mid-1960s for opening up the field of painting to include a more conceptual and process-oriented approach. Her central concerns have been to clarify and articulate the most mysterious and elusive aspects of the artistic process. Her series of images includes everyday objects, photographs of war and disasters and images of nature. There are works by her in the Los Angeles County Museum of Art, the National Gallery of Art, Washington, DC, the Museum of Modern Art and the Whitney Museum of American Art, New York.

During her time at John Herron, Celmins travelled with friends to New York to see the work of the Abstract Expressionists, and was influenced by Ad Reinhardt's article, "Twelve rules for a new academy" (*Art News*, lvi, May 1957, pp.37–8, 56), which advocated the elimination of texture, brushwork, calligraphy, sketching and drawing. She decided to become a painter at the Yale summer school in 1961, when she met Chuck Close, Brice Marden and Jack Tworkov. Her early work was in the style of the Abstract Expressionists, but other influences included the paintings of Jasper Johns, Magritte and Giorgio Morandi, as well as those of Cézanne and Velázquez, which she had seen on her visit to Europe in 1962.

Celmins's subsequent move to California coincided with a rejection of the New York School; instead, she sought a less "worked-out" way of making art and began to consider the objects at hand in her Venice studio: a chair, a goose-neck lamp, a television, a heater, a gun and a bowl of soup. Such objects were not chosen for psychological, sociological, political or symbolic reasons, however, nor did she consider them to be "private" or "personal". Their "meaning" as anything other than simple objects to be painted did not interest her. Her painting concerns were now based on observation and process, rather than led by convention or idea.

In her early paintings objects are given human attributes, appearing benign while simultaneously evoking a feeling of danger. Their intense character stems from the earlier influence of the Abstract Expressionists, and the emphasis is on form rather than surface appearance. Painted life-size, works such as *Lamp No.1* (1964; artist's collection) and *Hotplate* (1964; David McKee Gallery, New York) show centrally placed objects in non-specific spaces, painted in oils in tonal ranges of grey. In *Hotplate* only the heated electrical rings are coloured, manifesting the energy that passes through them. The straightforward, simple presentation of the homely image of the television set in *TV* (1964) contrasts with the image on the screen, which shows two fighter planes engulfed in smoke and falling through the sky. Other works from this period are the hand-painted replicas of houses in California and Indiana, *House No.1* (collection Betty Asher, Beverly Hills) and *House No.2*

(1965). Disturbing images painted on their walls – a gun being fired, a steam train emerging, a spreading fire – contrast with the intimate and private spaces within: *House No.2* opens to reveal a fur-lined interior. Celmins also explored the relation of two- to three-dimensional space in such works as *Puzzle* (1964; oil on wood; collection Mr and Mrs Melvin Hirsh, Beverly Hills), the pieces of which construct the image of a bowl of steaming stew. Later works include a series based on childhood objects, such as *Pencil* (1966; collection Betty Asher) and *Pink Eraser* (three versions). *Comb* (1969–70; lacquer and epoxy on wood; Los Angeles County Museum of Art) is unique in its direct reference to Magritte's *Personal Values* (1952). In these works, Celmins explores the essential mechanics of metaphor: seeing one thing in terms of another.

From 1966 Celmins used photographs as subjects for painting, and began to explore the formal and conceptual problems of this process. Both *Revolver* (1968; Odyssia Gallery) and *Plane* (1968; Clayton Garrison, Laguna Beach, CA) are carefully rendered to give as much physical evidence of the photograph as of the object represented, which is set against an ambiguous background. In *Revolver* the photograph is shown folded and crumpled from much usage; its bottom edge is torn and there is a slight shadow along two sides. Time is also suggested: the present by the matter-of-fact depiction of the photograph on a surface, and the past by the exact moment the picture was taken and by its history and usage by previous owners. The layering of intricate tonal marks across the paper creates a unified surface of graphite.

Celmins's use of photographs derived from her daily life. Some of her first pictures were taken while driving to work, when her camera was balanced on the steering wheel. Others, taken during evening walks with her dog along Venice beach, formed the basis of numerous images of the ocean. *Untitled (Ocean)* (1968; graphite on acrylic ground on paper) shows the undulatory mass of waves and their choppy surfaces; the image is built up through layers of small, integral marks, conveying its structure and form, its weight, surface quality and response to light. In each of these works Celmins explores a new formal problem, reinvestigating and going over an aspect of the construction of the image. Subsequent works include various views of nature: the sea, desert and constellations, all of which are based on photographs, with no humans or man-made artifices within them. Painted and drawn works include *Star Field No.1* (1982; collection Mr and Mrs Harry W. Anderson), *Star Field III* (1983; Edward R. Broida Trust Collection) and *Night Sky Painting No.1* (1991; David McKee Gallery), all of which are stunning visual depictions of expansive spaces in nature. One of Celmins's most visually and conceptually challenging works is *To Fix an Image in Memory* (1977–82; Edward R. Broida Trust Collection), a series of eleven acrylic-painted cast bronzes and stones, described by her as an "exercise in looking". Of the stone she said: "I developed this desire to try and put them in an art context. Sort of mocking art in a way, but also to affirm the act of making: the act of looking and making as a primal act of art" (Bartman 1992).

CECILE SOLIZ JOHNSON

Charmy, Emilie
French painter, 1878–1974

Born in Saint-Etienne, near Lyon, 1878. Lived with relatives in Lyon after being orphaned in her early teens; trained as a school teacher, then in the late 1890s took private art lessons in the studio of Jacques Martin, a local painter. Moved with her brother Jean to Saint-Cloud, near Paris, c.1902–3, renting a studio in the Place Clichy, Paris; moved to Rue de Bourgogne, Paris, 1908. Spent summer in Corsica with Fauve painter Charles Camoin, 1906. Began affair with painter Georges Bouche, 1912; son born 1915; married Bouche, 1935. Exhibited at Salon des Indépendants, from 1904, Salon d'Automne, from 1905. Chevalier, Légion d'Honneur, 1927. Died in Paris, 1974.

Selected Individual Exhibitions

Galerie Clovis Sagot, Paris: 1912
Galerie Berthe Weill, Paris: 1913, 1919 (with Jean Chabaud and Edmond Amédée Heuzé), 1923 (with André Favory), 1957
Galerie André Pesson, Paris: 1919
Galeries d'Oeuvres d'Art, Paris: 1921
Galerie Barbazanges, Paris: 1926
Galerie Druet, Paris: 1927
Galerie Jeanne Castel, Paris: 1932, 1936, 1948
Galerie Charpentier, Paris: 1935
Galerie Katia Granoff, Lyon: 1941
Galerie Bellecour, Lyon: 1943
Galerie Raspail, Paris: 1946
Galerie Bernheim, Paris: 1952
Galerie Katia Granoff, Paris: 1955
Galerie Paul Petridès, Paris: 1963
Patrick Seale Gallery, London: 1980 (retrospective)

Bibliography

Charmy: Toiles, exh. cat., Galeries d'Oeuvres d'Art, Paris, 1921
Quelques toiles de Charmy – quelques pages de Colette, exh. cat., Galerie d'Art Ancien et Moderne, Paris, 1926
Emilie Charmy, 1877–1974, exh. cat., Patrick Seale Gallery, London, 1980
Emilie Charmy, 1878–1974, exh. cat., Kunsthaus Bühler, Stuttgart, 1987
Emilie Charmy, 1878–1974, exh. cat., Kunsthaus Bühler, Stuttgart, 1991
Gill Perry, Women Artists and the Parisian Avant-Garde, Manchester: Manchester University Press, and New York: St Martin's Press, 1995

Although widely reviewed in the French press in the 1910s, 1920s and 1930s, Emilie Charmy's work is little known to a post-war audience. What are perhaps the most interesting periods of her work, including those spent in Lyon and Paris before World War I, were little documented before the 1980s. While living in Lyon in the 1890s she produced a series of works influenced by Impressionist and Post-Impressionist techniques in which she adopts and reworks subjects traditionally associated with a "feminine" iconography including many scenes of respectable, middle-class domestic life. Around the same time, however, she was also producing representations of the seedier side of modern bourgeois life, including one canvas titled La Loge (c.1900–03; see illustration), which suggests the interior of a brothel, a subject more often associated with the male avant-garde.

After moving to Paris around 1903, Charmy developed a strong, brightly coloured style, close to that of Matisse and the so-called Fauve group (see, for example, Woman in a Japanese Dressing Gown, 1907, repr. Perry 1995, colour pl.15 and cover). Through her experiments with colour, thickly applied paint and seemingly crude brushwork she produced a series of bold and technically innovative paintings. Surprisingly, these works were rarely discussed in contemporary art criticism partly because, like many women artists at the time, she did not exhibit with the relevant modernist groups. Although she was very friendly with Matisse and his circle, formed a close relationship with Camoin, and showed in many of the Salon des Indépendants and Salon d'Automne exhibitions now renowned for their Fauve exhibits, her works were hung separately and attracted relatively little attention. However, her paintings in the Salon des Indépendants of 1905 were spotted by Berthe Weill, one of the first women dealers to patronise the work of (then) little-known modern artists. Weill played a significant role in promoting Charmy's work, exhibiting it regularly in the 1910s.

From the 1910s onwards Charmy's work became increasingly remote from avant-garde interests and closer to the fringe modernist styles now identified with the "School of Paris". During the 1920s her canvases were featured regularly in gallery shows on the Left and Right Banks and her shows were well documented by critics. In 1921 the art critic Louis Vauxcelles described Charmy as "one of the most remarkable women [artists] of our time" (Eclair, 23 June 1921), although such critical acclaim was tempered by the assumption that the work of women artists (usually known in contemporary criticism as les femmes peintres) should be judged according to different criteria from that applied to the work of their male colleagues. Like many of his contemporaries, Vauxcelles was preoccupied with the notion of a "feminine" style, distinguished by its particular "sensibility" and "refinement". Yet Charmy's work confounded many critics who associated a bold, vigorous application of paint with a "masculine" form of creative expression. She became renowned for her use of thick impasto, heavily applied, causing the writer Roland Dorgelès to comment that Charmy "sees like a woman and paints like a man" (Paris 1921).

The theme of portraiture, still life and the female nude were important throughout her long career, although she rarely painted the mother and child subjects that are often associated with "women's art" around the turn of the 19th and 20th centuries, echoing perhaps her own ambivalence towards motherhood. Her only child, Edmond, who was born in 1915, was sent away in the care of nurses until the age of 14. Her unconventional attitudes went against the cult of maternité so popular in France after World War I, and which became a recurring theme in the work of better-known male artists from the period, such as Picasso, Derain and Léger. Charmy's enduring preoccupation with the theme of the female nude suggests some contradictory interests, both in terms of the forms of sexuality they reveal, and the public for which they were produced. While many of her exhibition pieces on this theme reveal marketable images of passive reclining nudes as erotic objects of a (male) gaze, there are many paintings of female nudes from the 1920s and 1930s that suggest a more active and threatening female sexuality, and in which women seem to

Charmy: *La Loge*, *c.*1900–03; oil; Galerie Bernard Bouche, Paris

pursue or reveal their own sexual pleasure (e.g. *Nude Holding Her Breast*, mid-1920s; repr. Perry 1995, colour pl.29). These latter works have been seen as a possible visual equivalent to the forms of female sexuality championed in the writings of Colette, who was a friend and admirer of Charmy's work.

Charmy's longevity has contributed to the ignorance and confusion that has surrounded her work. By the 1960s, when she was in her eighties, critical interest in her work had faded. By then much of her interesting and original work from her earlier Lyon and Paris periods was little known or inaccessible, and most of these canvases are now in private collections. A small number of her works can be found in the reserve sections of French public collections in Paris and Lyon. Since World War II the later canvases, particularly those painted when she was already in her seventies and eighties, were more likely to pass through the hands of French dealers. But access to a broader range of her works – most in private collections – has shown that her paintings provide rich material for study. They reveal a complex and sometimes contradictory relationship to those styles and conventions associated with the male avant-garde, and to those associated with "women's art".

GILL PERRY

Charpentier, Constance
French painter, 1767–1849

Born Constance Marie Blondelu in Paris, 1767. According to 19th-century dictionaries, studied under Wilk (?Wille), David, Lafitte, Gérard and Bouillon. Recipient of prix d'encouragement, 1788; gold medal, Musée Royal, 1819. Died in Paris, 3 August 1849

Principal Exhibitions

Paris Salon: 1795, 1798, 1800–01, 1804, 1806, 1808, 1810, 1812, 1814, 1819

Bibliography

Clara Erskine Clement, *Women in the Fine Arts*, Boston: Houghton Mifflin, 1904; reprinted New York: Hacker, 1974

Charles Sterling, "A fine 'David' reattributed", *Metropolitan Museum of Art Bulletin*, ix, 1951, pp.121–32

French Painting, 1774–1830: The Age of Revolution, exh. cat., Grand Palais, Paris, and elsewhere, 1974

Women Artists, 1550–1950, exh. cat., Los Angeles County Museum of Art, and elsewhere, 1976

Viktoria Schmidt-Linsenhoff, "Gleichheit für Künstlerinnen?", *Sklavin oder Bürgerin? Französische Revolution und Neue Weiblichkeit, 1760–1830*, exh. cat., Historisches Museum, Frankfurt am Main, 1989, pp.114–32

Although Constance Charpentier exhibited about 30 works at the Paris Salons in the period 1795 to 1819, only one painting, *Melancholy* (1801; see illustration), can be firmly attributed to her today. This painting shows the obvious influence of the artists Jacques-Louis David and François Gérard with whom Charpentier had studied. The profile pose of the figure of Melancholy is that of David's Camilla in his famously successful history painting the *Oath of the Horatii* (1784; Louvre, Paris). The landscape setting of Charpentier's dejected female figure, resting by a pool of water in front of a weeping willow is, however, very different to that of the history painting.

Melancholy, first exhibited at the Paris Salon of 1801, has no obvious narrative cause and is of a more generalised abstract and emblematic nature than that of the history painting. It does not incorporate a specific action, gesture or

Charpentier: *Melancholy*, 1801; oil on canvas; 130 × 165 cm.; Musée de Picardie, Amiens

passion, but explores and communicates mood and mystery. The passive, limp pose of the woman can be associated with 18th-century tomb sculpture, but it can also be linked forward to Romanticism and the pleasures of sensibility that might be induced from an observation of the outward expression of inner pain and emotion. Another, now lost, painting on the same subject by François Vincent was also exhibited at the Salon of 1801 and contemporary critics made associations between these visual images and the lyrical poetry of the Abbé Delille.

On the basis of this work, an engraving by Monsaldy and Devisme of the Salon of 1801 and the register of deliveries to the jury of that Salon, Charles Sterling (1951) proposed that a portrait of *Mademoiselle Charlotte du Val d'Ognes* (1801; Metropolitan Museum of Art, New York) should also be attributed to Charpentier. This portrait, though, is much more contrived; there is a challenging mystery about it and its luminosity is more transparent and complex. The fluent, abstract contours of the sitter, her attenuated anatomy, smoothly chiselled flesh and illuminated silhouette are all features of the mannered and discordant trend associated with the Primitifs, a group of students who had emerged, as rebels, from David's studio.

Mlle du Val d'Ognes is shown in the bare room of an artist's studio, looking up at the spectator as if she is using him or her as a model for the drawing she is in the process of producing. Behind her, a broken window pane is a *tour de force* of the painter's art distinguishing, in its *trompe-l'oeil* effect, the view of the scene outside as to be seen as only partly through glass. The unglazed area encompasses the two small figures of a seemingly compliant woman and her seemingly masterful male companion on the terrace of an austere building. The figure of Val d'Ognes is lit from behind with much of her body in shadow, but she has a transparency, grace and fragility that give an unsettling, almost surreal quality to the work as a whole. Sterling noted that the anatomy and certain anecdotal details of the contemporary setting and draperies can be compared to that of the figure of *Melancholy*. The handling of the anatomy is mannered – the legs and thighs are too long, the shoulder and wrist joints are weak and unconvincing, and both women have similarly curved backs and fingertips bent back. White draperies trail on the ground, while the tassels of Melancholy's shawl and the tapes of the drawing portfolio of Mlle du Val d'Ognes are specifically similar, as is the violet colour used for shoes and sash.

Although no further paintings have been attributed to Charpentier, we can still situate her as a woman artist who benefited from the greater exposure that the open Salon exhibitions of the Revolution offered to women, and from the greater public recognition that could be gained thereby. In his review of the Salon of 1801, the critic Ducray-Duminil commended the works of this pleasing painter for their firm and decisive execution, the arrangement of the poses and the choice of mass formations (*Les Petites Affiches de Paris*, September 1801). *Melancholy* was purchased by the State after the Salon of 1801.

Charpentier apparently received three times a week young artists who wished to hear her advice on painting and drawing, and in 1819, the year of her last Salon, she was awarded the gold medal by the Musée Royal. Salon catalogue entries reveal that she specialised in portraits, particularly of women and children, and in sentimental genre scenes. An entry to the Salon of 1806, *A Blindman, Surrounded by His Children, Is Consoled by the Four Other Senses*, and one to the Salon of 1808, the *First Cure of a Young Doctor*, indicate that she was concerned to invent her own iconography and does not necessarily conform to Sterling's damningly faint appraisal and highly gendered conclusion:

> Meanwhile the notion that our portrait of Mlle Charlotte may have been painted by a woman is, let us confess, an attractive idea. Its poetry, literary rather than plastic, its very evident charms, and its cleverly concealed weaknesses, its ensemble made up from a thousand subtle artifices, all seem to reveal the feminine spirit [Sterling 1951].

VALERIE MAINZ

Chase-Riboud, Barbara
American sculptor and writer, 1939–

Born Barbara DeWayne Chase in Philadelphia, 26 June 1939. Studied sculpture at Tyler School of Art, Temple University, Philadelphia (BFA 1957); worked for *Charm* magazine, New York; spent a year at the American Academy in Rome on John Hay Whitney fellowship, 1958–9; studied design and architecture at Yale School of Art and Architecture, New Haven, under Josef Albers (MFA 1960). Lived abroad from 1960, mainly in Paris. Married (1) journalist-photographer Marc Riboud, 1961; two sons; divorced; Riboud died 1981; (2) art dealer Sergio Tosi, 1981. Recipient of National Endowment for the Arts (NEA) grant, 1973; Kafka prize for best fiction written by an American woman, 1979; Academy of Italy gold medal, 1979; Carl Sandburg poetry prize, 1988; honorary doctorates from Temple University, 1981, and Muhlenberg College, Allentown, Pennsylvania, 1993. Lives in France.

Selected Individual Exhibitions
Galerie Cadran Solaire, Paris: 1966
Bertha Schaefer Gallery, New York: 1970
Massachusetts Institute of Technology, Cambridge: 1970
Betty Parsons Gallery, New York: 1972
University Art Museum, Berkeley, CA: 1973
Detroit Institute of Arts: 1973
Kunstmuseum, Düsseldorf: 1974
Musée d'Art Moderne de la Ville de Paris: 1974
United States Information Service, Washington, DC: 1975 (touring)
PS 80, New York: 1980
Stampatori Gallery, New York: 1981
Pasadena College of Art, CA: 1990
Galerie Flora, Espace Kiron, Paris: 1994

Selected Writings
From Memphis and Peking: Poems, New York: Random House, 1974
Sally Hemings, New York: Viking, 1979 (novel)
Valide, New York: Morrow, 1986 (novel)
Portrait of a Nude Woman as Cleopatra, New York: Morrow, 1987 (poems)

"Why Paris?", *Essence*, xviii, October 1987, pp.65–6
Echo of Lions, New York: Morrow, 1989 (novel)
Les Nuits d'Egypte, Paris: Félin, 1994
The President's Daughter, New York: Crown, 1994 (novel)

Bibliography

Chase-Riboud, exh. cat., University Art Museum, Berkeley, CA, 1973
Elsa Honig Fine, *The Afro-American Artist: Search for Identity*, New York: Holt Rinehart, 1973
Barbara Chase-Riboud: Zeichnungen, exh. cat., Kunstmuseum, Düsseldorf, 1974
Chase-Riboud, exh. cat., Musée d'Art Moderne de la Ville de Paris, 1974
Chase-Riboud: Skulpturen, Zeichnungen, exh. cat., Kunstverein, Freiburg im Breisgau, 1976
Irene Waller, *Textile Sculptures*, London: Studio Vista, 1977
Eleanor Munro, *Originals: American Women Artists*, New York: Simon and Schuster, 1979
Marjorie Elliott Bevlin, *Design Through Discovery*, 5th edition, New York: Holt Rinehart and Winston, 1989
Charlotte Streifer Rubinstein, *American Women Sculptors*, Boston: Hall, 1990
Mara R. Witzling, ed., *Voicing Today's Visions: Writings by Contemporary Women Artists*, New York: Universe, 1994

Barbara Chase-Riboud is noted as both a sculptor and a writer. Her sculpture is characterised by a unique blending of seemingly disparate materials: bronze, marble and fibre. Her written work is also diverse, including historical novels and volumes of poetry. Although American by birth, Chase-Riboud has pursued her career in Europe, primarily Paris, where she has lived for the full period of her artistic maturity. Her writing and visual art have both been informed by her African-American heritage. Most of her novels are reinterpretations of history in which black protagonists are given central place and voice. The format of her sculptures is derived from African mask-making traditions where soft and hard, permanent and impermanent materials are freely combined.

Barbara DeWayne Chase was the only child in a middle-class African-American family from Philadelphia. She took art classes throughout her childhood. Offered several college scholarships, she decided to attend Tyler School of Art, receiving a BFA in 1957. Upon graduation she moved to New York, having won the *Mademoiselle* guest-editorship award and, shortly thereafter, she was offered a position at *Charm* magazine. During her study year in Rome at the American Academy she was introduced to non-European art when, on a whim, she travelled to Egypt, where she ended up spending three months. Chase-Riboud then returned to the USA to pursue graduate studies at the Yale School of Art and Architecture, studying under Josef Albers. By the time she received her MFA, she had already developed her own ideas about making art, to wit, that she need not restrict herself to the Western mode. After leaving Yale, Chase-Riboud went back to Europe where she has resided ever since. While in Paris she met and then married the journalist Marc Riboud with whom she had two sons. There was a hiatus in her work during which she was more involved with bringing up her children and travelling with the family than in the production of art. When she went back to making images in 1967 her style had gone through a major change. Whereas her earlier works were figural images, in her work of a decade later she deliberately eschewed figural reference in

Chase-Riboud: *The Cape*, 1973; multi-coloured bronze, hemp rope, copper wire on aluminium support; 182.9 × 147.3 cm.; Collection Lannan Foundation, Los Angeles

order to imbue her sculptures with the magical presence of African masks.

During the early 1970s her first mature style emerged when Chase-Riboud developed a method of combining with bronze knotted and wrapped ropes made of silk or wool that cascaded curtain-like to the floor. By eliminating the visible "legs" of her bronze sculptures she was able to hide their structure. One unexpected aspect of these pieces in which Chase-Riboud delighted was that the rope, the softer and more pliable substance, seemed to be supporting the bronze, and hence became the "strong element" of the work. As her work developed, she deliberately attempted to imitate the visual effects of the bronze with the fibre sequences, thus creating a visual unity out of contradictory material elements, as in *Confessions for Myself* (1972; University Art Museum, Berkeley, CA). By combining these media, Chase-Riboud subverts the traditional hierarchy in which fibre is associated with craft – a lesser, "feminine" medium – while bronze-casting has its virile, heroic history within western art. Bronze is also associated with the African Benin sculptural tradition. Many works in this style, including several of *Malcolm X*, were exhibited together in 1973 in Chase-Riboud's first important solo exhibition at the University Art Museum, Berkeley.

Chase-Riboud's next stylistic development was stimulated by her reaction to a newly discovered Chinese burial suit that was made from a myriad of small jade pieces stitched together. She felt a special affinity with the concept of sewing hard, non-pliable materials, a feature of her own works. In *The Cape* (1973; see illustration) she pieced together with copper wires many small squares of bronze, individually cast with variegated patinas, to create a looming, ceremonial form. In a slightly earlier sculpture, *Bathers* (1972), she had already experimented with the idea of piecing her work from smaller elements.

During the 1980s, a time of personal change, in which she divorced her first husband and married the Italian art dealer Sergio Tosi, Chase-Riboud continued to piece together smaller segments to build works that were now characterised by an incorporation of architectural elements: neo-classical doors, columns and windows. In *Cleopatra's Door* (1983) she combined small, variegated bronze pieces with beams of wood, as in earlier works playing off the contradictions between soft and hard, rigid and pliable. Instead of reflecting the softness and irregularity of rope, however, the bronze is merged with a wooden post-and-lintel doorway.

Barbara Chase-Riboud is a prolific writer with four novels and two volumes of poetry to her credit. The relationship between her art work and poetry is especially close, and several poems and sculptures appear to be variations on the same theme. The sculpture *Cleopatra's Door* relates to her book of narrative poems, *Portrait of a Nude Woman as Cleopatra* (1987), Cleopatra's door being the portal to the feminine, to Africa. Chase-Riboud is interested in retelling history through black narrators and protagonists, such as Sally Hemings, Thomas Jefferson's "slave wife". With her sculpture *Harrar: The Middle Passage Memorial* (1994), Chase-Riboud has proposed a monument consisting of two bronze obelisks, each 15.5 metres high, to commemorate the victims of the African diaspora.

MARA R. WITZLING

Chéron, Elisabeth-Sophie
French painter and printmaker, 1648–1711

Born in Paris, 3 October 1648, to Henri Chéron from Meaux, a Calvinist, and Marie Le Fèvre, a Catholic; brother Louis and younger sister Marie also became artists. Taught by her father, a miniature painter, enamellist and engraver, and by Charles Le Brun. Educated at the convent of Ferté-sous-Jouarre from 1662. Converted to Catholicism, 1668. Married royal engineer Jacques le Hay(e), 1692(?); retained her own name. Received a pension of 500 livres from Louis XIV. Also an accomplished poet and musician, and translator of religious texts into French. Member, Académie Royale de Peinture et de Sculpture, Paris, 1672; Accademia dei Ricovrati, Padua, 1699. Died in Paris, 3 September 1711.

Principal Exhibitions
Paris Salon: 1673, 1679, 1699, 1704

Selected Writings
Essay de pseaumes et cantiques mis en vers, Paris: Brunet, 1694; as *Pseaumes nouvellement mis en vers françois*, Paris, 1715 (this edition contains an ode to the glory of the artist by Boutard)

La Coupe du Val-de-Grâce [Anonimiana ou mélanges de poésie d'éloquence et d'érudition], Paris, 1700; reprinted Paris, 1880, and Geneva: Slatkine, 1969 (response to a pamphlet by Molière)

Les Cerises renversées: Poème héroïque, Paris, 1717 (translator, from Virgil's *Georgics*)

Ode: Description de Trianon, 1745 (translation of the Abbé F. Boutard's Latin ode "Trianaeum")

Bibliography
Antoinette Deshoulières, *Réflexions morales sur l'envie immodérée de faire passer son nom à la postérité*, 1693–4

De Vertron, *La Nouvelle Pandore*, Paris, 1698

Jean Baptiste Fermel'huis, *Eloge funèbre de Madame le Hay*, Paris: Fournier, 1712; reprinted in *Archives de l'Art Français*, 2nd series, i, 1861, pp.370–411

Guérin, *Description de l'Académie Royale des Arts de Peinture et de Sculpture*, Paris, 1715; reprinted Geneva: Minkoff, 1973

Roger de Piles, *Abrégé de la vie des peintres*, 2nd edition, Paris, 1715

Niceron, *Mémoires des hommes illustres*, 1731

Lambert, *Siècle littéraire de Louis XIV*, 1751

François-Marie Arouet Voltaire, *Le Siècle de Louis XIV*, 2 vols, 1751; as *The Age of Louis XIV*, 2 vols, London, 1752

Antoine Joseph Dézailler d'Argenville, *Abrégé de la vie des plus fameux peintres*, iii, 1752

Jean Piganiol de la Force, *Description de Paris*, 1765

J. de la Porte and J.F. de la Croix, *Histoire littéraire des femmes françaises, ou lettres historiques et critiques*, Paris, 1769

Joseph Strutt, *A Biographical Dictionary Containing an Historical Account of All the Engravers from the Earliest Period of the Art of Engraving to the Present Time*, 2 vols, London, 1785–6

Robert Dumesnil, *Le Peintre-graveur français*, iii, Paris, 1838

P.J. Mariette, *Abecedario*, 1851–3; reprinted Paris: Nobele, 1966

Charles Le Blanc, *Manuel de l'amateur d'estampes*, 2 vols, Paris, 1854

Elizabeth Fries Lummis Ellet, *Women Artists in All Ages and Countries*, New York: Harper, 1859

"Réponse de Mlle Chéron à M. de Vertron", *Nouvelles Archives de l'Art Français*, i, 1872, p.121

Paul Lacroix, *La Coupe du Val-de-Grâce: Réponse au poème de Molière avec deux notices par le bibliophile Jacob*, Paris, 1880

Octave Fidière, *Etat-civil des peintres et sculpteurs de l'Académie Royale: Billets d'enterrement de 1648–1713*, Paris, 1883

——, *Les Femmes artistes à l'Académie Royale de Peinture et de Sculpture*, Paris, 1885

G. de Leiris, "Les femmes à l'Académie de Peinture", *L'Art*, xlv, Paris, 1888

Henry Jouin, *Charles Le Brun et les arts sous Louis XIV*, Paris, 1889

Catalogue of a Collection of Engravings, Etchings and Lithographs by Women, exh. cat., Grolier Club, New York, 1901

Léon Gréder, *Elisabeth-Sophie Chéron*, Paris: Jouve, 1909

Ernst Lemberger, *Meisterminiaturen aus funf Jahrhunderten*, Stuttgart, 1911

Ernesto Sarasino, *L'amatore di miniature su avoiro*, Milan: Hoepli, 1918

Jean Gabriel Goulinat, "Les femmes peintres du XVIIIe siècle", *L'Art et les Artistes*, 1926

Henri Clouzot, *La Miniature sur émail en France*, Paris, 1928

Pierre Lespinasse, *La Miniature en France au XVIII siècle*, Paris and Brussels, 1929

Roger-Armand Weigert, *Inventaire du fonds français: Graveurs du XVIIe siècle*, iii, Paris, 1954

Leo Schidloff, *The Miniature in Europe in the 16th, 17th, 18th and 19th Centuries*, 4 vols, Graz, 1964

La Femme: Peintre et sculpteur du XVIIe au XXe siècle, exh. cat., Grand Palais, Paris, 1975

Women Artists, 1550–1950, exh. cat., Los Angeles County Museum of Art, and elsewhere, 1976

Elsa Honig Fine, *Women and Art*, Montclair, NJ: Allanheld and Schram, 1978

Germaine Greer, *The Obstacle Race: The Fortunes of Women Painters and Their Work*, London: Secker and Warburg, and New York: Farrar Straus, 1979

Judith Brodsky, "Rediscovering women printmakers, 1550–1850", *Counterproof*, i, Summer 1979, p.7

Marie-France Hilgar, "The Val-de-Grâce cupola in painters' and writers' quarrels", *Laurels*, lii, Fall 1981, pp.171–80

Das Verborgene Museum I: Dokumentation der Kunst von Frauen in Berliner öffentlichen Sammlungen, exh. cat., Akademie der Künste, Berlin, 1987

Marie-France Hilgar, "Les multiples talents d'Elisabeth Sophie Chéron", *Cahiers du Dix-Septième*, ii, Spring 1988, pp.91–8

"Hommage à Elisabeth Sophie Chéron: Texte et peinture à l'âge classique", *Prospect* (Paris), no.1, 1992

Elisabeth-Sophie Chéron was one of the first women to be admitted to the Académie Royale de Peinture et de Sculpture. On 11 June 1672 her teacher Charles Le Brun introduced her with two portraits (one of them a self-portrait; now Louvre, Paris) to the academy members, who recognised "this rare work, surpassing all the ordinary power (force) of her sex". In his funeral eulogy to her (1712), Fermel'huis, Chéron's physician and a doctor of the University of Paris, ranked her alongside "Lavinia Fontana, Marietta Tintoretta, Anna Anguscioli de Cremone, Minerva Anguscioli, la célèbre Fede Galitia, Mesdemoiselles Boulogne et Madame Girardon". Antoinette Deshoulières (1693) referred to Chéron as a "wise painter", while Antoine de la Fosse ("Sur les peintures de Mademoiselle Chéron: A l'occasion de son portrait fait par elle-même") compared her to Circe. She was sung about by the poet Bosquillon, and in 1698 de Vertron, the court historian, compared her with Apelles. Chéron was also an accomplished musician, playing several instruments, and was well-known as a poet. In 1699 she was elected a member of the Accademia dei Ricovrati in Padua, under the name of the muse Erato, and Dézailler d'Argenville (1752) called her the "Sappho of her time". In his *Siècle de Louis XIV* (1751) Voltaire mentioned that the king awarded her a pension of 500 livres. At the age of 21 Chéron wrote a poem, *La Coupe du Val-de-Grâce* (published 1700), against a pamphlet published by Molière (this had praised Nicolas Mignard's painted ceiling in the church of the Val-de-Grâce, and was itself a response to Perrault's poem *La Peinture*, written to the glory of Mignard's rival Le Brun). The context was the debates between the proponents of classicism and the "Rubenistes" over the relative importance of line and colour in painting. In her poem, which is seen as an important source for the debates, Chéron defends her teacher Le Brun at Mignard's expense.

Like many female artists, Chéron was first instructed by her father. At the early age of 14 she painted portraits of noble fellow-pupils at the convent boarding school she attended at Ferté-sous-Jouarre, as well as a portrait of the abbess, Henriette de Lorraine, who may have introduced her to royal circles. Chéron returned home after the flight of her father in 1664, which was probably for religious reasons (he was a Calvinist). She not only supported her family from the proceeds of her work, but also enabled her brother, Louis, to spend some years of study in Rome. On 25 March 1668 she and her younger sister Marie converted to Catholicism in the church of Saint-Sulpice in Paris, where she is registered as a painter. At this time she was producing drawings and etchings on copper, translating religious writings and poetry and composing verse. She probably married the royal engineer Jacques le Hay(e) in 1692 but she retained her own name after their marriage, because she regarded it as a *union philosophique*.

Portraits formed the largest part of Chéron's oeuvre, but most of these are known only from descriptions. Among the works she exhibited at the Salon of 1699 were a portrait of herself as an artist and portraits of her sister as a singer, *Mlle Bélo as a Vestal Virgin*, *M. Morel de la Musique du Roi* and *Mme Dacier*. In 1704 she exhibited 12 paintings, including portraits of *Mme Mansard*, *Mme de Barbézieux*, the *Prior of Cordenoy*, *Mme de La Guette*, *Mlle de Villefranche in the Guise of Psyche about to Kill Cupid* and *Mme de Monaco*; two genre scenes, *Girl Drawing* and *Two Girls Tuning a Harpsichord*; and a *Descent from the Cross* (all untraced). According to Fermel'huis, she painted portraits of *Mlle de Montpensier*, *King Kasimir of Poland* and the royal princes. He also mentioned further full-length portraits with background landscapes: Mme Morin as Sappho with her daughter as Genius and as a naiad, and the Marquise d'Ussé with her daughter, chasing a bird.

Chéron is said to have rejected the opportunity of going to Vienna to paint portraits of the Emperor Joseph and the grand duchesses, but she did receive casts from which to execute them. Dézailler d'Argenville mentioned a number of portraits, including those of *Hardouin de Beaumont de Péréfixe, Archbishop of Paris* (1670), of the Carmelite friar *Sebastien Truchet* (1703; engraved by Thomassin *fils* in 1720), of *Madeleine de Scudérie* (engraved by Johann Georg Wille; Kunsthalle, Hamburg), of *Mme de Maintenon*, *Marie-Catherine le Jumel de Berneville, Comtesse d'Aulnoi* (engraved by Paison), *Jeanne-Marie Bouvières* (engraved by Aubert), two portraits of *Pierre Nicole* (engraved by P. Dupin and E. Desroches), the Jesuit and collector *Louis Bourdaloue* (engraved by Pierre de Rochefort), a portrait of *de Plattemontagne*, of *Mme Deshoulières*. Surviving works attributed to Chéron include *St Mary Magdalene Holding a Perfume Jar* (Musée des Beaux-Arts et d'Archéologie, Rennes), inscribed "Dilexit multum", and a portrait of *Jeanne-Marie Bouvier de la Motte Guyon* (Pushkin Museum, Moscow). According to the *Mémoires pour l'Histoire des Sciences et des Beaux-Arts* of March 1713, Chéron painted in her youth a portrait of *Dona Hipolita d'Aragon* solely from a description, as well as a posthumous portrait from memory of the Calvinist minister *Pierre du Moulin* (d. 1658).

Chéron's self-portraits (Louvre; Musée de Versailles; Musée des Beaux-Arts, Dijon; Kupferstichkabinett, Berlin; the last accompanied by a four-line verse by Santeuel and engraved by François Cherau) reveal that she saw herself as an artist, poet and musician in equal measure. There is another self-portrait in the graphics collection of the Kunsthalle, Hamburg, and one reproduced by Dézailler d'Argenville is similar to an engraving in the Kupferstichkabinett, Dresden.

Chéron also executed a large number of history paintings, which demonstrate her often-mentioned knowledge of antiquity, as well as religious subjects. Among others Dézailler d'Argenville lists a *Flight into Egypt* with the Virgin and Child depicted against a "beautiful landscape background"; *Cassandra Consulting a Guardian Spirit about the Fate of Troy*; an *Annunciation*; a *Lamentation* (for engraving, see illustration), painted with the help of wax models by Gaetano Zumbo; and a *St Thomas Aquinas* for the Jacobins in Paris. He

Chéron: *Lamentation*, engraving; 48.9 × 60.6 cm.; Kupferstichkabinett, Dresden

mentions that there were many large paintings by her in Parisian private collections.

Fermel'huis praised Chéron's study of antiquity, the confidence of her drawing, the elegance of outline, the characterisation of her figures, her colouring and chiaroscuro; in Chéron one could find a number outstanding qualities united "that normally are found parcelled out among several famous men". Dézailler d'Argenville emphasised Chéron's understanding of harmony and drapery, the ease of her brushwork and her extensive knowledge of antiquity, which manifested itself especially in her drawings of cameos. He also commented that she retained the character, drawing and brushwork of the old masters in her copies of their works.

In 1706 Chéron published her *Livre de dessin composé de testes tirées des plus beaux ouvrages de Raphael*, a collection of 36 engravings of drawings after heads by Raphael. The *Mémoires pour l'Histoire des Sciences et des Beaux-Arts* of October 1706 includes a review of Chéron's sketchbook of these drawings, which included an "Antique Flora". Twelve pages from her folio with copies of Raphael's Stanza della Segnatura in the Vatican are listed by Dumesnil (1838). The drawing of *A Grape Harvest* (British Museum) after Michelangelo and the above-mentioned sketchbook point to a

possible stay in Italy (Fidière), although this was rejected by Gréder (1909).

Besides portraits and biblical subjects, Chéron concentrated mainly on copying and making engravings, particularly of antique cameos. The works are undated and show no stylistic variation, but it is probable that she took on these commissions in order to support her family after the flight of her father. Dézailler d'Argenville notes that three prints in the suite of engravings of antique cameos (*Pierres antiques gravées, tirées des principaux cabinets de France*, Paris?, 1706?) after Chéron's drawings were engraved by the artist herself: *Bacchus and Ariadne*, *Mars and Venus* and *The Night that Scattered Poppies* (1710; Kupferstichkabinett, Berlin; Kupferstichkabinett, Dresden), the last based on a blood jasper in the royal collection. The rest were engraved by her nieces Ursule and Jeanne de la Croix and other printmakers (*Scipio's Restraint*, a portrait of *Julius Caesar*, a portrait of three unknown figures and one of an unknown man are in the British Museum, London). In 1710 Chéron and her husband published *Remarques sur la manière de graver et d'éxpliquer les pierres antiques, faites à l'occasion de deux estampes de la cornaline du Roi appelée le cachet de Michel-Ange.*

Many of Chéron's works were engraved after her death, and it can thus be assumed that they were popular collectors' items. In 1746 the Kupferstichkabinett, Dresden, held 41 works by Chéron and her brother Louis engraved by Moitte; in 1764 the number of their works had increased to 82 (55 by Elisabeth and 27 by Louis). Typical of Chéron's style in the scenic prints is the use of parallel or diagonal hatching for the background; cross-hatching in the middle ground; and point-hatching for the modelling of foreground figures. The antique-style portrait cameos, on the other hand, are mainly executed in parallel hatching. Chéron instructed her nieces Jeanne and Ursule de la Croix in the art of copper engraving and allowed them to etch many of her drawings. She is also said to have taught her sister Marie and sent her to a different teacher to learn other disciplines. Her own salon was a meeting place for intellectuals. Shortly before her death, Chéron completed a translation of psalms, the songs of Habbakuk, and the second ode of the first book of Horace's *Odes*; she had also begun to translate Sophocles' *Oedipus* into French. Besides her work as a draughtswoman and engraver Chéron was also one of the earliest important pastel painters in France.

ULRIKE BOLTE

Chicago, Judy
American multi-media artist, 1939–

Born Judy Cohen in Chicago, Illinois, 20 July 1939. Studied at University of California, Los Angeles, 1960–64 (BA 1962, MFA 1964). Married (1) writer Jerry Gerowitz, 1961; killed in a road accident, 1962; (2) sculptor Lloyd Hamrol, 1969; (3) photographer Donald Woodman. Adopted name Chicago, 1970. Taught at University of California Extension, Los Angeles, 1963–9; University of California Institute Extension, Irvine, 1966–9; California State University, Fresno, 1969–71 (founded first Feminist Art Program); California Institute of the Arts, Valencia, 1971–3 (moved Feminist Art Program here and co-directed it with Miriam Schapiro, and with students produced *Womanhouse*, exhibited in Los Angeles in 1972). Co-founder, Feminist Studio Workshop and Woman's Building, Los Angeles, 1973. Recipient of Woman of the Year award, *Mademoiselle* magazine, 1973; National Endowment for the Arts (NEA) grants, 1976 and 1977; honorary doctorate, Russell Sage College, Troy, New York, 1992. Lives in New Mexico.

Selected Individual Exhibitions
Pasadena Art Museum, CA: 1969 (as Judy Gerowitz)
Faculty Club, California State College, Fullerton, CA: 1970
Jack Glenn Gallery, Corona del Mar, CA: 1972
Artemisia Gallery, Chicago: 1974
JPL Fine Arts, London: 1975
San Francisco Museum of Modern Art: 1979– (*Dinner Party*, touring)
Parco Gallery, Japan: 1980
Fine Arts Gallery, Irvine, CA: 1981
Musée d'Art Contemporain, Montreal: 1982
ACA Galleries, New York: 1984, 1985, 1986
Schirn Kunsthalle, Frankfurt am Main: 1987
Spertus Museum, Chicago: 1993– (*Holocaust Project*, touring)

Selected Writings
"Female imagery", *Womanspace Journal*, i/1, Summer 1973, pp.11–17 (with Miriam Schapiro)
Through the Flower: My Struggle as a Woman Artist, New York: Doubleday, 1975; 2nd edition, New York: Doubleday, and London: Women's Press, 1982
The Dinner Party: A Symbol of Our Heritage, New York: Doubleday, 1979
Embroidering Our Heritage: The Dinner Party Needlework, New York: Doubleday, 1980 (with Susan Hill)
The Birth Project, New York: Doubleday, 1985
The Dinner Party, New York: Atheneum, 1987
Holocaust Project: From Darkness into Light, New York and London: Viking Penguin, 1993
Beyond the Flower: The Autobiography of a Feminist Artist (in preparation)

Bibliography
Lucy R. Lippard, "Judy Chicago talking to Lucy R. Lippard", *Artforum*, xiii, September 1974, pp.60–65; reprinted in Lucy R. Lippard, *From the Center: Feminist Essays on Women's Art*, New York: Dutton, 1976
Arlene Raven and Susan Rennie, "Interview with Judy Chicago", *Chrysalis*, no.4, 1978, pp.89–101
Lucy R. Lippard, "Judy Chicago's 'Dinner Party'", *Art in America*, lxviii, April 1980, pp.114–26
Judy Chicago: The Second Decade, 1973–1983, exh. cat., ACA Galleries, New York, 1984
Judy Chicago: Powerplay, exh. cat., ACA Galleries, New York, 1986
Hilary Robinson, ed., *Visibly Female: Feminism and Art: An Anthology*, London: Camden, 1987; New York: Universe, 1988
Moira Roth, ed., *Connecting Conversations: Interviews with 28 Bay Area Women Artists*, Oakland, CA: Eucalyptus Press, 1988
Mara R. Witzling, ed., *Voicing Our Visions: Writings by Women Artists*, New York: Universe, 1991; London: Women's Press, 1992
Norma Broude and Mary D. Garrard, eds, *The Expanding Discourse: Feminism and Art History*, New York: Icon, 1992
Judy Chicago: Holocaust Project: From Darkness into Light, exh. cat., Spertus Museum, Chicago, and elsewhere, 1993
Norma Broude and Mary D. Garrard, eds, *The Power of Feminist Art: The American Movement of the 1970s*, New York: Abrams, and London: Thames and Hudson, 1994
Amelia Jones, ed., *Sexual Politics: Judy Chicago's Dinner Party in Feminist Art History*, Berkeley: University of California Press, 1996

Since its first installation at the San Francisco Museum of Modern Art in 1979, Judy Chicago's monumental *Dinner Party* (see illustration) has come to be one of the most controversial works in the history of Western art. Supporters and critics of the piece alike, however, have tended to neglect the rich diversity of Chicago's oeuvre.

In the late 1950s the artist moved to Los Angeles from Chicago, where she had taken art classes from the age of five. By the mid-1960s her nascent feminism began to simmer in the context of her exploration of "finish fetish", the particular fusion by Los Angeles artists of Minimalist and Pop forms and techniques, involving the use of plastics, bright local colour, vacuum technologies and abstract forms. Chicago's spray-painted *Car Hood* (1964; Collection Mr and Mrs Radoslar L. Sutnar, Los Angeles) showed her mastery of such technical skills as auto-body painting. Signalling her conviction that women artists must demonstrate their competence in the crafts of art-making, this mastery gave Chicago the authority to compete with her male colleagues.

Chicago: *The Dinner Party*, view from Emily Dickinson's place setting, 1979; artist's collection

In connection with an exhibition of her work at California State College, Fullerton, in 1970, Chicago publicly proclaimed her intention of challenging discrimination in the art world. Overtly parodying the machismo of "The Studs", the name half-seriously adopted by her male finish-fetish colleagues, Chicago posed in short hair and boxer shorts, standing aggressively in the corner of a boxing ring, for a full-page advertisement for the show in *Artforum* (December 1970). The entrance wall of the exhibition itself was inscribed: "*Judy Gerowitz* [the surname of her first husband] hereby divests herself of all names imposed upon her through male social dominance and freely chooses her own name *Judy Chicago*".

Motivated by her rage at the discrimination she experienced in the art world and driven by a new conviction that her experience as a woman and her sexuality were central to her art, Chicago began openly to express her goal of forging a feminist art practice. The next decade of her career would be shaped by her attempt to define the particularity of this experience through abstract and then increasingly recognisable representational forms. This turn towards "content" was an explicit attempt to expose the biases behind the formalist privileging of the transcendent "universality" of male abstraction.

Chicago's pictures of the late 1960s, abstract and highly polished in appearance, were nascent formulations of the hotly debated theory of "central core" that she would develop with Miriam Schapiro (q.v.) in the early 1970s. The abstracted, centralised forms of *Pasadena Lifesavers*, *Star Cunts* and *Donut* series (all 1968–70) were theorised as expressive symbols of the central "cavity" that defines women's experience of sexuality. The 15 *Lifesaver* paintings, informed by Chicago's interest in using colour to evoke particular emotional states, are particularly subversive in that they feminise the slick, high-tech hipness of finish-fetish works: each consists of an enormous slab of acrylic on which hover four throbbing, radiating wheels of colour.

During this transitional period Chicago also experimented with pyrotechnics, another process that conventionally excludes women practitioners. After studying with a fireworks company, Chicago produced a series of *Atmospheres* (repr. Lippard 1976, p.225), performances documented through photographs that involved the firing of colour flares in strategic patterns in natural or cultural public sites (see *Pasadena Museum Atmosphere*, 1970). Chicago saw these dramatic plumes of coloured smoke as feminising the landscape, an effect she exaggerated with pieces that included naked women performing goddess-rituals (*Goddess*, 1970; all documentation in artist's collection).

In the early 1970s Chicago also created several photographically-based lithographs exploring explicitly feminist subject matter. *Red Flag* (1971) depicts a woman pulling a bloody tampon (tinted a vibrant red) from her vaginal canal; *Love Story* (1970; both artist's collection) presents a sado-masochistic text from *The Story of O* underneath the unsettling image – in deep blue – of a man's hand holding a gun up to a woman's naked rear end. *Love Story* complicates the view of Chicago's work developed later by some anti-essentialist feminists who criticised her for producing only positive images of women without critiquing patriarchy.

One of Chicago's important contributions to the feminist art movement has been her conviction that women must develop strategies of making, exhibiting, teaching and writing about art in order to transform mainstream art institutions. Offered a teaching job at California State University, Fresno, in 1970, Chicago established a "Feminist Art Program" there, moving her students (all women) off campus in the hopes of establishing an environment in which they could express themselves more freely. Merging principles of cooperative education, involving aggressive interpersonal exploration through consciousness-raising techniques, with confidence-building strategies and technical training, Chicago developed a groundbreaking, multi-faceted approach to art pedagogy. During the Fresno period she produced two series of paintings that expanded on the techniques and abstract symbology of her earlier work: the *Fresno Fan* and *Flesh Garden* paintings were large-scale sprayed acrylic bands of modulated colour on acrylic (e.g. *Desert Fan*, 1970–71; Collection Mary Ross Taylor, Houston). With the other members of the Feminist Art Program, Chicago also developed a number of performances, including her slapstick send-up of patriarchal sex-roles, *Cock and Cunt Play* (1970; script in *Through the Flower*).

In 1971 Chicago, at the invitation and with the support of her collaborator Miriam Schapiro, moved the Feminist Art Program with the Fresno students to the California Institute of the Arts in Valencia, where they were joined by art historian Paula Harper, designer Sheila de Bretteville, and aided by student assistants Faith Wilding, Suzanne Lacy and Sherry Brody. After the Program's climactic staging of *Womanhouse*, a derelict house in Los Angeles that they transformed into a feminist environment in 1972, Chicago became increasingly convinced that such an alternative program could not develop fruitfully within the confines of such an institution. In 1973 she withdrew from the Cal Arts faculty, moving on to co-found the Feminist Studio Workshop (with Arlene Raven and de Bretteville), an independent studio program in Los Angeles.

Chicago's works of the mid-1970s, which show a gradual development of the iconography that would come to be so controversial in the *Dinner Party* plates, are visually compelling attempts to arrive at a positive and explicit "female imagery". In her central core *Through the Flower* series and four *Great Ladies* paintings of 1973, she explored both the symbolic effects of abstracted, centralised forms (as expressive of women's sexual experience) and, with *Great Ladies*, the idea of using works of art to reinstall important women in history. In the "great lady" *Marie Antoinette* (whereabouts unknown; related piece from *Great Ladies* series repr. Lippard 1976 and *Through the Flower*), in which intense, pulsating orange rays radiate from a soft open core, Chicago uses the title to give the abstracted form a specific historical content. She has been criticised for this attempt to construct a "universal" sign for femininity, particularly in that it might be seen to imply that women's experiences can be summed up through the morphology of their sexual anatomy.

This contentious issue of central core, as well as the question of attempting to legitimate women through masculinist notions of "greatness", came to the fore with the *Dinner Party*. Aided by hundreds of assistants, Chicago laboured for five years on the project, which quickly expanded to a grand-scale installation modelled loosely after the exclusively male Last Supper. Introduced by large woven banners calling for a utopian merging of differences, the three-sided equilateral table is a large centralised form that symbolises the egalitarianism that Chicago saw as one of the goals of feminism (the 13 settings on each side also refer to the number of men at the Last Supper and the number of members of a witches' coven). A porcelain floor with an additional 999 women's names broadens Chicago's revised history of the Western world.

As the general concept of the piece grew, so did Chicago's ambitions for the plates and for the needlework runners surrounding them and her need for assistance (though she never claimed the project to be collaborative as far as its authorship was concerned, she has been criticised for her hypocrisy in depending on the help of volunteers). Ultimately, each place setting was completed to include an elaborately modelled and painted porcelain plate, 35.5 centimetres in diameter (designed by Chicago and executed by Leonard Skuro and a team of ceramists), placed on an exquisite needlework runner representing Chicago's vision of each woman's special contribution to history (these were completed by teams headed by Susan Hill in stitches common to the period of the woman commemorated). Running from the "Primordial Goddess" through Greek culture (Sappho) up to the Enlightenment (Mary Wollstonecraft) and the 19th century (Sojourner Truth – one of the few women of colour at the table – Susan B. Anthony and others), the final "guest" is Georgia O'Keeffe (q.v.) – served by a floral plate with flesh-coloured, labial folds lunging off the surface – an artist whose flower paintings Chicago found particularly inspirational.

The *Dinner Party* has been shown in venues across Europe, North America and Australia (a 15th public exhibition of the piece took place in 1996 at the UCLA/Hammer Museum). By and large rejected by the art world for its unabashed populism, many of these venues have been non-museum sites; the exhibitions were organised by international networks of supporters (initially spearheaded by Diane Gelon, who lectured and raised money for the piece). In this sense, the piece is a successful realisation of Chicago's attempt to expand the reception of art beyond an art-world elite.

As the *Dinner Party* made its rounds, Chicago began to organise another cooperative, alternative art work: the *Birth Project* (1980–85). Growing out of her new-found interest in designing patterns for needlework and her desire to counter the iconographic void surrounding the birth process, the *Birth Project* drew on the extensive network of supporters that had arisen in response to the *Dinner Party*. Chicago designed more than 150 needlework patterns, sent these out to women to stitch in their homes and worked closely with them in the completion of each piece. The most monumental of these, a tapestry entitled *Creation of the Universe* (1984; 107 × 427 cm.; Collection Judy Chicago and Audrey Cowan), was designed by Chicago and executed by Cowan, who had assisted her on the *Dinner Party*. This is a dramatic, decorative scene of an abstracted female body, legs spread, absorbing the vitality of the sun and earth around her to nurture a foetus.

While completing the *Birth Project*, Chicago began another series of works: *Powerplay*, which shifts the focus of her feminism to an interrogation of masculinity. Produced this time primarily in her own studio, *Powerplay* includes prismacolour drawings, tapestries (woven by Cowan), sprayed acrylic paintings and cast paper and bronze reliefs. Here, anguished male bodies and faces are depicted in various violent acts, as in *Trying to Kill the Woman Inside Him* (1983; whereabouts unknown, repr. New York 1986) and *Crippled by the Need to Control* (1983; artist's collection). The iconographically direct *Three Faces of Man* (1985; artist's collection) is composed of three images of male heads grimacing in violent rage, malevolent glee and painful anguish. "Man" is shown here not as singular abuser of power but as himself riven from within, subject to the violence of patriarchy.

Extending her exploration of masculinity and the abuse of power in *Powerplay*, Chicago's most recent project explores the patriarchal ideology underlying the Holocaust. Produced in collaboration with her husband, the photographer Donald Woodman, the *Holocaust Project: From Darkness into Light* consists of a number of painting/photo combines on photo-linen, a tapestry (woven by Cowan) and a stained-glass piece (executed by several artisans). Merging painting with Woodman's manipulated pictures of Holocaust sites and other historical imagery, Chicago highlights particular intersections among various modes of oppression – misogyny, homophobia, white racism, anti-semitism, class warfare – in order to expose the larger systems of injustice out of which she believes the Holocaust emerged.

In this traumatic but ultimately hopeful project, Chicago complicates her feminist identity by exploring her relationship to the Jewish tradition, relating her desire to "teach through art" to the Jewish concept of *tikkun*, the "process of healing and repairing the world". Depicting struggling Jews, women and homosexuals, piles of bones and bodies, and Nazis committing atrocities, the piece as a whole is a dark rumination on the human potential for evil, but also – especially with the utopian image of inter-ethnic harmony in the final stained-glass panel of the piece, *Rainbow Shabbat* – proposes, optimistically, that the feminine can be "an essential step toward the humanization of our world" (*Holocaust Project* 1993, pp.3 and 11).

Chicago's ambitious project intervenes in the history of the Holocaust in a controversial way. Using her signature crude representational style, developed as a counter to what she perceives to be the elitist, coded language of modernist practice, Chicago deliberately simplifies a complex history to present a bold – some would say reductive – message about the ideology of fascism. Her linking of Nazism to sexism or even more broadly defined modes of oppression (the imagery includes pictures from the Vietnam War, the US slave trade and animal testing) raises the important question of whether such connections defuse and dehistoricise the specificity of the Holocaust.

As a contemporary version of historical allegory, such a project clearly fulfills Chicago's career-long goal of reaching a broad audience with work that is both accessible and polemical. At the same time, the very directness with which she approaches complex and highly charged issues (the utopianism of her desire to speak transparently through visual symbols in order to change consciousness) just as clearly creates discomfort within an art audience now critical of such transformative ideals. It is not surprising, then, that Chicago's *Holocaust Project*, like her *Dinner Party*, has not been fully appreciated by the art world. But it may well become a major monument in the popular imagination.

AMELIA JONES

See also Training and Professionalism survey 10

Chryssa
American sculptor, 1933–

Born in Athens, Greece, 31 December 1933; later naturalised US citizen. Took a bachelor's degree in sociology in Athens, then studied under Greek painter Anghelos Prokopion. Studied at Académie de la Grande Chaumière, Paris, 1953–4; California School of Fine Arts, San Francisco, 1954–5. Settled in New York, 1955. Exhibited at Documenta, Kassel, Germany, 1968 and 1977. Recipient of Guggenheim fellowship, 1973. Lives in New York.

Selected Individual Exhibitions
Solomon R. Guggenheim Museum, New York: 1961
Museum of Modern Art, New York: 1963
Institute of Contemporary Art, University of Pennsylvania, Philadelphia: 1965
Pace Gallery, New York: 1966, 1968
Department of Fine Arts, Harvard University, Cambridge, MA: 1968
Walker Art Center, Minneapolis: 1968
Galerie Rive Droite, Paris: 1968
Galerie Der Spiegel, Cologne: 1969
Graphic Arts Gallery, San Francisco: 1970
Galleria d'Arte Contemporanea, Turin: 1970
Whitney Museum of American Art, New York: 1972
Musée d'Art Contemporain, Montreal: 1974
Galerie Denise René, Paris: 1974
André Emmerich Gallery, Zürich: 1974, 1975
Musée d'Art Moderne de la Ville de Paris: 1979
Pinacothèque Nacional Museum Alexandre Soutzos, Athens: 1980
Albright-Knox Art Gallery, Buffalo: 1982
Leo Castelli Gallery, New York: 1988, 1991

Bibliography
10 American Sculptors, exh. cat., Walker Art Center, Minneapolis, 1964
Chryssa, exh. cat., Galerie Denise René, New York, 1973
Sam Hunter, *Chryssa*, New York: Abrams, and London: Thames and Hudson, 1974
Pierre Restany, *Chryssa*, New York: Abrams, 1977 (contains bibliography)
Chryssa: Oeuvres récents, exh. cat., Musée d'Art Moderne de la Ville de Paris, 1979
Chryssa: Urban Icons, exh. cat., Albright-Knox Art Gallery, Buffalo, NY, 1982
The Tremaine Collection: 20th-Century Masters: The Spirit of Modernism, exh. cat., Wadsworth Atheneum, Hartford, CT, 1984
Miranda McClintic, "Chryssa: Cityscapes and icons", *Arts Magazine*, lxii, Summer 1988, pp.74–5
Donald Kuspit, "Chryssa", *Art in America*, lxxvi, September 1988, p.189
Chryssa: Cityscapes, New York: Thames and Hudson, 1990
Charlotte Streifer Rubinstein, *American Women Sculptors*, Boston: Hall, 1990
Amei Wallach, "Chryssa retraces her steps", *Newsday*, 3 February 1991, part ii, p.17

By 1955, as America enjoyed post-war prosperity, Chryssa had left her homeland, Greece, for Paris and had settled in New York. The effects of this move immediately manifested themselves in the artist's work. The influence of American commercial culture became apparent in *Cycladic Books* (1955; several casts made; private collections, repr. Restany 1977, figs 3, 55 and 56), where Chryssa poured plaster into a packaging box. The subsequent cast is barely three-dimensional (foreshadowing Minimalism) except for the presence of a T-shaped ridge. This ridge reminded Chryssa of the forms found on ancient Cycladic figures, allowing the work to illustrate the confluence of contemporary American and ancient Greek cultures.

The bright lights and visual language of Manhattan became a dominant source of inspiration for Chryssa's art. In *Arrow: Homage to Times Square* (1958; Empire State Collection, Albany, NY) Chryssa used small bars of aluminium to form an arrow shape. Each bar casts a shadow, which allowed her to experiment with the "static light" of the piece. In *Study of Light* (1958; painted aluminium; private collection, *ibid.*, fig.65) she cast a relief that looks like alphabet soup. When the light hitting the work changes, different forms are produced by the letters. Chryssa continued to study the structural potential of lettering in her oil painting *Newspaper No.3* (1961; Solomon R. Guggenheim Museum, New York), which is part of a series exploring patterns in newspapers. By working with such banal subject-matter, she echoed Pop Art's irreverence towards the separation of "popular" culture from "fine" art. She anticipated Warhol's multiple images with *Car Tires* (1958–62; Harry N. Abrams Family Collection, New York), in which she employed a stamp to repeat the image of a tyre within a grid.

On deciding to work with signboards in the early 1960s, Chryssa apprenticed herself to a sign maker. In *Times Square Sky* (1962; see illustration) she created an unintelligible message by layering decontextualised metal letters on to the wall. To balance the mélange, she used blue neon to write the word *air* above the work. Not only does this mark the first occurrence of neon in a sculpture (Hunter 1974, p.11), but it also points to Chryssa's strategic use of language. Henceforth, she experimented with the many artistic possibilities of neon. Symbols and letters were analysed via multi-coloured neon, as in *Five Variations on the Ampersand* (1966; Museum of

Chryssa: *Times Square Sky*, 1962; neon, aluminium, steel; Walker Art Center, Minneapolis

Modern Art, New York). Each ampersand stands over 60 centimetres high and is encased in grey Plexiglas, which creates a night-time effect. Emphasising the processes of the work, and her ability to control them, Chryssa exposed the mechanisms required to operate the neon. This manoeuvre complemented her claim that her sculptures are not dependent on technology, because they remain complete even after the transformers break down (*ibid.*, p.12).

In preparation for her *Gates to Times Square*, Chryssa produced a series of neon studies, most of which became individual works of art. Although *Clytemnestra II* (moulded

plastic tubes with inserted neon and timer; Nationalgalerie, Berlin) began as study No.14, this neon *S*, 4.57 metres high, caused a sensation when it was exhibited at Documenta IV in 1968. Unusually expressive, the work was inspired by Irene Papas's portrayal of Clytemnestra in Euripides' tragedy *Iphigenia in Aulis*. As Chryssa relates, when the protagonist learned of her daughter's sacrifice, the curves of her body convoluted as she screamed in horror (Restany 1977, p.69). The escalating sound of anguish is visually echoed by the sculpture, which requires several timed sequences before the boldly coloured neon is completely perceivable.

Combining the knowledge gained through her studies with her interest in the city, Chryssa started to build the *Gates to Times Square* (1964–6; Albright-Knox Art Gallery, Buffalo). As she has stated: "America is very stimulating, intoxicating for me ... The vulgarity of America as seen in the lights of Times Square is poetic" (Hunter 1974, p.10). For two years of intense activity, she worked to integrate metal, signs, neon and plastic into a three-metre cube that pays homage to communication, advertising and hence to the visual mechanics of capitalism. Art and technology unite in order to produce a light that is now dynamic. At both the entrance and the exit stands a giant letter *A*, which provides structural and symbolic support to the jumble of unreadable signs. Thus, what might be understood as chaotic, becomes logical (poetic) in form.

Works of the early 1970s are dominated by a triptych that furthers the analysis of linguistic codes. In one segment entitled *That's All* (1970–73; Plexiglas, neon, electrodes, asbestos, paper; Metropolitan Museum of Art, New York) Chryssa employed coloured neon to draw fragmented letters. The result, suggests Restany, is purely gestural, for the meaning of the fractured letters is suppressed by the visuality of the irregular lines. Although the triptych contains neon tubing and cut-aluminium shapes, the two-dimensionality of the work is emphasised through fields of colour. This graphic aesthetic reappears in a commission Chryssa received to transform the interior of a castle, known as the *Metternich Project* (1973–89; Schloss Adelsleben, Germany). After eliminating all natural light from the space, she recreated the exterior landscape by fabricating the passage of time. Cool blue and white neon is superimposed over warm yellows and foggy, grey-coloured paint to evoke the sensation of evening and daylight. The synthetic environment is then brought to life by a timer that moves the neon to a slow rhythm.

Chryssa continued to explore the use of language and light in New York. In addition to Times Square, she was newly inspired by Chinatown. Throughout the 1980s she produced paintings and large wall reliefs based on Chinese calligraphy and Roman script, as in *Mott Street No.2* (1985; sheet metal, mixed media, metallic paint; artist's collection, repr. *Chryssa: Cityscapes* 1990, fig.14). Instead of neon, she relied on aluminium to convey the structural qualities of the Chinese characters, while the highly polished surfaces reflect the surrounding light independently. By the 1990s Chryssa had returned to the topic of time with *Summer* (1988–90; honeycomb aluminium, paint, neon; artist's collection, repr. Wallach 1991). This complex sculpture, however, does not refer to the "natural" season, but rather, Vivaldi's musical construction.

Light, form, language and culture remain the constant themes in Chryssa's diverse work. Yet her concerns extend beyond that of the formal. By exploring language, she repossesses a domain once considered "masculine". Moreover, when she connotes the artificiality of "nature", she is actually questioning the presumption of an inherent "female" nature. Indeed, Chryssa may be seen as an overt feminist in the scream of *Clytemnestra* but, more subtly, she repeatedly contradicts theories of essentialism with her gender-neutral art. Quite often, the only way one could ascertain that Chryssa is a *woman* artist is by her unjust lack of art-historical recognition.

DEBRA WACKS

Churberg, Fanny (Maria)
Finnish painter, 1845–1892

Born in Vaasa, Österbotten, 12 December 1845. Educated at Emma Peranders's boarding school for girls, Porvoo, 1857–9, and in Viborg, 1860–61. Studied art privately in Helsinki under Finnish painters Alexandra Frosterus, Emma Gyldén and Berndt Lindholm, 1865–6; in Düsseldorf under landscape painter Carl Ludwig, 1867–8 and 1871–4; in Paris under Swedish landscape painter Wilhelm von Gegerfelt, 1876. Painted in Finland, 1877–80. Visited the Paris Exposition Universelle, 1878. Stopped painting, 1880; devoted herself to the Finska Handarbetets Vänner (Friends of Finnish Handicraft) and campaigned for an improvement in taste; wrote reviews and art criticism for Finnish newspapers and magazines, 1886–92. Lived, unmarried, partly with her brother's family in Sweden and partly in Finland. Died in Helsinki, 5 May 1892.

Principal Exhibitions
Finnish Art Society, Helsinki: 1869, 1879–80 (first prize 1879)
Art Exhibition, Kuopio: 1891
Stenman Gallery, Helsinki: 1919 (retrospective)

Selected Writings
"Konstföreningens exposition hösten, 1887" [The Art Association's autumn exhibition], *Finland*, 30 October 1887
"Konstföreningens årsexposition, 1888" [The Art Association's annual exhibition], *Finland*, 25 November 1888
"Atelier-besök" [Studio visit], *Finland*, 6 February 1889
"Konstexpositionen i Ateneum, 1889" [The art exhibition in the Ateneum], *Finland*, 23 and 26 October 1889

Bibliography
Carl Gustaf Estlander, "Konstföreningens exposition" [The Art Association's exhibition], *Finsk Tidskrift*, 1877, pp.383–5
—, "Finska Konstföreningens exposition" [The Finnish Art Association's exhibition], *Finsk Tidskrift*, 1878, p.460
J. Ahrenberg, "Ofversigt: Bildande konst" [A survey: Didactic art], *Finsk Tidskrift*, 1879
J.J. Tikkanen, "Finska konstföreningens exposition" [The Finnish Art Association's exhibition], *Finsk Tidskrift*, 1880
Fredrik Ahlstedt, "Fanny Maria Churberg", *Finska Qvinnor på olika arbetsområden* [Finnish women in different spheres], Helsinki: Finnish Women's Association, 1892
Signe Tandefelt, "Fanny Churberg", *Arena* (Helsinki), no.1, 1920
Sigrid Schauman, "Fanny Churbergs teckningar" [Fanny Churberg's drawings], *Svenska Pressen* (Helsinki), 11 February 1922
Helena Westermarck, "Fanny Churberg: Anteckningar om hennes insats i vår målarkonst" [Fanny Churberg: Notes on her contribution to our painting], *Finsk Tidskrift*, 1935, p.315
—, *Tre konstnärinnor: Fanny Churberg, Maria Wiik och Sigrid af Forselles* [Three women artists: Fanny Churberg, Maria Wiik and Sigrid af Forselles], Helsinki: Söderström, Förlagsaktiebolag, 1937
Aune Lindström, *Fanny Churberg: Elämö ja teokset*, Porvoo, 1938
Målarinnor från Finland: Seitsemän Suomalaista Taiteilijaa [Women painters from Finland], exh. cat., Nationalmuseum, Stockholm, and elsewhere, 1981
Leena Ahtola-Moorhouse, *Fanny Churberg: Myttin ainekset*, Helsinki, 1988

The last decades of the 19th century were a turbulent time for art in the Nordic countries. Artists rebelled against ingrown traditions in cultural life. Fanny Churberg belonged to the

Churberg: *Moonlight, Study,* 1878; oil; 37.5 × 52 cm.; Museum of Finnish Art Ateneum, Helsinki

generation that started this process, but she ended her painting career when she was 35 years old. She had been chastised by critics for her almost brutal paintings and dramatic visions. Although she did enjoy some measure of success, her self-confidence was shattered and in 1880 she put away her brushes for good. She continued with art by writing articles and she was the organiser and one of the founders in 1881 of the Friends of Finnish Handicraft, an organisation that helped women in particular to get an economic basis of their own. She also worked for the "Fennomanien", encouraging the Finnish people to accept their culture, language and country. She never married.

In the late 1870s Churberg tried to live as a free artist. She was strong-willed, had considerable creative powers and took great pleasure in her work. Her high moral standards did not allow her to compromise and accept half-hearted work, but neither Finnish society nor that of Germany or France could accept a woman of such strong character. Churberg accepted the consequences and stopped painting, turning her creative talents to social ends. Her breakthrough as a painter did not come until 1919, when a retrospective exhibition was held in Helsinki by the eccentric art dealer Gösta Stenman. By that time Churberg had been dead for almost 30 years. At her death her brother took care of what he thought was a bunch of worthless paintings. He kept them, but had almost forgotten their existence when Stenman happened to ask him if he knew

of the whereabouts of any of Churberg's paintings. Today her works have a firm place in Finnish art history.

Churberg was able to study painting because her family had sufficient money: her father was the town doctor in Vaasa. Both her parents died before she was 20 years old, but they left their children financially secure. After some years of private art training in Helsinki, in 1867 she headed for Düsseldorf in Germany, where the landscape painter Carl Ludwig became her private teacher. She remained his pupil until 1874, spending the summers in Finland. Churberg was a romantic soul with a passionate temperament and a great love for the Finnish landscape, particularly in late autumn and winter. She had a predilection for the dramatic in nature and loved the wild forests with rocks and broken trees and water.

In 1875–6 Churberg studied in France. It was not the work of the Impressionists as such that turned her mind to Paris, but the opportunity to paint her beloved nature in plein air. She chose the Swedish landscape painter Wilhelm von Gegerfelt as her teacher. In Paris she discovered the combination of light and colour values and the intensity of the still-life motifs in the work of the 18th-century painter Chardin. In 1876 she painted *Still Life with Vegetables and Fish* (Ateneum, Helsinki) and the following year *Still Life with Mushrooms* (Österbottens Museum of Vaasa), both technically extremely well painted and with that extra light in the colours that gives even a dead fish or a freshly-picked mushroom a soul.

Churberg's career as a painter was short. She painted for only ten years, yet almost 300 paintings by her are known. In a way she was a rebel. She was energetic, passionate and expressionistic. Her touch was free and uncurbed and far from the academic style she must have learned in Düsseldorf. The fact that she was a non-conformist may have given her the opportunity to go her own way. In the end it was too much of a burden for her to continue alone.

Although she never knew the work of Vincent van Gogh, who started his ten-year career at the time she ended hers, in their feelings and wild expression they are close to each other, although different in the landscapes they chose to paint. Churberg saw the unique and barren beauty of Finnish nature, and painted the heavy grey climate of the north (e.g. *Moonlight, Study*, 1878; see illustration; *Winter*, 1880; Ateneum). No one expected anything of her, which gave her a certain freedom to do what she most wanted. She felt strongly about her work and overstepped the bounds of convention. She never completed her paintings in a realistic or naturalistic way, but left them with stormy skylines, captured the open air and powerful emotions. She was romantic in one way, but never sentimental. Churberg inspired artists for generations after her; Helene Schjerfbeck (q.v.) saw her paintings in the exhibitions of 1879–80 in Helsinki and never forgot them.

LENA HOLGER

Clark, Lygia
Brazilian artist, 1920–1988

Born Lygia Pimentel Lins in Belo Horizonte, Minas Gerais, Brazil, 23 October 1920. Married Aloizio Clark c.1938; one daughter, two sons; divorced. Studied under landscape architect Robert Burle Marx in Rio de Janeiro, 1947, and under Fernand Léger, Dobrinsky and Arpad Szénes in Paris, 1950–52. Member of the Brazilian Concrete Art group, Grupo Frente, Rio de Janeiro, 1954–6. Founder-member, Neo-Concrete group, Rio de Janeiro, 1959–61. Lived in Rio de Janeiro for most of the 1960s. Taught courses on "gestural communication" at St Charles I, Sorbonne, Paris, 1970–75. Returned to Rio, 1976; began referring to herself as a therapist. Recipient of artist of the year award, Rio de Janeiro, 1952; Augusto Frederico Schmidt prize, Rio de Janeiro, 1953; first prize, Primeira Exposição Nacional de Arte Abstrata, Petrópolis, Rio de Janeiro, 1953; acquisition prize, São Paulo Bienal, 1957; Guggenheim fellowships, 1958 and 1960; best national sculpture, São Paulo Bienal, 1961; first prize, Bahia Bienal, Salvador, 1966; honorary doctorate and gold medal, Parma, Italy, 1980. Died in Rio de Janeiro, 1988.

Selected Individual Exhibitions
Galerie de l'Institut Endoplastique, Paris: 1952 (retrospective)
Ministério da Educação e Cultura, Rio de Janeiro: 1952
Galeria Bonino, Rio de Janeiro: 1960
Museu de Arte Moderna, Rio de Janeiro: 1963, 1968
Technische Hochschule, Stuttgart: 1964
Signals Gallery, London: 1965
Venice Biennale: 1968 (retrospective)
Galeria Ralph Camargo, São Paulo: 1971
Galeria Funarte, Rio de Janeiro: 1980
Gabinete de Arte Raquel Arnaud, São Paulo: 1982
Galeria Paulo Klabin, Rio de Janeiro: 1984
Salão Nacional de Artes Plásticas da Funarte, Paço Imperial, Rio de Janeiro: 1986 (touring retrospective, with Hélio Oiticica)
São Paulo Bienal: 1994 (retrospective)

Selected Writings
Book-Oeuvre, limited edition A–Z, 1964–83, private collections (Portuguese original)
"Un mythe moderne: La mise en évidence de l'instant comme nostalgie du cosmos", *Robho*, no.4, 1965, p.18
"L'homme, structure vivant d'une architecture biologique et céllulaire", *Robho*, no.5–6, 1969, p.12
"Le corps est la maison-sexualité: Envahissement du 'territoire' individuel", *Robho*, no.8, 1971, pp.12–13
"L'art, c'est le corps", *Preuves*, 1975, p.138
"De la suppression de l'objet", *Mácula*, 1976
"The relational object in a therapeutic context", *Flue*, ii/3, Spring 1983, pp.26–7

Bibliography
29 Esculturas de Lygia Clark, exh. cat., Galeria Bonino, Rio de Janeiro, 1960
Lygia Clark: Abstract Reliefs and Articulated Sculpture, exh. cat., Signals Gallery, London, 1965
Guy Brett, *Kinetic Art: The Language of Movement*, London: Studio Vista, and New York: Rienhold Book Company, 1968
Gaelle Basser, *La Quête de la mère dans l'oeuvre de Lygia Clark*, MA thesis, Ecole de St Charles, Paris, 1978
Suely Rolnyk, *La Mémoire du corps*, MA thesis, VER de Sciences Humaines Cliniques, Sorbonne, Université de Paris VII 1978
Lygia Clark, exh. cat., Galeria Funarte, Rio de Janeiro, 1980
Daisy Ribeiro de Resende, *Dedans et dehors: Evolution de l'oeuvre de Lygia Clark*, MA thesis, VER d'Arts Plastiques, Université de Paris, VII, 1984
Lygia Clark e Hélio Oiticica, Salão Nacional de Artes Plásticas da Funarte, Paço Imperial, Rio de Janeiro, and elsewhere, 1986
Guy Brett, "Lygia Clark: The borderline between art and life", *Third Text*, no.1, Autumn 1987, pp.65–94
Art in Latin America: The Modern Era, 1820–1980, exh. cat., South Bank Centre, London, and elsewhere, 1989, pp.264–6
Maria Alice Milliet, *Lygia Clark: Obra-Trajeto*, São Paulo: Editora da Universidade de São Paulo, 1992
Brasil: Segni d'Arte: Libri e video, 1950–1993, exh. cat., Fondazione Scientifica Querini-Stampalia, Venice, and elsewhere, 1993
Latin American Artists of the Twentieth Century, exh. cat., Museum of Modern Art, New York, 1993
Ultramodern: The Art of Contemporary Brazil, exh. cat., National Museum of Women in the Arts, Washington, DC, 1993
Guy Brett, "Lygia Clark: In search of the body", *Art in America*, lxxxii, July 1994, pp.56–63, 108
Yves Alain Bois, "Lygia Clark: Nostalgia of the body", *October*, no.69, Summer 1994, pp.85–109 (includes extracts from Clark's writings)
Paula Terra Cabo, *Resignifying Modernity: Clark, Oiticica and Categories of the Modern in Brazil*, PhD dissertation, University of Essex, 1996

Lygia Clark's unorthodox attitude towards art combined analytical rigour and philosophical questioning with a transgressive practice based on existential, sensorial, ludic and psychological experiences. Her work, which is unclassifiable, has touched upon all the pressing questions of recent art: of movement, the body, the environment, the relation of the visual to other senses, space-time, authorship, the status of the object and, above all, art's relationship with the viewer (see

Brett 1987, p.65). In her trajectory each future work can be seen as the next step of a self-contained process and each rupture as an analytical development of the preceding stage.

In the 1950s she produced a series of constructive paintings: *Compositions* (1954–5), *Modulated Surfaces* (1956–7), *Constellations* and *Unities* (1958; all private collections). In *Compositions* she broke away from the conventional schemes of perception and representation by incorporating the frame into the work. In *Modulated Surfaces* (repr. Washington 1993, p.9; New York 1993, p.209) there is no longer any distinction between painting and frame or figure and background. She abolished the use of colour and texture and changed medium and technique – from oil on canvas to nitro-cellulose paint airbrushed on to veneer.

Clark's experimentation with the dynamics of the surface soon led her to reduce surfaces to black and white; she achieved complete emptiness of surface in *Constellations* and *Unities* (1958). The last of these, called *Egg* (private collection, repr. London 1989, p.264), represents a conceptual development of her experiences of visual perception in relation to other senses. In *Egg*, a circular black surface incompletely enclosed by a white border, she explored the idea that if an almost complete circle is presented on a surface our visual perception will tend to close the circle, according to gestalt laws, but the "outline of a light line in actual space" prevents us from doing so. Expressing her concerns with the way the object occupies space and the traditional notions of the object-subject relationship, she said: "what I wanted was for the spectator to take an active part in this created space: to have the sensation of being himself within it, experiencing it as an organism" (*Book-Oeuvre*, 1964–83, see Venice 1993, p.35).

In the early 1960s Clark's work extended beyond painting. In the earliest wall-reliefs planes were juxtaposed, overlapped and unfolded to surge forth over space, as in *Cocoon* (iron; 30.4 × 30.4cm.; private collection, repr. Washington 1993, pp.44–5). In the manifesto of the Neo-Concrete movement the art critic Ferreira Gullar, inspired by Clark's work, defined the concept of non-object as a "quasi corpus". As examples of the quasi-corpus, Clark's *Beasts* (1959–64; private collections, repr. London 1989, p.265; New York 1993, p. 210) – hinged manipulable planar structures, interweaving clusters of aluminium sheets – are designed to be unfolded, brought to life, by the spectator.

Her production in the 1960s marked a point in her trajectory when the values of intuition, of active perception, of the re-introduction of expressive forces into art assumed a crucial role, reflecting a change of perception about the role played by Subject and Object. Painting was then replaced by wall-sculptures (*Cocoon*, 1958; *Rubber Grubs*, 1964), objects (*Beasts*, 1959–64; *Air and Stone*, 1966; *Sensorial Masks*, 1967–9), vestiary sculptures (*Ceasarean*, 1967; *I and You*, 1967), environments (*The House is the Body*, 1968; whereabouts unknown) and propositions/dematerialised art (*Going*, 1964; *Dialogue of Hands*, 1966; *Breathe with Me*, 1966; *Mandala*, 1969; repr. Brett 1987, Brett 1994 and Bois 1994).

In the trajectory of her work from abstract-geometric painting in the 1950s through participative art from the mid-1960s to the end of the 1970s – when her work developed into a form of psychotherapy – the issue of the "status of the object" was always addressed. The object itself assumed an

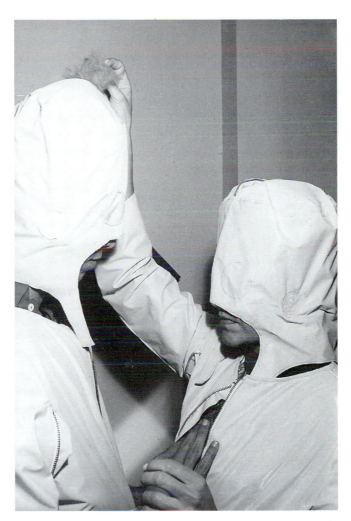

Clark: *I and You/Clothing-Body-Clothing*, 1967

increasingly secondary and incomplete role. Working in close collaboration with other Neo-Concrete artists such as Hélio Oiticica, Clark reinvested what can be called "conceptual" art with existential, psychological and ethical meanings. In *Going* (1964) the object's material existence was only an excuse for spectator action. This ephemeral work is made of a white strip of paper about 40cm. wide, to be twisted and its ends joined to form a Moebius strip, and to be continually cut with scissors from the centre of the strip along its length. In Clark's words: "the *Going* left me in a kind of void: the immanence of the act, the abandonment of any transference to the object, the dissolution even of the concept of 'the artist's work' produced in me a very deep crisis" ("About the act" in *Book-Oeuvre*).

The "crisis" to which she refers is not only "hers" but a broader crisis of modern art, of the "object itself" and even the crisis of a traditional model of opposition between signifier and signified, and the Moebius strip is the subversive model of these paradoxes. After the disintegration of the object the next step was to question the subject's relationship to the world, the continuity between the Ego and the Other. Clark proposed that "the artist loses his or her uniqueness and expressive power. He or she is content to propose to others that they be themselves, that they achieve the singular condition of art without art" (quoted in Bois 1994, p.102).

In the *I and You/Clothing-Body-Clothing* (1967; see illustration) vestiary sculptures, Clark uses clothing to denude the body. The work consists of two plastic suits, which are put on by a blindfolded couple, who, by opening the zippers, make all sorts of sensorial discoveries, including that of their gender. From that stage onwards the body incorporates the object and the body's expression assumes the essential role. As Clark wrote:

> in the sensorial phase of my work ... the object was still an indispensable medium ... Then, I incorporated the object by making it disappear ... and what remains of the object (some elastic bands, sheet of plastic, jute bags, string) is quite empty of meaning and can only be brought to life with human support [quoted in Brett 1987, p.85].

From the early 1970s until 1984 Clark worked with "group-propositions" and developed a kind of psychotherapy that involved the senses and the body. Although she developed the major part of her work called *Body Phantasmatic* in Paris (1968–75), and particularly the group experiences during the time she taught at the Sorbonne (*Biological Architecture*, 1972; *Cannibalism*, 1973; *Anthropophagic Dribble*, 1973; *Tunnel*, 1973; artist's estate, on loan to Museu de Arte Moderna, Rio de Janeiro; *Net of Elastic Bands*, 1974; repr. Brett 1994, pp.61–3), her position differed substantially from other forms of "participation art" or "body art". She discussed how both tendencies failed to address fully the crucial question of the prevailing notion of the artist in "De la suppression de l'objet" (1976, p.118). At this stage notions of object-subject, the art object and authorship were meaningless to her. She started referring to herself as a therapist and producing what she afterwards called "relational objects". According to the theories of Donald Winnicott and Melanie Klein, the relational object only exists within the relationship with the subject, becoming a depository of the subject's affections, fears, emotions and phantasies.

Clark's works from 1976 to 1984 were explorations of human subject issues, such as the precarious limits of personal memory and collective experiences. The relational objects – stones of a great variety of textures and heaviness, mattresses, shells, air bags, elastic strips, mirrors, cotton sacks – were a way of facilitating the reparative impulses of the participants by re-awakening their senses, the "memories" of the body, the pre-verbal experiences. Although she was not a qualified psychotherapist, Clark's therapeutic method of establishing the phenomenological contact between the participant and the relational-object, the subject and the other, rescued many "borderliners", as she called her patients, from their psychological disturbances. Affirming the subjective character of human lived-through experience as a non-codifiable one and the impossibility of translating primal experiences into verbal signs, Clark, with the relational objects, re-affirms the possibility of dissolving the boundaries between art and life.

The development of the artist, who led a provincial life as a socialite, daughter of a distinguished judge, wife of a successful engineer and mother-of-three, changed radically after she left her home town of Belo Horizonte in the late 1940s. She spent several years in psychoanalysis. Each rupture in her search to define art-without-art was lived through as an existential-psychological crisis, and this quality was intrinsic to her development. Certainly the work she produced over almost four decades has a broader significance for the changing condition of art even if it does not fit easily into galleries (see New York 1993, Brett 1994 and Bois 1994, p.85).

PAULA TERRA CABO

Clarke Hall, Edna
British painter, 1879–1979

Born Edna Waugh in Shipbourne, Kent, 29 June 1879; father a non-conformist minister and founder of the National Society for the Prevention of Cruelty to Children (NSPCC). Studied at Slade School of Fine Art, London, under Henry Tonks, part-time 1893–7, full-time, on Slade scholarship, 1897–9; Central School of Art and Design, early 1920s. Visited Florence, autumn 1897. Married barrister William Clarke Hall, 1898; two sons, born 1905 and 1910; husband died 1932. Lived at Great House, Upminster, Essex, 1902–79. Exhibited at New English Art Club from 1901; Allied Artists Association, 1908; Alpine Club Gallery, London, 1906–16 (with Friday Club); included in *Modern Pictorial Advertising*, Royal Academy, London, 1931. Visited Egypt, 1926. Died in Upminster, Essex, 16 November 1979.

Selected Individual Exhibitions
Chenil Gallery, London: 1914
Redfern Gallery, London: 1924, 1926, 1930, 1932, 1934 (with Mary Potter), 1941
City Art Gallery, Manchester: 1939 (retrospective)
Anthony d'Offay Gallery, London: 1971
New Grafton Gallery, London: 1979
Graves Art Gallery, Sheffield: 1985 (retrospective)

Selected Writings
Poems, London: Benn, 1926
Facets: A Book of Poems, London: Elkin Matthews and Marrot, 1930

Bibliography
Malcolm Salaman, *Fine Prints of the Year*, London: Benn, 1923
R.H. Wilenski, *Draughtsmen*, London: Benn, and McPherson, KS: Smalley's, 1924
"Drawings by Edna Clarke Hall", *The Studio*, cvi, 1933, pp.212–15
Campbell Dodgson, *Modern Drawings*, London: Studio, 1934
Edna Clarke Hall, 1879–1979: Watercolours and Drawings, exh. cat., Graves Art Gallery, Sheffield, 1985
Alison Thomas, "Edna Clarke Hall", *Antique Collector*, lvii, March 1986, pp.82–5
——, *Portraits of Women: Gwen John and Her Forgotten Contemporaries*, Cambridge: Polity Press, 1994

"With some, and I am one such, it is in the common life one finds the profoundest inspiration and in the everyday manifestations are woven the threads of eternal beauty" (letter to Malcolm Salaman, mid-1920s). With these words Edna Clarke Hall neatly captured the essence of her art – an expression of her deep involvement with her family and friends and the common world of their shared experience.

Clarke Hall was above all a superb draughtswoman. Her early drawings, with their carefully modulated cross-hatching, a technique that owes much to her Slade training, describe every nuance of light and shade. Her assurance in handling tone and line, which gives her drawings their strength, is perhaps most evident in a fine set of portrait drawings of her fellow Slade students. Seen together, these provide an insight into the ambition – and sometimes vulnerability – of subsequently famous friends, as in the bearded image of *Augustus John* (1897; conté) and the slightly aloof profile of *Gwen John* (1897; pen and ink; both National Museum of Wales, Cardiff). Years later, when her natural inclination towards line led her to etching, she returned to these drawings for subject matter. In this medium they lose none of their vitality, as in *Ida Nettleship* and *Ambrose McEvoy* (both 1922; National Museum of Wales).

Drawing for its own sake remained an important part of Clarke Hall's oeuvre and over the years her line became bolder and more economical. This stylistic development is well illustrated in the series of powerful drawings and etchings inspired by Emily Brontë's *Wuthering Heights* – a theme that repeatedly occupied Clarke Hall at different phases of her life. The earliest of these, as in the delightful *Catherine and Heathcliff* (1902; pen and ink; Tate Gallery, London) and *Children on the Hill* (1902; etching; Victoria and Albert Museum, London), are characterised by a careful realism, made appealing by a close attention to compositional structure and modelling. They quietly evoke mood. By contrast, the bold blue or sepia ink lines and washes of the later illustrations, such as *A Young Couple* (1924; Ashmolean Museum, Oxford), more vividly portray the tense drama of Catherine and Heathcliff's turbulent love, their spontaneity serving to heighten the emotional impact. Indeed these illustrations were born out of strong emotions: the initial set of 1902 were an outpouring of Clarke Hall's despair at the lack of emotional fulfilment in her recent marriage. She had married immediately after leaving the Slade in 1898, but very soon discovered profound differences between her successful barrister husband and herself, particularly in his disregard of, and at times hostility to her work. The personal dilemma that she experienced in trying to reconcile her husband's traditional domestic expectations with her artistic ideals cannot be exaggerated. A series of self-portraits (e.g. a pencil drawing of 1900; City Art Gallery, Sheffield) bears poignant witness to this struggle. While Clarke Hall was never actually prevented from drawing and painting, it became an increasingly personal and private activity, shared with only a few intimate friends.

Clarke Hall and her husband made their home at Great House, a 17th-century Essex farmhouse. The house and its farm buildings, together with the surrounding fields and gently rolling hills, soon began to be reflected in her work, as did the birth of her two sons, Justin and Denis, in 1905 and 1910 respectively. Clarke Hall rarely asked children to sit formally; instead she preferred to capture them while in unconscious absorption in their own pursuits, as in *Girl and Two Boys Beside a Boat* (1913; watercolour; Victoria and Albert Museum). The result is seen in work of great tenderness that nevertheless avoids overt sentimentality. Much of the work produced at this time was executed in watercolour.

From her student days Clarke Hall handled watercolour with great sensitivity, as can be seen in *Roses* (1897) and *Piano at Great Tomkins* (1902; both City Art Gallery, Sheffield) and *Self-Portrait in a Green Dress* (1898; see illustration). In their controlled arrangement of tones these watercolours hint at influences absorbed from James McNeill Whistler and regular student visits to the New English Art Club. Ten years later, however, all *fin-de-siècle* restraint was abandoned; her vivacious watercolours sparkle with energy to achieve an immediate visual impact. They are boldly and fluidly drawn, making use of atmospheric washes, as in *Catherine* (1912; Laing Art Gallery, Newcastle upon Tyne) and *Katie Glidden* (1912; National Museum of Wales). In other works, such as *Girl Leaning on a Gate* (1915; Tate Gallery), the brush is drawn almost dry across the paper in rapid, excited strokes. She displayed great versatility as a watercolourist, both in style and in choice of subject, as in a series of *Goat* paintings (1912; Victoria and Albert Museum) and seascapes painted at Vaucotte and West Wittering.

Overall the human condition was always Clarke Hall's greatest interest and increasingly a new theme dominated her work – that of the link between figure and landscape. Previously, her figures had generally dominated their landscape setting. Now, although the person standing atop the cliffs or hill might be recognisable as a Cornish friend or Edna herself, the subject's identity is no longer important. It is the harmony, even communion between the figure and the landscape that holds our attention, for example *Girl and Boy on Cliff* (c.1913; Tate Archives, London). This search to define the individual's place within the order of things attracted many British artists in this period, especially after the horrors of World War I. Such work often slips into romanticism, as with Augustus John and James Dickson Innes. Clarke Hall's watercolours, by contrast, evince simplicity and directness; her figures remain truly integral with the landscape.

Some of the boldest and profoundest of her works were painted at a time of increasing personal unhappiness that finally overwhelmed her and stilled her paintbrush – if not her pen. At this time, around 1920, Clarke Hall's troubled emotions found release in poetry (*Poems*, 1926) and, as in her paintings, there is spontaneity, a mood momentarily caught and transfixed in verse. Some years later she did in fact combine the two disciplines in a highly distinctive series of *Paintings with Poems*. In these works, which are clearly indebted to William Blake, Clarke Hall complements lines of her own poetry by swirling arabesques of colour and lyrical flowing figures. The original *Paintings with Poems* (all in private collections) were executed in gouache and characterised by a highly expressive use of colour. Later she reproduced some in lithographic and etched prints, for example *Female Nude* (1926; Victoria and Albert Museum, London) and *Facets* (1930).

For Clarke Hall, humankind and its world were always represented naturalistically. Over the years there is a gradual reshaping of the reality portrayed, away from the traditional ideas of her Slade training to something that in its expressive use of line and bold blocks of primary colour recalls the Expressionists, or even the Fauves. Nevertheless, it remains uniquely her own vision, where her primary concern was not with the artistic process itself but whether her work directly

Clarke Hall: *Self-Portrait in a Green Dress*, 1898; private collection, Graves Art Gallery, Sheffield

and simply conveyed the impulse of its creation.

ALISON THOMAS

Claudel, Camille
French sculptor, 1864–1943

Born in Fère-en-Tardenois, Aisne, 8 December 1864; father a government official, brother the writer Paul Claudel. Moved to Paris with her family, c.1881. Studied sculpture at the Académie Colarossi and in an independent studio shared with Jessie Lipscomb and other sculptors, where Alfred Boucher and Rodin came to give tuition. Later became assistant in Rodin's studio; relationship with him broke up by 1893. Took first independent Paris studio, 1888, moving to Quai Bourbon, 1899. Sociétaire, Société Nationale des Beaux-Arts, Paris, 1895. State of health declining by 1907. Confined to a mental asylum at Ville-Evrard, 10 March 1913, eight days after her father's death; remained in mental institutions for the rest of her life. Died in the Montdevergues asylum, near Avignon, 19 October 1943.

Principal Exhibitions

Paris Salon: 1882–3, 1885–9, 1903, 1905 (honourable mention 1888)
Société Nationale des Beaux-Arts, Paris: 1892–9, 1902
Exposition de la Libre Esthétique, Brussels: 1894
Salon de l'Art Nouveau, Paris: 1896
Exposition Universelle, Paris: 1900 (bronze medal)
Salon de la Plume, Paris: 1900
Salon d'Automne, Paris: 1904–5
Galerie Eugène Blot, Paris: 1905 (with Bernard Hoetger), 1907, 1908 (both individual)
Salon des Femmes Artistes Modernes, Paris: 1934
Musée Rodin, Paris: 1951 (retrospective)

Bibliography

Gustave Geffroy, La Vie artistique, 8 vols, Paris: Floury, 1892–1903
Roger Marx, "Les salons", Le Voltaire, 10 May 1893
Mathias Morhardt, "Mademoiselle Camille Claudel", Mercure de France, March 1898, pp.709–55
Roger Marx in Revue Encyclopédique, 15 July 1899, p.560
Exposition d'oeuvres de Camille Claudel et de Bernard Hoetger, exh. cat., Galerie Eugène Blot, Paris, 1905
Paul Claudel, "Camille Claudel, statuaire", Occident, August 1905
Camille Claudel, exh. cat., Musée Rodin, Paris, 1951 (with introduction by Paul Claudel)
Paul Claudel, Mémoires improvisés, Paris: Gallimard, 1969
Anne Delbée, Une Femme, Paris, 1982 (novel and play)
Anne Pingeot, "Le chef-d'oeuvre de Camille Claudel: L'Age mûr", Revue du Louvre et des Musées de France, xxxi (i.e. xxxii), 1982, pp.287–95
Anne Rivière, L'Interdite: Camille Claudel, 1864–1943, Paris: Tierce, 1983
Camille Claudel (1864–1943), exh. cat., Musée Rodin, Paris, and Musée Sainte-Croix, Poitiers, 1984
Louise R. Witherell, "Camille Claudel rediscovered", Woman's Art Journal, vi/1, 1985, pp.1–7
Camille Claudel, exh. cat., National Museum of Women in the Arts, Washington, DC, and elsewhere, 1987
Jacques Cassar, Dossier Camille Claudel, Paris: Séguier, 1987
Renate Flagmeier, "Camille Claudel: Bildhauerin", Kritische Berichte, xvi/1, 1988, pp.36–45
Bruno Nuttyen, Camille Claudel, film, 1988
Reine-Marie Paris, Camille: The Life of Camille Claudel, Rodin's Muse and Mistress, London: Aurum, and New York: Seaver, 1988 (contains extensive bibliography; French original, 1984)
"'L'Age mûr' de Camille Claudel", exh. cat., Musée d'Orsay, Paris, and Musée des Beaux-Arts, Lyon, 1989
Claudine Mitchell, "Intellectuality/sexuality: Camille Claudel, the fin de siècle sculptress", Art History, xii, 1989, pp.419–47
C. Claudel, exh. cat., Fondation Pierre Gianadda, Martigny, 1990
Reine-Marie Paris and Arnaud de la Chapelle, L'Oeuvre de Camille Claudel: Catalogue raisonné, 2nd edition, Paris: Biro, 1991
Anne Higonnet, "Myths of creation: Camille Claudel and Auguste Rodin", Significant Others: Creativity and Intimate Partnership, ed. Whitney Chadwick and Isabelle de Courtivron, New York and London: Thames and Hudson, 1993, pp.14–29
Octave Mirbeau, Combats ésthetiques, Paris: Séguier, 1993
Gail McIntyre and Mike Kenny, The Waltz, Leeds, 1994 (play)
J.A. Schmoll, Auguste Rodin and Camille Claudel, Munich: Prestel, 1994 (German original)

In the Paris of the mid-1890s Camille Claudel was hailed as one of the five outstanding sculptors in the age of Rodin. Those who promoted her works believed that she had brought to sculpture a dimension of intellectuality and pathos usually found only in poetry. Her reputation rested on her imaginative compositions and the expressive and narrative technique that she developed to convey emotions and concepts.

Claudel's career – the period in which she exhibited regularly, sold her sculptures and was written about – spans a period of 25 years, from the mid-1880s, when she began to exhibit regularly at the annual Paris Salons, until 1910. Her first works, as was customary with young sculptors, included modelling sections of the human body, Torso (1884–8; private collection, repr. Paris and de la Chapelle 1991, no.5), and a series of portrait busts for which she enlisted the collaboration of relatives and anonymous models. She immediately attracted the attention of a private collector, Baron de Rothschild, who bought My Brother (1884; bronze; Musée d'Art, Toulon) and continued to purchase her works, donating them to public collections. By 1888 she was capable of contrasting the male and female nudes in one composition entitled Sakountala (plaster; Musée de Châteauroux). Drawn from the epic poem of the Hindu writer Kālidāsa, it represents the reunion of the heroine with her husband who rescues her from a spell. In choosing an unfamiliar mythological subject Claudel made claim to originality and intellectual sophistication.

The rendering of a famous artist signalled a sculptor's status, in 1892 Claudel exhibited the portrait of a sculptor few of her colleagues had tackled, so eminent had he become: Rodin. Her effigy of Rodin (1892, plaster; 1895, bronze; Musée Rodin, Paris), transposed in lithograph and published many times, attested to the esteem in which she was held in professional circles. She had studied under him in the 1880s and subsequently joined his workshop as an assistant. This was a period of intense passionate relationship for both of them. In 1892 Claudel had determined to set up an independent practice. Rodin honoured her in prefacing the first monograph on Claudel with the words: "I showed her where to find gold, but the gold she finds is her own" (Morhardt 1898, p.709).

In the 1890s Claudel contributed sculptures on the themes of fate, love and destiny, death's omnipresence and the

Claudel: *Maturity (L'Age mur)*, Musée Rodin, Paris

importance of mental and private experience, for which she was ranked as an outstanding contributor to Symbolist art. Fate was represented by her in a sculpture named *Clotho* (1893; plaster; Musée Rodin) after Greek mythology, as a woman rendered skeletal with age. In 1893 *Clotho* (plaster) was coupled with *The Waltz* (plaster), and in 1899 *Clotho* (marble) with *Maturity* (plaster; both untraced). *The Waltz* represented the human couple embracing face to face in a sculpture where equilibrium is attained at the limits of balance, while *Maturity* symbolised destiny. As she explained to her brother: "I am still working hard at my group of three ... to represent destiny."

In all these sculptures the human body is envisaged as a signifying process. In *The Waltz* (1895; bronze; Musée Rodin) the illusion of movement freed from gravity relates thematically to the portrayal of a relationship signified in the sculpture by facial expressions, physical contact and yet restraint. The fact that the man's lips no more touch the woman's flesh than his hands are shown pressing into it and the elegant gesture of their hands displaying self-control contribute to an expression of love as a spiritual as much as a physical union. The narra-

tive techniques that Claudel elaborated give much scope for interpretation. Contemporary art critics who valued her work responded accordingly by publishing narrative descriptions showing that, like poetry, her sculptures were open to interpretation in a chain of associated ideas. The writer Octave Mirbeau interpreted *The Waltz* as narrating an escape from the material world: "Voluptuous and chaste they fly away, lost in the exaltation of their soul and flesh, closely united towards love or towards death" (*Journal*, 9 May 1893). The writer Léon Daudet considered *Clotho* a potent symbol for *fin-de-siècle* culture, calling to mind Baudelairian imagery of mental suffering and decay.

The figure of *Clotho* placed to the left of *Maturity* (1903; bronze; Musée d'Orsay, Paris; another cast after 1913; see illustration) is shown leading forward an ageing man; in the male nude the ageing process is registered by rendering flabby tissues and stiff articulations. To the right of the composition the figure of a young woman is shown kneeling, a version of which was first completed as the *Lost God* (private collection, repr. Paris and de la Chapelle 1991, no.44), a title referring to the myth of Psyche. When the Inspector of Fine Art, Silvestre, discovered the composition in the artist's studio in 1895, he strongly recommended its purchase by the State as a good example of Symbolist art that "represents maturity as a man drawn forward by Old Age while Youth sends a last farewell." *Maturity* interweaves connoted meanings and narrative to the allegory of life decoded by Silvestre. The base, an integral part of the sculpture, depicts patterns of waves rising or breaking on the seashore. The sea imagery combines with the floating drapery to evoke the image of a ghost ship, recurrent symbol of fate in Western art. The compositional structure itself has a symbolic meaning with the movement from left to right underlying the passage of time, while the oblique line described in space by the gaze of the young woman towards the departing group signifies the cycle of life. To spell out that her sculpture did not represent a scene in its moment of occurrence but a "vision", a figment of the artist's mind, Claudel subtitled *Maturity* "un groupe fantastique". These three sculptures fulfilled the demand that art, across disciplines, should give form to an anxious questioning of the individual's relation to existence, the characteristic mode of consciousness in *fin-de-siècle* culture.

Claudel elaborated a series of unprecedented scenic compositions, in which small-scale figures were placed within a sculptural environment that promised new departures. In the first of these, *The Gossip* (1897; onyx; Musée Rodin), two slabs positioned at right angles define an intimate corner where four naked women sit on opposite benches. One of them signals that she is about to speak by raising her hands to her mouth, and the way in which her companions stretch to gaze at her lips explains that her speech will remain a whisper. Narrative combines with the indeterminate nature of the environment to convey an overall climate of secrecy, mystery and potential threat. When exhibiting the plaster version in 1895, Claudel called it *Sketch from Nature* and confirmed in an interview (Morhardt 1898) that this work was based on a scene she observed while travelling by train. The creative process for Claudel did not, however, consist in recording such visual data as the naturalist ethos would require, but in transforming concrete material into conceptual rather than visual reality. Thus from her repertory of female figures she created two very different works *The Gossip* and *The Wave* (1900; onyx and bronze; Musée Rodin). The latter integrates three of the figures of the former, with a few modifications, in a construction suggestive of a huge wave rising nearly vertically and about to fall. The facial anatomy of these figures as well as their more compact sculptural volumes reveal Claudel's interest in Eastern art studied at the Musée Guimet, as does the image of the wave, inspired by Hokusai's famous print. It is this capacity for transforming figurative art into an imaginative experience that won her the admiration of eminent critics of the Symbolist era, such as Roger Marx who celebrated in 1899 the "tragic and fantastic imagination that enthrals us", as well as some emerging advocates of formalism such as Louis Vauxcelles, who praised "the tragic power that emanates from her art" (*Gil Blas*, 10 July 1913).

Claudel specialised in small-scale works that would find a suitable environment in the homes of private collectors. In Rodin's studio she learned of sculpture practised in the tradition of the workshop system, whereby the process of making the definitive plaster model on the basis of the clay designed by the sculptor, as well as the work of transferring the plaster model into durable material, were subcontracted to specialised technicians. The quality of the sculpture might depend on how well she or he supervised the work but the "sculptor" was not expected to carry out the carving. Claudel pioneered a new definition of sculpture in carrying out a greater part of the technical processes herself and demanding that her "originality" be evaluated on the carving technique she deployed. Through her exhibition policies she forced attention on this issue, for instance when coupling a version of *The Gossip* in onyx, a brittle material reputedly difficult to carve, with a portrait of *Mme D* (marble; untraced), publicised as "carved by herself in front of the model" (Geffroy 1897). Involving a time-consuming method, the viability of her practice depended on her ability to enrol a network of clients to finance the transfer of her designs into durable material. Most of her famous sculptures were indebted to private sponsorship, for instance the onyx version of *The Gossip*, commissioned by the banker Peytell, *Maturity*, commissioned in bronze by Capitaine Tissier, and the marble of *Sakountala* and *Perseus and the Gorgon*, both by Comtesse Maigret. The editor Mathias Morhardt organised several sponsorships on her behalf, the marble of *Clotho* and the edition of her bust of *Rodin*. Financial viability in the practice of sculpture came from the sale of bronze multiple editions. The art dealer Eugène Blot, whom she met in 1900, undertook the edition of 12 of her designs from the 1890s. Besides permanent display of some of her works in his Paris gallery, Blot organised much publicity for Claudel with private shows held in 1905, 1907 and 1908. According to Blot, Claudel did not prove a financial success, in spite of the low prices he conceded. In 1907 some critics and administrators felt it proper to call attention to the precarious situation in which she found herself.

As Claudel understood her career, her major difficulty was to establish the originality of her practice in relation to Rodin. In 1893 she decided to isolate herself, and so that no-one could say he helped produce her work, let it be known that he never visited her studio. Her other strategy was to claim authorship for the entire production of a sculpture, carving included. Rodin caused problems to many young practitioners because of his very stature, his work and persona, seemingly a constant subject of preoccupation in French culture. As "Rodin's student" her position was particularly insecure, and an easy target for his opponents anxious to detect his pernicious influence. Hostility to Claudel, directed both towards her expressionist technique and her themes, noticeably increased at the time when the French cultural establishment violently split over Rodin's *Balzac* (1898–9).

A major area of difficulty for Claudel was the sexual dimension of her work in a period when women's claims of access to the public debate on sexuality were a source of conflict and institutionalised oppression. The proposal to exhibit *Sakountala* in Châteauroux Museum in 1895 caused a public uproar echoed in the Parisian press. *The Waltz* fell under censorship from the State art establishment as Inspector Dayot advised that the sculpture should not be exhibited in a public gallery without added draperies because of "the violent accent of reality which comes from it … the proximity of the sexes being conveyed with a surprising sensuality of expression" (Archives Nationales, F21 4299). A clear sign of

Claudel's insecure position in culture was the contrast between the high esteem in which she was held in professional circles and the recurrently oppressive attitude of the State establishment towards her. Her request for the purchase of *Sakountala* (1888) and *Petite Châteleine* (1894) was rejected; the contracts for commissioning the bronze of *The Waltz* and *Maturity* drawn in March 1893 and June 1899 were never signed; *Clotho* offered on Rodin's behalf to the Musée du Luxembourg in 1905 somehow got lost. More damaging to her career, *Maturity* and a bust she considered particularly important works were refused at the art section of the Exposition Universelle of 1900, thus depriving her of a unique opportunity to receive the international recognition she deserved. The set of problems that Claudel encountered at the turn of the century while she was trying to secure her career was brutal enough to provoke a state of mental depression. Her illness, signs of which were evident in her correspondence of 1907, was never treated as such. On 10 March 1913 she was confined to a mental asylum, and remained in the custody of such institutions for the rest of her life.

In 1951 her brother, the famous poet Paul Claudel, in the introduction to the catalogue of her retrospective at the Musée Rodin, offered a biographical interpretation of her work that contradicted his Symbolist interpretation of 1905. This text has inspired many imaginative interpretations of Claudel's work and life in the 1980s. In 1914 Rodin agreed to Morhardt's idea that a room of the projected Musée Rodin should be dedicated to Claudel to exhibit the work left in her studio. This became a reality long after her death, thanks to donations of the Claudel family and purchases, the latest being *The Wave* put *in situ* in February 1995.

CLAUDINE MITCHELL

Clausen, Franciska
Danish painter, 1899–1986

Born in Åbenrå, 7 January 1899. Studied at the Grossherzogliche Sächsische Hochschule für Bildende Kunst, Weimar, under Robert Weise, 1916; Frauenakademie, Munich, under Walter Püttner, 1918–19; Royal Danish Academy of Fine Arts, Copenhagen, under Sigurd Wandel, 1920–21; further studies under Hans Hofmann in Munich, 1921–2; László Moholy-Nagy in Berlin, 1922; Constructivist sculptor Alexander Archipenko in Berlin, 1923. Moved to Paris, 1924; studied at Académie Moderne under Fernand Léger, 1924–5; refused Léger's invitation to put on a solo show in Paris, 1928. Associated with Mondrian, Arp, Sophie Taeuber-Arp (q.v.) and other artists of the Cercle et Carré group, c.1930. Returned to Denmark, 1931. Settled in Åbenrå, 1932. Turned to portrait painting to earn a living. Resumed exhibiting career in the 1950s. Died 5 March 1986.

Principal Exhibitions

Individual
Bingers Kunsthandel, Copenhagen: 1932 (retrospective)
Central Library, Flensborg: 1962 (touring retrospective)
Kunstforeningen, Copenhagen: 1964, 1978 (retrospective)

Folkehjem, Åbenrå: 1974
Maison du Danemark, Paris: 1978 (retrospective)
Randers Kunstmuseum: 1984 (retrospective)

Group
Grosse Berliner Kunstausstellung, Berlin: 1923
Maison Watteau, Paris: 1924 (*Les Artistes scandinaves de l'atelier Fernand Léger*)
L'Art d'Aujourd'hui, Paris: 1925
Salon des Indépendants, Paris: 1926–8
Galerie d'Art Contemporain, Paris: 1926
Société Anonyme, Brooklyn Museum, NY: 1926 (*International Exhibition of Modern Art*, touring)
Kunstnerforbundet, Oslo: 1927 (*8 skandinaviske kubister* [Eight Scandinavian Cubists])
Cercle et Carré, Paris: 1930
Salon des Surindépendants, Paris: 1931
Den frie udstilling, Copenhagen: 1935 (*International kunstudstilling: Kubisme-Surrealisme* [International Art Exhibition: Cubism-Surrealism])
Skånska Konstmuseum, Lund: 1937 (*Surrealisme i Norden* [Surrealism in Scandinavia])

Bibliography

Oscar Reutersvärd, "Franciska Clausen: Constructiviste, cubiste et neoplasticienne danoise", *L'Art d'Aujourd'hui*, no.7, 1953
M. Stein, "La peinture abstraite au Danemark", *ibid.*
Troels Andersen and Gynther Hansen, *Franciska Clausen*, Copenhagen, 1964
Franciska Clausen, exh. cat., Kunstforeningen, Copenhagen, 1964
Women Artists, 1550–1950, exh. cat., Los Angeles County Museum of Art, and elsewhere, 1976
Obliques, no.14–15, 1977 (special issue: *La Femme surréaliste*)
Franciska Clausen, exh. cat., Maison du Danemark, Paris, and elsewhere, 1978
L'altra metà dell'avanguardia, 1910–1940: Pittrici e scultrici nei movimenti delle avanguardie storiche, exh. cat., Palazzo Reale, Milan, and elsewhere, 1980
Mødested Paris: Franciska Clausen: Malerier, gouacher og tegninger, 1922–1932 [Rendez-vous Paris: Franciska Clausen: Paintings, gouaches and drawings, 1922–1932], exh. cat., Randers Kunstmuseum, 1984
Marie-Aline Prat, *Peinture et avant-garde au seuil des années 30*, Lausanne, 1984
Finn Terman Frederiksen, *Franciska Clausen*, 2 vols, Randers, 1987–8
Mødested Paris: Sonia Delaunay, Sophie Taeuber, Franciska Clausen [Rendez-vous Paris …], exh. cat., Randers Kunstmuseum, 1992

At the time of Franciska Clausen's birth, her home town of Åbenrå (German: Appenrade) belonged to German Schleswig. She consequently received her artistic training in Germany, in both Weimar and Munich. In 1920, after a referendum, the part of Schleswig where she lived was reunited with Denmark, and for a short period she studied at the Copenhagen Academy. Her inclination, however, was to follow the avant-garde, and she returned to Germany, where she studied under Hans Hofmann in Munich and at the Atelier Archipenko in Berlin, where she was also influenced by the Constructivist work of László Moholy-Nagy. She had seen an exhibition of Picasso's Cubist still lifes in 1921, and also dated her knowledge of Kandinsky's abstractions to this period, when she made her own first abstract or "informal" construction (1922; artist's estate), after a rather expressionistic start in Munich. Under the influence of Moholy-Nagy she took to making collages and smaller paintings in a crisp, Constructivist style

Clausen: *Circle and Square*, 1929–30; Statens Museum for Kunst, Copenhagen

(*Step Ladder*, 1922; artist's estate). In 1924 Clausen settled in Paris, where she joined Fernand Léger's Académie Moderne. She went on to work as an assistant of Léger's, often doing the manual work of translating his sketches into large-scale paintings. During her Paris years she also had to make a living by taking on decorative art, making patterns for wallpaper, designs for automobile carpets and sketching posters. Léger profoundly influenced her drawings and paintings of this period (e.g. *Eléments mécaniques*, gouache, 1926; artist's estate; painted version, 1959; Aabenraa Museum, Åbenrå; *The Screw*, 1926; Skive Kunstmuseum; *Vase and Pipes*, 1929; Aarhus Kunstmuseum, Århus), which featured the nude model in the studio and scenes from Parisian cafés. In 1924 Clausen exhibited at the Maison Watteau with the Swedish painters Otto Carlsund and Erik Olson in a show of Léger and his Scandinavian followers. Towards the end of the 1920s Clausen's interests changed towards the "purist" and "neo-plasticist" artists, among them Amédée Ozenfant, and in 1930 she exhibited with the group Cercle et Carré in a show that also included Piet Mondrian, who temporarily replaced Léger as the main inspiration on her art (*Circle and Square*, 1929–30; see illustration). Franciska Clausen had her first one-woman show in 1932, in Copenhagen, but it was not a success.

During her long stays outside Denmark, Clausen had no means of obtaining a studio of her own, and therefore many of her ideas for paintings were only executed in gouache or watercolour. Paintings from these sketches were then carried out as late as the 1950s and 1960s, while she sometimes dated her works from the time of the invention of a theme, not its actual execution; to her way of thinking, the concept had priority over the performance. Having settled in Åbenrå in 1932, Clausen worked for many years outside the mainstream of contemporary Danish art, but in 1935 she was included in a great Surrealist exhibition in Copenhagen, since through Erik Olson she had come into contact with the major Danish Surrealist, Vilhelm Bjerke-Petersen. She did not, however, consider herself at any time a Surrealist artist.

After World War II Clausen earned her living as a portrait painter in a vaguely Neo-Impressionist vein (*Queen Ingrid*, 1980; oil; Graasten Castle), quite opposed to her abstractions of the Cercle et Carré period or the more realist, Foujita-like work she had arrived at by c.1935 (*Portrait of a Young Girl*, 1934; drawing; Collection Charlotte Christensen). A retrospective in her home area in 1962 and a one-woman show in Copenhagen in 1964 again brought Clausen into the public eye. She continued to work in two warring styles, creating portraits in a lyrical mode of, among others, the Danish queen, *Margrethe II* (1977; Marselisborg Castle, Århus), as well as composing collages that have a taste of Pop art out of cut-outs from women's magazines (*Upper Level of the Garbage Bin of the Welfare Society*, 1967; Sønderborg Castle).

Clausen's connections to the Danish art scene continued to be marginal, although she experienced late recognition of her pioneer work when almost her entire production was acquired by Danish and Swedish museums, and in 1978 she was given major retrospectives at the Maison du Danemark in Paris and at the Kunstforeningen (Artists Association) in Copenhagen. Clausen was included in the important exhibition *L'altra metà dell'avanguardia*, 1910–1940, curated by Lea Vergine, which opened in Milan in 1980 and was shown in Stockholm in 1981.

CHARLOTTE CHRISTENSEN

Claxton, Florence (Anne)
British painter and illustrator, 1840–after 1879

Born 1840, to Sophia Hargrave and the painter Marshall Claxton; younger sister Adelaide also an artist. Trained by her father, and travelled with him to Egypt, India and Australia, 1850–57. Worked in Leeds and London. Signed the petition for women's admission to the Royal Academy Schools, 1859. Married Mr Farrington of Romsey, 1868. Date of death unknown.

Principal Exhibitions
Society of Female Artists, London: 1857, 1859, 1863
Royal Academy, London: 1859, 1863, 1865–7
National Institution, London: 1860–61
Royal Society of British Artists, London: 1865, 1867, 1869–70, 1873

Selected Writings
The Adventures of a Woman in Search of Her Rights, London: Graphotyping Company [1871]

Bibliography
Ellen C. Clayton, *English Female Artists*, 2 vols, London: Tinsley, 1876
William E. Fredeman, "Pre-Raphaelites in caricature: The *Choice of Paris: An Idyll* by Florence Claxton", *Burlington Magazine*, cii, 1960, pp.523–9
Frances Bonner and others, *Imagining Women: Cultural Representations and Gender*, Cambridge: Cambridge University Press, 1992
A Struggle for Fame: Victorian Women Artists and Authors, exh. cat., Yale Center for British Art, New Haven, 1994

Florence Claxton was trained by her father, the painter Marshall Claxton, alongside her younger sister Adelaide. Although working in Leeds and London, Florence had travelled widely with her father between 1850 and 1857 in his search for employment, to Egypt, India and Australia (Pamela Gerrish Nunn, "The woman question in the work of Florence and Adelaide Claxton", unpublished paper, which the author has kindly allowed me to read; see also Clayton 1876). On her return to London, she worked with her sister providing engravings for the popular press and attempting to attract patronage for painting within the fine art market. Her first wood engravings to be published were accepted by the *Illustrated Times* in 1859 – according to Ellen Clayton the first time that any woman had worked for a weekly paper in this way. Florence and her sister continued to engrave for a large number of magazines such as *London Society*, the *Englishwomen's Domestic Magazine* and *The Period*. Following her marriage to a Mr Farrington in 1868, however, her productivity decreased.

Claxton belonged to the generation of women who in the late 1850s campaigned for women's suffrage and rights in education and marriage (with her sister she signed the petition of 1859 seeking women's admission to the Royal Academy

Claxton: *Women's Work, A Medley*, exhibited 1861; oil; private collection

Schools). Although she covered a wide range of views and subjects in her commercial work, she was occasionally able to use her strong bent for graphic comedy in a campaigning mood. For instance, she made a series of drawings satirising the position of women in *Scenes from the Life of a Female Artist* (1858), *Scenes from the Life of an Old Maid* and *Scenes from the Life of an Old Bachelor* (1859) and *Scenes from the Life of a Governess* (1863). She also explored the possibilities of using oils to analyse women's position.

In 1861, aged 21, Claxton exhibited a small arch-topped oil painting entitled *Women's Work: A Medley* (see illustration), which was probably a feminist response to Ford Madox Brown's *Work*, which he had begun in 1852. Whereas his allegory had shown men's physical labour as representing all the work of humanity, Claxton showed women's unrecognised work in servicing men, and the current campaigns by women to widen the scope of women's work. The National Institution catalogue provided a lengthy explanation of the picture (the entry was presumably written by Florence herself):

> The four ages of man are represented: in the centre, youth, middle age and old age are reposing on an ottoman, infancy being in the background. The sugar plums dropping from the bon-bon box represent the airy nothings alone supposed to be within the mental grasp of womankind. A wide breach has been made [to the left] in the ancient wall of Custom and Prejudice, by Progress – Emigration – who points across the ocean. Three governesses, seen in the [left] foreground, apparently ignorant of the opening behind them, are quarrelling over one child. The upright female figure to the right is persuaded by Divinity [a parson], and commanded by Law [a lawyer], to confine her attention to legitimate objects. Another female has sunk, exhausted, against a door, of which the medical profession holds the key; its representative not perceiving that the wood is rotten and decayed in many places. An artist Rosa B[onheur] has attained the top of the wall (upon which the rank weeds of Misrepresentation and the prickly thorns of Ridicule flourish) – and others are following [Bonner and others 1992, p.174].

Claxton rebutted Misrepresentation with her own Ridicule – most powerfully of all in the central object in this allegory, which she tactfully did not allude to in her catalogue description: the statue of the biblical Golden Calf, the false god that the Israelites had worshipped before Moses reproved them. Women, she argues, should not worship men as if they were gods. This small painting bids fair to be called the first consciously feminist allegory.

The subversive streak in Claxton's work, often hidden beneath her necessarily milder commercial activities, is emphasised by her virulent pictorial attack in 1860 on the pretensions of the Pre-Raphaelites who had attained success during the previous decade. This picture, entitled the *Choice of Paris: An Idyll* (collection Ralph Dutton, Hinton Ampner; engraving in

Illustrated London News, 2 June 1860), derided the Pre-Raphaelites for making the commonplace and the ugly into the objects of representation, and also satirised the way in which they had criticised artistic reliance on the precedents of such artists as Raphael and van Dyck only to declare themselves – Millais, Ruskin and Hunt – as the new models to follow (Fredeman 1960).

CATHERINE KING

Clissold, Joyce
British textile designer and artist, 1903–1982

Born in Scarborough, Yorkshire, 24 July 1903. Studied print-making at the Central School of Arts and Crafts, London, 1924–7. Joined Mrs Eric Kennington's Footprints Studio at Durham Wharf, Hammersmith, 1927; took over management of workshop, 1929. Moved Footprints to Brentford, Middlesex, mid-1930s; reopened it after a period of closure during World War II, 1947. Died in London, 23 March 1982.

Principal Exhibitions
Dorland Hall, London: 1933 (*British Industrial Art in Relation to the Home*)
Watermans Art Centre, Brentford: 1984 (retrospective)

Bibliography
Stephen Clissold, "'Jo': A memoir by her brother", undated manuscript, Textile Department, Central St Martin's College of Art, London

Joyce Clissold: Textiles, Collages, Drawings, 1932–1982, exh. cat., Watermans Art Centre, Brentford [1984]

Mary Schoeser, *Fabrics and Wallpapers*, New York: Dutton, and London: Bell and Hyman, 1986

Alan Powers, *Modern Block-Printed Textiles*, London: Walker, 1992

Hazel Clark, "Joyce Clissold and the 'Footprints' textile printing workshop", *Women Designing: Redefining Design in Britain Between the Wars*, exh. cat., University of Brighton Gallery, 1994, pp.82–8

Bold Impressions, Block Printing, 1910–1950, exh. cat., Central St Martin's College of Art, London, 1995

It was the study of wood engraving, lino cutting and printing at the Central School of Arts and Crafts that inspired Joyce Clissold's interest in block printing on fabric. In 1929 she took over Footprints, a small textile-printing workshop on the Thames outside London, where she had helped out as a student. She turned it around from an *ad hoc* artists' studio to a successful small business. A unique aspect of Footprints was its predominantly female workforce. Each employee served an informal apprenticeship that began with the more menial tasks and progressed to making up dyes and printing. Clissold was solely responsible for the creative input of designing and block cutting. In the mid-1930s she relocated Footprints to enable her to live and work on the same premises. The new situation reflected the tradition of textile production by women at home. Household and workshop activities intermingled. The kitchen became known as the "lab". But the domestic setting belied the fact of an effective business. In its heyday there were 40–50 employees involved in the production, making up, distribution and sale of printed fabrics.

The first Footprints shop opened in New Bond Street, London, in 1933 to sell dress and furnishing fabrics; it moved to a more stylish location in 1936, near to furriers, milliners and gown makers. An additional shop was established in 1935 in fashionable Knightsbridge. Footprints' textiles provided interesting alternatives to predictable modernist trends and appealed to artistic customers such as Gracie Fields and Yvonne Arnaud. The hand-block process was slow and the products expensive, but it allowed freedom for experimentation, which was Clissold's forte. To enable different effects to be tried out, interesting fabric was often bought retail. Footprints rarely produced in large quantity, preferring piece prints, scarves and small repeats that could be varied. The patterns were not typical of the so-called modern trends favoured in the 1930s. *Bedroom Window*, for example, involved seven to ten interchangeable lino blocks. In one version, a chest of drawers is shown next to a curtained bedroom window that looks out on to grazing sheep. The whimsical, narrative design reflects images familiar from contemporary British book illustration. Simplified figurative elements prevailed over the more abstract shapes preferred by such textile designer craftswomen as Enid Marx (q.v.) and Barron and Larcher. Many of Clissold's patterns were inspired by her life and her often unusual travels. In the 1930s she and a friend organised four Punch and Judy tours on the beaches of English south-coast resorts. These journeys were recorded in Clissold's many sketchbooks and illustrated diaries. Another adventure, involving travel in a horse-drawn buggy, was featured in the national newspapers.

Footprints exhibited regularly during the 1930s. At the Dorland Hall exhibition of 1933 an imitation patchwork on printed linen was composed of more than 40 of their smaller designs. Another design, *Brittany*, a bedspread 0.8 metres square, designed and painted on linen by Clissold, priced at 15 guineas, was exhibited at the Arts and Crafts Society's 16th exhibition at Dorland Hall in 1935. Work was also shown at Heal's Mansard Gallery, the Society of Women Artist and Designers, the Crafts Centre and the Medici Gallery in London, and the Red Rose Guild in Manchester.

In 1940 Clissold had to close the shops due to the lack of essential supplies and the female employees being required for war work. The workshop managed to re-open after the war, but with fewer printers and a more modest range. The popular georgette scarves continued to be retailed through several dozen smallish outlets nationwide. Some of the earlier designs continued to be reproduced after World War II. *Riviera*, made up as a ladies' smoking jacket, was featured in the London *Evening Standard* in October 1954. The naive and colourful design, featuring sunbathers under palms, makes visual reference to modern painting. The subject is also a reminder that Clissold's middle-class background and business income together provided her with the inclination and the means to travel.

Less ambitious products were sold at fairs and country shows. "Miss Footprints" was a popular figure at the Horse of the Year Show, Crufts, Badminton and other country events. The merchandise was cheap, comprising aesthetically dubious "pot boilers". The aprons, tray cloths and children's games

Clissold: Fabric sample showing parachutist design, mid-1920s; machine-embroidered cotton voile; 15.5 × 14.5 cm.

revealed Clissold's sense of humour, but were quickly and poorly printed. Many items were bought retail and overprinted with images such as a dog or a horse's head. Such works were an indication of a change in the market – the high quality and expensive "bridge coats" and other items sold before the war were well beyond the pockets of those who patronised her stalls at the fairs. But they provided a modest income that allowed Clissold to channel her energies into making textile collages, which became her main creative activity. The collages were figurative, made of scraps of material and paper stuck on to backing board showing landscapes and events from Clissold's life and that of her friends; they were exhibited in London at the Everyman's Theatre, Hampstead, Imperial College and Grosvenor Gallery, and at the Primavera Gallery, Cambridge.

As a textile designer Joyce Clissold helped to perpetuate and invigorate the traditional craft of block printing. Her designs reveal a liveliness that was absent from many of the modern abstract patterns and revivalist florals favoured by the trade. She brought the eye of the artist to her designs and the tradition of women working together to their production. She did not favour repetitive and non-creative work; her inspiration was in the new and spontaneous, and her images were frequently amusing and often irreverent. She continued to create until her death and even during her final stay in hospital she was producing sketches and limericks that revealed her disdain at the frailty of the human body through her characteristic use of humour. Examples of printed textiles, garments,

blocks and associated ephemera are to be found in the Victoria and Albert Museum and Central St Martin's College of Art, London, and the Bath Museum of Costume and Fashion Research Centre.

HAZEL CLARK

Clough, Prunella
British painter, 1919–

Born Prunella Clough Taylor in London, 1919. Studied sculpture and graphics part-time at Chelsea Polytechnic School of Art, London, 1938–9. Worked as a draughtswoman and clerk during World War II. Subsequently attended Victor Pasmore's classes at Camberwell School of Arts and Crafts, London. Worked in London and East Anglia, 1946–9. Teaches at Wimbledon College of Art, London. Lives in London.

Selected Individual Exhibitions
Leger Gallery, London: 1947
Roland Browse and Delbanco Gallery, London: 1949
Leicester Galleries, London: 1953
Whitechapel Art Gallery, London: 1960 (retrospective)
Grosvenor Gallery, London: 1964, 1967
Graves Art Gallery, Sheffield: 1972 (retrospective)
New Art Centre, London: 1973, 1975, 1976, 1979, 1982
Serpentine Gallery, London: 1976
National Gallery of Modern Art, Edinburgh: 1976 (retrospective)
Fitzwilliam Museum, Cambridge: 1982
Warwick Arts Trust, London: 1982
Annely Juda Fine Art, London: 1989, 1992, 1993
Arthur Anderson, London: 1992
Camden Arts Centre, London: 1996

Bibliography
Prunella Clough, exh. cat., Whitechapel Art Gallery, London, 1960
Prunella Clough: New Paintings, 1979–82, exh. cat., Warwick Arts Trust, London, 1982
Malcolm Yorke, *The Spirit of Place: Nine Neo-Romantic Artists and Their Times*, London: Constable, 1988; New York: St Martin's Press, 1989
Prunella Clough, exh. cat., Annely Juda Fine Art, London, 1993
Judith Bumpus, "Prunella Clough", *Contemporary Art*, Winter 1993–4, pp.10–14
Bryan Robertson, "Happiness is the light", *Modern Painters*, Summer 1996, pp.16–20

Essentially a still-life artist, Prunella Clough's contribution to the genre resides in the imaginative processing of her experience of urban landscape. When she first became known in the late 1940s she was making still, tightly constructed, figurative pictures of industrial scenery. Moving gradually into abstraction in the 1960s she developed a distinctive voice whose expressive range she has explored with infinite variations over the past 35 years. In her mature work she employs a surprising and rarely repeating repertoire of everyday objects, or the abstracted qualities of things about her, to create decorative configurations. The characteristically elegant and celebratory interpretation of her visual sources often belies their commonplace origin, relating her more closely to 20th-century French Post-Impressionist painting than to English Neo-romanticism.

Clough: *Black Peony*, 1991; oil on canvas; 142 × 152.5 cm.; Annely Juda Gallery, London

In 1938 Clough began her education part-time in the Art School of Chelsea Polytechnic and there, in the design classes of James de Holden Stone and the commercial designer Edwin Calligan, she developed an appreciative understanding of and liking for the technical discipline and formal power of commercial design. She also studied life drawing, and enrolled in Henry Moore's sculpture class. Graham Sutherland, then teaching illustration at Chelsea, was an active and guiding presence. At the time Clough's interests were mainly practical and craft-oriented. Later, when they were directed into painting, her training in modelling and carving informed her three-dimensional and spatial thinking on the flat canvas. The outbreak of World War II put an end to her education in 1939 when, swept into the war effort, her technical precision as a draughtswoman was employed in cartography and engineering.

After the war Clough began seriously to paint, engaging, as did many contemporary writers and artists, with the tough reality of work. In search of a means of formulating her own ideas, she joined Victor Pasmore's classes at Camberwell School of Arts and Crafts, deriving inspiration from imagery as diverse as the townscapes seen in Italian Renaissance paintings and the works of Fernand Léger, as well as from the real world of post-war Britain. She worked independently in various fishing ports in East Anglia, including Lowestoft, and the resulting canvases of harbour scenes with boats and fishermen, such as *Fishermen with Sprat Nets, No.1* (exh. 1949; Pembroke College, Oxford) and *Fishermen in a Boat* (1949;

Aberdeen Art Gallery), were couched in the decorative, Neo-romantic idiom made fashionable by such artists as Sutherland.

Clough first came to prominence at this time as one of a younger generation of Neo-romantics. Many of her near contemporaries, with whom she was associated – John Minton, Michael Ayrton, John Craxton, Robert Colquhoun and Robert MacBryde – depicted a romanticised view of people in their working environment. Her own painting in this manner was distinguishable by its deliberate organisation of the canvas into a tightly interlocking surface pattern. Her large oil painting *Lowestoft Harbour* (1951; Arts Council of Great Britain) was characteristic. Commissioned by the Arts Council for inclusion in a touring exhibition, *60 Paintings for '51*, to mark the Festival of Britain's post-war celebration of national life and culture, it helped to establish Clough's reputation as an eloquent portrayer of aspects of shoreline industry and of its still-life accoutrements. Typical motifs included fish, anchors, nets for trawling and drying, bones and broken bottles. Her interest in the visual possibilities of the working landscape and its machinery, however, was already much wider, and early in the decade she began, as Minton had done, to explore the activities of London's shabby dockland at Shadwell and Wapping. Lorries and cranes and their drivers, telephone engineers, run-down factory buildings, workshops, scrap metal yards and industrial plant featured in exterior and interior scenes of industrial life along the River Thames. Typical of such themes are *Telephone Engineer* (1950; Aberdeen Art Gallery) and *Printer Cleaning Press* (1953; exh. 1953 in *Figures in Their Setting* as *Printer Cleaning Forme*; Ken Powell).

Clough's first retrospective exhibition, at the Whitechapel Art Gallery in London in 1960, charted the change that was taking place in her work towards the end of the 1950s under the influence of abstraction and, in particular, of American Abstract Expressionism. She began to interpret the facts of industrial life more selectively and subjectively, using a "murky" and moody palette appropriate, she felt, to the English climate. As figurative painting became unfashionable, Clough reduced her peopled landscapes to their material essentials, sometimes taking close-up photographs of their details as an *aide-mémoire* rather than as a working reference. Plucked from their context, the generally disregarded and discarded accoutrements of industrial life, such as an abandoned duty glove or wire mesh fencing, became themes for meditation and metamorphosis. A fellow artist, Michael Middleton, described this process in his catalogue essay to Clough's retrospective of 1960 as "the still, small voice" of "the perfectionist, determined to find the exact pictorial form for her thought" (London 1960).

In the course of the 1960s, although Clough was still primarily concerned with visual facts and the sensations imparted by particular places, her topography changed. The details of, say, an underground journey might linger in her mind. Later, a painting such as the two-part *District Line* (1964; Newcastle University) resulted from a re-assembling and elaboration of her dimmed memories on the canvas, usually over a long period. The wholly invented spaces in *Side Elevation* (1970; Aberdeen Art Gallery), with its undefined shapes suspended in a brown colour field, offered a visual equivalent to urban wasteland. Increasingly, in creating these spaces, she exploited the pictorial potential of atmospheres, textures and urban objects, by no means all of them industrial products, nearer home. Clough's 20th-century urban landscape has always included its softer, natural features, its plants, gardens, hedges and canals, as well as its fences and city lights. Since the 1970s she has found almost all these ideas in her immediate domestic surroundings, in her studio, or in the shops and streets of Fulham in southwest London where she has spent most of her professional career.

During the 1970s she painted her most sparsely abstract and most purely evocative canvases. Their very titles and dates, *Inside and Outside* (1970–75; Arts Council), *Recollection Inside/Outside* (1974–6), *Almost Erased* (1971–4), suggest something of their slow and considered evolution. The human figure, where it reappears in a number of Subway paintings in the late 1970s and early 1980s is no more than a "transient image of a human being, almost a trace", as she explained in an interview with Bryan Robertson (London 1982, p.3).

Clough is neither a moralist nor a social realist. Her meditative and more colourful paintings of the 1980s and 1990s continue to reflect, rather than comment on, the facts and features of a fast-moving, fragmented and consumer-led society in which tawdry objects are displayed in an abraded and crumbling environment. A candy wrapper, a plastic toy or paper flower is enough to prompt the recollection of a whole experience to unfold on the canvas in *Toypack: Sword* (1988; private collection, Germany), *Black Peony* (1991; see illustration) and *Cave* (1990; Manchester City Art Galleries). As Clough says, her paintings are many-layered, unconsciously bringing together disparate memories into a complex pattern of colours, shapes and textures. Her real experience of city life is invariably reworked and transformed in this way; her titles are never more than suggestive. Where Pop Art was of its time, consciously and blatantly vulgar, Clough's moody and beautifully refined compositions are quintessentially poetic.

JUDITH BUMPUS

Collot, Marie-Anne
French sculptor, 1748–1821

Born in Paris, 1748. Studied under Jean-Baptiste Lemoyne, then Etienne-Maurice Falconet. Accompanied Falconet to St Petersburg, Russia, 1766. Married Falconet's son, Pierre-Etienne, 1777; one daughter. Returned to Paris, 1778; brought legal action against her husband for abusive behaviour; remained estranged from him until his death in 1791. Joined her father-in-law in The Hague, Netherlands, 1779. Moved back to Paris, 1782; nursed Falconet after a stroke until his death in 1791. Moved to Lorraine and purchased an estate at Marimont, 1791. Member of the St Petersburg Academy. Died in Nancy, 23 February 1821.

Bibliography

Levesque, *Oeuvres complètes d'Etienne Falconet*, 3 vols, 3rd edition, Paris, 1808; reprinted Geneva: Slatkine, 1970

Antony Valabrègue, *Madame Falconet: Une artiste française en Russie, 1766–1778*, Paris: Rouam, 1898

Louis Réau, ed., *Correspondance de Falconet avec Catherine II*, Paris: Champion, 1921

Louis Réau, "Une femme sculpteur française au XVIIIe siècle: Marie-Anne Collot (1748–1821)", *Bulletin de la Société de l'Histoire de l'Art Français*, 1924, pp.219–29

——, "Les bustes de Marie-Anne Collot", *La Renaissance*, xiv, 1931, pp.306–12

Denis Diderot, *Correspondance*, ed. Georges Roth, 16 vols, Paris: Minuit, 1955–70

——, *Salons*, ed. Jean Seznec and Jean Adhémar, 4 vols, Oxford: Clarendon Press, 1957–67

Hal Opperman, "Marie-Anne Collot in Russia: Two portraits", *Burlington Magazine*, cvii, 1965, pp.408–13 (earlier works containing references to Collot listed in footnote 6)

La Femme artiste d'Elisabeth Vigée-Lebrun à Rosa Bonheur, exh. cat., Musée Despiau-Wlerick, Donjon Lacataye, Mont-de-Marsan, 1981

La France et la Russie au siècle des lumières: Relations culturelles et artistiques, exh. cat., Grand Palais, Paris, 1986

"I do not want to exaggerate her talent, but your Majesty knows that it is singular and that she is the only one of her sex who has devoted herself to the difficult profession of cutting marble and of cutting it successfully." So the sculptor Falconet described his student, Marie-Anne Collot, to Catherine the Great in 1771. Indeed, Collot is one of the few women before 1800 known to have practised sculpture as a profession, and she earned her living by what contemporaries saw as "indefatigable industry".

Born in Paris in 1748, Collot reputedly worked first with Jean-Baptiste Lemoyne, a prominent portraitist and noted teacher. She entered the atelier of Etienne-Maurice Falconet in 1763 when she was 15. Why (and if) Collot changed studios is not certain, nor do we know how as a young woman she came to enter any sculpture studio at all. But by 1766 Collot had made five or six portrait busts, including those of *Grimm*, the actor *Préville*, the Russian minister *Galitzine* and *Denis Diderot* (all untraced). In his *Salon of 1767* Diderot remarked on the portrait of himself, which replaced a less successful piece by Falconet: "When Falconet saw the bust his student had made, he took a hammer and broke his own in front of her. That was truthful and courageous."

Falconet's regard for Collot's talents is well documented, and he entrusted her with making the head of *Peter the Great* for the equestrian monument commissioned by Catherine II (completed 1782; St Petersburg). In 1766 Collot accompanied Falconet to St Petersburg; she was still a minor but apparently had been abandoned by her father. Her travel and work with Falconet predictably provoked gossip, even though her relation to the sculptor seems to have been one of dutiful daughter (and later daughter-in-law).

Falconet arranged for Catherine's patronage of Collot; he brokered her commissions and interceded on her behalf. During the 12 years she spent in Russia, Collot executed various portrait busts and medallions of the Empress, all of which were repeatedly replicated, often by Collot herself. Many of the extant works are now in the Hermitage, St Petersburg. Catherine also commissioned portrait medallions of her son *Paul Petrovich* and his first wife, *Natalya Alexeyevna*, in 1775. In addition, she ordered a medallion of *Count Orlov*, commemorating his relief of the plague-stricken in Moscow. This work suggests something of the collaboration between Collot and Falconet. Having educated himself in the classics, Falconet devised the iconography for the portrait, and wrote to Catherine on 17 November 1771: "This medallion must not only represent M. le Comte, but also characterise his great, memorable and humane act". He goes on to say that the ancients gave the oak crown to a citizen who had saved the life of another, but that Orlov's generous actions saved many lives. Falconet argued that no attribute could make the tribute clear, and suggested instead the inscription: "to the citizen who saved his country". Two branches of oak entwined in the border would indicate an action worthy of commemoration.

Collot's most famous collaborative work with Falconet is undoubtedly the monument to *Peter the Great*. She was involved with many aspects of the work, as Falconet suggested to Catherine in October 1776:

> Your Majesty knows that it is standard to save a small model of an equestrian statue from which one can make small bronzes. The model that I made to begin my work has been broken, and anyway, its proportions were too large. Mlle Collot has been busy for a long time making studies relative to that object … I would have liked to make the model myself, if my eyesight still allowed me to model in a small scale, but Mlle Collot who knows my work perfectly, who has followed all its operations, and who will work under my direction, will complete it successfully.

Collot is generally viewed, however, as having made only the portrait head (indeed, the small bronzes of the work, such as that in the Tretyakov Gallery, Moscow, are rarely attributed to her). In modelling the head (bronze cast, 1770; State Russian Museum, St Petersburg) she worked from Rastrelli's mask of the tsar. She idealised the features, but also stressed the intense gaze and furrowed brow, which convey an energetic determination that contributes to the overall effect. In making the head of Peter, Collot followed a procedure that she had used in several other "retrospective" portraits commissioned by Catherine, which included busts of *Henry IV* and *Sully*. In describing the genesis of these works, Falconet referred to Collot "dreaming" them. Although certainly drawing on her imaginative faculties, the artist also depended on portrait masks sent from Paris by Lemoyne.

If Collot dreamed for Catherine the images of past rulers, that of *Falconet* (1773; see illustration) she rendered for the Empress from life. The bust shows Collot's teacher informally dressed and wigless and, with high forehead, upturned eyes and deeply drilled pupils, the portrait invokes conventions for depicting the artist. Despite the conventional aspects, Falconet's features appear mobile – the smile is about to break, the eyebrows are lifted slightly – and Collot devised a lively and subtle expression that seems liable to change.

In addition to the portraits produced for Catherine, Collot also worked on private commissions. Her bust of *Mary Cathcart*, daughter of the British ambassador, exists in three examples: a finished work in marble (signed and dated 1772; State Russian Museum), an unfinished marble version (Musée des Beaux-Arts, Nancy) and a plaster bust (signed and dated 1768; Louvre, Paris). An anonymous "Eloge" to Collot praises the bust as "one of the prettiest that you can imagine" and

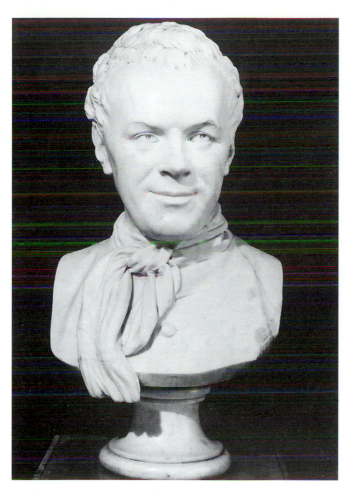

Collot: *Etienne-Maurice Falconet*, 1773; marble; Hermitage Museum, St Petersburg

remarks on its modest expression that lends truth and interest to the work. In contrast to the strikingly individual and animated features of her bust of *Falconet*, those of Miss Cathcart establish the contemporary ideal of fragile and vulnerable femininity. That ideal is evident in the perfected, generalised traits and downcast eyes, which allow viewers to look freely, sure that this young girl is not the sort who would brazenly return the gaze. For the same family Collot exercised her talents in retrospective portraiture, executing from memory a posthumous, life-size marble medallion of *Jane Hamilton, Lady Cathcart* (1772; Collection of the Earl Cathcart, Sandridge).

Few known works by Collot are dated after she returned to Paris from Russia in 1778. Those extant or recorded in literary sources include a bust of her husband *Pierre-Etienne Falconet* (Musée des Beaux-Arts, Nancy), that of the *Chevalier d'Eon*, whom she had known in Russia, and a third of *Charles-Godefroy de Villetaneuse*. In 1779 Collot joined her father-in-law in The Hague, leaving Paris after her husband's abusive and irrational behaviour provoked her to file an official complaint. During her sojourn in the Netherlands she executed marble busts of *William V* and his wife (1782; Mauritshuis, The Hague), and one in bronze of the physician *Camper* (1781; destroyed in a fire, 1907), which she gave to him in gratitude for saving her daughter.

It is not clear when and why Collot's production ended, but always the dutiful daughter, she spent the years between 1783 and 1791 in Paris nursing her father-in-law who was partly paralysed from a stroke. Both her husband and father-in-law died in 1791, and Collot retreated to Lorraine. The writer Levesque, an acquaintance of Falconet, went to visit Collot in 1808 and reported: "Madame Falconet, after having spent eight years in the sad and respectable profession of sick nurse, did not believe she could take up again an art that she had neglected for so long" (Levesque 1808, p.21). Even if she had wanted to return to her work, the problem of seeking out new patrons, as well as both the difficulty and expense of obtaining materials and founding a studio, would have been considerable, especially for a woman past her 50th year. Moreover, with her own earnings and her considerable legacy from Falconet, Marie-Anne Collot was financially secure – so secure that she married her daughter, Marie-Lucie, to the Baron de Jankowitz, a Polish nobleman established in Lorraine. It was Marie-Lucie who preserved the memory of Collot's art in France, donating her works and papers to the State in the hope that her mother might find a place in the national *patrimoine*.

MARY D. SHERIFF

Colman Smith, Pamela *see* Smith

Colquhoun, Ithell
British painter and writer, 1906–1988

Born in Shillong, Assam, India, 1906. Studied at the Slade School of Fine Art, London, under Henry Tonks and Randolph Swabe, 1927–31; subsequently studied privately in Athens and Paris. Read Paul Neagoc's *What is Surrealism?* in 1931; heard Salvador Dalí lecture in London and joined the Surrealists, 1936. Included in *Living Art in England* at London Gallery, 1939. Split from organised Surrealist Group, 1940. Married critic and writer Toni del Renzio, 1940; divorced late 1940s. Lived in Hampstead, London. Moved to Cornwall, 1950s. Died in Cornwall, 11 April 1988.

Selected Individual Exhibitions
Cheltenham Municipal Art Gallery: 1936
Fine Art Society, London: 1936
Liberty's and Heal's Mansard Gallery, London: 1937
Whiteley's and Everyman Theatre, London: 1938
Mayor Gallery, London: 1939 (with Roland Penrose), 1947, 1948
London Gallery, London: 1939
Heffer Gallery, Cambridge: 1953
Gallery I, London: 1959(?)
Newlyn Art Gallery, Cornwall: 1961 (retrospective), 1967, 1971
Kunstamt Wilmersdorf, Berlin: 1969
Galerie für Zeitgenossiche Kunst, Hamburg: 1969
Bristol Arts Centre: 1970
Exeter City Art Gallery: 1972 (retrospective)
Orion Gallery, Penzance, Cornwall: 1973
Leva Gallery, London: 1974
Newlyn Orion Galleries, Cornwall: 1976 (retrospective)
Parkin Gallery, London: 1977

Selected Writings

"The double village", *London Bulletin*, no.7, December 1938–January 1939

"The moths", *London Bulletin*, no.10, February 1939

"What do I need to paint a picture?", *London Bulletin*, no.17, 15 June 1939, p.13

"The volcano", *ibid.*, p.15

"The echoing bruise", *ibid.*, p.17

Contributions to *View*, 1940–47; *Arson*, March 1942 and 1944; *VVV*, nos 1–4, 1942–4; *New Road*, 1943; *Free Unions Libres*, 1946

"The Mantic Stain", *Enquiry*, no.2, October–November 1949, pp.15–21

"Children of the Mantic Stain", *Athene*, May 1951, pp.29–34

The Crying of the Wind: Ireland, London: Owen, 1955

The Living Stones: Cornwall, London: Owen, 1957

The Goose of Hermogenes, London: Owen, 1961

"L'Ile de la fleur nocturne", *Fantasmagie*, no.9, March 1962, pp.16–17 (prose poem)

"The schooner Hesperus/La goelette Etoile de Mer", *Soleils*, 1963

"Kurt Schwitters en Angleterre", *Fantasmagie*, no.29, February 1971

"Aperçu sur l'origine du collage", *Fantasmagie*, no.31, December 1971

Grimoire of the Entangled Thicket, Stevenage, Herts: Ore, 1973

Sword of Wisdom: MacGregor Mathers and the Golden Dawn, London: Spearman, and New York: Putnam, 1975

Osmazone, Orkelljunka, Sweden, 1983

Bibliography

Ithell Colquhoun, exh. cat., Mayor Gallery, London, 1948

Paul C. Ray, *The Surrealist Movement in England*, Ithaca, NY: Cornell University Press, 1971

Ithell Colquhoun, exh. cat., Exeter City Art Gallery, 1972

Ithell Colquhoun: Surrealism, exh. cat., Newlyn Orion Galleries, Cornwall, 1976

Dawn Ades, "Notes on two women Surrealist painters: Eileen Agar and Ithell Colquhoun", *Oxford Art Journal*, iii/1, 1980, pp.36–42

Whitney Chadwick, *Women Artists and the Surrealist Movement*, London: Thames and Hudson, and Boston: Little Brown, 1985

Angels of Anarchy and Machines for Making Clouds: Surrealism in Britain in the Thirties, exh. cat., Leeds City Art Galleries, 1986

La Femme et le surréalisme, exh. cat., Musée Cantonal des Beaux-Arts, Lausanne, 1987

Brigitte Libmann, "British women Surrealists: Deviants from deviance", *This Working Day World: Social, Political and Cultural History of Women's Lives, 1914–45*, ed. Sybil Oldfield, London: Taylor and Francis, 1994, pp.156–8

Ithell Colquhoun only briefly associated herself with the manifestation of Surrealism in London in the late 1930s, although she is often identified exclusively as a woman Surrealist artist. She took part in only one Surrealist exhibition, and submitted a variety of automatic prose and critical writing to the *London (Gallery) Bulletin*. In the same magazine's review of the *Living Art in England* exhibition (1939), she chose to describe herself as an "independent" rather than a Surrealist artist. In 1940 she split from the British Surrealist group, which was organised around E.L.T. Mesens and the London Gallery, because she could not agree with the three principles that Mesens argued for at the notorious Barcelona restaurant meeting in 1940 (see Ray 1971, pp.227–8, and the artist's own account in Newlyn Orion 1976). She nevertheless maintained contact with André Breton, leader of the French Surrealist group, and gave readings of Surrealist poetry at the International Art Centre, London, in 1942 and 1944. Her work is nearly always discussed in relationship to Surrealism because of her interest in automatism, the use of chance techniques, the occult and alchemy.

Colquhoun was drawn into contact with the British Surrealist Group after hearing Salvador Dalí deliver his infamous lecture, *Fantomes paranoiaques authentiques*, dressed in a diving suit at the *International Surrealist Exhibition* of 1936 in London. Dalí's technique, she argued, took root naturally after her education at the Slade where

> one was taught to draw like Michelangelo but to paint like the French Impressionists. I could not see how to combine these two disparate modes so I painted to match the drawing in monochrome with super-imposed glazes of colour. The themes of my early work reflect those set for Slade compositions, which were usually taken from classical or biblical mythology alongside portraits [Newyln Orion 1976].

Her early work also included studies of exotic plants developed into a form of magic realism, as in *Gouffres Amers* (1939; Glasgow University), where the landscape is transformed into the shape of an old river god, a parody of conventional masculinist associations of women with the landscape. In *Scylla* (1938; Tate Gallery, London) the crushing rocks that threatened Ulysses become flesh, literally a woman's legs rising from a bath, in what is a dreamlike transubstantiation. In this image she merges the "poetic projections of unconscious desires" – including women's sexual desires – with Breton's "fixing of dream images" in a form of magic realism. At her Mayor Gallery exhibition of 1939, Colquhoun showed a series of seven paintings called *Mediterranée*, which included *Rivières Tièdes/Tepid Waters* (1939; see illustration), in which strange rivulets run from the closed door of a church, a metaphor for the collapse of the Republican Government and the establishment of Franco's regime in Spain. In the same exhibition she also showed two Surrealist objects, *Death's Head and Foot* and *Heart* (repr. Ades 1980), where dripping lips were moulded on to a heart-shaped object.

In the summer of 1939 Colquhoun visited Breton in France. She always remained sceptical of his professed adoration of women, but was impressed by his discussion of automatism. Her essay "The Mantic Stain" advocated automatism for the first time in a British context and resulted in the artist's giving several lectures and demonstrations of the process (Oxford Art Society, 1950; Cambridge Art Society, 1951; Working Men's Institute, Crowndale Road, London, 1953; BBC TV programme *Fantastic Art*, n.d.). Her work as both a poet/writer and painter in the late 1930s developed through using automatic techniques and exploring the chance effects of a variety of paint processes including delcalcomacia (e.g. *Dreaming Leaps: A Tribute to Sonia Acquistain*, 1945; Collection Michel Remy, Nancy) and sfumage (e.g. *Bride of the Pavement*, 1942; repr. Chadwick 1985). Her painting *The Pine Family* (1941; Museum Collection: Arturo Schwarz, Milan) is regarded as a mock parody of male sexuality and a female reversal of the usual Surrealist emphasis on women as muse/*femme-enfant*. *Visitation I* (1945; Collection James Birch) develops another theme in her work – "psycho-morphology", where images are created through blind impulse or involuntary action. In 1942 she contributed a print, *Zodiac*, to *Salvo for Russia* (National Art Library, Victoria and Albert

Colquhoun: *Tepid Waters (Rivières Tièdes)*, 1939; oil on wood; 91.1 × 61.2 cm.; Southampton City Art Gallery

Museum, London), a limited edition of poems and etchings made for the Comforts Fund for Women and Children of Soviet Russia.

Colquhoun's novels written after the 1940s are both semi-autobiographical and topographical. *The Crying of the Wind* (1955), for example, is a travelogue of Ireland containing some surreal-type passages and strange chance encounters. The book also highlights her continuing interest in flowers/plants, topography/landscape for their roles in both myth and Celtic history. *The Goose of Hermogenes* (1961) evokes the statue woman Vellanserga, daughter of Atlantis, known more commonly as Britannia. This novel has been described by Paul C. Ray as an "occult picaresque", a first-person narrative that "recounts encounters of objective chance with their attendant shocks of recognition – encounters to produce their effect must be experienced" (Ray 1971, p.300). In Dawn Ades's assessment (1980), her early writings read "like accounts of dreams in which a stream of narrative fantasy replaces the striking juxtapositions of images in Surrealist automatic texts".

Other works exhibited in the 1940s, *Tendrils of Sleep, Arethusa, Gorgon* and *Garden of Adonis* (repr. London 1948), use Classical mythology to tell different and often surreal stories. Her meeting with the Dadaist Schwitters, when he was living in Hampstead, London, at the beginning of World War II, led after 1942 to experiments with Merz-type collages and reliefs (repr. Exeter 1972 and all Newlyn Gallery catalogues). Colquhoun also took part in A. Pasque's group Poésie Fantasmagie, which exhibited in Europe during the 1960s and early 1970s. At this time she began working with enamel paint in a semi-automatic way (*Volcanic Landscape*, 1969; repr. Exeter 1972).

KATY DEEPWELL

Cooper, Susie

British ceramic designer, 1902–1995

Born Susan Vera Cooper in Burslem, Staffordshire, 29 October 1902. Studied at Burslem School of Art, 1919–22/3. Designer for A.E. Gray & Co. Ltd, Hanley, 1922/3–9. Opened own decorating factory, the Susie Cooper Pottery, George Street, Tunstall, 1929; moved to Chelsea Works, Moorland Road, Burslem, 1930; to Crown Works, Burslem, 1931–80; established Susie Cooper China Ltd at Jason Works, Longton, 1950–58; both businesses merged with R.H. and S.L. Plant, 1958, and with Josiah Wedgwood and Sons Ltd, 1966. Worked as designer for Williams Adams and Sons Ltd after the closure of her pottery, 1980–86; moved to the Isle of Man and worked as freelance designer, 1986–95. Married architect Cecil Barker, 1938; son born 1943; husband died 1972. Recipient of honorary doctorate, Royal College of Art, London, 1987. Royal Designer for Industry, 1940; Order of the British Empire (OBE), 1979. Died in Douglas, Isle of Man, 28 July 1995.

Principal Exhibitions

Exposition Internationale des Arts Décoratifs et Industriels Modernes, Paris: 1925
Exposition Internationale, Paris: 1937
Victoria and Albert Museum, London: 1946 (*Britain Can Make It*)
Royal Pavilion, South Bank, London: 1951 (*Festival of Britain*)
Sandersons, London: 1978 (*Elegance and Utility*, retrospective)
Victoria and Albert Museum, London, and City Museum and Art Gallery, Stoke-on-Trent: 1987 (*Susie Cooper Productions*, retrospective)

Bibliography

Ann Eatwell, "Susie Cooper: Her pre-war productions, 1922–1939", *V&A Album*, v, 1986, pp.224–36
Susie Cooper Productions, exh. cat., Victoria and Albert Museum, London, and City Museum and Art Gallery, Stoke-on-Trent: 1987
Cheryl Buckley, "Pottery women: A comparative study of Susan Vera Cooper and Millicent Jane Taplin", *View from the Interior: Feminism, Women and Design*, ed. Judy Attfield and Pat Kirkham, London: Women's Press, 1989, pp.71–89
——, *Potters and Paintresses: Women Designers in the Pottery Industry*, London: Women's Press, 1990
Andrew Casey, *Susie Cooper Ceramics: A Collector's Guide*, Stratford upon Avon: Jazz, 1992
Adrian Woodhouse, *Susie Cooper*, 1992

Cheryl Buckley, "Design, femininity and modernism: Interpreting the work of Susie Cooper", *Journal of Design History*, vii, 1994, pp.277–93

Bryn Youds, *The Ceramic Art of Susie Cooper*, London: Thames and Hudson, 1996

Susie Cooper was the most important and influential designer to emerge from the British ceramic industry in the 20th century. She owned and managed her own business from 1929 to 1980 and was solely responsible for the creation of almost 5000 designs for table and ornamental wares. For many years she was the only woman in this position in the Potteries (English Midlands). Throughout her long career she continually sought new challenges. She never stopped experimenting to develop techniques of decoration or introduce higher standards of quality into manufacturing. Nor was she afraid to try out new concepts in design as tastes changed, while remaining true to her basic belief in functionality, value for money and a style that has become a classic of ceramic design. Streamlined, clean and practical shapes effectively combined with simple, plain patterning in pale pastel colours were the essence of this style. Although the contemporary design theory that informed her work was essentially modernist, it was not the bleak and stark modernism of the Continental model but one that was adapted to encompass the best traditions of the British industry and the need that she correctly perceived in her market for good-quality patterns. Examples of the pieces described here can be seen in major British public collections of ceramics, such as the Victoria and Albert Museum, London, and the City Museum and Art Gallery, Stoke-on-Trent.

At her first job, as designer for Gray's Pottery, Cooper came to appreciate the quality and versatility of hand-painted decoration. She steered the company away from the less practical lustre wares towards floral, banded and geometric patterns. The *Ginger Jar* (Victoria and Albert Museum, London), painted by her around 1926 as an exhibition piece, illustrates a technique (of breaking down the blocks of colour into more easily controlled layers) and a subject matter (stylised leaping deer) developed at Gray's but used in her later work. If the leaping deer and the Cubist-inspired geometric patterns, though of the highest quality, were very much of their day, the expansion of banding from a border device to form the entire pattern was Cooper's own innovation. The style was copied all over the world and used with increasing sophistication by Susie Cooper Pottery.

In the 1930s Cooper introduced new shapes such as Kestrel, Curlew and Wren and expanded the range of decorative techniques to include underglaze painting, crayon designs such as Crayon Loop, carved patterns on jugs and bowls, tube lining, sgraffito, aerographing and lithography. Some, such as crayon, were her own invention, but with others she took an existing method such as sgraffito and, as with banding, found an endless source of inspiration. The resulting polka dots, stars, loops and dashes of her diverse techniques, combined with banding or lithography, formed well-spaced and restrained designs that became Cooper's hallmark. The rich variety of her patterning could not be matched by any other designer or design studio in the Potteries. Nor were other designers as conscientious in their control over the design process – while one can be certain that Cooper designed the

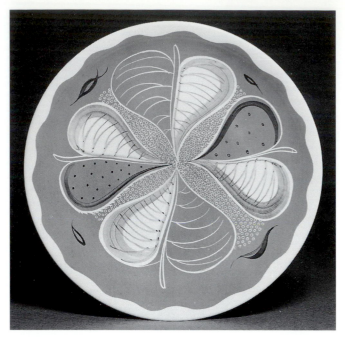

Cooper: Earthenware plaque, designed *c.*1950–51; inglaze design, aerographed in green with sgraffito and painted decoration; made by Wood and Sons Ltd; Victoria and Albert Museum, London

ceramics that issued from her factory, the same could not be said for Clarice Cliff, another prominent ceramic designer.

By 1933 the popularity of Cooper's products had led to an expansion from the original six paintresses (women pottery painters) to a workforce of more than 40 and she was already exporting abroad. Recognised as a force of some originality among her contemporaries, she took an informed part in the debates at the local branch of the Society of Industrial Artists, demonstrating an understanding of the topical debates on design quality and the more pragmatic concerns of a manufacturer. Her style was an intelligent response to several factors, not least of which was the varying abilities of her paintresses. The youngest could be trained to use colour and space on a pattern such as Polka Dots, supplying saleable wares in a very short time. A thoughtful balancing of the paintresses' capabilities, the need to produce maximum quantity from minimum capital outlay and an imaginative approach to design were the bases of her success in the ceramic industry. Attention to detail and an emphasis on quality distinguished her work from that of her rivals. As one commentator wrote: "Susie Cooper Pottery might be said to be the result of a studio instinct which has been judiciously steered into commercial channels" (*Pottery Gazette*, June 1931, p.819). Young designers starting out in the post-war period, such as Jessie Tait, were inspired by Cooper's success as a woman and a designer in a largely male-dominated industry.

In 1950, in her late forties, an age when many designers might have looked back on the rich body of their work and prepared to coast to retirement, Cooper reinvented herself. She bought a porcelain factory and started to manufacture for the first time. Previously Wood and Sons had supplied earthenware products to her design. She had designed only rarely for porcelain and the new departure revitalised her. She produced some of the most exciting post-war ceramic designs of the 1950s and 1960s. The bone china body developed at the Jason Works with the assistance of her husband, the architect Cecil Barker, was of a particularly delicate and translucent type. Cooper's earliest designs emphasised this fragility and elegance. Shapes such as Quail, with its curving lines, and such patterns as Spiral Fern were typical of this period. In the late 1950s Quail was replaced by the Can shape, a straight-sided and functional design so successful that it is still being used by the Wedgwood factory today. Few Staffordshire designers in the 1950s and 1960s could compete on the world market in terms of good contemporary design . Of those that did Cooper was the most significant. While most British manufacturers were looking to America and later to Scandinavia for inspiration, Cooper's original and intriguing modern floral and abstract patterns, such as Assyrian Motif, Harlequinade and Sunflower, earned her credibility as an important designer both at home and abroad. The more robust shapes and patterns of the 1960s and early 1970s developed an expression of classical modernity. The treatments confirmed that she had moved a considerable distance from the entrenched perception within the ceramic industry of porcelain as merely a vehicle for very traditional design.

Throughout her long working life, Cooper was able to remain in the forefront of British ceramic design through a combination of business acumen, design talent and market foresight. She had an unerring instinct for creating her products a sensible distance ahead of the taste of her markets, and ahead of the best efforts of her competitors. The styles and types of ceramics were designed to suit the lives and aspirations of her consumers, the middle-class professionals, who had "more dash than cash". She developed smaller service ranges, stacking products and multi-purpose items. Her designs were not only unfailingly aesthetically pleasing but also functional – such as the tureen lid that could become an extra serving dish. As her first advertisement had promised: "Elegance combined with utility. Artistry associated with commerce and practicality". This was the *raison d'être* behind the work of Susie Cooper.

ANN EATWELL

Coster, Anne *see* Vallayer-Coster

Cosway, Maria

British painter, illustrator and printmaker, 1760–1838

Born Maria Louisa Caterina Cecilia Hadfield in Florence, Italy, 1760; father ran fashionable inns. Copied paintings in Florence, 1773–8; elected member of the Accademia del Disegno, Florence, 1778. Visited Rome and Naples, 1778–9. Moved to London with her family, 1779. Married painter Richard Cosway in London, 1781; daughter born 1790 (d. 1796). Visited Paris and toured Flanders with husband, 1786; met Thomas Jefferson. Visited Paris alone, 1787. Lived alone in Venice and Genoa, 1790–94. In London with Richard Cosway, 1794–1801. Close association with the London-based print publisher Rudolph Ackermann, 1800–03. In Paris alone, copying in the Louvre, 1801–3. Established "a college for young ladies" at Lyon under the patronage of Joseph Fesch, Archbishop of Lyon and later Cardinal, 1803–9. Founded school for girls at Lodi, Lombardy, with the support of Francesco Melzi d'Eril, vice-president of the Cisalpine Republic and later Duke of Lodi, 1812; college re-established under the religious order of the Dame Inglesi, 1830. Visited Richard Cosway in London, 1815; stayed with him from 1817 until his death in 1821; arranged five auctions of his collections. Toured Scotland, 1822. Returned to Lodi, 1822; lived there for the rest of her life. Arranged publication of a selection of Richard Cosway's drawings, engraved by Paolo Lasinio, Florence, 1826. Created a Baroness by the Austrian emperor Francis I, 1834 (group portrait of *Baroness Maria Cosway, Surrounded by Sisters and Pupils, Listening to an Oration by Vittoria Manzoni* painted by Gabriele Rottini *c*.1835; Fondazione Cosway, Lodi). Died in Lodi, 5 January 1838.

Principal Exhibitions

Royal Academy, London: 1781–9, 1796, 1800–01

Bibliography

Anthony Pasquin [John Williams], *The Royal Academicians: A Farce as It Was Performed to the Astonishment of Mankind by His Majesty's Servants, at the Stone House, in Utopia, in the Summer of 1786*, London, 1786

"Cenni biografici sopra la Baronessa Maria Hadfield Cosway ...", (a pamphlet inserted in the) *Gazzetta Privilegiata di Milano*, 11 February 1838

Frederick B. Daniell, *A Catalogue Raisonné of the Engraved Works of Richard Cosway, RA*, London: Daniell, 1890

George C. Williamson, *Richard Cosway RA and His Wife and Pupils, Miniaturists of the Eighteenth Century*, London: Bell, 1897; revised as *Richard Cosway RA*, 1905

E. Fletcher, ed., *Conversations of James Northcote RA with James Ward on Art and Artists*, London: Methuen, 1901

Alfred Whitman, *British Mezzotinters: Valentine Green*, 3 vols, London: Bullen, 1902

E.L.G. Charvet, "Enseignement public des arts du dessin à Lyon, 1804", *Bulletin du Comité des Sociétés des Beaux-Arts des Départements (Réunion des Sociétés des Beaux-Arts des Départements)*, xxxv, 1912, pp.79–112

Emma Ferrari, "Di alcuni documenti riguardanti Riccardo Cosway nella biblioteca di Lodi", *Archivio Storico per la Città di Lodi*, xxxii, 1913, pp.171–86; xxxiii, 1914, pp.25–48, 75–93

P. B[arghazi], "Dalla corrispondenza di lettere con Madama Baronessa Maria Hadfield Cosway", *Archivio Storico per la Città e i Comuni del Circondario e della Diocesi di Lodi*, xliv, 1925, pp.109–20

Arthur T. Bolton, ed., *The Portrait of Sir John Soane RA (1753–1837), Set Forth in Letters from His Friends (1775–1837)*, London: Sir John Soane's Museum, 1927

Helen Duprey Bullock, *My Head and My Heart: A Little History of Thomas Jefferson and Maria Cosway*, New York: Putnam, 1945

Fawn M. Brodie, *Thomas Jefferson: An Intimate History*, New York: Norton, and London: Eyre Methuen, 1974

John Ford, *Ackermann, 1783–1983: The Business of Art*, London: Ackermann, 1983

Maurizio Lozzi and Angelo Stroppa, *Il Collegio Cosway ieri e oggi*, Lodi, 1985

John Walker, "Maria Cosway, an undervalued artist", *Apollo*, cxxiii, 1986, pp.318–24

Elena Cazzulani and Angelo Stroppa, *Maria Hadfield Cosway: Biografia, diari e scritti della fondatrice del Collegio delle Dame Inglesi in Lodi*, Orio Litta: L'Immagine, 1989; reviewed by Stephen Lloyd, *Burlington Magazine*, cxxxii, 1990, p.799

Philippe Bordes, "Jacques-Louis David's anglophilia on the eve of the French Revolution", *Burlington Magazine*, cxxxiv, 1992, pp.482–90

Stephen Lloyd, "The accomplished Maria Cosway: Anglo-Italian artist, musician, salon hostess and educationalist (1759–1838)", *Journal of Anglo-Italian Studies*, ii, 1992, pp.108–39

Ann Bermingham, "The aesthetics of ignorance: The accomplished woman in the culture of connoisseurship", *Oxford Art Journal*, xvi/2, 1993, pp.3–20

Richard and Maria Cosway: Regency Artists of Taste and Fashion, exh. cat., Scottish National Portrait Gallery, Edinburgh, and National Portrait Gallery, London, 1995 (contains extensive bibliography)

Maria Cosway was the most significant woman artist to exhibit her work publicly in London during the last two decades of the 18th century, after the departure of Angelica Kauffman (q.v.) for Rome in 1781. The contemporary reputation of her work was based on three factors: the history paintings and portraits shown at the Royal Academy; their reproduction as prints by major engravers such as Valentine Green and Francesco Bartolozzi; and between 1800 and 1803 her close association with the art entrepreneur Rudolph Ackermann, who published a number of prints after her paintings as well as various series of her etchings and illustrations. Until recently Cosway's artistic production and career received little critical study, in contrast with the attention given to her brilliant but eccentric husband Richard Cosway. For instance, it is still commonly assumed that she was a miniaturist, although there is no evidence for this. Cosway has been and will always be best known for her romance with Thomas Jefferson (*Jefferson in Paris*, film by Merchant Ivory Productions, 1995), which was just one of the many intense relationships that marked her fascinating life.

In 1787 one of the three self-portraits (all untraced) that Maria Cosway painted and exhibited at the Royal Academy in the 1780s was engraved in mezzotint by Green (see illustration). At the time of the print's publication Cosway was in her late twenties, at the height of her success as an artist and between two visits to Paris. This self-portrait, which was titled *Mrs Cosway*, is perhaps the strongest composition of her career, and has a clarity reminiscent of the work of Elisabeth Vigée-Lebrun (q.v.). The artist chose to present herself three-quarter length within a fictive window or picture frame, seated confidently and strongly lit against an open background of sea and dark sky, shown either at sunrise or sunset. The assertive pose adopted is notable for the crossed arms, which while acting as a neat device to conceal the hands, also help lend an air of forthright determination to the image. This aspect of Cosway's character was noted by the painter James Northcote, who cited her as the only individual apart from his master (Reynolds) who was superior to circumstances: "I knew her when she was in the greatest distress; I knew her when she was in high prosperity, and visited by the Prince of Wales, but at both periods her behaviour was exactly the same" (quoted in Fletcher 1901, pp.79–80). In the *Self-Portrait* Cosway turns

Cosway: Valentine Green, after Maria Cosway, *Mrs Cosway*, 1787; mezzotint; Royal Collection © Her Majesty Queen Elizabeth II

her head to face the viewer with a gaze of wide-eyed intensity and unaffected seriousness. This is achieved despite her fashionable appearance with puffed and powdered hair, offset by a characteristic turban. She decided against including any props, such as a palette or harp, which might have referred to her activities as an artist or musician. The emphasis is very much on her appearance and presence. She depicted herself wearing a cross at the end of a dark ribbon choker, tied at the front of the neck with a heart-shaped locket. This was both a fashionable piece of decorative jewellery and an overt reference to her strong Catholicism, the deep impact of which is vital for an understanding of her biography and artistic production.

Maria Hadfield's career as an artist was based on her training in Florence during childhood and adolescence. As she recorded in an autobiographical letter to Sir William Cosway (1830; National Art Library, Victoria and Albert Museum, London, MS Eng.L.961–1953), she began drawing at eight years of age; she was trained by Violante Cerroti; and she is known to have copied paintings in the galleries of the Uffizi and Palazzo Pitti in the years 1773–8. Among the works that Maria Hadfield studied were those of Correggio, van Meiris, Trevisani and Reynolds. Copies from this period of Raphael's *Large Cowper Madonna*, Correggio's *Virgin and Child with St Jerome* and Rubens's *Four Philosophers* are still preserved in the Fondazione Cosway, Lodi. Cosway was also taught by

Zoffany and received lessons from Wright of Derby. On her visit to Rome in 1778–9 she did not attend formal classes but made sketches from "all that was high in painting and sculpture". She also met a number of the major artists including Batoni, Mengs and Maron, as well as many of those visiting from Britain. She was greatly impressed by Fuseli's "extraordinary visions".

The paintings that Cosway exhibited at the Royal Academy were much influenced by Kauffman and Fuseli in terms of style, handling and range of subject matter. Her interest in spiritual iconography was part of an increasing trend during the 1780s that was dominated by Fuseli, but which received a mixed critical response. Horace Walpole recorded in his Royal Academy catalogue of 1783 that "of late Barry, Romney, Fuseli, Mrs Cosway, and others, have attempted to paint deities, visions, witchcrafts, etc., have only been bombast and extravert, without true dignity" (quoted in Martin Postle, *Sir Joshua Reynolds: The Subject Pictures*, Cambridge, 1995, p.265). Cosway's paintings comprised some notable "in character portraits", but they were principally ambitious subject pictures with mythological, literary and biblical themes drawn from such sources as Homer, Virgil, Diodorus Siculus, Petrarch, Spenser, Shakespeare, Pope, Gray, Rogers, Macpherson (*Works of Ossian*) and Hannah Cowley as well as the Bible. Her most successful work was the portrait of *Georgiana, Duchess of Devonshire as Cynthia* (1782; Duke of Devonshire and Chatsworth Settlement Trustees) based on Spenser's *Faerie Queene*. This dramatic, full-length portrait shows the Duchess flying through the night sky directly towards the viewer. One critic praised the "elegant compliment" paid to the sitter, noting the painting's originality and delicacy, and also asserted that Cosway was "the first of female painters" and among the male sex only inferior to her husband and Reynolds (*Morning Chronicle*, 9 May 1782). Other untraced paintings such as *Eolus Raising a Storm* (exh. Royal Academy 1782), *Samson* (exh. Royal Academy 1784), *The Deluge* (exh. Royal Academy 1785) and *A Vision* (exh. Royal Academy 1786), stylistically influenced by Fuseli, were generally considered failures by the reviewers. It is notable that all four of these compositions are included in the caricature etching of Cosway entitled *Maria Costive at Her Studies* (1786; British Museum, London). More successful was the painting of *The Hours* (1783; untraced), which was engraved in stipple by Bartolozzi (1788; British Museum) for Thomas Macklin's *British Poets* series. An impression of the print was sent to Jacques-Louis David, who in a letter to Cosway praised both the composition and the artist very warmly.

David's influence can be seen in the arrangement of figures and prominent use of gesture in an unusual painting by Cosway of the *Death of Miss Gardiner* (1789; Musée de la Révolution Française, Vizille), although it also shows handling and lighting characteristic of Reynolds. One of the few signed and dated works by Cosway to survive, this is also one of the finest. The subject is typical of sentimental taste across Europe, and reflects the spiritual interests of Cosway, who, like her husband, was a follower of Swedenborgian doctrines. Miss Gardiner, who is shown dying while being supported by her aunt Lady Townshend, had a vision of her deceased mother, and expressed a desire to join her. In the painting Cosway gave particular emphasis to Miss Gardiner's raised arm. Philippe

Bordes (*Revue du Louvre*, v–vi, December 1994, p.102, no.30) has plausibly described this painting as offering a specifically feminine vision of death, where emotional expressiveness contained within a private space may be contrasted with masculine stoic heroism set in public, which for instance Cosway would have seen in David's *Death of Socrates* (1787; Metropolitan Museum of Art, New York).

The following decade was one of disruption and great emotional turmoil for Cosway, and she exhibited only one painting at the Academy, in 1796. In that year the Cosways' only daughter Louisa died of a fever aged six. Cosway became increasingly religious and involved with girls' education, concerns that were eventually to dominate the rest of her life. Among the compositions that survive from this period, a number shows grieving or prostrate women, which suggests that these works may be revealing of her psychological state. The first and most important of these is the image of the dissolving water nymph *Lodona*, taken from Pope's poem *Windsor-Forest*, which was engraved in stipple by Bartolozzi (1792; British Museum) from an untraced oil painted for Macklin's *Poets Gallery*.

At the end of the decade Cosway painted for the Catholic Salvin family a huge altarpiece of the *Exultation of the Virgin Mary, or the Salvation of Mankind, Purchased by the Death of Jesus Christ* (1799; Croxdale Hall, Co. Durham), which was exhibited under that title at the Royal Academy in 1801. A smaller replica exists (c.1799; Fondazione Cosway, Lodi), and it was engraved in mezzotint by Green as the *Descent from the Cross* (1801; British Museum). The intensely emotional treatment of this subject – with its vivid colouring and broad handling – places particular emphasis on the Virgin, who is shown raising both her arms in triumph. This painting heralded a final surge of activity in Maria Cosway's career, which continued until her departure from Paris for Lyon in 1803. Seven paintings were exhibited at the Academy in 1800, with three more shown the following year. The most significant was perhaps the *Birth of the Thames* (c.1800; private collection, Ireland), which was engraved by P. W. Tomkins (1802; British Museum). In this highly unusual and original subject the River Thames is shown as a baby being raised above the bulrushes by a chorus of water nymphs and a swan.

This print was published by Ackermann and his influential print-selling business, *Repository of Arts*. Ackermann went on to publish many more of Cosway's projects, among which were a drawing book of her etchings after a selection of Richard Cosway's drawn sketches, entitled *Imitations in Chalk* (1800; Yale Center for British Art, New Haven); two series of moral illustrations known as the *Progress of Female Progress* and the *Progress of Female Dissipation* (1800; British Museum), which were engraved by A. Cardon; and the series of 12 pen and wash illustrations to Mary "Perdita" Robinson's pathetic autobiographical poem *The Winter Day* (c.1803; New York Public Library), which were etched in aquatint (1803; Courtauld Institute Galleries, London) by Caroline Watson (q.v.). The poem and the accompanying designs contrast "the evils of poverty and the ostentatious enjoyment of opulence". Ackermann in his introduction to the poem aptly described Cosway's style as demonstrated in these illustrations, and his criticism can be taken as referring to much of her other work:

Mrs Cosway's designs, it must be admitted, are sometimes eccentric, but it is the eccentricity of genius, and we have seen instances where she has snatched a grace beyond the reach of art. That extravagance carried to excess is an error, cannot be denied, but we prefer the artist who rather overcharges his figure, to him who touches the canvas with a timid feeble pencil, and leaves the imagination of the spectator to express what he cannot or dare not express. We prefer the extravagance of Michelangelo to the highest finishing of a dull Dutch artist. The horse that outstrips his competitors may be curbed; but the animal who is sluggish and incapabable of exertion cannot be spurred into speed.

Of all the artistic projects in which Cosway was involved around 1800, the most ambitious and demanding was that undertaken in Paris between 1801 and 1803. This was to copy and etch Dominique Vivant-Denon's display of the newly arrived old master paintings in the Musée Central or the Grand Gallery of the Louvre, with descriptive texts being provided by the entrepreneur Julius Griffiths. Eight folio-sized plates of the *Galerie du Louvre* (1802; British Museum) were published in Paris and made available to subscribers either monochrome or coloured. The original presentation volume of coloured etchings with the names of the French and British subscribers survives (1801–3; Fondazione Cosway). Despite signing the volume at the head of the Bonaparte family, Napoleon himself was disparaging about the quality of Cosway's copies, a judgement with which she herself concurred.

In her paintings Cosway wholeheartedly followed the impulse of her imagination, but her career as an artist was encouraged and affected by her husband. Richard Cosway portrayed his wife on many occasions, but in only one portrait drawing of her (c.1789; Fondazione Cosway) – shown with a bust of Leonardo da Vinci – did he represent her with palette and brushes. Moreover, he refused to allow her to sell her work, which, as she admitted in the letter of 1830, had a damaging effect on its quality: "had Mr C. permitted me to paint professionally, I should have made a better painter, but left to myself by degrees instead of improving, I lost what I had brought from Italy of my early studies." This honest statement is highly revealing of the problems that talented women artists encountered in having their activities and production recognised with professional status. This fact should not, however, detract from further study of one of the most accomplished women artists working in Europe in the late 18th century and at the beginning of the 19th.

STEPHEN LLOYD

Courtauld, Louisa
British goldsmith, 1729–1807

Born Louisa Perina Ogier in Spitalfields, London, 1729, to Peter Ogier II, silk weaver, and his wife Catherine Rabaud, both originally from Poitou, France. Married Samuel Courtauld, silversmith, at St Luke's, Old Street, London, 1749: three sons and four daughters. Succeeded to her

husband's business at his death in 1765. First mark entered 1765. Went into partnership with George Cowles and entered second joint mark, c.1768. Third joint mark with her son Samuel entered 1777. Sold business and retired to Clapton, Essex, 1780. Died 12 January 1807.

Bibliography
Edward A. Jones, *Some Silver Wrought by the Courtauld Family of London Goldsmiths in the Eighteenth Century*, Oxford: Shakespeare Head Press, 1940
Robert Rowe, *Adam Silver, 1765–1795*, London: Faber, and New York: Taplinger, 1965
E.J.G. Smith, "The Courtauld family of silversmiths", *Collector's Guide*, February 1970
Christopher Lever, "The Courtauld family of goldsmiths", *Apollo*, c, 1974, pp.138–41
J.F. Hayward, *The Courtauld Silver*, London and New York: Sotheby Parke Bernet, 1975
London Silver, 1680 to 1780, exh. cat., Museum of London, London, 1982
J. Banister, "Three generations in silver: Courtauld silver at the Museum of London", *Country Life*, clxxi, 3 June 1982, pp.1628–9
T. Murdoch, "The Courtaulds: Silversmiths for three generations", *Proceedings of the Silver Society*, iii/4, 1983
Philippa Glanville, *Silver in England*, London: Unwin Hyman, and New York: Holmes and Meier, 1987
Philippa Glanville and Jennifer Faulds Goldsborough, *Women Silversmiths, 1685–1845: Works from the Collection of the National Museum of Women in the Arts, Washington, DC*, London: Thames and Hudson, 1990
Arthur Grimwade, *London Goldsmiths, 1697–1837: Their Marks and Lives*, 3rd edition, London, 1990

Louisa Courtauld was a member by marriage of one of the most famous families of 18th-century goldsmiths. The Courtaulds were a part of the influx of French Protestant, or Huguenot, craftsmen who were forced out of France by religious persecution after the revocation of the Edict of Nantes in 1685 and who settled in England where they became enormously influential members of the artistic community. The activities and impact of the Huguenots have been thoroughly explored in the exhibition *The Quiet Conquest: The Huguenots, 1685–1985* (Museum of London, 1985). The Courtaulds' contact with the goldsmithing industry began with Augustin Courtauld, whose father apprenticed him to the goldsmith Simon Pantin (also a Huguenot and the father of another notable woman goldsmith, Elizabeth Godfrey, q.v.), after settling in London in 1687. In 1708 Augustin entered his mark and established his own workshop in St Martin's Lane. The business prospered, supplying a wide range of objects to aristocratic patrons, in particular silver vessels for the fashionable new hot drinks, tea, coffee and chocolate, and grand two-handled presentational cups. However, the workshop also produced more run-of-the-mill objects for a less wealthy market, such as casters, candlesticks and cruets. By 1734 Augustin was supporting a number of Huguenot apprentices, among whom was one of his sons, Samuel, who set up independently in 1746 in Chandos Street, just off St Martin's Lane. It was during this period that he married Louisa Perina Ogier, the daughter of another member of the Huguenot community, Peter Ogier II; a silk weaver from Spitalfields, his family was as important in its sphere as the Courtaulds were in theirs.

Samuel inherited his father's business in 1751, including (as was usual at the time) all his tools, patterns and apprentices. It was perhaps this expansion that prompted his move to new premises, and it was possibly due to connections made through his wife that they were in the heart of the City at Cornhill. The workshop continued to prosper under his management and to attract new clients such as the Clothworkers' Company as the new Rococo style was successfully adopted.

Samuel died in 1765, and as was usual practice in the goldsmiths' trade, his widow Louisa took over the business and added her own mark to his. The inheritance comprised the lease of the house and shop, her husband's stock-in-trade and the workshop, including his senior apprentice George Cowles, who did not become Louisa's second husband, although such an arrangement was quite common for women in this position. Rather, after Cowles's marriage to Samuel Courtauld's niece in 1768 Louisa took him into partnership and a joint mark was entered. Like her husband, Louisa's tradecard described her as a "goldsmith and jeweller", the term "goldsmith" indicating one made free of the Goldsmiths' Company, but also encompassing the work of a silversmith. Significantly, by the mid-18th century the term seems to have implied someone who was both a member of the Company and a retailer, whereas the title "silversmith" suggested an artisan. This distinction is borne out by Louisa's portrait (private collection, repr. Glanville and Goldsborough 1990), one of the few images of a woman goldsmith, painted around 1770 and attributed to Zoffany, but probably by Nathaniel Dance. It gives a sense both of the prosperity of the firm and Louisa's role within it. It is hardly the image of a craftsman, but rather that of an affluent business-woman, fashionably dressed and in apparently luxurious surroundings. The portrait also serves to emphasise that women goldsmiths did not necessarily practise the craft themselves, although some aspects were undertaken by women, such as burnishing and finishing. In general, women who entered a mark were acting rather as managers, employing competent artisans, overseeing the output of the firm, dealing with clients and the Goldsmiths' Company and managing the finances. In this respect, Louisa was carrying out the same function as many of her male counterparts in the trade, the structure of which was highly complex by the 18th century. The mark on a piece of silver did not indicate the craftsman, but rather the sponsoring firm, or even the retailer. Much of the work of producing an object could be contracted out to a number of subsidiary businesses specialising in particular skills such as engraving. Some of the major firms did not even have their own workshops as such, but used a web of other businesses, merely stamping their mark as retailer on the finished item.

The Courtauld-Cowles partnership maintained the highly successful family tradition, producing a steady output of work through the 1770s. This must be due in large measure to the ability of the workshop to continue to adapt to new styles. Just as Samuel had introduced Rococo patterns, it was under Louisa that the transition to Neo-classical designs was made. The impact of the style and the assurance with which it was handled can be seen on a series of objects produced by the firm from 1770 onwards, for example a two-handled cup and cover of 1771 in the Victoria and Albert Museum, London. Among the most striking products of the workshop was a series of vases inspired by Josiah Wedgwood's First Day Vases made to commemorate the opening of the Etruria Factory in 1769, and indicative of the revival of interest in the Antique that was such a vital feature of the Neo-classical style. The Wedgwood vases were decorated with scenes of Hercules in the Garden of Hesperides taken from the "Collection of Etruscan, Greek and Roman Antiquities from the Cabinet of the Hon. William Hamilton" published by François Hugues d'Hancarville in 1766, a collection acquired later by the newly founded British Museum. The Cowles and Courtauld vases were based on the same source, and notable for the quality of the silver engraving and the innovatory satin-finished surface. A set of three was supplied to Nathaniel Curzon, 1st Baron Scarsdale, in 1771 (now in Museum of Fine Arts, Boston) and a single version is now in the Courtauld Collection (on loan to the Victoria and Albert Museum). The urn form was one that had been long in the Courtauld family repertoire, but Courtauld and Cowles also proved that they could produce excellent designs for a whole range of objects such as teapots and tea caddies, catering to a middle-class as well as an aristocratic market.

An intelligent, restrained use of ornament and high-quality execution remained one of the trademarks of the firm after 1777 when the partnership with Cowles was ended and Louisa entered a joint mark with one of her sons, Samuel II, who must have been trained in the family workshop although there is no record of his apprenticeship. This lasted only three years, for in 1780 Louisa retired to Clapton in Essex and Samuel emigrated to America where he set himself up as a merchant. Her other son, George, revived the family links with the textile industry through an apprenticeship with a silk thrower in Spitalfields, leading ultimately to the fortune on which was founded the Courtauld Institute of Art in 1931, and Courtaulds PLC, the international textile company that maintains the most important and comprehensive collection of three generations of Courtauld silver.

PIPPA SHIRLEY

Croce, Suor Maria Eufrasia della

Italian painter, 1597–1676

Born Flavia Benedetti, 1597. Entered the Discalced Carmelite convent of San Giuseppe a Capo le Case, Rome, 3 May 1627; professed a year later; lived in strict enclosure for the rest of her life. Documentary evidence indicates that she also became prioress (Madre Priora) of the convent, but it is not clear when or for how long. Died 4 April 1676; buried in the convent.

Bibliography

"Libro delle vestizioni" and "Libro delle defunte", manuscripts, Convent of San Giuseppe, Rome

Filippo de Rossi, Ritratto di Roma moderna, Rome: Moneta, 1645

Giovan Antonio Bruzio, "Theatrum romanae urbis sive romanorum sacrae aedes, xv: Chiese, conservatori e monasteri di monache della città di Roma", 1655/61–c.1680, Biblioteca Apostolica Vaticana, Rome, MS Vat.Lat.11884, fol.224

Croce: *Mary Magdalene, the Virgin and St John*, upper choir wall, convent of San Giuseppe, Rome

Carlo Pietrangeli, "Chiesa e Monastero di S. Giuseppe a Capo le Case", *Guide Rionali di Roma Colonna III*, Rome: Palombi, 1980, p.68

Filippo Titi, *Studio di pittura, scoltura et architettura nelle chiese di Roma, 1674–1763*, ed. Bruno Contardi and Serena Romano, 2 vols, Florence: Centro Di, 1987

Franca Trinchieri Camiz, "'*Virgo-non sterilis*': Nuns as artists in 17th-century Rome", *Picturing Women in Renaissance and Baroque Italy*, ed. Sara Matthews Grieco and Geraldine Johnson (in preparation)

Contrary to the traditional assumption that the "art of nuns" essentially implied only miniature painting or embroidery, Suor Maria Eufrasia della Croce's paintings provide important and rare evidence that nuns did paint on a large scale. Her works include altarpieces on canvas, as well as murals (oil on plaster) in her convent of San Giuseppe a Capo le Case, Rome. These wall paintings were conceived for spaces of strict enclosure, viewed only and exclusively by the nuns; they present a significant iconography of images intended to inspire, and sustain prayer and private meditation.

Maria Eufrasia's activity as a *monaca pittrice* ("painting nun") is known essentially through 17th-century guide books (de Rossi, Titi and Bruzio), although these refer only to Maria Eufrasia's public altarpiece, a *Nativity of Christ* (untraced), in the church of San Giuseppe. In the convent proper, paintings (oil on plaster) depicting a *Noli me tangere*, the *Last Supper*, *Christ and the Woman from Samaria* and the *Transverberation of St Teresa*, which were once in the Refectory, were destroyed in the 1930s and survive only in the form of faded photographs. Paintings of *God the Father*, the *Annunciation*, *Christ and the Woman of Samaria* – wearing the jewels and elegant contemporary dress that the nuns renounced – and a humble, unsensual *Repentant Mary Magdalene* can now still be seen on walls that framed a former communion window (*comunichino*) behind the right side wall of the church's altar. They have in part been heavily restored. A larger and more accomplished mural – could it have been painted later? – depicting a tearful *Mary Magdalene, the Virgin and St John*, within an illusionistic architectural framework of receding columns and a theatrically staged sky torn by sudden light (see illustration), adorned the nuns' former inner choir (also called *coro d'inverno*). This mural was unknown until January 1995, when the convent was opened to the public as a renovated Galleria Comunale d'Arte Moderna. Originally, these grieving figures served as a painted backdrop for a three-dimensional sculpted *Crucified Christ* (probably the late 16th-century polychromed wooden example presently in the church). A *St

Teresa and Maria Maddalena de' Pazzi Contemplating the Cross as Fons Vitae, depicted in the lower left corner of the wall, is all that is left of a series of scenes that must have flanked the Crucifixion. Since all the surviving paintings of the convent are fairly consistent in medium, gestures, facial types and drapery patterns, it is likely that they were all painted by Maria Eufrasia della Croce. Moreover, these are very similar to a large painting in oil on canvas of *St Teresa Protecting Carmelite Nuns* (in the present convent of San Giuseppe), which has traditionally been attributed to her (except for modern additions of large lilies!).

Unfortunately, no-one from the outside, much less men, could see or describe the paintings within the convent's enclosure; the restrictions of enclosure combined with the regrettable loss of a large part of the convent's early archives have thus resulted in a lack of any specific documentation – besides the paintings themselves – on Maria Eufrasia's activity as a painter. In the 17th century Filippo de Rossi referred to her only known work, the *Nativity*, as painted by a "most excellent nun and painter of the place" (de Rossi 1645, p.305); Bruzio in his appraisal stated: "even if it is by a woman it is not a displeasing work" (fol.224). In recent times, the paintings of the *comunichino* have been assessed as, at best, "naïve", at worst, "crude" or "dilettante".

Maria Eufrasia was the daughter of a well-to-do patrician and the sister of the Abate Elpidio Benedetti, an art collector and amateur architect who submitted a plan for the Spanish Steps, and it is likely that she had formal lessons in drawing and painting before taking the veil, although this is only a matter of conjecture. She had, however, no experience in fresco technique, which explains why she chose to paint on walls in the less complex medium of oil on plaster. Once in her convent, her contacts with art would have been extremely limited except for the many prints – "saints on paper" – that once hung in the cells and corridors. That she made use of Counter-Reformation devotional prints as compositional models is particularly evident in her wall painting of the inner choir.

The iconography of the works relates closely to the writings of St Teresa, who expressed particular interest in the story of Christ and the Woman from Samaria and who invoked Mary Magdalene especially "when taking communion"; these are the subjects that Maria Eufrasia painted on the walls framing the window through which the nuns received the Eucharist. The theme of the Blood of Christ as redeeming nourishment, seen in her *Fons Vitae*, was also central to the thinking of St Theresa and Maria Maddalena de' Pazzi, as well as to other female mystics. Maria Eufrasia's images appear to us, therefore, as refreshingly sincere, unsophisticated and direct, and powerfully functional in their spiritual and devotional impact.

FRANCA TRINCHIERI CAMIZ

Cronqvist, Lena
Swedish painter, graphic artist and sculptor, 1938–

Born in Karlstad, 1938. Studied at the University College of Arts, Crafts and Design, Stockholm, 1958–9, and the Royal Academy of Fine Arts, Stockholm, 1959–64; subsequently travelled widely. Married writer Göran Tunström; son the theatre producer Linus Tunström. Recipient of Unga Tecknare (Young Draughtsmen) award, Nationalmuseum, Stockholm, 1973. Lives mostly in Stockholm.

Selected Individual Exhibitions
Galeri Pierre, Stockholm: 1965, 1967, 1970
Galerie Belle, Västerås: 1971, 1974, 1977, 1978
Galleri Doktor Glas, Stockholm: 1972, 1975, 1977
Centre Culturel Suédois, Paris: 1975
Konstmuseet, Norrköping, and Moderna Museet, Stockholm: 1979
Galleri 1, Göteborg: 1984
Konstakademien, Stockholm: 1987–8 (touring retrospective)
Galleri F15, Moss: 1988 (touring)
Prins Eugens Waldemarsudde, Stockholm: 1989
Galleri Langegaarden, Bergen: 1990
Galleri Lars Bohman, Stockholm: 1991, 1994, 1995
Värmlands Museum, Karlstad: 1992 (retrospective)
Liljevalchs Konsthall, Stockholm: 1994 (touring retrospective)

Bibliography
C.-J. Bolander, ed., *Lena Cronqvist*, Västerås, 1979
Maj-Brit Wadell, "Om att söka sitt jag: Ett tema i Lena Cronqvists konst" [On finding yourself: A theme in the art of Lena Cronqvist], *Konsthistorisk Tidskrift*, lv, 1986, pp.27–37 (with English summary)
Sune Nordgren, *Lena Cronqvist*, Århus: Kalejdoskop, 1990
Lena Cronqvist: Målningar, 1964–94 [Lena Cronqvist: Paintings, 1964–94]), exh. cat., Galleri Lars Bohman, Stockholm, 1994
Lena Cronqvist: Teckningar, 1969–79 [Lena Cronqvist: Drawings, 1969–79]), exh. cat., Galleri Lars Bohman, Stockholm 1994
Swedish Samples: A Conversation on Contemporary Art. AICA Congress, 1994, Trelleborg, 1994
Lena Cronqvist: Skulpturer, 1994–95 [Lena Cronqvist: Sculptures, 1994–95], exh. cat., Galleri Lars Bohman, Stockholm, 1995

In her art Lena Cronqvist has a never-ceasing link to art history, and to all the memories of her life. She creates from a chaos of impressions, and is earnest in her task. She does not copy, but uses earlier art as a resource. Her painting *The Betrothal* (1974–5; private collection) was inspired by Jan van Eyck's *Arnolfini Portrait* (1434; National Gallery, London), *Red and Green* (1986; Länsmuseet, Gävle) by Henri Matisse's *The Dance* (1911); and in her series of paintings of *Girls in New York* (1995), the girls stand on squares inspired by Piet Mondrian. Cronqvist picks out an idea and transforms it into her own paintings of daily life.

Nature is a source, an opportunity for the artist to get outside herself. Nature is wild, sensual, inspiring and enticing. *Compost Heap* (1974; Östergötlands Länsmuseum, Linköping) represents an aspect of nature in which no-one is especially interested, except artists and possibly wild animals. But Cronqvist sees beauty in nature even when an animal lies dead, as in *Foetus in the Desert Sand* (1976). She learned how to see and paint landscape from the Swedish painter Inge Schiöler, among others.

Cronqvist has travelled extensively all over the world, and has lived for several months in Mexico, Latin America, India and Egypt, as well as in Koster and Öland, two islands off the Swedish coast, and in London, Paris and New York. In the 1970s she often travelled with her husband and son. The places she visited and their atmosphere are reflected in her works.

Cronqvist: *Tell Tale II*, 1991; 144 × 117 cm.; Moderna Museet, Stockholm

When she has been unable to paint, she has done drawings, for example those published in *Mitt indiska ritblock* (My Indian sketchbook; Västerås, 1978). Ten years later, in Paris in 1988, she transformed her ideas of August Strindberg's drama *Ett drömspel* (A dream play) into graphic art. This is a series of 30 lithographs, commissioned by the Parisian publisher and gallery owner Édouard Weiss, who wanted Cronqvist's version of Strindberg's text (1916). The lithographs were also published in a catalogue when they were exhibited at the Prins Eugens Waldemarsudde, Stockholm, in 1989.

Cronqvist uses herself and her family relationships as models in her art. She concentrates on painting and drawing, but now and again also works as a sculptor. She brings the drama of her private life with all its difficulties and joys into a universal art. She has painted girls as monsters or goddesses, for example *Tell Tale II* in 1991 (see illustration), a terrible, innocent first view of a situation in which an older sister tries to drown a younger one in the blue sea. Her series of paintings from 1980 when her father lay dying in hospital, *Night Vigil* to *The Deathbed* (private collection), invites us all to share her sorrow and the necessity of parent and child being linked together, and then separated into responsible adults. Her compositions are vibrant with conflicts and held together by her wilful and bold technique.

In the autumn of 1984 Cronqvist saw two performances in Stockholm by the German choreographer Pina Bausch and the group Wuppertal Tanztheater. By that time she had painted herself through her childhood and adult life back and forth, transposing time as in a film. She was ready for the next step in life, and was struck by Bausch's intense work. She painted a series of pictures with a searching woman in focus. In *Yellow Dress* the model tries to hide in wall mirrors or go into or through them; instead she is shown from three sides. The artist seems to investigate the atmosphere and surroundings of a woman's life.

One of the pictures in Cronqvist's series of *Girls in New York* (1995) is *Girl with a Skipping-Rope* (Galleri Lars Bohman, Stockholm), a memory from her childhood, when she was six to seven years old in the 1940s. The work depicts a girl standing on her left foot on a white square, balancing with her other foot against the white square of wall, her arms outstretched and swinging a skipping-rope over her head. The little girl has a problem balancing in life, but is happy when she is standing. The grey spot next to her left foot is like life itself, it becomes whatever colour you want most. There is always a sense of contamination in Cronqvist's pictures, as in life – an unconscious danger. She also produced sculptured versions of the New York girls, first in wax and then cast into small bronze figures, happily playing around.

A gifted artist such as Cronqvist is able to make her own private experiences inexhaustible and of universal validity. Her life turns into ours. She paints what we all have inside, but do not dare to show. She has meant a lot to the younger generation of Swedish artists. Her work is represented in numerous Swedish museums, including the Nationalmuseum and Moderna Museet, Stockholm.

LENA HOLGER

Cunningham, Imogen
American photographer, 1883–1976

Born in Portland, Oregon, 12 April 1883. Studied chemistry at University of Washington, Seattle, 1903–7. Worked in Seattle studio of photographer Edward S. Curtis, 1907–9. Won scholarship to study photographic chemistry at the Technische Hochschule, Dresden, 1909. Opened portrait studio on return to Seattle, 1910. Married Roi Partridge, February 1915; son born December 1915, twin sons born 1917; divorced 1934. Moved to San Francisco, 1917. Resumed commercial portrait business, 1921; occasionally carried out assignments for *Vanity Fair* magazine, 1931–6. Founder-member, with Edward Weston and Ansel Adams, of Group f/64, San Francisco, 1932–5; participated in *Group f/64* exhibition at M.H. de Young Memorial Museum, San Francisco, 1932. Also included in the exhibitions *Film und Foto*, Deutscher Werkbund, Stuttgart, 1929, and *Photography, 1839–1937*, Museum of Modern Art, New York, 1937. Taught photography at California School of Fine Arts, San Francisco, 1947–50; San Francisco Art Institute, 1965–7 and 1973. Founded Imogen Cunningham Trust, 1975. Recipient of honorary doctorates from California College of Arts and Crafts, Oakland, 1969, and Mills College, Oakland, 1975; Guggenheim fellowship, 1970; Artist of the Year award, San Francisco Art Commission, 1973; Summa Laude Dignatus award, University of Washington, Seattle, 1974. Fellow, American Academy of Arts and Sciences, 1967. Died in San Francisco, 23 June 1976.

Selected Individual Exhibitions
Brooklyn Institute of Arts and Sciences, NY: 1914
Portland Art Museum, Oregon: 1914
M.H. de Young Memorial Museum, San Francisco: 1931, 1970
Los Angeles County Museum of Art: 1932
Dallas Art Museum: 1935
San Francisco Museum of Art: 1951, 1964
Mills College Art Gallery, Oakland: 1953
Cincinnati Museum of Art: 1956
Oakland Art Museum: 1957, 1974
International Museum of Photography, George Eastman House, Rochester, NY: 1961
Art Institute of Chicago: 1964
Henry Gallery, University of Washington, Seattle: 1965, 1974 (retrospective)
Stanford University Art Gallery, CA: 1967, 1976 (both retrospectives)
Museum of History and Technology, Smithsonian Institution, Washington, DC: 1968
California College of Arts and Crafts, Oakland: 1968
Atholl McBean Gallery, San Francisco Art Institute: 1971
Seattle Art Museum: 1971
Metropolitan Museum of Art, New York: 1973
San Francisco Art Commission "Capricorn Asunder" Gallery: 1973 (*Artist of the Year*)

Selected Writings
"Photography as a profession for women", *Arrow*, xxix/2, January 1913, pp.203–9

Bibliography

Flora Huntley Maschmedt, "Imogen Cunningham: An appreciation", *Wilson's Photographic Magazine*, li, March 1914, pp.96–9, 113–20

Minor White, "An experiment in 'reading' photographs", *Aperture*, v, 1957, pp.66–71

Edna Tartaul Daniel, ed., *Imogen Cunningham: Portraits, Ideas and Design*, Berkeley: University of California Regional Cultural History Project, 1961

Minor White, ed., *Imogen Cunningham*, Rochester, NY: Aperture, 1964

Margery Mann, "Imogen Cunningham", *Infinity*, xv, November 1966, pp.25–8

Imogen Cunningham: Photographs, 1921–1967, exh. cat., Stanford University Art Gallery, CA, 1967

Elizabeth Borden, "Imogen Cunningham", *US Camera World Annual*, 1970, pp.60–65, 206

Margery Mann, ed., *Imogen Cunningham: Photographs*, Seattle: University of Washington Press, 1970

[Bill Jay], "Imogen Cunningham", *Album*, no.5, June 1970, pp.22–38

Imogen! Imogen Cunningham Photographs, 1910–1973, exh. cat., Henry Gallery, University of Washington, Seattle, 1974

Imogen Cunningham: A Celebration, exh. cat., Stanford University Art Gallery, 1976

Margaretta Mitchell, ed., *After Ninety*, Seattle: University of Washington Press, 1977

Barnaby Conrad III, "An interview with Imogen Cunningham", *Art in America*, lxv, May–June 1977, pp.42–7

Thomas Joshua Cooper and Gerry Badger, "Imogen Cunningham: A celebration", *British Journal of Photography Annual*, 1978

Judy Dater, *Imogen Cunningham: A Portrait*, Boston: New York Graphic Society, and London: Gordon Fraser, 1979

Reclaiming Paradise: American Women Photograph the Land, exh. cat., Tweed Museum of Art, University of Minnesota, 1987

The Eclectic Spirit: Imogen Cunningham, 1883–1976, exh. cat., Glasgow Museums and Art Galleries, 1990

Amy Rule, ed., *Imogen Cunningham: Selected Texts and Bibliography*, Boston: Hall, and Oxford: Clio, 1992

Richard Lorenz, *Imogen Cunningham: Ideas Without End: A Life in Photographs*, San Francisco: Chronicle, 1993

Unpublished correspondence and writings are in the Imogen Cunningham Papers, Archives of American Art, Smithsonian Institution, Washington, DC, and the Imogen Cunningham Archives, Imogen Cunningham Trust, Berkeley, CA (the latter also contains Cunningham's original photographs and negatives).

Imogen Cunningham was one of the pre-eminent forces in 20th-century photography. Throughout her long career – she exhibited professionally from 1914 until her death in 1976 – she continued to expand the boundaries of the medium both technically and aesthetically. Cunningham majored in chemistry at the University of Washington in Seattle, where she had lived from the age of six. After graduating, she worked in the portrait studio of Edward S. Curtis, whose romanticised portrayals of Native American life had won great renown. In 1909 she travelled to Dresden to study photographic chemistry with Robert Luther at the Technische Hochschule and did research on various printing processes, the results of which she published the following year. On her trip back to Seattle, she met Alvin Langdon Coburn in London, and Alfred Stieglitz and Gertrude Käsebier (q.v.) in New York, photographers with whom she remained in professional contact for years. Other contemporaries with whom she had significant artistic dialogue included Roi Partridge (to whom she was married

from 1915 to 1934), Dorothea Lange (q.v.), Beaumont Newhall, Lisette Model (q.v.), Edward Weston and Ansel Adams.

One of Cunningham's first and most daring contributions to the field of fine art photography was her exploration of the nude male figure in the landscape. *The Bather* (1915), a nude image of her husband contemplating his reflection, Narcissus-like, at the edge of a pond, created a local scandal. But, as her biographer Richard Lorenz asserted:

> Cunningham's intention to deliberately devise shock value in her art, her willingness to transgress the boundaries of bourgeois morality, indicates a courageous, adventurous talent just beginning to bloom as well as a determination to advance the critical acceptance of photography [Lorenz 1993, p.20].

Although she experimented with "pictorial" photography – the use of the medium to echo conservative academic painting conventions – in such early works as *Marsh, Early Morning (Marsh at Dawn)* (1905–6) and in the hazy focus of *The Bather*, Cunningham was soon drawn to "straight" photography. With Weston and Adams, among others, she founded the influential Group f/64, a name chosen to indicate their shared preference for realistic photography executed with small apertures to achieve detailed images. The *Magnolia Blossom* (1925), which draws the viewer into intimate, erotic encounter with the undulating, fleshy petals of a single white blossom, recalls both Weston's clarity of detail and the vital, luxuriant canvases of sensual flowers by Georgia O'Keeffe (q.v.). (It should be noted that Cunningham did not meet O'Keeffe until a trip to New York in the 1930s.)

In the 1930s Cunningham began to photograph celebrities. She started with Martha Graham, the innovative expressionist dancer and choreographer, who found Cunningham to be the first photographer with whom she could collaborate. Of the two portraits that appeared in *Vanity Fair* magazine in December 1931, *Martha Graham 44* positions the dancer shadowing her lowered face with raised, bent arms, as brilliant light angles across her bare breasts. Later in the decade, the magazine commissioned Cunningham to photograph such Hollywood stars as James Cagney, Spencer Tracy and Cary Grant. The stark, precise realism of these images stands in marked contradistinction to the idealisation of most studio photographs.

In 1934 the University of California professor Paul Taylor invited Cunningham and Dorothea Lange to provide visual documentation for his research on migrant workers. The invitation led to what Cunningham called her "stolen pictures", images of the disenfranchised in American culture, such as the two troubled youths who loiter in a doorway in *Rebecca's Boys, Hume, Virginia* (1934) and the *Watchers of the Evangel Meeting, San Francisco* (1936). At the same time, Cunningham began experimenting with double exposures and photomontage. Certainly this was influenced by Cubism and other avant-garde movements in Europe, as evidenced in the overlaid multiple views of the head in *Gertrude Stein, San Francisco 2* (1935).

Although rarely aligned with organised feminist groups, as early as 1913 Cunningham had published an article entitled "Photography as a profession for women" in which she

Cunningham: *Self-Portrait, Denmark*, 1961; Imogen Cunningham Trust, Berkeley, California

wondered "Why women for so many years should have been supposed to be fitted only to the arts and industries of the home ...". Referring to the early years of her marriage, when she brought up her young sons, Cunningham later said of herself:

> she had a skill with the camera, which she was not willing to sacrifice to maternity, so she turned her camera to use and photographed the things she had around her – her own children of course and plants that she cultivated. It is quite easy to do a bit of gardening work and yet attend children. It is not as easy to do good photographic work, but it can be done. She did both [interview with Edna Tartaul Daniel for the Regional Cultural History Project, University of California, Berkeley, June 1959].

Cunningham's letters during the break-up of her marriage indicate that she resented her husband's traditional gender expectations, and she chose to live independent of a male partner for the rest of her life. In her seventies, that is, in the 1950s, the artist joined the San Francisco Society of Women Artists and turned increasingly to women's subjects. As Lorenz noted of her *Pregnant Nude* (1959), which he described as "startling" in its objectivity: "Cunningham's choice of the pregnant nude as a subject – during a decade when the word was not even allowed to be spoken on television – was a refreshingly candid challenge to the societal taboos of the Eisenhower years" (Lorenz 1993, p.50).

Imogen Cunningham continued to create compelling photographs throughout the 1960s and 1970s. Her *Self-Portrait, Denmark* (1961; see illustration) presents a dark reflection of the aged artist, her face partially obscured by two fashionable girdles displayed in a shop window. A canny commentary on how women's very identities are veiled by the constraints of culturally imposed ideals of beauty, the *Self-Portrait* demonstrates the pertinence of the text on the Chinese chop or seal with which the artist, later in life, described and labelled her oeuvre: "Ideas without End". (Prints of all cited works are in the collection of the Imogen Cunningham Trust, Berkeley, California.)

BETTY ANN BROWN

D

Dahl-Wolfe, Louise
American photographer, 1895–1989

Born Louise Emma Augusta Dahl in San Francisco, 19 November 1895. Enrolled at the San Francisco Institute of Art, 1914, studying design and colour under Rudolph Schaeffer, painting under Frank Van Sloan. Worked as an electric sign designer, met photographer Annie Brigman and took up photography, 1921. Studied interior decorating and architecture in New York, 1923. Became assistant to Beth Armstrong of the San Francisco interior decorating firm Armstrong, Carter and Kenyon, 1924. Travelled in Europe with photographer Consuelo Kanaga, 1927; bought movie camera and made films in France and Italy. Met sculptor Meyer "Mike" Wolfe in Tunisia; married him in New York, 1928; he died 1985. Returned to San Francisco and became a professional photographer, shooting rooms designed by interior decorators, 1929. Spent summers in Gatlingburg and took portraits of Tennessee mountain people, 1932. Moved to New York, did freelance photography for *Woman's Home Companion*, Saks Fifth Avenue and Bonwit Teller, 1933. Secured Crown Rayon advertising account, 1934. Staff photographer for *Harper's Bazaar*, 1936–58; travelled widely. Took photographs for *Sports Illustrated*, 1957–62, and *Vogue*, 1959. Retired from photography, 1960. Moved to Frenchtown, New Jersey, 1961. Recipient of honorary doctorate, Moore College of Art, Philadelphia, 1987. Died in Ridgewood, New Jersey, 11 December 1989.

Principal Exhibitions
Museum of Modern Art, New York: 1937 (*Photography, 1839–1937*)
Country Art Gallery, Westbury, Long Island: 1965 (with Meyer Wolfe)
Grey Art Gallery, New York University: 1983 (retrospective)
Cheekwood Fine Arts Center, Nashville: 1984 (retrospective)
Museum of Contemporary Photography of Columbia College, Chicago: 1985 (retrospective)
National Museum of Women in the Arts, Washington, DC: 1987 (retrospective)

Selected Writings
A Photographer's Scrapbook, New York: St Martin's Press, and London: Quartet, 1984

Bibliography
Margaretta K. Mitchell, *Recollections: Ten Women of Photography*, New York: Viking, 1979
Vicki Goldberg, "Profile: Louise Dahl-Wolfe", *American Photographer*, June 1981, pp.38–47
Owen Edwards, "Exhibitions: Dahl-Wolfe was the universal fashion photographer", *American Photographer*, December 1983, pp.24–31
Louise Dahl-Wolfe: A Retrospective Exhibition, exh. cat., National Museum of Women in the Arts, Washington, DC, 1987
John A. Cuadrado, "The fashion image: Louise Dahl-Wolfe", *Architectural Digest*, September 1988, pp.66–80

Louise Dahl-Wolfe is best known for her work as a fashion photographer. During her long association with *Harper's Bazaar*, she published 86 covers, some 600 colour photographs and thousands of black-and-white shots. She was at the height of her success in the 1940s, and is credited with helping to introduce a new naturalness into fashion photography, "The New American Look" (Goldberg 1981, p.42). She used models who were lithe and strong, who even smiled, as opposed to photographers of the 1930s who favoured an icy artificiality, featuring models in stiff poses who wore "blank, inhuman" masks (*idem*). Despite Dahl-Wolfe's success as a fashion photographer, she admitted candidly that she was a "frustrated painter" (*A Photographer's Scrapbook* 1984, p.2) and that, "if left to [her] own devices" at the outset of her career, would have preferred photographing "still lifes and portraits" (*ibid.*, p.19).

The daughter of Norwegian-born parents who settled in San Francisco, she was named Louise Emma Augusta Dahl (LEAD) because her mother "heard it was good luck if a child's name spelled a word" (*ibid.*, p.1). Like many women photographers, Dahl-Wolfe began as an art student (at the San Francisco Institute of Art) hoping to become a painter, or failing that, an interior decorator. She first became interested in the possibilities of the camera after an invitation to the studio of Pictorialist Annie Brigman. "Bowled over" by Brigman's allegorical nudes posed in the High Sierras and among Monterrey cypresses, she and her friends, who had all decided to become photographers, posed "in the nude for each other". She began by using a Brownie box camera and had her "film developed at the drugstore" (*ibid.*, p.4). She practised and experimented – even devising her own enlarger – and graduated to better and better equipment. By 1929 she was a professional photographer working in San Francisco and shooting rooms designed by interior decorators. She also did portraits of Tennessee mountain people when she spent the summer of 1932 there with her husband (the following year she published a portrait of a mountain woman, Mrs Ramsay, in *Vanity Fair*). It was only after she moved to New York in 1933 that Dahl-Wolfe decided to give fashion photography a try. In order to train herself in the new genre, she arranged with a friend who worked at Milgrim's department store to shoot the store's showroom models and clothes in exchange for photographs. The challenge was to devise lighting and exposures that would make 40-year-old models appear "chic, elegant, beautiful, and yet natural" (*ibid.*, p.19). In 1934 she landed her first advertising account (Crown Rayon) for which she was paid $100 for one advertisement a week.

Dahl-Wolfe's independent nature, no doubt encouraged by her family, was evident in the personal and career choices she made. After spotting American artist Meyer Wolfe from a train window while travelling in North Africa, for example, she thought "Gee, that's for me" (*ibid.*, p.7), and married him that same year in New York (1928). During the Depression, she turned down a secure position with Frank Crowninshield, editor of *Vanity Fair*, and later declined a retainer of $40,000 from the advertising executive J. Walter Thompson because she "could never work in someone else's studio ... I need my own surroundings" (*ibid.*, p.13). "I have to have my own place where I can walk out if I feel like it. There's nothing like liberty" (Goldberg 1981, p.40).

Carmel Snow was the editor of *Harper's Bazaar* when Dahl-Wolf began her career at the magazine in 1936. The photographer described Mrs Snow as "the greatest magazine editor ever", and "felt fortunate" (*A Photographer's Scrapbook*, p.21) to have worked under her. Mrs Snow assembled a talented staff, trusted them and, most importantly for the fiercely independent Dahl-Wolfe, did not interfere with their work. She had creative freedom and control over her photographs – how they were to be cropped, etc. – the only thing art director Alexey Brodovitch told the photographer was "which pages would face one another" (*idem*).

A fashion photographer is not a free agent. The job is first to help sell a garment or its designer's ideas, but it is also to define, transmit and help create current notions of what is beautiful, or at least, what is chic. For Dahl-Wolfe this task became particularly difficult if the designer was "third-rate" or the dress to be photographed was uninspired or shapeless. Dahl-Wolfe attributed her ability to overcome such limitations to her art school training, where she learned to solve problems in design, composition and light and to appreciate the differences between male and female bodies in form and movement. She traced her keen sense of colour, which she studied "like the scales of a piano", to Rudolph Schaeffer's course, which was a "profound experience" (*ibid.*, p.2) for her. Indeed, the photographer is particularly noted for her colour images, which are subtle and often luxurious. One example, offering up a feast of colour, is a photograph of 1949 showing a svelte model wearing a ruby velvet evening suit with long fuchsia gloves and heels. The figure, spotlighted from the left, is silhouetted against a sumptuous tapestry of huge off-white and rose-coloured flowers and pale green leaves, set against a deep black

ground (*The Covert Look*, 1949; Fashion Institute of Technology, New York).

A love of the fine arts is evident in Dahl-Wolfe's work. She posed models in the Museum of Modern Art, New York, next to works that would complement the line or intention of a dress. One model is seen contemplating Brancusi sculptures (*Schiaparelli's Tunic Dress*, 1938); another, bending forward squeezing her long hair dry, is photographed in a Japanese bathroom (*Japanese Bath*, 1954), which was reproduced in Dahl-Wolfe's studio after an example in the museum. Inspired by Matisse, her sculptor-husband Mike (who was a great help and support to her in her career) made cut-outs within which a model is framed – her back to the viewer so as not to distract from the photograph's overall design. A model in a bathing suit stands near a copy of the Medici Venus in a pose echoing that of the statue. And there are references to Toulouse-Lautrec, Rubens, Paolo Veronese and others.

Louise Dahl-Wolfe was also an accomplished portraitist. She created memorable images of such literary figures as Christopher Isherwood, W.H. Auden, Carson McCullers, Eudora Welty, Truman Capote, Jean Stafford, Dylan Thomas, Marianne Moore and Randall Jarrell, when *Harper's Bazaar* began to publish new fiction. She also photographed noted Hollywood figures – Orson Welles, Paul Muni, Tallulah Bankhead, Spencer Tracy and others – and it was her cover of March 1943 that introduced Betty (Lauren) Bacall to Hollywood. (Louise Dahl-Wolfe's colour work is at the Fashion Institute of Technology, New York; her black-and-white images are at the Center for Creative Photography, University of Arizona, Tucson.)

HELEN GOODMAN

Damer, Anne Seymour
British amateur sculptor, 1748–1828

Born 1748, to Field Marshal Henry Seymour Conway and Lady Caroline Ailesbury. During her parents' sojourns abroad, lived under the care of writer and patron Horace Walpole. Married the Hon. John Damer, 1767; he committed suicide in 1776, leaving debts of some £7000. Subsequently began serious study of sculpture, having a jointure of £2500 a year and no children. Honorary Exhibitor at the Royal Academy. Lived at Strawberry Hill, Twickenham, as Walpole's residuary legatee, 1797–1811, also maintaining a town house in London with studios at both sites. Supported the Whig cause throughout her life, canvassing in the Westminster election (1784) for Charles James Fox. Produced Mary Berry's play *Fashionable Friends*, 1801. Visited France with Berry during the Peace of Amiens (1802) and presented Napoleon with her bust of *Fox*. Lived at York House, Twickenham, from 1811, continuing to work in studio there despite failing health. Died at London house in Upper Brook Street, 28 May 1828; buried in Sundridge, Kent, with her sculptor's tools and the ashes of her favourite dog.

Damer: *Bust of Isis*, exhibited Royal Academy, *c.1789*; Victoria and Albert Museum, London

Principal Exhibitions

Royal Academy, London: 1784–5, 1787–90, 1795, 1799–1800, 1803–6, 1810, 1813–14, 1816, 1820
Leverean Museum, London: 1794 (statue of George III)

Selected Writings

Belmour, 1801 (novel)

Bibliography

Horace Walpole, *Anecdotes of Painting*, ed. James Dallaway, iv, London, 1827
Allan Cunningham, *The Lives of the Most Eminent British Painters, Sculptors and Architects*, iv, London: Murray, 1830
Mary Berry, *Extracts of the Journals and Correspondence of Miss Berry*, ed. Theresa Lewis, 3 vols, London: Longman, 1865; reprinted New York: AMS Press, 1971
Percy Noble, *Anne Seymour Damer: A Woman of Art and Fashion, 1748–1828*, London: Kegan Paul Trench Trubner, 1908
Mary Berry, *The Berry Papers: Being the Correspondence Hitherto Unpublished of Mary and Agnes Berry, 1763–1852*, ed. Lewis Melville, London: Lane, 1914
Rupert Gunnis, *Dictionary of British Sculptors, 1660–1851*, 2nd edition, London: Abbey Library, 1968
Susan Benforado, *Anne Seymour Damer (1748–1828), Sculptor*, PhD dissertation, University of New Mexico, Albuquerque, 1986
Margaret Whinney, *Sculpture in Britain, 1530–1830*, revised edition by John Physick, London and New York: Penguin, 1988

Anne Seymour Damer's output of sculpture was immensely varied but always exemplified her pursuit of the classical ideal. While her efforts to pursue this art were lampooned in popular prints and derided by contemporaries such as Joseph Farington, she was, nevertheless, the only woman sculptor to be included in Cunningham's *Lives of the Most Eminent … British Sculptors …*, published in 1830. Here she was placed alongside Banks, Flaxman and others, and although the author criticised her work, hinting that it was often carved by others and that it lacked "poetic feeling", he singled out her achievement "as a woman" in this pantheon of the British school. By her death in 1828 she was established as the leading woman sculptor of her day. While there were other women who had successful professional careers as makers of sculpture in wax or artificial stone, Damer was recognised in Britain for her single-minded pursuit of the "high" style. She was an Honorary Exhibitor at the Royal Academy exhibitions, where she showed 32 works; the title denoted her "amateur" status, appropriate to her class. There is little evidence that she sold her work for profit or pursued business interests as was the case with other contemporary professional sculptors. She was therefore not constrained by the demands of patrons or by the need to earn a living from her art.

Damer's contributions to the Royal Academy exhibitions included 20 ideal and idealised portrait busts. One of the earliest of these was her marble head of *Lady Melbourne* (1784; private collection), a skilful rendition that was praised by Erasmus Darwin in *The Economy of Vegetation* (1791). Several of her publicly exhibited works represented actors and actresses and included *Mrs Siddons as Melpomene* (before 1794; untraced), *Mrs Elizabeth Farren as Thalia* (c.1788; National Portrait Gallery, London) and *Master Betty* (exh. Royal Academy 1805; untraced). She also sculpted busts of *Admiral Nelson* (1798; several versions, earliest terracotta untraced) and *Joseph Banks* (British Museum, London), the former being taken from life during a stay in Naples. An ideal bust of *Isis* (exh. Royal Academy c.1789; see illustration), which she executed in a severe "Greek" style and carved in Greek marble, is a prime example of her ability to respond to the demands of the true and correct style. An early example of her Neo-classicism is the *Self-Portrait* (1778; Uffizi, Florence) that she gave to the royal gallery in Florence and which was placed in the hall of Ancient and Modern Painters; the sole example of a sculpted self-portrait in this important collection. For Boydell's Shakespeare Gallery she made two terracotta reliefs (untraced) that placed her work in the company of leading British exponents of history painting. Engravings after these lost works show her assimilation of Neo-classicism in their representation of scenes from *Antony and Cleopatra* and *Coriolanus*.

There are few remaining examples of her public sculpture, apart from the statue of *George III* (1794; ht 2.43 m.) made for the Register House, Edinburgh. This severe, almost schematic representation of the monarch was alleviated by the introduction of a metal crown and sceptre. She was reputed to have modelled and cast in bronze a statue of *King Joseph I of Portugal* (1791) in Lisbon. A colossal statue of *Apollo* (c.1792; destroyed 1809), executed for Drury Lane Theatre, London, is now known only through contemporary prints. Smaller-scale works included terracotta and marble versions of animal sculptures, for which she was over-praised by Walpole and for which she is now chiefly remembered. These are, however, misleading if understood to be representative of Damer's oeuvre as a whole, which is dominated by a more austere response to the classical ideal.

As the only child of an aristocratic family, Damer grew up in a privileged environment that was predominantly Whig. She was reputedly challenged to take up sculpture by her father's secretary, David Hume. Her education as a sculptor was the result of private tuition, notably from Giuseppe Ceracchi, who made a full-length statue of her as the *Muse of Sculpture* (c.1777; British Museum), and John Bacon RA. She also had anatomy lessons from Dr William Cumberland Cruikshank. Her support for Charles James Fox was well known and in 1802 she presented Napoleon with a plaster bust of the hero (untraced), which was followed by a marble version in 1812 (Louvre, Paris). She corresponded with the Empress Josephine, with whom she exchanged botanical specimens. She was friendly with Princess Caroline of Brunswick (who practised sculpture as an accomplishment art), executing a terracotta bust of her in 1814 (Ranger's House, London).

Horace Walpole, one of Damer's most enthusiastic supporters, encouraged her early interest in sculpture and was to make her his residuary executrix. Through Walpole she met Mary Berry with whom she developed a close and passionate friendship, recorded in letters and journals of the 1790s. It is not known that they had a physical relationship, but her reputed lesbianism had been made public in the 1770s by the publication of *A Sapphick Epistle from Jack Cavendish to the Honourable and Most Beautiful Mrs D.* (c.1770).

Damer was well-educated, speaking several languages and, like Mary Berry, was tutored in ancient Greek and Latin. In many ways the range of her intellectual and literary pursuits links her with the Bluestockings. These included: the publication of a novel, *Belmour*; her association with the writer

Joanna Baillie as well as with Agnes and Mary Berry; and her friendship with Princess Daschkow, whose salon in Rome attracted several artists including Gavin Hamilton. Damer performed in amateur theatre, both at the Duke of Richmond's private theatre and that at Strawberry Hill, Twickenham. She made many lengthy trips abroad, travelling in France, Portugal, Spain and Italy. During these she set up studios to continue working on her sculpture. In Naples, as a close friend of Sir William Hamilton, she was able to persuade Nelson to sit for his portrait in 1799, following his victory at the battle of the Nile. This became her best-known work – she presented the City of London with a version (Guildhall, London) following Nelson's death at Trafalgar in 1805 when she took the opportunity of offering to make the Guildhall monument to him at no charge. Thomas Hope, following its inclusion in the Royal Academy exhibition of 1804, praised Damer's achievement in the *Morning Post*. Here he described the bust as having "that very breadth of style ... discarding every incidental minutiae of feature". Casts of Damer's bust of *Nelson* were advertised in the newspapers in November 1805 and he was to be the subject of her last sculpture, a bronze bust (Royal Collection) for the Duke of Clarence, completed shortly before her death.

ALISON YARRINGTON

Danko(-Alekseyenko), Natalya (Yakovlevna)

Russian ceramist and sculptor, 1892–1942

Born in Tiflis (now Tbilisi, Georgia), 1892. Attended the Stroganov School of Art and Industrial Design, Moscow, 1900–02; studied at State Art School, Vilnius, and in the studio of Yalmar Yanson, 1906–8. Employed in the workshop of Marya Dillon and in studio of sculptor Leonid Sherwood (Leonty Shervud), St Petersburg, 1908–9. Worked under sculptor Vasily Kuznetsov from 1909; assistant to Kuznetsov at Imperial Porcelain Factory from 1914; head of sculpture workshop at renamed State (later Lomonosov) Porcelain Manufactory, 1919–41. Died in Irbit, Sverdlovsk, 18 March 1942.

Principal Exhibitions

Individual
Leningrad: 1929, 1946 (retrospective)

Group
Esposizione Nazionale, Rome: 1911
Esposizione Internazionale, Turin: 1911
Exposition Internationale des Arts Décoratifs et Industriels Modernes, Paris: 1925 (gold medal)
Trade and Industrial Fair, Lyon: 1926
Art and Design Exhibition, Monza: 1927 (gold medal)
State Russian Museum, Leningrad: 1932 (*Artists of the RSFSR over 15 Years, 1917–1932*)
Exposition Internationale, Paris: 1937 (gold medal)

Bibliography

I. Grabar, *Danko-Alekseyenko*, Moscow, 1934
Yu. Ebin, *N.Ya. Danko, 1892–1942*, Moscow, 1955
Yu.M. Ovsyannikov, *Skulptor v krasnom khalate* [Sculptor in red overalls], Moscow, 1965
L'altra metà dell'avanguardia, 1910–1940: Pittrici e scultrici nei movimenti delle avanguardie storiche, exh. cat., Palazzo Reale, Milan, and elsewhere, 1980
Art into Production: Soviet Textiles, Fashion and Ceramics, 1917–1935, exh. cat., Museum of Modern Art, Oxford, 1984
David Elliott and Valery Dudakov, *100 Years of Russian Art, 1889–1989*, London: Lund Humphries, 1989
Nina Lobanov-Rostovsky, *Revolutionary Ceramics: Soviet Porcelain, 1917–1927*, London: Studio Vista, and New York: Rizzoli, 1990
Agitation zum Glück: Sowjetische Kunst der Stalinzeit, exh. cat., Documenta-Halle, Kassel, and elsewhere, 1993

Natalya Danko was responsible for the revival of the production of porcelain figures in Russia after the Revolution, adapting a taste for 18th-century-style table pieces and figurines to Socialist aims and a feel for the life of the people, in simplistic, optimistic propaganda pieces.

The political interests that were to be so important to her work were derived from her childhood in a family of political revolutionaries in Tiflis. She studied in the St Petersburg studio of the sculptor Vasily Kuznetsov, working on his sculptures for the façades of buildings such as the Azov-Don Trading Bank (now the Central Telegraph), but she felt uncomfortable with the "bourgeois" nature of the commissions. When Kuznetsov moved to the Imperial Porcelain Manufactory in 1914 she went as his assistant, and considered that her artistic career began when she discovered porcelain.

The Mir Iskusstva (World of Art) movement had been responsible for something of a revival in the production of porcelain figurines, so popular in the 18th century. Danko produced her first figures in 1914 (surtout-de-table with dancers), followed in 1915 by *Woman with a Parrot* (in collaboration with Kuznetsov), but these were largely elegant pieces, still influenced by the traditions of the World of Art. As she mastered the new technique, however, and studied the clay statues of traditional Russian folk art, she rejected the training of Kuznetsov and Yevgeny Lansere and produced her first independent works (*Dancing Women*, 1916), revealing her own tastes and character in the link with serf art, the desire to reflect the life and energy of ordinary people in her depictions of buxom women rather than elegant ladies. From early in her career, Danko made the decision – perhaps influenced by her experience in working with monumental sculpture – not to paint her figures herself, feeling that this interfered with her approach to the material. All her figurines throughout her career were painted by her sister, Yelena Danko, who joined her at the manufactory.

The Revolution wrought radical changes in the production of the factory, and Danko's approach was in keeping with the political emphasis of the new regime. In 1919 she became head of the sculpture studio of the newly renamed State (later Lomonosov) Porcelain Manufactory. Political concerns played a major role in determining what she designed, with an initial demand for everyday objects that would be affordable to the populace (butter dishes, sugar bowls, an umbrella handle in the form of an odalisque, brooches, pipes), but perhaps her most startling work from this period was the openly agitational *Reds and Whites* chess set (1922; see illustration), in which the white king was a figure of death, the knight an imperial Hussar

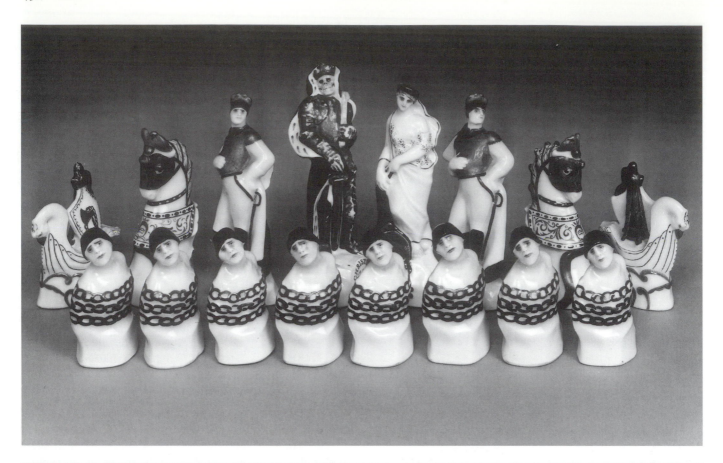

Danko: *Whites* and *Reds* chess set, 1922; Manchester City Art Galleries

and the pawns were slaves, while the red king was a heroic worker, the knight a Red Army soldier and the pawns happy peasants with sickles and sheafs of rye.

This made its political point somewhat heavy-handedly and had few artistic pretensions, but Danko seems genuinely to have had an implicit belief in the political aspect of her work. It was through a series of figures of popular dancers such as *Nijinsky* (1920) and *Anna Pavlova as the Dying Swan* (1923) that she gradually developed a surer feeling for the material, balancing its finesse and fragility with her images of solid, earthy characters. By 1933–4 the revolutionary theme almost totally dominated her output, changing its emphasis as the new country changed: she moved from the purely political subject (*Sailor with Banner*, 1921) to the expression of inner fervour being directed towards the building of a new, fair society of equal rights and opportunities (*Working Woman Making a Speech*, 1923; *Building Worker*, 1927). Socialist aims were depicted not just in her busts of *Lenin* (1925), but also in the bookstand *Liquidation of Illiteracy: Lessons by Radio* (1932).

Much of this work was produced for propaganda purposes and was aimed not at Soviet citizens but for show at the European international exhibitions. This was highlighted when White emigrés smashed a case of Soviet porcelain at the Brussels exhibition. None the less, Danko's works were highly popular both at home and abroad and their importance was recognised by the government in terms of propaganda and the money they brought in, and in 1925 she was put in charge of the export of artistic porcelain to Europe and America.

The decree of 1932, by the Central Committee of the Communist Party, which effectively imposed Socialist Realism as the only acceptable style of art, did not present Danko with any problems. She simply moved ever closer to representations of the life of ordinary people, both peasants and workers. The darling of the masses, in the 1930s Danko produced series of portrait figurines of actors from the Comedy Theatre in scenes from plays, often watching performances dozens of times and modelling as she sat in the auditorium, her sister making sketches nearby. But she appealed not only to town dwellers, and in 1934 on receipt of a request from a peasant on a collective farm to do something for their Party meeting room, she created a typically simplistic image of a cowherd: a fair, happy girl with a cow and calves, whose carefree smile reveals that work under the new regime is honourable and a joy, not heavy drudgery as under tsarism. This marked the start of a series of pieces on rural subjects.

The Stalinist architectural style of the 1930s brought new demands for the wide use of sculptural elements using a variety of materials. Danko was commissioned in 1936 to produce porcelain capitals for the Kievskaya Station of the Moscow Metro, as well as glazed porcelain bas-reliefs (1.5 m. high) with folk musicians and dancers from the republics of the Soviet Union for the Ploshchad Sverdlova Station. The latter presented serious technical problems in terms of size and how they were displayed, and both the bas-reliefs and fruit swags are lost in the setting, creating the impression of mass-produced ornament rather than individual works of art.

The unsuccessful return to monumental work convinced Danko that she was right in her choice of preferred medium, and she was much happier – both politically and artistically – in producing a series of table pieces to celebrate the issuing of a new Constitution in 1936 (*Soviet Constitution in Uzbekistan*, 1937; series of six multi-figure groups), and objects that affirmed the victory of Socialist ideas (vase, *Right to Education*; ashtray, *Right to Rest*). These later works were highly coloured, partly reflecting a change in the nature of the subject, partly the demands of the market. Early in 1940 an experimental laboratory for artistic glass was opened and the first work they put into production was, predictably, a piece by Danko, a small bust of a *Red Army Soldier*. But with the outbreak of war and the start of the Siege of Leningrad in 1941 all work at the factory was stopped, and Danko died of starvation and exhaustion in early 1942.

CATHERINE PHILLIPS

Darboven, Hanne
German artist, 1941–

Born in Munich, 29 April 1941. Studied at the Hochschule für Bildende Kunst, Hamburg, under Wilhelm Grimm and Almir Mavignier, 1963–5. Lived in New York, 1966–8. Recipient of Edwin Scharff prize, 1986. Lives in Hamburg.

Selected Individual Exhibitions
Galerie Konrad Fischer, Düsseldorf: 1967, 1968, 1970, 1971, 1978
Galerie Art & Project, Amsterdam: 1970, 1974, 1976 (with Roy Colmer)
Westfälischer Kunstverein, Münster: 1971 (retrospective)
Leo Castelli Gallery, New York: 1973, 1974, 1976, 1978 (in conjunction with Sperone-Westwater, New York, and Galerie Konrad Fischer, Düsseldorf), 1980, 1981, 1984, 1986, 1988, 1990
Kabinett für Aktuelle Kunst, Bremerhaven: 1974, 1975
Stedelijk Museum, Amsterdam: 1975
Galerie Liliane et Michel Durand-Dessert, Paris: 1976, 1979
Galerie Paul Maenz, Cologne: 1979, 1987, 1989
Städtisches Museum Abteiberg, Mönchengladbach: 1983
Musée d'Art Moderne de la Ville de Paris: 1986
Kunstraum München, Munich: 1988
Renaissance Society, University of Chicago: 1989
Goldie Paley Gallery, Moore College of Art and Design, Philadelphia: 1990

Selected Writings
Ein Jahrhundert, Amsterdam, 1971
"*Atta Roll*", Lucerne: Kunstmuseum, 1975
New York Diary, New York: Castelli/Sperone, 1976

Bibliography
Hanne Darboven: Een maand, een jaar, een eeuw [Hanne Darboven: A month, a year, a century], exh. cat., Stedelijk Museum, Amsterdam, 1975
Hanne Darboven: Bismarckzeit, exh. cat., Rheinisches Landesmuseum, Bonn, 1979
L. Arici, *Hanne Darboven: Schreibzeit/Existenzzeit: Von der Zahl der Weltbewältigung*, dissertation, University of Zürich, 1980
Donald B. Kuspit, "System as desire: Hanne Darboven", *Art in America*, lxviii, Summer 1980, pp.118–19
Amine Hasse, "Hanne Darboven", *Gespräche mit Künstlern*, Cologne, 1981
Annelie Pohlen, "Hanne Darboven's time: The content of consciousness", *Artforum*, xxi, April 1983, pp.52–3

Darboven: *24 Chants (Gesänge – B Form)*, 1974; ink on paper; 48 panels; Stedelijk Museum, Amsterdam

Hanne Darboven: "Histoire de la Culture", 1980/1983: "24 chants", exh. cat., Musée d'Art Moderne de la Ville de Paris, 1986

Coosje van Bruggen, "Today crossed out", *Artforum*, xxvi, January 1988, pp.70–73

Hanne Darboven: Primitive Zeit/Uhrzeit – Primitive Time/Clock Time, exh. cat., Goldie Paley Gallery, Moore College of Art and Design, Philadelphia, 1990 (contains extensive bibliography)

Isabelle Graw, "Marking time: Time and writing in the work of Hanne Darboven", *Artscribe International*, no.79, 1990, pp.68–71

Hanne Darboven: Die Geflügelte Erde Requiem, exh. cat., Deichtorhallen, Hamburg, 1991

Hanne Darboven, exh. cat., Kunsthalle, Basel, 1991

Hanne Darboven, exh. cat., Goethe Institute, London, 1994

Hanne Darboven writes. Since the end of the 1960s she has written not poetic, literary texts, but visual art. She writes numbers, in figures or letters, by hand or on a machine, and copies out long texts, adding images from daily life collected over the years. Although Darboven herself claims not to read: "I write but don't read", her work allows itself to be read, which is to say that the eye makes its way through the image. Through writing she measures time: the date, the time taken by the writing, the time required for contemplating the whole and the time of history.

Darboven removes from numbers their function as denotating quantities or units; from texts, their function as simple interpretations; and from words, their function as a currency of meaning. Numbers and letters become drawing. They stand by themselves, not serving as signs for anything outside themselves. A strict sense of order and an almost obsessive discipline underlie her work. It is therefore not surprising that Darboven's first training was not in the visual arts but in music. Since 1979 she has written musical compositions and scores that, like Bach's fugues, are based on a mathematical system and a clearly articulated harmonic rhythm. *24 Chants*

– *B Form* (1974; see illustration) leads ultimately to *Epic-Musical-Didactic Work for Peace – Beginning '80* (1980), which contains political quotations and musical notes, written as numbers.

After her studies in Hamburg, in 1965 Darboven left for New York, driven there by the need to separate herself from post-war Germany. She became friends with such artists as Carl André and Sol LeWitt, through whose efforts she had her first solo exhibition in 1967 at Konrad Fischer in Düsseldorf. Once in New York she produced the graphite *Constructions* (1966), linear, geometric constructions on graph paper, in which the printed lines were as important as the drawn ones. The rules underlying the sequences of rectangular and square compartments (*Kästchen*) that are built up are explained in the margin or on separate sheets; these are the indices. *Existence 66–68: 1st Part*, a work also begun in New York, is a collection of diaries in which Darboven has made notes – practical, personal and aesthetic – on her thoughts and actions. The significance of the diaries lies in the fact that from them emerges the idea of time and space combining with each other: "I thought of dates, since we concern ourselves on a daily basis with the sense or nonsense of things" (Darboven in conversation with Amine Haase, quoted in Haase 1981). Since then the word "Heute" (Today) has begun to occur in her work, struck through to register past time.

Although the *Constructions* were still reminiscent of diagrams, since 1968 the numbers themselves, as sign and as meaning, have become the material for Darboven's representations. In *A Month* (1968; paper and ink; 31 panels, each 180×40 cm.), *A Year* (1974; paper and ink; 31 panels, each 180×40 cm.) and *A Century* (1970–73; various subdivisions, paper, typescript, ink) she adds up the days of the year: for example, the number of the day, the month and the last two numbers of the year. The result is written in figures or letters, or else each unit is rendered as a *Kästchen*, symbolised by the letter K. The date 3.1.74, for instance, becomes 15K. She also uses U-shapes to draw the units, an abstract manner of writing without letters. By adding up this data she discovers that within one century a particular result occurs more often than any other, and that the rising and falling of the numbers thus obtained runs diagonally. Many variations on this *Numerical Language* occur in her work. Besides these, since the 1970s Darboven has also developed the *Word Language* and the *Pictorial Language*, systems of references to things that concern her. To register the distinction between quotations and her own thoughts or additions she uses the word *Gedankenstrich*, or the sign " – ", a dash.

Darboven's most distinguished works from the 1970s and 1980s consist of critical examinations of Western history, as is evident from their subjects/titles: *Odyssey* (1971), *For J.P. Sartre* (1975), *In the Time of Bismarck* (1978), *For Rainer Maria Fassbinder* (1982–3), *Cultural History, 1880–1983* (1980–83), *Evolution –86–* (1986) and *Primitive Time/Clock Time* (1990). In her most important works, *Time of Writing* (1975–80) and *Cultural History, 1880–1983*, Darboven combines the personal with the universal, and individual with world history. *In the Time of Bismarck*, of more than 900 pages, is an attempt to understand history, in this case the history of Germany; it is also a reflection on the universal history of humanity. Darboven connects the era of Bismarck, 1850–90, with 1978, the year of the work's creation. Biographical sketches of Bismarck and his political opponent August Bebel are combined with carefully selected quotations on political morality from Ludwig Reiners's biography of Bismarck, and with fragments characterising the social and cultural climate of the time from Rudolf Malsch's cultural history. A text by Willy Brandt from the political review *Sozialdemokratmagazin* on Bismarck's anti-social legislation is also included. By copying these fragments of text, Darboven possesses and reflects on them. The third part of the work consists of a "documentary": "insignificant" photographs that give an insight into daily life and culture. Her *Evolution –86–* of 1986, 500 pages in 100 frames with combinations of *Pictorial Language* and *Numerical Language*, gives pictorial form to evolution using historical documents, not represented heroically but prosaically, for example, the invention of a lavatory seat. In this way Darboven makes it clear that history may be documented not only from a universal, spiritual and technical point of view, but also from a personal one. It is difficult to comprehend the system of these large-scale works, or to see them all at once, and although an understanding of that system can aid their viewing, it is more important to respond to them emotionally, for as Darboven says: "there is nothing to understand, my secret is that I don't have one".

Through her personal way of visualisation Darboven attempts to make us aware of the world and all its mutations. Because she does not employ any of the current artistic idioms her work is considered difficult; nevertheless, since 1967 she has taken part in many large international avant-garde exhibitions, such as the Guggenheim International, and has had solo exhibitions in European and American museums.

MARJA BLOEM

Darwin, Gwen *see* Raverat

De Dominici, Suor Maria *see* Dominici

De Graag, Anna Julia
Dutch graphic artist, 1877–1924

Born in Gorinchem, 18 July 1877. Moved to The Hague with her family, *c.*1900. Studied at Academie voor Beeldende Kunsten (Academy of Fine Arts), The Hague (teaching certificate in drawing and handicraft *c.*1900). Attended the courses of H.P. Bremmer from 1901. Moved to Laren, 1904. Trip to Rothenburg in eastern Germany with a group of artist friends, 1922. Exhibited several times with the graphic art association Vereniging tot bevordering der grafische Kunst, Wassenaar. Died in The Hague, 2 February 1924.

Principal Exhibitions
Gallery De Zonnebloem, The Hague: 1917, 1924 (retrospective)
Gallery W. Walrecht, The Hague: 1917, 1924

Selected Writings
"Het ontwerpen van borduur patroontjes" [The development of embroidery patterns], *De vrouw en haar huis*, viii, 1913–14, pp.239–40

Bibliography
H.P. Bremmer in *Beeldende Kunst*, iv, 1917, pp.13 and 121; v, 1918, p.97; vi, 1919, p.49; ix, 1922, p.73; xii, 1925, p.17; xv, 1928, p.49
B. van Hasselt, "Julie de Graag: Overleden in februari 1924" [Julie de Graag: Died in February 1924], *Elseviers Geïllustreerd Maandschrift*, xxxiv, 1924, pp.294–6 (obituary)
A. de Ranitz, "Bij het werk van Julie de Graag" [With the work of Julie de Graag], *Maandblad voor Beeldende Kunsten*, iv/8, 1927
W.C. Feltkamp, *Zien en Verstaan* [Seeing and understanding], Amsterdam: Van Mantgem en de Does, 1952
Bloemen uit de kelder [Flowers from the cellar], exh. cat., Gemeentemuseum, Arnhem, 1989
L. Heyting, *De Wereld in een dorp* [The world in a village], Amsterdam, 1994

In the 20 years of her career Anna Julia De Graag produced an oeuvre consisting for the most part of woodcuts, but also of drawings, applied art and a handful of paintings, all of which testify to her considerable skill and force of personality. Unfortunately, her health was poor, and she died aged only 46. About 60 woodcuts survive, averaging 17.5×15 centimetres in size, although a few are larger, 30×20 centimetres, and the smallest, of little animals such as rabbits and ducks made at the end of her life, measure 4×5 centimetres. Besides these, she left behind about 100 drawings. Her subjects were animals, plants, landscapes and portraits. De Graag had an exceptional talent for making woodcuts, possessing the patience and dedication necessary for the minute working of hardwood. The revival of the technique in the first quarter of the 20th century provided a stimulus for her work. The technique lends itself to ornamental purposes on book-jackets and illustrations, then newly in vogue thanks to the influence of Art Nouveau. From her youth De Graag did many varieties of illustration, and later designed book-plates, calendar illustrations and vignettes to order (Haags Gemeentemuseum, The Hague; Provinciaal Museum van Drenthe, Assen). Most of her woodcuts were designed as independent art works, however, and do not belong to the realm of applied art.

Around 1900, while at The Hague Academy, De Graag obtained her teaching certificate. For a time she gave drawing lessons, a few hours each week. As a result of this teaching experience she wrote a short article on embroidery patterns (educational reform was much under discussion at the time). Her teachers at the Academy were Kuyper, who taught her woodcutting, and J.J. Aarts, from whom she learned drawing; she remained in contact with Aarts after leaving the Academy. She also made the acquaintance of another lecturer, the painter and critic H.P. Bremmer, and attended his courses throughout her career, first in The Hague and later in Laren, North Holland, after her move there. He directed her both technically and aesthetically, and mediated in the sale of her work to dealers and other clients. Bremmer promulgated a view of art in which the art was central; the intentions and concerns of the maker were an essential part of the work, capable of being read via the image, provided that the maker possessed sufficient artistic ability. De Graag took this view as her guiding principle.

Bremmer's courses brought her into contact with a number of other women artists, for example Cor J. Pabst, Anna W.E.M. Egter van Wissekerke, Truus G.M. van Hettinga Tromp and Bertha J.R. van Hasselt, who also worked in The Hague and/or Laren. They had all studied at The Hague Academy and came from the same well-to-do milieu as De Graag. They belonged to the generation of Dutch women whose mothers, unless they came from artists' families, had not been inclined to practise painting as a profession. They acted as a powerful stimulus for each other and enjoyed professional and friendly contact similar to that which existed among the Amsterdamse Joffers, the group that included Coba Ritsema (q.v.). At that time many artists had established themselves in provincial and as yet unspoiled Laren. There De Graag came into contact with the sculptor Joseph Mendes da Costa and the painter Bart van der Leck, and was influenced by the work of both. In the first quarter of the 20th century Mendes da Costa produced stylised sculptures, whose sober forms were superimposed on to those of Art Nouveau. Van der Leck (in 1917 a co-founder of the journal *De Stijl*) carried through an even more extreme stylisation in his paintings of 1912–18. De Graag's mature work, that produced from about 1917, must be placed in this context.

Two Crayfish (Gemeentemuseum, Arnhem) and *Tortoise* (Boijmans Van Beuningen Museum, Rotterdam) belong to De Graag's early woodcuts. These delicate prints are decorative and lively in design. Their realism and wealth of detail reveal the influence of her time at the Academy. Many of her early drawings were lost in a fire at her home in 1908; later examples, such as *Still Life with Skull and Pistol* (1913; Rijksmuseum Kröller-Müller, Otterlo) and *Dunes at Groet* (1914; Boijmans Van Beuningen Museum), are independent works and not preparatory studies for woodcuts. The

De Graag: *White Cat*, 1917; woodcut in green and black; 96 × 65 cm.; Museum voor Moderne Kunst, Arnhem

landscape is rendered in an expressive hand. Among the works of her productive years is a coloured woodcut *White Cat* (1917; see illustration), a highly stylised image without any details that depicts the animal as majestic. The only colour, green, is reserved for the background; the composition is powerful and the contours convey a striking tension. The woodcuts *Dog's Head* (1920; Gemeentemuseum) and *Two Owls* (1921; Rijksmuseum, Amsterdam) are even more stylised and convey the fierce gaze of the male owl and the somewhat fearful one of his mate convincingly. The chalk drawing *Farm in the Snow* (1918; Rijksmuseum Kröller-Müller) relies on the same technique. These works reveal an intensity of experience and an earnestness of temperament.

After 1914, in addition to the subject matter already mentioned, De Graag turned to portraiture. She produced characterful, realistic portrait-heads of women of lowly background who came from the neighbourhood of Laren. These include the Indian ink drawing *Mietje Pommer of Eemnes* and the woodcuts *Geertje Kuyer of Laren* and *Dina Klaver* (all 1916; Boijmans Van Beuningen Museum). She also produced a portrait of her mentor, *Bremmer* (1916; Boijmans Van Beuningen Museum), a good likeness, judging by contemporary photographs. The face is striking, with the emphasis on the contemplative gaze. All these portraits show great sensitivity.

From 1918 De Graag produced various multi-coloured woodcuts of flowers, including *June Rose* (1918), *Godetia* (1919) and *Cyclamen* (1920; all Boijmans Van Beuningen Museum). They are highly stylised and very decorative, the lines revealing a firm hand. While travelling in eastern Germany in 1922, she produced a number of black chalk townscapes, such as *View of a Walled Town* and *Townscape with a Group of Old Houses* (both Rijksmuseum Kröller-Müller), with compact compositions, the houses standing close to one another. Dark in tone, they speak of an intense and earnest view of things.

Morbid subjects occur frequently in De Graag's work, among them the woodcut *Memento mori* (1916; Boijmans Van Beuningen Museum), the pencil drawing *Dead Mole* (1917; Rijksmuseum Kröller-Müller) and the colour woodcut *Little Dead Bird* (1919; Gemeentemuseum), all sensitive works, which betray De Graag's depressive nature. Her tendency towards depression seems to have derived not from a lack of appreciation but from a lack of vitality and drive. Her work was always very positively received in her lifetime. It was shown at galleries in The Hague and at the exhibitions organised by the Society for the Promotion of the Graphic Arts, and was promoted by Bremmer in his monthly journal *Beeldende Kunst*. After her death in 1924, commentators spoke of De Graag's small but rich oeuvre as the product of a truly artistic mind.

ROSELLA M. HUBER-SPANIER

de Heer, Margaretha *see* Heer

Dehner, Dorothy
American sculptor and printmaker, 1901–1994

Born in Cleveland, Ohio, 23 December 1901. Studied under Gilmor Brown at the Pasadena Playhouse, 1918–21; drama major at University of California, Los Angeles, 1921–2. Moved to New York, 1922, to study at the American Academy of Dramatic Arts and to pursue a career in theatre, 1922–4. Travelled alone to Europe, 1925, visiting Italy, Switzerland and France; saw the Paris World's Fair of 1925. Enrolled at the Art Students League, New York, September 1925, studying drawing under Kimon Nicolaides and painting under Kenneth Hayes Miller. Married artist David Smith, 1927; separated 1950; divorced 1952. Studied with Smith under Jan Matulka at the Art Students League, 1929–31. Lived in Bolton Landing, New York, 1940–50. Attended Skidmore College, Saratoga Springs, New York, 1951–2 (BA). Began making prints at Stanley William Hayter's Atelier 17, New York, 1952. First sculpture produced in 1955; first solo exhibition of sculpture at Willard Gallery, New York, 1957; also exhibited in New Sculpture Group with Peter Agostini, Reuben Kadish, Philip Pavia, George Sugarman and others. Invited to become a member of the Federation of Modern Painters and Sculptors, and Sculptors Guild, 1957.

Married New York publisher Ferdinand Mann, 1955; he died 1974. Recipient of Yaddo Foundation fellowship, 1970; visiting artist, Tamarind Lithography Workshop, 1971; honorary doctorate, Skidmore College, 1982; Women's Caucus for Art award for outstanding achievement in the visual arts, 1983; award of distinction, National Sculpture Conference: Works by Women, University of Cincinnati, 1987. Died in New York, 22 September 1994.

Selected Individual Exhibitions
Albany Institute of History and Art, NY: 1943 (with David Smith), 1952
Rose Fried Gallery, New York: 1952
Art Institute of Chicago: 1955
Willard Gallery, New York: 1957, 1959, 1960, 1963, 1966, 1970
Columbia University (Avery Hall), New York: 1961
Jewish Museum, New York: 1965 (retrospective)
Hyde Collection, Glens Falls, NY: 1967
City University of New York: 1970, 1991 (retrospective)
Jane Voorhees Zimmerli Art Museum, Rutgers University, New Brunswick: 1984 (with David Smith, touring)
Wichita Art Museum, KA: 1985
Muhlenberg College, Allentown, PA: 1988
Phillips Collection, Washington, DC: 1990
Katonah Museum of Art, NY: 1993–4 (touring retrospective)
Boulder Art Center, Boulder, CO: 1994
Cleveland Museum of Art: 1995 (retrospective)

Selected Writings
"Plexiglas relief for the Great Southwest Industrial Park, Atlanta, Georgia", *Leonardo*, ii, 1969, pp.171–3
"Introduction" in John P. Graham, *Systems and Dialectics of Art*, Baltimore: Johns Hopkins University Press, 1971
"Medals for dishonor: The fifteen medallions of David Smith", *Art Journal*, xxxvii, Winter 1977–8, pp.144–50

Bibliography
Joan Marter, "Dorothy Dehner", *Woman's Art Journal*, i/2, 1980–81, pp.47–50
Judd Tully, "Dorothy Dehner and her life on the farm with David Smith", *American Artist*, xlvii, October 1983, pp.58–61, 99–102
Dorothy Dehner and David Smith: Their Decades of Search and Fulfillment, exh. cat., Jane Voorhees Zimmerli Art Museum, Rutgers University, New Brunswick, and elsewhere, 1984
Charlotte Streifer Rubinstein, *American Women Sculptors*, Boston: Hall, 1990
Dorothy Dehner: Sixty Years of Art, exh. cat., Katonah Museum of Art, NY, and elsewhere, 1993
Between Transcendence and Brutality: American Sculptural Drawings from the 1940s and 1950s, exh. cat., Tampa Museum of Art, FL, 1994
Mara R. Witzling, ed., *Voicing Today's Visions: Writings by Contemporary Women Artists*, New York: Universe, 1994

Dorothy Dehner Papers are in the Archives of American Art, Smithsonian Institution, Washington, DC.

Dorothy Dehner is recognised as one of the few women artists to be associated with the Abstract Expressionist generation. She created innovative abstract drawings and prints, and used wax to form sculptures at a time when most of the male artists were creating direct metal constructions.

From the beginning of her career, Dehner intended to be a sculptor but, as she acknowledged, it was impossible to make sculpture during her marriage to David Smith. In 1931 Dehner and Smith travelled to the Virgin Islands where they both made

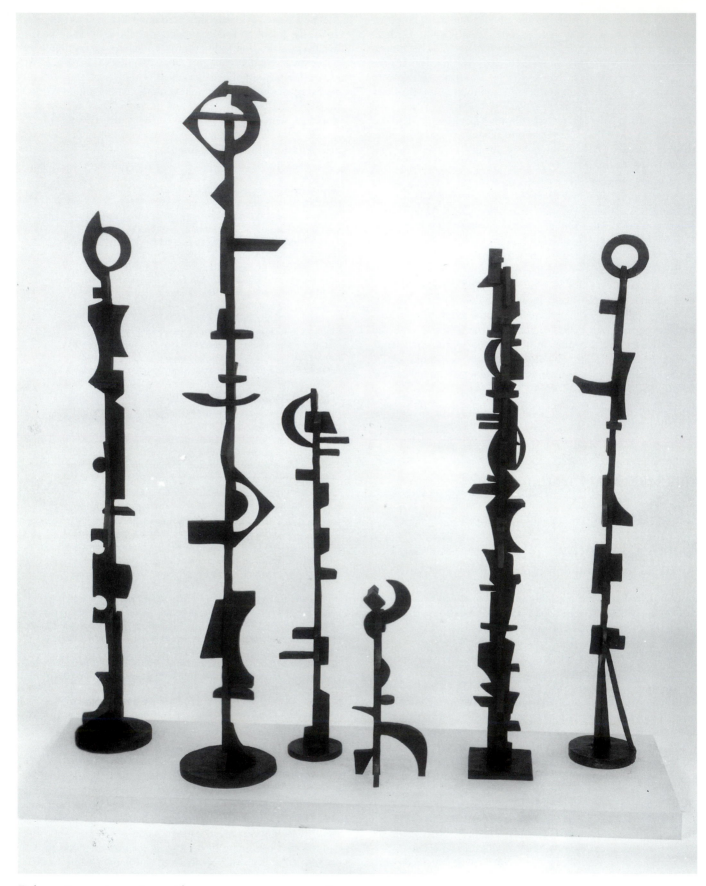

Dehner: *Encounter*, 1969; cast bronze; 124.5 × 110.5 × 31.8 cm.

still-life paintings. Dehner's paintings were accomplished abstractions, still indebted to Synthetic Cubism, but with organic forms predominating – particularly shells and marine life. A trip to Europe in 1935 was to have a lasting impact on her art. She and Smith went to Paris, Brussels, Greece, and later the Soviet Union and Britain. They spent six months in Greece, where Dehner made sketches in black and white. By the late 1930s she had abandoned abstraction for a representational approach, a miniaturist style based on her interest in illuminations in medieval manuscripts. While many of her works of these years were lost, the *Life on the Farm* series survives (Storm King Art Center, Mountainville, NY). These tempera paintings depict Dehner's life at Bolton Landing, including scenes of the daily chores on a farm she and Smith had purchased near Lake George, New York.

Dehner and Smith were closely involved in their creative activities during the 1940s. She gave titles to his sculpture, posed for some of his works and participated in the progress of his welded metal constructions. Both Dehner and Smith were inspired by the same images: the skeleton of a prehistoric bird from the American Museum of Natural History was the basis for Dehner's drawing *Bird of Peace* (1946), Smith's *Royal Bird*, *Jurassic Bird* and several other examples. For both artists the prehistoric creature assumed the appearance of a menacing predator, indicative of their political views in the post-war years. But for Dehner, *Country Living (Bird of Peace)* (1946; Snite Memorial Art Gallery, University of Notre Dame) held personal associations: the spectral presence of the skeletal creature and the barren, jagged peaks below it alluded to the anguish of her private life. The series of dramatic works on paper made in the 1940s are among the most provocative drawings of Dehner's career. The *Damnation Series* (artist's estate) consists of skilfully rendered pen and ink studies of nude figures, accompanied by vultures, bats and other animals. *Suite Moderne* (artist's estate) includes ghoulish figures dancing gigues, fandangos and gavottes, all of which become "dances of Death". Such images relate to post-war tensions, but have more to do with Dehner's state of mind in these final years of her marriage to Smith.

Dehner exhibited her work only a few times in the 1940s. She was in a number of group exhibitions in these years, and in 1946 the Audubon Artists awarded her a first prize for drawing. In this period she found a copy of Ernst Haeckel's seminal study of natural forms, *Kunstformen der Natur* (1904), and embarked on a series of drawings of microscopic organisms. She gained confidence in this new direction for her art, and created many successful abstractions in gouache and ink. In these works on paper Dehner introduced a repertory of biomorphic forms that related to Paul Klee, Joan Miró and Mark Rothko, among others. Unlike the Surrealists, Dehner did not emphasise the disquieting aspects of her imagery, but celebrated the animate energy of these unicellular forms of life. An innovative approach to watercolour can be found in drawings of this period: working wet on wet, the artist allowed for spontaneity and a full range of visual effects by applying water to the paper surface before brushing on colour, and then allowing liquid elements to blend in rich and lively variations.

In 1950 Dehner left Bolton Landing, and she was divorced from Smith two years later. She came to New York, where she taught at various schools, including the Barnard School for Girls, studied engraving at Stanley William Hayter's Atelier 17 and began experimenting in wax, with the intention of making three-dimensional works. Dehner's imagery was derived from her earlier abstract drawings and paintings, even going back to the organic abstractions of the 1930s. Sculpture dominated Dehner's production from 1955 until her death. Her work always emphasised contour rather than mass: she assembled sculptures of disparate parts and approached the use of wax as a constructivist using planar elements. Textural effects were explored: in *Low Landscape Sideways* (1962; Hyde Collection, New York), for example, she braised and drew on the wax slabs, introducing other textures by adding small pieces of metal. To create a lively visual effect, she used faceted elements to form planes that shimmer when reflecting light.

While Dehner's sculptures are abstract, they consistently make reference to the natural world. Vertical compositions evoke a totemic presence, while the horizontal format can be viewed as a landscape. *Encounter* (1969; see illustration), a work consisting of six separate sculptures, alludes to a chance meeting of people both in composition and in concept. The disparate totemic forms relate to one another, as individuals of varying sizes and proportions. This work and others suggest human gestures or evoke journeys through time. Her abstract sculptures represent a personal iconography that recurs over the decades. Imagery of circles, moons, ellipses, wedges and arcs abound. Like other artists of the New York School, Dehner acknowledges in her art that abstract symbols can communicate content that is private, but with universal implications.

By 1970 both the scale and monumentality of Dehner's sculpture had increased. She evoked architectural forms, and some of the totems became human-scale. In 1974 she changed her medium from cast metal to wood, and made constructed pieces using small wooden elements. While the bronzes have textured surfaces, the wooden constructions rely solely on variations of the graining to create lively surfaces. These wooden constructions have a strong association with architecture, and works that Dehner referred to as "toy-like" can also be considered to include fragments of memory and time. *Gateway* (1979; Metropolitan Museum of Art, New York) includes various woods with different grainings and tonalities. The architectonic structures of her wooden ensembles, with thrusting verticals or stacked elements, resemble the skyline of a fanciful city.

In the early 1980s Dehner began a new series of works of heroic proportions in corten steel. These powerful sculptures were fabricated, and were based on earlier works from the 1960s and 1970s that were originally cast in bronze from wax models. *Demeter's Harrow* (1990; artist's estate) attests to Dehner's long-standing involvement with imagery rich with personal associations. In the corten steel construction, polygonal and circular forms extend outwards in a sculptural composition that suggests a dynamic interplay of space and mass. Dehner's years at Bolton Landing must have offered many opportunities to see fields broken up and levelled by spike-tooth harrows or harrows with sharp-edged discs. With this sculpture she alludes to a farm implement, but also to the Goddess of the Corn, who made the fields rich with fruits, flowers and leaves, and instructed man about the sowing of corn. Demeter was also the sorrowing mother of Persephone, maiden of the spring and summer, who died every year and returned to the underworld. Demeter was therefore associated with the earth's fecundity, but was also a goddess who mourned for her beloved child. Thus, the mythological reference seems fitting for Dehner herself, who had known mourning from her earliest years, and worked as an artist to sustain herself in times of personal anguish. Her sculptures are like silent witnesses, enduring testimony to a life dedicated to art and to the pursuit of a visual equivalent to life's journeys.

JOAN M. MARTER

de Kooning, Elaine

American painter, 1919–1989

Born Elaine Marie Catherine Fried in Sheepshead Bay, Brooklyn, New York, 12 March 1919. Studied at Leonardo da Vinci Art School and American Artists School, New York, late 1930s; met Willem de Kooning, and became his student. Married de Kooning, 1943 (separated 1957–76). Accompanied husband to Black Mountain College, North Carolina, 1947. Contributed art criticism to *Art News*, c.1948–88. Spent summers in East Hampton from 1952, in Bridgehampton from 1954. Retained New York studio until 1974, then moved to Alewives Brook Road, Long Island, New York. Taught at University of New Mexico, Albuquerque, 1957–62, and later at many other universities and colleges, including Yale University Graduate School, New Haven, Pratt Institute, New York, and University of Pennsylvania, Philadelphia; also Lamar Dodd chair, University of Georgia, Athens, 1976–8; Mellon chairs at Carnegie Mellon Institute, Pittsburgh, 1969–70, and Cooper Union, New York, 1976; Milton and Sally Avery chair, Bard College, Annandale-on-Hudson, 1982. Visited cave paintings of Dordogne, France, 1983, of Altamira, Spain, 1985. Travelled to China as consultant for film on Willem de Kooning, 1987. Recipient of honorary doctorates from Western College, Oxford, Ohio, 1964; Moore College of Art, Philadelphia, 1972; Adelphi University, New York, 1985; Maryland Institute, Baltimore, 1986; Long Island University, Southampton, 1988. Fellow of Rhode Island School of Design, Providence, 1981. Died in Southampton, New York, 1 February 1989.

Selected Individual Exhibitions

Stable Gallery, New York: 1954, 1956
Tibor de Nagy Gallery, New York: 1957
Graham Gallery, New York: 1960, 1963, 1965, 1975
Roland de Aenlle Gallery, New York: 1961
Peale House Gallery, Pennsylvania Academy of the Fine Arts, Philadelphia: 1964
Montclair Museum of Art, NJ: 1973
Merwin Gallery, Illinois Wesleyan University, Bloomington: 1975
Gruenebaum Gallery, New York: 1982, 1986
Arts Club of Chicago: 1983
Gallerie Sylvia Menzel, Berlin: 1986
Flossie Martin Gallery, Radford University, VA: 1987
Fischbach Gallery, New York: 1988
Georgia Museum of Art, Athens: 1992–3 (touring retrospective)

Selected Writings

"Painting a portrait of the President", *Art News*, lxiii, Summer 1964, pp.37, 64–5
The Spirit of Abstract Expressionism: Selected Writings, ed. Rose Slivka, New York: Braziller, 1994

Bibliography

Lawrence Campbell, "Elaine de Kooning paints a picture", *Art News*, lix, December 1960, pp.40–44
Gerrit Henry, "The artist and the face: A modern American sampling", *Art in America*, lxiii, January–February 1975, pp.34–41
Elsa Honig Fine, *Women and Art*, Montclair, NJ: Allanheld and Schram, and London: Prior, 1978
Eleanor Munro, *Originals: American Women Artists*, New York: Simon and Schuster, 1979
Charlotte Streifer Rubinstein, *American Women Artists from Early Times to the Present*, Boston: Hall, 1982
Rose Slivka, "Elaine de Kooning: The *Bacchus* paintings", *Arts Magazine*, lvii, October 1982, pp.66–9
Lawrence Campbell, "Elaine de Kooning at Gruenebaum", *Art in America*, lxxi, January 1983, p.119
H. Harvard Arnason, *History of Modern Art*, 3rd edition, Englewood Cliffs, NJ: Prentice Hall, 1986
Rose Slivka, "Painting paleolithic", *Art in America*, lxxvi, December 1988, pp.134–9
Cecile Shapiro and David Shapiro, *Abstract Expressionism: A Critical Record*, Cambridge and New York: Cambridge University Press, 1990
Daniel Wheeler, *Art since Mid-Century: 1945 to the Present*, Englewood Cliffs, NJ: Prentice Hall, and London: Thames and Hudson, 1991
Elaine de Kooning, exh. cat., Georgia Museum of Art, Athens, and elsewhere, 1992
Lee Hall, *Elaine and Bill: Portrait of a Marriage: The Lives of Willem and Elaine de Kooning*, New York: HarperCollins, 1993
Jonathan Fineberg, *Art since 1940: Strategies of Being*, New York: Abrams, and London: Laurence King, 1995

A prominent figure within the New York School of the 1940s and 1950s, Elaine de Kooning is too often excluded from histories of this major development in art. Although her career was multi-faceted, including portrait painting, non-representational painting and art criticism, her achievements have been overshadowed by the reputation and celebrity status of her husband, Willem de Kooning. Consequently, information about her contributions to this significant period in the history of art is, regrettably, sparse.

As an eager young student, Elaine de Kooning disdained the social realist and American Scene directions of the 1930s, and aligned herself instead with the non-representational art of the American Abstract Artists. This group was determined to forge an important American modernist movement at a time when the Paris-based international Cercle et Carré and Abstraction-Création groups were dispersing as Fascism menaced Europe. One of her private tutors during the late 1930s was Willem de Kooning, whom she married in December 1943. After their marriage, the couple became the most visible exemplars of the emerging Abstract Expressionism of the New York School. Young, handsome and vibrant, the de Koonings established criteria for aspiring artists to mimic, both in lifestyle and artistic goals. Although they worked daily, the 1940s were lean years during which many New York School artists, including the de Koonings, lived illegally in lofts allocated for

de Kooning: *JFK No.7*, 1963; charcoal on paper; 83.8 × 64.1 cm.; Washburn Galleries, New York

commercial use. Rented as studios, the lofts were typically spacious but unheated and unfurnished. The de Koonings shared living and working space in a large loft at 143 West 21st Street, and later in another at 156 West 22nd Street. In 1947 they went to Black Mountain College in North Carolina, the influential art school that attracted such significant figures as Merce Cunningham, Franz Kline, Buckminster Fuller and John Cage. While at Black Mountain, Elaine de Kooning painted biomorphic abstractions on brown wrapping paper, a body of work that was later, in 1991, exhibited at the Joan Washburn Gallery in New York.

Following the hardships they endured during the 1940s, both de Koonings experienced success in the 1950s. Willem's achievements are familiar, while Elaine became known for her distinctive portraits painted with bold colours and vigorous brush strokes, and for the critical reviews she wrote for *Art News*. A strong psychological likeness of Willem de Kooning, her *Portrait of Bill* (1956; artist's estate) is painted with the bold strokes and strong colours of Abstract Expressionism. Among her portrait commissions was that of *President John F. Kennedy*, who sat for her at his Palm Beach house known as the winter White House. Captivated by the vigorous, handsome young president, she attempted, in numerous studies (see illustration), to capture on canvas his courtly demeanour and strong personality. At the time of Kennedy's assassination on 22 November 1963, de Kooning had taken the sketches to New York, intending to complete the painting there. The shock of his death, however, was so profound that she did not work again for a year (one of the portrait studies is in Harry S. Truman Library, Independence, Missouri; another in John F. Kennedy Library, Boston; all other sketches, artist's estate). Another well-known portrait is that of Harold Rosenberg, *Harold Rosenberg No.III* (1956; 220 × 128 cm.; artist's estate), the art critic who identified Willem de Kooning as the new and creative artist-hero, and who encouraged Elaine de Kooning's career as an artist-critic. *Fairfield Porter* (1956; artist's estate) and *Aladar No.2* (1986; Marberger Collection) are frontal studies of her subjects, both of whom are seated and gaze directly at the viewer. A standing portrait of *Frank O'Hara* (1963; 236 × 107 cm.; Collection Ariel Follett O'Hara and J. Philip O'Hara) eliminates facial detail but still captures the sensitivity of the poet.

Although their marriage weathered the difficulties of poverty, it could not survive the later combination of fame, adequate incomes and the birth of Lisa de Kooning to Joan Ward in 1956. After their separation in 1957, Elaine de Kooning took her first trip west and accepted the sculptor Robert Mallary's invitation to become a visiting professor of art at the University of New Mexico, Albuquerque. A gifted teacher, she encouraged students to use the brighter colours and larger canvases and brushes of the New York School artists. In 1960 her experience with the academic world expanded when she was appointed visiting professor of art at Pennsylvania State University where she taught two days a week in return for a salary and a studio. During the 1960s she accepted teaching positions at 15 universities, and subsequently held various visiting professorships.

During her first visit to Europe in 1976, de Kooning lived in Paris, taught summer school classes for American students and discovered the sculpture of *Bacchus* in the Jardin du Luxembourg. Obsessed with the dynamic intertwining figures and the idea of the god of wine and revelry, she made numerous sketches from which the later *Bacchus* series paintings were derived. Using acrylic paints for the first time, these paintings captured the exuberance she had responded to in her studies of the sculpture. Shown at the Gruenebaum Gallery, New York, in 1982, this series was favourably reviewed by Rose Slivka for *Arts Magazine* (1982). Following the success of the *Bacchus* series, de Kooning went to see the prehistoric cave paintings in the Dordogne Valley in France. In the caves at Lascaux, particularly, she found a kinship between the scale and spontaneity of the Paleolithic paintings of animals and the processes explored by her own contemporaries, the artists of Abstract Expressionism. The approaches of the prehistoric artists, who superimposed small animals over large ones, and the immediacy of their images seemed entirely comprehensible to de Kooning. The absence of illusionistic techniques and the relationship of the images to the uneven surfaces of the cave walls was consistent with her method of allowing forms to emerge from backgrounds of active surfaces.

De Kooning was one of the first artists to write critical reviews of contemporary art exhibitions, and her analytical insights were respected by such widely read critics as Clement Greenberg and Meyer Schapiro. She began writing small reviews for *Art News* in 1948, and later submitted full-length articles that were well received by editors, artists and critics. John Canaday, art critic for the *New York Times*, referred to her as Abstract Expressionism's mascot, sibyl and recording secretary. Her witty essays intuitively captured the spirit of the New York School artists who valued her interpretations of their work. It was Elaine de Kooning who perhaps best described the nature of Abstract Expressionism when she wrote: "The main difference, then, between abstract and nonabstract art is that the abstract artist does not have to choose a subject. But whether or not he chooses, he always ends up with one."

The de Koonings were reconciled in 1976, primarily because Willem de Kooning's deteriorating health required that he have constant care. Elaine de Kooning spent the remainder of her life ministering to him and administering his business affairs. Her own illness, however, claimed her life in 1989; her husband is, at this writing, still living.

MARY F. FRANCEY

Delany, Mary
British amateur artist, 1700–1788

Born Mary Granville in Coulston, Wiltshire, 14 May 1700; elder daughter of Colonel Bernard Granville. Spent early years in London. Moved with her family to Buckland Manor in the Cotswolds, Gloucestershire, 1713. For financial and political reasons, forced into an arranged marriage with Alexander Pendarves, MP for Launceston, Cornwall, 1717; lived at Penryn, Falmouth, Cornwall, and in London; husband died 1725. Visited Ireland, 1731–3, and became acquainted with Jonathan Swift. Married Swift's friend Dr Patrick Delany, Dean of Down and tutor at Trinity College,

Delany: Flowers on overskirt of Mrs Delany's court dress, embroidered by her with silks on a background of black silk, 1760s; 10 × 14 cm.; private collection

Dublin, 1743; lived at Delville, Glasnevin, Dublin; spent summers at Hollymount and later at Mount Panther, both near Downpatrick. Made many visits to England, principally to her sister Anne Dewes at Wellesbourne, Warwickshire; to her brother Bernard Granville at Calwich Abbey, Staffordshire; and to her friend the Duchess of Portland at Bulstrode, Buckinghamshire. Settled in London after husband's death in 1768, spending several months each year at Bulstrode. Moved to Windsor, 1785. Died 15 April 1788; buried at St James, Piccadilly, London.

Selected Writings

A Catalogue of Plants Copied from Nature in Paper Mosaic ... and Disposed in Alphabetical Order, According to the ... Names of Linnaeus, 1778

The Autobiography and Correspondence of Mary Granville, Mrs Delany, ed. Lady Llanover, 6 vols, London: Bentley, 1861–2; reprinted New York: AMS Press, 1974

Letters from Georgian Ireland: The Correspondence of Mary Delany, 1731–68, ed. Angélique Day, Belfast: Friar's Bush Press, 1991

Bibliography

Roger Granville, *The History of the Granville Family*, Exeter, 1895

Caroline Gearey, *Royal Friendships: The Story of Two Royal Friendships (Queen Anne and the Duchess of Marlborough, Queen Charlotte and Mrs Delany), as Derived from Histories, Diaries, etc.*, London: Digby Long, 1898

C. E. Vulliamy, *Aspasia: The Life and Letters of Mary Granville, Mrs Delany, 1700–1788*, London: Bles, 1935

Simon Dewes, *Mrs Delany*, London: Rich and Cowan, 1940

C. P. Curran, *Dublin Decorative Plasterwork of the Seventeenth and Eighteenth Centuries*, London: Tiranti, and New York: Transatlantic Arts, 1967

Stella Mary Newton, "Mrs Delany and her handiwork", *Magazine Antiques*, xcvi, 1969, pp.100–05

Ruth Hayden, *Mrs Delany: Her Life and Her Flowers*, London: British Museum Publications, 1980; revised as *Mrs Delany's Flower Collages*, 1992

Mary Delany was one of the most talented women of the 18th century, particularly in the applied arts. Her skills covered needlework, shell decoration, silhouettes, paper collages, japanning, drawing and painting in oils and watercolours. She studied botany, mineralogy and astronomy. Her letters comment on landscape design, architecture, social habits and fashion in clothes; because she moved in the circles of those who set the trends and influenced society, her letters provide a rich source of social history.

She was taught by private tutors in English, French, music, needlework and dancing. Beginning as a small child to cut silhouettes, she chose as her subjects family groups, children at play and pastoral scenes. A small book at Windsor Castle shows the royal family cut in paper; it is recorded in Queen Charlotte's own hand that it was presented to her in 1781. Mrs Delany also learned fine needlework at an early age, and as a young married woman spent hours sewing by the side of her sick husband, who was nearly 40 years her senior; over the years she developed an artistry esteemed by her contemporaries and exalted to this day. Taking flowers as her subject, she embroidered cushion and chair covers, (neck) handkerchiefs, quilts, knotting bags and kneelers. Her most magnificent embroidery was her own court dress (see illustration), which she designed and worked herself in the 1760s; it is composed of hundreds of large and small plants worked mostly in long and short stitch in silks on black silk, and in the Rococo style. She also made clothes for the poor in Ireland, as well as dolls' clothes and dresses for her niece.

Mrs Delany's interest in seashells began when she was in Cornwall. In Ireland, in 1732, she helped to build a grotto at Killala and decorated it with shells. Similar grottoes, none of which survive, were built and decorated at Northend, Fulham, London, at Delville and Calwich Abbey; at Bulstrode, she designed and helped to build a grotto, though it appears not to have been decorated with shells. She was a subscriber to Thomas Wright of Durham's book on designs for grottoes. She used shells to decorate the walls of a bath-house (restored) at Walton, Warwickshire, and ornamented interiors of houses with them at Wellesbourne (two mantelpieces survive), Calwich Abbey, Bulstrode and Delville (none of her decorations survive).

When widowed and still only in her twenties, as Mrs Pendarves, she was much sought-after in society. Living in the heart of London in Brook Street, she entertained her neighbour, the composer George Friedrich Händel. In an age when morals among men were lax, she was indignant at the harsh judgements imposed on women and deplored the insecure financial position of women on marriage. Brought up with strong Christian beliefs, she was offended by the frivolity and lack of purpose that seemed to fill the lives of so many. After her marriage to Dr Patrick Delany she lived happily at Delville and Downpatrick, pursuing her artistic creations and increasing her knowledge of botany.

The lifelong friendship that Mrs Delany formed with Margaret Cavendish Bentinck, wife of the 2nd Duke of Portland, became a mutual blessing when both women were widowed and in old age. Sharing an interest in the arts, botany, astronomy, conchology and mineralogy, they naturally drew many distinguished people with diverse interests to Bulstrode, the Duchess's country house in Buckinghamshire; among them were the botanists and explorers Sir Joseph Banks, D. Solander and C. Alstromer; the botanical artist Georg Dionys Ehret, the horticulturist G. Miller and the actor David Garrick, as well as members of the royal family. It was at Bulstrode that Mrs Delany began her "paper mosaicks", a collection of nearly 1000 botanically correct plants in coloured cut paper, which she produced between the ages of 72 and 82. With the plant set before her, and if possible another of the same species that she dissected for close examination, she cut particles of coloured paper to represent each part of the plant; using lighter and darker paper for shading, she stuck them on to paper with a black ground, to form a type of collage. Sometimes several hundred pieces of paper were used for one plant alone; occasionally roots, berries and seed-pod were represented. Mrs Delany also recorded the Linnaean classification, the place where the work was executed, the date, the donor and the provenance of the plant. Many plants came from the king's own private garden at Kew; other places to supply her were the Vineyards, Hammersmith; Dr Pitcairn's garden in Islington; Dr John Fothergill's at Upton, Essex; Lord Bute's at Luton Park; and the Chelsea Physic Garden, London. With a few exceptions the pictures measured 25×36 centimetres, with the plants cut to life size. They were placed in loose leafs in ten volumes, with an index of Latin and English names. The collection was bequeathed to the British Museum, London, by Mrs Delany's great-great-niece, Lady Llanover, in 1896.

After the death of her second husband, Mrs Delany spent the winter months at her house at 33 St James's Place, London, when she attended gatherings of the Bluestockings with the Duchess of Portland, and was venerated by Horace Walpole and Hannah More. Retaining her house in London, she moved in 1785 to a grace and favour house in Windsor, where she became a favourite of the royal family and entertained the novelist Fanny Burney. Her portrait was painted by Barber, Zincke (1740), Opie and Benjamin West.

RUTH HAYDEN

See also Copyists and Amateur Artists surveys

Delaunay, Sonia (Ilinichna)
Russian painter and designer, 1885–1979

Born Sarah Stern in Gradiesk, Ukraine, 14 November 1885; called Sonia. Moved to St Petersburg to live with her maternal uncle, 1890; adopted his surname Terk. Studied under Ludwig Schmid-Reutter in Karlsruhe, 1903–5. Made her first trip to Paris, 1905; studied at La Palette; met the artists Amédée Ozenfant and Segonzac. Marriage of convenience to German critic and collector Wilhelm Uhde, 1908; divorced 1910. Married French painter Robert Delaunay, 1910; one son, born 1911; husband died 1941. Established studio with Robert on the rue des Grands-Augustins, Paris, working there until 1935. Close friendships with the poets Blaise Cendrars and Guillaume Apollinaire, c.1912–13. Moved to Madrid at the outbreak of World War I; stayed in Portugal, 1915–16; met Sergei Diaghilev in Madrid, 1917; designed costumes for Diaghilev's production of *Cleopatra* in London, 1918. Back in Paris, 1920; made contact with members of the Dada group and future Surrealist movement. Opened fashion atelier with Jacques Heim, 1924. Concentrated on textile design, 1920s. Member of Abstraction-Création group, 1932. Helped to organise first exhibition of the Réalités Nouvelles group at Galerie Charpentier, Paris, 1939. Moved to Grasse, Provence, after Robert's death, 1941; lived near Jean Arp and Sophie Taeuber-Arp (q.v.); returned to Paris, 1945. Founder-member of Groupe Espace, 1953. Donated works to Musée National d'Art Moderne, Paris, 1963; Musée de l'Impression sur Etoffes, Mulhouse, 1971; Centre Georges Pompidou, Paris, 1976; Bibliothèque Nationale, Paris, 1977. Recipient of Grand Prix de l'Art Féminin, Salon International de la Femme, Cannes, 1969; Grand Prix, Ville de Paris, 1973. Chevalier des Arts et Lettres, 1958; Officier, Légion d'Honneur, 1975. Died in Paris, 5 December 1979.

Principal Exhibitions

Individual

Galerie Notre-Dame-des-Champs, Paris: 1908
Nya Konstgalleriet, Stockholm: 1916 (with Robert Delaunay)
Galerie Fermé la Nuit, Paris: 1929
Galerie des Deux Iles, Paris: 1948 (with Sophie Taeuber-Arp, Jean Arp and Alberto Magnelli)
Galerie Bing, Paris: 1953, 1954 (with Sophie Taeuber-Arp and Alberto Magnelli), 1957 (with Robert Delaunay)
Rose Fried Gallery, New York: 1955
Kunsthaus, Bielefeld: 1958
Musée des Beaux-Arts, Lyon: 1959 (with Robert Delaunay)
Galerie Denise René, Paris: 1962
Musée du Louvre, Paris: 1964 (*Donation Robert et Sonia Delaunay*)
Galerie Minima, Paris: 1964
National Gallery of Canada, Ottawa: 1965 (with Robert Delaunay)
Musée National d'Art Moderne, Paris: 1967 (retrospective), 1975 (*Hommage à Sonia Delaunay*)
La Demeure, Paris: 1970
Fundaçao Calouste Gulbenkian, Lisbon: 1972 (with Robert Delaunay and friends)
Musée d'Art Moderne de la Ville de Paris: 1972 (retrospective)
Galerie Gmurzynska, Cologne: 1975
Bibliothèque Nationale, Paris: 1977 (with Robert Delaunay)

Group

Galerie Der Sturm, Berlin: 1913 (*Erster deutscher Herbstsalon*), 1920
Salon des Indépendants, Paris: 1914, 1922
Salon d'Automne, Paris: 1925, 1939
Exposition Internationale des Arts Décoratifs et Industriels Modernes, Paris: 1925 (with Jacques Heim)
Société des Artistes Indépendants, Grand Palais, Paris: 1926 (*Trente ans d'art indépendant, 1884–1914*)
Union des Artistes Modernes, Musée des Arts Décoratifs, Paris: 1930
Abstraction-Création, Paris: 1932
Exposition Internationale, Paris: 1937 (gold medal, with Robert Delaunay)
Salon des Réalités Nouvelles, Paris: from 1939
Galerie René Drouin, Paris: 1945 (*Art concret*)
Galerie Denise René, Paris: 1947 (*Tendances de l'art abstrait*)
Galerie Maeght, Paris: 1949 (*Premiers maîtres de l'art abstrait*)
Musée National d'Art Moderne, Paris, 1953 (*Cubisme, 1907–1919*)

Selected Writings

"Tissus et tapis", *L'Art International d'Aujourd'hui*, no.15, Paris: Moreau, 1929
Compositions, couleurs, idées, Paris: Moreau, 1930
"Les artistes et l'avenir de la mode", *Revue de Jacques Heim*, no.3, September 1932
"Collages de Sonia et Robert Delaunay", *XXe Siècle*, no.6, January 1956, pp.19–21
The New Art of Color: Writings of Robert and Sonia Delaunay, ed. Arthur A. Cohen and others, New York: Viking, 1978
Nous irons jusqu'au soleil, Paris: Laffont, 1980 (memoirs)

Bibliography

André Lhôte and others, *Sonia Delaunay, ses objets, ses tissus simultanés, ses modes*, Paris: Librairies des Arts Décoratifs, 1925

Jacques Damase, *Sonia Delaunay: Rhythms and Colors*, Greenwich, CT: New York Graphic Society, and London: Thames and Hudson, 1972 (French original, 1971)
Arthur A. Cohen, *Sonia Delaunay*, New York: Abrams, 1975
Sonia Delaunay, exh. cat., Galerie Gmurzynska, Cologne, 1975
Cindy Nemser, *Art Talk: Conversations with 12 Women Artists*, New York: Scribner, 1975
Sonia et Robert Delaunay, exh. cat., Bibliothèque Nationale, Paris, 1977
Künstlerinnen der Russischen Avantgarde/Russian Women Artists of the Avant-Garde, 1910–1930, exh. cat., Galerie Gmurzynska, Cologne, 1979
Joan M. Marter, "Three women artists married to early modernists: Sonia Delaunay-Terk, Sophie Taüber-Arp and Marguerite Thompson Zorach", *Arts Magazine*, liv, September 1979, pp.88–95
Sonia Delaunay: A Retrospective, exh. cat., Albright-Knox Art Gallery, Buffalo, NY, and elsewhere, 1980
Bernard Dorival, *Sonia Delaunay: Sa vie, son oeuvre, 1885–1979*, Paris: Damase, 1980
J.C. Marcadé, ed., "La correspondance d'A.A. Smirnov avec S.I. Terk (Sonia Delaunay), 16 Septembre 1904–8 Avril 1905", *Cahiers du Monde Russe et Soviétique*, July–September 1983, pp.289–327
Isabelle Anscombe, *A Woman's Touch: Women in Design from 1860 to the Present Day*, London: Virago, and New York: Viking, 1984
Annette Malochet, *Atelier Simultané de Sonia Delaunay, 1923–1934*, Milan: Fabbri, 1984
Delaunay (Sonia et Robert), exh. cat., Musée d'Art Moderne de la Ville de Paris, 1985
Peter-Klaus Schuster, *Delaunay und Deutschland*, Cologne: DuMont, 1985
Sonia Delaunay, exh. cat., La Boetie, New York, and elsewhere, 1986
Elizabeth Morano, ed., *Sonia Delaunay: Art into Fashion*, New York: Braziller, 1986
Axel Madsen, *Sonia Delaunay: Artist of the Lost Generation*, New York: McGraw-Hill, 1989
Jacques Damase, *Sonia Delaunay: Fashion and Fabrics*, London: Thames and Hudson, and New York: Abrams, 1991 (French original)
Sonia & Robert Delaunay: Künstlerpaare-Künstlerfreunde/Dialogues d'artistes-résonances, exh. cat., Kunstmuseum, Bern, 1991
Whitney Chadwick, "Living simultaneously: Sonia and Robert Delaunay", *Significant Others: Creativity and Intimate Partnership*, ed. Whitney Chadwick and Isabelle de Courtivron, New York and London: Thames and Hudson, 1993, pp.30–49
Stanley Baron and Jacques Damase, *Sonia Delaunay: The Life of an Artist*, New York, Abrams, and London: Thames and Hudson, 1995
Gill Perry, *Women Artists and the Parisian Avant-Garde*, Manchester: Manchester University Press, and New York: St Martin's Press, 1995

Sonia Delaunay should be remembered in equal measure as a studio artist and as a designer. Throughout her long career, she worked with many media – easel painting, needlework, scenography, industrial design; and, in fact, she came to her mature style of painting around 1910 after concentrating on embroidery (she had earlier painted in a Fauvist manner under the influence of van Gogh and Gauguin). Delaunay's peculiar collocations of bold colours and her repetition of motifs and figures in rhythmic cycles often bring to mind the craft of quilts and plaids – an association that Delaunay herself emphasised and cultivated. Even her confrontations with the written and published word – that is, her visual perception of language – constitute a patchwork of genius. Delaunay's designs for Guillaume Apollinaire's poem *Zone* (1913) and Blaise Cendrars's *La Prose du Transsibérien et de la petite Jehanne de*

Delaunay: *Electric Prisms*, 1914; oil on canvas; 250 × 250 cm.; Musée National d'Art Moderne, Centre Georges Pompidou, Paris

France (1913), for example, cannot be classified as mere "illustrations", for they are an organic part of the literary whole and continue a synthetic tradition reinforced by the French and Russian Symbolists, in particular. But at the same time, with their borders and sectioning, they also bring to mind the traditional crochet and embroidery of her homeland, the Ukraine.

Delaunay elaborated her Simultanist concept of painting through a variety of engagements: the decorative arts, Fauvism, Cubism, Futurism, the topical fascination with electric illumination, and intense discussions with fellow artists and critics in Paris such as Apollinaire, Cendrars, Marc

Chagall and, of course, her husband Robert. Consequently, inspired by many concepts and conditions, Delaunay's paintings sometimes elicit associations with concurrent works by other artists. Her decorative arrangements for the *Bal Bullier* of 1912–13, for example, remind us of Gino Severini's *Bal Tabarin* (1912; Museum of Modern Art, New York), while her compositions of the 1930s such as *Composition No.38* (1938; gouache on paper; 105 × 74.5 cm.; ex-artist's collection) bring to mind certain abstract works of Giacomo Balla and Lyubov Popova (q.v.). Delaunay, however, developed her own special vision, and her exercises in luminosity and refractivity remain unmatched in their vigorous and radical resolutions of colour and movement.

The painting *Electric Prisms* (1914; see illustration), shown at the Salon des Indépendants in 1914, is a case in point. Not only did it confirm that Delaunay "liked electricity. Public lighting was a novelty. At night, during our walk, we entered the era of light, arm-in-arm" (*Nous irons jusqu'au soleil* 1980, p.43). But in some sense also, *Electric Prisms* can be regarded as a visual manifesto of intent, for the interpenetrating planes of colour, the evocation of solar and planetary bodies, and the juxtaposition of solidity, translucency and dissolution, are elements identifiable with much of Delaunay's work and with her fundamental conception of rhythm. They recur in other master paintings such as the *Rhythm in Colour* series of the 1960s and provide the driving force behind so much of her design work – for fabrics and textiles, for the stage (e.g. the *Quatre Saisons* ballet of 1928–9) and for interiors (e.g. the projects for the Air Pavilion, Paris, 1936). As she asserted: "Rhythm is based on numbers because colour can be measured by its vibrations. This was a completely new concept that opened infinite horizons for painting and could be used by anyone who felt and understood" (*The New Art of Colour* 1978, p.197).

Although Delaunay left Russia for Paris as a very young woman and never returned there, she – and her husband Robert – maintained close communication with Russian artists, choreographers, impresarios and designers, especially during the 1910s and 1920s. Indeed, a number of Delaunay's experimental undertakings done in Paris found immediate parallels among the avant-garde communities in Moscow and St Petersburg. For example, as early as 1904–5 she was exchanging ideas on sound and colour with the literary historian and musicologist Alexander Smirnov and her Simultanist colour accompaniments to Cendrars's *La Prose du Transsibérien et de la petite Jehanne de France* were held in high regard by both the French and the Russian Cubists. Even her bold fabric designs of the 1920s are curiously similar to those of the Constructivists Popova and Varvara Stepanova (q.v.) done in Moscow – something that became clear from the parallel exhibits at the Paris Exposition of 1925. The connections between the Delaunays in Paris with their theory of Simultanism and the colour theories of Aristarkh Lentulov and Georgy Yakulov in Moscow are also striking, even though the latter maintained that Simultanism was his invention (Lassaigne in Cologne 1979, p.79). In any case, what critics called Orphism in the context of Robert Delaunay's paintings of 1912 and what Sonia then absorbed into her theory of Simultanism is applicable to the work of many artists of the time: "Light in Nature creates color movement. Movement is provided by relationships of uneven measures, of color contrasts among themselves that make up Reality. This reality … becomes rhythmic simultaneity" (Robert Delaunay, "Über das Licht" (1913), quoted in Roger Lipsey, *An Art of Our Own: The Spiritual in Twentieth-Century Art*, Boston: Shambala, 1988, p.97).

Primarily, Sonia Delaunay is now remembered for her clothes and textile designs, although she was also active as a stage designer, especially just before and after 1920. In 1918 she designed the costumes for Sergei Diaghilev's production of *Cleopatra* in London; in 1919 she designed the inaugural revue for the Petit Casino in Madrid; and in 1923 she designed the *Soirée du Coeur à Barbe* directed by Ilya Zdanevich (Ilyadze) and Serge Romoff for the Cherez group in Paris. In this way, Delaunay established a fruitful relationship with the Paris Dada circle, leading, for example, to her fanciful costumes for Tristan Tzara's *Le Coeur à Gaz* in 1924. In these spectacles, Delaunay applied her notion of Simultanism, which one critic has defined succinctly as "based on colour relations that can be observed in their action on one another … contrasts are completed by harmonies based on dissonances" (Lassaigne in Cologne 1979, p.79). In her fabric designs for *Cleopatra* Delaunay demonstrated her radical position *vis-à-vis* the more conventional patterns in cloth design of her time. Here she substituted traditional ornamentation with geometric motifs and erotic imagery, and her bright, contrasting colour combinations, coupled with graduated tints and harmonies, anticipated a central direction of future fashion. Cyril Beaumont, who attended the production at the Coliseum, recalled:

> There was also a new costume for Cleopatra, designed by Sophie [sic] Delaunay; it was another vivid conception in yellow, red and gold not improved by a segment of mirror-glass affixed to the girdle, which winked like a heliograph every time it caught the light … [Cyril Beaumont, *The Diaghilev Ballet in London*, London: Maclehose, 1940, pp.109–10].

Like Alexandra Exter (q.v.), Delaunay transferred some of her lessons from stage design directly to fashion design. In this discipline she worked on several levels – providing total, "simultaneous" ensembles (from purse to gown to automobile) for the wealthy Parisienne as well as simple *tissu-patrons* or cut-out patterns that the working woman could use. While applying Simultanist devices to her dress creations, as evidenced by her concentration on colour rhythm and rotational pattern, Delaunay concerned herself with "liberating" the female body and she was an enthusiast of the "sack". In the words of André Lhôte (1925), she covered the "sweet undulations of the human body with geometric architectures". With her unabating artistic curiosity and *joie de vivre*, Delaunay continued to elaborate these initial ideas throughout her long and active career. With her bold colour resolutions and emphasis on dynamic interplay of forms, she anticipated – and contributed to – the Op Art and Kinetic movements of the 1960s.

JOHN E. BOWLT

Della Croce, Suor Maria Eufrasia *see* Croce

Demont-Breton, Virginie
French painter, 1859–1935

Born Virginie Elodie Breton at Courrières, Pas de Calais, 26 July 1859. Trained by her father, the painter Jules Breton. Married Adrien Demont, a landscape painter from Douai,

1880; settled at Montgéron, Seine-et-Oise; three daughters, born 1886, 1888 and 1901. Spent summers at Wissant, Pas-de-Calais, from c.1891. Promoted art education for women from the 1880s; elected president of the Union des Femmes Peintres et Sculpteurs, Paris, 1894. Member, 1894, and active member, 1913, Académie Royale, Antwerp; Sociétaire, Société des Artistes Français; Société des Gens de Lettres; Société des Poètes Français. Chevalier, 1894, and Officier, 1913, Légion d'Honneur, France, 1894; Chevalier, Ordre de Léopold de Belgique, 1898. Died in Wissant, 10 January 1935.

Principal Exhibitions

Paris Salon: from 1880 (honourable mention 1880, third-class medal 1881, second-class medal and exemption from jury 1883)
International Colonial Exhibition, Amsterdam: 1883 (gold medal)
Union des Femmes Peintres et Sculpteurs, Paris: 1887, 1890–91
Exposition Universelle, Paris: 1889 (gold medal), 1900 (gold medal)
Woman's Building, World's Columbian Exposition, Chicago: 1893
Exposition Internationale d'Anvers, Antwerp: 1894 (medal of honour)
New Gallery, London: 1898

Selected Writings

Les Maisons que j'ai connues, 4 vols, Paris: Plon, 1926

Bibliography

Edmond About, Quinze journées au salon de peinture et sculpture, Paris: Librairie des Bibliophiles, 1883
G. Maroniez, Virginie Demont-Breton, Paris, 1895
Lee Baron, "A painter of motherhood: Virginie Demont-Breton", Century Magazine, liii (new series xxxi), 1896–7, pp.210–15
Emile Langlade, Artistes de mon temps, ii, Virginie Demont-Breton, Paris, 1933
Revue de l'Art Ancien et Moderne, lxvii, 1935, p.110 (obituary)
J. Diane Radycki, "The life of lady art students: Changing art education at the turn of the century", Art Journal, xlii, Spring 1982, pp.9–13
Charlotte Yeldham, Women Artists in Nineteenth-Century France and England, 2 vols, New York: Garland, 1984
Annette Bourrut Lacouture, "Egyptomanie fin de siècle: Le Typhonium demeure des peintres Adrien Demont et Virginie Demont-Breton", Bulletin de la Société de l'Histoire de l'Art Français, 1989, pp.277–96
Susan Waller, Women Artists in the Modern Era: A Documentary History, Metuchen, NJ: Scarecrow Press, 1991
Tamar Garb, Sisters of the Brush: Women's Artistic Culture in Late Nineteenth-Century Paris, New Haven and London: Yale University Press, 1994

As the second woman artist to be awarded the Légion d'Honneur, Virginie Demont-Breton was officially recognised for her paintings, and as the second president of the Union des Femmes Peintres et Sculpteurs, she used her public recognition to campaign for women's entry into the Ecole des Beaux-Arts and other official institutions.

Her father Jules Breton, who was well known for his paintings of peasant life, encouraged her interest in art from an early age and gave her formal instruction from the time she was 14. In 1880 she made her debut at the Salon, for which she was awarded an honourable mention, and married Adrien Demont, a pupil of her uncle Emile Breton, who was also a painter. With her husband, Demont-Breton spent her summers in Wissant in Normandy, and many of her works represented the people of this fishing community. On the Beach, for which she was awarded a second-class medal and hors concours status (exemption from jury) at the Salon of 1883, is typical of her paintings of the 1880s. It represents a young mother in peasant dress seated with her four children on the sandy shore. Although the small boats behind the group allude to the day-to-day concerns of their community and the absent, labouring husband and father, this mother and her children are effectively removed from those concerns: the two older boys rough-house in the sand as their mother and two siblings sit idly in the placid natural setting. With its smooth finish and careful composition, the painting respects academic conventions. On the Beach was Demont-Breton's first State purchase; other works were purchased for the Musée Municipal, Douai, the Musée des Beaux-Arts, Lille, and public collections in Amiens, Antwerp and Amsterdam.

Views of peasants enjoyed a vogue in the French Salons of the 1880s and were painted by British and North American as well as French artists. A number of other artists who specialised in peasant subjects – including Jules Breton – chose to emphasise the religious customs and the "primitive" aspects of peasant life that were giving way to modern farming methods in many parts of France, especially Brittany. Demont-Breton's concentration on the Normandy fishing community served simultaneously to distinguish her work from and associate her work with that of her well-known father. In writing about On the Beach, such critics as Edmond About attributed Demont-Breton's choice and treatment of her subject to her gender: "[there is] no trace of insipidity, nothing to betray a feminine hand, except perhaps the vague caress of the brush on the tender nudity of the children" (About 1883, p.31). In concentrating on themes of maternity, Demont-Breton reinforced and naturalised conventional ideas of the family and women's role within it at a time when these ideas were increasingly called into question by some feminists.

In the 1880s Demont-Breton became active in the Union des Femmes Peintres et Sculpteurs, which Mme Léon Bertaux (q.v.) had founded in 1881 to create an opportunity for women artists to exhibit without prejudice or a jury. Demont-Breton participated in their exhibitions and became active in the campaign for women's admission to the Ecole des Beaux-Arts that Bertaux had initiated. Opposition to women's admission to the Ecole des Beaux-Arts centred on their access to the nude model in life-drawing classes, which brought to the fore questions about the contemporary conventions of feminine behaviour. In 1890 Bertaux and Demont-Breton, then vice-president of the organisation, met the members of the Conseil Supérieur des Beaux-Arts, which had been appointed to consider women's admission to the Ecole. In her memoirs Demont-Breton recounted the exchange, which concluded with the commitment in principle to state funding for women's art education, although it was not until 1897, after a protracted campaign by the Union des Femmes Peintres et Sculpteurs, that the first women students were admitted to the school.

In her speeches on behalf of women's admission to the Ecole, in paintings such as On the Beach and Dipped in the Sea (untraced, repr. Baron 1896, p.212), and in her public persona after 1886, when her first daughter was born, Demont-Breton reiterated rather than challenged traditional norms of femininity. She believed that women who were educated as artists

Demont-Breton: *Les Tourmentées*, 1890; Musée des Beaux-Arts, Lille

would contribute an instinctive femininity to art, in which motherhood would play a major part: "Maternity is the most beautiful, healthiest glory of woman; it is a love dream in palpable form and comes smilingly to demand our tenderness and our kisses; it is the inexhaustible source whence feminine art draws its purest inspirations" (quoted in Baron 1896, p.212).

Demont-Breton did not, however, want to limit women's work to genre paintings of motherhood. The intention of gaining women's admission to the Ecole des Beaux-Arts was to open to women the field of history painting – the highest genre of art within the French academic tradition and the genre that most directly depended on the study of the nude model. Within her own work, Demont-Breton carefully negotiated the contradictions of such an ambition, turning to images of heroic women, particularly mystics and saints. *Jeanne at Domrémy* (1893; Musée des Beaux-Arts, Lille, repr. Garb 1994, p.138) shows Joan of Arc as a child, kneeling in the field and ignoring the sheep that graze behind her as she hears the voices that urge her to take up arms against the English. *Stella Maris* (1895; untraced, *ibid.*, p.14, and Yeldham 1984, ill.188), which was painted after the death at sea of one of Demont-Breton's former models, represents a man and a boy who have lashed themselves to the mast of their fishing boat in a storm. The mast, which takes the shape of a cross, holds the two slack figures just above the water, and in the distance in a halo of light appears a vision of the Virgin holding the Christ Child. The torsos of the semi-nude male figures sink into the water: their masculinity is effectively hidden from view and Demont-Breton's conventional femininity is secure.

SUSAN WALLER

De Morgan, Evelyn
British painter, 1855–1919

Born Mary Evelyn Pickering, 1855; father Percival Pickering QC. Studied at the Slade School of Fine Art, London, under Edward Poynter, 1873–5 (Slade scholarship); studied in Italy, 1875–7. Subsequently established own studio in London. Often visited her uncle, the painter John Roddam Spencer-Stanhope, in Tuscany. Married William Frend De Morgan, art potter and later novelist, 1887; settled in Chelsea, London. Spent winters in Florence on account of husband's health, 1893–1914. Pottery business closed down, 1905. Completed two of husband's novels left unfinished at his death (1917). Died in London, 2 May 1919.

Principal Exhibitions
Grosvenor Gallery, London: 1877–88

Liverpool Autumn Exhibitions: 1884, 1888, 1890–93, 1897–1905, 1908
New Gallery, London: 1888–92, 1900–01, 1908–9
Bruton Galleries, London: 1906 (individual)
Red Cross Benefit, London: 1916 (individual)

Bibliography

The De Morgan Collection of Pictures and Pottery to which are Added a Few Pictures by Roddam Spencer-Stanhope and other Pre-Raphaelite Artists, London: Ryling, n.d.

Walter Shaw Sparrow, "The art of Mrs William De Morgan", *The Studio*, xix, 1900, pp.220–32

Isabel McAllister, "In memoriam: Evelyn de Morgan", *The Studio*, lxxix, 1920, pp.28–33

A.M.W. Stirling, *William De Morgan and His Wife*, London: Thornton Butterworth, and New York: Holt, 1922

Theodore Crombie, "Paintings from the De Morgan Foundation at Cragside", *National Trust Studies*, 1981, pp.17–26

The De Morgan Foundation at Old Battersea House: Paintings and Drawings by Evelyn De Morgan, Roddam Spencer-Stanhope and William De Morgan, Ceramics by William De Morgan, London: Wandsworth Borough Council, 1983

Pamela Gerrish Nunn, *Victorian Women Artists*, London: Women's Press, 1987

Jane Sellars, *Women's Works: Paintings, Drawings, Prints and Sculpture by Women*, Liverpool: National Museums and Galleries on Merseyside, 1988

Jan Marsh and Pamela Gerrish Nunn, *Women Artists and the Pre-Raphaelite Movement*, London: Virago, 1989

The Last Romantics: The Romantic Tradition in British Art: Burne-Jones to Stanley Spencer, exh. cat., Barbican Art Gallery, London, 1989

Deborah Cherry, *Painting Women: Victorian Women Artists*, London and New York: Routledge, 1993

A Struggle for Fame: Victorian Women Artists and Authors, exh. cat., Yale Center for British Art, New Haven, 1994

Catherine Gordon, ed., *Evelyn De Morgan: Oil Paintings*, London: De Morgan Foundation, 1996

Evelyn De Morgan created a strange and beautiful world in her paintings. A brilliantly coloured land peopled by sinewy female figures, often entwined, forming convoluted human friezes, with their bodies shrouded in a swirling arabesque of drapery. The serpentine whorls, the fearful, wistful, sometimes expressionless faces, interpreted her recurrent themes of depression, struggle, darkness and light, regret, yearning, sleeping and dreaming, all derived from literary and mythological subjects. The settings of her pictures describe an enclosed world with a strangely airless quality, often incorporating the drama of the sea, the mountains, vivid sunrise and the impenetrable night sky.

Her compositions are frequently bisected, as if to denote one dreamworld and the next. The scale of her work is large and ambitious; her palette has a Pre-Raphaelite brilliance and her sharply linear draughtsmanship shows a striking debt to Burne-Jones – her painting *Aurora Triumphans* (1886; 116 × 172cm.; Russell-Cotes Art Gallery, Bournemouth) was for 20 years misattributed to Burne-Jones because of a forged monogram signature – but the greatest influence on her was Italian art, especially that of Botticelli. De Morgan was one of the first generation of women to study at the Slade School of Fine Art, with Mary Huxley, Mary Kingsley, Dorothy Tennant and Mary Stuart Wortley. She was a distinguished pupil, in her first year winning the prize for painting from the antique, and in her second the prize for painting from life and one of the first

Slade scholarships to be awarded. She was also taught by her uncle John Roddam Spencer-Stanhope, with whom she spent much productive and inspirational time at his villa near Florence. In 1883 De Morgan was nominated by Charlotte Weeks in her article "The Slade girls" for the *Magazine of Art* (p.329) as having obtained a position of standing among the artists of the day.

All the accounts of De Morgan's life and work mention her tremendous industry, her passion for painting and her joy in her art. Her friend May Morris (q.v.), for example, wrote:

> Her pictures have an epic quality and are spacious in conception, while [in her later work] showing an almost exaggerated insistence on decorative detail. They are remarkable for the beauty of drapery design, for vigorous and delicate drawing and for sumptuous colour, for great enjoyment of textures. She had astonishing physical endurance and Power of work [quoted in *The De Morgan Foundation … 1983*].

Yet the pictures themselves seem to speak more of a woman imprisoned.

The artist's long and happy partnership with her husband, the potter William De Morgan, gave her work pragmatic purpose: the income from the sales of her pictures was essential to prop up her husband's uncertain business. She never exhibited at the Royal Academy, but instead at the more avant-garde Grosvenor and New galleries, and in the big provincial shows in Manchester and Liverpool. Some work was sold through the Fine Art Society and on commission. She developed an aversion to showing her work, setting each canvas aside as soon as she had finished it and immediately beginning to paint another.

De Morgan's biographer, her sister Wilhelmina Stirling, gives a full account of the artist's struggles to gain an education and work as a painter (Stirling 1922). De Morgan kept a journal when she was 16, in which she wrote obsessively about her feeling that a moment not spent painting was a part of her life wasted. She bitterly resented the tedious demands made on her time by the petty routines and enforced idleness of daily life. A Sunday entry reads: "Got up late; dawdled over dressing, went to Church; in the afternoon walked. Dawdled, dawdled, dawdled through a great deal of precious time". On her 17th birthday she wrote: "Art is eternal, but life is short, and each minute idly spent will rise, swelled to whole months and years, and hound me in my grave."

De Morgan found her subjects in literary sources, from Classical mythology, the Bible, medieval and contemporary poetry, in verse by Shelley and Tennyson, from Hans Christian Andersen's fairy-tales. She painted for an audience that almost ceased to exist with the end of the Victorian age, one who knew well the stories of Hero and Leander, Cadmus and Harmonia, Boreas and Orithyia, Cassandra and Helen of Troy, and who recognised every biblical reference or a quote from Tennyson's poetry. The 20th-century viewers' bafflement at these unfamiliar themes makes De Morgan's painted world seem yet more remote today: we do not know the stories, and the morals of the tales elude us. To the modern viewer, the subtext of the late Victorian woman artist struggling with her ambition and her dreams is the subject that leaps to the eye.

De Morgan: *Flora*, 1894; De Morgan Foundation

The largest collection of De Morgan's paintings and drawings belongs to the De Morgan Foundation, established in the early 1930s at Old Battersea House, London, by Wilhelmina Stirling. Substantial parts of the picture collection are on display there and also in appropriate late-Victorian settings at Cardiff Castle and Knightshayes Court, Devon, both houses designed by William Burges, and at Cragside, Northumbria, the house designed for Lord Armstrong by Norman Shaw. This group of works spans De Morgan's lifetime, from the first picture she exhibited, *Ariadne on Naxos*, at the Grosvenor Gallery in 1877, to her war painting *The Red Cross*. An overview of them reveals that De Morgan's compositional range was not great: the single female figure draped horizontally across the picture plane (*Port after Stormy Seas*, 1905), or standing like a sculpture in a vertical niche (*The Dryad*, 1884; *Helen of Troy*, 1898); a frieze-like procession of many figures, linked by gestures of hand and arm (*Grey Sisters*, 1880–81; *St Christina Giving Her Father's Jewels to the Poor*, 1904) and, at her most ambitious, a maelstrom of floating, crouching women (*The Kingdom of Heaven Suffereth Violence*, *The Captives*, *Daughters of the Mist*).

All the energy in De Morgan's pictures is contained in the individual poses of her figures that, despite the ever-linking hands and arms, seem curiously separate from each other. For this reason, De Morgan's most successful works are those of her single female subjects, such as *Medea* (1889; 150 × 89 cm.; Williamson Art Gallery and Museum, Birkenhead), in which the fearsome murderous character of Greek mythology is depicted as a more benign sorceress, standing reed-like within the marbled corridor of a Renaissance palace, and *Flora* (1894; see illustration), probably her masterpiece, painted in Florence as a homage to Botticelli's *Primavera* (Uffizi, Florence) and commissioned originally by an enthusiastic patron, the Liverpool shipowner, William Imrie. De Morgan is least successful, but wonderfully ambitious in scale, in such pictures as *Life and Thought Have Gone Away* (1893; 165 × 293 cm.), one of the earliest pictures by a woman artist to be bought by the Walker Art Gallery in Liverpool (1901). The vast canvas depicting lines from Tennyson's poem "The Deserted House" seems to consist, typically, of two unrelated picture planes – the symbolic figures of a knight and his lady in front of a tomb on the left, and the flurry of highly coloured angels on the right, intact in their own Pre-Raphaelite landscape.

De Morgan lived to see the beginnings of modern art and was bewildered by it. On seeing an exhibition of Cubist and Futurist art she commented: "… if that is what people like now, I shall wait for the turn of the tide". By the time of her death in 1919, her elaborate Symbolist pictures (e.g. *The Red Cross*, *Scrap of Paper* and *Coming of Peace*) already seemed to belong to another age. During World War I De Morgan frightened visitors to her studio with the notes of tragedy and evil to be found in her pictures, in which she symbolised the conflict. She willed these works to be auctioned with the rest of her studio contents after her death (the sale never took place) to raise funds for soldiers blinded in action – a fate that to the artist Evelyn De Morgan seemed worse than death.

JANE SELLARS

Derkert, Siri
Swedish painter and sculptor, 1888–1973

Born in Stockholm, 30 August 1888. Studied at Althin's art school, Stockholm, from 1904; Royal Academy of Fine Arts, Stockholm, 1911–13. In Paris, 1913–14; studied at Académie Colarossi, Académie de la Grande Chaumière and Académie Russe; met Finnish painter Valle Rosenberg; visited Algiers in winter 1914. Returned to Sweden, autumn 1914. Trip to Sicily with Rosenberg, 1915; son born in Naples, summer 1915. Returned to Sweden alone to raise money, 1916; forced to remain there because of World War I. Met Swedish artist Bertil Lybeck, 1917; two daughters, born 1918 and 1920 (elder daughter died 1938); married Lybeck, 1921; divorced 1925. Designer and buyer in fashion industry, 1918–21. Lived in Stockholm, but spent long periods with her children at Simpnäs by the Åland Sea, 1924–32. Moved to Lidingö near Stockholm, 1931; lived there until her death. Trip to Paris, 1936–7; studied at the Académie Lhôte and at Académie Colarossi under Marcel Gromaire and Gimond. Study trip to Amsterdam, 1948. Worked in Iceland, 1949–50; visited Moscow and Warsaw, 1950. Died 28 April 1973.

Principal Exhibitions

Individual
Svensk-Franska Konstgalleriet, Stockholm: 1932
Stenmans Galleri, Stockholm: 1944
Konsthallen, Göteborg: 1944
Skånska Konstmuseum, Lund: 1946
Samlaren, Stockholm: 1958
Moderna Museet, Stockholm: 1960 (touring retrospective)
Stedelijk Museum, Amsterdam: 1962 (retrospective)
Galleri F 15, Moss: 1969 (touring)

Group
Den frie udstilling (Free exhibition), Copenhagen: 1919
Lunds Universitets Konstmuseum, Lund: 1919
Liljevalchs Konsthall, Stockholm: 1921
Stockholmutställningen (Stockholm exhibition), Stockholm: 1930
Galerie Denise René, Paris: 1953 (L'Art suédois, 1913–53)
Venice Biennale: 1962 (Swedish representative)

Bibliography

Edvard Wallenqvist, "Siri Derkert", Konstrevy, no.3, 1939, pp.110–11
I betong [In concrete], exh. cat., Samlaren, Stockholm, 1958
Bo Lindwall, "Siri Derkert", Konstrevy, ii, 1958
Siri Derkert, exh. cat., Moderna Museet, Stockholm, 1960
Elisabeth Lidén, Expressionismen och Sverige [Expressionism and Sweden], Lund, 1974
Rolf Söderberg, Siri Derkert, Stockholm: Sveriges Allmänna Konstförening, 1974
Nytt sumhälle, ny kultur [New society, new culture], exh. cat., Arkiv för dekorativ konst, Lund, 1979
Ulf Linde, Siri Derkert, 2nd edition, Stockholm: Bonniers, 1981 (with English summary)
Ingrid Ingelman, "Women artists in Sweden: A two-front struggle", Woman's Art Journal, v/1, 1984, pp.1–7
B. Lärkner, Det internationella avantgardet och Sverige, 1914–1925 [The international avant-garde and Sweden, 1914–1925], Malmö, 1984
T. Sandqvist, Han finns, förstår du: Siri Derkert och Valle Rosenberg [He exists, you understand: Siri Derkert and Valle Rosenberg], Stockholm, 1986
A. Öhrner, "Siri Derkert och Halldor K. Laxness, 'Den goda fröken och huset'" [Siri Derkert and Halldor K. Laxness, "The good miss and the house"], Den goda fröken och huset, Stockholm, 1989, pp.101–11
Scandinavian Modernism: Painting in Denmark, Finland, Iceland, Norway and Sweden, 1910–1920, exh. cat., Göteborgs Konstmuseum, Göteborg, and elsewhere, 1989
Fogelstadkvinnor: En porträttutställning Gripsholms slott [Fogelstad women: A portrait exhibition at Gripsholm Castle], exh. cat., Nationalmuseum, Stockholm, 1990
"Den otroliga verkligheten": 13 kvinnliga pionjärer ["The incredible reality": 13 women pioneers], exh. cat., Prins Eugens Waldemarsudde, Stockholm, and elsewhere, 1994

Manuscript collection is in the Kungliga Biblioteket, Stockholm.

Siri Derkert's art spans a large part of the 20th century. Her early drawings show an elegant draughtsmanship. During the 1910s she worked in a Cubist style, and thus outside the principal stream within Swedish modernism that related to Matisse. Around 1920 she worked for a fashion house in Stockholm, designing models. Her expressive drawing technique and use of colour were developed during the 1930s and 1940s. During that time she also explored the human face more profoundly as a subject. In the 1950s she began to experiment in different techniques and media, such as iron bands, iron reliefs, coloured concrete and aluminium reliefs. Her works of greatest significance are public commissions, in which she experimented with engraving in cement and concrete. The great decoration of Östermalm underground station in Stockholm (1962–5) is one of her most innovatory works, in which all the walls of the 145-metre-long station are decorated in sand-blasted concrete. Here she combined lightness of touch with the coarseness of the material.

In 1915–16, in Italy, Derkert executed small, poetic landscapes and still lifes in a sensitive Cubist style. They were influenced by the Parisian milieu and by the Finnish painter Valle Rosenberg, with whom she fell in love, and by whom she had a son. Colour is toned down to grey, green and blue tones. In one of the foremost examples, Still Life with Teapot (1915; see illustration), the various elements of the composition float in the picture space. The teacup is placed in the centre, on a table that appears to be turned up against the picture surface. A black form pushes forward over the subject up to the picture surface towards the left, and seems to balance the subject and to hold its parts in place. Much of Derkert's work from this period has been lost.

Dance and music were already central concerns of Derkert from an early date. She herself performed experimental dance, inspired by Emile Jacques Dalcroze and Isadora Duncan. In 1917, with some friends, she organised a performance at the Intima Teatern in Stockholm, designing the costumes with them and Rosenberg. After a while she received a commission to design women's clothes from the Birgitta School, a fashion house in Stockholm. From 1918 until 1921 she travelled to Paris regularly to study fashion and buy fabrics and plumes. Her designs are clean and simplified, with high waists and a slim silhouette. During the later 1920s Derkert lived a more withdrawn existence, and her three children and their friends became her main subject matter. Rosenberg had died in 1919, and in 1925 Siri Derkert was divorced from the painter Bertil Lybeck. Sara with Three Friends in Simpnäs (1927; private

Derkert: *Still Life with Teapot*, 1915; oil; 61 × 47 cm.; Moderna Museet, Stockholm

collection, repr. Söderberg 1974, p.75) combines an intensity of expression in the figures, exactness of observation and a displacement of the picture's elements. During the next decade her depiction of people became more psychological and her style increasingly expressionistic.

During this time Derkert developed her serial working method, in which the composition emerged from an intensive drawing phase, each sketch having its own intrinsic significance, at the same time leading on to new drawings and paintings in an unhierarchical flow. Even if the many figurative drawings are not aimed at traditional portraits, the individual portrait drawings are striking studies of the psychological and physiognomical make-up of the sitter. This tendency is also apparent in the small clay sculptures on which Derkert began to work in the 1940s.

Derkert became increasingly politically involved, and was particularly interested in peace and feminist issues. In 1943 she made contacts with the feminist group Fogelstadgruppen, which organised courses in culture and sociology for women from different social classes. Derkert followed these courses until 1954. She sketched women, and they eventually became one of the main subjects of her oeuvre (e.g. portrait drawing of *Honorine Hermelin*, 1950s; Statens porträtt samling, Gripsholms Slott, repr. Stockholm 1990, cover). Between 1956 and 1958 she produced *Women's Pillar*, which was placed in the T-Centralen station of the Stockholm underground. The work comprises a square pillar clad in 12 subjects, representing prominent feminists, such as the Fogelstad women, as well as women in different professions. The motifs were engraved in wet, uncoloured concrete, which had been mixed with sand and marble, the result of a great deal of experimentation with different concrete mixtures. Derkert also worked on large-scale collage, which she exhibited at the Venice Biennale of 1962 as Sweden's representative.

During the succeeding years Siri Derkert was to execute a large number of works in concrete and cement, on both large and small scale. The large *Engravings in Natural Concrete* (1962–5) for Östermalm underground station in Stockholm was the last in this exploration of materials. Derkert prepared for the underground wall by composing drawings, then photographing, enlarging and recomposing them. There is a strong link here between her serial drawing method and her collage technique. The drawings were applied in a rhythmic composition on the concrete walls, which was then sandblasted to expose the underlying black stone. Siri Derkert came to call the decoration of Östermalm underground station her "Life's frieze". The programme is the struggle for freedom and for women's liberation and the struggle against the destruction of the environment. Drawn and written symbols for these struggles are crammed with symbols of love and *joie de vivre*, dancing children and flute-players. (There are works by Derkert in the Moderna Museet and Nationalmuseum, Stockholm; Statens porträtt samlingar, Gripsholms Slott; and Skissernas Museum, Lund.)

ANNIKA ÖHRNER

Desmarquest, Pauline *see* Auzou

Dewing, Maria Oakey
American painter, 1845–1927

Born Maria Richards Oakey in New York, 27 October 1845, to William Francis Oakey, a New York importer, and Sally Sullivan, writer on household management. Trained at Cooper Union School of Design for Women, New York, under William Rimmer, George Butler, Edwin Forbes and R. Swain Gifford, 1870. Attended Antique School of the National Academy of Design, New York, 1871–5; also studied under John La Farge. Subsequently worked in Boston with William Morris Hunt, then studied in Paris under Thomas Couture, 1876. Married painter Thomas Wilmer Dewing, 1881; son born 1882 (died in infancy), daughter born 1885. Lived in New York, spending summers in Cornish, New Hampshire, 1885–1905. Contributed articles on painting to *American Magazine of Art* from 1915. Died in New York, 13 December 1927.

Principal Exhibitions
Daniel Cottier Gallery, New York: 1875 (organised by John La Farge)
Society of American Artists, New York: from 1878
World's Columbian Exposition, Chicago: 1893 (bronze medal)
Pan-American Exposition, Buffalo, NY: 1901 (bronze medal)
Pennsylvania Academy of the Fine Arts, Philadelphia: 1907 (individual)
Knoedler and Co., New York: 1914 (individual)

Selected Writings
From Attic to Cellar: A Book for Young Housekeepers, New York: Putnam, 1879
Beauty in Dress, New York: Harper, 1881
Beauty in the Household, New York: Harper, 1882
"Flower painters and what the flower offers to art", *Art and Progress*, vi, 1915, pp.255–62
"Kenyon Cox: An appreciation", *American Magazine of Art*, x, 1919, p.304
"The ninety-fourth Annual Exhibition of the National Academy of Design", *ibid.*, pp.297–301

Bibliography
Francis Duncan, "An artist's New Hampshire garden", *Country Life in America*, xi, 1907, pp.516–20, 554, 556, 558
An Exhibition of the Paintings by Maria Oakey Dewing, exh. cat., Pennsylvania Academy of the Fine Arts, Philadelphia, 1907
Arthur Edwin Bye, *Pots and Pans, or, Studies in Still-Life Painting*, Princeton: Princeton University Press, and London: Oxford University Press, 1921
Flowers: Fourteen American, Fourteen French Artists, exh. cat., Marie Harriman Gallery, New York, 1940
Philip R. Adams, "Paintings of the later nineteenth and earlier twentieth centuries", *Cincinnati Art Museum Bulletin*, viii/4, 1968, pp.8–9
American Pupils of Thomas Couture, exh. cat., University of Maryland Department of Art, College Park, 1970
Jennifer Martin, "The rediscovery of Maria Oakey Dewing", *Feminist Art Journal*, Summer 1976, pp.24–7, 44
Jennifer M. Bienenstock, "Portraits of flowers: The out-of-door still-life paintings of Maria Oakey Dewing", *American Art Review*, vi, December 1977, pp.48–55, 114–18
Jennifer Martin, "Royal Cortissoz and Maria Oakey Dewing's *Rose Garden*", *Yale University Library Gazette*, lii, 1977, pp.84–8

Sarah Lea Burns, *The Poetic Mode in American Painting: George Fuller and Thomas Dewing*, PhD dissertation, University of Illinois at Urbana-Champaign, 1979

Ella M. Foshay, "Charles Darwin and the development of American flower imagery", *Winterthur Portfolio*, xv, 1980, pp.299–314

William H. Gerdts, "The artist's garden: American floral painting, 1850–1915", *Portfolio*, iv, July–August 1982, pp.44–51

——, *Down Garden Paths: The Floral Environment in American Art*, Rutherford, NJ: Fairleigh Dickinson University Press, 1983

Reflections of Nature: Flowers in American Art, exh. cat., Whitney Museum of American Art, New York, 1984

Susan Hobbs, "Thomas Dewing in Cornish, 1885–1905", *American Art Journal*, xvii, Spring 1985, pp.2–32

In Pursuit of Beauty: Americans and the Aesthetic Movement, exh. cat., Metropolitan Museum of Art, New York, 1986

Kathleen A. Pyne, *Immanence, Transcendence and Impressionism in Late Nineteenth Century American Painting*, PhD dissertation, University of Michigan, Ann Arbor, 1988

Virginia Tuttle Clayton, "Reminiscence and revival: The old fashioned garden, 1890–1910", *Magazine Antiques*, cxxxviii, 1990, pp.893–905

May Brawley Hill, "'Grandmother's garden'", *Magazine Antiques*, cxlii, 1992, pp.726–35

For most of her life, Maria Dewing was able to balance all her interests and skilfully achieve her goals: she published books and articles on art, colour and the home while studying painting; she became an amateur botanist and gardener while perfecting her particular style of flower painting; she wrote, produced and acted in amateur plays while maintaining a philosophical and aesthetic dialogue with her husband and nurturing her child.

Exceptional people are often, through accidents of birth, provided with the proper environment for growth. Maria Richards Oakey was born to a successful New York businessman father and a well-educated and travelled mother, who supported her desire to become an artist. Armed with financial backing and family support, Maria found herself in an enviable position for a woman of the 1860s. Not only was she able to study painting at the Cooper Union School of Design for Women and at the National Academy of Design and to travel to Italy and France (where she studied with Thomas Couture) but with her friend Helena DeKay she took an artist's studio on Broadway, where the two devoted themselves to painting and to the company of their fellow artists and teachers. Dewing was strongly influenced by her instructor John La

Dewing: *Garden in May*, 1895; oil on canvas; 60.1 × 82.5 cm.; National Museum of American Art, Smithsonian Institution, Washington, DC

Farge, a noted flower painter, and especially by his investigations into Japanese aesthetics; this influence would later result in her innovative use of colour and composition, and ultimately caused critics to compare her work to that of the Japanese painter Sotatsu.

With her marriage to the painter Thomas Wilmer Dewing in 1881, Maria Dewing made several concessions, one of which was to abandon figure painting in order to devote herself strictly to the art of flower painting. The Dewings spent their summers with a group of painters, sculptors and writers in Cornish, New Hampshire. Cornish became an artists' colony with summer homes of such notable contemporaries as August Saint-Gaudens, Annie Lazarus, Charles Platt and the Parrishes; Dewing adapted easily to this way of life by integrating the precepts of her teacher, La Farge. Following his lead, she cultivated her own lavish garden, growing flowers that she would later paint. Dewing's canvases provided the eye-level view of the gardener at work, as she herself expressed in an article in *Art and Progress*: "The flower offers a removed beauty that exists only for beauty, more abstract than it can be in the human being, even more exquisite" ("Flower painters and what the flower offers to art", 1915). *Garden in May* (1895; see illustration) exemplifies the unique quality of her light brushwork paired with shimmering colours, thus creating the illusion of a light breeze moving through the buds and grasses. Her original perceptions are evident in the painting *Bed of Poppies* (1909; Addison Gallery of American Art, Andover, MA), where the viewer glides through the greens and reds to focus on the beauty of the individual blooms growing in a garden setting. Dewing expressed her respect for the order of nature by painting in combinations those flowers that actually grew together and harshly criticised painters who depicted unnatural or inorganic arrangements of flowers. *Rose Garden* (1901; private collection, repr. Martin 1977, p.85) and *Lilies* (1882; repr. Kennedy Galleries cat. 267, 10–11 January 1947, no.185) also take the viewer on a visual journey passing the masses of flowers, leaves and vines.

Earlier in her career, in 1879, Maria Oakey had published *From Attic to Cellar*, a book on household management that resembled some of the articles her mother had written for *Scribner's* and other magazines. This was not a consuming interest for her since at this point in her life she had had no real experience as a housekeeper. In her next volume, *Beauty in Dress* (1881), she articulated basic ideas on colour and form by categorising women as types. Any present-day reader can easily identify this classification scheme as the "colour me beautiful" craze that was rampant in the USA and elsewhere in the 1980s. More importantly, the information on colour is as applicable to painting as it is to dress or for that matter to decoration. In 1882 Dewing tackled interior decoration with *Beauty in the Household*. Her publications were not an attempt to launch a new career but rather an integration of her life as a painter – she translated her work with colour on canvas to words on paper with ease. She wrote throughout her life, plays, diaries, poems and more. Her writings and reading influenced everyone with whom she came into contact, especially her husband Thomas, whose drawing *Summer* accompanied his wife's poem of the same title (both were published in *Century Magazine*). The Dewings also collaborated on a more substantial piece, a wedding present for the architect Stanford

White and his new bride entitled *Hymen* (gold leaf and oil on panel; Cincinnati Museum of Art), signed by both artists: the figure is by Thomas and the background by Maria. *Hymen* represents Thomas Dewing's idealised concept of womanhood pictured in front of Maria's background of massive green leaves and delicate flowers on an ethereal ground. Here she successfully employs her close-ups of lush greenery, which never betray location or orientation.

Dewing began exhibiting her canvases as early as the 1870s and in 1893 was awarded a bronze medal at the World's Columbian Exposition in Chicago and in 1901 again won a bronze medal for her submission to the Pan-American Exposition in Buffalo. One-woman exhibitions of her paintings were mounted in 1907 and 1914. Throughout her adult life, she exhibited individual pieces in group exhibitions at various galleries and institutions; these works were usually favourably reviewed by contemporary critics. Royal Cortissoz proclaimed Maria Dewing as one of the most talented flower painters of the day. Despite this acclaim, she harboured some regrets near the end of her life, wishing that she had spent more time on figurative painting. In 1926 she exhibited *Girl with Pomegranates* and in 1927 *Mother and Child* at the National Academy of Design's annual exhibitions; neither painting was well received, which made her regrets that much stronger. She died in her New York studio in 1927. The major public collections of her work are in the Addison Gallery of American Art, Andover, Massachusetts, and the National Museum of American Art, Washington, DC.

LAMIA DOUMATO

Díaz [Dieç], Teresa
Painter active in northern Spain, c.1316

Bibliography
José Camón Aznar, "Los murales góticos de Santa Clara de Toro", *Goya*, no.82, 1968, pp.214–19

J. Navarro Talegón, *Catálogo monumental de Toro y su alfoz*, Zamora, 1980, pp.169–75

José María Azcárate, *Arte gótico en España*, Madrid: Cátedra, 1990, p.285

Teresa Díaz is known for her signature on the choir frescoes of Santa Clara in Toro, Zamora (see illustration). These frescoes, major sections of which are still preserved, were discovered and removed from Santa Clara in 1955 and, after a period in storage and conservation, were placed on public view in the neighbouring church of San Sebastián. The ensemble is now recognised as one of the most extensive and significant monuments of Gothic painting to survive in Spain.

The Toro frescoes were probably painted for Santa Clara shortly after the completion of a reconstruction of that building in 1316. The fresco ensemble includes several scenes of the *Infancy* and *Resurrection of Christ*, extensive cycles of the *Lives of SS Catherine of Alexandria and John the Baptist*, and individual depictions of various additional saints. The paintings are executed in a graceful linear Gothic style, which in its decorative rhythms, incipient naturalism and close alliance with French models may be compared with several

Díaz: Choir frescoes of Santa Clara in Toro, Zamora, *c*.1316

contemporary ensembles in northeast Spain, among them the frescoes painted by Juan Oliver in 1332 in the refectory of Pamplona Cathedral (now in Museo de Navarra, Pamplona).

The signature of Teresa Díaz is found in a fragmentary image depicting St Christopher. It reads: TERESA DIEÇ ME FECIT, or "Teresa Díaz made me". Teresa's adoption of the formulaic phrase "me fecit", a convention of authorship used widely in the Middle Ages, would seem to identify her conclusively as the creator of the frescoes. None the less, at least one scholar has been hesitant to attribute the ensemble to a female hand, citing an unidentified crest that appears below Teresa's name as evidence that instead she may have been the donor of the frescoes. In the absence of more specific evidence, however, this suggestion remains difficult to substantiate.

Teresa Díaz's signature of the frescoes at Toro establishes her as the earliest female artist in Europe who is known to have worked in a monumental medium, as opposed to the smaller-scale media more commonly associated with medieval women

artists. The inscription also marks Díaz as the second female artist in medieval Spain, after the 10th-century illuminator Ende (q.v.), for whom a major signed work is known.

PAMELA A. PATTON

Dietzsch, Barbara Regina
German painter, 1706–1783

Born in Nuremberg, 22 September 1706; eldest child of the landscape painter Johann Israel Dietzsch, who taught her to paint with body colours on vellum. Declined offers to become a court painter; remained unmarried, living in the family home in the former milk market in Nuremberg and working with her parents, her five brothers and sister Margaretha Barbara. Suffered a stroke in 1775, but continued working

Dietzsch: *Blooming Pomegranate Branch*, undated; Kupferstichkabinett, Berlin

until two years before her death. Died in Nuremberg, 1 May 1783.

Bibliography

Michael Gröll, *Sendschreiben an Herrn Michael Keyl von den rühmlichen und nützlichen Bemühungen einiger Nürnbergischer Künstler dieses Jahrhunderts*, Dresden, 1753

Johann Georg Meusel in *Miscellaneen artistischen Inhalts*, xxiii, 1784, pp.302–5; *Neue Miscellaneen artistischen Inhalts für Künstler und Kunstliebhaber*, iii, 1796, pp.382–3

Christoph Gottlieb von Murr, text in *Journal zur Kunstgeschichte und zur Allgemeinen Literatur*, xii, 1784, pp.27–8

Friedrich Carl Gottlob Hirsching, *Historisch-Literarisches Handbuch berühmter und denkwürdiger Personen*, ii, Leipzig, 1795, p.17

Germaine Greer, *The Obstacle Race: The Fortunes of Women Painters and Their Work*, London: Secker and Warburg, and New York: Farrar Straus, 1979

Flowers of Three Centuries: One Hundred Drawings and Watercolors from the Broughton Collection, exh. cat., International Exhibitions Foundation, Washington, DC, 1983

Deutsche Zeichnungen des 18. Jahrhunderts: Zwischen Tradition und Aufklärung, exh. cat., Kupferstichkabinett, Berlin, 1987

Madeleine Pinault, *The Painter as Naturalist from Dürer to Redoute*, Paris: Flammarion, 1991

Heidrun Ludwig, *Nürnberger naturgeschichtliche Malerei im 17. und 18. Jahrhundert*, PhD dissertation, Technische Universität, Berlin, 1993

Barbara Dietzsch specialised in highly finished paintings of still lifes. She carefully painted flowers, birds and shells with body colour on vellum. Her finely executed, small cabinet pieces show a strong fidelity to nature due to an intense pictorial light, a detailed three-dimensional finish and a skilful handling of varicoloured layers of transparent glazes and opaque colours. By presenting her motifs in front of monochrome grounds – usually of chocolate brown, but sometimes white or light-coloured – Dietzsch intensified the colours and plastic effects, adding a precious impression to the natural objects depicted. The repertoire of her motifs is limited. Single flowers are most common in her oeuvre, but there are also arrangements with three or five flowers as well as bouquets in vases on stone tables, sometimes placed in front of a niche. Usually small insects and butterflies sit on leaves and blossoms or fly around the flowers. She also executed bird paintings, either of stuffed "live" birds set in front of stereotyped landscapes or of dead birds hanging on nails in front of chocolate-brown coloured walls. A few still lifes of shells can be attributed to her as well.

Except for two plates in Georg Wolfgang Knorr's *Deliciae naturae selectae* (part 1, Nuremberg, 1751), Dietzsch did not illustrate natural history books. But because of their specific beauty and their fidelity to nature her paintings were engraved and used for plates in such natural history books as Christoph Jacob Trew's *Hortus nitidissimus* (Nuremberg, 1750–86) and Adam Ludwig Wirsing's *Sammlung meistens deutscher Vögel* (Nuremberg, 1772–7). Knorr used six of her flower arrangements as shining examples for the art of flower painting in his *Auserlesenes Blumen-Zeichenbuch für Frauenzimmer* (Nuremberg, c.1740–50), a drawing book of flowers for women.

Dietzsch's paintings were usually arranged as companion pieces. Because of their standard size (c.29 × 21 cm. and 35 × 27 cm.) they could equally well be collected and combined in an unlimited number. In the 18th century collectors would hang them closely packed on the walls of cabinets. There are reports describing the garden-like effect that Dietzsch's flower pieces developed within such hangings. Sometimes her paintings were assembled in books and then used within a painted natural history collection.

There is a specific combination in Dietzsch's pictures of a faithful imitation of nature (*mimesis*) on the one hand and artistic idealisation on the other; her paintings fall in between the genres of still life and natural history illustration. Her pieces are rooted in the splendid 17th-century flower books or *florilegias*, which were usually painted for wealthy clients. Dietzsch worked for an educated middle-class clientele, usually merchants, Protestant theologians and art lovers as well as some noblemen, who were interested in both pictorial quality and natural history. For them, Dietzsch usually depicted objects life size, took notice even of the smallest details and arranged her motifs in such a way that everything of importance would be visible. Compared with botanical illustrations, her flower paintings do not show separately painted details such as seeds, and she selected motifs for their beauty, not for their rarity. This purely aesthetic view of nature was shared by many of her contemporaries. Like most Nuremberg artists involved in natural history painting, Dietzsch can be considered a follower of physico-theology, an important 18th-century Protestant movement in natural history. The physico-theologists tried to prove the existence of a good God from the perfect order and beauty of nature. They believed that, through endowing nature with beauty, God demonstrates his power and good will towards humankind, the summit of creation formed in his image. Therefore all Christians are obliged to honour God unceasingly by contemplating the beauty of his creation. One of the functions of Dietzsch's pictures was to assist in the praise of God.

Dietzsch's pictures of flowers and birds sold well in the German lands and were also exported to England, Holland and France. Because of their success, several Nuremberg painters started to work in her manner. Some of them were able to imitate her style so well that it is difficult to attribute the paintings, especially since only a few of these gouaches are signed. Dietzsch's brothers Johann Siegmund and Johann Jacob painted single fruits and vegetables floating on dark-brown grounds; Johann Christoph and Johann Albrecht – both of them shell collectors – seem to have participated in the production of miniature still lifes of shells. Margaretha Barbara Dietzsch, having been taught by Barbara Regina, painted flowers and birds in her manner, but unlike her older sister she was able to etch and engrave her designs herself. The closest follower of Dietzsch outside her own family was Ernst Friedrich Carl Lang, who preferred to paint stuffed birds. Elisabeth Christina Höll, sister of the engraver Katharina Prestel and student of both Dietzsch sisters, followed the manner of her teachers closely. She married the painter Christoph Nicolaus Matthes and moved to Hamburg, where she continued to paint in this style. Johann Christoph Bayer, the painter of the Flora Danica porcelain in Copenhagen, painted flower pieces in Dietzsch's manner as did Jan Karell, who also illustrated natural history books and painted flower pieces in oil. There were more followers of Dietzsch, most of them unknown, but all of them prove the popularity of the

Dietzsch manner in the second half of the 18th century. During the course of the 19th century, Barbara Regina Dietzsch's fame was lost, and nowadays her pictures are known only to a few specialists and collectors. Paintings by Dietzsch and her followers can be found in most departments of prints and drawings in Germany (Germanisches Nationalmuseum, Nuremberg; Kupferstichkabinett, Staatliche Museen zu Berlin; Kunsthalle, Bremen; Staatsbibliothek, Bamberg), the Netherlands (Rijksprentenkabinet, Amsterdam; Teylers Museum, Haarlem) and Britain (Fitzwilliam Museum, Cambridge).

HEIDRUN LUDWIG

Dismorr, Jessica
British painter, 1885–1939

Born Jessie Stewart Dismorr in Gravesend, Kent, 1885. Attended the Slade School of Fine Art, London, 1902–3; studied under Max Bohm at Etaples, c.1905–8; studied at La Palette, Paris, under Jean Metzinger, André Segonzac, John Duncan Fergusson and Jacques Emile Blanche, c.1910–12. Worked in Chelsea, London, and Paris, 1913–14. Signed Vorticist Manifesto in June issue of *Blast* and exhibited with Vorticists, 1914. Contributed to *Blast* and Rebel Art Centre. Voluntary war worker in France during World War I. Associate and patron of Wyndham Lewis, 1913–25. Only woman to exhibit with Group X, 1920. Began to exhibit under the name Jessica, 1924. Elected member of London Group, 1926; member, Seven and Five Society, 1926–31. Acquired studio flat in Alfriston, Sussex, 1928; moved back to London, mid-1930s. Died in Hampstead, London, 29 August 1939.

Principal Exhibitions
Stafford Gallery, London: 1912
London Salon of the Allied Artists Association: 1912–14, 1916
Salon d'Automne, Paris: 1913
Doré Galleries, London: 1915 (*Vorticist Exhibition*)
Penguin Club, New York: 1917 (*Vorticists*)
Heal's Mansard Gallery, London: 1920 (with Group X)
London Group: 1924, 1926, 1928, 1929–37
Mayor Gallery, London: 1925 (individual)
Seven and Five Society, London: 1926, 1927, 1928
Salon des Indépendants, Paris: 1927
Artists' International Association, London: 1937

Selected Writings
"Poems and notes", *Blast*, no.2, July 1915
Contributions to *Little Review*, January 1918, March 1918 and August 1919
"Critical suggestions", *Little Review*, September 1919
"Some Russian artists", *Tyro*, no.2, 1922

Bibliography
Jessica Dismorr, 1885–1939: Paintings and Drawings, exh. cat., Mayor Gallery, London, 1965
Della Dellman, "Kate Lechmere: 'Recollections of Vorticism'", *Apollo*, xciii, 1971, pp.52–3
Jessica Dismorr and Her Circle, exh. cat., Archer Gallery, London, 1972
W.C. Wees, *Vorticism and the Avant-garde*, Manchester: Manchester University Press, 1972; as *Vorticism and the English Avant-garde*, Toronto: University of Toronto Press, 1972
Jessica Dismorr, 1885–1939, exh. cat., Mercury Gallery, London, 1974
Richard Cork, *Vorticism and Abstract Art in the First Machine Age*, 2 vols, London: Gordon Fraser, and Berkeley: University of California Press, 1976
L'altra metà dell'avanguardia, 1910–1940: Pittrici e scultrici nei movimenti delle avanguardie storiche, exh. cat., Palazzo Reale, Milan, and elsewhere, 1980
Isabelle Anscombe, *Omega and After: Bloomsbury and the Decorative Arts*, London: Thames and Hudson, 1981; New York: Thames and Hudson, 1982
Jane Beckett and Deborah Cherry, "Women under the banner of Vorticism", *ISAC Cahier*, no.8–9, December 1988, pp.129–43

Jessica Dismorr participated in nearly every avant-garde grouping in London between 1912 and 1937. Her work was exhibited with the English Fauves (Stafford Gallery, 1912), the Allied Artists Association, the Vorticists (Doré Galleries, 1915), the Seven and Five Society and the London Group; she was the only woman contributor to Group X, and she was included among abstract artists at the Artists' International Association exhibition of 1937. She contributed both illustrations and poems to a wide variety of avant-garde publications of the same period: *Rhythm* (1911), *Blast* (no.2, 1915) and *Axis* (no.8, 1937), in addition to those listed above. Around 1934 she also wrote two unpublished articles for *Art*, one on Wyndham Lewis and the other on Henry Moore (both believed lost). Dismorr was also part of a close circle of women painters that included Catherina Giles, Helen Saunders and her cousin Gertrude Leese. She and Saunders appear in William Roberts's group portrait, *Vorticists at Restaurant de La Tour Eiffel, 1915* (1961–2; Tate Gallery, London), and were reputedly nicknamed by Kate Lechmere, co-founder and the financial backer of both the Rebel Art Centre and *Blast*, as Wyndham Lewis's "little lap-dogs who wanted to be Lewis' slaves and do everything for him" (Cork 1976, p.150).

Dismorr was a woman with a private income and the means to travel extensively across Europe. She was educated in Paris, was well read in contemporary avant-garde literature, and was a serious and committed painter whose friends were largely fellow-poets and artists. She is often, however, falsely regarded as a pupil or acolyte, rather than the patron and associate of Lewis that she really was. As Quentin Stevenson remarked: "If she is often regarded as a mere footnote to Wyndham Lewis, it is because the works on which her Vorticist reputation rests are so few. Her connection with Lewis has perhaps stood in the way of rather than encouraged the wider recognition her work deserves" (London 1974). She met Lewis in 1913 and worked on *Blast* as both a contributor and editor. Of her Vorticist work only a small number of paintings and drawings is known: *Abstract Composition* (1915; Tate Gallery), several works purchased by John Quinn and shown in the exhibition of his collection in New York in December 1916, *The Engine* (untraced, repr. *Blast* 1915 and Cork 1976, p.414) and *Landscape: Edinburgh Castle(?)* (c.1914–15; ink and watercolour; Victoria and Albert Museum, London). Dismorr's contributions to the Vorticist exhibition are listed as *Shapes*, *Interior*, *Movement* and *Design* (all untraced). Her contributions to *Blast* use strong diagonal compositions and

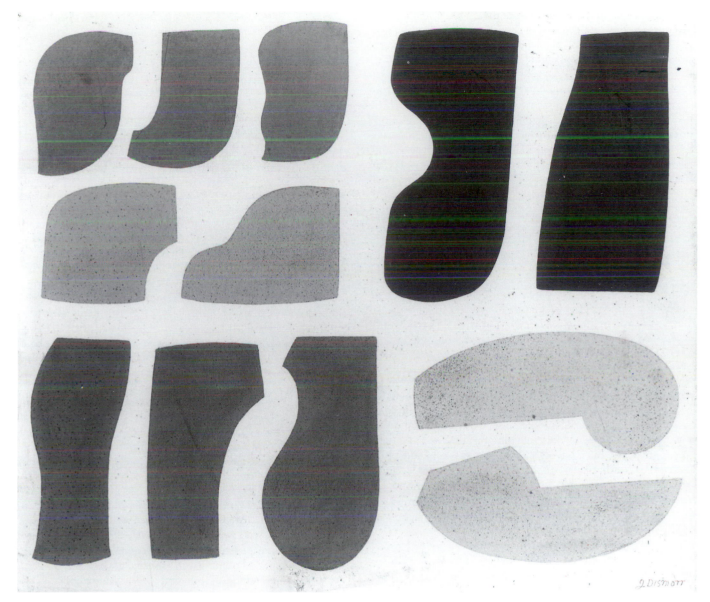

Dismorr: *Related Forms*, *c*.1936–9; tempera on board; Arts Council Collection, Hayward Gallery, London

contrasting masses of black and white. Cork acknowledged her bold design but regarded them as "crude" and derivative of Lewis's geometric Vorticism, although he was forced to acknowledge her comprehension of a quasi-Futurist, geometric vision of the modern city summoned up in her poetry (*ibid.*, pp.414–16). Lewis quarelled with Dismorr in 1925 when she would not purchase one of his drawings to supplement his meagre income. Although they were never again close friends, there appears evidence of a rapprochement between them around 1928, when Lewis borrowed and repaid money from Dismorr, and in 1934 when she introduced Lewis and T. S. Eliot to her young friend Roger Roughton.

Dismorr's lack of recognition is also attributed to her character, her modesty, reticence and lack of public ambition, alongside bouts of both mental and physical ill-health, yet she is also regarded as typifying the "New Woman" of the Edwardian era. Her other work from the 1910s and early 1920s includes Fauve-style landscapes in oil on panel

(*Landscape with Cottages*, 1912, and *Monument with Figures*, 1911–12, *ibid.*, p.151). In 1924 she began a series of water-colours of music-hall personalities; some of the subjects are associated with the Bedford music-hall that had been a popular subject among the Camden Town Group. At her only one-woman exhibition during her lifetime, in 1925, she showed a series of watercolours painted in Italy, the south of France, northern Spain, Scotland and England. One of these, *Pyrenean Town*, where a view of the town street is simplified into a geometricised, Fauve-like composition, was submitted to the Seven and Five Society exhibition in 1926 and reproduced in reviews of the show.

Between 1929 and 1934 Dismorr exhibited a series of oil portraits, alongside line drawings of her subjects, at the London Group and Seven and Five Society. The portraits encompass several pointillist self-portraits in light, bright pastel colours, portraits of her mother and her female friends, and a series of simplified and tightly executed line drawings of ten young poets including *Dylan Thomas*, *William Empson*, *Cecil Day Lewis* and *Charles Madge* (repr. London 1972 and London 1974). Her modernist approach is summed up by the statement: "Representative art is a contradiction in terms ... Beauty is the result of a certain arrangement of forms ... Real form has always to be invented as well as recognised – no construction without invention" (quoted by Quentin Stevenson in London 1974). Between 1935 and 1938 Dismorr moved into experiments with abstraction, as in *Related Forms* (see illustration; another version of 1937 in Tate Gallery) and *3 Tempos*, of which there are three versions. *Related Forms* juxtaposes free-floating vertical forms in a monochrome tonal composition.

KATY DEEPWELL

do Amaral, Tarsila *see* Amaral

Dominici, Suor Maria de
Maltese sculptor and painter, 1645–1703

Born in Vittoriosa, Malta, 6 December 1645, into a family of artists. In Rome by May 1684. Probably became a Carmelite tertiary in Malta before that date; in Rome her spiritual ties were with the Carmelite church of Santa Maria in Traspontina. Died in Rome, 18 March 1703; buried in Santa Maria in Traspontina.

Bibliography

Fra Giovan Francesco Abela, *Malta illustrata*, ed. Giovanntonio Ciantar, 2 vols, Malta, 1780

Bernardo de Dominici, *Le vite dei pittori, scultori ed architetti napolitani*, iv, Naples, 1846, pp.107–10, 200–03 (life of Mattia Preti)

Francesco Bologna, *Dizionario biografico degli Italiani*, xxxiii, Rome: Istituto dell'Enciclopedia Italiana, 1987, pp.619–32 (entries on Raimondo, Bernardo and Gian Paolo Dominici)

Mario Buhagiar, *The Iconography of the Maltese Islands, 1400–1900: Painting*, Malta: Progress Press, 1987

Dominic Cutajar, "The followers of Mattia Preti in Malta", *Report Account*, Valletta, 1988, pp.29–30, 49

P. Martin D. Schembri, "Id-devozzjoni u l-arti", *Programm tal-festa tal-Madonna tal Karmnu*, Valletta: Zabbar Verita Press, 1993, p.30

Dominic Cutajar, "Sulla scia del maestri i seguaci di Mattia Preti a Malta", *Dal segno al colore: Mattia Preti*, ed. Erminia Corace, Rome: Poligrafia del Vaticano, 1996, pp.228–30

Franca Trinchieri Camiz, "'Virgo-non sterilis': Nuns as artists in 17th-century Rome", *Picturing Women in Renaissance and Baroque Italy*, ed. Sara Matthews Grieco and Geraldine Johnson (in preparation)

Maria de Dominici was born in Malta into a family of artists. Her father Onofrio was a goldsmith and an official appraiser of valuables for the Knights of Malta; two of her brothers, Raimondo and Francesco, were painters. Her nephew Bernardo, Raimondo's son, wrote the "Lives" of Neapolitan painters, sculptors and architects, in which he also pays tribute to Maria. He informs us that while in Malta she was the pupil of Mattia Preti, who, observing her propensity for sculpture, encouraged her to go to Rome and study the works of antiquity and of Gianlorenzo Bernini, the most renowned sculptor of the time, who died in 1680. It is not known when she arrived in Rome, possibly in 1682. There is documentary evidence that in May 1684 her painting in honour of St Andrea Corsini was hung in the Roman church of the Calced Carmelites, Santa Maria in Traspontina. At that date she was already regarded as a Carmelite tertiary nun (*pizzochera*) who had the freedom to live, at least in the 17th century, not only outside the enclosed walls of the convent but also without the constraints of family ties. In fact, beginning in 1690, she lived with a woman companion and had her studio in Vicolo dell'Agnello, near the church of San Giovanni dei Fiorentini. In Rome she is said to have created public works both in sculpture and in painting, some of which were engraved by Charles de la Haye and Andrea Magliar. Most praised among her works, according to her nephew Bernardo, was a sculpture of the *Transverberation of St Teresa* (untraced), possibly a copy of the famous work by Bernini.

In Malta, Maria de Dominici is said to have made portable cult figures used for street processions on religious feast days; an *Ecco Homo* in wood and papier-mâché is recorded for the Good Friday celebrations of 1675. She also made a polychromed wooden *Virgin of the Immaculate Conception* for the Collegiate Church of Cospicua as well as a second version of the same subject in painted stone. Her wooden *Virgin* was either lost or destroyed at the beginning of the 20th century and survives only in an old photograph. A painted stone *Virgin*, now in the church crypt of the St Catherine Convent in Valletta, is believed to be her stone version even if there are no documents to support this attribution. The *Visitation*, now in the sacristy of Zebbug parish church, is considered to be her earliest painting (Abela 1780, i, p.295). It is a work that, in recent years, has been severely judged as "badly drawn and artistically uninspiring" (Buhagiar 1987, p.111). A newly discovered painting of the *Beato Franco* (see illustration) in the Carmelite church of Valletta, attributed to Maria de Dominici in various early sources, is more accomplished, but also closely resembles, in its composition, dark tonality and dramatic light effects, Mattia Preti's as yet unpublished portrayals of two other Carmelite saints in the same church. This painting was discovered in 1989 during restoration; in 1754 it had been completely repainted by Antonio Zammit in order to include an additional figure (Schembri 1993, p.30). Other altarpieces in various churches throughout Malta have been attributed to Maria de Dominici, but these are still problematic since they either have no stylistic affinity with this newly found painting or they appear to be by Mattia Preti. Attributed to her also is a drawing of the *Annunciation* in the Cathedral Museum of Valletta (A. Azzopardi, *Elenco dei disegni del Museo della Cattedrale di Malta*, Malta, 1980, no.258).

That Maria de Dominici was a strong-willed, determined and versatile artist, however, is easily surmised by two wills she drafted. The first, dated 20 July 1699 (Archivio di Stato, Rome, 30 not. cap., uff. 6, not. H. Sercamilli, Testamenti 1693–1723, fols 447–448v, 477–478), was subsequently annulled by a second one of 1 March 1703 (Archivio di Stato, Rome, 30 not. cap., uff. 10, not. E. Gattus, Testamenti

Dominici: *Beato Franco*, Carmelite church of Valletta, Malta

1695–1703, xi, fols 453r–453v, 474r–474v). The executor of these wills was the Marchese Marcello Sachetti, the Ambassador of the Knights of Malta in Rome, her special benefactor for whom she had made a marble bust of the *Virgin*. For his family, she states that she painted several portraits and an image of *St Stanislaus*. These wills list *gessi*, dies, clay or wax *modelli* and casting moulds, which give proof of her continuous interest in sculpture, particularly in bronze. Drawings were important to her, for she willed her collection, including examples that Mattia Preti had given her, to her brother Raimondo. In the spirit of a true professional, Maria de Dominici also recorded prices: 38–40 scudi in money and furniture for an altar depicting *St Teresa*, a modest sum with which she was dissatisfied, to the extent that she asked her heirs to have her work reappraised. Simone, the surgeon of Prince Borghese, is mentioned as still owing her money, beyond the 15 *giulii* and three barrels of wine she had already received, for a painting of "Queen Sofonisba".

Of particular interest, however, is the postscript to her first will that expresses her concern that the Carmelite brothers of Santa Maria in Traspontina wanted to remove her painting on the altar of St Andrea Corsini; she also records having appealed to the Sacred Congregation of Bishops and Regulars,

which decreed that the painting could not be taken down under penalty of excommunication. Hers was an admirable attempt, therefore, vigorously to defend her right as an artist to be represented on a major altar of her own church. Yet the brothers had, in 1698, donated the chapel to the Corsini family who, in renovating the chapel, replaced Maria de Dominici's picture (most likely in 1703) with a painting by G.P. Melchiorre, a pupil of Carlo Maratta, the most famed and prominent artist of the time. Melchiorre's work reflected the style of his master and must have carried greater prestige than a painting by a Carmelite tertiary nun, a situation not at all unusual in the history of art made by women. In a competitive market that distinguished then, as it still does today, betwen "major" and "minor" works of art, Maria de Dominici's artistic identity became obscured. What was the fate of her altar? Church inventories indicate that it hung in the church sacristy or choir until at least 1911; its present whereabouts are, however, unknown.

FRANCA TRINCHIERI CAMIZ

Donagh, Rita
British painter, 1939–

Born in Wednesbury, Staffordshire, 30 April 1939. Attended evening classes in life drawing at Bilston College of Further Education, 1954–6; studied fine arts at University of Durham, 1956–62 (BA). Taught full-time at Fine Art Department, University of Newcastle upon Tyne, 1962–4; School of Fine Art, University of Reading, 1964–72; part-time at Slade School of Fine Art, London, 1973; Goldsmiths' College School of Art and Design, London, 1976–8; Ruskin School of Drawing and Fine Art, University of Oxford, 1983–9; Royal College of Art, London, 1989–94. Prizewinner, John Moore's Exhibition, Liverpool, 1972. Member, Prix de Rome Selection Committee, 1972–9; Arts Council Performance Art Committee, 1975–6; Visual Arts Panel, Greater London Arts Association, 1978; Board of Trustees, Tate Gallery, 1977–84; Board of Studies, Slade School, 1990. Lives in Oxfordshire.

Selected Individual Exhibitions
Nigel Greenwood Gallery, London: 1972, 1982
The Gallery, London: 1975
Whitworth Art Gallery, Manchester: 1977 (touring, organised by Arts Council of Great Britain)
Orchard Gallery, Derry: 1983
Institute of Contemporary Arts, London: 1984 (with Richard Hamilton)
Central School of Art and Design, London: 1989 (organised by Association of Art Historians)
Cornerhouse, Manchester: 1994–5 (touring retrospective)

Bibliography
Rita Donagh: Paintings and Drawings, exh. cat., Whitworth Art Gallery, Manchester, 1977
Hayward Annual '78 , exh. cat., Arts Council of Great Britain, London, 1978
A Cellular Maze, exh. cat., Orchard Gallery, Derry, 1983

Sarat Maharaj, *Rita Donagh*, London: London Institute, 1989

Writing on the Wall: Women Writers on Women Artists, exh. cat., Tate Gallery, London, 1993

Rita Donagh: Paintings and Drawings: 197419841994, exh. cat., Cornerhouse, Manchester, and elsewhere, 1994

Ursula Szulakowska, "Rita Donagh", *Art Monthly*, December 1994, p.30

Bernadette Buckley and Jamie Stapleton, "Rita Donagh", *Circa*, no.72, Summer 1995, p.49

Rita Donagh's work has to be counted among the foremost post-war attempts to bring a more conceptual, self-reflexive approach to the practice of painting. From her early works of the mid-1960s through to the 1990s, she came to elaborate a distinctive painterly language in analytical key. She took on board the lessons and liberties of abstraction, keeping at a distance Abstract Expressionist rhetoric, remaining sceptical of its "claims to authenticity", its tendency to give almost exclusive value to seeing and the eye over thinking and the mind. Her work is deeply concerned with the force of painting itself: how is pigment, surface quality, facture, brushmark to be handled in relation to mass-media representation, photography, film and photocopier?

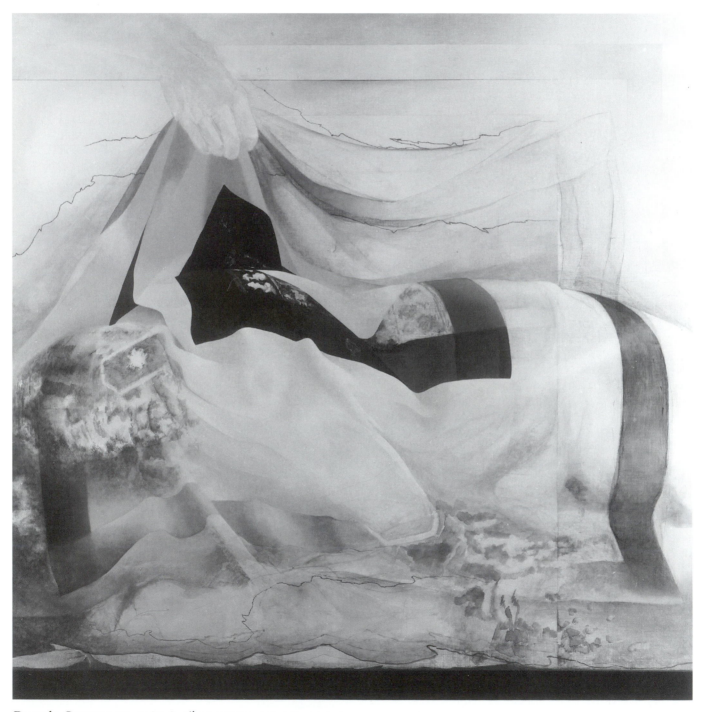

Donagh: *Counterpane*, 1987–8; oil on canvas; 152.4 × 152.4 cm.

This gives her work its performative edge: we can follow the pulse of her thinking step by step through the passage of her brush strokes across the canvas. What emerges from tracking the processes of her hand is a quiet critique of painting through painting itself. This is matched by the understated, critical focus of her subject matter and content. Donagh's works are thus both abstract and representational, as is evident from some of her earliest pieces: in *Shadow* (1964–5) and *42nd Street* (1965–6) she is as much concerned with the texture of the everyday world, the dark drama of contemporary experience as featured in *Life* magazine, as she is with the grain and structure of the printed image, with paring down photographic lushness into contours and outlines, translating them into schematic, graphic terms.

Donagh's approach – mulling over each brush stroke without making heavy weather of her probing – cannot be separated from her influential contribution as a tutor in several renowned centres of art education in England and Northern Ireland. She encouraged students to think through their art practice not only by means of ideas and concepts but through the materials at hand. We see this in operation at Reading University in *Reflection on Three Weeks in May 1970* (1970–71), which brought under scrutiny personal experience and group interaction, a questioning of time, duration, interior space and the outer world of political events, the location of the body and the means of communication. The project took off from mapping and marking but ventured beyond painting and drawing – a signpost for any history of installation, performance work and related experimental forms. The trial and error tone of her approach contributed to the atmosphere at Goldsmiths' College in the mid-1970s – to the famous "Backfields site", hotbed for the beginnings of conceptualism in Britain.

Reflection on Three Weeks in May 1970 includes a response to news of the shooting of student demonstrators against the Vietnam war at Kent State University. The concern with civil liberties, human rights, the quest for a personal sense of free expression remain central to Donagh's work. But these themes are always evoked in the course of an ongoing search – never as a fixed political stance or slogan. Thoreau's *Walden* – meditations on civil disobedience, on the ethical and creative life, language and nature – inspired *"Taking the Trouble to Sound It"* (1970–71), *New Bearings* (1971–2) and related drawings. They reveal Donagh's manner of tackling things: sizing up the pros and cons of a representation, taking the measure of its implications – so much so that we feel that more than one side of an argument is being looked at and aired.

This inquiring, non-dogmatic way of seeing and thinking informs one dimension of Donagh's abiding involvement with the theme of "Ireland"; her personal, emotional bond with the place through family links another. In *Lough Neagh* (1984; repr. Manchester 1994) the cultural memory of an ancient site intersects with intimations of the conflict in Northern Ireland – the lurid sky evokes a sense of turmoil, impending disaster, a bloody history. It also recalls how the media colours events by sensationalising accounts of the subject. Landscape turns into history painting as space, standpoint and perspectives are explored in their own right and articulated to suggest devices of control and check, a kind of policing force. With *Shadow of*

Six Counties (1980; *ibid.*), the map of post-partition Ulster, its borders and boundaries – lines of explosive clash and potential flashpoints – are literally inked, painted over and blurred. In *Long Meadow* (1982; *ibid.*) and *Compound* (1985; *ibid.*) from high up, in a bird's eye view, through cloud and mist, we catch glimpses of ghostly projections of the Maze Prison buildings, dividing walls and courtyards, the notorious H-Block cells and units in which prisoners were housed.

No other artist in Britain has brought such an unbroken focus to bear on the tragic events and episodes that make up the 25 years of the "Troubles". We see Donagh sounding out the details and facts of media representations of the conflict in *Evening Papers Ulster, 1972–4* (1973–4; *ibid.*) – trying to square versions of it, reports on the event, rumours, differing ways of recounting what happened. Does the coverage of the Troubles amount to a kind of cover-up? Does the way the story gets told in the media override the personal tragedy – the pitiful sight of the covering up of the bomb victim's body on the pavement with sheets of newspaper? *Bystander* (1977; *ibid.*) and *"Morning Workers Pass"* (1978; *ibid.*) bring a surging emotional undertow to the cool, spare abstract rendering. The calm, normal surface of the everyday is shattered by snapshots of violence and its debris, suffering and pain – the images all the more horrifying for their smallness against the canvas's abstract expanse. *Declaration* (1994) is a touched-up front-page newspaper photo of the Irish and British prime ministers standing in front of a festooned Christmas tree announcing the cease-fire of 1994 – an image Donagh had found by chance on the train that historic night. The ephemeral broadsheet aura of the piece – a photocopier print potentially reproducible in an infinite series by anyone who might wish to do so – holds back from monumentalising the occasion while it salutes the first tentative/shaky steps out of the Troubles.

Journey (1972) obliterates and redefines the real map used by the artist on a coach trip around Ireland, the last visit she was to make with her mother, who had never travelled in her own homeland. *Counterpane* (1987–8; see illustration) fuses the image of a personal memento – a threadbare patchwork quilt found in the empty and neglected dwelling in which her mother was born in Leitrim – with a public, media-derived one of a victim of the 1982 Regent's Park bomb. The powerful if restrained force of the personal sensed throughout her work comes more to the fore by the 1990s. *Slade* (1994; *ibid.*), a self-portrait of the genre "woman artist at her job", touches on issues of gender and representation, the relationship between media techniques and brushmark, abstraction and representation. The Slade School style is given a gentle, ironic once-over in what amounts to a reflective long-view on the state of painting and a comment on traditions of art education and its institutional force.

Examples of Rita Donagh's work may be found in the collections of the Arts Council of Great Britain; British Council; City Art Gallery, Leeds; Hunterian Museum, Glasgow; Tate Gallery, London; Ulster Museum, Belfast; and the Whitworth Art Gallery, Manchester.

SARAT MAHARAJ

Dorn, Marion
American textile designer, 1896–1964

Born in San Francisco, 25 December 1896. Studied graphic art at Stanford University, California (BA in education 1916). Married Henry Varnum Poor, 1919; divorced 1923. Lived with illustrator and poster artist Edward McKnight Kauffer from 1923; married him, 1950; he died 1954. Settled in London and began work as a freelance designer, 1923; established own company, Marion Dorn Ltd, in London, 1934. Freelance designer in New York from 1940. Honorary fellow, Society of Industrial Artists of Great Britain, 1957. Died in Tangier, Morocco, 23 January 1964.

Principal Exhibitions

Arthur Tooth Gallery, London: 1929 (with Edward McKnight Kauffer)
Dorland Hall, London: 1933 (*British Industrial Art in Relation to the Home*), 1934 (*Contemporary Industrial Design in the Home*)
Burlington House, London: 1935 (*British Art and Industry*)
Exposition Internationale, Paris: 1937

Bibliography

Dorothy Todd and Raymond Mortimer, *The New Interior Decoration*, New York: Scribner, and London: Batsford, 1929
Dorothy Todd, "Marion Dorn: Architect of floors", *Architectural Review*, lxxii, 1932, pp.107–14
Anthony Hunt, "The artist and the machine", *Decoration in the English Home*, January–March 1938, pp.28–33
Ann Thackeray, "Marion Dorn and carpets in the 1930s", *Leisure in the Twentieth Century*, London: Design Council, 1977, pp.14–19
Valerie Mendes, "Marion Dorn, textile designer", *Journal of the Decorative Arts Society, 1890–1940*, no.2, 1978, pp.24–35
Thirties: British Art and Design Before the War, exh. cat., Arts Council of Great Britain, London, 1979
Isabelle Anscombe, *A Woman's Touch: Women in Design from 1860 to the Present Day*, London: Virago, and New York: Viking, 1984
Christine Boydell, "Women textile designers in the 1920s and 1930s: Marion Dorn, a case study", *A View from the Interior: Feminism, Women and Design*, ed. Judy Attfield and Pat Kirkham, London: Women's Press, 1989, pp.57–70
——, *Marion Dorn: A Study of the Working Methods of the Female Professional Textile Designer in the 1920s and 1930s*, PhD dissertation, University of Huddersfield, 1992 (contains extensive bibliography and catalogue raisonné)
——, "The decorative imperative: Marion Dorn's textiles and modernism", *Journal of the Decorative Arts Society, 1850–the Present*, no.19, 1995, pp.31–40
——, *The Architect of Floors: Modernism, Art and Marion Dorn Designs*, Coggeshall, Essex: Schoeser, 1996

Marion Dorn is best known for her work as a textile designer in Britain in the inter-war period and for her efforts to elevate the status of textiles as a component of the interior. She designed batiks, rugs, printed and woven fabrics, wallpapers and illustrations. In the 1930s Dorn was a pioneer in the design of fabrics using the new hand-screen printing process. She worked as a freelance designer in Britain and the USA, establishing her own company, Marion Dorn Ltd, in 1934. Her work is notable for its bold patterning and exploration of technique – qualities that appealed particularly to modernist architects, who frequently incorporated her work into their buildings. The Victoria and Albert Museum, London, and the Warner Fabrics Archive, Milton Keynes, contain major collections of Dorn's work.

Dorn produced many designs for the hand-screen printing process that began to be used commercially in Britain in the early 1930s. It had advantages over the other available techniques (hand-block and mechanised roller printing) in that it allowed the faithful reproduction of the original design, including brush strokes. This is well illustrated in a design by Dorn of flowers and architectural motifs, *Column* (1942; Warner Fabrics Archive). Her designs were characterised by the use of bold outlines overlaid with broad unsynchronised patches of colour that floated across motifs, suggesting the colour of the object rather than describing it overtly. This technique can be seen in three hand-screen printed cottons for Warner and Sons of 1935: *Acorn and Oakleaf*, *Butterfly and Rose* and *Hand and Poppy* (all Warner Fabrics Archive) and it is also evident in her illustrations for William Beckford's novel *Vathek*, published by the Nonesuch Press (1929; see illustration).

Dorn drew on her experience of painting and the production of batiks to produce effective modern designs that were sought after to furnish modern interiors. After graduating from Stanford University, Dorn practised as a painter before concentrating on batik from c.1920. Her experience as a painter provided a perfect grounding for batik, which allowed for the creation of designs that could be drawn freely on to the fabric. On settling in London in 1923, Dorn produced decorative panels described as "a happy substitute for pictures" (*Vogue*, Early May 1925, p.50), but unlike her contemporaries she also produced large batik hangings for specific locations. Each piece was a unique creation and often produced to commission; during the 1920s Dorn's customers included Noel Coward and the Countess of Lathom. Batiks, such as a pair of curtains with a design of ships (repr. *Vogue*, Late October 1925, p.48), were reviewed favourably by the press and compared to tapestries or murals. Generally these batiks were patterned with figurative elements and included dramatic sea scenes (repr. Todd and Mortimer 1929, pl.87) or birds and animals (repr. *Vogue*, Early May 1925, pp.50–51), while a few contained classical architectural imagery (repr. *Studio Yearbook of Decorative Art*, 1928, p.182). Dorn's batik work marked a transition between her experience as a fine artist and her establishment as a freelance designer. By the end of the 1920s her work had changed dramatically: the batiks moved away from large pictures to small repeating geometric patterns (repr. *Architectural Review*, lxvii, 1930, p.37), more suited to mass production techniques.

Dorn's method of working when it came to rug design was to set the pattern of her professional practice for the rest of her career: she concentrated on design while contracting out the making of the rugs; alternatively, she worked on a freelance basis. Her first major exhibition of rugs was held at the Arthur Tooth Gallery in 1929, where her work was shown alongside rugs by her future husband Edward McKnight Kauffer – all the exhibits had been made by Wiltons. The success of this exhibition led to many commissions, including work for London hotels (the Savoy, Claridges' and the Berkeley), for shipping companies (Cunard and the Orient Line) and for architects, interior designers and private individuals. She often designed a rug as an individual piece, or as one of a limited edition of six or seven. The designs can be divided into two main categories:

Dorn: Illustration to William Beckford's *Vathek*, 1929

those that incorporate figurative motifs, such as wheat sheaves (*c*.1936; Victoria and Albert Museum), or those that are entirely abstract. Most of her rug designs are of this latter type and include a design for a rug with interlocking circles (*c*.1937; private collection, repr. *Architectural Design and Construction*, March 1937, p.179). Dorn would often incorporate her name within the construction of the rug to suggest authenticity and to maintain the association with painting. Her designs are characterised by a subtle use of colour: she had 500 shades of wool specially dyed, and instead of shading she often used tonal spots or flecks of colour to transfer from one area of pattern to the next. When using a restricted palette she would concentrate on textural variations in order to create further interest. This was achieved by combining flat weaving with hand-knotting and is evident in a number of rugs, some of which also utilised her technique of superimposing one pattern over another. A rug of 1936 (private collection, repr. London 1979, p.146) combines a blue abstract shape over a series of incised parallel lines. Dorn's habit of maximising aesthetic interest through the use of texture meant that her work was extremely popular with modernist architects and designers who required textiles that would enhance predominantly simple interior spaces.

Dorn produced designs for both printed and woven fabrics for some of the leading manufacturers of the day. She worked as a freelance designer for Warner and Sons, Old Bleach Linen, Edinburgh Weavers and Donald Brothers, who like many companies saw the commercial value of buying designs from "artist-designers"; such was the cachet of the "art" label that manufacturers such as Old Bleach Linen advertised Dorn's textile *Chorale* (1936; National Archive of Art and Design, London) alongside the work of others under the heading "Modern Artists Design for Old Bleach …". Her printed fabric *Magnolia* (1936; Victoria and Albert Museum) for Edinburgh Weavers was marketed as a "First Edition Fabric".

Marion Dorn continued to work as a freelance designer when she returned to the USA in 1940. At the heart of her success was her ability to draw on the European avant-garde in painting while simultaneously exploiting the commercial possibilities of her work. She led the way in re-evaluating the status of textiles in the interior and her approach to design resulted in textiles that were regarded by critics as "truly modern in spirit".

CHRISTINE BOYDELL

Dubourg, Victoria
French painter, 1840–1926

Born in Paris, 1 December 1840; spent some early years in Frankfurt am Main, where her father taught French. Married painter Henri Fantin-Latour, 1876; he died 1904. Lived in Paris, spending summers at Buré in Lower Normandy from 1878. Died in Buré, 30 September 1926.

Principal Exhibitions

Paris Salon: 1868–84, 1887–1902 (honourable mention 1894, third-class medal 1895)

Royal Academy, London: 1882–3, 1886–7, 1893, 1895–6
Royal Society of British Artists, London: occasionally 1882–99
Grosvenor Gallery, London: 1890

Selected Writings

Editor (as Mme Fantin-Latour), *Catalogue de l'oeuvre complet (1849–1904) de Fantin-Latour*, Paris: Floury, 1911; reprinted New York: Da Capo, 1969

Bibliography

The Realist Tradition: French Painting and Drawing, 1830–1900, exh. cat., Cleveland Museum of Art, and elsewhere, 1980
Elizabeth Kane, "Victoria Dubourg", *Woman's Art Journal*, ix/2, 1988–9, pp.15–21
Elisabeth Hardouin-Fugier and Etienne Grafe, *French Flower Painters of the 19th Century: A Dictionary*, London: Wilson, 1989

The still-life paintings by Victoria Dubourg have been overlooked in favour of those by her husband, Fantin-Latour, with which they have often been confused. So similar are some of their works that it is unlikely that they will ever be successfully attributed. Paradoxically, however, given the resemblance, this has been used by commentators to suggest that Dubourg was the inferior painter. The Irish writer George Moore, who had trained as a painter in Paris in the 1870s, examined the issue of sexual difference in his book *Modern Painting* (1893). He suggested that woman painters have tended to parody men:

[they] astonish us as much by their want of originality as they do by their extraordinary powers of assimilation. I am thinking now of the ladies who marry painters, and who, after a few years of married life, exhibit work identical in execution with that of their illustrious husbands – Mrs E.M. Ward, Madame Fantin-Latour, Mrs Swan, Mrs Alma-Tadema. In a word, what Manet used to call *la peinture à quatre mains*.

Most commentators have dismissed Dubourg in this way: as someone who was not in the same league as her husband and who gladly adopted his style as her own. The essential ingredient, according to Moore, which Fantin possessed and Dubourg lacked, was that of originality, which from the middle of the 19th century onwards was increasingly regarded as the prerogative of genius. In trying to draw a distinction between two painters whose work is so close, Moore has manufactured an apparent difference that is based on gender alone.

Nor do the facts support Moore's argument. Fantin and Dubourg first met in 1866, when they both belonged to the circle around Manet. Dubourg, however, had produced her first still life two years previously, and Fantin did not exhibit his first still life at the Salon until 1866, so it would appear that Dubourg discovered the genre independently. The two did not marry until 1876, by which time Dubourg had already exhibited still lifes at eight Salons. In fact, the interest of both painters in the genre was fuelled by a much larger still-life renaissance in France in the middle of the 19th century, which gained greater impetus when several fine still lifes by Chardin were bequeathed to the Louvre in 1870. Dubourg's *Still Life* (1884; Musée de Peinture et de Sculpture, Grenoble) depicts a Chardinesque table-top. It has the same indistinct setting, the same reliance on humble vegetables and utensils and the compositional device of the white napkin artlessly falling over the edge of the table to one side.

Dubourg: *Corner of a Table*, 1901; Musée d'Orsay, Paris

Fantin's frustration at having to paint still lifes instead of the higher genres is clear from his letters and recorded comments, but his paintings of flowers and fruits were immensely popular, especially with an English audience, and he produced them for economic reasons. Dubourg, on the other hand, specialised exclusively in still lifes and exhibited at the Salon from 1868. Apart from a portrait of her sister Charlotte painted in 1870 (Musée de Peinture et de Sculpture, Grenoble), she appears to have shown no interest in other genres, and in favouring the still life she was following a convention familiar to many other women who wished for some success at the Salon. Since they were denied access to the Ecole des Beaux-Arts until 1897 and few life classes (especially those using the nude male model) were open to them, women were effectively discouraged from producing history paintings or those that depended on the study of models. The still life needed no models, required very few props and could be set up in a rela-

tively confined domestic setting. By colonising the lowest genre, women posed no threat to their male counterparts at the Salon and there seems to have been a tacit agreement that their niche lay in painting still lifes and flowers. Yeldham has noted that at the Salon of 1870, 85 paintings of still lifes and flowers were by women (Charlotte Yeldham, *Women Artists in Nineteenth-Century France and England*, 2 vols, New York: Garland, 1984). Many critics commented, with some surprise, that more women than men appeared to be represented by still lifes. As well as these professional women, many of whom earned a living painting still lifes, the genre was debased by young women for whom it was an accomplishment, helpful in attracting suitors but essentially amateur in nature. Octave Uzanne in *La Femme à Paris* (1894) noted scornfully that "girls in society generally devote themselves to landscapes and flowers". With such associations, most serious male artists disdained such paintings.

Dubourg, however, continued to paint after her marriage and to exhibit at the Salon. *Corner of a Table* (1901; see illustration) betrays its destination as a Salon painting in its reliance for effect on the careful distinction between the different textures of the crisp white tablecloth, fruit, carnation and gleaming silver and glassware and a subject matter that is more identifiably drawn from a bourgeois home.

After Fantin's death in 1904, Dubourg collated the material and wrote a catalogue raisonné of her husband's work, which was published in Paris in 1911. In working so diligently to preserve his posthumous reputation, she may have done so at the expense of her own, for there is no comprehensive catalogue of her work, few works by her are in public collections and her paintings continue to be mistaken for those of her husband.

LESLEY STEVENSON

Duckworth, Ruth
American ceramist and sculptor, 1919–

Born Ruth Windmüller in Hamburg, Germany, 10 April 1919. Denied art education in Germany due to Jewish origins. Emigrated to Britain, 1936. Studied sculpture and painting at Liverpool School of Art, 1936–40. Travelled around northern England with own puppet show, 1940. Worked in a munitions factory during World War II, resulting in physical and nervous collapse. Moved to London, *c.*1944–5. Began psychoanalysis, and studied stone carving at Kennington School of Art, 1946. Subsequently worked for a short time as a monumental mason. Married sculptor Aidron Duckworth, 1949; divorced 1966. Studied ceramics at Hammersmith School of Art, London, 1955; Central School of Arts and Crafts, London, under Dora Billington and Gilbert Harding-Green, 1956–8. Moved to USA, at invitation of University of Chicago, 1964. Taught at Midway Studios, University of Chicago, 1964–5 and 1968–77; also at various summer schools and as visiting artist. Made annual visits to Europe. Visited Central America to study pre-Columbian pottery, 1965. Recipient of honorary doctorate, DePaul University, Chicago, 1982. Lives in Chicago.

Selected Individual Exhibitions
Primavera Gallery, London: 1960, 1962, 1967
Crafts Centre of Great Britain, London: 1964 (with Peter Collingswood)
Renaissance Society, University of Chicago: 1965
Agra Gallery, Washington, DC: 1965
Matsuya Department Store, Tokyo: 1967
Jacques Baruch Gallery, Chicago: 1972
Kunstkammer Ludger Köster, Mönchengladbach: 1973
Calgary School of Art, Alberta: 1973
Exhibit A, Gallery of American Ceramics, Evanston, IL: 1974 (with Richard de Vore), 1977, 1980, 1982, 1984
Museum für Kunst und Gewerbe, Hamburg: 1976
Moore College of Art, Philadelphia: 1979 (with Claire Zeisler)
Museum Boymans-van Beuningen, Rotterdam: 1979
Helen Druitt Gallery, Philadelphia: 1986
British Crafts Centre, London: 1986 (with Janet Leach)
Bellas Artes, Santa Fe, NM: 1991, 1993
Dorothy Weiss Gallery, San Francisco: 1992
Schleswig-Holsteinisches Landesmuseum, Rendsburg: 1994

Bibliography
Thomas W. Collins, "Ruth Duckworth: Clay artist", *Ceramics Monthly*, xvii, September–October 1969, pp.18–21
"Ruth Duckworth, Richard de Vore", *Ceramics Monthly*, xxiii, January 1975, pp.35–7
Tony Birks, *The Art of the Modern Potter*, 2nd edition, London: Country Life, 1976; New York: Van Nostrand Reinhold, 1977
Ruth Duckworth, exh. cat., Exhibit A, Gallery of American Ceramics, Evanston, IL, 1977
Alice Westphal, "The ceramics of Ruth Duckworth", *Craft Horizons*, xxxvii, August 1977, pp.48–51
Ruth Duckworth: Ceramiek 1979, exh. cat., Museum Boymans-van Beuningen, Rotterdam, 1979
Ruth Duckworth/Claire Zeisler, exh. cat., Moore College of Art, Philadelphia, 1979
"Ruth Duckworth exhibition", *Ceramics Monthly*, xxviii, February 1980, pp.48–51
Garth Clark, *American Ceramics, 1876 to the Present*, New York: Abbeville, 1987
Tanya Harrod, "Free spirit", *Crafts*, no.85, March–April 1987, pp.32–5
Elaine Levin, *The History of American Ceramics, 1607 to the Present*, New York: Abrams, 1988
Stephen Luecking, "Ruth Duckworth", *New Art Examiner*, January 1991, p.40
Influential Europeans in British Craft and Design, exh. cat., Crafts Council, London, 1992
Judith Raphael, "Ruth Duckworth", *Art Journal*, liii, Spring 1994, pp.43–4 (interview)

A sculptor in clay, Ruth Duckworth combines a subtle understanding of scale with great sensitivity towards her chosen material. Refused permission to attend art school in Hitler's Germany, she moved to Britain in 1936 to study sculpture and painting at Liverpool School of Art. She later set up a sculpture workshop in Mortlake, Surrey, with Aidron Duckworth, carving tombstones three days a week to eke out a living. One of her most successful sculptures was a commission, the *Stations of the Cross*, for St Joseph's, New Malden. Intrigued by clay and the possibility of making ceramics, she studied at first at Hammersmith School, but finding the teaching too doctrinaire soon transferred to the comparative freedom of the Central School of Arts and Crafts before opening her own pottery studio.

With a clear understanding of design, Duckworth produced a range of finely made tablewares in stoneware and porcelain. In addition to pots with delicate, thin walls thrown on the wheel, she also made a range of forms that included a cruet set made by slip-casting clay in plaster of Paris moulds. With their matt, creamy-yellow glaze, the pieces took on a sculptural strength. Coffee cups and saucers, equally simple in form, had a distinctly modernistic feel, successfully echoing that of contemporary design.

The sight of Mexican pots in the British Museum tempted Duckworth to try making forms using hand-building techniques, such as coiling rolls of clay and joining them to create the form, a process then little used in studio pottery. Duckworth's vessels, rounded and organic, were reminiscent of pebbles, rocks and the natural world, an impression heightened by the use of matt glaze poured on to the pot to create neutral-coloured surfaces. Her work made no attempt to

Duckworth: *Form*, December 1979–February 1980; white porcelain vase; Collection Museum Boijmans Van Beuningen, Rotterdam

disguise the ceramic processes, and in consequence her forms took on a life of their own, their massive, sometimes monumental sculptural qualities breaking new ground in studio pottery. Because of the excitement and interest in the hand-built work, Duckworth soon abandoned tablewares to concentrate on more decorative forms.

In contrast to the powerful stoneware pieces, Duckworth also produced objects in porcelain that were smaller in size and had a lighter, more mischievous air in the way they used the space around them. These pots have a delicacy and sensitivity that give them unique qualities of lightness and movement. One porcelain piece, made in 1966 (Victoria and Albert Museum, London), has a slightly flattened oval form on the top of the cylindrical base, reminiscent of an "eye", giving the piece an almost Surrealist quality. Buckinghamshire County Museum, Aylesbury, holds a major collection of Duckworth's ceramics.

At the invitation of the University of Chicago, Duckworth moved to the USA in 1964, first temporarily, then eventually to settle permanently. In America, Duckworth's work became larger and more sculptural. She continued to look at the concept of the vessel as container, in small-scale and delicate porcelain pieces, some of which have complex double forms that defy their apparent simplicity. There was also the opportunity to explore the idea of more abstract sculptural pieces in the form of murals. Some of these were independent objects, others were site-specific, and commissioned for particular buildings. The relationship between sculpture and architecture, one of the concerns with which Duckworth was involved, was

fully explored in *Clouds over Lake Michigan* (1976), a commission for the Dresdener Bank in Chicago. This was 25 square metres in size, and took Duckworth in a direction in which her skills as artist and maker were creatively united. The commission illustrates one of the differences between Britain, where such commissions are rare and unusual, and the USA, where there is a more open attitude to integrating fine art and architecture.

In one way, it would be accurate to describe Duckworth as a potter in Britain and a sculptor in America, but such a superficial reading of the work of this artist would ignore the sculptural dimensions of the pots she made in Britain, and her use and awareness of clay in the sculptural commissions. With great tenacity, Duckworth has continued to push at and challenge conventional concepts of what makers or artists should do, whether with pots, such as the white porcelain vase *Form* (1979–80; see illustration), or in sculptural forms. The tablewares she made were modern in concept and looked forward rather than back; her rough, powerful and sombre stoneware vessels, with their clear allegiance to the sculptural forms of landscape, had great strength and identity at a time when the popular mood was for functional pots rather than vessels that had a decorative or ritual significance. Duckworth's porcelain vessels, with their intimate, often involved forms, tell a different story, one in which the pot serves both as object and metaphor. But it is in the breadth and scale of her sculptural installations that Duckworth has found a medium that most clearly breaks away from the vessel and the idea of containment. Her forms not only retain references to the organic world and extend our understanding of what clay can do, but also make thoughtful use of its qualities.

EMMANUEL COOPER

Dumitrescu, Natalia
Romanian painter, 1915–

Born in Bucharest, 20 December 1915; naturalised French citizen, 1965. Graduated from the School of Fine Arts, Bucharest, 1939. Married painter Alexandru Istrati, 1939. Moved with Istrati to Paris, 1947; established a studio next door to the sculptor Constantin Brancusi; beneficiary, with Istrati, in Brancusi's will (he died 1957). Recipient of Groupe Espace award, Paris, 1952; Kandinsky prize, 1955; Amateurs et Collectionneurs d'Art prize, Paris, 1957; Carnegie prize, Pittsburgh, 1959; first prize, Salon International de la Femme, Paris, 1969. Lives in Paris.

Selected Individual Exhibitions
Galerie Breteau, Paris: 1950
Galerie Arnaud, Paris: 1952, 1954, 1956
Palais des Beaux-Arts, Brussels: 1956
Kölnischer Kunstverein, Cologne: 1960
Galerie Cavalero, Cannes: 1962, 1965, 1970, 1975
Städtische Kunsthalle, Mannheim: 1963
Alliance Gallery, Copenhagen: 1972
Artcurial, Paris: 1976, 1985, 1989 (with Alexandru Istrati), 1994
Tokoro Gallery, Tokyo: 1981
Musée d'Art Contemporain, Chamalières: 1986

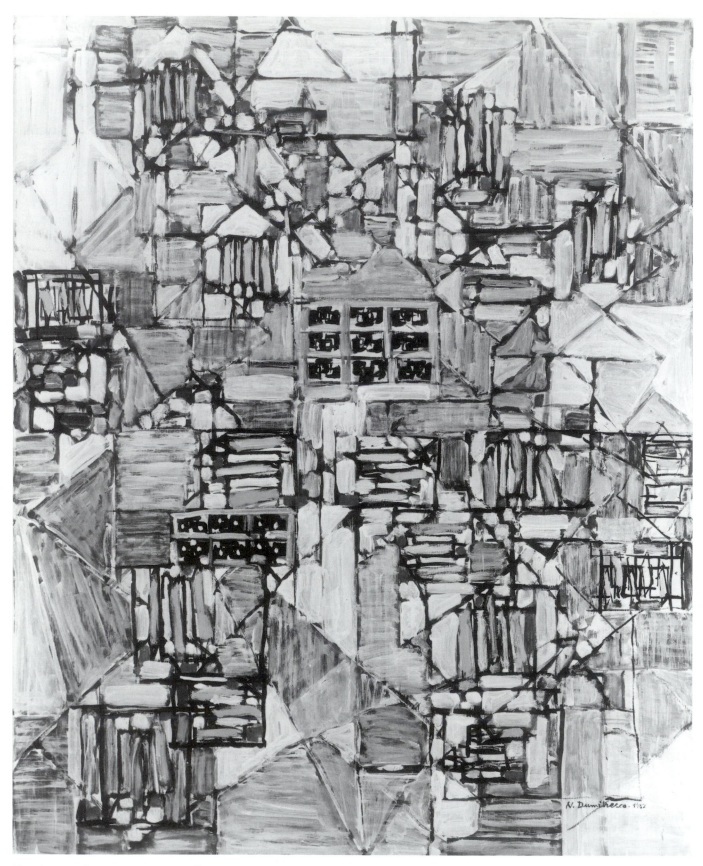

Dumitrescu: *Composition*, 1982; oil on canvas; 100 × 81 cm.

Musée des Arts Décoratifs, Paris: 1987 (retrospective)
Maison des Arts Georges Pompidou, Cajarc: 1991 (*Regards*, with Alexandru Istrati)
Musée d'Art Contemporain, Pérouges: 1994 (with Alexandru Istrati)

Selected Writings

(all with Alexandru Istrati)

"Neuf années auprès de Brancusi", *C. Brancusi: Plastiken, Zeichnungen*, exh. cat., Wilhelm-Lembruck Museum, Duisburg, and elsewhere, 1976

"Introduction", *Constantin Brancusi*, exh. cat., Tokoro Gallery, Tokyo, 1977

"Brancusi photographie ses oeuvres", *Brancusi: Photographies*, exh. cat., Tokoro Gallery, Tokyo, 1978

"Brancusis Grosser Hahn", *Artis: Das aktuelle Kunstmagazin*, June 1980, pp.24–5

Brancusi, Paris: Flammarion, 1986; New York: Abrams, 1987; London: Faber, 1988; 2nd edition, 1995 (with Pontus Hulten)

Bibliography

Roland de Renéville, "Natalia Dumitrescu", *La Jeune Ecole de Paris*, ed. Jean-Clarence Lambert, Paris: Fall, 1958

Michel Seuphor, *A Dictionary of Abstract Painting*, London: Methuen, 1958 (French original, 1957)

Ecole de Paris 1960, exh. cat., Galerie Charpentier, Paris, 1960

Michel Seuphor, *Abstract Painting*, New York: Abrams, 1962

Michel Ragon and Michel Seuphor, *L'Art abstrait, 1945–1970*, iv, Paris: Maeght, 1974

Dictionnaire universel de la peinture, Paris: Robert, 1975–6

Colin Naylor, ed., *Contemporary Artists*, London: St James Press, and New York: St Martin's Press, 1977

Olga Busneag, *Natalia Dumitrescu/Alexandru Istrati*, Bucharest: Meridiane, 1985

The award of the Kandinsky prize to Natalia Dumitrescu in 1955 gave recognition to an artist who had been living in Paris, searching for her own personal style of painting. This was a difficult process for an artist whose vocabulary had evolved from figuration to abstraction. Dumitrescu had studied at the School of Fine Arts in Bucharest under Professor Francisc Sirato, a painter whose work was primarily figurative. In the seven years that she worked and exhibited in the city, her husband Alexandru Istrati began experimenting with abstraction. She was captivated by the force and expression of his work and became dissatisfied with the figurative aesthetic.

Thus, during the 1950s, after her move to France, Dumitrescu abandoned figuration. She was encouraged to continue in this direction when she received the Amateurs et Collectionneurs d'Art prize in 1957 and the Carnegie prize in 1959. She further defined her artistic language by developing a mature style, different from that of her husband, with whom she shared a studio. Soon after, Dumitrescu began to travel and discover other countries, recording her impressions on large canvases in the form of abstract lines and colours. She began to reconstruct the cities she had seen in a lyrical and luminous manner. Her compositions evoke journeys between the real and the imaginary. Although her paintings may resemble architects' drawings, she was not influenced by them; she created her cities using linear structures of criss-crossing roads that form channels of communication. She constructs her paintings of faceted geometric forms – small squares, rectangles and triangles.

Line is of primary importance in Dumitrescu's work. Colour, in most cases primary colour, is used uniquely to define surface, as in *The Cathedral* (1982), where blue fills in drawn-in space, creating a mosaic-like effect. Even more colourful, *Rose Window* (1974) resembles stained glass. Dumitrescu, on occasion, uses images that haunt her memory, as in *Letter* (1964), a composition filled with red, blue and black squares, as in a deck of cards. Almost all of Dumitrescu's paintings have titles that give form to otherwise "abstract" compositions, thus eliminating ambiguous interpretations: *Los Angeles Freeway* (1973), *Agglomeration* (1979), *Joyous City* (1981), *White Town* (1980). Her paintings radiate optimism and joy. Her understanding of urban constructions and her love of the three-dimensional led her to create painted objects. She transformed everyday objects (a pair of scales, boxes, plates, eggs) into works of art by combining and then painting them in an unusual manner. These combinations culminated in her polychrome polyester pieces: *White Column* (1981), *Blue Column* (1980), *Yellow Column* (1982), *Windows I* (1978). Such works reveal her playfulness – a playfulness that enables her to create true miniature architectural constructions. Dumitrescu takes pleasure in understanding and mastering her materials.

In 1969 Dumitrescu received first prize at the Salon International de la Femme, confirming her reputation in the art world. The book on Brancusi that she wrote with Istrati and Pontus Hulten (1986) remains an important reference for his work. Her ten years working in close proximity to Brancusi enabled her to learn not only about her craft, but about the art world as well. His passion for work served as an example to her, but he did not otherwise influence her because he had no desire to interfere in her work. In 1977 Dumitrescu and her husband participated in the reorganisation of Brancusi's studio at the Musée National d'Art Moderne, Centre Georges Pompidou, Paris. As the legal heir to Brancusi's estate, she is preparing the publication of part of his archives.

DOÏNA LEMNY

Duncombe, Susanna

British amateur artist, 1725–1812

Born Susanna Highmore, 1725, daughter of the artist Joseph Highmore. Married the Revd John Duncombe, 1761; one daughter; husband died 1786. Lived in Kent after marriage. Died in Canterbury, Kent, 28 October 1812.

Bibliography

Anna Barbauld, ed., *The Correspondence of Samuel Richardson*, 6 vols, London: Phillips, 1804

Rowland Freeman, *Kentish Poets: A Series of Writers in English Poetry*, 2 vols, Canterbury, 1821

John Cole, *Memoirs of Mrs Chapone*, London: Simpkin Marshall, 1839

Dictionary of National Biography, vi, 1885

C.R. Beard, "Highmore's scrapbook", *Connoisseur*, xciii, 1934, pp.290–97

A.S. Lewis, *Joseph Highmore, 1692–1780: An Eighteenth-Century English Portrait Painter*, Cambridge, MA: Harvard University Press, 1975

Warren Mild, *Joseph Highmore of Holborn Row*, Ardmore, PA: Kingswood, 1990

Jacqueline Riding, *Susanna Duncombe: A Quintessential Female Artist in Eighteenth-Century England?*, MA thesis, Birkbeck College, University of London, 1994

The Highmore family archive is in the Tate Gallery Archives, London.

"The illustration of books has not, for some reason, found much favour at the hands of women. Hitherto the only female artist in England who had done anything in that line was Angelica [Kauffman]" (Ellen C. Clayton, *English Female Artists*, London: Tinsley, 1876, i, p.370). The career of the illustrator and poet Susanna Duncombe has been largely forgotten, as the above quotation suggests. The renown she enjoyed in her lifetime, although difficult to measure, resulted in her inclusion in the *Dictionary of National Biography* (1885) and prompted the antiquarian William Upcott to include one of her letters in a collection of literary miscellany entitled *Eminent Women* (Evelyn Collection, Christ Church College, Oxford, i, p.98). The fullest sources concerning Duncombe remain the biographies of her father, the prominent society painter Joseph Highmore. Although Charles Beard in his article in the *Connoisseur* (1934) dismissed her compositions as "insipid", "feeble" and "guileless", it is not constructive to compare the work of a painter such as Highmore with a few sketches by his young daughter, and there is no evidence to suggest that Susanna desired or expected such comparison; her art was produced with limited expectation, undoubtedly in response to the constrictive attitudes towards women during this period, particularly that within the middle classes towards female "accomplishments" (Davidoff and Hall, *Family Fortunes: Men and Women of the English Middle Class, 1780–1850*, London and New York: Routledge, 1992).

Duncombe's career should be seen in the light of a talented amateur, schooled by her father in the rudiments of drawing and supplying illustrations for the miscellaneous publications of predominantly, but by no means exclusively, her husband, friends and relatives. Her significance is as a representative of the majority of female art producers in the 18th century who remained non-professional and, with regard to the production of art itself, removed from the public sphere. Unlike other artists' daughters, such as Mary Moser (q.v.) and Angelica Kauffman (q.v.), Duncombe either did not choose or was not encouraged to follow her father into the artistic mainstream; her amateur status was probably considered by the Highmore family as an indication of their social standing. Furthermore, despite spending her youth attached to the busy studio of her father's London home in Lincoln's Inn Fields, actual references to Susanna's contact with the artistic circles in which her father moved are limited, and she seems to have formed stronger ties with his literary friends, in particular Samuel Richardson and Elizabeth Carter. She also moved on the periphery of the genteel literary "Bluestocking" set, of which her childhood friend Hester Chapone was a major participant. Her friendship with Carter, the subject of one of Dr Johnson's most pertinent comments on female accomplishments ("A man is in general better pleased when he has a good dinner on his table than when his wife talks Greek. My old friend, Mrs Carter … could make a pudding as well as translate Epictetus from the Greek, and work a handkerchief as well as compose a poem"), is perhaps the most significant indication of Susanna's aspira-

tions and social background. In a letter of 1756 from Elizabeth Carter to Susanna (unpublished, Deal Town Hall, Kent) Carter writes:

> And so you are an arrant frequenter of plays and opera, and leave the poor Abbé du Bos to moulder on his shelf … you will be mighty glad to have recourse to his Company in a few weeks when plays and operas will be no more, and you will be reduced to the lamentable Amusement of wandering in solitary contemplation round the Basin in Lincolns Inn Field.

Duncombe's relatively leisured existence is often further alluded to in her correspondence with Richardson (Barbauld 1804).

Duncombe's artistic pretensions are acknowledged in Highmore's portrait of her (*c*.1745–50; National Gallery of Victoria, Melbourne). She appears as a handsomely attired gentlewoman, staring confidently out of the canvas and holding up for the viewer's benefit a miniature taken from the collection of sketches and designs laid out on the table before her. Her early drawings (*c*.1750) in the "scrapbook" (consisting predominantly of sketches executed by members of the

Duncombe: Title page of "Letters by John Hughes", *Siege of Damascus, Act IV, Scene II*, 1773

Highmore family; Tate Gallery, London) of cupids, pilgrims and lovers in rural idylls show the influence of the Rococo *fête champêtre*. The classical, gothick and exotic subjects of her mature work reflect the eclecticism of the later 18th century. Stylistically, her strongest influence was Joseph Highmore, whose elegantly elongated figures and overall simplicity and clarity of composition (i.e. within his *Pamela* series) are echoed in her illustration for John Hughes's *Siege of Damascus* (1773; see illustration). Duncombe created designs for some of the most popular publications of the 18th century (those for *Orlando Furioso* and *The Castle of Otranto* are in the scrapbook), but despite the hand-written addition of "S. Duncombe delint." to many of the drawings in the scrapbook (a device in printmaking to indicate the designer of an engraving), few appear to have been published. Authorship within the scrapbook is invariably indicated by a monogram, and it may be that Susanna promoted her work by sending designs on a speculative basis to publishers and authors.

Duncombe's move to Kent after her marriage signalled a period of increased activity in the production and publication of illustrations. All her known published designs date from these years, and they include topographical (J. Duncombe, "The history and antiquities of Reculver and Herne" in *Bibliotheca topographica Britannica*, 1779) as well as figurative work (J. Duncombe, ed., *Letters from Italy in the Years 1754 and 1755 by the Late Right Honourable John Earl of Corke and Orrery*, London, 1773; E. Hasted, *The History and Topographical Survey of the County of Kent*, Canterbury, 1778; *The Works of Horace in English Verse by Several Hands*, translated by W. and J. Duncombe, 4 vols, 2nd edition, London, 1767). A reference by Rowland Freeman in his *Kentish Poets* (1821, i, p.342) to the illustrations designed for the work by Duncombe suggests that, amateur or no, the artist maintained a professional interest in the translation of her designs into engravings. He writes: "of the miserable engraving of those designed to ornament the four volumes of Horace, she very justly complains in a manuscript now before the writer". The main collections of drawings and engravings after Susanna Duncombe are held at the Tate Gallery. These are in the process of being catalogued, but a small catalogue of all known engravings after her designs can be found in Riding 1994.

JACQUELINE RIDING

Duparc, Françoise
French painter, 1726–1778

Baptised in Murcie, Spain, 15 October 1726; daughter of Antoine Duparc, a sculptor from Marseille, and his Spanish wife, Gabrielle Negrela. Moved to Marseille with her family, 1730. Said to have studied under Jean Baptiste van Loo, who was living in nearby Aix-en-Provence in 1735–6 and 1742–5. Moved to Paris with a younger sister, also an artist, who died soon afterwards. Subsequently said to have stayed in London; assumed to be the artist of similar name who exhibited there in the 1760s. Returned to Marseille by 1771; made a member of the local Academy, 1776. Died in Marseille, 11 October 1778.

Principal Exhibitions
Free Society, London: 1763 ("Mrs Dupart")
Society of Artists, London: 1766 ("Duparc")

Bibliography
Philippe Auquier, "An eighteenth-century painter: Françoise Duparc", *Burlington Magazine*, vi, 1904–5, pp.477–8
Joseph Billioud, "Un peintre de types populaires: Françoise Duparc de Marseille (1726–1778)", *Gazette des Beaux-Arts*, 6th series, xx, 1938, pp.173–84
Les Femmes peintres au XVIIIe siècle, exh. cat., Musée Goya, Castres, 1973
Women Artists, 1550–1950, exh. cat., Los Angeles County Museum of Art, and elsewhere, 1976
Nancy G. Heller, *Women Artists: An Illustrated History*, 2nd edition, New York: Abbeville, 1991

It was only at the beginning of the 20th century that Françoise Duparc became known in her own country and started to be included in exhibitions. She received her first public recognition in London in 1763. During her time there she exhibited various works at both the Free Society and the Society of Artists. As she did not sign or date her works, most are unknown today, with the exception of four paintings that she bequeathed to the town hall in Marseille (all now Musée des Beaux-Arts, Marseille), although there were reported to be 41 paintings in her studio at her death. The surviving documented works, usually of working people, "genre portraits", have earned her a comparison with Chardin. Yet, unlike Chardin and Greuze, who both had a tendency to moralise, Duparc's aim appears to have been the simple depiction of people from southern France, her immediate environment.

Coming from an artistic family – her brother and sister were also artistically precocious – Françoise received her early art education from her sculptor father, Antoine Duparc. Undoubtedly, her most formative place of study was the studio of Jean Baptiste van Loo. She is thought to have been in his studio in Aix-en-Provence either before or after his stay in England (1737–42). He insisted that she be quoted as one of his pupils and thus it can be assumed that he was impressed by her talent (Billioud 1938, p.174). Despite the frequent comparisons made between Duparc's work and that of Chardin and Greuze, van Loo was surely the biggest influence on her artistic development.

The sensitivity and humility of Duparc's works suggest a familiarity with either the sitters themselves or their social contexts. It is this focus solely on the figures, rather than objects and interiors, that gives her work its strength. Her work is both simple and direct, it does not shift into the realm of nostalgia. In her works we glimpse a brief moment of working lives, as Ann Sutherland Harris acknowledged: "Duparc had an exceptional gift for capturing a fleeting moment of evocative expression" (Los Angeles 1976, p.173).

Although Duparc did not date her work, which makes it difficult to trace her stylistic development with certainty, there are nevertheless clear distinctions among her surviving paintings. The three portraits, *Man with a Sack*, *Tisane Seller* and *Old Woman* (see illustration), bear certain common characteristics. All are half-length portraits with minimal backgrounds. Each of the sitters gazes out at the viewer, but their gaze is not challenging; it is almost as if they see through us. In spite of

Duparc: *Old Woman*, oil; Musées des Beaux-Arts, Marseille

this, the portraits possess a very intimate feel, and, although definitely staged, they preserve a sense of spontaneity. The *Tisane Seller* depicts a woman in grey dress with starched white apron, out of which emerges a blue striped scarf. She carries an urn upon her back, the tap in her right hand and the cup in her left. She makes her living selling her wares on the street and yet she does not look jaded. Her head is slightly tilted as if the weight of the urn is weighing her down. Similarly, the *Old Woman* gazes out at the viewer. Her arms are crossed at her belt, her shoulders covered with a scarf. Although she is called *La Vieille*, her face is neither young nor old (*ibid.*, p.172). Her posture, however, appears to be that of an elderly woman, drawn in on herself. It has been suggested that she is a symbol of after-work rest, for she is still in her work clothes (*idem*). She epitomises the perceived image of working life in the French countryside. Her clothes and the chair on which she rests are the only objects that could possibly distract from the sitter, but they do not do so. Attention focuses entirely on her and all she embodies. Much the same can be said about *Man with a Sack*. All the works share an anonymity reinforced by the nature of their titles.

The fourth work, *La Tricoteuse*, while sharing this sense of anonymity, is markedly different. Unlike the other works, the subject is absorbed. She gazes not at the viewer, but at her knitting. She is a young girl, her head bent down towards the wool resting on her lap. This work has been aptly subtitled "Poésie du travail incarnée", for she is completely engrossed in her work. Duparc focuses little on the actual domestic interior; the sitter remains her main concern. But unlike the other works, the knitter has become the passive object of the viewer's gaze, her space intruded.

Our preoccupation with Duparc's place in art history as a "female Chardin" is symptomatic of a wish to fill in the gaps and make sense of this woman who could so effectively portray unaffected figures. Her works are undated and unsigned: so much in the artistic as well as personal life and career of Françoise Duparc remains a mystery.

UTE KREBS and ESMÉ WARD

Duprè [Dupré], Amalia
Italian sculptor, 1842–1928

Born in Florence, 26 November 1842. Trained by her father, the sculptor Giovanni Duprè. Transformed Giovanni's studio into a museum after his death (1882). Died in Florence, 23 May 1928.

Principal Exhibitions
Exposition Universelle, Paris: 1867
Esposizione Beatrice, Florence: 1890

Selected Writings
"Un fiore sulla tomba paterna", *Giovanni Duprè: Scultore (1817–1882)*, ed. Giovanni Rosadi and others, Milan: Alfieri & Lacroix, 1917, pp.39–41

Bibliography
Augusto Conti, *Ricordi del proposto Giuseppe Conti e miei e opere di Amalia Duprè nella Cattedrale di S. Miniato*, Florence: Celline alla Galileiana, 1871 (extract from *Gioventù, Rivista dell'Istruzione Pubblica*, ii)

Giovanni Duprè, *Scritti minori e lettere con un'appendice ai suoi ricordi autobiografici per Luigi Venturi*, Florence: Successori Le Monnier, 1882

—, *Thoughts on Art, and Autobiographical Memoirs*, Edinburgh: Blackwood, 1884 (Italian original, 2 vols, 1879–82)

P. Antonio Fioresi (delle Scuole Pie), *Amalia Duprè*, Florence: Ciardi, 1886

Giovanni Duprè, *Lettere familiari a Tito Sarrocchi*, Siena: Lazzeri, 1917

Charles Marcel-Reymond, *La Sculpture italienne*, Paris: Van Oest, 1927

Silvio Vigezzi, *La scultura italiana dell'Ottocento*, Milan: Ceschina, 1932

Ettore Spalletti, "Il secondo ventennio di attività di Giovanni Duprè", *Annali della Scuola Normale Superiore di Pisa*, iv, 1974, pp.537–612

Gastone Tamagnini and Giuseppe Adani, eds, *Carmela Adani, scultrice*, Cinisello Balsamo, Milan: Amilcare Pizzi/Cassa di Risparmio di Reggio Emilia, 1975

Sandro Gattei and others, eds, *Molise*, Milan: Electa, 1980

Dizionario biografico degli italiani, xlii, Rome: Istituto dell'Enciclopedia Italiana, 1993

Vincenzo Vicario, *Gli scultori italiani dal Neoclassicismo al Liberty*, 2nd edition, Lodi: Pomerio, 1994

Family papers, including letters to Amalia Duprè from her student Carmela Adani, 1922–5, are in the archives of the Villa Duprè, Fiesole.

As is the case with most other women sculptors of the 19th century, the widespread fame of Amalia Duprè in her own day has been followed by the virtual erasure of her life and works from modern art history. While having the illustrious sculptor Giovanni Duprè as father may initially have assisted her career by providing her with the best in training and studio production facilities, this early supporting presence overshadowed Amalia Duprè's memory later on as her works came to be attributed to her father, and rare mentions of her in textbooks appeared only within larger discussions of Giovanni Duprè's career. To compound the injury, repeated occupations of the Duprè family home in Fiesole during World War II by both sides destroyed archives and damaged art works, while the great flooding of the Arno in 1966 led to the collapse of part of the family library, losing still more of Amalia Duprè's correspondence and papers.

None the less, enough remains in the family's possession today to sketch the outlines of a fascinating portrait of this early Italian woman sculptor. In his somewhat romanticised *Autobiographical Memoirs* (1884) Giovanni Duprè reports that Amalia manifested an early inclination for sculpture and thus began training at her own request quite young. Duprè was greatly pleased by his new student, and apparently nothing was prohibited to Amalia in her training, including access to nude models. Giovanni and Amalia Duprè worked together closely, and after Giovanni's death Amalia finished his last works: *St Zenobius* for the central façade portal of Florence Cathedral and *St Francis* for Assisi Cathedral. To these she added the companion pieces of *St Riparata* (c.1887) and *St Clare* (1888) respectively.

Duprè: *Giotto as a Boy*, exhibited 1862; private collection

In addition to meeting the pre-eminent artists of the day in her father's studio, Duprè accompanied Giovanni to Turin, Rome and Paris, thereby being exposed to a wide range of artistic influences. She exhibited a marble version of her gesso of 1862, *Giotto as a Boy* (see illustration), alongside her father's works at the Paris Exposition Universelle of 1867 with "discrete success" (*Dizionario biografico degli italiani*, 1993). The plaster original (Villa Duprè, Fiesole) demonstrates the artist's acute observation of the supple curve of her boy model's back and of the youth's gaunt wiriness.

Amalia Duprè's correspondence reveals a cultivated circle of friends, including such leading female intellectuals as Contessa Negroni-Prati (sister of the patriot Emilio Morosini and part of Giuseppe Verdi's circle). Although no letters from women sculptors are included in her extant correspondence, other than those of her student, Carmela Adani, the fact that Giovanni Duprè's *Autobiographical Memoirs* was translated by Edith M. Peruzzi, daughter of the Rome-based American sculptor William Wetmore Story and friend of Harriet Hosmer (q.v.) and Emma Stebbins (q.v.), is a tantalising indication that Duprè may have had some acquaintance with the American women sculptors in Rome.

Duprè's early work can be described as strictly neo-classical, in reference both to that of Giovanni and of the period. Her relief panels of five *Saints*, the *Virgin* and the *Risen Christ*, for the marble pulpit of San Miniato Cathedral, Tuscany (installed before 1871), show clear and direct forms, with simple profiles and uncomplicated drapery against plain backgrounds. The relief of the bodies is extremely shallow, with only the heads and sometimes the feet protruding further from their background. Four funerary monuments in the nave underscore the extreme cleanliness of line and spatial form that Amalia Duprè was trying to achieve. Each monument consists of a framed relief with inscriptions and themes referring to the career of the deceased, whose bust appears above. Again, the relief figures are highly classicising in form, proportion, costume and coiffure, and all are shown in rigid profile against a plain background. The portrait busts, however, attract much more attention for their vividness and individuality.

The contrast in Duprè's skill in these areas is demonstrated in a monument designed for her father, never translated out of plaster (Villa Duprè, Fiesole). Her own description of the monument ("Un fiore sulla tomba paterna", 1917) reveals both the almost religious reverence she paid to her father (referred to with the personal pronouns capitalised, as is the convention for deities) and the didactic intent of this memorial. Giovanni Duprè is represented life size and in modern dress, as a mature but not yet ageing man. The "idealised realism" of the figure in the round contrasts starkly with the rendering of figures in the bas-relief panels. Although the panels, of significant scenes from Giovanni's life, are sculpted in medium depth, the scenes retain an almost cartoon-like quality that recalls the stylised compositions, stasis and truncated proportions of late Imperial and early Christian relief carving.

Other late works are in a neo-15th-century style that is frequently called "purist" today, and to which some critics refer to as "Robbian" (see Gattei and others 1980, p.178). Two of Amalia Duprè's loveliest surviving works in this more mature style, executed after 1890, are the *Virgin and Child* in the parish of Casacalenda and the *Madonna of the Rosary* in San Marco, Florence, both painted terracotta, life-sized figures in the round. Both the extreme rigidity of her early neo-classicism and the emotionalism of her more romantic tendencies seem to have been tempered in these works to yield moving but not maudlin devotional figures.

Although religious works predominate in Duprè's oeuvre, she also executed portrait busts and secular themes. Pious to an extreme, Duprè did little to promote herself and her work. Her correspondence indicates a certain reluctance even to participate in public exhibitions: Angelo De Gubernatis, director of the Esposizione Beatrice of 1890, a national exhibition of women's arts and industries marking the 600th anniversary of the death of Dante's Beatrice, wrote to Duprè repeatedly in the most flattering of tones, begging her to contribute to the exhibition. One letter reads:

If it won't be too much trouble, I would like to stop by your studio on Saturday around three in the afternoon, not only to discuss the two statuettes of your great father, but also to convince his worthy daughter to give as generously as possible to the Exhibition. The work and genius of the Italian woman must triumph in every greatest way, and no-one better than you can help me realize this supreme goal [Duprè archives, Florence, *c*.April 1890; my translation].

Giovanni Duprè reports that Amalia worked primarily for pleasure and frequently donated her work to churches and religious groups, which may be a further contributing factor in her disappearance from the annals of professional artists.

The fact that Duprè had no need to support herself by sculpting also meant that she was free to sculpt most of her work herself, rather than having to resort to the support of skilled artisans. This intimacy with materials and their carving led to an increasing freeness in the rendering of both poses and surfaces, best seen in the plaster maquettes of her late works the *Three Cardinal Virtues* and *Baptism* (Villa Duprè), and introduced a modernist dynamism to traditional religious themes. In addition, Duprè had all the skills necessary to become a teacher, taking on the young sculptor Carmela Adani as her student for three summers between 1922 and 1925. The letters from Adani to Duprè (Duprè family archives) reveal the profound importance for Adani of this relationship with her ageing teacher. Duprè's influence can also be seen in the career of her great-great-niece and namesake, Amalia Ciardi-Duprè, who works largely with Christian imagery and themes.

NANCY PROCTOR

Durant, Susan (D.)
British sculptor, active 1847–73

Born in Devon, 1820s. Studied sculpture in Rome and under Baron Henri de Triqueti in Paris. Independent studio in London from 1847; also made frequent trips to France, apparently working in Triqueti's studio. Introduced to the court of Queen Victoria, c.1865; instructed Princess Louise in sculpture. Died of pleurisy at Triqueti's house in Paris, 1 January 1873.

Principal Exhibitions
Royal Academy, London: 1847–53, 1856–60, 1863–4, 1866–9, 1872–3
Great Exhibition, London: 1851
Manchester Art Treasures Exhibition: 1857
Society of Female Artists, London: 1858, 1863
British Institution, London: 1860

Bibliography
Art Journal, 1873, p.80 (obituary)
"Susan Durant: The sculptor", *Queen*, 11 January 1873, p.27
Charlotte Yeldham, *Women Artists in Nineteenth-Century France and England*, 2 vols, New York: Garland, 1984
Shannon Hunter Hurtado, *The Company She Kept: Susan D. Durant, a Nineteenth-Century Sculptor and Her Feminist Connections*, MA thesis, University of Manitoba, Winnipeg, 1994

Durant Papers are in the Royal Archive, Windsor Castle, Berkshire.

Susan Durant was one of the few female sculptors in Victorian Britain to achieve critical and financial success in what Zola described as the "most manly" of the arts. She was best known for her portraiture, which combines a quality of smooth, abstract classicism with a remarkable facility for conveying likenesses. She also produced a substantial body of ideal works, in low relief and in the round, which represented figures from English and Classical literature and the Bible. In general, her work was well received by critics who praised her handling of both form and composition. Most of her exhibited pieces were produced in marble, attesting to her confidence that they would find ready buyers. Unfortunately, much of her oeuvre is now lost either due to accidental destruction or insufficient records, making it difficult to trace her development as an artist. Similarly, a significant portion of biographical data has been lost, leaving many questions about Durant's life unanswered.

During a winter spent in Rome with her family, the young Durant took sculpting lessons at local studios and resolved to become a professional sculptor. There, surrounded by the monuments of antiquity and the Renaissance, she developed a taste for the classical style which can be seen in her works of the 1850s and early 1860s. Calm facial features, blank, unfocused eyes and simple drapery (or none at all) characterise these works. Her later pieces reflect the influence of Baron Henri de Triqueti, the sculpting master from whom she received the bulk of her training. In his studio she encountered the vestiges of French romantic historicism, with its attention to accurately rendered costumes composed of variously textured fabrics. She was also introduced to Triqueti's use of multi-coloured marble inlay, or *tarsia*, and carving in precious materials such as ivory. From 1866 onwards, Durant's work displays detailed contemporary costume and some experimentation with polychromy.

Although her portraiture is characteristically formal, it is softened by elegant modelling with a hint of graceful naturalism. The celebrated bust of *Harriet Beecher Stowe* (1857; plaster; Castle Howard, Yorkshire; marble; see illustration) established Durant's reputation. A contemplative Stowe is garlanded with grape leaves and dressed in a softly gathered tunic and shawl fastened with a cameo of her husband. Durant's medallion of *George Grote* (1863; marble; University College, London) displays a Flaxman-like sensitivity to the curving line of the historian's profile, which is set in moderate relief against a plain oval background. Together, these works comprise her earliest extant portraits. Both show a Neo-classical simplification of composition that soon gave way to more elaborate treatments of costume and jewellery as Durant adopted a more naturalistic style.

Durant was commissioned by Queen Victoria to sculpt high-relief medallions of the royal family for the Albert Memorial Chapel at Windsor Castle (1866–9). Conceived as part of a larger commemorative programme involving *tarsia* murals by Triqueti, the Windsor medallions differ markedly from the Grote portrait. Set in roundels of polychrome marble surrounded by inlaid floral motifs, the white marble reliefs are deeply undercut and overlap their frames, rendering the figures nearly three-dimensional. Though the faces are generally smooth, sagging jowls, under-eye bags and faint expression lines are subtly conveyed. In a further concession to naturalism, the images of Queen Victoria and the Prince Consort have coloured stone eyes. The varied textures of lace, military braid, jewels, ribbons and tresses of hair are rendered with consummate skill. Bronze reductions of these medallions were struck for use as official gifts (National Portrait Gallery, London).

The latest of Durant's extant works, a portrait of *Nina Lehmann* (1871; marble with hardstone inlay; private

Durant: *Harriet Beecher Stowe, c.*1863; marble; Harriet Beecher Stowe Center, Hartford, Connecticut

collection, England), is an adventuresome adaptation of the programme of polychrome inlay work of the Albert Memorial Chapel. In this piece, elements that had been purely decorative at Windsor are transformed into a coherent scene. The child Nina, carved in white marble, leans out of an arched casement of dark marble. A colourful inlay of climbing flowers and leaves follows the curve of the frame above the girl. While the bold use of coloured stone might seem to prefigure the work of Alfred Gilbert or George Frampton, the portrait itself remains anchored in the style of the royal medallions.

Only one ideal figure by Durant can now be located. The *Faithful Shepherdess* (1863; marble; Mansion House, London) was commissioned by the City of London as part of a series of sculptures intended to celebrate the great works of English literature. Durant's contribution illustrates a passage from the playwright John Fletcher's retelling of the story of Daphnis and Chloe. Her restrained handling of the pose and facial expression of the *Shepherdess* is characteristic of the cool Neo-classicism of her earliest surviving works. The bunched and copiously folded drapery shows an affinity with Classical Greek conventions rather than the diaphanous wet drapery prevalent in the succeeding Hellenistic period.

Queen Victoria also engaged Durant to execute a monument to *King Leopold of the Belgians* (1867; marble; Esher Church, Surrey). The naturalistic disposition of the king's body, lying as though asleep with one hand resting on a tame-looking lion, echoes funeral effigies of *Ferdinand, Duc d'Orléans*, sculpted by both Pierre Loison and Triqueti. The French sculptors had initiated this departure from the more formal treatment of royal personages on commemorative monuments (Philip Ward-Jackson, "The French background of royal monuments at Windsor and Frogmore", *Church Monuments*, viii, 1993).

Determined to attain a place "amongst the great thinkers and workers of the day" (*Queen* 1873), Durant strove to overcome the disadvantages attached to her gender by acquiring both technical expertise as a sculptor and a firm intellectual grasp of the history of art and of the classical tradition. Once established in her profession, she used her reputation to promote the work of other women artists by contributing to the annual exhibitions of the Society of Female Artists. She advocated equal access for women to education, the professions and the vote, and used her art as a vehicle for expressing her feminist convictions. Demonstrating this, images of strong women, such as the women's rights proponents *Harriet Beecher Stowe* and *Dr Elizabeth Garrett Anderson* (1872; medium and whereabouts unknown) and the heroic figures of *Ruth* (1869; marble; untraced), *Constance* (1866; medium and whereabouts unknown) and the *Faithful Shepherdess* drawn from great literature, feature prominently in Durant's oeuvre.

SHANNON HUNTER HURTADO

Dymshits-Tolstaya, Sofya (Isaakovna)

Russian painter and graphic designer, 1886–1963

Born Sofya Isaakovna Dymshits in St Petersburg (later Petrograd/Leningrad), 23 April 1886. Studied in St Petersburg under Sergei Egornov and subsequently in Elizaveta Zvantseva's studio under Leon Bakst, Mstislav Dobuzhinsky and Kuzma Petrov-Vodkin, 1906–7. In Paris, 1908–9; studied at La Palette under Jacques Emile Blanche, Guérin and Henri Le Fauconnier. Subsequently travelled frequently between Paris and St Petersburg until the outbreak of World War I. After the Revolution, directed the Organisational Department and later the All-Russian Bureau of Exhibitions of IZO Narkompros (Fine Arts Section of the People's Commissariat of Enlightenment), Moscow. Organised festivities for the second anniversary celebrations of the October Revolution in Moscow, 1919. Moved to Petrograd, 1919. Directed International Bureau of the Arts and solicited essays for unrealised journal, *Internatsional iskusstv* (International of the Arts), 1920. Appointed head of editorial department of the IZO Narkompros. Editor of journals *Rabotnitsa* (Woman Worker) and *Krestyanka* (Peasant Woman), 1925–35. Member, Union of Artists of the USSR; received award from the Union, 1934. Married to writer Aleksei Tolstoy (second marriage), 1907–14; daughter born 1911; married architect Guermain Pessati, 1921; son born 1922. Died in Leningrad, 30 August 1963.

Principal Exhibitions

Mir Iskusstva (World of Art): 1912–13, 1915–16
Bubnovy valet (Jack/Knave of Diamonds), Moscow and St Petersburg: 1913
Moscow: 1915 (*Exhibition of Paintings, "The Year 1915"*, *"1915 god"*), 1916 (*Futurist Exhibition: The Store*)
Esposizione Internazionale, Venice: 1919
Petrograd/Leningrad: 1922 (*New Tendencies in Art*), 1923 (*Painting by Petrograd Artists of All Tendencies*), 1934 (*Commemorative Exhibition, 1917–1934*), 1934 (*Women in the Building of Socialism*)
Venice Biennale: 1924
Leningrad Artists, Leningrad: 1935–7
Leningrad Division of the Union of Artists (LOOSX): 1953–9

Selected Writings

"Dokladnaya zapiska Moskovskoy Khudozhestvennoy Kollegiy pri Narodnom Komissariate po Voprosam Prosveshcheniya k Sovetu Narodnykh Komissarov o postanovke v Moskve 50 pamyatnikov velikim lyudyam v oblasti revolyutsionnoy i obshchestvennoy deyatelnosti, v oblasti filosofiy, literatury, nauk i iskusstv" [Memorandum of the Moscow Artistic Collegium of the People's Commissariat of Education to the Council of People's Commissars, on the erection in Moscow of 50 monuments to outstanding figures in the area of revolutionary and social activity in philosophy, literature, sciences and the arts], *Iskusstvo*, no.2 (6), August 1918, p.15 (with Vladimir Tatlin)
"Intuitsiya-osnova zhivogo tvorchestva" [The intuition of living creation], manuscript, 1920, Russian State Archives of Literature and Art, Moscow
"Doklad o muzeye sovremennogo iskusstva" [Speech on Museum of Contemporary Art], manuscript, 1920, Russian State Archives of Literature and Art, Moscow (with Vladimir Tatlin)
"Vospominaniya khudozhnitsy S.I. Dymshits-Tolstoy" [Memoirs of the artist S.I. Dymshits-Tolstaya], manuscript, 1950s–1961, State Russian Museum, St Petersburg
Contributor to *Vospominaniya ob Alekseye Nikolayeviche Tolstom* [Reminiscences of Aleksei Nikolayevich Tolstoy], Moscow and Leningrad: Sovetskiy Pisatel, 1973

Sofya Dymshits-Tolstaya was born into a wealthy and prominent Jewish-Russian family in St Petersburg. Although her family encouraged her to study medicine, one of the few professions open to young women of the intelligentsia in Russia at the turn of the 19th and 20th centuries, she quickly decided on a career in art. Her early training in St Petersburg and her marriage to Count Aleksei Tolstoy (then an art student and fledgling writer) established her within the various avant-garde literary and artistic milieux of Moscow and St Petersburg before the revolutions of 1917. For this reason, her unpublished autobiography (1950s–1961) provides crucial insight into the social culture of Russia's "Silver Age".

Following the February and October Revolutions, Dymshits-Tolstaya devoted herself entirely to the cultural campaigns of the Bolshevik and then Soviet State, both as an artist and an administrator. Her activities within the IZO Narkompros indicate that she was valued as an organiser and financial manager, as she was from its inception (1918–20) in charge of accounts for that department, working with the artist Vladimir Tatlin (Chair of the Moscow Collegium of the IZO), Anatoly Lunacharsky (Commissar of the Narkompros) and Nadezhda Krupskaya. She is perhaps best known for her work during this period with Tatlin, both at the IZO Narkompros and as a member of the collective that constructed the model for his most famous and incomplete project, the *Monument to the Third International*. Among the artist's proudest achievements was the organisation of the fireworks display of October 1919 in Moscow, the second commemoration of the Revolution in that city. Dymshits-Tolstaya gives every indication in her writings of being both personally and politically self-conscious of her position as a woman artist. In this respect, her career followed the course of Russian feminism, from its radical aspirations before 1917, through gradual submission to Bolshevik and Soviet social and economic policies. Thus, in the early 1900s she appears to have had contact with anarchism; whereas in the 1920s she adapted to the demands of collectivisation in her editorial work for the journals *Rabotnitsa* (Woman worker) and *Krestyanka* (Peasant woman). In the 1930s she ceased administrative work and concentrated for the first time exclusively on art.

The art of Dymshits-Tolstaya remains unexplored, in part as a consequence of Soviet cultural policies until 1986. Unfortunately, another obstacle is the absence of documented works by the artist, who in her various IZO Narkompros capacities managed to have much of her work sent to Russian provincial museums, where they may have been lost or destroyed or remain unidentified. From early works such as *Tartar Woman* (1912; untraced), it is apparent that she was broadly familiar with the work of West European modernists, particularly the French Fauves and Cubists. Her subject matter before 1915 consists of still lifes, landscapes and portraits of people within her milieu but also of peasants and workers. After 1915, and documented by her selection of works for the exhibition "*The Year 1915*" in Moscow, she consistently advances her dialectical understanding of the relationship between the illusionism and the material substance of paint and support. This concern first emerges in a series of works painted in tempera on canvas in 1915 that she subtitled *Glass Mirages*, and includes the painting *Aquarium* (State Russian Museum, St Petersburg).

At the critical avant-garde exhibition *The Store* (Moscow, 1916), she presented her first painted glass reliefs. Dymshits-

Dymshits-Tolstaya: *Compass*, 1920; oil, string and sand on canvas; 69 × 53 cm.; State Art Museum, Samara

Tolstaya's familiarity with Malevich's Suprematism and particularly Tatlin's counter-reliefs must have encouraged her shift in focus; yet her choice of glass as both metaphor and material support is unique. According to the artist, her interest in glass as a support extended from her work on *faktura* (structure) in painting, and the denial of the illusionistic space of the canvas: "it is a planar surface and at the same time three-dimensional, when worked on from both sides. In this way I achieved material transparency while working on a planar surface" (Memoirs, p.129). After the October Revolution, she produced *Agitational Glass Reliefs*, which incorporated words or word fragments. Only three of her glass reliefs survive, and none at present can be accurately dated, though they must all precede 1921. A relief (repr. *De grote utopie/Die grosse Utopie/The Great Utopia*, exh. cat., Stedelijk Museum, Amsterdam, and elsewhere, 1992) in the State Russian Museum reveals that she used pieces of glass as much as 5 centimetres thick. The painting on both surfaces of this relief establishes the contradictory duality of the transparency and material density of glass as does her incorporation of many other materials including oil paint and foil. Transparency here conveys both visual illusion and the inherent, organic properties of the material while denying exclusive significance to either (one sees through to the back of the glass because it is painted and thereby rendered palpable).

Between 1917 and 1921 Dymshits-Tolstaya returned to painting on canvas, and the few works that survive appear significantly enriched by her earlier work with other materials. Both *Circus* (c.1917–20; State Russian Museum) and *Compass* (1920; see illustration) represent objects, yet the force of each work results from a complex embedding of materials into pigment and support. In *Circus* plaster or marble dust thickens sectors of the painting, which contrast with the slicker varnished sectors. In *Compass*, undoubtedly the best of her works on canvas, string is woven into an abstract surface, the curvilinear forms of which only barely suggest the implement that is the work's subject. As in her glass reliefs, the duality of materials explored for their organic properties and their capacity to suggest illusion are both irreconcilable and inseparable, revealing her particular utopian vision of the role of art in society. These works attempt to integrate contradictory values into a single system of representation, an achievement that was meant to mirror the ambition, if not the success, of the Russian revolution.

Dymshits-Tolstaya's graphic work of 1925–33 for *Rabotnitsa* and *Krestyanka* is typical of many agitational efforts of the years immediately preceding the Congress of Soviet Writers (1934). Using photomontage and gouache together with graphic typography, she created images that celebrated women in agriculture and heavy industry. Her paintings from the mid-1930s through to the end of her life continued this concern to formulate a sustainable if idealised representation of women playing the roles assigned to them: they are heads of agitational brigades, and administrators. Adopting the formula of Socialist Realism of the AKhRR (Association of Artists of Revolutionary Russia), Dymshits-Tolstaya's images of this later period reveal her constant search for a style that would be both singularly her own and collectively responsive to her era.

JANE A. SHARP

E

Eakins, Susan Macdowell

American painter and photographer, 1851–1938

Born Susan Hannah Macdowell in Philadelphia, Pennsylvania, 21 September 1851; father an engraver. Studied at the Pennsylvania Academy of the Fine Arts, Philadelphia, 1876–82. Married painter Thomas Eakins, 1884; he died 1916. Member, Philadelphia Photographic Salon, 1898. Died in Philadelphia, 27 December 1938.

Principal Exhibitions

Pennsylvania Academy of the Fine Arts, Philadelphia: 1876–9, 1881–2, 1905 (Mary Smith prize 1879, Charles Toppan prize 1882)

Philadelphia Photographic Salon: 1898

Philadelphia Art Club: 1936 (works by Susan Macdowell Eakins, her sister Elizabeth, Thomas Eakins and followers)

Bibliography

Lloyd Goodrich, *Thomas Eakins: His Life and Work*, New York: Whitney Museum of American Art, 1933

Susan MacDowell Eakins, 1851–1938, exh. cat., Pennsylvania Academy of the Fine Arts, Philadelphia, 1973

Lloyd Goodrich, *Thomas Eakins*, 2 vols, Cambridge, MA: Harvard University Press, 1982

American Women Artists, 1830–1930, exh. cat., National Museum of Women in the Arts, Washington, DC, 1987

Until the 1970s the artistic accomplishments of Susan Macdowell Eakins were virtually unknown in the academic and museum worlds. Before marriage, Macdowell had studied at the renowned Pennsylvania Academy of the Fine Arts, which, in spite of restrictions women faced in the use of the nude life model, fostered a creative atmosphere that nurtured the training or careers of various women artists such as Mary Cassatt (q.v.), Alice Barber Stephens (q.v.), Cecilia Beaux (q.v.) and Emily Sartain. She was the daughter of a distinguished engraver who, with his wife, created a progressive and artistic home environment for their eight children. Another sister, Elizabeth, also painted, and Susan Macdowell went to study at the Academy in 1876, first under the conservative tutelage of Christian Schussele and then with the more radical Thomas Eakins, whom she met in 1877. Macdowell attended portrait, life and antique classes and from the outset was supportive both of Eakins's teaching abilities and of the need for decent life-class training for art students. She exhibited intermittently from 1876 at the Academy and in 1879 submitted seven works, one of which won her the first Mary Smith prize, given to the best work by a Philadelphia female artist. This was followed in 1882 by the Charles Toppan prize, awarded to an outstanding male or female student at the Academy for the most accurate drawing.

In her own paintings, especially those executed during her student years at the Academy, the subject matter is of a private and domestic nature, with sitters primarily drawn from the insular world of family and friends. Both she and her husband painted her father's strong features on various occasions, and her solid drawing, sombre hues and characterisation in individual portraits were all indebted partly to Eakins's own aesthetic and techniques. During this early period Macdowell's talents as a watercolourist also evinced themselves in examples such as *Chaperone* (private collection, repr. Philadelphia 1973, p.17) and *Roseanna Williams* (private collection), each dated 1879. Both use Eakinsesque subject matter of a solitary, introverted figure (often a contemplative female reading or knitting) as well as kindred technique, combining refined colour harmony, a beautiful range of textures and sensitive modelling of the face. In oil paintings such as her *Portrait of a Gentleman and Dog* (c.1878–9; private collection, *ibid.*, p.9), Macdowell's firm handling and solid anatomical construction are blended with generally dark tonalities. This work was chosen to be engraved for an article by William C. Brownell on Philadelphia art schools ("The art schools of Philadelphia", *Scribner's Monthly Illustrated Magazine*, xviii, 1879, pp.745 and 749), an obvious *coup* for the young artist. Another of her best works of this period, and of her entire career, was *Portrait of a Lady* (1880; private collection, repr. Philadelphia 1973, p.20), a probing, skilfully rendered portrait of an introspective female dressed in shades of pale blue and cream.

Macdowell married Thomas Eakins in January 1884 and thereafter she devoted much of her time to domestic issues and the maintenance of her husband's career over her own artistic pursuits. Apart from her addition of her spouse's portrait to his *Agnew Clinic* (University of Pennsylvania, Philadelphia) in 1889 and her assistance with his portrait of *Dr Spitzka* (1913; private collection), the two were not known to collaborate or interfere with one another's paintings. Portraiture became a main preoccupation in her middle years (after her departure from the Academy until 1916), mostly of friends, relatives and

Eakins: *Thomas Eakins*, c.1920–25; oil on canvas; 127 × 102.6 cm.; Philadelphia Museum of Art: Gift of Charles Bregler

others in their personal circle. Described as a very loyal and generous friend by contemporaries, she was also an accomplished pianist and shared her husband's interest in music as well as photography. She was a photographer even before the time she and Eakins met, and was among the first members of the Philadelphia Photographic Salon, founded in 1898. Occasionally she exhibited her work in this medium: *Child with Doll*, for example, was in the photography salon of 1898 at the Academy. Like her spouse, she is also known to have used photographs as an aid for her own paintings, especially for portraits.

After the death of her husband in 1916 Macdowell Eakins began to paint on a regular, often daily basis and continued doing so until her death in 1938. Her late style generally reflected a weakening solidity of three-dimensional form and more acid, higher-keyed colours, both indicating movement away from a purely Eakinsesque practice and palette. In the 1920s and 1930s her production was erratic in quality, although there was considerable pictorial freshness conveyed, for example, in her portraits of the *Lewis Sisters* and *The Bibliophile* (both 1932; private collections, *ibid.*, pp.32 and 34). Occasionally she produced still lifes that seemed influenced by the example of such artists as Maria Oakey Dewing (q.v.) and J. Alden Weir, but it was her portraiture that was her pre-eminent contribution to American art. The only exhibition of her work in any quantity occurred in 1936, when 20 paintings by the artist, in addition to those by her husband, her sister Elizabeth and various Eakins followers were displayed at the Philadelphia Art Club. In the end, the final phase of her own career coincided with the decreasing power of the Eakins tradition among followers.

Macdowell Eakins also appeared in a number of her husband's paintings as a somewhat haunting, enigmatic figure, testimony to the melancholic mood with which he often imbued his female sitters. In addition to various photographic portraits of her, the artist's best-known images of his wife are found in his *Portrait of a Lady with Setter Dog* (*c.*1885; Metropolitan Museum of Art, New York) and the portrait of *Mrs Thomas Eakins* (*c.*1899; Hirshhorn Museum and Sculpture Garden, Washington, DC). Her posthumous portrait of *Thomas Eakins* (*c.*1920–25; see illustration) aged about 45 in a shadowed studio corner mirrors her own adaptation of this theme. Most of Macdowell Eakins's surviving paintings are in private collections in the USA, although scattered examples may be found in a few American museums.

SUSAN P. CASTERAS

Eardley, Joan
British painter, 1921–1963

Born at Bailing Hill Farm, Warnham, Sussex, 18 May 1921. Studied at Goldsmiths' College School of Art, London, 1938–9; Glasgow School of Art, under Hugh Adam Crawford, 1940–43 (diploma; Sir James Guthrie prize for portraiture); Patrick Allan-Fraser School of Art, Hospitalfield, near Arbroath, under James Cowie, 1947; took up post-diploma scholarship at Glasgow School of Art, 1948; went to France and Italy on travelling scholarship, 1948–9. Began to visit Corrie, Arran, *c.*1943; first visited Catterline on north-east coast of Scotland, 1951; spent increasing time there from 1956. Spent summer in Cologne du Gers, France, and visited Pyrenees, 1951. Member, Society of Scottish Artists, 1948; associate member, 1955, and member, 1963, Royal Scottish Academy. Died at Killearn Hospital outside Glasgow, 16 August 1963.

Selected Individual Exhibitions
Glasgow School of Art Museum: 1949
Gaumont Cinema, Aberdeen: 1951
St George's Gallery, London: 1955
Scottish Gallery, Edinburgh: 1955, 1958 (with William Gillies), 1961
'57 Gallery, Edinburgh: 1959
Festival Exhibition, Edinburgh: 1963 (*Four Scottish Painters*, with William MacTaggart, Robin Philipson and Anne Redpath, organised by Arts Council of Great Britain Scottish Committee)
Roland, Browse and Delbanco, London: 1963
Art Gallery and Museum, Kelvingrove, Glasgow: 1964 (touring retrospective, organised by Arts Council of Great Britain Scottish Committee)

Bibliography
R.H. Westwater, "Joan Eardley", *Scottish Art Review*, vi/2, 1957, pp.2–6
Emilio Coia, "Joan Eardley", *Scottish Art Review*, ix/3, 1964, pp.2–7, 29
Joan Eardley, RSA (1921–1963): A Memorial Exhibition, exh. cat., Arts Council of Great Britain Scottish Committee, Glasgow, 1964
Three Scottish Painters: Maxwell, Eardley, Philipson, film directed by Laurence Henson, Templar Film Studios, 1964; Scottish Film Archive, Glasgow
David Irwin, "The work of Joan Eardley", *New Saltire*, no.11, April 1964, pp.21–4
Douglas Hall, "Drawings by Joan Eardley, RSA", *Connoisseur*, clix, 1965, pp.178–82
Edwin Morgan, "To Joan Eardley", *The Second Life*, Edinburgh: Edinburgh University Press, 1968 (poem)
Joan Eardley, exh. cat., University Art Gallery, Stirling, 1969
Cordelia Oliver, "Joan Eardley and Glasgow", *Scottish Art Review*, xiv/3, 1974, pp.16–19, 31
Joan Eardley, exh. cat., Scottish Arts Council and Third Eye Centre, Glasgow, 1975
William Buchanan, *Joan Eardley*, Edinburgh: Edinburgh University Press, 1976
Edward Gage, *The Eye in the Wind: Scottish Painting since 1945*, London: Collins, 1977
Douglas Hall, *Joan Eardley*, Scottish Artists in the National Gallery of Modern Art, no.3, Edinburgh, 1979
Joan Eardley, RSA, exh. cat., Talbot Rice Centre, Edinburgh University, 1988
Joan Eardley at Work, exh. cat., Aberdeen Art Gallery, 1988
Cordelia Oliver, *Joan Eardley, RSA*, Edinburgh: Mainstream, 1988
Fiona Pearson, *Joan Eardley, 1921–1963*, Edinburgh: National Galleries of Scotland, 1988
Scottish Art since 1900, exh. cat., Scottish National Gallery of Modern Art, Edinburgh, and elsewhere, 1989
William Hardie, *Scottish Painting, 1837 to the Present*, London: Studio Vista, 1990
Duncan Macmillan, *Scottish Art, 1460–1990*, Edinburgh: Mainstream, 1990
Andrew Gibbon Williams and Andrew Brown, *The Bigger Picture: A History of Scottish Art*, London: BBC Books, 1993
Emmanuel Cooper, *The Sexual Perspective: Homosexuality and Art in the Last 100 Years in the West*, 2nd edition, London and New York: Routledge, 1994

There is an archive of letters and photographs in the Scottish National Gallery of Modern Art, Edinburgh.

Although Joan Eardley was born in England, her early move to Scotland and her training, subject matter and vigorous handling of paint place her in the line of Scottish painting. This line contains some who worked, as she did, under the open sky, and one, William McTaggart, who faced, like her, the oncoming waves on an exposed beach. In Eardley's landscapes and seascapes at Catterline, a village to the south of Aberdeen, and in her paintings of the children of the Glasgow slums at Townhead she transcended mere locality to create universal statements about the force of the elements and the forces of life. She worked in the countryside, at the edge of the sea and also, in sharp contrast, among the crowded, rundown tenements of a huge city, but she felt at home in all these, she said, for each was a tight community.

Eardley was a skilful draughtswoman using ink, chalk, wax crayon and pastel, the last sometimes on glasspaper. She made many tender drawings of children: *Study of Child in Pink Jersey* is one in a group of various subjects in Aberdeen Art Gallery. Her oil paint was at first thinly applied, as in *Cornfield at Nightfall* (1952), but later, as in *High Tide – Winter Afternoon* (1961; both Aberdeen Art Gallery), it is thick and applied with fluent, powerful, gestural marks. For Eardley, the medium itself was always an important element. Although most of her works are in oil, on a support of canvas or board, in a few works she followed the practices of collage, incorporating flower stalks in *Seeded Grasses and Daisies, September* (1960) and slips of newspaper and burnished sweet wrappings in *Children and Chalked Wall III* (1963; both Scottish National Gallery of Modern Art, Edinburgh).

Eardley was first attracted to the back streets of the city while at Glasgow School of Art. She later found a studio in Glasgow. Her early works, such as *Back Street Bookie* (1952; Edinburgh University), are now labelled social realist, but the streets are full of playing children, depicted with the greatest compassion and understanding. Her art records and celebrates the harsh life of tough children who know little of care or comfort, far less of cleanliness. She treated with humour and affection the *Little Girl with a Squint* (1962; Gracefield Arts Centre, Dumfries). In the large *Glasgow Back Street with Children Playing* (c.1960; private collection, repr. Buchanan 1976, p.29), almost 1.8 metres long, she showed them playing in front of a graffiti-laden wall (the graffiti had been carefully photographed for the record). She noted the restraining hand of an older brother in *Brother and Sister* (1955; Aberdeen Art Gallery) and in *Children, Port Glasgow* (1955; private collection, repr. Oliver 1988, p.54.) she caught the exchange between a group of boisterous, gleeful boys as they pass two girls already burdened down with the care of a baby in a pram.

Eardley: *A Stormy Sea, No.1*, 1960; oil on hardboard; 96.5 × 145.5 cm.; Glasgow Museums: Art Gallery and Museum, Kelvingrove

Eardley had a special relationship with a family of about a dozen children, and *Some of the Samson Family* (1961; private collection, repr. Buchanan 1976, p.45) is a formal portrait of five of them. Rarely does she show children totally downtrodden, as is the sad pair, probably sisters, in *Glasgow Children* (*c.*1958; private collection, repr. Westwater 1957, p.20). Painters, especially women, who paint children run the risk of being accused of sentimentality, but Eardley's paintings of children are so wholly truthful that they do not allow sentiment. She never set them up in the contrived and mawkish situations used by some minor, male, Victorian artists.

Catterline still clings to its cliff tops. The remnants of its fishing days are seen in *Salmon Net Posts* (1962; Tate Gallery, London). On the headland, at the farthest end of the line, is No.1 The Row, the tiny gale-battered cottage where Eardley had a studio. The view from its door, down and over the bay, is depicted in *Winter Sea, IV* (1958; Aberdeen Art Gallery). Here she found everything she needed. The more she knew a place, even a particular spot, the more she found to paint. Having set up, with her paints left out overnight, the whole summer would pass in that same spot. In *A Field of Oats* (1962; Arts Council of England, London) and *A Field by the Sea, Summer* (1962; Royal Scottish Academy, Edinburgh), both painted on the cliff top, Eardley fused wind, sky and vegetation in luscious pigment with wild flowers becoming tiny points of sharp colour. More than a landscape painter she was a consummate recorder of the weather and the seasons, as in *Summer Grasses and Barley on the Cliff Top* (1962; City Art Centre, Edinburgh), *Catterline in Winter* (1963; Scottish National Gallery of Modern Art) and *Winter Sun* (*c.*1963; Birmingham Art Gallery).

Eventually Eardley joined battle with the icy North Sea pounding the stony beach below. She painted on large boards, often in the worst weather with her easel weighted down with stones. These seascapes became huge. *A Stormy Sea, No.1* (1960; see illustration) is almost 1.5 metres long, *Summer Sea* (*c.*1962; Royal Scottish Academy) is 1.8 metres long, and *Salmon Nets and the Sea* (1960; University of Glasgow) is almost 2.3 metres in length. At first sight the works look abstract and there is some disagreement about the influence of Abstract Expressionism on her work. She probably saw de Staël's work in Edinburgh in 1956, and in one interview (*The Scotsman*, 19 August 1961) she spoke of her interest in Jackson Pollock and the Tâchistes, but made it clear that she would never go as far as abstract or action painting. She stated: "I believe in what the subject matter makes you do. I believe in the emotion which you get from what your eyes show you, and what you feel about certain things" (taped interview, Scottish National Gallery of Modern Art).

The late seascapes are full of the roar of wind and sea, full of fury and turmoil. There was also turmoil, and probably fury, within the artist, for Eardley was now gripped by cancer. In what was to be the last year of her life her reputation was being consolidated. She was elected Academician of the Royal Scottish Academy; she was included in the exhibition *Four Scottish Painters* mounted by the Scottish Committee of the Arts Council at the Edinburgh Festival, and also in *Fourteen Scottish Painters* at the Commonwealth Institute, London; she appeared in the film *Three Scottish Painters*, which showed her at work in Glasgow and Catterline; and her exhibition at

Roland, Browse and Delbanco in London was both a critical and financial success. Joan Eardley flourished as an artist for 15 totally dedicated years before her cruel, early death.

WILLIAM BUCHANAN

Eberle, Abastenia St Leger
American sculptor, 1878–1942

Born in Webster City, Iowa, 6 April 1878; father a physician. Moved to New York, enrolling at the Arts Students League, 1899; trained under Charles Y. Harvey, George Grey Barnard and Kenyon Cox. Shared apartment in Manhattan with Anna Vaughn Hyatt, later Huntington (q.v.), *c.*1903–6. Went to Italy, to have works cast in bronze at a Naples foundry, 1907 and 1908. Established studio in Greenwich Village, New York, 1907. Lived in New York, but spent summers at "Pooh's Hill", Woodstock, New York, 1909–13, and at "Hedgerow", Westport, Connecticut, from 1931. Visited Paris, 1913. Health deteriorated after 1919, limiting her work. Member, Woman's Art Club of New York; National Sculpture Society, 1906; Associate member, National Academy of Design, 1920. Donated works to Kendall Young Library, Webster City, Iowa, 1922. Died in New York, 26 February 1942.

Principal Exhibitions

Society of American Artists, New York: 1904, 1905 (both with Anna Vaughan Hyatt)
Louisiana Purchase Exposition, St Louis: 1904 (bronze medal, with Anna Vaughan Hyatt)
Pennsylvania Academy of the Fine Arts, Philadelphia: occasionally 1905–41
National Academy of Design, New York: occasionally 1907–32 (Helen Foster Barnett prize 1910)
Macbeth Gallery, New York: 1907–13 (annuals), 1914 (with Chester Beach and Mahonri Young), 1915 (*The Dance as Interpreted by American Sculptors*), 1921 (individual)
National Sculpture Society, New York: 1908 (Baltimore), 1923, 1929 (San Francisco)
Theodore B. Starr Gallery, New York: 1913 (individual)
International Exhibition of Modern Art, "Armory Show", New York: 1913
Gorham Galleries, New York: 1914, 1919 (annual women's exhibitions)
Panama-Pacific International Exposition, San Francisco: 1915 (bronze medal)

Bibliography

R.G. McIntyre, "The broad vision of Abastenia St Leger Eberle", *Arts and Decoration*, iii, 1913, pp.334–7
Christina Merriman, "New bottles for new wine: The work of Abastenia St Leger Eberle", *Survey*, xxx, 3 May 1913, pp.196–9
"A sculptor who is different", *New York Evening Sun*, 28 May 1913
"A sculptress who has caught the American rhythm", *Current Opinion*, lv, August 1913, pp.124–5
Abastenia St Leger Eberle: Sculptor (1878–1942), exh. cat., Des Moines Art Center, IA, 1980
The Woman Sculptor: Malvina Hoffman and Her Contemporaries, exh. cat., Berry-Hill Galleries, New York, 1984

Janis Conner and Joel Rosenkranz, *Rediscoveries in American Sculpture: Studio Works, 1893–1939*, Austin: University of Texas Press, 1989

Charlotte Streifer Rubinstein, *American Women Sculptors*, Boston: Hall, 1990

Unpublished correspondence is in the Archives of American Art and Corcoran Gallery of Art, Washington, DC; Brookgreen Gardens, Murrells Inlet, SC; and Peabody Institute Archives, Johns Hopkins University, Baltimore; a scrapbook is in Kendall Young Library, Webster City, IA.

The pulsating life of the New York streets and the joys and troubles of the city's crowded and noisy immigrant neighbourhoods inspired the finest work of Abastenia St Leger Eberle. From her schooling in the academic tradition at the Art Students League in New York, Eberle mastered the principles and craft of sculpture but rejected the allegorical and imaginative subject matter espoused by her instructors. "An artist must not shut himself up in an attic but get out into life, for art is rooted in life", she later explained, "it cannot be separated from it, nor can it improve upon it" ("A sculptor who is different", 1913). Following the lead of Bessie Potter Vonnoh (q.v.), Eberle principally created small bronzes and showed a decided preference for modelling images of women and children. She did not, however, imitate Vonnoh; she brought a strikingly fresh perspective to these subjects, finding great poignancy in the lives of the working classes while avoiding sentimentality. In their matter-of-fact simplicity, Eberle's works are replete with profound dignity and affection.

Eberle's first attempt at a genre subject was a tender group in plaster of a mother holding a clinging infant to her shoulder (Kendall Young Library, Webster City, IA), modelled in 1901 in Puerto Rico while visiting her parents who had temporarily settled there. Sharing a studio in New York with Anna Vaughn Hyatt (later Huntington, q.v.), Eberle collaborated with her on at least two large-scale sculptures, for which she modelled the figures and Hyatt the animals. Their *Men and Bull* (1904; untraced), emblematic of the struggle of man to control nature, was awarded a bronze medal at the Louisiana Purchase Exposition of 1904, bringing the two young sculptors into the public light.

Supporting herself principally through the sale of bronze tobacco jars, bookends and other decorative pieces, Eberle soon modelled a pair of statuettes that anticipated her later efforts: *Girl Skating* (1906; see illustration) and *Girls Dancing* (1907; Corcoran Gallery of Art, Washington, DC). Cast in multiple versions in bronze, the two little sculptures of New York children captured the buoyancy and vitality that Eberle found in the urban streets. Her figures, with their generalised features, are analogous to the images of street urchins pervading the popular media at the time and also paralleled paintings by the artists grouped around Robert Henri, such as George Luks and George Bellows, who sought their gritty subjects in city neighbourhoods. In the sculptor's exuberant *Girl Skating* and *Girls Dancing* the exaggerated upward curves of limbs, hair and drapery evoke an uncanny sensation of dynamic movement. The palpable feeling of unadulterated pleasure and joyful abandon made these two works instant critical successes.

Produced at a time when concern for the plight of urban children was on the rise, Eberle's sympathetic sculptures effectively drew attention to the poor without moralising or appearing threatening. Under the influence of the writings of Jane Addams and reformist friends such as Lillian Wald, Eberle was deeply committed to social causes, from women's suffrage to settlement houses, leading her to espouse an art that might improve people's lives. She felt that it was the artist's obligation to humanity to address reality in a forthright manner. In topical works such as *Unemployed* (1911; untraced, repr. Des Moines 1980, fig.b) and *White Slavery* (1913; untraced, *ibid.* fig.d) Eberle provoked discussion of prevalent social problems. *White Slavery* shows a lecherous man selling a naked, vulnerable young woman into prostitution. The auctioneer's grotesquely exaggerated form heightens the impression of his depravity. Addressed in a plethora of newspaper and magazine articles, novels and plays, white slavery was among the most hotly contested issues of its day. When a photograph of Eberle's sculpture appeared on the cover of the leftist magazine *The Survey*, the editor was surprised to receive letters from readers incensed by its display in so public a forum. Recognising the propagandist nature of this work, Eberle subsequently reduced the potency of the image by eliminating the figure of the auctioneer and re-naming the work *Pinioned*.

Few of Eberle's works were as polemical as *White Slavery*. In 1910 she modelled one of her best-known sculptures, *Windy Doorstep* (Worcester Art Museum, MA), a supremely dignified statuette of a working woman, in which the sculptor balances the curve of the wind-blown drapery with the opposing axis of an anchoring broom. To be closer to her favourite subjects, in 1914 Eberle moved into a studio on Madison Street in the heart of Lower East Side, Manhattan, the Jewish quarter of the city. She opened her studio to the neighbourhood children, offering toys for their amusement and a refuge from the dangers of the streets. Many of Eberle's works from that time, such as *Playing Jacks* and *Mud Pies* (both 1914–16; Kendall Young Library), portray individual little girls rapt in solitary play. Their small rounded bodies, in the thin and worn clothing that Eberle claimed made them better subjects for the sculptor than wealthy children in stiff garments, were modelled in solid, compact compositions. She also continued to produce more open, spirited sculptures, such as her rhythmic *On Avenue A* (1914; Kendall Young Library), which like her earlier *Girls Dancing* shows a pair of girls engaged in street performance probably to the tune of a hand organ.

Only 18 months after moving into her Madison Street studio, Eberle, who had long suffered from a weak heart, began to experience declining health. Finding city life increasingly arduous, and desiring serenity, she later bought a barn in Westport, Connecticut, where she produced several portraits and garden sculptures of traditional subjects. An artist of firm convictions and an abiding sense of responsibility, Eberle created a distinctive body of work characterised by her keen sympathy for the people she took for her subjects. She must have derived some satisfaction in the art and writings of the social realists of the 1930s, who advanced the very tenets she had earlier championed.

JULIE ARONSON

Eberle: *Girl Skating*, 1906; bronze; Metropolitan Museum of Art, New York; Rogers Fund, 1909 (09.57)

Edelson, Mary Beth
American artist, c.1934–

Born Mary Beth Johnson in East Chicago, Indiana, c.1934. Studied at School of the Art Institute of Chicago; DePauw University, Greencastle, Indiana (BA 1955), and New York University (MA 1959). Lived in Indianapolis and Washington, DC, before settling in New York, 1975. Has lectured widely and been artist-in-residence at several universities. Recipient of National Endowment for the Arts (NEA) grant, 1973; honorary doctorate, DePauw University, 1992. One son, one daughter. Lives in New York.

Selected Individual Exhibitions
Henri Gallery, Washington, DC: 1973, 1975
AIR Gallery, New York: 1975, 1977, 1979, 1983
Mandeville Art Gallery, University of California at San Diego: 1977
Franklin Furnace, New York: 1978
Albright-Knox Art Gallery, Buffalo, NY: 1980
Wright State University Galleries, Dayton, OH: 1981–2 (touring)
Hewlett Gallery, Carnegie-Mellon University, Pittsburgh: 1983
Ewing Gallery, University of Tennessee: 1988–90 (*Shape Shifter*, touring retrospective)
Washington Project for the Arts, Washington, DC: 1989
Nicole Klagsbrun Gallery, New York: 1993
Creative Time, New York: 1995

Selected Writings
"Pilgrimage/see for yourself: A journey to a Neolithic goddess cave, 1977: Grapceva, Hvar Island, Yugoslavia", *Heresies*, no.5, 1978, pp.96–9 (Great Goddess issue)
Seven Cycles: Public Rituals, New York: AIR, 1980 (introduction by Lucy R. Lippard)
"See for yourself: Feminist spirituality in holistic art", *The Politics of Women's Spirituality: Essays on the Rise of Spiritual Power Within the Feminist Movement*, ed. Charlene Spretnak, New York: Doubleday, 1982, pp.312–26
Seven Sites: Painting on the Wall, New York: Edelson, 1988
"Objections of a 'Goddess artist': An open letter to Thomas McEvilley", *New Art Examiner*, xvi, April 1989, pp.34–8
Shape Shifter: Seven Mediums, New York: Edelson, 1990

Bibliography
Jack Burnham, "Mary Beth Edelson's Great Goddess", *Arts Magazine*, l, November 1975, pp.75–8
"Goddess imagery in ritual: Interview with Mary Beth Edelson", *Women's Culture: The Women's Renaissance of the Seventies*, ed. Gayle Kimball, Metuchen, NJ: Scarecrow, 1981, pp.91–105
Lynn Zelevansky, "Is there life after performance?", *Flash Art*, no.105, December 1981–January 1982, pp.38–42
Gregory Battcock and Robert Nickas, eds, *The Art of Performance: A Critical Anthology*, New York: Dutton, 1983
Mary Beth Edelson: New Work: An Ancient Thirst and a Future Vision, exh. cat., Hewlett Gallery, Carnegie-Mellon University, Pittsburgh, 1983
Lucy R. Lippard, *Overlay: Contemporary Art and the Art of Prehistory*, New York: Pantheon, 1983
To Dance: Paintings and Drawings by Mary Beth Edelson with Performance in Mind, exh. cat., Patrick King Contemporary Art, Indianapolis, 1984
Committed to Print: Social and Political Themes in Recent American Printed Art, exh. cat., Museum of Modern Art, New York, and elsewhere, 1988
Mark Levy, "The Shaman is a gifted artist: Klein, Beuys, Edelson, Finley", *High Performance*, Fall 1988, pp.54–61
Vanishing Presence, exh. cat., Walker Art Center, Minneapolis, and elsewhere, 1989
Heide Göttner-Abendroth, *The Dancing Goddess: Principles of a Matriarchal Aesthetic*, Boston: Beacon Press, 1991 (German original)
Sprung in Die Zeit, exh. cat., Berlinische Galerie, Berlin, 1992
Jan Avgikos, *Firsthand: Photographs by Mary Beth Edelson, 1973–1993 and Shooter Series*, New York: Edelson, 1993
Mark Levy, *Technicians of Ecstasy: Shamanism and the Modern Artist*, Norfolk, CT: Bramble, 1993
Eleanor Heartney, exhibition review, *Art in America*, lxxxi, October 1993, pp.128–9

When curator Charlotte Robinson teamed pioneering feminist artist Mary Beth Edelson with embroidery specialist Marie Griffin Ingalls to create a work for her landmark exhibition *The Artist and the Quilt* in 1983, she elicited *Woman Rising*, a significantly iconic piece that serves to summarise Edelson's visionary imagery. Its centrally located abstract orant surrounded by flamelike flowers, representations of elemental energy and celestial bodies, its flanking runic figures and litany of names of goddesses and contemporary women, create a paean to potential empowerment on both physical and spiritual planes. Edelson's triumphant image embodies a revitalised metaphor that suggests continuing cultural transformation. She has, in fact, often taken this ancient prayerful position in her performances, which she has called *Private Rituals*.

Edelson once said that she wants her art to express "multiplicity rather than linear elitism", a statement indicating her desire to alter deep-seated exclusionary patterns. While her journey as woman and artist has recovered archetypal symbols for feminine re-integration into Western mainstreams, it has also engaged her in a career-long battle with outmoded dichotomous beliefs (culture versus nature chief among them) and a hierarchical structure that was, until recently, the systemic paradigm. Struggling against a rigid artistic structure that had excluded all but a few lucky and/or tenacious women, leaving few models for distaff artists to emulate, Edelson had developed a synthesis of Jungian archetypal theories, archaeological and prehistoric data and socio-political action that placed her in the forefront of the emergent feminist art movement. Flowering in the early 1970s, this widespread movement reflected the accelerating paradigm shift towards social inclusivity and artistic pluralism that were being anticipated by Edelson's artistic strategies.

Beginning as a painter with a master's degree from New York University, the artist made her first impression in 1973 with the massive collaborative exhibition held at the Henri Gallery in Washington, DC, entitled *22 Others*, based on suggestions solicited over a two-year period from local artists and critics. The seeds of this show grew into her famous poster *Some Living American Women Artists/Last Supper* (see illustration), created for the First National Conference on Women in the Visual Arts held in Washington in 1972. Recasting Leonardo da Vinci's *Last Supper* into a feminine feast whose participants overflowed into the poster's margins, Edelson celebrated the presence of her peers at the table of high art with a work that probably inspired the *Dinner Party* by Judy Chicago (q.v.).

While the artist has continued to produce paintings, drawings and prints, such as the life-sized silkscreens placed in

SOME LIVING AMERICAN WOMEN ARTISTS

Edelson: *Some Living American Women Artists / Last Supper*, c.1972; offset poster; 66 × 96.5 cm.

doorways in her series *Athena of the Hallways* (1993; artist's collection), she first established her reputation for provocative allusion in the over-painted photographs of *Private Rituals* (1975–7; artist's collection) and in installations and their accompanying purgative group performances. No matter what the medium or mixture, Edelson's work has consistently avoided traditional categorisation, being at once suggestively poetic in its exploration of a lost mythos revolving around feminine spiritual power and covertly political in its often aggressive challenge to patriarchy. Her pivotal installation of 1977, *Your 5000 Years are Up!*, comprised photographs from her earlier rituals in natural settings, including the coastal self-portraits (variously collaged, montaged and vividly painted) from *Woman Rising* as well as those from prehistoric caves in Yugoslavia and North America where local legends spoke of goddess worship. Although these earlier rituals were enacted unclothed for the single eye of her camera, later ones such as *Fire Flights in Deep Space* (also 1977) were swathed in robes, creating a more poetic, even mystical aura on film, which required no post-production manipulation. During the exhibition of *Your 5000 Years* in La Jolla, California, Edelson led similarly robed enactors of both sexes in purifying performances centred within a ring of fire.

This mutative and cleansing element was likewise central to her *Proposal for Memorials to the Nine Million Women Burned as Witches in the Christian Era* (1977), an installation entered through a free-standing portal crowned by Minoan bull's horns and protected by the ancient sign of the "fig of triumph" that traditionally wards off evil. More historicist in its allusions than any of her previous works, *Proposal* was solidly grounded in research into the punitive history of women's alternative spiritual activities. With the inclusion of cards for its viewers' own stories – either familial or regional – that recounted such tragedies, this work continued her early project *Outward/Inward*, which had requested audience response to specific themes of domestic interaction. A perpetually burning ladder in the centre of the round table in *Proposal* reminded viewers in the darkened space of the support on which victims often met their end, an ascension to a higher realm cut short by the flames of execution.

The artist's return in the 1980s to painting was not, like so much art-world activity in that decade, driven by marketing demands for commodities, but by the need to explore further the mythos of female power. A series of large canvases resulted, based on well-known fragments of Greco-Roman goddesses ensconced in the world's museums. Each of them – the Winged Victory of Samothrace, a broken head of Athena, or an armless Venus – was caught in an expressionistically painted vortex, and many featured assemblaged wings that extended the reach of each embellished image. Such devices not only unified the exhibition (1983) in the gallery space but, more importantly, suspended these antique metaphors in potential and continuing movement.

If the socio-political backlash of the 1990s, following hard on the economic downturn of the late 1980s, has caused feminism to seem more embattled than ever, Edelson has not allowed the cooling climate to slow her commitment to women's potential, meeting the challenge with a number of performances such as *Safe Sex* and *Backlash* (both held in New York in 1992), the latter sporting the leading, lengthy subtitle *Masked, Manipulated, Depressed, Double-Voiced, Trivialized, Gagged and Erased*, a reflection of contemporary efforts at repression.

Mary Beth Edelson's well-developed persona, ever at the centre of her work, is a projection of the paradigmatic shift that continues to survive – and revive – despite ongoing setbacks. Since she evokes and visualises feminine strength, Edelson inevitably provokes criticism, fear and scorn from some traditional power-brokers, whose influence she eludes by being an accomplished and canny shape-shifter. Indeed, like the fragmented myths contained in her works, Edelson has emerged again and again in new guises – lecturer, defender of the faith in feminism, activist (notably in the founding of WAC, the New-York-based Women's Action Committee, which typically mutated into another group currently addressing the art world in its larger national context) and multimedia provocateur – that make her, as Alan Moore has proclaimed, a "spiritual Prometheus".

LINDA F. MCGREEVY

Ellenrieder, Marie

German painter, 1791–1863

Born in Konstanz (Constance), 20 March 1791. Took lessons with the miniature painter Joseph Einsle, c.1810–13. Studied under Johann Peter von Langer at the Munich Academy, the first woman to receive training there, 1813–16. Invited to the Hohenzollern court in Sigmaringen, 1818. Stayed at the Fürstenberg court in Donaueschingen, 1819. Invited to the Baden court in Karlsruhe, 1820. Worked in Rome, 1822–4; associated with Friedrich Overbeck and the Nazarenes. Appointed court painter at Baden by Grand Duke Ludwig I, 1829. Second journey to Italy, 1838–40. Subsequently retired to Konstanz; died there, 5 June 1863.

Bibliography

Cotta's Kunstblatt, Stuttgart and Tübingen, 1820–40, 1845, 1848, 1858

Friedrich Pecht, *Recensionen über bildende Kunst*, 1863, p.159

Hermann Uhde, ed., *Erinnerungen und Leben der Malerin Louise Seidler: Selbstbiographie*, Berlin, 1874; revised editions, 1875 and 1922; abridged edition, Weimar, 1964

Oscar Gehrig, "Maria Ellenrieder", *Die Christliche Kunst*, 1912–13, pp.292ff

Klara Siebert, *Marie Ellenrieder als Künstlerin und Frau*, Freiburg im Breisgau, 1916

Friedrich Noack, *Das Deutschtum in Rom*, i, Stuttgart, 1927; reprinted Aalen: Scientia, 1974

Margarete Zündorff, *Marie Ellenrieder: Ein deutsches Frauen- und Künstlerleben*, Konstanz, 1940

Otto Kähui, "Marie Ellenrieder in der Ortenau", *Ekkhart, Jahrbuch für das Badner Land*, 1959

Friedhelm Wilhelm Fischer and Sigrid von Blanckenhagen, *Marie Ellenrieder: Leben und Werk der Konstanzer Malerin*, Konstanz: Thorbecke, 1963 (contains catalogue raisonné)

Arthur von Schneider, *Badische Malerei des XIX. Jahrhunderts*, Karlsruhe: Muller, 1968

Jan Lauts and Werner Zimmermann, *Katalog neuere Meister 19. und 20. Jahrhundert: Staatliche Kunsthalle Karlsruhe*, 2 vols, Karlsruhe: Staatliche Kunsthalle, 1971

Women Artists, 1550–1950, exh. cat., Los Angeles County Museum of Art, and elsewhere, 1976

Baden und Württemberg im Zeitalter Napoleons, exh. cat., 2 vols, Württembergisches Landesmuseum, Stuttgart, 1987

Das Verborgene Museum I: Dokumentation der Kunst von Frauen in Berliner öffentlichen Sammlungen, exh. cat., Akademie der Künste, Berlin, 1987

Gottfried Sello, *Malerinnen aus fünf Jahrhunderten*, Hamburg: Ellert und Richter, 1988

Kunst in der Residenz, exh. cat., Staatliche Kunsthalle Karlsruhe, Heidelberg, 1990

"… und hat als Weib unglaubliches Talent" (Goethe): Angelika Kauffmann (1741–1807), Marie Ellenrieder (1791–1863), exh. cat., Rosgartenmuseum, Konstanz, 1992

Marie Ellenrieder diaries and archive are in the Rosgartenmuseum, Konstanz.

"All things considered, Marie Ellenrieder must be one of the most important German female artists of modern time", was the judgement of the painter and art writer Friedrich Pecht on her death in 1863. Even in her lifetime Ellenrieder was highly regarded: she was the first woman to be trained as an artist at a German Academy. The Grand Duke Ludwig von Baden appointed her court painter in 1829 after she had already been awarded a gold medal of art and science by the Baden artists' society – the first woman to be so honoured. Ellenrieder is known as a representative of the Nazarene style. Within this style, which was based on Renaissance and medieval German art, her works show an individual character to which her deep religiosity and sensitive perception strongly contributed. Her excellent painting technique distinguishes her works from those of other Nazarenes. Ellenrieder also left extensive diaries that reveal a sensitive artist who reacted strongly to the contemporary religious morality and its inherent contradictions. Ellenrieder has received only scant attention in art history, which does justice neither to her nor to her work.

Ellenrieder studied for three years under the Konstanz miniature painter Joseph Einsle before beginning her studies at the Munich Academy. In 1813, with the help of her patron and mentor Ignaz Heinrich, Freiherr von Wessenberg, a Konstanz church official, she was accepted into the Munich Academy, where she studied under the classicist painter Johann Peter von Langer. Von Langer recognised her exceptional talent for portrait painting and gave her strong support. Influenced by the Baroque, Ellenrieder's early works show a preference for the deliberate use of light emerging from a dark background. Some studies of male heads executed with a broad brush and lively, strong colours reveal an impressive vividness and force. She created technically excellent etchings – mostly copies of old masters – in the period 1815–16, making use of varied crosshatching (a method used in Baroque copper engravings), which she also employed in her later pastel works, a genre in which she was especially talented and in which she created her most beautiful and lively works.

The period 1817–22 is now seen as the most productive of Ellenrieder's career. Her works from that time display an enthusiasm and sensitivity that allowed her to capture the particular qualities of the people she painted. Through the deepening of spiritual expression, Ellenrieder was in advance of the realistic portraiture of the second half of the 19th century. Her early portraits, mostly half-length and partly in profile, were created in the middle-class milieu of her family and home on Lake Konstanz. Psychological characterisation is their most important feature. The portraits of her parents (1819; Rosgartenmuseum, Konstanz) are among the best. The portrait of *Baron von Wessenberg* (1819; Wessenberg-Galerie, Konstanz) conveys the sensitive character of the sitter with freshness and immediacy.

For many of her portraits, Ellenrieder prepared pastel drawings, which show an even greater degree of liveliness. She very much enjoyed painting portraits of children. The sketch for the portrait of *Prince Carl von Hohenzollern-Sigmaringen, Heir to the Throne* (c.1818; Wessenberg-Galerie) as well as the portrait of the *Artist's Nephews* (c.1818–19, private collection, repr. Konstanz 1992, ill.3) and the *Daughters Thurn-Valsassina* (1818; private collection, Kunsthaus, Zürich, *ibid.*, ill.23) are among Ellenrieder's most beautiful portraits of children, showing them refreshingly unself-conscious. It is only in the later portraits that she portrayed children as ideals of angelic goodness. She portrayed herself as a vivacious, self-confident and merry young woman in two self-portraits (1818; Staatliche Kunsthalle; Karlsruhe; 1819; Rosgartenmuseum), whereas her later portraits (e.g. *Self-Portrait*, 1827; Staatliche Kunsthalle; *Self-Portrait, Head Study with Bonnet*, 1827; Rosgartenmuseum) document the increasing loss of these characteristics and her retreat to an inner life of self-doubt.

From 1818 onwards Ellenrieder received princely commissions, painting the portraits of *Princess Jablonowska* (1818; Rosgartenmuseum) and *Carl Egon II and Amalie von Fürstenberg* (1819; private collection, *ibid.*, ill.24), and then began to portray the sitters half- and full-length. In 1820 she was called to the Baden court at Karlsruhe to paint the portraits of *Margrave Leopold and Margravine Sophie von Baden* (private collection, *ibid.*, p.193). In these portraits Ellenrieder managed to combine the public with the private, the representation of a public figure with the characteristics of an individual.

Ellenrieder's first religious canvases, *St Cecilia* (1816; Rosgartenmuseum) and *St Jerome* (c.1817; Wessenberg-Galerie), show a strong reliance on Baroque art in content, form and manner of representation. One can see here the excellent results of her academic studies and the flowering of her talent for colour and composition, as well as her sensitivity and liveliness. She used quick and firm brush strokes and light to model the figures and give depth to the surroundings. In 1820 she was the first woman to receive a commission for the decoration of a Catholic church, the Pfarrkirche zu Ichenheim (Baden), for which she painted three altarpieces: the *Virgin Mary Enthroned*, *St Nicholas*, the church's patron saint, and a *Resurrection* (all *in situ*). In these paintings a retreat from the liveliness of her earlier work towards the coldness of Neo-classicism is first apparent. This tendency mirrored her own incessant religious soul searching for purity and idealism.

Ellenrieder: *Virgin Mary with the Christ Child*, completed 1824; Staatliche Kunsthalle, Karlsruhe

Ellenrieder left Konstanz in 1822 to travel to Italy, where she stayed for several years. In Rome she stayed with the Weimar artist Louise Seidler (q.v.), who introduced her to the colony of German artists around Friedrich Overbeck. The art theories of the Nazarenes had an impact on Ellenrieder, a deeply religious woman who had a tendency towards self-denial and asceticism. Her manner of painting changed completely as a result of their influence and her impressions of the art of Raphael and Perugino; at the same time she perfected her technical skills. The paint surface of her works now attains the quality of smooth enamel, the range of colours is lighter, the plasticity of the figures and the sense of depth are gone, and the faces are highly idealised. The luminous enamel of the colouring generates a lyrical continuation of transcendental rapture. The figures move to the foreground of the picture plane as if stepping out of a flood of divine light. With these painterly techniques, Ellenrieder gave her paintings the static timeless quality that is associated with the works of the Nazarenes.

Ellenrieder's drawing technique also changed completely under the influence of the Nazarenes, who saw drawings and cartoons as works of art in themselves, which in their opinion embodied the purest depiction of truth, a notion that Ellenrieder took on board. Whereas she used a mixed and differentiated technique for her early works – soft and fine modelling and open outlines were characteristic of this – she now laid a strong emphasis on contour. Her mixed technique is rectified and large areas of light now contrast with deep shadows.

Her main work of this period is an almost life-size painting of the *Virgin Mary with the Christ Child* (completed 1824; see illustration). The structure, forms and colouring of the work reveal intensive study of the works of Raphael. The painting was highly praised by contemporary critics. It was of lifelong importance to the artist, who kept it in her studio. The harmony of a mystical radiant power and human closeness is an artistic quality of Ellenrieder's work that makes her paintings stand out from that of the other Nazarenes. There is, however, an inherent danger in such a harmony of sentimentality that Ellenrieder did not always avoid.

Her stay in Italy brought about a break from her former life. Disappointed by the lack of acknowledgement from other German artists in Rome, Ellenrieder returned to Konstanz via Florence, where her tendency towards depression became more prominent. She left Italy with the intention of putting her art in the service of religion and only accepted commissions for portraits if they came from the court of the Grand Duke. In 1827 she painted the *State Portrait of the Grand Duke Ludwig von Baden* (private collection, repr. Konstanz 1992, ill.25), with whose family she enjoyed a friendly relationship. In 1832 Ellenrieder received a commission for a family portrait of the *Grand Duchess Sophie von Baden with Her Five Children* (completed 1834; private collection, ex-Zähringersammlung, Neues Schloss, Baden-Baden). The clarity of drawing, balance of composition and the delicate harmony of the colours make this painting one of the finest family portraits of the 19th century. In these images one can increasingly detect Ellenrieder's efforts to create idealised portraits and bestow upon the sitters an individuality and quasi-religious meaning. Especially in her portraits of children, she attempted to show the pure and childlike "angelic soul" (Ellenrieder) and their proximity to God.

Ellenrieder became the most popular female religious artist in southwest Germany. In 1828 she received the honourable commission of painting an enormous work for the high altar of the Stadtkirche St Stephan in Karlsruhe, the *Martyrdom of St Stephen* (4.7 × 3.2 m.; now Pfarrkirche St Stephan, Konstanz). She was the first and only woman to create a work of such huge dimensions. The structure of the work is reminiscent of Italian Renaissance paintings. She avoided the common but brutal depiction of the stoning of the saint since art was meant to contribute to the "ennobling and edification of the beholder" (Ignaz Heinrich von Wessenberg, *Die christlichen Bilder, ein Beförderungsmittel christlichen Sinnes*, Konstanz, 1827, pp.42, 155, 186 and 201). The work signifies an important step in Ellenrieder's career as well as being of great importance in her oeuvre as a whole. It was decisive in her appointment as court painter. The largest commission she received from the Grand Duke Ludwig was the decoration of the castle chapel in Langenstein (1828) with life-size biblical scenes, including the *Feeding of the Five Thousand* and the *Blessing of*

the Children, a theme that she particularly liked and executed more than once.

Ellenrieder's depression in the years after 1834 was accompanied by a waning in creativity. In 1838 she again went to Italy on a journey from which she hoped to be inspired and encouraged. Despite the praise her work received in these years – especially the *Blessing of the Children* (1839; Rosgartenmuseum) and *Angel with a Bowl of Tears* (second version 1842; Kloster Lichtenthal, Baden-Baden) she returned to Konstanz in 1840 disappointed and depressed. The following years were marked by illness, depression and diminishing creativity. She painted many small, sometimes miniature-like works with religious subjects that were always in demand. She also received some commissions for large-scale works. In 1847 and 1849 she executed two large religious paintings for Queen Victoria (*St Felicitas and Her Sons* and *Christ in the Temple*; Royal Collection, Osborne House, Isle of Wight). In the last decade of her life she had a renewed burst of creativity, painting some altarpieces and at least 23 oil paintings, but the artistic quality of her earlier years seems to have been lost. She created one more masterpiece in the genre of portraiture with the pastel portrait of the *Three Young Countesses Douglas* (private collection, repr. Konstanz 1992, p.200).

Marie Ellenrieder had no artistic successors. She did not have many students because she found them disruptive, and the artistic taste of the second half of the 19th century took a different direction. The continuation of her style led to the sickly sweet devotional art that makes it so difficult to judge Ellenrieder's work justly and without prejudice. Soon after her death she disappeared into increasing obscurity. In three important exhibition catalogues of the art of the Nazarenes (1977, 1981 and 1989) her name is not even mentioned, although many of her technically excellent compositions should be recognised as masterpieces in the Nazarene tradition. In order to award Ellenrieder her just and valid place within art history one should consider especially her early works, which were influenced by the spirit of Romanticism. Ellenrieder must be counted among the best artists of southwest Germany.

KARIN STOBER

See also Court Artists survey

Emes, Rebeccah [Rebecca]

British goldsmith, active 1808–c.1829

Early details of her life unknown. Widow of John Emes, silversmith, who died in 1808. First mark, as a plateworker in partnership with William Emes, perhaps her brother-in-law, entered at Amen Corner, London, 30 June 1808. Second mark entered in partnership with her second husband, Edward Barnard, 14 October 1808. Three further marks entered with Barnard, the fifth on 29 October 1825. Presumably either retired or deceased by 25 February 1829, when Edward entered a new mark with his three sons, Edward, John and William, and the firm was re-titled Edward Barnard and Sons.

Bibliography

John Culme, *Nineteenth-Century Silver*, London: Hamlyn, 1977

Judith Banister, "Identity parade: Some people and pieces from the Emes and Barnard Ledgers", *Proceedings of the Society of Silver Collectors*, ii/9–10, 1980, pp.165–70

John Culme, *The Directory of Gold and Silversmiths, Jewellers and Allied Traders, 1838–1914*, Woodbridge, Suffolk: Antique Collectors' Club, 1987

Philippa Glanville, *Silver in England*, London: Unwin Hyman, and New York: Holmes and Meier, 1987

Philippa Glanville and Jennifer Faulds Goldsborough, *Women Silversmiths, 1685–1845: Works from the Collection of the National Museum of Women in the Arts, Washington, DC*, London: Thames and Hudson, 1990

Arthur Grimwade, *London Goldsmiths, 1697–1837: Their Marks and Lives*, 3rd edition, London, 1990

James Lomax, *British Silver at Temple Newsam and Lotherton Hall*, Leeds: Mancy, 1992

Edward Barnard and Sons, Ledgers, 1818–31 (Emes and Barnard), are in the Victoria and Albert Museum, Archive of Art and Design, London, AAD 5/14–1988 – 5/261–1988.

Although very few personal details about Rebeccah Emes are known, the partnership she established with Edward Barnard became one of the most successful of the 19th century. It was also a part of the oldest surviving goldsmiths' business in the world. The firm's roots can be traced back to Anthony Nelme who registered his mark in London *c.*1680. It then evolved through Thomas Whipham (*c.*1737–56), Thomas Whipham and Charles Wright (1756–75), Charles Wright (1775–85), Henry Chawner (1776–96), Henry Chawner and John Emes (1796–8) to John Emes alone (1798–1808). As Edward Barnard and Sons it survived into the 20th century before being absorbed into another firm. This history offers a glimpse into the close-knit pattern of the goldsmiths' craft in England that can be traced as a result of the Goldsmiths' Company regulations for every craftsman to register a mark at the Hall and present their wares for assay (or testing for the correct silver standard). In many ways it was a small world. Edward Barnard, for example, was not only John Emes's workshop foreman, but had been apprenticed to Thomas Chawner, taking his connection with the business back to 1773. Rebeccah Emes, in marrying her late husband's workshop manager and entering her own mark in partnership with him, was following a well-established practice for goldsmiths' widows to take over the business. She is unlikely to have been a practising goldsmith herself, but to have operated more as business woman and administrator (for a thorough examination of the role of women goldsmiths, see Glanville and Faulds Goldsborough 1990).

If Emes and Barnard were part of the oldest goldsmiths' business, they also made it one of the largest and most successful. The firm had expanded when John Emes, who had trained as an engraver, joined Thomas Chawner, which provided a firm base on which Emes and Barnard could build. The early 19th century was in any case a period during which industry was flourishing with the end of the Napoleonic Wars, and improvements in manufacturing and communications were made. Much information on the firm can be derived from the Barnard Ledgers, the earliest volumes of which, from 1818 to 1831, cover the latter years of the Emes and Barnard partnership. These Day Books not only show the kind of plate that

Emes: Weymouth Regatta cup, Victoria and Albert Museum, London

was made, but to whom it was sold and for how much. A complex manufacturing picture emerges from which it is clear that the firm was acting in the modern sense as a retailer rather than a producer, with a network of clients and other retailers to whom plate was supplied, often to be marked with their own mark for sale or export. The network was wide, with outlets all over the country from Portsmouth and Exeter to Manchester, Newcastle upon Tyne, Edinburgh and Aberdeen. There was also a flourishing overseas trade through agents to America and India, notably Calcutta. The Day Books record a wide variety of these transactions, the entries often marked "unfinished" or "not hallmarked" when the piece was to be marked with the customer's stamp. These records have been analysed in detail (see Banister 1980) and the names of many of the most prominent goldsmiths' firms appear as clients, for example Rundell, Bridge and Rundell, the famous London silversmiths and retailers, and Joseph Rodgers and Co. of

Sheffield. The trade was not only in complete objects. It is also clear that Emes and Barnard bought in objects in their turn and, in common with other similar firms, had a flourishing trade in repairs, often described in the Day Books as "taking out the bruises", tinning, polishing and the refurbishment of plate chests.

The firm had a wide output of everyday items, such as coffee- and teapots, saucepans, bread baskets, soup and sauce tureens, cruets, dishes, plates and inkstands, but they also specialised in grand presentational plate. For example, they supplied all the Doncaster Gold Cup race prizes from 1821 to 1829. The 1828 model (Temple Newsam, Leeds) is an exact, reduced replica of the famous antique Buckingham Vase, excavated from Hadrian's villa near Rome. The Weymouth Regatta cup (see illustration) is another example of this output. The firm was also responsive to changes in fashion and the developments of new types of plate. Thus, after the introduction of toast as part of the buffet breakfast in the early 19th century, they started to manufacture toast racks, often out of silver wire which was both elegant and practical. In stylistic terms, and in common with other major manufacturers of the period, Emes and Barnard drew on an eclectic range of patterns and ornament and was responsive to changes in fashion rather than setting the pace. Much of their output was competently Neo-classical, such as the Leeds Doncaster cup, but by the latter years the partnership was producing items with the dense decoration characteristic of the Rococo revival, sometimes slightly uncomfortably married with Neo-classical elements. The Weymouth Regatta cup is a case in point; the form and use of acanthus is Neo-classical, at odds with the naturalistic vine wreath and floral handles. In all respects, the firm was typical of its period, being a profitable business, supplying an expanding market with good-quality, conservative wares.

PIPPA SHIRLEY

Ende
Illuminator active in northern Spain, AD 975

Bibliography

Dorothy Miner, *Anastaise and Her Sisters: Women Artists of the Middle Ages*, Baltimore: Walters Art Gallery, 1974

José Camón Aznar, "Art in the Beatos and the Codex of Gerona", *Beati in Apocalipsin: Codex Gerundensis* (facsimile with commentaries), Madrid, 1975, pp.17–178

Annemarie Weyl Carr, "Women artists in the Middle Ages", *Feminist Art Journal*, V/1, Spring 1976, pp.5–10

John W. Williams, *The Illustrated Beatus: A Corpus of the Illustrations of the Commentary on the Apocalypse, II: The Ninth and Tenth Centuries*, London: Harvey Miller, 1994 (contains comprehensive bibliography on the Girona Beatus)

The 10th-century manuscript painter Ende is the earliest securely documented female artist in Spain. She is known for her illumination of the Beatus of Girona (Girona Cathedral, MS 7), one of the finest and most complete copies of the *Commentary on the Apocalypse* of Beatus of Liébana. The manuscript, which is dated by inscription to "ERA 1013", or AD 975, was brought to the cathedral from León in the 11th century. Ende's name is inscribed, with that of her male colleague Emeterius, in the manuscript's colophon (fol.284r), which reads: ENDE PINTRIX ET D(E)I AIUTRIX FR(A)TER EMETERIUS ET PR(E)S(BITE)R; or, "Ende, paint[ress] and helper of God; Emeterius, brother and priest". Some disagreement exists regarding the transcription of the artist's name, which may be read either as "Ende pintrix" or "En depintrix"; however, the relative frequency with which the former term, usually in its more common form, "pictor", is used in medieval texts suggests that "Ende pintrix" is probably correct.

Ende's life dates are unknown, and the inscribed date that appears in the Girona Beatus colophon offers the only chronological datum that can be attached to her activity as a painter. The appellation "dei aiutrix" suggests that she may have been a nun, although there is no indication to which foundation she might have belonged. Because her colleague Emeterius can be traced to the monastery of Tábara in León, where with his master Maius he produced an earlier Beatus manuscript dated AD 970 (Archivo Histórico Nacional, Madrid, MS 1097B), it has been supposed that Ende too was based in León, perhaps in a foundation affiliated with Tábara.

In spite of the fact that the Girona Beatus colophon names Ende specifically as a painter, disagreement has persisted regarding the extent of her work on the manuscript. Many scholars have assumed that Emeterius, a male artist known to have worked on a previous Beatus codex, was the work's primary illuminator, and have ascribed to Ende those illuminations displaying appropriately "feminine" qualities, such as decorativeness, delicacy, and even spelling and grammatical errors (as in the *Crucifixion* scene of fol.16v, where the names of the two thieves crucified beside Christ are exchanged and misspelled; see illustration). A more effective attempt to distinguish Ende's hand, however, may be made through comparison of the Girona manuscript with the fragmentary Tábara Beatus of Emeterius and Maius, so that any contrasting features found in the former codex might be evaluated as the result of Ende's intervention.

Whereas the Tábara illuminations are characterised by a predominantly warm palette and a restrained and delicate handling of form, the Girona codex often displays an exuberant colourism and formal vigour that might well be attributed to Ende. The Christological cycle that precedes the Girona text (fols 15r–18r) includes, in addition to the traditional *Annunciation*, *Nativity* and *Adoration of the Magi*, scenes showing the *Flight into Egypt* (pursued by Herod), *Illness of Herod*, *Christ Before Caiaphas*, *Denial of Peter*, *Crucifixion*, *Holy Women at the Tomb with Christ*, *Judas Hanged*, *Holy Women at the Tomb with Joseph of Arimathea*, *Descent into Hell* and *Resurrection*, which are not found in other Beatus texts of the 10th and 11th centuries. These non-traditional scenes, apparently inspired by northern European precedents, thus constitute an innovation for which Ende might be credited. Although these suppositions necessarily remain speculative, they suggest that Ende's significance stems not only from her status as one of the first known female artists in Europe, but also from her achievements as one of the most expressive and innovative painters of her era.

PAMELA A. PATTON

Ende: *Crucifixion,* *Commentary on the Apocalypse* of Beatus of Liébana, fol.16v, 975; Girona Cathedral Archives

Epps, Laura see Alma-Tadema

Eriksen, Gutte
Danish potter, 1918–

Born Gudrun Agnete Tryde Eriksen in Rødby, 20 November 1918. Studied at the Kunsthåndværkerskolen (School for Applied Arts), Copenhagen, 1936–9; student apprenticeships during the summers of 1937–9. Worked at Hegetslund earthenware factory, 1940. Shared a workshop with Åse Feilberg and Christian Frederiksen in Hareskov, 1941–2. Established own workshop in Kastrup, 1942. Visited England to work with Bernard Leach in St Ives, and France to work with Pierre Lion in Saint-Armand and Vassil Ivanoff in La Borne, 1948. Worked with Felix Möhl in Allerød, 1951–3. Established workshop in St Karlsminde, Hundested, 1953. Married painter Preben Hansen, 1951; daughter born 1952, son born 1955. Taught at the Jutland Kunstakademi in Århus, 1968–78. Made study visits to Japan, 1970 and 1973. Lives near Hundested.

Principal Exhibitions

Individual
Den Permanente, Copenhagen: 1955
Kunstforeningen, Copenhagen: 1969, 1987 (retrospective)
Höganäs Museum, 1976
Nyköpings Museum: 1979
Hetjens Deutsches Keramikmuseum, Düsseldorf: 1985
Gummesons Konstgalleri, Stockholm: 1988
Galerie Epona, Paris: 1989
Besson Gallery, London: 1990
Galleri Lejonet, Stockholm: 1991

Group
Nationalmuseum, Stockholm: 1942 (*Dansk kunsthåndværk* [Danish applied art])
Concorso Internazionale delle Ceramiche, Faenza: 1942, 1954
Musée du Louvre, Paris: 1958 (*Formes scandinaves*)
Victoria and Albert Museum, London: 1968 (*Two Centuries of Danish Design*), 1972 (*International Ceramics*)
National Museum of Modern Art, Kyoto: 1970 (*Contemporary Ceramic Art*, touring)
Nagoja, Kyoto and Tokyo: 1973–5 (*International Exhibition of Ceramic Art*)
Frechen Museum, Germany: 1976 (*Samtida Europeisk Keramik*)
Palmer Museum of Art, Pennsylvania State University, University Park: 1981 (*Danish Ceramic Design*)
Maison du Danemark, Paris: 1983 (*Créations et art danois*)
Seoul, Korea: 1986 (*International Exhibition of Creative Art*)
Kunstindustrimuseet, Copenhagen: 1990 (*Brændpunkter: Dansk keramik, 1890–1990* [Firing points in Danish ceramics, 1890–1990])

Bibliography
Skandinavische Keramik: Sammlung Thiemann, Hamburg, exh. cat., Focke Museum, Bremen, 1972
Danish Ceramic Design, exh. cat., Palmer Museum of Art, Pennsylvania State University, University Park, 1981
Gutte Eriksen: Sonderausstellung, exh. cat., Hetjens Deutsches Keramikmuseum, Düsseldorf, 1985
Françoise Espagnet, "Gutte Eriksen", *Revue de la Céramique et du Verre*, xxv/11–12, 1985, pp.10–11
Gutte Eriksen 50 års keramiske arbejder [Gutte Eriksen: 50 years of ceramic works], exh. cat., Kunstforeningen, Copenhagen, 1987
Brændpunkter: I dansk keramik, 1890–1990 [Firing points in Danish ceramics], exh. cat., Kunstindustrimuseet, Copenhagen, 1990
Dansk keramik 1991: Arbejder fra 22 værksteder Århus Kunstforening af 1847 [Danish ceramics, 1991: Works from 22 workshops, Århus Art Association of 1847], exh. cat., Århus Kunstbygning, Aarhus, 1991
Mailis Stensman, ed., *Gutte Eriksen*, Stockholm: Lejonet, 1991
Danish Ceramics/Deense Keramiek, exh. cat., Boymans-van Beuningen Museum, Rotterdam, 1995

Gutte Eriksen and her husband, the painter Preben Hansen, live and work in an early 19th-century former school-house outside Hundested, a small port city on the northwest coast of Sjaelland. The setting of their home and work-place has a sense of the sea in its proximity to the Kattegat, the strait between the Baltic and the North Sea. The thatch-roofed building has been adapted and enlarged for the two artists with a wing for each that forms two sides of a courtyard overlooking a pond and wooded background. The pottery, which is slightly detached from the main house, is entered through a generous covered space that holds an outcropping of bamboo and is the setting for several very large vessels by Eriksen. The uniqueness of these pieces as well as those one encounters within the studio lies in their shaping, but even more in their surfaces. And it is in the particular character of Eriksen's glazes that a significant part of her strong signature quality lies.

Eriksen first became aware of an uncomplicated glaze formula based on borax and quartz through Michael Gill, a British pottery apprentice who worked with her in 1950, and, after experimenting with it during the intervening years, she has used it exclusively since 1955. The addition of clays and ashes produces colours that range from the subtle to the dynamic, tending to blues, reds and greys – often with surprising accents of white. They defy standard colour definitions in their complexity and under different lighting conditions will subtly change. The body under the glaze is a high-fired earthenware that Eriksen has used throughout most of her career. It consists of halfred clay from the island of Bornholm and half clay from La Borne in France, a pottery centre where she worked for a time. To this she adds sand and a trace of chalk. Given these quite common materials, there could be reason to wonder how interesting her work might be. In fact, Eriksen has created and continues to create some of the most arresting and sophisticated ceramic vessels of our time – an oeuvre that has made her the most internationally recognised Danish potter. (Her work may be found in numerous public collections, including the Kunstindustrimuseet, Copenhagen; Hetjens-Museum, Deutsches Keramikmuseum, Düsseldorf; Palmer Museum of Art, University Park, Pennsylvania; Nationalmuseum, Stockholm; and the Victoria and Albert Museum, London.)

The milieu in which any young artist matures and develops skills is an important factor in setting the standards for a career. Clearly, the training of craftspeople in Denmark has been of a very high order throughout the 20th century, and the studios of the two great porcelain factories in Copenhagen have provided an appropriate grounding for clay artists. Given this background, Eriksen's training at the Kunsthåndværkerskolen, her internships in smaller ceramic factories, her

Eriksen: Pot with five handles, 1989; earthenware; artist's collection

studies with Bernard Leach in England, Pierre Lion and Vassil Ivanoff in France, and Felix Möhl in Denmark, the disciplines for a successful career were in place. Examples of her work from 1937 until the mid-1950s are not well-known, but several of these earlier pieces were shown at the retrospective celebrating her 50-year career in Copenhagen in 1987. A lively and fascinating variety of forms and decor evidenced the early exploration of ideas leading to her later work.

After 1953, when Eriksen set up her present workshop, her development of the borax-quartz glaze was intensified. This major element of her signature work was destined to undergo continuing experimentation and refinement throughout her career. Additions of elements such as ashes and clay have played their part in this, but an important factor is the firing process itself. Absolute control by the potter is forgone during the firing and results, while generally foreseeable, may at times produce surprises ranging from the greatly fulfilling to utter disaster. Among the controls that do exist are temperature and timing, and this master potter has made increasing use of reduction (starving the fire of oxygen) – not easily accomplished in the electric kilns she uses.

A significant characteristic of decor used extensively by Eriksen since c.1955 until the 1960s – and occasionally since then – is a repeated stamped pattern to define a shape further. These small stampings might be placed around the interior side of a bowl or on the shoulder of a teapot or jug. Her glaze, falling over the small crevices of the stamping, produces a subtle and satisfying result. It is tempting to term these years as her "classic" period; the lines of her shapes have an essentially

European character and indeed show occasional references to Classical Greek forms.

The two study trips to Japan in 1970 and 1973 brought about a subtle and continuing oriental feeling to Eriksen's oeuvre both in form and texture. While she has not made shapes that can be termed Japanese, the freedom of form found in her later work seems to emanate from that experience. The quality of her later glazes, which are more closely bonded to the body, probably also developed from these visits. Some of her most recent and captivating work has the quality of *yakisugi* (overfiring) that is sometimes found in the most hauntingly enigmatic and sought-after pieces of Japanese master potters.

The range of sizes in Eriksen's work has grown over the years, and since the late 1970s numerous very large vessels have emerged. Several shapes could be cited, but the most compelling of these is the five-handled *krukke* form, examples of which can be seen in major museums including the Victoria and Albert Museum in London. They range up to 72 centimetres in height, and, while they are purely the artist's creation, might be likened to the Mei P'ing vase form that came to perfection in Song Dynasty China. A form that has developed in the 1980s also deserves comment. Eriksen terms it a lotus bowl, but it is purely her designation since it bears no resemblance to traditional oriental forms of that name. It is a low, flat-bottomed vessel with straight sides that are shaped into a quatrefoil. The interior of the bottom tends to be white, as do the exterior sides; the rim is burned to a near black. The effect is unforgettable.

The art of Gutte Eriksen, like that of any strong and focused potter, is at once discernible as hers. She brings to her medium an intelligence and sensitivity filtered through a thorough knowledge of an art measured in many millennia. An authentic portion of that time is represented by a Tamba pot from the Momoyama period in Japan (1573–1638) given to her by her friend, Bjørn Winblad, which stands in front of the window by her throwing wheel. It is a metaphor for timeless craftsmanship, the quality that Eriksen's art represents.

WILLIAM HULL

Ermolaeva, Vera *see* Yermolayeva

Escallier, Eléonore
French painter and ceramist, 1827–1888

Born Eléonore Caroline Légerot in Poligny, Jura, 1827. Married Pierre Joseph Augustin Escallier, 1846; one son, one daughter. Trained in Dijon under Claude-Jules Ziegler, director of the Ecole des Beaux-Arts. Worked for the ceramist Théodore Deck, c.1859–74, then joined the Manufacture Nationale de Sèvres. Among her students were her daughter Marguerite and Jeanne Magnin, sister of Maurice Magnin whose collection now forms the Musée Magnin, Dijon. Died in Sèvres, 14 June 1888.

Principal Exhibitions

Paris Salon: 1857, 1861, 1863–70, 1872–5, 1877, 1880 (medal of
honour for painting on faience 1868)
Exposition de Troyes: 1860 (silver-gilt medal)
Exposition Universelle, Paris: 1867, 1878
Exposition Universelle d'Anvers, Antwerp: 1885 (gold medal)
Manufacture Nationale de Sèvres: 1888 (retrospective)

Bibliography

L'Art en France sous le Second Empire, exh. cat., Grand Palais, Paris,
1979
Elisabeth Hardouin-Fugier and Etienne Grafe, *French Flower Painters
of the 19th Century: A Dictionary*, London: Wilson, 1989

Eléonore Escallier was one of the very few women to achieve a
national reputation as a painter of flowers and birds, combining easel painting with a career as a ceramics designer and
decorator. The application of her considerable talents as an
artist to painting on faience for Théodore Deck brought her
instant success and, foreseeing the expansion of the decorative
arts that occurred from the 1850s onwards, she became a
pioneer in the teaching of flower design and painting to girls.
In 1874 she joined the Manufacture Nationale de Sèvres,
where she remained until her death.

Escallier was trained in Dijon by the artist Claude-Jules
Ziegler, the director of the Ecole des Beaux-Arts and curator of
the museum there. Ziegler had himself at one time given up
painting to become a potter and his example must surely have
inspired Escallier. Her earliest works were naturalistic paintings of flowers and birds. In 1857 she made her debut at the
Paris Salon with two items, *Vase of Flowers* and a large canvas,
The Irises (1856; archives of Manufacture Nationale de Sèvres;
damaged in 1871 during the Commune), which depicted a life-
like scene of a kingfisher drinking from a stream from which
grow iris plants. These paintings may have caught the eye of
Deck who was making a name for himself as the most innovative potter in Paris. Deck employed several Salon artists, and
Escallier must have started working for him soon after her
Salon debut. By 1859 her virtuoso paintings on faience had
established her as one of Deck's leading associates. From this
time on she followed a dual career, regularly exhibiting her
studio paintings at the Salon while working as a ceramist.

Deck had developed a method of modelling by laying on the
enamel very thickly. The effect of his designs was enhanced by
his brilliant colours and glazes, most famously a rich turquoise
known as *bleu Deck*. Escallier immediately adopted his procedures, demonstrating a natural affinity with the clay. Deck was
preoccupied with the development of designs and colours
based on Middle Eastern – mainly Iznik – and Chinese wares.
He was also enthusiastic about the prints and other Japanese
objects that had started to arrive in Paris. Escallier too admired
both Iznik and Japanese styles, and used both as sources of
inspiration.

Escallier's lustrously coloured plaques featured prominently
in Deck's display at the Paris Exposition Universelle of 1867,
one observer describing them as "magnificent". Of the two
that were purchased there by the South Kensington Museum
(now Victoria and Albert Museum, London), one was decorated with lilies and passion flowers, their deep-blue leaves and
stems set against a *bleu Deck* ground. The second plaque (see
illustration) depicted an exotic bird, a Central American

quetzal, perched on a branch of flowering prunus above a
broad-leafed plant. Its white ground and asymmetrical
arrangement owed much to Japanese influence, and Escallier
may have copied the design of the bird from a printed source.
Another plaque, with two male quetzals, a hellebore plant and
laburnum and plum branches, was bought by the Musée des
Arts Décoratifs, Paris. It seems that Escallier made other
versions as a similarly decorated plaque (private collection)
appeared in the exhibition *L'Art en France sous le Second
Empire* of 1979 (cat. no.IV–16).

Escallier continued to exhibit a variety of subjects at the
Salon throughout the 1860s, still lifes, naturalistic paintings of
gardens, flowers and birds and, on one occasion, a self-
portrait. Some were purchased by the State, although apparently she had to haggle hard about the payments offered. Her
flower paintings were distinguished by her attention to detail
and, as the decade advanced, the designs – often depicting
flowering branches of prunus or apple blossom asymmetrically
placed – reflected her continuing interest in Japonisme. In
1868, instead of the usual canvases, her Salon exhibit consisted
of two faience plaques, *Flowers and Birds*, for which she won
a medal of honour. These may perhaps have followed the
designs that she had shown so successfully at the Exposition
Universelle of 1867.

A marked change in style appeared on a large plaque
painted in 1871 that depicted a brilliantly coloured parrot
perched on a branch of flowering apple blossom (Musée
National Adrien Dubouché, Limoges). The dramatically posed
bird, its wings outstretched and grasping a twig in its beak,
occupied the whole of the central area of the plaque, unlike the
serene compositions typified by the quetzals exhibited in 1867.
Escallier may well have drawn the blossom directly from
nature since she is known to have painted such a tree in the
garden of Deck's pottery in Paris in the spring of 1871.
Naturalistic compositions such as *Peaches and Grapes of the
Jura* were probably also made in plein air. This work was
exhibited at the Salon in 1872 and was acquired for the Dijon
museum (mairie d'Arnay-le-Duc).

By 1875 her flower studies were so much admired that one
critic, reporting on the Salon that year, described her as "one
of the masters of the style" (*Gazette des Beaux-Arts*, 2nd
series, xii, 1875, p.33). Her exhibit there, a reflection of her
considerable reputation, consisted of four decorative panels
(Palais de Salm, Paris), which had been commissioned by the
Légion d'Honneur. The massed naturalistic flower arrangements and Rococo settings of the panels demonstrate
Escallier's ability to design for a particular location, in this case
the salon of an 18th-century palace.

In 1874 Escallier joined the Manufacture Nationale de
Sèvres. There she had to adapt to working on hard-paste
porcelain and to learn the *pâte-sur-pâte* technique, a decorative
method of applying a cameo-like image to porcelain by the
application with a brush of very thin layers of porcellanous
slip. Each layer, which had to be completely dry before the next
could be applied, was then smoothed and carved with a modelling tool. The process, which was very time-consuming and
required a high degree of skill, hitherto had been almost exclusively a male preserve. With her natural talent for devising
patterns entirely appropriate to the shapes she was required to
decorate, she quickly established her reputation. An English

Escallier: Faience plaque, exhibited 1867; Victoria and Albert Museum, London

visitor to the Exposition Universelle of 1878 was particularly attracted by one of her designs, *Vase of the City of Paris*, which he described as "a bird's-eye view of Paris, seen through vistas formed by branches of peony and woodbine, nestling among which are some charmingly painted pigeons" (*Society of Arts Artisan Reports*, London, 1879, p.35). The piece shows Escallier's ability to transform a French motif into a Japanese-inspired composition.

Escallier's final Salon exhibit, in 1880, was the design for a Beauvais tapestry for the main staircase of the Palais du Luxembourg in Paris. Despite the onset of a serious illness she continued to work at Sèvres. One of her last works there was a vase she designed and decorated in *pâte-sur-pâte* with comic and tragic masks – a work full of symbolism, according to one observer. This symbolism may have related to Escallier's illness, which was now terminal. When she died in 1888,

Champfleury, the deputy administrator of the Manufacture and curator of the Sèvres museum, observed in a graveside tribute that she had "been given the priceless gift of knowing how to decorate a vase, and that this gift had been bestowed on her by nature" (*Courrier de Versailles*, 30 September 1888).

BERNARD BUMPUS

Exter, Alexandra
Russian painter and designer, 1882–1949

Born Alexandra Alexandrovna Grigorovich in Belestok, near Kiev, Ukraine, 6 January 1882. Attended Kiev Art Institute, 1901–7. Married lawyer Nikolai Exter, 1908; he died 1918.

Frequently visited Paris and other European cities from 1908; studied at Académie de la Grande Chaumière, Paris, under Charles Delval, 1908. Took part in several Kiev exhibitions including David Burlyuk's Zveno (The Link), the first of many involvements with the avant-garde. Moved to St Petersburg, 1912. Began professional theatre work with designs for *Thamira Khytharedes* produced by Alexander Tairov at the Chamber Theatre, Moscow, 1916. Founded her own studio in Kiev, 1918; many artists of later fame, such as Isaak Rabinovich, Alexander Tyshler and Pavel Tchelitchew, studied there. Stage designer at the Theatre of the People's House, Odessa, 1920. Turned to textile and fashion design for the Atelier of Fashions, Moscow, 1923. Emigrated to Paris, 1924; worked for the Ballets Romantiques Russes with Léon Zack and Pavel Tchelitchew; taught stage design and painting at Fernand Léger's Académie d'Art Moderne. Continued to work on stage and interior design, 1920s and 1930s. Died in Fontenay-aux-Roses, near Paris, 17 March 1949.

Principal Exhibitions

Individual
Galerie Der Sturm, Berlin: 1927–8
Galerie Quatre Chemins, Paris: 1929
Prague: 1937

Group
Zveno (The Link), Kiev: 1908
Izdebsky Salon, Odessa: 1909–10 (*International Exhibition*, touring)
Soyuz molodyozhi (Union of Youth): 1910, 1913
Bubnovy valet (Jack/Knave of Diamonds), Moscow: 1910–17
Salon des Indépendants, Paris: 1912, 1914
Moscow: 1914 (*Exhibition of Paintings No.4*), 1916 (*Futurist Exhibition: The Store*), 1918 (*First Exhibition of Paintings of the Professional Association of Artists*), 1921 (*5 × 5 = 25*, with Rodchenko, Stepanova, Popova and Vesnin)
Koltso (The Ring), Kiev: 1914
Galleria Sprovieri, Rome: 1914 (*Libera mostra internazionale futurista di pittura e scultura*)
Petrograd: 1915 (*Tramway V: First Futurist Exhibition of Paintings*)
Galerie van Diemen, Berlin: 1922–3 (*Erste russische Kunstausstellung*, touring)
Museum of Decorative Painting, Moscow: 1923 (*Moscow's Theatrical and Decorative Art, 1918–1923*)
Venice Biennale: 1924
Exposition Internationale des Arts Décoratifs et Industriels Modernes, Paris: 1925
Cercle et Carré, Paris: 1930

Selected Writings
(as A.E.), "Novoye vo frantsuzskoy zhivopisi" [What's new in French painting], *Iskusstvo*, 1912, no.1–2, p.40

Bibliography

5 × 5 = 25, exh. cat., Moscow, 1921
Yakov Tugendkhold, *Alexandra Exter*, Berlin: Zaria, 1922
Alexander Tairov and others, *Alexandra Exter: Décors de théâtre*, Paris: Quatre Chemins, 1930
Alexandra Exter, exh. cat., Galerie Jean Chauvelin, Paris, 1972
Artist of the Theatre: Alexandra Exter, exh. cat., Center for the Performing Arts, Lincoln Center, New York, 1974
Alexandra Exter: Marionettes, exh. cat., Leonard Hutton Galleries, New York, 1975
Ronny H. Cohen, *Alexandra Exter and Western Europe: An Inquiry into Russian-Western Relations in Art, Theater and Design in the Early Twentieth Century*, PhD dissertation, New York University, 1979
Künstlerinnen der russischen Avantgarde/Russian Women Artists of the Avant-Garde, 1910–1930, exh. cat., Galerie Gmurzynska, Cologne, 1979
Alexandra Exter: Marionettes and Theatrical Designs, exh. cat., Hirshhorn Museum and Sculpture Garden, Washington, DC, 1980
Alexandra Exter, exh. cat., CTM, Moscow, 1988
Alexandra Exter, exh. cat., Odessa Art Museum, 1989
M. Kolesnikov, "Alexandra Exter i Vera Mukhina", *Panorama iskusstv*, no.12, Moscow, 1989, pp.89–110
M.N. Yablonskaya, *Women Artists of Russia's New Age, 1900–1935*, New York: Rizzoli, and London: Thames and Hudson, 1990
Alexandra Exter e il teatro da camera, exh. cat., Museo d'Arte Moderna e Contemporaneo di Trento, Rovereto, 1991 (contains exhibition list and extensive bibliography)
G. Kovalenko, *Alexandra Exter*, Moscow: Galart, 1993
D. Gorbachev, "Exter in Kiev – Kiev in Exter", *Experiment*, no.1, 1995, pp.299–320

Painter, book illustrator, teacher and above all stage designer, Alexandra Exter was a primary member of the international avant-garde and, like many of her colleagues in Russia and the Ukraine, she was in close contact with artists and writers in Kiev, Moscow, St Petersburg, Paris and Milan. But like Kazimir Malevich, Lyubov Popova (q.v.) and Vladimir Tatlin, Exter managed to integrate the principles of Cubism and Futurism with her own indigenous traditions (such as Ukrainian folk art) to produce distinctive interpretations of Cubo-Futurism, Suprematism and Constructivism.

Exter spent long periods in France and Italy, studied Cubism and Futurism, and was especially close to such artists as Robert and Sonia Delaunay (q.v.) and Ardengo Soffici. Robert Delaunay's Orphism also left a permanent imprint on her early work, and in her article on French painting she even promoted his ideas, using a Futurist terminology to explain his system: "instead of one plane he presents simultaneously several constructive planes mutually intersecting at the angle like the sides of a prism" ("Novoye vo frantsuzskoy zhivopisi", 1912). Indeed, Exter might well have been describing her own Cubo-Futurist paintings of 1912–15, for such works as *City at Night* (1913; see illustration), *Florence* (1914–15; 109 × 144 cm.) and *Composition* (1914; 90.7 × 72.5 cm.; both Tretyakov Gallery, Moscow), all oil on canvas, incorporate recognisable elements of the Delaunays' polychromatic system, evident in the street lamps reverberating as coloured discs. In turn, the refractive and rhythmic concentrations of Exter's paintings recur in those of her Ukrainian colleagues such as Vladimir Baranov-Rossiné and Alexander Bogomazov. Certainly, paintings such as *City at Night* are powerful gestures to the combined forces of French Cubism and Italian Futurism but, for Exter, they were only laboratory experiments that culminated in her non-objective paintings of 1916 onwards. While indebted to her formal training in Paris, such abstract compositions as *Non-Objective Composition* (1917–18; State Russian Museum, St Petersburg) derive from many other pictorial sources, not least Kazimir Malevich's Suprematist system (1915 onwards), and some scholars even contend that Exter's move towards abstraction was also stimulated by the rich patterns of Ukrainian decorative arts (e.g. Gorbachev 1995). In any case, by 1915–16 the non-objective aesthetic was of primary importance to Exter; she joined Malevich's Supremus

Exter: *City by Night*, 1913; State Russian Museum, St Petersburg

group, and contributed Suprematist works to the *0.10* exhibition in Petrograd. Just before and after the October Revolution of 1917, with Ivan Klyun, Malevich, Lyubov Popova and Tatlin, Exter was at the forefront of the Russian abstract movement – evidenced by colourful and dynamic canvases such as *Construction of Planes along Movement of Colour* (1918; Wilhelm Hack Museum, Ludwigshafen) and *Colour Construction* (1921; Radishchev Museum, Saratov).

Ultimately, however, Exter achieved an international reputation as a stage designer rather than as an easel painter. While trained as a studio artist, Exter came to the world of the theatre through her deep interest in the applied arts, contributing designs for dresses, scarves and cushions to Moscow design exhibitions in the 1910s. This was an interest that derived from her innate concern with fabric, material, pattern, colour application, sewing and weaving – an aspect of her career that tends to be overshadowed by the more familiar Cubism and abstract paintings. Although of a later generation, Exter was much indebted to the basic theatrical concept formulated by Leon Bakst – that a stage design must transcend the confines of the pictorial surface and organise forms in interaction with space. Exter's awareness of this interaction became especially evident in her first collaborations with Alexander Tairov at the Chamber Theatre in Moscow (where she also collaborated with Vera Mukhina, q.v.): the productions of *Thamira Khytharedes* (1916), *Salome* (1917) and *Romeo and Juliet* (1921). Aware of the principles of Edward Gordon Craig, Adolphe Appia and Sergei Volkonsky (Appia's apologist in Russia), Tairov and Exter conceived of the stage for *Thamira Khytharedes* as a volumetrical, constructive space where actors and scenery had equal roles and where, as Tairov himself recalled, the guiding force of the sets and costumes was "the Apollonian rhythm inherent in the figure of Thamira" (A. Tairov, "Zapiski rezhissyora" [Director's notes], *A.Ya. Tairov o teatre*, ed. P. Markov, Moscow: VTO, 1970, p.163).

Exter's concentration on what her friend the critic Yakov Tugendkhold called an "organic connection between the moving actors and the objects at rest" (Ya. Tugendkhold, "Pismo iz Moskvy" [Letter from Moscow], *Apollon*, 1917, no.1, p.72) pointed to her Constructivist costume designs for ballets performed by Bronislava Nijinska's Théâtre Chorégraphique in Britain and Paris (see *Bronislava Nijinska: A Dancer's Legacy*, exh. cat., Cooper-Hewitt Museum, New York, and elsewhere, 1986) and to her designs for the science-fiction film *Aelita*, released in 1924. Indeed, perhaps Exter attained the high point of her scenic career in the dynamic medium of film, where focus and sequence change constantly, where formal contrast is transmitted by a rapid variability of light, and where light itself plays a constructive role. *Aelita* was Exter's only major commitment to the art of film, although sources mention her involvement in others such as *Daughter of the Sun*, and she also created, with Nechama Szmuszkowicz, marionettes in 1926 for a film projected, but not produced, by Peter Gad in Paris. With *Aelita*'s easy plot, box office stars (Yuliya Solntseva as Aelita and Yury Zavadsky as Gor) and futuristic costumes by Exter, this "cosmic Odyssey" (V. Rakitin, "Marsiane A. Exter", *Dekorativnoye iskusstvo*, 1977, no.4, p.29), anticipated such recent space fantasies as *Star Wars*.

In the 1920s Exter continued to investigate the "dynamic use of immobile form" (Tugendkhold *op. cit.*), filling her Constructivist scenographies with staircases and platforms, manipulating planes and solids, and juxtaposing verticals with diagonals. Exter's experiments with stage lighting and her general emphasis on the dynamic and architectonic possibilities of the stage influenced a number of younger stage designers in Russia and the Ukraine such as Anatoly Petritsky, Isaak Rabinovich and Alexander Tyshler, and even the Surrealist Pavel Tchelitchew, remembered now for his canvas *Hide and Seek* (Museum of Modern Art, New York), started his career as a student of Exter in Kiev.

Exter continued to experiment throughout her Paris years, applying her ideas to ballets, revues and books – she illustrated a number of de luxe limited editions such as Marie Collin-Delavaud's *Panorama de la montagne* and *Panorama de la côte* (both Paris: Flammarion, 1938) and her own *Mon jardin* (Paris: Flammarion, 1936). In 1925 she even invented "epidermic costumes" for a ballet project in which the dancers were painted, not dressed (for a photograph of three performers wearing these costumes, see *Il contributo russo alle avanguardie plastiche*, exh. cat., Galleria del Levante, Milan, 1964, p.31). As Tyshler said: "In her hands, a simple paper lampshade turned into a work of art" (quoted in O. Voronova, *V.I. Mukhina*, Moscow: Iskusstvo, 1976, p.43).

JOHN E. BOWLT

F

Fahey, Jacqueline
New Zealand painter, 1929–

Born in Timaru, South Canterbury, 1929. Studied at University of Canterbury School of Fine Arts, Christchurch, 1947–51 (DFA). Moved to Wellington, 1951. Married psychiatrist Fraser McDonald, 1956; three daughters, born 1959, 1960 and 1967. Lived in Melbourne, 1960–61, then returned to Wellington, moving to Auckland in 1965. Visited New York on Arts Council of New Zealand travel grant, 1980. New Zealand representative for *Perspecta* exhibition, Art Gallery of New South Wales, Sydney, 1985. Part-time lecturer in fine arts, Elam School of Fine Arts, Auckland, 1989–93. President, New Zealand Society of Sculptors and Associates, 1984–5. Lives in Auckland.

Selected Individual Exhibitions

Victoria University, Wellington: 1973
John Leech Galleries, Auckland: 1974
Barry Lett Galleries, Auckland: 1978
RKS Art, Auckland: 1982, 1986, 1990
Galerie Legard, Wellington: 1983
Auckland City Art Gallery: 1983 (*Artist in Focus*)
Brooker Gallery, Wellington: 1988
Aberhart North Gallery, Auckland: 1995

Selected Writings

"Nineteen painters and their favourite works", *Islands*, no.10, Summer 1974, pp.394–5
"Letter to Alison Mitchell", *Spiral*, no.1, 1976, p.16
"Painting Christchurch red", *Beyond Expectations: Fourteen New Zealand Women Write about Their Lives*, ed. Margaret Clark, Wellington: Allen and Unwin, 1986, pp.68–81
"Eric", *Writing a New Country*, ed. James Ross, Linda Gill and Stuart McRae, Auckland, 1993, pp.165–8
"Two responses to the 'Rembrandt to Renoir' exhibition", *Landfall*, new series, i, Spring 1993, pp.187–93

Bibliography

Anthony Stones, "The paintings of Jackie Fahey", *Mate*, no.6, December 1960, pp.25–8
Juliet Batten, "New Zealand feminist artists", *Broadsheet*, no.110, June 1983, pp.19–36
Alexa Johnston, "Jacqueline Fahey", *Anxious Images*, exh. cat., Auckland City Art Gallery, 1984, pp.22–7
Pat Rosier, "Painting her life: Jacqueline Fahey, feminist artist", *Broadsheet*, no.117, March 1984, pp.29–33
Elizabeth Eastmond and Merimeri Penfold, *Women and the Arts in New Zealand: Forty Works, 1936–1986*, Auckland: Penguin, 1986
Elizabeth Eastmond, "Jacqueline Fahey: Artist and self-image", *Art New Zealand*, xlii, Autumn 1987, pp.55–60
Jillian Lloyd, *The Paintings of Jacqueline Fahey*, MA thesis, University of Canterbury, Christchurch, 1988
Lita Barrie, "The female impersonator in the suburbs", *alter/image: Feminism and Representation in New Zealand Art, 1973–93*, exh. cat., Wellington City Gallery and elsewhere, 1993
Anne Kirker, *New Zealand Women Artists: A Survey of 150 Years*, 2nd edition, Tortola, BVI: Craftsman House, 1993

Jacqueline Fahey stands out among her contemporaries in New Zealand because of her involvement in social and political issues. Unlike many artists of her generation who worked in landscape or upheld abstraction and the self-referential modernist creed, Fahey's commitment to figurative painting as a means of commenting on contemporary concerns has remained constant throughout her career. She has drawn on a diversity of styles and sources to develop an expressive technique, and produced paintings with dramatic visual impact that express her feminist and socialist attitudes to a range of problems confronting society. In her exploration of women's experience and analysis of female identity, social and artistic mythologies, Fahey, like other feminist artists of her generation, prefigured many of the aims of the Women's Art Movement in New Zealand.

Fahey's vivid autobiographical writing (which complements her painting) distances her from New Zealand's Protestant tradition and describes a childhood surrounded by conversation, books and music, and a Catholic education rich in religious rituals and images, which had a powerful influence on her visual imagination. At the University of Canterbury School of Fine Arts she was influenced less by the School's landscape tradition than by Russell Clark's depictions of Maori, which raised the possibility of a social role for art. Based in Wellington during the 1950s and 1960s, where the pursuit of internationalism led to an experimentation with modern styles, Fahey painted works that reflect her interest in Rouault and Picasso. In a group of untitled paintings dealing with domestic isolation, known as the *Suburban Neurosis Series* (1958–9; repr. Johnston 1984, pp.22–3), anonymous Picassoesque women are imprisoned within a shallow picture space, trapped by an assortment of familiar household objects that take on

Fahey: *Final Domestic Exposé – I Paint Myself*, 1981–2; Auckland Art Gallery Collection

symbolic significance. At this time, Fahey's reading of Simone de Beauvoir's *Day by Day in America* and *The Second Sex*, combined with marriage and the arrival of her first child when she was 30, heightened her awareness of how post-war social ideologies returned women to the home and away from the workforce. While Anthony Stones acknowledged her gendered perspective, asking: "Could the male painter have noticed this enormous world of frustration in the sprawl of Suburbia?" (Stones 1960, p.25), the failure of women artists to find a sympathetic gallery response brings into view the incomprehension that her paintings with specifically female themes found in this period.

Fahey painted sporadically during the next decade. In 1960–61 she accompanied her husband to Melbourne where she discovered an expressive social realism in the work of Arthur Boyd and his Australian contemporaries. After her return to New Zealand, reinforced by her contact with the older women artists Juliet Peter and Rita Angus (q.v.), Fahey painted *Interior with Artist at Work* (c.1972; private collection, repr. Eastmond 1987, p.56), a reflection on the personal struggle she faced at this time to define herself as an artist. She depicts herself with brush in hand, her face partly obscured, and surrounded by a jumble of children's dolls and family belongings that define her domestic/artistic working space. In this painting elements of her mature style take their place: her preference for constricted and crowded spaces, telling compositions, saturated colour, opulent surfaces, symbolic still life and loaded decorative detail.

Self-portraiture features frequently in Fahey's imagery, providing a pretext and means for an analysis of female identity and the imposition of sexual and behavioural roles. The controlling power of the male gaze was dealt with in *Drinking Couple: Fraser Analysing My Words* (1977; University of Auckland Medical School), where she depicts herself and her husband, the psychiatrist Fraser McDonald, in conversation. In *Fraser Sees Me, I See Myself* (1975; private collection, *ibid.*, p.57) the witty representation of Fraser's face viewing her – and seen by the artist – through the distorting lens of a magnifying glass deflates the male viewpoint as the sole authority. In *Final Domestic Exposé – I Paint Myself* (1981–2; see illustration) Fahey depicts herself naked, unidealised and surrounded by household clutter, thus undermining a long artistic tradition of the female nude at the same time as she explodes myths of an idealised femininity and ordered domesticity. This was followed by *Luncheon on the Grass*, in which Fahey appropriated images from the history of Western art and recast male and female roles in the manner of Sylvia Sleigh (q.v.), producing a radical revision of Manet's modernist masterpiece, *Le Déjeuner sur l'herbe*.

Whatever limits female experience imposes, Fahey turns to advantage in paintings of domestic life. Her return to regular work began with *In Memoriam* (1969; repr. Johnston 1984, p.24), a painting that dealt with her father's death and mother's grief and which prompted broader reflections on the meaning of life and the presence of death. This theme was developed in *Birthday Party* (1974; *ibid.*, p.27), which, with its realistic symbolism – candle, balloons – constituted an elaboration of a Baroque *vanitas* theme. Fahey has described the home as "the battlefield of the psyche", and likened it to a stage where a gamut of human emotions, comedies and tragedies is privately enacted. She dealt with its conflicts and dramas in *Mother and Daughter Quarrelling* (1980; Robert McDougall Art Gallery, Christchurch) and *My Skirt's in Your Fucking Room* (1978–9; repr. Eastmond and Penfold 1986, pl.9), where the brush became a weapon for painting messages of protest and subversion.

In the mid-1980s in a series of paintings based on the Auckland Domain, Fahey explored how landscape has served as a site for human drama; these include *Hill of Bitter Memories* (1981–2; repr. Johnston 1984, p.25), in which Fahey locates the war memorial in a disturbing and surreal landscape, making a powerful statement against war. In more recent work, the landscape at her home at French Bay, near Auckland, the bush in *Sisters Communing* (1990; Aigantighe Art Gallery, Timaru) and the beach in *Ben at French Bay* (1993; private collection) become active participants in her transformation of personal experience into themes with more universal significance.

JULIE KING

Falkenstein, Claire
American sculptor, 1908–

Born in Coos Bay, Oregon, 1908. Studied art, philosophy and anthropology at University of California, Berkeley (AB in Letters and Science), then sculpture under Alexander Archipenko at Mills College, Oakland; also briefly attended Stanley William Hayter's Atelier 17, New York. Taught sculpture at the California School of Fine Arts, San Francisco, late 1940s. Moved to Paris, 1950. Returned to USA, 1962, settling in Venice, California. Recipient of Woman of the Year for Art award, *Los Angeles Times*, 1969; Guggenheim fellowship, 1978; National Women's Caucus for Art achievement award, 1981; Vesta award, Woman of the Year in Art, Los Angeles, 1985; Distinguished Artist Forum, San Francisco State University, 1988. Lives in Venice, California.

Selected Individual Exhibitions
Galerie Stadler, Paris: 1955, 1960, 1985 (retrospective)
Martha Jackson Gallery, New York: 1960, 1963, 1965
Esther Robles Gallery, Los Angeles: 1963, 1964, 1965
Il Canale, Galleria d'Arte, Venice: 1965
Phoenix Art Museum: 1967
Fresno Arts Center, CA: 1969 (retrospective)
Palm Springs Desert Museum, CA: 1980
University of California, Riverside: 1984 (retrospective)
Jack Rutberg Fine Arts, Los Angeles: 1984, 1986 (retrospective), 1989
Stanislaus University, CA: 1987–8 (touring)

Bibliography
Michel Tapié, *Claire Falkenstein*, Rome: De Luca Art Monographs, 1958 (French original)
Sidney Tillim, "Claire Falkenstein", *Arts Magazine*, xxxiv, October 1959, p.60
Claire Falkenstein, exh. cat., Galerie Stadler, Paris, 1960
Michel Tapié, "The formal universe of Claire Falkenstein", *Prolégomènes à une esthétique autre de Michel Tapié*, ed. Francesc Vicens, Barcelona: Centre International de Recherches Esthétiques, 1960, pp.131–2
Claire Falkenstein, exh. cat., Phoenix Art Museum, 1967
Claire Falkenstein: The Formative Years, exh. brochure, Fresno Arts Center, CA, 1969
Painting and Sculpture in California: The Modern Era, exh. cat., San Francisco Museum of Modern Art and elsewhere, 1976
The Americans in Paris: The 50s, exh. cat., California State University at Northridge, 1979
Claire Falkenstein: In San Francisco, Paris, Los Angeles and Now, exh. cat., Palm Springs Desert Museum, CA, 1980
David Rubin, "Americans in Paris: The 50s", *Arts Magazine*, liv, January 1980, p.19
Ora Lerman, "Claire Falkenstein invites us to 'complete the circle'", *Arts Magazine*, lvi, January 1982, pp.64–7
Thomas Albright, *Art in the San Francisco Bay Area, 1945–1980*, Berkeley: University of California Press, 1985
Moira Roth, ed., *Connecting Conversations: Interviews with 28 Bay Area Women Artists*, Oakland: Eucalyptus Press, 1988
Claire Falkenstein: Chance and Choice, exh. cat., Jack Rutberg Fine Arts, Los Angeles, 1989
Charlotte Streifer Rubinstein, *American Women Sculptors*, Boston: Hall, 1990
Maren Henry Henderson, *Claire Falkenstein: Problems in Sculpture and its Redefinition in the Mid-20th Century*, PhD dissertation, University of California at Los Angeles, 1991
Michael Plante, "Sculpture's *autre*: Falkenstein's direct metal sculpture and the *Art autre* aesthetic", *Art Journal*, liii, Winter 1994, pp.66–72
Wendy Slatkin, *Women Artists in History: From Antiquity to the Present*, 3rd edition, Upper Saddle River, NJ: Prentice Hall, 1997

Over the course of a lengthy and prolific career, Claire Falkenstein has created an extensive oeuvre of highly innovative abstract sculpture. Executed in a range of materials, her works illustrate universal forces and processes as understood by 20th-century science and philosophy. In her efforts to depict concepts of the cosmos, her works may be seen as metaphors for universal forces that, in an earlier epoch, might be identified as belonging to the realm of the divine.

Falkenstein was born in a small rural community in Oregon, but her family moved to the San Francisco Bay area early in her life. Her early intellectual interests in anthropology and philosophy, which she studied at the University of California at Berkeley, would persist throughout her career and serve as sources for her aesthetic systems. The first famous sculptor with whom Falkenstein studied was Alexander Archipenko, whose interest in the expressive possibilities of negative spaces, although still tied to the human form, was influential for her. She would pursue her exploration of sculptural form, freed from enclosing volumes, throughout her career. Another influence was the noted Abstract Expressionist painter Clifford Still, who was on the faculty of the California School of Fine Arts while Falkenstein was teaching sculpture there in the late 1940s.

A turning point in Falkenstein's career occurred in 1950, when she moved to Paris. She matured as a sculptor during her years in Europe, creating a significant body of works of great originality. As Maren Henderson noted: "no other artist used metal as ingeniously and variously as she did" (Los Angeles 1989, p.3). In the welded wire sculptures known as *Sun Series* (artist's collection) Falkenstein created works that demonstrate her rejection of the closed, defined and measurable world of Euclidean geometry in favour of an active curved space illustrative of her understanding of "topology". The flowing and continuously expanding forms of topological space are related directly to Falkenstein's understanding of Einstein's theory of relativity. One underlying principle of her art is never to create objects or images that imply that one can entrap and separate space from the unity of the natural world. This conception of a space that flows and extends uninterruptedly moved logically in Falkenstein's oeuvre into metaphors of infinite expandability.

Falkenstein: *U as a Set*, 1965; copper tubing; Washington University Technology Associates, Inc.; Collection of University Art Museum, California State University, Long Beach

One of her symbols of infinity is the "never-ending screen". Inspired by Brancusi's *Endless Column* (1918), the "never-ending screen" has the intellectual potential to express endless expansion. During her years in Europe Falkenstein pioneered a technique in which large chunks of coloured glass are melded into networks of metal. She called these works *Fusions*. This technique was used for one of her major works, the Grotto Gates of the Villa of Princess Pignatelli (1957), which opened directly on to the Tyrrhenian Sea. Impressed by this work, Peggy Guggenheim, in 1961, commissioned Falkenstein to create the doors for her palazzo in Venice, which now houses the Guggenheim Collection. The "never-ending screen" first appeared on a major scale in the design of these gates. In that remarkable work, large chunks of Murano glass are entrapped in a web of welded linear elements that articulate the screen.

The most complete expression of the "never-ending screen" in an architectural context was the artist's contribution to St Basil's church on Wilshire Boulevard, Los Angeles. Eight doors and 15 enormous stained-glass windows (ranging from 24.3 to 39.6 m.) were created from her quarter-scale models. This architectural ensemble demonstrates Falkenstein's ability to juxtapose colour, light and the linear "never-ending screen" in a work of great beauty and spirituality. When the "never-ending screen" is expressed three-dimensionally, it takes the form of the "truss". Falkenstein's most recent monumentally scaled work developed from this system is a sculptural complex on the campus of California State University at Dominguez Hills, the *Forum: Memorial to A. Quincy Jones.*

Using Port Orford cedar logs, selected for their ability to survive outdoors, Falkenstein has created a beautiful complex that functions as a metaphor of the cosmos. In this work Falkenstein evokes the principles of nature, on a vast scale.

Another recurring formal element used by Falkenstein, which illustrates sculpturally the Einstein-derived principle of the expanding universe, is the "U". The "U" is a curved, open linear shape flattened at both ends. In her monumental sculpture, *U as a Set* (1965; see illustration), a mass of U-signs made of copper tubing have been welded into a gigantic shape, which is also a "U", more than 6 metres long. It is placed against a "wall" of fountain jets and isolated in its own reflecting pool on the campus of California State University in Long Beach. The interaction of active linear forms in the sculpture and the shooting sprays of water provide two parallel references to the motion of natural forces.

Falkenstein's most important works are monumental public installations, rather than portable objects. Her works have enriched a variety of public spaces in southern California, ranging from sites as diverse in purpose as a shopping mall or the Los Angeles Department of Motor Vehicles to St Basil's church. Most of her works on public view, however, are housed on the campuses of the universities of the region. Falkenstein's works constantly surprise and confound programmed expectations of sculpture, painting or architecture. Although she came to maturity in the era of "second-generation" Abstract Expressionism, her works do not fit easily or securely within a specific period, movement or group.

Emerging from a firm philosophical basis, their quality resides in a high level of distinctive, individual expression.

WENDY SLATKIN

Fantin-Latour, Mme *see* Dubourg

Fargue, Maria Margaretha, La *see* La Fargue

Fauveau, Félicie de

French sculptor, 1801–1886

Born in Florence, 1801, to French parents who had left France at the Revolution; father a banker, mother an aristocrat. Returned to Paris with her family, *c*.1813, after her father suffered severe financial losses; subsequent years spent in Limoux (Aude), Bayonne and Besançon. Began professional career after father's death in 1824, moving to Paris; encouraged by her mother, an amateur artist; received some drawing lessons from Louis Hersent and Bernard Gaillot. Became involved in royalist conspiracies against the revolutionary government after the overthrow of Charles X; imprisoned, 1830; sentenced to life imprisonment *in absentia*, 1832; left France, travelling to Italy via Belgium, settling in Florence with her mother and brother, 1833. Visited Rome, 1840. Died in Florence, 1886.

Principal Exhibitions

Paris Salon: 1827 (second-class medal), 1842, 1852
Exposition Universelle, Paris: 1855

Bibliography

"Beaux-Arts: Salon de 1831; M. Henri de Triqueti", *L'Artiste*, 1st series, ii, 1831, pp.13–14

"Le Miroir de la Vanité", *Magasin Pittoresque*, vii, May 1839, pp.137–8

Baron de Coubertin, "Mademoiselle de Fauveau", *Gazette des Beaux-Arts*, 2nd series, xxxv, 1887, pp.512–21

Stanislas Lami, *Dictionnaire des sculpteurs de l'Ecole française*, ii, Paris: Librairie Ancienne Honoré Champion, 1916

Luc-Benoist, *La Sculpture romantique*, Paris: La Renaissance du Livre, 1928

Le Style troubadour, exh. cat., Musée de l'Ain, Bourg-en-Bresse, 1971

Touraine néo-gothique, exh. cat., Musée des Beaux-Arts, Tours, 1978

Curiosità di una reggia: Vicende della guardaroba di Palazzo Pitti, exh. cat., Palazzo Pitti, Florence, 1979

The Romantics to Rodin: French Nineteenth-Century Sculpture from North American Collections, exh. cat., Los Angeles County Museum of Art, and elsewhere, 1980

Juliette Barbotte, "La dague de Félicie de Fauveau", *Revue du Louvre et des Musées de France*, xxxiii, 1983, pp.122–5

Gert Schiff, "The sculpture of the 'Style Troubadour'", *Arts Magazine*, lviii, June 1984, pp.102–10

Charlotte Yeldham, *Women Artists in Nineteenth-Century France and England*, 2 vols, New York: Garland, 1984

La Sculpture française au XIXe siècle, exh. cat., Galeries Nationales du Grand Palais, Paris, 1986

Un âge d'or des arts décoratifs, exh. cat., Exposition de Paris, 1991

When Baudelaire proclaimed the ascendancy of painting over sculpture in 1846, Félicie de Fauveau had already been sculpting in a decidedly "painterly" mode for two decades, which bespoke her early training in drawing and painting with Louis Hersent, Bernard Gaillot, Delaroche and – for two days – Ingres. Gert Schiff has dubbed several of Fauveau's works sculpture in the "Style Troubadour" (Schiff 1984), noting their affinity with the anecdotal history paintings popular in France at the beginning of the 19th century. In a relatively anti-heroic vein – and hence "Romantic" rather than "Neo-classical" – the Troubadour style focused on the sentimental and "human" moments of the lives of great figures from history and legend. While Fauveau's first major work, a plaster relief of *Christina of Sweden Refusing to Spare the Life of Her Equerry Monaldeschi* (second-class medal at the Salon of 1827; Musée Municipal, Louviers), shows the queen in the dramatic moment of punishing her lover for his political treason, it represents Christina on a "human scale", indistinct from the surrounding figures. Instead, she forms part of one of two figural groups that are spatially distant against the neutral background and unhierarchised with respect to each other, yet linked by the intersecting gazes of Christina and Monaldeschi, which mark them as the central figures. The overall effect is one of a theatrical scene, enclosed in its shallow, boxlike space, rather than an allegory of the queen's social and political role.

It is perhaps surprising that the politically reactionary Félicie de Fauveau, supporter of the Bourbon dynasty, should adopt such a democratic approach to the representation of her figures. In fact, her motivation was probably more art-historical than political. Working from the compositional formulae of Neo-classicism, Fauveau's interest in medieval iconography and biblical legend led her to use Gothic forms and themes in her own work. On her exile from France in 1833 Fauveau settled in Florence (actually her birthplace) and quickly became an expert on medieval Florentine art. Her home, a former convent, offered ample space both for Fauveau's studio and for her collection of Florentine art. The Troubadour style embraced the themes and figures that interested Fauveau, and permitted her to work to the level of almost fetishistic detail that she admired in her Gothic models.

Fauveau's notebooks (private collection) record her fascination with and deep study of medieval costume, architecture and heraldry, and her original designs chart her refashioning of medieval iconography for patrons drawn from European aristocracy. Fauveau was commissioned to carve busts in marble of the *Duchesse de Berry*, the *Duc de Bordeaux* and of the daughters of the Duc de Rohan (dates and whereabouts unknown). For Baroness Gros, widow of the painter, she produced a *Monument to the Memory of Baron Gros* (1847; Musée des Augustins, Toulouse) and a marble high-relief of *Judith Speaking to the People of Bethlehem* (untraced). The latter piece was refused at the Salon of 1841, but in the following year a marble bas-relief on the same theme, *Judith Showing the Head of Holofernes to the People of Bethlehem, Assembled in the Public Square*, was exhibited at the Salon of 1842. At the

Fauveau: *Monument to Louise Favreau*, 1856; height of figure 180 cm. (approx.), overall height 450 cm. (approx.); Santa Croce, Florence

Salon of 1852 Fauveau exhibited the bronze bas-relief, *Combat of Jarnac with La Châtaigneraie*, and three of her works were shown at the Exposition Universelle of 1855: a silver crucifix, a marble group in an architectural frame representing the *Martyrdom of St Dorothy* and a marble fountain adorned with a mer-boy, putto and decorative fish (all untraced; designs and photographs in notebooks).

Perhaps largely as a result of her expatriation, Fauveau became a truly international artist, working for Continental nobility including the Grand Duchess of Tuscany, the Queen of Naples and the court of Nicholas I of Russia (according to Barbotte, a fountain by Fauveau commissioned by the Tsar still exists in the hanging gardens of the Hermitage in St Petersburg, see Barbotte 1983, no.2). For Lord Londonderry, Fauveau created an extraordinary wooden relief representing the angels of peace and war above a battlefield, after the battle (date and whereabouts unknown; designs and photograph in notebooks). Her close friendship with the family of the Earl of Crawford led to several works in Scotland: two marble fireplaces at Dunecht House (1858 and 1860) and several funerary memorials for the Crawford-Lindsay family. Fauveau executed many such funerary monuments, among them one for the Graf von Sansst's family of Turin (1835; Sansst family chapel, Turin), and others for the families of expatriate aristocrats who had died in Florence, such as *Sir Charles Lyon Herbert* (1856; Protestant Cemetery, Florence), *Sir Fleetwood Broughton* (1862) and *Comte Henri de Larderel* (1865; Pozzo Latico).

One of the most impressive of these works is the monument to *Louise Favreau* (1856; see illustration) in Santa Croce, Florence. (The young woman, born in Guadeloupe, had died in 1850 at the age of 17.) Fauveau and her brother Hippolyte produced a raised sarcophagus with a sculptural backdrop in high relief. Hippolyte was trained by Félicie and charged with the architectural detailing of most of her large pieces, thus the architectural frame was probably his work; but Félicie is certainly the author of the central female figure (suggested by Pinto to be a portrait of the deceased, see Florence 1979, p.147, no.1) that seems to fly out of the backdrop above the sarcophagus. A striking blend of Neo-classical technique, particularly in the drapery, and Neo-gothic sensibility, the extreme relief of the figure represents a true *tour de force* of the artist's skill in carving: the figure's shoulders and arms are completely freestanding, and the back of the head touches only slightly the swathe of drapery behind.

From the medieval tomb monuments of Florence, Fauveau drew the design for her *Monument to Dante* (conceived 1830, finished 1836), representing two scenes from the tale of Paolo and Francesca from Dante's *Divina commedia*: the moment at which they pause in their reading, and the scene of their punishment in Hell. The monument has come under criticism for its heavily ornate architectural frame, but this somewhat neglects the intended context for the piece – a specially designed chapel in the mansion of the Comte de Pourtalès in Paris. The frame was again probably the work of Hippolyte de Fauveau, while Félicie executed the interior sculptural groups. Only photographs of the frame exist, but the figures survive (Cuvillier Collection, Paris). Fauveau's choice of theme again references contemporary French painting: Francesca and Paolo at the moment of their discovery by Francesca's husband was painted five times by Fauveau's former friend and erstwhile teacher, Ingres (reportedly, Fauveau left his tutelage impatient with Ingres's didactic technique of setting her to copy Classical works; politically, their ways parted after the Revolution of 1830).

Fauveau did not spurn work in the decorative arts, and was in fact well known for the quality of her metal-working in such pieces as the silver letter-opener in the shape of a dagger with relief figures of Romeo and Juliet (1850; Louvre, Paris), created for Marie Nicolaïevna, Duchess of Leuchtenberg, daughter of Nicholas I of Russia, and a decorative bronze collar-piece (1831; Musée des Beaux-Arts, Tours) executed for Fauveau's compatriot in the Vendée rebellion, the Comtesse de la Rochejaquelein. For the latter, Fauveau worked in nearly every medium, producing designs for stained-glass windows and decorative inlaid wooden ceilings for the Château at Ussie, as well as a holy water basin in marble, *St Louis* (1851; Palazzo Pitti, Florence). Fauveau's designs for a silver suit of armour for Count Zichy of Hungary, including breastplate, cloak-clasp, épée, belt and spurs, executed in 1851 and 1852 (untraced; see Barbotte 1983), also derive from her interest in medieval armour and heraldry designs. With her brother, Fauveau even produced a terracotta sundial with figures of "the feminine genius of Truth" and "the masculine genius of the Middle Ages" (date and whereabouts unknown; designs in notebooks). The high art/low art politic did touch Fauveau, however, when she submitted an ornately carved, wooden mirror (*Le Miroir de la vanité*, 1839; untraced) to the Salon only to have it rejected as "nothing more than a piece of furniture". None the less, Fauveau's supporters were unwavering: Gabriel Falampin presented the piece in his widely attended salon ("Le Miroir de la vanité" 1839).

Considering her success in both monumental sculpture and the decorative arts, Félicie de Fauveau's contemporaries would probably have been surprised by the complete silence that has surrounded this artist's work since the late 19th century. The popularity of the two bas-reliefs that she exhibited at the Salon of 1827, the *Christina and Monaldeschi* and *Scène de l'abbé* (after Walter Scott's novel), was noted by Alexandre Dumas (*Memoirs, 1802–1830*, ed. Robert Lieffont, Paris, 1989, pp.847–8, 1183). The young artist Bonnassieux, on his way to the French Academy at Rome, stopped in Florence in 1837 and was received by the Fauveau household. He wrote to his teacher Dumont:

> Mademoiselle de Fauveau showed me her atelier and what she had begun; she has, without doubt, much talent and taste for *romanticism* … Though she be a political volcano, Mlle de Fauveau reasons very well … I don't like the mania that she has for dressing like a man, that is to show disdain for her sex; she wore a man's topcoat and her hair cut short. Nevertheless, I am enchanted to have made her acquaintance; when I return to Florence, I must show her my work [quoted in Antoinette Le Normand, *La Tradition classique et l'esprit romantique: Les Sculpteurs de l'Académie de France à Rome de 1824 à 1840*, ii, Collection Académie de France à Rome, Edizioni dell'Elefante, 1981, p.143; my translation].

NANCY PROCTOR

Fell, Sheila

British painter, 1931–1979

Born in Aspatria, Cumberland, 20 July 1931, into a mining family. Studied at Carlisle School of Art, 1947–9; St Martin's School of Art, London, under Vivian Pitchforth and John Napper, 1949–51. Met her great friend and supporter, L.S. Lowry, 1956; painted with him at Maryport and in the surrounding countryside of Cumberland. Daughter by the Greek sculptor Takis Vassilakis born 1957. Travelled to Greece on Boise scholarship, 1958. Taught at Chelsea School of Art, London, 1958; guest lecturer, Royal College of Art, London, 1967. Prizewinner, John Moore's exhibition, Liverpool, 1957; recipient of Arts Council of Great Britain Purchase award, 1967; Austin Abbey award for research into mural painting, 1970. Associate, 1969, and Member, 1974, Royal Academy. Fellow, Royal Society of Arts, 1976. Died in London after falling down a flight of stairs, 15 December 1979.

Principal Exhibitions

Individual

Beaux Arts Gallery, London: 1955, 1958, 1960, 1962, 1964
Middlesbrough Municipal Art Gallery: 1962
Abbot Hall Art Gallery, Kendal: 1965
Queen's Square Gallery, Leeds: 1965
Stone Gallery, Newcastle upon Tyne: 1967, 1969
New Grafton Gallery, London: 1979
South Bank Centre, London: 1990–91 (touring retrospective)

Group

Stone Gallery, Newcastle upon Tyne: 1966 (*Painters of the North*)
Royal Academy, London: 1977 (*British Painting, 1952–77*)

Selected Writings

Text in *Painter and Sculptor*, iv, Summer 1961
Chapter in *Breakthrough: Autobiographical Accounts of the Education of Some Socially Disadvantaged Children*, ed. Ronald Goldman, London: Routledge, 1968

Bibliography

Alan Bowness, "Leaning out of the dream", *The Observer*, 21 January 1962

Fell: *Skiddaw, Summer 1964*, oil on canvas; 72.1 × 91.4 cm.; Collection Drs A. and K. Dalzell, Broughton Park, Threapwood

"Miss S.M. Fell (obituary)", *RSA Journal*, cxxviii, March 1980, p.237

Sheila Fell, exh. cat., South Bank Centre, London, and elsewhere, 1990

Anna Adams, "Sheila Fell, 1931–1979: A retrospective", *Green Book*, iii/9, 1991, pp.49–52

In her paintings and drawings Sheila Fell concentrated almost entirely on the landscape of northwest England, becoming one of the leading British landscape painters of her generation. Rather than choosing the traditional Lake District views of Derwent or Grasmere, however, she concentrated on the less well-known areas around the small mining town of Aspatria where she had spent her childhood. She retained this deep attachment to Cumbria throughout her life.

A number of artists have become inextricably linked with the particular places where they worked – perhaps the most famous instance being Cézanne's Mont Sainte-Victoire. Sheila Fell found that Cumbria had an overwhelming attraction for her, even after she left to go to college in London, and returned only for visits. She described it as "not like the rest of England. It is like no other place" (*Cumbria, Lakeland Life and Literature*, September 1960). Fell steadfastly followed her impulse to paint landscape, ignoring to a large extent the influence of the "kitchen sink" painters, whose work she would have seen in London in the 1950s.

Her early work is characterised by the dark, brooding forms of the Lake District landscape and particularly its imposing mountains, which she appreciated for the first time after she returned from a school trip to the Netherlands:

> The mountains, after the flatness of Gelderland, seemed to force themselves, black and hostile, almost through the window of the carriage. Slab over slab they rose up and enveloped us like a gigantic frightening wall nearly touching the glass and shutting out the sky. They hung over the train like great forlorn prehistoric animals [*Breakthrough* 1968, p.69].

There is a feeling of considerable solidity in these paintings, which echo the rhythms of the landscape and point to the influence of Cézanne. The colours of Fell's early works are earthy olives, ochres and browns. A typical painting is *Skiddaw, Summer 1964* (see illustration), in which the mountains cover almost the entire length of the canvas. The same subjects dominate her powerful charcoal drawings, which are marked by a great economy of line.

Although Fell continued to paint landscapes of this type for the rest of her career, in the mid- to late 1960s her work gradually became more expressive. *Silage Heap near Drumburgh II* (1964; Swindon Art Collection, Borough of Thamesdown) has swirls of vibrant orange and yellow paint in the almost abstract foreground. During these years her paintings often incorporated fewer topographical elements and the paint became thicker, with raised areas of impasto and vigorous brush strokes. Her paintings of the late 1960s and 1970s, unlike her earlier works, were nearly always horizontal, and in some works, such as *Maryport* (1966; private collection, *ibid.*, p.27), she lightened her colours. Although all of these works focus on a particular place, her concerns extended beyond the essence of the place to the actual paint.

At this time she was probably influenced by the Belgian painter Constant Permeke, whose work she had seen and admired. Although Fell enjoyed the friendship and support of the painter L.S. Lowry, she was probably most influenced by the work of Vincent van Gogh, and this is reflected in her paintings of potato-pickers and workers in fields (*Potato Picking – Clouds*, 1979; private collection, *ibid.*, p.37). In these years she again spent time painting in Maryport and Aspatria, and the following words perhaps encapsulate her own view of her work:

> I have no interest in any painting which does not have its roots in reality ... The closeness of my relationship with Cumberland enables me to use it as a cross section of life. All the landscape is lived in, modulated, worked on and used by men [*Painter and Sculptor*, iv, Summer 1961].

ANN JONES

Ferlov, Sonja
Danish sculptor, 1911–1984

Born in Copenhagen, 1 November 1911. Studied in Copenhagen at the Kunsthåndværkerskolen (School for Applied Arts) under Bizzie Høyer, 1930–32; Royal Danish Academy of Fine Arts under Aksel Jørgensen, 1933–5. Founder member, with Ejler Bille and Richard Mortensen, of the group Linien (the Line), 1937. Studied at the Ecole des Beaux-Arts, Paris, 1937–8; studio in the same building as sculptor Alberto Giacometti; met black South African painter Ernest Mancoba, 1938. Forced to return to Denmark at outbreak of World War II in 1939, but went back to Paris almost immediately; married Mancoba, 1942; one son. Lived in Denmark with husband and son, 1947–51. Became member of Høstudstillingen (Autumn Salon) and was drawn into Cobra group through Asger Jorn. Lived in Ogny-en-Valois, Aisne, 1951–61. Moved to Paris, 1961; started using the name Sonja Ferlov Mancoba. Recipient of Thorvaldsen medal, Copenhagen, 1971. Died in Paris, 17 December 1984.

Principal Exhibitions

Individual
Galerie Birch, Copenhagen: 1952 (with Grete Inge Petersen and Ernest Mancoba)
Holstebro Kunstmuseum: 1968 (with Erik Heide and Kirsten Dufour)
Horst Halvorsen, Oslo: 1969 (with Jan Groth)
Aarhus Kunstmuseum, Århus: 1969 (with Ernest Mancoba and Jan Groth)
Maison du Danemark, Paris: 1970
Kunstforeningen, Copenhagen: 1977–8 (touring retrospective, with Ernest Mancoba)
Kunstforeningen, Sophienholm: 1980 (with Alberto Giacometti)

Group
Kunstnernes Efteraarsudstilling, "KE" (Artists' Autumn Salon), Copenhagen: 1935–6, 1939–40
Odense: 1935 (*Den surrealistiske udstilling* [Surrealist exhibition])
Fyns Forum, Odense: 1936 (*Dansk kunststævne* [Danish Art Festival])
Linien (the Line), Copenhagen: 1937, 1939
Høstudstilling (Autumn Salon), Copenhagen: 1948–9

Kunstnernes Kunsthandel, Copenhagen: 1961 (*Cobra*)
Salon des Réalités Nouvelles, Paris: 1962
Musée Rodin, Paris: 1962 (*La Jeune Sculpture*)
Musée de l'Art Moderne de la Ville de Paris: 1964 (*La Jeune Peinture*)
Dallas, TX: 1964 (*Danish Abstract Art*, touring)
Museum Boymans-van Beuningen, Rotterdam: 1966 (*Cobra, 1948–51*)
Den frie udstilling (Free exhibition), Copenhagen: 1968–71, 1974, 1978, 1980–82, 1984–5
Hôtel de Ville, Brussels: 1974 (*Cobra*)

Bibliography

Herman Madsen and Niels T. Mortensen, *Dansk Skulptur* [Danish sculpture], Odense: Skandinavisk Bogforlag, n.d.
Ejler Bille and Richard Mortensen, "Om den spontane metode til irrationel erkendelse" [About the spontaneous method for irrational knowledge], *Julefluen* (Copenhagen), December 1935, p.26
Ejler Bille, "Abstrakt dansk skulptur" [Abstract Danish sculpture], *Helhesten*, ii/5–6, 1944
Christian Dotremont, "Sonja Ferlov", *Cobrabibliotheket*, i/9, 1950
Cobra, exh. cat., Kunstnernes Kunsthandel, Copenhagen, 1961
Troels Andersen, "Sonja Ferlov Mancobas tegninger" [Sonja Ferlov Mancoba's drawings], *Hvedekorn*, no.3, 1962
——, "Sonja Ferlov Mancoba", *Signum*, ii/3, 1962, pp.42–52
Robert Dahlmann Olsen, "Sonja Ferlov Mancoba", *Arkitekten*, no.25, 1963
Michel Ragon, "Cobra", *Jardin des Arts*, no.101, 1963
Danish Abstract Art, exh. cat., Dallas, TX, and elsewhere, 1964
Cobra, 1948–51, exh. cat., Museum Boymans-van Beuningen, Rotterdam, 1966
Louisiana Revy, no.1, August 1966
Gunnar Jespersen, *De abstrakte*, Copenhagen: Berlingske Forlag, 1967
Sonja Ferlov Mancoba, Ernest Mancoba and Jan Groth, exh. cat., Aarhus Kunstmuseum, Århus, 1969
Den frie udstilling [Free exhibition], exh. cat., Copenhagen, 1969
Sonja Ferlov Mancoba, exh. cat., Maison du Danemark, Paris, 1970
Robert Dahlmann Olsen, *Sonja Ferlov Mancoba*, Copenhagen: Gyldendal, 1971
Gertrud Købke Sutton, "Sonja Ferlov Mancoba", *Kunst og Kultur*, lxi, 1978, pp.79–90
Troels Andersen, *Sonja Ferlov Mancoba*, Copenhagen: Borgen, 1979 (with English and French summaries)
Sonja Ferlov Mancoba, Ernest Mancoba and Alberto Giacometti, exh. cat., Kunstforeningen, Sophienholm, 1980
Troels Andersen, text in *Eksempler og motiver* [Examples and motifs], Copenhagen, 1988, pp.102–7
Rolf Læssøe, *Stille vækst* [Silent growth], Copenhagen, 1992

Sonja Ferlov was initially trained as a painter, under the Danish woman artist Bizzie Høyer. She went on to study at the Royal Danish Academy of Fine Arts in Copenhagen in 1933, and made her debut at the Kunstnernes Efterårsudstilling (Artists' Autumn Salon, often initialled KE) in 1935 with two sculptures in plaster, *A Bird with Its Young* (1935; Louisiana Museum of Modern Art, Humlebæk), a very abstract, slightly Max Ernst-like work, and *Two Living Creatures*. Her artistic milieu was the abstract-surrealist movement of the mid-1930s, grouped in an artists' association named Linien (the Line). Its most prominent male members were the Surrealist painter Vilhelm Bjerke-Petersen, who had attended classes at the

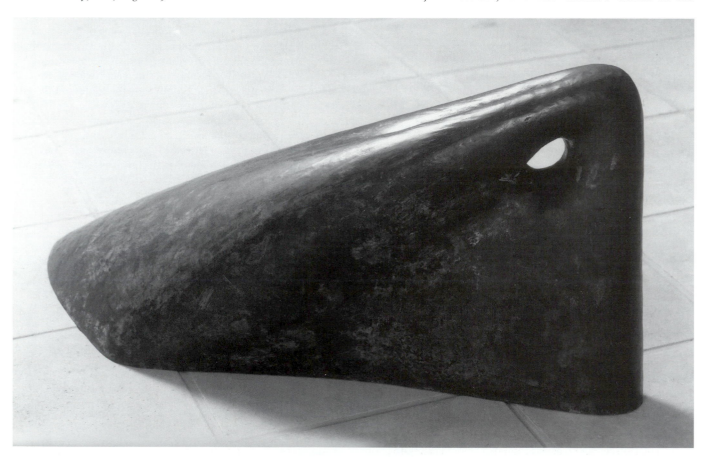

Ferlov: *Sculpture*, 1940–46; height 50 cm.; Statens Museum for Kunst, Copenhagen

Bauhaus, as well as the painter and sculptor Ejler Bille and the painter Richard Mortensen, who were both interested in the work of Picasso and in the abstract movement. Ferlov's paintings and drawings were very radical in their degree of abstraction when compared with the output of her Danish contemporaries. Her earliest assemblages of twigs and *objets trouvés* (1935; untraced) are related to Dada sculptures by Hans Arp and Kurt Schwitters, which were known in Denmark mainly through photographs in international art reviews. In 1936 she exhibited the sculpture *The Owl*, which she later destroyed. Throughout her career, Ferlov was extremely critical of her own work, and in consequence few works were finished. In 1937 Ferlov joined the Linien group, but emigrated to France that same year.

Ferlov made the acquaintance of Alberto Giacometti and Max Ernst, who influenced her sculpture to a great degree, as well as a black South African artist, Ernest Mancoba, whom she married in 1942. Non-European art had interested Ferlov from her early days in Copenhagen, and she went on to study it in the collections of the Musée de l'Homme in Paris. In France during World War II, when Ernest Mancoba was interned in a camp for enemy aliens, she worked on one single work, an abstract, triangular, very slightly zoomorphic sculpture, rising from a plinth (*Sculpture*, 1940–46; see illustration; other versions in Louisiana Museum of Modern Art, Humlebæk, and Moderna Museet, Stockholm). In 1947 she returned to Denmark, where she took part in a few major exhibitions of contemporary art. After settling in France again in 1951 Ferlov was largely forgotten in Denmark, but there was a revival of interest in her work after 1961, and in the 1960s and 1970s she received the principal Danish artists' awards. The high esteem in which she was held by Danish artists and art historians was expressed by the mounting of a retrospective at the Kunstforeningen (Artists' Association), Copenhagen, in 1977, and in acquisitions of her sculpture by all the leading museums of contemporary art in Denmark, as well as by the Moderna Museet, Stockholm.

Apart from a Constructivist period around 1948, the sculpture of Sonja Ferlov Mancoba is organic, with zoomorphic or anthropomorphic traits (e.g. *Elan vers l'avenir*, 1966; Sønderjyllands Kunstmuseum, Tønder; *A l'écoute de silence*, 1969; Statens Museum for Kunst, Copenhagen; *Mask*, 1977; Botanical Gardens, Copenhagen). Non-Western influences can be seen in certain mask-like forms and strong, symmetrical lines, whereas the profound humanity of her work bears witness to the interest she felt in the kindred spirit of Giacometti.

CHARLOTTE CHRISTENSEN

Ferrara, Jackie
American sculptor, 1929–

Born Jackie Hirschhorn in Detroit, Michigan, 17 November 1929. Attended Michigan State University, East Lansing, for six months in 1950. Moved to New York, 1952. Married jazz musician Don Ferrara (second marriage), 1955; separated 1957. Lived in Tuscany, Italy, 1959–60. Recipient of Creative Artists Public Service (CAPS) grants, New York State Council on the Arts, 1971 and 1975; National Endowment for the Arts (NEA) grants, 1973, 1977 and 1987; Guggenheim fellowship, 1976; design excellence award for Flushing Bay Promenade, Queens, New York, Art Commission of the City of New York, 1988; Institute Honor, American Institute of Architects, 1990. Lives in New York.

Selected Individual Exhibitions
A. M. Sachs Gallery, New York: 1973, 1974
Daniel Weinberg Gallery, San Francisco: 1975
Max Protetch Gallery, Washington, DC: 1975
Max Protetch Gallery, New York: 1975, 1976, 1977, 1978, 1979, 1981, 1982, 1983, 1984
San Francisco Art Institute: 1980
University Gallery, University of Massachusetts, Amherst: 1980 (touring)
Laumeier Sculpture Park Gallery, St Louis: 1981
Galleriet Lund, Lund, Sweden: 1983
Ackland Art Museum, University of North Carolina, Chapel Hill: 1983
Moore College of Art, Philadelphia: 1987
Michael Klein Inc., New York: 1991, 1994
John and Mable Ringling Museum of Art, Sarasota, FL: 1992–3 (touring retrospective)
Hudson River Museum, Yonkers, NY: 1993
Freedman Gallery, Albright College, Reading, PA: 1993

Bibliography
David Bourdon, "Jackie Ferrara: On the cutting edge of a new sensibility", *Arts Magazine*, l, January 1976, pp.90–91
Robert Pincus-Witten, "Jackie Ferrara: The feathery elevator", *Arts Magazine*, li, November 1976, pp.104–8
Kate Linker, "Jackie Ferrara's Il-lusions", *Artforum*, xviii, November 1979, pp.57–61
Jackie Ferrara, exh. cat., Lowe Art Museum, University of Miami, Coral Gables, 1982
Phil Patton, "Jackie Ferrara: Sculpture the mind can use", *Art News*, lxxxi, March 1982, pp.108–12
Charlotte Streifer Rubinstein, *American Women Sculptors*, Boston: Hall, 1990
Avis Berman, "Public sculpture's new look", *Art News*, xc, September 1991, pp.102–9
Jackie Ferrara Sculpture: A Retrospective, exh. cat., John and Mable Ringling Museum of Art, Sarasota, FL, and elsewhere, 1992
Jackie Ferrara: Traversing Space, exh. cat., Freedman Gallery, Albright College, Reading, PA, 1993

Since 1974 Jackie Ferrara has been a sculptor of abstract, systematic wood structures, having affinities with Minimalist sculpture of the 1960s but diverging significantly from it by being more complex, unfabricated and associative. Before reaching artistic maturity in the mid-1970s, Ferrara passed through several phases that functioned as self-education in the absence of formal art training. Her works from the late 1950s to the early 1970s included wax figures in groups, constructed boxes with macabre contents, and hanging pieces, such as tail-like objects of jute and canvas panels covered with cotton batting and hung in rows. Ferrara's interest in assembling and repetition in many of these sculptures pointed ahead to her mature works; the same is true of her building of fixtures and furniture for her New York studio, which she renovated over the course of a year, beginning in 1971.

Ferrara's solo exhibitions in New York in 1973 and 1974 revealed significant developments in her work, ones that

Ferrara: *A148 T Pyramid*, 1975; plywood; 122 × 122 × 122 cm.; Davis Museum and Cultural Center, Wellesley College, Wellesley, Massachusetts: Gift of Phyllis Noble Smith (Class of 1948)

established the general direction she still follows. The show of 1973 presented mainly layered, simplified sculptures – cubic or resembling stairs, obelisks or pyramids. The scale ranged from 0.6 to nearly 2.7 metres in height; the modular units of the works were made of wood or cardboard and covered with cotton batting. In the subsequent show Ferrara used only bare wood (nailed or glued) and thereby achieved greater clarity over all, technical precision and a stronger sense of mathematical order with her unitary sequences. The works were "pyramids" of various types, with stepped walls, truncated tops and sometimes curved sides, as in *B Pyramid* (1974; Sol LeWitt Collection, on loan to Wadsworth Atheneum, Hartford, CT). Although they evoke ancient pyramids, Ferrara conceived of

her sculptures as abstractions and not as models of architectural structures.

From 1975 until the late 1970s Ferrara made her stepped pyramids increasingly complex. Not only do the grainy ends of the narrow wood slats (of standard thickness) create a counterpoint pattern where they meet other slats at an edge, but now the pyramids no longer have four identical sides. Some, such as *Sepsected Pyramid* (1975; Baltimore Museum of Art), possess bilateral symmetry – having a different front and back (due to varying angles) but matching sides, which are occasionally straight rather than inclined. Ferrara further complicated these pyramids with sequences of openings in the slats, thus producing geometric patterns along the contours. She also cut away parts of the front contour of some pyramids, creating court-like planes or a deep recess from the top to bottom, as in *A148 T Pyramid* (1975; see illustration). Drawings on graph paper accompany Ferrara's works on exhibition and also testify to her methods of elaboration.

In the late 1970s a number of Ferrara's sculptures became tower-like, with openings in the slats still forming patterns and sometimes with whole contours of alternating slats and openings. Measuring in height from 1.32 to 2.43 metres, these works are imaginatively varied in their overall shapes and individually may evoke a high-rise building or a defensive tower. *Tower Beck* (1979; Mobil Oil Collection, Fairfax, VA) suggests a kiln tapering up to a chimney stack at the top. Sculptures such as this overcame the height restrictions of the stepped pyramid format, which would have required a huge base in order to be taller.

In 1981 Ferrara began a series of small-scale works that she called "wallyards" and "courtyards". Looking like models that could serve as the basis for large-scale outdoor works, these pieces have rectangular decks, flanked by one or more walls; they also sometimes include stairways and geometric motifs that mirror others on the opposing plane. After often choosing two shades of plywood for the wallyards, Ferrara in 1982 started using stains, which she limited to black, red and yellow and diluted so as to leave the grain of the wood visible. Colour allowed for more complicated patterning and geometry, as in *Wall Set/Yellow* (1983; Steven Goldberg collection, New York). Like many works by Ferrara from this and other periods, this sculpture derives some of its complexity from being composed of more than one type of wood (pine and poplar here).

Dating from the mid- to late 1980s, Ferrara's "places" evolved from the wallyards and courtyards. Also small in scale, these works suggest building models and are sometimes overtly temple-like, with a court in the front, as in *Traces* (1985; Mr and Mrs Edward C. Ellis collection, Los Angeles). Defying specific historical dating, however, they seem simultaneously ancient, modern and even futuristic in some cases.

Although Ferrara continued to produce indoor sculpture during the early 1990s (including strongly tapered pyramids of varying contour angles, pattern and colour), much of her creative activity since the 1980s has focused on commissions for outdoor settings. Her earliest outdoor works, the first one going back to 1973, were not site-specific but rather wood pieces of some scale that were placed outdoors. In 1979, when the expanding field of public art often encouraged site-specificity, Ferrara created her first site-specific sculpture, *Tower and Bridge*, for Castle Clinton in Battery Park, New York (see Linker 1979, p.61). This large, angular work of cedar, in two parts, had more associations with its context (a 19th-century fortress) than have her subsequent outdoor pieces with theirs. In step with the functionality of much contemporary public art since the late 1970s, Ferrara in 1986–7 did a series of wood seats for various locations. In *Stone Court* (1988; General Mills Sculpture Garden, Minneapolis) she shifted from sited wood forms to environments and, in this case, created a limestone work based on her small wallyards.

Ferrara's public environments from the late 1980s into the 1990s (some done in collaboration with architects) deal primarily with surface – floor areas, walkways and platforms – and the arrangement of geometric patterns. Whether outside, as in *Garden Courtyard* (1989; Fulton County Government Center, Atlanta), or inside, as in *Meeting Place* (1989; Washington Convention and Trade Center, Seattle), Ferrara has favoured the use of tiles (granite, slate and terracotta, for example) to compose such elements as chequerwork, triangles and bands of various sizes that traverse space in sometimes unpredictable directions.

TRUDIE GRACE

Fetti, Lucrina
Italian painter, active 1614–73

Born Giustina Fetti, sister of the painter Domenico Fetti. Entered a convent of Poor Clares, Sant'Orsola, Mantua, 3 December 1614; assumed the name of Lucrina. Died in Mantua, June 1673.

Bibliography

Giovanni Baglione, *Le vite de' pittori, scultori et architetti dal Pontificato di Gregorio XIII del 1572 in fino a' tempi di Papa Urbano Ottavo nel 1642*, Rome: Fei, 1642; reprinted Bologna: Forni, 1975–6

Filippo Baldinucci, *Notizie de' professori del disegno da Cimabue in qua*, Florence, 1681–1728; reprinted Florence, 1751, and in *Opere di Filippo Baldinucci*, 14 vols, Milan, 1808–12

Pellegrino Orlandi, *Abecedario pittorico ...*, Bologna, 1704; reprinted Venice, 1753, i, p.145

Giovanni Cadioli, *Descrizione delle pitture, sculture ed architetture che si osservano nella città di Mantova, e ne' suoi contorni*, Mantua, 1763, pp.71–3, 76; reprinted Bologna: Forni, 1974

Gaetano Susani, *Nuovo prospetto delle pitture, sculture ed architetture di Mantova e de' suoi contorni*, Mantua, 1818; reprinted Mantua, 1830, pp.55, 134

V.P. Bottoni, *Mantova numerizzata ...*, Mantua, 1839, pp.171–3

Carlo d'Arco, *Delle arti e degli artefici di Mantova ...*, Mantua, 1857, ii, pp.213–14, 245–6; iii, p.81; reprinted Bologna: Forni, 1975

G.B. Intra, "Le due Eleonore Gonzaga imperatrici ...", *Gazzetta di Mantova*, no.121, 8–9 May 1891

—, "Il monastero di Santa Orsola in Mantova", *Archivio Storico Lombardo*, 3rd series, iv, 1895, pp.167–85

Vittorio Matteucci, *Le chiese artistiche del Mantovano*, Mantua, 1902, pp.373–5

G. Matthiae, *Inventario degli oggetti d'arte d'Italia, provincia di Mantova*, vi, Rome, 1935, pp.57–60

E. Marani and C. Perina, *Mantova: Le arti*, iii, Mantua: Istituto Carlo d'Arco, 1965, pp.465–6

"Nota delle pitture più celebri" [from "Diario per l'anno 1749"], *Civiltà Mantovana*, ii, 1967, p.174

Dizionario enciclopedico Bolaffi dei pittori e degli incisori italiani, iv, Turin: Bolaffi, 1973

D. Wilkins, "Women as artists", *The Roles and Images of Women in the Middle Ages and Renaissance*, ed. Douglas Radcliff-Umstead, iii, Pittsburgh: Center for Medieval and Renaissance Studies, 1975

Women Artists, 1550–1950, exh. cat., Los Angeles County Museum of Art, and elsewhere, 1976

Splendours of the Gonzaga, exh. cat., Royal Academy, London, and elsewhere, 1981

I. Bini, "S. Barbara di Lucrina Fetti", *Quadrante Padano*, ii/3, September 1981, pp.18–23

Myriam Zerbi Fanna, "Lucrina Fetti pittrice", *Civiltà Mantovana*, new series, no.23–4, 1989, pp.35–53

Eduard A. Safarik, *Fetti*, Milan: Electa, 1993
S. Balbi de Caro, *I Gonzaga: Moneta, arte, storia*, Milan, 1995

Giustina Fetti, sister of the famous painter Domenico Fetti, was probably born in Rome in the last decade of the 16th century. This is based on the fact that in 1614 she entered Sant'Orsola, the exclusive Mantuan convent of Poor Clares founded by Margherita Gonzaga, the powerful aunt of Ferdinando IV Gonzaga, Duke of Mantua, who had invited Domenico Fetti to his court. The painter was joined in Mantua by his father, also a painter, his mother and sisters. Giustina assumed the monastic name of Lucrina (Mantova, Archivio di Stato, A.G., Camerale Antico, Rogiti Instrumenti iurium 1600–19, 3/12/1614), painted decorations for the convent and made portraits of the Gonzaga princesses and Mantuan noblewomen who were educated there. The personal and artistic life of the nun-painter is closely linked to that of her brother. Baglione met her during his stay in Mantua in 1621–2, and wrote in his *Vite* that Lucrina had learned from her brother, who was Cigoli's pupil, how to paint in a "good manner", but he does not mention any works by her.

The duke himself gave Lucrina a dowry to enter the convent of Sant'Orsola. She painted for the convent and its church the works that make up the first nucleus of her unfortunately scanty oeuvre. Sources mention eight scenes of the *Life and Passion of Christ* attributed to Lucrina. Originally marked with the initials S.L.F.R.F.S.O. ("Suor Lucrina Fetti Romana fecit Sant'Orsola"; or, the nun Lucrina Fetti from Rome made Sant'Orsola) and the date 1619, only the *Annunciation*, the *Crowning with Thorns* (both oratory of Ospedale di San Camillo, Mantua), the *Visitation* and the *Agony in the Garden* (both private collections, Mantua, repr. Zerbi Fanna 1989, pp.48, 47) are known, while the others (*Adoration of the Shepherds*, *Adoration of the Magi*, *Scourging of Christ* and *Road to Calvary*) are lost. In these paintings Lucrina repeats standard narrative conventions but with a domestic tone. The paintings show an elementary manipulation of different styles and a simplified transcription of elements taken from Domenico's compositions. They reveal a lack of experience in the rules of perspective and colour, and share an artificial, rigid stylisation of drapery folds and muscles.

Another *Annunciation* (Palazzo Ducale, Mantua), also from Sant'Orsola, is painted on two separated panels with the Archangel Gabriel and the Virgin, showing, apart from some perspective incoherence, a nice grace in the flowing movement of the draperies and a refined decorative sense in the details of gems, pearls and embroidery that embellish the clothing. This characterises the best elements in Lucrina's artistic production. A similar attention to detail and ornament can be found in the only certain portrait by Lucrina, *Eleonora I Gonzaga* (signed and dated 1622; see illustration), painted in the year of Eleonora's marriage to Emperor Ferdinand II. Lucrina skilfully reproduced the brilliance of embroidery interwoven with golden thread that wraps around the figure, the neat lace of starched ruffs, the richness of the jewellery and the silver-glazed satin lining of the white brocade dress, but her understanding of anatomy is weak. The stiffness of the sitter reflects the trend of official portrait painting at the Mantuan court, where works by such Flemish painters as Frans Pourbus and Justus Sustermans (who also painted a portrait of *Eleonora I*

Fetti: *Eleanora I Gonzaga*, 1622; Palazzo Ducale, Mantua

Gonzaga, which Lucrina's closely resembles) were fashionable and much appreciated. Lucrina exalts the social importance of the Empress, fixed in a solemn pose, by emphasising the magnificence of her costume. It is the character and not the person that she brings out in each portrait. Lucrina's hand may also be recognised in a *St Helen* (Palazzo Ducale) in regal clothes holding the cross with a landscape background, which has many features in common with the portrait of *Eleonora*.

The deep qualitative discrepancy compared with the rest of Lucrina's work makes it unlikely that she painted *St Barbara* (Strinati collection, Rome) from the church of Sant'Orsola, even though her name appears under that of Domenico at the bottom of the painting with the date, 1619, and many scholars do attribute it to her. According to the early historians, Lucrina learned the art of painting from her brother, copied his works and helped him in his numerous assignments, but her hand in the *St Barbara* may perhaps be recognised only in the weaker aspects such as the hair and the motionless face. Accompanying the *St Barbara* in the church of Sant'Orsola was a *St Mary Magdalene* (now San Martino, Mantua), both pictures "retouched by Domenico", according to the sources, while other pictures such as the *Nativity*, *Deposition* and *Christ in the Tempest Awakened by the Apostles* from

Sant'Orsola were lost after Napoleon's suppression of the convent and its conversion into a civic hospital. Similar stylistic solutions to the *St Mary Magdalene* are also visible in a *St Francis* (San Martino), which again shows Lucrina adopting Domenico's themes and models and rendering them in simplified formulas that are typical of her repertoire.

It is impossible to establish the nun's artistic development, since there are very few works attributed to her for certain and a reliable chronology is lacking. Her work wavers between an ingenuous rendering of religious subjects in a domestic atmosphere and a sincere approach to court etiquette in the official portraits, in which she shows a natural inclination for the accurate description of decorative details. She is a great describer of costumes, a fashion reporter of the Mantuan courtly style of her time, as seen from the aristocratic convent under its Gonzaga abbess. Lucrina Fetti was highly appreciated by her contemporaries. Baldinucci relates that "with praises persevering …till the end of her days she always painted". In Baglione's *Vite* (original volume in Rome, Biblioteca Accademia dei Lincei 31 E 15), where he writes about Lucrina, there is a very interesting hand-written marginal note by Bellori where he records her death in June 1673, adding that her funeral oration was done by Giovanni Alessandro Martinelli, the same orator who pronounced the panegyric for Domenico Fetti at his death and also eulogies for some of the dukes. This demonstrates that Giustina/Lucrina, the nun-painter, must have been truly held in high esteem in the Mantua of the Gonzaga.

MYRIAM ZERBI FANNA

Fini, Leonor
Italian painter, 1908–1996

Born in Buenos Aires, 30 August 1908, to parents of mixed European and Argentinian origin. Grew up in mother's home town of Trieste, Italy, from 1920; expelled from every school she attended; moved in intellectual circles, meeting writers James Joyce, Italo Svevo and Umberto Saba. Self-taught in art, studying old and modern masters in museums, and drawing corpses at the morgue. Participated in a group exhibition in Trieste at age 17, earning a commission in Milan. Moved to Paris, 1936. Made friends among the Surrealists, exhibiting with them in London (1936), New York (1936) and Tokyo (1937), but never became an official member of the group. Visited New York, 1939. Lived in Monte Carlo and Rome during World War II, returning to Paris in 1946. Died in Paris, 18 January 1996.

Selected Individual Exhibitions
Julian Levy Gallery, New York: 1939
Palais des Beaux-Arts, Brussels: 1949
Galleria-Galatea d'Arte Contemporanea, Turin: 1957, 1966
Kaplan Gallery, London: 1960
Galerie Iolas, Paris: 1965
Hanover Gallery, London: 1967
Galerie Brockstaedt, Hamburg: 1969
Yomiuri Shimburu, Tokyo: 1972 (touring retrospective)
Galerie Proscenium, Paris: 1978, 1982, 1991
Musée Ingres, Montauban: 1981 (touring retrospective)
Galerie Artcurial, Paris: 1981
Galleria Civica d'Arte Moderna, Ferrara: 1983 (retrospective)
Sago, Yokohama: 1985–6 (touring retrospective)
Musée du Luxembourg and Galerie Proscenium, Paris: 1986
Galerie Guy Pieters, Belgium: 1988
Mussavi Gallery, New York: 1989
Galerie Bosquet, Paris: 1991
Musée St Roch, Issoudun: 1991
CFM, New York: 1992
Galerie Dionne, Paris: 1992, 1993, 1995
Maison du Loir et Cher, Blois: 1992

Selected Writings
Histoire de Vibrissa, Paris: Tchou, 1973
Le Livre de Leonor Fini, Lausanne: Clairefontaine, and Paris: Vilo, 1975; 2nd edition, 1979
"Surtout les puanteurs", *Sorcières*, no.5 [c.1975]
Mourmour, conte pour enfants velus, Paris: Editions de la Différence: 1976
Le Miroir des chats, Lausanne: Guilde du Livre: 1977
L'Onëiropompe, Paris: Editions de la Différence, 1978
Rogomelec, Paris: Stock, 1979
Les Chats de Madame Helvétius, Paris: Navarra, 1985
Chats d'atelier, ed. Guy Pieters, Paris: Trinckvel, 1988; 2nd edition, 1994
Les Passagers, Paris: Dionne, 1992
Entre le Oui et le Non, Paris: Dionne, 1994

Bibliography
Paul Eluard, "Le tableau noir", *Donner à voir*, Paris: Gallimard, 1939 (poem dedicated to Leonor Fini)
Marcel Brion, *Leonor Fini et son oeuvre*, Paris: Pauvert, 1955
Leonor Fini, exh. cat., Kaplan Gallery, London, 1960
Leonor Fini, exh. cat., Casino Communale, Knokke-le-Zoute, 1964
Yves Bonnefoy, *Leonor Fini, ou, La Profondeur délivrée*, Montpellier: Leo, 1965
Leonor Fini, exh. cat., Galleria-Galatea d'Arte Contemporanea, Turin, 1966
Constantin Jelenski, *Leonor Fini*, Lausanne: Clairefontaine, 1968 and 1972
Xavière Gauthier, *Leonor Fini*, Paris: Musée de Poche, 1973
Obliques, no.14–15, 1977 (special issue: *La Femme surréaliste*)
Jean-Claude Dedieu, *Leonor Fini*, Paris: Birr, 1978
Jacques Audiberti and others, *Leonor Fini*, Paris: Hervas, 1981
Pierre Borgue, *Leonor Fini, ou, "Le Théâtre de l'imaginaire"*, Paris: Lettres Modernes, 1983
Leonor Fini, exh. cat., Galleria Civica d'Arte Moderna, Ferrara, 1983
Whitney Chadwick, *Women Artists and the Surrealist Movement*, Boston: Little Brown, and London: Thames and Hudson, 1985
Guy Pieters, ed., *Leonor Fini*, Paris: Trinckvel, 1986
Tiziana Villani, *Parcours dans l'oeuvre de Leonor Fini*, Paris: Trinckvel, 1986
La Femme et le surréalisme, exh. cat., Musée Cantonal des Beaux-Arts, Lausanne, 1987
Martine Antle, "Picto-théâtralité dans les toiles de Leonor Fini", *French Review*, lxii, 1989, pp.640–49
Georgiana M.M. Colvile, "Beauty and/is the beast: Animal symbology in the work of Leonora Carrington, Remedios Varo and Leonor Fini", *Surrealism and Women*, ed. Mary Ann Caws and others, Cambridge: Massachusetts Institute of Technology Press, 1991, pp.159–81
Leonor Fini: The Artist as Designer, exh. cat., CFM, New York, 1992
Leonor Fini peintures, Paris: Trinckvel, 1994
Peter Webb, *Leonor Fini* (in preparation)

Fini: *The Mutants*, 1971; private collection, Paris

Whether or not Leonor Fini should be considered a Surrealist remains an ongoing debate. She herself never wanted to be one, in spite of her friendships with numerous members of the group. She also refused to be isolated as a "woman artist" and was quite convinced that women's art and literature should be integrated with men's rather than constitute a separate corpus. Nevertheless, as Fini has been included in a number of exhibitions and critical volumes on Surrealism, whether on women or both genders, it seems most appropriate to classify her as an individual, independent artist with Surrealist tendencies.

Fini's early paintings tended to be slightly uncanny compositions principally involving female figures (*Black Room*, 1938; private collection, repr. Jelenski 1968) or portraits (*Anna Magnani*, 1949; Collection Anna Magnani, *ibid.*, *Jean Genet*, 1949; private collection, Turin, *ibid.*). She then increasingly represented her favourite mythical monster, the sphinx, and her personal totem creature, the cat, in conjunction with hybrid animal, plant or alchemical female figures, as in *Sphinx Amalburga* (1942; private collection, *ibid.*), *World's End* (1949; private collection, *ibid.*) and *Guardian of Phoenixes* (1954; private collection, *ibid.*), all small-scale oil paintings. Later, Fini experimented more with brighter colours, as in *Heliodora* (1964; private collection, Cannes, *ibid.*), developed the themes of woman as sorceress, often poised as a threat to a weak male, and especially the cat motif in both drawings and paintings (*The Mutants*, 1971; see illustration). Like those of Remedios Varo (q.v.), most of her figures have her own face.

Fini's traditional, carefully crafted and precise draughtmanship (she has been frequently accused of slickness) can be considered as contrary to Surrealism's liberation of form and yet makes her work comparable, at a certain level, to that of Max Ernst, Salvador Dalí, René Magritte and Remedios Varo. Like them, she subverts the content of her compositions, sometimes by means of a single detail, for example, in *La Belle Dame sans merci* (1969), in which a young woman takes a footbath and one of her feet, depicted as a monstrous, bulbous club-foot in dark hues contrasting with the otherwise pastel tones, undercuts the aesthetic harmony of the painting. *Les Invitées* (1971; private collection, New York, *ibid.*) shows two greedy female guests devouring platefuls of a pink substance, while their hostess hides her face: it soon becomes apparent that what they are eating must be her face.

Fini's work is strikingly decorative. She created the sets for more than 20 plays, including Jean Genet's *Les Bonnes* (1961) and *Le Balcon* (1969), and designed the costumes for two films: Renato Castellani's *Romeo and Juliet* (1963) and John Huston's *A Walk with Love and Death* (1969). For many years she loved to dress up in outlandish costumes and masks with her friends. These outfits and the theatrical poses they inspired no doubt provided her with visions of the majestic, either lavishly draped or proudly naked women who inhabit the world of her art. During the 1950s Fini produced an important series of canvases, in which a regally robed woman with shaved head guards a large alchemical egg varying in colour, or displays an ovoidal shape as part of her body (*Silence Enveloped*, 1955; Alexander Iolas Collection, New York; *Guardian with a Red Egg*, 1955; Suzanne Flon Collection, Paris; *Oval Lady*, 1956; private collection, Lausanne, *ibid.*).

During the late 1950s and early to mid-1960s Fini's paintings underwent a radical change: an explosion of colour and a blurring of form are conveyed by extremely delicate brushwork and the elaborate floral backgrounds, sometimes even foregrounds, evoke such Pre-Raphaelite works as John Everett Millais's *Ophelia* (1852; Tate Gallery, London), with discreet human and animal figures emerging from a floral jungle, as in *The Dew* (1963; private collection, Paris, *ibid.*) and *Trough of Night* (1963; artist's estate). Soon Fini's preference for clear forms and self-imposing personae re-emerged, while she retained the delicate and brightly coloured backgrounds of flowers, greenery or aquatic turquoise. In the late 1960s the dominant beautiful women are often enhanced by the presence of Art Nouveau objects: in *Guardian of the Wells* (1967; private collection, Milan, *ibid.*), a lovely young lady with feline eyes, ivory skin and red hair decked with flowers watches over a set of delicate, multi-coloured Lalique-style vases.

By 1969–70 the lush backgrounds become less frequent and Fini's compositions often stage a strange surreal scene with mythical implications and erotic undertones. In *Capital Punishment* (1969; private collection, *ibid.*) three women make ready for a sinister ritual: one with red hair, wearing nothing but turquoise thigh-boots, sits with legs apart, revealing a red mound of venus, and looks coldly at a half-naked, brown-haired servant kneeling before her, holding a white, limp, sacrificial goose, while a third, fair-haired and straight out of an Impressionist painting, in a high-necked white dress and lacy hat whose broad rim hides her eyes, brandishes a castrating knife. Fini's most mythical canvas, *Narcissus* (1971; private collection, Basel), with a beautiful background of turquoise water and waterlilies, provides a perfect illustration for Pausanias' version of the Narcissus story, in which the young man nourishes an incestuous passion for his twin sister, and after her death mistakes his own image in a pool for hers. To the left of Fini's picture, the young naked Narcissus sits by a pool in which he is clearly reflected, legs apart, genitals displayed; next to him, a standing figure, also naked, has been cut off mid-thigh by the frame, so that the person's sexual identity remains concealed, though the legs look masculine; the corresponding reflection, however, reveals a complete and clearly female body, thus creating a climate of ambiguous androgyny.

Fini's passion for cats and her identification with them inspired much of her writing and other people's writing about her, as well as the most important single motif to appear in her painting from the early days to the mid-1990s. Xavière Gauthier tells a remarkable story, according to which until the age of four Leonor Fini had vertical pupils like a cat! (Gauthier 1973, p.88). *The Mutants* represents three little girls on a swing, with such feline features that they appear to be turning into cats. As an additional Freudian *Witz*, such as the Surrealists enjoyed, each child is holding a large, live "pussy" (*chatte*) between her legs. Fini represented herself in *Ideal Life* (1950) as sitting on an exotic throne, surrounded by splendid Persian and other rare felines; she and the animals have the same cold, head-on stare. A visitor would find the artist in that same position, surrounded by a dozen similar long-haired cats of different colours. The animals inspired several of her later paintings, such as *Tigrana* (1994) and *Sunday Afternoon* (1980; both artist's estate). Her shows at the Galerie Dionne in Paris in the 1990s included many pen-and-ink drawings of cats, some of which were used to illustrate her feline children's story *Mourmour* (1976). Fini's last work, apart from the numerous cat pictures, consisted of a series of faces (*Passengers*, 1992; Galerie Dionne, Paris), as well as theatrical grotesques. Leonor Fini deservedly achieved considerable fame throughout Europe and continued to lead a very productive, though retired life, near the Palais Royal in Paris until her death.

GEORGIANA M.M. COLVILE

Fish, Janet
American painter, 1938–

Born in Boston, Massachusetts, 18 May 1938. Studied at Smith College, Northampton, Massachusetts (BA 1960); Yale University School of Art and Architecture, New Haven, 1961–3 (BFA, MFA); Skowhegan School of Art, Maine, summer 1962. Moved to New York, c.1964. Has taught at various schools nationwide, including the School of Visual Arts, New York; Skowhegan School of Art; Institute of Fine Arts, Santa Fe; and Vermont Studio Center, Johnston. Recipient of MacDowell fellowships, 1968, 1969 and 1972; Harris award, Chicago Biennial, 1974; Australian Council for the Arts travel and lecturing grant, 1975; Albert Dorne visiting professorship, University of Bridgeport, Connecticut, 1991. Associate member, American Academy of Arts and Letters, 1994. Lives in New York and near Rutland, Vermont.

Selected Individual Exhibitions

Ours Gallery, New York: 1969
55 Mercer Street Gallery, New York: 1971
Kornblee Gallery, New York: 1971, 1972, 1973, 1974, 1975, 1976
Galerie Alexandra Monett, Brussels: 1974
Tolarno Gallery, Melbourne, Australia: 1975, 1977
Phyllis Kind Gallery, Chicago: 1976, 1979, 1980
Robert Miller Gallery, New York: 1978, 1979, 1980, 1983, 1985, 1987, 1989, 1991
Delaware Art Museum, Wilmington: 1982
Texas Gallery, Houston: 1983, 1985, 1988
Columbia Museum of Art, Columbia, SC: 1984
Smith College Museum of Art, Northampton, MA: 1986
Marsh Gallery, University of Richmond, VA: 1987
Marianne Friedland Gallery, Toronto: 1987, 1989, 1990, 1992
Gerald Peters Gallery, Santa Fe: 1991, 1993
Orlando Museum of Art, FL: 1992
Museum of Arts and Sciences, Macon, GA: 1993
Aspen Art Museum, CO: 1993
Grace Borgenicht Gallery, New York: 1994, 1995

Bibliography
Linda Nochlin, "Some women realists, part 1", *Arts Magazine*, xlviii, February 1974, pp.46–51
David L. Shirey, "Through a glass, brightly", *ibid.*, p.27

Cindy Nemser, "Conversation with Janet Fish", *Feminist Art Journal*, v/3, Fall 1976, pp.4–10

Wolf Kahn, "The subject matter in New Realism", *American Artist*, November 1979, pp.50–55

Barry Yourgrau, "Janet Fish: New paintings", *Arts Magazine*, lv, December 1980, pp.96–7

Contemporary American Realism since 1960, exh. cat., Pennsylvania Academy of the Fine Arts, Philadelphia, 1981

Real, Really Real, Super Real: Directions in Contemporary American Realism, exh. cat., San Antonio Museum, TX, 1981

Jane Cottingham, "Janet Fish: Perceptual realist", *American Artist*, October 1982, pp.44–9, 90, 94–5

From the Heart, video, Santa Fe: Gihon Foundation, 1982

Paul Gardner, "When is a painting finished?", *Art News*, xxxiv, November 1985, pp.89–100

Gerrit Henry, *Janet Fish*, New York: Burton and Skira, 1987

Charles Le Clair, *Color in Contemporary Painting*, New York: Watson-Guptill, 1991

Elaine Steiner, "Gardens: Janet Fish, the artist, cultivates her palette on a Vermont hillside", *Architectural Digest*, August 1992, pp.64–8

Janet Fish, exh. cat., Yellowstone Art Center, Billings, MT, 1995

Janet Fish emerged as a painterly realist, specialising in still life, during the burgeoning of American realism in the 1960s and 1970s. Through the years, she has combined the description of objects – most often made of glass – with a pronounced concern for abundant chromatic and light effects, all captured in oil with a gestural and tactile technique. A modernist in approach, Fish has also shown a keen interest in the formal issues of arrangement and shape and, throughout most of the 1970s, used the close-up view in a shallow space. Although she has always worked from life, she has favoured larger scale formats than are customary for the still-life genre, with accessibility and the assertion of the stroke as important results.

The scale and surface qualities of Fish's still lifes derive from Abstract Expressionism, an idiom in which she worked in 1961 while a painting student in her first year at Yale University School of Art and Architecture. Her break with abstraction occurred during the summer of 1962 when she was studying at the Skowhegan School of Art in Maine. Ready for a new direction and encouraged by the visiting critic Alex Katz, one of her teachers at Yale, Fish began to paint landscapes. After returning to Yale, she made her definitive move to still lifes.

In the late 1960s Fish was painting enlarged fruit and vegetables, which she viewed up close and generalised using a fluid stroke. By 1969, the year of her first solo exhibition in New York, she had moved on to still lifes of supermarket-packaged fruit and vegetables – in cardboard boxes and, importantly for Fish, wrapped in cellophane. The taut, thin plastic allowed for many reflections; these, in turn, transformed the volumes below, as in *Box of Four Red Apples* (1969–70; Port Authority of New York and New Jersey Art Collection, New York).

In the early 1970s Fish added new complexities to her treatment of light by painting glass jars and bottles, usually with liquid contents, such as vinegar, soft drinks and liquor. The translucency of the glass and liquids offered the possibility of multiple reflections and refractions, which she increased by setting her objects on mirrors and observing the action of light over an extended period (a perceptual technique still used by her in the 1990s). As in *Eight Vinegar Bottles* (1972–3; Dallas Museum of Art), she typically filled the canvas with larger-than-life-size forms, increased the overall scale of the format (in this case, 135 × 183 cm.) and complicated the spatial relationships through the overlapping of the reflective and translucent surfaces. Although Fish's jars and bottles, most of which are labelled, have a kinship with Pop imagery of the 1960s, their selection and treatment were determined by formal concerns rather than an interest in social commentary.

By the mid-1970s Fish had purified her still lifes by focusing only on glasses – of various types, sizes and shapes, with smooth surfaces or having cut or moulded designs, and usually partly filled and placed on a mirror. The light effects, observed over the course of a day and for up to a month, were now more intricate and lively than before, with the activity sometimes concentrated more within the glasses than on their surfaces and often reaching near abstraction in some areas. Fish continued to make her objects bold presences by keeping them large and for a time used a reduced palette, thereby emphasising the action of the brush in such works as *Wine and Cheese Glasses* (1975; Indiana University Art Museum, Bloomington). Soon, though, she interjected more, often lustrous colour by depicting crimson, deep blue and other coloured glasses.

Fish proceeded in the late 1970s to open up and enlarge the backgrounds of her still lifes, after using them earlier only as slight framing devices for the glasses. The views were frequently of lustreless buildings, which provided Fish with contrasts to her highly reflective foregrounds. In *Decanters and Factories* (1978; Amy A. Weinberg collection, Louisville) and other works she furthermore merged the close and distant by recording the distortions of buildings seen through glass and their inverted reflections in glass-held liquids.

Beginning in the late 1970s and throughout the 1980s, Fish displayed a profusion of different objects in her still lifes, such as flowers in vases, tablecloths and curtains, fruit and many types of glassware, including stacks of colourful, translucent plates. Altered by light, colour seemed to undergo endless variation, with often luminous results. Gestural energies were still present and usually fluid, although not as active as earlier. Fish generally accommodated many forms and allowed for complexity of arrangement by using an exaggeratedly horizontal format (335 cm. across in some works) or an angled view. The colours were extraordinarily rich in numerous works, including *Raspberries and Goldfish* (1981; see illustration), which has a deep green cloth as the surface, a bowl of raspberries, a stack of lemon-yellow plates, an indigo vase, a dark-blue piece of thick glass under a goldfish bowl, and deep red, yellow and blue nasturtiums.

In the 1980s Fish also produced figurative works. The earliest examples show fairly static poses, with considerable emphasis given to the figures as formal elements within compositions otherwise filled with foliage or many colourful and varied objects covering desks or tables. The people in Fish's paintings of the mid-1980s were more active and usually happily engaged in outdoor activities in sunny country settings. The naturalism that prevailed in these works made them more traditional than any earlier works by Fish, but light remained an important element – usually having a high outdoor intensity that energised the many colours. *Sarah Swimming* (1986; private collection, Boca Raton, repr. Henry 1987, p.117) even contains multiple coloured reflections on a large area of water.

Fish's still lifes of the early to mid-1990s still often feature glassware and frequently include richly patterned cloths. The colour schemes of the paintings range from delicate to intense. Humour is evident in some works, as in certain aspects of Fish's earlier still lifes (the over-sized scale of the bottles and glasses or the stacking of plates, for instance). In *Dog Days* (1993; Grace Borgenicht Gallery, New York) several dogs rest or play on an arid stretch of sand behind a foreground still life that includes lemonade and water-melon slices – cooling treats appropriate for the "dog days" of summer.

TRUDIE GRACE

Fish: *Raspberries and Goldfish,* 1981; oil on canvas; 189.9 × 162.2 cm.; Metropolitan Museum of Art, New York; Purchase, Cape Branch Foundation and Lila Acheson Wallace Gifts, 1983 (1983.171)

Flack, Audrey

American painter and sculptor, 1931–

Born in Washington Heights, New York, 30 May 1931. Studied at Cooper Union, New York, 1948–51; Yale University, New Haven (BFA 1952); Institute of Fine Arts, New York University, 1953; Art Students League, New York. Subsequently worked as a part-time teacher in New York: at Pratt Institute and New York University, 1960–68; Riverside Museum Master Institute, 1966–7; School of Visual Arts, 1970–74; National Academy of Design, from 1987; also Albert Dorne Professor, University of Bridgeport, Connecticut, 1975, and Mellon Professor, Cooper Union, 1982. Married H. Robert Marcus in 1970 (second marriage); two daughters from previous marriage born 1959 and 1961. Recipient of award of merit, Butler Institute of American Art, Youngstown, Ohio, 1974; Citation and honorary doctorate, Cooper Union, 1977; Saint-Gaudens medal, Cooper Union, 1982; Artist of the Year award, New York City Teachers Association, 1985. Member of the Board of Directors, College Art Association of America, 1989–94. Lives in New York.

Selected Individual Exhibitions

Roko Gallery, New York: 1959, 1963
French and Co., New York: 1972
Louis K. Meisel Gallery, New York: 1974, 1976, 1978, 1983, 1991, 1995 (retrospective)
Joseloff Gallery, University of Hartford, CT: 1974
Carlson Gallery, University of Bridgeport, CT: 1975
Fine Arts Gallery, University of South Florida, Tampa/Art and Cultural Center, Hollywood, FL: 1981
Armstrong Gallery, New York: 1983
Hewlett Art Gallery, Carnegie-Mellon University, Pittsburgh: 1984
Cooper Union, New York: 1986–8 (*Saints and Other Angels*, touring)
Belk Building, Town Center Mall, Rock Hill, SC: 1990
Parrish Art Museum, Southampton, NY: 1991
Frederick S. Wight Art Gallery, University of California, Los Angeles: 1992–3 (*Breaking the Rules*, touring retrospective)

Selected Writings

"Luisa Ignacia Roldán", *Women's Studies*, vi, 1978, pp.23–33
Audrey Flack on Painting, New York: Abrams, 1981
"On Carlo Crivelli", *Arts Magazine*, lv, June 1981, pp.92–5
Art and Soul: Notes on Creating, New York: Dutton, 1986
Audrey Flack: The Daily Muse, New York: Abrams, 1989

Bibliography

Cindy Nemser, *Art Talk: Conversations with 12 Women Artists*, New York: Scribner, 1975
Audrey Flack: "The Gray Border Series", exh. cat., Louis K. Meisel Gallery, New York, 1976
Louis K. Meisel, *Photorealism*, New York: Abrams, 1980
Eileen Guggenheim-Wilkinson, *Photo-Realist Painting*, PhD dissertation, Princeton University, 1982
Charlotte Streifer Rubinstein, *American Women Artists from Early Times to the Present*, Boston: Hall, 1982
Thalia Gouma-Peterson, "Icons of healing energy: The recent work of Audrey Flack", *Arts Magazine*, lviii, November 1983, pp.136–41
Audrey Flack: A Pantheon of Female Deities, exh. cat., Louis K. Meisel Gallery, New York, 1991
Laurie S. Hurwitz, "A bevy of goddesses: Paintings and sculptures by Audrey Flack", *American Artist*, September 1991, pp.42–7, 85–7
Breaking the Rules: Audrey Flack: A Retrospective, 1950–1990, exh. cat., Frederick S. Wight Art Gallery, University of California, Los Angeles, and elsewhere, 1992 (contains extensive bibliography)
Louis K. Meisel, *Photorealism since 1980*, New York: Abrams, 1993
Mara R. Witzling, ed., *Voicing Today's Visions: Writings by Contemporary Women Artists*, New York: Universe, 1994
Patricia Mathews, "Goddess Redux", *Art in America*, lxxxii, March 1994, pp.88–91, 124–5
David R. Brigham, "The new civic art: An interview with Audrey Flack", *American Art*, ix, Winter 1994, pp.2–21

Audrey Flack was one of the first artists of the 1960s to use photographs as the basis for painting, yet her subject matter differed greatly from that of her male photo-realist colleagues – jewellery and perfume bottles, Hispanic Madonnas and narrative still lifes rather than the shiny surfaces of cars and motorcycles. Over the years she has been interested in imbuing her works – first paintings and then sculpture – with richly resonant layers of symbolic meaning. As a student at Cooper Union, she was recruited by Josef Albers to participate in the fine arts program at Yale University, although in contrast to his purist aesthetic she was captivated by the rich, lush surfaces of Baroque art. After graduation from Yale in 1952, she moved back to New York and studied anatomy with Robert Beverly Hale at the Art Students League, in response to her felt need to paint realistically, a technique that had been ignored in her previous art education.

During the 1950s Flack abandoned the Abstract Expressionist idiom used in her earliest paintings because of her belief that art's purpose was to communicate. Soon after she began her studies with Hale, recognisable imagery appeared in her work. One of a series of still lifes painted during this period, *Still Life with Apples and Teapot* (1955; private collection, repr. Los Angeles 1992, p.15), shows Flack's interest in recording the things of this world while retaining some elements of Abstract Expressionism. She also painted a series of self-portraits, very private images that she did not exhibit and through which she began to work out her conflict regarding both style and content. Beginning with the Abstract Expressionist *Self-Portrait* (1952) and culminating in *Self-Portrait: Dark Face* (1960; both Miami University Art Museum, Oxford, OH), her work shows an increasingly stabilising image of the artist, executed with broad, sometimes dripping, painterly strokes.

The 1960s represented a period of artistic consolidation for Flack. She abandoned her own image as a subject, painting instead those of her daughters, Melissa and Hannah. In the mid-1960s she branched away from the private sphere, basing her compositions on photographs pertaining to documentary news, focusing on such public figures as Roosevelt, Rockefeller, even Hitler. *Kennedy Motorcade* (1964; private collection, *ibid.*, p.53), her first work based on a colour photograph, showed President and Jackie Kennedy and the Texas governor John Connally, just moments before Kennedy was shot. This work confirmed the future direction of her art in terms of subject matter and style, as well as in her working method, which became increasingly based on photographic images.

The most important breakthrough for Flack occurred during the painting of the *Farb Family Portrait* (1969–70; Rose

Flack: *Queen*, 1976; acrylic on canvas; 203.2 × 203.2 cm.

Art Museum, Brandeis University, Waltham, MA), when her impatience to move beyond the preliminary stage of blocking the drawing on to canvas with charcoal led her to project a slide directly on to canvas and to apply colour through the projected image. This technique quickly led to her mature style, in which she applied paint in layers with an airbrush, mixing primary colours directly on the surface of the painting, in order to achieve a more intense luminosity than through conventional means. After the Farb portrait, Flack experimented with this photo-realist technique in works built from easily recognisable imagery. Her complex, monumental still lifes of the 1970s may be seen as the culmination of these endeavours.

In the early 1980s Flack underwent another period of intense self-questioning, which resulted in her changing her primary artistic medium, from painting to sculpture. She describes the change as a response to the felt need for "something solid, real, tangible. Something to hold and to hold on to" (*Art and Soul* 1986, p.26). Her earliest piece was a small bronze putto, *Angel with Heart Shield* (1981; Ari Ron Meisel collection, New York). She soon executed a somewhat larger work in clay, *Black Medicine* (1981–2; Pamela Rosenau collection, New York), whose model was a 75-year-old black woman. This was the first of a series of diverse, heroic women and goddess figures – many of them in bronze – that formed the major part of Flack's output over the next decade, culminating in her commission of 1990–91 for the Rock Hill City Gateway, South Carolina, four "visions" of female strength, each 3.9 metres high. In the early 1990s she was also commissioned to make a colossal statue of *Queen Catherine of Braganza* (the founder of the New York borough of Queens) to stand opposite the United Nations. Flack's women depart from conventional images of femininity in that they are athletic, older, fierce. As Flack describes them: "they are real yet idealized ... the 'goddesses in everywoman'" (lecture at the University of New Hampshire, May 1993).

Flack's sculptures bear a deep connection to her earlier work, particularly in their relation to femininity and its construction. The tension between woman as artist and woman as subject was a leitmotif in the series of self-portraits executed during the 1950s, particularly the *Anatomy Lesson* (1953; Miami University Art Museum) – a reference to Rembrandt's *Anatomy Lesson of Dr Tulp* (1632; Mauritshuis, The Hague) – and *Self-Portrait in Underpants* (1958; Miami University Art Museum), in which she stands at the easel, one hand on her tilted hip, confronting the viewer head on. When Flack began painting in a photo-realist style, women were a central subject of her art: Harry Truman's teachers, nuns leading a march, two women grieving over Kennedy, Carroll Baker, Marilyn Monroe. Flack also dealt with the construction of femininity in her monumental still lifes, without painting the actual likeness of a specific woman. A work such as *Jolie Madame* (1972; National Gallery of Australia, Canberra) presents in hot, lush, red tones the accoutrements of self-adornment of the beautiful woman. These works enabled her to explore the reflective surfaces that male photo-realists had found so captivating, yet their subject matter – "women's things" – is one that has been trivialised, seen as less appropriate or valuable, in our culture.

From the time she abandoned Abstract Expressionism, Flack sought a means of communicating expressive content through her work. While other photo-realists claimed that the subjects of their works were irrelevant, Flack chose to base her paintings on photographic imagery that communicated a particular socio-political point of view, culminating in the *Vanitas* series, including *Marilyn* (1977; University of Arizona Art Museum, Tucson) and *Wheel of Fortune* (1977–8; Louis K. Meisel Gallery collection, New York). These works make direct reference in both structure and motif – the candles, the hourglass – to the *vanitas* paintings of the Baroque period, with their didactic, symbolic purpose and engagement with broad philosophical issues, such as the passage of time and the meaning of life. Flack continued to explore "iconic images for a secularized age" in such works from the early 1980s as *A Course in Miracles* (Linnea S. Dietrich collection) and *Fruits of the Earth* (private collection, repr. Los Angeles 1992, p.96), in which she deliberately attempted to create a harmonious integration of paths towards spirituality. Flack's sculptural works fulfil the purpose of her artistic endeavour in that they make a comprehensible statement through manipulation of "readable" iconographic elements. Her goddesses are all given symbolic and mythological attributes – the *Egyptian Rocket Goddess*

(1990; private collection, Ontario, *ibid.*, p.109) wields a snake, *Islandia* (1987; Samuel P. Harn Museum of Art, University of Florida, Gainesville) offers a conch, an eagle perches atop the head of *American Athena* (1989; Donna and Neil Weisman collection). Some of these figures, like the *Rocket Goddess*, are hybrids, synthesised by Flack; others, like *Athena*, *Diana* and *Medusa* are reinterpretations of traditional mythological figures, from a contemporary, feminist perspective.

MARA R. WITZLING

Flöckinger, Gerda
British artist jeweller, 1927–

Born in Innsbruck, Austria, 8 December 1927. Emigrated to England with her family, 1938; naturalised British, 1946. Studied at St Martin's School of Art, London, 1945–50; Central School of Arts and Crafts, London, 1950–56. Established own studio/workshop in London, 1955–6. Lecturer at Hornsey College of Art, London, 1962–8. Commander, Order of the British Empire (CBE), 1991. Lives in London.

Selected Individual Exhibitions
Crafts Centre of Great Britain, London: 1968
Victoria and Albert Museum, London: 1971, 1986, 1991 (Crafts Council shop)
City of Bristol Museum and Art Gallery: 1971
Dartington Cider Press Gallery, Dartington, Devon: 1977

Bibliography
International Exhibition of Modern Jewellery, 1890–1961, exh. cat., Goldsmiths' Hall, London, 1961
Schmuck/Jewellery/Bijoux: International Ausstellung, exh. cat., Hessisches Landesmuseum, Darmstadt, 1964
Tarby Davenport, "Craftsmen in modern jewellery", *Design*, no.228, December 1967, pp.33–7
Susan Causey, "Modern jewellery in a new idiom", *Design*, no.245, May 1969, pp.56–9
Flöckinger/Herman, exh. cat., Victoria and Albert Museum, London, 1971
Alastair Best, "Sam & Gerda", *Design*, no.266, February 1971, pp.36–41
Brian Beaumont-Nesbitt, "Gerda Flöckinger's jewellery", *Connoisseur*, clxxxiv, 1973, pp.28–32
——, "Attitudes to jewellery", *Art and Artists*, x, October 1975, pp.11–17
Barbara Cartlidge, *Twentieth-Century Jewelry*, New York: Abrams, 1985
Gerda Flöckinger, exh. cat., Victoria and Albert Museum, London, 1986
Catherine McDermott, "Gerda", *Crafts*, no.82, September–October 1986, pp.20–23
Anna Beatriz Chadour and Andreas Freisfeld, eds, *SchmuckStücke: Der Impuls der Moderne in Europa*, Munich: Klinkhardt und Biermann, 1991
Clare Beck, "Gerda Flöckinger CBE", *Goldsmiths Review*, 1993–4, pp.30–32
Peter Dormer and Ralph Turner, *The New Jewelry: Trends and Traditions*, 2nd edition, New York: Thames and Hudson, 1994
David Watkins, *The Best in Contemporary Jewellery*, London: Batsford, 1994

Flöckinger: Necklace; private collection

Important developments have taken place in jewellery during the second half of the 20th century in terms of its techniques and materials as well as in fundamental attitudes towards its purpose and significance. Gerda Flöckinger's work in the 1950s and 1960s effectively opened the debate on whether jewellery should be recognised as a serious art form, smoothing the path for the now accepted role of the artist-jeweller. One of the finest jewellers of her time, Flöckinger has been both uniquely individual in her creative output and profoundly influential.

During the 1950s the idea that jewellery might be viewed as art was novel, and jewellers were regarded largely as skilled technicians. Flöckinger began by studying fine art at St Martin's School of Art, London, but went on to study etching,

and then jewellery and enamels, at the Central School. She began exhibiting jewellery in 1954 at the Institute of Contemporary Arts, London; there was then no specific outlet or venue for the display of modern jewellery. These exhibitions continued annually for some ten years. Her work at that time was principally of silver, copper and brass. Graham Hughes began to purchase pieces for the collection of the Goldsmiths' Company from as early as 1956. In 1961 the Worshipful Company of Goldsmiths organised what they described as the world's first international exhibition of modern jewellery, in which Flöckinger's work already attracted attention (London 1961, nos 283–8; no.283, enamelled ring, 1958, pl.64, is wrongly attributed to Desmond Clen-Murphy in the caption). Her first solo show was in 1968 at the Crafts Centre of Great

Britain. In 1971 she became the first living jeweller to be given a one-person show at the Victoria and Albert Museum, London, followed by another at the same venue 15 years later in 1986. Flöckinger's jewellery is included in a number of significant public collections including the Schmuckmuseum, Pforzheim; the Worshipful Company of Goldsmiths, Victoria and Albert Museum and Crafts Council, London; the Castle Museum, Nottingham; and the National Museums of Scotland.

Flöckinger's establishment of an experimental course in jewellery at Hornsey College of Art in 1962 marked a watershed in the post-war regeneration of jewellery design. The course concentrated on the interplay and interdependence of design and technique, a pioneering approach for its time, which fundamentally influenced the direction of jewellery in the following decades. Flöckinger proved to be an inspirational teacher, attracting and developing a remarkable generation of jewellers including, for example, Charlotte de Syllas and David Poston. Flöckinger's importance extends far beyond her influence on others, however, for her own output is of the highest calibre both technically and aesthetically. In the mid-1960s her work began to develop an intensely individual character that has been painstakingly and seamlessly refined over the following decades. (For examples of her work prior to the mid-1960s, see necklace, 1963–4; Collection of the Worshipful Company of Goldsmiths, London, repr. Chadour and Freisfeld 1991, fig.92; and necklace, 1964; Worshipful Company of Goldsmiths, repr. Darmstadt 1964, fig.50.)

Flöckinger's earliest years were spent in Austria among the dramatic mountain scenery around Innsbruck. She learned to ski and skate by the age of four, and summers were spent swimming and boating in the lakes. The dappling of light and the glint of sun on the water, the reeds thickly obscuring the banks of the lakes, the gentle movement of leaves in the breeze and the heat of the molten Austrian landforms find resonances in the distinctive surfaces of Flöckinger's jewellery. A unique contribution has been the development of new techniques using the controlled fusion of gold and silver rather than soldering. These methods, combined with low-relief scrolls, sinuous wires and scatters of tiny granules, result in the characteristic textures and movement of the surfaces of her work.

She uses naturally inspired forms that seem organically created. Each piece or pair of pieces employs a perfectly conceived asymmetry, often embellished with the subtle movement of drops, pendants and decorated rods (e.g. earrings, 1971, repr. London 1986, no.3; earrings, 1977, ibid., no.16; finger ring, 1977, ibid., no.19). Rings often have offset bezels (1978, ibid., no.24; 1979, ibid., no.31; 1983, ibid., no.50; 1985, ibid., no.63) and stones pour gently over the edges of bands (1983, ibid., no.51; 1986, ibid., nos 70–72). From the 1970s her work also explored openwork, which delicately breaks up the surface. This, combined with the encrusted textures and subtle colourings, produces a foamy quality (necklace, 1971, repr. Cartlidge 1985, no.153; two necklaces, both 1975–86, repr. London 1986, no.7 and front cover). Materials are chosen for their inherent characteristics – their colours, shapes, textures or reflective qualities – rather than any traditional notions of value or preciousness. Diamonds are scattered to glint across encrusted surfaces, pale matt metal

heightens the iridescent gleam of pearls, stones are set like coloured pools in the midst of tiny molten landscapes. Flöckinger cuts and polishes her stones herself to ensure their shape. Typical choices include opals, amethysts, tourmalines, moonstones, topaz, turquoise and amber, usually cabochon cut, together with subtly coloured baroque pearls and tiny brilliant diamonds. She also gives some stones – such as topaz, amethyst and fire opal – a remarkable matt finish, for the soft gleam produced in combination with her metallic surfaces (see, for example, the finger rings, 1979, ibid., no.32; 1983, ibid., no.50; 1984, ibid., no.58).

Successful execution requires meticulous processes of control and decision making and the finest balance of line and texture, metal and stone. Despite the effortless appearance of the finished product, Flöckinger's involvement with her work is deeply emotional and involves a painstaking degree of commitment, to the point of obsession. Each surface, back or front, is treated with equal care and attention; no detail is considered unimportant. She works surrounded by hundreds of drawings, which she executes rapidly and fluently (for an example from a sketchbook, 1976, see London 1986, p.9), but the actual creation of the jewellery is more improvised, beginning with a basic idea then following a complex route until the piece feels right. She describes it as like composing and performing simultaneously.

Flöckinger's work has a timeless appeal. She has a remarkable understanding of the meaning and potential of jewellery and, most crucially, its relationship to its eventual wearer. She has proved to be that rare combination of instinctive artist and superb creator. Her work gives profound pleasure to look at and touch, wear and possess, and can arouse a passion in its owners that perhaps only jewellery, the most personal and intimate of arts, can provide.

ELIZABETH GORING

Flögl, Mathilde
Austrian craftworker and designer, 1893–1958

Born in Brünn (now Brno, Czech Republic), 9 September 1893. Studied at the Kunstgewerbeschule, Vienna, under Strnad, Böhm, Anton von Kenner and Josef Hoffmann, 1909–16. Member of the Wiener Werkstätte, 1916–31; head of leather workshop, c.1925. Own studio in Vienna, 1931–5. Took up an apprenticeship in Czechoslovakia, 1935. Returned to Vienna, 1941; taught at the Frauengewerbeschule (Women's Craft School) in the Mollardgasse, and worked in Hoffmann's section of the experimental workshops of the Kulturamt der Stadt Wien. Worked full-time with Hoffmann at the Künstlerwerkstättenverein (Association of Artists' Studios), Vienna, from 1945. Taught drawing in Salzburg from 1951. Founder-member, 1914, and committee member, 1928, Österreichischer Werkbund; member, Wiener Frauenkunst. Died in Salzburg, 23 July 1958.

Principal Exhibitions

Bibliography

Die Wiener Werkstätte: Modernes Kunsthandwerk von 1903–1932,
exh. cat., Österreichisches Museum für angewandte Kunst,
Vienna, 1967

Waltraud Neuwirth, *Wiener Keramik: Historismus-Jugendstil-Art
Deco,* Braunschweig: Klinkhart und Biermann, 1974

——, *Die Keramik der Wiener Werkstätte,* i: *Originalkeramiken,
1920–1931,* Vienna, 1981

Isabelle Anscombe, *A Woman's Touch: Women in Design from 1860
to the Present Day,* London: Virago, and New York: Viking, 1984

Traude Hansen, *Wiener Werkstätte: Mode, Stoffe, Schmuck,
Accessoires,* Vienna: Brandstatter, 1984

Werner J. Schweiger, *Wiener Werkstätte: Designs in Vienna,
1903–1932,* New York: Abbeville, and London: Thames and
Hudson, 1984 (German original, 1982)

Angela Völker, *Wiener Mode und Modefotographie: Die
Modeabteilung der Wiener Werkstätte, 1911–1932,* Munich:
Schneider-Henn, 1984 (catalogue of the Österreichisches Museum
für angewandte Kunst, Vienna)

Astrid Gmeiner and Gottfried Pirhofer, *Der österreichische
Werkbund,* Salzburg: Residenz, 1985

Eduard F. Sekler, *Josef Hoffmann: The Architectural Work,* Princeton:
Princeton University Press, 1985 (German original, 1982)

Jane Kallir, *Viennese Design and the Wiener Werkstätte,* New York:
Braziller, and London: Thames and Hudson, 1986

Wiener Werkstätte: Atelier viennois, 1903–1932: Europalia, exh. cat.,
Brussels, 1987

Wien um 1900, exh. cat., Sezon Museum of Art, Tokyo, and elsewhere, 1989

Ruperta Pichler, *Wiener Werkstätte: Lederobjekte, Bestandskatalog
des Österreichischen Museums für angewandte Kunst,* Vienna,
1992

Angela Völker, *Textiles of the Wiener Werkstätte, 1910–1932,*
London: Thames and Hudson, 1994; as *The Wiener Werkstätte
Textiles,* New York: Rizzoli, 1994 (German original, 1990)

Manuscript collection is in the Archiv der Wiener Werkstätte, Österreichisches Museum für angewandte Kunst, Vienna.

From 1909 to 1916 Mathilde Flögl received the "classic"
education of a craftworker of her time at the Kunstgewerbeschule, Vienna. Under Böhm, Anton von Kenner, Strnad and
Josef Hoffmann she was trained in interior design, textile
design, design in general, applied graphics and creative enamelling. Hoffmann was to have an even greater influence on
Flögl's career: in 1916 he admitted her to the Wiener
Werkstätte, at first as a member of the newly founded artists'
workshop, in which artists of all different types could work
freely. Any outstanding designs and finished objects were
bought by the Werkstätte. In the same year Flögl became a
permanent member of the Werkstätte and soon proved herself
to have been a perfect choice: leather, ivory, wood, enamel,
glass, metal and textiles – she could work in all these media,
forming or decorating them in her own moderately avant-
garde style. In the ceramics department she proved her talent
for Expressionist sculpture by creating numerous small groups

Flögl: *Curzola,* textile fragment; length 24 cm.

of animals, as well as vessels and dinner services, which
brought out her special talent for surface decoration.

In 1918 Flögl was admitted to the textiles department. With
more than 120 designs, she became one of the most productive
members of the department, thus making a substantial contribution to the style of fabric patterns in the period between the
wars. Dagobert Peche's fantastic, delicate surface decoration
was a source of inspiration to her, as were the clear geometric
patterns of Maria Likarz-Strauss (q.v.). Flögl acquired a wide
repertoire of decorative elements, from stylised plant shapes to
more severe ornamentation composed of straight lines. As
demanded by the creative trends of the Wiener Werkstätte, her
work varied from large, striking designs to tiny, intricate
patterns. Many of her fabrics were later used as samples in the
fashion department, where they exerted a considerable influence on the cut of the clothes. Her more practical talents,
which did not tend to extremes, also predestined Flögl for large
decorative tasks.

In 1928 she was entrusted with the decorative revamping of
the murals in the Graben Café bar, which had been painted by
Hoffmann in 1912. Following the stepped form of the ceiling,

she created a homogeneous design that united architecture and arts and crafts. In her final version – asymmetrical, restless and brightly coloured – she introduced trends from avant-garde painting to the interior by placing the areas of colour in an irregular fashion with ornamental details scattered about. Around the same time Flögl designed a mural for the "tea room" at the *Die neuzeitliche Wohnung* (Modern homes) exhibition in the Österreichisches Museum für Kunst und Industrie in Vienna. Her design was relaxed and calm, appropriate to the room's function, the composition broken up by widely spaced horizontal motifs and enlivened with plants, animals and figures. The shaded material used for the upholstery put the final touches to the room. Flögl's freehand, stencilled murals were very fashionable – good reason for her to be entrusted with a task of this nature.

In order to reach a wider public, in 1928 Flögl produced a new wallpaper collection with the Salubra Works: *Kleid für die Wand*. The name, "Garments for the walls", suited the era: a room had to be "dressed" and "adorned" with fabrics; walls had to be "clothed". The mixing of a variety of patterns in a room was not only propagated by Hoffmann and his circle, but was also frequently practised by the Wiener Werkstätte. These innovations in interior design, to which Flögl made a measurable contribution, did not enjoy a general breakthrough until the 1930s.

From 1925 there is evidence of Flögl's work in the leather workshops of the Wiener Werkstätte, but her involvement did not intensify until her later years. The starting point of her designs was the use of materials of different colours. She decorated all sorts of objects with arrows, triangles and other geometric shapes. She also broke new ground in the field of posters and advertisement design. In 1927 she was given the responsibility for designing the exhibition catalogue of the Kunstschau. The lower-case typography, the arrangement of pictures and the broad, ribbon-like horizontal divisions reveal her sources of inspiration: the work of such avant-garde artists as El Lissitzky, László Moholy-Nagy and Theo van Doesburg. Her posters for the fashion department complete the picture.

In 1928 Flögl was given the prestigious commission to design the publication celebrating the Wiener Werkstätte's 25th anniversary, published by Krystallverlag: *Die Wiener Werkstätte 1903 bis 1928: Modernes Kunstgewerbe und sein Weg*. With the aid of silkscreen printing to transfer the photographs, she created a layout that was extraordinary in every way. The geometric, coloured divisions of the pages create a balanced relationship between areas of colour, photographs and text. The geometry of the cover is carried through to the inside of the book, according to the wishes of the artist. The press reviewed the book as "something that could never have happened at any time but in 1928, nor anywhere else but in Vienna". The journal *Der Tag* commented that it was: "typographically unusual; untrodden territory. The book is really a document of Peche's eclecticism and Russian Expressionism, the charm of Old Vienna and the taste for indulgent sumptuousness – truly the spirit of the Wiener Werkstätte". This success linked Mathilde Flögl still closer to the Wiener Werkstätte, and she stayed with the firm until it disbanded. After World War II she worked even more closely with Hoffmann at his Künstlerwerkstättenverein. Here, too, the bulk of her work consisted of designs for interiors,

furniture, textiles, lamps and crockery. After she moved to Salzburg, her main source of income was from her post as a drawing teacher.

GABRIELE FABIANKOWITSCH

Florence, Mary Sargant
British painter, 1857–1954

Born Mary Sargant in London, 21 July 1857; sister of the sculptor F.W. Sargant; father a barrister. Studied art in Paris under Luc-Olivier Merson; in London at the Slade School of Fine Art under Alphonse Legros. Married American musician Henry Smyth Florence, 1888; one son, one daughter; husband died 1892; retained a house in Nutley, New Jersey, an artists' and musicians' colony, until 1921. Founder-member, Society of Mural Decorators, 1901. Taught fresco painting at the Slade, 1912; also took private pupils. Died in Twickenham, Middlesex, 14 December 1954.

Principal Exhibitions
New English Art Club, London: from 1910
Burleigh House, Stamford: 1923 (*Decorative Art*)
Royal Academy, London: occasionally 1930–51

Selected Writings
"Fresco painting", *Papers of the Society of Painters in Tempera*, 1901–7, pp.53–68
"The influence of material on style", *Arts and Crafts Quarterly*, i/2, 1920, pp.13–20
"Frescoes in the Old School at Oakham", *Papers of the Society of Mural Decorators and Painters in Tempera*, 1907–24, pp.42–54
"Decorative perspective", *Papers of the Society of Mural Decorators and Painters in Tempera*, 1925–35, pp.79–86
"Survey of the Society's development", *ibid.*, pp.136–140
Colour Co-ordination, London: Lane, 1940
Militarism Versus Feminism: Writings on Women and War, ed. Margaret Kamester and Jo Vellacott, London: Virago, 1987 (with Catherine Marshall and C.K. Ogden)

Bibliography
Walter Bayes, *The Art of Decorative Painting*, London: Chapman and Hall, and New York: Scribner, 1927
The Times, 16 December 1954 (obituary)
Mary Chamot, Dennis Farr and Martin Butlin, *Tate Gallery Catalogues: The Modern British Paintings, Drawings and Sculpture*, London: Oldbourne Press, 1964
Keith Spence, "A country refuge from Bloomsbury: Lord's Wood, Marlow", *Country Life*, cliv, 15 November 1973, pp.1579–84
John Russell Taylor, *The Art Nouveau Book in Britain*, Edinburgh: Harris, 1979
Alan Powers, "The fresco revival in the early 20th century", *Journal of the Decorative Arts Society, 1850 to the Present*, no.12, 1988, pp.38–46
——, "Private faces in public places", *The Last Romantics: The Romantic Tradition in British Art: Burne-Jones to Stanley Spencer*, exh. cat., Barbican Art Gallery, London, 1989, pp.63–9

Mary Sargant Florence was one of the most powerful women artists of her generation, breaking away from the techniques of academic art to specialise in fresco. Due to the dispersal of her studio after her death, her work is hard to find apart from her

Florence: *Suffer the Little Children*, 1912–14; drawing, study for a fresco at the Bourneville School, West Midlands; Tate Gallery, London

murals, and of these important examples have been destroyed or covered over. The content of her paintings does not, however, relate to her feminist activities, although her independent attitude to life and art shows her determination to compete with men on an equal footing. Her son Philip, later Professor of Commerce at Birmingham University, wrote of his mother: "She was in revolt against the pampered place of grand bourgeois girls. She hated to have to lie in bed till called, be dressed up for church etc., and loved Paris where she could escape all that" (manuscript, Alan Powers collection).

Florence's illustrations for *The Crystal Ball* (1894) include firmly drawn decorative initials, making what John Russell Taylor called "one of the most altogether attractive books of the 1890s", although she appears to have done no other illustrating. In 1899–1900 she built a house, Lord's Wood, Marlow, Buckinghamshire, which, although outwardly conventional, was internally unplastered and, in Italian style, had curtains rather than doors between rooms. There were no water closets, because she believed strongly in the value of returning night-soil to the vegetable garden. The house contained a large fresco by her of *Les Aveugles*, based on a story by Maeterlinck, showing the blind, robed figures of women and a child in a wood (now painted over).

It was probably shortly before 1900 that Florence became interested in fresco painting. She was involved in the foundation of the Tempera Society in 1901 under the initial chairmanship of Lady (Christiana) Herringham who in 1899 had published a new edition of Cennino Cennini's *Craftsman's Handbook*. The Society was interested in various traditional painting techniques as an alternative to the domination of oil painting. In 1900 Florence began her work on frescoes for the

Old School, Oakham, a simple Elizabethan building, which was the origin of a small public school where her brother was headmaster. Eight large panels were carried out and completed in 1907. This was the largest cycle to be completed in genuine fresco (i.e. direct painting into wet plaster) as opposed to "Spirit fresco" (the Gambier-Parry medium) since the works of G. F. Watts in the 1850s. The subject was the story of Gareth from Sir Thomas Malory's *Le Morte Darthur*. The figures are mostly placed close to the picture plane to form a friezelike effect, but with greater animation than is found in the work of other fresco and tempera painters such as Joseph Southall, or such followers of Puvis de Chavannes as F. Cayley Robinson. The result is a convincing narrative with psychological tension in which the period trappings of medievalism do not obtrude. Technically, the paintings required long planning and experiment in acquiring and laying lime plaster. A restricted palette composed mainly of earth pigments was used to unify the effect and ensure permanence. The artist emphasised the importance of work on cartoons to allow for freedom and breadth of execution in the final painting. She wrote:

the actual painting should be full of spontaneous pleasure, the final expression in terms of colour of the original conception, and the worker freed by all the preceding labour to enjoy the supreme delight of the colourist in exquisite grading of a single hue by the simple handling of the brush, or the interweaving of many tints in harmonic concord and contrast [1924].

Four of the panels were damaged by building work in the 1950s. Despite strong protests, the whole scheme was covered over by panelling in 1994 at the order of Oakham School.

Florence joined the New English Art Club in 1910 and exhibited a tempera panel on wood, *Children at Chess* (Tate Gallery, London), an unsentimental picture of her two children in a complex rhythmical composition. In 1912 she entered the competition at Chelsea Town Hall for mural panels portraying famous residents of Chelsea. Her panel, *Religion, the Genius of Science and the Art of Music*, is the strongest and most original of the four selected designs and was recognised as such at the time. It was painted in oil and remains *in situ*. The last major fresco work by her was in the hall of Bourneville School, West Midlands (1912–14; *in situ*). The commission was given in the first instance to Mary Creighton, daughter of the Bishop of London. Florence was asked for her technical advice and carried out seven of the paintings, half the total. The works are rectangular in shape, horizontally placed and well composed in cool colours (two cartoons in Tate Gallery; see illustration).

Florence was an advocate for fresco and other alternatives to oil painting. She taught fresco at the Slade School in 1912 and taught private pupils at Lord's Wood, including Daphne Pollen (née Baring) and Beatrice Playne, who went on to be a pupil of Diego Rivera in Mexico City. She also tried to influence the painting faculty of the British School in Rome to demand more attention to materials and technique. Her complex work on colour theory was published at the end of her life.

ALAN POWERS

Fontana, Lavinia
Italian painter, 1552–1614

Baptised in Bologna Cathedral, 24 August 1552, daughter of the painter Prospero Fontana and his wife Antonia de Bonardis. Married Gian Paolo Zappi of Imola, 1577; eleven children, 1578–95; only three children were living in 1607. In Rome by 28 April 1604. Died in Rome, 11 August 1614; buried in Santa Maria sopra Minerva.

Bibliography

Raffaello Borghini, *Il Riposo*, Florence, 1584; reprint, ed. Mario Rosci, Milan, 1967

Francesco Cavazzoni, *Pitture et sculture ed altre cose notabili che sono in Bologna e dove si trovano*, Bologna, 1603; ed. Ranieri Varese in "Una guida inedita del seicento bolognese", *Critica d'Arte*, xvi, 1969, no.103, pp.25–38; no.104, pp.31–42; no.108, pp.23–34

Giulio Mancini, *Considerazioni sulla pittura* (c.1617–28), ed. Adriana Marucchi and Luigi Salerno, 2 vols, Rome: Accademia Nazionale dei Lincei, 1956–7

Giovanni Baglione, *Le vite de' pittori, scultori et architetti dal Pontificato di Gregorio XIII del 1572 in fino a' tempi di Papa Urbano Ottavo nel 1642*, Rome: Fei, 1642; reprinted Bologna: Forni, 1975–6

Antonio di Paolo Masini, *Bologna perlustrata*, Bologna, 1666

Carlo Cesare Malvasia, *Felsina pittrice: Vite dei pittori bolognesi*, Bologna, 1678; reprint, Bologna, 1969

——, *Le pitture di Bologna*, Bologna, 1686; reprint, ed. Andrea Emiliani, Bologna: ALFA, 1969

Luigi Lanzi, *Storia pittorica della Italia*, v, Bassano, 1819; as *The History of Painting in Italy*, London, 1828

Giordano Gaetano, *Notizie sulle donne pittrici di Bologna*, Bologna, 1832

Antonio Bolognini Amorini, *Vita de' pittori ed artefici bolognesi*, i/3, Bologna, 1843

Giovanni Gozzadini, "Di alcuni gioielli notati in un libro di ricordi del sec. XVI e di un quadro di Lavinia Fontana", *Atti e memorie della Reale Deputazione di storia patria per le province di Romagna*, i, Bologna, 1883, pp.1–16

Laura M. Ragg, *The Women Artists of Bologna*, London: Methuen, 1907

Tancred Borenius, "A portrait by Lavinia Fontana", *Burlington Magazine*, xli, 1922, pp.41–2

Bice Viallet, *Gli autoritratti femminili delle R. Gallerie degli Uffizi in Firenze*, Rome: Alfieri e Lacroix, 1923

Romeo Galli, *Lavinia Fontana, pittrice, 1552–1614*, Imola: Galeati, 1940

Paolo Della Pergola, "Contributi per la Galleria Borghese", *Bolletino d'Arte*, xxxix, 1954, pp.134–40

Eleanor Tufts, "Ms Lavinia Fontana from Bologna: A successful 16th-century portraitist", *Art News*, lxxiii, February 1974, pp.60–64

Women Artists, 1550–1950, exh. cat., Los Angeles County Museum of Art, and elsewhere, 1976

Eleanor Tufts, "L. Fontana: Bolognese humanist", *Le arti a Bologna e in Emilia dal XVI al XVII secolo: Atti del XXIV congresso internazionale di storia dell'arte: Bologna, 1982*, pp.129–34

Liana Cheney, "Lavinia Fontana: Boston *Holy Family*", *Woman's Art Journal*, v/1, 1984, pp.12–15

Angela Ghirardi, "Una pittrice bolognese nella Roma del primo seicento: Lavinia Fontana", *Carrobbio*, x, 1984, pp.149–61

Jean Owens Schaefer, "A note on the iconography of a portrait medal of Lavinia Fontana", *Journal of the Warburg and Courtauld Institutes*, xlvii, 1984, pp.232–4

The Age of Correggio and the Carracci: Emilian Painting of the Sixteenth and Seventeenth Centuries, exh. cat., Pinacoteca Nazionale, Bologna, and elsewhere, 1986

Vera Fortunati Pietrantonio, *Pittura bolognese del '500*, 2 vols, Bologna: Grafis, 1986

Maria Teresa Cantaro, *Lavinia Fontana bolognese, "pittore singolare", 1552–1614*, Milan: Jandi Sapi, 1989

Myriam Chiozza, *Lavinia Fontana: La rittratistica di committenza bolognese*, tesi di laurea, University of Bologna, 1993–4

Lavinia Fontana, 1552–1614, exh. cat., Museo Civico Archeologico, Bologna, 1994

Caroline P. Murphy, "Lavinia Fontana: The making of a woman artist", *Women of the Golden Age*, ed. Els Kloek and others, Hilversum: Verloren, 1994, pp.171–81

——, *Lavinia Fontana: An Artist and Her Society in Late Sixteenth-Century Bologna*, PhD dissertation, University of London, 1996

——, "Lavinia Fontana and female life-cycle experience in late sixteenth-century Bologna", *Picturing Women in Renaissance and Baroque Italy*, ed. Sara Matthews Grieco and Geraldine Johnson (in preparation)

Lavinia Fontana was the first female painter in Western Europe to have practised professionally not in a court or a convent, but as an equal among men in a city. In her lifetime she acquired an international reputation, and her works were sent to Spain, Germany and Persia. Fontana has the largest remaining oeuvre (more than 100 paintings) of any woman artist before the 18th century, producing small devotional paintings, large-scale altarpieces, portraits and mythological works.

She was the only surviving child of Prospero Fontana, an artist well-known in his day in Bologna, who taught her to paint. No indication has been found that Lavinia Fontana was a member of the painters' guild in Bologna, but her father was elected its head several times and this association may have allowed her to practise in the city without formal membership. Although Vasari knew Prospero, he makes no mention of his daughter in the second edition of his *Lives of the Artists* (1568), although he does mention Fontana's almost exact contemporary Barbara Longhi (q.v.); this would suggest that Fontana was at least in her late teens when she began her artistic education. Prospero ran a workshop frequented by a number of prominent Bolognese painters (Ludovico and Agostino Carracci, Denis Calvaert, Lorenzo Sabbatini and Orazio Sammachini), but it is not known whether Fontana learned and worked alongside them or if her father taught her privately. The difficulty with which she expressed her knowledge of anatomy in her paintings would suggest that anatomical drawing was not the focus of her training. Judging from her earliest works, from the early 1570s, it seems most likely that Prospero taught her to paint by setting her to work on small devotional paintings for domestic use, works for which there was a significant and steady demand in Counter-Reformation Bologna.

Gabriele Paleotti, Bishop of Bologna and a patron of Fontana, stated in *Il discorso intorno alle imagini sacre e profane* (1581), his treatise on sacred images, that religious paintings must be theologically correct, their messages clear and easy to understand. Fontana conformed to these injunctions. The *Mystic Marriage of St Catherine with SS Joseph, John the Baptist and Francis* (signed, c.1574; oil on copper; private collection, New York, repr. Cantaro 1989, p.56) is stylistically imbued with a sweetness and grave simplicity. The *Annunciation* (signed, c.1575; oil on copper; Walters Art Gallery, Baltimore) emphasises Mary's humility by contrasting her simple costume and downcast gaze with a dazzling and exotically clad angel. Both of these works show Fontana's taste at this time for a delicate and jewel-like colouring; she used soft blues, greens and pinkish tones. As she developed her artistic skills, her palette grew richer and her colours bolder. That these early pictures are both on copper, an expensive support, suggests that Fontana had already attracted a well-to-do clientele. She continued to paint such pictures on copper, but most of her subsequent work was on canvas. Her early works also reveal that she was much more influenced by Correggio and painters of the post-Tridentine era such as Federico Barocci and Scipione Pulzone than she was by her own father, who favoured a more acidic palette and grandiose rhetorical style. Clearly her father did not attempt to mould her in his own image.

Fontana also began to work on portraits of children during this period. Her earliest signed and dated work (1575) is a painting of a small boy holding a carnation (untraced, *ibid.*, p.63) which, with its warm tones, the bright orange of the boy's jerkin and his thoughtful, engaged expression, suggests that she may have used Venetian models for portraiture rather than the prevalent, rather chilly Bolognese portrait style typified by Bartolomeo Passerotti. Children's portraiture (including post-mortem portraits) is a genre that Fontana practised throughout her career.

In 1577 Fontana married Gian Paolo Zappi, a member of a minor noble family from Imola (after which she changed the signature on her paintings to Lavinia Fontana de Zappis). The change in marital status allowed her to expand her client base.

She became the portrait painter of choice for scholars at the University of Bologna and over the next decade garnered a reputation as a painter of famous intellectuals. She represented these subjects in three-quarter profile, seated at a desk, perhaps in the throes of composition, as in *Portrait of a Scholar* (signed and dated 1581; Pinacoteca Nazionale, Bologna), or with their publications, correspondence and students in the background, as in the portrait of the historian *Carlo Sigonio* (signed, c.1578–9; Museo Civico, Modena). These men are given the appearance of being deep in thought, looking beyond the viewer with pensive expressions of psychological depth. The rendering of their academic robes reveals Fontana's great skill in the depiction of fabric, for which the Bolognese held her in great esteem.

Scholars' portraits also helped to establish Fontana's reputation outside Bologna. Men of letters were part of international scholarly networks – Carlo Sigonio had friends such as Fulvio Orsini in Rome, who expressly requested Sigonio's portrait to be painted by Fontana. In 1584 she was described by Borghini in *Il riposo* as a painter of both public and private works, whose paintings had been sent to Rome and elsewhere, where they were greatly prized. About this time Fontana also began to work for the Bolognese nobility and to forge particularly close relationships with Bolognese noblewomen. In 1584 she undertook a commission for a family portrait from Laudomia Gozzadini, a member of a prominent family. The portrait of the *Gozzadini Family* (signed and dated 1584; see illustration) depicts Laudomia with her dead sister Ginevra with their husbands and dead father. The painting, some 2.1 × 2.4 metres, was innovative in Bologna in terms of size alone. As far as one can tell, no portrait in that city had ever been so large. The figures are life-size and are situated against an architectural background that is perspectively rendered. It was designed, when hanging on a wall, to give the illusion that the sitters were in the same room as the viewer. The production of the portrait cemented a long-standing relationship between Fontana and Laudomia Gozzadini, who gave her many more commissions and was godmother to her son Severo in 1586.

Laudomia was probably responsible for helping to launch Fontana as the fashionable Bolognese society portraitist and for the next 20 years of her career, the Bolognese nobility, and in particular Bolognese noblewomen, would be the staple of Fontana's income. As in the case of her paintings of scholars, she developed a successful pictorial formula for the depiction of noblewomen. They were usually posed either seated or standing in a half- or three-quarter-length portrait format, with a three-quarter profile view. They are invariably accompanied by a small dog, a popular companion for Bolognese noblewomen and a symbol of fidelity, a virtue in womanhood. Every detail of lavish, ornate dresses and jewels is recorded by Fontana. The personality of the women is an important feature of these portraits too – their gazes meet that of the viewer, their expressions are lively and intelligent – as can be seen in the portraits of *Costanza Alidosi Isolani* (two versions, both in private collections, c.1587, repr. Cantaro 1989, pp.172–3), *Isabella Ruini* (signed and dated 1593; Galleria Palatina, Palazzo Pitti, Florence) and the widowed *Ginevra Aldrovandi Hercolani* (c.1595; Walters Art Gallery). All these women were well-known personalities and beauties in their day in Bologna

Fontana: *The Gozzadini Family*, 1584; oil on canvas; Pinacoteca Nazionale, Bologna

and were part of the same social group, which thus facilitated the creation of a patronage network for Fontana.

Fontana was also employed as a portraitist to visiting dignitaries in Bologna. In 1585 she painted *Francesco Panigarola* (signed and dated 1585; Galleria Palatina), a Franciscan prelate, later Bishop of Asti, who had been invited to preach in the cathedral of San Petronio that year. Her most elaborate work of this type is a picture of the *Queen of Sheba's Visit to Solomon* (National Gallery, Dublin), in which the figures are believed to be the Mantuan duke and duchess Vincenzo and Eleonora Gonzaga with their retinue, whose likenesses were taken by Fontana during one of their visits to Bologna in 1598 and 1600. The portrait-like heads were clearly painted at a different time from the bodies, judging from the uneasy relationship between the two. This disjuncture suggests that Fontana was painting the visiting subjects with the knowledge that they would soon be gone from the city.

Fontana appears to have been the first woman painter to produce a considerable number of large-scale altarpieces. Her first was *Christ in the House of Martha and Mary* (c.1580; Conservatorio di Santa Marta, Bologna) for the church of Santa Marta Zitella in Bologna, possibly painted in collaboration with her father (he was most likely responsible for the figure of Christ, while she herself painted the two women). Iconographically it is an unusual rendering of the subject, in part due to its focus on the women, because Mary occupies the centre of the canvas, a space usually reserved for Christ. She is also presented as an earnest young girl, rather than a sensual penitent. Another Fontana altarpiece in which the female emphasis is striking is the nocturnal *Birth of the Virgin* (signed, c.1590; SS Trinità, Bologna). The painting has a genre-like character: the young girls in the foreground are totally occupied in bathing and swaddling the newborn child, while in the background food is given to the new mother.

Some of Fontana's most prestigious commissions were in the form of altarpieces. In 1589 she painted the *Holy Family with Sleeping Christ Child and Infant St John the Baptist* (signed and dated 1589; Escorial, Madrid). Philip II of Spain paid the huge sum of 1000 ducats for this picture, which arrived at the Escorial in 1593 and is now in the burial chapel of the Spanish Infanti. Whether Philip II commissioned this picture, or purchased it on the advice of one of his agents, is not known, but what is documented is Lavinia Fontana's association with the collector Alonso Ciacono, a friend of Francesco Pacheco, painter and artistic adviser to Philip II.

In 1599 Fontana received her first public commission in Rome, when she painted the *Virgin Appearing to St Hyacinth* for Cardinal Ascoli's chapel in Santa Sabina (signed and dated; *in situ*). This commission won her great praise in Rome and probably helped facilitate her move there in 1604, after which she became a portraitist at the Vatican court of Pope Paul V. Among the court dignitaries impressed by her artistic virtuosity was the Persian ambassador, who wrote a madrigal in her honour and claimed that of all the wonders he had seen in Rome, Lavinia Fontana was by far the greatest. In 1611 Fontana received another honour, when an Imolese medallist, Felice Antonio Casoni, cast a bronze portrait medal of her image (Biblioteca Communale, Imola). Its recto shows Fontana in a profile portrait, presented as a respectable matron, while its verso depicts her in a muse-like guise, seated at her easel,

her painting instruments around her and her hair tussled, an indication of her inspired creativity.

Fontana also appears to have been the first woman artist to paint female nudes, of which three survive. The earliest of these, *Venus and Cupid* (signed and dated 1585; private collection, Venice, *ibid.*, p.136), has a chaste and moralising quality more usually seen in northern versions of this subject. Venus and Cupid, depicted full length, negate each other's erotic powers: Cupid clasps a pink train over Venus's pudenda, while Venus has taken Cupid's bow away from him. It is, however, still a sensual image: Venus caresses Cupid, the pink cloth and a gold veil contrast with the whiteness of her skin, and the jewels that adorn her body invite comment on the comparison between their hard lustre and the softness of her flesh. Venus is bedecked in a similar fashion in a half-length *Venus and Cupid* (signed and dated 1592; Musée des Beaux-Arts, Rouen). Here she has taken Cupid's arrow away from him, rendering him powerless, but what is most interesting is the Venus's striking similarity to Fontana's portrait of the famous local beauty, *Isabella Ruini*.

The last of her trio of nudes and the last known painting by her is perhaps the most interesting of all: *Minerva in the Act of Dressing* (dated 1613; Galleria Borghese, Rome), which was executed for the Borghese family who had been enthusiastic patrons of Fontana. As with the *Venus and Cupid* of 1585, this work is not an overtly erotic one. The goddess is shown from the side, so her body is visible only in silhouette. Around her lie her shield, cuirass, helmet, her instruments of war, now abandoned for the courtly robe she is about to don. The goddess, perhaps weary of war, invites comparison with Fontana's own state of mind. According to Mancini (c.1620, i, p.235), she had never recovered from the death of her only daughter in 1605, whom she had been training as a painter. In 1609 she wrote to a patron declaring that she was overburdened with work and that her hands were "broken" (Cantaro 1989, document 5a 24, p.314), suggesting that now in pain she was weary of the profession she had pursued for more than 40 years. She died the year after *Minerva* was painted. The woman painter, like the woman warrior, had finally laid down her tools.

CAROLINE P. MURPHY

Forbes, Anne
British painter, 1745–1834

Born in Scotland, 1745. Living in Edinburgh, 1767. Studied in Rome, c.1768–71. Returned to Edinburgh briefly, 1771. Worked in London, 1772. Settled in Edinburgh, 1773. Appointed Portrait Painter to Society of Antiquaries of Scotland, 1788. Died in Edinburgh, 1834.

Principal Exhibitions

Royal Academy, London: 1772

Bibliography

Duncan Macmillan, *Scottish Art, 1460–1990*, Edinburgh: Mainstream, 1990

This article is based on the late Basil Skinner's transcripts from the Robertson Aikman Papers (Scotland) and the Chalmers Papers (courtesy of Brodie's, Solicitors, Edinburgh). The transcripts are in the archive of the Scottish National Portrait Gallery, Edinburgh; there are photocopies in the Sir Brinsley Ford Archive of the Grand Tour in the Paul Mellon Centre for British Art, London.

Through her mother, Margaret Aikman, Anne Forbes was the granddaughter of a successful Scottish portraitist, William Aikman, who had studied in Rome for three years before settling in Edinburgh in 1712, and then moving to London in 1723. He was an extremely accomplished portraitist, from a family directly related to the Clerks of Penicuik and the Aikman banking family. Surviving family papers provide extensive information about Forbes's reasons for becoming an artist, the patronage that enabled her to train abroad, and the commissions she received there and on her return to Britain.

In 1767 Forbes was living with her widowed mother and two elder sisters in "genteel poverty" in Edinburgh. That year, Robert Chalmers, a friend of the family, had seen some of her drawings in crayons (pastels), and felt that she showed enough skill to be sent to Italy to improve her work. He offered to settle a yearly sum on her and knew that the Aikmans and at least one other friend were also willing to support this venture, providing £200 per year for three years. Financial considerations were to the fore in this proposal – the family considered that in this way Forbes could support her family by her own work within three years, about the time her brother John Forbes was due to resign his lieutenant's commission, and at half the expense of living in London or Edinburgh. Forbes herself hoped by this means to acquire "as great fame and as much money as Miss [Katharine] Read" (q.v.).

Settled in Rome with her mother as chaperone by March 1768, Forbes was being advised in her studies by the artist and antiquarian Gavin Hamilton, an old friend of the Aikmans, and by another Scot, James Nevay, and one or two others. She began by copying drawings of heads in chalks and would soon be allowed to start in oils, which is significant. She had originally set upon the scheme of coming to Italy in order to compete with Katharine Read who drew in crayons, which Anne already did quite well while still in Scotland. Once in Italy she seemed to be following the more ambitious course set out for portrait and history painters in oil. Perhaps it was felt that if she were to succeed, it must be in a manner that had an edge over Miss Read, and to be a professional and earn money meant painting in oil.

Forbes was a novelty in Rome for a short time after her arrival there, all the British residents and visitors calling on her in the evenings, particularly Scots visitors, but also the envoy to Naples, Sir William Hamilton, who gave her a portrait of *George III* to copy, which he showed to all the British virtuosi. She had managed to take up oil painting by the beginning of the summer, but it proved to be the hottest for 40 years, and she was forced to give up working in oils in the heat. She suffered violent headaches from working to finish drawing from paintings that she had been lent to copy for a limited time, and eventually at the end of the summer was reduced to sketching from prints.

She failed to master the Italian language and was thus forced to rely on instruction in oil painting from the British resident artists, all very busy once the summer was over. James

Ann Forbes: *John Forbes*, private collection, Scotland

Nevay, however, was faithful in his instruction, visiting at least once, sometimes two or three times a day, to give advice on her progress in oils. Andrew Lumsden obtained for her important access to collections of old masters which she was permitted to borrow in order to make copies. Once she had finished these copies, some of which were being done on commission, she would begin to paint portraits from life.

Nevay's faithfulness in his instruction, however, had by that time caused its own problems, rumours of her being about to marry a struggling artist in Rome having reached patrons in Scotland. Mrs Forbes wrote to her other daughter:

> As miracles are ceased, nobody must expect to be a painter in 30 months … Annie had expected that her own Genius and the Air of Rome was to make her a Paintress even in less time. I'm really in the devil of a situation, longing of all things to be home, and yet frightened out of my wits as the time approaches for our return. I know nothing can save us from making a foolish appearance but Annie to get a good husband as soon as she sets foot on British ground.

Nevay stopped advising her on her painting, but Forbes progressed through the following summer to copying old masters in oil and painting half- and full-length portraits from life. John Forbes sold his commission and came to Rome with one of his sisters to escort them back to Edinburgh in March 1771.

A series of letters from Forbes in London from July to December 1772, addressed to Robert Chalmers, relates her progress once she was established in London and competing with other professional portraitists there. They mention commissions begun in Scotland, now being completed and sent up to the purchasers there, and later letters reveal that many of the portraits Forbes had begun in Edinburgh were to be paid for by Chalmers and given to the sitters as gifts – almost what we would term promotional gifts today.

In response to Chalmers's request for a list of what Forbes was working on, the stage they were in and how much she was charging, Forbes's sister sent a list of 23 portraits, head and half-lengths, totalling £404.5s. Forbes was certainly attracting sitters, especially Scots in London and people she had met in Italy; in fact she even hoped some would put off their decisions to have their portraits painted because she already had 13 in hand and it was all she could cope with. She had shown four works at the Royal Academy where one, a portrait of an *Italian Girl*, attracted the attention of John Raphael Smith who requested that he be permitted to produce a mezzotint of it. This led to his producing another of a portrait by Forbes of *Alexander Hume, Viscount Polwarth*, which had not been shown at the Royal Academy, but which Smith must have seen in her studio before it was sent up to Scotland later that year. On the evidence of the print after this portrait and one or two others now in private collections in Scotland, she was as good an artist as many, but simply could not produce them, particularly the drapery and the "filling up", with the facility and speed of other artists.

In Forbes's defence, her sister wrote: "Amongst all the paintings we saw both in France and Italy, [portrait and history painting] were both properly distinct, but here the Misses are not pleased without they be flying in the air, or sitting on a cloud or feeding Jupiter's Eagle." Forbes's training simply had not been sufficient for this. In addition, she lost weight, appetite and spirit in attempting to complete the numerous commissions she had obtained, which her mother noted would have been nothing to a man "or even to the famous Miss Angelica [Kauffman], who, added to her great facility, has such a constitution that she is able to work from 5 in the morning till sunset in the summer, and during the whole daylight in winter." And, finally, Forbes herself wrote:

> I am mortified to find what I can do is really only equal to living in this place, even in the recluse manner we live, which is more like nuns than anything else. I would with pleasure relinquish the idea of making a fortune, which I am now fearfully convinced I never can, could I make a comfortable living at home which I flatter myself I might be able for …

Forbes fell seriously ill in October 1772 and when she recovered she wrote to Chalmers giving additional reasons why they would be returning to Edinburgh in the spring. Sitters in London were too busy to give her the necessary time for sittings, arriving three hours late, staying less than an hour and not returning often enough. The English were not coming to sit for her, and those few who came to visit her studio complained that there were not enough pictures to view and they did not recognise any of the people in the paintings she had done. In other words she was not painting the famous, so the fashionable were not interested. To date, Forbes had earned £246 for finished pictures, but she and her mother had laid out £500 in expenses. For her to make money she needed a drapery painter, but without one, she could not afford to hire one. The last letter in this group to Robert Chalmers was dated December 1772.

When Forbes returned to Scotland she regained her health and continued to paint for Scottish patrons, mainly the same group that had patronised her from the beginning, and her work for them remains mostly in private hands (photographs of some of them can be consulted in the photographic archives of the Witt Library, Courtauld Institute of Art, London, and the Scottish National Portrait Gallery, Edinburgh). Her style in these works (see illustration) seems closer to that of David Allan, another Scottish artist who spent time in Italy, having been sent there by a group of patrons, but who could not make a living in London and also returned to Scotland. Like him, Forbes appears to have eked out a living by making conversation-piece portraits, helped out by her appointment (on the Earl of Buchan's motion, 2 December 1788) to the office of Portrait Painter to the Society of Antiquaries of Scotland. She never married and died in 1834. Lacking sheer physical stamina and the patronage of the powerful and fashionable, Anne Forbes had been unable to keep up in London. In Scotland she was able to make a living, but no great reputation.

KIM SLOAN

Forbes, Elizabeth
Canadian painter and printmaker, 1859–1912

Born Elizabeth Adela Armstrong in Kingston, Ontario, 29 December 1859; father a government official. Studied at the South Kensington School of Art, London, c.1875; Art Students League, New York, c.1877; then studied in Munich, in Pont-Aven, Brittany (1882), and in Zandvoort, near Haarlem, the Netherlands (summer 1884). Settled in Newlyn, Cornwall, with her mother, autumn 1885. Married painter Stanhope Alexander Forbes, 1889; son born 1893. Stayed in Brittany with Stanhope Forbes, 1891; opened a painting school in Newlyn with him, 1899. Exhibited widely throughout her life, both in London and the provinces. Associate member, Society of Painter-Etchers, 1883; member, New English Art Club, 1886; associate member, Royal Institute of Painters in Watercolours, 1899. Died 22 March 1912.

Principal Exhibitions
Royal Academy, London: 1883–98, 1900–06, 1908–12
Royal Institute of Painters in Watercolours, London: 1883
Society of Painter-Etchers, London: from 1883
Grosvenor Gallery, London: 1885–6, 1888–90
World's Columbian Exposition, Chicago: 1893 (gold medal)
Fine Art Society, London: 1900 (individual)
Leicester Galleries, London: 1904 (individual)

Selected Writings
"On the slope of a southern hill", *The Studio*, xviii, 1899, pp.25–34
"An April holiday", *The Studio*, xliii, 1908, pp.191–9

Bibliography

E.B.S., "The paintings and etchings of Elizabeth Stanhope Forbes", *The Studio*, iv, 1894, pp.186–92

Gladys B. Crozier, "Elizabeth Stanhope Forbes", *Art Journal*, lxvi, 1904, pp.382–5

Mrs Lionel Birch, *Stanhope A. Forbes ARA, and Elizabeth Stanhope Forbes ARWS*, London: Cassell, 1906

Arthur K. Sabin, "The dry-points of Elizabeth Adela Forbes, formerly E.A. Armstrong (1859–1912)", *Print Collector's Quarterly*, ix, 1922, pp.75–100

Denys Val Baker, "A Cornish art colony", *Connoisseur*, ccii, 1979, pp.161–9

Painting in Newlyn, 1880–1930, exh. cat., Barbican Art Gallery, London, 1985

The Last Romantics: The Romantic Tradition in British Art: Burne-Jones to Stanley Spencer, exh. cat., Barbican Art Gallery, London, 1989

Deborah Cherry, *Painting Women: Victorian Women Artists*, London and New York: Routledge, 1993

Caroline Fox, *Stanhope Forbes and the Newlyn School*, Newton Abbot: David and Charles, 1993

Elizabeth Forbes's clearest impressions of Canada were of the changing seasons, and although much of her life was spent in England she retained and captured this childhood view of nature in many of her prints and paintings. While in her early teens, the artist travelled to London with her mother and began classes at the South Kensington School of Art (she was one of the youngest students in the School). Her education there was cut short by her father's death, however, and she and her mother had to return to Canada. Instead of continuing with her European training, she decided to stay closer to home and enrolled at the Art Students League in New York (she was 18 years old). Later she spent an unhappy few months studying in Munich then, again with her mother, went to Pont-Aven in Brittany where she began the kind of work that would blend her childhood interest in nature with new experiments in plein-air painting. Back in London in 1883, she explored and developed her aptitude for drypoint, becoming an Associate of the Society of Painter-Etchers.

Elizabeth Forbes: *Blackberry Gathering*, 1912; Walker Art Gallery, Liverpool

Forbes's prints are among her strongest works, demonstrating her highly skilled technical abilities as well as her sensitivity and insights into the personalities of her sitters. Her *Self-Portrait* (1882; Victoria and Albert Museum, London), made when she was about 23 years of age, shows her proficiency with the medium as well as giving the viewer a picture of an intelligent and determined young artist. After 1888, mostly due to difficulties in having her plates printed after she settled in Cornwall, she turned her attention and energies to the establishment of a school (with Stanhope Alexander Forbes whom she married in 1889), and to her painting.

In 1899 Forbes wrote about a bicycle trip "among the hills of the Low Pyrenees" seeking peaceful and picturesque places where the tourists might set up their easels and "unfurl" their "sketching umbrellas" ("On the slope of a southern hill", 1899, p.25). The artist's poetic descriptions of the area and her search for romantic, pastoral sights confirm her subject matter as almost exclusively representative of "tourism". This visual selection informs her work whether it be of people or of landscape, and her capturing of the image always maintains her position as outsider-artist. For example, the young men she drew in the Pyrenees were "often beautiful as Greek athletes, trained to free supple movement by their national *jeu de paume*" (*ibid.*, p.31).

Her students at the Newlyn Art School were taught to observe and paint in and from nature: "let us shoulder our painting kit and go forth, let us celebrate the advent of the jocund Spring, if not with garlands and dances, at least with the brightest hues of our palette" ("An April holiday", 1908, p.192). Many of Forbes's initial sketches were made in her "portable studio". Thus she was able to capture the "local atmosphere", which was "unusually bright and clear on sunny days" (Crozier 1904, p.382). Oil paintings such as *At the Edge of the Wood* (1894; Wolverhampton Art Gallery, repr. *The Studio*, 1895, p.189), exhibited at the Royal Academy in 1894, *"Take, O Take Those Lips Away"* (exh. Royal Academy 1902; repr. *The Studio*, xxvi, 1902, p.34), *The Winter's Tale: "When Daffodils Begin to Peer"* (1906; National Gallery of Canada, Ottawa) and *Blackberry Gathering* (1912; see illustration) take the viewer into a pastoral, rustic and timeless nature where peacefulness is present, unrest and poverty absent. When she did choose to represent poverty, as in her early painting *A Zandvoort Fisher Girl* (1884; Newlyn Art Gallery), she conferred dignity on her subject by her ability to characterise and capture the human form and personality in the large strong hands and direct proud gaze of the "fisher girl".

Her activity at Newlyn, where she settled with her mother in the late 1880s, has been well documented, and her role as a teacher at the school of art founded with Stanhope Forbes remains a legacy to early 20th-century British art. Forbes is remembered as "one of the intellectuals of the group [of Newlyn artists], writing poetry and criticism, as well as for the local theatre" (Baker 1979, p.162). Although Forbes became a mother in 1893, she continued to work, and the same year won a gold medal in the oil painting section of the Chicago exhibition (Fox 1993, p.44). Thus she negotiated the tensions between her social role as woman and her activity as artist (Cherry 1993, p.184). Nevertheless, and although she did paint landscape, she remained within the ascribed realm for women artists of Victorian and Edwardian Britain, and her production consistently speaks of that realm.

JANICE HELLAND

Forner, Raquel
Argentinian painter, 1902–1987

Born in Buenos Aires, 1902. Studied at Academia Nacional de Bellas Artes, Buenos Aires (qualified as drawing teacher, 1922); first exhibition at Salón Nacional, 1924. Lived in Paris, attending courses at the Scandinavian academy under Emile Othon Friesz, 1929–31. Returned to Buenos Aires to establish Cursos Libres de Arte Plástico, the first private academy of modern art in Argentina, 1932. Married Argentinian sculptor Alfredo Bigatti, 1936. Visited Europe and North America on several occasions. Recipient of gold medal, Exposition Internationale, Paris, 1937; first prize, 1942, and Gran premio de honor, 1956, Salón Nacional de Bellas Artes, Buenos Aires; Palanza prize, Academia Nacional de Bellas Artes, Buenos Aires, 1947; press prize, Bienal de Arte Interamericana, Mexico, 1958; Gran premio de honor, Bienal Americana de Arte Córdoba, 1962. Member, Royal Society of Arts, London, 1951. Died in Buenos Aires, 1987.

Selected Individual Exhibitions
Galería Müller, Buenos Aires: 1928, 1946, 1947
Galería Bonino, Buenos Aires: 1952, 1953, 1954, 1955, 1957, 1960, 1967
Pan-American Union, Washington, DC: 1957
Museu de Arte Moderna, Rio de Janeiro: 1960
São Paulo Bienal: 1961, 1979
Museo de Arte Moderno, Buenos Aires: 1962, 1972
Galería Wildenstein, Buenos Aires: 1973
Corcoran Gallery of Art, Washington, DC: 1974 (*Space Mythology*, touring)
UNESCO, Paris: 1978 (touring)
Museo Nacional de Bellas Artes, Buenos Aires: 1983 (retrospective)

Bibliography
Geo Dorival, *Raquel Forner*, Buenos Aires: Losada, 1942
Antonio Berni, "Raquel Forner", *Revista Ars* (Buenos Aires), 1946
Juan Merli, *Raquel Forner*, Buenos Aires: Poseidón, 1952
Guillermo de Torre, "Una pintora argentina", *Revista Cuadernos* (Paris), 1955
Giampiero Giani, *Raquel Forner*, Milan: La Conchiglia, 1960
Gyula Kosice, *El viaje sin retorno: Raquel Forner*, Buenos Aires: Galería Bonino, 1965
"El políptico de Raquel Forner", *Revista Caballete* (Buenos Aires), September 1965
Raquel Forner, exh. cat., Drian Galleries, London, 1967
Max Wykes-Joyce, "Raquel Forner", *Arts Review*, April 1967
Rafael Squirru, "Raquel Forner", *Revista Américas* (Washington, DC), 1968
Vicente Caride, "El mundo de Raquel Forner", *Revista Decoralia* (Buenos Aires), April 1969
José Gómez Sicre, "Raquel Forner: La precursora", *Revista Fascinación* (Caracas), December 1975
Córdova Iturburu, *80 años de pintura argentina: Del pre-impresionismo a la novísima figuración*, Buenos Aires: La Ciudad, 1978
Eduardo Jantus, *Raquel Forner en Canadá, 1974–77*, Ottawa, 1978
Oscar F. Haedo, "Raquel Forner: Su mitología espacial", *Revista La Actualidad en el Arte* (Buenos Aires), June 1979

Forner: *Desolation*, 1942; oil on canvas; 93.7 × 72.7 cm.; Museum of Modern Art, New York; Inter-American Fund

Luisa Rosell and others, *Forner*, Buenos Aires: Centro Editor de America Latina, 1980

Guillermo Whitelow, *Raquel Forner*, Buenos Aires: Arte Gaglianone, 1980

Raquel Forner: Retrospectiva, exh. cat., Museo Nacional de Bellas Artes, Buenos Aires, 1983

The work of the Argentinian painter Raquel Forner can be divided into two phases: subjects preoccupied with human suffering and oppression, especially as victims of war, and themes concerned with human destiny and the enigmas of the universe. It was the Spanish Civil War that first impressed the young artist with its tragic cruelty, and she responded with paintings that expressed the human drama through colour and anguished figuration. As a student at the Academia Nacional in Buenos Aires she had exhibited a natural propensity for drawing, and graduated as a drawing teacher. Colour was also integral to her work in the early years, and she learned to use it for its emotional effects both as an addition to drawings and as the basis for paintings. Colour was at the essence of her visual language and a persistent and characteristic element in her work throughout her career.

An early painting, *Women of the World* (1938; private collection), was painted on Forner's return to Buenos Aires from an extended visit to Europe to see the great museums and familiarise herself with modern art. She was particularly impressed with the artists of France who freely combined elements from different cultures, Western and non-Western, in their work. The influences of Picasso and Léger are evident in this painting, as well as the monumentality and emotionalism that she encountered in the early Renaissance fresco cycles of Italy. The central figure is America, at peace but listening for the impending noise of war. Behind her, China and Spain are tragic muses surrounded by suffering figures. War machines pierce the sky, shrapnel litters the earth.

A visit to southern Argentina in 1942 had a profound effect on Forner's work and confirmed her need to visualise her concerns for the plight of humans and their suffering. The primitive isolation of the landscape with its calcified trees evoked feelings of war and destruction and the torture of human existence, themes that would affect her images, even as they were transferred from the terrestrial to the extra-terrestrial world over the years.

The desolation of the land portends her fascination with moonscapes and planetary exploration. In *Desolation* (1942; see illustration) the trees take on an anthropomorphic character as they writhe in pain, the last vestiges of life on the barren earth. As her subjects became more complex, Forner's painting style and compositional arrangements also changed. Working confidently with form and colour, she changed her focus from the tragic and dramatic to the investigation of earth, rocks and astral bodies, and astronauts searching the universe for peace. This fascination with outer space and its exploration by human voyagers was fully developed by the late 1950s when she began to produce large works with such titles as *Combat of the Astrobeings No.2* (1961; J.F. Kennedy Center for the Performing Arts, Washington, DC), *Conquest of the Moon Rock* (1968; private collection) and *Return of the Astronaut* (1969; National Air and Space Museum, Washington, DC). Her works became more abstract, colourful and dynamic, as if infused with a new energy inspired by the excitement of space

travel and exploration, rocket ships and satellite contacts. In works of the 1960s human figures are distorted, mutated, transformed in paint and colour into strange figments from space-comic books floating without gravity. Looking at the figures encased in their space helmets, one wonders if the astronaut is the hero or another victim in the artist's symbolic repertoire.

By the 1970s, Forner's spacemen had acquired an identity as astrobeings and she continued their mutation into something confused as animal, vegetable and mineral. She saw these mutated beings as prophetic of what will take place in the creatures of the earth in the future, a step in the process of evolution and necessary for humanity's eternal quest for survival and adaptation. The *Series of Space Mutations* (1971; San Francisco Museum of Modern Art) traces the formation of this new specimen of humanity from its birth in boundless space to its growth as a new being with the assistance of astrobeings; earthling and astrobeing give life to a new species. The last period of Raquel Forner's artistic production continued with the visualisation of her personal cosmos of mutants, astrobeings and earthlings described in vibrant canvases of brash expressionistic colour and free spontaneous brush strokes. The *Earthmen Series* (1979; private collection) is the culmination of her obsession with hybrids and mutations and her vision of the future of human beings. Whirling in space, earthlings tangle in a confusion of colour with mutant creatures as they approach their destiny and seek their future.

CAROL DAMIAN

Forster, Gela

German sculptor, 1892–1957

Born Angelica Bruno-Schmitz in Berlin, 1892; father the architect Bruno Schmitz. Founder-member, Dresdner Sezession: Gruppe 1919; resigned from group by 1920. Married Russian sculptor Alexander Archipenko, 1921; moved with him to Berlin, where he established an art school. Emigrated with Archipenko to the USA, 1923; settled in New York City and Woodstock, New York. Died 1957.

Principal Exhibitions

Dresdner Sezession: Gruppe 1919, Dresden: 1919 (spring and summer)

Galerie Der Sturm, Berlin: 1921 (*Hundertste Ausstellung*)

Bibliography

Will Grohmann, "Dresdner Sezession 'Gruppe 1919'", *Neue Blätter für Kunst und Dichtung*, i, March 1919, pp.257–60

Alfred Günther, "Vor Bildwerken von Gela Forster", *Menschen: Buch-Folge Neuer Kunst*, ii, 4 May 1919, pp.1–7

Theodor Däubler, "Gela Forster", *Neue Blätter für Kunst und Dichtung*, ii/3, June 1919, pp.51–3; reprinted in Theodor Däubler, *Dichtungen und Schriften*, Munich: Kösel, 1956; English translation in Los Angeles 1983, pp.30–33

Donald H. Karshan, ed., *Archipenko: International Visionary*, Washington, DC: Smithsonian Institution Press, 1969

Dresdner Sezession, 1919–1925, exh. cat., Galleria del Levante, Milan and Munich, 1977

Joachim Heusinger von Waldegg, "Plastik", *Deutsche Kunst der 20er und 30er Jahre*, ed. Erich Steingräber, Munich: Bruckmann, 1979, pp.236–303

L'altra metà dell'avanguardia, 1910–1940: Pittrici e scultrici nei movimenti delle avanguardie storiche, exh. cat., Palazzo Reale, Milan, and elsewhere, 1980

German Expressionist Sculpture, exh. cat., Los Angeles County Museum of Art, and elsewhere, 1983

Alexander Archipenko: A Centennial Tribute, exh. cat., National Gallery of Art, Washington, DC, and elsewhere, 1986

German Expressionism, 1915–1925: The Second Generation, exh. cat., Los Angeles County Museum of Art, and elsewhere, 1988

Magdalena Bushart, "Der Formsinn des Weibes: Bildhauerinnen in den zwanziger und dreissiger Jahren", *Profession ohne Tradition: 125 Jahre Verein der Berliner Künstlerinnen*, exh. cat., Berlinische Galerie, Berlin, 1992, pp.135–50

Erich Ranfft, "Expressionist sculpture, c.1910–30, and the significance of its dual architectural/ideological frame", *Expressionism Reassessed*, ed. Shulamith Behr and others, Manchester: Manchester University Press, 1993, pp.65–79

——, "German women sculptors, 1918–1936: Gender differences and status", *Visions of the "Neue Frau": Women and the Visual Arts in Weimar Germany*, ed. Marsha Meskimmon and Shearer West, Aldershot: Scolar Press, 1995, pp.42–61

Gela Forster's artistic career lasted apparently only from 1919 to 1921: to date, nothing is known of her training or career before 1919, it seems that she was not included in any exhibitions after 1921, and there is little to indicate that she continued to produce art in the USA. Only six sculptures are known to us – from the years c.1918–20 – and these have since been lost or destroyed. Yet her works remain among the most powerful and significant examples of Expressionist sculpture in Germany of the period c.1910–25. She was a founding member and the only woman artist of the radical, Expressionist group of Dresden artists, the Dresdner Sezession: Gruppe 1919. She was also the only sculptor to represent the Gruppe 1919 in its first exhibition in 1919, which brought her instant fame. Although her work was forgotten for many decades, since the mid-1970s the relevance of her work within Expressionist sculpture has been continually reaffirmed. Forster is today considered to be one of the most important German women sculptors involved in Expressionism, alongside Milly Steger (q.v.), Emy Roeder (q.v.) and Katharina Heise (q.v.).

Forster's first three works – *Conception*, *Awakening* and *The Man* (c.1918–19; repr. Los Angeles 1983, pp.31–3) – were exhibited in the first showing of Gruppe 1919 and reproduced in the Dresden Expressionist periodicals *Neue Blätter für Kunst und Dichtung* and *Menschen* in 1919. These were accompanied by rapturous critical acclaim from Will Grohmann, Theodor Däubler and Alfred Günther. For the second Gruppe 1919 exhibition in 1919, Forster showed *Pyramid (Female Nude)* (1919), which was not reproduced, and little is known of this work. Her last two known sculptures, *The Tree (Male and Female)* and *Sculpture (The Form)* of c.1919–20, were reproduced in *Neue Blätter für Kunst und Dichtung* (iii, 1920, pp.51 and 57 respectively; see illustration), but without any critical appraisals.

Forster's sculptures represent anonymous torsos, with *The Tree* as the sole figural group, and only *The Tree* and *Sculpture* incorporate a base. The exact sizes and material(s) of Forster's works are unknown; to date, near life-size dimensions and the

Forster: *The Tree (Male and Female)*, c.1919–20; from *Neue Blätter für Kunst und Dichtung*, iii, 1920, p.51

use of plaster or stone have been indicated. The formalist vocabulary of Alexander Archipenko, Forster's future husband, is apparent in the sculptures (except for *Awakening*) in the use of reductivist body parts and a diagonal axis along the torsos' shoulders. With its non-symbolic formal traits, the female figure of *Sculpture (The Form)* suggests a studied homage to Archipenko.

Forster's work is largely indebted to the thematic and stylistic manifestations of post-war utopian Expressionism, particularly Dresden's "ecstatic", visionary aims. For example, her work can be read in terms of the ideological, architectural frame of Expressionist sculpture and its function within the "total work of art" to embody the essence of all art and the regeneration of mankind into the "new man". Alfred Günther described Forster as "a master at building", and categorised the female figures of *Conception* and *Awakening* as a "pyramid" and a "tower". Forster undoubtedly sought to propagate such allusions with her titles *Pyramid* and *The Tree (Male and Female)*.

Related to the theme of Christian and mystical regeneration was the belief in a vitalist and primeval union of the spiritual and the erotic. In *Conception* and *Awakening* Forster depicts a pregnant woman to symbolise the birth of the Christian "new man" (this should be compared with the introspective *Pregnant Woman* of 1919 by Emy Roeder, and its crucial ideological basis). The female's sexuality in *Conception* is accentuated by the protruding position of her heavily swollen womb (outward from a legless lower body) and by the placement of her breasts in opposing directions along the harsh diagonal axis of her shoulders. The "rawness" and distortion of the forms extend an image of "primitive" or prehistoric woman. For *Awakening*, Günther described the body as "clumsily stretched, animalistic, the hanging arm of a gorilla, the face a terrifying mask, a vision from the underground of all earthly [things]" (Günther 1919). He was intimating Forster's interpretation of the "primitive" as African sculpture, which greatly inspired many of the Dresden Expressionists. Moreover, her treatment of the female bodies of *Conception* and *The Tree* as massive and voluptuous echoes the prehistoric *Woman from Willendorf*. This trait also characterised the work of other Dresden Expressionists, and was seen to symbolise a maternal and erotic vitalism. Similar types of female figures appear in the sculptural oeuvre of Katharina Heise from the 1920s.

The figural grouping of *The Tree (Male and Female)* can also be read as a symbolic birth of the "new man": the "tree" in the form of the female body signifies the source of life, out of which the "male" is born and pushes himself into the world. This feminine role relates to numerous representations of "Mother Earth" in Expressionism. From the title Forster asserts the importance of female experience in the light of the suggestive theme of a struggle between the sexes and man's domination over the woman, as he clings over her, enveloping her head. Similar figural groupings by male Expressionist sculptors, such as Rudolf Belling and Oswald Herzog, however, present this "struggle" only in terms of the sexual act.

In Theodor Däubler's commentary on *The Man*, depicting a forward-leaning, male figure with half an arm and no legs, he envisages the post-war reality of the "spiritual and sexual agitation" of Expressionism's "new man": "The sculptor has reduced the head to its most primitive, the egglike shape of the skull: it has become the bearer, we can even say the revealer, of a tragic mouth ... The entire sculpture climaxes in a cry" (Los Angeles 1983, p.30). In Forster's "cold-blooded and controlled manner" (Däubler 1919) she evokes the semblance of a war cripple, a theme with which Dresden artists were especially preoccupied, in what the art historian Dietrich Schubert has termed "socialist Expressionism".

Little is known of the reasons why Gela Forster's artistic career was so short-lived, but her status as an extraordinary woman sculptor at the time was certain; "extraordinary" also in the sense of her position within the heroic, male order of Expressionism:

It remains incomprehensible that it could be the hands of a woman, which wrestle with nature so violently. It is surprising that a woman should have such strength, to explode sculpture out of the still so mute forms to [gain] such incredible expression, that she could subordinate the statue of the human body in order to work with it in superiority. What a temperament! ... In the midst of the small group of those who truly create the sculptural expression of this time, is this woman! [Günther 1919].

ERICH RANFFT

Fortescue-Brickdale, Eleanor *see* Brickdale

Fox, Ethel (Carrick)
Australian painter, 1872–1952

Born Ethel Carrick in Uxbridge, Middlesex, England, 7 February 1872. Studied at the Slade School of Fine Art, London, under Henry Tonks, c.1898–1903. Married Australian painter Emmanuel Phillips Fox, 1905; he died 1915. Settled in Paris, but also travelled widely; stayed in Australia in 1908, 1913–16, 1925, 1933–4, c.1940–45, 1948–9 and 1952. Sociétaire, 1911, and jury member, 1912–c.1925, Salon d'Automne, Paris. Vice president, International Union of Women Artists. Member, Latin Quarter Association; Union Internationale des Beaux-Arts et des Lettres; Les Quelques group. Died in Melbourne, Australia, 17 June 1952.

Principal Exhibitions

Individual
Bernard's Gallery, Melbourne: 1908
Guildhall, Melbourne: 1913
Anthony Horden's Art Gallery, Sydney: 1913
Athenaeum Gallery, Melbourne: 1914, 1944 (both with E. Phillips Fox)
Everyman's Lending Library, Melbourne: 1933
Melbourne Bookclub Gallery: 1949

Group
Salon d'Automne, Paris: occasionally c.1906–30
Société Nationale des Beaux-Arts, Paris: occasionally c.1906–37
Melbourne Society of Women Painters and Sculptors: 1942–55

Bibliography
"Mrs Phillips Fox", *The Lone Hand* (Melbourne), 1 November 1913, pp.37–8
Ethel Carrick (Mrs E. Phillips Fox), exh. cat., Geelong Art Gallery, Geelong, Victoria, and elsewhere, 1979
Len Fox, *E. Phillips Fox and His Family*, Potts Point, NSW: privately printed, 1985
Juliet Peers, *More Than Just Gumtrees: A Personal, Social and Artistic History of the Melbourne Society of Women Painters and Sculptors*, Melbourne Society of Women Painters and Sculptors in association with Dawn Revival Press, 1993
Elin Howe, "Ethel Carrick Fox: The cheat or the cheated?", *Wallflowers and Witches: Women and Culture in Australia, 1910–1945*, ed. Maryanne Dever, St Lucia: University of Queensland Press, 1994, pp.105–14
John Pigot, "Les femmes orientalistes: Hilda Rix Nicholas and Ethel Carrick Fox in the East", *Strange Women: Essays in Art and Gender*, ed. Jeanette Hoorn, Melbourne: University of Melbourne Press, 1994, pp.155–68
Elin Howe, "Ethel Carrick Fox", *Heritage: The National Women's Art Book*, ed. Joan Kerr, Sydney: Dictionary of Australian Artists/Craftsman House, 1995

Family papers, including Ethel Carrick Fox's correspondence, are held privately by Len Fox.

Ethel Carrick Fox summed up her aesthetic with a quotation from Alfred de Musset printed in the catalogue of her solo exhibition in Melbourne of 1913. Loosely translated, the quotation, "her glass was a small one, but it was hers and she must drink from it", was thought to refer to her confidence in her paintings, which were small-scale and progressive in contrast to the academic late-Impressionist set-pieces of her husband. Her works are rarely dated, but her favourite subjects – public gardens, markets and beach scenes – appear consistently over three decades, so that the sequence can be inferred from rising hemlines and diminishing hats. The compass of her chosen aesthetic was modest but cohesive. Fox's career was characterised by a ceaseless dedication to professionalism, although with little institutional backing from the 1920s onwards. She was also active in art politics and organisations in France and Australia.

From a prosperous family, Fox was regarded with uneasy awe by her relatives due to her forthrightness and independence, qualities not considered proper for a "lady". She began art classes relatively late, first studying music, then taking lessons from Francis Bate. Later (c.1898–1903) she trained at the Slade School of Fine Art in London under Henry Tonks. She met her Australian-born husband, the artist Emmanuel Phillips Fox, while painting at St Ives in Cornwall.

After her marriage in 1905, Fox quickly developed a consistent style. From a base as a plein-air painter she moved to a mild form of Post-Impressionism, reducing forms to block-like shapes and expressing effects of light through sharp contrasts of colour. The simplification of subjects creates an abstract patterning and a progressive edge to her work. Between 1905 and 1913 she and her husband travelled widely, to fashionable resorts in France, Venice, North Africa and Spain. In 1908 they made an extended tour to Australia, where she was given a formal reception by women artists in Melbourne.

Works produced on a trip to North Africa in 1911 are among her most intense and Fauve-like, with abstraction of colour and form at its most extreme. Drawing and definition are largely subordinated to broad, flat areas of bright colour and impasto surface. According to some writers, however, these works betray a certain condescension towards her subjects, typecasting them as exotic and "other" in the manner of European orientalism. By 1910 another sub-group of works had emerged, a pure cloisonné style with forms defined by a dark line (e.g. *Flower Market*; private collection, Melbourne). Perhaps the most fully developed example of this style is *Manly Beach – Summer Is Here* (1913; oil on canvas; Manly Art Gallery), which was extremely progressive in comparison to Australian art of the period. It was awarded a diploma of honour at the Bordeaux exhibition of 1928.

Living in Paris, Fox exhibited annually at the Société Nationale des Beaux-Arts and the Salon d'Automne, and her reputation developed rapidly. For a woman artist she played a prominent role: she was regularly among the few women on official committees and in major exhibitions (*Lone Hand*, Melbourne, 1 November 1913, p.38). In 1911 she was elected a Sociétaire of the Salon d'Automne, and the following year she served on its jury, a measure of her prestige, particularly considering her gender and foreign birth; she was still serving on this jury c.1925. Before World War I she was vice-president of the International Union of Women Artists and a member of the Latin Quarter Association, the Union Internationale des Beaux-Arts et des Lettres and a small group of Paris-based women artists, Les Quelques.

The Foxes visited Australia in 1913 and Tahiti the following year. Her husband's death in 1915 led to period of uncertainty, but by the 1920s she was re-creating the pre-war ambience in her old apartment, on Boulevard Arago in Paris. She taught American as well as Australian students and was recommended as a teacher for still life by the staff of the Académie de la Grande Chaumière. She often acted as agent for Australian-based artists, such as Violet Teague, in negotiations with Salon juries.

In the 1920s she painted some impressionist studies with many figures and a broad outlook, such as *Flower Market, Nice* (c.1920s; oil on canvas; Art Gallery of New South Wales, Sydney). In many works the radical impetus is diminished in favour of a safer academic plein-air painting, although the Australian subjects document the relaxing of social mores, especially the beach scenes. Flower studies appeared in the 1920s; highly coloured if unimaginatively composed, they hint at an expressionist energy of brushwork markedly different from the conventional low-toned still lifes shown in inter-war Australia. Her lithographs of the 1930s are accomplished, but the vision of France, for example, views of the Seine, often reflects the nascent tourist industry and the works of Maurice Utrillo.

Fox's residence in Paris was punctuated with periods overseas: in Australia and, in the late 1930s, briefly in India. As the widow of a Jew, she would have been at risk in occupied France, and she spent the war years in Australia. The vibrant atmosphere of wartime Melbourne stimulated a burst of activity, and she enjoyed considerable respect, especially among women artists. A lively series of figurative oils, clearly impressionist in their treatment of light, documented female war workers and their workplaces. For nearly four decades Fox continued to promote her husband's work, as well as actively encouraging Australian women artists to present themselves publicly as professionals.

JULIET PEERS

Francés y Arribas, Fernanda

Spanish painter, 1862–1939

Born in Valencia, 26 February 1862. Studied painting under her father, the painter Plácido Francés y Pascual, from an early age. Competed for and won the post of painting tutor (female section) at the Escuela de Artes y Oficios, Madrid, 1888; later went on to teach at the Escuela del Hogar, Madrid. Married another tutor, landscape painter José Cayetano Vallcorba, 1892. Died in Madrid, 21 April 1939.

Principal Exhibitions

Exposición Circulo de Bellas Artes, Madrid: 1881, 1890–91, 1893, 1896–8, 1900–03
Internationale Kunstausstellung, Munich: 1883
Exposición Nacional de Bellas Artes, Madrid: occasionally 1884–1915 (honourable mention 1887, third-class medal 1890, second-class medals 1897 and 1910, decoration 1912)
Exposition Universelle, Paris: 1889

Bibliography

"Relación de las obras que con esta fecha se entregan a la casa de transportes Garrante y Ballesteros para la Exposición Internacional de Münich", undated manuscript, Academia de Bellas Artes de Madrid, 66–1/5

J. Bahamontes, *Mentor crítico de la Exposición Nacional de Pintura y Escultura de 1884*, Madrid, 1884

V. de la Cruz, *Catálogo comentado de la Exposición de Bellas Artes de 1884*, Madrid, 1884

Fernanflor, "La Exposición Nacional de Bellas Artes, *La ilustración española y americana*, xxvi, 15 June 1887

J.D. Picon, *Exposición Nacional de Bellas Artes*, Madrid, 1890

Pedro de Madrazo, "La Exposición Nacional de Bellas Artes de 1892", *La Ilustración Española y Americana*, xliii, 21 November 1892

Francisco Alcántara, *La Exposición Nacional de Bellas Artes*, Madrid, 1897

L.M. Cabello y Lapiedra, *La Exposición de Bellas Artes de 1897*, Madrid, 1897

Catálogo provisional del Museo de Arte Moderno, Madrid, 1899

L. Gabaldón, *Revista cómica de la Exposición Nacional de Bellas Artes de 1901*, Madrid, 1901

Documentos relativos a la compra por el Estado del cuadro "Mariscos" de Fernanda Francés, manuscript, 14 December 1905, Academia de Bellas Artes de Madrid, 177–1/5

Aureliano Beruete, *Historia de la pintura española en el siglo XIX*, Madrid, 1926

Julio Cavestany, *Floreros y bodegones en la pintura española*, Madrid: Palacio de la Biblioteca Nacional, 1940

Carmen G. Perez-Neu, *Galería universal de pintoras*, Madrid: Nacional, 1964

Bernardino de Pantorba, *Historia y crítica de las Exposiciones Nacionales de Bellas Artes celebradas en España*, Madrid: Garcia-Rama, 1980

Estrella de Diego, *La mujer y la pintura del XIX español*, Madrid: Universidad Computense de Madrid, 1987

J. Gutierrez Burón, *Las Exposiciones Nacionales de Bellas Artes*, Madrid, 1987

Fernanda Francés's career initially developed within the family circle, as both her father and brother were painters. She was first taught by her father, Plácido Francés – an Academician of the San Carlos Academy in Valencia – who enjoyed greater fame and prestige than she did, although the quality of his works was no better than hers. Francés was also taught by other artists, such as Salvador Viniegra, an important painter known primarily for his work in the *costumbrista*-realist genre (the term designates genre scenes of Spanish life taking place in the streets, markets or taverns with characters dressed in typical costume, as well as themes relating to middle-class life), and Sebastián Gessa, a well-known flower painter. The lack of surviving documentation concerning Francés means, however, that she is generally held to have been exclusively a disciple of her father. Her desire to make painting both a career and a way of life later led to her becoming a teacher, as was customary for Spanish female artists in the 19th century. Indeed, the teaching of painting to young middle-class girls increased enormously in Spain during the second half of the century. Francés was extremely successful in this aspect of her chosen career: she had a good critical reputation and enjoyed a certain amount of fame, and thus had numerous students, although none of them became famous artists. Francés's professional career developed within the academic world, which meant that most of the exhibitions she participated in were the Exposiciones Nacionales

Francés y Arribas: *Vase of Lilac*, 1896

de Bellas Artes of the second half of the 19th century. There is no evidence that she ever had a solo exhibition.

Much of her work has disappeared, but it formed part of the Madrid realist *costumbrismo* of the turn of the century. Francés's paintings conformed to the bourgeois values of modesty and discretion demanded of women painters of the time, and therefore in some ways are conservative. To begin with, the themes are conventional: the artist was renowned for her still-life paintings, a genre common to women, depicting the objects closest to hand, such as flowers, shellfish, her kitchen window, her garden, etc. Her paintings are often intimate, sometimes anecdotal, almost a personal diary expressed in pictures of small dimensions. This scale attracted the interest of a public that had begun to reject large-format works after the Exposición Nacional of 1887 and the Paris Exposition Universelle of 1889. Francés's predilection for still lifes is not unusual, because the study of human anatomy was not available to women painters at that time.

There are few changes in either form or content over the course of Francés's career. Her academicism meant that her work stayed within established canons. Her overall vision is characterised by the elegance and good taste that earned her much success. An ordered composition is fundamental to her pictures; she tended to separate the subject from its surroundings, locating it against a plain background, following the classical tradition of still-life paintings. Her works also reveal a concern with the depiction of light, which is rendered with academic virtuosity, heightening the impression of volume in the painted objects. Motifs are rendered in great detail with small, precise brush strokes that become looser towards the end of her career. Her painting *Vase of Lilac* (1896; see illustration) is a perfect example of her command of drawing as well as conforming perfectly to the middle-class fashion for flower painting, abounding with a lyricism that was both imposed and socially presumed to be typically female.

This virtuosity in the depiction of details is the aspect most discussed in articles on Francés. The critic Francisco Alcántara said that her pictures were so precise that they might almost be not the depiction of reality but reality itself, had they not been executed with the singular personality and style that made them unmistakable and unique. Another critic, Fernanflor, said that Francés's pictures were "purely and simply, perfection". As in the case of other famous 19th-century women artists, the critics – obviously male – were always gallant towards her, and often remarked on her skill in rendering reality and her liking for flowers: these were considered to be as delicious as women, and to accord with their emotions and sentiments. Some critics, such as Pedro de Madrazo, with bad taste and even worse judgement, explained this preference with one brief sentence: *mens blanda in corpore blando* (a bland mind in a bland body).

As a result of the Exposiciones Nacionales, where Francés won prizes, the State acquired some of her works; some of these are documented as belonging to the Museo de Arte Moderno, Madrid (the Prado), although the present location of most of these is unknown. There is also a record of Francés's proposal to the State for the acquisition of her work *Shellfish* (1904; 34 × 46 cm.; repr. *Catálogo de la Exposición Nacional de Bellas Artes*, 1904). This was rejected because it was considered that the State already owned a good piece that was repre-

sentative of the artist's work: *Oysters and Birds* (1897; 50 × 95 cm.; repr. Alcántara 1897, p.171).

KARINA MAROTTA PERAMOS

Francis, Mary *see* Thornycroft

Frankenthaler, Helen
American painter and sculptor, 1928–

Born in New York, 12 December 1928. Studied at Bennington College, Vermont, 1946–9 (BA); Graduate School of Fine Arts, Columbia University, New York, 1949. Married (1) artist Robert Motherwell, 1958; divorced 1971; (2) Stephen Dubruel, 1994. Taught at New York University, 1959–61; Yale University, New Haven, 1966, 1967 and 1970; Hunter College, New York, 1970; Princeton University, 1971; Harvard University, Cambridge, Massachusetts, 1976. Represented USA at Venice Biennale, 1966. Recipient of first prize, Paris Biennale, 1959; gold medal, Pennsylvania Academy of the Fine Arts, Philadelphia, 1968; Garrett award, Art Institute of Chicago, 1972; Arts and Humanities, Yale University, New Haven, 1976; New York City Mayor's Award of Honor for Arts and Culture, 1986; Lifetime Achievement award, College Art Association, 1994; and numerous honorary doctorates. Member, Fulbright Selection Committee, 1963–5; Board of Trustees, Bennington College, 1967–82; National Institute of Arts and Letters, 1974; National Council on the Arts (NEA), 1985–92; American Academy of Arts and Letters, 1990 (Vice-Chancellor 1991); American Academy of Arts and Sciences, 1991. Lives in New York.

Selected Individual Exhibitions
Tibor de Nagy Gallery, New York: 1951, 1953, 1954, 1956, 1957, 1958
André Emmerich Gallery, New York: 1959, 1960, 1961, 1963, 1965, 1966, 1968, 1969, 1971, 1972, 1973, 1975, 1977, 1978, 1979, 1981, 1982, 1983, 1984, 1986, 1987, 1988, 1989, 1990, 1991, 1993
Jewish Museum, New York: 1960 (retrospective)
Kasmin Gallery, London: 1964
Whitney Museum of American Art, New York: 1969 (touring retrospective, organised by International Council of Museum of Modern Art)
Janie C. Lee Gallery, Houston: 1975, 1976, 1978, 1980, 1982
Corcoran Gallery, Washington, DC: 1975 (touring)
Solomon R. Guggenheim Museum, New York: 1975, 1985–6 (touring)
Jacksonville Art Museum, FL: 1977–8 (touring)
Knoedler Gallery, London: 1978, 1981, 1983, 1985
Sterling and Francine Clark Art Institute, Williamstown, MA: 1980–81 (touring)
Rose Art Museum, Brandeis University, Waltham, MA: 1981
Museum of Modern Art, New York: 1989–90 (touring retrospective)
M. Knoedler & Co., New York: 1992, 1994, 1995
National Gallery of Art, Washington, DC: 1993–4 (touring)

Bibliography

E. C. Goosen, "Helen Frankenthaler", *Art International*, 5 October 1961, pp.76–9

Henry Geldzahler, "An interview with Helen Frankenthaler", *Art Forum*, iv, October 1965, pp.36–8

Gene Baro, "The achievement of Helen Frankenthaler", *Art International*, xi, September 1967, pp.33–8

Barbara Rose, "Paintings within the tradition: The career of Helen Frankenthaler", *Art Forum*, 7 April 1969, pp.28–33

Lawrence Alloway, "Frankenthaler as pastoral", *Art News*, 10 November 1971, pp.67–8, 89–90

Hilton Kramer, "Helen Frankenthaler", *New York Times*, 1 December 1973, p.27

E.A. Carmean, Jr, "On five paintings by Helen Frankenthaler", *Art International*, xxii, April–May 1978, pp.28–32

Irving Sandler, *The New York School: The Painters and Sculptors of the Fifties*, New York: Harper, 1978

Barbara Rose, *Frankenthaler*, 3rd edition, New York: Abrams, 1979

John Russell, "Recent paintings by Helen Frankenthaler", *New York Times*, 13 November 1981, p.C26

Karen Wilkin, *Frankenthaler: Works on Paper, 1949–1984*, New York: Braziller, 1984

H.H. Arnason, *History of Modern Art: Paintings, Sculpture, Architecture, Photography*, 3rd edition, revised by Daniel Wheeler, New York: Abrams, 1986

John Elderfield, *Frankenthaler*, New York: Abrams, 1989

Helen Frankenthaler: A Paintings Retrospective, exh. cat., Museum of Modern Art, New York, and elsewhere, 1989

Helen Frankenthaler: Prints, exh. cat., National Gallery of Art, Washington, DC, and elsewhere, 1993

Pegram Harrison and Suzanne Boorsch, *Frankenthaler: A Catalogue Raisonné: Prints, 1961–1994*, New York: Abrams, 1996

In 1953 Helen Frankenthaler had a solo exhibition at the Tibor de Nagy Gallery, an important New York gallery, featuring a landmark painting, *Mountains and Sea* (1952; artist's collection), and a good review in a major art journal, *Art Digest*. Although this was still a coup for a young female painter in New York – she had just turned 24 – Frankenthaler was well prepared. The third daughter of New York State Supreme Court Justice Alfred Frankenthaler and his wife Martha, she had been educated at Dalton School in New York (where she studied with Rufino Tamayo) and graduated from Bennington College in Vermont. By 1950, she had met the artists Lee Krasner (q.v.), Willem and Elaine de Kooning (q.v.), Franz Kline and Barnett Newman, and the following year visited the studios of David Smith and Jackson Pollock. In 1952 she travelled to Nova Scotia and Cape Breton in Canada in the summer, and in the autumn turned to paintings based on watercolours from that trip.

One of those autumn works, *Mountains and Sea*, is, historically, the most famous of the artist's works. The imagery, although abstracted, is still present in the composition, with the green and orange wooded peaks of the Nova Scotia mountains placed in contrast to the horizontal blues of the ocean. The palette of the picture is almost Cézanne-like in its pale tones, and reflects her summer watercolours. Most noteworthy – and also probably inspired by watercolours – was the application of paint, thin washes of oil spread on and thus soaking into unprimed canvas. Furthermore, whole areas were left unpainted, leaving even the artist to question when working on the painting: "Is it finished? Is it a complete picture?"

Frankenthaler: *For E.M.*, 1981; acrylic on canvas; 151.5 × 198.1 cm.; private collection

Mountains and Sea soon led to the creation of a whole school of painting, a first, historically speaking, for a female painter. Shortly after its first exhibition, two painters in Washington, DC, Kenneth Noland and Morris Louis, travelled to Frankenthaler's studio to see it, Louis calling it a "revelation". When they returned home, they adopted Frankenthaler's staining technique to more serial-type imagery – Noland's *Targets* and Louis's *Veils and Unfurleds*, and with these works established the so-called Color-Field School.

With this influence, Frankenthaler was considered a key member of the Color-Field School as it was recognised and then widely exhibited during the 1950s and 1960s. Her work, however, was decidedly different from the movement, remaining individual – rather than serial – and less than abstract. In such pictures as *Mother Goose Melody* (Virginia Museum of Fine Arts, Richmond) she used open drawing and stained passages to suggest that she and her sisters were being read to in a nursery, while in *Arden* (1961; Whitney Museum of American Art, New York) she employed an interweaving of areas of colour to suggest the forest in Shakespeare's play *As You Like It*. This latter connotation of an imaginary landscape gave way in the mid-1960s to works such as *The Bay* (1963; Detroit Institute of Arts), where the imagery is reflective of actual environments, in this instance Provincetown Bay where Frankenthaler had a summer studio.

As if in reaction to this direction in her own work, during the later 1960s and early 1970s there was a dramatic change in her painting, towards a nearly total abstraction. Now, simple block-like shapes of colour are abutted, or simple long lines of colour employed, in works whose only reference could be to heraldry or flags, as in *Summer Banner* (1968; collection Mr and Mrs Fayez Sarofim). In the mid-1970s Frankenthaler acquired a new summer/weekend studio and residence in Connecticut, in addition to those maintained in New York. As Frankenthaler worked beside Long Island Sound, the role of nature as seen returned to her work in pictures such as *Ocean Drive West No.1* (1974; private collection), which abstractly captures the sense of water and horizons seen from her studio. This aspect of her works – she also continued making less "relational" paintings – can also be seen in large canvases done in response to her experience of the great American Southwest – pictures such as *Natural Answer* (1976; Art Gallery of Ontario, Toronto), where the earthlike tones and horizontal strata link the work to the 19th-century American tradition of grand landscape painting.

From time to time in her career, Frankenthaler has chosen to paint works that can be seen as variations on those of the old masters. Her early *Las Mayas* (1958; Collection Norman and Irma Braman) is seen as an abstract composition until one realises that it is an inverted variation on Goya's *Mayas on a Balcony* (Metropolitan Museum of Art, New York). In a similar manner, her large abstract painting of 1981, *For E.M.* (see illustration), is in fact a response to Edouard Manet's *Still Life with Carp* (Art Institute of Chicago).

Frankenthaler's career is also distinguished by her works in other media besides painting. In 1972, in Anthony Caro's studio in London, she created nine extraordinary works in welded sculpture, an interest she continued in 1975 in ceramic works made at Syracuse University. She has also worked extensively in printmaking and in illustrated books, and in 1985

designed the sets and costumes for the Royal Ballet's production of *Number Three* at Covent Garden, London. Works on paper – drawings and paintings – play the second largest role in her art, beginning in the 1950s and continuing today. Indeed, such recent large sheets as *Aerie* (1995; M. Knoedler & Co., New York) have approached the impact of her works on canvas.

E.A. CARMEAN, JR

Frémiet, Sophie *see* Rude

Frink, Elisabeth
British sculptor, 1930–1993

Born in Thurlow, Suffolk, 14 November 1930. Studied at Guildford School of Art, 1947–9; Chelsea School of Art, London, under Bernard Meadows, one of Henry Moore's assistants, and Willi Soukop, 1949–53. Exhibited with the London Group, 1952; exhibited at the Venice Biennale, 1952; included in *Open Air Exhibition*, Royal Academy, London, 1957. Taught at Chelsea School of Art, 1953–61; St Martin's School of Art, London, 1954–62; visiting instructor, Royal College of Art, London, 1965–7. Married (1) Michel Jammet, 1955; son born 1958; divorced 1963; (2) Edward Pool, 1964; divorced 1974; (3) Alexander Csáky, 1974. Lived in the Camargue, southern France, 1967–73; moved to Dorset, 1976. Recipient of Student prize, Unknown Political Prisoner competition, London, 1953; honorary doctorates from University of Surrey, 1977; University of Warwick, 1983; Open University, 1983; University of Cambridge, 1988; University of Exeter, 1988; University of Oxford, 1989; University of Keele, 1989; University of Manchester, 1990; University of Bristol, 1991; doctorate, Royal College of Art, 1982. Associate, 1971, and member, 1977, Royal Academy. Member of Royal Fine Art Commission, 1976–81; Trustee, British Museum, 1977; Welsh Sculpture Trust, 1981. Commander, 1969, and Dame Commander, 1982, Order of the British Empire (CBE, DBE); Companion of Honour, 1992. Died in Dorset, 18 April 1993.

Selected Individual Exhibitions
St George's Gallery, London: 1955
Waddington Galleries, London: 1959, 1961, 1963, 1965, 1967, 1968, 1969, 1971, 1972, 1976, 1977
Bertha Schaefer Gallery, New York: 1959, 1961, 1964
Felix Landau Gallery, Los Angeles: 1961, 1964
Kettle's Yard Gallery, Cambridge: 1973
Maltzahn Gallery, London: 1974
Waddington Fine Arts, Montreal: 1977
Galerie D'Eendt, Amsterdam: 1977
Terry Dintenfass Gallery, New York: 1978, 1983
Open Air Exhibition, Winchester, Hampshire: 1981
Yorkshire Sculpture Park, Bretton Hall: 1983, 1994 (retrospective)
Royal Academy, London: 1985 (retrospective)
Fitzwilliam Museum, Cambridge: 1985
David Jones Art Gallery, Sydney, Australia: 1986
Coventry Cathedral: 1987

Hong Kong Festival: 1989
Lumley Cazalet, London: 1989, 1992
National Museum of Women in the Arts, Washington, DC: 1990
Galerie Simonne Stern, New Orleans: 1991
Beaux Arts Gallery, London: 1993

Bibliography

Edward Mullins, *The Art of Elisabeth Frink*, London: Lund Humphries, 1972; Park Ridge, NJ: Noyes Press, 1973

Hayward Annual '78, exh. cat., Arts Council of Great Britain, London, 1978

Elisabeth Frink: Sculpture in Winchester, exh. cat., Wolvesey Castle, Winchester, 1981

Peter Shaffer, Bryan Robertson and Sarah Kent, *Elisabeth Frink Sculpture: Catalogue Raisonné*, Salisbury: Harpvale, 1984 (contains bibliography)

Elisabeth Frink: Sculpture and Drawings, 1952–1984, exh. cat., Royal Academy, London, 1985

Elisabeth Frink: Sculpture and Drawings, 1950–1990, exh. cat., National Museum of Women in the Arts, Washington, DC, 1990

Elisabeth Frink Memorial Exhibition, exh. cat., Yorkshire Sculpture Park, 1994

Edward Lucie-Smith, *Elisabeth Frink: Sculpture since 1984 and Drawings*, London: Art Books International, 1994

——, *Frink: A Portrait*, London: Bloomsbury, 1994

Emma Roberts, "Frink again", *Women's Art Magazine*, no.62, January–February 1995, pp.22–3

The talent of Elisabeth Frink emerged early. Trained at the Guildford and Chelsea Schools of Art, she was still a student when, in 1952, the Tate Gallery bought a small bronze, *Bird of Prey*. Its attenuated, brittle planes were typical of the style of one branch of British sculpture of the day, and were a summation of Frink's concerns with the aggressive yet vulnerable male, human or animal. In 1953 she won the Student prize in the International Unknown Political Prisoner competition.

Early influences were the paintings of Grünewald, the sculptures of Rodin, Giacometti, Degas, Matisse and Germaine Richier (q.v.). Reg Butler, Paolozzi and other sculptors ten years older than Frink had recently returned from World War II. Their images displayed a disenchantment with war that she, too young to have seen active service, did not entirely share. *Warrior's Head* (1954; artist's estate) shows a young helmeted hero, aggressive but not brutal, harking back to Greek myth rather than the recent combat. Frink's style changed during her career, but the subjects she chose – the male nude and the male animal – did not. Hers was always to be an objective view, seen with compassion. She eschewed the vogue for abstraction. Expressionistic and imaginative, her sculpture is always figurative, though sometimes enigmatic (examples in Tate Gallery, London, National Gallery of Victoria, Melbourne, and Museum of Modern Art, New York).

Nor was there a change in technique. Frink worked quickly, building up forms in wet plaster on an armature, smoothing the surface, breaking it up when dry, often reintegrating discarded pieces into the finished work. This process was repeated until all the forms were simplified. Early on, these forms were rough, almost hacked away. Later the simplification was more pronounced. Less and less "fracturing" led to the boneless appearance of works of the late 1960s and beyond (e.g. *Paternoster (Shepherd with Sheep)*, 1974; Paternoster Square, London), sculptures that owe more to Degas and Matisse than to her contemporaries. From that time on, Frink was very much her own woman, with early influences assimilated and developed in a distinctive, personal way.

During the 1960s, Frink concentrated on two main themes: the spinning, falling man and the predatory bird. *The Cock* (1961; private collection, repr. Shaffer, Robertson and Kent 1984) is the essence of power and menace. He crows at full voice, strident, ready to strike, yet the thin, stiff legs could be snapped in one blow. Her male figures began to be less mythical, more archetypal. Elongated torsos spiral horizontally, with no stand to break their fall. These two themes are united in the Alcock and Brown Memorial at Manchester Airport, *Horizontal Birdman* (1962), which portrays the helplessness of a falling body whose tattered wings cannot save it.

A deep and lasting concern with man's inhumanity to man was revealed in the early 1960s when the busts and partial figures were replaced by monolithic standing male nudes. *Judas* (1963; see illustration) is still brutish and rough, but blindfold; the horizontal, emaciated *Dying King* (1963; artist's estate) wards off a blow. *First Man* (1964; Collection Lord McAlpine of West Green, Perth, Australia) is smoother in style and ushers in a series of male figures that stand in bewilderment at a vision of life, yet are monumental and eternal. These develop in the 1980s into groups of *Running Men*. Seen together, these figures seem to run noiselessly with the sense of an unknown quest.

The feeling of bewilderment and vulnerability engendered with *Judas* is seen in a later series of men moving ponderously with white painted faces: *Riace* (1986–9; artist's estate), suggested by recently discovered Greek sculptures from under the sea. But Frink did not abandon the huge portrait head of the male. *Tribute Heads* (1975–7), another series, and *In Memoriam* (1981; both artist's estate) depict the suffering stoicism of the martyr or victim, sometimes blindfold, with closed eyes, or gazing introspectively into an unknown distance. A visit to Algiers brought to Frink's attention the appalling activities of the terrorist Ben Oufkir. The huge heads now become the *Goggle Heads*, creatures of menace behind gleaming bronze glasses, only the mouth betraying the insecurity that Frink clearly sees behind all brutality. This concern with violation and abuse led to her close involvement with the human rights organisation Amnesty International for the rest of her life.

Frink's love of animals, particularly horses, is demonstrated in many bronzes in which she seeks not anatomical accuracy, nor anthropormorphism, but captures the spirit of the beast she portrays. She saw horses as loyal, resilient, affectionate and courageous, attributes that she also saw in men, despite their aggression and vulnerability. For her, they also shared speed and beauty. All these attributes are united in *Horse and Man* (1974; Dover Street, London). The aggressive and mythical birds of the early years largely disappear. The later animal sculptures are filled with a great love, understanding and sensitivity, immensely sensual and always male.

Not the least of Frink's achievements are the drawings made in preparation for maquettes and lithographs, which retain the vivid sense of life and the broken forms of her early work, one image often overlapping another. Commissions to illustrate *Aesop's Fables* (London, 1968), Chaucer's *Canterbury Tales* (London, 1972) and the *Iliad* and the *Odyssey* (London, 1978)

Frink: *Judas*, 1963

appealed to her sense of the mythical and the eternal and are, again, full of life, conviction and her own evident enjoyment.

Her many sculptures for public places reflect Frink's deep religious convictions. The *Risen Christ* (1964; Our Lady of the Wayside, Solihull) fumbles his way towards the light, sharing the bewilderment of First Man. *St Edmund* (1976; Bury St Edmunds), slender and hyper-sensitive, averts his head but clutches the cross to his heart. The eagle of the lectern of Coventry Cathedral (1962), a cast of which was used for the John F. Kennedy Memorial, Dallas, looks hewn from the rock on which it stands. This is perhaps Frink's best-known image and shares the indomitability of spirit and soaring optimism of her own religious belief. It is no coincidence that her one female figure, *Walking Madonna* (1981; Salisbury Cathedral), strides out across the green like Mother Courage, gaunt but single-minded towards her unseen goal. A close inspection shows something shared with all Frink's sculptured heads: an element of self-portraiture that is very revealing of the serenity and strength of the woman within the sculptor.

BRIDGET CROWLEY

Frishmuth, Harriet Whitney
American sculptor, 1880–1980

Born in Philadelphia, 17 September 1880; father a physician. Spent several years with her mother and sisters in Europe, attending schools in Paris and Dresden. At age 19, studied sculpture in Paris, briefly with Rodin, then at the Académie Colarossi under Jean-Antoine Injalbert and possibly Henri Gauquié. Spent two years in Berlin, working with Cuno von Euchtriz, before returning to USA. Studied at the Art Students League, New York, under Gutzon Borglum and Hermon A. MacNeil (won Augustus Saint-Gaudens prize). Worked as assistant to sculptor Karl Bitter and performed dissections to understand anatomy better at College of Physicians and Surgeons, New York. Moved with her mother to Sniffen Court, New York, c.1913, living there for many years. Returned to the Philadelphia area, c.1937. Moved to Connecticut, 1967. Remained unmarried; Ruth Talcott was secretary-companion from 1940s. Member, National Sculpture Society, 1914; Associate member, 1925, and Member, 1929, National Academy of Design. Died in Connecticut, 1 January 1980.

Principal Exhibitions
Paris Salon: 1903
National Academy of Design, New York: occasionally 1908–49 (Helen Foster Barnett prize 1915, Elizabeth N. Watrous gold medal 1922, Julia A. Shaw memorial prize 1923)
Pennsylvania Academy of the Fine Arts, Philadelphia: occasionally 1908–39
Art Institute of Chicago: occasionally 1912–25
Gorham Galleries, New York: 1912 (women sculptors), 1928 (*Famous Small Bronzes*)
Panama-Pacific Exposition, San Francisco: 1915 (honourable mention)
National Sculpture Society, New York: 1923 (*American Sculpture*)
Woman's World's Fair, Chicago: 1925
Grand Central Art Galleries, New York: 1928 (individual)

National Sculpture Society, California Palace of the Legion of Honor: 1929
Black, Starr and Gorham, New York: 1946 (individual)

Bibliography
Famous Small Bronzes, exh. cat., Gorham Galleries, New York, 1928
Brookgreen Gardens: Sculpture by Harriet Whitney Frishmuth, Brookgreen Gardens, SC, 1937
Beatrice Gilman Proske, *Brookgreen Gardens Sculpture*, 2nd edition, Brookgreen Gardens, SC, 1968
"Harriet Whitney Frishmuth, American sculptor", *The Courier* (Syracuse University Library Associates), ix/1, October 1971, pp.21–35
Charles N. Aronson, *Sculptured Hyacinths*, New York: Vantage Press, 1973
Ruth Talcott, ed., "Harriet Whitney Frishmuth, 1880–1980", *National Sculpture Review*, xxix, Summer 1980, pp.22–5
American Bronze Sculpture, 1850 to the Present, exh. cat., Newark Museum, NJ, 1984
The Woman Sculptor: Malvina Hoffman and Her Contemporaries, exh. cat., Berry-Hill Galleries, New York, 1984
Beatrice Gilman Proske, "Harriet Whitney Frishmuth, lyric sculptor", *Aristos: Journal of Esthetics*, ii, June 1984, pp.1–6
Janis Conner and Joel Rosenkranz, *Rediscoveries in American Sculpture: Studio Works, 1893–1939*, Austin: University of Texas Press, 1989
Charlotte Streifer Rubinstein, *American Women Sculptors*, Boston: Hall, 1990

Harriet Frishmuth Papers are in the George Arents Research Library, Syracuse University, Syracuse, NY.

Harriet Whitney Frishmuth, like Janet Scudder (q.v.), Anna Vaughn Hyatt Huntington (q.v.) and Malvina Hoffman (q.v.), belonged to the generation of talented women sculptors of the first decades of the 20th century whose work was strongly influenced by the lingering Beaux-Arts style.

During the early years of her career, Frishmuth earned an income by producing a variety of small decorative objects, such as the popular *Girl and Frog Ashtray* (1910) and *Pushing Men Bookends* (1912). In addition to these extremely popular bronzes, many of which were cast by Gorham, Frishmuth established a reputation for life-size figures and playful fountains, which were also successful subjects for numerous other women artists, especially after World War I. Among the most popular of these was *Joy of the Waters*, which Frishmuth sculpted in two sizes (1917; ht 161cm.; Dayton Art Institute, OH; 1920; ht 112cm.; National Academy of Design, New York). The exuberance of *Joy of the Waters* was recaptured in a statuette entitled *Crest of the Wave* (1925), which was later enlarged (Reading Public Museum and Art Gallery, PA). Her spirited *Call of the Sea* (1924; ht 117cm.; Brookgreen Gardens, Murrells Inlet, SC) represents a slender nude riding a fish, while *Playdays* (1925; Dallas Museum of Art) shows a standing nude tickling a frog's back with her toe. More whimsical, but a popular type of subject among artists, was *Trio* (c.1928), "... three lazy frogs, clinging to the lily pads ..." (New York 1928, p.77). The popularity of such skilfully crafted garden sculptures was partly due to the rediscovery of the work of the Renaissance sculptors Donatello and Verrocchio.

Frishmuth's most significant subject matter was that of the nude female figure in motion, and there is a lyrical quality to these bronzes that distinguishes her work. Like other artists,

Frishmuth: *The Vine*, bronze; height 212.1 cm.; Metropolitan Museum of Art, New York, Rogers Fund, 1927 (27.66)

Frishmuth relied on dancers for models (the popularity of dancing figures can be attributed in part to the efforts of Isadora Duncan and her followers), and around 1916 she made the acquaintance of Desha, who would become her favourite model and the inspiration for several sculptures, such as the *Joy of the Waters*. *L'Extase* (1920; ht 50 cm.; Wadsworth Atheneum, Hartford, CT), for example, represents Desha's reaction to Scriabin's music: the figure seems to express the spiritual uplifting of the dancer. Some years later, Desha is supposed to have struck a pose that inspired Frishmuth's *Sweet Grapes* (1922; ht 50 cm.; repr. Proske 1984, p.5), a bacchante whose more restrained pose recalls such work as *Reflections* (1930; ht 147 cm.; repr. Talcott 1980, p.22). Two rare bronzes for Frishmuth are the small *Slavonic Dancer* (1921; Wadsworth Atheneum) and *The Dancers* (1921; repr. Proske 1984, p.4), since both contain male figures and both seem more directly oriented towards the specific subject of the dance. *Fantaisie* (1922; ht 26 cm.; Fine Arts Museum of San Francisco) depicts Desha and Leon Barté, who also modelled for *The Dancers*, in the guise of a nymph and satyr.

One of Frishmuth's finest achievements is *The Vine*, which was executed in two sizes (1921; ht 32 cm.; Brookgreen Gardens, Murrells Inlet, SC; 1923; life-size, see illustration). Accounts vary, but according to *The Courier* (1971, p.27), Frishmuth modelled the first version when Desha struck the pose in the artist's studio class. The large version developed about two years later, when members of the National Sculpture Society agreed to contribute life-size works to their exhibition of 1923; the same year it won the Julia A. Shaw memorial prize at the National Academy of Design.

The life-size version of *The Vine* exemplifies Frishmuth's lyrical figures at their best. The lithe female nude, her body raised upon her toes, extends her left arm and arcs her body in a manner that suggests fluid upward motion (the grapes she holds symbolise the vineyards along the Hudson River). The statue was designed to present strong visual effects from several angles. Frishmuth recalled the advice given to her by Rodin (*The Courier* 1971, p.22): "First, always look at the silhouette of a subject ... second, remember that movement is the transition from one attitude to another ..." Nevertheless, *The Vine* remains anchored in the academic tradition. Frishmuth's delicate figure, for instance, recalls Augustus Saint-Gaudens's slender *Diana* (1893–4; Metropolitan Museum of Art), both in the smooth modelling and the penetration into space. (She would have also learned the technique of polished surfaces from Hermon A. MacNeil, who had studied in Paris.) Also, although the surfaces are more richly modelled and the corkscrew composition more reminiscent of the Beaux-Arts revival of the Baroque, Frederick MacMonnies's life-size *Bacchante and Infant Faun* (1893; Metropolitan Museum of Art) must have impressed Frishmuth, especially in its exuberance.

Around 1922 Frishmuth modelled a plaster entitled *Speed*, which is known only from photographs (Rubinstein 1990, p.156); the subject was inspired by watching Michel Fokine dance. Although Frishmuth disliked the term Art Deco, it best describes this beautifully stylised subject – certainly one of her best sculptures. *Speed* was popularised by the Gorham Company, which cast it in two small sizes intended for use either as radiator caps for fine automobiles or as athletic trophies (New York 1928, p.23). During the 1920s in France, the Lalique Company popularised a wide variety of glass radiator decorations, and their highly stylised *Victoire* (1925) recalls the dynamic spirit of Frishmuth's work. Frishmuth's *Speed* may have been enlarged to a marble relief for one of the former telephone company buildings in Erie, Pennsylvania (Rubinstein 1990, p.155).

Frishmuth also executed a variety of other significant work, which is less known: a bust of *President Woodrow Wilson* (1924; Virginia State Capitol, Richmond), done in the style of bland realism characteristic of most mid-20th-century portraiture, *Roses of Yesterday* (1923; Hacksensack, NJ), the idealised, dreamy figure of a girl holding a sundial and flowers, *The Christ* (1927; Denver), the *Dill Memorial* (1929; Bridgewater, MA) and *Peter Pan* (1936; Laurel Hill Cemetery, Philadelphia). According to several sources (Rubinstein 1990, p.156; Proske 1984, p.5), Frishmuth's output declined after a fall; this and the death of her mother combined to depress her spirits. Then, too, the demand for small academic bronzes declined sharply in the 1930s, and Frishmuth had a distaste for contemporary art. Nevertheless, there seems to be a renewed interest in her work: *The Vine* now stands in the American wing of the Metropolitan Museum of Art; Frishmuth has been included in several recent scholarly publications on American sculpture; and her work is again beginning to command attention at auction houses.

KENT AHRENS

Fritsch, Elizabeth

British potter, 1940–

Born in Shropshire, 11 September 1940. Studied harp and piano at Birmingham School of Music and Royal Academy of Music, London, 1958–64. Started to make hand-built pots at home after birth of son in 1966 (second child, a daughter, born 1980). Studied ceramics at Royal College of Art, London, 1968–71 (MA; silver medal and Herbert Read memorial prize for thesis). Worked at Bing and Gröndahl factory, Copenhagen, Denmark, 1972–3. Studio in Gestingthorpe, Suffolk, 1973–6; in Digswell, Hertfordshire, 1976–85; in East London, from 1985. Visiting lecturer at various art colleges, 1975–90. Recipient of major prize, Royal Copenhagen Porcelain Jubilee Competition, 1972; gold medal, International Ceramics Competition, Sopot, Poland, 1976; gold medal, Internationalen Handwerksmesse *Visuelle Spiele*, Munich, 1993. Lives in London.

Selected Individual Exhibitions

Bing and Gröndahl Porcelain, Copenhagen: 1972
Crafts Council, London: 1974, 1994
Amalgam Art, London: 1975 (with Anya Barnett)
British Craft Centre, London: 1976
Temple Newsam House, Leeds City Art Galleries: 1978 (*Pots about Music*, touring)
Victoria and Albert Museum, London: 1979
Royal College of Art, London: 1984
Künstlerhaus, Vienna: 1986 (solo room, *British Art and Design*)
Midland Arts Centre, Birmingham: 1989 (retrospective)

Galerie Besson, London: 1989
Royal Museum of Scotland, Edinburgh: 1990
Hetjeus Museum, Düsseldorf: 1990 (retrospective)
Pilscheur Fine Art, London: 1992 (retrospective)
New York Crafts Council: 1993
Northern Centre for Contemporary Art, Sunderland: 1993–4 (*Vessels from Another World*, touring)

Selected Writings

"Juggling into jugs", *Crafts*, no.41, November–December 1979, p.26
"Pots from nowhere", *Crafts*, no.71, November–December 1984, pp.20–21
"Notes on time in relation to the making and painting of pots", *Crafts*, no.97, March–April 1989, pp.18–19
"Metaphysical vessels", *Ceramic Review*, no.148, 1994, pp.27–31 (with others)

Bibliography

Ceramic Forms: Recent Works by Seven British Potters, exh. cat., Crafts Council, London, 1974
Elisabeth Cameron and Philippa Lewis, eds, *Potters on Pottery*, London: Evans, and New York: St Martin's Press, 1976
Jon Catleugh, "Recent pots by Elizabeth Fritsch", *Ceramic Review*, no.44, 1977, p.7
Elizabeth Fritsch: Pots about Music, exh. cat., Temple Newsam House, Leeds City Art Galleries, and elsewhere, 1978
Peter Inch, "Pots about music", *Crafts*, no.35, November–December 1978, p.47
British 20th-Century Studio Ceramics, exh. cat., Christopher Wood Gallery, London, 1980
Pots from Nowhere, exh. leaflet, Royal College of Art, London, 1984
Peter Dormer and David Cripps, *Elizabeth Fritsch: A View*, London: Bellew, 1985
Philip Rawson, "Pots from nowhere", *Crafts*, no.73, March–April 1985, pp.46–7
Elizabeth Fritsch: Vessels from Another World: Metaphysical Pots in Painted Stoneware, exh. cat., Northern Centre for Contemporary Art, Sunderland, and elsewhere, 1993
Oliver Watson, *Studio Pottery: Twentieth-Century British Ceramics in the Victoria and Albert Museum Collection*, London: Phaidon, 1993 (originally published as *British Studio Pottery*, Oxford: Phaidon, 1990)

Elizabeth Fritsch left the Royal College of Art in 1971. Almost immediately, her name became linked with a number of other potters, such as Glenys Barton (q.v.), Alison Britton and Jacqui Poncelet, whom the Crafts Council championed for the originality of their work, which was seen to be taking craft in new

Fritsch: left, *Dark Windows*; centre, *Collision of Particles*; right, *Spiral*; all 1992

directions. In later years, ironically, Glenys Barton and Jacqui Poncelet severed their connections with the craft world, instead asserting their right to be considered as fine artists. Fritsch has not taken such a stance, though this might have been expected of her. Instead, she has kept company with makers, pursuing the ethic and using the language of contemporary craft. She continues to make vessels – containers – and to call them "pots".

Fritsch's pots, however, are containers of contradictions. Their capacity is metaphorical: for the artist, the principle that they should be capable of use is crucial, but this does not imply any intention of actual use. She associates them with other vessels whose use is formal or ceremonial (lachrymatories or funerary urns) or obscure (the acquisitions of archaeologists and ethnographers). They are situated in that debatable land between the territories of the craftsman potter and the ceramic sculptor. In this, Fritsch continues the tradition of Hans Coper and Lucie Rie (q.v.), her mentors at the Royal College of Art. Her style, however, is entirely original, taking little from her teachers, owing nothing to contemporaries. Instead, she draws her inspiration largely from her eclectic reading, which ranges from archaeology, through world literature, to quantum physics. Considering the depth of intellectual background to these works, they have a remarkably immediate appeal. Her clean, elemental forms and clear fresco colours attract and hold the most casual viewer. This is no superficial seductiveness: the pots invite an examination that rewards both brain and eye.

There is a further contradiction between the sense of order and composure suggested by the works, and the level of improvisation that goes into their making. There are no preliminary sketches. Fritsch works directly and intuitively, and if the result does not satisfy her she effaces it and starts again. She likens herself to a jazz musician – in extremely slow motion. Although her repertoire of forms, her patterns and palette are not given to radical change, she rarely repeats herself except under pressure and finds copying more arduous than originality. Paradoxically, it is her most lively pots, those that most evoke a sense of spontaneity, that are likely to have been the most laborious to make (e.g. *Collision of Particles*, 1992; see illustration). At an emotional level, her work suggests a cool serenity that few human beings achieve in reality. They bear no traces of the competition for their maker's time from modern living, family responsibilities and the incessant demands of the telephone. They represent a classical tranquillity, to aspire to rather than to grasp. Edward Lucie-Smith, writing in *Vessels from Another World* (1993), speaks of their "completeness", and they share more than merely the colours of a Piero painting – Piero della Francesca, whom Fritsch so much admires; there is a similar sense of perfect composition, to which any addition would be a detraction.

The contradiction between reality and illusion is at its clearest in the forms of the pots themselves. From her student days, Fritsch has worked in what she calls two-and-a-half dimensions: bottles, bowls, cups and goblets in low relief that suggest a fully circular shape. They are not *trompes-l'oeil*: there is no attempt at deception. Rather, they depict three-dimensional vessels just as a two-dimensional artist might portray a still life. They are pots about pots. One clear area of development in Fritsch's work is her increased mastery of the half dimension.

Her earlier works were designed to be viewed from the front, later also from the back. Now, every angle offers its own perspective. The decoration may follow the actual form, or the apparent form, or be set in deliberate opposition to both – rectangles apparently protruding from the surface like ceramic holograms. Here, perhaps, can be seen the outcome of Fritsch's early interest in Surrealism: the creation of objects that fail to fulfil the function they describe, and which challenge conventional expectations. Unlike Magritte's *"Ceci n'est pas une pipe"*, however, her pots indisputably *are* pots.

Fritsch suffers from a contradiction (or rather a conflict) that has afflicted makers for more than a century: by putting a realistic price on their work, they severely limit the number of people who can afford it. This has not been greatly remedied by the acquisition policies of museums and art galleries, many of which seem to have difficulty in placing her either as a maker or as an artist, so that the greater part of her output is in private hands. There are exceptions. The Crafts Council in London has a fine collection of her work from the mid-1970s, although it has not made subsequent purchases. Lotherton Hall, Leeds, has an outstanding group dating from 1978, when Leeds City Art Galleries organised the first major touring exhibition of her work. Birmingham has a pair of pots from the 1980s, Bolton and Norwich each have one. Aberdeen Art Gallery, Liverpool Museum and the Laing Art Gallery, Newcastle upon Tyne, all bought works from the touring exhibition of 1993–4, *Vessels from Another World*. Generally speaking, however, one unfortunate contradiction is that while Fritsch's work, visually, is extremely accessible to a wide range of people, physically, it remains largely inaccessible.

MIKE HILL

Fuller, Meta Vaux Warrick

American sculptor, 1877–1968

Born Meta Vaux Warrick in Philadelphia, 9 June 1877. Studied at Pennsylvania School of Industrial Art (later Philadelphia College of Art), 1894–9 (scholarships; George K. Crozier and metalwork prizes 1899); Ecole des Beaux-Arts and Académie Colarossi, Paris, under Jean-Antoine Injalbert and Rollard, 1899–1903; also studied under Rodin in Paris. Attended Pennsylvania Academy of the Fine Arts, Philadelphia, 1907. Married psychiatrist Solomon Carter Fuller, 1909; three sons born 1910, 1911 and 1916; husband died 1953. Lived in Framingham, Massachusetts, after marriage. Most early work destroyed in a fire, 1910. Recipient of second prize, Massachusetts branch of Women's Peace Party, 1915. Fellow, Academy of the Fine Arts, Philadelphia. Member, Boston Art Club; American Federation of Arts; Federation of Women's Clubs, Wellesley Society of Artists; Civic League; Framingham Women's Club; honorary member and chair, Art Committee, Business and Professional Women's Club; chapter president, Zonta; honorary member, Alpha Kappa Alpha and Aristo Club, Boston. Died in Framingham, 13 March 1968.

Fuller: *Awakening of Ethiopia*, 1914; bronze; Art and Artifacts Division, Schomburg Center for Research in Black Culture, New York Public Library, Astor, Lenox and Tilden Foundations

Principal Exhibitions

Paris Salon: 1898–9, 1903
Pennsylvania Academy of the Fine Arts, Philadelphia: 1906, 1908, 1920, 1928
Jamestown Tercentennial Exposition: 1907 (gold medal)
Emancipation Proclamation Exposition, New York: 1913
New York Public Library: 1921
Boston Public Library: 1922
Art Institute of Chicago: 1927
Harmon Foundation, New York: 1931, 1932, 1933
Augusta Savage Studio, New York: 1939
Chicago: 1940 (*American Negro Exposition*)
Howard University, Washington, DC: 1961 (*New Vistas in American Art*, silver medal and citation)
Framingham Center Library, Framingham, MA: 1964 (individual)
City College of New York: 1967

Bibliography

Lorado Taft, *The History of American Sculpture*, 3rd edition, New York: Macmillan, 1930
Benjamin Brawley, *The Negro Genius: A New Appraisal of the Achievement of the American Negro in Literature and the Fine Arts*, New York: Dodd Mead: 1937
James A. Porter, *Modern Negro Art*, New York: Dryden Press, 1943; reprinted New York: Arno Press, 1969
Sylvia G.L. Dannett, "Meta Warrick Fuller", *Profiles of Negro Womanhood*, ii, Yonkers, NY: Educational Heritage, 1966, pp.31–46
Allan Morrison, "(Black) women in the arts", *Ebony*, August 1966, pp.90–94
The Evolution of Afro-American Artists, 1800–1950, exh. cat., City College of New York, 1967
Ten Afro-American Artists of the Nineteenth Century, exh. cat., Howard University Gallery of Art, Washington, DC, 1967
Ralph L. Harley, Jr, "A checklist of Afro-American art and artists", *Serif*, vii/4, 1970, pp.3–63
Elton Fax, *Seventeen Black Artists*, New York: Dodd Mead, 1971
Eleanor Tufts, *Our Hidden Heritage: Five Centuries of Women Artists*, New York and London: Paddington, 1974
Two Centuries of Black American Art, exh. cat., Los Angeles County Museum of Art and elsewhere, 1976
Samella S. Lewis, *Art: African American*, New York: Harcourt Brace, 1978; revised edition as *African American Art and Artists*, Berkeley: University of California Press, 1990
An Independent Woman: The Life and Art of Meta Warrick Fuller (1877–1968), exh. cat., Danforth Museum of Art, Framingham, and elsewhere, 1984
The Harlem Renaissance: Art of Black America, exh. cat., Studio Museum in Harlem, New York, 1987
Charlotte Streifer Rubinstein, *American Women Sculptors*, Boston: Hall, 1990

A sculptor of the Victorian era whose style ranged from romanticism to realism, Meta Fuller was one of the most prolific precursors of the Harlem Renaissance. Born to a middle-class family in Philadelphia, the daughter of a barber and a hairdresser, she attended the Pennsylvania School of Industrial Art for five years (1894–9), gaining recognition as the "sculptor of horrors" for her clay *Head of Medusa* and a figure of *Christ*. These works already indicate her absorption with heroic themes of sacrifice, slavery and suffering. By 1899 she was in Paris, studying at the Académie Colarossi and the Ecole des Beaux-Arts, and with artists including Rodin. Critics and historians have identified her with an elite group of African-American artists that included Henry Ossawa Tanner, William Edward Scott and May Howard Jackson. An alternative African-American art world was developing at the turn of the 19th and 20th centuries, and Fuller's stay in Paris reflected a pattern among many artists of colour to escape the restrictions of segregated, provincial America and seek training and exhibition opportunities in Europe.

For the Tercentennial Exposition in Jamestown of 1907 Fuller was commissioned to produce a 15-piece sculpture highlighting the history of African Americans. The African-American spokesman W.E.B. Du Bois commissioned a sculpture, *Emancipation Proclamation* (1913; plaster; Museum of the National Center of Afro-American Artists and Museum of Afro-American History, Boston), for the Emancipation Proclamation Exposition in New York of 1913. Fuller explained the subject thus:

> I represented the race by a male and a female figure standing under a tree, the branches of which are the fingers of Fate grasping at them to draw them back into the fateful clutches of hatred ... Humankind [is] weeping over her suddenly freed children who, beneath the gnarled fingers of Fate, step forth into the world, unafraid ... The Negro has been emancipated from slavery but not from the curse of race hatred and prejudice [quoted in Rubinstein 1990, p.202].

Fuller's *Awakening of Ethiopia* (1914; see illustration) is composed of a partially wrapped mummy, bound from the waist down but with the hair and shoulders of a beautiful African woman, wearing the headdress of an ancient Egyptian queen: "in title and spirit ... unquestionably the image of Ethiopia, mythical symbol of Black Africa" (David Driskell in New York 1987, p.108). The work became emblematic of the Harlem Renaissance and the New Negro Movement and was associated with what the historian Alain Locke described as a rebirth of consciousness rooted in African art. Widely exhibited and acclaimed, this shrouded female figure reflected the contemporary obsession with Egyptian culture.

In 1915 Fuller was awarded second prize by the Women's Peace Party for her group sculpture *Peace Halting the Ruthlessness of War*. American racism presented her with the challenge of reconciling aesthetics and social advocacy, as in *Mary Turner (A Silent Protest Against Mob Violence)* (1919;

painted plaster; Museum of Afro-American History), which commemorated a silent parade of 10,000 black workers in New York in 1917 to protest against continued violence against blacks. Fuller's piece was prompted by accounts in the *New York Times* and *Crisis* magazine, edited by Du Bois, of the lynching in Georgia of Mary Turner, a black woman accused of planning to murder a white man. Racial violence and the evasion of prosecution by whites was a major theme for UNIA (United Negro Improvement Association) and other political organisations of the period.

Fuller's involvement with the international tendency of the time is reflected in her marriage to the Liberian psychiatrist Dr Solomon Carter Fuller in 1909. The couple settled in Framingham, Massachusetts, and had three sons. She constructed a studio and continued to sculpt, despite a suspicious fire in 1910. Working primarily in plaster and bronze, she paid tribute to distinguished black Americans including *William Monroe Trotter*, *Samuel Coleridge Taylor*, *Frederick Douglass* and *Sojourner Truth*. Later works include *Talking Skull* (1937; bronze; Museum of Afro-American History), in which a nude black man kneels on the ground, gazing at a skull in front of him, and *Refugee* (1940; painted plaster; private collection), showing a refugee Jew trudging forward with a walking-stick. Fuller continued to exhibit until her death, and in 1984 the first retrospective exhibition was held at the Danforth Museum of Art in Framingham, curated by Joy L. Gordon, with works from the Meta Warrick Fuller Legacy founded by her family. Her work was also featured in the major exhibition *The Harlem Renaissance: Art of Black America*, held at the Studio Museum in Harlem in 1987.

Fuller's compositional power and aesthetic drive have been praised in many texts on American art, sculpture, women's art and African-American art. She led an active civic life and was a pioneer in combining a family and a career as a professional artist. She and her husband were honoured posthumously by the Framingham City Council and historical society in 1995 with the rededication of a city school as the Solomon and Meta Fuller Middle School.

ROBIN M. CHANDLER

G

Gág, Wanda (Hazel)

American graphic artist and illustrator, 1893–1946

Born in New Ulm, Minnesota, 11 March 1893. Studied at St Paul School of Art, 1913–14; Minneapolis School of Art, 1914–17; Art Students League, New York, 1917–18. Made first prints, had several drawings published in the magazines *Broom* and *The Liberator* and worked as a commercial artist, 1918–22. Drew and made prints in Connecticut and New York, 1923–4. Most productive period spent drawing and printmaking at "Tumble Timbers", Glen Gardner, New Jersey, and in New York, 1925–9. Moved to Milford, New Jersey, 1931. Married Earle Marshall Humphreys, 1943. Recipient of purchase prize, Metropolitan Museum of Art, New York, 1942; J. and E.R. Pennell purchase prize, Library of Congress, Washington, DC, 1944. Died in New York, 27 June 1946.

Principal Exhibitions

Individual
New York Public Library: 1923, 1924
Weyhe Gallery, New York: 1926, 1928, 1930, 1940 (retrospective)
Union College Library, Schenectady, NY: 1927 (with Adolf Dehn), 1928, 1931
Minneapolis Institute of Arts: 1927 (with Adolf Dehn and Richard Lahey)
American Association of University Women: 1944–6 (touring)

Group
American Print Makers, New York: 1927–36, 1939
American Institute of Graphic Arts Fifty Prints of the Year, New York: 1927–32, 1938, 1944
Bibliothèque Nationale, Paris: 1928 (*Gravure moderne américaine*)
Universidad Nacional de México, Escuela de Bellas Artes, Mexico City: 1929 (*Acuareles, dibujos, litografías y grabados originales de artistas franceses y norteamericanos*)
Whitney Museum of American Art, New York: 1933, 1936 (biennials), 1938–41 (annuals), 1942 (*Between Two Wars: Prints by American Artists, 1914–1941*)
Institut Propagandy Sztuki/Institut de Propagande de l'Art, Warsaw: 1936 (*Exposition internationale de gravures originales sur bois*)
Exposition Internationale, Paris: 1937
American Artists Congress, New York: 1937–40
Musée du Jeu de Paume, Paris: 1938 (*Trois siècles d'art aux Etats-Unis*)
Museum of Modern Art, New York: 1939 (*Art in Our Time*)
New York World's Fair: 1939
Metropolitan Museum of Art, New York: 1941 (*Artists for Victory*)

Selected Writings

"These modern women: A hotbed of feminists", *The Nation*, 1927, cxxiv, pp.691–3 (published anonymously)
Millions of Cats, New York: Coward McCann, 1928; London: Faber, 1929 (for children)
The Funny Thing, New York: Coward McCann, 1929; London: Faber, 1962 (for children)
Snippy and Snappy, New York: Coward McCann, 1931; London: Faber, 1932 (for children)
The ABC Bunny, New York: Coward McCann, 1933; London: Faber, 1962 (for children)
Gone is Gone; or, The Story of a Man Who Wanted to Do Housework, New York: Coward McCann, 1935; London: Faber, 1936
Growing Pains: Diaries and Drawings for the Years 1908–1917, New York: Coward McCann, 1940; reprinted St Paul: Minnesota Historical Society Press, 1984
Nothing at All, New York: Coward McCann, 1941; London: Faber, 1942 (for children)

Bibliography

Marya Mannes, "Wanda Gág: Individualist", *Creative Art*, i, December 1927, pp.xxix–xxxii
Anne Herendeen, "Wanda Gág: The true story of a dynamic young artist who won't be organized", *Century Magazine*, August 1928, pp.427–32
Ruth Howe, "Wanda and six other Gágs", *Woman's Journal*, xiv, January 1929, pp.25, 48
The Checkerboard, exh. cat., Weyhe Gallery, New York, 1930
Art in Our Time, exh. cat., Museum of Modern Art, New York, 1939
Carl Zigrosser, *The Artist in America: Twenty-Four Close-ups of Contemporary Printmakers*, New York: Knopf, 1942; reprinted New York: Hacker, 1978
Horn Book Magazine, May–June 1947 (Wanda Gág memorial issue)
Alma Scott, *Wanda Gág: The Story of an Artist*, Minneapolis: University of Minnesota Press, 1949
William S. Lieberman, ed., *Manhattan Observed: Selections of Drawings and Prints*, Greenwich, CT: New York Graphic Society, 1968
Michael Patrick Hearn, *65 Years of Wanda Gág's Millions of Cats*, New York: Putnam and Grosset, 1992
Audur H. Winnan, *Wanda Gág: A Catalogue Raisonné of the Prints*, Washington, DC: Smithsonian Institution Press, 1993 (contains bibliography)
Karen Nelson Hoyle, *Wanda Gág*, New York: Twayne, 1994
Doug Hanson, "Wanda Gág", *Window*, ii, January 1995, pp.4–9

Manuscript collections are in the Department of Special Collections, Van Pelt Library, University of Pennsylvania, Philadelphia;

Gág: *Interior: Studio – My Shack on the Hill at Tumble Timbers*, 1928; brush and ink on sandpaper; 50.5 × 40.8 cm.; Philadelphia Museum of Art; Purchase: Lola Downin Peck Fund, from the Carl and Laura Zigrosser Collection

Philadelphia Museum of Art; Kerlan Collection, University of Minnesota, Minneapolis; and Archives of American Art, Washington, DC, and New York.

During the years 1923–9 Wanda Gág produced a body of work of extraordinary originality and vitality based on her own theories, meticulously developed and documented in her diaries (Van Pelt Library, University of Pennsylvania). A major figure in the New York art world of the 1920s, Gág was progressive and innovative. Her alterations to traditional printmaking techniques broke new ground.

Living in New York from 1917, Gág felt the need to get closer to nature. In the early 1920s she began spending several months of the year in primitive conditions in the countryside, first in Connecticut, then in New Jersey. With great zeal she studied the forms of trees, rocks and clouds: "trying to extract from them the marvelous, inexhaustible secrets of their existence" (diary entry, autumn 1922). Gág's passion was drawing, which she extended to include prints and watercolours. As a printmaker she explored most of the matrices and media of the time. She mastered drawing on zinc plates, notoriously difficult to handle, and invented the use of sandpaper as a matrix for lithographs (1923–4). In *Upright Landscape* (1926; lithograph on sandpaper plate; Philadelphia Museum of Art) Gág's concern is renewal and decline, a deeply felt subject throughout her life. There is a geometry to the print, in both its construction and meaning. At the heart of the sheet is inscribed a square, the sides of which correspond to the distance between the dying and the living trees. Within this square is the vital, the living and the imagined. *Nude* (1924; lithograph on sandpaper plate; Philadelphia Museum of Art) depicts the figure of a youthful woman, sensual and primitive. It contradicts Gág's claim that doing fashion illustrations in the early 1920s ruined her ability to draw the human body.

Applying her "theory of the form of the atmosphere around objects", Gág strove to make energy visible in her work. Visualisation of a flowing energy is evident in *Upright Landscape* as well as in *Spring in the Garden* (1927; lithograph on zinc plate; repr. Winnan 1993, cat. no.38), *Rain* (1926; brush and ink drawing on sandpaper; Philadelphia Museum of Art) and in numerous other compositions. "A still life is never *still* to me, it is solidified energy – and space does not impress me as being empty", she wrote (application for a Guggenheim fellowship, 1938, Kerlan Collection, University of Minnesota). Sometimes inspired by moonlight, at other times by light from a kerosene lamp or a wood-burning stove, Gág frequently portrayed the changing appearance of light, shadow and mood. *Lamplight* (1929; lithograph on stone; *ibid.*, cat. no.72) is a stark work, in which light from a shaded kerosene lamp engulfs the darkened passageway, a framed opening suggests entrapment and edges of objects dissolve in the light with tenuous agitation. In *Moonlight* (1926; lithograph on zinc plate; *ibid.*, cat. no.26) perspective and an inventive use of mood combine the diverse elements of a nocturnal landscape. It illustrates Gág's thoughts on perspective: "To me, perspective is more than a mechanical set of rules – I see in it the potentialities for rhythmic forcefulness and even emotional significance" (application for Guggenheim fellowship, *op. cit.*).

Gág's stylistic language was replete with symbols, her drawing style spirited and quirky. One of her largest drawings is *Interior: Studio – My Shack on the Hill at Tumble Timbers* (1928; see illustration), which brings together many of Gág's icons: the patterned shadows, tilted walls, visible energy, kerosene lamp, cloth on the wall, wooden chair and gourds for a touch of nature. A group of tiny watercolours entitled *Urformen der Natur* (Nature's original forms; 1934; Van Pelt Library, University of Pennsylvania, Philadelphia) shows her detailed study of nature and some of her quasi-erotic symbols. By using sandpaper as a support for brush-and-ink drawings and for watercolours, Gág achieved texture, sparkle and an altered perception of light unmatched in other media. Among several examples in the collection of the Philadelphia Museum of Art are study drawings for the lithographs *Tumble Timbers* (1925–6) and *Stone Crusher* (1927), and the watercolours *Ceiling of the Paramount Theater* (1928), *Mushrooms* (undated) and *In the Year of Our Lord* (c.1936–7), the last two related to lithographs of the same titles.

Gág is also well known as the author and illustrator of children's books. With *Millions of Cats*, first published in 1928 and still in print, she pioneered the format of composing two facing pages as one single design. In the 1930s most of Gág's creative energy was devoted to writing and illustrating children's books. They were popular and earned her substantial royalties during the Depression when the art market had all but disappeared. Her plan was to produce the books only as needed in order to support long periods of drawing and painting. Much to her dismay, the inspiration to draw, "the drawing mood", eluded her year after year. She felt uneasy about her work and agonised that her later drawings lacked the power of her work of the 1920s. In her diary she wrote about feeling disjointed, restless, anchorless, and of being in need of a new period of expression. Gág's declining health and the interruption caused by her books are among the probable reasons for the impediment. She continued to make prints, often based on her earlier sketches. Three lithographs on zinc plates, *Grandma's Parlor* (1930; repr. Winnan 1993, cat. no.78), *Grandma's Kitchen* (1931; *ibid.*, cat. no.82) and *Uncle Frank's Workshop* (1935; *ibid.*, cat. no.106) reflect Gág's Minnesota Old World background and fond memories of her maternal grandparents and aunts and uncles. In *Ploughed Fields* (1936; lithograph on zinc plate; *ibid.*, cat. no.109) her emotional ties to the land are strongly felt as a great winged cloud hovers over freshly ploughed fields like a spirit. Aversion to billboards, red nail polish and the trappings of motoring prompted *Progress* (1936; lithograph on zinc plate; *ibid.*, cat. no.110), while the collapse of reason and the horrors of war provoked *In the Year of Our Lord* (1937; lithograph on zinc plate; *ibid.*, cat. no.112). During the 1940s Gág produced *Growing Pains* (1940), further children's books and a group of tempera paintings, a medium that she rarely engaged in before 1940. She was afflicted with multiple health problems during the early years of the decade and in 1945 lung cancer was diagnosed. She died the following year.

Wanda Gág's early work was predominantly figurative but, except for self-portraits, people rarely appear in her mature work. An urge to portraiture, however, is often apparent in her work, for example in the prints *Macy's Stairway* (etching, 1929; Philadelphia Museum of Art; lithograph on zinc plate, 1940–41; *ibid.*, cat. no.117), *Backyard Corner* (1930; lithograph on stone; *ibid.*, cat. no.80) and *Philodendron* (1944;

lithograph on zinc plate; *ibid.*, cat. no.121). Gág painted sporadically in oil but was not pleased with the results. The paintings were never exhibited, and it is believed that she destroyed most of them.

AUDUR H. WINNAN

Galizia, Fede
Italian painter, *c.*1578–*c.*1630

Born *c.*1578; father Nunzio Galizia, a miniature painter from Trento who was active in Milan. Last recorded 21 June 1630, the date of her will, made in Milan.

Bibliography

Giovanni Paolo Lomazzo, *Idea del tempio della pittura*, Milan, 1590; reprint, ed. Robert Klein, 2 vols, Florence, 1974

Paolo Morigia, *La nobiltà di Milano*, Milan, 1595, p.282

Stefano Ticozzi, *Dizionario degli architetti, scultori, pittori …*, 4 vols, Milan, 1830–33

Luigi Malvezzi, *Le glorie dell'arte Lombarda, ossia illustrazione storica delle più belle opere che produssero i lombardi in pittura, scultura ed architettura dal 1590 al 1850*, Milan, 1882, p.212

Gino Fogolari, "Artisti trentini a Milano: Nunzio e Fede Galizia", *Tridentum*, i, 1898, pp.307–18

Curt Benedict, "Osias Beert", *L'Amour de l'Art*, xix, September 1938, pp.307–14

Roberto Longhi, "Un momento importante nella storia della 'natura morta'", *Paragone*, i/1, 1950, pp.34–9

G. De Logu, *Natura morta italiana*, Bergamo, 1962

Stefano Bottari, "Fede Galizia", *Arte Antica e Moderna*, vi/24, 1963, pp.309–18

——, *Fede Galizia pittrice (1578–1630)*, Trent, 1965

Renato Ruotolo, "Un dipinto ignoto di Fede Galizia", *Paragone*, xix/215, 1968, pp.65–6

Dizionario enciclopedico Bolaffi dei pittori e degli incisori italiani, Turin: Bolaffi, 1972–6

Women Artists, 1550–1950, exh. cat., Los Angeles County Museum of Art, and elsewhere, 1976

M. Rosci, "Italia", *Natura in posa: La grande stagione della natura morta europea*, Milan, 1977, pp.83–112

M. Bona Castellotti, "Due aggiunte al catalogo di Fede Galizia", *Arte Lombarda*, no.49, 1978, pp.30–32

Charles Sterling, *Still Life Painting from Antiquity to the Twentieth Century*, revised edition, New York: Harper, 1981 (French original, 1952)

Italian Still-Life Paintings from Three Centuries, exh. cat., Centro Di, New York, and elsewhere, 1983

Natura morta italiana/Italienische Stillebenmalerei aus drei Jahrhunderten: Sammlung Silvano Lodi/Italian Still-Life Painting from Three Centuries: The Silvano Lodi Collection/Tre secoli di natura morta italiana: La raccolta Silvano Lodi, exh. cat., Alte Pinakothek, Munich, and elsewhere, 1984

Luigi Salerno, *La natura morta italiana, 1560–1805/Still Life Painting in Italy, 1560–1805*, Rome: Bozzi, 1984

Giacomo Berra, "Alcune puntualizzazioni sulla pittrice Fede Galizia attraverso le testimonianze del letterato Gherardo Borgogni", *Paragone*, xl/469, 1989, pp.14–29

M. Natale and A. Morandotti, *La natura morta in Lombardia*, i, 1989, pp.196–317

Francesco Porzio, ed., *La natura morta in Italia*, 2 vols, Milan: Electa, 1989

Giacomo Berra, "La natura morta nella bottega di Fede Galizia", *Osservatorio delle Arti*, no.5, 1990, pp.55–62

Flavio Caroli, *Fede Galizia*, 2nd edition, Turin: Allemandi, 1991

——, "Aggiunte a Sofonisba Anguissola e Fede Galizia", *Notizie da Palazzo Albani*, xx/1–2, 1991, pp.143–8

Giacomo Berra, "Appunti per Fede Galizia", *Arte Cristiana*, lxxx/748, 1992, pp.37–44 (with English summary)

It is not certain that Milan was Fede Galizia's city of birth: according to some writers she arrived there as a small child with her father Nunzio Galizia, a miniature painter of some repute from Trento, who was called to the city to execute some works; according to other sources, she was born when her father was already in Milan. What is certain is that her development as a painter took place in Milan and thus in Lombardy, which in this period was under the domination of Spain and the Counter-Reformation, with consequences that in figurative art brought a return to educative and devotional religious painting, to comply with the requirements of the Church. But, paradoxically, some painters abandoned religious painting to take refuge in genre painting, which allowed them to adhere to a realistic vision of life and thus to continue the Lombard pictorial tradition.

Fede Galizia was not a follower of any particular school, but her antecedents are the greatest representatives of the Lombard spirit of realism, such as Moretto da Brescia, Gian Girolamo Savoldo and Vincenzo Campi. She must have turned to Lorenzo Lotto for her introspective portraits, while her theories on the motions of the soul derive from Giovan Paolo Lomazzo. She developed a personal style that nevertheless in her religious pictures reflects the late Mannerism of Emilia and in her portraits the naturalism and interest in psychological analysis typical of Lombardy.

According to a late supposition (Ticozzi 1830), followed by many later 19th-century critics, in the early years of her career Galizia painted miniatures, but nothing is known of these today. In 1590, when the child prodigy was only 12 years old, Lomazzo, the celebrated painter and historian of the period, recorded his admiration for her copies after the best Italian painters. Accomplished equally in painting and in drawing, and considered a most excellent artist, Galizia impressed the critics of the day with her portraits, which were regarded as miraculous for the accuracy of their likeness.

The Jesuit historian Paolo Morigia, who mentioned Galizia in his *Nobiltà di Milano* (1595) as among the most distinguished people of the period, recorded some works by her that are now untraced, including a *Portrait of the Father and Mother of the Painter* and portraits of *Paolo Morigia* (1595), *Maria Giron de Velasca* and *Camilla Ferraro*. Among other documented works, also untraced, were those commissioned from Galizia by the Emperor Rudolph II. Her portraits were never idealised, but resulted from a desire to render reality, the basis of which lay in the studies of physiognomy developed in the 16th century and which revolutionised portraiture. In 1596 she painted another portrait of *Paolo Morigia* (Pinacoteca Ambrosiana, Milan), with an inscription stating that she was 18, from which her date of birth has been deduced. The historian is depicted after having written a poem about the painter and the painting itself. The pensive expression of the sitter is achieved through the reproduction of his characteristic expressions: mouth firmly closed and deep wrinkles on the forehead, lively eyes and the patient expression of someone doing his best to hold a pose; the lenses that reflect the room record the optical experiments typical of northerners; and the volume of the *Nobiltà di Milano*, on the left of the picture, reflects the fashion for portraying scholars, flanked by a still life of heaped books, an inkstand and a manuscript. The portrait of *Pietro Martire Mascheroni* (1622; Ospedale Maggiore, Milan), the benefactor of the Milan hospital, which is documented in the hospital's register of expenses of 1623 with a note of the artist's remuneration, reveals in the ruff the care that Galizia paid to details. The portrait of *Ludovico Settala* (collection Mina Gregori, Florence, repr. Caroli, *Fede Galizia*, 1991, fig.28), with an old inscription on the back that credits it to the painter, is one of the paintings that Galizia executed for the gallery of the noble Milanese family of Settala. A probable self-portrait is the signed *Woman Dressed as Diana* (c.1590s; private collection, Milan, *ibid.*, fig.l of appendix), in which the embroidery on the dress, the jewels and the smooth face resemble other female figures by Fede. A painting such as *St Carlo in Ecstasy* (San Carlo alle Mortelle, Naples), signed and dated (1611) at the bottom, recalls the moving devotional paintings of Giovanni Battista Crespi in the expressions of the saint, and the Lombard tradition for the background landscape and the angel chorus in the upper right of the canvas, while the saint's cope and the ecclesiastical dress are reproduced with the telling detail typical of the artist.

The Leonardesque landscape and Correggesque Emilian accents that Galizia introduced into her religious painting are found in the *Noli me tangere* (Santo Stefano, Milan), a signed painting executed in 1616 for the high altar of the church of the Maddalena in Milan. The realist tendency of Galizia's portraits was sacrificed in her pictures of religious themes to comply with the moral exigencies of the period and to pursue a model of ideal beauty: the figure of Christ, wrapped in a white cloth, is too rounded in bulk and has a mannered pose; the Magdalene, sinuously kneeling and elegantly dressed, flaunts a flowing blond head of hair. The flowers beside Christ, painted with the precision typical of the artist, form a counterbalance to the background landscape.

Perhaps it was feminine sensibility that caused Galizia to identify herself with the heroine Judith and to paint several versions of *Judith with the Head of Holofernes*. Of these, we know of a painting on canvas (Ringling Museum of Art, Sarasota. FL), which bears, inscribed on the knife in Judith's left fist, the signature and date (1596). Galizia's careful execution of the jewels and fabrics in this work is particularly notable – a precision in the rendering of detail that derives from her probable training as a miniature painter with her father. There is also a version on panel (private collection, Milan, *ibid.*, fig.4), datable to c.1620. Another version, executed by Galizia in 1601, is now in the Galleria Borghese, Rome. In this work, echoes of Emilian Late Mannerism are so obvious that until the discovery of the signature and date (1601) the painting was attributed to Lavinia Fontana (q.v.). The style, compared to the Sarasota version, is softer, the jewels and the dress differ subtly, and the whole scene is less disturbing due to the fact that Judith gazes in a different direction in relation to the viewer.

There is little documentation about Galizia, her private life was free from great events, and it is only thanks to 20th-century scholars that she is known as a painter of still lifes. This happened following a discovery, published by Curt

Galizia: *Peaches in a Ceramic Basket*, oil on panel; 30 × 41.5 cm.; Collection Silvano Lodi, Campione d'Italia, Switzerland

Benedict (1938), of a still life signed and dated 1602, the *Tazza with Plums, Pears and a Rose* (ex-Anholt collection, Amsterdam, *ibid.*, fig.5). This is now untraced, but a slightly larger version (private collection, Bassano, *ibid.*, fig.6) is the model for stylistic comparison for other still lifes assigned to the painter. In some cases Galizia's still lifes have been confused with those of Panfilo Nuvolone, a contemporary painter, but closer observation reveals a more sculptural style, more spacious composition and a more meticulous rendering of the modelling. True still lifes, introduced into Italy and Milan at the end of the 16th century, about the time of the one secure still life by Galizia, are few indeed: the *Basket of Fruit* (c.1596; Pinacoteca Ambrosiana) by Caravaggio, which marks the difference from the Flemish still lifes executed in Italy by Jan Bruegel, and the *Peaches on a Dish*, dated 1595, the only still life by the Milanese painter Ambrogio Giovanni Figino. Galizia, in this light, can be seen as an artist of the avant-garde, present at the moment in which objects of nature became autonomous subjects in painting.

Simple, balanced compositions, never excessive, few objects depicted, frontal and slightly raised viewpoint, and dark backgrounds characterise her still lifes: above all not analytic nor herbalistic research, but a sensitive representation of the object. A central tazza, of a type common in Lombardy, with few surrounding elements, is frequently repeated by Galizia: the example from the Anholt collection, like the copy in Bassano, is slightly assymmetrical and includes some perfectly formed fruit, almost unreal, and at the bottom a blackened half pear next to another pear that is half bright red and half yellow, counterbalanced with a slightly faded rose, symbol of the transience of beauty.

The *Glass Tazza with Peaches and Apples* (Museo Civico, Cremona), often copied (French and Co., New York, ex-Vitale Bloch collection; private collection, *ibid.*, fig.12; private collection, Bassano, *ibid.*, fig.13; Silvano Lodi collection, Campione d'Italia, *ibid.*, fig.2 of appendix), for which a probable pendant is *Apples, Basket with Chestnuts and a Rabbit* (Museo Civico, Cremona), also copied (private collection, *ibid.*, fig.60; private collection, Milan, *ibid.*, fig.61), has a more monumental setting, but also is lightened by the glass tazza and the delicate jasmine. It is interesting to note, in the *Wicker Basket with Peaches and Jasmine* (private collection, New York, ex-Sperling collection, *ibid.*, fig.23), the absence of the front part of the supporting plane that usually appears in the still lifes of Galizia and the clean cut of the flower on the lower right, suggesting a late reduction in size of the panel to give greater emphasis to the roundness of the fruit. *Peaches in a Ceramic Basket* (see illustration) can be seen as a *vanitas* because of the three stages of fruit represented: to the left the unripe plums, in the centre the mature peaches and to the right the slightly faded plums. The ceramic basket, another motif that occurs frequently in her still lifes, stands out in the centre against a very dark background.

After a period of new experiments with more casual compositions to which she added irregularly formed vegetables, Galizia recovered the balance that had been characteristic of her still lifes, which were now more interesting due to her increased confidence and experience. The forms, constructed by reflections of light, and the composition, balanced yet varied, made even more expressive and intimate the relationship between the painter and her works. Datable to this last period are the *Tazza with Pears* (ex-Lorenzelli collection, Bergamo, *ibid.*, fig.21), in which Galizia used the corner of a table as a support, and *Grapes and Plums in a Ceramic Basket* (private collection, Italy, *ibid.*, fig.34) and its pendant, *Grapes in a White Ceramic Bowl* (private collection, *ibid.*, fig.35). Versions of the two preceding works are *Grapes and Plums in a Ceramic Basket* (private collection, Switzerland, repr. Caroli, *Notizie da Palazzo Albani*, 1991, fig.8) and *Grapes in a White Ceramic Bowl* (private collection, Switzerland, *ibid.*, fig.9), discovered a few years ago.

Roberto Longhi (1950) was correct when he defined the still lifes of Fede Galizia as "careful" but "sad"; like the artist, they are pious, balanced and silent. The religious fervour of the painter is also evident from the will she made in 1630, probably when there was an outbreak of plague in Milan: she asked that her bequests, almost exclusively paintings, should be given to the religious order of Theatines, to which she was particularly linked, and to her cousin and nephew, her only relatives.

DOMENICA SPADARO and FLAVIO CAROLI

Gardner, Elizabeth

American painter, 1837–1922

Born in Exeter, New Hampshire, 4 October 1837. Graduated from Lasell Female Seminary, Auburndale, Massachusetts, 1856. Taught French at Worcester School of Design and Fine Arts, Massachusetts, late 1850s–early 1860s. Left for Paris with former teacher Imogene Robinson, July 1864; studied privately under J.-B.-A. Tissier and Hugues Merle; took classes at the drawing school, Manufacture Nationale des Gobelins et de la Savonnerie; studied at Académie Julian under Jules Lefebvre and William-Adolphe Bouguereau. Became engaged to Bouguereau, 1879; married him, 1896; he died 1905. Died in Saint-Cloud, France, 28 January 1922.

Principal Exhibitions

Paris Salon: 1868–9, 1872, 1874–5, 1877–97, 1906, 1909 (honourable mention 1879, third-class medal 1887)
Williams and Everett, Boston: 1876
Exposition Universelle, Paris: 1889 (bronze medal)

Selected Writings

"Letter from Paris", *Boston Evening Traveller*, 11 and 26 December 1871, 2 and 17 January, and 17 February 1872
"Paris-notes and news of the Univ. Expo.", *Cincinnati Daily Gazette*, 12 June 1878, p.5, columns 3–4

Bibliography

Clara Erskine Clement and Laurence Hutton, *Artists of the Nineteenth Century*, 2 vols, Boston: Houghton Osgood, 1879
The Portfolio, 1879, p.36
John Denison Champlin, Jr, and Charles C. Perkins, *Cyclopedia of Painters and Painting*, ii, New York: Scribner, 1886
Jean d'Albret, "The masterpiece of Elizabeth Gardner", *Boston Sunday Journal Supplement*, 19 July 1902, p.1
Lida Rose McCabe, "Mme Bouguereau: Pathfinder", *New Times Book Review and Magazine*, 19 February 1922, p.16
Margaret Parsons, "The thwarted romance of a Worcester lady of Civil War days", *Worcester Telegram*, 27 December 1937, section 5, p.8
Charlotte Streifer Rubinstein, *American Women Artists from Early Times to the Present*, Boston: Hall, 1982
Madeleine Fidell-Beaufort, "Elizabeth Gardner Bouguereau: A Parisian artist from New Hampshire", *Archives of American Art Journal*, xxiv/2, 1984, pp.2–9
Evalyn Edwards Milman, *The Letters of Elizabeth Gardner Bouguereau: Pathfinder Artist*, MA thesis, Hunter College, NY, 1985
Lois Marie Fink, *American Art at the Nineteenth-Century Paris Salons*, Washington, DC: Smithsonian Institution Press, and Cambridge: Cambridge University Press, 1990

Letters from Gardner to her family in New England are in the Elizabeth Gardner Papers, Archives of American Art, Smithsonian Institution, Washington, DC (on microfilm).

Elizabeth Gardner's career typifies the aims and aspirations of the generation of American artists who studied figure painting in France after the American Civil War. In Paris she pursued her career with a single-minded energy soon rewarded by official acceptance. With paintings accepted in 25 of the 19th-century Salons, Gardner was one of the most frequent American exhibitors. Her paintings were appreciated and her reputation was such that in 1893 Mrs Potter Palmer asked Gardner to execute murals for the Women's Building at the World's Columbian Exposition in Chicago. By this point in her career the artist felt that she was no longer physically able to accept such a challenge, and Mary Cassatt (q.v.) was awarded the commission instead.

Gardner left important records of her experience as a student and professional artist in France. In letters to her family in Exeter, New Hampshire, she discussed problems and working conditions for women art students. She wrote about the pictures that she was working on for the Salons, as well as her clients. Over the course of her long career, Gardner also acted as an art agent and adviser, helping friends and acquaintances, such as Jonas Gilman Clark, to acquire contemporary paintings. A former French teacher, Gardner had mastered the language, which facilitated her assimilation and acceptance by French academic artists and art dealers. Most of Gardner's

Gardner : *Ne bougez-pas (He Careth)*, *c.*1883; Philbrook Museum of Art, Laura A. Clubb Collection, Tulsa

work is now in private hands. The best records of it are the black-and-white photographs taken at the time the paintings were exhibited at the Salon. These photographs cannot, however, provide an accurate indication of the quality and colour of her highly finished paintings. She produced approximately four paintings a year during a career spanning approximately 30 years.

Gardner arrived in Paris in July 1864 accompanied by Imogene Robinson, her former teacher from Lasell, who had been an art student in Düsseldorf in 1856. They both had commissions to copy paintings in the Louvre and Musée du Luxembourg. Copy registers in the Louvre archives indicate that Gardner worked on diverse kinds of painting, from historical and mythological subjects to marine scenes, as well as portraits by a variety of artists from different periods. By the autumn of 1864 Gardner was also attending private classes in the studio of Jean-Baptiste-Ange Tissier, where she had access to live models four days a week. Her letters home in 1865 mention that she was working with other women who hired their own models and studied together in the evenings. In the Salon catalogue of 1868 she listed artist Hugues Merle as her teacher; in 1875 Merle's name was followed by that of Jules Lefebvre; William-Adolphe Bouguereau joined the list in 1877. It was Bouguereau's style that she preferred, and this was well before their engagement and marriage. Gardner sought access to life-drawing classes wherever she could find them. In 1873 she requested permission from the Paris Préfecture de Police to wear men's clothing so that she could attend the all-male classes at the Gobelins school. Although permission was granted, neither the length and nature of her studies there nor the classes she attended at an art school in the Jardin des Plantes – or even at the Académie Julian – are recorded.

Poetry and other literary sources frequently inspired Gardner, who portrayed heroines from antiquity and depicted mythological figures as well as anonymous women in Classical dress, as seen in an historical genre work such as *Dove Fanciers* (1883; Haussner's Restaurant, Baltimore). In the late 1870s and early 1880s several of Gardner's heroines were inspired by the American poets Henry Wadsworth Longfellow and John Greenleaf Whittier. She also depicted biblical subjects such as *David the Shepherd* (1895; National Museum of Women in the Arts, Washington, DC). Many of Gardner's paintings portray idealised subjects with single figures of peasant women drawing water or involved in farmyard activities. The theme of childhood showing peasant mothers or big sisters occupied with younger children, as in *Ne bougez-pas*, also known as *He Careth* (c.1883; see illustration), frequently appears, as do compositions depicting well-mannered children playing together out of doors, as in *Dans le bois* or *Bird's Nest* (1889; Norton Museum, Palm Beach), *Judgement of Paris* (1893; Lasell Junior College, Newton, MA) and *Crossing the Brook* (c.1894; Exeter Historical Society, NH).

Contemporary Salon critics praised Gardner's work for its freshness, its poetic feeling, its true sentiment and its careful imitation of nature. Her compositions were described as being graceful; her colour was judged to be charming, tender and rich. The finish of her pictures was presented as proof of her industry, labour and earnestness. Most of Gardner's paintings

appear to have found buyers easily. The French dealer Goupil began to acquire her Salon pictures during the 1870s, and her work was sold by Goupil's associates, Knoedler's Gallery, in New York. In Boston her work was handled by the dealers Noyes and Blakeslee, and Williams and Everett. Collectors from the American Midwest were among her most faithful clients.

MADELEINE FIDELL-BEAUFORT

See also Training and Professionalism survey 10

Garthwaite, Anna Maria
British textile designer, 1690–1763

Born in Grantham, Lincolnshire, 14 March 1690, to the Revd Ephraim Garthwaite and his wife Rejoyce Hansted; she was the second of three daughters. Moved to Spitalfields, London, with her sister Mary, 1730. Died in London, 1763.

Bibliography
Malachy Postlethwayt, *Universal Dictionary of Trade and Commerce*, 2nd edition, London, 1757 (entry on engraving)

Peter Thornton, *Baroque and Rococo Silks*, London: Faber, and New York: Taplinger, 1965

Natalie Rothstein, "Planning a careless air: Rococo in English silk design", *Country Life*, clxxvi, 30 August 1984, pp.563–5

—, *Silk Designs of the Eighteenth Century in the Collection of the Victoria and Albert Museum, London*, London: Thames and Hudson, and Boston: Little Brown, 1990

Deborah Kraak, "18th-century English landscape architecture and floral silk design", *CIETA Bulletin*, no.72, 1994, pp.70–79

By the 18th century fashion was international, and for over 30 years the designs of Anna Maria Garthwaite reveal its progress. The few facts known about her family, who were not poor, cannot explain why she should have become a silk designer – and an accomplished one. She was certainly talented artistically. A very fine paper-cut dated 1707 with her name on it recently came to light and was acquired by the Victoria and Albert Museum, London. The technical expertise needed to design a woven fabric successfully is not something that she could have picked up without tuition. Yet few of the silks woven from her designs have had more than minor alterations.

Her first designs in the 1720s include a group annotated "In York, before I came to London", which suggests that after her father's death in 1719 she joined her sister Mary, married to the Revd Robert Danny, rector of Spofforth in Yorkshire. After Danny's death in March 1729/30, the sisters moved to London, possibly to live with an aunt, but in a house in the heart of Spitalfields, surrounded by Huguenot immigrants.

Garthwaite's earliest designs show the influence of other techniques, especially embroidery and paper-cutting. She quickly adopted the current fashionable "lace pattern" styles and then the revolution in woven design that sought to replace flat surface effects in rich gold, silver and coloured silks with a totally different aim: three-dimensional effects. Although this

Mr Vanteir. June 16. 1744

Garthwaite: Design for woven silk, 1744; pen and watercolour on paper; Victoria and Albert Museum, London

startling change derived from the work of several Lyon designers, it was Garthwaite who was credited by Postlethwayt with introducing the "principles of painting into the loom". She possessed a collection of "Patterns by Different Hands" as well as a set of "French Patterns". Between 1730 and 1734 the transformation in style may be seen through the medium of her designs and in 1735 the introduction of *points rentrées* from the Lyon designer Jean Revel. She owned a key design by him dated 1735 and immediately adopted his method, by which colours were dovetailed, giving an uncanny illusion of three-dimensional form. The scale of designs grew ever larger until 1742, when there was another abrupt change.

Garthwaite's work was then divided into two books of designs for most years, all dated, with the type of silk given, as well as the name of the weaver and/or mercer who had bought the design. Most of her customers were the leading mercers and weavers of their day, selling their silks to the most fashionable in London. She prepared about 80 patterns every year, revealing changes season by season. All are for dress silks – most furnishing silks came from Italy. The cut of dress changed fairly slowly at this time, while the patterns on the silk itself changed rapidly. Garthwaite seems to have sold the point-paper with which the weaver could enter his drawloom, while retaining a fair copy for herself. The latter are now in the Victoria and Albert Museum; most were acquired in 1868 from a "Mr Sheriff of Streatham"; those for 1743 and half of 1744 were bought with the help of a public subscription in 1971. Designs for 1746 and 1750 are still missing.

Garthwaite appears to have been a pioneer in introducing botanically accurate flowers into her designs, a phase that lasted from 1742 to 1747. In 1743 and 1744 she even gave the names of the most important plants or flowers, and sometimes drew their roots. From 1743 her work epitomises English Rococo, with Hogarth's *Line of Beauty* first appearing in designs of October and November 1743. His *Industrious and Idle Apprentices* were, of course, Spitalfields weavers (perhaps he had seen her designs or at least silks woven from them?). Interest in natural history, natural form, flowers and gardens was an important aspect of this period. From about 1742 until the early 1750s English silk design developed independently from that of France. The industry itself was growing and English silks were being exported to English markets in northern Europe and, above all, to the American colonies. Thus, there are Garthwaite silks with an 18th-century provenance in Norway, Denmark and Boston, Massachusetts.

Botanical interest faded in the late 1740s. Instead, the grounds of silks were enriched with elaborate, self-coloured patterns. Garthwaite's last large-scale designs were for damasks – whose repeat of 100 cm. or more could take up the whole of a sack-back dress. She also drew many small warp-patterned designs for "tobines", fashionable in the early 1750s. The designs from 1754 to 1756 are her last. She died in 1763. Her name was preserved until the early 19th century as a trademark for a brand of point-paper. She was then virtually forgotten until the 20th century.

N. K. A. ROTHSTEIN

Garzoni, Giovanna
Italian painter, 1600–1670

Born 1600, probably in Ascoli Piceno, Marche, to Giacomo Garzoni and Isabetta Gaia, who came from a family of artists of Venetian origin. In Venice c.1615–30, perhaps not continuously. In Naples, in the service of the Spanish viceroy, the Duque de Alcalá, 1630. In Turin, in the service of Cristina of France, wife of Vittorio Amedeo I, Duke of Savoy, 1632–7. In Florence, working for the Medici, 1642 and c.1646–51. Settled in Rome permanently, 1651. Made a will in 1666, bequeathing her estate to the painters' guild in Rome, the Accademia di San Luca, on condition that they erect her tomb in their church, SS Luca e Martino. Died in Rome between 10 and 15 February 1670 (monument designed by Mattia de' Rossi, with portrait and inscription by Giuseppe Ghezzi of Ascoli, erected in SS Luca e Martino, 1698).

Bibliography
Lione Pascoli, *Vite de' pittori, scultori et architetti moderni*, 2 vols, Rome: Antonio de' Rossi, 1730–36; ed. Alessandro Marabottini, Perugia: Electa Umbri, 1992

La natura morta italiana, exh. cat., Palazzo Reale, Naples, 1964

Angela Cipriani, "Giovanna Garzoni miniatrice", *Ricerche di Storia dell'Arte*, i, 1976, pp.241–54

Women Artists, 1550–1950, exh. cat., Los Angeles County Museum of Art, and elsewhere, 1976

Italian Still-Life Paintings from Three Centuries, exh. cat., Centro Di, New York, and elsewhere, 1983

Sylvia Meloni, "Giovanna Garzoni miniatora medicea", *FMR*, no.15, 1983, pp.77–96

Immagini anatomiche e naturalistiche nei disegni degli Uffizi sec. XVI e XVII, exh. cat., Galleria degli Uffizi, Florence, 1984

Natura morta italiana/Italienische Stillebenmalerei aus drei Jahrhunderten: Sammlung Silvano Lodi/Italian Still-Life Painting from Three Centuries: The Silvano Lodi Collection/Tre secoli di natura morta italiano: La raccolta Silvano Lodi, exh. cat., Alte Pinakothek, Munich, and elsewhere, 1984

Marco Rosci, "Giovanna Garzoni dal Palazzo Reale di Torino a Superga", *Scritte di storia dell'arte in onore di Federico Zeri*, ii, Milan, 1984, pp.565–7

Luigi Salerno, *La natura morta italiana, 1560–1805/Still Life Painting in Italy, 1560–1805*, Rome: Bozzi, 1984

Silvia Meloni, "The gentle genre: Giovanna Garzoni", *FMR America*, no.11, 1985, pp.105–24

Il seicento fiorentino: Arte a Firenze da Ferdinando I a Cosimo III, exh. cat., 3 vols, Palazzo Strozzi, Florence, 1986

Francesco Porzio, ed., *La natura morta in Italia*, 2 vols, Milan: Electa, 1989

Gerardo Casale, *Giovanna Garzoni, "Insigne miniatrice", 1600–1670*, Milan: Jandi Sapi, 1991 (contains extensive bibliography)

Although the Baroque artist Giovanna Garzoni produced religious, mythological and allegorical paintings in her early years (examples of the latter genres all untraced), from the 1640s she specialised in still life. Little is known of her early artistic training; it is possible that she began her apprenticeship with her maternal uncle, Pietro Gaia, a painter and engraver in her home town of Ascoli Piceno. By c.1620 Garzoni had contributed a *St Andrew* (Accademia, Venice) to a series of the *Apostles* painted for the church of the Ospedale degli Incurabili in Venice, an important commission that suggests that she had been studying there with an influential master,

Garzoni: *Still Life with Artichokes*, c.1650–62; Galleria Palatina, Palazzo Pitti, Florence

perhaps even Jacopo Negretti, known as Palma il Giovane, whose style permeates the *St Andrew*. Soon afterwards, however, Garzoni abandoned the monumental style and rich colourism of the Venetian manner and began to work on an intimate scale, using water-based paint on parchment.

The *Portrait of a Gentleman* (Stichting Historische Verzamelingen van het Huis Oranje-Nassau, The Hague), signed and dated 1625, Venice, on the reverse, shows Garzoni's delicate stippled technique that, combined with carefully handled gradations of colour, results in an extremely refined and luminous surface. Garzoni's early interest in decorative design and naturalistic motifs can be seen in a book of calligraphic studies (Biblioteca Sarti, Rome), in which she illuminates a capital letter with fruit, flowers, birds and insects. The drawing is executed with graceful, flowing lines, subtle colouration and a fine pointillist technique, all characteristic of her mature style.

Garzoni never married; she pursued her artistic career with intensity, enjoying a life of steady work and constant success. In the few lines devoted to her in the *Vite* (1730–36) Lione Pascoli comments on Garzoni's productivity, and on the fact that she sold her works "for whatever price she wished", counting among her patrons the Medici in Florence and the

powerful Barberini family in Rome. In 1632, after a year in Naples in the service of the Spanish viceroy, Garzoni was persuaded by Cristina of France, Duchess of Savoy, to move to Turin, where she came into contact with Netherlandish and northern Italian paintings; the portrait of *Vittorio Amedeo, Duke of Savoy* (Uffizi, Florence) shows Garzoni's preoccupation with the naturalism and meticulous attention to detail of the northern schools, as well as her knowledge of the English portrait tradition.

Between 1646 and 1651 Garzoni resided in Florence. To these years dates the quaint portrait of a *Lap Dog with Biscuits and a Cup* (Galleria Palatina, Palazzo Pitti, Florence), commissioned by Vittoria della Rovere, wife of Grand Duke Ferdinand II de' Medici, a work that attests to Garzoni's familiarity with Dutch painters. For her Florentine patrons she also produced paintings on the popular theme of a vase of flowers; both casual arrangements set in a simple glass vase (*Vase with Tulips and Hyacinths*; Uffizi), in the tradition of the Roman followers of Caravaggio, and much more elaborate bouquets, decorated with butterflies, insects and exotic shells (*Vase with Various Flowers Resting on a Marble Ledge, with a Shell on Either Side and Several Butterflies Above*; Gabinetto Disegni e Stampi degli Uffizi, Florence), reminiscent of compositions by the

Dutch painter Ambrosius Bosschaert. In 1651 Garzoni moved to Rome, well-known, wealthy and closely connected with the Accademia di San Luca (opinions vary as to whether she had actually been elected to the Academy, although she did leave her estate to it and was buried in its church; cf. Casale 1991, p.11, with Harris in Los Angeles 1976, p.135).

Garzoni is best known today for the series of 20 small tempera still lifes of fruit and vegetables that she completed for Ferdinand II de' Medici between c.1650 and 1662 (all Galleria Palatina). The illustration of agrarian bounty was a traditional theme for the decoration of country villas, and Garzoni's elegant and refined interpretation of such ordinary subjects was well suited to her aristocratic patrons. *Dish with Plums, Jasmine and Walnuts* shows the characteristic composition of a central dish of fruit, here resting on a stippled, rocklike surface. In the front of the picture plane, to add interest to the composition, the artist introduces another single flower, or split fruit, or sometimes a bird or insect. In this example, jasmine and morning glory are intertwined with the delicately coloured plums, while a cracked walnut decorates the foreground. The composition is sophisticated and deceptively simple. Garzoni skilfully modulates shapes, textures and colours to evoke the sense of smell and touch, as well as vision – a preoccupation with the senses that was characteristic of 17th-century Dutch and Flemish art. The works of such Lombard painters as Fede Galizia (q.v.) and Panfilo Nuvolone, which Garzoni had seen in Turin, were also a strong influence. Galizia's small still lifes of, for example, a dish of peaches, centrally placed and set on a shallow stage, show a similar concern with representing reality through reference to the senses.

Another important model for Garzoni were the natural science illustrations by the Veronese artist Jacopo Ligozzi, who around 1576 was working in Florence for Francesco I de' Medici. Ligozzi's elegant and precise tempera drawings exhibited a refinement and formal clarity evident in Garzoni's later still lifes and botanical drawings; in fact, several of Garzoni's works, including *Still Life with Birds and Fruit* (Cleveland Museum of Art), were thought to be by Ligozzi until Mina Gregori corrected the misattribution (Gregori in Naples 1964, p.28). Although Garzoni was predisposed early on to naturalism and close observation, with the possible exception of a herbal (c.1650–55; Dumbarton Oaks, Washington, DC) containing 49 highly naturalistic botanical drawings, her works do not strictly fit the category of scientific illustration (for a discussion of the herbal, see Paola Lanzara in Casale 1991, pp.34–44). *Hyacinth Plant with Four Cherries, a Lizard and an Artichoke* (Uffizi), one of a series of four botanical studies dating to the end of the 1640s, exemplifies Garzoni's particular talent of combining naturalistic observation with a strong sense of the decorative and the aesthetic. The plant is drawn in minute detail, botanically accurate with flower, stem, bulb and roots, but the combination of the four subjects on the page is purely aesthetic. There is no natural correlation between them; they are a study in shapes and textures. A large fly is posed on the cut stem of the artichoke – reminiscent of Dutch still lifes – and the unnatural position of the lizard's legs suggests that it has been drawn not from life, but from a dead specimen.

Dish with an Open Pomegranate, a Grasshopper, a Snail and Two Chestnuts (Galleria Palatina) shows a variation on the theme that unites the 20 temperas cited above, and further illustrates Garzoni's interest in showing the variety of the natural world in all its precise detail, but only in so far as it suited her artistic aims. With its grainy-textured terrain continued into the background, the unnaturally large grasshopper and the subtly modulated colour contained within crisp outlines, the little picture vibrates with a living energy; the effect is charming and poetic, a fantasy still life, despite microscopic attention to detail. The awkward perspective, which adds to the abstract quality of the picture, may be due to Garzoni's use of the convex mirror, a standard artist's aid of the time. The *Old Man of Artimino* (?1648–9; Galleria Palatina) shows Garzoni's idiosyncratic use of perspective and proportion, as well as her consistently fine technique.

ELIZABETH MULLEY

Gasc, Anna Rosina de *see* Lisiewska

Geddes, Margaret *see* Carpenter

Geddes, Wilhelmina (Margaret)
Irish stained glass and graphic artist, 1887–1955

Born in Drumreilly, Co. Leitrim, 25 May 1887. Studied at Belfast Municipal Technical Institute, c.1901–13; Metropolitan School of Art, Dublin, c.1911–12. Joined An Túr Gloine (Tower of Glass), Dublin, 1912; subsequently worked in Dublin and Belfast. Lived in Belfast, 1922–5. Worked independently in London, based at the Glass House, Fulham, from 1925; taught the technique of stained glass to Evie Hone (q.v.). Member, Belfast Art Society, 1907–10 and 1925–8; Guild of Irish Art Workers, 1917; Ulster Academy, 1932. Died in London, 10 August 1955.

Principal Exhibitions
Arts and Crafts Society of Ireland, Dublin: 1910, 1917, 1921, 1925
Royal Hibernian Academy, Dublin: 1913–14, 1916, 1930
Whitechapel Gallery, London: 1913 (*Irish Art*)
British Empire Exhibition, Wembley, London: 1914
Musée du Louvre, Paris: 1914 (*Arts décoratifs de Grande Bretagne et d'Irlande*)
Royal Dublin Society Art and Industries Show: 1921
Galerie Barbazanges, Paris: 1922 (*L'Art irlandais*)
John Magee's Gallery, Belfast: 1924 (with Rosamond Praeger)
Arts and Crafts Exhibition Society, England: from 1926
Design and Industries Association, Leipzig: 1927
Society of Scottish Artists, Edinburgh: 1929

Selected Writings
"Making stained glass windows", *Belfast News-letter*, 25 September 1930

Bibliography

Stephen Gwynn, "The art of Miss W. M. Geddes", *The Studio*, lxxxiv, 1922, pp.208–13

Charles J. Connick, "Modern glass: A review", *International Studio*, lxxx, October 1924, pp.40–52

Bernard Rackham, "Stained glass windows by Miss W. M. Geddes", *The Studio*, xcviii, 1929, pp.682–3

Joan Howson, "Obituary", *Journal of the British Society of Master Glass Painters*, xii/1, 1955–6, pp.68–70

Anthea Callen, *Angel in the Studio: Women in the Arts and Crafts Movement, 1870–1914*, London: Astragal, 1979; as *Women Artists of the Arts and Crafts Movement, 1870–1914*, New York: Pantheon, 1979

Nicola Gordon Bowe, "Wilhelmina Geddes: Ireland's extraordinary artist", *Quarterly of the Stained Glass Association of America*, lxxvi, Spring 1981, pp.41–3

——, *Irish Stained Glass*, Dublin and Belfast: Arts Councils of Ireland, 1983 (text and fully documented slide pack)

The Dublin Arts and Crafts Movement, 1880–1930, exh. cat., Edinburgh College of Art, 1985

Women Artists of the Arts and Crafts Movement, exh. cat., William Morris Gallery, Walthamstow, 1985

Nicola Gordon Bowe, "Cats are my favourite animals: Wilhelmina Geddes (1887–1955)", *New Perspectives: Studies in Art History in Honour of Anne Crookshank*, ed. Jane Fenlon and others, Dublin: Irish Academic Press, 1987, pp.207–18

——, "Women and the Arts and Crafts revival in Ireland, c.1886–1930", *Irish Women Artists from the Eighteenth Century to the Present Day*, exh. cat., National Gallery of Ireland, Dublin, and elsewhere, 1987, pp.22–7

——, "Wilhelmina Geddes", *Irish Arts Review*, iv/3, Autumn 1987, pp.53–9

Centenary Exhibition of Wilhelmina Geddes, exh. cat., Arts Council of Northern Ireland, Belfast, 1987

Nicola Gordon Bowe, "Wilhelmina Geddes, 1887–1955: Her life and work – a reappraisal", *Journal of Stained Glass*, xviii, 1988, pp.275–301

——, "Wilhelmina Geddes, Harry Clarke and their part in the Arts and Crafts movement in Ireland", *Journal of Decorative and Propaganda Arts*, no.8, Spring 1988, pp.58–79

Nicola Gordon Bowe, David Caron and Michael Wynne, *Gazetteer of Irish Stained Glass*, Dublin: Irish Academic Press, 1988

Nicola Gordon Bowe, "Two early twentieth century Irish Arts and Crafts workshops in context: An Túr Gloine and the Dun Emer Guild and Industries", *Journal of Design History*, ii, 1989, pp.193–206

Katherine Shaw, *Wilhelmina Geddes and Her Laleham Window*, BA thesis, West Glamorgan Institute of Higher Education, 1989

Fiona Ciaran, *Stained Glass in Canterbury, New Zealand, 1860–1988*, PhD dissertation, University of Canterbury, Christchurch, 1992

Nicola Gordon Bowe, "Wilhelmina Geddes (1887–1955): Stained glass designer", *Women Designing: Redefining Design in Britain Between the Wars*, exh. cat., University of Brighton Gallery, 1994, pp.64–70

Shirley Anne Brown, "Wilhelmina Geddes' Ottawa window", *Irish Arts Review* 1994, ix, pp.180–88

When Wilhelmina Geddes was 32, her stained-glass war memorial for the Duke of Connaught, erected in St Bartholomew's, Ottawa, after exhibition in Dublin and London, assured her of an "enviable position among modern artists". Charles Connick, the American stained-glass artist and writer, admired "the spiritual beauty, the poetry and the youthful audacity wrought into ... glass, lead and iron". Geddes's unstinting courage, "outstanding artistry and crafts-manship", "strong expressive drawing", sober richness of colour and "power of simplifying without loss of meaning" were qualities that led her contemporaries to see in her work "a revival of the mediaeval genius".

Geddes had a rare ability to synthesise the earthy, smouldering colours and textures she selected in her glass with a uniquely loose, painterly technique and a direct, deeply spiritual integrity of vision. This was all the more remarkable when applied to the demanding architectural context and scale of the traditionally male-oriented craft of stained glass. Her work was consistently figurative throughout her career. She was an avid and sharply intelligent reader (and writer), who easily absorbed the influences of Archaic, Classical, Romanesque and Assyrian sculpture, progressive black-and-white illustration and northern European medieval stained glass. Providentially, the glowing watercolour *Cinderella Dressing the Ugly Sister* (1910; Hugh Lane Municipal Gallery of Modern Art, Dublin) was brought to the attention of Sarah Purser (q.v.), who had set up a co-operative stained-glass workshop, An Túr Gloine, in Dublin in 1903 and who was to become her lifelong mentor. Founded along progressive Arts and Crafts lines, its aim was to counter inferior foreign imports and to provide a base for Irish artists trained in the newly established stained-glass classes at the Dublin School of Art to work in a fresh, original, evocatively Irish mode in the spirit of the Celtic Revival. The finest materials were to be an intrinsic aspect of style, and commissions were to be undertaken throughout by one artist, according to their own interpretation but in a modern idiom.

Geddes's first stained glass essay for Purser, the anguished El Greco-like triptych, *St Colman MacDuagh* (1911–12; Hugh Lane Municipal Gallery of Modern Art), immediately revealed her aptitude for the medium. In 1912 her first window, the *Angel of Resurrection* (St Ninidh's, Inishmacsaint, Co. Fermanagh), showed that she could sustain dramatic compositions on a large scale, while integrating juxtapositions of inventive decorative detail to enhance the play of light so that it seemed trapped mysteriously within the surface of the glass. Her tightly draped figures, attenuated, lilting and intent, seem lost in meditation, displaying her "gift for the simple rendering of essential action"; this, whether in glass, linocut or pen-and-ink illustration.

The series of Archangel windows, *St Michael* (1918; St Anne's, Dawson Street, Dublin), *St Michael the Archangel and Soldier Saints* (1919; St Bartholomew's, Ottawa) and *SS Michael, Gabriel and Raphael* (1920; destroyed; repr. Bowe in *Irish Arts Review* 1987, p.54) for All Saints', Blackrock, Dublin, mark Geddes's early artistic maturity. Her instinctive choice and use of both glass and leadlines, her expressionist brushwork and consummate understanding of the limitations and potential of the stained-glass technique were and still are rare. The lithe, almost defiant figures, frozen in angular poses in poignant variations of scale, and the unusual colour combinations give these windows an original, dramatic intensity. The small figures in glowing colours meandering through a stage-set forest in the rich tapestry window, the *Leaves of the Tree Were for the Healing of the Nations* (1920; St John's, Malone Road, Belfast), give only a hint of the metamorphosis evident in her next work, the monumental *Crucifixion* window (1922; St Luke's, Wallsend-on-Tyne), where the full-scale figures seem intent on bursting their architectural confines. In the *SS Patrick and Columba* window (1923; Church of Ireland, Larne, Co.

Geddes: *Rhoda Opening the Door to St Peter*, 1934; Ulster Museum, Belfast

Antrim) the rough-hewn saints are barely contained in each light, as they persevere on their physically tough and spiritually demanding missions.

In 1922 Geddes formally left An Túr, dogged by emotional and artistic misgivings and undermined in health. The ensuing period of self-doubt is reflected in the contortions and introspection of her figures, whether in book illustrations (Harrap's *One Act Plays of Today*, 1924, 1926 and 1927; Harrap's *Essays of Today*, 1923; Bruce Graeme's *The Return of Blackshirt*, 1927) or in linocut portraits of her family and cat. She continued to exhibit with the Arts and Crafts Society of Ireland, for which she designed a fiercely graphic cover, *The Saint* (repr. Bowe in *Irish Arts Review* 1987, p.58), and more occasionally elsewhere, with a joint show in Belfast with Rosamond Praeger, her other mentor and old family friend, of 33 items – drawings, book illustrations, linocut portrait studies, designs for windows, stained glass and embroidered panels.

Geddes left Ireland for good in 1925 and rented a studio in the purpose-built Glass House in Fulham. Here, a growing band of devotees saw the painstakingly slow process of her windows before they were dispatched for installation. She abandoned the *St Brendan* window, the design for which was exhibited in the Basilica of the British Empire Exhibition at Wembley, for completion by her Dublin An Túr colleagues. Before she left, she had continued to design small wooden-framed panels for her sister to embroider; she would make them in glass and they would exhibit together. A version of one of these, somewhat Cubist in treatment, *Rhoda Opening the Door to St Peter* (1934; see illustration), is one of her few stained-glass cabinet panels to have survived. The watercolour designs (private collections, *ibid.*, p.57) demonstrate what a loss they are; subjects included Dr Johnson and Boswell, the Scottish Border Ballads and Charles Lamb's *Essays of Elia*. In 1930 the Ulster Museum commissioned a staircase window illustrating the ancient legend of the *Children of Lir* (1930; in storage, repr. Michael Wynne, *Irish Stained Glass*, Dublin: Eason, 1977, back cover), which consisted of a series of enchanting and dramatic narrative panels. Geddes took with her to London several Ulster commissions, including a second window for Larne, *Christ with Martha and Mary* (1927), where large pieces of ruby, purple and blue glass seem to resonate and the women's gesturing profiles introduce an arresting new element in the iconography of stained glass. Sadly, her four visionary windows of 1929 for Rosemary Street Presbyterian Church, Belfast, were destroyed in 1944.

Geddes's first English window, small but monumental and executed in flaming hues, portrayed a titanic *St Christopher* with a crew-cut St Cecilia flexing her forearms and red-legginged St Hubert looming large above the angling organist commemorated, wearing amber oilskins (1926; All Saints', Laleham, Middlesex). It recalls Raphael's Cartoons (Victoria and Albert Museum, London) and works by Michelangelo in its monumentality, but so disturbed the congregation that it was removed to the back of the church. Critics were stunned by the "virile, almost alarming strength" in Geddes's work, reflecting "the religion of power and fighting", and admired her "fine, bold drawing, afraid of nothing, even brutal at times".

In the 1930s, still varying the scale of her figures within a window and lightly inscribing seemingly incidental notes around the sketched-in, masklike features, Geddes would contrast growing areas of grisaille with gloriously orchestrated gold, pinks, purples, greens and yellows, as in the *Joseph of Arimathea* window (1933; Otterden Place Church, Kent). In *St Francis of Assisi Preaching to the Birds* (1930; Northchapel parish church, near Petworth, Sussex) the little figures seem to float, while in *Psalm 100* (1934; Egremont United Reform Church, Wallasey) the small figures appear suspended against a fishing net that covers the surface of the window.

Geddes was unstinting in her pursuit and acceptance of only the "right" piece of glass for each window. Such dedication cost her her health, particularly in the most demanding of all her commissions, the huge *Te Deum* rose window commissioned by the British Army and Royal Air Force to commemorate the King of the Belgians, finally erected in 1938 in the rebuilt cathedral of St Martin, Ypres. At the end of her life, her sight almost gone but her artistic and technical powers unim-

paired, her work was imbued with an elemental gentleness, warmth and deeply moving spiritual quality, seen in the *Virgin and Child* (1952; All Hallows', Greenford, Middlesex) and *St Elizabeth, the Virgin and St Mildred* (1954; St Mildred's, Lee, Kent). It is surely only because Geddes worked in the inaccessible and breakable medium of stained glass that her extraordinary artistic achievement is so little known.

NICOLA GORDON BOWE

Gengembre, Sophie *see* Anderson

Gentileschi, Artemisia
Italian painter, 1593–1652/3

Born in Rome, 8 July 1593, to the painter Orazio Gentileschi and Prudentia Montone. In March 1612 Orazio sued the painter Agostino Tasso for the rape of his daughter, initiating a seven-month trial; Artemisia was tortured to verify her testimony; case dismissed October 1612. Married Florentine painter Pietro Antonio di Vincenzo Stiattesi in Rome, 29 November 1612; at least four children, all born in Florence, two sons, born 1613 and 1615, two daughters, born 1617 and 1618; separated from husband c.1626. Member of the Accademia del Disegno, Florence, by 19 July 1616; remained in Florence until February 1620. In Rome, 1620, 1622 and 1624–6; visited Venice by 1627. In Naples by August 1630; left November 1637. In England, in the service of Queen Henrietta Maria, by December 1639. Subsequently in Naples. Died 1652/3.

Bibliography

Giovanni Baglione, *Le vite de' pittori, scultori et architetti dal Pontificato di Gregorio XIII del 1572 in fino a' tempi di Papa Urbano Ottavo nel 1642*, Rome: Fei, 1642; reprinted Bologna: Forni, 1975–6 (life of Orazio Gentileschi)

Joachim von Sandrart, *L'Accademia todesca della architectura, scultura e pittura: Oder Teutsche Academie der edlen Bau-, Bild- und Mahlerey-künste*, 2 vols, Nuremberg, 1675–9; ed. A.R. Peltzer, Munich, 1925; reprinted Farnborough: Gregg, 1971

Filippo Baldinucci, *Notizie de' professori del disegno da Cimabue in qua*, Florence, 1681–1728; reprinted Florence, 1751, and in *Opere di Filippo Baldinucci*, 14 vols, Milan, 1808–12

Giovanni Battista Passeri, *Vite de' pittori, scultori ed architetti che anno lavorato in Roma: Morti dal 1641 fino al 1673*, Rome, 1772; reprinted in *Die Künstlerbiographien von Giovanni Battista Passeri*, ed. Jacob Hess, Leipzig and Vienna, 1934

Roberto Longhi, "Gentileschi padre e figlia", *L'Arte*, xix, 1916, pp.245–314; reprinted in *Scritti giovannili, 1912–1922*, i, Florence: Sansoni, 1961, pp.219–83

Vincenzo Ruffo, "La Galleria Ruffo (appendice)", *Bollettino d'Arte*, xii, 1919, pp.43–56

R. Ward Bissell, "Artemisia Gentileschi: A new documented chronology", *Art Bulletin*, l, 1968, pp.153–68

Eva Menzio, *Artemisia Gentileschi/Agostino Tassi: Atti di un processo per stupro*, Edizione delle Donne, xxxvi, Milan, 1981

Roberto Fuda, "Un'inedita lettera di Artemisia Gentileschi a Ferdinando II de' Medici", *Rivista d'Arte*, xli, 1989, pp.167–71

Mary D. Garrard, *Artemisia Gentileschi: The Image of the Female Hero in Italian Baroque Art*, Princeton: Princeton University Press, 1989

Mina Gregori, "Una nota per Artemisia Gentileschi", *Paragone*, xli/487, 1990, pp.104–6

Artemisia, exh. cat., Casa Buonarroti, Florence, 1991; review by John Spike, *Burlington Magazine*, cxxxiii, 1991, pp.732–4

Susanna Stolzenwald, *Artemisia Gentileschi: Bindung und Befreiung in Leben und Werk einer Malerin*, Stuttgart and Zürich: Belser, 1991

Elizabeth Cropper, "Artemisia Gentileschi, La 'Pittora'", *Barocco al Femminile*, ed. G. Calvi, Rome: Laterza, 1992, pp.191–218

——, "New documents for Artemisia Gentileschi's life in Florence", *Burlington Magazine*, cxxxv, 1993, pp.760–61

Mary D. Garrard, "Artemisia Gentileschi's 'Corisca and the Satyr'", *Burlington Magazine*, cxxxv, 1993, pp.34–8

Artemisia Gentileschi was born in Rome. Her father was the Pisan painter Orazio Gentileschi, who had married a Roman woman, Prudentia Montone. Artemisia was the oldest of three surviving children, but as the only girl it was unlikely that she would become her father's artistic heir. The death of her mother in 1605 changed her life completely. Left alone with her younger brothers, she could no longer rely on the normal protection of family life. Her father seems to have been a solitary man, utterly devoted to his work, and the Gentileschi moved house often in the artists' neighbourhood around the Piazza della Trinità and the Via Margutta. Orazio's most important artistic relationship was with Caravaggio, whose practice of working directly from the model had a profound impact on Orazio's more ideally mannered style, and at the very moment when Artemisia was beginning to take a serious interest in painting.

In 1612 Orazio reported to the Grand Duchess of Tuscany that Artemisia had learned so much in three years that she had no equal. Such recognition, and the public life of a successful painter, presented unusual problems for an unmarried woman whose personal honour was vested in her virginity. When her mother died Artemisia was 12, and could normally have looked forward to contracting a marriage in three or four years. Meanwhile, Orazio taught her to paint. He was able to do this because he worked in the studio at home. In 1610 (or possibly in the early months of 1611, if like many Tuscans the Gentileschi kept to the calendar *ab incarnatione* even in Rome), after working beside her father for several years, Artemisia completed her first known masterpiece, *Susanna and the Elders* (see illustration).

Artemisia was 17, and reaching the age when marriage was imperative. At this delicate moment Orazio was embarking on fresco commissions on the Quirinal in collaboration with Agostino Tassi. He was out much of the time, leaving Artemisia without a chaperone. In 1611 Orazio tried to solve this problem by proposing to a woman called Tuzia, who lived opposite, that the two households move into new quarters together. His other proposal that Artemisia become a nun was completely unsuccessful. It was soon after the move, while Artemisia was supposedly under Tuzia's supervision, that she was raped by her father's colleague Agostino Tassi.

Much about Orazio's charges against Tassi almost a year later in 1612 can be understood in terms of legal convention. The suit was delayed in the hope that another way out would be found – the usual solution was marriage to the aggressor, or

Gentileschi: *Susanna and the Elders*, 1610(?); oil on canvas; Schloss Weissenstein, Pommersfelden

the latter's provision of a dowry to make possible marriage to another man. Artemisia's claim that she had been deflowered (which was surely true) included the required mention of blood. She testified, as the law expected and as was also surely true, that she had resisted Tassi by attacking him with a knife.

Tassi had promised to marry Artemisia, and consequently they had had regular sexual relations in Gentileschi's house for about eight months. Orazio's decision to go to court was the result of further events that pushed the threat to the family's honour beyond breaking point. Tassi already had a wife when he made his promise to Artemisia, and he almost certainly had her murdered. Events had finally got out of hand during carnival of 1612, when Artemisia and Tassi had sexual relations in the house of friends, making the affair a public scandal. In his petition Orazio cited not only rape and fornication, but also the theft from his daughter of some paintings, and especially a large *Judith*. There is no agreement about which of several versions of the subject this was, or whether it was in fact painted by father or daughter. But Artemisia had almost certainly represented herself either as Judith or as her servant in a scene in which a chaste and powerful virago kills or has just killed the man who has tried to seduce her.

At stake for Orazio was the ability to continue his profession as a painter, for which he needed to keep an open house without sacrificing his reputation. This was also critical for

Artemisia. *Susanna and the Elders* was almost certainly completed before the rape; but so much sexually charged gossip circled around her independently of that act of violence that the picture demands to be read as a powerful commentary by the 17-year-old Artemisia on the salacious curiosity she aroused. In her version of the story two whispering and conspiratorial men in modern dress lean over the wall of the pool where the naked Susanna bathes. Her body facing us, she turns away from them and holds up her arms in protection against their voices as much as against their gaze.

Artemisia's apprenticeship to her father caused prurient commentary. In various Roman workshops it was claimed that Orazio did not want her to marry, made her pose in the nude and liked people to look at her. Muse, whore and daughter, Artemisia was the object of such male fantasies because of the extraordinary fact that she was a painter. She was painting when Tassi came to rape her. He snatched away her palette and brushes and threw them away, saying, she reported: "Not so much painting, not so much painting".

In November 1612 Artemisia was married to Pietro Antonio di Vincenzo Stiattesi. The couple's first child was born in Florence in September of the following year, and the family would remain there until February 1620. Aurelio Lomi, Orazio's half-brother, had also returned to Florence in 1613, and Artemisia would adopt the Tuscan family name of Lomi for works executed in her Florentine period. She produced a number of small religious works in Florence, but the more ambitious group of the *Penitent Magdalene* (*c*.1618; Palazzo Pitti, Florence), *Jael and Sisera* (signed and dated 1620; Szépművészeti Múzeum, Budapest), and *Judith Beheading Holofernes* (Uffizi, Florence; surely completed before early 1621, but perhaps sent from Rome), all indicate a renewed commitment to the vividly naturalistic portrayal of strong women in morally justified opposition to men that had begun with the *Susanna* and the stolen *Judith*. Their production also reflects Artemisia's reputation for this sort of painting in Florence, where the Caravaggesque manner was still novel and her feminist version of it all the more so.

Artemisia's first known Florentine commission was in a different mode. In 1615 Michelangelo Buonarroti the Younger asked her to paint an *Allegory of Inclination* for the ceiling of the Casa Buonarroti. She produced a luminous fleshy female nude so natural and alluring that Buonarroti's great-nephew would later have Volterrano cover it with painted draperies. That she was paid more than the other artists for allegories of similar size reflects her superior reputation, but also reveals Buonarroti's understanding of her difficulties. In November 1615, for example, Buonarroti's servant delivered money in response to Artemisia's plea that she was in great need because she was in childbed. In fact she produced four children in five years in Florence.

Artemisia was constantly in debt. One tradesman to whom she owed money was the carpenter who produced the furnishings for her studio, whose account began on 24 October 1614. More serious were the debts incurred by her husband without her knowledge. On 5 June 1619 she appealed to the Grand Duke Cosimo II de' Medici through the Accademia del Disegno, explaining that her husband was indebted to a shopkeeper who had obtained a judgement against her that Stiattesi had also concealed. She begged the Academy to reconsider, and

to suspend the seizure of her goods on the grounds that a woman could not take on a debt while her husband was living with her.

Artemisia Gentileschi was the first woman member of the Accademia del Disegno, and so the first to pose this problem of responsibility for debts. Her inscription, probably under the sponsorship of her patron the grand duke, passed without comment. She paid her initial matriculation fee on 19 July 1616, but only as her debts mounted did she realise the privileges and responsibilities of membership.

In addition to supporting Artemisia in court, the grand duke also patronised her by buying paintings. In February 1619 a *Bath of Diana* (untraced) entered the Medici collection. She received an advance for another painting, and in January 1620 she requested a supply of ultramarine to use in a *Hercules* (untraced). But the trials of surviving as painter, mother and wife had taken their toll. In February 1620 Artemisia wrote to Cosimo II asking permission to spend some months in Rome.

The *Jael and Sisera* and *Judith Beheading Holofernes* already cited were to be followed by the forceful *Lucretia* (*c*.1621; Palazzo Cattaneo-Adorno, Genoa), the frankly nude *Cleopatra* (1621–2; Collection Amedeo Morandotti, Milan) and the last great version of *Judith and Her Maidservant* (*c*.1625; Detroit Institute of Arts). With the exception of the first, all bespeak a renewed contact with the vigorous tradition of Roman painting in the 1620s, and especially the work of Vouet. The signed and dated *Susanna and the Elders* (Burghley House, Stamford) of 1622 also reflects her knowledge of Guercino. But the subjects and the vision of these paintings, with their powerful women so directly described, set them apart.

The portrait of a *Knight of the Order of SS Maurice and Lazarus* (Pinacoteca Nazionale, Bologna), also signed and dated in Rome in 1622, is more indicative of Artemisia's later commissions than are these violent images of strong women. She became famous as a portraitist, and would secure fame through noble patronage. She was befriended by Cassiano dal Pozzo, who in turn brought her work to the attention of the Barberini. Artemisia's decision to go to Naples was probably the result of having sold several paintings in Rome in 1626 to the Duke of Alcalá, who then served as viceroy from 1629 to 1631. In the summer of 1630 she wrote to Dal Pozzo, reporting that she was making some paintings for the sister of the King of Spain. She received important ecclesiastical commissions, such as the *Annunciation*, probably for San Giorgio de' Genovesi, and three large works (Museo di Capodimonte, Naples) for the choir of Pozzuoli Cathedral. But she also painted for the palace of the King of Spain at Buen Retiro, for Charles Lorraine, Duc de Guise, for Cardinal Antonio Barberini and for Francesco I d'Este in Rome, among other princes. Her years under the protection of the grand duke in Florence had prepared her for the ways of the court; most important of all, Artemisia had gained control over her own affairs by learning to write letters.

This skill made it possible for Artemisia to participate in both the world of law and contract and in the culture of courtly artistic diplomacy. She was also skilful in creating her own reputation. In a letter to Galileo dated 9 October 1635 (cited in Garrard 1989, pp.383–4) she refers to her collection of gifts and letters from the kings and rulers of Europe,

Gentileschi: *Self-Portrait as La Pittura, c.*1640; Royal Collection © Her Majesty Queen Elizabeth II

expressing her displeasure at having received no favour from the Grand Duke Ferdinando II in Florence. Artemisia had learned to play upon the notion of herself as a vassal of princes offering gifts of love and courtesy, a powerless woman who served the greatest powers in Europe.

These skills did not secure Artemisia's hoped-for return to Florence in the mid-1630s, when she began to find Naples unbearably dangerous and expensive; instead, she took up a long-standing royal invitation to join her father in London, where he had been working since 1626. The atmosphere at court was highly charged, as suspicions rose that Queen Henrietta Maria and her advisers were working to convert Charles I and the kingdom to Catholicism (with art and artists not the least of their weapons). Plague was rife. None the less, Artemisia agreed to help Orazio with his commission to decorate the ceiling (now at Marlborough House, London) of the Queen's House at Greenwich.

Artemisia probably arrived in 1638. Within a year of her arrival her father was dead. The queen helped her to re-establish her contacts in Italy by sending a painting to Francesco I d'Este in Modena, but at this point the historical record of Gentileschi's life is broken by a nine-year silence. During most of this time she was probably in Naples, for she was well established there when she struck up her correspondence with Don Antonio Ruffo, the celebrated Messinese collector.

The 13 letters from Artemisia to Ruffo, dating from January 1649 to January 1651, provide a glimpse of the relationship between the painter and her patron. They also reveal tensions inherent in the new market for paintings. In her arguments with Ruffo over prices, Artemisia never hesitated to charge him with underestimating her because she was a woman. "The reputation of a woman stands in doubt until her work is seen", she wrote in 1649 in connection with the *Galatea* (untraced), and in response to her sense that Ruffo felt sympathy rather than admiration for her. Later, writing about the ambitious *Hunt of Diana* (untraced), with its eight figures, two dogs and landscape, she promised that she would make him see "what a woman can do". Her delay in completing the work in the summer's heat led Ruffo to demand a reduction in its price. This aroused Artemisia's fury at having to serve her "noviciate" all over again for a patron to whom she was charging less than she had the chamberlain of the King of Spain. She would rather give her work away, and believed that she had foolishly diminished her own value by asking too low a price because she needed cash.

Artemisia also explained why she had to have some money in advance. For each figure in the *Diana* she needed a model, and female models were especially difficult to find: they were expensive and she found that for every fifty who stripped only one was any good. In this work, she reminded him, she could not use a single model because there were eight figures, which had to be beautiful in different ways. Artemisia's own style had become more idealising, but the mode of production and vision she had learned in Rome had not changed. She still needed models for the paintings of female bodies that had become her speciality.

In addition to her dedication to the natural model, Artemisia took pride in her ability to invent on a given theme. Nicolas Poussin was also famous for this, defining invention in the terms used by Tasso, not as the discovery of wholly new themes, but as the disposition of something already known. Remarkably, Artemisia gave a similar response to the specification by a client that his *Galatea* be different from Ruffo's. In a letter to Ruffo of 13 November 1649 (Garrard 1989, pp.397–8) she replied tersely that he was dealing with a woman who had never repeated so much as a hand. She refused to set a price, and further refused to send a drawing because she had had her ideas stolen in the past. In one case a patron had saved money by giving her composition to another artist to execute. Artemisia claimed that this would never have happened to a man, but in fact several of her male counterparts were engaged in the same dilemma concerning their intellectual property rights.

In the allegorical self-portrait that Artemisia probably painted in London around 1640 (see illustration), sometimes dated c.1630, she presents herself as the figure of *La Pittura* – immortally young, proudly displaying her snowy breasts at the centre of the canvas, her gold chain a sign of princely honours, and her unruly locks representing her untrammelled thoughts. Painting's right hand is poised to begin the work of execution on the empty canvas, but it pauses there as "Arte-mi-sia" (or "May art be me") turns her gaze expectantly towards the light of the inventive intellect. The artist's colours are earthy, Neapolitan, Caravaggesque; her attitude is rhetorical, inquiring, closer to the world of Cassiano dal Pozzo and Tuscany. The confidence in her claim to fame is her own.

More than any other contemporary woman painter, Artemisia Gentileschi made her own career in the marketplace. But although she protected her daughters by marrying them within the aristocracy (as well as teaching them to paint), her own honour remained fragile, and misogynist anger against her talent persisted. The erotic legend around Artemisia was already being propagated by 1653, when, in a volume of satirical epitaphs (*Cimiterio, epitafi giocossi di Giovan Francesco Loredano e Pietro Michele*, Venice, 1653, cited in translation in Garrard 1989, p.137), she was made to say "Ne l'intagliar le corna a mio marito/Lasciai il pennello, e preso lo scalpello" (or, "To carve my husband's horns I put down my brush and took up a knife"). This satirical joke, which is our only evidence for the date of Artemisia's death, confirms that she invoked fears of castration beyond the grave.

Gentileschi persisted because of her talent, but also because she had the strength and intelligence to adapt to social circumstances, and because she determined to secure the fame reserved for men. Her painting reflects a similar path: the vulnerability of the early *Susanna* was superseded by a manner in which directness was combined with the detailed depiction of rich stuffs and fine jewels; in the end she painted with detachment, giving collectors what they wanted in the form of beautiful female nudes. The distinction between Artemisia's own body and her representations of the female nude necessarily widened with age. The exposed body of the female painter, putting her first foot in the water, is defenceless against gossip in the early *Susanna and the Elders*, whereas the women in the late *Bathsheba* and the *Tarquin and Lucretia* (both Neues Palais, Potsdam; late 1640s, with uncertain attribution) are rhetorical figures derived from the bodies of those models whom Artemisia accused of fleecing her. In this regard, the self-portrait as *La Pittura* marks a turning point in Artemisia's ability to conceive of herself as subject and object, to fashion a self through metaphor. Although her sexual identity determined everything in her life, Artemisia did not continue to identify with the female bodies she presented to the male gaze. As a result her late work has been quite misunderstood, considered empty, and its authenticity questioned.

ELIZABETH CROPPER

Gérard, Marguerite
French painter and printmaker, 1761–1837

Born in Grasse, Provence, 28 January 1761; father a perfume distiller. Probably moved to Paris after her mother's death in 1775; lived with her sister and brother-in-law, the painter Jean-Honoré Fragonard; looked after nephews after sister's death in 1824. Died in Paris, 18 May 1837.

Principal Exhibitions
Paris Salon: 1799 (prix du 5ème classe), 1801 (prix d'encouragement), 1802, 1804 (gold medal), 1806, 1808, 1810, 1814, 1817, 1822, 1824

Bibliography
Jeanne Doin, "Marguerite Gérard (1761–1837)", *Gazette des Beaux-Arts*, 4th series, viii, 1912, pp.429–52

George Levitine, "Marguerite Gérard and her stylistic significance", *Baltimore Museum of Art Annual*, iii, 1968, pp.21–31

Carol Duncan, "Happy mothers and other new ideas in French art", *Art Bulletin*, lv, 1973, pp.570–83

Women Artists, 1550–1950, exh. cat., Los Angeles County Museum of Art, and elsewhere, 1976

Sally Wells-Robertson, "Marguerite Gérard et les Fragonard", *Bulletin de la Société de l'Histoire de l'Art Français*, 1977, pp.179–89

——, *Marguerite Gérard*, PhD dissertation, New York University, 1978

Alexandre Ananoff, "Propos sur les peintures de Marguerite Gérard", *Gazette des Beaux-Arts*, 6th series, xciv, 1979, pp.211–18

Consulat-Empire-Restauration: Art in Early XIX Century France, exh. cat., Wildenstein and Co., London, 1981

Fragonard, exh. cat., Grand Palais, Paris, and Metropolitan Museum of Art, New York, 1987

Jean-Pierre Cuzin, *Jean-Honoré Fragonard: Life and Works: Complete Catalogue of the Oil Paintings*, New York: Abrams, 1988

Thanks to the research of Sally Wells-Robertson, the works of Marguerite Gérard have been rescued from the obscurity that enshrouded them after the artist's death in 1837. In her own lifetime, Gérard's paintings were anything but obscure, and LeBreton's official report detailing the state of French art (1808) claims that by 1789 Gérard's reputation matched those of Anne Vallayer-Coster (q.v.), Adélaïde Labille-Guiard (q.v.) and Elisabeth Vigée-Lebrun (q.v.). What sets Gérard apart from them is that she was not a member of the Academy, and she first showed her work at the Salon in 1799, six years after the exhibition was opened to all artists. Nothing indicates that Gérard ever sought or desired academic recognition, and her close association with Jean-Honoré Fragonard, himself a renegade from the royal institution, suggests that his support may

have compensated for a lack of institutional backing. As part of the Fragonard household, and sister to the painter's wife, Gérard was trained in the family atelier, a circumstance long common to both male and female artists. That Fragonard had entrée to private collections throughout Paris and that his lodgings were located in the Louvre allowed Gérard access to both art works and artistic community. He launched her on a career that brought the proverbial fame and fortune.

Marguerite Gérard came to Paris from Grasse in 1775, and in that year joined the Fragonard household. Only three years later she produced her first etching, the *Swaddled Cat*, made after a drawing by Fragonard and signed "first plate of Mlle Gérard, aged 16, 1778". Two more etchings of children's play followed, and Gérard returned to themes of childhood throughout her career. Indeed, she is best known today for painting mothers and children and depicting joyous family life. Works such as *Beloved Child* (1787–90) and *First Steps of Childhood* (1780–83; both Fogg Museum of Art, Harvard University) have suggested Gérard's role in propagating Rousseauian themes. Such images constitute a sizeable percentage of her production; they hang in public collections and have attracted recent commentary. But equally important are Gérard's depictions of female intimacy, feminine ritual and heterosexual lovemaking, which despite their presence in a few prominent collections (e.g. *Bad News*, c.1804; Louvre, Paris) remain less well known. Moreover, Gérard's range of subjects is not obvious because so many of her works are either lost or in private hands. Particularly keen is the loss of works that show the artist experimenting with a variety of subjects; her *Clemency of Napoleon*, exhibited in 1808 and bought by the Emperor for Josephine's private collection at Malmaison, is among those paintings whose recovery would give us a more complex picture of Gérard's artistic production.

Although Gérard's representations of motherhood seem to exemplify normative female behaviour, not all are as simple as they appear. One critic's remark points towards other possible readings: "Always a mommy with her little darling, always a dog, a maid, a cat, a cradle, a bird and some dolls" (*Revue du Salon de l'An X*, Paris, 1802, Collection Deloynes, no.1769, p.30). The critic suggests what becomes evident in looking at a selection of these images – cherished children, pampered pets, fetishised objects – all seem to hold the same importance in the visual and emotional world of Gérard's painting. For example, the cuddled babe in *First Caresses of the Day*, engraved by Henri Gérard in the 1780s, seems interchangeable with the Persian cat in *Triumph of Minette*, engraved by Vidal in 1786. The *Triumph of Raton* (1800–04; untraced, known only through reproduction) shows the performing dog as much an object of affection as the children cavorting around it, and the mother, holding centre stage, displays a ring biscuit – the prop that both Fragonard and Clodion rhymed with the female genitals in their overtly erotic images of women playing with lapdogs. These observations suggest that at least some of Gérard's images critique the conventions and pleasures of elite motherhood. Moreover, the high artifice of Gérard's paintings – their constant referral to other works of art (by herself, Fragonard, Greuze, Dutch genre painters, Prud'hon, Vigée-Lebrun and so forth) – undercuts any attempt to read her images as transparent to life. As much as "real" domesticity, Gérard's images signal artifice and the cabinet piece, the sort of art sought by

Gérard: *The Reader*, 1783–5; oil on canvas; 64.8 × 53.8 cm.; Fitzwilliam Museum, Cambridge

the collector who valued sensuous surface effects and bravura handling.

It is perhaps for this market that Gérard perfected what has become known as her "Metsu manner", a style reminiscent of the detailed, precisely finished and highly glazed surfaces wrought by that 17th-century Dutch painter. The *Music Lesson* (1782–3), known only through written descriptions and a detailed wash study (private collection), suggests that in the early 1780s Gérard was already producing elegant images of women in activities related to love (here, making music) inspired by such artists as Metsu. Gérard developed this subject and handling in advance of such artists as Boilly, who were credited with originating the neo-Dutch mode. In addition to genre scenes, Gérard made her career by painting portraits and portrait miniatures, and works produced in the 1780s and 1790s (e.g. the portrait miniature of a woman of 1785; Louvre) with their looser and less meticulous paint handling suggest that Gérard had an impressive control over the technical skills of her art.

Although interpreters have readily acknowledged the erotic content of images by Fragonard, Boilly and Schall, Gérard's renderings of love letters (*Billet Doux*, 1795–1800; untraced), music making (*The Concert*, 1800–05; private collection, New York) and female intimacy (*The Reader*, 1783–5; see illustration; *The Confidantes*, Musée des Beaux-Arts, Bordeaux) are usually considered innocent – or, as the critic Eméric David suggested of *Reading a Letter* (exh. Salon 1817; untraced), as showing a decency in their conception. Yet traditionally the iconography chosen by Gérard carried an erotic charge, sometimes carefully concealed, in the symbolic meaning of accoutrements, in the comparison between musical instruments and the female body, in the lap-dog or cat as surrogate lover. As a woman artist, Gérard's use of erotic subjects and symbols would of necessity be subtle, veiled or distanced through historical disguise. Her setting of love scenes in the courtly Middle Ages (as in the *Art of Love*, 1785–90; engraved by Henri Gérard in 1792) heralds the Troubadour style developed in the first half of the 19th century by such artists as her nephew Evariste Fragonard. Rather than promoting an exact historical reconstruction, Gérard's work is suffused with the theatricality of the Rococo pastoral and often uses the courtly tradition to signify a delicacy of sentiment, and perhaps also an imagined moment of woman's ascendancy.

The proliferation of love themes in Gérard's work and her reliance on well-established conventions of erotic depiction suggest that the thoughts of her women protagonists may not be as "decent" as moralising critics would have it. Recent feminist considerations of painted and textual images of female friendship, as well as recent work on women's literature, also suggest that Gérard's images transgress the decency seen by male Salon writers. Women's literature of the same period often exploited the unacknowledged sexual overtones of female friendship. Such friendships could be looked on with apprehension in the dominant culture, which feared that bad advice and moral corruption could be passed along in the exchange of confidences between women. Even Gérard's images of maternal bliss, as Wells-Robertson perceptively noted, can have erotic overtones. By representing bared breasts and joyful – even ecstatic – mothers, images such as *Nursing Mother* (c.1804; Musée Fragonard, Grasse) solicit male voyeurism. They also, however, underwrite the promise of sexual excitation that many writers on breast feeding guaranteed women as a happy by-product of fulfilling their maternal duty. Taking into account the eroticism of Gérard's art, we can more easily understand why she was commissioned to illustrate both Louvet de Couvray's *Les Amours du Chevalier de Faublas* (1798; examples in British Museum, London, and Bibliothèque Nationale, Paris) and Choderlos de Laclos's *Les Liaisons dangereuses* (1796; examples in Bibliothèque Nationale and Musée Fragonard).

It is both ironic and predictable that tradition would cast Marguerite Gérard as lover to the artist who was her teacher and her sister's husband, and at the same time find in her images only virtuous women. Wells-Robertson has shown the affair between Fragonard and Gérard to be pure fantasy; on the other hand, there is reason to suggest that Gérard's art, like that of Fragonard, was invested less in moral example and more in passion, pleasure and sensual appeal. Whereas such "authorities" as Rousseau generally held women susceptible to infatuation and physical stimulation, they also believed them incapable of *representing* love. "I would bet anything", wrote Rousseau, "that the *Lettres portugaises* were authored by a man". He would probably say the same of Gérard's impassioned *Geneviève de Brabant* (engraved by Augustin Le Grand, 1790) and her sensuous *Married Couple Re-reading Their Love Letters*, works that only recently have been recognised as the work of this woman artist.

MARY D. SHERIFF

See also Printmakers survey

Gerowitz, Judy *see* Chicago

Ghisi, Diana *see* Mantuana

Gillies, Margaret
British painter, 1803–1887

Born in London, 7 August 1803; father a Scottish merchant working in London. Brought up by her uncle, Lord Gillies, an Edinburgh judge, after mother's early death. Returned to London to pursue a professional career in art, receiving some training from Frederick Cruikshank, c.1830. Studied under Henri and Ary Scheffer in Paris, 1851. Lived in London with her sister, the writer Mary Gillies, and with Thomas Southwood Smith from the late 1830s until his death in 1861. Travelled widely, 1860s–70s. Lady member, Old Watercolour Society, 1852. Died of pleurisy at The Warren, Crockham Hill, Kent, 20 July 1887.

Principal Exhibitions
Royal Academy, London: 1832–61
Society of British Artists, London: 1834, 1837–9, 1842
Royal Scottish Academy, Edinburgh: occasionally 1834–52

Liverpool Academy: occasionally 1839–49
British Institution, London: 1846, 1853
Royal Manchester Institution: occasionally 1852–69
Old Watercolour Society, London: 1852–84, 1887
Society of Female Artists, London: 1858–61, 1863–5
Glasgow Institute of Fine Arts: occasionally 1867–77
Grosvenor Gallery, London: 1877–81

Bibliography

Alaric Watts, ed., *Men of the Time: Sketches of Eminent Living Characters*, 2 vols, London: Bogue, 1856

Ellen C. Clayton, *English Female Artists*, 2 vols, London: Tinsley, 1876

Lady Lindsay, "Some recollections of Miss Margaret Gillies", *Temple Bar*, lxxxi, 1887, pp.265–73

The Times, 26 July 1887, p.7 (obituary)

The Academy, no.795, 30 July 1887, pp.75–6 (obituary)

English Woman's Review, 15 August 1887, pp.369–70 (obituary)

Mary Howitt, *An Autobiography*, 2 vols, London: Isbister, 1889

John-Lewis Roget, *A History of the "Old Watercolour" Society*, 2 vols, London: Longman, 1891

Mrs C.L. Lewes, *Dr Southwood Smith: A Retrospect by his Granddaughter*, Edinburgh: Blackwood, 1898

Frances Blanshard, *Portraits of Wordsworth*, Ithaca, NY: Cornell University Press, and London: Allen and Unwin, 1959

Charlotte Yeldham, *Women Artists in Nineteenth-Century France and England*, 2 vols, New York: Garland, 1984

Pamela Gerrish Nunn, *Victorian Women Artists*, London: Women's Press, 1987

Deborah Cherry, *Painting Women: Victorian Women Artists*, London and New York: Routledge, 1993

Charlotte Yeldham, *Margaret Gillies, RWS: Unitarian Painter of Mind and Emotion, 1803–1887*, New York and Lampeter: Edwin Mellen Press, 1997

Unitarian in belief and committed, as were many Unitarians, to social reform, particularly the reform of women's education and political status, Margaret Gillies used art for highly motivated purposes during the greater part of her career. Her convictions sprang from, or were reinforced by, her association with the Unitarian and sanitary reformer Thomas Southwood Smith, with whom she lived from 1837 until 1861, and her links with the social group that formed around the Unitarian periodical, the *Monthly Repository*, in the 1830s. The moral, spiritual role of the arts emerges as a major theme from this publication and Gillies's work may be seen as a unique visual realisation of its ideals.

In the 1830s and 1840s most of Gillies's exhibited works were large, richly coloured portrait miniatures in watercolour on ivory in the style of Frederick Cruikshank (in turn a pupil of Andrew Robertson), from whom she received some instruction around 1830. She also executed a few portraits in oil in the 1840s and 1850s. Unlike Cruikshank and most contemporary portraitists, she distanced herself from the common practice of seeking aristocratic commissions and devoted herself to the portrayal of the bourgeoisie, charging from ten to twenty guineas for a miniature, according to its size. The portraits to which she attached most importance – and several of these were not commissions but works undertaken at her own request – were those of men and women of "genius" whom she wished to set up as "the guide and standard of human action" (Luther A. Brewer, *My Leigh Hunt Library: The Holograph Letters*, Iowa: University of Iowa Press, 1938, p.232). Among numerous examples are *Harriet Martineau* (1832; engraving in

British Museum, London), *James Henry Leigh Hunt* (1839; National Portrait Gallery, London), *William Wordsworth* (1839–40; Dove Cottage, Grasmere, and Rydal Mount, Ambleside), *Richard Hengist Horne* (1846; National Portrait Gallery), *Charles Dickens* (1844; engraved for *The New Spirit of the Age*, ed. R.H. Horne, London: Smith Elder, 1844) and *William and Mary Howitt* (1846; Castle Museum, Nottingham). A number of these portraits were reproduced in two publications that epitomised this ideal of creators and reformers as social exemplars: Richard Hengist Horne's *The New Spirit of the Age* of 1844 and the *People's Journal* (the *People's Portrait Gallery*) of 1846. Critics praised Gillies's miniatures for their truth to nature, for their rendering of intellectual expression and for boldness of effect (see, for example, *Art Union*, i, 1839, p.85, and *The Athenaeum*, no.657, 1840, p.436). Another more practical example of her use of art as a moral instrument in the 1840s is provided by her anonymous illustrations for a Government Report on Children in the Mines produced by the Children's Employment Commission in 1842. These shocked both Government and public and helped to produce subsequent legislation.

From the 1850s, by which time photography was threatening the career of the miniaturist, Gillies concentrated on larger, subject compositions, which represent a small but significant group in her previous work, and in that decade executed her most successful paintings, several of which were engraved. The influence of Ary Scheffer, in whose Paris studio she worked in 1851, is discernible in these. Occasionally in oil, these were more often watercolours in which an effect of oil was produced by an original sketch in scarlet and white and high finish; this practice and her depiction of large figures in watercolour were part of a broader, upgrading tendency in watercolour art of the period. Women, often from literature, history and the Bible, were her main subjects. Her most important compositions of this type were not merely narrative or anecdotal, but focused on emotional scenes, often trials, revealing the moral strength and religious faith of heroines such as the Martyr of Antioch, Vivia Perpetua, Ruth, Portia, Jeanie Deans (Sir Walter Scott) and Jennie (*The Ballad of Auld Robin Grey*). Most highly acclaimed were her allegorical paintings, examples of which include *Trust* (1860; see illustration) and *Hope and Faith* (engraving of 1864 in British Museum), in which female figures set against a broad expanse of sky personify an abstract idea.

Seen in the context of Gillies's ideological background and the contemporary intellectual perception of morality as an essentially feminine principle, her figurative oeuvre appears not only as a countervailing display of women's experience and achievements, but also as an attempt to diffuse moral principles through female example. Her reputation reached its peak from 1855 to 1861, when a reviewer referred to "that quasi-classic art in which she seems to stand without a competitor" (*Art Journal*, 1861, p.173). It rested chiefly on her ability to convey emotion and intellectual expression, but also on her effective use of colour and portrayal of drapery (see, for example, *Art Journal*, 1854, p.174; 1855, p.185; 1859, pp.83–4; 1860 pp.85–6 and 174–5). Her pictures sold rapidly to a mainly middle-class clientele (a maximum asking price, soon to be exceeded, was £52 10s. for *Vivia Perpetua* at the Society of Female Artists in 1859).

Gillies: *Trust*, 1860; watercolour; Victoria and Albert Museum, London

The death of Southwood Smith in 1861 had a profound effect on Gillies's life and work. Over the next 15 years she travelled widely, sketching rural life in Ireland, Arran, Italy, Scotland, France and the south of England. In these scenes, for example *Shepherdess Herding* (1863; British Museum), she depicted large figures, usually women or children, with an emphasis on features and expression, and paid particular attention to local scenery and costume. Her major works were characterised by idealising retrospection to the faith and chivalry of the Middle Ages, a period already favoured by the Pre-Raphaelites. Knights, ladies and pilgrims were the subjects of watercolours that critics praised for their historical accuracy (*Art Journal*, 1865, p.68). The work by which Gillies chose to be represented at such important exhibitions as the Exposition Universelle of 1878 in Paris and the Royal Jubilee Exhibition of 1887 in Manchester was *The End of the Pilgrimage* (1873; Cheltenham Art Gallery), which was bought for £105 at the Liverpool Autumn Exhibition in 1875. Known also as *Cercando Pace*, this was a typically religious work, in three compartments, showing the death of a pilgrim in Italy. Her work was effectively summarised in 1885:

Miss Gillies' chief characteristics are breadth and power, and she always paints with a high motive, seeking to inspire for good all who come within her sphere of influence, and endeavours to make art minister to the highest and best feelings of mankind [Frances Hays, *Women of the Day*, London: Chatto and Windus, 1885, pp.77–8].

CHARLOTTE YELDHAM

Ginnasi, Caterina
Italian painter, 1590–1660

Born 1590, birthplace unknown; niece of Cardinal Domenico Ginnasi, Dean of the College of Cardinals in Rome. Studied painting under Gaspare Celio, then under Giovanni Lanfranco. Member of the Accademia di San Luca, Rome, by 1638, when she is recorded as having paid her dues for one of its feasts. Died in Rome, 1660.

Bibliography

Giovanni Antonio Bruzio, "Theatrum romanae urbis sive romanorum sacrae aedes, xv: Chiese, conservatori e monasteri di monache della città di Roma", 1655/61–*c*.1680, Biblioteca Apostolica Vaticana, Rome, MS Vat.Lat.11884, fols 241v–247v

Raffaello Soprani and Carlo Giuseppe Ratti, *Vite de' pittori, scultori ed architetti genovesi*, i, Genoa, 1768, p.127; reprinted Bologna: Forni, 1969

Gian Battista Passeri, "Vita dell'Ill.ma Caterina Ginnasij pittrice", *Die Künstlerbiographen*, ed. Jacob Hess, Leipzig: Keller, and Vienna: Schroll, 1934, pp.257–8

Giacinto Gigli, *Diario Romano, 1608–1670*, ed. Giuseppe Ricciotti, Rome: Tumminnelli, 1958, p.171

Erich Schleier, *Giovanni Lanfranco: Das Römische Werk, 1602–1634*, PhD dissertation, University of Hamburg, 1966, pp.1404–13

——, "Charles Mellin and the Marchese Muti", *Burlington Magazine*, cxviii, 1976, pp.837–44 (p.842, note 36)

Franca Trinchieri Camiz, "'*Virgo – non sterilis*': Nuns as artists in 17th-century Rome", *Picturing Women in Renaissance and Baroque Italy*, ed. Sara Matthews Grieco and Geraldine Johnson (in preparation)

Caterina Ginnasi was encouraged in her proclivity for art by her uncle, Cardinal Domenico Ginnasi, who arranged for her to study painting, first with Gaspare Celio and subsequently with Giovanni Lanfranco. Even if she was never professed, she rejected marriage and lived a nunlike life. Operating in the tradition of pious women patrons, she convinced her uncle to found and build, within the Ginnasi palace in Rome, a convent of Discalced Carmelite nuns (1637); according to Bruzio (fol.245v), she even assisted the architect Orazio Torianni in designing the new church, Santa Lucia alla Botteghe Oscure (rebuilt 1630; destroyed 1936). For this church she painted the high altarpiece, *St Lucy Being Dragged off to Martyrdom* (now on the high altar of the Ginnasi palace chapel), as well as an altarpiece of *St Blaise Healing a Boy* (untraced) – the saint's head being a portrait of her uncle – which was present in the church until its destruction in 1936. Ginnasi also commissioned two important tombs, one for her uncle sculpted by Cosimo Fancelli, the other for her mother, Faustina Gottardi, carved by Cosimo and Antonio Fancelli (both in the Ginnasi palace chapel). She might be portrayed in a bust attributed to Cosimo Fancelli in the Victoria and Albert Museum, London (repr. John Pope-Hennessy, *Catalogue of Italian Sculpture in the Victoria and Albert Museum*, ii, London, 1964, cat. no.649, fig.645).

Ginnasi was the only woman painter that the biographer Gian Battista Passeri chose to include in his *Lives* of 17th-century artists. Her example, Passeri states, showed that "women were never scarce in intellect, and we can see, as they put into practice, that when they receive instruction they are capable of all that they have been taught" (Passeri 1934, p.258). He implies that she was commendable in that she had learned well the art of her master, Lanfranco, and could paint in his style. More specifically, Lanfranco is said to have assisted her, before leaving for Naples (1633), in painting the *St Lucy* for the high altar of Santa Lucia; most other references describe this painting as based on the "disegno" of Lanfranco. More recently, Erich Schleier (1976) cited Ginnasi as an example of "collaboration between a professional painter as a teacher and a noble amateur as a pupil", concluding that the *St Lucy* altar "must have been executed practically by Lanfranco himself". He deemed to be entirely by her hand only a *Last Supper* (now in the sacristy of the Ginnasi palace chapel), the original altarpiece of Santa Lucia before the church was rebuilt in 1630, subsequently cut down to fit a lunette of the new altar, over the *St Lucy*. Parts of the *Last Supper* are weak and seem painted by an inexperienced hand.

In addition to her works for Santa Lucia, Ginnasi also painted an altarpiece of the *Virgin and Child and Velletri's Four Protector Saints* and two side pictures for the Ginnasi chapel in Velletri Cathedral, as well as the chapel's cupola (in oil or fresco) and four corner *Evangelists*. In 1824 her paintings at Velletri were deemed as being in very poor condition and were consequently either removed or completely repainted. Other works painted by her are listed in the inventories of both Domenico and Caterina Ginnasi's belongings (17 March 1639; 7 December 1660): "A Standing St Catherine with the Wheel", an "Assumption of the Madonna", a "St Michael Archangel", a large "Madonna with Four Protector Saints of Velletri" (a copy of, or a model for her altarpiece in the Ginnasi chapel, Velletri), a "Madonna with St Teresa" and an unfinished "Custodian Angel".

Ginnasi had the relative advantage of operating in the more private realm of a noble family's pious commissions. Although her social position afforded her more respect as an artist, the confines of the private world of the Roman elite greatly decreased her chances of gaining widespread public recognition in her lifetime. As Passeri indicated, Caterina Ginnasi the painter seems to have been acceptable as an imitator but found wanting in originality or real talent, a judgement commonly directed towards women artists. Yet, as much as we might like to form our own opinion of her artistic achievement, we are hampered by the fact that only two pictures have survived from the several that she is known to have painted. One of them closely resembles the style of her teacher; the other represents an earlier, weaker and less successful work. All her other works are lost, unknown even to the Ginnasi family descendants.

FRANCA TRINCHIERI CAMIZ

Gluck
British painter, 1895–1978

Born Hannah Gluckstein in London, 1895. Attended classes at St John's Wood School of Art, 1913–16. First visited Lamorna, Cornwall, meeting Laura Knight (q.v.) and Dod Procter (q.v.), 1916. Subsequently left home, called herself Gluck and worked briefly at Selfridge's department store, London, painting portraits. Relationship with decorator Constance Spry, early 1930s, with writer Nesta Obermer, from 1936. Lived in London, then at The Chantry House, Steyning, Sussex, early 1940s. Died 10 January 1978.

Selected Individual Exhibitions
Dorien Leigh Galleries, London: 1924
Fine Art Society, London: 1926, 1932, 1937, 1973 (retrospective), 1980 (retrospective)

Selected Writings
"The dilemma of the painter and conservator in the synthetic age", Museum Association Conference, London, 1954
"The impermanence of paintings in relation to artists' materials", Royal Society of Arts Lecture, London, 1964
"On the quality of paint", *Tempera: Yearbook of the Society of Painters in Tempera*, 1969, pp.2–4

Bibliography
Gluck, 1895–1978, exh. cat., Fine Art Society, London, 1980
Painting in Newlyn, 1880–1930, exh. cat., Barbican Art Gallery, London, 1985
British Art in the Twentieth Century: The Modern Movement, exh. cat., Royal Academy, London, and elsewhere, 1987
Diana Souhami, *Gluck, 1895–1978: Her Biography*, London: Pandora, 1988
Emmanuel Cooper, *The Sexual Perspective: Homosexuality and Art in the last 100 Years in the West*, 2nd edition, London and New York: Routledge, 1994

Gluck received her only systematic artistic training during World War I, when she travelled to Lamorna, Cornwall, to study with the creative community associated with the so-called Newlyn School. These artists specialised in idyllic, pastoral and often meticulously literal landscapes and genre scenes of the surrounding Cornish life. Gluck's move to Lamorna was also a retreat from her prominent and wealthy London family, founders of the caterers J. Lyons and Co. Refusing her given name, Hannah Gluckstein, was only the first of many ruptures that characterised her troubled connection to a social milieu that she found personally repressive but to which she remained inextricably linked throughout her life and career. While her family's name and reputation guaranteed social acceptance, her lesbian sexuality and determined self-presentation in masculine clothing ensured that such acceptance was always conditional and limited. Gluck's training in a carefully naturalistic style and her relation to a sophisticated, wealthy post-Edwardian society are the crucial elements from which her paintings emerged. Throughout her career Gluck ignored the modernist trend towards abstraction and remained faithful to a naturalistic style that agreed with the more conservative, traditional tastes of her upper-class associations. At the same time she permeated her works with a utopian rhetoric of essences into which the subject of her lesbian identity occasionally erupted.

In 1926 Gluck had her first major solo exhibition at the Fine Art Society in London, called *Stage and Country*. The title and format signified the dichotomy of her social position, including landscapes and genre scenes of Cornwall, where she lived as a "rebel", a freely expressive artist, as well as paintings of the self-consciously sophisticated and artificial world of the London stage to which she had privileged access through her family's commercial venues. The "country" works centred on local Cornish events such as the Buryan races or views of the surrounding countryside. *Phoebus Triumphant* (c.1920; private collection, repr. Souhami 1988, p.46), with its huge expanse of sky and low horizon, typifies Gluck's landscapes, always marked by a pastoral stillness and idealised calm. In contrast to the idyllic ideology of the countryside, with her "stage" paintings Gluck underscores the blurred lines between theatrical performance and the performative artifice of London's theatre society. Alongside paintings of individuals of this wealthy and seemingly carefree world, Gluck exhibited specific depictions of London stage entertainers, including 15 images of the famous C.B. Cochran revues staged at her family's Trocadero Restaurant. Performers appear either on stage under intense spotlights or in more complex images in which Gluck seemed to be particularly interested in the theatre's interplay of reality and artifice. In such paintings as *Massine Waiting for His Cue* (c.1926; Victoria and Albert Museum, London) and *On and Off (Teddie Gerard on Stage at the Duke of York Theatre)* (c.1924; private collection, *ibid.*, p.57) Gluck contrasts the dimly lit wings of the theatre with the bright stage lights and includes custodians, actors and patrons engaged in backstage activities. The uncharacteristically complicated spatial arrangements of these works suggest a playful ambiguity and a knowing artifice that enveloped theatrical culture. In these paintings everything and everyone remain behind masks, costumes, screens and props under the harsh glare of public scrutiny.

Despite their diverse subjects, these paintings had a stylistic and conceptual unity to which Gluck adhered throughout her 50-year artistic career. Often small in scale, her paintings have a monumentality, meticulous rendering and sparse, geometrically schematic compositions. Within her closely observed naturalism there is, however, a simultaneous suppression of incidental detail that creates a sense of isolated utopia and suggests a symbolic layering of meanings behind the seemingly scrupulous attention to facts. Her notes on landscape painting signal clearly this dual trajectory:

> The sky is a bowl, not a flat backcloth, and its colour and light reflect in every blade of grass, every twig ... a landscape is chameleon to the light ... Will [the landscape's unique] note have reached you so clearly that no matter what changes and interruptions occur you will, like a good tuning fork, continue to vibrate to that note unerringly? [*ibid.*, p.42].

The duality of purpose between incident and symbol becomes an artistic credo for Gluck, and her writings often repeat this theme in relation to portraiture, genre scenes and flower paintings.

Gluck's portraits of the early 1920s almost immediately

Gluck: *Self-Portrait*, 1942; National Portrait Gallery, London

established a formula that forever defined her portraiture. Her sitters invariably appear alone, with frank, usually unsmiling faces and direct looks, against minimal backgrounds that sometimes contain objects or patterns that suggest an attribute, symbolic marker or allegorical icon. Her *Self-Portrait* (1942; see illustration) confirms this formula and also concisely engages the often contradictory aspects of her work: the construction of a defiant and isolated individualism but with the unmistakable marks of social privilege, articulated through a meticulously naturalistic aesthetic. Gluck presents herself with an unflinching look and tightly closed mouth to suggest both rebellion and control. The intensive attention to surfaces and details records each sign of age and passing time. Her severely cropped hair and stiffly binding collars both record her habitual masculine style and echo the unwavering control that pervades her face. Gluck's personal style is one specifically associated with the male British landed gentry of the early 20th century, and her slightly elevated viewpoint, forbidding gaze and clenched jaws suggest a position of superiority, privilege and judgement. The portrait simultaneously implies a potentially subversive sexuality and an aristocratic heritage and address. Thus the hermetic isolation of the artist's face is nevertheless permeated by the intersecting networks of individual agency and social context.

Gluck's other sitters are subjected to the relentless fidelity and intensity of observation with which she treated her own image. Among others, she painted the eminent psychiatrist *Sir James Crichton-Browne* (1930), the art patron *Lady Mount*

Temple (c.1936), the architect *Sir Edward Maufe* (1940) and *The Rt Hon. Sir Raymond Evershed, Master of the Rolls* (1951; all private collections, *ibid.*, pp.68, 145, 184 and 241 respectively). Together they are a record of Gluck's movements within particular strata of British society throughout her career, facilitated by the financial freedom to choose her sitters. They also reveal a very modern conception of self-sufficient individuality placed within an airless and remote atmosphere that recalls 19th-century Symbolism.

In the early 1930s Gluck's subject matter changed substantially, but the paintings remain intimately linked to her quotidian associations within a British class system. This change coincided with her relationship with the decorator Constance Spry, whose innovative flower arrangements became virtual requirements in the homes of wealthy, upper-class Londoners. Floral still lifes dominated Gluck's work (e.g. *Chromatic*, *ibid.*, p.91) and often she based her compositions on the unique and "modern" arrangements that made Spry famous. At this time, Gluck also developed and patented the three-tiered "Gluck frame" to achieve an integrated effect of picture and decorative scheme. Because it reflected contemporary ideas combining artistic form with practical utility, the Gluck frame became very popular and was used both in fashionable interiors as well as two major British Art in Industry exhibitions in the 1930s.

After her relationship with Constance Spry ended in 1936, Gluck painted fewer flower pictures. She became involved with the writer Nesta Obermer and soon produced two paintings that marked a dramatic departure from her established artistic interest. The two paintings, *Medallion* (1936; private collection, *ibid.*, p.8) and *Noel* (1937; private collection, *ibid.*, p.125), are an interjection of lesbian experience into Gluck's work that is uncommonly explicit and personal, a change perhaps due to the intensity of the relationship. Gluck considered that she and Nesta were married, and painted *Medallion* to commemorate their wedding ceremony in 1936 (Nesta was already involved in a heterosexual marriage of convenience, a common arrangement in early 20th-century European culture that allowed prominent society members to retain the necessary veneer of social respectability while not appearing to sanction homosexual relationships, particularly among women). In this painting Gluck presents her profile matched and surrounded completely by Nesta's; both figures are ambiguously androgynous and idealised. Gluck called the painting "YouWe", signalling her belief in the total merging of two individuals into a single being by an intensity of mutual feeling. This collapsing together of language, of distinct identities, of genders, is part of the larger utopian project that characterises Gluck's work. In *Medallion* she attempts to visualise symbolically a union that was illegible to the dominant British culture in which she and Nesta lived. That the two women continued the heterosexual terms of marriage – referring to each other as husband and wife – while visualising themselves as outside such conventions points to the irreconcilable demands of conformity that pervaded the contemporary British class and gender systems. *Noel* is less provocative but no less a commemorative painting to the women's relationship. The picture is an elaborate still life of decorations and desserts that celebrates the first Christmas they spent together. Through the scrupulously realised textures and surfaces and the solid armature of the composition, Gluck arrests time at a particular moment in

their lives, creating a memorial of mundane objects that are infused and coded with the lesbian relationship that stands unseen behind them.

A decade-long gap in Gluck's production resulted from her self-proclaimed "paint war", a crusade against inferior artists' materials that brought her into conflict with the British Board of Trade and commercial paint producers and eventually led to the formation of the British Standards Institution Technical Committee on Artists' Materials, which for the first time published standards for naming and defining pigments. After her return to painting in the 1960s, Gluck became preoccupied with time once again, specifically the passage from life to death and the consolation of the cycle of life. As in her earlier paintings, ordinary objects are suffused with implications of symbolic meanings that cling to the picture's surface and hover just below an explicit reading. The dead bird of *Requiem* (1964; private collection, *ibid.*, p.287), the solitary flight over the landscape in *Homeward* (1964; private collection, *ibid.*, p.286), the decaying fish in the surf from *Rage, Rage Against the Dying of the Light* (1970–73, private collection, *ibid.*, p.295): all are permeated with a mystical sense of the presence of death that Gluck called "beautiful and calming".

JOE LUCCHESI

Godfrey, Elizabeth [Eliza]
British goldsmith, silversmith and jeweller, active c.1720–58

Probably born in London between 1700 and 1705; daughter of the silversmith Simon Pantin. Learned trade in her father's workshop. Married her father's godson, the silversmith Abraham Buteux, 1720; entered her first mark at Goldsmiths' Hall in 1731 after Buteux's death. Married Benjamin Godfrey, 1732; entered a mark alone in 1741 after his death. Active until about 1758.

Bibliography
Eric J.G. Smith, "Women silversmiths", *Antique Dealer and Collectors' Guide*, xxiii, May 1969, pp.67–71, 81
Philippa Glanville and Jennifer Faulds Goldsborough, *Women Silversmiths, 1685–1845: Works from the Collection of the National Museum of Women in the Arts, Washington, DC*, London: Thames and Hudson, 1990
Arthur Grimwade, *London Goldsmiths, 1697–1837: Their Marks and Lives*, 3rd edition, London, 1990

Elizabeth Godfrey was the most outstanding woman goldsmith of her generation. The work that bears her mark shows the highest level of achievement in technical and design terms. She worked in London for the most sophisticated of clients, including the aristocracy, in the latest styles and on an equal footing with her – largely male – competitors.

The daughter of the distinguished Huguenot silversmith, Simon Pantin, Godfrey must have gained her initial experience and understanding of the goldsmith's craft in her father's workshop. Her first husband, Abraham Buteux, may have begun his career under Pantin's tutelage. As the daughter of a silversmith it is likely that Godfrey assisted her husband with the business.

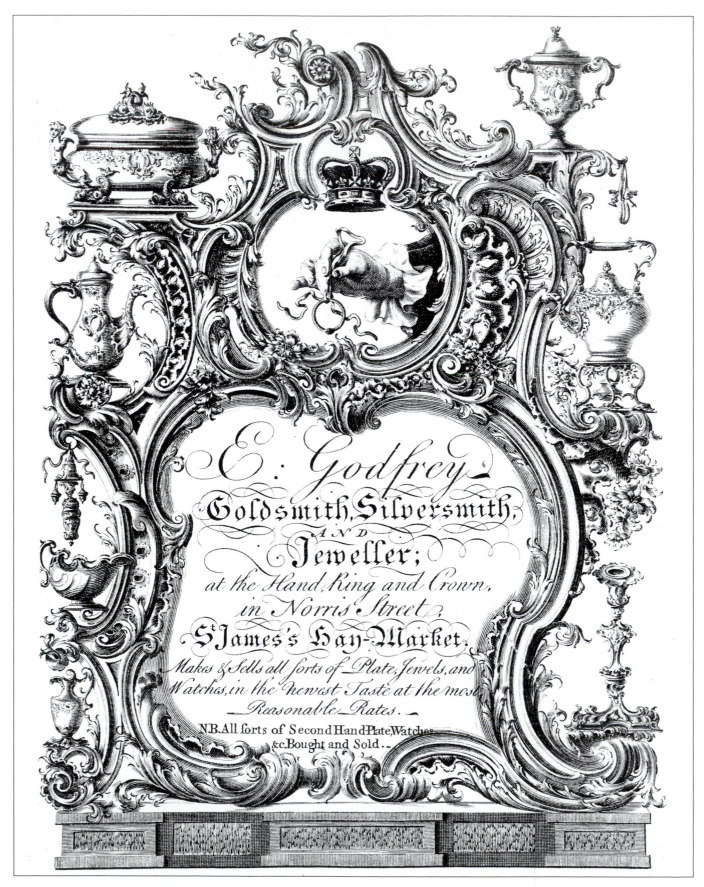

Godfrey: Trade card, British Museum, London

The connections of birth and training linking the two workshops is nowhere more clearly seen than in the similar types of production, chiefly plain cups, other hollow-wares and salvers. Given her background, it is not surprising that on the death of her husband Godfrey should have had the confidence, expertise and business skills to continue the firm as a widow.

She married again barely three months after registering her first mark at Goldsmiths' Hall. Her new husband, Benjamin Godfrey, had probably been working for her as a journeyman. After his death, Elizabeth Godfrey registered her second mark in 1741 and continued to run a successful workshop at Norris Street, Haymarket, London, until about 1758. The high quality of silver with her mark and the responsiveness of her business to changing fashion enabled her to operate at the top end of the market. She was patronised by, among others, the Duke of Cumberland. The silver ordered by her clients was always in the latest style and the numerous pieces that survive demonstrate, through their expression of the best Rococo design, that the confidence shown in her ability by high society was not misplaced.

It is doubtful, given the new understanding of the organisation of the trade, that Godfrey herself would now be credited with the manufacture of her silver. The mark entered at Goldsmiths' Hall signified a wider business relationship which is now known to have implications beyond a direct connection with a maker. Although the standards of workmanship, the design of the silver and the administration of the firm were probably the sole responsibility of Elizabeth Godfrey, she employed silversmiths to make her products. In addition to her own workshop's output, silver could be ordered from other suppliers. The common practice of overstriking the mark of these outworkers with her own demonstrates that her firm was the senior partner, buying in the skills of various manufacturing businesses to supplement that of her craftsmen. Godfrey is also known to have supplied some of the most prestigious goldsmithing firms, such as Parker and Wakelin, with silver from her workshops.

ANN EATWELL

Goldschmidt, Hilde

German painter and printmaker, 1897–1980

Born in Leipzig, 7 September 1897. Studied book design at the Leipzig Academy under Hugo Steiner-Prag, 1914–17; took private painting classes with Professor O.R. Bossert, 1917; studied at the Dresden Academy under Oskar Kokoschka, 1920–23. Worked in New York, 1923; stayed in Paris and Sanary-sur-Mer, south of France, 1926–7; Italy, 1929; Munich, 1932–3; moved to Kitzbühel, Austria, 1933. Moved to London, 1939; settled in English Lake District, on Langdale estate, near Ambleside, 1942–50. Returned to Austria, settling permanently in Kitzbühel, 1950. Several stays in Venice, 1957–72; trips to south of France, 1966; Israel, 1968; Gozo and Malta, 1971–3. Died in Kitzbühel, 7 August 1980.

Selected Individual Exhibitions

Galerie Caspary, Munich: 1932
Galerie Würthle, Vienna: 1934
Manchester: 1949
Ben Uri Art Gallery, London: 1959
Galerie Wolfgang Gurlitt, Munich: 1960
Tiroler Kunstpavillon, Innsbruck: 1962, 1966, 1974
Molton Gallery, London: 1962
Nora Studio, Jerusalem: 1968
Annely Juda Fine Art, London: 1969
Innsbruck University: 1972
Abbot Hall Art Gallery, Kendal, Westmorland: 1973 (touring retrospective)
Künstlerhaus, Vienna: 1975
Camden Arts Centre, London: 1976
Tiroler Landesmuseum Ferdinandeum, Innsbruck: 1977

Bibliography

Hilde Goldschmidt, exh. cat., Abbot Hall Art Gallery, Kendal, and elsewhere, 1973
Josef Paul Hodin, *Way of Life: Life and Work of the Painter Hilde Goldschmidt*, Portland, OR: Encore, 1976 (German original)
Hilde Goldschmidt, exh. cat., Tiroler Landesmuseum Ferdinandeum, Innsbruck, 1977
Elke Wagner, *Die Malerin Hilde Goldschmidt*, PhD dissertation, Innsbruck, 1978

Hilde Goldschmidt was brought up in a wealthy middle-class Jewish family, and in an artistic environment, complemented by a deep friendship with the cultivated White Russian Kallin family who were neighbours. Her early enthusiasms were for van Gogh, Gauguin, Cézanne and the painters of Der Blaue Reiter. From 1914 she spent three years in Hugo Steiner-Prag's book-design class at the Leipzig Academy, where she learned to make woodcuts and lithographs in the Expressionist style, with an influence from Edvard Munch visible in certain later works (*In the Wood, St Peter*, 1930; repr. Hodin 1976, pl.7). She was to abandon this early direction and took private classes in watercolour and oils with O.R. Bossert, who ran the painting class at the Academy. She wrote poetry, went to the theatre and was a keen student of the Dalcroze method of dance, taking lessons in the ballet school of the Leipzig Opera. The dancer Mary Wigman performed in Dresden shortly after Goldschmidt's move to the Academy there in 1920, and they became friends. The Dresden Academy had been reformed and opened to women after the revolution of 1918. Here Goldschmidt studied with Oskar Kokoschka, an inspirational tutor. After an important nine-month stay in New York, she established a pattern, journeying to Paris in the spring with her close friend from the Academy, the painter F.K. Gotsch (with whom she travelled to the south of France and Italy), summering in St Peter on the North Sea and returning home to Leipzig for the winter. Despite this cosmopolitanism, the sketches she made in Kitzbühel in the early 1930s demonstrate her empathy with peasant life and its relationship to nature.

In 1932 Goldschmidt's first solo show, at the Galerie Caspary, Munich, was cut short, and she moved under the shadow of the rise of Nazism from Munich to Kitzbühel in Austria, emigrating there officially with her mother in 1936. She was advised to leave the country after the Anschluss of 1938, and in March 1939 she left for Britain. After a period in which she founded the Golly Studios, making fur mittens to sell in London, she went by chance for a holiday to the Lake

District, and moved there with her mother in the autumn of 1942 to escape the bombing. Golly Studios moved too, and Goldschmidt set up leatherwork evening classes in Ambleside. She thus became part of a lively arts community that would include such figures as the philosopher Olaf Stapledon and the dancer Rudolph von Laban, as well as the exiled Kurt Schwitters, who was about to build his last Merzbarn on the Langdale estate. Her Expressionist pastel landscapes, such as *Elterwater* (1943; Abbot Hall Art Museum, Kendal), which may be compared with Kokoschka's contemporary Scottish landscapes, prove how Schwitters's return to realism was by no means an aberration, but part of a community of practice. Schwitters particularly admired Goldschmidt's painting *Awake and Dreaming* (1947; repr. Hodin 1976, pl.28): "I'm envious that you can express your dreams and thoughts in your paintings, whereas I, for this purpose, have had to follow a different path." *Awake and Dreaming*, with its doubled, introspective woman, governed by the different pulls of sun and moon, demonstrates Goldschmidt's still, Expressionist, Kokoschka-like style in oils, and as far as the subject is concerned, her intense, often melancholic introspection, as revealed in her detailed personal diaries and correspondence. Her *Self-Portrait* of 1952 (Abbot Hall Art Gallery, Kendal) shows how, after leaving Britain, her work assumed a bolder, more structured composition, in which the influence of celebrated contemporary School of Paris painters such as Alfred Manessier and Edouard Pignon is mixed with her Expressionist heritage: heavy, cloisonné black lines often separate boldly applied blocks of colour.

In 1950 Goldschmidt returned to Austria, where her attempts to run a guest house interfered with work, her only solace and strength. In 1954 she took another class with Kokoschka, which gave new energy and direction to her work, and inspired her also to teach students from Paris, the USA, Britain, Austria and even Cape Town and Hawaii. She drew additional inspiration from important trips to Venice in the 1960s and to Israel in 1968, which inspired the silkscreen print series *Venice* and *Israel: Man and Country*. Israel was the fulfilment of a lifelong dream, although orthodox Judaism had only been observed in her home during her grandfather's lifetime.

The art historian and critic Josef Paul Hodin, also an émigré and exile in Britain, and an expert on Kokoschka and Munch, was particularly drawn to Goldschmidt's work. He wrote the preface to the catalogue of her important retrospective exhibition, which opened in the Lake District at the Abbot Hall Art Gallery, Kendal, in 1973 and toured the north of England, and also produced a small monograph, which was published in English in the USA in 1976. Here he sketched her relationship with the complex networks of the avant-garde in Germany and Austria before World War II, and quoted extensively and movingly from her diaries and letters. His preface concluded: "Thus Hilde Goldschmidt takes her place among the most respected woman painters, such as Paula Modersohn-Becker, Kaethe Kollwitz [sic], Mary Cassat [sic], Berthe Morisot, Marie Laurencin and Sonja Delaunay [sic]".

SARAH WILSON

Golubkina, Anna (Semyonovna)
Russian sculptor, 1864–1927

Born in Zaraysk, Ryazan province, 28 January 1864. Studied painting and sculpture in Moscow, 1889–94, and at the Academy of Arts, St Petersburg, under sculptor V.A. Beklemishev, 1894–5. Trip to Paris to study at Académie Colarossi, 1895–6; met and worked with Rodin during second trip to Paris, 1897. Taught sculpture in Moscow, 1901–3. Trip to Paris and London, 1902–4. In Moscow from 1905; active in revolutionary movement; imprisoned, then released on bail, 1907. Taught workers' classes in sculpture, 1913. Held solo exhibition to aid war wounded, 1914. Taught sculpture at Svomas (State Free Art Studios), Moscow, 1918–20; professor at Vkhutemas (Higher State Artistic and Technical Workshops), Moscow 1920. Health declined from 1924, but continued to work and exhibit. Took part in the organisation of the ORS (Society of Russian Sculptors), 1926. Died in Zaraysk, 7 September 1927.

Principal Exhibitions
Moscow Society of Art Lovers: 1898, 1913
Moscow Association of Artists: 1898
SRKh (Union of Russian Artists), Moscow: 1898
Mir Iskusstva (World of Art), St Petersburg: 1898, 1913
Salon de Printemps, Paris: 1899 (third-class medal)
Moscow: 1913 (*Twentieth Exhibition of Watercolours*), 1925 (*Women in Russian Art*), 1925 (*Drawings by Contemporary Russian Sculptors*), 1944 (retrospective)
Museum of Fine Arts, Moscow: 1914 (individual)
Moscow Salon: 1917, 1923
Grand Central Palace, New York: 1923–4 (*Russian Art*, touring)

Selected Writings
Mastera iskusstva ob iskusstve [Masters of art on art], ed. A. Fyodorov-Davydov and G. Nedoshivin, vii, Moscow: Iskusstvo, 1970 (selections from Golubkina's letters and book)
Pisma. Neskolko slov o remesle skulptora. Vospominaniya sovremennikov [Letters. Some words on the sculptor's craft. Reminiscences of contemporaries], ed. N.A. Korovich, Moscow, 1983 (*Neskolko slov o remesle skulptora* first published 1923)

Bibliography
Boris Nikolayev (Ternovets), "Anna Semyonovna Golubkina", *Iskusstvo*, no.3, 1939, pp.117–21
Anna Golubkina: Yubileynaya vystavka [Anna Golubkina: Jubilee exhibition], exh. cat., Moscow, and elsewhere, 1964
Elena Murina, "Anna Semyonovna Golubkina", *Dekorativnoye iskusstvo*, no.6, 1964
Trois sculpteurs soviétiques: A.S. Goloubkina, V.I. Moukhina, S.D. Lebedeva, exh. cat., Musée Rodin, Paris, 1971
Ksenya V. Ardentova, *Anna Golubkina*, Moscow: Izobrazitelnoye Iskusstvo, 1976
Aleksandr Abramovich Kamensky, *Anna Golubkina: Lichnost, epokha, skulptura* [Anna Golubkina: Her personality, epoch, sculpture], Moscow: Izobrazitelnoye Iskusstvo, 1990
M.N. Yablonskaya, *Women Artists of Russia's New Age, 1900–1935*, New York: Rizzoli, and London: Thames and Hudson, 1990

Anna Golubkina was among the most highly acclaimed sculptors of early 20th-century Russia. From a provincial peasant background, self-taught until she began her artistic training, Golubkina identified strongly with Russia's common people.

Politically active, she spent time in prison and was often without food and money, but she gave away large amounts when she could. Her subjects ranged from portraits of major cultural figures to painful images of loneliness and old age. A down-to-earth fascination with the sculptor's materials combined with a bold fantasy gave Golubkina's work an unusually broad stylistic range and wide appeal.

Golubkina was born in 1864 in the town of Zaraysk, south of Moscow. Her grandfather was a serf who purchased his freedom, her father sold produce at the local market and died young, and Golubkina worked in the family garden until she was 25. With no chance of formal education, she read books in the library of a local merchant, and began drawing and modelling clay on her own. She decided to go to Moscow in 1889, with the modest ambition of learning to paint porcelain dishes, but she soon realised that she could do more. At the Moscow School of Painting, Sculpture and Architecture she studied under the painter Sergei Ivanov and the sculptor S.M. Volnukhin, and in 1894 transferred to the Academy of Arts in St Petersburg, where she worked under the sculptor V.A. Beklemishev. Golubkina appreciated Beklemishev's ability to teach without forcing pupils to emulate him, but in 1895 she left for Paris, hoping to work under Auguste Rodin.

Golubkina studied in Paris for more than a year; she did not meet Rodin during this trip, but worked in the studio of Filippo Colarossi. She returned to Paris in 1897 and established her own studio there. She did not study with Rodin formally, but consulted him and later called herself his pupil. Golubkina was not, however, overwhelmed by the master's enormous prestige and authority. When she used models or themes similar to Rodin's, she found emphatically different interpretations. The model who had posed for Rodin's statuette the *Helmet-Maker's Wife* (mid-1880s) became the subject for Golubkina's life-sized figure *Old Age* (1897; see illustration). Rodin's work, based on a ballad by François Villon, expressed a lament for lost beauty. Golubkina avoided this story-telling element: her old woman crouches defensively, an arm barely supporting her heavy head. The artist's empathy with the woman's physical and psychological condition reaches beyond symbolism. Exhibited at the Salon de Printemps in Paris in 1899, the work announced Golubkina's artistic maturity.

A large bronze sculpture, *Walking Man* (1903; Golubkina Studio Museum, Moscow), recalls Rodin's *Walking Man* (1877–8; Musée Rodin, Paris) and *Age of Bronze* (1875–7; Musée d'Orsay, Paris), but her treatment of the material emphasises potentially explosive strength. To Maxim Gorky and other contemporaries, the figure presaged the proletarian uprising of 1905. A later companion work, *The Slave* (1909; Golubkina Studio Museum), seemed to personify the State's repression of peasants and workers. Such interpretations were entirely in keeping with Golubkina's experience of poverty and commitment to revolutionary goals.

Golubkina accepted a commission for the first Russian bust of *Karl Marx* (1905; Tretyakov Gallery, Moscow), and she donated her fee to a fund for homeless workers. She opened her home as a temporary hospital and distributed revolutionary pamphlets. Arrested in 1907, she argued that urging the peasants to overthrow the tsar was no crime. In prison she went on a hunger strike, and illness resulted in an early release

Golubkina: *Old Age*, 1897; bronze; Golubkina Studio Museum, Moscow

on bail. During this time of intense political involvement, Golubkina acknowledged Rodin's role in liberating her potential as an artist, writing to him:

> I dreamed of creating something good and enduring, and thought that ... I could express my gratitude to you. Now I have no hope of doing this. ... I am writing now because our country is going through alarming times and no-one knows how it will turn out. They are throwing everyone into prison, and I have been in prison once. In the autumn I will have a new trial, and I fear that you will never know how much I venerate you ... While I live I shall always revere you as a great artist and as the person who gave me the possibility of life [Musée Rodin, reprinted in Fyodorov-Davydov and Nedoshivin, eds, 1970, pp.287–8].

A decade after her encounter with Rodin, Golubkina invoked not his stylistic influence but rather his image as a heroic personification of the power of sculpture.

Golubkina's subjects included well-known figures in Russian culture such as the writers *Andrei Bely* (1907; State Russian Museum, St Petersburg), *Alexei Remizov* and *Alexei Tolstoy* (both 1911; Tretyakov Gallery) and the art patrons

Savva Morozov (1902; Golubkina Studio Museum) and *E. Nosova-Ryabushinskaya* (1911; State Russian Museum). She also portrayed simple people whose faces express recognisable experiences and feelings: her grandfather *Polikarp Golubkin* (1892), the frail little girl *Manka* (1898) and the *Old Woman* (1907; all Tretyakov Gallery), whose piercing gaze makes her seem like an ancient prophet. Golubkina worked in a range of materials, starting with clay, plaster and bronze, studying techniques of marble sculpture during another trip to Paris in 1902 and exploiting the graining of wood for her portrayal of Remizov. Her book of 1923, *Neskolko slov o remesle skulptora*, discussed both techniques and reasons for working in specific materials. Golubkina understood how to use textures and other physical qualities of material in order to convey atmosphere or mood, and her work is usually identified with impressionism in sculpture. While emphasising the solidity of the underlying structures of the human form, Golubkina was also attuned to the more ephemeral, visionary aspects of symbolism. Her relief panel for the entrance of the Moscow Art Theatre, *In the Waves* (1902; *in situ*), and other, smaller works contain layers of form, human faces and abstract, swirling textures suggesting a cosmic environment.

In 1914–15 Golubkina held a personal exhibition of 150 sculptures in order to raise money for the victims of World War I. Critics compared her to Michelangelo, and rejoiced that Russian sculpture had at last attained independence from painting, had become more than decoration and could express the full range of human experience. Golubkina fell seriously ill in the 1920s; forced to stop working on large-scale sculptures, she executed miniature cameos in highly inventive forms. She also taught (as she had early in her career, and sporadically before and after the Revolution), but she was too exacting to enjoy teaching, and her best service was through her book on the sculptor's craft. During the last five years of her life, Golubkina created her most expressive and spiritually rich works, an imagined portrait of the writer *Lev Tolstoy*, posed as a sage with one finger to his brow, and *Little Birch-tree* (both 1927; Tretyakov Gallery), in which the figure of a young girl stands erect as a brisk wind sweeps her garments diagonally across her body, evoking ancient Russian folk beliefs about the female spirits dwelling in birch-trees. Both works, the spiritual portrait and the animistic fantasy, combine a solid, realist approach to the human figure and the mystical tones of symbolism; they are both a departure from and a culmination of Golubkina's earlier work. After her death in 1927, Golubkina's niece inherited her house and studio, and managed to preserve and restore the buildings as a permanent studio museum.

ALISON HILTON

Goncharova, Natalya (Sergeyevna)

Russian painter, printmaker and stage designer, 1881–1962

Born in the village of Negayevo, Tula Province, 21 June (Old Style calendar)/4 July (New Style calendar) 1881. Studied at the Moscow School of Painting, Sculpture and Architecture, c.1898–1910. Initially studied sculpture, but took up painting after meeting Mikhail Larionov, with whom she lived and worked for the rest of her life. Founder-member, Bubnovy valet (Jack/Knave of Diamonds) exhibition society, 1910; seceded with Larionov to found Osliny khvost (Donkey's Tail) group, 1912. Invited by Diaghilev to join the Ballets Russes as a stage designer; visited Paris to supervise designs for the ballet *Le Coq d'Or*, 1914. Left Russia with Larionov to join Diaghilev in Switzerland, 1915. Toured with the Ballets Russes to France, Spain and Italy, 1916–17. Settled permanently in Paris, working as a painter, stage designer and graphic artist, 1919. Made designs for the ballets *Les Noces*, 1923, and *The Firebird*, 1926. Worked as a stage designer for many different ballet companies after Diaghilev's death in 1929. Became a French citizen, 1936. Married Larionov, 1955. Died in Paris, 17 October 1962.

Principal Exhibitions

Individual

Obshchestvo svobodnoye estetiki, Moscow: 1910
Art Salon, Moscow: 1913
Art Bureau Dobychina, St Petersburg: 1914
Galerie Paul Guillaume, Paris: 1914 (with Mikhail Larionov)
Galerie Sauvage, Paris: 1918 (with Mikhail Larionov)
Galerie Barbazanges, Paris: 1919 (with Mikhail Larionov)
Kingore Galleries, New York: 1922 (with Mikhail Larionov)
Galerie Shiseido, Tokyo: 1923 (with Mikhail Larionov)
Galerie des Deux-Iles, Paris: 1948 (with Mikhail Larionov)
Galerie de l'Institut, Paris: 1956 (with Mikhail Larionov)
Arts Council of Great Britain, Leeds: 1961 (with Mikhail Larionov, touring)
Musée d'Art Moderne de la Ville de Paris: 1963 (with Mikhail Larionov, retrospective)

Group

Salon d'Automne, Paris: 1906 (*Exposition de l'art russe*)
Zveno (The Link), Kiev: 1908
Zolotoye runo (The Golden Fleece), Moscow: 1908–10
Soyuz molodyozhi (Union of Youth), St Petersburg: 1910–12
Bubnovy valet (Jack/Knave of Diamonds), Moscow: 1910–11
Der Blaue Reiter, Munich: 1912
Grafton Galleries, London: 1912 (*Second Post-Impressionist Exhibition*)
Osliny khvost (Donkey's Tail), Moscow: 1912
Mishen (Target Group of Artists), Moscow: 1913
Galerie Der Sturm, Berlin: 1913 (*Erster deutscher Herbstsalon*)
Moscow: 1914 (*Exhibition of Paintings No.4*), 1915 (*Exhibition of Paintings, "The Year 1915", "1915 god"*)
Museum of Modern Art, New York: 1936 (*Cubism and Abstract Art*)

Selected Writings

"Pismo k redaktsiyu" [Letter to the editor (on Cubism)], *Stolichnaya molva*, no.230, 20 February 1912, p.5 (English translations in Loguine 1971, pp.21–3, and Bowlt 1988, pp.77–8)
"Indusskiy i persidskiy lubok" [The Hindu and Persian "lubok"], *Vystavka ikonopisnykh i podlennikov lubkov* [Exhibition of icon paintings and "lubok" woodcuts], exh. cat., Khudozhestvenny Salon, Moscow, 1913, pp.11–12
"Luchisty i budushchniki: Manifest" [Rayists and Futurepeople: Manifesto], *Osliny khvost i Mishen* [Donkey's Tail and Target], Moscow: Ts. Myunster, 1913, pp.9–48 (English translation in Bowlt 1988, pp.87–91) (with Mikhail Larionov and others)
Radiantismo giudizi raccolti e tradotti dal Francese e dal Russo da N.A., Rome, 1917 (with Mikhail Larionov)

Les Ballets Russes de Serge de Diaghilew: Décors et costumes, Paris: Galerie Billiet, 1930 (with Michel Georges-Michel and Waldemar George)

"The creation of 'Les Noces'", *Ballet*, viii/3, 1952, pp.22–6

Serge de Diaghilew et la décoration théâtrale, Belvès, Dordogne: Vorms, 1955 (with Mikhail Larionov and Pierre Vorms)

Bibliography

Eli Eganbyuri (pseudonym Ilya Zdanevich), *Natalya Goncharova, Mikhail Larionov*, Moscow: Ts. Myunster, 1913

Osliny khvost i Mishen' [Donkey's Tail and Target], Moscow: Ts. Myunster, 1913 (essays by S. Khudakov, pp.125–53, and Varsanofy Parkin, pp.49–82)

V. Songaillo, *O vystavke kartin N.S. Goncharovoy* [On the exhibition of paintings by N.S. Goncharova], Moscow, 1913

Vystavka kartin Nataliy Sergeyevny Goncharovoy, 1900–1913 [Exhibition of the paintings of Natalya Sergeyevna Goncharova], exh. cat., Khudozhestvenny Salon, Moscow, 1913 (foreword by Goncharova translated in Bowlt 1988, pp.54–60)

Yakov Tugendkhold, "Vystavka kartin Nataliy Goncharovoy" [The exhibition of paintings by Natalya Goncharova], *Apollon*, no.8, October 1913, pp.71–3

Nikolai Khardzhiyev, "Pamyati Nataliy Goncharovoy i Mikhaila Larionova" [To the memory of Natalya Goncharova and Mikhail Larionov], *Iskusstvo knigi, v, 1963–1964*, 1968, pp.306–18

Tatiana Loguine, *Gontcharova et Larionov: Cinquante ans à Saint Germain-des-Prés*, Paris: Klincksieck, 1971

Mary Chamot, *Nathalie Gontcharova*, Paris: Bibliothèque des Arts, 1972

Susan P. Compton, *The World Backwards: Russian Futurist Books, 1912–16*, London: British Museum, 1978

Mary Chamot, *Goncharova: Stage Designs and Paintings*, London: Oresko, 1979

Abstraction: Towards a New Art: Painting, 1910–1920, exh. cat., Tate Gallery, London, 1981

Anthony Parton, "Russian 'Rayism': The work and theory of Mikhail Larionov and Natalya Goncharova, 1912–1914: Ouspensky's four-dimensional super race?", *Leonardo*, xvi, 1983, pp.298–305

——, "'Goncharova and Larionov': Gumilev's pantum to art", *Nikolai Gumilev, 1886–1986*, Oakland, CA: Berkeley Slavic Specialities, 1987, pp.225–42

John E. Bowlt, ed., *Russian Art of the Avant-garde: Theory and Criticism, 1902–1934*, 2nd edition, London and New York: Thames and Hudson, 1988

Alison Hilton, "Natalia Goncharova and the iconography of revelation", *Studies in Iconography*, xiii, 1989–90, pp.232–57

Marina Tsvetaeva, *Nathalie Gontcharova: Sa vie, son oeuvre*, Paris: Hiver, 1990 (Russian original)

M.N. Yablonskaya, *Women Artists of Russia's New Age, 1900–1935*, New York: Rizzoli, and London: Thames and Hudson, 1990

John E. Bowlt, "Natalia Goncharova and futurist theater", *Art Journal*, xlix, Spring 1990, pp.44–51

L'Avant-garde russe, 1905–1925, exh. cat., Musée des Beaux-Arts, Nantes, and elsewhere, 1993

Elena Basner, "Natalya Goncharova i Ilya Zdanevich" [Natalya Goncharova and Ilya Zdanevich], *Iskusstvo avangarda yazyk miravogo obshcheniya* [The universal language of avant-garde art], Ufa, 1993, pp.68–80

Anthony Parton, *Mikhail Larionov and the Russian Avant-Garde*, Princeton: Princeton University Press, 1993

Jane Sharp, "Redrawing the margins of Russian vanguard art: N. Goncharova's trial for pornography in 1910", *Sexuality and the Body in Russian Culture*, ed. Jane T. Costlow and others, Stanford, CA: Stanford University Press, 1993, pp.97–123

Nathalie Gontcharova, Michel Larionov, exh. cat., Musée National d'Art Moderne, Centre Georges Pompidou, Paris, 1995

The work of Natalya Goncharova first received critical attention in 1906 when she exhibited a series of impressionist pastel landscapes at the Salon d'Automne in Paris. Goncharova's work at this time was principally inspired by that of her teachers at the Moscow School of Painting such as Konstantin Korovin, as well as that of members of her peer group, such as Mikhail Larionov and Pavel Kuznetsov. In 1907 Goncharova fell under the influence of Symbolism and became friendly with the painter and financier Nikolai Ryabushinsky, who publicised both the Symbolist poets and the painters in his luxurious art magazine *Zolotoye runo* (Golden Fleece) of 1906–10. This magazine played an important role in the development of Russian art at this time and not least in Goncharova's own development. In 1908 *Zolotoye runo* sponsored a major exhibition of modern and contemporary French art that featured not only the work of French Symbolist painters but also the work of van Gogh, Gauguin, Cézanne, Matisse and the Fauves. The impact of this exhibition upon Goncharova cannot be overstated and during the next two years she began to assimilate these diverse approaches to modernism in her own work. In addition she began to study the impressive collections of French painting that were then being assembled by Ivan Morozov and Sergei Shchukin.

Goncharova's attention was principally attracted by the work of Gauguin, and in 1909 she executed a series of figure paintings entitled *God of Fecundity* (Larionov Goncharova Museum, Moscow) that emulated Gauguin's painting *Blue Idol* (Hermitage, St Petersburg). Several of Goncharova's paintings were exhibited at the Society of Free Aesthetics in March 1910, but the exhibition was criticised in the press as being "pornographic" and Goncharova was subsequently taken to court by the authorities on a charge of indecency. Although she was acquitted, this event was significant not only because it introduced Goncharova and Russian modernism into the public domain, but also because, as Jane Sharp has argued, from a feminist perspective it may be seen as the first response of the male art establishment to the work of a female artist that broke the accepted canons. From this point on Goncharova was to find herself at odds with and lampooned by society not only because of her staunch affiliation to the principles of the avant-garde but also because of her sex. The press, in particular, proved biting in their many caricatures of Goncharova and jibes at her expense (for the question of Goncharova's relationship with the Russian press, see Basner in Paris 1995).

Although these first figure paintings were deliberately calculated to shock the public, Goncharova entertained serious painterly interests at this time. *God of Fecundity* demonstrates not only the impact of Gauguin, but in the overall fracturing of the background plane also reveals a study of early Cubism. Indeed, in an interview with the press Goncharova declared that, in common with Picasso and Braque, she was attempting to find "sculptural distinctiveness" in her work (*Stolichnaya molva*, no.115, 5 April 1910, p.3). Having said this, the example of Gauguin remained important for several years. Like Gauguin, Goncharova associated rural life with moral regeneration, and she frequently returned to the provinces, where she mixed with the peasants on and around her parents' estate. Her first-hand experience of peasant life shaped a strong interest both in the subject of the peasantry and in their innate feeling for colour, composition and decoration, which found expression in her paintings. Works such as *Spring Gardening* (1909; Tate Gallery, London), which portrays the peasant women on the estate as they plant flowers, are characteristic of Goncharova's approach to art at this time. The stylisation of the figures, the Cubist fracturing of surface and the rich colours and garlands of blossom that decorate the surface of the painting idealise the life of the Russian peasantry in a similar way to Gauguin's paintings of the Tahitians among whom he lived.

During 1910, however, one may discern a clear development in Goncharova's peasant paintings. In *Washing Linen* (Tretyakov Gallery, Moscow) she abandoned the stylised forms of the peasant women and the rich colouring that had characterised her earlier work. Here, the figures are more crudely delineated, the colouring is more naturalistic and the rough texture of the paint seems to act as a metaphor for the mean life of provincial peasant women. From a feminist perspective it is interesting to note that during this period Goncharova executed many paintings specifically featuring women at work. Several such as the *Bread Seller* (1911; Musée National d'Art Moderne, Paris) are the more shocking because they represent a critique of the socio-economic circumstances in which the Russian peasantry found themselves. Here, the "picturesque" aspects of peasant life, alluded to in the bright colouring and decorative features of the background, act as a foil against which is set the vacant, lifeless and harrowing face of the bread seller.

While it is difficult to know what was Goncharova's precise political persuasion at this time, she did entertain socialist sympathies. She was friendly, for example, with the Russian socialist poet Mikhail Tsetlin, whose portrait she painted in 1910 (untraced). It seems likely that her political views played an important role in the development of her work since she also painted the "outcasts" of Russian society, in particular the Jews. In this, Goncharova's work must be seen in the context of that of her colleagues: Larionov, for example, who painted the prostitutes, Gypsies and common soldiers of the provinces, and Malevich, who worked closely with Goncharova at this time and stated categorically that the peasant paintings executed by himself and Goncharova were meant to function on a social plane.

Several of Goncharova's peasant paintings were exhibited at the Jack of Diamonds show of 1910–11. Shortly afterwards, however, Goncharova and Larionov seceded from the group on the grounds that it was necessary to break with Western artistic conventions and to develop a truly Russian school of modernist painting. To this end, they adopted what they called a Neo-primitive style, in which the subjects of the Russian peasantry and the urban workforce were expressed in the style of the visual traditions of the Russian people. During the next two years there followed an enormous series of Neo-primitivist paintings. Larionov was particularly inspired by the conventions of the Russian popular print (*lubok*) and whereas this traditional form of popular art impinged upon Goncharova, she turned more towards the conventions of icon painting and the provincial signboard. Goncharova's series of *Evangelists* (State Russian Museum, St Petersburg) are among the best known of her Neo-primitive paintings that emulate the icon tradition, whilst the bright colours and crude forms of her

series *The Harvest* (Tretyakov Gallery; State Russian Museum; Musée National d'Art Moderne; and elsewhere) owe an obvious debt to the tradition of hand-painted signboards to be found in the Russian provinces.

Although Goncharova's Neo-primitivism proposed a genuine reinvestigation of the indigenous visual traditions of the Russian people, the style was deliberately calculated to offend, since "cultivated" Russian society found the artefacts of the Russian peasantry boorish and disgusting. Consequently, Goncharova's Neo-primitive work was frequently criticised in the press and her religious paintings were impounded by the police on two occasions. In common with other members of her generation, Goncharova's socialist sympathies were mixed with an interest in religion and mysticism. In the years before World War I, for example, Goncharova was in correspondence with Kandinsky, whose famous series *Compositions* of 1911–13 adopted the theme of judgement as described in the biblical book of Revelation. It is interesting that in 1911 Goncharova executed a series of nine panels entitled the *Grape Harvest* (Tretyakov Gallery; Musée National d'Art Moderne; and elsewhere), which were also based on the divine judgement of society as described in Revelation. Goncharova's panels (assembled for the first time since 1913 in the exhibition *Nathalie Gontcharova, Michel Larionov*, see Paris 1995) are based on the style of signboard painting and seem to narrate a very contemporary judgement on the evils of her own society. Indeed this was a theme that Goncharova adopted again during World War I in a folio of lithographs *Misticheskiye obrazy voyny* (Mystical images of war; Moscow, 1915), when it was possible to identify the war with that of the Last Battle described in Revelation.

During the years 1912–14 Goncharova's interest in mysticism also found expression in a series of abstract and non-objective compositions painted in Larionov's innovative Rayist style, which represented a response to Analytical Cubism, Italian Futurism and Simultanism as practised by Robert and Sonia Delaunay (q.v.) in Paris. According to Larionov's theory of Rayism, which was publicised in several manifestoes during 1913–14, rays of light reflected from three-dimensional objects are able to create spatial forms in the atmosphere that represent a higher reality, identified by Larionov with the fourth dimension of space. It was this higher reality that Larionov attempted to interpret in his Rayist work by fragmenting the picture surface and presenting the spectator with an ambiguous and shifting surface of interconnecting planes. Goncharova undoubtedly played a role in the development of Rayism and, according to her statement in the catalogue to her one-woman exhibition in 1913, she subsequently elaborated the style. Typical of Goncharova's Rayist works is her painting *Cats: Rayist Perception in Rose, Black and Yellow* (1912; see illustration), in which the picture surface is shattered by sharp rays and fragmented planes, a formulation that recalls Cubist example. Goncharova's most important series of Rayist paintings, however, is entitled *Rayist Forest* (1912–14; Staatsgalerie, Stuttgart; Thyssen-Bornemisza Collection, Madrid; and elsewhere). It is these that principally express Goncharova's metaphysical and mystical philosophy relating as they do to the Eastern concept of the "world soul" and more specifically to the philosophy of Pyotr Ouspensky who, in his book on the subject of the fourth dimension entitled *Tertium organum* (St

Goncharova: *Cats: Rayist Perception in Rose, Black and Yellow*, 1912; oil on canvas; 85 × 86 cm.; Solomon R. Guggenheim Museum, New York

Petersburg, 1911), which was popular among the Russian avant-garde, identified the Forest as an example of the "fourth state of life activity". Despite the theoretical and philosophical depth of the Rayist style, which also relied on scientific developments such as the development of X-ray photography and the writings of Marie Curie, the critics invariably described Rayism as a degenerate form of Cubism. Rayism, however, was of historic importance in that several of Larionov's and a few of Goncharova's paintings were completely non-objective and were hence the forerunners of the non-objective tradition in modern Russian art.

In addition to Rayist paintings, Goncharova also practised in what has since become known as a Cubo-Futurist style, which amalgamated the stylistic devices of the French Cubist and Italian Futurist movements. Representative of Goncharova's work in this genre is *Woman in Hat* (1913; Musée National d'Art Moderne). Here, aspects of the portrait such as the nose, mouth and eyes are repeated across the canvas according to Futurist example, while the use of stencilled letters in the composition and the restricted palette testify to Cubist practice. The range of Goncharova's work in 1913 was particularly diverse and her one-woman exhibition in Moscow of that year represented more than 700 works. The exhibition clinched her reputation as one of the leading members of the Russian avant-garde, which was strengthened throughout the year by her lively participation in Russian Futurist activities. She illustrated Russian Futurist books for the poets Alexei Kruchyonykh, Velimir Khlebnikov, Sergei Bobrov and Konstantin Bolshakov, she painted her face and paraded the Moscow streets in the company of Larionov and Ilya Zdanevich, performed in a Futurist theatre called The Pink Lantern, and finally starred in a Russian Futurist film entitled *Drama in the Futurists' Cabaret No.13*.

It was partly due to Goncharova's popular notoriety that the impresario Sergei Diaghilev invited her to make the designs for his forthcoming production of the ballet *Le Coq d'Or*, which was to be staged in Paris in 1914. Goncharova accepted the commission and from 1914 onwards began to practise principally as stage designer for the Ballets Russes. In June 1915 Goncharova and Larionov left Russia to join Diaghilev in Switzerland, where the two artists were engaged to design new ballets for his repertoire. In 1916 Goncharova followed Diaghilev to Spain, which proved an important visit in the development of her work over the next two decades. The inspiration that Goncharova drew from her time there is embodied in a diverse series of *Espagnoles* (Musée National d'Art Moderne). The hieratic figures of Spanish women dressed in elaborate national dress and bedecked with tall mantillas appear in many of Goncharova's easel paintings and painted screens of the period, where they are treated in figurative, stylised and abstracted modes of representation. The *Espagnoles* are related to Goncharova's previous Russian work in that they show a monumental approach to figure painting. The works are often executed on a large scale and the figures almost fill the available picture space. Moreover, their format recalls that of the icon style of the years 1910–12, particularly that of the *Evangelists*. Although the *Espagnoles* represent a new and secular theme of Spanish ladies in their festival finery, they operate on the same principle as some of Goncharova's earlier peasant paintings, which use the monumental scale of the figure and quotations from the icon tradition in order to elevate the humble peasantry to the rank of saints and angels. In this sense the *Espagnoles* represent a reprise, though in different guise, of earlier work.

Unfortunately, Goncharova's painterly work in the West suffered a critical failure. First, she exhibited infrequently, and while exhibitions at the Galerie Sauvage (1918) and the Galerie Barbazanges (1919) established her reputation as a contemporary stage designer, they failed to promote her painterly work. Second, contemporary critical literature was almost exclusively devoted to her theatrical work. Third, from the late 1920s interest was focused principally on Goncharova's paintings from the Russian period at the expense of her contemporary work. Goncharova's initial critical success in the West might have been sustained had she been supported by the dealer system but she shunned any association with dealers, preferring to sell her work either in the Paris Salons or in small Parisian galleries. Despite her aggressive self-promotion during the Futurist years in Moscow, Goncharova was modest in terms of promoting her work. She also had an aversion to selling her work, preferring to give her paintings away. Consequently, it is only comparatively recently that

Goncharova's original contribution has been properly assessed and her Russian work singled out as having played a crucial role in the development of Russian modernism.

ANTHONY PARTON

Gonzalès, Eva
French painter, 1849–1883

Born in Paris, 19 April 1849, daughter of the novelist Emmanuel Gonzalès, later honorary president of the Société des Gens de Lettres. Studied in Paris under Charles Chaplin, 1866–7, then in the studio of Edouard Manet. Married engraver Henri Guérard, 1879. Died 6 May 1883, after giving birth to a son. Her sister Jeanne, also a painter, became Guérard's second wife.

Principal Exhibitions
Paris Salon: 1870, 1872, 1874, 1876, 1878–80, 1882–3
Salon des Refusés, Paris: 1873
Cercle Artistique et Littéraire, Paris: 1882 (*Exposition spéciale des oeuvres des artistes femmes*)
Salons de la Vie Moderne, Paris: 1885 (retrospective)

Bibliography
Maria Deraismes, "Une exposition particulière de l'Ecole réaliste", *L'Avenir des femmes*, 5 July 1874
Eva Gonzalès, exh. cat., Salons de la Vie Moderne, Paris, 1885; reprinted in *Modern Art in Paris, 1855–1900*, no.40, New York: Garland, 1981
Eva Gonzalès, exh. cat., Galerie Bernheim-Jeune, Paris, 1914
Etienne Moreau-Nélaton, *Manet raconté par lui-même*, 2 vols, Paris: Laurens, 1926
Eva Gonzalès, exh. cat., Galerie Marcel Bernheim, Paris, 1932
Paule Bayle, "Eva Gonzalès", *La Renaissance*, xv, June 1932, pp.110–15
Eva Gonzalès, exh. cat., Galerie Daber, Paris, 1950
Claude Roger-Marx, *Eva Gonzalès*, Saint-Germain-en-Laye: Neuilly, 1950
François Mathey, *Six femmes peintres*, Paris: Editions du Chêne, 1951
Pierre Courthion and Pierre Cailler, eds, *Portrait of Manet by Himself and His Contemporaries*, London: Cassell, 1960
John Rewald, *The History of Impressionism*, 4th edition, London: Secker and Warburg, 1973
Women Artists, 1550–1950, exh. cat., Los Angeles County Museum of Art, and elsewhere, 1976
Charlotte Yeldham, *Women Artists in Nineteenth-Century France and England*, 2 vols, New York: Garland, 1984
Tamar Garb, *Women Impressionists*, Oxford: Phaidon, 1986
Marie-Caroline Sainsaulieu and Jacques de Mons, *Eva Gonzalès, 1849–1883: Etude critique et catalogue raisonné*, Paris: La Bibliothèque des Arts, 1990
Les Femmes impressionistes: Mary Cassatt, Eva Gonzalès, Berthe Morisot, exh. cat., Musée Marmottan, Paris, 1993
Albert Boime, "Maria Deraismes and Eva Gonzalès: A feminist critique of *Une loge aux Théâtre des Italiens*", *Woman's Art Journal*, xv/2, 1994–5, pp.31–7

Until quite recently, Eva Gonzalès was marginalised by modern scholars as little more than a beautiful model and student of the French realist painter, Edouard Manet. But to many of her

Gonzalès: *L'Espagnole*, pastel; Eastlake Galleries, New York

peers Gonzalès's position as a woman painter in Paris in the era of the Impressionists was a formidable one.

The daughter of a well-known French novelist, Eva Gonzalès grew up surrounded by illustrious members of Parisian literary and artistic circles. Through Philippe Jourde, publisher of the journal Le Siècle, she met Charles Chaplin, a popular academic painter who had instituted a woman's programme in his studio and would later teach Mary Cassatt (q.v.). In 1866, at the age of 17, Gonzalès began her formal training in Chaplin's studio. Tea (private collection, repr. Sainsaulieu and Mons 1990, cat. no.6), an early genre painting executed in a tight realist style, probably dates from her brief tenure as Chaplin's student. Yet the intimate subject, a graceful interior that includes such emblems of gender as the gilded mirror, diminutive tea set, delicate furniture, fan, flowers and pink, unsealed letter, links the painting as well to a larger feminine visual culture that legions of amateur women painters would perpetuate in their work. Berthe Morisot (q.v.) among others would embrace this refined, protected world in her paintings of interiors in the following decade. One of Gonzalès's first pastels, The Fan (1869; Minneapolis Institute of Arts), again depicts the "feminised interior", but in the freer technique and lighter palette she would often explore in this more ephemeral medium.

By 1869 Gonzalès had met Manet and started to work in his studio. With his encouragement, she began to submit her work on a regular basis to the annual Salons. Her Salon debut in 1870 (in which she exhibited three works), however, was dramatically overshadowed by her presence at the same Salon as a subject in Manet's portrait of Mlle E.G. (National Gallery, London). Suffering a critical fate common to women artists who worked with older, established male painters, Gonzalès's public persona often revolved around critics' perceptions of her as dark-haired and fashionable, a subject and decorative acolyte of Manet's rather than as a professional artist in her own right. In an attempt to combat this perception, Gonzalès listed herself as a student of Chaplin, but few Salon viewers were fooled. Her own major submission, the life-sized Little Soldier (Musée Gaston Rapin, Villeneuve-sur-Lot), was an unmistakable reference to Manet's infamous Fife Player (1866; Musée d'Orsay, Paris). In her painting, however, Gonzalès subtly transformed Manet's radically two-dimensional figure into a once-more volumetric form, whose slightly turned pose, soft modelling and extended cast shadows re-establish the space and realist figural tradition that Manet had boldly flattened. The few critics who responded to Gonzalès's work recognised only her debt, not her response to Manet. Even they, however, could not separate their assessment of the actual woman painter from the image of elegant dilettante that Manet's portrait had established. As one review wrote condescendingly of Little Soldier: "It is an astoundingly strong statement from such a pretty little author" (Louis Leroy, Le Charivari, May 1870).

Undaunted, however, Gonzalès continued to work in a sober realist manner reminiscent of Manet's earlier Spanish period and began to enjoy some success. A small circle of critics, several of whom were also loyal admirers of her father, Emmanuel Gonzalès, applauded her efforts, and in particular a series of large genre works for which her sister Jeanne posed. Such paintings as Indolence (Sainsaulieu and Mons 1990, cat.

no.39) and the smaller pastel Favourite Plant (ibid., cat. no.40), both accepted for the Salon of 1872, were lavishly praised by Emile Zola, Jules Castagnary and others in their reviews, and established the subject of the contemplative, self-absorbed modern woman as a focus of Gonzalès's oeuvre. A more formal portrait of her sister from the same period (collection Judith and Alexander M. Laughlin, New York), which the dealer Durand-Ruel held briefly, exhibited the broad, summary handling, flattened space and black-and-white palette that characterise many of her early works and that critics quickly likened to Manet.

Although like Manet Gonzalès chose not to participate in the group exhibitions of the Impressionists, her painting did not escape their influence. Several small landscape studies from the early 1870s already suggest an awareness of the emerging Impressionist style. Beach at Dieppe (Musée Château, Dieppe), painted in Normandy in 1870–71, when the Gonzalès family sought refuge there from the Franco-Prussian war, uses the high bird's-eye viewpoint, flattened expanses and sunlit palette that had characterised Monet's views of Sainte-Adresse a decade earlier. Likewise, the luminous green tonality, sketch-like brushwork and motif of a reflective pond in Osier Beds (Kunsthistorisches Museum, Vienna) owed much to the plein-air technique and palette of early Impressionist landscapes. Even Gonzalès seemed to sense this new, if momentary affinity. When Osier Beds was rejected from the Salon of 1873, she did not hesitate, in this instance, to part company with Manet and to exhibit with Renoir and countless others at the Salon des Refusés, re-instituted that year to compensate for an unusually hostile Salon jury.

The fate of Gonzalès's work at the Salon of 1874, which opened shortly after the first Impressionist show closed, offers a revealing glimpse of the gendered discourse that would become commonplace in Impressionist art criticism. Her small pastel toilette scene The Nest (Musée d'Orsay), executed with smooth blended strokes and a muted pastel palette, was accepted as a sketch and widely acclaimed. Critics had previously likened the artist's pastels to those of the noted 18th-century pastellist Rosalba Carriera (q.v.), and in The Nest, as in traditional pastels, traces of a thin red line still rim the edges of the figure's hands, the mirror and still life. Gonzalès's fascination here with the fall of light on translucent fabric, conveyed with a subtle mixture of white, pink and soft blue sketch-like strokes, also aligns her work with the Impressionist Edgar Degas's earliest studies in pastel. But in Salon reviews The Nest became a paradigm of "feminine technique": Castagnary, for example, lauded its "seductive harmony" and "simple, natural grace" ("Le Salon de 1874", Le Siècle, 26 May 1874, p.2). Ironically, although such observations might seem to limit her "public" role as artist, the longstanding belief that the ephemeral medium of pastel was uniquely suited to the assumedly more delicate sensibilities of women artists actually allowed Gonzalès a unique freedom to experiment.

In contrast, Gonzalès's other submission in 1874, the monumental realist painting Box at the Théâtre des Italiens (Musée d'Orsay), was rebuffed by the Salon Jury. No doubt its ambitious scale (98 × 130 cm.), deemed more appropriate to the heroic subjects and aspirations of better established (male) painters, would have rendered problematic Gonzalès's elegant modern genre scene of a woman and her male escort at the theatre. The inclusion of a sumptuous floral bouquet – in the eyes of many viewers a pointed allusion to the analogous flowers (and erotic symbolism) in Manet's scandalous *Olympia* (1863; Musée d'Orsay) – only added to the painting's contentiousness. But it was above all her solid and forceful brushwork, in which critics detected a surprisingly "masculine vigour", that led to the work's rejection. As the feminist Maria Deraismes noted in her crucial essay on Gonzalès ("Une exposition particulière de l'Ecole réaliste", 1874), Gonzalès's painting was refused in 1874 not only because of its visible attachment to Manet, who still provoked controversy in some quarters, but also because it boldly defied gender-polarised conceptions of feminine delicacy. The painting seemed strident and defiant, while her more quietly venturesome pastel work appeared to sustain the status quo. When *Box at the Théâtre des Italiens* was finally shown at the Salon of 1879 – at the very moment that Mary Cassatt was exploring the same subject in her work – the skill and power of Gonzalès's painting still surprised her critics (quoted in Bayle 1932).

Several of Gonzalès's subsequent paintings, works that were not exhibited during her lifetime, embraced the kind of intimate genre themes favoured by Cassatt and Morisot and also illustrate a gradual loosening of her technique. In *The Awakening* (Kunsthalle, Bremen), one of two pendant paintings of c.1877–8 depicting her sister Jeanne reclining in bed, the potentially erotic subject in this instance provides only a pretext for the artist to respond to the animate surface of the setting, describing a vast range of pale pinks, violets, greys and blues reflected off diaphanous white fabrics. Equally subdued in theme but rich in tonal values is the related sketch-like canvas *The Convalescent* (Ordrupgaardsammlingen, Charlottenlund). In the paintings she produced at this point for public exhibition, however, Gonzalès attempted to reconcile her earlier realism with scattered Impressionist effects, and the results were often less successful. *Miss and Baby* (private collection, repr. Sainsaulieu and Mons 1990, cat. no.41), shown at the Salon of 1878, is her first full-scale landscape painted in plein air, and depicts a fashionable woman and child in a shady garden in Dieppe. But it is also a thinly disguised reworking of Manet's *Railroad* (National Gallery of Art, Washington, DC) and, lacking the spatial and psychological tensions of Manet's masterful prototype, suffers in comparison. More successful is Gonzalès's landscape from Grandcamp, *Brother and Sister* (c.1877; National Gallery of Ireland, Dublin). In this painting, the tactile brushwork and axial placement of the foreground still-life recall a favourite spatial ploy of Manet's. But Gonzalès's new attentiveness to surface effects and her depiction of a vast sunlit marine landscape, loosely sketched with a brightened palette, draw her at the same time closer to the Impressionist aesthetic. And in the *Donkey Ride* (c.1880; Museum and Art Gallery, Bristol), a small figure painting whose triangular composition and genre format recall the earlier *Box at the Théâtre des Italiens*, Gonzalès displays a combination of disparate techniques – thin oil washes, calligraphic lines and highly finished painterly details – that reveal the intense experimentation her painting as a whole underwent at this point.

After a decade in public view, Gonzalès seems finally to have hit her full stride in her late work, stepping forth from the shadow of Manet that hovered so long over her art. Her growing sense of self-assertion is especially evident in a series of radiant pastel portraits, including the portrait of *Mademoiselle S.* [Sarrasin] (Wadsworth Atheneum, Hartford, CT), exhibited at the Salon of 1879. A charming image of a young girl in fancy dress, it anticipates Cassatt's many later pastel portraits of well-dressed children. Against a luminous background through which the texture of the paper is allowed to sparkle, Gonzalès built up the child's face and bodice with pastel strokes that augmented the medium's traditional delicacy with a new vigour. Even more assured is the technique in *Woman in Pink* (c.1879; private collection, *ibid.* cat. no.99), a profile portrait of her sister. Gonzalès's interspersed hatchings of vibrant pink, blue and salmon overlay vestiges of a red pastel outline in this work, suggesting an intimate knowledge of Degas's work from the same period and drawing attention to its highly animated overall surface with confident self-awareness. In *L'Espagnole* (see illustration), a late and particularly dazzling pastel portrait on canvas, the full breadth of Gonzalès's mastery of the medium is evident. She exploits the bare patches to enhance the work's luminosity and texture, and also employs the hatching technique as a vivid compositional element. The downcast line of the model's gaze, the angle of her jawline, the slanted edge of her barely limned fan and the plaited lines of her coiffure all subtly reinforce the diagonal hatchings of the artist's pastel marks.

By the end of her brief career, Gonzalès's kinship with Degas and the Impressionists extended beyond questions of technique. In such works as the large and exquisitely rendered pastel, *A Milliner* (c.1882; Art Institute of Chicago), she took up a favourite Degas theme, one in which the worlds of female vanity, commercial display and the urban working woman intersect. Yet in her intimate focus on the milliner, as fashionable herself as the luxurious fabrics and flowers that surround her, Gonzalès paints not an urban type but an elegant modern portrait and thus pointedly avoids the dialectics of class and gender that infuse the work of so many of her Impressionist peers. Perhaps recognising the significance of this work to her woman-centred oeuvre, as well as its highly politic approach to a popular contemporary subject, Gonzalès showed it in 1882 at a special women's exhibition at the Cercle de la rue Volney, frequented by the more conservative painters of the Union des Femmes. In 1883, the year of Gonzalès's death, it represented the artist at the annual Salon.

MARY TOMPKINS LEWIS

Gordine, Dora
Russian sculptor, (?)1898–1991

Born in Russia, 13 April (?)1898. Moved to Paris to complete her education, 1920. Started sculpting in Paris, c.1925. Worked in Singapore and the Far East, 1929–35. Married a diplomat, the Hon. Richard Hare, later Professor of Russian Literature at School of Slavonic and East European Studies, London University, 1936; he died 1966. Settled in Britain after marriage, living at Dorich House, Kingston-upon-Thames, Surrey. Worked in USA, 1947 and 1959. Associate, 1938, and Fellow, 1949, Royal Society of British Sculptors.

Member, Society of Portrait Sculptors. Died in Kingston-upon-Thames, 29 December 1991.

Principal Exhibitions
Salon des Tuileries, Paris: 1926, 1933
Leicester Galleries, London: 1928, 1933, 1938 (all individual), 1945 (with William Roberts and Henry Lamb), 1949 (individual)
Royal Academy, London: 1937–41, 1944–50, 1952–60
Battersea Park, London: 1948 (*Open-Air Exhibition of Sculpture*, organised by Arts Council of Great Britain)
Fine Art Society, London: 1986 (*Sculpture in Britain Between the Wars*)

Bibliography
Marie Dormoy, "Dora Gordine, sculpteur", *L'Amour de l'Art*, viii, 1927, p.166
"Paris notes", *Drawing and Design*, new series, iv, February 1928, pp.33–5, 59
Luc Benoist, "Dora Gordine", *L'Amour de l'Art*, x, 1929, pp.172–6
Pawel Barchan, "Dora Gordina", *Deutsche Kunst*, October 1929, pp.46–50
Richard O. Windstedt, "The language of plastic beauty", *Straits Times*, 5 August 1932
Arthur Symons, "A triumph of sculptural form: The work of Dora Gordine", *Spectator*, 4 November 1938; reprinted in *Connoisseur*, cxlii, 1958, pp.233–7
"This is the house a sculptor built", *Ideal Home*, October 1946, p.36
E.H. Ramsden, *Twentieth-Century Sculpture*, London: Pleiades, 1949
Mary Sorrell, "Dora Gordine", *Apollo*, xlix, 1949, pp.113–14
George A. Nicholls, "Beauty in bronze", *Figure Quarterly* (US edition), xiii, 1956, pp.4–11
Mary Chamot, Denis Farr and Martin Butlin, *Tate Gallery Catalogues*, iv: *The Modern British Paintings, Drawings and Sculpture*, 1964
Nancy Wise interview for Radio 4, 1972, National Sound Archives, London
Sculpture in Britain Between the Wars, exh. cat., Fine Art Society, London, 1986
Obituaries in *Daily Telegraph*, 2 January 1992, p.17; *The Times*, 3 January, 1992, p.12; *The Independent*, 4 January 1992, p.10; 7 January 1992, p.11; 14 January 1992, p.25

Oral history is in the archives of Tate Gallery, London, and at Dorich House, Kingston University, Kingston-upon-Thames, Surrey.

Dora Gordine was a notable figure in the pre-war era, her work first attracting attention for its maturity and power when it was exhibited at the Salon des Tuileries in Paris in 1926. She attributed the intensity, maturity and feeling of her work to the experiences of her early years, when she left her parents in Estonia and travelled to Paris with her oldest brother, Leo, to study art and music. During the lonely holidays she recalled visiting the museums and art galleries of Paris, spending many fascinating hours at the Valsuani foundry where she was inspired to try modelling in clay (Tate Gallery interview). Throughout her life Gordine claimed to be self-taught and to have worked alone in Paris for several years to perfect her art. She was, however, encouraged by Aristide Maillol during this time; he advised her to continue working alone, saying that she already knew all that an art school could teach her and need only develop what was within her (*La Rumeur*, 22 July 1928). Her style of convex and well-rounded forms changed little over the years, apart from the surface texture, which is smooth in such early works as *Chinese Philosopher* and *Javanese Dancer*, and marked with cross-hatching and clay pieces in later ones.

Gordine: *Chinese Philosopher*, exhibited 1926; Dorich House Collection, Kingston, Surrey

The body of work that remains in numerous collections and in Dorich House, Kingston-upon-Thames, shows Gordine to be one of the many serious sculptors of the time, who, while clearly aware of modernist trends in technique and form, preferred a high degree of stylisation to abstraction, reflecting the sculptor's fascination with the art and philosophies of the East.

During her time in Paris, Gordine probably gained early inspiration from the many current exhibitions and lectures on Chinese and Asiatic art, particularly at the Musée Guimet. She first received acclaim for her Eastern heads, notably *Chinese Philosopher* (see illustration), exhibited in Paris in 1926. The critic Marie Dormoy (1927) wrote that Gordine had put "all the firmness, solidity and grandeur of that race" into one head. *Mongolian Head* was deemed to have "a rare power" (*ibid.*) and was bought by the National Gallery of British Art (now Tate Gallery) from Gordine's first solo exhibition at the Leicester Galleries in London in 1928, when reportedly all her works were sold. Full-length figures from this early period include nude male and female torsos, showing an allegiance to Maillol. In 1930 the Council of the City of Singapore commissioned Gordine to make six heads for the new City Hall, representing the different races that were living in Singapore. The commission gave her the opportunity to travel around the Far East, visiting Beijing and Bangkok and the recently discovered site of Angkor. One is reminded of its ancient sculptural forms in the life-size figure entitled *Pagan* (1935–8; Dorich House, Kingston-upon-Thames), a seated female nude.

Gordine had a sound working knowledge of casting and patination techniques, and worked exclusively in bronze in an age when sculptors were experimenting with new materials such as plastics and nylon (Naum Gabo), iron (Gonzales), collage (Picasso) and objets trouvés (Paul Nash). Although she was a contemporary of such sculptors as Chana Orloff (q.v.), Barbara Hepworth (q.v.) and Henry Moore, Gordine believed in representational "pure art". She regarded the revival of direct carving techniques and concerns with abstraction as frivolous, saying that "one should never follow fashion in art" (Nancy Wise interview, 1972). For Gordine, sculpture was a permanent, timeless art and she worked passionately to produce a work of "pure form" (Tate Gallery interview, 1990) that captured the spirit of her subjects as well as physical representation. Sitters for portrait heads were required to spend many hours in her studio, chatting and socialising, so that she could get to know them better, and it was her own perception of the sitter's character that she strove to express in the simple form of the finished bronze.

Throughout her life, inspiration came from all kinds of dance and music. Her bronzes of dancers capture the lyrical quality and movement of the dance (e.g. *Houri*; Dorich House) and are some of her most successful smaller figures. An early over-life-size bronze depicts the figure of a female *Javanese Dancer* (Dorich House) and a later series, exhibited at the Leicester Galleries in 1949, depicts ballet dancers observed from life in rehearsals. Other subjects for sculpture were frequently inspired by literature. Her bronzes have a distinctive patination. She felt that colour was an important part of the interpretation of the unique character of each individual work and for each piece she demanded from the foundry a specific colour according to her own perception of the subject. Thus she would seek to achieve a warm apricot or brown colour for what she saw as a warm personality and a calm green for a tranquil one.

After her marriage to the Hon. Richard Hare in 1936, Gordine settled in Kingston-upon-Thames, Surrey, and designed their home, Dorich House (its name was a conflation of their names). As well as living accommodation, the house incorporates two studios and a gallery, influenced by Gordine's Paris studio, which was designed in 1929 by Auguste Perret, a close friend. Richard Hare was Gordine's greatest supporter, encouraging many of his diplomatic associates to become sitters for portrait heads and promoting her work throughout his life. She accompanied him twice to the USA; to the Hoover Institution at Stanford University and Indiana in 1947, and to Hollywood, California, where he was a visiting Professor of Russian Studies, in 1959. During her time in America Gordine continued to work, taking commissions for portrait busts and giving lectures on Indian art.

Gordine's work had little affinity with that of other sculptors working in Britain in the 1930s. The solid, stylised forms continued to show the impact of the ancient Cambodian sculpture she had recently seen, and the spiritual calmness of the oriental mind. During the 1940s and 1950s a humorous and joyful element enters Gordine's work, although it loses the intensity and power of such early bronzes as *Pagan* and

Chinese Philosopher. Like many sculptors of the immediate post-war period, Gordine seemed to be searching for a new direction, although there seems to be no evidence of any move towards abstraction. Bronzes from these years are mainly smaller figures based on Western sources. Titles such as *Above Cloud* (1943–5; Dorich House), a male torso of an ex-RAF pilot, and *Mischief* and *Great Expectations* (both 1949; Dorich House), female nudes of young women, reflect Gordine's sharp and perceptive appreciation of her sitters' characters. Other titles such as *Sea Rose* and *World's Delight* (from the short stories of Somerset Maugham) and *Carmen* reflect her love of literature, and of opera, which she visited frequently with her husband and friends. Portrait busts included connoisseurs from the London art world, for example *John Pope-Hennessy* (1938–9), director of the Victoria and Albert Museum, and *Professor F. Brown* (1938), head of the Slade School of Fine Art; personalities from the entertainment world, *Dame Beryl Grey, Dame Edith Evans* (1937–8), *Emlyn Williams* (1940), *Sian Phillips* and *Dorothy Tutin*; and debutantes and society figures such as *H.E. The Egyptian Ambassador, Amr Pasha* (1949; all Dorich House). Her last public work was the *Mother and Child* (l. 27 m.), a "health-giving" sculpture commissioned for the entrance hall of the Royal Marsden Hospital in Surrey in 1963. Other public works are a bas-relief plaque to *Sun Yat-sen* (1946; 4 Gray's Inn Place, London), another to *General Mikhailovich* (Serbian Church, London) and a bas-relief of *Power* (1960; ht 2.1 m.) for the Milford Haven Refinery of the Esso Petroleum Company.

Gordine's sculpture was exhibited regularly at the Royal Academy, from 1937, and at the Society of Portrait Sculptors. She was elected a Fellow of the Royal Society of British Sculptors in 1949. Three of her oriental heads (*Chinese Philosopher, Kwa Nin*, the Chinese Lady of Peace, and *Malay Sultana*) were shown in the Fine Art Society's exhibition *Sculpture in Britain Between the Wars* in 1986. Four Eastern heads are held in the Tate Gallery, London, two portrait busts in the Royal Institute of British Architects and a striding male torso in Senate House, University of London. Other bronzes are in Holloway Prison, London; Herron Museum of Art, Indianapolis; the J.G. Stickney collection, California; the Parliament Building, Singapore; and in numerous private collections throughout the world. A major collection is in the sculptor's home, Dorich House, which has been renovated by Kingston University and holds a permanent display of Gordine's work, as well as an extensive archive (access on application to Kingston University).

BRENDA MARTIN

Gosse, (Laura) Sylvia
British painter and printmaker, 1881–1968

Born in England, 1881; father the literary critic Edmund Gosse; mother's sister was the painter Laura Alma-Tadema (q.v.). Educated in France. Studied at St John's Wood School of Art, London, 1903–6; Royal Academy Schools, London, 1906–8. Attended Walter Sickert's evening classes at

Gosse: *Rural Postmen, Mantes-La Jolie,* oil; York City Art Gallery

Westminster Technical Institute, 1908, and his etching classes at Rowlandson House, London, 1909–10. Managed Rowlandson House school for Sickert as joint business partner, 1910–14. Exhibited at the Allied Artists Association, 1909 and 1912; New English Art Club, 1911–27; Royal Academy from 1912; London Group, 1914–20 (member 1914). Included in the exhibitions *The Camden Town Group*, Brighton Art Gallery, 1913, and *Twentieth-Century Art*, Whitechapel Art Gallery, London, 1914. Associate member, 1917, and member, 1926, Royal Society of Painter-Etchers and Engravers; associate member, Royal Society of British Artists, 1928. Nursed Sickert's wife Christine at Envermeu, Dieppe, then Sickert himself after his wife's death, 1920–22. Organized "Sickert Fund" to free Sickert from financial worries, 1934. Moved to Ore, near Hastings, 1951. Died 6 June 1968.

Selected Individual Exhibitions

Carfax Gallery: 1914, 1916
Birmingham Repertory Theatre: 1918
Goupil Gallery, London: 1919, 1922, 1925
Walker's Gallery, London: 1922 (*Sickert Girls*)
P.D. Colnaghi, London: 1925, 1926
Arthur Tooth and Sons, London: 1927
Alex, Reid and Lefevre, London: 1931
Beaux Arts Gallery, London: 1937
Kensington Art Gallery, London: 1948
Redfern Gallery, London: 1951 (*French Paintings*, with Sidney Nolan and Vera Cunningham)
Hastings Museum and Art Gallery: 1978 (retrospective)

Bibliography

Hugh Stokes, "The etchings of Sylvia Gosse", *Print Collector's Quarterly*, xii, 1925, pp.314–38
London Group Retrospective, 1914–1928, exh. cat., New Burlington Galleries, London, 1928
Elliott Seabrooke, "The London Group", *The Studio*, cxxix, 1945, pp.33–44
London Group, 1914–1964, exh. cat., Tate Gallery, London, 1964
Marjorie Lilly, *Sickert: The Painter and His Circle*, London: Elek, 1971
The Sickert Women and the Sickert Girls, exh. cat., Michael Parkin Fine Art, London, 1974
Kathleen Fisher, *Conversations with Sylvia: Sylvia Gosse, Painter, 1881–1968*, ed. Eileen Vera Smith, London: Skilton, 1975
Wendy Baron, *Miss Ethel Sands and Her Circle*, London: Owen, 1977
Sylvia Gosse: Painter and Etcher, 1881–1968, exh. cat., Hastings Museum and Art Gallery, 1978
Wendy Baron, *The Camden Town Group*, London: Scolar Press, 1979
Sylvia Gosse, 1881–1968: Paintings and Prints, exh. cat., Michael Parkin Gallery, London, and elsewhere, 1989

Sylvia Gosse is often referred to as Walter Sickert's "favourite and best-known" pupil, as if her only relation to him was that of a follower. Many women who were friends and associates of Sickert have suffered the same fate, as is indicated by their more familiar acknowledgement as the "Sickert Girls and Women". Gosse's relationship with Sickert was extremely complex and lasted from 1908 until his death in 1942, moving from a very brief and early attendance at his evening classes where she first studied etching, to acting as his business partner at Rowlandson House, his nurse after the death of his first wife and, at the end of his life, his benefactor and supporter through her work to create the "Sickert Fund" in 1934, and occasional anonymous purchases of his work. Gosse admired Sickert's work and adopted his methods of working but she pursued an independent creative life as a painter in an undaunted fashion. A drawing by Gosse of *Rowlandson House* (1912; British Museum, London) shows a group of all-women students drawing in the garden, arranged in a semicircle around their subject, a shrub. Significantly, the master is nowhere in sight; what is shown is her overall view of this community of women students at work.

Gosse's work uses subject matter, colours and painting technique that are frequently identified only generically as "School of Sickert". The intellectual property and origin of the technique is attributed to the master and must (it is rather too automatically assumed) be only derivative in the work of his pupils. Gosse's subject matter, like Sickert's, primarily consists of scenes of working life – townscapes, domestic interiors with figures, music halls, street sellers – as well as still lifes and the occasional nude, cast not in an imaginary setting but in a dreary, north London bedsit. Her approach to what was common subject matter among the Camden Town Group is closest to Sickert's, as is her method of working from sketches to squared-up drawings in the studio, to a form of late Impressionist/Post-Impressionist painting where colour is applied in patches and blocks across carefully constructed tonal compositions. Sickert's technique also emphasised the importance of drawing as notes for compositions (Gosse's drawings are in the British Museum and Victoria and Albert Museum, London, Ashmolean Museum, Oxford, and Hanley Museum and Art Gallery, Stoke-on-Trent). A late work, *Lilies and Fruit* (1933; Manchester City Art Galleries), is unusual in that it was painted directly from the subject, whereas most of her other compositions were from studies worked up slowly in the studio. There are, however, good grounds for regarding the exchange as mutual rather than one-way in later life, although Sickert himself liked to boast that he finished the education of a large number of women artists. A reviewer in *The Times* (6 October 1925) wrote of Gosse's exhibition at Colnaghi's as "like a feminine retort in conversation" with Sickert's technique, and continued by attributing this to "deep unconscious 'difference', independent of opinion, which is generally lost in acquired expression" but in Gosse's case had been retained.

Around 1914 Gosse shared models and regularly painted with Harold Gilman. Gilman, supported by Sickert, opposed membership for women of the Camden Town Group – a rule that was dropped when the Camden Town Group amalgamated with the London Group. The supposed reason behind this was that the men feared that wives and girlfriends would wish to join the group, and pressure might be brought to bear even when their work might not be up to standard. There were nevertheless several single, independent women who also wished to join, among them, Nan Hudson, Ethel Sands and Sylvia Gosse. Gosse was elected to the London Group in 1914, although she tended not to mix socially with the group.

Many of Gosse's works depict scenes in and around Dieppe from the two years she spent there with Sickert and his wife (e.g. *Dieppe*; Gloucester City Museum and Art Gallery; *Envermeu under Snow*, Hastings City Art Gallery; *Dieppe: Moules Frites*, Bristol City Art Gallery; *Street Scene: Dieppe*,

Southampton City Art Gallery). She was reputed to have been a joint favourite with Thérèse Lessore (q.v.), her close friend who did marry him in 1926, to become Sickert's second wife. There is no evidence to suggest that she ever desired marriage, in spite of her evident devotion. On the contrary, her own views, according to Kathleen Fisher (1975, p.74), were that a woman painter should never contemplate marriage and that she had determined from an early age not to marry, because painting was of far greater importance to her. Gosse's mother had had similar ambitions for an independent life as a painter, and for a long time had refused to marry Edmund Gosse. Her desire for independence is perhaps also indicated by the fact that she signed her work "Gosse", thus depriving the viewer of any obvious attribution of gender.

In later life Gosse also used photography, particularly newspaper photography, as the basis for a series of documentary subject paintings. Here, her method of working preceded Sickert's own use (Gosse's *Madrid Crowd*, 1931, is compared with Sickert's *The Miner*, 1935, to illustrate this point in Baron 1979). After Sickert's death in 1942, she continued to paint until her own failing eyesight forced her to abandon work in 1961. Her work of these last 20 years is generally regarded to have blossomed in its technique, which is characterised both by a spare touch and a bold sense of design. A late series of genre paintings/character studies is another indication of her lack of dependence on Sickert, for example, *L'Oncle Josef at Versailles* (1947), *Balloon-Seller, Venice* (1951; repr. Fisher 1975) and *Old Venetian Woman* (Northampton Art Gallery).

KATY DEEPWELL

Graag, Anna Julia De *see* De Graag

Grant, Mary

British sculptor, 1831–1908

Born at Kilgraston, near Bridge of Earn, Perthshire, 1831, the elder daughter of John Grant and his second wife, Lady Lucy Bruce. Initially worked and exhibited from the family home at Kilgraston. Studied under Odoardo Fantachiotti in Florence, early 1860s; also reputed to have been a pupil of John Gibson in Rome. Further studies in Paris under Michel Louis Victor Mercier. Returned to London and established first independent studio at 64 Great Titchfield Street, 1868. Worked under the direction of John Henry Foley, 1868–9. Trip to USA, 1887. Never married. Died in London, 20 February 1908.

Principal Exhibitions

Royal Scottish Academy, Edinburgh: 1864, 1877, 1880, 1889
Royal Academy, London: occasionally 1866–92
Exposition Universelle, Paris: 1878

Bibliography

"Notes about Miss Mary Grant's works of art", undated manuscript in the possession of the artist's descendants; photocopy of the manuscript entitled "A list of the works of Mary Grant" in Conway Library, Courtauld Institute of Art, London

The "Journal" Guide to Dunfermline, Dunfermline, n.d., pp.26, 87–9

Art Journal, new series, xviii, 1879, p.106; new series, 1881, p.284

"Miss Mary Grant", *Ladies' Field*, 15 July 1899, pp.248–9 (with illustration)

M.H. Spielmann, *British Sculpture and Sculptors of Today*, London: Cassell, 1901

Clara Erskine Clement, *Women in the Fine Arts*, Boston: Houghton Mifflin, 1904; reprinted New York: Hacker, 1974

The Times, 29 February 1908, p.6 (obituary)

Maurice Harold Grant, *A Dictionary of British Sculptors*, London: Rockliff, 1953

Robin Lee Woodward, *Nineteenth-Century Scottish Sculpture*, PhD dissertation, University of Edinburgh, 1977 (contains bibliography and partial list of works)

Benedict Read, *Victorian Sculpture*, New Haven and London: Yale University Press, 1982

The manuscript correspondence of Mary Grant with Charles Chapman Grafton, Bishop of Fond-du-Lac, is in the Archives of St Paul's Cathedral, Diocese of Fond-du-Lac, Wisconsin, USA.

In 1899, when the *Ladies' Field* published a celebrity feature article on Mary Grant, she had recently completed a posthumous bust of *Gladstone* (her last recorded work) and had actually reached the zenith of her public career as a portrait and monumental sculptor over a decade earlier. In seeking to rationalise this phenomenon, the *Ladies' Field* highlighted her privileged social status, which should have predisposed her towards a dynastically advantageous marriage and which, in simultaneous defiance of and deference to convention, she had consistently exploited for her own professional advancement.

Grant's immediate family circumstances were exceptionally conducive towards the vocational as well as recreational development of artistic ability. Her maternal grandfather, the 7th Earl of Elgin, had achieved fame as the collector of the Parthenon sculptures or "Elgin Marbles". Her father, a Perthshire laird, practised as an amateur portrait and landscape painter, while her aunt, Mary Anne Grant, had studied with the Scottish landscape painter and dealer Andrew Wilson. Above all, the achievements of the sculptor's uncle, Francis Grant, a pupil and collaborator of John Ferneley, set a compelling precedent for the gifted aristocratic (male) amateur. Having exhausted his patrimony by his mid-twenties, Grant had embarked on a prolific and lucrative career as a professional portraitist without any obvious detriment to his social standing (see John Steegman, "Sir Francis Grant, PRA, the artist in high society", *Apollo*, 1964, pp.479–85). In 1866 his niece celebrated Grant's election to the Presidency of the Royal Academy by contributing a bust of him to the Academy's annual exhibition, thereby advertising her own influential connections and making a declaration of intent. Ten years later she presented this bust, rendered in marble, to the Academy.

By 1856, when she executed a bust of her brother *Charles Grant* (private collection, Scotland; record photograph in Scottish National Portrait Gallery archives, Edinburgh), Mary Grant had already attained a level of untrained competence indicative of higher potential. Family circumstances notwithstanding, her determination to accomplish the transition from amateur to professional met with vigorous opposition (see *Ladies' Field*). Ultimately and quite remarkably, she was afforded every opportunity for studio-based instruction with established British and Continental practitioners of portrait and ideal figure sculpture in the early 1860s. Her choice of John Gibson (see *The Times* obituary, 1908) was astute in terms of prestige and prospective patronage – as the elder statesman among British expatriate sculptors in Rome he attracted numerous pupils including Harriet Hosmer (q.v.) – and probably confirmed Grant's aptitude for portraiture. Her dedication to portraiture and, by extension, to monumental "public" sculpture must also have been reinforced by her subsequent training with Foley, apparently at his invitation.

Throughout her career Grant evidently depended on specialist carvers to translate her models into marble (for her copy of Woolner's bust of *Tennyson*, commissioned by the National Portrait Gallery in 1893, see Richard Ormond, *Early Victorian Portraits*, London, 1973, pp.450–51). Equally, her perseverance with such varied and extended training suggests that she was convinced of the need for formal technical proficiency, combined with the judicious deployment of social connections, as a vital prerequisite of professional independence for the woman sculptor. In this respect, as also in her audacious decision to base her career in London rather than in Scotland, and, presumably, in so doing, to maximise any advantages accruing from her uncle's position, she stood alone among her female compatriots, such as Amelia (Paton) Hill and Isabella Smith of Jordanhill.

From 1870 Grant began to reap the benefits of intensive studio training and obtained extensive patronage from both the English and Scottish aristocracy, periodically with an international dimension. Among the most prestigious commissions was a group of busts executed for the Rajah of Kapurthala in the Punjab and unveiled in 1874. These included a colossal bust of *Queen Victoria*, shown at the Royal Academy in 1871, and for which Grant received sittings at Windsor; posthumous likenesses of *Viscount Canning* and the *Prince Consort*; and, perhaps most tellingly, a bust of *General Sir James Hope Grant* (photograph of one example, privately owned, in Scottish National Portrait Gallery archives), Grant's uncle, who had recently retired after a brilliant military career in India. The precise context of these commissions is not recorded, but it is conceivable – even likely – that she owed them to the mediation of the General or to connections of her maternal uncle, the late 8th Earl of Elgin, who had served as Governor-General of India.

As an adjunct to bust portraiture, Grant favoured large-scale *alto relievo* medallions of a type exemplified by the Henry Fawcett Memorial on Thames Embankment, London, inaugurated in 1886 (plaster in the National Portrait Gallery, London). She had begun to experiment with this decorative genre as early as 1862 (medallion of *Georgiana Moncreiffe, later Countess Dudley*; private collection, Scotland) and showed a clear stylistic and formal affiliation with the work of the Pre-Raphaelite associate Alexander Munro (on Munro see Benedict Read and Joanna Barnes, eds, *Pre-Raphaelite Sculpture*, London, 1991, pp.11–30 and 46–65).

While portraiture remained her forte and staple source of income, Grant's submission to the Exposition Universelle in Paris in 1878 – at the request of the Prince of Wales – was an ideal sculpture representing *St Margaret of Antioch* (reviewed and illustrated in *Art Journal*, 1879, p.106; 1881, p.284). In 1897 Grant presented this sculpture to her old friend and

Grant: Reredos of the *Crucifixion*, St Mary's Episcopal Cathedral, Edinburgh

spiritual adviser Bishop Grafton of the Diocese of Fond-du-Lac, Wisconsin, where it is still located in the Cathedral of St Paul (in 1887, while on a two-month tour of the USA, she had corresponded with Bishop Grafton about her – unrealised – ambitions to open an American studio). Her alternative preoccupation with ideal sculpture also gave rise to occasional speculative projects such as a marble statuette of *Queen Margaret of Scotland*, sculpted in 1875, and of which versions were acquired by Lady Thurloe and Lady Monson. As late as 1904, Grant corresponded with Bishop Grafton about her abortive aspirations to have a larger version of this group commissioned by the Carnegie Trust for the royal burgh of Dunfermline (the example of the statuette now in Dunfermline City Chambers was presented to Dunfermline Corporation in 1946 by Lieutenant-Colonel J.P. Nisbet Hamilton Grant, the sculptor's nephew).

Less predictably, Grant appears to have discovered a second vocation and perfect mode of self-expression – which reflected her own intense Christian faith – through a series of important ecclesiastical projects on which she was engaged from the 1870s. At Kilgraston (now Kilgraston School, Society of the Sacred Heart) there is a plaster maquette for an unlocated quadripartite reredos comprising bas-reliefs of the *Life of St John the Baptist*, probably dating from the 1870s and related to a bas-relief of *The Baptist Preaching in the Wilderness*, which was shown at the Royal Academy in 1873. In 1880 she completed a marble reredos of the *Crucifixion* for St Mary's Episcopal Cathedral in Edinburgh (see illustration). This almost certainly prompted further commissions for architectural sculpture for Lichfield Cathedral (Read 1982, p.269) and for historical statuary (*Bishop Ken* and *Izaak Walton*) for the restored reredos at Winchester Cathedral, erected by 1884 and 1891 respectively. The extent to which inside influence, as distinct from proven skill, was instrumental in securing these commissions is open to speculation. In 1863 the sculptor's aunt, Lady Augusta Bruce, who was in the service of the Duchess of Kent and Queen Victoria successively, had married

Dean Stanley of Westminster. On his wife's death the Dean ordered from Grant a memorial for Dunfermline Abbey (as reported in *Art Journal*, 1876, p.208). In 1884 Mary Grant received final confirmation of royal favour in the form of a commission for a memorial relief bust of *Dean Stanley* for the private chapel at Windsor (repr. *Ladies' Field* 1899, p.249).

HELEN SMAILES

Graves, Nancy (Stevenson)
American sculptor and painter, 1940–1995

Born in Pittsfield, Massachusetts, 23 December 1940. Studied at Vassar College, Poughkeepsie, New York, 1957–61 (BA in English Literature); School of Art and Architecture, Yale University, New Haven, 1961–4 (BFA, MFA). Received Fulbright-Hayes grant for study in Paris, 1964. Lived and worked in Florence, Italy, 1965–6. Settled in New York, 1966. Taught at Fairleigh-Dickinson University, Rutherford, New Jersey, 1966–8. Resident, American Academy in Rome, 1979. Recipient of Vassar College fellowship, 1971; National Endowment for the Arts (NEA) grant, 1972; Creative Artists Public Service (CAPS) grant, 1974; Skowhegan medal for drawings/graphics, 1980; Yale University Distinguished Artistic Achievement award, 1985; New York Dance and Performance Bessie award for sets for Trisha Brown's *Lateral Pass*, 1986; Vassar College Distinguished Visitor award, 1986; American Art award, Pennsylvania Academy of the Fine Arts, 1987; honorary doctorates from Skidmore College, Saratoga Springs, 1989; University of Maryland, Baltimore, 1992; Yale University, 1992. Member, American Academy and Institute of Arts and Letters, 1991. Died in New York, 21 October 1995.

Selected Individual Exhibitions
Whitney Museum of American Art, New York: 1969
Museum of Modern Art, New York: 1971
Institute of Contemporary Art, University of Pennsylvania, Philadelphia: 1972–3 (touring), 1979
La Jolla Museum of Contemporary Art, CA: 1973
André Emmerich Gallery, New York: 1974, 1977
Knoedler and Co., New York: 1978, 1979, 1980, 1981, 1982, 1984, 1985, 1986, 1988, 1989, 1991, 1993, 1995
Albright-Knox Art Gallery, Buffalo, NY: 1980–81 (touring)
Vassar College Art Gallery, Poughkeepsie, NY: 1986 (touring)
Hirshhorn Museum and Sculpture Garden, Washington, DC: 1987–8 (touring retrospective, organised by Fort Worth Art Museum, TX)
Fine Arts Gallery, University of Maryland Baltimore County: 1993–4 (touring)

Bibliography
Gregory Battcock, "Camels today", *New York Free Press*, 2 May 1968, pp.8, 11
Nancy Graves: Sculpture, Drawings, Films, 1969–1971, exh. cat., Neue Galerie, Aachen, 1971
Hilton Kramer, "Downtown scene: A display of bones", *New York Times*, 19 January 1971, p.5
Nancy Graves: Sculpture and Drawings, 1970–1972, exh. cat., Institute of Contemporary Art, University of Pennsylvania, Philadelphia, and elsewhere, 1972
Lucy R. Lippard, "Distancing: The films of Nancy Graves", *Art in America*, lxiii, November–December 1975, pp.78–82; reprinted in Lucy R. Lippard, *From the Center: Feminist Essays on Women's Art*, New York: Dutton, 1976
Mimi Crossley, "Nancy Graves: Recent paintings, watercolors and sculptures", *Houston Post*, 24 November 1978, p.9AA
John Russell, "Art people", *New York Times*, 26 January 1979, p.C16
Nancy Graves: A Survey, 1969–1980, exh. cat., Albright-Knox Art Gallery, Buffalo, NY, and elsewhere, 1980
John Russell, "Nancy Graves makes art of science", *New York Times*, 1 June 1980, p.D25
Nancy Graves: Painting and Sculpture, 1978–82, exh. cat., Santa Barbara Contemporary Arts Forum, CA, 1983
Michael Edward Shapiro, "Nature into sculpture: Nancy Graves and the tradition of direct casting", *Arts Magazine*, lix, November 1984, pp.92–6
Nancy Graves: Painting, Sculpture, Drawing, 1980–85, exh. cat., Vassar College Art Gallery, Poughkeepsie, NY, and elsewhere, 1986
Avis Berman, "Nancy Graves' new age of bronze", *Art News*, lxxxv, February 1986, pp.56–64
E.A. Carmean, Jr, and others, *The Sculpture of Nancy Graves: A Catalogue Raisonné*, New York: Hudson Hills Press, 1987
Amy Fine Collins and Bradley Collins, Jr, "The sum of the parts", *Art in America*, lxxvi, June 1988, pp.112–119
Thomas Padon, *Nancy Graves: Excavations in Print: A Catalogue Raisonné*, New York: Abrams, 1996

A descendant of Cotton Mather, a founding New England patriarch, Nancy Stevenson Graves grew up immersed in her father's world of a small western Massachusetts museum that exhibited both art and natural science. This pairing – and the urge to merge them together – marked virtually all of Graves's mature work, following her graduate studies and degrees from Yale University. Highly educated and learned, she began her career in Florence in 1965. Influenced by the wax models of the 18th-century anatomist Clemente Susini, Graves first made two life-sized sculptures of *Camels*, placing pelts over an internal structure of her own design. Although the first pair was destroyed before she left Italy, she resumed the camels when she returned to New York in 1966, eventually creating a total of 25, of which only five remain intact, including *Camels VI, VII* and *VIII* (all National Gallery of Canada, Ottawa). When these three were first shown at the Whitney Museum of American Art in New York in 1969, they quickly established Graves as an important new artist.

From 1969 until 1971 Graves's sculpture focused on bones of animals and on abstract constructions that seemingly recreated ancient rituals, the latter including *Shaman* (1970; Museum Ludwig, Cologne). But after this intensive period of work, she turned to other media, first filmmaking, such as *Izzy Bourir* shot in Morocco in 1971, and then, in 1972, she resumed painting and began making prints. While these two-dimensional works continued to draw upon the natural world, they did so less directly, being based on abstract renderings or topographic maps.

In 1979 and 1980 Graves returned to sculpture in a major fashion, working on a larger scale and in collaboration with fabricators first at the Johnson Atelier in Princeton, New Jersey, and then with Lippincott, in North Haven, Connecticut. Her real breakthrough, and the start of her mature career, came when she began working with Richard Polich and the Talix Foundry in Peekskill, New York. Now using the lost wax

Graves: *Metaphore and Melanomy*, 1995; bronze and patina; Brooks Museum of Art, Memphis; Collection of Robert F. and Martha H. Fogelman

technique, she began casting natural forms in bronze, creating elements ranging from leaves and bananas to turkey bones and sardines. Following in the path of the American sculptor David Smith, Graves welded these varying cast materials into open, abstract compositions of increasing complexity and ever-larger physical size, until her untimely death at the age of 54.

As the critic Robert Hughes observed, a key aspect of Graves's sculpture is its "subversiveness". In her art, forms take on unexpected permutations. First, in the material itself, cast bronze, which challenges the identity of many objects and their assumed "natural" weight. Casting also allows for changes in "normal" sizes, while the open, welded structure often affords unusual placements or unexpected rhythms. Colour in the sculpture is also subversive, being "unreal" and created using four different methods: unaltered, natural surfaces; patina; glass enamelling; being painted with polyurethane.

A distinguishing factor about Graves's sculpture was her ability to work at widely different sizes, from small intimate pieces to constructions that tower at heights of 2.4 metres. Medium-size works also began to influence her paintings, and by the mid-1980s she had begun adding flat relief sculptures to her paintings so that they jutted outwards from the two-dimensional surfaces. In turn, in her later works, Graves began making sculptural reliefs proper, through dimensional structures intended to hang on the wall.

Graves's sculpture of the mid-1990s is marked by two fundamental changes – the palette is more restrained, and other new elements are introduced – quotations from other works of art, such as the Venus de Milo and Michelangelo's figure of Adam from the Sistine Chapel ceiling. All of this comes together in Graves's last sculpture, *Metaphore and Melanomy* (1995; see illustration). Soaring to 3 metres in height and nearly 3 × 3 metres across, it is the largest of her interior works. The sculpture colour is now subtle, largely a golden bronze patina, with only a hint of colour – pale pink, green and blue. Her cast baseball bat and a cheese grater are joined by the Head of Nefertiti and Venus de Milo and the pointing finger of the Sistine Adam. The title of the work alludes to the shifting references of her sculptured vocabulary and an acknowledgement that this would be her final, heroic work.

E.A. CARMEAN, JR

Gray, Norah Neilson

British painter, 1882–1931

Born in Helensburgh, Scotland, 16 June 1882, to George William Gray, a Glasgow shipowner, and his wife Norah Neilson. Trained with Miss Park and Miss Ross in Helensburgh, then at Glasgow School of Art, 1901–6. Taught fashion-plate drawing at the School, from 1906; also taught at St Columba's School for Girls, Kilmacolm, until April 1918. Own studio in Glasgow by 1910. Worked as Voluntary Aid Detachment nurse at Royaumont Abbey, outside Paris, spring 1918. Member, Royal Scottish Society of Painters in Watercolour, 1914; first woman to be appointed to the hanging committee of Royal Glasgow Institute of Fine Arts, 1921. Died of cancer in Glasgow, 27 May 1931.

Principal Exhibitions

Royal Academy, London: occasionally 1905–26
Royal Scottish Academy, Edinburgh: occasionally 1907–30
Royal Scottish Society of Painters in Watercolour, Edinburgh: 1909–32
Royal Glasgow Institute of the Fine Arts: 1909–31
Warneuke's Gallery, Glasgow: 1910 (individual)
Société Nationale des Beaux-Arts, Paris: from 1913
Paris Salon: occasionally 1921–30 (bronze medal 1921, silver medal 1923)
Gieves Art Gallery, London: 1926 (individual)
McLellan Galleries, Glasgow: 1932 (retrospective)

Bibliography

Memorial Exhibition of Pictures by the Late Norah Neilson Gray RSW, exh. cat., McLellan Galleries, Glasgow, 1932
Norah Neilson Gray (1882–1931), exh. cat., Dumbarton District Libraries, 1985
Jude Burkhauser, ed., *Glasgow Girls: Women in Art and Design, 1880–1920*, 2nd edition, Edinburgh: Canongate, and Cape May, NJ: Red Ochre, 1993

The correspondence between Norah Neilson Gray and E.A. Taylor is in the Merle Taylor Estate, Special Collections, University of Glasgow; the correspondence between Norah Neilson Gray and Mr Yockney is in the Imperial War Museum archives, London.

Norah Neilson Gray's early life as the second youngest daughter of a family of seven was spent at Carisbrook, a large villa in Helensburgh by the river Clyde, some 32 kilometres from Glasgow. It had a large garden that stimulated her love of flowers and growing things. Another early influence was a Highland nurse who told the three youngest girls wonderful legends and fairy stories; their effect on Gray can be seen in the imaginative fantasies she painted in watercolour later in life. The family moved to Glasgow in 1901, and she studied at the Glasgow School of Art under Francis Newbery and a recent addition to his staff, Jean Delville from Belgium, later to become known as a Symbolist painter. Gray joined the staff herself after her training to teach fashion-plate drawing, which helps to explain the emphasis on design in her portraits, using simplified areas in a single tone and colour that does not compromise the form. Her pupils at St Columba's School for Girls at Kilmacolm called her "Purple Patch" because she asked them to look for colour in shadows. In 1910 Gray moved into her own studio in Bath Street, Glasgow, and held her first exhibition at Warneuke's Gallery that same year. To the dismay of everyone, she covered the maroon walls of the gallery with light-coloured scrim, and toned down the gold frames of her pictures. In answer to her critics she said: "It is my exhibition". One of the pictures exhibited was a portrait of her mother dressed in black, as her father had died the previous year.

The independence of spirit and strength of will shown in the arrangement of her exhibition, which seemed at odds with her slim, elegant and impeccable appearance, are seen particularly in the paintings Gray did during World War I. An understanding of his feelings is seen in the face of the strongly painted *Belgian Refugee* (1916; see illustration), which speaks for all refugees, while an appreciation of the watching and waiting of

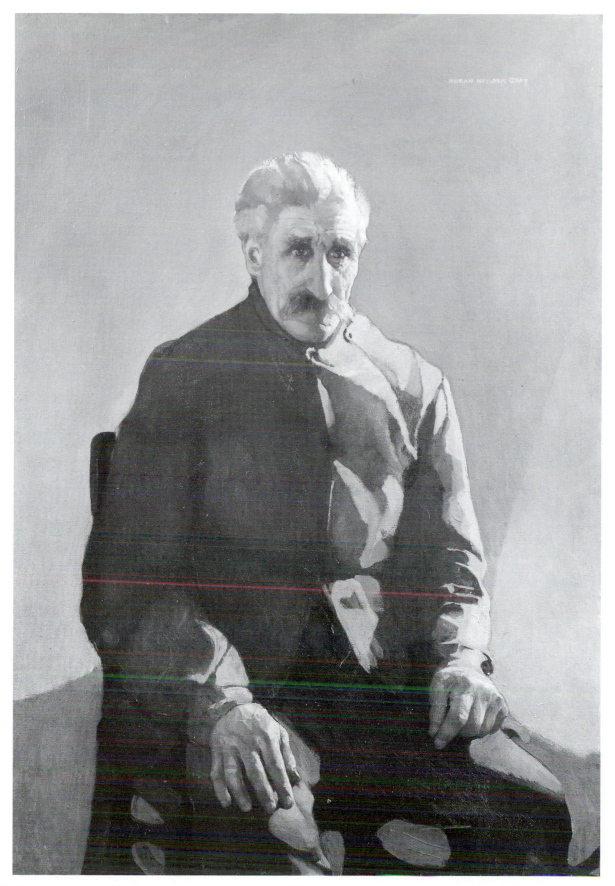

Gray: *Belgian Refugee*, 1916; oil on canvas; 125.7 × 87 cm.; Glasgow Museums: Art Gallery and Museum, Kelvingrove

women is seen in the watercolour *Missing Trawler* (1915; Glasgow Art Gallery). In April 1918, on her own initiative, Gray went to work as a Voluntary Aid Detachment nurse at a French Red Cross Hospital at Royaumont Abbey near Paris, which was staffed entirely by women of the Scottish Women's Hospitals. The hospital was very busy during the last German advance on Paris, and despite little free time, she painted the casualty-receiving area in the abbey crypt in *Hôpital Auxiliaire d'Armée 301 – Abbaye de Royaumont* (Dumbarton District Libraries and Museums). This painting was offered to the Imperial War Museum, but instead she was commissioned to paint the *Scottish Women's Hospital* (Imperial War Museum, London), which included portraits of the staff. As a painting it is rather stiff compared with the feeling of immediacy of her earlier work.

After the war Gray resumed her career as a portraitist, particularly of young women and children. Though she never married, and was by nature somewhat cool, withdrawn and shy, except with her own family, she had a natural affinity with children and succeeded in the notoriously difficult art of child portraiture (*Little Boy with Oranges*, c.1927; Glasgow Museums and Art Galleries). Very often flowers formed part of the composition in her decoratively designed canvases. The decorative approach was used also in commissioned portraits of men, such as *Professor E.P. Cathcart* (?1927; University of Glasgow) wearing his bright red graduation robes. Many of these canvases were large (usual size 127 × 89 cm.; some full-length portraits 183 cm.) and were regularly exhibited not only in Scotland and London, but also abroad, especially in Paris, where she gained bronze and silver medals and was acclaimed in the press, She was better known in France, where her work was reproduced in the magazine *L'Illustration*, than in Britain.

When she was asked by E. A. Taylor, who was writing for *The Studio* in 1912, whether she preferred painting in oil or watercolour she replied: "... I prefer oil as it is a much wider field and I'm desperately interested in people's faces. Doing a few of these watercolour drawings is a pleasure but if I do too many they become feeble and unspontaneous" (letter from Gray to E. A. Taylor, 7 October 1912). There are, however, dangers in using oil paints as a medium, and traps into which Gray fell – overpainting areas that were not quite dry and varnishing too soon – which has resulted in the later poor condition of her work. This weakness stemmed from the same determination and self-confidence that always characterised her work.

She herself, perhaps, realised the limitations of her earlier watercolour fantasies of a never-never land peopled with fairies and cherubs, which are sometimes given haloes like angels. Her illustrations to William Wordsworth's *Ode on Intimations of Immortality from Recollections of Early Childhood* (1913) do not match his images, but are poetic miniatures in their own right. Her later landscape watercolours, however, have real power and innovation. Washes were laid over pointillist touches with a small brush or pencil to build up a finely wrought surface and imbue it with a brooding romantic character. *July Night, Loch Lomond* (c.1923; private collection, Scotland) is a very romantic treatment of a familiar scene in an Art Nouveau style.

Norah Neilson Gray was an artist of real quality. She had something to say in painting, and it was in her own way, a resolute but feminine way. She was acknowledged in her own day, especially in France, and was reaching the height of her career when she died of cancer at the age of 49. Since her death her work has been undeservedly neglected.

AILSA TANNER

Grebber, Maria de *see* Guilds and the Open Market survey

Greenaway, Kate
British illustrator and painter, 1846–1901

Born Catherine Greenaway in Hoxton, London, 17 March 1846. First trained by her father, a wood engraver. Attended evening classes at Female School of Art, Clerkenwell, 1853–9, then day classes at Finsbury School of Art, under National Course of Art Instruction scheme; awarded national art competition prizes for drawings. Studied at South Kensington School of Art, 1865–9 (silver medal); subsequently took life classes at Heatherley's; enrolled at Slade School of Fine Art, 1871. Began career as freelance illustrator and painter with studio in Islington, London, 1870; worked for a number of publishers including Marcus Ward, Frederick Warne, Edmund Evans, Macmillan, George Routledge, Chatto and Windus, as well as her father's publishers, Griffith and Farran, Cassell, and Petter and Galpin. Began lifelong correspondence with John Ruskin, 1882. Member of the Royal Institute of Painters in Watercolours, 1889. Died in London, 6 November 1901.

Principal Exhibitions
Dudley Gallery, London: from 1868 (watercolour)
Royal Society of British Artists, London: 1870, 1872–5
Royal Academy, London: 1877–80, 1890, 1895
Fine Art Society, London: 1891, 1894, 1898 (all individual), 1902 (retrospective)
World's Columbian Exposition, Chicago: 1893
Royal Institute of Painters in Watercolours, London: 1893, 1895–7

Bibliography
"Art in the nursery", *Magazine of Art*, vi, 1883, pp.127–32
John Ruskin, "In fairyland", *The Art of England: Lectures Given in Oxford ... During His Second Tenure of the Slade Professorship*, Orpington: Allen, 1883
Austin Dobson, "Kate Greenaway", *Art Journal*, 1902, pp.33–6, 105–9
M.H. Spielmann, "Kate Greenaway: In memoriam", *Magazine of Art*, xxvi, 1902, pp.118–22
M.H. Spielmann and G.S. Layard, *Kate Greenaway*, London: A. & C. Black, 1905; reprinted New York: Blom, 1969
Austin Dobson, *De Libris: Prose and Verse*, London: Macmillan, 1908; New York: Oxford University Press, 1923
Jeanne Doin, "Kate Greenaway et ses livres illustrés", *Gazette des Beaux-Arts*, 4th series, iii, 1910, pp.5–22
Kate Greenaway Pictures, London: Warne, 1921
Anne Carroll Moore, *A Century of Kate Greenaway*, London and New York: Warne, 1946

Frances Paul, "A collection of children's books illustrated by Walter Crane, Kate Greenaway and Randolph Caldecott", *Apollo*, xliii, 1946, pp.141–3

Edward Ernest, ed., *The Kate Greenaway Treasury: An Anthology of the Illustrations and Writings of Kate Greenaway*, Cleveland: World Publishing, 1967; London: Collins, 1968

Kate Greenaway, 1846–1901, exh. cat., Bolton Art Gallery, 1975

Rodney Engen, *Kate Greenaway*, London: Academy Editions, and New York: Harmony Books, 1976

Bryan Holme, ed., *The Kate Greenaway Book*, New York: Viking, and London: Warne, 1976

Susan Ruth Thomson, *A Catalogue of the Kate Greenaway Collection, Rare Book Room, Detroit Public Library*, Detroit: Wayne State University Press, 1977

Kate Greenaway, exh. cat., Hunt Institute for Botanical Documentation, Carnegie Mellon University, Pittsburgh, 1980

Rodney Engen, *Kate Greenaway: A Biography*, London: Macdonald, and New York: Schocken, 1981

Thomas E. Schuster and Rodney Engen, *Printed Kate Greenaway: A Catalogue Raisonné*, London: Schuster, 1986

Ina Taylor, *The Art of Kate Greenaway: A Nostalgic Portrait of Childhood*, Exeter: Webb and Bower, 1991

During a career that spanned three decades, and included illustrations for more than 150 books and 90 periodicals, as well as 49 exhibited paintings, Kate Greenaway founded a tradition of children's illustration that continues even today. The Greenaway style has been reproduced and imitated on merchandise ranging from clothes to tea-sets, playing cards to paper dolls, ceramic tiles to wallpaper (the only product she ever authorised), and she has correctly been described as the most exploited, imitated and promoted artist of the Victorian period. After more than a century of these often saccharine spin-offs, the original strength of Greenaway's work can be difficult to appreciate. But considered within the context of the garishly coloured, over-produced and poorly designed books that dominated the children's market of the 1870s, her appeal regains its forcefulness. With Walter Crane and Randolph Caldecott, she was at the forefront of a movement to supply well-designed and well-produced children's books to a market that was booming under the influence of Forster's Education Act of 1870.

Greenaway was born in northeast London to lower-middle-class parents. During periods of financial hardship the Greenaway children spent time with relatives in the Northamptonshire countryside; her idealised memories of these visits provided her with the material for her first major collection of drawings and verse, *Under the Window* (1879), and continued to serve as a source of inspiration throughout her career. Encouraged by her father, a professional engraver with whom she would later share illustration projects, Greenaway undertook ten years of formal study on the National Course of Art Instruction, eventually attending the South Kensington School of Art, where she shared a studio with Elizabeth Thompson, later Lady Butler (q.v.). Greenaway excelled under the highly structured National Course, and her mature style retained its emphasis on linear draughtsmanship and decorative design, despite additional training at Heatherley's and the Slade School of Fine Art. The South Kensington focus on professional craftsmanship combined with economic necessity to encourage Greenaway to adopt a commercial approach to her career.

Even before she left school Greenaway began to receive illustration commissions. Her specialisation in scenes of childhood was established early, beginning in 1867 with the frontispiece for a nursery guide, *Infant Amusements*, and continuing with a series of fairytale books and numerous drawings of children for magazines such as *Cassell's* (1873–4), *Illustrated London News* (1874–9) and *Little Folks* (1876–9). Similar subjects were undertaken in her exhibited paintings as well. *A Flower Girl* (exh. Royal Society of British Artists, 1874; private collection, repr. Taylor 1991, p.21) and *Misses* (exh. Royal Academy, 1879; Walker Art Gallery, Liverpool) are characteristic of her early finished watercolours in their full-length frontal portrayal of young girls against a shallow background. Illustration and exhibition were linked for Greenaway from her first show at the Dudley Gallery (1868), when the Revd William Loftie purchased a series of fairy paintings for inclusion in his *People's Magazine*. Through Loftie she established a connection with the publisher Marcus Ward, for whom she designed 32 separate sets of greeting cards between 1868 and 1877, when his repeated exploitation of her designs without further payment led her to sever their connection. The cards served a triple purpose for Greenaway: they provided a steady income, they gave her work public visibility, and they furnished a forum in which to develop the "Greenaway child" that would become her hallmark. Despite the rather garish colours employed in Ward's early chromolithographs, samples preserved in the greeting-card collection of the Victoria and Albert Museum, London, show both the evolution of Greenaway's style and its departure from other exceedingly mawkish cards then on the market. The valentine *Disdain* is a notable example. An especially popular greeting card, it was repackaged with other designs by Greenaway and Walter Crane and sold as a book, *The Quiver of Love* (1876). Its Pre-Raphaelite tone would resurface more forcefully in much later paintings, such as the *Fable of the Girl and Her Milk Pail* (1893; private collection, repr. Engen 1981, p.176).

The connection with Walter Crane was reinforced in 1878, when Greenaway entered into partnership with the printer Edmund Evans, who was already producing a series of toybooks by Crane and Randolph Caldecott. The collaboration between Greenaway and Evans was auspicious for both of them. His three-colour woodblock printing technique was highly accurate in its reproduction of both the subtle colours and the refined outlines of the original watercolours. The quality of the printing itself contributed to the astounding success of their initial venture, *Under the Window*, which sold more than 100,000 copies. But Evans's impact should not be overstated, as it has sometimes been. Comparison of the paintings for *Mary, Mary Quite Contrary* and *Polly Put the Kettle On* (photographs in Witt Library, Courtauld Institute of Art, London) with the printed versions in *Mother Goose* (1881) reveals an engaging fluidity that Evans could not capture. The *Art Journal* found the prints to be "as moonlight unto sunlight compared with the original drawings" (Dobson 1902, p.109), and the *Illustrated London News* acknowledged in the watercolours a "delicacy and sense of humour which defy reproduction" (1891, p.215).

The publication of *Under the Window* ushered in a decade of intense work. Greenaway's *Birthday Book for Children* (1880) included 382 drawings, and in the same year there were

Greenaway: *May Day*, pen and watercolour; Huntington Art Gallery, San Marino, California

further illustrations in 18 books, eight journals and a calendar. With the exception of *The April Baby's Book of Tunes* (1900), all of Greenaway's major illustration projects were published between 1879 and 1889. She continued to illustrate other authors' writings, most notably Robert Browning's *The Pied Piper of Hamelin* (1888), but gave preference to her own collections of verse and prose. In her annual almanacs and books of songs, games, rhymes and stories she persistently focused on scenes of children's play. There is frequent emphasis on the ceremonial aspects of childhood pursuits, apparent in such pen and watercolour drawings as *May Day* (see illustration). While her earlier paintings of flower girls and watercress sellers bore traces of Victorian social realism, her book illustrations were completely devoid of class differences and political concerns. Only in one unusual drawing from 1886, *White Rose and White Lily* (photograph in Witt Library), do we see the transformative social power of the Greenaway pen, as a group of impoverished, ragged children is magically transformed through the agency of two maiden fairies into a stream of gay and gleaming girls and boys.

Stylistically, Greenaway's delicate lines, minimal shading, spare lay-out and pastel colours spoke with a clarity and freshness that captivated a book-buying public newly influenced by the Aesthetic movement. Aesthetic sensibilities were further engaged by details of subject matter such as blue-and-white china, rush-bottom chairs, sunflowers and flowing clothes. The high-waisted dresses and mob-caps coincided with a nascent 18th-century revivalism; the idyllic rural settings resonated with the pastoral nostalgia of industrialised England; the solemn, sexless, pretty children reinforced the cult of childhood innocence. The combination was to prove tremendously appealing. In the estimation of John Ruskin (1883), Greenaway's art had "the radiance and innocence of re-instated infant divinity ... All gold and silver you can dig out of the earth are not worth the kingcups and daisies she gave you of her grace".

Formally, Greenaway's drawing had certain weaknesses. Her scene of the *Four Princesses*, from *Marigold Garden* (1885), reveals a persistent difficulty with perspective. The feet of her figures were often disproportionately large, and their fingers stick-like. Most notably, the limbs of her subjects sometimes seemed detached from their bodies, giving them an awkwardness readily apparent in *Boy and Girl with a Cat* (Lady Lever Gallery, Port Sunlight). Her adviser and fellow artist Henry Stacy Marks admonished Greenaway for the way in which the girl descending *Pippin Hill* (*Mother Goose*, 1881) defied physical laws: "How about the centre of gravity, madam?" (Engen 1981, p.81). Intriguingly, however, these flaws do not seriously detract from the overall effect of her scenes. In this politely ordered world, where children are always good and the hedges are always perfectly trimmed, acceptance of an awkward pose here and there is by no means the greatest suspension of disbelief that viewers are asked to make. Such details may even contribute to the fantasy quality of "Greenaway land".

Writing in the *Art Journal*, Greenaway's colleague Austin Dobson enumerated the pleasures of this land, where the "most attractive environment of flower-beds or blossoming orchards, and red-roofed cottages with dormer windows" was peopled by children "so gentle, so unaffected in their affectation, so easily pleased, so innocent, so trustful, and so confiding" that no real children could compare (Dobson 1902, pp.33–4). Yet while Dobson readily conceded the unreality of these imaginary beings, many critics and historians have been eager to attribute the personal qualities of these fantasy children to Greenaway herself. "Never was an artist's self more truly reflected on to her paper" wrote her biographer M.H. Spielmann (1902), emphasising Greenaway's modesty, purity, simplicity and grace of mind. More recently, Ina Taylor has suggested that "to understand Kate Greenaway's early life is to understand her art, for she virtually painted her autobiography" (Taylor 1991, p.11). Critical assessment of the work and skills of women artists have often been subsumed within the details of their domestic and emotional lives. In Greenaway's case this approach combined with her focus on children and her unmarried status to create a perception of the artist as essentially childlike. John Ruskin described her as a mixed child and woman, and Greenaway herself encouraged the image, relating how she hated to be grown-up, and cried when she had her first long dress. One of the results of this construction was that it led even such staunch admirers as Spielmann to devalue the intense labour she put into her art, concluding that her talent arose "as much from intuition as from scholarly training" (Spielmann 1902, p.121).

Another biographical detail that Greenaway repeatedly asserted was the happiness of her childhood. In searching for a source of her idealised, idyllic creations, biographers have frequently quoted her account of childhood as "one long continuous joy – filled … with a strange wonder and beauty" (Greenaway Correspondence, Carnegie Mellon University Library, Pittsburgh). "I had such a happy time when I was a child", she wrote, "and curiously, was so very much happier than my brothers and sisters, with exactly the same surroundings" (Engen 1981, p.15). But, in fact, one aspect that repeatedly troubled critics was the sadness that so often appeared on the faces of Greenaway's children. In *Under the Window* a procession of children files out from school to the rhyme "School is over, oh, what fun!" Yet while the children in the distance fulfil their promise to run and laugh, the expressions of the main figures are unmistakably morose. Though Greenaway acknowledged that this sadness was perceived as a flaw, she was either unable or unwilling to change the tone of her work. It is revealing to note that Edmund Evans sometimes made the changes for her.

In 1890 Kate Greenaway decided to stop illustrating books and to pursue a gallery career. In this decision she was partly influenced by her intimate and often tumultuous friendship with Ruskin, who wished her to "make more serious use of her talent, without any reference to saleableness" (Engen 1981, pp.109–10). In contrast to her other close adviser, the poet Frederick Locker-Lampson, Ruskin felt that Greenaway's ornamental style was a weakness; he urged her to be truer to nature, as he did with all his protégés, and set her technical exercises such as the *Study of Moss, Rock and Ivy* (1885; Ruskin Gallery, Sheffield). Some evidence of an increasing naturalism may be seen in the illustrations of 1886 to Bret Harte's *The Queen of the Pirate Isle*.

Greenaway was also disillusioned by the widespread plagiarism of her work, which led to financial difficulty. Already by the time of *Marigold Garden* (1885) she had tired of the grind of publishing demands. From that point, illustration would be little more than an economic necessity for her. In 1889 she became a member of the Royal Institute of Painters in Watercolours, and renewed her friendship with her former classmate Helen Allingham (q.v.). Their sketching trips into the countryside provided the initial inspiration for an exhibition at the Fine Art Society in 1891, and subsequent one-woman shows were held in 1894 and 1898. Perceiving her own over-dependence on Allingham's style and technique (see the *Old Farm House*, Victoria and Albert Museum) she abandoned their working association, but isolated in her studio she lacked the influx of new ideas that might have facilitated the creative rejuvenation she sought. She exhibited at the Royal Academy and struggled with oil techniques, but such late paintings as *The Muff* (untraced, repr. Engen 1981, p.204) were largely stilted elaborations of themes that she had expressed more convincingly in her earlier illustration.

KRISTINA HUNEAULT

Greene, Gertrude
American sculptor and painter, 1904–1956

Born Gertrude Glass in Brooklyn, New York, 1904. Attended evening classes at the Leonardo da Vinci Art School, studying under Cesare Stea, 1924–6. Married painter Balcomb Greene, 1926; accompanied him on his studies in Europe. Set up first studio to make sculpture in Dartmouth, New Hampshire, 1930. Returned to Paris to study contemporary art, 1931–2. Settled in New York, 1933. Co-founder, 1933, and first salaried employee, 1936–7, American Abstract Artists (AAA); coordinated their first exhibition in 1937. Participated in Federal Art Project (FAP), 1934–9. Helped to form Artists Union. Divided time between Pittsburgh and Montauk, Long Island, 1947–56; also had a studio in New York. Member, Painters and Sculptors Guild; Federation of Modern Painters and Sculptors. Died of cancer in New York, autumn 1956.

Principal Exhibitions

American Abstract Artists, New York: 1937–46
Solomon R. Guggenheim Collection, New York: 1937
Museum of Living Art, New York: 1937
Helena Rubinstein New Art Circle Gallery, New York: 1942 (*Masters of Abstract Art*)
Museum of Modern Art, New York: 1951 (*Abstract Painting and Sculpture in America*)
Grace Borgenicht Gallery, New York: 1951 (individual)
Bertha Schaefer Gallery, New York: 1955 (individual), 1957 (retrospective)

Bibliography

American Abstract Artists: Letters, Minutes, Lists, microfilm roll NY 59–11, New York: Archives of American Art, 1936–44
American Abstract Artists: Three Yearbooks (1938, 1939, 1946), reprinted New York: Arno Press, 1969

Susan C. Larsen, "The American Abstract Artists: A documentary history, 1936–41", *Archives of American Art Journal*, xiv/1, 1974, pp.2–7

—, "Going abstract in the 30s", *Art in America*, lxiv, September–October 1976, pp.70–79

American Abstract Artists, exh. cat., University Art Museum, University of New Mexico, Albuquerque, 1977

Robert Beverly Hale and Nike Hale, *The Art of Balcomb Greene*, New York: Horizon Press, 1977

Jacqueline Moss, *The Constructions of Gertrude Greene: The 1930s and 1940s*, MA thesis, Queens College, City University of New York, 1980

Gertrude Greene: Constructions, Collages, Paintings, exh. cat., ACA Galleries, New York, 1981

Jacqueline Moss, "Gertrude Greene: Constructions of the 1930s and 1940s", *Arts Magazine*, lv, April 1981, pp.120–27

Susan C. Larsen and John R. Lane, eds, *Abstract Painting and Sculpture in America, 1927–44*, New York: Abrams, 1984

Charlotte Streifer Rubinstein, *American Women Sculptors*, Boston: Hall, 1990

Gertrude Greene is considered to be one of the first American artists to create totally abstract, non-objective sculpture and, according to fellow artist Ilya Bolotowsky, she may have been the first American to make painted wood-relief constructions. Greene was primarily a self-taught artist whose interest in art was stimulated after she opened a kindergarten in 1924, which prompted her to enroll at the Leonardo da Vinci Art School, founded by Italian émigré artists. They provided an essentially conservative art education, which involved drawing from plaster casts for two years before working from the model. Greene, however, was attracted to a more radical group within the school who sought out the modernist art exhibited at Alfred Stieglitz's Intimate Gallery.

This same year, 1924, Greene met John Wesley (name later changed to Balcomb) Greene, the son of a liberal Methodist minister, while visiting the Egyptian galleries at the Metropolitan Museum of Art. The couple married shortly after his graduation from Syracuse University in 1926, and travelled to Vienna, where Balcomb Greene had a fellowship in psychology. In 1927, when the fellowship was transferred to Columbia University, New York, the couple stopped in Paris to see art on their way home. Gertrude followed her husband to his various positions, first at Dartmouth College (1928–31), where she erected her first studio and resumed her sculpture, completing several plaster casts. She continued her study of European art during visits to New York at the Museum of Living Art, opened by the artist and collector Albert Eugene Gallatin in 1927 at New York University, and at the Museum of Modern Art, opened in 1929.

In 1931–2 the Greenes managed to return to Paris for an extended period to pursue their interest in contemporary European art. Of the many artistic influences circulating in Paris, it was the Constructivism of the Abstraction-Création group that appealed most to Gertrude Greene. Her idealism and romanticism found refuge in the group's attempt to create a pure, new abstract art for a new society. She responded to an abstraction based on pure colour, line and form, designed to unite art and society. When she returned to New York in 1933 she began her own abstract sculpture constructing works in iron, copper and aluminium. She acquired a forge that she installed in her fireplace. These earliest works in the round combined wood with metal components (*La Palombe*, 1935–6;

wood and Monel metal; 29.9 × 48.2 cm.; Collection Ahmet Ertegun, New York). Very few survived Greene's discriminating editing, but Balcomb always photographed her work, providing a record of her entire production.

When in 1934 the artist Burgoyne Diller, the first American disciple of Mondrian, became administrator for the mural project of the Federal Art Project (FAP), the government-sponsored art relief program, both Balcomb and Gertrude were awarded commissions for abstract murals. This period was also marked by Greene's social activism evidenced in her efforts to form the Unemployed Artists Group, later renamed the Artists Union, and her participation in strikes and demonstrations aimed at gaining government support for artists. When in 1936 the *Cubism and Abstract Art* exhibition at the Museum of Modern Art failed to include any American artists, the Greenes and a group of friends formed their own group, American Abstract Artists (AAA), both to exhibit works and to gain official institutional approval for American abstraction. In 1937 Gertrude coordinated the AAA's first exhibition at the Squibb Gallery, where she also exhibited, and was the group's first paid employee. During that year Baroness Hilla Rebay included a sculpture by Greene in the opening show of the Solomon R. Guggenheim Collection and A.E. Gallatin put one of her wooden relief sculptures on permanent view in his Museum of Living Art, making it her first work to enter a public collection.

Greene cut out wooden shapes and then glued or screwed them to the textured sides of compressed wooden sheets. She built up two to three layers of wood, integrating colour and form on several levels. The Arp-like shapes combined a biomorphic vocabulary with geometric compositions. Her interchange of geometric and amoebic shapes created an intricate system of solids and voids, as in the wood construction *Composition* (1937; 50 × 101 cm.; Berkshire Museum, Pittsfield, MA). While the earlier works relied on preparatory sketches, these constructions were first tested by cutting up pieces of coloured paper and gluing them into the desired configurations. Given the artist's small output, these small-scale collages remain the best way to enjoy her artistic process (*Untitled*, 1937; collage; 20.3 × 30.4 cm.; private collection, repr. New York 1981, fig.9).

When in 1942 Balcomb accepted a teaching position in art history and aesthetics at the Carnegie Institute of Technology in Pittsburgh, Gertrude began to divide her time between two studios, a routine that lasted for the rest of her life. This situation profoundly influenced her art-making since it became too difficult to transport supplies and tools on crowded war-time trains. She was compelled to reduce the number of her compositional elements and focus instead on the interplay of linear and spatial concerns. Mondrian's strict geometry also influenced her work at this time (e.g. *Space Construction*, 1942; wood; 100.3 × 69.6 cm.; Whitney Museum of American Art, New York); he had moved to the USA in 1940 and became a supporting member of the AAA. The inaccessibility of all but the most rudimentary of tools caused Greene to simplify her approach and eventually led to a renewed interest in painting. By 1946 she reintroduced biomorphic shapes as painted, not wooden forms, with edges less precise and more painterly (*Angular Rhythms*, 1946; oil on canvas; 60.9 × 81.2 cm.; private collection, *ibid.*, fig.15).

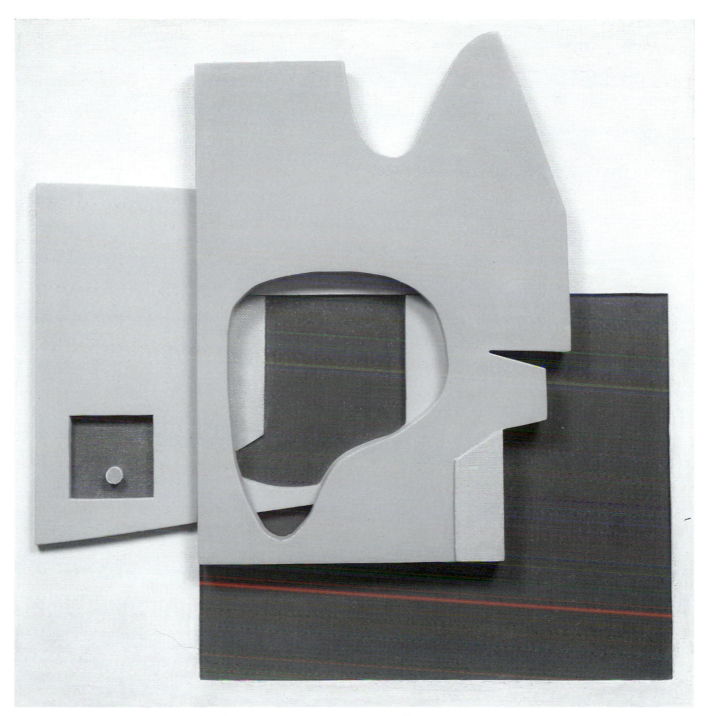

Greene: *Construction Square*, wood and paint; 77.5 × 77.5 cm.; private collection

In the late 1940s the Greenes purchased a tract of land high on a cliff on the far east end of Long Island where they built by hand a flat-roofed house of heavy beams and cement blocks. They spent increasing time there. The late 1940s and early 1950s marked Gertrude Greene's evolution from sculpture to painting. She combined formal geometry with a painterly abstraction (*Structure and Space*, 1950; oil on canvas; Newark Museum, NJ). She rejected the label Abstract Expressionist, however, a term that applied to the work of many fellow Long Island artists, such as Jackson Pollock and Willem de Kooning, because she considered her work as carefully calculated compositions evolved from oil sketches. They were intended as solutions to formal, not personal problems. Also by 1950 she had abandoned the brush in favour of the palette knife. The work of Gertrude Greene provided an important link between 20th-century European artistic movements and post-war abstraction in the USA. Her career was prematurely curtailed by her death from cancer in 1956.

AMY J. WOLF

Greenwood, Marion

American painter and graphic artist, 1909–1970

Born in Brooklyn, New York, 6 April 1909. Studied at the
Art Students League, New York, under George Bridgman,
F.V. DuMond and John Sloan, 1924–8, and at Académie
Colarossi, Paris, 1929–30; also studied lithography with Emil
Ganso and mosaic technique with Alexander Archipenko in
Woodstock, New York. Lived in Mexico, 1932–6, returning
briefly to New York in 1934, when employed on Public
Works of Art Project (PWAP) with elder sister Grace. Worked
on Treasury Relief Art Project, 1936–8. Appointed US
government artist-correspondent during World War II.
Married Captain Charles Fenn, 1939; divorced. Worked in
China and Hong Kong, 1946–7. Subsequently divided time
between New York and Woodstock; also travelled abroad.
Professor of fine arts, University of Tennessee, Knoxville,
1954–5; visiting professor, Syracuse University, New York,
1965. Recipient of second prize, Carnegie Institute National,
1944; first Lippincott figure prize, Pennsylvania Academy of
the Fine Arts, Philadelphia, 1951; Grumbacher prize,
National Association of Women Artists, New York, 1959.
Member, National Academy of Design, New York, 1959.
Died after a road accident in Woodstock, 20 February 1970.

Selected Individual Exhibitions

Associated American Artists Gallery, New York: 1944, 1947
Associated American Artists Gallery, Chicago: 1948
Associated American Artists Gallery, Knoxville: 1955
Milch Galleries, New York: 1959
Mint Museum of Art, Charlotte, NC: 1960
University of Maine Art Gallery, Orono: 1965 (organised by
    Associated American Artists)
Woodstock Artists Association, Woodstock, NY: 1972 (memorial)

Bibliography

Josephine Herbst, "The artist's progress", *Mexican Life*, March 1935
Guillermo Rivas, "Mexican murals by Marion Greenwood",
    Mexican Life, no.12, January 1936, pp.24–5, 61
Grace Pagano, *Contemporary American Painting: The Encyclopaedia
    Britannica Collection*, New York: Duell Sloan and Pearce, 1945
De Witt Mackenzie, *Men Without Guns, Illustrated with 137 Plates
    from the Abbott Collection of Paintings Owned by the United
    States Government*, Philadelphia: Blakiston, 1945
Marion Greenwood, exh. cat., Associated American Artists Gallery,
    New York, 1947
Henry Salpeter, "Marion Greenwood: An American artist of original-
    ity and power", *American Artist*, xii, January 1948, pp.14–19
Ralph M. Pearson, *The Modern Renaissance in American Art,
    Presenting the Work and Philosophy of 54 Distinguished Artists*,
    New York: Harper, 1954
Richard Case, "SU Campus gives birth to a mural", *Empire*, 26
    September 1965, pp.1, 4–5
Francis V. O'Connor, "New Deal murals in New York", *Artforum*,
    vii, November 1968, pp.41–9
Orlando S. Suárez, *Inventario del muralismo mexicano*, Mexico City:
    Universidad Nacional Autonoma de Mexico, 1972
7 American Women: The Depression Decade, exh. cat., Vassar
    College Art Gallery, Poughkeepsie, NY, 1976
Charlotte Streifer Rubinstein, *American Women Artists from Early
    Times to the Present*, Boston: Hall, 1982
*The Latin American Spirit: Art and Artists in the United States,
    1920–1970*, exh. cat., Bronx Museum of the Arts, NY, and else-
    where, 1988
Robert Henkes, *American Women Painters of the 1930s and 1940s:
    The Lives and Works of Ten Artists*, Jefferson, NC: McFarland,
    1991

Coming into prominence in the 1930s through receiving three
mural commissions in Mexico, Marion Greenwood was an
artist whose 40-year career as muralist, easel painter and
printmaker was dominated by the depiction of those whose
lives differed radically from her own. Frequent and extended
periods of travel permitted her to create a thick file of racial
and ethnic representations that served both as a collected
oeuvre and as an image bank for her own future use. Her final
mural, the *Tribute to Woman* (1965; originally in Slocum Hall,
Syracuse University; canvas removed to the University Art
Gallery after vandalisation in 1982; see illustration), based as
it is on a grouping of previously developed figures from China,
Haiti, Africa, Portugal and Mexico, offers a rapid means of
surveying this file, although the African American, a frequent
and highly regarded subject of her work in the early 1940s, is
strangely absent.

Perhaps prompted by the example of John Sloan, one of her
teachers at the Art Students League, the young Greenwood
joined the migration of artists to the American Southwest in
1930. Two years later she crossed the border into Mexico,
where her developing skills in rendering "the ethnic and
exotic" were quickly put to use. Selected in 1934, with her
older sister Grace, to work on the massive Mercado Abelardo
L. Rodriguez project in Mexico City, she contributed a
vibrantly coloured, solidly draughted 140-square-metre section
entitled the *Industrialisation of the Countryside*. Using the
organisational strategies of the medieval narrator as modified
by Diego Rivera, Greenwood packed her portion of the staircase walls (repr. *American Art Review*, February–March 1994,
p.127) with a myriad of labouring agricultural workers and the
suited or uniformed overlords who profited from their sweat.
Her composition was linked to her sister's with a banner that
translates as "Workers of the World Unite".

The sturdy, unbroken contour lines and the heavily loaded
colours of the Mexican murals continued to assert themselves
in the work undertaken by Greenwood for a number of problematic Depression-era government projects in the USA. Of
these, the *Blueprint for Community Life* (1940; Red Hook
Housing Community, Brooklyn; fresco covered over, repr.
Henkes 1991, p.68) permitted her, albeit temporarily, to render
visually her belief in the benefits of harmoniously designed
environments, a conviction that already in 1937 had led her to
band together with the architect Oscar Stonorov, the sculptor
Isamu Noguchi and a dozen other artists into the short-lived
Architects, Painters and Sculptors Collaborative.

Greenwood effectively abandoned mural work in 1940,
returning to it only twice again in her career. Turning to
portable formats that were hers to control artistically, she
enthusiastically engaged in a period that she characterised as
an American Renaissance: "instead of fussing with cute and
fancy nudes and pretty-pretty things" artists concentrated on
the depiction of "the life of America, whether it be industry,
farming or just plain people" (*New York World Telegram*, 3
November 1944). She worked for the Army Medical Corps,
documenting the rehabilitation of wounded soldiers, created
paintings for the George Abbott Laboratories, reproductions

Greenwood: *Tribute to Woman*, 1965; Syracuse University Art Collection

of which were used to advertise cold remedies and vitamin pills, and produced a series of paintings of African-American life, which were often re-issued in lithographic editions of up to 250. *Mississippi Girl* (1943; Maurice Wertheim Collection, repr. *Art Digest*, 15 October 1944), a painting destined to receive second prize in the Carnegie Institute exhibition the following year, was the best known of this latter genre. It abandoned the thick, closed contour lines of the murals in favour of broken, undulating lines, which, in combination with a palette that shifted between muted browns and brilliant reds and oranges, resulted in a portrait of a seated young black woman whose momentary repose was felt by contemporary critics barely to hide the sitter's nervous, high-strung personality. Considered equally powerful in its evocation of mood was the painting *Rehearsal for African Ballet* (c.1945; Encyclopaedia Britannica Collection), which in a dramatically highlighted frieze composition recorded the artist's responses to what she described as a Harlem group's study of "ancestral dance forms, chants and drumbeats of Africa" (Pagano 1945, p.45).

In partnership with her husband Captain Charles Fenn, who appears to have been a US intelligence operative in the closing years of World War II, Greenwood travelled and worked in China and Hong Kong. On her return to the USA, she began to show the products of her ever-expanding world, beginning with a solo exhibition at Associated American Artists, the catalogue for which contained a short, highly favourable essay by her friend Sir Julian Huxley, the Director-General of UNESCO. In much of this work, most especially in the wash and Chinese brush drawings on rice-paper, an enhanced calligraphy of line conveyed very effectively the presence of the will to live within the depicted figures, no matter how trying the circumstances they may have encountered. A gouache of 1946, *The Toilers* (Smith College, Northampton, MA), a complex and colourful assembly of figures seen from the back, pushing a heavily loaded cart, is a painted image from the war-torn Far East that speaks, through its lyricism of line, to a human capacity for survival, as does the gut-wrenching *Lament* (1952; Joseph P. Hirshhorn Collection, repr. *Art*

Digest, April 1952, p.8) of a Chinese mother for the dead child she clutches.

Notwithstanding their praise, it is clear that Greenwood's "foreign" imagery gave rise to a degree of uncertainty among her contemporaries. Some praised her work for its advocacy of the individual and its refusal to create types, while others claimed for her the capacity to move beyond particulars, to reach a statement of universal humanity. A New York journalist, writing in 1947, directly if somewhat problematically confronted the issue of representing the "other":

> Miss Greenwood draws the Chinese the way they look to Americans, but plunged no deeper … How could she? She is not native and could not tap the hidden springs. The Chinese, who are a polite people, were astonished that she came so near them as she did, but must have been equally astonished at what she left out [unidentified clipping, Woodstock Artists' Association Archives].

More recent critics have tended to pass over such questions, frequently simply labelling her imagery as "trite" or "outdated".

Settling into a somewhat less peripatetic existence from the early 1950s, Greenwood divided much of her time between New York and the artists' community of Woodstock that she had frequented off and on since childhood. Trips overseas and within North America refreshed her stock of imagery: a number of young Portuguese faces – male and female – are known to have enchanted her, as did the grace of a young American dancer. The recurrent renditions of youthfulness in her late paintings and lithographs are epitomised in the image of the blonde American student, swinging her open bag, who stands to the far left in *Tribute to Woman*, a work that the artist said focused on the "eternal role of woman as the bearer of life" no matter what her "age, race, occupation [or] privilege" (press release, *Syracuse University News*, 1965). With the exception of the centralised caucasian Madonna, however, all the women's faces in this final mural are solemn and knowing. Greenwood's version of reality, not bland optimism, is to be read into them – whether young or old – just as it is also evoked in a *Self-Portrait* (1960s; whereabouts unknown, repr. *Woodstock Times*, 14 September 1972), with its predominantly blue palette and its resolute refusal to mask the effects of life on a face that art critics had been unable to resist describing as staggering in beauty and on which those who remember her still comment. Pronounced in her dissatisfaction with what she regarded as the modern tendency to fear representation, she continued to probe her concern for what she considered to be the challenges confronting "the human element".

CATHERINE MACKENZIE

Grotell, Majlis [Maija]
Finnish ceramist, 1899–1973

Born in Helsinki, 19 August 1899. Studied at Central School of Arts and Crafts (Ateneum), Helsinki. Emigrated to USA, 1927. Instructor, Inwood Pottery Studios, New York, 1927–8; Union Settlement, New York, 1928–9; Henry Street Settlement, New York, 1929–38; instructor and research assistant, School of Ceramic Engineering, Rutgers University, New Brunswick, New Jersey, 1936–8; head of Department of Ceramics, Cranbrook Academy of Art, Bloomfield Hills, Michigan, 1938–1966. Elected master craftsman, Society of Arts and Crafts, Boston, 1938. Recipient of Charles Fergus Binns medal, Alfred University, New York, 1961; Cranbrook Founders medal, 1964; Cranbrook Academy of Art Faculty medal, 1966. Died 6 December 1973.

Principal Exhibitions
Exposición Internacional, Barcelona: 1929 (diploma di colaborador)
American Ceramic Society Exposition, Cleveland: 1931 (certificate of excellence)
National Ceramic Exhibition, Museum of Fine Arts, Syracuse, NY: 1933–60 (honourable mention 1933, 1934 and 1941, second prize 1936, Encyclopaedia Britannica prize and special commendation for group 1946, G.R. Croker and Co. prize 1949)
Society of Arts and Crafts, Boston: 1935 (honourable mention)
Exposition Internationale, Paris: 1937 (silver medal)
Wichita Art Association: 1947 (first prize), 1951 (Purchase prize), 1954 (honourable mention)
Michigan Artist Craftsman Exhibition: 1949 (Lillian Henkel Hass prize), 1950 (Material and Design prize), 1951 (Mr and Mrs Harry L. Winston prize), 1953 (Founders Society prize), 1955 (Mr and Mrs Lawrence A. Fleischman Purchase prize)
Michigan Academy of Science, Arts and Letters: 1949, 1950, 1951 and 1956 (award of merit of the first class in ceramics for each year)
Cranbrook Academy of Art, Bloomfield Hills, MI: 1967–8 (individual, touring)

Bibliography
Marion H. Bernis, "Maija Grotell decorates a pot", *Ceramics Monthly*, v, May 1957, pp.18–19, 32
Maija Grotell, exh. cat., Cranbrook Academy of Art, Bloomfield Hills, MI, and elsewhere, 1967
Jeff Schlanger, "Maija Grotell", *Craft Horizons*, xxix, November–December 1969, pp.14–23
Elaine Levin, "Pioneers of contemporary American ceramic art: Maija Grotell, Herbert Sanders", *Ceramics Monthly*, xxiv, November 1976, pp.48–54
Tamara Préaud and Serge Gauthier, *Ceramics of the Twentieth Century*, Oxford: Phaidon, 1982
Elaine Levin, "Maija Grotell", *American Ceramics*, i, Winter 1982, pp.42–5
Martin Eidelberg, "Ceramics", *Design in America: The Cranbrook Vision, 1925–1950*, exh. cat., Detroit Institute of Arts, Metropolitan Museum of Art, New York, and elsewhere, 1983, pp.213–36
Barbara Perry, ed., *American Ceramics: The Collection of the Everson Museum of Art*, New York: Rizzoli, 1989

Manuscript collection is in the Bird Library, Syracuse University, NY.

Maija Grotell's career as a ceramist and teacher at Cranbrook Academy of Art had a profound impact on the development of the "vessel aesthetic" in American ceramics in the period after World War II.

At the Central School of Arts and Crafts in Helsinki, Grotell studied painting, design and sculpture, and learned ceramics from the Belgian-British ceramist Alfred William Finch, known as the "father of Finnish ceramics". His use of incised and slip decoration on restrained forms laid the foundation for Grotell's aesthetic. Emigrating to the USA in 1927, Grotell

Grotell: *Vase*, c.1943; stoneware; height 34.3 cm., diameter 35.6 cm.; Cranbrook Art Museum, Michigan

taught at a number of institutions in the New York area, most notably at the Henry Street Settlement. The work that she developed in her first decade in New York was predominantly low-fire ware with pictorial designs in a Moderne style. Using a Cubist-derived geometry or a fluid Matisse-like line, she painted scenes from urban New York, or picnickers and deer, in striking and sophisticated colour combinations, such as turquoise and black or lemon and silver. An earthenware vase from 1935 shows a silver and grey scene of abstracted smokestacks and skyscrapers (repr. Eidelberg 1983, p.218). This body of work was represented and honoured in ceramic exhibitions in Cleveland and at the prestigious National Ceramic Exhibition at the Syracuse Museum, and attracted the attention of her compatriot, the architect and designer Eliel Saarinen, who was President of Cranbrook Academy of Art in Bloomfield Hills, Michigan.

Grotell was invited to join the Cranbrook faculty in 1938, and it was there that she developed her mature style. The facilities at Cranbrook allowed her to experiment with high-fire ware and glazes, and the institutional situation enabled her to balance teaching and her own work. Initially she developed vessels with clear, volumetric forms that she decorated with raised geometric patterns, building up designs in low relief. A stoneware vase (1939; Metropolitan Museum of Art, New York) of pale grey and black contrasts a crisp chequerwork pattern on the neck with narrow incised stripes encircling the swelling body. In the 1950s experiments with glazes became increasingly important to her work: those she developed

included a blue glaze, a bright orange glaze that could replace the uranium glaze that was no longer available, and a bubbled Bristol glaze over Albany slip. Characteristic of this period is a simple, open-throated vessel of 1951 (Cranbrook Academy of Art Museum): its profile is echoed in the brilliant orange and black Vs that repeat across the surface against a contrasting bubbling stone glaze. Grotell, like many of her contemporaries in the post-war period, had little interest in utilitarian ceramics, so it was with some reluctance that she agreed to be pressed into service by Saarinen to develop the brilliant glazes used on the ceramics for the exterior walls of the General Motors Technical Center in Warren, Michigan, constructed 1945–56. Her own work evolved towards more organic, curvilinear or amoeboid forms, often executed in slip decoration and rich colours, but always shaped by her concern for the close relationship of form and decoration. Her interest in experimentation was balanced by the discipline of repetition: if an experiment did not achieve what she hoped, she would continue to make similar pieces until she was satisfied. She explained how she persisted in refining her experiments with glazes and form:

> I always have something I am aiming at, and I keep on … I do not sketch on paper, I sketch in clay. So if it is not what I want, I make another one and keep on. In that way I have many similar pieces. My reason is not for repeating but for improving [quoted in Schlanger 1969, p.15].

Grotell's works (examples in Cranbrook Academy of Art Museum; Metropolitan Museum of Art, New York; Everson Museum of Art, Syracuse; Detroit Institute of Arts) were important in the shift from production pottery to the individual studio system and in the development of a "vessel aesthetic" in American ceramics. When she first arrived at Cranbrook, students were particularly interested in sculptural ceramics, but following the example of Grotell's powerful and large thrown vessels, the emphasis changed. Because in her first years at Cranbrook students were less experienced, her teaching was formal and more basic. In the years after World War II, however, as more experienced students came to the academy, her pedagogy evolved into an individual and personal mode. Critiques were private conversations rather than public performances. With humour and the occasional pointed remark, she advised students to develop technical skills and personal style before experimenting. Although she encouraged students to look at natural phenomena, which was important to her own work, she did not force an aesthetic upon them. Her students remember that what she would not say was as important as what she would say. She is quoted as suggesting: "The best thing you can do for students is to make them independent so they do not miss you" (*ibid.*, p.21). Under Grotell, the Cranbrook Academy became one of the major centres for ceramic education in the USA. Although there was never a unified stylistic approach, her students are some of the most important American ceramists of the later 20th century, including Toshiko Takaezu, Harvey Littleton, Leza McVey, Richard de Vore, Howard Kottler, John and Susanne Stephenson and Margie Hughto.

SUSAN WALLER

Grundig, Lea
German graphic artist, 1906–1977

Born in Dresden, 23 March 1906, into the Jewish family of
shop owners Moritz Langer. Studied at the
Kunstgewerbeschule, Dresden, 1922–3, then at the art school
"Der Weg – Kunstschule für Gestaltung" (The Path – Art
School for Design) founded by Edmund Kesting, 1923–6.
Joined the Communist Party, 1926. Stayed in Heidelberg and
Vienna, 1927. Married artist Hans Grundig, 1928. Founder-
member of the Dresden ARBKD (Association of
Revolutionary Artists in Germany), 1929. Banned from
working by the National Socialists, 1935; went to
Switzerland with husband and met exiled artists and writers;
arrested for political activities on return, 1936; imprisoned
for six months, 1938. Emigrated to Palestine on release,
returning to Dresden in early 1949 to rejoin husband, who
had been in a concentration camp. Appointed professor at the
Dresden Academy, 1950. Member, Deutsche Akademie der
Künste, Berlin, 1961; president, Verband Bildender Künstler
der DDR, 1964–70. Member of the central committee of the
SED, 1967. Died during a Mediterranean cruise, 10 October
1977.

Selected Individual Exhibitions
Galerie Joseph Sandel, Dresden: 1930
Tel Aviv, Haifa, Jerusalem: 1941–2
Galerie Manes, Prague: 1948
Żydowskie Towarzystwo, Warsaw: 1949
Museum der Bildenden Künste, Leipzig: 1951 (with Hans Grundig)
Staatliche Kunstsammlungen, Albertinum, Dresden: 1958 (with Hans
    Grundig, touring), 1962 (Der Mensch – mein Bruder, touring),
    1967 (touring), 1976 (retrospective)
Hermitage, Leningrad: 1959 (with Hans Grundig, touring)
Deutsche Bücherstube, Berlin: 1961
Pavillon der Kunst, Berlin: 1961
Herbert Art Gallery and Museum, Coventry: 1963
Musée des Beaux-Arts, Lyon: 1963 (with Hans Grundig)
Ladengalerie, Berlin: 1964, 1969, 1973
Museo Nacional de Bellas Artes, Buenos Aires: 1967 (with Hans
    Grundig)
Galleria del Levante, Milan and Munich: 1969
Square Gallery, Milan: 1972 (with Hans Grundig)
Ausstellungszentrum am Fernsehturm, Berlin: 1975–6 (touring)

Selected Writings
"Bezirksausstellung in Dresden", Bildende Kunst, viii, 1954,
    pp.20–23
"Zu meinen Illustrationen der Grimmschen Volksmärchen", ibid.,
    pp.23–6
Gesichte und Geschichte, Berlin, 1958
"Der Weg des Faschismus: Zu einem Triptychon von Hans Grundig",
    Bildende Kunst, xii, 1958, pp.170–72
"Über das Phantastische im Werk Hans Grundigs", Junge Kunst,
    no.5, 1959
"China: Unermessliches Erlebnis", Die Arbeiterin, no.3, 1961,
    pp.76–80
"Ich mache nicht einen Strich, wenn ich nicht hingesehen habe",
    Junge Kunst, no.2, 1962, pp.10–26
"Wir wollen die Schönheit des Menschen zeigen: Gedanken zum
    Nationalkongress", Bildende Kunst, xvi, 1962, pp.471–4
"Ansprache an einen alten Freund: Über den Maler Eric Johansson",
    Bildende Kunst, xxii, 1968, pp.369–72
"Vom Wert der Graphik", Graphik in der DDR, exh. cat., Dresden,
    1969, pp.17–19

Kunst unserer Zeit: Bild- und Leseheft für die Kunstbetrachtung,
    Berlin, 1972
"Zeit sich zu erinnern: Anlässlich des 50. Jahrestags der Gründung
    der ASSO", Bildende Kunst, xxxi, 1977, pp.587–92

Bibliography
Lea Grundig-Langer, exh. cat., Galleria del Levante, Milan and
    Munich, 1969
Lea Grundig: Zeichnungen, Graphik, exh. cat., Ausstellungszentrum
    am Fernsehturm, Berlin, and elsewhere, 1975
Peter H. Feist, "Lea Grundig", Dresdner Kunstblatter, xx/2, 1976,
    pp.34–47
Lea Grundig: Arbeiten der zwanziger und dreissiger Jahre, exh. cat.,
    Bonner Kunstverein, Bonn, and elsewhere, 1984 (contains exten-
    sive bibliography)
Das Verborgene Museum I: Dokumentation der Kunst von Frauen in
    Berliner öffentlichen Sammlungen, exh. cat., Akademie der
    Künste, Berlin, 1987
Domesticity and Dissent: The Role of Women Artists in Germany,
    1918–1938, exh. cat., Leicester Museum and Art Gallery, and
    elsewhere, 1992
Marsha Meskimmon and Shearer West, eds, Visions of the "Neue
    Frau": Women and the Visual Arts in Weimar Germany,
    Aldershot: Scolar Press, 1995

Lea Grundig's long career centred on the socio-critical graphics that she produced from the 1920s until her death in 1977.
Except during the traumatic years of the Third Reich and
World War II when she was exiled from Germany as a politically active Jew, Grundig lived all of her life in Dresden. Her
works are characterised by the combination of her political
commitment, strong use of the figurative realism associated
with the Neue Sachlichkeit (New Objectivity) and a sensitive
rendering of working-class life. She described herself not as an
artist, but as "an agitator" (Bonn 1984, p.33).

The context of Grundig's production in the period before
her exile in the late 1930s is the critical realism of the Weimar
Republic. Like many radical artists of the period, she refused
the apocalyptic extremes of Expressionism and its associations
with "art for art's sake" in favour of the veristic wing of the
Neue Sachlichkeit that sought to make art a tool for working-
class revolution. Grundig was particularly associated with the
Dresden artists Otto Griebel and Hans Grundig (whom she
married in 1928) – artists who produced what came to be
known as "proletarian-revolutionary" works, that is, positive
representations of the politically unified and self-conscious
working-classes.

Grundig lived her politics. Having been brought up in a
strict Jewish household, she was obliged to go against her
family's wishes in order to become an artist. Furthermore, she
lived in the working-class areas of Dresden and joined the
Communist Party in 1926. Even her marriage to Grundig was
one of the new Kameradschaftsehe or "companionate
marriages" much discussed in radical social circles of the
period. Hans and Lea Grundig acted as partners, supporting
one another's work and engaging together in political activities. In 1929 the Grundigs founded the first Dresden chapter of
the ARBKD (Association of Revolutionary Artists in
Germany), which linked their artistic region to others across
the country in the service of radical politics. The Grundigs
were forced to flee Germany under the Third Reich and were
both imprisoned for their views in 1938–9.

Grundig: *Comrade Elsa Fröhlich and Sonni*, 1935; drawing; Landesmuseum, Oldenburg

The significance of this biographical detail lies in its relationship to Grundig's work. Her work is characterised by a strong identification with her subjects, even an "identity politic", and the viewpoint of a working-class woman of the period. In addition to producing "realist" work that was meant to be stylistically intelligible to a mass audience and using graphic techniques in order to ensure mass production and dissemination of the work, Grundig employed themes that spoke of the lives of the workers in the period. More particularly, her focus was on the lives of working-class women and the politics of that sphere.

In her works Grundig represented many working-class mothers and children. Her approach to the theme was neither purely critical, producing caricatures of the "oppressed masses", nor simply propagandistic, espousing the strength of the proletariat. Rather, Grundig approached the theme of working-class mothers and children with sensitivity and an even-handedness; in works such as *Comrade Elsa Fröhlich and Sonni* (1935; see illustration), for example, the sobriety of Grundig's technique leaves us in no doubt that these people are poor, but they are not sentimentalised. The title, which gives the names of the sitters and refers to the woman as "comrade", further grants a dignity to the working classes rarely found in representations of the period.

Grundig was concerned with every aspect of the lives of working-class women, and in her series of etchings *Woman's Life* (1936; Ladengalerie, Berlin) she attempted to document this and set it into the context of the socio-political situation of the day. She represented, in the series, women nursing their dying children, lovers at night in an industrial landscape, a tired and bored woman at rest in the kitchen and mothers with children looking at a shop window. The variety of the individual works is especially remarkable at this time, when male artists, even politically committed ones, tended to reduce their representations of women to images of depraved prostitutes and deprived mothers. Grundig shows the range of experiences of working-class women and the variety of both public and private spaces they frequented. Furthermore, she politicised this by, for example, exploring the oppression of these economically powerless groups in a system that was marketing actively to women. Nowhere could that be made more clear than in the *Shop Window* piece from the *Woman's Life* series in which a group of poor women and children gaze longingly at the commodities offered, but not actually available to them.

Obviously, the works and politics of the Grundigs were unacceptable to the Nazis. Having travelled in exile from 1936 to 1949, Lea Grundig was able to return to Dresden only after the "two Germanies" were established. From this point, she became a powerful figure in the East German art scene including holding a Professorship at the Dresden Academy and travelling widely as a cultural ambassador. She received acclaim for the commitment her work had shown to the lives of the proletariat, to the communist cause and for having resisted Hitler. In the period after World War II Grundig continued to produce sensitive working-class portraits and socio-critical graphics (examples in Kunstsammlungen, Dresden).

MARSHA MESKIMMON

Guiard, Mme *see* Labille-Guiard

Guinness, May
Irish painter, 1863–1955

Born Mary Catherine Guinness in Rathfarnham, Co. Dublin, 1863. Educated privately. Due to family commitments, began to paint only when in her forties. Studied in Paris, 1905–7; returned there from Dublin intermittently over the next 20 years or so, working under Kees van Dongen, Hermen Anglada-Camarosa and, from 1922 to 1925, under André Lhôte. Served as a military nurse in the French army during World War I, winning the Croix de Guerre. Led a more withdrawn existence in her later years. Died in Dublin, 11 August 1955.

Principal Exhibitions

Individual
United Arts Club, Dublin: 1913
Dublin Painters' Gallery: 1922, 1935
Dawson Hall, Dublin: 1924, 1956 (retrospective)
Paris: 1925, 1930
Egan Gallery, Dublin: 1926
Barrett's, Molesworth Street, Dublin: 1930
Mills Hall, Dublin: 1932

Combridge Gallery, Dublin: 1938
Waddington Gallery, Dublin: 1946

Group

Royal Hibernian Academy, Dublin: 1897, 1901–2, 1911
Whitechapel Art Gallery, London: 1913 (*Irish Art*)
L'Art d'Aujourd'hui, Paris: 1925
Irish Exhibition of Living Art, Dublin: 1943–5, 1947
Municipal Gallery of Modern Art, Dublin: 1953 (*Irish Painting,
    1903–1953*)

Bibliography

May Guinness: Memorial Exhibition, exh. cat., Dawson Hall,
    Dublin, 1956
Irish Art, 1900–1950, exh. cat., Crawford Municipal Art Gallery,
    Cork, 1975
*The Irish Impressionists: Irish Artists in France and Belgium,
    1850–1914*, exh. cat., National Gallery of Ireland, Dublin, 1984
Irish Women Artists from the Eighteenth Century to the Present Day,
    exh. cat., National Gallery of Ireland, Dublin, and elsewhere,
    1987
Patricia Butler, *Three Hundred Years of Irish Watercolours and
    Drawings*, London: Weidenfeld and Nicolson, 1990
Kenneth McConkey, *A Free Spirit: Irish Art, 1860–1960*,
    Woodbridge, Suffolk: Antique Collectors' Club-Pyms Gallery,
    1990
S.B. Kennedy, *Irish Art and Modernism, 1880–1950*, Belfast:
    Institute for Irish Studies, 1991
Images and Insights, exh. cat., Hugh Lane Municipal Gallery of
    Modern Art, Dublin, 1993

May Guinness was one of the most innovative Irish painters of
her generation. Although she did not begin to study art until
she was 42 years of age, she soon made a niche for herself as
an experimental painter at a time when the art scene in Ireland
was conservative in the extreme. She was one of the first of a
number of Irish women artists to study in Paris during its
heyday as the art capital of the world, and from her teachers,
Kees van Dongen and Hermen Anglada-Camarosa, she developed a Fauvist-inspired palette of bright colours and a technique of great expressiveness. Later, as a pupil of André Lhôte,
she came briefly under the influence of Cubism. During World
War I she distinguished herself as a military nurse in the French
army and was awarded the Croix de Guerre for bravery during
the bombardment of Verdun in 1915. After the war she settled
at her family home, Tibradden House, near Dublin, and
remained there, apart from frequent visits to France, for the
rest of her life. While in Paris she amassed a small but distinguished collection of avant-garde French paintings by
Bonnard, Dufy, Matisse, Picasso and Rouault and these she
displayed at Tibradden, where she gathered around her a
group of admirers both of her own work and of avant-garde
art in general.

The development of Guinness's work is difficult to plot.
There are three main reasons for this difficulty: first, the fact
that she rarely, if ever, dated her works; second, the relatively
short span of her mature career (about 30 years); and, third,
throughout her career she exhibited a mixture of recent and
past works in various styles so that even the catalogues and
reviews of her exhibitions are of little help in tracing her developing technique. Despite these difficulties, however, her career
may be thought of as falling into three phases, namely the early
period (pre-1922), the Cubist period (1922–5) and the late
period (post-1925).

Guinness: *Still Life*, 1922–5; Hugh Lane Municipal Gallery
of Modern Art, Dublin

Guinness's early work was greatly influenced by French
Fauvism, the predominant style at about the time of her first
visit to Paris, and in particular the paintings of Matisse, which
she admired for their decorative qualities. The *Cathedral of
Diest* (Hugh Lane Municipal Gallery of Modern Art, Dublin)
and *Procession at Josselin* (National Gallery of Ireland,
Dublin), for example, both date from her early period and are
characterised by the use of strong colours and an emphasis on
the mood and atmosphere of the scene, the whole being set
down with bold brushwork.

But from 1922 until 1925, when she studied intermittently
with Lhôte, she came under the influence of Cubism and
produced a number of still lifes in which stylised forms are
used to make bold patterns, but with a residue of recognisable
imagery. *Still Life* (1922–5; see illustration), one of the most

successful of these works, is notable too for its restrained range of colours. Guinness's use of thin films of paint and, frequently, a paste-like appearance to the surface of the canvas also distinguish her work of this period and separate it from the more painterly approach of her earlier, and later, work. She was, too, at this time capable of a certain aridity of both concept and execution, as can be seen in her *Mother and Children* (private collection), a genre scene, produced, one feels, more as the result of the application of a formula than of any aesthetic conviction.

Her natural inclinations, however, were for gaiety and, probably around 1924 or early 1925 – by which time she was already in her sixties – she returned to a more spontaneous, essentially Fauvist method of painting. Occasionally in her later work the influence of Cubism reappeared, as in the splendidly colourful and forceful *Russian Cossack* (Church of Ireland Representative Church Body, Dublin). In 1925 she summed up her career, saying that she had been "through all the phases, and had now settled down to 'stylisation' ... the flat and rhythmic arrangements of line and colour" (*Sphere Magazine*, 17 October 1925).

Her late period, after 1925, was, however, her happiest and most assured and her best works of the time, *Outside a Paris Café* (Limerick Art Gallery) and *Mardi Gras* (Drogheda Corporation), have a lyricism reminiscent of Marie Laurencin (q.v.) whose work Guinness would have seen in Paris. In these late works the existential act of painting and the inherent qualities of the medium itself assume an importance far greater than the subject matter or any aesthetic theories and, occasionally, in pastel drawings such as *Athenian Evening* (Church of Ireland Theological College, Dublin) and *Les Amis* (Waterford Art Gallery), and in such watercolours as the splendid *Roses in a Jug* (private collection, Dublin), there is a *joie de vivre* not seen in her earlier work.

Despite her position as one of the most innovative Irish painters of her generation, Guinness remained, like many of her fellow countrywomen, essentially a conservative painter who, in style and concept, never progressed beyond the tenets of the School of Paris of the early years of the 20th century. She was reticent by nature and exhibited relatively infrequently, but by her example and through the presence of her own collection of modern paintings she inspired and encouraged a generation of Irish painters.

S.B. KENNEDY

Guro, Elena [Eleanora]

Russian painter and graphic artist, 1877–1913

Born in St Petersburg, 26 December 1876 (Old Style calendar)/10 January 1877 (New Style calendar). Studied at the Drawing School of the Society for the Encouragement of the Arts, 1890–93; studied in the studio of Jan Ciaglinsky, 1903–5; at the Zvantseva School, 1906–7, all in St Petersburg. Co-founder, Soyuz molodyozhi (Union of Youth) society of artists, 1909. Organiser of Hylaea, a literary group, 1912. Married Mikhail Matyushin, violinist, painter and co-founder of the Union of Youth, c.1906. Died of leukaemia in Uuskirkko, Finland, 6 May 1913.

Principal Exhibitions
St Petersburg: 1909 (*The Impressionists*)
Triangle, St Petersburg: 1910
Soyuz molodyozhi (Union of Youth), St Petersburg: 1913 (retrospective)

Selected Writings
Sharmanka [Hurdy-gurdy], St Petersburg, 1909
Osenniy son [Autumn dream], St Petersburg, 1912
Nebesnyye verblyuzhata [Baby camels in the sky], Petrograd, 1914
Elena Guro: Selected Prose and Poetry, ed. Anna Ljunggren and Nils Ake Nilsson, Stockholm: Almqvist & Wiksell, 1988

Bibliography
N. Khardzhiyev and others, *K istoriy russkogo avangarda* [Towards a history of the Russian avant-garde], Stockholm, 1976
K.B. Jensen, *Russian Futurism, Urbanism and Elena Guro*, Aarhus: Arkona, 1977
E. Kovtun, "Elena Guro: Poet i khudozhnik" [Elena Guro: Poet and artist], *Pamyatniki kultury, Novyye otkrytiya. Yezhegodnik 1976* [Cultural memorials, new openings: 1976 annual], Moscow, 1977, pp.317–26
Z. Ender: "Elena Guro: Profilo biografico", *Rassegna Sovietica*, no.24, 1978, pp.67–93
Jeremy Howard, *The Union of Youth: An Artists' Society of the Russian Avant-Garde*, Manchester: Manchester University Press, 1992
A. Sarabyanov, *Neizvestnyy russkiy avangard* [The unknown Russian avant-garde], Moscow, 1992
Milica Banjanin, "Between symbolism and futurism: Impressions by day and by night in Elena Guro's city series", *Slavic and East European Journal*, xxxvii/1, 1993, pp.67–84

In many respects Elena Guro's art took up where that of Elena Polenova (q.v.) and Marya Yakunchikova (q.v.) had left off. For she continued their tradition of immersion in the local landscape and organic nature, fairy-tales and folk art, and the expression of a childlike perception that was to infuse a sense of spontaneity, intimacy and intuitive response to an integrated visual and literary art. In addition, like Yakunchikova, her increasingly disabling illnesses (she suffered from pernicious anaemia and neuritis of the heart, and died of leukaemia) stimulated a highly sensitive quest for the self in relation to the surrounding world. At the same time she went further in her abstractions, using impressionistic stream-of-consciousness, *Japonist* and primitivist techniques in her painting, graphic art and writing, but without any striving after national identity. As such, and through her inspirational role in the new St Petersburg groups Triangle, the Union of Youth and Hylaea, Guro emerged as a vital figure in the development of Russian modernism, moving it forward from Symbolism towards Futurism.

In the late 1900s Guro developed the art of the fragment – this as she sought to express the free rhythms that she regarded as comprising the substance of life, both physical and spiritual. Her monistic world view allowed for the interpenetration of the material and psychological realms, and hence her prose and accompanying sketches frequently consist of a-sequential observations and fanciful visions in which the external environment is personified. She believed that every object had a

Guro: *Woman in a Headscarf (Scandinavian Princess)*, 1910; State Russian Museum, St Petersburg

soul and insisted on a form of art that represented both the beauty of the surrounding world and her own subjective experience of it. As a result she developed a pantheistic and synaesthetic approach closely akin to that of her associate, the psychologist-turned-artist Nikolai Kulbin.

Many of her early subjects involve fragments of street life as they enter a city room where the division between the perceiver and the perceived becomes blurred. This can be seen in *Woman in a Headscarf (Scandinavian Princess)* (1910; see illustration), with the characteristic depiction of a young woman seated beside a window where the night lights and shadows of the city appear as much in the glass as beyond it. The image of a

woman by a window was to recur consistently throughout Guro's work, the mixture of inner and outer worlds being most effectively conveyed in her ink illustrations to the *Poor Knight* (1911; Museum of the History of St Petersburg). There the apparition of an ethereal weak youth is dissolved into a tree with *Japonist* lightness of touch.

Guro's search for the inner, unifying life of all objects meant a concentration on such elements as pine trees, roots, branches, stumps, fungi, stones and shorelines, as in *Waterlilies* (c.1912) and *The Shore* (c.1909; both Central State Archive for Literature and Art, Moscow) – the nature that was closest to her at her dacha on the wooded banks of the Gulf of Finland, west of St Petersburg. In these, there is a lyrical, fragmentary feeling of nature that suggests the free interpenetration of the sensual and the concrete. She loved to make the inanimate come alive, to break down the boundaries between objects by, for instance, turning a cucumber into a man or a cloud into a baby camel. Through such means she felt that she evoked a sensation of the fourth dimension, her experience of a higher order of reality.

Description was anathema; narrative largely absent. Instead Guro presented fleeting images, many of which were impressions of conventional *début-de-siècle* subjects – the spring, youth, dreams, urban life, night, movement, natural growth, lilies, the soul. These, which primarily concerned the earth's cycles, were conveyed in several booklets and numerous oil sketches, watercolours and pen-and-ink studies. The intimacy that she revealed suggested that expression derived more from feeling than sight. Hence volume, modelling and perspective are ignored; objects, where they are still recognisable, are frequently cut off by the picture edge; colours are abstracted from physical reality; and line is given a tremulous life of its own. Features such as these characterise *Fawn* (c.1909) and *Still Life with Blue Cups* (1912; both Central State Archive for Literature and Art). Through such means, with the young deer and cups cut off and set against the flowing, ambiguous organic forms of a landscape, Guro strove to express a profound communion with nature.

The first published combination of visual and literary images in which mimesis of neuro-psychological nature was paramount was Guro's *Sharmanka* or hurdy-gurdy (1909). There vignettes of life in the city and countryside, together with childish and medievalist fantasies, were interspersed with simple, small drawings of stars, a bucket and drainpipe, lanterns, leaves, circles, stairs, a window and trees. The impression is one of a kaleidoscopic, miniature theatre where colours, sounds and movement are freely collated and where the sum is an animated picture, often of St Petersburg. In the course of this emerging picture, Guro relishes the crudely appetising signboards of bakers' shops and taverns, subsequently favourite sources for the Russian Neo-primitivists, most of whom were to collaborate with the Union of Youth that Guro co-founded with her husband Mikhail Matyushin in 1909. In association with this tendency, Guro made several designs for signboards as well as an ink drawing, *Hairdresser's Window* (1900s; Museum of the History of St Petersburg). This, with its display of female wigs and bent drainpipe, appeared to be a paraphrase of the *Barber's Window* (1906; Tretyakov Gallery) by her teacher, Mstislav Dobuzhinsky.

On occasion Guro's primitivism, with its attempt to reveal alternative states of consciousness, clearly coincided with that of her more flamboyant colleagues, such as the Burlyuks, Filonov and Malevich. This was evident in the calligraphic, "trans-rational" drawings and projected "abstract" cover for the unpublished fourth issue of *Soyuz molodyozhi* (Union of Youth; 1913; Museum of the History of St Petersburg); in her writing – which could employ scattered elements of peasant dialects, Finnish sounds and children's speech; and, more conventionally, in the paintings *Morning of the Giant* (1910; State Russian Museum), with its crude depiction of Russian ceramic and wooden dogs, and *Tea Drinking* (c.1910; Orel Art Gallery), with its *muzhik* and young lady seated around a table composed of Fauvist-style ambiguous colour space, and roughly contoured, generalised forms.

JEREMY HOWARD

Gustafsson-Nyman, Gunnel *see* Nyman

H

Hale, Ellen Day
American painter, 1855–1940

Born in Worcester, Massachusetts, 1855. Studied in Boston under William Rimmer, 1873, then under William Morris Hunt. Attended classes at Pennsylvania Academy of the Fine Arts, Philadelphia, 1878–9. First trip to Europe, 1881; studied in Paris at Académie Colarossi, under Jean-Jacques Henner and Emile-Auguste Carolus-Duran, and at Académie Julian; further studies at Académie Julian on second trip to Paris, 1885; also taught etching in Paris by Baltimore artist Gabrielle de Veaux Clements. Spent summers on Cape Anne, Massachusetts, from 1880s. Lived in Santa Barbara, California, 1892–3; subsequently lived and taught art in Boston; after much peripatetic wandering, moved to Washington, DC, in 1902. Travelled widely. Died in Brookline, Massachusetts, 1940.

Principal Exhibitions

Centennial Exposition, Philadelphia: 1876
Pennsylvania Academy of the Fine Arts, Philadelphia: occasionally 1876–1936
Boston Art Club: from 1878
Royal Academy, London: 1882
Paris Salon: 1883, 1885
World's Columbian Exposition, Chicago: 1893

Bibliography

Clara Erskine Clement, *Women in the Fine Arts*, Boston: Houghton Mifflin, 1904; reprinted New York: Hacker, 1974
Nancy Hale, *The Life in the Studio*, Boston: Little Brown, 1969
Christine Jones Huber, *The Pennsylvania Academy and Its Women, 1850–1920*, Philadelphia: Pennsylvania Academy of the Fine Arts, 1973
Frederic A. Sharf and John H. Wright, *William Morris Hunt and the Summer Art Colony at Magnolia, Massachusetts, 1876–1879*, Salem, MA, 1981
Martha J. Hoppin, "Women artists in Boston, 1870–1900: The pupils of William Morris Hunt", *American Art Journal*, xiii, Winter 1981, p.40
American Women Artists, 1830–1930, exh. cat., National Museum of Women in the Arts, Washington, DC, 1987

Ellen Day Hale was born into a family that was a very distinguished one in Boston and in American history. The artist's father Edward Everett Hale was a famous orator and author of *The Man Without a Country*, her aunt Catherine Beecher was a renowned educator and her aunt Harriet Beecher Stowe was internationally known for her book *Uncle Tom's Cabin*. Another aunt, Susan Hale, served as Hale's first art instructor. Her brother Phillip was a painter, as was his wife Lilian Westcott Hale.

In 1873 Hale studied with William Rimmer and then the acclaimed Boston painter William Morris Hunt and his assistant Helen Knowlton. She also went to classes with a friend at the Pennsylvania Academy of the Fine Arts. In 1878 the first exhibition of her paintings occurred at the Boston Art Club, where Knowlton, Susan Hale and other women were represented. Some of these artists were also included in what has been called the first American sale of works by women artists in 1881 in Boston at the auction house of Lewis J. Bird and Company. The same year Ellen Day Hale and Knowlton took a trip to Europe before Hale's matriculation in a women's class at the Académie Colarossi. This was followed in 1882 by study in another class offered to women by Jean-Jacques Henner and Emile-Auguste Carolus-Duran. After more European travel, Hale returned to Paris to begin classes at the Académie Julian. On a subsequent trip to Paris in 1885 Hale re-enrolled there, and while abroad also learned etching from a fellow American artist and friend named Gabrielle de Veaux Clements.

After her return to America, Hale exhibited at the Pennsylvania Academy of the Fine Arts, one of the more progressive places for women artists of the period. She also contributed a work to the Royal Academy, London, in 1882 and to the Paris Salons of 1883 and 1885. Most of her works, however, were exhibited in the USA in Boston, other Massachusetts venues and in Philadelphia. Like those of many contemporary artists of note, her pictures were among the fine arts on display at the Philadelphia Centennial Exposition (1876) and the World's Columbian Exposition in Chicago (1893).

In two separate trips to the West, Hale produced portraits of Native Americans and settled in Santa Barbara, California, for a year-long sojourn in 1892. Most of her summers from the 1880s onwards were spent on Cape Anne in Massachusetts, in a house next to her sister-in-law Lilian Westcott Hale. By the early 1890s Hale shared a house and studio there with Gabrielle Clements. In addition to family support, Hale earned a living painting portraits and teaching art in Boston, as well as by selling etchings and decorating some church interiors in

Hale: *Self-Portrait*, 1885; oil on canvas; 72.4 × 99.1 cm.; Museum of Fine Arts, Boston: Gift of Nancy Hale Bowers

New England, notably a *Nativity* for the South Congregational Church in Boston. Among her prizes was an award from the Mechanics' Charitable Association.

While living in Washington, DC, where her father served as chaplain to the United States Senate, Hale made a drawing of *President Theodore Roosevelt* (untraced) and painted other portraits, including a commissioned one of *John G. Carlisle* (untraced), Speaker of the House of Representatives. The artist continued her travels and in 1929 went to Palestine and Syria. She remained devoted to painting even as an octogenarian and after being disabled with a broken hip. She died in a nursing home in Brookline, Massachusetts.

Hale's early style was influenced by the palette and technique of William Morris Hunt, particularly his elimination of distracting details and integration of cool light and pellucid atmosphere with facile brush strokes to create graceful, even statuesque figures. Some of Hale's works were quite avant-garde and suggest an affinity both with Mary Cassatt (q.v.) and Whistler, as is evident in a commanding *Self-Portrait* of 1885 (see illustration), which shows Hale confidently gazing at the viewer as she holds a huge ostrich feather fan. While she produced some genre subjects and landscapes as well as numerous prints, portraits were her forte. In later years she shifted to a more impressionistic style, as in *Morning News*

(1905; National Museum of Women in the Arts, Washington, DC), a genre subject with a handsomely silhouetted woman shown reading a newspaper in beautiful morning light. Another work that reveals Hale's penchant for painting solitary women in light-filled chambers and absorbed in everyday activities is *June* (c.1905; Holladay Collection, Washington, DC).

SUSAN P. CASTERAS

Halicka, Alice

French painter, graphic artist and designer, 1895–1975

Born in Kraków, 20 December 1895; lived with maternal grandparents in Austria after mother's early death. Studied at the Munich Academy under Hungarian painter Simon Hollosy. Moved to Paris, 1912; studied at Académie Ranson under Maurice Denis and Paul Sérusier. Married Polish artist Louis Marcoussis, 1913; one daughter; husband died 1941. Exhibited at Salon des Indépendants, 1914 and 1920–21; Salon d'Automne, Salon des Tuileries and Salon des Surindépendants, all in Paris, from 1920. Visited Poland and

London, early 1920s. Lived in USA, 1935–8; provided publicity material for Helena Rubenstein and designed ballet sets in New York, including *Jardin Publique*, performed at the Metropolitan Opera, New York, and Covent Garden, London. Lived in Vichy, France, during World War II, then returned to Paris. Toured India, 1952; visited USSR, 1960. Died in Paris, 1975.

Selected Individual Exhibitions

Zborowsky Gallery, London: 1914
Galerie Berthe Weill, Paris: 1922
Galerie Druet, Paris: 1924
Galerie Georges Petit, Paris: 1930
Leicester Galleries, London: 1934
Marie Harriman Gallery, New York: 1935
Julien Levy Gallery, New York: 1937
Galerie Pascaud, Paris: 1938
Galerie de l'Elysée: Paris: 1945
Galerie Colette Allendy, Paris: 1947
Galerie Berri, Paris: 1954
Club International de la Presse et du Livre, Warsaw: 1956
Galerie Mariac, Paris: 1958
Galerie Ste Croix, Nantes: 1971 (with Louis Marcoussis)
Galerie 22, Paris: 1973

Selected Writings

Hier, souvenirs, Paris: Du Pavois, 1946

Bibliography

Maurice Raynal, *Anthologie de la peinture en France de 1906 à nos jours*, Paris: Montaigne, 1927
Guillaume Apollinaire, *The Cubist Painter: Aesthetic Meditations, 1913*, New York: Wittenborn, 1944 (French original, 1913)
Cyril W. Beaumont, *Ballet Design, Past and Present*, London: Studio Publications, 1946
Raymond Cogniat, *Les Décorateurs de théâtre*, Paris: Librairie Théâtrale, 1955
Stravinsky and the Dance: A Survey of Ballet Productions, 1910–1962, exh. cat., New York Public Library, 1962
Jeanine Warnod, "Alice Halicka et ses souvenirs", *Terre Europe*, no.48, May 1974
L'altra metà dell'avanguardia, 1910–1940: Pittrici e scultrici nei movimenti delle avanguardie storiche, exh. cat., Palazzo Reale, Milan, and elsewhere, 1980
Louis Marcoussis/Alice Halicka, exh. cat., Musée de Pontoise, 1986
Jeanine Warnod, *Le Bateau-Lavoir*, Paris: Mayer, 1986
Alice Halicka (1895–1975): Période cubiste (1913–1920), exh. cat., Salle de la Restauration, Vichy, 1988
Artystki polskie, exh. cat., National Museum, Warsaw, 1991
Gill Perry, *Women Artists and the Parisian Avant-Garde*, Manchester: Manchester University Press, and New York: St Martin's Press, 1995

The daughter of a doctor, Alice Halicka had a middle-class upbringing in Kraków and with her grandparents in Vienna after her mother's death. Passionately interested in Polish and French literature as well as painting, she went to Munich to study, where she discovered the work of El Greco, van Gogh and Picasso. In 1912 she moved to Paris and enrolled at the Académie Ranson, where Maurice Denis and Paul Sérusier were teaching. She met the Polish artist Louis Marcoussis, whom she married the following year, and his circle of avant-garde painters and poets such as Apollinaire, Max Jacob, Tristan Tzara, Juan Gris, Picasso, Braque and Dufy. These young painters, according to Apollinaire, had "but one aim: pure painting ... an entirely new plastic art". The friends met at the Bateau-Lavoir to talk about painting; they liked parties, holidays, jazz and the circus. The war separated them. Marcoussis went to the front and Halicka painted a great deal in order to support herself. After the war she deferred to her husband and abandoned Cubism, becoming more of a decorative artist than a painter. Marcoussis died in 1941, and life was difficult during the German occupation. In 1945 she published her memoirs, *Hier*. Halicka liked all forms of art and was very productive until her death. She is buried in Vichy, with Marcoussis.

From her first public appearance, at the Salon des Indépendants with Marcoussis and his friends known as "Cubists", Halicka exhibited and made a name for herself. Apollinaire, the sacred "mouthpiece of the avant-garde", acknowledged her "masculine talents", a compliment for a female artist, as well as her realist gifts, "which enabled her to build up a picture intelligently without spoiling the shape of the composition". Of course the two were friends, since meeting at the Bateau-Lavoir: "in all the world, one of the places where the spirit [of inspiration] breathed most superbly" (Jean Cassou).

Apollinaire's compliments are justified, not only by the still lifes Halicka exhibited but also by those painted by 1914, which were certainly known to him. Halicka belonged to the "revolutionary" school of painting, the "art of painting new compositions with formal elements taken not from visual reality but from the reality of ideas", as Apollinaire defined the Cubism practised by Braque, Picasso, Gris, Marie Blanchard (q.v.) and Marie Laurencin (q.v.) as well as Marcoussis and Halicka. In her still lifes Halicka showed great mastery in handling and understanding of the subject. Critics called her "the most gifted woman painter of her time" (Waldemar George) and acknowledged her "undeniable artistic talents accompanied by lyricism and wit" (Elie Faure, C. Roger Marx). These critics were capable of seeing the rigour and sensitivity she retained in her work throughout her life. Such qualities were already apparent in her Cubist period (1913–20), in the way she fragmented an object in order to reconstruct it without distortion, above all recapturing its essence. Light plays an important role in her Cubist compositions, whether it is strongly focused in the centre of the painting (*Composition with a Book and Sheet of Paper*), or falls horizontally, so that the objects reflect one another (*Composition with Bottle and Glass*; both 1914; oil on canvas; private collection, Paris), or enters through an opening in the composition and plays over the whites, reds and yellows; in one work (*Composition with Mirror, Glass and Pipe*, 1914; private collection, Paris), the white highlights on a pipe are reflected in the mirrors in the picture. There is a real sense of space within the canvas, even if the pictorial values by which this is achieved are different from those of the 19th century. Halicka's still lifes (in the literal sense of the English term) give a sense of silent life as well as her pleasure in painting.

If it seems regrettable that Halicka gave up this style at the request of Marcoussis, she did retain these plastic qualities throughout her work, as well as her appetite for creation and untiring imagination. She perfectly suited the atmosphere of her time. "All the artists want to be craftsmen capable of various, large-scale activities ...", wrote Cassou, "Modern Art

Halicka: *No.10*, 1914; oil on canvas; 61 × 50 cm.; Collection Guy and Christiane de Aldecoa, Paris

is a human art, a social art". Although money was an important motivation, she responded to commissions with talent, for example from Bianchini, for whom she designed fabrics and wallpapers.

Halicka also invented "little pictures, a mixture of painting, low relief, buttons, scraps of material, collage, bits of wire, and feathers, dubbed 'romances captionnées' [padded romances] by the Princess Murat and René Crevel" (Halicka). She said she used them to express "without false shame and without constraint, all the ideas, sometimes romantic, sometimes poetic, sometimes a bit crazy, that come into my head". Her little pictures "have none of the popular Epinal imagery (but) do have a hidden philosophy ... She cuts out her fleeting emotions and colours them ... If her lyricism is oriental, her wit is that of Montmartre" (Princess Murat). These quotes are a perfect commentary on her work: for example the small-scale picture of *Circus Act* (1925), in which she sculpted from material a circle of horses, led by a trainer and controlled by a rider standing on one of them. Its range of grey tones is brightened by a collage of red tartan. The composition of *Roland at Roncesvaux* (1930), with a mountain background, is very dynamic, punctuated by swords. It reveals the extent of her curiosity.

Every technique interested Halicka. During a stay in Warsaw, she sketched in gouache, capturing, in a small scale, picturesque views of the life of the ghetto (1925). With her knowledge of composition and use of light to create facial expressions and scenic depth, she caught the essence of the area. She learned lithography, and with her skill as a draughtswoman, her imagination and taste for colour, produced a series of prints in five colours of the *Place de la Concorde* (1949). The "realist" depiction of the architecture formed the backdrop to a dream image of a mermaid as high as the central obelisk, which dominates the composition. In her arms the mermaid carries a large, brightly coloured fish. This lithograph takes its place in the sphere of the prevailing Surrealism.

Halicka explored many different forms of original artistic expression. She published drawings in magazines as diverse as *Annales*, *Harper's Bazaar*, *Lettres Françaises* and *Vu*. The same free approach is evident in her illustrations commissioned for books (author portraits, of Gide and Crevel, vignettes for Zangwill). Her talent and imagination showed also in decorative art. In 1935 she produced publicity panels for Helena Rubenstein. The Comte de Beaumont and others ordered costumes and masks from her for balls in 1938. In the interwar period, like other artists including Picasso, Braque and Gris, she designed costumes and sets. For George Balanchine's version of the ballet *Baiser de la Fée* (New York, 1937), she dressed the dancers in Russian folk costume. In the second scene, for example, two pine trees framed a mountain landscape, and flounced, printed curtains were wrapped around the set, adding an ornamental touch.

Her work as a decorative artist showed that she was capable of undertaking all forms of art work. "The merit of painting lies in its eloquence, in the subject it depicts and in the power of its depiction on the mind" (Félibien). And that is exactly what Halicka communicates, because she knew that "art is not only the study of positive reality; it is a search for the ideal truth" (George Sand). Above all, as she herself pointed out: "a work of art remains alive only by the spirit".

HENRIETTE BESSIS

Hall, Edna Clarke *see* Clarke Hall

Hambling, Maggi
British painter, 1945–

Born in Sudbury, Suffolk, 1945. Studied under Lett Haines and Cedric Morris, then at Ipswich School of Art, 1962–4; Camberwell School of Arts and Crafts, London, 1964–7; Slade School of Fine Art, London, 1967–9. Visited New York on Boise travel award, 1969. Recipient of Arts Council of Great Britain award, 1977; joint winner, with Patrick Caulfield, Jerwood prize, Royal Academy, 1995. First artist-in-residence, National Gallery, London, 1980–81. Lives in Clapham, London.

Selected Individual Exhibitions
Hadleigh Gallery, Suffolk: 1967
Morley Gallery, London: 1973
Warehouse Gallery, London: 1977
National Gallery, London: 1981
National Portrait Gallery, London: 1983 (*Pictures of Max Wall*, touring)
Serpentine Gallery, London: 1987
Richard Demarco Gallery, Edinburgh: 1988
Arnolfini Gallery, Bristol: 1988–9 (*Moments of the Sun*, touring)
Bernard Jacobson Gallery, London: 1990, 1992
Yale Center for British Art, New Haven: 1991
Christie's Contemporary Art Galleries, London: 1993
Northern Centre for Contemporary Art, Sunderland: 1993–4 (*Towards Laughter*, touring)
Marlborough Fine Art, London: 1996

Selected Writings
"Velázquez: The reality of paint", *Modern Painters*, ii/4, 1989, pp.19–25

Bibliography
Judith Bumpus, "The artist at work", *Art & Artists*, no.198, March 1983, pp.20–22
The Hard-won Image, exh. brochure, Tate Gallery, London, 1984
Judith Bumpus, "In celebration", *Art & Artists*, no.228, September 1985, pp.18–21
Peter Fuller, "London: Maggi Hambling", *Burlington Magazine*, cxxix, 1987, pp.760–61
Maggi Hambling: Paintings, Drawings and Watercolours, exh. cat., Serpentine Gallery, London, 1987
Mary Rose Beaumont, "Maggi Hambling: Serpentine Gallery", *Arts Review*, xxxix, 9 October 1987, p.689
Elaine Feinstein, "Maggi Hambling", *Modern Painters*, i/2, 1988, pp.27–32
Maggi Hambling: Moments of the Sun, exh. cat., Arnolfini Gallery, Bristol, and elsewhere, 1988
Elizabeth Claridge, "Against generalization", *London Magazine*, xxvii, February 1988, pp.45–53

Hambling: *Professor Dorothy Hodgkin*, 1985; National Portrait Gallery, London

Maggi Hambling: An Eye Through a Decade, 1981–1991, exh. cat., Yale Center for British Art, New Haven, 1991

Frances Carey, "Maggi Hambling's monotypes", *Print Quarterly*, ix, 1992, pp.187–91

Maggi Hambling: Towards Laughter, exh. cat., Northern Centre for Contemporary Art, Sunderland, and elsewhere, 1993

Emmanuel Cooper, "Maggi Hambling: Christie's Contemporary Art Galleries, London, June", *Ceramic Review*, no.143, September–October 1993, pp.24–5

Despite the range of subjects and artistic media that Maggi Hambling has selected over the past 35 years, she has seldom strayed from the representation of the identifiable moment. Her techniques range from the exuberant use of colour, loosely handled, to detailed draughtsmanship. But whether she is capturing the spirit of a clown, painting the myth of Pasiphaë, celebrating a magnificent sunset or working on a drawing of her mother after death, Hambling's usually figurative works develop from direct observation, the recording of a particular narrative. The result is always a telling image, often of poverty, old age or some fallen social condition, but always including elements of celebration and poignancy.

As a student of Lett Haines and Cedric Morris in the 1960s, Hambling was admonished to "be yourself. Never follow the tide" (Claridge 1988). She took the advice to heart, and has never been much tempted by the abstract idiom, even in its dominant heyday. Although she did experiment with audio-visual and conceptual techniques after her studies at the Slade, by 1972 she had returned to painting. During the 1970s she began to paint people, focusing on a way to represent ruined lives without relying on the macabre. By the mid-1970s sympathy for the frailty of the human condition could be read in her work, but her figures were always specific people, not generalised "types". By 1980–81 Hambling had become the first artist-in-residence at the National Gallery, London, a position that gave her a high public profile. Shortly after her tenure there she completed a celebrated series of paintings of the clown, comic and serious actor, Max Wall, exhibited at the National Gallery in 1983.

While the painting of any portrait usually requires the rendering of a likeness, Hambling is distinguished by her ability to empathise with the sitter's inner life. She never uses photographs when creating portraits, but begins by drawing her subject to find the pose that the final work will retain. In *Max Wall and His Image* (1981; Tate Gallery, London) Wall is balanced precariously, seated on an unstable stool, heels on a table, while behind him his shadow has a life of its own. The shadow's persona is of Wall's character Professor Wallofski, a monster perhaps, haunting the scene and reminding both Max and the viewer of the two lives the actor juxtaposes, on and off stage. This portrait grew into a series of 15 paintings and 25 drawings, all being unique combinations of pathos and the healing effects of laughter.

In 1985 Hambling was commissioned by the National Portrait Gallery, London, to execute a portrait of *Professor Dorothy Hodgkin* (see illustration), winner of the 1964 Nobel Prize for Chemistry. Hambling portrayed the eminent scientist at her desk concentrating and absorbed in her work with not two but four hands busy, symbolising her constant motion. Despite the informality of the figure and its surroundings,

Hambling projects the intellectual importance of Hodgkin's work.

During the period 1983–7, Hambling's subject matter diversified significantly, and she did not show a substantial body of work. Her subsequent exhibition at the Serpentine Gallery in 1987 reflected this new diversity in a wealth of landscapes, people, religious, mythological, animal and political subjects. Alongside the portraits of neighbourhood people for which she was so well known, she now included members of the animal kingdom, both real and mythical. The spectacle of a bullfight that she had witnessed in Barcelona in 1977 influenced a series of paintings of the struggle between man and beast, with Hambling taking a sympathetic view of the bull's noble but futile struggle. *Descent of the Bull's Head* (1985; artist's collection, repr. Beaumont 1987) shows the unfortunate creature falling through four stages of death into its own blood. The true story of the bullfight led Hambling to the myth, and she painted the story of Jupiter disguised as a bull mating with Pasiphaë in *Pasiphaë and the Bull: Conception of the Minotaur* (1987; Tim Curry collection, repr. Feinstein 1988, p.31), a scene that Hambling manages to convey as affectionate. The unfortunate creature born of this union, the flesh-eating Minotaur, appears in *Minotaur Surprised while Eating* (1986–7; Tate Gallery), and he too is represented as paradoxically unthreatening, even in the middle of the ghastly act of eating human remains (Beaumont 1987).

This period of extensive production generated a series of almost abstract renditions of the sunrise and sunset in most vivid colour. In *Dragon Sunrise* (1986; artist's collection and Bernard Jacobson Gallery, London) the sun itself becomes a mythical beast, multi-coloured and powerful, joyful but violent. The works were done in Hambling's home town in Suffolk, where she has returned over the years to watch the sun rise and set over a specific spot. She recorded the scene on the spot in watercolour and recreated it later in her studio in oil (repr. Claridge 1988, p.52).

After 1988 Hambling began to work in monotype, an unpredictable medium in which the speed and skill of the artist determine the cohesiveness of the resulting image. The monochromatic colour schemes of the work contrast specifically with the colourful exhilaration of the sunrises and sunsets. *Standing Figure from behind with Hands on Hips* (from the first *Jemma* series, 1990; artist's collection, repr. Carey 1992, p.190) demonstrates Hambling's control of the monotype medium and her ability to use it "as a mediator between drawing and painting [rather] than as part of any print-making process" (*ibid.*, p.187).

In 1993 Hambling produced work in a medium that was new for her: ceramics. She created a mixture of mythical, three-dimensional creatures, highly glazed in bright colours, based on dragons, goddesses and a beaver. The clay was worked directly and spontaneously, resulting in some rather joyful effects. *Ancient Egyptian Goddess* (1993; private collection, repr. Cooper 1993, p.25) is part of the menagerie, a four-legged construction, 41 centimetres tall, that represents Hambling's continuous willingness to experiment with the new while remaining true to her own path and never being persuaded by fashion or fad.

JANICE ANDERSON

Hamilton, Letitia
Irish painter, 1878–1964

Born at Hamwood, Dunboyne, Co. Meath, 1878, younger sister of the painter Eva Hamilton. Studied at Metropolitan School of Art, Dublin, under Sir William Orpen, then at Chelsea Polytechnic, London, under Frank Brangwyn. Travelled widely in Europe, notably in France, Yugoslavia and Italy, 1920s and 1930s; came under the broad influence of the School of Paris. Recipient of silver medal, Board of Education, 1912; bronze medal, Olympic Games "Sport in Art" section, 1948. Founder member, 1920, and President, late 1950s, Society of Dublin Painters. Associate member, 1934, and member, 1944, Royal Hibernian Academy. Died August 1964.

Principal Exhibitions

Individual
Dublin Painters' Gallery: 1920, 1922, 1923, 1924 (with Eva Hamilton) 1927, 1928, 1929

Walker's Art Gallery, London: 1931
Waddington Gallery, Dublin: 1943 (twice), 1945, 1948
Dawson Gallery, Dublin: 1960

Group
Royal Hibernian Academy, Dublin: 1909–26, 1928–30, 1932–65
Royal Academy, London: 1922, 1924, 1935
Society of Dublin Painters: 1931, 1933–5, 1938

Bibliography

Irish Art, 1900–1950, exh. cat., Crawford Municipal Art Gallery, Cork, 1975

Irish Women Artists from the Eighteenth Century to the Present Day, exh. cat., National Gallery of Ireland, Dublin, and elsewhere, 1987

Patricia Butler, *Three Hundred Years of Irish Watercolours and Drawings*, London: Weidenfeld and Nicolson, 1990

Kenneth McConkey, *A Free Spirit: Irish Art, 1860–1960*, Woodbridge, Suffolk: Antique Collectors' Club-Pyms Gallery, 1990

S.B. Kennedy, *Irish Art and Modernism, 1880–1950*, Belfast: Institute of Irish Studies, 1991

Hamilton: *Donkeys*, 1930–32; Ulster Museum, Belfast

Images and Insights, exh. cat., Hugh Lane Municipal Gallery of Modern Art, Dublin, 1993

Letitia Hamilton was one of a number of Irish women artists of her generation – others included her elder sister, Eva, May Guinness (q.v.), Mary Swanzy (q.v.), Evie Hone (q.v.) and Mainie Jellett (q.v.) – who, with a modicum of private means, were able to devote much of their time to foreign travel; thus they encountered at first hand many of the developments of early modernism in European art and, through their own work, introduced these developments into Irish art. In particular, Hamilton adopted a plein-air approach, to which she brought an emphasis on strong light, atmosphere and colour, which she derived from Impressionism. Her whole technique of painting placed great emphasis on spontaneity, and the use of a palette knife and heavy impasto are also characteristics of her mature style. Yet in many respects, although her manner was free from the rigidity of academic painting, she too often lacks a sense of direction. Thus her development as an artist is difficult to plot.

Hamilton's early work is characterised by a simplification of forms and shapes and by the use of a limited palette, influences that may have come from her fellow-countryman Paul Henry. Her later compositions are generally more cluttered, her colour richer if, at times, a little fussy. Until the mid-1920s Hamilton painted mainly in Ireland, travelling about the countryside recording the ordinary everyday events that she witnessed. Country fairs and markets, often in the towns of the midlands, were her principal subject matter at the time. *An Irish Market Scene* (c.1923; Ulster Museum, Belfast) and *Donkeys* (1930–32; see illustration) are typical of such works and, in their directness of execution, show her ability to capture the atmosphere of the country and its people. In about the autumn of 1923 Hamilton went for the first time to Venice, on a painting holiday with her sister, and, on her return the following February, she and Eva held a joint exhibition of paintings at the Dublin Painters' Gallery. The works, which included Letitia's splendidly atmospheric *Venice* (private collection, Dublin), showed how the strong Italian sunshine had transformed her ability to handle bright colours, which she now did with great assurance, especially when using a palette knife. Henceforth these features (although at times in a lower tonal key) were to typify her work even of the Irish landscape. Her use of clear, unmuddied colours and her palette knife technique can be seen to perfection in the delightful *Snow in County Down* (c.1940; Hugh Lane Municipal Gallery of Modern Art, Dublin), where the wintry atmosphere of the scene is set down virtually in monochrome, the heavy snow on the drooping branches of the fir trees in the foreground being admirably rendered in simple swathes of thick paint laid on with a palette knife. This picture represents Hamilton at her very best.

While landscapes were her principal subject matter, Hamilton produced occasional interior scenes, such as *Interior at Cheyne Walk, Chelsea* (c.1936–7) and *The Window* (c.1940s; both private collections, Dublin). In these and other similar compositions the sense of space in the room is precisely regulated by the arrangement of the furniture, ornaments and other objects. In the former composition the elaborate patterning of the carpet and other furnishings produce an almost Matisse-like decorative quality, while in the latter the vase of flowers in the foreground provides ample opportunity for the artist to display her fine powers as a colourist. Both pictures are permeated by a quality of light that is characteristic of much of Hamilton's work.

As an artist Letitia Hamilton painted mainly to please herself rather than a wider audience. At her best she was an artist of considerable subtlety. It is a pity, however, that she was not more disciplined in her work, for in the Ireland of her time she had the potential to be a constructive influence on what was too frequently a doggedly conservative scene.

S.B. KENNEDY

Hammond, Harmony

American artist, 1944–

Born in Chicago, Illinois, 8 February 1944. Studied at the Junior School of the Art Institute of Chicago, 1960–61; Milliken University, Decatur, Illinois, 1961–3; University of Minnesota, Minneapolis, 1963–7 (BFA); also studied at the Alliance Française, Paris, summers 1967–9. Moved to New York, 1969. Subsequently participated in numerous feminist activities. Founder member of AIR Gallery, the first women's cooperative gallery in New York, 1972. Curated and participated in *A Lesbian Show* at 112 Greene Street Gallery, the first exhibition dedicated to lesbian art in New York, 1978; participated in the *Great American Lesbian Art Show*, Women's Building in Los Angeles, 1979; visiting artist there, 1980. Co-founder of Heresies Collective and contributor to its journal, *Heresies: A Feminist Publication of Art and Politics*, 1976–8. Gave several courses at the Feminist Art Institute in New York, 1980. Moved to New Mexico, 1984. Taught at University of Arizona, Tucson, from 1988 (tenured professor 1990). Recipient of National Endowment for the Arts (NEA) grants, 1979 and 1983; Creative Artists Public Service (CAPS) grant, New York State Council for the Arts, 1982; Pollock-Krasner Foundation fellowship, 1989; Guggenheim fellowship, 1991. Lives in Galisteo, New Mexico.

Selected Individual Exhibitions

AIR Gallery, New York: 1973, 1982, 1984
La Magna Gallery, New York: 1976
PS 1 Gallery, Long Island City, Queens, NY: 1979
Lerner Heller Gallery, New York: 1979, 1982
WARM Gallery and Glen Hanson Gallery, Minneapolis: 1981 (retrospective)
Real Art Ways, Hartford, CT: 1982
Luise Ross Gallery, New York: 1984
Matrix Gallery, Wadsworth Atheneum, Hartford, CT: 1984
Bernice Steinbaum Gallery, New York: 1986
Jonson Gallery, University of New Mexico, Albuquerque: 1987
Linda Durham Gallery, Santa Fe: 1988
Trabia-MacAffe Gallery, New York: 1988
Center for Contemporary Art, Santa Fe: 1992
Tucson Museum of Art: 1993
Fox Fine Art Center, University of Texas, El Paso: 1995

Selected Writings

Wrappings: Essays on Feminism, Art and the Martial Arts, New York: TSL Press, 1984

"The mechanics of exclusion", *THE Magazine*, April 1993, pp.41–3

"A space of infinite and pleasurable possibilities: Lesbian self-representation in visual art", *New Feminist Criticism*, ed. Joanna Frueh and others, New York: Icon, 1994

"A lesbian show", *In a Different Light*, exh. cat., Art Museum, University of California, Berkeley, 1995

The Art of Lesbian (Re)Presentation (in preparation)

Bibliography

Carter Ratcliff, "On contemporary primitivism", *Artforum*, xiv, November 1975, pp.57–65

Lucy R. Lippard, *From the Center: Feminist Essays on Women's Art*, New York: Dutton, 1976

Harmony Hammond: Ten Years, 1970–1980, exh. cat., WARM Gallery and Glen Hanson Gallery, Minneapolis, 1981

Lucy R. Lippard, "Binding/bonding", *Art in America*, lxx, April 1982, pp.112–18

Janice Willard, "Harmony Hammond: Collecting, reclaiming, connecting", *Fiberarts*, ix/4, July–August 1982, pp.58–60

Sandra L. Langer, "Harmony Hammond: Strong affections", *Arts Magazine*, lvii, February 1983, pp.122–3

Harmony Hammond, typescript exhibition guide, Wadsworth Atheneum, Hartford, CT, 1984

Judy Collischan van Wagner, "Harmony Hammond's painted spirits", *Arts Magazine*, lx, January 1986, pp.22–5

Harmony Hammond: Radiant Spirits, exh. cat., Jonson Gallery, University of New Mexico, Albuquerque, 1987

Arlene Raven, *Crossing Over: Feminism and Art of Social Concern*, Ann Arbor: UMI Research Press, 1988

Neery Malkonian, "Interview with Harmony Hammond", *THE Magazine*, October 1992, pp.9–11

Harmony Hammond: Farm Ghosts, exh. cat., Tucson Museum of Art, 1993

Emmanuel Cooper, *The Sexual Perspective: Homosexuality and Art in the Last 100 Years in the West*, 2nd edition, London and New York: Routledge, 1994

Mary D. Garrard and Norma Broude, eds, *The Power of Feminist Art: The American Movement of the 1970s*, New York: Abrams, and London: Thames and Hudson, 1994

Mara R. Witzling, ed., *Voicing Today's Visions: Writings by Contemporary Women Artists*, New York: Universe, 1994

Study of Harmony Hammond's professional chronology establishes that she participated in many of the landmark events in the history of the feminist art movement in the USA, but even this remarkable list belies the scope of her accomplishments. She has had more than 30 individual exhibitions since her first solo show at the University of Minnesota in 1963, and has participated in more than 60 group exhibitions throughout the USA, Europe and Latin America. She has lectured and given workshops in a vast array of prominent arts and educational institutions, and has also written criticism for the New Mexico periodicals, *THE Magazine* and *Artspace*.

Consistent with her feminist politics, in the early 1970s Hammond began to explode conceptual polarities such as male/female and art/craft that have formed the basis for art-historical hierarchies. In 1974 she exhibited *Floor Piece VI (Sculpture)* (artist's collection), a braided and painted simulacrum of a hooked rug. While her title ironically alluded to titles used by (male) minimalist artists who presented abstract geometric forms in industrial materials such as steel, Hammond's source was a traditional women's craft form. In celebrating art that was not valued by the dominant culture

Hammond: *Hunkertime*, 1979–80; cloth, wood, acrylic, gesso, liquid rubber, Rhoplex, metal; nine units varying in height from 152.4 to 210.8 cm.; artist's collection

and commemorating artists who were obscured by anonymity, Hammond began a career-long commitment to give voice to the silenced, to use her work to honour those disenfranchised because of class, race, gender or sexuality.

Hammond achieved wide renown for such wrapped sculptures as *Hunkertime* (1979–80; see illustration), a cluster of ladders ranging in size from 1.5 to 2 metres that huddle together in anthropomorphic embrace. The ladders are thickly wrapped with cloth and painted with skinlike strips of rubber so that their rectilinearity is veiled. Instead of resembling rigid strips of wood, the slats allude to limbs, legs and other body parts. The obsessive labour required by the wrapping is reiterated by flurries of paint marks, which the artist refers to as "spirit dots for protection". Occasional projections of stiff, ruffled wings "perversely feminize the minimal seriousness". It is clear that Hammond's process echoes the quilting, embroidery and tapestry techniques of historic women's arts. A related work, *Kudzu* (1981; Wadsworth Atheneum, Hartford), presents two surreal beings whose arcing arms project out to grab, caution or perhaps hug the viewer. *Radiant Affections* (c.1982; Metropolitan Museum of Art, New York), another wrapped work, pairs two immense ovals whose mouths/vaginas/orifices call/beckon/threaten the viewer.

Painting has been an ongoing interest for Hammond. Throughout her time in New York, she created small works with humorous allegorical figures, such as the whimsical *Fan Lady* (1980; Walker Art Center, Minneapolis), a version of which she used as the cartoon for a collaboration with quilt-maker Bob Douglas: *Fan Lady Meets Ruffled Waters* (1983; Collection Philip Morris Companies, Inc.)

Since moving to New Mexico in 1984, the artist has turned her focus increasingly towards large-scale, mixed-media works. She has retained an involvement with mass and space by combining richly textured surfaces with found objects from abandoned farms of the American Southwest, and juxtaposing Western painting with non-traditional materials such as leaves, roots, hair and other found materials. *Bitter Harvest* (1993; Roswell Museum, NM) is a diptych of oil and latex rubber on canvas painted in movingly expressive earth tones. The amber panel on the left is marked by 16 projections of dried roots, which resemble knotted threads of weavings or the fragile braids of hair that Hammond has also employed in her work. The panel on the right is crimson with blood-red wounds; the artist has often used her art surfaces as metaphors for human skin. Uniting the two painted panels is a pair of rusted, warped water gutters. Arranged as a cross, the dried gutters transcend sentimentalised nostalgia for a romanticised past to symbolise the arteries – the vessels – of self and culture. Reaching from the blood/body/red on the right to the fabric/artefact/gold on the left, the re-valued discarded objects point to the connective and healing role of art. Hammond uses paint as a poultice to heal wounds in the rusted metal or worn linoleum with which we mark our social spaces. She continues to use her work to trace the construction of identity and to explore what it means to be female, lesbian, rural and "other" in a society that values the male, heterosexual, urban and conformity.

BETTY ANN BROWN

Hamnett, Nina
British painter, 1890–1956

Born in Tenby, Pembrokeshire, 14 February 1890. Led an itinerant childhood, attending classes at Portsmouth School of Art, 1903, and Dublin School of Art, 1906, until her father, an army captain, lost his money. Subsequently trained at Pelham School of Art, South Kensington, under Sir Alfred Cope, and London School of Art under Frank Brangwyn, John Swan and William Nicholson, 1907. First visited Paris, 1912. Employed in Omega Workshops, London, 1913–19; also taught at Westminster Technical Institute. Married Norwegian artist Edgar de Bergen (adopted name Roald Kristian), 1914; son born prematurely and died, 1915; lost touch with husband when he was deported as an alien, 1917. Lived and worked in Paris and London. Exhibited at Salon d'Automne and Salon des Indépendants in Paris, and in London with the Allied Artists Association, 1913–14; Friday Club, 1914–15; Grafton Group, 1914; Goupil Gallery Salon; included in *Artists of Fame and Promise* exhibitions at Leicester Galleries, London. Died in London, after falling from apartment window, 16 December 1956.

Selected Individual Exhibitions
Cambridge Magazine Art Gallery, Cambridge: 1918
Eldar Gallery, London: 1918, 1919
Independent Gallery, London: 1919
Galerie Lucien Vogel, Paris: 1923
Claridge Gallery, London: 1926, 1927 (illustrations for Seymour Leslie's *The Silent Queen*)
Tooth Gallery, London: 1928
Prince Vladimir Galitzine's Gallery, London: 1930
Zwemmer Gallery, London: 1932
Redfern Gallery, London: 1948

Selected Writings
Laughing Torso: Reminiscences, London: Constable, 1932; reprinted London: Virago, 1984
Is She a Lady? A Problem in Autobiography, London: Wingate, 1955

Bibliography
Mrs Gordon-Stables, "Nina Hamnett's psychological portraiture", *Artwork*, i, 1924, pp.112–15
Judith Collins, *The Omega Workshops*, London: Secker and Warburg, 1983; Chicago: University of Chicago Press, 1984
Nina Hamnett and Her Circle, exh. cat., Michael Parkin Fine Art, London, 1986
Denise Hooker, *Nina Hamnett: Queen of Bohemia*, London: Constable, 1986
Teresa Grimes, Judith Collins and Oriana Baddeley, *Five Women Painters*, London: Lennard, 1989

Nina Hamnett made a significant contribution to the modern movement in London in the years around 1915–32. A self-appointed artistic ambassador between London and Paris, she benefited from her first-hand knowledge of the avant-garde movements in both cities to develop her own individual style while remaining independent of the competing factions that proliferated in those years. Friends and mentors included Henri Gaudier-Brzeska, Amedeo Modigliani, Walter Sickert, Roger Fry and Augustus John.

It was as a draughtswoman that Hamnett excelled. In his introduction to her first solo exhibition in 1918, Sickert

Hamnett: *Ossip Zadkine*, 1914; oil on canvas; 78.8 × 78.8 cm.; private collection, on loan to Cartwright Hall, Bradford

acutely observed: "I cannot see her drawing not leading her to sustained practice in sculpture, sculpture being merely the multiplication by a theoretic infinity of the sharp silhouette that her uniform and sensitive line defines with such expressiveness and such startling virtuosity" (*Cambridge Magazine*, 8 June 1918, pp.770–71). Sculptors figured prominently among Hamnett's friends, and she drew from the model alongside Gaudier-Brzeska and Modigliani. She met Gaudier-Brzeska when they were both exhibiting with the Allied Artists

Association in 1913, and they posed naked for each other. The ease and fluidity of Hamnett's line, her pared-down simplification of form, had much in common with Gaudier's style. In Paris in 1914 she admired Modigliani's sculptures and drawings of elongated heads with highly simplified, stylised features. His bold, fluent contour and purity of form had a lasting influence on her. The pronounced sculptural quality of Hamnett's drawings also appeared in her oil paintings. Her portrait of the sculptor *Ossip Zadkine* (1914; see illustration) was one of her most accomplished works of this time. Thickly painted in sombre tones, Zadkine's features are solidly modelled with a multitude of subtly differentiated brush strokes. The contrast between his lively, intelligent face and the anguished mood of the sculpture behind him is used to great psychological effect.

At Fry's Omega Workshops, Hamnett carried out decorative work, such as painting designs on candlesticks and a mural on the theme of contemporary London life for the art dealer Arthur Ruck at 4 Berkeley Street in 1916. Apart from portraits, in 1916 she began to depict rooftops and the backs of houses – subjects much favoured by the Camden Town Group. Influenced by Fry and French art, particularly Cézanne, Hamnett's solution to the problem of translating perceived reality into paint was to concentrate on its underlying formal structure. In *Housetops* (*Colour* magazine, January 1917) the view from a window of backyards with washing hanging on a line is seen in terms of severely simplified geometric planes and volumes. Hamnett also painted several strong, spare still lifes in the years 1915–20, emphasising the abstract spatial relationships and volumetric qualities of the objects depicted (e.g. *Der Sturm*; collection Edward Booth-Clibborn, repr. Grimes, Collins and Baddeley 1989, p.90).

Hamnett was not, however, concerned with abstract form for its own sake and declared: "I am more interested in human beings than in landscapes or in still life" (Gordon-Stables 1924). She painted and drew what she saw and felt about the people and scenes around her with a sharp eye for the underlying human comedy. Her subject matter wittily reflected her fascination with life: café and pub scenes, the circus, the boxing ring and the park bench. Fry commented on her "alert and slightly disillusioned, but never ill-natured, awareness of the general character and situation of human beings" (*The Nation & The Athenaeum*, 11 May 1926).

Hamnett's ambition was "to paint psychological portraits that shall represent accurately the spirit of the age" (Gordon-Stables 1924). Her sitters included many of the leading artistic personalities of the time, such as *Walter Sickert, Horace Brodzky, Edith Sitwell, Osbert Sitwell* (1918; National Portrait Gallery, London), *W.H. Davies, Rupert Doone* (1922–3; Doncaster Museum and Art Gallery) and *Alvaro Guevara*. Her portraits are strong, bold statements of character rather than exact likenesses. Features are simplified and exaggerated to express her concise view of the sitter's personality. The combination of fine draughtsmanship with well-defined modelling of forms gives the portraits an almost sculptural solidity. Her richly low-toned palette is relieved by well-placed details of colour.

Hamnett was always attracted to people and places with any kind of oddity value. In 1928 she collaborated with Osbert Sitwell on *The People's Album of London Statues* (London: Duckworth), a book of drawings that are among her best works. She infused even the most solemn official statue with humour, vitality and movement, wittily capturing respected dignitaries from unexpected angles. Augustus John wrote of "her light, savant and malicious touch" and praised "her perfectly original talent which (in the case of her drawings) falls into line with the grand tradition of British humouristics" (*Vogue*, April 1928).

By the mid-1930s Hamnett's talent was in decline and despite a brief revival of artistic energy in the late 1940s and early 1950s, she produced little work beyond quick portrait sketches. Distracted by life, she failed to develop her style and technique. Always willing to tell another anecdote in return for the next drink, gradually Nina Hamnett the celebrated bohemian personality took over from the respected artist she had once been.

DENISE HOOKER

Hansen, Frida
Norwegian textile artist, 1855–1931

Born Frederikke Bollette Petersen in Stavanger, 8 March 1855. Taught drawing by the Norwegian painters Kitty Kielland (q.v.) and Johan Bennetter, 1871. Married land- and ship owner Wilhelm Severin Hansen, 1873; three children, one surviving infancy; husband died 1919. Started an embroidery shop after husband went bankrupt in 1883. Introduced to weaving on a vertical loom by Kjerstina Hauglum, Lærdal in Sogn, 1888; set up studio for handmade Norwegian tapestries in Stavanger, 1890. Moved to Christiania (Oslo), 1892; set up studio for weaving and dying with vegetable colours; consultant, designer and supplier of vegetable-dyed wool for Norwegian Association of Handicraft (Den Norske Husflidsforening, "DNH"). Visited World's Columbian Exposition, Chicago, on Norwegian government grant, 1893. Left DNH and went to Cologne to study in museums, 1894; drew from life in the studio of Puvis de Chavannes, Paris, spring 1895. Opened independent studio in Christiania, 1895. Became artistic director of Norwegian Atelier for Tapestry Weaving (Norsk Aaklæde og Billedtæppevæveri, "NABV") and patented the technique of transparent weaving, 1897; patented an improved vertical loom, 1899. NABV changed name to Det Norske Billedvæveri, "DNB", 1899; premises moved to Hansen's home in Bestum outside Christiania, 1904; closed down, 1906. Retained studio and continued weaving until her death; taught several pupils. Recipient of gold medal of King Umberto of Italy, 1901; King of Norway's gold medal of merit, 1915. Officier d'Académie, France, 1901; associée, Société Nationale des Beaux-Arts, Paris, 1906. Died in Oslo, 12 March 1931.

Principal Exhibitions
World's Columbian Exposition, Chicago: 1893
Blomqvist, Christiania: 1896, 1897, 1898, 1901, 1902 (touring), 1903, 1904, 1906, 1909, 1915, 1922, 1925 (all individual)
Stockholm: 1897 (*Allmänna konst- och industriutställningen* [Universal art and industry exhibition])
Bergen: 1898 (*Landsutsstillingen* [National exhibition], gold medal)
Wangs Kunstutstilling, Christiania: 1900 (individual)
Earls Court, London: 1900 (*Women's Exhibition*, gold medal)
Exposition Universelle, Paris: 1900 (gold medal)
Glasgow International Exhibition: 1901
Esposizione Internazionale d'Arte Decorativa Moderna, Turin: 1902 (gold medal)
Krefeld: 1903 (*Die nordische Kunstausstellung*, gold medal)
Société Nationale des Beaux-Arts, Paris: 1906–7, 1909, 1927
Kunstindustrimuseet, Christiania: 1913 (*Norsk tekstilkunst* [Norwegian textile art])

Christiania: 1914 (*Jubileumsutstilling, 1814–1914* [Jubilee exhibition])

Selected Writings

"Vor gamle nationale Tæppevævning" [Our old national tapestry weaving], *Morgenbladet*, 25 October 1891

"Norske Kvinders Udstilling i Kvindernes Bygning i Chicago" [Norwegian women's exhibition in the Women's Building in Chicago], *Aftenposten*, 9 May 1893

Husflid og kunstindustri i Norge [Handicrafts and applied art in Norway], Christiania, 1899

"Gerhard Münthes dekorative Kunst set fra et faglig standpunkt" [Gerhard Munthe's decorative art seen from a professional viewpoint], *Morgenbladet*, 10 January 1902

"Billedvæv og Gobelin" [Tapestry and Gobelin], *Aftenposten*, 11 February 1913

"Om Göteborgutstillingen kunstindustri i almindelighet og tekstilkunst i særdeleshet" [About the Göteborg exhibition, applied art in general and textile art in particular], *Aftenposten*, 11 August 1923

"Billedvæv og Gobelin" [Tapestry and Gobelin], *Oslo Aftenavis*, 12 May 1927

Bibliography

Ann Margret Holmgren, "Om den gamla norska bildväfnadskonsten och dens pånyttfødelse" [About the old Norwegian art of tapestry and its renaissance], *Ord och Bild*, viii, 1900, pp.469–75

Anna Rogstad, "Frida Hansen", *Kjente menn og kvinner* [Famous men and women], ii, 1926, pp.25–37

Astrid Bugge, "Litt om transparente portierer" [Something about transparent curtains], *By og Bygd: Årbok*, xvi, 1963, pp.133–8

Gabriele Howaldt, *Bildteppiche der Stilbewegung*, Darmstadt, 1964

Marta Hoffman, "1880–årenes nye billedvev i Norge og litt om utviklingen senere" [The new tapestry in Norway of the 1880s and something about later developments], *Vestlandske Kunstindustrimuseums Årbok, 1963–68*, Bergen, 1969, pp.66–106

Frida Hansen: Europeeren i norsk vevkunst [Frida Hansen: A European in Norwegian textile art around 1900], exh. cat., Kunstindustrimuseet, Oslo, 1973 (with English summary)

Madeleine Jarry, *La Tapisserie: Art du XXe siècle*, Paris, 1979

Jan-Lauritz Opstad, *Norsk Art Nouveau* [Norwegian Art Nouveau], Oslo, 1979

Ruth Gronwoldt, *Art Nouveau Textil-Dekor um 1900*, Stuttgart, 1980

Alf Bøe, "Kunsthåndverket 1870–1914" [Applied art, 1870–1914], *Norges Kunsthistorie*, v, 1981

Anniken Thue, "Ny kunst: Frida Hansens transparenter" [New art: Frida Hansen's transparents], *Fortidsvern*, no.3, 1985, pp.35–7

——, *Frida Hansen: En europeer i norsk tekstilkunst omkring 1900* [Frida Hansen: A European in Norwegian textile art around 1900], Oslo, 1986

——, "En kamp om det nasjonale: Norske tekstilkunst ved århundreskiftet 1900" [A fight about the national: Norwegian textile art at the turn of the 19th century], *Tradisjon og fornyelse* [Tradition and innovation], exh. cat., Nasjonalgalleriet, Oslo, 1994, pp.294–8

Frida Hansen is today regarded as an important representative of Art Nouveau, and at the same time as one of the pioneers of modern textile art. The revival of tapestry weaving in Europe – and Norway – in the last decades of the 19th century was dominated by male artists (William Morris, Otto Eckmann, Gerhard Munthe, among others), but none of them had Hansen's technical knowledge and interest in weaving. She was responsible for both design and weaving, and she achieved remarkable results through her improvements to the traditional Norwegian vertical loom to make it a delicate tool for her intricate modern compositions. She based her work on Norwegian textile traditions (technique and use of vegetable-dyed wool), but her style was at the same time typical of the international Art Nouveau.

In Norway, however, Hansen was an outsider on the artistic scene. The revival of tapestry weaving in Norway in the 1880s and 1890s was linked to the development of a national consciousness in the same years (Norway, then in union with Sweden, became independent in 1905). Old tapestries were collected as examples of something specifically "Norwegian". Instead of starting a new development, however, this renewed interest in weaving led to rather dogmatic attitudes and debates about national characteristics, decorative art and tapestry weaving. The decorative style of the painter Gerhard Munthe was regarded as the true expression of national identity by museums and leading artists; Hansen was seen as too "Japanese", too "modern", too much like "the new style in Europe". As a result, none of the Norwegian museums bought any of her tapestries or ornamental works. All her important pieces are in the large European museums of applied art (e.g. Museum für Kunst und Gewerbe, Hamburg; Museum Bellerive, Zürich; Victoria and Albert Museum, London; Det Danske Kunstindustrimuseum, Copenhagen; Nordiska Museet, Stockholm; Österreichisches Museum für angewandte Kunst, Vienna; Iparművészeti Múzeum, Budapest). She created 30 large tapestries and approximately 170 patterns for transparent curtains, wall-hangings, carpets and cushions. (Her tapestries are signed F. Hansen or Frida Hansen [also *NABV, 1897–9; *DNB, 1899–1906], and her ornamental pieces F.H. or F. Hansen [also *NABV, 1897–1906, *DNB, 1899–1906; both with pattern numbers in Roman numerals], all with the year.)

Hansen started her career by struggling to master the weaving technique and experimenting with vegetable dyes, as well as looking for a manner of expression suited to the textile medium. After having translated Knud Bergslien's painting of the *Birkebeiner Skiing with the Young King Haakon Haakonsen Across the Mountains* (private collection, Norway) into a tapestry in 1890, she was convinced that the pure translation of paintings into weaving – like the French Gobelins – was not the answer. The drawing of the motifs had to be simplified. Her trip to Cologne and Paris in 1894–5 was vital to her development. She drew from life in the studio of Puvis de Chavannes, and also saw how such artists as Eugène Grasset, Alphonse Mucha and Paul Berthon created a decorative, expressive style through an emphasis on line and colour surfaces. On her return to Norway she made two large tapestries in which this new approach is apparent (*Mermaids Igniting the Moon*, 1895, and *Dance of the Mermaids*, 1896; both private collections, Norway). Her choice of themes also heralded a new development, because earlier tapestries had used motifs from Norwegian folk-tales and songs (*Olaf Liljekrans*, 1894; private collection, Norway). In Paris Hansen made a sketch for what was to become her most important work, *The Milky Way* (1898; see illustration). The motif is taken from Genesis 1:15, about the creation of light in heaven and earth. The daring cutting-off of the motif and the rhythmic movement through the tapestry make it a pure representative of Art Nouveau. This was evident when it was exhibited in

Hansen: *The Milky Way*, 1898; tapestry, wool, silk; Museum für Kunst und Gewerbe, Hamburg

Paris in 1900 and for that reason bought by the Hamburg museum; when it was displayed in Norway in 1898 it was not sold, for the same reason.

The largest display of Hansen's works was at the Paris Exposition Universelle of 1900. She was then artistic director of the Norwegian Atelier for Tapestry Weaving. In addition to two of the largest tapestries she ever made (7 m. long), the exhibition consisted of two tapestries based on designs by Gerhard Munthe, and a large collection of transparent curtains, wall-hangings, etc., based on Hansen's designs. She had enormous success with her so-called transparent curtains, the technique for which was patented in 1897. The invention lay in the use of warp where areas were left free to create a transparent contrast to the woven parts (usually flowers and leaves).

The *Five Wise and Five Foolish Virgins* (1900; sold to an Italian princess and lost during World War I) and the *Dance of Salome* (1900; Museum Bellerive, Zürich) are pendants, with motifs taken from 16th-century Norwegian tapestries. Hansen treats them in a modern fashion, however, under the influence of the painters Albert Moore and Mucha, but it is interesting to note that in the *Salome* tapestry the erotic undertones are absent. Women in Hansen's tapestries are neither victims nor fragile. As early as 1893 she had made a tapestry for the Women's Pavilion in Chicago, where the motif was a *Dandelion* (private collection, Norway), which was meant to symbolise survival and eternal life. The tapestry was ordered by the Feminist Association in Christiania. In 1905 she made another important statement as a female artist in the tapestry *Semper Vadentes* (private collection, France), in which four women wearing magnificent robes and carrying different objects (flowers, pearls, a lit candle and purse) choose different paths in life. The flowers and candle symbolise art and true love, the pearls and purse vanity and wealth.

Hansen, once one of the richest women in Norway, lost everything when her husband went bankrupt in 1883, but she found a new direction as a textile artist, which gave her life meaning. Around 1900 she was probably one of the most renowned Norwegian artists in Europe. Like many Art Nouveau artists, she went into oblivion between the wars, but with the new interest in Art Nouveau she was re-established as an important textile artist with a large retrospective exhibition in Oslo in 1973.

ANNIKEN THUE

Hanssen Pigott, Gwyn
Australian potter, 1935–

Born Gwyn John in Ballarat, Victoria, 1 January 1935. Studied for a fine arts degree at University of Melbourne. Worked as assistant to Ivan McMeekin at Sturt Pottery, Mittagong, New South Wales, 1954–7. Went to Britain, 1958. Worked with Ray Finch at Winchcombe Pottery, Gloucestershire; with Bernard Leach in St Ives, Cornwall; then as assistant to Michael Cardew at Wenford Bridge, Cornwall. Married poet Louis Hanssen, 1959; he later died. Set up pottery with him in Portobello Road, London, 1960; rented a workshop in Achères, France, 1963. Ran Cardew's pottery at Wenford Bridge during his visit to Africa, 1964–5. Revisited Australia, 1965; toured New Zealand, 1966. Lived in Achères, 1967–73; also tutor at Harrow School of Art, London, 1969–71; visiting lecturer in the Netherlands, USA and France, 1971–3. Returned to Australia, 1973. Established pottery in Tasmania with John Pigott, 1974; married him, 1976; divorced 1980. Workshop at Kelvin Grove, Queensland, from 1981; also at Netherdale, Central Queensland, from 1989. Recipient of Mayfair ceramic award, Meat Market Crafts Centre, Melbourne, 1980; Gold Coast ceramic award, Queensland, and city of Brisbane craft award, 1982; North Queensland ceramics award, Townsville, 1983; Fletcher Brownbuilt pottery award, Auckland, and Darling Downs First National ceramic award, Toowoomba, 1984; National Craft award, Darwin, 1991. Lives in Queensland.

Selected Individual Exhibitions

Primavera, London: 1961, 1963, 1965
Les Deux Tisserands, Paris: 1972
Jam Factory Gallery, Adelaide: 1981 (with John Pigott), 1988
Blackfriars Gallery, Sydney: 1983
Victor Mace Fine Art, Brisbane: 1983, 1986
Casson Gallery, London: 1984
Distelfink Gallery, Melbourne: 1986
Garry Anderson Gallery, Sydney: 1987, 1989, 1990
Devise Arts, Melbourne: 1988 (with Michael Casson)
Fremantle Art Centre, Western Australia: 1989
Margaret Francey Gallery, Brisbane: 1990, 1991
Narek Gallery, Canberra: 1990, 1991
Pro-Art Gallery, St Louis, USA: 1991, 1993
Galerie Besson, London: 1992
Crafthouse Gallery, Vancouver, Canada: 1993
Garth Clark Gallery, New York: 1993

Selected Writings

"The potters of Haut-Berry", *Pottery in Australia*, viii/2, 1969, pp.7–13

Bibliography

Michael Casson, *Pottery in Britain Today*, London: Tiranti, and New York: Transatlantic Arts, 1967
Emmanuel Cooper and Eileen Lewenstein, "Gwyn Hanssen talking", *Ceramic Review*, no.11, 1971, pp.4–6
Peter Lane, *Studio Ceramics*, London: Collins, and Radnor, PA: Chilton, 1983
Margaret Tuckson, "Gwyn Hanssen Pigott: Seeking perfection", *Ceramic Review*, no.89, 1984, pp.26–31
Victor Margrie, "Influence and innovation", *Ceramic Review*, no.100, 1986, pp.4–11
Jeff Shaw, "Integrity of function", *Craft Arts*, no.9, June–August 1987, pp.73–5
Janet Mansfield, *A Collector's Guide to Modern Australian Ceramics*, Seaforth, NSW: Craftsman House, 1988
Paul Rice and Christopher Gowing, *British Studio Ceramics in the 20th Century*, London: Barrie and Jenkins, and Radnor, PA: Chilton, 1989
Martina Margetts, ed., *International Crafts*, London: Thames and Hudson, 1991
Grace Cochrane, *The Crafts Movement in Australia: A History*, Sydney: University of New South Wales Press, 1992
The Raw and the Cooked, exh. cat., Barbican Art Gallery, London, and elsewhere, 1993
Oliver Watson, *Studio Pottery: Twentieth-Century British Ceramics in the Victoria and Albert Museum Collection*, London: Phaidon, 1993 (originally published as *British Studio Pottery*, Oxford: Phaidon, 1990)

To describe Gwyn Hanssen Pigott as a potter is like saying that Picasso was a painter – definitions that give little or no idea of the scope, ambition and importance of their work. In many ways Hanssen Pigott has remained true to her beliefs of wanting to make pots that are an intimate and integral part of daily life; pots to be used and enjoyed as superb examples of 20th-century hand-making. The idea of the domestic environment as an appropriate site for the expression and enjoyment of works of art has become obscured in the later part of the 20th century by the move towards large-scale work, much of it intended for the gallery and the anonymity of the corporate market. In contrast, Hanssen Pigott's unswerving desire to seek a wider relevance in the pots she makes, and to use beautifully made table and kitchen wares as a commentary on the value of daily life has been one of the important guiding principles of her work.

Although working in what can be loosely called the Leach tradition in the use of high-temperature stonewares and porcelains fired in a flame-burning kiln, Hanssen Pigott has adopted and reinterpreted the processes to create her own style. In Australia she worked with Ivan McMeekin, who had earlier worked with Michael Cardew in England. With McMeekin she learned to appreciate the qualities of classic Chinese forms and to find inspiration in their simplicity. In Britain she worked with, among others, Bernard Leach at St Ives, and Michael Cardew at Wenford Bridge, learning the skills of accurate, fast throwing, and absorbing some of their ideas about the unification of life and work. Her own pots reflected little of their influence, and she was as inspired by the fine and precisely made work of Lucie Rie (q.v.) as she was by the more robust qualities espoused by Leach and Cardew. Her inclination was to relatively simple, well-thought-out shapes, with minimal decoration.

At her first pottery, in Notting Hill, London, the shapes were rounded and full, functional and delightful to hold, with emphasis on form rather than decoration – characteristics that have continued to dominate her work. Above all, it was the quality of their making that gave them their unique identity. In contrast to the prevailing taste for quickly thrown and chunky pieces, Hanssen Pigott's pots were thoughtful and delicate, each one carefully made, the walls thin and the rims slim and linear. After throwing, each pot was returned to the wheel to have the foot trimmed and the surplus clay removed to give it an ideal balance when handled. As much attention was given

Hanssen Pigott: *Still Life, Bottle, Beaker and Bowl*, 1992; porcelain; height (bottle) 20.5 cm.; Galerie Besson, London

to the underside as to any other part of the pot, whether it be a plate, a jug, a teapot, a casserole or a mug. It was this concern with the whole pot that marked out her work as special.

Although she has produced a standard range of pots, Hanssen Pigott has never shown any feeling of hurry or speed in her work, and her degree of care and attention to detail has never faltered. This care was brought out more fully when in the late 1960s Hanssen Pigott moved to France and set up her workshop at Achères, near the traditional pottery-making town of La Bourne. Here she built a three-chamber kiln, and was able to make full use of the reaction between the local, high-temperature clay and the long, slow firing in the wood-burning kiln. She made a range of tablewares that included plates, bowls, teapots and casseroles, all superbly thrown and finished. During the firing, the simple glazes, often made from a mixture of wood ash and local clay, united the body and the surface of the pot in a rich and satisfying combination. During the firing, any iron speckles were brought to the surface, adding to the effect, with material and process allowed to convey some of their natural characteristics. Ironically, if the speckles became too pronounced, she would complain that this detracted from the overall unity of shape, surface and texture. In later pots, great care was taken to ensure that much of the iron was removed.

Since returning to Australia, Hanssen Pigott has found inspiration in the still-life paintings of the Italian artist Giorgio Morandi. She was particularly inspired by the way in which Morandi's gentle, lyrical paintings imbued everyday objects with metaphysical significance. The close juxtaposition of the objects seemed to Hanssen Pigott to be emblematic in suggesting the intimacy and importance of physical and spiritual communication. In consequence, she began to create groups of objects using domestic forms such as beakers, bowls and jugs in highly refined porcelain. In these assemblies she combines the familiar and ordinary with the exotic and highly charged. The pots themselves can be used individually, their functional qualities adding to their accessibility, but they are at their most evocative when seen in groups, their rims in close proximity, or even touching. Her work is well represented in the Art Gallery of South Australia, Adelaide; Civic Art Gallery Museum, Brisbane; National Gallery of Australia, Canberra; and the Victoria and Albert Museum, London.

In her assemblies, quiet and contemplative rather than loud and assertive, Gwyn Hanssen Pigott offers her own solution to the role of the studio potter in the late 20th century, heightening and intensifying our awareness of the world in which we live.

EMMANUEL COOPER

Hartigan, Grace
American painter, 1922–

Born in Newark, New Jersey, 28 March 1922. Married (1) Robert Jachens, 1941; son born 1942; divorced 1947; (2) artist Harry Jackson (Shapiro), 1949; marriage annulled 1950; (3) Long Island gallery owner Robert Keene, 1958;

divorced 1960; (4) Dr Winston Price, research scientist at Johns Hopkins University, Baltimore, 1960; he died 1981. Studied mechanical drawing at Newark College of Engineering, New Jersey, 1942; subsequently worked as mechanical draughtswoman, and studied painting privately under Newark artist Isaac Lane Muse. Moved to New York, 1945; met Jackson Pollock, Willem de Kooning and other members of the New York School. Selected by Clement Greenberg and Meyer Schapiro for *New Talent* exhibition at Kootz Gallery, New York, 1950; exhibited in avant-garde *Ninth Street Show*, 1951. Moved to Baltimore, 1960. Artist-in-residence, Maryland Institute College of Art, Baltimore, from 1965; Avery Chair, Bard College, Annandale-on-Hudson, 1983. Recipient of *Mademoiselle* magazine merit award for art, 1957; Childe Hassam purchase award, National Institute of Arts and Letters, 1974; honorary life trustee, Baltimore Museum of Art; honorary degrees from Moore College of Art, Philadelphia; Goucher College, Towson, Maryland, and Maryland Institute College of Art. Lives in Baltimore.

Selected Individual Exhibitions
Tibor de Nagy Gallery, New York: 1951, 1952, 1953, 1954, 1955, 1957, 1959
Vassar College, Poughkeepsie, NY: 1954
Gres Gallery, Washington, DC: 1960
Chatham College, Pittsburgh: 1960
Martha Jackson Gallery, New York: 1962, 1964, 1967, 1970
University of Minnesota, Minneapolis: 1963
Maryland Institute College of Art, Baltimore: 1967, 1990
University of Chicago: 1967
Gertrude Kasle Gallery, Detroit: 1972, 1974, 1976
American University, Washington, DC: 1975, 1987 (retrospective)
C. Grimaldis Gallery, Baltimore: 1979, 1981, 1982, 1984, 1986, 1987, 1989, 1990, 1993, 1995
Baltimore Museum of Art: 1980 (touring), 1990
State University of New York, Plattsburgh: 1980
University of Maryland, College Park: 1980
Fort Wayne Museum of Art, IN: 1981 (retrospective)
Lafayette College, Easton, PA: 1983, 1990
Gruenebaum Gallery, New York: 1984, 1986, 1988
Kouros Gallery, New York: 1989 (retrospective)
ACA Galleries, New York: 1991, 1992, 1994
Skidmore College, Saratoga Springs, NY: 1993

Selected Writings
"An artist speaks", *Carnegie Magazine*, February 1961
Statement for exhibition at Martha Jackson Gallery, New York, 1964; typescript in Martha Jackson Papers, Archives of American Art, Smithsonian Institution, Washington, DC

Bibliography
Twelve Americans, exh. cat., Museum of Modern Art, New York, 1956; artist's statement reprinted in *The New American Painting*, exh. cat., Museum of Modern Art, New York, 1959, p.44
"Women artists in ascendance", *Life*, xlii, 13 May 1957, pp.75–6
Harold Rosenberg, *The Tradition of the New*, New York: Horizon Press, 1959; London: Thames and Hudson, 1962
Grace Hartigan, exh. cat., Martha Jackson Gallery, New York, 1962
Barbara Flanagan, "Lively artist rebels at labeling and doesn't like to be lionized", *Minneapolis Tribune*, 24 September 1963; press clipping in Grace Hartigan Papers, George Arents Research Library, Syracuse University, Syracuse, NY
Three American Painters, exh. cat., Grand Rapids Art Museum, MI, 1968

Allen Barber, "Making some marks", *Arts Magazine*, xlviii, June 1974, pp.49–51 (interview)

Cindy Nemser, *Art Talk: Conversations with Twelve Women Artists*, New York: Scribner, 1975

Frank O'Hara, *Standing Still and Walking in New York*, ed. Donald Allen, Bolinas, CA: Grey Fox Press, 1975

Irving Sandler, *The New York School: The Painters and Sculptors of the Fifties*, New York: Harper, 1978

Eleanor Munro, *Originals: American Women Artists*, New York: Simon and Schuster, 1979

Laurence Campbell, "To see the world mainly through art: Grace Hartigan's *Great Queens and Empresses* (1983)", *Arts Magazine*, lviii, January 1984, pp.87–9

Robert S. Mattison, "Grace Hartigan: Painting her own history", *Arts Magazine*, lix, January 1985, pp.66–72

Stephen Westfall, "Then and now: Six of the New York School painters look back: Grace Hartigan", *Art in America*, lxxiii, June 1985, pp.118–20

Ann Schoenfield, "Grace Hartigan in the early 1950s: Some sources, influences and the avant-garde", *Arts Magazine*, lx, September 1985, pp.84–8

Eleanor Heartney, "How wide is the gender gap?", *Art News*, lxxxvi, Summer 1987, pp.139–45

Grace Hartigan: Four Decades of Painting, exh. cat., Kouros Gallery, New York, 1989

Robert S. Mattison, *Grace Hartigan: A Painter's World*, New York: Hudson Hills Press, 1990

Terence Diggory, "Questions of identity in *Oranges* by Frank O'Hara and Grace Hartigan", *Art Journal*, lii, Winter 1993, pp.41–50

Frank O'Hara, "Second avenue", *The Collected Poems*, ed. Donald Allen, Berkeley: University of California Press, 1995, pp.139–50

Although she is usually described as a leading representative of the "second generation" of New York School artists, Grace Hartigan has always resisted assimilation to any movement. Despite her love for the abstraction of Jackson Pollock and Willem de Kooning of the late 1940s, she gave up abstraction in 1952 to engage in a "struggle with content" that would test her right to claim the forms of Abstract Expressionism for herself (Sandler 1978, p.113). Then, after returning to abstraction, a decade later she "left expressionism" (New York 1962), although she refused to adopt the dead-pan objectivity of Pop or Minimalism, the emerging alternatives to Expressionism. Painting must have emotion, Hartigan insisted, but it must belong to the painting, not necessarily to the artist. A similar distinction informed her reluctance to enlist in the women's art movement that arose in the 1970s. "To be truthful I didn't much think about being a woman", she explained, "I thought about how difficult it was to paint" (Nemser 1975, p.150). Such an attitude aligns Hartigan most closely with Harold Rosenberg's theory of "action painting" free of all prior commitments: "action painting is painting in the medium of difficulties" (Rosenberg 1959, p.33).

For Hartigan, the New York School was a school in the literal sense of being the site of her education in art. She arrived in New York in 1945 with some experience in mechanical drawing, a sporadic history of evening art classes and a strong creative urge that began to assume definite direction as she visited galleries and museums and met the painters, poets and musicians whose paths criss-crossed the world of the avant-garde as if it were a tiny village. Her membership in that community was confirmed in 1950 when the landmark *New Talent* show, selected by Clement Greenberg and Meyer Schapiro for the Kootz Gallery, exhibited Hartigan's *Secuda*

Esa Bruja (1949; artist's collection). This work proves her already committed to the formal ideals of "all over" composition and integrity of surface that Hartigan has upheld ever since. It also points to concerns beyond formalism in its quasi-surrealist, non-representational figuration. White wind-sock shapes seem to ascend in an up draught fanned by a sheet of orange and yellow flame. The title, which Hartigan translates as "The Witch is Flying" (Mattison 1990, p.13), points to a later statement in which she identifies witchcraft with the painter's power to transform what she cannot bear in her environment (Flanagan 1963). Unlike her friend Jackson Pollock, who tended to identify the creative self with nature, Hartigan often claims a demonic power.

Appropriately, in 1952, Hartigan reversed the canvas she had used for *Secuda Esa Bruja* and painted *Frank O'Hara and the Demons* on the other side. While the "demons" in this picture retain some of the abstract quality of the earlier work, the figure of O'Hara is loosely representational in a manner that Hartigan was just beginning to employ. The rebellion against the orthodoxy of abstraction that occurred among a number of "second generation" painters at this time is often traced to the example of de Kooning's *Women* paintings, which Hartigan had seen evolving in his studio before they were first exhibited in 1952. For Hartigan in particular, however, the example of O'Hara's poetry may have been equally important, for in poetry the image served the purpose not only of representation but of transformative "witchcraft", through the device of metaphor (Grand Rapids 1968). In *Oranges No. 6* (1952–3; Gallery K, Washington, DC), one of a series of paintings incorporating text by O'Hara, Hartigan portrays a young girl who appears immobilised by the weight of an absurdly "feminine" bow, while at her feet her dolls stir with a lurid sexuality. Through this demonic twist on the conventional image of woman as doll, the picture acquires a metaphoric density that matches its "packing" of forms, a technique that Hartigan connects both with de Kooning's painting *Excavation* (1950; Art Institute of Chicago) and with O'Hara's poem "Second Avenue" (1953; remarks at a reading from the poetry of Frank O'Hara, Skidmore College, Saratoga Springs, 24 March 1993).

Another lesson for which Hartigan credits O'Hara is the possibility of drawing on popular culture as a source of imagery (Irving Sandler, "Artists talk on art series", public interview with Grace Hartigan, Fulcrum Gallery, New York, 11 November 1994). *Grand Street Brides* (1954; Whitney Museum of American Art, New York), perhaps Hartigan's best-known painting, exemplifies the resulting fusion of "high" and "low", for like many of Hartigan's paintings at this time it has a source in art history, in this instance the court scenes of Velázquez and Goya, but it also responds to the display windows of bridal shops that lined Grand Street on New York's Lower East Side, where Hartigan lived and worked (Mattison 1990, pp.33–4). Perhaps in reaction to the flatness of the figures, viewers have been tempted to read some form of critique into this painting's use of popular imagery. In his influential article, "Nature and new painting" (1954), O'Hara claimed that Hartigan's brides "face without bitterness the glassy shallowness of American life which is their showcase" (O'Hara 1975, p.45). Two decades later Cindy Nemser invited Hartigan to read *Grand Street Brides* in terms of the

Hartigan: *Hollywood Interior*, 1993; oil on canvas; 167.6 × 198.1 cm.

roles that society imposes on women, but Hartigan demurred (Nemser 1975, pp.157–8). Such interpretations mistakenly emphasise weakness while Hartigan's paintings are primarily about power: an artist's power to give life to shop-window mannequins, or a woman's power to multiply roles and thus extend rather than limit the range of self-expression. For example, throughout 1954 Hartigan exhibited under the name "George"; sometimes describing this practice as a homage to George Sand and George Eliot, Hartigan has always denied that she was conforming to a male-dominated art world. Only recently has she offered the fuller explanation that she was "camping", playfully crossing gender lines in the spirit of the homosexual men she met at the Tibor de Nagy Gallery (Diggory 1993, p.49).

According to Hartigan, gender discrimination became an issue in the New York art world only in the latter half of the 1950s, as the prospect of money and fame began to intensify competition among artists (Heartney 1987, p.141). At first, Hartigan's career seemed to prosper in this new atmosphere. In 1956 Dorothy Miller selected her work for inclusion in the exhibition *Twelve Americans*, spotlighted at the Museum of Modern Art. From this show, Nelson Rockefeller purchased Hartigan's *City Life* (1956; National Trust for Historic Preservation, Nelson A. Rockefeller Collection), a work incited, like *Grand Street Brides*, by "that which is vulgar and vital in American modern life", as Hartigan expressed it in her catalogue statement. In 1957 *Life* magazine placed Hartigan, as the "most celebrated of the young American women painters", at the head of a list that included Nell Blaine, Joan Mitchell (q.v.), Jane Wilson and Helen Frankenthaler (q.v.) ("Women artists in ascendance"). In 1958 the International Program of the Museum of Modern Art, where O'Hara worked, included Hartigan in the show that defined "The New American Painting" on a tour of eight European countries.

Although she benefited from the accompanying media attention, Hartigan began to resent the attempt to define her with her paintings. Marriage (her fourth) to Dr Winston Price in 1960 provided the satisfaction of love untainted by art-world politics as well as the opportunity to put some breathing space between herself and New York. She joined Price in Baltimore, where he pursued medical research at Johns Hopkins University, and where, in 1967, Hartigan began teaching at the Maryland Institute College of Art.

In Hartigan's paintings of the late 1950s the recognisable imagery of the "city life" paintings disappears, while broader planes of colour and more expansive brushwork seem to open up the surface area, an effect reinforced by extending the dimensions of the canvases to as much as 2.4 metres. Hartigan was responding to the landscape of eastern Long Island as well as to the contemporary work of de Kooning and Franz Kline, who reinforced the suggestion of landscape by using place names in their titles, as Hartigan did, for example, in *Montauk Highway* (1957; Sarah Campbell Blaffer Foundation, Houston) and *Interior – "The Creeks"* (1957; Baltimore Museum of Art). Technically, these are gorgeous, often breathtaking paintings, but they capture a moment after the creative struggle has been won, rather than recording the process of that struggle, which has always been Hartigan's chief aim.

To return to that aim, Hartigan began to reintroduce imagery from the visible world. At first, however, in such work as *Phoenix* and *Lily Pond* (both 1962; collection Mr and Mrs H. Perry, Germantown, NY), the mood seemed too "lyrical" – a judgement that for Hartigan implied an acceptance of visible beauty as given rather than achieved through creative transformation (Martha Jackson Gallery statement, 1964). *Marilyn* (1962; collection Mr and Mrs H. Perry) marks a significant turning point. When this work was first shown in 1962 by Martha Jackson, Hartigan's new dealer in New York, some viewers, including Frank O'Hara (O'Hara 1975, p.143), read it as a surrender to the new Pop trend, but in retrospect the mood is clearly different from the contemporary *Marilyns* of Warhol or Rosenquist. Although we see only human fragments – white teeth gleaming through red lips at the top of the canvas, an elegant hand extended at the bottom – the painter's fluid gestures recompose these fragments and assert a life force that Pop's irony drains away. Thematically, the same life force can be traced throughout this period in Hartigan's engagement with a variety of heroic female personae, from the mythical *Dido* (1960; McNay Art Museum, San Antonio) and *Pallas Athena – Earth* (1961; National Museum of American Art, Smithsonian Institution, Washington, DC) to the historical *Duchess of Alba* (1963; Collection Dr and Mrs S.E. Harris, Baltimore) and the archetypal *Mountain Woman* (1964; Huntington Art Gallery, University of Texas, Austin). These works remain essentially abstract, however. Stylistically, the promise of *Marilyn* is not realised until the later 1960s, when recognisable imagery, once again often drawn from popular culture, decisively re-emerges in such paintings as *Modern Cycle* (1967; National Museum of American Art).

At this point, Hartigan seems to have struck the balance that she wanted between image and abstraction. Although the battle still has to be refought in the process of composing each painting, she seems secure in her confidence that the image will emerge in the end without violating the surface. Her subsequent development focuses on expanding her range of techniques for unfurling the surface itself as a space that is not illusionistic, in the sense of suggesting three-dimensional depth, but rather metaphoric, in the way that a poem creates a space in the mind. A first step in this direction, already evident in *Modern Cycle*, was the use of line "like a lasso" to surround and define images as specific yet at the same time as flat (Barber 1974, p.50). A second step, offering a counter-statement to the reassertion of drawing, was the staining of primed canvas by rubbing it down with a sheepskin mitt steeped in pigment. This technique proved especially effective for evoking the quality of remembered images, as in *Black Velvet* (1972; Flint Institute of Art, Michigan), an elegy for Hartigan's father, and *Autumn Shop Window* (1972; Baltimore Museum of Art), which is in part a lament for her husband's slow decline towards his death in 1981 (Mattison 1990, pp.90–93). To pose the tension of drawn line and stained field within a single work, Hartigan began in the late 1970s to permit line to bleed colour that drips down the canvas in rivulets, partially hiding the images yet making their presence all the more tantalising. The related themes of costume and role-playing, harking back to *Oranges No.6* and *Grand Street Brides*, resurface in two series of the 1980s that both employ the "drip" technique: the *Paper Dolls* portraying film stars of the past, for instance, *Constance* [Bennett] (1981; collection Dolly Fiterman, Minneapolis), and the *Great Queens and Empresses*, for example, *Theodora* (1983; Solomon R. Guggenheim Museum, New York).

Hartigan's several styles have developed through expansion rather than succession. Rather than one style replacing another, all remain simultaneously available for the artist to call upon in response to the demands of a particular painting, just as she feels free to call upon and combine the images of "high" and "low" culture. Among the works included in her show at the ACA Galleries in New York in 1994, *Hollywood Interior* (1993; see illustration) gives fullest expression to this complex freedom. Like most of the other works in the exhibition, it employs a technique of overpainting to produce an effect of multiple exposure, as in photography. One of the figures, at the upper right, playfully recalls Caravaggio's *Bacchino Malato* (1593–4; Galleria Borghese, Rome), already the inspiration for Hartigan's *Bacchus* (1985; collection Mick Jagger and Jerry Hall, New York). In *Hollywood Interior* the figure is reversed in lateral position (left to right), in gender (male to female) and in level of iconography (the grapes that the classical god Bacchus holds in his upraised hand are replaced by the starlet's telephone). If the allusion to Hollywood directly refers to role-playing, the presence of multiple figures suggests multiple roles. In an interview, Hartigan proposed that such multiplicity may distinguish her images of women from those of male contemporaries such as de Kooning or Dubuffet, who essentially portray one woman. Explaining that all of the women in her paintings are aspects of her "many selves", she has speculated: "maybe it takes a woman to know the many faces of Eve" (Hartigan interview with Sandler, 1994, *op. cit.*).

TERENCE DIGGORY

Hasse, Sella

German graphic artist and painter, 1878–1963

Born Sella Schmidt in Bitterfeld, Saxony, 12 February 1878. Studied at the Berlin Academy under Walter Leistikow and Lovis Corinth from 1896. Married mathematician Robert Hasse; daughter born 1899 (d. 1928); husband died 1919. Met Käthe Kollwitz (q.v.), 1902. Lived in Hamburg, 1904–10; Wismar, 1910–30; Berlin from 1930. First visited Paris, 1912. Art declared "degenerate" by the National Socialists, 1937; 15 works confiscated. Lived in Alsace, 1943–5; subsequently in East Berlin. Recipient of numerous prizes including silver medal, Internationale Graphische Kunst-Ausstellung at the Internationale Ausstellung für Buchgewerbe und Graphik, Leipzig, 1914; Käthe Kollwitz prize, 1962. Member, Deutscher Künstlerbund, 1912; honorary member, Verband Bildender Künstler der DDR, 1955; Deutsche Akademie der Künste, Berlin, 1962. Died in Berlin, 27 April 1963.

Principal Exhibitions

Individual
Emil Richter, Dresden: 1916
Landesmuseum, Schwerin: 1947
Museum der Bildenden Künste, Leipzig: 1948, 1963
Städtische Kunstsammlung, Karl-Marx-Stadt: 1955, 1959
Kupferstichkabinett, Staatliche Museen, Berlin: 1958
Museum der Stadt Rostock: 1958
Schlossmuseum, Gotha: 1961
Nationalgalerie, Berlin: 1978 (retrospective)

Group
Berlin Secession: from 1902
Deutscher Künstlerbund, Bremen: 1912
Deutscher Künstlerbund, Hamburg: 1913 (*Graphische Ausstellung*)
Kunsthaus, Zürich: 1919

Selected Writings

Zur sozialen Wertung der weiblichen Fortpflanzungsorgane, Leipzig: Xenien, 1918

Bibliography

Sella Hasse, exh. cat., Landesmuseum, Schwerin, 1947
Sella Hasse: Arbeit und Rhythmus, exh. cat., Museum der Bildenden Künste, Leipzig, 1948
Hildegard Dennewitz, "Ihre Welt – die Welt der Arbeit: Zum 80. Geburtstag von Sella Hasse", *Bildende Kunst*, vi, 1958, pp.126–30
Georg Mielke, *Sella Hasse*, Dresden: Verlag der Bildenden Kunst, 1958
Rudolf Karnahl, "Ein Leben für die Darstellung der arbeitenden Menschen", *Mitteilungen der Akademie der Künste der DDR*, xii/3, 1974, pp.21–4
Sella Hasse zum 100. Geburtstag, exh. cat., Nationalgalerie, Berlin, 1978
Das Verborgene Museum I: Dokumentation der Kunst von Frauen in Berliner öffentlichen Sammlungen, exh. cat., Akademie der Künste, Berlin, 1987

That Sella Hasse is so little known in the Western art world is confirmation of the impact of recent German history: since she chose to live in the former German Democratic Republic for the last 20 years of her life, and having devoted her art to representations of the proletariat, she was widely known in the

Hasse: *Rhythm of Work*, 1912–16; woodcut; Kupferstichkabinett, Berlin

Eastern bloc yet virtually ignored in the West. She came by her political convictions easily, being born into a well-educated family of committed Social Democrats; in her memoirs she wrote that, as a little girl, she had sat on Wilhelm Liebknecht's knee. She demonstrated an early aptitude for art, mastering the pastel technique at the age of 12. Encouraged by her family, she studied in Berlin with Walter Leistikow and Lovis Corinth; it was at Corinth's school that she met the older Käthe Kollwitz (q.v.), who became her close friend and artistic comrade.

While her earliest works show evidence of the sentimental compositions of Heinrich Vogeler (whom she met in 1908 in the artists' colony at Worpswede), she soon developed a hard-edged graphic style more suited to her concentration on themes of manual labour. She also worked as a newspaper illustrator, whereby she perfected her ability to sketch quickly and on the spot; some of her first published pieces resemble Honoré Daumier's illustrations in theme and composition. Her most important work was her cycle of linoleum- and woodcuts, the *Rhythm of Work* (see illustration), completed between 1912 and 1916 and dedicated to Kollwitz. In her images of dockworkers, wood-carriers and bricklayers, Hasse concentrated on the beauty of physical labour, emphasising the rhythmic co-ordination of bodies and implements in motion. Upon finishing a woodcut of a telegraph worker, she wrote: "They do not know, these creators, what a beautiful effect their movements have, reaching up to the sky" (quoted in Mielke 1958, p.58).

While Hasse's aesthetic was frequently compared with that of Kollwitz, the images of this cycle indicate that her compositions were more clearly informed by the jagged, rough-edged Expressionist technique and a greater commitment to unsentimentalised yet optimistic depictions of urban workers without the specifically polemical message and elegant realism of the older artist's work. In many ways she is more stylistically aligned to the graphic works of other left-wing artists such as Conrad Felixmüller and Alice Lex-Nerlinger. None the less, Hasse's political sympathies were often apparent; she created many images protesting against World War I, and she enthusiastically applied her artistic skills in support of the cause of women's rights. In 1918 she even produced a book, *Zur sozialen Wertung der weiblichen Fortpflanzungsorgane* (On the social value of the female sexual organ), in which she exhorted the need for equality between the sexes. Like other "artists of the proletariat" of her time, she travelled to the heavy-industrial regions of the Rhineland and the Ruhr to experience the workers' lives directly; she wrote that hers was an art of observation rather than contemplation. Her many graphic portraits of famous contemporaries demonstrate her great ability to capture the essence of their character by using simple contrasts of black and white and rugged delineation of forms (*Gustav Landauer*, woodcut, 1918). While Hasse was best known publicly for her graphic works, she continued throughout her career to paint watercolours and oils that express not only her familiar themes of work, but also more intimate depictions of landscape and family.

Naturally an artist so firmly identified with proletarian causes would be included among those labelled "degenerate" by the Nazis; her works were removed from museums, and she was forbidden to exhibit. That she and her family chose to return after World War II to the supposed "workers' paradise" of East Germany indicates the strength of their political convictions. She continued to depict working people, becoming in Communist countries highly renowned and profusely exhibited. Her last work, a linoleum-cut of an East German industrial worker, appeared in 1951; an accident in 1953 confined Hasse to a wheelchair for the last 12 years of her life. For the anniversary of her 100th birthday in 1978, the National Gallery of East Berlin mounted a major retrospective, comprising more than 250 of her works on paper.

ERIKA ESAU

Haverman, Margareta

Dutch painter, 1693–after 1723

Born in Breda, 1693. Studied under Jan van Huysum. Married architect Jacques de Mondoteguy (variants given as Mondotiguy, Mondotigny, Mondotegny, Mondotige, Monte-Dotigny). Elected member of Académie Royale, Paris, 1722; expelled the following year. Date and place of death unknown.

Bibliography

Jan van Gool, *De nieuwe schouburg der Nederlandsche kunstschilders en schilderessen* [The new theatre of Netherlandish male and female painters], ii, The Hague, 1751; reprinted Soest: Davaco, 1971, pp.31–3

Gottfried Winkler, *Historische Erklärungen der Gemälde, welche Herr Gottfried Winkler in Leipzig gesammelt*, Leipzig, 1768, p.141, no.355 (artist's name erroneously listed as N.N. Havermanns)

Christian Josi, "Jan van Huyzum", *Collection d'imitations de dessins d'après les principaux maîtres hollandais et flamands*, ed. Cornelius Ploos van Amstel, Amsterdam and London, 1821

Christiaan Kramm, *De levens en werken der Hollandsche en Vlaamsche kunstschilders, beeldhouwers, graveurs en bouwmeesters* [The lives and works of the Dutch and Flemish painters, sculptors, engravers and architects], ii, Amsterdam, 1859

Henry James, "The Metropolitan Museum's '1871 purchase'", *Atlantic Monthly*, June 1872; reprinted in *The Painter's Eye*, ed. John L. Sweeney, Cambridge, MA: Harvard University Press, 1956, p.65

Louis Vitet, *L'Académie Royale de Peinture et de Sculpture*, Paris, 1880, p.358

Antoine de Montaiglon, *Procès-verbaux de l'Académie Royale de Peinture et de Sculpture, 1648–1793*, iv, Paris, 1881, pp.328 and 331; Table, published 1909, p.109

Octave Fidière, *Les Femmes artistes à l'Académie Royale de Peinture et de Sculpture*, Paris, 1885, p.27

Alfred von Wurzbach, "Haverman, Margareta", *Niederländisches Künstler-Lexikon*, i, Vienna and Leipzig: Halm & Goldmann, 1906, p.651

Hippolyte Mireur, *Dictionnaire des ventes d'art faites en France et l'Etranger pendant les XVIIIe et XIXe siècles*, 7 vols, Paris, 1911–27, iii, p.414 under "Haverman, Margareta"; iv, p.96 listed incorrectly as "Kavermann, Margaretta"

Margaretta Salinger, "Early flower paintings", *Metropolitan Museum Bulletin*, viii, 1950, pp.259–60

Maurice H. Grant, *Jan van Huysum, 1682–1749*, Leigh-on-Sea: Lewis, 1954

Poul Gammelbo, *Dutch Still-Life Painting from the 16th to the 18th Centuries in Danish Collections*, Copenhagen: Munksgaard, 1960

Christopher White, *Flower Drawings by Jan van Huysum*, Leigh-on-Sea: Lewis, 1964

Peter Mitchell, *European Flower Painters*, London: A. & C. Black, 1973

Women Artists, 1550–1950, exh. cat., Los Angeles County Museum of Art, and elsewhere, 1976

Germaine Greer, *The Obstacle Race: The Fortunes of Women Painters and Their Work*, London: Secker and Warburg, and New York: Farrar Straus, 1979

Margareta Haverman was the only known student of the noted Dutch flower painter Jan van Huysum. Details of her life are as scarce as her works, and her name has survived primarily through literature on van Huysum. Jan van Gool was the first biographer to discuss Haverman at any length, although he did not record her first name and did not know her personally. He described her as the pleasant and lively young daughter of a schoolmaster, who had evidently moved his family to Amsterdam around 1700. Van Gool noted that Haverman's father was acquainted with van Huysum in Amsterdam, and succeeded in convincing him to accept his daughter as a pupil even though the artist was extremely reluctant to share his professional secrets with anyone. Later writers (Josi 1821, White 1964 and Mitchell 1973) credit van Huysum's uncle, not Haverman's persuasive father, with arranging for Margareta's instruction. All biographers concur, however, in their characterisation of van Huysum as a secretive and jealous artist who feared that someone might discover his incomparable techniques for painting flowers and who employed no assistants.

As van Huysum's student, Haverman copied his work, worked from nature, and also produced flower pieces that were free interpretations of his style. Art enthusiasts who saw her student efforts marvelled at her mastery of van Huysum's

Haverman: *Vase of Flowers*, 1716; oil on wood; 79.4 × 60.3 cm.; Metropolitan Museum of Art, New York: Purchase, 1871 (71.6)

manner. The dates and length of time that Haverman studied with van Huysum are not recorded, although the fact that "the girl" had succeeded in making beautiful paintings in his style suggests that she studied with him over a period of years. According to van Gool, Haverman weathered her teacher's jealous and uncomfortably curt manner only through great perseverance. Van Huysum regularly devised reasons for getting rid of her, and finally found an excuse to dismiss her after she committed a misdeed (*slechte daet*, according to van Gool), the nature of which is uncertain. Kramm suggested, quite plausibly, that it was art related. French writers translated *slechte daet* as *faiblesse* or "weakness", and this was subsequently interpreted as an unhappy love affair. Grant and Mitchell suggested that the romance was with van Huysum himself, but he was already married in 1704.

By 21 January 1722, the date that she became a member of the notoriously chauvinistic Académie Royale, Haverman was living in Paris and married to an architect named Jacques de Mondoteguy. She was admitted by unanimous vote on the basis of a previously completed flower and fruit piece. The minutes of the Academy record that she was explicitly requested to produce another painting of similar subject and style to serve as her reception piece, but she was apparently expelled the following year. The Academy's records provide no account of the matter. Various writers maintained that she was accused of passing off a work by van Huysum as her own. Some have proposed that she did so, others that the accusation was false. It is unclear how this rumour originated, and she may well have been dismissed simply for failing to submit a diploma piece. The painting in question has never been securely identified.

Nothing is known for certain about Haverman's life after her expulsion from the Academy. Van Gool alluded to the expulsion in the vaguest of terms: "a case that threw her household into ruin". He also noted that although he had seen some of her work in Dutch collections (*c*.1750), he had met no-one who knew what had become of her. Kramm commented that Haverman had finished some of van Huysum's drawings after his death in 1749, which seems unlikely. Mitchell, Greer and White claimed that Haverman enjoyed a wealth of patronage in Paris, with Greer identifying her as the specific link between van Huysum and the generation of late 18th-century flower painters working in Paris (such as Gérard and Cornelis van Spaendonck, Paul Theodor van Brussel and Jan Frans van Dael). According to Kramm, Haverman was still alive in 1750. Some 20th-century writers – for instance, Grant, White and Greer – report that she died in 1795, but again this seems unlikely; had she lived to the advanced age of 102 years, the fact would no doubt have been noticed and recorded.

Only two works by Margareta Haverman are known today. The smaller and more modest of the two is a signed, undated flower piece on canvas (Statens Museums for Kunst, Copenhagen; on deposit at Fredenborg Castle), which depicts a mixed bouquet of summer flowers in a vase upon a brown stone table against a plain dark background. The signature, "M. Haverman Fec", appears in dark script on the lower right edge of the table. The bouquet is constructed of large blossoms that are tightly packed together into a vertical column that gestures slightly to the right and is illuminated from the left.

Along this linear mid-section Haverman displayed insects – ants on an open hollyhock and a red admiral butterfly on a pendant rose. By placing the arrangement of glowing blossoms against an inky backdrop, Haverman relied upon the dramatic device for achieving heightened three-dimensionality that Jan Davidsz. de Heem developed in the mid-17th century.

These features of the Copenhagen painting show great similarities with the flower paintings that Jan van Huysum produced around 1710–14, particularly a bouquet (*c*.1710; National Gallery, London) that also features hollyhocks as the most dominant floral specimen. Haverman's design is more deliberate in the way in which the highlighted flowers form a rigid row in the composition, causing spatial relationships to read a little awkwardly. None the less, this very characteristic suggests that the Copenhagen composition is Haverman's own, not a verbatim copy of a work by her teacher.

The other painting by Haverman, the more ambitious of the two, inscribed "Margareta Haverman fecit/A°/ 1716" at lower right on the edge of a shelf, is the artist's only known signed and dated work (see illustration). A tall, showy bouquet of different floral varieties and growing seasons stands in a footed ornamental urn on a ledge inside a niche. A grouping of red and white grapes and a peach attached to a twig are included to the right. The construction of the bouquet is much more complex than in the Copenhagen work, with many spindly stems of delicate flowers and grasses filling out the arrangement, softening its edges and counterbalancing the weight of the denser flowers (roses, marigolds, iris, tulips, passion flower, primulas, hollyhocks, carnations and poppies). The tonality has brightened up somewhat, and the palette has taken on a bluish cast, particularly in the leaves. The peculiar "metallic" quality of this blue, found also in works by van Huysum, Willem van Aelst and particularly Simon Verelst, suggests that Haverman must have used tinted spot varnishes to "glaze" these areas, and that they were removed at some point when the painting was cleaned. While light illuminates this bouquet from the left, as it did in the Copenhagen work, it also bounces off the right side of the niche and silhouettes the blossoms in that area – creating a sophisticated second light source. The new primary focus of this complex bouquet is the bright flame tulip near the apex. The presence of a fly heightens the sculptural quality of this flower.

Ralph Warner (letter of 23 November 1933, curatorial files, Metropolitan Museum of Art, New York) and other scholars have questioned the date of the work, arguing that it is painted in van Huysum's late manner and that the third digit of the date is a partially obliterated "5", but conservators at the Metropolitan Museum have determined conclusively that both the signature and the date of 1716 are in the old paint layer. The painting is compositionally similar to two undated paintings by van Huysum probably from the period *c*.1716–20 (Nelson-Atkins Museum, Kansas City; Liechtenstein collection).

The Metropolitan painting originally had a pendant of similar composition and subject, but with a bird's nest rather than fruit on the table. The two works were together in Paris in the 19th century when they were described in two sales: Louis Fould (1860) and Edouard Fould (1869). The pendants were undoubtedly split up either at the Edouard Fould sale, or shortly afterwards by the Parisian art dealer, Léon Gauchez, who might have purchased them both. (At the Edouard Fould sale, the Metropolitan painting sold for 2100 francs and its lost pendant for 2050.) Gauchez sold the 2100-franc panel to the Metropolitan in 1870, shortly after the museum opened. The description of the lost pendant suggests that it was probably very close in appearance to two paintings on panel by or attributed to van Huysum, both of which are the same size as the Metropolitan painting (Statens Museum for Kunst, Copenhagen; Dulwich Gallery, London).

Various old French, Dutch and German sales catalogues contain descriptions of paintings by Margareta Haverman. Works by her appeared in the following sales: Pieter Testas the Younger (Amsterdam, 29 March 1757), Diderick Smith, a friend of van Huysum (Amsterdam, 13 July 1761; flower-piece sold to Gottfried Winkler of Leipzig who published a description of it in a 1768 catalogue of his collection), Baron Mathieu de Faviers, senior army officer (Paris, 11 April 1837), Louis Fould (Paris, 4 June 1860), Edouard Fould, (Paris, 5 April 1869) and the Marquis de la Rochebousseau, the fictitious name of the art dealer Gauchez (Paris, 5–8 May 1873). Few of these works can be matched up with existing paintings. None the less, the descriptions yield interesting information about Haverman's artistic methods and patrons, and annotations reveal that her work generally sold for sums comparable to middle-range van Huysums. She used both wood and canvas supports for her paintings, which ranged in size from 40 × 32 to 79 × 60.5 centimetres (the larger being a dimension often used by van Huysum). In at least two instances she produced pendant still lifes. She painted floral bouquets in glass and ornamental (gilded, marble) vases as well as baskets, on stone and marble tabletops, and in niches as well as against plain dark backgrounds. Occasionally she placed fruit on the ledge beside the bouquet, but it is unclear whether she depicted fruit alone or placed any of the arrangements against garden settings and light backgrounds as van Huysum did regularly after 1720. In general, her paintings seem to resemble van Huysum's work from 1710 to 1720, which suggests the period of time she studied with him.

The catalogues sometimes specifically compare her work with that of van Huysum, and the descriptions sound very similar to his work. One painting, for example, was described as "a fresh flower arrangement … placed in a glass container on a marble ledge. The colors are organized in Van Huysum's manner, with shining dew and numerous insects throughout" (Smith sale, later Winkler collection). A pair of pendants, each depicting a variety of flowers and fruit, was described as being "painted with a care, precision and charm which rivals the most beautiful works of van Huysum" (de Faviers sale).

With so few known paintings by her hand, it is extremely difficult to determine Haverman's development as a painter, or to identify stylistic idiosyncrasies that set her apart from van Huysum as a distinct artistic personality. As many biographers have suggested, some of her works are probably hiding under van Huysum's name, since his oeuvre has never been the subject of a thorough art-historical evaluation. Ironically, almost three centuries later, Margareta Haverman's artistic achievements continue to be at the mercy of van Huysum's: not

until his work is carefully studied can her oeuvre begin to be substantially reconstructed.

MARIANNE BERARDI

Hawarden, Clementina, Viscountess
British photographer, 1822–1865

Born at Cumbernauld House near Glasgow, 1 June 1822, to the Hon. Charles Elphinstone Fleeming, an admiral, and his wife Catalina Paulina Alessandro of Cádiz. Married Cornwallis Maude, 1845; ten children, one son and seven daughters surviving infancy. Husband succeeded to title as 4th Viscount Hawarden, with estate at Dundrum, near Cashel, Co. Tipperary, Ireland, 1856; family moved there, 1857. Started taking photographs at Dundrum, late 1857 or early 1858. Moved to 5 Princes Gardens, South Kensington, London, 1859. Member, Photographic Society of London, 1863. Died of pneumonia, 19 January 1865.

Principal Exhibitions
Photographic Society of London: 1863 (silver medal for best contribution by an amateur), 1864 (silver medal for best composition from a single negative)

Bibliography
British Journal of Photography, x, 1863, pp.69, 79

Journal of the Photographic Society, ix, 1864, p.69

Photographic News, viii, 1864, pp.303, 348

O. G. R[ejlander], "In memoriam", *British Journal of Photography*, xii, 1865, p.38

Helmut Gernsheim, *Lewis Carroll: Photographer*, London: Parrish, and New York: Chanticleer Press, 1949; reprinted New York: Dover, 1969

Charles Lutwidge Dodgson, *The Diaries of Lewis Carroll*, ed. Roger Lancelyn Green, i, London: Cassell, and New York: Oxford University Press, 1954

Helmut Gernsheim, *Creative Photography: Aesthetic Trends, 1839–1960*, London: Faber, and Boston: Boston Book and Art Shop, 1962

"From Today Painting Is Dead": The Beginnings of Photography, exh. cat., Arts Council of Great Britain and Victoria and Albert Museum, London, 1972

Graham Ovenden, ed., *Clementina, Lady Hawarden*, London: Academy Editions, and New York: St Martin's Press, 1974

R. Aspin, "Oh, weary, neutral days: The photographs of Lady Hawarden", *British Journal of Photography*, cxxix, 28 May 1982, pp.564–6

Mark Haworth-Booth, ed., *The Golden Age of British Photography*, Millerton, NY: Aperture, 1984

Michael Bartram, *The Pre-Raphaelite Camera*, London: Weidenfeld and Nicolson, and Boston: Little Brown, 1985

Virginia Dodier, "Haden, photography and salmon fishing", *Print Quarterly*, iii, 1986, pp.34–50

Helmut Gernsheim, *The Rise of Photography, 1850–1880*, 3rd edition, London and New York: Thames and Hudson, 1988

Virginia Dodier, "Clementina, Viscountess Hawarden: Studies from life", *British Photography in the Nineteenth Century: The Fine Art Tradition*, ed. Mike Weaver, Cambridge and New York: Cambridge University Press, 1989, pp.141–50

Michael Hallett, "Lady of noble talents", *British Journal of Photography*, cxxxvi, 21 September 1989, p.25

Hawarden: *At the Window/Study from Life (Isabella Grace, 5 Princes Gardens, South Kensington),* *c.*1864; albumen print; Gernsheim Collection, Harry Ransom Humanities Research Center, University of Texas at Austin

Domestic Idylls: Photographs by Clementina, Lady Hawarden, exh. cat., J. Paul Getty Museum, Malibu, CA, 1990

Lady Hawarden: Photographe victorienne, exh. cat., Musée d'Orsay, Paris, 1990

Virginia Dodier, "Portraits in the mirror", *Antique Collector*, lxi, July 1990, pp.68–71

——, "From the interior: Photographs by Clementina, Viscountess Hawarden", *Magazine Antiques*, cxxxix, 1991, pp.196–207

In 1939 the descendants of Clementina, Viscountess Hawarden presented 776 of her photographic prints made between 1857 and 1865 to the Victoria and Albert Museum, London. Although recognised for her photographs by awards in 1863 and 1864, Lady Hawarden's early death from pneumonia at the age of 42 terminated a promising career. As most of her photographs were privately held, it was not until the bulk of her work reached a public collection that the extent and quality of it could be assessed, and it was not until the 1990s that individual exhibitions of Lady Hawarden's work were held, in London, Paris, the J. Paul Getty Museum in California and the Museum of Modern Art in New York, among others.

Although her photographs were appreciated in her own time, by awards and by praise from such photographers as Lewis Carroll and O.G. Rejlander, Hawarden's work is in many ways very different from typical Victorian photographs. She did not photograph celebrities or hire models but used her family, especially her two oldest daughters, as her subjects. Instead of proper Victorian young ladies, she revealed adolescent dreams and fantasies. Narrative elements are at a minimum. In her frequent use of mirror and window images, Hawarden's photographs show a preoccupation with the formal possibilities of composition. This is reinforced by her experimentation with variations on a composition, such as her series of her daughter Clementina Maude in vaguely medieval costume standing next to a mirror that reflects profile or full-face poses in different combinations, and also a series of her daughters in oriental dress in a variety of poses (all Victoria and Albert Museum). This interest in mirror imaging was also a preoccupation of 19th-century painters such as Berthe Morisot (q.v.), Mary Cassatt (q.v.) and Edouard Manet, among others.

One of the main elements in Hawarden's work is her use of light. Several studies are taken by windows, and while the concentration of light would obviously aid in the production of the photograph itself, the diffuse lighting often seems to become an element of mood within the composition. In her interest in defining and dissolving objects and scenes through lighting conditions, Hawarden shows obvious parallels with the preoccupations of the Impressionist painters a decade later. Another element in Hawarden's photographs that has parallels in the work of other Victorian photographers is the depiction of subjects in fancy dress or exotic costume. There are a number of period costume pieces, and even a few studies in "beggar rags" with bare feet (Victoria and Albert Museum). Although this delight in dressing up can be found in the photographs of such contemporaries as Lewis Carroll, Julia Margaret Cameron (q.v.), David Wilkie Wynfield and Roger Fenton, with Lady Hawarden, it is just an element in composition rather than a complete tableau or narrative.

Very little is known about Lady Hawarden's formal training as a photographer. It was not until her husband inherited his title and estate in 1856 that she could afford the expense of photographic equipment. Some of the influences on her work may have been the pictorialist photographer O.G. Rejlander and Charles Thurston Thompson, who was the official photographer of the South Kensington Museum and taught photography there. It is possible that she was one of Thompson's students, especially as she showed and sold her photographs at a bazaar in 1864 for the benefit of female artists at the South Kensington Museum school. Her first camera may have been a stereoscopic one, because a number of her early photographs are in stereopticon double image format. She produced albumen prints made from wet collodion on glass negatives, the largest size of her prints being approximately 9. × 11 inches (24 × 38 cm.).

Hawarden's first photographs were stereoscope views of the house and park at Dundrum and of her family and labourers on the Irish estate. Her early studies of trees are particularly striking, although not unique. In her South Kensington home Hawarden had the use of the first floor with its French windows and terrace for her photographic work. At this time she began to concentrate mainly on studies of her two eldest daughters, either singly or together, usually in interiors, until around 1862. The costume pieces and mirror images date mainly from her late work of 1862–4. Here Hawarden explored such oppositions as inside/outside, back/front images, as in *Study from Life* (1864; Victoria and Albert Museum), in which Isabella Grace Maude and Clementina face each other on two sides of a French window at 5 Princes Gardens. Hawarden also used mirror images reflecting another aspect of the model, and window images with light streaming in, sometimes in the same photograph, suggesting two aspects of women's experience – inner reflection and the exterior world.

One of the questions that arises in connection with Hawarden's work is whether it can be called Pre-Raphaelite. Michael Bartram included Lady Hawarden in his book *The Pre-Raphaelite Camera* (1985) and pointed to such Pre-Raphaelite elements as loosened long hair, flowing gowns, mirror imagery and costume pieces. Contemporaries, however, denied that she was anything but a photographer of natural settings (O.G.R. 1865). Julia Margaret Cameron with her medieval references fits more easily into the Pre-Raphaelite category. It is interesting to note that contemporaries such as Lewis Carroll, commenting on Hawarden's and Cameron's work, vastly preferred Lady Hawarden's; in a diary entry of 23 June 1864 he proclaimed that the best photographs in the Photographic Society exhibition were by Lady Hawarden, and later purchased five of her photographs for his collection (Gernsheim 1949, p.57).

In her brief career Lady Hawarden produced more than 800 photographs. Her mature work reveals a fascination with inner and outer reflections, of light dissolving form and of the dimensions of female experience. Although she shared many interests with her Victorian contemporaries, her photographs with their formal oppositions and suggestions of interior life are timeless and untraditional, haunting in their mystery and their intimations.

ALICIA CRAIG FAXON

Hay, Elisabeth-Sophie le *see* Chéron

Hébert, Hélène *see* Bertaux

Heemskerck, Jacoba van

Dutch painter, printmaker and stained-glass designer, 1876–1923

Born in The Hague, 1 April 1876. Initially taught by her father, Jacob Eduard van Heemskerck van Beest; attended classes in painting at The Hague Academy, 1897–1900; moved to Laren and received training in graphics by F. Hart Nibbrig, 1901–3; visited Paris and trained in the studio of Eugène Carrière, 1904–5. Alternated between The Hague and Domburg; use of studio in the garden of the villa Loverendale, Domburg, owned by art patron Marie Tak van Poortvliet, 1906–14. Visited Berlin with van Poortvliet, 1913; met art dealer and publisher Herwarth Walden. Attended Rudolf Steiner lecture cycle in The Hague, 1913. Corresponded with German Expressionist critic and writer Dr Adolf Behne, who collected her works, 1916. Approximately 14 works destroyed or damaged in a fire at a warehouse of *Der Sturm* in Berlin, 1917. Conducted controlled experiments on children with medical student F.W. Zeylmans van Emmichoven on the psychological and emotional effects of colour, 1918. Commissions for her lead and coloured-glass experiments secured by the architect Jan Buijs, 1919. Died in Domburg, 3 August 1923.

Principal Exhibitions

Salon des Indépendants, Paris: 1911–14
Moderne Kunstkring [Modern Art Circle], Amsterdam: 1911–13
Galerie Der Sturm, Berlin: 1913 (*Erster deutscher Herbstsalon*), 1914 (with Marianne Werefkin), 1915 (individual)
London Salon of the Allied Artists Association: 1913
Der Sturm, Berlin: 1916 (2nd exhibition), 1920 (83rd exhibition), 1921 (102nd exhibition), 1924 (129th exhibition, *Gedächtnis-Ausstellung*)
Kunstzalen d'Audretsch, The Hague: 1916 (*Expressionisten, Kubisten*)

Bibliography

"R", "Kunst te Domburg", *Domburgsch Badnieuws*, xxx/8, 1912
Adolf Behne, *Zur neuen Kunst*, Der Sturm, 1915 (Sturm-Bücher vii), first edition, 1916
F.W. Zeylmans van Emmichoven, "De geestelijke richting in de nieuwe schilderkunst: Jacoba van Heemskerck" [The spiritual direction of the new art: Jacoba van Heemskerck], unpublished article, 1917
Marie Tak van Poortvliet, *Jacoba van Heemskerck*, Sturm Bilderbuch, vii, Berlin, 1924
Nell Walden and Lothar Schreyer, *Der Sturm: Ein Erinnerungsbuch an Herwarth Walden und die Künstler aus dem Sturmkreis*, Baden-Baden: Klein, 1954
A.B. Loosjes-Terpstra, *Moderne Kunst in Nederland, 1900–1914*, Utrecht: Dekker & Gumbert, 1959
Jacoba van Heemskerck, 1876–1923: Kunstenares van het Expressionisme [Jacoba van Heemskerck, 1876–1923: Woman artist of Expressionism], exh. cat., Haags Gemeentemuseum, The Hague, 1982
Georg Brühl, *Herwarth Walden und "Der Sturm"*, Cologne, 1983
Shulamith Behr, *Women Expressionists*, Oxford: Phaidon, and New York: Rizzoli, 1988
K. Winskell, "The art of propaganda: Herwarth Walden and 'Der Sturm', 1914–1919", *Art History*, xviii, 1995, pp.315–44

Jacoba van Heemskerck was one of the few women artists to emerge as a major abstractionist in the second decade of the 20th century. Interaction with avant-garde groups in Paris and Berlin between 1911 and 1923 secured her familiarity with the fundamental tenets of early modernism. Moreover, the impact of the ideas of Rudolf Steiner, who enjoyed a substantial following in the Netherlands during this period, reinforced van Heemskerck's belief in the ability of the work of art to transmit spiritual values.

Her contact with the Berlin-based art dealer and publisher Herwarth Walden and his wife, the Swedish artist Nell Roslund, contributed to her celebrated reception within German Expressionist circles. Above all, however, it was her friendship with the patron Marie Tak van Poortvliet, a major collector and publicist of modern art in Holland, that gave the artist the continued security to pursue an agenda that isolated her from her Dutch contemporaries. Although these features of van Heemskerck's career suggest that she engaged exclusively in activities consistent with male avant-garde practice at the time, it is interesting to note that she exhibited at the Union des Femmes Peintres et Sculpteurs while in Paris and was treasurer for the Sub-committee of Fine Arts that formed to organise the large exhibition *De Vrouw, 1813–1913* (The woman, 1813–1913).

As the daughter of a well-known seascape painter, Jacob Eduard van Heemskerck van Beest, van Heemskerck received a traditional training. Evidence of this can be found in her small-scale character portraits, such as the coloured crayon drawing of the *Old Fisherman* (1906–7; Haags Gemeentemuseum, The Hague), which reveal her forceful command of linear configuration. Experimenting, as well, with graphic techniques, her lithographs of farmers and genre interiors demonstrate a finely tuned handling of realist detail united by a compositional use of chiaroscuro (e.g. *Farmer's Interior*, 1906–7; Haags Gemeentemuseum).

While these works testify to van Heemskerck's identification with the regionalism of the Hague School, it is evident that her acquaintance with the artists' colony at the Domburg coastal retreat turned her attention to landscape painting. Participating in summer exhibitions in Domburg, she was reviewed favourably by a certain "R" in the *Domburgsch Badnieuws* (1912):

Also, it can be seen that Miss van Heemskerck van Beest leans in the direction of Cubism which, by this time, she can express by preference. The form is already her own, that she handles without much difficulty and, with her diligence and good will, she will also master the exact colour.

In such oil paintings as *Mountain Landscape with Trees* (1912–13; Haags Gemeentemuseum) van Heemskerck exploited geometrical fragmentation while retaining forceful, linear definition of the shapes. Seemingly, however, the

Heemskerck: Jacoba van Heemskerck in her studio, 1915; Haags Gemeentemuseum, The Hague

reviewer seized on the powerful effects of colour that differentiated her works from the tonal investigations of Analytical Cubism. By exhibiting annually with the Moderne Kunstkring in Amsterdam between 1911 and 1913, the artist firmly associated herself with a form of internationalism currently being promoted by Herwarth Walden. Already in 1912, his Sturm gallery had organised exhibitions in The Hague, Amsterdam and Rotterdam that included works by the Futurists, Wassily Kandinsky and Franz Marc, a pattern that gathered pace due to German Foreign Office approval and Holland's neutrality during World War I.

By 1915 van Heemskerck's technical radicalism became more pronounced; she abandoned the practice of giving titles to her paintings and drawings, preferring to allocate numbers. Her seascape and harbour scenes (e.g. *Painting No.23*, 1915; Haags Gemeentemuseum) were reduced to a rhythmic repetition of quasi-geometric motifs and colours – dark, symmetrically placed trees, inverted white sails on red triangular-shaped bases, pyramidal mountain peaks – enlivened by the contrasting whiplash tendrils of the branches. Her works aroused much interest when exhibited from 1915 in Berlin at the Sturm galleries and, until 1920, her production was exclusively distributed through Walden's dealership. At least 21 of her abstracted woodcuts were illustrated in the journal *Der Sturm* between 1914 and 1921, the dramatic use of the medium suit-

ably reinforcing the emblematic content of the landscape motifs.

Due to her intensified activities in Steiner's anthroposophic movement, van Heemskerck became preoccupied with the mystical and expressive components of colour and, by 1920, this became the most powerful feature of her paintings. In *Painting No.105* (1920; Haags Gemeentemuseum) the reference to residual landscape imagery is almost dissolved as the autonomous painterly surface dominates the composition. Dispensing with the quasi-geometric forms, she explored the values of organic and aura-like shapes of saturated coloration. The artist's interest in colour symbolism received further impetus from her circle of friends in the Netherlands as she turned her attention to creating coloured-glass and lead compositions. Through the agency of the architect Jan Buijs, she received her first commission for the Wulffraat villa in Wassenaar in 1919 (The Hague 1982, cat. no.102). Inspired by her reading of Paul Scheerbart's book *Glasarchitektur* (1914), she aspired to achieve glowing, coloured light consistent with the demand for heightened spirituality in the Expressionist interior.

Following van Heemskerck's untimely death, van Poortvliet secured the artist's reputation by dedicating a book to her in 1924 and by bequeathing 37 of her works to the Haags Gemeentemuseum (1936). Subsequent bequests to this museum, for instance by Jan Buijs (woodcuts, drawings and lithographs), resulted in eventual public recognition of van Heemskerck in the early 1960s and acknowledgement of the crucial role that she played in the history of Dutch modernism.

SHULAMITH BEHR

Heer, Margaretha de
Dutch painter, active 1603–50

Born in Leeuwarden, Friesland, before 1603, to the glass painter Arien Willems de Heer and his wife Elisabeth Gerritsdochter; her brother Gerrit was also a glass painter (there is no evidence that she was the sister of the artists Willem and Simon de Heer). Married painter Andries Pieters Nijhoff, 21 September 1628. Worked in Groningen with Nijhoff between c.1635 and 1646, then in a number of places including Leeuwarden, where the couple bought a house on the Bagijnenstraat, 14 October 1650. Probably dead by 25 January 1665, when her husband sold this house with the consent of their two children, Catrina and Pytter (Margaretha is not mentioned in the transaction).

Bibliography

Christiaan Kramm, *De levens en werken der Hollandsche en Vlaamsche kunstschilders, beeldhouwers graveurs en bouwmeesters* [The lives and works of the Dutch and Flemish painters, sculptors, engravers and architects], iii, Amsterdam, 1859

W. Eekhoff, *De Stedelijke kunstverzameling van Leeuwarden* [The municipal art collections of Leeuwarden], Leeuwarden, 1875

Dessins hollandais du siècle d'or: Choix de dessins provenant de collections publiques et particulières néerlandaises, exh. cat., Bibliothèque royale Albert Ier, Brussels, 1961

D.J. van der Meer, "Sibben fan Gysbert Japix, Sijcke Salviusdr. en Margaretha de Heer" [The relationships between Gysbert Japix, Sijcke Salviusdr. and Margaretha de Heer], *It Beaken*, xxvi, 1964, pp.37–63

Women Artists, 1550–1950, exh. cat., Los Angeles County Museum of Art, and elsewhere, 1976

Peter Kartskarel, "Margaretha de Heer en haar 'stukjes'" [Margaretha de Heer and her "little pieces"], *Tableau*, i, 1978, pp.37–9

——, "Eekhoffs geschiedenis van de schilders, tekenaars en graveurs in Friesland tot 1875" [Eeckhoff's history of the painters, draughtsmen and engravers in Friesland before 1875], *Eekhoff en zijn werk: Leven en werk van Wopke Eekhoff (1809–1880)*, ed. C.P. Hoekema and others, Leeuwarden, 1980

P.H. Breuker, *It wurk fan Gysbert Japix* [The works of Gysbert Japix], 2 vols, Leeuwarden: Fryske Akademy, 1989

In contemporary sources Margaretha de Heer is only very rarely referred to as a painter. That she nevertheless enjoyed some fame is evident from a number of eulogies by the Friesland poet Gysbert Japix. The precise relationship between de Heer and Japix is not known, but in a letter of 1656 he calls her his "cousin". The anthology *Klioos Kraam* (Clio's Stall), published in 1656, includes a poem entitled: "To the artful Margarita de Heer. On the eye's delight at her miracle-working". In these lines her depictions of different kinds of animals ("Peewit, Jackdaw, Rabbit, Cow, Horse, Hart, Hind, Hound, Hare or Pig"), as well as trees and flowers, earn her the denomination "bright star". The same poem also includes the line: "I have heard many speak of your art ...", though whether this should be understood as recording Japix's actual experience or rather as a rhetorical flourish is open to question. The same anthology also contains a eulogy to de Heer by the poet Sibylle van Griethuysen: "Celebrated Margariet de Heer, whose Paint-Brush transmits your Renown as far as the Sun his beams, your praise is flying on the wings of Fame. Ay! paint us a lively Death, and the obsequies of this great Messenger." Besides de Heer, this last poem also cites as Frisian women painters Eelkje van Bouricius and Margaretha van Haren.

De Heer's oeuvre comprises at least 50 works, of which, according to Peter Kartkarel, 37 may still be conclusively assigned to her. This is in direct contrast to the work of her husband, who is referred to in official documents as "painter", but to whose hand not a single work can as yet be attributed. Her work is very diverse, and is not confined to watercolours of flowers and birds, the genre usually associated with her – for example, a signed and dated *Still Life with Insects and Shells* (1654; Wadsworth Atheneum, Hartford, CT), a sheet with a tulip and some little animals (Museum voors Stad en Ommelanden, Groningen) and another gouache on parchment of twigs with insects (1658; Fries Museum, Leeuwarden). It also includes genres far removed from the characteristic forms of amateur art practice, for example a canvas with *Brawling Beggars* (see illustration) and a *Farmyard* (Stedelijke Kunstverzameling, Leeuwarden). In Hoorn (Westfries Museum) two panel paintings of henneries are attributed to her. The Fries Museum has a gouache on parchment showing Diana spied on by a satyr. Literary sources also refer to a self-portrait (on which Sibylle van Griethuysen composed a poem: "Thus Margriet de Heer captured her living likeness, At whose command of handling and wonderful invention, The spirits of our age do truly shake and tremble, choking in rage at the brilliance of her brush"), and several history paintings. Nine works by de Heer were in the collection of the jurist Petrus Wierdsma, auctioned in 1813. Besides the *Diana* mentioned above, these included landscapes, a canvas with a "Fortune Teller telling a child's fortune", and an "Andromeda" chained to the rocks. As regards technique, de Heer confined herself to the use of gouache, mostly on parchment, and worked occasionally in oil. Her works were always small in scale.

De Heer is exceptional among the better-known women artists of the northern Netherlands. As far as can be determined, she had no direct connections with any official painters' organisations (unlike, for example, Judith Leyster, q.v.), yet her work is too atypical for her to be considered solely an amateur. Genre paintings, for instance, are highly unusual in the oeuvres of 17th-century women artists. Then again, her album illustrations of flowers and insects are closely related to works by other Netherlandish women such as Anna Maria van Schurman (q.v.) and later Maria Sibylla Merian (q.v.).

KATLIJNE VAN DER STIGHELEN

Heinrich-Salze, Karl Luis *see* Heise

Heer: *Brawling Beggars*, gum tempera on panel; 36.3 × 28.5 cm.; Leicester Museum

Heise, Katharina

German sculptor, painter and graphic artist,
1891–1964

Born in Gross Salze (now Schönebeck-Salzelmen), 3 May
1891. Trained alongside her older sister, Annemarie Heise,
who also became a professional artist. Studied at the
Kunstgewerbeschule, Magdeburg, before 1912; Dorsch
Malerinnschule (Art School for Women), Dresden, 1912;
Académie Ranson, La Grande Chaumière and La Palette,
Paris, 1913–14. Opened a studio with her sister in Berlin-
Moabit, autumn 1914. Adopted the pseudonym Karl Luis
Heinrich-Salze (and variations thereof), 1916–c.1931.
Concentrated on sculpture from 1917; self-taught, with
advice from Hugo Lederer, professor of sculpture at the
Berlin Academy. Member, 1920s, and secretary, 1925,
Frauenkunstverband (Women's Art Union), Berlin; also served
as vice-president. Taught life drawing at the Staatliche
Kunstschule, Berlin, 1926. Member, Social Democratic Party
of Greater Berlin, 1927; Künstlervereinigung Berliner
Bildhauer (Artists' Association of Berlin Sculptors), 1927;
Deutscher Lyceumsclub (German Lyceum Club), Berlin, late
1920s. Worked for Ernst Niekisch's magazine *Resistance:
Paper for National Revolutionary Politics* from 1929. Art
declared "degenerate" by the National Socialists, 1933;
works in museums confiscated and some of her public sculpture destroyed; prohibited from exhibiting or accepting public
commissions. Moved back to parents' home in Schönebeck-
Salzelmen after Berlin studio destroyed by bombing, 1942.
Died in Schönebeck-Salzelmen, 5 October 1964.

Principal Exhibitions

Individual
Gallery of *Die Aktion* magazine, Berlin: 1918
Berlin studio: 1931
Kulturhistorisches Museum, Magdeburg: 1961 (with Annemarie
    Heise)

Group
Berlin Secession: 1916
Magdeburg: 1916 (*Magdeburg Expressionisten*)
Die Kugel group, Magdeburg: 1919, 1921
Novembergruppe, Berlin: 1919–21
Kestner-Gesellschaft, Hannover: 1922
Freie Secession, Berlin: 1923 (*Frühjahrausstellung*)
Juryfreie Kunstausstellung, Berlin: 1925
Staatliche Kunstgewerbeschule, Hamburg: 1927 (*Frauenschaffen des
    20. Jahrhunderts*)
Grosse Berliner Kunstausstellung, Berlin: 1927, 1928, 1930
Museum Folkwang, Essen: 1929
Haus der Juryfreien, Berlin: 1931 (*Frauen in Not*, touring)
Galerie Billiet, Paris: 1931
Prussian Academy, Berlin: 1934 (*Sechs Jahrtausende Töpfertum*)
(West) Berlin: 1953 (*The Unknown Political Prisoner*, for
    International Sculpture Competition, London)

Bibliography

Theodor Däubler, "Kunstausstellung 'Die Aktion'", *Berliner Börsen-
    Courier*, no.129, first supplement, 15 March 1918, p.6
Paul Friedrich, "Das Tier in der modernen Plastik", *Kunst der Zeit*,
    i/7, April 1930, pp.162–7
Fritz Schiff, "Frauen in Not", *Der Weg der Frau*, no.6, 1 November
    1931, pp.16–17
*Revolution und Realismus: Revolutionäre Kunst in Deutschland,
    1917 bis 1933*, exh. cat., Nationalgalerie and Kupferstichkabinett,
    Berlin, 1978
Die Aktion: Sprachrohr der expressionistischen Kunst, exh. cat.,
    Städtisches Kunstmuseum, Bonn, 1984
Katharina Heise: Druckgrafik, exh. cat., Galerie erph, Erfurt, 1985
Thomas Rietzschel, ed., *Die Aktion, 1911–1918: Eine Auswahl*,
    Cologne: DuMont, 1987
German Expressionism, 1915–1925: The Second Generation, exh.
    cat., Los Angeles County Museum of Art, and elsewhere, 1988
Renate Ulmer, *Passion und Apokalypse: Studien zur biblischen
    Thematik in der Kunst des Expressionismus*, Frankfurt am Main:
    Lang, 1992
Anita Beloubek-Hammer, "Wider die 'Stand- und Spielbein'-
    Skulptur", *Novembergruppe*, exh. cat., Galerie Bodo Niemann,
    Berlin, 1993, pp.29–48
*"Die Kugel": Eine Künstlervereinigung der 20er Jahre:
    Spätexpressionistische Kunst in Magdeburg*, exh. cat., Kloster
    Unser Lieben Frauen, Magdeburger Museen, Magdeburg, 1993
Erich Ranfft, "German women sculptors, 1918–1936: Gender differ-
    ences and status", *Visions of the "Neue Frau": Women and the
    Visual Arts in Weimar Germany*, ed. Marsha Meskimmon and
    Shearer West, Aldershot: Scolar Press, 1995, pp.42–61

Until the mid-1980s Katharina Heise was a forgotten artist,
but more recent research has begun to reveal a significant artistic production and involvement with artists' associations
during the Weimar era in Berlin from 1918 to the early 1930s.
Her contributions to German Expressionist art in the period
after World War I, and to the socialist and feminist aims of
subsequent Weimar art and culture, place her among the most
important women artists working in Germany during this
period. It is important to recognise that Heise's career and life
in Berlin were inextricably bound to that of her younger sister
Annemarie Heise, also a professional artist (painter and
draughtswoman). They shared studios, frequently exhibited
together and actively involved themselves in women's artistic
associations. Käthe Kollwitz (q.v.) was also a close friend and
was to have a profound and long-lasting effect on Heise's artistic development and political outlook.

From the beginnings of her professional career in 1916 until
the early 1920s, Heise worked in various two-dimensional
media: watercolours, paintings (oils on canvas, tempera on
paper), but predominantly graphics (with at least 30 woodcuts,
ten etchings and five lithographs). She soon became well-
known for her woodcuts (c.1917–20), primarily because 18
were published in the spring of 1918 in *Die Aktion*, the most
radical left-wing Expressionist magazine in Berlin. The
imagery and stylistic approaches of the woodcuts typify the
"ecstatic" qualities of late Expressionism. A strong use of
linear and abstract patterning pervades her image of a Christ
figure above a multitude of worshippers (repr. Erfurt 1985,
p.44), and a sense of immediacy through angular spatial movement informs *Dance* (or *Death and the Maiden*) (Staatliche
Galerie Moritzburg, Halle). In *Mourning* the sheer simplification of the figural forms of a dead Christ in white against a
backdrop of lamenting women in black evokes a truly harrowing and empathetic drama (see Ulmer 1992, p.207). Published
as a front cover of *Die Aktion*, this woodcut equally symbolised the mourning of the fallen soldier in World War I. Another
front cover image with political significance was her portrait of
Karl Marx (repr. Rietzschel 1987, pp.903–4).

Heise: *Massacre of the Innocents, c.*1919; sandstone relief; Kloster Unser Lieben Frauen, Magdeburg

In 1917 Heise began to devote herself to sculpture on the recommendation of Kollwitz. Heise remained self-taught but received guidance from Hugo Lederer, a Berlin Academy professor of sculpture. She worked primarily in clay and plaster and casting in bronze, and periodically with various crafts media and architectural materials. Several polychromed reliefs in sandstone (*c.*1917–19) initiated an expressionistic phase until *c.*1924. They related closely to the woodcuts, with their similar working process, formal devices and subject matter. *Massacre of the Innocents* (see illustration), for example, depicts exaggerated figural forms of a male swooping over a mother who clings to her child.

Heise then produced statuette-size figures in "ecstatic" themes and reductivist form, such as her portraits of the "Expressionist dancers" *Harald Kreutzberg* (1919–20) and *Charlotte Bara* (1922; both bronze; Staatliche Galerie Moritzburg). These were followed by female figures that were more robust and voluptuous (under the influence of Alexander Archipenko), and marked by expressions of sorrow – beginning with *Small Striding Woman* (1922; ht 43 cm.; bronze;

Staatliche Galerie Moritzburg) and life-size variations (e.g. *Large Striding Woman, c.*1922–4; plaster?; private collection, Magdeburg, repr. Erfurt 1985, p.12). These voluptuous women signified a maternal and erotic vitalism, not unlike sculptures by Gela Forster (q.v.). Heise's imposing, large-scale figures became the focus of many laudatory reviews of her work after 1925; at one point she was affectionately nicknamed "the fat lady" in Berlin art circles.

Between 1925 and 1933 Heise pursued socialist themes in her sculptures, emphasising clothed figures in more naturalistic styles. The theme of motherhood and its struggles found particular resonance in a number of life-size works. For the State Medical Insurance building in Berlin she produced a standing figure of a mother with suckling infant (*c.*1925; vitrified clay; *idem*). In contrast, *Over-Abundance* (before 1927; plaster; repr. Ranfft 1995, pl.10) presented a lounging female figure (nude and very voluptuous) with several infants struggling to feed from her breasts. Heise's concerns found their clearest ideological platform in the international exhibition *Frauen in Not* (1931), which addressed itself to Germany's current abortion laws and to the social plight of working-class women burdened by pregnancy and motherhood. Her showing of a sculpture of a saddened pregnant mother with child (*c*.1927–30) was reviewed as one of the best works in the exhibition (see Schiff 1931, p.16).

During this period Heise also produced portrait busts of various celebrities of the Berlin arts scene, for example, the conductor *Arthur Nikisch* (1927) and the painter *Max Liebermann* (1931; both repr. Erfurt 1985, p.19). Additionally, she made a number of animal sculptures, such as several dogs, a swan and centaur (e.g. *Great Dane*, 1928–30; bronze; Staatliche Galerie Moritzburg; version in porcelain, repr. Friedrich 1930, p.166).

From 1916 to *c*.1931 Heise worked professionally under the pseudonym of "Karl Luis Heinrich-Salze" (and its variations in print, such as "K.L. Heinrich"). It is intriguing that Heise perpetuated her masquerade as a male artist – to what extent was her career dependent on the existence of "Heinrich-Salze"? To what extent did she separate the masculine identity from her solidarity with other women artists, particularly as she was closely involved with the Frauenkunstverband (Women's Art Union)? Undoubtedly she showed her solidarity and even stronger commitment by mirroring the disenfranchised in the very construction of her pseudonym: it asserted her right as a fully qualified artist, for adding one's birthplace to one's name (in her case, formerly "Gross Salze") was traditionally the birthright of men.

Heise's identification with masculine identity reflected the constructs of the Weimar "Neue Frau" and its discourses on bisexuality and androgyny. Comparisons can be made with the feminine/masculine roles of her Berlin colleagues, the famed women sculptors Milly Steger (q.v.) and Renée Sintenis (q.v.) (see Ranfft 1995, pp.51–4). Several sculptures, at least, by Heise asserted elements of androgyny: in the Berlin Freie Secession exhibition of 1923 she showed a work entitled *Hermaphrodite* (untraced); and in *Over-Abundance* the pose of the mother figure suggests male genitalia from the position of one of the infant's legs.

Heise probably discarded her pseudonym under the pressures exerted by encroaching National Socialist ideologies, which entrenched traditional gender roles according to patriarchal domination. Between 1933 and 1945 her art was declared "degenerate" by the Nazis, her works were confiscated from museums and some of her public sculptures destroyed. She was also prohibited from exhibitions or public commissions, and in 1942 her studio was destroyed in bombings. Thereafter Heise moved back to her parents' home in Schönebeck-Salzelmen (later part of East Germany), where she continued to work, in relative isolation, until the early 1960s. During the 1950s she produced religious works for churches in Nachterstedt and Magdeburg. She also renewed socio-political themes, as in the ceramic relief panel, *Rebuilding* (after 1947; repr. Erfurt 1985, p.21), which represents a group of figures sorting through the rubble of a ghostly cityscape. In 1945 and 1947 she designed memorials for those sacrificed at the hands of Fascism, and in 1959 sculpted a portrait bust of *Anne Frank* (whereabouts unknown).

ERICH RANFFT

Hemessen, Catharina [Catherina, Caterina] van [de]

South Netherlandish painter, 1528–after 1565

Daughter of the Antwerp painter Jan Sanders van Hemessen. Married the musician Chrétien de Morien, and went with him to Spain in the entourage of Queen Mary of Hungary, 1556.

Bibliography

Lodovico Guicciardini, *Descrittione di tutti i paesi bassi, altrimenti detti Germania Inferiore*, Antwerp, 1567; 2nd edition, 1588

Giorgio Vasari, *Le vite de' più eccellenti pittori, scultori ed architettori*, Florence, 1568; ed. Gaetano Milanesi, vii, Florence: Sansoni, 1881, p.588; as *Lives of the Most Eminent Painters, Sculptors and Architects*, 10 vols, London: Macmillan-Medici Society, 1912–15, ix, p.269; reprinted New York: AMS, 1976

Johan van Beverwyck, *Van de wtnementheyt des vrouwelicken geslachts* [On the excellence of the female sex], Dordrecht, 1639

Christiaan Kramm, *De levens en werken der Hollandsche en Vlaamsche kunstschilders, beeldhouwers, graveurs en bouwmeesters* [The lives and works of the Dutch and Flemish painters, sculptors, engravers and architects], ii, Amsterdam, 1859

Elizabeth F.L. Ellet, *Women Artists in All Ages and Countries*, New York: Harper, 1859

F. Joseph Van den Branden, *Geschiedenis der Antwerpsche Schilderschool* [History of the Antwerp school of painting], Antwerp, 1883

Exposition de la Toison d'or à Bruges, exh. cat., Bruges, 1907

Felix Graefe, *Jan Sanders van Hemessen und seine identification mit dem Braunschweiger monogrammisten …*, 2 vols, Leipzig, 1908

Kurt Erdmann, "Notizen zu einer Ausstellung flämischer Landschaftmalerei im 16. und 17. Jahrhundert", *Repertorium für Kunstwissenschaft*, xlix, 1928, pp.211–19

Jean Denucé, *Inventare von Kunstsammlungen zu Antwerpen im 16. u. 17. Jahrhundert*, Antwerp: De Sikkel, 1932

Le Portrait dans les Anciens Pays-Bas, exh. cat., Musée Communal des Beaux-Arts (Musée Groeninge), Bruges, 1953

Flandres, Espagne, Portugal du XVe au XVIIe siècle, exh. cat., Galerie des Beaux-Arts, Bordeaux, 1954

Simone Bergmans, "Le problème Jan van Hemessen, monogrammiste de Brunswick: Le Collaborateur de Jan van Hemessen: L'Idendité du monogrammiste", *Revue Belge d'Archéologie et d'Histoire de l'Art*, xxiv, 1955, pp.133–57

——, "Note complémentaire à l'étude des De Hemessen, de van Amstel et du monogrammiste de Brunswick", *Revue Belge d'Archéologie et d'Histoire de l'Art*, xxvii, 1958, pp.77–83

Le Siècle de Bruegel: La Peinture en Belgique au XVIe siècle, exh. cat., Musées royaux des Beaux-Arts de Belgique, Brussels, 1963

Simone Bergmans, "Le problème du Monogrammiste de Brunswick", *Bulletin Musées Royaux des Beaux-Arts de Belgique*, xiv, 1965, pp.143–62

Irmgard Hiller and Horst Vey, *Katalog der Deutschen und Niederländischen Gemälde bis 1550 … im Wallraf-Richartz-Museum und im Kunstgewerbemuseum der Stadt Köln*, Cologne: Wallraf-Richartz-Museum, 1969

Gert von der Osten and Horst Vey, *Painting and Sculpture in Germany and the Netherlands, 1500–1600* (Pelican History of Art), Harmondsworth and Baltimore: Penguin, 1969

Eleanor Tufts, *Our Hidden Heritage: Five Centuries of Women Artists*, London: Paddington Press, 1974

Max J. Friedländer, *Early Netherlandish Painting*, xii, New York: Praeger, and Leyden: Sijthoff, 1975 (German original, 1935)

Arthur van Schendel and others, *All the Paintings of the Rijksmuseum in Amsterdam: A Completely Illustrated Catalogue*, Amsterdam: Rijksmuseum, 1976

Hemessen: *Portrait of a Man*, 1552; National Gallery, London

Women Artists, 1550–1950, exh. cat., Los Angeles County Museum of Art, and elsewhere, 1976

Jeannine Lambrechts-Douillez, "The Ruckers family and other harpsichord makers in Antwerp in the sixteenth and seventeenth centuries", *Connoisseur*, cxciv, 1977, pp.266–73

Henri Hymans, ed., *Le Livre des peintres de Carel van Mander (1548–1606)*, 2 vols in 1, Amsterdam: Hissink, 1979 (van Mander discusses Jan van Hemessen but not Catharina; Hymans includes her in his commentary, p.77)

The Women's Art Show, 1550–1970, exh. cat., Nottingham Castle Museum, 1982

Burr Wallen, *Jan van Hemessen: An Antwerp Painter Between Reform and Counter-Reform*, Ann Arbor, MI: UMI Research Press, 1983

Martin Davies, *Early Netherlandish School*, National Gallery Catalogues, 4th edition, London, 1987 (revised edition by Lorne Campbell in preparation)

Mary Ann Scott, *Dutch, Flemish and German Paintings in the Cincinnati Art Museum: Fifteenth Through Eighteenth Centuries*, Cincinnati: The Museum, 1987

Catalogus Schilderkunst: Oude Meesters [Catalogue of painting: Old masters], Koninklijk Museum voor Schone Kunsten, Antwerp, 1988

Maria van Hongarije, 1505–1558: Koningin tussen keizers en kunstenaars [Mary of Hungary, 1505–1558: Queen among emperors and artists], exh. cat., Zwolle, 1993

Karolien De Clippel, *Catharina van Hemessen*, PhD dissertation, University of Leuven (in preparation)

Catharina van Hemessen was the daughter of the Antwerp painter Jan Sanders van Hemessen. The earliest reference to her is in Guicciardini's *Descrittione de tutti i paesi bassi*, first published in Antwerp in 1567. She is included among four living women artists considered to be famous not only in the Netherlands, but in much of the world. Guicciardini mentions that she was the wife of the musician Chrétien de Morien, that the couple went to Spain with Queen Mary of Hungary, and were well provided for at her death (1588 edition, pp.130–31). Vasari gives a similar account in the second edition of his *Vite* (1568), although he lists her among miniaturists in his chapter on *Divers Flemings* (Vasari 1976, ix, pp.268–9); based on Vasari, she is sometimes erroneously cited as a miniaturist. Catharina is mentioned also in Johan van Beverwyck's *Wtnementheyt des vrouwelicken geslachts* of 1639. He includes the four artists mentioned by Guicciardini (among others) and much of the same information, but adds that Catharina learned her art from her father (fols 290–91). At least one work by Catharina, a portrait of a man, is recorded in an Antwerp collection in the 17th century (Denucé 1932, p.107).

Specific dates are not given in these early sources. Mary, younger sister of the emperor Charles V and married to Louis II of Hungary, was widowed in She returned to the Netherlands and took over as governor-general in 1531 after the death of her aunt Margaret of Au1526. stria. Her primary residence was at the palace in Brussels, and a court ordinance of 1555 lists "kleine Catheline" as lady-in-waiting, among other court functionaries (Zwolle 1993, pp.189 and 202). Charles V abdicated in 1555 and the following year Charles, Mary and their sister Eleanor left for Spain, with Catharina and her husband in the entourage. In 1558, after Eleanor's death and at the urging of Charles and the Spanish monarchs, Mary agreed to return to the Netherlands where her expertise was needed in the conflicts with the French. Charles died in

September and, as Mary prepared to leave Spain the following month, she too died. At this time we have no documents or sources to indicate exactly what Catharina might have painted while in Spain, and whether she and her husband left immediately after Mary's death for the return trip to the Netherlands. The following year the Cremonese painter Sofonisba Anguissola (q.v.) was invited to join the court of the new Spanish queen Elisabeth (later Isabel) of Valois as lady-in-waiting, but there is no evidence that Catharina was still there or that the two artists met in Spain.

Catharina's date of birth was determined by the inscription and date on the *Self-Portrait* of 1548: EGO CATERINA DE HEMESSEN ME PINXI 1548 ETATIS SVÆ 20 (31 × 25 cm.; Kunstmuseum, Basel). Catharina presents herself here as a serious painter, seated at her easel as she looks out at the viewer while working on a framed panel with a face visible in its upper-left corner. From the same year, the painting of a young woman at the virginal (32.2 × 25.7 cm.; Wallraf-Richartz-Museum, Cologne: CATERINA DE HEMESSEN PINGEBAT 1548 ÆTATIS SVÆ 22) probably represents her sister Christina. As noted in Los Angeles 1976 (p.105), there is a strong resemblance between the two sitters, they face each other and the panels are almost identical in size, suggesting that they may have been intended as pendants. Catharina's father portrayed a young girl playing a clavichord (1534; Worcester Art Museum, Worcester, MA), also about three-quarter length but set in a more elaborate room. The instruments in both are precisely portrayed, and the virginal in Catharina's painting is decorated with a printed dolphin design on paper with a partial inscription that is identical to one on an existing instrument of 1644 (see Lambrechts-Douillez 1977). A slightly smaller portrait of a young woman is sometimes also considered a self-portrait, but the inscription does not establish this and the resemblance is not convincing (24 × 17 cm.; Rijksmuseum, Amsterdam: CATHERINA DE HEMESSEN PINXIT 1548).

The other portraits signed by Catharina van Hemessen or attributed to her are similar in size, with three-quarter-length figures, hands visible, set against plain backgrounds and dressed in fashionable clothes. They accord with the direction that her father's portrait style took in the 1540s, which was to be developed in the work of Antonis Mor in his portraits for Habsburg patrons, including Mary of Hungary. Pendant portraits of 1549 (*Portrait of a Man*: CATHERINA DE HEMESSÉ PINGEBAT 1549 ÆTATIS SVÆ 42; *Portrait of a Woman*: CATHERINA DE HEMESSEN PINGEBAT 1549 ÆTATIS SVÆ 30; both 22 × 17 cm.; Musées royaux des Beaux-Arts de Belgique, Brussels) follow this format. The couple is portrayed with quiet dignity and an easy naturalism; only the hands betray some weakness in drawing. Two separate portraits in the National Gallery, London, are of elegantly dressed sitters, and the anatomy is now somewhat more expertly rendered. The lady holds an equally elegant dog under her right arm (22.7 × 175 cm.; CATHARINA DE HEMESSEN PINGEBAT 1551), while the man grasps a sword hilt in his right hand (CATHARINA.FILIA IOANNIS DE HEMESSEN PINGEBAT. 1552. "over another, apparently similar inscription or signature", as noted in Davies 1987, p.67; see illustration). An attributed *Portrait of a Young Woman* (20 × 15 cm.; Koninklijk Museum voor Schone Kunsten, Antwerp) is described as once having the monograms CJGF and

CHF visible, but this would seem to be atypical. Another version of this painting was on the art market in 1939 (17.8 × 13.8 cm.; American Art Association sale, Anderson Galleries, Inc., 20 April 1939; listed as Catherina Hemessen and said to be accompanied by a signed certificate of endorsement by Max J. Friedländer). Other attributed portraits include: *A Lady* (36.8 × 27.9 cm.; Holburne Museum and Crafts Study Centre, Bath; attributed to Zucchero in the 19th century), elaborately dressed in what appears to be court costume, *A Young Lady* (30.4 × 22.9 cm.; Baltimore Museum of Art: c.1560 suggested), *A Woman* (33 × 25 cm.; Fitzwilliam Museum, Cambridge) and *A Man* (34 × 25.2 cm.; Rhode Island School of Design, Providence).

Catharina is best known as a portrait painter, and the most frequently reproduced works are the two portraits of 1548. She also painted religious subjects, three of them signed (and possibly one more, the *Crucifixion*). A *Rest on the Flight into Egypt* (74.5 × 64 cm.; Musée de la Vie Montoise, Maison Jean Lescarts, Mons; once mistakenly recorded as signed 1555, see Erdmann 1928, pp.211–12) carries the inscription CATERINA DE HEMESSEN PINGEBAT but no date. The unusually large panel shows the Virgin seated with the Christ Child standing on her lap, situated on a rise in front of a tree with an extensive landscape background. It recalls several compositions attributed to Catharina's father (repr. Friedländer 1975, figs 197–202). *Christ and Veronica* is signed CATHARINA DE HEMESSEN PINGEBAT (30 × 40 cm.; Convent des Pères Redemptoristes, Mons; see Brussels 1963, p.110, cat. no.127, ill.121). Bergmans states here that if a work is not signed as on this painting, it cannot be attributed to the artist. As we have seen, however, the spelling of the name varies, and certainly there may be works that were not signed or with now lost inscriptions. The painting shows a standing Christ carrying the cross followed by a crowd of figures, with the kneeling Veronica at the lower left. A signed and dated *Flagellation* (21.6 × 34.9 cm.; CATHARINA FILIA IOANNIS DE HEMESSEN PINGEBAT 1555) from a private collection was in a Christie's sale of 20 October 1988 (lot 127). The three main figures are large and set close to the picture plane, their bodies twisted in Mannerist torsion and strongly reminiscent of some of her father's figures. Indeed, in this inscription, Catharina again proudly proclaims herself daughter of Jan.

On the other hand the three figures in the *Crucifixion* are calm in pose and project a quiet sorrow (ex-Palais des Beaux-Arts, Brussels; Brussels Keyaerts sale, 18–19 November 1946, lot 260; according to a photograph in the Rijksbureau voor Kunsthistorische Documentatie, The Hague, the work was signed CATHARINA; no other information available). Other works are sometimes mentioned as all or in part by Catharina, for example a diptych of *SS Peter and Catherine* in the Catharinaconvent, Utrecht, and the *Tendilla Retablo* (open: 3.55 × 4.57 m.; Cincinnati Art Museum: Jan Sanders van Hemessen, studio, with Catharina van Hemessen). In this large altarpiece of *Scenes from the Old and New Testaments*, comprising 13 panels, four different hands can be identified. The panels attributed by the Cincinnati Museum to Hand B are closest to van Hemessen's style in the *Crucifixion* and in the portraits in London and Brussels. While probably painted for a Spanish patron, these panels are considered to date from just before her departure from the Netherlands rather than from the years in Spain, and it is suggested that she may have carried the panels with her when she left (Wallen 1983, pp.123–4; Scott 1987, pp.69–73).

Efforts have been made to detect Catharina's hand in the backgrounds of some of her father's compositions, and to identify the Brunswick Monogrammist as Jan, Catharina or another artist (see Bergmans 1955, 1958 and 1965; von der Osten and Vey 1969, p.199; Friedländer 1975, pp.44–52, 136–8). These questions have hardly been resolved and require further investigation.

Catharina van Hemessen was honoured by mention in her lifetime and by the court position she secured. She left signed and dated works to document her activity. Yet much remains to be done fully to understand her career and her contributions to the art of 16th-century Flanders. Archival research in Habsburg court documents may reveal other references to the artist and her duties for Mary of Hungary, and records in Spain may also yield information. It is surely premature to say that she did not paint after her marriage, or that her role as lady-in-waiting precluded painting for the queen and her court. The existence of signed and dated works presents the opportunity for scientific examination of the known paintings in order to establish a basis for authenticating attributed works – for example, the new technique of infra-red reflectography could provide the "handwriting" of the artist's underdrawing for comparison purposes.

Van Hemessen's portraits exhibit changes in the 1550s towards a severe yet elegant and sophisticated style, different from the naive and intimate early works, no doubt reflecting the demands of court patronage. The humanistic and artistic atmosphere at the court, and Mary of Hungary's contacts with Erasmus and Luther and the ideas of the Reformation have been documented (Zwolle 1993). Jan van Hemessen's art was affected by the turbulent religious currents of the time, and may have had an impact on his daughter's attitudes and prospects (Wallen 1983). The impact of the painters, architects, sculptors and musicians resident there, as well as the books and manuscripts that were available in the court libraries, should also be evaluated. We would then be able to add valuable evidence for the contributions of women artists in the Netherlands of the 16th century.

LOLA B. GELLMAN

See also Court Artists and Amateur Artists surveys

Henderson, Louise

New Zealand painter, 1902–1994

Born Louise Sidonie Sauze in Paris, 21 April 1902; father once Rodin's secretary. Attended the Ecole des Arts Industrielles, Paris, 1920–21. Employed as embroidery and interior designer on *Madame* magazine, 1921–7; also contributed embroidery designs to Belgian journal *La Femme et la Home*. Married Hubert Henderson and moved to Christchurch, New Zealand, 1925; daughter born 1933; husband died 1963. Taught embroidery and design at Canterbury School of Art, Christchurch, from 1925 (honorary diploma of fine arts 1931). Exhibited with the

New Zealand Society of Artists, 1933–4; first exhibited with The Group, Christchurch, 1935. Moved to Wellington, 1941. Taught needlework and established new course in embroidery at New Zealand Correspondence School, 1942–5. Taught art and craft at the Wellington Teacher's College, 1944–50. Attended classes at Victoria University, Wellington, 1945–9. Moved to Auckland with her family, 1950; attended classes at Elam School of Fine Arts under Archibald Fisher and began working in John Weeks's studio. Exhibited with the Thornhill Group, 1951. Visited London, then stayed in Paris, studying at the Atelier Frochot under Jean Metzinger, 1952. Returned to New Zealand, 1953. Only woman to be included in Colin McCahon's *Object and Image* exhibition, Auckland City Art Gallery, 1954. Accompanied husband (educational adviser to UNESCO) to the Middle East, 1956–8, also visiting London and Paris. Taught full-time at Elam School of Fine Arts, and taught classes at Auckland City Art Gallery, 1959–60. Taught painting and design at Darlinghurst School of Art, Sydney, 1961. Travelled to Brussels, Paris and London for openings of exhibition with Milan Mrkusich, 1965–6. During 1970s, tutored in painting and design in Auckland and other places in New Zealand. Married Thomas Lücke, 1985. Dame Commander, Order of the British Empire (DBE), 1994. Died in Auckland, 27 June 1994.

Selected Individual Exhibitions

Wellington Public Library: 1948
Auckland City Art Gallery: 1953, 1959 (with Colin McCahon and Kase Jackson), 1991 (retrospective)
Architectural Centre, Wellington: 1955
Macquarie Galleries, Sydney: 1959, 1960
Centre Gallery, Wellington: 1961, 1964
John Leech Gallery, Auckland: 1963, 1979, 1980, 1981, 1982, 1983 (retrospective)
Dunedin Public Art Gallery: 1965
Ikon Gallery, Auckland: 1965–6 (*Elements: Air and Water*, touring, with Milan Mrkusich's *Emblems*)
New Vision Gallery, Auckland: 1966 (with Jean Horsley), 1968, 1970, 1971, 1972, 1973, 1974, 1975, 1976
Vincentore Gallery, Brighton: 1967 (with Rosemary Brabant)
Canterbury Society of Arts Gallery, Christchurch: 1972
Court Gallery, Copenhagen: 1979
Charlotte H. Gallery, Auckland: 1987, 1988

Selected Writings

"Embroidery, a living art", *Art in New Zealand*, xiv, September 1941, pp.37–8
The Story of Knitting, Wellington: Owen, 1953 (for children)

Bibliography

Colin McCahon, "Louise Henderson", *Home and Building* (Auckland), February 1954, pp.40–41, 69
C.K. Stead, "The development of Louise Henderson's vision: A personal note", *Artis*, i/3, 1971, pp.25–6
Elizabeth Eastmond and Merimeri Penfold, *Women and the Arts in New Zealand: Forty Works, 1936–86*, Auckland: Penguin, 1986
Elizabeth Grierson, "Louise Henderson", *Art New Zealand*, no.46, 1988, pp.77–81
——, *The Art of Louise Henderson, 1925–1990*, MA thesis, University of Auckland, 1990
Louise Henderson: The Cubist Years, 1946–1958, exh. cat., Auckland City Art Gallery, 1991
Anne Kirker, *New Zealand Women Artists: A Survey of 150 Years*, 2nd edition, Tortola, BVI: Craftsman House, 1993

The French-born New Zealand artist Louise Henderson is significant for her contribution to the development of modernism in New Zealand art, most notably in the 1950s and 1960s. In particular, she introduced a Cubist-derived painting practice that confidently and elegantly dealt with still lifes, figure studies, urban scenes and portraiture at a time when the predominant subject matter in New Zealand art was landscape. During these decades she was linked with major experimental painters – Colin McCahon, Milan Mrkusich, Michael Nicholson and John Weeks – and was singled out for critical attention by such contemporary critics as Janet Paul, E.H. McCormick and I.V. Porsolt.

Although her painting career began in the 1920s in Christchurch, where she took up the characteristic flat, painterly style of the Canterbury School, Henderson's mature style can be recognised only once she began painting full-time after her move to Auckland in 1950. Here she came under the influence of John Weeks, a significant painter and teacher, whose modest, semi-abstract compositions, deriving from his study of the work of Cézanne and his time spent in the studio of André Lhôte, had shaped the outlook of an emerging generation of Auckland painters. *Still Life, Glass and Painted Cloth* (1950; private collection, repr. Auckland 1991, p.9), though uncharacteristically an oil painted on glass, clearly reveals her debt to Weeks, with its pattern-like play of colour and texture and its overlapping planes bounded by heavy black lines.

Weeks encouraged Henderson to undertake further study in London and Paris. Her time spent in the Atelier Frochot (in 1952) under the tutelage of Jean Metzinger was critical in the development of her work. Metzinger's late Cubist compositions provided her with a model that was at once both abstract and strikingly rational in its classicising clarity. She was able to find a way in which to combine her interest in accurate observation from life with her desire to transform her subject matter into two-dimensional compositions. Henderson's solo exhibition at the Auckland City Art Gallery on her return to New Zealand in 1953 shows the extent of her development. Here she exhibited a cohesive group of paintings, drawings and pastels based on her studies in Paris. Thinly painted, to accentuate the linear play of her draughtsmanship and to highlight the overlapping of colour planes, the works were remarked on for their clarity of drawing, the subtlety of their colour and for their sophisticated reference to a Cubist manipulation of form. In *Maori Matrons* (1953; private collection, *ibid.*, p.12) Henderson's new interest in the human form is evident. Interestingly, she turned her attention to local subject matter, investing her figures with a statuesque grandeur that is indebted as much to Gauguin as to Metzinger. Henderson's exhibition, the first one-person show by a contemporary artist at the Auckland City Art Gallery, was a significant moment in New Zealand art history. Her work was especially selected for this auspicious event because, to a community struggling to achieve cultural maturity, her stylised late Cubist idiom represented "modernity". As the reviewer Tom Bolster put it, her work was "so well ahead of most of that being done in New Zealand, so technically accomplished, so imaginative, original and exploratory that only those who had recently been abroad could appreciate the level she had reached" (quoted in *ibid.*, p.25).

Henderson: *Jerusalem Series No.4*, 1957; Auckland Art Gallery Collection

Henderson participated in the crucial *Object and Image* exhibition organised by Colin McCahon at the Auckland City Art Gallery in 1954. This exhibition, which brought together such abstract artists as McCahon, Mrkusich, Kase Jackson and Nicholson, was the first to set out a programme for modern art in New Zealand. In a review of her work, McCahon applauded Henderson's ability to synthesise her observations of nature into the unified field of the picture surface, which he, like his contemporaries, believed was the aim of the contemporary artist (McCahon 1954, p.69). At this moment McCahon and Henderson had these aims in common, although McCahon's interests lay with landscape, atmospheric conditions and light, while Henderson concentrated almost exclusively on the linear or planar massing of built or human forms. In the later 1950s, after spending time in the Middle East, she completed the *Jerusalem Series* (1957–8), the works of which demonstrate the logical continuation of such thinking (e.g. *Jerusalem No.4*, 1957; see illustration). Their hard-edged linearity and syncopated interplay of light against dark owe something to contemporary French art, most particularly that of the Abstraction-Création group whose work Henderson had seen at the Denise René Gallery in Paris (1956–7).

After a brief respite from painting in the early 1960s, Henderson began to paint on a larger scale in a far looser, more expressive manner. In *The Lakes* (1965; Auckland City Art Gallery) her characteristic blocks of colour are almost obscured by sweeping brush strokes and areas in which wet pigments run together. Almost purely abstract, the work evokes a watery realm in which the horizon is almost obliterated. *The Lakes* is a vestigial landscape. It signals her return to nature, which, with her ongoing fascination for the human figure, remained the predominant motif in her work from this date.

Henderson played a central role in these years in bringing abstraction into the arena of contemporary art in New Zealand. Her reputation has, however, suffered, partly because of the so-called decorative nature of her work and partly because of her refusal to subscribe to nationalist (or feminist) agendas. In a long and productive career – she continued to paint into her nineties – she proved the seriousness of her endeavour. She has also served as an example of the vagaries of critical attention; as the emphasis has shifted between the poles of nationalism and internationalism, abstraction and realism, she has occupied both central and peripheral positions in the discourses of New Zealand art history. Her work is represented in all major public galleries in New Zealand.

CHRISTINA BARTON

Henri, Florence
American photographer and painter, 1893–1982

Born in New York, 28 June 1893. Lived in various European capitals, 1895–1905, with her father, the director of an oil company, after her mother's early death; lived on the Isle of Wight, England, 1906–8. Studied music at the Accademia di Santa Cecilia, Rome, and met avant-garde musicians, writers and painters, 1909–11. Studied piano in Berlin under Egon Petri and later Ferruccio Busoni, 1912–13; abandoned music for painting, 1914; met art historian and critic Carl Einstein, who became a mentor. Lived in Berlin during World War I. Studied painting in the studio of Johannes Walter-Kurau, Berlin, 1922–3. Trip to Italy with Einstein, 1923. Married house servant Karl Anton Koster in Switzerland, acquiring Swiss citizenship, which enabled her to move to France, 1924; divorced 1954. Studied at the Académie Moderne, Paris, under Fernand Léger and Amédée Ozenfant, c.1925–7; attended summer session at the Bauhaus, Dessau, studying under László Moholy-Nagy, Wassily Kandinsky and Paul Klee, 1927. Decided to pursue a career in photography, 1928. Joined Michel Seuphor's group Cercle et Carré, Paris, which championed abstract geometric art, 1929. Opened commercial photographic studio in Paris, c.1929–30. Stayed in Paris during World War II; photographic production curtailed. Moved to Bellival, Compiègne, 1962. Died in Laboissière-en-Thelle, Oise, 24 July 1982.

Principal Exhibitions

Individual
Studio 28, Paris: 1930
Museum Folkwang, Essen: 1933
Galerie de la Pléiade, Paris: 1934
Galerie Wilde, Cologne: 1974
Galleria Martini & Ronchetti, Genoa and New York: 1974–5
Westfälischer Kunstverein, Münster: 1976 (touring)
Musée d'Art Moderne de la Ville de Paris, 1978 (retrospective)
Musée d'Art et d'Histoire, Geneva: 1981
Museum of Modern Art, San Francisco: 1990–92 (touring retrospective)

Group
Syndicat des Antiquaires, Paris: 1925 (L'Art d'aujourd'hui)
Salon d'Automne, Paris: 1925
Galerie d'Art Contemporain, Paris: 1926, 1931
Deutscher Werkbund, Stuttgart: 1929 (Film und Foto, touring)
Museum Folkwang, Essen: 1929 (Fotografie der Gegenwart, touring)
Munich: 1930–31 (Das Lichtbild, touring)
Art Center, New York: 1931 (Foreign Advertising Photography, honourable mention)
Julien Levy Gallery, New York: 1932 (Modern European Photography)

Bibliography

m-n [László Moholy-Nagy], "Zu den Fotografien von Florence Henri", I 10, no.17–18, 20 December 1928, pp.117–18

H.K. Frenzel, "Florence Henri: Paris", Gebrauchsgraphik: International Advertising Art, xiii, June 1936, pp.40–45
Romeo E. Martinez, "The woman as photographer: Florence Henri, a grande dame of photography", Camera, xlvi, September 1967, pp.4–19
D. Seylan, "Florence Henri", Creative Camera, no.97, July 1972, pp.234–41
Franz Roh and Jan Tschichold, eds, Foto-Auge/Oeil et photo/Photo-Eye: 76 Fotos der Zeit, New York: Arno, 1973; London, 1974 (German original, 1929)
Florence Henri, exh. cat., Galerie Wilde, Cologne, 1974
Florence Henri, exh. cat., Galleria Martini & Ronchetti, Genoa and New York, 1974
Maurizio Fagiolo dell'Arco, Florence Henri: Una riflessione sulla fotografia, Turin: Martano, 1975
Women of Photography: An Historical Survey, exh. cat., San Francisco Museum of Art, and elsewhere, 1975
Florence Henri: Photographies, 1927–1938, exh. cat., Musée d'Art Moderne de la Ville de Paris, 1978
Claudio Marra, "Le fotografie alla seconda di Florence Henri", G7 Studio, iv, January 1979, pp.4–7
Avant-Garde Photography in Germany, 1919–1939, exh. cat., Museum of Modern Art, San Francisco, and elsewhere, 1980
Herbert Molderings, "Florence Henri, 1893–1982", Kunstforum International, lii, August 1982, pp.137–9 (obituary)
Bauhausfotografie, exh. cat., Institut für Auslandsbeziehungen, Stuttgart, and elsewhere, 1983
Attilio Colombo and Romeo Martinez, Florence Henri: I grandi fotografi, Milan: Fabbri, 1983
Beatrice Laurent, Florence Henri: Peintre et photographe des années 20, MA thesis, Institut d'Art et d'Archéologie, Paris, 1986
Christiane Herzig, Florence Henri: Das fotografische Werk der 20er und 30er Jahre, MA thesis, Ludwig-Maximilians-Universität, Munich, 1989
Jeannine Fiedler, ed., Photography at the Bauhaus, Cambridge: Massachusetts Institute of Technology Press, 1990 (German original)
Florence Henri: Artist-Photographer of the Avant-Garde, exh. cat., Museum of Modern Art, San Francisco, and elsewhere, 1990
Naomi Rosenblum, A History of Women Photographers, New York: Abbeville, 1994
Florence Henri, exh. cat., Villa Aurélienne, Fréjus, 1995

Florence Henri was born in the USA but spent most of her life in France, where she was closely associated with the major figures of European modernism. Initially a student of painting at André Lhôte's Académie Montparnasse and from c.1925 to 1927 a member of the Académie Moderne directed by Léger and Ozenfant, she quickly became a gifted and knowing participant in the most advanced art movements of the time – late Cubism, Purism and Constructivism. In 1928, having spent the summer of 1927 at the Bauhaus in Dessau, she turned to the camera and moved swiftly from the avant-garde of one art form to the avant-garde of another. When Henri adopted photography as her new medium, the modernist ideas that had stimulated her as a painter continued as a vital base for her formal and structural aesthetic. For a heady ten years before the interruption of World War II, she created a rich body of work – still lifes, abstract compositions, advertising photographs, portraits, self-portraits, nudes, street photographs and photo-montages – that contributed to the development of geometric abstract art and of New Vision photography in France.

Significant in forming Henri's approach to photography was her period of study at the Bauhaus, where Neues Sehen (New Vision) photography was promulgated by one of the

Henri: *Still-Life Composition, No.76 (Mirrors and Ball)*, 1929; gelatin-silver print; 26.2 × 36.5 cm.; Museum of Modern Art, New York; John Parkinson III Fund

institution's most prescient and controversial *Formmeisters*, László Moholy-Nagy. Henri attended individual classes at the Bauhaus offered by Moholy-Nagy, Kandinsky and Klee, but as an older student with considerable previous training, she did not enroll in the full programme. The Bauhaus instruction of most importance to Henri was the *Vorkurs*, the two-part, year-long foundation course, the first segment of which was taught by Josef Albers and the second by Moholy-Nagy. Even though photography was not formally taught at the Bauhaus during the period of Henri's attendance there, experiments using photography were carried out in Moholy-Nagy's portion of the *Vorkurs*. It was in the exhilarating setting of the Bauhaus that Henri made her first photographs. For Henri, photography reinvigorated the issues that had been important in her painting: the use of simple, rectilinear forms, the rhythmic interplay of flat planes and a predilection for a language of geometric abstraction. She identified with the formal language of Constructivism, already predominant at the Bauhaus and then taking root in Paris, and viewed the photographic image as a "constructed" object in which the hand, and even more the intellect of the artist, is always self-consciously present.

Spurred by the Bauhaus debate on the viability of easel painting in the machine age, Henri's primary focus would

centre on photography soon after her return to Paris. She settled in Montparnasse, the dynamic centre for a small but energetic group of artists dedicated to the cause of geometric abstract art, and although she turned to photography, Henri's ties to painting remained strong. Her circle continued to consist of Léger and students from the Académie Moderne, while it expanded to include the Dutch-born Piet Mondrian, the Belgians Michel Seuphor and Georges Vantongerloo, the Uruguayan Joaquín Torres-García, the Alsatian Jean (Hans) Arp and his Swiss wife, Sophie Taeuber-Arp (q.v.), and the French Robert Delaunay and his Russian-born wife, Sonia Delaunay (q.v.). These artists, either members of the Cercle et Carré group or affiliated with the publications *L'Art Contemporain* and *Abstraction-Création*, formed the milieu in which Henri moved and nurtured her dedication to non-objective principles.

Like others imbued with the spirit of New Vision photography, Henri experimented with radical new methods. The most distinctive aspect of her photography in its early period is her extensive use of the mirror. It figures prominently in Henri's early portraits, still lifes and abstract compositions of the late 1920s and would continue as a major visual and metaphorical preoccupation until the early 1930s. Henri's manipulation of two-dimensional space by way of mirrors and the camera lens allowed her to extend the formal inventions of Cubism and Constructivism. Conceptual as well as perceptual, her pictorial conundrums were metaphors for the complexity of modern life as well as philosophical investigations into the nature of art and photography's special connection to the real.

Between 1928 and 1930 Henri's still lifes and abstract compositions were created in the spirit of the machine age. During the period 1931–2, however, she reinvented these genres with a sensibility that revealed a new connection to nature. At the same time she adopted the technique of collage as a complement to her construction of complicated pictorial spaces. If in Henri's hands the mirror was the ideal instrument for manipulating space and form to create pictorial ambiguity, it also provided the perfect tool for the analysis of self. Her own image is a recurrent theme in Henri's photographic oeuvre and the mirror figures in almost every self-portrait she made.

The stock market crash of 1929 having reduced her allowance, Henri was forced to establish a commercial photographic studio, where she made advertising photographs for such products as Lanvin perfume and La Lune pasta. She also sought income through commissioned portraiture. At the same time she continued her personal work in the genre. If defining the modern woman and artist guided Henri in her self-portraiture, it was the *raison d'être* for her striking portraits of other women.

By the early 1930s Henri also began making urban excursions to photograph life in the street. Like many artists who had emigrated to Paris, she was charmed by the city and experimented with the theme, photographing its people and environs. Throughout Henri's street and documentary photography her concern for composition remains consistent, as does her regard for the beauty of geometric form. In 1931, increasingly comfortable in using the camera as a documentary tool, she began making photographs of the architectural and sculptural ruins of Italy. The straightforward images she continued to produce over the next four years became the raw material for the creation of a series of dreamlike montages that express a new kinship with Neo-classicism and the Italian Novecento artists.

As the 1930s progressed, Henri's production waned in proportion to the growing social and political turmoil in Europe. With the outbreak of World War II, her work was hampered by the scarcity of photographic film and paper and was finally disrupted by the Nazi prohibition of photography during the Occupation. After the war Henri made photographic portraits on occasion, but essentially she returned to painting. Her canvases, now predominantly street scenes and landscapes, not abstractions, were inspired by travels to her favourite places – Italy, Spain, Greece and the Canary Islands. She also found a new interest – quilt-making – to which she could, in the manner of her friend Sonia Delaunay, apply the lessons of modernism in terms of colour and design.

In 1962 she moved to Bellival, a small village in the Compiègne region northeast of Paris, where she lived until her death in 1982. While Henri never regained the energy and inventiveness that marked the years between the wars, she spent her last decade making an extensive series of non-objective collages of cut paper, works reminiscent of those she had created at the Bauhaus in 1927. She also supervised the

enlargement and transfer of her signature photographs to photo-sensitised linen.

DIANA C. DU PONT

Henry, Grace
Irish painter, 1868–1953

Born Grace Mitchell in Peterhead, near Aberdeen, Scotland, 10 February 1868, to the Reverend John Mitchell and his wife Jane. Took up painting in her mid-twenties and began to exhibit at the Society of Aberdeen Artists' annual exhibitions. Studied under Ernest Blanc-Garrins in Brussels, 1899. Moved to Paris, and enrolled as a student in the atelier of Delacluse, 1900. Married Irish painter Paul Henry in London, 1903; separated 1930 (exhibited as "Mrs Paul Henry" until the marriage failed). Moved to Achill Island, off the extreme west coast of Ireland, 1910. Settled in Dublin, 1919; during the following decade studied intermittently in France under the Spanish artist Garrido, and under François Guelvec and André Lhôte. Lived a rootless existence in Ireland after separating from Paul Henry, but frequently returned to continental Europe, painting around the northern Italian lakes. Member, Society of Dublin Painters, 1920–c.1950s. Honorary member, Royal Hibernian Academy, 1949. Died in Dublin, 11 August 1953.

Principal Exhibitions

Individual
Cooling Galleries, London: 1929
Dublin Painters' Gallery, Dublin: 1930, 1934
Brook Street Galleries, London: 1933
Waddington Gallery, Dublin: 1939, 1941, 1943, 1945
Calman Gallery, London: 1939
Dawson Gallery, Dublin: 1946

Group
Royal Hibernian Academy, Dublin: occasionally 1910–52
Whitechapel Art Gallery, London: 1913 (*Irish Art*)
Society of Dublin Painters: occasionally 1920–35
Galerie Barbazanges, Paris: 1922 (*L'Art irlandais*)
New Irish Salon, Dublin: 1924–7
Hackett Galleries, New York: 1929 (*Irish Art*)
Leicester Galleries, London: 1930 (*Irish Art*)
Palais des Beaux-Arts, Brussels: 1930 (*L'Art irlandais*)
Irish Exhibition of Living Art, Dublin: 1943, 1947–9
Rhode Island School of Design, Providence: 1950 (*Irish Art*, touring)
Municipal Gallery of Modern Art, Dublin: 1953 (*Irish Painting, 1903–53*))

Bibliography

Mairin Allen, "Contemporary Irish artists, 15: Grace Henry", *Father Mathew Record*, xv, November 1942, p.4
Irish Art, 1900–1950, exh. cat., Crawford Municipal Art Gallery, Cork, 1975
The Irish Impressionists: Irish Artists in France and Belgium, 1850–1914, exh. cat., National Gallery of Ireland, Dublin, 1984
Irish Women Artists from the Eighteenth Century to the Present Day, exh. cat., National Gallery of Ireland, Dublin, and elsewhere, 1987

Kenneth McConkey, *A Free Spirit: Irish Art, 1860–1960*, Woodbridge, Suffolk: Antique Collectors' Club-Pyms Gallery, 1990

S.B. Kennedy, *Irish Art and Modernism, 1880–1950*, Belfast: Institute of Irish Studies, 1991

The Paintings of Paul and Grace Henry, exh. cat., Hugh Lane Municipal Gallery of Modern Art, Dublin, 1991

Images and Insights, exh. cat., Hugh Lane Municipal Gallery of Modern Art, Dublin, 1993

Grace Henry lived for the greater part of her life in the shadow of her husband, the landscape painter Paul Henry. In recent years, however, she has been recognised for her own qualities and, in Ireland, is increasingly seen as a painter of considerable ability and diversity. Grace Henry's career may be divided into three different phases: her early or Achill period, 1910–19, Dublin period, 1920–30, and late period, post-1930. In none of these periods is her work fully resolved; rather it suggests always a fluidity and restlessness determined, no doubt, by her temperament, which, characteristically, alternated between periods of gregariousness and introversion. By the time of her arrival on Achill Island, she was already in her forties and thus well beyond her formative years. As a young woman at home in Aberdeen she had been brought up in considerable comfort in a large, well-to-do family, but from the time of her father's death in 1895 her circumstances became greatly reduced. With her husband on Achill she led a frugal existence, a shortage of money always being a problem. In the end the strains imposed by such a life, combined with the loneliness that she felt on the island, destroyed her marriage.

Little of Henry's early work survives, but her *Girl in White* (*c*.1900–10; Hugh Lane Municipal Gallery of Modern Art, Dublin), with its closely modulated tones and limited range of colours, is distinctly Whistlerian in quality and illustrates the development of her work before she went to the west of Ireland. Little survives even from her early Achill period, but that which does is genre in character, representing the island people going about their everyday lives. *Top of the Hill* (1914–15; Limerick Art Gallery), for example, has a strong narrative element and is executed in a semi-illustrative manner – the picture, originally entitled *Achill Women*, depicts a group of three shawled women gossiping over something or other. The tendency that can be seen here to outline forms with a dark line also characterises much of Henry's work until the 1920s. Other compositions done in these years, such as *Mallarany* (private collection, Dublin) and the *Black Shawl*, which also have a genre quality, show in the juxtaposition of strong complementary colours the influence of Fauvism, which she would have encountered in Paris. Her landscapes of the same period, the Fauvist *Country of Amethyst* (private collection, Dublin) and *Landscape with Three Cottages* (Ulster Museum, Belfast), being excellent examples, are characterised by great economy of means both in conception and execution. In the latter work, the bold forms of the composition and the severely limited palette, with the blue sky and mountain in the background contrasting with the warm orange-yellows of the cottage roofs and cornfield, illustrate her debt to recent French painting.

By the 1920s Henry had become more experimental with a distinctly expressionist manner as can be seen, for example, in the splendidly vivacious *Spring in Winter, No.9* (*c*.1922–5;

private collection, Belfast). Here the tight precision of her earlier compositions has given way to a gusto of emotions that are set down with great spontaneity. This change of technique no doubt resulted from her deteriorating relationship with her husband, and the composition can be read as a *cri de coeur* for the anguish within her. At some time in 1924 Henry went to Paris and, so far as we know, remained there for almost a year. She studied briefly under the Cubist painter André Lhôte – who had an immense influence on a number of Irish women painters at this time – but seems to have been little swayed by him and her own free manner prevailed.

In 1930, amid considerable acrimony, Grace Henry, then aged 62, and her husband Paul separated, and although they were never divorced they agreed henceforth to go their own ways. Yet, the separation notwithstanding, Grace retained an affection for Paul that was unrequited, so that the remaining years of her life had a melancholy that she never overcame. Despite her domestic problems, the 1930s were a fruitful period for Henry. She spent long periods in continental Europe, painting landscapes in France, Spain and Italy and, stimulated by the bright sunshine of the south, produced some of her best-remembered pictures. As in *Red House at Mougins* (private collection, Belfast), these late works are characterised by the use of strong vibrant colours applied with fervour. Her favourite painting spots at the time included the northern Italian lakes and Venice, and she delighted in painting sun-drenched buildings, harbours with light shimmering on the water and the bright sails of boats. She also produced a number of still lifes in these years, all characterised by the use of strong colours and vigorous brushwork; stylistically, these recall the Fauvist-inspired work of her early years.

As the clouds of war approached in the late 1930s, Henry settled in Ireland, where she continued her semi-nomadic existence, moving from house to house and friend to friend. Her last years were lonely, yet she continued to paint and exhibited regularly at the Royal Hibernian Academy, of which she was elected an honorary academician in 1949, and held a number of solo exhibitions at the influential Waddington Gallery in Dublin. After her death in 1953, her reputation declined, but happily recovered in the 1970s. She is now, rightly, seen in an Irish context as an experimental painter of considerable ability.

S.B. KENNEDY

Hepworth, Barbara
British sculptor, 1903–1975

Born in Wakefield, Yorkshire, 10 January 1903. Won scholarship to Leeds School of Art, where first met Henry Moore, 1920; studied sculpture at Royal College of Art, London, 1921–4 (diploma). Awarded Yorkshire County Council travelling scholarship, 1924; lived in Florence and Siena. Married sculptor John Skeaping in Florence, 1925; lived in Rome for 18 months before moving to London, where son Paul born 1929 (killed in air crash while serving in the Royal Air Force, 1953); divorced 1933. Triplets, one son, two daughters, by artist Ben Nicholson born 1934; married Nicholson, 1936; separated 1951. Member, Seven and Five Society, London,

1931–6; Abstraction-Création group, Paris, 1933–5; only woman member, Unit One, London, 1934. Visited France frequently, 1932–6; met Picasso, Braque, Mondrian, Brancusi, Gabo, Herbin and Hélion. Moved to Cornwall with her family, 1939; purchased Trewyn Studio, St Ives, 1949. Founder-member, Penwith Society of Arts, Cornwall, 1949. Recipient of gold medal for sculpture, Hoffman Wood Trust, Leeds, 1951; second prize, Unknown Political Prisoner competition, London, 1953; Grand Prix, São Paulo Bienal, 1959; Lion of St Mark plaque, International Festival of Films on Art, Venice, 1962; Foreign Minister's award, Tokyo Biennale, 1963; Grand Prix, Salon International de la Femme, Nice, 1970; honorary doctorates from University of Birmingham, 1960; University of Leeds, 1961; University of Exeter, 1966; University of Oxford, 1968; University of London, 1970; University of Manchester, 1971. Trustee of Tate Gallery, 1965–72. Freedom of Borough of St Ives, 1968; Bard of Cornwall, 1968. Honorary fellow, St Anne's College, Oxford, 1968; senior fellow, Royal College of Art, London, 1970; honorary member, American Academy of Arts and Letters, 1973. Commander (CBE), 1958, and Dame (DBE), 1965, Order of the British Empire. Died in a fire at studio in St Ives, 20 May 1975. Barbara Hepworth Museum opened in St Ives, 1976.

Selected Individual Exhibitions

Beaux Arts Gallery, London: 1928
Arthur Tooth Gallery: 1930 (with John Skeaping), 1932 (with Ben Nicholson)
Reid and Lefevre Gallery: 1933 (with Ben Nicholson), 1937, 1946, 1950, 1952, 1954
Temple Newsam, Leeds: 1943 (retrospective, with Paul Nash)
Wakefield City Art Gallery: 1944, 1951 (both touring retrospectives)
Venice Biennale: 1950 (retrospective)
Whitechapel Art Gallery, London: 1954, 1962 (both retrospectives)
Walker Art Center, Minneapolis: 1955–6 (touring retrospective)
Gimpel Fils, London: 1956, 1958, 1961, 1964, 1966, 1972, 1975
São Paulo Bienal: 1959–60 (touring retrospective)
Moderna Museet, Stockholm: 1964–5 (touring, organised by British Council)
Rijksmuseum Kröller-Müller, Otterlo, Netherlands: 1965–6 (touring retrospective)
Tate Gallery, London: 1968 (retrospective)
Hakone Open-Air Museum, Kyoto: 1970 (touring)
Abbotsholme, Uttoxeter: 1970–71 (touring, organised by Arts Council of Great Britain)
Marlborough Fine Art, London: 1972

Selected Writings

"The sculptor carves because he must", *The Studio*, civ, 1932, pp.332–3
"Sculpture", *Circle*, ed. J.L. Martin, Ben Nicholson and Naum Gabo, London: Faber, 1937, pp.113–16; reprinted 1971 and in Witzling 1991
Statement in *Unit 1*, London, 1943, pp.17–25
"Approach to sculpture", *The Studio*, cxxxii, 1946, pp.100–01
Carving and Drawings, London: Lund Humphries, 1952 (with Herbert Read)
"Greek diary", *J.P. Hodin: European Critic*, ed. Walter Kern, London: Cory, Adams and Mackay, 1965
A Pictorial Autobiography, Bath: Adams and Dart, and New York: Praeger, 1970; 3rd edition, London: Tate Gallery, 1985

Bibliography

Lillian Browse, ed., *Barbara Hepworth: Sculptress*, London: Faber, 1946
A.M. Hammacher, *Barbara Hepworth*, London: Zwemmer, 1958; New York: Universe, 1959 (Dutch original)
Edouard Roditi, *Dialogues on Art*, London: Secker and Warburg, 1960; interview with Hepworth reprinted in Prosyniuk 1992, pp.256–8
J.P. Hodin, *Barbara Hepworth: Life and Work*, London: Lund Humphries, and Boston: Boston Book and Art Shop, 1961
Michael Shepherd, *Barbara Hepworth*, London: Methuen, 1963
Alan Bowness, *Drawings from a Sculptor's Landscape*, London: Cory, Adams and Mackay, and New York: Praeger, 1966
Barbara Hepworth, exh. cat., Tate Gallery, London, 1968
Alan Bowness, ed., *The Complete Sculpture of Barbara Hepworth, 1960–69*, London: Lund Humphries, 1971
A.M. Hammacher, *The Sculpture of Barbara Hepworth*, 2nd edition, London: Thames and Hudson, and New York: Abrams, 1987
Barbara Hepworth: The Art Gallery of Ontario Collection, exh. cat., Art Gallery of Ontario, Toronto, and elsewhere, 1991
Mara R. Witzling, ed., *Voicing Our Visions: Writings by Women Artists*, New York: Universe, 1991; London: Women's Press, 1992
Joann Prosyniuk, ed., *Modern Arts Criticism*, ii, Detroit: Gale Research, 1992
Barbara Hepworth: A Retrospective, exh. cat., Tate Gallery, Liverpool, and elsewhere, 1994
Margaret Gardiner, *Barbara Hepworth: A Memoir*, revised edition, London: Lund Humphries, 1994
Sally Festing, *Barbara Hepworth: A Life of Forms*, New York and London: Viking, 1995
Re-presenting Barbara Hepworth, Liverpool: Tate Gallery and University of Liverpool Press, 1996 (contains extensive bibliography)

Hepworth–Read correspondence is in the Herbert Read Archive, University of Victoria, Canada; some of Barbara Hepworth's files of correspondence with dealers, art galleries and institutions are in the Tate Gallery Archive, London; the rest remain with the Estate.

Barbara Hepworth's working career covered a full 50 years, from 1925 to 1975. Thus, although Hepworth tends to be earmarked for certain contributions, it is important to remember that her career was a long one, and more diverse than is commonly realised. The context in which she is most often placed is that of the group of British and Continental modernists who came together in Hampstead, London, in the decade before World War II. By this time Hepworth was living with her second partner, the painter Ben Nicholson, and they were close to Henry Moore and the critic Herbert Read. Read promoted Hepworth and Moore as the first of a new generation of direct carvers, sculptors who returned to the block of stone in the manner of medieval or non-Western carvers. In fact, Hepworth had been carving direct since the mid-1920s, and with her first husband, John Skeaping, was part of a recognised group of stone carvers by the end of that decade.

Skeaping was an important contact for Hepworth in terms of educating her about carving, because the technique was by no means part of the contemporary syllabus for a fine art training. It may be that Hepworth was able to learn something about carving from the craft teachers at the Royal College of Art, but she was actually enrolled in the sculpture school, whose teachers still believed in modelling from life in clay or plaster before turning over the work to the foundry or the stonemason. An early work such as *Doves* (c.1927; Manchester City Art Galleries) typifies the context of the

Hepworth: *Mother and Child*, 1934; grey stone; Tate Gallery, London

mid-1920s, in which carvers tended to use animal and bird subjects as a way of escaping the constraints of the figurative tradition. It also demonstrates a concern to show the stone from which the carving emerges (in which it probably draws still from the treatment of Rodin's marbles). Hepworth and Skeaping made a series of animal carvings in the late 1920s, and these found favour with a group of patrons in London who were otherwise associated with oriental studies and collections. It would seem that the appreciation of form in the non-Western tradition allowed a greater tolerance of these first steps towards an appreciation of form for form's sake in sculpture. Other works, for example, *Mask* (1928), *Kneeling Figure* (1932; both Wakefield City Art Gallery), *Head* (1930; Leicester Art Gallery) and *Torso* (1932; Aberdeen Art Gallery), show Hepworth's knowledge of and interest in the non-Western traditions of carving that she found in the British Museum.

World War I had caused a significant hiatus in British sculpture, and thus in Hepworth's early works we can see her consolidating some of the steps that had been made earlier by Jacob Epstein and Eric Gill. *Mother and Child* (1927; Art Gallery of Ontario, Toronto), which is actually signed Barbara Skeaping, is of the same date as *Doves* but reveals a greater interest in the block of stone itself. Whereas the concern of the traditional 19th-century or Edwardian sculptor was to create an illusion by setting the carving free of its block, the new creed sought to bring attention to the stone itself, and to the symbiotic relationship between the medium and the image within.

The *Mother and Child* of 1927 should probably be seen as much in the light of Henry Moore's development of this theme as in Hepworth's. It is the first "Maternity" in her work, and prefigures the important series she made from 1932 to 1934. Hepworth's own pregnancies frame, rather than coincide with, her work on the maternity theme. She had her first child in the summer of 1929, and her triplets in the autumn of 1934, and shortly afterwards began to make her first really abstract work. It is through her "Mother and Child" carvings that Hepworth began to work out her tendency to pierce the stone and to group pieces in relation to each other. In many ways the removal of stone at the centre of the figure, and its apparent fashioning into the small dependent form, seem integrally bound up with the development of the hole in modern sculpture. It is somewhat difficult to mark out which of Hepworth's works should be included within this series, partly because of the possibility of including even abstract compositions with larger and smaller components, and also because a number of works from this period are now lost or destroyed. There are eight works from 1932 to 1934 that bear the title, but the only readily accessible example is the carving of 1934 in grey Cumberland stone acquired by the Tate Gallery, London, in 1993 (see illustration). This piece probably post-dates Hepworth's first pierced work by three years, and shows her instead developing the conceit of the "hole" being the "baby", the form that is removed from the main body of the stone and now balanced precariously on the knee of the parent stone.

Thereafter Hepworth's compositions of two or three forms become less organic and much more regular; they are now spheres or polyhedrons arranged on grounds of the same material. In 1934–5 she made over half a dozen variations on *Two Forms*, and two *Three Forms* compositions (both Tate Gallery). By this point, however, the theme had expanded well beyond that of the mother and child, and should be seen to include also such works as *Discs in Echelon* (1935; Museum of

Modern Art, New York) and the more mathematical groupings of segments and spheres. This turn in Hepworth's work can be referred to the increasingly disciplinarian approach taken by the small group of like-minded artists who saw themselves as making concrete abstract art, and the fact that the grouping in Hampstead came to include further continental European immigrants, such as Naum Gabo and Mondrian, who brought with them the more austere approach of Constructivism, in contrast to the organic or Surrealist aspect of Moore's carving. Although the bringing together of forms on one plane was to remain important to Hepworth, another motif, which also first made its appearance in the mid-1930s, is perhaps of greater significance for her later oeuvre. This is that of the "Single Form", which by 1937 had assumed its distinctive role within Hepworth's production (see *Single Form* of 1937–8; holly wood; Leeds City Art Gallery).

Hepworth continued her exploration of the single, double and triple form motifs throughout the 1930s. Reintroducing wood into her range of materials allowed her greater freedom in this exploration, and probably encouraged the trend away from the predominantly horizontal compositions in carved stone towards the verticality of the single form. When World War II broke out in 1939 and Adrian Stokes offered Hepworth, Nicholson and their children accommodation near St Ives in Cornwall, this rhythm was abruptly broken. Although Hepworth never intended to settle there, and at first yearned to return to London, she was to stay in Cornwall for the rest of her life, for the next 35 years. In many ways St Ives marks her gradual separation from Nicholson, who was to spend a good deal of time in London, and by 1950 they had definitely fallen out. The war separated many erstwhile close colleagues, and thus Moore moved to Hertfordshire, and Read to Yorkshire. From now on Hepworth was much more on her own, and developed her own vision more or less in isolation. Though physically isolated, she was not cut off. She not only enjoyed a regular correspondence with Read for the rest of his life, but was also actively in contact with galleries, patrons and commissioners. In St Ives Hepworth steadily developed a business concern that was able to deal with and put out sculptures to any part of the world. This, however, was to evolve gradually, and in many ways only after the 1940s.

The 1940s are a distinctive period in that Hepworth was unable to get to work for much of the war, and when she did, she produced a stunning, but ultimately limited collection of abstract sculptures, which refine her pre-war ideas in combination with the stimulus of the Cornish landscape. This group of works is marked by its spherical or conical tendency, as opposed to the vertical feel of her work thereafter. The sculptures are mainly in wood, and set off by the stringing that Hepworth had introduced to her work in 1940 (which she and Gabo both used at this time) and by their painted interiors. Here Hepworth effectively sets up a sustained discourse between interior and exterior, having artificially created the effect of an interior that is separate from its exterior casing. In this group one might well locate some of Hepworth's greatest achievements: *Oval Sculpture* (1943; Pier Gallery, Stromness), *Wave* (1943–4; on loan to Scottish National Gallery of Modern Art, Edinburgh), *Landscape Sculpture* (1944; Hepworth Museum, St Ives) and *Pelagos* (1946; Tate Gallery).

In many ways, however, one can see this group as the delayed culmination of her earlier work, because it is also clear that while she was living in St Ives, the war and some of the post-war initiatives in the art world set Hepworth on to a new agenda. It is possible to read her reaction to the war as a positive one, which led her to set aside the isolation of the Hampstead group, in the face of her feeling that a collective approach was now not only desirable, but also possible. She understood abstraction as always to have been on the side of socialism, but now she felt herself to be really part of a community (St Ives), and able to respond to the new opportunities for an artist to be part of the reconstruction of society. Hepworth was certainly one of those avant-garde artists espoused by the new bodies set up for the encouragement of the arts in Britain: the Arts Council and the British Council chief among them, but reflected also in the development of the New Towns, educational planning and building, and the schemes of the London County Council.

A new period in Hepworth's career began with her commission in 1949 to make a large outdoor sculpture for the Festival of Britain site of 1951. This work – *Contrapuntal Forms*, 3 metres high, and now in Harlow New Town, Essex – marks the beginning of Hepworth's career as a public sculptor. With this commission came also the beginning of the press and public attention that put Hepworth up alongside (but still, at this point, secondary to) Britain's established public sculptors: Epstein, Moore and Dobson. Her recognition within the new artistic establishment being created by the two Councils is revealed by the fact that, after Moore was shown at the Venice Biennale of 1948, Hepworth was chosen for the Biennale of 1950. What should, however, have been a triumph, turned out badly for her. The 1950 Biennale as a whole was much less well received than that of 1948 (which was the first after World War II), and, for Hepworth, its particular timing meant that she was thereafter seen as Moore's disciple.

It is likely that it was the new interest in the human figure and humanitarian values brought on by the war that encouraged Hepworth to turn back to figuration. This tendency is most overt in her drawings of the period 1947–53, but visible too in her carvings. Those in stone attempt to integrate a human profile into an otherwise abstract whole (*Biolith*, 1948–9, and *The Cosdon Head*, 1949; both Birmingham City Art Gallery; *Hieroglyph*, 1953; Leeds City Art Gallery), while those in wood tend towards a broadly human form in their monolithic disposition (*Rhythmic Form*, 1949; British Council; *Figure (Churinga)*, 1952; Walker Art Center, Minneapolis; *Two Figures*, 1954–5; Art Institute of Chicago).

It was in 1956 that Hepworth first used metal, at first in the form of copper sheet, and thereafter in the more traditional bronze. Because she (like Moore) had previously attacked so fiercely this indirect way of making sculpture, one has to assess what her reasons might have been for this volte-face. It goes without saying that making bronzes not only made the work of a public sculptor more practicable (essentially quicker) but also allowed larger work to be supported through the sale of smaller-scale spin-offs in edition. It is also known from Hepworth's correspondence that in their touring programme the British Council preferred to use bronzes because they were more resistant to damage. It is also clear that she was increasingly aware of how well Moore was doing, and it is likely that she would have identified bronze as a way of giving herself a greater advantage in the competition. But metals were also the materials of post-war sculpture, and by using them Hepworth was also placing herself in a new generation, and a new sensibility. Moreover, bronze offered her creative opportunities in terms of opening up her work. Some of her most significant public commissions, *Meridian* (1958; originally for an office on High Holborn, London; now at Pepsico, USA) and *Winged Figure* (1957–62; John Lewis, Oxford Street, London), show how bronze allowed Hepworth to make stronger, lighter works. Her crowning achievement within the stakes of public sculpture, however, is a monolithic bronze, 6.6 metres high, outside the Secretariat building of the United Nations in New York. This work, *Single Form*, which was unveiled in 1964, reveals its origins instead in an earlier wood-carving. Its significance lies as much in Hepworth's relationship with the man it commemorates – Dag Hammarskjöld, the Secretary General of the UN – and their common concern to make order out of chaos.

For ten years Hepworth's use of bronze mirrors her career as a maker of large-scale works for public sites. During the last decade of her career, however, she returned to carving in marble and slate, and to smaller-scale, grouped compositions along the lines of her pre-war works. She was increasingly ill in this period, and would have been unable to produce these works without her assistants. Nevertheless, it is clear that in such pieces as *Three Part Vertical* (1971), *Two Rocks* (1971; artist's estate) and *Fallen Images* (1974–5; Hepworth Museum) the sculptor is returning not only to the tradition of Brancusi and modernist carving, but also to her own early works, such as the *Doves* of 1927 and *Three Forms* of 1934.

PENELOPE CURTIS

Hermes, Gertrude
British artist, 1901–1983

Born in Bromley, Kent, 18 August 1901. Studied at Beckenham School of Art, 1919–21; Leon Underwood School of Painting and Sculpture, London, 1922–5 (finalist in engraving, Prix de Rome, 1925). Married Blair Hughes-Stanton, 1926; daughter born 1927, son born 1929; divorced 1932. Lived in Chiswick, London, until basement flat flooded, destroying work, 1928; moved to Hacheston, Suffolk, 1928; Tregynon, Wales, 1930; Chiswick, 1932. Contributed to literary magazine the *Island*, edited by Joseph Bard, 1931. Exhibited with English Wood Engraving Society, London, 1925–31; London Group from 1934. Admitted to National Register of Industrial Designers, 1938. Selected to represent Britain at Venice Biennale of 1940 (cancelled). Taught life-drawing at Camberwell School of Arts and Crafts and Westminster School of Art, London, before World War II. In New York and Montreal with her children, 1940–45; undertook war work as a draughtswoman for shipyards and aircraft factories, 1942–5. Taught printmaking at Camberwell School of Arts and Crafts, 1939 and 1945–7; St Martin's School of Art, 1939 and after 1945; Central School of Art, 1945–65; Royal Academy Schools, 1965–76, all in London.

Councillor, Print Faculty, British School in Rome, 1952–65. Recipient of Giles Bequest purchase award, Victoria and Albert Museum, London, 1951 and 1961; Jean Davidson medal for sculpture, Society of Portrait Sculptors, 1967. Fellow, 1951, Royal Society of Painter-Etchers and Engravers; honorary member, Printmakers Council, 1977. Associate, 1963, and member, 1971, Royal Academy. Officer, Order of the British Empire (OBE), 1982. Gave up art after a stroke, 1968. Died in Bristol, 9 May 1983.

Selected Individual Exhibitions
St George's Gallery, London: 1928 (with Blair Hughes-Stanton, William McCance and Agnes Miller-Parker)
Winchester Art Club: 1934
Heal's Mansard Gallery, London: 1937
Art Association, Montreal Museum of Fine Art, Canada: 1940, 1945
Towner Art Gallery, Eastbourne: 1949–51 (touring)
Metropole Art Centre, Folkestone: 1963 (retrospective), 1982
Whitechapel Art Gallery, London: 1967 (retrospective)
Peterloo Gallery, Manchester: 1968 (with Elisabeth Vellacott, touring)
Printmakers Council at Oxford University Press, Ely House, London: 1973 (retrospective)
Portsmouth City Museum and Art Gallery: 1974 (touring)
Oban Art Society, Scotland: 1975
New Art Centre, London: 1976
Cootes Gallery, Lewes, Sussex: 1978
Royal Academy, London: 1981 (touring retrospective)

Bibliography
John Gould Fletcher, "Gertrude Hermes and Blair Hughes-Stanton", *Print Collector's Quarterly*, xvi, 1929, pp.183–98
C. Leighton, "Wood-engraving of the 1930s", *The Studio*, 1936, pp.55–65 (special winter issue)
Robert Ayre, "Visitor to Canada: Gertrude Hermes", *Canadian Art*, iii/3, April–May 1946, pp.115–17
Gertrude Hermes: Bronzes and Carvings, Drawings, Wood Engravings, Wood and Lino Block Cuts, 1924–1967, exh. cat., Whitechapel Art Gallery, London, 1967
Gertrude Hermes, RA, exh. cat., Royal Academy, London, 1981
Patricia Jaffe, *Women Engravers*, London: Virago, 1988
Anne Stevens, "Flowers in the wood", *Craft History*, no.2, April 1989, pp.74–81
Penelope Hughes-Stanton, *The Wood Engravings of Blair Hughes-Stanton*, Pinner: Private Libraries Association, 1991
Ten Decades: Careers of Ten Women Artists Born 1897–1906, exh. cat., Norwich Gallery, Norfolk Institute of Art and Design, Norwich, 1992
Judith Russell, ed., *The Wood-Engravings of Gertrude Hermes*, Aldershot: Scolar Press, 1993 (contains list of illustrated books)
James Hamilton, *Wood Engraving and the Woodcut in Britain, c.1890–1990*, London: Barrie and Jenkins, 1994

Gertrude Hermes is most celebrated as a printmaker and "book decorator", as she liked to call herself, but she also produced sculptures in both wood and bronze and a large body of architectural and industrial design decorations, including car mascots, door fittings, inn signs, fountains and weather-cocks. She began wood-engraving in 1922 with fellow students Marion Mitchell (later Stancioff) and Blair Hughes-Stanton while at Leon Underwood's school. With Hughes-Stanton, she showed first at the Society of Wood-Engravers (1924) and then established the English Wood Engraving Society, which in the years 1925–31 was her main place of exhibition, alongside Agnes Miller-Parker and William

McCance. These four printmakers are regarded as linking British wood-engraving to the modern movement. All emphasise a symbolic dimension both in their representations of the natural world and in figurative compositions, employing bold, flat designs, a calligraphic approach to mark-making and using the stark contrasts of black ink against a white page. Prints by Hermes of this period include *The Swimmers* (1924; British Museum, London, and Whitworth Art Gallery, Manchester), *Work (The Studio)* (1925; British Museum and National Gallery of Canada, Ottawa) and *The Fishers* (1924–5; National Art Gallery, Wellington, New Zealand).

Hermes's work as a printmaker is linked to her sculpture, both thematically, in terms of her numerous studies of animals and motifs from nature, and in her emphasis on line, mass, strong curves and dynamic compositions. Many of her early prints and woodblocks were lost when her basement flat was flooded in 1928. With her husband, McCance and Miller-Parker, she moved to Tregynon in Wales to work on a series of books that included *A Florilege* (1929) and four illustrations for *The Pilgrim's Progress*, including the *Slough of Despond* (1928; Ashmolean Museum, Oxford, and Whitworth Art Gallery; see illustration). Although her prints for *A Natural History of Selbourne*, studies of flowers laid out in rich, dense, almost abstract patterns, were produced at this time, they were not published until 1981 (plates in National Library of Wales, Cardiff).

In the 1930s, after separating from her husband and returning to London, Hermes exhibited for the first time at the Royal Academy Summer exhibition (1932) and with the London Group (1934). Among her prints of this period were *Jonah and the Whale* (1933; Ashmolean Museum and Portsmouth City Art Gallery), *One Person* (1937; Tate Gallery) and *Fathomless Sounding* (1934; Tate Gallery and Ashmolean Museum). She also began making more sculpture, developing her initial interest in wood-carving from 1924 when she was inspired by the work of Constantin Brancusi and Henry Gaudier-Brzeska. Her earliest sculptures were of animals and simplified forms that emphasised the dynamic movement of insects or the human figure (*Butterfly Carving*, 1937; repr. Russell 1993; *Baby*, 1932; Tate Gallery, London). *The Frog* was first exhibited at the Third International Exhibition of Contemporary Industrial Art, Museum of Fine Arts, Boston, in 1930. Bryan Robertson aptly described her work as demonstrating "a continual and agreeable tension between sobriety and verve, classical order and sensual impulse" (London 1967, n.p.). Hermes's first portrait commission, a bronze of *A.P. Herbert*, came from her friends and patrons Gwen and A.P. Herbert in 1931, and other commissions followed for these skilfully produced if robustly conventional portrait busts, modelled in clay and cast in bronze (*Lady Herbert*, 1951; *Kathleen Raine*, 1954; both Tate Gallery; *E. Maxwell Fry*, 1965; National Portrait Gallery, London).

In 1925 Hermes had assisted Hughes-Stanton with the murals for the restaurant in the British Pavilion at the Exposition Internationale des Arts Décoratifs et Industriels Modernes in Paris, which marked the beginning of a developing interest in decorative and industrial art. In the late 1920s she started working on road signs and with architects on interior decorations for inns, as well as undertaking a few small commissions for friends for individually designed door knockers and letterboxes, based on animal or figurative motifs. In

Hermes: *Slough of Despond*, 1928; woodcut, from *The Pilgrim's Progress*; private collection, Ashmolean Museum, Oxford

1932 she designed a mosaic floor, a carved centre stone for a fountain and door furniture for the Shakespeare Memorial Theatre, Stratford-upon-Avon. She designed a 9.1-metre sculptured glass window with the "Britannia" motif for the British Pavilion at the Paris Exposition Internationale of 1937, and in 1939 designed three glass panels for the British Pavilion at the New York World's Fair.

In 1937 Hermes's work was represented at an exhibition of the British Society of Wood-Engravers in San Francisco. She was selected in 1939 for the Venice Biennale of 1940 but the exhibition, like her part-time teaching posts in London, was cancelled due to the outbreak of war. Work undertaken during the war years spent in North America included six tempera panels for the British Booth at the Women's Exhibition at Grand Central Palace, New York (1942). On her return to Britain in 1945, Hermes taught printmaking at several London art schools, and began working on large figurative linocuts and woodcuts, adding colour to her images but retaining an interest in both narrative and symbolic compositions. In 1954 she began work on a portfolio, *The Yoke* (1954–75; Tate Gallery), which was conceived as a response to the memorial competition "To the Unknown Political Prisoner".

In 1966, soon after her election as an Associate, she wrote a letter of protest to the Royal Academy that resulted in women academicians being permitted to dine at the Academicians' Banquet, a privilege that had previously been barred to women. In her letter, she states: "no, I am not a feminist, nor have I ever felt the need to fight for rights, or anything like that. Just an artist and as such I cannot accept sex discrimination in the world of Art" (letter to H. Brooke, 8 December 1966, Royal Academy Archives, London). She became one of the first women Associates to teach at the Royal Academy Schools. In the 1960s she carved a large relief mural for the RMS *Empress of Canada* liner and undertook several sculptural commissions, including *Three Swans* (1960) for the London County Council, Ashburton Estate, Wandsworth, and *Peacock* (1961) for Ordsall School. Although she was unable to work after a severe stroke in 1968, she still continued to send in work for exhibition.

KATY DEEPWELL

Herrad
Abbess of Hohenbourg, *c.*1178–*c.*1196

Bibliography

Rosalie Green and others, *Herrad of Hohenbourg: Hortus Deliciarum*, 2 vols, London: Warburg Institute, and Leiden: Brill, 1979 (contains bibliography)

B.S. Eastwood, "The diagram *spera celestis* in the *Hortus deliciarum*", *Annali dell'Istituto e Museo di Storia della Scienza di Firenze*, vi/1, 1981, pp.177–86

Robert Will, "La reconstitution des miniatures de l'*Hortus deliciarum*: A la recherche des sources", *Cahiers Alsaciens d'Archéologie, d'Art et d'Histoire*, xxvi, 1983, pp.99–116

M. Curschmann, "Herrad von Hohenburg (Landsberg)", *Theologische Realenzyklopädie*, xv, Berlin and New York: de Gruyter, 1986, pp.162–4 (contains further bibliography)

Robert Will, "La reconstitution des miniatures de l'*Hortus deliciarum*", *Cahiers Alsaciens d'Archéologie, d'Art et d'Histoire*, xxx, 1987, pp.207–10

Thérèse B. McGuire SSJ, "Monastic artists and educators of the Middle Ages", *Woman's Art Journal*, ix/2, 1988–9, pp.3–9

P.C. Mayo, "*Concordia discordantium*: A twelfth-century illustration of time and eternity", *Album Amicorum Kenneth C. Lindsay: Essays in Art and Literature*, ed. Susan Alyson Stein and George D. McKee, Binghamton: State University of New York, 1990, pp.29–56

Herrad was appointed abbess of the Augustinian convent on the Odilienberg (popularly known as Hohenbourg) in Alsatia before or during 1178; she died in or after 1196. Even by medieval standards, this is a life of obscurity. The date and place of her birth are unknown: the legend that she was a member of the aristocratic von Landsberg family and born in the ancestral castle near Strasbourg is late and probably invented by the family itself. All that is known of her early years is that she was brought up in the convent by her predecessor, the abbess Relindis. There is fragmentary documentation of her administrative abilities, and circumstantial evidence of the high reputation of her house: when the Emperor Henry VI exiled Queen Sibylla of Sicily and her daughters in 1195, it was in Herrad's convent that they took refuge. But it is not as an administrator that Herrad is remembered; it is as the compiler of one of the most celebrated illuminated manuscripts of the Middle Ages: the *Hortus deliciarum*.

A large book (nearly 700 pages over 50 cm. high), the *Garden of Delights* is a retelling of the biblical story of salvation, from the fall of Lucifer to the last judgement. It is told in Latin prose, in verse, in song and in pictures; Herrad's intention, stated on the title-page, was that "the little group of young women should be continually delighted" by her work, and the nuns, as well as reading the book and singing the songs, will have enjoyed exploring the intricate pictures – especially the last, which is a group portrait of all of them, each identified by name. This is a charming, if somewhat self-indulgent painting; the others are of a different and quite unusual character. They are not simply illustrations to the text, but restatements of it in visual form. Often passages from the main text are repeated on the pictures, so the reader has the choice of being informed by word alone, or by word and image. The use of visual aids for teaching was common in the Middle Ages; what is uncommon here is the high quality of the art work, the novelty of the designs and the relative complexity of the ideas represented.

The text is not an original composition, but a collection chosen by Herrad from the work of other writers. Its originality resides in the way it is organised: while the historical narrative provides a solid framework, it is told from various points of view, and Herrad digresses freely into other subjects whenever appropriate. Thus the Genesis account of the creation of the heavenly bodies leads to a discourse on astronomy, which in turn leads to geography before getting back to Genesis and the story of Adam and Eve. In this way the volume acquires some of the qualities of an encyclopedia, and would have provided Herrad's community with a good all-round education.

There is no precedent for a book like this; others had assembled illustrated anthologies; none had done so with Herrad's clear sense of structure, nor with the assistance of such outstanding artists as those she employed. It is not known if these were men or women; the poets of the verses that were specially written for the book were men. Nor is it clear what Herrad's role in the design of the imagery was; in her preface she says only that she was responsible for the text, but it is hard to believe that she was not also involved in what is such a vital part of the *Hortus deliciarum*.

The pictures are of two kinds, narrative and dogmatic. The dogmatic ones are overtly the more remarkable: they present in pictorial form the Church's teaching on such matters as sin, redemption, the Eucharist, and the Christian's proper attitude to classical learning and literature. The illustrations employ symbols, especially symbolic animals, and are often laid out in the circular format that was characteristic of classroom visual aids. The most elaborate of these designs epitomises contemporary ethical teaching as a battle for the soul between medieval knights, and combines dogma with a pictorial chivalric narrative.

Most of the narrative pictures are of biblical subjects, usually arranged in three zones and illustrating the Old Testament selectively and the New Testament exhaustively. Compared with the dogmatic pictures, this may seem like a conservative pictorial programme; but when medieval artists illustrated the Bible, they generally chose from a restricted repertory of familiar subjects: the beginning and the end of Christ's life, for instance, received much more attention than

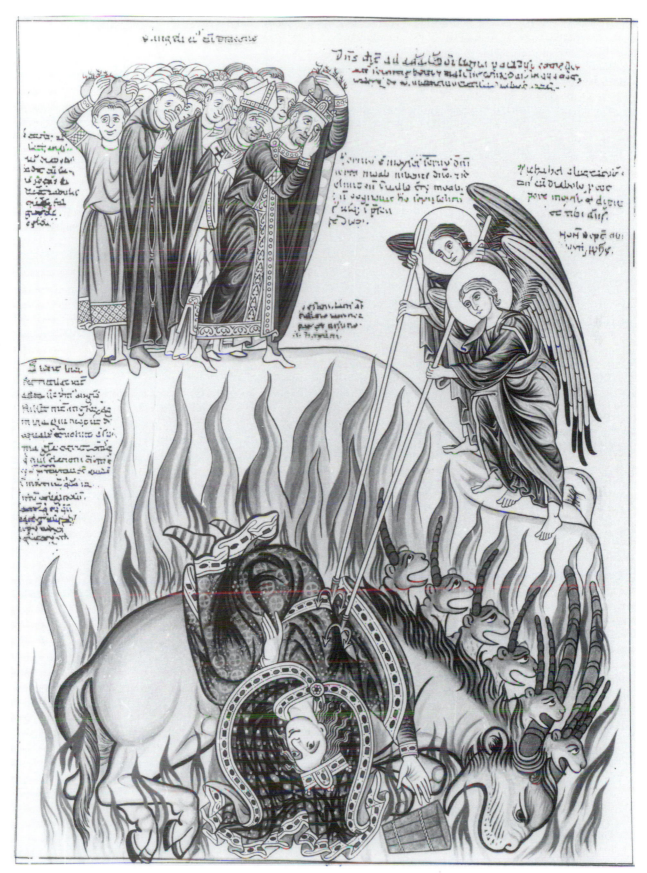

Herrad: *Overthrow of the Whore of Babylon*; photo-montage of 19th-century copy (Paris, Bibliothèque Nationale facsimile fol.8 (xi), pl.18) of *Hortus deliciarum*, fol.258v, with reconstructed text superimposed

his ministry. Herrad's artists were innovative, depicting the miracles and parables in as much detail as the infancy and passion. The artists must have gone to considerable trouble to find prototypes for these pictures, searching through Greek as well as Latin manuscripts to build up an unrivalled collection of New Testament scenes; and what they could not find, they invented. Such topics as the parable of the houses built on rock and sand and St Peter healing with his shadow are otherwise unknown in medieval iconography.

The arrangement in three zones is not invariable; particularly towards the end of the book there are single scenes filling the whole page, and it is these that demonstrate best the quality that, with iconographic originality, characterises Herrad's book: a monumentality that evokes wall-painting or even sculpture. Both qualities are evident in the painting of the overthrow of the whore of Babylon. At the top, the whore's devotees lament her downfall. They face two burly angels with well-developed wings, who thrust the whore, and the beast with seven heads on which she rides, into the pit of hell, where she is engulfed in almost palpable tongues of fire. The figure of the whore falling headlong in her finery is an extraordinary invention, at once fantastic and convincing.

This account of Herrad's work has been misleading in using the present tense. The book was burned in Strasbourg in 1870; all that remains are 19th-century copies of varying quality: fortunately the finest copyist recorded the page described above.

MICHAEL EVANS

Hesse, Eva

American sculptor, painter and graphic artist, 1936–1970

Born in Hamburg, Germany, 11 January 1936, into a Jewish family. Left Germany with elder sister Helen, 1938; joined parents and emigrated to New York, 1939 (later naturalised). Mother committed suicide, 1946. Studied at Pratt Institute (advertising design course), 1952–4; Art Students League, 1953; and Cooper Union, 1954–7, all in New York; at Yale Summer School, Norfolk, Connecticut, 1957; Yale School of Art and Architecture, New Haven, under Josef Albers, Rico Lebrun and Bernard Chaet, 1957–9 (BFA). Moved back to New York, 1959. Married sculptor Tom Doyle, 1961; separated 1966. Lived in Kettwig-am-Ruhr, West Germany, 1964–5; returned to New York, 1965. Began teaching at School of Visual Arts, New York, 1968. Died of a brain tumour in New York, 29 May 1970.

Selected Individual Exhibitions
Allan Stone Gallery, New York: 1963
Kunsthalle, Düsseldorf: 1965
Fischbach Gallery, New York: 1968, 1970
Solomon R. Guggenheim Museum, New York: 1972 (retrospective)

Bibliography
Robert Pincus-Witten, "Eva Hesse: Post-Minimalism into sublime", *Artforum*, x, November 1971, pp.32–44

Eva Hesse: A Memorial Exhibition, exh. cat., Solomon R. Guggenheim Museum, New York, 1972
Robert Pincus-Witten, ed., "Eva Hesse: Last words", *Artforum*, xi, November 1972, pp.74–6
David Shapiro, "The random forms in soft materials and string by the late young innovator Eva Hesse", *Craft Horizons*, xxxiii, February 1973, pp.40–45, 77
Cindy Nemser, *Art Talk: Conversations with 12 Women Artists*, New York: Scribner, 1975
Lucy R. Lippard, *Eva Hesse*, New York: New York University Press, 1976 (contains bibliography)
——, *From the Center: Feminist Essays on Women's Art*, New York: Dutton, 1976
Eva Hesse: Sculpture, exh. cat., Whitechapel Art Gallery, London, and elsewhere, 1979
Eva Hesse: A Retrospective of the Drawings, exh. cat., Allen Memorial Art Museum, Oberlin College, OH, and elsewhere, 1982
Marytha Smith-Allen, *The Art of Eva Hesse, Mel Bochner and Vito Acconci as Indicative of Shifts in Mainstream Art Between 1966 and 1973*, PhD dissertation, New York University, 1983
Ellen H. Johnson, "Order and chaos: From the diaries of Eva Hesse", *Art in America*, lxxi, Summer 1983, pp.110–18
Eva Hesse: The Early Drawings and Selected Sculpture, exh. cat., Rose Art Museum, Brandeis University, Waltham, 1985
Bill Barrette, *Eva Hesse: Sculpture: A Catalogue Raisonné*, New York: Timken, 1989
Charlotte Streifer Rubinstein, *American Women Sculptors*, Boston: Hall, 1990
Eva Hesse: A Retrospective, exh. cat., Yale University Art Gallery, New Haven, and elsewhere, 1992
Eva Hesse, exh. cat., IVAM Centre Julio González, Valencia, and Galerie Nationale du Jeu de Paume, Paris, 1993
Robert Taplin, "Vital parts", *Art in America*, lxxxi, February 1993, pp.70–75
Eva Hesse: Drawing in Space/Bilder und Reliefs, exh. cat., Ulmer Museum, Ulm, and elsewhere, 1994
Anne M. Wagner, "Another Hesse", *October*, no.69, Summer 1994, pp.49–84
Mara R. Witzling, ed., *Voicing Today's Visions: Writings by Contemporary Women Artists*, New York: Universe, 1994
Anne M. Wagner, *Three Artists (Three Women): Modernism and the Art of Hesse, Krasner and O'Keeffe*, Berkeley: University of California Press, 1996

Eva Hesse Archives are in the Allen Memorial Art Museum, Oberlin College; Hesse's diaries and Papers, 1955–1970, are in the Archives of American Art, Washington, DC.

Eva Hesse's career is distinguished not only by the innovative work that she produced between 1960 and her untimely death ten years later, but by an equally impressive mythology that now seems inseparable from it. Labelled an "Abstract Inflationist", "Stuffed Expressionist" and "Eccentric Abstractionist", Hesse never occupied stylistic niches comfortably. Like any discourse developing in a non-defined gap, her work fought against easy classification. While navigating within the formal boundaries of Minimalism, she veered towards extremes that transfigured the minimal object. It is impossible to dissociate the work she did – paintings, painted constructions, sculptures and works on paper – from its critical milieu; her receptiveness to work by Sol LeWitt, Mel Bochner, Donald Judd, Carl André and Agnes Martin (q.v.) was balanced by a deep respect for the work of Jackson Pollock, Willem de Kooning, Claes Oldenburg, Lee Bontecou (q.v.) and Lucas Samaras. Her uneasiness about the cool constraint of the former was tempered by the (sometimes fetishistic) exuberance of the latter. Her own work evolved through empirical processes yet still maintained, as its generative basis, a rigorous order. Courting the notion of absurdity through repetition and the marriage of bipolar tendencies, Hesse's art occupies an important place within the greater history of art of the 1960s; at the same time it continues to influence subsequent generations of sculptors. That she was also a woman who died tragically young, leaving behind candid diaries that reveal her personal trials, adds yet another dimension to the story.

Early on Hesse decided to become an artist. Given the circumstances leading up to this decision – her family's flight from Nazi Germany, her father's remarriage and mother's subsequent suicide – it is not surprising that she gravitated towards a profession that indulged cathartic self-expression. By the time she entered Yale School of Art and Architecture at the age of 21, she was determined to paint, as though painting, rather than sculpture, was a discipline of the highest calling. But from the beginning she struggled with the medium, which seemed to resist her best intentions. And still she persisted. Time and time again she wrote in her diary about "wanting to paint", "needing to paint", "fighting to paint" (New Haven 1992, pp.21 and 22). Apparently, painting was the one thing she felt she had to master, even though at times the task seemed daunting. Her role models then were the first-generation Abstract Expressionists – Jackson Pollock and Willem de Kooning – and in both her painted abstractions and works on paper she emulated their activated surfaces and bravura. Some of the most intriguing pictures from Hesse's postgraduate period (1960–63) are a series of introverted, frontal self-portraits, several of which – *Untitled* (1960; Museum of Modern Art, New York), *Untitled* (1960; Collection Galerie Sophia Ungers, Cologne) and *Self-Portrait* (1961; Collection Ruth and Samuel Dunkell) – were included in the Yale retrospective of 1992. In each of these small-scale pictures, the head dominates the composition. Its features are distorted; eyes are rendered askew, mouths as a bright patch of colour or eliminated entirely. These are troubled images not only for their confrontational distortion but for the struggle with paint that seems to characterise their making. Hesse truly wanted to find her own voice through painting. "I should like to achieve free, spontaneous painting", she wrote, "delineating a powerful, strong, structured image. One must be possible with the other" (*ibid.*, p.23). But her tendency to belabour execution, to rework an idea until structure superseded spontaneity, sometimes compromised the integrity of the image and ultimately made painting a frustrating endeavour.

A combination of spontaneity and structure was more possible with drawing, which became Hesse's breakthrough medium, even though for years she considered it preliminary to painting. Drawing allowed for more process-oriented images. It was fluid, like paint, but capable of greater delicacy and nuance; it allowed the artist's subconscious to bleed through. And Hesse was burdened by it, probably because, in her mind, it did not carry the same historical weight. She could afford to take chances with drawing, and did. More like writing, drawing was a natural extension of her diaristic tendencies, an imagistic counterpart to her ongoing self-analysis.

The drawings reveal a great deal about the origin of many of Hesse's ideas. Ellen H. Johnson, the first person comprehensively to assess Hesse's preoccupation with drawing, noted:

> From the beginning, drawing was close to the centre of Hesse's creativity. It was in her drawings that she first achieved a personal style – and recognition of it. From start to finish, she was a better painter in her drawings than in her work on canvas; and it was finally through her use of line that she discovered she was a sculptor [Oberlin 1982, p.9].

Many of the works on paper executed between 1960 and 1962 are unpretentious studies, whose diminutive scale (one of the largest sheets measures only 27 × 22 cm.) in no way diminishes their importance. Conceived in ink, wash and, in some cases, gouache, some of these images, such as *Untitled* (1960; private collection, repr. New Haven 1992, p.151) and *Untitled* (1961; private collection, *ibid.*, p.153), recall a similar figuration found in Hesse's contemporaneous painting; others, including *Untitled* (1961; Lucy R. Lippard) and *Untitled* (1961; Ellen H. Johnson), explore motifs that later became sculpture.

In 1964 Hesse accompanied Tom Doyle, then her husband, to Kettwig-am-Ruhr, Germany, where they stayed for 15 months as guests of F. Arnhard Scheidt, a German textile manufacturer and art collector interested in Doyle's work. It was a difficult period for Hesse, whose apprehension about returning to a Germany she was forced to leave as a young child, and intermittent bouts of pain at the time, made working difficult. When painting once again seemed impossible, she drew. This time the results were revelatory. About a year before going to Germany, she had been given a solo drawings exhibition at the Allan Stone Gallery, New York. Stylistically, these works ranged from a free-form abstraction – sheets filled with graffiti-like scrawls, patches of colour and, sometimes, geometric forms and arrows – and sparser images in which the repetition of various motifs, mostly boxes and circles, created a more ordered progression. She seemed to be investigating a personalised abstraction, marking more expansive sheets with colour washes, dense linear patterns or crisp outlines, as though they were symbolic microcosms, an arena for enacting scenes of struggle, confrontation and dialogue.

In Germany Hesse explored several graphic styles simultaneously. Drawing liberated her at this juncture, as a catalyst beyond painting. She wrote to her good friend Sol LeWitt back in New York:

> I have done drawings. Seems like hundreds, although much less in numbers. There have been a few stages. First kind of like what was in past, free crazy forms – well done and so on. They had wild space, not constant, fluctuating and variety of forms, etc ... 2nd Stage. Contained forms somewhat harder often in boxes and forms become machine like, real like, and as if to tell a story in that they are contained ... 3rd Stage. Drawings – clean, clear – but crazy like machines, forms larger and bolder, articulately described. So it is weird. They become real nonsense [*ibid.*, p.33].

A recurring motif in the German drawings is the square or rectangle – what Hesse later described as a "box" or "window". It appears in many variations and contexts (in some cases only implied through the inherent dimensions of

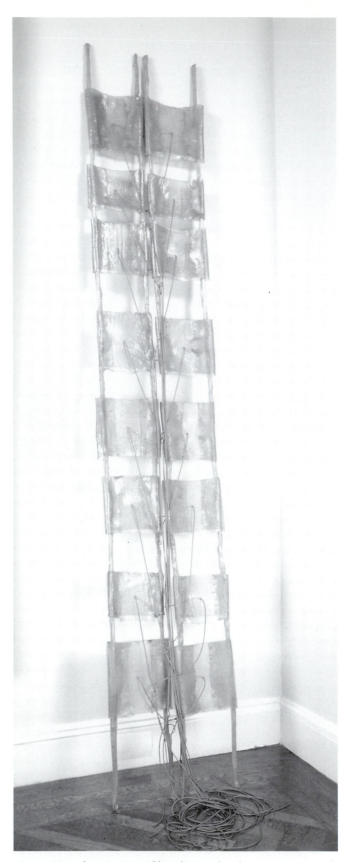

Hesse: *Vinculum I*, 1969; fibreglass and polyester resin, vinyl tubing and metal screen; each of two units, 264.2 × 21.6 × 5.1cm.; Collection of Mrs Victor W. Ganz

the actual sheet) and becomes a leitmotif in both her works on paper and sculptures. Several writers have discussed the significance of this motif (Lippard, *Eva Hesse*, 1976, p.158; Ellen Johnson in Oberlin 1982, p.22; Anna Chave in New Haven 1992, pp.110–12; Wagner 1994, pp.71–5), whose multivalent associations Hesse mined. In one well-known drawing from this period, *And He Sat in a Box* (1964; Barbara Gross Galerie, Munich), the box functions literally as metaphor for self-imposed isolation. This drawing, and others like it, has a diagrammatic quality, like a flow chart with a personal story to tell. In another, *Untitled* (1965; Wiesbaden Museum), the partitioning of the sheet into frames filled with fantastic biomorphic shapes suggests the narrative sequence of a story-board.

The box or window signified many things for Hesse: a frame through which to self-project; an image that may have symbolised her mother's suicide and Doyle's residual presence in her life; a comfort zone; and a continued reference to painting. But other associations are possible as well. Considering Hesse's early training with and admiration for Josef Albers, it is probably no coincidence that the square vehicle for Albers's colour theories became central to her own work. Hesse described herself as "Albers's little color studyist" (New Haven 1992, p.20), and her persistent use of the box (or, for that matter, any variation on the square) would seem inseparable from this formative encounter.

Hesse's interpretations, however, are both a homage and a violation. Her forms are far from perfect. Drawn freehand, stretched and warped, they resonate eccentrically. The box, like the circle, offered Hesse a formal starting point for her own variations and, ultimately, a departure from Minimalism's more austere incarnations. Although formal perfection was compatible with her aesthetic, as some of her exquisitely executed "target" drawings from 1966–7 attest, it was the notion of imperfection, what she later referred to as the "ugly zone", that preoccupied her. Courting the absurd meant avoiding the beautiful and decorative for something clumsy, unresolved, even chaotic.

Hesse returned from Germany to New York in 1965 having produced an impressive number of drawings, as well as 14 wood-and-masonite reliefs, many of which remained with F. Arnhard Scheidt. These painted constructions, first assembled with cord, plaster and, in some cases, discarded machine parts, are technically her first sculptures. Many evolved out of a series of bold contour drawings that recall Francis Picabia's and Marcel Duchamp's biomechanistic morphologies of the 1910s. In their quirky constitution, unlikely combination of organic and geometric forms and labour-intensive execution, works such as *Ringaround Arosie* (1965; Martin Bernstein), *Tomorrow's Apples* (or *5 in White*) (1965; Tate Gallery, London) and *Cool Zone* (1965; Audrey and Sidney Irmas, Los Angeles) set the tenor for subsequent sculptures.

From 1965 until her death Hesse worked primarily as a sculptor. With the confidence of someone who had finally found her calling, she began a protean production, experimenting with new materials such as fibreglass, latex, sculpt-metal and polyester resin and stretching the formal limits of Minimalism. Merging oppositional principle – male/female, resilience/vulnerability, hard/soft, perfect/imperfect – was important to her. So was working the gap between painting and sculpture. She explored a range of images. Some – *Untitled("Bochner Compact")* (1966; Mel Bochner, New York), *Untitled ("Vollmer Balloon")* (1966; Museum of Modern Art, New York), *Compass* (1967; Marilyn Cole Fischbach, New York) and *Iterate* (1966–7; Dr Robert Pincus-Witten, New York) – breastlike and phallic, are smaller scaled and intimate, in some cases studies for larger variations. Others were conceived as more monumental installations. Hesse probed the viability of an idea through what she called "test pieces". Independent works in their own right, and akin to the traditional maquette or bozetto, these preliminary experiments with materials and process initiated some of her most ambitious projects: *Accretion* (1968; Rijksmuseum Kröller-Möller, Otterlo), *Expanded Expansion* (1969; Solomon R. Guggenheim Museum, New York), *Right After* (1969; Milwaukee Art Center), *Contingent* (1969; National Gallery of Australia, Canberra) and *Seven Poles* (1970; Centre Georges Pompidou, Musée National d'Art Moderne, Paris).

There is nothing tentative about Hesse's sculptural statements. And yet a strange fragility permeates much of the work. This sense of vulnerability, due in part to the materials she used, also has to do with the way in which many pieces suspend and extend physically and emotionally. Hesse never intended her sculptures to appear dematerialised or inert, as objects transcending their environment. *Vinculum I* (1969; see illustration) requires a wall to lean against; its origin on the wall and termination on the floor, where rubber tubing falls helter-skelter, highlights the ambiguity between painting and sculpture and plots a progression from order to disorder. *Metronomic Irregularity I* (1966; Wiesbaden Museum) addresses similar issues: two painted panels systematically pierced and gridded are overlaid with skeins of sculptmetal and wire that randomly interconnect the diptych.

Towards the end of her life Hesse investigated a less structured, more amorphic image. In some of her last works on paper – *Untitled* (1969; Gioia Timpanelli) and *Untitled* (1969–70; private collection, Germany, repr. New Haven 1992, p.203) – luminous passages of gouache and watercolour hover within a shifting frame of activated ink lines and shadings. And an untitled rope piece (1970; Whitney Museum of American Art, New York) is the sculptural analogue for controlled chaos. In her last works Hesse moved beyond a discernible motif, what had always been her base ground, a formal and psychological centre. Her late drawings transcended the box by dissolving its borders; a sculpture such as *Right After* (1969; Milwaukee Art Museum), with its skeins of fibreglass cord suspended from the ceiling, yields a different configuration with each installation. It was Robert Pincus-Witten who first noted Hesse's reclamation of an earlier Abstract Expressionist tenet and her transition to another place altogether. "In her last year Eva Hesse discovered the sublime", he wrote, "another place and time at which the critic only guesses and of which the historian maps only these superficial paths" (Pincus-Witten 1971, p.43). That Hesse achieved this state as a sculptor rather than as a painter makes her accomplishment all the more poignant.

DOUGLAS DREISHPOON

Hester, Joy
Australian draughtswoman, 1920–1960

Born in Melbourne, 31 August 1920. Studied at Brighton Technical School, 1936; National Gallery School, Melbourne, 1937–8 (Drawing Head from Life prize 1938). Founder-member of Contemporary Art Society, Melbourne, 1938; exhibited with the group from 1939. Also wrote poetry. Married painter Albert Tucker, 1941; son born 1945. Left Tucker to live with painter Gray Smith, 1947; son born 1951, daughter born 1954; married Smith after divorce from Tucker, 1959. Diagnosed with Hodgkin's disease, 1947; condition deteriorated from 1955. Died in Melbourne, 4 December 1960.

Selected Individual Exhibitions
Melbourne Bookclub Gallery: 1950
Mirka's Café, Melbourne: 1955
Gallery of Contemporary Art, Melbourne: 1957
Museum of Modern Art and Design of Australia, Melbourne: 1963 (retrospective)

Bibliography
Joy Hester: Commemorative Exhibition of Her Drawings, exh. cat., Museum of Modern Art and Design of Australia, Melbourne, 1963

Barrie Reid, "Joy Hester: Draughtsman of identity", *Art and Australia*, iv, 1966, pp.45–53

Janine Burke, *Australian Women Artists, 1840–1940*, Collingwood, Victoria: Greenhouse, 1980

Richard Haese, *Rebels and Precursors: The Revolutionary Years of Australian Art*, Sydney: Penguin, 1981; London: Allen Lane, 1982

Joy Hester, exh. cat., National Gallery of Victoria, Melbourne, 1981

Janine Burke, *Joy Hester*, Melbourne: Greenhouse, 1983

Angry Penguins and Realist Painting in Melbourne in the 1940s, exh. cat., Hayward Gallery, London, 1988

Michael Kean, *An Unsettling World*, North Caulfield, Victoria: Malakoff Fine Art Press, 1993

In the 1940s Joy Hester was the only woman member of "Angry Penguins", a group of young Expressionist painters that included her husband Albert Tucker, as well as Sidney Nolan, John Perceval and Arthur Boyd. It was a period when the art world was divided by rowdy arguments about the function of art and vitriolic exchanges about the moral imperatives of painting and the role of the artist. Melbourne art politics in the war years were not for the faint-hearted. Joy Hester's gift was drawing and, from her student days, she chose to draw rather than to paint, marking her expression through a sure, rapid manner of execution. Drawing was an unusual choice, singling out Hester from her contemporaries, but one apposite for her skills and temperament. Her materials were the cheapest and most accessible; they facilitated speed. She also wrote poetry, creating an evocative and sensuous world in words. In this sense, too, Hester marked out fresh territory for herself. She would be the only artist in her circle to consolidate her literary interests into a body of work.

Despite a truncated art education, Hester's style, even as a young artist, was mature and distinctive. Expressive distortions of form and space were handled easily in her life drawings of the late 1930s. Heavily modelled, then outlined with

Hester: *The Lovers*, *c*.1958; gouache, brush and ink, synthetic polymer paint on card; 101.5 × 63.4 cm.; Art Gallery of South Australia, Adelaide: South Australian Government Grant, 1972

brush and ink, the male and female nudes are among Hester's first works to convey a plastic power independent of the small area they cover. She was uniquely placed to benefit from a diverse number of influences. In the early 1940s Social Realism had a pervasive rather than a distinctive effect on her work, while Surrealism, the other major current, surfaces in one or two drawings. Hester drew street scenes, often peopled with women. Their melancholy expressions, combined with a tender and implicit bond, indicate her true interests – the intimate and private aspects of relationships, disturbed states of mind and the human face.

In 1945 Hester's work developed the psychological and formal power that distinguished her maturity. The head and eyes became the focus in drawings that no longer hint at disturbed states of mind but portray them abrasively. Suddenly Hester could exploit the dramatic qualities of brush and ink to their full potential. The turning point for her was the newsreel footage of the concentration camps liberated by the Allies in 1945 – first Auschwitz by the Russians in January, then Bergen-Belsen by the British in April – which was soon screened worldwide. Hester drew on the films directly, the only Australian artist to do so. In *A Frightened Woman* (1945; Collection Albert Tucker, Melbourne) Hester concentrates and achieves what was essential to her art and what would subsequently direct it: the eye as carrier of meaning. Significantly, it is one of the few works from this period that she signed, dated and titled. Crazed pin-wheel eyes register the depths of violence and injury that a human being can experience, a point at which the essence of being human is itself on the verge of shattering and dissolving.

Hallucinatory masks of terror, passion and love delivered in black and white would now become the subject of Hester's work. Series such as *From an Incredible Night Dream*, *Gethsemane* (both *c*.1946) and *Faces* (1947–8; examples from these series in Museum of Modern Art at Heide, Melbourne, and National Gallery of Australia, Canberra) indicate the intensity of emotion that Hester saw shaping life and relationships. The exaggerated, staring eye not only came to symbolise feeling, but was the stylistic and compositional focus of her drawings. Bliss, suffering and revelation are all suggested by the upward-gazing eye. In the *Love* series (1949; examples in Museum of Modern Art at Heide, National Gallery of Australia and National Gallery of Victoria, Melbourne) Hester drew lovers, their eyes merged – sight unified in the sexual embrace. She conveyed the trembling edge of feeling, a place of extremes, of conflict, change and loneliness. What is most human about her work is also its most abstract quality, the essence of expression, feeling at its most concentrated.

In April 1947 Hester's life changed dramatically. She left Melbourne for Sydney, abandoning her marriage and her two-year-old son. Her companion was Gray Smith, with whom she would spend the rest of her life. She would hear from a specialist in Sydney what she had already been told in Melbourne: that her illness, Hodgkin's disease, a cancer of the lymph glands, was terminal. Hester had never enjoyed the solitude and contemplation of a studio or the luxury of expensive materials. She was used to working fast with whatever came to hand, putting down everything she had to say with speed, clarity and economy: it served her well now. A symptom of Hodgkin's disease was night sweats, when Hester would wake in fright, shaking and drenched in perspiration. Some of the *Faces* series have the quality of a nightmare emerging from a shadowy background, yet their resolution as images, as coherent and moving works of art, firmly grounded in human experience, means that they are more than either a therapeutic exercise or a diary of sensations of distress.

In 1948 Hester entered a period of remission that would last for eight years. She returned to Victoria, to live in the country outside Melbourne. Her next major series, *The Lovers* (begun 1955; National Gallery of Australia, Art Gallery of South Australia, Adelaide, and Art Gallery of Western Australia, Perth; see illustration), depict sites of passion between men and women. Voluptuous sexual abandon, the moment of orgasm, is celebrated as well. Hester was the only Australian woman artist before the late 1960s to celebrate the pleasures of the flesh and the contradictions of love. Her view of the relations between men and women is bleak and unflinching. Love is a battle that must be fought as a primary way of realising the self. Within it, Hester suggests, there can be not only tenderness and fulfilment but also violence that borders on madness and annihilation. Women are constrained, watched and shadowed by men. They are radiant but vulnerable, sexually potent but powerless once in the embrace. Desire involves rapture, but also dissolution. Keeping a distance, maintaining autonomy, are pictured as important but nearly impossible in these drawings. Love is the enactment of a tragedy.

After a move back to the suburbs precipitated by the renewal of the symptoms of Hodgkin's disease, Hester began to draw on her experience of the bush. She probed neither its "romance" nor its anecdotal aspects, both of which she appreciated: she isolated the figure, usually a child, in an empty space where it clutched an animal: a chicken, a lizard, a small bird. *Girl with Turkey* (1957; private collection, Melbourne, repr. Burke 1980, p.163) and *Girl with Hen* (1956; National Gallery of Australia) show the Child protecting that which cannot be saved, an animal about to be slaughtered. They are images of loss and betrayal, richly toned in golds and browns, large, confident, controlled – Hester's final statements as an artist.

Although Hester went on making drawings and poems until the last months of her life, she felt defeated about her status as an artist. At the time of her death in December 1960, her audience was a small group of artists and friends. Her solo exhibitions in the 1950s received uneven reviews and no sales. It was only in 1963 at Hester's Commemorative Exhibition at the Museum of Modern Art in Melbourne that her drawings first received critical praise (there are major collections in the National Gallery of Australia, Canberra, and National Gallery of Victoria, Melbourne).

JANINE BURKE

Hicks, Sheila
American textile artist, 1934–

Born in Hastings, Nebraska, 24 July 1934. Studied under Josef Albers at Yale University, New Haven, 1954–9 (BFA 1957, MFA 1959). Travelled in South America on Fulbright scholarship, 1957–9. Established studio in Taxco el Viejo, Mexico, 1960; settled in Paris, 1965. Married (1) Henrik Schlubach, 1959; divorced; (2) Enrique Zanartu, 1965; two children. Taught at University of Santiago, Chile, 1958; University of Mexico, Mexico City, 1962; Bath Academy of Art, England, 1964 (lecturer in thread exploration); The Hague, 1978; Middlebury College, Vermont, 1979; Fontainebleau, France, 1981–8. Chief editor, *American Fabrics and Fashions* magazine, New York, 1980–83. Directed art programme for new King Saud University, Riyadh, Saudi Arabia, 1983–5. Recipient of gold medal for craftsmanship, American Institute of Architects, 1974; honorary doctorate, Rhode Island School of Design, Providence, 1985; silver medal, Académie de l'Architecture, Paris, 1986. Honorary fellow, Royal Academy of Art, The Hague, 1975; fellow, American Crafts Council, 1983. Lives in Paris.

Selected Individual Exhibitions

Galeria Antonio Souza, Mexico City: 1962
Knoll Associates, Chicago: 1963–7 (touring)
Galerie Nationale de Bab Rouah, Rabat, Morocco: 1971
Musée des Arts Décoratifs, Château des ducs de Bretagne, Nantes: 1973
Stedelijk Museum, Amsterdam: 1974 (retrospective)
Modern Masters Tapestries Gallery, New York: 1974
Israel Museum, Jerusalem: 1980
Evanston Art Center, IL: 1982
Lunds Konsthall, Lund: 1986
Musée des Beaux-Arts, Pau: 1987
Octagon Gallery, Belfast: 1988
Matsuya Ginza Gallery, Tokyo: 1990
Seoul Art Center, Seoul: 1991
Walker's Point Center for the Arts, Milwaukee: 1992
Perimeter Gallery, Chicago: 1995

Bibliography

Betty Werther, "Radical rugs from Rabat", *Design*, no.270, June 1971, pp.48–53
——, "Sheila Hicks at Rabat", *Craft Horizons*, xxxi, June 1971, pp.30–33
Sheila Hicks, exh. cat., Musée des Arts Décoratifs, Château des ducs de Bretagne, Nantes, 1973
Monique Lévi-Strauss, *Sheila Hicks*, London: Studio Vista, 1973; New York: Van Nostrand Reinhold, 1974 (French original, 1973)
Gilles Plazy, "Sheila Hicks", *Cimaise*, no.158, May–June 1982, pp.17–28
Barbaralee Diamonstein, *Handmade in America: Conversations with Fourteen Craftsmasters*, New York: Abrams, 1983
Nancy Koenigsberg, "Sheila Hicks: An affinity for architecture", *Fiberarts*, xii, September–October 1985, pp.60–61
Debra Brehmer, "Collaboration: Sheila Hicks' cross cultural trapeze", *Fiberarts*, xix, September–October 1992, pp.12–13

Sheila Hicks has used fibre as the medium of her work since the late 1950s, and she is considered to be one of the founders of the contemporary movement that has come to see work in fibre recognised as art rather than as something created solely for decorative or practical purposes. Her years of practice – during which she has never strayed far from the fibre medium – have produced works ranging from the monumental to the miniature, each one seeking a way in which to imbue the fabric itself with the capacity to strike a resonant chord, to elicit an emotional and human response from the viewer.

As a student at Yale University in the 1950s, Hicks was influenced by Josef Albers, whom she credits with encouraging her ideas concerning "color, clarity. Articulateness, reverence, room to create" (Diamonstein 1983, p.93). At this time she began to seek a medium and style that would provide a personal contradiction to the then dominant and masculine world of Abstract Expressionism so prevalent in New York. In reacting against the ascendancy of the abstract idiom, she was prompted to begin travelling around the world, seeking practical experience in the fabric arts of indigenous cultures. To the present day, she has continued this search for knowledge of the thread-use traditions of other cultural heritages, and persists in the quest for ways to integrate old customs with modern designs. This search began between 1957 and 1959 when a Fulbright scholarship provided the means for Hicks to travel extensively in Chile, Venezuela, Colombia, Ecuador, Peru, Bolivia and Brazil, and by 1963 she had established a workshop in Mexico for the investigation of pre-Incan weaving techniques, including knotting, double-weaving and wrapped warp.

In the 1960s Hicks began to show her fibre constructions and concluded that "if a painter does paintings, an artist working in thread creates directly from the thread" (Colin Naylor, ed., *Contemporary Artists*, 3rd edition, New York and London, 1989, p.405). Work such as the *Principal Wife Goes On* (1968; National Museum of American Art, Smithsonian Institution, Washington, DC) reflects Hicks's interest in the interpretation of ancient techniques and how they might be incorporated into the modern discourse of contemporary practice. In this piece, linen and synthetic fibres hang in lengths of 4.57 metres, draped across a horizontal bar, and are combined with the ancient and simple technique of "wrapping" to create a monumental effect. The fabric is gathered and wrapped at intervals with bright colours, a technique previously unseen in a North American context.

In 1970 Hicks was asked by the government of Morocco to put her considerable skill in combining time-honoured craft-making practices and her own contemporary aesthetic to practical use. She would help to revitalise the country's traditional rug-making industry in order to broaden international markets. Hicks chose workshops in Tangier and Rabat to produce her designs. In contrast to the traditional Moroccan use of a planar surface finish, Hicks's rugs were constructed of pile in varying depths to emphasise the design, which was built of only three or four colours instead of the traditional nine or more. The subtle result combined the obviously modern with themes inspired by traditional Moroccan culture such as the prayer rug and a Moslem arch. This blend of ancient and modern resulted in work such as the hand-knotted prayer rug series *Sejjada* (1971; Philadelphia Museum of Art). This work, which reproduced the shape of the arch and structured it with long, overlapping tassels against striped, flat backgrounds, invoked a comparison between the texture of the work and the environment in which it was shown.

By the late 1970s and early 1980s Hicks's interest had turned more to the interpretation of fabric that had had some sort of previous life. During this period she took various objects such as hospital linen, soldiers' uniforms, sheets and baby clothes and piled them up, shaped them, tied them together and appropriated their previous uses. In the monumental *Back from the Front* (1979; artist's collection, still exhibited, repr. Plazy 1982, p.24), for example, a towering column of knotted Israeli soldiers' uniforms reaches from floor to ceiling and continues in a line across the ceiling to the far corner of the room. This consolidation of contemporary idiom with a material infused with human memories linked the viewer with the fabric itself, and with its position and meaning in our ethnological history.

In seeming contrast to much of the monumentality of her work, Hicks also shows miniature, more personal pieces, made with various materials such as bones, paper and fabric, bound together and placed in boxes or displayed between sheets of Plexiglas. The simple and elegant technique, combined with the choice of humble materials, creates an unspoken bridge between the technologically advanced and machine-oriented Western ethos and the more rooted-in-the-ground idiom of less technologically advanced cultures that is so typical of Hicks's work.

In an installation at Walker's Point Center for the Arts in 1992, Hicks specifically addressed issues of collaboration, challenging the traditional Western construction of the artist as a solitary worker. The work, *Cross Cultural Trapeze* (repr. Brehmer 1992), began with the stringing of fishing nets from the ceiling of the exhibition space, a task in which Hicks was aided by university students, who assisted in creating the elements and who signed their names to the work alongside that of Hicks. Children from the neighbourhood added chalk drawings to the gallery floor, illustrating an underwater theme. The activity gave the children the opportunity to redefine their concepts of the art gallery as a place for looking, and to think of it instead as a place for doing. Gallery visitors were invited to contribute their own little wrapped objects to the wrapped balls of fabric and yarn that Hicks had included. Consequently, the distance between the artist and the viewer was distinctly narrowed.

Since the early years of her practice, Hicks's work has continuously softened the parameters, not simply of what constitutes art and art practice, but of how the viewer can be included in the art-making process and who that viewer should be. She has challenged concepts of what constitutes the "correct" location for a work of art, and incorporated ideas of how the multi-cultural can become an integral part of the art-making process. "In art, everything is permitted", says Hicks. "There are no 'nos'" (*ibid.*, p.13).

JANICE ANDERSON

Highmore, Susanna *see* Duncombe

Hildegard of Bingen

German illustrator, writer and musical composer,
1098–1179

Born near Mainz, 1098, the tenth child of a noble couple,
Hildebert von Bermersheim and Mechthild. Presented by her
parents at the age of eight as an oblate to a cell attached to
the Benedictine monastery of Disibodenberg in the basin of
the Nahe and Glan, southern tributaries of the Rhine.
Brought up there by an anchoress, Jutta of Sponheim, who
gradually attracted more daughters of nobility as followers.
Became leader of this community after Jutta's death in 1136.
Continued her studies in Latin under a monk, Volmar, who
encouraged her to write a book recording her visions; illustrations to this work, the *Scivias*, were at some time completed
under her direction; the unfinished text was shown to Pope
Eugenius III and St Bernard of Clairvaux at the Synod of
Trier in 1147–8, and they endorsed her continuation of it;
Volmar acted as her mentor and scribe until his death in
1173. Other preserved writings include a book on the
rewards and punishments of good and evil (1158–63), a
treatise on the workings of God in the universe (*Liber
divinorum operum*, completed 1174), a medical treatise and
one on natural science, two saints' lives, the first known
morality play (with music), about 400 letters, and a commentary on the Rule of St Benedict. Also invented a language
with its own alphabet. Founded two Benedictine houses for
women, one in 1150 at Rupertsberg near Bingen on the
Rhine, where she served as *Magistra* (Mother Superior) until
her death, and another in 1165 at Eibingen. Biography
written by Gottfried, a monk of Disibodenberg and her secretary at Rupertsberg until his death in 1175/6; completed by
Theodorich, a monk of Echternach. Died 1179, at the age of
81. Often called a saint, but never officially canonised.

Manuscripts and Reproductions

Scivias (lost), formerly Wiesbaden, Hessisches Landesbibliothek, MS
1; attributed to Rubertsberg, c.1165
Louis Baillet, "Les miniatures du 'Scivias' de Sainte Hildegarde
conservé à la bibliothèque de Wiesbaden", *Académie des
Inscriptions et Belles Lettres, Monuments et Mémoires*, xix, 1911,
pp.49–149 (reproductions of the lost *Scivias* illuminations)
Rheinisches Bildarchiv, Cologne; complete set of black-and-white
negatives of the illustrations in the lost Rupertsberg manuscript,
taken about 1925
Complete copy of the Rupertsberg *Scivias*, made under the direction
of Josepha Knips, 1927–33, Abtei St Hildegard, Eibingen,
Codex 1
Maura Böckler, *Hildegard of Bingen, Wisse die Wege, Scivias*,
Salzburg, 1928 (with photographs of the original *Scivias* manu-
script; unfortunately, the later editions of 1954 and 1963 use the
modern copy)
Adelgundis Führkötter, *The Miniatures from the Book Scivias –
Know the Ways – of St Hildegard of Bingen from the Illuminated
Rupertsberg Codex*, Turnhout, 1977 (facsimile of the Knips copy
of the *Scivias*)

Liber divinorum operum, Biblioteca Governativa, Lucca, MS 1942,
c.1220–30 (black-and-white photographs and slides available
from the library)
Calderoni Masetti, Anna Rosa Calderoni and Gigetta dalli Regoli,
Sanctae Hildegardis revelationes manoscritto 1942, Lucca: Case di

Risparmio di Lucca, 1973 (facsimile of illuminated pages from the
Lucca manuscript and introductions)
Matthew Fox, tr., *Hildegard of Bingen's Book of Divine Works*,
Santa Fe: Bear, 1987 (with drawings after the Lucca manuscript
by Angela Werneke)
Liber divinorum operum, ed. Albert Derolez and Peter Dronke,
Corpus Christianorum Continuatio Mediaevalis, 92, Turnhout:
Brepols, 1996 (complete text and colour illustrations)

Selected Writings

"Sanctae Hildegardis Abbitissae opera omnia" in *Patrologia Latina*,
ed. J.-P. Migne, cxcvii, Paris, 1855; reprinted Turnhout: Brepols,
1976
Hildegardis Scivias, ed. Adelgundis Führkötter and Angela
Carlevaris, Corpus Christianorum Continuatio Mediaevalis, 43
and 43a, Turnhout: Brepols, 1978 (with plates from the modern
copy of the Rupertsberg manuscript)
Ordo virtutum, ed. Audrey Ekdahl Davidson, Kalamazoo, MI:
Medieval Institute Publications, 1984 (performance edition, with
English translation)
*Symphonia: A Critical Edition of the Symphonia Armonie Celestium
Revelationum*, ed. Barbara Newman, Ithaca, NY: Cornell
University Press, 1988
Scivias, ed. Mother Columba Hart and Jane Bishop, New York:
Paulist Press, 1990 (with plates by Placid Dempsey redrawn from
the copy of the Rupertsberg manuscript)
Epistolarium, ed. Lieven van Acker, Corpus Christianorum
Continuatio Mediaevalis, 91 and 91a, Turnhout: Brepols, 1993
The Letters of Hildegard of Bingen, ed. Joseph L. Baird and Radd K.
Ehrman, i, Oxford and New York: Oxford University Press, 1994
Liber vitae meritorum, ed. Angela Carlevaris, Corpus Christianorum
Continuatio Mediaevalis, 90, Turnhout: Brepols, 1995
Physica, ed. Irmgard Müller, Corpus Christianorum Continuatio
Mediaevalis (in preparation)

Bibliography

Primary sources

Anna Silvas, "Saint Hildegard of Bingen and the *Vita Sanctae
Hildegardis*", *Tjurunga*, xxix, 1985, pp.4–25; xxx, 1986,
pp.63–73; xxxi, 1986, pp.32–41; xxxii, 1987, pp.46–59
Monika Klaes, ed., *Vita Hildegardis*, Corpus Christianorum
Continuatio Mediaevalis, 126, Turnhout: Brepols, 1993

Secondary sources that discuss Hildegard's artistic involvement

Charles Singer, "The visions of Hildegard of Bingen", *From Magic to
Science: Essays on the Scientific Twilight*, London: Benn, and New
York: Boni and Liveright, 1928, pp.199–239
Rita Otto, "Zu den gotischen Miniaturen einer Hildegardhandschrift
in Lucca", *Mainzer Zeitschrift*, lxxi–lxxii, 1976–7, pp.110–26
Christel Meier, "Zum Verhältnis von Text und Illustration im über-
lieferten Werk Hildegards von Bingen", *Hildegard von Bingen,
1179–1979: Festschrift zum 800. Todestag der Heiligen*, ed.
Anton P. Brück, Mainz: Mittelrheinische Kirchengeschichte, 1979,
pp.159–69
Karl Clausberg, "Mittelalterliche Weltanschauung im Bild, z.b. die
Visionen de Hildegard von Bingen, oder: Mikrokosmos-
Makrokosmos 'reconsidered' und auf den neuesten (Ver-)Stand
gebracht", *Bauwerk und Bildwerk im Hochmittelalter*, ed. Karl
Clausberg and others, Giessen: Anabas, 1981, pp.236–58
Otto Pächt, *Book Illumination in the Middle Ages: An Introduction*,
London: Harvey Miller, 1986
Marilyn R. Mumford, "A feminist prolegomenon for the study of
Hildegard of Bingen", *Gender, Culture and the Arts*, ed. Ronald
Dotterer and Susan Bowers, Selinsgrove, PA: Susquehanna
University Press, 1993, pp.44–53
Carolyn Wörman Sur, *The Feminine Images of God in the Visions of
Saint Hildegard of Bingen's Scivias*, Lewiston, NY: Mellen Press,
1993

Madeline H. Caviness, "Anchoress, abbess and queen: Donors and patrons or intercessors and matrons?", *Women's Literary and Artistic Patronage in the Middle Ages*, ed. June Hall McCash, Athens: University of Georgia Press, 1996, pp.113–17

——, "Gender symbolism and text image relationships: Hildegard of Bingen's *Scivias*", *Translation Theory and Practice in the Middle Ages*, ed. Jeanette Beer, Kalamazoo, MI: Medieval Institute Publications, 1997, pp.81–123

Other useful sources

Werner Lauter, *Hildegard-Bibliographie: Wegweiser zur Hildegard-Literatur*, 2 vols, Alzey: Rheinhessischen Druckwerkstätte, 1970–84

Albert Derolez, "Deux notes concernant Hildegarde de Bingen", *Scriptorium*, xxvii, 1973, pp.291–5 (on the *Scivias* portrait)

Peter Dronke, *Women Writers of the Middle Ages: A Critical Study of Texts from Perpetua to Marguerite Porete*, Cambridge and New York: Cambridge University Press, 1984

Bernhard W. Scholz, "Hildegard von Bingen on the nature of woman", *American Benedictine Review*, xxxi, 1984, pp.361–83

Prudence Allen, *The Concept of Woman: The Aristotelian Revolution, 750 BC–AD 1250*, Montreal: Eden Press, 1985

Janet Martin and Greta Mary Hair, "*O Ecclesia*: The text and music of Hildegard of Bingen's sequence for St Ursula", *Tjurunga*, xxx, 1986, pp.3–60

Barbara Newman, "Divine power made perfect in weakness: Hildegard on the frail sex", *Medieval Religious Women, ii: Peaceweavers*, ed. Lillian Thomas Shank and John A. Nichols, Kalamazoo, MI: Cistercian Publications, 1987, pp.103–21

——, *Sister of Wisdom: St Hildegard's Theology of the Feminine*, Aldershot: Scolar Press, 1987; Berkeley: University of California Press, 1989

Elisabeth Gössmann, "Hildegard of Bingen", *A History of Women Philosophers*, ed. Mary Ellen Waithe, ii, Dordrecht: Kluwer, 1989, pp.27–65

Kathryn Kerby-Fulton, *Reformist Apocalypticism and Piers Plowman*, New York: Cambridge University Press, 1990

Anne Clark Bartlett, "Miraculous literacy and textual communities in Hildegard of Bingen's Scivias", *Mystics Quarterly*, xviii, 1992, pp.43–55

Audrey Ekdahl Davidson, *The Ordo Virtutum of Hildegard of Bingen: Critical Studies in Early Drama, Art and Music*, Kalamazoo: Medieval Institute, 1992

Helen J. John, "Hildegard of Bingen: A new twelfth-century woman philosopher?", *Hypatia*, vii/1, Winter 1992, pp.115–23

Laurence Moulinier, *Le Manuscrit perdu à Strasbourg: Enquête sur l'oeuvre scientifique de Hildegarde*, Paris: Presses Universitaires de Vincennes, 1996

Hildegard's inclusion in a dictionary of artists depends on my firm attribution to her of the designs for the illuminations in the lost Rupertsberg *Scivias* (Caviness 1996). Most recent authors had prevaricated on this issue, suggesting that she played some more distant role (Pächt 1986, pp.159–60; Newman, *Sister of Wisdom*, 1987, pp.17–18; Sur 1993, pp.17–19). I also contend that the Lucca manuscript of the *Liber divinorum operum* has illuminations copied from a recension that Hildegard designed (Caviness, work in progress). Once her artistic role is accepted, she becomes the only "great master" of the Middle Ages, comparable to such Renaissance figures as Leonardo da Vinci in the breadth of her achievements and in the originality of her images. Unlike the 12th-century metalworkers Godefroid de Claire of Huy and Nicholas of Verdun, her only rivals for fame and production, she was responsible for a very significant corpus of writings and musical compositions, and her life is closely documented not only by a contemporary biography, but also through letters

Hildegard of Bingen: *The Trinity*: formerly Wiesbaden, Hessisches Landesbibliothek, MS 1, fol.172 (Book III, vision 7)

and mentions in chronicles. Although highly appreciated as a German mystic and even as an artist earlier in the 20th century, it is only during a recent 40-year campaign of rigorously editing, studying and translating her writings that she has emerged as a medical scientist, philosopher and theologian (Allen 1985; Gössmann 1989; Bartlett 1992; John 1992). Making pictures is now definitively added to those logocentric activities. And her musical works are increasingly available on compact disc.

In such a brief article, it will be useful to examine one of Hildegard's original compositions for the way in which the text mediates the visionary image, particularly in relation to its authority in matters of the highest theological import. The illustration for Book III vision 7 in the lost *Scivias* manuscript of *c.*1165 depicts the *Trinity* (see illustration). It is of particular interest because it demonstrates the non-figural mode of Hildegard's visions; in most other cases, although the primary visual experience she describes is non-figural, these dynamic schematas incorporate figures at a later stage in the text, as part of her explanation of their metaphorical meanings. In this case, a vast seamless column at one corner of a building has three sharp metallic ridges, and she explains the configuration as the Trinity: "Thus the Father, the Son and the Holy Spirit testify that they are in no way disunited in power, even though they are distinguished in Persons, because they work together in the unity of the simple and immutable substance".

Hildegard did not image the Trinity in any of the standard 12th-century ways, which included the identical bearded pair with a dove that Christina of Markyate had seen in a vision some 25 years earlier, even though she refers several times to

Christ's becoming human, and once to the Holy Spirit as a dove (*Scivias*, ed. Hart and Bishop 1990, pp.411–21). She construed her vision as having a particular relationship to non-Christians: the straw scattered to the southwest (our right) represents heretics, the severed wings (or feathers as drawn) to the northwest (left) are Jews, and the excised dead branches in the west (centre) are pagans. She finishes with a long passage describing the punishment of one who "obstinately sought out what he should not have sought out", indicating her awareness of heretical beliefs concerning the Trinity, probably including those of the famous theologian, Abelard. She had submitted her own text to St Bernard of Clairvaux, who was well known to have judged Abelard. She also preached against the Cathars (a heretical dualistic sect), yet the non-figural rendering of the Godhead might have fitted their precepts as well as those of the Cistercians. Lest we doubt her authority (and her text provides the usual humility *topoi*), a reference here to the Holy Spirit coming to the Apostles "openly in tongues of fire" resonates with the author portrait at the beginning of the work, in which Hildegard herself is shown receiving tongues of flame from heaven and making a record on tablets like those of Moses.

Many of the lost *Scivias* compositions are characterised not only by irregular, non-representational forms (Book I, vision 3; Book III, vision 1), but also by a variety of human figures. Some gigantic, majestic, frontal figures may hold diminutive humans in their arms (e.g. Ecclesia, Book II, visions 3 and 4, and Synagogia, Book I, vision 5). When these are half-length, the suggestion of immense size is all the greater – like the column of the Trinity that disappears out of sight above and below. Other humans are reduced to truncated heads (Book I, visions 1, 4–6; Book III, vision 11), or even a headless body (Book I, vision 1). Architectural motifs, especially common in Book III, are drawn at unusual angles, conveying something like a cornerwise bird's-eye view. Bright elements in silver or gold (whether stars or fragmentary people) are counterchanged black or purple, and tiny white dots on the contours make them shimmer. Most of these effects mimic the scintillating scotomas experienced by patients before the onset of a migraine headache (Singer 1928; Caviness 1997). This confirms Hildegard's hand in the first stage of design, since autobiographical and biographical accounts of her sickness and pain accord well with a migraine disorder of early onset (at three or four) that was particularly severe in her forties, presumably around menopause, at the time she was composing the *Scivias*. Her ability to jot down the compositions and colours of these visual disturbances accords with her claim: "My outward eyes are open. So I have never fallen prey to ecstasy in the visions, but I see them wide awake, day and night. And I am constantly fettered by sickness, and often in the grip of pain so intense that it threatens to kill me" (Newman, *Sister of Wisdom*, 1987, p.6). Her images in the lost *Scivias* are unlike any others in the visionary tradition, such as Apocalypse or Beatus illustrations, or 12th-century images of divine order that have regular geometries.

The illuminations in the Lucca manuscript of the *Liber divinorum operum* are somewhat more conventional, whether because they were "normalised" in the course of posthumous copying from a recension made under Hildegard's direction, or because she (en)visioned the microcosm and macrocosm in somewhat traditional terms. Yet the disjunctures of human scale, fragmentation, oddly angled architecture, androgynous nudes and specific motifs such as a profile head with large wings suggest common authorship. As if to reinforce her agency in the design of the illuminations, Hildegard appears below most of the cosmic spheres, her eyes open to the flaming light that descends on her, her tablets in hand. It is excellent that the Corpus Christianorum text edition also includes the images that are integral to it. Although modernist categories and definitions tended to exclude Hildegard from all the canons, she may fare better in the post-modern era.

MADELINE H. CAVINESS

Hiller, Susan
American mixed-media artist, 1942–

Born in Tallahassee, Florida, 1942. Studied at Smith College of Art, Northampton, Massachusetts (AB 1961), and Tulane University, New Orleans (MA in anthropology 1965). Subsequently carried out field research in Mexico, Guatemala and Belize. Moved to Europe, late 1960s; resident in Britain from 1969; also long stays in North Africa, India and the Far East. Artist-in-residence, University of Sussex, Brighton, 1976. Recipient of Gulbenkian fellowships, 1976 and 1977. Currently professor of fine art, University of Ulster, Belfast. Lives in London.

Selected Individual Exhibitions
Gallery House, London: 1973
Garage Art, London: 1974
Gardner Centre for the Arts, University of Sussex, Brighton: 1976
Serpentine Gallery, London: 1976
Hester van Royen Gallery, London: 1976, 1977, 1978
Kettle's Yard, Cambridge, and Museum of Modern Art, Oxford: 1978
Matt's Gallery, London: 1980, 1991
Gimpel Fils, London: 1980, 1984, 1988, 1992, 1994
Ikon Gallery, Birmingham, and A Space, Toronto: 1981–2 (touring)
Gimpel, Hannover/André Emmerich, Zürich: 1982
Orchard Gallery, Derry: 1984
Third Eye Centre, Glasgow: 1984, 1990
Institute of Contemporary Arts, London: 1986 (retrospective)
Pat Hearn Gallery, New York: 1987, 1989, 1990, 1991
Nicole Klagsbrun Gallery, New York: 1991
Kettle's Yard, Cambridge: 1992
Sigmund Freud Museum, London: 1994
Tate Gallery, Liverpool: 1996 (retrospective)

Selected Writings
Dreams: Visions of the Night, London: Thames and Hudson, 1975; New York: Avon, 1976 (with David Coxhead)
Compiler, *Rough Sea*, for *Dedicated to the Unknown Artists* exhibition, Gardner Centre Gallery, University of Sussex, Brighton, 1976
"Sacred circles: 2000 years of North American Indian art", *Studio International*, December 1977; reprinted in *Art and Society History Workshop Papers*, 1979
Editor, *The Myth of Primitivism: Perspectives on Art*, London and New York: Routledge, 1991
"Hélio Oiticica: Earth, wind and fire", *Frieze*, November–December 1992, pp.26–31
"O'Keeffe as I see her", *Frieze*, Summer 1993, pp.26–9

Bibliography

Hayward Annual '78, exh. cat., Arts Council of Great Britain, London, 1978

Susan Hiller: Recent Works, exh. cat., Kettle's Yard, Cambridge, and Museum of Modern Art, Oxford, 1978 .

"Ten months", *Block*, no.3, 1980, p.27

Monument, exh. cat., Ikon Gallery, Birmingham, and elsewhere, 1981

Rozsika Parker, "Dedicated to the unknown artist", *Spare Rib Reader*, ed. Marsha Rowe, Harmondsworth and New York: Penguin, 1982

Susan Hiller, 1973–83: The Muse My Sister, exh. cat., Orchard Gallery, Derry, and elsewhere, 1984

Annette Van den Bosch, "Susan Hiller: Resisting representation", *Artscribe*, no.46, May–July 1984, pp.44–8

Susan Hiller: "Belshazzar's Feast", London: Tate Gallery, 1985

Sarah Kent and Jackie Morreau, "A conversation with Susan Hiller", *Women's Images of Men*, London and New York: Writers and Readers, 1985

Susan Hiller, exh. cat., Institute of Contemporary Arts, London, 1986

John Roberts, "Different pleasures", *Artscribe International*, no.58, June–July 1986, pp.40–41

Lisa Tuttle, *Heroines: Women Inspired by Women*, London: Harrap, 1988

Susan Butler, "Dream documents: Photographs by Susan Hiller", *WASL Journal*, no.29, 1989, pp.26–7

The Revenants of Time, exh. cat., Matt's Gallery, London, and elsewhere, 1990

John Roberts, *Postmodernism, Politics and Art*, Manchester: Manchester University Press, 1990

Signs of the Times, exh. cat., Museum of Modern Art, Oxford, 1990

Guy Brett, "Susan Hiller's shadowland", *Art in America*, lxxix, April 1991, pp.136–43, 187

Barbara Einzig, "Within and against: Susan Hiller's nonobjective reality", *Arts Magazine*, lxvi, October 1991, pp.60–65

Guy Brett, "That inner vision thing at Freud's", *The Guardian*, 16 April 1994, p.29

Susan Hiller's Brain, exh. cat., Gimpel Fils Gallery, London, 1994

Stuart Morgan, "Beyond control: Susan Hiller interviewed by Stuart Morgan", *Frieze*, no.23, Summer 1995, pp.52–7

Susan Hiller, exh. cat., Tate Gallery, Liverpool, 1996

Barbara Einzig, ed., *Thinking About Art: Conversations with Susan Hiller* (in preparation)

Susan Hiller's work is informed by her training and subsequent – albeit relatively brief – practice as an anthropologist. Her disillusionment with academic anthropology focused on the impossibility of the "participant/observer" position expected of the practitioner. Desirous of finding a way "to be *inside* all [her] activities", she turned to art. Her materials are the found object, the cultural artefact, and language. As she has said: "The thing that unites everything is the use of cultural artefacts from our society as starting points" (Morgan 1995). Her works have an investigative character – they explore, uncover, recover or re-present; for Hiller the world is "a series of marks to be deciphered". Using the analytic tools of anthropology – and its collecting/classifying activities – Hiller has endeavoured to find a practice that acknowledges that we are "simultaneously participant and spectator, author and reader, singular and plural".

Apart from her application of methodologies drawn from anthropology, Hiller has claimed that her origins as an artist lie in Minimalism: "I take a minimalist grid to represent a non-hierarchical orderly way of arranging things, so I use it as a basic principle quite often … I'm not interested in aesthetics or aestheticizing" (interview with Rozsika Parker, quoted in Derry 1984). Indeed this grid supplies the structural framework for most of her work, from *Dedicated to the Unknown Artists* (1972–6), where it serves to emphasise both similarity and divergence, *Fragments* (1976–7), where the horizontal floor-laid grid resembles an archaeological map of "finds", *10 Months* (1977–9), a chart of progression and development, *Sentimental Representations* (1980–81; Arts Council of Great Britain), a patchwork quilt, or collage, with its slightly misaligned panels, and *Monument* (1980–81), an imposing cruciform format of abutting panels. This passing acknowledgement of Minimalism (and of Fluxus) is the closest Hiller comes to alignment with any movement. She has preferred to remain marginal, unassimilated by any programme, any defining tendency, a stance that is certainly informed by her empathy with the "Other" and by her insistence on crossing the boundaries between disciplines.

The found object has been the raw material for Hiller's artist practice almost from the beginning. *Dedicated to the Unknown Artists* presents an exhaustive typological series of postcards that share a subject and a title: "Rough Sea". These were collected by Hiller over a long period and from many locations around Britain. These anonymous cards are a modest form of vernacular image-making, given an enhanced status by the gallery context, and by being seen as part of a "series", albeit a series created by Hiller herself as collector and curator. They mock the pretensions of one of the sacred-cow categories of British art – landscape painting. But they also engage with Hiller's interest in the contradictions between words and images, and the fact that "words don't explain images, they exist in parallel universes".

In *10 Months* this balance between text and image is made explicit in the structure. The piece presents aspects of Hiller's personal experience of pregnancy. In the first half she dwells on the physical changes and so the images – blown-up photographs of her growing belly – appear above the text panels, extracts from her journals of the time. In the later months thinking and reading dominated, and this is reflected in the second half by placing the text above the image. Exploring this phenomenon in later works, Hiller elides words and images, as in the pieces based on automatic scripts – *Sisters of Menon* (1972) and *Elan* (1982; Gimpel Fils, London), and in *Monument*, photographs of commemorative ceramic plaques. Here she melds verbal and visual, for the images *are* words. The originals are Victorian memorials in an East London park; they commemorate a number of people who died in the act of saving, or attempting to save, the lives of others. The photographs of these plaques are arranged, edges abutting, in a cruciform pattern on the wall; a park bench is set in front, but faces out from the wall. One spectator at a time sits on the bench and listens to a tape of the artist's voice reflecting and speculating on these 41 forgotten individuals. The lives of these local heroes have been reduced to a brief account of the circumstances of their deaths. Their identities have been effaced, overlaid with a narrative of undifferentiated heroism and self-sacrifice. Hiller is interested in the ways in which identity – individual and social – is fashioned, and in its mutability, its susceptibility to erasure and decline into anonymity. And death itself is a recurrent subject for Hiller: not only is it hedged around with cultural taboos, it also marks a transition to a state where identity is no longer self-created but is under the control of others.

Hiller has repeatedly tried to give a social visibility to anonymity, from the obscure heroes of *Monument* to the unnamed and unknown potters who produced the sherds in *Fragments*. To this end she began her ten-year series of *Photomat Portraits* with the discarded photo-booth images that their subjects had either rejected or abandoned, progressing to images of friends who deliberately disrupted the mechanically and culturally imposed constraints of the medium, and moving finally to making self-portraits. The photomat offers "photography for everyone", a democratisation of portraiture; although formally limited, it offers a simple method of self-presentation unmediated by the vision of another. In her photomat self-portraits Hiller resists the blank defining gaze of the camera, and beyond that the scrutiny of the viewer, by presenting instead fragments of her body, back views, shoulders, gesticulating hands. The hand, of course, signals the artist as maker, and connects with later photo-portraits in which the artist's face is overlaid, masked, by skeins of automatic writing. For Hiller, the self-portrait is exclusive, for *herself*, not for us; she subverts the notion of portrait as a means of revealing identity; it becomes instead a site of resistance, erasure and anonymity.

The expressive gesturing hand that appears in these photomat portraits (and also in the *Lucid Dreams* series of 1982–3, in which she attempted "to erode the supposed boundary between dream life and waking life") connects with Hiller's ongoing engagement with automatism. Automatic writing, described by André Breton as the "interior language", has associations with the irrational, the unconscious and the feminine. Hiller's work addresses the contradictions existing in Western cultures between rational and irrational, empiricism and intuition, dream life and waking life, and attempts the recuperation of the "feminine" side of these dichotomies. Thus for Hiller automatic writing, with its unintelligibility and its marginality, is a potent symbol of female speech. Hiller had admired the Surrealists' use of automatism as "spontaneous" and as a democratic creative act, something that "everyone can do". Her first experiments with automatic writing were undertaken while staying in France in 1972. The message that emerged expressed a powerful female solidarity. Later presented as the work entitled *Sisters of Menon*, these scripts asserted a multiple or collaborative identity that led Hiller to question the notion of "self", for the marks she made in this automatic mode were neither in her handwriting nor in her "voice" (i.e. her characteristic tone or mode of speech). Automatism is, of course, associated, especially in women, with madness and mediumship, both states in which the author has broken through the boundaries of their known personality. In this context it appeared a uniquely liberating process. These scripts allowed Hiller the fulfilment of utterance without the distortion of a recognisable categorisable language – the language of a male-dominated culture. "Menon" is an anagram for "no men" (inscribed when a male collaborator attempted to act as the transmitter), but also for "nomen" or "name": the invisible and anonymous crying out for visibility and identity.

Hiller at first described the signs as crypto-linguistic, that is "representing language", but in an interview in 1983 she said

that she was at the point of claiming these automatic works as "a new language". She felt that she was taking automatic writing beyond the point of being seen in purely pictorial terms to being accepted as a form of patterned utterance. Automatic writing was incorporated into many subsequent projects including *Sometimes I Think I'm a Verb Instead of a Pronoun* (1982; Gimpel Fils Gallery, London), *Gatwick Suite* (1983; artist's collection), *Midnight, Baker Street* (1983; Arts Council) and the *Lucid Dreams* series (1982–3), but it was the primary medium for *Elan* (1980–81). "Elan" – "ongoing energetic principle" – is the one decipherable word in the automatic script that comprises this work. As in several of Hiller's other works, the visual is complemented by the verbal. Speakers transmit the artist's voice, producing a wordless improvised singing, alternating with extracts from a famous experiment – the Raudive Recordings (1960s), in which the psychologist Konstantin Raudive left a tape-recorder running in an empty room, and claimed the amplified tapes as records of voices from the past. Where the "noises" on the Raudive tapes were attributed to specific identifiable individuals from history, Hiller's script and her singing are open to a wider interpretation.

Concerned to extend language to "outsiders", the culturally disenfranchised and the unheard, especially women, Hiller produced various collaborative *Group Investigation* pieces in the 1970s. These ranged from a large-scale community performance in London, *Street Ceremonies* (1973), *Draw Together* (1973), an experiment in telepathy, and *Dream Mapping* (1974), which involved a small group in the deliberate "incubation" of dreams, and the production of dream maps to create a composite picturing the shared consciousness of an "organic community". Much of her subsequent work might also be described as collaborative – with the dead, the unnamed, with other "selves". *Fragments* (1978) is a complex key work in which sherds of pottery by Pueblo Indian women were integrated into an installation about the abyss between cultures and the colonisation of archaeological material (it was indirectly a critique of the *Sacred Circles* exhibition of Native American art at the Hayward Gallery, London). Throughout her career Hiller has rejected the dominance of a unifying discourse, and has instead worked with the fragment as a non-hierarchical unit of meaning. In using fragments and found objects she engages in a process of reclamation and retrieval of the suppressed, repressed, unknown or rendered invisible, and her practice is thus central to the feminist agenda of the 1970s and 1980s.

In much of Hiller's work there is a deliberate avoidance of an "I", a controlling, identifiable ego. She attempts to deconstruct the traditional notion of the artist as an identity imposed on the work. In *Midnight, Baker Street* and the other works in that series, by veiling her blurred face with automatic script she is simultaneously obscuring her physical identity and asserting the identity of an "inner self" through the surfacing of an indecipherable personal language.

A continuity of concerns can be observed in all Hiller's work, regardless of the medium. Her first video piece, *Belshazzar's Feast* (1983), used the television set as a metaphor for the communal hearth; on the screen flames represent an uncontrollable nature threatening to burst from the confines of culture. The title refers to "the writing on the wall" that appeared at this biblical feast, and the subtitle "What the fire said" alerts us to reading the video as parable, with the flames resembling the glyphs of automatic writing, overlaid with a tape of commentary and incoherent singing. A more recent video piece, *An Entertainment* (1990), was included in the *Rites of Passage* exhibition of 1995 at the Tate Gallery. It explores the hidden or suppressed meanings of the traditional Punch and Judy show. Hiller noticed that this entertainment, though designed for children, is in fact profoundly and shockingly violent. Children saw this but their parents ignored it, thus "acculturating the children to an acceptance of this kind of violence". By making a room-sized multi-screen video collage of this puppet theatre, with clarified amplified dialogue, Hiller aimed to reveal to adults the true nature of the show.

An installation at the Freud Museum in 1994, part of "The Reading Room" project, continued the archaeological theme in Hiller's practice. Cardboard boxes of the kind used for sorting "finds" contained two or three objects and a fragment of text. The piece constituted a "dialogue" with its setting, a response to Freud's own collection of artefacts. Each box contained fragments of myth and memory, with themes that encompassed Judaica, Classical mythology and gender, among others. The context for this exhibition is perhaps especially pertinent for Hiller. She has always held that art is a "first-order practice – as important as sociology, psychology, physics, politics or whatever. "Artists", she believes, are not only "entertainers" but also "explainers" and "experts in their own culture". The knowledge they produce has a value of its own, and art cannot be reduced to the status of illustration for ideas constructed in other disciplines.

GEORGINA BUCKLAND

Hirsch Pauli, Hanna
Swedish painter, 1864–1940

Born Hanna Hirsch in Stockholm, 1864; father a music publisher. Studied in Stockholm at August Malmström's School for Women Painters, 1876–80; Technical School, 1880–81; Royal Academy of Fine Arts, 1881–5 (medal 1885); in Paris at Académie Colarossi, under Dagnan-Bouveret and Raphael Collin, 1885–7. Married Swedish painter Georg Pauli, 1887; three children; husband died 1935. Trip to Italy, 1887–8. Settled in Stockholm, 1888. Taught at Valand Art School, Göteborg, 1893–7. Moved back to Stockholm c.1900. In Italy, 1906–10. Trip to North Africa, 1920–21. Died in Stockholm, 1940.

Principal Exhibitions
Paris Salon: 1887
Göteborgs Konstnärsförbund (Göteborg Federation of Artists): 1887
Exposition Universelle, Paris: 1889, 1900
World's Columbian Exposition, Chicago: 1893

Bibliography
Kvinnor som malat [Women who painted], exh. cat., Nationalmuseum, Stockholm, 1975
Lena Söderlund, *Hanna Hirsch-Pauli: En kvinna i Konstnärsförbundet* [Hanna Hirsch-Pauli: A woman in the Artists Association], BA seminar paper, Institute of Art History, University of Uppsala, 1979
Vi arbetar för livet [We work for life], exh. cat., Liljevalchs Konsthall, Stockholm, 1980
Ingrid Ingelman, "Women artists in Sweden: A two-front struggle", *Woman's Art Journal*, v/1, 1984, pp.1–7
1880-årene i nordisk maleri [The 1880s in Nordic painting], exh. cat., Nasjongalleriet, Oslo, and elsewhere, 1985
De drogo till Paris: Nordiska konstnärinnor på 1880-talet [They went to Paris: Nordic women artists in the 1880s], exh. cat., Liljevalchs Konsthall, Stockholm, 1988
Hanna Pauli, Siri Tathsman, Anna Sjödahl, exh. cat., Göteborgs Konstmuseum, Göteborg, 1989

Best known for her intense and powerful portraits, Hanna Hirsch Pauli was one of the very few Nordic women artists of her generation who did not relinquish her career after marriage. While she produced a number of remarkably innovative works, her attention was constantly shifting; her works evidenced little consistent development. This may have been partly due to her independent economic status – liberated from the constraints of earning a livelihood, the only person that Hirsch Pauli had to please was herself. While this gave her great freedom, it also may have diffused her attention.

Hirsch Pauli was a child of Stockholm's Jewish middle class. Her general education was progressive, supervised as it was by Ellen Key, the prominent feminist socialist, who was retained as the Hirsch girls' private tutor. At the age of 12 Hirsch Pauli began taking art lessons with the academic painter August Malmström, highly regarded at the time for his evocations of Nordic prehistory. Malmström's students made costume studies from live models (no nude modelling occurred) and landscape studies out of doors. Three years later Hirsch Pauli continued her studies at the Technical School in Stockholm, and was admitted to the Royal Academy of Fine Arts in 1881. There she concentrated on portrait and landscape painting. It is not clear whether she did so for personal reasons or whether the more prestigious category of history painting was considered the exclusive purview of male artists. In 1885, her final year at the Academy, Hirsch Pauli won a medal for her painting *By Lamplight* (untraced), depicting three figures gathered around the glow of a lamp. Already her technical virtuosity and power of observation were evident in this unpretentious, realist motif.

The late 1880s was for Hirsch Pauli an exhilarating period of personal and artistic growth. In the autumn of 1885 she joined the flight of Swedish artists to Paris. She associated with the tightly knit community of several dozen Nordic artists, settling in Montparnasse, where she shared a room with the Finnish painter Venny Soldan-Aho, who became a lifelong friend. There she executed an arresting portrait of *Venny Soldan-Aho* (1887; see illustration). Its unusual subject and composition evidenced the freedom enjoyed by Nordic women artists in Paris.

Instead of bowing to conventional feminine roles, Hirsch Pauli depicted her friend literally down-to-earth, as an artist seated on the floor of her studio, a clump of clay in her hand. In this post-Courbet realist portrait, the artist chose to throw in her lot with the working classes, instead of high society, as Elisabeth Vigée-Lebrun (q.v.) had done in her self-portraits. The spartan setting reflected the life-style embraced by Hirsch Pauli and her colleagues in Paris, and Soldan-Aho's unflinching

Hirsch Pauli: *Venny Soldan-Aho*, 1887; 125.5 × 134 cm.; Göteborgs Konstmuseum, Sweden

eye-contact with the viewer evidenced the self-assured independence of sitter and artist. In this context, it is important to keep in mind that this painting was the product of a female relationship, and the presence of a male audience is nowhere suggested.

Hirsch Pauli studied at the Académie Colarossi, where men and women worked side by side. Five days a week students worked from a nude model from 8 a.m. until 12 p.m. and from a clothed model from 1 p.m. until 5 p.m. On the sixth day, either Dagnan-Bouveret or Raphael Collin came to criticise their work. The latter visited Hirsch Pauli's studio frequently during the period she was working on *Venny Soldan-Aho*. He played an instrumental role in ensuring the favourable

placement of the portrait on the crowded walls at the annual Paris Salon, where it received favourable reviews from French critics. In Sweden, on the other hand, critics were shocked by this depiction of a modern, liberated woman freed from the socially defined relationships that usually constrained her.

Marriage to fellow Swedish painter Georg Pauli in 1887 guaranteed her future as an artist. In marriage she was able to ignore the traditional expectations of her own family and to continue circulating in the artistic and intellectual circles she found so energising. Unlike most of her female Swedish colleagues, Hirsch Pauli played an active role in the National Romantic movement on her return to Sweden in 1888. She, her husband, Ellen Key and others believed that it was essential for

Swedes to create for themselves a national identity based on shared traditions and values, perpetuating it in all facets of life. Her dramatic portrait of the National Romantic poet *Verner von Heidenstam* (1893; Prins Eugens Waldemarsudde, Stockholm) communicates the emotional intensity that National Romantics wanted to elicit in their compatriots with thoughts of Sweden. Silhouetted against a rugged and stormy landscape, Heidenstam appears as a fierce Nordic god enveloped by powerful natural forces.

In *Princess at the Gate* (1896; Nasjonalgaleriet, Oslo) Hirsch Pauli executed a fairy-tale image of the sort that was the stock-in-trade of her teacher Malmström. By this time she had also seen the fanciful paintings of the Danish painter Agnes Slott-Møller (q.v.), and may have derived inspiration from them, a possibility suggested by the similarity in subject matter and execution. The image is intended to evoke nostalgia for an imagined earlier (medieval) era of harmony and simplicity that National Romantics sought to rekindle in modern Swedish society. Hirsch Pauli and her husband were profoundly concerned with reforming society along egalitarian and utopian lines, and she was the only female Swedish painter of her generation to promote social change actively.

MICHELLE FACOS

Hjertén, Sigrid
Swedish painter, 1885–1948

Born in Sundsvall, 27 October 1885; father a vice-district judge; mother died when Hjertén was aged two. Sent to school in Stockholm, 1897. Graduated as a drawing teacher from the Advanced School for Arts and Crafts, Stockholm, 1908; initially specialised in textile art. In Paris, autumn 1909–spring 1911; studied at the Académie Matisse; belonged to a group of Swedish painters in Paris, including Isaac Grünewald, who also trained at the Académie Matisse. Returned to Stockholm, and married Grünewald, 1911; son Iván, also a painter, born November 1911; divorced 1937. Only female member, De Åtta (the Eight) group, 1912. Trips to Gilleleje, 1917, and Fanø, 1918, both in Denmark; Italy, Austria and Germany, 1920. Lived in Paris with son, 1920–32, then returned to Sweden because of signs of mental illness; recovered temporarily, and went to France, 1933, and Sicily, 1934. Ceased painting, and admitted to Beckomberga Mental Hospital, 1938. Died after brain surgery, 24 March 1948.

Principal Exhibitions

Individual
Hallins Konsthandel: 1913 (with Isaac Grünewald and Einar Jolin)
Stadsgårdsateljén, Stockholm and Oslo: 1913 (with Isaac Grünewald)
Valand Academy, Göteborg: 1916 (with Isaac Grünewald)
Galleri Ny Konst, Göteborg: 1918 (with Nils Dardel)
Konsthallen, Göteborg: 1935 (with Isaac and Iván Grünewald)
Malmö Museum: 1935 (with Isaac Grünewald)
Royal Academy of Fine Arts, Stockholm: 1936 (retrospective)
Skånska Konstmuseet, Lund: 1938
Galerie Moderne, Stockholm: 1940 (with Iván Grünewald)
Nationalmuseum, Stockholm: 1949 (touring retrospective)

Group
Salong Joel, Stockholm: 1912 (*De Åtta* [the Eight])
Malmö: 1914 (*Baltiska utställningen* [Baltic exposition])
Galerie der Sturm, Berlin: 1915 (*Schwedische Expressionisten*)
Den frie udstillingsbygning, Copenhagen: 1916 (*Moderne svensk kunst* [Swedish modernism])
Liljevalchs Konsthall, Stockholm: 1917 (*Föreningen Svenska konstnärinnor* [Association of Swedish women artists]), 1918 (*Expressionistutställningen* [Expressionist exhibition]), 1919 (*Stockholm i bild* [Stockholm in pictures]), 1921 (*Aprilutställningen* [April exhibition]), 1927 (*Unionalen*), 1948 (*Nordiska konstnärinnor* [Nordic women artists])
Göteborg: 1923 (*Nordisk konst* [Nordic art])
Nordiska Museet, Stockholm: 1941 (*Barnet i konsten* [The child in art])
Nationalmuseum, Stockholm: 1944 (*Den unga expressionismen* [Young Expressionism])

Selected Writings
"Modern och österländsk konst" [Modern and oriental art], *Svenska Dagbladet*, 24 February 1911
"Paul Cézanne: Något om hans lif och verk" [Paul Cézanne: Something about his life and work], *Svenska Dagbladet*, 24 September 1911

Bibliography
"Intervju med Sigrid Hjertén" [Interview with Sigrid Hjertén]", *Idun*, 23 November 1924
Célie Brunius, "Jag målar mitt livs bilderbok" [I paint my life's picture book], *Bonniers Månadstidning*, no.4, 1934
Carl Palme, *Sigrid Hjertén*, Stockholm, 1936
Ingrid Rydbeck, "Sigrid Hjertén", *Konstrevy*, xii/3, 1936
Lars-Erik Åström, "Sigrid Hjertén: Randanteckningar till en minnesutställning" [Sigrid Hjertén: Annotations to a commemorative exhibition], *Konstrevy*, xxv/2 1949
Tor Bjurström, "Sigrid Hjertén", *Paletten*, x/2, 1949
Sigrid Hjertén: Minnesutställning [Sigrid Hjertén: Commemorative exhibition], exh. cat., Nationalmuseum, Stockholm, and elsewhere, 1949
Gösta Lilja, *Det moderna måleriet i svensk kritik, 1905–1914* [Modern painting in Swedish criticism, 1905–1914], dissertation, Malmö, 1955
Maj Bring, *Motljus* [Against the light], 1960
Sigrid Hjertén, 1885–1948, exh. cat., Moderna Museet, Stockholm, 1964
L'altra metà dell'avanguardia, 1910–1940: Pittrici e scultrici nei movimenti delle avanguardie storiche, exh. cat., Palazzo Reale, Milan, and elsewhere, 1980
Elisabet Haglund, "Kvinnan i den röda rullgardinen" [The woman in the red roller blind], *Moderna Museet*, no.4, 1982
Marit Werenskiold, "Sigrid Hjertén som ekspresjonist: En analyse av 'Självporträtt' 1914" [Sigrid Hjertén as an expressionist: Analysis of the self-portrait of 1914], *Konsthistorisk Tidskrift*, lii/1, 1983, pp.31–43
Elisabet Haglund, *Sigrid Hjertén*, Stockholm: 1985; revised edition, Stockholm: Raster, 1991
Nina Weibull, "Sigrid Hjertén eller en annan bild av människan" [Sigrid Hjertén or another picture of man], *Liv*, no.4, 1985
Shulamith Behr, *Women Expressionists*, London: Phaidon, and New York: Rizzoli, 1988
Folke Lalander, "Sverige och modernismen: 10-talets konst" [Sweden and modernism: The art of the 1910s], *Modernismens genombrott* [The breakthrough of modernism], exh. cat., Nordiska Ministerrådet, Copenhagen, 1989
Scandinavian Modernism: Painting in Denmark, Finland, Iceland, Norway and Sweden, 1910–1920, exh. cat., Göteborgs Konstmuseum, Göteborg, and elsewhere, 1989

Anita Goldman, *I själen alltid ren: Om Sigrid Hjertén* [In the ever-pure soul: About Sigrid Hjertén], Stockholm: Natur & Kultur, 1995

Maria Lind, "Sigrid Hjertén och Isaac Grünewald: Melankoli och virtuositet" [Sigrid Hjertén and Isaac Grünewald: Melancholy and virtuosity], *Dubbelporträtt: Konstnärspar i seklets början* [Double portrait: Artist couples at the beginning of the century], ed. Ingamaj Beck and Barbro Waldenström, Stockholm: Natur & Kultur, 1995

Sigrid Hjertén, exh. cat., Liljevalchs Konsthall, Stockholm, 1995 (contains extensive bibliography)

When Sigrid Hjertén entered the Académie Matisse in 1909 she was already trained as a designer of tapestries. It was only during her years of study in Paris that she received a proper education in painting and aesthetics. Some of her fellow students have given evidence of Henri Matisse's high appreciation of her painting, especially her independent attitude: "She was very gifted" (Bring 1960, p.125). *Still Life with Ginger Jar* (1910–11; private collection, repr. Stockholm 1995, pl.1 and p.154), a composition representing a private rather than a traditional choice of objects and painted in brilliant, light colours, bears witness to the strong impression that Cézanne's method of combining and analysing objects in a restricted space had made on Hjertén. Following Cézanne she combined jars and fruit with statuettes, but chose women nudes in contrast to Cézanne's plaster cast of *Cupid*. A sensuous humour prevails in her *Female Nude* (1910; Moderna Museet, Stockholm, *ibid.*, pl.1).

On a small scale Hjertén continued to design tapestries, such as *Adam and Eve* (1912; long-pile rug; Sveriges Radio, *ibid.*, pl.23), and furniture and to decorate ceramics, but she was never engaged by the art industry. Her verbal-analytical competence, held back in favour of her painterly-intuitive activity, was expressed in two articles published in *Svenska Dagbladet* in February and September 1911. Here she introduced the life and art of Cézanne to the Swedish public, and further presented her reflections on principles of composition in old Oriental as compared to modern French painting. She articulated her observations of "elementary laws" in Chinese religious painting, thereby declaring her own aesthetic programme and bearing witness to Matisse's strong influence:

> Some of these laws are: the consistent simplification of lines in order to obtain the greatest possible expressiveness, the subordination of proportion to the demands of the composition, concentration on the strongest moments of a movement on the part of the figure performing the movement, the supremacy of colour over tone. The movement of the figure is now compressed within the curve of one single line. The curve is the tune of the work, and its consistency must in no way be disturbed by the figure ["Modern och österländsk konst", 1911].

Such paintings as *Brunette and Blonde* (1912; Sundsvalls Museum, Sundsvall, repr. Stockholm 1995, pl.7), *Dora and Iván* and *Elder Tree* (both 1913; private collection, *ibid.*, pls 11 and 8) follow this aesthetic programme. The elastic outline is accentuated and brought into a full, rhythmic effect. The weight and volume of a dominating figure are set to play against a secondary one, added at an angle to the first as an element acting with alternative effects within the confined space. The subject matter in Hjertén's painting of the 1910s often combines, as rivalling principles, modernism's interest in depicting the model as an impersonal arrangement of volume, line and colour, and the traditional genre of middle-class home interiors filled with an emotionally condensed content. *Brunette and Blonde* is a good example of a modernist subject. The "Brunette", dressed in bright green, is engaged in sewing or reading. Her large but intimate figure is pushed into the background by the dominating "Blonde", characterised by golden hair, sensuously naked shoulders and arms, and heavy legs clad in sky-blue stockings. Draperies of ruby red and black, pale purple and white fill the surrounding space. Two later paintings, *Iván Sitting in an Armchair* (1915; private collection, *ibid.*, pl.19) and *Iván Asleep, or, The Balcony* (1915; Svenska Handelsbanken, *ibid.*, pl.12), may well illustrate the traditional genre. The room is a nicely furnished interior, dominated by warm red and yellow, but opening up to a cool and remote exterior seen through a large window. The small, solitary figure of Iván, Hjertén's four-year-old son, is made the very focus of the room, but he has powerful competitors for our attention, in the bric-à-brac and energetically patterned drapery that lines the living-room window.

Hjertén has been said to "anticipate the home ideal of our time, with the window wide open to society" (Carlo Derkert, *Nordisk Målarkonst*, Stockholm, 1951). But the relationship between her studio/living room and the vast room of society glimpsed through her window was one of tense contrast rather than of ideal harmony. In *View of the Locks* (1919; Moderna Museet, Stockholm; repr. Behr 1988, pl.24) Hjertén grasps the panoramic view from her studio overlooking the Old Town of Stockholm north of the locks, transforming its dynamic forces represented by pointed church towers, edgy buildings, steamers, trains and tram-cars, into a decorative zigzag pattern. The spectacle to be seen outside the low balcony railing is converted into a flat screen invaded by constant movement and a pulsating interplay of hot red-yellow tones and cold blue-green. A small doll on the balcony in the foreground has her back turned to the shallow space of the city behind her. Hjertén's singular choice of colours was described by the art critic August Brunius in 1918: "Her signature is a dry, hot nuance of red combined with a cool, moist one, the colours approaching each other with dangerous refinement". Recurring combinations of colour in the 1910s are pale purple, vermilion, bright pink, rose terra, golden ochre, ultramarine and cobalt blue and turquoise green, all colours often blended with white.

In 1913 a competition was held for the decoration of the Wedding Room in the Stockholm City Law Courts. Hjertén painted four sketches for which she, in a style close to a parody of Cézanne, chose three themes: the wedding ceremony, modern city and nakedness (Skissernas Museum, Lund, repr. Stockholm 1995, pls 91–3). But unlike Isaac Grünewald she never participated in the contest. With an ambiguous effect Hjertén places her husband's sketch as a halo to her face in her large *Self-Portrait* (1914; Malmö Konstmuseum, repr. Haglund 1985, pl.8). A drawing of the composition was published as cover picture of *Der Sturm*, no.7–8, 1915, in connection with the exhibition *Schwedische Expressionisten*. Little Iván acts as a link between his father's project behind him and the frail and extremely elongated figure of his mother, who is seated on a

Hjertén: *Studio Interior*, 1917; oil; 176 × 203 cm.; Moderna Museet, Stockholm

chair to work on an unseen canvas. Her face is white with a disquieting expression of painful abandon under the plumed hat. She wears an ice-green blouse and a vermilion red skirt, and on her breast a red bow of conspicuous size. In this large and important self-portrait Hjertén seems to confront her growing difficulties of being an artist, a wife and the mother of an unplanned child.

The dynamic, diagonal scheme of the *Self-Portrait* recurs in a number of large paintings depicting family and social life, such as *Tea Time* (1915; sold Sotheby's 1989, private collection, *ibid.*, p.17) and *At the Theatre* (1915; private collection, repr. Stockholm 1995, pl.24), a playfully naïve portrait of the dreaming, effeminate and orientalised Grünewald, and behind him Hjertén, confronting the passionate drama performed on the brightly illuminated stage. *Interior/Black Boot* (1917; sold Bukowski, 26 October 1995, lot 497, *ibid.*, pl.35) depicts a

"chez-nous" of both intimacy and tension. Child and husband turn their backs on the slender, barely dressed Hjertén. Compositionally her high-heeled black boot extends Grünewald's figure; Iván's blue toy trailer and its counterpart, the grapes in the drapery pattern behind Hjertén, form a second focal point. The arrangement of dynamically opposed figures is brought to a climax in the important *Studio Interior* (1917; see illustration). Is the subject to be understood as an ironic depiction of artistic social life, as a mythologising, split self-portrait, or as a bold expressionist arrangement of curved lines, flattened volumes and opposed colours in a room defined by planes, not by perspective? Hjertén sits by the large window in the company of her husband and the painter Einar Jolin; behind them is a sculptured nude woman and a painted Gypsy mother and child. A glamorous, anonymous woman, dressed in black and accompanied by the painter Nils Dardel, whose colour is pale mauve, dominates the foreground and the entire room. She has been interpreted as Hjertén's other self (Haglund 1985), but also as a figuration of "the Other", an impersonal imaginary representation of Hjertén's extreme opposite, perhaps experienced as a threat to her own self by the artist (Weibull 1985).

In 1916 Wassily Kandinsky wrote in a letter to Gabriele Münter (q.v.): "You must not envy Mme Grünewald on account of her talent for composition – the lady's paintings are beautiful, but not sufficiently powerful. Your paintings are much more serious, deep, enduring." Hjertén and Münter met as artists and friends in Stockholm in 1917, and in Copenhagen in 1918–19. Münter described Hjertén's painting as "harder" than that of her husband's, showing "a cool Nordic and naïvist tendency". Münter may allude to the degree of distortion of the body that Hjertén allowed herself in her search for decorative qualities, as in her arrangement of swinging dancers in The Masquerade (1916; private collection, repr. Stockholm 1995, pl.28). In Red Blind (1916; Moderna Museet, ibid., pl.26) the element of distortion is brought to an extreme and even parodic expression (Behr 1988, p.54). The aggressively twisted position of the stiff, tanned body of a nude reclining on a chaise longue in a cramped bedroom, the atmosphere of which is heightened by an exploding table lamp, suggests a site of desperately blocked sexual energy rather than an intimate chamber promising erotic pleasures. The brass bedpost resembles a boxing glove raised to crush the red blind that closes the window. Only the cool, silver-blue tones of the bedcover and the model's hair offer some relief from the claustrophobic atmosphere. It has been suggested that the red colour of the blind is metonymically identical to the red of the Matisse-looking Turkish Drapery (1923; private collection, repr. Stockholm 1995, pl.57), indicating female sexuality, here kept in place by a pale turquoise-green framework (Tom Sandqvist in ibid., p.178).

Blocked sexuality is the manifest subject of the almost surrealistic Harlequin (1928; private collection, ibid., pl.60). Brought together in an easy chair, a large female plaster torso, a squint-eyed male doll and a folded umbrella form a composition of undeniably symbolic dimension. The close background shows a harlequin-patterned drapery, softly painted in grey, green, pale purple and blue, rich red and bright yellow, as a striking contrast to the rigidity of the objects. The picture may well be seen as an expression of a situation of disharmony and lack, but its painterly qualities and sad, uncanny mood lift it above the private level. In a letter of 1927 to Grünewald, still formally her husband, Hjertén wrote: "I understand that you accept the artistic erotic feeling that is mine, but that you confuse it with the feeling that you experience yourself and which does not spring from the same source". A few years earlier she had commented on her situation: "I do not work much nowadays, I am absorbed in the work of my husband. His success, adversities, dreams and aspirations are mine, and then I also have the boy and the housekeeping. That is enough, and I take pleasure in it. I now paint only for my pleasure" (Idun, 1924). Significant paintings from the Paris years are Berthe Darning Socks (1922; private collection, repr. Haglund 1985, pl.39), In the Garden (1922; private collection, repr. Stockholm 1995, pl.49), both scenes of domestic intimacy reminiscent of the art of "Les Nabis", and The Nunnery (1922;

Göteborgs Konstmuseum, Göteborg, repr. Haglund 1985, pl.36).

A fine expression of Hjertén's "artistic erotic feeling" is The Beach (1917; Göteborgs Konstmuseum, repr. Stockholm 1995, pl.31), one of a number of spontaneous, sensual studies of sunbathers. In a later version she drew a sharp line splitting the scene in two, one part glowing with golden sunlight, the other chilled with blue shadow (Beach and Shadow, 1918; private collection, ibid., pl.44). In the Chalk Cliff, St Aubin (1921; private collection, ibid., pl.46) she contrasted the luminous monumentality of the cliff wall and the cool, cloudy sky with the small boats and human figures. Twelve years later she painted the subject anew, but as a screen of glowing, contrasting colours, the intensity of which seems to reveal a mental state of anguish rather than of pleasure (Chalk Cliffs in Brittany, 1933; private collection, ibid., pl.67).

The playfully futuristic Harvesting Machines in Stadsgården (1915; ibid., pl.18) can be instructively compared to a number of paintings dating from 1934, such as Large Red Crane (private collection, repr. Haglund 1985, pl.58), Steamers in Stadsgården (private collection, ibid., pl.62) and Wooden Horses and Cock (1934; Stockholms Konstråd, ibid., pl.65). Through her work Hjertén privileges the vermilion, cadmium and red-lead tones, in the 1910s using it as a signifier of intense, often sexually connoted, disciplined energy, in the 1930s loading it with an unconscious, anguished meaning. Her painting manifests a gradual shift from the communication of symbolic language to the dissolved flow of materialised colour that refers to nothing but itself.

From the very beginning Hjertén's art was treated with an almost entire lack of understanding, not to say frank disdain, by most Swedish art critics. In 1912 even Brunius, who was to become one of her few supporters, wrote: "The paintings by Mrs Grünewald have a mild and amiable clang of echo." The critique aimed at her art can be summarised in three points: her work was compared to that of her husband and considered a weak and affected copy; when her art was described as "feminine" or "primitive" it was always in a derogatory sense; her paintings were attacked as perverse and even insane. It was not until the large exhibition of 1935 in Göteborg and her first solo exhibition, in 1936, at the Royal Academy of Fine Arts in Stockholm that her art was recognised as being deeply original, securing her a distinguished position in her generation of artists. Today the work of Sigrid Hjertén is greatly appreciated in Sweden, and regarded as an uncompromising, vigorous, sensitive and very bold expression of her time and being.

NINA WEIBULL

Hobson, Diana

British glass artist and sculptor, 1943–

Born in Stoke-on-Trent, Staffordshire, 9 April 1943. Trainee designer for Clarice Cliff (Ceramics), 1958. Studied at Stoke-on-Trent School of Art, 1959–64 (NDD ceramics). Designer for Howard Pottery Ltd, 1965–71. Enamellist to jeweller Wendy Ramshaw (q.v.), 1972–3; studied metalworking at Royal College of Art, London, 1973–6 (MA). Attached to

Ateneum School of Art and Design, Helsinki, Finland, on British Council scholarship, 1976–7. Lecturer in metalwork, Camberwell School of Arts and Crafts, London, 1979–87; taught workshops at Pilchuck Glass summer schools, near Seattle, USA, 1987, 1988, 1990 and 1991; visiting lecturer, Royal College of Art, London, 1995. Practical research into the technique of *pâte de verre* glass, 1980–81. Recipient of Second Coburg glass prize, 1985; Rakow Commission, Corning Museum of Glass, New York, 1989. Lives in London.

Principal Exhibitions

Coleridge, London: 1983 (with Anne Dickenson)
Galerie d'Amon, Paris: 1984 (*Pâte de verre actuelles*)
Paskine de Gignoux, Strasbourg: 1984 (*Verre contemporain en Europe*)
Crafts Council Gallery, Victoria and Albert Museum, London: 1986 (individual)
Clara Scremini, Paris: 1988 (with Tessa Clegg and Keith Cummings)
Hokkaido Museum of Modern Art, Japan: 1988 (*World Glass Now 88*)
Japan and Australia: 1988–9 (*Contemporary British Crafts, 1988–9*, touring, organised by British Council)
Corning Museum of Glass, NY: 1989 (*Copper the Colour of Magic*)
Kurland Summers Gallery, Los Angeles: 1990 (individual)
Crafts Council Gallery, London: 1993 (*Glass Show*), 1995 (*Influence of Nature on Craft and Design*)

Selected Writings

"Breaking the mould", *Crafts*, no.64, September–October 1983, pp.36–9

Bibliography

Dan Klein, "Pâte de verre Britannique", *Revue de la Céramique et du Verre*, no.38, January–February 1988, pp.40–43
—, "Diana Hobson", *New Work Magazine*, Fall 1988
Susanne Frantz, *Contemporary Glass: A World Survey from the Corning Museum of Glass*, New York: Abrams, 1989
Dan Klein, *Glass: A Contemporary Art*, London: Collins, and New York: Rizzoli, 1989
Jeremy Theophilus, "Sources of inspiration", *Crafts*, no.113, November–December 1991, pp.44–7
Wendy Ramshaw, "Seven steps: Neue Arbeiten der Keramikkünstlerin Diana Hobson", *Art Aurea*, January 1993, pp.86–9

Diana Hobson is best known as a glass artist who developed the ancient glass technique of *pâte de verre*, first using the vessel form, then later using glass together with other materials in sculpture. She starting exhibiting *pâte de verre* work in 1983 in London, and has since exhibited throughout Europe and North America and has work in many private and public collections, including the Victoria and Albert Museum, London, Musée des Arts Décoratifs, Paris, Corning Museum of Glass, New York, and Museum of Modern Art, Hokkaido.

Hobson's fragile, irregularly shaped yet balanced objects – thin-walled bowls around 15–20 centimetres in height – appear to be made of sculptured sugar, a froth of milky opalescent glass, delicate with areas of dense colour patterns, and seem to float on the exhibition stands. *Paté de verre* is a glass-making technique that consists of placing minute fragments of crushed glass in a mould, then firing them in a kiln to a temperature at which the glass starts to melt and the pieces fuse

together without melting, thus retaining opalescence rather than transparency. The process originated in ancient Egypt and Rome and enjoyed a revival in various forms in late 19th-century France, when there was a vogue for reviving ancient techniques.

Hobson is one of a number of artist-craftworkers who profited from the excellent art college facilities in Britain in the 1960s and 1970s. The launching of the Crafts Council and *Crafts* magazine promoted recognition that valid and meaningful art objects embodying profound truths could be made in materials that did not fall into the traditional fine art categories. Hobson trained as a silversmith, but it was while working with enamels on silver during her post-graduate studies at the Royal College of Art that she arrived at *pâte de verre*. Jewellery enamel comprises finely ground glass that is layered on to a metal surface and heated until the enamels melt and bond to the metal base. Hobson's need to create shapes that were delicate and ethereal led to experiments with the use of fused enamel without the metal base. The vessel form was chosen not as an end in itself but as a starting point for her ideas – hollow forms enclosing space like a seed pod, both the inside and the outside of the bowls being important.

The development of old techniques to express new ideas is a challenge not without its problems. Much experimentation was necessary to enable Hobson to keep the walls of the bowl very fine – thicker walls present fewer problems but were not considered appropriate vehicles for her ideas. The problems of glass breakages in firing frequently caused Hobson to question her use of glass, particularly *pâte de verre*, but the delicacy and transparency of the medium, suggesting light sources and intangibility, have always been important and relevant to her work. There are now a number of glass artists working in *pâte de verre* who have profited from her researches.

Multi-Coloured Form (1983; ht 15 cm.; Victoria and Albert Museum, London) is characteristic of Hobson's early period. It has a wide, brittle-looking rim, the remainder of the bowl being ornately decorated with dense areas of small-scale, brightly coloured patterns. The rims have always been a significant area in Hobson's vessels, forming a strong line to emphasise the shape, sometimes below a fragmented top, or with projecting stone fragments. Hobson worked in this way until 1984, using bright enamels and making small vessels in irregular, yet balanced shapes, the interior spaces of which were as important as the space surrounding them. She has always resisted the ever-present temptation of making "pretty objects" that sell well.

A visit to Crete in 1986 marked the next stage in Hobson's development. The rich colours of the soil and texture of stone used in sacred artefacts and in the colourful restoration work at Knossos made Hobson aware of a need for her work to be less ethereal and more earthbound, "harnessing", she said, "the energies of the land we all move in". She continued with the vessel, but in a more classical form, as, for example, in an inverted cone-shaped piece (Corning Glass Museum, NY) with regular geometric patterns in which she used ceramic body stains and Cretan sand to achieve a denser, more earth-bound look. Another piece of this period (1986; Victoria and Albert Museum) with a pronounced rim is in opalescent *pâte de verre* with small squares of perforated metal fired into the surface in a geometric pattern. A characteristic of artists exploring ideas

Hobson: *New Texture Series No.1*, 1987; *pâte de verre*; height 20 cm.; private collection

outside the traditional fine art area is an intense interest in the quality of materials themselves, constantly exploring but without allowing the materials to dominate.

During the next stage in Hobson's development the shape and surface of the vessels became rougher and more elemental, like unhewn rocks, shapes battered by the elements, the patterns irregular, and the colours – browns, ochres and greens – almost opaque. She mixed coloured earths brought back from Crete with the crushed glass, breaking down the traditional barriers between glass and ceramics. These objects inhabit an in-between area, almost opaque but at the same time retaining some of the ethereal quality of glass, incorporating pebbles around the pronounced rims.

The next phase of Hobson's work was marked by a move away from the container form. Pieces now combined found objects, stones with cast glass and cast metal forms. Several years of teaching at the Pilchuck Glass summer school near Seattle, and of travel in North America, put Hobson in touch with different peoples. Hobson does not embrace any formal religion, but she is fascinated by mythology, the spiritual dimensions common to all cultures, particularly the myths concerning creation and the sources of knowledge. *Copper, the Colour of Magic*, commissioned by the Corning Museum of

Glass in 1989, is a work from this period. The mythical "Copper woman" was washed up in a coracle as a small child on the uninhabited shores of Vancouver Island, became the guardian of Native American knowledge and created the first man and woman of that culture. Using a naturally split, smooth and egg-shaped stone, Hobson placed a white *pâte de verre* bird symbol, wearing a crown of bronze feathers representing flight and spirit, together with a simple boat form made in *pâte de verre* with bands of strong colours, using American earth to colour the glass.

Since the mid-1990s Hobson's work has become much larger. One piece (artist's collection) incorporates branches of juniper tree (collected during a year spent in Finland), made permanent in bronze and combined with cast circles and spirals of opalescent glass to define volumes of diffused light. Hobson was impressed with the silent beauty, peace and sense of infinity engendered by the remote Lapland landscape situated within the Arctic Circle. She has moved on from the creative restrictions of the *pâte de verre* process to rethink the role of glass in her work, which now makes more use of symbols and stands on the floor to dominate a greater space around it.

KATE BADEN FULLER

Höch, Hannah
German artist, 1889–1978

Born Johanne Höch in Gotha, Thuringia, 1 November 1889. Enrolled at the Kunstgewerbeschule, Berlin, and studied glass design under Harold Bengen, 1912. Travelled to Cologne to see the Werkbund exhibition, 1914. Studied graphic art at the Staatliche Lehranstalt des Kunstgewerbemuseum (State School of the Arts and Crafts Museum) under Emil Orlik, 1915. Affair with artist Raoul Hausmann, 1915–22. Worked three days a week as a designer of handiwork patterns at the Ullstein Verlag, Berlin, 1916–26. Associated with the Berlin Dada circle from 1917. Met and collaborated with Kurt Schwitters, 1919. Visited Venice and Rome, 1920. Accompanied Hausmann and Schwitters on their performance tour "Anti-Dada-Merz-Tournee" to Prague, 1921. Travelled to Paris for the first time, 1924; met Mondrian. Lived with Til Brugman in The Hague, Netherlands, 1926–9; contact with De Stijl group. Moved back to Berlin with Brugman, 1929. Married Kurt Matthies, 1938; separated 1942; divorced 1944. Forbidden to exhibit by the National Socialists. Moved to Heiligensee in north Berlin, 1939. Guest at Villa Massimo, Rome, 1962. Died in Berlin-Heiligensee, 31 May 1978.

Principal Exhibitions

Individual
Kunsthuis de Bron, The Hague: 1929 (touring)
Kunstzaal d'Audretsch, The Hague: 1934, 1935
Brno, Czechoslovakia: 1934
Galerie Gerd Rosen, Berlin: 1946, 1957
Galerie Nierendorf, Berlin: 1964
Marlborough Gallery, London: 1966
Berlin Academy: 1971 (retrospective)

Höch: *Cut with the Kitchen Knife Dada, Through the Last Weimar Beer-Belly Cultural Epoch of Germany,* 1919–20; Nationalgalerie, Berlin

National Museum of Modern Art, Kyoto: 1974
Musée d'Art Moderne de la Ville de Paris: 1976 (touring retrospective)

Group
Graphisches Kabinett I.B. Neumann, Berlin: 1919 (*Dada*)
Novembergruppe, Berlin: 1920–23, 1925–6, 1930–31
Kunsthandlung Dr Otto Burchard, Berlin: 1920 (*Erste Internationale Dada-Messe*)
Moscow: 1924 (*Allgemeine deutsche Kunstausstellung*)
Onafhankelijken group, Netherlands: 1928–9
Deutscher Werkbund, Stuttgart: 1929 (*Film und Foto*, touring)
Grosse Berliner Kunstausstellung: 1930–31
Staatliche Kunstbibliothek, Berlin: 1931 (*Fotomontage*)
Haus der Juryfreien, Berlin: 1931 (*Frauen in Not*, touring)
Palais des Beaux-Arts, Brussels: 1932–3 (*Exposition internationale de la photographie*, touring)

Bibliography

Dada – Hannah Höch – Dada, exh. cat., Galleria del Levante, Milan and Munich [1963]
Hannah Höch, exh. cat., Marlborough Gallery, London, 1966
Heinz Ohff, *Hannah Höch*, Berlin: Mann, 1968
Hannah Höch: Collagen aus den Jahren 1916–1971, exh. cat., Akademie der Künste, Berlin, 1971
Hannah Höch Fotomontagen und Gemälde, exh. cat., Kunsthalle, Bielefeld, 1973
Suzanne Pagé, "Interview mit Hannah Höch", *Hannah Höch: Collages, peintures, aquarelles, gouaches, dessins*, exh. cat., Musée d'Art Moderne de la Ville de Paris, and elsewhere, 1976, pp.23–32
Hannah Höch zum Neunzigsten Geburtstag, exh. cat., Galerie Nierendorf, Berlin, 1979
Götz Adriani, ed., *Hannah Höch*, Cologne: DuMont, 1980
Jula Dech, *Schnitt mit dem Küchenmesser DADA durch die letzte Weimarer Bierbauchkulturepoche Deutschlands: Untersuchungen zur Fotomontage bei Hannah Höch*, Münster, 1981
Hannah Höch, 1889–1978, exh. cat., Fischer Fine Art, London, 1983
Helen Serger, *Hannah Höch, 1889–1978*, New York: La Boetie, 1983
Hannah Höch, 1889–1978: Collagen, exh. cat., Institut für Auslandsbeziehungen, Stuttgart, 1984 (with English text)
Hannah Höch, 1889–1978: Ihr Werk, Ihr Leben, Ihre Freunde, exh. cat., Berlinische Galerie, Berlin, 1989
Hannah Höch: Eine Lebenscollage, 2 vols, Berlin: Berlinische Galerie, 1989
Jula Dech and Ellen Maurer, *Da-da zwischen Reden zu Hannah Höch*, Berlin: Orlanda-Frauenverlag, 1991
Maud Lavin, *Cut with the Kitchen Knife: The Weimar Photomontages of Hannah Höch*, New Haven and London: Yale University Press, 1993 (contains extensive bibliography)
Marsha Meskimmon, *The Art of Reflection: Women Artists' Self-Portraiture in the Twentieth Century*, London: Scarlet Press, and New York: Columbia University Press, 1996

Hannah Höch had a long and varied career from the time of her association with the Berlin Dada group to the end of her life in 1978. She was a pioneer of photomontage, worked with graphics, photography, painting, collage and even produced puppets (Dada dolls). She was also responsible, during the Nazi period, for salvaging the work and papers of the Berlin Dada group that would have been confiscated and destroyed by the Reichskulturkammer because of their subversive political content. Despite the fact that she was forbidden to exhibit during the Third Reich, she remained in Berlin throughout the war years. Her position as a woman artist in the period makes her works fascinating studies of the gender politics of the day, and her development throughout her career of the themes of gender and racial boundaries and their disruption marks her out as an artist whose contemporary relevance is only beginning to be recognised fully.

Höch began her art training in 1912 at the Kunstgewerbeschule in Berlin. Her early training was decidedly that of a craftswoman; within the arts and crafts school, she studied glass painting. The outbreak of World War I spelt a break in her training and in 1915 she entered the graphics class of Emil Orlik at the Kunstgewerbemuseum school. Again, although this was not a fine art background *per se*, she would exploit the graphics training successfully in her Dada years. By 1919 she was active within the Berlin Dada group, whose membership included Raoul Hausmann, Johannes Baader, Hans Richter, George Grosz, John Heartfield and Wieland Herzfelde.

This politicised group formed the core of an anarchic practice that centred on the use of mass media and montage; both of these forms suited Höch's own aesthetics perfectly. However, the subtle themes in Höch's work differentiated her from the rest of the group, who mainly produced blatant forms of political propaganda and social criticism. Such subtle differences are apparent in such works as *Cut with the Kitchen Knife Dada, Through the Last Weimar Beer-Belly Cultural Epoch of Germany* (1919–20; see illustration) and *Da Dandy* (1919; private collection, repr. Lavin 1993). In these works Höch used the photomontage common to the Dada group in order to explore particular ideas of gender politics within the wider socio-political realm. In *Cut with the Kitchen Knife*, for example, she included a variety of male politicians from the government of the Weimar Republic, such as President Ebert, Reichswehrminister Noske and General von Pflazer-Baltin, but placed them with reference to a host of images concerned with the phenomenon of the *neue Frau* (New Woman). On one level, the work associated the right-wing and moderate politicians with "anti-Dada"; the social criticism of this placement is explicit and over-determined. Ebert and the others share space with Kaiser Wilhelm II and Friedrich von Hindenberg at the upper right of the work, while the Dadaists sit at the lower right with Karl Marx.

On another level, however, Höch's juxtapositions of these politicians and male artists with popular icons of the New Woman, such as Niddy Impekoven, Asta Nielsen and Pola Negri as well as the head of the well-known woman artist Käthe Kollwitz (q.v.), take this photomontage out of the simple realms of party politics and critique. Such popular images of female dancers and artists represented the possible liberation of women in the period through their newly acquired access to the public sphere. As Maud Lavin has noted: "Women occupy the principal revolutionary roles in *Cut with the Kitchen Knife*, often signified by dramatic or assertive physical movement, such as dancing or ice skating" (1993, p.23). The "kitchen knife" of the title further suggests the way in which the domestic, feminine sphere could enact the decisive cutting through of sterile, masculine party politics.

Höch's use of mass-media images derived from journals particularly concerned with a female audience (that new phenomenon, the "woman's magazine", exemplified by *Die Dame*) also heightened the gender implications of her recontextualising montages. It is not insignificant that between 1916 and 1926 she worked at the Ullstein Verlag, one of whose main publication interests was the woman's magazine. Her graphics background and knowledge of photographic technique meant that she was well suited to her work at Ullstein, while their publications were clearly of great interest to her. Throughout her life, Höch collected mass-media images, which she kept in journals and scrapbooks. Her scrapbooks from the Weimar Republic practically document the publications aimed at a female audience.

Da Dandy examined these images further. In this work Höch montaged a series of fashion plates of the New Woman into a work that both critically examines and celebrates this image. The way in which the figures of the women are composed of a number of isolated sections drawn from photographs of women parodies the fetishisation of women in mass-media advertising and exposes the mythical nature of the "ideal" woman. But this work also experiments with recombinations that are aesthetically pleasing in their own right and address the spectator in a very direct manner. Such multivalent uses of popular imagery were to characterise Höch's oeuvre throughout her life.

Höch's reputation during the Dada years was overshadowed by those of her male contemporaries and especially by the fact that she was romantically linked to Hausmann. In Hans Richter's memoirs of the Berlin Dada group, for example, Höch is consistently referred to as peripheral to the group, despite her activities within it. Most of the literature on Dada has tended until recently to marginalise Höch's contribution and ignore her integral participation in such events as the infamous *Erste Internationale Dada-Messe* of 1920 in Berlin and her collaborations with the Hannoverian Dadaist Kurt Schwitters. Höch produced photomontages and dolls that were displayed alongside works by the male members of the Berlin Dada group and, in a form of three-dimensional montage, Höch added two "grottoes" to the now-destroyed *Merzbau* that Schwitters produced during the 1920s.

Clearly, the emphasis on women's roles and the domestic sphere in Höch's Dada works also served to distance her from the centre until recent feminist re-evaluations of the period sought to explore these themes. Works such as the watercolour *Bourgeois Bridal Couple* (1920; private collection) and *My House-Sayings* (1922; Galerie Nierendorf, Berlin) are particularly concerned with the domestic roles performed by middle-class women in the period. While they provide brilliant critiques of these roles, their very domesticity in content marked Höch's distinction from the rest of the Berlin set. *Bourgeois Bridal Couple* uses the image of the bride as a mannequin, so commonplace in advertising images of women in the period, to suggest the mindlessness and emptiness of the role of the wife in contemporary society. This is represented by a large church, a series of houses and a huge coffee grinder in addition to the figure of the groom, in order to play out the masquerade. *My House Sayings* takes the form of the guest book kept by middle-class housewives for their visitors to write in. Höch's guest book parodies this trite convention by having Dada sayings written all over it, such as "Death is a thoroughly Dadaist affair" by Richard Huelsenbeck. Furthermore, the montaged images, which include a self-portrait of Höch and ball bearings next to bits of lace and needlepoint diagrams, underlie the critical eye with which the artist approached such domestic fancies.

By the mid-1920s Höch's associations with the members of the Berlin Dada group had mainly ended, as had her relationship with Hausmann. She was far more involved artistically during this period with Kurt Schwitters in Hannover and with Jean Arp and Sophie Taeuber-Arp (q.v.), Theo and Nelly van Doesburg and Til Brugman in the Netherlands. From 1926 until 1929 Höch lived with Brugman in Holland and worked closely with the Bauhaus and De Stijl circles. Again, these ties were with the part of the avant-garde that most thoroughly integrated fine and mass production, the arts and the crafts. Höch's work continued to be conceived from this very union between fine art and mass media. From this point, the more subtle themes of androgyny and ethnicity that would characterise her late work entered into her production.

In such works as *The Coquette I* (1923–5) and *Half-Caste* (1924; both Institut für Auslandsbeziehungen, Stuttgart) Höch manipulated the conventions of gender and race in order to produce works that explored the boundaries of those concepts and their social and political meanings. *The Coquette I* shows the stylish body of a woman being fêted by a "man-bear" and "man-dog", two composite representations derived from images of humans and animals. The fashionable female figure is surmounted by a man's head. Hence, the very standard poses of the coquette and her suitors are turned back upon themselves and confounded by the viewer's inability to fix any gender or biological identities to the figures. *Half-Caste* suspends our ability to determine racial identity in much the same way. Placed in the centre of an Asian female face is a pair of "Clara Bow" lips, a white woman's lips in the fashionable red lipstick of the period. Such imagery not only points to the construction of gender and racial identity as mere image, but parodies our attempts to fix these and mediate between people based on such false constructs. Given the period in which these were produced, when the politics of fixed gender and racial identity were so critical to power relations, Höch's work can be seen to be decidedly anarchic and subversive.

These themes were also explored as a means towards redefining canons of beauty and aesthetics. Looking at the two works *Strange Beauty* (1929; private collection, *ibid.*) and *Strange Beauty II* (1966; private collection, repr. Stuttgart 1984), the production of which was separated by almost four decades, reveals the way in which such multiplication of meaning remained a constant source of inspiration to Höch in her work. *Strange Beauty* placed a reclining, white female nude body into communion with a montaged African "fetish" head; both blurred gender and racial boundaries are again suggested in the piece. The work, however, also queries beauty itself as an operative visual category. By indicating estrangement, Höch was able, like Brecht, to distance the viewer critically and insist that new strategies of looking be defined. The sheer appeal of this work and its counterpart, *Strange Beauty II*, with its voluptuous colours and textures, confronts us with an alternative space for pleasure.

Such subtle refinements in concepts of seeing and reading work have made Hannah Höch one of the best-known and most discussed women artists of the last two decades. She has been subject to a number of outstanding critical reviews and her works have been shown widely. Her training, association with the avant-garde and sophisticated questioning of gender stereotypes all make her an ideal topic for feminist re-evaluations of the art produced by women in the 20th century.

MARSHA MESKIMMON

Hodgkins, Frances
New Zealand painter, 1869–1947

Born in Dunedin, South Island, 28 April 1869; father a solicitor and amateur painter. Took classes with visiting Italian painter Girolamo Pieri Nerli, 1893. Attended Dunedin School of Art, 1895–6. First visited Europe, 1901, travelling in England, France, Italy, Morocco and the Netherlands; attended Norman Garstin's sketching classes at Caudebec and Dinan, France, summers 1901 and 1902. Returned to New Zealand, 1903, opening studio in Wellington. Second visit to Europe, 1906; stayed in the Netherlands, 1907–8, before settling in Paris; first woman teacher at Académie Colarossi, 1910. Returned to New Zealand for the last time, 1912–13, then settled permanently in Europe. Lived in St Ives, Cornwall, during World War I, then divided time between Britain and France, painting in Spain, 1932–3 and 1935–6. Died at Herrison House, a psychiatric hospital near Dorchester, Dorset, 13 May 1947.

Principal Exhibitions

Individual
Claridge Gallery, London: 1928
Bloomsbury Gallery, London: 1929 (with Vera Cunningham)
St George's Gallery, London: 1930, 1948 (retrospective)
Lefevre Gallery, London: 1933, 1937, 1940, 1943, 1946 (retrospective)
Leicester Galleries, London: 1935, 1941
Wertheim Gallery, London: 1936
Manchester City Art Gallery: 1947

Group
New Zealand Academy of Fine Arts, Wellington: 1892, 1898, 1900
Otago Art Society, Dunedin: 1890, 1895–6, 1898, 1900–02
Doré Gallery, London: 1902
Royal Academy, London: 1903–5, 1915–16
Fine Art Society, London: 1903
Paris Salon: 1909
Société Nationale des Beaux-Arts, Paris: 1911–12
International Society, Grosvenor Gallery, London: 1915–19
Women's International Art Club, London: 1919, 1924
London Salon of the Allied Artists Association: 1920–21
Salon d'Automne, Paris: 1924, 1938
London Group: 1927, 1929
New English Art Club, London: 1927–8, 1932–3
Seven and Five Society, London: 1929, 1931, 1932, 1933, 1934
Lefevre Gallery, London: 1938 (*New Paintings*), 1945 (with Francis Bacon, Henry Moore, Matthew Smith and Graham Sutherland), 1946 (*British Painters Past and Present*)
London Gallery, London: 1939 (*Living Art in England*)
National Gallery, Wellington: 1939 (*Centennial Exhibition of International and New Zealand Art*)
Hertford House, London: 1940 (*Paintings Selected for Inclusion in the 22nd Biennale di Venezia*)
Musée du Jeu de Paume, Paris: 1946 (*Tableaux britanniques modernes appartenant à la Tate Gallery*, organised by British Council)
Albright Art Gallery, Buffalo: 1946 (*British Contemporary Painters*)

Selected Writings
Letters of Frances Hodgkins, ed. Linda Gill, Auckland: Auckland University Press, 1993

Bibliography
John Piper, "Frances Hodgkins", *Horizon*, iv/24, 1941, pp.413–16
Eardley Knollys, "Obituaries: Frances Hodgkins", *Burlington Magazine*, lxxxix, 1947, pp.197–8
Geoffrey Gorer, "Remembering Frances Hodgkins", *The Listener*, 19 June 1947, p.968
Myfanwy Evans, *Frances Hodgkins*, Harmondsworth: Penguin, 1948
Arthur Rowland Howell, *Frances Hodgkins: Four Vital Years*, London: Rockliff, 1951
Ethel Walker, Frances Hodgkins, Gwen John: A Memorial Exhibition, exh. cat., Tate Gallery and Arts Council, London, 1952
E.H. McCormick, *The Expatriate: A Study of Frances Hodgkins*, Wellington: New Zealand University Press, 1954
—, *Works of Frances Hodgkins in New Zealand*, Auckland: Auckland City Art Gallery, 1954
Ascent, 1969 (Frances Hodgkins commemorative issue)
Charles Brasch, "Frances Hodgkins at one hundred", *Landfall*, no.92, 1969, pp.265–76
Frances Hodgkins, 1869–1947: A Centenary Exhibition, exh. cat., Auckland Art Gallery, and elsewhere, 1969
J. Rothenstein, *Modern English Painters: Sickert to Smith*, 2nd edition, London: Macdonald and Jane's, 1976
E.H. McCormick, *Portrait of Frances Hodgkins*, Auckland: Auckland University Press, 1981
Katy Deepwell, "Women in the Seven and Five Society", *Women Artists Slide Library Journal*, no.22, April–May 1988, pp.10–12
Frances Hodgkins, 1869–1947, exh. cat., Whitford and Hughes, London, 1990
Michael Dunn, *A Concise History of New Zealand Painting*, Sydney: Craftsman House, 1991
Frances Hodgkins: The Late Work, exh. cat., Minories Art Gallery, Colchester, and elsewhere, 1991
Anne Kirker, *New Zealand Women Artists: A Survey of 150 Years*, 2nd edition, Tortola, BVI: Craftsman House, 1993
Iain Buchanan, "Frances Hodgkins and Neo-romanticism", *Writing a New Country: A Collection of Essays Presented to E.H. McCormick in his 88th Year*, ed. James Ross, Linda Gill and Stuart McRae, Auckland, 1993, pp.155–64
R.D.J. Collins, "A long attachment: Frances Hodgkins in France", *ibid.*, pp.84–95
Women's Suffrage Exhibition, exh. cat., Museum of New Zealand, Te Papa Tongarewa, Wellington, 1993
Iain Buchanan, Elizabeth Eastmond and Michael Dunn, *Frances Hodgkins: Paintings and Drawings*, Auckland: Auckland University Press, 1994; London: Thames and Hudson, 1995
Pamela Gerrish Nunn, "Frances Hodgkins: A question of identity", *Woman's Art Journal*, xv/5, 1994–5, pp.9–13
Influence and Originality: Ivon Hitchens, Frances Hodgkins, Winifred Nicholson: Landscapes, c.1920–1950, exh. cat., Djanogly Art Gallery, University of Nottingham, and elsewhere, 1996

Unpublished correspondence, 1875–1946, is in the Alexander Turnbull Library, Wellington; Frances Hodgkins Papers are in the Tate Gallery Archives, London.

Frances Hodgkins was a key figure in the context of British art of the 1930s and 1940s. Her early career developed with the support of her father, the watercolourist William Matthew Hodgkins, and alongside that of her initially more successful sister Isabel. Her great achievement, after absorbing the possibilities available in New Zealand's then provincial and colonial situation, and after several decades of persistent work, travel and experimentation in Europe and Britain, was to contribute significantly to British modernism. From about the age of 60 until the year before her death she held numerous solo exhibitions in London and exhibited with such avant-garde groups as the Seven and Five Society. She was invited to join Unit One (but withdrew), was one of the artists chosen to represent Britain at the Venice Biennale of 1940, exhibited at the Lefevre Gallery with Francis Bacon, Henry Moore, Matthew Smith and Graham Sutherland in 1945, and took part in a number of Neo-romantic group exhibitions and other international exhibitions.

Hodgkins's career can be roughly divided into three main phases: the period up to 1913, when she left New Zealand for the last time; the period from 1914 to c.1929; and the period from c.1929, when she first exhibited with the Seven and Five Society, until 1946, the year before her death. Her early works of the 1890s in New Zealand show the influence of her father, but figure subjects, not landscapes, predominate. The teaching of an Italian expatriate, Girolamo Pieri Nerli, was an important influence at this stage. The intimate qualities and loose watercolour technique of such portraits as the *Girl with the Flaxen Hair* (1893; Museum of New Zealand, Te Papa Tongarewa) can be linked to Nerli's portraiture of young women. Her genre scenes, such as *A Goose Girl* (1893; private collection, New Zealand, repr. McCormick 1981, p.22), show the artist adopting a conventionally sentimental approach to rural activity of the kind common in the work of certain late 19th-century European and European-influenced artists such as Helen Allingham (q.v.). Hodgkins also produced a number of works based on Maori subjects, mainly studies of women and children. *Maori Girl* (1896; Dunedin Public Art Gallery), which displays her proficiency at laying on wet-on-wet watercolour washes, has the girl's head isolated against the ground; the treatment of the subject again somewhat romanticises and arguably decontextualises (as with other artists' treatment of related subjects) Maori in terms of their then marginal and underprivileged social status. Depicting Maori as "exotic" connects works of this kind with the practice of such European artists as Jules Bastien-Lepage (whose work was known in New Zealand) in his paintings of peasants and peasant labour.

From 1901 to 1912 Hodgkins's work became, through her travels, more directly inspired by European art, although this inspiration was still Impressionist-based rather than a response to the European avant-garde of the first decade of the 20th century. She spent several years in France and in 1910 taught a class in watercolours at the Académie Colarossi. Paintings from this period, such as *Orange Sellers, Tangier* (1903; Olveston, Dunedin), can be related to similar subjects by Frank Brangwyn and Arthur Melville, while the breezy plein-air spirit of *Hill Top* (c.1908; Museum of New Zealand), with its group of women interacting with relaxed intimacy, its windswept outdoor setting and the spontaneous, vigorous brushwork, can be read as signifying something of the atmosphere of contemporary emancipation. The theme of women together, or of women with children, often treated in a way that iconographically and stylistically explores notions of intimacy, is a feature of several works throughout Hodgkins's career, and is an emphasis that connects some of her more Impressionist-related works of the pre-1920s with the women Impressionists Berthe Morisot (q.v.) and Mary Cassatt (q.v.). One of her last works

in this style is *At the Window* (c.1912; Art Gallery of South Australia, Adelaide), which prefigures a major thematic preoccupation of her late phase: the still-life landscape.

The war years of 1914–18, when Hodgkins was based in St Ives, corresponded to a major shift in her practice. She moved away from watercolour, Impressionist-influenced plein-air paintings to a series of often large-scale figurative works in oil. In *Loveday and Anne* (1916; Tate Gallery, London) the figures are posed informally in an interior domestic setting. Stylistically there is now more in common with the Post-Impressionists and with such Intimists as Bonnard and Vuillard, while Hodgkins conveys her increasingly individual painterly approach by engagingly free brushwork and a subtle and witty response to the different personalities of the figures. She links them in a formal and symbolic sense in terms of their relationship and femininity by the dominant motif and vivid colours of the foreground basket of flowers. Hodgkins was friendly with the older members of the Cornish School (Norman Garstin, Moffat Lindner, Stanhope Forbes), although her art was far less conservative. Later, as a result of the visit of Cedric Morris and Lett Haines in 1919–20, she probably came into contact with younger, rather more progressive artists such as Laura Knight (q.v.). The themes of Sickert's work appear to have exerted an influence in the choice of some of her subjects around 1919–20 (e.g. *My Landlady*, c.1920; Auckland City Art Gallery), while during the early to mid-1920s, when she was often based in France, she experimented with Post-Impressionism (portrait of *Lett Haines*, c.1920; untraced, repr. Buchanan, Eastmond and Dunn 1994, fig.21) and Cubism (*Red Cockerel*, 1924; Dunedin Public Art Gallery), and produced a dynamic series of black chalk drawings of the Provençal landscape (*Olives, St Tropez*, c.1921; Hocken Library, Dunedin).

The years 1925–7 were spent in Manchester, where Hodgkins worked for a time for the Calico Printers' Association. Little is known of her work for them, although the Association sent her to the Exposition Internationale des Arts Décoratifs et Industriels Modernes in Paris (1925), where she would have seen the work of such artist-designers as Dufy and Sonia Delaunay (q.v.). *Double Portrait* (1922–5; Hocken Library) displays rich, Matissean decorative effects that probably reflect her textile work. A spectacular, large-scale drawing of this time, *Seated Woman* (c.1926; Tate Gallery), also displays a brilliant handling of both bold and subtle decorative effects. While in Manchester Hodgkins met one of her most important collectors, Lucy Wertheim, a gallery owner who also frequently exhibited Hodgkins's work of the later 1920s.

From 1928 to 1930 Hodgkins developed a strong, consistent personal style, focused on figure and landscape subjects. She began to experiment with what was to become a frequent theme in her art into the 1940s: the still-life landscape. In 1929 she exhibited for the first time with the Seven and Five Society, and in 1930 her crucial solo exhibition at St George's Gallery established her as an important British modernist whose sensuous French School-inspired colour was her strong suit. The *White House* (c.1930; Art Gallery of New South Wales, Sydney) is an early example of the still-life landscape combination. Painted in France, it demonstrates Hodgkins's rich, fluid paintwork and sensuous colour typical of this period. A little later, outstanding works such as *Wings over Water* (1931–2;

Hodgkins: *Spanish Shrine*, 1933–4; Auckland Art Gallery Collection

Tate Gallery), *Arum Lilies* (*c*.1931; private collection, Britain; repr. Buchanan, Eastmond and Dunn 1994, pl.26), which was much reproduced in the 1930s, *Spanish Still Life and Landscape* (1932–3; Robert McDougall Art Gallery, Christchurch) and the watercolour *Enchanted Garden*, also known as *Cornish Garden* (1932; Sheffield City Art Galleries), continue to explore this conflation of genres in diverse ways.

From the early 1930s until her death Hodgkins was based in Britain, with much of the last ten years spent in or near Corfe Castle in Dorset. The period included sojourns at Bradford-on-Tone, Somerset, trips to Wales and two significant periods of work in Spain: 1932–3 in Ibiza and 1935–6 in Tossa de Mar. Her work, with its highly individual approach to colour and continual exploration of new kinds of increasingly calligraphic brushwork, moved through a succession of phases of selective and intelligent response to current movements in the arts: from the lyrical naturalism and *faux-naïveté* associated with the Seven and Five Society, to New Classicism of the 1920s, to Surrealism, through to Neo-romanticism, always tempered by her interest in major artists of the French School such as Matisse, Picasso and Dufy. The aesthetics of other cultures and times were also important to her: Chinese art, medieval art and child art, for instance, while her paintings of

the 1940s show concerns similar to those of Paul Nash and John Piper.

While the combination of the still-life and landscape genres is not confined to Hodgkins, her persistent and individual exploration of variations on this theme is unique. Her still-life landscapes demonstrate a concern for transgressing boundaries of genre and setting in their varied plays on interior/exterior spaces, and her selection of still-life motifs is often strongly suggestive and with clearly symbolic overtones. Early examples such as *Wings over Water* (1931–2; Tate Gallery) have the still-life elements (here lushly painted large-scale shells) set on a ledge overlooking a coastal view, while a later example such as *Walled Garden with Convolvulus* (1942–3; private collection, New Zealand, *ibid.*, pl.21) places the still life within a landscape setting and merges the two elements by adopting an overall calligraphic painterly approach bordering on abstraction. Still-life-related motifs are also a feature of one of the few large-scale figure compositions of Hodgkins's late work: *Spanish Shrine* (1933–4; see illustration). Eric Newton praised the balance achieved here between "the world of her eye and the world of her mind's eye … The picture is both a symbol and a description and the two are interwoven" (Eric Newton, "Frances Hodgkins", *The Listener*, 2 October 1941, p.473). Begun, if not completed in Ibiza in 1933, the painting's two neo-primitivising figures of women carrying on their heads, respectively, a barrel and a basket of fruit flank a mysterious, grisaille depiction of a statue of a woman with closed eyes. There are echoes of Rouault and Picasso, while the dynamic achieved between the three iconic, frontally positioned figures and the marvellously subtle array of shifting patches of salmon pinks, pale aquamarines and bronzes contributes to the painting's unique quality.

In the mid-1930s Hodgkins produced two innovative paintings that combine the genres of still life and self-portraiture. In one, *Self-Portrait: Still Life* (c.1935; Auckland City Art Gallery), a table-top is tilted vertically to frame various objects chosen by the artist to speak for her presence: a central bowl and pink rose, symbols of femininity; a belt, suggestive of the absent body; an amusingly frivolous pink high-heeled shoe and a mass of patterned scarves. This painting makes an intriguing addition to the range of self-representations made by women artists in the inter-war period.

Works of the later 1930s painted in Spain, such as the gouache *Pumpkins and Pimenti* (c.1935–6; Fletcher Challenge Art Collection, New Zealand; once owned by Sir Kenneth Clark), show that the artist was alert to Surrealism – distant mountains appear to erupt through the table and around the effectively sombre greys, sharp blues and reds of this Mediterranean still-life landscape. Hodgkins's one major experiment in printmaking was also produced in these years: the buoyant and boldly designed *Arrangement of Jugs* (1938), which was published by Contemporary Lithographs Ltd and printed at the Curwen Press. Hodgkins's last major figure painting was also done at this time: the Picassoesque *Double Portrait No.2 (Katharine and Anthony West)* (1937–9; oil; Museum of New Zealand). Hodgkins, a close friend of the Wests, here produced a variant on her longstanding interest in the double portrait by focusing on a male/female couple rather than her customary double portraits of women.

A significant number of Hodgkins's works of the war period, mostly highly individual and superbly painterly transformations of specific landscapes, show her connections with the Neo-romantics. She exhibited frequently both with established Neo-romantics such as Moore, Nash, Sutherland and Piper and also with the younger group, including John Minton, and the "two Roberts", Colquhoun and McBryde. But while the connections in terms of subject (e.g. *Broken Tractor*, 1942; gouache; Tate Gallery) and colour are clear, what set Frances Hodgkins apart from her colleagues (apart from gender and age) was the individual painterliness of her approach, with its continuing allegiance to the French School. As she herself put it, it was "that universality I ever strive after ... between the Ecole de Paris & FH" (letter from Frances Hodgkins to Duncan Macdonald, 11 April 1943). Many of Hodgkins's works from 1935 onwards are in gouache, a medium she exploited successfully in her increasingly free approach to colour, line and form. *Church and Castle, Corfe* (1942; Ferens Art Gallery, Hull City Museums and Art Galleries) includes typically Neo-romantic motifs of ruined castle and local church amidst an overall free surface play of ambiguous graphic effects, which renders these sites barely recognisable as a result of her increasingly abstract approach. A small group of major late works were, however, done in oil. These include the series based on the courtyard outside her studio at Corfe

Castle, of which the darkly dramatic *Courtyard in Wartime* (1944; University of Auckland Art Collection) is one important version. Another outstanding late oil is *Spanish Well, Purbeck* (1945; Auckland City Art Gallery). Both works combine a highly personal response to the idiosyncracies of place with a freely inventive formal approach verging on abstraction. The rather more highly keyed colouring of *Spanish Well, Purbeck* links it with her last post-war works, ebullient gouaches such as *Cherry Tree at the Croft* (1946; private collection, Britain, repr. London 1990, pl.32), painted at the age of 77.

Frances Hodgkins's important late work was generally highly regarded in her lifetime: besides representation in the exhibitions cited above, she was favourably reviewed by the critics Eric Newton, Raymond Mortimer and John Piper; she was included in John Piper's *British Romantic Artists* (London, 1947), and Myfanwy Evans's *Frances Hodgkins* (Harmondsworth, 1948) in the Penguin Modern Painters series was underway before her death. But the subsequent evaluation of her art has been somewhat uneven: she is widely recognised in New Zealand as one of the country's most important expatriate artists, and a major retrospective was held there in 1969, followed by several smaller exhibitions. But little of substance, until recently, has been written on her work (see Buchanan, Eastmond and Dunn 1994). In common with some other women artists, her situation as an "exceptional" woman has resulted in a focus on her life (McCormick 1981) and, as a successful expatriate New Zealander, as an exemplar of the complexities associated with expatriatism (McCormick 1954). The publication of Linda Gill's *Letters of Frances Hodgkins* (1993) has provided further invaluable material for both biographical and art historical study on this artist. In Britain, while some small recent exhibitions have signalled renewed interest in Hodgkins, and while she is covered in Frances Spalding's *British Art since 1900* (1989), such exhibitions as *British Art in the 20th Century* at the Royal Academy (1987) and *A Paradise Lost: The Neo-Romantic Imagination in Britain, 1935–55* at the Barbican, London (1987), did not include her. Neither did such major feminist resources on women artists as Germaine Greer's *The Obstacle Race* (1979) and *Women Artists, 1550–1950*, the catalogue of an exhibition held at the Los Angeles County Museum of Art in 1976.

ELIZABETH EASTMOND

Hoffman, Malvina

American sculptor, 1885–1966

Born in New York, 15 June 1885; father a concert pianist. Attended classes at Women's School of Applied Design and Art Students League, New York, 1899; studied sculpture under Herbert Adams and George Gray Barnard, painting under John White Alexander. Travelled to Europe with her mother after father's death in 1909. Worked for Janet Scudder (q.v.) as studio assistant in Paris and studied in Rodin's studio, 1910–11; continued to work with Rodin intermittently until outbreak of World War I. Enrolled in anatomy classes at College of Physicians and Surgeons, New York, 1911. Married musician Samuel Grimson, 1924;

divorced 1936. Studied equestrian sculpture under Yugoslav artist Ivan Mestrovic in Zagreb, 1927. Spent much time abroad, retaining a studio in Paris (Villa Asti) and travelling widely, particularly after receiving "Living Races of Man" commission from Field Museum of Natural History, Chicago, 1930. Recipient of first prize, Société Nationale des Beaux-Arts, Paris, 1912; first prize, American Art Students Club, Paris, 1913; Julia A. Shaw memorial prize, 1917, and Helen Foster Barnett prize, 1921, National Academy of Design, New York; George Widener gold medal, Pennsylvania Academy of the Fine Arts, Philadelphia, 1920; honorary degrees from Mount Holyoke College, South Hadley, and University of Rochester, 1937; Northwestern University, Evanston, 1945; Smith College, Northampton, 1951; Bates College, Lewiston, 1955. Member, National Academy of Design, 1931; American Institute of Arts and Letters, 1937; "Woman of the Year", American Association of University Women, 1957; fellow, National Sculpture Society, 1958. Chevalier, Légion d'Honneur, France, 1951. Died in New York studio, 10 July 1966.

Selected Individual Exhibitions
Grand Central Art Galleries, New York: 1928–30 (touring), 1934–6 (*Races of Man*, touring), 1936–8 (*Races of Man*, touring)
Corcoran Gallery, Washington, DC: 1929
Musée d'Ethnographie, Palais du Trocadéro, Paris: 1933 (*Les Races humaines*)
Robert C. Vose Galleries, Boston: 1937
Virginia Museum of Fine Arts, Richmond: 1937 (retrospective)

Selected Writings
"A sculptor goes head-hunting", *Asia*, xxxiii, 1933, pp.423–9, 450–52
Heads and Tales, New York: Scribner, 1936
Sculpture Inside and Out, New York: Norton, and London: Allen and Unwin, 1939
Yesterday Is Tomorrow: A Personal History, New York: Crown, 1965

Bibliography
Pauline Carrington Bouvé, "The two foremost women sculptors in America: Anna Vaughn Hyatt and Malvina Hoffman", *Art and Archaeology*, xxvi, September 1928, pp.77–82
Arsène Alexandre, *Malvina Hoffman*, Paris: Pouterman, 1930
Henry Field, *The Races of Mankind: An Introduction to Chauncey Keep Memorial Hall*, 4th edition, Chicago: Field Museum of Natural History, 1942
The Partial Figure in Modern Sculpture from Rodin to 1969, exh. cat., Baltimore Museum of Art, 1969
Joshua C. Taylor, "Malvina Hoffman", *American Arts and Antiques*, xi, July–August 1979, pp.96–103
Malvina Hoffman (1885–1966), exh. cat., FAR Gallery, New York, 1980
A Dancer in Relief: Works by Malvina Hoffman, exh. cat., Hudson River Museum, Yonkers, NY, 1984
The Woman Sculptor: Malvina Hoffman and Her Contemporaries, exh. cat., Berry-Hill Galleries, New York, 1984
Linda Nochlin, "Malvina Hoffman: A life in sculpture", *Arts Magazine*, lix, November 1984, pp.106–10
American Women Artists, 1830–1930, exh. cat., National Museum of Women in the Arts, Washington, DC, 1987
Janis Conner and Joel Rosenkranz, *Rediscoveries in American Sculpture: Studio Works, 1893–1939*, Austin: University of Texas Press, 1989
Pamela Hibbs Decoteau, "Malvina Hoffman and the 'Races of Man'", *Woman's Art Journal*, x/2, 1989–90, pp.7–12
Charlotte Streifer Rubinstein, *American Women Sculptors*, Boston: Hall, 1990

Malvina Hoffman Papers are in the Archives of the History of Art, Getty Center for the History of Art and the Humanities, Malibu.

Malvina Hoffman was one of the most successful, prolific and now neglected American sculptors of the inter-war period. Resources for her monumental production and adventurous life are found in her two autobiographies, *Heads and Tails* (1936) and *Yesterday Is Tomorrow* (1965).

Hoffman recounts her development in New York with a supportive family and formative training at the Women's School of Applied Design and the Art Students League. Gutzon Borglum, the sculptor of Mt Rushmore, saw Hoffman's portrait of her father, *Richard Hoffman*, and encouraged her to submit the plaster cast to the National Academy of Design (1910), and to carve it in marble. In the same year her bust of her future husband, the violinist *Samuel Grimson*, was shown at the Paris Salon. Her father, a pianist with the New York Philharmonic, died in 1909, leaving Hoffman with little more than high ideals. Determined to find avenues for self-support, she and her widowed mother sailed for Europe, first to Italy, then to France, where she camped on Rodin's doorstep until he finally accepted her as a student. During the years 1910–14, when she came to artistic maturity, the influence of the diverse, progressive styles of Paris was resolved in works that show remarkable skill and an astute observation of human form. Inspired by Rodin's fluent, energetic figures, the poetry of Gertrude Stein and above all by the prima ballerina, Anna Pavlova, who later became her close friend, Hoffman's naturalistic forms were endowed with graceful gestures, intense inner spirit and complex compositional arrangements. She avoided the neo-classicism of previous sculptors and sought instead to manifest the innate qualities of the subject, endowing representational details with brilliance of design, as in the bronze figure of Nijinsky in *L'Après-midi d'un faune* of 1912. Here the body is languidly prone, attired with horns, hoofs and light drapery over mid-section, with one leg over the other, the spiral movement of torso and shoulders imparting a faunlike grace. Sharing a similar artistic vision are *Russian Dancers*, depicting Anna Pavlova and Mikhail Mordkin as a dancing pair (exh. Paris Salon 1911; a monumental bronze version, *Bacchanale Russe*, was installed in the Jardin du Luxembourg in 1919 but destroyed in World War II), *Pavlova in La Gavotte* (1915; repr. Rubinstein 1990, p.179) and *Bacchanale*, a low-relief frieze of dancers (completed 1924).

On her return to New York in 1911 Hoffman took Rodin's advice and began anatomy classes in dissection with Dr George Huntington at the College of Physicians and Surgeons. She also acted on the suggestion of the Yugoslav sculptor Ivan Mestrovic that she become technically superior to her male competitors, and worked at foundries developing professional skills in casting and finishing bronze and bending metal. In the early 1920s she executed the war memorial, *The Sacrifice* (1920–22; Caen limestone; Harvard Memorial Chapel, Cambridge, MA), as well as bronze portraits of *John Keats* (University of Pittsburgh) and the pianist and Polish patriot *Ignacy Paderewski*. Two limestone figures, *England* and

Hoffman: *Tamil Climbing a Palm Tree*, 1933, from the *Races of Mankind* series; height 205.7 cm.; Field Museum of Natural History, Chicago

America, each 4.6 metres high, were commissioned in 1924 by Irving Bush for the nine-storey Bush House office building in London to represent Anglo-American friendship – the figures hold torches over a Celtic altar in the façade tympanum. The sculptures were insufficiently visible after installation, so Hoffman spent five weeks on a small platform high above the ground, deepening the relief. A bronze bust of *Anna Pavlova* (ht 33 cm.) resulted from the ballerina's tour to New York in 1928. The head is turned slightly to the right in a thoughtful pose, the drapery folding in from below the shoulder to converge on the clasped hands in front. In 1928 an exhibition of 105 pieces of Hoffman's sculpture was held at the Grand Central American Galleries in New York, followed by a tour of museums around the country.

After a trip to Africa, Hoffman produced a head of a *Senegalese Soldier* (1928; black marble; ht 50.8 cm.; Brooklyn Museum, NY) rendering it in a more cubic mode: the face is cut in simplified, angular planes, with sharp abstraction of the contours of cheeks and eyes. This, and the head of the *Girl from Martinique*, attracted the attention of officials of the Chicago Field Museum of Natural History. Hoffman persuaded them to assign to her, and cast in bronze, the largest sculpture project of the time to be granted to an individual sculptor: 110 life-size figures representing the *Races of Mankind* for the Hall of Man. She began the project in 1931

and completed it, near exhaustion, in 1933 in time for it to be shown as a centrepiece at the Chicago World's Fair. Peoples from French colonial territories had been assembled at the Colonial Exposition in Paris of 1930–31, and Hoffman was able to use them as models for her project in her Paris studio.

In pursuit of other models, she recounts her adventures to such distant lands as New Guinea, Africa and East Asia, as well as the Southwestern USA. Accompanied by her husband, a servant and an assistant to make plaster casts of her clay models, she travelled by all types of ship, from Chinese junks to South Sea outriggers, staying in dwellings ranging from mud huts to castles. The project comprises varying bust-length portraits, full-length single figures and family groups. Each image is lively and factual, showing meticulous attention to realistic surface detail. No artistic style foreign to the naturalism of the subject has been allowed to intrude on the objective scientific record of racial characteristics and authentic cultural lineage. In each figure references to communal rituals in clothing, body art, weaponry and pottery are preserved. The graceful *Dancing Sara Girl* from Chad rests on slightly bent legs and extends an arm in an elegant gesture. The bust-length *Eskimo Woman* reveals her heritage through braided hair, high cheekbones and almond eyes. The *Sicilian Man*, holding a fishing net and wearing very short trousers, shows masterly anatomical definition, as does the *Family of Pygmies* – a woman and child watch the hunter husband fire an arrow, his feet gripping the earth, fingers taut on the bow. *Tamil Climbing a Palm Tree* (see illustration) is aided in his quest by a pot slung at his side, his body roped into the tree for support. Almost all the sculptures are signed on the base: Malvina Hoffman, Art Institute, Chicago. The original moulds for the works were discovered in storage at the Chicago Field Museum of Natural History in 1995.

Of her later works, two major sculptures from 1948 include the *American World War II Memorial* at Epinal, France, for the US Fine Arts Commission, and the *History of Medicine* panels for the façade of the Joslin Clinic, Boston, executed in a simplified style to harmonise with the structure. Hoffman died at the age of 81 of a heart attack at her New York studio.

JANET A. ANDERSON

Hone, Evie
Irish painter and stained glass artist, 1894–1955

Born in Roebuck Grove, Co. Dublin, 22 April 1894, a descendant of the 18th-century painter Nathaniel Hone. Lived at intervals in continental Europe after being crippled with infantile paralysis at age eleven. During World War I, studied at the Byam Shaw School of Art, London, then at Westminster School under Walter Sickert; later studied briefly under Bernard Meninsky, who advised her to go to Paris. Studied with her friend Mainie Jellett (q.v.) under André Lhôte in Paris, 1920, then from 1921 under Albert Gleizes; worked for a time each year under Gleizes until the early 1930s. Member of Seven and Five Society, London, 1926–31; Abstraction-Création group, Paris, 1931. Turned from painting to stained glass, c.1933. Converted to Catholicism, 1939.

Hone: Stained-glass window with Crucifixion and Last Supper, 1949–52; Eton College, Berkshire

Member, Society of Dublin Painters, 1922–c.1950; White Stag Group, Dublin, 1940–41. Founder-member, with Jellett, of the Irish Exhibition of Living Art, 1943. Died in Rathfarnham, Co. Dublin, 13 March 1955.

Principal Exhibitions

Individual

Dublin Painters' Gallery: 1924 (with Mainie Jellett), 1929, 1931
Contemporary Picture Galleries, Dublin: 1941
Dawson Gallery, Dublin: 1945, 1947, 1957
University College, Dublin, and Tate Gallery, London: 1958–9 (retrospective)

Group

Dublin Painters' Gallery, Dublin: 1924 (*Cubist Paintings*)
Salon des Surindépendants, Paris: 1930–31
Abstraction-Création, Paris: 1931
Royal Hibernian Academy, Dublin: 1931–5, 1937
Contemporary Picture Galleries, Dublin: 1940 (*Académie Lhôte Irish Students*)
Irish Exhibition of Living Art, Dublin: from 1943

Bibliography

Mairin Allen, "Contemporary Irish artists, 17: Miss Evie Hone", *Father Mathew Record*, xxxvi, March 1943, p.7
C.P. Curran, "Evie Hone: Stained glass worker", *The Studio*, xliv, 1955, pp.129–42
Stella Frost, ed., *A Tribute to Evie Hone and Mainie Jellett*, Dublin: Browne and Nolan, 1957
Eileen MacCarvill, ed., *Mainie Jellett: The Artist's Vision: Lectures and Essays on Art*, Dundalk: Dundalgan Press, 1958
Irish Art, 1900–1950, exh. cat., Crawford Municipal Art Gallery, Cork, 1975
The Irish Impressionists: Irish Artists in France and Belgium, 1850–1914, exh. cat., National Gallery of Ireland, Dublin, 1984
Irish Women Artists from the Eighteenth Century to the Present Day, exh. cat., National Gallery of Ireland, Dublin, and elsewhere, 1987
Kenneth McConkey, *A Free Spirit: Irish Art, 1860–1960*, Woodbridge, Suffolk: Antique Collectors' Club-Pyms Gallery, 1990
S.B. Kennedy, *Irish Art and Modernism, 1880–1950*, Belfast: Institute of Irish Studies, 1991
Images and Insights, exh. cat., Hugh Lane Municipal Gallery of Modern Art, Dublin, 1993

Evie Hone's early career as a painter closely paralleled that of her friend and compatriot Mainie Jellett (q.v.); they both studied under, and later worked alongside, the French Cubist painter Albert Gleizes. With Jellett, Hone was largely responsible for introducing to Ireland in the early 1920s a first-hand knowledge of Cubism. She was thus for a time one of the most innovative of Irish painters.

Hone's brand of Cubism, which laid emphasis on the unity of matter in compositional terms, was in fact more nearly related to abstraction proper than to any of the theoretical principles of Cubism *per se*. Her compositions consist of rectangles and other geometrical shapes arranged, to begin with, concentrically and then turned about a central axis on the picture plane – a process that she and Jellett termed "translation" and "rotation", the overall intention being to produce an "organic" composition in which each element led the eye back into the unity of the whole. *Composition* (c.1924–5; National Gallery of Ireland, Dublin) exemplifies this development. Hone first exhibited pictures such as this, in a joint show

with Jellett, at the Dublin Painters' Gallery in June 1924, and met with considerable obloquy from the critics of the press. Both she and Jellett persevered, however, and over the following decade they held a number of similar exhibitions, eventually gaining a grudging acceptance for the validity of their approach.

In these years Hone also maintained contact with certain avant-garde movements outside Ireland. From 1926 until 1931 she was a member of the London-based Seven and Five Society and in 1931, in Paris, became a member of the Abstraction-Création group, the aim of which was to promote the purest form of non-objective art. But, despite these contacts, Hone grew tired of the somewhat arid abstraction that she had developed and seems to have suffered some crisis of conscience – in 1925 she joined for a time a community of Anglican nuns in Truro, Cornwall. Then, from the late 1920s, in compositions such as *A Cherry Tree* (c.1931; National Gallery of Ireland), representational imagery began to appear in her work. Reviewing her solo exhibition at the Dublin Painters' Gallery in 1931, the *Irish Times* remarked that she had "advanced from the earlier austere form of Cubism … and the result", it said, "is to lend a stronger atmosphere of life and mobility to her work" (*Irish Times*, 5 May 1931). Later, at the end of the 1930s, she abandoned Cubism completely.

Around 1933 Hone turned aside from painting and, working for a time with Wilhelmina Geddes (q.v.), took to stained glass, a medium that gave free rein to her growing powers as a colourist. Here she found her true métier in a medium that allowed her to develop her talents more naturally and completely than painting had done. She worked for a time alongside Michael Healy at An Túr Gloine, the Dublin glass house run by Sarah Purser (q.v.), and in 1938 produced her first important stained-glass window, *My Four Green Fields*, a large abstract composition done for the Irish Pavilion at the New York World's Fair of 1939. This piece was followed by a number of others, of which those at University Hall, Dublin (1947), St Stanislaus College, Tullabeg (1946; notably the *Nativity* and the *Beatitudes*), and St Mary's, Kingscourt (1947–8; *The Ascension*), are perhaps the most important of her works in Ireland, being especially notable for the simplicity and directness of the compositional technique. The success of these windows brought her the commission for what is her masterpiece, a large commemorative window in the chapel of Eton College, Berkshire (1949–52; see illustration).

Despite turning to stained glass, Hone did not give up painting completely, but her later paintings are largely expressionist in technique, and usually have a religious theme. In her later years she was influenced by Rouault, whom she admired for his simplicity of concept and spirituality; her Stations of the Cross at Kiltulla, Co. Galway (1946), for example, with their great pathos, have much in common with Rouault's work. In all its aspects Hone's art, in C.P. Curran's words: "was enclosed in her spiritual heroism and was fed and sustained by it" (Curran 1955). In 1943 Hone was a founder-member of the Irish Exhibition of Living Art and exhibited there regularly until the 1950s.

S.B. KENNEDY

Horenbout, Susanna *see* Guilds and the Open Market, and Court Artists surveys

Horn, Rebecca

German sculptor, performance artist and film-maker, 1944–

Born in Germany, 1944. Studied at the Hamburg Academy, 1964–9; St Martin's School of Art, London, 1971–2. Lived in New York, 1972–81; guest lecturer, California Art Institute of the University of San Diego, 1974. Divided time between New York and Paris from 1981. Professor of sculpture, Hochschule der Künste (Academy of Arts), West Berlin, from 1989. Recipient of Deutscher Akademischer Austauschdienst (DAAD) grant, 1971; Deutscher Kritikerpreis (German Critics award), for the film *Berlin-Übungen in neun Stücken*, 1977; Glockengasse art prize, Cologne, 1977; Böttcherstrasse art prize, Bremen, 1977; Documenta prize, Kassel, 1986; Carnegie prize, Carnegie International, Pittsburgh, 1988; Kaiserring, Goslar and Medienkunstpreis (Media art prize), Karlsruhe, for achievements in technology and art, 1992.

Selected Individual Exhibitions

Galerie René Block, Berlin: 1973
Galerie René Block, New York: 1974, 1976
Neuer Berliner Kunstverein, Berlin: 1975
Kölnischer Kunstverein, Cologne: 1975, 1977 (touring)
Saman Galleria, Genoa: 1975, 1976, 1981
Kestner-Gesellschaft, Hannover: 1978–9 (*Der Eintänzer*, touring), 1991
Salvatore Ala Gallery, New York: 1979
Staatliche Kunsthalle, Baden-Baden: 1981
Gewad, Vereniging Aktuele Kunst, Ghent: 1982
Galerie Eric Franck, Geneva: 1983, 1985, 1990
Centre d'Art Contemporain, Geneva: 1983–4 (touring)
Marian Goodman Gallery, New York: 1986, 1988, 1994
Musée d'Art Moderne de la Ville de Paris: 1986
Galerie Elisabeth Kaufmann, Zürich: 1987
Galerie de France, Paris: 1988, 1991, 1992
Artsite Gallery, International Festival, Bath: 1989
Museum of Contemporary Art, Los Angeles: 1990
Galerie Franck + Schulte, Berlin: 1991
Fundació Espai Poblenou, Barcelona: 1992
Solomon R. Guggenheim Museum, New York: 1993–5 (touring retrospective)

Selected Writings

Text in *Körpersprache*, exh. cat., Haus am Waldsee, Berlin, 1975
"Paradise-widow: Vedovanza, delicato strumento di martirio", *Saman* (Genoa), no.4, December–January 1976
Dialogo della vedova paradisiaca/Dialogue of the Paradise Widow, Genoa: Samanedizioni, 1976
"Maschera di gallo", *Saman* (Genoa), no.5, February–March 1976
"Cadacù", *Saman* (Genoa), no.6, May–June 1976
"Dialogo tra due altalene", *Saman* (Genoa), no.21, January–February 1980
"Reflections from the innermost earth to the outermost constellations", *Artforum*, xxvi, March 1988, pp.100–02
Rebecca Horn: La Lune Rebelle, Ostfildern: Cantz, 1993

Bibliography

Lea Vergine, *Il corpo come linguaggio*, Milan: Giampaolo Prearo, 1974
Timothy Baum, *Rebeccabook I*, New York: Nadada, 1975
Lucy R. Lippard, "The pains and pleasures of rebirth: Women's body art", *Art in America*, lxiv, May–June 1976, pp.73–81
Rebecca Horn: Arbeiten von 1968 bis 1977: Die Aktionsobjekte in ihren Reisekoffern, exh. cat., Haus am Waldsee, Berlin, 1977
Rebecca Horn: Zeichnungen, Objekte, Video, Filme, exh. cat., Kölnischer Kunstverein, Cologne, and elsewhere, 1977
Rebecca Horn: Der Eintänzer, exh. cat., Kestner-Gesellschaft, Hannover, and elsewhere, 1978
Rebecca Horn: La Ferdinanda: Sonate für eine Medici-Villa, exh. cat., Staatliche Kunsthalle, Baden-Baden, 1981
Bettina Gruber and Maria Vedder, *Kunst und Video*, Cologne: DuMont, 1983
Rebecca Horn, exh. cat., Centre d'Art Contemporain, Geneva, and elsewhere, 1983
Von hier aus: Zwei Monate neue deutsche Kunst in Düsseldorf, exh. cat., Messegelände Halle 13, Düsseldorf, 1984
Germano Celant, "Rebecca Horn: Dancing on the egg", *Artforum*, xxiii, October 1984, pp.48–55
Rebecca Horn: Nuit et jour sur le dos du serpent à deux têtes, exh. cat., Musée d'Art Moderne de la Ville de Paris, 1986
Bice Curiger, "Zarte Übertragungen/Gentle transference", *Parkett*, no.13, August 1987, pp.48–56
Skulptur Projekte Münster, exh. cat., Westfälisches Landesmuseum für Kunst und Kulturgeschichte, Münster, 1987
Rebecca Horn, exh. cat., Galerie de France, Paris, Marian Goodman Gallery, New York, and Carnegie International, Pittsburgh, 1988
Andreas Franzke, "New German sculpture: The legacy of Beuys", *Art and Design*, v/9–10, 1989, pp.29–33
Rebecca Horn: Missing Full Moon, exh. cat., Artsite Gallery, International Festival, Bath, 1989
Laura Cottingham, "The feminine de-mystique: Gender, power, irony and aestheticized feminism in '80s art", *Flash Art*, no.147, Summer 1989, pp.91–5
Rebecca Horn: Diving Through "Buster's Bedroom", exh. cat., Museum of Contemporary Art, Los Angeles, 1990
Künstlerinnen des 20. Jahrhunderts, exh. cat., Museum Wiesbaden, 1990
Rebecca Horn: Filme, 1978–1990, exh. cat., Kestner-Gesellschaft, Hannover, 1991
Bice Curiger, *Rebecca Horn: Buster's Bedroom: A Filmbook*, Zürich, Frankfurt am Main and New York: Parkett, 1991
Rebecca Horn, exh. cat., Solomon R. Guggenheim Museum, New York, and elsewhere, 1993 (contains extensive bibliography)

Rebecca Horn's art originated in the context of the early 1970s, when women artists referred to their bodies using performance, film and video as fresh means of expression. However, her early body sculptures, made from cloth, did not derive from contemporary art debate but from autobiography. A longish stay in a lung sanatorium as an art student led her to stop producing sculpture in polyester and fibreglass and begin an examination of the body. After this period of isolation, she used the body, the interface of personal and social experiences, as the medium to make contact with other people, including the opposite sex, in an experimental way. The attempt to relate art in its formal and historical structures to the experiencing subject – thus to the viewer as well – is apparent from her early performances, and continues throughout her oeuvre. Repeatedly, autobiographical links are crucial for the examination of specific themes and pictures, structured in form and content, whose sources are difficult to trace.

Horn extended the action of the body and its sensory and tactile abilities in such early performances as *Arm Extensions* (1968) and *Unicorn* (1970–72), which originated in a private circle of friends, using body fans, glove fingers and walking sticks, so-called body extensions. With these aids, Horn, increasingly acting herself, investigated space and its limitations and at the same time related these experiences in films. *To Touch the Wall with Both Hands at the Same Time* (1974–5; film still, private collection) is a sequence from her film *Berlin – Exercises in Nine Parts* of 1974–5. She also restricted her body and its energies with bandages and used it as an object-machine in *Flowing Over* (1970). The early body works received considerable attention and led to her participation in the Documenta V exhibition in Kassel.

Starting from these early body sculptures, psychic experiences and constellations became increasingly important, depicted and fixed with ritualised and instrumentalised body actions. Masks and feather dresses, which veil the body and thus isolate it from its surroundings, as in *Paradise Widow* (1975; on loan to Kunstmuseum, Bonn), demonstrate the dialectic of protection and injury, communication and isolation, extension and limitation. In this way Horn expressed the manifold net of connections in which the body is entangled.

These ambivalent psychic constellations are especially well conveyed by film. While her early films simply document performances, making it possible to experience the actions of the body in their ritual sequence, later films, such as *La Ferdinanda: Sonata für eine Medici Villa* (1981), approach the quality of feature films, with the scenario of human communication taking place in selected spaces outside museums. In this different medium Horn dedicated herself to the tension of rooms and the humans acting in them, caught in their own obsessions. These films for the first time show object-sculptures like the tango-dancing table in the film *Der Eintänzer* (Professional dancing partner) of 1978 or the peacock machine spreading its feathers in *La Ferdinanda*, through which human or animal actions are carried out by mechanical objects. In later works, such as *Forest of the Outlawed Singers* (1991; Kunst- und Ausstellungshalle der Bundesrepublik Deutschland, Bonn), the artificiality of the mechanical objects is more prominent as equipment such as binoculars isolate and potentiate the human visual faculty.

Towards 1980 the mechanically driven objects, which in the films enact roles within sequences and fulfil rituals, are emphasised as autonomous works of art. Objects, rather than humans, measure the room and demonstrate spatial experiences in *Hanging Fan* (1982; private collection) and *Drawing Radii* (1982; private collection), actions previously reserved for humans in her performances. Painting and drawing machines take over artistic activities. Her installation *Chinese Fiancée* (1976; private collection) is regarded as the key work in this new phase in which the interaction is transferred to the machines and the audience: the viewer enters a hexagonal temple and is exposed to darkness and whispering voices.

Horn's multi-part kinetic sculptures, which on one hand function as autonomous objects like the *Peacock Machine* (1982; Collection Eric Franck, Geneva) and on the other serve the allusive description of specific places in stationary installations, repeatedly refer to certain constructions and materials –

water, pendulum and metronome, ostrich eggs and needles – which, in combination, suggest psychic constellations like injury and penetration. Fixed on each other, in their repeated movements they meet briefly, reach a brief climax and fall back exhaustedly, as in the *Kiss of the Rhinoceros* (1989; Centre Georges Pompidou, Paris), or narrowly miss one another. The possibility of action and the physical strength contributed by the mechanics thus always carries an aspect of futility as well. "The tragic or melancholy aspect of machines", which Horn emphasised in an interview with Stuart Morgan (New York 1993), marks an aspect of her work that is committed to the idea of animation, unification and renewal in a poetic and symbolic way. Her inclusion of materials associated with alchemy, such as sulphur, coal or mercury, also should be interpreted in this way.

In her complementary use of film, installation and mechanically driven sculptures, Horn increasingly turned against a concept of art whose limitations already had been undermined by Marcel Duchamp and Joseph Beuys. Both artists influenced her: Beuys with the performance-based aspect of his work and Duchamp with his ironic examination of alchemy and eroticism. In the *Prussian Bride Machine* (1988; Collection Sylvio Perlstein, Antwerp), a new interpretation of Duchamp's *Large Glass* (1915–23), she breaks the male dominance through the introduction of a female element. An artist who repeatedly rejected dualities and confining sexual identities in a symbolic way, Horn professed a complex disposition in her installation *Orlando* (1988; Tate Gallery, London), named after Virginia Woolf's novel.

For her stationary installations in the mid-1980s Horn increasingly used spaces outside museums. In *El rio de la luna* (1992) she explored the theme of love through artistic intervention in the rooms of a former brothel hotel in Madrid. The energies inherent in places and things are the starting point of her dramatic *mise-en-scène*. A sanatorium is the central arena of her feature film, *Buster's Bedroom*, filmed in 1989. It is dedicated to the actor Buster Keaton, like Franz Kafka and Oscar Wilde, a figure with whom she identified. Her preference for these artists is due in large part to their expressive pictorial repertoire "that speaks about being lost and helpless, about rising and fighting against a hostile world …" (interview with Germano Celant, *ibid.*).

BEATE REESE

Hosmer, Harriet (Goodhue)
American sculptor, 1830–1908

Born in Watertown, Massachusetts, 9 October 1830; father a physician. Educated as a boarder at Mrs Charles Sedgwick's School for Girls in Lenox, Massachusetts, 1846–9. Had a private studio at the family home and studied under the Boston sculptor Peter Stephenson. Took lessons in anatomy at Missouri Medical College, St Louis, 1850. Lived in Rome, 1852–1900; pupil of John Gibson, the leading British sculptor there, 1852–c.1859; established own studio at 116 Via Margutta, early 1860s. Defended status as a professional sculptor with regard to her authorship of *Zenobia*, 1863–5.

Production of sculpture declined from the 1880s; became involved in scientific experimentation. Close link with the feminist movement in USA, 1890s. Returned to her home town of Watertown, 1900. Member, Accademia, Rome, 1858. Died of pneumonia in Watertown, 1908.

Principal Exhibitions

Royal Academy, London: 1857
International Exhibition, London: 1862
New York, Boston and Chicago: 1864–5 (*Zenobia*, touring)
International Exhibition, Dublin: 1865
Colnaghi's Gallery, London: 1878
World's Columbian Exposition, Chicago: 1893
California Midwinter International Exposition, San Francisco: 1894

Selected Writings

Letter in *Art Journal*, new series, iii, 1 January 1864, p.27
"The process of sculpture", *Atlantic Monthly*, xiv, December 1864, pp.734–7
Harriet Hosmer: Letters and Memories, ed. Cornelia Crow Carr, New York: Moffat Yard, 1912

Bibliography

Elizabeth Fries Ellet, *Women Artists in All Ages and Countries*, New York: Harper, 1859

Lorado Taft, *The History of American Sculpture*, 3rd edition, New York: Macmillan, 1930

Van Wyck Brooks, *The Dream of Arcadia: American Artists and Writers in Italy, 1760–1915*, New York: Dutton, and London: Dent, 1958

The White Marmorean Flock: Nineteenth-Century American Women Neoclassical Sculptors, exh. cat., Vassar College Art Gallery, Poughkeepsie, 1972

Joseph Leo Curran, ed., *Harriet Goodhue Hosmer: Collected Sources*, 7 vols, 1974, Watertown Free Public Library Collection, Massachusetts, microfilm, Archives of American Art, Smithsonian Institution, Washington, DC

Andrea Hoffman, *Harriet Hosmer's Life and Work*, PhD dissertation, University of Southern California, Los Angeles, 1979

Barbara S. Groseclose, "Harriet Hosmer's tomb to Judith Falconnet: Death and the maiden", *American Art Journal*, xii, Spring 1980, pp.78–89

Alicia Faxon, "Images of women in the sculpture of Harriet Hosmer", *Woman's Art Journal*, ii/1, 1981, pp.25–9

Philipp P. Fehl, "A tomb in Rome by Harriet Hosmer: Notes on the rejection of gesture in the rhetoric of funerary art", *Ars auro prior: Studia Ioanni Białostocki sexagenerio dicata*, ed. Juliusz A. Chróścicki and others, Warsaw: Państwowe Wydawnictwo Naukowe, 1981, pp.639–49

Andrea Mariani, "Sleeping and waking fauns: Harriet Goodhue Hosmer's experience of Italy, 1852–1870", *The Italian Presence in American Art, 1760–1860*, ed. Irma Jaffe, New York: Fordham University Press, 1989, pp.66–81

Carol Zastoupil, "Creativity, inspiration and scandal: Harriet Hosmer and *Zenobia*", ibid., pp.195–207

Joy S. Kasson, *Marble Queens and Captives: Women in Nineteenth-Century American Sculpture*, New Haven and London: Yale University Press, 1990

Charlotte Streifer Rubinstein, *American Women Sculptors*, Boston: Hall, 1990

Dolly Sherwood, *Harriet Hosmer: American Sculptor, 1830–1908*, Columbia: University of Missouri Press, 1991

Mara R. Witzling, ed., *Voicing Our Visions: Writings by Women Artists*, New York: Universe, 1991; London: Women's Press, 1992

The Lure of Italy: American Artists and the Italian Experience, 1760–1914, exh. cat., Museum of Fine Arts, Boston, 1992

Wendy Slatkin, *The Voices of Women Artists*, Englewood Cliffs, NJ: Prentice Hall, 1993

Harriet Hosmer's career as a sculptor is notable for her single-minded adherence to the classical ideal. Her first major works produced in the 1850s established her international reputation as a maker of ideal sculpture and gallery pieces. In the main these took up themes of women, noble in their suffering and differing from other interpretations of similar subjects in their dignity and chaste decorum. *Oeone* (c.1855), *Beatrice Cenci* (1853–7; both St Louis Mercantile Library) and *Zenobia, Queen of Palmyra* (1859; original untraced; reduced marble version, Wadsworth Atheneum, Hartford, CT; see illustration) are major examples of her high style which was popular both with British and American patrons until the 1880s. Her oeuvre also included commissions for public sculpture, notably the statue of *Thomas Hart Benton* (1860–68; Lafayette Park, St Louis, MI), fountains and busts, as well as smaller-scale gallery pieces, such as the popular *Puck* (1856; Wadsworth Atheneum) and *Will-o'-the Wisp* (1858; Chrysler Museum, Norfolk, VA). Her sculpture for the tomb of *Judith Falconnet* (1857; Sant'Andrea delle Fratte, Rome) is a notable interpretation of the popular form of 19th-century church monument in which the deceased is shown as though sleeping. Hosmer's portrait statue conveys the fragility and the pathos of the subject with its references to 15th-century Italian tomb sculpture. When unveiled it was the only example of a church monument in Rome executed by an American sculptor. Hosmer's works were often reproduced in reduced form, including small replicas in terracotta, which were popular in America.

Unusually for a woman of her generation, Hosmer's education as a sculptor included anatomy lessons and the study of the life model. Her first lessons in sculpture, which began around 1849, were from Peter Stephenson and she also took modelling classes in Boston. At this time she worked from her own studio in the family home in Watertown. In her ambition to become a professional sculptor she was encouraged by the British actress Fanny Kemble, whom she had first met while at Mrs Sedgwick's school. In the autumn of 1850 her father (a doctor) asked the Boston Medical Society that Hosmer be allowed to study anatomy, a vital element in any sculptor's training. This request was refused, and as a result she left her home town in order to study under the direction of Dr Joseph Nash McDowell at the Missouri Medical College, St Louis. Evidence of her anatomical studies is found in surviving drawings. In St Louis she lived with her school friend Cornelia Crow Carr, who was later to become her biographer. Cornelia's father, Wayman Crow, was to be one of Hosmer's first and most loyal patrons, subsidising her career by providing her with money after her father's financial crisis of 1854 seemed to threaten her attempts to establish her own sculptural practice in Rome. His financial support continued until his death in 1885.

Hosmer's lifelong adherence to the Neo-classical idiom was first fostered by the sculptor John Gibson, whose promotion of this "true" and "correct" style continued while many of his British contemporaries were moving towards a more natural interpretation of the human form. For a period of some seven years dating from 1852, when she was admitted as a pupil in

Hosmer: *Zenobia, Queen of Palmyra*, after 1859; Wadsworth Atheneum, Hartford, Connecticut; Gift of Mrs Josephine M.J. Dodge (Arthur E.)

his Via Fontanella studio in Rome, she gained technical expertise in modelling and carving under his direction, as well as being able to pursue her own study of ancient sculpture at first hand. This continuing close attention to canonical works from antiquity is most overt in a work such as the *Sleeping Faun* (1865; Forbes Collection, New York). This modern interpretation of the Barberini *Faun* was shown at the Dublin International Exhibition of 1865, where it excited positive critical responses, some of which pointed to connections with Nathaniel Hawthorne's novel *The Marble Faun* (1860).

Hosmer's natural talent and her passionate enthusiasm for sculpture were nurtured by Gibson who promoted her career well beyond any training in sculptural method. He introduced her to influential figures in the art world and was responsible for showing some of her early sketch models to Christian Rauch. (He had earlier helped Mary Thornycroft, q.v., by recommending her to Queen Victoria.) In Gibson's studio Hosmer was able to study from the life model, which she relished. Her interest in studying the human form at first hand included taking casts from the entire body of a woman model. In July 1854 her compatriot, the sculptor Thomas Crawford, reacted to the inappropriateness of such study, primarily on the grounds of gender: "Miss H[osmer's] want of modesty is enough to disgust a dog" (cited in Sherwood 1991, p.346, note 18).

Hosmer's lack of feminine decorum reaped its rewards. Her sculpture shows control of the medium as well as an in-depth knowledge of the human form. In her sculpture, although she was interested in decorative and poetic elements, she was never distracted by the minutiae of surface detail. She always reduced this to a minimum in order to create an overall harmony through the use of expressive contour. She maintained her preference for the calm grandeur and noble simplicity of the Neo-classical ideal throughout her career and, later in life, she openly criticised the naturalism evident in much late 19th-century sculpture. She is thought to have "tinted" some of her sculptures, following the example of Gibson. The *Sleeping Faun* and *Zenobia* both had a discreet, creamy, fleshlike tint, less overtly stated than in Gibson's polychromed works.

Hosmer's reputation as a professional sculptor came under public scrutiny in 1863 with the questioning of her authorship of *Zenobia*, the 2.43-metre-high statue that had been a major success at the London International Exhibition of 1862 and subsequently toured to New York, Boston and Chicago. The mostly positive critical response to *Zenobia* and the popularity of copies and reductions of the work, including that in Parian ware, confirm that she was establishing her professional status in Europe and America. A defamatory challenge to this was first raised publicly in the *Art Journal* (new series, ii, 1 September 1863, p.181) and *The Queen*. At this time Hosmer was in the process of setting up her own studio at 116 Via Margutta, where in future years she was to employ up to 24 studio assistants. She responded to the accusation that *Zenobia* was the work of her assistants in a letter to the *Art Journal* (1864). This provides important details of Hosmer's working methods on this statue, not least that she spent eight months perfecting the half-size clay model before it was transferred to marble. In her claims to authorship she was backed by Gibson, William Wetmore Story and Hiram Powers. She then published a detailed account of her working practice in "The process of sculpture" (1864), which demonstrates that her working methods were similar to those then employed by the majority of sculptors. Like them she concentrated most upon the creation of the original model, leaving the transfer and working of the marble to her studio assistants. In this sense the accusations against her had some foundation, but applied equally to the established studio practices of her contemporaries. Hosmer used her article as publicity for her case when *Zenobia* was exhibited in New York and Boston. She remained convinced that the attack upon her was prompted by her gender, and there is evidence that this was partly the case. She identified her fellow American sculptor Joseph Mozier as the perpetrator of the slander against her and was supported in her position by Gibson, Story and Powers. Later she was to support Vinnie Ream (q.v.), who in 1871 was similarly accused of over-reliance upon studio assistants in her sculpture. In 1874 she also became peripherally involved in retaliating to a more general attack – raised by Stephen Weston Healy – relating to the authenticity of sculpture emanating from Italian studios at that time. In the 1860s her reputation was further enhanced by the success of her bronze statue of *Thomas Hart Benton*, unveiled in 1868. A portrait statue of *Maria Sophia, Queen of Naples*, exiled to Rome after the fall of Gaeta, was another major commission on which she was working around 1868–9, all visual records of which are now lost. In many ways this work seems to have formed the modern counterpart to the heroism encapsulated in the figure of *Zenobia*.

In the early years in Rome Hosmer attracted a circle of men and women who were involved in the arts. From 1853 she developed a close friendship with Elizabeth Barrett Browning and Robert Browning, making a life cast of their joined hands (1853). The friendship with Robert waned after Elizabeth's death in 1861. Sophia and Nathaniel Hawthorn were other acquaintances and she also formed a lifelong friendship with Frederic Leighton. Her aristocratic British patrons included Lady Marian Alford and Lady Louisa Ashburton.

Hosmer became identified with the women's rights movement in later life as an example of a successful woman with a professional practice and international reputation. She supported women's suffrage and was particularly closely connected with the feminist movement in Chicago during the early 1890s. She was commissioned to execute a statue of *Queen Isabella of Castile* by the Daughters of Isabella, a Chicago suffragist group, but opposed the placement of her (plaster?) statue in the Woman's Building of the World's Columbian Exposition, preferring instead that it be located outside the California Pavilion (Sherwood 1991, p.325; repr. p.326). A version of the statue (destroyed c.1906) was exhibited at the California Midwinter Exposition in 1894. *Queen Isabella* shows the extent to which Hosmer absorbed the more decorative and imaginative surface prevalent in *fin-de-siècle* sculpture by the end of her career. Her last years were spent in scientific investigations. She returned to her home town in 1900, remaining there until her death.

ALISON YARRINGTON

Hoxie, Vinnie Ream *see* Ream

Hoy, Anita [Agneta]

British potter and ceramic designer, 1914–

Born in Southall, London, 3 November 1914, to Danish parents who had moved to London in 1910. Brought up in Denmark. Studied at the Copenhagen College of Arts and Crafts (Kunstværskole), 1933–6 (diploma in pottery design). Studio potter and designer under Gerhard Nielson at Holbæk Stoneware, 1937–8; under Natalie Krebs of Saxbo, 1938–9. Visited family in Britain, 1939; stayed there when war broke out. Designer for Bullers Ltd, Stoke-on-Trent, Staffordshire, 1939–52; for Doulton & Co., Lambeth, London, 1952–6. Opened own studio in Acton, London, 1952; also taught at West Surrey College of Art and Design, Farnham, 1961–83. Lives in London.

Principal Exhibitions

Craftsmen Potters Association, London: 1960 (individual)
Victoria and Albert Museum, London: 1973, 1979
Primavera, Cambridge: 1975
Gladstone Pottery Museum, Stoke-on-Trent: 1977 (*Art among the Insulators*)
Gunnersbury Park Museum, London: 1980, 1981, 1982

Selected Writings

"An adventure in porcelain", *Pottery and Glass*, August 1947
"New stoneware from Lambeth", *Royal Doulton Magazine*, June 1953
"Art among the insulators", *Ceramic Review*, no.69, May–June 1981, pp.10–11

Bibliography

Art among the Insulators: The Bullers Studio, 1932–52, exh. cat., Gladstone Pottery Museum, Stoke-on-Trent, 1977
Cheryl Buckley, *Potters and Paintresses: Women Designers in the Pottery Industry, 1870–1955*, London: Women's Press, 1990
Influential Europeans in British Craft and Design, exh. cat., Crafts Council, London, 1992
Oliver Watson, *Studio Pottery: Twentieth-Century British Ceramics in the Victoria and Albert Museum Collection*, London: Phaidon, 1993 (originally published as *British Studio Pottery*, Oxford: Phaidon, 1990)

The relationship between the modest, relatively small-scale world of the studio potter and industry has always been uneasy in Britain. Studio potters have tended to emphasise the importance of understanding material and process, and have allowed this to affect the final product, while industrial production inclines towards the anonymous and uniform, engendering suspicion and mistrust on both sides. Much of this unease was resolved in the innovative and highly creative work of the designer and potter Anita (Agneta) Hoy, an artist who combined the strength and technical expertise of industrial production with the sensitivity of hand-made ceramics.

One of the most notable responses from the ceramics industry to ways of making use of the ideas and methods of the studio potter came from Bullers Ltd in Stoke-on-Trent, manufacturers of electrical insulators and chemical containers for industry, made in high-temperature porcelain. In the early 1930s Gordon Forsyth, Principal of Burslem School of Art, impressed by the potential of Bullers' hard-paste porcelain, obtained supplies of the firm's porcelain clay for experimental use, and established the basis of a creative collaboration. Technical and aesthetically successful trials were carried out and fired in Bullers' kilns, with experiments made to achieve classical Chinese glazes such as celadons, chuns, oil-spot and *sang de boeuf*. In 1934 Bullers agreed to set up a small studio under the direction of the modeller Anne Potts; she used the

Hugo: Illustration for collection of poems, *Placard pour un chemin des ecoliers*, August 1937; Bibliothèque Nationale, Paris

Looking at the Rose with Crystals and Stars (1935; Musée d'Art et d'Histoire, Saint-Denis) was also inspired by Breton's introduction to *Le Peu de réalité* of 1927, where he speaks of a crystal labyrinth.

Hugo's group portrait, *The Surrealists* (1932–48; Collection H. Matarasso, Nice), is further evidence of her obsession with Breton. This mythical image depicts Paul Eluard, Tristan Tzara, René Char, René Crevel and Breton, who emanates rays of poetic light. Ganymede and Zeus, nude *femmes-enfants* ("child-women") and dreamy clouds enhance this mystical constellation of men, each of whom is in the process of transforming matter, of creating the marvellous. Hugo's tribute to these poets is masterfully executed in its combination of collage and portraiture. Her portrait of *Rimbaud* (1933; repr. de Margerie 1983, p.79), exhibited at the Palais des Beaux-Arts, Brussels, in 1934 and later in 1954 at the Bibliothèque Nationale, Paris, also shows a disembodied poet, with a supernatural gaze and alchemical powers. Hugo's love of the Symbolists, evident in her style since 1909, found its greatest outlet here as she captured what the Symbolists referred to as the "alchemy of the verb".

The third phase of Hugo's career was book illustration, mainly for Paul Eluard. Hugo was always very close to Eluard although they were never romantically involved. In 1938 he praised her art for "discovering the richness of words". She illustrated his *Appliquée* (1937), *Les Animaux et leurs hommes* (1937), *Médiuses* (1939), *Blason de fleurs et de fruits* (1940), *Corps mémorable* (1947) and more (she was to provide an illustration for his celebrated *La Liberté* in 1942 but broke her arm – hence the commission went to Fernand Léger). These collections were portrayed in highly stylised, romanticised lithographs. Even Hugo's eight illustrations for a special edition of the Marquis de Sade's *Eugénie de Franval* (Paris: Artigues, 1948) are remarkably romantic in style, presenting rape with the melodramatic poise of a Pre-Raphaelite affair (see *Obliques* 1977). The only publication that Hugo herself ever succeeded in finishing was *Fido Caniche* (Paris: le Prat, 1947), a story for children about a poodle with suitably comic illustrations.

The 1950s were financially hard for Hugo. When her mother died in 1953 she had to borrow funeral money from Dominique Eluard. In 1955 she had to sell Victor Hugo's travelling album, one of her last prized possessions. She lived meagrely on commissions for social portraits, such as those of *Myrtille Hugnet* (1954; Collection M. Hugnet). Most conformed to a romantic profile with floral details. On 4 July 1963 Yvonne Zervos organised an exhibition, *Hommage à Valentine Hugo de ses amis peintres, sculpteurs et compositeurs*, at Galliéra in Paris. Artists including Louis Aragon, Jean Cocteau, Salvador Dalí and Pablo Picasso donated at least one work to this show, the proceeds of which went to Hugo. After her death in 1968, at the age of 81, this money was established as a trust, making annual awards to a promising artist, writer or composer in Hugo's name – a fitting tribute to a woman who believed that friends were one's greatest asset and who had collaborated with each aspect of the arts to bring design and illustration into a calibre of its own.

ALYCE MAHON

Huntington, Anna Vaughn Hyatt
American sculptor, 1876–1973

Born Anna Vaughn Hyatt in Cambridge, Massachusetts, 10 March 1876, to Alpheus Hyatt II, distinguished professor of palaeontology and zoology at Massachusetts Institute of Technology and Boston University, and Audella (Beebe) Hyatt, an amateur landscape painter. Studied briefly under sculptor Henry Hudson Kitson in Boston, 1898. Moved to New York, 1902; studied at Art Students League under George Grey Barnard, Hermon Atkins MacNeil, Gutzon Borglum, Gertrude Vanderbilt Whitney (q.v.) and Malvina Hoffman (q.v.). Shared a studio on East 33rd Street, New York, with Abastenia St Leger Eberle (q.v.) from 1903. Travelled to France to study art, 1907; took a studio at Auvers-sur-Oise, then in 1908 rented a studio on the Impasse du Maine, Paris. Married philanthropist Archer Milton Huntington, 1923; he died 1955. The couple purchased the estate of Brookgreen, South Carolina, and surrounding plantations in 1930, and planned a nature reserve and outdoor museum for sculpture. Recipient of honorary doctorate, Syracuse University, 1932. Member, American Academy of Arts and Letters, 1932; National Sculpture Society and National Academy of Design. Chevalier, 1922, and Officier, 1933, Légion d'Honneur, France. Died 4 October 1973.

Selected Individual Exhibitions
Boston Art Club: 1902
Gorham Galleries, New York: 1914
Detroit Institute of Arts: 1916
St Botolph Club, Boston: 1917
American Academy of Arts and Letters, New York: 1936 (retrospective)
USA: 1937–9 (touring)
National Arts Club, New York: 1952 (retrospective)
Hispanic Society of America, New York: 1957, 1974

Bibliography
Dorothy Seckler, "Interview with Anna Hyatt Huntington", transcript, Archives of American Art, Smithsonian Institution, Washington, DC, n.d.
Bertha H. Smith, "Two women who collaborate in sculpture", *Craftsman*, viii, 1905, pp.623–33
Anna Coleman Ladd, "Anna V. Hyatt: Animal sculptor", *Art and Progress*, iv, 1912, pp.773–6
Royal Cortissoz, "Recent works by two American sculptors", *New York Tribune*, 1 February 1914, section v, p.6
Grace Humphrey, "Anna Vaughn Hyatt's statue", *International Studio*, lvii, 1915, pp.xlvii–l
Charles H. Caffin, "Miss Hyatt's statue of Joan of Arc", *Century Magazine*, xcii, 1916, pp.306–11
Cecilia Morrow, "An artist-patriot: A sketch of Anna Hyatt Huntington", *Touchstone*, v, 1919, pp.286–93
Frederick Newlin Price, "Anna Hyatt Huntington", *International Studio*, lxxix, 1924, pp.319–23
Pauline Carrington Bouvé, "The two foremost women sculptors in America: Anna Vaughn Hyatt and Malvina Hoffman", *Art and Archaeology*, xxvi, September 1928, pp.74–7
Kineton Parkes, "An American sculptress of animals, Anna Hyatt Huntington", *Apollo*, xvi, 1932, p.66
Jean Royère, *Le Musicisme sculptural: Madame Archer Milton Huntington*, Paris: Messein, 1933
André Devaux, "Anna Hyatt-Huntington", *L'Esprit Français*, ix, 10 May 1933, pp.23–7

Carol Deambrosis Martins, *Una gran escultora nort-americana: Diario de la marina*, 4 June 1933

Exhibition of Sculptures by Anna Hyatt Huntington, exh. cat., American Academy of Arts and Letters, New York, 1936

Leila Mechlin, "Anna Hyatt Huntington, sculptor", *Carnegie Magazine*, xi, June 1937, pp.67–71

Emile Schaub-Koch, "L'évolution de l'art animalier: Madame Anna Hyatt-Huntington", *Nouvelle Revue*, clv, 15 June 1938, pp.241–52

Anna Hyatt Huntington, New York: National Sculpture Society and Norton, 1947

Beatrice G. Proske, "Anna Hyatt Huntington", *Brookgreen Gardens Sculpture*, Murrells Inlet, SC: Brookgreen Gardens, 1968

Anna Hyatt Huntington, 1876–1973: Small Bronzes and Sketches, exh. cat., Hispanic Society of America, New York, 1974

Susan Harris Edwards, *Anna Hyatt Huntington: Sculptor and Patron of American Idealism*, MA thesis, University of South Carolina, 1983

American Figurative Sculpture in the Museum of Fine Arts, Boston, Boston: Museum of Fine Arts, 1986

Beatrice G. Proske, "A sculptor in New York", *SITES: A Literary/Architectural Magazine*, xvi–xvii, 1986, pp.30–36

Myrna G. Eden, *Energy and Individuality in the Art of Anna Huntington, Sculptor, and Amy Beach, Composer*, Metuchen, NJ: Scarecrow, 1987

Janis Conner and Joel Rosenkranz, *Rediscoveries in American Sculpture: Studio Works, 1893–1939*, Austin: University of Texas Press, 1989

Charlotte Streifer Rubinstein, *American Women Sculptors*, Boston: Hall, 1990

Anna Hyatt Huntington Papers are in the Archives of American Art, Smithsonian Institution, Washington, DC, and in the George Arents Research Library for Special Collections, Syracuse University, Syracuse, NY.

Anna Hyatt Huntington, one of America's foremost *animaliers* of the early 20th century, is noted for her essays in romantic naturalism that include intimate portraits of domestic and wild animals, as well as heroic equestrian monuments. She was equally capable in figurative sculpture, as confirmed by the scores of frolicking nymphs, goddesses and children that appear on her numerous garden commissions.

Huntington's career flourished during the first four decades of the 20th century, and she continued to produce sculptures until a few days before her death at the age of 97. Working in the conventions established by the French *animaliers* Antoine Louis Barye and Emmanuel Frémiet, Huntington created works that bridged the gap between the traditional, academic productions of the late 19th century and modern abstract sculpture. Her earliest pieces were of pets or farm animals, but Huntington's interests soon broadened to include wild animals, which she observed in live animal shows and zoo collections. An early group, the small-scale, granite *Elephants Fighting* (1905–12; Museum of Fine Arts, Boston), illustrates her unique response to the confrontation of competing concepts – the encounter of the lively surface effects and rich modelling of the Beaux-Arts style with the more abstract and often stylised forms of those artists working on the brink of modernism. In the piece, the modelled forms of the elephants are simplified to the essential, while a sense of anatomical accuracy is maintained to portray the tension and power of the battling beasts. The even more abstracted anatomy of the carved stone *Reaching Jaguar* (1906; Metropolitan Museum of Art, New York) successfully unites simplification of form with anatomical precision to emphasise the powerful musculature of the pouncing animal.

From the beginning, critics acknowledged Huntington's ability to portray anatomy with great accuracy in her animal characterisations, a skill that can be attributed to the early training in observation that she received from her scientist father, Alpheus Hyatt, and to the many hours the artist spent studying animals at first hand. Huntington's attention to detail is epitomised by her most famous work, the massive equestrian monument, *Joan of Arc* (1915), a bronze depiction of the Maid of Orléans in full armour with raised sword, rising up in the stirrups of a formidable mount (original on Riverside Drive, New York; copies in Blois, France; Gloucester, MA; on the Plains of Abraham, Quebec; and in San Francisco). In 1909, to begin the colossal undertaking, Huntington rented the former Paris stable-studio of the French sculptor Jules Dalou, and then set about thoroughly investigating the history of Joan of Arc, while searching for the perfect horse as model. She settled on a magnificent percheron borrowed from the Magazins du Louvre, bringing the animal to her studio for further study. Huntington began the final version of the tightly modelled, formal monument in 1914, on the family farm in Annasquam, Massachusetts. The local fire department donated a horse as model for the mount, and her niece posed on a barrel for the young maid. As meticulous in attention to period details as she was to human and animal anatomy, Huntington sought the assistance of Basford Dean, then curator of armour at the Metropolitan Museum, to assure the historical correctness of the horse's and rider's accoutrements.

Huntington's most adventurous characterisations are found in her garden sculptures. The idealised, over-life-size *Diana of the Chase* (1922; Brookgreen Gardens, SC), for example, represents the goddess of the wilderness in a complex spiralled composition. Although hardly revolutionary in terms of style, *Diana of the Chase* combines decorative stylisation with academic form, promising a viable alternative to modernism. Yet Huntington's sculptural language, although seemingly modern, falls far short of the stripped-down abstraction of Jacques Lipchitz, or the severe archaism of Paul Manship. A youthful Diana cavorts weightlessly on a small globe, as she twists back to look skyward over her shoulder towards the imaginary arrow just loosed from her bow. An equally stylised hunting dog – a strong compositional element – leaps frantically upwards from the bottom of the composition, emphasising and reinforcing the upward stretch of the goddess, while contributing to the active narrative of the ensemble. The following year Huntington produced an even more stylised version of Diana, on a bronze fountain commissioned for the estate in Gloucester, Massachusetts, of Mrs John Hays Hammond, a Boston socialite. This bronze, a prepubescent *Young Diana* (1923; ht 1.8 m.), balances with bow in hand on a base made up of a shell supported by twisted dolphins.

In the same year Anna Hyatt married Archer Huntington, the heir to an enormous railroad fortune and founder of the Hispanic Society of America. The sculptor came to share her husband's interest in Spanish culture, creating a dozen figures and groups for the plaza of the Society in New York, a project she worked on until the mid-1930s. The centre of the group was an equestrian statue of *El Cid Campeador*, the legendary warrior. The formal presentation depicts the Spanish hero riding into battle on a steed reminiscent of Renaissance prototypes. Huntington's ensemble included a second equestrian statue, *Don Quixote*, which shows the artist's preoccupation with fitting horse to rider. Unlike the powerful mounts of El Cid and Joan of Arc, this gallant knight's horse is emaciated, with hanging head.

In 1927 Huntington contracted tuberculosis, which slowed her production. Three years later the sculptor and her husband purchased Brookgreen, a large estate in Murrells Inlet, South Carolina, the culmination of the artist's search for a suitable climate in which to recover. Huntington also found in Brookgreen an ideal setting for her work, and soon opened the grounds to more than 200 American sculptors. By 1934, having regained her health, she attacked her work with renewed vigour to produce dozens of new sculptures, many of which were made of cast aluminium. This modern lightweight material made the works highly portable, resistant to effects of the weather, and allowed the freedom to create dynamic compositions. Through the 1950s Huntington exhibited widely, and during the 1960s and 1970s continued to produce new sculptures for frequent exhibitions.

PAMELA POTTER-HENNESSEY

Hyatt, Anna Vaughn *see* Huntington

Hydman-Vallien, Ulrica

Swedish glass artist, painter and designer, 1938–

Born Ulrica Hydman in Stockholm, 24 March 1938. Studied ceramic and glass at the National College of Art, Craft and Design, Stockholm, 1958–61. Studied in the USA and Mexico, 1962–3. Married crystal designer and sculptor Bertil Vallien, 1963; two sons. Established own painting and glass studio, Åfors Glassbruk, in Eriksmåla, 1963. Glass designer for Kosta Boda AB, Sweden, from 1972; ceramics designer, Rörstrand AB, Lidköping, 1984–6; also freelance designer for various firms. Guest lecturer at Pilchuck Glass School, Seattle, USA, 1981–8; Bildwerk, Frauenau, Germany, 1989. Recipient of Young Artists award, Nationalmuseum, Stockholm, 1972; Major State Scholarship, Stockholm, 1973 and 1974; Swedish National Artists award, 1980; Emmaboda district cultural award, 1981; prize, *Women in Design International*, New York, 1983; first prize, *Svensk Design*, Nationalmuseum, Stockholm, 1983; Swedish Artists' Council scholarships, 1983–7; Coburg Glaspreis, 1985; *Excellent Swedish Form* awards, 1985 and 1987; Design Plus Competition, Internationaler Frankfurter Messe Ambiente award, 1992. Lives in Eriksmåla.

Selected Individual Exhibitions

Bonniers, New York: 1974
Norrköpings Museum, Norrköping: 1976
Galleri Doktor Glas, Stockholm: 1976, 1984, 1991, 1994
Habatat Gallery, Pontiac, MI: 1980, 1981
Heller Gallery, New York: 1983, 1989, 1990, 1996
New Glass Gallery, New York: 1985
Kalmar Konstmuseum, Kalmar: 1987
Traver-Sutton Gallery, Seattle: 1988
Sanske Gallerie, Zürich: 1991
Centre Culturel Suédoise, Paris: 1992
Azabu Art Museum, Tokyo: 1992
Galleri Altes Raathaus, Inslingen: 1992
Örebro Castle, Örebro: 1995 (retrospective)
Galleri Glas 1, Stockholm: 1996
SOFA Art Fair, Chicago: 1996

Selected Writings

"In context: Poems and paintings by Ulrica Hydman-Vallien", *Glass Magazine*, no.51, Spring 1993, pp.44–7
Apekatt och vilde [Monkey-cat and savage], 1996 (for children)

Bibliography

Design in Sweden, exh. cat., Swedish Institute, Stockholm, 1972
Helena Dahlbäck Lutteman, *New Glass from Sweden*, Uppsala, 1982
Scandinavian Modern Design, 1880–1980, exh. cat., Cooper-Hewitt Museum, New York, and elsewhere, 1982
Un art du feu: La verrerie contemporaine en Suède, exh. cat., Centre Culturel Suédoise, Paris, 1985
Karen S. Chambers, "Bertil Vallien and Ulrica Hydman-Vallien: Designs for art and living", *New Work*, no.21–2, 1985
Ann-Marie Herlitz-Gezelius, *Kosta: Glaset och konstnärerna* [Kosta: The glass and the artists], Lund: Bokförlaget Signum, 1987
Susanne Frantz, *Contemporary Glass: A World Survey from the Corning Museum of Glass*, New York: Abrams, 1989
Mailis Stensman, *Ulrica Hydman-Vallien*, 1990
Swedish Art in Glass, 1900–1990: An Important Private Collection, Vänersborg: Knutsson Art and Antiques, 1991
Walter Lieberman, "Bertil and Ulrica in the kingdom of glass", *Scandinavian Review*, Spring–Summer 1991
World Glass Now, '91, exh. cat., Hokkaido Museum of Modern Art, Sapporo, Japan, and elsewhere, 1991
"Die Hexe von Åfors", *Harper's Bazaar*, March 1992
Tsuji Kazumi-Aoki Tomako, "Ulrica Hydman-Vallien", *Glasswork Magazine*, no.15, July 1993, pp.10–17 (interview)
Lena Katarina Swanberg, "The queen of the kingdom of crystal", *Månadsjournalen*, no.1, January 1993, pp.16–23
The Art of Painted Glass, exh. cat., Habatat Galleries, Pontiac, MI, 1995
Ulrica Hydman-Vallien, exh. cat., Örebro Castle, Örebro, 1995
Kavita Daswani, "Snakes in the glass", *Sunday Morning Post* (Hong Kong), 21 April 1996

Ulrica Hydman-Vallien has characterised herself more perceptively than could her biographers: as a tree with its highest branches blowing back and forth in a storm. She states that she has "too much adrenaline. I explode without warning". This explosive artistic temperament is channelled into images suffused with a restless energy and vigour, in paintings, ceramics and in her more widely-known medium of glass. Her characteristic subjects of women, men and children, often combined with serpents and other reptilian creatures, decorate glass vessels and sculptural forms painted in bright primary colours with sooty contours.

Hydman-Vallien came to glass from a training in painting at the National College of Art, Craft and Design in Stockholm. She subsequently trained in the USA and in Mexico. Memories of the bright colours of Mexican art and some of its images might account for her almost childlike paintings of the 1980s, such as *Beneath the Star of Bethlehem* (1980; private collection), in which the family is arranged in a pyramidal grouping

Hydman-Vallien: *Cat Man*, paint and mixed media; 60 × 45 cm.

against a broadly painted landscape dotted with conical hills; a menacing dog and a serpent also lurk nearby. Hydman has said:

> I have a strong desire to paint. My paintings are my feelings. I paint the strong woman that I sometimes am, the security of being a mother and wife. I paint the single woman, jealousy … Feelings of tenderness, anxiety, love, hopes, fears, laughter and strength.

These conflicting emotions can be sensed in a more complex composition, *A Try for Love* (1984; private collection), which depicts an interior with figures engaged in ambiguous activities, drawn in strict profile and painted in an expressive, flamboyant style reminiscent of German Expressionist painting or the contemporary work of the Scottish painter John Bethany. Radios and televisions often appear in her paintings, and the characters visible on the screens both continue the pictorial space and actively engage with the figures within it, as in *A Try for Love*. Animals are transformed by horns and breasts growing from their bodies, and the characteristic serpent usually appears, insinuating itself around the figures. The serpent reappears as a sculptural addition to champagne flutes in her *Cleopatra* series for Kosta Boda: apparently this image

refers back to her early experience of crawling into a snake's nest at the age of three.

For Hydman-Vallien, serpents "symbolise treachery, danger. Temptation. I often paint yellow snakelike eyes on my figures". Her interest in the theme of the serpent (of which she has owned a number as pets) first appeared in her glass designs in 1975, and in a sculptural form at the Pilchuck Glass School, where she taught between 1981 and 1988.

Although her extravagant designs (and her *horror vacui* – perhaps resulting from a fear of empty surfaces, which "are cold and melancholy") were initially slow to be appreciated, and met with resistance from some colleagues at Kosta Boda, where she has been head designer since 1972, she has stated: "I was before my time back then, but I never gave in to pressure". None the less, Erik Rosen at Kosta Boda supported the innovative designs she produced for the firm, and her *Poem* series of the mid-1970s was a commercial success. In 1986 her glass *Caramba* achieved even wider national notoriety after its appearance on a television programme, while such series as *Inca* and *Tulipa* are among Kosta Boda's most popular sellers. Hydman-Vallien's most recent works, the *Adam and Eve* glasses (1992), have gold paint decoration, while the *Nevada* series (1993) shows a more earthy palette. Although her largest market is still in Sweden, her designs have also met with great acclaim in the USA and Japan, where she exhibits regularly.

By the mid-1980s Hydman-Vallien's distinctive images of wolves and serpents began to appear on, and within, glass vessels and sculptures, often made from chiselled glass blocks in clear and coloured glass produced by the Oxelösund glassworks. Exploiting the pictorial potential of glass, for her *Kabale* sculptures (1980–90) she also adopted the Graal glass technique developed at Orrefors in 1916. The glass ingot is built up of successive layers of transparent and coloured glass, which the artist is then able to decorate by a number of methods, such as sandblasting or cutting. Finally the ingot is reheated and the shape formed, thereby also distorting the image as the glass is blown and expands. Great skill, and a steely nerve, are required for this technique, but the vibrantly painted ingot trapped deep beneath layers of clear crystal, which intensifies the colours of the design, justifies the risk of the process.

Other designs are painted straight on to blown glass in the valuable enamel paints that Hydman-Vallien rescued from old glassworks, for instance the rectangular design for the decanter *You and Me* (1980), which consists of a floating couple, the female figure sporting a feathered headdress, around which marine creatures circle menacingly. The contrast between the naive drawing and the delicate, milky glass is marked, a contrast that often characterises her glass vessels.

Hydman-Vallien's style has often been linked with that of the German Expressionists, an appropriate parallel, for she describes herself as "like an animal ... I always react quick as lightning and intuitively", and this spontaneous reaction is transferred into her designs. Whether in her enigmatic paintings, or in the sculptural rocklike glass such as the *Cat Man* (see illustration), this urgency of artistic expression is expressed through bold lines, vibrant colour and a refreshing disregard for the refined lines so often associated with Swedish design. Indeed, as she herself claims: "there is nothing typically Swedish about my work: it is typically me". Examples of Ulrica Hydman-Vallien's work may be found in the National Museum of Modern Art, Tokyo; Corning Museum of Glass, New York; Victoria and Albert Museum, London; and the Nationalmuseum, Stockholm.

ANTONIA BOSTRÖM

I

Iakunchikova, Maria *see* Yakunchikova

Ironside, Adelaide
Australian painter, 1831–1867

Born in Sydney, 17 November 1831. Grew up in St Leonard's, a North Shore suburb, in a cultural milieu around Dr John Dunmore Lang and Daniel Henry Deniehy; contributed articles and verse to local papers. Moved to Europe with her mother to study art professionally, 1855. Settled in Rome, 1856, becoming known both as a painter and a medium. Granted an audience with Pope Pius IX, 1861, receiving permission to copy pictures in the Vatican and study fresco painting at a Camaldolese monastery in Perugia, Umbria. Became a member of the Accademia dei Quiriti, Rome, and awarded its diploma, 1862. Stayed in London and met John Ruskin, 1865; subsequently corresponded with him. Died of tuberculosis at the Palazzo Albano, Rome, 15 April 1867.

Principal Exhibitions
Exposition Universelle, Paris: 1855 (honourable mention)
International Exhibition, London: 1862 (gold medal)
International Exhibition, Dublin: 1865

Bibliography
William Sharp, *The Life and Letters of Joseph Severn*, London: Sampson Low, 1892
W. Dixon "Notes on Australian Artists", *Journal of the Royal Australian Historical Society*, vii/4, 1921, pp.212–16
William Moore, *The Story of Australian Art*, Sydney: Angus and Robertson, 1934; reprinted 1980
M. Preston, "Some pioneer women artists", *The Peaceful Army: A Memorial to the Pioneer Women of Australia, 1788–1938*, ed. Flora S. Eldershaw, Sydney: Women's Executive Committee and Advisory Council of Australia's 150th Anniversary Celebrations, 1938
Cyril Pearl, *Brilliant Dan Deniehy: A Forgotten Genius*, Melbourne: Nelson, 1972
Eve Buscombe, *Artists in Early Australia and Their Portraits*, Sydney: Eureka Research, 1978
Ruth Teale, ed., *Colonial Eve: Sources on Women in Australia, 1788–1914*, Melbourne: Oxford University Press, 1978
Janine Burke, *Australian Women Artists, 1840–1940*, Collingwood, Victoria: Greenhouse, 1980
Caroline Ambrus, *The Ladies' Picture Show: Sources on a Century of Australian Women Artists*, Sydney: Hale and Iremonger, 1984
E. A. Martin, *The Life and Speeches of Daniel Henry Deniehy*, Melbourne: Robertson, 1984
D. W. A. Baker, *Days of Wrath: A Life of John Dunmore Lang*, Melbourne: Melbourne University Press, 1985
"Adelaide Ironside and the Wentworths", *Historic Houses Trust of New South Wales: Newsletter*, [September 1987]
J. Poulton, *Adelaide Ironside: The Pilgrim of Art*, Sydney: Hale and Iremonger, 1987
Patricia Clarke, *Pen Portraits: Women Writers and Journalists in Nineteenth-Century Australia*, Sydney: Pandora, 1988
Pamela Bell, "The Marriage at Cana of Galilee", *Heritage: The National Women's Art Book*, ed. Joan Kerr, Sydney: Dictionary of Australian Artists/Craftsman House, 1995

Adelaide Ironside Papers and J.D. Lang Papers are in the Mitchell Library, Sydney.

Many are the firsts claimed for Adelaide Ironside: she was the first professional woman artist in Australia; she was the first Australian-born artist to go overseas to study; and she was, with a handful of male artists, among the first Australian artists to exhibit overseas. It seems churlish then to describe her work as a curious blend of the outmoded and the inferior: she early adopted, and stuck to, a type of painting – religious art – that had once been considered superior to other art forms but which was, by the mid-19th century, outdated and irrelevant and, in the art of Ironside, sentimental and clichéd. But perhaps worse than this, despite spending eleven years in Rome, her talent never rose above being that of a competent copyist.

Brought up and educated by an adoring mother, Adelaide became fluent in several languages and was probably self-taught in art, though she possibly had some training with the artists James Armstrong Wilson and Conrad Martens. Her extant art work from this period consists of copies of insipid women from engraved plates after Hayter and Ross and a few drawings of native flowers (Mitchell Library, Sydney). Drawings such as *Ideal* (1855; Newcastle Regional Art Gallery) and *Twin Sisters* (1850; after Hayter; National Gallery of Australia, Canberra) were, however, admired by some of her circle and included in the first collection of Australian art ever to be exhibited overseas, when a collection of her pencil drawings – a mixture of religious subjects,

Ironside: *Marriage at Cana of Galilee*, 1861; oil on canvas; 101 × 145 cm.; Art Gallery of New South Wales, Gift of Warden and Fellows of St Paul's College, University of Sydney, 1992

portraits and flower studies – was shown at the Paris Exposition Universelle of 1855.

It was perhaps strange then, for a Protestant involved in the Sydney Republican movement of the 1850s, to seek Catholic Rome as a destination, but this she did, presenting her *Maiden War Banner* (now lost) to the First Volunteer Corps of New South Wales a week before her departure on 20 June 1855. Through the connection of their London physician, Sir James Clark, Ironside and her mother were introduced in Rome to the British sculptor John Gibson and his circle, which included the American sculptor Harriet Hosmer (q.v.). Doors everywhere flew open and they enjoyed an exciting and busy life in Rome for the next eleven years. Ambitious to return to Australia to fresco the walls of the new Houses of Parliament, Ironside and her mother visited Perugia in 1859, after which she completed *St Catherine of Alexandria as Patroness of Philosophy* (Art Gallery of New South Wales, Sydney), her first work in oil. In this painting, Ironside turned to the work of Perugino, Raphael's teacher, whose frescoes in the lower area of the Sistine Chapel she later so admired. Her use of the rich reds and golds and the symbology of a palm (for martyrdom) and a book (for learning) are a tribute to the artist. On the lapel of the cloak is the Catherine wheel – the instrument by

which the saint was tortured. The same year Ironside received a visit from the Prince of Wales, who reputedly (see Poulton 1987) bought a painting from her for 500 guineas, though its title and whereabouts are unknown.

In the next few years Ironside completed three more oils, *St Agnes* (1860; untraced), *Ars Longa, Vita Brevis*, also known by the title the *Pilgrim of Art, Crowned by the Genius of Art* (1859–60; destroyed), in which she portrayed herself as the Pilgrim and her mother as Genius, and the *Marriage at Cana of Galilee* (1861; see illustration). All were exhibited, with *St Catherine*, for which Ironside won a gold medal, in the New South Wales court at the International Exhibition in London in 1862. Her last known painting, the *Adoration of the Magi*, also known as the *Manifestation of Christ to the Gentiles* (1864; untraced), was exhibited at the Dublin International Exhibition in 1865.

The *Marriage at Cana of Galilee* is undoubtedly Ironside's most important extant work and, despite recent attempts by historians to elevate its quality (see Bell 1995), it remains an enfeebled painting, largely through the artist's inability to arrive at her own style. It was reputedly copied from works, mainly by Raphael and Perugino, in the Pope's private collection that Ironside had first seen when she had an audience with

Pius IX at the Vatican earlier that year. Borrowing some of the compositional elements of Renaissance painting – a triangular arrangement being uppermost (see Burke 1980, p.21) – and what the artist described as "the Hebrew and Egyptian [style]", the painting is a mélange of borrowed elements, which fails as a work; a "major intellectual effort" (Bell 1995) perhaps, but a failed one. For finally, Ironside is unable to invest any depth or sense of character to any of the figures in the painting. They remain adolescent copies of Hayter engravings, all the women (and some of the men) idealised with the delicate but vapid beauty of the young Queen Victoria. The Italian patriot Garibaldi was, as Ironside wrote, the bridegroom of the painting, but this too was most likely to have been taken from an engraving as there is no evidence that he ever sat for the artist. And while it is right to recall, as Bell suggests we do, that women artists at this time did not have access to life classes, neither did many male artists. They instead drew from Classical statuary, and here lies Ironside's principal weakness – her figures are flat, like so many cardboard cut-outs; they have no mass or solidity. They remain fatally imitative and without any imaginative power.

Ironside herself felt it to be "laborious work" to attempt so many figures; although she was only 30 years old at the time, she was a petite woman with a nervous and romantic temperament who was already seriously ill with the tuberculosis that would finally kill her a few years later. But she always had her supporters in the colony, some of whom organised an exhibition of 100 works in Sydney in 1870. The three major oils were hung again in 1880 at the opening of the Art Gallery of New South Wales and then were allowed to deteriorate until only the *Marriage at Cana of Galilee* survived.

CANDICE BRUCE

Izquierdo, María
Mexican painter, (?)1902–1955

Born in San Juan de los Lagos, Jalisco, Mexico, 30 October (?)1902. Married (1) Cándido Posados, 1917; three children; divorced 1927; (2) Raúl Uribe Castille, 1944; divorced 1953. Studied at Escuela Nacional de Bellas Artes (Academia de San Carlos), Mexico City, under Germán Gedovius, 1928–9. Taught painting at Escuela de Pintura y Escultura of the Secretaría de Educación, Mexico City, 1931. Art critic for newspaper *Hoy*. Lived and worked with artist Rufino Tamayo, 1929–33. Died in Mexico City, 2 December 1955.

Principal Exhibitions

Individual
Galería de Arte Moderno, Mexico City: 1929, 1956 (retrospective)
Art Center, New York: 1930
Galerie René Highe, Paris: 1933
Galerie van den Berg, Paris: 1937
Stanley Rose Gallery, Los Angeles: 1938
Galería de Arte Mexicano, Mexico City: 1939
Sala del Seminario de Cultura Mexicana, Mexico City: 1943

Group
Metropolitan Museum of Art, New York: 1930 (*Mexican Arts*)
Museum of Modern Art, New York: 1940 (*Twenty Centuries of Mexican Art*)

Bibliography
Antonin Artaud, "La pintura de María Izquierdo", *Revista de Revistas* (Mexico City), 23 August 1936
——, "Le Mexique et l'esprit primitif", *L'Amour de l'Art*, no.8, 1937
——, "Mexico y el espiritu feminino: María Izquierdo", *Revista de la Universidad de México*, xxii/6, 1968
Justino Fernández, *A Guide to Mexican Art*, Chicago: University of Chicago Press, 1969
María Izquierdo y su obra, exh. cat., Museo de Arte Moderno, Mexico City, 1971
María Izquierdo, exh. cat., Museo Regional, Monterrey, 1977
Margarita Michelana and others, *María Izquierdo*, Guadalajara: Departamento de Bellas Artes, 1985
Carlos Monsiváis and others, *María Izquierdo*, Mexico City: Casa de Bolsa Cremi, 1986
Imagen de Mexico, exh. cat., Museo Regional, Monterrey, and elsewhere, 1987
María Izquierdo, exh. cat., Centro Cultural de Arte Contemporáneo, Mexico City, 1988
Art in Latin America: The Modern Era, 1820–1980, exh. cat., South Bank Centre, London, and elsewhere, 1989
Oriana Baddeley and Valerie Fraser, *Drawing the Line: Art and Cultural Identity in Contemporary Latin America*, London and New York: Verso, 1989
Raquel Tibol, "Mariá Izquierdo", *Latin American Art*, i, 1989, pp.23–5
Art d'Amérique latine, 1911–1968, exh. cat., Musée National d'Art Moderne, Centre Georges Pompidou, Paris, 1992
Latin American Artists of the Twentieth Century, exh. cat., Museum of Modern Art, New York, 1993

María Izquierdo began painting in Mexico City in the 1920s at the beginning of the revolutionary era of the Mexican muralists. Determined to instill a spirit of national pride into the indigenous people of their country, the Mexican muralists led by Diego Rivera rejected the dominant academic approach to art and used a style described as Social Realism to introduce nativist themes and pre-Hispanic subject matter into grandiose programmes of murals painted on public buildings. In keeping with the traditional Mexican attitude that women belonged in the home, the mural projects excluded women, although many women shared the same commitment to social advancement and to art as a source of public information. Women artists were forced to produce works on a small scale for a limited audience. María Izquierdo defied the governing attitude of the muralists to produce large works of a propagandist and political nature and maintained her own anti-academic approach to painting based on a personal vocabulary of indigenous imagery.

Izquierdo had only one year of formal training at the Escuela Nacional in Mexico City in 1928–9; she found it too conservative and restrained. She was seriously committed to developing her art professionally, however, and secured a teaching position with the Ministry of Education. She also worked as an art critic for the newspaper *Hoy* in her effort to establish a reputation in the cultural community of the city. She was the first Mexican woman to have a one-person exhibition in New York (1930), and in the same year was included in the exhibition *Mexican Arts* at the Metropolitan Museum of Art. As a member of the Liga de Escritores y Artistas Revolucionarios, she dedicated herself to the

Izquierdo: *Altar of Sorrows*, 1943; oil on canvas; 74 × 59 cm.; Galeria de Arte Mexicana, Mexico

advancement of women and women artists. She knew the struggles of women at first hand, constantly encountering obstacles to her own advancement as an artist in a male-dominated art environment. Determined to succeed by creating works that celebrated the beauty of her land and culture (*Landscape*, 1930; collection Luis Felipe de Valle Prieto, Mexico City), she mastered a style of painting that was appropriately modern and recognisably "Mexican".

Influential to the development of Izquierdo's career and her sense of independence was a four-year relationship with the Mexican master Rufino Tamayo, from 1929 to 1933. In a daring act of personal liberation in a conservative country, she decided to share her life and studio with Tamayo. The collaboration encouraged their common vision of creating a purely Mexican art in style and substance. The relationship ended when Tamayo married another woman and Izquierdo's work of this period of heartbreak and pain reflects her grief. Women crying in desperation can be seen in paintings of the late 1930s and early 1940s. *La Dolorosa* (1947; collection Francisco and Laura Osio) demonstrates her skill in painting sculpturesque and volumetric forms, while her use of colours at full intensity is reminiscent of the popular arts and crafts of her people; it also shows the Mexican preoccupation with death and cemeteries that informs her work of this period.

In marked contrast to painful subjects, yet still with a sense of poignancy, Izquierdo frequently produced paintings that focus on the subject of the circus with acrobats, horses and clowns. Interesting and complex, the circus performers in *Circus Rider* (1932; private collection) and *The Cart* (1940; private collection) are as disturbing as they are humorous, and appear to be involved in a melancholy rather than a celebratory scene. They retreat into the glitter of the circus rather than participate in the reality of the world's problems, and transform a usually happy scene into an allegory replete with symbolism of universal importance.

In the 1940s the inclusion of elements drawn directly from Izquierdo's own culture and popular or folkloric crafts in still-life arrangements resulted in a sophisticated group of paintings. The objects depicted in works entitled *alacena* (cupboard) include fruit, flags, ceramic statues and unidentifiable objects arranged on shelves and domestic altars (e.g. *Alacena*, 1943; Galería de Arte Méxicano, Mexico City). *Altar of Sorrows* (1943; see illustration) includes an assortment of crafts and souvenirs arranged before an image of the weeping Virgin, typical of domestic altars found in many homes in Mexico dedicated to the Virgin Dolorosa. For these still-life arrangements, Izquierdo borrowed elements from numerous sources, both European and Mexican. The nostalgia for everything "Mexican" associated with childhood memories and the remnants of family traditions, fiestas, ceremonies and religious ritual that were part of her own upbringing appear in numerous works, including portraits of her friends and family.

The poignancy of these accumulations of personal objects in works of the late 1940s and 1950s (*Alacena*, 1952; Museo de Arte Moderno, Mexico City) may also reflect a particularly difficult incident in Izquierdo's career that occurred in 1945, when she was denied a large mural commission for the National Palace, already contracted for, when Diego Rivera and David Alfaro Siqueiros decided that she was too inexperienced for the project. It was only one of many incidents that left her bitter, but more determined to succeed where others had failed, and to create an art that was different from the propagandist style espoused by the muralists. She produced paintings that reflected her own Mexico in her own unique style.

The paintings from the last years of Izquierdo's life demonstrate an affinity for European methods of personal expression found in the works of Giorgio de Chirico and the Surrealists. She explores spatial relationships in deserted landscapes with strange perspectives and menacing shadows. The ground littered with an odd accumulation of objects in the foreground of *Naturaleza viva* ("living nature"; 1946; private collection, Monterrey) and *Landscape* (1953; private collection) contrasts with the empty landscape and desolate mood to comment on the still-life tradition of Spanish art described with titles of *naturaleza muerta* ("dead nature"). In 1953 María Izquierdo suffered her final indignity when a stroke left her partially paralysed and her marriage disintegrated. She filed for divorce and continued to work by training her left hand. She produced about 20 works before her death in 1955.

CAROL DAMIAN